DUKES' PHYSIOLOGY OF DOMESTIC ANIMALS | NINTH EDITION

Melvin J. Swenson, *Editor*
R. Scott Allen
Bengt E. Andersson
Erik Andresen
Harpal S. Bal
Gary K. Beauchamp
Emmett N. Bergman
James E. Breazile
Marvin P. Bryant
William H. Burke
Homer E. Dale
William M. Dickson
Robert W. Dougherty
Harry G. Downie
Gary E. Duke
H. Hugh Dukes
Joseph H. Gans
Ernest D. Gardner
Patricia A. Gentry
Darrel E. Goll
E.S.E. Hafez
Peter Hall
Robert L. Hamlin
William Hansel
Virgil W. Hays
Williamina A. Himwich
T. Richard Houpt
Ainsley Iggo
Norman L. Jacobson
M.G.M. Jukes
Morley R. Kare
William R. Klemm
Kenneth McEntee
Paul F. Mercer
Andrew T. Phillipson
Jack H. Prince
Richard M. Robson
L. Evans Roth
Alvin F. Sellers
David L. Smetzer
C. Roger Smith
Sedgwick E. Smith
Charles E. Stevens
Marvin H. Stromer
S. Marsh Tenney
William J. Tietz, Jr.
A. Robert Twardock
Robert H. Wasserman
Daniel C. Williams

To H. Hugh Dukes, teacher extraordinary, benefactor to veterinarians throughout the world, this edition is gratefully dedicated.

DUKES' PHYSIOLOGY OF DOMESTIC ANIMALS

NINTH EDITION

EDITED BY

MELVIN J. SWENSON D.V.M., M.S., Ph.D.

CBS Publishers & Distributors Pvt. Ltd.

New Delhi • Bengaluru • Chennai • Kochi • Kolkata • Mumbai

Hyderabad • Nagpur • Patna • Pune • Vijayawada

ISBN: 81-239-1067-3

First Edition: 1933
Second Edition: 1934
Third Edition: 1935
Fourth Edition: 1937
Fifth Edition: 1942
Sixth Edition: 1947
Seventh Edition: 1955
Eighth Edition: 1970
Ninth Edition: 1977
Second Printing: 1982
First Indian Reprint: 1992
Reprint: 2000, 2002, 2004

Published by **Satish Kumar Jain** and produced by **Varun Jain** for
CBS Publishers & Distributors Pvt. Ltd.,
4819/XI Prahlad Street, 24 Ansari Road, Daryaganj, New Delhi - 110002
delhi@cbspd.com, cbspubs@airtelmail.in • www.cbspd.com
Ph.: 23289259, 23266861, 23266867 • Fax: 011-23243014

Corporate Office: 204 FIE, Industrial Area, Patparganj, Delhi - 110 092
Ph: 49344934 • Fax: 011-49344935
E-mail: publishing@cbspd.com • publicity@cbspd.com

Branches:

- ***Bengaluru:*** 2975, 17th Cross, K.R. Road, Bansankari 2nd Stage, Bengaluru - 70 • Ph: +91-80-26771678/79 • Fax: +91-80-26771680 E-mail: cbsbng@gmail.com, bangalore@cbspd.com
- ***Chennai:*** No. 7, Subbaraya Street, Shenoy Nagar, Chennai - 600030 Ph: +91-44-26681266, 26680620 • Fax: +91-44-42032115 E-mail: chennai@cbspd.com
- ***Kochi:*** Ashana House, 39/1904, A.M. Thomas Road, Valanjambalam, Ernakulum, Kochi • Ph: +91-484-4059061-65 Fax: +91-484-4059065 • E-mail: cochin@cbspd.com
- ***Kolkata:*** 6-B, Ground Floor, Rameshwar Shaw Road, Kolkata - 700014 Ph: +91-33-22891126/7/8 • E-mail: kolkata@cbspd.com
- ***Mumbai:*** 83-C, Dr. E. Moses Road, Worli, Mumbai - 400018 Ph: +91-9833017933, 022-24902340/41 • E-mail: mumbai@cbspd.com

Representatives:

- Hyderabad: 0-9885175004
- Patna: 0-9334159340
- Vijayawada: 0-9000660880
- Nagpur: 0-9021734563
- Pune: 0-9623451994

Printed at:
Neekunj Print Process, Delhi (India)

Contents

Preface

Since 1933, H. Hugh Dukes' *The Physiology of Domestic Animals* has been indispensable as a textbook for undergraduate veterinary and agricultural students. Graduate students and research workers in veterinary medicine and animal science have also used it extensively. Dr. Dukes kept the book up to date through seven editions, but several years ago he relinquished further responsibility for it.

The purpose of the ninth edition continues in the same tradition as that expressed in the Preface to the first: "This book, based on years of experience in the field of animal physiology, represents an attempt to provide students of veterinary medicine with a suitable textbook for their courses in physiology. I believe also, on the basis of experience, that much of the book will be useful to students of animal science. Furthermore, I venture the opinion that practitioners of veterinary medicine who wish to keep up with the trend in physiology will find the book helpful."

This new edition has been thoroughly revised, rewritten, and updated. Some chapters are completely new, and there are many new illustrations. Special attention has been given to developing the book as a teaching tool; to that end, and without loss of essential material, the text has been somewhat shortened and less emphasis has been placed on research. In addition, a more compact format makes the information more accessible to the reader.

Chapter outlines are provided to aid instructors in making specific assignments to students. In turn students should be able to find reading assignments quickly.

Many people have given assistance in the preparation of the book. It has been a joy to work closely with Dr. Dukes and to receive his wise counsel, encouragement, and suggestions. The editor appreciates especially the time and effort the contributors have devoted to their chapters; they have worked hard to provide useful and accurate information while shortening many of the chapters.

The editor obtained constructive suggestions for each chapter from faculty members at various colleges of veterinary medicine who used the eighth edition. He sent these suggestions to each contributor, and many of them have been incorporated into the ninth edition. The advice of these reviewers has been a valued service.

The staff of Cornell University Press has provided continuous help and guidance. Working with them in the preparation of the ninth edition has been a great pleasure.

The editor acknowledges with special gratitude the patience and understanding of his wife, Mildred, and his family, who have encouraged him and contributed much during the preparation of this book.

M.J.S.

Ames Iowa

The Authors

R. Scott Allen, B.S., M.S., Ph.D. Professor and Head, Department of Biochemistry, Louisiana State University (Author of Chapters 26, 27, 28, and 29)

Bengt E. Andersson, V.M.D. Professor and Head, Department of Physiology, Karolinska Institutet, Stockholm (Author of Chapter 49)

Erik Andresen, D.V.M., Ph.D. Associate Professor, Department of Animal Genetics, The Royal Veterinary and Agricultural University, Copenhagen (Author of Chapter 4)

Harpal S. Bal, B.V.Sc., M.S., Ph.D. Associate Professor, Department of Veterinary Anatomy, Pharmacology, and Physiology, College of Veterinary Medicine, Iowa State University (Author of Chapter 38)

Gary K. Beauchamp, Ph.D. Associate Member and Assistant Professor, Monell Chemical Senses Center and Department of Otorhinolaryngology and Human Communication, University of Pennsylvania (Coauthor of Chapter 51)

Emmett N. Bergman, B.S., D.V.M., M.S., Ph.D. Professor of Physiology, Department of Physiology, Biochemistry, and Pharmacology, New York State College of Veterinary Medicine, Cornell University (Author of Chapter 30)

James E. Breazile, B.S., D.V.M., Ph.D. Professor, Department of Veterinary Anatomy-Physiology, College of Veterinary Medicine, University of Missouri (Author of Chapters 42 and 44)

Marvin P. Bryant, B.S., M.S., Ph.D. Professor of Microbiology, Departments of Dairy Science and Microbiology, University of Illinois (Author of Chapter 23)

William H. Burke, B.S., M.S., Ph.D. Associate Professor, Department of Animal Science, University of Minnesota (Author of Chapter 55)

Homer E. Dale, D.V.M., M.S., Ph.D. Professor, Department of Veterinary Anatomy-Physiology, College of Veterinary Medicine, University of Missouri (Author of Chapter 31)

William M. Dickson, D.V.M., M.S., Ph.D. Professor, Department of Veterinary Anatomy, Physiology, and Pharmacology, College of Veterinary Medicine, Washington State University (Author of Chapter 52)

Robert W. Dougherty, B.S., D.V.M., M.S. Formerly Head, Physiopathology Laboratory, National Animal Disease Center, presently Collaborator, NADC (Author of Chapter 24)

Harry G. Downie, D.V.M., M.V.Sc., M.S., Ph.D. Professor and Chairman, Department of Biomedical Sciences, Ontario Veterinary College, University of Guelph (Coauthor of Chapter 3)

Gary E. Duke, B.A., M.S., Ph.D. Associate Professor, Department of Veterinary Biology, College of Veterinary Medicine, University of Minnesota (Author of Chapters 16 and 25)

H. Hugh Dukes, B.S., D.V.M., M.S., D.H.C., D.Sc. (Hon.). Professor of Veterinary Physiology, Emeritus, Cornell University (Author of Appendix and first seven editions)

Joseph H. Gans, V.M.D., Ph.D. Professor, Department of Pharmacology, College of Medicine, University of Vermont (Senior author of Chapter 37)

Ernest D. Gardner, B.Sc., M.D. Professor of Neurology, Orthopaedic Surgery, and Human Anatomy, Department of Neurology, College of Medicine, University of California, Davis (Author of Chapter 35)

Patricia A. Gentry, B.Sc., Ph.D. Associate Professor, Department of Biomedical Sciences, Ontario Veterinary College, University of Guelph (Senior author of Chapter 3)

Darrel E. Goll, B.S., M.S., Ph.D. Professor and Head, Department of Nutrition and Food Science, University of Arizona (Senior author of Chapter 39)

E.S.E. Hafez, Ph.D. (Cantab.). Professor, Department of Gynecology-Obstetrics, School of Medicine, Wayne State University (Author of Chapter 47)

Peter Hall, M.B., Ch.B., F.F.A.R.C.S. Associate Professor, Department of Physiology and Biophysics, College of Veterinary Medicine and Biomedical Sciences, Colorado State University (Coauthor of Chapter 48)

Robert L. Hamlin, B.S., D.V.M., M.S., Ph.D. Professor, Department of Veterinary Physiology and Pharmacology, College of Veterinary Medicine, Ohio State University (Senior author of Chapters 5, 6, and 7 and coauthor of Chapters 8, 9, 10, 11, 12, and 13)

William Hansel, B.S., M.S., Ph.D. Professor of Animal Physiology, Department of Animal Science, Cornell University (Senior author of Chapters 53 and 54)

Virgil W. Hays, B.S., Ph.D. Professor and Chairman, Department of Animal Sciences, University of Kentucky (Senior author of Chapter 33)

Williamina A. Himwich, B.S., M.S., Ph.D. Research Professor of Psychiatry and Professor of Biochemistry, Departments of Biochemistry and Psychiatry, College of Medicine, University of Nebraska (Author of Chapter 14)

T. Richard Houpt, V.M.D., M.S., Ph.D. Professor of Veterinary Physiology, Department of Physiology, Biochemistry, and Pharmacology, New York State College of Veterinary Medicine, Cornell University (Author of Chapter 36)

Ainsley Iggo, B.Sc., M.Agr.Sc., D.Sc., Ph.D., F.R.S.E. Professor and Dean, Department of Veterinary Physiology, Royal (Dick) School of Veterinary Studies, University of Edinburgh (Author of Chapters 41 and 43)

Norman L. Jacobson, B.S., M.S., Ph.D. Professor of Animal Science, Department of Animal Science, Associate Dean, Graduate College, Iowa State University (Author of Chapter 56)

M.G.M. Jukes, M.A., B.Sc., D.M. (Oxon.). Professor of Veterinary Physiology, Department of Physiology, Royal Veterinary College, University of London (Author of Chapter 46)

Morley R. Kare, B.S.A., M.S.A., Ph.D. Professor of Physiology and Director, Monell Chemical Senses Center, University of Pennsylvania (Senior author of Chapter 51)

William R. Klemm, D.V.M., Ph.D. Professor, Department of Biology, Texas A & M University (Author of Chapters 40 and 45)

Kenneth McEntee, D.V.M. Professor of Veterinary Pathology, Department of Large Animal Medicine, Obstetrics, and Surgery, New York State College of Veterinary Medicine, Cornell University (Coauthor of Chapters 53 and 54)

Paul F. Mercer, D.V.M., Ph.D. Associate Professor, Department of Physiology, University of Western Ontario (Coauthor of Chapter 37)

Andrew T. Phillipson, M.A., Ph.D., M.R.C.V.S., F.R.S.E. Late Professor of Veterinary Clinical Studies, Department of Clinical Veterinary Medicine, School of Veterinary Medicine, University of Cambridge. Deceased 1977. (Author of Chapter 22)

Jack H. Prince, F.B.O.A., F.R.M.S., F.Z.S. Balgowlah, N.S.W. Formerly Associate Professor, Department of Ophthalmology and Institute for Research in Vision, Ohio State University (Author of Chapter 50)

Richard M. Robson, B.S., M.S., Ph.D. Associate Professor, Departments of Animal Science and Biochemistry and Biophysics, Iowa State University (Coauthor of Chapter 39)

L. Evans Roth, A.B., M.S., Ph.D. Vice Chancellor for Graduate Studies and Research, University of Tennessee (Senior author of Chapter 1)

Alvin F. Sellers, V.M.D., M.S., Ph.D. Professor of Physiology, Associate Dean for Research, New York State College of Veterinary Medicine, Cornell University (Author of Chapters 19, 20, and 21 and coauthor of Chapter 17)

David L. Smetzer, B.S., D.V.M., M.S., Ph.D. Associate Professor, Department of Veterinary Anatomy, Physiology, and Pharmacology, College of Veterinary Medicine, University of Illinois (Senior author of Chapter 8)

C. Roger Smith, D.V.M., M.Sc., Ph.D. Professor and Dean, College of Veterinary Medicine, Ohio State University (Senior author of Chapters 9, 10, 11, 12, and 13 and coauthor of Chapters 5, 6, 7, and 8)

Sedgwick E. Smith, B.S., Ph.D. Professor, Department of Animal Science, Cornell University (Author of Chapter 32)

Charles E. Stevens, B.S., D.V.M., M.S., Ph.D. Professor and Chairman, Department of Physiology, Biochemistry, and Pharmacology, New York State College of Veterinary Medicine, Cornell University (Author of Chapter 18 and senior author of Chapter 17)

Marvin H. Stromer, B.S., Ph.D. Professor, Departments of Animal Science and Food Technology, Iowa State University (Coauthor of Chapter 39)

Melvin J. Swenson, D.V.M., M.S., Ph.D. Professor, Department of Veterinary Anatomy, Pharmacology, and Physiology, College of Veterinary Medicine, Iowa State University (Author of Chapter 2, coauthor of Chapter 33, and editor)

S. Marsh Tenney, A.B., M.D. Professor and Chairman, Department of Physiology, Dartmouth Medical School (Author of Chapter 15)

William J. Tietz, Jr., B.A., M.S., D.V.M., Ph.D. Professor and Dean, College of Veterinary Medicine and Biomedical Sciences, Colorado State University (Senior author of Chapter 48)

A. Robert Twardock, B.S., D.V.M., Ph.D. Professor of Veterinary Physiology, Associate Dean for Academic Affairs, College of Veterinary Medicine, University of Illinois (Author of Chapter 57)

Robert H. Wasserman, B.S., M.S., Ph.D. Professor, Department of Physical Biology, New York State College of Veterinary Medicine, Cornell University (Author of Chapter 34)

Daniel C. Williams, B.S., Ph.D. Senior Electron Microscopist, Lilly Research Laboratories, Eli Lilly & Co. (Coauthor of Chapter 1)

DUKES' PHYSIOLOGY OF DOMESTIC ANIMALS | NINTH EDITION

CHAPTER 1

Introduction: Intracellular Organization and Physiology

by L. Evans Roth and Daniel C. Williams

The cell is the basic unit of life. All living cells display a fundamental similarity, since each consists of a nucleus that directs its complex activity, cytoplasm that carries this activity out, and membranes that enclose and divide it. At the simplest level, in such organisms as bacteria and protozoa, a single microscopic cell carries on all the functions by which life is defined—the conversion of food into energy, growth, and reproduction. At higher levels cells are combined in specialized tissues that permit the whole organism to sustain life, and a creature such as man contains many millions of them. But the functions of all its specialized systems, such as respiration and circulation, are still realized at the level of the cell. It is here that the blood, or specifically the cellular elements in it, delivers its oxygen and picks up its waste; it is here that the basic metabolic processes of the organism, including the synthesis of enormously complicated molecules, are performed.

Thus it is that the student must first understand the cell and how it works before he or she can understand the functioning of an organ such as the heart or liver, or of a whole organism or of a whole species.

THE CELL CONCEPT

The development of cell theory in the eighteenth and nineteenth centuries caused biological research to flourish at all levels. Early development of the cell concept centered around the studies of the German physiologist Johannes Müller (1801–1858). His student Theodor Schwann in 1830, at the age of 29, synthesized the work of earlier and contemporary scientists—among them, Robert Hooke, Lorenz Oken, Robert Brown, and M.J. Schleiden—in a definitive formulation of cell theory, demonstrating that the cell is the basis of animal as well as plant tissue. Schwann also was one of the first to consider the physicochemical level of life processes. He demanded a modification of vitalism (the belief that a vital principle apart from such processes sparked life) toward the modern philosophical position that the body functions as a machine with interdependent parts—a view so effectively championed by the French physiologist Claude Bernard. Albert von Kölliker, also Müller's student, applied the cell concept to embryology and histology and studied cell duplication, which later was termed *mitosis* by another German, Walther Flemming. During the same period, Rudolf Virchow extended the cell concept and applied it to pathology, while Theodor Boveri and Oskar Hertwig developed basic cell studies on chromosomes and fertilization. E.B. Wilson, the American zoologist noted for his work on the function of the cell in heredity, summarized the progress in cell research in his classic and still useful book *The Cell in Development and Heredity* (1928).

As new techniques are the foundations on which new concepts are built, so nineteenth-century biologists were dependent on developments in optics. The pioneering seventeenth-century work of Marcello Malpighi in Italy, Antony van Leeuwenhoek and Jan Swammerdam in Holland, and Robert Hooke in England developed the light microscope to the degree necessary for making the observations on which Schwann's concept was later based. In 1886 Ernst Abbe and Carl Zeiss developed much improved lenses, the apochromat objectives, that allowed detailed studies of pathology and intracellular structure. Gardner (1964) and Hughes (1959) give full accounts of these historical developments.

Technical developments since 1925 similarly are the basis for an information explosion that has produced highly modified and elaborated cell concepts. The phase-contrast microscope, developed by Zernicke, allowed more careful study of living cells; interference, polarizing, and ultraviolet microscopes have allowed other uniquely beneficial observations. Electron microscopy is now being developed through high-voltage instruments (Glauert 1974) and for element analysis. Many non-microscopic methods have also been vitally important, for example, X-ray diffraction, cell fractionation, microelectrical measurement, and in vitro biochemistry. Methods for laboratory culture of both cells and tissues have also opened many new avenues of research and diagnosis.

The instruments most significant in cell research have been the electron microscopes, which provide a vital link between histological and molecular levels of structure. Two types of electron microscopes are used, the scanning electron microscope (SEM) and the transmission electron microscope (TEM). Both image electrons rather than light and thus achieve increased resolution over the light microscope. The SEM has greater depth of field and is used primarily for observing surfaces (Fig. 1.1). It has a resolution limit of about 20 nm (1 nm, or nanometer, equals 10^{-9} meters), whereas the TEM has significantly greater resolving power (about 1 nm). Thereby small molecular aggregates and macromolecules may be visualized directly, and precise descriptions of normal and altered cell organelles can be made and compared. (An organelle is a part of a cell having specific functions, distinctive chemical constituents, and characteristic morphology; an organelle is to a cell as an organ is to an animal.)

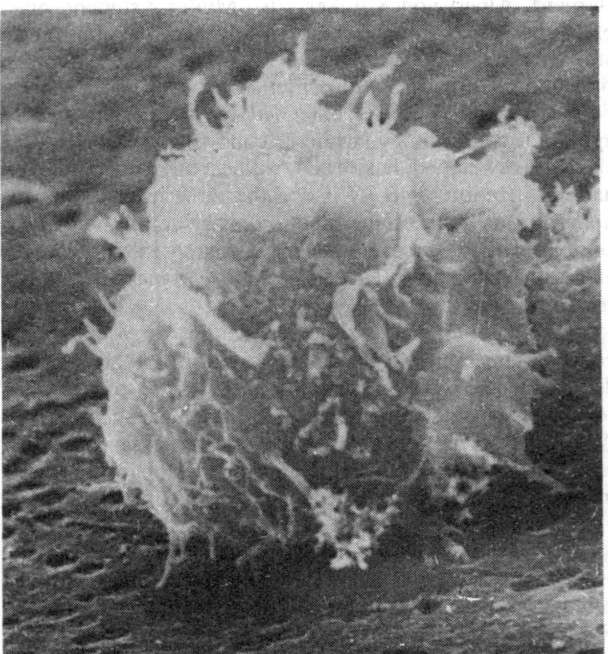

Figure 1.1. Scanning electron micrograph of a whole cultured human lymphocyte. Many cells show both villuslike and sheetlike protrusions of their surfaces, and changes in these surface elaborations are constantly taking place. ×3000; micrograph by L.E. Roth and R.S. Slesinski.

Since the cell is such a highly organized unit of molecular interaction and production, physiological and molecular precision in research and definition is both a modern necessity and a modern achievement. And many of these techniques were used in the work recognized by the Nobel Prize in Physiology in 1974. The award went to Albert Claude, Christian deDuve, and George Palade for their elucidation of cytoplasmic functions.

Since the cell is the basic unit of life, an understanding of the organization of cells is valuable preparation for studying the physiology of organs and organisms. Thus at the beginning it is helpful to present the structure of cells along with certain relevant physiological phenomena and biological principles.

THE EUCARYOTIC CELL

The typical cell of the metazoa or multicellular animals is the eucaryotic cell (*eu,* good; *karyo,* nucleus; i.e. having a visible nucleus). The nucleus is large, membrane-limited, and centrally located (Fig. 1.2 N). Surrounding it is the cytoplasm which contains numerous organelles and fills the remainder of the cell. Thus the eucaryotic cell is clearly divided into a nucleus and cytoplasm and into still other, smaller enclosures by membrane-partitions. In fact, one of the most conspicuous features of these cells is the ubiquity of membranes that form function-limiting compartments.

Membrane systems

The cell boundary is usually formed by a single membrane, the plasma membrane (Fig. 1.2 PM), which is the barrier between the surrounding fluid and the cytoplasm. At higher magnification, this membrane has the appearance of two dark lines uniformly separated by a light space of similar width; the entire membrane is usually no more than 10 nm thick but still has a considerable tensile strength and is similar in appearance to intracellular membranes (Fig. 1.3). The plasma membrane may be joined to its neighboring cell membrane by anchoring structures called junctional complexes.

The inner boundary of the cytoplasm is formed by two membranes that are separated by a space of variable width and that are together called the nuclear envelope (Fig. 1.2 E). These two membranes join at many points resulting in pores of about 40 nm diameter (Figs. 1.3, 1.7, P), each of which contains a pipelike annulus. These pores and their annuli are probably closed much of the time by single membranes but allow passage of selective ions and molecules. In thin sections, the nucleus appears to be enveloped by two dark lines when cross sectioned

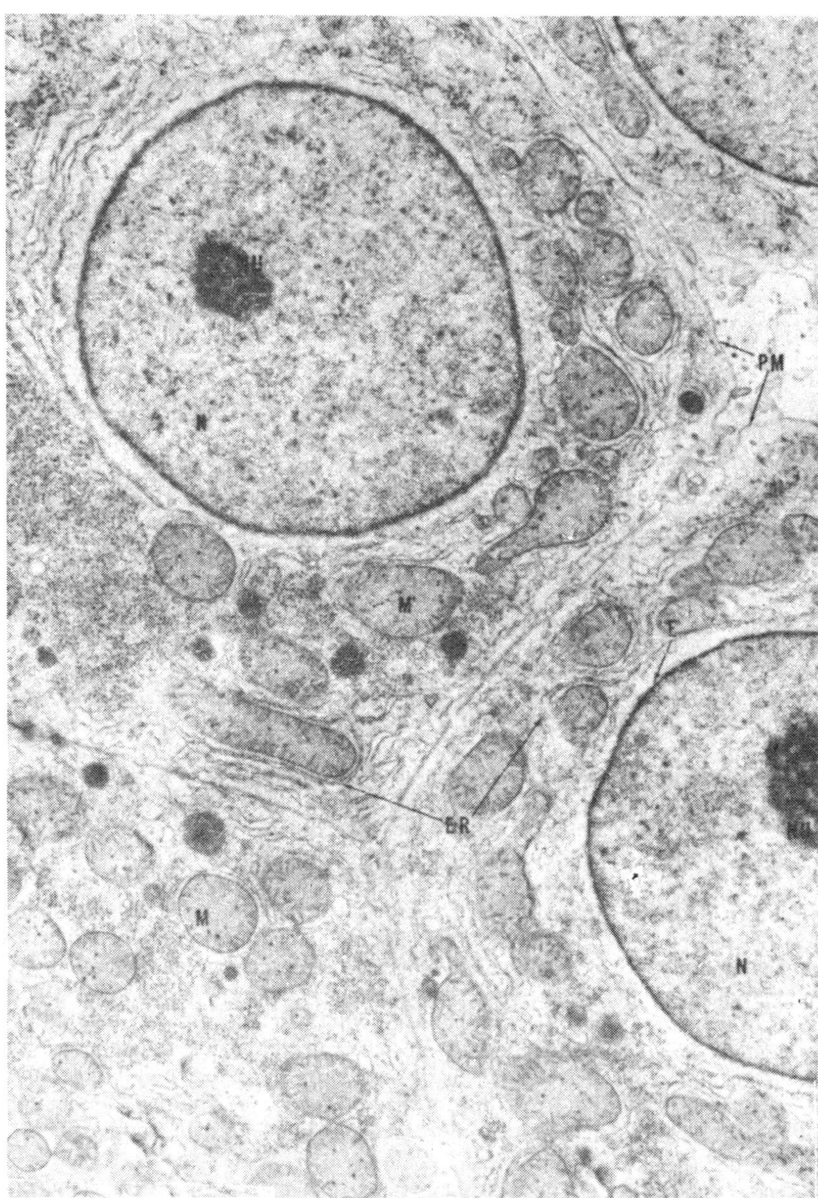

Figure 1.2. A transmission electron micrograph of a thin section showing the organelles of typical cells. The large circles are nuclei (N) with their nucleoli (NU) and nuclear envelope (E). In the cytoplasm, numerous mitochondria (M), the endoplasmic reticulum (ER), and granular regions of carbohydrate storage are visible. The cell boundary is the plasma membrane (PM). From normal dog liver ×8000. (From Stein, Richter, and Brynjolfsson 1967, *Exp. Mol. Path.* 5:195–224.)

(Fig. 1.3) or by a series of circles (the annuli) when tangentially sectioned (Fig. 1.4 EF). If the plane of section is oblique, the envelope is not seen but is still present.

The cytoplasm, lying between the plasma membrane and the nuclear envelope, has several important organelles that are essentially membrane-bounded compartments of smaller size and specialized function. Most conspicuous are mitochondria (Figs. 1.2, 1.7, M), which are usually 0.3–2.0 μ in size, are rather dense, and are numerous in all cells utilizing oxygen. Each mitochondrion has two membranes: the internal one folded into lamellae called cristae or tubules (unlettered arrows) and the external one more smoothly contoured. Internally a space enclosed by both membranes is filled with a finely granular matrix (Figs. 1.4, 1.5, MS).

Mitochondria are the sites for numerous biochemical reactions including amino acid and fatty acid catabolism, the oxidative reactions of the Krebs citric acid cycle, respiratory electron transport, and oxidative phosphoryla-

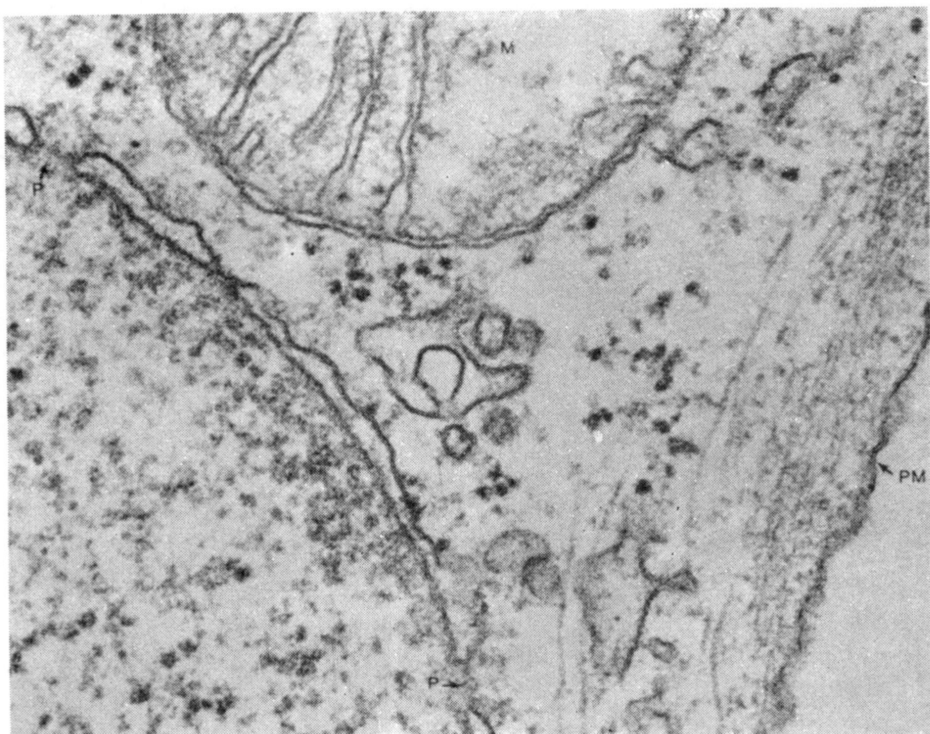

Figure 1.3. Transmission electron micrograph of a portion of a thin section of a cultured mouse fibroblast. The nucleus at the lower left has pores (P) in its nuclear envelope. A portion of a mitochondrion at the top (M) shows typical membrane configurations and a central matrix. To the right is the plasma membrane (PM) of the cell containing numerous microfilaments. ×20,400; micrograph by D.C. Williams.

tion. As a result of these reactions, mitochondria are the major producers of the high-energy compound adenosine triphosphate in aerobically grown cells. Separation of these reactions is maintained by localizing them to specific areas within the mitochondrion (Harmon et al. 1974); the Krebs cycle enzymes and fatty acid oxidation enzymes are found in the matrix, the electron-transport chain is found on the inner membrane, and monoamine oxidase is associated with the outer mitochondrial membrane. In addition to its enzymatic components, the mitochondrial matrix also has been shown to contain genetic material (DNA) and the necessary cellular machinery for protein synthesis (DeRobertis 1970, Racker 1970).

Another prominent membrane-bounded organelle associated with enzymatic activity is the lysosome (Fig. 1.6). Quite variable in size and shape, they are bounded by a single membrane, generally stained electron dense by TEM procedures, and are characterized by the presence of hydrolytic enzymes. They are best distinguished from other membrane-bounded vesicular organelles by the presence of enzymes such as acid phosphatase. Lysosomes are thought to be sites of intracellular digestion and storage of insoluble material. In addition to their presence in tissues of an endocytotic nature (e.g. macrophages or osteoclasts) where they function in the digestion of extracellular material, they may also function in autolysis (self-digestion) of other organelles within the cell. Thus their acccumulation may be significant in aging and pathology relating to tissues such as myocardium, liver, and kidney (Allison 1967).

Membrane-enclosed sacs (vesicles or vacuoles) are found in animal tissues. These are often associated with the storage or secretion of specific products within the cell, e.g. yolk granules, pigment granules, mucous droplets, or zymogen granules. Nonmembrane-bounded storage materials such as glycogen or lipid droplets are also frequently found within some cell types. In addition, however, there are other membraneous organelles within the cell which do not form a discrete body, but rather have the form of membrane arrays. The two most important are the Golgi apparatus and the endoplasmic reticulum.

The Golgi apparatus is composed of several flattened, often cup-shaped, closely stacked membranes that are closed vesicles. At their edges, small spherical vesicles are usually plentiful (Fig. 1.7 G). The Golgi apparatus functions in the packaging of materials into membrane-bounded vesicles for secretion (e.g. zymogen granules, mucous droplets) and for intracellular uses (e.g. yolk granules, lysosomes, pigment granules); in polysaccharide synthesis and the coupling of polysaccharides to proteins; and, in plant cells, for the formation of the cell plate during cell division (Beams and Kessel 1968).

The primary site of cytoplasmic protein synthesis is the

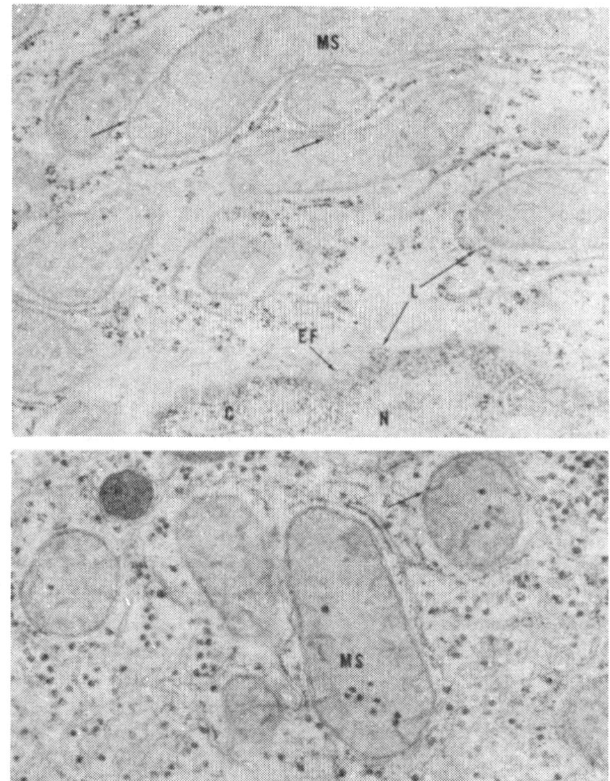

Figures 1.4 (above) and 1.5 (below). The outer mitochondrion membrane is smooth, while the inner is folded into lamellae called cristae (unlettered arrows); the result is several membrane surfaces serving as reaction sites, an intracristal space between the membranes, and an intramitochondrial space (MS). The endoplasmic reticulum is present both as rough surfaced (above) and smooth surfaced (ER, below); ribosomes in polysome configurations are included (L). The nuclear envelope sectioned tangentially, above, shows the annuli (EF) contained within the pores, and surrounds the nucleus (N), with its DNA-containing chromatin (C). From normal dog liver × 19,525 and 17,435 respectively; micrographs by W.R. Richter.

ribosome. These small organelles are about 20 nm in diameter, contain concentrations of ribose nucleic acid (RNA) as high as 60 percent, and are present in high numbers either on membranes for the production of exported proteins, or free in the cytoplasm for the production of internally used proteins. In both cases, the ribosome is the place where two other RNA's converge and result in protein synthesis by their interaction. The first of these two is transfer-RNA, which carries amino acids that it has activated for assembly into proteins; the second is messenger-RNA, which carries the code to determine the sequence of amino acids and which therefore specifies what protein will be produced. Several ribosomes may use the same messenger-RNA molecule at once, so that linear or circular associations result, which are called polyribosomes and look like beads on a string (Fig. 1.4 L).

In the endoplasmic reticulum membranes are elaborated in the inner cytoplasm of certain cells to form a continuous reticulum (Porter 1953). Many small, dense ribosomes then grow on these membrane surfaces and contribute to the synthesis and export of protein (Siekevitz and Palade 1959; Ernster, Siekevitz, and Palade 1962). The granular or rough endoplasmic reticulum appears as flattened membrane sacs with attached ribo-

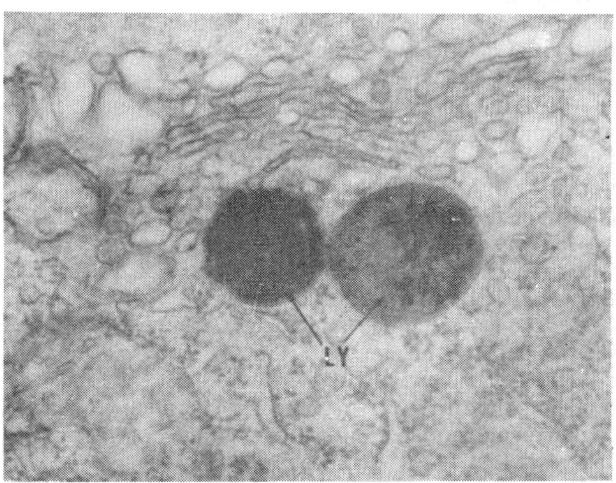

Figure 1.6. Lysosomes (LY) are membrane-bounded compartments for intracellular digestion. The single membrane encloses material whose origin is no longer recognizable here. From mouse liver × 50,000; micrograph by T.F. McDonald.

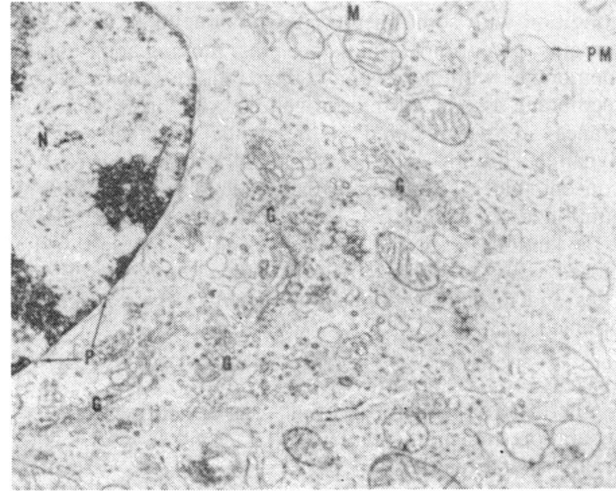

Figure 1.7. The Golgi apparatus (G), composed of numerous flattened vesicles, characteristically occupies a position near the nucleus (N). Pores (P) in the envelope, the plasma membrane (PM), and mitochondria (M) are also shown. Cultured cell from bovine testis × 12,770; micrograph by R.A. Jenkins.

somes (Figs. 1.2, 1.5, ER). It is highly developed in liver and pancreatic exocrine cells. The smooth (or agranular) endoplasmic reticulum is more tubular in form and lacks attached ribosomes (Fig. 1.5 ER). It is particularly well developed in cells producing steroid hormones, synthesizing lipids, and inactivating certain drugs.

Protein synthesized at ribosomes moves across the reticulum membrane and accumulates in the lumen. Passage of the protein through the reticulum follows and includes a progressive agglomeration into formed granules by the Golgi apparatus, from which the protein moves out of the cell. This sequence is one of the major biological discoveries of the last decade (Bosch 1972, Nanninga 1973).

A variety of both lipids and proteins is present in these membrane systems; lipid molecules outnumber protein but, since the protein molecules are larger, their contribution is nearly equal. Carbohydrates are also present (Nicholson and Singer 1974, Marchesi et al. 1972).

Membranes have a relatively high electrical resistance, withstand mechanical disruption well, and can be stretched to several times their normal dimension. Certain enzymes affect their structural integrity. Charges are present on most membranes, resulting in a small potential, the zeta potential, between the surface and the surrounding fluid; the plasma membrane usually carries a negative charge, while internal membranes carry positive charges.

The most widely accepted membrane model is the fluid mosaic model (Singer and Nicholson 1972). It depicts a lipid bilayer with the hydrophobic hydrocarbon ends inside and the polar regions at the membrane surfaces. The bilayer is thought to be in a relatively fluid and dynamic condition with some membrane components (e.g. glycoproteins, glycolipids, lipids, proteins) moving about in the membrane, while others have their mobility restricted by membrane-associated interior cellular structures. If membranes are remembered as molecular arrangements in dynamic equilibrium, the above information conveys a concept that is useful even though it is probably highly simplified (Capaldi 1974, Roth et al. 1971, Steck 1974).

To summarize, in the eucaryotic cell, membranes form closed vesicles within closed systems in several organelles and must be thought of as aggregates of precisely oriented molecules.

Physiology of membranes

There are six generalized functions of cell membranes: separation, transport, regulation, structural support, coordination, and fusion.

Membranes form compartments that *separate* functional areas within the cell. In the endoplasmic reticulum, membranes are involved in the separation of synthesized protein from the site of synthesis in ribosomes; they remove the reaction product so that the reaction continues without inhibition. The nuclear envelope also functions as a separating barrier controlling the entry of messenger-RNA into the cytoplasm and thereby exerting a controlling influence on protein synthesis. The nuclear envelope is important in maintaining and perhaps producing considerably different conditions of pH, ion concentration, gelation, and concentrations of several compounds between the cytoplasm and nucleoplasm. In this regard, the pores in the nuclear envelope are probably open only infrequently.

Although membranes are barriers, they also function in *transport*. Ions and molecules may pass through a membrane with varying degrees of ease. Diffusion, charge interaction, and active ion passage against concentration gradients are all involved. Transport should be considered in terms of passage through pores as needed, of lipoidal substances being dissolved in or fusing with the lipids of membranes, of reactions with membrane-bounded proteins which may act as carriers, or of combinations of these three. The selectivity of transport must be emphasized; in addition, the membrane is actively involved, so that energy is used in some transport phenomena (see Chapter 26).

Recent studies have shown how membranes contribute toward the *regulation* of biological processes. Studies of energy transformations involving mitochondria, chloroplasts, and visual photoreceptors and the study of the endoplasmic reticulum suggest that chemical reactions take place at membrane surfaces or perhaps within membranes. The inference is that membranes provide, either internally or immediately surrounding themselves, specialized environments allowing or favoring reactions that cannot be carried out in typical cellular conditions. For example, membrane-associated pH gradients probably exist. In addition, membranes may provide further for fixed arrangements or critical spatial concentrations of enzymes so that a multistep synthesis may follow a "production line."

Membranes also contribute to regulation when they restrict the access of compounds to reactive sites. For example, the nuclear envelope serves as a barrier to the entry into the cytoplasm of compounds synthesized intranuclearly. Similarly, regulative functions are performed by membrane systems in striated muscle (see Huxley 1971 and Chapter 39).

Another regulative capacity of membranes relates to mitosis and cellular motility. In a way not yet understood, contact of one cell with another has an inhibitory effect on mitosis; this phenomenon, called contact inhibition, is being carefully studied, since the absence of such inhibition is a characteristic of cells cultured from malignant tumors (Pollack and Hough 1974).

Membranes also provide *structural support* and anchor intracellular structures. Studies of striated muscle show that intracellular filament bundles are anchored to membranes; the continuous fibers thus formed are many cells long but function as a single unit. Similarly, cells in metazoan organs are attached firmly to each other by membrane specializations called junctional complexes (Goodenough and Revel 1970).

Enough information is available to infer that membranes serve in *coordination* (Naitoh and Echert 1969). The concept of semiconduction, important in physics and engineering, has been applied to biology with the result that numerous vital biological compounds have been shown to have semiconductor capabilities.

The ease and frequency with which membranes *fuse* and separate lead to several functional involvements. There is, in fact, the inference that all membranous structures are derived from pre-existing membranes by pinching off and fusing. Although membrane surfaces may enlarge often and quickly by the apparent insertion of molecules into existing membranes, no cases are yet demonstrated where any type of membranous vesicle arises *de novo*. Pinocytosis or, as it was first understood, cell drinking, is a remarkable case of membrane pinching-off that is important for intake of ionized solutes. For example, Roth (1960) has shown its importance in emptying the food vacuoles of amebas and suggests the necessity for each square micron of vacuole membrane to be replaced each minute. The plasma membrane is able to give off many small vesicles which are carried into the cytoplasm or transported through the cell, as in capillary walls (Fig. 1.8), and released by fusion with the plasma membrane on the other side. Of course, the material is no more accessible to the cytoplasm in small vesicles, but more surface is available for transport and these

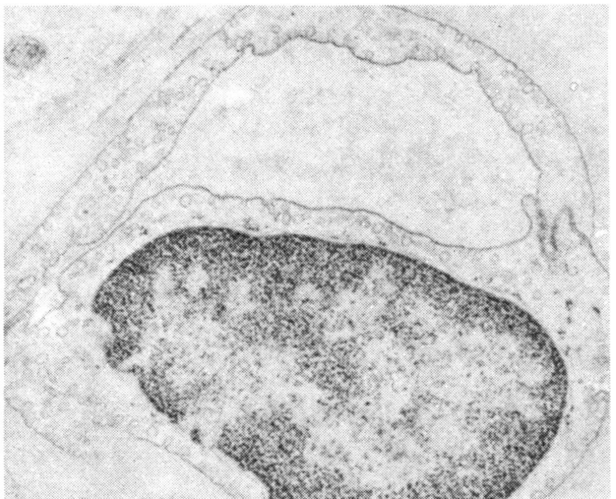

Figure 1.8. Membranes are dynamic and capable of pinching off and fusing. Here numerous vesicles have been pinched off by the process of pinocytosis and are carrying material across a capillary wall. From dog muscle × 7600; micrograph by W.R. Richter.

vesicles may undergo membrane changes allowing different transport properties.

Interestingly, the fertilization of an egg by a sperm is ultimately dependent on membrane fusion. In marine invertebrates, two steps of membrane fusion result in the plasma membrane of the zygote incorporating both the sperm plasma membrane and the membrane of another vesicle, the acrosome, that originated from the Golgi apparatus of the spermatocyte. A common cytoplasm forms and contains the two nuclei which move together and fuse, probably again by membrane fusion.

These cases of membranes joining are basically end-to-end fusions. Less frequently, lamination by surface fusion may also take place and is important in the many-layered myelin sheath of nerve cells. Here membranes are apparently wrapped around the axon in "jelly-roll" fashion and fuse their surfaces on contact. In contrast to this phenomenon, it should be emphasized that surface contact of membranes does not usually result in fusion.

The coatings of the exterior surfaces are currently being studied in several contexts. Their importance in embryonic processes of cell recognition and inhibitory control of cell division is now well established (Bernfield et al. 1972, Toole and Gross 1971). Such coatings are characteristically modified, usually reduced, in transformed cells cultured from malignant tissue (Warren et al. 1972) and apparently need to be modified in order for the membrane fusion of certain viruses with their host cells to achieve infection (Poste 1972). Further evidence shows that numerous normal processes such as cell fusion of gametes at fertilization may also depend on such surface modifications, either by removal of coatings from mature cell surfaces or by formation of nascent membrane areas that do not yet have their full coating (Vollet and Roth 1974).

Additional functions of membranes are transport and electrical conduction (see Chapters 39, 40).

Movement or filament systems

Movement systems are intracellular, filament arrays. All major movement systems show remarkably similar organization.

The movement system studied in greatest detail is striated muscle (see Chapter 39). This muscle is composed primarily of two kinds of filaments, the primary thick, myosin-containing filament and the more numerous, thinner, actin-containing, secondary filament. A precise arrangement is often present with six secondary filaments evenly spaced around each primary one. The feature that distinguishes this system from other movement systems is that neither filament is thought to be continuous through the sarcomere, the functional unit of striated muscle.

Actin is also thought to be the major component in microfilament aggregations (Fig. 1.9). The constriction

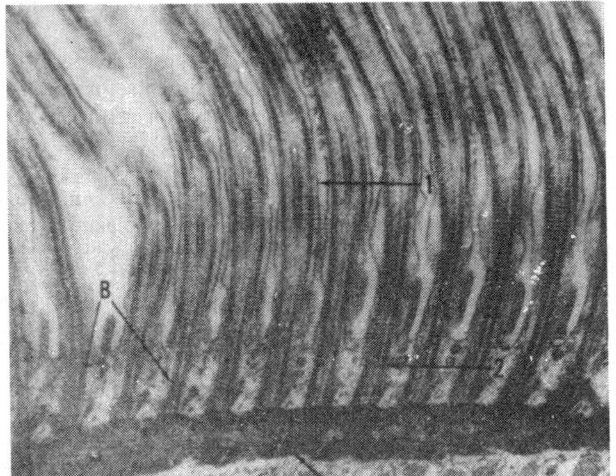

Figure 1.9. Cilia are filament-containing organelles of movement. They are anchored in the cytoplasm by their basal bodies (B) which are also attached to rootlets (RO). The shaft is about five times as long as indicated, beats with a whiplike action, and is covered by a membrane. Arrow 1 indicates the approximate level of the cross sections in Fig. 1.10 and arrow 2 the level of cross sections in Fig. 1.11. × 24,600. (Reprinted by permission of The Rockefeller Institute Press, from L.E. Roth and Y. Shigenaka 1964, *J. Cell Biol.* 20:249–70.)

furrow in cell division has been shown to contain a microfilament array that probably functions as a sphincter (Schroeder 1972). Microfilaments also appear as linear arrays and networks in the cytoplasm of cells that are moving and that are growing long nerve axons (Yamada et al. 1970) and are involved in cytoplasmic streaming. Presumably most of these systems participate in contractile activity via a sliding interaction in ways similar to those now understood for striated muscle (Spooner 1975, Murray and Weber 1974).

The other component of skeletal muscle, myosin, is also found in some of these filament systems (Nachmias 1972). It is highly significant, however, that both actin and myosin are present, from amebas and slime molds to mammals, in comparatively few array patterns.

The ubiquity and recurrence of certain molecules and structural and biochemical relationships are the basis for the principle of minimal mechanisms in physiology. When subcellular levels are studied, so many common molecules, metabolic pathways, and cell structures are found that an overwhelming unity of life processes is obvious; examples are the genetic code, the mechanism of protein synthesis, many biochemical reactions, and ubiquitous cell structures and organelles.

Another ubiquitous organelle is the microtubule composed of tubulin, a molecule rather similar to actin. In contrast to skeletal muscle, where filaments are not continuous across a functional unit, microtubules are usually uninterrupted along their lengths. For example, cilia in protozoa and metazoan epithelia and flagella in protozoa and sperm tails are essentially continuous from base to tip. Cilia and flagella are usually about one-half micron in diameter, are several to many microns long (Fig. 1.9), and contain a precise filamentous complement that is almost identical in all animal phyla except one and in many plant genera (Satir 1974). The shaft has two types of microtubules: nine peripheral ones of essentially doublet cross section and two central filaments of circular cross section (Fig. 1.10). An extension of the plasma membrane surrounds the microtubules. The cilium is anchored by being inserted about one micron in the cell (Fig. 1.9 B); this basal body is composed of extensions of only

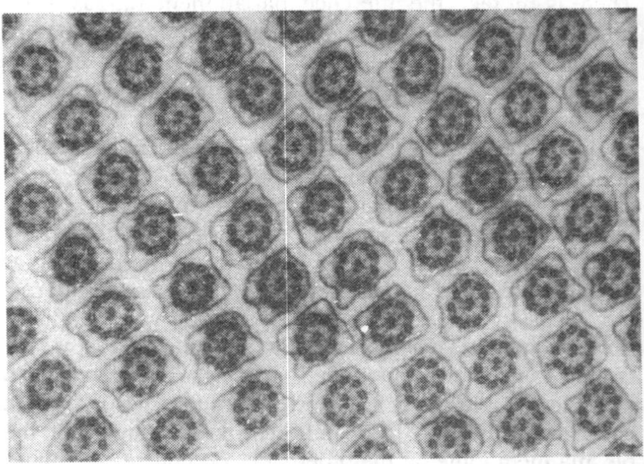

Figure 1.10. Cross sections of cilia showing the regularity of their arrangement and of filament grouping. Each cilium is composed of a membrane which appears as two parallel lines, of nine peripheral filaments each with a figure-eight cross section, and of two central filaments with circular cross section. From the rumen protozoan, *Diplodinium ecaudatum*, × 36,900; micrograph by L.E. Roth.

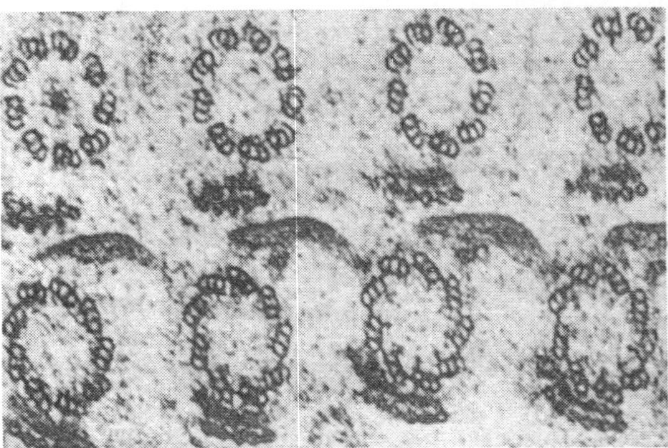

Figure 1.11. Cross sections of ciliary bases showing that each peripheral filament is now triplet in cross section and that the central filaments are missing. *Ophryoscolex* = 77,900. (Reprinted by permission of The Rockefeller Institute Press, from L.E. Roth and Y. Shigenaka 1964, *J. Cell Biol.* 20:249–70.)

the peripheral microtubules, each of which is now tripartite (Figs. 1.9, 1.11). At their tips, cilia taper as each peripheral microtubule is reduced to a circular cross section and then ends; thus peripheral microtubules are triplet, doublet, and circular in cross section from base to tip.

Another microtubular organelle is the centriole (Figs. 1.12, 1.14) found at the poles in certain types of dividing cells. A remarkable similarity exists between the structure in the basal bodies of cilia (Fig. 1.11) and in centrioles.

Extending as rootlets from many cilia are microtubules

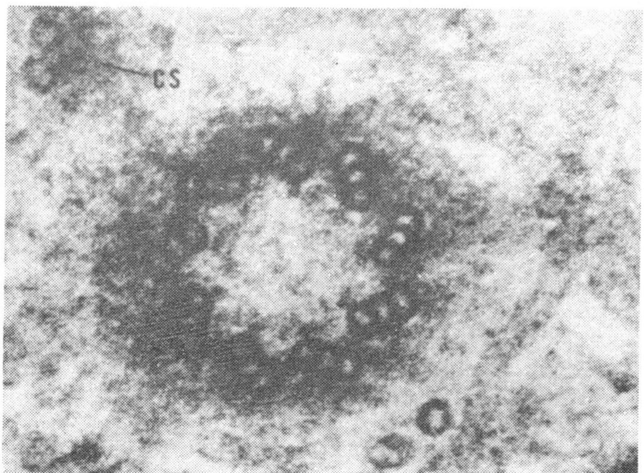

Figure 1.12. Cross section of a centriole showing its nine-part structure similar to that of ciliary basal bodies. In addition, centrioles have satellites (CS) which are thought to be the focal points of filaments as the centriole functions in the mitotic apparatus (see Fig. 1.13). From chick embryo pancreas × 147,600; micrograph by J. Andre.

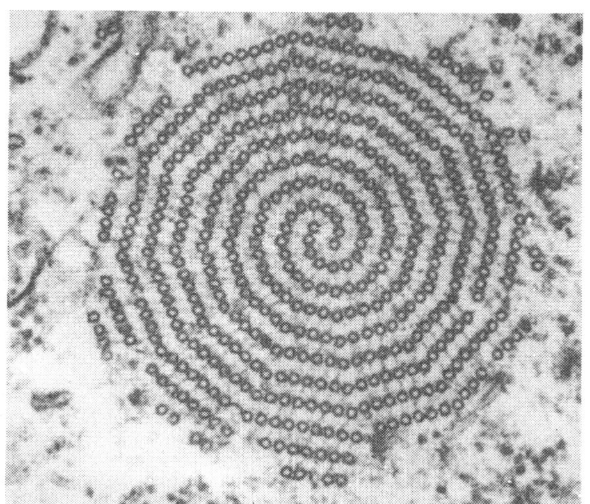

Figure 1.13. Microtubules in cytoplasm as found in numerous cells. From the fresh-water protozoan, *Echinosphaerium nucleofilum*, × 93,000; micrograph by L.E. Roth.

of circular cross section with diameters of 15–22 nm and with arrangements in bundles or sheets and in more random patterns (Fig. 1.13). They are being found in increasing numbers in protozoa, spermatozoa, nerve axons, platelets, erythrocytes, and embryonic movement systems, where they seem to be involved in movement or maintenance of form. Bacterial flagella are also microtubules of this general type.

All of these microtubules are quite stable to fixation in alkaline osmium-tetroxide solutions for electron microscopy. However, another group of microtubules is much more labile, requires additional fixation conditions with aldehydes, and is degradable by hydrostatic pressure, near-freezing temperatures, and treatment with colchicine, vincristine sulfate, and other chemicals.

A similar microtubular system is responsible for chromosome movement in mitotic cells (Figs. 1.14, 1.15, F). The predominate, nonchromosomal component of the mitotic apparatus is a microtubule that has a circular cross section and a diameter usually of 15–25 nm. Comparison of Figures 1.2 and 1.14 will show that this component spreads through a major portion of the cell at the time of division and that the dividing cell must be considered physiologically enucleated because of major changes in the nuclear material and dedifferentiated because of reduced membranous organelles.

The manner in which microtubules cause movement is now beginning to be understood in cilia and the mitotic apparatus. Sliding of one microtubule past another with interactions mediated by cross bridges (Fig. 1.14) is currently held to be the mechanism (McIntosh 1974, Satir 1974). Also, the addition or subtraction of monomer tubulin molecules can accentuate the movement in some systems (Bryan 1974).

The nucleus

The nucleus is largely concerned with the hereditary continuity and control of the cell. A modern concept of cell syntheses involves the trinity, DNA (deoxyribose nucleic acid), RNA, and proteins, of which DNA is largely localized in the nucleus in the chromosomes, which are most easily seen when condensed during division (Figs. 1.14, 1.15, C). Except for the specialized polytene and lampbrush chromosomes, chromosomes throughout interphase are massed together and visible only as chromatin (Fig. 1.4 C), which contains DNA, basic proteins, and divalent cations such as calcium. Linear integrity is maintained nevertheless because the long helical DNA molecules maintain the hereditary information in codons formed by three-unit sequences of four possible nucleotides (Clark and Marcker 1968). Colinearity of DNA nucleotides and protein amino acids has been established by repeated studies and has established beyond doubt the coding function of DNA.

The molecule that carries information from the DNA

"file cabinet" to the protein "production line" is messenger-RNA, which is synthesized in a DNA-dependent, intranuclear reaction. Although other RNA's are also synthesized in the nucleus for activation of amino acids and for ribosomes, messenger-RNA is the specific agent for the DNA command of protein synthesis. Whole volumes have been written in this large and recently expanded area of cell research (see De Robertis et al. 1970, Luria 1971).

Another intranuclear organelle, the nucleolus, is defined by its content of RNA (Fig. 1.2 NU). Cells usually have only one or two nucleoli, which are most clearly recognized by their granular, ribosome component and by their lack of membranes. The occurrence of nuclear ribosomes suggests their intranuclear synthesis with subsequent movement to the cytoplasm either through the pores in the envelope or at the time of mitosis when the envelope breaks and the nucleoli disappear.

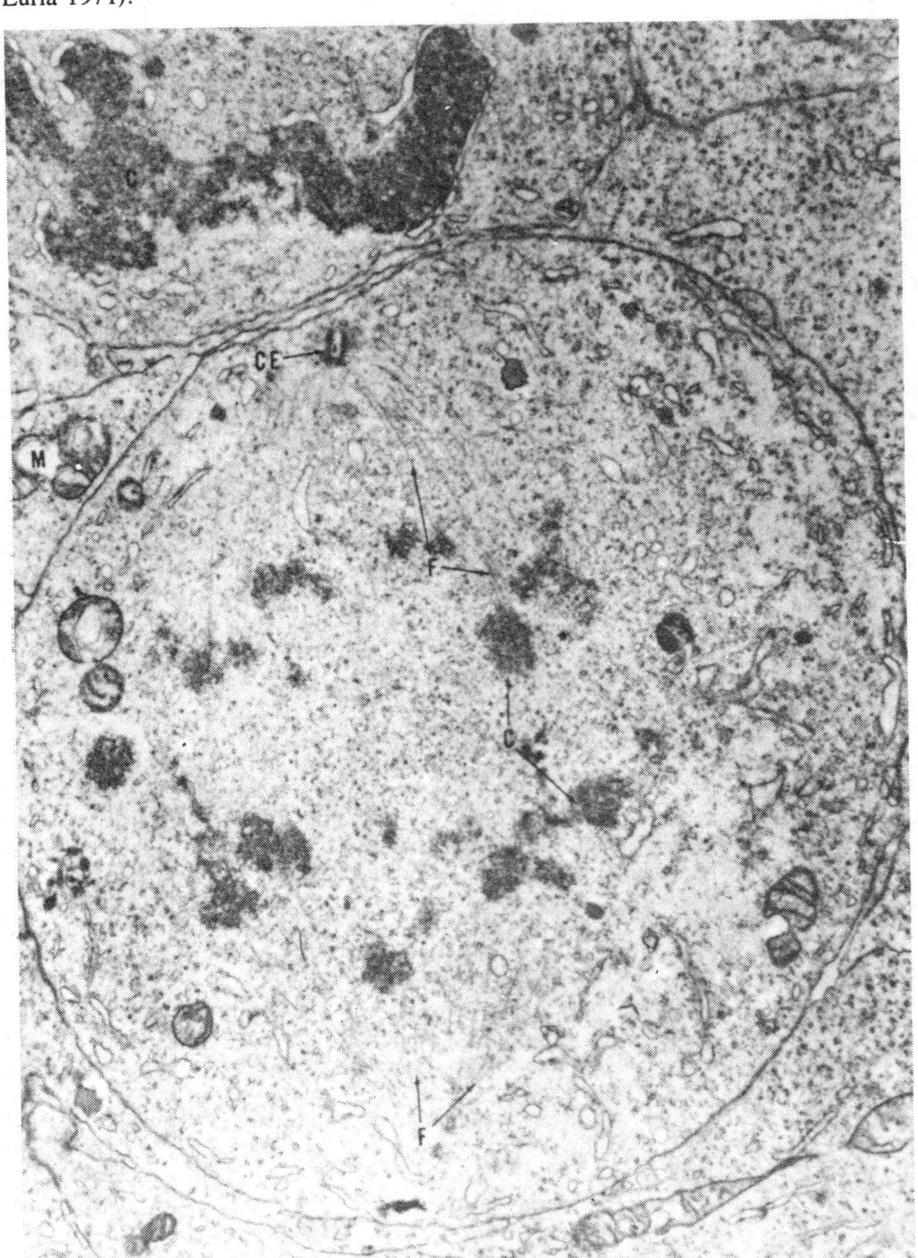

Figure 1.14. Survey section through dividing cells during anaphase. The chromosomes have separated into two sets and are seen in an early stage of movement (C, lower cell) toward the centrioles (CE) and in a late stage when movement is completed (C, upper cell) and the nuclear membranes are reappearing. Microtubules (F) extend from near the centriole to the chromosomes or from near one centriole to the other. From chick embryo neural tube ×15,100; micrograph by A.L. Allenspach and L.E. Roth.

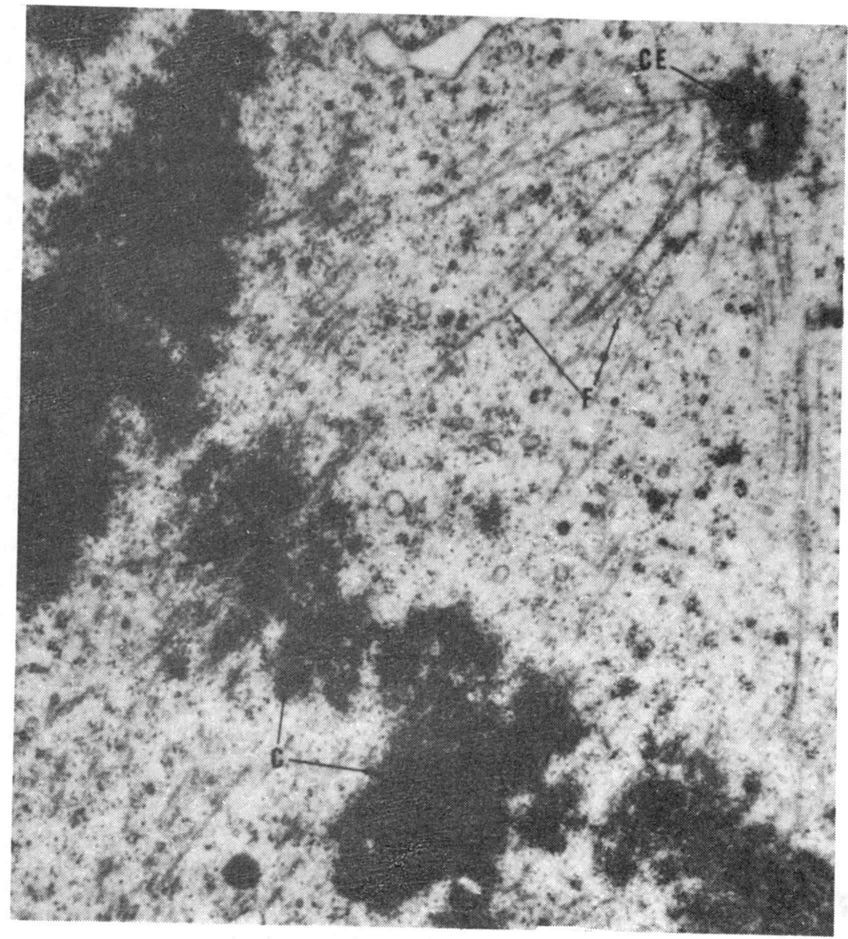

Figure 1.15. The metaphase mitotic apparatus has a centrosome composed of a centriole (CE) surrounded by other material, microtubules (F), and many ribosomes that appear as dark dots. Chromosomes (C) are dark because of a stain. From chick embryo mesenchyme ×31,500; micrograph by A.L. Allenspach and L.E. Roth.

In addition to chromosomes and nucleoli, the nucleoplasm has other constituents, many of which are precursors for the reactions taking place there. The entire nucleoplasm is in a more highly gelated condition than the cytoplasm, probably with relatively high concentrations of calcium and at a more alkaline pH.

THE PROCARYOTIC CELL

In contrast to the eucaryotic cell, bacteria and blue-green algae do not have true nuclei. The DNA-RNA-protein trinity is still functional, but there is a remarkable reduction in separation of these compounds and in the membranes present. The DNA is present in somewhat localized areas called nucleoids that are without a regular pattern and without envelope-membranes (Fig. 1.16 C). Ribosomes are present but not associated with membranes since these cells do not export synthate. The bacterial cell contains only one chromosome which is thought to be in a circular form. An elaborate mitotic apparatus is therefore not needed in bacterial division.

One of the newly discovered and striking similarities between procaryotic and eucaryotic cells is that mitochondria and chloroplants, like bacteria, contain circular DNA molecules (Fig. 1.17) and ribosomes that participate in a protein production partially autonomous from nuclear DNA. Thus, these two eucaryotic organelles are quite similar to the procaryotic cell.

The usual cytoplasmic membranous and filamentous organelles are largely lacking. The plasma membrane is present (Fig. 1.16 PM) with external additions of cell-wall layers including, in the gram-negative bacteria, another membrane (Fig. 1.16 CM). In addition, small membrane-whorls, called mesosomes, have been shown to contain elementary particles like those in mitochondria and to have respiratory activity.

Thus the procaryotic cells are thought to be primitive with a rather low level of organization, intracellular localization, and structural modification. Considering the eucaryotic and procaryotic cells together, it is apparent that a great diversity of physiological variation requires

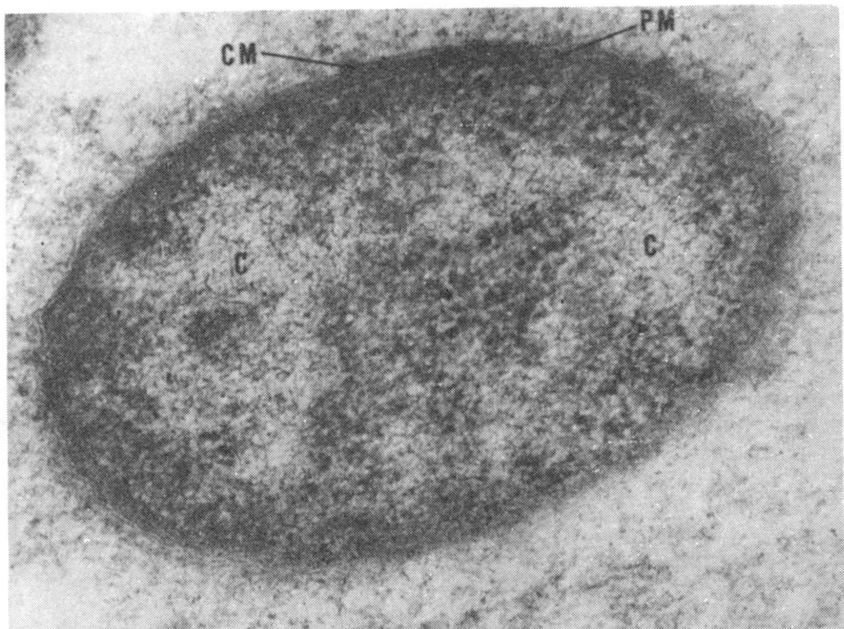

Figure 1.16. Bacteria conspicuously lack intracellular membranes. The chromosomal material (C) is not enclosed by membranes, and the cytoplasm lacks the membranous organelles of the eucaryotic cell. A plasma membrane (PM) and, in gram-negative organisms, a cell wall (CM) largely composed of another membrane are present. From *Acetobacter suboxydans* sectioned × 102,400. (Reprinted by permission of The Rockefeller Institute Press, from G.W. Claus and L.E. Roth 1964, *J. Cell Biol.* 20:217–33.)

an elaborate and complex organization. Only in the eucaryotic cells, which far exceed the procaryotic cells in functional capabilities, has the complexity become significant enough for great diversity.

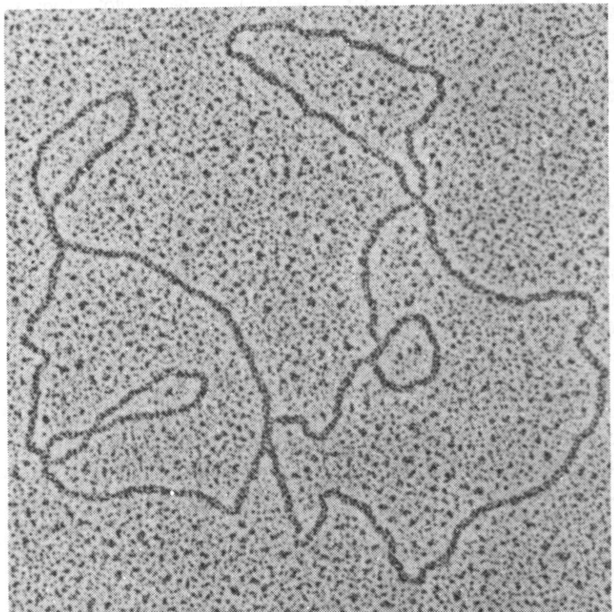

Figure 1.17. Isolated DNA molecule. The circular forms are typical of DNA isolated from both bacteria and mitochondria. From oocyte in *Xenopus laevis* × 85,000. (Reprinted by permission of the Cambridge University Press, from I.B. Dawid and D.R. Wolstenholme 1967, *J. Mol. Biol.* 28:233–45.)

VIRUSES

Viruses are the smallest living substances; they are usually less than a micron in size. The chemical trinity is no longer present, so that the virus is more primitive and contains only RNA and one or a few proteins or only DNA and protein (Fraenkel-Conrat 1962). The viruses are so simple that they are not reproductively self-sufficient. They must enter a cell and force it into alien metabolic pathways which result in the formation of new viruses; this seeming lack of independence is also a point of security, since viruses are so closely related to normal cell metabolism that the means of eradicating a virus infection may also adversely affect the host cell. In spite of the reduction in the number of chemical compounds present, viruses show considerable morphological variation (Dalton and Haguenau 1973).

SUMMARY

Certain major biological concepts are illustrated in the organization of cells: (1) The mechanisms of life processes are intracellular chemical reactions. (2) The organization of cells allows various optimal conditions for the numerous chemical reactions involved in normal life processes. (3) Only a few mechanisms with few modifications are utilized by cells to perform their vital functions. (4) Physiology at its fundamental levels must deal with ions, molecules, and reactions. Therefore biology must be cast in molecular and cellular terms if the basic processes are to be considered.

REFERENCES

Allison, A. 1967. Lysosomes and disease. *Scien. Am.* 217(5):62–67.

Baker, P.C., and Schroeder, T.E. 1967. Cytoplasmic filaments and morphogenetic movements in the amphibian neural tube. *Devel. Biol.* 15:432–50.

Beams, H.W., and Kessel, R.G. 1968. The Golgi apparatus: Structure and function. *Internat. Rev. Cytol.* 23:209–76.

Bernfield, M.R., Banerjee, S.D., and Cohn, R.H. 1972. Dependence of salivary epithelial morphology and branching morphogenesis upon acid mucopolysaccharide-protein (proteoglycan) at the epithelial surface. *J. Cell Biol.* 52:674–89.

Bosch, L. 1972. *The Mechanism of Protein Synthesis and Its Regulation.* Foundation of Biology, vol. 27. Elsevier, New York.

Bryan, J. 1974. Biochemical properties of microtubules. *Fed. Proc.* 33:152–57.

Capaldi, R.A. 1974. A dynamic model of cell membranes. *Scien. Am.* 230(3):26–33.

Clark, B.F.C., and Marcker, K.A. 1968. How proteins start. *Scien. Am.* 218(1):36–42.

Conrad, G., and Williams, D.C. 1974. Polar lobe formation and cytokinesis in fertilized eggs of *Ilyanassa obsoleta*. I. Ultrastructure and effects of cytochalasin B and colchicine. *Devel. Biol.* 36:363–78.

Dalton, A.J., and Haguenau, F. 1976. *Ultrastructure of Animal Viruses and Bacteriophages: An Atlas.* 6th ed. Academic Press, New York.

De Robertis, E.D., Nowinski, W.W., and Saez, F.A. 1970. *Cell Biology.* 5th ed. Saunders, Philadelphia.

Ernster, L., Siekevitz, P., and Palade, G.E. 1962. Enzyme-structure relationships in the endoplasmic reticulum of rat liver. *J. Cell Biol.* 15:541–62.

Fraenkel-Conrat, H. 1962. *Design and Function at the Threshold of Life: The Viruses.* Academic Press, New York.

Gardner, E.J. 1964. *History of Life Sciences.* Burgess, Minneapolis.

Glauert, A.M. 1974. The high voltage electron microscope. *J. Cell Biol.* 63:717–48.

Goodenough, D.A., and Revel, J.P. 1970. A fine structural analysis of intercellular junctions in the mouse liver. *J. Cell Biol.* 45:272–81.

Harmon, H.J., Hall, J.D., and Crane, F.L. 1974. Structure of mitochondrial cristae membranes. *Biochim. Biophys. Acta* 344:119–55.

Hughes, H. 1959. *A History of Cytology.* Abelard-Schuman, New York.

Huxley, H.F. 1971. The activation of striated muscle and its mechanical response. *Proc. Roy. Soc.*, ser. B, 178:1–28.

Luria, S.E. 1971. *Molecular Biology of the Gene.* 2d ed. Benjamin, New York.

Marchesi, V.T., Tillach, T.W., Jackson, R.L., Sergrest, J.P., and Scott, R.E. 1972. Chemical characterization and surface orientation of the major glycoproteins of the human erythrocyte membrane. *Proc. Nat. Acad. Sci.* 69:1445–51.

Mazia, D. 1961. Mitosis and the physiology of cell division. In J. Brachet and A.E. Mirsky, eds., *The Cell.* Academic Press, New York. Vol. 3, 80–412.

——. 1974. The cell cycle. *Scien. Am.* 230(1):54–64.

McIntosh, J.R. 1974. Bridges between microtubules. *J. Cell Biol.* 61:166–87.

Moscona, A.A. 1968. Cell aggregation: Properties of specific cell-ligands and their role in the formation in multicellular systems. *Devel. Biol.* 18:250–77.

Murray, J.M., and Weber, A. 1974. The cooperative action of muscle proteins. *Scien. Am.* 230(2):58–71.

Nachmias, V.T. 1972. Electron microscopic studies on myosin from *Physarum polycephalum*. *J. Cell Biol.* 52:648–63.

Naitoh, Y., and Echert, R. 1969. Ciliary orientation: Controlled by cell membrane or by intracellular fibrils? *Science* 166:1633–35.

Nanninga, N. 1973. Structural aspects of ribosomes. *Internat. Rev. Cytol.* 35:135–88.

Nicholson, G.L., and Singer, S.J. 1974. The distribution and assymetry of mammalian cell surface saccharides utilizing ferritin-conjugated plant agglutinins as specific saccharide stains. *J. Cell Biol.* 60:236–48.

Pollack, R.E., and Hough, P.V.C. 1974. The cell surface and malignant transformation. *Ann. Rev. Med.* 25:431–46.

Porter, K.R. 1953. Observations on a submicroscopic basophilic component of cytoplasm. *J. Exp. Med.* 97:727–41.

Poste, G. 1972. Mechanisms of virus-induced cell fusion. *Internat. Rev. Cytol.* 33:157–252.

Racker, E. 1970. *Membranes of Mitochondria and Chloroplasts.* Van Nostrand Reinhold, New York.

Roth, L.E. 1960. Electron microscopy of pinocytosis and food vacuoles in Pelomyxa. *J. Protozool.* 7:176–85.

Roth, S., McGuire, E.J., and Roseman, S. 1971. Evidence for cell-surface glycosyltransferases: Their potential role in cellular recognition. *J. Cell Biol.* 51:536–47.

Satir, P. 1974. How cilia move. *Scien. Am.* 231(4):44–52.

Schroeder, T.E. 1972. The contractile ring. II. Determining its brief existence, volumetric changes, and vital role in cleaving *Arbacia* eggs. *J. Cell Biol.* 53:419–34.

Siekevitz, P., and Palade, G.E. 1959. A cytochemical study of the pancreas of the guinea pig. IV. Chemical and metabolic investigation of the ribonucleo-protein particles. *J. Biophys. Biochem. Cytol.* 5:1–10.

Singer, S.J., and Nicholson, G.L. 1972. The fluid mosaic model of the structure of cell membranes. *Science* 175:720–31.

Spooner, B.S. 1975. Microfilaments, microtubules, and extracellular materials in morphogenesis. *Bioscience,* in press.

Steck, T.L. 1974. The organization of proteins in the human red blood cell membrane. *J. Cell Biol.* 62:1–19.

Stein, R.J., Richter, W.R., and Brynjolfsson, G. 1967. Ultrastructural pharmacopathology. I. Comparative morphology of the livers of the normal street dog and purebred beagle. *Exp. Mol. Path.* 5:195–224.

Stern, H., and Nanney, D.L. 1971. *The Biology of Cells.* Wiley, New York.

Toole, B.P., and Gross, J. 1971. The extracellular matrix of the regenerating newt limb. *Devel. Biol.* 25:57–77.

Vollet, J.J., and Roth, L.E. 1974. Cell fusion by nascent-membrane induction and divalent-cation treatment. *Cytobiologie* 9:249–62.

Warren, L., Fuhrer, J.P., and Buck, C.A. 1972. Surface glycoproteins of normal and transformed cells: A difference determined by sialic acid and a growth-dependent sialyl transferase. *Proc. Nat. Acad. Sci.* 69:1838–42.

Wessells, N.K., Spooner, B.S., and Luduena, M.A. 1973. Surface movements, microfilaments, and cell locomotion. In *Locomotion of Tissue Cells.* Ciba Found. Symp. 14. Associated Scientific Publishers, Amsterdam. Pp. 53–77.

Wilson, E.B. 1928. *The Cell in Development and Heredity.* Macmillan, New York.

Yamada, K.M., Spooner, B.S., and Wessells, N.K. 1970. Axon growth: Roles of microfilaments and microtubules. *Proc. Nat. Acad. Sci.* 66:1206–12.

PART I BLOOD CIRCULATION AND THE CARDIOVASCULAR SYSTEM

CHAPTER 2

Physiological Properties and Cellular and Chemical Constituents of Blood | by Melvin J. Swenson

The blood in an animal serves as a transport medium. It carries nutrients from the digestive tract to the tissues, the end products of metabolism from the cells to the organs of excretion, oxygen from the lungs to the tissues, carbon dioxide from the tissues to the lungs, and the secretions of the endocrine glands throughout the body. The blood also helps to regulate body temperature, maintain a constant concentration of water and electrolytes in the cells, regulate the body's hydrogen ion concentration, and defend against microorganisms.

Both the cells of the blood and its fluid components assist in these functions. The cells called leukocytes defend the body; the cells called erythrocytes contain hemoglobin, which transports oxygen and carbon dioxide. The extracellular constituents include water, electrolytes, proteins, glucose, enzymes, and hormones. Maintenance of uniformity and stability in this extracellular fluid is called *homeostasis*. In this environment cells function at their optimum. Homeostasis is maintained by physiological processes such as the use of diffusion, pressure gradients, concentration gradients, active transport, and by regulatory mechanisms controlled by the nervous and endocrine systems.

BLOOD CELLS, PLASMA, AND SERUM

Three classes of blood cells (corpuscles) are recognized—erythrocytes (red cells), leukocytes (white cells), and thrombocytes (platelets). The red color of blood is caused by the hemoglobin in the erythrocytes. All these cells are suspended in the fluid called *plasma*.

Plasma itself is yellow to colorless, depending on the quantity, the species of the animal, and its diet. When examined as a thin film, plasma is always colorless. In some species, such as cats, dogs, sheep, and goats, it is colorless or only slightly yellow in larger quantities; in cows and especially horses it is usually darker. The color results chiefly from varying concentrations of a pigment called bilirubin, although carotene and other pigments are contributing factors.

In coagulation, blood lost from the body becomes a gelatinous mass (see Chapter 3). Following coagulation, the blood clot retracts, thereby forcing from the clot a clear, watery fluid called *serum*. Serum is similar to plasma except that fibrinogen and other clotting factors have been removed.

Plasma may be obtained by adding to whole blood an anticoagulant to prevent clotting and letting the cells settle out, since they are heavier than plasma. By centrifuging the blood and thus hastening the settling of the cells, plasma may be obtained more readily.

Anticoagulants

Many anticoagulants can be used to obtain blood samples free from clots for transfusion and for analytical work. Heparin, a conjugated polysaccharide, is a natural anticoagulant, produced by basophils (a kind of leukocyte) in the blood and by mast cells throughout the body. Mast cells are part of the connective tissue surrounding capillaries in the lungs and other organs. From this tissue, heparin is released and passes into the capillaries. A concentration of 0.2 mg of heparin per ml of blood is used as an anticoagulant. However, 1 mg of heparin will prevent the coagulation of 100–500 ml of blood at 0°C and 10–20 ml at room temperature. One unit of heparin is approximately 0.01 mg of heparin sodium.

An anticoagulant commonly used for blood transfusions in animals is sodium citrate. The citrate combines with calcium ions of the plasma, forming an insoluble calcium salt. One must be careful not to give too much citrate because citrate can combine with sufficient calcium ions to produce tetany, and thus interfere with the functioning of nerves and of skeletal and cardiac muscles. Sodium citrate and similar salts are used in concentrations of 0.2–0.4 percent of blood to prevent coagulation. Potassium salts are not used in transfusions because of the possibility of producing heart block.

Other useful anticoagulants are sodium, potassium, and ammonium salts of oxalates and fluorides. Chelating compounds such as ethylenediaminetetraacetic acid (EDTA) are also used (Schmidt et al. 1953, Strumia 1954). Ammonium salts are not recommended when compounds containing nitrogen are being determined quantitatively, because of nitrogen in the anticoagulant.

In calculating mean corpuscular volume (MCV), mean corpuscular hemoglobin (MCH), and mean corpuscular hemoglobin concentration (MCHC) as diagnostic aids, it is essential to try to maintain the cell size as it existed in the circulating blood when the packed cell volume (PCV) was determined.

Heparin or EDTA is generally thought to keep the size of erythrocytes constant. Ammonium salts increase the size of cells; potassium salts decrease the size. Heller and Paul (1934) found that 6 mg of ammonium oxalate and 4 mg of potassium oxalate inhibited the coagulation of 5 ml of blood and kept the cell size constant. A comparison of various anticoagulants is given by Schalm et al. (1975).

ERYTHROCYTES

Erythrocytes in the circulating blood of mammals are nonnucleated, nonmotile cells. They appear as biconcave, circular discs varying in diameter and thickness according to species and nutritional status of the animal, but are capable of undergoing changes in shape while passing through capillary beds. The dog erythrocyte is markedly biconcave; cat and horse erythrocytes are slightly concave. The erythrocytes of the ruminants (cattle, sheep, goats) and of pigs are discoid. On the other hand, the red blood cells of most animals below mammals are elliptical in shape and possess nuclei.

Origin

In early fetal development nucleated red blood cells are produced in the yolk sac. Later the liver, spleen, and lymph nodes are involved. After birth the formation of red cells (erythropoiesis) takes place in the bone marrow. In birds the spleen also forms erythrocytes to a small extent. Under certain pathological conditions in postnatal life the liver, spleen, and lymph nodes may again assume their fetal function of erythropoiesis.

In the bone marrow, erythropoiesis goes on continuously, and corpuscles are poured into the blood stream at a rate to balance the destruction of red cells. Therefore the total number in the blood does not fluctuate greatly. The entrance of the newly formed corpuscles into a bone marrow capillary has been likened to the penetration, without rupture, of the film of a soap bubble by a needle; no stoma or opening is necessary. The erythrocyte, being nonmotile, may enter the capillary by diapedesis (the passage of a cell through the unruptured blood vessel wall). According to another view, erythrocytes develop intravascularly. There are, according to this theory, two kinds of capillaries in bone marrow: collapsed ones, which are erythrogenic, and open ones through which blood flows. The young erythrocytes are forced into the

Table 2.1. Developmental stages of various blood cells

Series	Cells
Erythrocytic	Rubriblast
	Prorubricyte
	Rubricyte
	Metarubricyte
	Reticulocyte
	Erythrocyte
Granulocytic	Myeloblast
	Progranulocyte
	Myelocyte
	Metamyelocyte
	Band cell
	Neutrophil
Lymphocytic	Lymphoblast
	Prolymphocyte
	Lymphocyte
Monocytic	Monoblast
	Promonocyte
	Monocyte
Thrombocytic	Megakaryoblast
	Promegakaryocyte
	Megakaryocyte
	Thrombocyte or platelet

blood stream as the erythrogenic capillaries become active and patent.

The metarubricyte, the bone marrow cell which is the immediate forerunner of the erythrocyte, is nucleated, whereas the mammalian adult erythrocyte is not (Table 2.1). The nucleus of the latter is lost by extrusion or by absorption before the corpuscle enters the blood stream. Normally 1–3 percent of the erythrocytes are reticulocytes (young red blood cells that contain the remains of a nucleus). These may increase greatly in number in some anemias when the bone marrow is more active in producing a greater number of erythrocytes. In hemorrhagic, hemolytic, or other anemias, which tend to be regenerative, nucleated red blood cells and reticulocytes are found in the blood of most animals, the horse being an exception.

Composition

Erythrocytes in adult animals contain 62–72 percent water; the approximately 35 percent remaining are solids. Of the solids, hemoglobin constitutes about 95 percent. The major solids of the other 5 percent are proteins in the stroma and cell membrane; lipids such as phospholipids (lecithin, cephalin, sphingomyelin), free cholesterol, cholesterol esters, and neutral fat; vitamins functioning as coenzymes; glucose for energy; enzymes such as cholinesterase, phosphatases, carbonic anhydrase, peptidases, and those concerned with glycolysis; and minerals such as phosphorus, sulfur, chlorine (principal intracellular anion), magnesium, potassium, and sodium.

Sodium is the principal cation in extracellular fluid. Cations and anions within and outside the cell help in establishing and maintaining electrical gradients across cell membranes by the sodium pump, by active transport of cations and anions, and by diffusion. These physiological processes help in maintaining a steady-state of electrolytes within cells (see Chapter 36).

Potassium is the principal cation of erythrocytes from most species of domestic animals except the dog and cat (Abderhalden 1898, Davson 1958) and cattle, goats, and sheep. The potassium and sodium concentrations vary with genetically different sheep (Tosteson 1963, Evans 1954), goats, and cattle (Evans and Phillipson 1957). Kerr (1937) reported on potassium and sodium content of erythrocytes (mM/1000 g red blood cells) from 20 species of animals. The erythrocyte potassium and sodium values he found for the dog are 8.7 and 107; cat, 5.9 and 103.7; cow, 21.8 and 79.8; goat, 18.4 and 93.2; sheep, 18.4 and 83.5, 64.2 and 15.6, 58.1 and 46.0; pig, 99.5 and 10.8; chicken, 97.3 and 7.1; and turkey, 99.5 and 9.7, respectively.

Size and hemoglobin content

The diameter of erythrocytes has been measured frequently. For most domestic mammals the mean diameters from dry smears vary from 4 μ for the goat to 7 for the dog (see Table 2.3 below). There are shortcomings in this measurement: (1) the cells in a dry smear (or in a moist state but losing water) are smaller, (2) very few cells are measured from the blood sample taken, and (3) the depth of the cell or third dimension is left out of account. For these reasons diameters of erythrocytes are less important than their cubic volume, which should be used to measure cells. The following formulas will give mean corpuscular volume, hemoglobin, and hemoglobin concentration in erythrocytes (for abbreviations of measures see below):

MCV in cu μ or fl

$$= \frac{\text{PCV} \times 10}{\text{no. of erythrocytes per cu mm blood} \times 10^6}$$

MCH in $\mu\mu$g or pg

$$= \frac{\text{hemoglobin in g \%} \times 10}{\text{no. of erythrocytes per cu mm blood} \times 10^6}$$

MCHC in % or g/100 ml

$$= \frac{\text{hemoglobin in g \%} \times 100}{\text{PCV}}$$

Prefixes commonly used in physiology with gram (g), meters (m), and liter (l or L) are as follows:

Prefix	Abbreviation	Quantity
deci	d	one tenth (10^{-1})
centi	c	one hundredth (10^{-2})
milli	m	one thousandth (10^{-3})
micro	μ	one millionth (10^{-6})
nano	n	one billionth (10^{-9})
pico	p	one trillionth (10^{-12})
femto	f	one quadrillionth (10^{-15})

Thus mμ = nm, $\mu\mu$m = pm, m$\mu\mu$m = fm; pg = $\mu\mu$g; μl = cu mm, dl = 100 ml, g/dl (or %) = g/100 ml, fl = cu μ; μm is often just written μ (micron).

These formulas are an aid in diagnosing various anemias. Iron deficiency in all mammals including man characterizes a microcytic type of anemia (very small cells). The MCV provides the average cell size in cubic microns. Pigs are usually born with large erythrocytes measuring 80–90 cu μ. MCH expresses the average weight of hemoglobin present in erythrocytes, while MCHC gives the average percentage of the MCV which the hemoglobin occupies. These values vary with species (Table 2.2). Pernicious anemia in man is macrocytic, but this anemia does not occur in domestic animals. In fact, pigs farrowed from sows on a vitamin B_{12} deficient ration had smaller erythrocytes (49 cu μ)—indicating a microcytic type of anemia—than control pigs, which had an average value of 69 cu μ (Swenson et al. 1955).

The variation in these values is considerable in domes-

Table 2.2. Erythrocyte size and hemoglobin content in adult domestic animals

Animal	MCV (cu μ)	MCH (pg)	MCHC (%)	References
Cat	51–63	13–17	32–34	Coffin 1953
Cattle	52	19	32	Drastisch 1928
	58	20	34	Wintrobe 1933
	46–54	15–20	32–39	Swenson et al. 1962
Chicken	115–125	25–27	21–23	Calculated from Swenson 1951
Dog	59–69	20–24	30–35	Ranges from 7 references cited by Wintrobe 1961
Goat	16	8	32	Drastisch 1928
	19	7	35	Wintrobe 1933
Horse	52	18	34	Drastisch 1928
	42	13	33	Macleod and Ponder 1946
Pig	58	19	33	Wintrobe 1961
At birth	64–96	21–31	32–34	Swenson et al. 1958
1 week	71–78	22–25	30–33	Swenson et al. 1958
3 weeks	61–75	20–23	29–33	Swenson et al. 1958
4–8 weeks	53–66	16–20	28–35	Swenson et al. 1958
Sheep	35	11	31	Drastisch 1928
	35	13	35	Wintrobe 1933
	30–44	10–14	27–36	Carlson et al. 1961

tic animals. Error in counting erythrocytes contributes to variations in MCV and MCH.

Number

The number of red blood cells varies greatly among species. The number varies also within species and within individuals of a species (because the cells are not uniformly distributed in the blood vascular system). Since plasma fluids are constantly being shifted across capillary walls, cell counts vary as well between arterial and venous blood samples. The following figures show the range of erythrocytes in blood of domestic animals and man:

Animal	Millions per cu mm
Cat	6–8
Cattle	6–8
Chicken	2.5–3.2
Dog	6–8
Goat	13–14
Horse (light or hot-blooded)	9–12
Horse (draft or cold-blooded)	7–10
Pig	6–8
Pigeon	3.5–4.5
Rabbit	5.5–6.5
Sheep	10–13
Man	5–6
Woman	4–5

Other factors affect not only erythrocyte counts but also hemoglobin concentration, PCV, and the concentration of other blood constituents: they are chiefly age, sex, exercise, nutritional status, lactation, pregnancy, egg production, excitement (release of epinephrine), blood volume (hemodilution or hemoconcentration), stage of

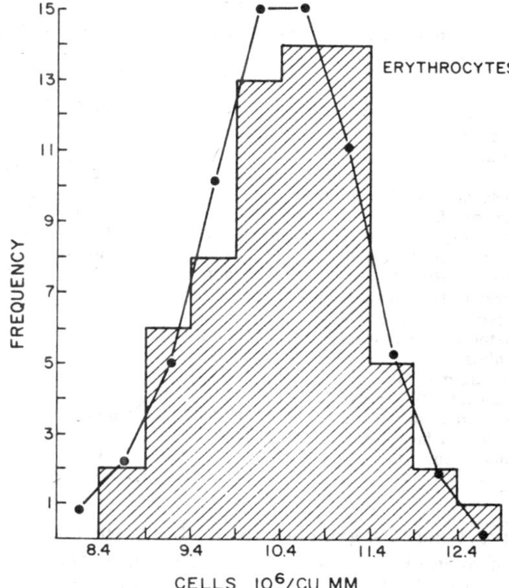

Figure 2.1. Number of erythrocytes (millions/cu mm) in blood of 65 Thoroughbred mares in foal. Average value is $10.52 \pm 0.102 \times 10^6$. Histogram shows the observed frequency distribution. Polygon shows the theoretical normal distribution. Other values are: hemoglobin, 14.9 ± 0.1 g/100 ml; PCV, 45.1 ± 0.4%; total leukocytes, $10{,}010 \pm 187$/cu mm. (From Hansen, Todd, Kelley, and Cawein 1950, *Ky. Ag. Exp. Sta. Bull.* 555.)

estrous cycle, breed, time of day, environmental temperature, altitude, and other climatic factors.

Figure 2.1 shows variation in red cell counts in pregnant Thoroughbred mares. All groups show higher red cell counts than for cold-blooded (draft) horses. The erythrocyte count for mules is practially the same as that for draft horses (Morris 1942).

Surface area

Total erythrocyte surface area can be estimated when blood volume, erythrocyte count, diameter, and thickness are known. The surface areas are amazingly large (Table 2.3). This surface area is of great importance to the respiratory or gas-transport function of the blood. A relatively constant value of erythrocyte surface area to body weight is maintained. For mammals it varies from 56 to 68 (sq m/kg). The value for the chickens, 44, is quite low compared with mammals. The estimated mean surface area per erythrocyte was calculated first from the dimensions reported on dry films (Altman and Dittmer 1961). This value was increased by 20 percent to arrive at the estimated wet erythrocyte surface area. The average thickness was calculated as 2 μ. Although considerable error may be introduced with this value and others used, they do provide some comparative values to help understand gas-transport mechanisms.

The figures for erythrocyte surface area are more im-

Table 2.3. Estimated values for calculating total erythrocyte surface area

Species	Man	Cattle	Goat	Sheep	Pig	Horse	Dog	Cat	Chicken
Weight (kg)	70	500	30	40	100	500	20	3	2
Blood volume (ml, calculated as 8% body wt.)	5600	40,000	2400	3200	8000	40,000	1600	240	160
Total RBC/cu mm blood × 10^6	5	7	14	11	7	10	7	7	3
Diameter of RBC (μ, dry films)	7.5	5.9	4	4.8	6	5.5	7	6	11.2 × 6.8
Total cu mm of blood × 10^6	5.6	40	2.4	3.2	8.0	40	1.6	0.24	0.16
Total no. of RBC × 10^{13}	2.8	28	3.4	3.5	5.6	40	1.1	0.17	0.048
Estimated surface area/RBC (sq μ) based on diameter and thickness (wet films)	162	110	50	66	113	84	121	113	183
Sq μ in 1 sq m × 10^{12}	1	1	1	1	1	1	1	1	1
Estimated total erythrocyte surface area (sq m)	4536	30,800	1680	2323	6328	33,600	1355	190	88
Erythrocyte surface area (sq m/kg body wt.)	65	62	56	58	63	67	68	63	44

pressive when compared with the body surface area. A man of average size has less than 2 sq m of body surface area, and a 500 kg cow somewhat less than 5.

Tonicity

In order to keep erythrocytes constant in size they must remain in an environment with the same osmolarity as blood plasma. When the osmotic pressure of plasma is lowered sufficiently, hemolysis (laking) of erythrocytes results. Hemolysis causes release of hemoglobin from red cells to the surrounding medium. Plasma osmotic pressure may be lowered by adding hypotonic salt solutions or water to blood. In such cases, water passes into the cell by osmosis through its semipermeable membrane, causing the cell to swell. This results in the stretching and eventual mechanical rupture of its membrane, with hemoglobin passing into the surrounding medium. The cellular stroma remaining is spoken of as a shadow or ghost corpuscle. Solutions osmotically weaker than plasma, causing hemolysis of red cells, are called *hypotonic*. Solutions similar to plasma in crystalloid osmotic pressure, into which erythrocytes may be placed without resulting in cell volume changes, are called *isotonic*. Solutions that exert a higher osmotic pressure than blood plasma are said to be *hypertonic;* they cause water to pass from the corpuscles by osmosis, and shrinking of the corpuscles results. Such erythrocytes are said to be crenated.

The isotonic solution of greatest interest is the physiological salt solution, known also as physiological saline—an aqueous solution of sodium chloride usually containing 0.85–0.9 percent sodium chloride. This concentration is satisfactory for practical use with mammalian blood cells. The extent to which the osmotic pressure of plasma can be lowered without causing hemolysis of all, or even of any, corpuscles is considerable, and it varies somewhat among different species. The concentration (%) of sodium chloride solution at which hemolysis begins indicates the osmotic resistance of the weakest corpuscles (minimum resistance). The concentration at which complete hemolysis occurs indicates the resistance of the strongest corpuscles (maximum resistance).

A test of erythrocyte fragility has some clinical application. The figures in Table 2.4 are erythrocyte fragility values for animals. A study of the osmotic resistance of sheep erythrocytes has been made by Stone et al. (1953). Perk et al. (1964) reported on the osmotic fragility of erythrocytes from 15 domestic and laboratory animals. Two erythrocyte populations, adult and fetal, were found in newborn pigs, rabbits, mice, hamsters, and guinea pigs. The first peak of minimum resistance came from the adult type.

It is not known whether hemolysis caused by lowering the osmotic pressure of the plasma plays a part in the destruction of erythrocytes in the body under normal condi-

Table 2.4. Erythrocyte fragility

	Strength of NaCl solution (g/100 ml)	
Animal	For initial hemolysis	For complete hemolysis
Cat (young)	0.58	0.47
Cat (adult)	0.69	0.5
Cattle	0.59	0.42
Chicken (male)	0.4	0.32
Chicken (female)	0.41	0.28
Dog	0.45	0.36
Goat	0.62	0.48
Horse	0.59	0.39
Pig	0.74	0.45
Rabbit	0.57	0.45
Sheep (young)	0.69	0.48
Sheep (adult)	0.6	0.45

From Altman and Dittmer, *Blood and Other Body Fluids*, Fed. Am. Soc. Exp. Biol., Washington, 1961

tions. However, knowledge of osmotic resistance is of practical importance in preparing solutions for intravenous injection. Large amounts of water may be injected into the blood stream at slow rates without producing any significant amount of hemolysis. In experiments on horses Roberts (1943) found that injections of over 4000 ml of distilled water or tapwater regularly produced a temporary hemolysis and hemoglobinuria. No hemolysis was observed in any horse receiving less than 2000 ml of distilled water or tapwater.

Additional items that cause hemolysis of erythrocytes are freezing and thawing, stirring or agitation, high temperatures, and substances that lower surface tension, such as saponins, soaps, and bile salts. Alcohol, ether, chloroform, and acetone also damage cell membranes and cause hemolysis.

It is possible to calculate what percentage solution of a compound is isotonic with erythrocytes by using the following formula:

$$\% \text{ solution (isotonic)} = \frac{0.03 \times \text{mol wt}}{\text{no. of ions per molecule in solution}}$$

The 0.03 is a constant. The number of ions for NaCl is 2; $CaCl_2$, 3; and organic compounds, 1. For sodium chloride the percentage is 0.8775, and for glucose it is 5.4.

Life span

The length of life for erythrocytes in man ranges from 90 to 140 days, averaging 120 days. For several small laboratory animals the life span is reported as much shorter (Burwell et al. 1953): life spans of 45–50, 45–50, and 20–30 days were found for the rabbit, rat, and mouse, respectively, by using ^{59}Fe tagged erythrocytes. Values of 62, 63, and 71 days for swine were found by using tagged erythrocytes in homologous transfusion, from another animal of the same species (Bush et al. 1955, Jensen et al. 1956, Hansard and Kincaid 1956, respectively). Bush et al. (1956) reported the half-life of erythrocytes to be 17 days. Talbot and Swenson (1963a) compared homologous with autologous (individual's own erythrocytes) transfusions using ^{51}Cr in determining the half-life of erythrocytes. The half-life for autologous cells was 28 ± 4 days, for homologous cells 13.8 ± 5.7 days. This study shows that erythrocytes from one animal infused into another of the same species do not live as long. With the autologous cells the length of life of erythrocytes in swine approaches the time reported for man.

Hawkins and Whipple (1938) studied the life span of erythrocytes in healthy dogs. The average was 124 days. Studies (in man and dog) in which isotopes of elements in the hemoglobin molecule were used have yielded a similar life span. The life span of erythrocytes of the hen, which are nucleated cells, was found to average only 28 days (Hevesy and Ottesen 1945).

Erythrocytes are destroyed in great numbers daily. The total number of erythrocytes in the body of a 450 kg animal with a blood volume of 8 percent of body weight is 300 trillion. If the average life of individual erythrocytes is 100 days, then 3 trillion must be destroyed (and formed) in the body every day, or about 35 million every second.

In iron-deficiency anemia, where erythrocytes become smaller in size, one might think that their life is prolonged, since younger cells are larger than older cells. The microcytic type of anemia, on the other hand, is the result of younger cells not being released into the circulating blood in sufficient quantities to replenish those being lost. (See Wintrobe 1961 and Medway et al. 1969 for classification of the anemias.)

Fate of erythrocytes

The cells of the reticuloendothelial system destroy the old, exhausted erythrocytes. These cells (known also as histiocytes, macrophages, or clasmatocytes) vary in size, shape, and location, but they possess the common property of ingesting particulate matter brought into relationship with them. Reticuloendothelial cells include the stellate, or Küpffer, cells found in the walls of the blood sinuses of the liver, similar cells in the spleen, and certain cells of the bone marrow and lymph nodes. As erythrocytes are destroyed, the iron-containing moiety of hemoglobin is conserved and the pigmentary part is converted into bile pigment, an excretory product. The liver and spleen are important storehouses of the iron that is not immediately used in the production of new hemoglobin (see Chapter 33).

The reticuloendothelial cells in different organs are important in the destruction of erythrocytes. In the dog, the main seat of bile pigment formations is the red bone marrow (Mann et al. 1951). The red bone marrow is the principal place of erythrocyte destruction. In man the spleen is probably of great importance; in the rabbit and guinea pig, less so; in birds, the liver is the main site (Krumbhaar 1926). In most species of animals the liver is also an important site. The protein portion of the hemoglobin molecule may enter the protein pool of the body and be used in the formation of new hemoglobin or other proteins.

Hematopoiesis

Hematopoiesis (the formation of blood or blood cells) is a continuous process. Many nutrients are essential for this process. Vitamin B_{12} (cyanocobalamin) contains one atom of cobalt in each molecule. It functions in the maturation of erythrocytes in a similar capacity as folic acid (pteroylglutamic acid). Both vitamins act as coenzymes in the synthesis of nucleic acids or their constituents, the purine and pyrimidine bases. Other vitamins that aid hematopoiesis are pyridoxine, riboflavin, nicotinic acid, pantothenic acid, thiamine, biotin, and ascorbic acid. When these vitamins are deficient, growth and development of erythrocytes are impaired. Pyridoxine deficiency in swine produces a microcytic, hypochromic anemia.

In addition to vitamins, nutrients such as minerals and amino acids, as well as water and energy, are needed for the synthesis of blood proteins. The minerals most commonly needed are iron, copper, and cobalt. Iron is built into the hemoglobin molecule, and copper is essential as a coenzyme or catalyst in hemoglobin synthesis. The body contains many iron- and copper-containing enzymes. Cobalt is a dietary essential for ruminants and is needed in the bacterial synthesis of vitamin B_{12} in the rumen. Cobalt given in excess will cause polycythemia. Animals placed at a high altitude may also show polycythemia because of the decreased oxygen pressure (Po_2).

With all the nutrients available for the maturation of erythrocytes there still remain various governing mechanisms for the production and release of these cells from the bone marrow. Normally about 1 percent of the red cells are replaced daily, based on the fact that they live approximately 120 days. The body has a reserve capacity for replenishing or producing many times this quantity as the need arises.

Nonregenerative anemias such as trichostrongylosis in cattle, anemia associated with chronic infection, neoplasia, or other cachetic diseases do not elicit the response for greater red cell production. On the other hand, hemorrhage, hemolytic diseases, blood-sucking parasites, and nutritional deficiencies elicit the response for greater red cell production. In hypoxic conditions caused either by an inadequate number or by improper functioning of erythrocytes, the tissues are not supplied with enough oxygen. As a result a humoral factor is released from the tissues which stimulates hematopoiesis. This substance is called erythropoietin, hemopoietin, or erythrocyte maturing factor. It is neither vitamin B_{12} nor the intrinsic factor of Castle. The kidney has been cited as producing this compound, but hypoxic tissue cells in general may produce it. It has been demonstrated that acute hypoxia, whether due to anemia or decreased oxygen pressure of the inspired air, will cause production and subsequent release of erythropoietin into the blood plasma. This compound has been found in the blood plasma of rats, mice, rabbits, dogs, cattle, sheep, swine, and man. It has been shown rather conclusively in mice that erythropoietin is produced by the spleen (de Franciscis et al. 1965). It is heat stable and is capable of producing a reticulocytosis when injected into animals.

PACKED CELL VOLUME

The volume of cells in the circulating blood is usually less than the plasma volume. Data for this relationship are readily obtained by using the hematocrit, a centrifuge in which is placed a small tube containing a sample of blood with the appropriate kind and quantity of anticoagulant (page 15). The Wintrobe hematocrit tube is centrifuged at 3000 rpm for 30 minutes; then the percentage of packed red cells is read from a scale or calculated. A layer of packed leukocytes occurs just above the packed erythrocytes. As a rule in normal animals the volume of packed red cells (PCV) is directly related to the erythrocyte count and hemoglobin content. It is a common practice in some laboratories to allow the hematocrit tube containing blood to stand vertically for an hour before centrifugation in order to obtain the erythrocyte sedimentation rate.

In recent years the microhematocrit centrifuge and tubes have been used widely to save time, values being obtained in 5 minutes. Microhematocrit tubes come with or without heparin.

The PCV is expressed as a percent volume of packed cells in whole blood after centrifugation. Most species of domestic animals have PCV values from 38 to 45 percent with a mean of 40. Cold-blooded (draft) horses usually have PCV values from 35 to 38 percent; lactating dairy cows 32–35; and chickens 30–33. Adult male chickens may reach 35–40. Hemoconcentration due to dehydration, asphyxia, or excitement causing release of erythrocytes concentrated in the spleen can result in abnormally high PCV values. In excitement the epinephrine causes splenic contraction.

HEMOGLOBIN

Hemoglobin, the pigment of erythrocytes, is a complex, iron-containing, conjugated protein composed of a pigment and a simple protein. The protein is globin, a histone. The red color of hemoglobin is due to heme, a metallic compound containing an iron atom. By itself heme does not contain water or globin, but hemoglobin does. Biosynthesis of hemoglobin starts in the erythroblasts and continues in the subsequent stages of cell development. As long as nuclear material is present in the cell, whether the cells are in the bone marrow or in the circulating blood, formation of hemoglobin may continue. Reticulocytes containing RNA in the fragmented nucleus have the ability to synthesize hemoglobin (see also Chapter 15). In hemoglobin synthesis the amino acid, glycine, and acetate coming from the tricarboxylic acid cycle form a four-carbon compound with additional glycine. This compound unites with glycine to form pyrrole.

```
HC——CH
‖    ‖
HC   CH
  \ /
   N
   H
```

Figure 2.2. Structural formula of heme and its combination with globin to form hemoglobin

Four pyrrole molecules come to form a protoporphyrin which, in turn, unites with iron to form heme. Four heme molecules unit with globin to form hemoglobin (Fig. 2.2).

Heme is widely distributed in the animal and plant kingdoms. It combines not only with globin to form hemoglobin but also with other nitrogenous compounds to form hemochromogens. Myoglobin is a combination of heme and muscle globin (see also Chapter 33).

The molecular weights of hemoglobin from most species are reported to vary from 66,000 to 69,000. Based on the iron content of hemoglobin as 0.334 percent and the atomic weight of iron being 55.84, a value of 16,700 as the minimal molecular weight of hemoglobin is obtained. Differences in the globin molecules among species probably account for the slight differences in their molecular weights.

When erythrocytes are hemolyzed in the blood stream by protozoa, toxins, or chemical agents, thereby releasing hemoglobin into the plasma, a hemoglobinuria may result. Hemoglobinuria will only occur when the plasma α_2-globulin, haptoglobin, is saturated with free hemoglobin in the plasma. Hb-haptoglobin complex cannot pass the glomerular filter, whereas free hemoglobin can (White 1972). The pores or fenestrae in the capillary endothelium in the glomerular tufts of the kidneys (Porter and Bonneville 1964) place the blood plasma in direct contact with the underlying basement membrane which permits passage of small proteins such as hemoglobin.

Fetal and adult

The hemoglobins of the fetus and adult differ in many species. These differences have been noted when the amino acid compositions, oxygen dissociation curves, electrophoretic mobilities, solubilities, and ultraviolet absorption spectrums were studied. The oxygen dissociation curve of fetal hemoglobin is steeper than that of adult hemoglobin (Fig. 15.15). At a given oxygen tension, fetal hemoglobin will take up more oxygen than adult hemoglobin. On the other hand, the passage of oxygen from the mother to the fetus is by diffusion, and the tension of oxygen in the blood of the umbilical vein is the same as the venous blood on the maternal side of the placenta. In the airless lungs of the fetus the blood vessels are bypassed, for the most part, and blood returns to the left atrium of the heart. Thus, a high percentage of the blood is shunted to the arterial side through vessels which normally become closed at birth or shortly after.

Fetal hemoglobin has been studied in cattle (Grimes et al. 1958). At birth fetal hemoglobin (F) makes up 41–100 percent of the total hemoglobin in calves. It diminishes rapidly after birth and is usually replaced with hemoglobin A (the more common adult type) in calves at 2–3 months of age. In some calves hemoglobin B (a less common adult type) appears in early life, and has the same electrophoretic mobility as fetal hemoglobin. Figure 2.3 shows the variation in the rate of disappearance of fetal hemoglobin in the blood of calves (see Chapter 4).

The production of fetal hemoglobin is dependent upon the presence and availability of amino acids at the site of formation and on the anatomical origin of the erythrocytes. Other factors are probably involved. Infants may be born with one half to three fourths of their hemoglobin of the fetal type. By the end of the first year fetal-type hemoglobin may reach 1 percent. The animal retains the ability to make fetal hemoglobin in adult life.

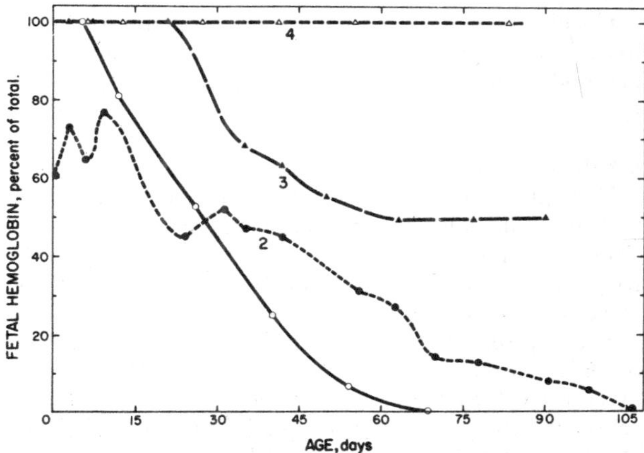

Figure 2.3. Variation in the rate of disappearance of fetal hemoglobin in the blood of calves. Curve 1, Holstein bull; curve 2, Holstein heifer; curves 3 and 4, Guernsey bulls. (From Grimes, Duncan, and Lassiter 1958, *J. Dairy Sci.* 41:1527–33.)

Hemoglobin is present in the blood of all mammals and of many animals far below mammals. In addition to variations in the hemoglobins within individuals (fetal and adult types) there are variations among species. The differences are in the globin part of the hemoglobin molecule, for heme does not vary in composition either in the animal or the plant kingdom.

Amount

The amount of hemoglobin in the blood is expressed as g/100 ml of blood. The quantity may vary within certain normal limits. As a rule in most mammals normal blood hemoglobin values are between 13 and 15 g/100 ml. Exceptions may be found with the lactating cow (11–12 g). The hemoglobin values from cold-blooded horses are usually lower, being 12–13. It is common to obtain values greater than 15 in some animals. Excitement may increase not only the hemoglobin concentration but also the PCV and erythrocyte numbers per unit of volume. These changes are due to the release of catecholamines (epinephrine and norepinephrine) causing an increase in blood pressure and the contraction of the spleen, which mobilizes erythrocytes into the circulatory system. They can easily be demonstrated in an anesthetized dog. The percent values for PCV may increase from 40 to 45 after a release or injection of epinephrine.

The hemoglobin concentration in avian blood is more difficult to determine. Various correction factors have been used in the past to adjust for the nucleated erythrocytes, which cause false high readings when conventional methods are used. A method has been devised to determine hemoglobin in the blood of chickens; the values obtained are similar to those when the iron method is used (Swenson 1951). The normal hemoglobin concentration in chicken blood ranges from 6.5 to 9 g/100 ml by this method.

Conditions that lower the oxygen content of blood, like elevated barometric pressure, cause an increase in the production of hemoglobin and the number of erythrocytes, and vice versa.

Oxyhemoglobin

Hemoglobin has important physiological relationships with oxygen. During the passage of the red corpuscles through the pulmonary capillaries, hemoglobin combines with oxygen to form oxyhemoglobin, which, as it traverses the systemic capillaries, loses its oxygen to the tissues and again becomes hemoglobin. Under appropriate conditions these reactions take place readily. Hemoglobin functions as the respiratory pigment of the blood. The red cells, the hemoglobin carriers, spend only about one second traversing a capillary. The relation between hemoglobin and oxygen may be expressed in its simplest form as follows: $Hb + O_2 \rightleftharpoons HbO_2$. Hemoglobin owes its oxygen-carrying power to the pigment it contains, and this in turn owes its oxygen-combining power to its iron content. The amount of iron in the blood is small, being about 0.334 percent of the hemoglobin molecule or 0.04–0.05 percent of the blood itself. The body carefully conserves the iron resulting from hemoglobin destruction, only a small amount being lost daily. The dietary iron needed for hemoglobin formation is therefore small.

When saturated with oxygen, one gram of hemoglobin carries about 1.36 ml of oxygen. As a result, 15 g of hemoglobin in 100 ml of blood may carry 20 ml of oxygen.

Oxyhemoglobin, its aqueous solutions, and arterial blood are bright red in color, whereas reduced hemoglobin, its aqueous solutions, and venous blood are purplish-red in color.

Myoglobin (myohemoglobin, muscle hemoglobin)

Myoglobin, or muscle hemoglobin, is a true hemoglobin, being composed of heme and globin. The heme is identical with that of blood. The globins of different species, like the globins of blood hemoglobins, differ somewhat because of variations in their amino acid content. Muscle hemoglobin contains only one heme group, and hence only one iron atom per molecule. Its molecular weight is approximately 16,700. The oxygen dissociation curve of muscle hemoglobin is hyperbolic, whereas that of blood hemoglobin in the body is S-shaped.

Myoglobin resembles blood hemoglobin in function. It serves as a brief oxygen store within the muscle fiber from one contraction to another. Myoglobin has a greater affinity for oxygen than blood hemoglobin and can release the oxygen with great rapidity when muscle fibers contract. Myoglobin is replenished with oxygen during the resting state.

Carboxyhemoglobin

Hemoglobin has the power of combining not only with oxygen but also with certain other gases, e.g. carbon monoxide. The resulting compound is carboxyhemoglobin, or carbonmonoxyhemoglobin. When carbon monoxide is present in the inspired air, it enters the blood and combines with hemoglobin to the exclusion of oxygen, for the affinity of hemoglobin for carbon monoxide is more than 200 times greater than for oxygen. Carbon monoxide attaches to the iron of heme in the same manner as oxygen. Carbon monoxide prevents hemoglobin from being a carrier of oxygen, thus interfering with hemoglobin supplying oxygen to the tissues. The breathing of air containing 0.1 percent of carbon monoxide will cause severe effects in 30–60 minutes, under which conditions some 20 percent of the hemoglobin will be converted to carboxyhemoglobin (HbCO). The carbon monoxide in combination with hemoglobin will be replaced with oxygen if the partial pressure of the latter is great enough. The replacement follows the law of mass action. The reaction $HbCO + O_2 \rightleftharpoons HbO_2 + CO$ will also be displaced to the right by an increase of carbon dioxide pressure.

Carboxyhemoglobin is a bright cherry red. Blood samples and tissues from animals poisoned with carbon monoxide may mislead one in thinking that the animal has had an abundant supply of oxygen.

Methemoglobin

Methemoglobin, a derivative of hemoglobin, is formed by the oxidation of the ferrous iron of hemoglobin to the ferric state. Methemoglobin is thus the true oxide of hemoglobin, whereas oxyhemoglobin is an oxygenated derivative. Methemoglobin is a nontoxic compound but it cannot combine with oxygen in the sense that hemoglobin does. Therefore it is useless as a respiratory pigment in the blood. Methemoglobin is formed in small amounts in the circulating blood, but reducing systems or compounds in the erythrocytes (ascorbic acid, glutathione) prevent its accumulation. Under some conditions, however, as after the administration of certain drugs (nitrites, aminophenols, acetanilid, sulfonamides, etc.), it may occur in the blood stream in larger amounts. Methemoglobin will form spontaneously in blood or in hemoglobin solutions kept in vitro. Partial deoxygenation of the samples favors its formation. Many chemical substances, including certain oxidizing agents, promote the conversion of hemoglobin to methemoglobin in vitro.

Absorption spectra

When white light is passed through a solution of hemoglobin or one of its derivatives, certain wavelengths are absorbed. The unit of light wavelength is 0.1 nm. The resulting spectrum is termed an absorption spectrum; the regions of absorption are known as absorption bands. They may be revealed by examining the solution with a spectroscope. When white light is examined spectroscopically, a series of colors known as the spectrum is obtained. The colors are red, orange, yellow, green, blue, violet, and indigo. When solutions of hemoglobin and its derivatives are examined in certain concentrations, absorption bands of definite size, appearance, and position appear (Table 2.5). Therefore spectroscopic examination identifies these pigments in solution.

LEUKOCYTES

Leukocytes, the white blood cells, are much less numerous than erythrocytes in the circulating blood. There are approximately 1300 erythrocytes to every leukocyte in the blood stream of goats; 1200 to 1 in sheep; 1000 to 1 in horses; 800 to 1 in cattle; 700 to 1 in man; 600 to 1 in dogs and cats; 400 to 1 in swine; and 100 to 1 in chickens. In anemia the number of erythrocytes may be reduced considerably. In bacterial infections the leukocytes, especially neutrophils, may be increased greatly (leukocytosis). In viral diseases the number of leukocytes, especially neutrophils, may be reduced (leukopenia). Leukopenia is also encountered with bacterial endotoxins, septicemia, and toxemia. In tumors (neoplasms) involving the lymphatic system the number of lymphocytes in the blood stream may show a marked increase, which changes the usual ratios of erythrocytes to leukocytes.

Leukocytes normally found in the blood are classified as granulocytes and agranulocytes. The granulocytes are characterized by specific granules in their cytoplasm. According to their staining reactions they are neutrophils, eosinophils, or basophils. The agranulocytes are lymphocytes and monocytes.

Granulocytes

Neutrophils

Neutrophils are comparatively numerous in the blood of most animals (Table 2.6). They have abundant, finely granular cytoplasm, and the granules stain with neutral dyes. The nucleus of each mature cell is generally divided into lobes or segments connected by filaments; such cells are called *segmented*. Those cells with a nucleus that appears as a curved or coiled band, rodlike or even deeply indented but without segmentation, are known as *band cells;* they are younger or immature

Table 2.5. Absorption of visible light by hemoglobin and derivatives

	Absorption bands, wavelengths in nm					
	Violet (400–475)	Blue (475–510)	Green (510–575)	Yellow (575–590)	Orange (590–620)	Red (620–700)
Hemoglobin	430		555			
Oxyhemoglobin	412–415		540–542	576–578		
Carbon monoxide-hemoglobin	418		538–540 568–572			
Methemoglobin						
pH<7	405–407	500				630
pH>7	411		540	577	600	
Cyanmethemoglobin	412–416		540			
Sulfhemoglobin						620

From Cantarow and Schepartz, *Biochemistry,* 3d ed., Saunders, Philadelphia, 1962, p. 131

Table 2.6. Total leukocytes per cu mm of blood and percentage of each leukocyte

Species	Total leukocyte count (range)	Percentage of each leukocyte				
		Neutrophil	Lymphocyte	Monocyte	Eosinophil	Basophil
Pig: 1 day	10,000–12,000	70	20	5–6	2–5	<1
1 week	10,000–12,000	50	40	5–6	2–5	<1
2 weeks	10,000–12,000	40	50	5–6	2–5	<1
6 weeks and older	15,000–22,000	30–35	55–60	5–6	2–5	<1
Horse	8000–11,000	50–60	30–40	5–6	2–5	<1
Cow	7000–10,000	25–30	60–65	5	2–5	<1
Sheep	7000–10,000	25–30	60–65	5	2–5	<1
Goat	8000–12,000	35–40	50–55	5	2–5	<1
Dog	9000–13,000	65–70	20–25	5	2–5	<1
Cat	10,000–15,000	55–60	30–35	5	2–5	<1
Chicken	20,000–30,000	25–30	55–60	10	3–8	1–4

forms. Neutrophils show ameboid activity and are active in phagocytosis to defend the body against infection or foreign matter, as they engulf bacteria and other small particles. They appear in large numbers at sites of inflammation.

In avian blood the comparable cell to the neutrophil is the heterophil. It contains large fusiform bodies which stain brilliantly with eosin.

Neutrophils are formed in the bone marrow from extravascular neutrophilic myelocytes (see Table 2.1). They enter the circulatory system through their ameboid action and by diapedesis.

Eosinophils

Eosinophils are large cells containing numerous large cytoplasmic granules that stain with acid dyes. The nuclei are less lobulated than those of neutrophils. Eosinophils originate in bone marrow, are very motile and slightly phagocytic. Although their numbers are normally small in the circulating blood, they may increase greatly in allergic conditions, anaphylactic shock, and certain parasitisms. Eosinophils participate in detoxification processes where histamine has been released. They are attracted to the site of antigen-antibody reactions, and after an animal has been sensitized to an antigen, its injection will cause eosinophils to appear in large numbers at the injection site. Eosinopenia follows stress conditions in which the hypothalamic-adenohypophyseal-adrenocortical response occurs or when exogenous ACTH (adrenocorticotropic hormone) is given. The eosinopenia is so consistent that it is used as a means of assaying the potency of adrenocortical hormones and ACTH. Epinephrine also produces an eosinopenia by causing a release of ACTH.

Basophils

Basophils have water-soluble cytoplasmic granules that stain with alkaline dyes. They originate in bone marrow and are closely related to tissue mast cells, which frequently are found near capillaries. Basophils resemble mast cells histologically, as both cells produce heparin and histamine—heparin to prevent the coagulation of blood, and histamine to attract the eosinophils that inactivate histamine. Basophils occur in normal blood only to a small extent. Phagocytic power is slight or absent.

Agranulocytes

Lymphocytes

Lymphocytes are relatively numerous in the blood of most species of domestic animals—most numerous in cattle, sheep, goats, swine, and chickens (see Table 2.6). They are formed in lymphoid tissue (e.g. lymph nodes, Peyer's patches, spleen, tonsils, and thymus) and are in fact the main constituent of this tissue. They produce antibodies, since their extracts contain γ-globulins. They are lost in large numbers by migration to the intestinal and respiratory mucous membranes. They are actively motile and show ameboid activity, but are not phagocytic.

Adrenocortical steroids (glucocorticoids) under the influence of ACTH cause an increase in antibody concentration in the blood through dissolution of lymphocytes in lymphoid tissue. Thus lymphopenia results from administering ACTH or cortisol, as it also comes from stress.

Monocytes

Monocytes originate in cells of the reticuloendothelial system in the spleen and bone marrow. They occur in normal blood only to a limited extent. They are relatively large, with a single nucleus and fairly abundant, faintly granular cytoplasm. They are motile and phagocytic. Monocytes have enzyme systems that are designed to engulf tissue debris from chronic inflammatory reactions.

Differential leukocyte counts

The values for each kind of leukocyte should be expressed as the number per cu mm of blood when differential leukocyte counts are made, rather than on a percentage basis. The percentage is needed with the total leukocyte count to arrive at the number of each kind of cell per cu mm of blood. From Table 2.6 the actual number of each kind of leukocyte per cu mm of blood can be obtained by multiplying the total count by the known percentage of each cell. If this is not done, one may be misled with relative values and make serious errors in conclusions.

For example, in cattle poisoned with trichloroethylene-extracted soybean meal or other bone marrow depressants, very few granulocytes are in the circulating blood. If one relies on the percentage only, a marked lymphocytosis may appear to be present (96–98%) with a marked neutropenia. The latter is correct, but the lymphocyte count may be normal (5000–6000 per cu mm in cattle blood). Also cattle with traumatic gastritis may have 70 percent neutrophils (mature and immature) and 20 percent lymphocytes. From these data one might conclude erroneously that neutrocytosis and lymphopenia are present. Actually the total leukocyte count may be 25,000; therefore the lymphocyte count is normal, but there are seven times as many neutrophils in the circulating blood as normal, whereas the percentages would show approximately three times as normal.

Total leukocyte counts

Various factors may contribute to physiological leukocytosis, such as time of day, a meal, exercise, epinephrine (endogenous or exogenous), ether anesthesia, and other stress conditions. Following exercise neutrophilia occurs. As a rule, epinephrine causes an increase in lymphocytes and neutrophils in the circulating blood and a decrease in eosinophils. With ether anesthesia, animals undergo an excitement period that causes epinephrine release, which contributes to a leukocytosis. Digestive leukocytosis occurs in some animals; however, with grazing and eating habits rather continuous in some animals, it is probably of less importance. Shifts of body water and secretions into the digestive tract during and following meals may provide a partial explanation for this phenomenon.

In the postnatal period marked changes take place in the number of circulating leukocytes. Some species of animals may be born with an increased number, but frequently the counts are comparable with those of adults or even less. In the newborn calf the number is similar to that found in the adult (Swenson et al. 1957). In the newborn pig (see Table 2.6) the number per cu mm of blood is approximately one-half that of adult swine (Swenson et al. 1955, 1958). At 5–6 weeks of age the number is similar to that found in blood of adult swine. During this 5- to 6-week period, counts made at weekly intervals may show a transitory rise at 1–2 weeks of age (Swenson et al. 1958). The reported rise is due to an increase in nucleated erythrocytes that are counted as leukocytes in the counting chamber of the hemacytometer. This error is introduced if the mathematical correction for the percentage of nucleated erythrocytes is not made.

Life span

The life span of leukocytes is not so easily measured as that of erythrocytes. The circulating blood transports the leukocytes to sites of action, where they function in an extravascular capacity. How long these cells live in the tissues is not known.

Lymphocytes have the ability to form fixed macrophages (histiocytes) and plasma cells. These cells engulf antigenic substances to form γ-globulin, as lymphocytes also can. Large numbers of lymphocytes enter the circulating blood daily. After lymphocytes are in the blood stream, they may degenerate and release γ-globulin. The turnover in lymphocytes is great; estimates of life span have been 1–4 days and also much longer. Drinker and Yoffey (1941) stated that the entire population of lymphocytes is replaced twice a day in the dog. Sanders et al. (1940) reported lymphocytes being replaced 0.5–3.5 times a day in the cat and about 5 times in the rabbit. It is thought that large numbers of lymphocytes are lost through the mucosa of the gastrointestinal tract.

In 1954, Ottesen found that most lymphocytes in man live 100–200 days, while 11–22 percent have a survival time of 3–4 days. Norman et al. (1965) reported that the mean life span of lymphocytes in women is 530 ± 64 days. The maximum length of time was 29 months. They also reported that a small number had a survival time of 3–4 days. It is possible that the short-lived ones serve their function early while others are retained longer.

The mean life span of the granulocytes in man is reported as 9 days. Granulocytes entering the blood stream are about 6 days old. Barely 5 percent of the granulocytes in the circulating blood are less than 5 days old and a few are older than 3 weeks (Ottesen 1954). The number of granulocytes in the circulating blood may decrease because of diminished production or because of their increased passage to tissues by diapedesis. Inflammatory processes hasten the passage of these cells to the site of infection. A decrease in bone marrow myeloid proliferation or impaired release of granulocytes from the marrow may cause a decrease in circulating granulocytes.

PLATELETS

Platelets (thrombocytes) are small, colorless, round or rod-shaped bodies in the circulating blood of mammals. In size they average about 3 μ in diameter, but in some cases are considerably larger. In chickens and other submammalian species they are nucleated cells usually oval in shape. In the chicken they range from 3–5 μ in width and 7–10 in length with a round nucleus in the center. Platelets are formed in fetal liver, spleen, and bone marrow. In adult mammals bone marrow is the principal source, where the platelets originate from the megakaryocyte (see Table 2.1). The lung also has been cited as a source of platelets. In birds megakaryocytes are not present, but it is thought that their thrombocytes originate in the bone marrow from large mononucleated cells.

Platelets are extremely numerous in the circulating blood—with considerable species variation. Venous and arterial platelet counts of the same individual also vary. In addition, variations have been found within the arterial or venous systems depending upon the blood vessel from which the sample is taken.

Many domestic mammals have blood platelet counts around 450,000 ± 150,000 per cu mm blood. The count for chickens usually ranges from 25,000 to 40,000. Draft horses usually have around 300,000 ± 150,000 per cu mm, while light horses have approximately one half this number. Platelets in pigs usually number 350,000 ± 150,000 (Rowsell et al. 1960, Rowsell and Mustard 1963).

There seems to be a variation between young and adult animals in some species. Lambs and calves have more than adults. The young dog has less than the adult. Infants have fewer platelets than adults. During the first 48 hours of life the number is considerably less than in adults. Usually at 3 months the infant has the number normally reported for adults. (For specific platelet counts, see Schalm et al. 1975).

The survival time of platelets is relatively short. It is thought that they survive 8–11 days in the circulating blood. The half-life of platelets is 2–3 days.

Platelets have numerous functions in the animal body. Their principal role is to prevent hemorrhage when blood vessels are injured (see Chapter 3).

SPLEEN

The spleen is the largest lymphoid organ in the animal body. More complex than other lymphoid tissue, it has been compared histologically to a large hemolymph node as found in ruminants. The spleen is abundantly supplied with blood. The splenic pulp consists of lymphoid cells primarily, but reticuloendothelial cells line the venous sinuses. Granulocytes and erythrocytes are also present. In the postnatal period the spleen usually produces lymphocytes and monocytes, but may produce erythrocytes, granulocytes, and megakaryocytes.

The more common functions of the spleen are as follows.

1. In the fetus the spleen is concerned with red blood cell formation. In the adult it forms lymphocytes, monocytes, and possibly other cells. Its fetal activity of erythropoiesis can be resumed under certain pathologic conditions. It may produce erythropoietin in some species.

2. The spleen is an important reservoir of blood, to be called upon when the body has a greater need for oxygen in the tissues. This may occur during exercise, following hemorrhage, in carbon monoxide poisoning, during the administration of certain anesthetics (chloroform, ether), and in emotional states. When an animal is excited, there is a release of catecholamines such as epinephrine and norepinephrine. Under these conditions there are increased values for erythrocyte counts, packed cell volumes, and hemoglobin values. The ability of the spleen to contract is reflected in the larger F_{cells} factor (Table 2.7). The blood values for red cell counts, hemoglobin, and PCV may be similar as during hemoconcentration. The size of the spleen in birds prevents it from serving as a blood reservoir.

3. The spleen is concerned with the destruction of erythrocytes; it removes aged and abnormal ones from the circulating blood. The numerous reticuloendothelial cells lining the venous sinuses and in the red pulp are active in this process.

4. The spleen helps the body to resist pathogenic organisms by lymphocytes and reticuloendothelial cells producing antibodies.

5. The spleen is of importance in the formation of bile pigment, in the storage of iron, and possibly in other phases of metabolism.

Hemal (*hemolymph*) *nodes,* found only in ruminants, are similar in structure and probably in function to the

Table 2.7. F_{cells} factors of various animals

Animal	F_{cells} factors	References
Cat		
normal	0.88–1.06	Farnsworth et al. 1960
splenectomized	0.76–0.80	Farnsworth et al. 1960
Dog		
normal	0.89	Clark and Woodley 1959
	1.02	Baker and Remington 1960
splenectomized	0.84	Baker and Remington 1960
	0.87–0.90	Reeve et al. 1953
	0.88	Rawson et al. 1959
Goat	0.90	O'Brien et al. 1957
Man	0.91	Gray and Frank 1953
infant	0.87	Chaplin et al. 1953
	0.73–0.95	Mollison et al. 1950
Monkey	0.83	Gregersen et al. 1959
Pig		
at birth	0.72	Talbot and Swenson 1963b
6 weeks	0.71	Talbot and Swenson 1963b
Rabbit	0.89	Zizza and Reeve 1958
Rat	0.74	Wang 1959

spleen. Erythropoiesis usually occurs in these nodes during the fetal period; granulopoiesis is more prevalent in the postnatal period.

SPECIFIC GRAVITY OF BLOOD

The specific gravities (with ranges) of whole blood of several species of domestic animals are as follows: horse, 1.053 (1.046–1.059); cattle, 1.052 (1.046–1.061); sheep, 1.051 (1.041–1.061); goat, 1.042 (1.036–1.051); pig, 1.045 (1.035–1.055); dog, 1.045–1.052; cat, 1.050 (1.045–1.057) (Altman and Dittmer 1961). The specific gravity of the corpuscles, especially the erythrocytes, is greater than the plasma. In cattle and sheep the erythrocytes have a specific gravity of 1.084 (1.079–1.090) and the serum 1.027 (1.021–1.029). The plasma protein concentration is largely responsible for the specific gravity of plasma or serum.

Because of the higher specific gravities of the cellular elements, the corpuscles of a sample of blood in which coagulation has been prevented will tend to settle out. The red blood cells gravitate to the bottom, the white blood cells occupy a thin intermediate zone, and the plasma rises to the top. This is the picture commonly seen when blood containing an anticoagulant is permitted to stand for a period of time. Other factors such as rouleaux formation of the erythrocytes also influence the settling of blood cells.

ERYTHROCYTE SEDIMENTATION RATE

The erythrocyte sedimentation rate (ESR) is a test performed on blood to help determine the health of an animal. An anticoagulant (Heller and Paul 1934, Schmidt et al. 1953) is used to keep the cell volume constant. ESR varies greatly among different species of animals (Table 2.8). It also increases with certain diseases. Microcirculatory changes occurring in disease are often manifested by "sludged blood" (partial or complete stasis of blood in capillaries).

Table 2.8. Erythrocyte sedimentation rates (vertical tubes)

Species	Mm	Time	PCV	References
Cat	53	1 hr	27	Didisheim et al. 1959
	15.4 (7–27)	1 hr	37.3 (34.5–41.0)	Schalm et al. 1975
	22.7 (0.5–51)	1 hr	38.7 (30–48.5)	Swenson 1966
Cattle	2.4	7 hr		Ferguson 1937
Chicken	0.5 (0–1)	30 min	30.6 (29.8–31.6)	Swenson 1951
	1.5 (1–3)	1 hr		
	6.7 (3–10)	3 hr		
	14.4 (10–18)	6 hr		
Dog	1–5	30 min		Coffin 1953
	6–10	1 hr		
Horse	2–12	10 min		Coffin 1953
	15–38	20 min		
Pig	0–6	30 min		Coffin 1953
	1–14	60 min		

It is not known specifically if sludged blood and an increased ESR are directly related, but an increased ESR is frequently found when microcirculatory changes such as sludged blood are present in morbid animals.

It is difficult to explain the marked variation of ESR among some species of animals. Erythrocytes of horse blood settle quickly, whereas those of ruminants settle very slowly. The ESR is measured, in standard tubes, by the distance in millimeters through which the uppermost layers of erythrocytes pass in a certain length of time.

Frequently one may observe a rapid ESR in newborn pigs; when not present at birth, it usually develops quickly if the pigs are not provided with adequate iron. The rapid ESR develops simultaneously with the anemia; however, an intramuscular injection of iron (iron-dextran) will usually correct the rapid ESR before the anemia is corrected.

The ESR is usually determined in standard tubes placed in a vertical position. Tubes held at a 45° angle will produce the maximum sedimentation rate of erythrocytes. This is advantageous when the ESR is needed quickly or the rate is slow. It is helpful with ruminant blood.

Fåhraeus (1929) made a detailed study of suspension stability of erythrocytes. He found that changes in the viscosity of the plasma, the specific gravities of the corpuscles or plasma, or the size of the erythrocytes had practically nothing to do with the sedimentation rate. The only factor of importance is the degree of agglutination of erythrocytes (size of sedimenting particles or rouleaux formation), and it is certain that the plasma proteins markedly influence this factor. According to some workers, it is an increase in the fibrinogen content of the plasma that hastens agglutination and settling, while according to others it is an increase in the globulin.

Horse erythrocytes will sediment rapidly even in ox and sheep plasma, and ox and sheep erythrocytes will sediment slowly in horse plasma (Fegler 1948). These findings indicate that the plasma is not the only factor determining the rapid ESR of horses.

Changes in the ESR are nonspecific reactions and do not indicate a pathological condition. The ESR is not pathognomonic for the diagnosis of a specific disease; it merely helps in the evaluation of the health status of the animal. At times a rapid ESR may be present and yet one is unable to make a diagnosis or observe symptoms of a disease. A rapid ESR may occur with normal hemoglobin and packed cell volumes.

Usually the rate is increased in acute general infections, in the presence of malignant tumors, in inflammatory conditions, in hypothyroidism, and also in pregnancy.

COMPOSITION OF BLOOD PLASMA

Plasma, which forms 55–70 percent of the blood, may be obtained from blood in which coagulation has been prevented. Chemical and physical analyses reveal that the composition of blood plasma is extremely complex. This is to be expected because blood has so many functions.

The chemical composition of blood plasma in the different mammals is similar; nevertheless, important quantitative differences have been discovered. The following list provides some of the plasma constituents:

Water

Gases
- Oxygen
- Carbon dioxide
- Nitrogen

Proteins
- Albumin
- Globulins
- Fibrinogen

Glucose, lactate, pyruvate

Lipids
- Fat
- Lecithin
- Cholesterol

Nonprotein nitrogenous substances
- Amino acids
- Urea
- Uric acid
- Creatine
- Creatinine
- Ammonia salts

Inorganic substances
- Sodium
- Potassium
- Calcium
- Magnesium
- Chloride
- Sulfate
- Phosphate
- Iron *
- Manganese *
- Cobalt *
- Copper *
- Zinc *
- Iodine *

Enzymes, hormones, vitamins, pigments

* Small amounts or traces

In recent years many reports on the composition of the blood of animals have been published (Table 2.9). (See also Altman and Dittmer 1961, 1964; Schalm et al. 1975; Sturkie 1965; Wintrobe 1961; Benjamin 1961; Kaneko and Cornelius 1970; Williams et al. 1972).

Plasma proteins

The plasma proteins have been identified as albumin, fibrinogen, and globulin fractions (α, β, γ). The γ-globulins contain most of the plasma antibody activity.

In man, sheep, goat, rabbit, dog, guinea pig, and rat, albumin predominates over the globulins; in the horse, pig, and cow the relative proportions of albumin and globulins are nearly equal or the globulins tend to predominate (Table 2.10).

In most newborn animals (except rodents and primates) plasma γ-globulin is either lacking or present in minute amounts since the placenta is impermeable to these protein molecules. The fetus is not capable of systhesizing them. To counteract this deficiency large quantities of γ-globulin are concentrated in the dam's colostrum. When the newborn ingests colostrum, the γ-globulin easily crosses the still imperfect intestinal barrier and provides the newborn with passive immunity in the form of antibodies.

Table 2.9. Usual ranges of some chemical constituents of the blood of mature domestic animals

	Whole blood (mg/100 ml)							Serum (mg/100 ml)	mEq/L serum		
	Glucose	Total nonprotein nitrogen	Urea nitrogen	Uric acid	Creatinine	Amino acid nitrogen	Lactic acid	Total cholesterol	Calcium	Phosphate	Chloride
Cow	40–70	20–40	6–27	0.05–2	1–2	4–8	5–20	50–230	4.5–6	2–5.2	80–100
Sheep	30–50	20–38	8–20	0.05–2	1–2	5–8	9–12	100–150	4.5–6	2–5.2	95–110
Goat	45–60	30–44	13–28	0.3–1	1–2			55–200	4.5–6	2–5.2	100–125
Pig	80–120	20–45	8–24	0.05–2	1–2	8		100–250	4.5–7.5	3.2–5.2	95–110
Horse	55–95	20–40	10–20	0.9–1	1–2	5–7	10–16	75–150	4.5–7.5	1.3–3.2	95–110
Dog	80–120	17–38	10–20	0.0–0.5	1–2	7–8	8–20	125–250	4.5–5.5	1.3–2.6	105–120
Cat	80–120							90–110			105–120
Chicken (laying)	130–290	20–35	0.4–1	1–7	1–2	4–9	20–98	125–200	8.5–19.5	4–6.4	110–120
Chicken (nonlaying)	130–260	23–36	0.4–1	2	1–2	5–10	47–56	125–200	4.5–6	2.6–5.2	110–120

Table 2.10. Types of plasma proteins (g/100 ml)

Animal	Total plasma protein	Fibrinogen	Total serum protein	Albumin	Globulin
Horse	6.84	0.34	6.50	3.25	3.25
Cow	8.32	0.72	7.60	3.63	3.97
Sheep	5.74	0.36	5.38	3.07	2.31
Goat	7.27	0.60	6.67	3.96	2.71
Dog	6.72	0.52	6.20	3.57	2.63
Cat			7.58	4.01	3.57
Pig			6.30	2.03	3.27

Data from Altman and Dittmer, *Blood and Other Body Fluids*, Fed. Am. Soc. Exp. Biol., Washington, 1961

The serum of laying hens contains 5.40 ± 0.71 g of protein per 100 ml. Serum of cockerels and nonlaying hens contains somewhat less (3.6 g/100 ml) and that of chicks still less. Simultaneous with the increase in plasma proteins in the laying hen is a marked increase in serum calcium. The nonlaying chicken has 4.5–6 mEq of calcium per liter of serum (9–12 mg/100 ml) while the laying hen has 6–18 mEq/L. The increase is attributed to the rise in estrogens from the follicles of the active ovary.

The concentration of electrolytes should be expressed in milliequivalents per liter (mEq/L) rather than milligrams per 100 ml (mg %), since the sum of all cations (sodium, potassium, calcium, magnesium, and so on) is equal to the sum of all anions (chloride, bicarbonate, phosphate, sulfate, protein, and so on). The use of this terminology emphasizes the electrical neutrality of the body fluids. When electrolytes are shown on a mg percent basis, this neutrality is not evident. The milliequivalent system indicates the capability for reactions and describes the concentration of a substance in terms of the reacting particles (ions or molecules) per volume. Milligrams per 100 ml (mg %) is converted to mEq per liter by the formula:

$$\text{mEq/L} = \frac{\text{mg \%} \times 10 \times \text{valence}}{\text{atomic weight}}$$

Origin

Plasma albumin, fibrinogen, and most of the globulins are formed in the liver. The balance of the globulins, especially γ-globulins, are formed extrahepatically in the lymph nodes and in other cells of the reticuloendothelial system of the spleen and bone marrow.

Plasma protein synthesis is markedly reduced in severe liver damage or prolonged dietary protein deficiency. This can reduce the plasma fibrinogen, resulting in increased prothrombin time and prolonged blood coagulation time (see Chapter 3). The prothrombin time is a liver function test. The normal plasma prothrombin times of most domestic animals by the one-stage method of Quick varies between 9 and 12 seconds, although for cattle, sheep, and chickens it ranges between 20 and 25 seconds.

The prothrombin time of newborn pups is prolonged during the first 48 hours of life, that of newborn lambs during the first 72 hours, and calves during the first week (Jones et al. 1956). Low levels of fibrinogen are found during this time (Field et al. 1951). Adult levels are reached after 1 day in the dog and 3 days in the lamb.

Functions

The plasma proteins, amino acids, and tissue proteins are in a state of equilibrium. When the amino acid concentration in tissue cells decreases below that in plasma, amino acids enter the cells and are used for synthesis of essential plasma and tissue proteins. The plasma proteins, formed chiefly by hepatic cells, may also be broken down into amino acids by reticuloendothelial cells and made available for the formation of cellular proteins, especially when the amino acid supply from the digestive processes is not adequate.

The plasma proteins help to maintain the colloid osmotic pressure of blood. The colloid osmotic pressure, not to be confused with crystalloid osmotic pressure of blood, amounts to 25–30 mm Hg (see Chapter 36). The proteins are colloidal and nondiffusible. The osmotic pressure produced by them opposes the hydrostatic blood pressure in the capillaries and thus prevents excess passage of fluid into the tissues, which might cause edema. The water-holding capacity of the blood depends on the concentration of the plasma proteins. A hypoproteinemia usually leads to edema. The albumins account for nearly 80 percent of the colloid osmotic pressure of the plasma—because of their abundance and smaller molecular weight. The osmotic pressure that each protein fraction contributes is inversely related to the molecular weight and directly related to its concentration in terms of number of particles in the plasma. The molecular weights of fibrinogen, albumin, and globulins are approximately 200,000, 70,000, and 180,000, respectively. Since the concentration of fibrinogen is low, the osmotic pressure exerted by this protein is likewise low. When the concentration of α-globulins and albumin is nearly the same, the albumin will contribute 2–3 times as much osmotic pressure as the globulins.

Other functions of plasma proteins are (1) to help maintain normal blood pressure by contributing to the viscosity of the blood, (2) to influence the suspension stability of the erythrocytes, (3) to help regulate the acid-base balance of the blood, (4) to provide antibodies (γ-globulins), (5) to affect the solubility of carbohydrates, lipids, and other substances held in solution in the plasma, and (6) to transport substances bound by plasma proteins, e.g. nutrients (Ca, P, Fe, Cu, lipids, fat-soluble vitamins), hormones (thyroxin, steroids), cholesterol, bilirubin, heme, and many others. Foreign substances such as T-1824 dye (used in measuring blood volume) and various therapeutic agents (sulfonamides, streptomycin, barbiturates, digitoxin) are united with the plasma proteins in the circulating blood.

REACTION OF BLOOD

The term "reaction" of blood usually refers to the pH of blood plasma in the intact animal. The balance of all cations against all anions is reflected in the hydrogen ion concentration. The negative logarithm of the hydrogen ion concentration is pH. For accurate measurements of pH, blood must be examined under conditions that prevent loss of its gases, particularly carbon dioxide. The reaction under these conditions is on the alkaline side of neutrality. Its average reaction is about pH 7.4. The pH fluctuates only within narrow limits. The mean blood pH values and ranges for several species (Altman and Dittmer 1964) are as follows:

cattle	arterial	7.38 (7.27–7.49)
sheep	venous	7.44 (7.32–7.54)
horse	venous	n.a. (7.20–7.55)
dog	arterial	7.36 (7.31–7.42)
cat	mixed	7.35 (7.24–7.40)
chicken	venous	7.54 (7.45–7.63)
man	arterial	7.39 (7.33–7.45)

Arterial blood is slightly more alkaline than venous blood. The plasma is more alkaline than the corpuscles. The limits of pH range of blood compatible with life are approximately 7.0 and 7.8.

A large amount of acid or alkali may be added to blood, in vitro or in vivo, without any considerable change in reaction. Some of the acids that are added to the blood in vivo as a result of normal metabolism are carbonic, lactic, pyruvic, phosphoric, sulfuric, and uric. Blood can maintain a constant reaction even with this acid metabolism primarily because of its buffer systems and secondarily because of its respiratory and renal mechanisms in eliminating carbon dioxide, ammonia, and hydrogen ions (see Chapters 15 and 37).

Alkali reserve

The capacity of blood to combine with carbon dioxide is the alkali reserve. It is conventionally expressed as the volume percent of carbon dioxide (ml CO_2/100 ml of plasma) that is obtained from a sample of plasma following its saturation with a gas mixture containing carbon dioxide with a partial pressure of 40 mm Hg, which is equivalent to alveolar air. About 95 percent of the carbon dioxide will unite with the bicarbonate in the plasma. The remainder will unite with the plasma proteins and in physical solution. The average carbon dioxide capacity of the blood plasma of several species of animals is as follows: mature cows, 62 volumes percent; calves, 73; sheep, 56; and horses, 64. The range of the carbon dioxide capacity of the horse is 55–75 volumes percent. In man the normal carbon dioxide capacity of blood plasma is 58 volumes percent. The carbon dioxide capacity of the plasma of birds is of the same order as in mammals.

The carbon dioxide content of blood plasma expressed in mM/L for man is 27 (25–29); cattle, 31 (29–33); sheep, 26.2 (21–28); horse, 28.1 (24–32); dog, 21.4 (17–24); cat, 20.4 (17–24); and chicken, 23 (21–26) (Altman and Dittmer 1964).

In maintaining the normal acid-base balance, and thus the alkali reserve, of the body it is essential that adequate electrolytes be ingested by the animal. The pH of the urine is affected by the constituents of the ration. Meat products containing chlorides, phosphates, and sulfates contribute to an acid urine in both ruminants and nonruminants. High protein diets typical of carnivores and some omnivores usually produce an acid urine. Citrus fruits and plant products containing abundant sodium and potassium make the body more alkaline and produce an alkaline urine. Sodium and potassium salts of strong bases and weak acids exist in citrus fruits. The anions of organic acids are metabolized, leaving the sodium and potassium for use by the body.

Frequently the pH of the urine in a sick animal may need to be changed. For example, normal cow urine is usually alkaline, while urine from a cow with ketosis is usually acid in reaction. Various salts can be used to change the reaction of urine. Salts of a strong base and a weak acid (sodium propionate, lactate, or acetate) will have an alkaline effect on the body and produce an alkaline urine. The sodium is retained by the body if needed and the organic anions are metabolized into carbon dioxide and water. Salts of a weak base and a strong acid (NH_4Cl) will produce an acid urine.

BLOOD VOLUME

The blood volume of an animal is an important consideration in understanding and interpreting packed cell volume, hemoglobin, red cell counts, plasma protein concentration, and other hematologic values. These values are altered when blood volume changes; they do not provide information on blood volume, and can even be misleading if hemoconcentration or hemodilution occurs. The status of blood volume in an animal is especially important when a blood transfusion is being considered, anemia diagnosed, or various kinds of anemia differentiated. PCV (the volume of packed red cells in a blood sample on a percentage basis) is preferred over the term *hematocrit* to express packed cell volume, since hematocrit also refers to a centrifuge. Changes in the volumes of red cells and blood plasma in the circulating blood will alter the PCV when increases or decreases in red cells and plasma are not proportional.

Methods of estimating blood volume

It is impossible to determine the volume of blood in the body merely by bleeding an animal to death. A considerable amount of blood is left in the vessels even after the animal dies of hemorrhage. Clotting and vasoconstrictor mechanisms retain a large amount of blood in the vessels. Attempts to wash out the blood retained in the vessels after bleeding have been used in the past; but the animal must be killed, and blood volume data obtained in this manner are not accurate and precise. In analytical work accuracy refers to closeness to the actual value, while precision concerns the repeatability of values obtained from a specific sample. Thus, one can have precision without accuracy.

Methods based on newer dilution procedures have greater accuracy and precision and can be repeated on the same conscious animal.

There are numerous indirect methods of estimating blood volume in the living animal. With these one may determine the plasma volume by injecting into the blood a foreign substance such as Evans Blue Dye (T-1824) or radioactive iodine (^{131}I) which combines with plasma proteins. Then one calculates the dilution the foreign substance has undergone in the plasma over a period of time by using the formula

$$\frac{\text{amount injected}}{\text{concentration/ml plasma}}$$

The erythrocyte volume may be determined in a similar manner by injecting radioactive phosphorus, iron, or chromium (^{32}P, ^{59}Fe, ^{51}Cr), which combines with erythrocytes, or by injecting red cells previously tagged either in vitro with ^{32}P, ^{59}Fe, ^{51}Cr or in a donor animal, and then, by measuring the dilution the tagged erythrocytes have undergone with time. After the plasma and red cell volumes are obtained, the blood volume can be calculated from the formulas

$$\text{plasma volume} \times \frac{100}{100 - \text{PCV}}$$

$$\text{or red cell volume} \times \frac{100}{\text{PCV}}$$

Blood is not homogenous; therefore to calculate blood volumes accurately, one must determine plasma volume and red cell volume and then use correction factors for true PCV and body PCV in the following formulas:

In calculating blood volume, multiply the correction factor for true PCV by that for body PCV to obtain the appropriate correction factor to be multiplied by the venous PCV. For example, when the correction factor for trapped plasma in arriving at the true PCV is 0.96 and F_{cells} factor in arriving at the body PCV is 0.90, the overall correction factor (0.864) is obtained by multiplying 0.96 by 0.90.

The *true PCV* of venous blood is the venous PCV minus the trapped plasma. It is impossible to centrifuge blood so that no plasma remains in the packed cells. Thus in blood volume determinations a correction must be made. The amount of plasma left in the packed cells varies with the time and force of centrifugation. Packed cell volumes obtained with a microhematocrit centrifuge usually contain less trapped plasma than those obtained with larger quantities of blood centrifuged for 30 minutes at 3000 rpm. A great variation is obtained among blood samples from anemic animals, normal animals, and animals having hemoconcentration. As a rule the smaller PCV values contain less trapped plasma on a percentage basis. Microhematocrit PCV values ranging from 13 to 20 percent contain 1.5–2.5 percent trapped plasma in the packed cells; 40–45 percent contain 4.5–5.5 percent; and 60–65 percent contain 7–8 percent (Albert 1964).

An additional factor regulating the amount of trapped plasma in the PCV is the size of the erythrocytes (Chien et al. 1965). As a rule the larger mean corpuscular volumes of erythrocytes have less trapped plasma in the PCV than the smaller cells. For example, the correction factors reported for trapped plasma in the PCV of elephant, man, dog, sheep, and goat were 0.96, 0.99, 0.97, 0.96, and 0.91, respectively, by the microhematocrit method. The mean corpuscular volumes on these same animals were 112, 91, 72, 37, and 18 cu μ. As a rule the smaller the cell the greater the amount of trapped plasma, a fact which may be partially explained by the greater amount of erythrocyte surface area per equal volume of packed cells. In order to arrive at the true PCV from the venous PCV, one must multiply the venous PCV by a correction factor such as 0.96.

The overall cell volume percentage or body PCV is the true PCV multiplied by the F_{cells} factor (obtained by dividing the body PCV by the venous PCV). The F_{cells} factor is used to correct the venous PCV and is based on a discrepancy between the true blood volume as actually

$$\text{blood volume} = \text{plasma volume} \times \frac{100}{100 - (\text{venous PCV})\,(\text{correction factor for true PCV and body PCV})}$$

$$\text{red cell volume} = \text{plasma volume} \times \frac{(\text{venous PCV})\,(\text{correction factor for true PCV and body PCV})}{100 - (\text{venous PCV})\,(\text{correction factor for true PCV and body PCV})}$$

$$\text{plasma volume} = \text{red cell volume} \times \frac{100 - (\text{venous PCV})\,(\text{correction factor for true PCV and body PCV})}{(\text{venous PCV})\,(\text{correction factor for true PCV and body PCV})}$$

Table 2.11. Reported blood volumes (ml/kg body wt.)

Animal	Plasma volume	Red cell volume	Total blood volume	References
Cat	47.7 (34–56)			Gregersen and Stewart 1939
	46.5 (34.3–65.8)			Conley 1941
	46.8		66.7	Spink et al. 1966
Cattle				
Beef			57	Hansard et al. 1953
Dairy	38.8 (36.3–40.6)		57.4 (52.4–60.6)	Reynolds 1953
	36.6		62	Dale et al. 1957
Chicken	55		83	Pappenheimer et al. 1939
Male		21		Rodnan et al. 1957
Female		10		Rodnan et al. 1957
2–5 weeks	65.6		95.5	Hegsted et al. 1951
1 week	87		120	Medway and Kare 1959
32 weeks	46		65	Medway and Kare 1959
Dog	(42–58)	38–43	83–101	Ranges from 17 references cited by Altman and Dittmer 1961
	52.8	34.1		Baker and Remington 1960
	48.3	26.4		Baker 1963
	41.6			Baker 1963
			81	Clark and Woodley 1959
	51.4	43	94.4	Parkinson and Dougherty 1958
	50.2	33.5		Deavers et al. 1960
	54		79	Courtice 1943
Goat	53		70	Courtice 1943
	55.9	14.7	70.6	Klement et al. 1955
Horse	51		72	Courtice 1943
Draft	43.2	28.5	71.7	Julian et al. 1956
	43.5	18.2	61.4	Marcilese et al. 1964
Thoroughbred	61.9	47.1	109.6	Julian et al. 1956
	63.3	39.8	103.1	Marcilese et al. 1964
Saddle	52.5	25.3	77.5	Marcilese et al. 1964
Pig				
0–2 months	48–81	13–33	74–100	Ranges from 8 references cited by Swenson 1975
2–12 months	35–59	21–27	52–69	
1–3 years			35–46	
Sheep			58	Schambye 1952
			57	Hansard et al. 1953
	61.9			MacFarlane et al. 1959
	44.6			Hodgetts 1961
	46.7	19.7	66.4	Hodgetts 1961

measured and the total blood volume calculated from the venous PCV. The venous PCV gives a higher value than actually exists as an overall or body PCV because most blood samples are taken from large veins and arteries, which have higher PCV readings than samples from capillaries, arterioles, and other minute vessels. The ratio of the endothelial surface area to the blood volume in small blood vessels is considerably larger than in large arteries and veins. When blood circulates, plasma passes near the endothelial lining more rapidly than erythrocytes do, granting that there may be "no slip" or passage of plasma in intimate contact with the endothelium. As a result, erythrocytes are more to the center of the blood vessels and plasma to the periphery; this hastens circulation. Thus, in the process of blood flow, capillaries and other small vessels having a greater ratio of endothelial lining to blood volume will have more plasma at the periphery and a lower PCV reading. The F_{cells} factor corrects this disparity.

Considerable variation exists in the F_{cells} factor among species of animals (see Table 2.7). The F_{cells} factor is influenced by the spleen, as shown by the fact that it is stable in cats and dogs after splenectomy. The spleen does not function as a large blood reservoir in humans; however, the F_{cells} factor is rather constant when it is compared in intact and splenectomized patients (Fudenberg et al. 1961).

It is generally thought that the venous circulation contains approximately 50 percent of the blood volume and the capillaries contain 5 percent. While an animal rests, only 10 percent of the capillaries may be patent in skeletal muscle. The volumes of the capillary beds in various tissues and organs are subject to change depending upon the needs of the cells for oxygen and nutrients. The status of the animal with regard to age, size, activity, health, excitement, and quantity of hemoglobin may affect the F_{cells} factor.

McLain et al. (1951) compared blood volume values in dogs and rabbits by bleeding and dye-dilution methods. The latter method gives larger volumes. Considerable variation, then, in blood volume values can be expected as a result of the methods used, species variation, and variations within species, such as age, nutrition, health of animal, degree of physical activity, lactation, sex, and environmental factors such as temperature and altitude. Larger blood volumes are present in lightweight horses (hot-blooded) than in draft horses (cold-blooded) (Julian et al. 1956). Animals that are more excitable and active usually have greater blood volumes (Table 2.11). The fluctuations of the plasma volume in lambs are greater than those of erythrocytes because of the passing of plasma fluids extravascularly in order to help maintain a constant intracellular environment (Fig. 2.4). In sheep, as pregnancy advances, increases in blood and plasma volumes occur (Fig. 2.5). The cellular volume decreases slightly. Thus the increase in blood volume is caused by the increase in plasma volume.

The plasma, erythrocyte, and total blood volumes vary greatly with age in swine. The plasma volume of newborn pigs is 53–55 ml per kg body weight and increases to 81 after nursing (McCance and Widdowson 1959). There is a progressive decrease in these percentage values as pigs and other animals grow and become fat. The percentage of total body water is likewise decreased as the body fat increases.

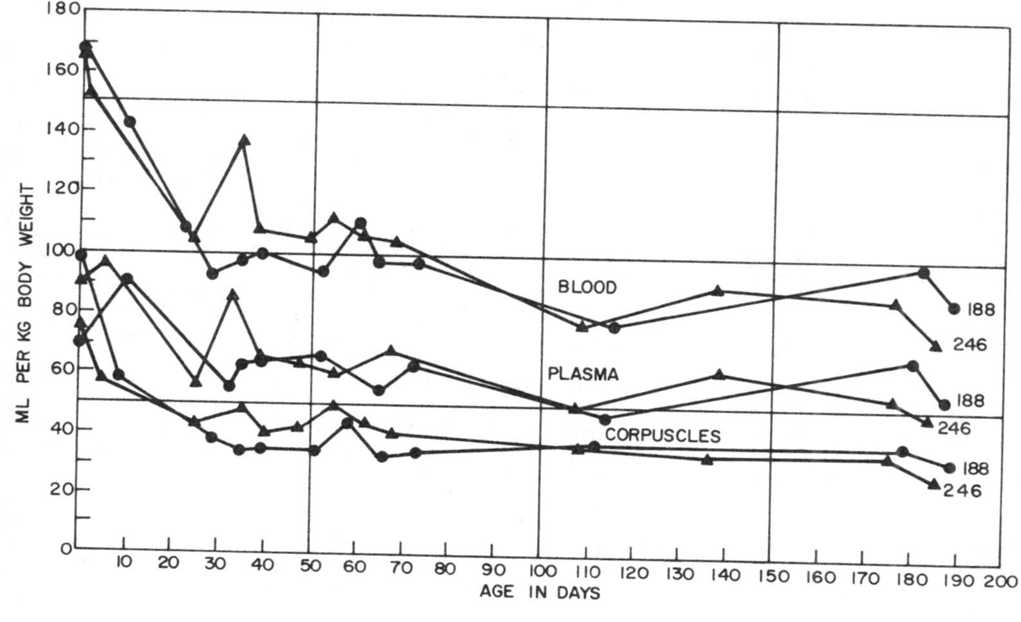

Figure 2.4. Volumes of blood, plasma, and red corpuscles per kg of body weight of lambs at different ages. Note that fluctuations of plasma are different from those of corpuscles. (Redrawn and slightly modified from Gotsev 1939, *J. Physiol.* 94:539–49.)

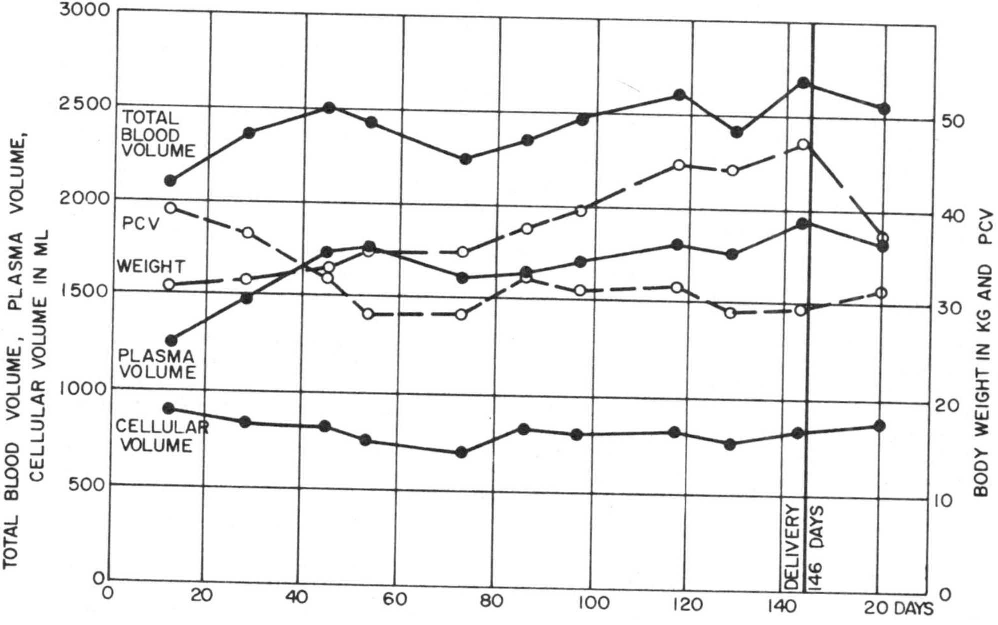

Figure 2.5. Total blood volume, PCV, plasma volume, cellular volume, and body weight of sheep. Note rise in blood volume and plasma volume as pregnancy advances. The cellular volume falls slightly; hence the increase in blood volume is due to an increase in plasma volume. (Redrawn and slightly modified from Barcroft, Kennedy, and Mason 1939, *J. Physiol.* 95:159–72.)

REFERENCES

Abderhalden, E. 1898. Zur Quantitativen Vergleichenden Analyse des Blutes. *Zeitschrift Physiol. Chem.* 25:65–115.

Albert, S.N. 1964. Blood volume. *Scintillator* 8(2):1–6.

Altman, P.L., and Dittmer, D.S. 1961. *Blood and Other Body Fluids.* Fed. Am. Soc. Exp. Biol., Washington.

——. 1964. *Biology Data Book.* Fed. Am. Soc. Exp. Biol., Washington.

Baker, C.H. 1963. Cr^{51} labeled red cell, I^{131}-fibrinogen, and T-1824 dilution spaces. *Am. J. Physiol.* 204:176–80

Baker, C.H., and Remington, J.W. 1960. Role of the spleen in determining total body hematocrit. *Am. J. Physiol.* 198:906–10.

Barcroft, J., Kennedy, J.A., and Mason, M.F. 1939. The blood volume and kindred properties in pregnant sheep. *J. Physiol.* 95:159–72.

Benjamin, M.M. 1961. *Outline of Veterinary Clinical Pathology.* 2d ed. Iowa State U. Press, Ames.

Burwell, E.L., Brickley, B.A., and Finch, C.A. 1953. Erythrocyte life span in small animals. *Am. J. Physiol.* 172:718–24.

Bush, J.A., Berlin, N.I., Jensen, W.N., Brill, A.B., Cartwright, G.E., and Wintrobe, M.M. 1955. Erythrocyte life span in growing swine—determined by glycine-2-C^{14}. *J. Exp. Med.* 101:451–59.

Bush, J.A., Jensen, W.N., Athens, J.W., Ashenbrucker, H.,

Cartwright, G.E., and Wintrobe, M.M. 1956. Studies on copper metabolism. XIX. The kinetics of iron metabolism and erythrocyte life span in copper-deficient swine. *J. Exp. Med.* 103:701–12.

Cantarow, A., and Schepartz, B. 1962. *Biochemistry*. 3d ed. Saunders, Philadelphia.

Carlson, R.H., Swenson, M.J., Ward, G.M., and Booth, N.H. 1961. Effects of intramuscular injections of iron-dextran in newborn lambs and calves. *J. Am. Vet. Med. Ass. 139:457–61.*

Castle, W.B. 1934–1935. The etiology of pernicious and related macrocytic anemias. *Harvey Lectures* 30:37–48.

Chaplin, H., Jr., Mollison, P.L., and Vetter, H. 1953. The body-venous hematocrit ratio: Its constancy over a wide hematocrit range. *J. Clin. Invest.* 32:1309–16.

Chien, S., Dellenback, R.J., Usami, S., and Gregersen, M.I. 1965. Plasma trapping in hematocrit determination: Differences among animal species. *Proc. Soc. Exp. Biol. Med.* 119:1155–58.

Clark, C.H., and Woodley, C.H. 1959. A comparison of blood volumes as measured by rose bengal, T-1824 (Evans Blue), radiochromium-tagged erythrocytes, and a combination of the latter two. *Am. J. Vet. Res.* 20:1067–68.

Coffin, D.L. 1953. *Manual of Veterinary Clinical Pathology*. 3d ed. Cornell U. Press, Ithaca, N.Y.

Conley, C.L. 1941. The effect of ether anesthesia on the plasma volume of cats. *Am. J. Physiol.* 32:796–800.

Courtice, F.C. 1943. The blood volume of normal animals. *J. Physiol.* 102:290–305.

Dale, H.E., Brody, S., and Burge, G.J. 1957. The effect of environmental temperature on blood volume and the antipyrine space in dairy cattle. *Am. J. Vet. Res.* 18:97–100.

Davson, H. 1958. Cellular aspects of the electrolytes and water in body fluids. In G.E.W. Wolstenholme and M. O'Connor, eds., *Water and Electrolyte Metabolism in Relation to Age and Sex*. Ciba Found. Colloquia on Ageing. Churchill, London. Vol. 4, 15–35.

Deavers, S., Smith, E.L., and Huggins, R.A. 1960. Control circulatory values of morphine-pentobarbitalized dogs. *Am. J. Physiol.* 199:797–99.

Didisheim, P., Hattori, K., and Lewis, J.H. 1959. Hematologic and coagulation studies in various animal species. *J. Lab. Clin. Med.* 53:866–75.

Drastisch, L. 1928. Ist die Konzentration des Blutfarbstoffes im Blutkörperchen bei allen Tieren Konstant? *Arch. f. g. ges. Physiol.* 219:227–32.

Drinker, C.K., and Yoffey, J.M. 1941. *Lymphatics, Lymph, and Lymphoidal Tissue*. Harvard U. Press, Cambridge.

Evans, J.V. 1954. Electrolyte concentrations in red blood cells of British breeds of sheep. *Nature* 174:931–32.

Evans, J.V., and Phillipson, A.T. 1957. Electrolyte concentrations in the erythrocytes of the goat and ox. *J. Physiol.* 139:87–96.

Fåhraeus, R. 1929. The suspension stability of the blood. *Physiol. Rev.* 9:241–74.

Farnsworth, P.N., Paulino-Gonzalez, C.M., and Gregersen, M.I. 1960. F_{cells} values in the normal and splenectomized cat: Relation of F_{cells} to body size. *Proc. Soc. Exp. Biol. Med.* 104:729–33.

Fegler, G. 1948. Haemoglobin concentration, hematocrit value, and sedimentation rate of horse blood. *Q. J. Exp. Physiol.* 35:129–39.

Ferguson, L.C. 1937. Studies on bovine blood. I. The sedimentation rate and percentage volume of erythrocytes in normal blood. *J. Am. Vet. Med. Ass.* 91:163–75.

Field, J.B., Spero, L., and Link, K.P. 1951. Prothrombin and fibrinogen deficiency in new-born pups and lambs. *Am. J. Physiol.* 165:188–94.

de Franciscis, P., de Bella, G., and Cifaldi, S. 1965. Spleen as a production site for erythropoietin. *Science* 150:1831–33.

Fudenberg, H., Baldini, H., Mahoney, J.P., and Dameshek, W. 1961. The body hematocrit/venous hematocrit ratio and the splenic reservoir. *Blood* 17:71–82.

Gotsev, T. 1939. Blood volume in lambs. *J. Physiol.* 94:539–49.

Gray, S.J., and Frank, H. 1953. The simultaneous determination of red cell mass and plasma volume in man with radioactive sodium chromate and chromic chloride. *J. Clin. Invest.* 32:1000–4.

Gregersen, M.I., Sear, H., Rawson, R.A., Chien, S., and Saiger, G.I. 1959. Cell volume, plasma volume, total blood volume, and F_{cells} factor in the Rhesus monkey. *Am. J. Physiol.* 196:184–87.

Gregersen, M.I., and Stewart, J.D. 1939. Simultaneous determination of the plasma volume with T-1824, and the available fluid volume with sodium thiocyanate. *Am. J. Physiol.* 125:142–52.

Grimes, R.M., Duncan, C.W., and Lassiter, C.A. 1958. Bovine fetal hemoglobin. I. Postnatal persistence and relation to adult hemoglobins. *J. Dairy Sci.* 41:1527–33.

Hansard, S.L., Butler, W.O., Comar, C.L., and Hobbs, C.S. 1953. Blood volume of farm animals. *J. Anim. Sci.* 12:402–13.

Hansard, S.L., and Kincaid, E. 1956. Red cell life span of farm animals. *J. Anim. Sci.* 15:1300.

Hansen, M.F., Todd, A.C., Kelley, G.W., and Cawein, M. 1950. *Six Blood Values in Thoroughbred Stallions, Mares in Foal, Barren Mares, and Weanlings*. Ky. Ag. Exp. Sta. Bull. 555. Lexington.

Hawkins, W.B., and Whipple, G.H. 1938. The life cycle of the red blood cell in the dog. *Am. J. Physiol.* 122:418–27.

Hegsted, D.M., Wilson, D., Milner, J.P., and Ginna, P.H. 1951. Blood and plasma volume and thiocyanate space of normal chicks. *Proc. Soc. Exp. Biol. Med.* 78:114–15.

Heller, V.G., and Paul, H. 1934. Changes in cell volume produced by varying concentrations of different anticoagulants. *J. Lab. Clin. Med.* 19:777–80.

Hevesy, G., and Ottesen, J. 1945. Life-cycle of the red corpuscles of the hen. *Nature* 156:534.

Hodgetts, V.E. 1961. The dynamic red cell storage function of the spleen in sheep. III. Relationship to determination of blood volume, total red cell volume, and plasma volume. *Austral. J. Exp. Biol.* 39:187–96.

Jensen, W.N., Bush, J.A., Ashenbrucker, H., Cartwright, G.E., and Wintrobe, M.M. 1956. The kinetics of iron metabolism in normal growing swine. *J. Exp. Med.* 103:145–59.

Jones, W.G., Hughes, C.D., Swenson, M.J., and Underbjerg, G.K.L. 1956. Plasma prothrombin time and hematocrit values of blood of dairy cattle. *Proc. Soc. Exp. Biol. Med.* 91:14–18.

Julian, L.M., Lawrence, J.H., Berlin, N.I., and Hyde, G.M. 1956. Blood volume, body water, and body fat of the horse. *J. Appl. Physiol.* 8:651–53.

Kaneko, J.J., and Cornelius, C.E. 1970. *Clinical Biochemistry of Domestic Animals*. 2d ed. Academic Press, New York. Vols. 1, 2.

Kerr, S.E. 1937. Studies on the inorganic composition of blood. IV. The relationship of potassium to the acid-soluble phosphorus fractions. *J. Biol. Chem.* 117:227–35.

Klement, A.W., Jr., Ayer, D.E., and Rogers, E.B. 1955. Simultaneous use of Cr^{51} and T-1824 dye in blood volume studies in the goat. *Am. J. Physiol.* 181:15–18.

Krumbhaar, E.B. 1926. Functions of the spleen. *Physiol. Rev.* 6:160–200.

Lawrie, R.A. 1950. Some observations on factors affecting myoglobin concentrations in muscle. *J. Ag. Sci.* 40:356–66.

MacFarlane, W.V., Morris, R.J.H., Howard, B., and Budtz-Olsen, O.E. 1959. Extracellular fluid distribution in tropical Merino sheep. *Austral. J. Ag. Res.* 10:269–86.

Macleod, J., and Ponder, E. 1946. An observation on the red cell content of the blood of the Thoroughbred horse. *Science* 103:73–75.

Mann, F.D., Shonyo, E.S., and Mann, F.C. 1951. Effect of removal of the liver on blood coagulation. *Am. J. Physiol.* 164:111–16.

Marcilese, N.A., Valsecchi, R.M., Figueiras, H.D., Camberos, H.R., and Varela, J.E. 1964. Normal blood volumes in the horse. *Am. J. Physiol.* 207:223–27.

McCance, R.A., and Widdowson, E.M. 1959. The effect of colostrum on the composition and volume of the plasma of newborn piglets. *J. Physiol.* 145:547–50.

McLain, P.L., Ruhe, C.H.W., and Kruse, T.K. 1951. Concurrent estimates of blood volume in animals by bleeding and dye methods. *Am. J. Physiol.* 164:611–17.

Medway, W., and Kare, M.R. 1959. Blood and plasma volume, hematocrit, blood specific gravity, and serum protein electrophoresis of the chicken. *Poul. Sci.* 38:624–31.

Medway, W., Prier, J.E., and Wilkinson, J.S. 1969. *Textbook of Veterinary Clinical Pathology*. Williams & Wilkins, Baltimore.

Mollison, P.L., Veall, N., and Cutbush, M. 1950. Red cell and plasma volume in newborn infants. *Arch. Dis. Childhood* 25:242–53.

Morris, P.G.D. 1942. Comparative blood picture of army mules and horses. *Vet. J.* 98:224–31.

Norman, A., Sasaki, M.S., Ottoman, R.E., and Fingerhut, A.G. 1965. Lymphocyte lifetime in women. *Science* 147:745.

O'Brien, W.A., Howie, D.L., and Crosby, W.H. 1957. Blood volume studies in wounded animals. *J. Appl. Physiol.* 11:110–14.

Ottesen, J. 1954. On the age of human white cells in peripheral blood. *Acta Physiol. Scand.* 32:75–91.

Pappenheimer, A.M., Goettsch, M., and Jungherr. E. 1939. *Nutritional Encephalomalacia in Chicks and Certain Related Disorders of Domestic Birds*. Conn. Ag. Exp. Sta. Bull. 229. Storrs.

Parkinson, J.E., and Dougherty, J.H. 1958. Effect of internal emitters on red cell plasma volumes of beagle dogs. *Proc. Soc. Exp. Biol. Med.* 97:722–25.

Perk, K., Frei, Y.F., and Herz, A. 1964. Osmotic fragility of red blood cells of young and mature domestic and laboratory animals. *Am. J. Vet. Res.* 25:1241–48.

Porter, K.R., and Bonneville, M.A. 1964. *An Introduction to Fine Structure of Cells and Tissues*. Lea & Febiger, Philadelphia.

Rawson, R.A., Chien, S., Peng, M.T., and Dellenback, R.J. 1959. Determination of residual blood volume required for survival in rapidly hemorrhaged splenectomized dogs. *Am. J. Physiol.* 196:179–83.

Reeve, E.B., Gregersen, M.I., Allen, T.H., Sear, H., and Walcott, W.W. 1953. Effects of alteration in blood volume and venous hematocrit in splenectomized dogs on estimates of total blood volume with P^{32} and T-1824. *Am. J. Physiol.* 175:204–10.

Reynolds, M. 1953. Plasma and blood volume in the cow using the T-1824 hematocrit method. *Am. J. Physiol.* 173:421–27.

Roberts, S.J. 1943. The effects of various intravenous injections on the horse. *Am. J. Vet. Res.* 4:226–39.

Rodnan, G.P., Ebaugh, E.G., Jr., and Fox, M.R.S. 1957. Red cell turnover rate in the mammal, bird, and reptile. *Blood* 12:355–66.

Rowsell, H.C., Downie, H.G., and Mustard, J.F. 1960. Comparison of the effect of egg yolk or butter on the development of atherosclerosis in swine. *Can. Med. Ass. J.* 83:1175–86.

Rowsell, H.C., and Mustard, J.F. 1963. Blood coagulation in some common laboratory animals. *Lab. Anim. Care* 13:752–62.

Sanders, A.G., Florey, H.W., and Barnes, J.M. 1940. The output of lymphocytes from the thoracic duct in cats and rabbits. *Brit. J. Exp. Path.* 21:254–63.

Schalm, O.W., Jain, N.C., and Carroll, E.J. 1975. *Veterinary Hematology*. 3d ed. Lea & Febiger, Philadelphia.

Schambye, A.P. 1952. Det cirkulerende Blodvolumen hos får bestemt med P^{32}-maerkede Erytrocyter og T-1824. *Nord. Vet. Med.* 4:929–61.

Schmidt, C.H., Hope, M.E., and Gomez, D.C. 1953. A new anticoagulant for routine laboratory procedures. *U.S. Armed Forces Med. J.* 4:1556–62.

Spink, R.R., Malvin, R.L., and Cohen, B.J. 1966. Determination of erythrocyte half life and blood volume in cats. *Am. J. Vet. Res.* 27:1041–43.

Stone, E.C., Adams, M.F., and Dickson, W.M. 1953. Electrophotometric determination of osmotic resistance of ovine erythrocytes. *Cornell Vet.* 43:3–9.

Strumia, M.M. 1954. The preservation of blood for transfusion. *Blood* 9:1105–19.

Sturkie, P.D. 1965. *Avian Physiology*. 2d ed. Cornell U. Press, Ithaca, N.Y.

Swenson, M.J. 1951. Effect of a vitamin B_{12} concentrate and liver meal on the hematology of chicks fed on all-plant protein ration. *Am. J. Vet. Res.* 12:147–51.

——. 1966. Erythrocyte sedimentation rates of cats. Unpublished data.

——. 1975. Composition of body fluids. In H.W. Dunne and A.D. Leman, eds., *Diseases of Swine*. 4th ed. Iowa State U. Press, Ames. Pp. 95–124.

Swenson, M.J., Goetsch, D.D., and Underbjerg, G.K.L. 1955. The effect of the sow's ration on the hematology of the newborn pig. *Proc. Book.* Am. Vet. Med. Ass., 92d Ann. Mtg., Minneapolis. Pp. 159–62.

——. 1962. Effects of dietary trace minerals, excess calcium, and various roughages on the hemogram, tissues, and estrous cycles of Hereford heifers. *Am. J. Vet. Res.* 23:803–8.

Swenson, M.J., Underbjerg, G.K.L., Bartley, E.E., and Jones, W.G. 1957. Effects of trace minerals, aureomycin, and other supplements on certain hematologic values and organ weights of dairy calves. *J. Dairy Sci.* 40:1525–33.

Swenson, M.J., Underbjerg, G.K.L., Goetsch, D.D., and Aubel, C.E. 1958. Blood values and growth of newborn pigs following subcutaneous implantation of bacitracin pellets. *Am. J. Vet. Res.* 19:554–59.

Talbot, R.B., and Swenson, M.J. 1963a. Survival of Cr^{51} labeled erythrocytes in swine. *Proc. Soc. Exp. Biol. Med.* 112:573–76.

——. 1963b. Plasma volume, erythrocyte volume, total blood volume, and F_{cells} factor in the suckling pig. *Fed. Proc.* 22(2), pt. I:682.

Tosteson, D.C. 1963. Active transport, genetics, and cellular evolution. *Fed. Proc.* 22(1), pt. I:19–26.

Wang, L. 1959. Plasma volume, cell volume, total blood volume, and F_{cells} factor in the normal and splenectomized Sherman rat. *Am. J. Physiol.* 196:188–92.

White, P. 1972. Degradation of hemoglobin. See Williams et al. below.

Williams, W.J., Beutler, E., Erslev, A.J. and Rundles, R.W. 1972. *Hematology*. McGraw-Hill, New York.

Wintrobe, M.M. 1933. Variations in the size and hemoglobin content of erythrocytes in the blood of various vertebrates. *Folia Haemat.* 51:32–49.

——. 1961. *Clinical Hematology*. 5th ed. Lea & Febiger, Philadelphia.

Zizza, F., and Reeve, E.B. 1958. Erroneous measurement of plasma volume in the rabbit by T-1824. *Am. J. Physiol.* 194:522–26.

CHAPTER 3

Blood Coagulation | by Patricia A. Gentry and Harry G. Downie

The development of a cardiovascular system and a blood supply circulating by virtue of large pressure differences confronted organisms with a considerable hazard, that of bleeding to death as the result of any break in the vascular wall. Spontaneous systems for reducing leakage thus became essential for survival.

The most obvious parts of this mechanism are coagulation of the blood, adhesion of blood platelets, contraction of damaged vessels, and adhesion of vessel walls, perhaps due to increased endothelial stickiness.

The biochemical mechanism of blood clot formation involves a complex sequence of protein-protein interactions. The majority of the plasma proteins which participate in the hemostatic process circulate in plasma as inactive proenzymes. The net result of the protein reactions is the sequential activation of these proenzymes to their active form.

Initially the various proteins, or factors, involved in the blood coagulation system were identified in humans congenitally deficient in the specific protein. As a result the proteins were assigned a variety of interesting but confusing names. In order to simplify and standardize the nomenclature system, the majority of proteins involved in the blood coagulation process are, by international agreement, designated by Roman numerals (Table 3.1).

INTRINSIC MECHANISM OF COAGULATION

Intrinsic mechanism refers to the sequence of enzymatic reactions which is initiated when blood comes into contact with a "foreign surface." Any surface other than the intact endothelial lining of the blood vessel walls is "foreign" to both the coagulation proteins and the blood cells. Consequently, damage to a vessel wall or exposure to air can initiate the clotting process. Once the clotting process has been initiated, the chain of reactions culminates in the generation of thrombin and the formation of an insoluble fibrin clot. It is convenient to consider the sequence of enzymatic reactions in several steps: (a) the contact phase, or activation of the clotting mechanism, (b) the activation of factor X, (c) the formation of thrombin, and (d) the formation of insoluble fibrin (Fig. 3.1).

Contact activation phase

The initial event is the conversion of the plasma protein factor XII to the active enzyme factor XIIa. A wide variety of substances may activate factor XII. It is well established that a wide range of insoluble particles bearing a negative charge, such as glass, celite, kaolin, asbestos, or collagen (Nossel, in Biggs 1972), will all convert factor XII to the active proteolytic enzyme form. Their surfaces may resemble damaged endothelium in

Table 3.1. Synonyms of Blood-Clotting Factors *

Factor	Synonym †
I	FIBRINOGEN
II	PROTHROMBIN
III	THROMBOPLASTIN TISSUE THROMBOPLASTIN
IV	CALCIUM
V	PROACCELERIN Labile factor Accelerator globulin (Ac-globulin)
VII	PROCONVERTIN Stable factor Serum prothrombin conversion accelerator (SPCA) Autoprothrombin I
VIII	ANTIHEMOPHILIC FACTOR (AHF) Antihemophilic globulin (AHG) Platelet cofactor I Antihemophilic factor A
IX	CHRISTMAS FACTOR Plasma thromboplastin component (PTC) Autoprothrombin II Platelet cofactor II Antihemophilic factor B
X	STUART FACTOR Stuart-Prower factor Autoprothrombin III
XI	PLASMA THROMBOPLASTIN ANTECEDENT (PTA)
XII	HAGEMAN FACTOR (HF) Contact factor
XIII	FIBRIN STABILIZING FACTOR (FSF) Laki-Lorand (L-L) factor Fibrinase Plasma transglutaminase

* Nomenclature recommended by the International Committee on Haemostasis and Thrombosis 1964, *Thromb. Diath. Haemorrh.* 13 (suppl.):455. A sixth factor was initially postulated but does not exist.

† The most common synonyms are in capital letters.

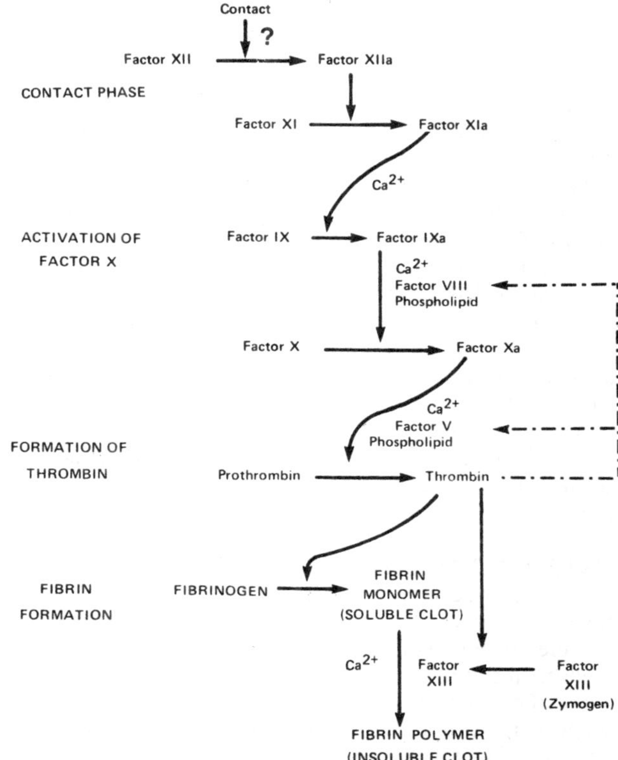

Figure 3.1. Intrinsic mechanism of blood coagulation illustrated as a modified cascade phenomenon. Solid lines represent the processes of activation, broken lines illustrate the auto-catalytic action of thrombin on the reaction sequence.

being "wettable surfaces." They appear to initiate the clotting process by causing a configurational change in the factor XII molecule which results in the exposure of an enzymatic site. Factor XIIa then perpetuates the coagulation process by converting factor XI to the active form, factor XIa.

Activation of factor X

Factor XIa exerts a proteolytic effect on the glycoprotein zymogen factor IX to convert it to factor IXa, an active enzymatic entity. The presence of calcium ions is obligatory for this reaction. In order for the activation of factor X by factor IXa to proceed at an adequately fast rate, two additional cofactors are required. One is a phospholipid component which is supplied by the blood platelets (see below) and the second is a large protein molecule, factor VIII. Factor IXa, factor VIII, phospholipid, and calcium combine to form a protein-phospholipid-calcium complex which rapidly converts factor X to factor Xa (Biggs, in Biggs 1972; Davie and Kirby 1973).

Formation of thrombin

Factor Xa, like factor IXa, is a proteolytic enzyme which can, in the presence of calcium ions, slowly convert prothrombin, the precursor of thrombin, to the active enzyme (Nemerson and Pitlick 1972). Again, this reaction requires the addition of two cofactors in order for thrombin to be formed at an adequate rate—a phospholipid component and factor V, a protein component. The cofactors stimulate the rate of reaction up to 1000 fold over that of the enzyme alone.

Formation of fibrin

Once thrombin has been generated, the fibrin clot can form. Thrombin is a serine protease enzyme which exhibits an unusually high degree of substrate specificity for its natural substrate fibrinogen. The enzyme converts fibrinogen to soluble fibrin by the hydrolysis of only two fibrinopeptide bonds. Thrombin first cleaves off two small peptide chains from each end of the fibrinogen molecule (Esnouf, in Biggs 1972). As a result of this proteolytic activity, the fibrinogen molecules lose their negative charges which have in effect been repelling each other. The altered fibrinogen molecules, since they now have no forces to prevent their adhering to each other, form a lattice. This structure is referred to as soluble fibrin since it is still permeable to the flow of blood because of the loose nature of the contact. The transformation of this soluble fibrin to the insoluble fibrin clot requires the formation of peptide bonds between the chains of the different fibrin molecules and across the chains of the same fibrin molecules. This transamination, or peptide bond forming reaction, is catalyzed by the enzyme factor XIII in the presence of calcium ions. As with the other enzymes involved in the coagulation process, factor XIII normally circulates in plasma in the form of an inactive proenzyme and is converted to the activate form by thrombin generated in the sequence of reactions described above.

Once the insoluble fibrin clot has formed, platelets, white cells, and red cells are trapped inside the mesh of fibrin strands and blood flow ceases.

EXTRINSIC MECHANISM

Extrinsic mechanism refers to the sequence of reactions which occur when the damage to the blood vessel is sufficiently traumatic to involve the surrounding tissues, with the resulting release of tissue juices. Tissues contain a specific lipoprotein, tissue thromboplastin, which can produce rapid fibrin formation when it enters the blood stream. Although the mechanism is not completely understood, it is known that tissue thromboplastin, in the presence of calcium ions and another plasma protein, factor VII, forms an active proteolytic enzyme complex (Fig. 3.2). This complex directly converts the proenzyme factor X to the active enzyme factor Xa (Nemerson and Pitlick 1972). In essence, the extrinsic clotting mechanism, by activating factor X directly, bypasses the initial stages of the intrinsic mechanism and produces fibrin formation at a faster rate than the intrinsic mechanism. This is advantageous to the animal since, when damage to a blood vessel is of sufficient severity to include damage to the surrounding tissues, the animal would require an extremely efficient clotting mechanism.

The intrinsic and the extrinsic mechanisms of blood coagulation should not be regarded as competing with each other but rather as complementary systems designed to cope with the everyday minor traumas to which the blood vessels are exposed. The two mechanisms are not in fact separated as distinctly in nature as has been described.

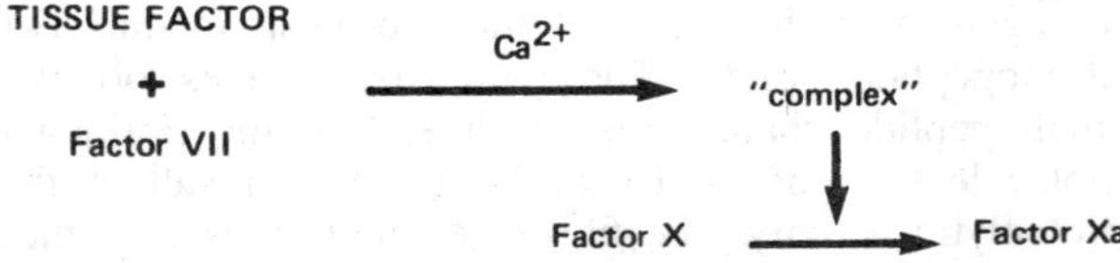

Figure 3.2. Extrinsic mechanism of blood coagulation

INTEGRATION OF INTRINSIC AND EXTRINSIC MECHANISMS

Recent data suggests that the intrinsic and extrinsic mechanisms of blood coagulation are linked through a second set of reactions in addition to the common activation of factor X. A clotting defect involving the initial stages of the intrinsic mechanism has been identified in a family named Fletcher. The Fletcher factor has been characterized as a prekallikrein which is converted to the active kallikrein by activated factor XII or by active fragments of factor XII (Fig. 3.3). Fletcher factor in its active kallikrein form is now known to participate in the coagulation sequence by converting factor XII to its active form (Schreiber and Austen 1973). Once the prekallikrein has been activated it generates additional active molecules by a feedback effect analogous to that described for thrombin below. This active kallikrein appears to form a link between the intrinsic and the extrinsic mechanisms of coagulation. The kallikrein, activated by factor XII, seems to interact with factor VII and produce a dramatic increase in its procoagulant activity (Stormorken et al. 1974). In effect, the kallikrein not only activates the intrinsic pathway but can also markedly accelerate the extrinsic pathway. In all probability the kallikrein is not a single entity but represents a group of enzymes which form kinins, small polypeptide molecules which can cause contraction of smooth muscle and vasodilatation. This seems especially likely when one considers that the plasma kallikreins have a wide range of effects on the cardiovascular system (Ratnoff 1969). In addition, the kallikreins have long been known to produce an increase in vascular permeability, to stimulate the contraction of smooth muscle, to cause a decrease in blood pressure, to induce leukocytes to adhere to small blood vessels, and to migrate into extravascular spaces.

AMPLIFICATION AND FEEDBACK STIMULATION

One aspect of the blood coagulation mechanism which is often confusing is the apparent complexity of the sequence of reactions. At present we do not understand why the coagulation profile evolved as it did. It is clear, however, that each reaction of the sequence represents an amplification point. Not only does the amount of each proenzyme normally present in the circulation get progressively larger as one goes down the sequence in the direction of thrombin generation, but also the rate at which each reaction proceeds becomes progressively faster. Thus one consequence of the chain of reactions is the generation of a relatively large amount of thrombin from a relatively small stimulus (Davie and Kirby 1973).

The amplification of the response of the coagulation mechanism to a small stimulus is still further enhanced by the multiple action of the thrombin molecules which are formed (Fig. 3.1). Thrombin reacts with the protein

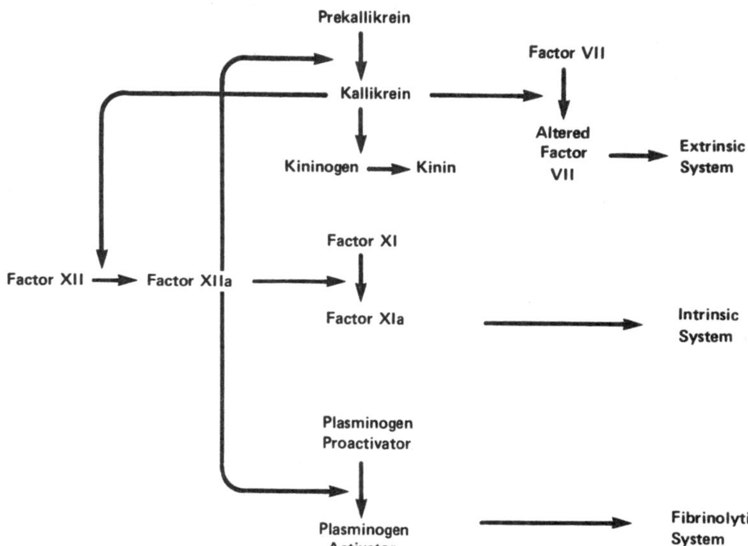

Figure 3.3. Activation of factor XII by plasma kallikrein and the interrelationship between the kinin, intrinsic, and fibrinolytic mechanisms. Also shown is the kallikrein pathway which can link the intrinsic and extrinsic mechanisms of coagulation through the activation of factor XII and factor VII.

cofactor factor VIII and modifies the molecule such that the reaction of factor IXa, phospholipid, calcium, and altered factor VIII (factor VIIIt) in converting factor X to its activated form proceeds at a greatly accelerated rate compared to the reaction with nonmodified factor VIII protein (Nemerson and Pitlick 1972). In an analogous fashion thrombin can interact with the other protein cofactor, factor V, and modify the molecule so that the complex between factor Xa, phospholipid, calcium, and factor Vt (thrombin modified) converts prothrombin to thrombin at a much faster rate. In this fashion the positive feedback effect of the first few molecules of thrombin generated leads to the consequent generation of more thrombin at an even faster rate.

LIMITATION OF FIBRIN CLOT FORMATION

Since thrombin can lead to the formation of more thrombin, it is pertinent to consider the limiting factors which prevent the coagulation mechanism from proceeding unchecked until either all the circulating prothrombin is converted to thrombin or all the available fibrinogen has been utilized. One important reason why this does not happen is that in the circulation there are normally present several specific inhibitors which can neutralize their respective active enzymes. Another limiting factor is that the coagulation reactions are effectively occurring in a microcirculation environment around the site of damage to the vessel wall, so that only a small portion of the coagulation proteins comes in contact with the damaged surface or the activated enzymes and hence are available to the reaction. Furthermore, the modified forms of factor VIII and factor V have a considerably shorter half-life than their unmodified parent molecules, and increased levels of thrombin can lead to the rapid destruction of factor VIII and factor V, which effectively blocks the coagulation process (Davie and Kirby 1973). Finally, once the fibrin mesh forms, the major portion of the active enzymes, especially thrombin, become trapped in the network of fibrin strands. Consequently, the procoagulant enzymes are not released into the general circulation and their active enzymatic forms quickly run out of substrate, so that clotting effectively ceases.

THROMBUS FORMATION

The body has another mechanism, in addition to the procoagulant activities described above, which is especially useful in the repair of small lesions in the blood vessel walls. This mechanism is dependent on the functional activity of platelets.

The platelet is a nonnucleated disc-shaped structure derived from the megakaryocyte (Table 2.1). As mentioned above, platelets participate in the coagulation mechanism; however, perhaps the most impressive function of the platelets is their ability to adhere to damaged endothelium and to each other. The term platelet adhesion is used to describe the interaction of platelets with a surface other than another platelet, and the term platelet clumping or aggregation refers to platelet-platelet interaction.

As with the intrinsic coagulation mechanism, the stimulus for platelet adhesion appears to be the contact of the cell with a "foreign surface," e.g. damaged endothelium, exposed extravascular tissues, or collagen fibrils. Figure 3.4 illustrates the typical platelet association with endothelium which occurs on minimal injury to the endothelial surface. Following contact with the surface the intact platelet undergoes a shape change. The platelet throws out pseudopods which enable it to adhere to the

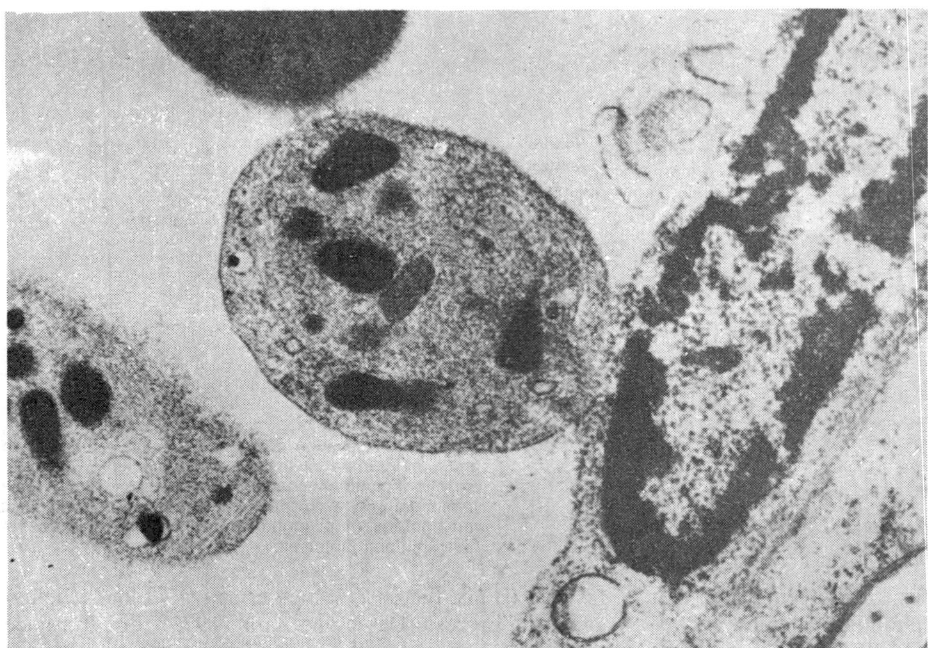

Figure 3.4. A single rabbit platelet attached to intact arteriolar endothelium which was minimally damaged by a laser. Note the lack of plasma membrane of both platelet and endothelium at the site of contact. The platelet has retained its shape and no pseudopods are visible; comparison with the second platelet (bottom left) reveals the cellular integrity. A red blood cell is visible at the top. (From T. Hovig, F.N. McKenzie, and K.-E. Arfors 1974, *Thromb. Diath. Haemorrh.* 32:695–703.)

surface (Figs. 3.5, 3.6). As the platelets change their shape they expell serotonin, calcium, adenosine triphosphate (ATP), and adenosine diphosphate (ADP) from their α-granules into the surrounding medium (Booyse and Rafelson 1972). The release enhances the formation of a platelet plug, since the released ADP is itself a powerful inducer of the release reaction and hence causes additional platelets to participate in the chain of events, while the released serotonin can produce local vasoconstriction, which slows the blood flow and assists hemostasis. During the initial shape change and the extrusion of small pseudopods it is possible for the platelets to revert back to their normal shape if platelet plug formation is not required; this phase represents reversible adhesion and aggregation. However, in the animal body, when platelets have once undergone the initial shape change, they usually proceed to the irreversible phase of aggregation in which the platelet throws out numerous pseudopods. Then more and more platelets accumulate around the platelet clump already formed at the site of injury until eventually a mass of platelet material has been deposited. By this time the platelets have lost their individual integrity and their contents have been released into the surrounding medium.

The platelet plug which forms in response to vessel wall injury can effectively stop the flow of blood through the damaged area. This hemostatic plug is markedly strengthened by the formation of fibrin around the platelet plug. Not only does damaged endothelium stimulate the activation of factor XII and initiate the clotting process, but platelets have also been shown to initiate the in-

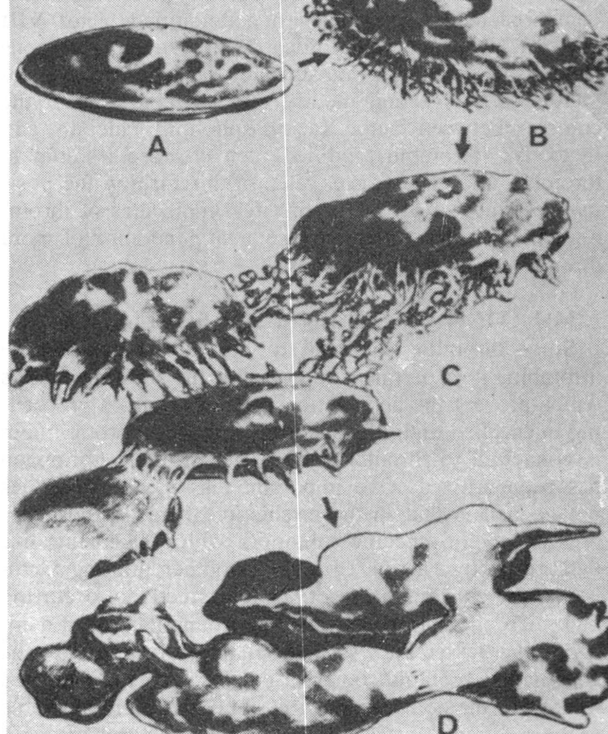

Figure 3.5. Illustration of changes in shape of blood platelets: A, normal platelet; B, initiation of pseudopod formation; C, further pseudopod formation, aggregation, and clumping of platelets; D, amorphous platelet mass following platelet deposition. (From Booyse and Rafelson 1972, *Ann. N.Y. Acad. Sci.* 201:37–60.)

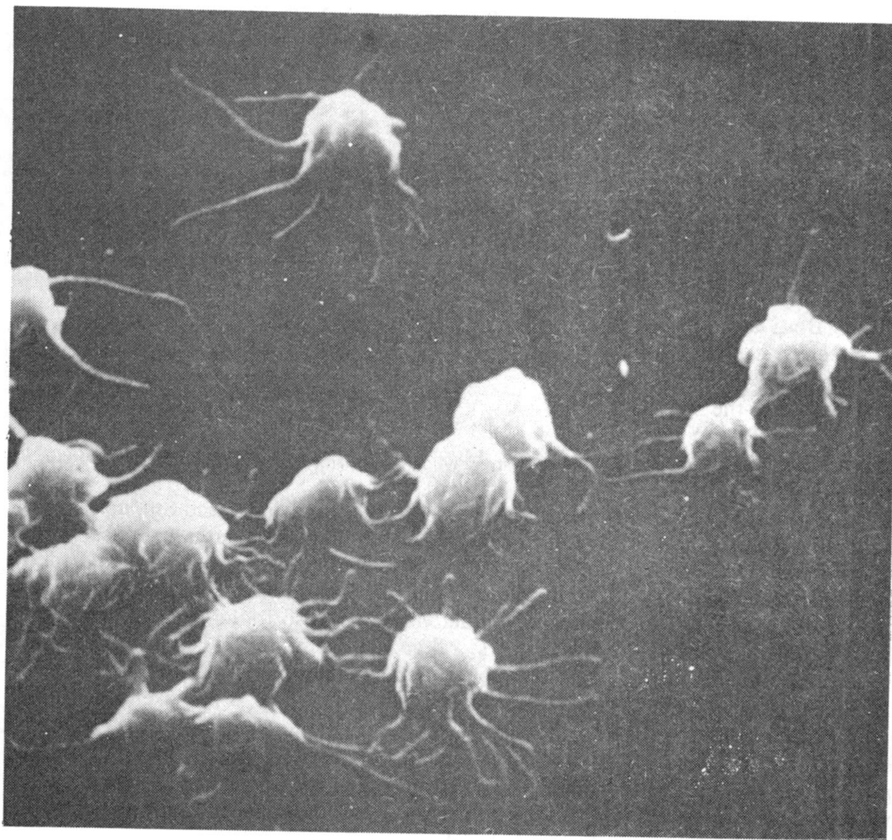

Figure 3.6. Collagen-treated platelets (×8400). Note the numerous pseudopods. The two-unit platelet aggregate at far right shows irreversible membrane fusion. (From M.I. Barnhart, R.T. Walsh, and J.A. Robinson 1972, *Ann. N.Y. Acad. Sci.* 201:360–90.)

trinsic coagulation mechanism even in the absence of the contact factors, i.e. factors XI and XII (Walsh 1972). This effect of platelets on the coagulation mechanism is in addition to the role of the phospholipid, platelet factor 3 (PF-3), which is released from the platelets to catalyze the reaction of factors VIII and IXa to activate factor X and the reaction of factors V and Xa to activate prothrombin. There is a close relationship between blood platelets and the coagulation proteins since in order to maintain normal hemostasis it is necessary for an animal to have both adequate numbers of functional platelets and adequate procoagulant activity. Just as fibrin formation helps to strengthen and stabilize a platelet plug, so do platelets help to strengthen and stabilize a fibrin clot. Indeed, there exists a close association between platelets and strands of polymerized fibrin. Furthermore, just as thrombin generated during the coagulation process can accelerate the rate of further thrombin generation, so does thrombin play an important role in the growth and stabilization of platelet plugs (Mustard and Packham 1971). Thrombin, in concentrations which do not cause gross fibrin formation, aggregates platelets by inducing the release reaction.

In addition to this vascular function the platelets also respond to nonhemorrhagic intimal lesions by forming a thrombus within the lumen. For thrombus formation to take place, other factors in addition to injury to the vessel wall, such as disturbance of blood flow, must occur. In the arterial circulation the thrombi which form are generally the result of platelet-platelet interaction. In animals this is invariably a positive reaction to a potential bleeding problem, but in man, where atherosclerotic plaques can develop on arterial walls, the white thrombi which form around such plaques can cause life-threatening stasis of blood flow. In the veins the most common type of thrombus is the result of platelet-fibrinogen interaction. The thrombus contains red cells and fibrin as well as platelets and may occur as a secondary effect of platelet plug formation or as a result of activation of the procoagulation factors locally in the vein (Mürer and Day, in Sherry and Scriabine 1974). This type of thrombus is, in many respects, similar both functionally and morphologically to the fibrin clot formed by either the intrinsic or the extrinsic mechanisms of coagulation.

DISSOLUTION OF THE FIBRIN CLOT

Although the formation of the fibrin clot is essential to stop bleeding, once the clot has formed, allowing the blood vessel to be repaired by tissue growth, the continued presence of the clot would impair normal blood circulation. Consequently, the body has two mechanisms for the reduction and eventual elimination of the fibrin clot—clot retraction and fibrinolysis.

Clot retraction

Platelets are essential for the process of clot retraction. If a fibrin clot is formed in the absence of platelets or if the platelets trapped in the mesh of fibrin strands do not function normally, no shrinking of the fibrin clot occurs. Not only are platelets necessary for clot retraction but to a great extent the concentration of functional platelets determines the amount of clot retraction (Born and Hardisty, in Biggs 1972). The ability of platelets to produce the retraction of formed fibrin strands requires energy, which is provided by platelet ATP, calcium, and the specific contractile protein thrombosthenin. It would appear that in the presence of ATP and calcium, thrombosthenin reacts in a fashion analogous to muscle actinomyosin. The ability of platelets to retract fibrin also depends on the generation of energy, in the form of ATP, by the processes of oxidative phosphorylation and anaerobic glycolysis (Niewiarowski, in Sherry and Scriabine 1974). Some evidence suggests that thrombosthenin may be located in or on the platelet membrane, which enables thrombosthenin and fibrin to react directly when the platelets lose their cellular integrity during irreversible aggregation. The net effect of the platelet thrombosthenin is to markedly reduce the size of the fibrin clot or of the thrombus. Since the plug is not removed from the site of damage, repair may proceed without completely impeding blood flow.

Fibrinolysis

The mechanism of fibrinolysis, or digestion of fibrin, can occur in the absence of clot retraction. As with the procoagulation mechanisms, the fibrinolytic mechanism involves a sequence of enzymatic reactions in which inactive proenzymes present in the circulation are converted to active proteolytic enzymes. The fibrinolytic pathway can be divided into two phases—the generation of the key enzyme plasmin and the action of plasmin on the formed fibrin strands.

Activation of plasmin

The initial steps in the formation of plasmin appear to be triggered by activated factor XII molecules. Factor XIIa converts a proenzyme known as plasminogen proactivator to plasminogen activator. This enzyme then converts plasminogen, the inert form of plasmin, to the activated form (Fig. 3.7). There are other circumstances which can cause the activation of the fibrinolytic mechanism (McNicol and Douglas, in Biggs 1972). For example, certain strains of hemolytic streptococci contain an enzyme, streptokinase, which triggers the fibrinolytic mechanism by converting the plasminogen proactivator

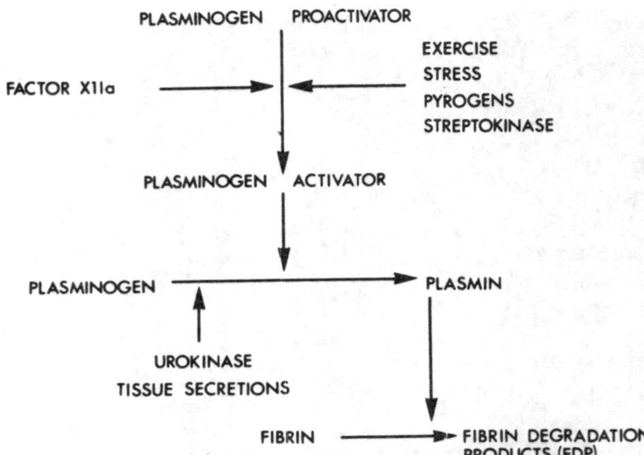

Figure 3.7. Fibrinolytic mechanisms of degradation of formed fibrin

to its active form. In addition, increased amounts of activator can be detected in plasma after exercise, emotional stress, surgical operations, epinephrine and nicotine injections, and administration of bacterial pyrogens. Plasminogen activators are also found in body secretions such as tears, saliva, and seminal fluid but not in sweat. The most potent activator is found in urine. This activator is a proteolytic enzyme called urokinase which does not act through an intermediate step as do the other activators described above. Urokinase acts directly on plasminogen converting the molecule to the active enzyme plasmin by the controlled cleavage of a limited number of peptide bonds.

Proteolytic digestion of fibrin

Plasmin cleaves the fibrin molecules into small fragments which are released from the fibrin clot into the circulation and completely broken down by the reticuloendothelial system. Since the fibrinolytic system can be activated by factor XIIa simultaneously with the activation of the procoagulant system, plasmin can become trapped in the fibrin network and hence can digest portions of the fibrin clot. In this manner plasmin can effectively digest the fibrin clot. The small fragments of fibrin, the platelet debris, and other cellular material released from the fibrin mesh are removed from the circulation by the reticuloendothelial system.

Although both the coagulation and fibrinolytic mechanisms are activated by a common pathway, the fibrinolytic system can be activated without the concomitant activation of the coagulation sequence. This situation produces a bleeding diathesis and is usually associated with a disease state such as a bacterial infection. Normally fibrin is the only substrate for plasmin since plasmin digests fibrinogen rather slowly. However, when plasmin is generated in such excess that the naturally occurring plasmin inhibitors cannot neutralize the enzyme, plasmin starts to digest fibrinogen. If the situation continues unchecked, the concentration of fibrinogen can be depleted and replaced with fibrinogen fragments which cannot be converted to fibrin by thrombin. Consequently, bleeding from damaged blood vessels cannot be stopped by the normal processes of blood coagulation, thus endangering the life of the animal. A similar type of situation is often encountered in an acquired coagulation defect known as disseminated intravascular coagulation, in which both the procoagulant and fibrinolytic mechanism are activated.

INHIBITORS OF BLOOD COAGULATION AND FIBRINOLYSIS

As mentioned, inhibitors present in the circulation can effectively neutralize the procoagulant activity and hence prevent the excessive generation of thrombin (Table 3.2). They can control blood clotting either by inhibiting the enzymatic activity of the various reactions leading to the generation of thrombin or by inhibiting the enzymatic activity of thrombin.

Table 3.2. Inhibitors present in the circulation and the enzymes inhibited

Inhibitor	Enzyme inhibited
Antithrombin III	Thrombin, factor Xa, factor IXa, factor XIa, plasmin
$C\bar{1}$ inactivator	Factor XIIa, factor XIa, kallikrein
α_2-macroglobulin	Thrombin, plasminogen activator, plasmin, kallikrein
α_1-antitrypsin	Thrombin, plasmin

One of the most important inhibitors is an α_2-globulin, antithrombin III. This protein has the capacity to slowly and irreversibly inhibit thrombin by forming an inactive protein-protein complex with the enzyme. Antithrombin III, in addition to being an inhibitor of formed thrombin, is also a potent inhibitor of thrombin generation, by neutralizing the activity of factors IXa, Xa, and XIa and plasmin. In all cases the inhibitory effect is markedly enhanced by heparin.

Another inhibitor present in plasma is an α_2-macroglobulin, which in addition to contributing 25 percent of the antithrombin activity present in plasma (Ratnoff 1974) also inhibits the fibrinolytic system through its action on both plasminogen activator and plasmin. This α_2-macroglobulin can also inhibit plasma kallikrein activity.

As with the other inhibitors, the first component of complement ($C\bar{1}$ inactivator) acts as an inhibitor of several plasma proteins, e.g. factors XIa and XIIa and plasma kallikrein (Schreiber and Austen 1973).

Since many of the inhibitors influence more than one enzyme, this indicates that the enzymes possess some similarities at their active sites. Since the proteolytic enzymes, especially factor Xa, thrombin, and plasmin have some similarity with the enzyme trypsin, the antitrypsin activity of plasma also plays a role, albeit a minor one, in the control or modulation of the hemostatic process.

There are three main categories of compounds, both naturally occurring and synthetic, which can act as anticoagulants.

Chelating agents

The simplest anticoagulants and those used most frequently in vitro are the chelating agents. When a chelating agent such as trisodium citrate, sodium oxalate, or EDTA (ethylenediaminetetraacetic acid disodium salt) is added to whole blood, all the calcium ions present are bound by these salts and hence are not available to participate in the coagulation reactions. Blood clotting will only occur when calcium ions, usually as calcium chloride, are added to the blood.

Heparin

Heparin is perhaps the most effective anticoagulant. It is present in mast cells in conjunction with histamine (Ehrlich and Stivala 1973). Since heparin is a highly negatively charged compound it probably exists in mast cells to neutralize the positively charged histamine and presumably is released into the general circulation when the mast cells are disrupted during the inflammatory process. Whether heparin so released exerts an anticoagulant action in vivo has yet to be determined. Nevertheless, heparin, intravenously administered, is one of the most widely used anticoagulants in human medicine. Heparin exerts its anticoagulant action at a number of steps in the coagulation sequence by greatly accelerating the reaction between antithrombin III and the various enzymes which it inhibits (Table 3.2). For example, not only is the rate of inhibition of thrombin much faster but also the complex of heparin–antithrombin III–thrombin which forms is completely undissociable. The other enzymes appear to be inhibited in an analogous fashion. Although heparin can inhibit factor XIa, factor IXa, and thrombin, it is probably the action of heparin on factor Xa which accounts for its potency as an anticoagulant. Since each molecule of factor Xa is capable of activating many molecules of thrombin, the inhibition of factor Xa can effectively prevent the formation of thrombin and hence blood coagulation. Consequently heparin is an anticoagulant which can inhibit both the generation of thrombin and also formed thrombin. The platelets possess an antiheparin activity, platelet factor 4 (PF-4), which is released from platelets during the process of aggregation along with serotonin and ADP. This PF-4, a protein distinct from antithrombin III, neutralizes heparin by forming a complex with the molecule.

Antagonists of vitamin K

The liver appears to be the only site of synthesis of the clotting factors of the prothrombin complex, namely factor II, factor X, factor VII, and factor IX. The synthesis of these proteins is dependent on the availability of adequate amounts of vitamin K and hence these can be considered to be vitamin K dependent and coumarin sensitive (O'Reilly, in Spaet 1974). The coumarin and indanedione group of oral anticoagulant drugs, whose effect is observed 36–48 hours after administration, antagonizes vitamin K and induces the synthesis of nonfunctional forms of the coagulant proteins. The nonactive proteins cannot participate normally in the coagulation reactions and this prevents blood clot formation.

HEMOSTATIC MECHANISM IN DIFFERENT SPECIES

When the overall coagulation profiles for different species are compared, there are striking similarities (Archer, in Macfarlane 1970). Most of the differences between species become evident in in vitro laboratory tests and are quantitative rather than qualitative. For example, when the clotting times obtained in a routine screening test such as the whole blood clotting time test are compared, the values obtained become progressively longer in the following order—cat; dog and pig; horse and sheep; cow; and finally, birds and chickens (Rowsell 1969). Variations are also found in the circulating activity of the specific coagulation proteins. In most studies, normal human plasma has been used as a reference. Abilgaard and Link (1965) reported that compared to man, horses had elevated levels of prothrombin complex factors and factor IX, equal levels of factor VIII, and reduced levels of factors XI and XII. As to cattle, Kociba et al. (1969) reported that, using the human reference standard, factors V and XII are elevated. Similarly, in sheep factors VII, VIII, and IX are elevated (Gajewski and Povar 1971) while in swine factors VIII and XII are grossly elevated (Bowie et al. 1973). The significance of the various levels is not clear, especially in relation to the in vivo activity.

A comparable situation is found when the fibrinolytic mechanism in different animals is compared by in vitro tests. For example, the bovine and ovine systems are reduced in comparison to man. It has been suggested that the slow fibrinolytic mechanism in sheep is due to an apparent lack of plasminogen proactivator and increased (above human values) antiplasmin activity. Indeed, it has been reported that among marsupials, primates, rodents, and carnivores the most variable factor was the level of circulating plasminogen activator (Hawkey, in Macfarlane 1970).

The most striking differences in the blood coagulation mechanism are found when clotting profiles of marine mammals, the avian species, and reptiles are compared with the terrestrial mammals. In marine mammals the in vitro clotting time of the blood is prolonged compared with man, apparently as a result of a total lack of factor XII (Lewis et al. 1969; Robinson et al. 1969). A similar situation has been documented in poultry except that in birds it appears that the entire contact phase is absent; that is, neither factor XI nor XII can be detected in the blood. Factor XII has also been reported to be absent from the blood of most reptiles (Ratnoff 1966). Since none of the animals, birds, or reptiles exhibit unusual hemorrhagic problems, it would appear that factor XII is not essential for the maintenance of adequate hemostasis.

The quantitative differences in the coagulation profiles not only exist between species but can also be found within them. The coagulation profiles of newborn cows, cats, dogs, guinea pigs, rabbits, and pigs exhibit marked differences from those of the comparable adult animal (Hathaway et al. 1964). In each of these species, reduced levels of factors II, V, VII, and X were found in relation to those of the comparable adult.

HEMORRHAGIC DISORDERS

Bleeding problems which may be encountered in veterinary medicine fall into two categories—congenital and acquired.

Congenital coagulation defects

The congenital coagulation defect which occurs most frequently in the human population is true hemophilia (hemophilia A), which is characterized by defective synthesis of the coagulation protein, factor VIII. Hemophilia A was the first defect reported in domestic animals and has now been identified in various breeds of dogs. It was first recognized in Irish setters (Field et al., 1946) and subsequently in Saint Bernards, Labradors, Shetland Sheepdogs, Beagles, Greyhounds, Samoyeds, mongrels, Vizslas, Weimaraners, and Chihuahuas (as reviewed in Hall 1972). The defect has also been found in Thoroughbred and standardbred horses (Archer 1961, Hutchins et al. 1967, Sanger et al. 1964). In horses the bleeding problems are severe and affected animals which are homozygous for the disorder have a poor survival rate. In dogs a wide spectrum of clinical severity is found: in the mild form animals may survive surgery such as tail docking and ear cropping without obvious hemorrhagic problems; in the severe form animals will bleed in response to minor trauma and also spontaneously. The clinical severity of the disorder appears to be correlated with the circulating functional factor-VIII activity, although bleeding episodes in larger breeds of dogs appear more often and are more severe than in small breeds of dogs despite similar factor VIII levels. The defect is transmitted in animals and man on the X-chromosome as a recessive trait (Barrow and Graham 1974). In animals, affected females are encountered as a result of mating an affected male with a "carrier" or heterozygous female. Heterozygous animals can be identified since they have approximately 50 percent of the normal level of functional factor VIII activity as determined in a biological in vitro assay system.

A second disorder which closely resembles hemophilia A is von Willebrand's disease (VWD). This disease was first identified in swine (Cornell and Mührer 1964, Hogan et al. 1941) and more recently in German shepherds (Dodds 1970). As with hemophilia A the bleeding diathesis can vary from mild to moderately severe. In addition, homozygous animals show an unusual response to transfusions of whole blood or plasma; the circulating factor VIII levels rise to above normal and far exceed the amount of factor VIII administered during the transfusion. In dogs the disorder is transmitted as an autosomal dominant trait while in the porcine it seems to be inherited as an autosomal recessive trait (Cornell et al. 1969).

Another coagulation disorder closely resembling hemophilia A is hemophilia B, which results from reduced functional factor IX levels in the circulation. This defect was first identified in cairn terriers and subsequently in black and tan coonhounds (Hall 1972). The genetic inheritance, clinical symptoms, and variation in severity resemble that of hemophilia A.

There are two other congenital defects which have so far only been identified in man and dogs. Hereditary factor VII deficiency has been reported in a number of families and colonies of beagles throughout North America and Great Britain. This autosomally transmitted disorder is expressed as a mild clinical condition requiring no therapy. Indeed some of the affected animals have only been identified as the result of routine laboratory screening (Spurling et al. 1972). Factor X deficiency in the dog is manifest as a severe bleeding diathesis in newborn and young adult dogs, although in those dogs which survive to maturity the disorder seems to be clinically mild unless the dogs undergo surgery (Dodds 1973). This disorder is transmitted as an autosomal dominant trait.

Factor XI deficiency is the only congenital coagulation disorder which has been reported in cattle (Gentry et al. 1975, Kociba et al. 1969). It has also been identified in springer spaniels (Dodds and Kull 1971). In the dog this defect is transmitted as an autosomal trait and affected animals exhibit mild bleeding, although again surgery can greatly increase the severity of bleeding.

Bleeding diathesis associated with defective platelets has also been reported in dogs. In one type of dysfunction identified in a family of otterhounds (Dodds 1967), the platelets exhibit an abnormal morphology—over 80 percent of the platelets of severely affected dogs are giant forms. The abnormal platelets do not adhere to glass surfaces, fail to aggregate in response to ADP, thrombin, and collagen, exhibit abnormal PF-3 release and hence cannot support normal thromboplastin generation, and finally, fail to sustain normal clot retraction. As a consequence of these problems homozygous animals exhibit a moderately severe bleeding diathesis which is aggravated by trauma or surgery. The defect is inherited as an autosomal dominant trait. A second platelet defect, reported in a family of Basset hounds (Lotz et al. 1972), is manifested by recurrent bleeding. Once again the platelets fail to aggregate in response to ADP or thrombin, but in this case the platelets respond to collagen and exhibit normal morphology. The biochemical nature of this defect may be related to defective platelet membrane function.

Acquired coagulation defects

Since vitamin K is essential for the synthesis of several of the normal functional proteins involved in the coagulation sequence (factors II, VII, IX, and X), any compound which acts as an antagonist of vitamin K will lead to defective synthesis of these proteins, with concomitant hemorrhagic diathesis like that associated with the congenital defects described above. The first account of such bleeding episodes was described by Schofield in 1924 as a result of cattle eating spoiled sweet clover. Perhaps the most commonly encountered problem is the result of accidental dicoumarol poisoning of dogs and cats. Many of the commercial rodenticides are warfarin (dicoumarol) derivatives designed to produce lethal bleeding in rodents. The accidental ingestion of these rodenticides can produce acute bleeding episodes in the animal, but it responds well to fresh blood transfusion and vitamin K therapy.

As the liver is the major site of synthesis of the coagulation proteins, especially factors II, VII, IX, and X, hemorrhagic problems are sometimes encountered as a result of liver dysfunction. The clinical severity of the bleeding episodes varies depending on the severity of the liver damage. This type of acquired defect can be differentiated from dicoumarol poisoning since in the latter case liver function tests will be normal.

Sometimes associated with liver malfunction is a rather complex hemorrhagic problem known as Disseminated Intravascular Coagulation (DIC). DIC is usually encountered following obstetrical complications, malignancy, and infections, although there are many other causes. Severe bleeding problems can be encountered due to excessive coagulation and excessive fibrinolysis. This disorder has been reported in dogs (Dodds, in Spaet 1974), swine (Lawson and Dow 1964), horses (Nordstoga et al. 1968), and cattle (Thomson et al. 1974).

Acquired platelet defects are also observed in domestic animals. Bruising or petechial hemorrhages as a result of reduced numbers of circulating platelets (thrombocytopenia) have been reported in dogs, swine, and cattle (Dodds, in Spaet 1974). When the disorder is of unknown etiology, or origin, it is referred to as idiopathic thrombocytopenic purpura (ITP). This is the most commonly reported type of thrombocytopenia; however, thrombocytopenia can occur secondarily to a variety of systemic diseases such as bacterial and viral infections. Thrombocytopenia and platelet function defects can also be drug induced. Aspirin, promazine-type tranquilizers, and local anesthetics are among the list of compounds which alter platelet function, generally by impairing proper platelet aggregation, which usually results in mild capillary bleeding.

LABORATORY TESTS FOR HEMOSTASIS

There are a number of screening tests which are available for the laboratory diagnosis of hemorrhages (for more detailed information see Biggs, in Biggs 1972; Bowie et al. 1971; Rowsell 1969).

Intrinsic system tests

These tests are designed to detect abnormalities in the intrinsic pathway. Any marked reduction in circulating activity of factors II, V, VII, IX, X, XI, XII, or XIII, in addition to fibrinogen or the presence of circulating anticoagulants, will result in prolonged clotting times.

The simplest test is the Whole Blood Clotting Time (WBCT) test which measures the time required for native blood to form a clot. Another screening test is the Recalcification Time or Plasma Clot Time test in which the time for plasma to clot after the addition of calcium chloride is measured. This test will detect coagulation factor abnormalities, the presence of anticoagulants, and also the absence of platelets, since the clotting time varies inversely with the plasma platelet concentration. A modification of this test is the Partial Thromboplastin Time (PTT) test which measures the intrinsic procoagulant activity of plasma independently of the platelet contribution. When an activating surface such as celite or kaolin is included in the system, the test is referred to as the Activated Partial Thromboplastin Time (APTT)test.

The Thrombin Time test measures the time required for a standard thrombin solution to convert fibrinogen to fibrin and detects any fibrinogen deficiency. This test will also give an abnormal result if heparin or a heparinlike anticoagulant is present or if the fibrinogen has been altered by a fibrinolytic condition. There are two tests which can be used to measure the efficiency of the generation of activated coagulation factors when the clotting has been initiated. The Prothrombin Consumption Test measures the procoagulant which remains in serum after clotting has occurred, and the Thromboplastin Generation Test (TGT) measures the rate at which the active enzymatic complex which converts prothrombin to thrombin is generated.

Extrinsic system tests

When measuring the coagulation factors which participate in the extrinsic mechanism it is necessary to add components which will allow clot formation to occur while bypassing the initial stages of the intrinsic system. In the One Stage Prothrombin Time (OSPT) test this is achieved by adding tissue thromboplastin to plasma before recalcification. This test will detect a deficiency of one or more of the factors II, V, VII, and X and of fibrinogen, and the presence of a coagulation inhibitor. An alternative test which does not require the presence of factor VII is the Stypven Time or Russell's Viper Venom Time (RVVT) test. Stypven, a commercial preparation of the venom from Russell's Viper interacts directly with factors V and X and PF-3 for the activation of prothrombin. This test will be prolonged if any of these factors are missing or if plasma fibrinogen is deficient.

Tests of fibrinolysis

The simplest test is the Whole Blood Clot-Lysis Time test which measures the time taken for a blood clot, incubated at 37°C, to lyse. This test is not a rapid test since normal clots generally take 12–24 hours to lyse. The time of clot lysis not only depends on the amount of plasmin generated in the system but also on the presence of platelets, which initiate clot retraction, and on the fibrinogen content of the sample.

Other tests include the specific determination of plasminogen, and the measurement of fibrinogen degradation products (FDP).

Tests for platelet function

Since an adequate number of functional platelets are necessary for the maintenance of normal hemostasis, perhaps one of the simplest tests is to perform a platelet count. In order to measure platelet function such tests as whole-blood clot retraction and RVVT, which requires PF-3, can be routinely used.

REFERENCES

Abilgaard, C.F., and Link, R.P. 1965. Blood coagulation and hemostasis in Thoroughbred horses. *Proc. Soc. Exp. Biol. Med.* 119:212–15.

Archer, R.K. 1961. True haemophilia (haemophilia A) in a Thoroughbred foal. *Vet. Rec.* 73:338–40.

Barrow, E.M., and Graham, J.B. 1974. Blood coagulation factor VIII (antihemophilic factor): With comments on von Willebrand's disease and Christmas disease. *Physiol. Rev.* 54:23–74.

Biggs, R., ed. 1972. *Human Blood Coagulation, Haemostasis, and Thrombosis.* Blackwell Scientific, Oxford.

Booyse, F.M., and Rafelson, M.E. 1972. Regulation and mechanism of platelet aggregation. *Ann. N.Y. Acad. Sci.* 201:37–60.

Bowie, E.J.W., Owen, C.A., Zollman, P.E., Thompson, J.H., and Fass, D.N. 1973. Tests of hemostasis in swine: Normal values and values in pigs affected with von Willebrand's disease. *Am. J. Vet. Res.* 34:1045–7.

Bowie, E.J.W., Thompson, J.H., Didisheim, P., and Owen, C.A.

1971. *Mayo Clinic Laboratory Manual of Hemostasis*. Saunders, Toronto.
Cornell, C.N., Cooper, R.G., Kahn, R.A., and Garb, S. 1969. Platelet adhesiveness in normal and bleeder swine as measured in a celite system. *Am. J. Physiol.* 216:1170–75.
Cornell, C.N., and Mührer, M.E. 1964. Coagulation factors in normal and hemophiliac-type swine. *Am. J. Physiol.* 206:926–28.
Davie, E.W., and Kirby, E.P. 1973. Molecular mechanisms in blood coagulation. In B.L. Horecker and E.R. Stadtman, eds., *Current Topics in Cellular Regulation*. Academic Press, New York. Pp. 51–86.
Dodds, W.J. 1967. Familial canine thrombocytopathy. *Thromb. Diath. Haemorrh.* 26 (suppl.):241—48.
——. 1970. Canine von Willebrand's disease. *J. Lab. Clin. Med.* 76:713–21.
——. 1973. Canine factor X (Stuart-Prower factor) deficiency. *J. Lab. Clin. Med.* 82:560–66.
Dodds, W.J., and Kull, J.E. 1971. Canine factor XI (plasma thromboplastin antecedent) deficiency. *J. Lab. Clin. Med.* 78:746–52.
Ehrlich, J., and Stivala, S.S. 1973. Chemistry and pharmacology of heparin. *J. Pharm. Sci.* 62:517–44.
Field, R.A., Rickard, C.G., and Hutt, F.B. 1946. Hemophilia in a family of dogs. *Cornell Vet.* 36:285–300.
Gajewski, J., and Povar, M.L. 1971. Blood coagulation values of sheep. *Am. J. Vet. Res.* 32:405–9.
Gentry, P.A., Crane, S., and Lotz, F. 1975. Factor XI (plasma thromboplastin antecedent) deficiency in cattle. *Can. Vet. J.* 16:160–63.
Hall, D.E. 1972. *Blood Coagulation and Its Disorders in the Dog*. Williams & Wilkins, Baltimore.
Hathaway, W.E., Hathaway, H.S., and Belhasen, L.P. 1964. Coagulation factors in newborn animals. *J. Lab. Clin. Med.* 63:784–90.
Hogan, A.G., Mührer, M.E., and Bogart, R. 1941. A hemophilia-like disease in swine. *Proc. Soc. Exp. Biol. Med.* 48:217–19.
Hutchins, D.R., Lepherd, E.E., and Crook, I.G. 1967. A case of equine haemophilia. *Austral. Vet. J.* 43:83–87.
Kociba, G.J., Ratnoff, O.D., Loeb, W.F., Wall, R.L., and Heider, L.E. 1969. Bovine plasma thromboplastin antecedent (factor XI) deficiency. *J. Lab. Clin. Med.* 74:37–41.
Lawson, G.H.K., and Dow, C. 1964. Production of the generalized Schwartzman reaction with Salmonella cholerae-suis. *J. Comp. Path.* 74:482–86.
Lewis, J.H., Bayer, W.L., and Szeto, I.L. 1969. Coagulation factor XII deficiency in the porpoise, Tursiops truncatus. *Comp. Biochem. Physiol.* 31:667–70.
Lotz, F., Crane, S., and Downie, H.G. 1972. A study of a specific congenital platelet functional abnormality in dogs. Prog. 3d Cong. Internat. Soc. Thromb. Haemostasis, Washington. P. 220.
Macfarlane, R.G., ed. 1970. *The Haemostatic Mechanism in Man and Other Animals*. Symp. Zool. Soc. Lond., vol. 27.
Mustard, J.F., and Packham, M.A. 1971. The reaction of the blood to injury. In H.Z. Movat, ed., *Inflammation, Immunity, and Hypersensitivity*. Harper & Row, New York. Pp. 528–607.
Nemerson, Y., and Pitlick, F.A. 1972. Tissue factor pathway of blood coagulation. In T.H. Spaet, ed., *Progress in Hemostasis and Thrombosis*. Grune & Stratton, New York. Vol. 1, 1–37.
Nordstoga, K., Sparboe, O., and Stokkan, M. 1968. Generalized Schwartzman reaction including extensive adrenal hemorrhage in a pregnant mare. *Nord. Vet. Med.* 20:330–37.
Ratnoff, O.D. 1966. The biology and pathology of the initial stages of blood coagulation. In E.B. Brown and C.V. Moore, eds., *Progress in Hematology*. Grune & Stratton, New York. Vol. 5, 204–45.
——. 1969. Some relationships among hemostasis, fibrinolytic phenomena, immunity, and the inflammatory response. *Adv. Immun.* 10:145–227.
——. 1974. Some recent advances in the study of hemostasis. *Circ. Res.* 35:1–14.
Robinson, A.J., Kropatkin, M., and Aggeler, P.M. 1969. Hageman factor (factor XII) deficiency in marine mammals. *Science* 166:1420–22.
Rowsell, H.C. 1969. Blood coagulation and hemorrhagic disorders. In W. Medway, J.E. Prier, and J.S. Wilkinson, eds., *A Textbook of Veterinary Clinical Pathology*. Williams & Wilkins, Baltimore. Pp. 247–81.
Sanger, V.L., Mairs, R.E., and Trapp, A.L. 1964. Hemophilia in a foal. *J. Am. Vet. Med. Ass.* 144:259–64.
Schofield, F.W. 1924. Damaged sweet clover: The cause of a new disease in cattle simulating hemorrhagic septicemia and blackleg. *J. Am. Vet. Med. Ass.* 64:553–75.
Schreiber, A.D., and Austen, K.F. 1973. Interrelationship of the fibrinolytic, coagulation, kinin generating, and complement systems. *Ser. Hemat.* 6:593–601.
Sherry, S., and Scriabine, A., eds. 1974. *Platelets and Thrombosis*. University Park Press, Baltimore.
Spaet, T.H., ed. 1974. *Progress in Hemostasis and Thrombosis*. Grune & Stratton, New York. Vol. 2.
Spurling, N.W., Burton, L.K., Peacock, R., and Pilling, T. 1972. Hereditary factor VII deficiency in the beagle. *Brit. J. Haemat.* 23:59–67.
Stormorken, H., Gjoennaess, H., and Laake, K. 1974. Interrelations between the clotting and kinin systems. *Haemostasis* 2:245–52.
Thomson, G.W., McSherry, B.J., and Valli, V.E.O. 1974. Endotoxin induced disseminated intravascular coagulation in cattle. *Can. J. Comp. Med.* 38:457–66.
Walsh, P.N. 1972. The role of platelets in the contact phase of blood coagulation. *Brit. J. Haemat.* 22:237–54.

CHAPTER 4

Blood Groups, Immunogenetics, and Biochemical Genetics | by Erik Andresen

During the first half of this century, the concept of *blood groups* was confined to the surface antigens of erythrocytes. Now it includes not only the differences due to antigens of red cells, white cells, platelets, and tissue cells, but also the distinctions based on hemoglobins, albumins, globulins, and various enzymes in the blood.

The nature of the cellular antigens is revealed by joint applications of immunological and genetic methods. This field of biology is therefore called immunogenetics. Although individual differences among proteins can be detected by immunological methods, they are usually studied by using procedures applied in biochemistry; this field is called biochemical genetics.

In the latter part of the nineteenth century experiments showed that an animal which had been depleted of blood could be saved by transfusion of blood from another animal of the same species (homologous transfusions), but not if the animal were from a different species (heterologous transfusions). Bordet (1896) showed why: red blood cells usually are clumped (agglutinated) and subsequently lysed by serum of a different animal species. By simple cross matching tests in vitro with blood and serum samples, Landsteiner (1900) discovered the ABO blood groups and the corresponding naturally occurring anti-A and anti-B antibodies in man. And Ehrlich and Morgenroth (1900), with the aid of isoimmunizations, discovered a number of individual varieties of goats' blood.

GENERAL PRINCIPLES

Blood group antigens

The red blood cells have many different blood group antigens thought to be arranged in a more or less regularly patterned mosaic structure on the cell surface (Fig. 4.1). They are classified by heredity studies, and antigens belonging to all blood group systems are represented on each red cell. Each system has separate locations, of which there are several thousand on each red cell surface. Blood group antigens also occur on white blood cells, blood platelets, sperm, and various tissue cells, and have been detected as soluble substances in blood plasma, saliva, milk, gastric juice, meconium, seminal fluid, and ovarian cyst fluid, in which they are highly concentrated.

Blood group antigens induce the formation of antibodies when injected into a suitable organism. These antibodies may react with the antigen both in vivo and in vitro. Such antigen-antibody reactions are almost the only means of distinguishing between various blood groups since few of the antigens have been chemically characterized. All blood group substances so far examined in man and domestic animals are glycoproteins or

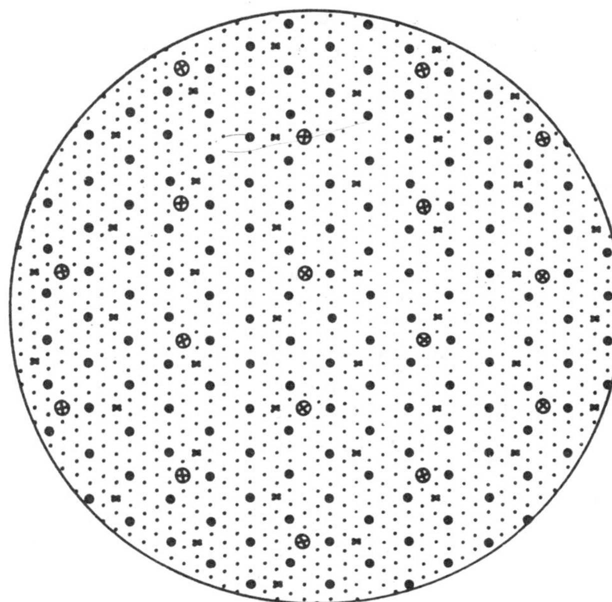

Figure 4.1. Hypothetical arrangement of some blood group antigens on the surface of the human erythrocyte: ● = ABO groups; x = MN groups; ⊗ = Rh groups; · = others, including human species-specific erythrocyte antigens. (From A.S. Wiener and I.B. Wexler, eds., *An Rh-Hr Syllabus: The Types and Their Applications*, 2d ed., Grune & Stratton, New York, 1963.)

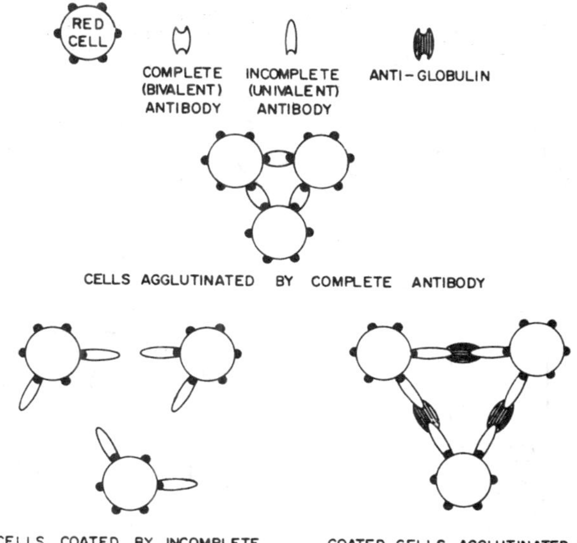

Figure 4.2. Agglutination reactions. (Modified from I. Dunsford and J. Grant, *The Anti-Globulin (Coombs) Test in Laboratory Practice*, Oliver & Boyd, Edinburgh, 1959.)

glycolipids, but the blood group antigenic specificities reside in the carbohydrate portions. Moreover, it is likely that blood group genes control the formation or functioning of specific glycosyl transferase enzymes that add sugar units from a donor substrate to the carbohydrate chains.

Serological reactions

The antibody effect on red blood cells having the corresponding blood group antigen is usually a clumping (agglutination) of the cells. Hence, such antibodies are called agglutinins, and they may be characterized further as complete agglutinins in contrast to incomplete agglutinins, which are produced frequently following blood transfusions (Fig. 4.2). Complete agglutinins are bivalent antibodies, that is, they have two combining sites, one at each end of the molecule. Incomplete agglutinins are univalent antibodies, since they merely attach themselves to the antigens but are not able to make a direct connection between two red cells. The bridge between the red cells may be completed, however, by adding anti-antibody (i.e. anti-globulin).

Certain antibodies (hemolysins) can damage red cells carrying the corresponding antigen. The hemoglobin then escapes from the cells. The phenomenon is called immune hemolysis, but it occurs only if complement is added. Guinea-pig serum contains the most potent source of complement for activating most hemolysins, although rabbit serum is frequently used also. Hemolytic tests require incubation at temperatures ranging from 25 to 30°C. In some instances good reactions are observed at temperatures ranging from about 20 to 37°C.

Production of specific antisera

Naturally occurring blood group antibodies have been found in normal sera of all domestic animals. They may be detected by the so-called checkerboard technique. That is, each serum of a certain number of individuals is tested with erythrocytes from each of the other individuals and also with its own erythrocytes. The latter reaction serves as a negative control. Anti-J in cattle, anti-R in sheep, and anti-A in pigs are naturally occurring isoantibodies that are found frequently in normal sera. Additional isoantibodies are rare, and they usually have a low titer (the reciprocal value of the highest serum dilution giving visible or a defined degree of reaction). It has therefore been necessary to resort to purposely induced immune antibodies against blood group antigens in order to reveal a maximal degree of individual blood group diversity within each species.

An antiserum containing a single, specific antibody population used for typing red cells is called a blood-typing reagent. The hypothetical isolation of a C reagent for blood-typing pigs (Fig. 4.3) is as follows: (1) Blood from a donor pig that has the blood group antigens A, B, and C is inoculated into another pig (the recipient) that has the A antigen but lacks the antigens B and C. (2) If the

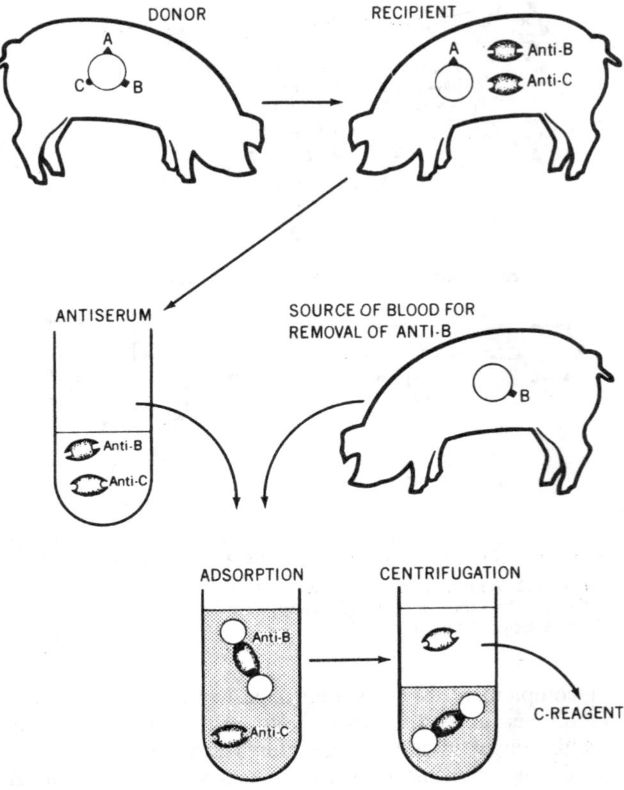

Figure 4.3. Production and isolation of a reagent for blood-typing pigs.

recipient is a good antibody producer, it produces anti-B and anti-C (anti-A is not produced because the A antigen is not foreign to the A-positive recipient). (3) Blood is withdrawn from the recipient when the antibody titer has reached its maximum. The antiserum is decanted following coagulation. (4) Erythrocytes are obtained from a pig that has the B antigen but lacks the C antigen. (5) When the B-positive red blood cells are mixed with the antiserum, the anti-B antibody will be adsorbed by the cells, whereas anti-C remains free in the serum. (6) Following the subsequent centrifugation, the supernatant fluid consists of serum containing only anti-C. This serum is called a C reagent.

INHERITANCE OF BLOOD GROUPS

Physical basis

With very few exceptions blood groups are inherited as Mendelian dominant characters, meaning the trait observed in one generation must have been present in each of the preceding generations—it never skips a generation. Thus red cell antigen in an offspring must be present in at least one of its parents, which shows why blood-typing is an aid in solving problems of questionable parentage.

The blood groups are the phenotypic products of corresponding genes in the chromosomes, just like all other inherited traits. The genes are made of DNA, and the direct function of DNA is to produce polypeptide chains. Thus, it is obvious that the antigenic specificities which reside in the carbohydrate portions of the antigens cannot be primary gene products. Nevertheless, the inheritance of each antigenic specificity can almost always be explained as if it depends on the presence of only one corresponding gene in the whole array of chromosomes in each cell (Fig. 4.4). In fact, it is likely that the genes for blood group antigens are genes for specific enzymes, that is, enzymes which add and arrange the components responsible for the serological specificity.

In somatic cells, as distinct from germ cells, there are two chromosomes of each kind, one received by the individual from its dam, the other from its sire. Only the sex chromosomes X and Y are different in size and shape. All the rest of the chromosomes are called autosomes. In mammals, males have both the X and Y chromosomes, while females carry two X's but no Y. Cytological studies have revealed that somatic cells in cattle contain a total of 60 chromosomes, consisting of 30 pairs, of which 29 pairs are autosomes and one is the sex chromosome pair. The total number, 60, is referred to as the diploid number or 2n. Since the germ cells contain only one member of each pair of chromosomes, the number is half that in somatic cells. This is called the haploid (or n) number. The diploid chromosome number in man is 46; pig, 38; horse, 64; dog, 78; and cat, 38.

With few exceptions all known blood group genes in mammals are located on the autosomes. However, the exact positions are entirely hypothetical. The loci for the C and J blood group systems in the pig (Fig. 4.4) are,

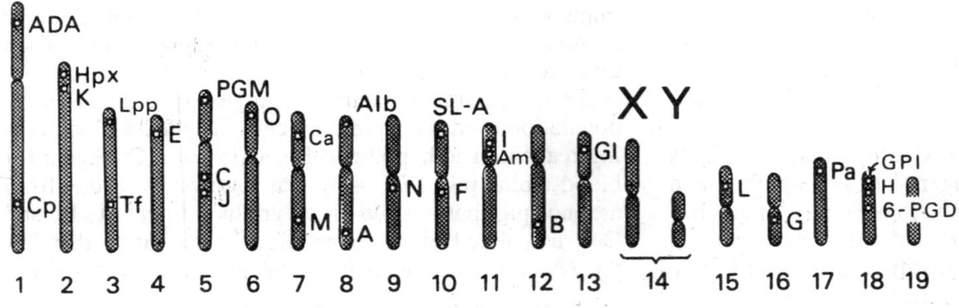

Figure 4.4. Chromosome ideogram showing the 18 autosomes and both sex chromosomes of the pig. Apart from a few established cases of linkage, the positions are entirely hypothetical.

however, known to be closely linked (close together on the same chromosome), as are the K blood group locus and the Hpx locus for hematin-binding β-globulins (hemopexin), and the loci for the I blood groups and for variants of serum amylase (Am). Finally, the H blood group locus is linked with loci for enzymes of both the Embden-Meyerhof pathway of glucose metabolism (i.e. glucose phosphate isomerase, GPI) and the pentose cycle (i.e. 6-phosphogluconate dehydrogenase, 6-PGD). In horses the locus for 6-PGD is linked with the K blood group locus; in cattle, the hemoglobin β-locus is linked with the A blood group locus.

Two-allelic systems

The inheritance of a red cell antigen (arbitrarily called A) is illustrated in Table 4.1, which summarizes the expected segregation ratios in dominant inheritance. The corresponding dominant gene is *A* and its allele *a*. Individuals which are A-positive will therefore have the genotype *AA* or *Aa*, whereas A-negative individuals are homozygous for the other allele, that is, they are *aa*. Note that segregation into A-positive and A-negative offspring occurs in only two out of the six genotypic parental combinations. The corresponding segregation ratios 1:1 and 3:1 illustrate expectations according to Mendel's first law of segregation.

Quite regularly the blood group antigen determined by the previously unidentified allele *a* is discovered. The new antigen invariably behaves as a straightforward dominant trait, and the two antigens are dominant together, that is, both antigens are expressed in the heterozygote. This phenomenon of codominance is illustrated well by the human blood group antigens M and N or the bovine F and V antigens. The previously unidentified alleles to *M* and *F*, namely *m* and *f*, are now designated as *N* and *V*. The two allelic genes *M* and *N* give rise to the three genotypes *MM*, *MN*, and *NN*. The corresponding phenotypes, M, MN, and N, indicate that red cells of human beings who have the phenotype M are agglutinated by anti-M but not by anti-N; MN-cells are agglutinated by both reagents, and red cells of type N persons are agglutinated by anti-N but not by anti-M. A similar description is valid for closed systems like the FV system in cattle (Table 4.2).

Table 4.1. Blood group inheritance based on a two allelic system with only one directly detectable antigen

Mating type	Genotypic combinations	Offspring	
		A-positive	A-negative
A-positive × A-positive	*A/A* × *A/A*	All	
	A/a × *A/A*	All	
	A/a × *A/a*	¾	¼
A-positive × A-negative	*A/a* × *a/a*	½	½
	A/A × *a/a*	All	
A-negative × A-negative	*a/a* × *a/a*		All

Table 4.2. Inheritance of bovine blood group antigens F and V (closed system)

Mating types		Offspring types		
Phenotypic combinations	Genotypic combinations	F(*FF*)	FV(*FV*)	V(*VV*)
F × F	*FF* × *FF*	All		
V × V	*VV* × *VV*			All
F × V	*FF* × *VV*		All	
FV × F	*FV* × *FF*	½	½	
FV × V	*FV* × *VV*		½	½
FV × FV	*FV* × *FV*	¼	½	¼

Three-allelic systems

Genes can occur not only in two but in several forms (multiple alleles), all created by mutations during the evolution of the species. Since chromosomes occur in pairs, a normal individual possesses no more than two alleles from the series: one maternal, the other paternal. These two alleles separate at meiosis into different gametes, and therefore segregate according to the first law of Mendel (see the third and fourth genotypic combinations in Table 4.1).

The first blood group system discovered, the human ABO system, provides the simplest example of inheritance by multiple alleles. Disregarding subgroups of the A antigen, there are only three alleles (*A*, *B*, and *O*). Since only anti-A and anti-B antibodies are available, but not anti-O, the *O* gene appears recessive to both codominant genes *A* and *B*. Therefore, the six possible genotypes *AA*, *AO*, *BB*, *BO*, *AB*, and *OO* correspond to the four phenotypes A, B, AB, and O. By using the method illustrated in Table 4.2 one could work out a similar table showing the expected segregation results from the ten possible parental phenotypic combinations.

Emergence of blood group systems

At its inception, a blood group system usually appears as a two-allelic system encompassing only one directly detectable antigen. But as time goes on additional blood-typing reagents are usually produced which detect previously unknown antigens. Ultimately all blood group systems may prove to include multiple allelic series. Quite often two or more antigenic specificities appear to be inherited together, as if they were determined by just one gene, or by a number of very closely linked genes. The bovine and ovine B systems, the porcine E system, and the Rh (Rhesus) system in man are striking examples of this phenomenon (see Table 4.4). The letter designations often reflect the order in which the discoveries were made.

BLOOD GROUP SYSTEMS

In cattle and sheep

Lytic techniques are used in cattle blood-typing because of an inherent inagglutinability of erythrocytes of certain individuals. This inagglutinability is probably due to the position of the antigens on the red cell surface rather than to an "incompleteness" of the antibodies. Possibly, the antigens are situated slightly below the outer margin of the cell periphery. They are still accessible to antibodies, but agglutination does not take place because the distance to the antigen of a second cell is too great (Coombs et al. 1951).

More than 100 specifically different lytic reagents for blood-typing cattle are now in use. Most reagents are obtained from isoimmune sera, but some are based on heteroimmunizations made by injecting cattle blood into rabbits, sheep, or goats. Very few blood group antibodies occur in normal serum of cattle. One, however, anti-J, occurs regularly.

Blood group antigens in cattle are products of genes at 12 loci (Tables 4.3, 4.4). In the complicated A, B, and C systems, two or more antigenic specificities appear to be transmitted as one unit from one generation to the next.

Eight blood-group systems are currently recognized in sheep. The antigens belonging to the R-O system are detected by naturally occurring antibodies. Normal sera from R-negative sheep frequently contain anti-R, whereas anti-O is rare. Antigens belonging to the other systems are detected by isoimmune antibodies or by antibodies produced by injecting sheep blood into rabbits. The B and C systems appear to be homologous with the complex B and C systems of cattle because ovine isoimmune antisera, used as sources of B-system reagents for sheep, frequently cross react with the B antigens of cattle. Conversely, B-system reagents for cattle may be used as a source for detecting B antigens in sheep. Similar cross reactions have been found with the C system reagents of ovine and bovine origin. The antigens in the two species are not identical, but the resemblances demonstrate the usefulness of blood-typing in taxonomic studies. The reagents for sheep blood-typing are used in lytic tests with the exception of anti-D, which is an agglutinin.

Table 4.3. Numbers of blood group systems known in man and some domestic animals in 1975

Species	Systems (loci)	Systems with more than two alleles	Largest no. of alleles at one locus
Man	14	9	28 (Rh)
Cattle	12	9	500+ (B)
Sheep	8	4	60 (B)
Horse	8	4	10 (D)
Swine	15	5	14 (E)
Dog	8	1	3 (A)
Rabbit	1	1	3 (Hg)
Mink	4	1	3 (A)
Chicken	12	10	35 (B)

In horses

Several early authors classified horses into four groups, A, B, AB, and O, based on reactions with two naturally occurring isoagglutinins in normal horse serum. Unlike the situation in man, however, there was no strict reciprocal relationship between agglutinins in serum and antigens on the red cells.

Renewed interest in horse blood groups was stimulated by the discovery that hemolytic disease in horses and mules could result from transplacental isoimmunization. Several blood-typing reagents have been isolated from sera obtained from mares that have given birth to foals afflicted with this disease. Blood-typing reagents are produced more effectively, however, by planned isoimmunizations or heteroimmunizations. A total of approximately 25 reagents are available at present. Some of these are applicable in agglutination tests, others require the lytic technique. Eight blood group systems are currently recognized in the horse.

In pigs

Contemporary studies of pig blood groups were primarily initiated to discover the exact pathogenesis of hemolytic disease of the newborn pig (Bruner et al. 1949). A few naturally occurring blood group antibodies have been found in normal serum of adult swine. But only one of these antibodies, anti-A, occurs frequently in A-negative pigs. This antibody is serologically related to the human anti-A and also to anti-R in sheep sera and anti-J in cattle serum. In fact, cattle anti-J hemolysin is used routinely as a source for detecting A-positive pigs. All other reagents for blood-typing pigs are isolated from isoimmune or heteroimmune sera and contain complete agglutinins, incomplete agglutinins, or hemolysins. More than 60 different blood-typing reagents have been produced, and these reagents detect antigens belonging to 15 blood group systems (Fig. 4.4).

In dogs

A knowledge of blood groups in dogs has been of interest primarily because dogs are frequently used in experimental physiology, pharmacology, and surgery, often involving blood transfusions.

Naturally occurring isoantibodies are found in less than 15 percent of randomly chosen dogs. Moreover, the most powerful antigen, A, does not have a naturally occurring counterpart, anti-A. The latter antibody is, however, easily produced following transfusion of A blood into A-negative recipients. Anti-A is a potent isolysin in vitro and in vivo. Additional immune antibodies (agglutinins) have been encountered following multiple transfusions.

The available reagents (possibly less than 10) detect antigens classified into 8 blood group systems.

BLOOD GROUPS AND LIVESTOCK IMPROVEMENT

Parentage problems

Problems of questionable parentage are relatively frequent in modern cattle and swine breeding. Often the problems are caused by mere recording mistakes, incorrect earmarking, accidental interchange of the newborn, or mixing of semen samples in artificial insemination. Dog and horse pedigrees have been confused by casual paternity.

Blood-typing is used primarily because red cell antigens are inherited in a simple manner, and almost all individuals have different blood types. In addition, the antigens are unchangeable throughout life, and their detection is reliable whenever good reagents are available.

Blood tests can be used to exclude parentage but cannot prove parentage. However, if only two males are known to be involved in a case of disputed paternity and one of these can be excluded, then the inference is obvious. For example, in Table 4.4 the calf has the antigens A_1, B12, and U_1H', all of which the cow lacks. These antigens have therefore been transmitted from the sire. Since bull 1 lacks A_1 and B12, this bull cannot have sired the calf. In contrast, bull 2 cannot be excluded because it not only has the three antigens A_1, B12, and U_1H', but the entire blood type of bull 2 is compatible with the calf's.

In Table 4.5 the blood types of a boar, a sow, and four presumptive offspring are indicated. Pig 2 has the antigens E_4, F_a, and K_b; pig 3 has the antigens E_4, H_c, and K_b. These antigens are not present in either of the alleged parents. Hence, they can be excluded as parents of pigs 2 and 3, but based on blood types alone they cannot be excluded as parents of pigs 1 and 4. If, however, the four pigs can be regarded as unquestionably full sibs, then all four pigs must have been "adopted."

Inclusion of additional inherited traits in parentage testing, such as hemoglobins, albumins, globulins, and various enzymes, considerably increases the possibility of detecting incorrect pedigrees.

Diagnosis of cattle twins

Two kinds of twins may be distinguished: monozygotic (MZ) or identical twins arise from a single fertilized egg; dizygotic (DZ) or fraternal twins result from the separate fertilization of two eggs. The MZ twins must always be of the same sex, but the DZ twins can obviously be of either sex, and the combinations occur with a frequency of approximately 0.25, both males; 0.50, one male and one female; and 0.25, both females. Since MZ twins have identical genotype, they are useful for determining the comparative importance of heredity and environment in milk yield, butterfat yield, size, growth, and various biochemical constituents of blood or milk. Moreover, by using one member of a MZ twin pair as a control and subjecting the other to a different diet or different therapy, those treatments can be studied without any complication from different genetic susceptibilities.

The frequency of twinning in cattle breeds is 2–3 percent. Only one tenth of twin calvings are monozygotic. As with parentage, it is not possible to prove monozygosity, but it is possible to eliminate most of the like-

Table 4.4. Blood-typing in a case of disputed paternity in cattle

Animal	Blood group systems										
	A	B*	C	F–V	J	L	M	N	S	Z	R′–S′
Bull 1	D/DH	B50/B62	C_1E/WX_2	F_1/F_1	J	L/	M_2/	N/	U_1H'/	–/–	S′/S′
Bull 2	A_1/D	B12/B252	EWX_2	F_1/F_1	J	–/–	–/–	–/–	U_1H'/	–/–	S′/S′
Cow	D/D	B62/B67	RWX_2/	F_1/F_1	J	L/–	–/–	N/	–/–	–/–	S′/S′
Calf	A_1/D	B12/B67	RWX_2	F_1/F_1	J	–/–	–/–	N/	U_1H'/	–/–	S′/S′

* B12 = $BGKO_xE_2'F'7$, O′; B50 = $O_1Y_1E_3'G'$; B62 = $O_3J'K'7$, O′; B67 = PY_2 (Stormont 1962)

Table 4.5. An example of disputed parentage in pigs

Animal	Blood group systems													
	A	B	C	D	E*	F	G	H	I	J	K	L	M	N	O
Boar	O/O	a/a	–/–	a/	1/3	–/–	a/a	a/a	b/b	–/–	a/	a/a	a/	a/	–/–
Sow	A/O	a/a	a/–	a/	1/2	–/–	a/a	a/a	a/b	a/–	a/	a/a	a/	–/–	a/–
Pig 1	A/O	a/a	a/–	a/	1/2	–/–	a/a	a/a	a/b	a/–	a/	a/a	a/	–/–	a/
Pig 2	A/O	a/a	–/–	a/	2/4	a/	a/a	a/a	a/b	–/–	a/b	a/a	a/	–/–	a/
Pig 3	O/O	a/a	–/–	a/	2/4	–/–	a/a	a/c	b/b	–/–	a/b	a/a	a/	–/–	a/
Pig 4	O/O	a/a	–/–	a/	1/2	–/–	a/a	a/a	b/b	–/–	a/	a/a	a/	–/–	–/–

* E_1=bdg, E_2=edg, E_3=aeg, E_4=efd

sexed twins of dizygotic origin by detecting genetic differences. More than 80 percent of like-sexed twins can be diagnosed as dizygotic by inspecting various morphological traits such as coat color, patterns in coat color, and hair whorls. Blood-typing tests are useful in separating the remaining DZ twins from the MZ twins.

Erythrocyte chimerism

In about 9 out of 10 cases of bovine twin fetuses there is a fusion of fetal membranes at an early stage of development followed by anastomosis of the chorionic blood vessels. The mixture of two kinds of blood in each twin is called erythrocyte chimerism, and this chimerism persists in each twin postnatally. Owen (1945) explained the phenomenon by proposing that the mixed erythrocyte precursors (i.e. primordial blood cells) settle and become established (take root) in the hematopoietic tissues of each twin. Such twins do not reject the stem cells from the co-twin because the ''grafting'' takes place before the individuals become immunologically mature. Consequently, the stem cells of the hematopoietic tissue in each twin continue to produce two antigenically distinct kinds of red cells, one corresponding to its own genotype and another corresponding to the genotype of the co-twin.

The mixture of two populations of red cells in each twin will cause identical blood types and thus simulate monozygosity. For example, if the genotype of one twin is

A/A, B/—, C/—, —/—, E/E

and the genotype of the other is

A/—, —/—, C/C, —/—, —/—

then, because red cells in each twin are A and C positive, complete lysis takes place in test tubes to which A or C reagents are added. But, when anti-B is added to the mixture, in which both B-positive and B-negative erythrocytes are present, only the former cells will lyse. The B-negative cells will form a deposit covered by reddish tinged supernatant. A similar weak (± placed above the designation for the reagent) reaction is observed in the test tubes to which anti-E is added. Thus identical blood types with one or more weak reactions are characteristic of chimerism. The mixed blood in each of the twins considered here will give reactions in the hemolytic blood-typing test according to the following phenotype:

$$A, \overset{\pm}{B}, C, —, \overset{\pm}{E}$$

In a chimeric twin, cells corresponding to the individual's own genotype may be present in any proportion, which usually does not change with age. In cases of extreme displacement of the cell proportions the weak reactions may be overlooked and a pair of dizygotic twins with chimerism (DZm) may therefore escape detection. Nevertheless, the use of blood-typing tests on those twins preliminarily classified as monozygotic (based on morphological tests) has proven to be an indispensable part of the diagnosis of zygosity among twins (Stormont 1954, Rendel 1958).

The cells that produce soluble J blood group substance in a J-positive calf fetus are not transplanted into the tissues of the J-negative co-twin. Thus permanent chimerism does not involve the J substance. The same is true for those cells that produce inherited variants of serum proteins. The latter traits have, however, increased the efficiency of distinguishing between twin types.

Bovine freemartins

The freemartin is a sterile female born co-twin with a male. About 90 percent of heifers born co-twin with a bull calf are freemartins. Freemartins develop only in the male-female combination of twins with communal circulatory systems during prenatal life (Lillie 1916). Male hormones, produced by the testes of the male fetus before the ovary of the female is fully developed, probably circulate through the female fetus and prevent normal development of the ovary and of the female reproductive tract. The assumption that the freemartin is a naturally occurring hormonic intersex is supported by the observation that androgen administration to pregnant females of several species may result in pseudohermaphroditism among offspring which are genetically female (van Wagenen and Hamilton 1943). Androgen administration does not produce intersexual change in the male embryo but merely accentuates male characteristics.

Since the freemartin and its male co-twin have a communal circulatory system during fetal life, such individuals have erythrocyte chimerism. Conversely, if a female calf, born co-twin with a bull calf, exhibits erythrocyte chimerism (DZm), this female is a freemartin. For this purpose blood-typing is particularly advantageous because of the difficulty in correctly diagnosing the young freemartin morphologically. The 10 percent of females that have a blood type distinctly different (DZo) from their twin are potentially fertile (Fig. 4.5).

In chimeric individuals the ''grafted'' stem cells not only produce red cell antigens according to their own genotype but they also produce hemoglobin molecules according to their own genotype (Stormont et al. 1964). Thus if one twin has the genotype for hemoglobin A and the co-twin has the genotype for hemoglobin B or AB, then a hemolysate of the mixed blood from each twin exhibits the phenotype AB. This phenomenon is called hemoglobin chimerism.

The primordial blood cells from one twin that take root in the hematopoietic tissue of a co-twin continue to pro-genes are found to be pleiotropic, and influence characters of economic importance, then there may be an advantage in using blood-typing in genetic improvement programs, that is, an advantage in addition to parentage control. So far, the search for such has not been encouraging but various associations have been detected. The problems connected with association studies have been discussed by Neimann-Sørensen and Robertson (1961), Smith (1967), and Bodmer (1972).

In cattle a small effect of alleles of the B blood group locus on butterfat production has been estimated (Neimann-Sørensen and Robertson 1961, Rendel 1961). In pigs the H blood group locus may have an effect on productive and reproductive traits (Jensen et al. 1968, Rasmusen 1972, Rasmusen and Hagen 1973). In addition, the chromosomal region in which the three genetic systems GPI, H, and 6-PGD are located (see Fig. 4.4) is associated with the porcine stress syndrome (PSS) and thereby with meat quality (Rasmusen and Christian 1976, Jensen et al. 1976).

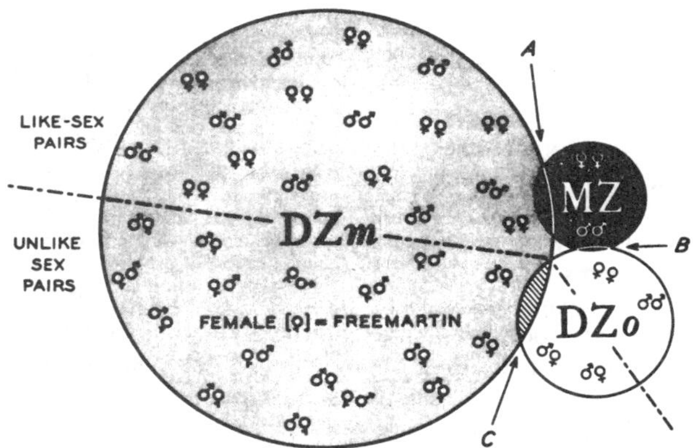

Figure 4.5. Relative frequencies of five categories of bovine twins: MZ, twins without chimerism, like in sex and blood groups; DZo, twins without chimerism, unlike in sex or blood groups or both; DZm, twins with chimerism, of like or unlike sex. Due to chance identical inheritance for all tested blood group factors, some DZ twins will be misclassified as MZ (overlaps A and B), and some freemartins will be misclassified as DZo (overlap C). (From Stormont, in Kempthorne, Bancroft, Gowen, and Lush, eds., *Statistics and Mathematics in Biology,* Iowa State U. Press, Ames, 1954; original drawing conceived and prepared by C.W. Cotterman.)

duce white cells, which can also be used to diagnose the freemartin. Since the freemartin is a female genetically, its cells have two X chromosomes, whereas those cells originating from the co-twin each have one X and one Y chromosome.

Twins and freemartins in sheep and pigs

Freemartinism accompanied by erythrocyte chimerism has been reported in sheep but the condition is rare (Stormont et al. 1953). Also, evidence for monozygotic twins in sheep is on record. Although intersexes are not rare in pigs, the causes of them have yet to be discovered. Embryological studies showed that chorionic vascular anastomosis occurs at rare occasions in pigs. Female fetuses that have a common circulation with males show structural modifications resembling those described for freemartins in cattle (Hughes 1928). Since chimerism may lead to female sterility, it is not surprising that chorionic vascular anastomosis occurs infrequently in multiparous mammals. Embryological studies have indicated that monozygotic twin fetuses occur with a frequency of about 0.1 percent (Schmitt 1959). The combined use of blood-typing and skin grafting did not reveal any monozygotic twins in a study comprising 172 litters (1384 pigs) of the Hampshire and Duroc breeds (Baker 1964).

Blood groups, production traits, and disease

Certain genes appear to have pleiotropic effects; that is, they act on two or more traits at once. If blood group

Blood group substances similar to those of the human ABO system occur in several mammalian species. The results of a study involving the O substance of sheep suggest that it may take part in the production of a certain serum phosphatase or may act as an essential mediator in the release of this enzyme into the serum (Rendel et al. 1964). Moreover, studies with chickens have indicated a possible influence of various levels of serum alkaline phosphatases on quantitative traits (Wilcox et al. 1963).

In sheep there is a direct relationship between red cell potassium levels and the M system of blood groups (Rasmusen and Hall 1966, Tucker and Ellory 1970). The L antigen of this system appears to act as an inhibitor of active potassium transport. Erythrocytes of sheep possessing antigen L have a low potassium concentration (less than 25 mM/1000 ml), whereas erythrocytes of sheep lacking the L antigen have a high potassium level (more than 75 mM/1000 ml).

Blood group loci (B and R) and resistance to leukosis in chickens are associated (Briles 1974). However, the B locus in chickens also serves as a major histocompatibility locus and (by analogy to the situation in man, mouse, and guinea pig) maybe as an immune response locus. Therefore, the observed association may reflect an effect of immune response (Ir) genes. An antigen of the R locus appears to act as a cell-surface receptor of certain avian leukosis-sarcoma viruses.

These and other studies suggest that many of the red cell membrane antigens serve as recognition codes for normal cell functions (Hubbert and Miller 1974). And it is possible that the developmental origin of certain blood group antigens reflects different environments in the various centers of racial development (Damian 1964). Moreover, since individual differences in histocompatibility antigens confer protection against dissemination of malignant disease within and between individuals this provides an explanation of the changes occurring in these antigens (Burnet 1969, 1974).

BLOOD TRANSFUSION

The purpose of blood transfusion is primarily to restore the blood volume after hemorrhage or to compensate for an insufficient supply of red cells in various anemias. Likewise, preoperative transfusion is used to prevent cardiac malfunction if more than trivial hemorrhage is anticipated or if the hemoglobin concentration is low. The substitution effects are obtained equally well with fresh and with stored blood. But the hemostatic effect requires the viable blood platelets in fresh blood (Jackson et al. 1959).

Obviously, the beneficial effect of a transfusion of normal blood is best achieved if each constituent of the donor blood maintains its capacity for normal physiological function in its new environment.

Plasma proteins

In man the albumin contributes about three fourths of the total colloid osmotic pressure while the globulin and fibrinogen account for the remaining 25 percent. In domestic animals the albumin contributes less than 75 percent but usually more than 50 percent. Albumin is therefore the most important protein in the transfused plasma. However, the globulin fraction of the donated plasma protein may contain blood group antibodies against the recipient's own erythrocytes.

In animals, though, natural isoantibodies do not occur as regularly as in man. And even when present, they usually have a low titer. More importantly, pigs, sheep, and cattle have a built-in mechanism that effectively protects them from the most common naturally occurring antibodies, anti-A, anti-R, and anti-J respectively. The corresponding blood group substances, A, R, and J, are present not only on the red cells of adult individuals but also in the plasma, from which the substances are acquired by the erythrocytes when the animals are 2–3 weeks old. Therefore, whenever blood or plasma containing one of these antibodies is injected into a recipient possessing the corresponding blood group substance, most of the antibodies, if not all, will be neutralized by the substances in the plasma before they reach the substances on the erythrocytes. This protective mechanism prevents agglutination or lysis of the recipient's erythrocytes. Thus transfusion reactions in animals following inoculation of whole blood are not associated with the donor plasma but are caused by incompatible donor erythrocytes.

Erythrocytes

The survival of donor erythrocytes in the circulatory system of a recipient can be measured by serological methods or by labeling the donor cells with radioactive tracers (Mollison 1961). The serological methods are time consuming and do not allow the subject's own erythrocytes to be studied. For these reasons labeling red cells is very valuable. Several tracers have been used but ^{51}Cr seems the most satisfactory.

This method consists of labeling the donor cells in vitro and, following intravenous inoculation of the labeled blood, measuring the radioactivity at intervals. The radioactivity in each sample is expressed as a percentage of the initial radioactivity, that is, the activity measured in a blood sample obtained as soon as the donor blood is well mixed with the recipient's blood (Figs. 4.6, 4.7). Chromium 51 is firmly bound to the hemoglobin. Any excess in the plasma is rapidly excreted and, in contrast to Fe-tracers, is not reutilized when new erythrocytes are formed. The "survival curve" therefore reflects fairly accurately the actual situation.

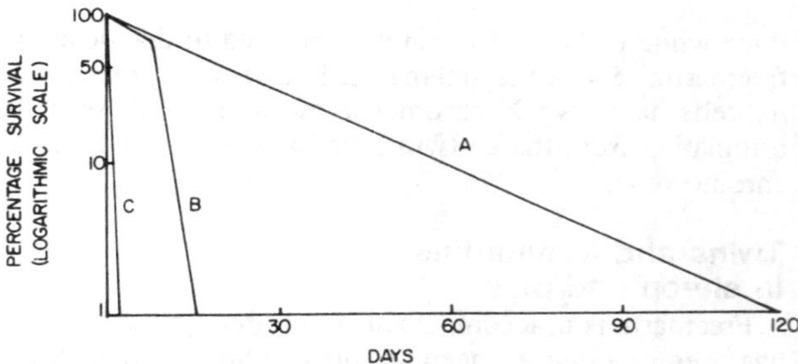

Figure 4.6. Hypothetical fate of donor erythrocytes in three recipients. A, survival of completely compatible donor blood. B, removal of donor cells caused by antibodies produced following transfusion. C, rapid destruction of donor cells by antibodies already present.

The plasma of recipient A (Fig. 4.6) does not contain antibodies against the donor cells. Consequently, the donor cells are treated as if they were the recipient's own cells. Since the antigenic composition of an individual differs from any other individual (except in the case of identical twins or members of a highly inbred strain), the donor cells will always possess some erythrocyte antigens not shared by the recipient. Antigens on the donor cells might stimulate production of the corresponding antibodies and thereby curtail their own survival as indicated by B. The removal of such donor cells is relatively slow (from one to several days) and will not cause outward signs of harmful effect. However, rapid removal of donor cells, accompanied by a transfusion reaction, will occur frequently if at the time of the transfusion the recipient has blood group antibodies against the donor cells (C). Such antibodies may be either naturally occurring or

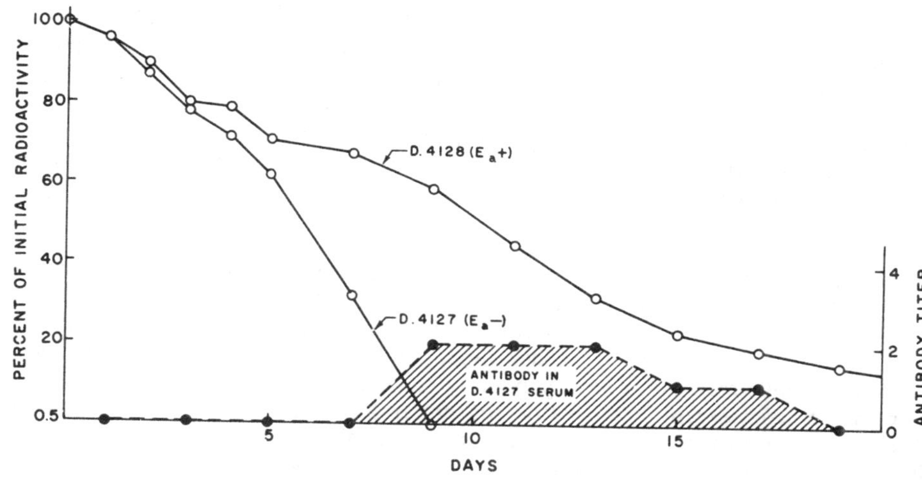

Figure 4.7. Survival of transfused ^{51}Cr-labeled E_a-positive erythrocytes in two 8-week-old pigs, one E_a-positive, the other E_a-negative. (From Andresen and Talbot 1965, *Am. J. Vet. Res.* 26:138–40.)

immune antibodies produced in response to previous immunizations.

Results corresponding with those in Figure 4.6 have been obtained in experiments with pigs (Talbot and Andresen 1964, Andresen and Talbot 1965). A mean half-life of 28 days was estimated when erythrocytes of young pigs were labeled with ^{51}Cr and reinjected (autologous or autotransfusions). A similar survival time of donor erythrocytes was measured following transfusion of compatible homologous blood (homologous or cross transfusions). But when E_a-positive donor blood was transfused into the same pigs whose plasma contained anti-E_a, a half-life of only one hour was observed.

Figure 4.7 indicates the survival of E_a-positive erythrocytes in two recipients devoid of blood group antibodies at the time of the transfusion. The survival of the donor cells in the E_a-positive recipient was normal (no correction because of growth was made) and antibodies were not produced. In contrast, the donor cells survived for only 8 or 9 days in the E_a-negative recipient, and anti-E_a was detected following the disappearance of the donor erythrocytes. The antibodies were obviously produced in response to the donor cells and were responsible for the removal of these cells from the blood stream. The first antibody produced by the E_a-negative recipient probably was cleared from the blood plasma by adsorption to the circulating donor cells. Hence free anti-E_a could not be detected in the plasma until the antibody-coated donor erythrocytes were removed from the blood stream.

General precautions

The following should be considered when a blood transfusion is required: (1) To prevent shock or early destruction of donor erythrocytes by naturally occurring isoantibodies (Fig. 4.6 C), transfusion with A-positive pig blood, J-positive cattle blood, R-positive sheep blood, or A-positive or C-positive horse blood should be avoided. (2) In cases where the donor blood has potent antigens (certain E and K antigens in pigs, the A antigen in dogs and horses, and certain B antigens in cattle and sheep) not shared by the recipient, a first-time injection might stimulate antibody production and thus curtail the life span of the donor erythrocytes (Fig. 4.6 B). (3) Repeated transfusions, given later than 4 days after the first transfusion, increase the risk of rapid removal of donor blood. (4) Maximum survival of donor blood is obtained if it does not possess red cell antigens which are absent in the recipient. However, a survival time approaching normal may be achieved if these donor antigens are weak. Finally, in certain clinical situations (e.g. first-time transfusions in animals) a blood transfusion may be regarded as successful if the donor erythrocytes survive for merely a few days.

HEMOLYTIC DISEASE OF THE NEWBORN

Under natural conditions newborn calves, foals, piglets, and puppies require passive immunity, which is provided by maternal antibodies in the colostrum, because maternal antibodies do not pass their placental barriers. Moreover, the developing fetuses rarely come in contact with foreign antigens and therefore do not make their own antibodies, although many of them can if exposed (Brambell 1970). In keeping with this the fetuses do not develop a so-called immunological memory, which ensures a rapid antibody production (secondary response) in connection with repeated antigenic exposure. Occasionally, though, passive immunity can have severe and even fatal consequences (Stormorken et al. 1963, Stormont 1972). One of these is hemolytic disease of the newborn.

This may be defined as a hemolytic anemia caused by maternal blood group antibodies in the circulatory system of the offspring possessing the corresponding red cell antigens. These antibodies are transmitted from the mother to the offspring either in utero or in the colostrum immediately after birth. The onset of the disease and also the events associated with antibody production in the females differ from species to species. In some domestic animals the blood group antigens can pass from the fetus to the mother. In order to be antigenic in the mother the red cells from the fetus must possess one or more antigenic determinants not present on the mother's red cells but inherited from the father alone.

In horses

The condition in newborn horse foals or mule foals is comparable to the disease in man with one major exception; instead of being transmitted across the placenta, antibodies in the mare are transmitted to the offspring exclusively through colostrum and early milk. The epitheliochorial placenta of the horse is impermeable to antibodies. The disease develops only if the foal receives the antibody in colostrum and early milk within the first 2 days. After that further passage of antibodies through the intestinal wall and into the circulatory system ceases. In fact, rearing the foals for a day or two on cow's milk and then returning them to the mares was a treatment applied with some success by the middle of the nineteenth century.

Comparable to the situation in man, one or two unaffected foals may be raised after successive potentially incompatible pregnancies before sufficient antibodies are formed to cause serious damage. Despite the 6-cell-layer barrier provided by the placenta the evidence indicates that the antibody production is caused by isoimmunization during pregnancy. Leakage of fetal material caused by placental hemorrhage may be the cause. Also, artificial antibody stimulation may occur when mares are inoculated with equine vaccines. For example, a rise in antibody titer has been observed following inoculation of equine virus abortion vaccine during pregnancy. This might be expected, since the vaccine is prepared from homogenized lung tissue from aborted fetuses and probably contains red blood cell antigens (Doll et al. 1952). Naturally occurring antibodies have not been encountered in hemolytic disease in the horse.

The incidence of the disease varies from one locality to another, probably depending primarily upon the local distribution of the blood groups responsible for the isoimmunizations. In the Newmarket area in England the frequency of hemolytic disease is about 1 percent of all Thoroughbred pregnancies, whereas it is 8–10 percent in the mule-breeding districts in France. This considerable difference may be due to a better opportunity of isoimmunization, possibly because of a particular manner of placentation when a horse carries a mule fetus, or because of a high frequency of the powerful antigens among donkeys. The results from Newmarket indicate that one antigenic factor (factor 6) is responsible for 80 percent of the isoimmunizations among Thoroughbreds (Franks 1962). However, only one in about 15 potentially incompatible pregnancies (i.e. 6 positive stallion × 6 negative mare) will cause harmful isoimmunization.

In pigs

In recent years evidence has been obtained for occasional transplacental isoimmunization of sows by red cells from the fetuses, resulting in hemolytic disease (Linklater 1968, 1971). Such naturally occurring cases were previously masked by the use of crystal violet vaccine (for hog cholera) of porcine origin, which was a major cause of the disease (Goodwin et al. 1955). The fact that specific blood group antigens (especially antigens of the E system) are primarily responsible for the disease has been demonstrated (Bruner et al. 1949, Andresen et al. 1965, Linklater 1968, 1971).

One might expect that the naturally occurring anti-A antibody in sows could cause hemolytic disease in newborn A-pigs whenever they are nursing colostrum with high anti-A titer. But the same mechanism that protects pigs from serious consequences of A–anti-A interactions in blood transfusions, namely the soluble A substance, also protects the newborn A-positive pigs against anti-A from the mother. Furthermore, such pigs are protected because the A substance is not present on the erythrocytes until the pigs are 1–3 weeks old. An additional factor is that the soluble A substance is present not only in the blood plasma but also in the gastric fluid. Thus it is possible that anti-A from the colostrum may be completely neutralized by the soluble A substance in the gastric secretion of newborn A-pigs (Goodwin and Coombs 1956).

In other species

Naturally occurring cases of hemolytic disease have not been observed in cattle, sheep, or goats. However, the disease has been detected in cattle following vaccination with a vaccine marketed under the trade name Anaplaz. This vaccine is made from cattle red cells infected with *Anaplasma marginale,* the cause of anaplasmosis. Stormont (1972) has shown that the vaccine in fact gives rise to antibodies in cattle which are specific for known blood group antigens in that species. This indicates that Anaplaz has a harmful side effect similar to that of the crystal violet vaccine. Hemolytic disease following blood transfusion has also not been observed in cattle, sheep, or goats. It is possible, therefore, that Anaplaz is particularly effective in provoking blood group antibodies that cause the disease. In newborn pups the disease appears to occur only when the bitch has produced blood group antibodies in response to a previous transfusion (Swisher et al. 1962). The hemolytic syndrome has been produced in several species of laboratory animals, e.g. rabbits, guinea pigs, mice, and rats.

OTHER EXAMPLES OF INDIVIDUALITY

Transplantation antigens

In 1945 Owen discovered erythrocyte chimerism in cattle and proposed that the grafted cells would continue to produce blood cells throughout the life of the host. It was later found that skin grafts exchanged between ordinary siblings were all sloughed off within two weeks after transplantation, but almost all grafts exchanged between twins survived. Thus, contrary to expectation, skin grafting was found to be of little value in distinguishing between monozygotic and dizygotic cattle twins (Anderson et al. 1951). The authors concluded that the cross transfusion of primordial blood cells in fetal life of most cattle twins destroys their power to recognize each other's skin as foreign. However, skin grafting may be an aid in detecting dizygotic twins without chimerism (DZo) if other methods are insufficient. It is therefore possible to reduce or eliminate the areas B and C in Figure 4.5 by using all available methods. Evidence indicates that antigens on leukocytes rather than erythrocytes are associated with histocompatibility, even though certain histocompatibility genes are responsible for antigens both on leukocytes and erythrocytes. In each species studied there has been one major histocompatibility locus, for example, H-2 in the mouse, HL-A in man, and the B blood group locus in chickens.

In pigs combined use of blood-typing and skin grafting has demonstrated the existence of potent histocompatibility antigens not determined by known blood group loci (Baker and Andresen 1964). This has been confirmed by the discovery of the major histocompatibility locus, SL-A, encompassing at least ten alleles (Vaiman 1974). The DL locus is a corresponding locus in dogs (Saison 1974). Among histocompatibility loci the H-2 locus of the mouse constitutes the best studied model for gene action, organization, and evolution.

Protein variants

Hemoglobins

The protein part of hemoglobin is called globin and consists of four polypeptide chains, each composed of about 140 amino acids. Study of the genetics of hemoglobin synthesis has been fundamental in formulating the current concept of gene action. Each gene determines the amino acid sequence of a polypeptide chain (that is, the primary structure of a protein). Moreover, more than one species of polypeptide chains, each with separate genetic control, may be combined in a single protein.

Mutations in man have given rise to more than 100 variants of hemoglobin, which are responsible for anemias of varying degrees of severity. Only a few hemoglobin variants are on record in domestic animals and none seem to be deleterious to its carrier. Deer is the only animal species in addition to man known to have a hemoglobin variant that causes sickling of red cells. But contrary to the situation in man, sickling in deer is apparently not associated with any disease. With sheep, some breeds seem to have only one type of "adult hemoglobin." In most breeds there are two types, designated as A and B. Individual sheep are phenotypically A, B, or AB. Erythrocytes of AB individuals contain a mixture of HbA and HbB. Since HbA has a higher anodic mobility than HbB at pH 8.6, the two types of hemoglobins can be separated by electrophoresis into two distinct bands. The three genotypes may be designated as Hb^AHb^A, Hb^AHb^B, and Hb^BHb^B.

Although sheep hemoglobins are inherited independently of erythrocyte potassium levels, both hemoglobin A and the gene for high potassium occur more frequently in hill breeds of sheep than in lowland breeds. Since sheep hemoglobin A has a higher oxygen affinity than sheep hemoglobin B, this alone might provide type A sheep with some adaptive advantages. Likewise, some cattle breeds have only one type of hemoglobin in adult life. But hemoglobin polymorphism does occur in several breeds such as Jersey, Guernsey, South Devon, Charolais, Brown Swiss, and various American, African, and Indian breeds. These breeds have two hemoglobins, A and B, which are controlled by codominant genes. A few breeds have a third hemoglobin, designated as hemoglobin C, which migrates at a position between HbA and HbB. Hemoglobin variants have also been detected in various breeds of horses (Braend 1968, Schleger and Mayrhofer 1973).

Hemoglobin types that exist predominantly or exclusively in prenatal life have been reported in several mammalian species. The major hemoglobin types recognized are embryonic (HbE) and fetal (HbF), and both are known to occur in cattle, man, pig, and sheep before adult hemoglobin appears. Production of HbE may be associated primarily with early intravascular erythropoiesis, i.e. during the first month of gestation. After this time extravascular hepatic erythropoiesis begins and thereby also the production of HbF, which is the only hemoglobin present during the remaining part of fetal life. The time of disappearance of HbF from blood may vary from 3 to 10 weeks after birth. Production of adult hemoglobin begins about the time of delivery.

A fourth type of hemoglobin can be detected in calves 1–2 weeks old, but not later. Therefore, it has been designated *neonatal* hemoglobin (Hubbert and Miller 1971). Differences between hemoglobins from fetuses and adults have not been detected in the horse and dog.

Serum proteins

The usual clinical method of separating serum proteins involves electrophoresis at pH values of about 8.5. Albumin migrates toward the anode and is followed by α-, β-, and γ-globulins. These four major components consist of many subfractions which can be detected by procedures of high resolving power such as starch gel electrophoresis or immunoelectrophoresis.

Haptoglobins are α-globulins that are able to combine with hemoglobin both in vivo and in vitro. The haptoglobin (Hp) in 100 ml of human plasma or serum can combine with approximately 100 mg of hemoglobin. This property is physiologically important, since hapto-hemoglobin complexes are not excreted by the kidney but are cleared from the blood by the reticuloendothelial system. The in vitro formation of Hp-Hb complexes permits identification of the haptoglobins, since a Hp-Hb complex usually remains intact during electrophoresis. The location of these complexes in the gel may be detected by a catalytic reaction based on the peroxidative activity of hemoglobin (e.g. benzidine test).

Apart from variants in dogs (Naik et al. 1971), haptoglobin polymorphism has not been detected in other domestic animals. A serum protein polymorphism in pigs was originally presumed to involve variants of haptoglobin (Kristjansson 1961). These proteins are β-globulins which do not bind fresh homologous hemoglobin, in contrast to haptoglobins in man. However, benzidine-stainable complexes are formed if the pig serum is mixed with aged hemolysate, alkaline hematin, or with methemoglobin (Hesselholt 1963, in *Annual Report*). Such heme- or hematin-binding proteins are called hemopexin. Genetic studies with pigs of the Danish Landrace breed have revealed a considerable number of phenotypes for variants of hemopexin (Hesselholt 1966, in *Annual Report*). This variation is caused by a series of at least six alleles. In contrast, inherited differences have not been observed within the α_2-globulin fraction (Hp-5) which corresponds to the haptoglobins in man (Brummerstedt-Hansen 1967). Hemopexin polymorphism has not been observed in cattle, sheep, and horses.

The iron-binding globulin which forms part of the β-globulin fraction of serum proteins is called transferrin. This protein occurs in various molecular forms exhibiting multiple band patterns on the stained gel after electrophoresis (Fig. 4.8). Transferrins are identified in electrophoresis by specific iron staining or by using a radioactive tracer (e.g. ^{59}Fe). Once their location is known, ordinary protein staining (e.g. amido black or nigrosin) may suffice. Transferrin polymorphism has been detected in all domestic mammals so far examined. In each species the genetic mechanism appears to be essentially the same. Each allele determines from three to five of the previously mentioned transferrin bands or zones.

Various investigations have indicated some association between transferrin types and reproductive performance in cattle, sheep, and pigs. However, if true associations do exist they are probably small (Fésüs and Rasmusen 1971a, 1971b; Rasmusen and Tucker 1973; Spooner 1974). On the other hand, in local populations specific associations may be very large (Imlah 1970).

Only a few association studies have been reported so far involving the protein variants considered in this section, and observed effects are small (Ashton 1972). Major effects are expected in cases of deficiency of specific proteins. For example, agammaglobulinemia is expected to be fatal in all mammalian species. Deficiency of various components of complement may likewise be deleterious.

Inherited variations have been observed in prealbumins of pigs, horses, and chickens (Kristjansson 1963, Gahne 1966, Stradil 1970), and in albumins and postalbumins of

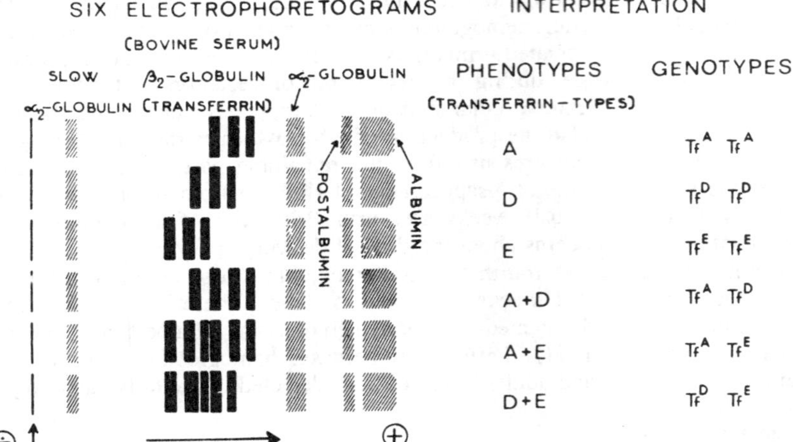

Figure 4.8. Bovine transferrin types (in black) as demonstrated by starch-gel electrophoresis. Cross-hatched areas represent other proteins. (Modified after G.C. Ashton 1958, *Nature* 182:370–72.)

cattle (Gahne 1963, Ashton 1963, 1964), horses (Stormont and Suzuki 1964), and pigs (Kristjansson 1966, Kúbek and Matoušek 1970). In pigs and cattle, genetic variants have been detected in the specific copper-binding protein, ceruloplasmin (Imlah 1964, Schröffel et al. 1968). Variants of slow α_2-globulins and low density lipoproteins have been detected in pigs (Schröffel 1964, Rapacz 1974). Immunoglobulin polymorphisms have been studied notably in man, rabbits, and mice, but similar studies have been initiated in the larger farm animals, e.g. cattle (Blakeslee et al. 1971) and pigs (Rasmusen 1965, Nielsen 1972).

Milk proteins

Some proteins are common to blood and milk, but the three major components of milk protein—casein, β-lactoglobulin and α-lactalbumin—are synthesized exclusively by the mammary gland. In most cattle breeds individual cows produce either a mixture of two electrophoretically distinct β-lactoglobulins (A and B) or only one of them. Two additional components (C and D) occur in the Jersey breed. The four lactoglobulins are determined by allelic, autosomal genes, Lg^A, Lg^B, Lg^C, and Lg^D. Another series of allelic genes governs the electrophoretic variability exhibited by casein. Each allele seems responsible for a specific pattern of α_{S1}-, β- , and κ-casein following starch-gel electrophoresis (Larsen and Thymann 1966, in *Annual Report*). Since different polypeptides are involved in the three casein components, the term "allele" should be regarded as describing a small chromosomal region (short DNA section) within which crossing over possibly takes place at rare occasions. Variants of casein have also been detected in other mammals including pigs (Gerrits et al. 1969). The casein and lactoglobulin of cow's milk have been subjected to detailed chemical analysis including amino acid sequence analysis (Grosclaude et al. 1972).

The milk of British and Danish cows of type Lg^ALg^A or Lg^ALg^B contains significantly more β-globulin (relative measurements) than milk from cows of type Lg^BLg^B (Aschaffenburg and Drewry 1957; Moustgaard, Møller, and Sørensen 1960, in *Annual Report*).

Enzyme Polymorphisms

In 1959 Markert and Møller introduced the term isozymes to designate proteins with the same enzymatic specificity but which can be resolved into different molecular forms by physicochemical techniques. The more descriptive term *isoenzyme* is often used. In 1969 Harris reported on 6 polymorphisms in human beings among 18 enzymes studied. These enzymes were chosen merely because they were easily accessible and because appropriate techniques could be devised. The conclusion from this investigation was that enzyme polymorphisms are relatively frequent not only in man but probably also in domestic animals. By 1975 about 40 enzyme polymorphisms had been detected in domestic and laboratory animals (McDermid et al. 1975).

The significance of most enzyme polymorphisms is not obvious, except when the allelic genes determine two or more levels of enzyme in blood or tissues. The extreme situation is the presence of a certain enzyme in some individuals and the complete absence of that enzyme in others. Lack of enzymes may lead to blocks at various points in the pathways of metabolism. For example, an enzyme deficiency may cause an accumulation of a metabolic precursor just proximal to the block, or it may result in lack of the normal metabolite distal to the block and without any accumulation of the precursor. Disorders caused by insufficient amounts of enzymes are called "inborn errors of metabolism." Congenital porphyria in cattle and pigs and congenital photosensitivity in sheep are examples in domestic animals, but several additional ones are known (Hutt 1964).

Variation in enzyme activity is to a large extent responsible for the individual susceptibility to various drugs and thus forms the basis for the important field of pharmacogenetics. For example, pharmacologists recognize that there is a normal variation in response to drugs by defining the *potency* of a drug as that dose which produces a given effect in 50 percent of a population. This variation, reflecting the normal, continuous curve, is expected if the response is due to the effect of many genes (polygenic inheritance) combined with a more or less pronounced environmental effect. However, in cases involving enzyme deficiencies, a discontinous response curve is observed.

In a study of arylesterase, Augustinsson and Olsson (1961) found that this enzyme in plasma of randomly sampled pigs may lead to a normal curve of activity. Nevertheless, the possibility of polygenic inheritance was excluded after a refined measurement of enzyme activity resulted in a discontinuous activity curve. Subsequent investigations showed that the various phenotypic activity levels were produced by one genetic locus with a set of multiple alleles, each determining a certain level of enzyme activity. Thus the phenotype of a pig was the result of the enzyme activities determined by the two alleles present.

Results with other enzymes have confirmed that an apparently normal curve in some cases may be regarded as a composite of a few overlapping "sub-curves" with different means and standard deviations.

REFERENCES

Anderson, D., Billingham, R.E., Lampkin, G.H., and Medawar, P.B. 1951. The use of skin grafting to distinguish between monozygotic and dizygotic twins in cattle. *Heredity* 5:379–97.

Andresen, E. 1963. *A Study of Blood Groups of the Pig*. Munksgaard, Copenhagen.

——. 1967. Sequential analysis of genetic linkage in pigs. In *Yearbook*

1968. Royal Veterinary and Agricultural U., Copenhagen. Pp. 1–11.

——. 1971. Linear sequence of the autosomal loci PHI, H, and 6-PGD in pigs. *Anim. Blood Grps. Biochem. Genet.* 2:119–20.

Andresen, E., Preston, K.S., Ramsey, F.K., and Baker, L.N. 1965. Further studies on hemolytic disease in pigs caused by anti-B_a. *Am. J. Vet. Res.* 26:303–9.

Andresen, E., and Talbot, R.B. 1965. Survival of transfused erythrocytes in pigs devoid of preformed isoantibodies against the donor cells. *Am. J. Vet. Res.* 26:138–40.

Annual Report. Sterility Research Institute, Royal Veterinary and Agricultural U. Mortensen, Copenhagen. (In Danish, English summaries.)

Aschaffenburg, R., and Drewry, J. 1957. Genetics of the beta-lactoglobulins of cow's milk. *Nature* 180:376–78.

Ashton, G.C. 1963. Polymorphism in the serum post-albumins of cattle. *Nature* 198:1117–18.

——. 1964. Serum albumin polymorphism in cattle. *Genetics* 50:1421–26.

——. 1965. Serum amylase (thread protein) polymorphism in cattle. *Genetics* 51:431–37.

——. 1972. Serum post-albumins and fertility in dairy cattle. *Anim. Blood Grps. Biochem. Genet.* 3:229–35.

Augustinsson, K.-B., and Olsson, B. 1961. Genetic control of arylesterase in the pig. *Hereditas* 47:1–22.

Baker, L.N. 1964. Skin grafting in pigs: A search for monozygotic twins. *Transplantation* 2:434–36.

Baker, L.N., and Andresen, E. 1964. Skin grafting in pigs: Evidence for a histoincompatibility mechanism. *Transplantation* 2:118–19.

Blakeslee, D., Rapacz, J., and Butler, J.E. 1971. Bovine immunoglobulin allotypes. *J. Dairy Sci.* 54:1319–20.

Bodmer, W. 1972. Associations between HL-A type and specific disease entities. In H.O. McDevitt and M. Landy, eds., *Genetic Control of Immune Responsiveness*. Academic Press, New York. Pp. 338–48.

Braend, M. 1968. Genetic variation of horse hemoglobin. *Hereditas* 58:385–92.

Braend, M., and Stormont, C. 1964. Studies on hemoglobin and transferrin types of horses. *Nord. Vet. Med.* 16:31–37.

Brambell, F.W.R. 1970. *The Transmission of Passive Immunity from Mother to Young*. Frontiers of Biology, vol. 18. Ed. A. Neuberger and E.L. Tatum. American Elsevier, New York.

Briles, W.E. 1974. Associations between the B and R blood group loci and resistance to certain oncogenic viruses in chickens. 1st World Cong. Genet. Applied Livestock Production, Madrid. Vol. 1, 299–306.

Brummerstedt-Hansen, E. 1967. *The Serum Proteins of the Pig: An Immunoelectrophoretic Study*. Munksgaard, Copenhagen.

Bruner, D.W., Brown, R.G., Hull, F.E., and Kinkaid, A.S. 1949. Blood factors and baby pig anemia. *J. Am. Vet. Med. Ass.* 115:94–96.

Burnet, M.F. 1969. *Self and Not-Self*. Cambridge U. Press, London, New York.

——. 1974. *Intrinsic Mutagenesis: A Genetic Approach to Ageing*. Medical & Technical, Lancaster, Eng.

Coombs, R.R.A., Gleeson-White, M.H., and Hall, J.G. 1951. Factors influencing the agglutinability of red cells. II. The agglutination of bovine red cells previously classified as "inagglutinable" by the building up of an "antiglobulin:globulin lattice" on the sensitized cells. *Brit. J. Exp. Path.* 32:195–202.

Damian, R.T. 1964. Molecular mimicry: Antigen sharing by parasite and host and its consequences. *Am. Natur.* 98:129–49.

Doll, E.R., Richards, M.G., Wallace, M.E., and Bryans, J.T. 1952. The influence of an equine fetal tissue vaccine upon haemagglutination activity of mare serums: Its relation to hemolytic icterus of newborn foals. *Cornell Vet.* 42:495–505.

Ferguson, L.C., Stormont, C., and Irwin, M.R. 1942. On additional antigens in the erythrocytes of cattle. *J. Immun.* 44:147–64.

Fésüs, L., and Rasmusen, B.A. 1971a. The distribution of transferrin and hemoglobin types in families of Suffolk and Targhee sheep. *Anim. Blood Grps. Biochem. Genet.* 2:39–43.

——. 1971b. Transferrin types and litter size in the pig. *Anim. Blood Grps. Biochem. Genet.* 2:57–58.

Franks, D. 1962. Horse blood groups and hemolytic disease of the newborn foal. *Ann. N.Y. Acad. Sci.* 97:235–50.

Gahne, B. 1961. Studies of transferrins in serum and milk of Swedish cattle. *Anim. Prod.* 3:135–45.

——. 1963. Inherited variations in the post-albumins of cattle serum. *Hereditas* 50:126–35.

——. 1966. Studies on the inheritance of electrophoretic forms of transferrins, albumins, prealbumins, and plasma esterases of horses. *Genetics* 53:681–94.

——. 1967. Some genetic variations of cattle and horse serum proteins. Ph.D. diss., U. of Uppsala, Sweden.

——. 1970. The genetic control of arylesterase activity in pig serum. *Anim. Blood Grps. Biochem. Genet.* 1:33–42.

Gerneke, W.H. 1967. Cytogenetic investigations on normal and malformed animals, with special reference to intersexes. *J. Vet. Res.* 34:219–300.

Gerrits, R.J., Kraeling, R.R., and Kincaid, C.M. 1969. Polymorphism in a casein fraction of sows' milk. *Biochem. Genet.* 3:335–58.

Goodwin, R.F.W., and Coombs, R.R.A. 1956. The blood groups of the pig. IV. The A antigen-antibody system and haemolytic disease in new-born piglets. *J. Comp. Path.* 66:317–31.

Goodwin, R.F.W., Saison, R., and Coombs, R.R.A. 1955. The blood groups of the pig. II. Red cell iso-antibodies in the sera of pigs injected with crystal violet swine fever vaccine. *J. Comp. Path.* 65:79–92.

Gordon, W.G., Basch, J.J., and Kalan, E.B. 1961. Amino acid composition of β-lactoglobulins A, B, and AB. *J. Biol. Chem.* 236:2908–11.

Grosclaude, F., Mahé, M.-F., Mercier, J.-C., and Ribadeau-Dumas, B. 1972. Caractérisation des variants génétiques des caséines α_{S1} et β bovines. *Eur. J. Biochem.* 26:328–37.

Harris, H. 1969. Enzyme and protein polymorphisms in human populations. *Brit. Med. Bull.* 25:5–13.

Hubbert, W.T., and Miller, W.J. 1971. Developmental polymorphism in bovine hemoglobin. *Am. J. Vet. Res.* 32:1723–30.

——. 1974. Immunogenetic ontogeny of cellular membrane function: A review. *J. Cell. Physiol.* 84:429–44.

Hughes, W. 1928. The freemartin condition in swine. *Anat. Rec.* 41:213–45.

Huisman, T.H.J. 1966. Hemoglobin types in some domestic animals. Proc. X Euro. Conf. Anim. Blood Grps., Paris. Pp. 61–75.

Hutt, F.B. 1964. *Animal Genetics*. Ronald, New York.

Imlah, P. 1964. Inherited variants in serum ceruloplasmins of the pig. *Nature* 203:658–59.

——. 1970. Evidence for the *Tf* locus being associated with an early lethal factor in a strain of pigs. *Anim. Blood Grps. Biochem. Genet.* 1:5–13.

Jackson, D.P., Sorensen, D.K., Cronkite, E.P., Bond, V.P., and Fliednen, T.M. 1959. Effectiveness of transfusions of fresh and lyophilized platelets in controlling bleeding due to thrombocytopenia. *J. Clin. Invest.* 38:1689–97.

Jensen, E.L., Smith, C., Baker, L.N., and Cox, D.F. 1968. Quantitative studies on blood group and serum protein systems in pigs. II. Effects on production and reproduction. *J. Anim. Sci.* 27:856–62.

Jensen, P., Staun, H., Nielsen, P.B., and Moustgaard, J. 1976. *Investigations on the Association between the H Blood Group System and Scores for Porcine Meat Colour*. National Institute of Animal Science, Copenhagen. Communication no. 83.

Kitchen, H., Putnam, F.W., and Taylor, W.J. 1964. Hemoglobin polymorphism: Its relation to sickling of erythrocytes in white-tailed deer. *Science* 144:1237–39.

Kristjansson, F.K. 1961. Genetic control of three haptoglobins in pigs. *Genetics* 46:907–10.

——. 1963. Genetic control of two pre-albumins in pigs. *Genetics* 48:1059–63.

——. 1966. Fractionation of serum albumin and genetic control of two albumin fractions in pigs. *Genetics* 53:675–79.

Kúbek, A., and Matoušek, J. 1970. Polymorphism of postalbumins in the serum of pigs and the ovarian follicular fluid of sows. *Anim. Blood Grps. Biochem. Genet.* 1:163–67.

Landsteiner, K. 1900. Zur Kenntnis der antifermentativen, lytischen, und agglutinierenden Wirkungen des Blutserums und der Lymphe. *Zentralblatt Bakt.* (sec. 1) 27:357–62.

——. 1901. Ueber Agglutinationserscheinungen normalen menschlichen Blutes. *Wien. klin. Wschr.* 14:1132–34.

Larsen, B. 1965. Test for linkage of the genes controlling haemoglobin, transferrin, and blood types in cattle. In *Yearbook 1966*. Royal Veterinary and Agricultural U., Copenhagen. Pp. 41–48.

Lillie, E.R. 1916. The theory of the freemartin. *Science* 43:611–13.

Linklater, K.A. 1968. Iso-immunisation in the parturient sow by foetal red cells. *Vet. Rec.* 83:203–4.

——. 1971. Iso-antibodies to red cell antigens in pigs' sera. II. The incidence of iso-antibodies to red cell antigens in the sera of adult pigs. *Anim. Blood Grps. Biochem. Genet.* 2:215–20.

Markert, C.L., and Møller, F. 1959. Multiple forms of enzymes: Tissue, ontogenetic, and species specific patterns. *Proc. Nat. Acad. Sci.* 45:753–63.

Matoušek, J., ed. 1965. *Blood Groups of Animals*. Czechoslovak Academy of Sciences, Prague.

McConnell, J., Fechheimer, N.S., and Gilmore, L.O. 1963. Somatic chromosomes of the domestic pig. *J. Anim. Sci.* 22:374–79.

McDermid, E.M., Agar, N.S., and Chai, C.K. 1975. Electrophoretic variation of red cell enzyme systems in farm animals. *Anim. Blood Grps. Biochem. Genet.* 6:127–74.

Mollison, P.L. 1961. *Blood Transfusion in Clinical Medicine*. 3d ed. Blackwell Scientific, Oxford.

Naik, S.N., Anderson, D.E., Jardine, J.H., and Clifford, D.H. 1971. Glucose-6-phosphate dehydrogenase deficiency, haptoglobin, and hemoglobin variants in dogs. *Anim. Blood Grps. Biochem. Genet.* 2:89–94.

Neimann-Sørensen, A. 1958. *Blood Groups of Cattle*. Mortensen, Copenhagen.

Neimann-Sørensen, A., and Robertson, A. 1961. The association between blood groups and several production characteristics in three Danish cattle breeds. *Acta Ag. Scand.* 11:163–96.

Nielsen, P.B. 1961. The M blood group system of the pig. *Acta Vet. Scand.* 2:246–53.

——. 1972. Isoantigens of the immunoglobulins in pigs. *Acta Vet. Scand.* 13:143–45.

Owen, R.D. 1945. Immunogenetic consequences of vascular anastomoses between bovine twins. *Science* 102:400–1.

Rapacz, J. 1974. Immunogenetic polymorphism and genetic control of low density beta-lipoproteins in swine. 1st World Cong. Genet. Applied Livestock Production, Madrid. Vol. 1, 291–98.

Rapacz, J., and Shackelford, R.M. 1966. The inheritance of seven erythrocyte antigens in the domestic mink. *Genetics* 54:917–22.

Rasmusen, B.A. 1964. Gene interaction and the A-O blood-group system in pigs. *Genetics* 50:191–98.

——. 1965. Isoantigens of gamma globulin in pigs. *Science* 148:1742–43.

——. 1972. Gene interaction and the A-O and H blood-group systems in pigs. *Anim. Blood Grps. Biochem. Genet.* 3:169–72.

Rasmusen, B.A., and Christian, L.L. 1976. H blood types in pigs as predictors of stress susceptibility. *Science* 191:947–48.

Rasmusen, B.A., and Hagen, K.L. 1973. The H blood-group system and reproduction in pigs. *J. Anim. Sci.* 37:568–73.

Rasmusen, B.A., and Hall, J.G. 1966. An investigation into the association between potassium levels and blood types in sheep and goats. Proc. X Euro. Conf. Anim. Blood Grps. Biochem. Polymorphisms, Paris. Pp. 453–57.

Rasmusen, B.A., and Tucker, E.M. 1973. Transferrin types and reproduction in sheep. *Anim. Blood Grps. Biochem. Genet.* 4:207–20.

Rendel, J. 1958. Studies of cattle blood groups. III. Blood grouping as a method of diagnosing the zygosity of twins. *Acta Ag. Scand.* 8:162–90.

——. 1961. Recent studies on relationships between blood groups and production characters in farm animals. *Zeitschrift Tierzucht. Zuchtbiol.* 75:97–109.

Rendel, J., Aalund, O., Freedland, R.A., and Møller, F. 1964. The relationship between the alkaline phosphatase polymorphism and blood group O in sheep. *Genetics* 50:973–86.

Saison, R. 1964. The blood groups of mink. II. The detection of an A-like antigen on the red blood cells of mink by the use of pig anti-A serum. *J. Immun.* 93:20–23.

——. 1974. The DL system and the reproducibility of cytotoxic histocompatibility sera (abstr.). *Anim. Blood Grps. Biochem. Genet.* 5(suppl. 1):40.

Sandberg, K. 1974. Blood typing of horses: Current status and application to identification problems. 1st World Cong. Genet. Applied Livestock Production, Madrid. Vol. 1., 253–65.

——. 1974. Linkage between the K blood group locus and the 6-PGD locus in horses. *Anim. Blood Grps. Biochem. Genet.* 5:137–41.

Schierman, L.W., and Nordskog, A.W. 1961. Relationship of blood type to histocompatibility in chickens. *Science* 134:1008–9.

Schleger, W., and Mayrhofer, G. 1973. Genetic relationships between Lipizzan horses, Haflinger, Noriker, and Austrian Trotters. *Anim. Blood Grps. Biochem. Genet.* 4:3–10.

Schmitt, J. 1959. Über das Vorkommen eineiiger Zwillinge beim Schwein. *Züchthygiene* 4:316–21.

Schröffel, J. 1964. Genetic determination of the serum "thread protein" and slow alfa fraction polymorphism in pigs (abstr.). Proc. IX Euro. Conf. Anim. Blood Grps., Prague.

Schröffel, J., Kúbek, A., and Glasnák, V. 1968. Serum ceruloplasmin polymorphism in cattle. Proc. XI Euro. Conf. Anim. Blood Grps. Biochem. Polymorphisms, Warsaw. Pp. 207–10.

Smith, C. 1967. Improvement of metric traits through specific genetic loci. *Anim. Prod.* 9:349–58.

Spooner, R.L. 1974. The relationships between marker genes and production characters in cattle, sheep and pigs. 1st World Cong. Genet. Applied Livestock Production, Madrid. Vol. 1, 267–71.

Stone, W.H., and Irwin, M.R. 1963. Blood groups in animals other than man. *Adv. Immun.* 3:315–50.

Stormont, C. 1954. Research with cattle twins. In O. Kempthorne, T.A. Bancroft, J.W. Gowen, and J.L. Lush, eds., *Statistics and Mathematics in Biology*. Iowa State U. Press, Ames. Repr. Hafner, New York, 1964.

——. 1962. Current status of blood groups in cattle. *Ann. N.Y. Acad. Sci.* 97:251–68.

——. 1972. The role of maternal effects in animal breeding. I. Passive immunity in newborn animals. *J. Anim. Sci.* 35:1275–79.

Stormont, C., Morris, B.G., and Suzuki, Y. 1964. Mosaic hemoglobin types in a pair of cattle twins. *Science* 145:600–601.

Stormont, C., and Suzuki, Y. 1964. Genetic systems of blood groups in horses. *Genetics* 50:915–29.

Stormont, C., Weir, W.C., and Lane, L.L. 1953. Erythrocyte mosaicism in a pair of sheep twins. *Science* 118:695–96.

Stormorken, H., Svenkerud, R., Slagsvold, P., Lie, H., and Lundevall, J. 1963. Thrombocytopenic bleeding in young pigs due to maternal iso-immunisation. *Nature* 198:1116–17.

Stradil, A. 1970. Prealbumin locus in chickens. *Anim. Blood Grps. Biochem. Genet.* 1:15–22.

Swisher, S.N., Young, L.E., and Trabold, N. 1962. *In vitro* and *in vivo* studies of the behavior of canine erythrocyte-isoantibody systems. *Ann. N.Y. Acad. Sci.* 97:15–25.

Talbot, R.B., and Andresen, E. 1964. Influence of blood group antibodies on survival of transfused erythrocytes in pigs. *Am. J. Vet. Res.* 25:1556–59.

Talbot, R.B., and Swenson, M.J. 1963. Survival of Cr^{51} labeled erythrocytes in swine. *Proc. Soc. Exp. Biol. Med.* 112:573–76.

Tucker, E.M., and Ellory, J.C. 1970. The M-L blood group system and its influence on red cell potassium levels in sheep. *Anim. Blood Grps. Biochem. Genet.* 1:101–2.

Vaiman, M. 1974. The major histocompatibility complex SL-A in swine. 1st World Cong. Genet. Applied Livestock Production, Madrid. Vol. 1, 273–90.

Van Wagenen, G., and Hamilton, J.B. 1943. The experimental production of pseudohermaphroditism in the monkey. In *Essays in Biology*. U. of California Press, Los Angeles. Pp. 583–607.

Wiener, A.S. 1962. *Blood Groups and Transfusion*. Hafner, New York.

Wilcox, F.H., VanVleck, L.D., and Harvey, W.R. 1963. Estimates of correlation between serum alkaline phosphatase level and productive traits. *Poul. Sci.* 42:1457–58.

CHAPTER 5

Basic Features of the Cardiovascular System

by Robert L. Hamlin and C. Roger Smith

Blood circulation
Cardiac cycle
Blood pressure
Types of blood vessels
  Windkessel vessels
  Arterial resistance vessels
  Exchange vessels
  Capacitance vessels
Volume flow
Velocity of flow

An understanding of the cardiovascular system is central to the study of nearly all physiology. The life of every body cell depends upon an adequate blood flow. In addition to supplying the metabolic needs of cells, blood flow is also the basis for the special functions of groups of cells or organs, for example, the formation of urine by the kidney and the thermoregulatory action of the skin. Finally, through the circulation the work of highly specialized but widely separated organs is made the common property of all tissues.

BLOOD CIRCULATION

Venous blood low in oxygen returns to the right atrium from capillaries of the head and thoracic limbs via the anterior vena cava; from capillaries of the pelvic limbs, tail, and abdominal viscera via the posterior vena cava, and from capillaries of the heart itself via the coronary sinus and the anterior cardiac veins (Fig. 5.1).

From the right atrium, blood traverses the right atrioventricular (A-V) valve (tricuspid valve) into the right ventricle, which ejects it through the pulmonary semilunar valve (pulmonic valve) into the main pulmonary artery. The main pulmonary artery bifurcates and carries blood to the left and right lobes of the lung, where it enters the pulmonary capillaries and exchanges carbon dioxide for oxygen with the pulmonary alveoli.

Blood is then collected by 4–8 pulmonary veins which carry it to the left atrium. From this chamber it traverses the left atrioventricular valve (mitral valve) into the left ventricle, which ejects it into the aorta.

From the aorta, blood enters either the coronary circulation to the myocardium, or the systemic circulation through arborization of the aorta into systemic capillaries. After traversing systemic capillaries, the blood returns again to the heart via veins.

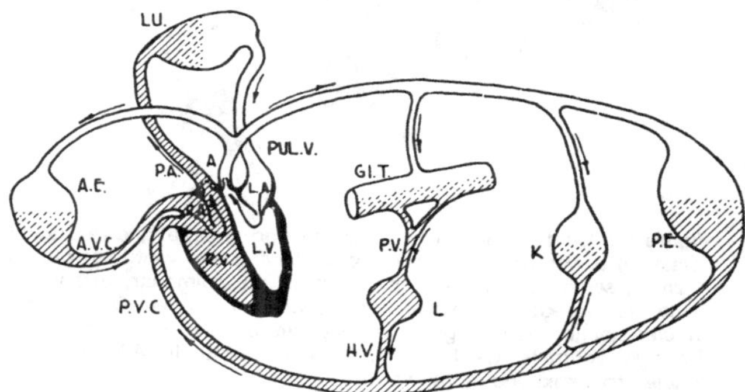

Figure 5.1. Mammalian blood circulation (heart rotated somewhat counterclockwise as viewed from above; venous side shaded): R.A., right atrium; R.V., right ventricle; L.A., left atrium; L.V., left ventricle; GI.T., gastrointestinal tract; K, kidney; P.E., posterior extremities; P.V., portal vein; L, liver; H.V., hepatic veins; P.V.C., posterior vena cava; A.E., anterior extremities; A.V.C., anterior vena cava; P.A., pulmonary artery; A, aorta; Lu., lungs; Pul.V., pulmonary veins.

Cardiac valves (Fig. 5.2) and valves within certain veins keep blood moving in one direction. Chordae tendineae, tough fibers extending from the apices of papillary muscles in the ventricles to the free edges of A-V valve leaflets, prevent the leaflets from inverting into the atria when ventricular pressure exceeds atrial pressure.

CARDIAC CYCLE

The cardiac cycle is measured from the onset of one ventricular contraction to the beginning of the next. It includes all events: electric, acoustic, pressure, flow, and volume changes. The cycle is divided into two principal

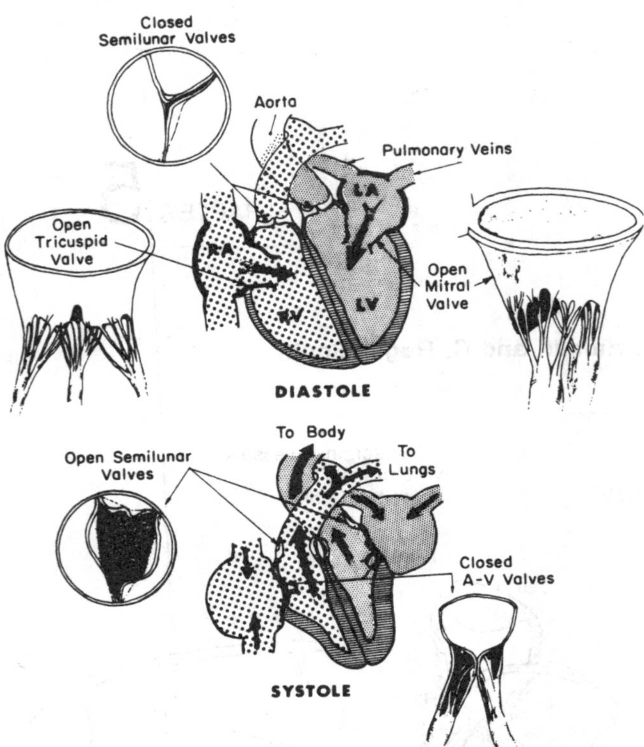

Figure 5.2. Cardiac valves during contraction (systole) and relaxation (diastole) of ventricles. When blood is flowing into ventricles during diastole, semilunar valves at the origin of the pulmonary artery and aorta are closed; tricuspid and mitral valves are open. During ventricular ejection (lower figure) the opposite occurs. RA, right atrium; RV, right ventricle; LA, left atrium; LV, left ventricle; A-V, atrioventricular (tricuspid and mitral) valves.

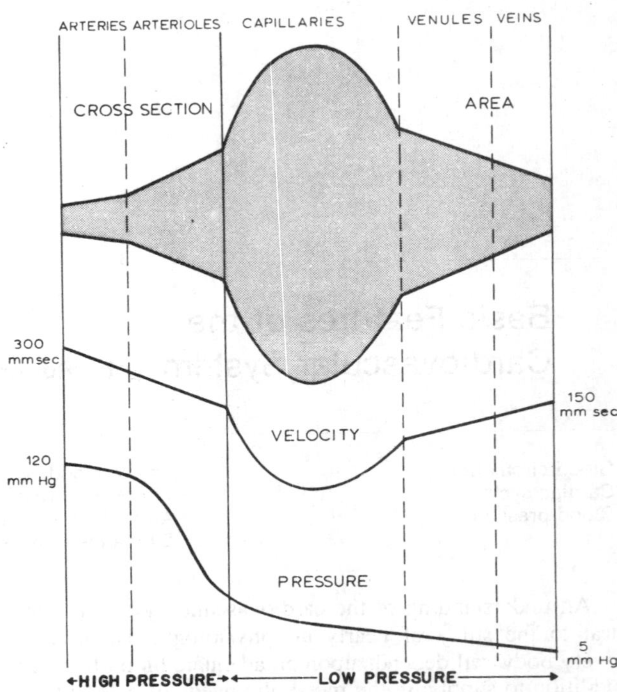

Figure 5.3. Cross section, mean blood pressure, and mean linear velocity of blood flow

phases: ventricular contraction and ventricular relaxation. Under basal metabolic conditions the contraction phase is shorter; its duration is altered only slightly by changes in heart rate. The relaxation phase is longer during the lowest heart rate but progressively shortens during cardiac acceleration and almost disappears at maximum heart rate. The beat interval, and thus the length of the cycle, is determined by a pacemaker, the sinoatrial node, located within the tissues of the right atrium.

BLOOD PRESSURE

Pressure refers to the force exerted upon the walls of the blood vessels. It is usually expressed in mm Hg. If the pressure is measured successively in the central aorta, the arteries, arterioles, capillaries, venules, veins, and right atrium, there is a pressure gradient (Fig. 5.3). Pressure is highest in the aorta and lowest in the right atrium. Blood flow depends upon this pressure gradient.

The circuit consists of two parts—a high pressure system (the arterial side) and a low pressure system (the capillaries and veins). The transition between them is abrupt: from high on the central side of the arterioles to low on their peripheral side (in the capillaries). This sudden reduction in pressure marks the arterioles as the principal site of resistance to flow in the systemic circuit.

TYPES OF BLOOD VESSELS

The vascular system consists of hollow tubes of varying diameter, wall thickness, and function. In general the caliber of individual veins is somewhat larger than that of corresponding arteries (Fig. 5.3) and their walls significantly thinner. Large arteries and veins have thicker walls than small ones. Veins are much more easily collapsible, not only because of their thinner walls, but also because venous blood pressure is so much lower. The lumens of all blood vessels are lined with thin, flat, epithelial cells which minimize frictional resistance to blood flow. Nerve fibers are distributed in the walls of arteries and veins; they are terminations of extrinsic nerves. Most are autonomic motor fibers connected to vascular smooth muscle. Some are sensory fibers connected to special receptor areas such as the aortic arch and carotid sinus. The walls of larger arteries and veins are supplied from a separate nutrient blood supply, the *vasa vasorum*.

The proportion of connective tissue to smooth muscle in the walls of vessels varies among different segments of the vascular system. The walls of veins are much less muscular, and they have less potential for active change in caliber. This apparent deficit is compensated for in part by the fact that venous pressures are much lower than arterial. In the arterial system, the walls of the aorta and large arteries have the largest amounts of elastic connective tissue and the least smooth muscle, while those of the small arteries and arterioles are predominately smooth muscle. Thus the larger arteries are the most elastic and passively distensible, while the smaller ones have the best-developed capability for active change.

The walls of most systemic blood vessels except capillaries have some smooth muscle. It is innervated by motor fibers of the autonomic nervous system. However, most vascular smooth muscle is capable of spontaneous rhythmic or sustained contraction independent of extrinsic innervation. (Periods of sustained contraction vary from a few seconds to as long as 60 minutes.) Vascular smooth muscle responds to remote stimuli originating in central nervous vascular coordinating structures or endocrine glands, as well as to those evolving in local vascular beds. Mechanically, the slow isotonic mode of contraction effects the caliber changes.

Blood vessels can be classified as distributing vessels, exchange vessels, or capacitance vessels. *Distributing vessels* are arteries which carry blood away from the heart to the tissues. Functionally, they are further subdivided into *windkessel vessels* and *resistance vessels*. *Exchange vessels* are the capillaries. Venules collect blood flowing out of the capillaries and veins return it to the heart. The venous vessels are termed *capacitance vessels* because they serve as a reservoir in which as much as 80 percent of the total blood volume is located.

Windkessel vessels

The aorta and the large- and medium-sized arteries constitute the windkessel vessels. Windkessel is a German word for a vessel which regulates a forcing pump. The heart is an intermittent forcing pump. This intermittent style of pumping creates an undulating pulse in the larger arteries. The windkessel vessels, because their walls contain a large component of elastic tissue, are distensible tubes. They in turn are connected to more muscular, smaller, much less elastic and more peripheral arterial resistance vessels which act like leaky stopcocks to the flow of blood into capillaries. The windkessel vessels progressively reduce the arterial pressure during ventricular systole by distending and storing approximately one half of the ejected volume. While the ventricle is relaxing and filling during diastole the elastic recoil of the windkessel vessels pushes the blood through the leaky stopcocks. Thus the elasticity of the windkessel vessels is almost entirely responsible for transforming the intermittent character of flow initiated by systole into an almost steady flow in the capillaries.

Increase in diameter by palpation is best detected in large arteries. Smaller peripheral arteries may move or straighten in rhythm with each beat of the heart, but such pulsation is not due to an increase in radius.

Arterial resistance vessels

The arterial resistance vessels are the muscular small arteries and especially the arterioles. These small-bore tubes account for approximately 75 percent of the total resistance to flow encountered in precapillary vessels. Their size is adjusted by smooth muscle in their walls: contraction is called *vasoconstriction* and increases resistance, relaxation is called *vasodilatation* and decreases it.

The arterial resistance vessels maintain and regulate the arterial blood pressure, and they regulate the volume and rate of blood flow through the capillary beds.

The arterial blood pressure depends upon the amount of blood being pumped into the arteries by the heart and the volume leaving them in the same length of time. The volume flowing from the arteries into the capillaries depends largely upon the resistance provided by the precapillary arterioles and small arteries. The relationship between resistance, pressure, and flow is called total peripheral resistance, calculated by dividing the mean arterial pressure by the mean blood flow. If blood flow remains constant while resistance increases, the arterial pressure will rise and outflow decrease.

Hypertensive disease is generally associated with a normal or low volume of blood being pumped into the arteries, a markedly elevated systemic arterial resistance, and a distinctly higher than normal blood pressure. The amount of resistance in the arterioles primarily determines the level of diastolic pressure. Blood also escapes from the arterial system during that interval when none is entering. Thus the more constricted the peripheral arterioles are, the more the resistance to flow, the less the blood escapes, and higher the arterial diastolic pressure.

The role of precapillary arterial resistance vessels in the regulation of regional blood flow is equally as important as their role in maintaining an optimum arterial blood pressure. Every tissue has arteriolar resistance vessels in its vascular bed. Normally, even when a tissue is at rest, arterial smooth muscle is in a state of partial contraction (called *tone*). The degree of contraction generally increases or decreases with the level of activity of the tissue.

Exchange vessels

Capillaries are the exchange vessels. Through the walls of capillaries nutrients leave the blood and enter the tissues by diffusion and filtration, while waste products leave the tissues and enter the blood by diffusion and osmosis. Blood is rapidly transported to and from capillaries, but in capillaries themselves the rate of flow is only a fraction of 1 percent of the rate in large arteries.

Capillaries are microscopic vessels. They connect terminal arterioles with small venules. Their diameter is so small it barely admits red blood cells whose thickness measures only 6–8 μ. Their total length ranges between 0.5 and 1.0 mm. The average rate of capillary flow is 0.5–1.0 mm/sec. This is several times faster than that required for exchanges to occur over the minuscule distances separating capillary blood from tissue cells.

Capillaries are exceedingly thin walled. In large part the capillary walls are a modified extension of the continuous flat endothelial lining of arteries and veins. There is almost no connective tissue and no true vascular smooth muscle. The thin walls are porous. The pores are visible under the electron microscope only as ultramicroscopic gaps. The size of the gaps varies some within a given capillary and more between capillaries of different beds. Pores convert the capillaries into a sort of screening device for the physical exchanges between tissue cells and the circulating blood.

Capillaries, though small, are fantastically numerous and remarkably close together. The distance separating adjacent capillaries may be no more than two times the capillary diameter itself. The tremendous density of capillaries means that every cell is in close proximity to slowly moving blood. Because they are so numerous capillary walls make up a large surface area for exchange of materials. In 100 g of cat skeletal muscle the total capillary surface area is approximately 7000 sq cm. Normally, all capillaries are not open at any given time, and there is a capillary reserve.

In certain vascular beds (e.g. cutaneous tissue of dog and cat paws, ears of sheep, fingers and toes of man, and stomachs and mesenteries) the capillaries may be bypassed by shunting vessels called *arteriovenous anastomoses*. They are wide-bore vessels which act as direct channels between arterioles and venules. They are not exchange vessels but rather they short-circuit exchange vessels. Flow-through then is nonnutrient. They are present in some tissues and not others, and are normally either completely open or closed. Generally, they open as terminal arterioles close and vice versa. In the skin, by permitting an increase in flow to extremities, they aid in the dissipation of body heat.

Capacitance vessels

Veins and venules are capacitance vessels. They collect the blood flowing out of the capillaries and keep it in relatively large quantities for pumping by the heart as needed. The voluminous venous compartment of the vascular system contains two thirds to three fourths of the total blood volume. Veins are capable of enlarging and contracting many times and still maintaining an almost constant pressure. This characteristic is called *plasticity*. Plasticity stems from the fact that veins, especially the larger ones, are normally not filled and have a flattened elliptical shape. As their volume increases, they become cylindrical with a rise in pressure of only a few mm Hg. As they become fully cylindrical, distensibility is markedly reduced and further increase in volume occurs only with much sharper rises in pressure.

The thin-walled veins and venules do have smooth muscle in their walls, although much less than arterial vessels. The musculature of venous vessels receives an adrenergic sympathetic vasoconstrictor nerve supply. The smooth muscle may constrict either reflexly over venomotor nerves, or by the action of vasoactive endogenous substances or drugs. *This capability for actively changing the size of the venous reservoir has real hemodynamic significance,* since the heart can pump only as much blood as flows into it from the veins. In this manner *the venous system acts as an important regulator of cardiac output*.

Veins are formed by the convergence of a number of venules. In contrast to the arterial system, blood flows progressively more rapidly from the periphery to the center. The functional resistance to blood flow is primarily in the moving blood itself. The larger the column of moving blood, the larger the central core and the smaller the resistance. The venous system thus presents only minimal resistance to forward flow and requires only a small pressure gradient. The opposite is true for backward flow.

Cardiac output is also an important determinant of venous return to the heart. The veins empty into the right atrium, whose pressure is a function of its blood volume. The emptier the right atrium, the lower the right atrial pressure and the steeper the pressure gradient between it and peripheral veins. For the venous system as a whole *the right atrial pressure is the single largest resistance to venous return*. Thus the level of blood transfer from the veins at the base of the heart to the pulmonary circuit is important in setting the central venous pressure, which in turn governs the rate of venous return to the heart. Normally, the central venous pressure varies only minimally because cardiac output is so well coordinated with the rest of the system. When there is failure of the right heart as an effective pump, blood accumulates within the veins, the veins become distended, central venous pressure rises, and venous return is impeded. In such instances the capillary beds feeding into the veins also become passively dilated and congested, with the development of edema in the tissues.

Many veins 1 mm or larger have valves which readily permit flow in the direction of the heart, but prevent it in the direction of capillaries. Valves are present in veins of limbs of the body, but not in those of the mesentery or the venae cavae. In the limbs, venous valves have special significance in two ways. First, when muscles contract and relax they have a massaging effect on surrounding soft-walled veins. When they contract, blood is thrust forward into large veins, due to both the valves and the lower flow resistance in the direction of the heart. When the muscles relax the veins fill from the capillary side and the cycle may be repeated. Long periods of muscular inactivity may be accompanied by venous pooling and edema. In upright man, pooling and diminished venous return to the heart from the legs, a fall in cardiac output, a fall in arterial pressure below that required to perfuse the brain against gravity, which causes fainting—all may occur when the muscle pump for venous return does not function. Second, valves in the long veins of extremities separate the continuous column of blood into small segments, lessening the effect of gravity and the degree of venous pooling.

VOLUME FLOW

The circulatory system is a closed circuit. The arteries, capillaries, and veins of the systemic and pulmonary circuits normally contain a characteristic and relatively constant fraction of the total blood volume. The volume of blood flowing per unit of time through a complete cross section of the system at any point is the same as that through a complete cross section at any other point. However, the linear velocity in different segments of the vascular tree varies inversely with the cross section.

VELOCITY OF FLOW

Three considerations affect the velocity of blood flow: (1) volume flow, just discussed, (2) the cross section of the vascular bed, and (3) the inverse relationship between velocity and cross section.

The cross section of the vascular bed at a given instant is the sum of the cross sections of all the vessels equally distant in time from the heart. The changes in cross section can be visualized by placing two funnels together mouth to mouth with the narrow parts pointing in opposite directions (Fig. 5.3.). One tubular extremity represents the aorta, the other the venae cavae. The point of junction of the two funnels represents the cross section of the capillary bed.

The inverse relationship between the velocity of flow and cross section indicates that as the area increases the velocity decreases and vice versa (Fig. 5.3). Velocity is highest in the aorta, progressively diminishes in the arteries as the distance from the heart increases, is minimal in the capillaries, and gradually increases again within the venous system.

[References for specific features of the cardiovascular system are in Chapters 6–14. See also *Handbook of Physiology,* sec. 2, W.F. Hamilton and P. Dow, eds., *Circulation,* 3 vols., Am. Physiol. Soc., Washington, 1962–1965.]

CHAPTER 6

Electrophysiology of the Heart | by Robert L. Hamlin and C. Roger Smith

PHYSICAL CHEMISTRY OF MYOCARDIAL CELLS

The heart beats because of a stimulus which originates at the sinoatrial node near the junction of the anterior vena cava with the right atrium. This stimulus first traverses the atria, then the ventricles.

Resting membrane potential

A hypothetical cell membrane 0.01 μ thick is pictured in Figure 6.1. In A it surrounds an internal environment of anions balanced by an equal number of positively charged potassium ions. The external environment is bathed continuously with the same number of positively charged sodium and negatively charged chloride ions. The membrane is impermeable and no electrical potential exists between the inside and the outside.

In the next phase (B) the resting cell membrane becomes slightly permeable to potassium ions, and they tend to diffuse to the lower concentration outside. This tendency to diffuse (F_d) may be expressed as

$$F_d = RT \ ln \frac{[K^+]\ i}{[K^+]\ o}$$

where R is the universal gas constant, T is the temperature (Kelvin), and $[K^+]i$ and $[K^+]o$ are concentrations of potassium ions inside and outside the membrane; ln is the natural logarithm (to the base e).

For example, when the potassium ion concentration outside the cell equals that inside, their ratio is 1, the logarithm (to any base) of 1 is 0, and F_d is 0. Since the resting cell has a ratio of potassium ions inside to outside of approximately 40 to 1, a marked tendency to diffuse outside exists.

There are forces which retain potassium ions within the cell. Whenever a positively charged potassium ion diffuses, it leaves behind an unbalanced anion which attracts positive ions. This attraction is expressed as $F_a = ZFE$, where Z equals the unit charge (valence) of the ion, F the Faradaic constant, and E the strength of the electric field, which either pushes the potassium ion back to the anion (if positive) or pulls it from the anion (if negative).

Thus at equilibrium in the resting cell just enough potassium ions diffuse from inside to outside that the F_d of concentration gradient and the F_a of electrostatic attraction become equal.

Since some potassium ions diffuse outside of the cell

	INSIDE					MEMBRANE			OUTSIDE				
	(+/−)	A−	K+	Na+	Cl−	EMF	P_{Na^+}	P_{K^+}	A−	K+	Na+	Cl−	(+/−)
A	0	10	10	0	0	0	0	0	0	0	10	10	0
B	−2	10	8	0	0	−80	0	++	0	2	10	10	+2
C	+1	10	8	3	0	+15	++++	++	0	2	7	10	−1
D	0	10	7	3	0	0	0	+	0	3	7	10	0
E	−2	10	5	3	0	−80	0	++	0	5	7	10	+2
F	−2	10	8	0	0	−80	0	++	0	2	10	10	+2

Figure 6.1. Hypothetical states of ion concentrations: A^-, negatively charged protein "ions"; P_{Na^+} and P_{K^+}, permeabilities to sodium and potassium respectively (0 for complete impermeability, 4+ for maximal permeability); EMF, voltage (mv) between the inside and outside of the membrane; +/−, relative dominance of either positive or negative ions.

until this equilibrium is attained, some negatively charged ions (anions) remain unbalanced and a resting membrane potential (Em) of approximately 80 mv is generated. Such a potential is called a potassium equilibrium potential, and the inside of the cell is negative with respect to the outside.

Voltage between inside and outside of a typical mammalian myocardial cell during potassium equilibrium may be approximated:

If $F_a = F_d$ then

$$ZFE = RT \ln \frac{[K^+]\,i}{[K^+]\,o}$$

$$E = \frac{RT}{ZF} \ln \frac{[K^+]\,i}{[K^+]\,o}$$

$$E = -60 \log \frac{[K^+]\,o}{[K^+]\,i}$$

Action potential

Depolarization

When a cell is stimulated membrane permeability to sodium ions may increase 500 fold (Fig. 6.1 C). Sodium ions—and to a lesser extent calcium ions—because of their high concentration outside of the membrane (approximately 15 to 1, see Chapter 2 for species differences) rush inside. The inside then contains: (a) more anions, (b) just slightly fewer potassium ions than are required to balance the anions, and (c) the sodium ions which have diffused. The sum of potassium and sodium ions now exceeds the negatively charged ions, and the inside of the cell becomes approximately 15 mv positive with respect to the outside (Fig. 6.2). The cell is now considered depolarized or active.

Depolarization requires 1–3 msec, the precise duration being determined by the ratio of sodium ions outside and inside of the cell, membrane permeability to sodium ions, and the previous resting potential.

Repolarization

Immediately following depolarization, internal cellular positivity and a rapid decrease in sodium permeability (sodium inhibition) stop further influx of sodium ions even though they are still more concentrated outside the cell. Internal positivity also accelerates the efflux of potassium ions (plus charges). The internal positive potential drifts fairly rapidly toward zero.

At this instant—peculiar to cardiac and smooth muscle, and distinct from skeletal muscle and nerve (Fig. 6.2)—permeability of the membrane to potassium decreases (Fig. 6.1 D), preventing any further efflux of potassium, and holding the membrane potential at a plateau near 0 mv for 0.1–0.4 seconds. During this plateau, calcium ions enter the cell and initiate contraction. No additional depolarization will occur. During this time the cell is in the period of absolute refraction, which persists for 0.1–0.3 seconds and corresponds roughly to the duration required for the ventricles to eject their blood and refill. Thus, not only can the myocardium not be tetanized by rapid repeated stimulation, but it cannot be "driven" to contract in such rapid succession that there is inadequate time for performing its task.

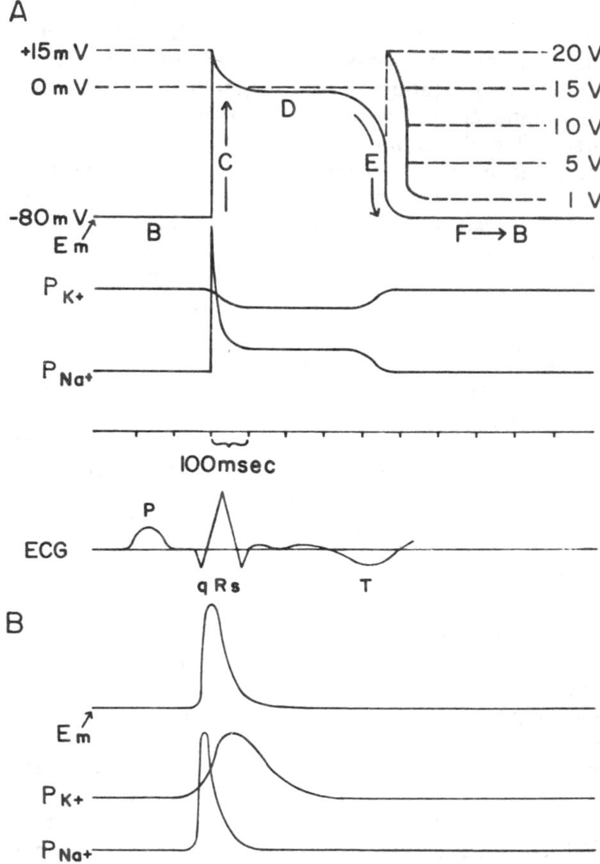

Figure 6.2. Two action potentials (Em). A, monophasic action potential from single ventricular fiber. Letters B, C, D, E, and F represent states equivalent to those in Figure 6.1. Upper righthand corner, typical curve for various voltages. B, action potential from single skeletal muscle fiber.

Potassium permeability increases next (Fig. 6.1 E). Potassium ions diffuse down their concentration gradient to the external environment, and the membrane potential returns (in 0.1–0.2 sec) to −80 mv because of the increase of anions. Depolarization may be elicited by a stronger than normal stimulus, and the cell is said to be in its period of relative refraction. The later in this period that the membrane potential approaches the pre-excitatory state of −80 mv, the less stimulus required to elicit a response (Fig. 6.2).

Next the sodium-potassium "pump" actively extrudes sodium ions (which entered the cell during depolarization) and reintroduces potassium ions (which left the cell during repolarization). Since few sodium ions are actually intracellular and few potassium ions are extracellular, the pump can quickly create an environment nearly identical to that immediately before depolarization (6.1 F).

If the heart beats so rapidly that this duration is abbreviated severely, or if the pump lacks adequate energy, the cell may become sodium-logged and/or potassium-deficient, and may cease to respond to stimuli by either electrical or mechanical means.

Although gradients and fluxes of potassium ions have been used here to explain the resting potential, one should remember that chloride ions contribute negativity and sodium and calcium ions contribute positivity in proportion both to their concentration gradients across the membrane and to the relatively low permeability of the resting membrane to them.

MYOCARDIAL CONDUCTIVITY

The dipole

Following depolarization and activation of one segment of a myocardial cell (Fig. 6.3), ion fluxes occur between this active segment (A) and adjacent resting segments (B). These fluxes increase permeability of the adjacent resting membrane to sodium ions, permitting influx of sodium ions and depolarization. If a large enough flux occurs, depolarization becomes self-propagating and traverses the cell mass from point of origin to its extremities. This is termed dromotropism or conductivity.

Although depolarization through a mass of skeletal muscle travels, in general, along the longitudinal axes of fibers, heart muscle depolarization proceeds radially in all directions from the point of stimulation because of transverse communications among adjacent myocardial fibers.

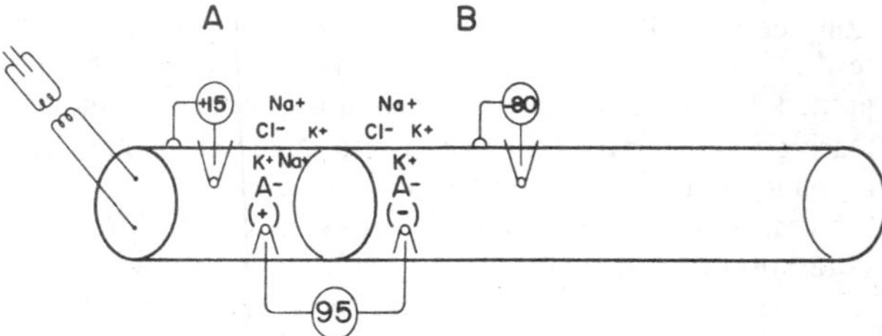

Figure 6.3. Single myocardial fiber stimulated by inductorium at left. Galvanometers record potential differences between the inside and outside of the cell at points A and B. The electrode to the positive input of the galvanometer is inside the cell whereas that to the negative input is outside. The galvanometer at the bottom measures the potential difference between the inside of the depolarized portion of the cell (A) and the inside of the resting portion (B).

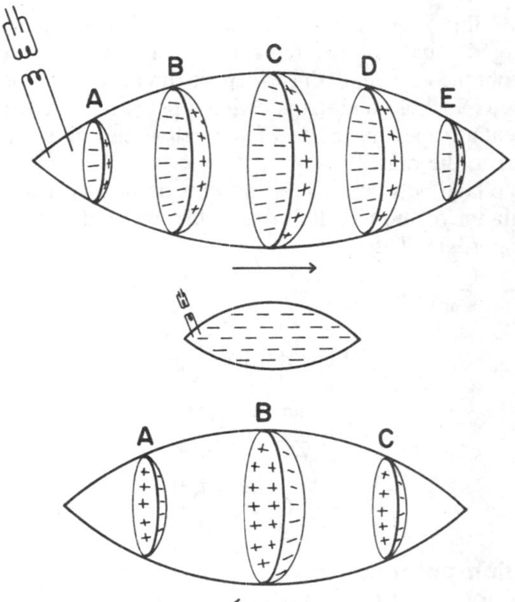

Figure 6.4. Volume of muscle stimulated by inductorium. Top figure, depolarization. Middle figure, totally depolarized volume of muscle; consequently it is comprised of an entirely negative zone. No boundaries between active and resting tissue exist because the muscle is all active. Bottom diagram, three instants of repolarization.

Waves of depolarization traversing either a single myocardial fiber or a syncytial volume behave as moving boundaries (interfaces or fronts) between resting and active myocardium, producing a potential difference of approximately 95 mv *across* the interface. This latter potential is the strength of the unit generator, dipole, thousands of which form the interface between resting and active tissue in a syncytial volume of myocardium.

Figure 6.4 shows the wave of depolarization traversing a volume of myocardium. Activity is frozen at instants A through E, showing configuration of the boundaries. In the volume of muscle, the boundaries are concave and the portion of the shell facing the stimulus has minus polarity while that facing the direction of the front has positive polarity.

The first area depolarized (A) becomes the first area repolarized. The potential difference across the membrane returns to the resting −80 mv, while the polarity in adjacent yet depolarized tissue is still +15 mv. A potential of 95 mv again exists across the boundary. However, the side of the boundary facing the area first repolarized is electrically positive and the opposite side is negative.

A map of boundaries between resting and active myocardium during many instances of excitation of atria and ventricles describes the pathways of cardiac activation. This forms the basis of electrocardiography.

Cardiac activation process

Depolarization

The entire heart is depolarized as if it were two functionally isolated units. One unit is composed of both atria and the other of both ventricles. They are connected by a bridge of conductive tissue, the atrioventricular (A-V) node (Fig. 6.5).

Pathways of cardiac activation (waves of depolarization) begin from the sinoatrial (S-A) node. They are emitted an average of 35 times a minute in elephants to 750 in bats (see Table 7.1).

The waves traverse the atria from S-A node to left atrium as if a pebble were dropped into still water (Fig. 6.6 A). Since the atrial walls are thin, depolarization travels nearly simultaneously through endocardium and epicardium, tangential to the surface of the atria. Velocity is approximately 1 m/sec; however, it varies with autonomic stimulation, temperature, and myocardial fiber size. Atrial depolarization requires from 0.08 seconds in the dog to nearly 0.10 seconds in the large atria of the horse.

Following traversal of the atria by these waves of depolarization, the atria contract and eject their contents into the ventricles. Normally, in the dog the atria are stimulated and contract approximately 0.1–0.2 seconds before the ventricles contract; in the horse the time is 0.2–0.5 seconds. This delay in activation results from an extremely low velocity of conduction (25 mm/sec) over portions of the ''bridge'' (A-V node).

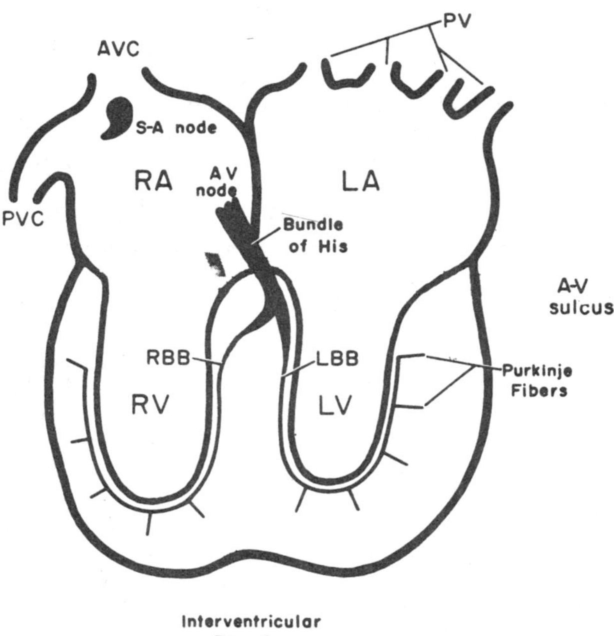

Figure 6.5. Chambers of the heart. Imaginary zones of ''insulation'' between the two atria and the ventricles and between the two ventricles are shaded. LBB, left bundle branch; RBB, right bundle branch.

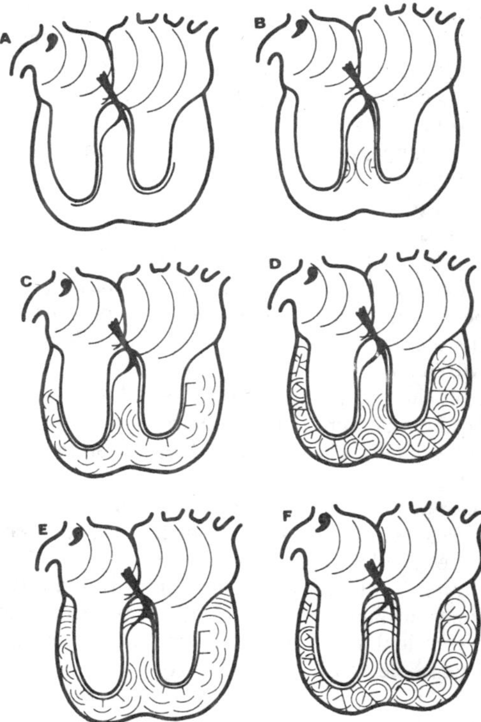

Figure 6.6. Waves of depolarization in the heart

The A-V node is comprised of three zones: (1) The atrial-nodal junction consists of an interface between fingerlike projections of A-V node and the right atrial musculature of the interatrial septum. (2) The body of the A-V node is located in the apex of the interatrial septum. (3) The nodal-His junction is a smooth continuum between the body of the node and the fibers of specialized conduction tissue (His bundle) which extends to the base of the interventricular septum.

The His bundle bifurcates into left and right bundle branches, which arborize further into small Purkinje fibers distributed from the endocardium to varying depths into subendocardium, subepicardium, or epicardium.

Species may be classified into two categories based upon the degree of endocardial to epicardial penetration. In the first (dog, cat, primates, rodents), fibers extend from one quarter to one half of the endocardial to epicardial distance (Fig. 6.6 C). In the second (ruminants, horses, swine, birds), fibers penetrate the entire distance in the free walls and base (D).

After the impulse is delayed because of slow conduction through the A-V node, it is accelerated (from 2.5 to almost 5 m/sec) in the bundle of His and the Purkinje fibers. From these points it begins to traverse myocardium in concentric rings. Conduction through the ventricles ranges from 300 to 800 mm/sec. The velocity of ventricular conduction is more rapid from apex to base, parallel to the longitudinal axis of the myocardial fibers, and from endocardium to epicardium, than in the opposite directions.

Depolarization begins in the apical third of the interventricular septum from both endocardial surfaces and proceeds toward the center of the septum (Fig. 6.6 B).

The next ventricular areas to be depolarized depend upon the species. In the first category both ventricular free walls are excited in a general subendocardial to epicardial direction (C). Following activation of the interventricular septum and both ventricular free walls, the bases of the interventricular septum and of both ventricles are excited, with fronts of depolarization traveling in general from apex to base (E).

Animals in the second category, because of the more general penetration of Purkinje fibers into the epicardium, have depolarization of both free walls in almost a single "burst," with no fronts of depolarization (D). The middle and terminal ventricular activiation occurs across the interventricular septum in general from apex to base and left ventricle to right ventricle (F).

Repolarization

Before atria or ventricles will respond again to stimulation, repolarization or restitution of the ionic concentration on the inside of the myocardial cell to a preexcitatory state must occur. Repolarization probably proceeds in the same sequence as depolarization.

ELECTROCARDIOGRAPHY

The normal ECG

The electrocardiogram is a recording of differences of electrical potentials generated by the waves of depolarization and repolarization traversing atrial and ventricular myocardiums. These electrical potentials project to points on the surface of the body.

The total system consists of a generator (the heart); a volume conductor (the saline-filled body); wires connecting points on the body surface to the electrocardiograph (leads); and an electrocardiograph (galvanometer which detects, amplifies, and records voltage changes).

A positive deflection is recorded when a wave (front) of depolarization is traveling toward that electrode on the body surface. A negative deflection is recorded if the front of depolarization is going away. No deflection is registered when the front is traveling at right angles to the point. Deflections of opposite sign are recorded in repolarization.

The amplitude of the deflection is determined by the density of unit dipoles comprising the front, the distance between the front and the electrode, and the number of dipoles the electrode "sees" (the number that face either toward or away from the point on the body surface).

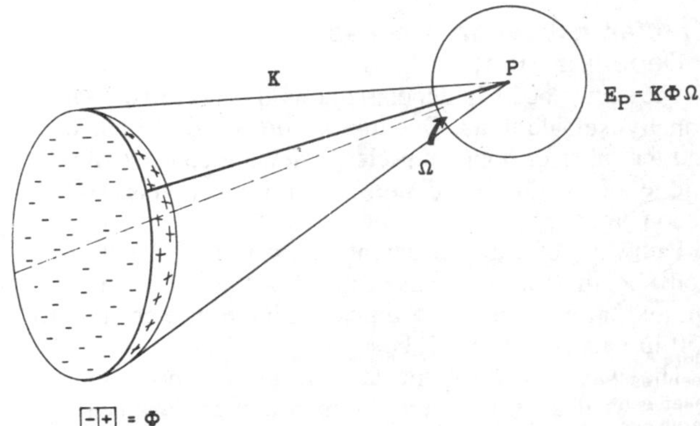

Figure 6.7. Electric potential at point P (E_p) on body surface. The sign of the potential will be positive because the positive face of the boundary faces the point. Ω, solid angle; K, resistance between the boundary of origin and the point from which the ECG is recorded.

To calculate the precise magnitude and sign of a potential inscribed from any point on the body surface, given the boundary between resting (positive) and active (negative) myocardia, construct a sphere of unit radius around the point (P) from which the potential is recorded. Then draw imaginary radii from the perimeter of the boundary to that point (Fig. 6.7). These radii subtend a solid angle within the sphere whose magnitude is proportional to the magnitude of the potential recorded.

The information required to predict the magnitude and sign of an ECG deflection is: (1) geometry of the boundary between resting and active myocardium at that instant, (2) the position of the heart within the thorax, (3) the position of the heart in the body volume, and (4) the position of the electrode on the body surface.

Figures 6.8, 9, and 10 show the heart and points ($P_{V_{10}}$, P_{VR}, P_{VF}) of electrical potential on the body surface. The

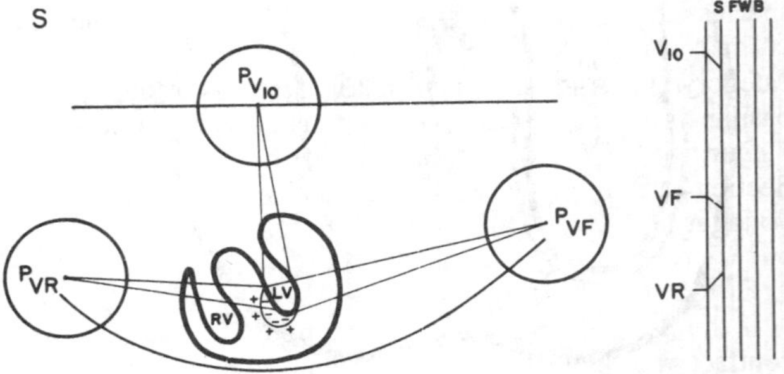

Figure 6.8. Left sagittal diagram of a canine thorax and points $P_{V_{10}}$ on the ventral portion of the thorax, P_{VF} on the left hind leg and P_{VR} on the right thoracic limb. ECGs at extreme right. The time line is labeled S since this boundary occurred during the initial excitation of the interventricular septum from left to right ventricle. Because point P_{VF} "sees" the negative portion of the boundary, it will inscribe a negative deflection. $P_{V_{10}}$ will inscribe a negative deflection; P_{VR} will inscribe a positive deflection.

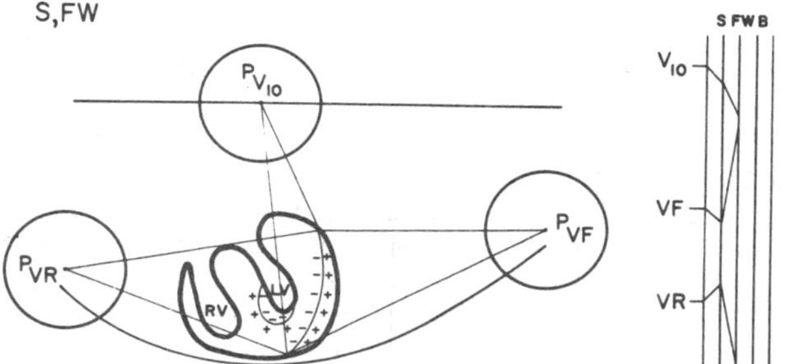

Figure 6.9. At an instant slightly later than Figure 6.8, the boundary between resting and active myocardium occurs in the epicardial third of the left ventricular free wall. P_{VF} will be positive. Since the boundary is a large one the potential is large. These voltages are labeled FW, since they represent excitation of the free ventricular walls.

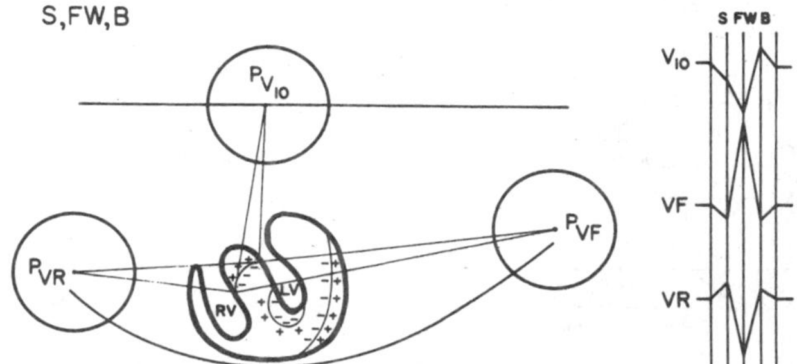

Figure 6.10. The last instant of ventricular excitation. A relatively small boundary between resting and active tissue exists in the basilar third of the interventricular septum. P_{VF} is negative. Because the boundary is small, the negative deflection will be small. P_{VR} and $P_{V_{10}}$ are positive. The deflection will be small since the boundary is small, but it will be slightly larger than that of the negative boundary in P_{VF} since the boundary is slightly closer to $P_{V_{10}}$.

magnitudes of the boundaries are approximated as in Figure 6.7. The geometry of boundaries between resting and active myocardium during cardiac activation is labeled S (septal), FW (free wall), or B (base).

During depolarization of the atrial syncytium, the P wave of the ECG is inscribed. Since this concerns a relatively small muscle mass, relatively few dipoles comprise the front and its magnitude is small.

The duration between onset of P wave and onset of the first deflections of the QRS complex (representing activation of the ventricles) is termed the A-V conduction time (PQ interval). This includes both conduction over the A-V node and over atria and Purkinje fibers.

During excitation of the interventricular septum from left ventricular endocardium to right (Fig. 6.9), a small deflection is generated as either a small positive or a small negative wave. Next a relatively high magnitude deflection is generated by the large fronts of depolarization traversing the ventricular free walls from endocardium to epicardium (Fig. 6.9) in hearts of species in the first category; the depolarization traverses the base of the interventricular septum from apex to base in hearts of species in the second category.

Final ventricular depolarization for species in the first category consists of apico-basilar activity through the basilar third of the interventricular septum (Fig. 6.10).

During ventricular repolarization, the T wave, a deflection of rather low magnitude and rate of change of voltage, is inscribed.

Sinoatrial node (the "pacemaker")

If the heart is removed from the body, it continues to contract rhythmically for some time. If blood or blood substitute containing oxygen, glucose, and various ions is perfused, it may continue to contract for hours. This capacity is termed *rhythmicity* or *automaticity*. The ability of the heart to spontaneously elicit waves of depolarization is termed *chronotropism*.

The S-A node is the region of greatest spontaneous rhythmicity in the mammalian heart. It is followed by the A-V node; however, the latter structure, in absence of the former, "drives" the heart at approximately one half the normal rate. Neither atrial nor ventricular myocardium normally possesses great rhythmicity.

Rhythmicity of both nodes probably results from inherently reduced permeability to potassium ions. In most myocardial cells a negative resting membrane potential is maintained by the fact that the efflux of potassium ions is countered through the reintroduction of potassium into the cells by the sodium-potassium pump. If the cell membrane becomes less permeable to potassium ions, the pump will reintroduce more potassium than can diffuse across the membrane. Positive charges tend to build up within the cell, fewer negatively charged anions remain unbalanced, and the membrane potential drifts toward positivity (Fig. 6.11). Such a steady drift is termed diastolic depolarization.

When the membrane potential slowly and spontaneously depolarizes to near −55 mv, the membrane becomes markedly permeable to sodium ions, and the normal rapid depolarization described previously occurs. If this results in a wave of depolarization, the region from which it originates is termed the pacemaker.

Rate of spontaneous diastolic depolarization, the degree of rhythmicity, is dependent upon the rate at which potassium ions build up within the cell. If the membrane becomes less permeable to potassium ions, these ions tend to remain within the cell; consequently the pump appears to be accelerating the influx of potassium ions and spontaneous diastolic depolarization is accelerated. If the resting membrane potential were normally only −60 mv instead of −80 mv, fewer potassium ions would be required to spontaneously depolarize the cell to the value of −55 mv, when the more rapid influx of sodium is permitted. Any or all of the above factors might account for more rapid decrease in intracellular negativity, thus producing a greater degree of rhythmicity.

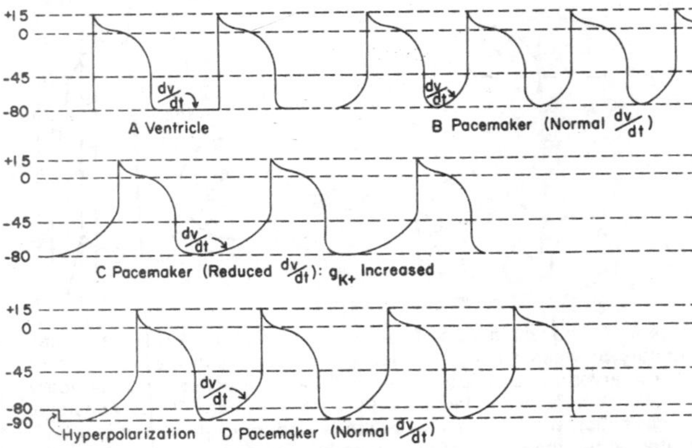

Figure 6.11. Monophasic action potentials from a single ventricular fiber and pacemaker fibers under three different conditions. In A, no voltage change occurs after the action potential returns to the −80 mv line (diastole). In B, C, and D, however, a slow period of diastolic depolarization exists and the fiber drifts steadily toward the −45 mv line, which will initiate a spontaneous depolarization. If dv/dt decreases because of an increase in potassium permeability, the heart rate will be slower. If the cell repolarizes past the −80 mv line to −90 mv, but the rate of change of voltage remains normal, then the rate will be reduced, since the diastolic depolarization must drift further.

Abolition of parasympathetic, or stimulation of sympathetic, nerves to the S-A node probably causes this node to elicit an increased number of spontaneous waves of depolarization (positive chronotropism) by a further decrease in permeability of the membrane to potassium ions. Also, slight decrease in membrane resting potential has been described. The increased heart rate may be a function of both factors.

Conversely, sympathetic blockade or parasympathetic stimulation causes either increase in membrane permeability to potassium ions or hyperpolarization of the resting membrane (further increase in negativity even beyond the normal resting −80 mv). The heart rate decreases (negative chronotropism) under these conditions.

Calcium ions affect the permeability of the cell membrane and so may alter the rate of diastolic depolarization. In concentrations slightly greater than normal, permeability is increased, the rate of potassium efflux is augmented, and the rate of spontaneous diastolic depolarization is decreased. This response is actually reversed by a greater concentration of calcium ions. Within a fairly large range potassium ions tend to inhibit or to reverse the effects of calcium ions on a stoichiometric basis.

Considerable confusion exists as to the role of potassium and calcium ions in regulating rhythmicity. The heart stops in relaxation (potassium inhibition) when concentrations of potassium ions exceed physiological limits (above 15 mEq/L of blood plasma). Conversely, the heart stops in contraction (calcium rigor) when concentration of calcium ions is increased above physiological limits (30 mEq/L).

The normal sequence of cardiac activation produces a normal ECG (Figs. 6.12, 6.13). Depending upon the species and upon the physiological state, a P wave precedes a QRS complex by 0.08–0.16 seconds in the dog and 0.08–0.50 seconds in the horse. Duration of the QRS also varies among species, but it too is fixed so as not to exceed normally 0.065 seconds in the dog and approximately 0.12 seconds in the horse.

The heart rate of a horse may vary from 20 beats per minute at rest to over 250 beats per minute during exertion. Thus the interval between subsequent QRS complexes (the deflection representing excitation of the ventricles) will vary from 3 seconds to less than 0.3 seconds. The heart rate of a dog may fluctuate nearly threefold (Fig. 6.14); during inspiration the QRS intervals are 0.4 seconds, while during expiration they may be 1.2 seconds.

Examples of pathological influences are prolongation of the interval between atrial and ventricular excitation (PQ interval) by disease of the A-V node, and disorientation by vectors representing forces generated during exci-

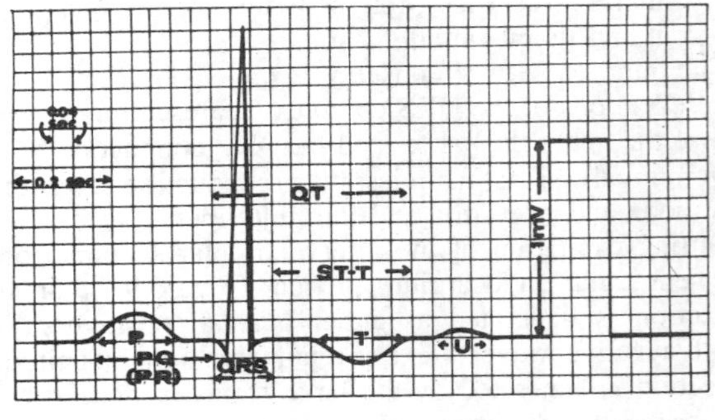

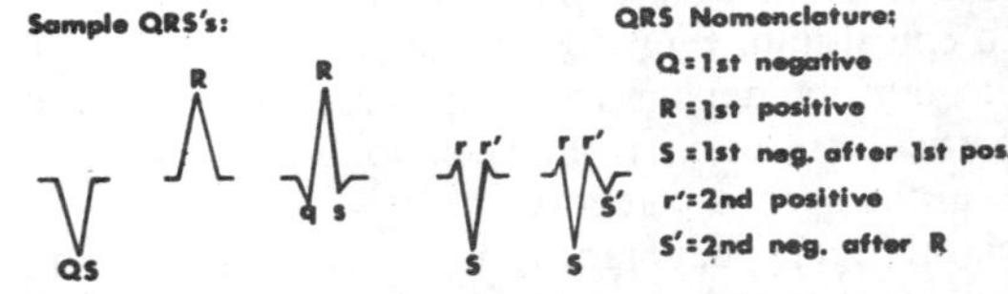

Figure 6.12. Schematic ECG showing the P, QRS, T, and U waves followed by a 1 mv calibration signal

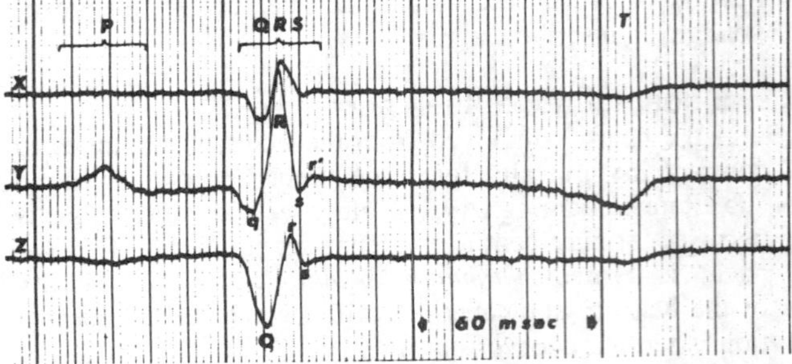

Figure 6.13. Three ECGs recorded simultaneously from a healthy dog

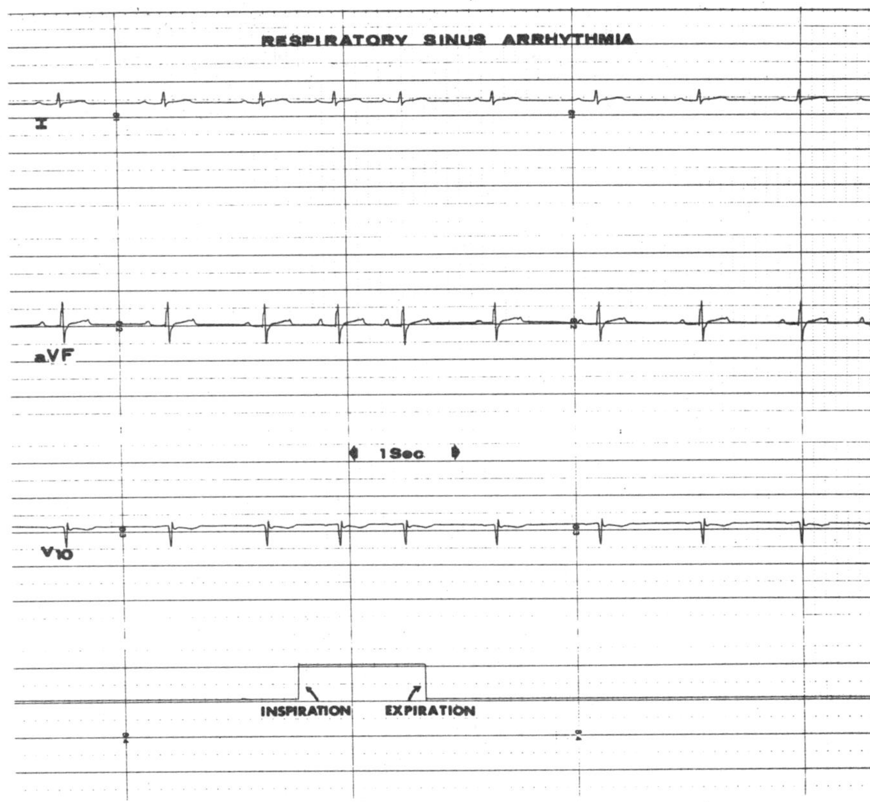

Figure 6.14. ECGs from three different leads during sinus arrhythmia in a healthy dog. During inspiration the heart rate accelerates (intervals between QRS are shortened) and during expiration it decelerates.

tation of the ventricles by right ventricular hypertrophy as a sequel to pulmonary stenosis.

ECG irregularities

Heat block

Heart block or A-V block (Fig. 6.15 D, E, F) is characterized by an abnormal association between the atria and the ventricles. In first-degree A-V block (D) the ventricles contract longer than normal after the atria contract, which is indicated by prolongation of the PR interval. In second-degree A-V block (E) the PR interval may be normal or it may be prolonged; however, more P waves exist than QRS complexes. In many instances 2, 3, or 4 P waves occur to each QRS complex, thus the atria beat 2, 3, or 4 times for each ventricular contraction. In third-degree or complete A-V block (F), no association between atrial contraction and ventricular contraction (P and QRS complexes) is observed. Normally the atria beat at a rate in excess of 90 beats per minute while the ventricles beat at a constant rate of 40–50 beats per minute. Although the atrial rate accelerates during the exercise, the ventricular rate accelerates much less.

Premature beats

Under abnormal conditions, either because the S-A node is suppressed or because other areas in the heart become hyperexcitable, other areas (ectopic or misplaced foci) initiate impulses which, while traversing the heart, generate abnormal ECG deflections and a beat which occurs out of phase with the normal sinus rhythm. Premature beats are classified according to their origin: supraventricular, when located in the atria; ventricular, when located in the A-V node or ventricular myocardium. Atrial premature beats may occur from any area in the atria. They are characterized by an early P wave; and, if the impulse originates from within the atrium but not the sinus node, the P wave is abnormal. Indeed if the ectopic impulse originates from within the left atrium, those leads in which the P wave is normally positive will be negative.

Ventricular premature beats occur in most normal dogs under thiobarbiturate anesthesia and arise for the most part from foci within the left ventricle. They are characterized (Fig. 6.15 C) by QRS complexes of increased magnitude and duration. In leads which have a positive QRS complex for a sinus-originated QRS complex, a premature beat initiated from the left ventricle (Fig. 6.16) usually induces a QRS complex of negative sign. If the beat originates from within the right ventricle (Fig. 6.17) the polarity of the QRS complex will be similar to that for the sinus beat, while the duration will be 2–3 times as long and the magnitude 1½–2 times greater. A premature

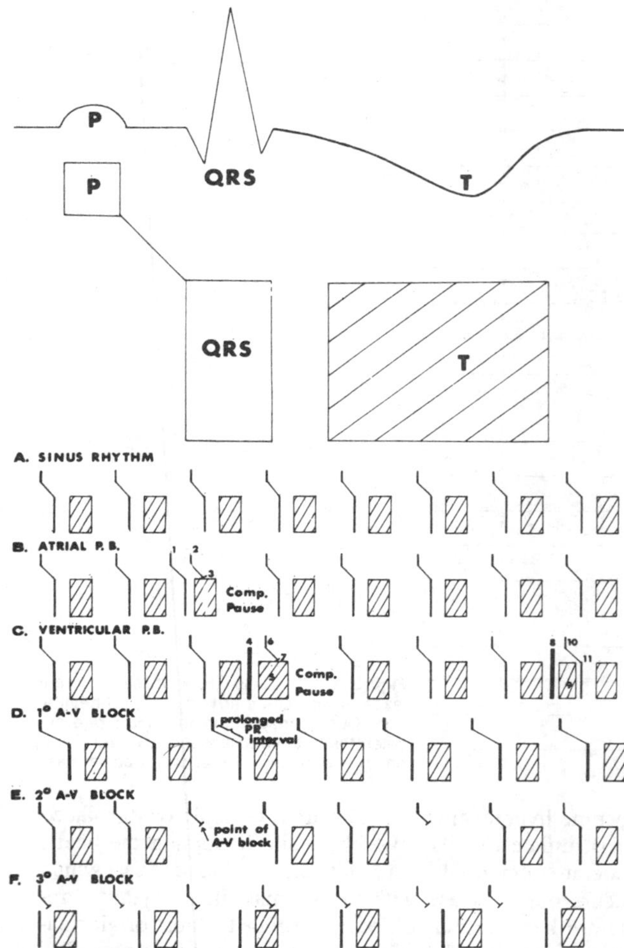

Figure 6.15. Schematic P, QRS, and T waves. Top trace, the ECG. Second trace, block diagram of each deflection (line connecting P to QRS "block" represents A-V conduction). In B normal sinus rhythm is interrupted by atrial premature beats (1), followed by QRS and T wave. Regular sinus-originated impulse (2) is conducted into A-V conduction system but is blocked before it can enter ventricles (3); no QRS follows and a pause exists until the next sinus-originated atrial beat. C demonstrates two types of ventricular premature beat. Premature beat (4) is followed by T wave during which ventricles are refractory to regular sinus impulse originating in atrium (6). It is blocked before it can enter ventricles after traversing A-V conduction system (7). This beat is followed by compensatory pause until next sinus-originated atrial impulse. Line (8) is ventricular premature beat interpolated between two sinus-originated beats. It does not interrupt rhythm since period of refractoriness is over before next sinus-originated beat.

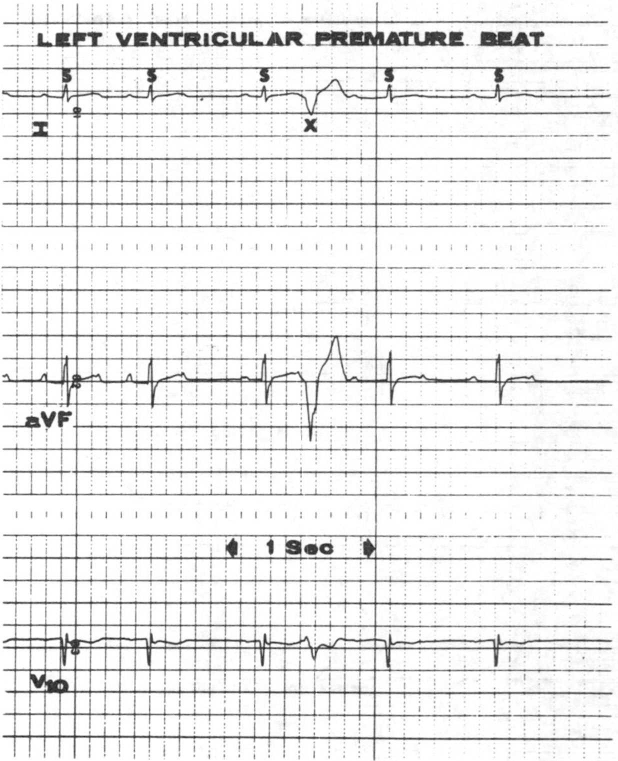

Figure 6.16. ECG from a normal dog in which a premature beat was induced from a left ventricular epicardial focus. The QRS complex is labeled X.

beat may be characterized also by a compensatory pause. This arises because a premature beat depolarizes ventricular myocardium so that when the normal sinus beat traverses the A-V node it reaches muscle in the absolute refractory period, and the muscle cannot respond until the next normal sinus QRS complex. Nodal premature beats, elicited from some area in the A-V node, are characterized by their premature but normal or only slightly abnormal configuration of QRS.

In addition, premature beats may occur in short bursts called *paroxysms* or for long periods called *tachycardias*. If the frequency of either atrial or ventricular premature beats is very high, close to 300 per minute, the arrhythmia is called a *flutter*. If the impulses do not arise from a single focus but arise from many foci and each individual focus has an island of tissue for which it serves as a "captain," the arrhythmia is called either *atrial fibrillation* (Fig. 6.18) or *ventricular fibrillation* (Fig. 6.19). Ventricular fibrillation is fatal, since the ventricular beat is uncoordinated, but it may be converted to a sinus rhythm by external countershock (ventricular defibrillation). In this, a large current traverses the total ventricular volume, thus depolarizing all of the myocardial fibers simultaneously and permitting them to repolarize simultaneously in preparation for an impulse originating from the S-A node.

Interventricular conduction disturbances are other abnormalities seen occasionally as a sequel to disease of the bundles of specialized conduction tissue in the interventricular septum. The purpose of these bundles is to ex-

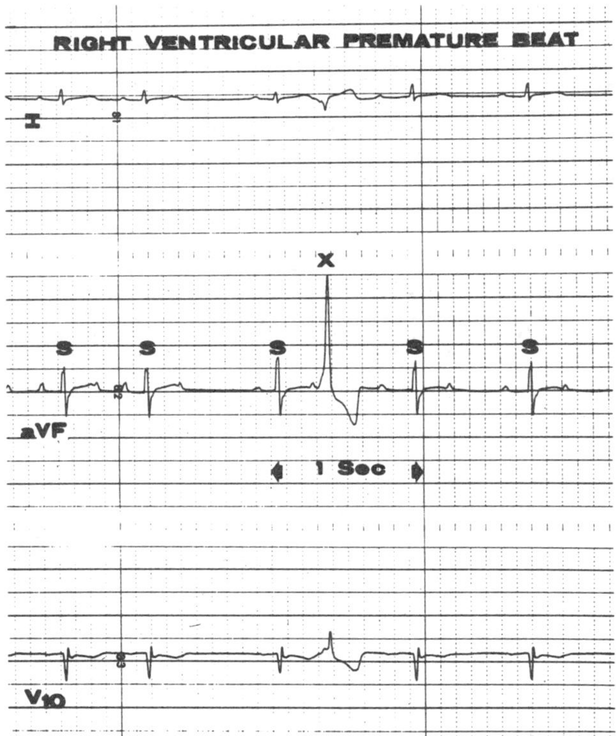

Figure 6.17. Premature beat induced from the epicardium of the right ventricle. The general deflection of the QRS is that from the sinus-originated beat in lead aVF.

pedite and coordinate the impulse so that both ventricles may contract relatively synchronously. In *right bundle branch block,* a lesion may occur there. The right ventricular myocardium becomes activated and contracts tardily. The QRS complex of right bundle branch block is characterized by waves of excitation oriented, in the dog, in a caudocranial direction. Because these forces are tardy, are unopposed, and traverse a larger volume of muscle, they are of high magnitude; and because they represent myocardial to myocardial spread rather than over the Purkinje system, they are of long duration.

Occasionally hypertrophy of the right ventricle or dilatation of the right ventricle with stretching of the moderator band within the right ventricle induces a QRS complex mimicking that of right bundle branch block. The reason may be that the hypertrophied muscle "outgrows" the Purkinje fibers, thus the muscle depolarizes from muscle fiber to muscle fiber. In left bundle branch block, just the opposite situation exists, and depolarization of the ventricles is deviated in its course, traversing the left ventricular free wall from endocardium to epicardium.

The QRS complex observed in right ventricular hypertrophy or right bundle branch block mimics that occurring after a left ventricular premature beat, because the waves of depolarization traverse the heart similarly. Likewise, the QRS complex in left bundle branch block mimics that of the right ventricular premature beat.

REFERENCES

Electrocardiography

Burch, G.E., and Winsor, T. 1960. *A Primer of Electrocardiography.* 4th ed. Lea & Febiger, Philadelphia.

Katz, L.N. 1941. *Electrocardiography.* Lea & Febiger, Philadelphia.

Sodi-Pallares, D. 1951. *Nuevas Bases de la Electriocardiografia.* Instituto Nacional de Cardiologia la Prensa Medica Mexicana, Mexico City.

Electrical properties of membranes

Hodgkin, A.L. 1951. The ionic basis of electrical activity in nerve and muscle. *Biol. Rev.* 26:339–409.

Hodgkin, A.L., and Huxley, A.F. 1952a. Currents carried by sodium

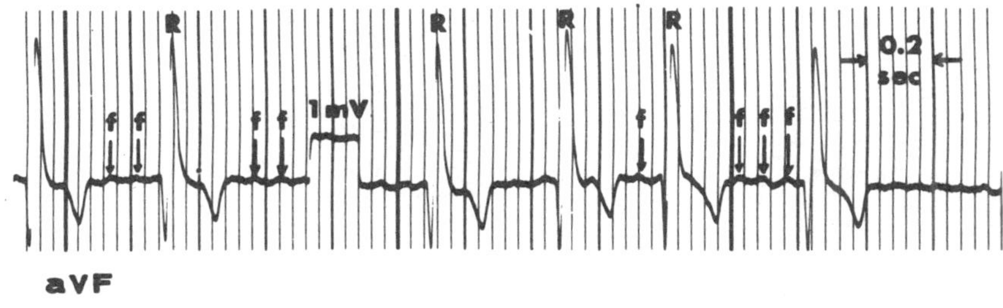

Figure 6.18. Atrial fibrillation demonstrating substitution of irregular fibrillation waves, f waves (undulations in baseline), for P waves and for rapid and arrhythmic ventricular complexes

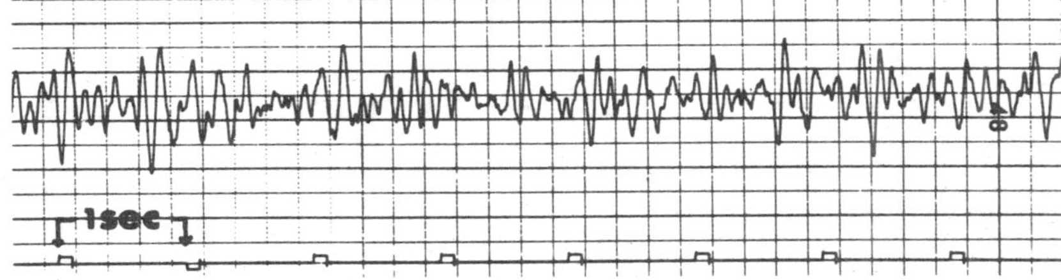

Figure 6.19. Ventricular fibrillation in which the base line is undulating without known cause. No P, QRS, or T waves are observed, and no large boundaries of depolarization are present.

and potassium ions through the membrane of the giant axon of Loligo. *J. Physiol.* 116:449–72.

——. 1952b. A quantitative description of membrane current and its application to conduction and excitation in nerve. *J. Physiol.* 117:500–544.

Hoffman, B.F., and Cranefield, P.F. 1960. *Electrophysiology of the Heart*. McGraw-Hill, New York.

Hoffman, B.F., and Suckling, E.E. 1953. Cardiac cellular potentials: Effect of vagal stimulation and acetylcholine. *Am. J. Physiol.* 173:312–20.

——. 1956. Effect of several cations on transmembrane potentials of cardiac muscle. *Am. J. Physiol.* 186:317–24.

Ling, G., and Gerard, R.W. 1949. The normal membrane potential of frog sartorius fibers. *J. Cell. Comp. Physiol.* 34:383–96.

Moe, G.K., and Mendex, R. 1951. The action of several cardiac glycosides on conduction velocity and ventricular excitability in the dog heart. *Circulation* 4:729–34.

Sano, T., Tasaki, M., Onon, M., Tsuchihashi, H., Takayama, N., and Shimamoto, T. 1958. Resting and action potentials in the region of the atrio-ventricular node. *Proc. Jap. Acad.* 34:558–63.

Weidmann, S. 1956. *Elektrophysiologie der Hermuskelfaser*. Huber, Bern.

Woodbury, J.W., and Hecht, H.H. 1952. Effects of cardiac glycosides upon the electrical activity of single ventricular fibers of the frog heart, and their relation to the digitalis effect of the electrocardiogram. *Circulation* 6:172–82.

General cardiac electrophysiology

Hecht, H.H. 1957. The electrophysiology of the heart. *Ann. N.Y. Acad. Sci.* 65:art. 6.

Hecht, H.H., and Detweiler, D.K. 1965. Comparative cardiology. *Ann. N.Y. Acad. Sci.* 127:art. 1.

CHAPTER 7

The Heart as a Pump, Hemodynamics, and Regulation of Cardiac Output

by Robert L. Hamlin and C. Roger Smith

VOLUME CHANGES

After the waves of depolarization the myocardial fibers of the chamber walls contract. Ability of the myocardium to respond to an electrical disturbance by contraction is termed contractility or *inotropism*. Thus, atrial contraction begins from the anterior vena cava and terminates, approximately 0.1 seconds later, in the extreme left atrium. Contraction occurs as a peristalticlike wave which "milks" blood from within the atria through the atrioventricular (A-V) orifices into the respective ventricles (Fig. 7.1). Because of the time sequence of atrial contraction, blood tends to flow into the ventricles with only minimal regurgitation into the veins.

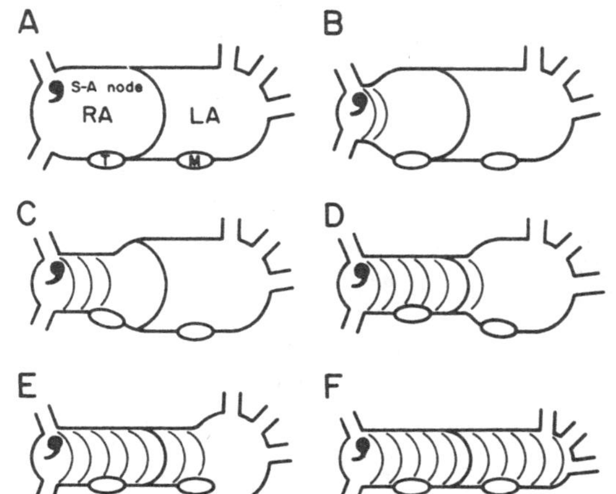

Figure 7.1. Right (RA) and left (LA) atria, tricuspid (T) and mitral (M) orifices, and veins returning blood to the chambers. Impulse from sinoatrial (S-A) node proceeds first through the right and then through the left atrium. A, resting phase; B and C, wave of excitation traverses the right atrium; D and E, it traverses the left atrium; F, both atria excited and contracted fully.

Following traversal of the A-V conduction system, waves of depolarization excite fibers of the ventricular syncytium. Because of the Purkinje system, the waves are propagated nearly simultaneously to all areas of the ventricles. All fibers of the ventricles respond by a nearly synchronous contraction, and blood is ejected into the great arteries through semilunar valves within 0.2 seconds.

Differences in modes of left and right ventricular contraction arise from anatomical variations. The left ventricle may be represented as a cylinder formed by muscle fibers originating from a fibrous skeletal ring (the A-V ring) on one face, and spiraling first toward the opposite face of the cylinder (the apex of the heart) and then back into the ring (Fig. 7.2).

Decreased left ventricular volume during contraction results partly from decreasing the length (from L_d to L_s), but more by slightly reducing the radius (from r_d to r_s), since the volume of a cylinder is a function of the radius squared and is only linearly related with length.

The right ventricle (Fig. 7.2) may be represented as a bellows, with the apex as the pivot and the interventricular septum and right ventricular free wall as movable faces. During contraction, the fibers of the right ventricular free wall (extending at near right angles to the axis) shorten and pull the free wall toward the septum, thus "collapsing" the bellows. Although both ventricles contract nearly synchronously, the left ventricle begins and ends sooner than the right.

Changes in volume during contraction and relaxation are studied easily in radiographs (Fig. 7.3). During sys-

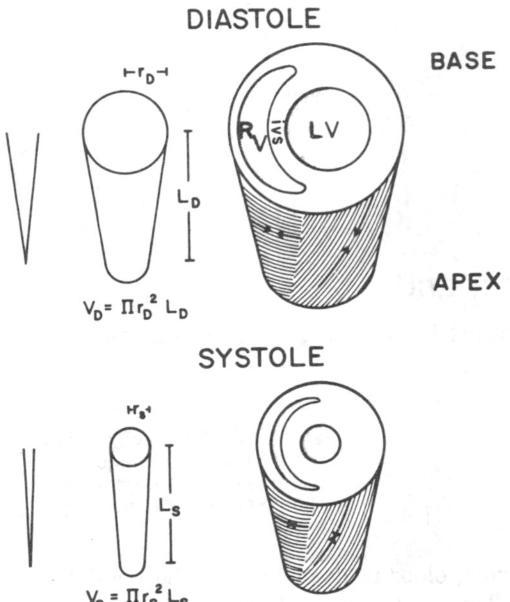

Figure 7.2. Bellow-shaped right ventricle (left), cylindrical left ventricle (center) and total heart (right). RV, ivs, and LV refer to right ventricle, interventricular septum, and left ventricle. Arrows on the outside surface run in direction that fibers shorten.

tole the A-V ring and apex move toward one another and the diameter of the left ventricular lumen decreases. The aorta becomes distended with blood and radiopaque medium is ejected by the left ventricle. Also, a considerable reserve remains in the ventricle after contraction, averaging 50–60 percent of the end-diastolic volume. Early in the period of ventricular relaxation, blood enters the ventricles from the atria and the atria become smaller. Later in the period, when the atria contract, they become even smaller as the ventricles are distended to their greatest volume (end-diastolic volume) immediately before contracting.

PRESSURE EVENTS

As the cardiac chambers contract and relax, fluctuations in pressure occur within their lumina and within lumina of great vessels leading to and away from them. These fluctuations in pressure create gradients of pressure which drive the blood.

Pressure variations are measured by inserting a hollow, fluid-filled tube (cardiac catheter) through a peripheral artery or vein into a lumen. The other end is attached either to a column of mercury or to an ultrathin diaphragm. Recently, miniature electronic pressure transducers in the tip of cardiac catheters have produced even better results.

Pressure is measured in physical terms as a force (dynes/sq cm) which distends the vessel or chamber wall (or elevates a Hg column). To convert from mm Hg to dynes per sq cm, multiply by 1330. After the wall is deformed, it then reacts, if it is elastic, by exerting a force on the contents and attempting to squeeze the contents either out of the chamber or down the blood vessel to a place of lower pressure.

For purposes of timing, pressure fluctuations are recorded simultaneously with the ECG (Fig. 7.4), since the ECG represents the waves of depolarization which initiate the contraction that elevates pressure. The following discussion refers to the schematic representations of pressure curves recorded from within the aorta, left ventricle, and left atrium. With only slight alterations these curves could represent the main pulmonary artery, right ventricle, and right atrium.

A cardiac cycle is initiated by waves of depolarization

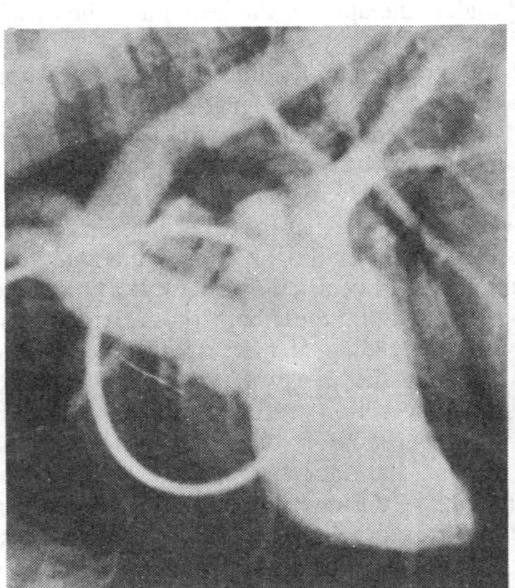

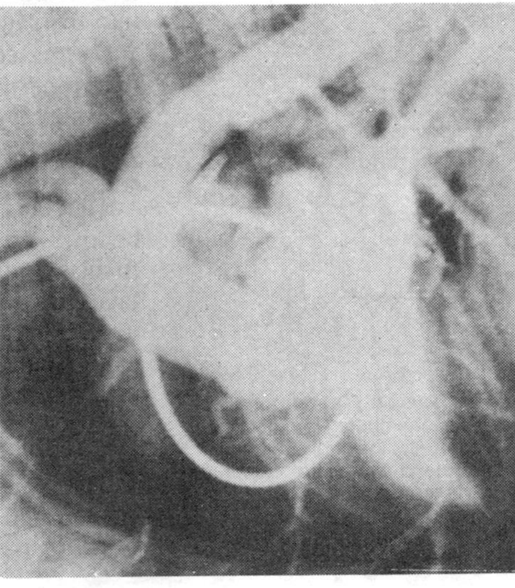

Figure 7.3. Left ventricular volume changes in a dog during diastole (left) and systole (right). During left ventricular diastole the left atrium (located immediately to the right of the tip of the cardiac catheter) is extremely small, the aorta extending from the left ventricle to the upper lefthand corner of the picture is rather small, whereas the left ventricle is very large. In left ventricular systole, the ventricle is very small, whereas the left atrium and the aorta are large.

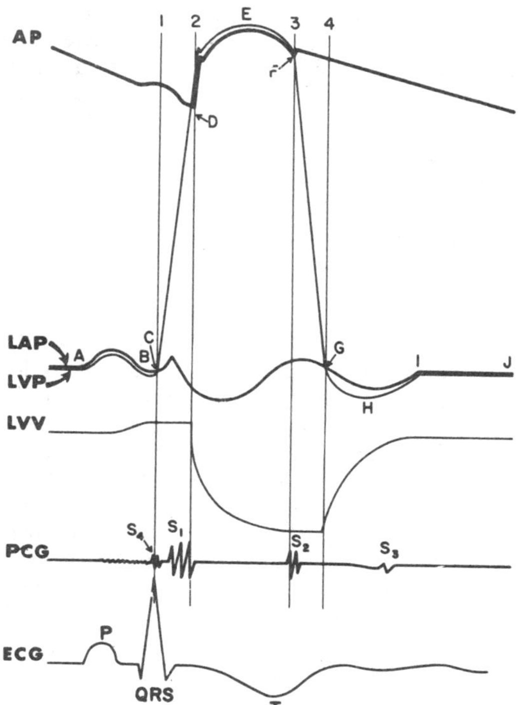

Figure 7.4. Pressure, acoustic, and electrical events during one cardiac cycle from a normal dog: aortic pressure (AP), left atrial pressure (LAP), left ventricular pressure (LVP), left ventricular volume (LVV), phonocardiogram (PCG).

which traverse the atrium and generate the P wave of the ECG. Following onset of the P wave by approximately 0.05 seconds (the electropressor latent period), myocardial fibers of the atrium begin to contract and pressure within rises from near 0 to 5 mm Hg. Since leaflets of the A-V (mitral) valve lie flaccid in the mitral orifice, they are opened maximally by blood as it is ejected from atrium into ventricle. Pressure within the ventricle rises to nearly the same height as that within the atrium. So long as the leaflets of the valve are not in apposition, both chambers form a single larger chamber with only slight pressure differences.

From the time the right atrium begins to contract (A) to the time the area of the left atrium most distal from the S-A node contracts (B) is approximately 0.1 seconds in the dog and 0.3 seconds in the horse. During atrial systole (Fig. 7.4), the pressure rise is termed the *a wave* (positive wave between A and B) of the intra-atrial pressure curve, or the atrial "kick" of the intraventricular pressure curve.

If atrial systole is not followed within 0.14 seconds in the dog or 0.28 seconds in the horse by ventricular systole, the elastic walls of the distended ventricles recoil, and pressure within the ventricle rises. This forces closure of the leaflets of the A-V valve, called presystolic closure.

After a delay created by the rather slow rate with which the A-V conduction system propagates the stimulus from atrium to ventricle, the ventricle is stimulated by waves of depolarization generating the QRS complex. Following approximately 0.02–0.04 seconds in the dog and 0.08 seconds in the horse, the left ventricle begins to contract vigorously (C). Pressure within this chamber rises quickly (C–D) from nearly 0 to 100 mm Hg in the cat and man to over 300 mm Hg in the turkey and giraffe. When ventricular pressure exceeds 3 mm Hg (C) it exceeds the pressure within the atrium and "cross over" occurs; leaflets of the A-V valves are forced into apposition, if they had not already been closed by atrial contraction and ventricular recoil. As they become tensed by a further increase in ventricular pressure, they bulge into the atrium. This gives rise to the *c wave* in the interatrial pressure curve. The valley between c and a waves is termed the *x wave*.

For approximately 0.05 seconds after closure of the A-V valves, pressure within the ventricle continues to rise rapidly (C–D), until it exceeds pressure in the aorta and the leaflets of the aortic semilunar valve are thrown open (D). The maximal rate of rise of pressure is an expression of vigor of contraction. When intraventricular pressure is rising most rapidly, the A-V valve is closed, the semilunar valve has not yet opened, and the ventricle is a closed cavity (1–2). Since volume within a closed cavity cannot change, even though the pressure is rising, the chamber is termed isovolumetric (also isometric or isovolumic), and this period is called *isovolumetric contraction*.

After the semilunar valve opens, blood is ejected, first very rapidly (D–E) and then at a reduced rate (E–F), into the aorta. The phase of rapid ejection persists for approximately 0.10 seconds in the dog to 0.18 seconds in the horse. The period of reduced ejection is slightly shorter. Together they constitute the period of *isotonic contraction* (D–F). During this time pressure within and tension on wall fibers remain fairly constant since blood is ejected into the arteries. With an acceleration in heart rate the periods of isovolumetric and isotonic contraction shorten only slightly, and vice versa.

During isotonic contraction the A-V annulus moves toward the apex of the heart and enlarges the atrium. This causes a rather sudden decrease in left atrial pressure (the x′ descent or wave) to nearly −3 to −5 mm Hg. During this instant most of the blood to be either ejected by the atrium during its systole or "aspirated" by the ventricle during the early stages of ventricular filling is drawn into the left atrium from the pulmonary veins.

As the ventricles begin to relax after contraction, intraventricular pressure falls (Fig. 7.4), first below that maintained within the arterial system by the recoiling elastic vessels (F), and then below that maintained by the return of blood into the atrium from the pulmonary veins (G). This generates the *v wave* of the intra-atrial pressure curve.

The instant intraventricular pressure falls below that within the aorta (F), leaflets of the semilunar valves are forced closed. Pressure within the ventricle continues to fall (F–G)—this time at its most rapid rate—for approximately 0.05 seconds. As in the case of contraction, the term isovolumetric is used.

After intraventricular pressure falls below that within the atrium (G), leaflets of the A-V valve are opened by blood proceeding from the atrium to the ventricle. Pressure built up within the atrium by blood returning from the lungs via pulmonary veins (vis a tergo), the elastic recoil of the great veins (vis a latere), plus a slight aspiration by the ventricles as they actively distend (vis a fronte) are probable causes. In addition, since during relaxation the A-V annulus moves from apex to base, the ventricle will actually move basilarly and engulf the volume of blood in the atrium.

Ventricular filling is divided into two rather poorly defined stages. During the approximately 0.1 seconds after opening of the A-V valve (G–H), the most rapid influx of blood occurs, termed *rapid ventricular filling*. Following this for a variable but much shorter duration is *reduced filling* (H–I). Together they constitute the period of isotonic relaxation. During the time immediately following the opening of the A-V valves, pressure within the atrium falls rapidly and the y descent or *y wave* of the intra-atrial pressure curve is inscribed.

Following ventricular filling, the ventricle, overdistended by the influx of blood from the atrium, recoils and generates a slight elevation of pressure which closes the A-V valve. This is analogous to the closure of the same valves following atrial contraction. Now neither atrium nor ventricle is in motion. Little blood moves until the next atrial systole. This period is termed *diastasis*. Intraventricular pressure curves obtained during prolonged periods of cardiac arrest show that ventricular pressures continue to rise very slowly until all pressures within the closed vascular system come into equilibrium; this *mean circulatory filling pressure* is obtained only after minutes of cardiac inactivity.

Duration of ventricular plus atrial contraction is fairly constant and decreases only slightly with increasing heart rate. Atrial systole lasts for 0.1 seconds, and ventricular systole for 0.2–0.3 seconds. If the heart beats once every one second, then 0.6–0.7 seconds remain for periods of ventricular filling and diastasis. If heart rate increases to one beat every 0.5 seconds and atrial and ventricular systole together still take only 0.3 seconds, then periods of ventricular filling and diastasis will last only 0.2 seconds. Since ventricular filling requires slightly over 0.1 seconds, this leaves only 0.1 seconds for diastasis. If the heart rate accelerates even more, the entire period of diastasis may be abolished. Still further increase in heart rate might impinge upon the time during which the ventricles fill, and the ventricles may not fill sufficiently to generate a subsequent contraction forceful enough to eject blood against the arterial resistance.

From closure of the A-V valves to closure of the semilunar valves is called ventricular or cardiac systole. From closure of the semilunar valves to closure of the A-V valves in the next cardiac cycle is termed *ventricular* or *cardiac diastole*.

The a, v, and c deflections of the pressure curve are between 3 and 5 mm Hg in amplitude. The x, x′, and y valleys are between 0 and −5 mm Hg. Nearly identical fluctuations occur within the right atrium. Since the right atrium is excited and contracts an instant before the left atrium, the right atrium's a wave occurs approximately 0.08 seconds sooner in the dog and 0.16 seconds earlier in the horse. Peak systolic pressure for the right ventricle equals approximately 20 mm Hg, or one fifth that of the peak left ventricular systolic pressure. Right ventricular peak pressure begins later than left ventricular peak presure but is maintained longer. Consequently, the pulmonic semilunar valve normally closes slightly later than the aortic semilunar valve. During inspiration even a longer duration exists.

CARDIAC FILLING

Of the blood ejected by the ventricles, approximately 85 percent enters during the 0.1 seconds following the opening of the A-V valve, while approximately 15 percent is contributed by atrial contraction immediately before ventricular contraction.

The atrial contribution is highly variable. In instances in which the major portions of the atria are removed or atrial fibrillation is present and the atria beat ineffectively, ventricular performance in the resting animal is not altered markedly. On the other hand, the ventricles respond with near maximal vigor only after being primed by the blood ejected from the atria.

For the dog, the optimal interval between atrial and ventricular contraction ranges between 0.10 to 0.14 seconds, while for the horse the interval ranges from 0.2 to 0.3 seconds. If the interval becomes much shorter than that, the atria do not have adequate time to eject their contents. On the other hand, if ventricular contraction begins too long after atrial contraction, the ventricles seem to lose the stimulating effect of the atrial "prime."

Among other reasons, ventricular filling occurs because the pressure within the atria tends to push the blood to the position of lower pressure in the ventricle (vis a tergo). This results from the blood being returned to the atria after traversing the entire systemic or pulmonic capillary circuit under the driving thrust of ventricular systole. The v wave of the intra-arterial and intravenous pressure curves probably results from this return.

The atria are also filled by various forces. The dominant portion of blood enters the atria during the period of isotonic ventricular contraction, when the A-V annulus moves apically, the atria are enlarged, the pressure within them falls, and blood is aspirated into their chambers. This decrease in pressure is manifested as the x′ descent of the interatrial or intravenous pressure curve.

As the ventricles relax, the A-V annulus moves basilarly during the period of isotonic relaxation (rapid ventricular filling) and the open valves surround the blood in the apex of the atria.

Blood is returned to the right atrium by skeletal muscular contraction which raises pressure within the belly of the muscle and squeezes blood out of the collapsible thin-walled veins within the muscle mass. Another factor is alteration in intrathoracic pressures during respiration. As the thoracic cage expands during inspiration, intrathoracic pressure falls and blood is aspirated into the thoracic structures through veins which empty into them. Only the thin-walled or easily distended structures may be filled in this manner. Since the left atrium and lungs are both thin-walled and lie within the thoracic cage, inspiration has little tendency to move blood from the lungs into the left atrium.

A final force tending to fill the right atrium results from the weight of the column of blood between the right atrium and all points in the venous system above the atrium. In the standing human being this hydrostatic pressure tends to drain blood from the anterior (superior) vena cava into the right atrium, but also tends to siphon blood from the right atrium into the posterior (inferior) vena cava. These forces seem to be of lesser significance in quadrupeds, since the craniocaudal axis of the thorax lies horizontal to the forces of gravity.

CARDIAC OUTPUT AND VELOCITY

The volume of blood each ventricle ejects is termed cardiac output. It may be expressed either as stroke volume (ml/beat) or as minute volume (ml or L/min). Cardiac output corrected for body weight may be written as ml/kg/min, or corrected for body surface area, as cardiac index, ml or L/sq m/min.

Measurements are usually indirect. One method uses a vessel which receives the entire ventricular output (either the main pulmonary artery or the aorta). If the diameter is known, then the cross section may be calculated and multiplied by average velocity to give the volume of blood traversing that cross section per unit time. The aortic flow so measured will equal the main pulmonary arterial flow minus coronary arterial flow.

Another method measures the amount of labeled material either added to or taken away from a segment of the vascular system to which all—or a representative aliquot of all—the blood flows. Knowing the amount of label either added or removed and the average carrying capacity of the blood for that substance, one may estimate cardiac output. This method utilizes the Fick principle (see below) and the labels added to the blood stream are either oxygen, through the pulmonary circuit, or dyes, by intravenous injection.

Velocity of blood flow is often measured with an electromagnetic flowmeter. A probe is placed around a vessel receiving the entire ventricular output. The probe impinges slightly upon the diameter of the vessel, thus holding it constant. Two points on contralateral surfaces of the probe emit electromagnetic waves at high frequencies. Two other points placed at right angles to the first pair register alterations in electromagnetic fluxes which are proportional to the blood flow through the probe.

A second method is to insert a very light ring which is held in the middle of the vessel by an umbrella-type apparatus which also holds the diameter of the vessel constant. The ring is attached to an equally light metal core which is placed between primary and secondary turns of an induction coil. As the flow of blood strikes the metal ring, it drives the core either deeper or shallower into the coil and alters the amount of current induced.

Peak velocity of flow occurs during the ascending or anacrotic limb of the aortic pulse curve, during the period of maximal ventricular ejection (Fig. 7.5). A reduced velocity is registered during the reduced ventricular ejection. During inscription of the incisura, flow actually reverses as blood forces the aortic semilunar valve closed. A second but rather low peak of velocity follows as the valve leaflets recoil from the ventricle and accelerate blood again downstream.

Certain pitfalls exist in using these types of flowmeters. Total flow is calculated by integrating the area under the velocity curve for any given duration. The area is then in units of cardiac output for that given time. Velocity is variable, however, not only between different

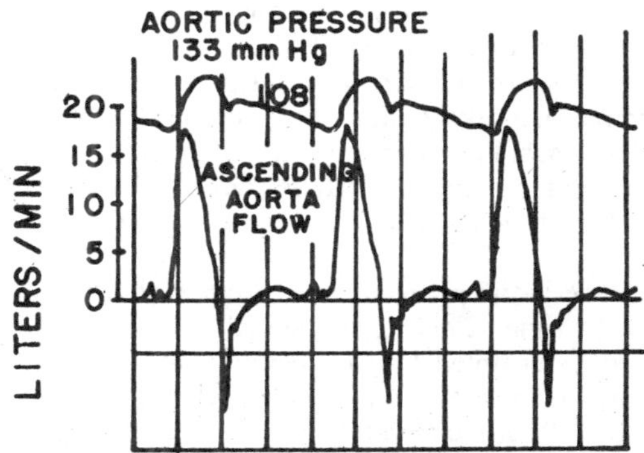

Figure 7.5. Aortic pressure curve and ascending aortic blood flow for a normal dog. (From Pieper 1965, *Cardiologia* 47:393–406.)

phases of ejection but also for different areas of cross section. In general, velocity is greatest toward the center of the stream because of less friction.

The best method of estimating cardiac output (C.O.) again utilizes the Fick principle. Oxygen content of arterial and mixed venous blood (taken from the main pulmonary artery) is measured by manometry and is expressed as ml O_2/100 ml whole blood (20 and 16 respectively). The amount of oxygen each 100 ml of blood can carry is calculated by subtracting the oxygen content in a mixed venous sample from that in the arterial sample (4 ml). This amount is termed the arteriovenous (A-V) oxygen difference. (Note that A-V elsewhere in these chapters refers to atrioventricular, however.) Total oxygen extracted during one minute's respiration is measured by spirometry (80 ml). If 100 ml blood carries 4 ml O_2, then how many ml blood carries 80 ml O_2? 2000 ml blood.

Ordinarily, mixed venous blood is taken from the main pulmonary artery, since the oxygen content of venous segments varies. Arterial blood is taken from any point in the vascular system downstream from the lungs, since oxygen is neither added nor subtracted from the vascular segment between pulmonary veins and capillaries. Oxygen consumption is recorded usually over a 6 minute period.

A modification of this method—the indicator dilution method—circumvents the necessity of measuring oxygen consumption and concentrations of oxygen in the venous and arterial blood, and permits integrating a sample over only 5–10 seconds. A known quantity of foreign substance is added to the venous circulation (e.g. chromium-tagged erythrocytes, indocyanine green, Evans blue dye, red dye, saline, or cold blood). It must be nontoxic and must be neither added nor subtracted from the vascular system during at least one complete circulation.

Blood is sampled continuously from an artery and the samples are analyzed constantly at no greater than one-second intervals. An indicator dilution curve results (Fig. 7.6). This curve represents the concentration of indicator in arterial blood between the time of injection and the time required for an aliquot of all or nearly all of the particles to traverse the sampling artery at least once. The concentration peaks within three seconds after the first particles reach the sampling site. It then falls, then increases again as the first particles have had time to recirculate through the system and return to the point of sampling.

After the initial peak one sees a logarithmic decay with respect to time. This decay would approach zero if it were not interrupted by the recirculation cycle. To circumvent superimposition of this recirculation on the curve of primary circulation, concentration may be replotted on semilogarithmic paper, from which we may answer the following questions:

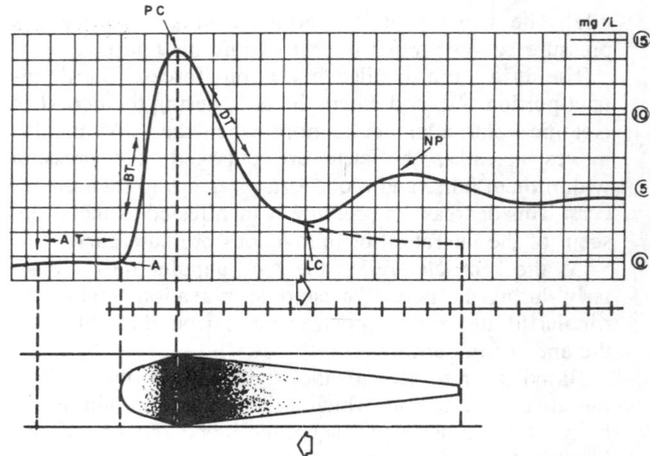

Figure 7.6. Indicator-dilution curve for normal dog, concentration along ordinate, time along abscissa (one-second intervals). Arrow left of AT marks injection of indicator. AT, duration between injection and arrival of first particles at point of sampling (A). BT, concentration increases from time of arrival (A) until its peak (PC). DT, concentration decreases from its peak to point where the most rapidly moving particles return, after traversing circulation once, to the site of sampling and will cause an increase in concentration. LC, between the peak concentration of the first circulation and the concentration of the new (recirculation) peak (NP). Below, section of arteries from which the blood samples may have been taken. Dots represent particles of indicator.

(1) What is the total time required for all the dye particles to traverse this sampling site?

(2) What is the average concentration of indicator over the entire curve of primary circulation?

The first question is answered simply by measuring the time between onset of the first particles of indicator (arrival time) and the time when the decay slope intersects the ordinate line representing 1 percent of peak concentration. The method is accurate except for the small amount of indicator excluded by the 1 percent cut off, and the time is accurate except for the time required for that small amount of unmeasured indicator to traverse the sampling site. Jugular to femoral artery arrival time varies depending upon cardiac output, from 3 to 15 seconds in the dog to over 30 seconds in the horse. The second question is answered by summing the measurements of concentration at each instant during which the primary curve is inscribed, and by dividing the sum by the number of seconds as measured in the first instance.

The Fick principle may then be applied to estimate cardiac output as follows. If 2.5 mg of indicator were injected, the average concentration of indicator in blood during the time the primary curve was inscribed would be 3.0 mg per liter, and a total of 20 seconds required for the entire curve to be inscribed. One may then calculate cardiac output by answering the question: If 1 L blood carries 3 mg dye (3 mg/L), then how many liters carry 2.5 mg dye? 0.83 L. But this was carried in only 20 seconds, so corrected for 60 seconds time we have 2.49 L/min.

Cardiac output varies with physiological state. For example, in healthy unanesthetized dogs it may vary from 90 to 240 ml/kg body weight/min, depending upon how excited the dog is. During second-degree A-V block in a horse, cardiac output may be 15 ml/kg body weight/min; while if standing but excited, the cardiac output may exceed 120 ml/kg/min. In general, for a dog under barbiturate anesthesia, cardiac output is 180 ml/kg/min; for a horse cardiac output is 90 ml/kg/min.

The profile of indicator particles in the vessel is dependent upon both differential velocity of flow between the center of the stream and the periphery, and upon the length of the route taken by the particle of indicator. That is, the particle which traveled the shortest route in the center of the stream would reach the sampling site soonest. Other indicators may be used to measure circulation. For example, ether injected into the cephalic vein may be smelled on the animal's breath after it has had time to travel from vein to pulmonary circulation, thus giving the arm-to-lung circulation time. Fluorescein may be injected into the cephalic vein and detected by shining an ultraviolet light on the sclera. The time measured is termed the arm-to-eye circulation time.

WORK, POWER, AND EFFICIENCY

The pressure-volume work is estimated as the product of the volume of blood ejected times the resistance against which it is ejected—the mean arterial pressure. Work performed to impart velocity is estimated as one half the product of the average velocity squared times the mass of the blood. Total work performed by a ventricle is the sum of both fractions:

$$W = P\Delta V + \frac{MV^2}{2}$$

The portion of the equation representing expenditure of kinetic energy ($MV^2/2$) is usually negligible—less than 5 percent—even at rather high velocities attained during exercise. Under unusual conditioning it may rise to 20 percent.

Considering only pressure-volume work of the heart, that of the left ventricle equals the stroke volume (2 ml/kg) times the mean systemic arterial pressure (approximately 100 mm Hg) or 200 mm Hg ml/kg. Since the right ventricle ejects an identical volume but against the mean main pulmonary arterial pressure (approximately 15 mm Hg), right ventricular stroke work is approximately one sixth that of the left.

Combined work of both ventricles equals, therefore, $^7/_6$ times the work of the left ventricle or approximately 230 work units. If volume ejected were expressed in cubic centimeters and mean arterial pressure were expressed in dynes per square centimeter, then work would be expressed in units considered dimensionally correct—gram centimeter.

Often work is expressed by merely multiplying $^7/_6$ stroke volume (i.e. not per kilogram) times mean arterial pressure.

Efficiency of ventricular work may be estimated by dividing the thermal equivalent of useful work by the potential work estimated to be available from the amount of oxygen consumed by the heart. Such calculations estimate the heart as a mechanical pump to be approximately 20 percent efficient.

Work per unit of time is power. Stroke power is the vigor of contraction: stroke work divided by the duration of isotonic ejection.

ARTERIAL PRESSURE

Contraction of the ventricle imparts energy to the blood within. One portion of this energy—kinetic energy—is expended to overcome viscous forces of friction between molecules of blood and between blood and the vessel wall. The other portion—potential energy—is expended in lateral pressure tending to deform the elastic walls of the arteries. After the blood performs work on the arterial walls, the walls expend the stored energy in passive recoil, exerting pressure and performing work on the blood. Thus blood is pumped actively not only by the ventricle, but also passively by the arterial walls.

Figure 7.7 shows the ventricular and arterial system: (a) the ventricle, the pump; (b) the aortic semilunar valve leaflets which lie passively in the orifice between left ventricle and aorta; (c) the aorta, a hollow elastic structure divided into three imaginary segments, each of which is long enough to accommodate approximately the

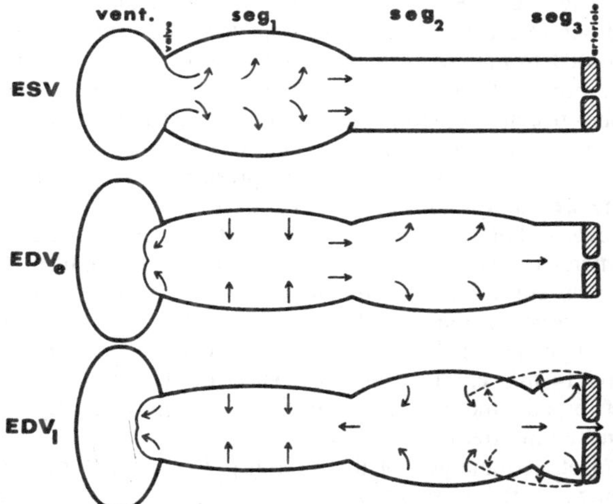

Figure 7.7. Ventricle, three segments of arterial tree, and the arteriole during three stages of the cardiac cycle: ESV, end-systolic volume, EDV_e and EDV_l end-diastolic volumes "early" and "late."

volume of blood ejected during one ventricular contraction; (d) the arterioles, extremely thick-walled valves at the terminus of the arterial system.

As the ventricle contracts it ejects blood into the first segment of the arterial tree, elevating pressure within the segment and deforming the elastic walls. Then the ventricle relaxes quickly and pressure within it falls to zero. But pressure within the artery is maintained as the arterial walls recoil and exert a force on the blood. This force closes the aortic semilunar valve and pushes blood downstream into the next segment of the arterial tree. The next segment responds to the augmented blood volume by distending, recoiling, and forcing blood downstream to still the next segment. The distal arterioles force blood in a rather smooth fashion through the capillary beds and it finally reflects back toward the left ventricle.

The height to which the arterial pulse pressure rises is dependent upon (a) vigor of ventricular contraction (the ventricular impulse), (b) elasticity of the arterial system, (c) arteriolar resistance, and (d) percent change in volume of the arterial segment during one systole (this factor depends upon initial volume of blood within the vascular system, as well as the stroke volume). Factors related to the arteries (excluding ventricular impulse and arteriolar resistance) may be summarized as:

$$\Delta P = E_m \frac{\Delta V}{V} \times 100$$

where ΔP is the change in pressure within the artery, ΔV is the change in volume from the resting volume (V), E_m is a measure of the elasticity of the artery. Assuming E_m is constant, then the change in pressure is proportional to the percent change in volume ($\Delta P \propto \Delta V/V$).

Although the mean pressure within a portion of artery closer to the heart is higher than the mean pressure recorded from a point more distal, the peak pressure may be higher distally because primary and reflected waves may become superimposed, and because the distal segment is narrower in diameter and less elastic.

The velocity with which the pressure wave traverses the arterial system in either direction is inversely proportional to both the elasticity of the arterial tree and the diameter of the vessels, while the ventricular impulse remains constant. An average velocity of propagation to the large arteries of the system is 4–5 m/sec, while through the smaller arteries the wave travels between 5 and 14 m/sec. This must be contrasted with the velocity of blood—the much slower rate of approximately 18 cm/sec in arteries.

Detailed analysis of the arterial pulse curve (Fig. 7.8) shows a rather rapid upstroke (anacrotic limb) with a rounded peak pressure reaching approximately 180 mm Hg in the dog, 100 mm Hg in the cat and man, and over 300 mm Hg in the giraffe and turkey. This peak is followed by an initial rapid decrease until, after a notch (incisura) occurs, a more gradual decrease continues to the diastolic level of from 80 mm Hg in man to approximately 120 mm Hg in the dog. The limb of this curve from the peak systolic pressure to the lowest pressure (diastolic pressure) is termed the *catacrotic limb*. The deflection which interrupts the catacrotic limb is the dicrotic notch, which is caused by closure of the aortic semilunar valves, their buckling back into the left ventricle (LV), and their recoiling from the ventricle back toward the aorta.

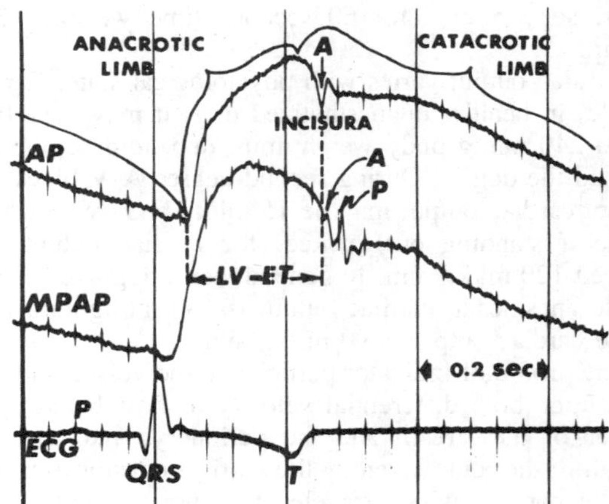

Figure 7.8. Pressures within the aorta (AP) and the main pulmonary artery (MPAP), and the concurrent ECG. Taken with catheter tip manometers, they are not distorted by catheter movement or time lag. The MPAP curve begins its positive deflection earlier and ends later than does the AP. Since both left and right ventricles eject the same amount of blood, the left ventricle behaves as a more vigorous pump (pumping the same amount in lesser time).

The small and rather slow increase in pressure after the incisura in the catacrotic limb is often termed the *standing wave*. The catacrotic limb then decreases in pressure gradually until immediately before ventricular contraction and the large increase in pressure. At this instant two small deflections are observed. The first arises during atrial systole and probably results from rotation of the entire heart and a tugging on the arterial tree. The second occurs during the period of isovolumetric contraction and may have an origin similar to that of the earlier deflection. In the horse, where atria may contract more asynchronously because of the relatively great distance between S-A node and left atrium, two atrial tugs may precede the pressure fluctuation representing isovolumetric contraction.

It should be emphasized that if the arterial system were more rigid, the peak systolic pressure would not be maintained by recoil and would fall to near zero. Thus this elastic tree (ET) generates a rather continuous flow of blood into the capillaries.

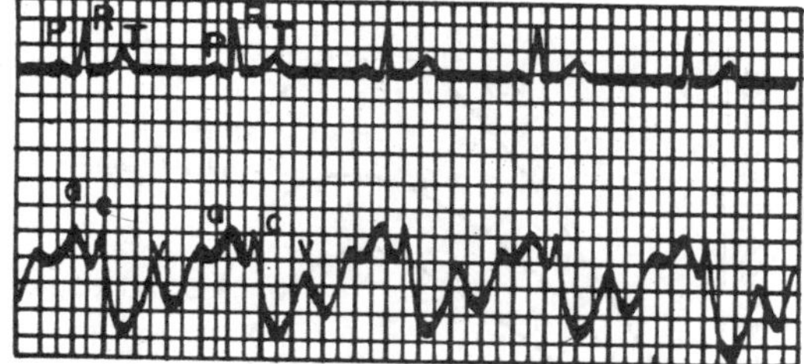

Figure 7.9. Simultaneous ECG (lead II) and jugular pulse of a man, using a crystal microphone and a string galvanometer—vertical time lines at 0.1 seconds. There is a slight lag in the jugular pulse tracing in comparison with the ECG because of the transmission time. (From Miller and White 1941, *Am. Heart J.* 21:504–10.)

VENOUS PRESSURE

As fluctuations of pressure within arteries are sequels to events of the cardiac cycle, so pressure fluctuations in the pulmonary and systemic veins are sequels to those in the arteries. (Fig. 7.9). In general, these fluctuations are similar in configuration but slightly lower in magnitude and slightly asynchronous with pressure fluctuations within the atria where they originate.

As the a, c, and v waves, and the x, x′, and y descents occur within the atria, they are transmitted well away from the heart toward the venules because of the absence of valves at the venoatrial junction. The greater the distance from the atrium, the more attenuated and the more asynchronous with atrial events the venous pressure fluctuations are.

PERIPHERAL RESISTANCE

According to Ohm's law the amount of current (I) flowing through a conductor is proportional to the electromotive force (E) of the current but inversely proportional to the resistance (R) of the conductor: $I = E/R$. A similar relationship holds true for flow of blood through a vessel. The volume (Q) of blood flowing through any tube is proprtional to the pressure difference (ΔP) between the two ends of the tube and inversely proportional to the resistance (R) to flow of blood through the tube

$$Q = \frac{\Delta P}{R}$$

Resistance may be estimated by combining factors. For example, the greater the length of the tube (L) the greater the resistance. Resistance is also proportional to the narrowness of the tube, or more correctly, inversely proportional to the radius (r) of the tube to the fourth power. Resistance is also directly proportional to the viscosity (η) of the fluid. Combining all these, we have

$$R = \frac{8\eta L}{\pi r^4}$$

Substituting this relationship for R in Ohm's equation gives us Poiseuille's equation

$$Q = \frac{\Delta P}{8\eta L/\pi r^4}, \quad Q = \frac{\Delta P \pi r^4}{8\eta L}$$

Because of the complicated dimensions used in expressing resistance (dynes sec cm^{-5}) most physiologists express it by dividing mean driving pressure exerted by the heart, during the time the semilunar valves are open, by volume of blood traversing the tube during that time or per minute. Some investigators derive that mean pressure by merely dividing the peak systolic pressure plus the diastolic pressure by 2. Others more correctly integrate the area under the pressure curve with respect to time and derive a true mean pressure. The results do not differ significantly.

Both right and left ventricles eject a similar volume of blood. Since mean systemic arterial pressure is approximately 100 mm Hg and mean pulmonary arterial pressure is approximately 15, then systemic vascular resistance must be nearly 7 times greater. For example, cardiac output for an average dog is 180 ml/kg/min. At an average heart rate of just below 100 beats per minute (Table 7.1) the stroke volume would be approximately 2 ml/kg/stroke. Then systemic and pulmonary vascular resistances must be 100/2 and 15/2 mm Hg/ml/kg/stroke, or 50 units and approximately 7 units.

Total systemic or pulmonary vascular resistance is determined by the number, length, and cross section of patent communications from the arterial systems into the

Table 7.1. Heart rates of animals in beats per minute

Animal	Mean	Range
Man	70	(58–104)
Ass	50	(40–56)
Bat	750	(100–970)
Camel	30	(25–32)
Cat	120	(110–140)
Cow		(60–70)
Dog		(100–130)
Elephant	35	(22–53)
Giraffe	66	
Goat	90	(70–135)
Guinea pig	280	(260–400)
Hamster	450	(300–600)
Horse	44	(23–70)
Lion	40	
Monkey	192	(165–240)
Mouse	534	(324–858)
Rabbit	205	(123–304)
Rat	328	(261–600)
Sheep	75	(60–120)
Skunk	166	(144–192)
Squirrel	249	(96–378)
Swine		(55–86)

From Spector, *Handbook of Biologic Data*, Saunders, 1956

capillaries. The greater the cross section, the less the resistance. The longer the vessels, the greater the resistance. However, resistance is only linearly related to length, whereas it is inversely related to the square of the cross section.

The greatest resistance arises from the great arteries and the arterioles, the resistance vessels. On the other hand, the greatest capacity for storage of blood is with the veins, the capacitance vessels. Although the capillaries provide by far the greatest cross section (by a factor of hundreds), they are extremely short vessels and contain only approximately 5 percent of the total blood volume. The arteries contain approximately 15 percent, the veins 50 percent, and the heart and pulmonary vessels approximately 30 percent.

Although a change in vessel length or viscosity of blood might alter the resistance, both viscosity and vessel length are not varied acutely during physiological stresses. Indeed, arterial driving pressure and cross section of the arterioles are the prime regulators of blood flow.

REGULATION OF VENTRICULAR CONTRACTION

Determinants of the force of ventricular contraction may be separated into extrinsic (neural or humoral) and intrinsic (autoregulatory). Increasing sympathetic efferent activity or decreasing parasympathetic efferent activity will cause the ventricles to contract more forcefully and usually more often, and the opposite is also true. An agent which alters force of contraction without changing the degree of stretch on myocardial fibers at end-diastole is termed an *inotrope*. A positive inotrope increases force while a negative inotrope decreases force. Waxing and waning of autonomic efferent activity originate from the hypothalamus which sends negative impulses over the vagus and positive impulses over augmentor nerves. Positive inotropic humors (norepinephrine, epinephrine) circulate from the adrenal medulla to the heart via the blood.

Autoregulation of the force of contraction may arise from two routes: heterometric, in which the force is altered by changing fiber length; or homeometric, in which the force is altered with no change in fiber length.

Heterometric autoregulation (Frank-Starling Law of the Heart)

All other factors being constant, the force of ventricular contraction increases with the stretch (preload) on the myocardial fibers at end-diastole. After fibers are stretched to such a degree that sarcomere lengths exceed 2.2 μ, force of contraction decreases with further stretch. If fibers are stretched so that sarcomere lengths are less than 2.2 μ the force of contraction decreases with the decrement in stretch (Fig. 7.10). In fact, ventricular

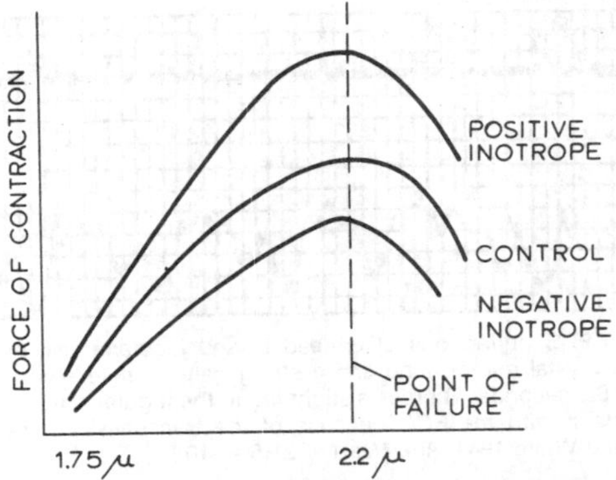

Figure 7.10. Force of contraction versus stretch on the myocardial fibers just before they are stimulated

function may be expressed by a series of Frank-Starling curves. Thus force of contraction may vary due to changes in fiber length during end-diastole, changes in contractility with a constant fiber length, or changes in both end-diastolic fiber length and contractility.

The basis for this length-force relationship resides in the ultrastructure of the myocardial contractile components comprised of interdigitation (cross bridge) between actin and myosin filaments. With introduction of calcium ions in the regions of interdigitation the extensions of actin and myosin ''grab'' on to each other and pull, thus sliding two Z bands together. This grab is permitted when Ca^{++} removes the protein complex, troponin-tropomyosin from between the actin and myosin cross bridge. If the sarcomeres are stretched to varying lengths, the degree of interdigitation will be varied (Fig. 7.11).

Homeometric autoregulation

In homeometric autoregulation, the ventricle responds to an increased outflow resistance in the presence of constant autonomic stimulation and end-diastolic volume by increasing vigor to maintain forward flow nearly constant. The phenomenon may be parallel to *treppe,* in which the increment in vigor follows alteration in the biochemical environment subsequent to the increased workload of ejecting blood against the higher resistance. Another expression of homeometric autoregulation arises from pacing the ventricles more rapidly than does the sinus pacemaker. During this augmented rate, augmented vigor occurs, called chronotropic inotropism. An alteration in intracellular chemistry—in particular a loss of potassium ion or a gain of calcium ion due to the abbreviated period of repolarization—may be the cause.

These three mechanisms for increasing or decreasing ventricular performance permit the heart to eject either an augmented venous return or a normal return against an increase in peripheral resistance. For example, homeometric autoregulation and sympathetic efferent activity

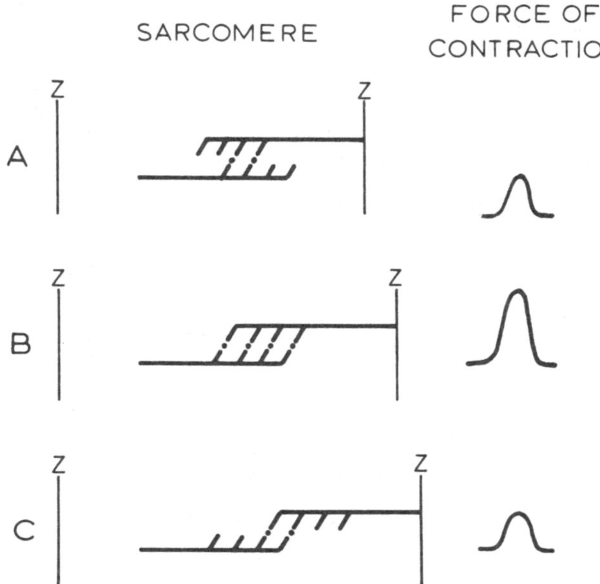

Figure 7.11. Sarcomere stretched to varying lengths (A, B, C) and force of contraction. Black dots represent potential sites for interaction between actin and myosin. Since B gives the greatest opportunity for interaction between coarse and fine filaments because of an optimal degree of stretch, then it will be the most forceful.

may increase both heart rate and vigor of contraction in the presence of a constant end-diastolic volume. However, if they fail, then an augmented end-diastolic pressure may add a yet more vigorous contraction.

In the denervated heart or in an adrenalectomized dog, cardiac output may rise to levels identical with that of an intact dog by, for the most part, increase in stroke volume with only slight increase in heart rate. Under conditions of normal stress, increase in ventricular performance results primarily from increase in heart rate and vigor of contraction.

Force-velocity relationship

Let us examine inotropic regulation through use of a force-velocity curve (Fig. 7.12). If an excessive load is placed on the muscle, some maximal force (F_m) will be produced (A). As the load is lightened until the muscle has to lift only itself, little force will be generated but the velocity of shortening will be increased. To ascertain what velocity of fiber shortening to expect at 0 load (when the muscle did not even have to lift itself) the curve is extrapolated to F_0, at which maximal velocity (V_m) of fiber shortening would occur. This is a measure of inherent myocardial contractility—the inotropic state.

Now let us examine force-velocity curves which represent varying inotropic states (B). The curve between V_3 and F_3 is for a positive inotropic state; that between V_1 and F_1 is for a negative inotropic state. For the positive inotropic state the muscle is capable of generating a greater force; while when permitted to contract against no load it is capable of generating a greater velocity. For the negative inotropic state the muscle generates a weaker maximal force; while when permitted to contract against no load a lesser maximal velocity of shortening is achieved. For these three examples, the preload (degree of stretch on the muscle just before it is stimulated) is constant.

In the force-velocity curves from a muscle that is sub-

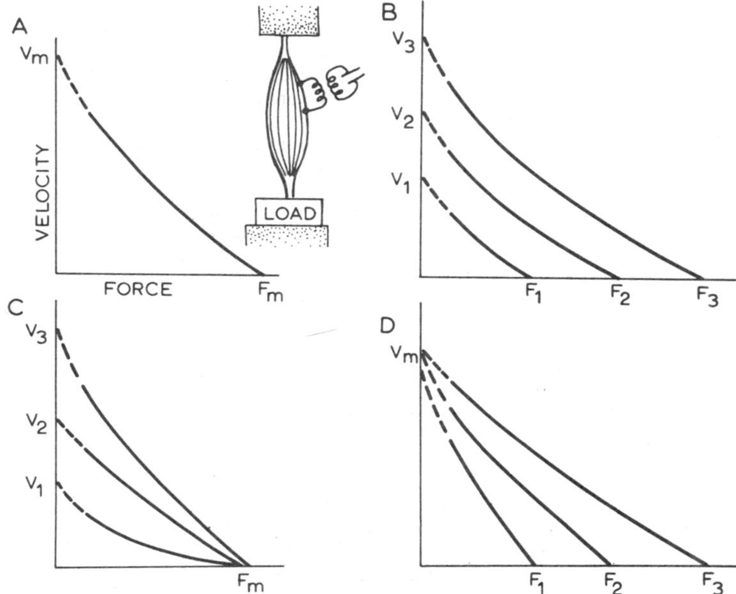

Figure 7.12. Velocity of muscular contraction versus force of contraction. A single force-velocity curve is shown in A. Three force-velocity curves are shown in B. Curves in C represent what might happen to a muscle if preload were varied enough to cause a constant maximal force generated. D demonstrates heterometric autoregulation.

jected to a positive inotropic influence (C) the preload is varied in a manner opposite to the inotropic influence. Muscle V_2-F_m is the unperturbed muscle. If one subjects that muscle to a positive inotropic influence (which should increase V_m) but stretches the muscle less during end-diastole (which should give a lesser F_m), one gets curve V_3-F_m. V_3 is greater but F_m is the same.

Finally, let us examine a muscle with a constant inotropic state but with varying preload—that is, a muscle with varying stretch on it during the period immediately preceding its stimulation (D). Curve V_m-F_2 is the unperturbed state. If the muscle fibers are stretched to a greater length in end-diastole, the force velocity curve representing the function of the muscle is given by the curve V_m-F_3; which shows that the maximal velocity of fiber shortening does not change but the maximal force generated is greater. Next stretch the fiber to a lesser degree; V_m is the same but F_1 is less than either for the unperturbed or stretched muscle.

REFERENCES

Volume changes

Brockman, S.K. 1963. Dynamic function of atrial contraction in regulation of cardiac performance. *Am. J. Physiol.* 204:597–603.

Hamilton, W.F., and Rompf, J.H. 1932. Movements of the base of the ventricle and the relative constancy of the cardiac volume. *Am. J. Physiol.*, 102:559–65.

Hamilton, W.F., Jr., Dow, P., and Hamilton, W.F. 1950. Measurement of volume of dog's heart by x-ray: Effect of hemorrhage, of epinephrine infusion, and of buffer nerve section. *Am. J. Physiol.* 161:466–72.

Harvey, W. 1949. *Anatomical Studies on the Motion of the Heart and Blood.* 3d ed. Thomas, Springfield, Ill. P. 40.

Holt, J.P. 1956. Estimation of the residual volume of the ventricle of the dog's heart by two indicator dilution technics. *Circ. Res.* 4:187–95.

Katz, A.M., Katz, L.N., and Williams, F.L. 1955. Registration of left ventricular volume curves in the dog with the systemic circulation intact. *Circ. Res.* 3:588–93.

Rushmer, R.F. 1955. Anatomy and physiology of ventricular function. *Physiol. Rev.* 36:400–410.

——. 1961. *Cardiovascular Dynamics.* 2d ed. Saunders, Philadelphia.

Spencer, M.P., and Greiss, F.C. 1962. Dynamics of ventricular ejection. *Circ. Res.* 10:274–79.

Wallace, A.G., Mitchell, J.H., Skinner, N.S., Jr., and Sarnoff, S.J. 1963. Hemodynamic variables affecting the relation between mean left atrial and left ventricular end-diastolic pressures. *Circ. Res.* 13:261–70.

Wiggers, C.J., and Katz, L.N. 1921–1922. Contour of ventricular volume curves under different conditions. *Am. J. Physiol.* 58:439–43.

Pressure events

Braunwald, E., Fishman, A.P., and Cournand, A. 1956. Time relationship of dynamic events in the cardiac chambers, pulmonary artery, and aorta in man. *Circ. Res.* 4:100–107.

Braunwald, E., Moscovitz, H.L., Amram, S.S., Lasser, R.P., Sapin, S.O., Himmelstein, A., Ravitch, M.M., and Gordon, A.J. 1955. Timing of electrical and mechanical events of the left side of the human heart. *J. Appl. Physiol.* 8:309–14.

Cournand, A., and Ranges, H.A. 1941. Catheterization of the right auricle in man. *Proc. Soc. Exp. Biol. Med.* 46:462–67.

Forssmann, W. 1929. Die Sondierung des rechten Herzens. *Klin. Wchschr.* 8:2085–90.

Frank, O. 1959. On the dynamics of cardiac muscle. *Am. Heart J.* 58:282–317, 467–78.

Hamilton, W.F., Attyah, A.M., Fowell, D.W., Remington, J.W., Wheeler, N.C., and Witham, A.C. 1947. Do the human ventricles eject simultaneously? *Proc. Soc. Exp. Biol. Med.* 65:266–68.

Holt, J.P., Rhode, E.A., and Kines, H. 1960. Pericardial and ventricular pressure. *Circ. Res.* 8:1171–81.

Little, R.C. 1951. Effect of atrial systole on ventricular pressure and closure of the A-V valves. *Am. J. Physiol.* 166:289–95.

Luisada, A.A., and Liu, C.K. 1958. *Intracardiac Phenomena in Right and Left Heart Catheterization.* Grune & Stratton, New York.

Mitchell, J.H., Gilmore, J.P., and Sarnoff, S.J. 1962. The transport function of the atrium: Factors influencing the relation between mean left arterial pressure and left ventricular end diastolic pressure. *Am. J. Cardiol.* 9:237–47.

Opdyke, D.F., Duomarco, J., Dillon, W.H., Schreiber, H., Little, R.C., and Seely, R.D. 1948. Study of simultaneous right and left atrial pressure pulses under normal and experimentally altered conditions. *Am. J. Physiol.* 154:258–72.

Remington, J.W. 1954. The relation between the stroke volume and the pulse pressure. *Minn. Med.* 37:105–10.

Rushmer, R.F. 1956. Initial phase of ventricular systole: Asynchronous contraction. *Am. J. Physiol.* 184:188–94.

Wiggers, C.J. 1923. *Modern Aspects of Circulation in Health and Disease.* Lea & Febiger, Philadelphia.

——. 1928. *The Pressure Pulses in the Cardiovascular System.* Longmans, New York.

Cardiac filling

Asmussen, E., and Nielsen, M. 1955. Cardiac output during muscular work and its regulation. *Physiol. Rev.* 35:778–800.

Bauereisen, E., Peiper, U., and Weigand, K.H. 1960. The diastolic suction effect of the cardiac ventricles. *Zeitschrift Kreislaufforsch.* 49:195–200.

Brecher, G.A., and Hubay, H.A. 1955. Pulmonary blood flow and venous return during spontaneous respiration. *Circ. Res.* 3:110–214.

Brecher, G.A., and Kissen, A.T. 1958. Ventricular diastolic suction at normal arterial pressures. *Circ. Res.* 6:100–106.

Buckley, N.M., Ogden, E., and Linton, D.S., Jr. 1955. The effects of work load and heart rate on the filling of the isolated right ventricle of the dog. *Circ. Res.* 3:434–46.

Buckley, N.M., Ogden, E., and McPherson, R.C. 1955. The effect of inotropic drugs on filling of the right ventricle of the dog heart. *Circ. Res.* 3:447–53.

Guyton, A.C. 1955. Determination of cardiac output by equating venous return curves with cardiac response curves. *Physiol. Rev.* 35:123–29.

Guyton, A.C., Lindsey, A.W., and Kaufmann, B.N. 1955. Effect of mean circulatory filling pressure and other peripheral circulatory factors on cardiac output. *Am. J. Physiol.* 180:463–68.

Hamilton, W.F. 1953. The physiology of the cardiac output. *Circulation* 8:527–36.

Hennacy, R.A., and Ogden, E. 1960. Factors affecting the filling of the frog's ventricle after isotonic contraction. *Circ. Res.* 8:825–30.

Kraner, J.C., and Ogden, E. 1956. Ventricular suction in the turtle. *Circ. Res.* 4:724–26.

Landis, E.M., Brown, E., Fauteux, M., and Wise, C. 1946. Central venous pressure in relation to cardiac "competence," blood volume, and exercise. *J. Clin. Invest.* 25:237–55.

Sonnenblick, E.H., Siegel, J.H., and Sarnoff, S.J. 1963. Ventricular distensibility and pressure-volume curve during sympathetic stimulation. *Am. J. Physiol.* 204:1–4.

Wetterer, E. 1937. Eine neue Methode zur Registrierung der Blutströmungsgeschwindigkeit am uneröffneten Gerfäss. *Zeitschrift Biol.* 98:26–34.

Cardiac output

Bingham, E.C., and Roepke, R.R. 1944. The rheology of blood. *J. Gen. Physiol.* 28:79–93.
Brecher, G.A., and Praglin, J. 1953. A modified bristle flowmeter for measuring phasic blood flow. *Proc. Soc. Exp. Biol. Med.* 83:155–57.
Cournand, A., Riley, R.L., Breed, E.S., Baldwin, E. de F., and Richards, D.W., Jr. 1945. Measurement of cardiac output in man using the technic of catheterization of the right auricle or ventricle. *J. Clin. Invest.* 24:106–16.
Dow, P. 1956. Estimations of cardiac output and central blood volume by dye dilution. *Physiol. Rev.* 36:77–102.
Katz, L.N., Wise, W., and Jochim, K. 1945. Dynamics of isolated heart and heart-lung preparation of dog. *Am. J. Physiol.* 143:463–78.
Marshall, E.K. 1926. The cardiac output of the normal unanesthetized dog. *Am. J. Physiol.* 77:459–73.
Pieper, H.P. 1965. Experiments on the autonomic control of the coronary system studied in intact dogs. *Cardiologia* 47:393–406.
Remington, J.W., Noback, C.R., Hamilton, W.F., and Gold, J.J. 1948. Volume elasticity characteristics of the human aorta and prediction of the stroke volume from the pressure pulse. *Am. J. Physiol.* 153:298–308.
Sheppard, C.W., Jones, M.P., and Murphree, E.L., Jr. 1961. Shapes of indicator-dilution curves obtained from physical and physiological labyrinths. *Circ. Res.* 9:936–44.
Spencer, M.P., and Denison, A.B., Jr. 1959. The square-wave electromagnetic flowmeter: Theory of operation and design of magnetic probes for clinical and experimental applications. *Trans. Inst. Radio Engrs. Med. Electronics* 6:220–26.
Visscher, M.B., and Johnson, J.A. 1953. The Fick principle: Analysis of potential errors in its conventional application. *J. Appl. Physiol.* 5:635–42.
Warner, H.R., Swan, H.J.C., Connolly, D., Tompkins, R.G., and Wood, E.H. 1953. Quantitation of beat-to-beat changes in stroke volume from the aortic pulse contour in man. *J. Appl. Physiol.* 5:495–501.
Zierler, K.L. 1963. Theory of use of indicators to measure blood flow and extracellular volume and calculation of transcapillary movement of tracers. *Circ. Res.* 12:464–71.

Work, power, and efficiency

Braunwald, E., Sarnoff, S.J., Case, R.B., Stainsby, W.N., and Welch, G.H., Jr. 1958. Hemodynamic determinants of coronary flow: Effect of changes in aortic pressure and cardiac output on the relationship between myocardial oxygen consumption and coronary flow. *Am. J. Physiol.* 192:157–63.
Pieper, H.P., and Ogden, E. 1964. Determinants of stroke work in the dog heart-lung preparation. *Am. J. Physiol.* 206:43–48.

Arterial pressure

Burton, A.C. 1951. On the physical equilibrium of small blood vessels. *Am. J. Physiol.* 164:319–29.
——. 1954. Relation of structure to function of the tissues of the wall of blood vessels. *Physiol. Rev.* 34:619–42.
Dow, P., and Hamilton, W.F. 1939. An experimental study of the velocity and the pulse wave propagated through the aorta. *Am. J. Physiol.* 125:60–65.
Franklin, D.L., Ellis, R.M., and Rushmer, R.F. 1959. Aortic blood flow in dogs during treadmill exercise. *J. Appl. Physiol.* 14:809–12.
Hamilton, W.F., and Dow, P. 1939. An experimental study of the standing waves in the pulse propagated through the aorta. *Am. J. Physiol.* 125:48–59.
Hamilton, W.F., Remington, J.W., and Dow, P. 1945. The determination of the propagation velocity of the arterial pulse wave. *Am. J. Physiol.* 144:521–35.
Remington, J.W. 1960. Contour changes of the aortic pulse during propagation. *Am. J. Physiol.* 199:331–34.

Venous pressure

Guyton, A.C. 1956. Factors which determine the rate of venous return to the heart. In *World Trends in Cardiology*. Hoeber, New York. Pp. 32–48.
Miller, A., and White, P.D. 1941. Crystal microphone for pulse wave recording. *Am. Heart J.* 21:504–10.

Peripheral resistance

Spector, W.S. 1956. *Handbook of Biologic Data*. Saunders, Philadelphia. P. 277.
Wiggers, C.J. 1925. The independence of electrical and mechanical reactions in the mammalian heart. *Am. Heart J.* 1:3–20.
Wiggers, H.C. 1944. Cardiac output and total peripheral resistance measurements in experimental dogs. *Am. J. Physiol.* 140:519–34.

Regulation of cardiac performance

Barger, A.C., Metcalfe, J., Richards, V., and Gunther, B. 1961. Circulation during exercise in normal dogs and dogs with cardiac valvular lesions. *Am. J. Physiol.* 201:480–84.
Chapman, C.B., Baker, O.B., and Mitchell, J.H. 1959. Left ventricular function at rest and during exercise. *J. Clin. Invest.* 38:1202–13.
Gleason, W.J., and Braunwald, E. 1962. Studies on the first derivative of the ventricular pressure pulse in man. *J. Clin. Invest.* 41:80–91.
Goodyer, A.V.N., Goodkind, M.J., and Landry, A.B. 1962. Ventricular response to a pressure load: Left ventricular function curves in intact animal. *Circ. Res.* 10:885–96.
Hamilton, W.F. 1955. Role of the Starling concept in the regulation of the normal circulation. *Physiol. Rev.* 35:161–68.
Holt, J.P., Rhode, E.A., Peoples, S.A., and Kines, H. 1962. Left ventricular function in mammals of greatly different size. *Circ. Res.* 10:798–806.
Mitchell, J.H., Linden, R.J., and Sarnoff, S.J. 1960. Influence of cardiac sympathetic and vagal nerve stimulation on the relation between left ventricular diastolic pressure and myocardial segment length. *Circ. Res.* 8:1100–107.
Mitchell, J.H., Wallace, A.G., and Skinner, N.S., Jr. 1963. Intrinsic effects of heart rate on left ventricular performance. *Am. J. Physiol.* 205:41–48.
Peiss, C.N. 1960. Central control of sympathetic cardio-acceleration in the cat. *J. Physiol.* 151:225–37.
Rushmer, R.F. 1955. Applicability of Starling's Law of the heart to intact unanesthetized animals. *Physiol. Rev.* 35:138–42.
——. 1958. Autonomic balance in cardiac control. *Am. J. Physiol.* 192:631–34.
——. 1959. Constancy of stroke volume in ventricular responses to exertion. *Am. J. Physiol.* 196:745–50.
Rushmer, R.F., and Smith, O.A. 1959. Cardiac control. *Physiol. Rev.* 39:41–68.
Rushmer, R.F., Smith, O.A., and Franklin, D.L. 1959. Mechanisms of cardiac control in exercise. *Circ. Res.* 7:602–27.
Sarnoff, S.J. 1955. Myocardial contractility as described by ventricular function curves: Observations on Starling's law of the heart. *Physiol. Rev.* 35:107–22.
Sarnoff, S.J., and Berglund, E. 1954. Ventricular function. I. Starling's law of the heart studied by means of simultaneous right and left ventricular function curves. *Circulation* 9:706–18.
Sarnoff, S.J., Brockman, S.K., Gilmore, J.P., Linden, R.J., and Mitchell, J.H. 1960. Regulation of ventricular contraction: Influence

of cardiac sympathetic and vagal nerve stimulation on atrial and ventricular dynamics. *Circ. Res.* 8:1108–22.

Sarnoff, S.J., Gilmore, J.P., and Mitchell, J.H. 1962. Influence of atrial contraction and relaxation on closure of mitral valve: Observations on effects of autonomic nerve activity. *Circ. Res.* 11:26–35.

Sarnoff, S., and Mitchell, J.H. 1961. The regulation of the performance of the heart. *Am. J. Med.* 30:747–71.

Sarnoff, S.J., Mitchell, J.H., Gilmore, J.P., and Remensnyder, J.P. 1960. Homeometric autoregulation in the heart. *Circ. Res.* 7:1077–91.

Shepherd, J.T., Wang, Y., and Marshall, R.J. 1959. Relative contribution of changes in heart rate and stroke volume to the increase in cardiac output in dogs during exercise. *Physiologist* 2(3):105–15.

Siegel, J.H., and Sonnenblick, E.H. 1963. Isometric time-tension relationships as an index of myocardial contractility. *Circ. Res.* 12:597–610.

Smith, O.A., Jr., Jabbur, S.J., and Rushmer, R.F. 1960. Role of hypothalamic structures in cardiac control. *Physiol. Rev.* 40:136–149.

Sonnenblick, E.H. 1962. Force-velocity relations in mammalian heart muscle. *Am. J. Physiol.* 202:931–39.

Warner, H.R., and Cox, A. 1962. A mathematical model of heart rate control by sympathetic and vagus efferent information. *J. Appl. Physiol.* 17:349–55.

CHAPTER 8

Cardiovascular Sounds

by David L. Smetzer, Robert L. Hamlin, and C. Roger Smith

Contraction of the normal heart generates vibrations by direct and indirect mechanisms. Many of these vibrations are transmitted to specific locations on the surface of the thorax, but only a portion possess sufficient frequency or amplitude to be audible.

Groups of audible vibrations are perceived as heart sounds when the ear or a stethoscope is placed at appropriate locations on the thoracic surface. This procedure is known as *cardiac auscultation*. Phonocardiography is also used for the same purpose, but to a lesser extent, mostly as a teaching aid. An electrocardiogram, and in some instances one or more pressure events, is recorded simultaneously with the phonocardiogram (PCG). This permits the student or clinician to visualize the temporal relationships among sound, electrical, and mechanical events of the heart beat (see the cardiac cycle in Chapter 7). The ability to judge the magnitude of the intervals separating sounds is essential to auscultation.

CLASSIFICATION

Traditionally, cardiovascular sounds have been categorized as normal or abnormal. However, no sound is an abnormality in itself; each "extra" sound has to be judged in view of the circumstances under which it occurs. While an audible third heart sound usually indicates heart disease in the dog, it is commonplace in normal horses. So-called innocent or functional murmurs are prevalent in apparently normal animals, particularly horses and puppies.

Categorizing all cardiovascular sounds as either transients or murmurs seems to be less ambiguous than the aforementioned classification. Transients are sounds of brief duration, such as the first, second, third, and fourth heart sounds. Murmurs are prolonged groups of vibrations that occur during normally silent intervals of the cardiac cycle.

TRANSIENT SOUNDS

Each normal heartbeat generates at least two transients, the first (S1) and second (S2) heart sounds. These are described onomatopoeically as *lub-dub*. In addition to S1 and S2, two other heart sounds sometimes occur during ventricular diastole. These are the third (S3) and fourth (S4) heart sounds.

The first sound occurs immediately after the onset of ventricular systole and is caused by closure of the atrioventricular (A-V) valves. The second sound occurs at the termination of ventricular systole and is caused by closure of the semilunar valves. The third sound occurs early in ventricular diastole and is associated with rapid filling of the ventricles. The fourth or atrial sound precedes S1 and is associated with atrial systole.

First heart sound

The first sound is longer and lower pitched than S2. Sudden development of tension in the A-V valves at the time of closure is generally cited as the major factor in its genesis. Factors of less importance include vibrations

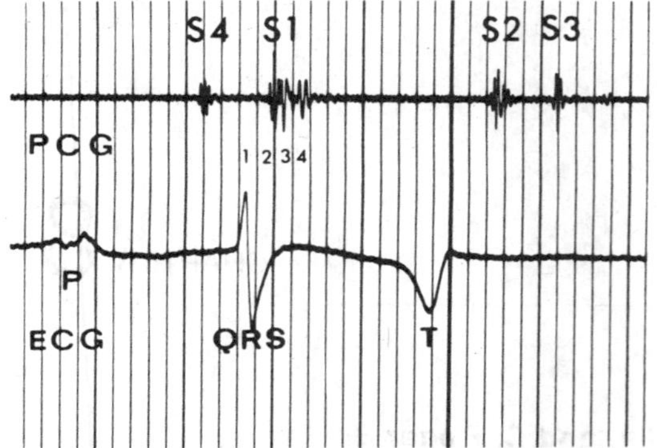

Figure 8.1. PCG and ECG from a normal house. The four components of S1 are indicated by numbers under it. The somewhat accentuated fourth component could be considered an ejection sound. Minimal splitting of S2 is observed. S3 follows the onset of S2 by 0.14 seconds. S3 is followed by a soft low frequency sound. Vertical lines occur at 0.04 second intervals in all figures.

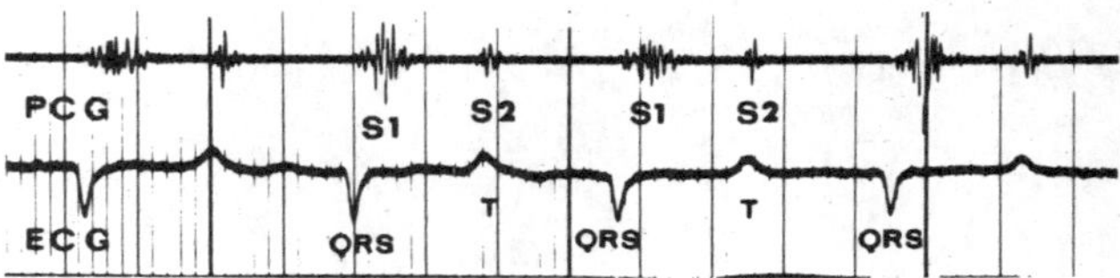

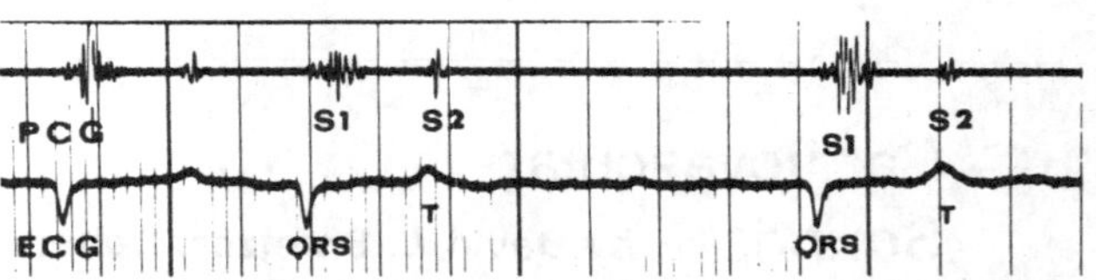

Figure 8.2. PCG and ECG from a mule with atrial fibrillation (bottom trace is continuation of top). Note the absence of P waves and the variation in the interval between QRS complexes. The beat-to-beat variation in S1 amplitude is typical. An early systolic murmur is discernible in most beats. The early vibrations of S1 resemble those of an S4, but they are not S4 because of the absence of effective atrial contractions.

generated within the contracting ventricular myocardium, opening of the semilunar valves, and vibrations generated within the wall of the aorta and pulmonary artery as blood is ejected into the arteries at the onset of systole.

Phonocardiographically, there are usually four components or groups of vibrations recognizable in S1 (Fig. 8.1). Vibrations of the first component are of low frequency and low amplitude. Vibrations of the second and third components, the most prominent part of S1, are of greater frequency and amplitude. Vibrations of the fourth component are of low frequency and low amplitude.

First component

At one time it was thought that vibrations of the first component were caused by atrial systole. However, since similar vibrations are found in phonocardiograms recorded from animals afflicted with atrial fibrillation, a condition obviously incompatible with effective atrial contraction and sound production (Fig. 8.2), other mechanisms should be considered. Alternative mechanisms include vibrations generated by the contracting ventricular myocardium, slight A-V valvular regurgitation occurring at the onset of ventricular systole, and coaptation of leaflets of the A-V valves prior to complete closure and distension.

Second and third components

It is generally believed that sudden development of tension in the closing mitral valve and then in the tricuspid valve generates the second and third components of S1, respectively. According to other investigators, though, development of tension in different parts of the contracting ventricular myocardium is responsible.

Because the second and third components tend to occur as distinct entities, some degree of splitting or doubling of S1 is detectable by auscultation in most normal animals. If excitation and contraction of the right ventricle are delayed because of right bundle branch block or ectopic beats of left ventricular origin, then pronounced splitting of S1 and S2 sometimes occurs (Fig. 8.3).

Fourth component

The fourth component of S1 occurs at the onset of ventricular ejection. It is probably caused by the sudden ejection of blood into the great arteries which generates vibrations within the walls. Dilatation of the pulmonary artery because of pulmonary hypertension or pulmonic stenosis (absolute or relative) can cause the fourth component to be accentuated. In this case, it is called an ejection sound or ejection click. A normal S1 and an ejection sound occurring in sequence can sound like pronounced splitting of S1 in auscultation.

Identifying S1 and determining the temporal relationship between it and other sounds and murmurs permits timing of murmurs, identification of "extra" sounds, and diagnosis of simple arrhythmias.

Intensity of first sound

In the dog, S1 is usually more intense than S2. The opposite is true for many horses under basal conditions. Furthermore, a marked beat-to-beat variation in intensity of S1 is not unusual in horses under basal conditions.

Numerous extracardiac and cardiac factors influence the intensity of S1 and other sounds. Obesity, degree of muscular development, length of hair coat, and excessive fluid in the thorax or pericardial sac are a few of the extracardiac factors. Since heart sounds tend to project to specific locations on the thoracic wall, proper placement of the stethoscope is also important.

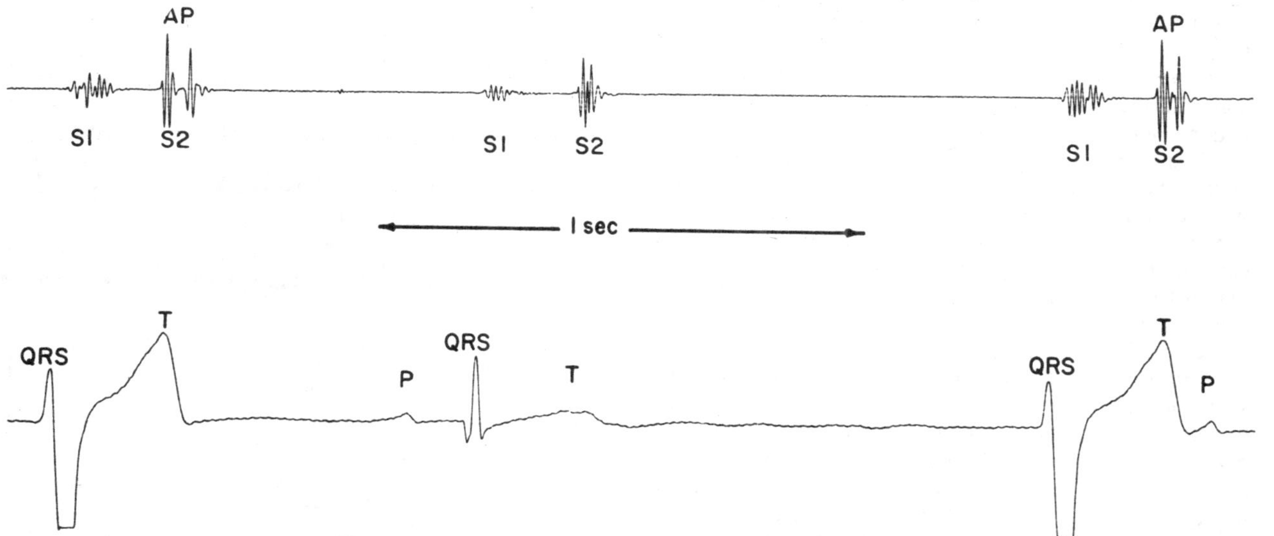

Figure 8.3. PCG and ECG (lead aVF) from a dog with sinus bradycardia and ventricular escape beats. The first and third beats are escape beats, probably originating in the left branch bundle. Note the widely split S2 on these beats. Presumably, tardy excitation of the right ventricle was responsible for the pulmonic (P) component being delayed relative to the aortic (A) component. Slight splitting of S1 is also apparent on the escape beats. Note the lack of splitting of S1 and S2 on the second beat, which was of sinus origin. The sequence of ventricular excitation was normal on this beat; therefore, closing of the pulmonic semilunar valve was not delayed as it was on the escape beats.

Cardiac factors influencing intensity of S1 include the distance the A-V valves move during closing and tensing, the force and speed with which the A-V valves are closed and tensed, and the physical characteristics of the A-V valves.

The A-V valves probably close solely as a consequence of atrial systole, provided that the interval between atrial systole and ventricular systole (A_s-V_s interval) is of sufficient duration. Presumably, a transient ventriculoatrial pressure gradient at the end of atrial systole is responsible for this valve-closing phenomenon. With a proper A_s-V_s interval, the A-V valves are in the closed or nearly closed position at the onset of ventricular systole. Therefore, the distance through which the A-V valves move in being tensed is minimal and the intensity of S1 is likewise minimal. If the A_s-V_s interval lengthens (recognized by a lengthened PR interval on the electrocardiogram), then the intensity of S1 increases. The A-V valves close once as a consequence of atrial systole and then drift open again before the onset of ventricular systole. Since the valves move a greater distance in closing, the intensity of S1 is increased. Intensity of S1 is also great if the A_s-V_s interval is relatively short. In this case, atrial systole is still maintaining the A-V valves in an open position at the onset of ventricular systole. As a consequence, the A-V valves move a considerable distance in closing and an intense S1 results. The relationship between the distance the A-V valves move in closing and intensity of S1 is exemplified in animals having either partial or complete A-V block.

Intensity of S1 is increased in animals during periods of excitement and immediately after exercise. More vigorous closing and tensing of the A-V valves related to increased sympathetic activity probably account for increased intensity of S1 under these circumstances.

Second heart sound

Closure of the semilunar valves causes S2. It occurs at the end of ventricular systole as pressure in the relaxing ventricles falls below that in the aorta and pulmonary artery. Each semilunar valve contributes to the generation of S2. Intensity of S2 seems to be related to arterial pressure since dogs afflicted with pulmonary hypertension tend to have a loud and snapping S2.

Splitting of second sound

Splitting or doubling of S2 occurs when the semilunar valves close out of phase. This is a respiratory-related phenomenon of normal human beings, appearing during inspiration and disappearing during expiration. During inspiration increased venous return to the right side of the heart occurs as a consequence of decreased intrathoracic pressure. The resultant lengthening of right ventricular ejection time causes pulmonic valve closure to occur late. Simultaneously, the act of inspiration hinders venous return to the left side of the heart and this in turn abbreviates left ventricular ejection time and causes the aortic valve to close early. During expiration, right ventricular ejection time returns to normal and left ventricular ejection time lengthens to handle the increased amount of blood delivered to the lungs during the preceding inspiration. Therefore S2 becomes a single sound.

Respiratory-related splitting of S2 is detectable in some normal dogs, particularly if the heart rate is slow and pronounced sinus arrhythmia exists. On the other hand, splitting of S2 is detectable by auscultation in most normal horses, and it tends to be fixed rather than vary with respiration.

Significant splitting of S2 is a characteristic of certain cardiac abnormalities in the dog (Fig. 8.3). These abnormalities include pulmonary hypertension, pulmonic stenosis, right bundle branch block, and interatrial septal defect. Splitting tends to be fixed in the latter.

Splitting of S2 during expiration rather than during inspiration is characteristic of abnormalities such as left bundle branch block and aortic stenosis. This phenomenon is called paradoxical splitting. Tardy closure of the aortic semilunar valve on every heartbeat contributes to this type of splitting. Since right ventricular ejection time is normally lengthened during inspiration, closure of the pulmonic semilunar valve coincides with closure of the aortic valve and a single sound results. During expiration, right ventricular ejection time shortens; therefore, splitting of S2 occurs.

Third heart sound

The third heart sound occurs near the end of the phase of rapid ventricular filling. Some investigators think S3 is caused by transient closing and tensing of the A-V valves. Others theorize that it is generated by vibrations arising in the walls of the ventricles. S3 occurs 0.12–0.14 seconds after the onset of S2.

Although S3 is detectable in phonocardiograms of apparently normal dogs, it is rarely audible. On the other hand, S3 is audible in many dogs afflicted with congestive heart failure. Occasionally, it is more intense than either of the two major heart sounds (Fig. 8.4). The third sound is readily audible in many apparently normal horses (Fig. 8.1). The sound is quite intense and clicking in some horses; in others, it is soft and dull. A beat-to-beat variation of intensity is not unusual. As in dogs, S3 in horses with congestive heart failure is frequently very intense.

Fourth heart sound

Although the fourth or atrial heart sound is seldom found in dogs, it is commonplace in apparently normal horses. When present, S4 precedes S1. Some investigators believe that S4 is generated by transient closing and tensing of the A-V valves. (A transient ventriculoatrial pressure gradient at the end of atrial systole is thought to be responsible for closure of the valves.) Others attribute the sound to vibrations generated within the walls of the ventricles as blood is pumped into the ventricles by atrial systole.

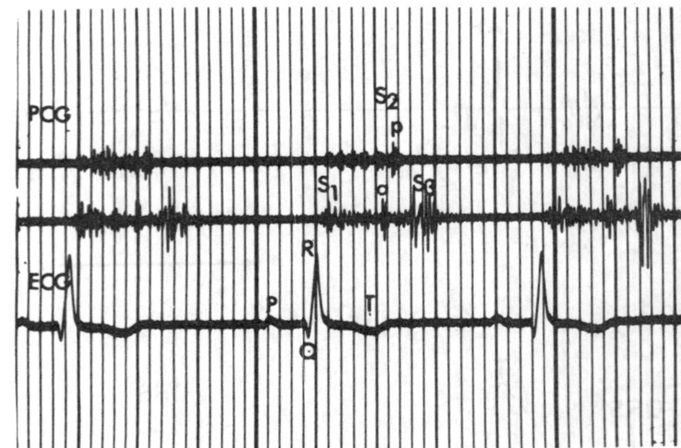

Figure 8.4. Two PCGs and an ECG from a dog with congenital mitral insufficiency and congestive heart failure. The bottom PCG was recorded from the left side of the thorax at the apex beat. The top PCG was recorded from an area two intercostal spaces anterior and slightly dorsal to the apex beat. Note the extremely intense S3 and the aortic (a) component of S2 in the PCG recorded at the apex. The pulmonic (p) component of S2 is apparent in the top PCG. A soft regurgitant type of systolic murmur is apparent in both PCGs.

Partial A-V heart block is found in many of the animals that have S4. Apparently, lengthening of the A-V conduction time allows for completion of the sequence of events leading to its generation. The interval between the P wave of the ECG and S4 in the PCG tends to remain constant at about 0.32–0.36 seconds in the horse (Fig. 8.1) and about 0.17 seconds in the dog (Fig. 8.5). If the A-V conduction time varies from one beat to the next, then the interval between S4 and S1 varies accordingly. Such a phenomenon is common in horses under resting conditions. Slight separation of S4 and S1 can be mistaken during auscultation for pronounced splitting of S1. When the timing of S4 is such that S4 extends into S1, the intensity of S1 is usually reduced. This finding indirectly supports the theory that S4 is generated by transient closing and tensing of the A-V valves. If an occasional atrial systole is not followed by a ventricular systole, as in second-degree A-V block, then S4 occurs as an isolated sound in the resulting pause in the ventricular rhythm.

Two components of S4 are apparent in phonocardiograms recorded from some horses. The second component is ordinarily the only one that is audible. The first component is usually inaudible and consists of low amplitude and low pitched vibrations. These vibrations might be generated either by blood flow through the A-V valves or by atrial contraction per se.

Diastolic gallop sounds

The third and fourth heart sounds are sometimes called ventricular and atrial gallop sounds, respectively, because either S3 or S4 in sequence with S1 and S2 resembles the sound of a galloping horse.

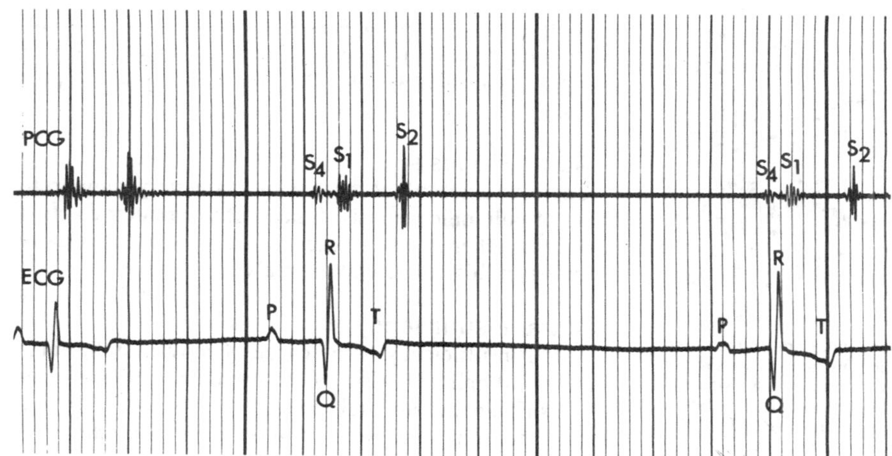

Figure 8.5. PCG and ECG from a dog with first-degree A-V heart block. Note that the PR interval of the second and third beats is 0.2 seconds. A prominent S4 occurs on these beats.

A mid-diastolic sound called a summation gallop sound occurs during tachycardia in some animals that normally have S3 and S4 at normal heart rates. As the period of diastole shortens with an increase in heart rate, atrial systole becomes superimposed upon the rapid filling phase of the ventricles. As a consequence S3 and S4 merge and form a single sound.

Other systolic sounds

One or two "extra" sounds sometimes occur between S1 and S2. One of these, the ejection sound or ejection click, is an accentuation of the terminal component of S1. It often coexists with abnormalities that cause dilation of either the aorta or pulmonary artery of the dog, but is common in seemingly normal horses.

Another "extra" sound, the systolic click, occurs during mid- or late systole of some animals. The systolic click is sometimes detectable in animals afflicted with mitral insufficiency. However, it is not unusual to hear a systolic click in a horse or dog with an apparently normal heart. Checking of adhesions between the pericardial sac and adjacent lungs coincident with the heartbeat is probably responsible for many of the systolic clicks heard in apparently normal animals. It is not unusual for the intensity or even the location of the systolic click to change from one beat to the next.

CARDIAC MURMURS

Turbulence in flowing blood is generally accepted as the major source of murmurs, or prolonged vibrations. Causes of turbulent blood flow include: (1) alteration of the morphology of any one of the four heart valves (stenosis or insufficiency), (2) abnormal communication between the two sides of the heart and/or great vessels (interatrial septal defect, interventricular septal defect, and patent ductus arteriosus), and (3) increased blood flow velocity through a normal valve orifice or vessel. Murmurs occur during systole, during diastole, or during both systole and diastole.

Diastolic murmurs

While pure diastolic murmurs are extremely rare in dogs, they are not uncommon in horses.

Atrioventricular stenosis

Although pathology of the A-V valves, particularly the mitral valve, leading to A-V stenosis is prevalent in human beings, it is virtually nonexistent in domestic animals. Accordingly, absolute A-V valvular stenosis can be discounted as the cause of a pure diastolic murmur (DM). On the other hand, lesions such as interatrial septal defect, mitral insufficiency, or tricuspid insufficiency can result in an increased rate of blood flow through the appropriate A-V valve during early diastole in domestic animals as well as in human beings. The resulting relative A-V stenosis can cause an early diastolic murmur. Although apparent in a phonocardiogram these murmurs are usually inaudible.

Pulmonic insufficiency

Diastolic murmurs due to pulmonic insufficiency are rare in animals. Occasionally, dilatation of the pulmonary artery with attendant incompetence of the pulmonic valve resulting from pulmonary hypertension is the cause of a diastolic murmur in the dog. Likewise, a diastolic murmur of pulmonic insufficiency sometimes appears after surgical correction of pulmonic stenosis. The murmur of pulmonic insufficiency tends to be soft and blowing.

Aortic insufficiency

Uncomplicated or pure aortic insufficiency is extremely rare in the dog, but common in old horses. Most are "noisy," that is, a blend of a wide range of vibration frequencies. They tend to be high-pitched and decre-

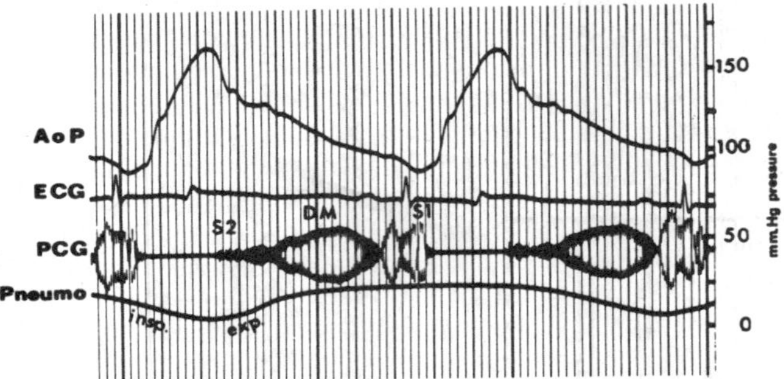

Figure 8.6. Aortic pressure, ECG, PCG, and pneumogram from a horse with a musical diastolic murmur of aortic insufficiency. Eversion of one cusp of the aortic semilunar valve (left coronary cusp) was the cause. Note the abrupt increase in amplitude and abrupt decrease in vibration frequency midway between the P wave and the QRS of the murmur. This accentuated presystolic component blends into S1.

scendo in configuration. Less frequently, the diastolic murmur of aortic insufficiency in the horse is "musical," that is, composed of a fundamental frequency and overtones of the fundamental frequency (Fig. 8.6). These murmurs have a groaning, whining, or buzzing quality. Some are decrescendo in configuration, others are crescendo in configuration, and some are most intense in mid-diastole. Some have both musical and noisy components.

Innocent diastolic murmurs

It is not unusual to find soft diastolic murmurs in apparently normal horses under five years of age. These are high-pitched and very brief in duration. They occur immediately after S2 and their cause is unknown.

Systolic murmurs

Pulmonic stenosis

Pulmonic stenosis is responsible for many of the loud systolic murmurs (SM) found in young dogs. This murmur is usually diamond shaped; that is, the intensity of the murmur increases until mid-systole and then decreases during the remainder of ventricular systole (Fig.

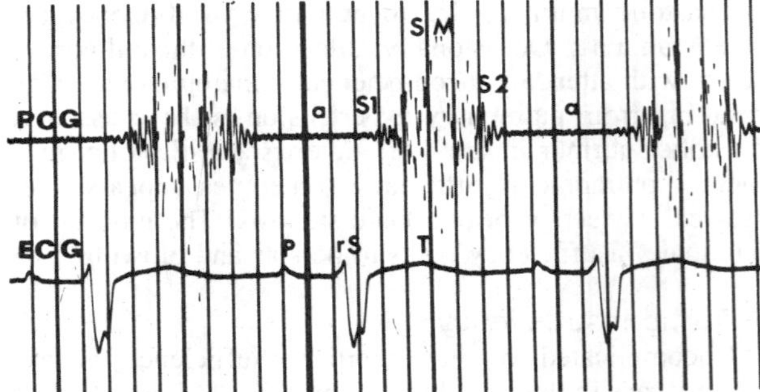

Figure 8.7. PCG and ECG from a dog with pulmonic stenosis. A small vibration (a) precedes S1. It is probably related to atrial systole. (Lowercase r indicates small deflection.)

8.7). It tends to have a very harsh quality. Since right ventricular ejection time is prolonged in the animal having pulmonic stenosis, splitting of S2 is usually pronounced.

Aortic stenosis

Characteristics of aortic stenosis are very similar to those of pulmonic stenosis. Since left ventricular ejection time is lengthened, paradoxical splitting of S2 is usually manifest in this congenital anomaly.

Mitral insufficiency

Mitral insufficiency is the cause of most systolic murmurs in old animals. Most of the murmurs caused by mitral insufficiency are high-pitched and blowing. In the dog the murmur tends to be of uniform intensity throughout its course (Fig. 8.4). The murmur is crescendo in configuration in many horses. Frequently, respiration influences the intensity of the mitral insufficiency murmur, causing it to increase during expiration and decrease during inspiration.

Tricuspid insufficiency

The characteristics of the systolic murmur of tricuspid insufficiency are very similar to those of mitral insufficiency. The intensity of the murmur of tricuspid insufficiency increases during inspiration and decreases during expiration.

Interventricular septal defect

The systolic murmur associated with an interventricular septal defect is generated as blood flows from the left ventricle into the right ventricle. This murmur tends to be of uniform intensity throughout its course; it is a regurgitant type of murmur like the systolic murmurs of mitral insufficiency and tricuspid insufficiency. It is usually high-pitched and blowing. The point of maximal intensity of the interventricular septal defect murmur is located on the right side of the thorax. Shunting of a large volume of blood through a large defect frequently causes an additional systolic murmur. This murmur is the most intense on the left side of the thorax at the pulmonic area and is caused by relative pulmonic stenosis.

Interatrial septal defect

A systolic murmur is associated with an interatrial defect. In this congenital anomaly, blood flows from the left atrium to the right atrium, thereby increasing the stroke volume of the right ventricle and causing relative pulmonic stenosis. Therefore, the systolic murmur is caused by relative pulmonic stenosis rather than by blood flow through the defect itself. Another rare congenital cardiac defect, anomalous pulmonary veins returning to the right atrium, causes a systolic murmur by the same mechanism as interatrial septal defect.

Functional systolic murmurs

Soft systolic murmurs are common in horses and puppies having apparently normal valve orifices and great arteries. Turbulent blood flow stemming from increased blood velocity is thought to be of prime importance in the generation of these innocent murmurs. Severe anemia also can cause a systolic murmur.

Continuous murmurs

Patent ductus arteriosus is the most prevalent abnormality which causes both a systolic and a diastolic murmur. Turbulence in blood flowing through the ductus arteriosus is responsible for generating the murmur. Since the abnormal blood flow is continuous during systole and diastole, the murmur is likewise continuous during systole and diastole. The intensity of the murmur increases during systole, attains a peak at the time of S2, and decreases during diastole. Near the end of the longer diastolic intervals the murmur becomes almost inaudible. The murmur of patent ductus arteriosus is frequently referred to as a "machinery murmur."

Patent ductus arteriosus is not the only abnormality which causes an audible systolic murmur and diastolic murmur. In some instances, an interventricular septal defect is located high in the septum and causes sagging of one cusp of the aortic valve. The resulting aortic insufficiency causes a diastolic murmur. The systolic murmur associated with the septal defect is essentially identical to the one associated with an uncomplicated interventricular septal defect. The two murmurs in combination have a to and fro quality.

REFERENCES

Detweiler, D.K., and Patterson, D.F. 1965. Heart sounds of the dog. *Ann. N.Y. Acad. Sci.* 127:322–40.

Eyster, G.E., Anderson, L.K., and Cords, G.B. 1976. Aortic regurgitation in the dog. *J. Am. Vet. Med. Ass.* 168:138–41.

Faber, J.J. 1964. Origin and conduction of the mitral sound in the heart. *Circ. Res.* 14:426–35.

Glendenning, S.A. 1964. A distinctive diastolic murmur observed in healthy young horses. *Vet. Rec.* 76:341–42.

Grant, C., Green, D.G., and Bunnell, I.L. 1963. The valve-closing function of the right atrium. *Am. J. Med.* 34:325–28.

Holmes, J.R. 1966. Equine phonocardiography. *Med. Biol. Illus.* 16:16–25.

Littlewort, M.C.G. 1962. The clinical auscultation of the equine heart. *Vet. Res.* 74:1247–56.

Luisada, A.A., Sakai, A., and Feigen, L. 1970. Comparative electrocardiography and phonocardiography in six species of animals. *Am. J. Vet. Res.* 31:1695–1702.

McKussick, V.A. 1958. *Cardiovascular Sound in Health and Disease.* Williams & Wilkins, Baltimore.

Patterson, D.F., and Detweiler, D.K. 1963. The diagnostic significance of splitting of the second heart sound in the dog. *Zentralblatt Veterinärmedizin* 10:121–32.

Patterson, D.F., Detweiler, D.K., and Glendenning, S.A. 1965. Heart sounds and murmurs of the normal horse. *Ann. N.Y. Acad. Sci.* 127:242–305.

Segal, B.L., ed. 1964. *The Theory and Practice of Auscultation.* Davis, Philadelphia.

Smetzer, D.L., Bishop, S., and Smith, C.R. 1966. Diastolic murmur of equine aortic insufficiency. *Am. Heart J.* 72:489–97.

Smetzer, D.L., and Breznock, E.M. 1972. Auscultatory diagnosis of patent ductus arteriosus in the dog. *J. Am. Vet. Med. Ass.* 160:80–84.

Smetzer, D.L., and Smith, C.R. 1965. Diastolic heart sounds of horses. *J. Am. Vet. Med. Ass.* 146:937–44.

Smetzer, D.L., Smith, C.R., and Hamlin, R.L. 1965. The fourth heart sound in the equine. *Ann. N.Y. Acad. Sci.* 127:306–21.

CHAPTER 9

Regulation of the Heart and Blood Vessels | by C. Roger Smith and Robert L. Hamlin

The functions of circulation fall into two categories: support of the metabolic requirements of each cell, and support of special, blood-flow dependent functions of individual organs. The latter category includes formation of filtrate by the kidney, exchange of gases by the lungs, and radiation and convection of heat by the skin. The requirements for nutrient flow among the various tissues or organs vary. Some tissues, for example, the brain, have a rather uniform metabolic rate and oxygen requirement. Others, such as skeletal muscle, have a wide range of cellular activity and oxygen requirement.

The circulatory control systems have the task of providing each organ with blood flow adequate to satisfy intrinsic nutritional needs; to subserve special functions, that is, nonnutrient needs which provide homeostasis of the entire body; and to guarantee flow to the critical organs during a crisis, even at the expense of other tissues. The heart and brain are excellent examples of such critical organs: they rapidly suffer irreversible damage under anaerobic conditions.

Table 9.1 shows how total flow (cardiac output) is distributed to the various tissues in the anesthetized dog. The fraction of the cardiac output received by a tissue depends upon the size or percent of the total body weight the organ or tissue represents, the density of the blood

Table 9.1. Blood flow in the anesthetized dog

Organ	Percentage of cardiac output	ml/kg/min	ml/organ g/min
Kidney	11.1	19	3
Heart	5.2	9	1
Liver	30	51	1.2
Arterial	10	17	0.4
Portal	20	34	0.8
Pancreas	1.6	1.7	1.6
Spleen	1.3	2.2	0.6
Gut	16.5	24.8	0.7
Stomach	2.5	8.3	0.4
Skin	4.9	8.4	0.07
Carcass	44.3	75.8	
Whole dog	100	169	0.17

Adapted from Sapirstein 1958, *Am. J. Physiol.* 193:161–68

vessels in the tissue, and the resistance to flow offered by the individual vascular beds. Of course, the absolute amount each tissue receives can increase or decrease with changes in cardiac output.

BASIC SCHEME

Poiseuille's equation

The work of the control mechanisms is summarized by Poiseuille's equation

$$Q = \frac{P_1 - P_2}{R}$$

Q is volume of flow in milliliters or liters per second. P_1 is the aortic pressure. P_2 is the pressure in the right atrium; in health it is so near zero the formula may be written $Q = P/R$. R is the resistance offered by the tubes and the liquid. It can be expressed as

$$R = \frac{8\eta L}{\pi r^4}$$

(see Chapter 7). Since in health all are constants except r, the formula can be rewritten $R = 1/r^4$. The radius is obviously the major determinant of resistance.

Laplace's equation for wall tension

The walls of a vessel subjected to the radius-expanding force of blood pressure are in a state of tension. In order to appreciate wall tension, visualize the force necessary to hold together the edges of a horizontal slit in a vessel subjected to transmural pressure. As the walls become more distended (tense and stiff), more force is required to change the radius.

The mechanical properties contributing to wall tension are the elasticity and viscosity of the tissue comprising the vessel wall. Another factor is wall thickness. Wall thickness and composition vary among different kinds of vessels and with disease, but in health remain constant for individual vessels. A third and physiologically very important determinant of wall tension is vessel size. The smaller the vessel the smaller the effect of any given pressure. If wall tension is T and distending pressure P, then $T = P \times r$ (Laplace's equation).

When the force of the distending pressure is just balanced by wall tension, the radius is unchanged. Active contraction of vascular smooth muscle increases wall tension while relaxation decreases it. According to the Laplace's equation the load against which vascular smooth muscle contracts depends upon both the net pressure acting on the wall *and* the prevailing radius. Because of this, and the effect of initial fiber length on contraction, wall tension is most effectively increased by contraction of vascular smooth muscle in the moderately distended blood vessel. Other factors contributing to the size of the lumen of vessels are the inherent passive elastic forces of wall tissue and structural alterations induced by vascular diseases.

BLOOD PRESSURE

Homeostasis

Homeostasis of blood pressure refers to the processes by which the normal level of arterial blood pressure is maintained. The principal mechanism is neural and basically reflex in nature. It is an extrinsic, central regulatory mechanism which is capable of balancing variations in cardiac output with variations in total peripheral resistance, so that the level of arterial pressure remains relatively constant. Physiological changes in body posture, mild to moderate exercise, environmental temperature changes, change in the functional activity of digestive organs or of the entire body (sleep and wakefulness) may be accompanied by changes in cardiac output, distribution of blood flow, and peripheral resistance without significant alteration of arterial blood pressure.

Many physiological and pathological cardiovascular behavior patterns cannot be explained by the basic, involuntary, automatic reflex mechanism responsible for pressure homeostasis. The term *regulation* refers more specifically to the maintenance of homeostasis. The term *control* refers to the adaptive behavior in which the usual homeostatic function may be altered in one way or another. The neural homeostatic reflexes are subject to modification by a hierarchy of connections within the CNS. These connections selectively adapt cardiovascular function to individual stimuli and environmental circumstances—fear, anxiety, hypoxia, high environmental temperature—and they can even be affected by learned control. The discreteness and differentiation of the nervous system become apparent in blushing in people; the redistribution of blood flow in anticipation of exercise, in hemorrhage, and in hot and cold environments; and the emergence of cardiac arrhythmias during emotionally stressful situations. These exemplify the precise control individual stimuli may exercise over the cardiovascular system. Only occasionally do adaptive reactions become so intense or sustained that they constitute signs of disease.

For healthy individuals of each species there is a normal resting blood pressure, which is maintained in the face of considerable stress. If a dog is tilted from horizontal to a 30-degree head-up position, the pressure, after a transient fall, returns to normal. Ten to twenty percent of the blood volume may be removed without a significant fall in blood pressure. The cardiovascular reflexes operate to adjust both cardiac output and peripheral resistance nearly simultaneously. If they are interrupted at any point in the arc, the blood pressure deviates from its normal level and circulatory stresses result in predictable changes. For example, if important cardiovascular reflexes are eliminated by section of sensory nerves (sinus and aortic nerves) or efferent nerves (sympathectomy or adrenergic blocking agents), postural hypotension occurs during appropriate posture changes, and death occurs after only a 15–20 percent instead of a 40–50 percent blood loss. In deeply anesthetized animals the reflexes may be depressed to the extent that hypotension may occur in any but the horizontal position. If the aortic and sinus nerves are cut in the dog and the animal is allowed to survive, a chronic hypertensive state may evolve.

There are several reasons to maintain an optimum stable pressure in the arterial vessels: (1) Flow through the exchange vessels would not occur without it. (2) If the perfusion pressure is held constant, variations in blood flow can be achieved by altering the resistance in vascular beds with a high potential for producing active changes in vessel caliber. (3) In vascular beds with a low potential for active changes in resistance, a stable and optimal arterial pressure per se is the major determinant of flow. (4) A minimal level is required for maintaining the patency and perfusion of vessels above the level of the heart. (5) A stable perfusion pressure is important for obtaining a normal balance between the intra- and extravascular fluid volumes.

Systolic, diastolic, pulse, and mean pressure

The pressure in the arteries oscillates during each cardiac cycle. *Systolic* pressure is the peak arterial pressure and *diastolic* the minimal. *Pulse* pressure is the difference between the two. The *mean* arterial pressure is an intermediate pressure between the systolic and diastolic pressures. The *true* or geometric mean pressure, used mainly in research, is nearer the diastolic than the systolic pressure. Sometimes it is estimated by adding one third of the pulse pressure to the diastolic pressure.

Measurement

There are two general methods for accurate measurement of blood pressure, one direct, using an inserted catheter, and one indirect, employing an exterior cuff. The mercury manometer is used in the oldest direct method (see Chapter 7). Because of excessive dampening, it is limited to laboratory measurement of slow changes. The most accurate direct method utilizes an electronic transducer with a high frequency response, usually a strain gauge transducer. In this device the arterial pressure acts upon a thin but stiff metal diaphragm whose movements result in changes in the flow of current. These electrical signals are then amplified to drive a writing recorder or oscilloscope. The strain gauge transducer is used extensively for the determination of blood pressure in anesthetized animal subjects.

The most familiar indirect method is that applied in the physician's office. The sphygmomanometer consists of an inflatable cuff placed around a limb or tail and connected to a mercury manometer or other pressure gauge. The manometer measures the external pressure required to just collapse an artery followed by that which just balances the lowest or diastolic pressure. By placing a stethoscope over the artery just distal to the cuff a series of Korotkoff sounds may be detected. Initially, the cuff pressure is made to exceed systolic pressure. The pressure is then gradually and slowly lowered. The point at which the first sounds make their appearance is the systolic pressure. The point at which the sounds pass from maximal intensity to a distinctly muffled sound and just before they become totally inaudible is the diastolic pressure. The distinctiveness of the sounds lessens as the size of the artery becomes smaller (peripheral arteries in the distal portion of limbs of animals), and often with limb shapes other than cylindrical. The most useful, current modification substitutes a specially designed transducer which detects changes in Doppler-shifted ultrasound generated by arterial wall motion for the stethoscopic detection of Korotkoff sounds. This overcomes the problem of small arteries. It has been applied in the dog, horse, and pony (Freundlich et al. 1972, Garner et al. 1972, Hahn et al. 1973).

In the healthy animal an independent and isolated change in heart rate affects diastolic more than systolic pressure, a change in stroke volume systolic more than diastolic, and a change in peripheral resistance diastolic more than systolic. It is unusual except under controlled laboratory situations to observe a change in only one factor. When arterial capacitance, defined as the slope of dv/dp, is decreased by age or disease, the mean arterial pressure, cardiac output, and total peripheral resistance may be normal, but the diastolic pressure is lower and the systolic pressure higher than normal. If peripheral resistance is increased while arterial capacitance is decreased, systolic pressure may be affected more than diastolic.

LEVELS OF CONTROL

Control of cardiac output and peripheral resistance is a highly complex meshing of local or intrinsic and remote or extrinsic regulatory mechanisms. The strictly local, intrinsic mechanisms are referred to as autoregulation. Autoregulatory mechanisms operate at the level of the myocardium in determining the size of the stroke volume (Chapter 7). They also help regulate the active tension of vascular smooth muscle and in so doing adjust vessel caliber and peripheral resistance (Chapter 10). Extrinsic control refers to the regulatory effects of extrinsic nerves and circulating chemicals on heart rate and stroke volume and on vascular smooth muscle. The autonomic nerves are a prime regulator of cardiovascular functions. However, in major departures from the normal metabolic state, circulating hormones or chemicals of remote origin may have marked effects.

The denervated heart

Studies on dogs (Donald et al. 1964) with chronic total denervation of the heart (extrinsic nerves) demonstrate that the intrinsic cardiac mechanisms are capable of meeting the requirements of even severe grades of exercise. Dogs achieved the same oxygen consumptions and cardiac outputs when exercised after denervation as before. The increase in heart rate was slower in reaching the maximum rate, the maximum rate was lower (140 percent of resting as compared to 220–260 percent); it tended to reach a plateau during exercise and decline more slowly following cessation of exercise. In dogs with normal cardiac innervation the rate varied considerably during exercise, in contrast to very slight variation following denervation. The increase in rate during exercise following denervation persisted after adrenalectomy and the administration of β-adrenergic blocking agents. Thus the rate increase does not appear to be due to circulating catecholamines. The increase in cardiac output prior to denervation was almost entirely due to an increase in rate. After denervation, increased stroke volume accounted for one half or more of the increase in cardiac output. The increase in stroke volume was accounted for by an increase in the end-diastolic volume rather than a decrease in the end-systolic volume as is the case in the normal, innervated heart.

In general these results agree with those of other investigations (Stinson et al. 1973, Kent and Cooper 1974). Light to moderate exercise is adapted to differently but adequately. Severe stresses on cardiac output cannot be accommodated through intrinsic mechanisms alone.

EXTRINSIC HUMORAL CONTROL

Humoral substances produced by the endocrine glands or other tissues extrinsic to the heart exercise little or no significant regulatory effect upon heart rate or stroke volume under basal physiological conditions. Minor or moderate fluctuations in blood pressure or blood flow in the general systemic circulation do not result in variations in the concentrations of catecholamines, thyroid hormones, or other similar substances in the circulating blood. The heart is one of the principal targets of the catecholamines. Epinephrine and norepinephrine are secreted by the adrenal medulla. In appropriate amounts both stimulate cardiac rhythmicity, conduction, contractility, and excitability. Epinephrine increases blood pressure largely because it increases cardiac output, norepinephrine because of vasoconstriction and increased peripheral resistance, although neither are restricted to these actions. The half-lives of the catecholamines in the circulation is rather short (less than 2 min). They are not cumulative. In fact, an *animal with its adrenal medulla removed does not normally suffer from deficiencies in the control of cardiac output*. However, in special responses such as fright, fear, anger, hostility, anxiety, hemorrhage, shock, anaphylaxis, or postural hypotension, the adrenal secretion of catecholamines becomes a part of the cardiac control mechanism integrated by the limbic system, hypothalamus, and other parts of the CNS.

There are a number of endogenous chemical substances capable of either stimulating or inhibiting vascular smooth muscle. They can alter peripheral resistance, distribution of blood flow, and blood pressure. Among these are the catecholamines, angiotensin II, vasopressin, prostaglandins, histamine, and bradykinin. None of the recognized specific vasoactive substances are established as regular, circulating, and essential participants in a centrally integrated mechanism for regulating peripheral resistance and blood pressure. Nor are any necessary for fixing the resting level of tone of peripheral resistance vessels. For example, a lack of vasopressin due to disease or experimental ablation of the posterior pituitary gland results in diabetes insipidus rather than hypotension. Removal of the adrenal medullary source of catecholamines does not result in a major loss of capability for regulating peripheral resistance and blood pressure or cause hypotension. And the effects on peripheral resistance elicited by direct stimulation of sympathetic secretomotor nerves to the adrenal medulla are negligible compared to those following equal stimulation of sympathetic vasoconstrictor nerves (Powis 1974).

Catecholamines

Epinephrine, norepinephrine, and dopamine are three endogenous catecholamines. Norepinephrine is principally found in the endings of adrenergic sympathetic nerves. To a variable extent, it is also found in the adrenal medulla. The adrenal medulla is the source of the hormone epinephrine. Dopamine, the immediate precursor of norepinephrine, is found in highest concentrations in sympathetic nerves and the adrenal medulla and serves as a neurotransmitter in some areas of the brain. The tissue concentrations of catecholamines are low and normally remain constant. In the circulating blood, their concentration is normally exceedingly small due to their slow rate of release and to their rapid inactivation in the liver by catechol-O-methyltransferase and monoamine oxidase. All three catecholamines produce their vascular effects by uniting with adrenergic receptors on the cell membrane of vascular smooth muscle. Stimulation of β-receptors produces vasodilatation. Stimulation of α-receptors produces vasoconstriction. All of the peripheral arterial system contains α-receptors and some of it also contains β-receptors. The arterial β-receptors appear to be fewer in number and are largely restricted to the skeletal muscle and myocardial vascular beds. The adrenergic receptors in the venous system are thought to be primarily the α-type. Norepinephrine stimulates α-receptors and produces vasoconstriction. Epinephrine stimulates both α- and β-receptors and can cause both vasoconstriction and vasodilatation. Likewise dopamine stimulates specific dopamine vasodilator receptors and α-receptors and thus can produce vasodilatation and vasoconstriction (Goldberg 1974). Higher doses of either epinephrine or dopamine produce an overall vasoconstrictor response which seems to support the concept that β- and dopamine arterial dilator-type receptors are much fewer in number than are α-constrictor receptors. Thus the diversity of vascular response to catecholamines in part depends upon the distribution and density of the specific kinds of adrenergic receptors. Also, when a given catecholamine combines with both α- and β-receptors it may have a greater affinity for one kind of receptor than the other.

The changing concentrations of endogenous catecholamines in the circulating blood ordinarily exert minimal regulatory effects upon peripheral resistance and blood pressure. In a number of disease states (e.g. tumors of catecholamine-secreting tissue, hypotensive shock, cardiac failure, and some forms of hypertensive disease), however, the levels of catecholamines in the blood are significantly elevated and do increase peripheral resistance and affect blood flow. Blood pressure may or may not be elevated depending upon the level of cardiac output.

Prostaglandins

Prostaglandins have been found in many of the body's tissues and cells. They are very potent in unusually low concentrations and they exhibit a wide range of effects. They are stored in tissues to a very limited extent, but are capable of rapid synthesis. Their concentration in most tissues varies from 0.35 to 35 ng/g. Smooth muscle including vascular smooth muscle is one of the important targets of the major prostaglandins. Many kinds of stimuli can provoke their release within tissues, including mechanical stimuli, nonneural humoral agents, sympathetic nerve stimulation (Horton 1973), inflammation, anaphylaxis, and cellular damage. Their principal vascular effects are limited to the tissue in which they are released. Their major vascular actions are upon regional peripheral resistance and blood flow. Their concentration in the arterial blood delivered to the peripheral resistance vessels is kept minimal by rapid metabolism in the tissue site of release and rapid inactivation during passage through the liver and lungs. A single passage through either organ removes substantial amounts of the blood prostaglandin content. *It appears unlikely that they behave as hormones* under normal physiological circumstances. Their most important effect is upon local blood flow.

Prostaglandins are 20-OH fatty acids with a cyclopentane ring produced from the corresponding polyunsaturated fatty acids by a microsomal synthetase system. The primary naturally occurring ones are divided into types PGA, PGB, PGE, and PGF. Each type is further subdivided into classes, PGA_1, PGA_2, etc. The PGE's and PGA's produce arteriolar vasodilatation in nearly all vascular beds. The PGF and PGB compounds are principally vasoconstrictors. Prostaglandins produce their vascular effects in two ways: by a direct stimulating or inhibiting effect upon vascular smooth muscle, or by augmenting (PGF and PGB) or inhibiting (PGE) the vasoconstrictor response to sympathetic nerve stimulation (Brody and Kadowitz 1974). Some species variations are encountered.

Angiotensin II

Angiotensin II is a naturally occurring vasoactive octapeptide which acts as a local tissue humoral within the kidneys and as a hormone on peripheral arteries and the adrenal gland. It has a role in the pathogenesis of hypertension. After removal of its source by bilateral nephrectomy the immediate effects upon blood pressure are negligible. It is a powerful arterial vasoconstrictor, being 10 times more potent in this respect than norepinephrine. Potency, however, does not necessarily reflect a major physiological role in homeostasis.

Angiotensin II production is initiated by the action of a kidney enzyme, *renin,* secreted into the renal vein. In the blood, renin acts upon a plasma globulin, angiotensinogen, normally present and produced by the liver, to form angiotensin I, which is physiologically inactive. Angiotensin I can be converted to active angiotension II in numerous body tissues, but the capillaries of the lungs are the major site. Transformation from the inactive to the active form in the lungs is important because it has the potential for making the entire cardiac output an angiotensin II distributor to all the systemic arterioles with little effect on venous vascular smooth muscle. The events in the animal body which lead to increased renal release of renin and then increased circulating levels of angiotensin II are acute reduction in blood volume or blood pressure and chronic sodium ion depletion (Davis and Freeman 1976). Events which compromise blood flow to the kidney (low arterial perfusion pressure, occlusive disease of the renal artery, fibrotic contraction of the kidney) increase renin release and activate the renin-angiotensin pressor system. Angiotensin II has a major regulatory role in the release of the adrenal cortical hormone aldosterone. The result of activation of this system is elevation of both angiotensin II and aldosterone.

Pipkin et al. (1974) found that lowering the blood pressure in sheep by hemorrhage or only in areas of the arterial system containing receptors sensitive to changes in pressure caused an increase in angiotensin II–like activity. In upright man, gravitational forces accompanying sudden posture adjustments cause falls in pressure in these same pressure sensory areas. An independent role of the renin-angiotensin pressor system in pressure homeostasis is further complicated by the knowledge that angiotensin may augment sympathetic nerve vasomotor activity as well as participate in the mechanism liberating catecholamines from the adrenal medulla.

Antidiuretic hormone

Antidiuretic hormone (ADH) is released by the posterior pituitary gland into the blood in active form. Its major physiological effect is to cause the kidney to retain water in excess of solute, thus lowering the osmotic pressure of the blood and other body fluids. A very sensitive intracerebral osmoreceptor is a most important regulator of ADH release. In addition to osmoreceptors, volume receptors in the large intrathoracic veins and left atrium, pressure sensitive receptors (baroreceptors) in the arterial system, drugs, endogenous humoral substances, and other factors affect its release. Diabetes insipidus occurs when ADH deficiency develops due to disease of the posterior pituitary gland, the superoptic nuclei, or the hypothalamo-hypophyseal tract.

ADH in relative large doses increases peripheral resistance and blood pressure by directly stimulating vascular smooth muscle. However, it probably is not secreted in sufficient quantities to have any appreciable role in normal blood pressure homeostasis. Hemorrhage is a potent stimulus for ADH release. Both ADH and angiotensin may significantly contribute to the prolonged and intense intestinal vasoconstriction following induction of hemorrhagic hypovolemic shock.

CARDIOVASCULAR REFLEXES

There are five essential components of any reflex arc: (1) receptors, (2) afferent or sensory neurons, (3) a reflex center within the CNS, the medulla oblongata, (4) efferent or motor neurons, and (5) effector organs, principally vascular smooth muscle of arteries and veins, atrial and ventricular muscle, sinoatrial (S-A) and atrioventricular (A-V) nodes, and Purkinje fibers. This most simple unit of neural organization accounts for the homeostasis of blood pressure. All are autonomic reflexes.

Negative feedback

The reflex regulation of blood pressure depends upon the stimulating action of blood pressure itself upon pressure sensitive receptors (baroreceptors) within the blood vascular system. These reflexes constitute negative feedback loops. This means that a rise in blood pressure, e.g. 10 mm, will initiate the opposite, a fall of approximately 10 mm, and conversely. The system consists of a sensing or detecting device (baroreceptor), an input loop (afferent neurons), a coordinating device (cardiovascular reflex centers), and an output loop (efferent neurons) to the effectors (vascular and cardiac muscle). The system continually adjusts cardiac output and total peripheral resistance. In unanesthetized animals the more important reflex effects are adjustments of heart rate and peripheral vascular resistance (Vatner and Braunwald 1975). The systemic arterial baroreceptor reflexes have been recently reviewed by Kirchheim (1976).

Efferent nerves to the heart

Sympathetic cardiac augmentor nerves

The heart receives its sympathetic fibers (postganglionic) via the cardiac nerves. The myocardium of both the atria and ventricles, the S-A node, and the A-V node all have sympathetic innervation. The action of the sympathetic nerves on the cardiac tissues is mediated by the release of norepinephrine from the sympathetic nerve endings which then combines with β-receptors of the heart tissues.

The effect of sympathetic nerves on the heart is often studied by stimulating the stellate ganglion or postganglionic fibers. The effects, which come on gradually, are: an acceleration of rate—positive chronotropic effect (Fig. 9.1); increased force of contraction of both the atria and ventricles—positive inotropic effect (Fig. 9.2); a shortening of the interval between atrial and ventricular contraction—positive dromotropic effect; and an increase in the excitability of myocardium. The sympathetic effects on the heart are opposite those of the parasympathetic system.

The resting heart rate of animals is only slightly controlled by tone of the sympathetic fibers. Bilateral removal of the stellate ganglia results in only a small decrease in resting heart rate. This is evidence for a small resting tone in accelerator nerves, and is substantiated by studies of the impulse traffic (electroneurography) in the sympathetic nerves to the heart. There is a continuous passage of impulses at a low frequency, less than 10 per second, which may be made to vary reflexly.

In departures from the basal state the positive chronotropic effect upon the S-A node and the inotropic effect

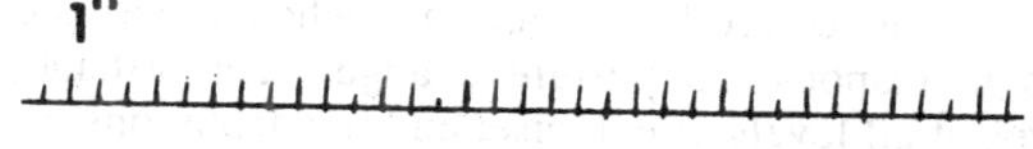

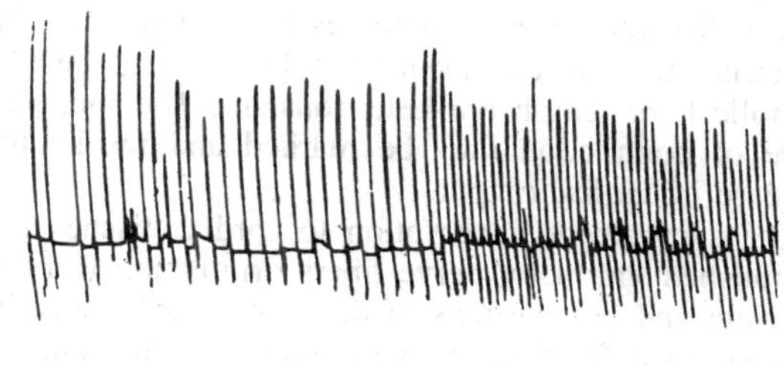

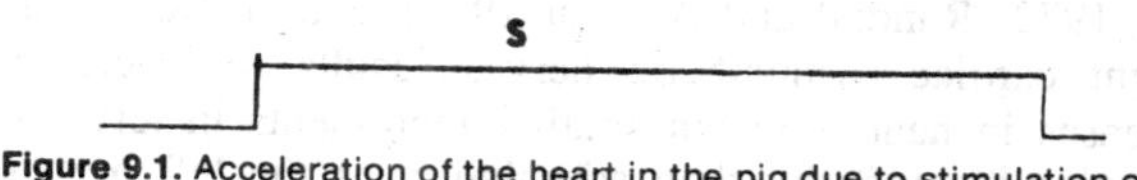

Figure 9.1. Acceleration of the heart in the pig due to stimulation of an accelerator nerve (filament of left cardiac plexus). There was a lag of about 13 seconds between the beginning of the stimulus and the beginning of the acceleration.

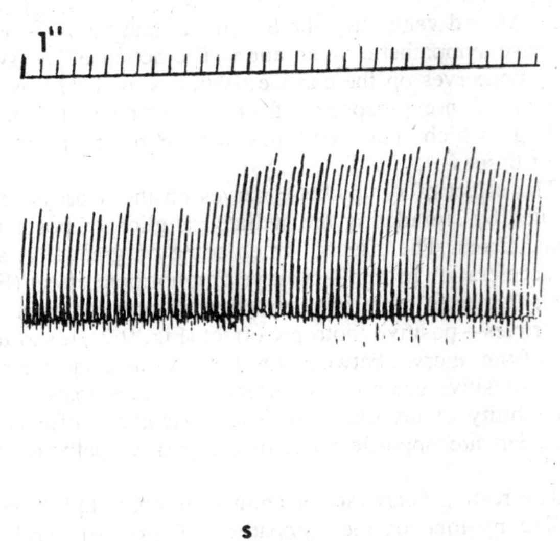

Figure 9.2. Augmentation of the heart beat due to stimulation of a branch of the cardiac plexus in the pig. S indicates duration of the stimulus. Note the absence of cardiac acceleration.

upon the auricular and ventricular myocardium are important. Direct stimulation of the accelerator nerves can increase the heart rate 2–3 times.

The sympathetic augmentor nerves also play an important part in controlling heart rate when blood pressure falls in response to posture changes, hemorrhage, and drugs; at all levels of exercise; and in adaptations to emotional stress and heart disease, e.g. chronic congestive heart failure (Black and Prichard 1973, Edkberg et al. 1971, Braunwald 1974). Their importance in controlling rate may vary with species (Scher et al. 1972). Reflex or direct stimulation of sympathetic nerves not only increases the rate but also increases the pumping ability of the atria and ventricles even when both the rate and end-diastolic fiber length are held constant. The increase in force of contraction may be marked and results in an increase in cardiac output.

The sympathetic innervation to cardiac tissues is accomplished via many nerve fibers originating from both the right and left portions of the spinal cord. Selectively stimulating a fraction of them results in different kinds (inotropic, chronotropic, bathmotropic) of responses, different magnitudes of given responses, and responses more localized to given regions of the heart (Randall et al. 1972, Randall and Armour 1974). Stimulation of the right cardiac sympathetic nerves results in larger increases in heart rate but smaller increments in left ventricular contractility than stimulation of the left nerves. Overlap in regions supplied by branches of sympathetic cardiac nerves does prevail, but the more precise mapping of innervation has revealed the possibility for a more highly localized sympathetic cardiac control system.

Sympathetic stimulation extends and supplements changes in heart rate and contractility beyond that available by vagal inhibition alone. It is a source of reserve pumping ability (increases in rate) in situations of severe stress or adaptation to the more unusual environmental stimuli.

Parasympathetic cardioinhibitory nerves

The cardioinhibitory fibers are contained in the vagus nerves of the cranial division of the parasympathetic nervous system. The vagal fibers are preganglionic. They synapse with postganglionic neurons located in the heart (Fig. 9.3). In mammals the cardiac tissues receiving parasympathetic fibers are the S-A node, the A-V node, the atrial myocardium, coronary blood vessels, and ventricular conduction system (Kent et al. 1974). What has

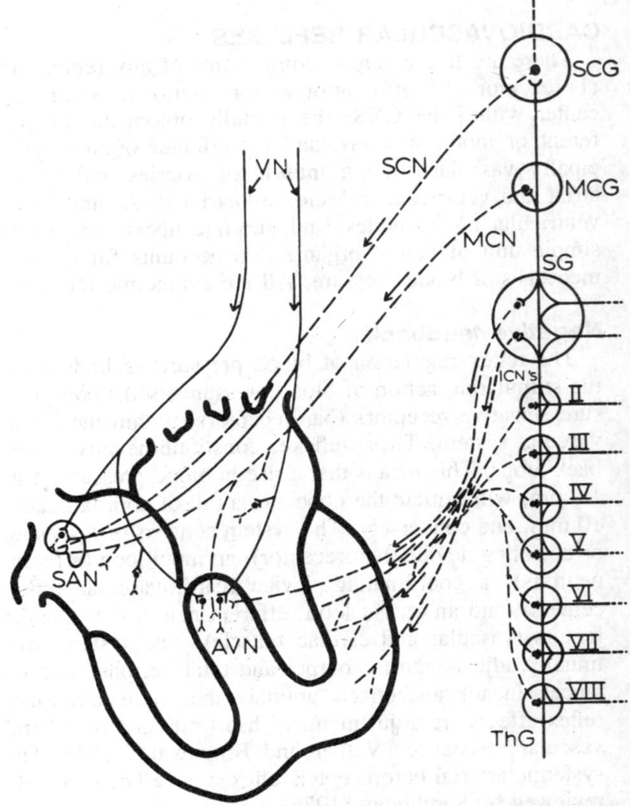

Figure 9.3. Autonomic nerves to the heart. VN (vagus nerves) to the sinoatrial node (SAN), atrioventricular node (AVN), and atrial musculature. Sympathetic nerves in interrupted lines from superior cervical ganglion (SCG), middle cervical ganglion (MCG), stellate ganglion (SG), and thoracic ganglia (ThG) to S-A and A-V nodes and auricular and ventricular myocardium. SCN, MCN, and ICN are the superior, middle, and inferior cardiac nerves.

been stated about localized myocardial responses to stimulation of smaller branches of the sympathetic cardiac nerves also applies to small vagal branches (Armour et al. 1975). The cardioinhibitory nerves are cholinergic. Atropine blocks and physostigmine augments the effects of vagal stimulation on the heart.

The direct effects of vagal stimulation on the heart in all mammals are dramatic and occur suddenly, in less than 1 second. They are exerted principally upon the S-A and A-V nodes and the atrial myocardium. Changes observed in ventricular rate are secondary to the vagal depression of the S-A node. A change in ventricular stroke volume also occurs as a function of rate; that is, as the rate slows, filling time and end-diastolic volume increase, and vice versa (Fig. 9.4).

Stimulation of the peripheral end of one vagus nerve in the anesthetized dog, after both vagi are cut, with frequencies between 0 and 25 per second will reduce the rate from 180 per minute to complete arrest. This slowing effect is called a negative chronotropic effect. It is the most important vagal effect in the regulation of cardiac output. The right vagus usually has a more marked negative chronotropic effect than the left (Figs. 9.5, 9.6). The different effects indicate that the S-A node receives more fibers from the right than the left vagus. The heart cannot be maintained in arrest by vagal stimulation; the ventricles soon commence to beat. This is called vagal escape and is due to a shift of the pacemaker from the S-A node to a ventricular site. Figures 9.4 and 9.7 illustrate the results of stimulation of the peripheral end (efferent fibers only) of the cut vagus nerve on heart rate and blood pressure. The fall in blood pressure is a consequence of a reduction in cardiac output.

Early observations of the reciprocal relationship of blood pressure to heart rate formed the basis for Marey's law: a rise in blood pressure is followed by a reflex slowing of the heart and vice versa. When pressure goes down, vagal inhibitory tone reflexly decreases and sympathetic augmentor tone increases. Recent research throws doubt on this, however. For example, in the dog (Scher et al. 1972) and horse (Hamlin et al. 1972) the reflex slowing of heart rate in response to a rise in blood pressure is principally a parasympathetic effect. The reflex speeding in response to a drop in arterial pressure is a mixed sympathetic-parasympathetic effect with some variation according to species.

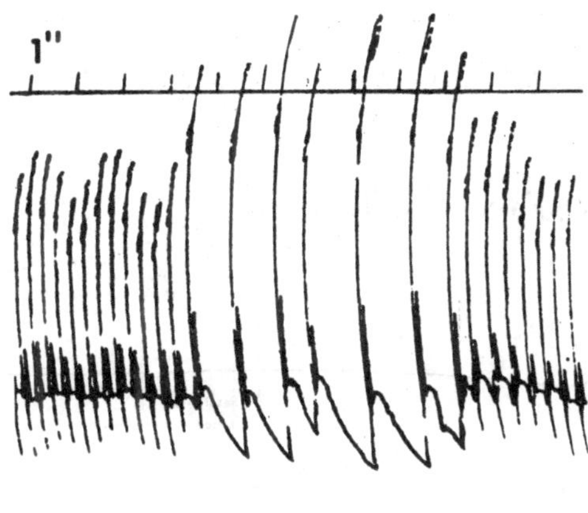

Figure 9.4. Slowing of the heart due to stimulation of the peripheral end of a cervical vagus nerve in the pig. The slowing of the heart was accompanied by larger beats. During the longer diastoles the ventricles were filled more completely and, in accordance with the Frank-Starling law of the heart, gave more forceful beats.

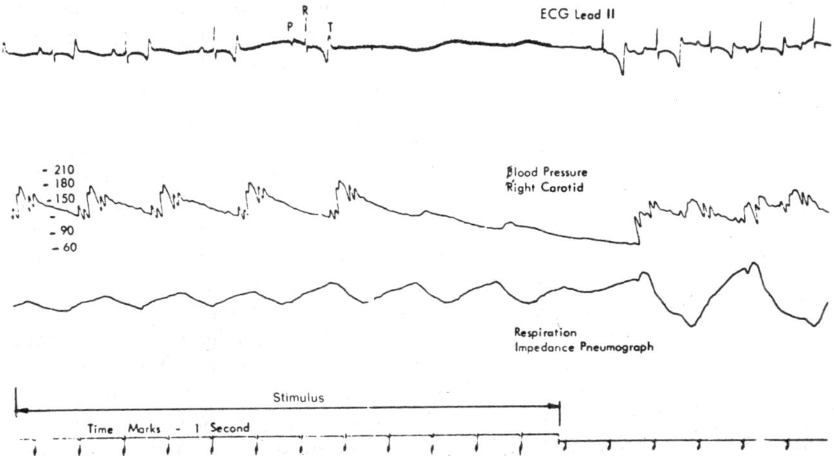

Figure 9.5. Right vagal stimulation in the horse. In the ECG note the slowing of the pacemaker (increase in distance between P waves) and the arrest of the pacemaker for about 5 seconds. (From Geddes, Hoff, and McCrady 1965, *Cardiovascular Res. Ctr. Bull.* 3:80–95.)

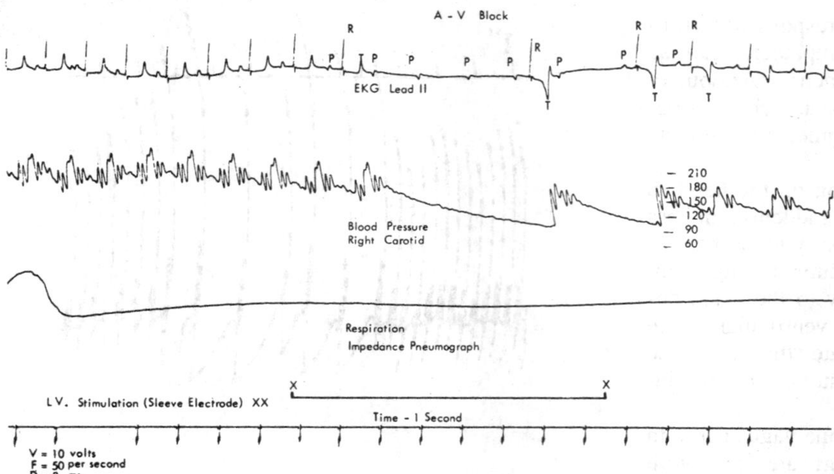

Figure 9.6. Left vagal stimulation in the horse. X-X indicates duration of stimulation. Block of conduction of impulses over A-V node is denoted by absence of ventricular complexes (QRS-T) following P waves. Pressure pulses are absent and blood pressure falls coincident with absence of PRS-T complexes. (From Geddes, Hoff, and McCrady 1965, *Cardiovascular Res. Ctr. Bull.* 3:80–95.)

In any event, Marey's law did not always hold. For example, in the response to physical exercise and emotional stress both blood pressure and heart rate are elevated.

Vagal stimulation prolongs the interval between the end of atrial contraction and the beginning of ventricular contraction. This is the result of the inhibitory action the

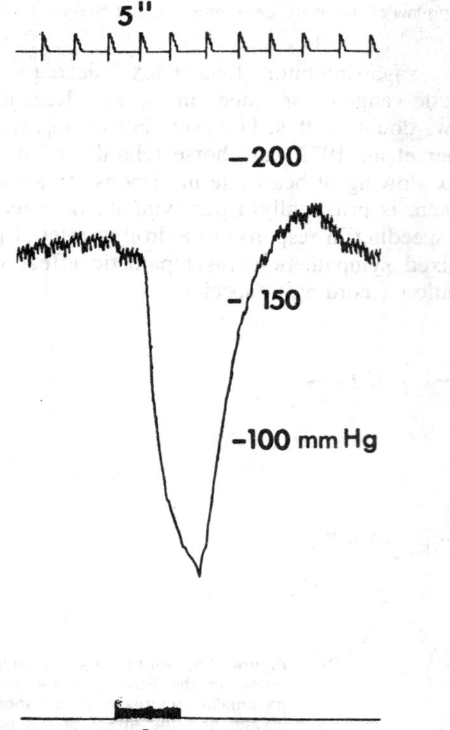

Figure 9.7. Effect of stimulation of the peripheral end of a vagus nerve (left) on the heart beat and blood pressure of a horse

vagi have on conduction of excitation from the atria to ventricles over the A-V node. It is most easily appreciated by examining an ECG during vagal stimulation (Fig. 9.6). Mild stimulation results in prolongation of the PR interval; that is, conduction over the A-V node is slowed. Moderate stimulation slows the ventricular rate more than the auricular rate. Some atrial contractions are not followed by ventricular contraction. This is due to failure of A-V conduction after some S-A node discharges. Strong stimulation may cause complete blocking of A-V nodal transmission. In this situation the atria beat at one rate and the ventricles at a slower rate. In complete A-V block there is not one pacemaker but two, one in the atria and a slower one in the ventricles. When the left and right vagi are similarly stimulated, the left may be found to have more effect upon the A-V node than the right. The difference is presumably due to the fact that the A-V node receives a larger percentage of inhibitory fibers via the left vagus nerve.

The vagi also have a direct depressing effect upon the strength of contraction of the atria, that is, a negative inotropic effect. The atrial myocardium, compared to the ventricular, has a dense parasympathetic supply. Vagal stimulation, by reducing the vigor of atrial contraction and hence ventricular filling, can indirectly diminish ventricular stroke volume. However, in normal situations ventricular filling is most dependent on atrial contraction at high heart rates when parasympathetic tone is low and sympathetic tone is high. At low heart rates the prolonged ventricular filling in diastole permits heterometric intrinsic regulation to work to increase ventricular stroke volume (Fig. 9.4). Vagal stimulation by way of its slowing effect on atrioventricular conduction can indirectly depress ventricular function in yet a different way. Depressed A-V conduction, by altering the synchronicity of atrial and ventricular contractions, tends to reduce ventricular filling and simultaneously reduce the efficiency of

Table 9.2. Changes in pulse rate with age

Animal	Age	Pulse rate
Horse	8–10 weeks	60–79
	6 months	60–71
	10–12 months	50–68
	2 years	44–65
	3 years	39–62
	4 years	36–59
	5 years	36–57
Ox	fetus	154–175
	newborn	118–148
	6–12 hours	115–136
	2–4 days	110–125
	8–14 days	105–115
	1 month	100–115
	3 months	90–105
	6 months	85–103
	1 year	80–98

Data from Ellinger as cited by R. Tigerstedt, *Textbook of Physiology*, New York, 1910

unidirectional emptying by interfering with closure of the A-V valves. The latter is most probable in heart block. The mammalian ventricles have a sparse parasympathetic innervation. Vagal stimulation can have direct but small negative inotropic effects.

The vagal inhibitory fibers are in a state of tone. When the parasympathetic fibers are blocked, the heart rate is increased markedly. The degree of vagal tone may be estimated by the injection of atropine which blocks parasympathetic effects or by cutting the vagi. The extent of resting vagal tone varies with age, with species, and with the physical fitness of the individual animal and with the environmental temperature. In young and aged animals vagal tone is less marked than in mature ones (Table 9.2). In the mature domestic rabbit, the control rate and rate following section of the vagi are respectively 205 and 321 beats per minute. In the wild hare the same rates were 64 and 264. In 30 aged draft horses, the injection of 30 mg of atropine sulfate increased the rate from 40–45 to 85–90 per minute. In the dog observed rates of 75–140 increased to 180–220 following section of the vagi. In unanesthetized dogs, observed for several weeks following cervical vagotomy, heart rates increased from an average of 75 to 160, began to decrease on the third day, and then slowly declined but continued to be elevated by an average of 50 beats per minute during the observation period. Vagal tone is an important reserve of immediate rapid cardiac acceleration.

Sympathetic-parasympathetic interactions

The actions of the two divisions of the autonomic nervous system on cardiac tissues are antagonistic (Higgins et al. 1973). Simultaneous stimulation of opposing divisions on cardiac effector cells results in algebraic summation of inhibition and excitation. Because parasympathetic cholinergic effects begin almost immediately following initiation of stimulation and are short lived, while sympathetic effects are delayed and more sustained, the initial, intermediate, and terminal effects of combined stimulation may vary. In the laboratory, combined stimulation is common since the vagus, its branches, and cardiac nerves often include both sympathetic and parasympathetic fibers. In controlled laboratory situations, equipotent concentrations of acetylcholine and norepinephrine at the receptor site of pacemaker cells always reveal a predominant, cholinergic, slowing effect. Under normal situations the cardiovascular reflexes operate so that when vagal tone is high, sympathetic tone is low and vice versa. Thus there is little opportunity for the liberation and presence of equipotent quantities of opposing neurotransmitters.

Interactions between the cholinergic and adrenergic cardiac nerves are further complicated by two additional observations: there are stores or depots of norepinephrine in cardiac postganglionic nerve fiber terminals; and acetylcholine and other cholinergic substances can effect the release of norepinephrine from such depots. Thus stimulation of cholinergic nerve fibers can be accompanied by the release of norepinephrine and norepinephrine-dependent effects.

Efferent nerves to the blood vessels

Vasoconstrictor fibers

All vasoconstrictor fibers are sympathetic nerves (Fig. 9.8). The neurohumoral mediator is norepinephrine. It causes the vessels to constrict by combining with excitatory α-adrenergic receptors of the smooth muscle fibers in the vessel walls. The order of potency of sympathetic α-receptors from high to low is: kidney, skin, mesentery, hepatic artery, and skeletal muscle. Sympathetic vasoconstrictor fiber control is high for skin, gastrointestinal tract, and kidney, moderate for skeletal muscle, and practically absent for brain, heart, and lung.

Other important characteristics in addition to distribution are: (1) they are all adrenergic fibers; (2) they all show some tone; (3) they are the only vasomotor fibers of the efferent limbs of the medullary pressor and depressor (aortic arch, carotid sinus) vasomotor reflexes (Fig. 9.9);

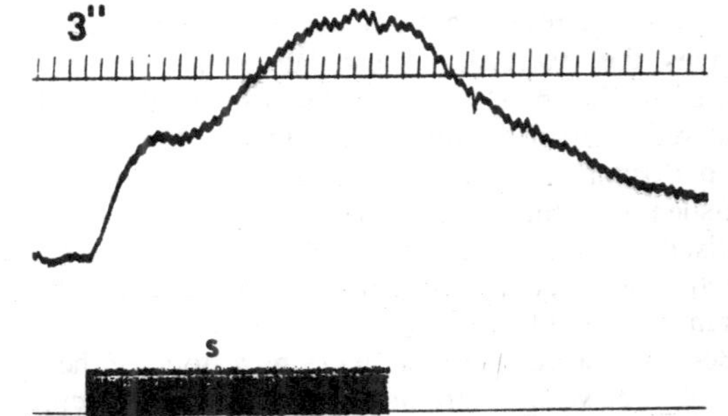

Figure 9.8. Effect of stimulation of the peripheral end of a splanchnic nerve on blood pressure (pig)

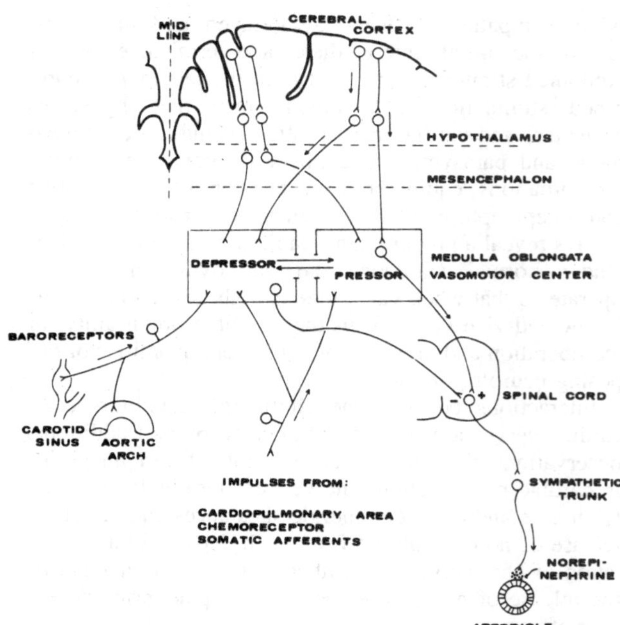

Figure 9.9. Afferent impulses to and efferent impulses from medullary vasomotor center. Impulses from medullary centers pass down the spinal cord to make excitatory (+) or inhibitory (−) synapse with preganglionic sympathetic fibers. Postganglionic vasoconstrictor fibers pass to the smooth muscle of arteries and veins.

(4) because of the above, they play a predominant role in the maintenance and regulation of total peripheral resistance and homeostasis; (5) they are distributed widely not only to resistance vessels but also to capacitance vessels; and (6) via the heat regulating center in the hypothalamus, they regulate heat loss from the skin.

The extrinsic sympathetic vasomotor fibers are important in baroreceptor-reflex blood pressure homeostasis and in cooperation with autoregulation in the distribution of blood flow in response to physical, thermal, and chemical (hypoxia) stress. Braunwald (1974) and Franklin et al. (1973) found during exercise increased vasoconstriction in renal and mesenteric vascular beds and decreased resistance in those of the limbs. Total systemic blood flow increased but because of selective resistance changes the exercising musculature flow is most increased while flow to other tissues remains relatively unaltered (dog) or is diminished (man). When the pumping performance of the heart and cardiac reserve is diminished or other circulatory reserve mechanisms are abolished (e.g. splenectomy and anemia in the canine), selective neurogenic vasoconstriction is even more important in circulatory adaptation to exercise.

Because vasoconstrictor fibers have tone, either vasodilatation or vasoconstriction may occur in a vascular bed entirely independent of any specific vasodilator nerve fiber supply. If the rate of transmission of nerve impulses over vasoconstrictor fibers decreases, vasodilatation occurs. If it increases, vasoconstriction occurs. Inhibition of sympathetic vasoconstrictor tone is the most common mechanism of reflex neurogenic vasodilatation. The medullary vasomotor reflexes which participate, along with the cardiac reflexes, in the maintenance of blood pressure, control peripheral resistance entirely over vasoconstrictor fibers. This would not be possible if they were not tonically active at normal blood pressure levels. The frequency of impulse transmission at normal resting blood pressure is 1–3 per second. Maximal vasoconstriction occurs when the frequency is about 8–10 per second.

Veins, or capacitance vessels, are also subject to control by vasoconstrictor fibers. Venules and veins have a sparser vasoconstrictor supply than arterioles and arteries. Veins are not supplied by specific vasodilator fibers. Venoconstriction is an important part of the central neurogenic cardiovascular control mechanism. When arterial blood pressure falls during hemorrhage, the direct reflex effects which operate to increase cardiac output, that is, increase in rate and contractility, are supplemented indirectly via a simultaneous reflex venoconstriction. Veins are reflexly reactive. Venoconstriction occurs upon exposure to cold, during emotional stress, muscular exercise, and posture changes. Venomotor reflex mechanisms are not as well defined as those involving resistance vessels. Stimulation of aortic and carotid baroreceptors and chemoreceptors produces only moderate and sometimes opposite responses to those observed in resistance vessels (Browse et al. 1966, 1967; Braunwald et al. 1963).

The neurohumoral mediator of vasoconstrictor fibers to veins is norepinephrine. This unites with a substance of the α-receptor site in the walls of the veins. The vascular smooth muscle fibers of veins do not seem to possess other adrenergic receptors, nor are they subject to local regulation. The capacitance function of larger veins is related to pressure homeostasis of the general circulation rather than perfusion of individual tissues.

Vasodilator fibers

Central baroreceptor or chemoreceptor reflex vasodilatation concerned with pressure homeostasis has nothing to do with *specific* vasodilator fibers. This is completely a matter of inhibition of the tonic activity of vasoconstrictor fibers. Specific vasodilator fibers are those whose stimulation increases the diameter of vessels. By distribution and function, they regulate local peripheral resistance of specific vascular beds and are concerned with regional blood flow. The three kinds of vasodilator fibers are sympathetic vasodilator fibers, parasympathetic vasodilator fibers, and dorsal root vasodilator fibers.

The characteristics of sympathetic vasodilator fibers are: (1) their distribution is limited to the arterioles of skeletal muscles; (2) while anatomically they are sympathetic, the chemical mediator is acetylcholine; (3) they do not possess tone; (4) they do not participate in carotid sinus and aortic arch vasomotor reflexes; (5) they are not activated by stimulation of the medullary depressor area; (6) they are a functionally distinct vasodilator mechanism; (7) while present in the dog, cat, and related species, they have not been demonstrated in rabbits, hares, seven primate species, and certain other mammals (Uvnäs 1966).

The receptor sites of smooth muscle to which the acetylcholine liberated by sympathetic vasodilator fibers attaches are termed *γ-receptor sites*. They are found only in association with the vascular smooth muscle of the vascular bed of skeletal muscle. Local intra-arterial injection of acetylcholine causes vasodilatation of these vessels of the skeletal muscle vascular bed. Atropine blocks both the vasodilator response to acetylcholine and stimulation of sympathetic vasodilator nerve fibers. Basal flow in muscle increases as much as fivefold following maximal stimulation. Since it may increase as much as twentyfold during exercise, such vasodilatation is less than that produced via other mechanisms.

Stimulation of vasodilatation via the sympathetic vasodilator fibers from electrodes placed in the medulla is abolished by decerebration. This is due to the degeneration of nerve fibers following their separation from the soma of the neuron and indicates that the vasodilator system originates cephalad to the medulla. The nerve cells are thought to be located in the mesencephalon and hypothalamus. Their fibers pass through the medulla without synapse. Since sympathetic vasodilator activity can be elicited by stimulation of the motor area of the cortex (dogs and cats), the hypothalamus, and mesencephalon, each of these areas probably participates in the integration of blood flow to skeletal muscle (Fig. 9.10).

Parasympathetic vasodilator fibers are distributed by both the cranial and sacral divisions of the parasympathetic nervous system to restricted areas. Tissues which receive parasympathetic vasodilator fibers include the tongue, salivary glands, urinary bladder, external genitalia, and large intestine. These fibers do not have tone and do not participate in the baroreceptor reflex regulation of blood pressure. They supply only arterioles.

The vasodilatation observed following stimulation of parasympathetic nerve fibers is not in all cases due to the direct action of the liberated acetylcholine on vascular smooth muscle. Stimulation of the parasympathetic nerves to the submaxillary salivary gland results in both an increase in the rate of secretion and vasodilatation. Atropine sulfate, which usually blocks the action of acetylcholine, will block the secretory but not the vasodilator effects. Acetylcholine has a direct uncomplicated stimulating action upon the gland cells but the vasodilator effect is due to a powerful vasodilator substance formed in the active tissues. The rate of formation of the vasodi-

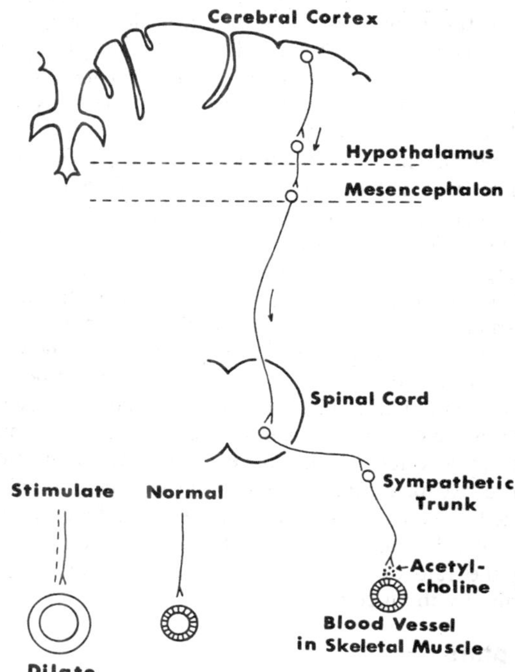

Figure 9.10. Sympathetic vasodilator fibers are controlled by a descending pathway within the CNS which begins in the cerebral cortex. The path includes relay stations at the level of the hypothalamus and mesencephalon.

lator substance depends upon the rate of tissue activity. In the case of the submaxillary salivary gland the vasodilator formed in the tissue fluid is a polypeptide called bradykinin. Bradykinins have a role in the production of functional vasodilatation in certain exocrine glands including the salivary, pancreatic, and sweat glands. They are rapidly degraded in the tissues and plasma to physiologically inactive fragments.

The parasympathetic vasodilator fibers to the external genitalia are cholinergic and the vasodilatation produced by their stimulation is abolished by atropine and augmented by physostigmine.

The peripheral branches of sensory nerves supplying pain receptors to the skin and mucous membranes may serve as vasodilator fibers. The fiber divides; one branch supplies a pain receptor, the other the vascular smooth muscle in cutaneous vascular bed. The nerve impulses generated by the pain receptor not only pass centrally to the spinal cord but also peripherally over the branch to a vasomotor ending of the cutaneous arteriole. The efferent and afferent pathways are formed by branches of a single nerve fiber. This is not a true reflex, as the five essential components of a true reflex are not present. The impulses passing backward to the vasomotor ending are called *antidromic vasodilator* impulses. The arc is called an *axon reflex*. The axon reflex is a special local vasomotor mechanism; it functions to increase the local blood supply following mechanical or chemical (inflammatory) stimulation of pain fibers of the skin and mucous membranes. Dorsal root dilator fibers are not activated reflexly from the CNS.

Nonneurogenic vasodilatation by circulating vasoactive chemicals is possible. The vascular beds of skeletal muscle, cardiac muscle, and to a lesser extent those of the mesenteric artery and spleen have a noninnervated β-adrenergic receptor. Isoproterenol is the most potent stimulator of the β-adrenergic receptor. Epinephrine in very small doses also stimulates the β-receptor. In the usual dose of epinephrine the β- or dilator response is masked by the predominant α-constrictor response. The effects of circulating adrenal catecholamines on vascular smooth muscle in healthy animals are minor compared to direct neural effects. They have little effect upon blood pressure except during circulatory crises such as shock. The medullary vasomotor center exerts its effect on blood vessels via the vasoconstrictor fibers rather than by regulating the rate of secretion of epinephrine and norepinephrine by the medulla.

Receptors

The cardiovascular reflexes are normally initiated by receptor organs located within the cardiovascular system itself. There are two kinds of intravascular receptors. The first and physiologically most important are sensitive to mechanical stimulation, that is, stretch or deformation. They are variously termed *pressoreceptors, baroreceptors,* or *mechanoreceptors*. The second class is sensitive to P_{O_2}, P_{CO_2}, and pH. These are called *chemoreceptors*. Chemoreceptors are of little significance for the homeostatic reflex regulation of pressure. They are more important for the control of the circulation under stressful conditions accompanied by hypoxia, e.g. hemorrhage and maximal physical exertion.

The baroreceptors are located at several sites. They are found in the systemic arteries, pulmonary arteries, central veins, and in the chambers of the heart. Those most important for the reflex regulation of blood pressure are the *systemic arterial baroreceptors* located in the *aortic* and *carotid arteries*. Mechanoreceptors are also located in the right and left atria, the pulmonary artery and veins, and right and left ventricular chambers, whose reflex functions are less well defined. They are not essential for reflex pressure homeostasis. They generate a variety of afferent or sensory impulse patterns associated with each heart beat in the cardiac cycle which functionally become more important in situations in which the filling and emptying of the heart are stressed (Kezdi et al. 1974, Hess et al. 1974, Chevalier et al. 1974, Uchida 1975, Lloyd 1975). They may reflexly affect heart rate, myocardial contractility, intravascular volume, or peripheral resistance in ways appropriate for sensing ventricular overload. They are particularly significant in the interpretation of cardiovascular responses accompanying diseases, e.g. cardiogenic shock, myocardial infarction, left ventricular failure, and arrhythmias.

Systemic arterial baroreceptors

The most important locations of arterial baroreceptors are the carotid sinus and the aortic arch. In man, dog, horse, and rabbit, the carotid sinus is a fusiform swelling of the internal carotid artery at its origin from the common carotid. In the horse there is a small bone, the intercarotid ossicle, in the adventia at the point of bifurcation of the common carotid. In ruminants, in the absence of an internal carotid artery, there is an occipital sinus at the origin of the occipital artery from the common carotid. There may be, as there are in the cat, baroreceptor areas or zones outside of the sinus and within the wall of the common carotid area between its origin and its bifurcation. In birds there is no carotid sinus; a segment of the wall of the common carotid artery just distal to the origin of the subclavian artery is its homologue. Systemic arterial baroreceptors are also found in the mesenteric arteries, but the role in pressure homeostasis is not well defined. In the cat, but not in the dog, occlusion of the mesenteric artery causes a marked increase in arterial blood pressure.

The stimulus for baroreceptor response is distortion or stretch of the vessel wall. Normally distortion results from the action of blood pressure, but the threshold value is not uniform. In the dog and cat, a pressure below 40 mm Hg is below threshold for the majority of the baroreceptors. Pressures in excess of 200 mm Hg do not provoke additional receptor discharge. Baroreceptors respond to the stretch produced by a steady pressure and to changing tension produced by a rise in pressure. During the upstroke of the pulse wave the firing of nerve impulses increases. The density of a barrage of impulses passing centrally over the sinus or aortic nerve increases rhythmically with each beat of the heart.

The impulses arriving at the medullary vasomotor reflex center excite the cardioinhibitory center and inhibit the vasoconstrictor center. When arterial pressure rises, the barrage of baroreceptor impulses increases in size and a depressor response occurs. Systemic vasodilatation and reduction in heart rate are established reflex responses to sinoaortic stretch receptor stimulation. When the pressure falls, the barrage decreases in size and a pressor response occurs.

The range of effective pressures just cited shows that there is always baroreceptor activity throughout the cardiac cycle in normal animals. There are no sinoaortic baroreceptors which respond to a fall in pressure. The reflex pressor response to a fall in pressure comes about because fewer baroreceptors are stimulated and fewer nerve impulses are transmitted to the reflex centers.

Chemoreceptors

The chemoreceptors of the carotid and aortic bodies are inspectors of the blood's chemical composition. They have their own blood supply and gram for gram have a larger blood flow (20 ml/g/min) than any other tissue in the body. They are stimulated by changes in P_{CO_2}, P_{O_2}, and pH. It is doubtful that changes in the chemical composition of the blood under physiological conditions are sufficiently large to exercise any reflex control of the circulation by the way of the chemoreceptors. They are primarily concerned with the homeostasis of blood gases by virtue of their participation in the reflex control of the respiration. Of the four types of anoxia (hypoxic, stagnant, histotoxic, and anemic) only anemic anoxia fails to induce chemoreceptor activity.

In hypoxia and hypercapnia the chemoreceptors exercise control over the cardiovascular system. The predominant chemoreceptor reflex response is vasoconstriction, increased peripheral resistance, and a rise in blood pressure.

Afferent nerves

The most important afferent nerves in the reflex regulation of the cardiovascular system are the aortic and sinus nerves. They are the only afferent limbs of cardiovascular reflexes whose surgical section results in a significant elevation of systemic arterial pressure in the normal animal. The aortic fibers are incorporated into the vagus in most animals.

Sinus and aortic nerves are purely sensory. They transmit nerve impulses from receptors in the carotid sinus and in aortic arch reflexogenic zones to reflex centers in the medulla. In the cat the sinus and aortic nerves contain about 700 and 450 individual nerve fibers respectively. The sinus nerve is a branch of the glossopharyngeal nerve. The aortic nerve is a branch of the vagus. In the rabbit the aortic and vagus nerves are separate in the neck.

Peripherally the aortic and sinus nerves do not terminate exclusively in baroreceptors. They also join the chemoreceptors in the aortic arch and carotid sinus areas. Chemoreceptors are grouped together in the aortic and carotid bodies. Chemoreceptor fibers may be distinguished from baroreceptor fibers by the uniformity of their discharge throughout the cardiac cycle and their response to changes in P_{O_2}, P_{CO_2}, pH, or the action of drugs (cyanide, lobeline) in the blood or perfusing medium. Baroreceptor fiber discharge increases simultaneously with each systolic rise in blood pressure.

Frequently the function of the aortic or sinus nerves in baroreceptor reflexes is demonstrated by isolating one or the other of the nerve trunks for stimulation while recording the blood pressure and/or heart rate. When the aortic nerve is stimulated, invariably the blood pressure falls because of diminished heart rate (cardiac output) and vasodilatation. The characteristic response of the aortic nerve to stimulation resulted in it being called the *aortic* or *cardiac depressor* nerve. Similar results follow stimulation of the sinus nerve.

The threshold for baroreceptors is far below that of normal arterial pressure. This means that there are, under normal circumstances, impulses continually passing to stimulate the medullary cardioinhibitory center and inhibit the vasoconstrictor center. The continual stream of impulses can be abolished by section of the aortic and sinus nerves or diminished by any procedure which lowers arterial pressure, such as hemorrhage, tilt from the horizontal to head-up position, or in the case of the carotid sinus, by clamping one or both of the common carotid arteries. The result of any of these procedures is a reflex rise in arterial blood pressure.

Medullary reflex centers

The medulla oblongata is essential for the maintenance and regulation of peripheral resistance. A maximal fall in blood pressure occurs only when the level of the medulla is reached during progressive transection of the brain from the cerebrum posteriorly. Both pressor and depressor reflexes can be elicited in animals after extirpation of the brain except the medulla. The medulla exerts a well-integrated control of the blood vessels and heart independently of higher nerve centers. Higher centers—the hypothalamus, mesencephalon, and cerebrum—exert their influence by associative neuronal circuits with medullary centers or by converging projections upon the spinal preganglionic cardiac and vasomotor sympathetic neurons.

The application of electrical stimuli to a rather extensive area in the lateral reticular formation of the medulla oblongata on either side of the midline causes an increase in blood pressure by increasing total peripheral resistance and cardiac output (increase rate and vigor of contraction). This is the *pressor* area. It consists of both a vasoconstrictor center and a cardiostimulator (cardioaccelerator) center. The vasoconstrictor center is continuously discharging efferent impulses. The cardiostimulatory center is relatively quiescent. The vasoconstrictor centers have tone; the cardiostimulator centers have very little tone.

In the medial and more posterior area of the medulla, electrical stimuli cause vasodilatation and decrease in the heart rate. This is the *depressor* area of the medulla. The vasodilatation is produced by inhibition of vasoconstrictor tone and not by activation of specific vasodilator fibers. Only in this sense can the depressor area be considered to include a vasodilator center. The inhibition of vasoconstriction is effected via reciprocal inhibitory circuits between the pressor and depressor areas and by convergence of both inhibitory (from the depressor area) and excitatory (from the pressor area) fibers upon the preganglionic sympathetic neurons in the spinal cord. The cardioinhibitory center slows the heart by increasing vagal tone.

The medullary areas utilize two efferent pathways for controlling heart action—sympathetic and parasympathetic. Regulation of blood vessels is accomplished over a single system of efferent pathways, the vasoconstrictor fibers.

Tonic activity is an important physiological feature of two medullary cardiovascular centers. Tone is manifested by the vasoconstrictor center and the cardioinhibitory center.

If by tone one means the resting or basal sustained degree of discharge by the centers, then the most important factors for it are the baroreceptor impulses from the carotid sinus and aortic arch and the P_{CO_2} of the blood. Section of the two sinus and two aortic nerves or reduction of carotid sinus or aortic pressure, by withdrawing stimulation from the cardioinhibitory center, will result in as much acceleration of the heart as will section of the vagus nerves themselves. Stimulation of the sinus and aortic nerves has the opposite effect. Similarly, the same procedures by release of the vasoconstrictor area from inhibitory baroreceptor impulses result in vasoconstriction and a rise in blood pressure. The vasomotor center is especially sensitive to the P_{CO_2} in the surrounding tissue fluid. As far as central vasomotor effects are concerned, carbon dioxide is a strong vasoconstrictor agent. A normal P_{CO_2} is necessary for preservation of the normal tone of the pressor area. If the P_{CO_2} is raised or lowered, parallel changes in the sympathetic vasoconstrictor impulse traffic occur.

The dynamic changes in cardiac and vasomotor function depend upon the normal tone of the medullary centers. The inflow of impulses from peripheral receptors in the heart, lungs, and venae cavae, from other visceral and somatic pain receptors, from the adjacent respiratory, and from the higher centers contributes to the increase or decrease of the efferent flow of impulses from the vasomotor and cardiac centers over the cardiac and vasomotor nerves.

Sinus arrhythmia is an example of the influence adjacent medullary centers may have on each other. In the resting healthy dog the heart rate increases with inspiration and decreases with expiration. This is due to the influence of the medullary inspiratory center on the cardioinhibitory center. The respiratory induced changes in the tone of the cardioinhibitory center are accompanied by a rhythmic waxing and waning in its efferent outflow over the vagal nerves to the heart. It is abolished by vagal nerve section but not by chemical blockade of the β-adrenergic fibers of the sympathetic nerves to the heart. Figure 9.11 illustrates that sinus arrhythmia is not dependent upon the stimulation of peripheral receptors by respiratory movements, as it persists following their arrest. It is a centrally induced change.

Summary of baroreceptor reflexes

The carotid sinus and baroreceptor cardiovascular reflexes are the most important neural mechanisms by which the normal level of the systemic arterial blood pressure is maintained. When arterial pressure falls, events occur that tend to increase both cardiac output and peripheral resistance. Cardiac output is favored by (1) increase in heart rate (decrease in inhibitory and increase in augmentor tone), (2) increased ventricular contractility (increased sympathetic tone), and (3) increased ventricular filling and end-diastolic pressure via venoconstriction and increased vigor of atrial contraction (increased sympathetic tone). Peripheral resistance is increased by increased sympathetic tone to the smooth muscle in arteries and arterioles. A rise in pressure is followed by the opposite sequence of events.

Normally both cardiac and vasomotor changes occur

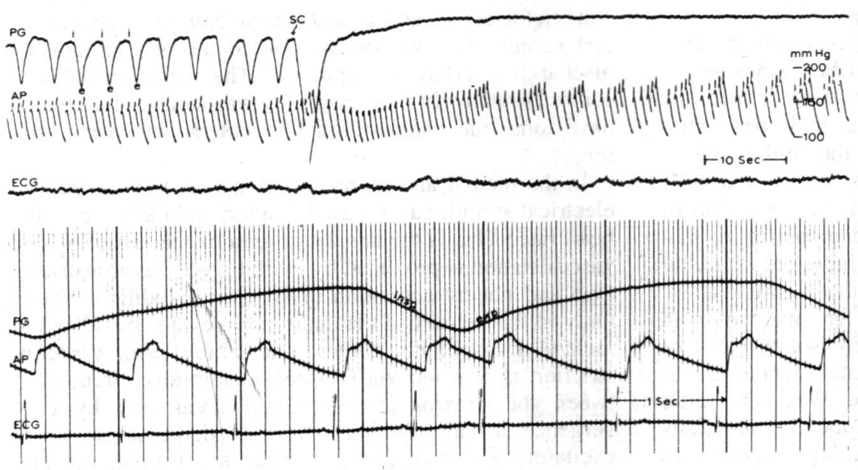

Figure 9.11. Sinus arrhythmia in the dog. Beginnings of inspiration and expiration are labeled i and e respectively. Respiratory movements arrested with succinylcholine at arrow (SC). In the upper trace sinus arrhythmia-induced blood pressure fluctuations occur regularly before arrest of respiratory movements, cease for 16 seconds following arrest, and return to a pre-arrest rate while respiratory movements are absent. (From Hamlin, Smith, and Smetzer 1966, *Am. J. Physiol.* 210:321–28.)

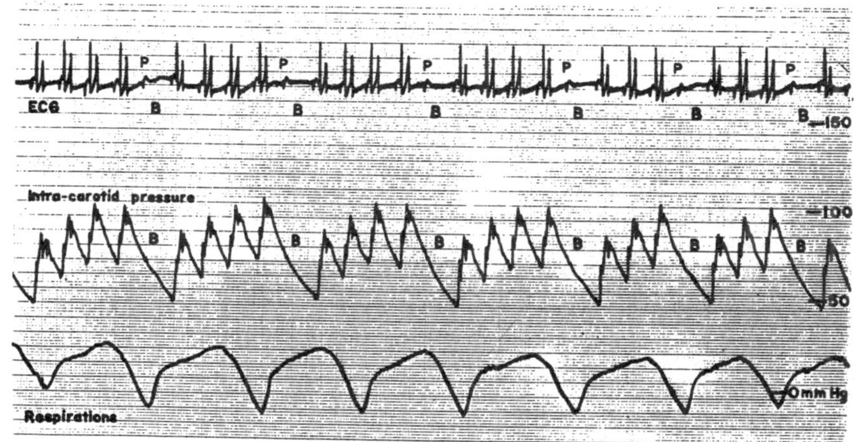

Figure 9.12. Second-degree A-V block in a horse. P, activation of the atria; B, blocked ventricular complexes in the ECG and missing pressure pulses in the blood pressure record.

nearly simultaneously in response to baroreceptor stimulation. Rapid compensatory cardiac responses to circulatory stresses are mediated via the vagal mechanism. Changes in heart rate occur within a second following the onset of vagal stimulation. The interval for sympathetic induced cardiac and vasomotor fibers is 15–20 seconds. Clamping of both common carotid arteries in the dog is followed by a pressor response both before and after cutting the vagi. Similarly, a fall in pressure is reflexly induced by stimulation of the central end of one cut vagus nerve when both vagi were previously cut. In the chronically totally sympathectomized dog, neither clamping of the common carotid arteries nor section of both the aortic and sinus nerves is followed by a pressor response. The relative importance of the cardiac and vasomotor effects for arterial pressure homeostasis varies with the species.

Second-degree heart block in the horse is a modified sinus arrhythmia in which the ventricular rate is controlled not only by a change in the rate of sinus node discharge, but also by the actual dropping of a ventricular beat. Since atropine restores a normal sinus rhythm, the rhythmic blocking of transmission over the A-V node is a vagal effect. The blocked P waves follow a steplike rise in arterial blood pressure (Fig. 9.12). No precise correlation between the phases of respiration and the blocked P waves is evident, which suggests that this block is a baroreceptor reflex.

Bainbridge and other minor baroreceptor reflexes

If in an anesthetized animal the venous return to the heart is suddenly increased, the heart rate increases (Bainbridge reflex). This occurs provided the control rate is slow, that is, if the vagal tone is high. The acceleration is presumably due to a reflex reduction in vagal tone, as it can be abolished by vagal section. When the control rate is high and vagal tone is already low, the reflex does not occur. Both afferent and efferent vagal fibers play a part in the Bainbridge reflex.

This reflex is difficult to demonstrate. Neither the nature of the stimulus nor the location of the specific receptors has been identified. Investigators have not been able to identify afferent vagal pathways from either the lungs or the heart whose stimulation results in tachycardia. However, weak stimulation of the central end of the vagus or of its pulmonary branches does sometimes produce cardiac acceleration. In unanesthetized dogs the Bainbridge reflex is readily demonstrable.

There are a number of minor depressor baroreceptor reflexes originating from the chambers of the heart and pulmonary arteries and veins which are important in disease, for example in hypotension (vasodilatation) and bradycardia due to stimulation of stretch receptors in the left atrium and ventricle, hypotension and bradycardia following a rise in pulmonary arterial pressure, and hypotension and bradycardia following the injection of veratrine into the coronary arteries or selectively increasing the pressure in the left ventricle (Bezold-Jarisch reflex). The baroreceptors located in the low pressure veins and in the heart chamber appear mainly to induce reflex cardioinhibition (vagal activation) and vasodilatation (vasoconstrictor inhibition). Table 9.3 summarizes baroreceptor and chemoreceptor reflexes. (The opposite response occurs when the change is in the opposite direction.)

Summary of chemoreceptor reflexes

In the normal central control of blood pressure the principal action of carbon dioxide is to directly stimulate the vasomotor center in the medulla. Peripherally, both CO_2 and O_2 participate in metabolic autoregulation. An increase in tissue P_{CO_2} has a vasodilative effect. Similarly a low P_{O_2}, either directly or more likely via a metabolite produced in the presence of a low tissue P_{O_2}, results in a local vasodilatation. Changes in the direction

Table 9.3. Cardiovascular reflexes

	Receptor site	Change	Afferent nerve(s)	Efferent nerve(s)	Reflex responses	
	Carotid bodies	Hypoxia	Sinus	Vagus	Slowing	
	Left atrium, rt. and left ventricles	Pressure↑	Vagus	Vagus	Slowing	Minor baroreceptor reflexes Systemic hypotension
Heart	Left ventricle	Pressure↑	Vagus	Vagus	Slowing	
	Rt. atrium	Pressure↑	Vagus	Vagus	Acceleration	Bainbridge reflex
	Aortic arch	Pressure↑	Aortic nerve	Vagus	Slowing	
	Carotid sinus	Pressure↑	Sinus nerve	Vagus	Slowing	Principal buffer reflexes for pressure homeostasis
Arteries and arterioles	Aortic arch	Pressure↑	Aortic nerve	Sympathetics	Dilatation	
	Carotid sinus	Pressure↑	Sinus nerve	Sympathetics	Dilatation	
	Aortic and carotid bodies	$Po_2\downarrow pH\downarrow Pco_2\uparrow$	Sinus and aortic nerves	Sympathetics	Constriction	
Venules and veins	Aortic arch	Pressure↓	Aortic nerve	Sympathetics	Constriction	Venous component of sinoaortic baroreceptor response to hypotension
	Carotid sinus	Pressure↓	Sinus nerve	Sympathetics	Constriction	

of an increase in Po_2 restore normal tone as the smooth muscle again regains its original length. These effects occur independently of vasomotor nerves.

Only when severe hypoxia, hypercapnia, or acidosis exists or is threatened do chemoreceptor reflexes significantly participate in the control of the cardiovascular system. When only the chemoreceptors are stimulated via hypoxia and hypercapnia the responses are vasoconstriction, increased peripheral resistance, a rise in blood pressure, and vagal slowing of the heart.

Under normal conditions, chemoreceptors do not act alone in the presence of hypoxia or hypercapnia. Arterial baroreceptors, central chemoreceptors, epinephrine from the adrenal medulla, receptors from the lung stimulated by hyperventilation, and perhaps others have input to the neural control of the circulation. The characteristic responses to systemic hypoxia are tachycardia, increased ventricular contractility, increased cardiac output, vasoconstriction, increased total peripheral resistance, and a rise in blood pressure. In contrast to mammals, systemic hypoxia in chickens results in a progressive fall in blood pressure (Sturkie 1970).

Other afferent pathways

Electrical stimulation of the central end of almost any visceral or somatic afferent nerve fiber, in addition to the aortic and sinus nerves, may cause a reflex pressor or depressor response. In the pressor response both cardiac augmentation (increase in rate and contractility) and vasoconstriction usually contribute to the elevation of blood pressure. In the depressor response diminished cardiac output and vasodilatation go hand in hand. The efferent nerves, sympathetics and parasympathetics to the heart and sympathetics to the vessels, are the same as those involved in the sinus and aortic baroreceptor and chemoreceptor responses. The absence of response—or its feebleness—of the cardiovascular system to afferent stimulation in the sympathectomized animal demonstrates the importance of sympathetic efferent fibers for both pressor and depressor reflexes.

HIGHER CENTERS AND CARDIOVASCULAR CONTROL

Reflex cardiovascular changes elicited by stimulation of baroreceptors and chemoreceptors are mediated at the level of the medulla. However, these medullary reflexes are subject to modification emanating from various brain areas (Hilton 1966, Eferakeya and Buñag 1974, Kumada et al. 1975, Miller 1969). Some observed differences in blood pressure and heart rate in various species can be attributed to facilitatory and inhibitory influences exercised by higher nerve centers upon medullary and spinal neurons.

The preganglionic autonomic fibers in the brain stem (vagal) and spinal cord (sympathetic and parasympathetic fibers) by which all central neurogenic control mechanisms exert their influence can be both stimulated and inhibited by the cerebrum and hypothalamus. They and the medullary centers converge upon the same final common paths.

Hypothalamus

An important relationship between the hypothalamus and the response of the heart and blood vessels during normal activity is evident. In departures from the basal state the central cardiovascular control mechanisms change so as to include not only the primary centers in the medulla but also those in the cerebrum and hypothalamus. The medullary cardiovascular areas and supramedullary sites probably act as lower and higher links in the same chain.

Some examples of the evidence for participation by the hypothalamus in the integration of cardiovascular responses are: (1) bradycardia, tachycardia, and other arrhythmias following hypothalamic stimulation; (2) pressor and depressor responses after the application of stimuli to hypothalamic nuclei; (3) changes in the magnitude and sign of baroreceptor and chemoreceptor reflexes following inactivation of selected areas of the hypothalamus; (4) distortion of the normal changes in blood pressure and heart rate accompanying eating and exercise after experimental hypothalamic lesions in the dog; and (5) exerciselike cardiovascular responses to the stimulation of discrete areas in the hypothalamus.

Cerebrum

Stimulation of motor, frontal, and temporal areas of the cerebral cortex may be followed by pressor, depressor, accelerator, or inhibitory responses. Such responses include: (1) a rise in cardiac output in dogs upon excitement which is comparable to that accompanying moderate physical exercise; (2) vasodilatation via sympathetic vasodilator fibers following stimulation of the cerebral cortex in dogs and cats; (3) the disappearance of sinus arrhythmia in the dog and second-degree heart block in the horse which accompanies disturbing environmental stimuli; (4) the tachycardia which appears in the cow upon arrival of investigators in an otherwise neutral environment; and (5) the hypotension, bradycardia, and vasodilatation which sometimes occurs in some people at the sight of blood. The influence of the cerebrum on the heart rate was observed by the authors while recording ECG's in horses. A telemetering system showed that the heart rate in an animal trained for racing and quietly standing in the stall increased to nearly the same extent in response to sound signals broadcast over the public address system at the racetrack as it did in response to actual racing. The animal had apparently developed a conditioned reflex which caused the cardiac acceleration. Operant conditioning of heart rate has been accomplished in man and animals.

REFERENCES

Armour, P.A., Randall, W.C., and Sinha, S. 1975. Localized myocardial responses to stimulation of small cardiac branches of the vagus. *Am. J. Physiol.* 228:141–47.

Black, J.W., and Prichard, B.N.C. 1973. Activation and blockade of β adrenoceptors in common cardiac disorders. *Brit. Med. Bull.* 29:163–67.

Bleecker, E.R., and Engel, B.T. 1973. A comparison of the cardiovascular responses to stimulation of the aortic and carotid sinus nerves of the dog. *Proc. Soc. Exp. Biol. Med.* 144:404–11.

Braunwald, E. 1974. Regulation of the circulation. *New Eng. J. Med.* 290:1124–29, 1420–25.

Braunwald, E., Ross, J., Jr., Kahler, R.L., Graffney, T.E., Goldbatt, A., and Mason, D.T. 1963. Reflex control of the systemic venous bed. *Circ. Res.* 12:539–50.

Brody, M.J., and Kadowitz, P.J. 1974. Prostaglandins as modulators of the automatic nervous system. *Fed. Proc.* 30:48–60.

Bronk, D.W., Pitts, R.F., and Larrabee, M.G. 1940. Role of hypothalamus in cardiovascular regulation. In *The Hypothalamus and Central Levels of Autonomic Function.* Williams & Wilkins, Baltimore. Pp. 323–41.

Browse, N.L., Donald, D.E., and Shepherd, J.T. 1966. Role of the veins in the carotid sinus reflex. *Am. J. Physiol.* 210:1424–34.

Browse, N.L., Shepherd, J.T., and Donald, D.E. 1967. Differences in response of veins and resistance vessels in the limb to same stimulus. *Am. J. Physiol.* 211:1241–47.

Chevalier, P.A., Weber, K.C., Lyons, G.W., Nicoloff, D.M., and Fox, I.J. 1974. Hemodynamic changes from stimulation of left ventricular baroreceptors. *Am. J. Physiol.* 227:719–28.

Davis, J.D., and Freeman, R.H. 1976. Mechanisms regulating renin release. *Physiol. Rev.* 56:1–56.

Edkberg, D.L., Drabinsky, M., and Braunwald, E. 1971. Defective cardiac parasympathetic control in patients with heart disease. *New Eng. J. Med.* 285:877–83.

Eferakeya, A., and Buñag, R.D. 1974. Adrenomedullary responses during posterior hypothalamic stimulation. *Am. J. Physiol.* 227:114–18.

Franklin, D., Vatner, S.F., Higgins, C.B., Patrick, T., Kemper, W.S., and Van Citters, R.L. 1973. Measurement and radiotelemetry of cardiovascular variables in conscious animals: Techniques and applications. In L.T. Harmison, ed., *Research in Animal Medicine.* HEW Pub. no. 72-333 (NIH), Washington. Pp. 1119–33.

Freundlich, J.J., Detweiler, D.K., and Hance, H.E. 1972. Indirect blood pressure determination by the ultrasonic doppler technique in dogs. *Current Therapeutic Res.* 14:73–80.

Garner, H.E., Coffman, J.R., Hahn, A.W., and Hartley, J. 1972. Indirect blood pressure measurement in the horse. *Am. Ass. Equine Pract. Proc.* Pp. 343–40.

Geddes, L.A., Hoff, H.E., and McCrady, J.D. 1965. Some aspects of cardiovascular physiology in the horse. *Cardiovascular Res. Ctr. Bull.* 3:80–96.

Goldberg, L.I. 1974. Dopamine: Clinical uses of an endogenous catecholamine. *New Eng. J. Med.* 291:707–10.

Hahn, A.W., Garner, H.E., Coffman, J.R., and Saunders, C.W. 1973. Indirect measurement of arterial blood pressure in the laboratory pony. *Lab. Anim. Sci.* 23:889–93.

Hamlin, R.L., Kepinger, W.L., Gilpin, K.W., and Smith, C.R. 1972. Autonomic control of the heart rate in the horse. *Am. J. Physiol.* 222:976–78.

Hamlin, R.L., Smith, C.R., and Smetzer, D.L. 1966. Sinus arrhythmia in the dog. *Am. J. Physiol.* 210:321–28.

Hess, G.L., Zuperku, E.J., Coon, R.L., and Kampine, J.P. 1974. Sympathetic afferent nerve activity of left ventricular origin. *Am. J. Physiol.* 227:543–46.

Higgins, C.B., Vatner, S.F., and Braunwald, E. 1973. Parasympathetic control of the heart. *Pharm. Rev.* 25:119–55.

Hilton, S.M. 1966. Hypothalamic regulation of the cardiovascular system. *Brit. Med. Bull.* 22:243–48.

Horton, E.W. 1973. Prostaglandins at adrenergic nerve-endings. *Brit. Med. Bull.* 29:148–51.

Kendrick, J.E., and Matson, G.L. 1973. A comparison of the cardiovascular responses to stimulation of the aortic and carotid sinus nerves of the dog. *Proc. Soc. Exp. Biol. Med.* 144:404–11.

Kent, K.M., and Cooper, T. 1974. The denervated heart: A model for studying autonomic control of the heart. *New Eng. J. Med.* 291:1017–21.

Kent, K.M., Epstein, S.E., Cooper, T., and Jacobowitz, D.M. 1974. Cholinergic innervation of the canine and human ventricular conducting system: Anatomic and electrophysiologic correlations. *Circulation* 50:948–55.

Kezdi, P., Kordenat, R.K., and Misra, S.N. 1974. Reflex inhibitory effects of vagal afferents in experimental myocardial infarction. *Am. J. Cardiol.* 33:853–60.

Kirchheim, H.R. 1976. Systemic arterial baroreceptor reflexes. *Physiol. Rev.* 56:100–176.

Kumada, M., Nogami, K. and Sagawa, K. 1975. Modulation of carotid sinus baroreceptor reflex by sciatic nerve stimulation. *Am. J. Physiol.* 228:1535–40.

Lloyd, T.C. 1975. Cardiopulmonary baroreflexes: Effects of staircase, ramp, and square-wave stimulation. *Am. J. Physiol.* 228:470–76.

Melmon, K.L. 1966. Kinins in medicine: Present and future. *Physiol. Pharmac. Physicians* 1(6):1–6.

Miller, M.E. 1969. Learning of visceral and glandular responses. *Science* 163:434–45.

Pipkin, F.B., Kilpatrick, S.M., Lumbers, E.R., and Mott, J.C. 1974. Renin and angiotensin-like levels in foetal, newborn, and adult sheep. *J. Physiol.* 241:575–88.

Powis, D.A. 1974. Comparison of the effects of stimulation of the sympathetic vasomotor nerves and adrenal medullary nerves on hind limb blood vessels of the rabbit. *J. Physiol.* 240:135–51.

Randall, W.C., and Armour, J.A. 1974. Complex cardiovascular responses to vagosympathetic stimulation. *Proc. Soc. Exp. Biol. Med.* 145:493–99.

Randall, W.C., Armour, J.A., Geis, P.W., and Lippincott, D.B. 1972. Regional cardiac distribution of sympathetic nerves. *Fed. Proc.* 31:1199–1208.

Sapirstein, L.A. 1958. Regional blood flow by the fractional distribution of indicator. *Am. J. Physiol.* 193:161–68.

Scher, A.M., Ohm, W.W., Baumgarner, J., Boynton, R., and Young, A.C. 1972. Sympathetic and parasympathetic control of heart rate in the dog, baboon, and man. *Fed. Proc.* 31:1219–25.

Stinson, E.B., Rahmoeller, G., Techlenberg, P.L., Colvin, S.B., Jones, K.W., and Pierce, J.E. 1973. Left ventricular hemodynamic and dimensional responses to treadmill exercises in normal and cardiac denervated dogs. In L.T. Harmison, ed., *Research in Animal Medicine*. HEW Pub. 72-333 (NIH), Washington. Pp. 429–35.

Sturkie, P.D. 1970. Circulation in Aves. *Fed. Proc.* 29:1674–79.

Uchida, Y. 1975. Afferent sympathetic nerve fibers with mechanoreceptors in the right heart. *Am. J. Physiol.* 228:223–30.

Uvnás, B. 1966. Cholinergic vasodilator nerves. *Fed. Proc.* 25:1618–22.

Vatner, S.F., and Braunwald, E. 1975. Cardiovascular control mechanisms in the conscious state. *New Eng. J. Med.* 293:970–76.

Zussman, R.M., Snyder, J.J., Cline, A., Caldwell, B.V., and Speroff, L. 1974. Antihypertensive function of a renal-cell carcinoma: Evidence for a prostaglandin-A–secreting tumor. *New Eng. J. Med.* 290:843–45.

CHAPTER 10

Microcirculation and Lymph

by C. Roger Smith and Robert L. Hamlin

MICROCIRCULATION

Living cells are constantly extracting from and adding to the tissue fluid which is their environment. But since the ratio of environmental volume to cellular volume is small, the effects of the activity of cells on their environment are normally counteracted by exchanges between interstitial fluid and capillary blood. The blood movement expands a rather limited cellular environment to one whose functional volume provides an almost inexhaustible supply of necessary metabolic substances and greatly dilutes potentially toxic metabolic end products.

The metabolic rate of cells varies with their activity. Since the composition of their environment remains constant, the exchange between it and the blood in capillaries must vary in a parallel fashion. The adjustments in exchange are principally a function of changes in the numbers of capillaries through which blood flows, which means a change in diffusion surface and capillary blood volume, and changes in the rate of blood movement through capillaries.

Anatomy

Individual capillaries

The explanation of the strength of capillaries lies in their extremely small radii. Laplace's equation, $T = P \times r$ (see Chapter 9), shows how such thin-walled structures can support pressure of 30 to 40 mm Hg without rupture. Although capillary pressure is one fifth to one third that of aortic pressure, capillary wall tension is approximately 10,000 times smaller.

The inner surface of the capillary consists principally of the cell membranes of the endothelial cells. The area between the cell boundaries comprises approximately 1 percent of the total internal surface area. Gaps between cells are filled by polysaccharide material which presumably does not hinder the passage of small molecules but acts as a filter and obstructs the passage of macromolecules. The endothelial cells rest upon a thin basement membrane, a fibrillar structure which acts as framework for the endothelial layer and, at least where complete, contributes to permeability. It blends continuously into the homogeneous ground substance of the tissues.

Microcirculatory bed

The term *microcirculation* refers to the whole system of small vessels less than 100 μ in diameter. Taken in order from arterial to venous side they are: arteriole, terminal arteriole, metarteriole, capillary, and venule (Fig. 10.1).

A varying fraction of total blood flow subserves nutrient and nonnutrient functions. A portion of the flow may bypass circulation through: (1) arteriovenous (A-V) capillaries or preferential channels which are a part of the intricate microcirculatory bed (nutrient flow), and (2) A-V shunts which are larger and bypass from arterioles to venules (nonnutrient flow).

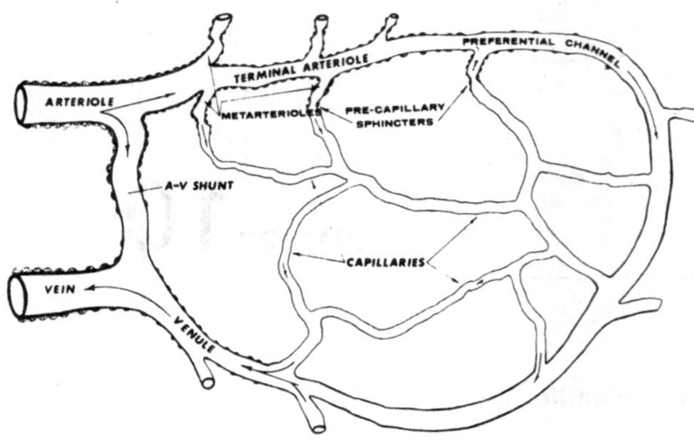

Figure 10.1. Terminal vascular bed

Arterioles have a single layer of circular smooth muscle and may have a diameter no larger than an erythrocyte. They communicate with one another freely. An arcuate pattern is formed by adjacent and anastomosing arterioles, the capillaries in the roughly circular area are mutually supplied from a circumscribing ring of arterioles. The arrangement preserves uniformity of flow and pressure in capillaries in spite of independent vasomotion by individual terminal vessels.

Terminal arterioles are the first extensions of the arterioles and are distinguished from them by less regular smooth muscle. Metarterioles are branches of the terminal arterioles, the least muscular of the precapillary vessels. They branch to form the nonmuscular capillaries. At the root of the branches a single elongate muscle cell coils around the origin of the capillary to form the precapillary sphincter. (These are the final contractile elements for regulating capillary flow.) Capillaries become venules at the site of the first appearance of muscle on the postcapillary vessel. Venules so formed are almost twice the size of capillaries and they in turn converge to form venules three times the size of the arterioles. The small veins formed from venules are twice as numerous and three times as large as small arteries. A-V capillaries (preferential channels) are formed by nonmuscular extensions of the metarterioles. They act as direct arterial-venous bridges, with only limited blood distribution through nutrient capillaries which arise from them.

Pressure and flow

Capillary blood pressure

Accurate measurements of capillary blood pressure have been made in a relatively few tissues by a micropipette technique. The mean blood pressure for systemic capillaries is about 25–30 mm Hg. Capillary pressure is normally quite variable.

Blood pressure decreases from the arterial to the venous end of the capillary. In systemic capillaries the respective pressures are 35 and 15 mm Hg. This pressure gradient is higher per unit length than in any other segment of the vascular system except for the arterioles. The gradient is an important determinant not only for capillary flow but also for exchange of fluid between the capillary and the tissue fluid (Gore and Bohlen 1975). Pulse pressures are damped out in the more proximal segments of the arterial system.

Mean capillary pressure is determined by the volume of blood flow, since the capillary walls have no smooth muscle and thus are relatively inelastic. Volume will vary if changes occur in the relationship between the resistance to flow in vessels upstream and downstream from the capillary: the *ratio* of postcapillary to precapillary resistance. The first value is small since the difference between normal mean capillary pressure (25 mm Hg) and mean peripheral venous pressure (6) is small (19). However, the second value is much larger because of the difference between the mean arterial pressure (100) and mean capillary pressure (25). Thus a change in postcapillary resistance has a much larger effect upon capillary pressure than the same change in precapillary resistance vessels (5–10 times).

Normally an autoregulatory mechanism stabilizes capillary blood pressure and flow by altering post- and precapillary resistance simultaneouly and thus maintaining a normal ratio. When venous resistance to capillary outflow increases, capillary pressure rises. The precapillary sphincter and arteriolar smooth muscle respond by active contraction of the inflow vessels, and as a result capillary pressure returns toward normal. This mechanism may be interrupted by potent vasoactive substances such as histamine or bradykinin.

Capillary blood flow

The total blood flow through the systemic capillary bed is usually equal to the cardiac output. In addition to being slow, capillary flow is remarkably nonuniform. Primary control of flow through and between individual capillaries resides in the spontaneous contractile activity of precapillary sphincters. They guard the entrances into the capillary network, and their contractions vary widely in both frequency and duration. Once blood has entered the capillaries, its flow is determined by various resistances within the complex anastomotic network. Transient pressure changes in venules draining some capillaries and variations in arterial pressure due to the activity of precapillary sphincters cause flow in capillaries to change, to reverse direction, or to bypass some routes.

Other factors may contribute to capillary flow. There is some intermittency due to variations in extramural pressure on thin-walled vessels during muscular contraction (e.g. in the heart). Occasional obstruction by leukocytes due to the ratio of capillary to leukocyte diameter occurs. Red cells, on the other hand, are deformed in passing through the small capillary lumen. Apparently such deformation is not injurious. Red cells have been observed to pass through artificial pores less than one half the size of their own diameters without incurring injury. Passing through the capillaries, the cells are oriented one after another single file with a volume of plasma between each. This has been referred to as bolus flow (Barton 1965).

There are fewer erythrocytes per 100 ml volume of blood in the capillaries than in the larger vessels feeding and draining them; that is, the packed cell volume is lower (see Chapter 2). There is a relative excess of plasma. Perhaps the remaining cells flow through A-V shunts. In addition the erythrocytes may move faster through the capillaries than does the plasma.

Cell aggregation has been described in various infections, shock, and during extracorporeal circulation of blood. It leads to trapping of cells in the microcirculation (a kind of anemia), stasis of flow in ordinary capillaries, and shunting of flow through A-V anastomoses. It is reversed by saline solutions and solutions of low molecular-weight dextrans.

Regulation of flow

Normally the pressure in the aorta and large arteries supplying the peripheral circulation is maintained at a relatively constant level. A series of reflexes maintain perfusion pressure homeostasis (see Chapter 9). In addition, peripheral vascular beds possess intrinsic control mechanisms. For example, exercise results in vasodilatation within the exercising muscles, and secretion of saliva is accompanied by increase in blood flow to the salivary glands. When functional activity subsides, flow diminishes. Even if the pressure in the large arteries transiently rises or falls, local mechanisms preserve the normal rate of flow. Blood flow in peripheral vascular beds is largely self regulated.

Tone

When a structure is said to have *tone,* it means that it is functioning in a continual, sustained way. A nerve fiber continually conducting nerve impulses possesses tone. A precapillary sphincter muscle contracting in a regular rhythmic fashion is in tone. An arteriole in whose walls a fraction of the total population of smooth muscle fibers are continually contracting, either in a tetanic or phasic manner, has tone. When all or nearly all the muscle fibers are contracting simultaneously and maximally, tone is very high. When only a few are actively contracting tone is low. In the microcirculatory bed, tone is best developed in the more muscular precapillary vessels.

The tone of peripheral vessels is variable, not only in the same vascular bed but also from bed to bed. The degree of tone can be estimated by comparing the average blood flow through a tissue to that occurring when the vessels are maximally dilated. The degree of tone in the microcirculation of a tissue at rest is a measure of its circulatory reserve. Release of vascular tone or the act of vasodilatation as a tissue moves from a state of relative rest to one of greater activity is a means of balancing variations in the tissue demands for metabolic exchanges and the amount of blood flow.

Because vascular and other smooth muscle has the inherent property of automaticity, and also because it may be innervated by vasoconstrictor nerve fibers, vascular tone can be myogenic in origin, neural, or both. Some or most of vascular tone persists following surgical or chemical interruption of all efferent vasomotor fibers and in the absence of circulating vasoactive chemicals. Tone of blood vessels due to myogenic automatic contractility is called *basal tone*. The magnitude of basal tone is inversely related to the density of vasoconstrictor fiber innervation. Basal tone is relatively high in the vascular beds of the brain, myocardium, and lungs, more moderate in skeletal muscle, splanchnic viscera, and kidneys, and very low or absent in the skin. Basal tone is subject to modulation by both extrinsic neural and local mechanisms (see Chapter 9).

The level of vascular tone depends upon the nature and intensity of the stimuli. These include impulses conducted over autonomic vasomotor nerves, vasoactive hormones originating in remote organs, and noncirculating vasoactive chemicals released locally and local physical stimuli. The principal physical stimulus is stretch. The magnitude of the stretching force is equal to the transmural pressure, which is calculated by subtracting the total collapsing force acting upon the external wall from the distending force of the blood pressure acting upon the internal wall. Transmural pressure varies with the level of hydrostatic blood pressure, the pressure of the tissue fluid, and the contractions of skeletal muscles.

Critical closure

In small muscular arterioles changes in blood pressure, active wall tension, and vessel radius sometimes lead to complete vessel closure. As blood pressure, the distending force, falls (active wall tension remaining constant), the vessel radius decreases, and, according to Laplace's law, the distending force per unit area also falls. Finally, when the radius becomes sufficiently small, wall tension exceeds the distending force and the vessel suddenly closes. Critical closure is thus a cessation of flow at a low nonzero A-V pressure difference. Critical closure may be significant in hypotensive shock, where there is partial obstruction in the principal arterial supply to a part or organ, or in diseases which reduce the size of vessel lumens.

Autoregulation

Autoregulation refers to the process of local intrinsic regulation of blood flow. By this process the concentration of cell nutrients and waste products is stabilized despite variations in perfusion pressure, the metabolic rate of cells, or the influence of extrinsic vasomotor nerves. Autoregulation of peripheral resistance vessels is important for the adjustment of the volumetric flow rate to the metabolic rate in individual tissues, and for the selective distribution of total blood flow among all the body tissues and organs.

There are two types of autoregulation, myogenic and metabolic. Their exact origin is uncertain: the myogenic hypothesis originally proposed by Bayliss says that the vascular smooth muscle responds by contraction when the vessel transmural pressure increases and relaxes when it decreases; the metabolic hypothesis proposes a mechanism capable of acting upon detected differences in the concentration of some chemical(s). In any event, tissue metabolism and vascular smooth muscle constitute a local control system. The membrane of the smooth muscle cell is a crossroad for the body's communication system.

Evidence of myogenic autoregulation has been obtained by perfusing denervated, isolated smooth muscle tissue in vivo, which eliminates known neural and hormonal vasoactive factors. The perfusion pressure in the arterial supply vessels can then be adjusted to any desired level. The result is that flow in resting tissue remains relatively constant when pressure is either increased or decreased within rather wide limits. A reduction in pressure is followed by vasodilatation, a rise by vasoconstriction. Myogenic autoregulation stems from the inherent automatic response of contraction when smooth muscle is stretched; the more stretch the more contraction and vice versa. Myogenic autoregulation is a perfusion pressure–initiated autoregulation. It preserves normal capillary pressure and flow in spite of moderate changes in arterial blood pressure.

In metabolic autoregulation, the concentration of some local chemical(s) alters the degree of contraction of vascular smooth muscle. The muscle may possess receptor sites to which metabolic vasodilator chemicals attach.

Microcirculatory autoregulation is well illustrated by experiments in which the blood supply to a muscle is totally occluded for a brief interval (Fig. 10.2). The increase in blood flow during the postocclusion period is called *reactive hyperemia*. Reactive hyperemia is due to metabolic factors, the accumulation of vasodilator waste products or the depletion of the oxygen necessary for normal smooth muscle contractility, which occur rapidly during occlusion. Both the intensity and duration of reactive hyperemia are directly related to the duration of occlusion.

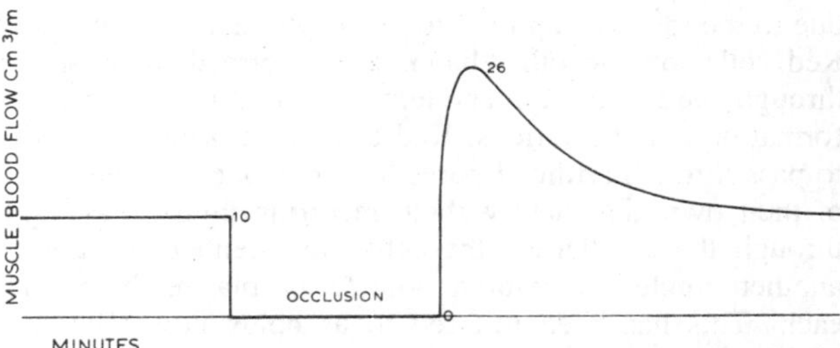

Figure 10.2. Reactive hyperemia. (From Green, Rapela, and Conrad, in *Handbook of Physiology,* sec. 2, Hamilton and Dow, eds., *Circulation,* Am. Physiol. Soc., Washington, 1963, vol. 2, 935–60.)

Exercise or *functional hyperemia* is another example of metabolic autoregulation. Venous blood draining from exercising muscle causes vasodilatation when collected and perfused through resting muscle. The principal metabolites shown to have a vasodilator effect are: (1) lack of oxygen, (2) hydrogen ion, (3) potassium ion, (4) hyperosmolarity, (5) adenine nucleotides (ADP, AMP, IMP), and (6) adenosine (Haddy and Scott 1975). None of the substances by themselves satisfactorily account for all the phases of exercise hyperemia. They probably act sequentially, some being more important in its initiation (potassium ions and hyperosmolarity), other in its continued maintenance (O_2 tension and pH) (Haddy and Scott 1975). The duration and intensity of exercise influence the extent of tissue hypoxia and may affect the rate and kind of vasodilator metabolites generated. Adenosine, adenine nucleotides, organic phosphates, and magnesium ions have been described as vasodilator metabolites in some experimental exercise hyperemias, but are less well estabished.

Oxygen plays a central role in most schemes of metabolic autoregulation. A rise in oxygen tension above normal produces vasoconstriction whereas a fall produces vasodilatation. It may act directly upon smooth muscle or indirectly by causing the release of vasoactive substances from parenchymal or other cells (Duling and Pittman 1975). There is also evidence that changes in oxygen tension produce different reactions in smooth muscle cells of different precapillary resistance vessels (Granger et al. 1975). In any event, oxygen is important to the intrinsic regulation of all tissues in situations resembling reactive hyperemia and in normal circumstances in some tissues with a high metabolic rate, e.g. the heart, brain, and exercising muscle.

Other substances assigned roles in intrinsic autoregulation include the locally produced prostaglandins, intrinsic histamine, serotonin, and bradykinin. Bradykinin, one of the vasoactive polypeptides, is involved in the functional hyperemia of the salivary glands and the pancreas.

Which kind of autoregulation occurs, myogenic or

metabolic, depends more upon the circumstances than upon the individual vascular bed. In experimental reactive hyperemia the initial vasodilatation is a myogenic response which later is augmented and dominated by a metabolic mechanism. Similarly, the initial autoregulatory vasodilatation occurring at the onset of muscular contraction prior to the development of vasoactive metabolites is myogenic in origin. It is thus possible that both myogenic alone and metabolic alone, but in a sequence, may be involved in peripheral vascular autoregulation (Johnson and Heinrich 1975).

In some vascular circuits having only a sparse vasomotor innervation, e.g. brain and kidney, autoregulation is functionally very well developed. The cutaneous vessels exemplify the opposite situation. In other vascular beds, central neurogenic and local autoregulatory mechanisms exist side by side with the blend varying (Table 10.1).

Table 10.1. Relative potentials of autoregulation (intrinsic) and neural (extrinsic) regulations

Vascular bed	Potency of vasoconstrictor nerves	Potency of autoregulation
Brain	−	++++
Heart	±	+++
Skeletal muscle	++	+++
Intestinal tract	+++	++
Hepatic (arterial)	+++	++
Kidney	++++	++++
Skin	++++	−

Central neural regulation is concerned with general overall hemodynamics, is more homogenous, is widely distributed, and is rapid in onset in contrast to the more diversified and more slowly responding autoregulatory mechanisms. What happens when both remote extrinsic and local mechanisms operate simultaneously is largely determined by the characteristics of the regulatory system. Neither are simple on and off devices and both can vary in degree. Strong stimulation of vasoconstrictor nerves can transiently overcome metabolically induced vasodilatation. Similarly, metabolic autoregulatory vasodilatation can break through neurally induced vasoconstriction; autoregulatory escape is an emergency mechanism for preserving the integrity and function of a tissue. However, autoregulation breaks down in shock, in prolonged periods of ischemia of tissues, and in inflammation.

Inflammation

Inflammation is a local process attended by local vascular changes including hyperemia. The increase in blood flow is excessive and causes redness and an increase in temperature. The porosity of capillaries increases which promotes edema of the tissues. Analysis of the lymph-draining sites of inflammation suggests that each substance associated with the inflammatory process has a definitive role at a certain stage in its course (Lewis 1975).

The inflammation site is relatively overperfused, as the redness and temperature indicate. Thus the hyperemia must have a somewhat different basis than does reactive or functional hyperemia. Among the vasodilators identified are prostaglandins, bradykinin, and histamine (Beavin 1976). These also increase capillary permeability. Numerous enzymes capable of hydrolyzing macromolecules are released from cellular lysosomes.

EXCHANGE BETWEEN BLOOD AND TISSUES

In the exchange of substances between the blood in the capillaries and the tissue cells, materials move from the lumen of the capillary through the capillary wall and finally through the interstitial fluid to reach the cell membrane, or vice versa. This occurs by two mechanisms: diffusion and ultrafiltration. The capillary membrane appears ideal for a free exchange of small molecules between the vascular and extravascular fluid and for confinement of the circulating blood volume within the vascular system.

The rate of diffusion depends upon the difference in the concentration of diffusible solutes across the capillary wall; the size of the effective diffusing surface area, that is, the number of open nutrient capillaries; and the permeability of the capillary membrane per unit of surface area. The first two factors are subject to vasomotor adjustments. Arteriolar vasomotion controls total blood flow through the microcirculatory bed. The rate of blood flow determines the concentration gradient along the lumen. If capillary flow were to become very rapid, for example, the concentration of diffusible solutes in the plasma would be more nearly the same throughout its length. Precapillary sphincters control the number of open capillaries and thus regulates the size of the diffusing membrane.

Filtration into and out of the capillaries maintains the balance between intravascular and interstitial fluid volume. It contributes very little to the exchange of nutrients and waste products. The rate of filtration depends upon the membrane porosity or its hydraulic conductivity, the effective filtration pressure, and the size of the filtering membrane. The last two are subject to vasomotor control. The effective filtration pressure depends heavily, but not solely, upon the capillary blood pressure. The volumetric flow rate through the individual capillaries per se does not exert a significant effect upon the net volume filtered because the latter is only a small percentage of total plasma flow. Total flow rate through a tissue relates to filtration only when total flow involves more or fewer capillaries than normal and thus alters the size of the filtering membrane.

Kinds of capillaries

Structural features concerning the endothelial layer, the basement membrane, and the pericapillary cellular investment (pericytes or Rouget cells) distinguish the capillaries in individual organs. On the basis of degree of completeness of the endothelial layer three major types of capillaries are recognized: continuous, discontinuous, and fenestrated (Fig. 10.3).

Continuous capillaries have a complete endothelial and basement membrane layer. They are found in adipose tissue, smooth, skeletal, and cardiac muscle, placenta, lung, and CNS. They have numerous small vesicles in the endothelial cells and tight junctions at the point where adjacent endothelial cells meet. The vesicles, 60–70 nm in diameter, are mostly located along luminal and basal borders of the cell.

The junctions between cells are particularly important. They are believed to have pores through which the major exchanges between the blood and tissue occur. These pores are not simple unobstructed slits between cells (Fig. 10.3). The potential pathway appears to be closed by the close contact of cell membranes. This near blending of the most superficial layer of the double-layered cell membrane forms what is call the tight junction.

Discontinuous capillaries are characterized by intercellular gaps and by the absence of a basement membrane or a basement membrane that is incomplete. This kind of capillary is usually referred to as a sinusoid. It is found in the liver, spleen, and bone marrow. Species variations are encountered; for example, in the calf liver, the capillaries are continuous rather than discontinuous. Discontinuous capillaries permit the passage of whole cells, macromolecules, and particulate matter. They are the most permeable of the several types of capillaries. The discontinuous capillary is the basis for the high volume (one quarter to one half the thoracic lymph flow) and high protein content of hepatic lymph.

The distinguishing features of *fenestrated capillaries* are: the endothelial cells are pierced with small windows or fenestrae, and the endothelial cells are thinner. In other respects the fenestrated capillaries are similar to the continuous capillaries. The fenestrae are 0.1 μ or less in diameter and except for glomerular capillaries are closed by a thin diaphragm. The fenestrae are thought to facilitate the rapid diffusion of solutes and water. Fenestrated capillaries are found in endocrine glands, tissues specialized for the secretion or absorption of fluids (e.g. kidney, pancreas, salivary gland, intestinal villus, gall bladder, synovial membrane, ciliary body, and choroid plexus), and the capillaries of countercurrent flow systems (e.g. renal medulla, fish eye, and swim bladder). The fenestrae morphologically appear to offer a direct pathway across the endothelium. Intravenously injected macromolecules appear in the lymph of tissues whose microcirculatory beds include fenestrated capillaries more rapidly than those having continuous capillaries.

Figure 10.4 summarizes the possible pathways between the capillary lumen and the tissue fluid: diffusion directly through the cell membranes and cytoplasm by gases and water, transfer by vesicles (cytopempsis), and transfer through intracellular gaps (fenestrae). Viruses cross tissue cell walls and also traverse capillary endothelial cells. However, material may diffuse around the tight junction, enter the slit beyond the tight junction via vesicle transport, or simply filter through the tight junctions as water and solutes do through pores in filter paper (Fig. 10.4).

The capillary membrane is a kind of molecular sieve. The mesh or pore size of the sieve ranges between 3 and

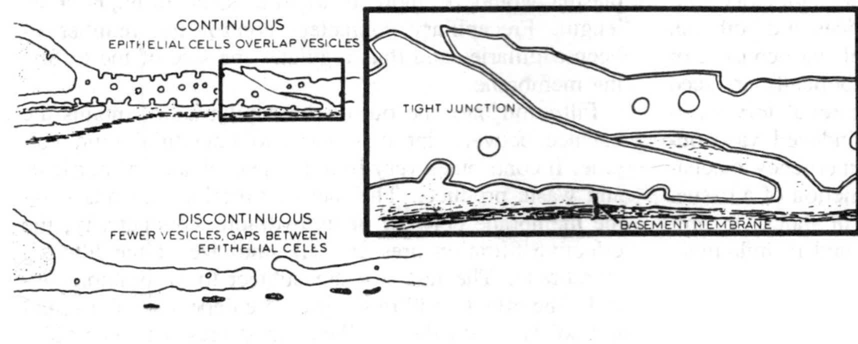

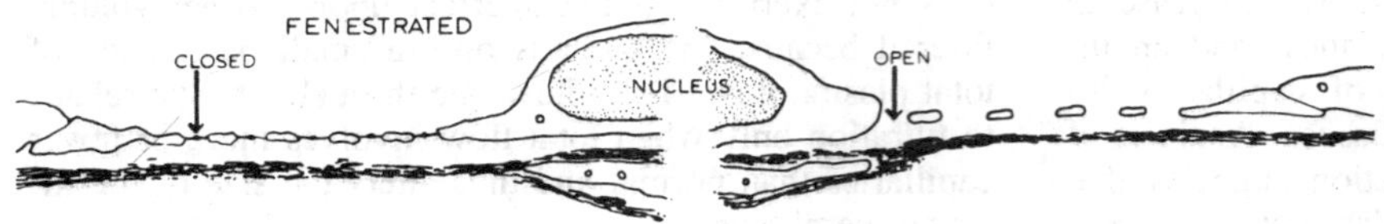

Figure 10.3. Three types of capillaries according to completeness of the endothelium. (Modified from Majno, in *Handbook of Physiology*, sec. 2, Hamilton and Dow, eds., *Circulation*, Am. Physiol. Soc., Washington, 1965, vol. 3, 2293–2375.)

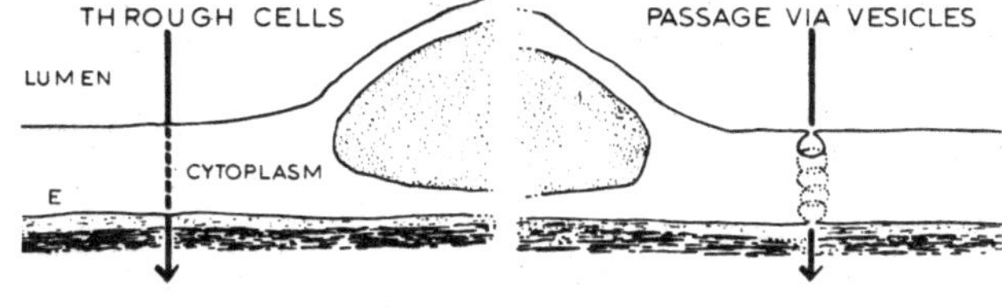

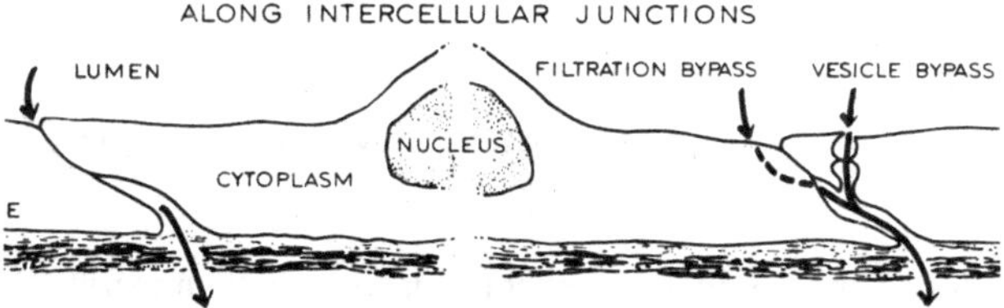

Figure 10.4. Possible passages to extravascular space. (Modified from Majno, in *Handbook of Physiology*, sec. 2, Hamilton and Dow, eds., *Circulation*, Am. Physiol. Soc., Washington, 1965, vol. 3, 2293–2375.)

5 nm for continuous capillaries. For discontinuous capillaries the pore size is larger so that even macromolecules (plasma proteins) disappear rapidly and reappear in the lymph vessels draining such tissues. The system of small pores in continuous capillaries occupies only about 0.1 percent of the endothelial surface. Besides these small capillary pores there appears to be a limited number of larger ones in the venous end of capillaries and small venules which permit the passage of molecules the size of plasma proteins. Permeability along the length of the capillary is thus not uniform.

Changes in capillary permeability

Permeability is estimated by determining the rate at which a labeled substance leaves the blood stream and/or enters the lymph, since lymph collected from tissues contains water and low molecular weight molecules in about the same concentration as plasma. Macromolecules are present in lower concentrations and the concentration varies with the tissue. (In a precise sense permeability should be used only for a specific substance and a specific capillary bed.)

Change in permeability is only one factor influencing rate of escape. Changes in the state of the circulation through an unchanged capillary wall also influence filtration and diffusion. Among these are vasoconstriction and vasodilatation. Arterial vasoconstriction decreases capillary blood pressure and flow and the size and number of open capillaries. Vasodilatation has the opposite effects. Venoconstriction diminishes the normal A-V capillary pressure gradient, slows blood flow, and increases the mean capillary pressure.

If the membrane is stretched by pressure, existing intercellular pores may be passively enlarged, or additional ones opened. Also, certain endogenous chemical substances when activated induce pathological increases in permeability. These include pharmacologically active amines (histamine and hydroxytryptamine), proteolytic enzymes, and products of protein breakdown. The latter includes plasmin, a serum globulin permeability factor, leukotaxine, and bradykinin, all of which accompany injury to tissues.

The effects of Pco_2, pH, and Po_2 on permeability have been studied by interruption of blood supply and by perfusion experiments. In general only extreme hypoxia increases permeability while more moderate degrees, those compatible with life, do not (Scott et al. 1967). Likewise, the capillary wall does not seem to be affected by normal pH and Pco_2 changes.

Diffusion

Diffusion is the spontaneous movement of molecules or discreet particles from regions of higher to lower concentration. It is due to the continuous but erratic random motion of particles in solution. By diffusion solutes migrate from regions of higher to lower concentration until equilibrium is established; solvent and solutes distribute themselves evenly within a volume of fluid. Diffusion over the minute distances involved in capillary–tissue cell exchanges is extremely rapid. It accounts for nearly all exchange of metabolic substrates and products between blood and other tissues.

In the case of blood and interstitial fluid, the two volumes can be considered a continuum by virtue of the submicroscopic water-filled pores in the junctions between cells. To diffuse through the endothelial cells, substances must be of small molecular size and soluble in the lipid layer of the cell membrane. For a small molecule to diffuse freely through the water-filled pores it need be only water soluble. Thus the total area available to a substance for diffusion is a function of its oil-water partition coefficient: solubility in lipid/solubility in water, and its molecular size.

Diffusion through the water-filled pores by lipid-insoluble small molecules (e.g. electrolytes, glucose, urea, water) occurs freely. The results of distribution studies of water, potassium ion, and sodium ion show that for some substances the capillary membrane acts as though it offered no physical barrier at all. It is an extremely rapid process. The rates at which glucose, urea, sodium chloride, and water diffuse across the capillary membrane are 10–80 times the rate at which they circulate. Diffusion for such substances is limited only by the rate at which they are presented to capillary surface, that is, by the rate of blood flow. For substances of small molecular size the rate of diffusion is sufficiently rapid to effect a state of equilibration between the blood in the venous end of the capillary and the interstitial fluid. Molecules with a molecular weight less than 5000 diffuse freely.

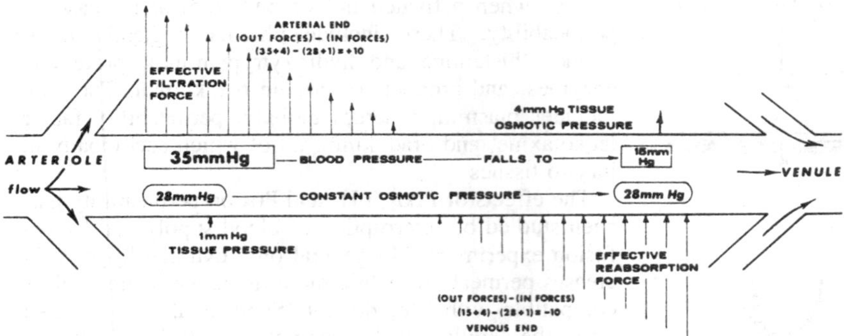

Figure 10.5. Capillary filtration and absorption

Filtration

Filtration is the process by which solutes that are smaller than the pores of a membrane pass from one side of the membrane to the other by virtue of a difference in the hydrostatic (fluid) pressure. It is largely responsible for maintaining fluid balance between the intravascular and interstitial compartments. In filtration there is a bulk passage of water and solute across the capillary membrane. The porous capillary membrane is the filter medium. Plasma water and solutes flow through the membrane at a rate which depends upon the effective filtration pressure and the resistance to flow, that is, the pore size. In the resting state the pore size tends to remain constant, so that effective filtration pressure governs the rate of filtration. The effective filtration pressure is the difference between the sums of (1) the blood pressure (35 mm Hg) plus the tissue colloid osmotic pressure (4 mm) and (2) the plasma protein osmotic pressure (28 mm) plus the tissue hydrostatic pressure (1 mm) (Fig. 10.5). Outward filtration occurs in the arterial end of the capillary. Because of the gradient of blood pressure, the effective outward filtration pressure diminishes to zero at the middle of the capillary.

Osmosis

When two volumes of pure water are separated by a semipermeable membrane, molecules of water, in accord with their random movement, pass through in both directions at equal rates. The addition of solute to one of the volumes disturbs the equilibrium of solvent passage. Each time a solute particle strikes the membrane surface, it prevents similar action by a solvent molecule. Thus solute and solvent molecules compete with each other for membrane passage. The result is a difference in the rate of passage of solvent molecules between the two volumes. This is osmosis, *the means by which molecules of solvent move from regions of lower to those of higher solute concentration.* If the membrane is permeable to the particles of solute the differences in solute concentration and solvent migration are progressively abolished and equilibrium is once again established.

Since the capillary membrane is relatively impermeable to plasma proteins, they are largely but not entirely confined to the intravascular fluid. Other solutes, largely sodium and its attendant ions, make up most of the osmotic pressure of both plasma and tissue fluids. Since the capillary membrane is freely permeable to them, they do not contribute to an osmotic pressure difference between the fluid compartments; the plasma proteins do. The difference normally amounts to about 25 mm Hg. The osmotic effect of plasma proteins exerts a restraining effect upon the escape of water from the plasma to interstitial fluid. This is called the *oncotic pressure* or *colloid osmotic pressure,* or sometimes simply the effective osmotic pressure of blood plasma. The colloid osmotic pressure is but a fraction of the total osmotic pressure of plasma, since the large protein molecules comprise but a small fraction of the total number of particles in solution. The total osmotic pressure for both plasma and interstitial fluid is approximately 310 milliosmoles (see Chapter 36).

Capillary absorption

At the venous end of the capillary, fluid enters from the extracellular fluid compartment. This is a reverse or inward filtration due to the plasma colloid osmotic pressure. Two factors are responsible for the force which determines the direction of net movement of water and solutes in the distal end of the capillary: the existence of a pressure gradient along the length of the capillary with the lowest pressure at the venous end, and the maintenance of a constant plasma protein osmotic pressure throughout the entire length of the capillary (Fig. 10.5). Absorption into the capillary occurs wherever the sum of the plasma protein osmotic pressure and pressure of the tissue fluid exceeds the sum of the capillary blood pressure and the protein osmotic pressure of the extracellular fluids.

Normally capillary filtration and absorption are balanced and changes in intravascular and extravascular fluid volume do not occur. However, there is a small net filtration; that is, the volume filtered at the arterial end of the capillary is slightly larger than the volume reabsorbed at the venous end. This excess of filtered fluid enters the lymphatic system for return to the blood vascular compartment. In the liver the net filtration is comparably high as is the volume of lymph flow. There are thus two extravascular fluid circulations: from the arterial end of the capillary into the extracellular fluid and back to the blood at the distal end of the capillary, and from the arterial end of the capillary into the extracellular fluid and back to the blood by the way of the lymphatics.

Capillary filtration and blood pressure

The role of capillary filtration and absorption in the regulation of intravascular pressure and volume is affected by (1) the direct relationship between volume and pressure in a closed tubular system, (2) the requirement that at equilibrium effective filtration pressure must equal effective absorption pressure, and (3) the buffering possibilities of the interstitial fluid volume based upon the nature and relative sizes (1:3) of the intravascular and extravascular compartments of the extracellular fluid volume. For example, should the blood volume be increased by the rapid infusion of fluid, the resulting increase in capillary pressure disrupts the balance between filtration and absorption, net filtration increases, and a fall in blood volume and capillary pressure accompanied by a temporary rise in the tissue fluid volume occurs. The opposite sequence takes place should the blood volume be reduced by hemorrhage or dehydration. The dynamics of fluid exchange at the capillary level tend to maintain the blood volume and pressure at the expense of the interstitial fluid.

LYMPH

Except for the liver and possibly the spleen, blood does not come into direct contact with tissue cells. Exchanges between the two occur via the interstitial fluid. In mammals some of the capillary filtrate (the net filtration volume) and some plasma substances (primarily plasma proteins) are returned to the blood vascular system by the lymphatic system. It is estimated that in a 24 hour period 50–100 percent of the plasma proteins leave the blood vascular system at the capillary level. The extravascular plasma protein cannot be reabsorbed directly into the blood capillaries; this occurs almost entirely via lymphatic capillaries. The lymphatic system is thus essential to the maintenance of the normal colloidal osmotic pressure of the blood plasma and the interstitial fluid. By absorption and return of the net filtration volume the lymphatic system also assists in regulating the volume and the hydrostatic pressure of the interstitial fluid. In addition, the lymphatic system transports long-chain fatty acids and vitamin K absorbed from the intestine to the blood. The maintenance of a normal cellular environment depends upon the cooperative functions of the vascular systems, blood, and lymph.

The lymph channels begin in the tissues as blind lymph capillaries, similar in structure to blood capillaries. They are approximately twice the size of the smaller blood capillaries. The basement membrane is not so complete, and cell junctions are more porous. Lymph capillaries converge to form larger lymph vessels. Their structure is similar to that of veins, although they have thinner walls. Ultimately all lymph vessels drain into either the thoracic duct or the right lymphatic duct, which empty into the venous system anterior to the heart. Lymph from the right side of the head and neck, the right foreleg, and the right side of the thorax is returned to the venous system by the right lymphatic duct; that from the rest of the body by the thoracic duct. Upon entering the venous system, the lymph mixes completely with the blood and loses its identity.

The density of the lymph capillaries in a tissue does not parallel that of the blood capillaries. Neither the bone marrow nor brain is supplied with lymph vessels. In the lungs the lymphatic capillaries do not extend to the alveoli but terminate at the alveolar openings. Variation in the distribution of lymph capillaries also occurs in the liver and spleen.

Function of lymph nodes

Lymph on its way to the blood stream via the system of lymph vessels must pass through one or more lymph nodes. Lymph nodes have at least two functions. One is the production of lymphocytes, which the lymph nodes contain in large numbers. These cells are added to the lymph current as it slowly passes through the node.

Another function of lymph nodes is to stop foreign material coming into them. This filtration is believed to be accomplished mechanically by the phagocytic activity of the reticuloendothelial cells. Drinker et al. (1934) showed that normal lymph nodes are very efficient filters. The "efficiency was so great as to make it fairly certain that in a part kept at rest early in an infection practically no microorganisms would escape the nodes in the line of drainage."

In gallinaceous birds and pigeons, lymph nodes are absent. In swimming birds they are present but not numerous. The bone marrow of birds, however, contains numerous nodules of lymphoid tissue, apparently to compensate in part for the absence of lymph nodes elsewhere (Jordan 1942). These medullary lymph nodules increase in number following splenectomy (Jordan and Robeson 1942). Various organs of normal chickens produce lymphocytes, e.g. thymus, bursa of Fabricius, spleen, wall of intestine, and periportal areas of liver.

Interstitial fluid and lymph

Interstitial or tissue fluid is located within the tissue spaces, distributed uniformly between the surfaces of cells, connective tissue fibrils, and blood and lymph capillaries in a film or layer approximately 1 μ thick. Its mass is equal to about 15 percent of the body weight. It is normally in free interchange with the blood plasma and lymph capillaries by simple diffusion and filtration. The large inulin molecule diffuses rapidly through this volume.

Other portions of the extracellular fluid are in (1) dense connective tissue such as bone, cartilage, and tendon; and (2) the vitreous and aqueous humor, cerebrospinal fluid, fluid in the serous cavities, fluid in the gastrointestinal tract and urinary bladder, and the synovial fluids. The second group is termed *transcellular fluids*. Cellular transport and/or secretion can contribute to the composition of transcellular fluid.

Lymph is fluid within the closed lymphatic system. It is often included as a part of the tissue fluid. In a strict sense it is not identical with tissue fluid although, except for location, it is similar. Lymph is a mixture of capillary filtrate and tissue fluid which has entered the lymph capillaries.

Composition and formation

The lymph resembles blood plasma except for a lower concentration of plasma proteins. The composition varies, especially in protein concentration, depending upon origin. The variation is an expression of differences in the capillary filtrate (capillary permeabilities) and in the function of tissues.

The composition of lymph also varies with the state of activity of the digestive organs. During fat absorption, intestinal lymph has a milky appearance because of the fat that it contains and is known as *chyle*. Ordinarily lymph is a clear, colorless, watery liquid having a specific gravity of about 1.015. It contains lymphocytes and normally a few red cells. Neutrophilic leukocytes are ordinarily absent; however, they may be present in great numbers in infections. Platelets are absent. Lymph does contain fibrinogen and prothrombin, and will clot slowly. The liquid part, after clotting has occurred, is designated lymph serum. Lymph contains water, gases, proteins, nonprotein nitrogenous substances, glucose, inorganic substances, hormones, enzymes, vitamins, and immune substances.

The proteins are the same as in blood plasma but the amount is less, especially in lymph from the limbs (Table 10.2). In a study of the rate of flow and the normal composition of the lymph from the forelegs of calves, the percentage of protein in the blood serum varied from 5.4 to 6.7, in the lymph from 2.2 to 3.1 (Glenn et al. 1943).

Since lymph is formed from blood by physical forces, the crystalloid content of lymph and blood plasma is very similar. There are some small quantitative differences, however, in the electrolyte pattern, which is affected by the lower protein content of lymph. Thus lymph shows higher chloride and bicarbonate concentrations than serum; these differences can probably be explained on principles of diffusion in the Donnan equilibrium. The freezing point of lymph is substantially the same as that of blood serum. The pH of lymph (cervical) is slighty higher than that of plasma.

Table 10.2. Protein content of blood serum and lymph

Species	Source of lymph	Protein (g/100 ml) Serum	Lymph
Lamb	Cervical lymphatics	5.81	3.64
Dog	Thoracic duct	6.25	4
Dog	Cervical lymphatics	6.25	3.63
Dog	Leg lymphatics	6.46	1.91
Dog	Intestinal lymphatics	6.23	3.98
Dog	Liver lymphatics	6.34	5.32
Rabbit	Thoracic duct		3.53
Monkey	Cervical lymphatics	5.12	3.48
Man	Deep pelvic lymphatics	7.8	5.5

From Drinker and Yoffey, *Lymphatics, Lymph, and Lymphoid Tissue*, Harvard U. Press, 1941

The amount of lymph flowing through the thoracic duct in nonruminants is approximately 2 ml/kg/hr and is somewhat higher in ruminants. In a 24 hour interval it is equivalent to the entire plasma volume.

Under normal conditions the effective filtration pressure for the entrance of fluid into the lymph capillaries is exceedingly small. Diffusion undoubtedly accounts for the entry of most of the lymph constituents; lymph capillaries are more permeable than blood capillaries. However, they are closed, and though porous, may represent somewhat of a barrier to substances from the interstitial fluid, especially macromolecules. After diffusion through the semipermeable lymph capillary, changes in extramural pressure (contracting muscle, arterial pulsations) express the lymphatic lumen content via hydrodynamic flow into succeeding segments of the lymphatic system where it is retained by valves, and by filtration back into the interstitial compartment. After filtration through the lymph capillary wall, the filtered fluid will contain less protein than that retained within the lumen. The protein concentration of lymph will increase in proportion. As the extramural pressure decreases (muscular relaxation), fluid and substances in the interstitial fluid again diffuse into the lymph capillary.

Circulation of plasma proteins

Plasma proteins escape from normal healthy capillaries by filtration. The average protein content of the capillary filtrate ranges from 0.7 to 2.1 percent. The return of protein to the blood vascular system is a function of the lymphatic vessels. Since at least 50 percent of the plasma protein escapes daily, the lymphatic return is essential for the normal effective osmotic pressure of the blood and for regulating the osmotic pressure of the interstitial fluid.

The passage of protein through the blood capillary walls provides for antibodies in controlling infections and for the transport of protein-bound hormones and drugs, and it is essential if plasma proteins are to be a useful source of cellular metabolic protein.

Flow

Tissue fluid is in communication with the blood in the capillaries, the intracellular fluid, and the lymph in the lymph capillaries. The latter remove from the tissue spaces materials that do not or cannot enter the blood capillaries. Water and crystalloids can move either way. Particulate matter and large molecules such as proteins and lipids cannot enter the blood capillaries but can penetrate the much more permeable walls of the lymph capillaries.

The flow of lymph in the lymph vessels is sluggish and in one direction only—from the tissues toward the heart. The factors concerned in lymph flow are: (1) the difference in pressure at the two ends of the lymph system, (2) the massaging effects of muscular movements, (3) the presence in the lymph vessels of valves which permit flow in one direction only, and (4) the propulsive contractility of lymphatic vessels (Campbell and Heath 1973). Lymphatic vessels are actively contractile and this is a major force of propulsion. The contractility is myogenic in origin and occurs independently of the extrinsic autonomic nerves with which lymph vessels are normally supplied. The observed frequencies of contractions range from 2 to 20 per minute accompanied by pressure pulses with amplitudes of 1–15 mm Hg. Active propulsive lymphatic motility has been described for sheep, dogs, horses, birds, and man.

With reference to the first factor, the pressure in the lymph capillaries is higher than the pressure at the entrance of the thoracic duct into the venous system. The latter pressure is still further lowered at every inspiration by the aspiratory action of the thorax. Lymph therefore flows toward the venous system. The flow of lymph toward the thorax is further augmented, during inspiration, by the backward movement of the diaphragm, which increases the pressure in the abdomen and thus assists in emptying its lymphatics toward the thorax. As for the second and third factors, the lymph vessels have very thin walls. It follows therefore that any outside pressure, such as that produced by the contraction of skeletal or smooth muscle, will tend to compress their walls and force lymph toward the heart.

The rate of lymph flow varies with the rate of formation of lymph. Normally the more active a tissue is, the greater is the net filtration volume. When a tissue becomes active, autoregulation increases the number of capillaries carrying blood. Thus the filtration surface increases; that is, a large filter begins to operate. With arterial dilatation, the capillary blood pressure increases and the effective filtration pressure increases. Independent of filter size, an increase in pressure augments the formation of lymph. A decrease in osmotic pressure of the plasma proteins via the intravenous injection of isotonic saline will decrease the effective osmotic pressure of the plasma (by dilating the plasma proteins) and increase the effective filtration pressure and the net filtration volume. Should the permeability of the capillaries increase by mechanical stretching due to increased intraluminal pressure, the action of an increased concentration of metabolites, drugs, or toxins will cause capillary filtration and lymph flow to increase.

Simultaneously with increased activity of an organ, the factors promoting lymph flow are augmented. Movement of muscles increases, tissue hydrostatic pressure tends to rise, pulsation of arterioles increases, and respirations become deeper and shorter.

Edema

Normally the volume of a tissue remains constant except for minor variations in capillary blood volume. The term edema refers to an increase of interstitial fluid volume.

This accumulation of tissue fluid occurs when the equilibrium between the rate of its formation and the rate of its removal is disrupted. Normally the fluid and protein that escape from the blood capillaries are returned in equal amounts by absorption into either the blood or lymph capillaries. When this occurs neither the blood nor the extravascular volumes change. *Increased capillary pressure, increased capillary permeability, decreased concentration of plasma proteins, or obstruction of lymph vessels may give rise to edema.*

Any increase in the capillary blood pressure increases the effective filtration pressure. An increase in venous pressure increases net filtration much more than a similar increase in arterial pressure. Increased venous pressure decreases venous outflow from the capillaries. The mean pressure in the capillaries increases and the gradient between the arterial and venous end is diminished. Absorption rate at the venous end decreases in proportion to the fall in the difference between the osmotic pressure of the plasma and the hydrostatic pressure. Thus a rise in venous pressure not only increases filtration but effectively decreases absorption. A rise in venous pressure is a common cause of edema. It occurs in hydropericardium (pericarditis), chronic congestive heart failure, intrahepatic obstruction to blood flow, or following the tight application of bandages.

Hypoproteinemia decreases capillary reabsorption and increases filtration. In severe hypoproteinemia, edema occurs. Hypoproteinemia may be caused by insufficient intake of dietary protein, digestive or absorption disturbances (parasitism, pancreatic deficiency, chronic diarrhea), excessive loss of protein as a result of burns, repeated paracentesis, chronic hemorrhage, dilution of plasma with protein-free fluid, or failure in synthesis of protein by the liver.

Inflammatory edema may involve increased capillary pressure (arteriolar relaxation, thrombosis of venules), increased capillary permeability, and obstruction or plugging of lymph vessels.

In quadrupeds, when the central venous pressure is raised as in chronic congestive heart failure, fluid accumulation is most marked clinically within the peritoneal cavity. Subcutaneous edema of the dependent extremities is much less common than in man. However, edema of the brisket or ventral abdominal area is frequently observed.

Ascitic fluid is formed in the abdominal cavity. If the hepatic portal vein is ligated, ascites does not occur unless the concentration of plasma proteins is low. If the hepatic veins are obstructed so that the liver is also congested, ascites occur regularly. Furthermore, if, following partial obstruction of the hepatic veins, the liver is moved from the abdominal to the thoracic cavity, hydrothorax instead of ascites results. Observation of the experimentally congested liver reveals the regular formation of drops of fluid at the surface of the liver. This fluid when collected and analyzed is similar to liver lymph and ascitic fluid obtained by paracentesis.

Salt metabolism plays a very dominant role in any form of edema. The retention of water is secondary to the renal retention of sodium. Retention of sodium produces edema, not increased concentration of sodium (hypernatremia). Sodium retention is increased by a hormonal system involving renin, angiotensin, and aldosterone. Whenever the perfusion of the kidney is threatened, the renin is released from the juxtaglomerular apparatus in the kidney. Renin acts upon a plasma globulin to form angiotensin. Angiotensin stimulates directly the aldosterone-producing cells of the adrenal cortex to increase the output of the sodium-retaining hormone, aldosterone. Aldosterone then acts to increase sodium retention by the kidney. Retention of sodium is accompanied by retention of water and expansion of the plasma volume. If expansion of the plasma volume is all that is required to return the circulation to normal, the increased secretion of renin is corrected. If normal circulatory dynamics are not restored, the hormonal mechanism continues to operate and capillary filtrate continues to enter the extravascular pool of fluid.

REFERENCES

Beavin, M.A. 1976. Histamine. *New Eng. J. Med.* 294:30–36, 320–25.

Burton, A.C. 1965. *Physiology and Biophysics of the Circulation*. Year Book Medical, Chicago.

Campbell, T., and Heath, T. 1973. Intrinsic contractility of lymphatics in sheep and in dogs. *Q. J. Exp. Physiol.* 58:207–17.

Drinker, C.K., Field, M.E., and Ward, H.K. 1934. The filtering capacity of lymph nodes. *J. Exp. Med.* 59:393–405.

Drinker, C.K., and Yoffey, J.M. 1941. *Lymphatics, Lymph, and Lymphoid Tissue*. Harvard U. Press, Cambridge.

Duling, B.R., and Pittman, R.N. 1975. Oxygen tension: Dependent or independent variable in local control of blood flow? *Fed. Proc.* 24:201–19.

Glenn, W.W.L., Muus, J., and Drinker, C.K. 1943. Observations on the physiology and biochemistry of quantitative burns. *J. Clin. Invest.* 22:451–60.

Gore, R.W., and Bohlen, H.G. 1975. Pressure regulation in the microcirculation. *Fed. Proc.* 34:2031–37.

Granger, H.J., Goodman, A.H., and Cook, B.H. 1975. Metabolic models of microcirculatory regulation. *Fed. Proc.* 34:2025–30.

Green, H.D., Rapella, C.E., and Conrad, M.C. 1963. Resistance (conductance) and capacitance phenomena in terminal vascular beds. In *Handbook of Physiology*. Sec. 2, W.F. Hamilton and P. Dow, eds.. *Circulation*. Am. Physiol. Soc., Washington. Vol. 2, 935–60.

Haddy, F.J., and Scott, J.B. 1975. Metabolic factors in peripheral circulatory regulation. *Fed. Proc.* 34:2006–11.

Jordan, H.E. 1942. Extramedullary blood production. *Physiol. Rev.* 22:375–84.

Jordan, H.E., and Robeson, J.M. 1942. The production of lymphoid nodules in the bone marrow of the domestic pigeon following splenectomy. *Am. J. Anat.* 71:181–205.

Krogh, A. 1922. *The Anatomy and Physiology of the Capillaries*. Yale U. Press, New Haven.

Lewis, G.P. 1975. A lymphatic approach to tissue injury. *New Eng. J. Med.* 293:287–91.

Majno, G. 1965. Ultrastructure of the vascular membrane. In *Handbook of Physiology*. Sec. 2, W.F. Hamilton and P. Dow, eds., *Circulation*. Am. Physiol. Soc., Washington. Vol. 3, 2293–2375.

Messina, E.J., Weiner, R., and Gabor, K. 1976. Prostaglandins and local circulatory control. *Fed. Proc.* 35:2367–75.

Scott, J.B., Daugherty, R.M., and Haddy, F.J. 1967. Effect of severe local hypoxemia on transcapillary water movement in the dog forelimb. *Am. J. Physiol.* 212:847–51.

CHAPTER 11

Regional Circulation | By C. Roger Smith and Robert L. Hamlin

The basic features of circulation in different organs and tissues are similar. However, there are some important, special features in most organs. These are related to differences in size (e.g. skeletal muscle versus CNS), how blood flow is related to organ function (e.g. kidney and skin), at what intensities and for what intervals of time that function occurs (e.g. myocardium versus myometrium), how homogeneous the organs are in structure and function (e.g. skeletal muscle versus intestinal tract), their capability for anaerobic energy production (e.g. skeletal muscle versus CNS), and the functional relationships among them (e.g. pituitary and hypothalamus) and with the entire body (e.g. lungs).

The maximal limit of exchange between the blood and a tissue depends upon the density of nutrient capillaries and the blood perfusion rate. While capillary permeability varies among different vascular beds, it normally remains largely unaltered in any given tissue. Functional hyperemia accounts for the matching of increases in metabolic need with blood flow. In some organs, e.g. the CNS and myocardium, the vascular bed is large enough at maximal dilatation and optimal perfusion pressures to meet maximal metabolic need. In others, e.g. skeletal muscle, the vascular bed even at maximal dimensions is too small to satisfy maximal nutritional requirements, and an oxygen debt accumulates which is repaid later. In still others where blood flow subserves special organ functions in addition to cell metabolic need, e.g. adipose tissue, skin, kidney, and other glands, the maximal dimensions of capillary surface area far exceed that required.

SKELETAL MUSCLE

Several structural and functional features of skeletal muscle and its vascular bed are special: (1) collectively, skeletal muscle is normally the largest organ in the body, (2) it is largely but not completely homogeneous, (3) flow through microcirculatory vessels is subject to changes in pressure exerted on their walls as muscle contracts and relaxes, (4) the range of its metabolic rate is more extensive and the flexibility in the control of blood flow more extensive than in most other tissues, (5) the architectural design of its vascular bed is relatively uniform, and (6) flow through its vascular bed is subject to dual control, i.e. extrinsic neural and intrinsic autoregulatory mechanisms.

Hemodynamic significance

Hemodynamically, muscle is one of the most important body tissues. Skeletal muscle comprises 40–50 percent of body weight. It may account for as little as 20 percent of the body's oxygen consumption or as much as 80 percent. Cardiac output varies from 17 percent at rest to 80–85 percent during maximal physical exertion. Skeletal muscle has a relatively high density of capillaries with only a relatively few patent (open) and functioning at a given time during rest. Exercise exerts a potent vasodilatory effect on precapillary resistance vessels. The number of patent capillaries increases 10–100 fold. While muscle vessels are relatively homogeneous, there is a difference between red or aerobic muscle (e.g. soleus) and white muscle. In most mammalian species, many muscles contain both some red and white fibers. Red muscle blood flow varies from 20–30 ml up to 115 ml/100 g/min. For white muscle the range is from 2–5 to 40–60 ml/100 g/min.

When compared to other tissues at rest, the volumetric flow rate through skeletal muscle is disproportionately low. In the dog the flow rates for the kidney, heart, pancreas, and intestine range from 0.7 to 3 ml/g/min, while for skeletal muscle it is only 0.2–0.3. At rest the vascular smooth muscle fibers of the small vessels in skeletal muscles which provide resistance to flow are nearly maximally constricted. Consequently the number of patent capillaries is relatively few and blood volume and blood flow are minimal. This situation is fortunate in terms of requirements for cardiac output. If all the capillaries in all skeletal muscle were maximally dilated at rest, the required cardic output would be 3–4 times as much as it actually is.

The low rate in resting muscles must be geared to the metabolic state. Each patent capillary can efficiently bring about exchange of solutes with only a limited domain of tissue fluid. When only a fraction of the total capillary population is open simultaneously, it is likely that some muscle fibers are ischemic. However, there is probably a rotation of perfusion by which the period of ischemia for each individual fiber is shortened. Nevertheless, the fact that nearly one half the glucose uptake from arterial blood can be accounted for by the increase in lactate in the venous drainage suggests a state of relative hypoxia for some skeletal muscle fibers at least part of the time. When the vascular bed is maximally dilated, exchange is facilitated by the decrease in the distance separating muscle cells and blood brought about by the opening of additional capillaries as well as by passive capillary dilatation.

Adjustments during exercise

During exercise the oxygen requirement of skeletal muscle increases in proportion to its rise in metabolic rate. The requirement is met by an increase in ventilation rate and by circulatory adaptations. The principal adaptations in the dog are: (1) 3–5 fold increase in cardiac output, (2) a threefold increase in the A-V (arteriovenous) O_2 difference, (3) a mobilization of blood from the spleen, and (4) a fall in the resistance to flow in the vascular beds of active muscle (see references for studies on the dog and the horse).

Exercise is usually accompanied by an increase in visceral vascular resistance which causes a shunting of flow to exercising muscle. In normal dogs exercising at near maximal capacity, such a pattern of redistribution was not observed (Millard et al. 1972, Franklin et al. 1973). Autoregulation kept mesenteric and renal blood flows near control levels, even though arterial pressure was moderately elevated. When the circulatory reserves were reduced by anemia or chronic heart failure, however, intense visceral vasoconstriction and marked reduction in visceral flow were recorded. In splenectomized dogs, exercise results in a compensatory reduction and diversion of visceral flow similar to that accompanying other experimentally created forms of circulatory deficiency. The spleen, by storing a significant mass of erythrocytes and plasma, is an important circulatory reserve mechanism in the dog. Thus differences in splenic reserve functions may be one explanation of species differences.

LIVER

The liver is a highly vascular organ. The fraction of cardiac output received by the liver for the dog and sheep respectively are 30 percent and 30–40 percent. Total hepatic flow amounts to 35–45 ml/kg of body wt./min in the dog, sheep, and calf.

The liver receives blood from two sources, the *portal vein* and the *hepatic artery*. The larger fraction, about two thirds, is supplied by the portal vein. It terminates in an enormous capillary bed which provides for nutritional requirements and also subserves the special effects that the hepatic parenchymal cells have on substances absorbed from the gastrointestinal tract. The blood distributed by the hepatic artery to the capillaries of the bile ducts and hepatic connective tissue is drained by venules emptying into portal vein branches. Perhaps the most important fraction of the hepatic artery flow is delivered directly, that is, without prior venous admixture, to the sinusoids at the level of the liver lobule. In the sinusoids the venous blood draining from the hepatic connective tissue and biliary system, some hepatic arterial blood, and the portal venous blood are all mingled.

The blood leaves the lobule (450,000–500,000 lobules in the pig) by the central vein. The central vein, via the hepatic veins, drains into the posterior vena cava. In the dog, but not in other common domestic animals, the hepatic veins at their caval ends have strong bundles of smooth muscles which have a sphincterlike effect.

Blood flow

Both the Fick and the dye-dilution principles are employed in intact animals to estimate hepatic blood flow. In the former, a test substance is used which is believed to be removed exclusively by the liver, e.g. radioactive chromic oxide or gold, bromsulfalein, rose bengal, or iodocyamine green. Blood flow can be estimated by dividing the overall amount of the test substance removed from the blood by the quantity removed from each milliliter of blood perfusing the liver. Inaccuracies in the Fick procedure stem from the effects of extrahepatic removal of tne test substance on the overall removal rate, and from allowing the samples drawn from a single hepatic vein to represent all venous blood draining the liver.

In animals prepared in advance, the dye dilution principle is used by injection of ^{51}CR-labeled erythrocytes into the splanchnic circulation upstream from the liver and rapid serial sampling obtained from the hepatic venous outflow. The concentration in the outflow following rapid injection is inversely related to the volume of blood flowing through the liver (see Chapter 7). By sampling from the portal vein the portal flow alone may be determined.

In acute experiments, collection techniques which include rapid return of the collected volume may be employed to measure flow through either the portal vein or hepatic artery. In both acute and chronic preparations, flow meters may be used.

Through the hepatic artery

The hepatic artery supplies about one third of the total liver blood flow. The arterial pressure (which is the same as that in other systemic arteries) is dissipated in presinusoidal vessels. Acute ligation of the hepatic artery in the normal animal has little or no effect upon sinusoidal or portal venous pressures. The functions of hepatic artery flow include serving as the principal blood supply to the bile ducts, assuring an adequate oxygen tension in the blood perfusing the liver parenchyma, and acting as a reserve blood supply to liver tissue whenever portal vein flow is reduced.

At least in the rabbit and dog, insuring an adequate oxygen supply to the liver cells is a vital function of the hepatic artery. The blood flowing through the portal vein has already lost some oxygen as it passed through one set of capillaries in other splanchnic viscera. There are, however, species differences in the oxygen content of portal blood. In the dog and rabbit, it has a relatively low oxygen concentration; in the cat, rat, and *Macaca mulatta*, oxygen concentration is relatively high. When the hepatic artery is ligated in the dog, death occurs in 24–48 hours accompanied by massive gangrenous necrosis of the liver. The rat, cat, and monkey survive acute ligation of the hepatic artery with no recognizable clinical illness and relatively minor structural damage limited to the biliary system.

Anaerobic bacteria can regularly be cultured from the normal livers of species susceptible to arterial ligation but not from others. Anaerobes thrive only in a hypoxic environment. The flow of oxygenated blood through the hepatic artery normally serves to check their growth. Partial arterialization of the portal blood by an A-V anastomosis preserves liver function and structure in the dog following hepatic artery ligation. Likewise the administration of antibiotics inhibits the growth of anaerobes in the hypoxic liver and prolongs survival.

Through the portal vein

The portal vein is the major source of blood supply to the liver. The functions of the portal blood flow are to carry absorbed substances from the intestine and stomach (in ruminants) to the liver, and to supply oxygen to the liver parenchyma. Acute occlusion of the portal vein is rapidly followed by death. The characteristics of the hepatic portal system are: (1) it has a high volume flow rate, (2) it is a low pressure system, even lower than the pulmonary system, (3) it is an afferent flow system carrying blood from which some oxygen has already been removed while traversing prehepatic capillary beds, (4) its flow rate is largely determined by extrahepatic (arterial vasomotion in vascular beds of the stomach, pancreas, intestine, mesenteries, and spleen) rather than by intrahepatic conditions, (5) it ends in a tremendously large system of intercommunicating and leaky discontinuous capillaries called sinusoids, and (6) the blood is not homogeneously mixed—that is, streamlining of flow occurs.

The original perfusion pressure for the pathway leading from the aorta via the portal vein to the liver is identical to that of other systemic circuits. In the case of the liver, however, 90 percent of the pressure is dissipated in the prehepatic vascular circuits of the splanchnic viscera. In the dog the pressures in the portal and hepatic veins respectively are 8 and 2 mm Hg. This leaves a pressure gradient across the liver of only 6. Nevertheless, it is sufficient to force a relatively large volume of blood through the liver vessels. In the sheep, the portal vein flow is 37 ml/kg body wt./min. The level of the perfusion pressure in the portal vein largely determines total blood flow through the liver.

Poiseuille's equation ($Q = P/R$) shows that resistance to flow through the liver is low. Small changes in portal pressure in response to neural or chemically induced changes in vasomotor tone in the prehepatic vascular beds can cause large changes in portal blood flow.

Resistance to hepatic outflow comes from intrahepatic vessels, extrahepatic efferent venous vessels, and pressure in the right atrium. The total is normally small. Because the pressure gradient from portal vein to right atrium is so small, slight changes in any component could result in relatively large changes in hepatic flow. Intrahepatic resistance to flow largely resides within the portal venules and sinusoids. In the dog, but not the sheep, cat, or goat, histamine reduces hepatic venous outflow and results in passive congestion of the liver and other splanchnic organs. The sinusoids appear more narrow at the ends than in the middle.

Blood storage

The veins comprise the largest part of the hepatic vascular tree and account for most of its volume. One important function of the veins is to form a low resistance pathway for blood flow. Another function is the distribution of blood volume. Veins receive vasomotor nerves. In response to the intensity of discharge over them, the volume increases or decreases. In this sense the liver acts as a blood storage organ. Should the need for additional blood volume in extrahepatic beds increase (e.g. during exercise when the functioning cross section of the muscle capillary beds increases), the veins of the hepatic and other splanchnic vasculature redistribute the blood volume by contraction. The sequestration of erythrocytes which occurs in the spleen does not occur to an appreciable extent in the liver.

Streamline flow

Blood within the portal vein is not homogenously mixed but is streamlined in character. It somewhat resembles the channeling of the Gulf Stream within the Atlantic Ocean. Due to hydrodynamics, flow in the portal vein is also streamlined, at least in some species.

Channeling permits different parts of the liver to receive portal blood from distinct visceral sources. In the dog, the left side of the liver receives portal blood from the stomach, upper duodenum, spleen, and most of the colon. The right side of the liver receives blood from the jejunum and ileum. Streamline flow may cause differences in the content of various parts of the liver, dependent upon differences in the composition of the blood being drained from prehepatic organs. It may also be related to the distribution pattern of hepatic metastases from visceral organs. In the sheep, the geometry of vessels converging to form the portal vein minimizes streamline flow and enhances mixing.

Interruption of portal flow

Portal vein flow may be forced to bypass the liver entirely. This is accomplished by establishing a shunt between the portal vein and posterior vena cava followed by ligation of the portal vein between the shunt and the liver. This does not alter the venous drainage of prehepatic organs, but does deprive the liver of its normal volume flow (hepatic ischemia). It also produces a type of hepatic insufficiency by diverting venous blood from the stomach, intestine, and other viscera directly to the systemic circuit without the alterations in composition normally imposed by the hepatic parenchyma.

Dogs prepared in this fashion survive for periods of 3–12 months. Hepatic ischemia is in part compensated by increased flow through the hepatic artery and an increase in the oxygen utilization coefficient. However, there is atrophy of the liver, progressive deterioration in the liver function, progressive loss of body weight, development of stupors, and finally attacks of coma, one of which proves fatal. The signs related to the abnormal function of the CNS depend upon chemical changes occurring in the blood. Changes in the concentration of ammonia and amino acid content are believed to be of great significance. The loss of liver mass and functional capacity at least in part depends upon the relative hepatic ischemia. If the normal blood volume flow is maintained but diversion of the portal blood around the liver is continued by transposing the portal vein and posterior vena cava, the liver structure and functional capacity remain normal.

Hepatic lymph

Compared to other tissues, the liver is a mass producer of lymph. Estimates of the volumetric flow rate based upon cannulation of the main hilar lymph vessels range from 0.35 to 0.6 ml/kg of liver tissue per minute. By contrast, rates for the dog heart, spleen, and thoracic limb are 0.08–0.3, 0.05–10.2, and 0.03–0.07.

The remarkable feature about the composition of hepatic lymph is its high protein concentration. The plasma contains only 10–20 percent more. Further, albumin and globulin are present in about the same proportion in the two fluids. Almost no erythrocytes and relatively few leukocytes are observed in the lymph. The sinusoidal epithelium filters the formed elements of the blood but is almost freely permeable to the plasma proteins.

There are no lymph capillaries in the hepatic parenchyma. They are found only in the connective tissue septa and capsule and in plexuses surrounding those segments of the vascular and biliary system outside the liver lobule.

Extravascular fluid

The metabolic functions of the liver make it the body's most important chemical factory. Between the hepatic parenchyma and the fluid input-output transportation systems is the interstitial fluid. Substances are delivered to it from extrahepatic tissues via the hepatic artery, the portal vein, and their associated capillary networks. Fluid and materials leave it by the way of the blood capillaries emptying into the hepatic veins, and by the biliary and lymphatic systems.

The principal site of extravascular fluid formation is the sinusoidal bed within the liver lobules. Here a large volume of blood is being propelled at low pressures through baggy endothelial tubes with large pores. Due to its unusual porosity, the sinusoidal endothelium is bathed on both sides by fluids with similar protein concentrations. This similarity reduces the effective osmotic pressure normally restraining the net outward movement of fluid and simultaneously renders the low sinusoidal hydrostatic pressure an effective outward moving force. This plus the fact that larger pores offer less flow resistance forms the basis for the rapid formation of extravascular fluid at the low pressures prevailing in the sinusoids.

The absence of the usual restraining force exerted by plasma proteins when confined to the intravascular fluid makes the rate of formation of extravascular fluid extremely unstable. The rate is sensitive to pressure changes of small magnitude. Increased resistance in the postsinusoidal vessels raises the sinusoidal pressure. It can occur passively, that is, in chronic congestive heart failure, or actively, by venoconstriction or contraction of hepatic vein sphincters. This sequence leads to fluid imbalance in the liver and ultimately to the accumulation of fluid in the peritoneal cavity (ascites).

The general direction of movement of the extravascular fluid is from lobule to hilus. In order to gain access to the lymphatic capillaries, fluid must percolate through the interstices of the parenchyma to the connective tissue investing and separating lobules and surrounding the vascular and biliary vessels. Extravascular fluid formed in normal amounts enters the lymphatic capillaries and leaves the liver via the main hilar lymphatic vessel. In the gap between the formation and flow through lymph vessels there are opportunities for modifications of composition by exchanges with fluid in the blood capillaries of the connective tissue and in the biliary system.

When the sinusoidal pressure rises, the rate of extravascular fluid formation increases and may exceed the rate it leaves the liver in the lymphatic drainage system. Under these circumstances, pressure gradients develop which move the excess fluid to the surface of the liver capsule where it is shed into the peritoneal cavity.

RUMEN

Blood flow to the rumen has been studied in unanesthetized cattle by Sellers (1965), who was concerned with the effects of feeding and of fermentation products, i.e. carbon dioxide and volatile fatty acids. Flow was estimated by chronically implanting an electromagnetic flow meter on the right ruminal artery. The results suggest an autoregulatory mechanism in which the local concentration of carbon dioxide and volatile fatty acids help determine flow.

Effects of feeding

Feeding is followed by an increase in blood flow to the rumen. If the normal rumen content is replaced by an equal volume of saline, the increase in blood flow above control values is limited to the interval during which ingestion occurs. If the rumen contains normal ingesta, the increase in blood flow persists for 90 or more minutes following cessation of eating. During the same interval, flow through the posterior mesenteric and hypogastric arteries occurs at the same rate as during the prefeeding control period. Thus the increase in flow following feeding appears specific for the rumen.

Volume and rumen motility

Emptying and rinsing of the ruminoreticulum are followed by depression of both ruminoreticular blood flow and contraction rate. Return of original rumen ingesta confined in a plastic bag (volume replacement) is followed by some increase in contraction rate but no increase in ruminal blood flow. When contact between ingesta and mucosa is established by opening and removing the bag, ruminal blood flow increases while contraction rate remains unaltered. This suggests that the increase in ruminal blood flow following feeding does not depend solely upon the mechanical effect due to the volume of rumen ingesta or increase in rumen contraction rate, but upon stimulation provided via contact between mucosa and constituents of the normal rumen contents.

Carbon dioxide and volatile fatty acids

Carbon dioxide and volatile fatty acids are two of the principal end products of rumen fermentation. An increase in the concentration of either of these appears to increase the ruminal blood flow independent of an increase in hydrogen ion concentration.

When carbon dioxide is bubbled through normal rumen content or a saline substitute for normal content, rumen blood flow increases. The carbon dioxide is introduced and allowed to escape via an open rumen fistula. Substituting nitrogen for carbon dioxide does not increase blood flow, nor does decreasing the pH by the addition of lactate, citrate, or phosphate. However, the addition of carbon dioxide to rumen content with a low pH does. Carbon dioxide probably brings about a dilatation of the resistance vessels in the rumen vascular bed.

Addition of volatile fatty acids to the saline-filled rumen increases rumen blood flow also. Increasing the concentration of butyrate from 5 to 20 mM results in a progressive increment in flow, but there is no regular relationship above 20 mM.

BRAIN

Afferent vessels

The blood supply to the brain is derived from four arteries, the paired carotid and vertebral arteries. The vertebral arteries are the main source of supply for the cerebellum, pons, and medulla and are somewhat separate from the carotid arteries, which supply the cerebrum. However, the terminal extensions of the vertebral arteries do unite with a major supply from the carotid arteries to form a vascular ring (the circle of Willis) on the surface of the base of the brain. Three pairs of cerebral arteries, the anterior, middle, and posterior, arise from this vascular ring to supply the cerebral hemispheres. There is wide species variation in the anatomical details of the arterial supply, including the relative importance of the vertebral arteries, the contribution of the internal as opposed to the external carotid arteries, the presence or absence of a *rete mirabile* between the cranial arteries and the vascular ring serving as a common trunk for the cerebral arteries, and the number and identity of extracranial arteries of the head which communicate with the circle of Willis.

In the cow, sheep, goat, and deer, occlusion of the common carotid arteries results in acute cerebral hypoxia. In these species the vertebral arteries are poorly developed or atresic; the carotid arteries are almost the exclusive supply to the cerebrum. In the horse the vertebrals are well developed, the carotid supply to the cerebrum poorly developed. In man both the vertebral and carotid arteries contribute substantially to brain perfusion. The dog tolerates ligation of both the internal carotid and vertebral arterial supply. In this case anastomotic connection between the anterior spinal arteries and major branches feeding the circle of Willis provides at least minimal brain blood flow.

In man and other primates the carotid supply to the brain is usually exclusively from the internal carotid arteries. In the cat family and ruminants the internal carotid arteries are atrophic, and the external carotids are the major source. In the domestic cat the internal carotids eventually become completely atresic with age. In these species there are anastomotic communications between branches of the external carotid arteries. In some animals—the dog for example—the internal carotids are present but poorly developed. In such cases branches of the internal and external carotids anastomose with each other. The complex anastomosis is called a *rete mirabile,* the splitting of a vessel into a plexus of smaller vessels which then reunite to form a single vessel which continues on its way to the circle of Willis. It is found in the cat, sheep, goat, cow, and pig and may serve as a pressure-regulating device. The *rete mirabile* is located extracranially in the cat and intracranially in ruminants.

The circulation to the brain has a considerable degree of independence from the blood flow to other regions, made possible by different regulating mechanisms. As in other vascular regions, the blood flow through the brain depends upon the perfusion pressure, that is, the difference in pressure in the cerebral arteries and veins at the level of the head; and the cerebral vascular resistance, which is controlled principally by autoregulation.

The brain capillaries together with surrounding tissue form the blood-brain barrier. The capillaries are continuous with complete endothelial and basement membrane layers. Further, the basement membrane blends with the web of neurogliar tissue to form one continuous sheet separating capillaries from neurons. The intact blood-brain barrier restricts and limits the interchange between blood and neurons, especially of proteins, lipids, and drugs with large molecular weights. The barrier maintains a constant chemical environment for the very responsive neurons, and it becomes an important consideration in the selection of drugs to treat diseases of the CNS (see Chapter 14).

Brain blood flow

There are several important features of cerebral circulation: (1) the brain is extremely dependent upon an uninterrupted nutrient blood flow; (2) the total demand for flow is relatively stable under a variety of conditions; and (3) flow occurs through an incompressible mass of tissues circumscribed by the rigid skull. Sensitivity to the interruption of blood flow is so high that a complete stoppage for 4–5 seconds results in unconsciousness while a 4–5 minute interval in the mature animal produces irreversible damage. Different parts of the brain have different volume flow rates.

The gray matter of the CNS is composed largely of the cell bodies of neurons. The volume flow rate through grey matter is approximately sixfold greater than that through white. With respect to blood flow the brain behaves as though it were a group of organs whose flows vary independently according to different and changing rates of oxygen extraction. Those components with the highest normal rates of oxygen consumption—the cerebral cortex, cerebellum, caudate nucleus, and thalamus—are commonly the first structues to incur damage in disease accompanied by chronic hypoxia.

The total amount of blood with normal P_{O_2} and P_{CO_2} perfusing the entire brain per unit of time remains remarkably constant even under such diverse conditions as sleep, muscular exercise, emotional stress, or, in man, marked mental effort. However, the normal rate varies with the species. In man 14 percent of the cardiac output flows through the vessels of the brain; in the dog only 8.

Cerebral perfusion pressure

The force which drives blood through the cerebral vessels is equal to the difference between the arterial and venous pressures at the head level. Normally the cerebral venous pressure compared with arterial pressure is very low and stable, and the arterial pressure can be taken as the perfusion pressure. The carotid sinus and aortic cardiovascular reflexes do not induce changes in resistance to flow in the arterioles of the brain. They do rigidly maintain blood pressure in the carotid arteries. The reflexes thus serve to preserve blood flow to the brain even under conditions in which total body flow (cardiac output) is reduced. The cardiovascular reflexes which provide for pressure homeostasis constitute the first impediment to a reduction in cerebral blood flow. There is a significant difference between the arterial pressures at the heart level in some species. However, when differences in the vertical distance between the heart and brain are taken into account, the cerebral perfusion pressures are quite comparable (Fig. 11.1).

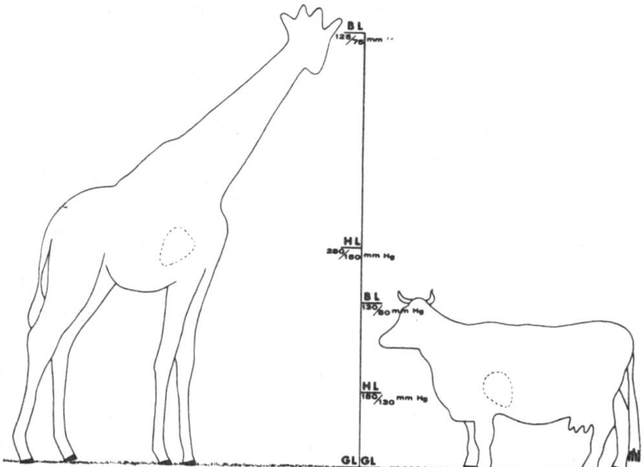

Figure 11.1. Cerebral perfusion pressure in the ox and giraffe. BL, brain level; HL, heart level. (From Patterson et al. 1965, *Ann. N.Y. Acad. Sci.* 127:393–413.)

Regulation

The vascular bed of the brain normally can distribute blood flow among its component parts in keeping with variations in nutritional demands. It likewise can adjust somewhat to extrinsic stresses such as hypotension, hypertension, hypoventilation (hypoxia and hypercapnia), and hyperventilation (hypocapnia). These capabilities are derived in large measure from well-developed autoregulatory mechanisms rather than from neural vasomotor reflexes (Kontos 1975, Rosenblum 1975). The precapillary resistance vessels and particularly the small arteries and arterioles of the microcirculatory bed are the responsive and active elements in matching the driving force of the blood at the head level with vascular resistance. There are limits to autoregulation and under some circumstances this ability is lost (Meyer and Marx 1971, Miller et al. 1973).

Neurogenic reflex regulation

Both adrenergic and cholinergic autonomic efferent fibers are distributed to pial and parenchymal arterial vessels of the brain, but there is controversy concerning their significance in the regulation of brain blood flow (Lluch et al. 1975, Raper et al. 1972, Wahl et al. 1972, D'Alecy and Fiegel 1972). The current consensus is that the potential for neural regulation exists but that its physiological role is negligible. Visual observations of exposed pial arteries and arterioles reveal that they constrict when norepinephrine is applied directly. The sensitivity to epinephrine is several times less than that found in other vascular beds. A reduced sensitivity to serotonin and other vasoactive humoral substances is also characteristic. The reduction in sensitivity may depend upon a low density of receptors or upon rapid inactivation or trapping of vasoactive substances. This relatively large freedom from extrinsic neural and humoral vasomotor forces isolates and enhances local blood flow regulation.

Metabolic autoregulation

In the process of intra-organ distribution of flow, metabolic autoregulation plays a dominant role. The very small arteries and arterioles of the microcirculatory beds are the active vessels. Selective individual vasoconstriction and vasodilatation of fractions of the total microcirculatory bed may occur without changing the gross cerebrovascular resistance.

Changes in tensions of carbon dioxide and oxygen in the extracellular fluid are the two most important stimuli in cerebral metabolic autoregulation. Of the two, changes in P_{CO_2} are commonly regarded as having the stronger influence. A rise in P_{CO_2} or a fall in P_{O_2} has a dilator effect. A fall in P_{CO_2} or a rise in P_{O_2} produces vasoconstriction. The changes act locally rather than remotely via reflex arcs or circulating hormones. The levels of P_{CO_2} and P_{O_2} influence local pH. Changes in hydrogen ion concentrations are known to be vasoactive. In addition to dependency upon local pH, the vasomotor effects of P_{CO_2} and P_{O_2} may involve the release of adenosine, acetylcholine, or other vasoactive substances from nearby neurons or nerve fibers.

While the effects of P_{CO_2} and P_{O_2} are important, both easily pass the blood-brain barrier, and local gaseous tensions may be affected by local vaso-occlusive disease, or by conditions remote from the brain per se, such as systemic hypo- or hypertension and hypo- or hyperventilation.

Intracranial pressure

The vasculature of the brain is passively subjected to pressure changes occurring within the confines of the rigid cranial cavity. Increases in cerebrospinal fluid pressure or space-occupying lesions such as brain edema, hemorrhage, or tumors tend to compress vessels, increase cerebrovascular resistance, and compromise brain blood flow. Rapidly occurring increases may result in intense cerebral ischemia and unconsciousness.

A systemic pressor response associated with sudden and extensive elevations of intracranial pressure (33 mm Hg or above) is referred to as the Cushing law or reflex. Elevation of intracranial pressure to or above that prevailing in the capillary and small precapillary vessels of the microcirculation causes a drastic reduction in blood flow, brain ischemia, and a rise in tissue P_{CO_2}. The medullary vasoconstrictor center is stimulated by the elevation of P_{CO_2}. Its stimulation causes systemic vasoconstriction, increased peripheral resistance, and a powerful rise in arterial blood pressure. The rise in pressure in vessels supplying the brain tends to restore and maintain brain blood flow while simultaneously it drastically reduces flow to abdominal viscera and the kidneys.

HEART

Morphology

In mammals two arteries, the right and left coronary arteries, supply blood to the heart. They are so designated because of their origin from the right and left aortic sinuses and their termination on the corresponding heart surfaces. There are species differences in their precise course, branching, and fraction of total heart blood flow. In ruminants and the dog, the left coronary artery is larger, supplies a greater amount of the myocardium, and carries approximately 80 percent of the total blood flow. In man and other primates a more highly developed right coronary pattern is evident. Most cardiac veins parallel the course of the analogous arteries on and within the heart (Anderson 1973, Heine et al. 1973).

The microcirculatory bed is extensive and well adapted to subserve the nutritional needs of the beating heart. Capillary density is approximately eight times that of skeletal muscle. At body rest only one half of the capillaries are open. As metabolic rate increases more capillaries are recruited into the functional circulatory bed. A normally high capillary density appears consistent with the stimulating effect on capillary endothelium of the normally low intracellular Po_2 (10 mm Hg) prevailing in myocardium, as well as the failure of additional capillary proliferation when the myocardial mass increases in cardiac hypertrophy.

Collateral circulation refers to circulation through secondary arterial channels when flow through primary vessels is diminished or abolished. The coronary arteries anastomose with each other during their course on the surface of the heart as well as within the heart. Collateral circulation is only a small fraction of normal flow and is not sufficiently developed to prevent death of some myocardial tissue when a primary arterial channel is suddenly and completely occluded. Limited further development of collateral circulation occurs during slow progressive restriction of flow through a primary branch of the coronary arteries (Helfant et al. 1971, Cibulski et al. 1973). In contrast to man, vaso-occlusive diseases of the more proximal and major extramyocardial branches of the coronary arteries are rare in common domestic and zoo animals and birds.

Myocardial oxygen demand and supply

Physiological mechanisms serve to balance oxygen supply with demand. Because of the obligatory aerobic nature of myocardial metabolism the rate of oxygen consumption can be used as a reliable index of energy production and utilization. Oxygen consumption may vary from 3–15 ml/100 g of ventricle per minute, which accounts for 8–10 percent of the body's total. Increases in heart rate, volume and dimensions of cardiac chambers, magnitude of pressure developed by a chamber, velocity of pressure development (i.e. the state of myocardial contractility), and amount of external mechanical work performed all increase myocardial oxygen consumption.

The supply of oxygen to the heart is dependent upon the blood flow rate and the amount of oxygen which can be extracted. The heart has a relatively high volume flow rate. In the resting dog, total coronary flow varies from 40 to 60 ml/100 g of tissue per minute, or 4–5 percent of total cardiac output. In addition, there is an ample blood flow reserve. In dogs coronary blood flow may increase more than 10 fold during severe physical exertion. The opposite is true for a reserve oxygen extraction capacity. Normally, the myocardium extracts 60–80 percent of the oxygen from arterial blood. This is the highest normal O_2 utilization coefficient of all body tissues. It leaves only a very small reserve oxygen supply.

Regulation

Coronary driving pressure

The anatomy of the coronary circuit promotes a favorable A-V pressure gradient. The circuit is relatively short, originates at the prime source of pressure in the root of the aorta, and terminates within its own right auricle. Flow remains relatively constant between arterial pressures of 60 and 180 mm Hg due to automatic compensatory changes in coronary vascular resistance through autoregulation. Coronary autoregulation has its normal limits and is itself subject to alteration by structural changes and the influence of unusual vasoactive substances created by disease.

Mechanical factors

Despite a favorable pressure gradient across the coronary vascular bed throughout the cardiac cycle, the heart's rhythmic contraction and relaxation interrupt what might otherwise be a relatively steady blood flow. During systole, vessel compression by myocardial tissue pressure impedes or stops flow in capillaries and precapillary intramyocardial vessels and empties corresponding veins. Compressive forces are not uniformly distributed over the wall thickness of a given chamber or among different chambers. They are largest in layers adjacent to the endocardium in the walls of the left ventricle.

Total coronary blood flow is lowest during systole because of the relative brevity of systole compared to diastole and the flow hindrance imposed by systolic compression of inflow vessels. For these reasons a slow heart rate, a normal duration of systole, and ejection against normal aortic and pulmonic artery pressures all favor a more optimal total coronary blood flow.

Neural regulation

The coronary arteries are innervated by both cholinergic and adrenergic nerve fibers. The adrenergic fibers terminate at both α-stimulating and β-inhibiting smooth-muscle receptor sites. By separate blocking of the two types of receptors sympathetic nerve stimulation may produce either coronary vasoconstriction or dilatation. Their simultaneous activation tends to moderate each other's influence. Stimulation of parasympathetic cholinergic fibers in the controlled and artifically paced heart produces vasodilatation.

Both divisions of the autonomic nervous system innervate the S-A (sinoatrial) node and control heart rate. β-adrenergic nerves innervate ventricular myocardial fibers and influence contractility. Both heart rate and contractility influence myocardial oxygen consumption and tissue Po_2. Normally tissue Po_2 via local metabolic autoregulation dominates coronary arterial vasomotion. Most of the neural effect seems to be exerted indirectly via its influence on metabolic rate and the subsequent effect on autoregulation. Since neural effects are exerted rapidly, the overall response may be a blending over time of both their direct neural and their indirect metabolic effects on arteriolar vasomotion.

Metabolic autoregulation

The myocardium can develop only a very small oxygen debt. Normally the A-V oxygen difference across the coronary vascular bed is high. The myocardium extracts most of the oxygen with which it is presented. Most of any increase in myocardial oxygen demand is satisfied by an increase in the coronary blood volume flow rate. The level of myocardial tissue Po_2 has the most influence on coronary vascular resistance and blood flow. It is a major regulator of blood flow. Increases in tissue Pco_2 and hydrogen ion concentration have similar but much less intense vasodilator effects. Changes in O_2 tension act locally via autoregulatory mechanisms.

REFERENCES

Anderson, W.D. 1973. A correlative study of the anatomy of the cardiovascular systems of man and animals. In L.T. Harmison, ed., *Research in Animal Medicine*. HEW Pub. no. 72-333 (NIH), Washington. Pp. 767–805.

Asheim, A., Knudsen, O., Lindholm, A., Rulcker, C., and Saltin, B. 1970. Heart rates and blood lactate concentrations of standardbred horses during training and racing. *J. Am. Vet. Med. Ass.* 157:304–12.

Barger, A.C., Richards, V., Metcalfe, J., and Gunther, B. 1956. Regulation of the circulation during exercise: Cardiac output (direct Fick) and metabolic adjustments in the normal dog. *Am. J. Physiol.* 184:613–23.

Bergstein, G. 1974. Blood pressure, cardiac output and blood-gas tension in the horse at rest and during exercise. *Acta Vet. Scand.* 48 (suppl.):1–88.

Cerretelli, P., Piiper, J., Mangili, F., and Ricci, B. 1964. Circulation in exercising dogs. *J. Appl. Physiol.* 19:29–32.

Cibulski, A.A., Lehan, P.H., and Timmis, H.H. 1973. Contribution of intramyocardial collaterals to anastomotic flow in mongrel dogs. *J Cardiovasc. Surg.* 14:275–81.

D'Alecy, L.G. and Feigel, E.D. 1972. Sympathetic control of cerebral blood flow in dogs. *Circ. Res.* 31:267–83.

Ehrlein, H.J., Hornicke, H., Engelhardt, W.V., and Tolkmitt, G. 1973. Die Herzschlagfrequenz während standardisierter Belastung al Mass für die Leitungsfähigkeit von Pferde. *Zentralblatt Veterinärmedizin*, ser. A, 20:188–208.

Franklin, D., Vatner, S.F., Higgins, C.B., Patrick, T., Kemper, W.S., and Van Citters, R.L. 1973. Measurement and radiotelemetry of cardiovascular variables in conscious animals: Techniques and applications. In L.T. Harmison, ed., *Research in Animal Medicine*. HEW Pub. no. 72-333 (NIH), Washington. Pp. 1119–33.

Heine, H., Tschirkov, F., and Manz, D. 1973. Über Beziehungen zwischen Herzmorphologie, Coronargefässtipp, and Herzenfalligikeit bei Saugetieren. *Klin. Wchschr*. 51:191–97.

Khouri, E.M., Gregg, D.E., and Rayford, C.R. 1965. Effect of exercise on cardiac output: Left coronary flow and myocardial metabolism in the unanesthetized dog. *Circ. Res.* 17:427–37.

Kontos, H.A. 1975. Mechanism of the regulation of the cerebral microcirculation. *Current Concepts Cerebrovascular Dis.: Stroke* 10(2):7–12.

Lluch, S., Gomez, B., Alborch, E., and Urquilla, P.R. 1975. Adrenergic mechanisms in cerebral circulation of the goat. *Am. J. Physiol.* 228:985–89.

Marsland, W.P. 1968. Heart rate response to submaximal exercise in the standardbred horse. *J. Appl. Physiol.* 106:689–715.

Meyer, J.S., and Marx, P. 1971. Cerebral autoregulation and "dysautoregulation" and their relation to cerebral vascular symptoms. *Current Concepts Cerebrovascular Dis.: Stroke*. 6:1–5.

Miller, J.D., Stanek, A.E., and Langfitt, T.W. 1973. Cerebral blood flow regulation during experimental brain compression. *J. Neurosurg.* 39:186–96.

Patterson, J.L., Goetz, R.H., Doyle, J.T., Warren, J.V., Gauer, O.H., Detweiler, D.K., Said, S.I., Hoernicke, H., McGregor, M., Keen, E.N., Smith, Jr., M.H., Hardie, E.L., Reynolds, E.L., Flatt, W.P., and Waldo, D.R. 1965. Cardiorespiratory dynamics in the ox and giraffe, with comparative observations on man and other animals. *Ann. N.Y. Acad. Sci.* 127:393–413.

Raper, A.J., Hermes, A.K., and Wel, E.P. 1972. Unresponsiveness of pial precapillary vessels to catecholamines and sympathetic nerve stimulation. *Circ. Res.* 31:257–66.

Rosenblum, W.I. 1975. Cerebral microcirculation: Selected topics. *Current Concepts Cerebrovascular Dis.: Stroke*. 10(1):1–6.

Rushmer, R.F., Smith, O., and Franklin D., 1959. Mechanisms of cardiac control in exercise. *Circ. Res.* 7:602–27.

Saltin, B. 1974. The physiological and biochemical response of standardbred horses to exercise of varying speed and duration. *Acta Vet. Scand.* 15:310–24.

Sellers, A.F. 1965. Blood flow in the rumen vessels. In R.W. Dougherty, R.S. Allen, W. Burroughs, N.L. Jacobson, and A.D. McGilliard, eds., *Physiology of Digestion in the Ruminant*. Butterworths, Washington. Pp. 171–84.

Van Citters, R.L., Kemper, W.S., and Franklin, D.L. 1966. Blood pressure responses of wild giraffes studied by radio telemetry. *Science* 152:384–86.

Wahl, M., Kuschinski, W., Bosse, O., Olesen, J., Lassen, N.A., Ingvar, D.H., Michaelis, J., and Thuran, K. 1972. Effect of L-norepinephrine on the diameter of pial arterioles and arteries in the cat. *Circ. Res.* 31:248–56.

Wittke, G., and Bayer, A. 1968. Die Herzschlagfrequenz von Pferden bei Vielseitigkeitsprüfungen. *Berl. Münch. Tierartzl. Wchschr.* 81:389–92.

CHAPTER 12

Pulmonary Circulation

by C. Roger Smith and Robert L. Hamlin

ANATOMY

The pulmonary and systemic circulatory systems may be regarded as two open circuits connected in series to form a single closed loop. A major function of the pulmonary circuit is to facilitate the exchange of gases occurring in the lungs. Although the average volume flow through the two circuits is almost the same, there are marked structural and dynamic differences. The pulmonary circulation is a relatively short, low resistance, low pressure system which conducts blood to and from a single but very dense capillary bed enveloping the pulmonary alveoli. It consists of the right ventricle, pulmonary arteries, pulmonary capillaries, pulmonary veins, and left atrium. Because the pulmonary vessels are very distensible they not only serve as a channel but also as a reservoir between the right and left ventricles.

The lung is not inert; it is an important metabolic organ (Bakhle and Vane 1974, Fishman and Giuseppe 1974). The squamous cells comprising the pulmonary capillary endothelium are involved in a major way in the uptake, storage, degradation, inactivation, and release of a large number of bioactive substances, including vasoactive chemicals. Because the lungs receive the entire cardiac output, the inactivation or synthesis of vasoactive chemicals is important for both the systemic and pulmonary circulation. Bradykinin, adenine nucleotides, and some prostaglandins are inactivated; inactive angiotensin I is converted to active angiotensin II; and histamine, kallikreins, and some prostaglandins are synthesized, stored, and discharged into the pulmonary circulation.

Right ventricle

The right ventricle functions as a "volume pump." It ejects almost the same volume (95%) per minute as does the left ventricle but against a much lower pressure. The normal right ventricle can be identified by the fact that the right ventricular free wall is only about one third as thick as the left. When dissected from the rest of the heart, the free wall has a triangular shape. Its normal attachment to the cylindrical surface formed by the interventricular septum and the free wall of the left ventricle results in a crescent-shaped right ventricular lumen of relatively large dimensions. The right ventricle is not normally required to develop a large driving force. Starr (1943) and Rodbard and Wagner (1949) eliminated the right ventricle as a pump and demonstrated that right atrial pressure alone suffices for lung perfusion when pulmonary resistance is normal.

Pulmonary vessels

The pulmonary vascular system, like the systemic, consists of a series of tubes. However, the large pulmonary arteries are short and rapidly subdivide into peripheral branches, which have thinner walls and wider lumens than their systemic counterparts and which in general resemble systemic veins more than arteries. The wall of the pulmonary artery is less than one third as thick as that of the aorta. Small arteries have only a thin media with relatively little smooth muscle. The small postcapillary venules are devoid of smooth muscle. Because the pressures throughout the pulmonary circuit are so low, even smaller amounts of vascular smooth muscle are capable of actively changing vessel radii.

Important features to consider in the dynamics of pulmonary circulation are: (1) the position within the negative but rhythmically variable pressure of the thorax, (2) the position between the right ventricle and the left atrium, (3) the relatively great distensibility and collapsibility of the vessels, (4) the effect that the interaction of intravascular and extravascular pressures has on easily collapsible and distensible vessels, pulmonary vascular resistance, and flow distribution within the lung, (5) the relative paucity of vascular smooth muscle and vasomotor nerves, and (6) the transport of venous blood in arteries and arterial blood (oxygenated) in veins in quantities per unit of time equal to that of the systemic circulation.

There are species differences in the morphology of the pulmonary vessels. In the rabbit the small pulmonary arteries are relatively muscular. In the cow a distinct muscular media occurs in both arteries and veins down to vessels with diameters as small as 20 μ (Hecht et al. 1962, Kuida et al. 1963, Alexander 1965). Among the species studied, the bovine has the best developed muscular coat in the arterioles. Differences in pulmonary vasoactivity among species correlate well with the degree of development of the vasculature of the pulmonary vessels.

In addition to the flow of venous blood delivered by the pulmonary artery to the alveoli for oxygenation, the lungs also receive a nutrient supply via the bronchial arteries. They supply oxygenated blood to the lung tissues at least to the level of the bronchioles. Normally the volume flow through the bronchial arteries amounts to no more than 1–2 percent of the cardiac output. The bronchial arteries resemble other systemic arteries. Part of the venous drainage from them is returned by systemic veins to the right atrium. The remainder drains into the pulmonary veins.

PRESSURES

Right ventricle pressures

For the right ventricle the highest systolic pressures occur in the horse, cow, and pig, the lowest in the dog. Intermediate systolic pressures are found in the goat and sheep. The higher pressures in larger animals are probably related to the higher resistances to flow encountered in larger lungs, especially in those with significant portions of the pulmonary vascular bed above the level of the heart. Diastolic pressures in large domestic animals are also usually higher than those in the dog and other small laboratory animals (Table 12.1). The higher diastolic pressures may be related to the weight of the column of blood (hydrostatic effect) between the ventricle and the head, that is, contained within the right atrium and the jugular veins. Spörri (1965) found that the diastolic pressure in cows is increased when the head is elevated and decreased when the head is lowered.

The pulse contour of the right ventricle differs from the left: (1) it is smaller in amplitude, (2) the rate of rise is smaller, (3) the peak pressure occurs early rather than late in the ejection period, and (4) the pressure falls rather rapidly following the early peak, in contrast to the plateau-peak sequence in the left ventricle pressure pulse (Fig. 12.1). The lower rate of rise of pressure, that is, dp/dt (the rate of change of pressure), is determined by the smaller myocardial mass of the right ventricle and the lower resistance and greater distensibility of the pulmonary circuit (Doyle et al. 1960). The fall in pressure following the early peaking is due to the rapid passage of

Table 12.1. Pressures in the pulmonary circulation (mm Hg)

	Right ventricle pressures			Pulmonary artery pressures			
Species	Systolic	Diastolic	Source	Systolic	Diastolic	Mean	Source
Cow	42–56	0–1	Doyle et al. 1960	33–46	19–21	24–31	Doyle et al. 1960
Horse	49 ± 11 (35–72)	14 ± 6 (7–24)	Gall 1967	36 ± 9 (25–51)	21 ± 5 (14–28)	28	Gall 1967
Calf	55 (51–60)	0	McCrady et al. 1968	45 (36–52)	16 (12–18)	26 (20–35)	McCrady et al. 1968
Pig	51	0	Wachtel et al. 1963	40	16 9–20	22.5	Maaske et al. 1965
Dog	24	2	Moscovitz et al. 1956	21	10	10	Moscovitz et al. 1956
Man	25 (17–32)	4 (1–7)	Dittmer et al. 1959	22 (11–29)	9 (4–13)	15 (9–19)	Dittmer et al. 1959
Goat	24.5 (24–32)	−1.5 (−3 to 0)	Spörri 1962				
Sheep	26.3 (18–37)	−3.1 (−6 to 0)	Spörri 1962			9	Halmagi et al. 1961
Cat	26	0	Tashjian et al. 1965	26–36	15–17		Grauweiler 1965

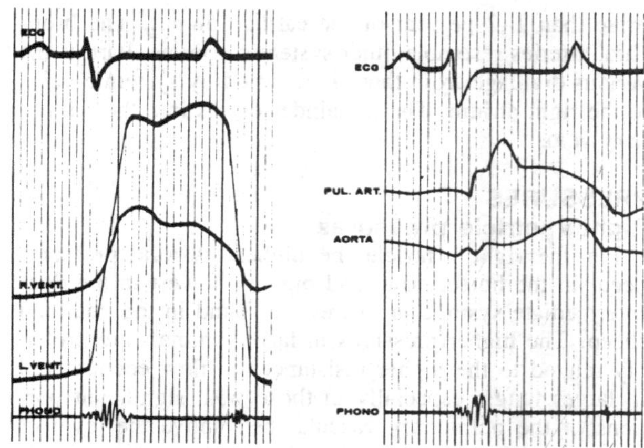

Figure 12.1. Contour of the pressure pulses in the right and left ventricles, aorta, and pulmonary artery in the ox. (From Spörri 1965, *Ann. N.Y. Acad. Sci.* 127:379–92.)

the blood from the relatively short pulmonary arteries. When conditions in the pulmonic circuit become more like those in the systemic, the pulse contours become more alike. In pulmonary hypertension, for example, the right ventricle hypertrophies and the pulmonary vascular resistance increases.

Pulmonary artery pressure

The mean pressure in the pulmonary artery is approximately one sixth that of the systemic. Pressures in man, dog, cat, calf, and sheep tend to be lower than those in the cow, pig, and horse (see Table 12.1). The pressures vary with age as well as with species. In utero, the pulmonary and systemic pressures are nearly equal as a result of the patent ductus arteriosus. In newborn calves the pulmonary artery pressure decreases in three stages: it falls below systemic pressure during the first 2 hours after birth; it falls rapidly during the period between the second and twelfth hours; and it slowly decreases further until the animal is 14 days old (Reeves and Leathers 1964).

In normal animals the output of the right ventricle and the pulmonary blood flow nearly equal the output of the left ventricle and the systemic blood flow respectively. Thus in Poiseuille's equation ($Q = P/R$), Q, or volume of flow, is very nearly the same for both pulmonary and systemic circuits. On the other hand, the short lengths and large radii of the pulmonary arteries yield a small value for resistance, approximately one fifth of the resistance to flow observed in the systemic arteries.

The direct effect of volume upon pressure is less marked in the pulmonary circuit than in the systemic too. The distensibility of the pulmonary arterial tree tends to prevent wide fluctuations in pressure in spite of rather marked variations in volume and flow. For example, a doubling or even a tripling of cardiac output during exercise increases the pressure no more than a few mm Hg. Likewise occlusion of one pulmonary artery in the mature dog increases the mean pressure by one third or less, and removal of more than one half of the lungs is required to produce pulmonary hypertension.

Contour of pressure pulse

The contour of the pulmonary arterial pressure pulse basically resembles that of the aorta (see Fig. 12.1). The pressure pulse is smaller in amplitude, peaks more sharply and earlier in systole, and begins to fall earlier and more steeply while systole is still in progress. Consequently the incisura occupies a lower position on the catacrotic limb of the pulse. The fall during diastole, that is, following the incisura, is more gradual than that of the central systemic circuit. The low absolute value of the pulse pressure is a reflection of the marked distensibility of the pulmonary arterial vessels, which permits easy accommodation to the right ventricular stroke volume without a marked rise in the pressure; and the low arteriolar resistance, which allows a larger fraction of the stroke volume to leave the arterial tree during each systole. The latter also accounts for the early fall during systole and the low position of the incisura on the descending limb of the pulse curve.

The ratio of pulse pressure to systolic pressure is higher than in the systemic circuit. Pulse pressure is one half or more of systolic pressure due to the fact that the stroke volume represents a relatively larger fraction of the blood in the pulmonary arteries. For example, blood volume in the pulmonary arteries of a 20 kg dog is approximately 60 ml; stroke volume is 20–30 ml. Were it not for the marked distensibility of the pulmonary arterial tree, the pulse pressure would be still larger.

Effect of respiration

During inspiration the intrapleural pressure falls, and the lungs are expanded. The reverse occurs during expiration. Pressures and flow in the pulmonary artery are both influenced by these events. If the pressures measured are atmospheric, pulmonary artery pressure will parallel the intrapleural pressure fluctuations, that is, fall during inspiration and rise during expiration. If they are intrapleural, that is, if the transmural pressures are measured, pressure rises during inspiration and falls during expiration. The inspiratory rise is due to the increased flow which follows increased cardiac output occurring concomitantly with an increased venous return during the inspiratory fall in intrapleural pressure. In the dog at rest, an increase in cardiac output during inspiration is also aided by an increase in heart rate during sinus arrhythmia. During expiration the opposite takes place.

Nonrespiratory pressure waves

Slow, noncardiac, and nonrespiratory rhythmic fluctuations in pulmonary arterial pressures are sometimes observed. They are most frequently found in association with systemic (Traube-Hering-Mayer) waves, with frequency and amplitude independent of the breathing pattern. They are the passive effects of fluctuations in pulmonary blood flow due to rhythmic changes in systemic vascular resistance and flow (Ferretti et al. 1965).

CAPILLARY FLOW

In marked contrast to the systemic circuit, the resistance to outflow from the pulmonary arteries is low. Further, the capacities of the pulmonary arteries and the right ventricular stroke output are nearly equal. Thus uneven or pulsatile capillary flow occurs. Pulsations of flow are accompanied by pressure pulsations of several mm Hg. These may at times affect whether a pulmonary capillary is open, closed, or partially collapsed. They also provide rhythmical stimulation to the vascular smooth muscle in the small precapillary arterioles.

Effect of hydrostatic pressure

The weight of a column of fluid in a vessel exerts force as hydrostatic pressure. For blood this increases approximately 7.4 mm Hg for each 10 cm of height. In mature large animals with large lungs or in man in the upright posture a significant portion of the pulmonary vascular bed may lie several times this distance above or below the level at which the main pulmonary vessels leave the heart. For levels above the heart, the hydrostatic pressure opposes the arterial perfusion pressure generated by the right ventricle. Thus the net pressure which distends vessels and propels blood is reduced. For levels below the heart, the opposite prevails. In man and upright bipeds the hydrostatic pressure is a major determinant of the distribution of pulmonary blood flow. In quadripeds in normal posture, such effects may be somewhat different since the most dorsal portion of the lung is not the apex (Will et al. 1973, Hamlin et al. 1974).

The combination of several conditions makes the effect of gravity so marked. First, all the pulmonary vessels do not lie in the same plane. Since the pulmonary vascular perfusion pressure is low, relatively small, directly opposing or augmenting pressures can either cancel or significantly increase its magnitude and effect on vessel size and blood flow. Second, all the pulmonary blood vessels including the arteries are easily collapsed or distended, which requires only small differences between intravascular and extravascular pressures. And finally, the alveolar microcirculatory vessels are surrounded by air spaces, rather than by fluid and tissue cells as in the systemic circuit. Since the specific gravity of air is negligible compared to that of blood and other tissue, the pressure exerted on the outside walls of alveolar vessels is a constant irrespective of the alveolus' location. This precludes the possibility of parallel changes in extravascular pressure which would balance those intravascular ones due to gravity. In addition, should the blood pressure in small vessels rise, it can attain levels beyond influence by alveolar air pressure. Positive pressure breathing, which creates high intra-alveolar pressures, increases such an influence.

In larger quadripeds and bipeds the effects of hydrostatic pressure bring about a considerable unevenness of alveolar perfusion from the top to the bottom of the lung. Generally three zones or regions are described. At the top of the lung, the pressure inside some of the arterial microcirculatory vessels may fall below the critical closing pressure, or be less than required for full distension. In this zone, flow is diminished in some vessels and arrested in others despite an A-V (arteriovenous) pressure gradient. At some lower point arterial but not venous pressure exceeds alveolar pressure. In this zone the alveolar pressure tends to pinch off venules, increase resistance, and decrease blood flow. At a still lower level, even the venous pressures exceed alveolar pressure. In this zone the pulmonary vessels are most distended, offering minimal resistance to flow. Also the blood flow rate is highest. Because both arterial and venous pressures are higher in this region than alveolar pressure, the latter does not play a role in the determination of resistance. In some situations all pulmonary intravascular pressures exceed alveolar pressures, for example, in exercise or in pulmonary hypertension. This minimizes inequalities in alveolar perfusion.

In health the inequalities in alveolar perfusion are not significant. In part this is due to the fact that alveolar ventilation also decreases from bottom to top of the lung although at a much lower rate. Regions of the lung in which the alveoli are relatively overperfused or underperfused contribute to the lung's dead space. This contribution expands when the effects of gravity are exaggerated (rapid acceleration or deceleration), when pulmonary hypotension exists, or during positive pressure breathing.

Transit time

The time estimated for the blood to traverse the pulmonary capillaries in the dog varies from 0.18 to 1 second. The more capillaries open for a certain volume flow, the longer the average capillary transit time. The time the blood remains in the capillaries is largely conditioned by the frequency and size of the right ventricle stroke output compared to the size of the pulmonary capillary blood volume. Normally blood does not accumulate in arteries, capillaries, or veins. With each heartbeat the stroke volume ejected replaces an equivalent volume in the pulmonary arteries, which is propelled onward to the succeeding segment. In a 15–20 kg dog the pulmonary capillary blood volume is about 20 ml, which also approximates the stroke volume. If these volumes are equal, the capillary transit time will equal the beat interval.

Normally the time spent by the blood in the capillaries is more than sufficient for oxygenation. When the pulmonary flow rate increases, as during exercise, oxygenation is still normal because: (1) usually it only requires a fraction of the time spent in the capillaries under basal conditions, and (2) when the beat interval is decreased, as it is when cardiac output increases during exercise, the number of patent capillaries increases and they all dilate. The stroke volume thus becomes smaller compared to the capillary volume and transit time occupies more than one beat interval. Only when flow volume and capillary volumes change in opposite directions is there danger of reducing the time spent in the capillaries below that required for oxygenation.

Pressures

Indirect measurements of pulmonary capillary pressures are made by passing a fine flexible catheter through the right heart and out into the pulmonary artery until its tip is firmly wedged into a peripheral branch. Wedge pressures, however, estimate venous pressure and left atrial pressure more accurately than capillary pressures. From a consideration of wedge pressures and the fact that mean capillary pressure is intermediate between mean arterial and venous pressures, a value between 5 and 10 mm Hg appears reasonable.

Normally the capillary pressure must be below the oncotic pressure of the plasma proteins (25 mm Hg) or else a bulk transfer of fluid from the capillaries to the alveoli of the lungs would occur. In the healthy animal, fluid does not accumulate in the alveoli but is rapidly absorbed.

PULMONARY EDEMA

The lung is unique in that alveolar gas spaces are included in its extravascular space. Normally this space is devoid of free fluid. The blood pressure in the lung capillaries, the filtering surface, is only 10 mm Hg. The plasma oncotic pressure is 25 mm Hg. These conditions favor retention of fluid within the intravascular compartment. However, normally some fluid leaves the vascular compartment, enters the interstitial space surrounding alveoli, and passes centrally to enter the nearby lymphatic capillaries in the interstitium surrounding respiratory bronchioles. Here the lymphatic vessels, which are contractile, serve as skimming pumps for maintaining the extravascular fluid volume. In mature, normal unanesthetized sheep weighing 30–40 kg, lung lymph flow is estimated to be 10 ml/hr. Normally the lung lymphatics can transport moderately increased fluid loads with only minimal increases in interstitial fluid volume and pressure. Only when they become overwhelmed does fluid accumulate and edema become evident.

The alveolar epithelial membrane keeps fluid from entering the alveolar gas spaces. The uninjured membrane is normally impermeable to the common solutes of body fluids which pass freely over the capillary wall. Entrance of fluid into the alveoli only occurs as the final event in lung edema.

For lung edema with alveolar flooding to occur, one or a combination of events must lead to an imbalance between the rate of formation of tissue fluid and the rate of its drainage. The rate of filtration of capillary fluid is determined by the capillary blood pressure, tissue oncotic pressure, permeability of the capillary wall, pressure of the environment surrounding the capillary, and oncotic pressure of the blood plasma. Increases in any of the first three or decreases in the last two favor more rapid filtration. Lymphatic obstruction or paralysis of lymphatic contractility decreases the rate of drainage and enhances its accumulation. In clinical situations, by far the most common cause of imbalance is increased capillary blood pressure.

The most frequent cause of pulmonary capillary hypertension and lung edema is a decrease in the pumping action of the left ventricle as occurs in chronic congestive heart failure or acute myocardial infarction. When the ventricle fails to empty, it accumulates blood, end-diastolic volume and pressure increase, and pressures more proximal to the lung in the left atrium and the pulmonary vessels rise. Obstruction to flow from the left atrium to the left ventricle (mitral stenosis) causes a similar chain of events. Noncardiac causes of pulmonary capillary hypertension include intravascular fluid overload, pulmonary veno-occlusive diseases, and congenital and acquired forms of venous narrowing or stenosis.

Increases in the permeability of the pulmonary microvascular and alveolar membranes can be a primary factor in lung edema. Often permeability factors which are also mediators of inflammation, coagulation, or embolism are involved. Pulmonary edema due to increased permeability may be seen in pneumonias, following inhalation of irritating gases, in radiation sickness, in uremia, following aspiration of foreign material, as a result of poisoning with snake venoms or organophosphate insecticides, and along with pulmonary microembolization which may accompany physical trauma, hemorrhagic and septic shock, hemodialysis, or cardiopulmonary bypass. (Pulmonary edema has been reviewed by Staub 1974, Robin et al. 1973, and Szidon et al. 1972.)

VASOMOTION

Because pulmonary vessels are thin walled and easily collapsible, passive mechanical forces, such as those associated with the consolidation of some pneumonias or with airless or atelectic areas, substantially increase resistance to flow. Contrawise, the structure of pulmonary vessels is not particularly well suited for active vasoconstriction. Neither pulmonary arteries nor veins have much vascular smooth muscle. There are species differences; cattle and swine have relatively more, while sheep and dogs have relatively less muscle in arterial walls. However, since pulmonary arterial pressure is so low, the contraction of small amounts of vascular muscle can cause constriction of vessels under normal circumstances.

The concentrations of oxygen and carbon dioxide in the alveolar gas spaces are the most powerful stimuli for pulmonary arterial vasomotion. In health not all alveoli are equally well ventilated, but much more significant unevenness of ventilation develops in pneumonias, bronchitis, emphysema, or other diseases in which some regional airway is obstructed. Either a fall in Po_2 or a rise in Pco_2 in an alveolus results in vasoconstriction of its arterial vessels. Extrinsic autonomic nerves are not required.

Autoregulation

Autoregulation is well developed in the pulmonary vascular system. Experimental observations on isolated artificially perfused and ventilated lungs, as well as in vivo experiments employing drugs which block autonomic nerves, reveal that the major vasomotor activity of resistance vessels depends upon local autoregulatory mechanisms rather than central neural reflex systems (Hyman and Kadowitz 1975).

The action of alveolar hypoxia is limited to very short segments of arteries less than 200 μ in diameter which are immediately adjacent to the alveolus. Carbon dioxide acts similarly but upon somewhat longer segments. It is the effect that the Pco_2 has upon the local hydrogen ion concentration rather than the Pco_2 per se which stimulates the vasomotion. The site of action is important in that it renders autoregulation effective down to the level of the individual alveoli. The vasoconstrictor effect of alveolar hypoxia or hypercapnia diverts blood flow from under-ventilated to more normally ventilated air spaces. *Hypoxia is a more potent vasoconstrictor than hypercapnia*.

There are a number of vasoactive substances which are either synthesized, stored, or activated by cells of the lung. Cells of the reticuloendothelial system, blood platelets, white blood cells, and those of the alveolar epithelium participate in the local production and destruction of vasoactive chemicals. Histamine, widely distributed in mast cells, is a powerful but rapidly inactivated pulmonary vasoconstrictor, although it has been reported to have a vasodilator action on the neonatal bovine circulation. Serotonin (5-hydroxytryptamine) is found in mast cells and blood platelets and also is a potent vasoconstrictor. Angiotensin II, formed from angiotensin I by a lung-converting enzyme, is also a vasoconstrictor. Bradykinin, a vasodilator, is both generated and destroyed in the lungs. The prostaglandin vasodilators PGE_1 and PGE_2 can be synthesized and stored in the lungs, but the vasoconstrictor PGF_2 is most abundant in lung parenchyma. These and others play important roles in a wide variety of pathological states (e.g. endotoxic shock, hemorrhagic shock, and anaphylaxis).

Vasomotor nerves

The pulmonary vessels receive some autonomic vasomotor nerve fibers, predominantly adrenergic sympathetic vasoconstrictors. Their stimulation can raise pulmonary blood pressure 10–15 percent. The capacious pulmonary vessels are one of the body's blood reservoirs, and the vasoconstrictor fibers function more in the reflex mobilization of blood, e.g. in hemorrhage, than in pressor or depressor pulmonary responses.

The presence of an adrenergic system within the lungs is confirmed by the actions of injected catecholamines in perfused, isolated lungs. Small doses of epinephrine produce either minimal vasoconstriction or vasodilatation. Larger doses produce definite vasoconstriction. Epinephrine binds to both α-constrictor and β-dilator receptors, but has a stronger affinity for the latter. The β-receptors are far fewer in number. Thus the larger the dose the more conspicuous the vasoconstrictor effect. Isoproterenol, a pure β-stimulator, regularly produces vasodilatation. Norepinephrine, a pure α-stimulator, regularly produces vasoconstriction. Catecholamines are synthesized and stored in adrenergic nerve endings, but their release may be initiated not only by nerve impulses but also by local chemicals. For this reason the presence of adrenergic receptors is not absolute proof of neural reflex regulation.

PULMONARY HYPERTENSION

The most important factors for the production and maintenance of pulmonary blood pressure are the rate of blood flow or the output of the right ventricle, the resistance to flow, the blood vessel volume, the expansiveness of the vascular system, and the blood viscosity. The pulmonary system is so extensive and capacious that increases in pulmonary blood flow and volume tend to be self-cancelling due to the recruitment of additional pathways. Since the arterial resistance vessels are relatively thin walled, pulmonary hypertension in the absence of lung or heart disease is less common than systemic hypertension. When primary pulmonary hypertension occurs, it is vaso-occlusive, that is, there is a curtailment of the pulmonary vascular bed or an impediment to flow through it. Vaso-occlusive pulmonary hypertension associated with a raised vascular resistance may be vasoconstrictive, a kind of functional vasospasm; obstructive, due to mechanical blockage of the vessel lumen by external pressure upon vessel walls or plugging by thrombi or emboli; or obliterative, due to primary destructive or occlusive diseases of the walls of arteries and capillaries with a reduction in total functional cross section. Often, several factors operate simultaneously or serially.

Often one mechanism recruits another. For example, the vaso-occlusion which accompanies obstruction by thrombi may be both mechanical and vasoactive because thrombi contain platelets, whch are a source of the vasoconstrictor serotonin. Also, some chemicals which promote thrombosis and embolism, besides being vasospastic agents, may also be vasculotoxic, inducing inflammation and destruction of vessels. In animals, 30–50 percent of the vascular bed must be occluded to evoke pulmonary hypertension in the absence of increased pulmonary blood flow, volume, or viscosity.

High altitude

At high altitudes, airway or ventilatory hypoxia occurs in the absence of any hypercapnic acidosis or CO_2 retention. Ventilatory hypoxia regularly elicits pulmonary arterial vasoconstriction and an elevated pulmonary arterial pressure in mammals. The hypertension is reversible when the hypoxia is relieved. The magnitude of the pressor response varies among species, being most pronounced in those having the most vascular smooth muscle (Tucker et al. 1975). Calves and pigs, with relatively more vascular smooth muscle, are especially responsive (Fig. 12.2). In normal calves, hypoxia increased the mean pulmonary artery pressure by 21 mm Hg (Vogel et al. 1963). Initially and during acute hypoxia, the pressor response is adaptive, that is, the higher pressures encourage more flow to alveoli at the top of the lung which are otherwise underperfused because of gravity.

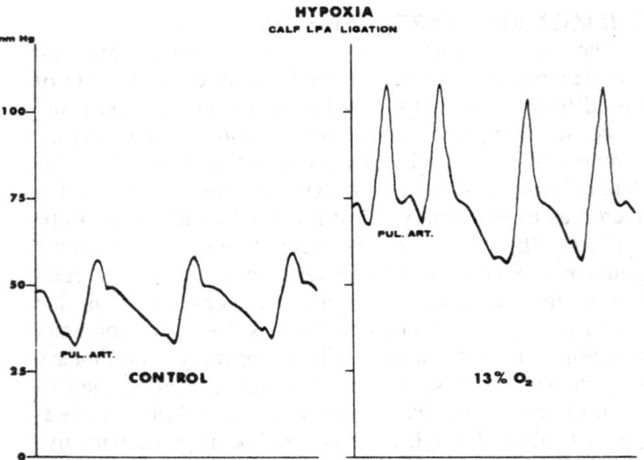

Figure 12.2. Effects of reduced oxygen in inspired air on pulmonary artery pressure in calves with unilateral pulmonary artery ligation. LPA, left pulmonary artery. Mean pulmonary artery pressure for control was 38 mm Hg; for reduced mixture, 84. (From Vogel, Averill, Pool, and Blount 1963, *Circ. Res.* 8:557–71.)

Brisket disease is a vasoconstrictive pulmonary hypertension due to alveolar hypoxia which is observed in some cattle kept at altitudes of 7000 feet or more above sea level. When pulmonary hypertension persists, it initiates responses in the right ventricle and systemic veins, capillaries, and tissues. The right ventricle hypertrophies, followed by right ventricular dilatation and failure, filling and distension of systemic veins, congestive edematous swelling of subcutaneous tissues, and ascites. Together, pulmonary hypertension, cardiac hypertrophy, and right heart dilatation and failure constitute *cor pulmonale,* a heart disease secondary to pulmonary hypertension. The clinical signs in cattle are principally those associated with right heart failure, including a dependent edematous swelling of the brisket region, a low exercise tolerance, tachycardia, distended and pulsating jugular veins, a loud pulmonic second heart sound, sometimes a systolic murmur due to incompetency of the tricuspid valve, ascites with congestion of the abdominal viscera, and profuse diarrhea. Pulmonary hypertension is the characteristic hemodynamic change which leads to right heart failure. The necropsy finds a hypertrophied and dilated right ventricle and hypertrophy of the vascular smooth muscle of pulmonary arteries.

Emphysema (heaves) in horses

Increased hindrance to airflow out of the lungs is common in chronic obstructive lung diseases, e.g. chronic emphysema and bronchitis. Increased pulmonary vascular resistance is particularly frequent in emphysema. The resulting pulmonary hypertension is vaso-occlusive. The primary lung disease results in destruction of vessels and thus a reduction in the overall radius of the pulmonary vascular system. Gillespie and Tyler (1973) demonstrated increased vascular resistance, pulmonary hypertension, and an apparent decrement in the density of capillaries in emphysematous horses. In emphysema, airway hypoxia and hypercapnia occur, both of which favor pulmonary vasoconstriction.

Hypertrophy and dilatation of the right ventricle secondary to the pulmonary hypertension of chronic obstructive lung disease have been reported in horses and cattle. And pulmonary vascular resistance and pulmonary arterial pressure are definitely elevated in emphysematous horses (Spörri 1962, Detweiler and Patterson 1963, Eberly et al. 1966). However, cor pulmonale secondary to pulmonary hypertension is not found frequently (Gillespie and Tyler 1969).

Heartworm disease in dogs

Pulmonary hypertension is characteristic of heartworm disease in dogs. Pulmonary artery pressures as high as 158/59 have been observed. Pulmonary vascular resistance is increased due to obstruction, narrowing, or closing of pulmonary vascular pathways. In large vessels this is the result of mature worms in their lumens. In the smaller vessels, mechanical obstruction is caused by thrombi containing fragments of disintegrating parasites, by emboli, and by fibroplasia involving the walls of arteries.

Right heart failure is common in dogs infested with *Dirofilaria immitis*. Such failure is not always purely secondary to pulmonary hypertension. Both mature worms (up to 15 cm long) and microfilariae may be widely distributed in the chambers of the heart and the vessels of the systemic circulation. Dozens of mature worms may be found in the venal cavae, lumens of the right atrium and ventricle, and orifices of the tricuspid and pulmonary semilunar valves. They obstruct flow into and out of the right side of the heart and hinder normal function of cardiac valves.

REFERENCES

Alexander, A.F. 1965. Normal morphology and pathology of the bovine pulmonary circulation at high altitude. *Ann. N.Y. Acad. Sci.* 127:640–45.

Bakhle, Y.S., and Vane, J.R. 1974. Pharmacokinetic function of the pulmonary circulation. *Physiol. Rev.* 54:1007–45.

Detweiler, D.K., and Patterson, D.F. 1963. Diseases of the blood and cardiovascular system. In J.F. Bone, E.J. Catcott, A.A. Gabel, L.E. Johnson, and W.F. Riley, eds., *Equine Medicine and Surgery*. American Veterinary, Santa Barbara, Calif. Pp. 338–97.

Dittmer, D.S., and Grebe, R.M. 1959. *Handbook of Circulation*. WADA Technical Report 59-593. Wright Air Development Center, Wright-Patterson Air Force Base, Ohio.

Doyle, J.T., Patterson, J.L., Warren, J.V., and Detweiler, D.K. 1960. Observations on the circulation of domestic cattle. *Circ. Res.* 8:4–15.

Eberly, V.E., Tyler, W.S., and Gillespie, J.R. 1966. Cardiovascular parameters in emphysematous and control horses. *J. Appl. Physiol.* 21:883–89.

Ferretti, R., Cherniack, N.S., Longobardo, G., Levine, R.O., Morkin, E., Singer, D.H., and Fishman, A.P. 1965. Systemic and pulmonary vasomotor waves. *Am. J. Physiol.* 209:37–50.

Fishman, A.P., and Giuseppe, G.P. 1974. Handling of bioactive materials by the lung. *New Eng. J. Med.* 291:884–89, 953–59.

Gall, C.M. 1967. Intra-carotid and right heart pressures. M.S. thesis, Ohio State U., Columbus.

Gillespie, J.R., and Tyler, W.S. 1969. Chronic alveolar emphysema in the horse. *Adv. Vet. Sci. Comp. Med.* 13:59–99.

——. 1973. Chronic obstructive lung disease in horses. In L.T. Harmison, ed., *Research in Animal Medicine*. HEW Pub. no. 72-333 (NIH), Washington. Pp. 223–27.

Grauweiler, J. 1965. *Herz und Kreislauf der Saugetiere*. Birkhaüser, Basel, Stuttgart.

Halmagyi, D.F.J., and Colebatch, H.J.H. 1961. Ventilation and circulation after fluid aspiration. *J. Appl. Physiol.* 16:35–40.

Hamlin, R.L., Weill, S., Gross, D.R. 1974. Perfusion discrepancies in the horse lung unexplained by "waterfall" effect. *Circulation* 49, 50 (suppl. 3):178.

Hecht, H.H., Kuida, H., Lange, R.L., Thorne, J.L., and Brown, A.M. 1962. Brisket disease: The clinical features and hemodynamic observations in altitude dependent right heart failure of cattle. *Am. J. Med.* 32:171–83.

Hyman, A.L., and Kadowitz, P.J. 1975. Effects of alveolar and perfusion hypoxia and hypercapnia on pulmonary vascular resistance in the lamb. *Am. J. Physiol.* 228:397–403.

Kuida, H., Tsagaris, T.J., and Hecht, H.H. 1963. Evidence for pulmonary venoconstriction in brisket disease. *Circ. Res.* 12:182–89.

Maaske, C.A., Booth, N.H., and Nielson, T.W. 1965. Experimental right heart failure in swine. In L.K. Bustad, R.O. McClellan, and M.P. Burns, eds., *Swine in Biomedical Research*. Frayn, Seattle.

McCrady, J.D., Hallman, G.L., McNamara, D.G., and Vogel, J.H.K. 1968. Effects of increased flow of pulmonary blood on pulmonary vascular resistance and structure in calves. *Am. J. Vet. Res.* 29:1539–47.

Moscovitz, H.L., and Wilder, R.J. 1956. Pressure events of the cardiac cycle in the dog. Normal right and left heart. *Circ. Res.* 4:574–78.

Reeves, J.T., and Leathers, J.E. 1964. Hypoxic pulmonary hypertension of the calf with denervation of the lungs. *J. Appl. Physiol.* 19:976–80.

Robin, E.D., Cross, C.E., and Zelis, R. 1973. Pulmonary edema. *New Eng. J. Med.* 288:239–46, 292–304.

Roobard, S., and Wagner, D. 1949. Bypassing the right ventricle. *Proc. Soc. Exp. Biol. Med.* 71:69–70.

Spörri, H. 1962. The study of cardiac dynamics and its clinical significance. In C.A. Brandly and E.L. Jungherr, eds., *Advances in Veterinary Science*. Academic Press, New York. Vol. 7, 1–41.

——. 1965. Studies of cardiodynamics in animals (horse, cattle, sheep, and goats). *Ann. N.Y. Acad. Sci.* 127:379–92.

Starr, J., Jeffers, W.A., Meade, R.H., Jr. 1943. The absence of twelve conspicuous increments in venous pressure after severe damage to the right ventricle of the dog, with a discussion of the relations between clinical congestive failure and heart disease. *Am. Heart J.* 26:291–301.

Staub, N.C. 1974. Pulmonary edema. *Physiol. Rev.* 54:678–811.

Szidon, J.P., Giuseppe, G.P., and Fishman, A.P. 1972. The alveolar and capillary membrane and pulmonary edema. *New Eng. J. Med.* 286:1200–1204.

Tashjian, R.T., Das, K.M., Palich, W.E., Hamlin, R.L., and Yarns, E.E. 1965. Studies on cardiovascular disease in the cat. *Ann. N.Y. Acad. Sci.* 127:581–605.

Tucker, A., McMurtry, I.F., Reeves, J.T., Alexander, A.F., Will, D.H., and Groover, R.F. 1975. Lung vascular smooth muscle as a determinant of pulmonary hypertension at high altitude. *Am. J. Physiol.* 228:762–66.

Vogel, J.H.K., Averill, K.H., Pool, P.F., and Blount, G.S., Jr. 1963. Experimental pulmonary arterial hypertension in the newborn calf. *Circ. Res.* 13:557–71.

Wachtel, W., Lyhs, L., and Lehmen, E. 1963. Measurement of blood pressure in pigs. *Arch. Exp. Vet. Med.* 17:335–60.

Will, J.A., Bisgard, G.E., Ruiz, A.V., and Grover, R.F. 1973. Models of cardiopulmonary function in calves. In L.T. Harmison, ed., *Research in Animal Medicine*. HEW Pub. no. 72-333 (NIH), Washington. Pp. 267–74.

CHAPTER 13

Circulatory Shock

by C. Roger Smith and Robert L. Hamlin

BASIC CONSIDERATIONS

Circulatory shock is characterized by arterial hypotension and a progressive and widespread hypoperfusion and hypoxia of tissues. When tissue hypoxia is sufficiently intense and prolonged hypotension and hypoperfusion become irreversible, death results. Time is an important determinant. The common critical feature in all circulatory shock is an acute, persistent, inadequately slow circulation of blood through nutrient capillaries. As tissue hypoxia develops, aerobic metabolism of cells is replaced by anaerobic, which results in metabolic acidosis, lowered tissue pH, slowing of glucose metabolism, depletion of cellular energy stores, cessation of protein synthesis, and breakdown of lysosomes accompanied by the release of enzymes.

Principal hemodynamic changes

Hypotension is a common feature of most forms of circulatory shock. Providing resistance remains unchanged, flow progressively falls as the perfusion pressure falls. In shock, with the exception of severe primary heart disease, the main reason for hypotension is a significant reduction in the effective intravascular blood volume. Other factors add to the complexities of shock, but they are largely secondary in all but the final irreversible stages.

The important blood volume in maintaining arterial blood pressure is that volume which is circulating at a normal rate, successively and continuously, through the heart, arteries, capillaries, venules, and veins. A severe depletion of the functional volume reduces cardiac output and arterial blood pressure. In circulatory shock, effective blood volume may be reduced by loss of whole blood (hemorrhage); sequestration of blood in stagnant, intravascular pools formed by malfunctioning capillaries, venules, and veins; or by shifts of fluid from the intravascular to the extravascular fluid volumes.

Circulatory disturbances

The living cells and other materials comprising the walls of microcirculatory vessels, plus the formed elements in the blood they contain, are the first parts of the cardiovascular system exposed to hypoxic tissue cells. The circulatory disturbances which follow such exposure may include: (1) impairment of vascular smooth muscle function; (2) sequestration and pooling of blood within the vascular compartment; (3) increased capillary permeability; (4) shift of fluid from intravascular to extravascular sites; (5) injury of the endothelial lining of blood vessels, leading to a generalized activation of the hemostatic mechanism, hypercoagulability of blood, and microembolization of small blood vessels; (6) a fibrinolytic response to microembolization, which converts blood plasma to a serumlike fluid incapable of coagulation and accompanied by hemorrhage; (7) deterioration and functional insufficiency of organs, e.g. lungs, kidneys, and liver; and (8) functional derangement and failure of vital central regulatory mechanisms. All disturbances stem from an inadequacy of normal tissue perfusion, i.e. a slow circulation time.

Classification

All types of shock are examples of acute, stagnant hypoxia. However, not all shock is precipitated by the same event; it may follow accidental, surgical, or disease-induced trauma of tissues and organs; hemorrhage; acute overwhelming infections; exposure to antigens followed by acute antigen-antibody responses; severe forms of dehydration; and acute myocardial disease. Accordingly, shock is most commonly classified on the basis of the initiating event: (1) cardiogenic, (2) hemorrhagic, (3) septic, toxic, or endotoxic, (4) traumatic, or (5) anaphylactic.

Sometimes shock is divided into only three classes: hypovolemic, septic, and cardiogenic. Hemorrhagic and traumatic shock are included in the hypovolemic class. Shock which follows acute septicemia is defined as septic shock even though hypovolemia may evolve via separation and pooling of plasma in tissues. All involve the activation of neural sympathetic, adrenal medullary (catecholamines), renal (angiotensin), and hypothalamic (vasopressin) pressor mechanisms in variable degrees.

The classification of shock according to etiology also has reference to therapeutics. Surgical (drainage) and antibacterial therapy are beneficial at the start in septic shock, digitalis may be in cardiogenic, epinephrine in anaphylactic, and volume replacement in hemorrhagic.

Clinical signs

Clinical signs of shock are detected by observation of the skin, mucous membranes, neuromuscular system, circulatory and respiratory systems, and body temperature. The skin, where exposed, is cold due to vasoconstriction. Visible mucous membranes are pale and cyanotic. The animal is indifferent to normally effective stimuli. Muscular weakness is evident. The animal lies quietly and fails to respond to painful stimulation. The breathing rate is rapid, the pulse is small in amplitude and the rate is high, the amplitude of the heart sounds, especially the second sound, is reduced. Urine flow is reduced as the blood flow to the kidney is decreased. The pupils are dilated and lacrimation may occur as a part of the increased sympathetic discharge. The body temperature falls as a result of reduced muscular activity and reduction in general body metabolism. Many of these signs may be either complicated or obliterated by anesthesia. They are especially significant if they become progressively more intense.

Toxic factors

Progressive shock can be divided into three stages. The first is a stage of ischemic hypoxia due to intense reflex peripheral arterial vasoconstriction. The second is a stage of stagnant hypoxia due to the gradual fading of precapillary vasoconstriction, sustained venular constriction, capillary pooling of blood, and progressive decline in venous return, cardiac output, and blood pressure. The third is the stage of irreversibility associated with the shift of fluid from the intravascular to the extravascular fluid volumes and microembolization of vessels due to hypoxic injury of capillary endothelium, blood platelets, white blood cells, and erythrocytes.

The peripheral microcirculation occupies a central position in all three stages. A large and complex number of endogenous substances which may be toxic are produced locally in the tissues, as well as by specific organs or glands, in response to hypotension, hypovolemia and depletion of functional body fluid, hemorrhagic tendency in tissues as a result of endothelial damage, tissue invasion by microbes, or the introduction of antigens. The accumulation or depletion of some substances is in part due to failure of organ function, e.g. in the liver (lactic acid, blood glucose), lung (CO_2 and O_2), or kidney (uremia).

CARDIOGENIC SHOCK

Cardiogenic shock is due to myocardial infarction. Myocardial infarction, which can lead to peripheral shock, is common as a primary lesion in the human but rare in other species. In acute myocardial infarction a mass of myocardium undergoes necrosis because of a critical difference between the oxygen demand of the tissue and the amount of oxygen being supplied via blood capillaries. It follows coronary artery diseases.

As to the reverse, in animals, acute peripheral circulatory shock seldom results in cardiogenic shock or lethal heart pathology. In the dog in hemorrhagic shock, coronary blood flow may fall to 30 percent of normal. One consequence is a rapid development of discrete areas of hemorrhage and necrosis of muscle fibers in the subendocardial layers of the ventricular myocardium (Hackell et al. 1973). The cessation of the heartbeat at death is secondary to peripheral circulatory failure in other tissues and organs.

HEMORRHAGIC SHOCK

Experimental inducement

Hemorrhage is one of the better methods of experimentally producing shock. The usual procedure involves withdrawing a volume of blood sufficient to produce and maintain the mean arterial pressure at a low level, e.g. 30–50 mm Hg for 90–130 minutes in the dog. This method assumes that the reduction in capillary perfusion is roughly proportional to the reduction in blood pressure. After this time reinfusion of all withdrawn blood fails to produce more than a transient rise in pressure, and 80 percent of the animals die within 6 hours or less of the reinfusion. This is called *irreversible shock.* In a variation of this method, blood is allowed to flow from a femoral artery into a heparinized reservoir elevated above the heart so as to produce and maintain a pressure of 30–35 mm Hg. If the blood is returned after 90–120 minutes, a maintained pressure response is observed and 80 percent of the animals recover. This is *reversible hypovolemic shock*. If transfusion is delayed until about 40 percent of the bleeding volume has been spontaneously transferred or taken up from the reservoir by the animal, then a return of the entire volume fails to permanently restore pressure and 80 percent of these animals die. The spontaneous uptake of blood from the reservoir is a sign of failure of compensatory mechanisms and the onset of irreversibility. In experimental hemorrhagic shock, two principal divisions of the interval from blood loss to death are available for study: that prior to the time of the reinfusion called *hypovolemic* or *oligemic shock*, and that following reinfusion called *normovolemic shock*.

The changes occurring during oligemic shock are *progressive*, and if the hypotension is sufficiently prolonged they are irreversible. The progressive nature of the changes prompted Wiggers to divide oligemic shock into three stages: simple hypotension or latent shock which can be reversed by reinfusion, an impending stage which may or may not be reversed by reinfusion, and a critical or irreversible stage.

Dynamics

The effective circulating blood volume can be depleted by (1) internal or external hemorrhage, (2) local fluid loss into a damaged area (as in burns, wounds, peritonitis, intestinal obstruction), (3) leakage of plasma from capillaries remote from an injured tissue, (4) pooling or sequestration of blood which is either stagnant or extremely slow moving, or (5) diversion of flow through nonnutrient channels in the peripheral circulation. As fluid is diverted from the active circulation, the venous volume and pressure fall.

A low venous pressure, especially the central venous pressure, is the hallmark of peripheral circulatory failure in shock, and is often the most important guide in planning therapy. Normally the veins serve as a reservoir for blood. As the reservoir is depleted, venous return is reduced, and the amount of blood transferred to the arterial system by the heart falls in proportion. Underfilling of the normally moderately overfilled arterial tree leads to arterial hypotension and a reduction in the force for propelling blood through the resistance vessels (arterioles) into the capillaries.

The healthy animal can tolerate a 20 percent loss of blood volume without developing signs of circulatory failure. The normal arterial pressure in such instances signifies that pressure is not always a reliable indication of the intravascular volume. Neither absolute reduction in volume nor efficiency of compensatory mechanisms alone determines whether shock will occur. Circulatory failure depends upon both. Since the residual volume remaining in the vascular system is more important than the absolute volume lost, the ratio of the lost volume to the total volume is a more accurate indicator.

Hypovolemic shock is a peripheral circulatory failure in which the deficit in circulating volume exceeds the maximal efficiency of the compensatory mechanisms. If a loss of 40 percent or more of the total blood volume constitutes an emergency, then one has a clue to the compensatory mechanisms. Cannon postulated that the sympathetic-adrenal mechanisms operate in emergencies. They are the result of overactive or augmented sympathetic-adrenal responses which are essential for immediate survival following massive hemorrhage. The compensatory mechanisms are of two general kinds. One involves adjustment of the intravascular volume toward normal by expulsion of blood from blood depots (splenic contraction) and by withdrawal of fluid from the interstitial fluid compartment. This withdrawal occurs automatically as a result of the fall in blood pressure within the capillaries and is the basis for the use of isotonic solutions in the therapy of shock. The other mechanism is the result of discharge over sympathetic nerves to the heart, arterioles, and veins, that is, cardiac stimulation, selective arteriolar constriction, and reduction in size of veins.

Early in the stages of shock the only volume deficit is that due to hemorrhage. As shock becomes progressive, the peripheral circulatory apparatus fails in such a way that a second depletion of volume begins within the vascular system itself.

Arterial blood pressure

Hypotension is characteristic of all stages of shock. In fact, surgical procedures during shock are practically bloodless. Sustained levels of 50 mm Hg or less in the dog are indicative of a drastically low circulating blood volume. This pattern is not entirely consistent, making single measurements of doubtful value. A consistently low and progressively declining blood pressure is a sign of progressive circulatory failure.

Heart rate

Tachycardia generally accompanies shock. The small venous return limits the stroke volume, so the heart beats more often. A small stroke volume during tachycardia generates only a small pulse pressure, i.e. a feeble pulse. The tachycardia is the result of the accelerating effect of baroreceptor reflex responses to arterial hypotension. In the terminal stages of shock, bradycardia develops even in atropinized dogs and is probably due to the effects of hypoxia on pacemaker tissue. Deceleration with well-established shock or declining arterial pressure is an indication of continued deterioration as is failure to slow heart rate following infusion. A decline in rate with a rise in pressure is a good sign.

Vasoconstriction

Constriction of the resistance and capacitance vessels occurs in response to hypotension via the usual carotid sinus and aortic chemoreceptor and baroreceptor reflexes and catecholamines. The levels of catecholamines in the peripheral blood increase 30–100 times during hemorrhagic hypotension in the dog.

In shock arteriolar constriction cannot preserve perfusion pressure because cardiac output is reduced. Furthermore, not only is perfusion pressure inadequate, resistance to flow is increased. In constricted peripheral vascular beds flow is reduced proportionately more than pressure.

Vasoconstriction is a natural first-aid measure. Initially it preserves perfusion pressure. As shock progresses the organs with intensely constricted arterioles are among the first to deteriorate (Hardaway 1973). Intense vasoconstriction of an organ's vascular bed produces an ischemia much like the application of a tourniquet to a limb. Flow through the pulmonary, coronary, and cerebral circuits is less restricted because these vessels do not participate in the reflex vasoconstrictor response.

Total peripheral resistance of the vascular circuit during irreversible hemorrhagic shock has been measured both before (hypovolemic) and after (normovolemic) reinfusion of the withdrawn blood. In general it is mildly or moderately increased during impending or progressive shock and tends to be inversely related to the input (cardiac output) into the arterial system except in the terminal stage.

Current shock therapy includes measures to reduce intense vasoconstriction by the administration of blockers, but only following effective restoration of intravascular volume. Similarly, subjects are not warmed until after transfusion because of heat's vasodilating and metabolic-rate effects on cutaneous tissue.

Failure in peripheral circulation

The definition of irreversible shock includes failure to respond favorably to the infusion of a volume of blood equal to the deficit. The reason for failure appears to be the appearance of a new opportunity for continuing the hypovolemia. A "lake" is formed beyond the arterioles by countless capillaries and venules which permit entrance but either no exit or exit below the rate of entrance. This is due to the opening and filling of capillaries normally empty, to the dilatation and filling of venules, and perhaps to the development of leaky capillary walls. Capillaries alone are capable of accounting for shock should they simultaneously dilate maximally, since normally 80 percent of the capillaries are closed. As shock progresses, more and more of the blood disappears into the trap, progressively reducing venous return. This reduction leads to an intensification of the already critical tissue hypoxia.

In the dog an important recognized site of trapping is the vessels of the small intestine and liver. The weight of the small intestine increases during shock. The intestinal mucosa is edematous, hemorrhagic, and necrotic. Often dogs dying of shock have a bloody diarrhea. Removal of the small intestine delays the appearance of irreversibility.

Suggested mechanisms for this trapping include paralysis of precapillary vessels and loss of balance of tone between pre- and postcapillary vessels of the microcirculation, with postcapillary vessel tone dominating in the terminal stages of shock. In the dog the musculature of the hepatic veins has a sphincterlike effect. In shock it appears to be sufficiently constricted to retard flow from the liver into the posterior vena cava. Portal venous pressure is increased and hepatic blood flow is decreased.

Disseminated intravascular coagulation

Disseminated intravascular coagulation is an acute transient coagulation occurring throughout the peripheral microcirculation. It almost always appears only in severe or refractory shock, and is one important mechanism whereby shock becomes irreversible. It has been observed in hemorrhagic, traumatic, and endotoxic shock, that is, circulatory states characterized by hypotension and hypoperfusion. It is always generalized but is more severe in the most constricted, stagnant circulatory beds. The flow obstruction causes tissue necrosis and organ failure (Hardaway 1973).

Hemorrhage can reduce clotting time to a fraction of normal. This is required for disseminated intravascular coagulation. The condition in shock which leads to the development of this hypercoagulable state is a slow-flowing acid blood, since heparin, the body's own anticoagulant, is ineffective at a pH of 7.2. But even hypercoagulable blood will not clot unless a thromboplastic triggering agent is present. In shock, thromboplastic factors may be generated as the result of hemolysis, exposure of blood to endotoxins, damaged endothelium or wettable foreign surfaces, or because of substances generated by injured tissue cells.

A coagulation defect exactly the opposite of hypercoagulability follows disseminated intravascular coagulation. The process is called *consumptive coagulopathy*. In the formation of countless numbers of miniature clots throughout the vessels of the microcirculation the plasma becomes a serumlike fluid totally incapable of coagulation. Blood transfusions which might have been effective prior to the onset of disseminated intravascular coagulation are ineffective following the development of consumptive coagulopathy.

The state of incoagulability following initiation of intravascular coagulation is the result of an exaggerated response by the body's fibrinolytic system, which acts to limit clotting. By dissolving fibrin and fibrinogen, the plasma enzyme plasmin forms fibrinogen degradation products which in turn inhibit thrombin. Hypofibrinogenemia often accompanies prolonged hypotensive states.

Disseminated intravascular coagulation is a known complication of shock in the dog, man, and lower primates. The canine normally has a short coagulation time.

TRAUMATIC SHOCK

Clinically, physical trauma is a mixed type of injury. It produces tissue damage by hemorrhage, crushing or maceration, interruption of blood supply (ischemia), and infection. Shock produced experimentally in anesthetized animals by bullet wounds, contusions, compression of the musculature of limbs, or tumbling in a drum may involve two or more of these factors. A more satisfactory method involves ischemia; hypotension follows the release of a tourniquet applied to the pelvic limbs of a dog for 4–10 hours. The shock is reversed by the infusion of plasma if ischemia is maintained for 4 hours or less and irreversible if its duration exceeds 8–10 hours. The desirable features of the limb ischemia method are: (1) tissue damage is caused by one factor, (2) the extent of injury can be controlled by varying the duration of ischemia, the amount of tissue deprived of blood flow, and the limb temperature, (3) the injury is reproducible, (4) muscle in different species is similar with respect to biochemistry and function, and (5) the changes in the injured muscle can be measured.

Traumatic shock is caused by the local loss of plasma into the injured area. Upon release of the tourniquets in limb ischemia the limbs swell and blood pressure progressively falls. The volume or mass increment of the limbs is directly related to the degree of hypotension. Prior to the release of the tourniquet, the hypoxia is localized to the tissues distal to the point of application of the ligature. Upon release of the tourniquet, hypoxia of all tissues develops as a result of inadequate tissue perfusion. If the resultant hypoxia is sufficiently intense and prolonged, the shock becomes irreversible. Traumatic shock is a hypovolemic shock. The hypovolemia occurs as a result of leakage of plasma into the interstitial volume of the damaged tissue. Although the visual appearance may not reveal it, a severely traumatized pelvic limb may hold as much as two thirds of a dog's normal total circulating blood volume.

SEPTIC SHOCK

In septic (endotoxic) shock, deterioration of the microcirculation, with prolonged reduction of capillary blood flow below the level required for normal cellular metabolism, leads to irreversibility. Circulatory shock from any cause may become septic shock if it persists long enough. Fine hypothesizes that deficiencies of oxygen and tissue nutrients and the accumulation of cellular metabolites render the body's reticuloendothelial (RE) system incapable of detoxifying bacterial cytotoxins; the shocked animal is 100,000 times as senstive as the normal animal. Bacterial endotoxins are constantly entering the body by absorption from the intestine. In the animal with shock they cause the release of a RE depressing substance which together with hypoxia and acidosis depresses the functional capability of the body's detoxifying and phagocytic mechanisms.

The direct injection of endotoxin into common laboratory animals produces an irreversible type of peripheral circulatory failure. The order of species susceptibility from high to low is cat, rabbit, dog, guinea pig, rat, and mouse. The puppy is more susceptible than the mature dog. The phagocytic activity of the RE system on a per gram of tissue basis in various animals is remarkably constant. In the dog the intravenous injection of 0.5 mg/kg of *E. coli* endotoxin results in a marked loss of intravascular fluid, hemoconcentration, hypotension, hypoperfusion, acidosis, and oliguria.

The deterioration of the microcirculation in septic shock is accelerated by a direct action of endotoxin on vascular endothelium and smooth muscle and upon blood and tissue cells. Endotoxins may cause hemolysis of erythrocytes and the release of histamine, ADP, and serotonin from blood platelets and mast cells. Other primary actions include the release of catecholamines from tissue stores and the adrenal medulla and the formation of kinins in plasma and prostaglandins in tissues.

The concentration of endotoxins in the tissues varies among individuals. There are also variations among individuals and species with respect to which organs or tissues are involved in the generation of chemical mediators of shock and the rapidity with which the generation occurs. In canine septic shock, pooling of blood in the splanchnic viscera, intestinal ischemia and necrosis, renal ischemia and oliguria, and failure of liver's glucostatic mechanisms are almost routine. In primates, intestinal venous pooling is not as universal or intense as in the dog. In the cat, pulmonary venous constriction, capillary pooling and transudation of fluid with pulmonary edema, dyspnea, and respiratory insufficiency are regular features. In the low pressure respiratory system, uniform venous constriction may result in a venous pressure equaling or exceeding pulmonary arterial pressure, with capillary pooling, stasis, and edema.

In the dog an early and late period of hypotension separated by a temporary period of near normotension occurs following the injection of a minimum lethal dose of endotoxin. The immediate and early fall in arterial pressure is due to a decrease in venous return as a result of pooling of blood in the liver and intestine. The early but not the late hypotension is absent in the eviscerated dog. The early pooling is caused by constriction of hepatic veins. In this stage central venous pressure, cardiac output, and arterial pressure are reduced but the net portal pressure is increased.

Following the initial hypotension there is a compensatory outpouring of epinephrine and norepinephrine which transiently restores blood pressure to normal. While such response does aid pressure homeostasis, the cost of it may also be perpetuation and intensification of the shock process. Endotoxins appear to potentiate the activity of catecholamines. Enhanced adrenergic activity alone can produce intestinal pooling of blood and hemorrhagic necrosis of the intestinal epithelium as well as a large plasma volume deficit, all of which occur also in endotoxin shock. Concomitant with the secondary fall in arterial pressure there is a fall in circulating plasma volume, a fall in the plasma protein concentration, and a rise in the packed cell volume. In canine experimental endotoxin shock, adrenergic α-receptor blockage has sometimes proved to be a beneficial kind of therapy. Selective surgical interruption of the vasoconstrictor nerves to the liver and spleen preserves arterial inflow, which protects the reticuloendothelial cells, preserves ability to detoxify endotoxins, and protects the animal against shock.

In calves pulmonary vascular hypertension is the principal hemodynamic response to the injection of endotoxin. Pressure increments of 30 mm Hg develop within 10 minutes and gradually subside over the next 60 minutes. The rise is principally due to pulmonary arterial constriction with a lesser component of venoconstriction. Pooling of blood in the lungs, lung edema, and respiratory insufficiency with hypoxemia and acidosis occur. One hour following endotoxin administration, systemic arterial resistance, after a moderate and transient rise, falls to normal or below. Systemic hypotension and tachycardia are consistent findings. Hemoconcentration and hepatosplanchnic congestion are not observed. Thus the evidence for intense systemic arterial vasoconstriction due to endotoxin is absent. In sheep and calves the pulmonary vasculature appears to be the primary target for bacterial endotoxin.

Volume replacement in all forms of shock characterized by systemic hypovolemia and hypotension is the first and most important measure in the correction of a diminished venous return, low cardiac output, and exaggerated reflex and catecholamine-mediated vasoconstriction. Restoration of the intravascular blood volume causes a release from the intense arterial baroreceptor stimulation responsible for the intense reflex vasoconstriction, tachycardia, and secretion of catecholamines. Venous return and cardiac output return to normal. The depressed central venous pressure becomes normal when a volume deficit is the primary reason for circulatory failure, but alone will not be a reliable guide for volume therapy when myocardial damage is responsible.

ANAPHYLACTIC SHOCK

Anaphylactic shock is characterized by hypotension. It is a kind of peripheral circulatory failure which in many respects resembles septic shock. However, anaphylactic shock is an immunological phenomenon. It may occur within minutes following the administration of a specific antigen to which an animal has been sensitized by prior exposure. The combination of antigen with antibody is accompanied by the explosive release of chemical mediators of shock. Anaphylaxis is serious because of this very rapid and often unexpected onset. Histamine, slow-reacting substance (SRA), and eosinophil leukocyte chemotactic factor (ECF) are primary mediators. Secondarily bradykinin and prostaglandins become involved. Histamine is a systemic vasodilator: it also increases capillary permeability, causes transudation of fluid and plasma proteins into tissues, and stimulates contraction of the smooth muscles of the respiratory bronchioles, urinary bladder, intestine, and uterus. There are pronounced species variations in the intensity of responses in the muscular and glandular visceral organs (Beaven 1976, Powell and Brody 1976). Like histamine, SRA enhances capillary permeability and stimulates visceral smooth muscle. Epinephrine is a physiological histamine antagonist useful in the treatment of anaphylaxis. It also effectively blocks the release of histamine in tissues. Antihistamines are reasonably effective as preventive therapy, but much less effective as treatment drugs.

In the dog during anaphylactic shock there is a sharp drop in blood pressure accompanied by vomiting, diarrhea, ataxia, prostration, dyspnea, coma, and if unattended, death in a matter of hours. In the blood there is a rise in packed cell volume and a decrease in coagulability and the number of white blood cells. The deficiency of flow is due to stagnation of blood in the portal circuit. The liberated histamine causes constriction of the hepatic veins so that as much as 60 percent of the blood volume is sequestered in the portal vascular bed. The decrease in cardiac output is due to a decrease in venous return rather than to myocardial weakening.

In the rabbit there is a fall in systemic pressure as a result of an obstruction to flow in the pulmonary circuit. The pulmonary arteries constrict, pulmonary pressure rises, and right heart failure occurs. The amount of blood returning to the left ventricle decreases cardiac output. In the guinea pig the principal feature of anaphylactic shock is violent bronchial constriction and death by asphyxia. In calves and sheep the lung is likewise the principal target during anaphylaxis. Bronchial constriction, dyspnea, and pulmonary edema are common and prominent.

REFERENCES

Aviado, D.M. 1965. Pharmacologic approacn to the treatment of shock. *Ann. Internal Med.* 62:1050–59.

Beaven, M.A. 1976. Histamine. *New Eng. J. Med.* 294:30–36, 320–25.

Bock, K.D., ed. 1962. *Shock: Pathogenesis and Therapy*. Academic Press, New York.

Bohlen, H.G., Hutchins, P.M., Rapela, C.E., and Green, H.D. 1975. Microvascular control in intestinal mucosa of normal and hemorrhaged rats. *Am. J. Physiol.* 229:1159–64.

Chien, S. 1967. Role of the sympathetic nervous system in hemorrhage. *Physiol. Rev.* 47:214–88.

Coleman, B., Kallal, J.E., Feigen, L.P., and Glaviano, V.V. 1975. Myocardial performance during hemorrhagic shock in depancreatized dog. *Am. J. Physiol.* 228:1462–67.

Corwin, D.S., Bottoms, G.D., and Roesel, O.F. 1975. Distribution of ^{3}H-hydrocortisone in dogs with hemorrhagic shock. *Am. J. Vet. Res.* 34:1015–19.

Errington, M.I., and De Silva, R.M., Jr. 1974. On the role of vasopressin and angiotensin in the development of irreversible hemorrhagic shock. *J. Physiol.* 242:119–41.

Essex, H.E. 1965. Anaphylactic and anaphylactoid reactions with special emphasis on the circulation. In *Handbook of Physiology*. Sec. 2, W.F. Hamilton and P. Dow, eds., *Circulation*. Am. Physiol. Soc., Washington. Vol. 3, 2391–2408.

Ferguson, W.W., Glenn, T.M., and Lefer, A.M. 1972. Mechanisms of production of circulatory shock factors in isolated perfused pancreas. *Am. J. Physiol.* 222:450–57.

Ferguson, W.W., and Wangensteen, S.L. 1974. The search for a toxic factor in circulatory shock. In T.I. Malinin, R. Zeppa, W.R. Drucker, and A.B. Callahan, eds., *Acute Fluid Replacement in the Therapy of Shock*. Stratton, New York.

Fine, J. 1965. Shock and peripheral circulatory insufficiency. In *Handbook of Physiology* Sec. 2, W.F. Hamilton and P. Dow, eds., *Circulation*. Am. Physiol. Soc., Washington. Vol. 3, 2037–69.

Hackell, D.B., Chang, J., Ratliff, N.B., and Mikat, E. 1973. Cardiac effects of hemorrhagic shock in dogs and other animals. In L.T. Harmison, ed., *Research in Animal Medicine*. HEW Pub. no. 72-333 (NIH), Washington. Pp. 813–16.

Halmagyi, D.F.J., Starzecki, B., and Horner, G.J. 1963. Mechanism and pharmacology of endotoxin shock in sheep. *J. Appl. Physiol.* 18:544–52.

Hardaway, R.M., III. 1973. Animal research in shock. In L.T. Harmison, ed., *Research in Animal Medicine*. HEW Pub. no. 72-333 (NIH), Washington. Pp. 21–28.

Hardaway, R.M., James, P.M., Jr., Anderson, R.W., Breedenberg, C.E., and West, R.L. 1967. Intensive study and treatment of shock in man. *J. Am. Med. Assoc.* 199:779–90.

Hinshaw, L.B., Acher, L.T., Black, M.R., Elkins, R.C., Brown, P.P., and Greenfield, L.J. 1974. Myocardial function during shock. *Am. J. Physiol.* 226:357–66.

Hinshaw, L.B., Emmerson, T.E., and Reins, D.A. 1966. Cardiovascular responses to the primate in endotoxin shock. *Am. J. Physiol.* 210:335–40.

Kezdi, P., Misra, J.N., Kordenat, R.K., and Smith, J.T. 1973. Studies of a cardiogenic shock model. In L.T. Harmison, ed., *Research in Animal Medicine*. HEW Pub. no. 72-333 (NIH), Washington. Pp. 61–74.

Kuida, H., Gilbert, R.P., Hinshaw, L.B., Brunson, J.G., and Visscher, M.B. 1961. Species differences in the effect of gram-negative endotoxin on circulation. *Am. J. Physiol.* 200:1197–1202.

Liao, J.C., Zimmerman, B.G., and Van Bergen, F.H. 1975. Adrenergic responses in canine cutaneous vasculature during acute hemorrhagic hypotension. *Am. J. Physiol.* 228:752–55.

Mills, L.C., and Moyer, J.H., eds. 1965. *Shock and Hypotension Pathogenesis and Treatment*. Grune & Stratton, New York.

Musa, E.E., Conner, G.H., Carter, G.R., Gupta, B.N., and Keahey, K.K. 1972. Physiologic and pathologic changes in calves given *Escherichia coli* endotoxin or *Pasturella multocidia*. *Am. J. Vet. Res.* 33:911–16.

Powell, J.R., and Brody, M.J. 1976. Identification and blockade of vascular H_2 receptors. *Fed. Proc.* 35:1935–41.

Reddin, J.L., Starzecki, B., and Spink, W.W. 1966. Comparative hemodynamic and humoral responses of puppies and adult dogs to endotoxin. *Am. J. Physiol.* 210:540–52.

Reece, W.O., and Wahlstrom, J.D. 1973. *Escherichia coli* endotoxemia in conscious calves. *Am. J. Vet. Res.* 34:765–69.

Seeley, S.F., and Weisiger, J.R., eds. 1961. Recent progress and present problems in the field of shock. *Fed. Proc.* 20(2), suppl. 9, pt. 3:1–268.

Spath, J.A., Gorczynski, R.J., and Lefer, A.M. 1974. Pancreatic perfusion in the pathophysiology of shock. *Am. J. Physiol.* 226:443–51.

Strawitz, J.G., and Grossblatt, N., eds. 1965. *Septic Shock*. Proc. Workshop Nat. Res. Council, Washington.

Tikoff, G., Kuida, H., and Chiga, M. 1966. Hemodynamic effects of endotoxin in calves. *Am. J. Physiol.* 210:847–53.

Tsagaris, T.J., Gani, M., and Lange, R.L. 1967. Central blood volume during endotoxin shock in dogs. *Am. J. Physiol.* 212:498–505.

Visscher, M.B. 1965. Physiological factors in bacterial endotoxin shock. *Physiol. Pharmac. Physicians* 3(8):1–5.

Wiggers, C.J. 1952. *Physiology of Shock*. Commonwealth Fund, New York.

CHAPTER 14

Cerebral Circulation, Blood-Brain Barrier, and Cerebrospinal Fluid | by Williamina A. Himwich

CEREBRAL CIRCULATION

In its microscopic anatomy the vascular supply of the brain is not significantly different from that of the other organs except that arteriovenous anastomoses do not occur. In *Placentalia* in contrast to *Marsupialia* the arteries of the brain are characterized by relatively few branches which come off the main trunk at narrow angles and in curved lines. The tributaries to the veins enter the main trunk in large numbers at more or less right angles (Scharrer 1940).

Arteries

In its gross anatomy the brain is different from other organs. It is not fed from a hilum or single vessel but from a series of vessels, including the paired vertebral arteries which empty into the single basilar artery. This vessel and the two internal carotid arteries with their connections form the circle of Willis at the base of the brain. From the circle of Willis, the large branches arise and send out the smaller pial arteries, which spread like a net over the surface of the brain and dip into it to supply the cerebral tissues. The arterioles arising from these arteries anastomose with one another, and the capillary beds which branch from the arterioles form a continuous interlacing mesh (Miller et al. 1964).

Although the anatomical structure of the circle of Willis allows complete mixing of the blood supply, usually the contents of one internal carotid artery are distributed almost wholly to the hemisphere of the same side. Such a segregation may be expected with equal blood pressure in both internal carotid arteries. Only when one of the component tributaries of the circle is occluded, at least partially, are the distributing potentialities of this structure realized, but even then its anastomoses may not supply an adequate volume of blood to all parts of the brain. The completeness of the circle of Willis and the direction of flow in its main branches vary from species to species. Several current lines of research suggest that structures similar to arterial valves which help to control flow are present in cerebral arteries. Thickening of the intima called *intimal cushions* may help to regulate both flow and pressure (Hassler 1962, Mchedlishvili 1959).

On the carotid side of the arterial supply to the circle, some species have a *rete mirabile,* consisting of an inflow artery that breaks up into a fine network of vessels which are gathered again into a single effluent vessel. This structure lies within a venous lake, usually the cavernous sinus. Although its functions are unknown, in the sheep the rete mirabile may act as a venous pump. Moreover, it appears to serve as an excellent heat-exchange mechanism allowing cerebral blood to be as much as 1°C below the central arterial blood. The most extensive available studies of the carotid rete and its associated arteries are those carried out by Daniel et al. (1953) and Ask-Upmark (1935), which described the arterial connections and the variations to be found in many species, including the cat, sheep, goat, ox, pig, rabbit, rat, and dog. The anastomoses between the internal and external carotid circulation in the dog, with a detailed description of the sources of blood and the connections between the carotid and vertebral system, have been presented by Jewell (1952).

The carotid circulation in the adult domestic cat differs from that of a number of other animals in that the internal carotid artery as a branch of the common carotid is usually absent. The internal carotid artery is present, however, and patent in the fetal kitten. In other members of *Panthera* the internal carotid may be patent more frequently than in *Felis* (Davis and Story 1943).

In the sheep the brain is supplied almost entirely by blood from the carotid arteries, and no direct connection exists between these arteries and the basilar artery. In this species, blood in the basilar artery actually flows in a caudad direction (Fig. 14.1). In the calf the arterial input is similar to that of the sheep but the rete receives a further large component from the basilar-occipital plexus formed by the vertebral and occipital arteries. Thus in the bovine species, vertebral blood probably enters the rete directly before passing to the circle of Willis. The changes occurring in cephalic and systemic blood pressure when the arteries supplying blood to the brain are clamped have been examined in the ox and sheep by Baldwin and Bell (1960, 1963).

In the dog the vertebral-basilar and carotid arterial systems are each supplied exclusively by their own arteries. But anastomoses between the vertebral arteries and the anterior spinal artery are often seen at each vertebra. The vascular supply of the vertebral structures of the rabbit and the monkey has been described by Stilwell (1959). The exact areas supplied by vertebral and carotid circulations vary greatly among species (Fig. 14.2). In the dog at least, the areas supplied can be separated effectively by ligation of the occipital artery.

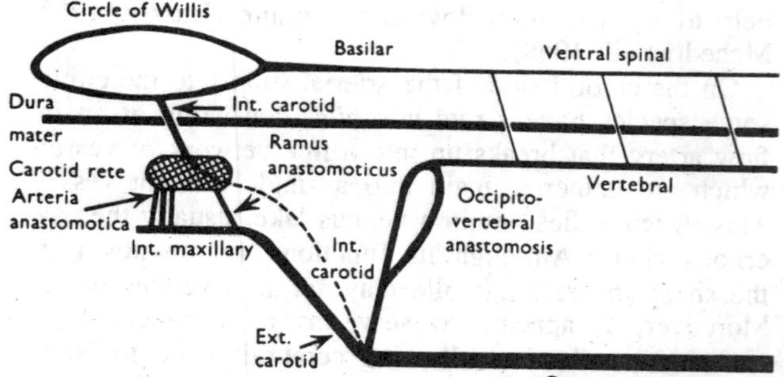

Figure 14.1. Arrangement of the cephalic arteries in the sheep. The dotted line indicates that the internal carotid does not persist in the adult. (From B.A. Baldwin and F.R. Bell 1963, *J. Physiol.* 167:448–62.)

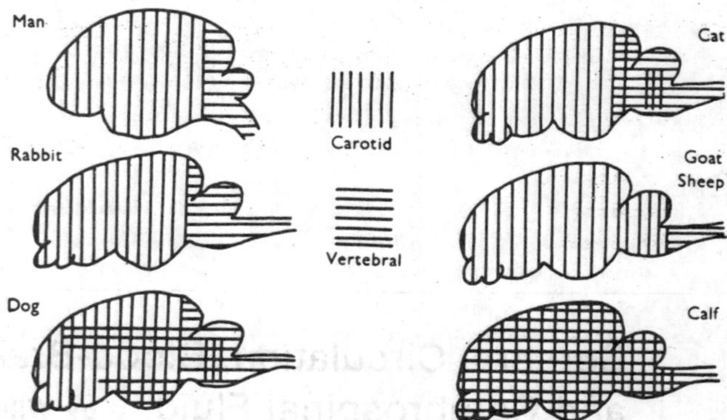

Figure 14.2. Approximate areas of the brain and anterior spinal cord supplied by carotid and vertebral blood. (From Baldwin and Bell 1963, *J. Anat.* 97:203–15, Cambridge University Press.)

In the dog more than in any other species investigated, there is a great ability to develop collateral circulation. This ability is particularly evident in the leptomeningeal circulation. Careful surgical occlusion of the middle cerebral artery results only in infarction in the basal ganglia. The development of collateral circulation between the anterior and middle cerebral arteries must be very rapid. In the majority of dogs both vertebral arteries and both common carotid arteries can be tied and cut simultaneously, or at least in the course of one surgical procedure, without ill effects. Not only do the animals not show any decrease in cerebral function at rest, but the circulation is not sufficiently reduced to cause difficulties when the animal is put under stress. The circulation does change,

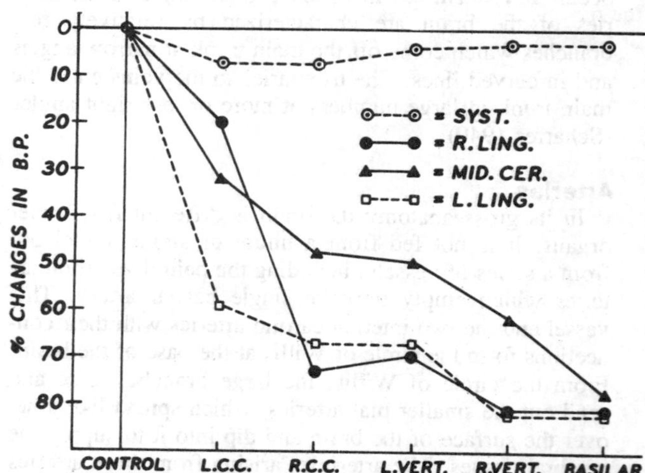

Figure 14.3. Percentage decreases in arterial blood pressure of normal dogs following occlusion in sequence of arteries indicated. SYST., systemic blood pressure; R.LING., right lingual artery; MID.CER., middle cerebral artery; L.LING., left lingual artery; L.C.C., left common carotid artery; R.C.C., right common carotid artery; L.VERT., left vertebral artery; R.VERT., right vertebral artery. (From Knapp, in Himwich and Schadé, eds., *Horizons in Neuropsychopharmacology: Progress in Brain Research*, Elsevier, Amsterdam, 1965, vol. 16, 285–96.)

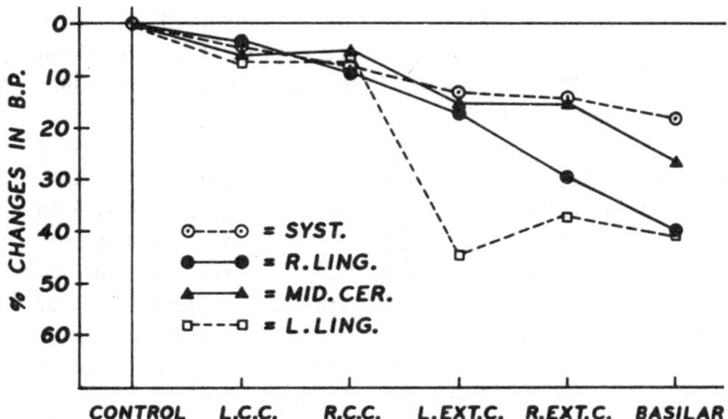

Figure 14.4. Percentage decreases in arterial blood pressure of the dog following occlusion in sequence of arteries indicated, with both common arteries and both vertebral arteries ligated in the neck approximately 4 months previously. L.EXT.C., left external carotid artery; R.EXT.C., right external carotid artery. (From Knapp, in Himwich and Schadé, eds., *Horizons in Neuropsychopharmacology: Progress in Brain Research,* Amsterdam, 1965, vol. 16, 285–96.)

however, as has been shown by Knapp (1965) (Figs. 14.3, 14.4). When the ligations were produced stepwise most of the collaterals were on the vertebral side, although collaterals may also arise on the carotid side.

Veins

The return flow from the brain is gathered in two groups of veins: one within the structure of the brain and the other on its surface (Fig. 14.5). Both groups empty into the intradural veins, so called because they lie within the folds of the thick dura mater which envelops the brain. The dorsal sagittal sinus, which drains a portion of the medial surfaces of the cerebral hemispheres and most of their convex surfaces, travels caudad to the occipital region and there in the sinuum confluens meets another intradural vein, the straight sinus, which also collects blood from the medial surfaces of the cerebral hemispheres, the choroid plexus, and most importantly, the basal ganglia. The sinuum confluens not only receives these two veins but also gives rise to the two lateral sinuses. After traversing the lateral sinuses, the venous blood leaves the cranial cavity chiefly by the internal jugular veins, but in part by the two vertebral veins. The same two paired veins (internal jugular and vertebral) drain the blood from the base of the brain. In general the blood collected from the internal jugular veins contains the return flow from bilaterally symmetrical portions of the brain.

The definitive work on the venous system and sinuses of the dog was completed by Reinhard et al. (1962) and extended through detailed study of the subcortical venous circulation (Armstrong and Horowitz 1971). For detailed descriptions of venous structure in other species see Hofmann (1901) and Heeschen (1958).

Vascularity and metabolism

A continual supply of nutrients of various types to the brain as well as the steady removal of the products of metabolism is the primary function of the blood supply. This function is actuated by the two-way exchange between the capillary blood and the cells supplied by the blood. The relation between the capillary supply or vascularity and metabolism has been extensively studied in the rat (Craigie 1955) but less well in domestic animals. It can be assumed, however, that the same situation which applied to the rat applies to other animals: the greater the metabolism of the area the more vascular it is. In the cat in general the capillary count for a specific area

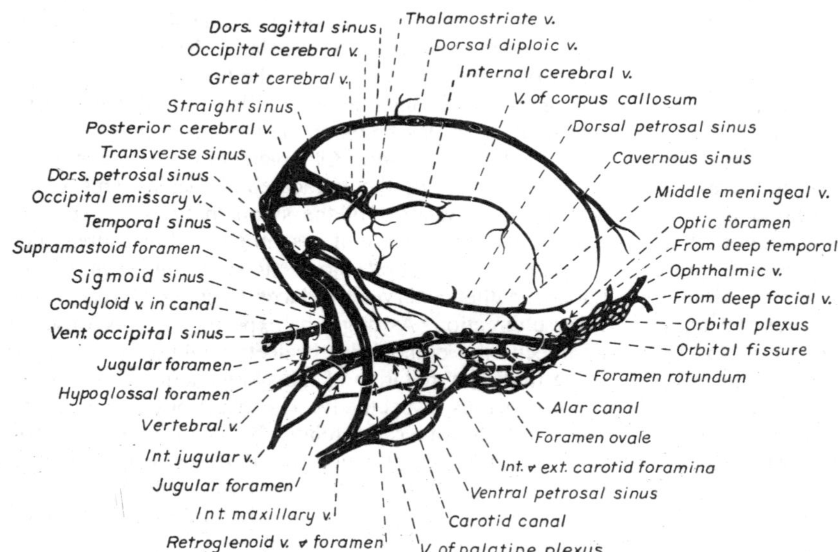

Figure 14.5. Cerebral venous drainage in the dog; intracranial channels and connections to major effluent veins are shown. (From fig. 3, K.R. Reinhard, M.E. Miller, and H.E. Evans 1962, *Am. J. Anat.* 111:67–87.)

paralleled the content of succinic dehydrogenase in its cells. This enzyme is considered a good indicator of oxidative metabolism. In a few nuclear structures the number of capillaries appears to be more closely related to the lactic acid dehydrogenase than to succinic dehydrogenase, suggesting a dependence on anaerobic rather than aerobic metabolism.

Control of cerebral blood supply

The brain is almost completely surrounded by a rigid skull which prevents any major change in its volume of blood. Though the skull confines the arterial blood to small changes in volume it does not prevent variations in the rate of blood flow, and in this way moderate vascular adaptations necessary for the acquisition of foodstuff and oxygen can be made.

A physical characteristic of blood, its viscosity, plays an important role in the regulation of the cerebral blood supply. For example, a slow blood-flow is observed with the increase of viscosity due to the large number of red blood cells in polycythemia vera. Conversely a fast flow and diminished viscosity are associated with anemia. Still another physical factor is the pressure of the cerebrospinal fluid (CSF), which aids in maintaining hemodynamics during sudden and extreme pressure alterations within the cerebral vessels. Pressure changes in the veins are communicated to the CSF and therefore to the cranial contents. Thus pressures both within and without the vessels may fluctuate together. With a precipitous rise of arterial and venous pressure, due to a cough or a strain of any kind, rupture of the finer vessels is prevented by a rise in pressure of the surrounding CSF.

Intracranial hypotension such as may be produced by a ventriculoatrial shunt increases cerebral blood due both to a decrease in differential pressure between precapillary arterioles and veins and to decreased external pressure.

Systemic blood pressure

Systemic blood pressure is the strongest extracerebral factor in the regulation of cerebral circulation.

The amount of blood passing through the brain at any given moment is the result of both volume and rate, acting simultaneously. The velocity of the blood is influenced by the pressure difference between the cerebral arteries and veins. Systemic pressure is important because it is proportional to that in the cerebral arterial system. Measurements of middle cerebral artery pressure show that it is somewhat lower than systemic pressure; the venous pressure is low and approaches zero in the erect position. Changes in intrathoracic pressure, whether due to respiration or other causes, such as a heavy load or the increased venous pressure associated with cardiac decompensation, are transmitted to the cerebral veins. Arterial blood pressure is an important determinant for cerebral blood flow and a precipitous fall of pressure may induce fainting due to a profound decrease in the cerebral blood supply. Within wide limits, however, physiological adaptations usually insure an adequate cerebral blood flow with various levels of long-maintained arterial pressure whether they are excessively high or moderately low. Animals with hypertension (about 200 mm Hg) and with the carotid sinus denervated show the most pronounced effects on cerebral circulation following the occlusion of one carotid. Conversely, in hypotensive animals under similar condition less effect is observed. When the carotid sinus is not denervated, the change in cerebral circulation following the clamping of one carotid is inversely proportional to the change in systemic blood pressure.

Arterial blood pressure remains in a constant relation to intracranial pressure. Cushing (1901) concluded that blood pressure establishes itself at a level above the pressure exerted on the medulla. Such a response prevents a persistent anemia of the medulla and thus protects the vital centers in that area.

Autonomic nervous regulation

Vasomotor reflexes, like those of the carotid sinus, which play a significant role in limiting alterations in blood pressure, are important for the stabilization of the cerebral blood flow. The vasomotor reflexes counteract changes in arterial blood pressure by appropriate alterations in heart action and peripheral vasomotor tone which increase with the fall of blood pressure and diminish with a rise. By virtue of these reflexes, with centers in the medullary and supramedullary regions, the brain takes part in the regulation of its own blood flow. This ability to control blood pressure subordinates the systemic circulation to maintenance of the cerebral blood supply.

Another important component in the regulation of cerebral blood flow, cerebrovascular resistance, is the end result of all factors that impede the flow of blood through the brain. The constriction or dilatation of the arteries and their arterioles helps counteract the influence of the systemic blood pressure. One element contributing to the steadying effect of the intracerebral mechanisms is observed on stimulation of the sympathetic nerves of animals. This causes a rise of systemic blood pressure which increases the cerebral blood flow. Stimulation of the parasympathetic nerves produces stronger effects in the reverse direction. As might be expected, the responses to an injection of epinephrine or acetylcholine are similar to those from a stimulation of the sympathetic and parasympathetic nerves respectively. The effect of epinephrine on the brain, however, is relatively small in comparison with its extracerebral action, perhaps due to its failure to cross the blood-brain barrier. Even when all buffer nerves are eliminated, the vessels still shrink as blood pressure rises and enlarge when pressure falls. The vessels seem to be sensitive to the pressure within them and thus tend to maintain cerebral blood flow within normal limits.

Intrinsic chemical regulation

An augmented cerebral blood flow following the rise of cerebral blood pressure may act impartially to bring more blood to all parts of the brain. In contrast the intrinsic chemical regulation is more concerned with the blood supply to individual cerebral regions. Whether chemical control is exercised synchronously with changes in blood pressure or separately, it affords a more equable distribution in accordance with the varied metabolic requirements of the cerebral regions, sequestering more blood for the active part than could come to it without the chemical regulation.

Carbon dioxide is the most powerful of the intrinsic influences. One way in which this dissolved gas operates effectively is through its synergistic action upon cerebral vasculature and systemic blood pressure to either raise or lower cerebral blood flow. The inhalation of carbon dioxide causes cerebral blood vessels to dilate and, at the same time, may increase systemic blood pressure by generalized vasoconstriction. Both of these responses accelerate cerebral blood flow. Conversely, pumping out the carbon dioxide from the brain, perhaps by hyperventilation, sharply limits blood flow because of the localized vasoconstriction, which may be intensified by a fall in systemic blood pressure. The cerebral vasomotor reactions to carbon dioxide are probably direct ones exerted on the walls of the vessels, and are not mediated by nervous impulses, as are the systemic changes actuated by receptors in the carotid sinus and body under the influence of the vasomotor centers in the medulla oblongata.

The remarkable sensitivity of the cerebral vasculature to carbon dioxide results in the following adaptive change: in response to stimulation, an area of the brain increases activity. The metabolism of that area must necessarily speed up to support the sudden burst of activity. The local manufacture and accumulation of carbon dioxide, which always follow any increase in metabolism, accelerate the flow of blood through the stimulated locus, thus satisfying the higher demand for oxygen and nutrients.

These physiological responses not only convey more oxygen to active tissue, but also diminish the range in fluctuations of CO_2 partial pressure within the brain. A high partial pressure hastens the cerebral blood flow, and by virtue of this acceleration the carbon dioxide produced in the brain is washed away, tending to reduce its pressure therein. With a decrease in carbon dioxide pressure to below normal, cerebral circulation is checked, which promotes an accumulation of carbon dioxide and therefore a rise of blood pressure toward normal. In a word, if there are changes in the CO_2 pressure in the brain, it is not because of the adaptive circulatory changes but despite them.

The effects of oxygen and carbon dioxide on cerebral circulation are opposite rather than complementary. In the first place, the two gases influence circulation in opposite directions; that is, a surplus of carbon dioxide accelerates the blood flow through the brain, a deficiency of oxygen exerts the same effect. Conversely, an excess of oxygen and a decrease of carbon dioxide diminish the blood flow. Not only does cerebral circulation differ qualitatively in its behavior to carbon dioxide and oxygen, but quantitatively also. The circulation of the brain is much more sensitive to small fluctuations of carbon dioxide than it is to similar changes in oxygen. Oxygen at abnormally high partial pressures slows cerebral blood flow by increasing cerebrovascular resistance. In contrast a diminution of oxygen does not greatly accelerate cerebral circulation until the hypoxia becomes intense.

When the brain is hypoxic any further deprivation of oxygen enhances the ability of carbon dioxide to increase cerebral blood flow and at the same time minimize the production of more carbon dioxide. But when oxygen levels are within normal limits, carbon dioxide exerts the controlling influence over the cerebral vasculature. It should be recognized that oxygen and not carbon dioxide is the gas required for generating cerebral energy, and that the great sensitivity of the brain and body to carbon dioxide facilitates the adaptation of the oxygen supplies to the needs of the brain. This relationship breaks down, however, when the O_2 supply of the brain becomes the critical factor.

Intrinsic chemical control is not limited to carbon dioxide and oxygen; other substances produced in cerebral metabolism become involved as the demands for energy grow more intense. The enhanced blood supply accompanying increased cerebral activity is not only a response to the more rapid formation of carbon dioxide but also to the local drop in O_2 partial pressure. If the enlarged supply is still not adequate to maintain cerebral oxidations, anaerobic energy sources are tapped, lactate and pyruvate accumulate, and consequently an acid shift in pH occurs. The local acidosis dilates the vessels and thus increases still more the oxygen supplement. The need for more blood is mediated by the production of a vasodilatator material.

These vascular adaptations are also regulated by indirect axon reflexes mediated by perivascular nerves. The combined reactions form the *nutritive reflex*, which is sensitive to many metabolites and precisely adapts blood supply to cerebral activity. Cerebral blood vessels apparently possess an inherent constrictor tone and are prevented from going into spasm by normally occurring vasodilator agents such as carbon dioxide. The intrinsic regulation of the cephalic vasculature, whether chemical or nervous (parasympathetic and perivascular), is predominantly dilator and overcomes the constrictor influences arising within the blood vessels. But the vascular reactions have their limits and cannot always assure a normal partial pressure of oxygen in the brain, a failure which occurs, for example, during convulsions. Nevertheless, the limitations imposed upon cerebral metabolism by blood flow are not absolute but may be ameliorated to some extent by the anaerobic utilization of energy, as occurs in the breakdown of cerebral glycogen stores to lactic and pyruvic acids and the concomitant cleavage of the energy-rich phosphate bonds, especially those in phosphocreatine, while adenosine triphosphate is broken down to adenosine diphosphate and inorganic phosphate. The changes in the acid-base equilibrium are also important determinants of the vascular reactions. The early alkaline shift may limit the flow of blood to the hyperactive part while the subsequent acid shift insures the continuation of the localized hyperemia until the acid metabolites are finally removed and the energy-rich phosphate bonds are regenerated.

Cerebral blood flow

Most anatomical studies of the cerebral circulation have utilized the injection of dye or resin after death. In the living animal, blood distribution has been followed with angiographic techniques. The disadvantage of all these studies is that injections are made at a pressure greater than the arterial blood pressure. Under such conditions the injected material fills all of the anastomotic channels that are patent irrespective of whether they are functional under normal conditions.

Many attempts have been made to study the circulation under more physiological or dynamic circumstances. Pressure measurements in the middle cerebral artery have been made in the dog and the monkey. In the calf and the sheep pressures and flow were recorded in the vertebral and carotid arteries. Blood flow in general has been studied less adequately than pressure changes because of the difficulties of measuring flow in small arteries. Only a few flow measurements have been made on vessels within the brain. Ideally pressure and flow must be followed simultaneously from approximately the same recording sites.

Cerebral blood flow has been estimated in the dog and goat using techniques developed by Kety (1960) for man. This method, based on the Fick principle, measures only total cerebral blood flow and not regional blood flows. Cerebral blood flow data as well as arteriovenous oxygen differences are necessary for the calculation of cerebral metabolic rate. Labeled iodine (^{131}I antipyrine) has been used to follow the changes in cerebral blood flow in the quiet unanesthetized cat and during visual stimulation. The method requires that the animal be decapitated, the brain frozen, and radioautographs made. In the rat other methods for cerebral blood flow have been developed by Sapirstein and Hanusek (1958). A number of additional techniques also appear to be of great promise for man but seem to be of limited use in experimental animals with large muscle masses in the head and neck regions and hence relatively large extracerebral blood flows in those areas. Sokoloff and his colleagues have used deoxyglucose to estimate cerebral metabolism in various nuclei in the brain (Kennedy et al. 1975).

BLOOD-BRAIN BARRIER

Evidence of a functional barrier

Paul Ehrlich reported in 1885 that some supravital dyes stain all the tissues of the body with exception of the brain. And although equilibrium is rapidly established between the vascular fluids and the interstitial fluids of most organs, many substances show a slow equilibration in the brain. Moreover, the brain is more accessible to certain substances if they are administered intrathecally than if given intravenously. For example, if sodium ferricyanide is given intravenously, it produces no symptoms even in fairly high concentrations, nor can it be detected in the brain although it penetrates all other tissues of the body. However, if small amounts of ferricyanide are introduced into the cerebrospinal fluid, the animal develops pronounced symptoms and may die of convulsions. These lines of evidence suggest that there is a functional barrier between the blood and the brain. Consideration of the blood-brain barrier is of great importance in many problems including the utilization of nutrients by the brain, the therapeutic use of drugs, and the pathological effects of viruses and toxins upon brain tissue. Actually, in discussing this problem one must consider the four fluid compartments in the brain (Fig. 14.6) and the barriers between them.

Acid aniline dyes fail to enter the brain although basic aniline dyes do so readily. Friedemann (1942) pointed out that acid aniline dyes carry a negative electric charge and stressed the fact that negatively charged particles meet resistance at the blood-brain barrier. On the other hand, positively charged substances such as basic aniline dyes penetrate the brain without hindrance. Not only the electronegatively charged dyes but also substances such as lactic acid and pyruvic acid containing electronegative carboxyl groups enter the brain slowly. The rate of entrance of these substances into the brain is considerably slower than that of glucose and is too slow to support brain metabolism. In contrast, observations on excised cerebral tissue reveal that lactic acid is as effective as glucose in maintaining brain metabolism. In excised tissues materials penetrate the brain easily at the cut surfaces.

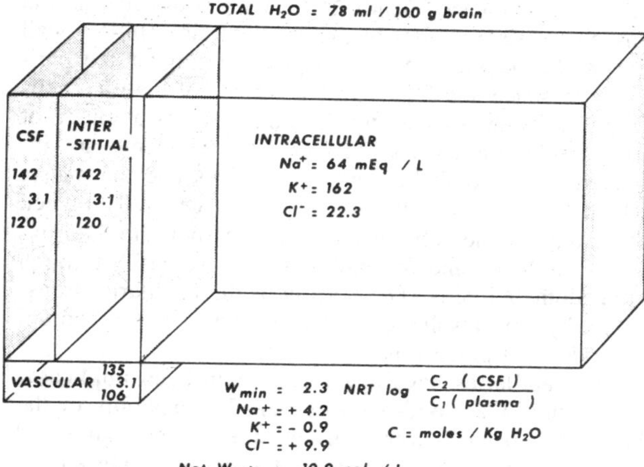

Figure 14.6. Fluid compartments of the CNS. Size of each rectangle is proportional to estimated volume of the compartment it represents. Concentrations of Na^+, K^+, and Cl^- in cerebrospinal fluid as well as calculations for W_{min} (thermodynamic work to form one liter of CSF) are from Flexner (1934). Intracellular concentrations are calculated on the basis of 15 percent interstitial volume. N, number of molecules of any substance; R, gas constant; T, absolute temperature. (From R.D. Tschirgi, Chemical environment of the central nervous system, in *Handbook of Physiology*, sec. 1, *Neurophysiology*, Am. Physiol. Soc., Washington, 1960, vol. 3, 1865–90.)

Permeability to toxins and viruses

The mode of action of toxins which produce symptoms of central origin, such as tetanus, diphtheria, botulinus, dysentery, cobra venom, lamb dysentery, and staphylococcus, is difficult to elucidate. Their effects on the CNS may be due to primary injury either of the nervous tissue or of the capillary bed. On the other hand, a toxin may fail to act because it lacks affinity for nervous tissue. It appears that the capillaries of the CNS are impermeable to these toxins.

The neurotropic viruses, such as those of rabies and endemic encephalitis, are thought to reach the CNS by neural pathways. Whether this means that the blood-brain barrier is impermeable to these viruses has been much debated.

Permeability to drugs, including antibiotics

The ability of drugs to enter the CNS has an important bearing not only on their therapeutic value but also on the side effects which they produce. The distribution of urea, isoniazid, phenobarbital, and acetazolamide has been studied in cat and monkey brains. Each compound has its own peculiarities of penetration. Phenobarbital, for example, penetrates white matter more slowly than gray with a clear anatomical distribution not consistently related to vascularity. The exposure of the animal to 25 percent carbon dioxide increased the concentration of phenobarbital in the brain. Penetration of salicyclic acid also increased under these circumstances. In the case of sulfate ion, auditory or visual stimuli appeared to promote the entrance of the sulfate into the brain.

The capillaries of the CNS are probably also impermeable to antibiotics. If, however, the antibiotic is given directly into the brain, it does penetrate the walls of the ventricles. Treatment of the animal with any procedure which will injure the blood-brain barrier, such as hyaluronidase, contrast media, heparin, or cold, will increase the entrance of antibiotics.

Epinephrine and theophylline will increase the permeability of the brain only for those substances to which it is normally permeable. The availability of transport systems may be a factor.

Permeability to amino acids, electrolytes, and ions

In general the amino acids have not been studied in great detail in terms of their ability to pass the blood-brain barrier. Only a few have been studied extensively, e.g. glutamic acid, leucine, isoleucine, lysine, tyrosine, tryptophan, and phenylalanine (Lajtha et al. 1963). The ability of these substances to penetrate the brain is greater in the young than in the adult. In the adult the ability of brain amino acids to exchange with those in the blood appears to be on a one-to-one basis. When an isotopic-labeled amino acid such as glutamic acid is given, it appears in the brain, although there is not an increase in the total amount of the amino acid. Each amino acid must be considered individually especially with regard to the function and the specificity of the transport system. Moreover, it is necessary to consider the age of the animal and its previous treatment as well as the individual amino acid entering the brain. One of the most exciting developments of recent years has been the demonstration that an increased blood level of one amino acid can influence the entrance of other amino acids into the brain, for example, the inhibition of the uptake of tryptophan and of tyrosine by a high blood-level of phenylalanine.

Most ions, whether cations or anions, require a relatively long period before equal concentrations are present in the blood and in brain tissue. Anions such as bromide, iodide, thiocyanide, and chloride have a short equilibration period, usually only a few minutes, between the circulatory fluids of the vascular tree and the interstitial fluids of the various organs. Yet equilibration with the brain may not be complete even in a period of three hours. Sodium and potassium are the classical examples of cations which enter the brain slowly. Radioactive sodium concentration, for example, equalizes throughout the vascular and interstitial fluid of the various organs of the body within 11 minutes and yet requires 62 hours to attain equilibrium between brain and blood. Though potassium enters interstitial fluid more rapidly than sodium, the rate is slower for the brain than for other organs.

Two additional points must be considered here: first,

not all parts of the brain are equally protected by the blood-brain barrier. A portion of the hypothalamus with pituitary and pineal glands, the choroid plexus, and the area postrema are more permeable than other areas. Second, the physiological status of the brain is also important. Any injury to the brain tends to reduce the resistance of the blood-brain barrier to penetration. Inflammation facilitates the passage of substances. Considerable evidence has accumulated that increase of carbon dioxide also reduces barrier function. There is also the possibility that the rate of permeability of the brain may be regulated in part by nonnervous tissue as shown by Geiger et al. (1952). They found that using the perfused brain of cats, the administration of glucose failed to revive the brain unless an extract of liver was added at the same time.

The existence of diffusional barriers in the spinal cord has been documented specifically for the Renshaw cells by Curtis and Eccles (1958). Their experiments using acetylcholine and anticholinesterase as well as other drugs applied to the immediate locality of the Renshaw cells led them to conclude that two barriers are present—the blood-brain barrier and another diffusional barrier closely associated with the synaptic terminations upon the Renshaw cells.

Nature of the barrier

It is becoming increasingly evident that what has been called the blood-brain barrier is not a generalized phenomenon. It is probably a summation of many factors only some of which are integral parts of the anatomical boundary between blood and brain. The active work in this field in the last fifteen years leads largely to the conclusion that there will be no generalized concept developed to fit all the phenomena and that each condition and each metabolite must be considered by itself (Edström 1964). Dobbing (1963) has suggested a unified hypothesis which postulates many factors including on one hand those which the brain has in common with other tissues, and on the other those which are unique to the brain. In the first group of factors, Dobbing includes electrical charge, molecular size, degree of dissociation, extent of protein binding, and lipid solubility. The second group consists of the negligible extracellular space in the brain, with the consequent necessity for transcellular transport, and the resistance to entry of substances into metabolically inert compartments. Brain metabolism, then, would dominate much of the transport of substances between blood and brain. Considered in this way, the blood-brain barrier would be a reflection of, rather than a limiting factor in, in vivo cerebral metabolism.

Anatomical explanation

In spite of the above, considerable research is still devoted to determining the exact location of the blood-brain barrier. Theoretically the barrier could function at any one of several sites beginning with the capillary wall and going outward to the peripheral lining of the perivascular space and finally to the surface of the glial cells (Fig. 14.7). In considering the capillaries as a source of the blood-brain barrier, two possible elements are involved—the endothelial cells themselves and the matrix which binds these cells together. It is generally agreed that lipid-soluble substances such as carbon dioxide, oxygen, urethane, and formaldehyde diffuse easily through the endothelial cells. The portion of the capillaries transversed by lipid-insoluble substances such as water, sodium chloride, and glucose is still disputed.

The capillaries have again and again been implicated as the site of a blood-brain barrier. The anatomy of the barrier has been "surprisingly elusive but the claims and counterclaims have developed a fervor exceeding almost any other aspect of the subject" (Tschirgi 1960). Two main theories have developed: the perivascular glia membrane theory and the capillary endothelial theory. In a classical experiment, Schaltenbrand and Bailey (1928) perfused hypertonic saline through one carotid artery in the dog and distilled water at equal pressure through the other carotid. The side of the brain perfused with saline was shrunken and dehydrated; the other side receiving distilled water was swollen and edematous. The authors concluded that the perivascular membrane was relatively impermeable to sodium chloride. This membrane consists of the invaginating pia which follows the vessels from the surface into the depth of the brain and is supported by

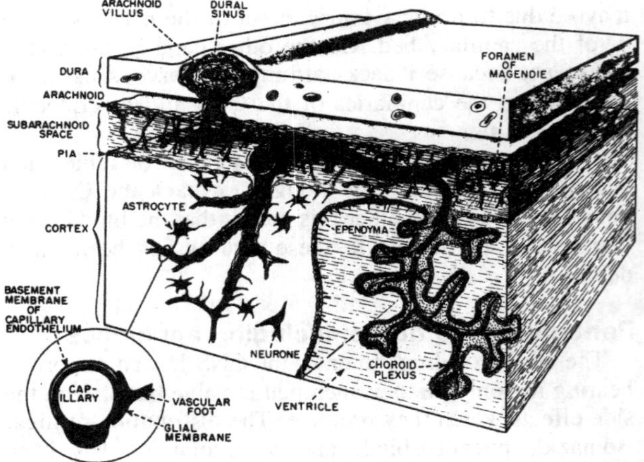

Figure 14.7. Section of CNS and investing membranes illustrating relationships of various fluid compartments and barriers. *Enlargement at lower left* illustrates three probable sites of blood-brain barrier action: capillary endothelium, basement membrane, and perivascular glia. Note that the invaginating pia does not accompany penetrating vessels beyond the larger branches. Astrocytes form an 85–90 percent complete sheath around blood vessels, although only a few are illustrated. (From R.D. Tschirgi, Chemical environment of the central nervous system, in *Handbook of Physiology*, sec. 1, *Neurophysiology*, Am. Physiol. Soc., Washington, 1960, vol. 3, 1865–90.)

a closely adherent layer of astrocytes. Standard histological techniques using light microscopy have failed to show whether this double membrane accompanies the blood vessels throughout. However, electron microscopy of cerebral capillaries clearly reveals astrocytic feet in association with most of the capillary surfaces. The expanded astrocytic processes form a single layer around the capillaries and do not appear to overlap one another. The "sheet" formed by these processes is incomplete and covers about 85 percent of the total capillary surface. On the other hand, many workers believe that the barrier lies in the capillary walls themselves. This view is strongly advanced by studies on the introduction of an aminoacridine dye into the brain. The dye did not enter the vascular endothelium of the cerebral blood vessels, although it entered the endothelial cells of other tissues.

Mention should also be made of the extensive work of Hess (1955), who believed that he had demonstrated the relation of the blood-brain barrier to the ground substance in the brain. What he called ground substance of the brain probably exists within the extraneuronal space rather than the extracellular space and may consist largely of glial processes.

In the last few years attention has turned to the relative lack of extracellular space in the brain as a possible explanation for the blood-brain barrier. The close packing of the cells in the brain results in a dearth of extracellular space, less than 5 percent being fairly well agreed upon, although some investigators believe this low value is the result of the fixation of tissue for electron microscopy. This situation would mean that material entering the brain would have to enter almost immediately into a cell rather than into extracellular fluid. In contrast, in organs such as kidney and liver the cells are surrounded by extracellular fluid which may make up as much as 30 percent of the organ. The function of astroglia in water and ion metabolism of the CNS was elucidated in one of the early electron microscopy studies: the volume of the astroglia can change by taking up water and salt, and the glial processes are similar in function to an extracellular space. The authors concluded that the astroglia function as a water-ion compartment for the CNS and that this compartment is involved in a selective transport of fluids and metabolites between blood and brain. These ideas led to the concept that the important factor in the blood-brain barrier is a combination of glial cells and extracellular space, the so-called extraneuronal space. In this regard it is interesting that in the brain the chloride space does not correspond to the extracellular space as in other organs.

Transport explanation

One of the most intriguing suggestions that has arisen from studies of the blood-brain barrier is that the barrier may have a functional rather than anatomical localization and may depend upon transport phenomena. The transport of materials can be either active or passive. Passive transfer would include processes such as dialysis and diffusion and might involve a carrier. Active transport requires a carrier substance (Fig. 14.8). Transport by a carrier has been vigorously studied in bacteria, and in many cases these ideas explain transfer phenomena in organs such as the kidney and muscle. Another type of active transfer linked to metabolic processes has been hypothesized to account for transfer between blood and brain, between brain and CSF, and between blood and CSF. The diagram of the brain and its membranes (see Fig. 14.7) suggests that a net movement of water and solutes from the vascular compartment into the extravascular compartments in the CNS could be balanced at least in part by a net movement of water and solutes from the subarachnoid space through the arachnoid villi into the blood stream. The chemodynamic analyses of such fluid formation depend upon the local elaboration of metabolic energy in order to explain the electrolyte composition of the CSF.

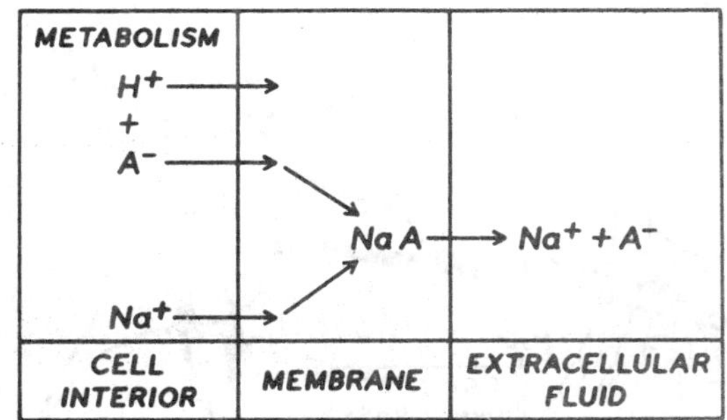

Figure 14.8. Active transport in which sodium combines with a transport substance across the membrane

Tschirgi has postulated in Figure 14.9 the mechanism whereby sodium and chloride might move from plasma to the extravascular fluids of the CNS by an exchange mechanism controlled by the carbon dioxide produced by metabolism. A fraction of the carbon dioxide produced by the cellular metabolism of the brain would not diffuse into the blood but would be rapidly hydrated to carbonic acid in the presence of carbonic anhydrase. This reaction, according to Tschirgi, would reasonably occur within the cellular structure adjacent to the capillary wall, that is, in the neuroglial perivascular membrane. He suggests further that within this membrane selective exchange can be made of the hydrogen and bicarbonate ions formed for other electrolytes, mainly sodium and chloride. The sodium and chloride ions thus obtained would enter the interstitial fluid of the nervous system.

On the basis of such a hypothesis the decrease in extracranial fluid formation after the administration of acetazolamide (a carbonic anhydrase inhibitor) could be explained. And this mechanism is essentially identical with that proposed for kidney tubular reabsorption of so-

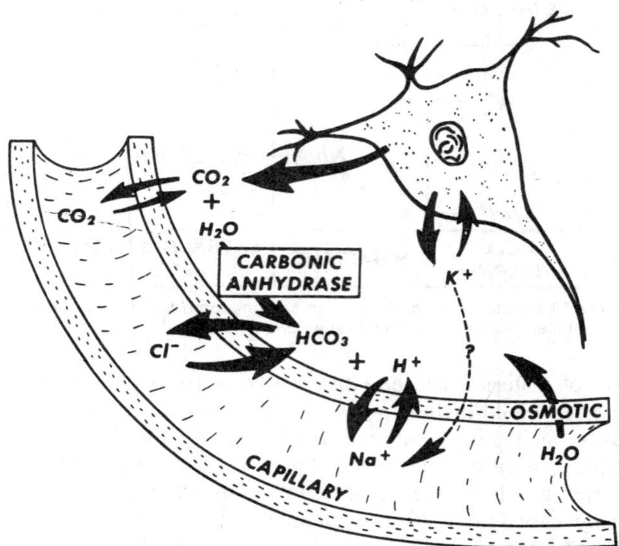

Figure 14.9. Proposed mechanism for converting metabolically produced CO_2 into carbonic acid, with subsequent exchange for plasma Na^+ and Cl^-. (From R.D. Tschirgi, Chemical environment of the central nervous system, in *Handbook of Physiology*, sec. 1, *Neurophysiology*, Am. Physiol. Soc., Washington, 1960, vol. 3, 1865–90.)

dium. In the kidney, however, the pump moves sodium and water from the extravascular fluid into the plasma, whereas in the brain, Tschirgi (1960) proposed that it moves these substances from the plasma into extracellular fluid. Interference by acetazolamide with the kidney tubular mechanism occurs in a manner apparently entirely analogous to that proposed for intracranial fluid formation. This interference is thought to be responsible for the lack of water reabsorption by the kidney and consequent diuresis produced by this compound. Since tubular secretion of potassium in exchange for sodium can occur in the kidney, and since potassium and hydrogen behaved similarly with respect to electrical potential difference across the blood-brain barrier, the possibility of potassium-sodium exchange across the barrier must also be considered. A further consequence of such a hypothesis is the prediction that acetazolamide should decrease the rate of accumulation of parenterally administered radioactive sodium in the CNS.

In considering the transfer of substances from the blood into the brain, one can compare it with the renal tubular transport apparatus in the case of glucose, where the sugar is reabsorbed by means of active transport from urine to blood. When organic acids are used to produce "overloading," they show various inhibiting potencies on the blood-brain barrier. A rough correlation can be drawn between their ability to inhibit blood-brain barrier transport and their maximal tubular rate of excretion. The evidence for a close analogy between renal tubular function and the blood-brain barrier has been marshaled by

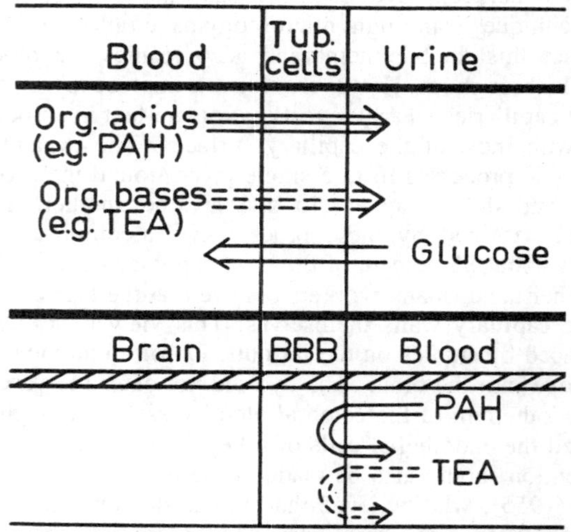

Figure 14.10. Hypothesized comparison between renal tubules and blood-brain transport. (From O. Steinwall 1961, *Acta Psychiat. Neurol. Scand.* 36 [suppl. 150]:314–18.)

Tschirgi, but, on the basis of data obtained from the isolated choroid plexus, has been questioned by Welch (1963).

The types of transfer involved in the blood-brain barrier have been summarized by Steinwall (1964) as shown in Figure 14.10.

Development

It is an intriguing possibility that during growth the brain is freely permeable to the nutrient substances required for its development and maturation but that after this time permeability decreases. In the adult animal only small amounts of substances other than glucose would be required by the brain and hence no mechanisms would be needed for their entrance into the brain. The relative lack of transport mechanisms would then result in the blood-brain barrier phenomenon. Such a teleological explanation has not been proven, however.

A definite change in the permeability of the barrier can readily be shown using radioactive phosphorus in rabbits (Fig. 14.11). Young animals of several species also show a marked diminution of brain permeability to various amino acids as the brain matures. The age at which the barrier "shuts down" appears to be related to the age at which the brain matures. In animals born relatively old, such as the colt, calf, guinea pig, and kid, the blood-brain barrier is probably well developed at birth. In other species in which the young are born immature—the rat, the rabbit, and the mouse, for example—the barrier is less adult in function. In the cat and dog the efficiency of the barrier may be at an intermediate level. It is possible that these differences are due only to differences in the maturity of the brain and hence are not true species differences. For example, the penetration of bilirubin ap-

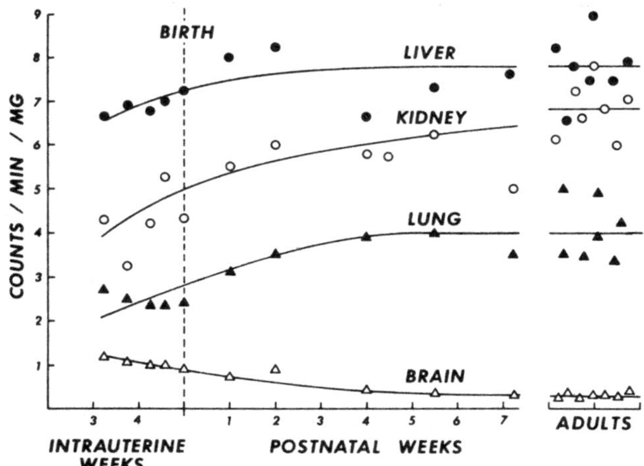

Figure 14.11. Concentration of ^{32}P in various organs of fetal, young, and adult rabbits 24 hours after injection. (From Bakay 1953, *Arch. Neurol. Psychiat.* 70:30–39.)

parently does not occur in the monkey, dog, and rabbit unless hypoxia or other injury is present. In the kitten, however, a high concentration of bilirubin in blood is apparently all that is necessary for the brain to become stained. Moreover, the brains of rat embryos are impervious to trypan blue administration as early as the tenth day of the gestation period. Normal body constituents are probably treated differently by both young and mature brains than are foreign substances. The gradual maturation of the blood-brain barrier has been related to the slow development of the ground substance (Hess 1955). If the ground substance is composed of glia and of the periglia sheaths, gradual development would be expected. The difference in uniformity of phenobarbital penetration in all parts of the brain in kitten and adult cat has been linked to myelinization.

CEREBROSPINAL FLUID–BRAIN BARRIER

The blood-brain barrier is a complex phenomenon partly because its function involves the CSF-brain barrier as well as the blood-CSF barrier. Although materials pass with more freedom between the CSF and the brain than between blood and brain, there still appears to be some barrier. If a substance is lipid-soluble, it can diffuse across lipoidal portions of cells at the brain-CSF boundary and enter the brain cells. The rate at which this occurs appears to be mainly dependent upon the lipid-solubility of the undissociated form of the substance and its dissociation constant. In addition, other substances may leave the CSF by specialized active processes. Isotopic materials injected into the cisterna magna of the rabbit or into a ventricle can be monitored to determine how much enters the brain from the CSF. Sulfhydryl-containing compounds are involved in the transfer of ^{32}P and possibly other isotopes from CSF to brain.

Even lipid-insoluble substances with molecules as large as sucrose can diffuse readily from the CSF to the interstitial space of the brain. This process, however, is important only for distances of 100 μ or less. Particles as large as ferritin when injected into the ventricles have appeared both within and between the cells. It therefore appears that substances placed in the ventricle can penetrate far enough to become directly available not only to glial cells and the neurons themselves but also in the synaptic endings.

If trypan blue is injected into the cisterna magna, it can be found in the base of the brain, midbrain, medulla, and cervical spinal cord. The dye seems to spread through the CSF and is absorbed by the surface of the brain which is in direct contact with the CSF.

BLOOD–CEREBROSPINAL FLUID BARRIER

If dyes such as the aminoacridines are injected into the blood, they penetrate the choroidal endothelium but do not enter the CSF. On this basis Rodriguez-Peralta (1957) proposed that the cell membrane of the choroidal endothelium facing the ventricular lumen constitutes the blood-CSF barrier. These results are in essential agreement with the earlier observations on trypan blue.

The barrier to movement of materials in the opposite direction is also important. This barrier controls the adequate removal of materials from the CSF—a process which depends upon their passage through the arachnoid villi and into the venous sinuses.

A relatively high rate of escape was found for substances such as ethyl thiourea, thiocyanate, and iodide. The rate for inulin was the lowest and the passage was probably almost exclusively by way of the arachnoid villi. These villi are highly porous structures which are permeable to proteins, colloidal gold, yeast cells, and erythrocytes among others (see below). The more rapidly escaping substances presumably pass also into nervous tissue and thence into the blood or are absorbed by the choroid plexuses. In cats evidence was obtained for the absorption of PAH (p-aminohippuric acid) from the lateral ventricles and from the third ventricle. Prockop et al. (1962) pointed out that lipid-insoluble substances such as inulin and dextran pass from blood to CSF very slowly but in contrast are released from CSF to blood quite readily. Thus, to enter the CSF, compounds must penetrate a boundary that is almost impermeable to lipid-insoluble substances; but on leaving the CSF they manage to circumvent this requirement. The passage of inulin from CSF to blood in rabbits in which the CSF pressure was lowered by the intravenous administration of urea provides a good example. Simultaneous recording of CSF pressure and of blood pressure from the dural venous sinuses revealed that the exit rates of inulin were directly related to the pressure differences between the two fluids. The results suggested that lipid-insoluble molecules in general could escape from the CSF by filtration per se through the arachnoid villi.

Several exit routes for drugs administered into the CSF are available, the route used being determined by the physical properties of the drug. All drugs apparently can leave by filtration across the arachnoid villi, their speed of exit depending only upon the rate at which CSF drains into the blood stream.

Phenol red and several other lipid-insoluble acids are actively transported directly from CSF to blood. Diodrast (iodopyracet) or PSP (phenolsulfonphthalein) in low concentrations can be removed from the ventriculocisternal perfusate by a process of active transport that resembles secretion by the proximal tubules of the kidney. The transfer maximum of 2–3 μg/min occurred at an inflow concentration of 20 μg/ml. Active transport appeared to occur in the region of the fourth ventricle and in the cisterna magna. If active transport was inhibited by drugs, passive transport also occurred, by diffusion as well as by absorption in bulk.

In the dog, spinal fluid iodide transport has been studied by the injection of radioactive iodide into the ventricular spinal fluid. Under these circumstances ^{131}I disappears rapidly from the spinal fluid and appears in the blood, indicating a carrier transport system. If perchlorate is administered systemically, it increases the movement of iodide from blood to CSF but decreases the movement in the opposite direction. It seems likely therefore that iodide is normally transported from spinal fluid to blood by a mechanism different from that of passive diffusion through a semipermeable membrane. The locus occurs largely in the choroid plexus. This transport system may be different from that described by Pappenheimer et al. (1961) for organic anions in the goat, since Becker (1961) has demonstrated that there is no mutually competitive inhibition.

The active transport of thiocyanate (CNS) out of the cerebrospinal fluid appears to maintain the observed concentration gradient of that substance between brain and cerebrospinal fluid. This gradient does not allow CNS in plasma and brain water to reach an equilibrium. If the transport process is blocked, however, so that there is no net flux between the blood, brain, and CSF compartments, it is then possible to make an accurate estimate of the thiocyanate space in the brain.

INJURY TO THE BARRIERS

The effects of injury to any of the barriers discussed above have been well documented. Drastic injury such as stab wounds, crushing blows, or cold destroys the barrier phenomenon only in the injured areas. Hypoxia affects the barriers in all parts of the brain; carbon dioxide has a potent influence on the barriers in all parts. In experimental animals including rabbits, guinea pigs, and cats carbon dioxide increases the permeability of the brain capillaries to substances such as trypan blue which normally do not pass the barrier. The accumulation of carbon dioxide may explain the barrier effects seen in some types of asphyxia.

Sulfhydryl-group inhibitors may cause metabolic injury, since mercurial poisons all influence the function of the various barriers. Hyaluronidase and heparin also have potent effects. High body temperatures such as occur in febrile diseases also decrease the efficiency of the blood-brain barrier and possibly of the other barriers as well. The effects of injuries in general were described by Steinwall (1964):

(1) Injuries	causing free diffusion or flow (mechanical, necrotizing or otherwise rupturing)
Indicators:	detectable native or foreign blood constituents in general
(2) Injuries	causing functional alteration of specific transfer mechanism(s)
Indicators:	substances presumed to be specifically handled by the actual mechanism(s)
Example	(a) general transport inhibition: decrease CNS uptake of glucose, "increased uptake" (abnormal blood-CNS passage) of acid dyes
	(b) selective (overloading) inhibition of CNS-blood extrusion of "waste acids": abnormal blood-CNS passage of acid indicators only.

PRACTICAL CONSIDERATIONS IN THE TREATMENT OF ANIMALS

The practical problems concerned with the barriers are numerous and difficult to codify in a few rules. The basic fact that no simple overall rule can be used is of great importance. In the adult animal only certain groups of drugs such as lipid-soluble drugs, anesthetics, analgesics, monoamine oxidase inhibitors, and psychoactive drugs in general are known to enter the brain. Other substances, urea, isoniazid, and acetazolamide, for example, also penetrate the brain. As noted, however, each substance has its own peculiarities of distribution and penetration. It is also probable that penicillin may be actively passed from CSF to blood. Such active absorption may account for the difficulty of maintaining therapeutic concentrations in the CSF even when the drug is given intrathecally. Higher concentrations might be obtained by the use of inhibitors, possibly PAH.

It is perhaps the reverse of this situation—how to treat infections of the brain and meninges—which is of the most importance to the veterinarian. The possibilities of infections entering the brain are of course greatly enhanced by any of the circumstances which alter the blood-brain barrier (including drugs). On the other hand, fever accompanying an infection may accelerate the entrance of antibiotics which normally do not penetrate the brain.

Considerable research on meningitis in man by Smith (1957) and his colleagues at Oxford has led them to support the intrathecal as well as the intramuscular administration of penicillin or streptomycin in such cases. Smith also pointed out that the use of cortisone in treating meningitis may restore the barrier just at the time when the maximum penetration of the drug is needed. Although these observations were made on man, there is no reason to believe that they should not apply to other animals.

A drug which appears to have central action may actually have a peripheral effect which in turn influences the CNS. For example, any drug which lowers blood pressure beyond the ability of the brain to compensate may appear to have a direct effect upon that organ, whereas the observed effect is really only secondary. Such responses should be viewed very conservatively. The proof of primary effect upon the brain rests in the last analysis on the demonstration of the drug in the brain.

Animals which suffer from head injuries may have enough brain damage, due to contrecoup if nothing else, to make changes in their barriers. Similar changes may arise from treatment with phenothiazines such as chlorpromazine, from hypoxia, or CO_2 inhalation. The use of mercurials may influence barrier phenomena due to the poisoning of sulfhydryl-containing enzymes. One reason for lowering body temperature in fever may be to restore the barriers toward normal efficiency. This procedure, however, may reduce the penetration of antibiotics.

In the young animal the barriers should be assumed to be more permeable than in the adult. Similarly, injuries to a young animal whether physical or metabolic may have a relatively greater effect than in the mature animal.

CEREBROSPINAL FLUID (CSF)

Meninges and the anatomical CSF pathway

The meninges are the membranes surrounding the brain and spinal cord. The outermost of these coverings is the thick, fibrous dura mater. Beneath this is the potential subdural space, containing a film of fluid. Forming the inner wall of this space is the arachnoid, which sends from its inner surface numerous delicate trabeculae or fibrous bands into the extensive subarachnoid space (see Fig. 14.7). These trabeculae extend down to the pia mater, a highly vascular membrane which closely invests the spinal cord and brain and adheres to them. The two innermost membranes, the arachnoid and the pia mater, are sometimes collectively designated as the leptomeninges or pia-arachnoid.

The subarachnoid space, its perivascular extensions, the ventricles of the brain, and the central canal of the spinal cord collectively constitute the cerebrospinal pathway, which contains the CSF. The subdural space has no anatomical and probably no physiological connection with the subarachnoid space. The subarachnoid space is unique for mammals. Phylogenetically it is first seen around the brain stem in warm-blooded birds. The passage of dye introduced into the lumbar subarachnoid space of pigs and sheep demonstrates that CSF passes along the spinal nerves.

Two factors govern the distribution of material injected into the ventricles. The first is the volume, which if insufficient will not allow the material to move downstream. The second is the failure of the solution to move anteriorly if injected downstream. The first factor becomes unimportant if the normal flow of CSF carries enough of the injected material to these areas. The second factor, however, may be used to determine a functional compartmentalization of the ventricular spaces.

Properties

The CSF is thin and watery and normally contains only the filterable constituents present in blood. It has been referred to as the "neural urine." The CSF has a much lower protein content than plasma but it is not just a dialysate of plasma. Sodium, chloride, and magnesium are higher than in a dialysate, and potassium, calcium, urea, and glucose are lower. The pH of the two fluids (plasma and CSF) is approximately the same. Cellular elements are normally absent from CSF except for a few lymphocytes, although in certain pathological conditions neutrophils may appear. Erythrocytes in the fluid indicate hemorrhage in some portion of the CNS (for the composition of CSF see Tables 14.1 and 14.2).

In infections such as meningitis the various barriers between brain and blood, brain and CSF, and blood and CSF are altered so that the CSF concentration of various substances approaches that in plasma. This generalization is called Cohen's law.

Functions

The CSF, which fills the central canal of the spinal cord, the ventricles of the brain, and the subarachnoid space, serves as a watery cushion of the brain and the spinal cord. This is its best known and perhaps most important function. Another function of the liquid is related to the perivascular and perineuronal spaces. In lieu of a true lymphatic system, the CNS may use these channels for the elimination of fluid into the subarachnoid space. Lastly, changes in the amount of blood in the cranium are balanced by changes in the amount of CSF. Thus the volume of the cranial contents remains constant (Monro-Kellie doctrine). In untreated animals the osmolarity of brain fluids is apparently slightly greater than that of the plasma. A rise or fall in plasma tonicity is accompanied by a change in osmolarity of tissue fluids of brain in the

Table 14.1. Chemical composition of CSF in some domestic animals (mg/100 ml)

Constituent	Cattle	Goat	Horse	Rabbit	Sheep [7]	Swine [7]
Calcium	(5.1–6.3) * [7] †		6.26 (5.55–6.98) [1]		577	
Carbon dioxide				(41.2–48.5) volume % [14]		
Chloride	(650–725) [7]	681 [9]	737 (691–792) [1]	(600–730) [7, 14]	832 (750–868)	
Magnesium			198 (1.06–2.95) [1]		2.86	
Phosphorus (inorganic)			1.44 (0.87–2.20) [1]			
Potassium	(11.2–13.8) [7]		12.66 (10.65–14.20) [1]			
Sodium						
Protein (total)	(16–33) [7]	12 [7, 9]	47.58 (28.75–71.75) [1]	(15–19) [7]	(8–70)	(24–29)
Albumin			38.64 (22.62–67.94) [1]	(15–19) [14]		(17–24)
Globulin			9.34 (3.37–18.37) [1]	0 [14]		(5–10)
Creatinine	1.4 [3]					
Nitrogen						
Nonprotein N	16 [3]		26.88 (13.72–39.20) [1]	(5.6–16.8) [7]	29 (9.6–42.0)	
Urea N	10.8 [3]					
Urea			(23–31) [8]			
Sugar	(35–70) [7]	71 [7]	57.2 (40–78) [1]	(50–57) [7]	(48–109)	(45–87)
Vitamin C			1.7 [6]			
Lactic acid				(1.4–4.0) [14]		

* Values in parentheses are ranges. † Numbers in brackets refer to references below.

1. Behrens, H. 1953. Der liquor Cerebrospinalis des Pferdes, seine entnahme, untersuchung, und diagnostische Bedeutung. *Proc. 15th Int. Vet. Cong.* 2(1):1031–34.
2. Byers, S.O., and Friedman, M. 1949. Rate of entrance of urate and allantoin into cerebrospinal fluid of Dalmatian and non-Dalmatian dogs. *Am. J. Physiol.* 157:394–400.
3. Carmichael, J., and Jones, E.R. 1939. The cerebrospinal fluid in the bovine: Its composition and properties with special reference to turning sickness. *J. Comp. Path. Ther.* 52:222–28.
4. Citron, L., and Exley, D. 1957. Recent work on the biochemistry of the labyrinthine fluids. *Proc. Roy. Soc. Med.* 50:697–701.
5. Citron, L., Exley, D., and Hallpike, C.S. 1956. Formation, circulation, and chemical properties of the labyrinthine fluids. *Brit. Med. Bull.* 12:101–4.
6. Errington, B.J., Hodgkiss, W.S., and Jayne, E.B. 1942. Ascorbic acid in certain body fluids of horses. *Am. J. Vet. Res.* 3:242–47.
7. Fankhauser, R. 1953. Der Liquor Cerebrospinalis in der Veterinärmedizin. *Zentralblatt Veterinärmedizin* 1:136–59.
8. Fedotov, A.I. 1937. Cerebrospinaljnaja zidkostj posadi. *Sborn. Rab. Leningrad Vet. Inst.*, pp. 263–273.
9. Fujisawa, Y. 1927. Supplemental findings on normal cerebrospinal fluid in experimental animals. *Osaka Igakkai Zasshi* 26:344–52.
10. Kabat, E.A., Wolf, A., Bezer, A.E., and Murray, J.P. 1951. Studies on acute disseminated encephalomyelitis produced experimentally in rhesus monkeys. *J. Exp. Med.* 93:615–33.
11. Kasahara, M., and Fujisawa, Y. 1930. Studien über liquor Cerebrospinalis. I. Uber die normale cerebrospinal Flüssigkeit der Versuchstiere. *Zeitschrift ges. Exp. Med.* 73:11–13.
12. Merritt, H.H., and Bauer, W. 1931. The equilibrium between cerebrospinal fluid and blood plasma. III. The distribution of calcium and phosphate between cerebrospinal fluid and blood serum. *J. Biol. Chem.* 90:215–232.
13. Perlstein, M.H., and Levinson, A. 1931–1932. Cerebrospinal fluid in dogs. *Am. J. Physiol.* 99:626–30.
14. Roeder, F., and Rehm, O. 1942. *Die Cerebrospinalflüssigkeit: Untersuchungsmethoden und Klinik für Ärtze und Tierätze.* Springer-Verlag, Berlin.
15. Teunissen, G.H.B., and Verwer, M.A.J. 1953. Cerebrospinal fluid in dogs. *Proc. 15th Int. Vet. Cong.* 2(1):1022–28.

same direction. The water movements produce variations in the bulk of the brain which might interfere with intracranial volume-pressure relationships. The brain is in part protected from these by the CSF.

Origin and circulation

Bering (1974) has designated as simplistic the view that CSF only arises and is completely formed at the choroid plexuses, and then flows steadily through the ventricles, out the subarachnoid spaces, and finally into the sagittal sinus. The whole process is much more complex, with the choroid plexuses, brain tissue, ventricular walls, and subarachnoid pial surfaces all contributing.

The choroid plexuses located in each of the four ventricles of the brain consist of highly vascular cores covered with a single layer of epithelial cells. Some workers maintain that the process is one of active secretion; others believe that it is essentially one of filtration, in which the filtering force is equal to the blood pressure in the capillaries of the choroid plexus minus the osmotic pressure of the blood colloids and the CSF pressure. In the latter view, the mechanism would be similar to lymph production and the initial formation of urine.

The CSF in each area must be in open communication with the extracellular fluid of that area. Thus it is not surprising that the CSF varies greatly in composition from area to area. Therefore only when the sampling site has been specified can data on the composition of the CSF be properly interpreted. Moreover, materials introduced into the ventricles probably penetrate by diffusion into the tissue surrounding the ventricles. The relation of these physiological functions are also part of the blood-CSF and brain-CSF barriers which were discussed above.

The ability of the CSF to circulate over the surface of the hemispheres, into and out of the subarachnoid space,

Table 14.2. Chemical composition of CSF in some laboratory animals (mg/100 ml)

Constituent	Cat	Dog	Guinea pig	Monkey
Calcium	6 [12] †		6.01 [4]	
Chloride	899 [7] 531.9 [5]	808 (761–883) * [15]	432.6 [5]	(420–500) [7]
Magnesium			2.43 [4]	
Potassium	23.1 [5]		15.6 [5]	
Sodium	372.5 [5]		344.9 [5]	
Protein	25 [5]	27.5 (11–55) [15]	20 [5]	lumbar (20–30) [7, 14] cisternal (8–15) [7]
Albumin		27 [15]		
Globulin		9 [15]		(0.4–6.3) [10]
Allantoin		0.3 (0.25–0.47) [2]		
Uric acid		0.23 (0.13–0.35) [2]		
Nitrogen nonprotein	20 [5]		21 [5]	
Sugar	85 [7]	74 (61–116) [15]		60 [7]
Vitamin C	3.8 [11]	6.6 [11]		2.3 [11]

* Values in parentheses are ranges. † Numbers in brackets refer to references in Table 14.1.

and through the spinal canal, as well as to bathe the roots of the cranial and cervical nerves, is an important part of its role. The pulsation of the CSF is obvious to neurosurgeons and neuroradiologists although this facet of CSF circulation is frequently played down. The pulsation follows the heartbeat. In man there is a flow of 13.75 ml per pulse or a total movement of about 2410 times the formation rate (0.3 ml/min) (Bering 1974).

The CSF from the lateral and third ventricles enters the fourth ventricle from which it passes out through the roof of the ventricle into the subarachnoid space, principally through the lateral foramina. A small volume also enters the central canal of the medulla oblongata and the spinal cord. After entering the subarachnoid space the ventricular CSF passes downward in the spinal subarachnoid space and upward over the brain, mixing as it flows with the fluid derived from the perivascular and perineuronal spaces. The relative proportion of fluid in the various areas depends upon the cardiac cycle. In systole as the brain expands, CSF is forced into the spinal canal and the ventricles from the subarachnoid spaces; in diastole on the contrary, the subarachnoid space enlarges, the ventricles shrink, and blood leaves the choroid plexuses. This arrangement protects the delicate brain tissue from injury, lying as it does in a rigid bony box.

The movement of CSF has been investigated using ^{131}I in autologous CSF which was injected intraventricularly and intrathecally. The labeled compound began to flow into the basal cisterns within a few minutes. After 12.24 hours most of the activity appeared along the superior longitudinal sinus. These data suggest a "transport" or "sweeping" phenomenon. Although an ebb and flow are present, there also appears to be a net forward progression. This forward movement may be due to vascular and choroid plexus pulsation, plus vis a tergo of the newly produced fluid. Although these observations were obtained in men, the same flow characteristics probably apply to all mammals.

The composition of CSF drawn simultaneously from the cisterna magna, one lateral ventricle, and the cortical and spinal arachnoid spaces in the dog showed an amazing difference. The concentration of potassium was less in cisternal and cortical subarachnoid fluids, due apparently to loss of potassium as the CSF passed over the cortex. The concentration of urea rose as the fluid passed down from the cisterna magna to the cortical subarachnoid space. Granholm and Siesjö (1967) have studied the lactic-pyruvate ratio in brain tissue, arterial blood, and CSF of cats. The concentrations of these two metabolites in the CSF were larger than those in the brain or the blood, but the ratios of these two substances were lower in CSF than in blood and brain.

The anatomy of the arachnoid villi and their function are still open to question. Electron micrographs show no apparent openings but experimental data suggest openings of some sort. The perfusion pressure required to produce a given flow increased during the experiment due to deterioration of the specimen. If a surface-active polysorbate (Tween 80) was added to the perfusion fluid, the level required for opening pressure was reduced (Fig. 14.12). In the reverse direction, flow at any pressure was slight and constant over a wide range of pressure. The flow of dog plasma was essentially the same as for saline.

Among the most interesting observations have been those on the anatomy of the villi. In both dog and monkey the majority of the villi project into the sinus when open but lie flat when collapsed. When open, a villus consists of a mesh of prolongations of mesothelial cells associated with fibers. In the dog, however, a second type of villus also occurs as a space (subendothelial with respect to the sinus) containing a loosely fastened ball of cells. This cellular ball has been considered a ball valve by Pollay and Welch (1962). Although such valves have not been demonstrated in the monkey, a valvular behavior was demonstrated by Welch and Friedman (1960).

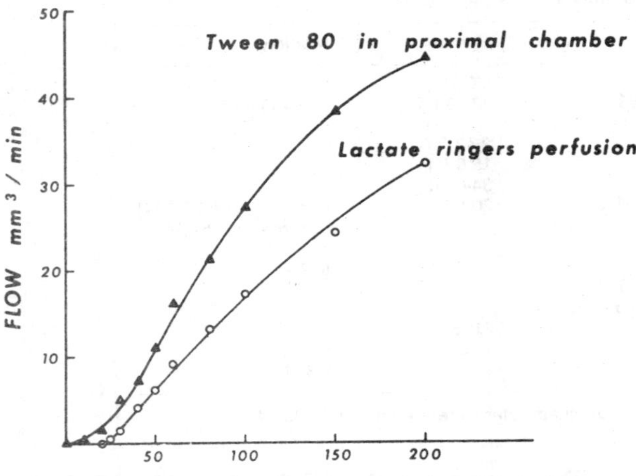

Figure 14.12. Effect of Tween 80 upon the flow-pressure relationship. (From Pollay and Welch 1962, *J. Surg. Res.* 2:307–11.)

Pressure

The CSF pressure exhibits cardiac and respiratory rhythms. It appears that the choroid plexuses transmit the arterial pulse to the CSF. Venous pressure changes, especially in the sagittal sinus or torcular, also affect CSF pressure. Posture or position of the animal has a marked effect; for example, an anesthetized animal in the horizontal position with a pressure of 120 mm may show a rise to 490 mm when tilted 30 cm with head down. In man no fixed relation can be seen between the pressure when recumbent and when sitting. The problems of CSF pressure are related to the so-called Monro-Kellie doctrine, which considered the cerebrospinal axis as a "closed box." However, the rigid skull is open both to the spinal canal and to the blood vessels and so is not strictly a closed box. The volume of the cranial cavity is *relatively* fixed and the cavity is completely filled at all times by CSF, blood, and brain. A variation in one component is compensated by changes in the other two. Because of the relatively fixed volume of the cranial cavity a small change in volume in the CSF results in a large change in pressure.

CSF pressure is also directly related to venous pressure. For example, in a dog with a CSF pressure of 120 mm of water, jugular compression increased pressure to 310 mm (the Quackenbush maneuver or sign). A block in the vertebral canal will prevent such a rise of pressure and the failure of the sign is thus diagnostic of such a condition.

An increase in intracranial tension may theoretically be produced by (1) obstruction of CSF drainage, (2) reduction of space in the cranial cavity due to an expanding lesion, (3) obstruction of CSF absorption, or (4) obstruction of the venous system draining the brain. The first factor is the most important. Among the symptoms of an increase of intracranial tension are headache, vomiting, stupor, and choked discs or papilledema. Papilledema arises because of interference with venous return from the eye; the eyegrounds are blurred at the margins of the discs, usually first on the nasal side.

CSF pressure has been measured usually by inserting a needle into the cisterna magna and connecting this needle to a manometer containing Ringer's solution or physiological saline. In anesthetized dogs pressures of 110–120 mm of Ringer's solution are commonly seen. In young cattle pressures ranging from 80–150 mm saline with an average of 105 mm have been observed. In vitamin A deficiency in this species the CSF pressure is elevated; at the terminal stage pressures 4–6 times normal may be seen (Moore and Sykes 1940, 1941; Sykes and Moore 1942). In anesthetized pigs 23–45 kg in weight, an average pressure of 110 mm of CSF has been observed. The range was 80–145 mm. Pigs deficient in vitamin A showed higher pressures (Sorenson et al. 1954). Considerably higher pressures have been found in horses than in other normal animals (Fedotov 1939, 1960). One of the problems in analyzing CSF pressure changes lies in the difficulties of obtaining accurate measurements in a chronic preparation. Recently Verdura et al. (1964) have recorded CSF pressures in an ambulatory, awake, unrestrained dog during various activities. As might be expected, barking increased CSF pressure markedly. In the anesthetized animal they obtained additional evidence of the effect of respiration upon CSF pressure.

Absorption

The constant formation of CSF implies its constant absorption. As it circulates in the subarachnoid spaces, it is brought into contact with the tiny arachnoid villi, through which it is removed into the adjacent venous sinuses. It is through these villi that the CSF is forced into the venous blood of the sinuses. In addition, a much less important slow drainage has been demonstrated in the perineural spaces of the spinal and cranial nerves to the lymphatic vessels. The force concerned in the absorption of CSF appears to be derived from the subarachnoid pressure and the osmotic pressure of the blood colloids less the opposing intracranial venous pressure.

Hydrocephalus, which occurs spontaneously in man and animals, is usually considered to be due to impaired absorption of CSF resulting from an insufficient amount reaching the absorption sites. Artificial hydrocephalus was produced experimentally by Dandy and Blackfan (1914) by blocking the aqueduct of Sylvius in the dog. The CSF pressure compared to blood pressure in a hydrocephalic dog is shown in Figure 14.13. Blockage occurring spontaneously may be due to many causes, among

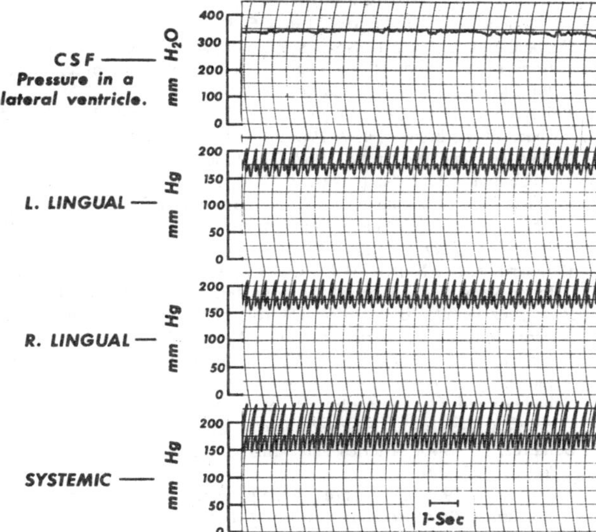

Figure 14.13. Relation of CSF pressure and arterial blood pressure in a hydrocephalic dog produced by the technique of Dandy. (From Cucciniello 1967, *Acta Neurol.* 22[1]:54–64.)

the commonest of which are congenital malformations. Post-traumatic or postinfectious scarring may also block the aqueduct or the foramina in the posterior fossa.

Amount and rate of formation

The amount of the CSF in man is some 60–80 ml. By cisternal puncture in horses, 170–300 ml of fluid can be obtained at a time (Fedotov 1939). Fluid may also be easily obtained by cisternal puncture in the dog and the rabbit.

In measurements of the rate of formation of CSF in dogs by open drainage from the cisterna magna, an average rate of 96 ml/24 hr for a dog weighing 20 kg has been found (Greenberg et al. 1943). This rate is about 0.2 ml/kg/hr. Probably values obtained by open drainage are not the same as those which would be found in the intact animal. Because of the technical difficulties involved, such observations have not been made except in the goat and cat (Heisey et al. 1962). In the goat the rate is estimated to be 0.16 ml/min and it has been shown that the net rate of formation is linearly related to total osmotic differences between plasma and CSF. Values for CSF ml/min/g choroid plexus for cat, dog, and goat are 0.37, 0.26–0.50, and 0.36 respectively. The observations in the dog were made using an isolated choroid plexus technique. CSF production rates have also been measured in the dog by ventriculo-cisternal perfusion with an inulin-containing buffer. Under these circumstances normal CSF production rate was 0.05 ml/min, which represents a turnover of 0.4 percent per minute. Intravenous administration of carbonic anhydrase inhibitors gave a 40–50 percent reduction of CSF production, underlining the role of carbonic anhydrase as postulated by Tschirgi in discussing the blood-brain barrier.

REFERENCES

Armstrong, L.D., and Horowitz, A. 1971. The brain venous system of the dog. *Am. J. Anat.* 132:479–90.

Ask-Upmark, E. 1935. The carotid sinus and the cerebral circulation. *Acta Psychiat. Neurol.* 6:1–4.

Bakay, L. 1953. Studies on blood-brain barrier with radio-active phosphorus. III. Embryonic development of barrier. *Arch. Neurol. Psychiat.* 70:30–39.

Baldwin, B.A., and Bell, F.R. 1960. The contribution of the carotid and vertebral arteries to the blood supply of the cerebral cortex of sheep and calves. *J. Physiol.* 151:9–10.

——. 1963. The anatomy of the cerebral circulation of the sheep and ox: The dynamic distribution of the blood supplied by the carotid and vertebral arteries to cranial regions. *J. Anat.* 97:203–15.

Becker, B. 1961. Cerebrospinal fluid iodide. *Am. J. Physiol.* 201:1149–51.

Bering, E.A., Jr. 1974. The cerebrospinal fluid and the extracellular fluid of the brain. *Fed. Proc.* 33:2061–63.

Bito, L.Z., and Davson, H. 1966. Local variations in cerebrospinal fluid composition and its relationship to the composition of the extracellular fluid of the cortex. *Exp. Neurol.* 14:264–80.

Bonakdarpour, A., Lynch, P.R., Murtagh, F., and Stauffer, H.M. 1966. High speed cinefluorography of cervicocerebral blood flow patterns in dogs. *Acta Radiol.* 5:114–26.

Clark, K. 1962. Isolation of the choroid plexus *in vivo*. *J. Neurosurg.* 19:1004–6.

Craigie, E.H. 1955. Vascular patterns of the developing nervous system. In H. Waelsch, ed. *Biochemistry of the Developing Nervous System*. Academic Press, New York. Pp. 28–49.

Cucciniello, B. 1967. L'idrocefalo sperimentale nel cane. *Acta Neurol.* 22(1):54–64.

Curtis, D.R., and Eccles, R.M. 1958. The effect of diffusional barriers upon the pharmacology of cells within the central nervous system. *J. Physiol.* 141:446–63.

Cushing, H. 1901. Concerning a definite regulatory mechanism of the vaso-motor centre which controls blood pressure during cerebral compression. *Bull. Johns Hopkins Hosp.* 12:290–92.

Dandy, W.E., and Blackfan, K.D. 1914. Internal hydrocephalus: An experimental, clinical, and pathological study. *Am. J. Diseases Children* 8:406–82.

Daniel, P.M., Dawes, J.D.K., and Prichard, M.M.L. 1953. Studies of the carotid rete and its associated arteries. *Phil. Trans. Roy. Soc. Lond.*, ser. B, *Biol. Sci.* 237:173–208.

Davis, D.D., and Story, H.E. 1943. The carotid circulation in the domestic cat. *Field Museum of Natural History, Zool. Ser.*, vol. 28, no. 1.

De Rougemont, J., Ames, A., III, Nesbett, F.B., and Hofmann, H.F. 1960. Fluid formed by choroid plexus: A technique for its collection and a comparison of its electrolyte composition with serum and cisternal fluids. *J. Neurophysiol.* 23:485–95.

Dobbing, J. 1963. The blood-brain barrier: Some recent developments. *Guy's Hospital Reports* 112:267–86.

Edström, R. 1964. Recent developments of the blood-brain barrier concept. In C.C. Pfeiffer and J.R. Smythies, eds., *International Review of Neurobiology*. Academic Press, New York. Vol. 7, 153–90.

Fedotov, A.I. 1939. Subokcipitaljnaja i cervikaljnaja punkcii subarahneidaljnogo prostranstva u krupnogo rogatogo skota [Spinal puncture in cattle]. *Vet. Bull.* 9:49.

Fedotov, A. 1960. *Cerebrospinal Fluid of Domestic Animals*. Trans. L. Saunders. Russian Translation Program, NIH, Bethesda.

Flexner, L.B. 1934. The chemistry and nature of the cerebrospinal fluid. *Physiol. Rev.* 14:161–87.

Friedemann, U. 1942. Blood brain barrier. *Physiol. Rev.* 22:125–45.

Geiger, A., Magnes, J., and Geiger, R.S. 1952. Survival of perfused cat's brain in absence of glucose. *Nature* 170:754–55.

Granholm, L., and Siesjö, B.K. 1967. Lactate and pyruvate concentrations in blood, cerebrospinal fluid and brain tissue of the cat. *Acta Physiol. Scand.* 70:255–56.

Greenberg, D.M., Aird, R.B., Boelter, M.D.D., Campbell, W.W., Cohn, W.E., and Murayama, M.M. 1943. A study with radioactive isotopes of the permeability of the blood-cerebrospinal fluid barrier to ions. *Am. J. Physiol.* 140:47–64.

Hassler, O. 1962. A systematic investigation of the physiological intima cushions associated with the arteries in five human brains. *Acta Societatis Medicorum Upsaliensis* 67:1–2.

Heeschen, W. 1958. Arterien und Venen am Kopf des Schafes. D.V.M. diss. Anatomischen Institut der Tierärztzlichen Hochscule, Hanover.

Heisey, S.R., Held, D., and Pappenheimer, J.R. 1962. Bulk flow and diffusion in the cerebrospinal fluid system of the goat. *Am. J. Physiol.* 203:775–81.

Hess, A. 1955. The ground substance of the developing central nervous system. *J. Comp. Neurol.* 102:65–76.

Hofmann, M. 1901. Zur Vergleichenden Anatomie der Gehirn und Rückenmarksvenen der Vertebraten. *Zeitschrift Morph. Anthropol.* 3:239–99.

Howarth, F., and Jowett, A. 1962. A technique for surgical encapsulation of a canine choroid plexus. *J. Physiol.* 162:20P.

Jewell, P.A. 1952. The anastomoses between internal and external carotid circulations in the dog. *J. Anat.* 86:83–94.

Kennedy, C., Des Rosiers, M.H., Jehle, J.W., Reivich, M., Sharpe, F., and Sokoloff, L. 1975. Mapping of functional neural pathways by autoradiographic survey of local metabolic rate with [^{14}C] deoxyglucose. *Science* 187:850–53.

Kety, S.S. 1960. Measurement of local blood flow by the exchange of an inert, diffusible substance. In H.D. Bruner, ed., *Methods in Medical Research*. Year Book Medical, Chicago. Sec. 3, vol. 8, 228–36.

Knapp, F.M. 1965. The cerebral circulation: Some hemodynamic aspects. In W.A. Himwich and J.B. Schadé, eds., *Horizons in Neuropsychopharmacology: Progress in Brain Research*. Elsevier, Amsterdam. Vol. 16, 285–96.

Lajtha, A., Lahiri, S., and Toth, J. 1963. The brain barrier system. IV. Cerebral amino acid uptake in different classes. *J. Neurochem.* 10:765–73.

Lajtha, A., and Toth, J. 1963. The brain barrier system. V. Stereospecificity of amino acid uptake, exchange, and efflux. *J. Neurochem.* 10:909–20.

Lorenzo, A.V., Fernandez, C., and Roth, L.J. 1965. Physiologically induced alteration of sulfate penetration into brain. *Arch. Neurol.* 12:128–32.

Mchedlishvili, G.I. 1959. An investigation of the localization of the "locking mechanisms" in the carotid and vertebral arteries. *Doklady Akademii nauk, SSSR*, vol. 124, no. 6.

Miller, M.E., Christensen, G.C., and Evans, H.E. 1964. *Anatomy of the Dog*. Saunders, Philadelphia.

Moore, L.A., and Sykes, J.F. 1940. Cerebrospinal fluid pressure and vitamin A deficiency. *Am. J. Physiol.* 130:684–89.

——. 1941. Terminal cerebrospinal fluid pressure values in vitamin A deficiency. *Am. J. Physiol.* 134:436–39.

Pappenheimer, J.R., Heisey, S.R., and Jordan, E.F. 1961. Active transport of Diodrast and phenolsulfonphthalein from cerebrospinal fluid to blood. *Am. J. Physiol.* 200:1–10.

Pollay, M. 1966. Cerebrospinal fluid transport and the thiocyanate space of the brain. *Am. J. Physiol.* 210:275–79.

Pollay, M., and Welch, K. 1962. The function and structure of canine arachnoid villi. *J. Surg. Res.* 2:307–11.

Prockop, L.D., Schanker, L.S., and Brodie, B.B. 1962. Passage of lipid-insoluble substances from cerebrospinal fluid to blood. *J. Pharmac. Exp. Ther.* 135:266–70.

Reinhard, K.R., Miller, M.E., and Evans, H.E. 1962. The craniovertebral veins and sinuses of the dog. *Am. J. Anat.* 111:67–87.

Rodriguez-Peralta, L.A. 1957. The role of the meningeal tissues in the hematoencephalic barrier. *J. Comp. Neurol.* 107:455–73.

Sapirstein, L.A., and Hanusek, G.E. 1958. Cerebral blood flow in the rat. *Am. J. Physiol.* 193:272–74.

Schaltenbrand, G., and Bailey, P. 1928. Die perivaskuläre Piagliamembran des Gehirns. *J. Psychol. Neurol.* 35:199–78.

Scharrer, E. 1940. Arteries and veins in the mammalian brain. *Anat. Rec.* 78:173–96.

Smith, H.V. 1957. Discussion on the penetration of drugs into the cerebral spinal fluid. *Proc. Roy. Soc. Med.* 50:964–66.

Sorenson, D.K., Kowalczyk, T., and Hentges, J.F. 1954. Cerebrospinal fluid pressure of normal and vitamin A deficient swine as determined by a lumbar puncture method. *Am. J. Vet. Res.* 15:258–60.

Steinwall, O. 1964. Blood-brain barrier dysfunction: Some theoretical aspects. *Acta Neurol. Scand.* 40(suppl. 10):25–29.

Stilwell, D.L., Jr. 1959. The vascular supply of vertebral structures: Gross anatomy, rabbit and monkey. *Anat. Rec.* 135:169–83.

Sykes, J.F., and Moore, L.A. 1942. The normal cerebrospinal fluid pressure and a method for its determination in cattle. *Am. J. Vet. Res.* 3:364–67.

Tschirgi, R.D. 1960. Chemical environment of the central nervous system. In *Handbook of Physiology*. Sec. 1, J. Field, H.W. Magoun, and V.E. Hall, eds., *Neurophysiology*. Am. Physiol. Soc., Washington. Vol. 3, 1865–90.

Verdura, J., White, R.J., and Albin, M. 1964. Chronic measurements of cerebrospinal-fluid pressure in the dog. *J. Neurosurg.* 21:1047–50.

Weed, L.H., and McKibben, P.S. 1919. Experimental alteration of brain bulk. *Am. J. Physiol.* 48:531–58.

Welch, K. 1963. Secretion of cerebrospinal fluid by choroid plexus of the rabbit. *Am. J. Physiol.* 205:617–24.

Welch, K., and Friedman, V. 1960. The cerebrospinal fluid valves. *Brain* 83:454–69.

Welch, K., and Pollay, M. 1963. The spinal arachnoid villi of the monkeys Ceropithecus aethiops sabaeus and Maca irus. *Anat. Rec.* 145:43–48.

Whisnant, J.P., Millikan, C.H., Wakim, K.G., and Sayre, G.P. 1956. Collateral circulation to the brain of the dog following bilateral ligation of the carotid and vertebral arteries. *Am. J. Physiol.* 186:275–77.

PART II RESPIRATION

CHAPTER 15

Respiration in Mammals

by S. Marsh Tenney

Respiration includes all those chemical and physical processes by which an organism exchanges gases with its environment. The principal exchange involves oxygen and carbon dioxide, the former taken from the atmosphere and required by the tissues of the body for oxidative metabolism, the latter, an important end product of that metabolism which must be eliminated from the body. Survival is dependent upon the maintenance of proper concentrations and quantities of carbon dioxide and oxygen in the tissues. In higher organisms there are specialized structures and processes which serve that purpose.

The gaseous exchange that occurs in the lung, between its contained air and the pulmonary capillary blood, is frequently referred to as *external respiration*. The exchange that takes place at the tissue level is called *internal respiration*. The act of bringing air into and expelling air from the lungs is not, strictly speaking, respiration; it is called *ventilation*—a bulk transport process. In the same manner the circulatory system delivers, by cardiac output, oxygen to the capillaries and carbon dioxide from the tissues to the lungs. The flow of oxygen and carbon dioxide between the air and blood in the lungs and between the capillary blood and the cells in the tissues is by physical diffusion.

Much of modern respiratory physiology is quantitative, and its treatment is facilitated by the use of accepted symbols and abbreviations. A complete list is given at the end of the chapter.

RESPIRATORY APPARATUS

Anatomy

The mammalian respiratory apparatus consists of the lungs and the airways leading to them, the thorax and its pleural sac(s), the diaphragm and muscles of the thorax, and the afferent and efferent nerves connected with these structures.

The airways are the nasal cavity, pharynx, larynx, trachea, and bronchi, which function as a continuous air tube to the lungs. The mucous membrane of the nasal cavity is moist and highly vascular, and contains numerous glands, thus adding warmth and moisture to the inspired air. The pharynx is a common passageway for the respiratory and digestive tubes. The larynx is a musculocartilaginous valvular structure serving as the principal organ of phonation and as a variable resistance for the air entering or leaving the lungs. The vocal cord and the arytenoid cartilage on each side form the boundary of the glottis, which may be completely closed by apposition of these structures. The trachea is kept open by the presence of incomplete rings of cartilage in its wall. Its membrane has numerous mucous glands and the epithelium is ciliated. The secretion of the glands and the motion of the cilia help to clear the trachea of dust and other foreign matter. The bronchi are similar in structure and function to the trachea.

The lungs are two elastic membranous sacs whose interior is highly modified by, and internal surface area enlarged by, partitioning into numerous alveoli. These are hemispherical outpouchings from the alveolar sacs. These sacs connect, by way of their atria, with the alveolar ducts, which are direct branches of the bronchioles. The bronchioles are fine divisions formed by a complex branching and rebranching of the two main bronchi after they enter the lungs (Fig. 15.1).

The alveolar ducts have a small amount of smooth muscle in their walls. Fine bronchioles have no cartilage but some muscular tissue in their walls. Large bronchioles have both cartilage and muscle. The bronchiolar musculature is regulated by bronchoconstrictor and bronchodilator fibers in the vagi and the sympathetic nerves respectively.

The alveolus wall is a single layer of epithelium. Gaseous exchange between the air in the alveoli and the blood in the dense network of overlying capillaries takes place across both this layer of cells and the endothelium of the capillaries. An O_2 molecule, in diffusing from the gas phase in the respiratory unit to the site of binding on the hemoglobin molecule, must traverse the following barriers: alveolar wall, capillary wall, blood plasma layer, and red cell membrane. The resistance encountered is small because the distance is only about 2 μ, a value that appears not to vary between species.

The thoracic cavity contains the lungs and mediastinal organs. It has no opening to the outside and is completely separated from the abdominal cavity by the diaphragm. The pleurae, two serous membrane sacs, line the thoracic cavity, one on each side. They form the lateral walls of the mediastinum (in animals such as man and sheep which have a complete one), and are reflected onto the lungs. A complete mediastinum prevents air and fluids passing from one pleural sac to the other. In the dog, however, with its incomplete mediastinum, bilateral pneumothorax will occur if the chest is opened on one side. The pleural "space" between the parietal and visceral parts of the pleura is occupied by a thin film of fluid, which moistens and lubricates the two pleural layers. The pressure in the pleural cavities is subatmospheric. Therefore, when a pleural cavity is opened air enters and the lung collapses.

Quantitative morphology

The basal oxygen requirement of mammals is not proportional to body weight, but is more nearly proportional to body surface area (Rubner's law). More precisely, basal O_2 consumption is proportional to body weight raised to the 0.74 power (Fig. 15.2). Since small mammals have very high oxygen requirements in comparison with large mammals, one can expect adaptations.

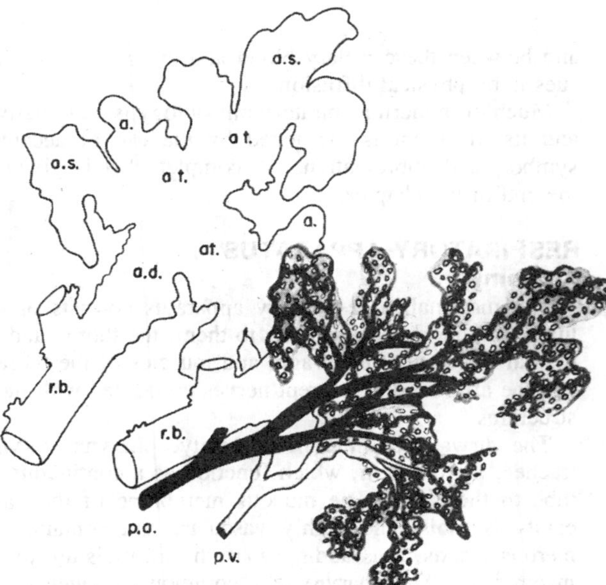

Figure 15.1. Schematic longitudinal section of primary lobule of the mammalian lung (upper left): r.b., respiratory bronchiole; a.d., alveolar duct; at., atrium; a.s., alveolar sac; a., alveolus. The dense overlying capillary network is shown lower right: p.a., branch of pulmonary artery; p.v., branch of pulmonary vein. (Modified after Miller, *The Lung*, Thomas, 1947.)

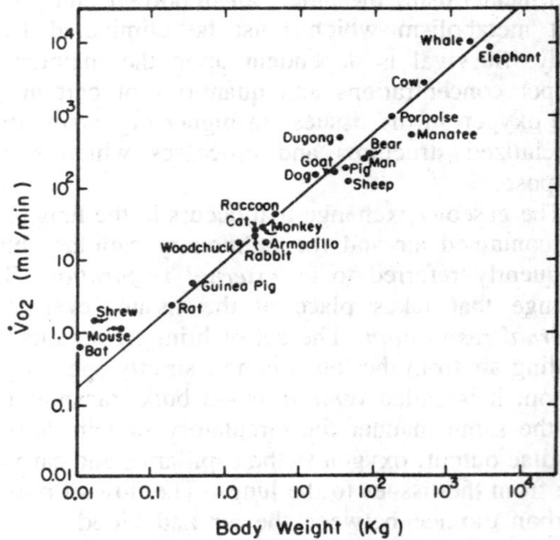

Figure 15.2. Basal O_2 requirements and body weight plotted logarithmically

In the functional design of the lungs there are two major mechanical considerations. The first includes the *physical properties of the conduits* through which air flows during the ventilatory cycle, where the important principles are largely aerodynamic. The other concerns the *elastic characteristics of the lung tissue*. Both mechanical properties impose important problems of energetics.

Another major consideration concerns the movement of oxygen from the air spaces of the lung into the pulmonary capillary blood. This movement follows the laws of physical diffusion. Hence the nature of the *anatomical diffusion barrier* has to be considered. As will be seen later, the total surface area across which diffusion exchange takes place in the lung is probably the single most important factor.

The primary respiratory anatomical correlate with animal size is the volume of the lungs. For all mammals, total lung capacity (volume of inflated air with maximal normal transmural distending pressure, about 20 cm H_2O) is proportional to body weight (Fig. 15.3). In other words, lung size, like the size of most organs, is a constant fraction of the body mass. Although the lungs might be predicted to vary in size with the demand for oxygen (i.e. with body surface area), this is clearly not the case. If in fact the size of the lungs varied in proportion to the resting oxygen consumption, the lungs in the very smallest animals would constitute well over half of the total body mass. Clearly, this could have created a grotesque body design, and nature solved the respiratory requirements in another way.

Ventilation is not necessarily seriously handicapped by restriction on lung size even though oxygen demand is disproportionately high in small animals. A primary restriction is the number of times the lungs can be filled and emptied per unit of time, as is the rate of the diffusion process by which oxygen moves across the alveolar boundary into the blood. In physical diffusion the resistance varies inversely with the area across which the exchange occurs. In animals the internal diffusing surface area varies directly and proportionately with the basal rate of oxygen consumption (Fig. 15.4). Increased diffusion is achieved by increased internal partitioning of the lungs in the smaller mammals, and they therefore have lungs with many small alveoli (Fig. 15.5). Although pulmonary capillary surface area is the true gas-exchanging interface in the lung, the diffusing surface area of the lungs may be regarded as nearly proportional

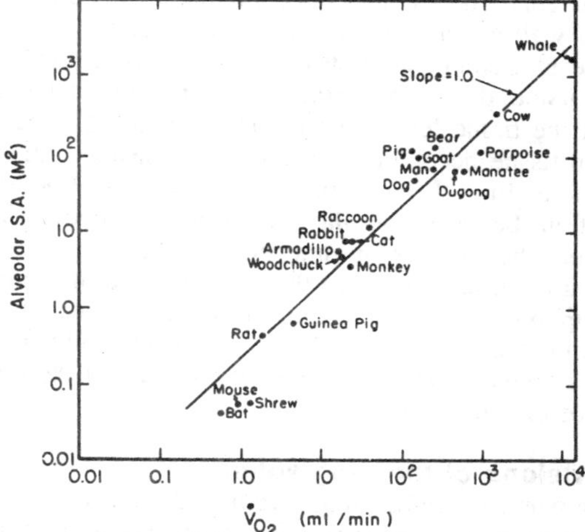

Figure 15.4. Total alveolar surface area in relation to metabolic rate (oxygen consumption). (From Tenney and Remmers 1963, *Nature* 197:54–56.)

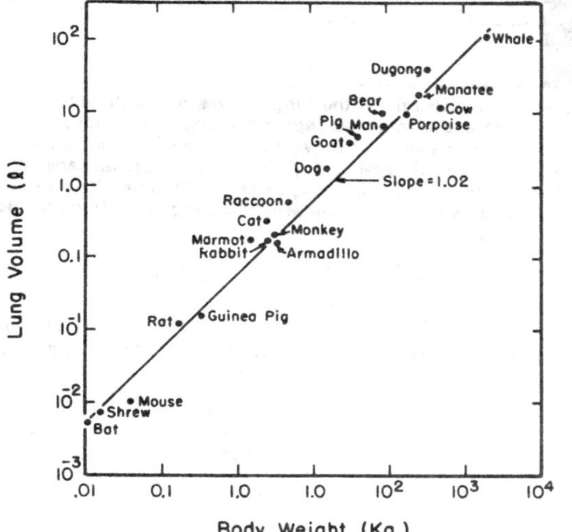

Figure 15.3. Total lung capacity as a function of body weight. (From Tenney and Remmers 1963, *Nature* 197:54–56.)

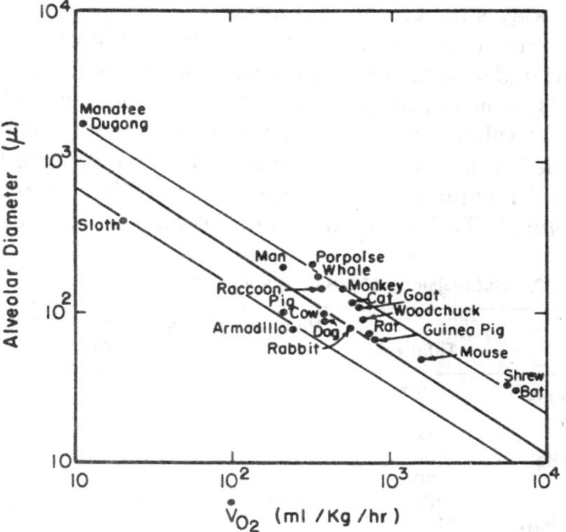

Figure 15.5. Alveolar size (diameter) in relation to metabolic rate. (From Tenney and Remmers 1963, *Nature* 197:54–56.)

Table 15.1. Capillary density in skeletal muscle and mitochondrial density in liver

Animal	Capillarity * (caps./fiber)	Mitochondrial density † (no./g dry wt.)
Rat	1.7	5.15
Guinea pig	2.7	
Rabbit	2.1	2.96
Cat	0.9	
Dog	2.2	
Sheep	2.1	2.45
Pig	2.0	
Cow	2.5	2.23

* From Schmidt-Nielsen and Pennycuick 1961, *Am. J. Physiol.* 200:746–50
† From Smith 1956, *Ann. N.Y. Acad. Sci.* 62:405–21

to the alveolar surface area since the major fraction of the alveolar wall is densely packed with capillaries.

There is a comparable structural relationship between the available diffusing surface area and the metabolic need at the tissue level (internal respiration). The capillaries in tissue occur in a more or less constant ratio to the cells, and for skeletal muscle there is no well-defined correlation between capillary density and body size. However, the number of mitochondria per unit of cell mass varies in proportion to the animal's rate of oxygen consumption, or inversely with body size (Table 15.1). In the mitochondria, then, the site of the intracellular oxidative enzymes, the final structural correlate in the utilization of oxygen emerges.

Subdivisions of the lung volume

Even when an animal lung is removed it does not completely empty itself of air, presumably because of the collapse of the outflow airway channels. This small volume of air is called the *minimal air*. In its normal situation, in situ, the lung cannot shrink to this value because of the bony structure of the thorax.

The remaining components of the lung volume are examined under normal physiological conditions in the animals. By convention, primary units of volume are called *volumes;* subdivisions made up of two or more volumes are called *capacities*. The air that remains in the lung following a maximal forceful expiration is called the *residual volume*. The maximal volume of air that can be expelled from the lungs following a maximal inspiration is called the *vital capacity*. The sum of the vital capacity and the residual volume is called the *total lung capacity* (Fig. 15.6).

During normal breathing, the volume of air that remains in the lungs at the end of expiration exceeds the residual volume. The amount of excess is called the *expiratory reserve volume*. The sum of the expiratory reserve volume and the residual volume is called the *functional residual capacity,* the total volume of air in the lungs at the end of each normal expiration. The volume of air introduced into and expelled from the lungs with each respiratory cycle is called the *tidal volume*. And finally, the additional volume of air that can be taken into the lungs, beginning at the normal end-inspiratory position, is called the *inspiratory reserve volume*. Clearly, the expiratory reserve volume, the inspiratory reserve volume,

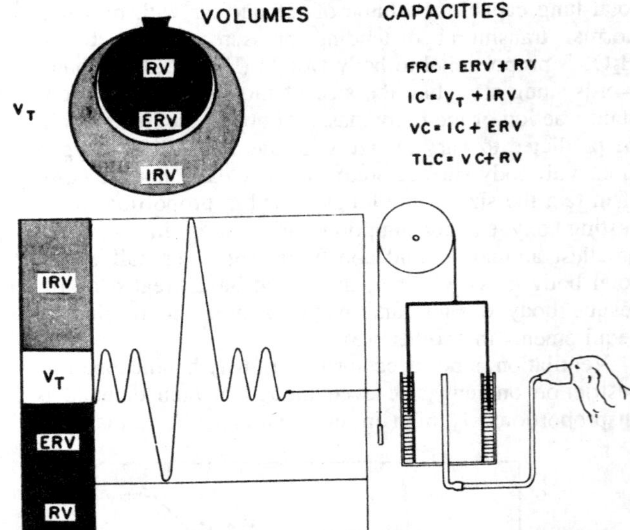

Figure 15.6. Subdivisions of the lung volume as illustrated on a spirometer record and a schematic spherical lung: RV, residual volume; ERV, expiratory reserve volume; V_T, tidal volume; IRV, inspiratory reserve volume; VC, vital capacity; FRC, functional residual capacity; IC, inspiratory capacity; TLC, total lung capacity. (Modified from Comroe, Forster, Dubois, Briscoe, and Carlsen, *The Lung*, Year Book Medical, Chicago, 1962.)

Table 15.2. Subdivisions of the lung volumes in ml (BTPS)

Animal	Tidal vol.	Vital capacity	Inspiratory reserve vol.	Inspiratory capacity	Expiratory reserve vol.	Residual vol.	Functional residual capacity	Total lung capacity
Guinea pig	3.7						4.75	
Rabbit	15.8						11.3	
Cat	34						66	
Dog (8 kg)	144						252	
Goat	310							
Man	400	4800	3100	3600	1200	1200	2400	6000
Cow (lying)	3100							
(standing)	3800							
Horse	6000	30,000	12,000		12,000	12,000	24,000	42,000

and the tidal volume, taken together, are equal to the vital capacity.

Because many of the measurements require cooperation, only the functional residual capacity and tidal volume can be measured accurately in most animals (Table 15.2).

By the time inspired air has reached the level of the major bronchi its temperature is already that of the body, and it is also completely saturated with water vapor. One can measure its volume with a spirometer if one corrects to BTPS (body temperature, atmospheric pressure, and saturated with water vapor). In accordance with the laws of Charles and Boyle, the volume of gas varies directly with absolute temperature and inversely with barometric pressure.

For example, if an experiment is carried out in a laboratory where the temperature is 20°C and the barometric pressure is 755 mm Hg, this will ordinarily also be the temperature and pressure of the spirometer. One can call the volume of air displaced at room temperature and pressure and saturated with water vapor V_{ATPS}, its volume at body temperature and pressure and saturated with water vapor V_{BTPS}. If the experimental animal is a normal dog, its body temperature, if not measured, may be assumed to be 38°C. The partial pressure of water vapor (P_{H_2O}) in a saturated sample of air varies with the temperature of the sample: at 20°, $P_{H_2O} = 17.6$ mm Hg; at 38°, 49.6 mm Hg. Then

$$V_{BTPS} = V_{ATPS} \times \frac{273+38}{273+20} \times \frac{755-49.6}{755-17.6}$$

MECHANICS OF VENTILATION

The lungs, because of their elasticity, tend to collapse toward the volume of minimal air. The chest wall, on the other hand, tends to spring out to a volume considerably in excess of the minimal lung volume. Therefore, the lung and chest wall taken as a unit, under normal physiological conditions, will come to a resting volume which is the equilibrium between the two opposing forces. If a bubble of air is placed in the pleural space, and this is connected to a manometer, it will record at equilibrium an *intrapleural pressure* which is subatmospheric. The pressure inside the lung, so long as the mouth and glottis are open and ventilation is arrested, is one atmosphere. The *transmural pressure gradient* across the lung is the difference between the pressure existing in the lumen of the lung (alveoli) and that on the outside of the lung but inside of the thorax (pleural space). At normal end-expiration this gradient is about 8 cm H_2O.

In order for the lung to expand, a force must be applied across the lung wall. This is accomplished by increasing the transmural (distending) pressure gradient by lowering intrapleural pressure (Fig. 15.7). Intrapleural

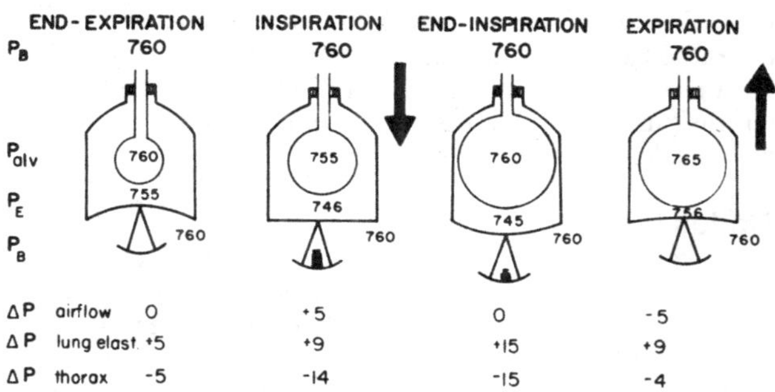

Figure 15.7. Lungs and chest wall represented as a balloon in a bottle. The base of the bottle is replaced by a rubber diaphragm whose position can be changed by suspending weights. With added weight the rubber diaphragm is stretched down, the pressure in the bottle surrounding the balloon (intrapleural pressure P_E) becomes subatmospheric, a transmural pressure gradient between balloon (alveolus) P_{alv} and intrapleural pressure P_E is created which distends the balloon, and air enters the balloon from the atmosphere (atmospheric pressure is P_B). Units are in cm H_2O and typical pressures are given. (In the living animal the diaphragm is always concave toward the abdomen except in extreme inspiration when it is flat.)

pressure is made more negative, that is, more subatmospheric, by contracting the respiratory muscles, which lowers the diaphragm and elevates the rib cage. The applied force causes the volume of the lung to increase with the result that intra-alveolar pressure will also become slightly subatmospheric. Now there is established a pressure gradient between air in the mouth and air in the lumen of the lungs; in other words, there is an energy gradient which will favor the flow of air into the lungs.

The total energy required to move air into the lungs must take into account that pressure which is required to stretch the *elastic* tissues of the system (P_{el}), an additional pressure required to induce air flow along the bronchial tree and to overcome frictional *resistance* to motion of the lung tissues (P_{res}), and finally an increment of pressure required to overcome inertia and to accelerate gas flow from zero velocity (P_{in}). These three forces are the necessary components for a complete description of the equation of motion. If P_{app} is designated as the applied pressure to the total pulmonary mechanism, then

$$P_{app} = P_{el} + P_{res} + P_{in}$$

is a statement of the balance of applied and opposing forces in accordance with Newton's Third Law of Motion.

If the following three linear relationships are assumed, $P_{el} = KV$, $P_{res} = K'\dot{V}$, $P_{in} = K''\ddot{V}$, then the total applied pressure, in terms of the volume of the lung (V), the rate of change of the volume of the lung ($\dot{V}$), and acceleration of the volume of the lung ($\ddot{V}$) is

$$P_{app} = KV + K'\dot{V} + K''\ddot{V}$$

K, K′, and K″ are constants of proportionality which depend on the physical characteristics of the system. The third term, $K''\dot{V}$, which deals with inertia, is measurable but insignificant in relation to the other two and need not be considered further.

Statics

In analyzing the elementary stress-strain relationship on the lungs and chest wall, the most useful physiological parameters are pressure and volume. Values may be determined by inflating the lungs in situ to several fixed volumes, arresting respiration, and measuring the distending pressure at each volume. The respiratory muscles must be in a relaxed state. Instantaneous measurements of pressure and flow during the respiratory cycle may be related at the moment when either inspiration or expiration reverses, because at those times the flow of air is zero (Fig. 15.8). What this maneuver accomplishes is to eliminate the term $K'\dot{V}$ in the equation above, thus making the total applied pressure equal to KV. Since we have assumed that the pressure required to stretch the elastic tissue of the system is proportional to the volume of the lung, the two points representing inspiration and expiration on a graph may be connected by a straight line. This provides a useful measure of the elastic properties of the lung-chest system, free of its resistive characteristics. The ratio $\Delta P/\Delta V$ defines the "elastance" of the respiratory system and is seen in our equation to be the coefficient K. The reciprocal of the "elastance" is also a useful concept (Fig. 15.9). It is referred to as *compliance* (expressed as $C = \Delta V/\Delta P$), and the absolute value depends on the size of the lungs (Table 15.3).

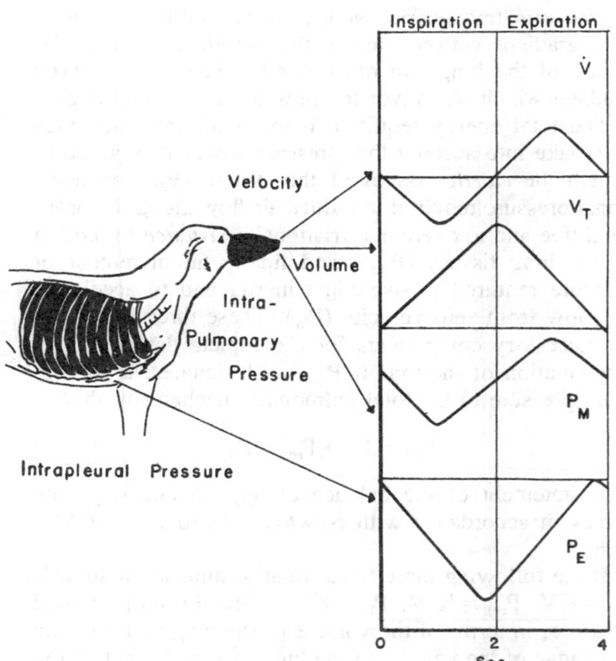

Figure 15.8. Schematic oscillograph tracing intrapulmonary (P_M) and intrapleural (P_E) pressures and airflow velocity ($\dot{V}$) and volume (V_T) recorded simultaneously

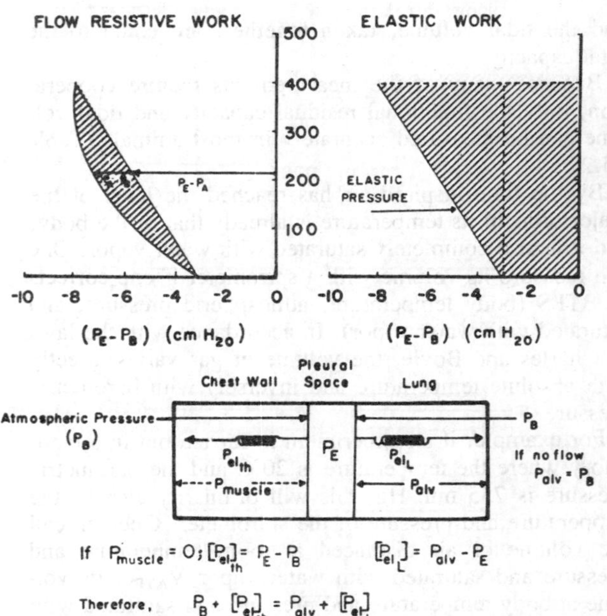

Figure 15.9. Mechanical equivalent portraying the forces acting on the lung and chest wall. Pressure-volume relationships shown above: static curve (right) with compliance line, dynamic curve (left) illustrating added energy required for airflow. Work indicated by shading. P_{el} is elastic pressure on thorax (th) or lungs (L), and P_{muscle} is muscle force.

Actually, the assumption that the compliance of the lung is linear over the full range of volume is not valid. The true curve is sigmoid in shape, although the mid portion, which represents the volumes and pressures normally utilized in the act of breathing, remains nearly linear. Therefore, the usefulness of the concept is not significantly affected. The gross nonlinearity which appears over the full range of pressures and volumes derives in

Table 15.3. Lung and chest wall compliance in anesthetized animals

Animal	FRC * (ml BTPS)	Lung compliance (ml/cm H_2O)	Chest wall compliance (ml/cm H_2O)
Cat	66	13.4	13.4
Dog	609	63	32
Guinea pig	4.75	1.3	3.66
Man		200	208
Monkey	87.5	12.3	7.3
Mouse	0.29	0.05	0.33
Rabbit	11.3	6.0	9.4
Rat	1.55	0.4	1.47

* Functional residual capacity

Data from Crosfill and Widdicombe 1961, *J. Physiol.* 158:1–14

large part from the structural nature of the so-called elastic tissue of the lungs. In point of fact, almost all biological tissues are not in the strict physical sense elastic solids and do not therefore obey Hooke's law over the full range of stress-strain relationships. The mixed composition of pulmonary tissue, which is made up of elastic and connective tissues, explains the sigmoid shape of the curve.

The second most important deviation from predicted behavior based on an ideal elastic solid is the property of *hysteresis*. That is to say, the curve relating pressure and volume during inflation of the lung is different from the curve obtained during deflation (Fig. 15.10). This important effect is due to properties of the gas-liquid interface. If the interfacial effect is eliminated by studying the pressure-volume curve of isolated lungs inflated with a physiological saline solution instead of air, hysteresis is eliminated. This curve approximates the deflation portion of the curve obtained with an air-filled lung.

In the air-filled lung there are potent intermolecular forces in the fluid lining the alveolar wall. This is the origin of *surface tension,* a property which tends to minimize the area of a surface. In the lungs the alveolar wall is concave to the airway, and thus surface tension promotes collapse. If each alveolus were treated as a sphere, surface tension (T) would be related to the transmural pressure at the alveolus (P) and the radius of the alveolus (r) by the expression $T = Pr/2$ (Laplace's law). If the surface tension at the fluid lining of the alveoli were equal to that of the blood plasma (55 dynes/cm), the surface tension law indicates that a transmural pressure gradient of 20 cm of water would be required to distend an alveolus of the dimensions measured in a dog's lung. This is a much higher pressure than is observed experimentally. Therefore some explanation is required.

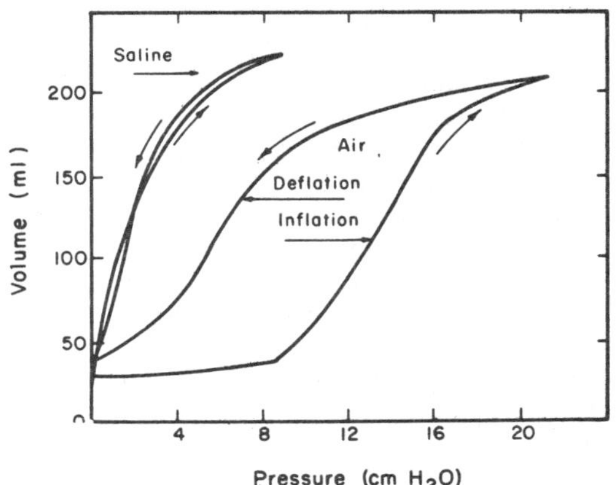

Figure 15.10. Pressure-volume curves of cat lung, comparing results obtained when the lung is inflated with air and when it is filled with saline. In the latter case the surface tension effect is eliminated. (Redrawn from Radford, in Remington, ed., *Tissue Elasticity,* Am. Physiol. Soc., Washington, 1957.)

If the fluid lining of the lungs is removed and spread out as a thin film which may be expanded and compressed, the relationship between the area of the film and its surface tension is nonlinear and shows pronounced hysteresis. The measured surface tension of the fluid lining of the alveolus is considerably below that of blood plasma, but it increases as surface area increases. The surface tension value is about 40 dynes/cm when stretched and 10 dynes/cm when compressed.

Surface tension dependency on film area is a characteristic of protein films. What lowers the surface tension of the fluid lining the alveoli is a phospholipid, mainly dipalmitoyl lecithin, and its synthesis occurs in the lung in specialized cells. The manner of destruction of pulmonary surfactant is not clear, but it includes the influence of the breathing motion itself. Important diseases like the respiratory distress syndrome are due to inadequate surfactant material.

The presence of a surface-tension lowering material in the alveolar lining decreases the probability of alveolar collapse at low lung volumes under small distending pressures, particularly during deflation. Also, it lessens the number of forces that cause fluid migration from pulmonary capillaries to alveoli. Because the alveolar surface tension increases with inflation, it contributes to the forces that limit peak alveolar size during inspiration.

In brief, the elastic character of the lung tissue is such that, as the lung volume decreases, the tendency to collapse decreases, but the relative contribution of surface tension to the retractive force of the lung increases. The greater the value of the surface tension the more pronounced this tendency will be. On the other hand, a low surface tension exerts a stabilizing influence. The hazard of alveolar collapse at small lung volumes is therefore minimized. When the lung volume is low, alveolar dimensions are decreased, and the Laplace relationship requires a larger distending pressure to hold the alveoli open. However, the compressed liquid lining the alveoli lowers its surface tension fourfold, and patency can be maintained at lower pressures. The increase in surface tension as the lung expands with inspiration checks the upper limit of the lung volume.

One half to three fourths of the bulk "elasticity" of the lungs when inflated with air, it is estimated, is due to their liquid lining. Whether there are important differences in the surface lining material among species is not known, but one can predict the surface tension relationship in lungs from different animals and with different alveolar radii (Fig. 15.11). As the alveolar radius becomes smaller, the distending pressure must become larger if the surface tension is to remain the same among species. In small animals this would mean an enormous extra burden to the work of breathing. Direct measurement of intrapleural pressure in several species in fact reveals very little difference, which probably raises

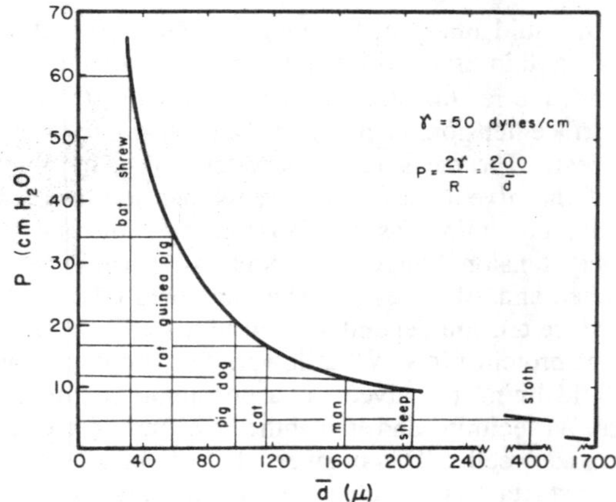

Figure 15.11. Alveolar opening pressure computed from Laplace's law and alveolar dimensions (d). Alveolar surface tension (γ) was measured in human lungs.

serious questions about mechanical deductions based on idealized alveolar models.

Respiration in the newborn

In the adult the chest wall tends to spring outward, but in the fetus its resting position is at the volume of the air-free lung. This results in an intrapleural pressure which is atmospheric and keeps the lungs from distending in utero and filling with liquid, obviously a serious hazard.

After birth, breathing begins and the pulmonary blood flow increases. The introduction of air into the lungs creates an air-liquid interface which, due to the surface tension effect, causes the lung to recoil. The opposing force of the chest wall on the lung increases during the first few breaths, and the intrapleural pressure gradually decreases. Chest wall compliance, which is very high in the newborn animal, decreases progressively with growth, but the compliance of the lung is less at birth than later on. The intrapleural pressure becomes more subatmospheric with growth and the functional residual capacity increases. The main change with growth is the increasing outward recoil of the chest, but its origin is not clear.

Dynamics

During the normal ventilatory cycle, work must be done, not only in distending the elastic structure of the respiratory apparatus, but also in overcoming the resistance offered by the bronchi to the flow of air. If the pressures in the alveolar space and at the mouth, together with the change of volume during a normal tidal excursion, are both measured and the volume is plotted against pressure, a loop is obtained. By connecting the terminal portions of the loop with a straight line, a curve of the *dynamic compliance* of the lung is obtained, and it will agree, under most circumstances, with the static compliance. The extra negative pressure required to inflate the lungs, beyond that predicted from the line of dynamic compliance, is a measure of the extra energy required to overcome pulmonary resistance. The major portion of this added work is needed to overcome airway resistance (see Fig. 15.9).

The total work done on the respiratory apparatus during inspiration is given by the area between the volume axis and the inspiratory portion of the pressure-volume curve (Table 15.4). Physical work is defined as force × distance, and this is readily seen to be dimensionally equivalent to pressure × volume, since pressure = force/area. That portion of the work done against elastic recoil during inspiration is given by the area between the static diagonal and the volume axis, and the difference between the two is the work done against nonelastic resistance (see Fig. 15.9). Expiration is largely passive and utilizes the potential energy stored in the stretched elastic system during inspiration. It can be measured as the area between the static diagonal and the volume axis. In a physical sense it appears that no work is done during the respiratory cycle, since the energy expended during inspiration is recovered during expiration, excepting what is liberated as heat. In a physiological sense, of course, this is erroneous, because the energy imparted to the system during inspiration is derived from chemical energy, and there is no restoration of this source during expiration. An estimate of the rate of work of breathing can therefore be made by multiplying the work of inspiration per breath by the number of breaths per minute.

Metabolic cost of breathing

The chemical energy required to perform physical work is usually measured in terms of oxygen consumption; the work of breathing normally requires about 1–2 percent of total body oxygen consumption in man. If the metabolic cost is related to physical work done, the efficiency of the system is found to be between 5 and 10 percent. As ventilation increases, for example, during muscular exercise, the work of breathing increases disproportionately, and beyond 50–60 percent of maximum attainable ventilation the metabolic cost rises precipitously. In this range the metabolic cost of an added increment in ventilation exceeds the added gas exchange, and hence no useful purpose is served. Normal regulatory mechanisms limit the maximal ventilatory volumes during exercise at about the largest values which do not compromise a net gain of oxygen for the body. This is an example of the principle of optima.

VENTILATION

Alveolar and dead space ventilation

Pulmonary ventilation ($\dot{V}_E$) is usually measured in liters expired per minute (Fig. 15.12). Values in excess of normal define a state of *hyperventilation*, and below,

Table 15.4. Resting respiratory frequencies and rate of work of breathing

Animal	Weight (kg)	Resp. rate (breaths/min)	Work * (g cm/min)	Work/body wt. (g cm/min/g)	Work/unit ventil. (g cm/min/L/min)
Hamster	0.091	74			
Rat	0.25	97	482	1.9	2940
Guinea pig	0.52	90	272	0.52	2090
Rabbit	2.4	39	1502	0.62	2370
Monkey	2.68	40	817	0.31	1157
Cat	2.95	26	1857	0.63	1900
Dog	12	22	6720	0.55	2350
Sheep	63	19			
Man	70	12	30000	0.43	4700
Cow (heifer)	144	34			
Cow (adult)	514	30			
Horse	696	12			

* From Crosfill and Widdicombe 1961, *J. Physiol.* 158:1–14

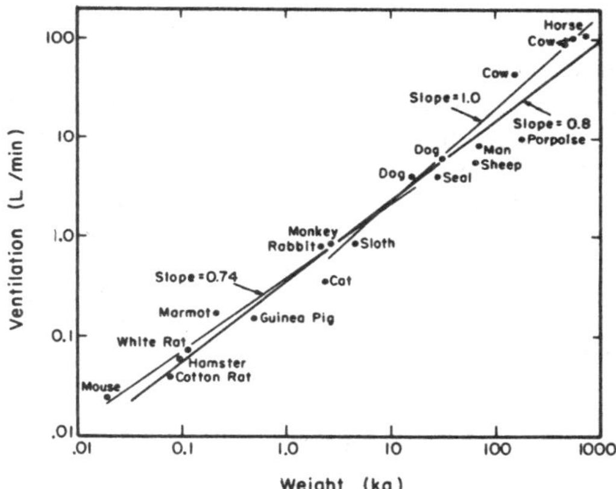

Figure 15.12. Resting minute volume of ventilation

hypoventilation. $\dot{V}_E$ is equal to the product of the tidal volume (V_T) and the respiratory frequency (f) in breaths per minute. However, only a portion of each tidal volume actually reaches the alveoli. This is because, at the end of a normal inspiration, the upper respiratory passages and the tracheobronchial tree are filled with fresh inspired air which will leave the lung during expiration without any change in its gaseous composition. At the end of expiration this same portion of the airway will remain filled with alveolar air and must be washed out with fresh air at the beginning of the next inspiration. Since it does not participate in gas exchange, the volume of the upper airway and tracheobronchial tree is referred to as the dead space volume (V_D). Tidal volume is thus composed of a dead space volume and an alveolar volume ($V_D + V_A$). Alveolar ventilation is, then, the difference between the total ventilation and dead space ventilation: $\dot{V}_A = \dot{V}_E - fV_D$.

Under most circumstances the volume of dead space may be inferred from direct measurements of the upper airway and tracheobronchial tree and has therefore been called the *anatomical dead space*. It may also be measured under living conditions using physiological techniques (and the Bohr formula). V_D varies directly with the end-inspiratory volume of the chest, a relationship which is probably based on a simple expansion of the tracheobronchial tree with inspiration.

There is also an important correlation of dead space volume with body weight in mammals (Fig. 15.13): like lung volume, it is directly proportional; hence the dead space volume–lung volume ratio is constant. Dead space ventilation, then, is proportional both to the magnitude of dead space volume and to the respiratory frequency. The normal respiratory frequency in mammals decreases as body size increases (Table 15.4). The general relationship, over a wide range of animal size, is that respiratory frequency varies inversely with body weight raised to the 0.28 power, that is, roughly, the cube root of body weight.

At this point the necessary data to clarify an important

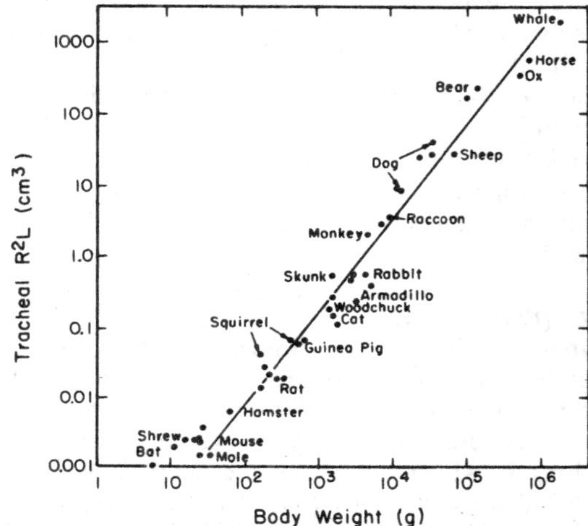

Figure 15.13. Tracheal volume as a function of body weight. The tracheal volume may be assumed to be proportional to dead space volume. (From Tenney and Bartlett 1967, *Resp. Physiol.* 3:130–35.)

principle are in hand. The act of breathing may be considered from two standpoints: the energy required to inflate the lungs, and the relationship between dead space volume and alveolar volume in each tidal volume. An increase of frequency, with alveolar ventilation maintained constant, requires a reduction of tidal volume. But at the same time an increased minute volume of ventilation ($f \times V_T$) has been imposed, because there is, of necessity, an associated increase in dead space ventilation ($f \times V_D$). However, work against nonelastic resistance is a function of the total minute volume of ventilation, and hence it will increase continuously as frequency increases. On the other hand, work against elastic resistance is much greater for a given minute volume of ventilation when made up of a few large breaths rather than a larger number of small breaths. There is, therefore, a particular respiratory frequency, for any given alveolar ventilation, at which the elastic work of breathing is minimal. If the frequency is too great, work increases because of wasteful ventilation of dead space; if frequency is too low more energy will be required to stretch the lungs for each tidal volume. Thus for a given alveolar ventilation, as frequency increases, work against nonelastic resistance increases continuously, while work against elastic resistance diminishes to a minimum and then increases again. The total work therefore also has a minimal value at a particular respiratory frequency.

Small animals, with their high metabolic rate, must have a large oxygen supply. They have achieved a large internal diffusing surface area by increased internal partitioning. But small alveoli result in a low pulmonary compliance, and work done against the elastic resistance of these small lungs could be proportionately higher, depending on the size of the tidal volume. From an energetic standpoint then, it is to the advantage of small animals to minimize the tidal volume and to allow the respiratory frequency to increase even though a proportionately large component of each tidal volume must then be utilized to wash out the dead space. This is one mechanical explanation for the inverse correlation between respiratory frequency and body size. It is also intuitively obvious that stroke size and pump size will be related, since it is not mechanically feasible to make many large strokes per unit time because of the high velocities required.

Descriptive terms

Eupnea is the state of ordinary quiet breathing—assumed to be effortless. *Dyspnea* is a condition of labored breathing (may be inferred from facial expressions or other behavioral traits). *Hyperpnea* is a condition of breathing in which the rate or the depth or both are increased. *Polypnea* is a rapid, shallow, panting type of respiration. *Apnea* is cessation of breathing.

Alveolar gas

The fractional concentration of carbon dioxide in alveolar air (normal inspired air contains none) will vary directly with the level of metabolic CO_2 production and inversely with the level of alveolar ventilation. (This relationship is expressed by the *alveolar ventilation equation.*) If metabolic rate is held constant, doubling alveolar ventilation will halve alveolar CO_2 concentration, or conversely, halving alveolar ventilation will double alveolar CO_2 concentration. Obviously, the same applies to the partial pressure of carbon dioxide.

The concept of how the fractional concentration (or partial pressure) of alveolar oxygen varies with the level of ventilation is more complicated than for carbon dioxide because the body is consuming oxygen and the inspired air contains oxygen. If for every molecule of oxygen taken up by the body one molecule of carbon dioxide were produced the matter would be a simple one. But this is the case only if the respiratory quotient (RQ) is equal to 1, and hence a correction factor must be introduced. Still, the idea of carbon dioxide replacing oxygen is qualitatively useful (Fig. 15.14).

If the metabolic rate increases, the alveolar gas pressure can be held constant only if there is a proportional

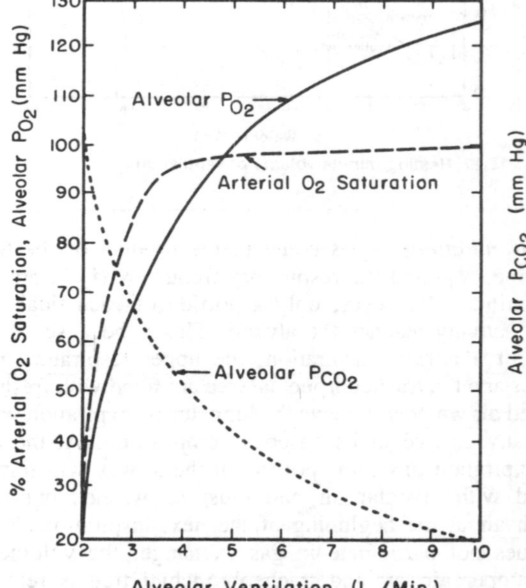

Figure 15.14. Relation between alveolar ventilation and alveolar P_{CO_2}, alveolar P_{O_2}, and oxyhemoglobin saturation. Oxygen uptake is held fixed at 300 ml/min and the respiratory exchange ratio is 0.8. Note that an increase of alveolar P_{O_2} beyond a ventilation of 4 L/min does not appreciably increase arterial O_2 saturation, due to the shape of the O_2 Hb saturation curve. Below 3 L/min arterial O_2 saturation is largely dependent on P_{O_2}. (Modified from Comroe, Forster, Dubois, Briscoe, and Carlsen, *The Lung,* Year Book Medical, Chicago, 1962.)

rise of alveolar ventilation. If carbon dioxide is added to the inspired air, ventilation will increase, but the alveolar P_{CO_2} must still rise.

The explicit statements of the alveolar ventilation equation must not be confused with, or taken to be contradictory to, the well-known fact that ventilation increases consequent to an increase in alveolar CO_2. In this case, the alveolar CO_2 must be increased by adding CO_2 to the inspired air, and ventilation now becomes the variable dependent upon the CO_2 pressure. When the variable which is regulated (P_{ACO_2}) is also the stimulus to the regulator (V_A), the system is said to be of the closed loop type.

HEMOGLOBIN AND OXYGEN TRANSPORT

If the tissues are to receive an adequate supply of oxygen, the requisite number of molecules must be delivered per unit of time, and the partial pressure of oxygen in the tissue capillaries must provide the necessary driving force for their diffusion. Since the transport system from lung to tissues is a liquid one, the first consideration is the solubility of oxygen in blood. The amount of gas in physical solution is directly proportional to its partial pressure, and the coefficient of proportionality is usually symbolized by α—the *solubility coefficient*. Its units are milliliters of gas, per milliliter of solvent, per atmosphere of pressure. In blood plasma the solubility coefficient of oxygen is 0.021. Since environmental air contains approximately one fifth of an atmosphere partial pressure of oxygen (about 150 mm Hg at sea level), enormous quantities of blood would have to be circulated if oxygen availability to tissues depended solely on its transport in simple physical solution.

In all mammals and most vertebrates, therefore, the major portion of the oxygen carried by the blood is not in physical solution but is associated with hemoglobin molecules inside the red cells. Since the red cells are suspended in the plasma, an oxygen molecule leaving the alveolar air in the lung must first traverse the plasma in physical solution before it enters the red cell to associate in a reversible combination with hemoglobin. At any one time there will be an equilibrium of the partial pressure of oxygen between plasma and red cells, but the amount of oxygen will be much greater inside the red cell, because the affinity of hemoglobin for oxygen is very large. Each hemoglobin molecule contains four heme groups, and in the reduced state each molecule is capable of combining with 1, 2, 3, or 4 molecules of oxygen, depending on the relative concentrations of hemoglobin and oxygen in the blood. Each heme group contains one iron atom in the ferrous state, but after its combination with oxygen the valency is not changed. For this reason it is said that when reduced hemoglobin has combined with oxygen, it has been *oxygenated* (not oxidized) and is then called *oxyhemoglobin*. The greater the concentration of hemoglobin in a given unit of blood, the greater the amount of oxygen the blood can carry.

It is useful to know not only the amount of oxygen in association with hemoglobin, but also how nearly saturated with oxygen the blood is. When the blood is fully saturated with oxygen, its oxygen content is called the *oxygen-carrying capacity*. Blood is nearly saturated if it is allowed to come into equilibrium with a partial pressure of oxygen at 150 mm Hg or more (the partial pressure of oxygen in atmospheric air). For that reason the oxygen capacity is normally determined by equilibrating the sample of blood with room air. If the whole-blood O_2 content is measured, and a correction is made for the amount of oxygen in simple physical solution in the plasma (based on knowledge of the solubility coefficient of oxygen and the partial pressure of oxygen in the room air), then the difference between total oxygen content and the oxygen in physical solution is the amount of oxygen carried as oxyhemoglobin. If blood from the same animal is analyzed to determine its *oxygen content* (e.g. after equilibration with a different partial pressure of oxygen, or as it was drawn from the arterial or venous circulation), one may determine the ratio of the particular oxygen content to the oxygen capacity. The ratio is called the *oxyhemoglobin saturation* (S_{O_2}) and is expressed as a percentile:

$$\frac{O_2 \text{ content} - \text{physically dissolved } O_2}{O_2 \text{ capacity} - \text{physically dissolved } O_2} \times 100$$

Oxyhemoglobin dissociation curve

If oxygen enters into association with hemoglobin in a simple reaction expressed as $Hb + O_2 = HbO_2$, with an equilibrium constant K, then the oxyhemoglobin dissociation curve, that is, a plot of the relationship between the partial pressure of oxygen and the percent oxyhemoglobin saturation, is a rectangular hyperbola. This is the case with myoglobin or muscle hemoglobin. However, with blood hemoglobin the curve is S-shaped (Fig. 15.15). The difference results from the nature of the processes through which oxygen becomes associated with hemoglobin. In the first place, the reaction is now known to occur in four stages, and each step in the oxygenation process has its own equilibrium constant—K_1, K_2, K_3, and K_4.

$$Hb_4 + O_2 = Hb_4O_2$$
$$Hb_4O_2 + O_2 = Hb_4(O_2)_2$$
$$Hb_4(O_2) + O_2 = Hb_4(O_2)_3$$
$$Hb_4(O_2)_3 + O_2 = Hb_4(O_2)_4$$

The equilibrium constants do not have exactly equal experimental values, although K_1 and K_3 do not differ by

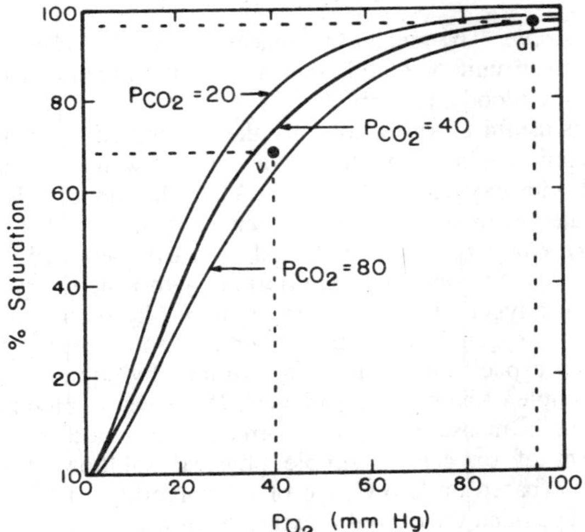

Figure 15.15. Oxyhemoglobin dissociation curves of whole blood. The normal positions of arterial and venous blood are signified by a and v.

very much. K_2 is slightly greater and K_4 about 20 times greater than K_1.

The explanation for this fact appears to lie in a change of configuration of the hemoglobin molecule which takes place during the process of oxygenation. The affinity of any heme group for oxygen is influenced by the number of its neighbors on the same molecule which have already combined with oxygen. The most important change occurs at the last step. Once three O_2 molecules have entered into association with hemoglobin, the affinity for the last is increased some 20 fold. Physicochemical evidence suggests that the configurational change of the hemoglobin molecule during the first three steps somehow results in exposure of the last iron atom through an unfolding and eversion.

The fundamental difference between the S-shaped curve and a rectangular hyperbola is that the steep portion has been shifted to the right on the pressure axis. This allows conservation of the available driving pressure gradient as molecular oxygen is given up to the tissues. Under normal circumstances blood leaving the lungs is 95–98 percent saturated with oxygen, and from inspection of the oxyhemoglobin dissociation curve this places the arterial point on the flat portion. In other words, beyond the normal arterial point, increases in P_{O_2} do not substantially increase the oxygen-carrying power of the blood (see Figs. 15.14 and 15.15). The hemoglobin is already almost fully saturated in arterial blood, and the most that could be expected would be that further oxygen would go into physical solution in accordance with Henry's law. As oxygen is unloaded from the blood to supply tissue needs, the oxygen saturation normally falls to about 70 percent in venous blood, although there are

Table 15.5. Partial pressures of respiratory gases in man or dog at rest (at sea level)

Sample	Partial pressure in mm Hg				
	O_2	CO_2	N_2	H_2O	Total
Atmospheric air *	158	0	596	6	760
Inspired air †	149	0	564	47	760
Expired air	116	29	568	47	760
Alveolar air	100	40	573	47	760
Arterial blood	95	40	573	47	755
Venous blood	40	46	573	47	706
Tissues	30 or less	50 or more	573	47	700

* P_{H_2O} arbitrarily assigned

† Saturated with water vapor at body temperature in region of bronchi

great differences between individual organs. The average effect is equivalent to unloading approximately 5 volumes percent of oxygen. This is the *arteriovenous oxygen content difference*. The P_{O_2} in the blood after it has given up its normal amount of oxygen is then about 40 mm Hg (Table 15.5). If the oxyhemoglobin dissociation curve had been hyperbolic instead of S-shaped, the venous oxygen pressure might have fallen well below 10 mm Hg.

While conservation of the partial pressure of oxygen in the veins is important to the delivery of oxygen, if oxygen delivery does not result in a considerable drop in oxygen pressure, there will not be a sufficient partial pressure gradient of oxygen between the alveolar air and the blood to accomplish the necessary loading quickly (Fig. 15.16). The actual exposure time in the pulmonary capillaries is less than one second at rest and is even less

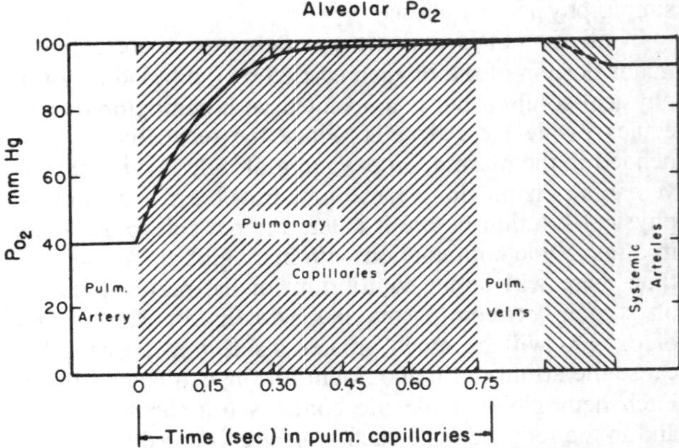

Figure 15.16. Loading of oxygen in the pulmonary capillaries. The change in P_{O_2} from mixed venous blood to pulmonary vein follows an exponential time course. Equilibrium between P_{O_2} in alveolar air and end-pulmonary capillary blood is assumed, but arterial blood has a drop in P_{O_2} of about 10 mm Hg due to contamination with deoxygenated blood via venous shunts or from poorly ventilated alveoli. (From Comroe, Forster, Dubois, Briscoe, and Carlsen, *The Lung*, Year Book Medical, Chicago, 1962.)

Table 15.6. Oxygen capacity, oxygen tension for half-saturation value, Bohr effect, and red-cell carbonic anhydrase concentration

Animal	Weight (kg)	O_2 capacity (μl O_2/ml @ pH 7.1)	P_{50} (mm Hg)	log P_{50} pH	Carbonic anhydrase (C.A.E.U./μl rbc)
Mouse	0.03	66.8	60	0.96	27.3
Guinea pig	0.57	43.2	50	0.79	12.8
Dog (chihuahua)	1.36	40.6	48.5	0.64	10.6
Rabbit	1.5	42.5	49	0.75	13.8
Dog (English setter)	27.2	51.4	42	0.65	
Man	62	35	40	0.62	9.5
Pig	102	45.5	39	0.57	8.5
Cow	454	31.6	36	0.52	13.79
Horse	544	76.0	35.5	0.68	2.4
Elephant	3140	33.5	32	0.38	

Data from Riggs 1960, *J. Gen. Physiol.* 43:737–52; Larimer and Schmidt-Nielsen 1960, *Comp. Biochem. Physiol.* 1:19–23; Drabkin 1950, *J. Biol. Chem.* 182:317–33

during exercise. Therefore, in recognizing the physiological advantage of the S-shaped oxyhemoglobin dissociation curve, it is important to reconcile the conflict of interest between the lung and the tissues. Any change that facilitates loading of oxygen in the lungs may compromise its unloading in the tissues, and vice versa.

Since species differ greatly in their oxygen requirements, it should not be surprising to discover that oxygen-carrying capacities of the blood also differ. The quantity of hemoglobin per unit of blood volume is more or less determined by the red cell mass, but the relevant factor is less the respiratory function of the blood and more its hemodynamic consequences. More hemoglobin, and therefore more red cells per unit of blood volume, increases the oxygen-carrying capacity of the blood and might at first appear to be a partial solution to the high O_2 requirements of small mammals. However, the viscosity of blood increases as the volume of red cell mass increases, and above 50 percent packed cell volume the effect is very large. An increase in viscosity imposes an added work load on the heart, and there would thus be no net gain to the organism. In fact, both the hemoglobin mass and the red cell concentration vary within rather narrow limits. However, the chemical properties of the oxyhemoglobin dissociation curve show considerable variation, and the partial pressure of oxygen required for half saturation (P_{50}) appears to vary directly with the resting oxygen consumption of the animal (Table 15.6).

The effect noted is also described as a displacement of the steep part of the oxyhemoglobin dissociation curve downward and to the right in animals with increased metabolic rates (Fig. 15.17). This effect is due to an increased red cell concentration of 2,3-diphosphoglycerate. Thus, in small animals an arteriovenous oxygen content difference comparable to that in large animals results in a higher venous partial pressure of oxygen. If this change is of adaptive significance, the weighting of factors favors preservation of tissue oxygen tension over loading in the lungs.

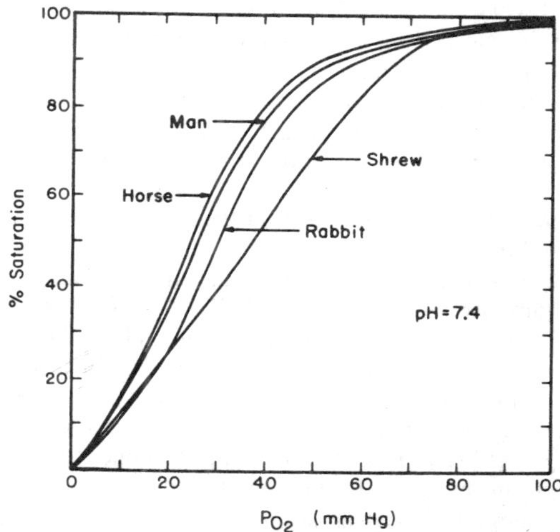

Figure 15.17. Representative oxyhemoglobin dissociation curves. (Data from Bartels and Harms 1959, *Pflüg. Arch. ges. Physiol.* 268:334–65; Ulrich, Hilpert, and Bartels 1963, *Pflüg. Arch. ges. Physiol.* 277:150–65; Schmidt-Nielsen and Larimer 1958, *Am. J. Physiol.* 195:424–28.)

Effect of carbon dioxide, pH, and temperature

The most important chemical effect on the oxyhemoglobin dissociation curve is that of carbon dioxide. If the oxyhemoglobin dissociation curve is determined by equilibrating a blood sample with a variety of O_2 pressures, but at several fixed CO_2 pressures, a family of oxyhemoglobin dissociation curves results. The effect of elevating the CO_2 pressure is to displace the oxyhemoglobin dissociation curve downward and to the right (see Fig. 15.15). Present evidence indicates that there are both hydrogen-ion and carbon-dioxide specific effects. In the tissues, as oxygen is unloaded, carbon dioxide is simultaneously taken up by the capillary blood, and through the action of carbon dioxide (and the attendant increase of hydrogen ion) on the position of the oxyhemoglobin dissociation curve, the unloading of oxygen from the hemoglobin is enhanced. For the same change in Po_2 more oxygen can be released than would be the case if no CO_2 were added. When the venous blood returns to the lung, carbon dioxide is rapidly eliminated from the blood into the alveolar air, a decrease in the blood Pco_2 occurs, the oxyhemoglobin dissociation curve is shifted up and to the left, and the oxygen loading process is enhanced.

The mechanism of the effect of CO_2 or of hydrogen ion on the oxyhemoglobin dissociation curve is called the *Bohr effect*. The physicochemical mechanism involves the heme groups in neighboring imidazole groups in the globin portion of the molecule. The α-chain is apparently responsible and unless hemoglobin is a heteropolymer the Bohr effect does not occur. Oxygenation of the heme group favors the liberation of hydrogen ions from the imidazole ring and a conformational change. Conversely, an increase in hydrogen ion concentration from any other source drives the reaction in the opposite direction and favors the uptake of hydrogen ions by the imidazole group and causes the liberation of oxygen from the heme group.

Another chemical influence on the position of the oxyhemoglobin dissociation curve is the intra-erythrocytic organic phosphates concentration, and the most important is 2,3-diphosphoglycerate (2,3-DPG). As red cell 2,3-DPG increases the curve shifts down and to the right, thus augmenting oxygen unloading in the tissues. The rate of synthesis of 2,3-DPG is increased by hypoxia (O_2 deficiency) and hypocapnia (CO_2 deficiency) and is inhibited by acidosis. The regulation of the concentration of 2,3-DPG in the red cell tends to stabilize the position of the oxyhemoglobin dissociation curve in acid-base disturbances.

Increase in blood temperature results in a shift of the oxyhemoglobin dissociation curve down and to the right; the effect is similar to that of carbon dioxide or hydrogen ion. Rise in temperature also favors the unloading of oxygen in tissues—an advantage since the tissue metabolic rate may be elevated as a result of local heating. However, oxygen loading in the lungs is impaired. As before, the biological action that has evolved gives priority to the tissues.

Comparative aspects of oxygen transport

Just as there are wide species differences in the position of the oxyhemoglobin dissociation curve and consequently in the half-saturation values, so too there is considerable variation in the magnitude of the Bohr effect. In general, the higher the metabolic rate of the animal, the greater the magnitude of the Bohr shift. Small animals not only have an oxyhemoglobin dissociation curve that is normally shifted down and to the right compared with the larger animals, but also, for every given increment of CO_2 loaded in the tissues, the physiological curve is shifted even farther. It would appear that this major adaptation favors oxygen unloading even more.

Diffusing capacity

The respiratory gases exchange across the alveolar-capillary barrier by diffusion. Although there is gaseous diffusion in the alveoli, the primary exchange occurs in a liquid phase, either in the membrane or in the plasma. Therefore, in considering the diffusivity of gases their solubilities must be taken into account. The thickness of the pulmonary diffusion barrier is estimated to be 1.5 μ, and the surface area across which exchange takes place varies as shown in Figure 15.4. The pulmonary capillary blood volume in man is about 100 ml, but in other species the normal value is not known.

The diffusing capacity of the lungs is the volume of gas which crosses the alveolar membrane per unit of time, per mm Hg difference of partial pressure. In man the value for oxygen is 20 ml/min/mm Hg.

The diffusing capacity increases several fold during muscular exercise; in diseases it may be markedly reduced. Any change in the pulmonary capillary blood volume, alveolar-capillary surface area, or thickness or physical character of the alveolar membrane will affect the diffusing capacity. If the diffusing capacity is reduced, alveolar air and end-capillary blood will not be in equilibrium and arterial hypoxemia (deficient oxygenation) will result.

CARBON DIOXIDE TRANSPORT

Compared with oxygen, carbon dioxide is about 20 times as soluble in blood plasma. In spite of this, less than 5 percent of the total CO_2 carried by the blood is in a simple physical solution. This is because carbon dioxide in aqueous solution forms carbonic acid which dissociates into hydrogen ions and bicarbonate ions until an equilibrium is established:

$$CO_2 + H_2O \leftrightharpoons H_2CO_3$$

$$H_2CO_3 \leftrightharpoons H^+ + HCO_3^-$$

$$H^+ + \text{protein}^- \ Na^+ \leftrightharpoons \text{H-protein} + Na^+$$

$$Na^+ + HCO_3^- \leftrightharpoons NaHCO_3$$

The first equation shows the hydration reaction of carbon dioxide. But because the reaction proceeds so slowly, it cannot reach equilibrium during the time capillary blood is exposed to alveolar air in the lung. The chemical hydration reaction itself would become a rate-limiting step and would impede both CO_2 elimination in the lung and CO_2 uptake in the tissues. There is, however, in the stroma of red blood cells an enzyme, carbonic anhydrase, which accelerates the hydration reaction about 500 times. Carbonic anhydrase is a zinc-containing protein of approximately 30,000 mol wt. It can be inhibited by the sulfonamides, for example acetazolamide, which causes a build-up of CO_2 in the blood and tissues.

The second equation comes to equilibrium very rapidly, probably in less than 0.001 sec, and is therefore not a rate-limiting reaction. The third and fourth equations represent examples of the powerful buffering action of the proteins in the blood plasma, and particularly in the red blood cells by hemoglobin. One important consequence of this buffering reaction as hydrogen ions are taken up by the protein anionic groups is to shift the reactions expressed in the first and second equations to the right, hence allowing more CO_2 binding through the formation of more bicarbonate.

Carbon dioxide absorption curve

The amount of CO_2 that can be carried in the blood, as a function of the partial pressure of CO_2 with which the blood has been equilibrated, can be determined by techniques comparable to those for the oxyhemoglobin dissociation curve. The resulting curve is called the *carbon dioxide absorption curve* (Fig. 15.18). And just as CO_2 tension affects the amount of oxygen that could be held in association with the hemoglobin molecule, the O_2 saturation of the blood affects the amount of carbon dioxide that can be held in chemical combination (Table 15.7). This analogue of the Bohr effect was discovered by Christiansen, Douglas, and Haldane and is known as either the *C-D-H effect,* or more commonly, the *Haldane effect*. The greater the oxygen saturation, the less the CO_2 carrying power. And graphically, removing oxygen from blood shifts the CO_2 absorption curve up and to the left. The mechanism of this reaction is the same as for the Bohr effect and concerns the oxylabile ionizing groups in hemoglobin. Each hemoglobin molecule has about 30 groups which ionize between pH 6 and 8. In other words, there are approximately 8 such groups per heme, and it is likely that 1 of these 8 groups is strongly influenced by the state of oxygenation of heme. The effect of oxygenation is to make hemoglobin a stronger acid and as such it is capable of binding more alkali. Conversely, reduced hemoglobin, being a weaker acid, effectively contributes to the alkaline pool of the blood. Reduced hemoglobin has an effective pK of 6.8; oxyhemoglobin 6.6.

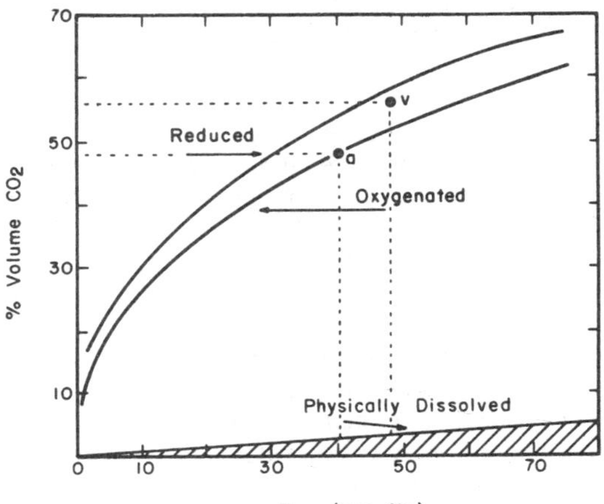

Figure 15.18. CO_2 absorption curve of whole blood. Fully saturated and deoxygenated curves indicate the change in CO_2 binding capacity after oxygenation.

Table 15.7. Distribution of CO_2 in 1 L normal human blood containing 8.93 mM hemoglobin and having a packed cell volume of 40 percent

	Arterial	Venous	Difference
Total CO_2 in 1 L of blood	21.53 mM	23.21 mM	1.68 mM
Total CO_2 in plasma of 1 L of blood (600 ml)	15.94	16.99	1.05
As dissolved CO_2	0.71	0.8	0.09
As bicarbonate ions	15.23	16.19	0.96
Total CO_2 in erythrocytes of 1 L of blood (400 ml)	5.59	6.22	0.63
As dissolved CO_2	0.34	0.39	0.05
As carbamino-CO_2	0.97	1.42	0.45
As bicarbonate ions	4.28	4.41	0.13

From H.W. Davenport, *The ABC of Acid-Base Chemistry,* 4th ed., The University of Chicago Press, Copyright 1958 by The University of Chicago

Physiologically, there are two CO_2 absorption curves, one for partially deoxygenated hemoglobin and the other for oxyhemoglobin—the former applying to veins and the latter to the arteries. By simultaneously unloading oxygen as CO_2 is loaded, the CO_2 carrying capacity of the blood is enhanced, and more CO_2 can be carried at the same partial pressure. The reverse pertains in the lung. There, as oxygen is loaded and the O_2 saturation of the blood increases, hemoglobin becomes more acidic, CO_2 carrying power is thus diminished, and removal of CO_2 from the blood into alveolar air is augmented.

Carbon dioxide as an acid

The CO_2 absorption curve is similar to a titration curve. The P_{CO_2} could be thought of as acid added, and the ordinate could be corrected to the alkali bicarbonate equivalent of the CO_2 content. The equation for the dissociation of H_2CO_3 may be rearranged as follows

$$[H^+] = K_1 \frac{[H_2CO_3]}{[HCO_3^-]}$$

In this expression the constant of proportionality, K_1, is the "true" first ionization constant. The concentration of H_2CO_3 is proportional to the partial pressure of CO_2, and in this case the constant of proportionality is the solubility (α) of CO_2 expressed as mM/L/mm Hg (0.0301 in plasma). Taking the logarithm of both sides of the equation and remembering that pH is defined as a negative reciprocal of the log of hydrogen ion concentration, we have

$$pH = pK_1' + \log\frac{[HCO_3^-]}{\alpha P_{CO_2}}$$

This is called the *Henderson-Hasselbalch equation,* and it expresses one of the most important relationships in the acid-base balance of the body. Using the same variables in the carbon dioxide absorption curve, one may express the change in pH which can be predicted from the log ratio of the bicarbonate and carbonic acid concentrations. The value for pK′ is determined by the pH when the bicarbonate–carbonic acid ratio is 1, since the logarithm of 1 is 0. Its value is about 6.1.

Gas transport and blood buffering

For purposes of acid-base analysis it is often more convenient to replot the basic information already contained in the conventional CO_2 absorption curve (Fig. 15.18). One can rearrange the graph so that pH is plotted along the horizontal axis and HCO_3^- along the vertical axis (Fig. 15.19). Now the effect of added alkali on pH appears as it would in a conventional buffer plot, and the *buffer curve* for whole blood appears as a straight line of negative slope. Furthermore, although a blood sample has many buffer curves depending on the state of oxygenation of the hemoglobin, the limits are defined by saturated and unsaturated hemoglobin. The former is the buffer line of arterial blood; the buffer line for venous blood lies nearer the unsaturated curve.

The fact that normal respiratory gas exchange involves loss of O_2 at the same time CO_2 is taken up means that through the Haldane effect blood is increasing its buffering capacity at the same time that it is taking on an acid load. This efficient intrinsic regulatory system serves to stabilize partially the pH change which would otherwise

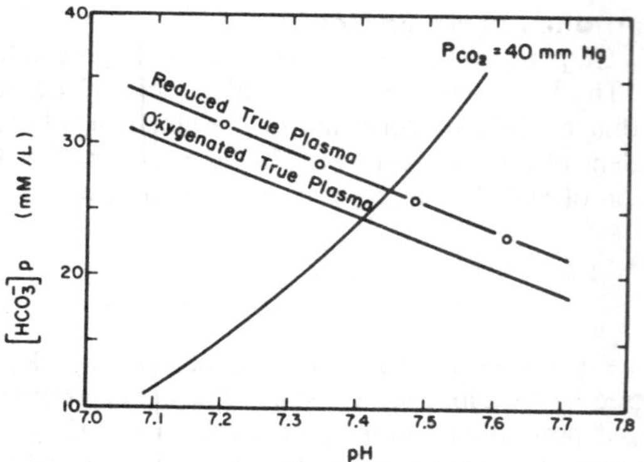

Figure 15.19. Buffer curves of oxygenated true plasma and reduced true plasma with the normal P_{CO_2} isobar. The pH is computed from the Henderson-Hasselbalch equation and replotted. (From H.W. Davenport, *The ABC of Acid-Base Chemistry,* 4th ed., The University of Chicago Press, Copyright 1958 by The University of Chicago.)

occur. In fact, if the amount of CO_2 taken up into the blood were about seven tenths of the O_2 removed from the blood, the change in the buffer capacity by means of the Haldane effect would be completely compensatory, and there would be no change in pH at all. Actually, with the normal exchange of O_2 and CO_2 there is a decrease in plasma pH from arterial to venous blood of about .06 units.

Carbamino compounds

Although most carbon dioxide carried in the blood is in the form of bicarbonate, and bicarbonate is divided between plasma and red blood cells in the ratio 2 to 1, there is also an extremely important fraction of CO_2 carried in the following way

$$HbNH_2 + CO_2 \rightleftharpoons HbN\begin{matrix}\diagup H\\ \diagdown COOH\end{matrix} \rightleftharpoons HbN\begin{matrix}\diagup H\\ \diagdown COO^-\end{matrix} + H^+$$

This reaction occurs most strongly with reduced hemoglobin and is responsible for some 20 percent of the total CO_2 transport. Further, the reaction is a very fast one and needs no enzymic acceleration. In the physiological pH range these compounds are closely identified with oxylabile ionizing groups, and this is probably the reason for the greater carbamino combining capacity of reduced hemoglobin. Although carbamino CO_2 constitutes a relatively small fraction of the total CO_2 content, it assumes a much larger role in the CO_2 exchange during the single respiratory cycle than does the bicarbonate transport system.

RESPIRATORY GAS EXCHANGE

Respiratory exchange ratio

The best assessment of the respiratory exchange process is usually arrived at by measuring the oxygen consumption and carbon dioxide production of the whole animal. This is most simply accomplished by analyzing the volume of air expired per unit of time and the differences between the inspired and expired concentrations of the respiratory gases (open circuit method). Since some of the oxygen consumed does not lead to the production of carbon dioxide but appears as water, the value for oxygen consumed does not ordinarily equal the value for carbon dioxide produced. The ratio of carbon dioxide produced to oxygen consumed in the steady state indicates whether the body's source of energy is primarily fat, carbohydrate, or protein. In this sense the ratio is called the *respiratory quotient* (RQ). On the other hand, it may be useful to measure this ratio under conditions other than the steady state. In that case the value does not indicate the metabolic substrate of the body; it is called the *respiratory exchange ratio* and is symbolized R. Under steady state conditions R = RQ. In fact, one of the uses of the respiratory exchange ratio is to determine whether or not one is dealing with a steady state.

Ventilation-perfusion ratio

The gas exchange process depends on ventilation of the alveoli and on blood flow to the alveoli. Either, in the absence of the other, creates a totally ineffective situation. The ratio between ventilation and perfusion ($\dot{V}_A/\dot{Q}$) greatly affects this exchange; normally a nearly one-to-one relationship is required.

Pressure in the pulmonary vascular system is low, peak systolic pressure being only about 20 mm Hg. So the hydrodynamic "lift" of systole is just adequate to propel blood to a height about 20 cm above the level of the right heart. Depending on orientation in the gravitational field, some portions of the lung may be beyond that limit: in a standing man the apices of the lungs are about 20 cm above the right heart. The apical alveoli then, even though they receive some fresh air with each inspiration, may not receive significant blood flow for exchange. These apical alveoli are normally the highest $\dot{V}_A/\dot{Q}$ population in the lung (if $\dot{Q}$ is zero, $\dot{V}_A/\dot{Q}$ will be infinity), but there will be other regions, especially in disease, where $\dot{V}_A/\dot{Q}$ will also be high. Collectively the high $\dot{V}_A/\dot{Q}$ alveoli contribute a dead space effect, and an estimate of an equivalent volume of wholly unperfused alveoli has come to be known as the *alveolar dead space*. It is a "virtual space," computed as if all of the high $\dot{V}_A/\dot{Q}$ alveoli have the effect of a hypothetical volume of alveoli with infinite $\dot{V}_A/\dot{Q}$ ratio. (The calculation is made with the Bohr formula by substituting arterial for alveolar P_{CO_2}, and alveolar for mixed expired P_{CO_2}.) The sum of this alveolar dead space and the anatomical dead space is the *physiological dead space*.

The arterial-alveolar P_{CO_2} difference indicates high $\dot{V}_A/\dot{Q}$ alveoli, and frequently that difference is used to calculate the alveolar dead space. Normally, the value of $P_{a_{CO_2}} - P_{A_{CO_2}}$ is close to zero, indicating that $\dot{V}_A/\dot{Q}$ is narrowly distributed around a statistical mean of 1. Pulmonary disease, however, frequently alters the picture drastically. The situation also changes normally with shifts of posture (Fig. 15.20). When man reclines, the apices are brought to the level of the heart, their blood supply is no longer compromised, and the alveolar dead space is less. In the large quadrupeds a similar problem exists in the dorsal areas of the lung. And tubercle bacilli tend to locate in these poorly perfused areas.

There are also in the lung populations of alveoli with $\dot{V}_A/\dot{Q}$ ratios below normal. It is easy to conceive of some alveoli which would be normally perfused but which, because of an obstructed airway or low wall compliance, might receive no ventilation, and would therefore have a $\dot{V}_A/\dot{Q}$ ratio of zero. The blood leaving such a region would not exchange with representative alveolar gas and would be added to pulmonary venous blood with an ef-

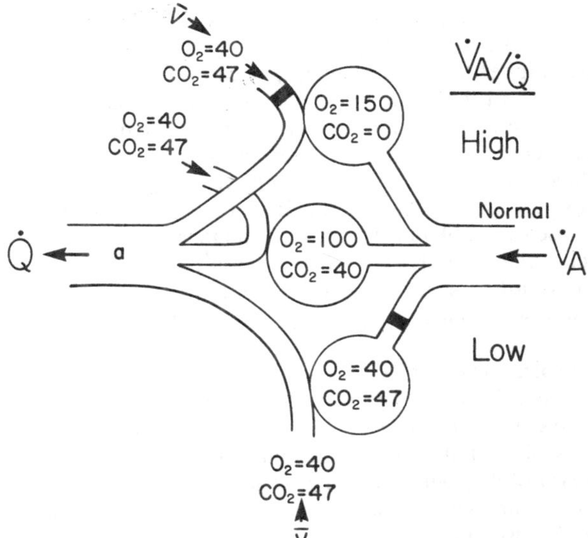

Figure 15.20. Diagram of extremes of $\dot{V}_A/\dot{Q}$. Blood with mixed venous composition enters each vessel that approaches an alveolus. Blood supply to top alveolus is shown obstructed, $\dot{V}_A/\dot{Q}$ is therefore infinite, and composition of alveolar gas is that of inspired air. Middle alveolus is normal and has normal composition. Bottom alveolus has obstructed airway, $\dot{V}_A/\dot{Q}$ is therefore zero, and alveolar gas is in equilibrium with mixed venous blood.

fect on the systemic arterial blood gas composition that would be the same as if there were a true anatomical shunt of venous blood into the arterial pool. Because of the shape of the oxyhemoglobin dissociation curve, and the fact that the normal arterial value is on the flat part, the shuntlike effect of low $\dot{V}_A/\dot{Q}$ alveoli is manifest P_{O_2} difference between alveolar air and arterial blood. If the mixed venous value is known, a virtual *shunt flow*, that is, the volume flow equivalent of a true anatomical shunt of venous blood, but due to low $\dot{V}_A/\dot{Q}$ alveoli, can be calculated. It is usually expressed as a fraction of the cardiac output.

It may not be immediately obvious why the $P_{a_{CO_2}} - P_{A_{CO_2}}$ difference reveals high $\dot{V}_A/\dot{Q}$ alveoli, and $P_{A_{O_2}} - P_{a_{O_2}}$ difference reveals low $\dot{V}_A/\dot{Q}$ alveoli. With high $\dot{V}_A/\dot{Q}$, the problem is dominated by consideration of ventilation, and for carbon dioxide the partial pressure in the alveolar space could vary from the usual normal value of 40 mm Hg down to zero (inspired value). On the other hand, for the shunt problem created by low $\dot{V}_A/\dot{Q}$ alveoli the dominant aspect is blood flow, and for oxygen the $P_{a_{O_2}} - P_{\bar{v}_{O_2}}$ difference is normally about 60 mm Hg, but the $P_{\bar{v}_{CO_2}} - P_{a_{CO_2}}$ difference is only 7 mm Hg. Hence the shunting of venous blood into arterial does not affect the arterial P_{CO_2} very much, but it does affect arterial P_{O_2}.

In man, the bases of the lungs are normally low $\dot{V}_A/\dot{Q}$ regions. The pulmonary vessels there tend to be distended by the hydrostatic weight of the blood column, and their resistance therefore is less than in the vessels higher in the lung. In addition, ventilation at the bases is also higher than at the apices, because the basal regions are less distended at functional residual capacity (FRC) and, due to the sigmoid shape of the pulmonary compliance curve, are more compliant at normal tidal volume. Nonetheless, even though both ventilation and blood flow are each higher at the base than the apex, the increase of ventilation is less than the increase of flow, and hence the ratio of $\dot{V}_A$ to $\dot{Q}$ is lower at the base. Similarly, the ventilation is low at the apex but the blood flow is lower still, hence $\dot{V}_A/\dot{Q}$ is higher (see Fig. 15.20).

Respiratory cycle

The following events occur simultaneously but with different rate constants. Carbon dioxide in the mixed venous blood returning to the lungs normally has a partial pressure of about 47 mm Hg. Thus on its exposure to alveolar air, whose partial pressure of CO_2 is approximately 40 mm Hg, there exists a 7 mm Hg P_{CO_2} gradient between blood and air. This gradient of pressure will drive CO_2 out of the blood. The instant the first molecule of CO_2 leaves the blood there will be a decrement in plasma P_{CO_2}, a rise in alveolar P_{CO_2}, and consequently a narrowing of the partial pressure gradient. Further, there will be a momentary disequilibrium created between the plasma, which will have been the source of the first CO_2 molecule given off into the alveolar air, and the CO_2 contained in the red blood cell (Figure 15.21). This will cause red cell CO_2 to diffuse into the plasma. As indicated previously, a large part of this red cell CO_2 will derive from carbamino CO_2. Because of the efflux of CO_2 into the alveolar air the plasma CO_2 equilibrium

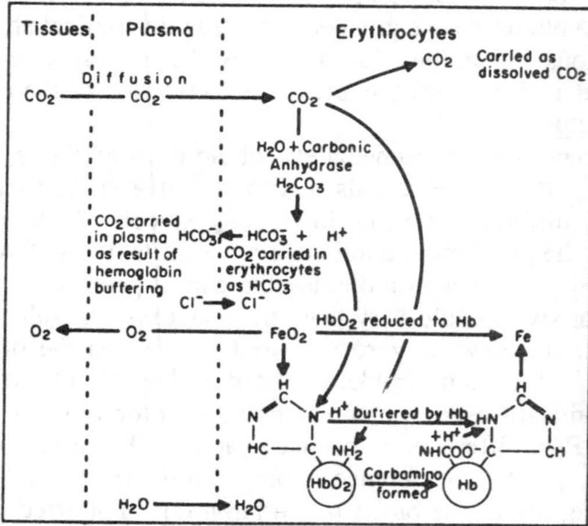

Figure 15.21. Diagram of CO_2 entry into the blood plasma and red cells from tissues and the reactions and processes associated with CO_2 transport. (From H.W. Davenport, *The ABC of Acid-Base Chemistry*, 4th ed., The University of Chicago Press, Copyright 1958 by The University of Chicago.)

($CO_2 + H_2O \rightleftharpoons H_2CO_3 \rightleftharpoons H^+ + HCO_3^-$) shifts to the left with a decrement in red cell bicarbonate (due to movement along the CO_2 absorption curve). A concentration gradient for bicarbonate ion is also established between red cell and plasma; bicarbonate moves into the red cell from the plasma. The acquisition of a negatively charged bicarbonate ion in the red cell interior creates an electric field. Since the red cell membrane is relatively more permeable to anions than it is to cations, the effect of the field is to draw anions into the plasma—chloride is the most abundant, making up the major part of migrating anions from the red cell—and the process continues until the ratio of chloride concentration in red cell to chloride concentration in plasma is equal to the ratio of bicarbonate concentration in red cell to bicarbonate concentration in plasma. This exchange process of bicarbonate and chloride between plasma and red cell is referred to as the *chloride* or *Hamburger shift*. The enzyme carbonic anhydrase increases these reactions so rapidly that the new arterial equilibrium is achieved faster than pulmonary capillary transit.

Venous blood returning to the lungs is normally about 70 percent saturated with oxygen and has a partial pressure of oxygen of about 40 mm Hg. Since alveolar air has about 100 mm Hg partial pressure of oxygen, there is a gradient for oxygen of approximately 60 mm Hg, or about 10 times that for CO_2. In spite of this, the relatively low solubility of oxygen (all gases must pass through an aqueous phase separating alveolar air and blood) limits the speed of O_2 flow into the plasma. The venous blood is more rapidly unloaded of its carbon dioxide than it is charged with oxygen; thus, the operative oxyhemoglobin dissociation curve along the major portion of the pulmonary capillary will have been shifted up and to the left of its venous position due to the Bohr effect. This means that more oxygen can be loaded for the same partial pressure of oxygen than would have been the case without the loss of CO_2. Under normal circumstances near-equilibrium is achieved in end-pulmonary capillary blood between alveolar and blood oxygen pressures. The oxygen entering the blood must, of course, first pass through the plasma, but it is rapidly taken up into the red cell interior, where it enters into association with hemoglobin. The change in saturation of hemoglobin will cause a shift in the CO_2 absorption curve through the Haldane effect, and by this mechanism some final extra unloading of CO_2 is achieved.

In the tissues these processes all occur in reverse but according to the same general principles (Fig. 15.21).

The problem of supplying oxygen to the tissues is largely one of geometry and of the diffusion resistance to the movement of oxygen molecules from within the capillary blood to the source of intracellular utilization at the mitochondria. There are critical regional oxygen pressures below which life cannot be maintained. Since the mean available oxygen pressure in the tissue region more nearly approximates the venous than the arterial pressure, the tissues "see" an oxygen pressure head of about 50 mm Hg. Whether or not this available pressure head is adequate to drive the necessary oxygen into any given cell will depend upon the distance that cell is from the source, and the rate of oxygen utilization along the diffusion path. In most cases it is important to consider more than one capillary, because tissues are designed so that a group of cells normally has two available sources. The relationship between regional capillary oxygen pressure and the pressure available to any cell is dependent upon the diffusion capacity of the tissue, the distance the cell is from the tissue capillary, the P_{O_2} within the capillary, and the radius of the capillary.

There are also variations among species whose tissues have different rates of oxygen consumption, even under conditions of rest, and in all animals when the available oxygen supply is compromised, for example at high altitude. One of the most readily available regulatory mechanisms under increased call for oxygen is the opening of capillary beds which, under resting conditions, are not perfused. In skeletal muscle, for example, it has been shown that the available capillary bed is considerably in excess of that which is normally used, until tissue O_2 demand increases. Upon the opening of more capillaries and increase of blood flow to the tissues the distance separating cells from the available capillary source is decreased. It is surprising how low the intracellular oxygen pressure is even under sea level conditions and at rest. The cell has been estimated to exist in an environmental partial pressure of oxygen of about 4 mm Hg, but more defined measurements in the region of the mitochondria show that the partial pressure may be below 1 mm Hg. These extremely low P_{O_2} values in tissues, upon which life depends, emphasize how great the need is for precise physiological regulatory mechanisms.

HYPOXIA

Classification

If the partial pressure of oxygen is below normal, the animal is in a state of *hypoxia*. Absence of oxygen is *anoxia*. Frequently, though mistakenly, anoxia and hypoxia are used synonymously.

Ambient hypoxia is characterized by a low partial pressure of oxygen in environmental air; it affects the body as a whole. It is seen at high altitudes or in a closed space or with an anesthetic agent. In certain diseases arterial blood may be deficient in oxygen, even if the inspired air is normal. The effect is the same as in true ambient hypoxia; it is therefore included in this category. All diseases that cause hypoventilation will cause arterial hypoxia.

Anemic hypoxia is the result of a decrease in the oxygen-carrying capacity of the blood because of a shortage of functioning hemoglobin. The partial pressure of oxygen is normal and the percentage saturation of the hemoglobin is also normal, but an insufficient volume of oxygen is delivered to the tissues. Anemic hypoxia is seen after hemorrhage, in various anemias, and in conditions where a part of the hemoglobin is changed to methemoglobin or is combined with carbon monoxide.

Stagnant hypoxia is caused by a general or local failure of the circulation. The oxygen content of the arterial blood is normal, but the tissues fail to receive enough oxygen because of diminished blood flow. In its slow movement through the capillaries the blood gives off a larger proportion of its oxygen than normal.

Histotoxic hypoxia follows if the tissues are unable to utilize oxygen in the physiological oxidations. The amount and the partial pressure of oxygen are normal in arterial blood but, because of the failure of the tissues to use oxygen, above normal in venous blood. Histotoxic hypoxia is typically seen in cyanide poisoning.

Oxygen decrements from environment to mitochondrion

Another useful way to look at hypoxia is from the standpoint of the identifiable decrements in partial pressure of oxygen as it is transported from nose to cell (Fig. 15.22). The value of this approach is that each major decrement occurs with an identifiable physiological process or function and with identifiable regulatory mechanisms.

1. Nose to alveolus. Since inspired air is saturated with water vapor before it reaches the lungs, the sum of the partial pressures of all other gases must be 47 mm Hg less than the barometric pressure (P_{H_2O} at 37°C is 47 mm Hg). Further, since the lungs contain not only the inspired oxygen but also whatever CO_2 has been produced

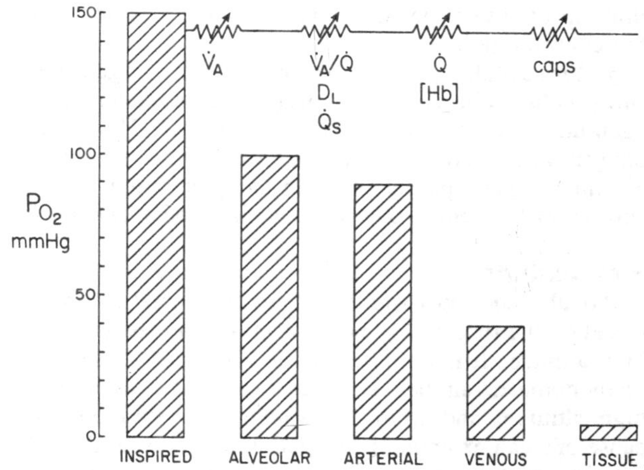

Figure 15.22. Oxygen conductance from ambient air to mitochondrion (average pressures for normal subject at sea level). The major controlling mechanisms are illustrated along the top at their site of action. Each step is shown as a variable resistance.

by metabolism, the fractional concentration, and hence the partial pressure of oxygen, will be diluted in accordance with the volume of CO_2 present. The most important regulatory mechanism that can affect this decrement is thus the magnitude of alveolar ventilation. The limiting oxygen pressure is the inspired value, and this could be achieved only with an infinite alveolar ventilation, at which point the alveolar CO_2 pressure would be zero (see Fig. 15.14).

2. Alveolus to arterial blood. The second drop in partial pressure occurs as oxygen moves across the alveolar capillary membrane. The diffusion resistance of the membrane is significant, particularly at low oxygen pressures. But of greater importance are two other phenomena: the "true" venoarterial anatomical shunts and the shuntlike effect produced by the ventilation $\dot{V}_A/\dot{Q}$ inequality throughout the lung. At sea level, these three processes together account for about 10 mm Hg partial pressure drop in oxygen.

3. Arterial to venous blood. As blood passes from the arteries to the veins the fall in oxygen partial pressure is determined by the rate of metabolism of the tissues and the rate of blood flow in accordance with the Fick principle, and by the portion of the oxygen dissociation curve over which these changes occur. This is sometimes called the *circulatory gradient*. Since most tissues are probably in some sort of equilibrium with the venous oxygen pressure, this value becomes an important index of mean tissue oxygenation.

4. Venous blood to cell. Other things being equal, the oxygen pressure in any cell will depend upon its relative distance from a nutrient capillary. In general, the mean Po_2 of the cell will depend upon the cell-capillary ratio. Increasing the capillary density of a tissue increases its oxygen capacity in a manner analogous to the relationship of the oxygen capacity of blood to its hemoglobin concentration.

5. Intracellular gradient. Distribution of oxygen pressures within cells depends upon internal gradients of oxygen utilization and distribution of enzymes. The critical oxygen value may be close to zero. In other words, by the time oxygen partial pressure has gone from nose to cell, almost the entire potential may have been expended.

High altitude

Probably the most significant environmental stress imposed on the respiratory mechanisms of animals is that of high altitude. It is important in an economic sense since many domestic animals are grazed, at least seasonally, at high altitude, and from a physiological standpoint because one can examine the responses to hypoxia. A characteristic picture of homeostasis in a situation of environmental stress is provided by the example of high altitude.

Ambient hypoxia provides the most comprehensive example of hypoxia since the fault lies at the oxygen source and therefore every step along the oxygen transport system is affected. Unless regulatory mechanisms are mobilized, an animal may not be able to survive, or at the least the ability to function will be seriously compromised. Slight elevations call for minor adjustments, while at extreme altitudes (probably over 18,000 feet) no long-term adaptation appears possible. Nonetheless, some animals domesticated over a long period, e.g. the llama, are able to live normal lives at altitudes over 15,000 feet. Some human beings cannot make the necessary physiological adjustments, and they suffer from chronic mountain sickness, and some domestic animals, particularly cattle, develop brisket disease, peculiar to high altitude. In these cattle a chronic hypertension in the pulmonary circuit develops, followed by right ventricular hypertrophy and congestive failure. Return to lower altitudes may be necessary for survival. The problems of other domestic animals are less well known, but some, like sheep, have no difficulty at all with a change of altitude.

Adaptations to ambient hypoxia may be brought about through any or all of the mechanisms by which the normal oxygen gradients arise (see Table 15.8). Emergency mechanisms, such as the oxygen stores of the body, are extremely important in meeting acute situations, but they are not adaptive processes.

One of the first adjustments to be described, but one that still remains unexplained in many basic aspects, is the ventilatory response. At high altitude, the lower arterial oxygen pressure is a potent stimulus to the carotid and aortic bodies, the chemoreceptor output is more vigorous, phrenic nerve discharge increases, and ventilation is increased. This response minimizes the partial pressure drop from the inspired air to the alveolar air, but during the first 7–10 days important changes occur in the controlling mechanisms. The hypoxia-evoked ventilatory response brings about a rapid fall of alveolar CO_2 pressure, and the resultant hypocapnia initially inhibites ventilation. The net effect is a balance between hypoxic stimulus and hypocapnic inhibition that results in a comparatively trivial increase in ventilation. However, the renal response to the uncompensated respiratory alkalosis is to conserve hydrogen ions and to excrete fixed base in the urine with gradual restoration of the pH of the blood to normal after about a week. Concurrently, the early alkalinity of the cerebrospinal fluid is corrected toward normal, and during this time ventilation and the sensitivity of response to carbon dioxide gradually increase. Pure oxygen administered to a subject who is hyperventilating during acute high altitude exposure results in a return of ventilation to normal sea level values. Following acclimatization, some decrease in ventilation following the administration of oxygen is still observed, but the value does not return to normal. Apparently, the processes of acclimatization shift ventilatory control back to the CO_2

mechanism, in large part through restoration of pH in blood and cerebrospinal fluid. Hypoxic control mechanisms remain intact, but an unexpected consequence of a lifetime at high altitude is attenuation of hypoxic ventilatory response. Nonetheless, chronic hyperventilation and increased ventilatory response to carbon dioxide is characteristic of long-term residents at high altitude, although it is less than in acclimatized sojourners. The system fails in a high altitude syndrome known as chronic mountain sickness, also called Monge's disease.

During exercise, the hypoxic stimulus is particularly apparent. The ventilations achieved when breathing air at a variety of altitudes, if plotted against work load measured as oxygen consumption, all fall on a common regression line if reduced to standard conditions. Thus the regulatory mechanism is concerned not with the volume of air moved but with the rate of oxygen molecule delivery.

There is no evidence of a change in the respiratory dead space volume, which would effectively increase the alveolar fraction of each tidal volume. There are, however, changes in other compartments of the lung volume which occur acutely and are still apparent in long-term native residents at high altitude: (1) increase in vital capacity, (2) increase in expiratory reserve volume, (3) increase in residual volume, and (4) a large increase in functional residual capacity.

There may be an increase in the alveolar capillary diffusing area, an adaptation which would be particularly important during exercise or other stress. The shape of the oxygen dissociation curve suggests a minimal contribution to the uneven ventilation-perfusion ratio distribution to the total alveolar-arterial oxygen gradient, but there is some evidence that even the anatomical venoarterial shunt may be diminished during the process of high altitude adaptation. The net result of all these factors is that the alveolar-arterial oxygen pressure difference, which in normal man at sea level is about 10 mm Hg, may, in a fully acclimatized individual, be so small as to be just measurable. In chronic mountain sickness, however, it is much exaggerated.

The circulatory gradient, normally about 60 mm Hg partial pressure of oxygen at sea level, is the largest component in the steps from inspired air to the cell. It has the potential, therefore, for important adaptive adjustment. To bring about an increase in cardiac output, however, the oxygen requirements of the myocardium have to be increased. Bearing in mind that the heart under normal circumstances has a larger arteriovenous difference than any other organ in the body, it is doubtful whether over a long period of time the combination of hypoxia and an increased work load on the heart would represent a satisfactory functional adaptation. Further, since both the mass and concentration of red blood cells increase during prolonged hypoxia, the resultant increase in blood viscosity adds a further burden on the circulatory pump. Nonetheless, under acute conditions, the response to hypoxia is characteristically an increase of cardiac output, probably elicited through stimulation of the sympathoadrenal system. The duration of the enhanced cardiac response may be dependent upon the supply of body catecholamine stores. After one week at high altitude, the cardiac output has decreased to below sea level values, and in fully acclimatized man the cardiac output and heart rate are low. So too is mean systemic blood pressure, but pulmonary arterial pressure is high.

Actually, the most important mechanism that conserves venous oxygen tension in the face of arterial hypoxia is reflected by the shape of the oxygen dissociation curve. As the oxygen pressure is lowered, the arterial point moves over the bend in the normal curve and a comparable arteriovenous oxygen content difference in the presence of arterial hypoxia is met with only a trivial decrease in the venous oxygen tension. This is because the respiratory exchange now takes place over the steep portion of the oxyhemoglobin dissociation curve. The combination of hypoxia and hypocapnia stimulates the synthesis of intra-erythrocytic 2,3-DPG, and this shifts the oxygen dissociation curve down and to the right with some saving of venous P_{O_2}.

The amount of hemoglobin available for the transport of oxygen is obviously important. And polycythemia after prolonged residence at high altitude was the first adaptive change to be described. The evidence for an erythropoietic stimulating factor in the plasma of most animals exposed to high altitudes (Chapter 2) is quite certain. The total blood volume expands, not merely the hemoglobin concentration; hence the total body hemoglobin mass increases. The increase in blood volume per se may open normally nonperfused areas of the capillary circulation. The distribution of the blood volume between the central and systemic reservoirs indicates that there is preferential distribution to the chest.

The increase in hemoglobin mass will increase the oxygen capacity of the blood, and the fall in partial pressure will be lessened. However, it is easy to overemphasize the importance of the polycythemic response, and the final effect on venous oxygen tension is surprisingly slight. An increase of muscle myoglobin may be of greater significance. The added burden of the increase in cardiac work due to the increase in the whole blood viscosity may be a more serious hazard to life than is worth the gain from increase in oxygen-carrying capacity. One of the perversions of this adaptation is seen in chronic mountain sickness where the polycythemic response is excessive.

Within a tissue, the oxygen pressure of its cells will be determined by the rate of metabolism and the ratio of tissue cells to capillary blood vessels. An important adjustment to combat the relative hypoxia of remote cells is to

Table 15.8. Common physiological measurements in normal human residents living at sea level (Lima) and at 14,900 feet (Morococha)

Measurement	Lima	Morococha
Barometer	750	445
Ventilation	8.24 L/min	9.73 L/min
Alveolar ventilation	5.0 L/min	6.0 L/min
Respiration frequency	14.7 per min	17.3 per min
Alveolar O_2 tension	104 mm Hg	50 mm Hg
Alveolar CO_2 tension	39 mm Hg	29 mm Hg
O_2 consumption	253 ml/min	230 ml/min
Red blood cells	5.11 millions/cu mm	6.44 millions/cu mm
Packed cell volume	46.6%	59.5%
Hemoglobin	15.64%	20.13%
Total blood volume	4.77 L	5.7 L
Plasma volume	2.52 L	2.23L
Vital capacity	4.92 L	5.35 L

From Hurtado, Velasquez, and Reynafarje 1956, U.S.A.F. Tech Rept. no. 56–1

increase the number of perfused capillaries. Evidence of this has been found in the pial vessels of the brain, in the retina, and less directly in skeletal and heart muscle.

There have been many efforts to prove that whole-body oxygen consumption, and more recently tissue oxygen consumption, is decreased with adaptation to high altitude. This would be an effective mechanism, although the biochemical implications would be profound. There is no unequivocal evidence for such a change (Table 15.8), but there are important differences in oxygen utilization during exercise when native residents at high altitude are compared with sea level residents. The altitude-acclimatized subject demonstrates a strikingly increased "efficiency," but it is not entirely clear whether this is biochemical or a matter of training.

There are undoubtedly important biochemical changes which could increase the efficiency of cellular metabolic processes. The acclimatized subject shows less of an increase in blood lactate than does the unacclimatized subject during muscular exercise, but at rest there is no difference. In the guinea pig, fully acclimatized to high altitude, there is an increase in tissue succinoxidase activity, but interestingly, in high altitude animals there are more cells per gram of tissue, and the amount of succinoxidase per cell may not be changed. High altitude animals show an increase in glycolysis and more ATPase activity, and their tissues contain higher concentrations of high-energy phosphate stores.

REGULATION OF BREATHING

The motor act of breathing originates with the rhythmic contraction of the muscles: the diaphragm, which is innervated by the phrenic nerves originating in spinal roots C_2, C_3, and C_4, and the intercostal muscles whose motor supply comes from T_1 through T_6. They are active during both inspiration and expiration; however, under

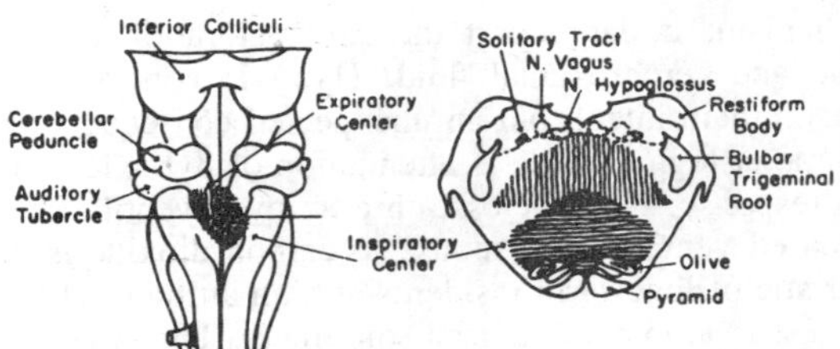

Figure 15.23. Inspiratory and expiratory neurons in the respiratory center of the cat. (Redrawn from Pitts, Magoun, and Ranson 1939, *Am. J. Physiol.* 126:673–88.)

normal resting conditions inspiratory activity far exceeds expiratory, since inspiration is active and expiration passive. There is a constantly maintained background tonus, with not only excitation of the appropriate units but also reciprocal inhibition of the others. During inspiration there is recruitment of motor units, with peak activity achieved at the end of inspiration, which is abrupt. The inspiratory motor units return to their background rate of activity, and tonic discharge in the expiratory units reappears. Many aspects of the act of breathing are integrated at cord level, but the origin of the rhythm and the limits of tidal volume and respiratory frequency are dependent upon neuronal pools in the medulla oblongata. These areas are vaguely defined and referred to collectively as the *respiratory centers* (Fig. 15.23). Into them flows information from peripheral receptors, chemosensitive areas in the brain, and higher nervous centers, including the cerebral cortex. From them flows the efferent impulse over the phrenic and intercostal nerves.

Respiratory centers

It has long been known that an animal will continue to breathe regularly even if all the cranial nerves have been cut and the brain stem has been transected above the pons. If the brain stem is sectioned along the lower border of the pons, the animal makes an inspiratory gasp and respiration is arrested in a sustained inspiratory position. This response is referred to as *apneusis* and is believed to originate through removal of the normal tonic inhibitory effect of the pneumotaxic center on the inspiratory neurons. The *pneumotaxic center* lies in the upper part of the pons, and through a periodic inhibiting influence it converts the continuing discharge activity of the inspiratory center into a rhythmic pattern.

If a further section is made at the level of the lower third of the medulla, all respiratory activity ceases. Both the *inspiratory and expiratory centers* lie in the medulla, the former in the ventral reticular formation immediately over the cephalic four fifths of the inferior olive, in the region of the entrance of the vagus nerve. The latter is a less well-defined group of neurons intermingling with the inspiratory center but extending cephalically and more

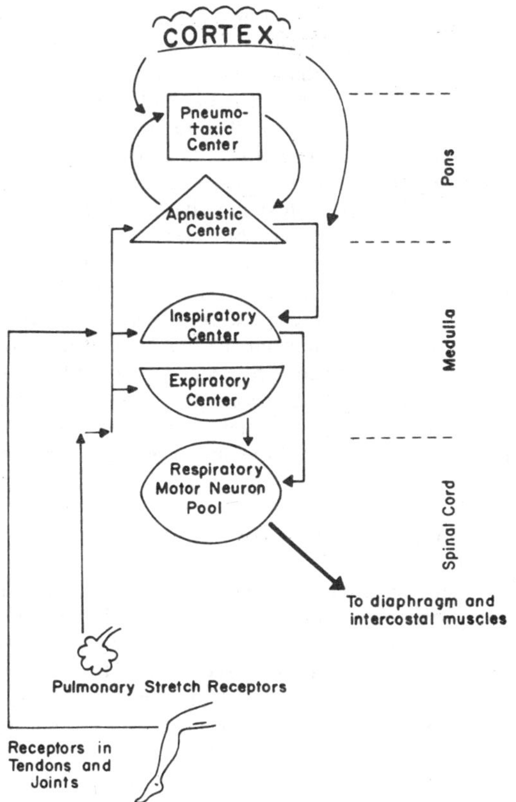

Figure 15.24. Principal circuits in the central respiratory control system of mammals and the most important afferent and efferent pathways. (Modified from Wang, Ngai, and Frumin 1957, *Am. J. Physiol.* 190:333–42.)

dorsally and is laterally placed with regard to the reticular formation.

There is considerable evidence that the pneumotaxic center, the inspiratory center, and the expiratory center make up a feedback circuit between the medulla and the pons (Fig. 15.24). According to this hypothesis, when the inspiratory center discharges, it not only sends efferent impulses to the spinal motor neurons, but also, by recurrent collaterals, a volley of impulses to the pneumotaxic center. The pneumotaxic center in turn sends impulses to the expiratory center which, when excited beyond a certain level, relays inhibitory impulses to the inspiratory center and thus brings about the end of inspiration. This termination of activity in the inspiratory center eliminates excitatory impulses to both the inspiratory muscles and to the pneumotaxic center, and thus also the effect of the pneumotaxic centers on the expiratory center disappears. The inspiratory center being normally dominant, it is once again free to exert its influence, and a new respiratory cycle begins.

Lung and chest-wall receptors

The vagus nerve carries afferent impulses that originate in receptors in the lung tissue which are sensitive to stretch. If both vagus nerves are cut, breathing becomes slower and deeper. If the pneumotaxic center is isolated from the respiratory center in the manner previously described, but if the vagi are left intact, breathing continues normally. These two observations, taken together with the apneustic pattern of breathing observed in the animal with a pontine section and cranial nerve denervation, show that the vagi exert an inhibiting effect on the inspiratory center not unlike that of the pneumotaxic center. This important vagal reflex is known as the *Hering-Breuer reflex,* and it appears to be more important in setting the normal rhythm of respiration than is the pneumotaxic feedback.

There is also an expiratory-excitatory reflex, particularly at lung volumes below the functional residual capacity. The afferent path for this reflex is also in the vagi, and its role is to promote inspiration.

The intercostal muscles are richly supplied with muscle spindles which act as length receptors and transmit information to the spinal cord and to the cerebrum. At cord level increased spindle activity with stretch elicits an excitatory reflex which augments efferent motor response. At supraspinal levels the same information is inhibitory and will terminate inspiration. The effect is analogous to the Hering-Breuer reflex.

Chemical control of breathing

By far the most important stimuli that regulate the volume of ventilation are the partial pressures of carbon dioxide and oxygen (Table 15.9). In man residing at sea level, the normal arterial partial pressure of CO_2 (about 40 mm Hg) provides a constant chemoreflex stimulus to the CNS; however, the arterial partial pressure of oxygen (about 100 mm Hg) acting at the carotid and aortic bodies provides only a very low intensity of background stimulus. Only if the P_{O_2} falls to about 65 mm Hg does the hypoxic chemoreflex drive assert itself in a major

Table 15.9. Relative net ventilatory response in man *

Condition	Ventil. (L/min)	Changes in arterial: P_{O_2}	P_{CO_2}	pH
Control (room air)	5	0	0	0
Hypoxia	12	↓	↓	↑
CO_2 inhalation	70	↑	↑	↓
Metabolic acidosis	35	↑	↓	↓
Moderate exercise	50	0	0	0
Severe exercise	120	0 or ↓	0 or ↓	↓

* 0, no change; ↑ increase; ↓ decrease
From Gray, *Pulmonary Ventilation and Its Physiological Regulation,* Thomas, 1950

way, even though the threshold for hypoxia is much higher.

The sites of excitation by low O_2 partial pressures are in specialized collections of nervous cells localized peripherally in the *carotid and aortic bodies* (Fig. 15.25). Carbon dioxide (and hydrogen ion) also act on the peripheral chemoreceptors but only mildly unless there is a concomitant hypoxemia. The principal excitatory locus for carbon dioxide is in the CNS, which has superficial cells near the floor of the fourth ventricle of the medulla that are chemosensitive. Cells deeper in the brain are also responsive. The superficial neurons probably sense cerebrospinal fluid (CSF) while those deeper in the substance of the brain are more likely to detect blood gas composition. The carotid and aortic bodies are critically poised in the arterial stream and are thus able to sense the partial pressures of O_2 and CO_2 in blood which has left the lungs. In this way they serve as monitoring devices. Since concentrations of CO_2 and O_2 in the alveolar gas are dependent upon the ratio of metabolic rate to magnitude of alveolar ventilation, if the ventilation is not adequate the alveolar P_{CO_2} will rise and arterial P_{O_2} will fall. The carotid body will as a consequence initiate excitatory impulses which will pass over the carotid sinus nerve into the respiratory centers of the medulla. Simultaneously, the arterial blood with its increased P_{CO_2} will signal chemosensitive neurons in the brain. Ventilation will increase and will continue above the normal value until the P_{CO_2} and P_{O_2} have been brought back to normal, and excitation in the carotid body and medullary neurons is reestablished at normal intensity. The basic arrangement is that of a negative feedback control system.

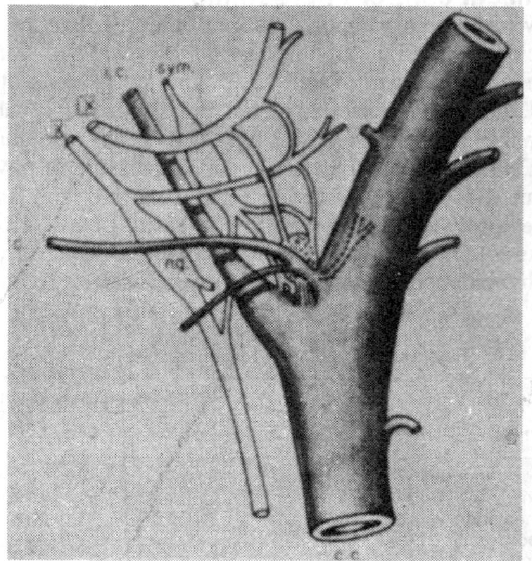

Figure 15.25. Simplified carotid body and adjacent structures in the dog: c.c., common carotid; i.c., internal carotid; e.c., external carotid; n.g., nodose ganglion; sym., sympathetic nerve; IX and X, ninth and tenth cranial nerves; occ., occipital artery. The carotid body is the stippled structure at the bifurcation of the common carotid. (Modified from Adams, *The Comparative Morphology of the Carotid Body and the Carotid Sinus*, Thomas, 1958.)

The carotid body consists of epithelioid cells surrounded by a rich network of sinusoidal blood vessels. The rate of metabolism of its cells is very high, and the blood supply to this organ is greater than to any other. How exactly its cells detect the change in their chemical environment is not known, but clearly the partial pressure, not the content, of oxygen is important. The rate of blood flow through the organ is important, and at low perfusion pressures the carotid body will be excited even though arterial P_{O_2} is normal. Both CO_2 and low O_2 may stimulate the receptor cells by means of some third agent, perhaps the local hydrogen ion concentration or a neurohumoral agent. Lastly, the chemoreceptor cells are under efferent nervous control, the major effect being inhibitory.

Response to carbon dioxide and hydrogen ions

The chemical control system that regulates the rate of breathing can detect minute changes in the balance between ventilation and metabolic need. Metabolism may be increased during exercise several fold, but the ventilation is so closely regulated that the arterial partial pressure of carbon dioxide is held at nearly its normal resting value.

On the other hand, the most common method to study the ventilatory response to carbon dioxide manipulates the CO_2 concentration in inspired air. This will increase the stimulus to breathe, but the alveolar P_{CO_2} will not be brought down to normal so long as the inspired air also contains CO_2. Therefore, the system will come to a steady state characterized by an increase in ventilation and an increase in arterial CO_2 pressure. Hence, a relationship may be defined between the stimulus, which is the arterial P_{CO_2}, and the response, which is ventilation measured during the steady state period. By using different inspired CO_2 pressures, a large number of paired values of arterial CO_2 and ventilation may be plotted (Fig. 15.26). The result is a nearly linear relationship between stimulus and response

$$V_E = mP_{A_{CO_2}} + k$$

a straight line whose slope is m. M is often referred to as the *sensitivity of the respiratory center* and is defined by the ratio $\Delta \dot{V}_E/\Delta P_{A_{CO_2}}$. In normal man ventilation is approximately doubled for every 2 mm Hg change in $P_{A_{CO_2}}$. (K is a constant whose value defines the intercept on the ventilation axis.) The equation also says that ventilation would be zero at some $P_{A_{CO_2}}$, called *threshold*. However, it is a difficult quantity to verify experimentally.

But it is naive to believe that the arterial (or alveolar) P_{CO_2} is little more than an index of stimulus intensity—

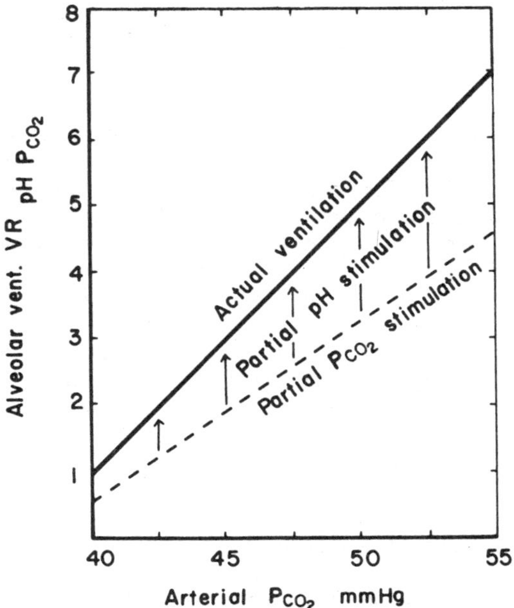

Figure 15.26. The alveolar ventilatory response to P_{CO_2} and pH in man. The effect of CO_2 is a combination of the specific action of CO_2 and the associated change of H^+ concentration, since CO_2 is an acid in solution. VR, ventilation ratio measured under test conditions. All absolute values of $\dot{V}_E$ for control period are reduced to VR = 1; test responses are then relative. (From Gray, *Pulmonary Ventilation and Its Physiological Regulation,* Thomas, 1950.)

the real stimulus would probably have to be measured at (or in) chemoresponsive cells of the brain. A closer index is probably the [H^+] of CSF (see below) but it is less readily accessible for measurement. If the inspired CO_2 pressure rather than the arterial pressure were used as an index of stimulus, the relationship would be nonlinear. For this reason it is less useful.

Since CO_2 in solution is an acid, the associated H^+ effect invariably complicates the interpretation of CO_2 as a respiratory stimulus. By the simultaneous administration of CO_2 and a blood buffer, the arterial pH can be controlled; it can be varied by administering acid, but in this case the increase of ventilation will drive the arterial P_{CO_2} down in accordance with the alveolar ventilation equation. Hence an experiment designed to study the "pure" H^+ stimulus to ventilation must add enough CO_2 to the inspired air to hold $P_{A_{CO_2}}$ at the normal value. The results of such experiments show that both CO_2 and H^+ are powerful stimuli and that the effects of the two are additive (Fig. 15.26).

CSF is also a determinant in ventilatory control. Changes of H^+ concentration or P_{CO_2} of the CSF are followed by ventilatory responses, and a more or less well-localized area on or beneath the floor of the fourth ventricle has been discovered as the chemosensitive site. The P_{CO_2} of CSF is in equilibrium with cerebral blood, probably venous. However, the CSF, being almost protein free, is less well buffered than blood, and its pH is normally well below the blood value. Nonetheless, although changes of P_{CO_2} in the blood are rapidly followed by comparable changes in the CSF, and with change of pH in both, the CSF pH is soon restored through change of its bicarbonate content. This can occur even against a bicarbonate concentration gradient between blood and CSF, and must of necessity therefore be ascribed to an active secretory pump.

CSF may be regarded as the extracellular fluid of the brain, and the remarkable constancy of its hydrogen ion concentration under a wide variety of acid-base changes of the blood suggests a well-developed homeostatic control system. Although the P_{CO_2} of CSF changes rapidly in response to a change of blood P_{CO_2}, and [H^+] of CSF will also change immediately, the blood-brain barrier is not very permeable to ions, and for that reason metabolic acid-base changes in the blood are more slowly reflected in CSF. The arterial receptor mechanisms—peripheral chemoreceptors and medullary chemosensitive neurons close to arterial supply—are geared for fast response, while the steady state responses, and especially those in compensated states of acidosis or alkalosis, can be understood only in terms of the hydrogen ion balance of CSF.

Response to hypoxia

Although chemoreceptor activity consequent to the normal P_{O_2} of arterial blood at sea level is very small, it probably does not completely disappear until the arterial partial pressure of oxygen is raised very high, probably to 500 mm Hg. Nonetheless, it remains unimportant until the arterial P_{O_2} reaches about 65 mm. Reduction to this level most commonly occurs if the partial pressure of oxygen in the inspired air decreases, for example at high altitude. With depression of P_{O_2} in the region of the carotid and the aortic bodies, ventilation will increase, and as a result the alveolar P_{CO_2} will decrease. The actual ventilation will therefore be an algebraic resultant dependent upon hypoxic stimulation and hypocapnic inhibition. This important balancing of concomitant excitatory and inhibitory influences makes the analysis of hypoxic stimulus to breathing extremely confusing unless, through the addition of carbon dioxide to the inspired air, the alveolar CO_2 tension is held constant and thus only the hypoxic stimulus remains under study. If this is done, and if either afferent discharge in the carotid sinus nerve is correlated with the arterial oxygen tension, or if ventilation is correlated with the arterial oxygen pressure at constant alveolar CO_2 pressure, the stimulus-response relationship is seen to be curvilinear (Fig. 15.27).

If the peripheral chemoreceptor areas are denervated by cutting the vagi and carotid sinus nerves, no excitatory effect is seen. There is only inhibition. It appears that the sole mechanism for hypoxic stimulation to venti-

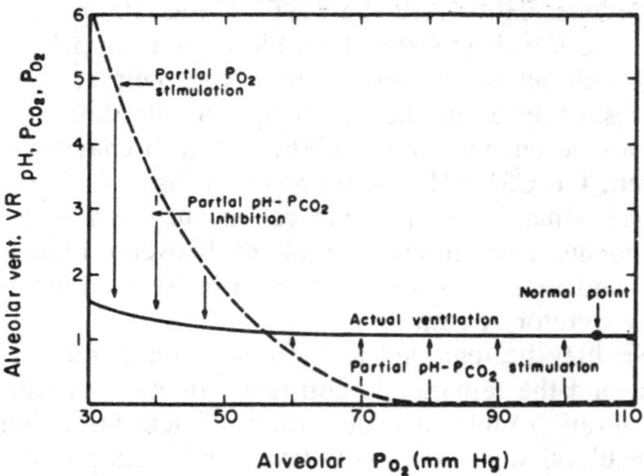

Figure 15.27. Ventilatory response to hypoxia in man. (From Gray, *Pulmonary Ventilation and Its Physiological Regulation*, Thomas, 1950.)

lation depends upon the peripheral chemoreceptor areas, and hypoxia acting on the CNS is a depressant.

The partial pressure of oxygen is the important stimulus, not the oxygen content or the oxygen saturation. In anemia and in carbon monoxide poisoning the arterial oxygen saturation is low, but the arterial oxygen tension is normal. There is no hyperventilation unless extreme degrees of arterial hypoxemia are produced.

Interaction of carbon dioxide and hypoxia

There is an important interaction between chemical stimuli to ventilation. If the alveolar oxygen pressure is held at several fixed values while the CO_2 pressure is varied over a wide range of values, the increment in ventilation achieved for each unit change in P_{CO_2} is dependent upon the prevailing oxygen pressure. The lower the alveolar oxygen pressure, the greater the sensitivity of response

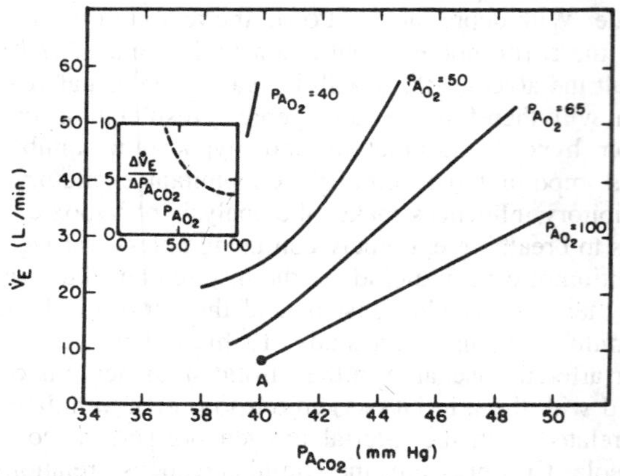

Figure 15.28. The effect of $P_{A_{O_2}}$ on the ventilatory response to CO_2. The vertical displacement of each response curve is indicative of hypoxic stimulation, and the change in slope of the individual curves is indicative of interaction effect (change in "sensitivity"). The insert plots magnitude of change of slope of CO_2 ventilatory response curve caused by increasing hypoxia. (From Tenney, Remmers, and Mithoefer 1963, *Q. J. Exp. Physiol.* 48:192–201, replotted.)

to CO_2 (Fig. 15.28). Similarly, the ventilatory response to hypoxia is augmented by increasing concentrations of alveolar CO_2. The observed responses are more nearly multiplicative. It appears that both peripheral and central processes are involved. The isolated carotid body whose afferent nerve discharge is quantitated against controlled chemical stimuli reveals unequivocal evidence of interaction. CNS phenomena are less readily analyzed, but the fact that hypoxic potentiation of ventilatory response to CO_2 is rarely seen in an anesthetized animal suggests strongly that the way the CNS handles the information it receives also determines, in part, whether or not interaction will occur. It is important to note that all searches for $[H^+]$-CO_2 interaction have been negative. Those responses are simply additive. Hypoxic-CO_2 or hypoxic-$[H^+]$ interactions are well established. The response with those combined stimuli cannot be predicted by adding the individual responses.

Integration of components

As a vital phenomenon, ventilation is peculiar in that it is subject to both voluntary and involuntary control. Willful stimulation or inhibition is obvious, but other manifestations of higher nervous control remain poorly understood. The importance of level of consciousness has long been appreciated, and the changing ventilatory pattern with sleep is well documented. The contribution of attentiveness, diversion, or emotion to ventilation is also familiar, and breathing may be thought of in terms of both automatic or vegetative function and behavioral function. There appear to be two different efferent pathways for mediating these two basic functions. Although breathing is mostly an unconscious act, conditional responses in ventilation have long been known, and deliberate controls imposed by well-trained athletes, presumably arrived at through trial and error, can override elementary stimuli up to a point.

The picture which emerges is one of a highly developed system of many component parts, nearly integrated into a functional unit. There are weak and potent physical and chemical stimuli, positive and negative feedback loops, slowly and rapidly responding units, and an array of defenses in an identifiable hierarchy.

A common experience such as exercise probably involves every process. The initial ventilatory response begins so promptly that none of the chemical changes occurring with exercise could have reached any known receptor site; and there is no known mechanical receptor that causes a potent enough stimulus to account for the observed immediate increase of ventilation. Receptors in the joints and tendons of the leg, when stimulated reflexly, excite ventilation, but they are weak. The conclusion which must be reached is that the animal anticipates the ventilatory need of exercise and does so with considerable accuracy.

The chemoreceptor system can be viewed as a reserve mechanism which backs up the higher nervous system. The placement of chemoreceptors in the arterial blood stream is adequate only if they can serve as "error correctors." This design provides maximum stability, but a temporal delay has been introduced, and this leads to oscillatory behavior, although of low magnitude.

Chemoreceptor areas in the brain, particularly those sensitive to the composition of CSF, probably do not regulate ventilation during very acute episodes, but in a manner of minutes, and certainly hours, their response will constitute an important part of the total process.

SYMBOLS AND ABBREVIATIONS

Primary quantities

P	pressure, or in the case of gases, partial pressure
Q	quantity of blood
C	content per unit volume of blood
V	volume of air
F	fractional concentration in air
α	solubility coefficient of a gas
f	frequency (per unit time, usually minute)
$\dot{Q}$, $\dot{V}$, $\dot{W}$	dot signifies time rate. Hence $\dot{Q}$ is cardiac output, $\dot{V}_E$ is minute volume of ventilation, $\dot{W}$ is rate of work (power)
v	velocity

Subscripts are used to particularize

V_A	alveolar volume
$\dot{V}_A$	alveolar ventilation
P_A	partial pressure of a gas in alveolar air
F_A	fractional concentration of a gas in alveolar air
F_E	fractional concentration of a gas in expired air
$\dot{V}_E$	minute volume of ventilation (expired)
P_B	barometric pressure
V_D	dead space volume
V_T	tidal volume
I	inspired
a	arterial
v	venous
$\bar{v}$	mixed venous (i.e. pulmonary artery)
$\bar{c}$	capillary
c	mixed capillary
STPD	standard temperature and pressure, dry
BTPS	body temperature and pressure, saturated with water vapor
ATPS	ambient temperature and pressure, saturated with water vapor

Sub-subscripts particularize further

$P_{A_{CO_2}}$	alveolar partial pressure of CO_2
$F_{E_{O_2}}$	fractional concentration of O_2 in expired air
$C_{\bar{v}_{CO_2}}$	mixed venous blood CO_2 content

Derived quantities

W	work = pressure × volume
$D_{L_{O_2}}$	diffusing capacity of lungs for O_2
$S_{a_{O_2}}$	arterial oxygen saturation
$\dot{V}O_2$	oxygen consumption (per minute, usually STPD)
$\dot{V}CO_2$	carbon dioxide production (per minute, usually STPD)
R	respiratory exchange ratio

For a complete listing see Glossary on respiration and gas exchange, *J. Appl. Physiol.* 34:549–58, 1973.

REFERENCES

General

Altman, P.L., Gibson, J.F., Jr., and Wang, C.C. 1958. *Handbook of Respiration*. Saunders, Philadelphia.

Comroe, J.H., Forster, R.E., Dubois, A.B., Briscoe, W.A., and Carlsen, E. 1962. *The Lung: Clinical Physiology and Pulmonary Function Tests*. 2d ed. Year Book Medical, Chicago.

Fenn, W.O., and Rahn, H., eds. 1964. *Handbook of Physiology*. Sec. 3, *Respiration*. 2 vols. Am. Physiol. Soc., Washington.

Haldane, J.S. 1917. *Organism and Environment as Illustrated by the Physiology of Breathing*. Yale U. Press, New Haven.

Rossier, P.H., Bühlmann, A.A., and Wiesinger, K. 1960. *Respiration: Physiologic Principles and Their Clinical Applications*. Trans. P.C. Luchsinger and K.M. Moser. Mosby, St. Louis.

Anatomy of lung

Adams, W.E. 1958. *The Comparative Morphology of the Carotid Body and the Carotid Sinus*. Thomas, Springfield, Ill.

de Reuck, A.V.S., and O'Connor, M., eds. 1962. *Pulmonary Structure and Function*. Ciba Found. Symp. Little, Brown, Boston.

Miller, W.S. 1947. *The Lung*. 2d ed. Thomas, Springfield, Ill.

Schulz, H. 1959. *Electron Microscopy of the Lung*. Trans. F. Dallenbach. Springer, Berlin.

von Hayek, H. 1960. *The Human Lung*. Hafner, New York.

Weibel, E.R. 1963. *Morphometry of the Human Lung*. Academic Press, New York.

Comparative physiology

Bartels, H., and Harms, H. 1959. Sauerstoff-dissoziationskurven des Blutes von Säugetieren. *Pflüg. Arch. ges. Physiol.* 268:334–65.

Crosfill, M.L., and Widdicombe, J.G. 1961. Physical characteristics of the chest and lungs and the work of breathing in different mammalian species. *J. Physiol.* 158:1–14.

Drabkin, D.L. 1950. The distribution of the chromoproteins, hemoglobin, myoglobin, and cytochrome C in the tissues of different species, and the relationship of the total content of each chromoprotein to body mass. *J. Biol. Chem.* 182:317–33.

Krogh, A. 1959. *The Comparative Physiology of Respiratory Mechanisms*. U. of Pennsylvania Press, Philadelphia.

Larimer, J.L., and Schmidt-Nielsen, K. 1960. A comparison of blood carbonic anhydrase of various mammals. *Comp. Biochem. Physiol.* 1:19–23.

Prosser, C.L., and Brown, F.A., Jr. 1961. *Comparative Animal Physiology*. 2d ed. Saunders, Philadelphia.

Radford, E.P., Jr. 1957. Recent studies of mechanical properties of mammalian lungs. In J.W. Remington, ed., *Tissue Elasticity*. Am. Physiol. Soc., Washington. Pp. 177–90.

Riggs, A. 1960. The nature and significance of the Bohr effect in mammalian hemoglobins. *J. Gen. Physiol.* 43:737–52.

Schmidt-Nielsen, K. 1972. *How Animals Work*. Cambridge U. Press, Cambridge.

Schmidt-Nielsen, K., and Larimer, J.L. 1958. Oxygen dissociation curves of mammalian blood in relation to body size. *Am. J. Physiol.* 195:424–28.

Schmidt-Nielsen, K., and Pennycuick, P. 1961. Capillary density in mammals in relation to body size and oxygen consumption. *Am. J. Physiol.* 200:746–50.

Smith, R.E. 1956. Quantitative relations between liver mitochrondria metabolism and total body weight in mammals. *Ann. N.Y. Acad. Sci.* 62:405–21.

Tenney, S.M. 1967. Some aspects of the comparative physiology of muscular exercise in mammals. *Circ. Res.* 20(suppl. 1):7–14.

Tenney, S.M., and Bartlett, D., Jr. 1967. Comparative quantitative morphology of the mammalian lung: Trachea. *Resp. Physiol.* 3:130–35.

Tenney, S.M., and Morrison, D.H. 1967. Tissue gas tensions in small wild mammals. *Resp. Physiol.* 3:160–65.

Tenney, S.M., and Remmers, J.E. 1963. Comparative quantitative morphology of the mammalian lung: Diffusing area. *Nature* 197:54–56.

Ulrich, S., Hilpert, P., and Bartels, H. 1963. Über die Atmungsfunktion des Blutes von Spitzmaüsen, weissen Maüsen und syrischen Goldhamstern. *Pflüg. Arch. ges. Physiol.* 277:150–65.

Control of respiration

Brooks, C.McC., Kao, F.F., and Lloyd, B.B., eds. 1965. *Cerebrospinal Fluid and the Regulation of Ventilation.* Blackwell Scientific, Oxford.

Cunningham, J.C., and Lloyd, B.B. 1963. *The Regulation of Human Respiration: The Proceedings of the J.S. Haldane Centenary Symposium, . . . Oxford.* Davis, Philadelphia.

Gray, J.S. 1950. *Pulmonary Ventilation and Its Physiological Regulation.* Thomas, Springfield, Ill.

Grodins, F.A. 1963. *Control Theory and Biological Systems.* Columbia U. Press, New York.

Heymans, C., and Neil, E. 1958. *Reflexogenic Areas of the Cardiovascular System.* Churchill, London.

Nahas, G.G., ed. 1963. Regulation of respiration. *Ann. N.Y. Acad. Sci.* 109:411–948.

Pitts, R.F., Magoun, H.W., and Ranson, S.W. 1939. Localization of the medullary respiratory centers in the cat. *Am. J. Physiol.* 126:673–88.

Porter, R., ed. 1970. *Breathing: Hering-Breuer Centenary Symposium.* Churchill, London.

Tenney, S.M., Remmers, J.E., and Mithoefer, J.C. 1963. Interaction of CO_2 and hypoxic stimuli on ventilation at high altitude. *Q. J. Exp. Physiol.* 48:192–201.

Torrance, R.W., ed. 1968. *Arterial Chemoreceptors.* Blackwell Scientific, Oxford.

Wang, S.C., Ngai, S.H., and Frumin, M.J. 1957. Organization of central respiratory mechanisms in the brain stem of the cat: Genesis of normal respiratory rhythmicity. *Am. J. Physiol.* 190:333–42.

Gas exchange and acid-base balance

Davenport, H.W. 1958. *The ABC of Acid-Base Chemistry.* 4th ed. U. of Chicago Press, Chicago.

Henderson, L.J. 1928. *Blood: A Study in General Physiology.* Yale U. Press, New Haven.

Peters, J.P., and Van Slyke, D.D. 1931. *Hemoglobin and Oxygen: Carbonic Acid and Acid Base Balance.* Repr. from *Quantitative Clinical Chemistry.* Vol. 1, *Interpretations.* Chs. 12, 13. Williams & Wilkins, Baltimore.

Rahn, H., and Fann, W.O. 1955. *A Graphical Analysis of the Respiratory Gas Exchange: The O_2–CO_2 Diagram.* Am. Physiol. Soc., Washington.

West, J.B. 1970. *Ventilation: Blood Flow and Gas Exchange.* 2d ed. Davis, Philadelphia.

Hypoxia and high altitude

Hurtado, A., Velasquez, T., and Reynafarje, C. 1956. Mechanism of natural acclimatization: Studies of the native resident of Morococha, Peru, at an altitude of 14,900 feet. U.S.A.F. School of Aviation Medicine, Tech. Rept. no. 56-1.

Vanliere, E.J. 1942. *Anoxia: Its Effect on the Body.* U. of Chicago Press, Chicago.

Weihe, W.H. 1964. *The Physiological Effects of High Altitude.* Macmillan, New York.

Methodology

Bartels, H., Bucherl, E., Hertz, C.W., Rodewald, G., and Schwab, M. 1963. *Methods in Pulmonary Physiology.* Hafner, New York.

Comroe, J.H., Jr., ed. 1950. *Methods in Medical Research.* Vol. 2, *Pulmonary Function Tests.* Year Book Medical, Chicago.

Consolazio, C.F., Johnson, R.E., and Pecora, L.J. 1963. *Physiological Measurements of Metabolic Functions in Man.* McGraw-Hill, New York.

CHAPTER 16

Respiration in Birds | by Gary E. Duke

ANATOMY OF THE RESPIRATORY SYSTEM

The avian respiratory system has several very distinctive features. The lungs are small and are attached to the ribs, making them relatively inexpansible. Large, discrete, poorly vascularized air sacs are present. Contraction of respiratory muscles occurs during both inspiration and expiration so that both phases are active. Air flow is primarily unidirectional and continuous through a system of primary, secondary, and tertiary bronchi. Gaseous exchange occurs across the walls of air capillaries which branch off the tertiary bronchi.

The respiratory system begins with the external nares which open into nasal cavities. These cavities are separated from each other by a septum in most birds but not all (e.g. vultures), and open into the mouth via a slit. The glottis leading to the trachea is at the base of the tongue. The trachea divides to form two primary bronchi; at this division is the syrinx, which is the vocal organ in birds. Contractions of syringeal muscles change the tension on tympaniform membranes attached to the luminal surfaces of the trachea and/or bronchi in the syrinx. Air passing over the membranes produces the variety of sounds characteristic of birds.

The two primary bronchi lead to the lungs where further branching forms secondary and tertiary bronchi (Fig. 16.1). The primary bronchi also pass through the lungs to connect directly to the abdominal air sacs. The lung is connected to the other air sacs via secondary bronchi which may arise from the primary bronchi or by the joining together of a group of tertiary bronchi. Recurrent bronchi lead from the air sacs back to the lung. This general description applies to most birds; however, there are many variations among species (King 1966, Duncker 1972). Likewise, a variety of terms have been used to describe the system (King 1966).

Air sacs

The air sacs lie outside the lungs in the body cavity (Fig. 16.2). They function principally as airways, and because they are so nearly avascular are capable of little gaseous exchange. The chicken, duck, pigeon, and turkey have nine air sacs, including five anterior ones (the unpaired interclavicular sac and the paired cervical and anterior thoracic sacs) and four posterior ones (the paired posterior thoracic and large abdominal sacs). Diverticula arise from the interclavicular sac, and the suprahumeral diverticulum (the most prominent one) connects to the humerus, which is markedly pneumatic. It is possible to ventilate the lung by way of the humerus, and the bird can draw air through the broken, opened humerus into the lung even though the trachea is occluded, provided that respiratory thoracic movements are maintained.

Since most of the so-called pneumatic or aerated bones of birds are not connected with the air sacs, they are not important in respiration.

Lungs and gaseous exchange

Within the lungs, air conduits provide a complicated system of anastomosing bronchi. The smallest conduits, the tertiary bronchi, are arranged as parallel connectors between the secondary bronchi within the lung. This arrangement permits the continuous flow of air between the secondary bronchi and through the lung. The functional respiratory exchange regions of the avian lung, the air capillaries, surround the tertiary bronchi and make up the bulk of the lung.

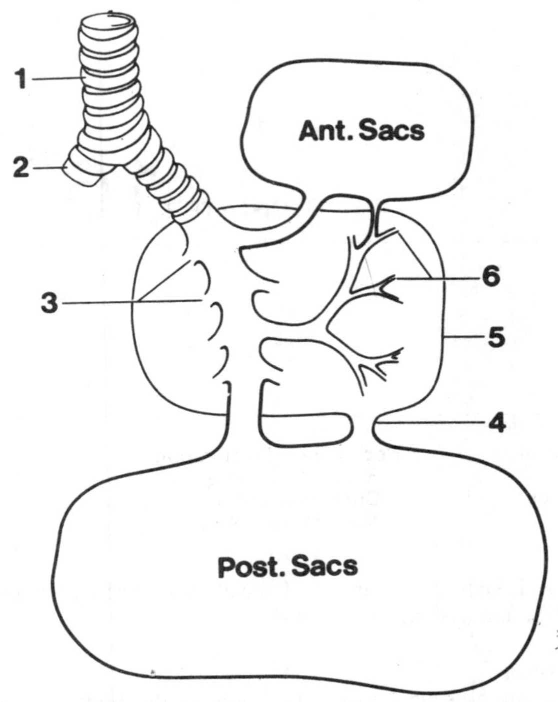

Figure 16.1. Simplified avian lung and air sac system: 1, trachea; 2, primary bronchus; 3, secondary bronchi; 4, recurrent bronchus; 5, lung; 6, tertiary bronchi (greatly enlarged). Ant. sacs include 1 interclavicular, 2 cervical, and 2 thoracic; post. sacs include 2 thoracic and 2 abdominal.

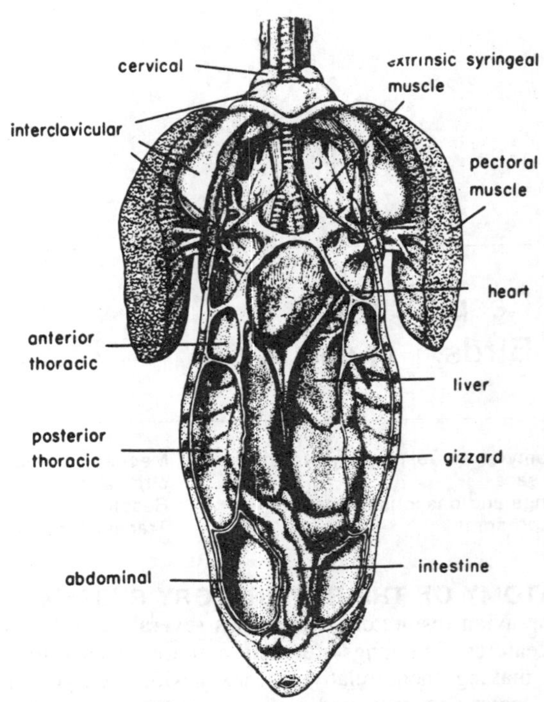

Figure 16.2. Location of air sacs in relation to other organs of the duck. (From G.W. Salt and E. Zeuthen, in A.J. Marshall, ed., *Biology and Comparative Physiology of Birds,* Academic Press, New York, 1960, vol. 1.)

The walls of tertiary bronchi are lined with spiral smooth-muscle bands (Fig. 16.3). Heavier bands of smooth muscle surround the entrances of tertiary bronchi. Both the spiral bands and the heavier bands constrict the bronchi to regulate air flow (King and Cowie 1969). Atria open off the spiral bands and air capillaries lead from the atria (Figs. 16.3, 16.4). The atria may divide into several smaller atria after branching off the tertiary bronchus (Fig. 16.5). Air capillaries extend perpendicularly either from the main atrium or from its subdivisions and connect with other air capillaries (Nowell et al. 1970). Blood capillaries lie adjacent to air capillaries but blood and air flow in opposite directions. This countercurrent flow permits a more thorough exchange of gases than is achieved in the alveoli of the mammalian lung (Scheid and Piiper 1970). As blood passes through the avian lungs it meets air of increasing oxygen tension and decreasing carbon dioxide tension (Fig. 16.6). Thus blood is able to pick up oxygen and release carbon dioxide throughout its passage through the lung.

Table 16.1. Respiratory rates and volumes for resting birds

Species	Body wt. (g)	Respiration rate (no./min) *	Tidal vol. (ml) †	Percentage of total respiratory system as ‡: lungs	abdom. air sacs
Ostrich	100,000	5	1350		
Chicken	5200	13	25.3	11.2	47
Pigeon	317	26	4.6	16.6	37
Robin	70	37			
House sparrow	25	59			

* Crawford and Schmidt-Nielsen 1967, Calder 1968, Hart and Roy 1966, Lewis 1967, Calder 1968 (reading down)
† Lasiewski and Calder 1971 ‡ Dunker 1972

The total number of tertiary bronchi in the chicken lung is estimated to be 300–500 (King and Cowie 1969). Stronger fliers (e.g. pigeons and ducks) have at least four times more tertiary bronchi per unit of lung tissue than chickens (Akester 1960). The total respiratory exchange surface area for chickens is approximately 18 sq cm/g body weight. This surface area is 2–4 times greater in stronger fliers (Duncker 1972). Lung volume is only about 10–15 percent of the volume of the entire respiratory system (Table 16.1).

Diaphragms

There are no structures homologous to the mammalian diaphragm in birds. Two membranes called the pulmonary aponeurosis and the oblique septum, which have some muscular components, occur in birds and function during respiration. Since these structures do not divide

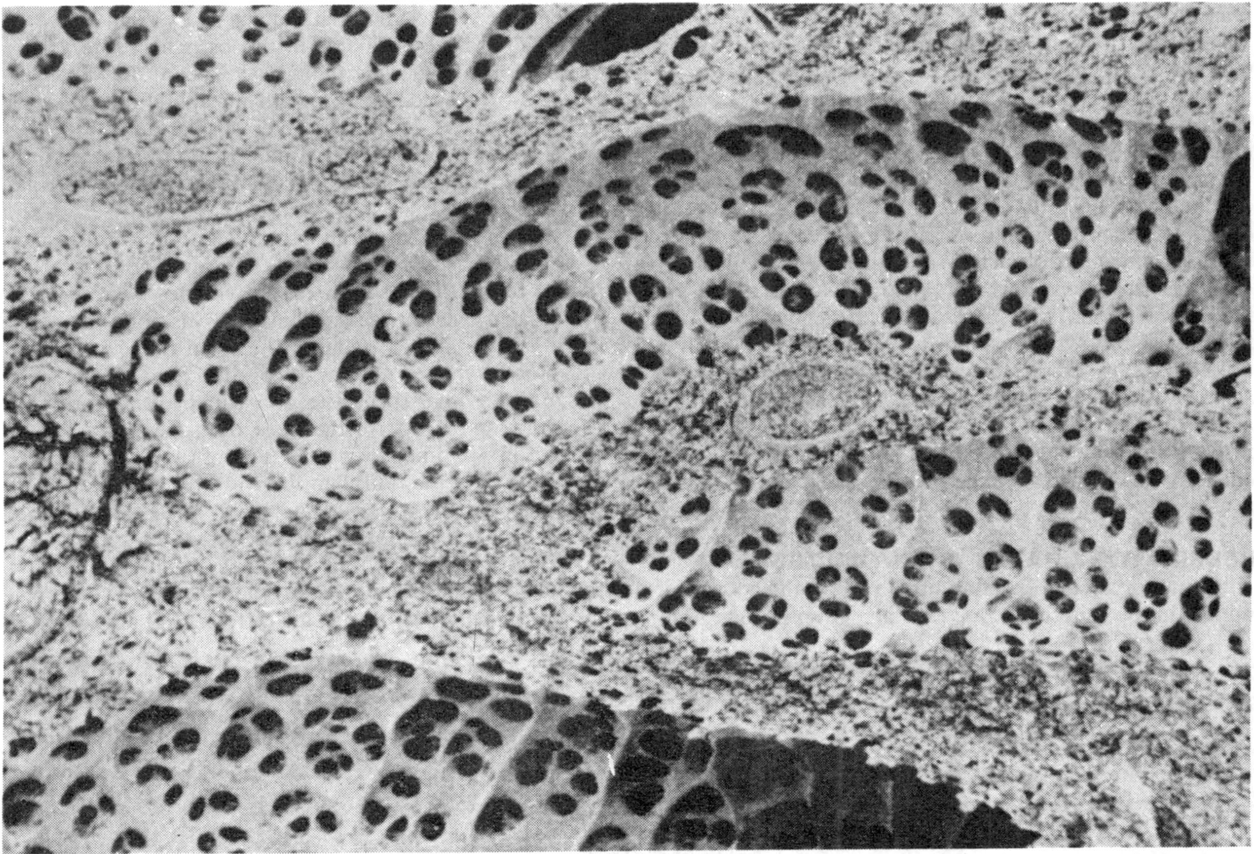

Figure 16.3. Scanning electron micrograph of tertiary bronchi in Japanese quail. Atria open off each bronchus. Oblique section ×95. (From J.A. Nowell, J. Pangborn, and W.S. Tyler, in *Scanning Electron Microscopy,* IIT Res. Inst., Chicago, 1970.)

the body cavity of the bird into thoracic and abdominal cavities, pressures occurring during the respiratory cycle are referred to as thoracoabdominal pressures.

MECHANICS OF RESPIRATION AND AIR CIRCULATION

During inspiration, the size of the thoracic area increases in both transverse and dorsoventral directions. The greatest increase occurs in the caudal portion of the thoracic area because the sternum and sternal ribs swing forward and downward while the vertebral ribs move forward and inward. During expiration, these movements are reversed, requiring active muscular effort. Also during expiration, the muscles of the pulmonary aponeurosis contract, expanding the lung (Fedde et al. 1963). In mammals, expansion of the lung occurs during inspiration.

Pressure drops in all air sacs during inspiration, that is their volume increases, and upon expiration pressure increases in all the sacs. These changes in volume cause the sacs to act as a ''bellows'' (Schmidt-Nielsen 1971). The lungs are compressed during inspiration and expand during expiration.

Knowledge of the mechanical changes in the size of the thoracic and abdominal areas and of pressure changes within the lungs and air sacs helps to explain how air moves through the respiratory system. In addition, the movement of air through the system has been directly studied by introducing a foreign gas marker or another airborne marker into the trachea or an air sac. Small airflow sensors have also been put into air conduits to detect direction of airflow.

A generalized concept of airflow in the avian respiratory system has been derived (Bretz and Schmidt-Neilsen 1971, Schmidt-Neilsen 1971, Lasiewski 1972), but airflow probably varies somewhat between species. Upon inhalation, all air sacs are filled and the lungs are emptied. The posterior sacs are filled primarily with ''fresh'' atmospheric air plus dead space air left in the trachea from the previous exhalation. The anterior sacs are filled primarily with air left in the lung from the previous respiratory cycle. Upon exhalation all sacs empty and the lungs are filled. The air in the posterior sacs goes into the lungs primarily, and air in the anterior sacs is exhaled through the trachea. Thus both the lungs and air sacs are thoroughly ventilated. However, the anterior air sacs are ventilated mainly with air that has gone through the lungs.

Anatomical valves to direct this airflow within the air conduits have not been found, but constriction of bronchi (by contraction of smooth muscles in the bronchial wall) and fluid dynamics of airflow are apparently involved.

Burger and Lorenz (1960) reported a system of artificial respiration which takes advantage of the unique features of the avian respiratory system. A hypodermic needle may be inserted between the last two ribs to gain access to the posterior thoracic air sac. The needle is then attached to an air line, and the air (or oxygen) thus perfused through the system escapes orally and provides adequate ventilation to maintain subjects during surgery or acute experiments.

RESPIRATORY RATES AND VOLUMES

Respiratory rates of resting birds vary from about 5 per minute in the ostrich to over 100 in small passerine birds (Calder 1968). Resting tidal volumes vary from a few ml in small birds to 1350 ml in the ostrich (Table 16.1). Metabolic rates during flying have been shown to increase 3–14.5 fold over standard metabolic rates (Farner 1970). Likewise, respiratory rates during flights are 3–18 times greater than at rest, but tidal volumes increase only 0.1–4 fold during flight (Hart and Roy 1966, Berger et al. 1970a).

As for the synchronization of wingbeats with respiration, a recent study of 10 species of birds (Berger et al. 1970b) found that respiration and wingbeat were usually coordinated but that the coordination was not obligatory. A 1:1 coordination (synchrony) existed only in pigeons and crows while 11 other types of coordination were found in the other species (e.g. 5 wingbeats/respiration). They reported that "for the most part, the beginning of inspiration was linked with the (end of) upstroke and the beginning of expiration with the end of downstroke."

TRANSPORT OF BLOOD GASES

Exchange of gases in the bird lung, as in the mammalian lung, results from diffusion and is governed by physical laws. While there are some differences in the manner

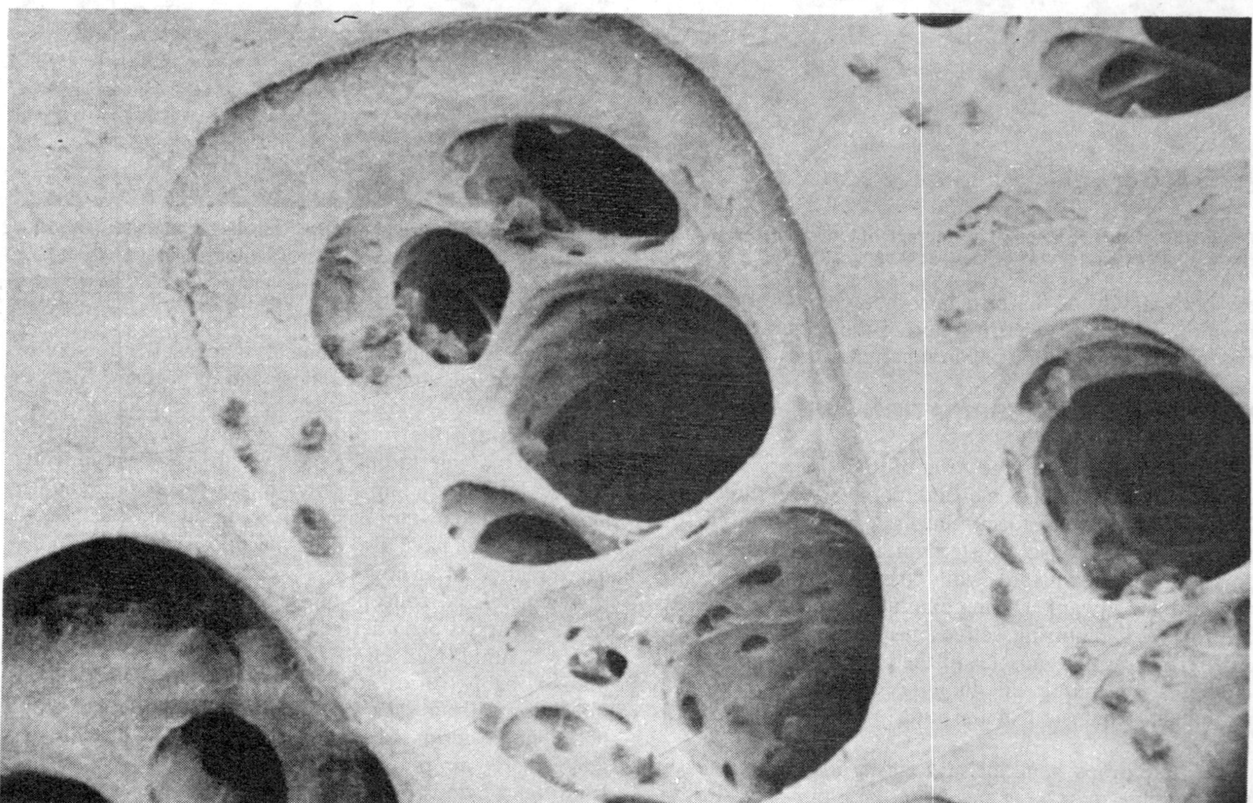

Figure 16.4. Scanning electron micrograph of atria in a depression in a spiral band of bronchial smooth muscle. Air capillaries open off each atrium. ×850. (From J.A. Nowell, J. Pangborn, and W.S. Tyler, in *Scanning Electron Microscopy,* IIT Res. Inst., Chicago, 1970.)

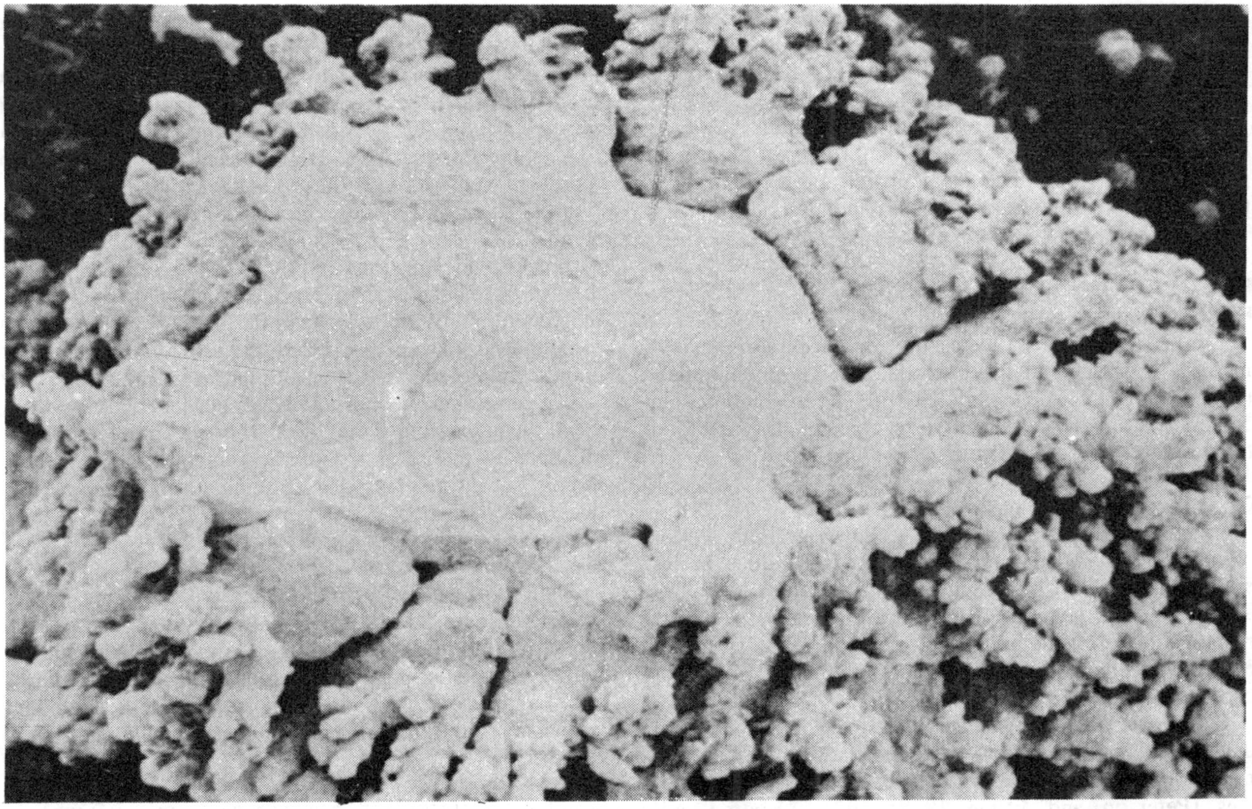

Figure 16.5. Scanning electron micrograph of tertiary bronchus in Japanese quail (transverse section of a latex replica). Atria, with subdivisions, extend perpendicularly off the tertiary bronchus. ×250. (From J.A. Nowell, J. Pangborn, and W.S. Tyler, in *Scanning Electron Microscopy,* IIT Res. Inst., Chicago, 1970.)

in which gases are transported and handled, the differences are not great.

Oxygen dissociation curves have been established for a number of avian species. According to most authors the shape of the curve for avian blood is similar to that of mammals (Fig. 15.15) except that it is to the right of the mammalian curve. However, Lutz et al. (1974) have evidence that avian and mammalian curves occupy similar positions. A position of the avian curve to the right of the curve for mammals would indicate that avian blood is less saturated with oxygen than mammalian blood at the same temperature and tensions for O_2 and CO_2, and that it would release its O_2 to the tissues more readily than mammalian blood, thus providing for greater oxygen utilization. The utilization of oxygen in most birds is high, ranging from 54 percent in the chicken to 60 percent in the duck and the pigeon. The figure for the goose, 26 percent, is much lower and of the same magnitude as mammals.

Oxygen saturation of arterial blood (88–90 percent) and venous blood (40 percent) in the chicken is lower than in mammalian blood (Chiodi and Terman 1965).

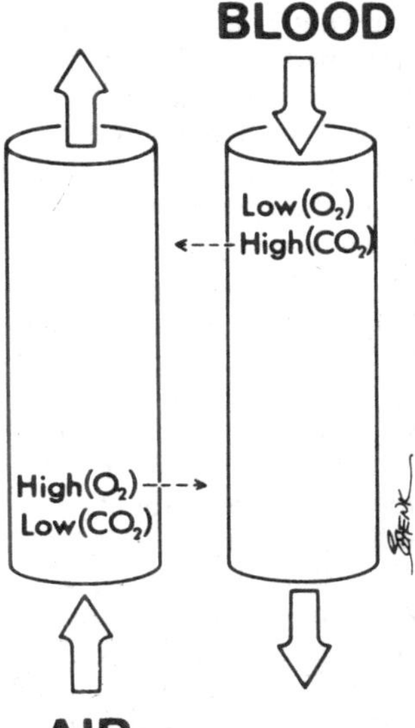

Figure 16.6. Countercurrent flow of blood and air in avian lung capillaries

The Po_2 for arterial blood ranges from 90 to 96 mm Hg for different avian species (Sturkie 1965, Chiodi and Terman 1965). The Pco_2 for fowl blood (28–34 mm Hg) is again lower than for mammals. This lower Pco_2 (and thus higher pH) is facilitated by the more thorough ventilation of the respiratory system of birds, particularly in panting birds, where the Pco_2 is lower and the pH higher than in panting mammals (Calder and Schmidt-Nielsen 1968).

REGULATION OF RESPIRATION

Respiratory center

Limited evidence indicates that the respiratory center in birds is located in the medulla, as it is in mammals (von Saalfeld 1936, Richards 1970). Like the mammalian center it is apparently sensitive to changes in pH, blood temperature, and other factors.

Chemoreceptors

In chickens, increases in CO_2 concentration or decreases in O_2 concentration from normal values in inspired gas result in increased respiratory rate, respiratory amplitude, and heart rate (Ray and Fedde 1969). These responses suggest the existence of chemoreceptors and of a reflex mechanism capable of responding to chemoreceptor stimulation.

Pulmonary receptors sensitive to carbon dioxide are apparently very important in the regulation of avian respiration. These receptors are present in several avian species (Peterson and Fedde 1968, 1971; Osborne and Burger 1971). Most of the receptors (95 percent) are in the caudal parts of the lung; none are in extrapulmonary airways (Fedde et al. 1974). The receptors detect CO_2 levels in lung air, not in the blood flowing through the lung. The afferent pathways from these receptors are in the vagus nerves and the maximal activity of these afferents is associated with the lowest concentrations of carbon dioxide in the lung (Fedde 1970). This is the opposite of the situation with arterial chemoreceptors, which increase their activity in response to high concentrations of carbon dioxide in arterial blood. Activity of these lung chemoreceptor afferents, however, inhibits respiration. Stimulation of these pulmonary chemoreceptors with low levels of carbon dioxide results in an increase in activity from the receptors over vagal fibers, which produces a rapid decrease in respiratory rate. In fact, unidirectional artificial respiration with a CO_2-free gas mixture produces apnea within 0.5 seconds (Peterson and Fedde 1968). Bilateral vagotomy abolishes the rapid response to low carbon dioxide but does not eliminate the sensitivity of chickens to changes in carbon dioxide levels (Peterson and Fedde 1968). Thus other CO_2-sensitive receptors apparently also exist in birds.

Carotid and aortic chemoreceptors have also been described in birds (Fedde 1970). Although physiological studies have been performed on the carotid bodies, the function of the aortic bodies has not been determined. In normal ducks, higher than normal arterial O_2 tensions produced decreased respiratory ventilation and lower than normal arterial O_2 levels caused increased ventilation (Jones and Purvis 1970). High arterial CO_2 tensions also increased ventilation in these ducks. Following denervation of the carotid bodies, the ducks no longer responded to changes in oxygen tensions and the response to high carbon dioxide tensions required 10–15 seconds longer than in intact ducks. It is not clear why pulmonary chemoreceptors did not respond in the latter situation. However, the response does indicate the probable existence of cranial chemoreceptors as are found in mammals.

Bouverot and Leitner (1972) recorded activity from vagal fibers arising from the carotid chemoreceptors in chickens. A constant activity was recorded during normoxia, activity increased in response to hypercapnia and decreased in response to hyperoxia.

Mechanoreceptors

The existence of mammalian-type Hering-Breuer stretch reflexes has not been clearly demonstrated in birds. Inhibition of inspiration following inflation of the pulmonary system has been demonstrated (e.g. Richards 1968) and recordings of vagal afferent activity associated with inspiration and expiration have been obtained (e.g. King et al. 1968, Jones 1969). However, interpretation of these results is complicated by the presence of intrapulmonary CO_2 receptors. Inflation with gas mixtures low in carbon dioxide might produce apnea while inflation with gases high in carbon dioxide might stimulate inspiration.

In a recent study, Leitner (1972) recorded the activity of vagal pulmonary afferent fibers in chickens and found three main types: (1) those which were activated by inflation of the respiratory system, (2) those which were activated by both inflation and deflation, and (3) those which were activated by deflation only. The activity of about half of the first two types of fibers was depressed when the bird was ventilated with a hypercapnic gas mixture, but the third type of fiber was unaffected by increased carbon dioxide tensions. Thus stretch receptors apparently are present in the avian pulmonary system, but, as suggested by Burger (1968), the activity of the stretch receptors (or of at least part of them) may be modulated by carbon dioxide; for example, an increase in carbon dioxide tension in pulmonary air decreases the inhibition that the stretch receptors might otherwise exert on inspiration.

Another type of mechanoreceptor was described by Graham (1940) who reported that outflow of air through the trachea of the chicken inhibited inspiration. He attributed this response to tracheal receptors and believed that the response ensured the completion of expiration once it had begun. However, Eaton et al. (1971) showed that blowing dry air at room temperature or air containing acid vapor through the trachea of chickens slowed respiration. They suggested, therefore, that "receptors in the trachea or upper respiratory tract which respond to such noxious stimuli as dry, room air and acid vapor, can influence respiration" rather than the airflow itself.

REFERENCES

Akester, A.R., 1960. The comparative anatomy of the respiratory pathways in the domestic fowl (*Gallus domesticus*), pigeon (*Columba livia*) and the domestic duck (*Anas platyrhyncha*). *J. Anat.* 94:487–505.

Berger, M., Hart, J.S., and Roy, O.Z. 1970a. Respiration, oxygen consumption, and heart rate in some birds during rest and flight. *Zeitschrift vergl. Physiol.* 66:201–14.

——. 1970b. The co-ordination between respiration and wingbeats in birds. *Zeitschrift vergl. Physiol.* 66:190–200.

Bouverot, P., and Leitner, L.-M. 1972. Arterial chemoreceptors in the domestic fowl. *Resp. Physiol.* 15:310–20.

Bretz, W.L., and Schmidt-Nielsen, K. 1971. Bird respiration: Flow patterns in the duck lung. *J. Exp. Biol.* 54:103–18.

Burger, R.E. 1968. Pulmonary chemosensitivity in the domestic fowl. *Fed. Proc.* 27:328.

Burger, R.E., and Lorenz, F.W. 1960. Artificial respiration in birds by unidirectional air flow. *Poul. Sci.* 39:236–37.

Calder, W.A. 1968. Respiratory and heart rates of birds at rest. *Condor* 70:358–65.

Calder, W.A., and Schmidt-Nielsen, K. 1968. Panting and blood carbon dioxide in birds. *Am. J. Physiol.* 215:477–82.

Chiodi, H., and Terman, J.W. 1965. Arterial blood gases of the domestic hen. *Am. J. Physiol.* 208:798–800.

Crawford, E.C., and Schmidt-Nielsen, K. 1967. Temperature regulation and evaporative cooling in the ostrich. *Am. J. Physiol.* 212:347–53.

Duncker, H.R. 1972. Structure of avian lungs. *Resp. Physiol.* 14:44–63.

Eaton, J.A., Fedde, M.R., and Burger, R.E. 1971. Sensitivity to inflation of the respiratory system in the chicken. *Resp. Physiol.* 11:167–77.

Farner, D.S. 1970. Some glimpses of comparative avian physiology. *Fed. Proc.* 29:1649–63.

Fedde, M.R. 1970. Peripheral control of avian respiration. *Fed. Proc.* 29:1664–73.

Fedde, M.R., Burger, R.E., and Kitchell, R. 1963. Electromyographic studies on certain respiratory muscles of the chicken (abstr.). *Poul. Sci.* 42:1269.

Fedde, M.R., Gatz, R.N., Slama, H., and Scheid, P. 1974. Functional localization of intrapulmonary CO_2 receptors in the duck (abstr.). *Physiologist* 17:220.

Graham, J.D.P. 1940. Respiration reflexes in the fowl. *J. Physiol.* 97:525–32.

Hart, J.S., and Roy, O.Z. 1966. Respiratory and cardiac responses to flight in pigeons. *Physiol. Zool.* 39:291–306.

Jones, D.R. 1969. Avian afferent vagal activity related to respiratory and cardiac cycles. *Comp. Biochem. Physiol.* 28:961–65.

Jones, D.R., and Purves, M.J. 1970. The effect of carotid body denervation upon the respiratory response to hypoxia and hypercapnia in the duck. *J. Physiol.* 211:295–309.

King, A.S. 1966. Structural and functional aspects of the avian lungs and air sacs. *Internat. Rev. Gen. Exp. Zool.* 2:171–267.

King, A.S., and Cowie, A.F. 1969. The functional anatomy of the bronchial muscle of the bird. *J. Anat.* 105:323–36.

King, A.S., Molony, V., McLelland, J., Bowhser, D.R., and Mortimer, M.F. 1968. Afferent respiratory pathways in the avian vagus. *Experientia* 24:1017–18.

Lasiewski, R.C. 1972. Respiratory function in birds. In D.S. Farner and J.R. King, eds., *Avian Biology*. Academic Press, New York. Vol. 2.

Lasiewski, R.C., and Calder, W.A., Jr., 1971. A preliminary allometric analysis of respiratory variables in resting birds. *Resp. Physiol.* 11:152–66.

Leitner, L.-M. 1972. Pulmonary mechanoreceptor fibers in the vagus of the domestic fowl. *Resp. Physiol.* 16:232–44.

Lewis, R.A. 1967. "Resting" heart and respiratory rates of small birds. *Auk* 84:131–32.

Lutz, P.L., Longmuir, I.S., and Schmidt-Nielsen, K. 1974. Oxygen affinity of bird blood. *Resp. Physiol.* 20:325–30.

Osborne, J.L., and Burger, R.F. 1971. Static and dynamic characteristics of CO_2-sensitive chemoreceptors in the avian lung (abstr.). *Fed. Proc.* 14:205.

Peterson, D.F., and Fedde, M.R. 1968. Receptors sensitive to carbon dioxide in lungs of chicken. *Science* 162:1499–1501.

——. 1971. Avian intrapulmonary CO_2-sensitive receptors: A comparative study. *Comp. Biochem. Physiol.*, ser. A, 40:425–30.

Ray, P.J., and Fedde, M.R. 1969. Responses to alterations in respiratory Po_2 and Pco_2 in the chicken. *Resp. Physiol.* 6:135–43.

Richards, S.A. 1968. Vagal control of thermal panting in mammals and birds. *J. Physiol.* 199:89–101.

——. 1970. A pneumotaxic center in avian brain. *J. Physiol.* 207:57–59P.

Saalfeld, F.E. von. 1936. Untersuchungen uber das Hacheln bei Tauben. *Zeitschrift vergl. Physiol.* 23:727–43.

Scheid, P., and Piiper, J. 1970. Analysis of gas exchange in the avian lung: Theory and experiments in the domestic fowl. *Resp. Physiol.* 9:246–62.

Scheid, P., Slama, H., and Piiper, J. 1972. Mechanisms of unidirectional flow in parabronchi of avian lungs: Measurements in duck lung preparations. *Resp. Physiol.* 14:83–95.

Schmidt-Nielsen, K. 1971. How birds breathe. *Scien. Am.* 225:72–79.

Sturkie, P.D. 1965. *Avian Physiology*. 2d ed. Cornell U. Press, Ithaca, N.Y.

PART III DIGESTION, ABSORPTION, AND METABOLISM

CHAPTER 17

Basic Characteristics of the Digestive System | by Charles E. Stevens and Alvin F. Sellers

Veterinary practitioners devote an important percentage of their time to the treatment of diseases involving the digestive system. A large number of infectious diseases have their primary effect on this system, e.g. Johne's disease in cattle, *E. coli* bacillosis in calves, viral gastroenteritis in pigs, feline panleukopenia, and salmonellosis in the dog. Many other infectious diseases have secondary effects. For example, renal damage from canine leptospirosis can result in digestive tract lesions due to excessive excretion of urea. The digestive system of many species also is subject to infestations with parasites—coccidia, nematodes, cestodes, and trematodes—and to invasion by a variety of neoplasms. In addition, it can be damaged by a diet it is not equipped to handle. This could account for many cases of gastric ulcers in swine and calves, enterotoxemia in lambs, equine colic, and bovine bloat, rumen atony, and abomasal displacement.

In recent years improved techniques have been developed for electron microscopy, biopsy, histochemistry, fluorescent antibody staining, electromyographic recording, and in vitro and in vivo studies of absorptive mechanisms. The rapid development of investigative tools has provided information that has significantly changed some concepts of digestive tract function and malfunction and resulted in a greater appreciation of the importance of digestive diseases. The economic loss to this country from digestive diseases of man in 1963 was estimated at $8 billion per annum or 1 percent of the Gross National Product (National Health Education Committee 1971). Although the evidence is not as well documented, there is little question that diseases of the digestive system represent a significant fraction of the economic losses from diseases of domestic animals as well.

BASIC FUNCTIONS

The digestive system includes the digestive tract and its associated glands. The tract itself is essentially a tubular structure for the ingestion and digestion of food. Its ultimate purpose is to provide for the efficient assimilation of nutrients necessary for life while rejecting dietary constituents unnecessary for or potentially harmful to the animal. The attendant salivary, gastric, pancreatic, biliary, and intestinal secretions are usually isotonic to blood and collectively provide mucus for lubrication and protection, enzymes which aid in digestion, and acid or base which helps establish an optimum pH for digestion.

Since the gastrointestinal tract provides the most readily accessible route for substances to enter the body, it carefully selects these substances through a variety of mechanisms, including food selection (palatability), rapid rejection of toxic substances (emesis or increased rate of passage), and gastric digestion of substances before they have access to the more permeable intestinal tract. The final and probably most critical determinant is the selective permeability of the digestive tract's epithelial barrier. The stomach is permeable to a few inorganic ions and to ethanol, water, and organic substances that remain in a lipid-soluble state at a low pH (e.g. very weak bases such as caffeine and weak acids such as aspirin and barbiturates). Even the intestine, which serves as the primary site of absorption, is quite selective. Its cell membranes, or the intercellular junctions and pathways, normally allow passive diffusion of a few substances such as H_2O, Cl^-, NH_3, urea, and CO_2 as well as larger lipid-soluble molecules that may be present. However, these membranes are relatively or entirely impermeable to the passage of most water-soluble substances, even to those minerals, vitamins, monosaccharides, and amino acids required as nutrients. These nutrients are transferred by mechanisms that provide for highly selective active transport across the intestinal mucosa. The mechanisms may be entirely incorporated into the lumen-facing membrane, or they may involve other portions of the cell as well. For example, the final digestion of peptides and disaccharides is carried out by enzymes in both the luminal brush border and the cytoplasm of the intestinal epithelium prior to transport of the resultant monosaccharides or amino acids into the blood.

DIGESTION OF CARBOHYDRATE, FAT, AND PROTEIN

Digestion includes a number of sequential, physicochemical processes which usually begin with the trituration (grinding) of the food into smaller particles. Although this is largely accomplished by the teeth in most vertebrates, in some species the stomach helps. In many birds and some mammals, the stomach is the major site of trituration. The stomach also serves to macerate (soften by soaking) ingesta. In most vertebrates the second step in this digestive process is enzymatic hydrolysis of the ingested material at the low pH of the stomach. The third step is enzymatic digestion in the small intestine at a pH that is relatively neutral (5.5–7.0).

Figure 17.1 outlines the sequential, enzymatic digestion of carbohydrate, fat, and protein in the stomach and small intestine.

Carbohydrates are attacked by a number of amylases, one of which is present in the saliva of some species, e.g. man and pig. In the stomach, HCl also may aid in the hydrolysis of polysaccharides. However, most of the hydrolysis is due to pancreatic and intestinal amylase. In mammals, pancreatic amylase is the more important of these two. Disaccharides (maltose, isomaltose, sucrose, and lactose) are digested by their respective disaccharidases. This is believed to take place primarily at the brush border of the intact mucosal cell.

Fat must be emulsified to provide sufficient surface area for efficient digestion of triglycerides, the principal components of dietary fat, by water-soluble lipase. Emulsification is initiated by bile salts, which act as anionic detergents. These are secreted by the liver, forming micelles into which cholesterol and phospholipids become incorporated. This incorporation lowers the osmotic activity of these substances in the bile and may allow a greater concentration of bile especially in animals that have a gallbladder. Bile salts also serve to keep the cholesterol in solution, that is, a decrease in the bile salt–cholesterol ratio can result in the formation of gallstones.

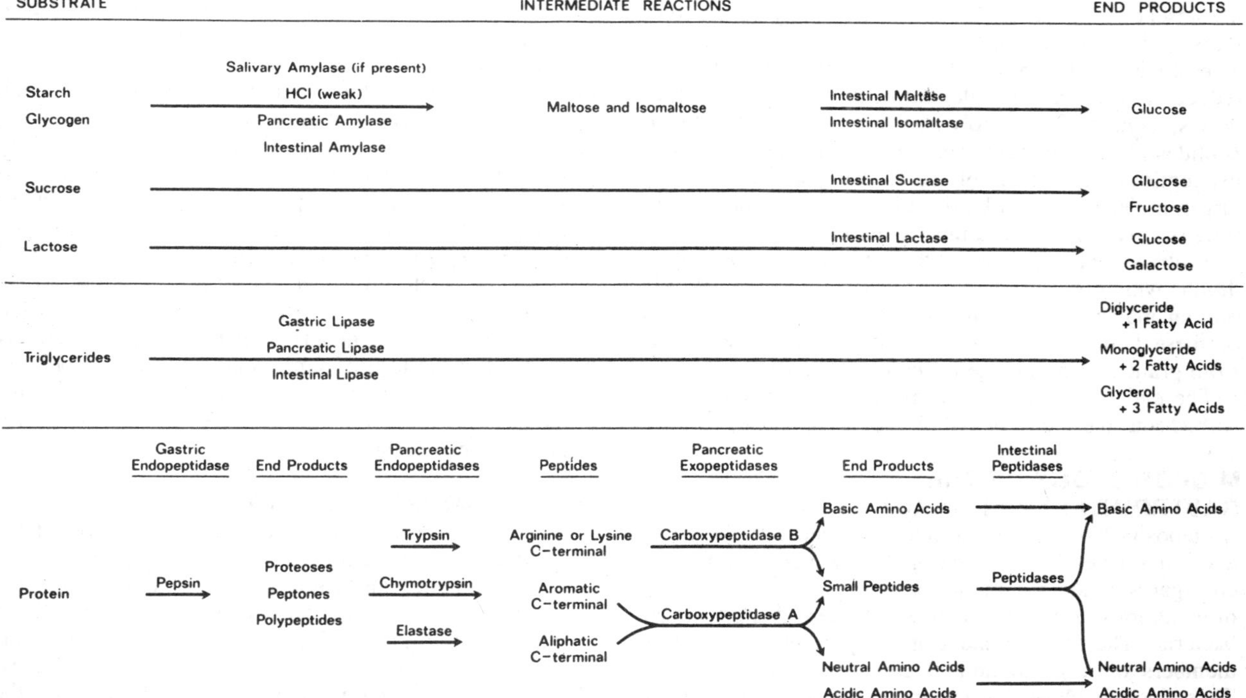

Figure 17.1. Enzymatic digestion of carbohydrate, fat, and protein under optimal conditions. The protein sequence is simplified; pepsin can produce relatively small polypeptides, pancreatic endopeptidases can digest protein, and carboxypeptidases can attack relatively large peptide chains. Therefore, loss of any one of these enzymes does not prevent protein digestion. Diagram does not include all pancreatic enzymes or intestinal oligosaccharides.

Within the intestine, these micelles incorporate the free fatty acid and glycerides which result from triglyceride hydrolysis by lipase. They also incorporate fat-soluble vitamins (A, D, E, and K). Enzymatic digestion of triglycerides is carried out by gastric, intestinal, and pancreatic lipase. Of these, pancreatic lipase is the most important. Thus diseases affecting the pancreas can result in fat malabsorption. Bile salts are normally reabsorbed by the lower small intestine and are recycled. Bacterial overgrowth in the small intestine can result in deconjugation of free bile acids, which decreases their ability to keep lipolytic products in micellar solution. Conditions which encourage this, e.g. blind-loop syndrome, can also result in malabsorption of fat.

Gastric and pancreatic enzymes involved in protein digestion are stored and secreted in an inactive form, in order to protect secretory cells from autodigestion. A number of pepsinogens have been described which differ in their site of origin and the optimal pH at which they are activated and act (Samloff 1969). However, the most important are believed to be secreted by the proper gastric (oxyntic glandular) mucosa and require a low pH for activation and activity. Trypsinogen is activated by enterokinase, an enzyme secreted by the intestinal mucosa. Trypsin then activates the remaining pancreatic proenzymes. Thus while protein digestion can be carried out in the absence of pepsinogen, e.g. following total gastrectomy, it is seriously impaired in cases of trypsinogen or enterokinase deficiency. The pancreatic endopeptidases reduce the protein molecule and its large fragments (proteoses, peptones, and polypeptides) to peptides. Small peptides and amino acids are then released by pancreatic exopeptidase hydrolysis of the C-terminal ends of these larger molecules. Small (di-, tri-, and quaternary) peptides are hydrolyzed to amino acids by the brush border and intracellular enzymes of the intestinal mucosa. Conditions which result in damage to these cells can result in protein malabsorption. Nontropical sprue in man is one of these conditions. It is believed to result specifically from grain gluten damage to the brush border.

The end products of these digestive processes are absorbed into the blood or lymph (see Chapter 26).

MICROBIOLOGY OF THE GASTROINTESTINAL TRACT

Dubos (1966) divides the flora indigenous to the gut of a given species into two categories. Autochthonous microorganisms are symbionts present under a wide range of conditions, e.g. lactobacilli and bacteroid and fusiform bacteria. The other broad class is present in nearly all members of a given animal colony but less constant. These include clostridia, enterococci, and enterobacteria. The type and number of microorganisms present in the digestive tract after weaning are affected by a number of conditions, including diet. Microbial populations may be little affected by marked changes in diet, however, if the change is not too rapid. This is especially true of those indigenous to the large intestine, which are protected by compensatory secretions and by digestion and absorption in the upper digestive tract. In fact, the normal balance of gastrointestinal microorganisms can be affected more by starvation or overfeeding than by the composition of the diet. Gut microorganisms are also affected by pH changes and the administration of antibiotics or other antimicrobial drugs.

Gastrointestinal microorganisms are capable of reduction, dehydration, ring fusion, and aromatization of a wide range of compounds. They can digest mucus, bilirubin, gastrointestinal enzymes, urea, protein, and other nitrogenous compounds, plus a wide range of drugs. They can produce organic acids, CO_2, H_2, and NH_3, as well as toxic amines and phenols. Studies of gnotobiotic (germ-free) animals show that the microflora normally present protect the gut from disease both by stimulation of immune mechanisms and by direct competition with pathogenic organisms. They are also capable of converting plant material of little direct nutritional value into readily usable nutrients.

In many vertebrates, digestion is aided by microbes indigenous to the foregut and hindgut. This occurs in the stomach of quite a wide range of mammals, and in the large intestine of an even wider range of species. It provides a means of digesting soluble as well as otherwise insoluble carbohydrate, e.g. cellulose and hemicellulose, into organic acids which can be readily absorbed and utilized as a source of energy. The microorganisms are also capable of synthesizing B vitamins and high-quality protein (in their own cell bodies) from nonprotein nitrogenous sources (see Chapters 22 and 23). An understanding of the conditions required for microbial digestion helps explain many of the structural and functional adaptations which have developed in the gastrointestinal tract of vertebrates. The primary requirements are anaerobic conditions, a means of maintaining a relatively neutral pH in the face of substantial organic acid production, and, since microbial digestion is a relatively slow process, provision for more prolonged contact of microorganisms and digesta.

NEUROHUMORAL CONTROL

The visceral efferent or autonomic innervation of the mammalian gastrointestinal tract is either parasympathetic or sympathetic. The parasympathetic division is often referred to as the craniosacral system, due to the origin of its preganglionic fibers. Cranial parasympathetic neurons provide innervation via the vagus nerve to the esophagus, stomach, small intestine, and proximal portion of the large intestine. The sacral segment of the spinal cord provides parasympathetic innervation to the distal portion of the colon, the rectum, and the internal anal sphincter.

This system is also referred to as cholinergic, due to the fact that acetylcholine is released at the terminals of its postganglionic fibers. Acetylcholine is generally considered to be stimulatory to motor (muscular) and secretory activity. Postganglionic neurons are located in plexuses situated in the submucosa, between the muscular layers, and in the subepithelial tissue of the tract. The preganglionic neurons of the sympathetic system originate in the thoracolumbar segments of the spinal cord. Its postganglionic neurons originate in ganglia outside of the viscera and supply the entire digestive tract. These are called adrenergic neurons since they release norepinephrine, which inhibits secretion and motility.

A third type of neuron, which is nonadrenergic and inhibitory, has more recently been described. The neurotransmitter it releases may be adenosine triphosphate (Satchell et al. 1969), and it may be responsible for some inhibitory reflexes, e.g. receptive relaxation of gastric muscle during swallowing.

Humoral control of gastrointestinal motility and secretion involves a relatively large number of hormones. Those generally listed are gastrin, secretin, cholecystokinin-pancreozymin (CCK-PZ), glucagon, enterogastrone, enterocrinin, and villikinin. Each of these is believed to be secreted by small intestinal mucosa, although the stomach is the primary site of gastrin secretion, and the pancreas (α-cells of the islets of Langerhans) is the primary site of glucagon secretion. This proclivity for hormone secretion led Nasset to label the duodenum as the pituitary gland of the digestive system.

New techniques, such as the fluorescent antibody procedure (which allows the localization of hormones) and sequential amino-acid analysis (which allows characterization of these hormones), have provided much new information on their sites of origin and activity. For example, secretin, originally believed to elicit only the flow of alkaline pancreatic juice, is now known to be (1) a polypeptide which consists of 27 amino acids, (2) chemically homologous to glucagon, (3) structurally similar to growth hormone, and (4) possibly capable of other activities, e.g. inhibition of gastric secretion. CCK-PZ, once believed to be two separate hormones which stimulated the secretion of pancreatic enzymes and contraction of the gallbladder respectively, is a polypeptide containing 33 amino acids with a C-terminal pentopeptide identical to gastrin. In addition it appears to stimulate the synthesis as well as the secretion of pancreatic enzymes; it also stimulates muscular contraction of the gallbladder. CCK-PZ has also been shown to delay gastric emptying. Gastrin, long known to be secreted by the stomach and to be stimulatory to gastric-HC1 and pepsinogen secretion, is also secreted by the upper small intestine and the pancreas. The latter discovery resulted from studies demonstrating that the Zollinger-Ellison syndrome in man is caused by the development of pancreatic, gastrin-producing neoplasms. An important action of gastrin is its tropic effect on the mucosae of the stomach and intestine (see Chapter 20). Gastrin can also increase the tonus of the cardiac sphincter, decrease the tonus of the ileocecal valve, and stimulate contraction of large-intestine muscle. However, the physiological significance of these results has been questioned by Walsh and Grossman (1975).

Previously, enterogastrone was believed to serve primarily as an inhibitor of gastric secretion and motility. These activities may now be accountable to secretin and CCK-PZ respectively. Villikinin is said to stimulate the motility of intestinal villi and aid in the transport of lymphatic fluid into the lymphatic ducts. Enterocrinin is believed to be the hormone that stimulates intestinal secretion. However, there is still considerable uncertainty over these and speculation over the presence of a number of newly discovered hormones (see Chapter 20). Grossman et al. (1974) provide a recent review of digestive system hormones.

Glucagon stimulates insulin secretion as well as glycogenolysis. Its recent experimental isolation from the wall of the duodenum may explain how the body provides an anticipatory redistribution of glucose prior to its actual absorption from the intestine into the blood.

ONTOGENIC DEVELOPMENT

The digestive system of all mammals shares one characteristic. At birth it receives a diet of milk, which tends to be relatively high in fat and low in carbohydrate. Upon weaning, this changes to one generally low in fat and high in carbohydrate. Hence changes in the digestive tract of mammals may be expected both at birth and weaning (Koldovský 1970).

The length and size of the digestive tract increase during prenatal development. Musculature develops in a craniocaudal sequence, circular muscle first. In species with complex stomachs, such as ruminants, compartmentalization may be evident quite early in gestation (Bryden et al. 1972). The large intestine tends to develop later. It initially terminates together with the renal system in a cloaca like that of lower terrestrial vertebrates. Outlets for the renal and digestive systems eventually separate, prior to birth in most mammalian species. Lymphatic tissue, e.g. Peyer's patches, also appears along the intestine well before birth.

Although the glandular tissue of the gastrointestinal tract appears fully developed at birth, the time of functional secretory activity varies with species. For example, gastric secretion of HC1 is well developed in the guinea pig prior to birth, so that the gastric contents of the newborn demonstrate a pH of 1–2. In man, the gastric pits and chief cells are well developed in the fetus, but gastric contents are usually neutral at birth, decreasing in pH rapidly the first day; the pH of rat stomach contents remains high (5–6.5) for a few days after birth. This species variation may help explain the variation in immunoglobulin absorption discussed below.

Both pancreatic and intestinal proteases increase in activity during gestation. Further increases are noted during the suckling period, for example, trypsin activity increases in human infants and calves the first week after birth, in pigs the first 5 weeks, and in rats (most rapidly) between the fourth and sixth week. Pancreatic amylase is evident in the prenatal human, horse, cow, and sheep. It increases postnatally, but most rapidly after weaning. Intestinal disaccharidase activity follows a somewhat similar pattern. Sucrase is present in the mucosa of the large as well as the small intestine of the 8-week human fetus. The milk of most mammals contains lactose as its major carbohydrate; at birth the activity of β-glucosidases, e.g. maltase, sucrase, and isomaltase, is low or absent while lactase and cellobiase activity is high. After weaning, β-glucosidase activity increases, and lactase and cellobiase activities decrease. Glycerol-ester specific lipase has been reported in the human fetus by the third month of gestation. Although nonspecific lipases are found in the intestinal epithelial cells and lumen of many species early in gestation, they are present in most body cells, and their importance to digestive tract function is highly questionable. Glycerol-ester specific lipase and the brush border disaccharidases are presumably most important to the digestion of fat and disaccharides.

Absorption of intact protein by the neonate represents one means for antibody transfer. Intact protein can be absorbed from the intestine during the first 24–36 hours after the birth of pigs, goats, sheep, cattle, and horses. It may be absorbed for a longer period by dogs and cats, up to 3 weeks after birth by mice and rats, up to 6 weeks by the hedgehog, and up to 27 weeks by the wallaby. Although intact protein absorption was observed prior to the birth of guinea pigs (Leissring and Anderson 1961), it was not noted after birth (Brambell 1970). Table 17.1 demonstrates the inverse relationship between a given

Table 17.1. Transmission of passive immunity *

Species	Prenatal	Postnatal
Horse	0	+++ (24 hr)
Pig	0	+++ (24–36 hr)
Ox, goat, sheep	0	+++ (24 hr)
Wallaby (*Setonix*)	0	+++ (180 d)
Dog, cat	+	++ (1–2 d)
Fowl	++	++ (<5 d)
Hedgehog	+	++ (40 d)
Mouse	+	++ (16 d)
Rat	+	++ (20 d)
Guinea pig	+++	0
Rabbit	+++	0
Man, monkey	+++	0

* 0, no absorption or transfer; + to +++, degrees of absorption or transfer. (From Brambell, *The Transmission of Passive Immunity from Mother to Young*, American Elsevier, New York, 1970.)

species' ability to transfer passive immunity (immunoglobulins) via the placenta and via intestinal absorption. Although the process of intestinal protein transport is still poorly understood, it does appear to be a specific, active mechanism. However, as Koldovský points out, this capability for transfer of immunity from dam to progeny also depends upon whether the immunoglobulin survives previous digestion. Animals that have a highly operative gastric secretion of HC1 and pepsinogen at or shortly after birth tend to digest these proteins in the stomach. In man, gastric pH has been shown to decrease within 20 minutes after birth. This explains, for example, the ineffectiveness of orally administered insulin beyond this time and supports the conclusion of many investigators that intestinal transfer of immunoglobulins is of little or no significance in human infants.

Smith and Crabb (1961) found similar microflora in the feces of nursing calves, lambs, pigs, rabbits, and human infants. Colonization of the digestive tract with bacteria begins shortly after birth. Schaedler et al. (1965) found *E. coli, Clostridium welchii*, and species of streptococci in the digestive tract of mice a few hours after birth. Lactobacilli and anaerobic streptococci became established in the nonglandular portion of the stomach in a few additional hours, and within 48 hours were found along the entire digestive tract. Their numbers continued to increase during the first few weeks of life. During the second week, the large intestine became colonized with *Bacteroides*, fusiform and spiral-shaped organisms; coliforms and enterococci were found along the entire gastrointestinal tract. As time progressed, lactobacilli became primarily confined to the lining of the gastric mucosa and anaerobes to the lining of the mucosa of the large intestine.

A stable microflora develops in the colon and feces of breast-fed infants within 3–4 days of birth. It consists primarily of *Lactobacillus bifidus*, with lesser numbers of coliforms, enterococci, and aerobic lactobacilli (Haenel 1970). The feces of bottle-fed infants also includes *L. acidophilus* and a number of nonsporulating anaerobes (Donaldson 1964). However, the stomach and small intestine of these infants were relatively sterile, except for the presence of some large-intestine organisms in the terminal ileum.

Following weaning, the gut microflora of mammals shows marked, species-specific changes due to the change in diet and changes in the gastrointestinal contents. For example, in contrast to breast-fed infants, the feces of children and adults demonstrate a higher pH, lower redox potential, and larger numbers (200–300 billion/g) of bacteria. The majority of the bacteria in the gastrointestinal tract of most species reside in the large intestine. However, an indigenous colony of gram-negative rods and cocci has been reported on villi of the rat ileum (Savage 1969).

REFERENCES

Brambell, F.W.R. 1970. *The Transmission of Passive Immunity from Mother to Young*. American Elsevier, New York.

Bryden, M.M., Evans, H.E., and Binns, W. 1972. Embryology of the sheep. II. The alimentary tract and associated glands. *J. Morph.* 138:187–206.

Donaldson, R.M. 1964. Normal bacterial populations of the intestine and their relation to intestinal function. *New Eng. J. Med.* 270:938–45, 994–1001, 1050–56.

Dubos, R. 1966. The microbiota of the gastrointestinal tract. *Gastroenterology* 51:868–74.

Gillette, D.D., and Filkins, M. 1966. Factors affecting antibody transfer in the newborn puppy. *Am. J. Physiol.* 210:419–22.

Grossman, M.I., and others. 1974. Candidate hormones of the gut. *Gastroenterology* 67:730–55.

Haenel, H. 1970. Human normal and abnormal gastrointestinal flora. *Am. J. Clin. Nutr.* 23:1433–39.

Koldovský, O. 1970. Digestion and absorption during development. In U. Stave, ed., *Physiology of the Perinatal Period*. Appleton-Century-Crofts, New York. Vol. 1, 379–415.

Leissring, J.C., and Anderson, J.W. 1961. The transfer of serum proteins from mother to young in the guinea pig. I. Prenatal rates and routes. *Am. J. Anat.* 109:149–55.

National Health Education Committee, comp. 1971. What are the facts about digestive diseases? In *Facts on the Major Killing and Crippling Diseases in the United States*. National Health Education Committee, New York.

Samloff, M. 1969. Slow moving protease and the seven pepsinogens. *Gastroenterology* 57:659–69.

Satchell, D.G., Burnstock, G., and Campbell, G.D. 1969. Evidence for a purine compound as of the transmitter in non-adrenergic inhibitory neurones in the gut (abstr.). *Austral. J. Exp. Biol. Med. Sci.* 47:P24.

Savage, D.C. 1969. Localization of certain indigenous microorganisms on the ileal villi of rats. *J. Bact.* 97:1505–6.

Schaedler, R.W., Dubos, R., and Costello, R. 1965. The development of the bacterial flora in the gastrointestinal tract of mice. *J. Exp. Med.* 122:59–66.

Smith, H.W., and Crabb, W.E. 1961. The faecal bacterial flora of animals and man: Its development in the young. *J. Path. Bact.* 82:53–66.

Walsh, J.H., and Grossman, M.I. 1975. Gastrin (first of two parts). *New Eng. J. Med.* 292:1324–34.

CHAPTER 18

Comparative Physiology of the Digestive System | by Charles E. Stevens

Knowledge of comparative physiology is a necessity for the veterinarian, who has always had responsibility for a wide range of companion and food-producing animals. Increasingly, there is a need for individuals trained in areas such as laboratory, zoo, and aquatic animal medicine, and the need for alternative sources of animal protein for human consumption will undoubtedly result in an even greater variety of species which require treatment. The reader should be reminded, however, that simplified overviews are always suspect, since conclusions are often based on limited information; that simplicity in a biological system does not necessarily imply that it is primitive; and that similarities in structure or function between two species may result from either inheritance or convergence on an efficient system.

COMPARATIVE ANATOMY AND PHYSIOLOGY

Invertebrates

Many structural and functional characteristics of the vertebrate digestive tract are also seen among invertebrates. Various species of protozoa demonstrate (1) a provision for prolonged contact between food and digestive system by the slow, tortuous passage of vacuoles through the organism, (2) absorption by both cellular membrane transport and pinocytosis, (3) a process of acid followed by alkaline hydrolysis in the vacuoles, with at least the latter aided by digestive enzymes, and (4) intracellular digestion by many of the enzymes previously noted in the vertebrate digestive system. Extracellular (intraluminal) enzymatic digestion occurs in the digestive tract of primitive metazoan species, where a wide range of functions still may be performed by the same cell type. These include secretion of mucus and enzymes, absorption, food storage, detoxification, and rapid regeneration of digestive-tract epithelia. In more advanced invertebrates, these functions become the property of special cells, which are aggregated into tissues and organs. For example, salivary glands are highly developed in many invertebrate species; the octopus and squid have a distinct pancreas and liver; the digestive tracts of the earthworm and of many insects demonstrate a relatively complex autonomic nervous system; insects have intestinal cells with a brush border and, in some species, the capacity for rapid intestinal epithelial-cell turnover.

Another relatively widespread characteristic of the invertebrate digestive system is the importance of symbiont microorganisms. Symbiont algae, bacteria, fungi, and protozoa can be critical to the growth or even the survival of the host. Buchner (1965) reviewed the widespread distribution of endosymbiosis. He described the inclusion of algae in the cytoplasm of *Paramecium bursa* which, with sufficient light, can supply nutrients and oxygen in quantities sufficient for survival of the protozoa in the absence of other food supplies. Algae also are present in cells lining the digestive tract of a wide range of metazoan invertebrates. They provide their host with oxygen and carbohydrate, a site for food storage, and mechanisms for utilizing excess carbon dioxide, phosphate, and nitrogenous wastes. Bacteria are normally present within some protozoa and within the intestinal cells of many other invertebrates. They can fix nitrogen, synthesize vitamins, and digest cellulose.

The location of symbionts within the invertebrate digestive tract varies. They are usually found either in the cells, in the contents of intestinal ceca, or in an enlarged segment of hindgut. Their presence in the intestinal cells of insects may provide for their continuity during periods of molt. The hindgut of some insects, e.g. cockroach and termite, contains bacteria and protozoa which very efficiently digest insoluble carbohydrate (cellulose, hemicellulose, pectin, etc.). In many invertebrates, symbionts that aid digestion are transmitted to the following generation by inclusion within the gamete, or by application to the egg shell. The newborn of some invertebrates (e.g. the ditch bug) appear to acquire their gut bacterial flora by ingestion of maternal feces.

Nonmammalian vertebrates

Fish show considerable variation in digestive-tract structure, including the absence (as in cyclostomes) or presence of movable jaws, and the absence of a stomach in primitive or even highly advanced species. Species that possess a stomach demonstrate gastric secretion of HCl and pepsinogen. Organization of pancreatic tissue varies from dispersal along the gut to isolation as a distinct organ. The digestive system of fish is regulated by both a visceral efferent nervous system and by digestive hormones. Bayliss and Starling (1903), in their early studies of secretin, demonstrated its presence in the dogfish, skate, and salmon. In fact, humoral control of the digestive system is quite highly developed in fish. Development of lymphatic tissue along the gut appears first among invertebrates as a protective mechanism. However, in fish there appears to be a lymphatic system capable of producing both a cellular immune response (Finstad et al. 1964) and antibodies (Hildemann and Thoenes 1969).

As for amphibians, their ontogeny includes changes in the digestive system from that of an aquatic, microphagous, and often herbivorous animal to that of a terrestrial, macrophagous carnivore. One of these changes is the development of an enlarged hindgut (large intestine). In some species it is separated from the upper intestine by a sphincter or valve. The hindgut terminates in a cloaca, a common site for excretion of urine and digesta.

Reptiles and birds demonstrate additional developments in the vertebrate digestive system. The reptilian digestive tract, which has received relatively little study, appears to represent the earliest use, by terrestrial vertebrates, of the large intestine as a major site for electrolyte and water absorption and for microbial digestion. The former is indicated by the ability of many reptilian species to survive in the desert. The capability for microbial digestion can be presumed in the now-extinct, herbivorous dinosaurs (e.g. *Brontosaurus,* estimated to have weighed 50 tons), and is still evident in a number of species of herbivorous lizards and turtles. Special characteristics of the bird digestive tract (see Chapter 25) are (1) division of the stomach's storage, secretory, and triturative functions into three distinct compartments (crop, proventriculus, and gizzard), (2) further development of the immunogenic system in the cloacal bursa of Fabricius, and (3) development of paired ceca in the large intestine of most species.

Figure 18.1 is a simplified diagram of the intestinal tract of the fish, amphibian, reptile, bird, and mammal. Most species of fish appear to have no distinct hindgut or large intestine. A short segment of the terminal intestine in some fish, e.g. the scup, *Stenotomus chrysops,* is lined with an epithelium which differs in both morphological and absorptive characteristics from more oral portions (Strauss and Ito 1969). However, the valvular separation, enlarged diameter, and presence of a cecal compartment—characteristics of the hindgut of most higher vertebrates—are absent from the fish intestine. As in the adult amphibian, the hindgut of reptiles and birds is distinctly enlarged, terminating in a cloaca which provides a common reservoir for both digesta and urine. Although the cloaca persists in the monotreme and a few other mammalian species (e.g. the mountain beaver *Aplodontia rufa*), in most mammals the digestive and urinary sys-

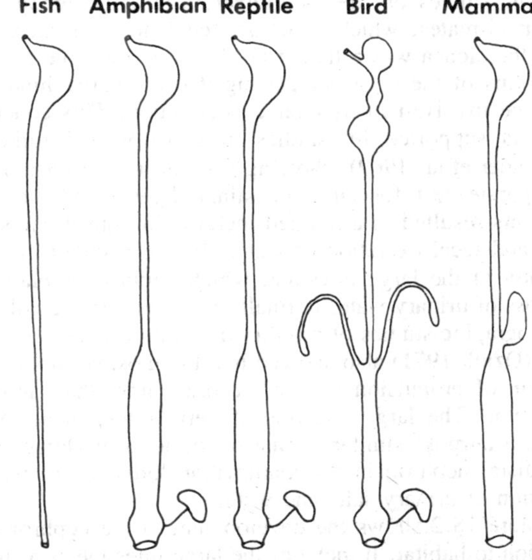

Figure 18.1. General characteristics of the vertebrate gastrointestinal tract. In fish the stomach is usually present and the tract shows no external characteristics indicative of a large intestine. Urine is usually excreted via a separate orifice. In the adult amphibian there is a distinct enlargement of the hindgut into a large intestine which terminates in a cloaca. The gastrointestinal tract of reptiles is similar to that of the amphibian, except that the most proximal segment of the large intestine may be dilated. The large intestine of most avian species contains paired ceca, although some species have only a single cecum and others none. The avian large intestine also terminates in a cloaca. With a few exceptions, mammals have a distinct large intestine, and digesta and urine are excreted separately.

tems are provided with separate exits. The intestine of some Cetacea, e.g. the porpoise, is similar to that of fish, with no distinct hindgut. This is believed to be a degenerative rather than a primitive characteristic. A large intestine and cecum are found in many aquatic carnivores (seal, walrus) and herbivores (manatee, dugong).

Thus the appearance of the hindgut in terrestrial insects and vertebrates was probably associated with the need to conserve electrolytes and water. It allowed retrieval of inorganic ions and water of dietary origin and, perhaps more important, retrieval of the large quantities of fluid secreted into the upper gastrointestinal tract (see Chapter 21). It also provided a means of retrieving electrolytes and water excreted by the urinary system. The mesonephrons of terrestrial insects terminate at or near the beginning of the hindgut, and the hindgut serves as the site for concentration of the dilute urine. The kidneys of amphibians, reptiles, and many birds are also limited in their ability to concentrate urine when compared to most terrestrial mammals. Minnich (1970) concluded that the desert iguana reabsorbs most of its urinary sodium and water prior to excretion, and suggested the cloaca as the site of absorption. However, Junqueira et al. (1966) concluded that in the snake, the colon also absorbs urinary ions and water. Ohmart et al. (1970) performed urographic studies on the roadrunner, a bird indigenous to desert climates, which demonstrated that urine excreted into the cloaca was refluxed up the large intestine to the very tips of the ceca, suggesting that the entire hindgut may be involved in its final concentration. This conclusion is supported by studies of colostomized turkeys (Scheiber et al. 1969), showing that surgical provision of a separate exit for large intestinal digesta and cloacal contents resulted in a marked increase in both the ingestion and fecal excretion of water. It also resulted in impaction of the large intestine, which could be explained by loss of urinary water normally refluxed into the colon. Radiographic studies of motility in the turkey large intestine (Dziuk 1971) also showed that the most common direction of propulsion was in the oral rather than aboral direction. The large intestine of vertebrates, then, may serve a purpose similar to that of the loop of Henle and the distal nephron in the mammalian kidney, i.e. reabsorption of urinary salts and water.

Figure 18.2 shows the development of the nephron in relation to habitat. It includes the large intestine as a subsidiary component of the reptile nephron, providing a supplementary mechanism for conservation of water. Fish handle the problem of water conservation by other means, and in most mammals urinary excretion of water is controlled by the countercurrent, concentrating mechanism of the kidney. The valvular separation from the small intestine, development of ceca, antiperistaltic motor activity, and absorptive capabilities of the large intestine all subserve this function. These characteristics

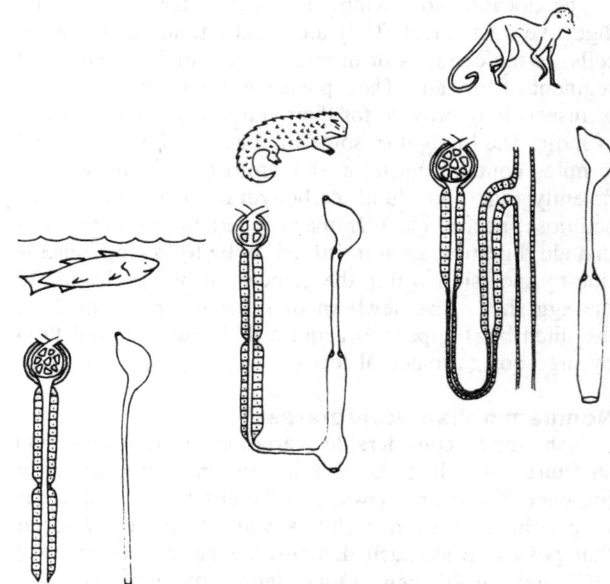

Figure 18.2. Development of the nephron and hindgut in relation to habitat. The nephron of the fish kidney is unable to concentrate urine. The nephron of terrestrial reptiles is also limited in its ability to conserve water. This function may be aided partly by salt glands, and through recovery of urinary electrolytes and water by the large intestine. A few terrestrial mammals have retained the cloaca. These species usually live in or near water. However, the majority of the terrestrial mammals excrete their digesta and urine via separate orifices. Conservation of urinary water is largely accomplished by the development of the loop of Henle and countercurrent multiplier system in the nephron. (Modified from Smith, *Lectures on the Kidney*, U. of Kansas Press, Lawrence, 1943.)

have been preserved in the mammalian large intestine, which conserves large amounts of electrolytes and water of both secretory and dietary origin.

Anatomical and functional characteristics, which prolong retention of large-intestine contents and allow for more efficient absorption of electrolytes and water, also provide one of the conditions necessary for microbial digestion. The significance of microbial digestion in reptiles and birds is uncertain, but Barnes (1972) concluded that the bacteria indigenous to the ceca of domestic fowl recycle urinary nitrogen by converting uric acid into more readily absorbed ammonia, and McBee and West (1969) concluded that approximately 30 percent of the basal energy requirement of the Willow Ptarmigan is supplied via microbial digestion in its voluminous ceca. Microbial digestion is one of the primary functions of the large intestine in many mammals.

As for neuroregulation, Burnstock (1969) pointed out that vagal innervation of the fish gastrointestinal-tract musculature extends only as far as the stomach and is entirely nonadrenergic and inhibitory. There is no sacral parasympathetic system and little or no hindgut for it to innervate. The sympathetic (thoracolumbar) innervation of the fish gastrointestinal tract is cholinergic, that is, opposite to that of the mammal. In the adult amphibian, the vagus nerve remains noncholinergic and inhibitory, but there is the additional appearance of a sacral parasympathetic nerve supply to the hindgut. Sympathetic innervation of the amphibian gut includes a mixture of both cholinergic excitatory and adrenergic inhibitory fibers. In reptiles, one finally sees the complete exchange of cholinergic excitatory function from the sympathetic to the parasympathetic outflow, the arrangement present in the mammal. Nonadrenergic inhibitory neurons have been described in the nerve supply to both the stomach and large intestine of mammals. The reasons for these changes are unknown, although parallel changes in the respiratory system have been suggested as one cause.

In addition to the above differences in the autonomic nervous system, the circulating catecholamines (epinephrine, norepinephrine, and dopamine), which also affect secretion and motility of the digestive system, are released by diffusely distributed chromaffin cells in lower vertebrates. However, the release of catecholamines comes under more direct nervous control in higher vertebrates via the adrenal glands. These major differences in the autonomic nervous system among vertebrates explain much of the confusion that has resulted from attempts to equate the mammalian system with that of lower vertebrates.

Mammals

Ingestion, mastication, and deglutition

Many of the structural and functional variations in the digestive tract of mammals are clearly related to diet and feeding habits. This is especially true of those associated with prehension and mastication of food. An animal may obtain its food by use of a prehensile forelimb (primate, raccoon), snout (elephant, tapir), tongue (anteater, ox), or lips (horse, sheep). Highly developed prehensile organs allow a more careful selection of food. The dental arrangement also can be related to diet, and varies from that of the relatively toothless edentates to the presence of large incisors, canines, and molars in carnivores and the even more highly specialized molars of herbivores.

The act of deglutition (see Chapter 20) shows little variation with diet. The effort required by the killer whale to ingest and swallow its prey is of course different from that required by microphagous whales, which strain their food prior to deglutition. Most carnivores swallow large pieces of prey; ruminants masticate fibrous material poorly during its initial ingestion; while many omnivores and herbivores tend to carefully masticate their food prior to deglutition. The esophagus varies in the extent to which its musculature is striated rather than smooth and in the effectiveness of the gastroesophageal junction in preventing reflux of gastric contents. (The importance of the latter to emesis, and the special case of rumination, will be discussed in later chapters.) These differences in esophageal musculature appear unrelated to diet.

The salivary glands, which secrete mucus as an aid to swallowing, seem most appropriately discussed in context with deglutition. Junqueira and de Moraes (1965) provide a comparative review of the vertebrate salivary gland. Only among mammals and various invertebrates do they often serve many additional purposes. In addition to mucus, the secretions of these glands contain components which aid anteaters in their capture of prey and vampire bats in preventing coagulation of ingested blood. In the dog and cat, evaporation of salivary water is an important aid in the loss of body heat. The saliva of a number of species contains digestive enzymes, e.g. amylase and various proteases. Secretions of bicarbonate and phosphate ions by the parotid salivary glands of many herbivorous species provide buffers to help neutralize organic acid produced in the stomach (for the ruminant parotid salivary gland see Chapter 22). Relatively large parotid salivary glands are present in many herbivorous mammals. For example, while many aquatic mammals such as the carnivorous seal have only vestigial salivary glands, these are well developed in the herbivorous manatee.

Major structural variations in the gastrointestinal tract

Tables 18.1 and 18.2 list some species variations in the dimensions and capacity of various segments of the gastrointestinal tract. Since these data were obtained at the postmortem examination the values for capacity are questionable; a considerable exchange of water can occur between body fluid spaces and gut contents after death. As noted below, digesta volume can also vary by several orders of magnitude with time after feeding. However, these tables demonstrate marked species differences, especially between carnivores and herbivores and among various species of herbivore.

Figures 18.3–18.6 illustrate the broad range of variations in the gastrointestinal tract of mammals. All animals, except the mink and kangaroo, were fed their conventional diet at 12 hour intervals for at least 6 weeks prior to sacrifice. All except the kangaroo were sacrificed 4 hours after feeding. The gastrointestinal tract was then dissected free of its attachments, arranged as indicated and drawn to scale, with special attention given to the structural characteristics of the stomach and large intestine. While removal of the gastrointestinal tract from its attachments can increase its length and obliterate many of the features used by anatomists to designate various segments of the intestine, it allows a more direct comparison of species variations in the relative size and length, compartmentalization, and sacculation. Furthermore, the volume and shape of individual segments can be affected as much by the time after feeding and by the diet as by

Table 18.1. Lengths of parts of the intestine at autopsy

Animal	Part of intestine	Relative length (%)	Average absolute length (m)	Ratio of body length to intestine length
Horse	Small intestine	75	22.44	1:12
	Cecum	4	1.00	
	Large colon	11	3.39	
	Small colon	10	3.08	
	Total	100	29.91	
Ox	Small intestine	81	46.00	1:20
	Cecum	2	0.88	
	Colon	17	10.18	
	Total	100	57.06	
Sheep and goat	Small intestine	80	26.20	1:27
	Cecum	1	0.36	
	Colon	19	6.17	
	Total	100	32.73	
Pig	Small intestine	78	18.29	1:14
	Cecum	1	0.23	
	Colon	21	4.99	
	Total	100	23.51	
Dog	Small intestine	85	4.14	1:6
	Cecum	2	0.08	
	Colon	13	0.60	
	Total	100	4.82	
Cat	Small intestine	83	1.72	1:4
	Large intestine	17	0.35	
	Total	100	2.07	
Rabbit	Small intestine	61	3.56	1:10
	Cecum	11	0.61	
	Colon	28	1.65	
	Total	100	5.82	

Adapted from G. Colin, *Traité de physiologie comparée des animaux*, Baillière, Paris, 1871

Table 18.2. Capacities of parts of the digestive tract at autopsy

Animal	Part of canal	Relative capacity (%)	Average absolute capacity (L)
Horse	Stomach	8.5	17.96
	Small intestine	30.2	63.82
	Cecum	15.9	33.54
	Large colon	38.4	81.25
	Small colon and rectum	7.0	14.77
	Total	100.0	211.34
Ox	Stomach	70.8	252.5
	Small intestine	18.5	66.0
	Cecum	2.8	9.9
	Colon and rectum	7.9	28.0
	Total	100.0	356.4
Sheep and goat	Rumen	52.9	23.4
	Reticulum	4.5	2.0
	Omasum	2.0	0.9
	Abomasum	7.5	3.3
	Small intestine	20.4	9.0
	Cecum	2.3	1.0
	Colon and rectum	10.4	4.6
	Total	100.0	44.2
Pig	Stomach	29.2	8.00
	Small intestine	33.5	9.20
	Cecum	5.6	1.55
	Colon and rectum	31.7	8.70
	Total	100.0	27.45
Dog	Stomach	62.3	4.33
	Small intestine	23.3	1.62
	Cecum	1.3	0.09
	Colon and rectum	13.1	0.91
	Total	100.0	6.95
Cat	Stomach	69.5	0.341
	Small intestine	14.6	0.114
	Large intestine	15.9	0.124
	Total	100.0	0.579

Adapted from Colin 1871

other variables. The effect of time after feeding is demonstrated in the drawings of the rat gastrointestinal tract (see Fig. 18.5), which compares the stomach and cecum from an animal sacrificed immediately after a meal to the same organs from an animal sacrificed 4 hours after feeding. Argenzio et al. (1974a) have shown that the large intestine of ponies undergoes a similar cyclic variation in cecal volume over a 12 hour period between meals. The volume measured 8 hours after feeding was more than three times that measured 12 hours after the meal. They also found a twofold difference between the volume of large-intestine contents in ponies fed two different diets (see below).

The digestive tract of the mink (Fig. 18.3) has a simple (noncompartmentalized) stomach and relatively short intestine. The terminal segment of intestine is larger, but it is nonsacculated and contains neither a cecum nor evidence of a sphincter or valve at its junction with the upper intestine. This general pattern is characteristic of arctoid (bearlike) carnivores. Some species in other mammalian orders (Insectivora, Edentata, Cetacea, Chiroptera, and Marsupialia) also have a simple stomach, no cecum, and little or no distinction between a small and large intestine.

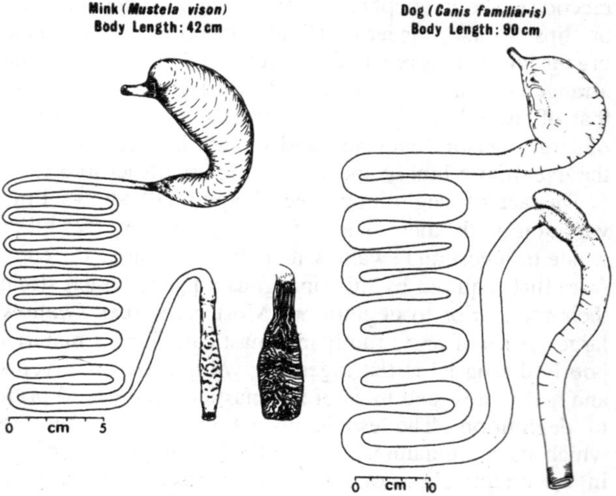

Figure 18.3. Gastrointestinal tracts of the mink and dog. Note simple, nonvoluminous large intestine. (Drawings by Erica Melack.)

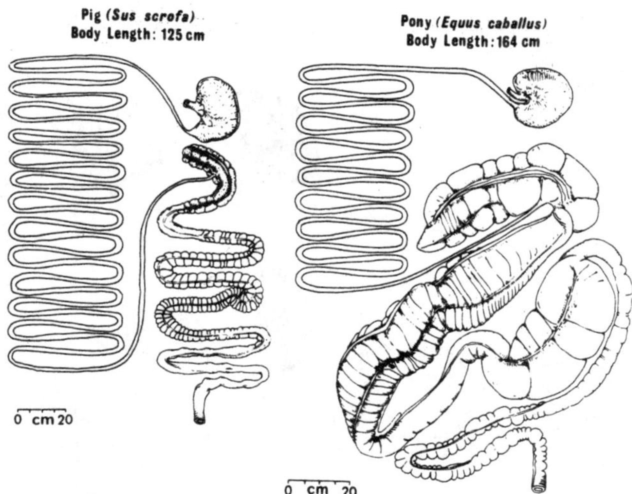

Figure 18.4. Gastrointestinal tracts of the pig and pony. A major portion of the colon of pigs and other Artiodactyla is arranged in two spirals. The centripetal (ascending) spiral reverses itself to form the centrifugal (descending) spiral, as indicated by the slight downward bend near the center of the colon. The cecum and colon of the pony are also sacculated. The cecum of the pony is relatively voluminous, but its ventral and dorsal large colon are developed into even more voluminous compartments. The general structure of the pony large intestine is characteristic of Perissodactyla. (Drawings by Erica Melack.)

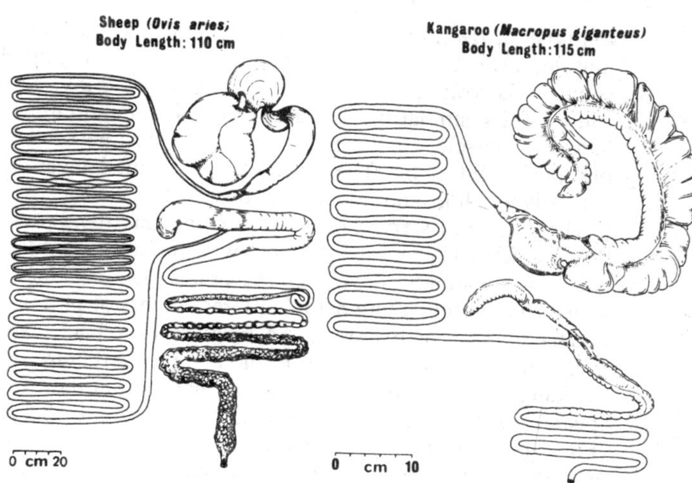

Figure 18.6. Gastrointestinal tracts of the sheep and kangaroo. The kangaroo drawing was prepared from a photograph supplied by Dr. I.D. Hume (U. of New England, Armidale, Australia) and the time between feeding and sacrifice is unknown. Note the similarity between the kangaroo stomach and the sacculated portions of the pig, pony, and rabbit colon. The point at which the spiral colon of the sheep reverses its direction is indicated in the same manner as that of the pig. (Drawings by Erica Melack.)

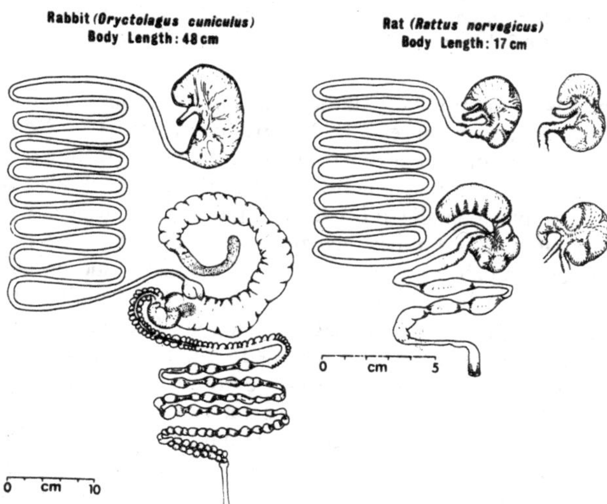

Figure 18.5. Gastrointestinal tracts of the rabbit and rat. The appearance of the rat gastrointestinal tract 4 hours after a meal suggests a noncompartmentalized stomach and relatively voluminous cecum. However, an animal sacrificed immediately after a meal (right) demonstrates a constriction near the midpoint of the stomach, which results in partial compartmentalization. It also shows that while the stomach is more voluminous at this time, the terminal segment of cecum is much reduced in size. (Drawings by Erica Melack.)

The digestive tract of the dog (Fig. 18.3) is relatively short and simple, like that of the mink, although it does contain an ileocecal valve and small cecum. The pig (Fig. 18.4) has a simple stomach. However, the relative length of both its small and large intestine is considerably greater than that of either the mink or dog. Furthermore, in the pig, the cecum and a considerable part of the colon are sacculated as a result of longitudinal bands of muscle. As we will see later, these sacculations or haustra ("buckets") may serve as one means of prolonging the retention of digesta. The pony stomach (Fig. 18.4) is similar to that of the pig, but its small intestine is much shorter in relative length, and its cecum and colon are much more voluminous. Equines demonstrate an extreme in colonic capacity.

The rabbit stomach is simple in structure (Fig. 18.5). However, its cecum is extremely voluminous, and both the cecum and proximal colon are sacculated. The rat cecum (Fig. 18.5) is also relatively voluminous, but its colon is neither sacculated nor particularly long. Furthermore, the rat stomach is partially compartmentalized. This characteristic, barely apparent in the rat, is extremely evident in the sheep and kangaroo (Fig. 18.6). The sheep small intestine appears to have the greatest relative length in comparison with the common domestic and laboratory mammals. However, its cecum and colon are neither sacculated nor particularly voluminous. The sacculated appearance of the lower colon and rectum in the rabbit, rat, and sheep appears to be due to the presence of pelleted feces rather than the result of the haustral-type structures associated with longitudinal bands of muscle, as noted in the pig and horse. The kangaroo stomach is voluminous and especially noteworthy because of its similarity, in sacculation and longitudinal bands of muscle, to the proximal large intestine of the pig, pony, and rabbit. The large intestine of the kangaroo is relatively short and nonvoluminous.

These species were chosen only to indicate the variation in the gastrointestinal tract of mammals. Parallel changes apparently developed separately among marsupials and within a number of different orders of placental mammals. For example, the marsupial stomach can range from simple (opossum) to the complex structure of the kangaroo, in a manner similar to that seen in the two species of the order Artiodactyla, the pig and sheep (Figs. 18.4, 18.6). Both simple and complex stomachs also are evident among other orders, such as those which represent the bats, edentates, rodents, and primates. Moir (1968) provides an excellent review of this subject. The large intestine shows similar variations in structure. These examples provide classical demonstrations of convergence, i.e. similar but lineally separate development of a common biological characteristic.

Stomach

The stomach serves as a reservoir and the initial site for digestion of protein and fat. Species of fish which have no stomach and simple-stomached herbivores, which have stomachs of relatively small capacity, tend to be continuous feeders. Differences in gastric capacity help explain why nondomesticated Proboscidea (elephants) and Perissodactyla (horse, rhinoceros, tapir) spend most of their day procuring food, while cattle spend only one third of their day feeding. The highly concentrated diet of carnivores would account for the fact that wild felines, which also are limited in their gastric capacity, have been observed to sleep 18 hours after rapidly feeding on their prey. A relatively large stomach may simply provide increased storage capacity, as is seen in some species of Insectivora (shrews), Chiroptera (fruit-eating and vampire bats), and Cetacea (porpoise, dolphins, whales). It also serves as a major site for microbial digestion in some species of the following mammalian orders: Marsupialia (kangaroo and wombat), Artiodactyla (peccary, hippopotamus, chevrotain, camelids, and the Pecora, or true ruminants), Rodentia (vole, lemming, hamster, muskrat), Sirenia (dugong, manatee), Edentata (sloth), and Primates (Colobus and Semnopithecus monkeys).

There are also species variations in the distribution and composition of the epithelium lining the stomach (Fig. 18.7). The simple stomachs of man and the dog are lined with three major types of tissue: cardiac mucosa, proper gastric (oxyntic) mucosa, and pyloric mucosa. Pyloric mucosa lines the aboral portion of their stomachs. Orad to this is a relatively large segment of proper gastric mucosa, which secretes both pepsinogen and HCl. Near the gastroesophageal junction the proper gastric mucosa blends into cardiac mucosa. The pig stomach is also a noncompartmentalized organ with the same orad progression of mucosal types, except that cardiac mucosa occupies a much larger percent of the stomach, and an additional small area of stratified squamous epithelium surrounds the gastroesophageal junction. The stomach of the horse is simple, but stratified squamous epithelium occupies a major part of its oral extremity. The distribution of gastric epithelium in the rat is similar to that of the horse. Due to a stricture at the junction of the cardiac glandular and stratified squamous epithelium, the rat stomach is partially divided into two compartments. The stomachs of the cow and llama are extremely enlarged and compartmentalized. In the bovine stomach, typical of Pecora, most of the additional surface area is lined with stratified squamous epithelium. The llama stomach, typically camelid, contains a large segment of cardiac mucosa in its third compartment as well as islands of this glandular epithelium within the areas of stratified epithe-

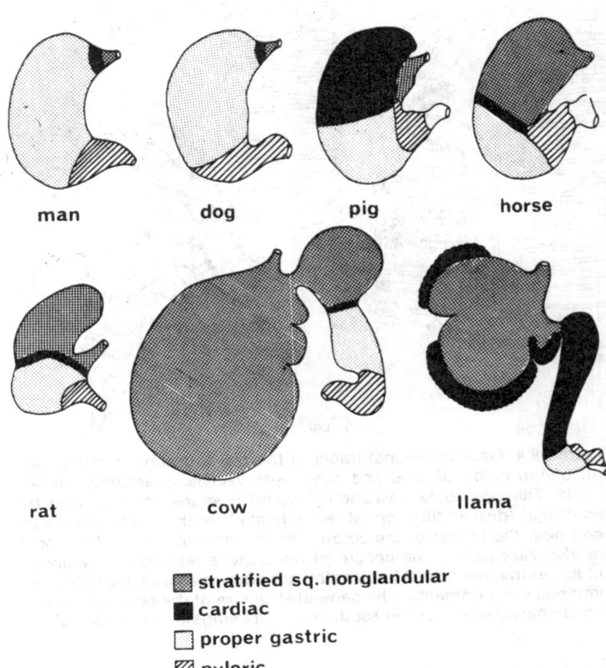

Figure 18.7. Variations in the type and distribution of gastric mucosa. Stomachs are not drawn to scale, for example, the capacity of the adult bovine stomach is approximately 70 times that of man, or 14 times the capacity per kg body weight. (Modified from Stevens, in Ussing and Thorn, eds., *Transport Mechanisms in Epithelia*, Munksgaard, Copenhagen, 1973.)

lium which line its first two compartments. A similar range in the composition and distribution of gastric epithelium can be seen among species belonging to the orders Rodentia, Marsupialia, and Primates. This led Oppel (1897) and Bensley (1902–1903) to propose that cardiac glandular mucosa may represent an intermediate stage in the evolutionary replacement of the proper gastric glandular tissue with nonglandular, stratified squamous epithelium.

The proper gastric mucosa contains the compound tubular glands which secrete HCl (parietal or oxyntic cells) and pepsinogen (neck chief cells). This area of mucosa is of critical importance to the gastric digestive process, and it has received extensive study in a wide range of species. Hogben et al. (1974) provided a quantitative histological comparison of gastric mucosa of man, dog, cat, guinea pig, and the frog. They described the relative percentages of parietal, chief, and mucous cells in the proper gastric region as well as the maximal rate of hydrogen ion secretion per unit weight of parietal cell. The glands of the pyloric region are said to secrete mucus and some pepsinogen (Davenport 1971). They also secrete a serous fluid low in bicarbonate and therefore presumably low in acid-neutralizing capacity.

It is generally thought that cardiac glands secrete only mucus. However, Höller (1970), who examined cardiac mucosal secretions in the pig stomach, concluded that these glands secreted bicarbonate ion and absorbed chloride ion. There is evidence for a similar exchange by the cardiac mucosa lining the glandular pouches in the forestomach compartments of the llama (Eckerlin and Stevens 1973). Höller further showed that the acid-neutralizing capability of the pig's cardiac glandular secretion was substantial. From results obtained by sham feeding (collecting ingested food via an esophageal fistula) and pentagastrin injection, he concluded that HCO_3^- secretion was inhibited by gastrin. On the basis of these results he proposed that HCO_3^- secretion may be inhibited during the period of gastrin-induced HCl secretion associated with feeding. The later increase in HCO_3^- secretion, after the meal, could thus serve as a mechanism for buffering excess HCl.

Information on the function of stratified squamous tissue is largely limited to studies of the forestomach of ruminants (see Chapter 22). In these animals it serves as a major site for absorption of volatile fatty acid (VFA), Na^+, and Cl^-. In addition, it may aid in the neutralization of these acids in rumen contents by secretion of HCO_3^- (Chien and Stevens 1972, Stevens 1973). Its stratified squamous structure is presumably protective, in the same sense as is the mucous secretion of the epithelium lining the remainder of the gastrointestinal tract.

Aukema and Breukink (1974) reviewed evidence showing that gastric ulcers in the pig, rat, and mouse are most commonly found in the stratified squamous region or at its junction with cardiac mucosal tissue, while those in cattle were largely found in the oxyntic mucosal region. In man, gastric ulcers are often located at the junction of the oxyntic and pyloric mucosae. Thus the structural and functional characteristics of the different types of mucosa and their interfaces may play an important role in the pathogenesis of ulcers.

Midgut

In the species most intensively studied, the rate of passage of gastric contents into the small intestine is affected by their physical consistency, osmolality, and composition. The pylorus appears to limit the size of particle which can enter the intestine, and particulate matter is subject to greater delay at the pylorus than fluids. The rate at which digesta leaves the stomach is under both neural and endocrine control.

The small intestine adds biliary, pancreatic, and its own secretions to the gastric chyme. In many species the bile is stored in a gallbladder. This allows for both concentration of the bile and its intermittent release into the small intestine. In many other species the gallbladder is absent (see Chapter 20). Biliary secretions contain bile salts, usually in an alkaline solution (for species variations see Haslewood 1968). They emulsify fat to allow more efficient digestion by the water-soluble lipases (see Chapter 17). Digestive enzymes have been reported in the bile of lower vertebrates but not in that of mammals.

The pancreatic juice of mammals is quite alkaline. The bicarbonate content of pancreatic, biliary, and intestinal secretions contributes to the neutralization of gastric chyme. The other critical contribution of pancreatic juice is its content of protease, carbohydrase, and lipase enzymes (see Fig. 17.1). As with the biliary system, the pancreas in various species differs in its size, position, and the arrangement by which the pancreatic ducts enter the intestine.

The small intestine serves as a major site for absorption of required nutrients, and for the synthesis and release of numerous hormones (see Chapter 20). Its secretory functions are poorly understood. Intestinal secretions include mucus and result in the release of bicarbonate, but whether bicarbonate release is due to direct secretion or to the absorption of hydrogen is not clear (Hubel 1974). The contribution of the intestinal mucosa to extracellular (intraluminal) digestion is similarly unclear. Small amounts of enzymes are undoubtedly released into the lumen. Whether these result from secretion or the release of intracellular enzymes from cells disrupted in the process of epithelial turnover is not clear. As indicated previously, much of the disaccharidase and peptidase activity takes place in the brush border and cytoplasm of intact intestinal mucosa cells rather than in the lumen.

The rate of digesta passage through the small intestine

of most species is rapid in comparison to passage through the stomach or large intestine. This helps account for the low concentrations of microbes normally found in small-intestine contents, even in those species which normally have large microbial populations in their stomach. That conclusion is supported by the fact that bacterial overgrowth commonly occurs following the development of crypts or *blind loops* in this section of the tract. The relative length of the small intestine with respect to the entire digestive tract varies considerably among species. In mammals, it appears that variations in the stomach and hindgut are greater than those seen in the midgut.

Hindgut

A primary function of the mammalian hindgut is absorption of inorganic electrolytes and water of both dietary and secretory origin (see Chapter 21). A second important function of the large intestine in most if not all mammals is that of microbial digestion (see below). It has been pointed out previously that both of these functions are aided by mechanisms which would prolong the retention of large-intestine contents. This may be accomplished by orad (antiperistaltic) propulsion of digesta, retention of contents in a cul-de-sac (cecum), retention of contents in compartmentalized and/or sacculated segments of colon, or by infrequent aborad propulsion of digesta.

DIGESTA PASSAGE

The efficiency of digestion and absorption is highly dependent on the rate at which digesta move through the gastrointestinal tract. The rate of passage can be estimated by the use of digesta "markers," substances which are not normally secreted, digested, or absorbed by the gut. Passage of fluid digesta can be estimated by the use of soluble markers, and the passage of particles by the use of insoluble particulate markers.

The feeding of conventional diets allows comparison of what happens under normal conditions. However, since the rate of passage through a given segment varies with both the diet and time after feeding, the diet and dietary regime should be held constant if one wishes to separate the effect of diet from other structural and functional variables.

Figure 18.8 shows the passage of fluid and particulate markers through the gastrointestinal tract of a carnivore, an omnivore, and a simple-stomached herbivore. Fluid passage was measured with polyethylene glycol (PEG). Passage of particles was measured using segments of plastic tubing 2 mm in diameter. The liquid marker left the stomach and traversed the small intestine of all three species quite rapidly. Particles were retained in the stomach much longer. Both fluid and particulate markers passed through the large intestine of the dog at approximately the same rate. Passage of fluid marker through the large intestine of the pig and rabbit was much slower. The spiral colon of the pig appeared to be the major site of fluid marker retention. The cecum was the major site in the rabbit. Passage of particles through the large intestine of the pig and rabbit was difficult to assess, due to their slow release from the stomach. However, particles were retained by the centripetal segment of the pig's colon. There was no evidence of particle retention by the cecum or any other segment of the rabbit's large intestine.

In experiments similar to those described above, fluid and particulate markers were administered directly into the cecum of rabbits via a fistula (Pickard and Stevens 1972). Fluid marker was retained by the cecum in a manner similar to that following its intragastric administration. Particles were rapidly expelled from the cecum and excreted in the feces. Cinefluoroscopic examination of these animals showed a periodic flux and reflux of barium between the cecum and proximal colon, suggesting that particles of the size used in these studies could readily leave the cecum but were not as readily refluxed from the colon into the cecum.

Argenzio et al. (1974a) studied passage of markers through the gastrointestinal tract of ponies under the same experimental conditions. Fluid marker also left the pony stomach very rapidly; less than 5 percent remained 2 hours after its administration with the meal. Passage of particulate markers through the upper gastrointestinal tract was not measured, but passage of both types of marker through the large intestine was determined by their direct administration into the large intestine via fistulae (Fig. 18.9). The ventral and dorsal large colon, rather than the cecum, served as the major sites for both fluid and particle retention. The retention time for particles was greater than that for fluid and increased with an increase in particle length.

Table 18.3 gives the calculations of gastric emptying time and measurements of the rate of fecal excretion of fluid and particulate markers in the above studies, plus measurements from an additional study of marker excretion in the feces of young pigs subjected to the same experimental conditions but fed a conventional, high-concentrate diet. Fluid marker was released most rapidly from the pony stomach and least rapidly from the stomach of the mature pig. The slow evacuation of particles from the pig and rabbit stomach is also evident. The dogs and young pigs showed the most rapid passage of particulate markers through their gastrointestinal tracts. Passage of particles through the rabbit gastrointestinal tract was considerably slower. Particulate markers were excreted in the feces of the rabbit more rapidly than fluid when these were administered into the stomach, and the results of intracecal administration support the conclusion that particles were retained by the stomach and fluid marker by the cecum. Comparison of the gastric-emptying times and fecal-excretion rates of the two markers by the adult pig indicate a similar retention of particles by

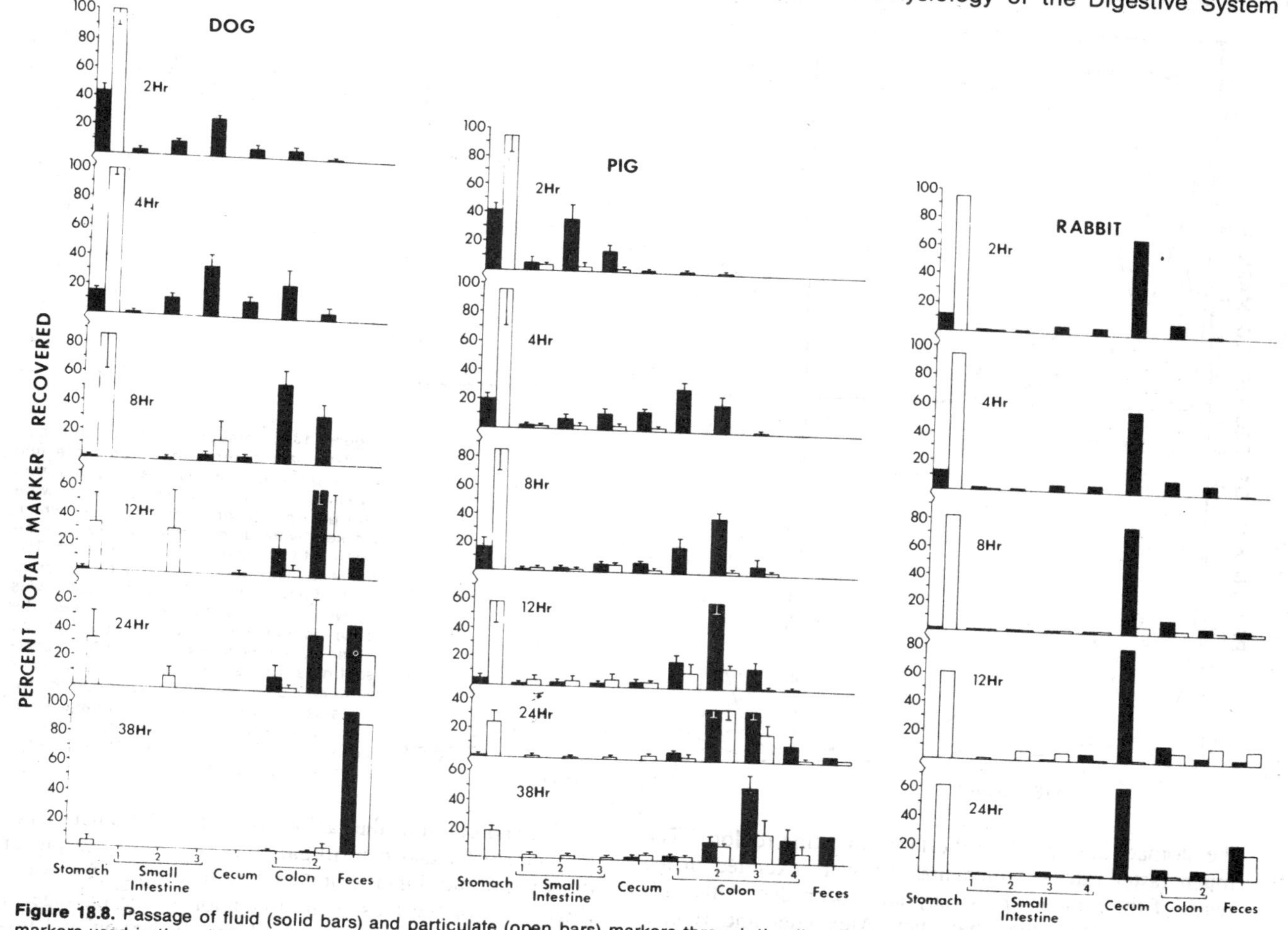

Figure 18.8. Passage of fluid (solid bars) and particulate (open bars) markers through the digestive tract of the dog, pig, and rabbit. Particulate markers used in the rabbit were 2 × 5 mm in size, those in the dog and pig 2 × 10 mm. Dogs were fed a conventional meat diet, pigs were fed a pelleted, low concentrate-high fiber diet, and rabbits were fed a conventional pelleted rabbit diet. All animals were fed at 12 hour intervals over a 6 week period prior to the experiment. Markers were administered via a stomach tube at the time of the morning meal, and three animals of each species were sacrificed at each indicated time. The gastrointestinal tract was then subdivided with ligatures into segments as indicated. Brackets indicate standard error (SE). (Modified from Banta, Clemens, Kronsky, and Sheffy, unpublished; Clemens, Stevens, and Southworth 1975, *J. Nutr.* 105:759–68; Pickard and Stevens 1972, *Am. J. Physiol.* 222:1161–66.)

Table 18.3. Species variations in gastric emptying time and fecal excretion of fluid (F) and particulate (P) markers *

Species	Diet	Gastric emptying half-time (hr)		Percentage excreted in feces (first 24 hr): Intragastric administration		Intracecal administration		References
		F	P	F	P	F	P	
Dog	chow	1.5	1.5	55	40			Banta et al., unpublished
Pig (young)	high concentrate			63	35			Argenzio and Southworth 1975
Pig (mature)	horse diet	2	10	7	2			Clemens et al. 1975
Rabbit	rabbit diet	1.3	12	25	54	30	96	Pickard and Stevens 1972
Pony	horse diet	0.3				7	2	Argenzio et al. 1974a

* Adult dogs, rabbits, and ponies were used. Young pigs had an initial body weight of 12.5 ± 3.1 kg and a final body weight of 67 ± 10 kg when sacrificed 9 weeks later. Mature pigs weighed an average of 176 ± 3.3 kg. Dogs, young pigs, and rabbits were provided with diets which are conventionally fed to each of these species. Ponies and the mature pigs were given a pelleted "choice" diet conventionally fed to horses. Fluid marker (PEG) and particulate markers (2 × 2 mm) were administered into the stomach or cecum at the time of feeding. Gastric emptying half-times and time chosen for comparison of fecal excretion are in reference to the time of marker administration. The values for gastric emptying time are approximations obtained by sacrificing animals in groups of three at 2, 4, 8, 12, and 24 hours after marker administration (see Figs. 18.8–18.10). All animals were subjected to the same feeding regime and general experimental procedures.

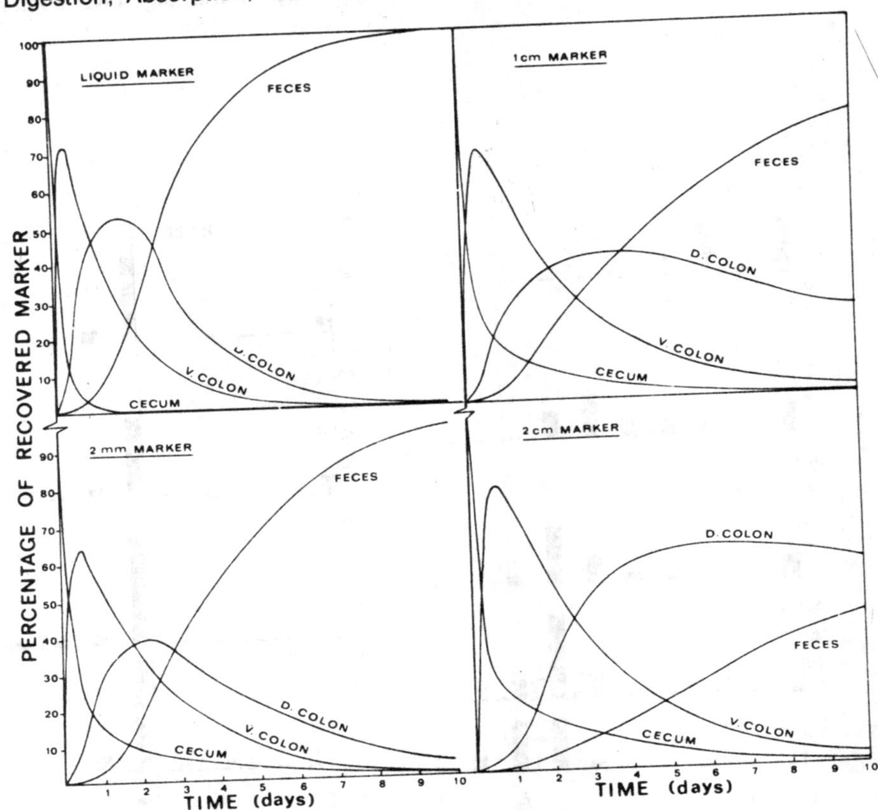

Figure 18.9. Passage of fluid and particulate markers through the large intestine of the pony. Curves representing retention by cecum, ventral, and dorsal colons were derived from a series of studies in which markers were administered via fistulae directly into the ileum, cecum, or colon. The curve labeled dorsal colon actually represents dorsal plus small colon, since it was derived from the difference between the dose administered and the sums of the other curves. Fecal excretion curves represent data from experiments in which feces were collected over a 10 day period following a cecal dose of markers; average variation was ±18% (SE). (From Argenzio, Lowe, Pickard, and Stevens 1974a, *Am. J. Physiol.* 226:1035–42.)

the stomach and fluid by the large intestine (colon). The much faster rate at which markers were excreted in the feces of the younger pigs may have been due to the differences of age rather than diet. Alexander and Benzie (1950) have shown that digesta passage through the gastrointestinal tract of the foal is much faster than in the mature horse. When mature pigs and ponies were fed the same diet, the rates at which they excreted both markers in the feces were quite similar.

The above comparisons indicate some substantial species differences in the rates of digesta passage through the gastrointestinal tract. It is equally obvious that the rate of passage in a given species can be affected to a considerable degree by differences in diet or age. The effect of these multiple variables underlines the need for either controlling or specifying them in species comparisons.

The rate at which digesta pass through given segments of the gastrointestinal tract should show some correlation with both anatomical structure and the degree of microbial digestion. Re-inspection of large-intestine structure in the dog, pig, pony, and rabbit (Figs. 18.3–18.5) shows that digesta tended to be retained in the sacculated segments. Digesta passage may also be slowed down by areas of constriction such as the junction between the cecum and colon of the rabbit, as well as the junctions of the centripetal and centrifugal spiral colon of the pig or the ventral and dorsal colon (pelvic flexure) of the pony. Regardless of the reason, prolongation in the passage of digesta allows greater time for both absorption and microbial digestion.

MICROBIAL DIGESTION

As mentioned in Chapter 17, the gastrointestinal tract is colonized with microorganisms shortly after birth. They become primarily restricted to the stomach and large intestine, presumably due to the slower rate of digesta passage through these parts of the tract. The small intestine is relatively sterile, although significant numbers of organisms can be found in the ileum of many species. This may be due to a slower rate of passage through the terminal intestine or occasional regurgitation of large-intestine contents into the ileum. These microorganisms serve a multitude of purposes. One major function in some species is to convert a poor-quality diet into more readily utilizable nutrients.

Production and absorption of organic acids

The nutritional importance of gastrointestinal microorganisms has been most clearly demonstrated by the extensive studies conducted on the ruminant forestomach (see Chapters 22, 23). In brief, microbes indigenous to the ruminant forestomach convert soluble carbohydrate, e.g. glucose and starch, as well as insoluble carbohydrate (cellulose, hemicellulose, pectin) into organic acids. Under normal conditions the principal end products of carbohydrate digestion are three volatile fatty acids (acetate, propionate, and butyrate), carbon dioxide, and methane. Only small quantities of other organic acids, including lactate, are normally produced. However, if sufficiently large amounts of soluble carbohydrate become available to the organisms, there is an increase in lactic acid production. The pH of forestomach contents is normally maintained within a relatively narrow range (5.5–7.0) in spite of the high concentrations of volatile fatty acid (VFA) produced. This is accomplished by buffers secreted in the saliva and, it appears, directly by the forestomach epithelium. It is also aided by the fact that most of the VFA produced within the forestomach is quite rapidly absorbed. Total absorption of VFA from the digestive tract of cattle has been estimated to provide 70 percent of the animal's basal energy requirements. Structural and functional characteristics of the forestomach aid in the retention of microbes, as well as fluid and especially particulate digesta, for the period of time required for the microbial digestive process. Fluid digesta and microbes are slowly released into the remainder of the digestive tract where microbes are digested, allowing assimilation of their protein and vitamin content.

Concentrations of VFA similar to those found in the ruminant forestomach have been described in the voluminous, compartmentalized stomachs of camelids (Williams 1963, Vallenas and Stevens 1971), kangaroos (Moir et al. 1956, Henning and Hird 1970), Colobus monkeys (Ohwaki et al. 1974) and the hippopotamus (Thurston et al. 1968). Substantial concentrations of VFA have also been measured in the stomach of the horse, pony, rabbit, and many rodents. Stomach contents of the horse, pig, rabbit, and guinea pig also have been shown to contain lactic acid (Alexander and Davies 1963). VFA are normally absent from the diet, except for those species which practice coprophagy (ingestion of feces). Lactic acid can be released into the gut as a result of carbohydrate metabolism within its mucosal cells; therefore, it is not necessarily an indicator of microbial digestion.

Elsden et al. (1946) and Phillipson (1947) measured concentrations of VFA in the gastrointestinal tract of the ox, sheep, deer, horse, pig, rabbit, rat, and dog (see Fig. 22.1). Low concentrations of VFA were found in the abomasum of ruminants and in the stomach of each of the other species. Relatively high concentrations of VFA were found in the large intestine of all of these species. VFA also have been shown to constitute a major portion of the anions in the feces of man (Torres-Pinedo et al. 1966, Rubinstein et al. 1969). Thus microbial digestion of carbohydrate similar to that seen in the ruminant stomach occurs in the stomach of a wide range of mammals and in the large intestine of an even wider range of species.

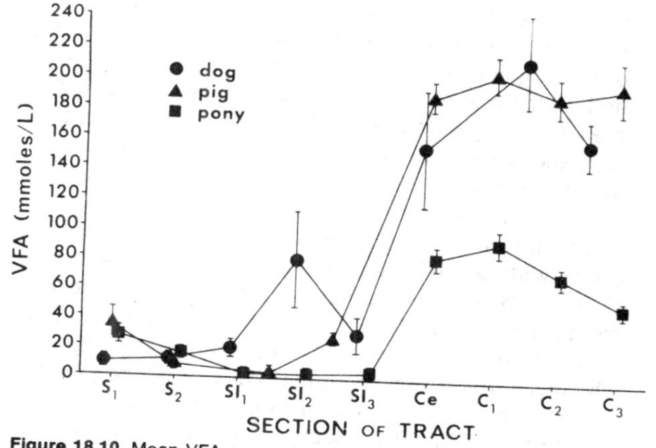

Figure 18.10. Mean VFA concentrations (±SE) in segments of the dog, pig, and pony gastrointestinal tracts. Each value represents the average from 12 animals, sacrificed in groups of three animals each at 2, 4, 8 and 12 hours after feeding. The sections of tract examined were the oral (S_1) and aboral (S_2) halves of the stomach; two or three equal segments of the small intestine, SI_1, SI_2, and SI_3; the cecum, Ce; and two or three segments of the colon, C_1, C_2, and C_3. The pig colon was divided into proximal (C_1), centripetal (C_2), and centrifugal plus terminal (C_3) segments. In the pony, C_1 represents the ventral large colon, C_2 the dorsal large colon, and C_3 the small colon. Dogs were fed a meat diet, pigs a high-concentrate diet, and ponies a conventional, pelleted horse diet. (Modified from Argenzio, Southworth, and Stevens 1974b, *Am. J. Physiol.* 226:1043–50; Argenzio and Southworth 1975, *Am. J. Physiol.* 228:454–60; Banta, Clemens, Kronsky, and Sheffy, unpublished.)

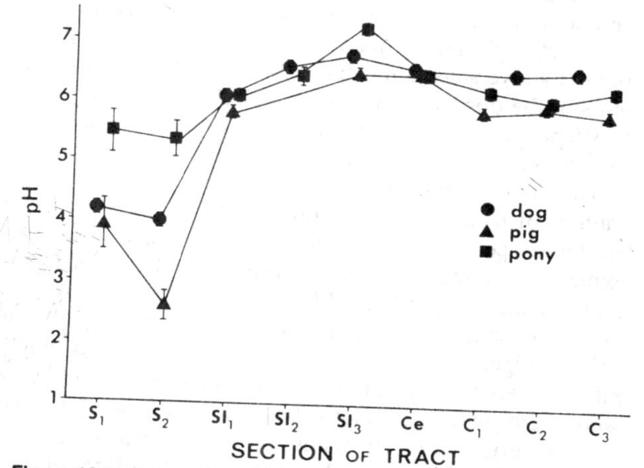

Figure 18.11. Mean pH (±SE) in segments of the dog, pig, and pony gastrointestinal tracts. Procedures, symbols, and diets are identical to those in Figure 18.10. The pH was measured anaerobically in the axial center of each segment except SI_1 and SI_3, where measurements were taken 5 cm below the pyloric valve and 5 cm above the ileocolonic junction respectively. These were the only two measurements made in the small intestine of the pig. (Modified from Argenzio, Southworth, and Stevens 1974b, *Am. J. Physiol.* 226:1043–50; Argenzio and Southworth 1975, *Am. J. Physiol.* 228:454–60; Banta, Clemens, Kronsky, and Sheffy, unpublished.)

Figures 18.10 and 18.11 give the mean values for concentrations of VFA and for digesta pH measured over a 12 hour period at various sites along the digestive tract of the dog, pig, and pony. Dogs were fed a meat diet, young pigs the conventional high-concentrate diet, and ponies a diet conventionally fed to horses. The stomach of the dog contained low concentrations of VFA; the oral half of the pig and pony stomach contained significantly higher concentrations (20–40 mEq/L). Lactic acid concentrations were lower than the VFA levels in the stomach of the pig, but 2–3 times higher than VFA levels in the pony stomach.

The mean pH of gastric contents was highest in the pony, with no difference between digesta in the oral and aboral halves. The average pH of digesta in the dog's stomach was much lower, but again there was no significant difference between the oral and aboral segments. The mean pH of digesta in the oral half of the pig stomach was approximately equal to that in the dog stomach, but the pH in the aboral segment of the pig stomach was significantly lower. This difference in pH between the two segments of the pig stomach could be explained by the secretion of bicarbonate by cardiac mucosa, noted by Höller, which could also account for the difference in VFA levels (microbial activity).

In the dog and most simple-stomached vertebrates, gastric secretion of HCl serves as a means of destroying ingested microorganisms. However the isolation of bacteria from the gastric mucosal surface of many species (see Chapter 17) and the presence of VFA in their gastric contents indicate that microorganisms do survive. This could be due to a microenvironment at the lumen surface maintained at a pH higher than that of bulk gastric contents, but the above studies indicated that the pH of gastric contents in the dog, pig, and pony was also sufficiently high to support microbial digestion throughout at least a portion of the period between meals.

The highest concentrations of VFA and lowest concentrations of lactic acid were found in the large intestine of all three species. Low values of lactic acid could be explained by the lower availability of soluble carbohydrate in the large bowel. Mean pH of cecal contents in the three species was practically identical. The pH of colonic digesta was highest in the dog and lowest in the pig. However, the fact that the variations of pH with time were kept within a relatively narrow range (5.5–7.0) suggests efficient mechanisms for their neutralization.

Figures 18.12 and 18.13 demonstrate the effect of dietary changes on gastrointestinal contents. Dogs were fed a dry (chow) diet, which contained more soluble carbohydrate and fiber than the meat diet. Mature pigs were fed the same diet as the ponies in the previous experiment, a diet which contained less soluble carbohydrate and more fiber than the diet fed the younger pigs. Ponies were fed a specially prepared diet which was higher in fiber, lower in protein, and contained 3 percent urea. These changes in diet resulted in some significant changes in the organic-acid concentrations and pH, demonstrating that gastrointestinal pH and VFA concentrations varied with diet as well as species.

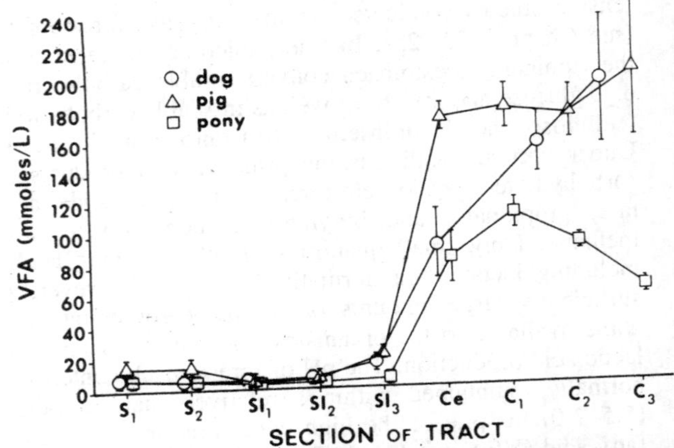

Figure 18.12. Mean VFA concentrations (±SE) in segments of the dog, pig, and pony gastrointestinal tracts. Procedures and symbols are identical to those in Figure 18.10, except for the diet (see text). (Modified from Argenzio, Southworth, and Stevens 1974b, *Am. J. Physiol.* 226:1043–50; Clemens, Stevens, and Southworth 1975, *J. Nutr.* 105:759–68; Banta, Clemens, Kronsky, and Sheffy, unpublished.)

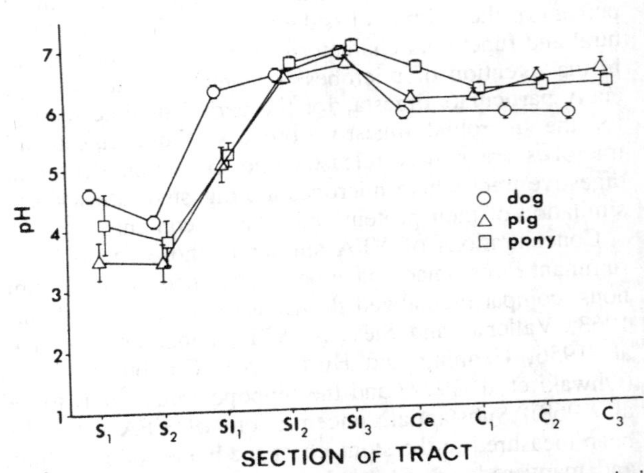

Figure 18.13. Mean pH (±SE) in segments of the dog, pony, and pig gastrointestinal tract. Procedures and symbols are identical to those in Figure 18.10. (Modified from Argenzio, Southworth, and Stevens 1974b, *Am. J. Physiol.* 226:1043–50; Clemens, Stevens, and Southworth 1975, *J. Nutr.* 105:759–68; Banta, Clemens, Kronsky, and Sheffy, unpublished.)

The above studies show that the conditions required for microbial digestion are present in the stomach and large intestine of the dog, pig, and pony. The physiological significance of this lies in its value to the nutrition of the animal and its effect on the secretion and absorption of other substances. The nutritional value of organic acids depends on the actual quantity absorbed by the animal. Table 18.4 gives the results of in vitro measurements of VFA transport across the epithelium lining the stomach and large intestine of the pig and pony. The difference between the quantity absorbed (loss, lumen side) and transported (gain, blood side) was due partly to the accumulation of VFA within the tissue and partly to metabolism of these organic acids by the tissue. The cardiac mucosa of the pig stomach transported VFA at approximately one half the rate measured with rumen epithelium under identical conditions (Stevens and Stettler 1966). The stratified squamous epithelium, proper gastric mucosa, and pyloric mucosa of the pig stomach transported VFA at rates less than 20 percent of that of rumen epithelium; the stratified squamous epithelium of the pony stomach was essentially impermeable to these organic acids. The area of cardiac mucosa in the pony stomach was too small to allow measurement, but the proper gastric and pyloric mucosa of the pony transported VFA at rates similar to those for the pig stomach. These results indicated that VFA would be absorbed from the stomach of both the pig and the pony. Measurements of the amounts transported and present in the tissue at the end of the experiments indicated that a substantial percentage of the VFA absorbed from the lumen bath was metabolized by the gastric mucosa of both animals.

The rate of VFA transport across the large-intestine mucosa of these two species was more rapid than that measured for their gastric tissue. The large-intestine mucosa of the pig transported VFA at a rate greater than that of rumen epithelium. The mucosa of the pony large intestine transported VFA at a rate approximately two thirds that of rumen epithelium. A substantial degree of VFA metabolism by large-intestine mucosa of both species was also indicated.

Other studies of ponies have shown that approximately 50 percent of the soluble carbohydrate in the diet reaches the large intestine (Hintz et al. 1971), and that VFA produced in the large intestine supplies a minimum of 25 percent of the animal's basal energy requirement (Argenzio et al. 1974b). Less is known about the quantities of VFA absorbed by the large intestine of the dog and pig.

In addition to its importance as a source of energy, VFA production in the large intestine of the pony also appears to be accompanied by a secretion of Na^+, HCO_3^-, and large volumes of water (Argenzio and Stevens 1975). Furthermore, Na^+ and VFA appear to be the major substances absorbed from the pony large intestine and therefore the primary solutes responsible for its absorption of water. Perfusion studies of the goat colon (Argenzio et al. 1975) showed that VFA was absorbed more rapidly than Na^+, and that Na^+ and water absorption were markedly inhibited when the VFA in the perfusate was replaced with Cl^-. Therefore it seems that there is a marked interdependency between microbial digestion and the retrieval of Na^+ and water by the large intestine of mammals (see Chapter 21).

Less is known about the fate of the lactic acid in gastrointestinal contents. Under in vitro conditions, lactate is released into solutions bathing the lumen surface of gastric and large-intestine mucosa of the pony (Argenzio et al., unpublished). This is the L(+) isomer. Rumen microorganisms produce both the L(+) and D(−) lactic acid. Both can be absorbed, but the D(−) isomer is less readily metabolized (Dunlop 1961).

Protein and vitamins

The significance of protein and vitamin synthesis by large-intestine microorganisms is poorly understood. In rodents and the rabbit there is substantial evidence that coprophagy allows the recycling of VFA, proteins, and vitamins through the normal digestive and absorptive processes of the upper gastrointestinal tract, providing an important addition of nutrients to the diet. There also is good evidence that urea excreted into the large intestine

Table 18.4. Transport of VFA across the gastric, cecal, and colonic mucosa (μmol/sq cm) *

Tissue	Pig		Pony	
	Loss, lumen side	Gain, blood side	Loss, lumen side	Gain, blood side
Stomach				
Stratified squamous	15.2 ± 6.0	1.0 ± 0.2	3.5 ± 3.5	0.1 ± 0.1
Cardiac	20.8 ± 4.6	2.8 ± 0.7		
Proper gastric	12.6 ± 2.5	0.8 ± 0.1	23.4 ± 9.4	0.6 ± 0.3
Pyloric	14.6 ± 2.7	1.3 ± 0.5	13.7 ± 3.4	1.0 ± 0.2
Large intestine				
Cecal	25.8 ± 7.3	10.7 ± 1.6	20.4 ± 2.0	4.0 ± 0.5
Proximal colonic	20.1 ± 1.9	9.3 ± 1.6	24.6 ± 3.5	4.4 ± 0.5
Distal colonic	24.4 ± 2.4	7.7 ± 0.6	16.3 ± 3.8	3.6 ± 0.4

* Means (± SE) of results during 2.5-hour experimental periods. Epithelial tissue was dissected free of underlying muscle. Ringer solution containing a 90 mM, equimolar mixture of acetate, propionate, and butyrate was used to bathe the lumen surface of the tissue. The blood-facing surface was bathed with normal Ringer. Both solutions were buffered at pH 7.4 with bicarbonate, gassed with 5% CO_2–95% O_2, and maintained at 39°C. Tissues were short-circuited to provide a zero transepithelial, electrical potential difference. (Modified from Argenzio, Southworth, and Stevens 1974b, *Am. J. Physiol.* 226:1043–50; Argenzio and Southworth 1975, *Am. J. Physiol.* 228:454–60.)

of man (Giordano et al. 1966) and the horse (Slade et al. 1970, 1971) is converted by microbial urease into ammonia. This can then be absorbed, providing a source of nitrogen for the synthesis of nonessential amino acids, or incorporated into microbial protein in the gut. Although it has been generally assumed that the large intestine is incapable of digesting protein and absorbing peptides or amino acids, recent evidence indicates that microbial protein is digested in the colon of the rabbit (Bonnafous and Raynaud 1968) and in the large intestine of the pony (Slade et al. 1971, Wootton and Argenzio 1975). Slade et al. (1971) have shown that both essential and nonessential amino acids, derived from hydrolysis of microbial protein synthesized in the cecum of the horse, can be directly absorbed from that organ. The question of whether the majority of the nitrogen leaves the large intestine of the equine and other species in the form of peptides, amino acids, or ammonia remains unanswered. Evidence that vitamins synthesized in the large intestine of noncoprophagous species are absorbed in significant quantities is equivocal.

Pathophysiology

As mentioned in Chapter 17, a number of gastrointestinal diseases in domestic animals can result from dietary change. Chapter 24 discusses the tympany (bloat), inflammation, and ulceration of ruminant forestomach mucosa which can result from the feeding of a high-concentrate ration to cattle or allowing these animals to engorge themselves on grain. This is believed to be due to the rapid fermentation of excessive quantities of soluble carbohydrate into VFA and lactic acid. The effect of grain engorgement on the bovine forestomach epithelium suggests that excessive feeding of soluble carbohydrate also may be responsible for gastric ulcers in the abomasum of cattle and the stomach of pigs on high-concentrate diets. The incidence of gastric ulcers in these two species is higher than that of most species other than man (Aukema and Breukink 1974), and Davenport (1964) has shown that gastric ulcers can be experimentally produced in dogs by oral infusion of acetate. Although the concentration of VFA normally found in the bovine abomasum or pig stomach is much lower than that found in the bovine forestomach, each unitary decrease in the pH of a solution containing VFA results in a tenfold increase in the percentage of undissociated acid. In this way, the concentration of this more permeating form could reach relatively high levels in the presence of HCl secretion.

Svendsen (1969) found that the abomasum of cattle fed a high-concentrate diet contained higher levels of VFA and showed a marked increase in the volume of gas produced or liberated *within* that organ. He found that increasing the concentration of VFA in abomasal contents also inhibited abomasal motility and that this, plus insufflation of this organ with gas, resulted in its dorsal displacement (torsion). Therefore, he proposed that abomasal displacement, a relatively common syndrome in cattle, could result from the feeding of high-concentrate diets. Van Kruiningen (1974) reviewed the incidence of acute gastric dilatation in dogs, monkeys, man, horses, and a variety of other species. He examined the microbial population and gas composition of stomach contents in dogs suffering from gastric dilatation and concluded that this syndrome, like that of abomasal displacement, may be due to excessive microbial digestion of soluble carbohydrates. He pointed out that "only domestication allows or forces animals to consume large meals of readily digestible carbohydrates after long intervals of fasting."

Dietary effects on microbial digestion in the intestine have received less study. Excessive feeding of carbohydrate to lambs can result in enterotoxemia, due to overgrowth of *Cl. welchii* in the small intestine. Although microbial populations of the large intestine are less vulnerable to dietary change, malabsorption of carbohydrate, e.g. lactase deficiency, by the small intestine of man can result in diarrhea. Direct infusion of solutions containing high concentrations of VFA has been shown to inhibit the motility of the cecum in cattle (Svendsen and Kristensen 1970) and sheep (Svendsen 1972). Allison et al. (1975) found that cecal contents of cattle and sheep, subjected to experimental grain engorgement, showed a marked increase in the number of lactic acid–producing bacteria and a marked decrease in pH, to levels as low as 4.66. Argenzio (1975) suggested that colic and a number of other diseases common to the large intestine of horses may result from a malfunction in the microbial digestive process. Visek (1974) has proposed that an excessive production of ammonia from high-protein diets may be responsible for the high incidence of human colonic cancer in the more affluent societies of the world.

The major point here is that microorganisms indigenous to the digestive tract are important symbionts. They help protect the animal from pathogenic organisms, provide an additional source of nutrients, and take part in a number of other normal digestive-tract functions. An imbalance of this symbiotic relationship, resulting from either a disease or its treatment, can result in serious malfunctions.

SUMMARY

Many of the species variations in the digestive system can be related to diet. Carnivores tend to have a short, nonvoluminous, minimally compartmentalized gastrointestinal tract which provides for brief storage of food in the stomach until it is prepared for relatively rapid passage through the intestine. These animals can eat rapidly and digest at leisure. At the other extreme, herbivores may spend up to 75 percent of the day eating to obtain an equivalent amount of nutrients from a larger volume of food. Their digestive tract contains a more voluminous, compartmentalized stomach and/or hindgut, allowing for both a greater capacity and a more prolonged retention of digesta. The increase in relative stomach size appears to involve expansion of the areas lined with cardiac mucosa and/or stratified squamous epithelium. Among herbivores, there tends to be an inverse relationship between the volume of the stomach and the large intestine. In simple-stomached herbivores the major site of microbial digestion may be either the cecum or the colon. In rodents, for example, the cecum is the primary site. The colon is the major site in animals such as the horse.

These functional-morphological relationships do not of course account for all species variations. An enlarged stomach can provide a nonherbivore, such as the vampire bat, with the option of less frequent feeding. And microbial digestion occurs in the stomach and large intestine of carnivores and omnivores as well as herbivores. While this has greater nutritional significance in herbivores, its effects on the secretion and absorption of electrolytes and water may be equally important in nonherbivores as well. Furthermore, a voluminous and/or highly compartmentalized large intestine may be a function of the need to conserve water rather than the ability to digest plant roughage. Omnivores show great variations in digestive-tract structure: the bear has a gastrointestinal tract similar to the mink in its simplicity, while in many respects the large intestine of the pig or man is no less complex than that of many herbivores. It is possible that some characteristics, such as the compartmentalized stomach of the porpoise and the degree of sacculation in the large intestine of man, are preserved from an earlier time and different diet. For example, the concept of early man as a vegetarian is supported by the fact that most primates are vegetarians or herbivores, and seems to be further corroborated in scripture (Genesis 1:28–29 and 9:2–4).

REFERENCES

Alexander, F., and Benzie, D. 1950. A radiological study of the digestive tract of the foal. *Q. J. Exp. Physiol.* 36:213–17.

Alexander, F., and Davies, E.M. 1963. Production and fermentation of lactate by bacteria in the alimentary canal of the horse and pig. *J. Comp. Path.* 73:1–8.

Allison, M.J., Robinson, I.M., Dougherty, R.W., and Bucklin, J.A. 1975. Grain overload in cattle and sheep: Changes in microbial populations in the cecum and rumen. *Am. J. Vet. Res.* 36:181–85.

Argenzio, R.A. 1975. Functions of the equine large intestine and their interrelationship in disease. *Cornell Vet.* 65:303–30.

Argenzio, R.A., Lowe, J.E., Pickard, D.W., and Stevens, C.E. 1974a. Digesta passage and water exchange in the equine large intestine. *Am. J. Physiol.* 226:1035–42.

Argenzio, R.A., Miller, N., and Engelhardt, W. von. 1975. Effect of volatile fatty acids on water and ion absorption from the goat colon. *Am. J. Physiol.* 229:997–1002.

Argenzio, R.A., and Southworth, M. 1975. Sites of organic acid production and absorption in gastrointestinal tract of the pig. *Am. J. Physiol.* 228:454–60.

Argenzio, R.A., Southworth, M., and Stevens, C.E. 1974b. Sites of organic acid production and absorption in the equine gastrointestinal tract. *Am. J. Physiol.* 226:1043–50.

Argenzio, R.A., and Stevens, C.E. 1975. Cyclic changes in ionic composition of digesta in the equine intestinal tract. *Am. J. Physiol.* 228:1224–30.

Aukema, J.J., and Breukink, H.J. 1974. Abomasal ulcer in adult cattle with fatal haemorrhage. *Cornell Vet.* 64:303–17.

Banta, C.A., Clemens, E.T., Kronsky, M.M., and Sheffy, B.E. Sites of organic acid production and pattern of digesta movement in the gastrointestinal tract of dogs. Unpublished.

Barnes, E.M. 1972. The avian intestinal flora with particular reference to the possible ecological significance of the cecal anaerobic bacteria. *Am. J. Clin. Nutr.* 25:1475–79.

Bayliss, W.M., and Starling, E.H. 1903. On the uniformity of the pancreatic mechanism in vertebrata. *J. Physiol.* 29:174–80.

Bensley, R.R. 1902–1903. The cardiac glands of mammals. *Am. J. Anat.* 2:105–56.

Bonnafous, R., and Raynaud, P. 1968. Mise en évidence d'une activité lysante du colon proximal sur les microorganismes du tube digestif du lapin. *Arch. Sci. Physiol.* 22:57–64.

Buchner, P. 1965. *Endosymbiosis of Animals with Plant Microorganisms.* Interscience, New York, London, Sydney.

Burnstock, G. 1969. Evolution of the autonomic innervation of visceral and cardiovascular systems in vertebrates. *Pharmac. Rev.* 21:247–324.

Chien, W., and Stevens, C.E. 1972. Coupled active transport of Na and Cl across forestomach epithelium. *Am. J. Physiol.* 223:997–1003.

Clemens, E.T., Stevens, C.E., and Southworth, M. 1975. Sites of organic acid production and pattern of digesta movement in the gastrointestinal tract of swine. *J. Nutr.* 105:759–68

Davenport, H.W. 1964. Gastric mucosal injury by fatty and acetylsalicylic acids. *Gastroenterology* 46:245–53.

——. 1971. *Physiology of the Digestive Tract.* 3d ed. Year Book Medical, Chicago.

Dunlop, R.H. 1961. A study of factors related to the functional impairment resulting from loading the rumen of cattle with high carbohydrate feeds. Ph.D. diss., U. of Minnesota.

Dziuk, H.E. 1971. Reverse flow of gastrointestinal contents in turkeys (abstr.) *Fed. Proc.* 30:610.

Eckerlin, R.H., and Stevens, C.E. 1973. Bicarbonate secretion by the glandular saccules of the llama stomach. *Cornell Vet.* 63:436–45.

Elsden, S.R., Hitchcock, M.W.S., Marshall, R.A., and Phillipson, A.T. 1946. Volatile acid in the digestion of ruminants and other animals. *J. Exp. Biol.* 22:191–202.

Finstad, J., Papermaster, B.W., and Good, R.A. 1964. Evolution of the immune response. II. Morphologic studies on the origin of the thymus and organized lymphoid tissue. *Lab. Invest.* 13:490–512.

Giordano, C., de Pascale, C., Balestrieri, C., Cittadini, D., and Crescenzi, A. 1966. The incorporation of urea-^{15}N into serum proteins of uremic patients on low nitrogen diets. *J. Clin. Invest.* 45:1013.

Haslewood, G.A.D. 1968. Evolution and bile salts. In *Handbook of Physiology.* Sec. 6, C.F. Code and W. Heidel, eds., *Alimentary Canal.* Vol. 5, *Bile, Digestion, Ruminal Physiology.* Am. Physiol. Soc., Washington. Pp. 2375–90.

Henning, S.J., and Hird, F.J.R. 1970. Concentrations and metabolism of volatile fatty acids in the fermentative organs of two species of kangaroo and the guinea-pig. *Brit. J. Nutr.* 24:145–55.

Hildemann, W.H., and Thoenes, G.H. 1969. Immunological responses of Pacific hagfish. I. Skin transplantation immunity. *Transplantation* 7:506–21.

Hintz, H.F., Hogue, D.E., Walker, E.F., Lowe, J.E., and Schryver, H.F. 1971. Apparent digestion in various segments of the digestive tract of ponies fed diets with varying roughage-grain ratios. *J. Anim. Sci.* 32:245–48.

Hogben, C.A.M., Kent, T.H., Woodward, P.A., and Sill, A.J. 1974. Quantitative histology of the gastric mucosa: Man, dog, cat, guinea pig, and frog. *Gastroenterology* 67:1143–54.

Höller, H. 1970. Untersuchungen über Sekret und Sekretion der Cardiadrüsenzone im Magen des Schweines. *Zentralblatt Veterinärmedizin*, ser. A, 17:685–711, 857–73.

Hubel, K.A. 1974. The mechanism of bicarbonate secretion in rabbit ileum exposed to choleragen. *J. Clin. Invest.* 53:964–70.

Junqueira, L.C.U., and de Moraes, F.F. 1965. Comparative aspects of the vertebrate major salivary glands biology. In W. Bothermann, ed., *Funktionelle und morphologische Organisation der Zelle: Sekretion und Exkretion*. Springer-Verlag, Berlin, Heidelberg, New York. Pp. 36–48.

Junqueira, L.C.U., Malnic, G., and Monge, C. 1966. Reabsorptive function of the ophidian cloaca and large intestine. *Physiol. Zool.* 39:151–59.

McBee, R.H., and West, G.C. 1969. Cecal fermentation in the willow ptarmigan. *Condor* 71:54–58.

Minnich, J.E. 1970. Water and electrolyte balance of the desert iguana, *Dipsosaurus dorsalis*, in its natural habitat. *Comp. Biochem. Physiol.* 35:921–33.

Moir, R.J. 1968. Ruminant digestion and evolution. In *Handbook of Physiology*. Sec. 6, C.F. Code and W. Heidel, eds., *Alimentary Canal*. Vol. 5, *Bile, Digestion, Ruminal Physiology*. Am. Physiol. Soc., Washington. Pp. 2673–94.

Moir, R.J., Somers, M., and Waring, H. 1956. Studies on marsupial nutrition. I. Ruminant-like digestion in a herbivorous marsupial (*Setonix brachyurus* Quoy & Gaimard). *Austral. J. Biol. Sci.* 9:293–304.

Ohmart, R.D., McFarland, L.Z., and Morgan, J.P. 1970. Urographic evidence that urine enters the rectum and ceca of the roadrunner (*Geococcyx californianus*) Aves. *Comp. Biochem. Physiol.* 35:487–89.

Ohwaki, K., Hungate, R.E., Lotter, L., Hofmann, R.R., and Maloiy, G. 1974. Stomach fermentation in East African Colobus monkeys in their natural state. *Appl. Microb.* 27:713–23.

Oppel, A. 1897. *Lehrbuch der vergleichenden mikroskopischen Anatomie der Wirbeltiere*. Sec. 2, *Schlund und Darm*. Gustav Fischer, Jena.

Phillipson, A.T. 1947. The production of fatty acids in the alimentary tract of the dog. *J. Exp. Biol.* 23:346–49.

Pickard, D.W., and Stevens, C.E. 1972. Digesta flow through the rabbit large intestine. *Am. J. Physiol.* 222:1161–66.

Rubinstein, R., Howard, A.V., and Wrong, O.M. 1969. *In vivo* dialysis of faeces as a method of stool analysis. IV. The organic anion component. *Clin. Sci.* 37:549–64.

Scheiber, A.R., Dziuk, H.E., and Duke, G.E. 1969. Effects of a chronic colostomy in turkeys. *Poul. Sci.* 48:2179–82.

Slade, L.M., Bishop, R., Morris, J.G., and Robinson, D.W. 1971. Digestion and absorption of ^{15}N-labelled microbial protein in the large intestine of the horse. *Brit. Vet. J.* 127:xi–xiii.

Slade, L.M., Robinson, D.W., and Casey, K.E. 1970. Nitrogen metabolism in nonruminant herbivores. I. The influence of nonprotein nitrogen and protein quality on the nitrogen retention of adult mares. *J. Anim. Sci.* 30:753–60.

Smith, H.W. 1943. The evolution of the kidney. In *Lectures on the Kidney*. Porter Lectures, ser. IX. U. of Kansas Press, Lawrence.

Stevens, C.E. 1973. Transport across rumen epithelium. In H.H. Ussing and N.A. Thorn, eds., *Transport Mechanisms in Epithelia*. Proc. Alfred Benzon Symposium V. Munksgaard, Copenhagen. Pp. 404–26.

Stevens, C.E., and Stettler, B.K. 1966. Transport of fatty acid mixtures across rumen epithelium. *Am. J. Physiol.* 211:264–71.

Strauss, E.W., and Ito, S. 1969. A fine structural study of lipid-uptake in the terminal intestine of the scup, *Stenotomus chrysops*. *Biol. Bull.* 137:414–15.

Svendsen, P. 1969. Etiology and pathogenesis of abomasal displacement in cattle. *Nord. Vet. Med.* 21 (suppl. 1).

——. 1972. Inhibition of cecal motility in sheep by volatile fatty acids. *Nord. Vet. Med.* 24:393–96.

Svendsen, P., and Kristensen, B. 1970. Cecal dilatation in cattle: An experimental study of the etiology. *Nord. Vet. Med.* 22:578–83.

Thurston, J.P., Noirot-Timothée, C., and Arman, P. 1968. Fermentative digestion in the stomach of *Hippopotamus amphibius* (Artiodactyla:Suiformes) and associated ciliate protozoa. *Nature* 218:882–83.

Torres-Pinedo, R., Lavastida, M., Rivera, C.L., Rodriguez, H., and Ortiz, A. 1966. Studies on infant diarrhea. I. A comparison of the effects of milk feeding and intravenous therapy upon the composition and volume of the stool and urine. *J. Clin. Invest.* 45:469–80.

Vallenas, A., and Stevens, C.E. 1971. Volatile fatty acid concentrations and pH of llama and guanaco forestomach digesta. *Cornell Vet.* 61:239–52.

Van Kruiningen, H.J. 1974. Acute gastric dilatation: A review of comparative aspects, by species, and a study in dogs and monkeys. *J. Am. Anim. Hosp. Ass.* 10:294–324.

Visek, W.J. 1974. Some biochemical considerations in utilization of nonspecific nitrogen. *J. Ag. Food Chem.* 22:174–84.

Williams, V.J. 1963. Rumen function in the camel. *Nature* 197:1221.

Wootton, J.F., and Argenzio, R.A. 1975. Nitrogen utilization within the equine large intestine. *Am. J. Physiol.* 229:1062–67.

CHAPTER 19

Genesis and Propagation of Motor Activity in the Digestive Tract | by Alvin F. Sellers

Multicellular organisms are dependent upon volume transport systems for homeostasis. Urinary, genital, digestive, and cardiovascular sytems all contain hollow-tube modifications capable of developing propulsive pressure gradients. Study of rates of volume flow of material in these organs is of considerable benefit in understanding normal and disease processes. The motor function of the digestive tract is performed by smooth muscle, except at its pharyngeal and anal ends. In order to understand the mechanisms for propulsion of food through the gut, it is necessary to understand the properties of gastrointestinal smooth muscle. For example, following transection of the small gut, as in therapeutic resection and anastomosis, the distal end develops an electrical rhythm of lower frequency and diminished motility. Massive resection may be followed by diarrhea and malabsorption.

GASTROINTESTINAL SMOOTH MUSCLE

The smooth muscles of the gastrointestinal tract generally show spontaneous (myogenic) activity, conduction of electrical impulses from fiber to fiber, and sensitivity to stretch. Their activity is modulated, but not initiated, by autonomic nerves. Exceptions to this are the ruminant forestomach and avian gizzard smooth muscles, which are primarily nerve activated (Prosser, in Daniel 1974). Within the cells are parallel myofilaments; individual filaments terminate at the cell wall at the tapering tips of the cell (Davenport 1971). Their contractions cause lateral indentations on the cell border, so that the cell seems to fold on itself like an accordion. The filaments may slide past one another, which accounts for the great range of length over which tension can be exerted, and in part for the decrease in wall tension subsequent to stretch (e.g. as in the stomach during eating). The latter is called *stress relaxation,* and can also be caused by inhibition of active contraction. That is, if tension is being maintained by active and regular spike discharge, stretch may inhibit spiking for a time, during which the muscle relaxes to accommodate to the new length.

Individual smooth-muscle cells are surrounded by a sheath of reticular fibers attached to neighboring connective tissue. The force of contraction is transmitted through the reticulum to the connective tissue. Groups of muscle cells are organized as bundles (fasciculi). These contain about 7000 cells each and constitute the functional effector units. They are attached to adjacent bands by connective tissue.

In smooth muscle, as in other excitable tissues, there is normally an electrical potential of about −50 mv (inside negative to outside) across the membranes of single cells. This fluctuates in two major ways: *slow waves* are spontaneous, slow, transient depolarizations of the membrane potential, apparently conducted varying distances along the tract (Basic Electrical Rhythm, BER); *spikes* are faster transient depolarizations, which can occur in bursts at the periods of maximal depolarization of a slow wave. These rapid transients precede and appear to initiate contraction (Fig. 19.1).

In the cat and rabbit, longitudinal smooth-muscle fibers may show, at the peak of slow waves, one or more prepotentials (or generator potentials) ahead of the spike. These have been likened to the prepotentials of cardiac pacemaker tissue, and probably represent ion (Na^+, Ca^{++}) conductance changes. Parasympathetic stimulation increases the rate at which these potentials depolarize the

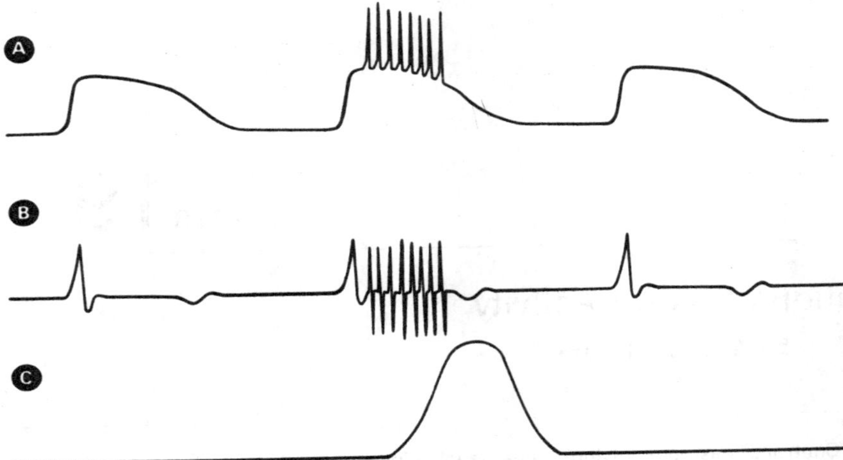

Figure 19.1. Diagram of relation between slow waves, spikes, and contractions. A, intracellular electrode, a burst of spike potentials appears on the second slow wave; B, extracellular electrode, configuration of recorded waves approximates a derivative of the membrane potential change; C, tension record, contractions are phased by bursts of spike potentials, which in turn are paced by slow waves. (From Christensen, reprinted, by permission, from the *New England Journal of Medicine* 285:85–98, 1971.)

membrane, thus increasing the rate of spike discharge. Sympathetic stimulation prolongs the rate at which the generator potential depolarizes the membrane, thus slowing the rate of spike discharge.

Slow waves set the maximal possible frequency of "segmental" contractions. The waves are generated in longitudinal muscle of the small bowel, but pass to circular muscle passively, possibly via thin connecting muscle strands. They are synchronized in a ring circumferentially, and travel for a few centimeters at about 1 cm/sec. This propagation is abolished if the circular muscle is transected. A sodium-potassium pump contributes to the resting potential; one hypothesis for slow waves is that they represent a rhythmic sodium pump (Prosser, in Daniel 1974). The nature of the primary pacemaker reaction is unknown.

Spikes are normally required to activate contractions, and involve inward calcium currents. Spikes are present in all vertebrate gastrointestinal muscles. Vagal stimulation results in bigger bursts of spikes and more vigorous contractions, as does the parasympathomimetic drug physostigmine. Sympathetic stimulation reduces spiking without affecting the slow waves; such stimulation reduces the rate at which the prepotentials depolarize the membrane and prolongs the intervals between spikes.

Figure 19.2 shows electrical events in the duodenum

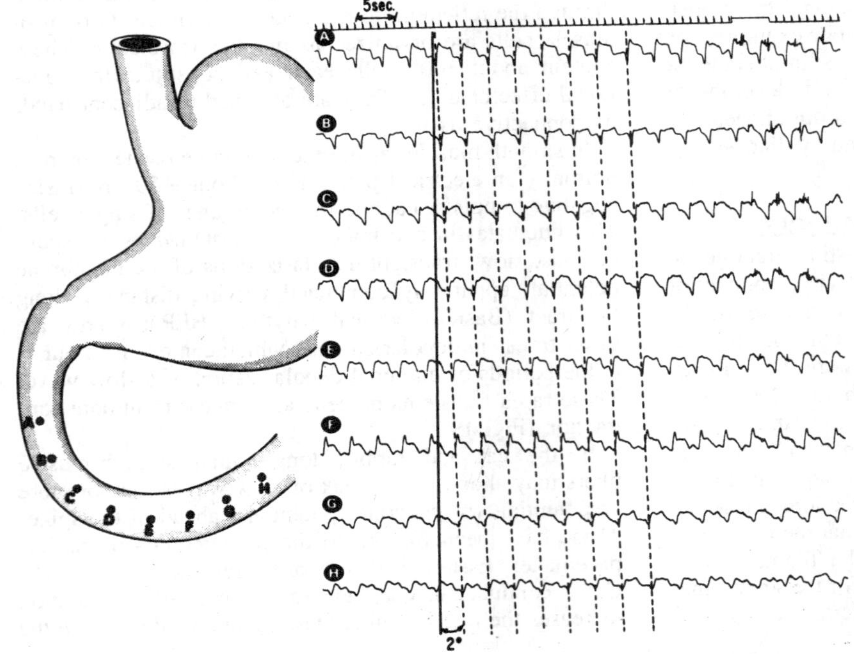

Figure 19.2. Electrical events in duodenum of unanesthetized cat. Note aboral progression of slow waves, and at right, superimposed spikes. (From Christensen, reprinted, by permission, from the *New England Journal of Medicine* 285:85–98, 1971.)

of an unanesthetized cat with chronically implanted needle electrodes.

PRESSURES IN HOLLOW ABDOMINAL VISCERA

The abdominal viscera are relatively mobile, and their specific gravity is approximately that of water. The physical result is that the viscera apply hydrostatic pressure to the serosal surface of a given hollow viscus (e.g. the stomach) proportional to their vertical height.

If the stomach contents, for example, have nearly the same specific gravity as the abdominal viscera, then the stomach will behave as a water-filled bag suspended in water, that is, the transmural pressure approaches zero (Davenport 1971). As the animal eats or drinks, stomach filling results in a rise in hydrostatic pressure within it. The intra-abdominal hydrostatic pressure rises at the same time. Thus the difference in pressure across the stomach wall (transmural pressure) is small. However, the volume of the organ is increasing, so that wall tension is rising, for in a hollow organ at constant transmural pressure (P), tension (T) in the wall is directly proportional to the radius (r)—Laplace's law. For a sphere (which the stomach approximates), $P = 2T/r$; for a cylinder (which the intestine approximates), $P = T/r$.

This tension increase, proportional to the radius, is sensed by mechanoreceptors in the wall (Iggo 1955, Leek 1972). For example, the afferent discharge of these receptors during active contraction of the organ is proportional to the developed tension and conveys the sensation of fullness (Fig. 19.3).

It is further apparent from Laplace's law that pressure in hollow organs is directly proportional to the tension in their walls. The tension in the wall of the digestive tract is maintained by active contraction of its muscle. Adjustments in active tension are the means by which pressure and volume are regulated (Davenport 1971). Stress relaxation occurs as the organ fills. This involves both sliding of myofibrils past one another and inhibition of spiking. These allow accommodation to the new volume, and transmural pressure falls toward the value obtaining before the volume increase. As the animal swallows, the gastric fundus also relaxes reflexly, along with the caudal esophageal sphincter, providing some additional volume for swallowed food (receptive relaxation).

MOVEMENTS OF THE STOMACH

In the dog, when the stomach is empty, electrical slow waves occur at about 4–5 per minute, with occasional superimposed spikes and corresponding contractions. When the animal eats, vagal tone to the stomach increases. Each slow wave may now bear spikes. Peristaltic waves now reach a maximum rate of 4–5 per minute (or a bit more, due to a slight increase in slow-wave frequency).

In the dog stomach, slow waves begin from a pacemaker high on the greater curvature in the longitudinal muscle. Aboral conduction is at first about 0.5 cm/sec, lasting about 1.5 seconds at any one point. In the pyloric antrum, the aboral conduction rate reaches 3–4 cm/sec. When spikes are superimposed on these slow waves, peristaltic waves about 2 cm wide follow the electrical waves over the body of the stomach and antrum. Two or three such waves are usually present at any one time.

The terminal antrum and pylorus contract almost simultaneously, but the pylorus closes early, so that the net result is that only a small quantity of liquid enters the

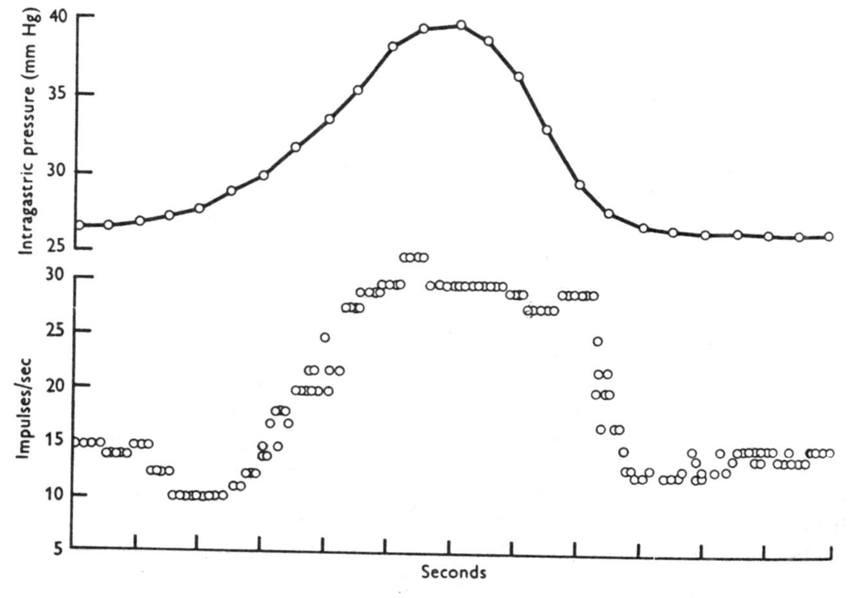

Figure 19.3. Intrareticular pressure, or reflex isometric contraction of reticulum (above), and frequency of discharge in single afferent vagal fiber (below) in the goat. (From Iggo 1955, *J. Physiol.* 128:593–607.)

duodenum with each wave. The rest of the liquid is retropelled into the proximal antrum. Then the terminal antral segment and pylorus relax until the next peristaltic wave comes down the antrum. The contraction of the antrum on its contents squeezes fluid in both directions but tends to force more fluid material into the duodenum and leaves solid material to be remixed in the body of the stomach. This also aids in the trituration of this material.

The first part of the duodenum is stimulated to contract by distension with chyme. Its contraction appears to displace the chyme in both directions—orally into antrum and aborally. Oral displacement appears to be limited by the fact that most duodenal contractions follow antral contractions. The antral basic electrical rhythm, whose frequency is much less than that of the duodenum, is conducted into the duodenal bulb by longitudinal muscle fibers which cross the pyloric junction, chiefly along the lesser curvature. The two electrical rhythms interact, with the result that every fifth or so duodenal depolarization is augmented by depolarization conducted from the antrum. Augmented duodenal depolarization is often followed by contraction.

Spike bursts are propagated in retrograde fashion orally from time to time in the duodenum of unanesthetized rhesus monkeys (Thouin et al. 1974) and sheep (Sellers and Code, unpublished). About 5 percent retrograde volume flow occurs in the sheep duodenum and 40 percent in the goat (Singleton 1961).

CONTROL OF GASTRIC EMPTYING

Duodenal intraluminal pressures of 10–15 mm Hg, attained by distension with chyme, reflexly reduce gastric motility via vagal efferents (enterogastric reflex), and in painful distensions by way of sympathetic efferents from the celiac ganglion. Fat in the duodenum of a dog profoundly inhibits the motility of a transplanted gastric pouch, and delays gastric emptying in intact dogs. Since fats in the duodenum are powerful releasers of cholecystokinin-pancreozymin (CCK-PZ) and, since pure CCK-PZ has been shown (Debas et al. 1975) to inhibit gastric emptying in dogs concurrent with pancreatic protein (enzyme) secretion and gallbladder contraction stimulation, inhibition of gastric emptying is thought to be one of the physiological actions of CCK-PZ (see Chapter 20). Gastric emptying may be completely suppressed for 24 hours by painful injuries. Hypertonic and hypotonic solutions (e.g. glucose) in the duodenum slow gastric emptying.

MOTILITY OF THE SMALL INTESTINE

In the cat and dog, a pacemaker in the longitudinal muscle of the duodenum near the entrance of the bile duct generates slow waves at about 17–18 per minute. Successively lower portions of the small gut have lower slow-wave rates. These are conducted aborally for short distances. (Vomiting is characterized by orad propagation; Weisbrodt and Christensen 1972, Tan and Code 1974.) Spikes and their resultant segmental contractions tend to be few during fasting, and increase with feeding, vagal stimulation, or cholinergic drugs. Atropine tends to diminish spike activity.

In fasted dogs and cats, and in fed sheep and rabbits, bands of spike potentials with accompanying segmental contractions sweep aborally over the small gut, taking about 1.5–2 hours to reach the terminal ileum (Szurszewski 1969; Carlson, Bedi, and Code 1972; Weisbrodt and Christensen 1972; Grivel and Ruckebusch 1972). Neither the continuity of the bowel wall nor the presence of intestinal contents is needed for this propagation. Propagation in normal aboral sequence successively involves separated intestinal loops with intact extrinsic nerve supply. Extrinsic nerves must be responsible for the coordinated propagation. Segmental contractions are propulsive, and differ only in degree from the more rarely occurring peristalsis (Grivel and Ruckebusch 1972). Peristalsis and segmentation differ only quantitatively in the cat jejunum (Bortoff and Sacco, in Daniel 1974).

THE ILEOCECAL JUNCTION

Relaxation of the ileocecal junction in dog and man occurs during ileal distension. During gastric emptying there is heightened ileal contraction, resulting in emptying of the ileum during and following eating (gastroileal reflex). Each time a propulsive wave travels along the ileum, a small amount of digesta is squirted into the cecum. In man during eating there is fall in the tonus of the junction muscle. This would favor ileal flow into the cecum. Distension of the cecum causes junction tonus to rise, delaying flow from the ileum.

LARGE INTESTINE

From study of a few domestic species (cat, pig, rabbit, horse, and turkey), the many uncertainties regarding both functions and diseases of the large gut are beginning to be resolved. It will be the author's intention first to set out common denominators, where known, among species, then to describe those species about which most is known.

Primary function and species comparison

In 1904, Elliott and Barclay-Smith studied large intestinal motility in a wide variety of species. They observed colonic antiperistalsis in the cat, rat, guinea pig, rabbit, hedgehog, and ferret, and demonstrated reflux of digesta from colon to cecum in all but the last two, which have no cecum. They postulated three functionally distinct colonic segments, best distinguished in the herbivores studied (e.g. rabbit, see Fig. 18.5): (1) a proximal segment with digesta similar in consistency to the cecum, and with predominantly antiperistaltic motor activity; (2) an intermediate segment in which formed feces first appeared, with predominantly peristaltic motor activity; and (3) a distal segment similar to the intermediate segment, except that it alone could be evacuated in a single movement by stimulation of the sacral parasympathetic nerves.

Present studies support their observations, and suggest that a primary function of colonic antiperistalsis may well be selective retention of water and microorganisms essential for fermentation in the large intestine. This is consistent with the presence of a large intestinal pacemaker some distance caudal to the ileocecal junction in most species studied (Christensen 1971).

Cat and horse

The cat has been especially well studied. In this carnivore, with a short, simple large intestine, distension of the proximal large gut during filling initiates antiperistalsis. The slow-wave frequency is higher in the distal colon than in the proximal part (about 4.5/min proximal, 6/min distal) and the slow waves are conducted orally in the proximal half of the colon. This polarity tends to produce orad flow, on the average, in the proximal half of the cat colon. Migrating spike bursts arise about the middle of the colon and progress aborally (70%) or orally (30%). Contractions accompany these spike bursts (Fig. 19.4).

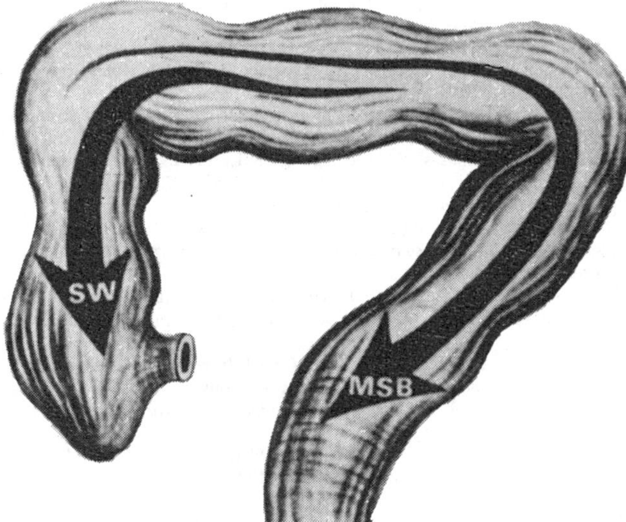

Figure 19.4. Proposed scheme for flow in the cat colon related to electrical events. Electrical slow waves (SW) are oriented in such a way that they appear to spread toward the cecum, away from a pacemaker whose position is highly variable but about midway along the colon. Since slow waves appear to pace rhythmic contractions, such contractions should produce flow with a polarity in the same direction (arrow, SW), although this polarity is probably not fixed. The migrating spike bursts (MSB) begin at a variable position in the middle or proximal colon and migrate toward the rectum. Since contractions accompany them, the contractions should produce flow with a polarity in the same direction (arrow, MSB). The migrating spike burst also has the capacity to reverse direction. (From Christensen, Anuras, and Hauser, *Gastroenterology* 66:240–47, © 1974, The Williams & Wilkins Co., Baltimore.)

Slow waves in the cat colon are generated in the circular muscle layer. Cholinergic drugs prolong the slow-wave duration and increase the incidence of spike bursts and thus of contractions. These effects are antagonized by atropine. Adrenergic drugs are inhibitory to spike activity in large doses (Wienbeck and Christensen 1971).

In cats with either spontaneous or induced diarrhea, instead of the usual point-to-point spread of the electrical excitation over the colon, many pacemakers arise in closely spaced segments. These segments then contract independently and the contractions spread only short distances. These contractions are so weak and the distances traversed so small that they are ineffective in generating intraluminal pressure changes. The colon becomes in effect a flaccid, low-resistance segment, poorly able to oppose flow of digesta entering it from the ileum (Christensen et al. 1972). In humans, diarrhea is often characterized by a flaccid colon, whereas in constipation, colon activity is increased over normal (Connell 1968, in *Handbook*).

The horse has also been studied in considerable detail. This strict herbivore, having a capacious, haustrated large intestine, derives a minimum of 25 percent of its daily maintenance energy requirement from volatile fatty acid (VFA) produced by microbial fermentation in the large gut (Argenzio et al. 1974).

Endoscopic observations by Dyce and Hartmann (1973) using cecal fistulae allowed study of the erectile *ileal papilla*. This projects into the cecal body at all times, with more pronounced projection accompanying ejection of ileal contents into the cecum. Cecal haustra were photographed in successively oral as well as aboral progression of contractions. *Mass movements* at times supervened, tumbling digesta from the cecal body aborally into the base of the cecum. This was followed by contraction of a dorsoventral fold of the cecal base which, by obliteration of the lumen at that point, effectively prevented reflux during the immediately supervening cecal-base contraction. The latter propelled digesta through the ceco-colic orifice.

Digesta-passage and water-exchange studies (Argenzio et al. 1974) indicated that major barriers to digesta flow existed at the junction between the ventral and dorsal large colon (pelvic flexure) and at the junction of the dorsal and small colon (transverse colon). The delay in transit thus imposed was somewhat more than 2 days, allowing cellulose hydrolysis with VFA production. Figure 19.5 shows, for example, that ventral-colon volume increase following feeding (some threefold) peaked at 8 hours. This increase was accompanied by an increase in total volatile fatty acid and net production. The total volume of transmucosal water movement into the entire large gut approximated 12 L (see Fig. 21.2). This could be almost entirely accounted for by the rise in osmotic pressure of the digesta consequent upon VFA production

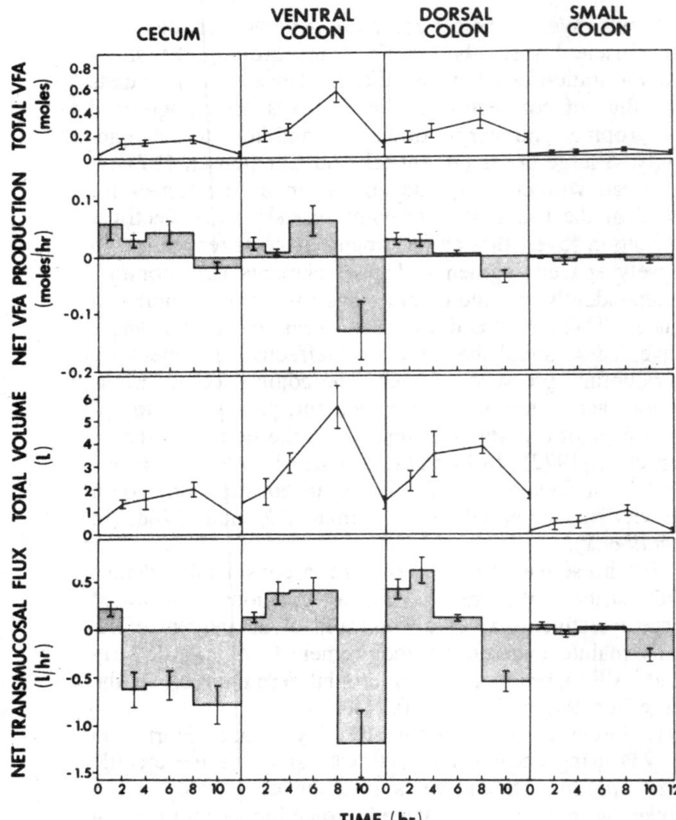

Figure 19.5. Volume, net transmucosal exchange of water, VFA content, and VFA net production in individual segments of large intestine as a function of time (pony). Animals fed at zero time; negative values designate net absorption. (From Argenzio 1975. *Cornell Vet.* 65:303–30.)

(Argenzio et al. 1974). Thus, using digesta transit or retention data, the effects of the motility patterns of this complex organ, e.g. on cellulose hydrolysis, may be inferred.

Dziuk (1971) noted that the predominant motor activity of the entire colon of the turkey was antiperistaltic. Hukahara and Neya (1968) described a colonic pacemaker area in the rat and guinea pig from which waves of antiperistalsis moved toward the cecum, and waves of peristaltic contraction moved along the distal colon. Pickard and Stevens (1972) found in the rabbit a periodic flux and reflux of digesta between the cecum and proximal colon. Clemens and Stevens (1974) noted prolonged retention of both fluid and particulate markers in, first the descending colon, then the ascending colon of swine, with accompanying VFA production.

DEFECATION

Defecation is a reflex act in which the feces are discharged from the terminal colon and rectum. It, like emesis, may be aided by abdominal press produced by muscle contraction with the glottis closed. It is subject to voluntary inhibition in trained animals and humans.

The efferent pathways of the defecation reflex are cholinergic. Thus parasympathomimetic drugs make the reflex more vigorous. Distension of the terminal colon and rectum is the normal stimulus for the reflex, which includes strong peristaltic movements of the terminal colon, contraction of the longitudinal muscle of the rectum, and relaxation of the internal and external anal sphincters.

Frightened animals frequently defecate, presumably by facilitation of the reflex by centers in the brain. In humans, cord damage above the lumbosacral region results in transient incontinence. The reflex soon returns, and autonomous evacuation follows mass movement in the proximal colon. The latter is strongly influenced by ileal outflow, and this in turn is affected by eating.

REFERENCES

Argenzio, R.A. 1975. Functions of the equine large intestine and their interrelationship in disease. *Cornell Vet.* 65:303–30.

Argenzio, R.A., Lowe, J.E., Pickard, D.W., and Stevens, C.E. 1974. Digesta passage and water exchange in the equine large intestine. *Am. J. Physiol.* 226:1035–1042.

Argenzio, R.A., Southworth, M., and Stevens, C.E. 1974. Sites of organic acid production and absorption in the equine gastrointestinal tract. *Am. J. Physiol.* 226:1043–50.

Carlson, G.M., Bedi, B.S., and Code, C.F. 1972. Mechanism of propagation of intestinal interdigestive myoelectric complex. *Am. J. Physiol.* 222:1027–30.

Christensen, J. 1971. The controls of gastrointestinal movements: Some old and new views. *New Eng. J. Med.* 285:85–98.

Christensen, J., Anuras, S., and Hauser, R.L. 1974. Migrating spike bursts and electrical slow waves in the cat colon: Effect of sectioning. *Gastroenterology* 66:240–47.

Christensen, J., Weisbrodt, N.W., and Hauser, R.L. 1972. Electrical slow waves of the proximal colon of the cat in diarrhea. *Gastroenterology* 62:1167–73.

Clemens, E.T., and Stevens, C.E. 1974. Digesta flow and organic acid concentrations in the gastrointestinal tract of the pig. *Physiologist* 17:197.

Daniel, E.E., ed. 1974. *Proceedings, Fourth International Symposium on Gastrointestinal Motility*. Mitchell, Vancouver.

Davenport, H.W. 1971. *Physiology of the Digestive Tract*. 3d ed. Year Book Medical, Chicago.

Debas, H.T., Farooq, H., and Grossman, M.I. 1975. Inhibition of gastric emptying is a physiological action of cholecystokinin. *Gastroenterology* 68:1211–17.

Dyce, K.M., and Hartmann, E.G. 1973. An endoscopic study of the cecal base of the horse. *Tijdschrift Diergeneeskunde* 98(20):957–62.

Dziuk, H.E. 1971. Reverse flow of gastrointestinal contents in turkeys. *Fed. Proc.* 30:610.

Elliott, T.R., and Barclay-Smith, E. 1904. Antiperistalsis and other muscular activities of the colon. *J. Physiol.* 31:272–304.

Grivel, M.L., and Ruckebusch, Y. 1972. The propagation of segmental contractions along the small intestine. *J. Physiol.* 227:611–25.

Handbook of Physiology. 1968. Sec. 6, C.F. Code and W. Heidel, eds., *Alimentary Canal*. Vol. 4, *Motility*. Am. Physiol. Soc., Washington.

Hukahara, T., and Neya, T. 1968. The movements of the colon of rats and guinea pigs. *J. Physiol.* (Tokyo), 18:551–62.

Iggo, A. 1955. Tension receptors in the stomach and urinary bladder. *J. Physiol.* 128:593–607.

Leek, B.F. 1972. Abdominal visceral receptors. In H. Autrum, ed., *Handbook of Sensory Physiology*. Vol. 3, pt. 1, E. Neil, ed., *Enteroceptors*. Springer-Verlag, Berlin, New York. Pp. 113–60.

Pickard, D.W., and Stevens, C.E. 1972. Digesta flow through the rabbit large intestine. *Am. J. Physiol.* 222:1161–66.

Singleton, A.G. 1961. The electromagnetic measurement of the flow of digesta through the duodenum of the goat and the sheep. *J. Physiol.* 155:134–47.

Szurszewski, J.H. 1969. A migrating electrical complex of the canine small intestine. *Am. J. Physiol.* 217:1757–63.

Tan, L., and Code, C.F. 1974. The effects of cholecystokinin on the canine gastrointestinal tract at different phases of the interdigestive myoelectric complex. *Physiologist* 17:341.

Thouin, A., Braitman, R.E., Chaddock, T.E., Hamilton, C.L., and Carlson, G.M. 1974. Interdigestive gastric and duodenal myoelectric activity in the unanesthetized rhesus monkey. *Physiologist* 17:345.

Walsh, J.H., and Grossman, M.I. 1975. Gastrin (first of two parts). *New Eng. J. Med.* 292:1324–34.

Weisbrodt, N.W., and Christensen, J. 1972. Electrical activity of the cat duodenum in fasting and vomiting. *Gastroenterology* 63:1004–10.

Wienbeck, M., and Christensen, J. 1971. Effects of some drugs on electrical activity of the isolated colon of the cat. *Gastroenterology* 61:470–78.

CHAPTER 20

Neurohumoral Regulation of Gastrointestinal Function—Secretion and Motility | by Alvin F. Sellers

Much of the activity of the digestive tract is expressed in variations in glandular secretion rates and hollow-organ contraction. These are largely controlled involuntarily by autonomic and hormonal agencies working in conjunction.

SALIVARY SECRETION

The presence of food in the mouth and its mastication are primary stimuli to increased saliva secretion, as is also taste perception. Afferents from the mouth, pharynx, olfactory area, and from the forestomach in ruminants, converge on salivary secretory centers in the medulla. Parasympathetic preganglionic efferents in cranial nerves VII, IX, and X synapse in or close to the glands. Their postganglionic fibers are distributed to the acinar secretory cells, where acetylcholine is liberated.

Stimulation of salivary gland cells to secrete, in the dog or cat, for example, involves change in magnitude of the transmembrane potential of the secretory cells. Thus during stimulation the resistance of the contraluminal secretory cell membrane decreases. Initially, loss of cell potassium ion occurs, and sodium ion enters the cell. (The changes in the transmembrane potential may be the result of these two conductance changes.) The concentration of potassium ion is now elevated in the saliva and in the venous blood draining the gland (e.g. dog submaxillary, Burgen 1956; sheep parotid, Coats et al. 1958). It is not clear how this is related to the accompanying secretion of fluid, other electrolytes, or protein, or to the accompanying elevation in metabolic rate of the gland (Schneyer et al. 1972).

In the excretory ducts, net reabsorption of sodium occurs, and is more complete when the rate of flow is slower. Secretion of potassium into the duct lumens appears to be coupled with sodium reabsorption.

Thus Heidenhain in 1878 noted that in the submaxillary and parotid glands of the dog increased strength of stimulus resulted in an increased rate of flow and an increase in salt concentration. Subsequent work has shown that a primary secretion is formed in the acini which is approximately isotonic to plasma and has a sodium concentration similar to plasma. The ducts then reabsorb Na and Cl in excess of water from this primary secretion; this is accompanied by a lesser duct secretion of K^+ and HCO_3^-. The rise in [Na] and [Cl] with progressive increase in flow rate (Fig. 20.1) is currently thought to be due to progressive saturation of the reabsorptive processes in the ducts (Schneyer et al. 1972).

In the sheep and man, the reabsorption of sodium and chloride in the ducts is under the control of the circulating aldosterone concentration. During sodium depletion, when increased aldosterone blood concentration obtains, the sodium content of the saliva and the volume of saliva secreted are both reduced (Blair-West, Coghlan, Denton, and Wright 1967, in *Handbook*). The salivary sodium is largely replaced by potassium.

When the parasympathetic nerve supply to the dog's submaxillary gland is stimulated or acetylcholine is given, the resting blood flow rate through the submaxillary gland (0.1–0.6 ml/g/min) rises about fivefold. However, there is no necessary relation between increased blood flow and secretion. With stimulation, oxygen and glucose consumption increase.

Sympathetic efferents from the cranial cervical ganglion are adrenergic, liberating norepinephrine or epinephrine, and are distributed to blood vessels and secre-

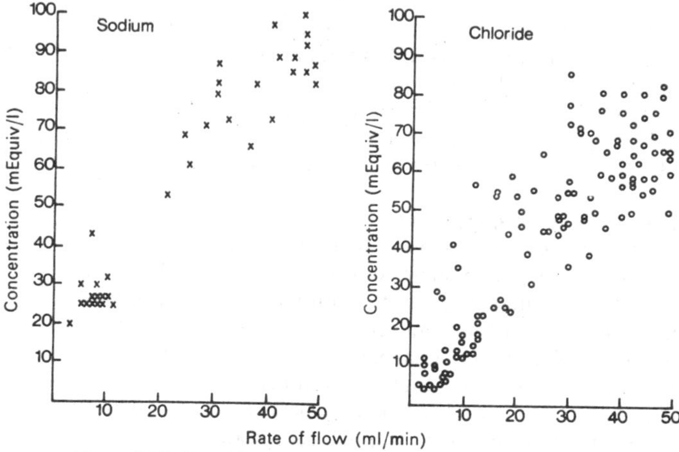

Figure 20.1. Parotid secretion in the conscious pony: relationship between rate of secretion and [Na] and [Cl] in saliva. (From Alexander and Hickson, in Phillipson, ed., *Physiology of Digestion and Metabolism in the Ruminant*, Oriel, Newcastle upon Tyne, 1970.)

tory cells. Stimulation of sympathetic fibers to all glands causes vasoconstriction. This results in a much lower rate of primary secretion from sympathetic than from parasympathetic stimulation (Emmelin 1955), but K^+ and HCO_3^- secretion by the ducts is stimulated almost to the same extent. Thus experimentally, the slower-flowing *sympathetic saliva* acquires a much higher [K] and lower [Na] in the final saliva than *parasympathetic saliva*.

ESOPHAGUS

The esophagus shows wide variations among species. In certain birds (doves, pigeons, flamingos) it produces a nutrient fluid for the young. In doves and pigeons (and presumably in flamingos) the holocrine "crop milk" is under the control of prolactin from the anterior pituitary. In some birds it serves a storage function, particularly in those with crops (e.g. chicken). Thus when a fasted chicken is fed, the first food is swept by peristalsis into the gizzard. Then the crop sphincter opens reflexly and subsequent food enters the crop; emptying of the crop is regulated reflexly by the degree of distension of lower portions of the tract.

The esophagus is in effect continuous with the reticular groove in ruminants. Suckling in young ruminants reflexly closes the groove, conducting the swallowed milk directly to the abomasum. Equids (horses, asses) possess a long, thick smooth-muscle terminal esophagus, with a well-marked cardiac sphincter (Fig. 20.2).

Afferents from palate, pharynx, and epiglottis connect tactile receptors in those organs to a swallowing center in the medulla. The compressive force exerted by the hyoid, lingual, and pharyngeal musculature drives the bolus into the upper esophagus. Near the nucleus ambiguus, motoneurons are found which innervate the striated muscle of the esophagus. These fire in overlapping sequence,

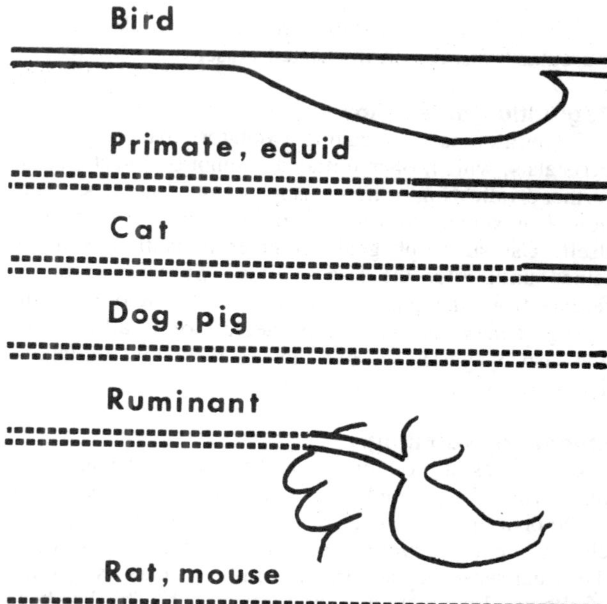

Figure 20.2. Distribution of esophageal striated muscle (dotted line) and smooth muscle (solid line) in some common species

causing a peristaltic wave to proceed aborally upon ingress of a bolus. The cardia relaxes upon the first swallow, remaining open during repeated swallowing and until the esophageal peristaltic wave reaches it after the last swallow.

Esophageal peristaltic waves arise in the absence of buccopharyngeal swallowing when the esophagus is distended at any point, inducing secondary peristalsis. This is accompanied by relaxation of the cardia just as with primary waves. A strong stationary afferent input, as with lodged food in the cervical or thoracic esophagus, initiates repeated peristaltic waves. These start at the cervical end of the esophagus but are inhibited distal to the point of distension (Doty 1968, in *Handbook*). The frequency of firing, the duration of discharge of the motoneurons, and the strength of the resultant contraction of the esophageal muscle are all proportional to the degree of distension.

In those species having an extensive area of esophageal smooth muscle cranial to the cardia (see Fig. 20.2) the effects of hormones and drugs on this muscle may be summarized as follows: (1) In general, cholinergic drugs (acetylcholine and other choline esters) cause caudal esophageal sphincter relaxation; this is blocked by atropine, which also tends to reduce the frequency or amplitude of balloon-induced peristalsis; (2) Epinephrine tends to produce caudal esophageal sphincter contraction.

In animals with predominantly striated muscle in the esophagus (e.g. sheep) movements are unaffected by atropine. However, movement ceases after administration of decamethonium or *d*-tubocurarine, which block neuromuscular transmission in striated muscle.

Deglutition or swallowing

Deglutition is a spreading excitatory pattern causing peristalsis, which, once initiated, cannot be forestalled by further swallowing or by glossopharyngeal nerve stimulation. It is subject to afferent control from the esophagus itself. Caudal esophageal sphincter relaxation is maintained until after the last swallow. Stimulation of afferents from the pharynx, larynx, and epiglottis in the laryngeal nerve is followed by deglutition in all animals, and also by gastric groove closure in young ruminants. The latter is annulled by atropine.

Emesis or vomiting

Carnivores and omnivores (except rodents) vomit easily. Swine, for example, frequently vomit with irritation of the pharynx or stomach, e.g. indigestion states, erysipelas, cholera. In ruminants, vomiting does not occur in the usual sense of the term, but rather occurs as ejection of abomasal contents into the forestomach. This has been noted in intestinal obstruction. Vomiting in the horse is extremely rare, apparently due to the marked tonus of the caudal esophageal sphincter. It is the only domestic species in which acute gastric dilatation can occur to the point of rupture of the stomach wall without vomiting.

A more detailed description of vomiting can be given for the cat (Smith and Brizzee 1961, Weisbrodt and Christensen 1972, McCarthy and Borison 1974). Electrical slow-wave amplitude in the duodenum decreases and is superseded by a long burst of intense spike activity spreading orad at about 3 cm/sec, driving a mass antiperistaltic movement. This empties the proximal small gut into the relaxed stomach. Repetitive inspiratory movements, with glottis closed, result in filling of the relaxed thoracic esophagus with gastric content. This is followed by reflux of contents from the thoracic esophagus into the stomach, in a repetitive rhythmic fashion called retching.

Retching drives the gastric contents forward and backward by inspiratory muscle contraction, with the glottis closed concurrent with rectus abdominis muscle contraction, followed by relaxation. The lowered intrathoracic pressure, concurrent with raised intra-abdominal pressure, aspirates gastric content into the thoracic esophagus. Each such contraction lasts about 0.1–0.3 seconds. Relaxation of the inspiratory and abdominal muscles then occurs, allowing reflux back into the stomach. Several such retching cycles precede the actual expulsive effort. Expulsion is brought about by a stronger, longer rectus abdominis muscle contraction occurring coincidentally with contraction of inspiratory muscles (including diaphragm) against a closed glottis, as before, but this time ending with sudden relaxation of the diaphragm. This allows the intrathoracic pressure to become positive rapidly by transmission of the pressure that has already been built up in the abdomen. Vomitus is expelled mostly through the mouth since the soft palate is elevated reflexly, closing off the posterior nares.

Eructation or belching

In man belching is associated with relaxation of the lower esophageal sphincter during inspiration. The gas is expelled by increased intra-abdominal and intrathoracic pressure via somatic muscle contraction. This occurs while the pharyngoesophageal sphincter is relaxed. In ruminants eructation is a highly developed reflex event, occurring once or twice a minute, closely integrated with forestomach contraction. Volume receptors in the rumen, stimulated during rumen contractions, initiate reflex relaxation of the cardia. Gas enters the esophagus as a result of rumen contraction and abdominal press. It is then expelled by antiperistalsis.

Regurgitation

Regurgitation is noted in ruminants and in certain birds such as owls. Unlike emesis, regurgitation is a normal physiological component of the animal's digestive process. In ruminants regurgitation is the first stage of rumination (see Chapter 22). It involves inspiration against a closed glottis which is simultaneous with submergence of the cardia. Ingesta thus aspirated into the lower esophagus are driven to the mouth by antiperistalsis. Less is known about this process in the few other species in which it is practiced.

STOMACH

Upon the sight, smell, or ingestion of food into the mouth, reflex vagal tone to the stomach increases; the blood flow, motor activity, and acid and pepsin secretion all increase. Increased blood flow following vagal stimulation or cholinergic drugs does not in itself stimulate secretion, but adequate flow is required if the stomach is to secrete (Jacobson 1967, in *Handbook*). The vagal stimulation causes release of gastrin from the pyloric mucosa. Gastrin is synergistic with acetylcholine liberated at vagal endings, causing increased gastric mucosal blood flow and HCl and pepsinogen secretion. Food in the stomach causes continued gastrin release.

Gastrin has a tropic effect on the mucosa of the stomach and intestine. This is evident from the profound atrophy of these mucosae during starvation in the rat or after antrectomy in the rat or human; the atrophy can be prevented by gastrin injection. Hyperplasia of the gastric mucosa occurs in humans with gastrin-secreting tumors of the exocrine pancreas, and in rats given large doses of gastrin over several weeks. In such rats, secretin counteracts the tropic action of gastrin on gastric mucosa. The pancreas of rats and probably of humans is also supported tropically by gastrin (Walsh and Grossman 1975).

As mentioned in Chapter 19, when gastric digesta enter the duodenum, gastric motility is reduced. This is accomplished reflexly, the efferent pathway being in part by way of vagal fibers (Thomas et al. 1934). Acidification of the proximal duodenum of dogs delays gastric emptying (Cooke 1974), as does cholecystokinin-pancreozymin (CCK-PZ) (Debas et al. 1975).

Animals differ greatly in the distribution of cardiac glandular epithelium in the gastric mucosa (see Chapter 18), the pig, for example, having a much larger cardiac glandular area than the dog, as do also the Camelidae (e.g. llama). The common denominator in all species so far studied seems to be that secretion of bicarbonate ion into the lumen occurs in exchange for chloride ion. This cardiac glandular epithelium thus resembles in this function the stratified squamous epithelium of the rumen (Stevens 1973).

Pepsinogens are synthesized and secreted by the chief cells of the oxyntic glandular area and are activated to pepsin by the HCl secreted by the parietal cells. The milk-clotting enzyme, rennin, which also is proteolytic, is present in the gastric juice of the calf, lamb, and kid (Taylor 1962). Pepsin can also coagulate milk, and presumably does this in the newborn of those species in which rennin has not been clearly demonstrated.

The precise mechanism of secretion of approximately isotonic HCl by the parietal cells is not clear. Energy for the process is derived from oxidation, probably of glucose. For every hydrogen ion produced, a bicarbonate ion equivalent enters the interstitial fluid and eventually the blood. This is due to neutralization of hydroxyl ions by carbonic acid. The latter is produced by hydration of CO_2 with the aid of carbonic anhydrase present in the parietal cells.

Once hydrogen ions have been secreted, the gastric mucosa contains them within the gastric lumen. It normally resists back-diffusion of (and damage from) them. In the dog stomach this barrier can be damaged by high concentrations of HC1, or by lower concentrations of weak organic acids (e.g. acetic, propionic, or butyric acid, or aspirin) which are largely undissociated (lipid-soluble) at the low pH of gastric contents (Davenport 1971).

Gastric acid secretion is inhibited by acidification of the duodenum via secretin production (Johnson and Grossman 1968) and reflexly (Konturek and Johnson 1971).

SMALL INTESTINE

The proximal duodenum of dogs appears to be more resistant to attack by acid chyme than is the jejunum. Experimental surgical bypass of this area, so that gastric contents empty directly into the jejunum, often results in ulceration of the jejunal mucosa (Davenport 1971). Brunner's gland secretion is stimulated by feeding, secretin, and possibly other stimuli (Hubel 1972). It has negligible acid-neutralization capacity, but the mucus may be a mechanical barrier.

The aqueous portion of the duodenal secretion is probably isotonic with blood. Pepsinogen is present in low concentration. Other enzymes, e.g. amylase and peptidases, are derived from desquamated cells. Many or all intestinal digestive enzymes derived from intestinal cells are intracellular, and are present in the juice only because cells desquamate. Jejunal and ileal secretions in dogs also are approximately isotonic with plasma; the chief electrolytes are sodium, chloride, and bicarbonate.

Strains of *E. coli* which produce enterotoxins pathogenic for swine and calves elicit increases in adenyl cyclase activity in the small gut, together with copious secretion of an isotonic fluid across a histologically intact epithelium. A similar noninflammatory *secretory diarrhea* or *overflow diarrhea* occurs in man from the exotoxin of *Vibrio cholerae* (Field 1974). The secretion occurs without either light- or electron-microscopic evidence of morphological damage to epithelial cells or disruption of the junctions between cells. The secretory changes are paralleled by changes in adenyl cyclase activity and cyclic AMP (adenosine-5-monophosphate) content of the intestinal mucosa. The effect of cholera toxin on intestinal ion transport can be reproduced in vitro by addition of cyclic AMP. Thus cholera toxin may increase the synthesis of cyclic AMP in the intestinal mucosa, and cyclic AMP then stimulates secretion, or unmask pre-existing secretion by inhibiting an active absorptive process, or produce a combination of these effects (Field 1974).

Blood flow through the intestine of an anesthetized dog averages 32 ml/min/100 g tissue, about that of skeletal muscle after vigorous exercise. The increase in blood flow which follows parasympathetic stimulation is probably secondary to increased motor and secretory activity. When systemic arterial pressure is varied experimentally over the range of 90–270 mm Hg, the intestinal blood flow tends to remain constant (autoregulation) (Davenport 1971).

Villi of the intestinal mucosa move to-and-fro and shorten abruptly at intervals. Some of their movement results from contraction of the muscularis mucosae. Lymph flow from the intestine is elevated during periods of increased activity of the villi.

Experimentally, acidification of the duodenum in dogs has been associated with contraction of the villi of resected jejunal loops perfused with the animal's blood (Kokas and Ludany 1933). This "candidate hormone," called villikinin, is one of several presumed to affect the digestive organs but not yet completely studied (Grossman and others 1974).

In man, the ileocecal junction pressure falls following eating, at which time ileal activity is reflexly increased, accompanying gastric emptying (Davenport 1971).

PANCREATIC EXOCRINE SECRETION

Neurohumoral regulation of the exocrine secretion of the pancreas is effected largely through the agencies of the vagus nerve and two hormones, secretin and CCK-PZ.

One currently plausible mechanistic theory is that, when stimulated, the pancreas secretes a fluid that is isotonic with plasma and contains sodium bicarbonate mixed with amylolytic, lipolytic, and proteolytic enzymes. As this fluid flows down the pancreatic ducts, passive reabsorption of some of its bicarbonate in exchange for chloride occurs (Davenport 1971).

In the pig (Hickson 1970) vagal stimulation caused a profuse flow of pancreatic juice, containing high concentrations of both bicarbonate and enzymes. Both vagal stimulation and acetylcholine were effective after resection (surgical removal) of the stomach and intestine, or in the intact animal, when the vagus distal to the stomach was stimulated. Hence liberation of gastrointestinal hormones was not responsible for the rise in secretory rate, and the vagal stimulation must have acted directly on the pancreas (Hickson 1970). No one appears to know whether the vagus acts directly on the pancreas in other species (Hubel 1972).

In the pig pancreas, vagal stimulation produced an intense vasodilatation, which preceded secretion and was not annulled by atropine. Smaller increases in blood flow followed CCK-PZ and secretin injections (Hickson 1970). In the dog, similar rises in pancreatic blood flow have been noted after introduction of HCl into the duodenum and after secretin injection (Hubel 1972).

In the horse, the resting secretion of the pancreas is profuse and apparently continuous (3–8 ml/min in 120 kg ponies), rising about fourfold within 2–3 minutes after feeding. The concentration of bicarbonate is low and does not exceed that of chloride at any rate of secretion. The output of enzymes is small compared with other species studied (Alexander and Hickson 1970).

LIVER

There are no structures in the liver and biliary tract analogous to renal glomeruli for hydrostatic filtration of water and solute directly from blood to bile. The perfused rat liver can secrete bile against hydrostatic pressures greater than the pressure of the perfusing blood. Therefore bile formation does not depend on mechanical energy supplied by the heart, but rather on intrahepatic chemical energy (Wheeler 1968, in *Handbook*). Active solute transport is the primary event in bile formation. The active secretion of bile salts is accompanied by an apparently passive flow of water and electrolytes into the bile, with the result that the volume as well as the bile salt concentration of the bile increases (Wheeler 1968, Davenport 1971). Bile salts are among the most potent choleretic agents (i.e. they stimulate bile secretion), whether given to the animal orally or parenterally. These compounds, which are salts of organic acids, are excreted in the bile in osmotically significant concentrations. In the dog, a direct quantitative relationship exists between bile flow and bile salt excretion (Fig. 20.3). In most species the interruption of the enterohepatic circulation of bile salts by diversion of bile to the exterior results in a significant reduction in bile flow. This is very striking in the dog and cat, and has also been described in the rat, sheep, and man (Wheeler 1968).

More than 95 percent of bile salts entering the duodenum are normally reabsorbed, chiefly in the ileum (Davenport 1971). The bile salt pool also is replenished by steady synthesis from cholesterol, the rate of synthesis normally being equal to the rate of loss. Bile salts lost to the colon are normally deconjugated and metabolized by the microbial population of the colon. If abnormally large amounts of bile salts reach the large intestine, they inhibit net absorption of sodium and water with resulting diarrhea (see Chapter 21).

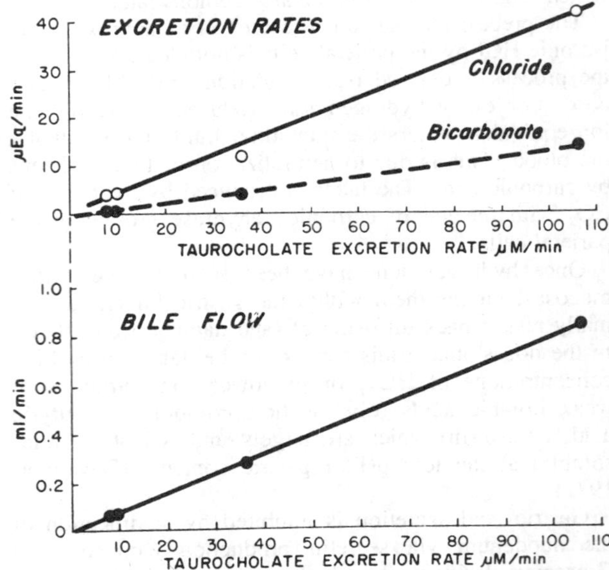

Figure 20.3. Relation between excretion rate of bile salt and the output of chloride, bicarbonate, and water in the dog during cholinergic blockade (pipenzolate methylbromide). Sodium taurocholate was infused intravenously at successive rates of 8, 40, 118, and 8 μM/min. Output of water (bile flow) appeared to be directly proportional to taurocholate excretion rate, as did the output of chloride and bicarbonate ions. (From Wheeler 1968, in *Handbook of Physiology*, sec. 6, C.F. Code and W. Heidel, eds., *Alimentary Canal*, vol. 5, 2409–31.)

In animals possessing a gallbladder, which concentrates and stores bile, the entry of bile into the duodenum does not parallel its secretion by the liver. The gallbladder utilizes metabolic energy to transport NaCl-$NaHCO_3$ and water in isotonic proportions from bile to blood (Dietschy 1964; Diamond 1968, in *Handbook*).

The pig, sheep, goat, and cow have gallbladders with low concentrating ability. The gallbladder has a high concentrating capacity in man, mouse, chicken, duck, dog, cat, and striped gopher. The gallbladder mucosa also secretes mucin. In the horse, which lacks a gallbladder, the sphincter of the hepatopancreatic ampulla has little resistance, and bile flow into the duodenum tends to be continuous. Other animals lacking a gallbladder include deer, elk, moose, giraffe, camel, elephant, pigeon, dove, and rat. In humans, the gallbladder begins to contract within the first half hour after a meal. The increase in vagal tone upon eating and the liberation of CCK-PZ from the duodenal mucosa are the controlling influences.

The choleretic effect of secretin causes increased bile flow without any increase in bile salts or pigments, with bicarbonate secretion by the intrahepatic bile ducts and ductules in the dog, cat, and man (Wheeler 1968, in *Handbook*). The qualitative similarity between the biliary and the pancreatic response to secretin with respect to bicarbonate output leads to a suspicion that the underlying mechanisms are similar (Wheeler 1968). Gastrin secretion (in response to vagal stimulation during eating) stimulates acid secretion by the gastric mucosa, which in turn elicits secretin secretion when the acidic gastric digesta reach the duodenum. Harrison (1962) observed an increase in hepatic bile secretion of sheep when gastric juice (pH 1.5) was introduced into the duodenum, from 12 ml/hr preinfusion to 65 ml/hr postinfusion. This was accompanied by a diminution in the concentration of total solids and chloride as well as a rise in pH consistent with a rise in bicarbonate output, presumably due to release of endogenous secretin.

The pigments which give the bile its color have no digestive function. Bilirubin is produced from hemoglobin porphyrin in the reticuloendothelial system. It is extracted from the plasma by the hepatic cells, conjugated with glucuronic acid, and excreted in the bile. In cattle, rapid oxidation to the greenish biliverdin occurs. In the large gut of all species, microbial conversion to urobilinogen occurs, coloring the feces brown. A small amount of intestinal urobilinogen is absorbed and secreted into the bile or excreted in the urine.

In addition to conjugated bilirubin, several other organic anions are secreted in bile in concentrations greatly exceeding that of plasma (Arias 1968). Examples are the bile salts, certain dyes (e.g. sulfobromophthalein or BSP), porphyrins (e.g. phylloerythrin, derived from chlorophyll), and certain drugs. Study of an inherited chronic nonhemolytic jaundice occurring in certain families of humans and Corriedale sheep (Dubin-Johnson syndrome) demonstrated that bile salt anions were excreted normally, while the excretion of other anions such as bilirubin and BSP was specifically impaired (Arias et al. 1964; Arias 1968, in *Handbook*). Thus different mechanisms exist in sheep for excretion of bile salt and conjugated bilirubin.

LARGE INTESTINE

The bicarbonate- and mucus-rich secretion is evidently parasympathetically controlled. Stimulation of the peripheral ends of the pelvic nerve, or central stimulation of one sectioned pelvic nerve with the other remaining intact, increases the motility, blood flow, and secretory rate. Parasympathomimetic drugs cause secretion and atropine blocks it. Stimulation of the sympathetic supply relaxes colonic movement, causes vasoconstriction, and reduces any ongoing secretion. Aldosterone stimulates sodium absorption, with concomitant chloride and water absorption. Under conditions in which adrenal secretion of aldosterone rises, as in sodium-depleted animals, fecal excretion of sodium falls.

Urinary water absorption occurs in the colon and ceca of birds, following retropulsion of cloacal urine into the lower bowel. For example, in 8–10-week-old turkeys normally excreting about 110 g HOH/day/kg body wt., about 450 g HOH/day/kg body wt. were excreted following rectal fistulation. This fourfold change gives an idea of the water recovery carried out by the large bowel to aid the kidney (Scheiber and Dziuk 1969, Dziuk 1971).

RENEWAL OF GASTROINTESTINAL EPITHELIA

In gastrointestinal epithelia, rapid proliferation provides a continuous renewal of cell population, as in skin and bone marrow. A nucleotide precursor, tritiated thymidine, which is incorporated into DNA, allows analysis of the precise rates of renewal of gastrointestinal epithelial cells by microautoradiography.

In recent years, interest has focused on (1) the nature of the critical events that lead intestinal cells through the proliferative cell cycle and cause further differentiation and functional specialization, (2) the controls that provide for the maintenance of optimum numbers of cells at a given time at a given location, (3) the controls that respond to a need for additional new cell production, and (4) the breakdown of certain of these regulatory mechanisms leading to disease (Lipkin 1973).

Proliferating layers have been studied in the basal layer of esophageal epithelium, in the isthmus between the gastric pits and the gastric glands, and in the lower parts of the crypts of the small and large intestine. In normal adult gastrointestinal mucosa, the rate of cell loss by death or migration is equal to the rate of cell production.

Gastrointestinal cells respond to certain stimuli (e.g. resection, vagotomy, anterior pituitary growth hormone) with production of new cells. At some point, DNA synthesis ceases, enabling differentiation into mature cells. In the normal small and large intestine, decreased thymidine kinase and increased adenine phosphoribosyltransferase activities accompany differentiation and migration.

During development of certain neoplastic diseases of the stomach and large intestine, morphologically well-differentiated epithelial cells develop which retain immature metabolic features related to proliferative activity. One of these metabolic features is persistent DNA synthesis, for example, in colon-surface epithelial cell tumors in man. A chemical carcinogen—1,2-dimethylhydrazine—produces the same metabolic abnormalities in the colon cells of rodents (Lipkin 1973).

REFERENCES

Alexander, F., and Hickson, J.C.D. 1970. The salivary and pancreatic secretions of the horse. In A.T. Phillipson, ed., *Physiology of Digestion and Metabolism in the Ruminant*. Oriel, Newcastle upon Tyne. Pp. 375–89.

Arias, I.M., Bernstein, L., Toffler, R., Cornelius, C.E., Novikoff, A.B., and Essner, E. 1964. Black liver disease in Corriedale sheep: A new mutation affecting hepatic excretory function. *J. Clin. Invest.* 43:1249–50.

Burgen, A.S.V. 1956. The secretion of potassium in saliva. *J. Physiol.* 132:20–39.

Coats, D.A., Denton, D.A., and Wright, R.D. 1958. The ionic balances and transferences of the sheep's parotid gland during maximal stimulation. *J. Physiol.* 144:108–22.

Cooke, A.R. 1974. Duodenal acidification: Role of first part of duodenum in gastric emptying and secretion in dogs. *Gastroenterology* 67:85–92.

Davenport, H.W. 1971. *Physiology of the Digestive Tract*. 3d ed. Year Book Medical, Chicago.

Debas, H.T., Farooq, H., and Grossman, M.I. 1975. Inhibition of gastric emptying is a physiological action of cholecystokinin. *Gastroenterology* 68:1211–17.

Dietschy, J.M. 1964. Water and solute movement across the wall of the everted rabbit gall bladder. *Gastroenterology* 47:395–408.

Dziuk, H.E. 1971. Reverse flow of gastrointestinal contents in turkeys. *Fed. Proc.* 30:610.

Emmelin, N. 1955. Blood flow and rate of secretion in the submaxillary gland. *Acta Physiol. Scand.* 34:22–28.

Field, M. 1974. Intestinal secretion. *Gastroenterology* 66:1063–84.

Grossman, M.I., and others. 1974. Candidate hormones of the gut. *Gastroenterology* 67:730–55.

Handbook of Physiology. 1968. Sec. 6, C.F. Code and W. Heidel, eds., *Alimentary Canal*, vols. 2, 4, 5. Am. Physiol. Soc., Washington.

Harrison, F.A. 1962. Bile secretion in the sheep. *J. Physiol.* 162:212–24.

Hickson, J.C.D. 1970. The secretion of pancreatic juice in response to stimulation of the vagus nerves in the pig. *J. Physiol.* 206:275–97.

——. 1970. The secretory and vascular response to nervous and hormonal stimulation in the pancreas of the pig. *J. Physiol.* 206:299–322.

Hubel, K.A. 1972. Secretin: A long progress note. *Gastroenterology* 62:318–41.

Johnson, L.R., and Grossman, M.I. 1968. Secretin: The enterogastrone released by acid in the duodenum. *Am. J. Physiol.* 215:885–88.

Kokas, E., and Ludany, G. 1933. Die hormonale Regelung der Darmzottenbewegung. *Pflüg. Arch. ges. Physiol.* 232:293–98.

Konturek, S.J., and Johnson, L.R. 1971. Evidence for an enterogastric reflex for the inhibition of acid secretion. *Gastroenterology* 61:667–74.

Lipkin, M. 1973. Proliferation and differentiation of gastrointestinal cells. *Physiol. Rev.* 53:891–915.

McCarthy, L.E., and Borison, H.L. 1974. Respiratory mechanics of vomiting in decerebrate cats. *Am. J. Physiol.* 226:738–43.

Scheiber, A.R., and Dziuk, H.E. 1969. Water ingestion and excretion in turkeys with a rectal fistula. *J. Appl. Physiol.* 26:277–81.

Schneyer, L.H., Young, J.A., and Schneyer, C.A. 1972. Salivary secretion of electrolytes. *Physiol. Rev.* 52:720–77.

Smith, C.C., and Brizzee, K.R. 1961. Cineradiographic analysis of vomiting in the cat. I. Lower esophagus, stomach, and small intestine. *Gastroenterology* 40:654–64.

Stevens, C.E. 1973. Transport across rumen epithelium. In H.H. Ussing and N.A. Thorn, eds., *Transport Mechanisms in Epithelia*. Proc. Alfred Benzon Symposium V. Munksgaard, Copenhagen. Pp. 404–21.

Taylor, W.H. 1962. Proteinases of the stomach in health and disease. *Physiol. Rev.* 42:519–53.

Thomas, J.E., Crider, J.O. and Morgan, C.J. 1934. A study of reflexes involving the pyloric sphincter and antrum and their role in gastric evacuation. *Am. J. Physiol.* 108:683–700.

Walsh, J.H., and Grossman, M.I. 1975. Gastrin (first of two parts). *New Eng. J. Med.* 292:1324–34.

Weisbrodt, N.W., and Christensen, J. 1972. Electrical activity of the cat duodenum in fasting and vomiting. *Gastroenterology* 63:1004–10.

CHAPTER 21

Water and Electrolyte Movements into and out of the Digestive Tract | by Alvin F. Sellers

ABSORPTIVE LOAD

Water and salt ingested orally make up only a fraction of the amount of these substances that the gastrointestinal tract must absorb to preserve homeostasis. Most of the absorptive load comes from secretions. Figure 21.1 shows the approximate daily volumes of these in fasting man. The total of 5.9 L entering is almost balanced by absorption, aggregating 5.8 L. Upon food intake the load does increase by the amount ingested, but it increases mainly through a two- to fourfold increase in the flow of salivary, gastric, biliary, and pancreatic secretions. Alexander and Hickson (1970) showed that in ponies pancreatic juice secretion of about 125 ml/hr rises to 500–600 ml/hr within a few minutes after feeding (Fig. 21.2).

In simple-stomached omnivores like man, jejunal absorption is of major importance. Thus in man, by the time an ordinary meal reaches the ileum, the total increment in luminal flow amounts to only one third of the original meal volume. By mid-jejunum (Fig. 21.1), of the some 5400 ml of the secretions entering the tract, about 2600 ml have been absorbed. This would indicate a mid-jejunal flow rate of about 2800 ml/24 hr (about 2 ml/min). Normally, after a small meal this flow may increase to about 3.5 ml/min; the small gut of man can distend (diameter increase) to accommodate volume flow rates up to 7–8 ml/min without changes in flow velocity.

Overflow diarrhea and extracellular fluid loss

At volume flow rates greater than 7–8 ml/min (as with excessive secretion volume) the luminal diameter remains constant and flow velocity increases, resulting in a reduction in time for absorption. This is *overflow diarrhea.* Clinical examples commonly encountered are the enteric colibacilloses of the pig, the human infant, and the calf. These conditions are characterized by abundant net movement of water and electrolytes into the lumen across a morphologically intact intestinal epithelium (Moon and Whipp 1971). Under these conditions, the normal absorptive capacity for water and electrolytes is essentially preserved, and diarrhea is due to overloading of the intestinal tract with excessive secretions. Affected individuals show the clinical signs of dehydration very rapidly (sunken eyes, inflexible skin, gaunt appearance), because the extracellular fluid has become rapidly depleted. Thus the first concern is for repair of the extracellular fluid and electrolyte deficit, regardless of whatever other treatment is required. As a rule of thumb, 15 percent volume loss from the extracellular fluid results in clinical signs in most species; 30 percent volume loss is almost always fatal.

Large intestine

The large intestine is a critical site for electrolyte and water absorption and secretion. Phillips and Giller (1973) found the following mean values for five human subjects on a standard diet:

	Ileal Content (24 hr)	*Feces (24 hr)*	*Colonic Absorption (24 hr)*
Vol. (ml)	1524	39	1485
Na (mEq)	196	0.6	195
K (mEq)	9.3	4.7	4.6
Cl (mEq)	102.9	0.3	102.6

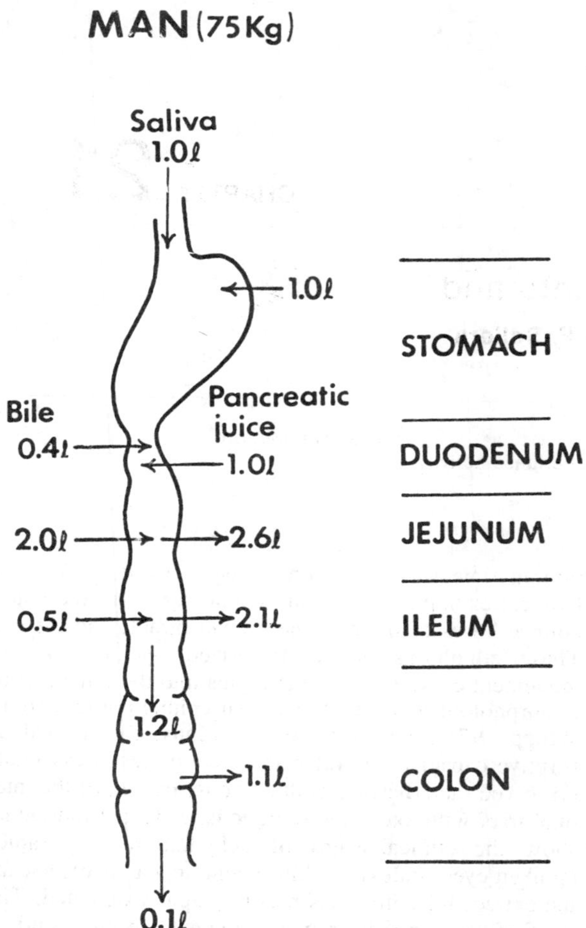

Figure 21.1. Secretion, absorption, and intraluminal flow (L/day) of gastrointestinal tract in fasting man. The numbers are approximate. (Adapted from Soergel and Hofmann, in Frohlich, ed., *Pathophysiology*, Lippincott, Philadelphia, 1972.)

Thus the colon absorbed more than 95 percent of the Na, Cl, and HOH, and 50 percent of the K traversing the ileocecal junction.

In the cecum and colon of the herbivorous pony, three- to fourfold volume changes occur diurnally (Argenzio et al. 1974). The net exchange of water between lumen and plasma is associated primarily with a cyclic change in digesta osmolality, resulting from a cyclic pattern of microbial digestion. Microbial digestion in the large gut results, for example, in the production of organic acids from carbohydrate. These are primarily volatile fatty acids (acetic, propionic, butyric). They collectively constitute a major fraction of the anions in the large-intestine contents of most mammals studied (see Chapter 18). The conversion, for example, of one molecule of glucose into two or three smaller molecules increases the osmotic

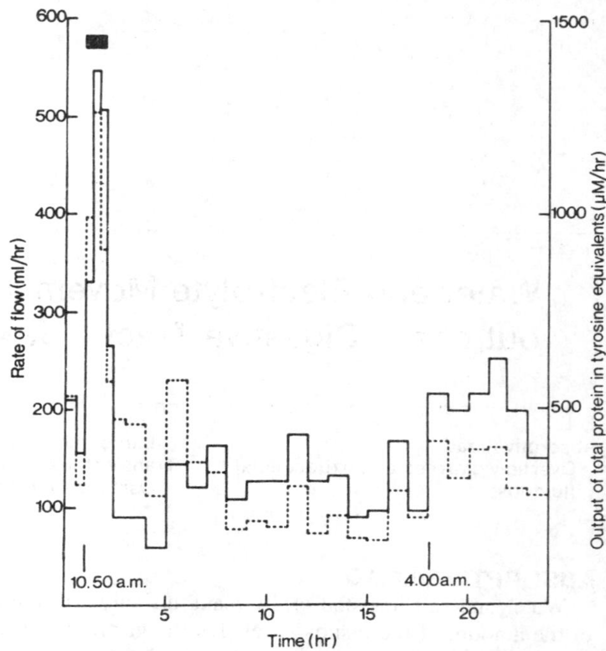

Figure 21.2. Pancreatic secretion in the conscious horse: effect of feeding oats and concentrates (indicated by bar) on the flow (solid line) and output of total protein (dotted line) in pancreatic juice during 24 hours. Food but not water was withheld for 15 hours beforehand, and withdrawn again for the remainder of the experiment after the test meal. Juice was returned to the duodenum continuously. (From Alexander and Hickson, in Phillipson, ed., *Physiology of Digestion and Metabolism in the Ruminant*, Oriel, Newcastle upon Tyne, 1970.)

pressure of large-gut luminal contents, tending to cause water to move into the large gut from the extracellular fluid when production of these acids exceeds their absorption. Conversion of larger polysaccharides, e.g. cellulose and hemicellulose, into volatile fatty acids (VFA) results in an even larger increase in particle numbers and thus in osmolality of the digesta. There is also evidence that, at least in the pony large intestine, VFA production is associated with a secretion of $NaHCO_3$ (Argenzio et al. 1974). Thus VFA production and the subsequent absorption of VFA and sodium largely account for the cyclic net exchange pattern for water in the large intestine (see Chapter 19 and Fig. 19.5).

In the large gut of a 160 kg pony, of the total volume entering (31.3 L) about 30 L are reabsorbed (Fig. 21.3). This very large exchange approximates the extracellular fluid volume (20% of body wt., 32 L). If, applying our 15 percent rule of thumb, about 4.8 L were not reabsorbed per day, clinical signs should appear, and a 9.6 L loss per day should result in death.

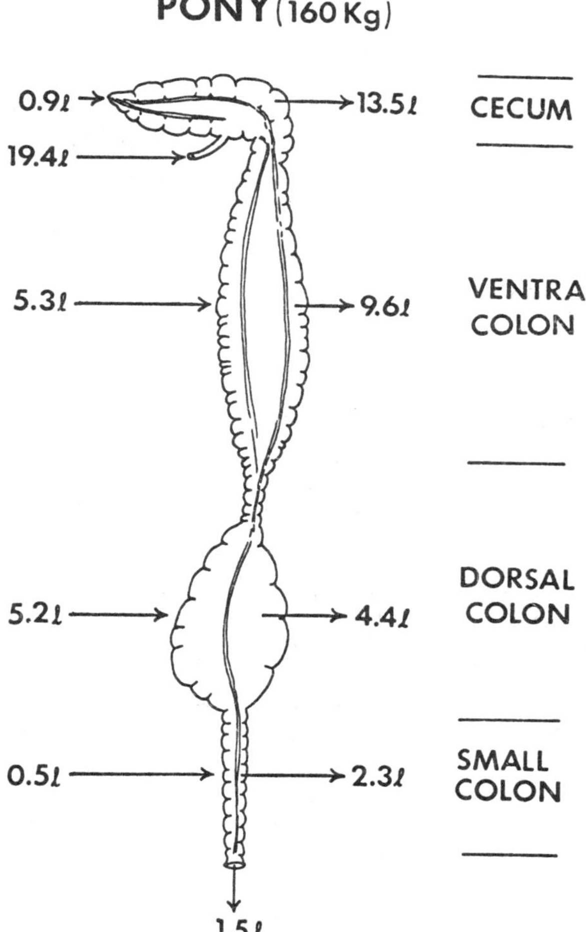

Figure 21.3. Net movement of water through the large intestine of a 160 kg pony. About 95 percent of the ileal outflow and net fluid secretion is absorbed, about 30 L/day. (Adapted from Argenzio, Lowe, Pickard, and Stevens 1974, *Am. J. Physiol.* 226:1035–42.)

TRANSIENT LOSS OF DISACCHARIDASE ACTIVITY

Osmotic diarrhea

In a variety of bacterial and viral enteric infections in man, transient loss of disaccharidase activity of the small-gut epithelium occurs (Soergel and Hofmann 1972, Donaldson and Gryboski 1973). For example, lactase activity may be nearly undetectable, while other enzymes (e.g. sucrase) may be reduced to 25 percent of their normal activity. As a result, increased amounts of ingested disaccharides are delivered to the large gut. Little mono- or disaccharide appears in the feces, since the resident flora ferment these carbohydrates to gas and organic acids. Therefore, water flows into the large gut from the extracellular fluid, increasing the feces volume and resulting in *osmotic diarrhea.* A large part of the total solute in fecal water in such cases is constituted by organic acids. Bicarbonate-ion buffering of the acid can result in a net loss of HCO_3^- to the body, producing systemic acidosis. In overflow diarrhea, the fecal water solute is comprised largely of inorganic ions. Thus with equal volumes of feces, osmotic diarrhea causes less sodium loss than overflow diarrhea (Soergel and Hofmann 1972).

ILEAL DYSFUNCTION

If the ileum (the main reabsorptive area for bile acids) malfunctions increased quantities of bile acids are found in the large gut. In humans (and presumably in other animals) excess bile acid in the large gut induces mucosal secretion of electrolyte and water (Mekhjian et al. 1971), with resultant diarrhea. In extensive ileal disease or resection, the body bile-acid pool also may become depleted to the point where jejunal bile-acid concentration is insufficient for normal micellar dispersion of ingested lipid, resulting in malabsorption of fat and steatorrhea (fat in feces). In addition, malabsorption of oleic acid by the small intestine can induce large-gut electrolyte and water secretion in a manner similar to ricinoleic acid, the active principle of castor oil (Hofmann and Poley 1972).

REFERENCES

Alexander, F., and Hickson, J.C.D. 1970. The salivary and pancreatic secretions of the horse. In A.T. Phillipson, ed., *Physiology of Digestion and Metabolism in the Ruminant.* Oriel, Newcastle upon Tyne. Pp. 375–89.

Argenzio, R.A., Lowe, J.E., Pickard, D.W., and Stevens, C.E. 1974. Digesta passage and water exchange in the equine large intestine. *Am. J. Physiol.* 226:1035–42.

Donaldson, R.M., Jr., and Gryboski, J.D. 1973. Carbohydrate Intolerance. In M.H. Sleisenger and J.S. Fortran, eds., *Gastrointestinal Disease: Pathophysiology, Diagnosis, Management.* Saunders, Philadelphia. Pp. 1015–30.

Hofmann, A.F., and Poley, J.R. 1972. Role of bile acid malabsorption in pathogenesis of diarrhea and steatorrhea in patients with ileal resection. I. Response to cholestyramine or replacement of dietary long chain triglyceride by medium chain triglyceride. *Gastroenterology* 62:918–34.

Mekhjian, H.S., Phillips, S.F., and Hofmann, A.F. 1971. Colonic secretion of water and electrolytes induced by bile acids: Perfusion studies in man. *J. Clin. Invest.* 50:1569–77.

Moon, H.W., and Whipp, S.C. 1971. Systems for testing the enteropathogenicity of Escherichia coli. *Ann. N.Y. Acad. Sci.* 176:197–211.

Phillips, S.F., and Giller, J. 1973. The contribution of the colon to electrolyte and water conservation in man. *J. Lab. Clin. Med.* 81:733–46.

Soergel, K.H., and Hofmann, A.F. 1972. Absorption. In E.D. Frohlich, ed., *Pathophysiology: Altered Regulatory Mechanisms in Disease.* Lippincott, Philadelphia. Pp. 423–53.

CHAPTER 22

Ruminant Digestion | by Andrew T. Phillipson

The principal feature of the ruminant digestive system is that fermentative digestion due to bacteria and protozoa occurs on a massive scale in the first two parts of the stomach, the rumen and the reticulum, and precedes hydrolytic digestion due to enzymes secreted in the digestive juices of the abomasum and intestine.

The suborder Ruminantia does not include all animals that ruminate. The process of regurgitating food for remastication is also a property of camels and other animals included in the suborder Tylopoda. The suborder Ruminantia includes the deer, elk, moose, chevrotain, reindeer, caribou, okapi, giraffe, eland, antelope, gazelle, musk ox, bison, buffalo, and chamois, in addition to the cattle, sheep, and goat. Suborder Tylopoda consists of the camel, dromedary, llama, alpaca, and vicuna. The stomach of the Tylopoda is similar to that of the ruminant except that the third part, the omasum, is absent or vestigial, and that areas of cardiac glands open into the ventral sacculated surfaces of the rumen and reticulum that form the so-called water cells.

The epithelium lining the first three parts of the stomach of ruminants is stratified, squamous, and keratinized, and the interior surface of the rumen is papillated. A study of 20 species of wild East African ruminants distinguishes between species that are predominantly grazing animals and those that have selective habits that include browsing, according to the number, size, and distribution of rumen papillae (Hofman 1968).

Fermentation in the stomach is not confined to the suborders that ruminate, for in animals that have a stomach constructed in a way that delays the passage of food, and in which the acid-secreting fundic glands are confined to a small caudal area, bacterial and possibly protozoan activity will occur. The kangaroo is an example. Some fermentation also occurs in the crop of the chicken, although this organ is not a gastric structure.

Fermentation is a characteristic of the large intestine in all ruminating and nonruminating species that have been studied. Its significance is determined by the nature of the food, the anatomy of the organ, and the organ's capacity. Fermentation in the cecum and colon is confined to food residues that escape hydrolytic digestion and to

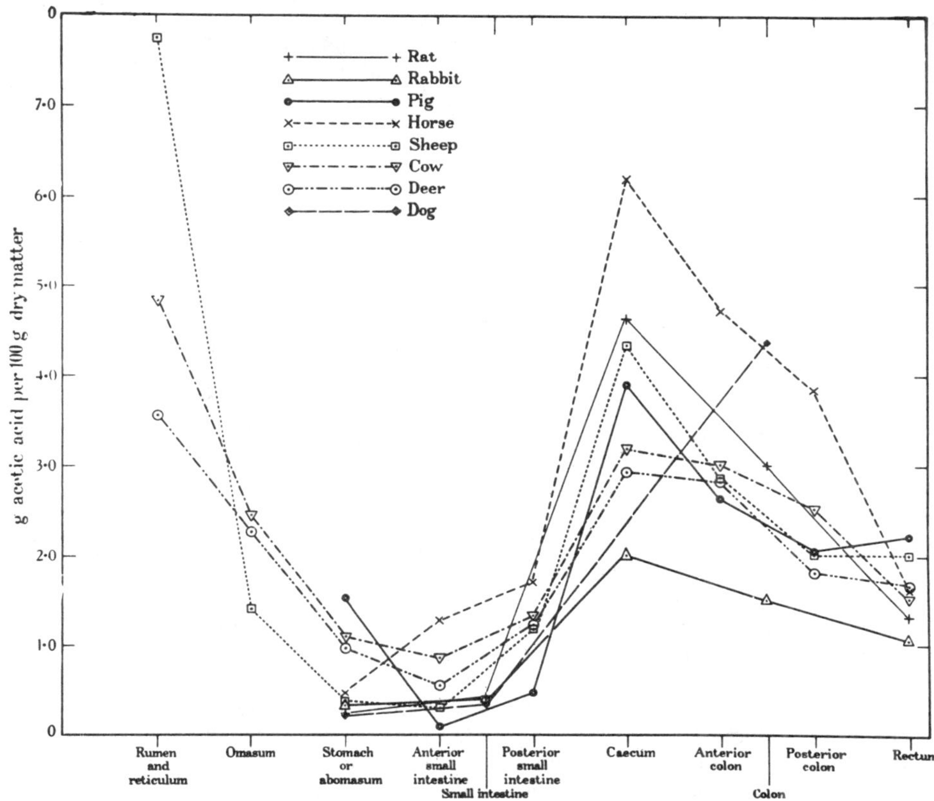

Figure 22.1. Average concentration of volatile fatty acids in the ingesta of different parts of the alimentary tract. (Adapted from Elsden, Hitchcock, Marshall, and Phillipson 1946, *J. Exp. Biol.* 22:191–202; Phillipson 1947, *J. Exp. Biol.* 23:346–49.)

food constituents that cannot be digested except by bacterial enzymes, such as plant fibers, in herbivorous animals that do not ruminate. These animals have, in consequence, a capacious large intestine (as in the horse) which has a similar function to the rumen, although, since it follows hydrolytic digestion, it does not have such a dominating role as the rumen.

The volatile fatty acids (VFA) are characteristic end products of fermentation, and their concentrations in the alimentary contents of domestic animals are shown in Figure 22.1.

The comparative measurements of the capacities of the main divisions of the alimentary tract given in Table 22.1 illustrate the difference in the relative capacities of the stomach and large intestines of ruminants, the horse, the omnivorous pig, the carnivorous dog, and the cat. The differences between the herbivores and the carnivores in the length of intestine in proportion to the body length and in the surface area of the gastrointestinal tract (exclusive of villi and papillae) compared with the body surface area reflect the greater alimentary capacities of the herbivores.

Table 22.1. Comparative measurements of the gastrointestinal tract

	Relative capacity (%)				Ratios	
Animal	Stomach	Small intestine	Cecum	Colon and rectum	Intestinal to body length	Gastrointestinal surface to body surface area
Ox	71	18	3	8	20:1	3.0:1
Sheep and goat	67	21	2	10	27:1	
Horse	9	30	16	45	12:1	2.2:1
Pig	29	33	6	32	14:1	
Dog	63	23	1	13	6:1	0.6:1
Cat	69	15		16	4:1	0.6:1

Adapted from G.C. Colin, *Traité de physiologie comparée des animaux*, Baillière, Paris, 1886

DEVELOPMENT OF THE RUMINANT STOMACH

In the development of the ruminant stomach in the embryo, the stomach is first a spindle-shaped enlargement of the primitive foregut as in other animals, and it is from this enlargement that the four parts of the stomach develop.

The stages of development indicate that the esophageal groove and the omasum correspond to the lesser curvature of the simple stomach, while the rumen and reticulum represent enlargements of the body of the simple stomach; the abomasum develops from the caudal part of the primitive spindle. This concept is supported by the courses taken by the abdominal roots of the vagus nerves in the ruminant, which are similar to those found in man and the dog except that more numerous and larger branches are given off to the first three parts of the stomach.

In its final stage the greater omentum is attached to the greater curvature of the abomasum and to the left side of the rumen, indicating that both these surfaces arise from the dorsal curvature of the primitive stomach spindle. A detailed account of the rotations and reflections undergone by the four parts of the stomach is given by Pernkopf (1931) and Warner (1958).

The rumen may be regarded as an S-shaped organ which opens at its anterior end into the reticulum. The anterior and posterior pillars are then seen to be strong muscular invaginations of the walls. Additional invaginations have occurred at the caudal extremities of the ventral and dorsal sacs, which are known as the ventral and dorsal coronary pillars respectively. These also have a well-developed musculature, and the areas caudal to them are known as the ventral and dorsal blind sacs of the rumen. The anterior and posterior pillars of the rumen continue on the lateral and medial walls as muscular thickenings known as the longitudinal pillars. They demarcate the rumen into an upper or dorsal sac and a lower or ventral sac (Fig. 22.2).

The rumen opens cranially to the reticulum, and an invagination of the musculature of the ventral surface occurs which forms the reticuloruminal fold. This invagination is projected upward on the lateral and medial walls of the organ. The reticulum lies under the dome of the diaphragm with its anterior surface against the diaphragm. The esophagus enters an area that lies above the proximal edge of the reticuloruminal fold, which is sometimes called the *antrum* of the rumen. The esophageal groove runs from the entrance of the esophagus almost vertically downward to the entrance of the omasum. The groove lies on the medial surface of the reticulum in front of the reticuloruminal fold, where the "honeycomb" structure that lines the reticulum meets the papillated area of the rumen.

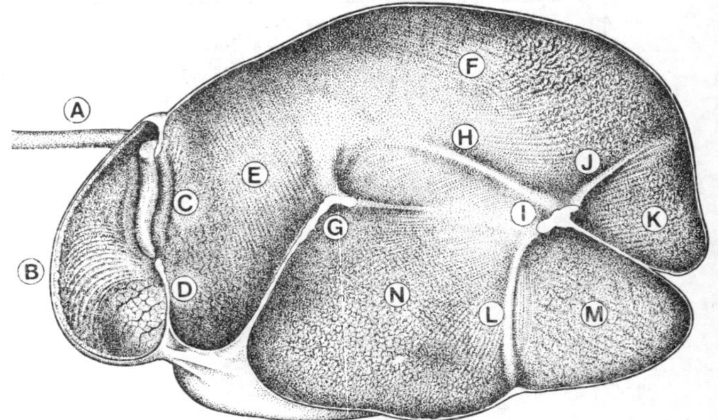

Figure 22.2. The reticulum and rumen of the sheep sectioned in the vertical plane to expose the internal structures. A, esophagus; B, reticulum; C, esophageal groove; D, reticuloruminal fold; E, anterior rumen sac; F, dorsal rumen sac; G, anterior pillar; H, longitudinal pillar; I, posterior pillar; J, dorsal coronary pillar; K, dorsal blind sac; L, ventral coronary pillar; M, ventral blind sac; N, ventral rumen sac. (Drawing by J.R. Fuller, based on R.E. Hungate, *The Rumen and Its Microbes*, Academic Press, New York, 1966.)

The orifice leading to the omasum is small, and the main body of this organ extends caudally from the canal joining the reticulo-omasal orifice with the omaso-abomasal orifice. This canal is often called the *omasal groove* or *sulcus*. The interior of the body of the omasum has numerous laminae, the largest of which extends from the greater curvature forward to the omasal groove. These laminae are of differing depths, and five principal sizes are recognized.

The opening from the omasum to the abomasum is large and oval. In the abomasum there are two folds on either side of the long axis of the orifice which may possibly act as "flap" valves. The omasum of cattle is larger in relation to the other compartments of the stomach than in sheep and goats. In the two main parts of the abomasum, the mucosa of the first part, the fundic area, is characterized by many folds and contains fundic glands similar to those of other animals. The second part, the pyloric antrum, is more muscular than the fundic area and is lined with pyloric glands.

At birth the rumen and reticulum have a smaller capacity in relation to the abomasum than in the adult, but these organs soon enlarge. By the time the animal is 6 months old the various compartments of the stomach have assumed the same relationship to each other as in the adult. The speed with which the capacities of the rumen, omasum, and abomasum change is influenced by the diet of the animal. Under the free-ranging conditions, calves and lambs start to nibble grass within 10–14 days of birth and are eating considerable quantities by the time they are 4 weeks old. Under these circumstances the development of the rumen and omasum is more rapid than

Table 22.2. The proportions of the compartments of the stomach of grazing lambs and calves as percentages of the weight of the whole stomach

Age (days)	Rumen and reticulum	Omasum	Abomasum	Whole stomach as percentage of whole alimentary tract
Lambs				
1	31	8	61	22
14	36	5	59	25
30	63	5	32	27
49	71	5	24	35
112	73	6	21	39
Adult	69	8	23	49
Calves				
1	34	10	56	
14	40	15	45	
28	55	11	34	
47	66	11	23	
100	70	18	12	
Adult	64	25	11	

Adapted from I.D. Wardrop and J.B. Coombe 1960, *J. Ag. Sci.* 54:140–43; N.W. Godfrey 1961, *J. Ag. Sci.* 57:173–75, 177–83

if the animals subsist on milk or gruels. The omasum in particular remains underdeveloped while the young animal is maintained on liquid foods.

The proportions of the various parts of the stomach of slaughtered lambs and calves of varying ages are given in Table 22.2.

ESOPHAGEAL GROOVE

When the lamb or calf sucks its mother the milk passes directly to the abomasum. The first recorded observation of this was by Tiedemann and Gmelin (1827), who rightly considered that the esophageal groove was the pathway that allowed this to occur. Flourens (1844) observed that the lips of the esophageal groove contracted to form an almost closed tube when the cervical vagus was stimulated. It was not until 1926 that the comprehensive series of experiments by Wester produced adequate evidence that closure of the groove was the result of a vagal reflex in which the afferent nerve endings were situated in the mouth and pharynx. Wester worked with calves in which he had created a rumen fistula large enough to allow him to put his hand inside the reticulorumen to feel the behavior of the esophageal groove. He noted (1) that the groove closed when the calf drank milk; (2) that closure of the groove did not occur if milk was given through a tube introduced into the cervical esophagus via the nasal canal; (3) that closure of the groove occurred in sham-fed calves when they drank milk even though the milk did not reach the stomach; (4) that anesthetization of the buccal and pharyngeal mucosa, by swabbing the mouth with a solution of cocaine, inhibited closure of the groove when the calf subsequently drank milk; and (5) that large doses of atropine inhibited closure of the groove. Radiological observations on lambs and kid goats (Czepa and Stigler 1926) provided visual evidence of the direct passage of fluid barium meals to the abomasum in the young animal. The esophageal groove reflex includes not only closure of the groove, but also dilatation of the reticulo-omasal orifice and opening of the omasal canal so that milk runs through the omasum to the abomasum (Watson 1941).

Reflex pathway

The essential reflex nature of the contractions of the esophageal groove was shown by Comline and Titchen (1951), who examined the afferent and efferent pathways in decerebrate lambs and calves in which the brain stem was transected at the level of the anterior colliculus.

Water introduced into the posterior parts of the mouth effectively stimulated the reflex. Stimulation of the central end of the cut anterior laryngeal nerve also produced swallowing and reflex contractions of the groove, although water was more effective. The efferent fibers passed to the stomach mostly in the dorsal abdominal root of the vagus. Inhibition of the reflex was demonstrated by stimulation of the central ends of the abomasal nerve, of the splanchnic nerves, or by the intravenous injection of epinephrine.

Transection of both abdominal roots of the vagi abolishes subsequent passage to the abomasum of radiopaque liquid meals sucked from a bottle in conscious lambs and calves (Duncan 1953, Newhook and Titchen 1974). Atropine, however, is only partly effective in lambs and somewhat more effective in calves in this respect. Hexamethonium, on the other hand, which blocks ganglionic transmission, inhibits the esophageal groove mechanism in both species, although epinephrine itself is without effect. The caudal end of the esophagus and the reticulo-omasal orifice are opened by vagal stimulation, and it is this effect that is not blocked by atropine (Newhook and Titchen 1974). These observations place the structures involved in the esophageal groove mechanism in line with the behavior of the simple stomach in that there is no clear division between the vagal and sympathetic effects that can be elicited.

Chemical stimulation of the reflex

Wester (1930) noticed that milk caused closure of the groove in calves older than 3 weeks while water did not. He examined many of the constituents of milk; all of them had some effect, but the most potent compounds were various sodium salts. Sodium chloride and bicarbonate (0.5 percent solutions) continued to stimulate closure of the groove in cattle up to 2 years old, but in older animals the effect was irregular or absent. He recommended the use of these agents as a means of closing the groove and so of conveying medicinal drugs or capsules directly to the abomasum. Wester's work attracted immediate interest, particularly in relation to the administration of an anthelmintic drug to young sheep (Clunies-Ross 1931), but sodium salts with these animals proved to be ineffective. Instead, various astringent salts had some effect, and the most potent were those of copper. The effect of copper, however, was irregular in animals that were more than 18 months old. Riek (1954) repeated Wester's work on cattle and confirmed the fact that sodium salts and especially sodium bicarbonate (60 ml of a 10 percent solution) effectively caused closure of the esophageal groove in 90 percent of young cattle but found comparable doses of copper salts to be much less effective.

Behavioral factors influencing closure

There is a short delay before the esophageal groove responds when the young animal sucks or drinks milk. In decerebrate calves, the interval is from 2 to 5 seconds. Schalk and Amadon (1928) describe the response in the conscious calf: "The pillars of the groove contract strongly and draw into close apposition; and the length of the groove is very much shortened by contraction of the longitudinal fibers." Comline and Titchen (1951) describe two stages in the movement. The first was similar to that given by Schalk and Amadon; the second stage occurred after a short pause and consisted of inversion of the lips of the groove and a twisting movement of the right lip, which drew the epithelium of the reticulum adjacent to it so that the left lip disappeared from view.

The manner in which the animal takes milk has an influence on the response of the groove. Wise and Anderson (1939), who studied calves taking milk or water from a nipple or a bucket, observed that a small quantity of milk entered the rumen and reticulum during the first few gulps when it was drunk from a bucket but little or none entered the organs when it was sucked from a nipple. With water, some occasionally entered the rumen and reticulum when it was sucked from a nipple, but large quantities entered these organs when it was drunk from a bucket. Watson (1944) concluded that the response of the groove to ingested fluids depended upon whether the animal exhibited the pattern of behavior that is associated with sucking its mother. When the animal showed eagerness for milk, rapid and efficient closure of the groove occurred no matter whether it drank or sucked either milk or water. Closure of the groove in response to swallowing fluid from the mouth is an inborn reflex and can be demonstrated in the lamb near full term (Duncan and Phillipson 1951) and in the newborn animal when it first sucks its mother. Watson's experiments suggest that the reflex can be conditioned to a variety of circumstances.

Normally the responsiveness of the reflex diminishes with age. In kid goats the responses to milk and water were similar until about 3 months of age, after which the response to both was usually lost (Czepa and Stigler 1926). Age by itself, however, is not necessarily associated with a loss of response to sucked milk; Watson (1941) found that, of 12 lambs, 10 sucked milk to the abomasum after weaning, and two continued to do so until they were 4 years old. The response seems to depend upon whether the animal retains a delight in taking milk, and the shift from the "sucking" pattern of behavior to a "thirst" pattern of behavior appears to be an outward sign of whether the groove will respond. In the adult, water seldom evokes the reflex when it is drunk and attempts to sensitize the reflex by withholding water do not influence the result.

SALIVATION

The parotid, submaxillary (mandibular), and sublingual glands are the principal ones that secrete saliva. In addition there are numerous other salivary glands that secrete into the mouth of ruminants. Both the sheep and the ox have two well-defined multilobular glands, the inferior molar glands, each lobule of which drains by a separate duct into the lower nonpapillated area of the cheek. Numerous small glands are also found in the cheek and surrounding the lateral areas of the lips—the buccal and labial glands respectively. In addition, numerous small glands, known as the palatine glands, are found in the posterior parts of the hard palate and in the soft palate, while a further group of glands occurs in the oral and laryngeal parts of the pharynx. These, together with additional glands in the lateral margins and root of the tongue, have together been called the pharyngeal glands (Kay 1960).

The salivary glands may be grouped according to their histological structure (Kay 1960) into (1) serous glands (parotid and inferior molar glands), (2) mucous glands (buccal, palatine, and pharyngeal glands), and (3) mixed glands (submaxillary, sublingual, and labial glands). Although mucous glands are not found in the secreting acini of the adult parotid gland, goblet cells occur in the ducts of the glands, while small groups of mucous cells have been found in the acini of the young ruminants (Bock and Trautmann 1914).

Activity of parotid glands

The parotid glands secrete continuously, but the flow of saliva varies greatly throughout the day and is particularly rapid during feeding and rumination. In cattle, one parotid gland may secrete at the rate of 30–50 ml/min when the animal is feeding (Bailey and Balch 1961). During rumination, the flow of parotid saliva from the side of the mouth in which the bolus is chewed is of the same order, but the response from the gland on the opposite side of the mouth is much less. The flow of parotid saliva when the animal is resting may be reduced to about 2 ml/min.

Stimulation of the parasympathetic nerve causes an increase in blood flow through the gland and profuse salivation. The relationship between blood flow and salivary flow, however, is not a linear one (Coates et al. 1956). Section of the parasympathetic and sympathetic nerves to the gland greatly reduces salivary flow but does not stop it, since the gland continues to secrete slowly (Kay 1958).

Stimulation of the cervical sympathetic nerve of sheep, after section of the parasympathetic nerve, causes the expulsion of a small quantity of saliva from the duct, followed by a compensatory pause in the flow before it returns to its resting rate. This effect is probably due to the contraction of the myoepithelial or "basket" cells that were found by Silver (1954) to surround the intercalated ducts of the parotid glands. A transient increase in salivary flow similar to that caused by stimulation of the cervical sympathetic nerve is produced when epinephrine is injected into the carotid artery after section of the parasympathetic nerve. A similar effect is produced by the injection of oxytocin. These observations support the concept that contractile myoepithelial cells are innervated by adrenergic fibers and expel saliva from the duct system when they contract (Comline and Kay 1955).

Reflex excitation of parotid salivation can be produced by mechanical stimulation of the mouth, thoracic esophagus, cardia, reticulo-omasal orifice, lips of the esophageal groove, adjacent walls of the reticulum, or the reticuloruminal fold in anesthetized sheep. Stroking the interior of the empty reticulum of conscious sheep and gentle dilating of orifices provoke parotid secretion. These structures are more sensitive than the various pillars and walls of the rumen in this respect. Infrequent responses are obtained from the posterior pillars of the rumen, but stimulation of the longitudinal and anterior pillars of the rumen produces responses somewhat more frequently (Ash and Kay 1959). Tactile stimulation or the distention of the thoracic esophagus (Clark and Weiss 1952) by fluid, gas, or other means is a potent stimulus to salivary secretion, but the effect can be inhibited by distention of the rumen with gas. The threshold at which inhibition occurs in anesthetized animals is when the intraruminal pressure is between 10 and 19 mm Hg (Kay and Phillipson 1959).

Other salivary glands

The reflex behaviors of the inferior molar glands and of the buccal and palatine glands are similar to those of the parotid glands. The total flow from these glands can be measured roughly by collecting the total secretions from the mouth when the secretions from the submaxillary and sublingual glands are excluded and the ducts of both parotid glands are cannulated. The flow may in some animals be as great as that from both parotid glands. The secretion is thick and viscid, as it is composed of secretions of both serous and mucous glands.

The submaxillary and sublingual glands behave as they do in other animals. The former secrete only when the animal is feeding, while the latter have a very slow resting rate of secretion, which shows a small response to distention of the thoracic esophagus.

Development of parotid secretion

The young ruminant secretes comparatively little saliva during the first few weeks of life. Thereafter the secretory activity of the parotid glands in lambs is strongly influenced by diet, while the remaining salivary glands develop more slowly. The most rapid development of parotid secretion was found in lambs grazing at pasture with ewes. Lambs maintained indoors on reconstituted milk developed parotid secretion slowly, although the addition of hay to the diet improved secretion (Wilson and Tribe 1961).

The resting secretion rate of kid goats increased when they were about 7 weeks old, although the stimulated rate of secretion did not reach adult proportions relative to the gland weights until they were 3 months old (Kay 1960).

The contribution of parotid saliva to the total salivary flow of adult sheep is about 60 percent, although at 3 months it represents about 75 percent, indicating a slower development of the remaining salivary glands (Tribe and Peel 1963).

Quantities of saliva secreted

The saliva secreted by a single parotid gland of the sheep may be from 1 to 4 liters per 24 hours (Denton 1957), although larger quantities have been recorded (Wilson 1963).

Estimates of the total salivary secretion of cattle based on the addition of water to swallowed boluses arriving at the cardia, the swallowed saliva during resting periods, and the calculated flow during ruminating periods suggest that the total secretion may vary from 90 to 190 liters per 24 hours (Table 22.3). If this is so then parotid saliva, which amounted to 44–48 liters per 24 hours for a hay-fed steer, is considerably less than half the total flow when compared to the values given by Bailey (1961) for total flow. Clearly diet influences salivation, although it is not related to the dry matter eaten by the animal either in cattle (Bailey 1961) or in sheep (Wilson 1963). The values in Table 22.3 are within the ranges for the outflow of rumen contents to the omasum made by Hyden (1961) and van't Klooster and Rogers (1969).

The slowest rate of secretion of mixed saliva occurs immediately after the cessation of feeding when the animals are resting; in addition the saliva secreted during

Table 22.3. Total daily salivary secretion of cows eating various diets

Diet	Dry matter eaten per day (kg)	Salivary flow during 24 hr (L) A	B	C	D	Mean total water swallowed per day (L, from food, drinking water, and saliva)
Cut grass	5.5	189	190	156		215
6.4 kg hay	5.5	146	173	140	137	170
3.6 kg hay 5.5 kg dairy cubes	7.7	130		115		148
18.2 kg alfalfa silage	7.7		121		98	148
0.9 kg hay 5.5 kg flaked maize 0.9 kg peanut cake	6.4	111			105	124

Adapted from Bailey 1961, *Brit. J. Nutr.* 15:443–51

ruminating periods that follow feeding is less than in subsequent periods. The general picture observed by Bailey and Balch (1961) was that the quantities of saliva entering the rumen and reticulum during resting and ruminating periods increased as the interval after feeding increased.

Composition of saliva

Parotid

The first comprehensive analysis of parotid saliva is that of McDougall (1948), who examined the saliva obtained by cannulation of the parotid duct (Table 22.4).

The parotid saliva has been described with some justification as a bicarbonate phosphate buffer, as these two anions form over 90 percent of the total anion content. The total cations amount to 186 mEq/L and total anions 173. The difference can be accounted for by the small quantity of mucus added in the parotid duct. The analysis assumes that the inorganic phosphate is present as HPO_4^- ions and that the total carbon dioxide is present as HCO_3^- ions, which at the pH of saliva measured at room temperature will be largely true. An increase in secretion from a resting rate of 0.2–0.5 ml/min to a maximal flow of 15–20 ml/min is accompanied by a small increase in the concentrations of sodium chloride and bicarbonate and a reciprocal decrease in the concentrations of potassium and inorganic phosphate. The concentrations of total cations and anions, however, do not alter significantly, while the osmotic pressure of the saliva is very close to that of plasma.

Table 22.4. Average composition of sheep parotid saliva

Composition	Parotid salavia
Dry matter	1.28 g/100 ml
Ash	0.97 g/100 ml
Nitrogen	20 mg/100 ml
Sodium	177 mEq/L
Potassium	8 mEq/L
Calcium	0.4 mEq/L
Magnesium	0.6 mEq/L
Inorganic phosphorus	52 mEq/L
Chloride	17 mEq/L
Total carbon dioxide	104 mEq/L
pH * (as secreted)	8.1

* Calculated from the Henderson-Hasselbalch equation, assuming the CO_2 tension to be the same as that for human arterial blood at 38°C

Adapted from McDougall 1948, *Biochem. J.* 43:99–109

The most striking change that can occur in the composition of parotid saliva is found when the animal is depleted of sodium. Under these circumstances the sodium content of the saliva is reduced and is replaced by potassium (Blair-West et al. 1965).

Sodium depletion reduces the volume of saliva secreted. The changes in the total cations in the saliva are relatively small, but there is a remarkable reduction in the quantity of sodium and potassium excreted in the urine. Sodium depletion is accompanied by an increase in the quantities of aldosterone entering the blood from the adrenal cortex. These changes do not occur in adrenalectomized sheep maintained by a constant and minimal quantity of aldosterone when sodium depletion is induced. When solutions of sodium salts are available, sheep drink sufficiently to rectify a sodium deficit (Denton and Sabine 1961, 1963).

Submaxillary

The concentrations of sodium, bicarbonate, and inorganic phosphate in the submaxillary saliva of sheep are much less than in parotid saliva, but they vary greatly with the rate of secretion (Kay 1960).

Sodium and bicarbonate, and to a lesser extent chloride, increase with the rate of secretion. The concentrations of potassium and inorganic phosphate, however, decrease abruptly when secretion is stimulated, and the viscosity of the saliva increases, indicating an increase in mucous content.

The electrolyte composition of saliva secreted by the inferior molar and the palatine glands is very similar to that of parotid saliva, while the saliva of the sublingual and labial glands are similar to the submaxillary glands.

Nitrogenous constituents

The saliva of ruminants contains appreciable concentrations of urea (McDonald 1948), and the concentrations are related to the concentration of ammonia in the rumen and to the concentration of urea in the blood (Somers 1961). A nondialysable fraction (4–22 percent) of nitrogen is present in the parotid saliva, which probably represents mucus secreted from the goblet cells of the ducts.

An unidentified nitrogenous fraction (10–26 percent) is also present. The mixed saliva that can be aspirated from beneath the tongue of adult cattle while feeding contains appreciably more nitrogen than the mixed saliva that can be collected from the cardia during resting (Phillipson and Mangan 1959). This is probably because it contains saliva from the submaxillary and sublingual glands which are quiescent or secreting very slowly during resting. Bailey and Balch (1961) found 3–14 mg/100 ml in the mixed saliva that arrived at the cardia of resting cows, of which urea represented about 77 percent of the total nitrogen.

RUMEN CONTENTS

The contents of the rumen and reticulum of sheep amount to about 4–6 kg; larger values have been recorded. The contents of these organs in fully fed adult cattle may weigh from 30 to 60 kg. These quantities vary with the diet, the time they are measured, and the rapidity with which fermentation occurs in the rumen. The rumen never empties, but with fasting the contents become more and more fluid. The dry matter of the well-mixed contents consequently may vary considerably, but for animals that are regularly fed it is likely to be in the region of 10–15 percent of the wet weight.

The rumen and reticulum form a fermentation vat into which food enters, in grazing animals, for about 8 hours of the 24. The bacteria and protozoa of the rumen live on the food the animal eats and cause extensive chemical changes. The soluble products of fermentation are largely absorbed, and the material leaving the rumen represents a mixture of food residues, bacteria and protozoa, and some soluble fermentation products dissolved in a buffered fluid. There is a continuous fluctuating flow of saliva into these organs and a fairly continuous flow of material from them to the omasum and thence caudally to the abomasum and intestines. As food is eaten, most of it passes back to the rumen and becomes slowly mixed with the residues of previous meals; under these circumstances the variation in the weight of the total contents throughout the 24 hours is not as great as might be expected. The residues of any one meal pass from the rumen over a considerable period (Usuelli 1933).

Fermentation of carbohydrates

The population of bacteria inhabiting the rumen may be as dense as 10^9 cells per gram when they are counted directly under the microscope in suitably diluted samples (Moir 1951). The largest viable counts, however, are less than direct microscopic counts (Bryant and Burkey 1953). A thriving population of ciliated protozoa is also present, and flagellated organisms can usually be found but are insignificant in number.

Some forms of bacteria are microscopically distinct (Smiles and Dobson 1956), but numerically they are insignificant when compared with the coccoid forms which make up about 90 percent of the bacterial population.

The speed at which carbohydrates are fermented in the rumen varies with their availability. Generally speaking, soluble sugars are rapidly fermented and starches are less rapidly fermented, while the structural components of plant tissues, namely cellulose and the hemicelluloses, are slowly fermented. The age of the plant and the degree of lignification are important. The chemical nature of the association of lignin with cellulose and hemicelluloses is not understood, but there is no doubt that lignification reduces the digestibility of cellulose and hemicelluloses.

Very little of the total carbohydrates of grasses can be digested by intestinal enzymes. The composition of common grasses varies with the age of the plant and between species. The soluble carbohydrates present are principally hexoses, sucrose, and fructosan (a polysaccharide composed of fructose units). They may form as much as 25 percent of the dry matter in early summer grass but only 4–5 percent in autumn grass. Of the three main components, fructosan is the largest in young grasses. Cellulose is associated with xylan, sometimes named cellulosan, which is regarded by some as an integral part of the cellulosic framework of the plant. Xylan in mature rye grass may be as much as 20–30 percent of the dry matter but is less in young grasses. The content of true cellulose after removal of cellulosan may be from 15 to 35 percent of the dry matter of grasses, the quantity increasing with the age of the plant.

The hemicelluloses have been defined as cell wall polysaccharides soluble in dilute alkalis but not in water, which may be hydrolyzed to sugar and sugar-acid units. The sugars derived are both pentose and hexose units, and they may be in combination with uronic acid, the usual combinations being galacturonic acid. The most abundant sugar derived from grasses is xylose (Buston 1934, Waite and Gorrod 1959). The hemicelluloses form as much as 14–25 percent of the dry matter of grasses.

Lignin is deposited between the microfibrils and micellar strands of cellulose. Its structure is not fully understood but it contains methoxyl groups and is thought to be a polyflavone compound. The lignin content of herbage may vary from 2 to 12 percent of the dry matter.

The methods of determining lignin are empirical, and there is doubt whether it is digested to a small extent or whether it is completely indigestible. Digestion, if it occurs, does not involve more than 15–20 percent of the lignin ingested.

In spite of the complexity of the carbohydrates ingested, the results of their fermentation are simple mixtures of VFA with carbon dioxide. The fermentation of purified cellulose, starch, or glucose in vitro by mixed rumen bacteria produces acetic and propionic acids in about equal proportions, but in the rumen acetic usually represents 60–70 percent, propionic 15–20, and butyric 10–15 of the fatty acid mixture in animals fed hay or other roughages. Branched-chain isomers of C_4 acids, and straight- and branched-chain C_5 acids as well, are usually present in small quantities, but these are associated with the deamination of amino acids and presumably are derived from their carbon skeletons.

The concentrations of propionic acid in the rumen are greatest in vivo when the diet contains large quantites of soluble sugar or starches, and least in animals fed on poor hay. The concentration of acetic acid varies in an inverse direction. It is common to find lactic acid in the rumen when animals are fed on root crops containing a large quantity of soluble sugar and when they are fed on high starch diets. Lactic acid, however, is unstable in the rumen. It may be present in quantity during the first few weeks after animals have been placed on rations high in starches or sugars, but later be present in only insignificant concentrations. Lactate in the rumen may be fermented to acetic and propionic acids and is therefore an intermediary product. It will accumulate or not according to the concentration of bacteria that can ferment it. Apparently it takes some time for these to develop.

Gas production

The gas mixture in the rumen is largely composed of carbon dioxide and methane. Some nitrogen appears, and traces of oxygen have been found as the length of time after feeding increases. Hydrogen is absent or is present only in traces, except when feeding is resumed after a period of fast (Pilgrim 1948), when it appears in quantity for a few days in place of methane. Methane is formed by the reduction of carbon dioxide by methanogenic bacteria. Hydrogen, formate, and succinate are hydrogen donators for this reaction (Beijer 1952), and this is probably one reason why they are virtually absent from the rumen or present only in small concentrations, although all are known to be metabolic products of various rumen bacteria.

In cattle, methane forms from 30 to 40 percent of the total gas present in the rumen, but carbon dioxide may vary greatly from 20 to 65 percent in cattle fed once in 24 hours. Usually carbon dioxide forms about 60 percent of the gas present in animals that are fed *ad libitum*

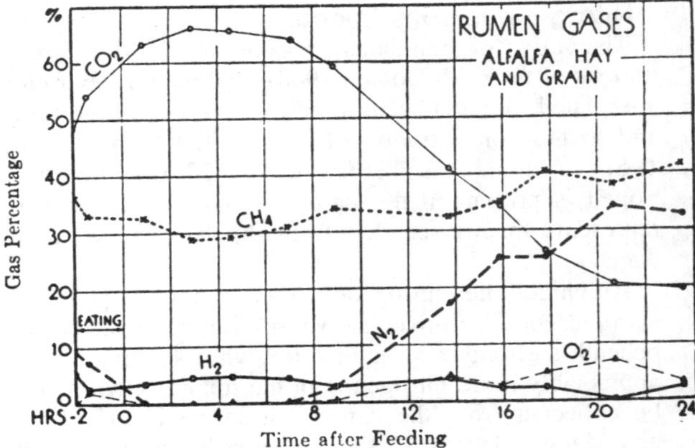

Figure 22.3. Composition of rumen gases (in a dairy cow) on a ration of alfalfa hay and grain. (From L.E. Washburn and S. Brody 1937, *Mo. Ag. Exp. Sta. Res. Bull.* 263.)

(Fig. 22.3). Carbon dioxide is evolved during the fermentation of carbohydrates and the deamination of amino acids. It also arises from saliva bicarbonate as a result of neutralization of fatty acids formed during fermentation and by exchange across the rumen epithelium during the absorption of fatty acids (see below).

The quantity and rate of gas evolved from the rumen of cattle vary considerably with the food. Feeding is followed by an increase of gas evolution that may be as much as 20 liters in 30 minutes in cattle, but this subsides to about 5–10 liters in 30 minutes after about four hours.

Protein digestion

Sym (1938) showed that proteolytic activity was present in the rumen contents. This activity is a property of suspensions of the mixed rumen bacteria of sheep. The nature of the protein of the diet of the donor sheep seems to have little influence on the proteolytic activity of such suspensions (Warner 1956). Proteins with different solubilities, however, cause widely different concentrations of ammonia to appear in the rumen, and the extent of ammonia formation is related to the solubility of the protein (McDonald 1952). When casein hydrolysates are introduced into a mixed suspension of rumen bacteria, the loss of α-amino nitrogen is accompanied by the formation of ammonia, carbon dioxide, and VFA as main products of the reaction in roughly equimolar proportions. The fatty acid mixture produced is similar to that in the rumen except that isomers of C_4 and C_5 acids are formed in greater quantities (el-Shazly 1952). The deaminase activity of rumen bacteria does not vary widely with the protein content of the diet (Warner 1956). Usually there is only a small quantity of amino nitrogen to be found in the rumen fluid, which is an indication of the rapidity with which fermentative deamination occurs, but with experimental diets as much as 10 mg percent may appear temporarily (Annison 1956). In vitro deamination can be inhibited by toluene, and under these circumstances amino nitrogen rather than ammonia has been shown to accumulate when protein is introduced into mixed suspensions of rumen bacteria. Leibholz (1965) has been able to identify individual amino acids in the supernatant of centrifuged rumen contents of sheep in small concentrations which increase temporarily after feeding. Isotopic studies with ^{14}C-labeled L-glutamate and L-aspartate show that the half-life is about one minute when exposed to mixed rumen bacteria; less than 10 percent is assimilated by the bacteria (vaz Portugal 1963).

The digestion of protein in the rumen, therefore, appears to proceed by a steady rate of hydrolysis. In Warner's view, this takes place in the usual way through peptides of decreasing chain length to free amino acids, which are largely destroyed by fermentative deamination with the production of carbon dioxide, ammonia, and short-chain fatty acids. Some peptides and amino acids may pass directly into bacterial cells, but the evidence suggests that many of the various species of rumen bacteria are able to synthesize their nitrogenous cell constituents using ammonia as a principal source of nitrogen, although some available sulphur and possibly certain carbon structures are necessary too. Some of the bacteria, however, have an amino acid requirement.

Ammonia is the principal soluble nitrogenous constituent of rumen fluid. Its concentration is influenced by the quantity and solubility of the dietary protein, the quantity of urea that enters the rumen in saliva, the diffusion of urea through the rumen wall, and the rate at which ammonia is absorbed from the rumen. Rumen fluid has a pronounced urease activity (Pearson and Smith 1943), so that urea entering is rapidly hydrolyzed to ammonia and carbon dioxide.

Increased quantities of sugars and starches in the diet decrease the concentrations of ammonia in the rumen (McDonald 1952), since the inclusion of rapidly fermenting carbohydrate substrates increases the speed with which organisms can incorporate ammonia nitrogen into their cell protoplasm.

Lipid hydrolysis

Triglycerides undergo hydrolysis in the rumen to glycerol and fatty acids. No mono- or diglycerides have been detected during the hydrolysis, so that if there are intermediary stages they are very transient (Garton et al. 1958). Hydrolysis of triglycerides is due to rumen microorganisms, and the glycerol derived from the hydrolysis is fermented principally into propionic acid (Johns 1953), although the transitory stages, succinic and lactic acids, have also been detected.

Phospholipids are similarly hydrolyzed (Dawson 1959). The most important change that occurs to the fatty acids derived from triglycerides is the hydrogenation of unsaturated fatty acids. Thus when unsaturated C_{18} acids (oleic, linoleic, or linolenic acids containing one, two, and three double bonds respectively) are incubated in rumen contents in vitro, appreciable portions are converted to the saturated C_{18} acid (stearic acid) (Shorland et al. 1957). *Trans* and positional isomers are formed during this process, and these are found in depot and butterfats. A *trans* acid is one in which the methyl groups on either side of a double bond are opposite in space to each other in contrast to the *cis* form in which both are arranged on the same side.

Synthesis of B vitamins

It is impossible to produce in adult ruminants the characteristic signs of deficiencies of any of the members of the B complex, as they were first understood, by feeding rations deficient in these factors. For example, Bechdel et al. (1926) found that a cow maintained throughout pregnancy on a deficient diet not only remained in perfect health but was able to bear and rear a calf satisfactorily. This showed that members of the B complex were synthesized somewhere in the cow.

Deficiencies of members of the B complex have been produced in young ruminants experimentally before the bacterial flora of the rumen have developed, and many alimentary bacteria are known to synthesize B vitamins. The concentrations of these vitamins are greater in the rumen contents than in the food when the food contains very little of them, although differences are small when the food contains adequate quantities (Porter 1961).

The total quantities of thiamine, riboflavin, and nicotinic acid in the rumen contents are much greater than the quantities eaten daily (Buziassy and Tribe 1960). Most of the thiamine is in solution (Phillipson and Reid 1957), and 40 percent or more of pantothenic acid, pyridoxine, and biotin is also extracellular (Porter 1961). B vitamins can be absorbed from the rumen (Rérat et al. 1958) so that their production in the rumen may be much greater than their concentrations suggest. Riboflavin, nicotinic acid, folic acid, and vitamin B_{12} are largely intracellular, and little absorption occurs from the rumen.

The only well-established B-vitamin deficiency of adult ruminants is that associated with insufficient cobalt in the diet; this element forms the prosthetic group of the cyanocobalamin known as vitamin B_{12}. Cobalt in common with other trace elements is concentrated within bacterial cells in the rumen, and the cobalamines, of which there are at least four known forms, are synthesized by bacteria. Lack of cobalt leads to inadequacy of vitamin B_{12} synthesis within the rumen, a depressed appetite, and poor growth in young ruminants. The severity of the condition depends on the degree of deficiency.

Pattern of chemical changes

The pH of the rumen does not deviate far from neutrality, and is usually within the range of 5.8–7.0. After feeding, the pH decreases, and the speed and extent of the decrease are related to diet. The decrease in pH is especially marked when the diet contains appreciable quantities of rapidly fermentable sugars. A strong inverse relationship exists between the concentration of VFA and lactic acid, on the one hand, and the pH of the contents, on the other (Briggs et al. 1957). During fasting the concentration of VFA steadily decreases, and the pH of the contents rises above pH 7 to a region close to that of blood (Phillipson 1942).

Values of 5.5 or less in pH are associated with lactic acid fermentation when cattle or sheep are allowed to eat diets high in starch or sugar and low in fiber. In extreme situations such a diet may cause death due to acidosis. The introduction of excessive amounts of urea into the rumen can induce alkalinity due to excessive ammonia formation, which may also be fatal.

The buffering capacity of the rumen fluid is considerable and does not depend entirely on the saliva secreted, as exchange across the rumen wall of un-ionized acid with bicarbonate accounts for about one half the acids absorbed (Ash and Dobson 1963). The role of salivary bicarbonate and phosphate in buffering the rumen contents has been examined by Turner and Hodgetts (1955); its buffering capacity is due principally to its bicarbonate content.

The concentrations of VFA in the rumen vary over a very wide range, but the total volatile acidity is usually within the range of 60–120 mEq/L. Exceptionally high values rising to 200 may occur when animals graze on young summer grass or when they are fed on starch-rich diets. Diets of hay produce smaller fluctuations throughout the day, and concentrations below 100 mEq/L are usual.

The concentrations of ammonia in the rumen vary greatly with the diet and may be anything from 2 to over 100 mg of ammonia nitrogen per 100 ml. The lowest concentrations occur in animals maintained on high starch rations (Chalmers and Synge 1954), and the highest have been found in sheep in New Zealand eating young summer grass (Johns 1955). The usual range of concentrations for animals fed mixed rations is 5–25 mg/100 ml. There are numerous studies on the concentrations of the VFA present in the rumen of cattle and sheep. Variations in the composition of the foods, and the times at which they are fed, do not allow easy comparison. The usual picture is that the individual acids are present in the following order: C_2 (acetic) > C_3 (propionic) > C_4 (iso- and n-butyric) > C_5 (iso- and n-valeric acid and α-methyl butyric acid) (Tables 22.5, 22.6).

PASSAGE OF FOOD THROUGH THE ALIMENTARY TRACT

The time spent by food residues in passing through the alimentary tract may be considered in two phases, the time spent in reaching the abomasum and the time spent in passing from the abomasum to the feces.

Lenkeit and Columbus (1934) observed that stained particles of straw given in milk consumed by kid goats or lambs were largely excreted in the feces during the next 24 hours. If the particles were given in milk by stomach tube, excretion was much delayed. The maximum excretion occurred at 36 hours or later and persisted for days. The difference between the rates of excretion was clearly due to closure of the esophageal groove when the animals

Table 22.5. **Proportions of fatty acids with different numbers of carbon atoms in the rumen, calculated as a percentage of the total VFA on a molecular basis**

Diet	No. of carbon atoms C_2	C_3	C_4	C_5	Reference
			Cattle		
High roughage with Low concentrate	65–75	15–21	5–14	2.5	Balch and Rowland 1957
	65–95	16–20	12	3	McClymont 1951
Low roughage with High concentrate	40–66	18–41	7–15	3–14	Balch and Rowland 1957
	52–61	17–30	10–18	3–5	McClymont 1951
Grass	63–68	17–20	10–12	3–5	Balch and Rowland 1957
			Sheep		
Lucerne hay	68–73	15–20	10–16		Gray et al. 1951
Wheaten hay	60–70	17–27	14–16		Ibid.
Grass hay (N 2.8%)	65–71	15–24	8–15	2–5	Johns 1955
Grass (summer and winter)	50–64	13–30	12–20	3–10	Ibid.
Low hay, high-flaked maize	51–68	23–42	3–14	1–2	Phillipson 1952

Table 22.6. Proportions of VFA in the rumen of sheep

Diet	Acetic	Propionic	Iso-butyric	n-butyric	Iso-valeric	2-methyl butyric	n-valeric
Dried grass	55–69	16–26	0.5–1.4	7.6–11.9	0.8–1.9		0.7–1.5
Grass silage	53–72	15–25	1.3–2.6	7.4–10.7	1.9–3.2		0.6–2.3
Hay	78–81	13–19	0.4–0.6	2.4–2.9	0.2–0.3	0.2–0.8	0.3–0.5
Hay + maize	41–56	18–35	0.2–0.5	8.9–28.9	0.3–1.8	0.1–1.2	0.3–3.7
Hay + maize + peanut	41–60	26–34	0.9–2.4	10.1–24.1	0.9–24.1	0.5–1.9	1.6–3.5

Adapted from el-Shazly 1952, *Biochem. J.* 51:640–53; E.F. Annison 1954, *Biochem. J.* 57:400–405

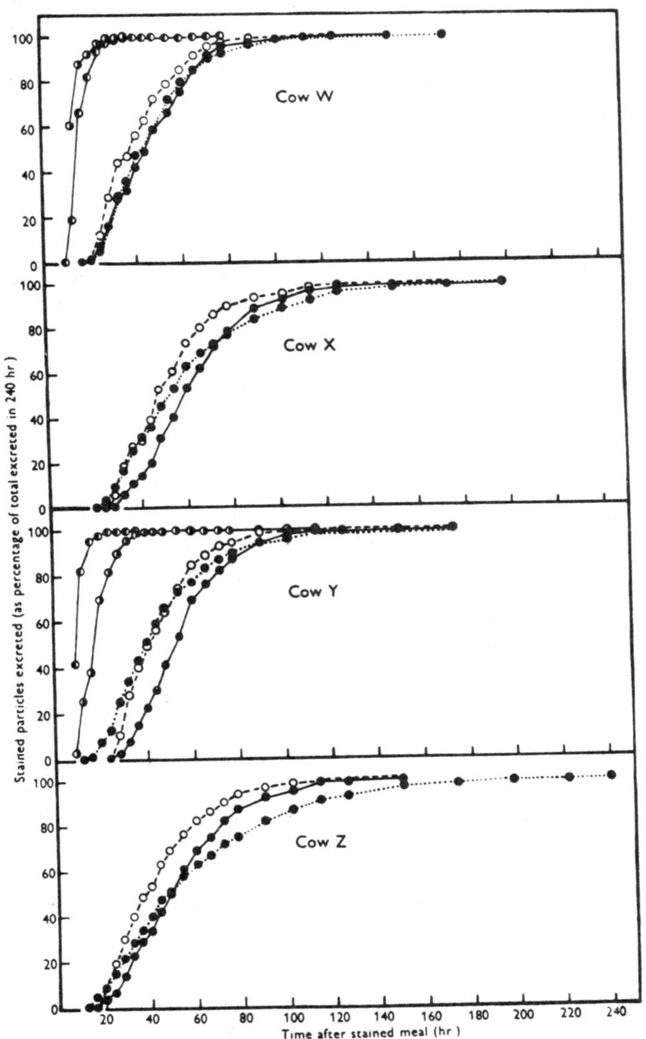

Figure 22.4. Excretion of undigested particles of stained hay and ground hay in two diets. ●——●, hay given in a hay diet; ○---○, ground hay in a hay diet; ●········●, ground hay in a ground-hay diet. Values for the fecal excretion of ground hay introduced into the abomasum through rumen fistulas are shown for cows W and Y: ◑——◑, hay diets; ◐——◐, ground-hay diets. (From Balch 1950, Factors affecting the utilization of food by dairy cows, *Brit. J. Nutr.* 4:361–88, published by Cambridge U. Press.)

spontaneously took milk. Balch (1950) showed in cows that 90 percent or more of stained straw particles were recovered in the feces about 30 hours after they were placed in the abomasum, while about 100 hours were needed for recovery when they were given by mouth (Fig. 22.4). These experiments leave no doubt that the rumen, reticulum, and omasum cause considerable delay to the passage of foodstuffs and that the rate of passage of ingesta from the abomasum caudally is similar to that of animals with a simple stomach.

After stained hay is added to a ration of hay, the concentration of stained particles in the rumen is halved after 40–48 hours and stained particles remain in the rumen for 5 days or more. The passage from the rumen of stained ground particles added to an all-hay diet is more rapid than that of stained long hay (Balch 1950).

There have been several ways of expressing the rate of excretion of food particles, and the method given by Castle (1956) is frequently used. The number of stained particles excreted in the feces is plotted as a cumulative curve against the percentage of the total excretion. The shape of the curve is expressed by taking the mean of the times needed for the excretion of 10 percent increases in the stained particles recovered in the feces, starting at 5 percent and ending at 95 percent (Fig. 22.5). The values

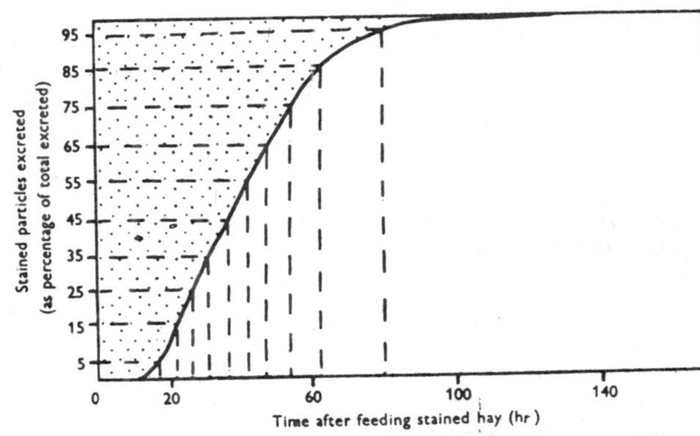

Figure 22.5. Rate of excretion of undigested residue of stained hay by an adult goat showing method of calculation of the R value (mean retention time). (From Castle 1956, The rate of passage of foodstuffs through the alimentary tract of the goat, *Brit. J. Nutr.* 10:15–23, published by Cambridge U. Press.)

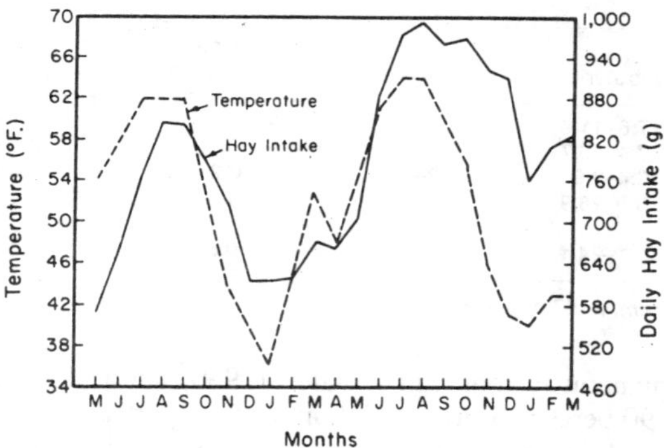

Figure 22.6. Relationship between environmental temperature and hay intake. (From J.G. Gordon 1964, *Nature* 204:798–99.)

(in hours) where each vertical line cuts the ordinate are added and divided by ten to give what is called "the mean retention time" (R). For adult goats these values varied from 32 to 40 hours when fed calf cubes (400 g) and meadow hay. Values for adult cattle when fed on varying quantities were from 65 to 93 hours (Campling et al. 1961). R values for the whole alimentary tract decrease as the quantity of roughage eaten increases, but the digestibility of the roughage decreases with retention time (Blaxter et al. 1956). These generalizations apply when roughages are consumed, but when meals alone are eaten the situation is less clear.

For roughage, there is evidence to indicate that enteroceptive reflexes play a positive role in controlling food consumption at least over short periods of time. However, the marked variation in the consumption of chopped hay by sheep over long periods (Fig. 22.6) can hardly be explained in terms of enteroception alone. Over two years, sheep at latitude 57°N varied the quantity of hay eaten by as much as 40 percent; they ate most during the summer and least during the winter. In addition, cattle fed on concentrated foodstuffs do not conform to the enteroception hypothesis. Enteroception is only one of many factors that influence the central control of food intake. Metabolic effects are equally if not more important.

MECHANICAL PROPULSION OF FOOD TO THE OMASUM

In cattle

The movements of the walls and pillars of the reticulum and rumen of cattle have been deduced from recordings of the pressure changes within the various parts of these organs and by palpation of those structures (Wester 1926, Schalk and Amadon 1928).

The essential features of the movements of the reticulum and rumen, with which subsequent investigations concur, are that the reticulum contracts in two stages. In the first stage the organ contracts to about one half of its size; this movement is followed by a relaxation and then a further contraction that is stronger than the first. The organ then relaxes and may dilate before finally assuming its resting form. The dilatation can sometimes be seen radiologically in sheep and goats. The whole movement is referred to as the *biphasic contraction* of the reticulum and occupies about 7–12 seconds. There has been much dispute whether or not a relaxation of the organ occurs between the two phases of contraction; all that can be said is that some relaxation occurs in sheep, but more usually it does not, while relaxation between the two stages of contraction is usual with cattle.

Reticulum contractions occur during feeding at about 35–45 second intervals. When the animal is resting or ruminating they occur at longer intervals—up to 75 seconds in cattle or even longer in sheep. The frequency when animals are standing but not eating is greater than when they are lying down (Balch 1952). The biphasic contraction is preceded by an extra contraction of the reticulum when animals are ruminating. These forms are referred to as *triphasic contractions* (Table 22.7).

Contraction of the main body of the dorsal sac of the rumen starts during the second part of the biphasic contraction of the reticulum and involves the anterior pillar, which contracts to form a prominent barrier between the anterior and posterior regions of the whole organ. The contraction spreads rapidly toward the posterior part of the dorsal sac and involves the posterior pillar, the dorsal coronary pillars, and finally the dorsal blind sac, so that the entire dorsal sac is in a contracted state. The contraction of the dorsal blind sac persists after the remainder of the dorsal sac has relaxed and is concurrent with the contraction of the main body of the ventral sac. This again involves the anterior pillar, which contracts into a low position along with the posterior pillar and the ventral coronary pillars. The ventral blind sac next contracts as the main body of the ventral sac relaxes. This sequence of events has been largely confirmed by Reid and Cornwall (1959) and is now referred to as the primary wave of contraction, the A wave (Reid 1962), or the backward-moving wave (Reid and Titchen 1965).

Following this phase, a second contraction of the dorsal sac of the rumen followed by a contraction of the ven-

Table 22.7. Numbers of bi- or triphasic contractions of the reticulum of cattle fed on varying amounts of hay or straw

Activity	Contractions per hour
Eating	79–100
Resting	47–80
Ruminating	55–76

Adapted from M. Freer, R.C. Campling, and C.C. Balch 1962, *Brit. J. Nutr.* 16:279–95

tral sac may occur. This secondary wave of contraction of the rumen, also called the B wave or forward-moving wave, originates in the posterior part of the organ. It occurs independently of the reticulum and is associated with eructation (Weiss 1953).

The events in the rumen often follow an alternating pattern; thus a biphasic contraction of the reticulum may be followed by the primary wave of pressure changes in the rumen and then by a secondary wave; the next biphasic contraction may be followed only by a primary wave of contractions, while the third biphasic contraction of the reticulum may be followed by primary and secondary waves of contraction in the rumen and so on (Fig. 22.7).

Reid and Cornwall (1959) observed that the behavior of the ventral sac of the rumen during rumination was quite distinctive. The ventral sac component of the primary wave was frequently absent or the pressure changes were much reduced, while the ventral sac component of the secondary wave was unusually strong and prolonged. An analysis of the patterns of pressure waves from four cows enables us to compare the frequency of dorsal and ventral sac activity (Table 22.8). The symbols used are as follows: D denotes the primary wave of pressure in the dorsal sac; V, a wave of pressure in the ventral sac; S, the secondary wave of pressure in the dorsal sac, which, at its peak, usually coincides with a sharp "spike" of pressure in the anterior and ventral sacs of the rumen and in the reticulum, and which accompanies belching. The classification under *a* represents the sequences of these changes and the incidence of each sequence in relation to the activity of the animal. About 10 percent of the sequences analyzed cannot be classified into the four categories listed.

The sequences rearranged under *b* indicate the incidence of primary waves (DV), modified primary waves in which the ventral sac shows no pressure change (D), and secondary waves (SV). The secondary wave associated with belching was only slightly modified by activity of the animal. The incidence of the primary wave, however, was greatly reduced during rumination and to a less extent during resting and was replaced by the modified primary wave.

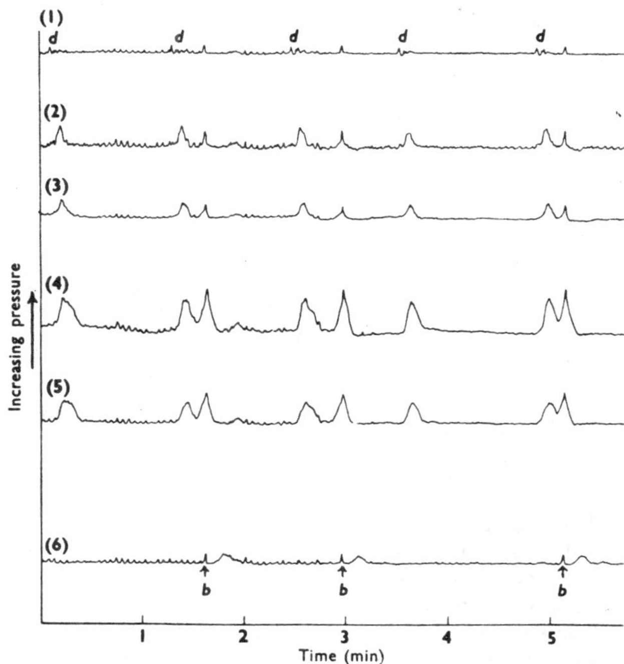

Figure 22.7. Pressure changes in the reticulum (1) and in the dorsal sac (2–5, anterior-posterior) and the ventral sac (6) of the rumen of a cow. The double contraction of the reticulum (d) is indicated. Belching (b) coincides with the peak of the secondary contraction of the rumen. The start of the secondary pressure wave occurs in tracing 5 before it can be seen in tracing 2, although the peak of the pressure wave is synchronous in tracings 2–5. (From C.C. Balch 1959, *Proc. Nutr. Soc.* 18:97–102.)

The pressure changes within the dorsal and ventral blind sacs are more complex than those in the main body of the rumen and more variable.

In sheep

The same patterns of pressure waves were found in the rumen of sheep by Ohga et al. (1965), although the incidence of modified primary waves was less than in cattle (Table 22.9). During fasting, movements of the dorsal and ventral sac overlap each other, and considerable vari-

Table 22.8. Percentages of pressure waves in the rumen of cows

	a*					b†		
Activity	D	DV	DSV	DVSV	Others	Primary (DV)	Modified primary (D)	Secondary (SV)
Feeding	1	27	5	56	11	55	4	41
Resting	10	35	25	22	8	41	25	34
Ruminating	22	28	37	6	7	25	43	32

* Total patterns analyzed, 5998
† Excludes the group "others" under *a*
From A.T. Phillipson and C.S.W. Reid 1960, *Proc. Nutr. Soc.* 19:xxvii

Table 22.9. Percentages of different sequences of pressure waves in the rumen of sheep

	a					b		
Activity	D	DV	DSV	DVSV	Others	Primary (DV)	Modified primary (D)	Secondary (SV)
Feeding	0	45	1	46	8	65	1	34
Resting	2	48	4	39	7	64	4	32
Ruminating	4	48	13	30	6	57	12	31

Modified from Ohga, Ota, and Nakatato 1965, *Jap. J. Vet. Sci.* 27:151–60, so that the results are comparable to those given in Table 22.8. These authors classify D, DV, DSV, and DVSV as D_1, D_1V_1, $D_1D_2V_2$, and $D_1V_1D_2V_2$ respectively. The values given under *b* are calculated in the same way as those in Table 22.8.

ation occurred in the ventral sac for about 10 minutes after feeding before settling down to the patterns described (Titchen and Reid 1965).

Rumination

The material entering the thoracic esophagus is semifluid in consistency. This is clear from radiological studies and means that recently eaten forages whose particle size is too great to be suspended in the rumen fluid are not included in the material that is rechewed. The transfer of fluid material to the esophagus depends on a pressure gradient that causes it to move in this direction. Such a gradient can be produced by an increase in pressure in the reticulum and rumen or by a decrease of pressure in the thoracic esophagus, or by a combination of both. There has been much dispute on these two possibilities.

Evidence presented by Colin (1886) showed that during the act of regurgitation the diaphragm contracts and the cardia dilates widely to form a funnel-like opening into which semifluid food moves rapidly. He suggested that the contraction of the diaphragm caused an increase in intragastric pressure that forced food into the thoracic esophagus. Toussaint (1875) recorded the pressure changes within the pleural cavity and trachea of ruminating cattle and the movement of the thoracic rib cage. He noted a decrease in pressure in both the pleural cavity and trachea that exceeded that of normal inspiration when the animal made an inspiratory effort at regurgitation. He found that air did not pass through the nostrils at this time, and he consequently concluded that the glottis was closed. He suggested that the decreased pressure induced in the thorax was translated to the lumen of the thoracic esophagus and that this produced the pressure gradient that caused food to flow into it. Bergman and Dukes (1926) and Stigler (1933) confirmed the occurrence of the events described by Toussaint, and Stigler was able to measure a fall in pressure into the thoracic esophagus itself at the moment of regurgitation.

Recently this hypothesis has come again under scrutiny because it has been shown in sheep (Webster and Cresswell 1957) that animals fitted with an open tracheal cannula can regurgitate easily. Colvin et al. (1957) made similar observations in cattle and found that animals had no difficulty in regurgitating with an open trachea, but they mention that an extra pressure occurred in the rumen when the tracheal cannula was open.

These observations do not necessarily contradict the hypothesis of Toussaint who also observed regurgitation in cattle with an open trachea but noted that extra activity of the abdominal muscles occurred under these circumstances. Instead they suggest that there is more than one way of causing food to flow into the esophagus.

During rumination an additional contraction of the reticulum occurs which precedes the normal biphasic contraction. The actual movement of food into the esophagus occurs during the later stages of this additional contraction and therefore precedes the following biphasic contraction with the closely following primary wave of movement in the rumen. Contraction of the reticulum is not an essential part of regurgitation, for cattle and sheep can still ruminate after the organ is immobilized by the administration of atropine (Wester 1926, Duncan 1953). However, Bell (1958) thought that increased pressure in the region of the antrum of the rumen in intact goats when they regurgitate corresponded to the first of the triphasic contractions of the reticulum. In contrast, Stevens and Sellers (1960) failed to find any appreciable increase in pressure on the gastric side of the cardia of cattle during regurgitation, although they recorded a sharp fall in pressure, 30–40 mm Hg within the lower part of the thoracic esophagus during the inspiratory effort.

Wester (1926) pointed out that, since the esophageal musculature was composed entirely of striated muscle, this organ could be expected to have brisk movements, and he proposed that the essential part of the regurgitating mechanism was a sharp longitudinal contraction of the esophagus together with contraction of the pillars of the diaphragm, the latter movement increasing the aperture through which the esophagus passes. This action of the esophagus could be aided by the decrease in intrapleural pressure that occurs when the animal inspires with a closed glottis. Wester's hypothesis has never been seriously investigated, but it does satisfy the known experimental evidence because, under these circumstances, an open trachea would not necessarily impede regurgitation, while denervation and immoblization of the diaphragm producing flaccid pillars, which does not prevent regurgitation (Bell 1958), would not impede a longitudinal contraction of the esophagus.

Two further observations are worth mentioning. The first is that Stigler, acting on a suggestion made by Mangold (Stigler 1933), dilated the cardia of cattle with a small speculum and found that some food passed into it without any of the activities associated with regurgitation. From this it can be concluded that for normal regurgitation, a large pressure gradient is not required for the rapid filling of the esophagus that occurs during regurgitation. The second is that regurgitation, although normally occurring during the first of the triphasic reticulum contractions, may occur at other times (Downie 1954) or, as the author has found, can be induced by obstructing the flow of food in the esophagus. Obstruction of the flow of food into the esophagus of a ruminating cow resulted in the cow making as many as four attempts at regurgitation between each triphasic contraction, and the activities concerned were those of the diaphragm and apparently the esophagus.

Radiological observations show that the thoracic esophagus rapidly fills with radiopaque fluid on regurgitation and has a dilated appearance. A contraction occurs about 3–4 cm anterior to the cardia. Fluid on the oral side of the contraction is rapidly propelled to the mouth, and the whole of the thoracic esophagus appears to contract in such a way as to obliterate its lumen. Fluid caudal to the initial contraction returns to the rumen. The studies of Dougherty et al. (1955, 1958) in relation to eructation suggest that the activity of the thoracic esophagus, when it is distended with gas, in much the same as when it is distended with fluid.

Rumination can easily be evoked in cattle with a rumen fistula by stroking the interior wall of the reticulum, the reticuloruminal fold, or the rumen in the region of the cardia. The coarseness of the food influences the time devoted to rumination; for example, Gordon (1958a) observed that the average time devoted to rumination by six sheep fed on ground-dried grass was only 5 hours out of 24, but when they received the same quantity of dried grass in the long or chopped state, they ruminated for 8½ or 9 hours. A diet consisting of concentrates alone caused rumination for only 2½ hours in contrast to a diet of the same weight of hay which provoked 8 hours of rumination during the 24. Habit also seems to affect the distribution of periods of rumination throughout the 24 hours irrespective of the feeding time in sheep (Gordon 1958b).

Nervous control

Section of both vagus nerves results in the loss of the major movements of the reticulum and rumen, stagnation of food within these organs, loss of rumination, and loss of the esophageal groove reflex. Sheep that have been maintained for 40 days by intra-abomasal feeding following thoracic vagotomy have shown some return of movement in the reticulum and rumen, but these have been weak and uncoordinated (Duncan 1953). Stimulation of the various branches of the abdominal vagus causes contraction of those parts of the stomach supplied by their fibers, and movements of the reticulum and rumen are suppressed following the injection of atropine. The dependence of the reticulum on its vagal innervation was shown best by Popow et al. (1933), who exteriorized both cervical vagi in loops of skin and showed that blocking conduction by the application of cold suppressed the biphasic contractions of the reticulum, which returned when the cold block was removed. Splanchnicotomy, however, has apparently no effect on the contractions of the reticulum and rumen (Duncan 1953).

This evidence demonstrates that discharges down efferent vagal fibers passing to the reticulum are responsible for the initiation of the major movements of this organ, although contraction of the reticulum can also be elicited by splanchnic stimulation or by the injection of epinephrine under certain circumstances (Titchen 1958a).

Intrinsic nerves

The presence of a myenteric plexus in the reticulum and rumen has been recognized for a long time; an exact description of it is given by Habel (1956) and Morrison and Habel (1964). They found a rich ganglion plexus in all compartments of the stomach of sheep and goats. The ganglia were composed of cells measuring 18–40 μ in diameter, while some larger cells (50–60 μ) were present. The smaller cells were most frequent in the esophageal groove, reticulum, and pillars of the rumen and omasum. The larger cells were most frequent in the abomasum. Synaptic connections between ganglion cells occurred, but axons derived from these cells could not be traced to either encapsulated pressure receptors or to tension spindles. The nonglandular part of the stomach did not contain a subepithelial ganglionic plexus. Histochemical studies by Comline and Message (1965) have shown cholinergic nerve fibers in the stomach of sheep, especially in the anterior and posterior pillars. Nerve fibers in the subepithelial region of the first three parts of the stomach were also demonstrated, some of which penetrated to the epithelium. It is improbable that they are afferent fibers; they may be concerned with blood vessels. Their nature suggests that they are vasodilatory fibers. Fine nerve fibers have been found in the conical papillae of the reticulum and in some rumen papillae (Leek 1972), yet electron microscope studies of appropriate areas of the epithelium have not revealed nerve fibers that penetrate the epithelial layers or evidence of specialized sensory nerve endings (Steven and Marshall 1972).

Gastric reflexes

The frequency of contractions of the reticulum of lambs is much reduced after they suck a barium meal from a bottle to fill the abomasum. Similarly, distention of the abomasum of the adult sheep with fluid or by mechanical means reduces the force and frequency of reticular contractions or may cause complete inhibition. Rumen movements, however, may be unaltered or continue in an irregular manner (Phillipson 1939). Tactile or stretch stimuli applied to the interior surfaces of the reticulum and rumen usually provoke increased reticular contractions and salivation. The anterior structures are more sensitive than the main body of the rumen (Ash and Kay 1959). Inhibition of all movement can be induced by filling the empty organs with solutions of VFA buffered to the region of pH 4, although similar solutions of acids that are not readily absorbed are ineffective (Ash 1959). This suggests that rapid penetration of the rumen epithelium is needed to produce inhibition and that acid-sensitive receptors may be present, since local application of acid vapor, which does not cause systemic changes in the blood, is also effective.

In decerebrate or anesthetized sheep and goats in which contractions of the reticulum are absent, stimulation of the central end of one of the cut cervical vagi or the cut ventral thoracic vagus or of its cut abdominal branches may evoke characteristic biphasic contractions of the reticulum (Iggo 1951, Titchen 1953, 1958a). In decerebrate preparations, spontaneous contractions of the reticulum may reappear after a lapse of time following laparatomy, or they may be evoked by afferent vagal stimulation. For example, Titchen was able to induce contractions of the reticulum by distension of the omasal canal, by reducing the pH of the abomasal contents to around 1, by mechanical stimulation of the lower part of the thoracic esophagus, or by stretching the reticulum by the inflation of a balloon within it. Distension of the abomasum or the introduction of saline into the abomasum inhibited the reticulum as in the conscious sheep; but section of the splanchnic nerves reversed this effect. Central stimulation of the cut splanchnic nerves inhibited contractions of the reticulum.

A study of the reflex activity of both the reticulum and rumen showed that the rumen was more susceptible to inhibition than the reticulum (Titchen 1960).

Potentials recorded from both efferent and afferent single vagal fibers passing to or arising from different parts of the stomach show that the resistance within the reticulum when it contracts modifies the frequency of discharge in efferent and afferent fibers (Iggo 1956, Iggo and Leek 1967). Efferent discharges related in time to the biphasic contractions of the reticulum and to the primary contraction of the rumen have been recorded (Dussardier 1958, Harding and Leek 1971), and areas in the reticulum, rumen, abomasum, and duodenum have been described that give rise to afferent discharges following mechanical or chemical stimulation (Harding and Leek 1972a,b). The conical papillae of the reticular ridges and some papillae of the rumen are examples of structures from which afferent discharges can be elicited (Leek 1972).

Role of the CNS

Stimulation of areas of the medulla in the region of the dorsal vagal nucleus provokes responses of the reticulum, rumen, and esophagus, and these are not abolished by section of the brain stem in the pontine area or of the spinal cord at the first cervical vertebra (Bell and Lawn 1955). Stimulation of the dorsal vagal nucleus by implanted electrodes in conscious goats causes complete cessation of the contractions of the reticulum and rumen, followed by intense activity when the stimulus is withdrawn (Andersson et al. 1959). Increased activity, however, is produced by stimulation of other areas.

Areas of the medulla close to the dorsal vagal nucleus that respond to efferent gastric inputs from different areas of the stomach have been mapped by Harding and Leek (1973). Partial overlapping of these areas occurred, and most of the responses are considered to be from interneurons. Regurgitation with subsequent remastication can also be produced by stimulation of the area lateral to the dorsal vagal nucleus. This area is quite distinct from the area that produces vomiting. Higher areas of the CNS may also affect gastric movement; for example, reticular and rumen contractions may be increased by the anticipation of food. Large changes in the concentrations of circulating glucose and VFA have been shown to modify rumen movements, although it remains to be seen whether physiological variations have such an effect. Titchen (1968) discussed this subject in detail and concludes: "The frequency and form of contractions of different parts of the ruminant stomach are determined by the efferent discharge from medullary centres. These centres are influenced by a wide spectrum of afferent impulses, many but not all of which are initiated by stimulation of receptors in the alimentary tract. These centres are in turn affected by influences from higher parts of the central nervous system; their excitability and that of sensory receptors and of affected organs may be directly or indirectly influenced hormonally, and by their immediate chemical environment due either to changes in the composition of the blood or to local metabolic activities."

Omasum

The contents of the omasum in the dead animal contain less water than the contents of the rumen and abomasum (Table 22.10).

Table 22.10. Average dry matter of the stomach contents of sheep and cattle (%)

Stomach	Sheep	Cattle
Reticulum and rumen	14	12
Omasum	22	16
Abomasum	11	9

Means represent 38 sheep fed on a variety of rations and 29 cattle fed on clover-timothy hay. (Data from Elsden et al. 1946, Garton 1951, Parthasarathy 1952, Boyne et al. 1956 for sheep, and Makela 1956 for cattle.)

It is usually considered that the principal function of the omasum is to reduce the particulate state of its contents to a fine degree of division, and this was shown to be true for calves up to 227 days old (Becker et al. 1963).

The mechanical activity can only be deduced from the pressure changes recorded within. Changes in position of the omasum, however, can be observed radiologically when the organ is viewed in the lateral position. It is rotated about its lesser curvature when the reticulum contracts, so that the lower pole moves slightly in a cranial direction and the upper pole slightly in a ventral direction.

A study of the movements of the reticulum, the lips of the esophageal groove, and the reticulo-omasal orifice in young sheep and cattle anesthetized with chloralose (Borgatti and Matscher 1958, Balch et al. 1951) showed that the omasal orifice moves in two phases. It closes during the first phase of the reticular contraction and remains closed until the reticulum is relaxing after the second phase of contraction, when it widely dilates. Spontaneous opening and closing movements of the reticulo-omasal orifice occur, and the orifice opens after vagal stimulation, following an initial closure. These activities are not abolished by atropine (Newhook and Titchen 1972).

Palpation of the reticulo-omasal orifice in cattle shows that during the relaxation of the reticulum, after the second phase of the contraction, the orifice opens and a flow of food can be felt to enter the omasum. Immediately after this, the orifice closes and an increase in pressure in the omasal sulcus, followed by a wave of pressure, occurs in the main body of the organ. Sometimes two waves of pressure occur in the body of the omasum between the biphasic contractions of the reticulum. The waves of increased pressure in the body of the omasum and in the sulcus at times occur regularly and at other times irregularly (Stevens et al. 1960).

Flow of food

The material entering the omasum is from the reticulum. This is frequently exchanged with the material in the anterior sac of the rumen and is usually more fluid than the rumen contents. The concentration of VFA in the contents of the reticulum is about 10 percent less than that of the ruminal fluid when these are compared in slaughtered sheep.

Table 22.11. Estimated passage of organic matter to the omasum of cows during 24 hours

Food	Daily intake of organic matter in kg	Weight of organic matter leaving the reticulum and rumen per day in kg
Straw	4.16	3.21
Hay	4.25	2.85
Hay	6.38	4.27
Hay	9.35	6.26
Dried grass *	9.58	5.69
Concentrates *	7.34	4.51

* Adapted from M. Freer, R.C. Campling, and C.C. Balch 1962, *Brit. J. Nutr.* 16:279–95; M. Freer and R.C. Campling 1965, *Brit. J. Nutr.* 19:195–207

Rough estimates of the quantities of organic matter passing to the omasum of cattle (Table 22.11) were made by removing, measuring, and sampling the contents of the rumen before feeding and then returning them to the rumen. This was repeated after feeding. Samples were then taken from the region of the omasal orifice throughout the day, and the loss of nutrients due to digestion was estimated, using lignin as a marker. The difference between the organic matter eaten and the organic matter digested, absorbed, or excreted as gas was taken as a measure of the organic matter passing to the omasum.

The flow of water is much greater than the flow of solid material. This has been estimated to be in the region of 0.9–1.8 liters per 100 g of organic matter in sheep (Weston and Hogan 1967) and 15–25 liters per kg dry matter in cattle (van't Klooster and Rogers 1969).

The outflow from the omasum to the abomasum can be measured by the use of a bell-mouthed cannula placed within the abomasum. This can be adjusted to direct the flow through the abdominal wall (Bouckaert and Oyaert 1954) and by exteriorizing the flow by re-entrant cannulas (Ash 1962a).

In spite of the consistency of the omasal contents when inspected postmortem, the material leaving the omasum collected by either method has a dry-matter content that does not exceed 8 percent. Ash (1962b) described the flow and nature of the material leaving the omasum as (1) oozes and trickles of small quantities of fluid devoid of solid matter that appear about the time of the reticulum contractions, (2) gushes of 20–30 ml containing appreciable amounts of finely divided plant material which occur at irregular intervals between the reticular contractions, and (3) slow extrusions of lumps of relatively solid matter which were washed through in small quantities of liquid. Sheep eating from 750 to 1100 g daily passed 1072–2075 ml/6 hours from the omasum. If the material collected was not returned to the abomasum, the flow from the omasum was about twice as great as when it was returned. The introduction of 2–4 liters of rumen fluid into the rumen caused a pronounced increase in flow from the omasum which persisted for 2 hours irrespective of whether the material collected from the omasum was or was not returned to the abomasum.

These observations show that the volume of contents in the abomasum has a controlling effect on flow through the omasum and that the volume of contents in the rumen also affects this flow. It is not clear whether there is a direct passage of food from the reticulum to the abomasum, but the evidence provided by the pressure changes within the omasum suggests that nearly all material entering the omasum is pressed into the interlaminal spaces and that excess fluid is squeezed from it and passes to the abomasum. It is clear that the limited capacity of the omasum means that it cannot retain either solids or liquids for more than a short time.

Chemical composition of contents

The concentrations of VFA and bicarbonate decrease from the rumen to the abomasum, while the concentration of chloride increases (Table 22.12). The concentrations of bicarbonate and chloride at various sites extending from the entrance to the exit of this organ in slaughterhouse material vary inversely with each other (Ekmann and Sperber 1952).

It appears as if there is exchange of chloride ions with bicarbonate and VFA within the omasum. The same changes in bicarbonate and chloride concentrations have also been found in the living animal in the fluid that passes from the omasum, when these are compared with the concentration present in the ruminal fluid (Oyaert and Bouckaert 1961). Lower concentrations for sodium and potassium also indicate absorption of those elements in the omasum (Table 22.13).

Water absorption (42–81 ml/hr) occurs from the omasum of anaesthetized sheep after ligation of its entrance and exit (Raynaud and Bost 1957), although the extent of water absorption in conscious animals is unknown. There is some evidence that the omasum is an important site for the absorption of magnesium. All aspects of omasal physiology are discussed by Bost (1970).

Table 22.12. VFA and chloride in the stomach contents of slaughtered sheep

	mEq/kg fresh contents	
	VFA	Chloride
Rumen	100	13
Omasum	57	47
Abomasum	5	100

Data from Elsden et al. 1946, Phillipson et al. 1949, Boyne et al. 1956, Badawy et al. 1958

Table 22.13. Average values for ruminal and omasal fluid of sheep

	mM			
Fluid	Sodium	Potassium	Total CO_2	Chloride
Ruminal	68	62	42	16
Omasal	53	54	24	47

From Oyaert and Bouckaert 1961, *Res. Vet. Sci.* 2:41–52

Abomasum

The abomasum is the only part of the stomach that secretes digestive juices. The secretion from innervated pouches of the sheep fundic area is similar to that of dogs in that it contains pepsin and hydrochloric acid (Table 22.14), while the secretion from the pyloric area is scanty and neutral in reaction.

Fundic juice is a watery fluid but may contain small quantities of mucus. The solid content of the juice is about 1 percent. The two major variable constituents are hydrogen and sodium ions, which replace each other. The pH of the juice from sheep feeding *ad libitum* may be from 1.05 to 1.32, but fasting often produces a decrease in the acidity. No particular pattern of secretion from innervated pouches of sheep can be detected either in the volume of juice or in its acidity when animals are fed *ad libitum*. This is due probably to the extended feeding habits of the animal, for when sheep or goats are restricted to feeds given either once or twice a day, which they consume in a short space of time, then clear responses to feeding are obtained (Hill 1960, Ash 1961a). The output of gastric juice from the fundic area of the abomasum was assessed at 4–6 liters per 24 hours.

The acidity of the juice from innervated pouches increases with the volume of juice secreted (Fig. 22.8).

The secretion of pepsin is much less variable than that of acid from innervated pouches; consequently, the total output varies with the volume of juice secreted (Hill 1961).

The output of juice from the pyloric region of the abomasum was assessed at about 200–400 ml/24 hr (Harrop 1974). The pyloric juice collected from innervated pouches is slightly alkaline and contains visible strands

Table 22.14. Composition of the gastric juice of sheep

Constituent	Concentration (mEq/L)	Reference
Hydrogen ions	Up to a maximum of 124	Ash and Kay 1963
Potassium	2–19	Ibid.
Sodium	21–167	Ibid.
Calcium	1.0–2.2	Storry 1960
Magnesium	0.5–0.9	Ibid.
Chloride	138–172	Ash and Kay 1963
Bicarbonate (when the abomasum is empty and the juice is neutral)	6–9	Ibid.
Nitrogen	15–33 (mg/100 ml)	Hogan 1957

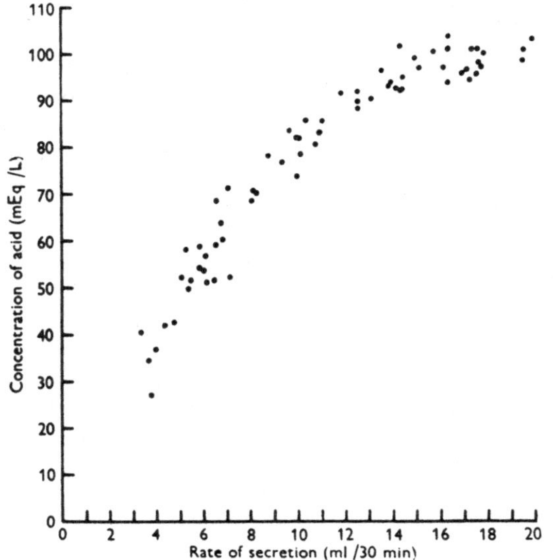

Figure 22.8. Relationship between the rate of secretion and concentration of acid in the juice secreted by innervated pouches of the fundic area of the abomasum of sheep. (From Ash 1961a, *J. Physiol.* 156:93–111.)

of mucus and clumps of epithelial cells. It exhibits peptic activity when adjusted to pH 2, although the activity per unit is much less than that of fundic juice (Harrison and Hill 1962).

Stimulation of abomasal secretion

It has been difficult to analyze the factors that cause the secretion of abomasal juice because of the continuous flow of contents through the abomasum. The acidity of the contents does not vary very much and usually remains close to pH 3 (Masson and Phillipson 1952). Emptying the rumen, and so stopping the flow of fluid through the abomasum, results in a marked reduction in the volume and acidity of the juice secreted by innervated pouches of the abomasum (Hill 1955). Secretion can be provoked by the injection of carbachol or histamine. Distension of the body of the abomasum provokes a small acid secretion from the fundic area. Buffered solutions of acetic, propionic, and butyric acids, however, promote copious secretion. Secretion, however, is inhibited when the contents of the abomasum is acidified to pH 2. Such experiments leave no doubt that the volume of material flowing into the abomasum and its fatty acid content are both concerned with the stimulation of acid secretion (Figs. 22.9, 22.10).

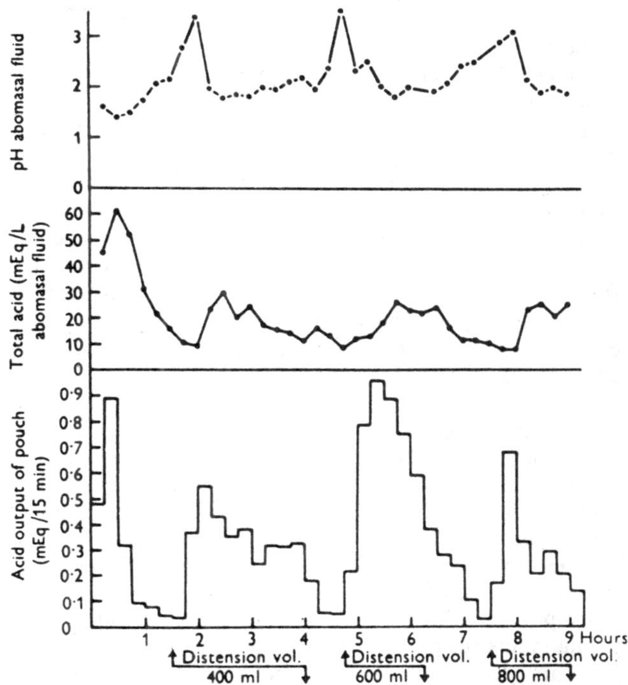

Figure 22.9. Effects on acid secretion of an abomasal pouch distended with a saline-filled balloon. Top and center, pH and total titratable acidity of the free fluid in the main body of the abomasum. The experiment was done on conscious sheep; the reticulorumen and abomasum were emptied the night before the experiment, and there was free flow between abomasum and duodenum. (From Ash 1961b, *J. Physiol.* 157:185–207.)

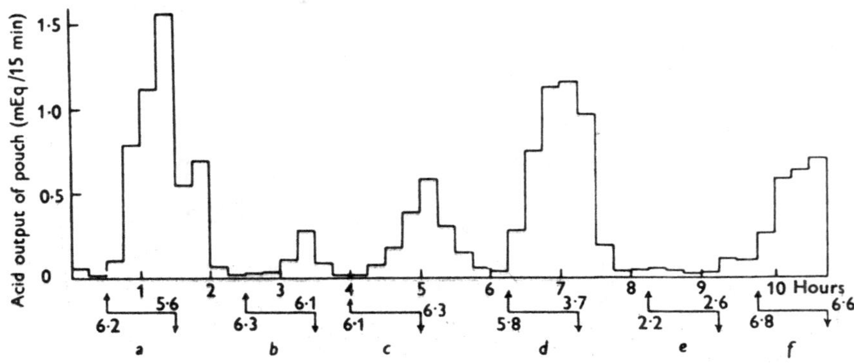

Figure 22.10. Comparison of the stimulating effects of different solutions on acid secretion from abomasum in conscious sheep: a, phosphate + 50 mM fatty acid; b, phosphate buffer alone; c, phosphate + 30 mM $NaHCO_3$ bubbled with 100% CO_2; d, phosphate + 50 mM fatty acid; e, phosphate-HCl + 50 mM fatty acid; f, rumen fluid. The numerals below and above the arrows indicate the pH values of the solution (all volumes 450 ml) introduced into the abomasum and drained respectively. The reticulorumen and abomasum were emptied on the morning of the experiment. Maximum acid output of the pouch during normal feeding was equivalent to 1.6 mEq/15 min on a diet of 750 g of food per day. (From Ash 1961b, *J. Physiol.* 157:185–207.)

The dependence of the abomasal glands upon parasympathetic stimulation is shown by the fact that carbachol stimulates and atropine inhibits secretion. The abomasum is a rich source of gastrin, suggesting that the humoral phase of secretion is prominent, and that gastrin release may be mediated by cholinergic fibers.

Teasing sheep with food before feeding causes secretion from innervated fundic pouches (McLeay and Titchen 1970). Hill (1960), on the other hand, considered the apparent physic effects to be due to an increased frequency of reticular contraction causing an increased flow of flood to the abomasum. This, however, does not explain the time relation between teasing and secretion in adult sheep.

Propulsion of food

The activity of the walls of the abomasum when the organs are filled with a radiopaque meal and screened fluoroscopically is mostly confined to the pyloric antrum. Strong waves of contraction pass over this part of the stomach, but the main body remains relatively inactive. Pressure tracings from the abomasum show bursts of activity probably due to activity of the pyloric antrum. In young lambs strong contractions of the body of the stomach can occasionally be seen before a meal when the lambs are hungry, while the reticulum lifts the part of the abomasum immediately adjacent to it when it contracts, owing to the thin muscular sheet which attaches it to the body of the abomasum.

The manner in which food passes to the duodenum can be studied in sheep where the flow in the first part of the duodenum is exteriorized (Hogan and Phillipson 1960, Singleton 1961). The food flow into the duodenum usually occurs in gushes as great as 30–40 ml at a time. A series of gushes of this magnitude may occur within 10–15 minutes followed by a period of rest in which nothing or only insignificant trickles of food are passed to the duodenum. The flow from the abomasum is much greater when the material collected is not returned to the duodenum than when it is, and periodicity in the flow may be accentuated by this method of measuring it. The quantity of material per hour passing to the duodenum of sheep, even when it is rapidly returned to the duodenum, may vary from 200 to 800 ml. When these measurements are continued over 24 hours, the mean value per hour for sheep weighing from 35 to 40 kg is about 400 ml. The total quantity collected from such sheep when fed on hay varied from 8.5 to 10 liters per 24 hours (Harris and Phillipson 1962). Higher values have been found when sheep consume green fodders (Hogan 1964). Singleton (1961) noted backflow from the duodenum to the abomasum when measuring the total flow through duodenal bypasses. In sheep the backflow amounted to some 10 percent of the total peristaltic flow, although it was more pronounced in goats.

The inhibition due to reintroducing the ejected abomasal contents into the duodenum appears to be a volume effect. The pH of the contents collected is usually around 3. Irrigation of the duodenum with a solution of hydrochloric acid does not markedly affect the quantity of food passed from the abomasum, but distension of the duodenum does. The discharge from the abomasum to the duodenum, therefore, appears to be controlled by the quantity of chyme in the duodenum.

The abomasal contents are slightly hypotonic to plasma in adult sheep; in milk-fed calves they are almost isotonic to plasma after feeding (Ash 1964). Inhibition of abomasal emptying occurs when hypo- or hypertonic solutions are placed in the organ (Bell and Razig 1973). This experiment suggests that osmo-receptors in the duodenum may materially influence the abomasal outflow of milk-fed calves.

Clotting of milk occurs rapidly in the abomasum, and the initial outflow is largely the whey of the milk.

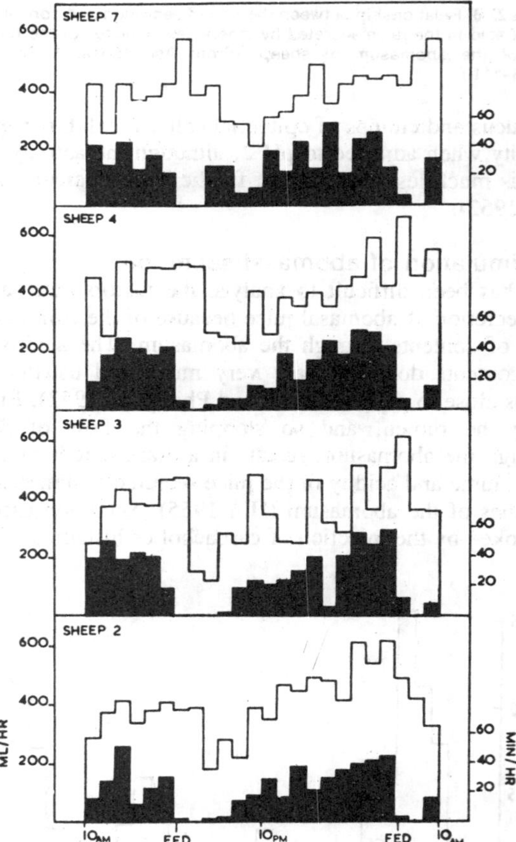

Figure 22.11. Abomasal contents of sheep (in ml) flowing to the duodenum per hour. The sheep were given 375 g hay twice daily. Each 24 hour series was made in two separate 12 hour periods. The time spent ruminating (min/hr) is shown in black. (From Harris and Phillipson 1962, *Anim. Prod.* 4:97–116.)

The flow to the duodenum is depressed in adults soon after feeding when the bulk of the food is hay. Although there is considerable individual variation, the results on four sheep measured on three occasions each over 24 hour periods show an underlying pattern that is related to feeding and rumination. Flow before and during feeding was at a maximum; following feeding the flow decreased for a short while and then gradually increased until the next feed. The relationship between rumination and outflow to the duodenum is not a close one when observations are made over daylight periods. Hourly observations through a 24 hour period, however, do reveal a relationship (Fig. 22.11).

Integration of flow

The flow of food through the abomasum and the secretion of abomasal juice are integrated so that the volume of the abomasal contents, although varying, is maintained as a fairly constant acidity. Boyne et al. (1956) found the average weight of the abomasal contents of sheep slaughtered at varying times after feeding to be 910 ± 488 g. The evidence indicating integration of passage to and from the abomasum with gastric secretion is as follows:

1. The strength and frequency of the reticular contractions are reduced if the abomasal content is increased.
2. The flow of digesta to the omasum occurs after every reticular contraction.
3. Increases in the volume of the rumen contents increase the omasal outflow.
4. The outflow from the omasum to the abomasum and from the abomasum to the duodenum is influenced by the quantities of material in the recipient organ.
5. The volume and acidity of the abomasal juice are influenced by the volume of material within the body of the abomasum and by the fatty acid content of the material entering the abomasum.
6. The secretion of acid in the abomasal juice is inhibited if the pH of the abomasal contents falls to the region of pH 2 and if acid is introduced into the duodenum.

These observations provide a framework for envisaging a control system that regulates the passage of food as far as the duodenum, and its acidity.

BILE AND PANCREATIC SECRETIONS

The bile and pancreatic secretions are discharged into the duodenum through a common duct; the union between the pancreatic and bile ducts occurs about 3 cm from their common opening into the duodenum. This arrangement makes it necessary to divert the flow of bile to the intestine if either the bile or the pancreatic secretions are to be studied separately. Descriptions of surgical preparations that overcome this difficulty are given by Hill and Taylor (1957), Magee (1961), Harrison (1962), and Sineschekov (1953).

Flow of bile

The flow of bile from a gallbladder fistula of sheep varies according to whether or not the bile is rapidly returned to the intestine. A flow of bile between 20 and 40 ml per hour was found by Harrison (1962) when bile was returned to the intestine. It reduced to between 10 and 20 ml per hour when it was not returned. The difference may be attributed to the cholagogue effect of bile salts, which increases both the flow and the solid content of the bile. The volume and the total solid content of bile were greater during the first hour of collection than during later periods, even when bile was returned to the intestine. The total solids and nitrogen content of bile withdrawn from the full gallbladder immediately after death were considerably greater than in bile secreted during the first hour of a collection and subsequent collections in the living animal (Table 22.15).

Table 22.15. Composition of the bile of sheep taken from the gallbladder after death or collected during experiments in which bile was not returned to the intestine

Bile of sheep	Gallbladder	First hour of collection	4–24 hours of collection (mean values)
Volume (ml/hr)		60	17
Total solids (g/100 ml)	8.7	5.9	2.9
Chloride (mEq/L)	74	83	122
Sodium (mEq/L)	197	179	154
Potassium (mEq/L)	8	7.6	6.7
Nitrogen (mg/100 ml)	248	150	76

Adapted from F.A. Harrison 1962, *J. Physiol.* 162:212–24

Harrison (1962) found that removing the contents of the reticulum and rumen and reducing the flow of food to the intestine to insignificant amounts considerably reduced the flow of bile and its total solid content, while feeding had no immediate effect on bile flow. The introduction of bile salts into the intestine increased the flow of bile as expected.

Pancreatic juice

The volume of pancreatic juice secreted by the ox is 2.2–4.8 liters per day (Colin 1886; Sheremet, in Sineschekov 1953) and 0.32–0.42 liters for sheep (Taylor 1962, Table 22.16). Fasting reduces the quantities secreted, and vagal stimulation causes a brief increase. Large responses are obtained by the injection of secretin and pilocarpine, although only secretin produces a juice with increased enzyme and bicarbonate contents. The introduction of buffered solutions into the duodenum also produces secretion which increases with the hydrogen ion concentration of the solutions used (Magee 1961).

Table 22.16. Composition of the pancreatic juice of sheep

	mEq/L
Sodium	135 –165
Potassium	3.9 – 5.4
Chloride	110 –126
Bicarbonate	15 – 30
Calcium	4.0 – 5.7
Magnesium	0.7 – 1.5
Nitrogen	0.48– 0.72 (mg/100 ml)
pH	7.2 – 7.8

From Taylor 1962, *Res. Vet. Sci.* 3:63–77

Pancreatic juice of ruminants has amylase, lipase, and protease activity, with roughly the same activities as those found in the pancreatic juice of the dog. However, the pancreatic juice secreted by the dog is about seven times greater in proportion to its weight than in the sheep, and so the total enzymatic activity is also considerably greater. Both deoxy- and ribonucleases are present in the pancreatic juice of sheep (Martinez-Arias 1974).

The chyme entering the duodenum has a pH of about 3, while the chyme at the lower end of the duodenum has a pH of 4–4.5 (Storry 1960). Under these circumstances, the discharge of secretin from the duodenal mucosa is likely to be continuous.

INTESTINES

Small intestine

Brunner's glands extend from the pylorus to the papilla of Vater. The secretions from the duodenal glands can be collected from sheep in which a re-entrant cannula has been inserted into the first part of the duodenum and into the last part, if, in addition, a Thomas-type cannula is inserted into the duodenum opposite the papilla of Vater so that the common pancreatic and bile duct can be cannulated. Harrison and Hill (1962) have collected the secretion from the duodenum isolated in this way, after it was washed with saline. The secretion collected had a pH of 6.7 and flowed at the rate of about 13 ml/hr in sheep fed once daily. This increased to an average of 26 ml/hr when the sheep were fed three times daily.

There is little information on the enzymes secreted by Brunner's glands of the ruminant. Extracts of mucosa from the duodenum have been found to possess greater amylolytic activity than extracts of other tissues (Bergman et al. 1924). The secretions of surgically isolated segments of the duodenum of goats exhibited only a weak proteolytic activity. The ribonuclease activity of duodenal juice is much greater than the activity present in pancreatic juice (Martinez-Arias 1974).

Studies with barium meals in lambs show that food passes rapidly through the small intestine, and barium can be seen in the cecum 4 hours after a radiopaque meal is given from a bottle. In the adult sheep, after the ingestion of a dry barium meal, the small intestine contains barium 4 hours after feeding, and some barium reaches the rectum 12 hours after feeding.

Table 22.17. The electrolyte composition of juice from the small intestine of sheep

	mEq/L	
Composition	Upper jejunum	Lower ileum
pH	7.1	8
Sodium	136	135
Potassium	8.1	9
Calcium	1.2	2.1
Magnesium	0.5	0.6
Chloride	134	105
Bicarbonate	11.8	41.5
Phosphate	1.5	

Adapted from Scott 1965, *Q. J. Exp. Physiol.* 50:312–29

The average composition of the secretions of intestinal loops temporarily isolated from the flow of chyme is given in Table 22.17.

The secretions of the lower ileum are slightly alkaline while those of the upper jejunum are practically neutral. The increase in the concentrations of bicarbonate in the secretion from the lower ileum is balanced by a decrease in the concentration of chloride. These changes are similar to those observed in the concentration of these two constituents in the intestinal contents of the horse, pig, rabbit, and guinea pig by Alexander (1962, 1965). The only other major difference is that the concentration of calcium is about two thirds greater in the ileal secretion than in the jejunal secretion.

The nitrogenous constituents of the jejunal secretion contribute from 250 to 300 mg of nitrogen per 100 ml, and of this about 90 percent is precipitated by trichloroacetic acid (Hogan 1957). Further investigations of the protein fractions of these secretions have shown that when plasma albumin labeled with ^{131}I is injected intravenously into sheep, protein appears in the secretions that behaves in an electrophoretic field in an identical manner to plasma albumin, although it is not possible from the data to say what proportion of the protein of the juice it constituted (Campbell et al. 1961).

Large intestine

The delay imposed on the passage of food residues by the large intestine is considerable. In lambs given radiopaque fluid meals from a bottle, barium can be seen entering the intestine within 5 minutes of the administration of the meal and entering the cecum about 4–8 hours later, while its appearance in the feces is delayed until 12–24 hours.

The passage of stained particles of hay through the intestine of adult sheep takes about 3 hours for the small and 18 hours for the large intestine, or about 21 hours for the whole intestine (Coombe and Kay 1965). About 2 hours are needed for a marker introduced into the duodenum to pass the terminal part of the ileum, and about 27 hours for the marker to be excreted in the feces after it was introduced into the terminal part of the ileum.

An increase in the food eaten by the sheep is accompanied by an increase in the rate at which the marker passes through both the small and large intestine.

Propulsive movements

Peristaltic and antiperistaltic movements of the cecum of lambs can be seen fluoroscopically when this organ contains radiopaque material. These movements originate at the ileocecal junction, pass to the apex of the organ, and return. According to Spörri and Asher (1940), peristaltic movements may pass to the first part of the colon. Phaneuf (1952) studied the pressure changes within the cecum of sheep and noted that these were periods of quiescence, periods of slow movement, and periods of great activity. During the latter periods, strong waves of increased pressure lasting 6–36 seconds occurred, and from 6 to 15 such movements could occur during a period of 10 minutes. The activity of the cecum showed no relation to either feeding or rumination.

This is in keeping with the observation of Goodall and Kay (1965), who found no relation between the passage of intestinal contents from the terminal ileum of the sheep to feeding or rumination. Flow of contents from this site to the cecum is spasmodic.

Peristaltic and segmentary movements can be detected radiologically in the spiral colon (Spörri and Asher 1940). Pellet formation occurs in the ansa spiralis. The radiological appearance of the large intestine of a goat is illustrated in Figure 22.12.

The extent of water absorption that occurs in the large intestine of goats is indicated by the dry matter of the intestinal contents (Spörri and Asher 1940). Dehydration of the contents of the large intestine of cattle is less extensive than in the small ruminants, as shown by the consistency of the feces (Table 22.18).

There is little information on the secretions that enter the large intestine; Phaneuf (1952) reports that the secretions into pouches of the cecum were of the order of 50–75 ml/12 hr, and the fluid had a pH of 8.0–8.2.

Van Weerdern (1961) has shown that the contents of the large intestine of cattle progressively become hypotonic to plasma and that this can be attributed to a progressive decrease in the concentrations of sodium, chlo-

Table 22.18. Dry matter (%) of the contents of the ileum and large intestine

	Goat *	Sheep †	Ox †
Terminal ileum	8.6	9.7	7.5
Cecum and colon up to ansa spiralis	11.7	14	9.1
Ansa spiralis, ascending	12.4	18.1	9.2
Ansa spiralis apex	16.3		
Ansa spiralis, descending	23	21.7	10
Terminal colon	31.6	23.7	12.1

* Adapted from Spörri and Asher 1940, *Schweiz. Arch. Tierheilk.* 82:243–64

† From Elsden, Hitchock, Marshall, and Phillipson 1946, *J. Exp. Biol.* 22:191–202

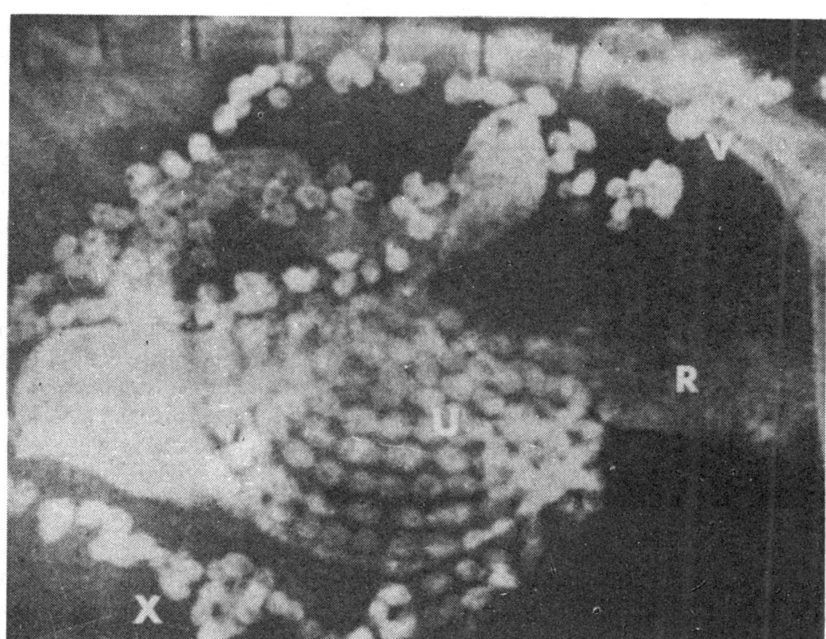

Figure 22.12. Left lateral view of a 4-month-old goat's large intestine filled with barium. R, apex on the cecum; U, spiral colon; V, rectum; X, distal colon. (From D. Benzie and A.T. Phillipson, *The Alimentary Tract of the Ruminant,* Oliver & Boyd, Edinburgh, 1957.)

ride, total carbon dioxide, volatile acids, and ammonia from the cecum caudally. The activity of the large intestine as an absorptive organ is considerable.

ABSORPTION

The epithelium lining the rumen, reticulum, and omasum is usually described as stratified and squamous. This description is misleading, for the cells of the basal layer are columnar in appearance although the overlying cells are transitional and cuboidal in appearance. The cuboidal type give way to flattened cells in which keratinization is occurring, and many of the keratinized cells become misshapen in the superficial layers. The keratinized layer of cells is thin and in some areas is replaced by vesiculated cells which also show some degree of keratinization (Dobson et al. 1956).

The basal columnar cells are intimately associated with fine blood vessels that penetrate between the papillary bodies. Injection of India ink into rumen vessels reveals that each of the rumen papillae contains arteries and veins in the central core of connective tissue, and removal of the epithelial layers shows a fine branching network of vessels spreading over the surface of the whole papilla. Capillary loops enter the indentations between the papillary bodies, and these indentations expand the area of the vascular inner surface to almost twice the area of the ruminal epithelium (Cheetam and Stevens 1966).

Intracellular bridges can be seen joining the cuboidal type of cells in the epithelium. The size of the spaces between the cells of the basal layer measured by electron microscopy is about 1 μ (Lindhé and Sperber 1959).

Development of ruminal papillae

Young ruminants maintained on milk diets for prolonged periods fail to develop normal-sized papillae (Warner and Flatt 1965). Mechanical stimulation of the interior of the rumen of milk-fed animals by the insertion of plastic sponges does not cause papillary development, but the inclusion of the VFA normally formed in the rumen produced papillary development when quantities in excess of those found in the rumen were used. Rumen fluid itself caused no papillary development (Flatt et al. 1958).

The reason for this effect of the VFA may be that some metabolism of these acids occurs in the rumen epithelium. Butyrate is metabolized in appreciable quantities and produces mainly acetoacetate; propionate metabolism is less extensive and produces lactate, while metabolism of acetate is least of all (Pennington 1952). This is of interest as Saunders et al. (1959) found that butyrate was more effective than propionate and propionate more effective than acetate in promoting papillary growth.

It should be noted that these VFA also increase blood flow to the rumen.

Absorption from rumen, reticulum, and omasum

Aggazzotti (1910) seems to have been the first to produce experimental evidence that absorption from any part of the ruminant's stomach was possible. His results showed that absorption of water can occur from the omasum. Trautmann (1933) showed conclusively that pilocarpine and atropine in solution were absorbed rapidly from the rumen, reticulum, and omasum of goats. Absorption was determined by the speed at which the salivary glands responded to these alkaloids. He also observed that the exposed epithelium of the rumen rapidly dried and that solutions placed in isolated pockets disappeared, indicating the absorption of water. Rankin (1940) confirmed his results and added iodide, strychnine, sodium cyanide, potassium, and glucose to the substances that could penetrate the epithelium. Later Barcroft et al. (1944a,b) showed that the radiopaque salt, sodium ortho-iodohippurate, was absorbed from the rumen of lambs and that acetate, propionate, and butyrate were absorbed from the rumen, reticulum, and omasum of adult sheep.

Absorption of VFA

The fact that VFA are absorbed to a considerable extent before the stomach contents reach the duodenum could be deduced, since their concentrations in the rumen are about 7–10 times greater than in the abomasum. They are reasonably stable end products of fermentation, and the addition of individual acids to the rumen does not cause a corresponding increase in their concentration in the abomasum (Phillipson 1942, Phillipson and McAnally 1942). At the usual pH of the rumen most of the VFA are in the anion rather than the free-acid form. The actual disappearance of these anions from the rumen, however, is not proportional to the concentrations appearing in the blood (Masson and Phillipson 1951). The low concentration of butyrate in the blood does not reflect a rate of absorption that is any less than that of acetate. The same effect is seen when the mixture of fatty acids in the blood leaving the rumen, after correction for acetate present in arterial blood, is compared with the VFA mixture in the rumen. There is a considerable reduction in the proportion of butyrate in the acids present in the venous blood from the rumen (Kiddle et al. 1951).

The metabolism of butyrate mainly to acetoacetate by isolated rumen epithelia occurs in vitro, as found by Pennington (1952), who also found excess ketones in the venous blood of the rumen when compared to arterial blood during butyrate absorption.

The rates at which acetic, propionic, and butyric acids are absorbed from the rumen increase as the pH of the solution within the rumen decreases. This has led to the concept that the undissociated acids penetrate the rumen epithelium more rapidly than their anions (Danielli et al.

1946, Gray 1948). It has been calculated that the rates of absorption of the undissociated acids are as follows: butyric > propionic > acetic.

The extent of metabolism of the fatty acids within the rumen epithelial is in the same order, and this suggests that the concentration gradients between rumen contents and the fluid within or without epithelial cells favors absorption of acids with a high rate of metabolism in the epithelium (Stevens and Stettler 1966). The loss of fatty acid from neutral solutions is accompanied by the accumulation of carbon dioxide (in all forms) in the solution in the rumen up to concentrations that exceed those of plasma. These must be largely in the form of bicarbonate, as the solutions in the rumen stay slightly above neutral. The quantities of carbon dioxide accumulating in the rumen are equivalent to about one half of the fatty acids absorbed (Masson and Phillipson 1951). Ash and Dobson (1963) observed that, when solutions containing no acetate were in the rumen, the steady state concentration of carbon dioxide in the rumen as such was greater than that of plasma, while for bicarbonate the steady state was less than that of plasma. The reverse situation was found when acetate was present, which indicates a consumption of carbon dioxide and a production of bicarbonate, with the corollary that a removal of hydrogen ions occurs, as is indicated by the lack of increased acidity (Fig. 22.13).

The evidence suggests that the exchanges occur within the rumen epithelium and, if this is so, at least one membrane between the solution in the rumen and the plasma is more permeable to the un-ionized fatty acids than it is to the ionized acids. Sodium and other strong electrolytes in smaller quantities are absorbed from the rumen in quantities that are sufficient to balance the loss of acetate (Dobson 1959), although the absorption of sodium occurs equally well when no acetate is present. It should be noted that acidic solutions of the fatty acids improve the blood flow to the rumen (Dobson and Phillipson 1956), which assists in maintaining a wide concentration gradient from the rumen to the blood.

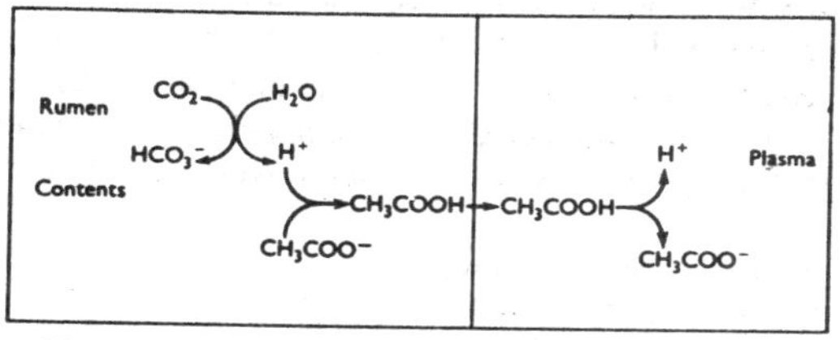

Rumen Contents: CO_2, H_2O, HCO_3^-, H^+, CH_3COOH, CH_3COO^- | Plasma: CH_3COOH, H^+, CH_3COO^-

Figure 22.13. Effect of the selective absorption of acetic acid upon CO_2 and HCO_3^- in the rumen. The position of the membrane within the layers between plasma and rumen contents is not defined. Acetic acid diffuses through the barrier down its concentration gradient. It ionizes continuously on the plasma side of the membrane, producing hydrogen ions and acetate. On the rumen contents side of the membrane the reverse process takes place. The supply of hydrogen ions is maintained by the conversion of CO_2 to HCO_3^-. (From Ash and Dobson 1963, *J. Physiol.* 169:39–61.)

Absorption of lactic acid

Excessive feeding with cereals or foods rich in sugar can cause large concentrations of lactic acid in the rumen, accompanied by unusually high concentrations of lactate in the blood. The inference has thus been drawn that lactic acid is absorbed from the rumen, which is not necessarily so. The appearance of lactate in the blood leaving the rumen in greater concentrations than the arterial blood (Shoji et al. 1964) is not conclusive proof of absorption, since the metabolism of propionate in the rumen epithelium leads to the formation of lactate (Pennington and Sutherland 1956). Lactic acid is absorbed from both neutral and acidic solutions, but the rate of absorption is about one tenth of the VFA introduced at the same concentration. Absorption was greater from acidic than from neutral solutions (Williams and Mackenzie 1965).

Absorption of ammonia

Ammonia is present in excess of the venous blood of those parts of the alimentary tract whose contents contain an appreciable concentration of ammonia (McDonald 1948). The manner in which it is absorbed has not been investigated in detail, but Hogan in 1961 presented evidence that ammonia is absorbed more rapidly than the ammonium ion. This concept is in keeping with studies on urea toxicity in sheep by Coombe et al. (1960), who found that signs of toxicity appeared only if the pH of the rumen rose to 7.3 and was not directly related to the concentration of ammonia (in both forms) in the rumen. High concentrations were well tolerated, provided that the pH was below neutral.

Absorption of inorganic ions

Studies of the absorption of chloride from Pavlov pouches of the rumen of goats and from the rumen of sheep show that chloride disappears against a concentration gradient (Sperber and Hyden 1952, Parthasarathy and Phillipson 1953). Phosphate, on the other hand, is absorbed only in traces even though its concentration is many times greater than that of plasma.

The behavior of chloride was shown to be influenced by the electrical potential gradient which exists between the rumen contents and the blood. This is usually between 30 and 40 mv in conscious sheep fed in a customary way (Dobson 1956), the blood being positive with respect to the rumen contents. Chloride moved in accordance with its electrochemical gradient (Dobson and Phillipson 1958). This gradient is composed of the ratio between the concentrations of chloride ions on either side of the rumen epithelium (in these experiments, represented by the concentrations of chloride in rumen fluid and in the plasma) expressed as mv plus the electrical potential difference. The chemical or diffusion potential between different concentrations of a negatively charged univalent ion at 39°C is expressed as

$$-62 \times \log \frac{\text{conc. in rumen}}{\text{conc. in plasma}}$$

Thus, if chloride behaves as a passive freely diffusing ion, a steady state between the rumen contents and the plasma should be achieved when the calculated chemical or diffusion potential is the same as the measured electrical potential, but with an opposite sign. When solutions containing electrolytes within the usual physiological range are used, the movements of chloride conform with the electrochemical gradient, and under these circumstances it behaves as a passive ion. This was not so when high concentrations of potassium were present in the rumen, for the small movements of chloride occurred against the electrochemical gradient (Dobson 1959).

The situation with sodium is different, as this ion is absorbed against its concentration gradient and the electrical potential. There is no doubt that absorption of sodium, which carries a positive charge, is due to an active process within the rumen epithelium (Dobson 1959). Movements of potassium into pouches of the rumen when potassium-free solutions are introduced were observed by Sperber and Hyden (1952), to a concentration of 27 mM, which is about six times the concentration of plasma. This could be explained if there was an electrical potential of 50 mv between the pouch contents and the plasma, which is at the upper end of the difference usually encountered. However, a similar movement of potassium has been found by Ferreira et al. (1964), using isolated rumen epithelium with the same salt solution on either side of the membrane when the potential difference is short circuited. The net movement of potassium from the plasma to the lumen side of the epithelium was only about one third of the net movement of sodium from the rumen to the plasma side of the membrane. These experiments and those of Ferreira et al. (1966a,b) confirm the active absorption of sodium and suggest that potassium is actively secreted into the rumen.

The potential difference is sensitive to lack of oxygen, and temporarily clamping the posterior aorta above the celiac artery in anesthetized sheep causes the potential difference immediately to decline to the region of 5 mv. It is restored when the clamp is released, unless this is delayed for longer than about 10 minutes, when restoration does not occur (Dobson and Phillipson, unpublished). Similarly, depriving isolated rumen epithelium of oxygen causes a rapid fall in potential difference (Ferreira et al. 1966a).

The concentrations of potassium found in the rumen fluid of normally fed sheep are always much greater than those in plasma, while sodium values are usually less in the rumen than in plasma (Table 22.19). A net absorption of potassium, therefore, occurs from the rumen, as a concentration of 25 mEq/L is slightly above the theoretical steady state for the usual range of potential differences between the rumen and the blood (Scott 1967).

The rumen epithelium is relatively impermeable to phosphate (Sperber and Hyden 1952), although very small quantities penetrate the epithelium in either direction when isotopic phosphate is used (Parthasarathy 1952).

The concentrations of calcium and magnesium in rumen fluid in an ultrafiltrable form are small (Storry 1961). For calcium they may vary from 4 to 11 and for magnesium from 4 to 9 mEq/L, which are insufficient to overcome the potential difference across the epithelium.

Absorption of water

There is considerable disagreement on the extent to which absorption of water from the rumen occurs. Studies with tritium-labeled water show that it can move freely in either direction across the rumen epithelium (von Engelhardt 1970), but this information does not provide a basis for deducing net movements of water.

The rumen contents are usually slightly hypotonic to plasma (Warner and Stacy 1965), although they become hypertonic after feeding (Parthasarathy and Phillipson 1953, Ternouth 1967). Under experimental circumstances net movements of water across the epithelium occur in either direction in relation to the osmotic gradient, although there is disagreement whether this holds true in the range of 265–325 m osmol/L. Von Engelhardt's work suggests that equilibrium exists within this range, while Dobson et al. (1970) found that net water movements varied in a linear manner with changes of osmolarity in the rumen; equilibrium was established when the osmolarity of solutions were 51 m osmol/L

Table 22.19. Concentrations of sodium and potassium in the rumen contents of sheep

	mEq/L		
Diet	Sodium	Potassium	Reference
Hay and meals	60–87	26–45	Parthasarathy 1952
Various diets including grass	20–140	25–110	Sellers and Dobson 1960
Hay and meals	80–110	25–35	Dobson and McDonald 1963
Young summer grass	30–70	60–110	Ibid.

Representative values for Na and K in plasma are 135 and 4.5 mEq/L.

above that of plasma if CO_2 and VFA were present and 26 m osmol/L if no CO_2 was present.

In undertaking absorption studies, solutions slightly hypertonic to plasma by some 50–60 m osmol/L have to be used if there is to be no measurable absorption of water. The loss of water from the rumen per hour when hypotonic solutions are present is not large; it represents about 5–10 percent of the solution.

Absorption from the omasum and abomasum

The large surface area offered by the omasal laminae suggests that absorption may occur from the organ. There is no doubt that VFA are absorbed, because their concentration in omasal contents is lower than in the rumen, and the venous blood leaving the organ contains substantially more of these acids than the arterial blood. Much speculation has been given to the absorption of water, because the dry-matter content of the material between the omasal laminae is substantially greater than it is in the rumen contents. Comparisons between the ratios of nitrogen to lignin in the various parts of the stomach led Gray et al. (1954) and Raynaud (1955) to conclude that appreciable absorption of water occurred from the omasum. Raynaud and Bost (1957) ligated the entrance and exit to the omasum in anesthetized sheep and goats and introduced water slowly over periods of 3–5 hours. They found that water was absorbed at the rate of 40–80 ml/hr, which confirmed the experiments of Aggazzotti (1910).

The epithelium of the omasum is histologically similar to that of the rumen. There is no doubt that the omasum is an absorptive organ, but the extent to which absorption occurs is not clear. The differential passage of material through it may mean that little change occurs in material flowing rapidly to the abomasum, but extensive changes occur in the more solid material that takes a slower passage via the interlaminal spaces.

The concentration of VFA entering the abomasum, although less than in the rumen, is greater than the concentration passing to the duodenum. The change is too great to be accounted for by dilution with gastric juice. The fact that VFA in the abomasum stimulate secretion of gastric juice (Ash 1961b) suggests that these acids penetrate the abomasal epithelium.

Digestion in the small intestine

Carbohydrates

The fermentation of starches and sugars in the rumen means that very little of these carbohydrates enters the small intestine. When hay alone is eaten, virtually no dietary carbohydrates, excluding cellulose and the hemicelluloses, reach the duodenum, although a few grams of polysaccharide that yield glucose leave the abomasum daily (Heald 1951). This is largely microbial polysaccharide. Sheep eating a diet containing 148 g of starch daily passed only about 8 g daily to the duodenum (Gray et al. 1954). An increase in the quantities of starch in the diet increases the quantities reaching the duodenum, while the proportions in relation to the quantities eaten decrease. Instances have been recorded where as much as 30 percent of the dietary intake enters the duodenum (Karr et al. 1966; Topps et al. 1968a,b; Tucker et al. 1968; MacRae and Armstrong 1969; Nicholson and Sutton 1969; Armstrong and Beaver 1969). The situation is complicated, since it is not clear whether the methods used always distinguish completely between dietary and microbial polysaccharides. Most of the starch entering the small intestine disappears before the cecum, and residual starch entering the cecum is fermented, as practically none has been found in feces.

Proteins

About 64–68 percent of the nitrogen leaving the abomasum is in the form of amino acids, about one third of which is in solution. The remainder of the nitrogen is made up of ammonia, small quantities of urea, and nucleic acids, together with nitrogenous constituents of the gastric juice which were recently characterized by Harrop (1974). About 55–75 percent of the nitrogen entering the duodenum disappears before the cecum, but this takes no account of the additions that are made to intestinal chyme from secretions entering the small intestine. The lowest value for disappearance was found in sheep eating low-nitrogen diets (Clark et al. 1966). This is an indication that a considerable part of the nitrogen entering the cecum is endogenous, and thus masks the disappearance of nitrogen of dietary or gastric origin that enters the duodenum. About 8–12 percent of the nitrogen entering the duodenum is present in nucleic acids, and about 80 percent disappears before the cecum is reached (Smith and McAllan 1971, Martinez-Arias 1974).

Fatty acids

Only small quantities of VFA enter the duodenum, and these are reduced in the jejunum. Increases found in ileal contents are due to fermentation that develops as the passage of digesta slows in this organ.

The distribution of long-chain fatty acids in the abomasum is similar in proportion to that in the rumen in that about 77 percent are unesterified, 20 percent are present in neutral lipids, and the remainder are phospholipids. The addition of bile in the duodenum decreases the free fatty acid content and increases the neutral and phospholipid content (Garton 1969).

Absorption of fatty acids depends upon pancreatic juice and bile. Deprivation of pancreatic juice reduces and deprivation of bile abolishes their absorption (Heath and Morris 1963). The mechanism seems to be that long-chain fatty acids are conjugated with bile salts and made soluble, and that this process is promoted by the presence of monoglycerides derived from triglyceride by the action of pancreatic lipase. The bicarbonate content of pancreatic juice increases the pH of the acid duodenal contents to around 6.5 in the upper jejunum. This allows partial ionization of fatty acids and favors the formation of lysolecithin, which assists solubilization of partly ionized fatty acids.

Most of the long-chain fatty acids are absorbed by the middle of the jejunum and appear as triglycerides in the thoracic lymph. About 20 g in sheep, 200 g in dry cows, and 400 g in lactating cows are transported per day to the blood stream in this way (Felinski et al. 1964, Hartmann and Lascelles 1966).

Inorganic elements

Measurements of the total quantities of calcium and magnesium entering and leaving the small intestine in the chyme give only small differences, indicating that the amount of entry due to secretion may be similar to the amount of exit due to absorption (Pfeffer et al. 1970). Substantial losses of sodium, potassium, chloride, phosphate, and water occur from the small intestine (Bruce et al. 1966), although overall increases in sodium have also been found.

Calcium and magnesium are present in the intestinal contents in an ultrafilterable form and as bound ions attached to a nitrogen-rich fraction (Storry 1961). Calcium in solution is absorbed in relation to the concentration introduced into temporarily isolated loops of the sheep jejunum. In ileal loops, however, this has not always been so. The electrical potential difference between the intestinal contents and the blood is about 13 mv in the jejunum and 7.5 mv in the ileum, the blood being positive to the lumen. For free diffusion of calcium ions to occur, a concentration of 8.1 and 5.4 mEq/L is necessary in the jejunum and ileum respectively (Scott 1965). The fact that these concentrations of ionized calcium seldom occur, however, suggests that an active process is concerned in absorption.

The behavior of magnesium is less predictable than calcium. There is no clear tendency for losses of magnesium at all levels of the small intestine to follow the concentration gradient. An increase in the magnesium content of isolated loops occurs frequently. Absorption of magnesium certainly can occur at all levels of the small intestine, and the inconsistency may be due to variability in endogenous secretion. Studies with ^{25}Mg indicate that absorption of this isotope is greatest in the middle third of the small intestine (Field 1961).

Digestion in the large intestine

Food residues that enter the cecum are subject to fermentation. The most abundant residues are cellulose and the hemicelluloses. Many estimates show that up to 10 percent of the total cellulose digestion may occur in the large intestine, although higher values have been recorded (Gray 1947, Goodall and Kay 1965, Topps et al. 1968a). Cellulolysis as measured by the loss of weight of cotton threads proceeds at the same rate in the cecum as in the rumen (Hecker 1971).

Appreciable quantities of nitrogenous substances enter the cecum, including amino acids, urea, and mucus. Proteolytic activity is stronger in cecal contents than in rumen contents. This may be due to the presence of trypsin. Deaminative and urease activities are less pronounced than in the rumen (Hecker 1971).

Both VFA and ammonia are present in substantial concentrations, and these products of bacterial metabolism are absorbed into the blood stream (Barcroft et al. 1944a, McDonald 1948).

One of the principal functions of the large intestine is the reabsorption of water and inorganic elements. Most of the sodium, potassium, and chloride entering the large gut is absorbed, but little further absorption of calcium, magnesium, or phosphorus occurs in the adult; in the young calf considerable absorption of dietary magnesium occurs until the animal is about 6 weeks old, when this ability is lost (Smith 1969).

BLOOD FLOW

The anterior and posterior veins of the rumen have well-developed semilunar valves close to their union with each other. These valves presumably prevent backflow of blood during major movements of the rumen. Fine valves may also be found in the veins draining the reticulum. In young animals valves are present in the epiploic veins into which the omasal and abomasal vessels open. These, however, are not functional in the adult. Fine valves are also found in the veins draining the cecum.

The blood flow from the rumen is influenced by the composition of its contents. Neutral solutions without VFA in the rumen are usually accompanied by a slow blood flow. The inclusion of acetate, propionate, or butyrate produces a larger flow of blood. If solutions of these fatty acids are acidified, blood flow is greatly increased. The effects of butyrate solutions are greater than those of propionate or acetate. Carbon dioxide also produces a very rapid blood flow (Dobson and Phillipson 1956, Sellers 1965).

The sight and smell of food increase arterial blood flow to the rumen slightly, while feeding causes a considerable increase. Emptying the rumen depresses blood flow (Sellers et al. 1964).

Measurements of portal blood flow show that this increases after feeding and subsequently declines (Fig. 22.14). Portal blood flow on an average ranges from 33 to 37 ml/min/kg body weight in sheep (Schambye 1955, Fegler and Hill 1958).

Comparisons of VFA and glucose in portal blood with the concentrations present in arterial blood show that for sheep eating hay or hay with oats, VFA pass to the liver

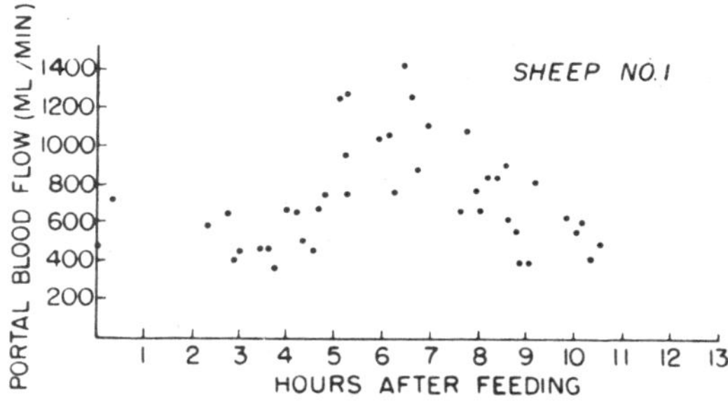

Figure 22.14. Portal blood flow in a sheep after feeding. (From A. Bensadoun and J.T. Reid 1962, *J. Dairy Sci.* 45:541.)

in greater quantity than glucose (Schambye 1951). The concentration of butyrate in relation to acetate and propionate is less than that in the rumen contents, and ketone bodies in portal blood may exceed those of peripheral blood (Annison et al. 1957).

There is no detectable uptake of glucose into the portal blood stream even when diets are 50 percent cereal (Bergman et al. 1970). However, since utilization of glucose by the abdominal viscera represents about one fifth of the total turnover of the body, some of this need may be met by glucose of intestinal origin. Estimates of the metabolism of VFA by the rumen epithelium are substantial; the quantities passing to the liver in the portal blood stream do not represent the quantities absorbed.

The liver removes most of the propionate and butyrate from the blood, and only traces of these acids appear in peripheral blood. Acetate represents 85–95 percent of the VFA in arterial blood. In addition, formate, or a volatile substance that has very similar properties, appears in arterial blood (Annison 1954).

Measurements of portal blood flow and the temperature of portal blood before and after feeding allowed Webster and White (1973) to assess the heat generated by abdominal viscera as a result of digestion. The total heat minus the heat due to aerobic metabolism, which was calculated from oxygen uptake, gave a remainder taken to be the exothermic heat engendered by anaerobic microbial metabolism. The values found were 4–9 percent of the digestible energy when dried green fodders were eaten by sheep. This range covers the value of 6 percent found by Marston (1948) in his in vitro studies of cellulose digestion. Lower values were found for barley-fed sheep (Webster et al. 1975).

CIRCULATION OF WATER, NITROGEN, AND IONS

In order to appreciate the extent of circulation of materials between the body and digestive tract of ruminants, quantitative data on flow of secretions and intestinal contents have to be compared. Ash and Kay (1963) assessed the turnover of water between the body and the digestive tract of sheep. The total secretions into the alimentary tract of sheep vary from 10 to over 20 liters per 24 hours; these amounts do not include any estimate of the water passing into the small intestine below the duodenum. As the quantity of water drunk by sheep is seldom more than 3 liters a day and as the quantity of water excreted in the feces is only a few hundred ml a day, it is clear that the flow of food through the alimentary tract is maintained by the large volumes secreted into the stomach and intestines and subsequently reabsorbed.

In the same way, sodium, chloride, and phosphate, and to a less extent potassium, are added to the stomach and intestinal contents and are reabsorbed (Fig. 22.15).

The recirculation of nitrogenous compounds between the body and the digestive tract is interesting from the point of view of nutrition. Nassett (1964) has emphasized the extent to which nitrogenous compounds are secreted into the intestine of dogs and rats. In sheep, quite apart from the contributions made by the abomasal and intestinal secretions, the quantity of nitrogen added to the rumen contents by the saliva in the form of urea and mucoproteins is considerable. Urea diffuses into the rumen through the epithelial lining from the blood stream (Houpt 1959, Ash and Dobson 1963), and the quantities of nitrogen reaching the rumen of sheep in these ways may be of the order of 1–5 g/24 hr. The urea concentrations of parotid saliva are related to the concentrations of urea in the blood (Somers 1961), and the ability of ruminants to conserve urea nitrogen when their diet is inade-

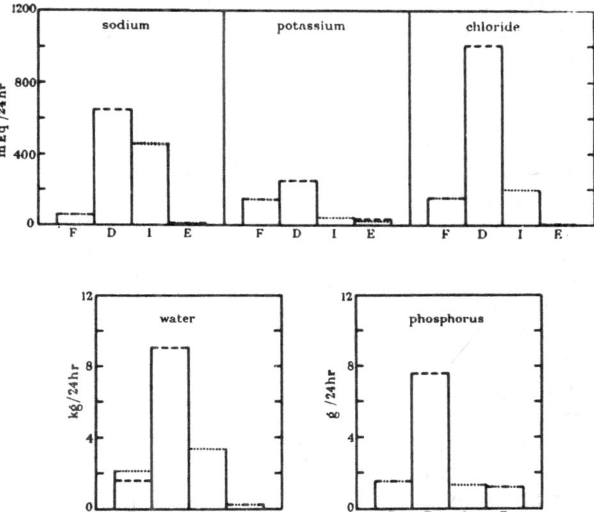

Figure 22.15. Amounts of sodium, potassium, chloride, water, and phosphorous in the food eaten, duodenal ingesta, ileal ingesta, and feces of sheep. The food values for sodium and chloride include the 50 mEq NaCl supplement. Ingesta and fecal values have been adjusted to give 100 percent recovery of chromium sesquioxide. Duodenals, broken line; ileals, dotted line. F, food; D, duodenal ingesta; I, ileal ingesta; E, feces. (From Bruce, Goodall, Kay, Phillipson, and Vowles 1966, *Proc. Roy. Soc.*, ser. B, 166:46–62; by permission of the Royal Society.)

quate in protein was demonstrated by Schmidt-Nielsen et al. (1957, 1958). Urea infused slowly into the blood stream of sheep in a negative nitrogen balance results in a greater proportion of it reappearing in the parotid saliva than when the sheep are in a positive nitrogen balance (Somers 1961). This procedure in fact turned a negative nitrogen balance into a small positive nitrogen balance.

The same effect has been found in cattle when slow urea infusions are given into the rumen of animals fed on straw (Campling et al. 1962). Under these circumstances the speed with which cotton threads suspended in the rumen are digested and with which food residues leave the rumen is enhanced. The overall digestion of cellulose is increased by some 10 percent, the appetite of the animals is improved, and again a negative nitrogen balance is converted to a small positive balance. The most reasonable explanation is that urea and other nitrogenous compounds entering the rumen provide a source of nitrogen which helps to maintain the bacterial population within the rumen, upon which the digestion of straw depends. The animal will therefore obtain more energy from its food. It may also increase to a small extent the supply of amino acid nitrogen reaching the intestine. Both effects would promote a better overall nitrogen balance by the animal.

The quantities of amino acids entering the duodenum of sheep do not bear a close relationship to the quantities eaten (Fig. 22.16). The interesting feature is that considerably more amino acid nitrogen entered the duodenum when the dietary supplies were small, while considerably less entered the duodenum when they were ample. The dietary range, in fact, had been reduced to one half by the time the food reached the duodenum. Losses of amino acids presumably are largely due to ammonia formation and absorption in the rumen.

The composition of the amino acid mixture leaving the omasum of cattle (Bigwood 1964) or entering the duodenum of sheep (Clark et al. 1966) is markedly different from and does not vary with the diet. This is an indication that a large part of the dietary protein is degraded in the rumen and its place taken by bacterial and protozoan protein (McDonald 1954, McDonald and Hall 1957, Weller et al. 1958).

Hutton et al. (1971) estimated that about half the amino acids entering the duodenum are of bacterial origin. Since protozoa represent nearly half of the microbial mass in the rumen (Warner 1962), a substantial part of the remainder is likely to be of protozoan origin. Endogenous nitrogen from abomasal secretions is also present (Harrop 1974).

Because of the considerable losses of nitrogen as ammonia that occur from the rumen when protein-rich foods are eaten, attention has been given to various ways of protecting dietary proteins from microbial attack. The use of formalin in dilute concentrations has proved successful

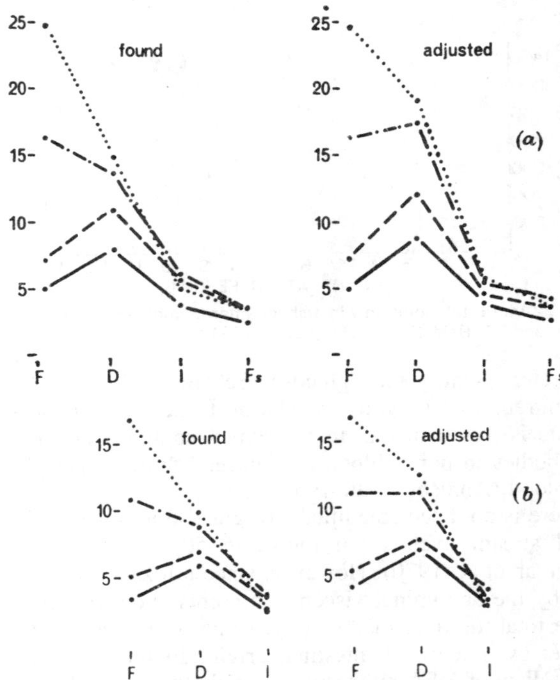

Figure 22.16. Total (g/24 hr) nitrogen (a) and amino nitrogen (b) ingested (F), passing to duodenum (D), from ileum (I), and in feces (Fs) before and after adjustment for recovery of Cr_2O_3. The sheep were fed on ——— hay, - - - - - - hay + maize, –·–·–·–·– hay + maize + soya protein, ········· hay + soya protein. (From Clark, Ellinger, and Phillipson 1966, *Proc. Roy. Soc.*, ser. B, 166:63–79; by permission of the Royal Society.)

in protecting casein and other foods. Treated casein given as a protein supplement has stimulated wool growth on account of the additional amino acids passing to the intestine (Ferguson et al. 1967). Formalinized casein has also been used experimentally to protect the unsaturated fatty acids of vegetable oils from hydrogenation in the rumen (Scott et al. 1971). Vegetable oils protected in this way result in an increase of unsaturated fatty acids in body and butter fat.

Fermentative digestion in the rumen results in the disappearance from the stomach of some 60–75 percent of the digestible organic matter. A further 20–30 percent disappears from the small intestine and the remainder from the large intestine.

The heat, methane, and VFA produced in the rumen are more than enough to account for the loss of organic matter (Nicholson and Sutton 1969). All the necessary measurements have not been done on the same animals at the same time, however, so balance sheets cannot be expected to be more than general indications.

Bergman et al. 1965 found that VFA production in the rumen estimated by a continuous isotopic technique accounted for 62 percent of the digestible energy of the ration. The relationship between VFA produced and organic matter digested is a close one for sheep consuming a variety of good and poor fodders (Weston and Hogan 1968); on an average 0.85 mol VFA, representing 242 kcal, are produced in the rumen for every 100 g of organic matter digested by sheep. Grazing sheep throughout the summer have been found to produce, in all, 3.4–5.3 mol VFA daily (Weller et al. 1969), and there is no doubt that VFA are the major source of energy derived by the animal.

The disadvantages of microbial digestion are that energy is lost in the form of heat and methane, and nitrogen is lost due to ammonia formation in the rumen. The assets of this form of digestion are that structural carbohydrates can be utilized as sources of energy, depending on the age of the plant; the food is enhanced by the synthesis of B vitamins, and recycling of urea to the rumen provides some compensation to the deaminative processes of the rumen, especially when the food is low in protein. These characteristics provide the ruminant with an alimentary system that has considerable survival value when food supplies are poor, even though it is a somewhat extravagant system when food supplies are good.

REFERENCES

Aggazzotti, A. 1910. Observations on absorption from the stomachs of ruminants. *Clin. Vet.* 33:53–57.

Alexander, F. 1962. The concentration of certain electrolytes in the digestive tract of the horse and pig. *Res. Vet. Sci.* 3:78–84.

——. 1965. The concentration of electrolytes in the alimentary tract of the rabbit, guinea pig, dog, and cat. *Res. Vet. Sci.* 6:238–44.

Andersson, B., Kitchell, R.L., and Persson, N. 1959. A study of central regulation of rumination and reticulo-ruminal motility. *Acta Physiol. Scand.* 46:319–38.

Annison, E.F. 1954. Studies on the volatile fatty acids of sheep blood with special reference to formic acid. *Biochem. J.* 58:670–80.

——. 1956. Nitrogen metabolism in the sheep: Protein digestion in the rumen. *Biochem. J.* 64:705–14.

Annison, E.F., Hill, K.J., and Lewis, D. 1957. Studies on the portal blood of sheep. II. Absorption of volatile fatty acids from the rumen of the sheep. *Biochem. J.* 66:592–99.

Armstrong, D.G., and Beaver, D.E. 1969. Post-abomasal digestion of carbohydrate in the adult ruminant. *Proc. Nutr. Soc.* 28:121–31.

Ash, R.W. 1959. Inhibition and excitation of reticulo-rumen contractions following the introduction of acids into the rumen and abomasum. *J. Physiol.* 147:58–73.

——. 1961a. Acid secretion by the abomasum and its relation to the flow of food material in the sheep. *J. Physiol.* 156:93–111.

——. 1961b. Stimuli influencing the secretion of acid by the abomasum of sheep. *J. Physiol.* 157:185–207.

——. 1962a. Omaso-abomasal re-entrant cannulae for sheep. *J. Physiol.* 164:4P.

——. 1962b. The flow of food material from the omasum of sheep. *J. Physiol.* 164:24–25.

——. 1964. Abomasal secretion and emptying in suckled calves. *J. Physiol.* 172:425–37.

Ash, R.W., and Dobson, A. 1963. The effect of absorption on the acidity of rumen contents. *J. Physiol.* 169:39–61.

Ash, R.W., and Kay, R.N.B. 1959. Stimulation and inhibition of reticulum contractions, rumination, and parotid secretion from the forestomach of conscious sheep. *J. Physiol.* 149:43–57.

——. 1963. Digestive secretions and the flow of food material in the sheep. In D.P. Cuthbertson, ed., *Progress in Nutrition and Allied Sciences*. Oliver & Boyd, Edinburgh. Pp. 127–40.

Badawy, A.M., Campbell, R.M., Cuthbertson, D.P., and Mackie, W.S. 1958. Further studies on the changing composition of the digesta along the alimentary tract of the sheep. III. Changes in the omasum. *Brit. J. Nutr.* 12:391–403.

Bailey, C.B. 1961. Saliva secretion and its relation to feeding in cattle. III. The rate of secretion of mixed saliva in the cow during eating, with an estimate of the magnitude of the total daily secretion of mixed saliva. *Brit. J. Nutr.* 15:443–51.

Bailey, C.B., and Balch, C.C. 1961. Saliva secretion and its relation to feeding in cattle. *Brit. J. Nutr.* 15:371–402.

Balch, C.C. 1950. Factors affecting the utilization of food by dairy cows. I. The rate of passage of food through the digestive tract. *Brit. J. Nutr.* 4:361–88.

——. 1952. Factors affecting the utilization of food by diary cows. VI. The rate of contraction of the reticulum. *Brit. J. Nutr.* 6:366–75.

Balch, C.C., Kelly, A., and Heim, G. 1951. Factors affecting the utilization of food by dairy cows. IV. The action of the reticulo-omasal orifice. *Brit. J. Nutr.* 5:207–16.

Balch, D.A., and Rowland, S.J. 1957. Volatile fatty acids and lactic acid in the rumen of dairy cows receiving a variety of diets. *Brit. J. Nutr.* 11:288–98.

Barcroft, J., McAnally, R.A., and Phillipson, A.T. 1944a. Absorption of volatile acids from the alimentary tract of the sheep and other animals. *J. Exp. Biol.* 20:120–29.

——. 1944b. The absorption of sodium ortho-iodo-hippurate from the rumen of lambs. *J. Exp. Biol.* 20:132–34.

Bechdel, S.I., Eckles, C.H., and Palmer, L.S. 1926. The vitamin B requirements of the calf. *J. Dairy Sci.* 9:409–38.

Becker, R.B., Marshall, S.P., and Arnold, P.T.D. 1963. Anatomy, development, and functions of the bovine omasum. *J. Dairy Sci.* 46:835–39.

Beijer, W.H. 1952. Methane fermentation in the rumen of cattle. *Nature* 170:576–77.

Bell, F.R. 1958. The mechanism of regurgitation during the process of rumination in the goat. *J. Physiol.* 142:503–15.

Bell, F.R., and Lawn, A.M. 1955. Localization of regions in the medulla oblongata of sheep associated with rumination. *J. Physiol.* 128:577–92.

Bell, F.R., and Razig, S.A.D. 1973. The effect of some molecules and ions on gastric function in the milk-fed calf. *J. Physiol.* 228:513–26.

Bergman, E.N., Katz, M.L., and Kaufman, C.F. 1970. Quantitative aspects of hepatic and portal-glucose metabolism and turnover in sheep. *Am. J. Physiol.* 219:785–93.

Bergman, E.N., Reid, R.S., Murray, M.G., Brockway, J.M., and Whitelaw, F.G. 1965. Interconversions and production of volatile fatty acids in the sheep rumen. *Biochem. J.* 97:53–58.

Bergman, H.D., and Dukes, H.H. 1926. An experimental study of the mechanism of regurgitation in rumination. *J. Am. Vet. Med. Ass.* 69:600–612.

Bergman, H.D., Dukes, H.H., and Yarborough, J.H. 1924. A study of the enzymatic action of extracts of the duodenal gland region of the domestic animals. *J. Am. Vet. Med. Ass.* 18:313–26.

Bigwood, E.J. 1964. Amino acid balance studies in the ruminant during lactation: Dietary lysine as an essential limiting factor in milk secretion. In H.N. Munro, ed., *The Role of the Gastrointestinal Tract in Protein Metabolism*. Blackwell, Oxford. Pp. 155–74.

Blair-West, J.R., Bott, E., Boyd, G.W., Coghlan, J.P., Denton, D.A., Goding, J.R., Weller, S., Wintour, M., and Wright, R.D. 1965. General biological aspects of salivary secretion in ruminants. In R.W. Dougherty, ed., *Physiology of Digestion in the Ruminant*. Butterworths, Washington. Pp. 198–220.

Blaxter, K.L., Graham, N. McC., and Wainman, F.W. 1956. Some observations on the digestibility of food by sheep, and on related problems. *Brit. J. Nutr.* 10:69–91.

Bock, E., and Trautmann, A. 1914. Die Glandula parotis bei ovis aries. *Anat. Anz.* 47:433–47.

Borgatti, G., and Matscher, R. 1958. Paths and significance of the oral reflex of the reticulum. *Arch. Ital. Biol.* 96:38–57.

Bost, J. 1970. Omasal physiology. In A.T. Phillipson, ed., *Physiology of Digestion and Metabolism in the Ruminant.* Oriel, Newcastle upon Tyne. Pp. 52–65.

Bouckaert, J.H., and Oyaert, W. 1954. A method of collecting fluid leaving the omasum of sheep. *Nature* 174:1195.

Boyne, A.W., Campbell, R.M., Davidson, J., and Cuthbertson, D.P. 1956. Changes in composition of the digesta along the alimentary tract of sheep. *Brit. J. Nutr.* 10:325–33.

Briggs, P.K., Hogan, J.P., and Reid, R.L. 1957. Effect of volatile acids, lactic acid, and ammonia on rumen pH in sheep. *Austral. J. Ag. Res.* 8:674–710.

Bruce, J., Goodall, E.D., Kay, R.N.B., Phillipson, A.T., and Vowles, L.E. 1966. The flow of organic and inorganic materials through the alimentary tract of the sheep. *Proc. Roy. Soc.*, ser. B, 166:46–62.

Bryant, M.P., and Burkey, L.A. 1953. Cultural methods and some characteristics of some of the more numerous groups of bacteria in the bovine rumen. *J. Dairy Sci.* 36:205–17.

Buston, H.W. 1934. The polyuronide constituents of forage grasses. *Biochem. J.* 28:1028–37.

Buziassy, C., and Tribe, D.E. 1960. The synthesis of vitamins in the rumen of sheep. I. The effect of diet on the synthesis of thiamine, riboflavin, and nicotinic acid. *Austral. J. Ag. Res.* 11:989–1001.

Campbell, R.M., Cuthbertson, D.P., Mackie, W., McFarlane, A.S., Phillipson, A.T., and Sudsaneh, S. 1961. Passage of plasma albumin into the intestine of the sheep. *J. Physiol.* 158:113–31.

Campling, R.C., Freer, M., and Balch, C.C. 1961. Factors affecting the involuntary intake of food by cows. II. The relationship between the voluntary intake of roughages, the amount of digesta in reticulo-rumen, and the rate of disappearance of digesta from the alimentary tract. *Brit. J. Nutr.* 15:531–40.

——. 1962. Factors affecting the voluntary intake of food by cows. III. The effect of urea on the voluntary intake of oat straw. *Brit. J. Nutr.* 16:115–24.

Castle, E.J. 1956. The rate of passage of foodstuffs through the alimentary tract of the goat: Studies on adult animals fed on hay and concentrates. *Brit. J. Nutr.* 10:15–23.

Chalmers, M.I., and Synge, R.L.M. 1954. The digestion of protein and nitrogenous compounds in ruminants. *Adv. Protein Chem.* 9:93–120.

Cheetham, S.E., and Stevens, D.H. 1966. Vascular supply to the absorptive surfaces of the ruminant stomach. *J. Physiol.* 186:56–58.

Clark, E.M.W., Ellinger, G.M., and Phillipson, A.T. 1966. The influence of diet on the nitrogenous components passing to the duodenum and through the lower ileum of sheep. *Proc. Roy. Soc.*, ser. B, 166:63–79.

Clark, R., and Weiss, K.E. 1952. Reflex salivation in sheep and goats initiated by mechanical stimulation of the cardiac area of the forestomachs. *J.S. Afr. Vet. Med. Ass.* 23:163–65.

Clunies-Ross, I. 1931. The passage of fluids through the ruminant stomach. *Austral. Vet. J.* 7:122–34.

Coates, D.A., Denton, D.A., Goding, J.R., and Wright, R.D. 1956. Secretion by the parotid gland of the sheep. *J. Physiol.* 131:13–31.

Colin, G.C. 1886. *Traité de physiologie comparée des animaux.* 3d ed. Baillière, Paris.

Colvin, H.W., Wheat, J.D., Rhode, E.A., and Boda, J.M. 1957. Technique for measuring eructated gas in cattle. *J. Dairy Sci.* 40:492–502.

Comline, R.S., and Kay, R.N.B. 1955. Reflex secretion by the parotid gland of the sheep. *J. Physiol.* 129:55–56.

Comline, R.S., and Message, M.A. 1965. The neuromuscular physiology of the ruminant stomach. In R.W. Dougherty, ed., *Physiology of Digestion in the Ruminant.* Butterworths, Washington. Pp. 78–87.

Comline, R.S., and Titchen, D.A. 1951. Reflex contraction of the oesophageal groove in young ruminants. *J. Physiol.* 115:210–26.

Coombe, J.B., and Kay, R.N.B. 1965. Passage of digesta through the intestine of the sheep. Retention times in the small and large intestines. *Brit. J. Nutr.* 19:325–38.

Coombe, J.B., Tribe, D.E., and Morrison, J.W. 1960. Some experimental observations on the toxicity of urea to sheep. *Austral. J. Ag. Res.* 11:247–56.

Czepa, A., and Stigler, R. 1926. Der Wiederkäuermagen im Röntgenbild. *Arch. f. d. ges. Physiol.* 212:300–356.

Danielli, J.F., Hitchcock, M.W.S., Marshall, R.A., and Phillipson, A.T. 1946. The mechanism of absorption from the rumen as exemplified by the behaviour of acetic, propionic, and butyric acids. *J. Exp. Biol.* 22:75–84.

Dawson, R.M.C. 1959. Hydrolysis of lecithin and lysolecithin by rumen microorganisms of the sheep. *Nature* 183:1822–23.

Denton, D.A. 1957. The study of sheep with permanent unilateral parotid fistulae. *Q.J. Exp. Physiol.* 42:72–95.

Denton, D.A., and Sabine, J.R. 1961. The selective appetite for Na^+ shown by Na^+-deficient sheep. *J. Physiol.* 157:97–116.

——. 1963. The behaviour of Na^+-deficient sheep. *Behaviour* 20:364–76.

Dobson, A. 1956. The movements of ions across the epithelium of the reticulorumen sac. Ph.D. thesis, U. of Aberdeen.

——. 1959. Active transport through the epithelium of the reticulorumen sac. *J. Physiol.* 146:235–51.

Dobson, A., and McDonald, I. 1963 Changes in composition of the saliva of sheep on feeding heavily fertilized grass. *Res. Vet. Sci.* 4:247–57.

Dobson, A., and Phillipson, A.T. 1956. The influence of the contents of the rumen and of adrenaline upon its blood supply. *J. Physiol.* 133:76–77P.

——. 1958. The absorption of chloride ions from the reticulorumen sac. *J. Physiol.* 140:94–104.

Dobson, A., Sellers, A.F., and Shaw, G.T. 1970. Absorption of water from the isolated ventral sac of the rumen of the cow. *J. Appl. Physiol.* 28:100–104.

Dobson, M.J., Brown, W.C.B., Dobson, A., and Phillipson, A.T. 1956. A histological study of the organization of the rumen epithelium of sheep. *Q. J. Exp. Physiol.* 41:247–53.

Dougherty, R.W., Habel, R.E., and Bond, H.E. 1958. Esophageal innervation and the eructation reflex in sheep. *Am. J. Vet. Res.* 19:115–28.

Dougherty, R.W., and Meredith, C.D. 1955. Cinefluorographic studies of the ruminant stomach and of eructation. *Am. J. Vet. Res.* 16:96–100.

Downie, H.G. 1954. Photokymographic studies of regurgitation and related phenomena in the ruminant. *Am. J. Vet. Res.* 15:217–23.

Duncan, D.L. 1953. The effects of vagotomy and splanchnotomy on gastric motility in the sheep. *J. Physiol.* 119:157–69.

Duncan, D.L., and Phillipson, A.T. 1951. The development of motor responses in the stomach of the foetal sheep. *J. Exp. Biol.* 28:32–40.

Dussardier, M. 1958. La comande motrice de l'estomac etudiée chez le mouton, par la technique de la suture pneumogastric-phrénique. *J. Physiol.* (Paris) 50:265–68.

Ekmann, J., and Sperber, I. 1952. The distribution of concentrations of bicarbonate (including carbon dioxide) and chloride in the omasum of cows. *Kunglia Lantbrukshögsk Ann.* 19:227–31.

Elsden, S.R., Hitchcock, M.W.S., Marshall, R.A., and Phillipson, A.T. 1946. Volatile acids in the digestion of ruminants and other animals. *J. Exp. Biol.* 22:191–202.

el-Shazly, K. 1952. Degradation of protein in the rumen of the sheep. I. Some volatile fatty acids, including branched-chain isomers, found *in vivo.* II. The action of rumen micro-organisms on amino-acids. *Biochem. J.* 51:640–47, 647–53.

Engelhardt, W. von. 1970. Movements of water across the rumen epithelium. In A.T. Phillipson, ed., *Physiology of Digestion and Metabolism in the Ruminant.* Oriel, Newcastle upon Tyne. Pp. 132–46.

Fegler, G., and Hill, K.J. 1958. Measurement of blood flow and heat production in the splanchnic region of the anesthetized sheep. *Q. J. Exp. Physiol.* 43:189–96.

Felinski, L., Garton, G.A., Lough, A.K., and Phillipson, A.T. 1964. Lipids of sheep lymph: Transport from the intestine. *Biochem. J.* 90:154–60.

Ferguson, K.A., Hemsley, J.A., and Reis, P.J. 1967. Nutrition and wool growth: The effect of protecting dietary protein from microbial degradation in the rumen. *Austral. J. Sci.* 30:215–17.

Ferreira, H.G., Harrison, F.A., and Keynes, R.D. 1964. Studies with isolated rumen epithelium of sheep: Transport of Na and K ions. *J. Physiol.* 175:28P.

——. 1966a. Observations on the potential across the rumen of the sheep. *J. Physiol.* 187:631–44.

Ferreira, H.G., Harrison, F.A., Keynes, R.D., and Nauss, A.H. 1966b. The potential and short-circuit current across isolated rumen epithelium of the sheep. *J. Physiol.* 187:615–30.

Field, A.C. 1961. Studies on magnesium in ruminant nutrition. III. Distribution of ^{28}Mg in the gastro-intestinal tract and tissues of sheep. *Brit. J. Nutr.* 15:349–59.

Flatt, W.P., Warner, R.G., and Loosli, J.K. 1958. Influence of purified materials on the development of the ruminant stomach. *J. Dairy Sci.* 41:1593–1600.

Flourens, L.J. 1844. *Mémoires d'anatomie et physiologie comparées.* Paris.

Garton, G.A. 1951. Observtions on the distribution of inorganic phosphorus, soluble calcium, and soluble magnesium in the stomach of the sheep. *J. Exp. Biol.* 28:358–68.

——. 1969. Digestion and absorption of lipids in the ruminant. *Proc. Nutr. Soc.* 28:131–39.

Garton, G.A., Hobson, P.N., and Lough, A.K. 1958. Lipolysis in the rumen. *Nature* 182:1511–12.

Goodall, E.D., and Kay, R.N.B. 1965. Digestion and absorption in the large intestine of the sheep. *J. Physiol.* 176:12–23.

Gordon, J.G. 1958a. The relationship between fineness of grinding of food and rumination. *J. Ag. Sci.* 51:78–80.

——. 1958b. The effect of time feeding upon rumination. *J. Ag. Sci.* 51:81–83.

Gray, F.V. 1947. The digestion of cellulose by sheep: The extent of cellulose digestion at successive levels of the alimentary tract. *J. Exp. Biol.* 24:15–19.

——. 1948. The absorption of volatile fatty acids from the rumen. II. The influence of pH on absorption. *J. Exp. Biol.* 25:135–44.

Gray, F.V., Pilgrim, A.F., and Weller, R.A. 1951. Fermentation in the rumen of the sheep. I. The production of volatile fatty acids and methane during the fermentation of wheaten hay and lucerne hay in vitro by micro-organisms from the rumen. *J. Exp. Biol.* 28:74–82.

——. 1954. Functions of the omasum in the stomach of the sheep. *J. Exp. Biol.* 31:49–55.

Habel, R.E. 1956. A study of the innervation of the ruminant stomach *Cornell Vet.* 46:555–627.

Harding, R., and Leek, B.F. 1971. The locations and activities of medullary neurones associated with ruminant forestomach motility. *J. Physiol.* 219:587–610.

——. 1972a. Rapidly adapting mechano-receptors in the reticulo-rumen which also respond to chemicals. *J. Physiol.* 223:32–33P.

——. 1972b. Gastro-duodenal receptor responses to chemical and mechanical stimuli, investigated by a 'single fibre' technique. *J. Physiol.* 222:138–39P.

——. 1973. Central projections of gastric afferent vagal inputs. *J. Physiol.* 228:73–90.

Harris, L.E., and Phillipson, A.T. 1962. The measurement of the flow of food to the duodenum of sheep. *Anim. Prod.* 4:97–116.

Harrison, F.A. 1962. Bile secretion in sheep. *J. Physiol.* 162:212–24.

Harrison, F.A., and Hill, K.J. 1962. Digestive secretions and the flow of digesta along the duodenum of sheep. *J. Physiol.* 162:225–43.

Harrop, C.J.F. 1974. Nitrogen metabolism in the ovine stomach. IV. Nitrogenous compounds of the abomasal secretions. *J. Ag. Sci.* 83:249–57.

Hartmann, P.E., and Lascelles, A.K. 1966. The flow and lipid composition of thoracic duct lymph in the grazing cow. *J. Physiol.* 184:193–202.

Heald, P.J. 1951. The assessment of glucose-containing substances in rumen micro-organisms during a digestion cycle in the sheep. *Brit. J. Nutr.* 5:84–93.

Heath, T.J., and Morris, B. 1962. The absorption of fats in sheep and lambs. *Q. J. Exp. Physiol.* 47:157–69.

——. 1963. The role of bile and pancreatic juice in the absorption of fat in ewes and lambs. *Brit. J. Nutr.* 17:465–74.

Hecker, J.F. 1971. Metabolism of nitrogenous compounds in the large intestine of sheep. *Brit. J. Nutr.* 25:85–95.

Hill, K.J. 1955. Continuous gastric secretion in the ruminant. *Q. J. Exp. Physiol.* 40:32–39.

——. 1960. Abomasal secretion in sheep. *J. Physiol.* 154:115–32.

——. 1961. Digestive secretions in the ruminant. In D. Lewis, ed., *Digestive Physiology and Nutrition of the Ruminant.* Butterworth, London. Pp. 48–58.

Hill, K.J., and Taylor, R.B. 1957. Collection of pancreatic juice from conscious sheep. *J. Physiol.* 139:26P.

Hofman, R.R. 1968. Comparisons of the rumen and omasum structure in East African game ruminants in relation to their feeding habits. In M.A. Crawford, ed., *Comparative Nutrition of Wild Animals.* Symp. Zool. Soc. Lond. 21. Academic Press, London, New York. Pp. 179–94.

Hogan, J.P. 1957. The transport of ammonia from the digestive tract of the sheep. Ph.D. thesis, U. of Aberdeen.

——. 1964. The digestion of food by the grazing sheep. I. The rate of flow of digesta. *Austral. J. Ag. Sci.* 15:384–96.

Hogan, J.P., and Phillipson, A.T. 1960. The rate of flow of digesta and their removal along the digestive tract of the sheep. *Brit. J. Nutr.* 14:147–55.

Houpt, T.R. 1959. Utilization of blood urea in ruminants. *Am. J. Physiol.* 197:115–20.

Hutton, K., Bailey, F.J., and Annison, E.F. 1971. Measurements of the bacterial nitrogen entering the duodenum of the ruminant using diamino-pimelic acid as a marker. *Brit. J. Nutr.* 25:165–73.

Hyden, S. 1961. The use of reference substances and the measurement of flow in the alimentary tract. In D. Lewis, ed., *Digestive Physiology and Nutrition of the Ruminant.* Butterworth, London. Pp. 35–47.

Iggo, A. 1951. Spontaneous and reflexly elicited contractions of reticulum and rumen in decebrate sheep. *J. Physiol.* 115:74–75.

——. 1956. Central nervous control of gastric movements in sheep and goats. *J. Physiol.* 131:248–56.

Iggo, A., and Leek, B.F. 1967. An electrophysiological study of single vagal efferent units associated with gastric movements in the sheep. *J. Physiol.* 191:177–204.

Johns, A.T. 1953. Fermentation of glycerol in the rumen of sheep. *New Zealand J. Sci. Tech.*, ser. A, 35:262–69.

——. 1955. Pasture quality and ruminant digestion. II. Levels of volatile acids and ammonia in the rumen of sheep on a high-production pasture. *New Zealand J. Sci. Tech.*, ser. A, 37:323–31.

Karr, M.R., Little, C.O., and Mitchell, G.E., Jr. 1966. Starch disappearance from different segments of the digestive tract of steers. *J. Anim. Sci.* 25:652–54.

Kay, R.N.B. 1958. Continuous and reflex secretion by the parotid gland in ruminants: The effects of stimulation of the sympathetic nerve and of adrenaline on the flow of parotid saliva in sheep. *J. Physiol.* 144:463–75, 476–89.

——. 1960. The rate of flow and composition of various salivary secretions in sheep and calves: The development of parotid salivary secretion in young goats. *J. Physiol.* 150:515–37, 538–45.

Kay, R.N.B., and Phillipson, A.T. 1959. Responses of the salivary glands to distension of the oesophagus and rumen. *J. Physiol.* 148:507–23.

Kiddle, P., Marshall, R.A., and Phillipson, A.T. 1951. A comparison of the mixtures of acetic, propionic, and butyric acids in the rumen and in the blood leaving the rumen. *J. Physiol.* 113:207–17.

' eek, B.F. 1972. The innervation of sheep forestomach papillae from which combined chemoreceptor and rapidly adapting mechanoreceptor responses are obtainable. *J. Physiol.* 227:22–23.

Leibholz, J. 1965. The free amino acids occurring in the blood plasma and rumen liquor of the sheep. *Austral. J. Ag. Res.* 16:973–79.

Lenkeit, W., and Columbus, A. 1934. Testing the oesophageal groove reflex: Physiology of the reflex. *Arch. wiss. prakt. Tierheilk.* 68:126–33.

Lindhé, B., and Sperber, I. 1959. A note on the structure of rumen epithelium. *Kunglia Lantbrukshögsk Ann.* 25:321–25.

MacRae, J.C., and Armstrong, D.G. 1969. Studies on intestinal digestion in the sheep. II. Digestion of some carbohydrate constituents in hay, cereal, and hay-cereal rations. *Brit. J. Nutr.* 23:377–87.

Magee, D.F. 1961. The investigation into the external secretion of the pancreas in sheep. *J. Physiol.* 158:132–43.

Mäkelä, A. 1956. Studies on the question of bulk in the nutrition of farm animals with special reference to cattle. *Suom. Maataloust. Seur. Julk.* 85:1–139.

Marston, H.E. 1948. The fermentation of cellulose in vitro by organisms from the rumen of sheep. *Biochem J.* 42:564–74.

Martinez-Arias, A.M. 1974. Studies on the digestion of nucleic acids in the digestive tract of sheep. Ph.D. thesis, Cambridge U.

Masson, M.J., and Phillipson, A.T. 1951. The absorption of acetate, propionate, and butyrate from the rumen of sheep. *J. Physiol.* 113:189–206.

——. 1952. The composition of the digesta leaving the abomasum of sheep. *J. Physiol.* 116:98–111.

McClymont, G.L. 1951. Identification of the volatile fatty acid in the peripheral blood and rumen of cattle and the blood of other species. *Austral. J. Ag. Res.* 2:92–103.

McDonald, I.W. 1948. The absorption of ammonia from the rumen of the sheep. *Biochem. J.* 42:584–87.

——. 1952. The role of ammonia in ruminal digestion of protein. *Biochem. J.* 51:86–90.

——. 1954. The extent of conversion of food protein to microbial protein in the rumen of the sheep. *Biochem. J.* 56:120–25.

McDonald, I.W., and Hall, R.J. 1957. The conversion of casein into microbial proteins in the rumen. *Biochem. J.* 67:400–405.

McDougall, E.I. 1948. Studies on ruminant saliva. I. The composition and output of sheep's saliva. *Biochem. J.* 43:99–109.

McLeay, L.M., and Titchen, D.A. 1970. Abomasal secretory responses to teasing with food and feeding in the sheep. *J. Physiol.* 206:605–28.

Moir, R.J. 1951. The seasonal variation with ruminal micro-organisms of grazing sheep. *Austral. J. Ag. Res.* 2:322–30.

Morrison, A.D., and Habel, R.E. 1964. A quantitative study of the distribution of vagal nerve endings in the myenteric plexus of the ruminant stomach. *J. Comp. Neurol.* 122:297–309.

Nassett, E.S. 1964. The nutritional significance of endogenous nitrogen to the nonruminant. In H.N. Munro, ed., *The Role of the Gastrointestinal Tract in Protein Metabolism.* Blackwell Scientific, Oxford. Pp. 83–96.

Newhook, J.C., and Titchen, D.A. 1972. Effects of stimulation of efferent fibres of the vagus on the reticulo-omasal orifice of the sheep. *J. Physiol.* 222:407–18.

——. 1974. Effects of vagotomy, atropine, hexamethonium, and adrenaline on the destination in the stomach of liquids sucked by milk-fed lambs and calves. *J. Physiol.* 237:415–30.

Nicholson, J.W.G., and Sutton, J.D. 1969. The effect of diet composition and level of feeding on digestion in the stomach and intestine of sheep. *Brit. J. Nutr.* 23:585–601.

Ohga, A., Ota, Y., and Nakatato, Y. 1965. The movement of the stomach of sheep with special reference to the omasal movement. *Jap. J. Vet. Sci.* 27:151–60.

Oyaert, W., and Bouckaert, J.H. 1961. A study of the passage of fluid through the sheep's omasum. *Res. Vet. Sci.* 2:41–52.

Parthasarathy, D. 1952. Some aspects of digestion in herbivora. Ph.D. thesis, U. of Aberdeen.

Parthasarathy, D., and Phillipson, A.T. 1953. The movement of potassium, sodium, chloride, and water across the rumen epithelium of sheep. *J. Physiol.* 121:452–69.

Pearson, R.M., and Smith, J.A.B. 1943. The utilization of urea in the bovine rumen. II. The conversion of urea to ammonia. *Biochem. J.* 37:148–53.

Pennington, R.J. 1952. The metabolism of short-chain fatty acids in the sheep. I. Fatty acid utilization and ketone body production by rumen epithelium and other tissues. *Biochem. J.* 51:251–58.

Pennington, R.J., and Sutherland, T.M. 1956. The metabolism of short-chained fatty acids in the sheep. IV. The pathway of propionate metabolism in rumen epithelial tissue. *Biochem. J.* 63:618–28.

Pernkopf, E. 1931. Die Entwicklung des Vorderdarmes, insbesondere des Magens der Wiederkäuer. *Zeitschrift ges. Anat.* 94:490–622.

Pfeffer, E., Thompson, A., and Armstrong, D.G. 1970. Studies on the intestinal digestion in the sheep. III. Net movements of certain inorganic elements in the digestive tract of rations containing different proportions of hay and rolled barley. *Brit. J. Nutr.* 24:197–204.

Phaneuf, L.P. 1952. Studies on the motor and secretory activity of the caecum and small intestine of the sheep. M.S. thesis, Cornell U.

Phillipson, A.T. 1939. The movements of the pouches of the stomach of sheep. *Q. J. Exp. Physiol.* 29:395–415.

——. 1942. The fluctuation of pH and organic acids in the rumen of the sheep. *J. Exp. Biol.* 19:186–98.

——. 1947. The production of fatty acids in the alimentary tract of the dog. *J. Exp. Biol.* 23:346–49.

——. 1952. The fatty acids present in the rumen of lambs fed on a flaked maize ration. *Brit. J. Nutr.* 6:190–98.

Phillipson, A.T., Green, R., Reid, R.S., and Vowles, L.E. 1949. The passage of food through the abomasum of the sheep. *Brit. J. Nutr.* 3:iii–iv.

Phillipson, A.T., and Mangan, J.L. 1959. Bloat in cattle. XVI. Bovine saliva: The chemical composition of the parotid, submaxillary, and residual secretions. *New Zealand J. Ag. Res.* 2:990–1001.

Phillipson, A.T., and McAnally, R.A. 1942. Studies on the fate of carbohydrates in the rumen of the sheep. *J. Exp. Biol.* 19:119–214.

Phillipson, A.T., and Reid, R.S. 1957. Thiamine in the contents of the alimentary tract of sheep. *J. Exp. Biol.* 11:27–41.

Pilgrim, A.F. 1948. The production of methane and hydrogen by the sheep. *Austral. J. Sci. Res.* 1:130–38.

Popow, N.A., Kudriatsev, A.A., and Krasovsky, W.K. 1933. On the question of the innervation and pharmacology of the stomachs of the ruminant. *Arch. Tierernähr. Tierz.* 9:243–52.

Porter, J.W.G. 1961. Vitamin synthesis in the rumen. In D. Lewis, ed., *Digestive Physiology and Nutrition of the Ruminant.* Butterworth, London, Pp. 226–34.

Rankin, A.D. 1940. A study of absorption from the rumen of sheep. M.S. thesis, Cornell U.

Raynaud, P. 1955. L'azote total dans les réservoirs gastriques des bovides. *Arch. Sci. Physiol.* 9:83–96.

Raynaud, P., and Bost, J. 1957. Preuves directes de la résorption d'eau par l'omasum chez les petits ruminants. *Pflüg. Arch. ges. Physiol.* 264:306–13.

Reid, C.S.W. 1962. The influence of the afferent innervation of the ruminant stomach on its motility. Ph.D. thesis, Cambridge U.

Reid, C.S.W., and Cornwall, J.B. 1959. The mechanical activity of the reticulo-rumen of cattle. *Proc. New Zealand Soc. Anim. Prod.* 19:23–35.

Reid, C.S.W., and Titchen, D.A. 1965. Reflex stimulation of movements of the rumen in decerebrate sheep. *J. Physiol.* 181:432–48.

Rérat, A., Molle, J., and Le Bars, H. 1958. Mise en évidence chez le mouton de la perméabilité du rumen aux vitamines B et conditions de leur absorption à ce niveau. *Compte rend. Acad. Sci.* 246:2051–54.

Riek, R.F. 1954. The influence of sodium salts on the closure of the oesophageal groove in calves. *Austral. Vet. J.* 30:29–37.

Saunders, E.G., Warner, R.G., Harrison, H.N., and Loosli, J.K. 1959. The stimulatory effect of sodium butyrate and sodium propionate on the development of rumen mucosa in the young calf. *J. Dairy Sci.* 42:1600–1605.

Schalk, A.F., and Amadon, R.S. 1928. Physiology of the ruminant stomach (bovine): Study of the dynamic factors. *N. Dak. Ag. Exp. Sta. Bull.* 216.

Schambye, P. 1951. Volatile acids and glucose in portal blood of sheep. II. Sheep fed hay and hay plus crushed oats. III. The influence of orally administered glucose. *Nord. Vet. Med.* 3:555–74, 748–62, 1003–14.

——. 1955. Experimental estimation of the portal vein blood flow in sheep. II. Chronic experiments in cannulated sheep applying infusion and injection methods. *Nord. Vet. Med.* 7:1001–16.

Schmidt-Nielson, B., and Osaki, H. 1958. Renal responses to changes in nitrogen metabolism in sheep. *Am. J. Physiol.* 193:657–61.

Schmidt-Nielson, B., Schmidt-Nielson, K., Houpt, T.R., and Jarnum, S.A. 1957. Urea excretion in the camel. *Am. J. Physiol.* 188:477–84.

Scott, D. 1965. Factors influencing secretion and absorption of calcium and magnesium in the small intestine of sheep. *Q. J. Exp. Physiol.* 50:312–29.

——. 1967. The effects of potassium supplements upon the absorption of potassium and sodium from the sheep rumen. *Q. J. Exp. Physiol.* 51:382–91.

Scott, T.W., Cook, L.J., and Mills, S.C. 1971. Protection of dietary polyunsaturated fatty acids against microbial hydrogenation in ruminants. *J. Am. Oil Chem. Soc.* 48:358–64.

Sellers, A.F. 1965. Blood flow in the rumen vessels. In R.W. Dougherty, ed., *Physiology of Digestion in the Ruminant.* Butterworths, Washington. Pp. 171–184.

Sellers, A.F., and Dobson, A. 1960. Studies on reticulo-rumen sodium and potassium concentrations and electrical potentials in sheep. *Res. Vet. Sci.* 1:95–102.

Sellers, A.F., Stevens, C.E., Dobson, A., and McCleod, F.D. 1964. Arterial blood flow to the ruminant stomach. *Am. J. Physiol.* 207:371–77.

Shoji, Y., Miyazaki, K., and Umezu, M. 1964. Studies on the metabolic conversion of volatile fatty acids in the rumen epithelium. I. Ruminal arterio-venous differences of the blood organic acids and lipids. *Tohoku J. Ag. Res.* 15:91–97.

Shorland, F.B., Weenink, R.O., Johns, A.T., and McDonald, I.R.C. 1957. The effect of sheep rumen contents on unsaturated fatty acids. *Biochem. J.* 67:328–33.

Silver, I.A. 1954. Myoepithelial cells in the mammary and parotid glands. *J. Physiol.* 125:8–9.

Sineschekov, A.D. 1953 (trans. 1964). *The Nutritional Physiology of Farm Animals.* National Lending Library for Science and Technology, Boston Spa, Yorkshire, Eng.

Singleton, A.G. 1961. The electromagnetic measurement of the flow of digesta through the duodenum of the goat and the sheep. *J. Physiol.* 155:134–47.

Smiles, J., and Dobson, M.J. 1956. Direct ultra-violet and ultra-violet negative phase-contrast micrography of bacteria from the stomach of the sheep. *J. Roy. Microsc. Soc.* 74:244–53.

Smith, R.H. 1969. Absorption of major minerals in the small and large intestines of the ruminant. *Proc. Nutr. Soc.* 28:151–60.

Smith, R.H., and McAllan, A.B. 1971. Nucleic acid metabolism in the ruminant. III. Amounts of nucleic acids and total and ammonia nitrogen indigesta from the rumen, duodenum, and ileum of calves. *Brit. J. Nutr.* 25:181–90.

Somers, M. 1961. Factors influencing the secretion of nitrogen in sheep saliva. *Austral. J. Exp. Biol. Med. Sci.* 39:111–56.

Sperber, I., and Hyden, S. 1952. Transport of chloride through the ruminal mucosa. *Nature* 169:587.

Spörri, H., and Asher, T. 1940. Röntgenologische Studien über die Motorite des Wiederkäuerdickdarmes. *Schweiz. Arch. Tierheilk.* 82:243–64.

Steven, D.H., and Marshall, A.B. 1972. Branching mononuclear cells in the forestomach epithelium of the sheep. *Q. J. Exp. Physiol.* 57:267–70.

Stevens, C.E., and Sellers, A.F. 1960. Pressure events in bovine esophagus and reticulorumen associated with eructation, deglutition, and regurgitation. *Am. J. Physiol.* 199:598–602.

Stevens, C.E., Sellers, A.F., and Spurrel, F.A. 1960. Function of the bovine omasum in ingesta transfer. *Am. J. Physiol.* 198:449–55.

Stevens, C.E., and Stettler, B.K. 1966. Factors affecting the transport of volatile fatty acids across rumen epithelium. *Am. J. Physiol.* 210:365–72.

Stigler, R. 1933. The mechanism of rumination. *Arch. Tierernähr. Tierz.* 4:613–94.

Storry, J.E. 1960. Calcium and magnesium contents of various secretions entering the digestive tract of sheep. *Nature* 190:1197–98.

——. 1961. Studies on calcium and magnesium in the alimentary tract of sheep. I. The distribution of calcium and magnesium in the contents taken from various parts of the alimentary tract. II. The effect of reducing the acidity of abomasal digesta in vitro on the distribution of calcium and magnesium. *J. Ag. Sci.* 57:97–102, 103–9.

Sym, E.A. 1938. Hydrolase activity of the contents of the caecum of the horse and of the rumen in cattle. I. Introduction: General methods and proteolytic action. *Acta Biol. Exp. Varsovie.* 12:192–210.

Taylor, R.B. 1962. Pancreatic secretion in the sheep. *Res. Vet. Sci.* 3:63–77.

Ternouth, J.H. 1967. Post-prandial ionic and water exchange in the rumen. *Res. Vet. Sci.* 8:283–93.

Tiedemann, F., and Gmelin, L. 1827. *Recherches experimentales physiologiques et chimiques sur la digestion.* Trans. A.J.L. Jourdan. Baillière, Paris, London. Vol. 1, 278–89.

Titchen, D.A. 1953. Reflex contractions of the reticulum. *J. Physiol.* 122:32P.

——. 1958a. Reflex stimulation and inhibition of reticulum contractions in the ruminant stomach. *J. Physiol.* 141:1–21.

——. 1958b. Partial exteriorization of the reticulum in sheep. *J. Physiol.* 143:35P.

——. 1960. The production of rumen and reticulum contractions in decerebrate preparations of sheep and goats. *J. Physiol.* 151:139–53.

——. 1968. Nervous control of motility of the forestomach of ruminants. In *Handbook of Physiology.* Sec. 6, C.F. Code and W. Heidel, eds., *The Alimentary Canal.* Am. Physiol. Soc., Washington. Pp. 2705–24.

Titchen, D.A., and Reid, C.S.W. 1965. The reflex control of the motility of the ruminant stomach. In R.W. Dougherty, ed., *Physiology of Digestion in the Ruminant.* Butterworths, Washington, Pp. 68–77.

Topps, J.H., Kay, R.N.B., and Goodall, E.D. 1968a. Digestion of concentrate and hay diets in the stomach and intestines of ruminants. I. Sheep. *Brit. J. Nutr.* 22:261–80.

Topps, J.H., Kay, R.N.B., Goodall, E.D., Whitelaw, F.G., and Reid, R.S. 1968b. Digestion of concentrate and of hay diets in the stomach and intestines of ruminants. II. Young steers. *Brit. J. Nutr.* 22:281–90.

Toussaint, H. 1875. Application de la méthode graphique à la determination du mechanisme de la rejection dans la rumination. *Arch. Physiol.* 7:141–76.

Trautmann, A. 1933. Contributions to the physiology of the ruminant stomach. VI. About absorption from the ruminant stomach. *Arch. Tierernähr. Tierz.* 9:178–93.

Tribe, D.E., and Peel, L. 1963. Total salivation in grazing lambs. *Austral. J. Ag. Res.* 14:330–39.

Tucker, R.E., Mitchell, G.E., Jr., and Little, C.O. 1968. Ruminal and postruminal starch digestion in sheep. *J. Anim. Sci.* 27:824–26.

Turner, A.W., and Hodgetts, V.E. 1955. Buffer systems in the rumen of the sheep. I. pH and bicarbonate concentration in relationship to pCO_2. *Austral. J. Ag. Res.* 6:115–24.

Usuelli, F. 1933. Time spent by food in the rumen of cattle. *Profilassi* 6:7–14.

van Weerden, E.J. 1961. The osmotic pressure and the concentration of some solutes of the intestinal contents and the faeces of the cow, in relation to the absorption of the minerals. *J. Ag. Sci.* 56:317–24.

van't Klooster, A.Th., and Rogers, P.A.M. 1969. Observations on the digestion and absorption of food along the gastrointestinal tract of fistulated cows. I. The rate of flow of digesta and the net absorption of dry matter, organic matter, ash, nitrogen, and water. *Meded. HandbHoogesch. Wageningen.* 69(11):3–19.

vaz Portugal, A. 1963. Some aspects of protein and amino acid metabolism in the rumen of the sheep. Ph.D. thesis U. of Aberdeen.

Waite, R., and Gorrod, A.R.N. 1959. The structural carbohydrates of grasses. *J. Sci. Food Ag.* 10:308–17.

Warner, A.C.I. 1956. Proteolysis by rumen micro-organisms. *J. Gen. Microbiol.* 14:749–62.

——. 1962. Enumeration of rumen micro-organisms. *J. Gen. Microb.* 28:119–28.

Warner, A.C.I., and Stacy, B.D. 1965. Solutes in the rumen of the sheep. *Q. J. Exp. Physiol.* 50:169–84.

Warner, E.D. 1958. The organogenesis and early histogenesis of the bovine stomach. *Am. J. Anat.* 102:33–63.

Warner, R.G., and Flatt, W.P. 1965. Anatomical development of the ruminant stomach. In R.W. Dougherty, ed., *Physiology of Digestion in the Ruminant.* Butterworths, Washington. Pp. 24–38.

Watson, R.H. 1941. Studies on deglutition in sheep: Observations on the course taken by liquids through the stomach of the sheep at various ages from birth to four years. *Austral. Vet. J.* 17:52–58.

——. 1944. Studies on deglutition in sheep. I. Observations on the course taken by liquids through the stomach of the sheep at various ages from birth to maturity. *Bull. Council Sci. Ind. Res.*, no. 180, 1–94.

Webster, A.J.F., Osuji, P.O., White, F., and Ingram, J.F. 1975. The influence of food on portal blood flow and heat production in the digestive tract of sheep. *Brit. J. Nutr.* 34:125–39.

Webster, A.J.F., and White, F. 1973. Portal blood flow and heat production in the digestive tract of sheep. *Brit. J. Nutr.* 29:279–92.

Webster, W.M., and Cresswell, E. 1957. New evidence on the regurgitation mechanism. *Vet. Rec.* 69:527–28.

Weiss, K.E. 1953. Physiological studies on eructation in ruminants. *Onderstepoort J. Vet. Res.* 26:251–83.

Weller, R.A., Gray, F.V., and Pilgrim, A.F. 1958. The conversion of plant nitrogen to microbial nitrogen in the rumen of the sheep. *Brit. J. Nutr.* 12:421–29.

Weller, R.A., Pilgrim, A.F., and Gray, F.V. 1969. Volatile fatty acid production in the rumen of the grazing sheep: Its use as an indicator of pasture value. *Brit. J. Nutr.* 21:97–111.

Wester, J. 1926. *Die Physiologie und Pathologie der Vormägen beim Rinde.* Richard Schoetz, Berlin. Pp. 1–110.

———. 1930. Der Schlundrinnenreflex beim Rinde. *Berl. Tierärztl. Wschr.* 36:397–402.

Weston, R.H., and Hogan, J.P. 1967. The digestion of chopped and ground roughages by sheep: The movement of digesta through the stomach. *Austral. J. Ag. Res.* 18:789–801.

——. 1968. Ruminal production of volatile fatty acids by sheep offered diets of ryegrass and forage oats. *Austral. J. Ag. Res.* 19:419–32.

Williams, V.J., and Mackenzie, D.D.S. 1965. The absorption of lactic acid from the reticulorumen of the sheep. *Austral. J. Biol. Sci.* 18:917–34.

Wilson, A.D. 1963. The effect of diet on the secretion of parotid saliva by sheep. XI. Variations in the rate of salivary secretion. *Austral. J. Ag. Res.* 14:680–89.

Wilson, A.D., and Tribe, D.E. 1961. The development of parotid salivation in the lamb. *Austral. J. Ag. Res.* 12:1126–38.

Wise, G.H., and Anderson, G.W. 1939. Factors affecting the passage of liquids into the rumen of the dairy calf. I. Method of administering liquids: Drinking from open pails versus sucking through a rubber nipple. *J. Dairy Sci.* 22:697–705.

CHAPTER 23

Microbiology of the Rumen

by Marvin P. Bryant

A study of the nutrition and physiology of ruminants requires some understanding of the intense microbial activity that occurs in the rumen. About 70–85 percent of the digestible dry matter of the usual diet is digested by microorganisms in the rumen (Gray 1947), with the production of volatile fatty acids (VFA) (the main source of energy for ruminants), carbon dioxide, methane, ammonia, and microbial cells. Major carbohydrate constituents of ruminant diets, such as cellulosic materials (not digested by mammalian enzymes) and starch and other carbohydrates (digested by mammalian enzymes), are all digested by rumen microorganisms. Since many of the microorganisms can synthesize the proteins and B vitamins required for their growth and metabolism from carbohydrates, certain organic acids, ammonia, and minerals, the ruminant can be maintained on diets free of otherwise essential B vitamins and amino acids.

The rumen differs from many other natural microbial habitats in its relative constancy and can be viewed as a highly efficient continuous culture apparatus for the propagation of anaerobic microorganisms. There is a relatively constant influx of food and water with constant mixing and passage of undigested food residues and microbial cells to the lower tract. The moisture content is relatively constant and the osmotic pressure is maintained close to that of blood. The temperature is usually 38–42°C. The pH, usually between 6 and 7, is buffered by the influx of quantities of saliva containing large amounts of bicarbonate and phosphate, by absorption into the blood stream of VFA and ammonia produced in the fermentation, and by the tendency toward an ionic equilibrium between the rumen contents and the blood stream. The contents are highly anaerobic with E_h (oxidation-reduction potential) values usually between -250 and -450 mv, depending on the diet, pH of contents, and method of measurement. E_h expresses the degree of oxidation or reduction compared with the hydrogen electrode. When the value is negative, greater reduction has taken place and the condition in the rumen is anaerobic, while a positive value shows oxidation or an aerobic environment. The gaseous phase of the dorsal rumen usually contains 50–70 percent of carbon dioxide; the remainder is chiefly methane with small amounts of other gases such as nitrogen and oxygen. The nitrogen and oxygen gain entrance mainly with the feed, but oxygen is very rapidly utilized by the microbial population. The cell-free fluid portion of rumen contents usually contains relatively large amounts of ammonia as the main nitrogen compound and VFA, carbon dioxide, or bicarbonate as the main carbon compounds. Carbohydrates and organic nitrogen compounds are mainly associated with the fibrous solids and microbial cells.

A very complex mixture of many species of microorganisms is present in the rumen of animals maintained on most dietary regimes. Variations in numbers with time after feeding and dietary regime, and differences in individual animals held under identical conditions make it difficult to generalize. However, under most conditions the anaerobic ciliate protozoa and a great variety of non-spore-forming anaerobic bacterial genera account for the

Table 23.1. Approximate average volumes and numbers of microbial groups in the rumen of sheep fed alfalfa and wheaten chaff

Organism	Av. individual cell vol. (cu μ)	No./ml	Percentage of total microbial vol.*
Ciliate protozoa			
Isotricha, Epidinium, Diplodinium sp.	1,000,000	1.1×10^4	33.55
Dasytricha, Diplodinium sp.	100,000	2.9×10^4	8.78
Entodinium sp.	10,000	2.9×10^5	8.79
Polymastigates	500	9.4×10^3	0.01
Oscillospiras, flagellates	250	3.8×10^5	0.26
Selenomonads	30	1.0×10^8	0.09
Small bacteria	1	1.6×10^{10}	48.52

* Total microbial vol. was about 0.036 ml per ml of rumen fluid.
Modified from data of Warner 1962a, *J. Gen. Microbiol.* 28:129–46

bulk of the microbial protoplasm and activity. Perhaps the best quantitative estimates on total counts of most major microbial groups present have been made in the direct microscopic studies of Warner (1962a). Table 23.1 indicates a microbial volume of about 3.6 percent of the volume of strained rumen fluid; this microbial volume contains about 50 percent ciliate protozoa and 50 percent small bacteria. However, under some conditions other groups of microorganisms might account for as much as 10 percent of the total microbial volume. Microbial protoplasm would rarely account for more than 10 percent of the volume of rumen fluid. In terms of metabolic activity per unit of cell volume, in general organisms with small individual cell volumes are much more active than those with large individual cell volume. Thus, though the total volume of small bacteria might be about the same as for the ciliate protozoa, their metabolic activity is undoubtedly much greater. Also, the bacteria grow and pass out of the rumen much faster than the ciliate protozoa (Weller and Pilgrim 1974).

In general similar microbial species and similar metabolic activities are present in the rumen of cattle and sheep, and presumably in most other ruminants. Hungate et al. (1959) indicated that fermentation rates per unit weight of rumen contents increase as the size of the ruminant species decreases and might be related to the fact that animal energy requirements are approximately equal to body weight to the ¾ power.

FUNCTIONS OF RUMEN MICROORGANISMS

While a great amount of excellent qualitative and semiquantitative information is available on the activities of rumen microorganisms, precise estimates of the various contributions to ruminant metabolism are not available. Obtaining a sample of rumen contents representative of the total, even at one time, is difficult, as the contents are far from homogeneous, with variation in both insoluble and soluble components of the ingesta in different areas. For example, Smith et al. (1956) found values for dry matter, crude fiber, ash, total nitrogen, ammonia, nonprotein nitrogen, and VFA to be higher in samples collected from the dorsal rumen than from the ventral rumen. Bryant and Robinson (1968) found that colony counts of total viable bacteria from the rumen of cattle fed chopped or ground hay or hay-grain diets were always much higher in dorsal than in ventral samples, while counts from ventral samples were almost identical with those obtained from the area adjacent to the reticulo-omasal orifice. Warner (1964a) gives an excellent discussion of problems involved in precise measurements of daily VFA production.

Metabolism of carbohydrates

Any carbohydrates entering the rumen are fermented by the microbial population with the production of microbial cells, VFA, carbon dioxide, and methane. (Figure 23.1 shows a simplified scheme of carbohydrate breakdown.) Major carbohydrates in the usual types of ruminant feeds include polysaccharides such as cellulose, fructosan, pentosans, pectic substances and other polyuronides, and starch; and sugars such as sucrose and glucose. The catabolism of polysaccharides by rumen bacteria involves extracellular degradation to sugars or short-chain oligosaccharides, which are transported into the cell, intracellular catabolism involving hydrolysis or phosphorylative cleavage of oligosaccharides to monosaccharides, and further catabolism of the pyruvate produced by glycolysis to VFA, carbon dioxide, and methane.

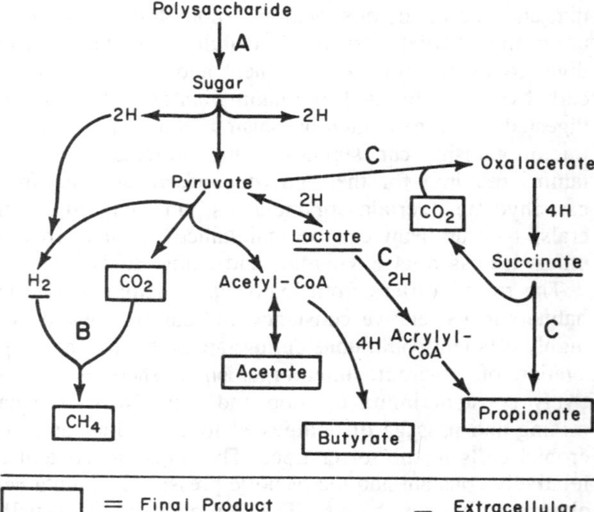

Figure 23.1. Complex foodweb of diverse bacterial species involved in carbohydrate fermentation. H, an electron plus a proton or electrons from reduced pyridine nucleotides; A, carbohydrate fermenting species; B, methanogenic species; C, lactate-fermenting species which often also ferment carbohydrates.

Polysaccharides

The microbial degradation of cellulose by microorganisms in general is not well understood; however, it is evident that even in one organism a complex system including a number of enzymes is involved (Hajny and Reese 1968). The degradation is divided into three phases, disaggregation, extracellular hydrolysis, and intracellular metabolism, based on the changes in the physical and chemical properties of the substrate.

The native cellulose fiber consists of numerous cellulose molecules aligned in a loosely organized manner in amorphous regions and in rigidly oriented crystalline regions. The amorphous, more hydrated regions of the fiber are hydrolyzed more rapidly than the crystalline regions, leaving an excess of the highly crystalline regions which change to more hydrated amorphous cellulose before much hydrolysis occurs. The content of lignin and a few other cell-wall constituents of forages shows strong inverse relationships to the amount of digestion of cellulose and hemicellulose that occurs (van Soest, in McDonald and Warner 1975).

Studies on rumen cellulolytic bacteria indicate that the cellulose degrading systems in these organisms are at least as complex as those in other microorganisms. Some strains attack only partially degraded cellulose, presumably shorter chained molecules from fibers with less crystallinity, while others rapidly degrade highly crystalline native cotton cellulose (Bryant 1973).

Pentosans and hemicelluloses are very actively digested by mixed rumen bacteria, and many species are known to ferment a commercial preparation of xylan and several other pentosans containing mainly xylosyl and/or arabinosyl units (Howard et al. 1960). In pentosan fermentation by mixed rumen bacteria and by strains of the genus *Butyrivibrio,* partially hydrolyzed pentosan yielded arabinose, xylose, xylose oligosaccharides from xylobiose to xylopentose, and oligosaccharides containing both arabinose and xylose.

Pectic materials are very rapidly degraded by enzymes produced by both rumen bacteria and protozoa (Wright 1961).

Starch granules are actively attacked by both bacteria and protozoa in rumen contents. The studies of Baker et al. (1951) indicate that the disintegration of intact granules by bacteria occurs only when bacteria are attached. Cooking or grinding the granules renders them more susceptible to bacterial attack. In addition to the amylases, maltase and isomaltase have been found in various rumen microorganisms (Bailey and Howard 1963).

Enzymes attacking many other polysaccharides have been demonstrated in rumen microorganisms. Rumen contents are one of the best sources of microorganisms that digest plant polysaccharides.

Although no quantitative and few qualitative estimates have been made, it seems certain that bacterial species not attacking the long-chain polysaccharides of ruminant feeds obtain a considerable amount of energy for growth from extracellular products such as hexoses, pentoses, and short-chain oligosaccharides, which are produced as extracellular intermediates by the polysaccharide-decomposing bacteria (Scheifinger and Wolin 1973).

Glycolysis

Until recently it was generally assumed that polysaccharides were metabolized extracellularly to the mono- or disaccharide stage and that these sugars were then further metabolized intracellularly. However, definite evidence for efficient intracellular metabolism of cellulodextrins containing up to at least six glucosyl moieties has been obtained with a nonruminal cellulolytic bacterium (Alexander and Sheth 1967). It seems probable that many rumen bacteria, possibly including species not attacking the long-chain polymers, will be found to utilize similar oligosaccharides from cellulose, pentosans, and other polysaccharides. Whether hydrolytic or phosphorylative cleavage of oligosaccharides occurs is a subject of interest, because phosphorylative cleavage would conserve the energy of the glycosidic bond for bacterial growth. Ruminococci utilize cellobiose but usually not glucose as an energy source and contain a cellobiose phosphorylase yielding glucose-1-phosphate and glucose. The inability of the organism to utilize extracellular glucose is probably due to impermeability, since cell extracts contain enzymes necessary for its glycolysis (Ayers 1958). A strain of the same organism utilizes exogenous xylobiose but not xylose, and the starch-digesting rumen bacterium *Bacteroides amylophilus* utilizes maltose but not glucose.

Studies to date indicate that the Embden-Meyerhof mechanism is the main pathway involved in hexose metabolism in the rumen (Wallnöfer et al. 1966). And the end products of hemicellulose or xylan fermentation by mixed rumen bacteria and ruminococci are similar to those formed from cellulose or cellobiose, suggesting that pentoses are metabolized mainly via a pathway involving hexose synthesis and the Embden-Meyerhof pathway.

End-product formation

The terminal pathways involved in production of the final end products of carbohydrate fermentation are quite complex and probably involve a large number of different reaction mechanisms. These lead from pyruvic acid or phosphoenolpyruvic acid plus reduced nicotinamide adenine dinucleotide (NAD)—the products of glycolysis—to carbon dioxide, methane, and acetic, propionic, butyric, and valeric acids (see Fig. 23.1). Acetic acid and carbon dioxide are each produced from carbohydrates by a large number of individual species of rumen organisms, and propionic, butyric, and valeric acids, by a smaller number. However, many of these individual species also produce one or more end products such as succinic, lactic, or formic acids, hydrogen gas, and ethanol, which are not final end products of the fermentation. Table 23.2 shows some typical end products of carbohydrate fermentation. These compounds, with the exception of ethanol, are further metabolized by other species resulting in the final end products.

Most of the rumen acetate is produced from pyruvate by pyruvate: ferredoxin oxidoreductase or similar enzymes yielding acetate, carbon dioxide, and reduced ferredoxin, or other carriers of low-potential electrons (Miller and Wolin 1973). These electrons are utilized by the cells producing them for the reductions required for production of excretory products such as succinate, propionate, lactate or butyrate, or they can be excreted as hydrogen gas or as formate (via carbon dioxide reductase).

Rumen methane is produced mainly by reduction of carbon dioxide (Kleiber 1953) with hydrogen gas being the main hydrogen donor (Hungate et al. 1970). Opperman et al. (1961) showed that only a small amount of the rumen methane could be produced from the methyl group of acetate, although this is the main precursor of methane in some anaerobic ecosystems.

Although the hydrogen gas produced in fermentation is utilized mainly in reduction of carbon dioxide to methane, it also functions as a hydrogen donor in the reduction of sulfate to sulfide and nitrate to ammonia, and probably in other reductions.

Two general pathways of propionic acid production in the rumen are known. The most important one involves carbon dioxide fixation to phosphoenolpyruvate to form oxalacetate and reduction through malate and fumarate to succinate. Succinate is a major end product of fermentation by many rumen species (see Table 23.2). The succinic acid excreted into the fluid is rapidly decarboxylated by species such as *Selenomonas ruminantium* (Scheifinger and Wolin 1973), yielding propionic acid and carbon dioxide. A variation of this general pathway includes propionic acid production from sugar, glycerol, or lactate by organisms such as *Selenomonas ruminantium*.

That most of the rumen propionate is produced via extracellular succinate is indicated by the studies of Blackburn and Hungate (1963) and Satter et al. (1964).

The second general pathway of propionate production involves the more direct reduction of pyruvate through the coenzyme A (CoA) derivatives of lactate and acrylate. This pathway is found in *Megasphaera elsdenii,* which is one of the more important lactate-fermenting organisms of the rumen, and is of greater importance in ruminants on high-grain diets (Baldwin et al. 1963).

Lactate is usually not a very important extracellular intermediate in carbohydrate fermentation in the rumen. Jayasuriya and Hungate (1959) studied the level of lactate present in rumen contents and its turnover rate, and estimated lactate to be an intermediate in the conversion of less than 1 percent of the feed digested in hay-fed cattle. When a high-grain diet was fed, it accounted for much more of the conversion.

Production of butyrate probably proceeds mainly via production of acetyl CoA from pyruvate and extracellular acetate and condensation of these to form butyrate via the CoA derivatives of acetoacetate, β-hydroxybutyrate, and

Table 23.2. Major fermentation products produced by pure cultures of rumen bacteria

		Fermentation products *								
Species	Energy source	Acetic	Propionic	Butyric	CO_2	Succinic	Lactic	Formic	Ethanol	Hydrogen
Lachnospira multiparus	Glucose	1.08			2.5		1.38	1.62	2.5	0.24
Ruminococcus albus	Cellobiose	1.25			†			1.45	1.2	0.83
Ruminococcus flavefaciens	Cellobiose	0.62			‡	1.47		0.66		0.10
Bacteroides succinogenes	Cellulose	0.61			−0.83	1.26		0.21		
Bacteroides amylophilus	Starch	0.59			−0.24	0.98		0.74		
Bacteroides ruminicola	Glucose	2.68			‡	4.2		1.25		
Succinivibrio dextrinosolvens	Glucose	0.78			−0.5	1.41		0.26		
Butyrivibrio fibrisolvens	Glucose	−0.14		1.1	2.17		0.43	0.42	0.07	0.76
Eubacterium ruminantium	Glucose	0.17		0.71	0.33		0.71	0.93		
Selenomonas ruminantium	Glucose	0.89	1.38		1.44		2.05	0.3		
	Lactate	3.03	5.44		†					
Megasphaera elsdenii	Lactate §	2.04	2.43	2.04	7.45					0.47
Streptococcus bovis	Glucose	†					7	†		
Lactobacillus vitulinus	Glucose						10.16			
Methanobacterium ruminantium	$CO_2 + H_2$ ‖				−1					−4
Succinimonas amylolytica	Glucose	0.09			−0.44	0.72				
Treponema sp.	Glucose	0.48			0.28	0.53	0.16	0.17	0.12	
Veillonella alcalescens	Lactate	4.38	5.27		3.17					1.33

* Molar ratios (usually in mM/100 ml medium) † Not determined but probably produced. ‡ Not determined but probably fixed.
§ Also, valeric acid, 2.58 mol, and caproic acid, 0.15 mol, are produced. ‖ Product is 1 mol of methane. It also utilizes formate.

crotonate (Barker 1956). Valerate is probably produced via an analogous reaction with propionate and acetate rather than from two moles of acetate. Gray et al. (1952) showed that acetate and propionate are utilized for butyrate and valerate synthesis by mixed rumen microorganisms.

The proportions of end products such as methane, acetate, and propionate are very important to the metabolism of the animal (see Chapters 22, 30, and 56), and an understanding of the factors involved requires knowledge of fermentation balance concepts (Wolin 1960; Demeyer and Van Nevel, in McDonald and Warner 1975). Diets containing finely ground forages, high levels of starch, sucrose, or other sources of readily available carbohydrates, and lush immature pasture, and diets fed in large amounts tend to cause lower rumen pH and greater production of propionate and less acetate and methane (Schwartz and Gilchrist, in McDonald and Warner 1975). When methanogenesis is more or less specifically inhibited by chemicals such as viologen dyes, chloral hydrate, chloroform, and other chlorinated or brominated methane analogues, the ratio of propionate to acetate increases, and hydrogen gas tends to accumulate. Other materials such as unsaturated fatty acid, nitrate, sulfate, and analogues of coenzyme M (2-mercaptoethane-sulfonic acid) also cause similar shifts (Demeyer and Van Nevel, in McDonald and Warner 1975; Taylor and Wolfe 1974).

This hydrogen gas ordinarily is very rapidly used by methane-producing bacteria and is maintained at a very low partial pressure in the rumen (Hungate 1967). The rapid use allows the hydrogen gas–producing, carbohydrate-fermenting bacteria to excrete more of the electrons generated in glycolysis as hydrogen gas. Therefore they produce more acetate and carbon dioxide from pyruvate and less of the reduction products such as propionate and succinate which otherwise must be produced in order to reoxidize (remove electrons from) the cellular reduced pyridine nucleotides. The detailed pathways and thermodynamics of the important concept of *interspecies hydrogen transfer* are discussed by Wolin (McDonald and Warner 1975). The concept helps to explain the increase in propionate when methanogenesis is inhibited and also the fact that, though many pure cultures of rumen bacteria produce much ethanol or lactate in pure culture (see Table 23.2), they produce little or none of these, and a larger amount of acetate, in the natural mixed-culture system where methanogenesis is active (Iannotti et al. 1973).

Significant amounts of ethanol are found in the rumen under adverse conditions such as excessive feeding of starch or sugar (Allison et al. 1964, Krogh 1959).

Some discussion of the amount of microbial cell substance (growth yields), and thus of the amount of protein, produced during catabolism of a unit amount of carbohydrate is in order. The amount of cell material produced depends on the amount of carbohydrate fermented, the amount of adenosine triphosphate (ATP) produced by the individual fermentation mechanisms, the growth rate, and the factors limiting the amount of growth (Isaacson et al. 1975; Smith, in McDonald and Warner 1975). For example, when the energy source is limiting growth, more cell material will be produced per unit of energy source fermented than when a carbon or nitrogen source required for cell synthetic reactions is limiting growth. When carbohydrate is fermented by a mixed population of rumen bacteria, the yield of dry weight of cells is equal to about 20–45 percent of the weight of carbohydrate fermented, and the latter is equal to about 92 percent of that used—the rest being incorporated into the cells. Recent research indicates that one of the main factors affecting the yield is the growth rate of the microbes. When the overall growth rate is high, and materials are more rapidly passing out of the rumen to the lower tract, yields of bacterial dry weight and therefore of bacterial protein (about 50 percent of the dry weight) are higher per unit amount of carbohydrate fermented. This is due to an energy requirement for maintenance of the population which utilizes more of the total energy (ATP) made available by fermentation when growth rate of microbes and passage out of the rumen are lower. The maintenance energy concept is quite complex but includes that energy which is required to maintain the integrity of microbial cells as well as that required to replace cells which autolyze or are destroyed by other microorganisms (Robinson and Allison 1975; Coleman, in McDonald and Warner 1975). Microbial growth yields are often discussed in terms of grams of cells produced per mole of ATP made available for growth via the fermentation of carbohydrate. In rumen bacteria, however, the amount of ATP produced in some of the specific fermentation reactions, e.g. those involved in propionate and methane formation, is not yet known. Changes in growth yields due to changes in proportions of fermentation end products, and thus in ATP production per unit of carbohydrate fermented, are probably small compared to changes in yield due to growth and passage rates.

Some of the carbohydrate utilized by rumen bacteria and protozoa is taken into the cells and converted to glycogen or amylopectinlike reserve material, which serves as the main source of energy via catabolism to organic acids when extracellular energy supply is low. Although the amount of these carbohydrate reserve materials in the microorganisms may reach as high as 30 per cent of their dry weight shortly after animals are fed, they usually account for much less. Heald (1951) estimated that 5–6 g of this material passed from the abomasum of sheep in 24 hours, a quantity of little importance. However, it is possible that under conditions of high-grain feeding as now carried out, or conditions causing increased rate of passage, a considerably larger amount may escape catabolism in the rumen. Build-up of these polysaccharide reserves from dietary carbohydrate shortly after the animal is fed, and their continued fermentation after much of the rapidly available extracellular energy supply has been utilized, probably allows the animal to consume larger amounts of carbohydrate without deleterious effects, since more rapid acid production and lowering of pH would take place if most of the carbohydrate was fermented immediately.

Metabolism of nitrogen

The microbial metabolism of nitrogen compounds of the diet and those such as urea which enter the rumen from the portal system and in saliva is very active, and the nature of the activity is of great importance to the efficiency of the animal's system (Allison 1970; Smith, in McDonald and Warner 1975). The general scheme is as follows: (1) proteinases and peptidases hydrolyze much of the protein to peptides and free amino acids; (2) these are taken into the cell, the peptides being hydrolyzed to amino acids; the amino acids are utilized directly for synthesis of protein and other microbial cell constituents such as cell-wall constituents and nucleic acids, or (3) they are catabolized to VFA and other acids, carbon dioxide, and ammonia; (4) urea is hydrolyzed to ammonia by potent urease activity; (5) compounds such as nitrate are reduced to ammonia; and (6) ammonia is utilized in synthesis of microbial cell components such as protein. The balance between the rate of production and utilization of ammonia by the rumen microorganisms in their catabolic and anabolic metabolism is of primary concern because ammonia in the rumen is rapidly absorbed into the blood and excreted in the urine mainly as urea. If rumen ammonia levels are high for long periods of time, the efficiency of utilization of dietary nitrogen by the animal is very low.

Varying proportions of the dietary protein nitrogen undergo rumen microbial digestion and conversion to microbial protein, excretion as urea, or passage to the lower gastrointestinal tract, where it is mainly digested by enzymes of the animal or excreted as fecal nitrogen. The proportion of the total dietary protein that is digested in the rumen varies from about 70–80 percent or more for many diets to 30–40 percent for some (Smith, in McDonald and Warner 1975). The rumen microbial protein is highly digestible and has a high biological value.

Protein breakdown

Hydrolysis of dietary proteins by mixed rumen microorganisms is quite rapid, and the amount digested appears to be closely related to the solubility of the individual protein in a mineral solution that approximates the minerals and pH in the rumen (Henderickx and Martin 1963; Smith, in McDonald and Warner 1975). Ordinarily the intermediate products of protein hydrolysis, that is, amino acids and peptides, are present in large amounts for only a short time after feeding, indicating a rapid destruction yielding ammonia or rapid fixation into microbial cells (Annison 1956).

The proteolytic enzymes have been only partially characterized. They are about equally present in rumen bacteria and protozoa (Blackburn and Hobson 1960), and the level of activity is about the same regardless of diet. The enzymes appear to be mainly cell or substrate bound since little proteolytic activity is present in rumen fluid which is centrifuged to remove microbial cells; however, the enzymes are easily liberated from microorganisms by cell disruption procedures.

Although many species of rumen bacteria are proteolytic, none of the major species so far studied are particularly active in this respect; most require carbohydrate for energy, and very few utilize amino acids as an energy source for growth. None of them are actively proteolytic or putrefactive as are organisms such as *Clostridium sporogenes*. One of the most actively proteolytic species is *Bacteroides amylophilus,* which is not able to either catabolize amino acids or utilize exogenous amino acids or peptides (Blackburn 1968).

The major products of extracellular protein hydrolysis that actually enter the microbial cell for their catabolic or anabolic metabolism are not well known. The ciliate protozoa have been seen to engulf and rapidly digest insoluble protein particles and bacterial cells and at least some ciliates can incorporate exogenous free amino acids into cellular substance. It seems possible that much of the nitrogen metabolized by the ciliates enters the cell as particulate material. In the case of bacteria, it is often assumed that protein is broken down to free amino acids before entering the cell for further metabolism; however, experiments of Warner (1955) suggested that peptides were efficiently incorporated into rumen bacterial cells. Studies on many pure cultures indicate that *Bacteroides ruminicola* is one of the most important rumen organisms in proteolysis and deamination of amino acids (Bladen et al. 1961). Pittman et al. (1967) indicated that most free amino acids cannot permeate its cells. However, peptides containing from about 4 to 20 or more amino acid residues are very rapidly utilized. The peptides enter the cell as such and then are hydrolyzed to amino acids before further metabolism occurs. Thus a considerable amount of relatively long-chain peptides is taken into rumen bacterial cells before further catabolism occurs (Wright 1967).

Amino acid catabolism

The principal end products of the catabolism of either whole protein or acid-hydrolyzed protein by mixed rumen microorganisms include ammonia, carbon dioxide, and VFA similar to those produced from carbohydrate, i.e. acetic, propionic, butyric, and n-valeric acids. In addition, the work of el-Shazly (1952) and Annison (1954) demonstrated that isobutyric, isovaleric, and D-2-methyl-n-butyric acids were produced in response to protein catabolism, and Scott et al. (1964) showed the production of *p*-hydroxyphenylacetic, phenylacetic, phenylpropionic, benzoic, and indolylacetic acids from aromatic amino acids. Skatole may also be an important product and is associated with pulmonary edema in cattle (Yokoyama and Carlson 1974).

The amounts of the total dietary amino acids metabolized in the rumen that are catabolized to these end products are not well known because the microorganisms are utilizing peptides, amino acids, and their catabolic products in synthetic reactions at the same time. However, evidence suggests that a relatively large part of the dietary amino acids are catabolized to the end products before being used in biosynthetic reactions. Portugal (1963) found very rapid degradation of ^{14}C-glutamic and aspartic acids in rumen contents, with most ^{14}C being recovered in carbon dioxide and short-chain fatty acids and little in amino acids of bacterial protein. Under similar conditions protein was being synthesized, as indicated by incorporation of ^{14}C from glucose into glutamic and aspartic acids of the protein. Other studies discussed below indicate most rumen bacteria can synthesize major cellular constituents including protein, using ammonia-nitrogen, and exogenous carbon sources such as certain VFA and organic acids, carbon dioxide, and carbohydrate; and many utilize these compounds in synthetic reactions in preference to extracellular amino acid and peptide mixtures. Also, ammonia is essential as the main nitrogen source for a significant number of bacterial species. Thus even when diets contain amino acids and peptides in amounts sufficient for rumen microbial protein synthesis, and adequate carbohydrate as an energy source for rapid protein synthesis, a considerable amount of the amino acids is catabolized to ammonia, carbon dioxide, and acids (Wright and Hungate 1967).

Work on mixed suspensions of rumen microorganisms indicated that, while proteolysis is little affected by the amount of protein in the animal's diet, the rate of deamination of hydrolyzed protein depends on the amount of readily digested protein (Warner 1956, Annison 1956). Whether this is due to induction of deaminative enzymes of the microbial population or to changes in the dominant species of microorganisms or both is not known.

The catabolism of amino acids in the rumen is carried out by both bacteria and ciliate protozoa (Allison 1970; Coleman, in McDonald and Warner 1975).

Studies on the production of ammonia from amino acids or protein hydrolysates by rumen bacteria indicate that only a few species are involved among the species predominating in mature cattle under usual conditions. *B. ruminicola* appears to be most active while selenomonads and *Megasphaera* are also active (Bladen et al. 1961). Most strains of selenomonads, *Megasphaera elsdenii*, and some strains of *B. ruminicola* are very active in production of sulfide from cysteine.

Some of the intermediates and final products of the catabolism of individual amino acids have been determined when mixed suspensions of bacteria and protozoa or bacteria alone were used. Some amino acids, such as arginine, serine, aspartic acid, threonine, cysteine, and glutamic acid, are metabolized by these suspensions at much faster rates than others (Sirotnak et al. 1953, Van Den Hende et al. 1963, Lewis 1955). El-Shazly (1952) showed that a Stickland reaction, a coupled deamination of two amino acids with one serving as a hydrogen donor and the other as a hydrogen acceptor, occurs involving proline and alanine as follows: 2 proline + alanine $+ H_2O \rightarrow 2\ \delta$-aminovalerate + acetate + CO_2 + NH_3.

Many of the amino acids appear to be deaminated via oxidative decarboxylation reactions as follows:

$$RCHNH_2COOH + 2H_2O \rightarrow RCOOH + CO_2 + NH_3 + 4H$$

Acids that are probably catabolized in this way and the corresponding carboxylic acids produced are alanine (acetate), valine (isobutyrate), leucine (isovalerate), isoleucine (D-2-methyl-n-butyrate), phenylalanine (phenylacetate), tryptophan (indolylacetate), and tyrosine (*p*-hydroxyphenylacetate). Tyrosine appears also to be further catabolized to phenylacetate, and most of it is broken down via another reaction which yields phenylpropionic acid (Scott et al. 1964). Lewis and Emery (1962) indicated further metabolism of tryptophan to indole and skatole.

Various amidases from rumen microorganisms have been studied by Warner (1964b), who found asparagine, glutamine, nicotinamide, and formamide to be rapidly attacked while acetamide and propionamide were only slowly attacked.

Formamide and glutamic acid are intermediates in the catabolism of histidine in the rumen, and glutamic acid is also catabolized, with production of ammonia, acetate, and small amounts of butyrate and propionate via mechanisms found in other anaerobic bacteria (Van Den Hende et al. 1963). Aspartic acid catabolism yields propionate, acetate, carbon dioxide, and ammonia (Sirotnak et al. 1954). Serine is actively catabolized too, with production of ammonia, carbon dioxide, and acetate; and also threonine, with similar products plus propionate (Lewis and Elsden 1955). Glycine yields ammonia, carbon dioxide, and acetate (Wright and Hungate, 1967). Lewis and Emery (1962) suggested that arginine, lysine, and proline are all degraded, with δ-aminovaleric acid being an intermediate; δ-aminovaleric acid is probably further catabolized, yielding ammonia and valeric acid.

Other nitrogen compounds

Nucleic acids or their purine and pyrimidine precursors are common constituents of ruminant diets and are produced by microorganisms, but studies of their catabolism in the rumen have been meager. Jurtshuk et al. (1958) showed the breakdown of purines by mixed bacterial suspensions, with ammonia, carbon dioxide, and acetate being major products.

Urea continually enters the rumen by crossing the rumen wall from the blood stream and in the saliva, if not as a dietary constituent, and is an important source of nitrogen for growth and protein synthesis by rumen bacteria. Pearson and Smith (1943) indicated that urea in rumen contents is rapidly broken down to ammonia and carbon dioxide by the enzyme urease and that ammonia is the nitrogen compound utilized in bacterial protein synthesis. They estimated that 40–80 g of urea per day could be converted to ammonia in a steer with 75 kg of rumen contents. The urease is synthesized by the rumen bacteria and is closely associated with cells, as differential centrifugation of rumen fluid reveals most urease activity to be associated with bacterial fractions, while little activity is found in cell-free rumen fluid, protozoal, or feed residue fractions (Gibbons and McCarthy 1957). Recent work on ruminal urease is summarized by Mahadevan et al. (1976).

Nitrate in the diet is rapidly reduced by rumen bacteria to ammonia, with nitrite being an intermediate which accumulates in the rumen under certain conditions. Nitrite is absorbed into the blood stream, where it converts hemoglobin to methemoglobin, which, if enough nitrite is present, will result in asphyxiation. Very few of the more numerous rumen bacteria reduce nitrate in pure culture; however, some strains of *S. ruminantium* reduce it with nitrite or ammonia production. Wolin et al. (1961) isolated *Vibrio succinogenes* in relatively low numbers from rumen fluid. This organism obtains energy for growth via nitrate reduction to ammonia with nitrite as an intermediate and uses hydrogen gas or formate as hydrogen donor. M. Bennick (unpublished data) recently isolated nitrate-reducing strains of *Desulfovibrio desulfuricans* from the sheep rumen.

Nitrogen compounds in microbial growth

The main extracellular nitrogen compounds utilized in the synthesis of rumen microbial protein and other cellular constituents are ammonia, amino acids, and peptides. The amounts of amino acids and peptides taken into the cells and utilized directly in synthesis of protein are about 30 percent or less of the cell nitrogen (Nolan, in McDonald and Warner 1975). A large amount of the preformed amino acids is catabolized with production of ammonia, and the ammonia is utilized as a major source of cellular nitrogen compounds. Studies of Warner (1955) and Phillipson et al. (1962) and others on incubations of rumen contents with ^{15}N ammonia showed that ammonia was a significant source of microbial protein even when supposedly adequate exogenous amino acids were available for protein synthesis. The more recent study of Portugal (1963) using ^{14}C-glutamic and ^{14}C-aspartic acids tends to confirm the ^{15}N studies in that most of the carbon of these amino acids was metabolized to VFA rather than being incorporated into amino acids of microbial protein. Studies on the nitrogen and other growth requirements of pure cultures of rumen bacteria also support the conclusions from these mixed culture studies. Bryant and Robinson (1962) found that 56 percent of 89 strains of predominating rumen bacteria that were cultured could be grown with either ammonia or enzymatically hydrolyzed protein as the nitrogen source, while ammonia was essential and the main nitrogen source for an additional 25 percent of the strains. Six percent of the strains required one or more amino acids, mainly methionine. With many strains free extracellular amino acids are not incorporated into cellular protein to a significant extent (Bryant and Robinson 1963). At least one species, *B. ruminicola,* will utilize either ammonia or peptides as the main nitrogen source but not free amino acids (Pittman and Bryant 1964), and other studies suggest that the cells are impermeable to many free amino acids but highly permeable to large peptides (Pittman et al. 1967) and to ammonia. A number of important species do efficiently utilize exogenous free amino acids as nitrogen and carbon sources (Bryant and Robinson 1963). However, exogenous peptide carbon and presumably peptide nitrogen are more efficiently converted into bacterial protein in whole rumen contents than is exogenous free amino acid carbon and nitrogen (Wright 1967).

The ciliate protozoa have limited ability to synthesize cell monomers such as amino acids and therefore utilize amino acids derived from dietary and bacterial protein, but some ammonia might be used (Coleman 1963, 1967, and in McDonald and Warner 1975).

Carbon sources in protein synthesis

Many of the rumen bacteria that efficiently utilize or require ammonia as the main nitrogen source require and/or efficiently utilize carbon sources, in addition to the carbohydrate energy source, in reactions leading to synthesis of amino acids and other important cellular constituents. Carbon dioxide is fixed into a large number of amino acids and into nucleic acid (Allison and Bryant 1963, Otagaki et al. 1955), and large amounts of acetate are used in synthesis of amino acids and long-chain fatty acids (Allison et al. 1966). Of particular interest are certain of the monocarboxylic acids that are produced by some rumen organisms which form certain amino acids via oxidative decarboxylation, yielding monocarboxylic acid, carbon dioxide, and ammonia (see above). Other rumen bacteria utilize pathways in reverse of these catabolic reactions in synthesis of the corresponding amino acid: $RCOOH + CO_2 + NH_3 + 4H \rightarrow RCHNH_2COOH + 2H_2O$. Amino acids synthesized in this general manner include leucine, isoleucine, valine, tryptophan, and phenylalanine; the acids of isovalerate, 2-methylbutyrate, isobutyrate, indoleacetate, and phenylacetate respectively are involved (Allison et al. 1966). Whether other amino acids are synthesized in this manner has not yet been studied. These acids are important in that many species of rumen bacteria require one or more of them for growth (Bryant and Robinson 1962).

Thus, while few rumen bacteria require amino acids for growth, the organic acids produced by the oxidative decarboxylation of certain amino acids, acetic acid, carbon dioxide, and carbohydrate are very important carbon sources for growth. And most species of rumen bacteria are involved in amino acid and protein synthesis and utilize ammonia nitrogen.

Other metabolic functions

The sulfur requirements of mixed rumen microorganisms for synthesis of essential cellular compounds such as cysteine and methionine can be supplied in the diet as inorganic sulfate (Loosli et al. 1949). However, only a few species of rumen bacteria appear to be capable of utilizing sulfate as the sulfur source (Emery et al. 1957). This apparent discrepancy is probably due to the fact that sulfate and sulfur are rapidly reduced to sulfide by some of the bacteria in rumen contents (Anderson 1956), since many rumen bacteria can synthesize all essential cellular sulfur compounds using sulfide.

Few studies are available on species of rumen bacteria capable of dissimilatory sulfate reduction, that is, sulfate reduction in which large emounts of sulfide are produced, as opposed to assimilatory sulfate reduction in which sulfate is reduced and incorporated into cellular sulfur compounds but excess sulfide is not produced. Emery et al. (1957) found small amounts of sulfate to be reduced and incorporated into organic sulfur compounds by a few species, but this was apparently of the assimilatory type, as little or no sulfide was produced from sulfate.

In studies on dissimilatory sulfate reduction by mixed rumen bacteria, Lewis (1954) showed that sulfate was reduced when hydrogen, glucose, lactate, pyruvate, formate, succinate, and a number of other compounds were added as hydrogen donors. Several recent studies show that *Desulfovibrio desulfuricans* is the main species involved.

The amino acids cysteine and methionine are other sources of sulfide.

Most of the bacteria can utilize sulfide, but not more oxidized forms of sulfur, as the sole source of sulfur. Although most species do not require organic sulfur compounds for growth, many strains of *Bacteroides ruminicola* require methionine and cysteine (Pittman and Bryant 1964), and some *Lactobacillus bifidus* strains require methionine (Gibbons and Doetsch 1959).

Rumen microorganisms have a great effect on dietary lipids (Garton 1961). Glycerides and phospholipids are hydrolyzed, and the glycerol is fermented mainly to propionic acid (Johns 1953).

The dietary fatty acids and those liberated by lipolysis in the rumen are not broken down; however, the unsaturated fatty acids such as linolenic, linoleic, and oleic acids are extensively hydrogenated by both bacterial and protozoal fractions of rumen contents (Chalupa and Kutches 1968). The fatty acids hydrogenated may be partially converted to the *trans* form, and shifts occur in the position of the double bond (Shorland et al. 1957).

Bacteria synthesize large quantities of long, odd-numbered-carbon, straight-chain and odd- and even-numbered-carbon, and branched-chain fatty acids which are important constituents of their phospholipds (Keeney et al. 1962). Some rumen bacteria are unable to synthesize these acids from carbohydrate or amino acid carbon but require acids such as n-valeric, isovaleric, 2-methylbutyric, or isobutyric. For example, *B. succinogenes* requires n-valeric acid and isobutyric acid for growth (Bryant and Doetsch 1955), and these acids are utilized mainly to synthesize *n*-pentadecanoic acid and isotetradecanoic acid respectively (Wegner and Foster 1963).

Ruminant body and milk fats tend to have larger amounts of saturated fatty acids, unsaturated fatty acids with double bonds in unusual positions, *trans* isomers of unsaturated fatty acids, branched-chain fatty acids, and odd-numbered-carbon straight-chain fatty acids than fats from nonruminant animals. These differences reflect the activities of rumen microorganisms.

The ruminant does not have any dietary requirement for vitamins of the B complex or vitamin K, after the rumen fermentation becomes developed in the young animal, because of their synthesis by rumen microorganisms (Porter 1961, Barnett and Reid 1961).

Bacterial species rather than protozoa are important in the synthesis of B vitamins, and most of the more numerous bacterial species contribute to their synthesis.

Most species require few vitamins. The most commonly required vitamin is biotin, and *p*-aminobenzoic acid is required by many. Smaller numbers require pyridoxine, vitamin B_{12}, folic acid, riboflavin, or thiamin. The B_{12} requirement of some is replaced by methionine.

Bacteroides ruminicola requires heme for growth and utilizes this compound for synthesis of a cytochrome (White et al. 1962).

BACTERIA

While adequate characterization of the functions of rumen bacteria involves the isolation of individual species in pure culture, direct microscopic studies have given valuable information on the effects of various factors such as the feeding regime on total numbers and on certain morphologically distinguishable groups of bacteria (Moir and Masson 1952, Warner 1962b). Microscopic studies have also given good information on the morphological forms of bacteria involved in decomposition of structural cellulose (Baker and Harris 1947) and starch (Baker et al. 1951) and have served as a useful guide in pure culture studies of morphologically distinct bacterial species. Fluorescent antibody techniques have helped identify and enumerate bacteria in rumen fluid after isolation of cultures so that antisera against certain serological types can be prepared (Jarvis et al. 1967).

Culture

Many species of bacteria present in the rumen are not functional but are merely casual passengers brought in with the food (Sijpesteijn 1948), and other species may be functional but be present in insignificant numbers (for example, *Streptococcus bovis* is very active in digestion of starch but often represents only 1 percent or less of the total starch-digesting bacteria).

Criteria used in determining an organism's significance in the rumen have been discussed by many authors (Bryant 1959). The most important criteria are that the organism be shown to grow in the rumen in significant numbers and have a metabolism compatible with rumen reactions and with the rumen environment.

It was not until about 1947 that unqualified success was obtained in growing pure cultures of functional bacteria (Hungate 1950, Sijpesteijn 1948). Hungate used culture media similar in composition to the rumen environment (i.e. habitat-stimulating media). The media contained agar and minerals including ammonium ions and bicarbonate, so that with a CO_2 gaseous phase a pH of about 6.7 was obtained. Sterile rumen fluid was added as a source of growth factors; finely dispersed cellulose was added as energy source; and the oxidation-reduction potential was kept low by adding small amounts of the reducing agents cysteine or sodium sulfide. Hungate showed that many colonies of noncellulolytic bacteria as well as cellulolytic bacteria developed on such media and that very high colony counts could be obtained when noncellulosic substrates such as glucose were used.

Two general types of culture media are now in use, including media more or less selective for enumeration and isolation of specific groups of bacteria, and relatively nonselective media for total viable counts and isolation of a wide variety of species. Although many different nonselective media have been used, those most successful in terms of the variety of species cultured with high and precise colony counts are anaerobic rumen fluid agar media similar to that of Hungate (1950), but with small amounts of glucose, cellobiose, and sometimes maltose, starch, or xylose added as energy sources in place of cellulose (Bryant 1959). One such rumen fluid-glucose-cellobiose-starch agar medium (Bryant and Robinson 1961) is used to grow most of the carbohydrate-fermenting bacteria that have been isolated in large numbers. Organisms which fail to grow on this medium include *Methanobacterium ruminantium* (Smith and Hungate 1958), which requires more extreme anaerobic conditions than most rumen bacteria and also requires hydrogen gas or formate as an oxidizable energy source, and other bacteria such as the lipolytic, glycerol-fermenting *Anaerovibrio lipolytica* (Hobson and Mann 1961) and lactate-fermenting *Veillonella alcalescens*, which do not utilize glucose, cellobiose, or starch as energy sources.

For the most part, only rather crude culture media have been developed for the selective or differential enumeration and isolation of species or physiological groups of rumen bacteria. Most of these media are selective only as to the main energy source, and they usually support considerable growth of other bacteria. Also, where rumen fluid has not been added, the failure of workers to add growth factors such as certain VFA and heme would not allow growth of some very numerous bacterial species within certain physiological groups (Caldwell and Bryant 1966). For further references to cultures see Hungate et al. (1964).

Species

The rumen contains a great variety of bacteria, many species of which are usually present in large numbers. For example, Moir and Masson (1952) catalogued 33 different types on the basis of microscopic observations alone; 29 genera and 63 species were mentioned in one of the more comprehensive reviews (Bryant 1959). Most of the predominant species are nonsporeforming anaerobes, although sporeforming anaerobes are occasionally found, and bacteria not requiring anaerobic conditions for growth, such as *Streptococcus bovis* and species of the genus *Lactobacillus*, are sometimes quite numerous (Hungate et al. 1964). Enteric bacteria such as *E. coli* and salmonellae represent a very small fraction of the total population and cannot be maintained in large numbers at least partially because of inhibition by free VFA (Wolin 1969). Also, the pathogenic sporeforming anaerobe, *Clostridium perfringens* type D, cannot be maintained and is rapidly destroyed when large numbers of cells are inoculated into the rumen, but the few cells which reach the small intestine multiply rapidly (Bullen et al. 1953).

Tables 23.2 and 23.3 show a few characteristics of some of the bacterial groups which are important components of the rumen flora. More detailed references to these and other species and methods of identification are given in reviews (Bryant 1959, 1963; Hungate et al. 1964). Most of the bacteria utilize one or more types of the major ruminant dietary carbohydrates as an energy source for growth. Others utilize the simpler carbohydrate hydrolytic products of these or major end products of the carbohydrate metabolism such as lactate, formate, or hydrogen (Table 23.2). Thus there is considerable overlapping of functions among the various bacterial species (also between bacterial and protozoal species). Because of this overlapping, it seems doubtful that the loss of any one or of a few microbial species from the rumen would have a deleterious effect on the host.

Another point of interest concerning the general properties of rumen bacteria is the degree of versatility in compounds utilized as energy sources. Some species are quite specific; for example, *Methanobacterium ruminantium* obtains its energy by reduction of carbon dioxide and utilizes only hydrogen gas or formate, and *Bacteroides amylophilus* obtains energy for growth only from starch and its hydrolytic products, dextrins and maltose. A number of other species such as *Bacteroides succinogenes, Ruminococcus* sp., and *Lachnospira multiparus* utilize only a limited number of energy sources. However, a number of the more numerous species are quite versatile. *Butyrivibrio fibrisolvens* and *Bacteroides ruminicola* strains often ferment saponin, grass levan, and many other sugars, glycosides, and polysaccharides in addition to those indicated in Table 23.3, and *Selenomonas ruminantium* ferments many of these carbohydrates. Some strains also ferment glycerol and lactate. Few of the species are able to utilize amino acids or peptides as the main source of energy for growth, and none are known to oxidize fatty acids.

Some rather large and morphologically distinct bacteria which are commonly seen on microscopic examination of rumen contents have not yet been studied in pure culture, so that little knowledge of their metabolism and function is available. These include *Oscillospira*, Quinn's oval, and "window pane" sarcina (Moir and Masson 1952). *Oscillospira* is a large cigar-shaped multicellular motile organism which has been enumerated by a number of workers (Warner 1962b, Eadie 1962a).

Table 23.3. Characteristics of anaerobic rumen bacteria

Species	Shape	Motility †	Gram stain	Energy sources *					
				Glucose	Cellulose	Xylan	Starch	Lactate	Glycerol
Bacteroides succinogenes	Rods to coccoid, sometimes pointed ends and curved, no chains	−	−	+	+	−	∓	−	−
Ruminococcus flavefaciens	Cocci, usually in chains	−	±	∓	±	±	−	−	−
Ruminococcus albus	Cocci, usually single and diplo	−	±	∓	±	±	−	−	−
Butyrivibrio fibrisolvens	Small curved rods, often chains and filaments	+ mono-trichous	−	+	∓	±	±	−	−
Eubacterium ruminantium	Small rods often coccoid	−	+	+	−	±	−	−	−
Bacteroides ruminicola	Long rods to coccoid, some chains	−	−	+	−	±	±	−	−
Bacteroides amylophilus	Rods to coccoid	−	−	−	−	−	+	−	−
Selenomonas ruminantium	Curved rods, crescentic	+ tufts, often attached concave side of cell	−	+	−	−	±	∓	∓
Lactobacillus vitulinus	Long to short rods, some branched	−	+	+	−	−	−	−	−
Streptococcus bovis ‡	Coccus, short chain	−	+	+	−	−	+	−	−
Lachnospira multiparus	Rods, curved, chains and filaments	+ mono-trichous	±	+	−	− pectin	∓	−	−
Succinimonas amylolytica	Short rod to oval	+ mono-trichous	−	+	−	−	+	−	−
Fusobacterium necrophorum	Rod to coccoid, some filaments	−	−	+	−	−	−	+	+
Succinivibro dextrinosolvens	Small curved rods, pointed ends	+ mono-trichous	−	+	−	−	−	−	−
Treponema sp.	Typical spirochete	+	−	+	−	−			
Megasphaera elsdenii	Large cocci in pairs to long chains	−	−	+	−	−	−	+	±
Veillonella alcalescens	Small cocci irregular masses	−	−	−	−	−	−	+	−
Methanobacterium ruminantium	Small oval rods in chains	−	+	− hydrogen or formic acid	−	−	−	−	−
Anaerovibrio lipolytica	Small curved rods	+ mono-trichous	−	− lipolytic	−	−	−	−	+

* +, all strains ferment; ±, most strains ferment; ∓, less than half ferment
† Also, type of flagellation where known
‡ Not a strict anaerobe.
See Hungate et al. 1964 for references.

Quinn's oval is a large yeastlike bacterium which is motile and divides by binary fission. It is commonly found in quite large numbers in sheep but has not been found in cattle.

Occurrence

Many of the predominant bacterial species have been found only in the rumen; however, the exacting anerobic culture procedures used for their isolation have not been extensively applied to many other anaerobic microbial habitats. Present information suggests that many similar or identical species are present in other habitats such as the gastrointestinal tract of nonruminant mammals, organic sediments of natural waters, and sewage sludge. Strains of the genus *Butyrivibrio* have been isolated from human, rabbit, and horse feces (Brown and Moore 1960). Cellulolytic ruminococci were found in the rabbit (Hall 1952) and guinea pig cecum. The guinea pig cecum also contains spirochetes culturally similar to the rumen *Treponema* sp. *M. ruminantium* was isolated from sewage sludge and human feces. *Selenomonas* species cultured from the rat cecum and the rumen are similar. Similar organisms are seen in intestinal contents of other mammals (Lessel and Breed 1954) and in river water. Definitive studies on human oral and fecal *Bacteroides* species (Loesche et al. 1964) suggest that *Bacteroides oralis* is very closely related to *B. ruminicola*.

In young ruminants

The development of a bacterial flora in young ruminants typical of that found in adult animals begins at a very young age. The nature and rate of development are greatly affected by the diet and to some extent by isolation from ruminants harboring organisms typical of the mature animal (Pounden and Hibbs 1950, Bryant and Small 1960, Eadie et al. 1959). Under relatively normal conditions where milk was fed through 9 weeks of age and alfalfa hay and grain feeding started at 10 days of age, Bryant et al. (1958) found the predominant culturable bacteria of 1-to-3-week-old calves to be most different from those of mature cattle. At 6 weeks of age, many groups of bacteria typical of mature animals were among the predominant bacteria, but several groups not found in mature animals remained. At 9–13 weeks of age, bacteria isolated were mostly typical of those in mature cattle on similar diets. Total culture counts of calves at all of these ages are in the range found for mature animals or higher. However, culture counts on specific groups of bacteria vary with age.

Cellulolytic bacteria were present in appreciable numbers in some calves at 1 week of age; numbers were similar to those of mature cattle at 3 weeks. This finding is of particular interest because the calves at 1 week received no cellulosic material except straw bedding. It indicates that the rumen fluid was an excellent enrichment medium. The relatively large numbers do not indicate particularly active growth and metabolism since the fluid is probably in a somewhat stagnant condition and even a low growth rate would maintain the numbers. Lactate-fermenting bacteria are present in very high numbers at 1 and 3 weeks, as are bacteria such as coliforms that are capable of growth under aerobic conditions. The large number of lactate-fermenters such as *M. elsdenii* in calves at about 3 weeks of age is correlated with large numbers of anaerobic lactate-producing lactobacilli and often with low pH of rumen contents and relatively high intake of grain as compared to hay (Eadie et al. 1959, Bryant et al. 1958). Strict isolation of calves from adult ruminants can delay the establishment of a completely normal bacterial flora (Bryant and Small 1960), but isolation has a much more drastic effect upon the ciliate protozoa. The ciliates may not become established in young ruminants unless they are maintained in close contact with animals harboring them or are inoculated. The presence or absence of ciliates has little effect on the establishment of the normal bacteria except that total numbers of bacteria are much higher in lambs and calves without ciliates than with ciliates (Bryant and Small 1960, Eadie and Hobson 1962). It seems unlikely that under any practical farm condition lack of appropriate rumen bacterial species would be a primary cause of poor health or growth in young ruminants.

Mann (1963) was able to isolate small numbers of *Ruminococcus, Veillonella, Eubacterium, S. bovis,* and *Lactobacillus* sp. from air in a cowshed, so airborne transfer is possible.

Dietary and other factors

The total number of bacteria per unit weight or volume as determined by direct microscopic studies is usually about 15–80 billion per ml. It varies depending on the diet, the feeding regime, the time after feeding, the individual animal, and the presence of ciliate protozoa.

However, the number of bacteria per unit weight of rumen contents may give little idea as to their total activity in the rumen because rumen ingesta volumes may vary a great deal under different feeding regimes, and metabolic activity per unit of cells can vary greatly depending on factors such as the growth rate. Also, the amounts of bacteria and rumen ingesta passing on to the abomasum are probably quite variable. The numbers of bacteria in the contents leaving the rumen need not be directly related to the numbers per unit weight of whole rumen contents (Bryant and Robinson 1968).

Numbers of bacteria per gram of rumen contents tend to be higher in animals fed on green pastures than in those fed dry rations (Gall et al. 1949, Moir 1951). Animals fed dry rations containing very high levels of starch concentrates tend to have larger numbers of viable rumen bacteria. When ciliate protozoa are absent, the bacterial population is considerably increased (Eadie and Hobson 1962), and particularly high viable counts of bacteria are obtained during high-grain feeding when the ciliate protozoa may be missing (Bryant et al. 1961). The effect of rate and method of feeding upon diurnal variation in the numbers of bacteria and ruminal function was studied by Moir and Somers (1957). In one of the few well-designed series of experiments that have been carried out, Moir and Harris (1962) showed that, when nitrogen intake was the only variable in a semipurified diet fed to sheep, bacterial counts and cellulose digestion were both positively and significantly correlated with nitrogen intake. Similar studies showed that, with low nitrogen levels in the diet, addition of starch depressed bacterial counts.

The direct microscopic studies of Warner (1962b), in which most microbial groups were counted, indicated that the level of roughage has little effect on numbers or kinds of microorganisms per unit volume of rumen contents except where it is fed in very low amounts. This study also indicated the magnitude of variations to be expected between animals and in the same animal on different days when a constant diet of roughage is fed; the effect of starvation on the microorganisms; and the great variation in time required for appearance of certain microorganisms after they disappear due to starvation.

The effect of the animal's diet on the proportional distribution of the small, metabolically more important, rumen bacteria of various species has received some study (e.g. Bryant et al. 1960, 1961). Because most of these bacteria can be enumerated and identified only by isolation and study of some of their characteristics in pure culture, a large amount of work is necessary to obtain good information even from one sample of rumen contents. A few generalizations can be made from studies on cattle. Certain species usually represent from about 1 to 30 percent of the culturable bacteria over a wide range of diets, such as hay only, hay-grain, silage, lush pasture, wheat straw, or diets consisting mainly of grain. These species include *Butyrivibrio fibrisolvens, Bacteroides ruminicola,* and others which are quite versatile in fermenting carbohydrates, and less versatile bacteria such as the cellulolytic organisms, *Bacteroides succinogenes* and the genus *Ruminococcus*. The relatively large numbers of these cellulolytic species in the rumen of cattle fed mainly grain are probably explained by the fact that cellulose is more slowly metabolized than starch, and would represent a larger proportion of microbial energy throughout the day than one might expect from the feed composition. Some species are a substantial percentage of the total only under certain conditions. For example, *Lachnospira multiparus* is usually 2 percent or less of the total but was 21 percent of isolates when cattle were pastured on clover having a high pectin content. *Succinivibrio dextrinosolvens* and *Megasphaera elsdenii* exist in large numbers in cattle fed large amounts of grain. In studies on animals fed similar diets, much greater variation in bacterial species between animals and between samples taken on different days occurs when diets consisting mainly of grain are fed as compared to diets containing considerable roughage. When sheep are rapidly changed from a high roughage diet to one consisting mainly of starch or sugars, a very rapid change in the flora and fauna occurs and the animal may develop acute indigestion. The sequence of change may vary somewhat, but usually the normal bacterial flora, ciliate fauna, and VFA are greatly depressed, and at the same time a great increase in *Streptococcus bovis,* lactic acid, ethanol, and hydrogen ion concentration occurs (Hungate et al. 1952, Krogh 1961, Allison et al. 1964). At a later stage, the streptococci rapidly fall in numbers, and lactobacilli become the dominant organisms. Allison et al. (1964) indicated that inoculation of the rumen with large amounts of fresh rumen contents of sheep conditioned to a diet containing a large amount of cracked wheat reduced the symptoms of acute indigestion in sheep which were abruptly switched to a cracked-wheat diet. This suggests that the more normal flora adapt to high-grain feeding if the switch from roughage to grain is not too rapid.

PROTOZOA

Species

Many different species of protozoa are active in the rumen. Ciliates usually represent the bulk of the microfauna, and very little has been done to enumerate or accumulate metabolic information on the flagellates or other species found (Becker and Talbot 1927). Flagellate species are often observed in the rumen and may be more numerous in young animals before the ciliate population becomes established (Eadie 1962a).

Most of the functional ciliates belong in one of two families: *Isotrichidae,* commonly called the holotrichs, and *Ophryoscolecidae,* commonly called the oligotrichs. There is considerable disagreement on the taxonomy of genera in the latter (Hungate 1966), but the holotrichs are represented by the genus *Isotricha* and the genus *Dasytricha*. These ciliates are superficially similar to paramecium, being more or less egg-shaped and having a cell surface covered with cilia.

The oligotrichs are represented by a great variety of species which exhibit a variety of sizes, shapes, and organelles. Some of them are the most morphologically complex of all ciliates. These ciliates are oval to elongate in shape and possess no cilia other than an adoral zone or both adoral and dorsal zones of brushlike membranelles. Although the different genera overlap somewhat in size, the genus *Entodinium,* with a mouth surrounded by a single adoral zone of membranelles, is the smallest, varying in size from about 22 by 40 μ to about 60 by 80 μ. Other genera of oligotrichs, including *Diplodinium, Epi-*

dinium, and *Ophyroscolex,* possess both adoral and dorsal zones of membranelles. In *Diplodinium* the dorsal zone is at or very near the anterior end, while in *Epidinium* the cell is more elongate, with the dorsal zone of membranelles back somewhat from the anterior end. One of the most obvious differences between these and *Ophryoscolex* is that in the latter the dorsal zone of membranelles surrounds about four fifths of the circumference of the cell somewhat anterior of the middle.

In the voluminous literature on rumen protozoa, many other generic names for ciliate protozoa are found. Most of these are often considered to be subgenera of the genus *Diplodinium* (Hungate 1966).

Culture

The growth of the rumen ciliate protozoa in culture media free from contaminating bacteria has not been completely successful (Coleman 1963, in McDonald and Warner 1975; Hungate 1966). Hungate (1943) was the first to successfully culture species of *Entodinium* and *Diplodinium* for long periods of time in the presence of bacteria. However, the techniques are very laborious.

Suspensions of protozoa for metabolic studies have been readily obtained by differential sedimentation from rumen fluid and washing to rid them of most bacteria (Oxford 1955, Hungate 1966), and bacterial metabolism can be kept to a minimum by including antibiotics in the suspensions. Because of the difference in size and density, the ciliates can be relatively easily freed of most bacteria, but separation of single species of ciliates from other ciliates may be very difficult. Eadie and Oxford (1957) found that sheep can be maintained free of ciliates by avoiding direct contact with animals harboring ciliates. The ciliates can be removed from the rumen by various procedures (Hungate 1966) but the simplest method appears to be by the use of aerosol OT (dioctylsodiumsulfosuccinate) (Abou-Akkada et al. 1968). One can then establish, by inoculation, single species of ciliates in the rumen. With animals containing the single species of ciliate, it is a relatively easy task to separate the ciliate from bacteria.

Metabolism

All of the rumen ciliate protozoa are strict anaerobes and obtain their energy by fermentation of carbohydrates, with the production of acetic, butyric, and lactic acids, carbon dioxide, and hydrogen gas. Small amounts of propionic acid are sometimes detected, and the holotrichs appear to produce more lactic acid and less volatile acid than others. All species produce large amounts of starch-like reserve polysaccharide during fermentation of exogenous carbohydrate, and this material is catabolized to the same end products as the exogenously supplied carbohydrates, but apparently at a slower rate (Oxford 1955). The holotrichs are particularly active in synthesizing the reserve polysaccharide, which has been identified as amylopectin.

The types of carbohydrate fermented vary with the individual species, but in general the holotrichs are concerned more with fermentation of soluble carbohydrates. However, *Isotricha* species ferment starch grains if they are small enough to be swallowed, although *Dasytricha* do not. The holotrichs probably compete with bacteria for soluble carbohydrates to a much greater extent than the other ciliates.

Species of oligotrichs have either a limited ability or no ability to ferment exogenously supplied soluble carbohydrates and are mainly restricted to fermentation of the carbohydrate in particulate material. Most of these species attack starch granules, and, although some species are very restricted in the number of carbohydrates fermented, many species ferment polysaccharides, such as pectin and hemicellulose, that are present in plant fragments, and cellulose is fermented by some species (Hungate 1966).

All of the ciliates engulf bacteria, and bacteria and particulate proteins in the animal's feed probably serve as the main source of nitrogen for growth (Coleman, in McDonald and Warner 1975).

Occurrence

In contrast to most rumen bacteria, the ciliate protozoa do not become established in young ruminants unless they have relatively direct contact with animals harboring ciliates (Eadie 1962a). This is in part because none of the rumen ciliates produce cysts or other resistant forms that remain viable when exposed to air or other adverse conditions for long periods. Also, rumen ciliates appear to be found only in ruminants, so that, in contrast to some rumen bacterial species, they cannot be obtained from natural sources other than rumen ingesta or materials such as saliva freshly contaminated with rumen ingesta.

Very little is known concerning the factors affecting the numbers or kinds of ciliates present in the rumen (Warner 1962a, Eadie 1962b), and animals maintained under similar conditions may have quite different faunas. The pH of rumen ingesta is quite important. Purser and Moir (1959) found few or no ciliates in the rumen when pH values of about 5.5 or lower were maintained for a considerable part of the day. This is often associated with the feeding of high levels of starch or sugar. According to Eadie, the pH of rumen contents is the most important factor in the establishment of ciliates inoculated into young ruminants. When rations are fed in ground form, few or no protozoa may be found, especially at a high level of intake (Christiansen et al. 1964). This is presumably due to both a greater acidity and a faster rate of passage of materials from the rumen. More frequent feeding results in larger numbers (Moir and Somers 1957). Antibiotics such as chlortetracycline, tylosin, or penicillin in the ration may also cause an increase in the protozoa (Purser et al. 1965, Bryant et al. 1961, Mann et al. 1954).

Significance

At least under some dietary regimes, the ciliate protozoa are quite beneficial to the host animal. The reasons for this are not yet clear, but results suggest that increases in digestibility and efficiency of utilization of organic matter and protein, and increased VFA production (especially of propionic and/or butyric acids) are important factors. The dietary conditions under which ciliates produce their maximum beneficial effect are little understood but appear to be those in which a considerable amount of grain is included in the diet and in which nitrogen content is relatively low.

Becker et al. (1930) indicated little or no effect on young ruminants raised without ciliate protozoa or in those from which ciliates were removed. However, Pounden and Hibbs (1950) and Eadie (1962a) found unfaunated calves to have rougher coats and to be more potbellied than controls. In most experiments, few animals were used, and in many the experimental design was not adequate to show small but significant differences in weight gains or other parameters.

In more recent studies of faunated and defaunated animals, the faunated animals have shown better average daily gains (Abou-Akkada and el-Shazly 1964, Christiansen et al. 1965) and better nitrogen retention (Abou-Akkada and el-Shazly 1965). Klopfenstein et al. (1966) suggested that the value of ciliate protozoa regarding nitrogen retention depends on the diet. With a low-nitrogen diet, faunated sheep retained significantly more nitrogen, whereas with a ration containing higher nitrogen, defaunated animals retained more nitrogen. When the ciliates are present, rumen ammonia levels are consistently higher (Klopfenstein et al. 1966). The reported effects of VFA produced have been variable, but some workers have reported higher VFA levels when ciliates are present (Christiansen et al. 1965) and increased propionate (Abou-Akkada and el-Shazly 1964), propionate and butyrate (Christiansen et al. 1965), or butyrate (Klopfenstein et al. 1966), and often lower proportions of acetate. Christiansen et al. (1965) indicated lower pH, and some studies suggest more extensive hydrogenation of fatty acids in faunated animals (Klopfenstein et al. 1966). The latter workers showed clearly that digestibility of dry matter and nitrogen was greater in faunated sheep as compared to defaunated sheep when high energy rations were fed, but no difference was evident when a relatively lower energy ration was fed.

The mixed protozoal-bacterial protein may be of better quality than bacterial protein alone in digestibility (McNaught et al. 1954) as well as in amino acid distribution (Holmes et al. 1953). With protozoa present, less of the feed protein may be converted to nitrogen compounds such as those present in nucleic acids (Oxford 1955) and cell-wall compounds, which are relatively high in bacteria and not efficiently used by the animal (Ellis and Pfander 1965). While the biological value of bacterial and protozoal protein is similar, the digestibility of protozoal protein is higher (Bergen et al. 1968a,b).

Regardless of whether bacteria can completely replace the ciliate protozoa in an efficient rumen fermentation, the volume of protozoa (see Table 23.1) is usually such that they must be of significance. Hungate (1955) estimated that, although numbers and kinds of ciliate protozoa in the rumen vary greatly, they may account for about 20 percent of the protein requirement and a similar amount of the acid fermentation products available to the animal.

REFERENCES

Abou-Akkada, A.R., Bartley, E.E., Berube, R., Fina, L.R., Meyer, R.M., Henricks, D., and Julius, F. 1968. Simple method to remove completely ciliate protozoa of adult ruminants. *Appl. Microbiol.* 16:1475–77.

Abou-Akkada, A.R., and el-Shazly, K. 1964. Effect of absence of ciliate protozoa from the rumen on microbial activity and growth of lambs. *Appl. Microbiol.* 12:384–90.

——. 1965. Effect of presence or absence of rumen ciliate protozoa on some blood constituents, nitrogen retention, and digestibility of food constituents in lambs. *J. Ag. Sci.* 64:251–55.

Alexander, J.K., and Sheth, K. 1967. Cellulodextrin phosphorylase from *Clostridium thermocellum*. *Biochim. Biophys. Acta* 148:808–10.

Allison, M.J. 1970. Nitrogen metabolism in rumen microorganisms. In A.T. Phillipson, ed., *Physiology of Digestion and Metabolism in the Ruminant*. Oriel, Newcastle upon Tyne. Pp. 456–73.

Allison, M.J., and Bryant, M.P. 1963. Biosynthesis of branched-chain amino acids from branched-chain fatty acids by rumen bacteria. *Arch. Biochem. Biophys.* 101:269–77.

Allison, M.J., Bucklin, J.A., and Dougherty, R.W. 1964. Intraruminal inoculation and adaptation to grain. *J. Anim. Sci.* 23:1164–71.

Allison, M.J., Bucklin, J.A., and Robinson, I.M. 1966. Importance of the isovalerate carboxylation pathway of leucine biosynthesis in the rumen. *Appl. Microbiol.* 14:807–14.

Anderson, C.M. 1956. The metabolism of sulfur in the rumen of the sheep. *New Zealand J. Sci. Tech.*, ser. A, 37:379–94.

Annison, E.F. 1954. Some observations on the volatile fatty acids in the sheep's rumen. *Biochem. J.* 57:400–405.

——. 1956. Nitrogen metabolism in the sheep: Protein digestion in the rumen. *Biochem. J.* 64:705–14.

Ayers, W.A. 1958. Phosphorylation of cellobiose and glucose by *Ruminococcus flavefaciens*. *J. Bact.* 76:515–17.

Bailey, R.W., and Howard, B.H. 1963. Carbohydrases of the rumen ciliate *Epidinium ecaudatum* (Crawley). II. α-galactosidase and isomaltase. *Biochem. J.* 87:146–51.

Baker, F., and Harris, S.T. 1947. Microbial digestion in the rumen (and caecum) with special reference to the decomposition of structural cellulose. *Nutr. Abstr. Rev.* 17:3–12.

Baker, F., Nasr, H., Morrice, F., and Bruce, J. 1951. Bacterial breakdown of structural starch and starch products in the digestive tract of ruminant and non-ruminant mammals. *J. Path. Bact.* 62:617–38.

Baldwin, R.L., Wood, W.A., and Emery, R.S. 1963. Conversion of glucose-C^{14} to propionate by the rumen microbiota. *J. Bact.* 85:1346–49.

Barker, H.A. 1956. *Bacterial Fermentations*. Wiley, New York.

Barnett, A.J.G., and Reid, R.L. 1961. *Reactions in the Rumen*. Edward Arnold, London.

Becker, E.R., Schultz, J.A., and Emmerson, M.A. 1930. Experiments on the physiological relationships between the stomach infusoria of ruminants and their hosts, with bibliography. *Iowa State Coll. J. Sci.* 4:215–41.

Becker, E.R., and Talbott, M. 1927. The protozoan fauna of the rumen and reticulum of American cattle. *Iowa State Coll. J. Sci.* 1:345–71.

Bentley, O.G., Johnson, R.R., Hershberger, T.V., Cline, J.H., and Moxon, A.L. 1955. Cellulolytic-factor activity of certain short-chain fatty acids for rumen microorganisms in vitro. *J. Nutr.* 57:389–400.

Bergen, W.G., Purser, D.B., and Cline, J.H. 1968a. Determination of limiting amino acids of rumen isolated proteins fed to rats. *J. Dairy Sci.* 51:1698–1700.

——. 1968b. Effect of ration on the nutritive quality of rumen microbial protein. *J. Anim. Sci.* 27:1497–1501.

Blackburn, T.H. 1968. Protease production by *Bacteroides amylophilus* strain H18. *J. Gen. Microbiol.* 53:27–36.

Blackburn, T.H., and Hobson, P.N. 1960. Proteolysis in the sheep rumen by whole and fractionated rumen contents. *J. Gen. Microbiol.* 22:272–81.

Blackburn, T.H., and Hungate, R.E. 1963. Succinic acid turnover and propionate production in the bovine rumen. *Appl. Microbiol.* 11:132–35.

Bladen, H.A., Bryant, M.P., and Doetsch, R.N. 1961. A study of bacterial species from the rumen which produce ammonia from protein hydrolyzate. *Appl. Microbiol.* 9:175–80.

Brown, D.W., and Moore, W.E.C. 1960. Distribution of *Butyrivibrio fibrisolvens* in nature. *J. Dairy Sci.* 43:1570–74.

Bryant, M.P. 1959. Bacterial species of the rumen. *Bact. Rev.* 23:125–53.

——. 1963. Symposium on microbial digestion in ruminants: Identification of groups of anaerobic bacteria active in the rumen. *J. Anim. Sci.* 22:801–13.

——. 1973. Nutritional requirements of the predominant rumen cellulolytic bacteria. *Fed. Proc.* 32:1809–13.

Bryant, M.P., Barrentine, B.F., Sykes, J.F., Robinson, I.M., Shawver, C.B., and Williams, L.W. 1960. Predominant bacteria in the rumen of cattle on bloat-provoking ladino clover pasture. *J. Dairy Sci.* 43:1435–44.

Bryant, M.P., and Doetsch, R.N. 1955. Factors necessary for the growth of *Bacteroides succinogenes* in volatile acid fraction of rumen fluid. *J. Dairy Sci.* 38:340–50.

Bryant, M.P., and Robinson, I.M. 1961. An improved non-selective culture medium for ruminal bacteria and its use in determining diurnal variation in numbers of bacteria in the rumen. *J. Dairy Sci.* 44:1446–56.

——. 1962. Some nutritional characteristics of predominant culturable ruminal bacteria. *J. Bact.* 84:605–14.

—— 1963. Apparent incorporation of ammonia and amino acid carbon during growth of selected species of ruminal bacteria. *J. Dairy Sci.* 46:150–54.

——. 1968. Effects of diet, time after feeding, and position sampled on numbers of viable bacteria in the bovine rumen. *J. Dairy Sci.* 51:1950–55.

Bryant, M.P., Robinson, I.M., and Lindahl, I.L. 1961. A note on the flora and fauna in the rumen of steers fed a feedlot bloat-provoking ration and the effect of penicillin. *Appl. Microbiol.* 9:511–15.

Bryant, M.P., and Small, N. 1960. Observations on the ruminal microorganisms of isolated and inoculated calves. *J. Dairy Sci.* 43:654–68.

Bryant, M.P., Small, N., Bouma, C., and Robinson, I.M. 1958. Studies on the composition of the ruminal flora and fauna of young calves. *J. Dairy Sci.* 41:1747–67.

Bullen, J.J., Scarisbrick, R., and Maddock, A. 1953. Enterotoxaemia of sheep: The fate of washed supensions of *Cl. welshii* type D introduced into the rumen of normal sheep. *J. Path. Bact.* 65:209–19.

Burchall, J.J., Niederman, R.A., and Wolin, M.J. 1964. Amino group formation and glutamate synthesis in *Streptococcus bovis*. *J. Bact.* 88:1038–44.

Caldwell, D.R., and Bryant, M.P. 1966. Medium without rumen fluid for nonselective enumeration and isolation of rumen bacteria. *Appl. Microbiol.* 14:794–801.

Chalupa, W., and Kutches, A.J. 1968. Biohydrogenation of linoleic-1-^{14}C acid by rumen protozoa. *J. Anim. Sci.* 27:1502–08.

Christiansen, W.C., Kawashima, R., and Burroughs, W. 1965. Influence of protozoa upon rumen acid production and liveweight gains in lambs. *J. Anim. Sci.* 24:730–35.

Christiansen, W.C., Woods, W., and Burroughs, W. 1964. Ration characteristics influencing rumen protozoal population. *J. Anim. Sci.* 23:984–88.

Coleman, G.S. 1963. The growth and metabolism of rumen ciliate protozoa. In P.S. Nutman and B. Mosse, eds., *Symbiotic Associations*. Cambridge U. Press, Cambridge. Pp. 298–324.

——. 1967. The metabolism of free amino acids by washed suspensions of the rumen ciliate *Entodinium caudatum*. *J. Gen. Mcrobiol.* 47:433–47.

Eadie, J. 1962a. The development of rumen microbial populations in lambs and calves under various conditions of management. *J. Gen. Microbiol.* 29:563–78.

——. 1962b. Inter-relationships between certain rumen ciliate protozoa. *J. Gen. Microbiol.* 29:579–88.

Eadie, J., and Hobson, P.N. 1962. Effect of the presence or absence of rumen ciliate protozoa on the total rumen bacterial count in lambs. *Nature* 193:503–05.

Eadie, J.M., Hobson, P.N., and Mann, S.O. 1959. A relationship between some bacteria, protozoa, and diet in early weaned calves. *Nature* 183:624–25.

Eadie, J., and Oxford, A.E. 1957. A simple and safe procedure for the removal of holotrich ciliates from the rumen of an adult fistulated sheep. *Nature* 179:485.

Ellis, W.C., and Pfander, W.H. 1965. Rumen microbial polynucleotide synthesis and its possible role in ruminant nitrogen utilization. *Nature* 205:974–75.

el-Shazly, K. 1952. Degradation of protein in the rumen of the sheep. II. The action of rumen microorganisms on amino acids. *Biochem. J.* 51: 647–53.

Emery, R.S., Smith, C.K. and Fai To, L. 1957. Utilization of inorganic sulfate by rumen microorganisms. II. The ability of single strains of rumen bacteria to utilize inorganic sulfate. *Appl. Microbiol.* 5:363–66.

Gall, L.S., Burroughs, W., Gerlaugh, P., and Edgington, B.H. 1949. Rumen bacteria in cattle and sheep on practical farm rations. *J. Anim. Sci.* 8:441–49.

Garton, G.A. 1961. Influence of the rumen on the digestion and metabolism of lipids. In D. Lewis, ed., *Digestive Physiology and Nutrition of the Ruminant*. Butterworth, London. Pp. 140–51.

Gibbons, R.J., and Doetsch, R.N. 1959. Physiological study of an obligately anaerobic ureolytic bacterium. *J. Bact.* 77:417–28.

Gibbons, R.J., and McCarthy, R.D. 1957. Obligately anaerobic urea-hydrolyzing bacteria in the bovine rumen. *U. Md. Ag. Exp. Sta. Misc. Pub.* no. 291, 12–16.

Gray, F.V. 1947. The extent of cellulose digestion at successive levels of the alimentary tract. *J. Exp. Biol.* 24:15–19.

Gray, F.V., Pilgrim, A.F., Rodda, H.J., and Weller, R.A. 1952. Fermentation in the rumen of the sheep. IV. The nature and origin of the volatile fatty acids in the rumen of the sheep. *J. Exp. Biol.* 29:57–65.

Hajny, G.J., and E.T. Reese. 1968. *Cellulases and Their Applications*. American Chemical Society, Washington.

Hall, E.R. 1952. Investigations on the microbiology of cellulose utilization in domestic rabbits. *J. Gen. Microbiol.* 7:350–57.

Heald, P.J. 1951. The assessment of glucose containing substances in rumen microorganisms during a digestive cycle in sheep. *Brit. J. Nutr.* 5:84–93.

Henderickx, H., and Martin, J. 1963. In vitro study of the nitrogen metabolism in the rumen. *Comptes rend. rech. Inst. Rech. Sci. Ind. Ag. Bruxelles,* no. 31.

Hobson, P.N., and Mann, S.O. 1961. The isolation of glycerol-fermenting and lipolytic bacteria from the rumen of the sheep. *J. Gen. Microbiol.* 25:227–40.

Holmes, P., Moir, R.J., and Underwood, E.J. 1953. Ruminal flora studies in the sheep. V. The amino acid composition of rumen bacterial protein. *Austral. J. Biol. Sci.* 6:637–44.

Howard, B.H., Jones, G., and Purdom, M.P. 1960. The pentosanases of some rumen bacteria. *Biochem. J.* 74:173–80.

Hungate, R.E. 1943. Further experiments on cellulose digestion by the protozoa in the rumen of cattle. *Biol. Bull.* 84:157–63.

——. 1950. The anaerobic mesophilic cellulolytic bacteria. *Bact. Rev.* 14:1–49.

——. 1955. The ciliates of the rumen. In S.H. Hutner and A. Lwoff, eds., *Biochemistry and Physiology of Protozoa.* Academic Press, New York. Vol. 2, 159–79.

——. 1966. *The Rumen and Its Microbes.* Academic Press, New York.

——. 1967. Hydrogen as an intermediate in the rumen fermentation. *Arch. Mikrobiol.* 59:158–64.

Hungate, R.E., Bryant, M.P., and Mah, R.A. 1964. The rumen bacteria and protozoa. *Ann. Rev. Microbiol.* 18:131–66.

Hungate, R.E., Dougherty, R.W., Bryant, M.P., and Cello, R.M. 1952. Microbiological and physiological changes associated with acute indigestion in sheep. *Cornell Vet.* 42:423–49.

Hungate, R.E., Phillips, G.D., McGregor, A., Hungate, D.P., and Buechner, H.K. 1959. Microbial fermentation in certain mammals. *Science* 130:1192–94.

Hungate, R.E., Smith, W., Bauchop, T., Yu, I., and Rabinowitz, J.C. 1970. Formate as an intermediate in the bovine rumen fermentation. *J. Bact.* 102:389–97.

Iannotti, E.L., Kafkewitz, D., Wolin, M.J., and Bryant, M.P. 1973. Glucose fermentation products of *Ruminococcus albus* grown in continuous culture with *Vibrio succinogenes:* Changes caused by interspecies transfer of H_2. *J. Bact.* 114:1231–40.

Isaacson, H.R., Hinds, F.C., Bryant, M.P., and Owens, F.N. 1975. Efficiency of energy utilization by mixed rumen bacteria in continuous culture. *J. Dairy Sci.* 58:1645–59.

Jarvis, B.D.W., Williams, V.J., and Annison, E.F. 1967. Enumeration of cellulolytic cocci in sheep rumen by using a fluorescent antibody technique. *J. Gen. Microbiol.* 48:161–70.

Jayasuriya, G.C.N., and Hungate, R.E. 1959. Lactate conversion in the bovine rumen. *Arch. Biochem. Biophys.* 82:274–87.

Johns, A.T. 1953. Fermentation of glycerol in the rumen of sheep. *New Zealand J. Sci. Tech.,* ser. A, 35:262–69.

Jurtshuk, P., Doetsch, R.N., and Shaw, J.C. 1958. Anaerobic purine dissimilation by washed suspensions of bovine rumen bacteria. *J. Dairy Sci.* 41:190–202.

Keeney, M., Katz, I., and Allison, M.J. 1962. On the probable origin of some milk fat acids in rumen microbial lipids. *J. Am. Oil Chem. Soc.* 39:198–201.

Kleiber, M. 1953. Biosynthesis of milk constituents by the intact dairy cow studied with C^{14} as tracer. In C.L. Comar, ed., *Atomic Energy Ag. Res.* (Oak Ridge), TID5115. P. 253.

Klopfenstein, T.J., Purser, D.B., and Tyznik, W.J. 1966. Effects of defaunation on feed digestibility, rumen metabolism, and blood metabolites. *J. Anim. Sci.* 25:765–73.

Krogh, N. 1959. Studies on alterations in the rumen fluid of sheep, especially concerning the microbial population when readily available carbohydrates are added to the food. I. Sucrose. *Acta Vet. Scand.* 1:74–97.

——. 1961. Studies on alterations in the rumen fluid of sheep, especially concerning the microbial composition, when readily available carbohydrates are added to the food. III. Starch. *Acta Vet. Scand.* 2:103–19.

Lessel, E.R., and Breed, R.S. 1954. *Selenomonas* Boskamp, 1922: A genus that includes species showing an unusual type of flagellation. *Bact. Rev.* 18:165–69.

Lewis, D. 1951. The metabolism of nitrate and nitrite in the sheep. II. Hydrogen donators in nitrate reduction by rumen microorganisms *in vitro. Biochem. J.* 49:149–53.

——. 1954. The reduction of sulfate in the rumen of the sheep. *Biochem. J.* 56:391–99.

——. 1955. Amino acid metabolism in the rumen of the sheep. *Brit. J. Nutr.* 9:215–21.

Lewis, D., and Elsden, S.R. 1955. The fermentation of L-threonine, L-serine, L-cysteine, and acrylic acid by a gram-negative coccus. *Biochem. J.* 60:683–91.

Lewis, T.R., and Emery, R.S. 1962. Metabolism of amino acids in the bovine rumen. *J. Dairy Sci.* 45:1487–91.

Loesche, W.J., Socransky, S.S., and Gibbons, R.J. 1964. *Bacteroides oralis,* proposed new species isolated from the oral cavity of man. *J. Bact.* 88:1329–37.

Loosli, J.K., Williams, H.H., Thomas, W.E., Ferris, F.H., and Maynard, L.A. 1949. Synthesis of amino acids in the rumen. *Science* 110:144–45.

Mahadevan, S., Sauer, F., and Erfle, J.D. 1976. Studies on bovine rumen bacterial urease. *J. Anim. Sci.* 42:745–53.

Mann, S.O. 1963. Some observations on the airborne dissemination of rumen bacteria. *J. Gen. Microbiol.* 33:ix.

Mann, S.O., Masson, F.M., and Oxford, A.E. 1954. Effect of feeding aureomycin to calves upon the establishment of their normal rumen microflora and microfauna. *Brit. J. Nutr.* 8:246–52.

McDonald, I.W., and Warner, A.C.I. 1975. *Digestion and Metabolism in the Ruminant.* U. of New England Pub. Unit, Armidale, Austral.

McNaught, M.L., Owen, E.C., Henry, K.M., and Kon, S.K. 1954. The utilization of non-protein nitrogen in the bovine rumen. VIII. The nutritive value of the proteins of preparations of dried rumen bacteria, rumen protozoan and brewers yeast for rats. *Biochem. J.* 56:151–56.

Miller, T.L., and Wolin, M.J. 1973. Formation of hydrogen and formate by *Ruminococcus albus. J. Bact.* 116:836–46.

Moir, R.J. 1951. The seasonal variation in the ruminal microorganisms of grazing sheep. *Austral. J. Ag. Res.* 2:322–30.

Moir, R.J., and Harris, L.E. 1962. Ruminal flora studies in the sheep. X. Influence of nitrogen intake upon ruminal function. *J. Nutr.* 77:285–98.

Moir, R.J., and Masson, M.J. 1952. An illustrated scheme for the microscopic identification of the rumen microorganisms of sheep. *J. Path. Bact.* 64:343–50.

Moir, R.J., and Somers, M. 1957. Ruminal flora studies. VIII. The influence of rate and method of feeding a ration upon its digestibility, upon ruminal function, and upon the ruminal population. *J. Ag. Res.* 8:253–65.

Opperman, R.A., Nelson, W.O., and Brown, R.E. 1961. *In vivo* studies of methanogenesis in the bovine rumen: Dissimilation of acetate. *J. Gen. Microbiol.* 25:103–11.

Otagaki, K.K., Black, A.L., Goss, H., and Kleiber, M. 1955. In vitro studies with rumen microorganisms using carbon-14-labeled casein, glutamic acid, leucine, and carbonate. *J. Ag. Food Chem.* 3:948–51.

Oxford, A.E. 1955. The rumen ciliate protozoa: Their chemical composition, metabolism requirements for maintenance and culture, and physiological significance for the host. *Exp. Parasit.* 4:569–605.

Pearson, R.M., and Smith, J.A.B. 1943. The utilization of urea in the bovine rumen. II. The conversion of urea to ammonia. *Biochem. J.* 37:148–53.

Phillipson, A.T., Dobson, M.J., Blackburn, T.H., and Brown, M. 1962. The assimilation of ammonia nitrogen by bacteria of the rumen of sheep. *Brit. J. Nutr.* 16:151–66.

Pittman, K.A., and Bryant, M.P. 1964. Peptides and other nitrogen sources for growth of *Bacteroides ruminicola. J. Bact.* 88:401–10.

Pittman, K.A., Lakshmanan, S., and Bryant, M.P. 1967. Oligopeptide uptake by *Bacteroides ruminicola. J. Bact.* 93:1499–1508.

Porter, J.W.G. 1961. Vitamin synthesis in the rumen. In D. Lewis, ed., *Digestive Physiology and Nutrition of the Ruminant*. Butterworth, London. Pp. 226–34.

Portugal, A.V. 1963. Some aspects of protein and amino acid metabolism in the rumen of the sheep. Ph.D. thesis, U. of Aberdeen.

Pounden, W.D., and Hibbs, J.W. 1950. The development of calves raised without protozoa and certain other characteristic rumen microorganisms. *J. Dairy Sci*. 33:639–44.

Prescott, J.M. 1961. Utilization of sulfur compounds by *Streptococcus bovis*. *J. Bact*. 82:724–28.

Purser, D.B., Klopfenstein, T.J., and Cline, J.H. 1965. Influence of tylosin and aureomycin upon rumen metabolism and the microbial population. *J. Anim. Sci*. 24:1039–44.

Purser, D.B., and Moir, R.J. 1959. Ruminal flora studies in the sheep. IX. The effect of pH on the ciliate population of the rumen in vivo. *Austral. J. Ag. Res*. 10:555–64.

Robinson, I.M., and Allison, M.J. 1975. Transfer of *Acholeplasma bactoclasticum* Robinson and Hungate to the genus *Anaeroplasma* (*Anaeroplasma bactoclasticum* [Robinson and Hungate] comb nov.): Emended description of the species. *Internat. J. Syst. Bact*. 25:182–86.

Satter, L.D., Suttie, J.W., and Baumgardt, B.R. 1964. Dietary induced changes in volatile fatty acid formation from α-cellulose-C^{14} and hemicellulose-C^{14}. *J. Dairy Sci*. 47:1365–70.

Scheifinger, C.C., and Wolin, M.J. 1973. Propionate formation from cellulase and soluble sugars by combined cultures of *Bacteroides succinogenes* and *Selenomonas ruminantium*. *Appl. Microbiol*. 26:789–95.

Scott, T.W., Ward, P.F.V., and Dawson, R.M.C. 1964. The formation and metabolism of phenyl-substituted fatty acids in the ruminant. *Biochem. J*. 90:12–24.

Shorland, F.B., Weenink, R.O., Johns, A.T., and McDonald, I.R.C. 1957. The effect of sheep rumen contents on unsaturated fatty acids. *Biochem. J*. 67:328–33.

Sijpesteijn, A.K. 1948. Cellulose-decomposing bacteria from the rumen cattle. Ph.D. thesis, U. of Leiden.

Sirotnak, F.M., Doetsch, R.N., Brown, R.E., and Shaw, J.C. 1953. Amino acid metabolism of bovine rumen bacteria. *J. Dairy Sci*. 36:1117–23.

Sirotnak, F.M., Doetsch, R.N., Robinson, R.E., and Shaw, J.C. 1954. Aspartate dissimilation reactions of rumen bacteria. *J. Dairy Sci*. 37:531–37.

Smith, P.H., and Hungate, R.E. 1958. Isolation and characterization of *Methanobacterium ruminantium n. sp*. *J. Bact*. 75:713–18.

Smith, P.H., Sweeney, H.C., Rooney, J.R., King, K.W., and Moore, W.E.C. 1956. Stratifications and kinetic changes in the ingesta of the bovine rumen. *J. Dairy Sci*. 39:598–609.

Taylor, C.D., and Wolfe, R.S. 1974. Structure and methylation of coenzyme M ($HSCH_2CH_2SO_3$). *J. Biol. Chem*. 249:4879–85.

Van Den Hende, C., Oyaert, W., and Bouckaert, J.H. 1963. The metabolism of amino acids by rumen bacteria. *Comptes rend. rech. Inst. Rech. Sci. Ind. Ag. Bruxelles*, no. 31.

Wallnöfer, P., Baldwin, R.L., and Stagno, E. 1966. Conversion of C^{14}-labeled substrates to volatile fatty acids by the rumen. *Appl. Microbiol*. 14:1004–10.

Warner, A.C.I. 1955. Some aspects of the nitrogen metabolism of the microorganisms of the rumen with special reference to proteolysis. Ph.D. thesis, U. of Aberdeen.

——. 1956. Proteolysis by rumen microorganisms. *J. Gen. Microbiol*. 14:749–62.

——. 1962a. Some factors influencing the rumen microbial population. *J. Gen. Microbiol*. 28:129–46.

——. 1962b. Enumeration of rumen microorganisms. *J. Gen. Microbiol*. 28:119–28.

——. 1964a. Production of volatile fatty acids in the rumen: Methods of measurement. *Nutr. Abstr. Rev*. 34:339–52.

——. 1964b. The breakdown of asparagine, glutamine, and other amides by microorganisms from the sheep rumen. *Austral. J. Biol. Sci*. 17:170–82.

Wegner, G., and Foster, E.M. 1963. Incorporation of isobutyrate and valerate into cellular plasmalogen by *Bacteroides succinogenes*. *J. Bact*. 85:53–61.

Weller, R.A., and Pilgrim, A.F. 1974. Passage of protozoa and volatile fatty acids from the rumen of the sheep and from a continuous in vitro fermentation system. *Brit. J. Nutr*. 32:341–51.

White, D.C., Bryant, M.P., and Caldwell, D.R. 1962. Cytochrome-linked fermentation in *Bacteroides ruminicola*. *J. Bact*. 84:822–28.

Wolin, M.J. 1960. A theoretical rumen fermentation balance. *J. Dairy Sci*. 43:1452–59.

——. 1969. Volatile fatty acids and the inhibition of *Escherichia coli* growth by rumen fluid. *Appl. Microbiol*. 17:83–87.

Wolin, M.J., Wolin, E.A., and Jacobs, N.J. 1961. Cytochrome-producing anaerobic vibrio, *Vibrio succinogenes, sp. n*. *J. Bact*. 81:911–17.

Wright, D.E. 1961. Bloat in cattle. XIX. The metabolism of pectin by rumen microorganisms. *New Zealand J. Ag. Res*. 4:203–15.

——. 1967. Metabolism of peptides by rumen microorganisms. *Appl. Microbiol*. 15:547–50.

Wright, D.E., and Hungate, R.E. 1967. Metabolism of glycine by rumen microorganisms. *Appl. Microbiol*. 15:152–57.

Yokoyama, M.T., and Carlson, J.R. 1974. Dissimilation of tryptophan and related indolic compounds by ruminal microorganisms in vitro. *Appl. Microbiol*. 27:540–48.

CHAPTER 24

Physiopathology of the Ruminant Digestive Tract | By Robert W. Dougherty

Functional aspects of the ruminant digestive tract cannot be fully understood without knowledge of some of the disturbances that lead to malfunction and changes in intermediary metabolism. Several of these conditions will be discussed here from a physiological standpoint.

TRAUMATIC RETICULITIS

This common disease is due to the ingestion of sharp metallic or nonmetallic objects by grazing and stall-fed animals. The incidence is compounded by the nondiscriminatory eating habits of cattle and the carelessness of man.

Symptoms occur as localized peritonitis or inflammation that develops around the area of perforation. The position and shape of the foreign object and the occurrence in late pregnancy and during parturition cause increased abdominal pressure and are thought to be contributing factors responsible for the penetration of foreign objects through the wall of the reticulum. Foreign objects of high specific gravity usually localize in the reticulum. This is due in part to the complicated nature of normal ruminoreticular motility. If the foreign object perforates and migrates to other organs, the disease can become extremely complicated and severe.

The blood picture of this disease was first studied by Dougherty (1939), who, after completing normal blood studies of fistulated cows, forced nails and wires through the wall of the reticulum. He noted that blood cytological changes occurred in 4 hours and that in 72 hours the blood pictures were beginning to return to their normal levels. The blood cell changes included a neutrophilic leukocytosis, with the band cells showing the greatest increase in numbers. Although these changes were distinct, they were not as marked as the leukocyte changes in man suffering from localized peritonitis; however, they are of definite diagnostic value. In severe experimentally induced traumatic pericarditis there was an increase in the erythrocyte sedimentation rate, and nucleated red cells were found in circulating blood. In most instances a pronounced eosinophilia developed.

Arthur (1946) studied clinical cases and confirmed some of the above conclusions. Kingrey (1955) gave capsules containing sharpened foreign bodies to cattle. Besides confirming the earlier blood studies, he included other facets of study such as heart rate, respiratory rate, grain and hay consumed, rumen contractions, milk produced, character of feces, and height of thoracic spine. Although he did not know the exact time of penetration, the results were fairly uniform with the other studies.

A number of seldom-mentioned facts relating to traumatic gastritis are worth discussing. First, the bacteria of the rumen, although they are technically not pathogens, can cause alarming lesions and symptoms when released into body cavities or tissues. Second, the usual decrease in rumen motility may soon shift to relatively normal motility *except near the point of foreign body penetration*. This rather remarkable reflex has an obvious and important purpose, that is, to immobilize the involved anatomical structures so that adhesions may circumscribe the infected area.

A number of methods of diagnosis have been described: examination of the blood picture, study of the pain reflex from the xiphoid region, X-ray examination of the area in and around the reticulum, use of magnets and metal detectors (Van Hoosen and Isham 1958).

Sharp foreign objects may penetrate the wall of the reticulum, or they may be found lying loose in the lumen of this compartment where they are a constant threat to the animal's health. This points to the recurring nature of the disease.

It has been observed (Dougherty 1939, Sharpe et al. 1969) that adult cattle can build up appreciable immunity to their own microflora. To produce pronounced cytological blood changes takes several months after rumen fistulas have been established surgically, or until the blood picture has returned to normal levels and the relatively transient partial immunity has subsided.

Mullenax et al. (1964) investigated the possibility of lung contamination by rumen microorganisms during the normal eructation process. Marker organisms were placed in the rumen and samples were taken from the trachea, the lungs, and the feces of one cow. seven sheep, and three goats. Two organisms not common to the environment of the rumen were used as markers, *E. coli* BT-3 bacteriophage and spores of *B. subtilis* var. niger. Both bacteriophage and *B. subtilis* organisms were recovered from the trachea and lungs in some but not all cases. That organisms can be carried to the trachea and lungs during normal eructation presents some intriguing possibilities and may be a mechanism by which ruminants build up partial immunity to their own microflora.

HYPOCALCEMIA

Pronounced atony of the ruminant digestive tract, whether primary or secondary, is a noticeable symptom of hypocalcemia and can be relieved very soon after intravenous injections of calcium have been initiated. Conversely, it has been demonstrated (Ringarp 1964) that the use of drugs which stimulate motility of the digestive tract in hypocalcemia-prone cows near parturition time may prevent the occurrence of hypocalcemia. Ringarp postulates that proper motility of the digestive tract is essential for absorption of adequate amounts of calcium. This important observation needs further conformation. If atony develops in these animals near parturition time, what is the direct cause of digestive tract stasis?

Boda and Cole (1954) suggested that the incidence of milk fever is reduced by feeding a low-calcium high-phosphorus diet to preparturient cows. Recent work (Goings et al. 1974) has shown that a low-calcium intake one or two weeks before parturition will reduce the incidence of hypocalcemia. It is postulated that the low-calcium intake at this time will stimulate mobilization of calcium from the bones, a process thought to be inhibited at or near parturition time.

GRAIN ENGORGEMENT SYNDROME

Studies of grain engorgement in ruminants were begun about 1940 by Turner and Hodgetts in Australia and reported annually from 1943 to 1959. Dougherty and Cello (1949) found that 3–4 pounds of grain (wheat, corn, rye, as well as starch and sugar) placed in the rumen of fistulated sheep would cause extreme sickness in 12 hours and death in 20–30 hours. In some lots of sheep nearly all of the animals died; in others, morbidity was high and mortality was low. There was a rapid decrease in pH of rumen ingesta, a disappearance of protozoa, and the presence of large amounts of lactic acid in the rumen ingesta. Symptoms in the experimentally engorged animals included ruminal stasis, abdominal distress, progressive dehydration, tachycardia, hemoconcentration, weakness, coma, and death in a large percentage of the overfed animals. If death did not occur in 20–30 hours, diarrhea and laminitis became prominent symptoms.

Two schools of thought have developed on the pathogenesis of engorgement toxemia. One group of workers (Dougherty and Cello 1952, Hungate et al. 1952, Dain et al. 1955) has expanded the hypothesis that toxins are formed in the rumen as the result of the presence of large amounts of available carbohydrates, changes in hydrogen ion concentration, and pronounced changes in rumen microbes. Rumen ingesta from overfed ruminants have been shown to be more toxic than that obtained from normal animals. Mullenax et al. (1966) demonstrated that bacterial endotoxins originating in the rumen have pronounced physiopathological effects when injected into normal animals. The other school of thought (Turner and Hodgetts 1943–1959, Dunlop 1961, Ryan 1964a,b) believes that the pathological effects due to grain engorgement are due mainly to the formation of large amounts of lactic acid in the rumen and the subsequent acidosis and other effects on intermediary metabolism. A preponderance of D(−) lactic acid has been demonstrated in the rumen ingesta of grain-engorged animals (Bond 1959).

Bond (1959) approached the acid indigestion syndrome from the standpoint of the ratio of D(−) and L(+) isomers of lactic acid, assuming that the D(−) form was not as readily metabolized. Later Dunlop (1961), using quantitative enzymatic methods, demonstrated that the lactic acid that accumulates in the rumen is a mixture of D(−) and L(+) isomers. The excess lactate that accumulates in the blood of overfed animals is largely the unnatural D(−) isomer. The D(−) lactate is slowly metabolized in cattle, whereas L(+) lactate is rapidly converted to pyruvate when it is introduced into the blood.

Turner and Hodgetts (1943–1959) found that grain engorgement also causes a pronounced hemoconcentration and that intravenous injections of isotonic saline may partially alleviate the symptoms of overeating toxemia.

As in many studies where opinions are divergent, both hypotheses may eventually be shown to be applicable, and no single theory may be adequate.

PRODUCTION OF TOXIC MATERIALS IN THE RUMEN

Quin (1929) and Sapiro et al. (1949) have shown that nitrates can be converted to nitrites and that severe intoxication (methemoglobinemia) may develop when nitrite concentrations reach high levels in the rumen and blood. The diet of the animals influenced the rate of reduction of intraruminal nitrates; lucerne and glucose accelerated the reaction until a high concentration of nitrites was reached.

The release of hydrocyanic acid from cyanogenic glucosides has been demonstrated by Van der Wath (1944) and Coop and Blakely (1949). Certain plants may become poisonous in this manner, while others such as birdsfoot trefoil are relatively harmless under natural feeding and grazing conditions. Dougherty and Christensen (1953) demonstrated that the plant juice extracted by pressure from six pounds of freshly cut birdsfoot trefoil was lethal when injected into the rumen of sheep. Under natural grazing conditions birdsfoot trefoil has not been known to be harmful.

It was shown by Dougherty and Lindahl (1957) that a significant reduction in blood volume in sheep has a marked effect in reducing motility of the ruminant digestive tract. The same effect may be induced by a significant reduction in functional hemoglobin.

PARAKERATOSIS OF THE RUMEN IN SHEEP

Jensen et al. (1958) described a hardening and enlargement of the rumen papillae, characterized microscopically by the accumulation of excessive layers of keratinized, nucleated squamous epithelial cells on the papillae. The keratinized areas are dark, almost black in appearance. These changes were associated with the feeding of pelleted rations.

Lindahl and Dougherty (1958) divided a large amount of good quality alfalfa hay into two equal parts. One part was pelleted, and the other half of the hay was coarsely chopped. Extreme care was exercised to prevent the addition of chlorinated hydrocarbons to the pelleted hay.

After feeding on the pelleted and chopped hay for several months, some of both groups of sheep were killed so that certain tissues could be examined grossly and histologically. All of the pellet-fed group had areas of keratinized papillae in the ventral part of the rumen. No lesions were seen in the group that was fed chopped hay.

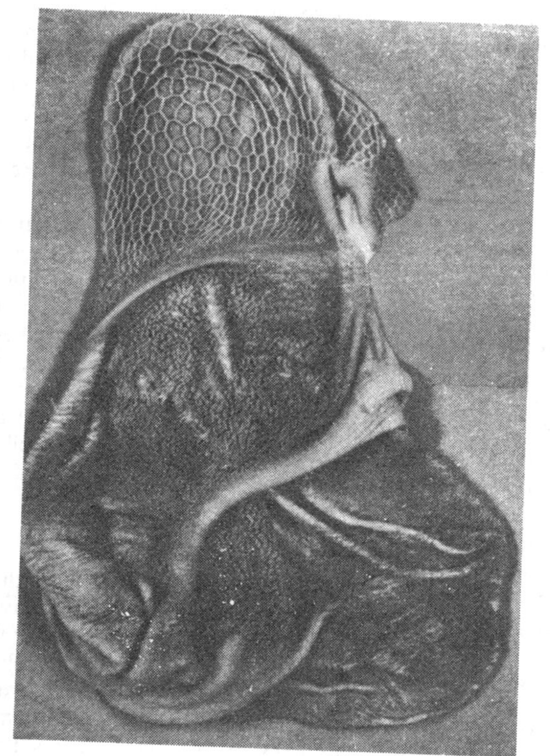

Figure 24.1. Reticulum and rumen of a normal sheep

Figure 24.2. Reticulum and rumen of a pellet-fed sheep. Note differences in the pillars and pigmentation of mucosa from those of the control in Figure 24.1.

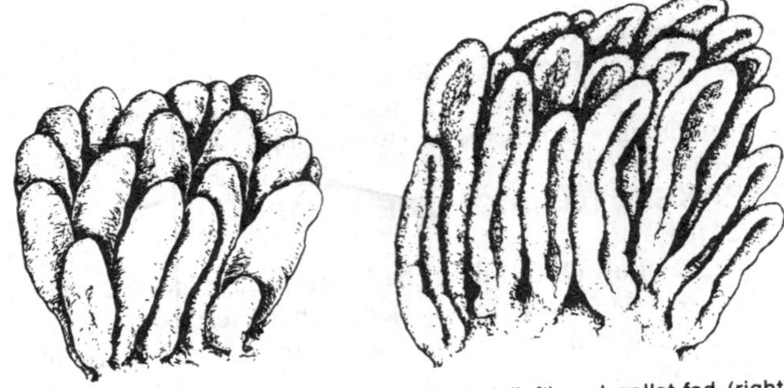

Figure 24.3. Rumen papillae from control (left) and pellet-fed (right) sheep. (Drawn by Marian Newson.)

The anterior pillar of the pellet-fed sheep seemed less well developed (Figs. 24.1, 24.2, 24.3). Changes occurred in the shape and length of the rumen papillae (Fig. 24.3).

Although the causes are unknown, it is of considerable interest to know that changes in the character of the feed and not the chemical composition may cause such changes. Harris (1964), using Ayrshire calves, stated that during the early development of parakeratosis volatile fatty acid (VFA) absorption is increased, but as the condition becomes more severe, VFA absorption decreases. However, the difficulties encountered in measuring VFA absorption quantitatively throw some doubt on the validity of the results obtained in the above experiments.

RUMENITIS

Jensen et al. (1954) reported that cattle transferred from a roughage ration to a high concentrate in a relatively short time developed significantly more rumenitis than animals in which the change was effected more slowly. Areas in the rumen wall showed vesication, necrosis, depapillation, hyperemia, and edema. When ulcerated areas healed, considerable scar tissue was evident. The exact etiology is unknown. These lesions reduce absorptive efficiency, permit facultative pathogens to enter the portal circulation, and cause liver abscesses.

ACUTE TYMPANY

Gas production in the ruminoreticulum proceeds at a high rate, is greater on some feeds than others, and is usually more rapid soon after eating. Hungate et al. (1955) have estimated that a 500 kg animal with 70 kg of rumen contents produced slightly more than 2 liters of gas per minute. If this gas can be released from countless bubbles so that it can accumulate in the dorsal part of the ruminoreticulum, and if the eructation mechanism is functioning normally, even these large amounts of gas are in no way deleterious.

McArthur and Miltimore (1961), using gas-solid chromatography, listed rumen gas in the following percentages: 65.35 CO_2, 26.76 CH_4, 7.00 N_2, 0.56 O_2, 0.18 H_2, and 0.01 H_2S. These relative amounts are subject to appreciable variations under different dietary regimes. Rumen gases are produced by bacterial metabolism and by release of carbon dioxide from salivary bicarbonate.

Rumen gas is eliminated by eructation, by absorption from the digestive tract, and by excretion with the feces. Normally, eructation occurs at the rate of 1–3 times per minute. The frequency of eructation is dependent upon the rate of gas formation.

Acute tympany or bloat results from inefficient gas elimination. Since a large proportion of the rumen-reticulum gas is eliminated by belching, a study of this physiological mechanism should enhance understanding of the bloat problem.

Dougherty et al. (1958, 1962a,b), Dougherty and Cook (1962), and Dougherty and Habel (1955) have studied eructation in sheep and in cattle. Since the mechanism is described elsewhere in this text, only those features that are related to bloat will be discussed in this chapter.

An area of the mucosa around the cardia contains receptors (Dougherty et al. 1958) which, when covered with water, ingesta, or foam, will initiate the eructation-inhibition reflex. This means that with the ruminoreticulum full of ingesta, a complex and coordinated type of motility of the rumen and reticulum must occur to clear this area of ingesta so that eructation can occur. If gas pockets exist over the ingesta, a type of movement must also be initiated which will move the gas located in the caudal part of the dorsal sac forward to the area around the cardia which has just been cleared. Weiss (1953b) first described this antiperistaltic movement of the rumen. It was later confirmed by Titchen and Reid (1965).

In many instances gas accumulates as foam with little or almost no gas existing in pockets. Bloat has been variously described as being due to the high soluble protein content of the rumen (Mangen 1959), to mucin in saliva (Van Horn and Bartley 1961), to insufficient amounts of saliva (Weiss 1953a), to bacterial slime, to the high saponin content of ingested plants (Lindahl et al. 1954), to specific eructation inhibitors (Dougherty et al. 1958), to lack of fiber in the plants (Cole and Kleiber 1948), to genetic weaknesses (Hancock 1953), and to other reasons. In general it might be said that there is no single cause, but rather bloating and foaming may be due to various factors and combinations of factors.

Studies of the eructation mechanism led to the finding that a large proportion of the normally eructated gas is recycled into the lungs and that certain components of the gas are absorbed (Dougherty et al. 1962b). Eructation then may influence milk flavor (Dougherty and Shipe 1960) and may contribute to certain pathological conditions of the lungs (Mullenax et al. 1964). It has been found (Dougherty et al. 1967) that $^{14}CO_2$, when given into the rumen in gaseous form, appears in the blood 4–5 seconds after an eructation, and radioactivity may soon be found in many tissues including the lactose fraction of milk.

Methane is absorbed principally from the lungs. Dougherty et al. (1967) demonstrated that methane introduced as $^{14}CH_4$ is metabolized by sheep. The amounts metabolized are too small to be considered as an important factor in energy metabolism.

EFFECTS OF ANTIBIOTICS

Turner and Hodgetts (1952) reported that chlortetracycline depressed digestion in adult sheep through its effects on the microflora of the rumen. Others reported that small doses had beneficial effects on calves (Bartley et al. 1951) and lambs (Jordan and Bell 1951), but not when fed to older animals (Bell et al. 1951). Later Barrentine et al. (1956) administered procaine penicillin to cattle on bloat-provoking pastures and prevented bloat. This was accomplished by producing changes in the microflora that did not significantly decrease digestion or milk production. Since microflora sometimes became resistant to the specific antibiotics, it was necessary to use other antibiotics alternately.

This work suggests that antibiotics can alter the microflora of the rumen and that, if used over prolonged periods, they might be deleterious to the health and productivity of ruminants.

EFFECTS OF RADIATION INJURY

The potential health hazard to ruminants grazing on pastures or ranges contaminated by radioactive fallout has been demonstrated experimentally by Sasser et al. (1969).

^{90}Y-labeled sand particles (88–176 μ), a fallout simulant with a specific activity of 5–12 mCi/g, were mixed with alfalfa pellets and fed to lambs weighing 30 kg for three days at the rate of 2.4 mCi/kg of body weight. Anorexia, diarrhea, and pyrexia were observed within one week. At necropsy, the ventral rumen mucosal surface contained large elevated areas of polyp- or cauliflowerlike masses of fibrino-necrotic exudate with relatively minor hemorrhage. The abomasum was usually edematous and inflamed with large focal areas of hemorrhagic necrosis of the mucosal surface. The serosal surface of both organs was adhered to adjacent tissues in severe cases. Intestinal alterations were minor. The effect on animal productivity and health was pronounced, but mortality was low.

DEFICIENCIES

Cobalt

Cobalt deficiency occurs in those parts of the world where the soils contain less than 2 ppm cobalt. Factors other than very low soil concentrations are known to cause this deficiency.

Cobalt is essential for the production of vitamin B_{12} (cyanocobalamin) by microorganisms of the digestive tract, principally of the rumen. The deficiency is characterized by anorexia and wasting in cattle and sheep. If the disease becomes advanced, sheep develop a pronounced anemia and loss of appetite. Blood volume and the concentration of protein in the plasma are reduced and the oxygen-carrying capacity falls to 30 percent of normal or even lower. The anemia is macrocytic with marked poikilocytosis, and eventually polychromasia supervenes. The syndrome that develops in cattle is similar though not as spectacular.

Small doses of cobalt given orally usually reduce the severity of the symptoms. Proper amounts of cobalt in the diet prevent the disease. This is a good example of the necessity of some trace elements for proper growth of rumen microorganisms as well as the synthesis of vitamin B_{12}, both of which are so important to the health of the animal.

Sulfur

Thomas et al. (1951) fed sheep on a synthetic diet in which urea was the sole source of nitrogen, but they had difficulty in maintaining the animals. This problem was solved when inorganic sulfur was added to the diet. Sulfur is necessary for the synthesis of the essential amino acid methionine. In these studies the 10 amino acids which are known to be dietary essentials for the rat were shown to be synthesized in the rumen of the lamb. Rumen bacteria can synthesize methionine when urea is the sole source of nitrogen and when inorganic sulfur is available. Conversely, in the absence of dietary sulfur, urea nitrogen was not efficiently utilized.

The sulfur-deficient lambs in the experiments of Thomas et al. (1951) exhibited gradual failure of appetite, loss of body weight, emaciation, and death. Wool growth seemed to have a greater priority on nutrients from the metabolic pool than tissue growth or even maintenance. The rate of wool growth was decreased, however, by sulfur deficiency.

TORSION OR DISPLACEMENT OF THE ABOMASUM

This disease, which has been more commonly diagnosed in recent years, is characterized by atony, distension, and frequently 180°–360° torsion of the abomasum. The cause has been variously described as being due to injuries of the vagus nerve supply to the abomasum, obstruction of the pylorus, and primary atony of the abomasal musculature. Displacement of the abomasum may occur without torsion. If the disease is acute and definite torsion occurs, death may occur unless the torsion is corrected by surgery or other means.

IMPACTIONS OF THE RUMEN, OMASUM, AND ABOMASUM

Impaction of one or more of these three compartments of the ruminant stomach may result from injuries to the vagus nerves supplying the structures, or it may be due to the eating of large amounts of indigestible material. Radical surgical treatment is quite often needed. The vagus-injury theory has many proponents, as well as some who do not give it much credence (Hoflund 1940). Insufficient water intake (Schalk and Amadon 1928) and the ingestion of large amounts of sand and soil particles from dry, sandy ranges may contribute to impactions, especially of the ruminoreticulum.

BOVINE PULMONARY EMPHYSEMA

This disease is characterized by extensive alveolar and less extensive interstitial emphysema. The immediate cause of the emphysema is a dilatation, thinning, and eventual rupture of the alveolar walls. The disease is widely distributed, having been reported in many countries. In the United States the incidence of the disease is increasing.

It has been reported in the literature under various names, such as acute alveolar emphysema and edema, fog or feg fever, aftermath disease, atypical interstitial pneumonia, bovine asthma, and pulmonary adenomatosis. There are some differences in the lesions which may be due to the rapidity with which the disease develops. In some of the western states the disease develops so rapidly that there is apparently insufficient time for the formation of adenomatosis lesions.

Primary pulmonary emphysema seems to be associated with drastic changes in diet, such as the sudden change from dry pastures to green, lush meadows. In some of the western states cattle are moved from high altitude ranges which are usually rather dry in late summer or early fall to lower altitude pastures that are lush and green. The disease is encountered in other parts of the country where the dry-pasture to lush-pasture situation is somewhat the same, but where altitude changes are minimal. Primary pulmonary emphysema may develop 4–10 days after the cattle are put on lush pastures.

In the varied and somewhat confusing descriptions of acute bovine pulmonary emphysema, there is one consistent factor, that is, there must be a sudden change in the kind, quantity, and condition of the food eaten. This would lead to changes in rumen microflora, which in turn could either directly or indirectly cause the disease. The work of Colvin et al. (1956), Dougherty and Cook (1962), Dougherty et al. (1962a,b), and Mullenax et al. (1964) has made it possible to develop new and intriguing etiological possibilities.

A sudden change in diet will cause drastic changes in the microflora and fauna of the ruminoreticulum. These changes may lead to the formation of new and possibly harmful products of microbial digestion. These products, in turn, either as an aerosol or in a volatile form, could reach the lungs during normal eructation. It is conceivable that they could cause the degenerative changes in the alveolar walls which cause alveolar emphysema. Mullenax et al. (1964) have shown that certain bacteria can be carried by eructated gas deep into the respiratory tree.

Carlson et al. (1968) and Dickinson et al. (1967) have produced pulmonary emphysema and pulmonary adenomatosis in cattle by placing fairly large amounts of tryptophan into the ruminoreticulum. Respiratory symptoms develop within 2–4 days, and the lung lesions are indistinguishable from those seen in clinical cases of pulmonary adenomatosis.

HYPERACTIVITY OF THE RUMINORETICULUM IN CATTLE

This condition, in which the rumen is contracting almost continuously, is extremely rare. A new wave of contraction begins before completion of the preceding one.

As far as is known, no detailed motility studies of these rare cases have been made. In a case observed by the author, the animal was found on autopsy to have an advanced case of lymphosarcoma. Humans with certain types of leukemia may have a greatly increased rate of metabolism. No published work can be found showing any relationship between metabolic rate and rate of motility of the ruminant stomach or between neoplasms of the hemopoietic tissue and the rate of stomach motility.

REFERENCES

Arthur, G.H. 1946. The diagnostic value of the blood leukocyte picture in traumatic reticulitis and pericarditis of bovines. *Vet. Rec.* 58:365–66.

Barrentine, B.F., Shawver, C.B., and Williams, L.W. 1956. Antibiotics for the prevention of bloat in cattle grazing ladino clover. *J. Anim. Sci.* 15:440–46.

Bartley, E.E., Wheatcroft, K.L., Claydon, T.J., Fountaine, F.C., and Parrish, D.B. 1951. Effects of feeding aureomycin to dairy calves. *J. Anim. Sci.* 10:1036.

Bell, M.C., Whitehair, C.K., and Gallup, W.D. 1951. The effect of aureomycin on digestion in steers, *Proc. Soc. Exp. Biol. Med.* 76:284–86.

Boda, J.M., and Cole, H.H. 1954. The influence of dietary calcium and phosphorus on the incidence of milk fever in dairy cattle. *J. Dairy Sci.* 39:360–72.

Bond, H.E. 1959. A study on the pathogenesis of acute acid indigestion in the sheep. Ph.D. diss., Cornell U. University Microfilms, Ann Arbor. No. 59–6204.

Carlson, J.R., Dyer, I.A., and Johnson, R.J. 1968. Tryptophan-induced interstitial pulmonary emphysema in cattle. *Am. J. Vet. Res.* 29:1983–89.

Cole, H.H., and Kleiber, M. 1948. Studies on ruminal gas formation and on consumption of alfalfa pasture by cattle. *J. Dairy Sci.* 31:1016–23.

Colvin, H.W., Cupps, P.T., and Cole, H.H. 1956. Eructation studies in cattle. In *Report of Conference on Rumen Function.* Agricultural Research Service, U.S.D.A., Chicago. Pp. 24–25.

Coop, I.E., and Blakeley, R.L. 1949. The metabolism and toxicity of cyanides and cyano-genetic glucosides in sheep. I. Activity in the rumen. *New Zealand J. Sci. Tech.* 30:277–91.

Dain, J.A., Neal, A.L., and Dougherty, R.W. 1955. The occurrence of histamine and tyramine in rumen ingesta of experimentally overfed sheep. *J. Anim. Sci.* 14:930–35.

Dickinson, E.O., Spencer, G.R., and Gorham, J.R. 1967. Experimental induction of an acute respiratory syndrome in cattle resembling bovine pulmonary emphysema. *Vet. Rec.* 80:487–89.

Dougherty, R.W. 1939. Induced cases of traumatic gastritis and pericarditis in dairy cattle. *J. Am. Vet. Med. Ass.* 94:357–62.

Dougherty, R.W., Allison, M.J., and Mullenax, C.H. 1964. Physiological disposition of C^{14}-labeled rumen gases in sheep and goats. *Am. J. Physiol.* 207:1181–88.

Dougherty, R.W., and Cello, R.M. 1949. A preliminary report on toxic factors in the rumen ingesta of cows and sheep. *Cornell Vet.* 39:403–13.

——. 1952. Studies of the toxic factors in rumen ingesta of cows and sheep. *Proceedings Book.* A.V.M.A. 89th Ann. Mtg., Atlantic City. Pp. 130–37.

Doughtery, R.W., and Christensen, R.B. 1953. *In vivo* absorption studies of hydrocyanic acid of plant juice origin. *Cornell Vet.* 43:481–86.

Dougherty, R.W., and Cook, H.M. 1962. Routes of eructated gas expulsion in cattle: A quantitative study. *Am. J. Vet. Res.* 23:997–1000.

Dougherty, R.W., and Habel, R.E. 1955. The cranial esophageal sphincter, its action and its relation to eructation in sheep as determined by cinefluorography. *Cornell Vet.* 45:459–64.

Dougherty, R.W., Habel, R.E., and Bond, H.E. 1958. Esophageal innervation and the eructation reflex in sheep. *Am. J. Vet. Res.* 19:115–28.

Dougherty, R.W., Hill, K.J., Campeti, F.L., and McClure, R.C. 1962a. Studies of the pharyngeal and laryngeal activity during eructation in ruminants. *Am. J. Vet. Res.* 23:213–19.

Dougherty, R.W., Lindahl, I.L., et al. 1957. Alfalfa saponins: Studies on their chemical, pharmacological, and physiological properties in relation to ruminant bloat. *U.S.D.A. Tech. Bull.* 1161.

Dougherty, R.W., O'Toole, J.J., and Allison, M.J. 1965. Metabolism of carbon-labeled methane by sheep. Unpublished data.

——. 1967. Oxidation of intra-arterially administered $carbon^{14}$-labeled methane in sheep. *Proc. Soc. Exp. Biol. Med.* 124:1155–57.

Dougherty, R.W., and Shipe, W.F. 1960. Technique for studying the effects of feed and environment on the flavor of milk. *J. Dairy Sci.* 43:859.

Dougherty, R.W., Stewart, W.E., Nold, M.M., Lindahl, I.L., Mullenax, C.H., and Leek, B.F. 1962b. Pulmonary absorption of eructated gas in ruminants. *Am. J. Vet. Res.* 23:205–12.

Dunlop, R.H. 1961. A study of factors related to the functional impairment resulting from loading the rumen of cattle with high carbohydrate feeds. Ph.D. diss., U. of Minnesota.

Goings, R.L., Jacobson, N.L., Beitz, D.C., Littledike, E.T., and Wiggers, K.D. 1974. Prevention of parturient paresis by a prepartum, calcium-deficient diet. *J. Dairy Sci.* 57:1184–88.

Hancock, J. 1953. Grazing behavior in relation to bloat. *New Zealand Soc. Anim. Prod. Proc.* 13:127.

Harris, Barney, Jr. 1964. Studies on ruminal parakeratosis in dairy calves. Ph.D. diss., Oklahoma State U. University Microfilms, Ann Arbor. No. 65–8729.

Hoflund, Sven. 1940. Untersuchungen über Störungen in den Funktionen der Wiederkäuermagen, verursacht durch Schädigungen des N. vagus. *Svensk Veterinärtidskrift,* vol. 45 (supp.).

Hungate, R.E., Dougherty, R.W., Bryant, M.P., and Cello, R.M. 1952. Microbiological and physiological changes associated with acute indigestion of sheep. *Cornell Vet.* 42:423–49.

Hungate, R.E., Fletcher, D.W., Dougherty, R.W., and Barrentine, B.F. 1955. Microbial activity in the bovine rumen: Its measurement and relation to bloat. *Appl. Microbiol.* 3:161–73.

Jensen, R., Connell, W.E., and Deem, A.W. 1954. Rumenitis and its relation to rate of change of ration and the proportion of concentrate in the ration of cattle. *Am. J. Vet. Res.* 15:425–28.

Jensen, R., Flint, J.C., Udall, R.H., Deem, A.W., and Seger, C.L. 1958. Parakeratosis of the rumens of lambs fattened on pelleted feed. *Am. J. Vet. Res.* 19:277–82.

Jordan, R.M., and Bell, T.D. 1951. Effect of aureomycin on growing and fattening lambs. *J. Anim. Sci.* 10:1051.

Kingrey, B.W. 1955. Experimental bovine traumatic gastritis. *J. Am. Vet. Med. Ass.* 127:477–82.

Lindahl, I.L., Cook, A.C., Davis, R.E., and Maclay, W.D. 1954. Preliminary investigation on the role of alfalfa saponin in ruminant bloat. *Science* 119:157–58.

Lindahl, I.L., and Dougherty, R.W. 1958. Effects of pelleted feed on rumen development. Unpublished data.

Mangan, J.L. 1959. Bloat in cattle. *New Zealand J. Ag. Res.* 2:47–71.

Marston, H.R. 1952. Colbalt, copper, and molybdenum in the nutrition of animals and plants. *Physiol. Rev.* 32:66–121.

McArthur, J.M., and Miltimore, J.E. 1961. Rumen gas analysis by gas-solid chromatography. *Can. J. Anim. Sci.* 41:187–96.

Mullenax, C.H., Allison, M.J., and Songer, J.R. 1964. Transport of aerosolized microorganisms from the rumen to the respiratory system during eructation. *Am. J. Vet. Res.* 25:1583–94.

Mullenax, C.H., Keeler, R.F., and Allison, M.J. 1966. Physiologic responses of ruminants to toxic factors extracted from rumen bacteria and rumen fluid. *Am. J. Vet. Res.* 27:857–68.

Quin, J.I. 1929. Further investigations into geeldikkop (Tribulosis ovis). *Ann. Rep. Director Vet. Sci. Onderstepoort* 15:765–67.

Ringarp, Nils. 1964. Personal communication. Royal Veterinary College, Stockholm.

Ryan, R.K. 1964a. Concentrations of glucose and low-molecular weight acids in the rumen of sheep following the addition of large amounts of wheat to the rumen. *Am. J. Vet. Res.* 25:646–52.

——. 1964b. Concentrations of glucose and low-molecular weight acids in the rumen of sheep changed gradually from a hay to a hay-plus-grain diet. *Am. J. Vet. Res.* 25:653–59.

Sapiro, M.L., Hoflund, S., Clark, R., and Quin, J.I. 1949. Studies on the alimentary tract of the Merino sheep in South Africa. XVI. The fate of nitrate in ruminal ingesta as studied *in vitro*. *Onderstepoort J. Vet. Sci. Anim. Ind.* 22:357–72.

Sasser, L.B., West, J.L., and Bell, M.C. 1969. Rumen pathological alterations in sheep ingesting radioactive sand particles (abstr.). Rumen Function Conference, Chicago, Ill. AEC, U. of Tenn., Oak Ridge, Tenn.

Schalk, A.F., and Amadon, R.S. 1928. Physiology of the ruminant stomach. *N. Dak. Ag. Exp. Sta. Bull.* 216.

Sharpe, M.E., Latham, M.J., and Reiter, B. 1969. The occurrence of natural antibodies to rumen bacteria. *J. Gen. Microbiol.* 56:353–64.

Thomas, W.E., Loosli, J.K., Williams, H.H., and Maynard, L.A. 1951. The utilization of inorganic sulphates and urea nitrogen by lambs. *J. Nutr.* 43:515–23.

Titchen, D.A., and Reid, C.S.W. 1965. The reflex control of the motility of the ruminant stomach. In R.W. Dougherty, ed., *Physiology of Digestion in the Ruminant.* Butterworths, Washington. Pp. 68–77.

Turner, A.W., and Hodgetts, V.E. 1952. Depression of ruminal digestion in adult sheep by aureomycin. *Austral. J. Ag. Res.* 3:453–59.

——. *Toxicity of Wheat for Stock.* Council for Scientific and Industrial Research, Australia, 17th Ann. Rept. (1943):22 through 22nd Ann. Rept. (1948):27.

——. *Toxicity of Large Rations of Wheat.* Council for Scientific and Industrial Research, Australia, 1st Ann. Rept. (1949):39 through 11th Ann. Rept. (1959):50.

Van der Wath, S.J. 1944. Some aspects of the toxicology of hydrocyanic acid in ruminants. *Onderstepoort J. Vet. Sci. Anim. Ind.* 19:79–160.

Van Hoosen, N., and Isham, R.R. 1958. The therapeutic use of magnets given orally for traumatic gastritis. *J. Am. Med. Ass.* 132:388–89.

Van Horn, H.H., Jr., and Bartley, E.E. 1961. Bloat in cattle. I. Effect of bovine saliva and plant mucin on frothing rumen contents in alfalfa bloat. *J. Anim. Sci.* 20:85–87.

Weiss, K.E. 1953a. The significance of reflex salivation in relation to froth formation and acute bloat in ruminants. *Onderstepoort J. Vet. Res.* 26:241–50.

——. 1953b. Physiological studies on eructations in ruminants. *Onderstepoort J. Vet. Res.* 26:251–83.

CHAPTER 25

Avian Digestion | by Gary E. Duke

ANATOMY OF THE ALIMENTARY CANAL

The anatomy of the avian alimentary canal is most notably different from that of mammals in the mouth area, in the presence of a crop in the esophagus, and in the presence of a muscular stomach or gizzard. The mouth and pharynx are not sharply delimited in birds, and in most species there is no soft palate. The hard palate communicates with the nasal cavities. Teeth are absent, their function being accomplished by the horny beak and the gizzard, and a great variety of tongue and beak adaptations exist. Salivary glands and taste buds are present, with their number and locations varying (Ziswiler and Farner 1972).

The size and length of the digestive tract vary considerably among species, depending upon dietary habits. In adult chickens, the length of the entire tract may be 210 cm or more (Table 25.1).

Table 25.1. Length (cm) of the digestive tract of chickens (5 birds)

	At 20 days	At 1.5 years
Entire digestive tract	85	210
Angle of beak to crop	7.5	20
Angle of beak to proventriculus	11.5	35
Duodenum (complete loop)	12	20
Ileum and jejunum	49	120
Cecum	5	17.5
Rectum and cloaca	4	11.25

Modified from Calhoun, *Microscopic Anatomy of the Digestive System of the Chicken,* Iowa State U. Press, Ames, 1954

The avian esophagus is generally comparatively long and rather large in diameter, being larger in species which swallow larger food items. A dilatation of the esophagus, the crop (Fig. 25.1), is present in most species although absent in some (e.g. insectivorous birds and owls). The form of the crop may vary from a simple enlargement of the esophagus to one or two pouches off the esophagus.

The glandular stomach or proventriculus (Fig. 25.1) of birds functions primarily in secretion, although it may also have a storage function in those birds lacking crops and in some fish-eating species. The muscular stomach is highly specialized for grinding in those species that eat hard foods, or for mixing digestive secretions with food in carnivorous species. In most species the muscular stomach is composed of two pairs of muscles called the *musculi intermedii* and *musculi laterales* (Mangold 1906), or more recently termed the thin and thick muscle pairs (Dziuk and Duke 1972) respectively (Fig. 25.1). These pairs of muscles are not present in most carnivorous birds (e.g. hawks, owls, herons).

The small intestine of birds has a duodenum like that in mammals, but beyond the duodenum there are no delimited areas like the jejunum and ileum of mammals. The vestige of the yolk sac (Meckel's diverticulum) may be found about midway in the small intestine. The small intestine is much longer in herbivorous birds than in carnivorous birds. The mucosa of the small intestine is like that of mammals except that the villi are in general taller, more slender, and more numerous in birds. Brunner's glands are absent in the chicken (Calhoun 1954), although in some species tubular glands that are homologous to Brunner's glands in mammals are present. Electron microscopic examination of chicken villi reveals a well-defined network of blood capillaries but no lacteals (Graney 1967).

Located at the junction of the small and large intestines are the ceca, which in birds, unlike in most mammals, are usually paired. Their size is influenced by dietary habits. The large intestine of birds is relatively short and is not sharply demarcated from the rectum and colon as in mammals.

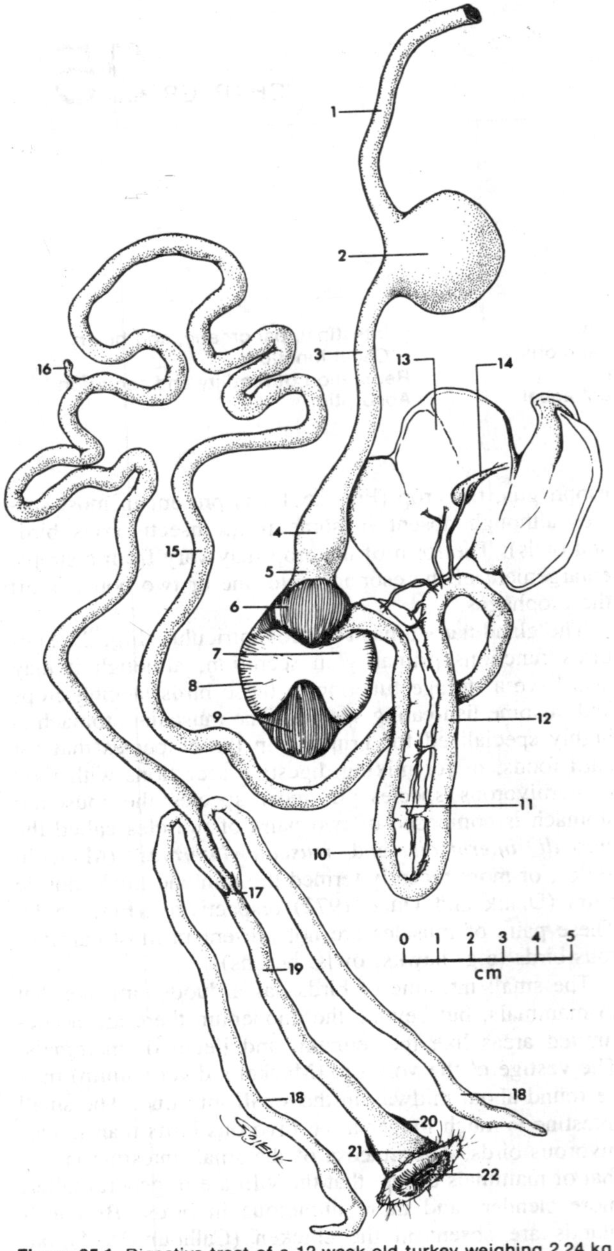

Another organ concerned with digestion is the liver, which is bi-lobed and relatively large in most birds; the left hepatic duct communicates directly with the duodenum, whereas the right duct sends a branch to the gallbladder, or it may be enlarged locally as a gallbladder. Gallbladders are present in the chicken, duck, and goose, but some other species including the pigeon do not have one. The gallbladder gives rise to bile ducts which empty into the duodenum near the distal loop. The pancreas lies within the duodenal loop. It consists of at least three lobes, and its secretions reach the duodenum via three ducts.

Figure 25.1. Digestive tract of a 12-week-old turkey weighing 2.24 kg. 1, precrop esophagus; 2, crop; 3, postcrop esophagus; 4, glandular stomach; 5, isthmus; 6, thin craniodorsal muscle; 7, thick cranioventral muscle; 8, thick caudodorsal muscle; 9, thin caudoventral muscle (6–9, muscular stomach); 10, proximal duodenum; 11, pancreas; 12, distal duodenum; 13, liver; 14, gall bladder; 15, ileum; 16, Meckel's diverticulum; 17, ileocecocolic junction; 18, ceca; 19, colon; 20, bursa of Fabricius; 21, cloaca; 22, vent.

REGULATION OF FOOD INTAKE

In birds as in mammals, hypothalamic centers are involved in the control of appetite. Ventromedial hypothalamic lesions produce hyperphagia and lateral lesions result in aphagia (Kuenzel 1972). A number of other factors affect feeding; for example, high environmental temperatures, high dietary energy levels, or high dietary protein levels all result in decreases in food consumption. If a diet is high in protein but low in energy value, food consumption will increase over normal levels. Apparently, energy content of a diet is a more important regulator of food intake than is protein content (Gleaves et al. 1968). The presence of lesions or small foreign bodies in the colon will cause a decrease in food intake (Sturkie and Joiner 1959).

MOTILITY

Deglutition and esophageal and crop motility

Extension of the neck and raising of the head apparently play a secondary role in swallowing in poultry. The tongue and hyoid apparatus (Pastea et al. 1968) and larynx (White 1969) actively move food or fluid into the esophagus. Stimulation of the pharyngeal roof by food results in reflex closure of the choanal slit. This mechanism may be different in pigeons since they can swallow without raising their heads, or perhaps the difference is related to the presence of a soft palate in pigeons.

Food is moved through the esophagus by peristalsis. According to several authors (see Ziswiler and Farner 1972), when a fasted chicken eats, the first food ingested goes directly into the stomach, and food subsequently swallowed mainly goes into the crop. The movement of ingesta from crop to stomach thereafter is reflexly controlled by the fullness of the stomach and intestines. In more recent observations in chickens (Pastea et al. 1968) and turkeys (Dziuk and Duke 1971), the stage of the gastric contraction cycle at the time that a bite of food was swallowed was believed to be the determinant of whether that food entered the crop or went to the stomach.

The contractions of the crop (peristaltic waves) vary considerably in rhythm and amplitude and are influenced by the nervous state of the bird, hunger, and other factors. The frequencies of these contractions, for chickens starved for 1.5, 10, and 27 hours, were 13, 55, and 75 per hour respectively (Groebbels 1932).

Gastroduodenal motility

A rhythmic contraction cycle can be observed in the muscular stomach even in the absence of extrinsic innervation. This inherent rhythmicity is apparently neurogenic. Also, the contractions of the glandular stomach and duodenum are dependent upon intrinsic neural connections with the muscular stomach (Nolf 1938, 1939). The latter situation accounts for the complex gastroduodenal contraction sequence seen in chickens (Mangold 1906) and turkeys (Duke et al. 1972). In this contraction sequence the pair of thin muscles of the muscular stomach (Fig. 25.1) contracts first. Secondly, two to three peristaltic waves pass through the duodenum. Next, the pair of thick muscles contract, and lastly a peristaltic wave passes through the glandular stomach. In the contractions of the thin and thick muscles, a wave of contraction proceeds in a counterclockwise direction (as viewed in Fig. 25.1) across each muscle.

During each gastroduodenal contraction sequence ingesta flow from the muscular stomach into the duodenum at the end of the contraction of the thin muscles and aborally into the glandular stomach during contraction of the thick muscles (Dziuk and Duke 1972). During contraction of the glandular stomach, ingesta are returned to the muscular stomach.

Two other aboral movements of luminal contents are associated with the normal function of the avian gastroduodenal apparatus. A reflux of duodenal and upper ileal contents into the muscular stomach occurs about four times per hour in turkeys (Duke et al. 1972). This apparently permits remixing of intestinal ingesta with gastric secretions. Predaceous birds (e.g. owls, hawks, herons) regularly egest a pellet of bones and hair or feathers of their prey from their stomach. Several species of birds egest gastric contents, apparently by vomiting (e.g. vultures), and various drugs have been widely used to produce emesis in species which do not normally vomit (Chaney and Kare 1966). The emesis of vultures appears to be a reaction to disturbance or fright rather than a part of their normal digestive process.

In the glandular and muscular stomachs of fowl 2–3 contractions per minute occur. Duodenal contraction frequency in turkeys is 6–9 contractions per minute, but 2–3 contractions occur in rapid succession in conjunction with each gastroduodenal contraction cycle. The mean amplitude of intraluminal pressure changes in the glandular stomach of turkeys was found to be approximately 35 mm Hg. Mean amplitudes measured in the muscular stomach of fowl range from 40 to 150 mm Hg with the higher average pressures being recorded during contraction of the thick muscle pair (Duke et al. 1972, 1975a). In the domestic goose (Kato 1914), common buzzard (Mangold 1911), and great horned owl (Kostuch and Duke 1975), amplitudes of 265–280, 8–26, and 60–175 mm Hg respectively have been reported. In the latter two species, mean amplitudes varied with the quantity eaten and with the time at which measurements were made after eating.

Hunger or starvation decreases the frequency of gastric contractions in fowl, and the duration of contractions tends to increase; the latter is decreased when fibrous or coarse food is ingested. The presence of grit in the gizzard increases the amplitude of contractions.

Inherent, myogenic, electric slow waves (basic electric rhythm), which are recorded from the mammalian gastrointestinal tract, have not been recorded from the stomach of turkeys. Slow waves have been recorded from the duodenum and ileum of turkeys, but they are not believed to have a regulatory (pacesetter) function in the duodenum because of the intrinsic neural system which coordinates motility in the stomach and duodenum. Slow waves may be regulatory in the ileum of turkeys (Duke et al. 1975a,b).

The esophagus, crop, proventriculus, and gizzard are innervated by the vagus, a parasympathetic nerve which is the principal motor nerve to these organs, and by sympathetic fibers. Stimulation of the peripheral end of the vagus increases motility, and ligation of it (particularly the left vagus) decreases motility.

Grit (i.e. small stones) is present in the muscular stomach of most graminivorous and herbivorous birds. It is used for grinding hard foods between the thick muscles of the muscular stomach. Grit is apparently not essential for normal digestion, but digestion of hard foods is slower and the total digestibility of a diet may be decreased without it. Grit is normally ingested regularly, but if it is not available food is retained longer in the muscular stomach.

Ileal, colonic, and cecal motility

Little is known about ileal motility in birds. Peristalsis and segmenting contractions have been observed radiographically. In the ileum of the turkey, contractions normally occur at a mean frequency of about four per minute with an average amplitude of about 16 mm Hg; however, periods of more intense activity, with contractions of higher amplitude and with a frequency of about six per minute have also been observed (Duke et al. 1975b). These latter periods apparently are the result of a migrating electric complex similar to that observed in the canine ileum.

The most striking feature of colonic motility is antiperistalsis, which is believed to occur nearly continuously (Yasukawa 1959, Dziuk 1971). This activity appears to have two functions: movement of urine from the cloaca into the colon and thence into the ceca for water absorption, and filling of the ceca. The antiperistaltic contractions arise from the cloaca and occur at a rate of 10–14 per minute in chickens and turkeys. Antiperistalsis ceases immediately prior to defecation, during which the entire colon appears to contract simultaneously.

Both peristalsis and antiperistalsis have been observed in the ceca. Fargeas et al. (1963) described high amplitude contractions occurring in conjunction with filling and emptying of the ceca and weaker contractions associated with mixing of the cecal contents. Yasukawa (1959) found that colonic antiperistaltic waves passed alternately into the right and left ceca and continued through both ceca. He also observed peristalsis, which usually terminated at the proximal ends of the ceca but sometimes proceeded into the colon. He termed these latter waves *mass peristalsis*. Although they occurred more often than cecal droppings, he believed that they were involved in the formation of these droppings.

Cecal droppings of most avian species can easily be distinguished from intestinal droppings by their chocolate brown color and homogenous texture. One or two cecal droppings occur per day in gallinaceous species, while 25–50 intestinal droppings are formed.

Oshima et al. (1974) found a diurnal rhythm in cecal motility with the highest daily contraction frequency (about 1 per minute) occurring in late afternoon and the lowest frequency (about 0.5 per minute) occurring just after lights were turned off in the holding rooms.

The time required for food to pass through the entire alimentary canal is generally longest in herbivores and shortest in carnivores and frugivores. The rate of passage may be influenced by the consistency, hardness, and water content of the food and by the amount consumed. Apparently age may also influence passage rate because food passes through young chicks faster than through adults. The rate of passage through the adult turkey is, however, similar to that of the adult chicken. Within 2.5 hours after feeding chromic-oxide marker to fowl (Dansky and Hill 1952) it can be detected in the excreta, and most of it can be recovered from the excreta within about 24 hours. Marked cecal excreta may, however, be detected for 2–3 days after feeding the marker (Duke et al. 1968).

SECRETION AND DIGESTION

Buccal, crop, and esophageal

The number and arrangement of salivary glands vary among species. In general, species that eat wet foods have fewer glands than those that eat dry food with little natural lubrication. The salivary glands of most birds have only mucous-secreting cells; however, serous cells have been reported in a few species (Warner et al. 1967), and amylase has been found in the saliva of poultry. In most avian species little maceration of food occurs, and food spends little time in the mouth. Hence, even if amylase is present in saliva, little digestion could occur in the mouth. Likewise, food passes quickly through the esophagus, and its major secretion is mucus for lubrication of this passage.

Mucus is also secreted by the crop of fowl, and amylase may be secreted as well. However, amylase found in the crop or on the crop mucosa may originate from the salivary glands, ingested food, bacteria in the crop, regurgitated duodenal contents, or from the crop mucosa itself.

Bolton (1965) believed that a significant amount of starch digestion occurred in the crop of chickens as a result of bacterial action. However, Pritchard (1972) collected crop contents of chickens, killed the bacteria therein with chloroform, and upon incubation of the contents found that sucrose was still digested; so nonbacterial digestion of carbohydrates apparently can occur in the crop.

Both serous and mucous-secreting glands occur in pigeons; and mucus, amylase, and invertase have been found in the crop mucosa of pigeons (Dulzetto 1930). Perhaps the crop of pigeons is more active in chemical digestion than that of fowl. In any case, after leaving the crop, ingesta receive much more thorough mechanical and chemical digestion in the stomach and intestines.

Gastric

Two types of glands predominate in the glandular stomach—simple mucosal glands secreting mucus, and compound glands secreting mucus, HCl, and pepsinogen. Apparently the compound glands are functionally homologous to both the chief and parietal cells of the mammalian stomach. Although gastric juice is secreted by the glandular stomach, preliminary acid proteolysis occurs mostly in the muscular stomach. Mechanical digestion also occurs predominantly in this organ in most species. The pH of gastric juice ranges from about 0.5 to 2.5, being slightly higher in omnivores and herbivores than in carnivores (Herpol 1967a), and is appropriate for good peptic activity. Values for gastric pH may also vary considerably depending upon method of collection and analysis of the juice, and upon the hunger of the bird.

Long (1967) indicated that the chicken secretes 8.8 ml per kg body weight per hour of gastric juice, which is considerably higher than for man, dog, rat, and monkey. Likewise, the acid concentration is higher, but the pepsin content per volume is lower than for most mammals. The total pepsin output, however, in pepsin units per kg per hour (2430) is higher than in mammals.

The avian muscular stomach has a unique lining which is formed by both secretory activity of tubular glands in the muscular stomach and by entrapment of sloughed epithelial cells and other debris. The lining is periodically sloughed off and replaced in most species, and it is thicker in species eating hard foods than in those eating soft foods.

Intestinal, pancreatic, and biliary

The small intestine is the primary site of chemical digestion, and a number of digestive enzymes are secreted by its cells. The intestinal mucosa has been shown to possess proteolytic activity in chickens (Kokas et al. 1967) and pigeons (Herpol 1967b), and amino peptidases and carboxypeptidases have been found in duodenal mucosa of chickens (DeRycke 1962). Intestinal amylase was found in chickens (Polyakov 1958, Kokas et al. 1967), and maltase and sucrase of intestinal origin have been found in a number of species (Zoppi and Schmerling 1969).

Intestinal pH ranges from about 5.6 to 7.2 in those species which have been tested (Herpol and Van Grembergen 1967). The pH of the avian intestinal tract increases from the oral to the aboral end, and the pH of each portion of the tract is maintained (i.e. regulated) by secretory activity within that portion (Hurwitz and Bar 1968). A pH of approximately 6–8 is optimal.

Digestion of nutrients in the intestine occurs as a result of pancreatic enzymes and microbial activity as well as by intestinal secretions. The pancreas secretes both digestive enzymes and an aqueous solution containing buffering compounds. The latter secretion acts to neutralize the acid chyme, thus providing a pH of 6–8. The pancreas is the major source of amylase, and pancreatic amylolytic activy has been found in several avian species (Polyakov 1958, Dandrifosse 1970). Pancreatic lipase has been demonstrated in chickens (Polyakov 1958) and pigeons (Schleucher and Hokin 1954) and probably is present in other species.

Pancreatic proteolytic activity has been found in several species. Highly purified chicken chymotrypsin and turkey trypsin have been extracted from the pancreas. Less purified samples of chicken trypsin and turkey chymotrypsin have also been obtained (Ryan 1965). Dipeptidase, aminopeptidase, and carboxypeptidase activities were found in pancreatic extracts of chickens (DeRycke 1962).

Kokue and Hayama (1972) have shown that the pancreatic secretory rate is relatively greater in fowl than in dogs, rats, and sheep and that it is less affected by fasting in fowl than it is in these mammals.

The secretion of bile into the duodenum aids in the neutralization of chyme. Bile salts are required for the emulsification of fats, a process which aids in their digestion. In fowl, as mammals, bile salts are reabsorbed in the lower ileum and recirculated to the liver to be used again.

Cecal function

Only about 10 percent of most diets eaten by Galliformes receives cecal action (Duke et al. 1968, 1969), and fowl survive well following cecectomy. Nevertheless, several important functions are believed to occur in the ceca (MacNab 1973), most notable of which is the microbial digestion of cellulose. The coefficient of digestibility of crude fiber for Galliformes was about 18 percent when ceca were intact, but was zero after removal of the ceca (Radeff 1928, Henning 1929). However, there is no conclusive evidence that the host derives any nutritive benefit from this breakdown of cellulose or from other nutrients made available upon breakdown of plant cell walls.

Urine is moved from the cloaca into the colon from which it may pass into the ceca. Absorption of water from the cecal contents appears to be a major function of the ceca. The moisture content of excreta is 1–2 percent higher after cecectomy (Thorburn and Wilcox 1965).

Microbial synthesis of vitamins also occurs in the ceca, but the vitamins are apparently not absorbed by the host. In studies by Coates et al. (1968), chicks were raised in both conventional and germ-free environments on diets lacking in various B-complex vitamins. Normal amounts of the omitted vitamins were subsequently found in the cecal contents of conventionally raised birds, but only negligible amounts were found in the ceca of germ-free birds. However, signs of dietary deficiency due to the omitted vitamins were no less severe in the conventionally raised birds, indicating that they derived little benefit from the vitamins synthesized by their cecal microbes.

REGULATION OF MOTILITY AND SECRETION

Salivary secretion increases in response to eating. Similarly, the presence of food in the esophagus stimulates secretion of mucus, and the presence of food in the mouth and in the esophagus initiates motility in these areas. Regulation of the movement of food into or out of the crop is more complex, but it is apparently controlled reflexly by the fullness of the rest of the tract below the crop.

Regulation of gastric activities is also very complex. In mammals and birds the nature and volume of duodenal contents can inhibit gastric activity. In mammals this happens via neural and humoral mechanisms (enterogastric reflex and enterogastrone respectively). In birds the mechanisms are unknown, but both neural and humoral elements may be involved. Distention of the duodenum caused decreased gastric secretion in chickens (Joyner and Kokas 1971) and decreased gastric motility in turkeys (Duke and Evanson 1972). Intraduodenal injections of small volumes of corn oil, 1600 mOsM NaCl (pH 7), 0.1 N HCl, and 10 percent amino acid solutions all inhibited gastric motility in turkeys. The inhibition required 2–3 minutes with oil but occurred immediately after injection of the other solutions, implying the existence of a humoral mechanism for the oil and a neural mechanism for the others (Duke and Evanson 1972, Duke et al. 1973). In other examples after chronic bilateral section of the vagal innervation of the glandular stomach of fowl, duodenal distention produced much less inhibition of gastric secretion than in normal birds, indicating a neural mechanism; and injections of mammalian enterogastrone, secretin, serotonin, and cholecystokinin-pancreozymin (CCK-PZ) caused some inhibition of gastric secretion, indicating a humoral regulatory mechanism (Kokas and Brunson 1969). Enterogastrone has not been isolated from the avian duodenum, but serotonin has been found, and it may act similarly to, or partly in place of, enterogastrone in avian gastric regulation. When the actions of endogenous serotonin were blocked (by injection of UML 491, a serotonin blocker) less inhibition of gastric secretion occurred following duodenal distention (Joyner and Kokas 1971).

Increased gastric secretion occurs also in chickens as a result of feeding (Farner 1941), and in turkeys there is a direct relationship between the protein content of a diet and the proteolytic activity and rate of production of gastric juice (Fedorovskii 1951). These results indicate the presence of a gastric phase in the control of gastric secretion, or of a mechanism similar to it, in birds.

Mammalian gastrin stimulates gastric secretion in chickens (Kokas and Brunson 1969); however, gastrin has not been isolated from any part of the gastrointestinal tract of fowl (Ruoff and Sewing 1970). Histamine has been isolated from the esophagus, crop, the glandular and muscular portions of the stomach, and the duodenum; the greatest concentrations were in the latter three organs (Ruoff and Sewing 1970). Injections of histamine produce increases in gastric secretion in chickens (Kokas and Brunson 1969, Burhol and Hirshowitz 1972), in pigeons (Ojha and Ahmed 1967), and in ducks (Keeton et al. 1920). Secretions of pepsin and HCl by fowl were equally stimulated by injections of mammalian pentagastrin and by histamine (Burhol and Hirschowitz 1970). Thus a gastric phase seems to be present in birds, but gastrin does not appear to be involved. Apparently another hormone, e.g. histamine, performs the role of gastrin.

A cephalic phase in the regulation of gastric secretion also probably exists in birds. The sight of food caused an increase in the volume of gastric secretion in ducks (Walter 1939) and an increase in acid secretion in barn owls (Smith and Richmond 1972). Sham-feeding of chickens resulted in increased gastric secretion according to Collip (1922) but yielded equivocal results in the studies of Farner (1941). Also in the latter study, the sight of food, even after prolonged fasting, did not stimulate increased gastric acid secretion.

Below the stomach, the inherent motility of the entire small intestine is increased by vagal stimulation. Intestinal secretion is also slightly increased by vagal action. But secretion is increased more by distention of the duodenum and by injections of secretin and extracts of the mucosa of the small intestine, including those from which secretin had been removed. The latter stimulus indicates the presence of another hormone or hormones (in addition to secretin) in the small intestinal mucosa capable of stimulating intestinal secretion (Kokas et al. 1967). Presumably, secretin and other humoral factors are released into the circulation when ingesta distend the intestine.

When a fasted chicken eats, pancreatic secretion begins immediately. If the bird is vagotomized at the pancreatic level, no immediate secretion occurs, although pancreatic secretion eventually increases. The delayed secretion is probably humorally induced (Kokue and Hayama 1972). Secretin, which is responsible for stimulation of the initial secretion of the aqueous component of pancreatic juice in mammals, has been isolated from the intestinal mucosa of turkeys (Dockray 1972). Pancreozymin, which causes prolonged secretion of both aqueous and enzyme components of mammalian pancreatic juice, has not been found in birds, but intravenous injections of mammalian CCK-PZ cause an increase in pancreatic secretion in the pigeon (Sahba et al. 1970). Although the regulation of avian pancreatic secretion is not completely understood, it is probably similar to regulation in mammals.

The rate of bile secretion in chickens increases upon eating, but the mechanism is unknown.

ABSORPTION

The absorption of nutrients from the intestines of chickens has been relatively well studied although the mechanisms involved have not received as much attention. The orad one fourth of the ileum has been shown to be the most important site for absorption of fats, carbohydrates, and proteins. Bile salts are absorbed largely in the lower ileum; amino acids coming from exogenous proteins are mostly absorbed in the upper half of the ileum; and the breakdown products from endogenous proteins are absorbed primarily in the lower half of the ileum (Crompton and Nesheim 1969).

The absorption of D-glucose, D-galactose, D-xylose, 3-methyl glucose, α-methyl glucoside, and possibly D-fructose is active. Seven other monosaccharides are apparently passively transported (Bogner 1960, Hudson and Levin 1966, Fearon and Bird 1968). Chickens possess a sodium-dependent mobile-carrier system for active transport of sugars similar to that of mammals (Alvarado and

Monreal 1967), and the system becomes functional before hatching (Hudson and Levin 1966).

The in vivo absorption of 18 L-amino acids into tied-off segments of the intestine of chickens was studied by Tasaki and Takahashi (1966); they observed that the absorption rate was not dependent on molecular weight but that those amino acids with large nonpolar side chains (e.g. methionine, valine, leucine) were absorbed more readily than those with polar side chains. Apparently most amino acids are actively absorbed, but not all have separate transport mechanisms. For example, L-methionine and L-histidine are both actively absorbed but share a common transport system and are absorbed more rapidly than their D-isomers (Paine et al. 1959). The absorption of leucine or phenylalanine is inhibited by methionine (Tasaki and Takahashi 1966).

Aramaki and Weiss (1962), who determined the concentration of glucose and amino nitrogen in the portal venous blood and wing vein blood, showed that within 15 minutes after eating there was a significantly higher concentration of these substances in the portal blood, indicating a high rate of digestion and absorption. The absorption of proteinaceous materials occurs more rapidly in young chicks than in older birds and in males as compared to females (Wakita et al. 1970).

Apparently the amount of fat digested and absorbed in birds and mammals is similar. The processes of absorption are, however, somewhat different between the two vertebrate classes. In mammals, fat is absorbed into the lymph lacteals of the villi, whereas in birds, fats are absorbed directly into the blood (Noyan et al. 1964). Approximately 80–95 percent of the fatty acids present in the intestine of adult chickens are absorbed (Noyan et al. 1964, Carew et al. 1972, Hurwitz et al. 1973), but newly hatched chicks absorb less (Carew et al. 1972).

REFERENCES

Alvarado, F., and Monreal, J. 1967. Na^+-dependent active transport of phenylglucosides in the chicken small intestine. *Comp. Biochem. Physiol.* 20:471–88.

Aramaki, T., and Weiss, H.S. 1962. Patterns of carbohydrate and protein digestion in the chicken as derived from sampling the hepatic portal system. *Arch. Internat. Physiol.* 70:1–15.

Bogner, P.H. 1960. Alimentary absorption of reducing sugars by embryos and young chicks. *Proc. Soc. Exp. Biol. Med.* 107:263–65.

Bolton, W. 1965. Digestion in crop. *Brit. Poul. Sci.* 6:97–102.

Burhol, P.G., and Hirshowitz, B.I. 1970. Single subcutaneous doses of histamine and pentagastrin in gastric fistula chickens. *Am. J. Physiol.* 218:1671–75.

——. 1972. Dose responses with subcutaneous infusion of histamine in gastric fistula chickens. *Am. J. Physiol.* 222:308–13.

Calhoun, M.L. 1954. *Microscopic Anatomy of the Digestive System of the Chicken.* Iowa State U. Press, Ames.

Carew, L.B., Machemer, R.H., Jr., Sharp, R.W., and Foss, D.C. 1972. Fat absorption by the very young chick. *Poul. Sci.* 51:738–42.

Chaney, S.G., and Kare, M.R. 1966. Emesis in birds. *J. Am. Vet. Med. Ass.* 149:938–43.

Coates, M.E., Ford, J.E., and Harrison, G.F. 1968. Intestinal synthesis of vitamins of the B-complex in chicks. *Brit. J. Nutr.* 22:493–500.

Collip, J.B. 1922. The activation of the glandular stomach of the fowl. *Am. J. Physiol.* 59:435–38.

Crompton, D.W.T., and Nesheim, M.C. 1969. Amino acid patterns during digestion in the small intestine of ducks. *J. Nutr.* 99:43–50.

Dandrifosse, G. 1970. Mechanism of amylase secretion by the pancreas of the pigeon. *Comp. Biochem. Physiol.* 34:229–35.

Dansky, L.M., and Hill, F.W. 1952. Application of the chromic oxide indicator method to balance studies with growing chickens. *J. Nutr.* 47:449–59.

DeRycke, P. 1962. Onderzoek over exopeptidasen bij het kuiken. *Natuurwet. Tijdschr.* 43:82–86.

Dockray, G.J. 1972. Pancreatic secretion in the turkey. *J. Physiol.* 227:49P–50P.

Duke, G.E., Dziuk, H.E., and Evanson, O.A. 1972. Gastric pressure and smooth muscle electrical potential changes in turkeys. *Am. J. Physiol.* 222(1):167–73.

Duke, G.E., Dziuk, H.E., and Hawkins, L. 1969. Gastrointestinal transit-times in normal and bluecomb turkeys. *Poul. Sci.* 48:835–42.

Duke, G.E., and Evanson, O.A. 1972. Inhibition of gastric motility by duodenal contents in turkeys. *Poul. Sci.* 51(5):1625–36.

Duke, G.E., Evanson, O.A., Ciganek, J.G., Miskowiec, J.F., and Kostuch, T.E. 1973. Inhibition of gastric motility in turkeys by intraduodenal injections of amino acid solutions. *Poul. Sci.* 52(5):1749–57.

Duke, G.E., Kostuch, T.E., and Evanson, O.A. 1975a. Gastroduodenal electrical activity in turkeys. *Am. J. Dig. Dis.* 20(11):1047–58.

——. 1975b. Electrical activity and intraluminal pressures in the lower small intestine of turkeys. *Am. J. Dig. Dis.* 20(11):1040–46.

Duke, G.E., Petrides, G.A., and Ringer, R.K. 1968. Chromium-51 in food metabolizability and passage rate-studies with the ring-necked pheasant. *Poul. Sci.* 47:1356–64.

Dulzetto, F. 1930. La funzione delle ghiandole del gozzo del colombo studiata mediante la fistola temporanea. *Arch. Sci. Biol.* 14:430–50.

Dziuk, H.E. 1971. Reverse flow of gastrointestinal contents in turkeys (abstr.). *Fed. Proc.* 30:610.

Dziuk, H.E., and Duke, G.E. 1971. Radiographic studies of deglutition in turkeys. Unpublished observation.

——. 1972. Cineradiographic studies of gastric motility in the turkey. *Am. J. Physiol.* 222(1):159–66.

Fargeas, M.J., Fargeas, J., LeBars, H., and Sevrez, C. 1963. Etude de la motricité caecale, chez la poule, par la technique de la fistule permanente. *Revue Med. Vet.* 114:693–707.

Farner, D.S. 1941. Some aspects of the physiology of digestion in birds. Ph.D. diss., U. of Wisconsin, Madison.

——. 1942. The hydrogen ion concentration in avian digestive tracts. *Poul. Sci.* 21:445–50.

Fearon, J.R., and Bird, F.H. 1968. Site and rate of active transport of D-glucose in the intestine of the fowl at various intestinal glucose concentrations. *Poul. Sci.* 47:1412–16.

Fedorovskii, N.P. 1951. Zobnoe i zheludochnoe pischevarenie indeek. *Soviet Zootekh.* 1:50–58.

Gleaves, E.W., Tonkinson, L.V., Wolf, J.D., Harman, C.K., Thayer, R.H., and Morrison, R.D. 1968. The action and interaction of physiological food intake regulators in the laying hen. I. Effects of dietary factors upon feed consumption and production responses. *Poul. Sci.* 47:38–67.

Graney, D.O. 1967. Electron microscopic observations in the morphology of intestinal capillaries in the chicken and the transcapillary passage of chylomicra during fat absorption. *Anat. Rec.* 157:250.

Groebbels, F. 1932. *Der Vogel, Erster Band, Atmungswelt und Nahrungswelt.* Gebruder Borntraeger, Berlin.

Henning, H.J. 1929. Die Verdaulichkeit der Rohfaser beim Huhn. *Landwirt. Versuchsstation* 108:235–86.

Herpol, C. 1967a. Zuurtegraad en vertering in de maag van vogels. *Natuurwet. Tijdschr.* 49:201–15.

——— 1967b. Etude de l'activité proteolytique des divers organes du système digestif de quelques espèces d'oiseaux en rapport avec leur régime alimentaire. *Zeitschrift Vergl. Physiol.* 57:209–17.

Herpol, C., and van Grembergen, G. 1967. La significance du pH dans le tube digestif de *Gallus domesticus*. *Ann. Biol. Anim. Biochem. Biophys.* 7:33–38.

Hudson, D.A., and Levin, R.J. 1966. Changes in the transmural potential difference associated with active hexose absorption during the development of the chick small intestine. *J. Physiol.* 186:112P–13P.

Hurwitz, S., and Bar, A. 1968. Regulation of pH in the intestine of the laying fowl. *Poul. Sci.* 47(3):1029–30.

Hurwitz, S., Bar, A., Katz, M., Sklan, D., and Budowski, P. 1973. Absorption and secretion of fatty acids and bile acids in the intestine of the laying fowl. *J. Nutr.* 103:543–47.

Joyner, W.L., and Kokas, E. 1971. Action of serotonin on gastric (proventriculus) secretion in chickens. *Comp. Gen. Pharmac.* 2:145–50.

Kato, T. 1914. Druckmessungen im Muskelmagen der Vogel. *Pflüg. Arch. ges. Physiol.* 159:6–26.

Keeton, R.W., Koch, F.C., and Luckhardt, A.B. 1920. Gastrin studies. III. The response of the stomach mucosa of various animals to gastrin bodies. *Am. J. Physiol.* 50:454–68.

Kokas, E., Phillips, J.L., Jr., and Brunson, W.D., Jr., 1967. The secretory activity of the duodenum in chickens. *Comp. Biochem. Physiol.* 22:81–90.

Kokas, E., and Brunson, W.D. 1969. Gastric secretion inhibition in chickens (abstr.). *Physiologist* 12:272.

Kokue, E., and Hayama, T. 1972. Effects of starvation and feeding on the exocrine pancreas of the chicken. *Poul. Sci.* 51:1366–70.

Kostuch, T.E., and Duke, G.E. 1975. Gastric motility in great horned owls. *Comp. Biochem. Physiol.* 51:201–5.

Kuenzel, W.J. 1972. Dual hypothalamic feeding system in a migratory bird, *Zonotrichia albicollis*. *Am. J. Physiol.* 223(5):1138–42.

Long, J.F. 1967. Gastric secretion in unanesthetized chickens. *Am. J. Physiol.* 212:1303–7.

MacNab, J.M. 1973. The avian caeca: A review. *World Poul. Sci. J.* 29:251–63.

Mangold, E. 1906. Der Muskelmagen der korner fressenden Vogel, seine motorischen Funktionen und ihre Abhangigkeit vom Nervensystem. *Pflüg. Arch ges. Physiol.* 111:163–240.

——. 1911. Die funktionellen Schwankungen der motorischen Tatigkeit des Raubvogelmagens. *Pflüg. Arch. ges. Physiol.* 139:10–32.

Nolf, P. 1938. Le système nerveux gastro-enterique. *Ann. Physiol. Physiochim. Biol.* 14:293–319.

——. 1939. Les éléments intrinsèques de l'anneau nerveux de gesier de l'oiseau granivore. *Arch. Internat. Physiol.* 48:451–52.

Noyan, A., Lossow, W.J., Brot, N., and Chaikoff, I.L. 1964. Pathway and form of absorption of palmitic acid in the chicken. *J. Lipid Res.* 5:538–41.

Ojha, K.N., and Ahmad, Q. 1967. The inhibitory effect of some thiazide diuretics and acetazolamide on the histamine-induced gastric secretory response in pigeons. *Indian J. Physiol. Pharmac.* 1:53–61.

Oshima, S., Shimada, K., and Tonoue, T. 1974. Radio telemetric observations of the diurnal changes in respiration rate heart rate. and intestinal motility of domestic fowl. *Poul. Sci.* 53:503–7.

Paine, C.M., Newman, H.J., and Taylor, M.W. 1959. Intestinal absorption of methionine and histidine by the chicken. *Am. J. Physiol.* 197:9–12.

Pastea, E., Nicolau, A., Popa, V., and Rosca, I. 1968. Dynamics of the digestive tracts in hens and ducks. *Acta Physiol. Acad. Sci. Hung.* 33:305–10.

Polyakov, I.I. 1958. Nekotorye dannye o podzheludochnom i kishernom soke kur. *Dokl. Mosk. Sel'skokhoz. Akad.* 38:238–333.

Pritchard, P.J. 1972. Digestion of sugars in the crop. *Comp. Biochem. Physiol.* 43A:195–205.

Radeff, T. 1928. Die Verdaulichkeit der Rohfaser und die Funktion der Blinddarme beim Haushuhn. *Arch. Geflügelkunde* 2:312–24.

Ruoff, A.J., and Sewing, K.F. 1970. Histamine, histidine decarboxylase, and gastrin in the upper gastrointestinal tract of chickens. *Arch. Pharmakologie* 265:301–9.

Ryan, C.A. 1965. Chicken chymotrypsin and turkey trypsin. I. Purification. *Arch. Biochem. Biophys.* 110:169–74.

Sahba, M.M., Morisset, J.A., and Webster, P.D. 1970. Synthetic and secretory effects of cholecystokinin-pancreozymin on the pigeon pancreas. *Proc. Soc. Exp. Biol. Med.* 134:728–32.

Schleucher, R., and Hokin, L.E. 1954. The synthesis and secretion of lipase and ribonuclease by pigeon pancreas slices. *J. Biol. Chem.* 210:551–57.

Smith, C.R., and Richmond, M.E. 1972. Factors influencing pellet egestion and gastric pH in the barn owl. *Wilson Bull.* 84:179–86.

Sturkie, P.D., and Joiner, W.P. 1959. Effects of foreign bodies in cloaca and rectum of the chicken on feed consumption. *Am. J. Physiol.* 197:1337–38.

Tasaki, I., and Takahashi, N. 1966. Absorption of amino acids from the small intestine of domestic fowl. *J. Nutr.* 88:359–64.

Thorburn, C.C., and Willcox, J.S. 1965. The caeca of the domestic fowl and digestion of the crude fibre complex. I. Digestibility trials with normal and cecectomized birds. *Brit. Poul. Sci.* 6:23–31.

Wakita, M., Hoshino, S., and Morimoto, K. 1970. Factors affecting the accumulation of amino acid by the chick intestine. *Poul. Sci.* 49:1046–49.

Walter, W.G. 1939. Bedingte Magensaftsekretion bei der Ente. *Acta Brevia Neerl. Physiol.* 9:56–57.

Warner, R.L., McFarland, L.Z., and Wilson, W.O. 1967. Microanatomy of the upper digestive tract of the Japanese quail. *Am. J. Vet. Res.* 28:1537–48.

White, S.S. 1969. Mechanisms involved in deglutition in *Gallus domesticus*. *J. Anat.* 104:177.

Yasukawa, M. 1959. Studies on movements of the large intestine. VII. Movements of the large intestine of fowls. *Jap. J. Vet. Sci.* 21:1–8.

Ziswiler, J., and Farner, D.S. 1972. Digestion and the digestive system. In D.S. Farner and J.R. King, eds., *Avian Biology*. Academic Press, New York. Vol. 2.

Zoppi, G., and Schmerling, D.H. 1969. Intestinal disaccharidase activities in some birds, reptiles, and mammals. *Comp. Biochem. Physiol.* 29:289–94.

CHAPTER 26

Absorption | by R. Scott Allen

Absorption is the process whereby digested foodstuffs are transferred from the lumen of the gastrointestinal tract to the blood and/or lymph. The absorbed materials are transported to the tissues for degradation, synthetic processes, or storage.

SITES OF ABSORPTION

Although no absorption of food or end products of digestion is known to take place in the mouth and esophagus, certain drugs may be absorbed from their epithelial surfaces. Meltzer (1896, 1899) showed that strychnine may be absorbed from the pharynx but only to a very limited extent from the esophagus.

In the stomach of the monogastric animal, absorption is very limited under normal conditions (see Chapter 22 for the ruminant). On the whole, food substances are not ready for absorption. Proteins are only partially degraded, fats are hydrolyzed only to a slight extent, and carbohydrate digestion is, in most animals, far from complete. Deuterium oxide (heavy water) can be absorbed from stomach pouches. However, it is doubtful that under ordinary circumstances water remains in the stomach long enough to undergo any significant reduction in volume. Inorganic salts are not absorbed in significant amounts, but certain drugs (such as ethanol) are absorbed from the monogastric stomach.

The small intestine is the chief site of absorption in carnivores and omnivores. It is also of great importance in herbivores.

The large intestine as an organ of absorption is of limited importance in carnivores and man except in the initial part of the colon, where water and electrolyte absorption occurs. Conversely, the large intestine in all herbivores is well adapted for absorption, particularly of short-chain fatty acids derived from fermentation of polysaccharides. However, bacterial proteins produced in the large intestine are not digested. This is especially true in single-stomached herbivores such as the horse, where extensive digestive changes occur in the large intestine. It is probably less true of ruminants, where digestion and absorption are so important in the anterior part of the digestive tract.

ABSORPTIVE SURFACES

The mucous membrane of the small intestine consists of numerous tiny fingerlike projections known as villi. These vary considerably in form and length in different animals, being longest in the carnivores, shorter in the solipeds, and shortest in swine and ruminants. In general, animals with the most rapid digestive and absorptive processes have a more highly developed system of villi to provide a greater surface area for absorption.

A villus is composed of a projecting core of lamina propria covered with a simple columnar epithelium. The luminal side of the epithelial cells is covered with fingerlike projections (microvilli) about 1.0–1.5 μ long and 0.1 μ wide (Fig. 26.1). Below the microvilli is an area called the terminal web, which contains many thin filaments. The epithelial cell is equipped with mitochondria, which tend to be oriented parallel to the long axis of the cell, Golgi apparati, two types (agranular and granular) of endoplasmic reticulum, lysosomes, and basally located nuclei.

The microvilli (often called the brush border) constitute the barrier through which absorbed materials must pass to gain entry into the mucosal cells (Crane 1968b).

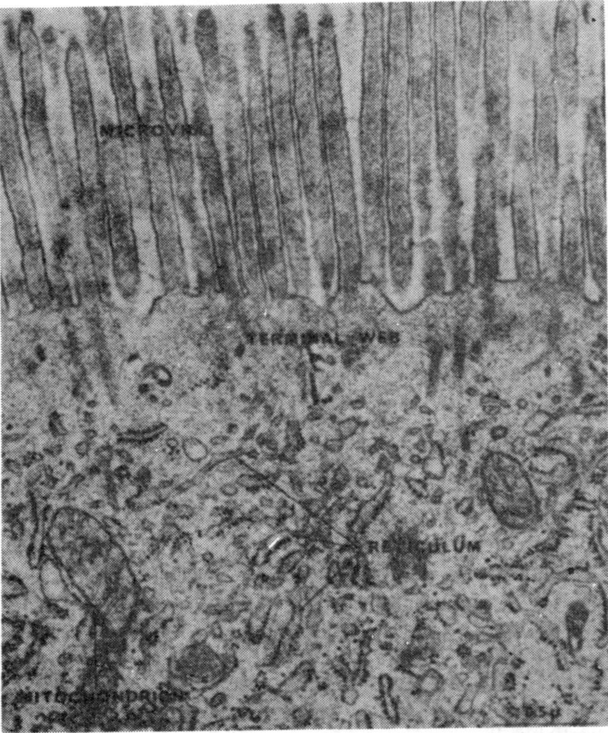

Figure 26.1. Electron micrograph of jejunal mucosa of a young dairy calf. (Courtesy of Dr. Peter R. Sterzing.)

The luminal surface includes a filamentous mucopolysaccharide layer (glycocalyx) capable of adsorbing proteins and binding them to its charged surface. Pancreatic enzymes may also bind to this surface and be functional there. Intrinsic to the microvilli are digestive disaccharidases, alkaline phosphatase, aminopeptidase, Na^+-K^+ – activated ATPase (adenosine triphosphatase) and possibly other hydrolases. The membrane matrix includes lipoidal materials and carrier proteins, both of which are involved in transport phenomena.

In the core of the villus is a large lymph capillary known as a lacteal. This capillary begins near the tip of the villus and enters a plexus of lymph vessels lying just on the inner side of the muscularis mucosae. Branches of this plexus enter the submucosa and there form a loose plexus of larger lymphatics. The latter pass through the muscularis externa into the mesentery.

Each villus contains several small arteries which enter the base of the villus and form a dense capillary network immediately under its epithelium. Near the tip of the villus one or two small veins arise from a capillary network and run downward where they anastomose and pass to the submucosa. These veins join with those of the submucosal plexus, then pass through the muscularis externa.

Strands of smooth muscle, which arise from the inner surface of the muscularis mucosae, extend toward the surface and are especially prominent in the core of the villi. Here they are arranged parallel to the axis of the villus around the central lacteal.

Villi undergo rhythmic (pumping) contractions, pendulum movements, and tonic contractions (Verzár and McDougall 1936). The movement of each villus appears to be independent of adjacent villi unless an intense stimulus is applied. During pumping movements the villi shorten quickly and lengthen more slowly, which results in removal of part of the contents from the central lacteals. Shortening of the villus is effected by contraction of the smooth-muscle fibers which are located along the axis of the villus; elongation of the villus probably is due to the elasticity of the connective tissue, the capillaries, and the muscles which bring the villus back to its original form.

Movements of the villi are in part under nervous control through the action of the submucosal plexus, which forms a continuous network between the muscularis mucosae and the submucosa. Stimulation of the sympathetic fibers excites the smooth-muscle fibers of the muscularis mucosae and results in increased activity of the villi. The parasympathetics, however, have little influence on movement of the villi.

King and Robinson (1945) reported that the submucosal plexus contains ganglionic cells with both adrenergic and cholinergic motor endings. Moreover, these workers felt that the rhythmic movements of the muscularis mucosae are primarily myogenic, but that they can be initiated or augmented by nervous control.

There is current evidence indicating that the movements of the villi are augmented by a hormone in the mucosa of the duodenum. This hormone, villikinin, is activated by hydrochloric acid.

Although the mucous membrane of the large intestine is devoid of villi, in herbivores it is well adapted for absorption, particularly of the short-chain fatty acids derived from the fermentation of polysaccharides.

ROUTES FOR ABSORBED FOODSTUFFS

The small intestine has extremely well-developed blood and lymphatic systems which function in absorption of the products of digestion.

Lymph

The lymph capillaries of the mucous membrane of the intestine, including the lacteals of the villi, drain into the larger lymph vessels of the submucosa. These penetrate the muscular coat of the small intestine and empty into the lacteal vessels of the mesentery, which are connected with mesenteric lymph nodes. The lacteal vessels of the mesentery proceed to and empty into the *cisterna chyli*. The latter vessel is continued forward as the thoracic duct, which empties into the venous system anterior to the heart. Glycerides, long-chain fatty acids, certain proteins (particularly the immune globulins during the first 24 hours of life), and cholesterol are absorbed by the lymphatic system. The rate of lymph flow increases after a meal.

Blood

The blood capillaries of the mucous membrane of the intestine, including those of the villi, unite to form venules and veins which drain into the portal vein via its mesenteric radicles. The portal vein enters the liver, where its blood is mixed with that of the hepatic artery. The hepatic veins convey the blood of the liver to the posterior vena cava.

Materials absorbed largely by the blood include water, inorganic salts, short-chain fatty acids, amino acids from protein digestion, monosaccharides from carbohydrate digestion, and the free glycerol which occurs during the digestion of certain fats.

The rapid flow of blood (about 600 times that of lymph) allows efficient absorption of these small molecular weight compounds. The rate of blood flow increases after a meal, but the increase is less than for lymph flow.

MECHANISMS OF ABSORPTION

The process by which products of digestion are transported across the epithelial cell wall has been investigated widely (for an excellent review see Curran and Schultz 1968). The possible mechanisms can be categorized into three general groups. First, noncarrier-mediated transport (passive diffusion) includes (1) solvent drag (interaction between the flow of a solute and the flow of a solvent); (2) single-file diffusion (movement via narrow channels, in the direction of a electrochemical potential difference); (3) nonionic diffusion (such as weak acids or bases); and (4) ion pair diffusion (anion and cation association at the membrane, followed by movement across the barrier as a neutral salt). Second, carrier-mediated transport involves (1) facilitated transfer (movement independent of metabolism, more rapid than simple diffusion, and in the direction of a concentration gradient); (2) exchange diffusion (exchange of a molecule on one side of a membrane for a molecule of the same species from the other side); and (3) active transport (net transfer of a substance against a concentration gradient or an electrochemical potential difference of that substance, a process which requires energy and involves direct coupling to metabolic reactions of the biological system). Third, the process of pinocytosis (transport of intact luminal materials in vacuoles into the mucosal cells).

Absorption processes are in large part dependent upon the structure of the compound being absorbed and upon the membrane structure. Kinetic studies suggest that in carrier-mediated processes the carrier, like an enzyme, possesses specific binding sites; but, unlike enzymes, no reaction beyond association appears to occur. The carrier may provide a specific means for water-soluble materials to cross the lipid matrix of cell membranes. Although active transport plays a major role in the absorption of glucose and amino acids, it is increasingly clear that facilitated transfer by mobile carriers also plays a significant role in the total absorption process. Noncarrier-mediated processes also are important, particularly in the absorption of some water-soluble vitamins, certain sugars such as fructose, short-chain fatty acids, inorganic salts, and many lipid-soluble compounds.

The significance of the pinocytotic process in mammals is not yet clear, but it appears to be related mostly to absorption of intact proteins and to some extent of intact triglycerides.

LIPID ABSORPTION

Dietary triglycerides (fats and oils) are converted to a coarse emulsion in the stomach. This emulsion is a result of mechanical movements and admixture with phospholipids and other chyme components. Although some lipolysis occurs in the stomach, the major digestive processes occur in the small intestine. Upon ejection from the stomach into the duodenum, the emulsion is mixed with bile and pancreatic juice. Triglycerides are attacked by pancreatic lipase at the 1- or 3-position (or α-positions) to yield diglycerides and monoglycerides successively. The result is the formation of free fatty acids and monoglycerides as principal products which then interact with conjugated bile acids (taurine and glycine types) to form microemulsions (micellar solutions). Lipid droplets decrease in size as hydrolysis of ester linkages continues. Although some glycerol may be produced in the lumen, its production depends primarily on the nature of the fatty acid residue remaining on the monoglyceride. Monoglyceride ester linkages involving short-chain fatty acids, such as those found in milk fat, are more readily hydrolyzed than those from plant and animal tissues with long-chain acids. Glycerol is quickly absorbed by passive diffusion and mostly enters the mesenteric venous blood. A small part, however, may be phosphorylated by enzymes of the intestinal cell cytoplasm and subsequently utilized for glyceride biosynthesis. Short-chain (up to C_{10}) fatty acids also are more water soluble and tend to be absorbed into the mesenteric portal blood.

Monoglycerides and long-chain fatty acids of the mixed micelles enter the microvilli (brush border) and the apical pole of the absorptive cells by simple diffusion (Porter 1969). The conjugated bile salts are not absorbed during lipid absorption but move along the tract and are absorbed in the lower region of the ileum. Dietschy (1968) showed that absorption of the conjugated bile salts involves an energy-requiring active transport system.

The lipid absorption process is thought to begin in the distal duodenum and to be completed in the proximal jujenum.

Within the epithelial cell, long-chain fatty acids are converted into fatty-acyl coenzyme A derivatives via reactions that involve coenzyme A (CoA) and adenosine triphosphate (ATP). These fatty acyl compounds react with monoglycerides to form diglycerides and then triglycerides as the major product (see Chapter 28.) The newly formed triglycerides may differ from the dietary fat or oil in that they contain essentially no fatty acid with less than 12 carbons in the chain. To a minor extent glycerol phosphate, derived primarily from glucose metabolism, may provide the glycerol residue for triglyceride synthesis. In addition, some phospholipids (needed for chylomicron formation) are formed by a process which involves cytidine diphosphate derivates as intermediates. To a minor extent cholesterol esters also are produced and include mostly unsaturated fatty acid residues. Prior to transfer of lipid from the epithelial cells, a small amount of protein is incorporated onto the surface of the lipid droplet. The finished products are chylomicrons (high triglyceride content and low levels of phospholipids, cholesterol, cholesterol esters, and protein), which leave the cells by reverse pinocytosis and enter the lateral intercellular spaces from which they pass into the lacteals. Subsequently, they are collected in lymphatic channels and transported via the thoracic duct into the blood for distribution to the tissues.

Cholesterol, endogenous and exogenous, is absorbed much less efficiently (generally 20–50 percent) than are triglycerides (with few exceptions, 95 percent or more). The presence of dihydrocholesterol and/or plant sterols in the lumen tends to inhibit cholesterol absorption.

Cholesterol can be absorbed only in the free form; cholesterol esters must first be hydrolyzed by pancreatic or brush border hydrolases. Absorption is enhanced by bile. Cholesterol enters the epithelial cell by displacement of the endogenous cholesterol of the brush border lipoprotein. Absorbed cholesterol is associated mostly with the microsomes. Before or during transfer from the epithelial cell to the lymphatics, as a part of the chylomicra, a major portion (80–90 percent) of the cholesterol is esterified. Certain physiologically active steroids (digitalis glycosides, cortisol, and vitamin D) are absorbed at rates sufficient to make them effective when administered orally.

Enzymes capable of hydrolyzing phospholipids are produced by the pancreas and the intestinal epithelium. It is now felt that a major portion of the phospholipids in the lumen is hydrolyzed to free fatty acids and lysophospholipids, and that the latter are absorbed as such by the intestinal mucosal cells and subsequently acylated. A small fraction, however, appears to be absorbed intact into the epithelial cells.

PROTEIN ABSORPTION

Proteins (dietary, endogenous, microbial, and shed mucosal) capable of being hydrolyzed by proteolytic enzymes (originating in the gastric musoca, pancreas, and intestinal mucosa) are degraded mostly to their amino acid components. Hydrolysis occurs in the lumen and also at the surface of the mucous membrane. The free amino acids are readily absorbed (chiefly in the small intestine) primarily by an active, energy-requiring system which has high structural specificity and requires sodium ions. The L-isomers (derived from plant and animal proteins) are more readily absorbed than the corresponding D-isomers, and there are marked differences in the rate of absorption among individual amino acids.

Wiseman (1968) reported that histidine and the neutral amino acids usually are very rapidly absorbed against a concentration gradiant. Tryptophan and the basic amino acids are actively absorbed only when their initial concentration is relatively low.

Glutamic and aspartic acids participate in transamination reactions within the mucosa which result in an increase chiefly in the level of alanine in the mesenteric veins.

Absorption rates are also influenced by the composition of the amino acid mixture at the site of absorption, presence of monosaccharides, general nutritional status, psychological state, dehydration, intestinal antiseptics, ethanol, and the condition of the intestinal mucosa. Jacobs (1965) reported that there is a dynamic bidirectional (both in and out) flux of amino acids across the intestinal mucosa.

Absorbed amino acids enter the circulation almost exclusively via the portal blood system.

Under some circumstances, native protein may be absorbed, possibly because of the altered morphology of the intestinal musoca associated mostly with age. Immune globulins from colostrum appear to be absorbed intact by the process of pinocytosis immediately after birth in some species, particularly in lambs, pigs, kids, calves, and pups. Transmission of the immune globulins in these species decreases progressively after birth and ceases after 24–36 hours (see Table 17.1). In other species, such as mice and rats, the ability to absorb intact proteins continues for a much longer period (10–18 days). Absorption of intact protein involves the lymph pathway almost exclusively.

CARBOHYDRATE ABSORPTION

The degradation of carbohydrates by digestive enzymes both in the lumen and on the external surface of the mucosal cells results in the formation of monosaccharides, whereas fermentation by bacteria often produces short-chain fatty acids (mostly acetic, propionic, and butyric). Monosaccharides are absorbed for the most part in the portal blood and are carried to the liver, although the lymph stream removes some sugar from the alimentary canal. Short-chain fatty acids are absorbed by the blood.

Short-chain fatty acids have been found in significant amounts in the blood draining from the cecum of the sheep, the cecum and colon of the pig, the colon of the horse, and the cecum of the rabbit. Blood coming from the small intestine does not contain significant amounts of short-chain fatty acids in any of these species, except the pig (Barcroft et al. 1944).

Although maltose, sucrose, and lactose are relatively soluble compounds, they are not absorbed as such except when consumed in very large amounts, and even then the extent of their absorption is slight. Disaccharides do not normally enter the blood stream because of the presence of their corresponding disaccharidases in the brush border of the mucosa of most species. These enzymes insure the conversion of disaccharides to monosaccharides during absorption. It has been suggested that absorption of intact disaccharide is mostly a measure of mucosal injury. When for any reason disaccharides appear in the blood stream, either by absorption or by parenteral introduction, they are largely eliminated unchanged in the urine.

Energy is expended during glucose absorption, and active transfer is involved. It was formerly thought that glucose was phosphorylated in the wall of the intestine and then was dephosphorylated before it entered the blood, but recent evidence indicates that the energy is expended in maintaining the sodium ion pump. Apparently these monosaccharides that are absorbed against a concentration gradient are transported across the cell barrier via a carrier which simultaneously moves both the sugar molecule and sodium ion (Crane 1968a). Energy is needed then to return the sodium ion to another carrier site. All phosphorylations and sugar interconversion reactions occur within the intestinal cell after absorption.

Monosaccharides are transported in the portal blood to the liver, where to a considerable extent they are converted to and stored as glycogen. Other tissues, notably the skeletal muscle, also form and store glycogen.

Numerous studies have shown that the rate of absorption of different sugars from the intestine is variable. Wilson (1962) summarized a number of experiments on comparative absorption rates of sugars. In most species, galactose is absorbed more rapidly than glucose. Fructose is taken up at a considerably slower rate (16–77 percent that of glucose). Mannose, xylose, and arabinose are poorly absorbed. Cori (1925) reported that the rate of absorption of glucose and other monosaccharides is fairly constant regardless of the amount of sugar ingested, the quantity determining the duration of absorption but not the rate. Concentration, however, does have a marked effect on absorption of sorbose, mannose, and xylose, probably because of an increase in simple diffusion with an increase in concentration. Crane (1968a) reported that care must be exercised in comparing rates of absorption when assurance of proper levels of sodium ion has not been made. Active transport of commonly occurring or natural sugars appears to be restricted to those of the D-pyranose structure with a hydroxyl group of the glucose configuration at carbon 2.

The rate of absorption of glucose from the intestine of the chick is more than twice that found in rats of similar size and over four times that found in dogs (Golden and Long 1942).

ABSORPTION OF SALTS AND WATER

Although sodium, potassium, and chloride ions normally are almost completely absorbed in the mammalian intestine, the sodium ion plays a highly significant role in the general function of the mucosa. Moreover, sodium ions are known to be involved in water transport and in the absorption (active transport) of monosaccharides, amino acids, pyrimidines, and bile salts.

A variety of experiments strongly indicate that sodium ion transfer across mucosal membranes of all segments of the intestine involves an active process. The active transport of sodium ions depends upon the potassium ion concentration in the cell; and there seems to be a coupling of the outward active transport of sodium with the inward transport of potassium. The major driving force for sodium transport in the duodenum and jejunum is the active transport of nonelectrolytes such as glucose and amino acids.

The Na^+-K^+–activated ATPase in epithelial membranes requires the presence of both cations for maximal activity. There is considerable evidence that this enzyme is intimately involved in active cation transport mechanisms. For example, a variety of metabolic inhibitors cause marked reductions in sodium absorption. However, potassium absorption appears also to occur passively.

Although the process of chloride ion transport is not entirely clear, most of the recent data tend to favor passive transfer. Some data, however, suggest that chloride may be absorbed from the small intestine against electrochemical potential differences. Bicarbonate absorption in the small intestine appears to be mediated by an active transport system; it is absorbed in preference to chloride.

The mechanism for water transport in the intestine has not been fully established. There is no compelling evidence in support of active transport.

The absorption of electrolytes is influenced significantly by diarrhea. As stool volume increases there is a progressive rise in the sodium content of stool water along with a corresponding fall in potassium content. This appears to result from diminished active sodium absorption due primarily to decreased contact time of intestinal contents with gut mucosa. In some diarrheal diseases, defective active transport in the ileum and colon has been noted. Acid-base balance disturbances ranging from alkalosis to acidosis have also been observed in diarrhea. These changes relate to levels of sodium, potassium, chloride, and organic acids in the stool water.

Intestinal absorption of calcium is slow in comparison to sodium and apparently involves active transport.

Vitamin D induces the presence of a mucosal calcium-binding protein, the level of which correlates with the extent of calcium absorption. Moreover, Ca^{++}-stimulated ATPase and alkaline phosphatase are involved in calcium transport in the small intestine. Although the absorption of magnesium appears to involve Mg^{++}-stimulated ATPase, this cation is rather poorly absorbed when the luminal levels are high, that is, when magnesium sulfate is employed as a laxative. The absorption of phosphate is probably an active process closely related to the simultaneous active transport of calcium. Recent evidence suggests that the calcium-binding protein of the brush border can also bind strontium and barium, suggesting at least a carrier-mediated transport system for these cations.

The absorption of iron from the intestine is regulated by mechanisms which are related to the level of ferrous iron in the mucosal cell. It has been proposed that absorption is limited by the binding capacity of apoferritin (a protein) for iron to form ferritin. Iron absorption appears to be an active transport process occurring mostly in the duodenum; however, when massive doses are administered the process appears to be one of simple diffusion.

Although some inorganic sulfate is absorbed from the intestine, little is known of the mechanism involved. Similarly, the mechanism of absorption of most of the trace minerals is not known. Only small amounts of copper are absorbed, mostly from the upper small intestine. Manganese and zinc are poorly absorbed, while cobalt and molybdenum are readily absorbed from the intestine.

Fat-soluble vitamins (A, D, E and K) pass through the intestinal mucosa primarily by passive diffusion through the lipid phase of the mucosal cell membrane. Also, most studies with water-soluble vitamins (except B_{12}) show that the major absorption process is passive diffusion. There is some evidence, however, that suggests active transport of some B-complex vitamins (folacin and thiamin) particularly when ingested at low levels. Physiological levels of vitamin B_{12} require an intrinsic factor, secreted by the stomach, for its absorption by an active transport process. Massive doses, however, result in passive diffusion even in the absence of the intrinsic factor.

REFERENCES

Barcroft, J., McAnally, R.A., and Phillipson, A.T. 1944. Absorption of volatile acids from the alimentary tract of the sheep and other animals. *J. Exp. Biol.* 20:120–29.

Booth, C.C. 1968. Effect of location along the small intestine on absorption of nutrients. In *Handbook*. Vol. 3, 1513–27.

Cori, C.F. 1925. The fate of sugar in the animal body. I. The rate of absorption of hexoses and pentoses from the intestinal tract. *J. Biol. Chem.* 66:691–715.

Crane, R.K. 1968a. Absorption of sugars. In *Handbook*. Vol. 3, 1323–51.

——. 1968b. A concept of the digestive-absorptive surface of the small intestine. In *Handbook*. Vol. 5, 2535–42.

Crosby, W.H. 1968. Iron absorption. In *Handbook*. Vol. 3, 1553–70.

Curran, P.F., and Schultz, S.G. 1968. Transport across membranes: General principles. In *Handbook*. Vol. 3, 1217–43.

Dietschy, J.M. 1968. Mechanism for the intestinal absorption of bile acids. *J. Lipid Res.* 9:297–309.

Fortran, J.S. 1967. Speculations on the pathogenesis of diarrhea. *Fed. Proc.* 26:1405–14.

Golden, W.R.C., and Long, C.N.H. 1942. Absorption and disposition of glucose in the chick. *Am. J. Physiol.* 136:244–49.

Handbook of Physiology. Sec. 6, C.F. Code and W. Heidel, eds., *Alimentary Canal.* 5 vols. Am. Physiol. Soc., Washington.

Jacobs, F.A. 1965. Bidirectional flux of amino acids across the intestinal mucosa. *Fed. Proc.* 24:946–52.

Johnston, J.J. 1968. Mechanism of fat absorption. In *Handbook*. Vol. 3, 1353–75.

King, C.E., and Robinson, M.H. 1945. The nervous mechanisms of the muscularis mucosae. *Am. J. Physiol.* 143:325–35.

Meltzer, S.J. 1896. On absorption of strychnine and hydrocyanic acid from the mucous membrane of the stomach: An experimental study on rabbits. *J. Exp. Med.* 1:529–36.

——. 1899. An experimental study of the absorption of strychnine in the different sections of the alimentary canal of dogs. *Am. J. Med. Sci.* 118:560–70.

Morris, I.G. 1968. Gamma globulin absorption in the newborn. In *Handbook*. Vol. 3, 1491–1512.

Oxender, D.L. 1972. Membrane transport. *Ann. Rev. Biochem.* 41:777–814.

Porter, K.R. 1969. Independence of fat absorption and pinocytosis. *Fed. Proc.* 28:35–40.

Rindi, G., and Venturi, U. 1972. Thiamine intestinal transport. *Physiol. Rev.* 52:821–27.

Schultz, S.G., and Curran, P.F. 1970. Coupled transport of sodium and organic solutes. *Physiol. Rev.* 50:637–718.

Treadwell, C.R., and Vahouny, G.V. 1968. Cholesterol absorption. In *Handbook*. Vol. 3, 1407–38.

Verzár, F., and McDougall, E.J. 1936. *Absorption from the Intestine.* Longmans, Green, London.

Wilson, T.H. 1962. *Intestinal Absorption*. Saunders, Philadelphia.

Wiseman, G. 1968. Absorption of amino acids. In *Handbook*. Vol. 3, 1277–1307.

CHAPTER 27

Carbohydrate Metabolism | by R. Scott Allen

In most mammalian species, dietary carbohydrates provide well over one half of the energy needs for performance of metabolic work, growth, repair, secretion, absorption, excretion, and mechanical work. The mechanism through which energy is developed, trapped, and delivered to the active functional machinery in the individual cells is termed intermediary metabolism, and it includes the sum total of these processes as related to the utilization of all nutrients (glucose, amino acids, fatty acids and other lipids, purines, pyrimidines, water, oxygen, and other substances).

Carbohydrate metabolism includes all of the reactions undergone by carbohydrates whether they are provided in the diet or formed in the body from noncarbohydrate sources. Most of the dietary carbohydrates are in the form of polysaccharides (starch, occasionally small amounts of glycogen, and in some species, cellulose, hemicellulose, and the pentosans). Other dietary carbohydrates include disaccharides (maltose, sucrose, and lactose) and monosaccharides (glucose, fructose, galactose, mannose, and certain pentoses). Except for small amounts of glucose and fructose, monosaccharides are not important dietary energy sources.

In nonruminants, starch and glycogen are hydrolyzed enzymatically, mostly to the disaccharide stage, in the gastrointestinal tract. Some monosaccharides are formed in the lumen of the small intestine by reaction with disaccharidases in mucosal cells which have been sloughed off. During absorption the disaccharides are hydrolytically degraded to monosaccharides by enzymes in the brush border of the mucosal epithelial cells, and the resulting monosaccharides pass into the portal vein for transportation to the liver. Monosaccharides in the lumen of the intestine also are absorbed by the portal system.

In herbivorous animals, cellulose, hemicellulose, and pentosans are converted, to the extent that they are digested, to the lower fatty acids by microbial fermentation in the alimentary canal. Acetic, propionic, and butyric acids predominate, the first two being most abundant, with relative amounts of these varying with time, diet, pH, and microbial composition of the ruminal contents. In adult ruminants and nonruminant herbivores relatively small amounts of dietary carbohydrates escape fermentation. Since ruminants derive the major portion of their energy from the lower fatty acids, glucose and other monosaccharides as such play only a secondary role in the metabolism of these animals.

BLOOD GLUCOSE

In mammalian species the characteristic sugar of blood and of other tissue fluids is glucose. Occasionally very small amounts of galactose and fructose may be present after absorption from the intestine and before their conversion to glucose. This conversion occurs both in the intestinal mucosa and in the liver.

Blood glucose and glucose in certain tissue fluids are drawn upon by all cells of the body to produce energy. The dependence of various tissues on circulating blood glucose varies greatly. Erythrocytes and the mature brain are critically dependent. However, the brain, under certain circumstances such as in starved animals, is able to utilize significant quantities of blood ketone bodies. Other tissues, such as skeletal muscle, are capable of deriving considerable amounts of their chemical energy needs from other nutrients (such as ketone bodies and fatty acids) and are not so highly dependent upon sustained blood glucose levels.

The level of glucose in the blood is also an important factor in determining the glucose concentration in the interstitial fluid, which in turn has an influence on the rate of transport of this sugar into individual cells.

Under postabsorptive conditions the ranges of blood glucose values vary considerably among species (see Chapter 2). Variability among animals of a given species is often observed too and may be related to nutritive state and to carbohydrate stores within the animal.

Blood glucose levels in mature ruminants are substantially lower than those in nonruminants. Though the newborn ruminant has blood glucose values that approximate those of nonruminant mammals, these values decrease sharply during the first few weeks of life and then more slowly up to about the sixth month, when approximately adult values are reached. In calves raised on an all-milk diet the blood glucose levels follow the same pattern as calves raised on high-forage diets.

Sources

Absorption of monosaccharides resulting from digestion of dietary carbohydrates constitutes a major, though variable, source of blood sugar in nonruminants. Digestive and absorptive rates may be highly variable, even among animals of the same species on the same dietary regimen. After a high carbohydrate meal the blood glucose levels may be considerably above the fasting state, but in a relatively short time they return to a prefeeding level.

A second continuing source of blood glucose results from endogenous synthesis from glucogenic materials, such as glycogen, glucogenic amino acids, glycerol, propionic acid, and others. The immediate precursor for blood glucose is glucose-6-phosphate, which undergoes hydrolysis in the presence of glucose-6-phosphatase in liver, kidney, and intestinal mucosa.

Uses

Subsequent to active transport of blood glucose into cells, a hexokinase reaction produces glucose-6-phosphate. This process seems to be based primarily upon the need for glucose-6-phosphate by the cells. This glucose derivative in turn can be converted into cellular glycogen, metabolized via pyruvic acid and the citric acid cycle to provide energy for the cell, metabolized via the pentose phosphate pathway, used in biosynthesis of other carbohydrate derivatives (glycolipids, nucleic acids, lactose, mucopolysaccharides), or converted into lipids for storage.

Normally only a trace of glucose is lost in the urine, even when a high-carbohydrate diet is fed. However, several diseases result in significant excretion of glucose in the urine (glucosuria). Under some circumstances the urinary glucose is even derived in part from non-carbohydrate materials such as certain amino acids. Disease conditions resulting in glucosuria often result from hormone imbalances (see Chapters 24, 30, and 56).

METABOLIC MECHANISMS

Although the pathways of carbohydrate metabolism are numerous, the present discussion will be limited to those most prominent in mammalian species: (1) glycolysis, (2) the citric acid cycle, (3) the pentose phosphate pathway, (4) glycogen formation and degradation, and (5) interconversions among monosaccharides. (For abbreviations see end of chapter.)

GLYCOLYSIS

Glycolysis involves the breakdown of glycogen, glucose, or other monosaccharides to pyruvic and lactic acids by enzymes in the cytosol (this term is used here interchangeably with cytoplasm). Although only a small part (about 5 percent) of the total available energy of free glucose becomes available by glycolysis, this process allows for rapid formation of energy in the form of ATP under anaerobic conditions. The energy may be used for muscle contraction and other functions and is particularly important during sudden strenuous exercise. Maximum attainable energy from glucose in the form of ATP can result only when pyruvic acid is oxidized to carbon dioxide and water via the citric acid cycle under aerobic conditions (see below).

In the first part of the glycolysis sequence (Fig. 27.1), glucose is converted to fructose-1,6-diphosphate by phosphorylation, isomerization, and a second phosphorylation reaction. Each phosphorylation step utilizes ATP. In the second phase, fructose-1,6-diphosphate is cleaved with aldolase to dihydroxyacetone phosphate and 3-phosphoglyceraldehyde. The latter is then oxidized (NAD^+) and phosphorylated (Pi) to form 1,3-diphosphoglyceric acid which is an acyl phosphate with a high energy-transfer potential. After transfer of the acyl phosphate to form ATP, the 3-phosphoglyceric acid undergoes phosphoryl shift and dehydration to produce phosphoenolpyruvate, which is a second compound with a high energy-transfer potential (the "ate" ending may be used interchangeably with "acid"). A transfer reaction then results in the generation of ATP and pyruvate.

Metabolic control of glycolysis is centered primarily on those reactions that are irreversible. Hexokinase is inhibited by glucose-6-phosphate. Phosphofructokinase is allosterically inhibited by ATP and citric acid, and is activated by AMP and ADP. Muscle pyruvate kinase is inhibited by high concentrations of ATP, whereas liver pyruvate kinase is inhibited by ATP, alanine, long-chain fatty acids, and acetyl CoA. The level of activity of phosphofructokinase is the primary control for the rate of

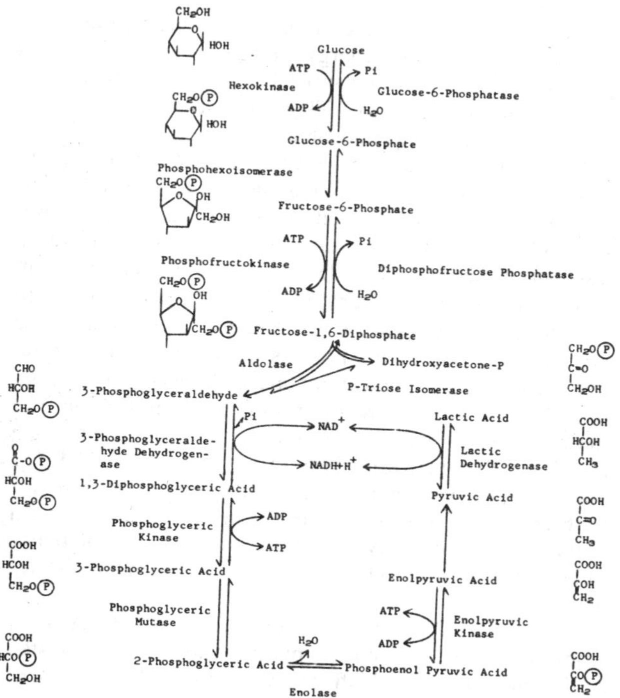

Figure 27.1. Reactions in glycolysis

glycolysis, for example, the low concentration of this enzyme is rate-controlling in the liver. In many systems the glycolytic chain of reactions terminates by the conversion of pyruvic acid to lactic acid. This step makes use of NADH, which was previously formed in the oxidation of 3-phosphoglyceraldehyde. In active skeletal muscle the rate of production of pyruvate exceeds its oxidation by the citric acid cycle. For glycolysis to continue, NAD^+ is needed for the oxidation of 3-phosphoglyceraldehyde. This is made available by the reduction of pyruvate to lactate. The resulting lactate readily diffuses in the blood and is transported to the liver where it is oxidized to pyruvate by the NAD^+ in cytosol. Subsequently, the pyruvate is converted to glucose for transport back to the skeletal muscle. The overall process is called the Cori cycle.

The conversion of lactic acid (and of other noncarbohydrate precursors) to glucose is called gluconeogenesis. The major site for this process is the liver; some occurs in the kidney. Gluconeogenesis is not a reversal of glycolysis because of the essential irreversibility of three reactions: (1) glucose to glucose-6-phosphate, (2) fructose-6-phosphate to fructose-1,6-diphosphate, and (3) phosphoenolpyruvate to pyruvate. Moreover, glycolysis is a highly exergonic process.

Circumvention of these virtually irreversible reactions is accomplished by (1) conversion of pyruvate to phosphoenolpyruvate via oxalacetate, (2) hydrolysis of fructose-1,6-diphosphate to form fructose-6-phosphate, and (3) hydrolysis of glucose-6-phosphate to produce glucose (Fig. 27.2). Pyruvate diffuses into and malate out of the mitochondria in the course of the gluconeogenic process. The balance of the reactions in gluconeogenesis are reversible reactions common to glycolysis. Glucose-6-phosphatase is present only in those tissues (liver, kidney, and intestinal epithelium) which provide glucose to the blood.

A total of six high-energy phosphate bonds are expended in the gluconeogenic conversion of pyruvate to glucose, whereas only two high-energy phosphate bonds are generated in glycolysis. The four extra bonds are required to shift the energetically unfavorable process (direct reversal of glycolysis) to a favorable one (gluconeogenesis). The extra energy for gluconeogenesis probably comes from the oxidation of fatty acids.

Gluconeogenesis is under nucleotide, metabolite, and hormone control. Four key enzymes are involved: pyruvate carboxylase, phosphoenolpyruvate carboxylase, fructose diphosphatase, and glucose-6-phosphatase. The first two are stimulated by acetyl CoA and inhibited by ADP. Both phosphatases are inhibited by AMP and ADP, but glucose-6-phosphatase is product inhibited by Pi and glucose. Slower rates of control are affected by insulin which suppresses and by cortisol which induces the synthesis of the four enzymes.

AEROBIC METABOLISM

Although special pathways for aerobic metabolism of carbohydrates exist in certain tissues, the major route in animal tissues begins with pyruvic acid produced primarily by glycolysis. The pyruvate diffuses into the mitochondria and is oxidatively decarboxylated to form acetyl CoA in an involved reaction that is catalyzed by the pyruvate dehydrogenase complex. This enzyme system is a highly integrated complex of three enzymes with cofactor requirements for NAD^+, TPP, FAD, CoA, and lipo-

MITOCHONDRIA

(biotin)
pyruvate + CO_2 + H_2O + ATP ⇌ oxalacetate + ADP + Pi + H^+
pyruvate carboxylase

oxalacetate + NADH + H^+ ⇌ malate + NAD^+
malic dehydrogenase

CYTOSOL

malate + NAD^+ ⇌ oxalacetate + NADH + H^+
malic dehydrogenase

oxalacetate + GTP ⇌ phosphoenolpyruvate + GDP + CO_2
phosphoenolpyruvate carboxykinase

fructose-1,6-diphosphate + H_2O → fructose-6-phosphate + Pi
fructose-1,6-diphosphatase

glucose-6-phosphate + H_2O → glucose + Pi
glucose-6-phosphatase

Figure 27.2. Key reactions in gluconeogenesis

amide. The acetyl unit is then oxidized to CO_2 by enzymes involved in the citric acid cycle

Acetyl CoA is an extremely versatile intermediary metabolite. In addition to being metabolized primarily by the citric acid cycle, it may be used in the formation of long-chain fatty acids, cholesterol, bile acids, steroid hormones, ketone bodies, and a variety of acetylated compounds.

Citric acid cycle

The citric acid cycle (also known as the Krebs cycle) is confined to the mitochondria in respiring tissues of all animals. The cycle (Fig. 27.3) is initiated by condensation of the acetyl unit with oxalacetate to form citric acid. An isomer of citric acid is then oxidatively decarboxylated to produce α-ketoglutarate which is subsequently oxidatively decarboxylated by a multi-enzyme complex resembling that of the pyruvate dehydrogenase complex described above. The resulting succinyl CoA is converted to succinate, a process which generates GTP. Succinate is oxidized to fumarate, which is then hydrated to produce malate. Finally, malate is oxidized to oxalacetate to complete the cycle.

In one turn of the cycle two carbons enter as the acetyl unit and two carbons leave as CO_2, four pairs of hydrogen atoms leave (three NAD^+ are reduced, one FAD is reduced), one high-energy phosphate bond (GTP) is generated, and two water molecules are consumed. GTP reacts with ADP to form ATP plus GDP, a reaction catalyzed by nucleoside diphosphate kinase.

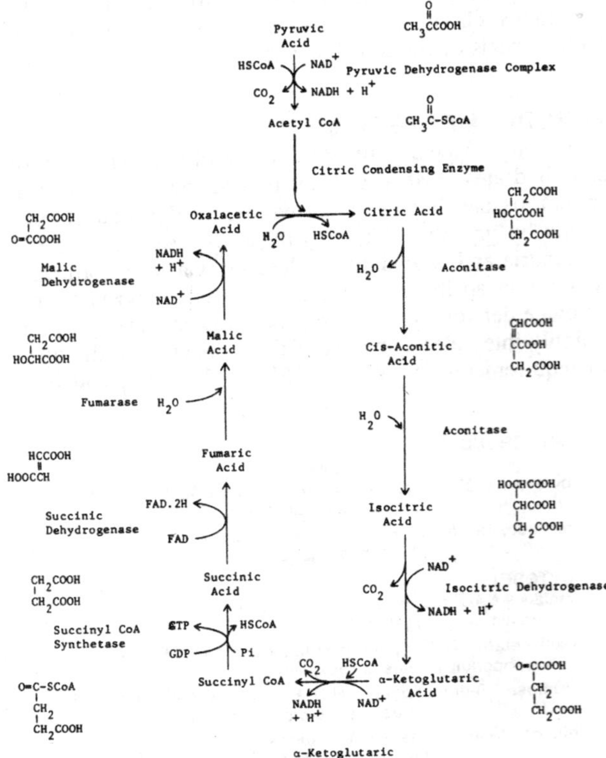

Figure 27.3. Citric acid cycle

Considerable energy in the form of ATP becomes available to the organism by oxidation of the reduced coenzymes produced in the citric acid cycle. Within mitochondria are localized enzymes, capable of electron transport functions, that deliver electrons derived from oxidizable substrates to oxygen. The energy derived from this transport process is conserved by coupling it to the formation of ATP. This process (oxidative phosphorylation) requires ADP and inorganic phosphate. The oxidative phosphorylation process results in the formation of 3 moles of ATP from each NADH and 2 ATP from each FAD·2H. The net result is the formation of 12 ATP (11 via oxidative phosphorylation, 1 from the GTP step) for each complete turn of the citric acid cycle, starting with acetyl CoA. Obviously, the citric acid cycle is of major importance in the production of energy for metabolic reactions.

The complete oxidation of glucose yields 36 ATP: 2 from glycolysis, 6 from the pyruvate to acetyl CoA step in the mitochondria, 24 from two turns of the citric acid cycle to oxidize two acetyl CoA, and 4 from the mitochondrial oxidation (involving a flavoprotein enzyme) of two glycerol-3-phosphates, which carries into the mitochondria electrons derived from the two cytoplasmic NADH. Most of the ATP, 32 of 36, are derived by oxidative phosphorylation. Under normal conditions, the rate of oxidative phosphorylation is determined by the need for ATP and the level of ADP.

The citric acid cycle is a central pathway which unifies and integrates total cellular metabolism. Both catabolism and anabolism of carbohydrates, lipids, and amino acids involve this vital aerobic reaction sequence.

Certain components of the citric acid cycle are products of catabolism and serve as points of entry for final oxidation and ATP generation. Acetyl CoA is derived from carbohydrate degradation via glycolysis, from oxidative breakdown of long-chain fatty acids, and from catabolism of ketone bodies and several amino acids. Oxalacetic acid, fumaric acid, succinyl CoA, and α-ketoglutaric acid also are produced in the degradation of amino acids.

Several citric acid cycle components play vital anabolic roles. Oxalacetic acid serves as a precursor for phosphoenolpyruvate in gluconeogenesis and is the carbon skeleton for aspartic acid and asparagine synthesis. Pyruvic acid, although not strictly a component of the citric acid cycle, serves as a carbon source for several amino acids. Citric acid, when produced at higher than normal levels, diffuses from the mitochrondria and is cleaved to oxalacetic acid (returning to the mitochondria after reduction to malic acid) and acetyl CoA (used in the cytoplasmic synthesis of long-chain fatty acids, sterols, and ketone bodies). Succinyl CoA is involved in some acylation reactions and in the biosynthesis of the porphyrin ring system of heme. α-ketoglutaric acid is readily converted to glutamic acid, a precursor for several other amino acids. Biosynthesis of purine and pyrimidine nucleotides also involves compounds derived from the citric acid cycle.

A variety of controls govern the pyruvate dehydrogenase complex and the citric acid cycle. Acetyl CoA and NADH, products of the oxidation of pyruvic acid, inhibit the pyruvate dehydrogenase complex, while CoA and NAD^+ stimulate it. The citric acid cycle is controlled at three sites: (1) ATP allosterically inhibits the citrate-condensing enzyme (citrate synthetase), (2) isocitric dehydrogenase is allosterically stimulated by ADP but is inhibited by ATP and NADH, and (3) α-ketoglutaric dehydrogenase is inhibited by succinyl CoA and NADH. The cyclic process is carefully adjusted to meet the need of ATP in the cell. When the mitochondrial level of ATP is high the acceptance of acetyl CoA into the cycle is reduced.

PENTOSE PHOSPHATE PATHWAY

The combined glycolysis and citric acid cycle reactions are primarily concerned with ATP production. Another type of metabolic energy, namely reducing power in the form of NADPH, is required for reductive biosyntheses. The major metabolic system utilized for generation of NADPH is called the pentose phosphate pathway. It also is called the hexosemonophosphate shunt, the pentose shunt, or the phosphogluconate oxidative pathway. The enzymes for this pathway are found in the cytoplasm of those cells in which this process is important, including the liver, adipose tissue, mammary gland (particularly during lactation), adrenal gland, erythrocytes, and the cornea and lens of the eye.

In the pentose phosphate pathway (Fig. 27.4), NADPH is generated by the oxidative conversion of glucose-6-phosphate to the pentose-5-phosphates. The pentose phosphate pathway also involves monoxidative interconversions of four-, five-, six-, and seven-carbon sugars.

Ribose-5-phosphate is a key intermediate in the formation of several important biomolecules, such as NAD^+, CoA, ATP, FAD, RNA, and DNA. When there is a need for more ribose-5-phosphate than NADPH, glucose-6-phosphate is converted to fructose-6-phosphate and 3-phosphoglyceraldehyde via the glycolytic pathway. Transketolase and transaldolase then convert these products to ribose-5-phosphate by reversal of the nonoxidative phase of the pathway.

Recycling of the pentose phosphates back to glucose-6-phosphate allows for complete oxidation of glucose-6-phosphate to CO_2 with the concomitant generation of NADPH. The NADPH serves primarily in the biosynthesis of long-chain fatty acids, in hydroxylations of fatty acids and steroids, and also in maintaining a cellular pool of reduced glutathione in erythrocytes.

Regulation of the pentose phosphate pathway involves primarily the dehydrogenation of glucose-6-phosphate. Diets with excess carbohydrates cause an increase in level of the dehydrogenase enzyme, while NADPH acts as a competitive inhibitor for the enzyme. However, ox-

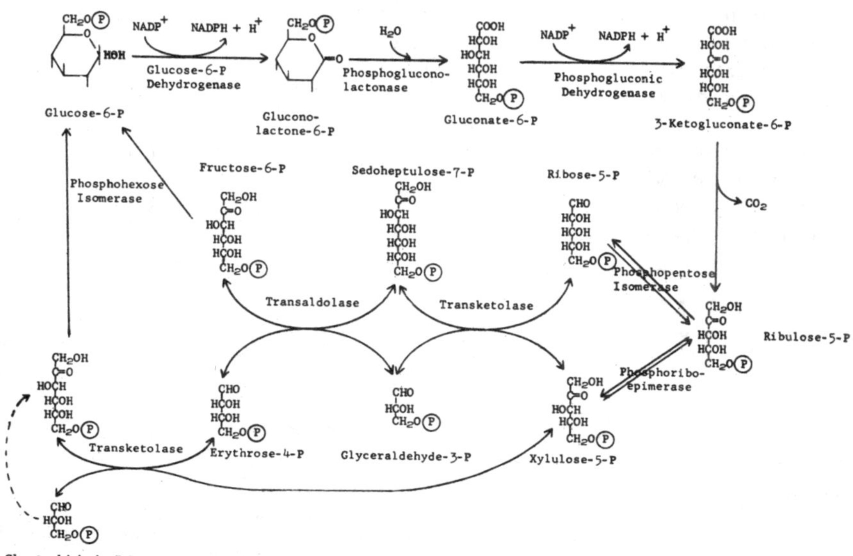

Figure 27.4. Pentose phosphate pathway

idized glutathione acts specifically to reverse this inhibition.

GLYCOGEN

Glycogen is a highly branched polymer of glucose that is stored in liver and muscle tissues. This polysaccharide serves as a reservoir for glucose when it is needed in metabolic processes.

Glycogenesis

In glycogenesis (Fig. 27.5), glucose, galactose, fructose, and mannose are readily converted to glycogen. Glucose-6-phosphate in the presence of phosphoglucomutase is reversibly converted to glucose-1-phosphate. In the presence of UDP-glucose pyrophosphorylase, glucose-1-phosphate reacts with uridine triphosphate (UTP) to form uridine diphosphate glucose (UDP-glucose) and pryophosphate (PP). Also, UDP-glucose is formed easily from UDP-galactose. The synthesis of the amylose chain of glycogen is catalyzed by glycogen synthetase and involves an interaction of UDP-glucose with the hydroxyl group of the number 4 position at the nonreducing ends of pre-existing polysaccharide chains (primers). The primer generally consists of a branched polysaccharide, the main linkages of which are α-1,4. Glycogen itself is the most efficient primer, and the synthetase is closely bound to it.

Glycogen has a highly branched structure; the branches result from α-1,6 bonds which occur every 8–12 glucose units. This highly branched structure is a result of the activity of a branching enzyme, amylo-(1,4$\rightarrow$1,6)-transglucosylase, which is found in liver, skeletal muscle, and brain. The transglucosylase cleaves fragments of the glycogen chain at α-1,4 linkages and transfers them to the same or another glycogen molecule to form α-1,6 linkages. Each chain is extended by the action of glycogen synthetase, and further branching and extension continue to produce the highly branched glycogen molecule.

Glycogen synthetase exists in two forms (independent and dependent). The independent form is most active and is produced by the action of a phosphatase on the dependent form. Conversion of the independent to the dependent form requires ATP and a kinase which is stimulated by cyclic AMP. The latter arises from the stimulatory effect of epinephrine (effect greatest in muscle) and of glucagon (response greatest in the liver) on adenyl cyclase, the plasma membrane enzyme responsible for cyclic AMP formation from ATP. The effect of these hormones is to switch off glycogen synthesis. In addition, high levels of glycogen inhibit the action of phosphatase on the less active form of glycogen synthetase. Insulin, however, activates glycogen synthetase.

Glycogenolysis

In contrast to the common hydrolytic fragmentation of polysaccharides in the gastrointestinal tract, glycogen is degraded within cells to glucose-1-phosphate by the action of inorganic phosphate in the presence of glycogen phosphorylase (Fig. 27.6). Phosphorylase degradation of glycogen begins at the nonreducing end of each chain, releasing glucose-1-phosphate successively until a branch point is approached. Here another enzyme (oligo transferase) redistributes the chain to leave a single glucose residue at the α-1,6 linkage. The resulting compound, called a limit dextrin, is then hydrolytically attacked at the α-1,6 linkage by amylo-1,6-glucosidase with the removal of free glucose. Subsequently phosphorylase action continues with release of glucose-1-phosphate until another branch point is approached. The transfer, hydrolysis, and phosphorylase reactions follow in order to pro-

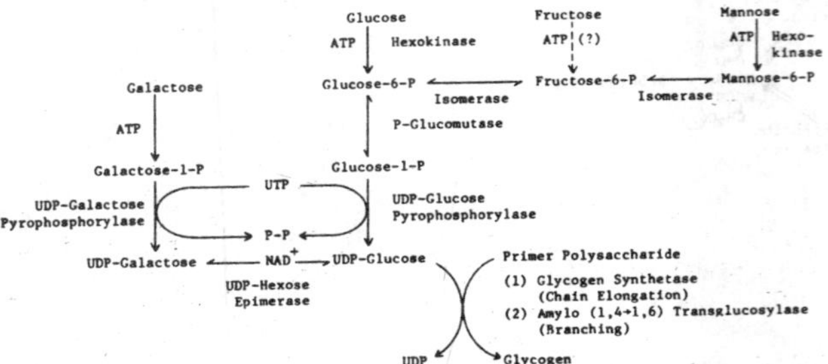

Figure 27.5. Glycogen synthesis

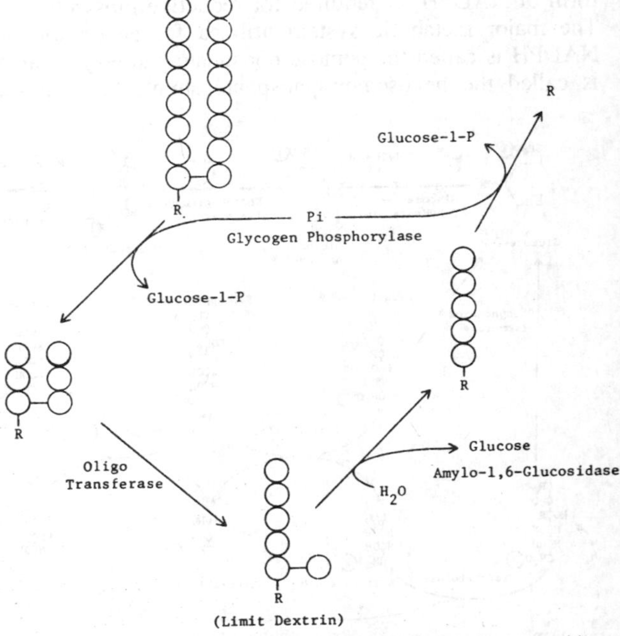

Figure 27.6. Glycogenolysis. Each circle represents a glucose residue. Only one set of the many terminal endings of glycogen is shown; R represents the remainder of the glycogen molecule.

duce mostly glucose-1-phosphate and a small amount of glucose.

Muscle glycogenolysis is under metabolite, nucleotide, hormone, enzyme, and cation control. Skeletal muscle has two forms of glycogen phosphorylase (*a* is active, *b* is inactive). The *b* form becomes active when AMP levels are high, whereas both ATP and glucose-6-phosphate inhibit phosphorylase *b*. In contrast, phosphorylase *a* is active regardless of the level of AMP, ATP, and glucose-6-phosphate, but is inhibited by UDP-glucose. Conversion of *a* to *b* is triggered by increased levels of Ca^{++} in the cytoplasm which both stimulates muscle contraction and the partial activation of a kinase. Subsequently, the epinephrine–cyclic AMP system stimulates the formation of fully active phosphorylated kinase which converts phosphorylase *b* to *a*. Deactivation of glycogenolysis results from the conversion of phosphorylase *a* to *b*.

Liver glycogenolysis is similar to that in muscle except that the principal hormone which stimulates cyclic AMP formation is glucagon. Liver phosphorylase *b*, however, is not activated by AMP.

Physiological role

Glycogen is present in practically all tissues in all species of animals. In various mammalian species it may occupy between 2 and 8 percent of the wet weight of the liver. It is relatively labile and may vary greatly depending upon the nutritional status of the animal. If an animal is fasted for 24 hours of longer, the liver may be almost depleted of glycogen. A dietary intake of glycogenic materials, such as glucose, results in a rapid biosynthesis of liver glycogen. In the normal animal, even when excess carbohydrate is available in the diet, the level of liver glycogen is relatively constant, but it is continuously being formed and degraded. Excess dietary carbohydrate is converted to and stored as fat.

Muscle glycogen content varies from about 0.5 to 1 percent by wet weight; due to the large muscle mass most of the total body glycogen is found in this tissue. In normal animals, muscle glycogen levels are more constant than in the liver. Muscle glycogen and the glycogen of other extraphepatic tissues are used extensively in metabolic processes and are restored primarily by synthesis from blood glucose. Not all of the muscle glycogen is synthesized from glucose originating directly from liver glycogen; some glucose absorbed from the alimentary tract may serve directly in the synthesis of muscle glycogen.

Both the quantity of food consumed and the composition of the diet have been shown to influence the quantity of liver glycogen. Animals on high-carbohydrate diets tend to have substantially higher liver glycogen levels than those on diets deficient in carbohydrates. Exercise reduces the quantity of glycogen in the liver. Abnormal conditions such as hypoxia and acidosis do also. In addition, the liver glycogen content is under endocrine regulation. Epinephrine and glucagon under normal circumstances have glycogenolytic activity. Insulin and the 11-oxysteroids favor accumulation of liver glycogen. The uptake of glucose from blood by skeletal muscle is dependent upon insulin, while uptake by liver is not, and therefore muscle glycogen increases more significantly following insulin injection than does liver glycogen.

ROLE OF THE LIVER

The liver plays a key role in the metabolism of carbohydrates. One of the unique and highly significant reactions is that catalyzed by glucose-6-phosphatase which converts glucose-6-phosphate to glucose. Through this reaction glycogen can contribute directly to blood glucose by way of glucose-1-phosphate and glucose-6-phosphate. The activity of glucose-6-phosphatase is subject to change: it is increased during fasting and in diabetes mellitus, and reduced by insulin. This hormone also induces the synthesis of glucokinase, which is used primarily when blood glucose levels are elevated. In addition to glycogen, blood lactate (resulting from muscle contraction) and several of the glucogenic amino acids may also serve as glucose-6-phosphate precursors.

The level of liver glycogen at any time is a result of the combined effects of synthesis and degradation. The blood sugar level is a major factor in determining the rates of glycogenesis and glycogenolysis.

Gluconeogenesis

The liver is the major site for significant conversion of various nutrients into carbohydrate. Although glycerol derived from fat hydrolysis may be converted to glucose, it is of relatively minor significance as a source of carbohydrate.

The chief gluconeogenic substances are the amino acids. Most amino acids may be converted to α-keto acids by deamination and transamination reactions (see Chapter 29). Pyruvic and oxalacetic acids are converted to glucose by the gluconeogenic reactions described above (see Fig. 27.2); α-ketoglutaric acid may contribute carbons to glucose subsequent to its conversion to oxalacetic acid via the citric acid cycle. In addition, several nitrogen-free compounds derived from amino acids by deamination may be converted to one of these α-keto acids and thus serve as carbohydrate precursors.

Lactic acid, produced in active skeletal muscle, also is an important gluconeogenic compound. After transport to the liver by the blood, it is oxidized to pyruvic acid and subsequently converted to glucose.

Propionic acid and other odd-carbon fatty acids tend to be glucogenic. Carbon atoms are removed from the longer odd-carbon fatty acids by β-oxidation, finally resulting in the formation of propionyl CoA. Propionyl

CoA is converted to succinic acid by carbon dioxide fixation and molecular rearrangement.

Of the lower fatty acids produced by microbial fermentation in the ruminant, propionic acid alone is glucogenic, while acetic and butyric acids tend to be ketogenic. Acetic acid is absorbed as such, while butyric acid is metabolized to a substantial extent in the rumen mucosa, where ketone bodies appear to be the major products formed.

During starvation, liver glycogen is soon depleted and thus cannot serve as a significant contributor to blood glucose. Moreover, extrahepatic glycogen does not directly yield glucose to the blood, but may serve indirectly by forming lactic acid, which returns to the liver to be converted to glucose. Gluconeogenesis, particularly from amino acids, becomes extremely important when dietary carbohydrates are not furnished and in ruminants where dietary carbohydrates are fermented to short-chain fatty acids. In ruminants, amino acids and propionic acids are the major precursors of blood glucose.

Gluconeogenesis occurs even when adequate dietary levels of carbohydrates are furnished. Shortly after a carbohydrate meal the capacity of glycogen storage is reached, and excess glucose is converted to and stored as fats. The gluconeogenic process becomes effective to help maintain adequate blood glucose levels between meals. Moreover, gluconeogenesis is in continuous operation in ruminants.

CARBOHYDRATE INTERCONVERSIONS

Some of the more significant hexose interconversions that occur in mammalian metabolism are summarized in Figure 27.7. Monosaccharides must first be phosphorylated by ATP to form hexose-6-phosphate or hexose-1-phosphate derivatives. Some interconversions among the hexose-6-phosphates occur. Nucleoside triphosphates react with hexose-1-phosphates, with the liberation of pyrophosphate and the formation of nucleoside diphosphate–hexose compounds. These derivatives undergo a variety of reactions including (1) epimerization (interconversion of UDP-glucose to UDP-galactose), (2) oxidation (conversion of UDP-glucose to UDP-glucuronic acid), (3) acetylation (conversion of UDP-glucosamine to UDP-N-acetyl-glucosamine), and several other reactions (such as decarboxylation, introduction of a lactic acid residue, and addition of amino acids) which are not illustrated.

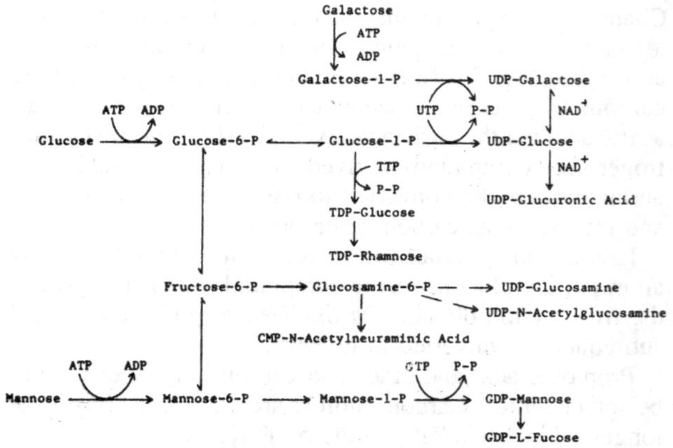

The nucleoside diphosphate sugars and their derivatives are utilized in the biosynthesis of glycoproteins (including some enzymes, immunoglobulins, epithelial mucins, and blood group substances) and of mucopolysaccharides (such as hyaluronic acid, chondroitin sulfates, heparin, and dermatan sulfate).

Figure 27.7. Interconversions of hexoses

ABBREVIATIONS

ACP	acyl carrier protein
ADP	adenosine diphosphate
AMP	adenosine monophosphate
ATP	adenosine triphosphate
CoA	coenzyme A
CTP	cytidine triphosphate
FAD	flavin adenine dinucleotide
FAD·2H	reduced flavin adenine dinucleotide
FMN	flavin mononucleotide
FMN·2H	reduced flavin mononucleotide
GDP	guanosine diphosphate
G-6-P	glucose-6-phosphate
GTP	guanosine triphosphate
HSCoA	coenzyme A (reduced form)
mRNA	messenger ribonucleic acid
NAD^+	nicotinamide adenine dinucleotide, often referred to as diphosphopvridine nucleotide (DPN^+)
NADH	reduced nicotinamide adenine dinucleotide
$NADP^+$	nicotinamide adenine dinucleotide phosphate
NADPH	reduced nicotinamide adenine dinucleotide phosphate
P, Pi	inorganic phosphate
PP, P-P	pyrophosphate
tRNA	transfer ribonucleic acid
THFA	tetrahydrofolic acid
TPP	thiamine pyrophosphate
UDP	uridine diphosphate
UTP	uridine triphosphate

REFERENCES

Dickens, F., Randle, P.J., and Whelan, W.J., eds. 1968. *Carbohydrate Metabolism and Its Disorders*. Academic Press, New York. Vols. 1, 2.

Fain, J.N., ed. 1975. Cyclic nucleotides and mammalian cells. *Metabolism* 24:235–456.

Goodwin, T.W., ed. 1968. *The Metabolic Role of Citrate*. Biochemical Soc. Symp. 27. Academic Press, London.

Heath, E.C. 1971. Complex polysaccharides. *Ann. Rev. Biochem.* 40:29–56.

Helmreich, E. 1969. Control of glycogen, starch, and cellulose. *Compreh. Biochem.* 17:17–92.

Lardy, H., Veneziale, C., and Gabrielli, F. 1970. Paths of carbon in gluconeogenesis. In A. Sols and S. Grisolina, eds., *Metabolic Regulation and Enzyme Action.* Academic Press, New York. Pp. 55–62.

Larner, J. 1971. *Intermediary Metabolism and Its Regulation.* Prentice-Hall, Englewood Cliffs, N.J. Chaps. 4, 8.

Leloir, L.F. 1971. Two decades of research on the biosynthesis of saccharides. *Science* 172:1299–1302.

Lowenstein, J.M. 1971. The pyruvate dehydrogenase complex and the citric acid cycle. *Compreh. Biochem.* 18(suppl.):1–55.

Marco, R., and Sols, A. 1970. Metabolic crossroads in gluconeogenesis and its enzymic regulation in liver. In A. Sols and S. Grisolia, eds., *Metabolic Regulation and Enzyme Action.* Academic Press, New York. Pp. 63–76.

Pigman, W., and Horton, D., eds. 1970 (vols. 2A, 2B), 1972 (vol. 1A). *The Carbohydrates: Chemistry and Biochemistry.* 2d ed. Academic Press, New York.

Pontremoli, S., and Grazi, E., 1969. Hexose monophosphate oxidation. *Compreh. Biochem.* 17:163–89.

Rose, I.A., and Rose, Z.B. 1969. Glycolysis: Regulation and mechanisms of the enzymes. *Compreh. Biochem.* 17:93–161.

Scrutton, M.C., and Utter, M.F. 1968. The regulation of glycolysis and gluconeogenesis in animal tissues. *Ann. Rev. Biochem.* 37:249–302.

Shreeve, W.W. 1974. *Physiological Chemistry of Carbohydrates in Mammals.* Saunders, Philadelphia.

CHAPTER 28

Lipid Metabolism | by R. Scott Allen

The absorption of lipids from the gastrointestinal tract (see Chapter 26) is a primary process in lipid metabolism. Most of the dietary lipids enter the lacteals as chylomicrons along with some very low-density lipoproteins. These complexes are formed in the intestinal mucosal cells and contain chiefly triglycerides. Dietary cholesterol also is included, mostly as cholesterol esters. The lymph enters the systemic blood via the thoracic duct. Short- and medium-chain fatty acids and the free glycerol resulting from complete hydrolysis of triglycerides are absorbed into the portal blood.

LIPID TRANSPORT AND DEPOSITION

Upon discharge of the chylomicrons into the venous blood, a rise in blood lipid content occurs. When this results after ingesting food high in lipids, the increase is termed *absorptive lipemia*. The chylomicrons consist of a central core of triglycerides and a thin coating of hydrophilic lipoprotein. The core also contains all of the cholesterol esters and some free cholesterol, while the lipoprotein envelope consists largely of phospholipids along with some protein (apolipoprotein) and free cholesterol. This envelope undergoes compositional change by exchange with lipids and proteins in the extracellular fluids.

Blood lipids

The lipids in the blood may arise from intestinal absorption of ingested lipids, mobilization of lipids from storage, or synthetic processes (especially in the liver). Most of the blood lipids are present as chylomicrons and other lipoproteins (very low density, low density, or high density). In addition, the nonesterified fatty acids are transported as a complex of fatty acid and albumin.

There are large differences in the blood lipid components among species, among individuals within species, and at various times. Factors influencing these lipid levels include the quantity and type of lipid in the diet, time after consumption of food, health and age of the subject, hormone balance, and energy needs. There is a tendency, however, for the cholesterol–cholesterol ester and the cholesterol-phospholipid ratios to be relatively constant within a given species. These ratios appear to be under hepatic control, whereas levels of triglycerides can vary greatly, depending in large part on dietary intake, storage in, or mobilization from, adipose tissues, and on synthesis by the liver.

Under normal conditions the levels of unesterified fatty acids are considerably below those of other plasma lipids. They are released to the blood from adipose triglycerides through the action of hormone-sensitive lipase. The fatty acids then physically bind to plasma albumin and are transported to the heart, skeletal muscles, liver, and other tissues where they are either oxidized as energy sources or incorporated into other lipids through esterification.

Although the plasma unesterified fatty-acid levels are low, the turnover rates are extremely rapid (1–3 minutes in most species).

While the heart utilizes these acids as a significant source of energy, the brain appears unable to utilize the unesterified fatty acids for energy. However, plasma unesterified fatty acids are transported into the brain and incorporated into polar lipids.

Transport and storage

A simplified scheme for the transport and storage of lipids is presented in Figure 28.1. (For abbreviations see Chapter 27.) Chylomicron triglyceride fatty acids are rapidly removed from the plasma by the extrahepatic tissues and to a limited extent by the liver. The mechanism in extrahepatic tissues involves a hydrolytic enzyme, lipoprotein lipase, which is present in the capillary wall and probably acts on or in epithelial cells. This enzyme is found in adipose tissue, heart and skeletal muscle, lactating mammary gland, spleen, lung and kidney medulla, but not the brain. Limited hydrolysis of chylomicron triglycerides occurs at the surface of liver parenchymal cells.

Very low-density lipoproteins are primarily of liver origin. They transport triglycerides to extrahepatic tissues where they, like chylomicron triglycerides, are hydrolyzed through the action of lipoprotein lipase. The liberated fatty acids are rapidly taken up and esterified by the tissues.

Unesterified fatty acids resulting from hydrolysis of adipose tissue triglycerides form complexes primarily with serum albumin and are transported in this form to other tissues.

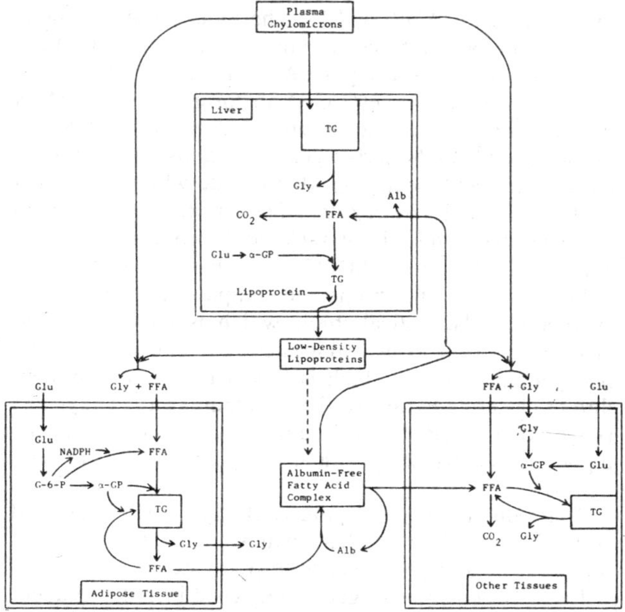

Figure 28.1. Transport, storage, and metabolism of lipids derived from plasma chylomicrons. TG, triglycerides; FFA, free fatty acids; Gly, glycerol; Glu, glucose; α-GP, α-glycerol phosphate; G-6-P, glucose-6-phosphate; Alb, albumin.

Storage of lipids as triglycerides occurs in virtually all tissues. Under normal circumstances, however, adipose tissue is most important quantitatively as a lipid storage depot. Stored triglycerides result primarily from reaction of fatty acids (from action of lipoprotein lipase on chylomicron and lipoprotein triglycerides) with α-glycerol phosphate (derived from glucose). Fatty acids also are synthesized from glucose in nonruminants and from acetate in ruminants. Triglycerides in tissues other than liver and adipose tissue result from reactions closely related to those in adipose tissue.

Adipose tissue

Adipose tissue is dynamic. It is (1) metabolically active, (2) capable of carrying out biosynthesis of fats from glucose, (3) capable of some alterations of fatty acids by chain lengthening or shortening and by saturation or desaturation, and (4) under nervous and endocrine control.

Stored triglycerides constitute a reserve supply of energy-producing material. Although previously thought to be a surplus depot, it is now clear that continuous deposition and mobilization of adipose triglycerides occur regardless of nutritional status. Triglyceride deposition is favored when food is plentiful and the animal is calm and resting. Fasting and the release of many different hormones into the blood cause rapid lipolysis of stored triglycerides, releasing unesterified fatty acids for transport to other tissues.

Within any species, the composition of depot triglycerides tends to be constant. However, by drastic change in type of dietary lipid the nature of stored fats may be altered. For example, pigs fed peanuts or soybeans deposit a somewhat more unsaturated fat than those fed a typical diet. On the other hand, pigs fed highly saturated fats tend to deposit fats which contain more unsaturated fatty acid residues. Thus there is a tendency for an animal either to saturate or desaturate fatty acids in an effort to deposit a fat typical of that species. Dietary alteration of depot lipids can best be accomplished after preliminary starvation. Also, prolonged feeding of atypical dietary lipids will result in marked changes in composition of stored triglycerides.

The conversion of glucose or glycogen to triglycerides within adispose tissue cells has been established. These cells have the full complement of enzymes needed for glycolysis and the pentose phosphate pathway, the formation of acetyl CoA, and for the synthesis of long-chain fatty acyl CoA from acetyl CoA. The latter process requires NADPH which is generated during the oxidative phase of the pentose phosphate pathway and also from the cytoplasmic conversion of malic acid to pyruvic acid and CO_2 by malic enzyme.

Several hormones are involved in controlling the process of lipogenesis (conversion of glucose to triglycerides) and of lipolysis in adipose tissue. Insulin stimulates lipogenesis primarily by increasing glucose permeation through the cell membrane and secondarily by increasing (probably at the gene level) the activity of several enzymes involved in fatty acid synthesis. This hormone also increases the influx of unesterified fatty acids into adipose tissue, presumably by activation of lipoprotein lipase.

Lipolysis of triglycerides and the subsequent release of unesterified fatty acids from adipose tissue are stimulated by many hormones. Norepinephrine, epinephrine, glucagon, and ACTH (adrenocorticotropic hormone) activate the hormone-sensitive lipase which catalyzes hydrolysis of triglycerides to produce diglycerides and fatty acids. Subsequently the diglycerides are hydrolyzed to fatty acids and glycerol through the catalytic action of adipose tissue lipase. These hormones combine with receptor sites on the cell membrane and activate adenyl cyclase which converts ATP to cyclic AMP. The latter activates a protein kinase which catalyzes a phosphorylation of inactive hormone-sensitive lipase to form the active enzyme. Thyroxine and growth hormone act more slowly, probably by increasing the synthesis of adenyl cyclase. Although adrenal glucocorticoids have no direct lipolytic effect, they facilitate the action of the other hormones which stimulate lipolysis. Prostaglandins inhibit lipolysis, probably by inhibiting adenyl cyclase.

In starvation and diabetes mellitus, where carbohydrate insufficiency exists at the tissue level, fatty acid and triglyceride syntheses are reduced sharply; hormone-sensitive lipase activity continues, resulting in increased levels of unesterified fatty acids which are transported to the liver and other tissues as albumin–fatty acid complexes; and the activity of adipose tissue lipoprotein lipase decreases.

The overall result of carbohydrate deprivation is a hyperlipemia that results primarily from increased levels of low-density lipoproteins. These are formed in the liver from fatty acids derived originally from adipose triglycerides. However, when carbohydrate metabolism is normal, glucose serves as a precursor for the glycerol residue in adipose triglycerides. The deposition of adipose lipid from carbohydrate, chylomicron, and lipoprotein sources proceeds readily, with a reduction in the formation of unesterified fatty acids.

TRIGLYCERIDE METABOLISM

Triglycerides are the most significant group of lipids from the standpoint of energy need. They may be provided by the diet or may be synthesized from nonlipid sources.

Biosynthesis of fatty acids

In avian and mammalian species fatty acids are synthesized in the cytoplasm (in liver, adipose tissue, mammary gland, heart, lung, and brain) from acetyl CoA, a substrate that may be derived from carbohydrates and amino acids as well as from fatty acids. Acetyl CoA is generated in the mitochondrion but cannot cross the inner mitochondrial membrane. Citric acid, the initial intermediate in the citric acid cycle, carries acetyl groups across the membrane. In the cytoplasm, citric acid is cleaved by citrate lyase, the enzyme that catalyzes the reaction of citric acid with ATP and CoA to produce acetyl CoA, oxalacetic acid, ADP, and Pi. The sequence of reactions involved in the synthesis of palmitic acid (the major fatty acid produced) from acetyl CoA is shown in Figure 28.2.

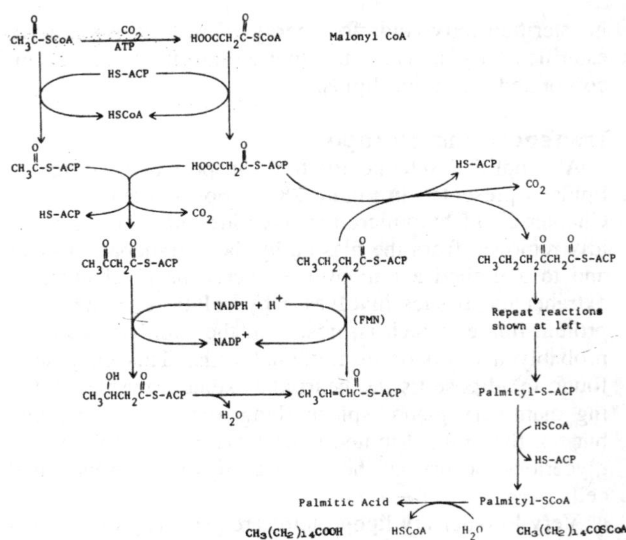

Figure 28.2. Biosynthesis of long-chain fatty acids

Carboxylation of acetyl CoA to form malonyl CoA is the rate-limiting reaction in fatty acid synthesis. The enzyme, acetyl CoA carboxylase, is allosterically regulated. Citric and isocitric acid stimulate while long-chain acyl CoA inhibits the enzyme. The enzyme system which catalyzes the synthesis of fatty acids from acetyl CoA, malonyl CoA, and NADPH in higher organisms is a tightly associated multi-enzyme complex called fatty acid synthetase. The critical thiol, which is attached to the growing acyl chain as a thioester, is contributed by 4′-phosphopantetheine, which is linked to a unique protein through a serine hydroxyl. This protein is called acyl carrier protein (ACP) and is analogous to but of somewhat higher molecular weight than the ACP of bacteria and plants.

The reduction steps require NADPH, which is derived from the pentose phosphate pathway and from the cytoplasmic oxidation of malate to pyruvate.

Each subsequent elongation sequence includes condensation with malonyl ACP, reduction, dehydration, and reduction again until palmityl ACP is formed. Palmitic acid is finally released by hydrolysis.

The biosynthesis of long-chain fatty acids is under nutritional, hormonal, and metabolite influences. During fasting or ingestion of high-fat diets the fatty acid synthesis is reduced to very low levels. High synthesis rates occur after ingestion of high carbohydrate or during intermittent eating (fasting followed by feeding). Insulin stimulates biosynthesis, while a diabetic state sharply reduces fatty acid synthesis. Metabolite levels affect the specific enzymes involved. For example, ATP stimulates citrate lyase, citrate and isocitrate stimulate acetyl CoA carboxylase, and palmityl CoA inhibits both acetyl CoA carboxylase and fatty acid synthetase.

Fatty acid interconversions

Enzyme systems in the mitochondria of heart, liver, and brain utilize acetyl CoA for the addition of two carbon atoms to elongate existing long-chain acyl CoA derivatives. Malonyl CoA is not involved in these reactions. The requirements for acyl CoA, NADH, and NADPH suggest the sequence of reactions outlined in Figure 28.3. This system can make use of intermediate-chain-length fatty acids (C_{12}, C_{14}, C_{16}) and also of some unsaturated fatty acids (palmitoleic, oleic, and others) to add two carbon atoms at the carbonyl end of the chain. Although NADPH does not appear to be a major product in mitochondrial metabolism, this reduced coenzyme probably arises through transhydrogenation from NADH.

Elongation also occurs in liver microsomes. Malonyl CoA provides the two-carbon fragment, and the resulting β-keto derivatives are reduced by NADPH. ACP is not involved. Both saturated and unsaturated fatty acyl CoA derivatives are elongated by this system; the unsaturated derivatives, however, are elongated more rapidly.

Both elongation and shortening of the chain length of fatty acids occur when ^{14}C-palmitic acid is fed. The body lipids contain the highest concentration of labeled palmitic acid, but labeled stearic and myristic acids also are formed. These and similar observations with other tagged fatty acids demonstrate interconversions involving gain or loss of two carbon atoms.

Desaturation reactions also occur in mammals. Feeding of stearic acid leads to the formation of some oleic acid, and palmitoleic acid is produced when palmitic acid is included in the diet. Each of these monoenoic acids is a 9,10-unsaturated compound. The desaturase system is associated with the microsomes in animal tissues and is dependent upon molecular oxygen and NADH.

A variety of unsaturated fatty acids is found in animal tissues; some acids are of dietary origin, others are produced in the tissues by a series of two-carbon additions and desaturation reactions. The essential fatty acids (linoleic and linolenic) cannot be synthesized by animal tissue. Elongation results in the addition of two carbons at the carboxyl end of the fatty acid; desaturation begins at the 9,10-position and subsequently moves three carbons toward the carboxyl end of the chain. Arachidonic acid, a potent acid for correcting fatty acid deficiencies in animals, can be biosynthesized from linoleic acid.

Triglyceride synthesis

Two general pathways have been proposed for the synthesis of triglycerides. The first (Fig. 28.4) involves phosphatidic acid as an intermediate, while the second (Fig. 28.5) does not include phosphorylated intermediates. In each case, activated fatty acids (fatty acyl CoA)

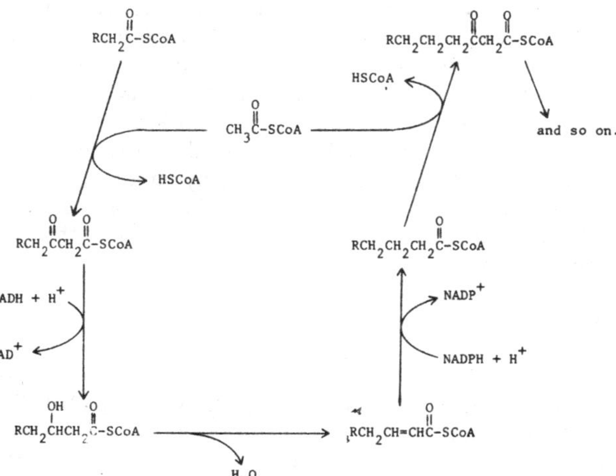

Figure 28.3. Elongation of fatty acids in the mitochondria

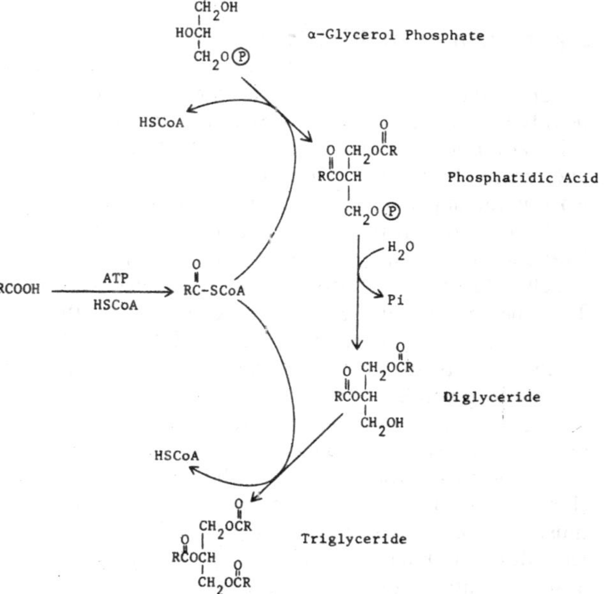

Figure 28.4. Biosynthesis of triglycerides via the phosphatidic acid pathway

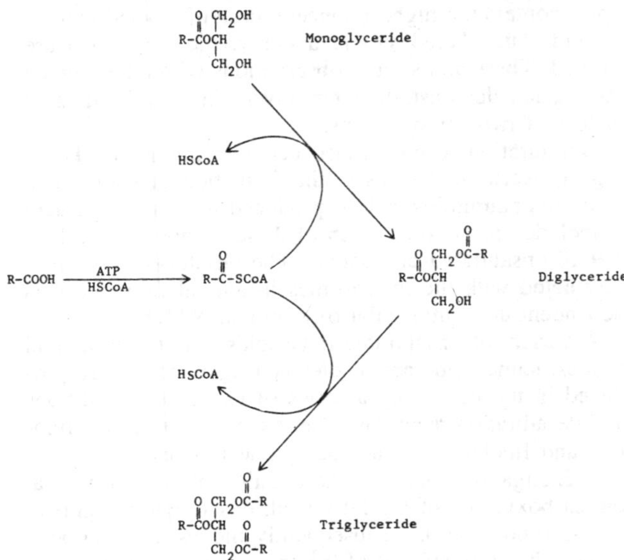

Figure 28.5. Biosynthesis of triglycerides by the monoglyceride pathway

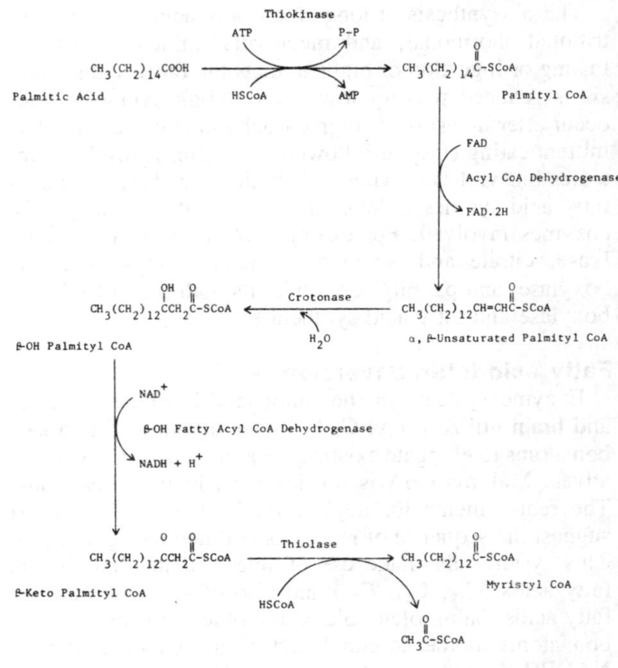

Figure 28.6. The initial sequence of β-oxidation of palmitic acid

are essential to the formation of glyceryl ester linkages. In both pathways, a diglyceride is produced and subsequently esterified to form a triglyceride. The phosphatidic acid pathway predominates in the synthesis of triglycerides in most tissues, whereas monoglycerides serve as major substrates for triglyceride synthesis in mucosal epithelial cells prior to formation of chylomicrons.

Catabolism of triglycerides

The liver plays a major role in the synthesis and degradation of fatty acids in the animal body. Depot lipids are readily hydrolyzed by tissue lipase, and the released fatty acids are transported in large part to the liver as albumin-unesterified fatty acid complexes. Accompanying this release is the appearance of free glycerol in the plasma.

Glycerol is transported to various tissues, particularly liver and kidney, that possess the enzyme glycerol kinase, which catalyzes the formation of α-glycerol phosphate. This metabolite can be used for glyceride synthesis or can be converted (by reduction with NADH) to dihydroxyacetone phosphate for use in energy metabolism or conversion to glucose.

Degradation of long-chain fatty acids proceeds by a process of β-oxidation, which brings about a stepwise removal of two carbons at the carboxyl end of the acid (Fig. 28.6). Before oxidation can begin, the fatty acid must first be activated by conversion to acyl CoA. At least three thiokinases are known, each being specific for a set of fatty acids. One requires short-chain (C_2–C_3), a second is specific for intermediate-chain (C_4–C_{12}), and a third acts on long-chain (C_{10}–C_{22}) fatty acids. Short-chain fatty acids diffuse across the outer and inner mitochondrial membranes into the matrix where they are activated by intramitochondrial thiokinase.

Activation of intermediate- and long-chain fatty acids occurs on the outer mitochondrial membrane, whereas the oxidation sequence involves mitochondrial matrix enzymes. Since the acyl CoA molecules cannot traverse the inner mitochondrial membrane, carnitine (γ-trimethylammonium-β-hydroxybutyrate) carries the acyl group across the membrane. The acyl group of acyl CoA is transferred to the hydroxyl group of carnitine to form acyl carnitine which diffuses across the inner mitochondrial membrane. On the matrix side the acyl group is transferred to CoA.

The saturated acyl CoA is degraded in a sequence involving oxidation (linked to FAD), hydration, oxidation (linked to NAD^+), and thiolysis by CoA to produce acetyl CoA and an acyl CoA with two carbons less than the starting compound.

The β-oxidation process may be repeated to completely degrade the original even-carbon fatty acids to acetyl CoA.

Acetyl CoA may be utilized in a variety of ways, including entry into the citric acid cycle, synthesis of long-chain fatty acids, acetylation reactions, steroid synthesis, and ketone body formation. Energy production from degradation of fatty acids comes from both the β-oxidation sequence (oxidation by the electron transport system of FAD·2H and NADH) and from the oxidation of acetyl CoA in the citric acid cycle.

Unsaturated fatty acids also are oxidized. The process involves all of the enzymes used in β-oxidation of saturated fatty acids and two additional ones, an isomerase and an epimerase. This combination of mitochondrial enzymes catalyzes the degradation of unsaturated fatty acids to acetyl CoA at rates comparable to those for saturated fatty acids.

Ketogenesis

Ketone bodies (acetoacetic acid, β-hydroxybutyric acid, and acetone) are produced primarily in liver mitochondria due to overproduction of acetyl CoA and its underutilization by the citric acid cycle. The high rate of fatty acid uptake and β-oxidation by the liver is a key factor in ketogenesis. Moreover, when carbohydrate degradation is reduced, the level of oxalacetate is inadequate to condense with acetyl CoA. Conditions which stimulate ketogenesis include fasting (or starvation), pregnancy, lactation, and diabetes. Ketone bodies diffuse from the mitochondria and are transported to peripheral tissues.

The first reaction in ketogenesis (Fig. 28.7) is catalyzed by thiolase and produces acetoacetyl CoA. This compound may undergo hydrolysis to form acetoacetic acid, or condensation with acetyl CoA to yield β-hydroxy-β-methylglutaryl CoA. The latter is more significant. Moreover, β-hydroxy-β-methylglutaryl CoA also serves as an important precursor in the synthesis of cholesterol. Splitting of acetyl CoA from β-hydroxy-β-methylglutaryl CoA yields acetoacetic acid, which may be decarboxylated to form acetone or reduced with NADH to β-hydroxybutyric acid. The availability of NADH appears to govern the production of β-hydroxybutyrate.

Ketolysis

The level of blood ketone bodies normally is low because of their efficient removal by peripheral tissues, especially skeletal muscle. These tissues may derive a significant fraction of their energy needs by degradation of the ketone bodies. Moreover, heart muscle and renal cortex utilize acetoacetate in preference to glucose. Although the brain utilizes glucose as the major fuel in a well-nourished animal, in starvation and diabetes it adapts to acetoacetate utilization.

In the conversion of ketone bodies to acetyl CoA (Fig. 28.8), β-hydroxybutyric acid is oxidized by NAD^+ to form acetoacetic acid, which is converted to acetoacetyl CoA by reaction with succinyl CoA or with ATP and CoA. Thiolysis with CoA yields acetyl CoA. Acetone may be oxidized to pyruvic acid or cleaved to give acetyl and formyl fragments.

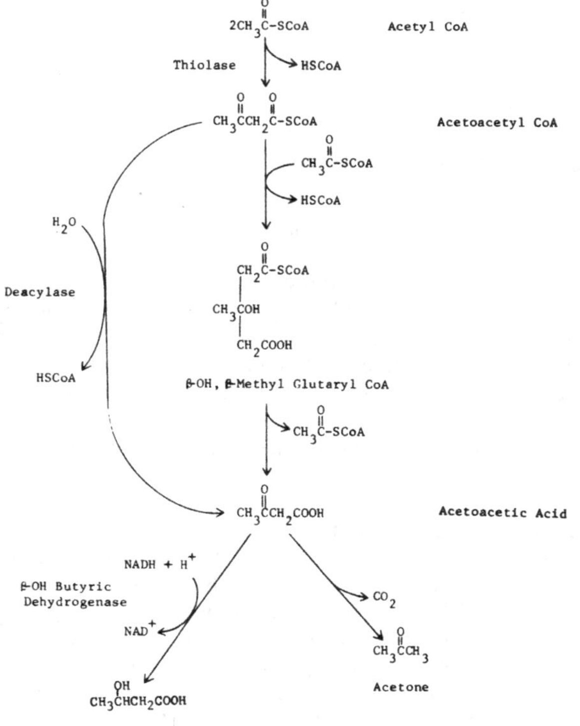

Figure 28.7. Liver ketogenesis

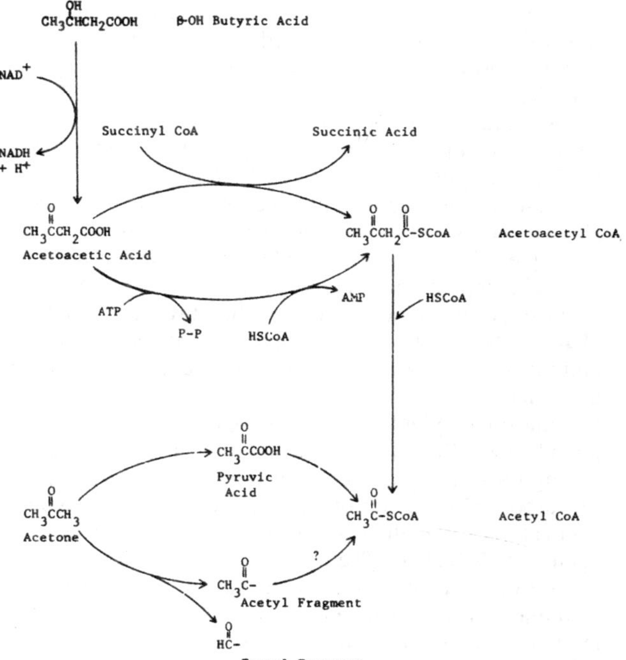

Figure 28.8. Ketolysis by extrahepatic tissues

When ketone body production significantly exceeds peripheral tissue utilization, blood levels and urinary excretion of these compounds rise. This is called ketosis. Since acetoacetic and β-hydroxybutyric acids are moderately strong acids whose loss causes equivalent cation (mostly Na^+) losses in the urine, acidosis sometimes results. Large volumes of fluid also are lost (see Chapters 30 and 56).

STEROID METABOLISM

Cholesterol is the most abundant sterol found in animal tissues. It may come from the diet, particularly in carnivores, and/or from biosynthesis from acetyl CoA. Most other mammalian steroids are derived from cholesterol, including vitamin D which is formed in the skin during exposure to ultraviolet light. Vitamin D, however, often is included in the diet, particularly in young animals.

Absorption of dietary cholesterol is solely by way of the lacteals and is dependent upon the bile salts in the lumen of the small intestine. In the brush border (microvilli) some free cholesterol is converted to cholesterol esters. Both the free and esterified forms of cholesterol subsequently appear in the lymph; the latter form generally predominates.

Cholesterol biosynthesis

Acetyl CoA serves as the sole precursor for biosynthetic cholesterol. Although the liver is the major site of cholesterol synthesis, many other tissues also synthesize this sterol, e.g. intestine, skin, adrenal cortex, and arterial wall. The enzymes involved are associated primarily with microsomes, but some necessary cofactors are in the cytoplasm.

The sequence of reactions for the synthesis of cholesterol has been largely resolved (Fig. 28.9). The formation of β-hydroxy-β-methylglutaryl CoA from acetyl CoA was described earlier. Upon reduction with NADPH, mevalonic acid is formed. Phosphorylation with ATP and subsequent loss of inorganic phosphate and carbon dioxide yield isopentyl pyrophosphate. A rearrangement catalyzed by an isomerase gives 3,3-dimethylallyl pyrophosphate. These two pyrophosphates interact with the elimination of pyrophosphate to produce geranyl pyrophosphate. The condensation of an additional C_5-pyrophosphate yields farnesyl pyrophosphate, a C_{15} compound. Two C_{15} pyrophosphates then interact under reducing (NADPH) conditions to form squalene, a C_{30} hydrocarbon. Conversion of squalene to lanosterol involves cyclization and methyl group transfers, and requires oxygen and NADPH. The formation of cholesterol from lanosterol is rather complicated and may involve more than one pathway. This process involves removal of three methyl groups, reduction of one double bond by NADPH, and migration of the other double bond to the

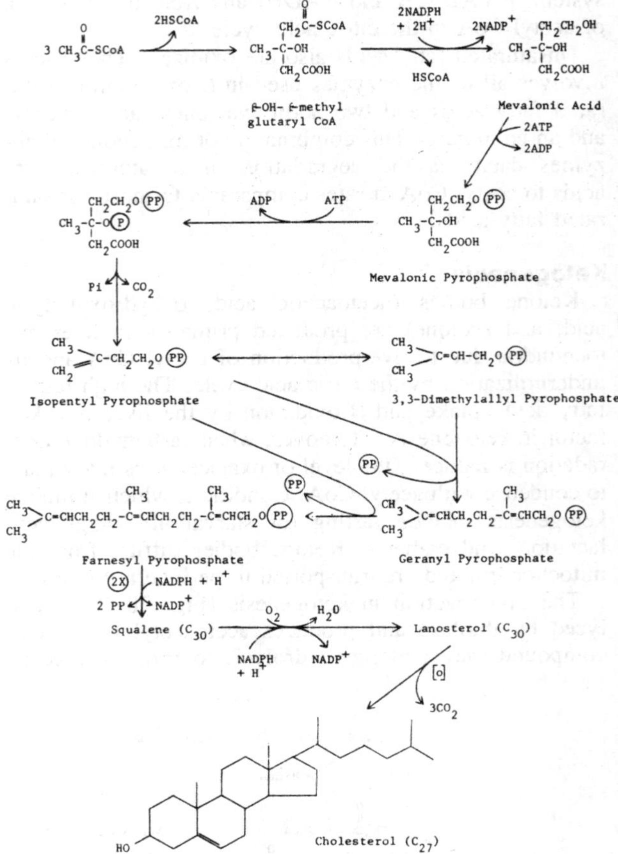

Figure 28.9. Biosynthesis of cholesterol

5,6-position. Methyl removal is oxidative, but the mechanism is not clear.

The biosynthesis of cholesterol is regulated in part by the supply of cholesterol. High dietary levels of cholesterol or the presence of cholesterol precursors result in depressed liver cholesterol synthesis. Low cholesterol levels stimulate biosynthesis. Cholesterol inhibits its own synthesis by blocking the synthesis of the reductase enzyme which is required for the formation of mevalonic acid from hydroxymethylglutaryl CoA.

Catabolism of cholesterol

The fates of cholesterol include (1) excretion as sterols in bile, (2) conversion to bile acids, (3) production of 18-, 19-, and 21-carbon steroid hormones, and (4) pathological deposit as in cholesterol calculi in the bile ducts and cholesterol-containing plaques in the arteries.

From a quantitative standpoint, the conversion of cholesterol to bile acids is most significant. This process, which occurs exclusively in the liver, includes shortening of the side-chain from eight to five carbons, oxidation of the terminal side-chain carbon to a carboxyl, saturation of the 5,6-position, inversion of the β-OH at carbon 3 to the α-orientation, and the introduction of one or two hydroxyl groups in α-orientation at carbons 3 and/or 12. The bile acids (as CoA derivatives) tend to conjugate with taurine or glycine. The conjugated bile acids are excreted in the bile, but are in large part reabsorbed lower in the intestinal tract after having participated significantly in lipid digestion and absorption.

Cholesterol is the precursor for many important steroid hormones. These include 21-carbon steroids (the corpus luteum hormone, progesterone, and the adrenal cortical hormones), the 19-carbon male androgens, and the 18-carbon estrogens (estradiol, estrone, and estriol). The biosynthesis of these hormones is presented in Figure 53.5.

METABOLISM OF PHOSPHOGLYCERIDES

Phosphoglycerides (also called phosphatides) include several types of compounds having unique solubility and functional characteristics. They tend to be soluble both in water and nonpolar solvents and thus may serve as structural bridges between protein and nonpolar lipids. These are essential components of cellular membrane systems. Phosphoglycerides are found only in traces in depot lipids, but are present in significant amounts in glandular organs (especially the liver), in blood plasma, and in specialized tissues (nervous system). They have widely differing turnover rates, ranging from half-lives of less than 1 day for liver lecithin to over 200 days for brain cephalins.

Biosynthesis

Lecithin (phosphatidyl choline) may be synthesized in vivo by two major pathways (Fig. 28.10): first by making use of choline directly, and second by methylation of phosphatidyl ethanolamine.

The choline pathway involves phosphorylation of choline with ATP to yield phosphorylcholine. This compound reacts with cytidine triphosphate (CTP) to produce pyrophosphate and cytidine diphosphate choline. The latter interacts with 1,2-diglyceride (derived by hydrolysis of phosphatidic acid) to generate phosphatidyl choline and cytidine monophosphate (CMP). The other pathway, which is confined to the liver, involves methylation of phosphatidyl ethanolamine with S-adenosylmethionine, wherein the methyl groups are successively introduced to form the monomethylethanolamine-, dimethylethanolamine-, and choline-containing phosphoglycerides.

The biosynthesis of phosphatidyl serine in mammalian tissue involves an exchange reaction between the ethanolamine of phosphatidyl ethanolamine and free serine (an amino acid found in many proteins).

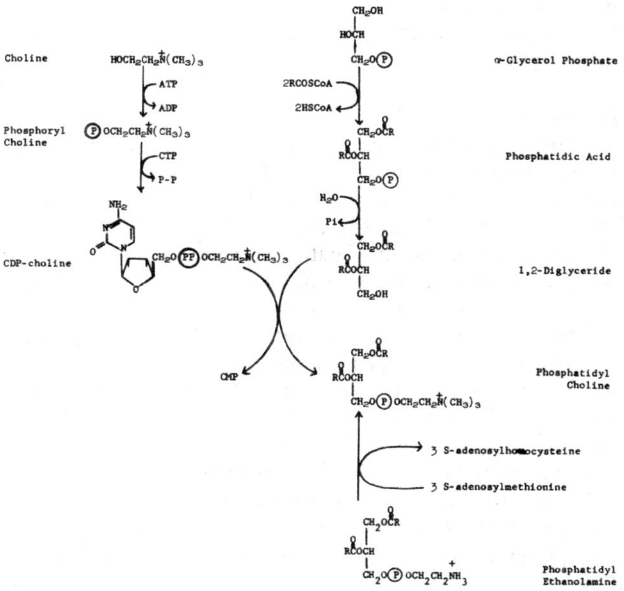

Figure 28.10. Pathways for biosynthesis of phosphatidyl choline (lecithin). CDP, cytidine diphosphate.

Phosphatidyl ethanolamine may be biosynthesized by two pathways (Fig. 28.11). The first involves phosphorylation of ethanolamine with ATP and subsequent reactions analogous to those for lecithin. The second is simply a decarboxylation of phosphatidyl serine by an enzyme which requires pyridoxal phosphate. The latter pathway is more important in mammalian tissues.

CDP-diglyceride serves as an essential precursor for several other phosphatides, including phosphatidyl inositol, phosphatidyl glycerol, and diphosphatidyl glycerol.

The enzymes involved in phosphoglyceride biosyntheses are localized primarily in liver mitochondria and

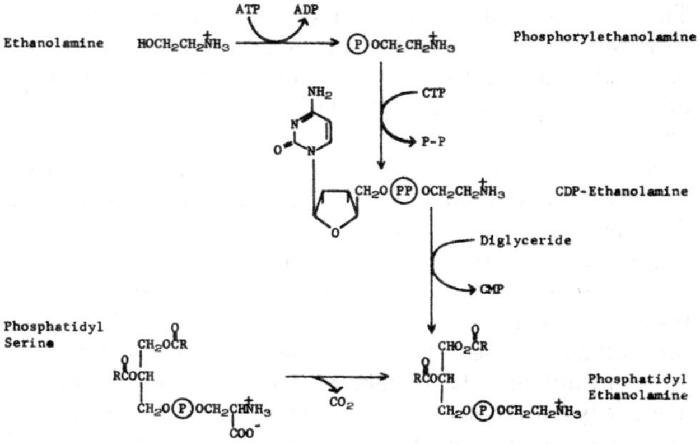

Figure 28.11. Formation of phosphatidyl ethanolamine

microsomes. Some syntheses also occur in the kidney, brain, intestinal mucosa, adipose tissue, lung, and skeletal muscle.

Function

Phosphoglycerides are present in all tissues and in the blood plasma and blood cells. For the most part they exist as lipoprotein complexes. These lipoproteins contribute significantly to the matrix of cell walls, the cell membranes, the myelin sheath, mitochondria, and microsomes. In this role, the phosphatides provide for the high permeability of nonpolar material.

The importance of phosphatides in mitochondrial electron transport has been demonstrated. Their removal from the enzyme protein inactivates it. Phosphoglycerides are also involved in blood coagulation by activating two factors involved in prothrombin formation.

Chylomicrons contain some phosphoglycerides in the form of lipoproteins. Moreover, plasma lipoproteins (ranging from very low density to high density) contain phosphoglycerides. Such lipoproteins serve in lipid transport.

Degradation

Hydrolytic reactions are prominent in phosphoglyceride degradation. Enzymes for catalyzing hydrolysis of both carboxy-ester and phosphate-ester linkages are located primarily in microsomes, mitochondria, and lysosomes in liver. Other tissues (kidney, brain, and intestinal mucosa) also are involved but to a limited extent.

Degradation may be illustrated with phosphatidyl choline. Fatty acid moieties are removed through the combined actions of phospholipases A_1 and A_2 and lysophospholipase. The A_1 enzyme promotes removal of the fatty acid from the α- or 1-position while A_2 catalyzes removal of the fatty acid from the β- or 2-position. The other product from each of the above reactions is lysophosphatidyl choline which is hydrolyzed through the action of lysophospholipase to form glycerylphosphorylcholine. The latter is further hydrolyzed to α-glycerol phosphate and choline in a reaction promoted by glycerylphosphorylcholine diesterase. Phospholipase C catalyzes hydrolysis of phosphatidyl choline to yield diglyceride and phosphorylcholine.

Similar hydrolytic reactions are observed with phosphatidyl ethanolamine and are thought also to occur with the other phosphoglycerides.

Degradation products may be metabolized in various ways. Liberated fatty acids are oxidatively catabolized for energy or reused for synthesis of various lipids. (Choline, ethanolamine, and serine are discussed in Chapter 29.) Inositol may be metabolized to produce glucuronic acid. Glycerol phosphate is readily converted to dihydroxyacetone phosphate, an intermediate in the glycolysis sequence, or used in tryglyceride or phosphatide synthesis.

SPHINGOLIPIDS

The sphingolipids are found in many tissues but are particularly significant in nervous tissues. Their structure involves sphingosine—$CH_3(CH_2)_{12}CH=CHOHCHNH_2CH_2OH$—rather than glycerol. This amino alcohol is synthesized by brain enzymes through condensation of palmityl CoA with serine and with the loss of CO_2, followed by reduction with NADPH and dehydrogenation by FAD to form a *trans* double bond. Acylation of the amino group of sphingosine by reaction with fatty acyl CoA provides ceramides. The terminal hydroxyl group of ceramides is substituted to form sphingolipids.

Ceramides react with CDP-choline to yield sphingomyelin and with UDP-glucose or UDP-galactose to form cerebrosides. In gangliosides, an oligosaccharide unit which contains at least one acid sugar (sialic acid) is linked to ceramide by a glucose residue.

Degradation of sphingolipids is initiated by specific hydrolases. Sphingomyelin yields phosphorycholine and ceramide. Cerebrosides are cleaved to sugars and ceramide. Gangliosides, through the sequential action of glycosyl hydrolases found in lysosomes, yield ceramide and monosaccharide (free and amino-derivative) units. The enzyme ceramidase promotes hydrolysis of ceramides to form free fatty acids and sphingosine. The latter may be utilized for sphingolipid synthesis or catabolized to palmitic acid.

RELATION OF LIPIDS TO OTHER NUTRIENTS

Figure 28.12 presents some of the relationships of the major types of lipids to other nutrients.

Acetyl CoA is the key component relating carbohydrate and lipid metabolism. The major sources of acetyl CoA are glucose, fatty acids (derived primarily from triglycerides), and amino acids. The major pathways of utilization of acetyl CoA are (1) oxidation via the citric acid cycle, (2) conversion to hydroxymethylglutaryl CoA and subsequent formation of ketone bodies and/or cholesterol (precursor for bile acids and steroid hormones), and (3) synthesis of long-chain fatty acids which are utilized in the formation of triglycerides.

When glucose catabolism is depressed (such as in insulin deficiency and fasting), acetyl CoA utilization by the citric acid cycle is decreased, and there is a marked tendency to convert available resources (particularly glucogenic amino acids (see Table 29.1) into blood glucose via gluconeogenesis. Other processes are affected as well. These include reduction in fatty acid synthesis, increase in lipolysis to provide fatty acids which are β-

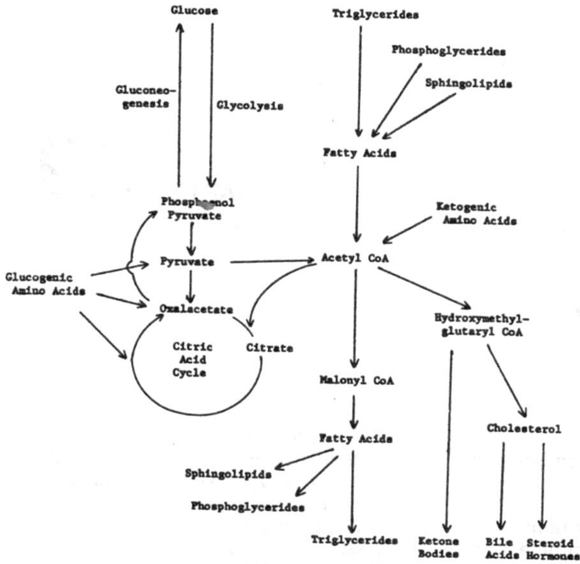

Figure 28.12. Metabolic relations of the major lipids to other nutrients

oxidized for the generation of ATP, and increase in ketone body formation from the acetyl CoA. Although ketone bodies and cholesterol both arise from hydroxymethylglutaryl CoA, cholesterol synthesis is under metabolic control; thus the great bulk of the excess acetyl CoA is converted to ketone bodies.

Under normal conditions an increase in blood glucose stimulates the release of insulin which increases glucose uptake by adipose tissue and also suppresses the activity of adipose tissue hormone-sensitive lipase. The consequences are decreased release of free fatty acids to the blood and increased triglyceride formation. Glucose catabolism in adipose tissue provides α-glycerol phosphate and acetyl CoA (used in the formation of long-chain fatty acids) for triglyceride synthesis. Ketone body formation is depressed when the rate of glucose metabolism is high.

REFERENCES

Bergström, S., and Danielsson, H. 1968. Formation and metabolism of bile acids. In *Handbook of Physiology*. Sec. 6, C.F. Code and W. Heidel, eds., *Alimentary Canal*. Am. Physiol. Soc., Washington. Vol. 5, 2391–2407.

Bressler, R. 1970. Fatty acid oxidation. *Compreh. Biochem.* 18:331–59.

Dempsey, M.E. 1974. Regulation of steroid biosynthesis. *Ann. Rev. Biochem.* 43:967–90.

Dhopeshwarkar, G.A., and Mead, J.F. 1973. Uptake and transport of fatty acids into the brain and the role of the blood-brain barrier system. *Adv. Lipid Res.* 11:109–42.

Fulco, A.J. 1974. Metabolic alterations of fatty acids. *Ann. Rev. Biochem.* 43:215–41.

Jensen, R.G. 1971. Lipolytic enzyme. In R.T. Holman, ed., *Progress in the Chemistry of Fats and Other Lipids*. Pergamon, New York. Vol. 11, 347–94.

Johnston, J.M. 1970. Intestinal absorption of fats. *Compreh. Biochem.* 18:1–18.

Larner, J. 1971. *Intermediary Metabolism and Its Regulation*. Prentice-Hall, Englewood Cliffs, N.J. Chaps. 4, 8.

Lennarz, W.J. 1970. Lipid metabolism. *Ann. Rev. Biochem* 39:359–88.

Marinetti, G.V. 1970. Biosynthesis of triglycerides. *Compreh. Biochem.* 18:117–55.

McMurray, W.C., and Magee, W.L. 1972. Phospholipid metabolism. *Ann. Rev. Biochem.* 41:129–60.

Packter, N.M. 1973. *Biosynthesis of Acetate-derived Compounds*. Wiley, New York.

Prescott, D.J., and Vagelos, P.R. 1972. Acyl carrier protein. *Adv. Enzymology* 36:269–311.

Robinson, D.S. 1970. The function of the plasma triglycerides in fatty acid transport. *Compreh. Biochem.* 18:51–116.

Scow, R.O., and Chernick, S.S. 1970. Mobilization, transport, and utilization of free fatty acids. *Compreh. Biochem.* 18:19–49.

Stoffel, W. 1971. Sphingolipids. *Ann. Rev. Biochem.* 40:57–82.

Stumpf, P.K. 1969. Metabolism of fatty acids. *Ann. Rev. Biochem.* 38:159–212.

Thompson, G.A. 1970. Phospholipid metabolism. *Compreh. Biochem.* 18:157–99.

van den Bosch, H. 1974. Phosphoglyceride metabolism. *Ann. Rev. Biochem.* 43:243–77.

Volpe, J.J., and Vagelos, P.R. 1973. Saturated fatty acid biosynthesis and its regulation. *Ann. Rev. Biochem.* 42:21–60.

Wakil, S.J., and Barnes, E.M., Jr. 1971. Fatty acid metabolism. *Compreh. Biochem.* 18S:57–104.

Zilversmit, D.B. 1967. Formation and transport of chylomicrons. *Fed. Proc.* 26:1599–1605.

CHAPTER 29

Protein Metabolism | by R. Scott Allen

Deamination
- Oxidative
- Nonoxidative

Transamination
Decarboxylation
Fate of ammonia
- Urea formation
- Biosynthetic reactions
- Direct excretion

Biosynthesis of amino acids
Fate of amino acids
Protein synthesis
Gluconeogenesis from amino acids
Ketogenic amino acids
Creatine and creatinine
Metabolism: alanine, glutamic acid, and aspartic acid; ornithine, proline, and hydroxyproline; serine and glycine; threonine; valine, leucine, and isoleucine; sulfur-containing amino acids; phenylalanine and tyrosine; lysine; histidine; tryptophan
- Nucleoproteins and nucleic acids: purine and pyrimidine nucleotides
- Hippuric acid
- Direct excretion

Essential amino acids
Protein quality
Protein quantity
- Nitrogen balance
- Protein sparers

Protein nutrition by intravenous injection

Proteins are essential organic constituents of all cells and constitute approximately 18 percent of the body weight. They are complex polymers ranging in molecular weight from about 5000 to one million. The monomer units of proteins are amino acids. These are linked together by peptide bonds in which nitrogen of the amino group of one acid is linked to the carbonyl group of a neighboring amino acid through the loss of water.

Dietary proteins are digested in the gastrointestinal tract by the action of endopeptidases, which catalyze hydrolysis of peptide fragments, and exopeptidases, which catalyze hydrolysis of terminal peptide bonds. The final products of their combined actions are free amino acids, which are absorbed almost entirely via the cells of the intestinal villi and pass for the most part into the portal blood. They are transported to the liver and in part from there into the systemic blood system which supplies other tissues and organs. In addition to this dietary supply, amino acids derived from tissue metabolism represent a significant quantity.

Although intracellular amino acids are not necessarily in equilibrium with circulating amino acids, the blood pool serves as a major source of specific amino acids for synthesis of protein. In addition, many other nitrogen compounds essential for proper tissue function are formed from amino acids drawn from the blood pool.

Free amino acids undergo catabolism in the intestinal mucosa, liver, skeletal muscle, and kidney. The catabolic process commonly involves deamination and utilization of the resulting α-keto acids for energy purposes. In most terrestrial vertebrates a large part of the released ammonia is converted into urea and excreted. In terrestrial reptiles and birds the ammonia is converted to uric acid for excretion. Many aquatic animals excrete the ammonium ion.

The use of labeled amino acids permits estimation of the following rates: absorption; degradation into urea, carbon dioxide, and water; and turnover of biosynthesized proteins and other anabolic end products. Those isotopes that have been most effective include ^{15}N, ^{14}C, ^{2}H, and ^{3}H.

DEAMINATION

Deamination is the removal of the amino group from an amino acid. It occurs in a variety of tissues, is particularly active in the liver and kidneys, and may be either oxidative or nonoxidative.

Oxidative

There are several specialized enzyme systems capable of oxidative deamination of amino acids. One of these is D-amino acid oxidase. This enzyme is widespread in animal tissues, is quite active, but is of little known significance in view of the shortage or almost complete ab-

Figure 29.1. Oxidative deamination by D- or L-amino acid oxidase

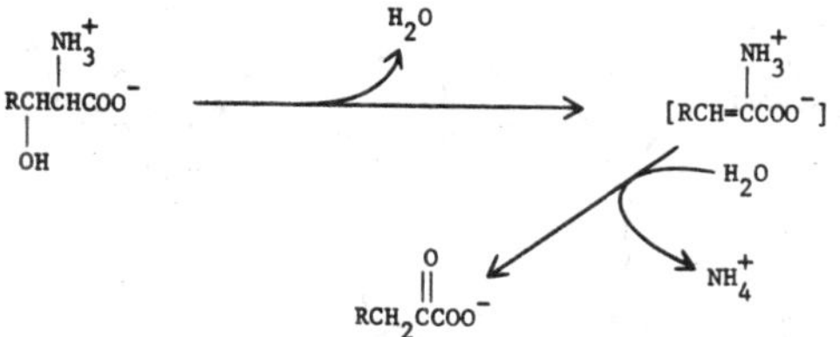

Figure 29.3. Deamination of hydroxyl-containing amino acid by amino acid dehydratase

Figure 29.2. Oxidative deamination by L-glutamate dehydrogenase

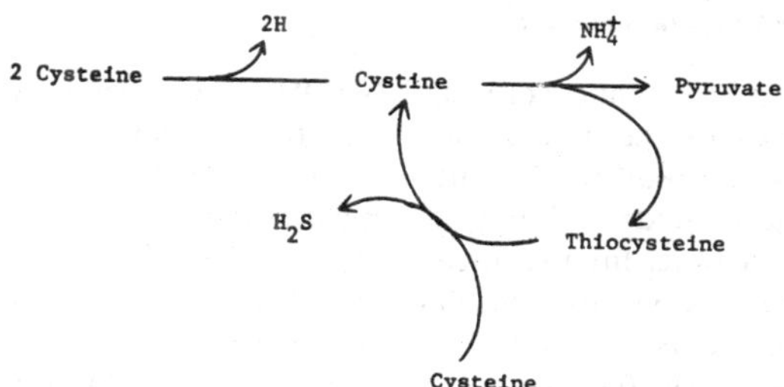

Figure 29.4. A mechanism for nonoxidative deamination of cysteine

sence of D-amino acids in mammalian tissues. Its counterpart, L-amino acid oxidase, on the other hand, has relatively little activity and has a restricted distribution in mammalian tissues. The D-amino acid oxidases are flavoproteins containing FAD, while the L-amino acid oxidases contain FMN as the coenzyme (Fig. 29.1). (For abbreviations see Chapter 27.) Subsequent to removal of two hydrogen atoms from the amino acid substrate, the hydrogen is passed to oxygen to form hydrogen peroxide, which subsequently is decomposed rapidly by cellular catalase.

A third enzyme involved in oxidative deaminations is L-glutamate dehydrogenase. It is widely distributed in mammalian tissues, is very active, and catalyzes a reversible reaction (Fig. 29.2). The activity of glutamate dehydrogenase is allosterically controlled; ATP and GTP are inhibitors, while ADP and GDP are activators. In the reverse of this reaction, a reductive amination of α-ketoglutaric acid yields glutamic acid.

Glycine also may undergo an oxidative deamination catalyzed by glycine oxidase. The mechanism is thought to be essentially the same as that for D- or L-amino acid oxidase.

Nonoxidative

A significant contribution to the total ammonia production results from the action of amino acid dehydratase, which requires the coenzyme pyridoxal phosphate. Substrates for this enzyme include serine and threonine (Fig. 29.3). Dehydration produces an unstable intermediate which reacts with water to produce an α-keto acid and NH_4^+. In an analogous reaction cysteine is converted to pyruvate, NH_4^+, and H_2S through the action of cysteine desulfurylase.

Cystine (the oxidation derivative of cysteine) may be nonoxidatively deaminated to produce pyruvate, NH_4^+, and unstable thiolcysteine, a reaction that is catalyzed by cystathionase in the cytoplasm. Thiolcysteine ($HSSCH_2CHNH_3^+COO^-$) reacts with cysteine to regenerate cystine and release H_2S (Fig. 29.4).

Amino group removal may also occur by a special mechanism. For example, histidine is deaminated by histidase to yield free ammonia and urocanic acid.

TRANSAMINATION

The process of amino acid-keto acid interconversion is termed transamination. In this process ammonia does not appear in the free state. The coenzyme for the transaminases is pyridoxal phosphate, which serves as a functional intermediate. The reaction is reversible and catalyzed by transaminase enzymes, which are widely distributed in animal tissues, especially in heart, brain, kidney, testicle, and liver. Some transaminases are mitochondrial, some are cytoplasmic, and others are found in both systems. In transamination (Fig. 29.5), pyridoxal phosphate acts as an acceptor for an amino group. The resulting pyridoxamine transfers the amino group to a new α-keto acid resulting in the regeneration of pyridoxal phosphate and the formation of a new amino acid.

The α-amino groups of most amino acids may be converted to ammonia by consecutive transamination with α-ketoglutaric acid and oxidation of the newly formed glutamic acid by L-glutamate dehydrogenase. The result is the formation of ammonia, an α-keto acid derived from

Figure 29.5. Transamination

the original amino acid, and NADH. The latter may be oxidized by the mitochondrial electron transport system, or may be reutilized in the reductive amination of α-ketoglutaric acid. Although the most common transamination reactions involve dicarboxylic amino or keto acids, transamination also occurs among pairs of monocarboxylic acids. In addition, transaminations have been observed with β-, γ-, and δ-amino acids. Moreover, transamination reactions of glutamine or asparagine with keto acids occur. The amide group of the newly formed α-keto acid is cleaved by hydrolysis. These amide transamination reactions, in contrast to the typical amino acid transaminase systems, tend to be irreversible because of rapid hydrolysis of the amide linkage.

DECARBOXYLATION

Many amino acids may be decarboxylated by amino acid decarboxylase enzymes which require pyridoxal phosphate as cofactors. The net result is the formation of primary amines and carbon dioxide. Several of these amines have strong pharmacological effects, while others are important as hormone precursors and as components of coenzymes and other active substances.

FATE OF AMMONIA

The fate of ammonia produced by various deamination reactions varies with the type of animal and its habitat. Since ammonia is very toxic, mammalian tissues are equipped with various mechanisms to convert ammonia into nontoxic materials, either for use by the animal or for excretion. The most significant methods for disposal are urea formation and excretion, biosynthesis of other nitrogen-containing compounds, and direct elimination in the urine.

Urea formation

Deamination of amino acids occurs primarily in the liver, and the resulting ammonia is converted to urea in most terrestrial vertebrates (Fig. 29.6). Ammonia and carbon dixoide (derived primarily from the citric acid cycle) interact with ATP to form carbamyl phosphate. In the liver of mammals, the enzyme carbamyl phosphate

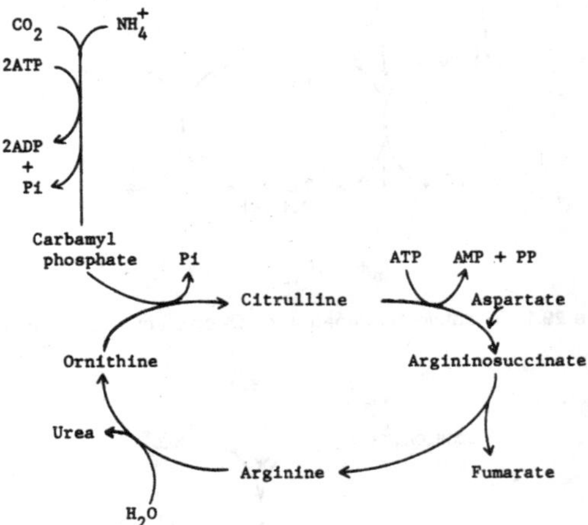

Figure 29.6. Urea cycle

synthetase requires N-acetylglutamate for activity. The enzyme system (carbamyl phosphate kinase) is able to bind ammonium ions even at very low concentrations.

The carbamyl group is transferred from carbamyl phosphate to ornithine to form citrulline, a reaction catalyzed by ornithine transcarbamylase. Argininosuccinate synthetase then catalyzes the condensation of aspartate with citrulline to produce argininosuccinate. This synthesis is driven by the cleavage of ATP into AMP and pyrophosphate, and the subsequent hydrolysis of pyrophosphate. Argininosuccinase then cleaves argininosuccinate into fumarate and arginine. The latter is hydrolytically cleaved by the enzyme arginase to form urea and ornithine, thus completing the cycle. Arginase is found only in the liver of animals which excrete urea. Fumaric acid formed in the arginylsuccinase reaction is readily hydrated to malic acid and reoxidized to oxalacetic acid.

Carbamyl phosphate synthetase and ornithine transcarbamylase are the only enzymes of the urea cycle found in the mitochondria.

Thus urea is formed from ammonia, CO_2, and the α-amino nitrogen of aspartic acid. The latter is provided by transamination of glutamic acid with oxalacetic acid. The glutamic acid is formed easily by transamination of α-ketoglutaric acid with most amino acids. Thus aspartic acid serves as a compound to channel α-amino nitrogen from amino acids to urea. The synthesis of urea is an energy-consuming process which requires the cleavage of four high-energy phosphate bonds.

Biosynthetic reactions

Part of the ammonia resulting from deamination of amino acids is utilized in the formation of biologically useful nitrogenous compounds. The processes involved are (1) reductive amination of α-ketoglutarate to form glutamate (reversal of reactions in Fig. 29.2), (2) amina-

$$^{-}OOCCH_2CH_2\overset{\overset{+}{NH_3}}{CH}COO^{-} \qquad NH_2\overset{O}{\overset{\|}{C}}CH_2CH_2\overset{\overset{+}{NH_3}}{CH}COO^{-}$$

$$\text{Glutamic Acid} \xrightarrow[\text{ATP} \rightarrow \text{ADP}, \; \text{Pi}]{\overset{+}{NH_4}} \text{Glutamine}$$

Figure 29.7. Glutamine synthesis

tion of glutamate to produce glutamine (Fig. 29.7), and (3) formation of carbamyl phosphate (see Fig. 29.6).

The amide-N of glutamine is incorporated into purines and into certain pyrimidines. Carbamyl phosphate is utilized in the synthesis of the pyrimidine ring system.

Direct excretion

Urinary ammonia is derived in kidney epithelial tissues from the hydrolysis of glutamine and from the deamination of α-amino acids. Glutaminase catalyzes hydrolysis of the amide linkage of glutamine to produce ammonia and glutamic acid. Amino acid oxidases play a lesser role in deamination of amino acids in the kidney. Excretion of ammonia helps conserve sodium ions, which is the chief cation in the regulation of electrolyte concentration and acid-base balance in the blood.

BIOSYNTHESIS OF AMINO ACIDS

Both nonessential and essential dietary amino acids are necessary for animal life. The essential amino acids must be provided in the diet because of the inability of the animal to synthesize adequate quantities. In addition, carnivores and omnivores make use of various animal proteins to help provide the essential amino acids. The principal reason for the inability of animals to synthesize these acids is the lack of the proper α-keto acids for transamination.

The biosynthesis of the nonessential amino acids in mammalian tissues requires precursors primarily from carbohydrate metabolism. These may be divided into three important groups: (1) those amino acids (serine, glycine, and cysteine) derived from phosphoglyceric acid, (2) those (glutamic acid, arginine, proline, and hydroxyproline) derived from α-ketoglutaric acid, and (3) those (alanine and aspartic acid) derived from pyruvic acid.

FATE OF AMINO ACIDS

Amino acids undergo a great variety of reactions. Some of the more significant ones include the synthesis of proteins, formation of peptide hormones, and production of special compounds such as detoxication derivatives, ketone bodies, nonpeptide hormones, glutathione, and many others. Also, deamination with the production of α-keto acids used in a variety of ways is important.

Protein synthesis

The animal body may store both glycogen and fat but has little capacity for reserve storage of proteins. Generally speaking, intake of protein beyond daily needs results in increased urea formation accompanied by the conversion of the carbon skeleton of most amino acids into carbohydrates and fats or in their metabolic degradation for energy purposes. On the other hand, if dietary intake is less than normal daily needs, catabolism of body proteins proceeds with a loss of body nitrogen until nitrogen balance at a lower level has been achieved.

The mechanisms of protein synthesis are complex. They may be considered in four phases: activation, initiation, elongation, and termination.

During the activation phase individual amino acids become attached by ester linkage to the ribose portion of the adenosine residue at the 3′-terminus of specific transfer RNA's (tRNA) by the action of specific aminoacyl-tRNA synthetases. This action is driven by ATP. For each amino acid there is at least one specific tRNA and activating enzyme.

The initiation phase includes dissociation of the ribosome into large and small subunits, binding of initiator-tRNA (formylmethionine-tRNA) to the small subunit–mRNA complex in response to the initiator codon (a nucleotide triplet) on the mRNA, and finally association of the large subunit with the small subunit–initiation complex. The initiator-tRNA occupies the P site on the ribosome. Hydrolysis of GTP is involved during the formation of the small subunit–initiation complex and formation of the final reassociation step.

The elongation phase starts with the binding of aminoacyl-tRNA at the other tRNA site (A site) on the ribosome, a process which requires GTP and an elongation factor. Peptidyl transferase, associated with the large ribosomal subunit, then catalyzes formation of the peptide bond between the amino group of the incoming aminoacyl-tRNA and the carbonyl of the formylmethionine carried by the initiator-tRNA. The dipeptidyl-tRNA now occupies the A site on the ribosome while the P site carries the deacylated tRNA. The dipeptidyl-tRNA then is translocated to the P site with concomitant release of the deacylated tRNA. This step requires GTP and another elongation factor. Another round of elongation occurs with the binding of another aminoacyl-tRNA as dictated by the next codon on the mRNA.

Termination of protein synthesis occurs when a stop signal (termination codon) on mRNA is recognized by the protein release factor. The termination codon activates a large ribosomal subunit enzyme which catalyzes hydrolysis of the bond between the polypeptide chain and tRNA at the P site. The polypeptide then leaves the ribosome, and the latter dissociates into two subunits for subsequent involvement in initiation of another sequence of protein synthesis.

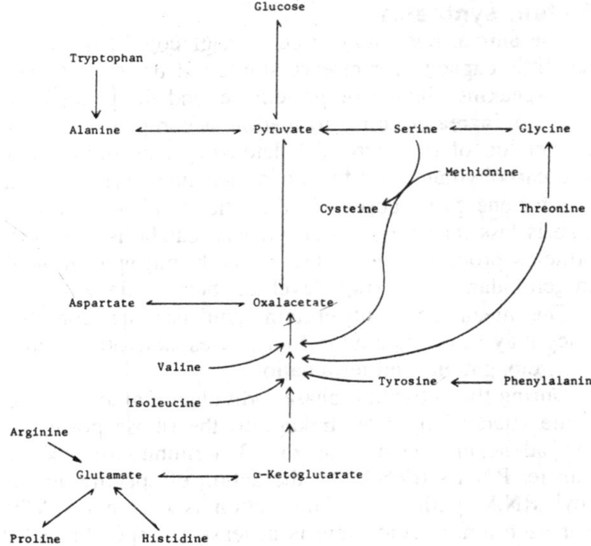

Figure 29.8. Gluconeogenesis from amino acids

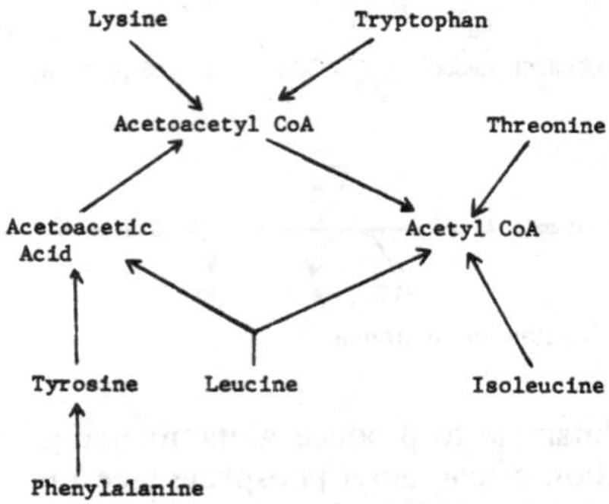

Figure 29.9. Ketogenic amino acids

The final protein product has no amino-terminal formylmethionine; the formyl group is hydrolyzed by a deformylase during or subsequent to synthesis of the polypeptide chain. Moreover, one or more of the amino-terminal residues may be removed through hydrolysis by aminopeptidases.

After protein synthesis is completed, certain modifications can occur: disulfide linkages are formed; lysine and proline residues are hydroxylated in certain proteins; sugars may be attached to aspartate, serine, and threonine residues to form glycoproteins; phosphorylation of some proteins occurs; and certain polypeptide chains may be cleaved to provide biologically active proteins.

Gluconeogenesis from amino acids

Glucose may be formed from most of the amino acids (Table 29.1). Figure 29.8 shows in outline the amino acids that may serve as precursors to carbohydrates. Alanine, aspartic acid, and glutamic acid are directly

Table 29.1. Classification of amino acids according to catabolic fates

Glucogenic	Ketogenic	Glucogenic and/or ketogenic
Alanine	Leucine	Isoleucine
Arginine		Lysine
Aspartic acid		Phenylalanine
Cysteine		Tyrosine
Glutamic acid		Threonine
Glycine		Tryptophan
Histidine		
Hydroxyproline		
Methionine		
Proline		
Serine		
Valine		

convertible by transamination to the corresponding α-keto acids. By a variety of other reactions, some of which are considerably less direct than might be inferred from this outline, the other amino acids may be metabolized to carbohydrate precursors.

Ketogenic amino acids

Although leucine is the only truly ketogenic amino acid, several other amino acids may be catabolized to form some acetyl CoA or acetoacetic acid (see Table 29.1). Figure 29.9 presents an outline of those amino acids that serve as precursors to these ketogenic compounds.

The glucogenicity or ketogenicity of an amino acid may be determined by administering amino acids to animals made diabetic either by pancreatectomy or by administration of phlorhizin, with subsequent measurements of urinary excretion of glucose and ketone bodies. Recent detailed studies, involving the use of isotopically labeled amino acids and of specific isolated enzymes, have confirmed the earlier observations with diabetic animals.

Creatine and creatinine

Creatine is methylguanidoacetic acid and is found mostly in skeletal muscle. It is derived by interaction between glycine and arginine in the kidney to produce guanidoacetic acid and ornithine. A reaction in the liver converts guanidoacetic acid to creatine by interaction with activated methionine (S-adenosylmethionine). The latter serves as a methyl donor in transmethylation reactions.

Creatine is readily converted to phosphocreatine, an important storage form of high-energy phosphate in skeletal muscle. Phosphocreatine is formed by interaction between creatine and ATP, a reaction which is readily reversible when there is a need for additional ATP elsewhere.

In mammalian species the normal excretory product of creatine is creatinine. Under normal conditions, phosphocreatine may lose phosphoric acid in a ring closure reaction and yield creatinine. Free creatine also may produce the same product by loss of water, but at a slower rate.

There is a steady creatinine production which is proportional to the total amount of creatine and phosphocreatine in the body and also proportional to the muscle mass. Thus creatinine is excreted in the urine at levels which are independent of diet and are remarkably constant in the individual animal. Moreover, the daily excretion of creatinine is little influenced by ordinary exercise or by urine volume.

Metabolism

Catabolism of amino acids commonly begins with the removal of the α-amino groups by transamination or by oxidative deamination. The resulting α-keto acids are used in a number of ways including oxidative degradation for energy needs, conversion to glucose or glycogen, conversion to and storage as fats, and formation of ketone bodies, cholesterol, bile acids, and steroid hormones.

Alanine, glutamic acid, and aspartic acid

Figure 29.10 summarizes the major reactions of these amino acids. Transamination results in the formation of α-keto acids which are normal compounds in carbohydrate catabolism. Glutamic acid is extremely versatile in that it may transaminate with a number of α-keto acids or may undergo oxidative deamination in the mitochondria through the action of L-glutamate dehydrogenase. Aspartic acid and alanine are readily transminated to yield oxalacetic acid and pyruvic acid respectively. The α-ketoglutaric acid is perhaps the most universal of all the acceptors of amino groups in transamination reactions.

Glutamic acid is involved in the biosynthesis of certain special products such as glutathione and glutamine. In addition, glutamic acid may be reduced to glutamic semialdehyde, which undergoes transamination to form ornithine, a compound of major importance in the urea cycle. Glutamic semialdehyde also may be converted to proline and hydroxyproline.

Aspartic acid is an essential reactant in the urea cycle, in the formation of anserine and carnosine (which are dipeptides found in muscle tissue), and in the biosynthesis of purines and pyrimidines.

Ornithine, proline, and hydroxyproline

Ornithine and proline are produced from glutamic acid through glutamic semialdehyde as an intermediate (see Fig. 29.10). These reactions are reversible. Hydroxyproline, derived by oxidation of proline, is catabolized to γ-hydroxyglutamic acid by a process that is a reversal of the types of reactions involved in the conversion of glutamic acid to proline. Transamination of γ-hydroxyglutamic acid yields α-keto-γ-hydroxyglutaric acid,

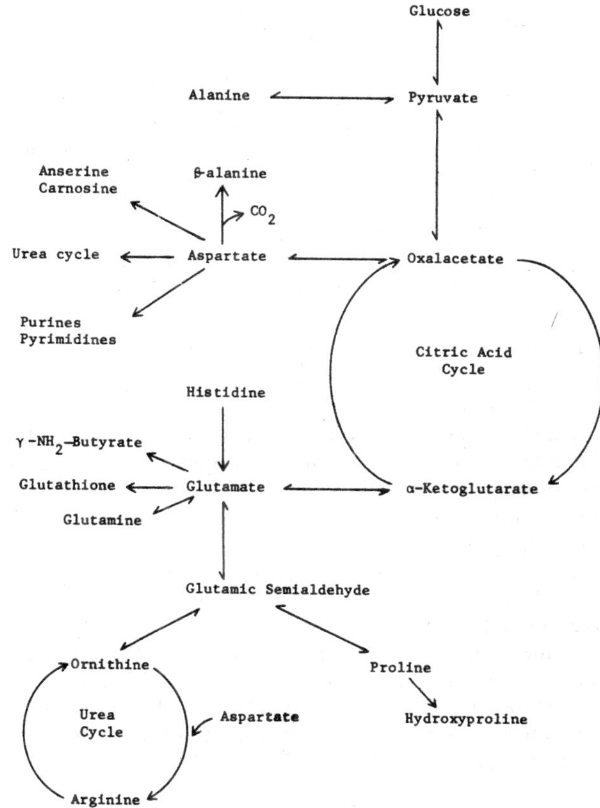

Figure 29.10. Metabolism of alanine, aspartic acid, and glutamic acid

which may be cleaved to form glyoxylic acid and pyruvic acid.

Serine and glycine

As shown in Figure 29.11 oxidative deamination of glycine with glycine oxidase yields free ammonia and glyoxylic acid. Glycine serves as an important component in the formation of glycocholic acid, glutathione, guanidoacetic acid, hippuric acid, purines, and porphyrins.

Serine may be deaminated either by transamination to produce hydroxypyruvate or by serine dehydratase to yield pyruvic acid. The biogenesis of several of the important phosphatides—including lecithins, cephalins, and sphingomyelins—and cerebrosides requires serine. In addition, serine is a precursor for cysteine, which results from an interaction of serine with homocysteine (derived from the degradation of methionine).

Interconversion of serine and glycine in the liver results through the action of serine transhydroxymethylase, which requires tetrahydrofolic acid (THFA) as a single carbon (C_1) carrier.

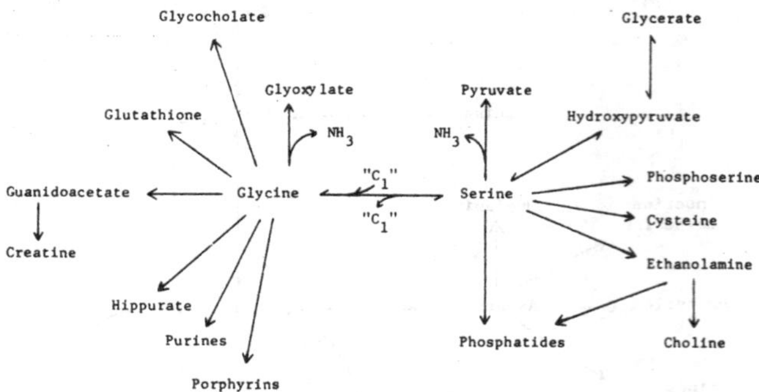

Figure 29.11. Major metabolic fates of glycine and serine

Threonine

There appears to be no transaminase that is specific for threonine; however, this amino acid may be degraded by two other pathways (Fig. 29.12). Under the catalytic action of threonine dehydratase, ammonia and α-ketobutyric acid are derived from threonine. The α-ketobutyric acid is oxidatively decarboxylated to yield propionyl CoA. The latter may be converted, by carbon dioxide fixation and rearrangement, to succinyl CoA.

In the other pathway, threonine is cleaved in the presence of threonine aldolase to produce glycine and acetaldehyde. The latter is oxidized to acetate and then converted to acetyl CoA. This pathway, however, appears to be the minor one.

Valine, leucine, and isoleucine

These branched-chain amino acids cannot be synthesized in mammalian tissues and thus are classified as essential. Each acid readily transaminates with α-ketoglutaric acid to produce the corresponding α-keto acid and glutamic acid (Fig. 29.13). Each α-keto acid undergoes oxidative decarboxylation to produce an acyl CoA by a mechanism thought to be essentially that described earlier for the oxidative decarboxylation of pyruvic acid (see Chapter 27). Subsequent reactions for each of the acyl CoA derivatives resemble β-oxidation of fatty acyl CoA compounds involved in fatty acid oxidation.

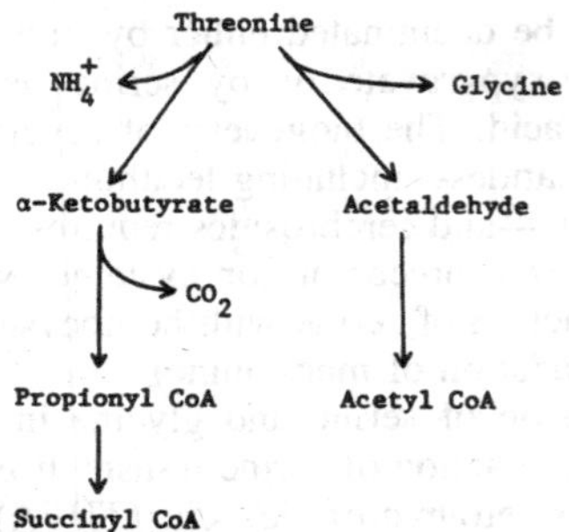

Figure 29.12. Catabolism of threonine

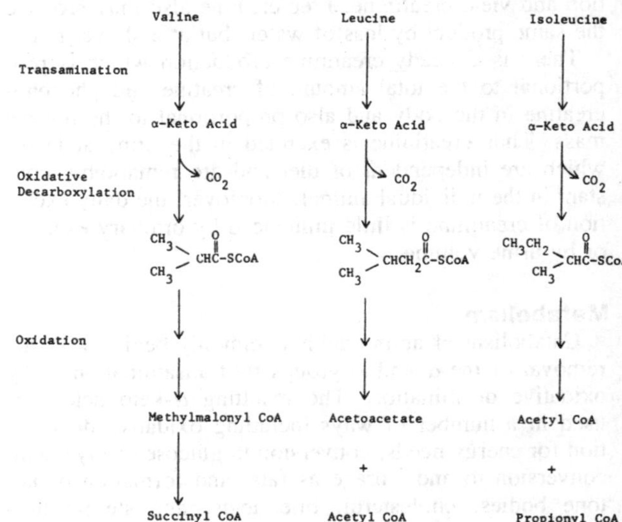

Figure 29.13. Degradation of the branched-chain amino acids

Valine oxidation yields methylmalonyl CoA, which is converted into succinyl CoA and completely oxidized by the citric acid cycle.

Acetoacetic acid and acetyl CoA are produced by oxidation of leucine. This amino acid, therefore, is strictly ketogenic.

Isoleucine oxidation results in the formation of acetyl CoA and propionyl CoA. The latter will fix CO_2 to form methylmalonyl CoA, which rearranges to produce succinyl CoA. Isoleucine, therefore, is both ketogenic and glucogenic.

Sulfur-containing amino acids

S-adenosylmethionine (active methionine) is formed by reaction of methionine with ATP (Fig. 29.14). It is important for transmethylation reactions. Some of the more important compounds which accept a methyl group from S-adenosylmethionine include guanidoacetic acid, nicotinamide, phosphatidyl ethanolamine, and norepinephrine. S-adenosylhomocysteine, which results from transfer of methyl groups to the methyl acceptors just listed, is hydrolyzed to yield homocysteine and adenosine. Homocysteine interacts with serine to form cystathionine, which in turn is cleaved to produce homoserine and cysteine. Homoserine is converted to α-ketobutyric acid by a dehydratase. Subsequent normal reactions of α-ketobutyric acid result in succinyl CoA formation.

Cysteine may be converted to (1) pyruvate by a variety of pathways, (2) cystine, and (3) taurine by a series of oxidation steps and a decarboxylation. The latter is utilized in forming taurine derivatives of bile acids. Cysteine also is a component of glutathione, an important tripeptide.

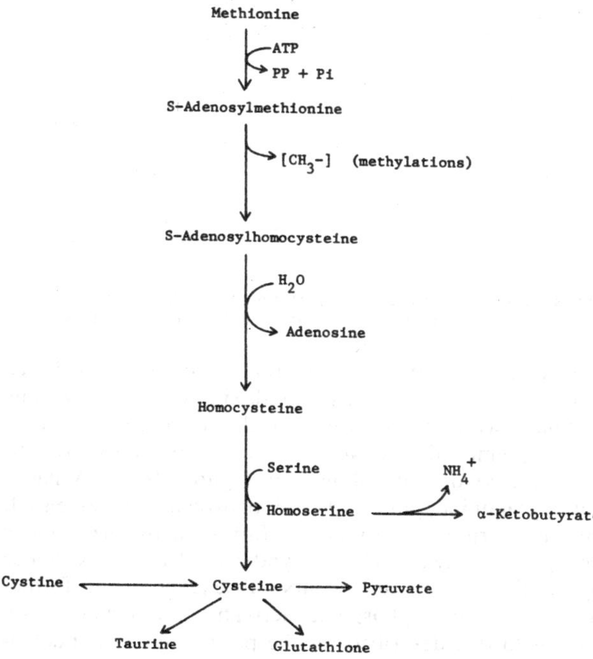

Figure 29.14. Metabolism of sulfur-containing amino acids

Phenylalanine and tyrosine

Under normal circumstances most of the phenylalanine metabolism is channeled through tyrosine by the action of phenylalanine hydroxylase, which requires NADPH and molecular oxygen (Fig. 29.15). However, when there is an inborn block to this reaction, phenylalanine is converted by transamination to phenylpyruvic acid. The latter may be excreted in the urine or converted to and

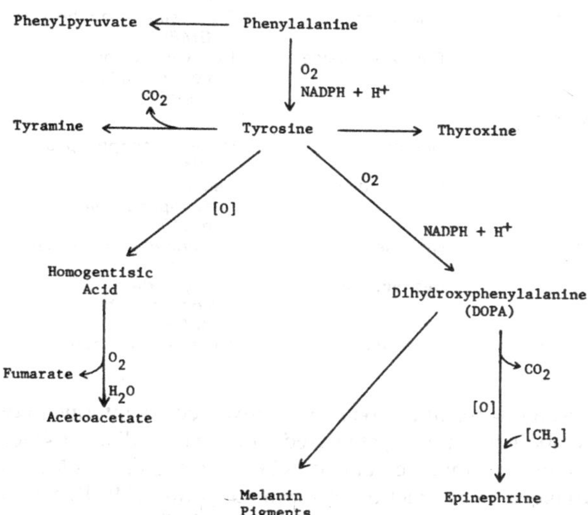

Figure 29.15. Catabolism of phenylalanine and tyrosine

excreted as phenyllactic acid or phenylacetic acid. The resultant abnormal condition is called phenylketonuria.

Tyrosine may undergo a number of different reactions. It may be (1) decarboxylated to produce tyramine, (2) iodinated to produce monoiodotyrosine, which in turn undergoes subsequent reactions eventually resulting in the formation of thyroxine, (3) hydroxylated to produce dihydroxyphenylalanine, which serves as a precursor for epinephrine or for melanin pigments, or (4) transaminated to yield *p*-hydroxylphenylpyruvic acid, which undergoes further oxidation to homogentisic acid. This compound is excreted in individuals with another inborn error in metabolism; this condition is called alcaptonuria. Under normal circumstances, homogentisic acid is further oxidized by homogentisic oxidase wherein molecular oxygen effects a cleavage of the aromatic ring between the side-chain and the adjacent hydroxyl group. The resulting compound, maleylacetoacetate, has a *cis* configuration which undergoes rearrangement to the *trans* compound (fumarylacetoacetate). Hydrolysis of the latter yields fumaric acid and acetoacetic acid. Thus tyrosine and phenylalanine are both glucogenic and ketogenic.

Lysine

Lysine, like threonine, apparently does not undergo typical transamination. However, in one of its major catabolic sequences deamination occurs through the catalytic action of L-amino acid oxidase in the liver, resulting in the formation of the α-keto acid. Subsequent reactions eventually result in the formation of acetoacetyl CoA which is cleaved with CoA to form acetyl CoA. Alternate pathways of catabolism yield the same products.

Histidine

Histidine undergoes a series of reactions (Fig. 29.16) including decarboxylation to form histamine, methylation to form several different methyl histidine derivatives, transamination to form imidazolepyruvic acid, and finally (and most importantly) deamination by the enzyme histidase to form urocanic acid. The latter undergoes a sequence of reactions finally resulting in the formation of α-formiminoglutamic acid. The formimino group is transferred to the N^5-position of THFA, resulting in the formation of the glutamic acid.

Tryptophan

Tryptophan undergoes a number of metabolic reactions, including (1) hydroxylation followed by decarboxylation to yield serotonin, a powerful vasoconstrictor; (2) decarboxylation to form tryptamine; (3) transamination to give indolepyruvic acid; and (4) conversion through a series of reactions to nicotinic acid, which reduces the level of dietary niacin required for optimum growth and function.

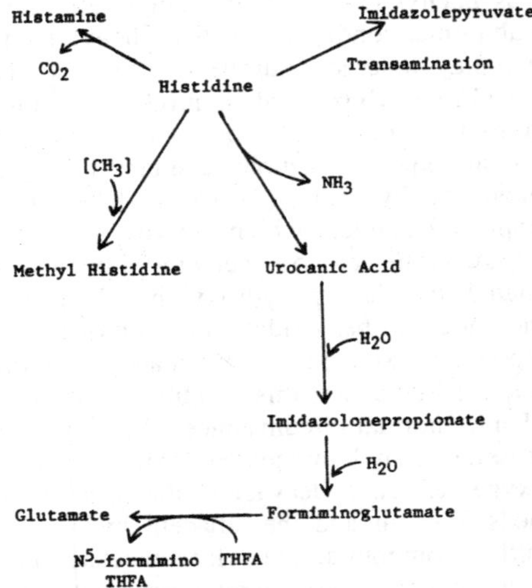

Figure 29.16. Catabolism of histidine

Nucleoproteins and nucleic acids

Nucleoproteins constitute a group of conjugated proteins wherein nucleic acids are combined with simple proteins, generally of basic character. The nucleoproteins make up a large part of the nuclear material of cells and also are present in cytoplasm. They are vitally concerned with cellular organization and function.

Nucleic acids are polynucleotides either of the deoxyribonucleic acid (DNA) or ribonucleic acid (RNA) type. Complete hydrolysis of nucleic acids yields a mixture of purines and pyrimidines, ribose and/or deoxyribose, and phosphoric acid.

Purine and pyrimidine nucleotides

Nucleotides are essential for the formation of RNA and DNA, both of which are involved in the synthesis of proteins. The direct precursors for the purine nucleotides are summarized in Figure 29.17. Glycine, aspartic acid, and glutamine furnish all of the nitrogens and some carbons in the purine ring synthesis. The ribose phosphate component is derived from the pentose phosphate pathway. Deoxyribonucleotides are synthesized subsequent to the formation of the ribose derivatives. The reductase system involved includes two proteins and requires ATP and

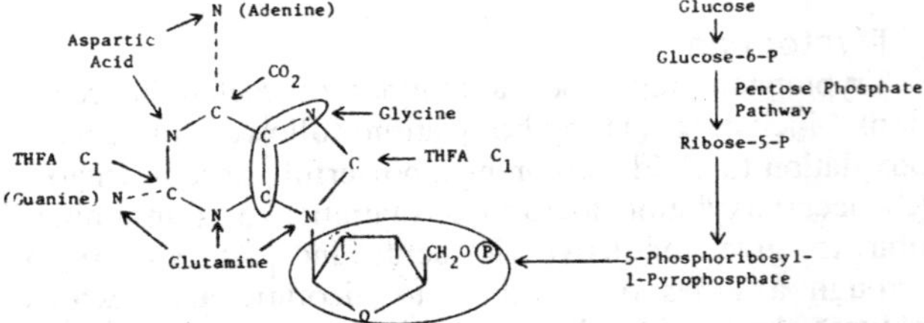

Figure 29.17. Biosynthesis of purine nucleotides. The 2′-deoxynucleotides are synthesized from the ribonucleotides.

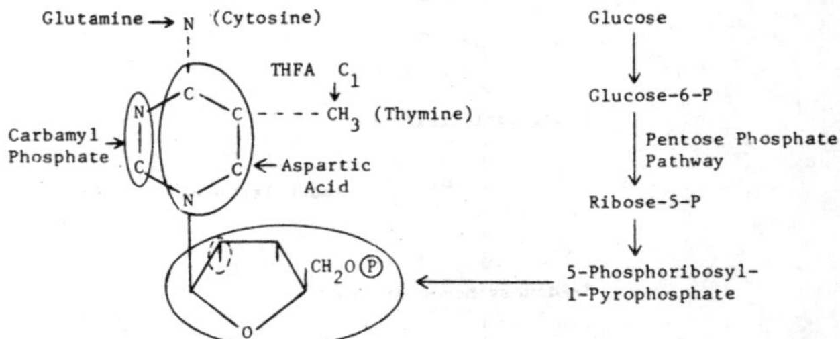

Figure 29.18. Biosynthesis of pyrimidine nucleotides. The 2′-deoxynucleotides are formed from the ribonucleotides in most cases.

magnesium ion for full activation. The actual hydrogen donor is a small protein (thioredoxin) with two cysteine residues, which is in addition to the reductase complex.

Compounds that serve as contributors to the pyrimidine nucleotides are shown in Figure 29.18. Aspartic acid, glutamine, and carbonyl phosphate are essential, and again ribose phosphate is furnished by the pentose phosphate pathway. The biosynthesis of the deoxyribose pyrimidine nucleotides occurs subsequent to the formation of the ribosephosphate derivative by a mechanism similar to that described for the purine deoxyribonucleotides.

Listed below are the names of the major purines and pyrimidines and their corresponding nucleosides and nucleotides. In addition to the monophosphate derivatives listed each of the nucleotides may exist also as di- and triphosphate derivatives.

Purine	*Nucleoside*	*Nucleotide*
Adenine	Adenosine	Adenosine monophosphate (AMP)
	Deoxyadenosine	Deoxyadenosine monophosphate (dAMP)
Guanine	Guanosine	Guanosine monophosphate (GMP)
	Deoxyguanosine	Deoxyguanosine monophosphate (dGMP)
Pyrimidine		
Uracil	Uridine	Uridine monophosphate (UMP)
	Deoxyuridine	Deoxyuridine monophosphate (dUMP)
Cytosine	Cytidine	Cytidine monophosphate (CMP)
	Deoxycytidine	Deoxycytidine monophosphate (dCMP)
Thymine	Thymidine	Thymidine monophosphate (TMP)

Several essential coenzymes involved in intermediary metabolism are synthesized in mammalian tissues through the involvement of ATP. For example, FMN is produced by interaction of riboflavin with ATP. Reaction with additional ATP produces FAD. NAD^+ is biosynthesized by interaction of ATP with nicotinamide nucleo-

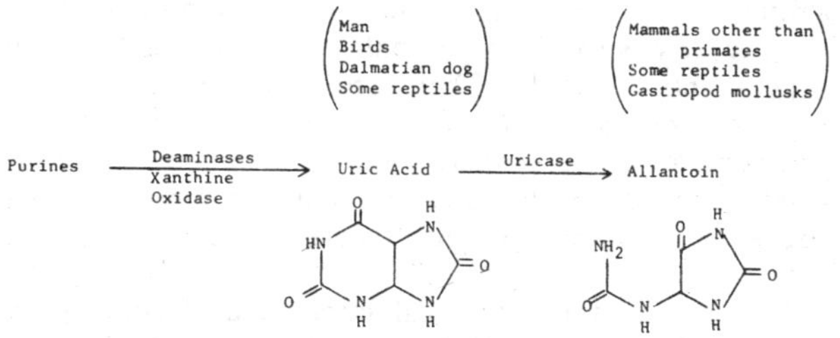

Man
Birds
Dalmatian dog
Some reptiles

Mammals other than primates
Some reptiles
Gastropod mollusks

Purines —Deaminases, Xanthine Oxidase→ Uric Acid —Uricase→ Allantoin

Figure 29.19. Excretory products derived from purines

tide. $NADP^+$ is produced by reaction of ATP with NAD^+. ATP contributes to a significant part of the CoA molecule. And thiamin, a B-complex vitamin, is converted to TPP by reaction with ATP.

The degradation of purine nucleotides by hydrolases, phosphorylases, pyrophosphorylases, and deaminases results in the formation of the purines hypoxanthine and xanthine. Hypoxanthine is converted to xanthine and xanthine to uric acid by the action of xanthine oxidase. The conversion of uric acid to allantoin in some species is catalyzed by the enzyme uricase. (Figure 29.19 summarizes these reactions.)

Catabolism of the pyrimidines yields NH_3, CO_2, β-alanine (from uracil and cytosine), and β-aminoisobutyric acid (from thymine).

Hippuric acid

The reaction of benzoic acid with glycine produces hippuric acid, which occurs in the urine of all mammals. However, the level of urinary hippuric acid is considerably greater in herbivores than in carnivores. Glycine serves as a detoxifying agent for benzoic acid, which results from the metabolism of plant components and normally is not oxidized further. The kidney seems to be the major site of hippuric acid formation in all species, but in some the liver makes an important contribution.

Direct excretion

Small amounts of free amino acids are normally found in the urine, suggesting that the kidney renal tubules do not completely absorb amino acids.

ESSENTIAL AMINO ACIDS

Mammalian organisms have lost, through the course of time, the ability to synthesize in adequate quantities the carbon chain of certain α-keto acids. Thus the corresponding α-amino acids are not formed by transamination reactions. Since all of the amino acids commonly found in proteins must be present for the biosynthesis of proteins, the diet must furnish these additional amino acids either as protein or as free amino acids. The amino acids which cannot be synthesized in adequate quantities to meet metabolic requirements are called essential amino acids. Those considered to be essential in all mammalian species include valine, leucine, isoleucine, threonine, methionine, lysine, phenylalanine, and tryptophan.

Arginine and histidine formerly were included in this list. However, it is now clear that these amino acids are synthesized in adequate quantities to meet minimum metabolic needs. In some species, however, better growth occurs when these amino acids are added to the diet.

The dietary needs for specific amino acids are considerably less important in ruminants (see Chapter 22). Rumen microorganisms are normally able to synthesize both essential and nonessential amino acids in sufficient quantities.

PROTEIN QUALITY

Even if highly digestible, certain proteins are nutritionally inadequate due to the absence or very low level of one or more of the essential amino acids. For example, gelatin contains no tryptophan, and zein from corn contains no lysine and is low in tryptophan. The quality of these proteins, therefore, is extremely low; they will not support normal growth and development in experimental animals. Feeding low-quality proteins will result in a substantial loss of nitrogen as urea in the urine and in poor utilization of amino acids for body protein synthesis. Although plant proteins in general are nutritionally inferior to those from animal sources, it is often possible by combinations of plant protein sources to provide a diet that is adequate.

The term *biological value* of protein indicates the value of the protein for maintenance and growth. It expresses the percentage of a protein that is actually used.

The biological value of several common protein sources has been determined for the rat by Mitchell (1927). Animal proteins (whole egg, 94; milk, 85; beef liver, 77) tend to have higher biological values than those of plant proteins (wheat, 67; potato, 67; whole corn, 60; cooked navy beans, 38). The biological value for mixed plant proteins often is higher than that for any one of the component plant proteins.

Because of protein synthesis in the rumen, the biological value for proteins appears to be different in ruminants than in monogastric mammals. Ruminants are able to perform well on so-called low-quality proteins so long as adequate levels of total dietary nitrogen (protein and some nonprotein nitrogen) are provided. Moreover, the biological value of dietary protein in cattle changes with level of intake. With 9, 11, 13, and 15 percent crude protein rations, biological values for the protein are 79, 70, 60, and 52 respectively (Lofgren 1964).

PROTEIN QUANTITY

The quantity of a good-quality protein needed for growth and maintenance may be determined by the nitrogen balance technique.

Nitrogen balance

When the protein intake by a healthy, well-nourished animal is gradually reduced, there is a corresponding decline in nitrogen loss in the excreta. The animal will have essentially equal values for intake and elimination (nitrogen balance) until a critical intake level is reached, below which the nitrogen balance becomes negative. On the other hand, if the consumption of good-quality protein is increased beyond maintenance and growth needs, the animal will remain in nitrogen equilibrium by simply excreting the excess.

Whenever the nitrogen intake exceeds excretion, a positive nitrogen balance exists. Some of the conditions that cause this include (1) growth, (2) recovery from fasting, starvation, or extended illness, and (3) pregnancy, mostly related to growth of the fetus.

Negative nitrogen balance occurs when more nitrogen is excreted than consumed. Conditions that result in this, primarily at the expense of body proteins, include (1) fasting, (2) starvation, (3) severe fever, (4) severe illness, (5) protein-free diets, (6) diets of low-quality protein or of protein lacking in essential amino acids, or (7) a shift from a high-protein to a low-protein diet. Certain cellular proteins contribute to the amino acid pool under these circumstances. The liver may lose as much as 50 percent of its total nitrogen, and skeletal muscle may also lose considerable nitrogen. Some enzymes may decrease in activity; others may increase. In severe protein restriction, certain peptide hormones may not be synthesized in adequate quantities, and endocrine disorders may appear.

If good health is to be assured, one must allow for about 10 percent wastage in the gastrointestinal tract and also allow for a possible overestimate in biological value. For most animals, the optimum is not known, but it is generally felt that crude protein needs should be set at four times the protein equivalent ($N \times 6.25$) of the urinary endogenous nitrogen.

Protein sparers

Endogenous protein catabolism may be kept at a minimum when carbohydrates and fats are readily available for energy needs. Carbohydrates are more effective than fats, due primarily to the elimination of the need for gluconeogenesis from amino acids. If both carbohydrates and fats are in short supply, body proteins are called upon to help maintain blood glucose levels via glucose formation from glucogenic amino acids.

PROTEIN NUTRITION BY INTRAVENOUS INJECTION

The parenteral administration of nitrogen in the form of whole blood, blood plasma, protein hydrolyzates, and amino acids has been successful in maintaining nitrogen balance or positive nitrogen balance in man and several experimental animals. There are many circumstances, such as those following serious surgery, serious burns, and certain diseases, where there is a marked loss of nitrogen from the body. Extra protein or amino acids are needed to maintain nitrogen balance or at least reduce serious loss.

Nutrient solutions for total intravenous feeding have been developed and used successfully. For example, beagle puppies (12 weeks of age) infused intravenously at a constant rate with a 30 percent nutrient solution over periods up to 36 weeks showed normal growth and development. Moreover, the total intravenous feeding system has been used successfully in human infants and adults recovering from serious surgery and certain diseases.

The nutrient solutions normally are about six times more concentrated than blood and usually consist of 20–25 percent glucose, 4–5 percent protein hydrolyzate, and 5 percent minerals and vitamins. Pure crystalline amino acids can replace the protein hydrolyzate.

REFERENCES

Bosch, L., ed. 1972. *The Mechanism of Protein Synthesis and Its regulation*. North-Holland, Amsterdam.

Dudrick, S.J., and Rhoads, J.E. 1971. New horizons for intravenous feeding. *J. Am. Med. Ass.* 215:939–49.

——. 1972. Total intravenous feeding. *Scien. Am.* 226(May):73–80.

Felig, P. 1975. Amino acid metabolism in man. *Ann. Rev. Biochem.* 44:933–55.

Haselkorn, R., and Rothman-Denes, L.B. 1973. Protein synthesis. *Ann. Rev. Biochem.* 42:397–438.

Krebs, H.A. 1964. The metabolic fate of amino acids. In H.N. Munro and J.B. Allison, eds., *Mammalian Protein Metabolism*. Academic Press, New York. Vol. 1, 125–76.

Larner, J. 1971. *Intermediary Metabolism and Its Regulation*. Prentice-Hall, Englewood Cliffs, N.J. Pp. 219–47.

Lofgren, G.P. 1964. How nutritious is your feed. *Feed Age* (Nov.):22–24.

Lucas-Lenard, J., and Lipman, F. 1971. Protein biosynthesis. *Ann. Rev. Biochem.* 40:409–48.

McLaughlan, J.M., and Campbell, J.A. 1964. Methodology of protein evaluation. In H.N. Munro and J.B. Allison, eds., *Mammalian Protein Metabolism*. Academic Press, New York. Vol. 3, 391–422.

Meister, A. 1965. *Biochemistry of the Amino Acids*. 2d ed. Academic Press, New York. Vols. 1, 2.

Mitchell, H.H. 1927. The protein values of foods in nutrition. *J. Home Econ.* 19:122–31.

Nyhan, W.L., ed. 1967. *Amino Acid Metabolism and Genetic Variation*. McGraw-Hill, New York.

Schepartz, B. 1973. *Regulation of Amino Acid Metabolism in Mammals*. Saunders, Philadelphia.

Truffa-Bachi, P., and Cohen, G.N. 1973. Amino acid metabolism. *Ann. Rev. Biochem.* 42:113–34.

CHAPTER 30

Disorders of Carbohydrate and Fat Metabolism | by Emmett N. Bergman

In domestic animals the principal metabolic disorders associated with carbohydrate, fat, and protein metabolism are bovine ketosis, ovine pregnancy toxemia, spontaneous hypoglycemias such as hypoglycemia of newborn pigs, diabetes mellitus of dogs, and numerous fatty liver syndromes affecting both mammals and birds.

RUMINANT KETOSIS

In ruminants, ketosis (acetonemia) occurs most frequently in high-producing dairy cows and in pregnant ewes (pregnancy toxemia, twin-lamb disease). Ketosis of varying intensity may occur in all animal species, however, and can be induced by starvation, high-fat and low-carbohydrate diets, impaired liver function, anesthesia, and endocrine disorders such as diabetes mellitus or hyperfunction of the anterior pituitary gland. Females of any species are more susceptible to ketosis than males, and this predisposition is exaggerated during lactation or pregnancy. The minimal number of fetuses required for the development of intense ketosis is two in the sheep (Reid 1968), three in the guinea pig (Bergman and Sellers 1960), and eight in the rat (Scow et al. 1964). The ketosis syndrome of the guinea pig and rat is very similar to that of sheep.

Ketosis usually affects cows within 6 weeks after calving. The mortality rate is low, but since ketosis causes a marked loss in milk production and body weight, it results in a great economic loss to the dairyman. Bovine ketosis has been classified into primary and secondary (or complicated) ketosis. Secondary ketosis may be induced or aggravated by a poor appetite resulting from any one of a variety of pathological conditions such as metritis, peritonitis, indigestion, displaced abomasum, mastitis, and nephritis (Fincher 1955). Ketosis of sheep usually occurs during the last month of pregnancy when fetal growth is the most rapid. It is most common in ewes carrying twins or triplets, and practically all of the ewes die unless parturition occurs or the lambs are removed by a Caesarean operation. Ketosis can often be produced experimentally in sheep by undernutrition during pregnancy (Fig. 30.1), but ketosis in cows is more difficult to induce. Giving thyroid hormones along with a low-energy or high-protein diet has been the only method found to produce severe ketosis in cattle (Hibbitt and Baird 1967).

Ketosis of cattle and sheep are not identical diseases, but they have at least three features in common (Bergman 1971, 1973): (1) a negative energy balance due to high production or inadequate food consumption, (2) a reduction of carbohydrate in blood (hypoglycemia) and liver (glycogen depletion), and (3) an increased fat metabolism. The first two features undoubtedly influence the third, and the body overshoots in the direction of excessive fat metabolism and ketosis.

Glucose metabolism

In ruminants, a blood glucose concentration of 30–60 mg/100 ml is required for normal physiological processes. It is needed by at least five tissues of the body: (1) nervous system, (2) fat, (3) muscle, (4) fetuses, and (5) mammary gland.

The nervous system, in particular, is completely dependent upon a regular supply of glucose for its oxidative

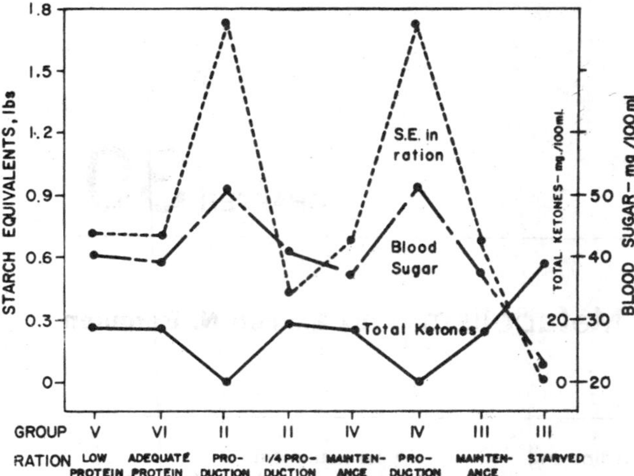

Figure 30.1. Relationship between food intake, blood sugar concentration, and blood ketone concentration in pregnant ewes. Note the inverse relationship between the caloric intake and blood sugar concentration, on the one hand, and the ketonemia on the other. S.E., starch equivalents. (From Fraser, Godden, Snook, and Thomson 1938, *J. Physiol.* 94:346–57.)

requirements. This is made quite clear by the coma resulting from severe hypoglycemia and the rapidity of recovery if glucose is injected. During prolonged glucose shortage or starvation the brain will begin to use ketone bodies and fatty acids, but considerable glucose still is required. Glucose also is indispensable as a glycerol precursor and reducing agent (in the formation of reduced nicotinamide adenine dinucleotide phosphate or NADPH) for the turnover and synthesis of body fat, and for producing muscle glycogen, which serves as an anaerobic energy supply during exercise.

The greatest demand for glucose is during late pregnancy and lactation. The placentas of all ungulates convert some of the glucose to fructose, and the glycogen content of the fetal liver, lung, and muscle increases to very high levels just prior to term. Further, the amounts are not greatly reduced by starvation of the mother. Lactation also poses a great demand for glucose since milk contains about 90 times as much sugar as does blood, and glycerol has to be synthesized for production of milk fat. By the infusion of isotopically labeled glucose it has been calculated that the glucose requirements for a heavily lactating cow are about 1700 g per day and that 60–85 percent is used for milk production. Similar studies on sheep have shown that normal sheep synthesize about 100 g of glucose per day, but during late pregnancy this basal rate goes up to about 180 g. When the rate of synthesis is too low, hypoglycemia develops, and the animal becomes ketotic (Bergman 1973).

In simple-stomached animals dietary carbohydrates such as starch and sucrose are sources of glucose. In roughage-fed ruminants, however, dietary carbohydrates, including cellulose, are fermented in the rumen to form volatile fatty acids (VFA). Thus only small amounts of glucose are absorbed, and gluconeogenesis, or a synthesis of glucose from nonhexose sources, is of prime importance for ruminant metabolism. The supply of glucose precursors and the organs that synthesize glucose can be limiting factors for the animal's overall productivity and even for its survival. The liver produces about 85 percent of the glucose in ruminants and the kidneys nearly all of the remainder (Bergman et al. 1974a,b). Only four groups of metabolites are important for glucogenesis in ruminants: propionate, protein, glycerol, and lactate. Other glucose precursors are present only in small amounts, and their contribution is limited (Fig. 30.2).

Acetic, propionic, and butyric acids are the most important of the VFA, but propionic acid is the only one that can be used for glucogenesis. It is the major source of glucose and glycogen in the ruminant. The percentage of the total glucose formed from propionate varies with the diet, from a maximum of about 70 percent under heavy grain feeding to none at all during starvation. Acetic and butyric acids, as well as longer-chain fatty acids, cannot contribute to a net synthesis of carbohydrate (Weinman et al. 1957).

Other than propionate, the most important source of glucose is protein. While some amino acids are ketogenic (lysine, leucine, and taurine), the vast majority are glucogenic. Recent estimates show that protein accounts for

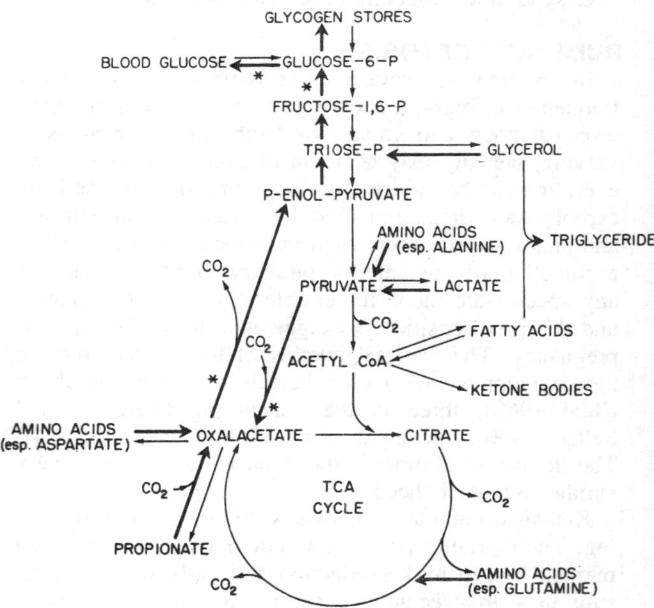

Figure 30.2. Major metabolic pathways in ruminant liver. Since insufficient glucose is absorbed, one of the main functions of the liver is gluconeogenesis. These reactions are shown by heavy arrows: four major pacemaker reactions are indicated by asterisks. TCA, tricarboxylic acid.

a range of about 25 percent of the glucose synthesis in feeding ruminants to about 70 percent during complete starvation (Wolff et al. 1972). Alanine and glutamine seem to be the principal amino acids involved since, in addition to being absorbed, they are formed from other amino acids in the muscles, after which they are released to the blood and removed by the liver for glucose formation (Bergman 1973). Aspartic acid also is highly glucogenic, but its blood concentration is too low to be significant.

Lactic acid and glycerol are sources of glucose but little is produced during normal digestion. During starvation, however, glycerol from mobilized body fat largely replaces propionate as an important glucogenic compound. The synthesis of glucose from the above compounds is controlled by several pacemaker reactions (see Fig. 30.2) which, in turn, are influenced by specific enzymes and hormones.

Fat metabolism

Rumen volatile fatty acids

Acetic, propionic, and butyric acids are the major VFA produced by rumen fermentation. Acetate is not used by the liver but is readily oxidized by the muscles and is used for synthesis of fat (lipogenesis) by the adipose tissue and mammary gland (Bergman and Wolff 1971). Its concentration in the blood during ruminant ketosis can be either higher or lower than normal. No specific defect in acetate utilization has been found in ketosis, and the probable reason for any decreased metabolism is that less acetate is being absorbed due to the decreased feed consumption. Long-chain fatty acids are mobilized from adipose tissue in ketosis and, due to their high concentration in the blood, would be metabolized in place of acetate. Under conditions of excessive fat metabolism and acetyl CoA (coenzyme A) formation, however, acetate sometimes can be released from the tissues (endogenously) in increased amounts, resulting in high blood concentrations (Aafjes 1964, Knowles et al. 1974).

Practically all of the absorbed propionate and butyrate are removed by the rumen epithelium and liver before they reach the general blood circulation. Propionate is glucogenic, whereas butyric acid is ketogenic. Some butyric acid is converted to ketone bodies by the rumen epithelium during absorption (Stevens 1970).

Adipose tissue and fat transport

The body's reserve of glucose and glycogen is limited, and in terms of calories it can sustain the animal for only a few hours. Adipose tissue, on the other hand, serves as a vast storage depot for calories. The major functions of adipose tissue can be summarized as follows: (1) synthesis of triglycerides, (2) storage of triglycerides, and (3) release of long-chain free fatty acids (FFA) and glycerol into the blood. The plasma FFA concentration therefore can be regarded as an index of fat mobilization and metabolism. The quantity of FFA in plasma is small but its turnover is extremely rapid (Armstrong et al. 1961).

Acetate is the major precursor of adipose tissue triglycerides in ruminants (Ballard et al. 1969), although dietary triglycerides (chylomicrons) and lipoprotein triglycerides (produced by the liver) also are involved. Glucose, however, still plays an essential role: (1) it forms α-glycerophosphate, which is the precursor of glycerol with which fatty acids are esterified for triglyceride storage. Adipose tissue has no glycerokinase and therefore free glycerol cannot be used. (2) Glucose furnishes NADPH via the pentose pathway; NADPH is specifically required as a reducing agent at recurring steps in the synthesis of fatty acids.

The processes of fat synthesis and degradation are under nervous and endocrine control. During periods of exercise, stress, or excitement, the body's energy requirements are temporarily increased. Therefore the sympathetic nerve supply and epinephrine release by the adrenal medulla increase the rate of lipolysis and release FFA to the blood stream. Thus the body tissues are flooded with an easily oxidizable substrate for their energy needs.

During starvation, and especially during hypoglycemia, there is a decreased rate of glucose utilization which results in a decreased synthesis of triglycerides. In addition, the pituitary gland increases its output of growth hormone (STH, somatotropic hormone) and adrenocorticotropic hormone (ACTH), which increase the rate of formation of FFA and glycerol from the stored triglycerides. The effect of decreased glucose utilization, which is especially marked during hypoglycemia, thus is to increase the rate of FFA release from adipose tissue cells. The liver is then flooded with FFA, much of which is oxidized to acetyl CoA. These two-carbon fragments condense into ketone bodies, which appear in the blood stream in increased concentrations. An increased plasma FFA concentration has been demonstrated quite clearly in both bovine and ovine ketosis (Reid and Hinks 1962, Adler et al. 1963) and has been called a primary factor for the development of ketosis by Bergman (1971).

Ketone body metabolism

In normal ruminants, the concentration of blood ketone bodies will be only 2–4 mg/100 ml. During hypoglycemia and increased fat mobilization, however, the ketone concentration will rise, and it is usually above 10 mg/100 ml when the animal shows clinical signs typical of the disease.

The ketone bodies (also called acetone bodies) are acetoacetic acid (CH_3-CO-CH_2-COOH), β-hydroxybutyric acid (CH_3-CHOH-CH_2-COOH), and acetone (CH_3-CO-CH_3). All of these compounds arise from acetoacetyl

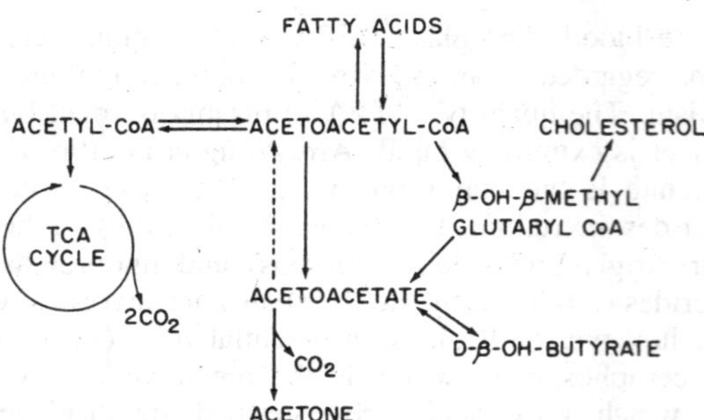

Figure 30.3. Major metabolic pathways in the formation, utilization, and interconvertibility of ketone bodies. The reaction indicated by the dashed line does not occur in liver.

CoA, which is a normal intermediate in fatty acid oxidation but which also is readily formed from acetyl CoA (Fig. 30.3). The liver is the primary site of ketone body production during ketosis, but once acetoacetate is formed the liver cannot reconvert it efficiently to acetoacetyl CoA. This is because the liver is deficient in the necessary activating enzyme system. In the normal ruminant, smaller amounts of ketone bodies also are produced from butyrate and acetate by the rumen epithelium during the process of absorption. Furthermore, certain feeds such as silage may at times have a high butyric acid content and therefore augment ketone body production (Adler et al. 1958).

Acetoacetate is the parent ketone body (see Fig. 30.3), but most of it is reduced to β-hydroxybutyrate by the coenzyme NADH. The reaction is reversible and the two compounds are interconvertible, but wide variations in the ratio of the two acids can be encountered. The conversion of acetoacetate to β-hydroxybutyrate may play a special role in the transport of ketone bodies by the blood, since acetoacetate is unstable (Krebs 1[illegible]). It undergoes an irreversible nonenzymatic decarboxylation to form acetone at a rate of about 5 percent per hour. Acetone metabolism is of little importance to the animal unless the ketosis is severe and of long duration.

Since ketone bodies are produced by the liver but are utilized by other tissues, ketosis could conceivably be the result of underutilization by the extra hepatic tissues, or overproduction by the liver. The underutilization theory was widely accepted at one time, but many studies have now demonstrated extensive extrahepatic utilization of ketone bodies even in severely ketotic states.

By the infusion of isotopically labeled ketone bodies it has been possible to estimate the production and oxidation of ketone bodies by the whole animal. These studies were made on sheep afflicted with pregnancy ketosis and are summarized in Figure 30.4; they show that the rates of turnover (production and utilization) and oxidation of ketone bodies in the ketotic animal are proportional to their concentration in the blood plasma but only up to an acetoacetate concentration of about 10 mg/100 ml (total ketone bodies would be about 20 mg/100 ml). Therefore, plasma ketone body concentrations up to about 20 mg/100 ml simply are a reflection of the rate of ketone production. Utilization, in turn, is regulated by the blood ketone concentration. Maximal ketone body utilization evidently occurs at about 20 mg/100 ml and thus, after reaching this maximum, small increments in production would entail large increases in blood concentration. The maximal utilization rate of ketone bodies in sheep seems to be about 8 g per hour (0.4 g/hr/kg¾), and it is about the same in naturally occurring ketosis as it is in artificial ketosis, that is, in normal animals injected with large quantities of acetoacetate. They also can derive at least 20 percent of their energy (carbon dioxide production) from ketone bodies.

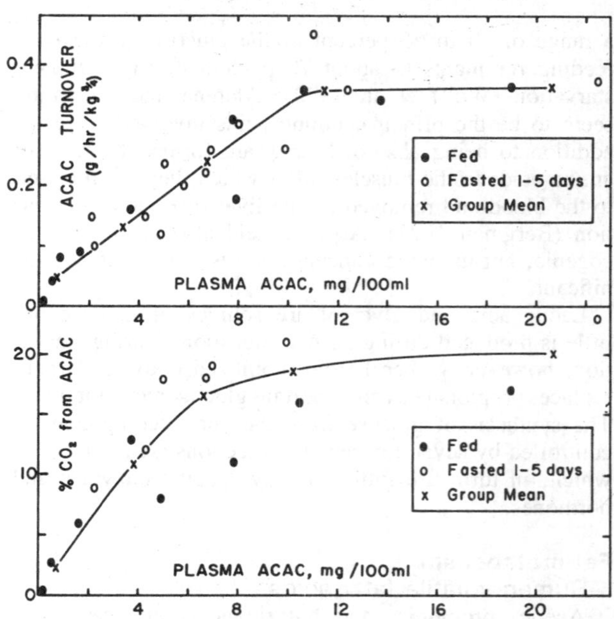

Figure 30.4. Production and oxidation of ketone bodies. *Above*, acetoacetic acid turnover rates per unit metabolic size (kg ¾) during varying degrees of spontaneous or fasting ketosis in twin-pregnant sheep. *Below*, percent of respiratory carbon dioxide derived from acetoacetic acid. (From Bergman and Kon 1964, *Am. J. Physiol.* 206:449–57.)

Ketone bodies are excreted mainly in urine (ketonuria) and milk. A third avenue is that of acetone via the breath. All are easily detectable by simple qualitative chemical tests or by the odor. The amount excreted varies with the severity of ketosis, and excretion in urine far exceeds that in milk or the breath. The total amount excreted, however, probably never exceeds 10 percent of that produced. Since ketone bodies are acids, an excessive accumulation in the body can produce a metabolic acidosis. The severity of the acidosis in ruminant ketosis, however, is much less than in diabetes mellitus (Katz and Bergman 1966). β-hydroxybutyrate by itself is nontoxic, but high concentrations of acetoacetate and acetone can result in depression of the CNS and contribute to the development of clinical signs. The concomitant hypoglycemia, however, probably is the major factor involved in the onset and development of the disease.

Metabolic interrelationships and control

The metabolism of glucose, fat, and ketone bodies is intimately related. When the concentration of blood glucose decreases to hypoglycemic levels, the ketone bodies increase, frequently to high but erratic concentrations.

Figure 30.5 shows that the plasma concentrations of FFA, which represent the mobilization of body depot fat, and glucose are inversely proportional to each other. In other words, when the blood glucose concentration is normal the FFA concentration is very low and of only minor importance, but as blood glucose falls to hypoglycemic proportions, the FFA concentration increases in a linear relationship. Figure 30.5 also shows the relationship of FFA to blood ketone bodies. Blood ketones increase as the FFA concentration increases, but the increase is not linear. When the FFA concentration becomes more than about 1.5 mEq/L, the ketone body concentration increases rapidly and can reach almost any magnitude. It is at this point that the body probably shifts from what is called a *physiological* ketosis to that of a *pathological* ketosis (Krebs 1966). Before this, ketogenesis is controlled merely by FFA mobilization from the adipose tissue, in response to low blood glucose, and with only part of the FFA forming ketone bodies. The more severe or pathological ketosis is most likely due to an hepatic factor, a shift in the pattern of FFA utilization in the liver itself (Bergman 1971).

The liver is a major utilizer of FFA. It removes about 25 percent regardless of the actual quantities released.

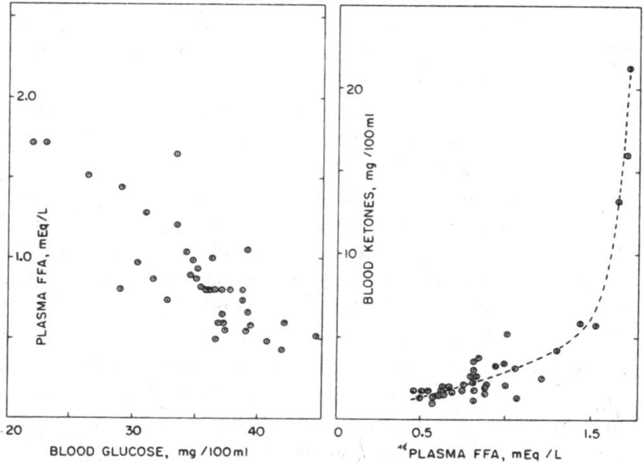

Figure 30.5. Relationship between plasma FFA, blood glucose, and blood ketone bodies in pregnant sheep. (Adapted from Reid and Hinks 1962, *Austral. J. Ag. Res.* 13:1124–36.)

However, there are only three major pathways for FFA catabolism in the liver (see Fig. 30.2): (1) oxidation to CO_2 in the tricarboxylic acid (TCA) cycle, (2) partial oxidation to ketone bodies, and (3) esterification to triglycerides. If the first FFA pathway is reduced, ketogenesis and liver fat formation increase out of proportion to the FFA being presented. If the condition also is of sufficient duration, a grossly fatty liver occurs. Reduced hepatic function associated with fatty livers occurs frequently in protracted cases of ruminant ketosis (Cornelius et al. 1958, Forenbacher and Srebocan 1963).

An important theory as to how the first FFA pathway (oxidation to CO_2) is reduced involves oxalacetate deficiency. Oxalacetate plays a dual role in gluconeogenesis and the production of CO_2 (see Fig. 30.2). It is needed to combine with acetyl CoA for CO_2 production and is involved in the metabolism of all glucose precursors except glycerol. Thus if oxalacetate becomes deficient, a shift in liver FFA metabolism to that of ketogenesis and fat formation occurs. There are several hypotheses for hepatic oxalacetate deficiency, but the most likely is that of precursor shortage (propionate, amino acids, or lactate).

Adequately fed ruminants should not be short of glucose precursors. If they are not eating, however, or if large amounts of feed are needed for high productivity, an excessive drain of precursors may occur and result in hypoglycemia. There is evidence that areas of the hypothalamus, and even of the digestive tract, respond to changes in concentrations of blood metabolites for regulating appetite or feed intake (Baile 1974). Feed intake may be reduced in ruminants showing clinical signs of hypoglycemia and ketosis, possibly because vital areas of the nervous system become depressed by the hypoglycemia, ketosis, or other metabolic disturbances.

Hormonal control

The hormonal control of metabolism is complex, and this is especially true during hypoglycemia and ketosis (Fig. 30.6). If hypoglycemia occurs, the first response is a reduced secretion of insulin, increased glucagon, and stimulation of the hypothalamus to increase the secretion of epinephrine. These will increase glycogenolysis in the liver and also cause a mobilization of glycerol and FFA from adipose tissue. Glycerol will increase glucose synthesis, and more FFA will provide an alternate fuel for oxidation by the body. Amino acid release from muscle also is stimulated, and thus additional glucose precursors, especially alanine and glutamine, become available for gluconeogenesis (Bergman 1973).

The above hormonal reflexes are rapid; if a glucose shortage persists, more long-range actions are necessary. The anterior pituitary secretes growth hormone (STH) and also ACTH, which increases glucocorticoid secretion by the adrenal cortex. These hormones all act in a "permissive role," but their overall effect is a maintained and

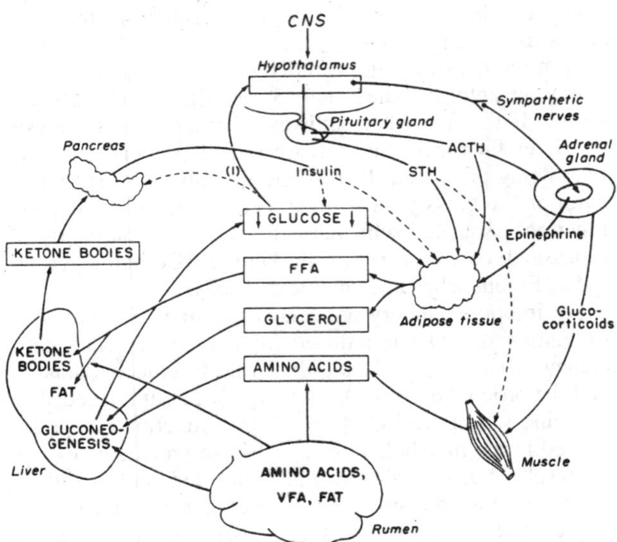

Figure 30.6. Metabolic interrelationships and hormonal control. Dashed lines indicate inhibition. Hypoglycemia initiates a complex of hormonal adjustments (1) that are mediated by the pancreas, hypothalamus, and pituitary gland. Direct effects of hormones on the liver are not shown. Epinephrine and glucagon accelerate glycogenolysis, and glucagon and glucocorticoids increase gluconeogenesis. Insulin may inhibit and glucagon increase amino acid release from muscle.

high release of glycerol, FFA, and amino acids from the peripheral tissues. The action of glucocorticoids probably is one of the most beneficial effects of the various hormones, since more amino acids are mobilized as precursors for gluconeogenesis. Glucocorticoid blood concentrations frequently are elevated in bovine and ovine ketosis (Robertson et al. 1957, Reid 1968), and they reduce milk secretion in lactating animals. They also inhibit glucose utilization so that the body can rely more on FFA and ketone metabolism for its caloric needs.

The hormonal regulation of metabolism within the liver itself also is important and there are four major rate-limiting or pacemaker enzymes involved (see Fig. 30.2): (1) glucose-6-phosphatase for release of free glucose into the blood; (2) fructose-1,6-diphosphatase; (3) pyruvate carboxylase for formation of oxalacetate from pyruvate; and (4) PEP carboxykinase for conversion of oxalacetate to P-enolpyruvate. All of these reactions are influenced by hormones as well as diet. Glucocorticoids and glucagon accelerate their rates, and insulin depresses them. The third reaction (pyruvate carboxylase) is of particular importance, since the enzyme is dependent upon acyl CoA compounds for activity. Propionate and butyrate are converted to propionyl CoA and butyryl CoA by the liver, and increases in these compounds, as occurs after feeding, will increase oxalacetate and thus gluconeogenesis. The reaction also is particularly sensitive to glucagon (Brockman and Bergman 1975). PEP carboxykinase activity probably is a major factor only in long-term adaptations of gluconeogenesis, such as occurs during fasting, diabetes, or prolonged glucocorticoid administration. It is not changed during ruminant ketosis (Butler and Elliot 1971).

Thus in ketosis there seems to be an insufficient production of oxalacetate within the liver to maintain the needed high rate of glucogenesis. The animal's ability to mobilize precursors seems inadequate. Further research is needed on the control of feed intake and on the control of the peripheral supply of precursors.

Therapy for ketosis

There are several forms of therapy for ketosis, but no single type is consistently successful. Clinical impressions are that bovine ketosis cases can recover without any treatment at all, but with a longer recovery time and a greater loss in milk production. Sheep, as a rule, respond poorly to treatment unless it is given in the early stages of the disease. This probably is due to irreversible damage to the CNS or other organs from the prolonged hypoglycemia. Termination of the pregnancy by Caesarean operation often is done and is the surest way to remedy the disease.

Any treatment which will raise or maintain a normal blood glucose concentration, with the exceptions noted above, is a logical measure for ketosis. The oral administration of sugar is of little or no value, however, since microorganisms in the rumen will ferment the compound into VFA. Glycerol and propylene glycol are commonly used since they resist fermentation and after absorption will form glucose and glycogen (Burtis et al. 1968). Intravenous injections of 500 ml of 50 percent glucose solutions are successful in a high percentage of cases of bovine ketosis, but more persistent cases require repeated injections usually at short intervals. The resultant hyperglycemia from a single injection is short lived and raises the blood sugar concentration for only about 2 hours. About 10 percent of the injected glucose is eliminated in the urine (Goetsch et al. 1956, Bergman and Roberts 1967). The administration of glucose by a continuous intravenous infusion for several days has practical limitations, but ketosis can be controlled successfully by this technique (Roberts and Dye 1951). Fructose or invert sugar has been suggested as a possible replacement for glucose since it is converted more rapidly into hepatic glycogen and slightly less is excreted in the urine (Goetsch et al. 1956).

ACTH and especially the adrenal glucocorticoid hormones are efficacious in the treatment of ketosis since they stimulate the animal to produce its own glucose at the expense of body protein (Kronfeld 1969, Braun et al. 1970). The action of these hormones in elevating the blood glucose is more prolonged than in the case of an intravenous injection of glucose. This is desirable, since considerable time may be required for metabolic adaptations.

In many instances ketosis may be prevented by increasing the feed intake, especially the grain ration, before inappetence has had a chance to occur. In the high-producing animal a deficiency of total digestible nutrients (TDN) can be a considerable factor in the onset of the disease. Swenson (1956) has calculated the energy requirements at the peak of lactation and believes that it is difficult, and in some cases impossible, for the cow to ingest enough TDN to meet these energy needs. Molasses when added to the ration may increase feed intake since it increases palatability. Sodium propionate has proved of some value in the prevention of ketosis. Propionate is a normal fermentation product in the rumen and is glucogenic. Only small amounts can be added to the feed, however, since it is relatively unpalatable (Schultz 1971).

SPONTANEOUS HYPOGLYCEMIAS

Spontaneous hypoglycemias occur in a variety of metabolic disorders. The severity of clinical signs depends upon both the degree and the duration of the hypoglycemia. Early signs, if the decrease in blood sugar is rapid, are largely attributed to epinephrine release. There can be trembling, chills, paresthesia, tachycardia, increased blood pressure, and dilated pupils. If the hypoglycemia is severe and develops more slowly, the CNS is affected, and nervous symptoms such as muscle twitching, impaired locomotion, visual disturbances, fainting, convulsions, and coma can occur. Prolonged and severe hypoglycemia will result in permanent cerebral damage.

Hypoglycemia of newborn pigs

Neonatal hypoglycemia can occur in all animal species, especially if the newborn is premature or of low weight. The liver and muscles of the fetus become high in glycogen near term, which helps to tide the newborn over the transitional period until efficient suckling is established (Dawes 1968). Thereafter, its principal fuel is fat, or otherwise stored fat and protein must become available to maintain metabolism.

Newborn pigs are more susceptible to hypoglycemia than are other species (Sampson and Graham 1943). The first week of life constitutes the critical period of susceptibility, especially if milk is not easily obtainable. The pig is unique in that it has only small amounts of adipose tissue at birth (about 1 percent of body weight), and that it can mobilize only limited amounts of FFA. There is no deficiency in hepatic glucogenic enzymes but, since the animal is forced to rely upon glucose metabolism, gluconeogenesis cannot keep pace with the glucose demands (Swiatek et al. 1968). Glucose therapy in early stages of the disease will alleviate the clinical signs, but in the terminal stages it is ineffective. Similar disorders have been produced experimentally by fasting for 36–48 hours or by injection of insulin (Fig. 30.7). Weanling pigs, however, show only a moderate fall in blood sugar level even when fasted for 3–4 weeks.

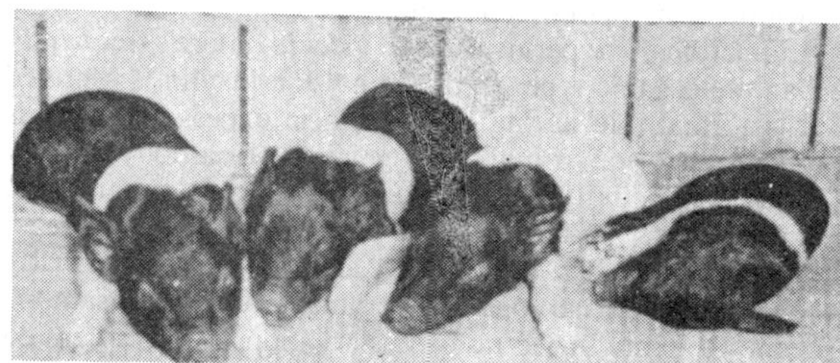

Figure 30.7 Hypoglycemia in newborn pigs. *Above*, severe spontaneous hypoglycemia; *middle*, hypoglycemic coma produced by fasting; *below*, hypoglycemic coma produced by insulin injection. Increasing stupor and finally coma are manifested as the blood glucose level continues to fall below 40 mg/100 ml. Convulsions may or may not be observed. The normal range of the blood glucose level of newborn pigs is 60–140 mg/100 ml. (Courtesy of Drs. Sampson, Hanawalt, Hester, and Graham, College of Veterinary Medicine and Agricultural Experiment Station, University of Illinois.)

Hyperinsulinism

Hyperinsulinism can be due to an organic structural change, for example, insular carcinoma, or due to a functional derangement. It has been diagnosed on many occasions in the dog, but only one case has been reported in the cow (Tokarnia 1961). It seems probable that, because of difficulties in diagnosis, the disorder occurs more frequently than is generally supposed.

Organic hyperinsulinism has been studied more completely in the human. The tumors arise from the islets of Langerhans of the pancreas and contain large numbers of β-cells. Tumors reported in the dog (Krook and Kenney 1962) usually have been malignant, and considerable metastases had occurred in the liver. Surgical extirpation of the tumor, if it is benign, will remedy the condition, but since most tumors in the dog have been malignant, the disorder usually will reappear after several months' time. The administration of alloxan, which leads to selective necrosis of the β-cells in the normal pancreas, has been unsuccessful as a therapeutic measure (Beck and Krook 1965). The condition in dogs is characterized by a persistent hypoglycemia, but at certain times, such as during fasting or exercise, the usual control mechanisms are overwhelmed and the hypoglycemia becomes more intense. Acute clinical attacks caused by the hypoglycemia can occur at any time but occur more often if the animal is fed only once a day or if exercise is particularly vigorous. The attacks are characterized by weakness, unresponsiveness, staggering, and convulsions. Injections of glucose temporarily relieve the attacks.

Functional hyperinsulinism occurs more frequently than the organic type. In this condition insulin is secreted at a normal rate during fasting but in excessive amounts after such usual stimuli as ingestion of carbohydrate or changes in activity of the autonomic nervous system. The hypoglycemic syndrome has been observed in dogs, especially the hunting breeds; affected animals usually have a highly nervous temperament and an insatiable desire to hunt. In the human, starvation is well tolerated but the blood glucose concentration falls to hypoglycemic levels 2–4 hours after ingestion of carbohydrate. Frequent feedings with a low-carbohydrate, high-protein diet will minimize the alimentary hyperglycemia and also minimize insulin secretion.

Miscellaneous hypoglycemias

Hypoglycemia can be caused by specific hormonal deficiencies; the anterior pituitary gland and adrenal cortex are classical examples. From Figure 30.6 it is apparent that ACTH, STH, and the glucocorticoids exert a physiological action on the mobilization of FFA and amino acids and also on gluconeogenesis. Furthermore, these factors are related to an endocrine balance involving a close relationship with insulin and glucagon. In deficiencies of the adrenal cortex or anterior pituitary gland gluconeogenesis is impaired. Fasting adrenalectomized animals, in contrast to normal animals, therefore undergo a rapid decline in liver glycogen and a development of hypoglycemia; in fact, a deficiency of the adrenal cortex (Addison's disease) may be easily mistaken for hyperinsulinism. Similar but more drastic disturbances occur in animals with an anterior pituitary deficiency.

Spontaneous hypoglycemia also occurs in a wide variety of liver diseases, if they are severe, and is due to an interference with the glycogenetic, gluconeogenetic, or glycogenolytic enzyme systems. Some diseases that can cause extensive liver damage are: viral hepatitis, cholangiolitic hepatitis, diffuse carcinomas, fatty degeneration, cirrhosis, and hepatic poisons such as phosphorus and carbon tetrachloride.

Glycogen storage (Von Gierke's) disease is a disorder characterized by an excessive deposition of glycogen in the liver, kidneys, muscle, and other tissues. It is primarily a hereditary disease of children, and symptoms include hypoglycemia, enlargement of the liver, and ketosis. Deficiencies of at least three liver enzymes have been found, among which glucose-6-phosphatase seems to be the most important. Bardens et al. (1961) reported a similar condition in puppies.

DIABETES MELLITUS

Diabetes mellitus is due to an absolute or relative lack of insulin. The disease can be brought about by one or more predisposing factors, including hereditary tendency; pancreatitis; neurogenic factors such as stress, overfeeding, and obesity; hyperfunction of the anterior pituitary gland or adrenal cortex; and any factor causing degeneration of the islets of Langerhans. Diabetes mellitus has been reported in cattle, horses, pigs, and sheep (Wilkinson 1957, Kaneko and Rhode 1964) but is most frequently found in dogs and cats (Krook et al. 1960). Herbivorous animals are more resistant and can live for longer periods without insulin (Reid et al. 1963, Procos and Clark 1963). In some species of birds hypoglycemia may occur.

Experimental diabetes mellitus

Diabetes mellitus can be produced by a number of experimental procedures which include pancreatectomy, production of an exhaustion or disuse atrophy of the β-cells, administration of alloxan, and large doses of anterior pituitary or adrenocortical hormones. A temporary diabetes lasting only a few hours can be produced by injection of anti-insulin serum or by injection of compounds that inhibit insulin release, such as D-mannoheptulose and 2-deoxyglucose.

Total pancreatectomy has been performed in many animal species, but it has been studied the most thoroughly in the dog and rat (Scow 1957). If as much as one eighth of the pancreas is left intact, however, the animal does not become diabetic. Feeding a high-carbohydrate diet or repeated administrations of glucose produce a permanent diabetes, especially if part of the pancreas has been removed or previously damaged. The increased glucose metabolism and hyperglycemia will overwork the remaining β-cells and produce an exhaustion atrophy. The injection of excessive amounts of insulin over several weeks' time can also produce diabetes by disuse atrophy.

The intravenous injection of alloxan leads to a selective necrosis of the β-cells of the pancreatic islets, and the secretion of glucagon and pancreatic juice remains undisturbed. Alloxan, therefore, provides a quick and easy method for producing experimental diabetes mellitus.

A temporary and in some cases permanent diabetes can be produced by the prolonged administration of STH, ACTH, or adrenal glucocorticoids. All of these hormones tend to produce hyperglycemia which will stimulate insulin secretions and produce an exhaustion and degeneration of the β-cells. In addition, anterior pituitary and adrenal hormones exert an anti-insulin effect and reduce the ability of the animal to utilize glucose. STH is the principal diabetogenic hormone and often produces a permanent diabetes, but large doses of ACTH or the glucocorticoids induce a diabeticlike hyperglycemia which usually is only temporary.

Metabolic alterations

The mechanism of insulin action is complex (see Chapter 52). There are many metabolic alterations in diabetes mellitus, but the central feature is hyperglycemia. It is due to reduced entry of glucose into adipose tissue and muscle, and increased glucose production by the liver. Thus there is an extracellular glucose excess but an intracellular glucose deficiency, or, a "starvation in the midst of plenty." In hyperglycemia (above 160 mg/100 ml) the renal tubules are unable to reabsorb all the filtered glucose, and glucose is excreted in the urine (glucosuria). This produces an osmotic diuresis, and the loss of water (polyuria) causes dehydration in spite of an increased thirst and water intake (polydipsia).

In severe insulin deficiency, mobilization of FFA occurs, and the concentration of blood ketone bodies greatly increases. These compensatory changes are similar to those responsible for ruminant ketosis (see Fig. 30.6) but are more marked. Severe ketoacidosis then occurs and this, together with the large urine volume, results in a depletion of electrolytes. The acidosis, dehydration, hyperosmolarity, and hypotension will eventually cause renal failure, hyperventilation, and deterioration of cerebral function. The plasma sodium concentration usually remains normal, however, because of the reduction in extracellular fluid volume. Plasma potassium may be increased because of the intracellular loss of amino acids for use in gluconeogenesis. In other cases plasma potassium is decreased (hypokalemia). With insulin administration, potassium re-enters the cells along with glucose, and it is not unusual for severe hypokalemia to occur. This is an inherent danger, and potassium may have to be administered along with insulin in the treatment of ketoacidosis.

Glucose tolerance tests are frequently used to test the ability of the animal to utilize glucose and are of great value in the diagnosis of diabetes mellitus or hyperinsulinism. In this procedure the animal is fasted for 24 hours and then given an intravenous injection of 0.5 g of glucose per kg body weight. The height of the blood sugar rise and its rate of return to normal are then measured. In the normal animal the preinjection glucose concentration is reached in about 2 hours, but if a decreased tolerance is present, which is indicative of diabetes, 3 or more hours may be required. An increased tolerance, or a faster rate of return to normal, is observed in hyperinsulinism, and the tolerance curve is followed by a hypoglycemic phase of at least one half hour in duration. The glucose tolerance curve tests primarily the ability of the pancreas to respond and provide additional insulin when needed.

FATTY LIVERS

The liver plays a major role in fat metabolism as well as in carbohydrate and protein metabolism. It removes much of the FFA released by adipose tissue and converts them into triglycerides which then are secreted into the circulation as lipoproteins. The synthesis of the protein moiety of the lipoproteins occurs only in the liver and is a rate-limiting step for the hepatic release of lipoproteins. Thus there is an active shuttle of fatty substances between liver and adipose tissue. Except for ruminants, the liver also actively participates in liponeogenesis from amino acids and glucose.

Fat normally constitutes about 5 percent of the liver weight, but in many instances it can rise to 30 percent or more. Excessive fat in the liver is sometimes called a fatty infiltration or fatty degeneration, but this accumulation is not a disease per se, but rather a symptom of deranged fat metabolism. One may think of the problem in the general statement that "fatty liver is to fat metabolism what hyperglycemia is to carbohydrate metabolism." It may be due to an overproduction or an underutilization, that is, an increased transport of fat to the liver or a defective transport of fat away from the liver.

Fatty livers may be caused by any one of the following: (1) high-fat or high-cholesterol diet; (2) increased liponeogenesis by the liver from excessive carbohydrate intake or excessive administration of certain vitamins, such as biotin and thiamine; (3) increased mobilization of fat from adipose tissue due to stress, starvation, insulin deficiency, hypoglycemia, hyperactivity of the sympathoadrenal system, or increased output of glucagon, STH, ACTH, and adrenal steroids; (4) liver damge due to hepatitis, cirrhosis, necrosis from vitamin E deficiency, or liver poisons such as carbon tetrachloride, phosphorus, and chloroform; and (5) deficient transport of fat from the liver due to excessive glucagon or to specific nutritional deficiencies such as lack of choline, inositol, protein, essential fatty acids, pyridoxine, and pantothenic acid.

The rate of transport of fat away from the liver depends upon the ability of the liver to synthesize phospholipids and also the protein moiety of the lipoproteins. Without this ability, fat cannot be released into the circulation. Substances which improve lipoprotein synthesis and thus prevent many nutritionally induced fatty livers are said to have a lipotropic action. Among these lipotropic factors are choline, inositol, and lipocaic, of which choline is the most generally effective. Methionine serves as a methyl donor and may replace choline to some extent. Inositol also is present in phospholipids and is effective against certain types of fatty livers. Lipocaic is a substance which has been extracted from the pancreas and is necessary along with insulin to prevent the development of fatty livers in depancreatized dogs. B-vitamin deficiencies are related primarily to the utilization of essential fatty acids for lipoprotein synthesis (McHenry and Patterson 1944).

Exposure to toxic chemicals or infections, or even deficiencies which cause fatty livers, eventually can lead to excessive production of fibrous tissue in the liver. This is called cirrhosis, and the liver is shrunken, distorted, and of an orange-brown color. It is commonly seen, for example, in cases of prolonged protein deficiency and begins after the central lobular cells have been ruptured by excessive fat. The ruptured cells have atrophied and left scars formed from their remnants. The scars may spread and even include areas around the large portal veins. A reduction in portal blood flow and portal hypertension can occur.

Fatty livers are commonly found in laying hens and are associated with a 30 percent decrease in egg production and a mortality rate as high as 2 percent per month. The fat content of the liver can exceed 50 percent, and the liver becomes so enlarged that hepatic hemorrhages and rupture frequently occur. The syndrome can be produced experimentally in high-producing flocks by feeding diets high in carbohydrate and energy. It also can be partially reversed by feeding more fiber, such as wheat bran, to reduce the intake of digestible carbohydrate and energy (Barton 1967, Couch 1968). In some societies, fatty goose livers are considered a delicacy and are deliberately produced by force-feeding large quantities of cereal grains.

The apparent mechanism for the development of fatty livers in birds is that the high-carbohydrate intake stimulates hepatic lipogenesis and triglyceride formation beyond the liver's maximal ability to synthesize lipoproteins for secretion into the plasma. Further, the hormone glucagon probably is involved. Glucagon is secreted by the avian pancreas to a much greater extent than in mammals, and has been shown to limit or even decrease the synthesis of the protein portion of the lipoproteins (DeOya et al. 1971). The major effect of glucagon on the liver, in addition to glycogenolysis, is to enhance protein catabolism for use in gluconeogenesis. This is an adverse effect as far as fat metabolism is concerned and could increase the incidence of fatty livers. In any case, both nutritional and hormonal factors are involved.

REFERENCES

Aafjes, J.H. 1964. Volatile fatty acids in blood of cows with ketosis. *Life Sci.* 3:1327–34.

Adler, J.H., Roberts, S.J., and Dye, J.A. 1958. Silage as a possible etiological factor in bovine ketosis. *Am. J. Vet. Res.* 19:314–18.

Adler, J.H., Wertheimer, E., Bartana, U., and Flesh, J. 1963. FFA and the origin of ketone bodies in cows. *Vet. Rec.* 75:304–7.

Armstrong, D.T., Steele, R., Altszuler, N., Dunn, A., Bishop, J.S., and deBodo, R.C. 1961. Regulation of plasma free fatty acid turnover. *Am. J. Physiol.* 201:535–39.

Baile, C.A. 1974. Control of feed intake in ruminants. In I.W. McDonald and A.C.I. Warner, eds., *Digestion and Metabolism in the Ruminant.* U. of New England Pub. Unit, Armidale, Austral.

Ballard, F.J., Hanson, R.W., and Kronfeld, D.S. 1969. Gluconeogenesis and lipogenesis in tissue from ruminant and nonruminant animals. *Fed. Proc.* 28:218–31.

Bardens, J.W., Bardens, G.W., and Bardens, B. 1961. A Von Gierke-like syndrome in puppies. *Allied Vet.* 32:4–7.

Barton, T.L. 1967. Fatty liver studies in laying hens. Ph.D. diss., Michigan State U.

Bassett, J.M. 1974. Dietary and gastrointestinal control of hormones regulating carbohydrate metabolism in ruminants. In I.W. McDonald and A.C.I. Warner, eds., *Digestion and Metabolism in the Ruminant.* U. of New England Pub. Unit, Armidale, Austral.

Beck, A.M., and Krook, L. 1965. Canine insuloma. *Cornell Vet.* 55:330–39.

Bergman, E.N. 1971. Hyperketonemia-ketogenesis and ketone body metabolism. *J. Dairy Sci.* 54:936–48.

——. 1973. Glucose metabolism in ruminants as related to hypoglycemia and ketosis. *Cornell Vet.* 63:341–82.

——. 1974. Production and utilization of metabolites by the alimentary tract as measured in portal and hepatic blood. In I.W. McDonald and A.C.I. Warner, eds., *Digestion and Metabolism in the Ruminant.* U. of New England Pub. Unit, Armidale, Austral.

Bergman, E.N., Brockman, R.P., and Kaufman, C.F. 1974a. Glucose metabolism in ruminants: Comparison of whole-body turnover with production by gut, liver, and kidneys. *Fed. Proc.* 33:1849–54.

Bergman, E.N., Kaufman, C.F., Wolff, J.E., and Williams, H.H. 1974b. Renal metabolism of amino acids and ammonia in fed and fasted pregnant sheep. *Am. J. Physiol.* 226:833–37.

Bergman, E.N., and Kon, K. 1964. Acetoacetate turnover and oxidation rates in ovine pregnancy ketosis. *Am. J. Physiol.* 206:449–52.

Bergman, E.N., and Roberts, S.J. 1967. Urinary glucose excretion and blood concentrations in ketotic cattle after treatment with glucose. *Cornell Vet.* 42:624–30.

Bergman, E.N., and Sellers, A.F. 1960. Comparison of fasting ketosis in pregnant and nonpregnant guinea pigs. *Am. J. Physiol.* 198:1083–86.

Bergman, E.N., and Wolff, J.E. 1971. Metabolism of volatile fatty acids by liver and portal-drained viscera in sheep. *Am. J. Physiol.* 221:586–92.

Braun, R.K., Bergman, E.N., and Albert, T.F., 1970. Effects of synthetic glucocorticoids on milk production and blood concentrations in normal and ketotic cows. *J. Am. Vet. Med. Ass.* 157:941–46.

Brockman, R.P., and Bergman, E.N. 1975. Effect of glucagon on plasma alanine and glutamine metabolism and hepatic gluconeogenesis in sheep. *Am. J. Physiol.* 228:1627–33.

Burtis, C.A., Troutt, H.F., Goetsch, G.D., and Jackson, H.D. 1968. Effects of glucagon, glycerol, and insulin on phlorizin-induced ketosis in fasted nonpregnant ewes. *Am. J. Vet. Res.* 29:647–55.

Butler, T.M., and Elliot, J.M. 1971. Effect of diet and glucocorticoid administration on liver phosphoenolpyruvate carboxykinase activity in the cow. *J. Dairy Sci.* 53:1727–33.

Cornelius, C.E., Holm, L.W., and Jasper, D.E. 1958. Bromsulfalein clearance in normal sheep and in pregnancy toxemia. *Cornell Vet.* 48:305–12.

Couch, J.R. 1968. Fatty liver syndrome. *Feedstuffs* 7:48–51.

Crone, C. 1965. The secretion of adrenal medullary hormones during hypoglycemia in intact, decerebrate, and spinal sheep. *Acta Physiol. Scand.* 63:213–24.

Dawes, G.S. 1968. *Fetal and Neonatal Physiology.* Year Book Medical, Chicago.

DeOya, M., Prigge, W.F., Swenson, D.E., and Grande, F. 1971. Role of glucagon on fatty liver production in birds. *Am. J. Physiol.* 221:25–30.

Felig, P., and Wahren, J. 1974. Protein turnover and amino acid metabolism in the regulation of gluconeogenesis. *Fed. Proc.* 33:1092–97.

Fincher, M.G. 1955. Diagnosis of acetonemia in dairy cattle. *Biochem. Rev.* 25:7–11.

Forenbacher, S., and Srebocan, V. 1963. On the part played by the liver in the transformation of tricarbonic acids, particularly pyruvic alpha-ketoglutaric, and lactic acid in ketosis of milch cows. *Vet. Arhiv.* 33:1–6.

Fraser, A.H.H., Godden, W., Snook, L.C., and Thomson, W. 1938. Influence of diet upon ketonemia in pregnant ewes. *J. Physiol.* 94:346–57.

Gerich, J.E., Martin, M.M., and Recant, L. 1971. Clinical and metabolic characteristics of hyperosmolar nonketotic coma. *Diabetes* 20:228–40.

Goetsch, D.D., Underbjerg, G.K.L., and Swenson, M.J. 1956. The utilization of intravenously administered glucose, invert sugar, and fructose in cattle. *Am. J. Vet. Res.* 17:213–16.

Hibbitt, K.G., and Baird, G.D. 1967. An induced ketosis. *Vet. Rec.* 81:511–17.

Kaneko, J.J., and Rhode, E.A. 1964. Diabetes mellitus in a cow. *J. Am. Vet. Med. Ass.* 144:367–73.

Katz, M.L., and Bergman, E.N. 1966. Acid-base and electrolyte equilibrium in ovine pregnancy ketosis. *Am. J. Vet. Res.* 27:1285–92.

Knowles, S.E., Jarrett, I.G., Filsell, O.H., and Ballard, F.J. 1974. Production and utilization of acetate in mammals. *Biochem. J.* 142:401–11.

Krebs, H.A. 1966. Bovine ketosis. *Vet. Rec.* 78:187–92.

Kronfeld, D.S. 1958. The fetal drain of hexose in ovine pregnancy toxemia. *Cornell Vet.* 48:394–404.

——. 1969. Bovine ketosis: The problems of treatment. *Mod. Vet. Prac.* 50:47–51.

Krook, L., and Kenney, R.M. 1962. Central nervous system lesions in dogs with islet cell carcinoma. *Cornell Vet.* 52:385–415.

Krook, L., Larsson, L., and Rooney, J.R. 1960. Interrelationship of diabetes mellitus, obesity, and pyometra in the dog. *Am. J. Vet. Res.* 21:120–24.

Leng, R.A. 1970. Glucose synthesis in ruminants. *Adv. Vet. Sci.* 14:209–60.

Manns, J.G., Boda, J.M., and Willes, R.F. 1967. Probable role of propionate and butyrate in control of insulin secretion in sheep. *Am. J. Physiol.* 212:756–64.

McHenry, E.W., and Patterson, J.M. 1944. Lipotropic factors. *Physiol. Rev.* 24:128–67.

Patterson, D.S.P., and Cunningham, N.F. 1969. Metabolic and hormonal aspects of bovine ketosis and pregnancy toxemia in the ewe. *Proc. Nutr. Soc.* 28:171–76.

Procos, J., and Clark, R. 1963. The effects of alloxan on ketone bodies and blood sugar levels of Merino wethers. *Onderstepoort J. Vet. Res.* 30:161–67.

Reid, R.L. 1968. The physiopathology of undernourishment in pregnant sheep with particular reference to pregnancy toxemia. *Adv. Vet. Sci.* 12:163–238.

Reid, R.L., and Hinks, N.T. 1962. Studies on the carbohydrate metabolism of sheep. *Austral. J. Ag. Res.* 13:1124–36.

Reid, R.L., Hinks, N.T., and Mills, S.C. 1963. Alloxan diabetes in pregnant ewes. *J. Endocr.* 27:1–30.

Roberts, S.J., and Dye, J.A. 1951. The treatment of acetonemia in cattle by continuous intravenous injection of glucose. *Cornell Vet.* 41:3–10.

Robertson, W.G., Mixner, J.P., Bailey, W.W., and Lennon, H.D. 1957. Determination of liver function, plasma and blood volumes in ketotic cows, using bromsulfalein. *J. Dairy Sci.* 40:977–80.

Sampson, J., and Graham, R. 1943. Experimental insulin hypoglycemia in the pig. *J. Am. Vet. Med. Ass.* 102:176–79.

Schultz, L.H. 1971. Management and nutritional aspects of ketosis. *J. Dairy Sci.* 54:962–73.

Scow, R.O. 1957. Total pancreatectomy in the rat. *Endocrinology* 60:359–67.

Scow, R.O., Chernick, S.S., and Brinley, M.S. 1964. Hyperlipemia and ketosis in the pregnant rat. *Am. J. Physiol.* 206:796–804.

Stevens, C.E. 1970. Fatty acid transport through the rumen epithelium. In A.T. Phillipson, ed., *Physiology of Digestion and Metabolism in the Ruminant.* Oriel, Newcastle upon Tyne. Pp. 101–12.

Swenson, M.J. 1956. Bovine ketosis complex. *Vet. Med.* 51:207–11.

Swiatek, K.R., Kipnis, D.M., Mason, G., Chao, K., and Cornblath, M. 1968. Starvation hypoglycemia in newborn pigs. *Am. J. Physiol.* 214:400–405.

Tokarnia, C.H. 1961. Islet cell tumor of the bovine pancreas. *J. Am. Vet. Med. Ass.* 138:541–47.

Weinman, E.O., Strisower, E.H., and Chaikoff, I.L. 1957. Conversion of fatty acids to carbohydrate: Application of isotopes to this problem and role of the Krebs cycle as a synthetic pathway. *Physiol. Rev.* 37:252–72.

Wilkinson, J.A. 1957. Spontaneous diabetes in domestic animals. *Vet. Rev. Annot.* 3:69–96.

Wolff, J.E., Bergman, E.N., and Williams, H.H. 1972. Gluconeogenesis from plasma amino acids in fed sheep. *Am. J. Physiol.* 223:455–60.

CHAPTER 31

Energy Metabolism | by Homer E. Dale

Various forms of energy manifested by the animal body are derived from chemical energy in the food that the animal eats. Chemical energy appears in animal products, such as meat, eggs, milk, or fiber; or chemical energy can be converted to heat, work, or electrical energy by oxidative processes. Energy metabolism is an accompaniment of life itself. When the energy of absorbed nutrients is insufficient, tissues are used for this purpose. It should be noted, however, that there is no unique source of animal energy; the animal body, like a nonliving system, conforms to the laws of thermodynamics.

UNITS OF HEAT

Energy metabolism is measured in units of heat. With varying degrees of efficiency the different forms of energy can be converted one to the other; all, however, can be converted completely to heat. The calorie is a common denominator. It is defined as the amount of heat required to raise the temperature of one gram of water 1°C. It is the equivalent of 4.185×10^7 ergs or 4.185 joules. The kilocalorie, or Calorie (Cal), is the unit commonly used in bioenergetics; it is equal to 1000 calories.

SOURCE OF ENERGY

Energy of the ration

Gross energy, or total energy of the food, is determined by bomb calorimetry of a food sample. Since this includes both digestible and nondigestible components, gross energy has little physiological significance, especially in animals that consume significant quantities of crude fiber.

Digestible energy may be estimated by subtracting fecal energy from gross energy. The energy of the feces, however, represents not only undigestible matter in the ration but also material that is lost from the body into the gastrointestinal tract. Also, digestible energy is not an accurate measure of the energy available to the animal body because it includes energy lost by fermentation in the gastrointestinal tract of herbivores and the energy of incompletely oxidized materials, chiefly urea, in the urine.

Metabolizable energy is energy available to the animal body. It represents digestible energy minus fermentation energy and the energy lost in the urine. Metabolizable energy is further subdivided into net energy, that which is available for productive processes, and specific dynamic action (SDA) energy, that which is unavoidably lost as heat when nutrients are added to the metabolic pool.

Chemical energy

Metabolizable energy is the chemical energy of carbohydrates, fats, and proteins that is liberated by oxidation in the animal body. The end products of this oxidation are carbon dioxide and water; the energy is available to the tissues through the synthesis of high-energy phosphate bonds.

Oxidation in the animal body is quite different from oxidation in the bomb calorimeter. Biological oxidations occur stepwise at a relatively low temperature in a fluid environment; in the bomb calorimeter oxidation occurs rapidly at high temperature in a gaseous environment. From a thermodynamic standpoint, however, these facts

Table 31.1. Heat of combustion (Calories per gram)

Ethanol	7.11	Palmitic acid	9.35
Glycerol	4.31	Stearic acid	9.53
Glucose	3.74	Oleic acid	9.41
Sucrose	3.94	Lactic acid	3.62
Starch	4.18	Urea	2.52
Acetic acid	3.49	Glycine	3.12
Propionic acid	4.96	Tyrosine	5.91
Butyric acid	5.95		

Data from Hodgman, ed., *Handbook of Physics and Chemistry,* Chemical Rubber Publishing, 1958

are incidental. The energy liberated by any oxidation depends on the reacting substances and the end products, not on the environment or intermediate steps by which the reaction proceeds (Hess's law). For these reasons, the physical and physiological heat values of a foodstuff, with the exception of protein, are the same.

The end products of protein oxidation in the body and in the bomb calorimeter are not the same. Waste products of protein metabolism, chiefly urea, are capable of further oxidation; the energy of these waste products is responsible for the difference between the physical heat value of protein, 5.6 Cal per gram, and the physiological heat value, 4.6 Cal per gram.

The heat of combustion for several biologically important compounds is shown in Table 31.1. In animal calorimetry it is customary to assume that a typical carbohydrate has a heat value of 4.1 Cal per gram, while a typical fat has a value of 9.3.

The chemical reactions of energy metabolism are stoichiometric; substrate and oxygen react in fixed proportion to yield predictable amounts of carbon dioxide, water, and energy. Because of this, changes in the respiratory gases can be used to estimate the metabolic rate, provided the source of energy is known. In turn, the proportion of carbohydrate, fat, and protein used for energy purposes can be adduced from the excretion of urinary nitrogen and from the respiratory quotient (RQ), the ratio of carbon dioxide produced to oxygen consumed.

METABOLIC RATE

Basal metabolism

In human medicine it is customary to measure the basal metabolic rate (BMR)—the intensity of energy metabolism of a resting, postabsorptive subject in a thermally neutral environment. Under these conditions the rate of energy metabolism as a function of body surface in man or metabolic weight ($kg^{.75}$) in animals is reasonably uniform. Energy metabolism in the basal state, however, does not represent an irreducible minimum; for example, sleep depresses the basal metabolic rate in man by approximately 10 percent.

Under basal conditions, essentially all of the energy released by the animal body appears as heat, and maintenance of body temperature is the only useful purpose served by this heat. It has been estimated that approximately 25 percent of the basal expenditure of energy is used for vital functions such as the circulation of blood, pulmonary ventilation, membrane potentials, and urine formation. Brody (1945) states that "the remaining basal metabolism energy represents the cost of maintaining the thermodynamically unstable and improbable living state and free-energy losses incidental to the purposeless enzyme activities (analogous to yeast enzymes which continue their catalytic activites after the death of the yeast), and maintaining the characteristic body temperature." The dynamic equilibrium of body constituents is a continuous process with no net gain or loss to the body, and appreciable amounts of energy are involved.

Resting energy metabolism

The basal state is seldom achieved with assurance in animals. Physical, mental, and emotional repose through voluntary cooperation of the subject requires a period of training, and even the best-trained herbivore may not be in such a state after fasting for the period of the time necessary to insure a postabsorptive condition, 2 or 3 days. Measurements of resting energy metabolism are more common in animals than are measurements of BMR.

Resting metabolism refers to heat production when the animal is at rest, usually recumbent. The measurement is made before the morning feeding under the usual farm or laboratory conditions. Many species are not in a postabsorptive state under these conditions, and they may not be in a thermally neutral environment either.

Measurement of metabolic rate

Resting energy metabolism differs from basal energy metabolism in that it includes variable amounts of SDA energy, energy used in productive processes, and possibly energy used in the regulation of body temperature. Under ordinary conditions, however, the difference is not great.

An animal in the basal state accomplishes little or no work in the physical sense of the word. All of the energy released, even that needed to carry out vital functions of the body, is degraded to heat and lost to the environment. Under these circumstances the intenstiy of energy metabolism can be estimated either by calculating heat production from the exchange of respiratory gases (indirect calorimetry) or by measuring the heat which is lost from the body by radiation, conduction and convection, and evaporation (direct calorimetry).

Because the energy released by oxidation is equal to heat loss unless physiological work is done or unless the heat content of the body changes, it is customary to use either direct calorimetry or indirect calorimetry but not both. Either technique supplies essentially the same information.

Direct calorimetry

Direct calorimetry is simple in theory, difficult in practice. Measurements of heat loss from the animal body must include not only the sensible heat of radiation, conduction, and convection, but also the insensible, latent heat of water vaporized from the skin and the respiratory passages. Sensible heat loss from the animal body can be measured with two general types of calorimeters, adiabatic and gradient. In both types the loss of heat by evaporation of water from the animal body must be estimated by determining in some way the amount of water vapor added to the air which flows through the calorimeter. It is this measurement, involving rate of air flow and change in humidity, which is the most difficult to accomplish.

In adiabatic calorimeters an animal is confined in a chamber whose heat loss is near zero. This may be accomplished by a box within a box. When the outer box or wall is electrically heated to the same temperature as the inner wall, heat loss from the inner wall to the outer wall is impossible. Water circulating in a coil absorbs the heat collected by the inner wall; the volume and change in temperature of the water can be used to calculate sensible heat loss from the animal. Such calorimeters have been constructed for both man and animals. Mount and co-workers, for example, have such a heat-sink calorimeter equipped as a pigpen capable of accommodating a group of animals for an extended period of time.

Gradient calorimeters permit the loss of heat through the walls of the chamber. When the walls are of uniform thickness and thermal conductivity, the amount of heat lost from the chamber is proportional to the thermal gradient, or temperature difference, between the inner and outer surface of the walls. The outer surface is maintained at a constant temperature with a water jacket; the temperature gradient is measured with thermocouples which line the inner and outer surfaces of the wall. By the use of appropriate techniques it is possible to measure separately the radiation component of the sensible heat loss. With thin walls of high thermal conductivity, the response time of such a device may be less than one minute.

Indirect calorimetry

Because the animal body ultimately derives all of its energy from oxidation, the magnitude of energy metabolism can be estimated from the exchange of respiratory gases. Such measurements of heat production are more readily accomplished than are measurements of heat dissipation by direct calorimetry. The respiratory exchange of animals of any size can be measured. Even isolated tissues, cells, and subcellular materials are amenable to the techniques of indirect calorimetry by the use of the microrespiration apparatus of Warburg.

Measurement of respiratory exchange

A variety of techniques are available for measuring the respiratory exchange; all ultimately seek to measure oxygen consumption and carbon dioxide production per unit of time. To measure these changes it is necessary either to confine the animal to a chamber where changes in the ventilating air can be determined, or else to connect the animal by face mask or tracheal cannula to some measuring device.

Open-circuit devices allow the animal to breathe atmospheric air. The effluent air, exhaust air from a chamber or expired air from a mask or cannula, is either collected or else metered and sampled, and then analyzed. The Haldane apparatus (Fig. 31.1) is an open-circuit device suitable for small laboratory animals; Figure 31.2 diagrams an open-circuit apparatus for cattle.

Analysis of biological gas mixtures has traditionally been accomplished with chemical and volumetric or manometric techniques. More recently methods of analysis based on physical properties of gases have been developed. Oxygen, for example, can be determined by its paramagnetic effect or with a mass spectrometer; carbon dioxide can be measured by infrared absorption or thermal conductivity. Such analytic devices commonly have

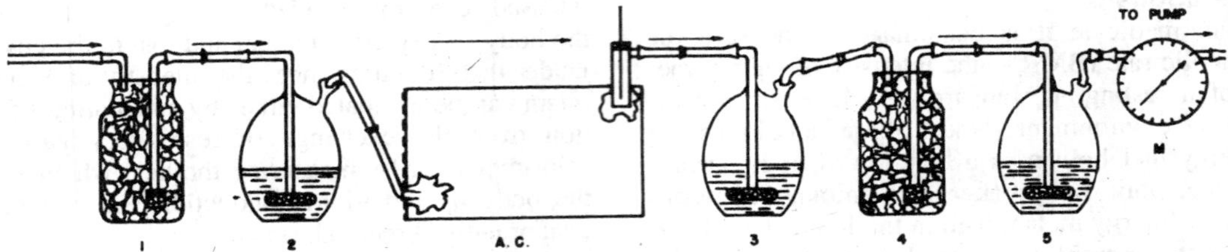

Figure 31.1. Haldane respiration apparatus. A.C., animal chamber; M, meter for measuring rate of ventilation. Bottles 1 and 4 contain soda lime (or caustic alkali) for absorption of carbon dioxide. Bottles 2, 3, and 5 contain sulfuric acid for absorption of water. Air entering the animal chamber is freed of carbon dioxide and moisture by passage through bottles 1 and 2. The animal gives off carbon dioxide and moisture, and these are collected in the bottles of the outgoing chain. Bottle 5 is necessary because soda lime gives off moisture. The gain in weight of bottles 4 and 5 represents the carbon dioxide production. The gain in weight of bottles 3, 4, and 5 minus the loss in weight of the animal and chamber represents the oxygen consumption.

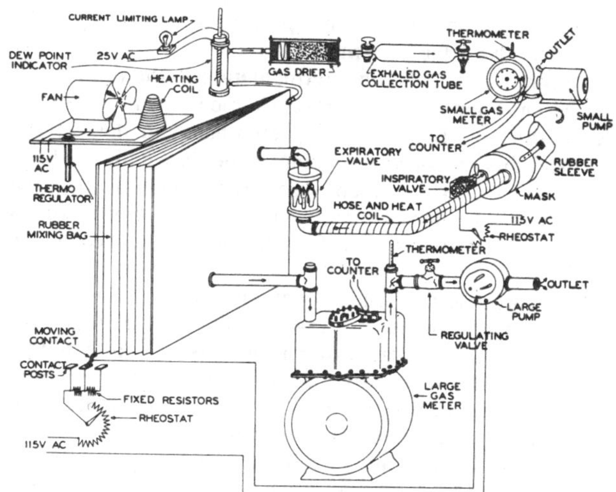

Figure 31.2. Open-circuit apparatus suitable for use with large animals. (From Kibler 1960, *Mo. Ag. Exp. Sta. Res. Bull.* 743.)

an electric output, and they are frequently used with a recording flow meter to provide a continuous record of the respiratory exchange.

Closed-circuit devices require the animal to rebreathe the same air. Carbon dioxide is removed with a suitable absorber which is weighed before and after use to determine its rate of production. The use of oxygen by the animal body decreases the volume of the respiratory gas mixture, and this change in volume is used as a measure of the rate of oxygen consumption. One of the most widely used types of this apparatus, the Benedict-Roth machine, employs a spirometer as a reservoir for the respiratory gases and records volume change on a recorder (Fig. 31.3).

Respiratory quotient and the caloric equivalent of oxygen

The amount of energy liberated in the animal body by the consumption of one liter of oxygen varies depending on the substrate being oxidized. Thus the oxidation of fat yields 4.69 Cal per liter of oxygen at standard temperature and pressure (STP); of protein 4.82, and of carbohydrate 5.04, values known as the caloric equivalent of oxygen. Similar values for the amount of carbon dioxide produced are: fat 6.6, carbohydrate 5.04, and protein 5.88. These caloric equivalents of carbon dixoide are quite variable, however, and do not have the same utility as the values for oxygen.

Precise knowledge about the substrate used for energy purposes depends upon measurement of the excretion of urinary nitrogen to estimate the amount of protein metabolized, and subsequent calculation of the nonprotein respiratory exchange to estimate the proportion of fats and carbohydrates metabolized.

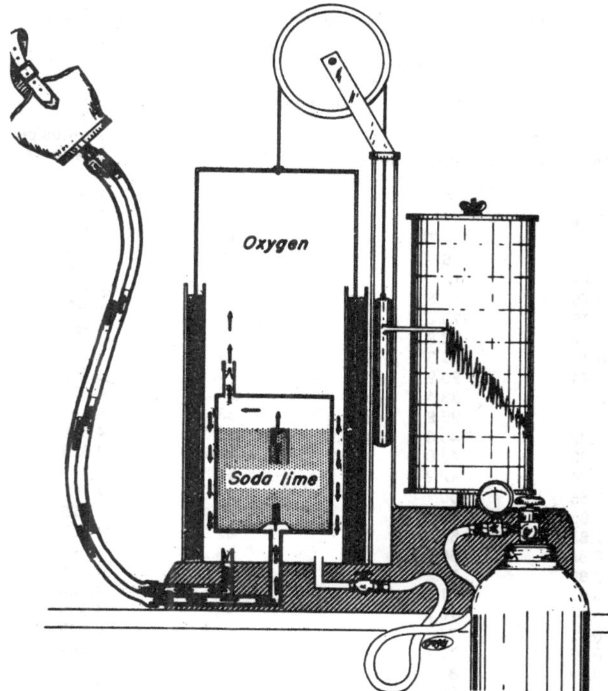

Figure 31.3. Benedict-Roth closed-circuit metabolism apparatus

The value of the respiratory quotient in indirect calorimetry is that it provides information about the proportion of fats and carbohydrates used for energy purposes and consequently enables the use of a more exact caloric equivalent of oxygen.

Equimolar amounts of any gas occupy the same volume (STP), and conversely equal volumes of gas contain the same number of molecules. Thus the RQ of any carbohydrate is 1, that of a typical fat, tripalmitin, is 0.7, and that of a typical protein is 0.8.

$$1 \text{ mole } C_6H_{12}O_6 + 6 \text{ mole } O_2 \rightarrow 6 \text{ mole } H_2O + 6 \text{ mole } CO_2$$

$$RQ = \frac{6 \text{ mole } CO_2}{6 \text{ mole } O_2} = \frac{6 \text{ vol. } CO_2}{6 \text{ vol. } O_2} = 1$$

$$1 \text{ mole } C_{51}H_{98}O_6 + 72.5 \text{ mole } O_2 \rightarrow 51 \text{ mole } CO_2 + 49 \text{ mole } H_2O$$

$$RQ = \frac{51 \text{ mole } CO_2}{72.5 \text{ mole } O_2} = \frac{51 \text{ vol. } CO_2}{72.5 \text{ vol. } O_2} = 0.703$$

On the assumption that all urinary nitrogen comes from protein and that protein contains 16 percent nitrogen, grams of metabolized protein can be calculated by multiplying grams of urinary nitrogen by 6.25. Liters of oxygen consumed in protein metabolism can be calcu-

Table 31.2. Analysis of the oxidation of mixtures of carbohydrate and fat

RQ	Percentage of total heat produced by		Calories per liter of O_2
	Carbohydrate	Fat	
0.7	0	100	4.686
0.71	1.1	98.9	4.69
0.72	4.76	95.2	4.702
0.73	8.4	91.6	4.714
0.74	12	88	4.727
0.75	15.6	84.4	4.739
0.76	19.2	80.8	4.751
0.77	22.8	77.2	4.764
0.78	26.3	73.7	4.776
0.79	29.9	70.1	4.788
0.8	33.4	66.6	4.801
0.81	36.9	63.1	4.813
0.82	40.3	59.7	4.825
0.83	43.8	56.2	4.838
0.84	47.2	52.8	4.85
0.85	50.7	49.3	4.862
0.86	54.1	45.9	4.875
0.87	57.5	42.5	4.887
0.88	60.8	39.2	4.899
0.89	64.2	35.8	4.911
0.9	67.5	32.5	4.924
0.91	70.8	29.2	4.936
0.92	74.1	25.9	4.948
0.93	77.4	22.6	4.961
0.94	80.7	19.3	4.973
0.95	84	16	4.985
0.96	87.2	12.8	4.998
0.97	90.4	9.58	5.01
0.98	93.6	6.37	5.022
0.99	96.8	3.18	5.035
1	100	0	5.047

From Lusk, *The Elements of the Science of Nutrition*, Saunders, Philadelphia, 1928

lated by multiplying grams of urinary nitrogen by 5.91; liters of carbon dioxide produced by multiplying grams of urinary nitrogen by 4.76. Subtraction of these volumes from the total leaves the nonprotein respiratory exchange. After the nonprotein RQ has been calculated, Table 31.2 will indicate the proportion of fat and carbohydrate used for energy purposes and provide an appropriate caloric equivalent of oxygen.

In the practice of animal calorimetry, the calculations implied by the preceding paragraphs are usually regarded as unnecessary and even undesirable insofar as they lead to a rigid interpretation of substrate used for energy metabolism. It is customary to assume a mixed respiratory quotient of 0.82 and assign oxygen a caloric equivalent of 4.825. Since the caloric equivalent of oxygen varies only from 4.7 at an RQ of 0.7 to 5.0 at an RQ of 1, a range of about 6 percent, the error introduced by the preceding assumption is probably seldom more than 3 percent.

Interpretation of the respiratory quotient

Although oxygen consumption is a valid measure of the rate of energy metabolism, the elimination of carbon dioxide is influenced by other processes, and RQ must be examined with these in mind.

In ruminants, anaerobic fermentation in the rumen produces large amounts of carbon dioxide and methane. At least some of these gases are eliminated in the expired air, and this carbon dixoide cannot be distinguished from that carbon dioxide which arises from metabolism in the tissues. Under these circumstances some correction is necessary before any significance can be attached to the RQ.

The carbonic acid–bicarbonate buffer system is important in regulation of the reaction of body fluids; consequently the elimination of carbon dioxide is affected by any factor which disturbs the pH of blood or interstitial fluid. In general, respiratory acidosis and metabolic alkalosis are characterized by retention of carbon dioxide, respiratory alkalosis and metabolic acidosis by loss of carbon dioxide. Under these circumstances the elimination of carbon dioxide does not reflect accurately the rate of production. For example, lactic acid, which accumulates during strenuous muscle exercise, is buffered with bicarbonate of the plasma. The carbon dioxide which is displaced from plasma bicarbonate is eliminated along with that of metabolic origin; and the RQ calculated from the exchange of pulmonary gases does not accurately reflect gaseous exchange in the tissues. Conversely, as this oxygen debt is repaid, lactate will be removed from the plasma, base will be available for the formation of bicarbonate, and the elimination of carbon dioxide will be less than the production. Again the RQ measured by exchange of respiratory gases may lead to an erroneous interpretation.

The metabolic interconversion of foodstuffs may also alter RQ. Synthesis of fat from carbohydrate changes an oxygen-rich substrate to an oxygen-poor substrate; the oxygen which is liberated substitutes for oxygen from respired air, and the respiratory quotient may be greater than 1. The reverse process, conversion of fat to carbohydrate, also occurs, and one result is a respiratory quotient less than 0.7. In a related sense it is very unlikely that an RQ of 1 means that carbohydrates are the exclusive source of energy or that one of 0.7 means fats are the only substrate; such values more likely represent the algebraic addition of several processes proceeding simultaneously within the cell.

In summary, the RQ may provide valuable information about the nutritional status of an animal, but not with the rigor implied by Table 31.2. The RQ is notorious for the accuracy of its estimation and the errors of its interpretation.

Comparisons of direct and indirect calorimetry

Respiration calorimeters, systems that permit simultaneous determinations by direct and indirect calorimetric techniques, have been constructed for both animals and

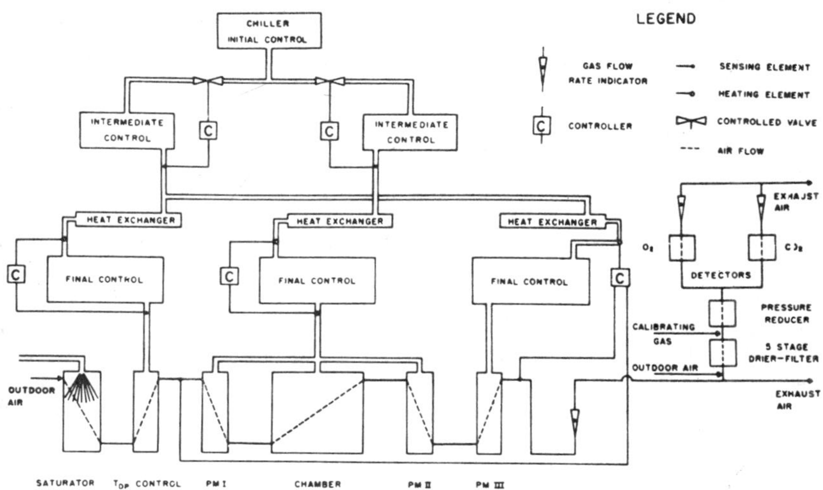

Figure 31.4. Respiration calorimeter used at Missouri Agricultural Experiment Station. Heat dissipation is measured with the gradient principle; respiratory exchange with a paramagnetic oxygen analyzer and an infrared carbon dioxide detector. (From M.D. Shanklin and A.F. Butchbaker, personal communication, 1964.)

man. Figure 31.4 is a schematic of the Missouri calorimeter, which permits simultaneous measurement of heat loss by the gradient principle and heat production by the respiratory exchange. Rabbits and other animals as large as sheep can be accommodated. In general such comparisons demonstrate good agreement between the two measurements, as indeed there must be if temperature and heat capacity of the body stay constant. The measurements of Rubner in this regard have particular significance. He demonstrated that the first law of thermodynamics applies to the animal body; the animal body has no source of energy other than food.

Calorimetry in ruminants

Fermentation in the rumen is an anaerobic process which converts carbohydrates to short-chain fatty acids, chiefly acetic, propionic, and butyric. In association with this transformation, heat is liberated which is dissipated with metabolic heat at the body surface, and carbon dioxide and methane are produced which, at least in part, are eliminated with the respiratory gases. Although the reactions in the rumen are outside of the animal body and are not part of metabolism, the end products of reactions in the rumen blend with the end products of metabolism and complicate both indirect and direct calorimetry.

Both the open- and closed-circuit types of indirect calorimeters need to make provision for the loss of methane in the expired air. In the closed-circuit apparatus methane accumulates in the spirometer and in part replaces the oxygen that is used. As a consequence the apparent rate of oxygen utilization is somewhat less than the actual rate of utilization. In the open-circuit type of apparatus it is customary to measure the volume of expired air and to calculate the volume of inspired air on the assumption that the quantity, although not necessarily the percentage, of nitrogen inspired and expired is the same. The amount of nitrogen in expired air is calculated by subtraction of oxygen and carbon dioxide; failure to subtract methane would overestimate the amount of nitrogen and hence the volume of inspired air.

The usual technique of indirect calorimetry in ruminants is to measure oxygen consumption and total carbon dioxide production; as might be expected the resultant RQ is close to 1 and the associated caloric equivalent is approximately 5 Cal per liter of oxygen (Kibler 1960).

Separation of the heat of fermentation in the rumen from heat production in the tissues (metabolic heat) can be accomplished, in theory at least, in two ways.

Heat production in the rumen has been estimated at 2.25 Cal per liter of methane produced (Krogh and Schmit-Jensen 1920). Fermentation heat then can be calculated from the rate of methane production. Subtraction of this value from total heat production leaves metabolic heat production.

While fermentation in the rumen does produce carbon dioxide, it apparently does not use oxygen. As a consequence, metabolic heat production can be estimated by calculation of tissue RQ, with the resulting assignment of a more realistic caloric equivalent to oxygen. Calculation of tissue RQ involves partition of expired carbon dioxide into fermentation and metabolic components. This partition has been based upon the ratio of carbon dioxide to methane produced by in vitro fermentation, 2.6:1 (Krogh and Schmit-Jensen 1920), and on the ratio of these gases found by analysis of rumen gas, 2.6:1 or higher immediately after feeding, and declining to less than 1:1 within 24 hours (Washburn 1937). Fermentation carbon dioxide calculated from methane production is subtracted from total carbon to yield the metabolic component; this and oxygen consumption then yield the metabolic RQ with its associated caloric equivalent of oxygen. As might be expected from the knowledge that fermentation in the rumen changes cellulose to short-chain fatty acids, this RQ is close to 0.8, and the associated caloric equivalent is approximately 4.8 Cal per liter of oxygen (Kibler 1960).

The second method of separating metabolic and fermentation heat depends upon an estimate of fermentation carbon dioxide based on the ratio of this gas to methane produced by in vitro fermentation or on the ratio found in rumen gas. Such ratios, however, are perhaps a more valid estimate of comparative production than of absorption and elimination. Diffusibility, directly related to solubility and inversely related to molecular weight, of carbon dioxide is approximately 10 times that of methane. As a consequence the production ratio may be quite different from the ratio eliminated in expired air.

FACTORS AFFECTING METABOLIC RATE

Body size

Large animals produce more heat than small animals; a 20 g mouse, for example, might produce 4 Cal per day, a 500 kg cow 7000 Cal per day. Since both have approximately the same body temperature, it might seem reasonable that heat production per unit of body weight would be the same. However, in fact the mouse produces 200 Cal per kilogram of body weight per day, the cow only 14. The search for a unifying biological principle to explain such discrepancies led to the expression of metabolic rate first as a function of the surface area of the body and more recently as a function of the *metabolic weight,* an exponential function of the body weight.

The expression of metabolic rate as a function of surface area was based on a rationale that related heat production to heat loss. As long as heat content of the body is constant, these two processes, production and loss, must be equal. Since heat is dissipated at the body surface, the amount of heat lost, and hence the amount produced, might be related more closely to the surface of the body than to the weight of the body. Such a relationship was first demonstrated by Rubner (1885) in dogs of different size, and since then it has been extended by other investigators to a variety of species.

The surface area of similarly shaped bodies is proportional to the two-thirds power of the body weight; the surface area of men, who are not all shaped alike, is calculated from a formula based on height and weight. In human medicine it is still customary to express metabolic rate as the number of Calories produced per square meter of body surface per hour.

The relationship between surface area and metabolic rate may have evolutionary significance in that such a proportionality enhanced the probability of survival in homeotherms. The two items, however, are not cause and effect, and the relationship is not as straightforward as once thought. Large animals, for example, produce more heat per square meter of body surface than do small animals. For this reason the physiological surface area, where heat loss can occur, varies even in the individual animal. Because surface area is difficult or impossible to measure accurately, metabolic rate is usually not expressed as a function of surface area in animals.

The straight-line relationship between the logarithm of heat production and the logarithm of adult body weight in a diversity of species (Fig. 31.5) has led to the concept of a *metabolically effective body weight,* denoted as an exponential function of body weight. Brody et al. (1928), dissatisfied with the relationship between surface area and metabolic rate, suggested that it might be simpler to relate heat production to an exponent of body weight; in a later examination of data from animals ranging in size from a mouse to a horse (1932), Brody estimated this metabolic weight as the body weight in kilograms raised to the 0.73 power ($kg^{.73}$). The basal 24-hour heat production by the adult of these different species averaged 70.4 Cal per $kg^{.73}$. Kleiber (1932) noted the same relationship and independently estimated the metabolic weight as $kg^{.75}$. His computation indicates that the metabolic level of adult homeotherms from mice to cattle averages 70 Cal per $kg^{.75}$ per day.

The difference between these two estimates of metabolically effective weight is not large. Kleiber's exponent has the advantage of easy computation. Expression of metabolic rate as a function of either exponent is preferable to relating metabolic rate to body surface. As Kleiber (1961) has emphasized, the three-quarter power relationship has been empirically derived from observations on a number of species and is not an approximation of the rationally derived surface area concept.

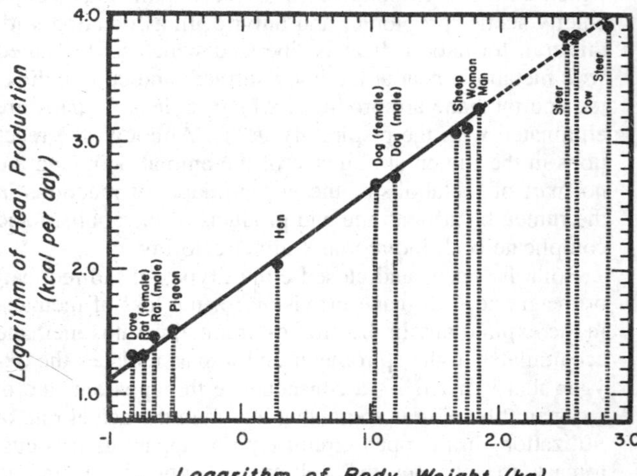

Figure 31.5. Relationship between logarithm of body weight and logarithm of heat production. (From Kleiber 1932, *Hilgardia* 6:315–53.)

Metabolic weight is a concept that derived from studies of energy metabolism; the concept, however, has much broader application. Since animals expend energy in proportion to kg$^{.75}$ they should be supplied with dietary energy on the same basis. Little animals need more calories per pound of body weight than do big animals. And it is not just energy metabolism; other activities of the body are affected in a similar way. The work of the heart, renal function, respiratory function, and various aspects of drug metabolism among other things are more closely related to metabolic weight than body weight per se.

Nervous and endocrine regulation

The rate of energy metabolism is regulated by both the nervous and endocrine systems. The role of the nervous system is, most obviously, one of regulating the activity of skeletal muscle. Under basal conditions, muscle tone contributes approximately 20 percent of total heat production. During strenuous exercise energy metabolism in skeletal muscle can increase many fold. In the horse, for example, intense muscle effort may increase the rate of oxygen consumption to 20 times the basal rate, while the rate of energy expenditure may increase 100 times. The difference is an oxygen debt that is repaid by an elevated rate of oxygen consumption after the effort terminates.

The endocrine system regulates energy metabolism chiefly through the action of two hormones, thyroxine and epinephrine. Thyroxine affects many cells of the body to increase the rate of energy metabolism. A total lack of thyroid hormone may reduce energy metabolism by 40 percent, while an excess may increase metabolic rate by 100 percent. In contrast to the relatively slow and persistent calorigenic effect of thyroxine, epinephrine has a rapid and fleeting effect. The administration of a single therapeutic dose may increase heat production by as much as 30 percent. There is also evidence that the adrenal medulla and the sympathetic nervous system play a part in the acute response to cold temperature (Hsieh and Carlson 1957).

This distinction between the nervous and endocrine regulation of body temperature is somewhat arbitrary. The secretion of epinephrine is controlled by preganglionic sympathetic fibers to the gland. The secretion of thyroxine is regulated by the thyroid-stimulating hormone from the anterior pituitary. The rate of secretion of this hormone is affected by temperature only if the hypophysis retains a direct vascular communication with the hypothalamus. At least one aspect of thyroid secretion, the response to temperature change, is controlled by the nervous system.

In a more general sense calorigenesis is regulated not only by thyroxine and epinephrine but also by a balance of hormones including principally those from the pituitary, gonads, pancreas, and adrenal cortex. It is quite possible that some of these regulators are responsible, in part, for long-term changes in metabolic rate, such as the declining rate of metabolism observed with advancing age in a variety of species.

Specific dynamic action

The ingestion of food is accompanied by an increased rate of heat production. A variety of names for the effect have been suggested, for example, specific dynamic action, specific dynamic effect, heat increment of a feeding, calorigenic effect of foods, and thermogenic effect.

SDA heat is a fraction of metabolizable energy. It is heat that is produced metabolically and should not be confused, in theory at least, with heat that is produced by fermentation in the rumen; practically it is difficult to separate the two. The work of digestion, glandular secretion, and movements of the gastrointestinal tract are responsible for only a small fraction of SDA heat. The effect is not duplicated, for example, by bulk cathartics and cholinergic agents.

SDA heat represents energy that is unavoidably lost as heat. It assists in the maintenance of body temperature in a cold environment, but at high environmental temperature it presents an added burden to the heat-dissipating mechanisms.

The amount of energy lost as SDA heat varies with a number of factors, but especially with the plane of nutrition and the balance of nutrients in the ration. Cattle fed at 50 percent of maintenance requirements lose about 10 percent of metabolizable energy as SDA heat. At full feed SDA heat may amount to almost 40 percent of metabolizable energy. In general, nutrient imbalance increases the amount of metabolizable energy lost as SDA heat. The total lack of a single essential amino acid may mean that body protein cannot be synthesized and that those amino acids present will be deaminated in the liver.

It is customary to express SDA heat as a percentage of the metabolizable energy. SDA is equivalent to about 30 percent of the metabolizable energy of proteins, 10–15 percent for carbohydrates, 5–10 percent for fats, and 15–20 percent for mixtures of short-chain fatty acids. These values, especially those for short-chain fatty acids (Blaxter 1962), are quite variable depending upon nutritional status and the amount of different foodstuffs consumed.

SDA is normally associated with the digestion and absorption of food. A similar effect, however, can be produced by the parenteral injection of the end products of digestion. The fact that an SDA is not observed after the administration of amino acids in the hepatectomized animal indicates that much of the SDA of protein is associated with deamination and the formation of urea. Approximately 80 percent of SDA heat originates in the viscera, only 20 percent in the peripheral tissues.

Temperature

Regulation of body temperature in a thermally neutral environment is achieved by adjusting heat loss to match heat production, or *physical regulation*. Below a critical temperature it becomes necessary to increase heat production to maintain a constant body temperature. This *chemical regulation* of body temperature is accomplished during acute exposure to cold by contraction of skeletal muscle, either shivering or voluntary movement, and by the release of epinephrine. During prolonged exposure to cold, heat production is increased by secretion of larger amounts of thyroid hormones.

The speed of chemical reactions, including those of metabolism, is affected by temperature: the rate of the reaction doubles with each 10°C rise in temperature, the van't Hoff effect. At low environmental temperature when, despite an increased rate of metabolism, body temperature falls, the hypothermia itself decreases the rate of heat production. Conversely when body temperature rises, whether from fever or from failure of heat dissipation to keep pace with heat production, the rate of metabolism is accelerated, and this in itself aggravates the hyperthermia (Fig. 31.6).

There is considerable species variation in the environmental temperatures which mark the various critical temperatures. In general the nonsweating domestic animals tolerate low temperature very well; they have difficulty regulating body temperature at high environmental temperature. The upper critical temperature, for example, where body temperature begins to increase because heat loss cannot keep pace with production, is about 27°C for cattle.

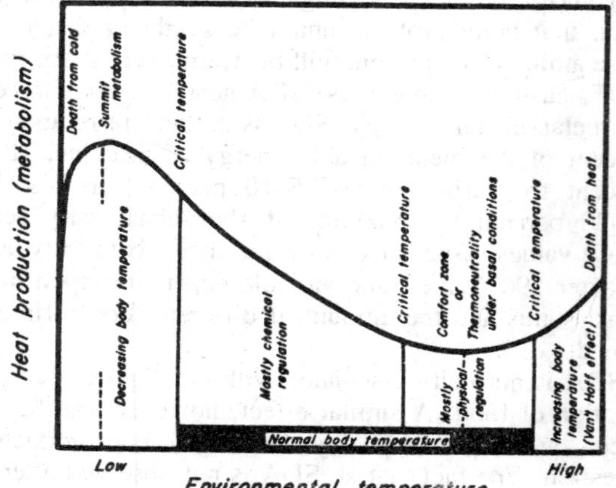

Figure 31.6. Relationship between environmental temperature and metabolic rate. (From Brody, *Bioenergetics and Growth*, Reinhold, New York, 1945.)

Work and productive processes

Animals do not live in the basal state or even in the resting state for extended periods of time. While some pets are kept at a maintenance level of energy exchange, most domestic animals are valuable only by virtue of some productive processes: either muscle work, meat, milk, egg, or wool production. All of these processes represent physiological work; none is accomplished at an efficiency of 100 percent. Not only energy metabolism but also heat production is increased.

The energy released by oxidation is coupled to productive processes by the synthesis of ATP. Oxidation of one mole of glucose to carbon dioxide and water releases energy equivalent to 673 Cal. When the mole of glucose is oxidized in the body, 266 Cal may be converted to phosphate bond energy of ATP, with 407 Cal being lost as heat. The efficiency of this energy transfer is 39 percent.

The magnitude of all types of physiological work and the associated change in energy metabolism are variable in the extreme. Some approximation, however, can be derived from the amount of work—either force times distance, or the caloric equivalent of meat, eggs, or milk—and the efficiency with which the process is accomplished.

Total or gross efficiency is the ratio between the caloric equivalent of the work accomplished and total energy metabolism. Net or partial efficiency is the ratio between the caloric equivalent of work and the energy expenditure above basal. Muscle work in horses is accomplished at a maximal gross efficiency of 25 percent. The gross efficiency of milk production is approximately 30 percent, that of egg production 16 percent, and that of growth varies from 35 percent shortly after birth to 5 percent in the later stages of beef production. Net efficiency, which does not include the cost of maintenance, is considerably higher and less variable, approximately 60 percent for all of the processes (Brody 1945).

REFERENCES

Albritton, E.C., ed. 1954. *Standard Values in Nutrition and Metabolism*. Saunders, Philadelphia.

Anon. 1964. Dietary protein content and heat production. *Nutr. Rev.* 22:156–58.

Benedict, F.G. 1938. *Vital Energetics: A Study in Comparative Basal Metabolism*. Carnegie Institute, Washington. Pub. 503.

Blaxter, K.L. 1962. *The Energy Metabolism of Ruminants*. Thomas, Springfield, Ill.

——. 1971. Methods of measuring the energy metabolism of animals and interpretation of results obtained. *Fed. Proc.* 30:1436–43.

Borsook, H. 1936. The specific dynamic action of protein and amino acids in animals. *Biol. Rev.* 11:147–80.

Brody, S. 1945. *Bioenergetics and Growth*. Reinhold, New York.

Brody, S., Comfort, J.E., and Matthews, J.S. 1928. Growth and development with special reference to domestic animals. XI. Further investigations on surface area with special reference to its significance in energy metabolism. *Mo. Ag. Exp. Sta. Res. Bull.* 115.

Brody, S., and Procter, R.C. 1932. Growth and development with special reference to domestic animals. XXIII. Relation between basal metabolism and mature body weight in different species of mammals and birds. *Mo. Ag. Exp. Sta. Res. Bull.* 166.

Brooks, G.A., Hittelman, K.J., Faulkner, J.A., and Beyer, R.E. 1971. Tissue temperatures and whole-animal oxygen consumption after exercise. *Am. J. Physiol.* 221:427–31.

Chambers, W.H., and Summerson, W.H. 1950. Energy metabolism. *Ann. Rev. Physiol.* 12:289–310.

Dale, H.E., Shanklin, M.D., Johnson, H.D., and Brown, W.H. 1967. Energy metabolism of the chimpanzee: A comparison of direct and indirect calorimetry. *J. Appl. Physiol.* 22:850–53.

DuBois, E.F. 1936. *Basal Metabolism in Health and Disease*. Lea & Febiger, Philadelphia.

Goodfield, G.J 1960. *The Growth of Scientific Physiology*. Hutchinson, London.

Hsieh, A.C.L., and Carlson, L.D. 1957. Role of adrenaline and noradrenaline in chemical regulation of heat production. *Am. J. Physiol.* 190:243–46.

Kibler, H.H. 1960. Environmental physiology and shelter engineering. LV. Energy metabolism and related thermoregulatory reactions in Brown Swiss, Holstein and Jersey calves during growth at 50° and 80°F temperatures. *Mo. Ag. Exp. Sta. Res. Bull.* 743.

Kleiber, M. 1932. Body size and metabolism. *Hilgardia* 6:315–53.

——. 1947. Body size and metabolic rate. *Physiol. Rev.* 27:511–41.

——. 1961. *The Fire of Life: An Introduction to Animal Energetics*. Wiley, New York.

Krogh, A., and Schmit-Jensen, H.O. 1920. The fermentation of cellulose in the paunch of the ox and its significance in metabolism experiments. *Biochem. J.* 14:686–96.

Lilly, J.C. 1950. Physical methods of respiratory gas analysis. In J.H. Comroe, ed., *Methods in Medical Research*. Year Book Medical, Chicago. Vol. 2.

Lusk, G. 1928. *The Elements of the Science of Nutrition*. Saunders, Philadelphia.

Mount, L.E., and Stephens, D.B. 1970. The relation between body size and maximum and minimum metabolic rates in the new-born pig. *J. Physiol.* 207:417–27.

Richardson, H.B. 1929. The respiratory quotient. *Physiol. Rev.* 9:61–125.

Stewart, R.E. 1957. Device isolates radiant heat for animal heat transfer studies. *Ag. Engin.* 38:734.

Vercoe, J.E. 1973. The energy cost of standing and lying in adult cattle. *Brit. J. Nutr.* 30:207–10.

Verstegen, M.W.A., Close, W.H., Start, I.B., and Mount, L.E. 1973. The effects of environmental temperature and plane of nutrition on heat loss, energy retention, and deposition of protein and fat in groups of growing pigs. *Brit. J. Nutr.* 30:21–35.

Washburn, L.E., and Brody, S. 1937. Growth and development. XLII. Methane, hydrogen, and carbon dioxide production in the digestive tract of ruminants in relation to the respiratory exchange. *Mo. Ag. Exp. Sta. Res. Bull.* 263.

Wilhelmj, C.M. 1963. The specific dynamic action of food. *Physiol. Rev.* 15:202–20.

CHAPTER 32

Vitamins | by Sedgwick E. Smith

Vitamin A
Vitamin D
Vitamin E
Vitamin K
Ruminal and intestinal synthesis of the B vitamins
Thiamin
Riboflavin
Niacin
Pyridoxine
Pantothenic acid
Vitamin B_{12}
Folacin
Biotin
Choline
Ascorbic acid
Antimetabolites

There is no completely satisfactory definition of vitamins. Certainly, they all are organic compounds, they function in small and in some cases extremely small quantities, they are chemically unrelated, and, for the most part, they function as metabolic catalysts usually in the form of coenzymes. They are both fat- (A, D, E, K) and water-soluble (the B complex and C). It appears that most if not all of the vitamins have been discovered, but research activity continues at a high level, particularly in detailing the role of vitamins in intermediary metabolism.

In considering the vitamin requirement of an animal, one should distinguish between a physiological and a dietary requirement. Presumably all of the vitamins are physiologically required by higher animals; that is, they play some essential role in metabolism. In some instances the needed vitamin is synthesized within the body tissues. This is the case for vitamin C in many animals. Especially significant is the synthesis of all members of the B-complex vitamins and vitamin K in the rumen by microorganisms, chiefly bacteria. For this reason, ruminants, after the first few weeks of life, are not dependent on dietary sources of the B vitamins or vitamin K. Even in nonruminants, intestinal synthesis of many vitamins occurs, but these for the most part are not readily available to the host. When synthesis of vitamins is inadequate, the animal is of course dependent on outside supplies, usually from the diet but in some instances from other sources, such as solar radiation in the case of vitamin D.

For the vitamin content of various feeds and foods see National Research Council (1971) and U.S.D.A. (1971). For requirements of vitamins by animals see National Research Council 1970–1973, 1971.

VITAMIN A

This vitamin, termed fat-soluble A by McCollum in 1913, is a dietary requirement of all animals so far studied. Vitamin A itself is a nearly colorless compound, which appeared to conflict with the early observation that vitamin A activity was associated with certain yellow-colored fats. The problem was resolved by Steenbock in 1919 when he showed that carotene fed to rats possessed vitamin A activity. The carotenes became known as provitamins A, since in the animal body they are converted to vitamin A. The alcohol form is referred to as retinol; the aldehyde as retinal; and the acid as retinoic acid. Owing to *cis-trans* isomerism at the double bonds, many stereoisomers of vitamin A are possible. By definition *all-trans* vitamin A has 100 percent activity, and all isomers so far studied have less activity.

In spite of intensive study, the precise mechanism whereby carotene is converted to vitamin A is uncertain (Glover 1960). It is generally agreed that the primary site of conversion is the mucosa of the small intestine, though

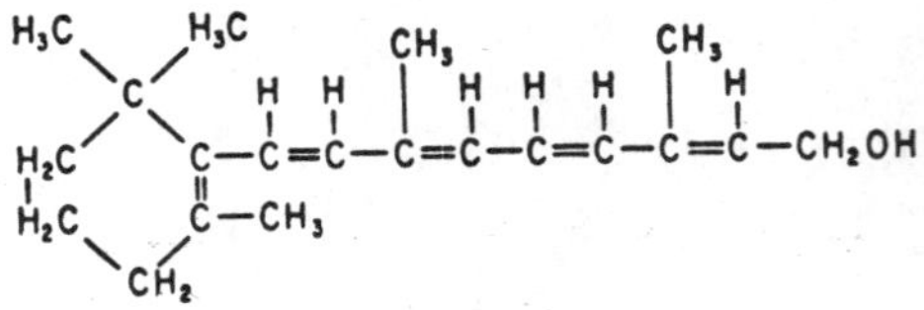

Vitamin A

some conversion can occur in other tissues. β-carotene, $C_{40}H_{56}$, has two β-ionone rings, and if the animal organism could split this molecule at the central double bond, two molecules of vitamin A would result. However, biological tests have consistently shown that pure vitamin A has twice the potency of β-carotene on a weight-to-weight basis. Thus only one molecule of vitamin A is formed from one molecule of β-carotene. Some evidence has been presented (Koehn 1948, Burns et al. 1951) that under ideal conditions and associated with optimum levels of vitamin E, β-carotene may be converted to vitamin A with 100 percent efficiency. The relative biopotency of the carotenoids based on a unit weight of vitamin A_1 (retinol, $C_{20}H_{30}O$) is as follows: vitamin A_1, 100; vitamin A_2 (dehydroretinol, $C_{20}H_{28}O$), 40; β-carotene, 50; α-carotene, 25; γ-carotene, 14; and cryptoxanthin, 29.

Vitamin A absorption is an energy-dependent reaction. It is transported from the small intestine exclusively as an ester with a higher fatty acid through the lymphatic system. A low-density lipoprotein in the lymph acts as a carrier to the liver, where vitamin A is deposited in the Küpffer cells. From the liver stores, vitamin A is transported, probably by another lipoprotein, as the free alcohol to the blood and other tissues (Roels 1967). The blood tenaciously maintains its level of vitamin A even at the expense of the last traces of liver stores. Thus the blood level of the vitamin is not a reliable indication of mild vitamin A deficiency.

Both vitamin A and the carotenoids are easily oxidized. Therefore, roughages lose a large percentage of their vitamin A activity during field-curing. During periods of luxury consumption, the animal can store large reserves of vitamin A and carotene, primarily in the liver but also in adipose tissue, to carry it over a period of many months if necessary (Riggs 1940).

A deficiency of vitamin A results in a wide variety of lesions in different species and even within species under different conditions.

Moore (1960) has pointed out that at least three basic lesions occur in avitaminosis A: (1) A lack of vitamin A, required in the form of its aldehyde for the formation of rhodopsin, causes defective dark adaptation. (2) Inadequate supplies of vitamin A generally lead to a keratinization of epithelial tissues, especially those of a columnar structure which are often associated with the secretion of mucus (Fig. 32.1). Wolbach and Bessey (1942) summarized these changes as "atrophy of the epithelium concerned, reparative proliferation of basal cells, and growth and differentiation of the new products into a stratified keratinizing epithelium." Tissues often affected include the salivary and buccal glands, respiratory and urogenital tracts, the eyes and associated structures, and even the intestinal tract. The damaged epithelium is subject to various infections, and as a result complicating, secondary infections often occur. Following the administration of vitamin A these epithelia return to normal. (3) During growth, a deficiency of vitamin A causes a defective modeling of bones, which become cancellous, weak, and excessively thick. This defect is generally held to account for the nervous lesions that often occur. There is a disparity in growth between the skeletal system and the CNS, which results in mechanical pressure on certain nerves, leading to distortion, herniation, and degeneration of the CNS. The increased cerebrospinal fluid pressure that also occurs is explained in a similar fashion.

In cattle, night blindness is one of the first clinical manifestations of vitamin A deficiency. Convulsions, total blindness, and degenerative changes in the kidneys occur later. Abortions and birth of weak calves have been noted under natural conditions of vitamin A deficiency (Guilbert and Hart 1935, Hart 1940–1941). Calves on diets low in carotene develop night blindness, papillary

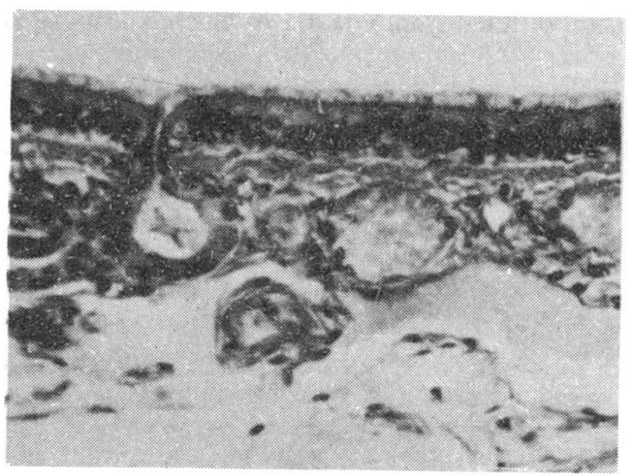

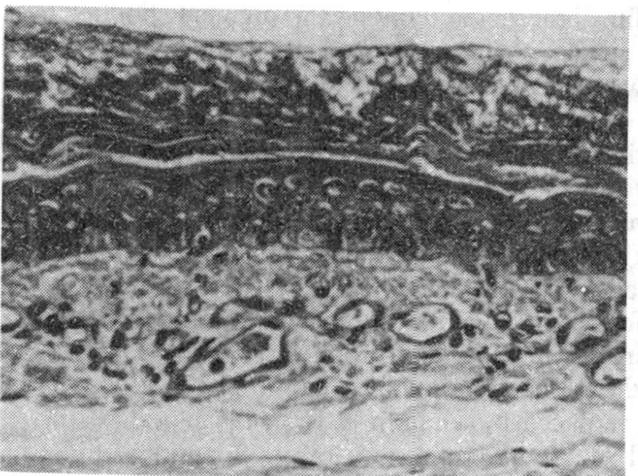

Figure 32.1. The tissue on the left is from the trachea of a normal mink, and that on the right from a vitamin A–deficient mink shows a squamous metaplasia of the normal ciliated, cylindric epithelium. Hematoxylin eosin. ×300. (Courtesy Prof. L. Krook, Cornell University.)

edema, permanent blindness associated with constriction of the optic nerve and elevated cerebrospinal fluid pressure (Moore 1939, Moore and Sykes 1940).

Studies on vitamin A deficiency in horses (Howell et al. 1941) found that night blindness, lacrymation, keratinization of the cornea and respiratory system, reproductive difficulties, capricious appetite, progressive weakness, and death occur quite regularly. Vitamin A deficiency is apparently not the cause of joint lesions in the horse (Hart et al. 1943). Histological changes in the retinas of horses showing vitamin A deficiency have also been studied (Andersen and Hart 1943).

In sheep vitamin A deficiency results in night blindness, nervous disorders, and reproductive troubles.

In pigs the absence of vitamin A results principally in nervous signs such as unsteady gait, incoordination, trembling of the legs, spasms, and paralysis. Eye lesions are seldom present (Hughes et al. 1928). Other troubles are night and day blindness and dead, weak, or malformed offspring. Elevated cerebrospinal fluid pressure has been observed (Sorensen et al. 1954).

In avitaminosis A in the dog, xerophthalmia, corneal changes, nervous disturbances, and bone malformations are seen.

In chickens lack of vitamin A in the diet causes slower growth, lowered resistance to disease, eye lesions, muscular incoordination, and other signs (Norris 1941).

Evidently the effects of vitamin A deficiency in different animals vary widely (Moore 1960).

It should be recognized that the signs of a deficiency of vitamin A, or for that matter of any other vitamin, are merely expressions of some defect(s) of more fundamental functions of the vitamin. In too many instances these basic functions have not been detected in spite of enormous research activities. Due to the brilliant studies of Wald (1960) and associates one function of vitamin A is now well established, that is, its role in the dark adaptation mechanism of animals. The rods, the receptors concerned in dim-light vision, contain the pigment rhodopsin or visual purple. When exposed to light, rhodopsin breaks down into the pigment retinene and a protein known as opsin. In the dark the reaction reverses and rhodopsin is re-formed. The change from rhodopsin to retinene and opsin is rapid; the reverse is slower. These changes are believed to be the photochemical basis of dark and light adaptation. Retinene, which is vitamin A aldehyde, and opsin undergo another reaction, the very slow transformation to a mixture of vitamin A and opsin. This mixture can regenerate to rhodopsin. During the reactions in the retina some of the vitamin A or retinene is lost and is replaced by vitamin A from the blood. If the blood level of vitamin A is too low, a functional night blindness will result. Iodopsin, a cone pigment, also undergoes similar cyclic changes in the retina. The pigment is the same in the two cycles but the opsins are different.

The intake of vitamin A considerably beyond requirements causes severe damage or toxicity. This fact explains the long recognized symptoms following the consumption of polar bear and some seal livers in the far north. The ingestion of 300–500 g of polar bear liver containing up to 18,000 International Units (IU) of vitamin A per gram causes an acute toxicity characterized by headache, vomiting, diarrhea, and giddiness, and, about a week later, desquamation of the skin and loss of some hair. The continued intake of smaller quantities leads to a chronic toxicity including such symptoms as scaly dermatitis, patchy loss of hair, anorexia, and pain in the skeletal system. The medical literature records death following the intake of a single dose of 1,000,000 IU in adults and 500,000 IU in children. Many of these same symptoms appear in swine under controlled studies (Anderson et al. 1966).

Vitamin A is found only in lipids of animal origin. A few of these, various fish liver oils, are very rich sources ranging from about 600 to over 350,000 IU per gram. Among common foods, milk fat, egg yolk, and liver are rated as rich sources. Plants of course contain no vitamin A but many, such as pasture, are rich in provitamin A.

Two reference standards are generally accepted. For vitamin A this is 0.344 μg of *all-trans* vitamin A acetate and for carotene, 0.6 μg of β-carotene. Each of these units equals one IU.

Unfortunately attempts to relate vitamin A requirement to some metabolic unit common to all animals have met with only limited success, and thus many exceptions exist. From limited data, the vitamin A requirement of mammals approximates 4 μg per kg of body weight per day for growth and about 12 μg per kg of body weight per day for storage and reproduction.

VITAMIN D

The fat-soluble, antirachitic factor was named vitamin D by McCollum in 1925. Earlier, McCollum had shown that it differed from vitamin A which is associated with it

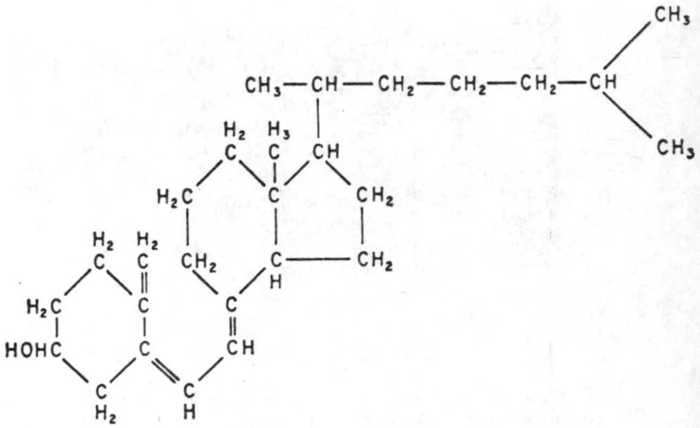

Vitamin D_3, irradiated 7-dehydrocholesterol

in cod liver oil. It soon became evident that vitamin D was not a single compound, and today almost a dozen different compounds are recognized as possessing vitamin D activity. Only vitamins D_2 and D_3, however, are important in usual foods. As in the case of vitamin A, certain compounds function as provitamins, acquiring vitamin D activity under the influence of ultraviolet light (230–300 nm) (Hess and Weinstock 1924, Steenbock and Black 1924). In plants, this provitamin is chiefly the sterol ergosterol, $C_{28}H_{43}OH$, which when irradiated by sunlight or ultraviolet lamps undergoes an internal molecular rearrangement involving the breakage of a carbon-to-carbon linkage to become vitamin D_2. Similarly, in animals 7-dehydrocholesterol is changed to vitamin D_3, $C_{27}H_{43}OH$. In the rat, dog, pig, calf, and man, vitamin D_2 approximately equals the biopotency of vitamin D_3, but in birds it is far less effective.

The outstanding deficiency disease of avitaminosis D is rickets, generally characterized by a decreased concentration of calcium and phosphorus in the organic matrices of cartilage and bone. In the adult osteomalacia is the counterpart of rickets and, since cartilage growth has ceased, is characterized by a decreased concentration of calcium and phosphorus in the bone matrix only. "Undoubtedly vitamin D is always required for the normal calcification of the growing bone, but the amount needed varies with the mineral relations in the diet and also with the species. More is required when the amount of either element or the ratio between them is suboptimum. But no amount will compensate for severe deficiencies of either mineral" (Maynard and Loosli 1962). The species difference in vitamin D requirements is illustrated by the fact that the rat will not develop rickets if the dietary calcium and phosphorus levels and ratios are optimum even though vitamin D supplies are very deficient. On the other hand, birds, puppies, and man do require vitamin D in addition to adequate calcium and phosphorus levels.

Clinical symptoms, a consequence of the fundamental bone lesions in rickets, differ somewhat in different animals. Generally the ends of long bones are enlarged; they may be bent, and in extreme deficiencies may be so soft as to be readily cut by a knife. Changes in the teeth are less complex and are related to the fact that here no resorption occurs. Areas of disturbed calcification may be noted in such rapidly growing teeth as the incisors. In dairy and beef calves there occurs a swelling in the region of the metacarpal and metatarsal bones, bending of the forelegs, stiffness of the joints, and arching of the back (Fig. 32.2). Swine, in addition, may suffer fracture of the vertebrae leading to a posterior paralysis. In poultry the beak may become soft in addition to the skeleton, and in mature birds the egg shell becomes thin and is followed by a decrease in both egg production and hatchability.

In all species rickets is accompanied by a decrease in the calcium and/or phosphorus in the blood plasma and an increase in the alkaline-phosphatase activity of the blood.

Figure 32.2. Calf suffering from clinical rickets (above). The same calf after having been on a rachitogenic diet and a vitamin D supplement for 6 months (below). (From Rupel, Bohstedt, and Hart 1933, *Wis. Ag. Exp. Sta. Res. Bull.* 115.)

Due to the excellent work of Wasserman et al. (1966, 1968) and Omdahl and DeLuca (1973) our knowledge of the function and metabolism of vitamin D has been greatly advanced. The vitamin is necessary for the synthesis of a specific calcium-binding protein in the intestinal mucosa which is involved in the active transport of calcium. This carrier protein has now been identified in a number of species and thus appears to be a general mechanism. Furthermore, the concentration of Ca-binding protein varies with the calcium needs of the body. Under calcium deficient intakes the carrier protein increases, thus increasing the absorption of calcium. This explains the previously known partial adaptation of animals to a dietary deficiency of calcium. Two metabolites of vitamin D_3 have been identified in the animal body, both of which are more active than the vitamin itself. 25-hydroxycholecalciferol (25-OH-D_3) is formed in the liver from vitamin D_3 and is some 1.5–5 times more effective than D_3 itself. It is stored in reserve in the liver and called upon as needed. Under the stimulus of low calcium concentrations in the blood plasma, 25-OH-D_3

is mobilized and circulated to the kidneys where it is hydroxylated to 1,25-dihydroxycholecalciferol [$1,25(OH)_2D_3$] which appears to be the form of vitamin D which acts directly on target organs. It is some 100 times as active as 25-OH-D_3. The formation of $1,25(OH)_2D_3$ responds to the need for calcium by the body and is stimulated by low blood serum calcium concentration; the transformation from 25-OH-D_3 is under the influence of parathormone (see Chapter 52). Vitamin D_3 and its metabolites are also involved in mobilizing calcium from bones, in addition to their effects on calcium transport.

Phosphorus, of course, is required for bone formation as well as calcium. Heretofore it had been thought that vitamin D had no direct effect on phosphorus absorption, but evidence is now accumulating for such a direct effect. Harrison and Harrison (1969) have verified the presence of a vitamin D–dependent active phosphate pump in the rat intestine, and this has been confirmed by others.

The intake of vitamin D in amounts considerably in excess of requirements leads to a toxicity termed hypervitaminosis D. In early stages calcification of bone may be accelerated, but in later stages bone resorption is increased leading to a demineralized and weakened skeleton. Extensive calcification of soft tissues takes place, such as in the joints, kidneys, myocardium, lungs, arteries, and other locations. The kidney damage is particularly serious, and most fatal cases terminate in uremia.

The distribution of vitamin D is limited in nature though provitamins D are widely found. The latter sterols when irradiated by sunlight form vitamin D. The effectiveness of sunlight depends on the length and intensity of the ultraviolet component reaching the body. These short rays do not pass through window glass, are maximum on the earth during the height of summer and minimum during the winter, and are filtered out by clothing, hair coat, or pigmented layers of the skin. Sunlight-activated vitamin D is probably the largest source of this vitamin for animals. Among the richest food sources of vitamin D are the various fish liver oils.

Vitamin D in the form of 25-OH-D_3 is stored in the liver and during times of luxury intake can be stored in amounts to last the animal for several weeks if not months.

One IU of vitamin D is equal to the biopotency of 0.025 μg of vitamin D_3. This is one vitamin in which physicochemical methods of assay have not supplanted bioassays, due to the multiple nature of vitamin D and the small amounts usually found in foodstuffs.

VITAMIN E

The failure of reproduction in rats fed certain purified diets was recognized by Evans and Bishop in 1922 as a vitamin deficiency. Vitamin E was isolated from wheat germ oil in 1936 and given the name by which it is now generally known, tocopherol, meaning "to bear offspring" (Evans 1962).

As in the case of vitamin D, the tocopherols make up a group of active compounds. Of these, α-tocopherol is the most common and active form found in nature. It has the formula of $C_{29}H_{50}O_2$, is an alcohol, possesses a 6-hydroxy-chroman nucleus, and of course is fat soluble. The relative biopotencies of the various forms are not well defined but for one method of bioassay (rat fetal resorption) are approximately as follows: α-tocopherol, 1; β-tocopherol, 0.5; γ-tocopherol, 0.2; δ-tocopherol, 0.1.

A dietary deficiency of vitamin E leads to a bewildering array of symptoms (Mason and Horwitt 1972) in various animals, which generally may be classified as (1) reproductive failures, (2) muscle degeneration, and (3) some functional and/or physical damage to cell membranes. In the rat, gestation is interrupted by death and resorption of the embryos. In the male rat, the testicular germinal epithelium degenerates, and such damage is permanent. Similar symptoms are found in the mouse, hamster, and guinea pig but not in certain other animals such as ruminants. The early recognition of an association between vitamin E deficiency and reproductive failure led to the term antisterility vitamin, which in retrospect was unfortunate since most of the metabolic activities of this vitamin appear to be associated, not with reproduction, but with the integrity of the muscular and other systems. In some 20 different animal species a deficiency of tocopherol leads to muscular dystrophy. Fundamentally this is a Zenker's degeneration of both skeletal and cardiac muscle fibers. The connective tissue replacement which follows is grossly observed as white

Vitamin E (α-tocopherol)

striations in the muscle bundles. Unfortunately, muscular dystrophy in man does not respond to vitamin E therapy. In chickens, encephalomalacia (an ataxia resulting from hemorrhage and edema in the cerebellum), exudative diathesis (a generalized edema), and muscular dystrophy, as well as reproductive failure, are deficiency signs. Other deficiency symptoms include a necrosis of the liver and an increased susceptibility of erythrocytes to hemolysis.

Since animals respond so variably to inadequate intakes of vitamin E, it is not surprising that the fundamental metabolic roles of the vitamin are unresolved. The tocopherols are, without question, excellent naturally occurring antioxidants, and a few researchers hold that this is their basic function. Most authorities, however, insist that in addition vitamin E plays a more specific role. The antioxidant function of the tocopherols is well illustrated in the peroxidative degradation of body fats (Tappel 1962):

$$R\cdot + O_2 \longrightarrow ROO\cdot$$

$$RH + ROO\cdot \longrightarrow ROOH + R\cdot$$

Here a lipid, RH, is oxidized to a peroxide, ROOH, by molecular O_2. The reaction is catalyzed by the free radicle $R\cdot$ or $ROO\cdot$. Such free radicles can interact at enzyme sites or damage structural membranes (Green 1972). An antioxidant, such as the tocopherols, can break this chain of reactions by combining with $ROO\cdot$ In this way, tocopherol supplies are used up, which explains the often observed fact that dietary unsaturated fats (susceptible to peroxidation) augment or precipitate a vitamin E deficiency, the so-called cod liver oil injury in ruminants and other herbivores. Again, the interruption of fat peroxidation by tocopherol explains the well-established observation that dietary tocopherols protect or spare body supplies of such oxidizable materials as vitamin A and the carotenes. Certain deficiency symptoms of vitamin E (encephalomalacia, experimental muscular dystrophy) can be prevented by supplementing the diet with other antioxidants, thus lending support to the antioxidant role of the tocopherols. On the other hand, certain other well-established symptoms of vitamin E deficiency, such as the fetal resorption syndrome, do not respond to antioxidant treatment or to selenium and thus support the concept of a unique role of the tocopherols.

Abundant data now show that the mineral element selenium (see Chapter 33) is somehow metabolically interrelated with vitamin E. Schwarz and Foltz (1957) showed that a selenium-containing compound effectively prevented a liver necrosis in rats that was induced by a vitamin E deficient diet. Later, other workers showed that additional vitamin E deficiency symptoms would respond to selenium treatment, notably, muscular dystrophy in a number of species and exudative diathesis in poultry. Selenium, however, does not effectively prevent the fetal resorption in rats nor encephalomalacia in chickens and thus is not a complete substitute for vitamin E.

The absorption of the tocopherols has been little studied. It is known that bile salts are required; that they enter the circulatory system as the free alcohols; that excretion is primarily by way of the feces; that storage occurs in many body tissues including adipose tissues, muscles, and liver; and that the animal body has the capacity to store large amounts.

One IU of vitamin E is equal to 1 mg of DL-α-tocopheryl acetate.

The tocopherols are widely distributed in nature, more so than any of the other fat-soluble vitamins. Animal products contain mainly α-tocopherol, the cereal grains about half α- and half non-α-forms, and legumes mostly non-α-forms. Most green plants and vegetable oils are rich sources, especially wheat germ oil. The whole grain cereals contain abundant supplies and so does egg yolk. Milk and dairy products are poor sources.

VITAMIN K

Chicks on a purified, ether-extracted diet were reported by Dam in 1934 to develop a hemorrhagic syndrome. In 1935, he showed that this disease was an avitaminosis and proposed the name vitamin K (for Koagulation). In 1939 Dam et al. isolated pure vitamin K from alfalfa and McKee et al. (1939) from putrefied fish meal. The vitamin from alfalfa and other plants is now termed vitamin K_1 ($C_{31}H_{46}O_2$) and that from bacterial synthesis as vitamin K_2 ($C_{41}H_{46}O_2$). These naturally occurring vitamin K's are derivatives of napthoquinone, are fat soluble, and are sensitive to light and oxidation. At present a large number of naturally occurring and synthesized homologues of vitamin K are known, as well as highly active, synthetic analogues, especially menadione ($C_{11}H_8O_2$). Some of the salts of menadione are water soluble and even more active than vitamin K_1.

In chicks and other birds, a deficiency of vitamin K is followed by a delay in the clotting time of the blood, anemia, and hemorrhage in many body tissues. This hemorrhage may occur spontaneously or as the result of trauma. The same syndrome occurs in other animals, including man, but usually as a result of some conditioning agent, that is, some factor interfering with vitamin K metabolism or synthesis. Other deficiency symptoms have been described but now appear to be secondary to the primary lesion—a reduced production of prothrombin.

Prothrombin, a protein, is manufactured in the liver and is the precursor of thrombin, which is required to catalyze the conversion of fibrinogen to fibrin in the blood clot. In the absence of vitamin K the prothrombin

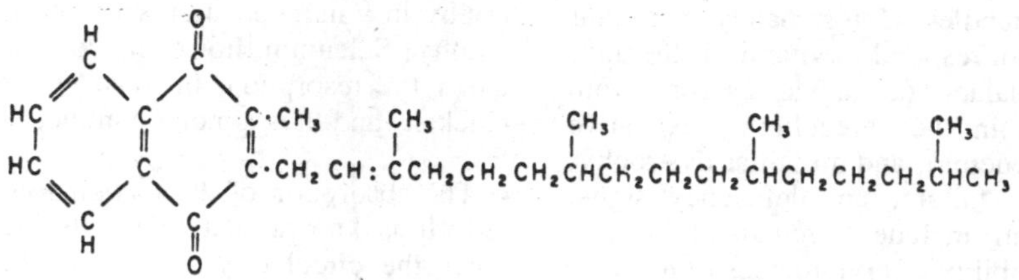

```
         H     O
         C     C
       //  \  /  \
    HC      C      C·CH3    CH3           CH3              CH3              CH3
    |       ||     ||        |             |                |                |
    HC      C      C·CH2 CH : CCH2CH2CH2CHCH2CH2CH2CHCH2CH2CH2CHCH3
       \\  /  \   /
         C     C
         H     O
```

Vitamin K_1 (2-methyl-3-phytyl-1,4-naphthoquinone)

level in the blood decreases, though how this is effected is still unknown. Some evidence indicates that vitamin K may act as a coenzyme for a prothrombin-synthesizing enzyme, while other evidence indicates that the vitamin may actually be a precursor of prothrombin. Whatever the fundamental mechanism, it does take place in the liver cell, for in the absence of the liver, vitamin K is not effective. In addition to its effect on prothrombin, vitamin K may also play some role in maintaining the activity of the plasma thromboplastin component and of factor VII, both part of the blood coagulation mechanism (Sebrell and Harris 1971) (see Chapter 3).

Vitamin K is one fat-soluble vitamin that is generally synthesized by bacteria in the gastrointestinal tract, even in birds. Its production in the rumen and subsequent passage along the small intestine, a region of active absorption, make such synthesized vitamins highly available to the host. In nonruminants, the site of synthesis is in the lower gut, an area of poor absorption, and thus vitamin K is available to the host in limited amounts only, unless the animal practices coprophagy, in which case the synthesized vitamin K is highly available. This probably explains the difference in species sensitivity to low dietary supplies of vitamin K. With the exception of birds, other animals are likely to obtain their needed vitamin K from that manufactured in the gut, and when a deficiency does occur it is probably due to some interference with vitamin K synthesis or metabolism, that is, a condition of avitaminosis K. A deficiency of bile, e.g. obstructive jaundice, will reduce vitamin K absorption. The prolonged administration of the sulfa drugs and some antibiotics will reduce intestinal synthesis of the vitamin and, as expected, several diseases of the liver will interfere with the key function of the vitamin. The presence of a vitamin K antagonist will occasionally lead to hemorrhages. One naturally occurring antagonist is dicoumarin, isolated in 1941 from spoiled sweet clover hay (Link 1959). Such hay or silage when fed to calves can cause massive internal hemorrhages and has been termed sweet clover disease. This dicoumarin is formed from coumarin by bacteria. (The anticoagulant effects of dicoumarin are used in medicine and as a rodenticide.) All of these conditioned vitamin K deficiencies can be prevented by increasing vitamin K supplies.

The standard for estimating the biopotency of vitamin K is the antihemorrhagic activity of 1 μg of menadione. Based on the chick assay the relative potency of menadione is 1000; vitamin K_1, 500; and vitamin K_2, 400 units per mg.

Information on food supplies of vitamin K is not as important as it is for most other vitamins, since intestinal synthesis of the vitamin normally supplies the needs of the animal, with an occasional exception in chickens.

RUMINAL AND INTESTINAL SYNTHESIS OF THE B VITAMINS

The various members of the vitamin B complex are of course physiologically required by all animals, but except for niacin (from tryptophan) and choline (from serine via aminoethanol), animal cells are incapable of their synthesis. It therefore follows that these vitamins must be presented to animals preformed in the diet or from microbial synthesis in the gastrointestinal tract.

Ruminal synthesis, by bacteria, of all the B vitamins is well established (Kon and Porter 1954). While many aspects remain unclear, especially the quantitative production, it appears that under most management conditions ruminants can and do receive most of their requirements from synthesis and are thus independent of dietary supplies of these vitamins. Other dietary components can and do influence the extent of synthesis. For example, cobalt is required for the synthesis of vitamin B_{12}, and if the diet is inadequate in this element the animal develops a vitamin B_{12} deficiency (Smith and Loosli 1957). For the first few days of life the young ruminant resembles a nonruminant in requiring dietary sources of the B vitamins (Barnett and Reid 1961). Beginning as early as 8 days and certainly by 2 months of age the ruminal flora have developed to the point of contributing significant amounts of the B vitamins as well as essential amino acids. The production of these vitamins at the proximal end of the gastrointestinal tract means they are highly available to the host as they pass down the tract through areas of efficient digestion and absorption.

In the nonruminant, including man, intestinal synthesis of the B vitamins is considerable (Mickelsen 1956) though not as extensive or as efficiently utilized as in ruminants. The low efficiency of utilization is probably related to several factors. Intestinal synthesis in nonruminants occurs in the lower intestinal tract, an area of poor absorption. In many cases the synthesized vitamins are held intracellularly by bacteria (Mitchell and Isbell 1942), and are swept from the body in the feces. In still other cases (thiamin), the synthesized vitamin exists extracellularly but in a form that is poorly absorbed (Wostmann and Knight 1961). Intestinally produced vitamins are more available to those animals (rabbit, rat, and others) that habitually practice coprophagy and thus recycle the products of the lower gut. In this event, significant amounts of the B vitamins are available to the host animal.

While excessive intakes of some fat-soluble vitamins may be toxic, this is rare with the water-soluble vitamins. Presumably the B vitamins and ascorbic acid are so readily excreted that harmful amounts seldom accumulate in the body.

THIAMIN

Beriberi, now a recognized thiamin-deficiency symptom, was described in Chinese literature several centuries ago. The researches on beriberi and its counterpart in birds, polyneuritis, are closely associated with the development of the vitamin concept. Thiamin ($C_{12}H_{17}N_4OSCl \cdot HCl$) consists of a molecule of pyrimidine and one of thiazole. It is highly soluble in water and is readily destroyed by heat, especially in the presence of alkali.

Absorbed thiamin is carried to the liver, where it is phosphorylated in the presence of adenosine triphosphate (ATP) to form a coenzyme, cocarboxylase, in which form it exerts its primary physiological function. Two such thiamin-containing coenzymes are known, thiamin pyrophosphate (cocarboxylase or TPP) and lipothiamide (LTPP). It is thus involved in the enzymatic decarboxylation of α-ketoacids such as pyruvic acid. In plants, pure or nonoxidative decarboxylations involving TPP occur. In animals, however, the decarboxylations are oxidative (actually dehydrogenation), two of which occur in the tricarboxylic acid cycle in the form of LTPP:

$$\underset{\text{Pyruvic acid}}{CH_3{-}\overset{\overset{O}{\|}}{C}{-}\overset{\overset{O}{\|}}{C}{-}OH} + \text{Coenzyme A (CoA)} + \text{Diphosphopyridine nucleotide (DPN)} \xrightarrow{\text{LTPP}} \underset{\text{Acetyl CoA}}{CH_3{-}\overset{\overset{O}{\|}}{C}{-}CoA} + DPN \cdot H + CO_2 + H^+$$

In a similar fashion, α-ketoglutarate is decarboxylated. Inasmuch as pyruvate stands at the crossroads in the degradation of carbohydrates, it is obvious that thiamin is closely associated with carbohydrate metabolism and in a still broader sense with energy metabolism in general.

Thiamin hydrochloride

The symptoms of a thiamin deficiency in various animals have much in common: lameness, convulsions (in birds accompanied by a head retraction and in rats by walking in a circle), a severe anorexia, bradycardia, and anatomical lesions in the heart muscle, peripheral nerves (birds), and CNS (Follis 1958). As would be expected, pyruvic acid or its derivative, lactic acid, accumulates in body tissues and fluids, accounting for many of the deficiency symptoms (Robinson 1966). In common with all B vitamins, thiamin is stored in the animal body in very limited amounts except in swine. This accounts for the relatively high thiamin content of pork muscle.

Thiamin utilization or availability is occasionally reduced by the dietary presence of interfering compounds. One of these is a chemically similar compound termed pyrithiamin. When added to a diet normally adequate in thiamin, a thiamin deficiency develops that is corrected by the addition of more thiamin. Pyrithiamine evidently competes with thiamin in the formation of cocarboxylase and thus antagonizes its function. Pyrithiamin is thus an antimetabolite and more specifically an antivitamin. A second type of antagonism involves the disease of foxes termed Chastek paralysis. Certain species of fishes, when fed raw to foxes and other animals, induce many of the symptoms characteristic of thiamin deficiency. Furthermore, these symptoms respond to thiamin therapy. Later work showed that a number of fishes, mostly freshwater species, clams, shrimp, and some mussels, contain an enzyme, thiaminase, that splits thiamin. The cooking of such fishes destroys the thiaminase. A thiaminase has also been observed in bracken fern, and, for example, horses fed a diet of these ferns develop a thiamin deficiency. Ruminants, presumably due to their abundant supply of thiamin, do not develop a thiamin deficiency when fed bracken fern but do develop a degeneration of the bone marrow which apparently is caused by a second toxic principle in the fern (Kingsbury 1964).

Pyrithiamin

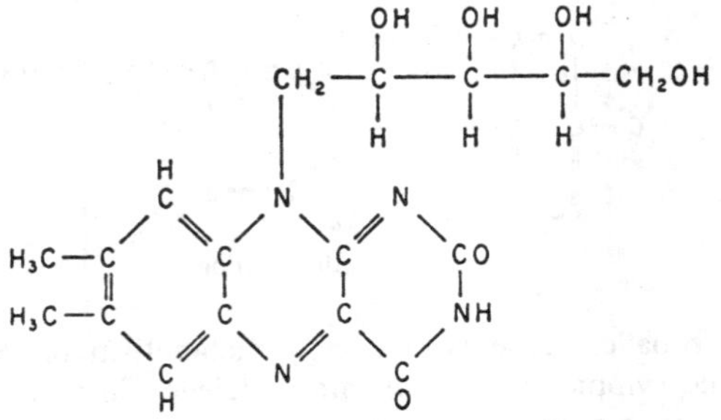

Riboflavin

The generally recognized official unit is the biopotency of 3 μg of pure thiamin hydrochloride.

Thiamin is present in significant quantities in a wide variety of foods. Brewer's yeast is an exceptionally rich source, while whole (but not polished) grain cereals, lean pork, liver, and egg yolk are very good sources.

RIBOFLAVIN

Riboflavin, a fluorescent yellow pigment, is a part of the "old yellow enzyme," a respiratory enzyme discovered by Warburg and Christian (1932). This vitamin was synthesized almost simultaneously by Karrer et al. (1935) and Kuhn et al. (1935). It is made up of ribose and isoalloxazine, from which its name is derived, has the formula of $C_{17}H_{20}N_4O_6$, is only slightly soluble in water, differs from thiamin in being relatively stable to heat in neutral solutions, and is highly sensitive to light, so much so that milk exposed to sunlight loses more than half of its content in two hours.

The symptoms displayed by various riboflavin-deficient animals differ considerably. Chickens develop a peculiar leg paralysis (curled-toe disease) and a decline in egg production and hatchability. In swine, dermatitis, crooked and stiff legs, and opacity or even cataract of the eye lens are prominent signs. The ragged coat of deficient rats is due to the generalized atrophy of the sebaceous glands and hair follicles. A deficiency during pregnancy leads to a number of congenital deformities in young rats—cleft palate and shortened, fused, or missing bones (Kalter and Warkany 1959).

Riboflavin, as a component of a coenzyme, functions in the transport of hydrogen or more strictly speaking, electrons. Ingested riboflavin is phosphorylated in the wall of the intestine, absorbed as such, and carried to body tissues where it is found either as the phosphoric acid ester or as a flavoprotein. These flavoprotein enzymes contain flavin mononucleotide (FMN) or flavin adenine dinucleotide (FAD) as the coenzyme. Both of these are closely associated in their function with coenzyme I, which is niacinamide adenine dinucleotide (NAD), and coenzyme II (NADP). One illustration of this cooperative function follows:

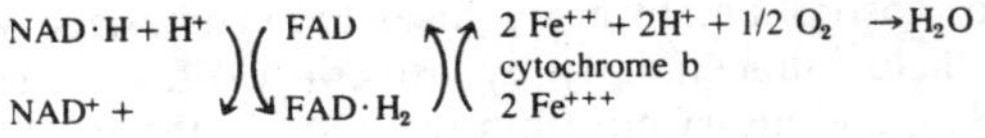

NAD·H + H⁺ / NAD⁺ + ⇄ FAD / FAD·H₂ ⇄ 2 Fe⁺⁺ + 2H⁺ + 1/2 O₂ → H₂O; cytochrome b; 2 Fe⁺⁺⁺

Here H^+, released for example from the oxidation of isocitrate in the tricarboxylic acid cycle, is successfully transported by three enzymes to its terminal oxidation to water by dissolved oxygen. It is thus obvious that riboflavin is significantly involved in the complexes of energy metabolism in the body. In addition to this role, riboflavin-containing enzymes are concerned with the oxidation of D- and L-amino acids and with purines through xanthine oxidase.

The chemical structure of riboflavin appears to be highly specific to its function, for even minor changes result in either a loss of vitamin activity or in the formation of an antagonist. The feeding of such derivatives as diethylflavin, isoriboflavin, dichloroflavin, and others completely inhibits the response of animals to riboflavin.

Riboflavin is synthesized by most higher plants, yeasts, and some bacteria, and thus it is widely found in nature. Yeast is very rich, while milk, eggs, liver, and growing leafy vegetables are among the best sources.

NIACIN

Niacin, previously termed nicotinic acid, was prepared in the laboratory in 1867 by oxidizing nicotine. Niacinamide was isolated from coenzyme II by Warburg and Christian (1934), who thus demonstrated its function in the hydrogen-transport system. Recognition of niacin as a vitamin, however, came later when Elvehjem et al. (1937) showed that it would cure blacktongue in dogs. Later other workers demonstrated that it was equally effective in curing pellagra in man. Chemically, niacin is one of the simplest vitamins, $C_6H_5O_2N$. It is a derivative of pyridine, is soluble in water, and is very stable in the dry state.

The discovery that niacin was the pellagra-preventing factor ranks with the great advances in human medicine. Pellagra symptoms are characterized by four D's—dermatitis, diarrhea, delirium, and death (Hundley 1954). The epithelial lesions, including ulceration, extend to internal surfaces such as the mouth (stomatitis) and the gastrointestinal tract. The oral lesions that occur in the dog are prominent and are known as blacktongue. In other species the symptoms are less specific. In addition to a growth depression, which of course eventually occurs

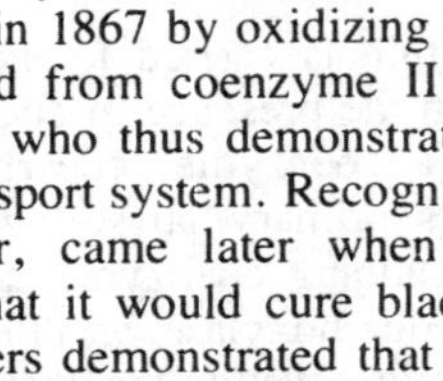

Niacin

with any nutrient deficiency, chickens display a stomatitis and occasional dermatitis; the pig a dermatitis, diarrhea with occasional vomiting, and a mild anemia; and the rat a poor hair coat with occasional porphyrin-caked whiskers and alopecia. However, these symptoms have not been specifically related to the well-established biochemical functions of niacin.

Ingested niacin is transformed (the site is still unsettled) to niacinamide, which becomes the physiologically active form of the vitamin. In the body niacinamide is found in only two coenzymes—coenzyme I and coenzyme II. The former has been termed diphosphopyridine nucleotide (DPN) but this has been superseded by the more chemically correct term of niacinamide adenine dinucleotide (NAD), while the second coenzyme (triphosphopyridine nucleotide or TPN) is called niacinamide adenine dinucleotide phosphate (NADP). NAD and NADP function in oxidation-reduction systems by their ability to accept hydrogen atoms (dehydrogenation) from selected substrates and to transfer these hydrogen atoms to other hydrogen acceptors such as the flavin enzymes discussed under riboflavin. In combination with different proteins, these two coenzymes serve the body in a large number of dehydrogenase activities of which more than 40 have been recognized, including anaerobic and aerobic oxidation of glucose (carbohydrate metabolism), fatty acid oxidation and synthesis (lipid metabolism), conversion of vitamin A to rhodopsin, and the incorporation of high-energy phosphate bonds in ADP and ATP. Thus niacin-containing enzymes serve the animal body in most fundamental ways.

In 1945, Krehl et al. showed that in the rat (later in other species) the amino acid tryptophan could substitute for niacin; that is, tryptophan is a niacin precursor. The conversion of tryptophan to niacin is not an efficient process (Firth and Johnson 1956), and obviously tryptophan must be present in excess of the animal's requirement for this essential amino acid. Some synthetic niacin antivitamins are known, such as 3-acetylpyridine and isonicotinic acid hydrazide, but none have been recognized in natural foods.

Niacin is well distributed in nature. Brewer's yeast is a very rich source, while good supplies are found in liver, muscle meats in general, peanuts, and some fishes.

PYRIDOXINE

Pyridoxine, vitamin B_6, was discovered by György (1934), who showed that the rat acrodynia (painful extremities) factor did not respond to the then-known vitamins. The name pyridoxine was coined in recognition of its pyridine structure. It is a relatively simple compound, $C_8H_{11}O_3N$ freely soluble in water, fairly stable to heat, but sensitive to light destruction. Three biologically active forms are now recognized—pyridoxine, the primary alcohol form; pyridoxal, the aldehyde form; and pyridoxamine, the amine form.

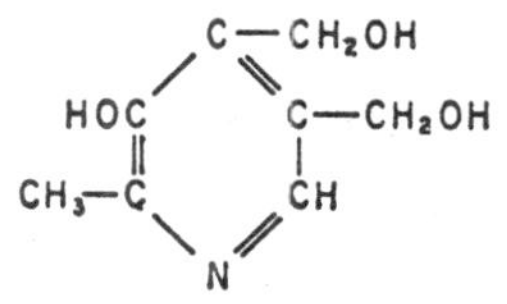

```
          C—CH₂OH
        /   \\
    HOC       C—CH₂OH
      ||      |
  CH₃—C       CH
        \   //
          N
```

Pyridoxine

The symptoms of an avitaminosis B_6 follow a reasonably uniform pattern among animal species: alterations in the skin and the erythropoietic and nervous tissues (Follis 1958). Lesions of the skin, often termed a dermatitis, are prominent in the rat but less so in other animals. This dermatitis is characterized by a hyperkeratosis, erythema, and edema. Anemia, usually microcytic and hypochromic, occasionally occurs in the deficient rat, more so in dogs, and is prominent in swine. Epilepticlike fits, hyperexcitability, or convulsions occur in almost all species so far studied and appear to be related to microscopic lesions in the nervous system.

Pyridoxine functions in the form of a coenzyme, codecarboxylase. All three forms of the vitamin are converted in the animal body to the active coenzyme, pyridoxal phosphate. In this form, pyridoxine is concerned with a wide variety of enzyme systems (Sauberlich 1968), many of which involve amino acids. Among these enzyme systems are: (1) amino acid decarboxylases, of which a number are known including arginine, lysine, and glutamic acid; (2) transaminases, which catalyze the exchange of amino groups between α-ketoglutarate and a variety of amino acids to yield glutamate and a corresponding keto acid; and (3) those specifically concerned with the metabolism of tryptophan. An end product of this latter action is the vitamin niacin. Under deficiency conditions, the degradation of tryptophan may be incomplete leading to the accumulation in the urine of the abnormal metabolite, xanthurenic acid, which can indicate the vitamin B_6 status of the animal. Several synthetic vitamin B_6 antagonists are known, of which one, deoxypyridoxine, appears to act by becoming phosphorylated and competing with pyridoxine for position on the surface of the apoenzyme (Umbreit 1954).

Pyridoxine is widely available in foods, so much so that naturally occurring deficiencies are rare. Most vitamin B_6 statistics are not satisfactory, especially the older ones, since several forms of the vitamin occur naturally and these have different activities or else the vitamin is bound to other compounds in unavailable forms. In a general way muscle meats, liver, vegetables, and whole grain cereals are among the best sources.

PANTOTHENIC ACID

The name pantothenic acid, meaning "from everywhere," was proposed by Williams et al. (1933) when

```
      CH₃  OH   O
   H   |    |   ||  H   H   H
HOC — C —— C —— C — N — C — C — COOH
   H   |    H           H   H
      CH₃
```

Pantothenic acid

they found it to be a component of *bios,* a factor essential for yeast. A series of studies on the chick antidermatitis factor culminated in the production of an active concentrate by Elvehjem and Koehn (1935), which on degradation was shown by Woolley et al. (1939) to contain β-alanine, a known component of pantothenic acid. Jukes (1939) showed that the calcium salt of pantothenic acid was indeed the antidermatitis factor. Later, pantothenic acid was shown to be a dietary requirement for a number of other animal species. This vitamin in pure form is a pale-yellow oil ($C_9H_{17}O_5N$), but the sodium, potassium, and calcium salts are crystalline and highly soluble in water.

Among the animal species studied, a deficiency of pantothenic acid has variously affected the skin, hair, reproduction, gastrointestinal tract, nervous system, and adrenal glands. In the chick, which played a significant role in the discovery of the vitamin, there occurs retardation of feather development, dermatitis including an exudate around the eyes, and scabbiness around the mouth and vent. On autopsy dark and patchy livers are observed as well as a myelin degeneration in the spinal cord. In mature hens, hatchability of eggs is depressed. In the rat, an alopecia and scaly skin around the eyes (spectacle alopecia) are prominent. Graying of the hair has been noted in the rat, mouse, and fox. Deficient pigs show a scurfy skin, thin hair, ulceration of the intestinal tract, degeneration of the dorsal root ganglion cells, reproductive failure, and a characteristic gait, termed "goose step" (Fig. 32.3).

Lesions in the adrenal glands have been noted in several species, which may indicate some relationship between pantothenic acid and steroid hormone production (Follis 1958, Briggs and Daft 1954).

The general and important metabolic role of pantothenic acid was apparent when it was found to be a component of coenzyme A (CoA), discovered by Lipmann (1945). The combination of CoA with two-carbon fragments is an essential step in activating these fragments for acetate transfer. Inasmuch as two-carbon fragments can arise from the degradation of carbohydrates, fats, and some amino acids, the formation of acetyl CoA (active acetate) is a necessary step in the intermediary metabolism, both breakdown and synthesis, of a large number of metabolites. Furthermore, CoA can activate carbon fragments larger than acetate so that it is in a more general sense involved in acyl transfers. The roles of CoA include the transfer of acetate from carbohydrate oxidation to the citric acid cycle; oxidation of ketoglutarate; synthesis of such amino acids as glutamic, proline, and others; through succinyl transfer, probable involvement with the synthesis of the pyrrole ring in the heme molecule; and involvement in the formation of acetoacetate, fatty acids, and cholesterol (Lipmann 1954). All living material studied contains CoA. Highest concentrations are located in the liver.

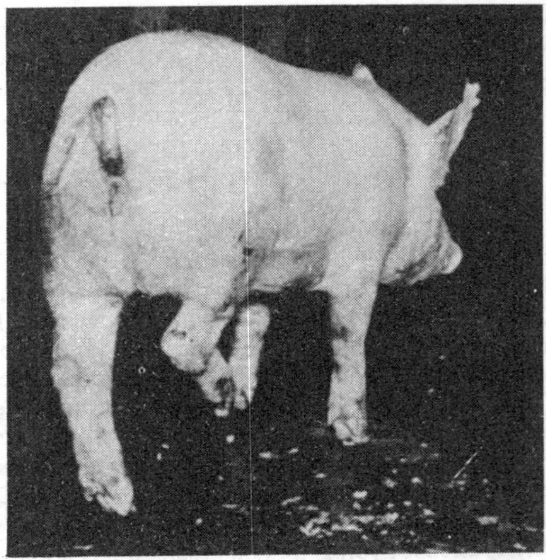

Figure 32.3. A pig with pantothenic acid deficiency walks with the exaggerated step termed "goose stepping." (Courtesy Prof. W.G. Pond, Cornell University.)

The generally accepted standard of reference is calcium pantothenate, 1.087 g of which equals 1 g of pure pantothenic acid. Pantothenic acid is widely distributed in nature, especially in liver, kidney, yeast, egg yolk, and fresh vegetables.

VITAMIN B_{12}

Castle et al. (1930) hypothesized that the effectiveness of liver extract in treating pernicious anemia in man was due to an erythrocyte maturation factor that was a combination of an intrinsic factor produced by the stomach and an extrinsic factor derived from the diet. The intrinsic factor is an enzyme secreted by the gastric and intestinal mucosa (Reisner 1968), but the extrinsic factor is vitamin B_{12}. The identification of this vitamin, involving various analytical techniques, electron density maps, crystallographic data, electron computers, and extensive team work is one of the fascinating achievements of present-day science (Smith 1960). Vitamin B_{12}, or cyanocobalamin, was isolated in 1948 but it was not until 1956 that its very complicated structure was ascertained. The empirical formula is $C_{63}H_{88}O_{14}N_{14}PCo$, and among its unusual features is the content of 4.5 percent cobalt.

A deficiency of vitamin B_{12} in man, usually if not always conditioned by a deficiency of the intrinsic factor

Vitamin B_{12} (cyanocobalamin)

necessary for its absorption, leads to pernicious anemia. In nonruminants, pernicious anemia, or in fact any anemia, is not characteristic of a vitamin B_{12} shortage. In rats, guinea pigs, swine, and poultry, vitamin B_{12} functions as a growth factor, although a mild normocytic anemia does occur in a small percentage of deficient swine. In addition, an inadequate intake of this vitamin interferes with hatchability of eggs and reproduction in swine and rats (Coates 1968).

In ruminants, a deficiency of vitamin B_{12} is usually indirect and related to a dietary shortage of cobalt, which is required by ruminal microorganisms to synthesize the vitamin. Here the deficiency signs include anorexia, depressed growth (Fig. 32.4), and a simple anemia (Smith and Loosli 1957).

One of the most important functions of B_{12} is its involvement in the metabolism of propionic acid:

$$\text{propionyl CoA} + CO_2 + \text{ATP} \xrightarrow{\text{Biotin}}$$

$$\text{methyl malonyl CoA} \xrightarrow{B_{12}\ \text{coenzyme}}$$

$$\text{succinyl CoA} \longrightarrow \text{Kreb's cycle}$$

In this way three-carbon fragments, particularly propionate in ruminants, are utilized. Vitamin B_{12} is also concerned with the synthesis of methyl groups from single-carbon units derived from formate, serine, or glycine. Such methyl groups are available for the formation of choline, methionine from homocysteine, and thymine from uracil. Thymine may then be converted to thymidine, which is utilized in the synthesis of deoxyribonucleic acid. Barker et al. (1958) reported the isolation of a vitamin B_{12} coenzyme which is required for the decomposition of glutamate to β-methylaspartate, while others have reported the isolation of vitamin B_{12} coenzymes from various sources whose functions are yet unresolved.

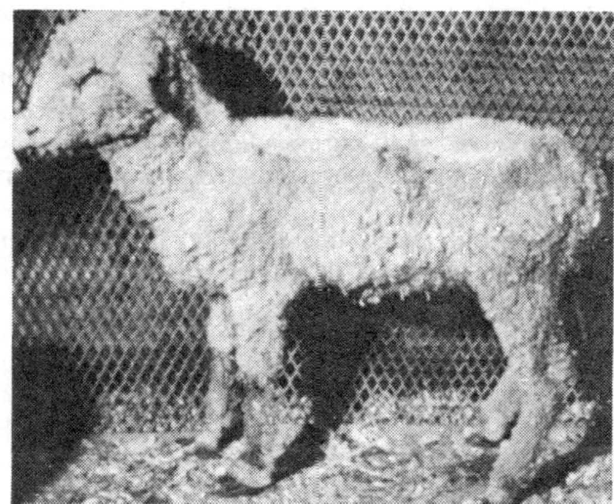

Figure 32.4. Vitamin B_{12} deficiency in the lamb induced by limiting the intake of cobalt. This lamb was approximately 50 percent of normal weight and severely anemic.

It seems likely that vitamin B_{12} in natural products is of microbial origin. Higher plants and animals apparently do not synthesize it. Assay of foods is difficult, for the vitamin exists in a number of substituted forms and as pseudovitamin B_{12} compounds, some of which have biological activity and some of which do not (Ford and Hutner 1955). Foods of animal origin are reasonably good sources—meat, liver, milk, eggs, and fish. Among the richest sources are fermentation residues often used to supplement animal diets.

FOLACIN

Mitchell et al. (1941) isolated a substance from spinach that proved to be a growth factor for *S. faecalis*. They named it folic (foliage) acid. This vitamin, whose present generic name is folacin, has a number of biologically active derivatives, notably folinic acid, or citrovorum factor, and pteroylglutamic acid. Folacin ($C_{19}H_{19}N_7O_6$) is made up of glutamic acid, para-aminobenzoic acid, and a pteridine nucleus and was synthesized by Angier et al. (1946). There is an imposing list of antagonists, such as aminopterin, which have been used to determine some of its functions.

In animals, this vitamin is in general concerned with erythrocyte formation, and in its absence there develops an anemia which in many species (Follis 1958) is macrocytic and therefore similar to pernicious anemia. In fact, folacin is an effective treatment of pernicious anemia but not of accompanying nervous symptoms. Further signs of a deficiency include leucopenia, and, in chickens, poor feathering and depigmentation of colored feathers.

The basic functions of folacin have only been incompletely resolved (Robinson 1966). There is evidence that it functions as a coenzyme in the form of tetrahydrofolic acid. Through various enzymatic systems it is involved in the transfer of single-carbon units and in this respect is similar to vitamin B_{12} with which it cooperates. Examples of this function are found in the interconversion of serine and glycine and the synthesis of methyl groups of methionine, choline, and thymine. Also, it is somehow involved with purine synthesis, a deficiency of which may account for the associated anemias (Hartman and Buchanan 1959).

Animal species vary considerably in their dietary requirement for folacin, in large part due to the availability of intestinally synthesized vitamin. The chick, monkey, and guinea pig develop avitaminosis folacin when fed diets deficient in the vitamin or one of its active derivatives, but the rat and pig need to be fed in addition one of the sulfa drugs that reduces the intestinal synthesis of folacin. In still other animals (dog) a deficiency develops only following the feeding of one of the folacin antagonists. Excellent natural sources of folacin are liver, dried beans, pork, kidney, spinach, asparagus, and some berries. Among livestock a dietary shortage is a problem only occasionally with chickens.

BIOTIN

The identification of biotin as a vitamin resulted from three lines of research involving a yeast growth factor, coenzyme R, which functions in the respiration of legume nodule bacteria, and vitamin H, a factor related to the disease called egg white injury. In 1940 duVigneaud et al. showed that these three factors were identical and two years later announced the structure of biotin ($C_{10}H_{16}O_3N_2S$). The first synthesis of biotin was announced by Harris et al. (1943). This vitamin is sparingly soluble in cold water.

Biotin is synthesized by microbes in the intestinal tract of all animals, usually in amounts adequate to meet the nutritional needs. To demonstrate a biotin deficiency in the rat, for example, requires treatment by a conditioning factor such as feeding sulfa drugs, preventing coprophagy, or administering an antivitamin. The only known naturally occurring antivitamin to biotin is heat-labile avidin in raw egg white. This compound is a protein secreted by the oviduct mucosa into the egg white and combines stoichiometrically with biotin to form an unabsorbable complex. The chick will respond to a biotin-deficient diet without the addition of a stressing agent.

In the rat and pig a biotin deficiency is characterized by progressive dermatitis and scaly skin accompanied by alopecia. In colored mice, depigmentation of the hair occurs. In addition to dermatitis, chicks may develop perosis, a syndrome that involves still other factors (György and Langer 1968).

Biotin is a functional constituent of various enzyme systems, presumably in the form of a coenzyme. It has a well-established role in carbon dioxide fixation; the reaction in reverse is a decarboxylation. An example of this

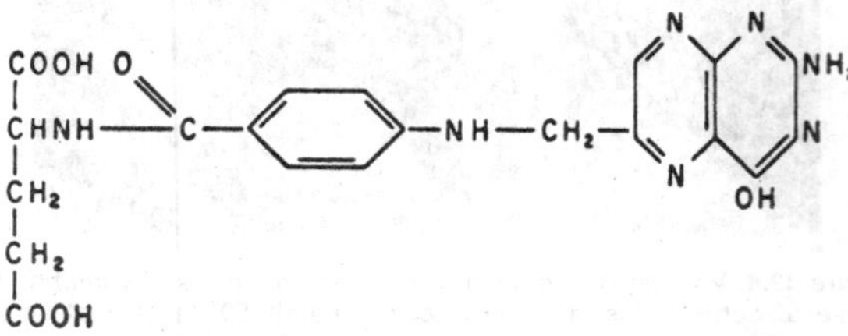

Folacin (liver *L. casei* factor)

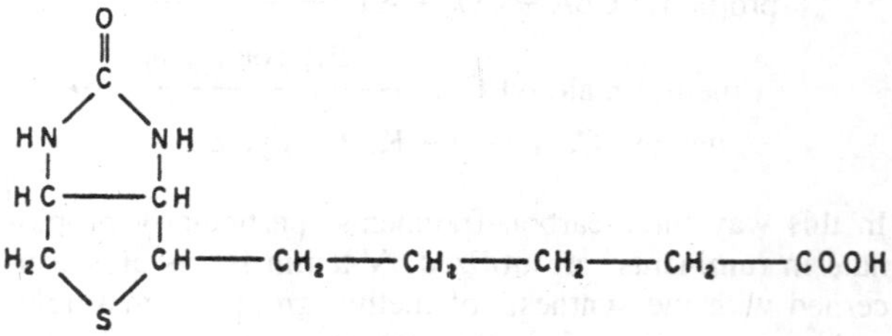

Biotin

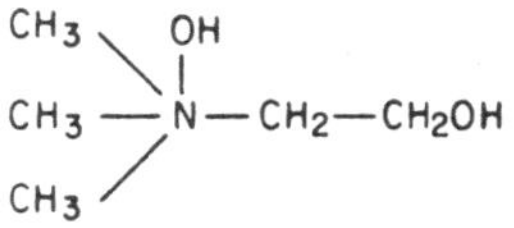

$$(CH_3)_3\overset{OH}{N}-CH_2-CH_2OH$$

Choline

reaction involves the formation of methylmalonate from propionate and carbon dioxide (see vitamin B_{12}). Another function concerns certain transcarboxylations such as the formation of oxalacetate from pyruvate. There is also evidence for a functional role in fat synthesis, aspartic acid formation, and in amino acid deamination (György and Langer 1968).

Rich food sources include milk, liver, meats generally, many vegetables, and whole grains. Except for chickens, a biotin deficiency is unlikely to occur naturally.

CHOLINE

The classification of choline as a vitamin is questionable inasmuch as it is not known to function as a metabolic catalyst and is a structural component of significant magnitude in such compounds as the phospholipids (lecithin) and acetylcholine. Choline is synthesized in the animal body and, under proper conditions, in amounts adequate to meet physiological requirements. Proper conditions stipulate the presence of precursors, such as ethanolamine (from serine), and labile methyl groups from compounds such as methionine. Excess dietary methionine can thus partly replace or spare a dietary deficiency of choline. Choline, in turn, can supply methyl groups to other compounds such as homocysteine to form methionine. This transfer of methyl groups between compounds is termed transmethylation (duVigneaud et al. 1950).

With a deficiency of choline, there is a deficiency of phospholipids, which are generally concerned with the transport from and oxidation of fatty acids in the liver (Artom 1953). As a consequence, fat accumulates in the liver in all species so far studied (Follis 1958). Compounds which prevent or cure the abnormal accumulation of fat are termed lipotropic substances. This includes choline and also inositol, which at one time was also classified as a B vitamin.

In poultry, a dietary shortage of choline is not only followed by fat accumulation in the liver but in addition by perosis—a syndrome related to other factors as well. For an excellent review see Griffith and Nye (1971).

ASCORBIC ACID

Scurvy, the deficiency disease of avitaminosis C, has been known for centuries. It occurred epidemically in times of wars, famines, and long voyages when there was a shortage of fruits and fresh vegetables. Pure vitamin C (ascorbic acid) was isolated by Waugh and King

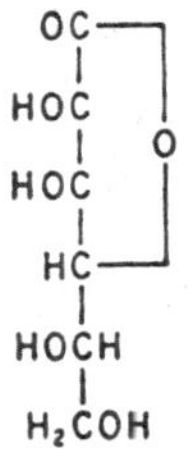

```
OC──┐
 |   |
HOC  |
 |   O
HOC  |
 |   |
HC──┘
 |
HOCH
 |
H2COH
```

L-ascorbic acid (reduced form)

(1932) and shown to be the antiscorbutic factor. Ascorbic acid, $C_6H_8O_6$, occurs as such in nature or in the oxidized form of dehydroascorbic acid. Both are biologically active. Further oxidation of dehydroascorbic acid produces diketogulonic acid, an inactive compound. This oxidation proceeds easily under conditions of heat and light and explains the ready destruction of vitamin C in foods. Vitamin C is highly soluble in water and in the cooking of foods much is lost by leaching.

Ascorbic acid was thought to be a dietary requirement of only man, monkeys, and guinea pigs, but now a large array of animals including a number of species of birds, fishes, fruit bat, flying fox, and some insects have been shown to require it (Chatterjee et al. 1961, Chaudhuri et al. 1969, Halver et al. 1969, and Gupta et al. 1972). The inability to synthesize ascorbic acid is apparently due to the absence of glucurono reductase and gulono oxidase, which enzymes are variously found in the liver and kidneys of those species that synthesize the vitamin from hexose sugars, and which are therefore not dependent on a dietary supply.

Scurvy in man is characterized by capillary fragility and thus widespread hemorrhages throughout the body, swollen and bleeding gums, a loosening of the teeth, weak bones, and anemia (Follis 1958). The capillary fragility and weak bones are related to the function of vitamin C in regulating the formation and maintenance of intercellular substances having collagen or related compounds as basic constituents. Defects, probably due to a failure to hydroxylate proline, are noted in collagen produced by fibroblasts, osteoid by osteoblasts, and dentine by odontoblasts in scorbutic animals (Reid 1954, Chatterjee 1967). Another function of ascorbic acid is that of an antioxidant. Ascorbic acid is so readily oxidized to dehydroascorbic acid that other compounds may be protected against oxidation. Whether the associated anemia is entirely the result of the extensive tissue hemorrhage or is due also to some more direct action of ascorbic acid is unclear. A unique function of ascorbic acid is its role, along with ATP, in the transfer of plasma iron and its incorporation into tissue ferritin, but whether or not this mechanism is involved in the anemia is unknown. Another and seemingly isolated function of this vitamin is its role in maintaining normal tyrosine oxidation. In ascorbic acid deficiency intermediate metabolites—hydroxyphenylpyruvic, hydroxyphenyllactic, and homogentisic acids—are excreted in the urine, and this observation is diagnostic of the deficiency. The healing of wounds is defective in scorbutic animals and is probably due to the defective formation of collagen and/or the mucopolysaccharides in the interfibrillar ground substance of connective tissue.

The best sources of vitamin C are fresh fruits such as guava, oranges, grapefruit, limes, strawberries, and leafy vegetables, particularly broccoli, turnip greens, brussels sprouts, and peppers.

ANTIMETABOLITES

A metabolite is a compound that plays some essential role in metabolic reactions, for example, vitamins, amino acids, fatty acids, and hormones. Antimetabolites have two distinguishing features: they resemble in chemical structure (analogue) some metabolite, and they specifically antagonize the biological action of the metabolite (Woolley 1959).

The antimetabolite concept crystallized with the discovery of Woods (1940) that the bacteriostatic action of some sulfonamides could be reversed by *p*-aminobenzoic acid. The latter compound is structurally very similar to these sulfa drugs and, since the bacteriostatic effect is overcome by corresponding increases in the supply of *p*-aminobenzoic acid, is an example of competitive inhibition. Another classical example involves the antimetabolite pyrithiamin and, since this specifically antagonizes the action of a vitamin, thiamin, is an example of an antivitamin. The addition of pyrithiamin to the diet of animals evokes the recognized symptoms of a thiamin deficiency. Further additions of thiamin prevent this antagonism. Antimetabolites, naturally occurring or synthetic, are now known for all vitamins except A and D, for most of the amino acids, and for several hormones as well as a few other metabolites.

It appears that an antimetabolite is sufficiently similar in structure to a metabolite to combine with a specific apoenzyme that normally would combine with the metabolite. The function of the abnormal enzyme thus formed is altered and the organism suffers accordingly. If the antimetabolite-apoenzyme combination is reversible, the addition of the normal metabolite will dislodge the antimetabolite and the antagonism is reversed. Should the antimetabolite-apoenzyme combination be irreversible, further additions of the metabolite are ineffective. Generally an apoenzyme prefers its normal substrate, but in a few instances antimetabolites have been constructed which an apoenzyme prefers over its normal substrate, and such compounds are especially potent biological materials.

Treatment of an animal with an antimetabolite is of course generally detrimental, but the concept has been employed to advantage in further determining the metabolic reactions in which a vitamin, for instance, functions in the body. Further, some progress has been made in using certain antimetabolites as chemotherapeutic agents (Woolley 1952, Martin 1951).

REFERENCES

Andersen, A.C., and Hart, G.H. 1943. Histological changes in the retina of the vitamin A deficient horse. *Am. J. Vet. Res.* 4:307–17.

Anderson, M.D., Speer, V.C., McCall, J.T., and Hays, W.V. 1966. Hypervitaminosis in the young pig. *J. Anim. Sci.* 25:1123–27.

Angier, R.B., Boothe, J.H., Hutchins, B.L., Mowat, J.H., Semb, J., Stokstad, E.L.R., Subbarow, Y., Waller, C.W., Cosulich, D.B., Fahrenbach, M.J., Hultquist, M.E., Kuh, E., Northey, E.H., Seeger, D.R., Sickels, J.P., and Smith, J.M., Jr. 1946. The structure and synthesis of the liver *L. casei* factor. *Science* 103:667–69.

Artom, C. 1953. Role of choline in the oxidation of fatty acids by the liver. *J. Biol. Chem.* 205:101–11.

Barker, H.A., Weissback, H., and Smyth, R.D. 1958. A coenzyme containing pseudovitamin B_{12}. *Proc. Nat. Acad. Sci.* 44:1093–97.

Barnett, A.J.G., and Reid, R.L. 1961. *Reactions in the Rumen.* Edward Arnold, London.

Briggs, G.M., and Daft, F.S. 1954. Pantothenic acid. IX. Effects of deficiency. In Sebrell and Harris. Vol. 2, 649–69.

Burns, M.J., Hauge, S.M., and Quackenbush, F.W. 1951. Utilization of vitamin A and carotene by the rat. I. Effects of tocopherol, Tween, and dietary fat. *Arch. Biochem. Biophys.* 30:341–46.

Castle, W.B., Townsend, W.C., and Heath, W.C. 1930. Observations on the etiologic relationship of achylia gastrica to pernicious anemia. III. The nature of the reaction between normal human gastric juice and beef muscle leading to animal improvement and increased blood formation similar to the effect of liver feeding. *Am. J. Med. Sci.* 180:305–35.

Chatterjee, G.C. 1967. Ascorbic acid: Effects of ascorbic acid deficiency in animals. In Sebrell and Harris. Vol. 1, 407–57.

Chatterjee, I.B., Kar, N.C., Ghosh, N.C., and Guha, B.C. 1961. Aspects of ascorbic acid biosynthesis in animals. *Ann. N.Y. Acad. Sci.* 92:36.

Chaudhuri, C.R., and Chatterjee, I.B. 1969. L-ascorbic acid synthesis in birds. *Science* 164:435–36.

Coates, M.E. 1968. Vitamin B_{12}: Deficiency effects in animals. In Sebrell and Harris. Vol. 2, 212–20.

Dam, H. 1934. Haemorrhages in chicks reared on artificial diets: New deficiency disease. *Nature* 133:909–10.

——. 1935a. The antihaemorrhagic vitamin of the chick. *Biochem. J.* 29:1273–85.

——. 1935b. The antihaemorrhagic vitamin of the chick: Occurrence and chemical nature. *Nature* 135:652–53.

Dam, H., Geiger, A., Glavind, J., Karrer, P., Karrer, W., Rothschild, E., and Salomon, H. 1939. Isolierung des Vitamins K in hochgereinigter Form. *Helv. Chim. Acta* 22:310–13.

Dam, H., and Schonheyder, F. 1934. A deficiency disease in chicks resembling scurvy. *Biochem. J.* 28:1355–59.

duVigneaud, V., Melville, D.B., György, P., and Rose, G.S. 1940. On the identity of vitamin H with biotin. *Science* 92:62–63.

duVigneaud, V., Ressler, C., and Rachele, J.R. 1950. The biological synthesis of "labile methyl groups." *Science* 112:267–71.

Elvehjem, C.A., and Koehn, C.J., Jr. 1935. Studies on vitamin B_2; The non-identity of vitamin B_2 and flavins. *J. Biol. Chem.* 108:709–28.

Elvehjem, C.A., Madden, R.J., Strong, F.M., and Woolley, D.W. 1937. Relation of nicotinic acid and nicotinic acid amide to canine black tongue. *J. Am. Chem. Soc.* 59:1767–68.

Evans, H.M. 1962. The pioneer history of vitamin E. *Vitam. Horm.* 20:379–87.

Fernholz, E. 1938. On the constitution of α-tocopherol. *J. Am. Chem. Soc.* 60:700–705.

Firth, J., and Johnson, B.C. 1956. Quantitative relationships of tryptophan and nicotinic acid in the baby pig. *J. Nutr.* 59:223–34.

Follis, R.H. 1958. *Deficiency Disease.* Thomas, Springfield, Ill.

Ford, J.E., and Hutner, S.H. 1955. Role of Vitamin B_{12} in the metabolism of microorganisms. *Vitam. Horm.* 13:102–36.

Funk, C. 1912. The etiology of the deficiency diseases. *J. State Med.* (Roy. Inst. Pub. Health, London), 20:341–68.

Glover, J. 1960. The conversion of β-carotene into vitamin A. *Vitam. Horm.* 18:371–86.

Goldblith, S.A., and Joslyn, M.A. 1964. *Milestones in Nutrition.* Avi, Westport, Conn.

Green, J. 1972. Tocopherols: Biochemical symptoms. In Sebrell and Harris. Vol. 5, 259–72.

Griffith, W.H., and Nye, J.F. 1971. Choline: Effects of deficiency. In Sebrell and Harris. Vol. 3, 81–123.

Guilbert, H.R., and Hart, G.H. 1935. Minimum vitamin A requirements with particular reference to cattle. *J. Nutr.* 10:409–27.

Gupta, S.D., Chaudhuri, C.R., and Chatterjee, I.B. 1972. Incapability of L-ascorbic acid synthesis by insects. *Arch. Biochem. Biophys.* 152:889–90.

György, P., and Langer, B.W. 1968. Biotin: Deficiency effects and requirements of animals. In Sebrell and Harris. Vol. 2, 336–47.

Halver, J.E., Ashley, L.M., and Smith, R. 1969. Ascorbic acid requirements of Coho salmon and rainbow trout. *Trans. Am. Fish. Soc.* 98:762.

Harris, S.A., Wolf, D.E., Mozingo, R., and Folkers, K. 1943. Synthetic biotin. *Science* 97:447–48.

Harrison, H.E., and Harrison, H.C. 1969. Intestinal transport of phosphate: Action of vitamin D, calcium, and potassium. *Am. J. Physiol.* 201:1007–12.

Hart, G.H. 1940–1941. Vitamin A deficiency and requirements of farm mammals. *Nutr. Abstr. Rev.* 10:261–72.

Hart, G.H., Goss, H., and Guilbert, H.R. 1943. Vitamin A deficiency not the cause of joint lesions in horses. *Am. J. Vet. Res.* 4:162–68.

Hartman, S.C., and Buchanan, J.M. 1959. Biosynthesis of the purines. XXVI. The identification of the formyl donors of the transformylation reactions. *J. Biol. Chem. 234:1812*–16.

Hess, A.F., and Weinstock, M. 1924. Antirachitic properties imparted to inert fluids and to green vegetables by ultra-violet irradiation. *J. Biol. Chem.* 62:301–13.

Howell, C.E., Hart, G.H., and Ittner, N.R. 1941. Vitamin A deficiency in horses. *Am. J. Vet. Res.* 2:60–74.

Hughes, J.S., Aubel, C.E., and Lienhardt, H.F. 1928. The importance of vitamin A and vitamin C in the ration of swine, concerning especially their effect on growth and reproduction. *Kan. Ag. Exp. Sta. Tech. Bull.* 23.

Hundley, J.M. 1954. Niacin. X. Effects of deficiency. In Sebrell and Harris. Vol. 2, 551–65.

Jansen, B.C.P., and Donath, W.F. 1926. On the isolation of the anti-beri-beri vitamin. *Proc. Roy. Acad. Sci. Amsterdam* 29:1390–1400.

Johnson, B.C., and Wolf, G. 1960. The function of vitamin A in carbohydrate metabolism: Its role in adrenocorticoid production. *Vitam. Horm.* 18:457–83.

Jukes, T.H. 1939. The pantothenic acid requirements of the chick. *J. Biol. Chem.* 129:225–31.

Kalter, H., and Warkany, J. 1959. Experimental production of congenital malformations in mammals by metabolic procedures. *Physiol. Rev.* 39:69–115.

Karrer, P., Morf, R., and Schöpp, K. 1931. Zur Kenntnis des Vitamins-A aus Fischtranen. *Helv. Chim. Acta* 14:1431–36.

Karrer, P., Schöpp, K., and Benz, F. 1935. Synthesen von Flavinen. *Helv. Chim. Acta.* 18:426–29.

Kingsbury, J.M. 1964. *Poisonous Plants of the United States and Canada.* Prentice-Hall, Englewood Cliffs, N.J.

Koehn, C.J. 1948. Relative biological activity of beta-carotene and vitamin A. *Arch. Biochem. Biophys.* 17:337–44.

Kon, S.K., and Porter, J.W.G. 1954. The intestinal synthesis of vitamins in the ruminant. *Vitam. Horm.* 12:53–68.

Krehl, W.A., Tepley, L.J., and Elvehjem, C.A. 1945. Corn is an etiological factor in the production of a nicotinic acid deficiency in the rat. *Science* 101:283.

Krehl, W.A., Tepley, L.J., Sarma, P.S., and Elvehjem, C.A. 1945. Growth-retarding effect of corn in nicotinic acid–low rations and its counteraction by tryptophane. *Science* 101:489–90.

Kuhn, R., Reinemund, K., Weygand, F., and Strobele, R. 1935. Uber die Synthese des Lactoflavins (Vitamin B_2). *Berichte deutsch. Chem. Gesellsch.* 68:1765–71.

Link, K.P. 1943–44. The anticoagulant from spoiled sweet clover hay. *Harvey Lectures,* ser. 39. Pp. 162–216.

——. 1959. The discovery of dicumarol and its sequels. *Circulation* 19:97–107.

Lipmann, F. 1945. Acetylation of sulfanilamide by liver homogenates and extracts. *J. Biol. Chem.* 160:173–90.

——. 1954. Pantothenic acid. III. Biochemical systems. In Sebrell and Harris. Vol. 2, 598–625.

Martin, G.J. 1951. *Biological Antagonism.* Blakiston, Philadelphia.

Mason, K.E., and Horwitt, M.K. 1972. Tocopherols: Effects of deficiency in animals. In Sebrell and Harris. Vol. 5, 272–92.

Maynard, L.A., and Loosli, J.K. 1962. *Animal Nutrition.* 5th ed. McGraw-Hill, New York.

McCollum, E.V. 1957. *A History of Nutrition.* Houghton Mifflin, Boston.

McCollum, E.V., and Davis, M. 1913. The necessity of certain lipids in the diet during growth. *J. Biol. Chem.* 15:167–75.

McCollum, E.V., Simmonds, N., Becker, J.E., and Shipley, P.G. 1925. Studies on experimental rickets. XXVI. A diet composed principally of purified foodstuffs for use with the "Line Test" for vitamin D studies. *J. Biol. Chem.* 65:97–100.

McKee, R.W., Binkley, S.B., MacCorquodale, D.W., Thayer, S.A., and Doisy, E.A. 1939. The isolation of vitamins K_1 and K_2. *J. Am. Chem. Soc.* 61:1295.

Mickelsen, O. 1956. Intestinal synthesis of vitamins in the nonruminant. *Vitam. Horm.* 14:1–95.

Mitchell, H.K., and Isbell, E.R. 1942. Intestinal bacterial synthesis as a source of B vitamins for the rat. *U. of Texas Pub.* 4237:125.

Mitchell, H.K., Snell, E.E., and Williams, R.J. 1941. The concentration of folic acid. *J. Am. Chem. Soc.* 63:2284.

Moore, L.A. 1939. Relationship between carotene, blindness due to constriction of the optic nerve, papillary edema and nyctalopia in calves. *J. Nutr.* 17:443–59.

Moore, L.A., and Sykes, J.F. 1940. Cerebrospinal fluid pressure and vitamin A deficiency. *Am. J. Physiol.* 130:684–89.

Moore, T. 1960. The pathology of vitamin A deficiency. *Vitam. Horm.* 18:499–514.

National Research Council. 1970–1973. *Nutrient Requirements of Domestic Animals,* I–X. Nat. Acad. Sci., Washington.

National Research Council. 1971. *Atlas of Nutritional Data on United States and Canadian Feeds.* Nat. Acad. Sci., Washington.

Norris, L.C. 1941. The nutritional deficiency diseases of chickens. *J. Am. Vet. Med. Ass.* 98:200–205.

Omdahl, J.L., and DeLuca, H.F. 1973. Regulation of vitamin D metabolism and function. *Physiol. Rev.* 53:327–65.

Reid, M.E. 1954. Ascorbic acid. VIII. Effects of deficiency in animals. In Sebrell and Harris. Vol. 1, 269–347.

Reisner, E.H. 1968. Vitamin B_{12}: Deficiency effects and physiology in man. In Sebrell and Harris. Vol. 2, 220–41.

Riggs, J.K. 1940. The length of time required for depletion of vitamin A reserves in range cattle. *J. Nutr.* 20:491–500.

Robinson, F.A. 1966. *The Vitamin Co-Factors of Enzyme Systems.* Pergamon, London.

Roderick, L.M. 1931. A problem in the coagulation of the blood: "Sweet clover disease of cattle." *Am. J. Physiol.* 96:413–25.

Roderick, L.M., and Schalk, A.F. 1931. Studies on sweet clover disease. *N. Dak. Ag. Exp. Sta. Bull.* 250.

Roels, O.A. 1967. Vitamin A and carotine: Biochemical systems. In Sebrell and Harris. Vol. 1, 167–245.

Rupel, J.W., Bohstedt, G., and Hart, E.B. 1933. Vitamin D in the nutrition of the dairy calf. *Wis. Ag. Exp. Sta. Res. Bull.* 115.

Sauberlich, H.E. 1968. Vitamin B_6 group: Biochemical systems and biochemical detection of deficiency. In Sebrell and Harris. Vol. 2, 44–80.

Schwarz, K., and Foltz, C.M. 1957. Selenium as an integral part of factor 3 against dietary necrotic liver degeneration. *J. Am. Chem. Soc.* 79:3292–93.

Sebrell, W.H., and Harris, R.S. 1971. Vitamin K group. In Sebrell and Harris. Vol. 3, 417–521.

Sebrell, W.H., and Harris, R.S. *The Vitamins: Chemistry, Physiology, Pathology, Methods.* Academic Press, New York. Vol. 1 (1967), vol. 2 (1968), vol. 3 (1971), vol. 5 (1972).

Smith, E.L. 1960. *Vitamin* B_{12}. Methuen, London.

Smith, S.E., and Loosli, J.K. 1957. Cobalt and vitamin B_{12} in ruminant nutrition. *J. Dairy Sci.* 40:1215–27.

Sorensen, D.K., Kowalczyk, T., and Hentges, J.F. 1954. Cerebrospinal fluid pressure of normal and vitamin A deficient swine as determined by a lumbar puncture method. *Am. J. Vet. Res.* 15:258–60.

Stahmann, M.A., Huebner, C.F., and Link, K.P. 1941. Studies on the hemorrhagic sweet clover disease. V. Identification and synthesis of the hemorrhagic agent. *J. Biol. Chem.* 138:513–27.

Steenbock, H. 1919. White corn vs. yellow corn and a probable relation between the fat-soluble vitamine and yellow plant pigments. *Science* 50:352–53.

Steenbock, H., and Black, A. 1924. The induction of growth-promoting and calcifying properties in a ration by exposure to ultraviolet light. *J. Biol. Chem.* 61:405–22.

Tappel, A.L. 1962. Vitamin E as the biological lipid antioxidant. *Vitam. Horm.* 20:493–510.

Umbreit, W.W. 1954. Pyridoxine and related compounds. IV. Biochemical systems. In Sebrell and Harris. Vol. 3, 234–42.

U.S.D.A. 1950. Composition of foods: Raw, processed, prepared. *Ag. Handbook* no. 8. Washington.

——. 1971. *Nutritive Value of Foods.* Washington.

Wald, G. 1960. The visual function of the vitamin A. *Vitam. Horm.* 18:417–30.

Warburg, O., and Christian, W. 1932. A new oxidation enzyme and its absorption spectrum. *Biochem. Zeitscrift* 254:438–58.

——. 1934. The problem of the coenzyme. *Biochem. Zeitschrift* 274:112–16.

Wasserman, R.H., and Taylor, A.N. 1968. Vitamin D-dependent calcium-binding protein. *J. Biol. Chem. 243:3987*–93.

Wasserman, R.H. Taylor, A.N., and Kallfelz, F.A. 1966. Vitamin D and transfer of plasma calcium to intestinal lumen in chicks and rats. *Am. J. Physiol.* 211:419–23.

Waugh, W.A., and King, C.G. 1932. Isolation and identification of vitamin C. *J. Biol. Chem.* 97:325–31.

Williams, R.J., Lyman, C.M., Goodyear, G.H., Truesdail, J.H., and Holaday, D. 1933. "Pantothenic acid," a growth determinant of universal biological occurrence. *J. Am. Chem. Soc.* 55:2912–27.

Williams, R.R., and Cline, J.K. 1936. Synthesis of vitamin B_1. *J. Am. Chem. Soc.* 58:1504–05.

Wolbach, S.B., and Bessey, O.A. 1942. Tissue changes in vitamin deficiencies. *Physiol. Rev.* 22:233–89.

Wolf, G., and Johnson, B.C. 1960. Vitamin A and mucopolysaccharide biosynthesis. *Vitam. Horm.* 17:439–55.

Woods, D.D. 1940. The relation of *p*-aminobenzoic acid to the mechanism of the action of sulphanilamide. *Brit. J. Exp. Path.* 21:74–90.

Woolley, D.W. 1952. *A Study of Antimetabolites.* Wiley, New York.

——. 1959. Antimetabolites. *Science* 129:615–21.

Woolley, D.W., Waisman, H.A., and Elvehjem, C.A. 1939. Nature and partial synthesis of the chick antidermatitis factor. *J. Am. Chem. Soc.* 61:977–78.

Wostmann, B.S., and Knight, P.L. 1961. Synthesis of thiamine in the digestive tract of the rat. *J. Nutr.* 74:103–10.

PART **IV** MINERALS, BONES, AND JOINTS

CHAPTER 33

Minerals

by Virgil W. Hays and Melvin J. Swenson

All forms of living matter require inorganic elements, or minerals, for their normal life processes. Minerals that have demonstrable bodily functions either in elemental form or incorporated into specific compounds are calcium, phosphorus, magnesium, sodium, potassium, sulfur, chlorine, iron, copper, cobalt, iodine, manganese, selenium, and zinc. In addition there is evidence that chromium, fluorine, molybdenum, nickel, silicon, tin, and vanadium play a functional role in animal physiology; however, their essentiality has not been established. Although aluminum, arsenic, barium, boron, bromine, cadmium, and strontium occur in animal tissue, their significance is unknown. Virtually all elements have been found in animal tissues, and several additional ones may possess physiological significance.

The functions of minerals in animal physiology are interrelated; seldom can they be considered as single elements with independent and self-sufficient roles. The definite relationship of calcium and phosphorus in the formation of bones and teeth and the interrelationships of iron, copper, and cobalt (in vitamin B_{12}) in hemoglobin synthesis and red blood cell formation are examples. Sodium, potassium, calcium, phosphorus, and chlorine serve individually and collectively in the body fluids. However, some elements serve very specific roles, such as iodine in thyroxine and cobalt as an integral part of vitamin B_{12}. Thyroxine and vitamin B_{12}, though, are intimately involved in processes related to many other organic and inorganic nutrients.

Cobalt, copper, iodine, and selenium deficiencies in the soil and flora in certain areas of the world have led to deficiencies of these minerals in domestic animals. Also, excesses of selenium in the soil may result in levels in plants which are toxic to animals. Nutritional disorders involving the mineral elements may arise as simple deficiencies or excesses of particular elements, but more often as deficiencies or toxicities conditioned by the extent to which other organic or inorganic nutrients are present in the diet. These conditioning factors may themselves be a reflection of the soils on which the plants are grown, or they may be related to the presence of specific plants which are seleniferous or goitrogenic.

CALCIUM AND PHOSPHORUS

Calcium and phosphorus serve as the major structural elements of skeletal tissue, with more than 99 percent of the total body calcium and more than 75 percent of the total phosphorus being found in the bones and teeth. They are present in the bone principally as apatite salt and as calcium phosphate and calcium carbonate. In addition to being the structural framework, bone also is the calcium and phosphorus reservoir of the body. The calcium and phosphorus found in the trabecular portion (substantia spongiosa) of bones are in dynamic equilibrium with that of body fluids and other tissues of the body. During periods of dietary deficiency or when the requirement is increased, such as during pregnancy and lactation, calcium and phosphorus are readily mobilized from the bones to maintain normal and near constant levels (especially of calcium) in blood and other soft tissue (see Chapter 52).

Normally, blood plasma or serum contains 5 mEq of

calcium per liter (9–11 mg % for most species). However, the laying hen has calcium levels between 15 and 20 mEq/L of plasma (estrogens increase plasma calcium). The levels of calcium in erythrocytes have been reported to vary from approximately 0.05 to 1.35 mEq/L of cellular water (Streef 1939, Valberg et al. 1965).

From 45–50 percent of the plasma calcium is in the soluble, ionized form, while 40–45 percent is bound with protein, primarily albumin and other plasma proteins. The remaining 5 percent is complexed with nonionized inorganic elements depending on blood pH. Plasma calcium is essential for the coagulation of blood (see Chapter 3). In cerebrospinal fluid, calcium is present in the diffusible (ionic) form and is equal in concentration to the ionic form in blood plasma. It is also required for membrane permeability, neuromuscular excitability, transmission of nerve impulses, and activation of certain enzyme systems. A reduced extracellular blood calcium increases the irritability of nerve tissue, and very low levels may cause spontaneous discharges of nerve impulses leading to tetany and convulsions. Hypocalcemia may cause weakness of the heart similar to that caused by hyperpotassemia. Excess calcium depresses cardiac activity and leads to respiratory and cardiac failure; it may cause the heart to stop in systole. Normally, though, calcium ions increase the strength and duration of cardiac muscle contraction.

Phosphorus has more known functions than any other mineral element in the animal body. In addition to uniting with calcium and carbonate to form compounds which lend rigidity to bones and teeth, it is located in every cell of the body and is vitally concerned in many metabolic processes, including those involving the buffers in body fluids. Practically every form of energy exchange inside living cells involves the forming or breaking of high-energy bonds that link oxides of phosphorus to carbon or to carbon-nitrogen compounds. Since every biological event involves gain or loss of energy, one can readily grasp the great physiological role of phosphorus.

Dietary calcium and phosphorus are absorbed chiefly in the upper small intestine, particularly the duodenum; the amount absorbed is dependent on source, calcium-phosphorus ratio, intestinal pH, lactose intake, and dietary levels of calcium, phosphorus, vitamin D, iron, aluminum, manganese, and fat. As is the case with most nutrients, the greater the need, the more efficient the absorption. Absorption increases somewhat, though not proportionally, with increased intake. Absorption of calcium and phosphorus is facilitated by a low intestinal pH which is necessary for their solubility. Thus normal gastric secretion of hydrochloric acid or H^+ is necessary for efficient absorption. Achlorhydria decreases absorption of these minerals. The low pH of the duodenum accounts for the greater absorption in that area. Lactose has also been reported to enhance the absorption of calcium.

A major and possibly the sole function of vitamin D is its role in the intestinal and cellular absorption of calcium (see Chapter 32). Growing, pregnant, and especially lactating animals require liberal amounts of calcium and phosphorus, and in some species the ratio may be critical. A ratio of calcium to phosphorus of 1:1 to 2:1 is usually recommended. The ratio is far more critical if the level of phosphorus is marginal or inadequate or if vitamin D is limited.

Insoluble calcium salts such as calcium oxalate formed from oxalic acid pass through the intestine without being absorbed. The amounts consumed by domestic animals fed natural feedstuffs are usually not great enough to cause serious problems. Plants known to concentrate oxalic acid are rhubarb (leaves), sheep sorrel, sour dock, curly dock, and greasewood. When these plants are eaten in sufficient quantities, poisoning may occur, with an increase in coagulation time of blood.

A large part (60–80%) of the total phosphorus of cereal grains and oil seeds exists organically bound as phytic acid. Phytic acid, the hexaphosphoric acid ester of inositol, is present in cereal and legume seeds primarily as the Ca-Mg salt called phytin. Phytic acid may form insoluble salts with free calcium. Zinc may also be complexed with the calcium-phytate and lead to inefficient utilization of dietary zinc. Liberal calcium intake will compensate for the reduced availability of calcium, but it aggravates the zinc deficiency. Such a relationship has frequently led to parakeratosis in pigs.

The organically bound phosphorus, phytin phosphorus, is largely unavailable to monogastric animals, whereas ruminants are capable of utilizing it relatively well. The species difference is explained by the presence of the enzyme phytase from rumen microorganisms, which hydrolyzes the organically bound phosphorus and renders it available for absorption. This in part, coupled with the slower growth rate of ruminants, accounts for the rather

Table 33.1. Some dietary mineral requirements

Species	Body wt. (kg)	Ca (%)	P (%)	Na (%)	Cl (%)
Chickens					
Starting chicks		1	0.7	0.15	0.19
Laying hens		2.75	0.6	0.15	0.19
Pigs	30	0.65	0.5	0.1	0.13
Lactating sows	200	0.75	0.5	0.1	0.13
Beef steers	275	0.37	0.27	0.1	0.13
Pregnant beef cows	500	0.16	0.16	0.1	0.13
Lactating beef cows*	500	0.27	0.22	0.1	0.13
Veal calves	100	0.55	0.42	0.1	0.15
Dairy herd replacement	400	0.34	0.26	0.1	0.15
Lactating dairy cows*	550	0.47	0.35	0.18	0.27

* Requirement varies depending on level of milk production.

Data from National Research Council, *Nutrient Requirements of Domestic Animals,* Nat. Acad. Sci., Washington, 1963–1968, 1970–1973.

large difference in phosphorus requirements of ruminant and nonruminant animals (Table 33.1).

An excess of dietary fat or poor digestion of fat also may reduce calcium absorption through the formation of insoluble calcium soaps; however, small amounts of fat may improve calcium absorption.

An excess of iron, aluminum, or magnesium interferes with phosphorus absorption through the formation of insoluble phosphates.

Calcium and phosphorus absorbed from the intestine by the portal route are circulated through the body and readily withdrawn from the blood for use by the bones and teeth during periods of growth. Some incorporation into bone occurs at all ages. The plasma calcium level is regulated by the parathyroid hormone and thyrocalcitonin (see Chapter 52). The plasma phosphorus level is inversely related to the blood calcium level. Thyrocalcitonin decreases plasma calcium and phosphate levels while parathyroid hormone increases them.

Excess calcium and phosphorus are excreted by the kidney. Calcium and phosphorus excreted in feces are largely the unabsorbed dietary minerals; some comes from the digestive juices, including bile.

Insufficient intake of calcium, phosphorus, or vitamin D will result in rickets in young animals. In adults, calcium deficiency may cause osteomalacia, a generalized demineralization of bones, not to be confused with osteoporosis, a metabolic disorder resulting in decalcification of bone with a high incidence of fractures (see Chapter 34).

Parturient paresis, or milk fever, in cows is also associated with calcium metabolism. The malady usually occurs with the onset of profuse lactation, and the most consistent abnormality is acute hypocalcemia with the blood calcium declining from the normal of 5 mEq/L to levels of 2–3. Serum magnesium levels may be elevated or depressed, low levels being accompanied by tetany and high levels by a flaccid paralysis.

The feedstuffs used markedly affect the adequacy of both calcium and phosphorus in animal diets. Grains are low in calcium for all livestock regardless of the soil. Forage crops are relatively high in calcium, with legumes containing 1–2 percent. The calcium-phosphorus ratio in legumes ranges from 6:1 to 10:1, which often upsets the balance of these two elements and increases the requirement for phosphorus.

Phosphorus-deficient areas are prevalent in the Great Lakes area and Pacific Northwest and extend into the Dakotas and Nebraska. The application of fertilizers to the soil and the movement of feedstuffs from one area to another alter the picture of localized mineral deficiencies to some extent. Fertilization of soil, however, may not always be accompanied by an improvement in quality or even by the maintenance of existing levels of minerals. Thus phosphorus supplements in livestock nutrition are of particular importance. Table 33.2 provides data on calcium and phosphorus supplements fed to livestock.

Table 33.2. Calcium and phosphorus supplements fed to livestock *

Supplement	Ca (%)	P (%)
Bone meal, steamed	24–28	12–14
Calcite	34	0
Calcium carbonate (limestone)	38	0
Curacao Island phosphate	34	14
Diammonium phosphate	0	20–23
Dicalcium phosphate	20–24	18.5
Disodium phosphate †	0	20.5
Defluorinated rock phosphate	32	18
Monocalcium phosphate	15–21	21
Monosodium phosphate ‡	0	22.4
Oyster shell	38	0
Phosphoric acid	0	24
Sodium tripolyphosphate §	0	25.3
Soft rock phosphate	18	9

* Analysis of feed grade products varies.
† Contains 32.4% sodium.
‡ Contains 19.2% sodium.
§ Contains 32.1% sodium.

MAGNESIUM

Approximately 70 percent of the magnesium in the animal body is in bone. In addition, cardiac muscle, skeletal muscle, and nervous tissue depend on a proper balance between calcium and magnesium ions. Magnesium is an active component of several enzyme systems in which thiamine pyrophosphate is a cofactor. Oxidative phosphorylation is greatly reduced in the absence of magnesium. Magnesium is also an essential activator for the phosphate-transferring enzymes myokinase, diphosphopyridinenucleotide kinase, and creatine kinase. It also activates pyruvic acid carboxylase, pyruvic acid oxidase, and the condensing enzyme for the reactions in the citric acid cycle (see Chapter 27).

Deficiency of magnesium was first studied intensively in the rat but has since been produced in other species. Acute magnesium deficiency results in vasodilatation, with erythema and hyperemia appearing after a few days on the deficient diet (Kruse et al. 1932). Neuromuscular hyperirritability increases with the continuation of the deficiency, and may be followed eventually by cardiac arrhythmia and generalized tremors. The symptomatology of magnesium deficiency resembles that of a low-calcium tetany (Kruse et al. 1933).

Tissue analysis of animals fed a deficient diet reveals a drop in serum magnesium levels to 30–50 percent of normal within 7–9 days. (Blood plasma concentrations of magnesium are normally 2–3 mEq/L.) The concentration in other soft tissue is not altered appreciably, however. Bone apparently acts as a reservoir for magnesium, but the mobilization from bone is relatively slow. Thus a dietary deficiency may result in a marked reduction in blood magnesium before the level in bone is affected. If the deficiency is sufficiently severe, tetany and other clinical symptoms may result. On continued deficiency, the magnesium content of bone decreases and the calcium content increases. The bone magnesium is rapidly replenished when the animals are fed a diet high in magnesium (Aikawa et al. 1962, Blaxter et al. 1954, Smith 1957, Duckworth and Godden 1941).

A common form of magnesium-deficiency tetany is called *grass tetany* or wheat-pasture poisoning. Although this condition closely resembles the magnesium-deficiency syndrome and can be corrected by the administration of magnesium salts, it is not a typical magnesium deficiency. The condition occurs in ruminants grazing on rapidly growing young grasses or cereal crops and develops very quickly. Unlike other magnesium deficiency conditions, the magnesium in the bone is not normally depleted in grass tetany. Instead, high potassium levels in young succulent plants create an imbalance with magnesium, thereby creating a condition where magnesium therapy is effective.

The magnesium content of the forages and soils where grass tetany occurs is within normal ranges. But a high level of crude protein in forages has been associated with magnesium deficiency symptoms characteristic of grass tetany and of the disease known as grass staggers, which suggests that a high rumen ammonia content may interfere with the absorption or utilization of magnesium. In support of this theory is the observation that feeding high levels of ammonium carbonate increases the ammonia content of the rumen and results in a condition similar to grass staggers (Ershoff 1948, Head and Rook 1955).

The prolonged feeding of a whole milk diet, which is deficient in magnesium, to calves results in a type of magnesium deficiency that is different from grass tetany and resembles classical magnesium deficiencies observed in other species. On continued feeding of the deficient diet, a reduction in serum magnesium occurs, and magnesium content of the bone may decline to one third of normal (McCandlish 1923, Moore et al. 1938, Blaxter and Sharman 1955).

The dietary requirement for magnesium has not been well established. The National Research Council (1963–1968) estimates a requirement of 400 ppm of the diet for the pig, 500 for the chick, and 500–750 for the calf. Most diets composed of natural ingredients contain sufficient quantities of magnesium.

SODIUM

Sodium is present in animals largely as the sodium ion. The major functions of the sodium ion concern regulation of crystalloid osmotic pressure, acid-base balance, maintenance of membrane potentials, transmission of nerve impulses, and the absorptive processes of monosaccharides, amino acids, pyrimidines, and bile salts (see Chapter 26). The role of sodium in osmotic pressure regulation may be typified by consideration of the electrolyte distribution of blood plasma in mEq/L which is approximated for man as follows:

$$\begin{aligned}&Na^+ + K^+ + Ca^{++} + Mg^{++}\\&155 + 5 \quad + 5 \quad + 3\\&\quad = Cl^- + HCO_3^- + \text{proteinate} + \text{other}\\&\quad\ \ 105 + 30 \quad + \quad 18 \quad + \quad 15\end{aligned}$$

The sodium ion is the chief cation of extracellular fluids. Intracellularly, potassium and magnesium are the principal cations. Of the osmotically effective bases of extracellular fluids, sodium makes up more than 90 percent of the total. Thus changes in osmotic pressure are largely dependent on the sodium concentration. Under stress conditions, a loss of sodium may be compensated for by an increase in potassium; but the organism is limited in its capacity to substitute bases, and major losses of sodium lead to a significant lowering of osmotic pressure, and therefore to a loss of water or dehydration. Restoration is incomplete until both the base and water are replaced.

The role of sodium in acid-base balance, though important, is secondary to its role in maintaining osmotic pressure. That portion of sodium equivalent to the bicarbonate present (about 30 mEq/L of plasma water as shown above) represents most of the available base which can be used for the neutralization of acids entering the blood stream, and in conjunction with carbonic acid it affects the pH of blood. It is more accurate, however, to regard acid-base balance changes in terms of the anions present than in terms of sodium. Thus an acidosis or alkalosis with variation in plasma bicarbonates and carbon dioxide tension can exist without significant changes in sodium content. (Acid-base balance and osmotic pressure regulation are more thoroughly covered in Chapter 36.)

Commonly used vegetable foodstuffs do not contain sufficient quantities of sodium to meet the animal's need of 0.10–0.18 percent of the diet (Table 33.1). This inadequacy is overcome by including sodium chloride, common salt, in their diet or by allowing them to consume salt *ad libitum*. Sodium is readily absorbed as the sodium ion and circulates throughout the body. Excretion takes place mainly through the kidney as sodium chloride or phosphate. There are appreciable losses in perspiration, and the quantities lost by this route vary rather markedly with the humidity of the environment.

Excessive intake of sodium chloride may result in salt toxicity. The sodium ion is primarily responsible for the toxicity, since sodium acetate or sodium propionate affects the animals in a manner similar to that of sodium chloride. The amounts required for toxicity vary tremendously and are largely dependent on the availability of water to the animals. Mature cows will tolerate more than 450 g per day without ill effects, and sows and chicks will tolerate 8–10 percent of the diet as salt, provided ample water is available. Toxicity most often results when animals are deprived of salt and then have access to a brine solution or loose salt without access to sufficient water.

POTASSIUM

Potassium is the major cation of body cells and apparently serves the same general functions relating to osmotic pressure regulation and acid-base balance in the cells as does sodium in the extracellular fluids. Blood plasma of man contains about 5–6 mEq of potassium per liter (Roy et al. 1959, Meyer et al. 1950). Approximately 75–80 percent of the cation content of red cells is made up of potassium (about 125–170 mEq/L of cellular water) in many animals. However, lesser amounts are present in the erythrocytes of dogs, cats, cattle, sheep, goats, and other animals (see Chapter 2). Potassium deficiency leads to an increase in the basic amino acid concentration of the tissue fluids and some increase in cellular sodium levels as a means of maintaining cation-anion balance.

Potassium functions in maintaining acid-base balance, regulating osmotic pressure, and developing cellular membrane potentials as does sodium. When the extracellular potassium is low, transmission of nerve impulses becomes impaired, and muscular paralysis develops. Potassium influences the contractibility of smooth, skeletal, and cardiac muscle and has an effect on muscular irritability that, like that of sodium, tends to antagonize the effect of the calcium ion. However, under conditions of salt restriction, calcium appears highly important in helping to maintain the potassium content of tissue. Potassium aids in the transfer of phosphate from ATP to pyruvic acid and probably has a role in numerous other basic cellular enzymatic reactions.

Since potassium is the major intracellular cation, its depletion is associated with many functional and structural abnormalities, including impaired neuromuscular functions of skeletal, smooth, and cardiac muscle, Cardiac arrhythmias and impaired carbohydrate tolerance are abnormalities seen in potassium deficiency. Altered electrocardiograms have been reported in potassium-deficient calves (Sykes and Alfredson 1940). A pronounced increase in the QRS duration was present, being twice the normal time. The increase in time for the QRS complex to form was due to degenerative lesions in the Purkinje fibers. Excess potassium causes dilatation of the heart. When extracellular potassium reaches three times the normal value, heart block develops. The heart stops in diastole. This is why inorganic potassium salts are seldom recommended for intravenous administration. The electrocardiogram shows a decrease in heart rate, increase in PR interval, and increase in QRS duration, and eventually leads to A-V block.

Potassium deficiency affects the collecting tubules of the kidney, resulting in an inability to concentrate urine, and also causes alterations of gastric secretions and intestinal motility (see References).

Because of their related roles in regulating cation balance and osmotic pressure in intracellular and extracellular fluids, it has been suggested that the relative quantities of sodium and potassium in the diet are critical. However, plant products contain many times as much potassium as sodium, yet animals do well on such diets. The potassium requirement of chicks and pigs is approximately 0.20–0.25 percent of the diet (Jensen et al. 1961, O'Dell and Savage 1957); the requirement is affected to some extent by the growth rate of the animal (Gillis 1948) and the protein level of the diet (Wooley and Mickelson 1954, Leach et al. 1959). The rapid-growing animals apparently have a higher requirement for potassium, and increasing the protein level increases the requirement. The turkey, for example, has a relatively high requirement for potassium (0.4–0.5% of the diet). The requirement of ruminants has not been established; however, the levels in natural feedstuffs normally preclude a deficiency.

CHLORINE

A close relationship exists between chloride and sodium ions. The principal anion in extracellular fluid is chloride. It is the chief anion of the gastric juice and is accompanied by the hydrogen ion in nearly equal amounts. The chloride of the gastric secretions is derived from blood chloride and is normally reabsorbed during later stages of digestion in the lower intestine.

Excessive depletion of chloride ions through losses in the gastric secretions or by deficiencies in the diet may lead to alkalosis due to an excess of bicarbonate, since the inadequate level of chloride is partially replaced or compensated for by bicarbonate. On a chloride-deficient diet, the excretion of chloride in the urine or perspiration is markedly reduced.

Chloride is involved in the regulation of extracellular osmotic pressure and makes up over 60 percent of the anions in this fluid compartment. Thus the chloride ion is important in acid-base balance. The concentration of the chloride ion is subject to more variation than that of sodium, since other anions, especially bicarbonates, can exchange for the chloride. The optimum dietary intakes of sodium and chloride approximate a 1:1 ratio. Excess chloride and a constant level of sodium can result in acidosis, whereas an excess of sodium and a constant level of chloride can result in alkalosis. (Cohen et al.

1972, Hurwitz et al. 1973). The ratios in Table 33.1 appear satisfactory, provided there is an adequate level of both elements in the diet.

Chloride is excreted in the feces, sweat, and urine primarily as sodium or potassium chloride, although it may be accompanied by ammonium ions when base needs to be conserved (see Chapter 36).

IODINE

Iodine functions in animals as a basic component in forming the thyroid hormones thyroxine and mono-, di-, and triiodothyronine (see Chapter 52). In the absence of pathological conditions, the major factor affecting the secretion of thyroxine and related compounds by the thyroid gland is the dietary intake and biological availability of iodine. The ion is freely diffusible, is readily absorbed from the gastrointestinal tract, and is excreted mainly in the urine at a relatively constant rate provided the dietary intake is sufficient. Plasma iodide is trapped by the thyroid gland and oxidized to a form available for incorporation into thyroxine by combination with thyroglobulin. Proteolysis results in release of thyroxine and its intermediates. Deiodination of the hormone intermediates supplies reactive iodine for reincorporation into the thyroglobulin protein. Much of the released iodine reenters the iodide pool, so that little is wasted, especially if the diet is limited in iodine.

Iodine deficiency has been stated to be the most widespread of all mineral deficiencies in grazing stock (Allman and Hamilton 1948). It can be due to a deficiency of iodine in the diet or the presence of dietary constituents which interfere with the use of iodine by the thyroid gland. As a result, the production and general health of farm animals are markedly affected.

Plants are highly variable in iodine content depending on the species, soil type including its iodine content, fertilizer, and climate. Iodine-deficient areas are found in the interior of all countries, especially in areas where wind or rainfall are unable to carry traces from the sea and where the soil has been depleted by leaching by heavy iodine-poor rains, or where there is little rainfall (Fig. 33.1). Feedstuffs or forages produced in these areas may be deficient in iodine and affect the growth and reproduction (see Chapter 52).

Animals fed a prepared feed or concentrate may be provided with supplemental iodine by incorporating iodine into the salt, mineral mixture, or other concentrates. It is more difficult to assure adequate intake by grazing animals. The most effective way is by incorporating potassium iodate into the salt offered the animals. The iodate, stabilized potassium iodide, or pentacalcium orthoperiodate is preferable because it is less subject to losses from leaching or volatilization.

Goitrogenic activity has been found in many plants, including virtually all cruciferous plants, soybeans, linseed, peas, and peanuts. The goitrogenic substances in the plant material include thioglycosides, thiocyanates, and perchlorates. Thiocyanate and perchlorate ions act by inhibiting the selective concentration of iodine by the thyroid (Wolff et al. 1946). Their actions are reversible with iodine. Thioglycosides from brassica seeds and other goitrogens of the thiouracil type act by inhibiting hormonogenesis in the thyroid gland, and their effects are either not reversible or only partly so with iodine supplementation.

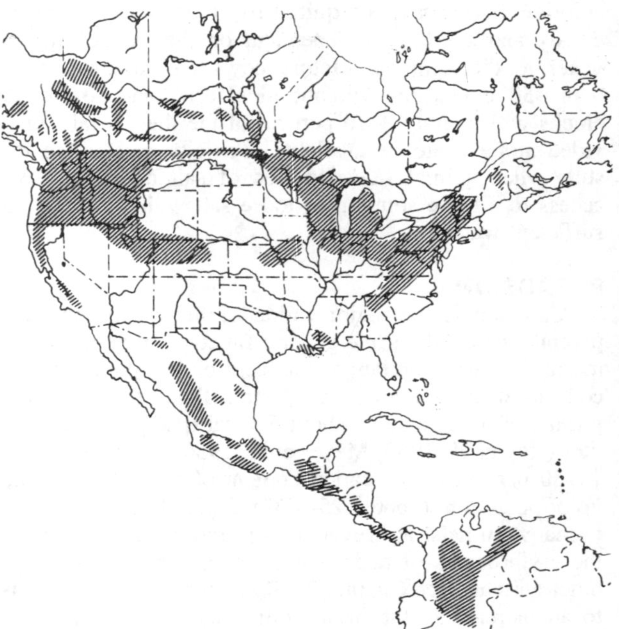

Figure 33.1 Areas of endemic goiter caused by deficiency of iodine in the United States and adjoining countries. (From Kelly and Snedden, *Endemic Goiter*, World Health Organization, Geneva, 1960.)

Goitrogens have been demonstrated in the milk of cows following their ingestion of cruciferous plants in grazing or as fodder (Clements and Wishart 1956, Clements 1957). The goitrogenic factor in the milk of such animals is not overcome by supplemental iodine. This could contribute to the endemism of goiter in areas in which the animals consume such feedstuffs and their milk is subsequently consumed.

The iodine requirement of animals has not been clearly established. Creek et al. (1954) placed the requirement of chicks at 0.3 ppm of the diet or the equivalent of 75 μg per 1000 Calories of metabolizable energy. Earlier work (Marine and Lenhart 1909a,b) arrived at an estimated requirement of 1–2 μg per day for rats, which, on a similar caloric basis as above, would be approximately 30–65 μg per 1000 Calories. In the absence of goitrogenic substances in the diet, 0.2–0.3 ppm appears sufficient at least for monogastric animals. The feeding of iodized salt containing 0.01 percent stabilized iodine or 0.0076 percent iodine at the rate of 0.25–0.50 percent of the diet or by allowing it *ad libitum* will prevent symptoms of iodine deficiency. The animals will tolerate 50–100 times the actual requirement without ill effects, and if feedstuffs include goitrogenic substances, dietary levels well above the minimum requirement may be not only desirable but necessary.

SULFUR

Sulfur is usually not considered in discussions of inorganic metabolism since only an insignificant part of the sulfur ingested is inorganic. By far the greatest portion of sulfur is in the amino acids, cystine and methionine, in protein molecules (see Chapter 29). Proteins vary widely in sulfur content, depending on their amino acid composition, but average about 1 percent sulfur. The sulfur amino acid requirement for the monogastric animals is approximately 3–4 percent of the total protein requirement. Thus the sulfur requirement would approximate 0.6–0.8 percent of the total protein. However, for metabolic purposes, this is necessary as the preformed amino acid; hence sulfur deficiencies are reflected as sulfur-containing amino acid deficiencies.

Ruminants depending largely on nonprotein nitrogen sources, such as urea, biuret, or ammonium phosphate, may need supplemental inorganic sulfur. This sulfur is utilized by the microorganisms for synthesis of methionine and cystine.

The end products of sulfur metabolism are taurine and sulfuric acid. The sulfuric acid is either neutralized and excreted as inorganic sulfates in the urine or conjugated with phenol, glucuronic acid, or indoxyl. The taurine is conjugated with cholic acid and excreted in the bile.

Other sulfur compounds of biological significance include cyanate (SCN) in saliva and other fluids, ergothioneine of the red blood cells, glutathione which is present in all cells, and chondroitin sulfate which serves a structural function in cartilage, bone, tendons, blood vessel walls, and so forth. The primary function of sulfur is as the disulfide linkage, -S-S-, of such organic compounds.

FLUORINE

Fluorine is an important mineral in the formation of bones and teeth. A proper intake is essential to achieve maximum resistance to dental caries. Fluorine deficiency in terms of soft-tissue lesions or specific metabolic functions has not been reported under natural conditions; however, there is recent evidence that low fluoride intake retards growth rate, reduces fertility, and results in anemia. Since these symptoms are rather nonspecific, the essentiality of fluoride is only tentative (Messer et al. 1974).

A fluorine concentration of about 1–2 ppm added to the drinking water will result in a marked reduction in dental caries in man. Apparently fluorine, which is deposited in the enamel of teeth during their formation, increases crystal size and perfection in the biological apatites, and reduces the solubility of enamel in the acids that are produced by the bacteria implicated in tooth decay. Fluorides may also inhibit bacterial action. In the growing animal, fluorine replaces the hydroxyl group in the formation of the apatite structure, but there is only limited metabolic exchange of fluorine in the previously formed bone. In the mature animal, the incorporation is apparently limited to the latter mechanism.

Intestinal absorption of fluorine is highly variable depending in a large part on the solubility of that ingested. Mammalian species differ little in their susceptibility to fluorine, but poultry have a higher tolerance due probably to a lower absorption and to increase excretion of the element. In general, animals will tolerate a considerably high level of fluorine in natural feedstuffs or in rock phosphate than in the highly soluble forms such as sodium fluoride (Table 33.3).

Fluorine is widely but unevenly distributed in nature. Water normally contains traces, but the fluorine content may vary markedly. Water high in fluorides is usually from deep wells in which the fluorine comes from deep rock formations and not from surface contaminations. Surface water rarely contains as much as 1 ppm and more often contains 0.1 ppm. By contrast the deep well water from the Texas Panhandle and Colorado, where chronic fluorine toxicity is endemic, may contain 2–5 ppm. If the water is allowed to stand in tanks, evaporation may result in a much higher concentration.

Fluorine content of the soil may affect the fluorine content of forages, though plant materials seldom contain more than 1–2 ppm, even though the soil or the phosphate fertilizers used may be considerably higher. Contamination of the plant material from soil being splashed or blown onto the plant or from irrigation water high in fluorine may leave fluorine deposits on the plants, and may result in fluorosis even though the actual plant material contains safe amounts of bound fluorine. Excessive fluorine intakes may also result from grazing too close,

Table 33.3. Safe levels of fluorine in the total diet (ppm)

Species	NaF or other soluble fluoride	Phosphatic limestone or rock phosphate
Dairy cow	30–50	60–100
Beef cow	40–50	65–100
Sheep	70–100	100–200
Chickens	150–300	300–400
Turkeys	300–400	
Swine	70–100	100–200

From National Research Council, *The Fluorosis Problems in Livestock Production,* Nat. Acad. Sci., Washington, 1960. For more detailed information see National Research Council, *Effects of Fluorides in Animals,* Nat. Acad. Sci., Washington, 1974.

when the animals actually consume sufficient amounts of soil or dust to result in fluorosis.

The more common fluorosis results when the animals consume foods that have been contaminated with or supplemented with fluoride-bearing minerals, or when they inhale or ingest fumes and dusts emitted from industrial plants. In the processing of rock phosphates, in smelting of aluminum and other ores, and in ceramic industries, dust or fumes containing fluorides may be given off. This fluorine in large amounts may result in increased concentrations in the forages and water in the surrounding area.

The principal fluorine-containing minerals in animal feeds are the phosphatic limestones or rock phosphate. Most of the rock phosphate used in animal feeds has been defluorinated to the extent that it will not result in toxic levels (Table 33.4). However, other ration components and water may contribute appreciable amounts.

The symptoms of fluorine toxicity are similar for all species. Quantities of fluorine that show no gross ill effects at first may eventually be harmful. The animal is protected by increased urinary excretion and by deposition in the skeletal tissue. When the upper limits of the protective mechanisms are reached, the soft tissues are flooded with fluorine, resulting in metabolic disturbances and finally death. Voluntary reduction in food intake occurs as the critical stage is reached. Thus typical symptoms of starvation are observed in acute fluorine toxicity.

Various clinical signs of fluorosis become apparent before the critical stage is reached. The teeth become modified in shape, size, and color; they become pitted; and the pulp cavities may be exposed due to fracture or wear (Fig. 33.2). These abnormalities occur only in animals exposed to excess fluorine prior to the eruption of the permanent teeth. Fluorine is an enzyme inhibitor. When this happens in odontoblasts and osteoblasts, teeth and bone deformities occur. Exostoses of the jaw and long bones develop and the joints become thickened and ankylosed, resulting in lameness. As these conditions become more advanced, there is a reduction in food consumption, accompanied by reduced growth or weight loss. Reproductive performance is not affected by fluorosis unless food intake is severely depressed. Signs of fluorosis are rarely seen in the newborn or suckling animals, as placental and mammary transfer of fluorine is limited.

Table 33.4. Levels of daily fluorine ingestion from raw rock phosphate compatible with growth

Species	F per kg body wt. per day (mg)
Cattle	2–3
Swine	8
Poultry	35–70

Data from National Research Council, *The Fluorosis Problems in Livestock Production*, Nat. Acad. Sci., Washington, 1960

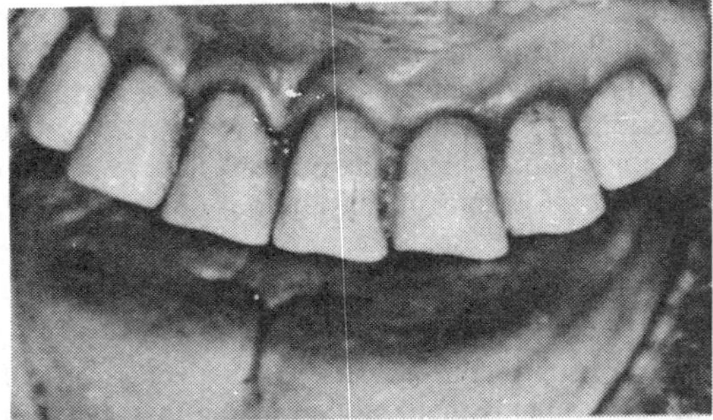

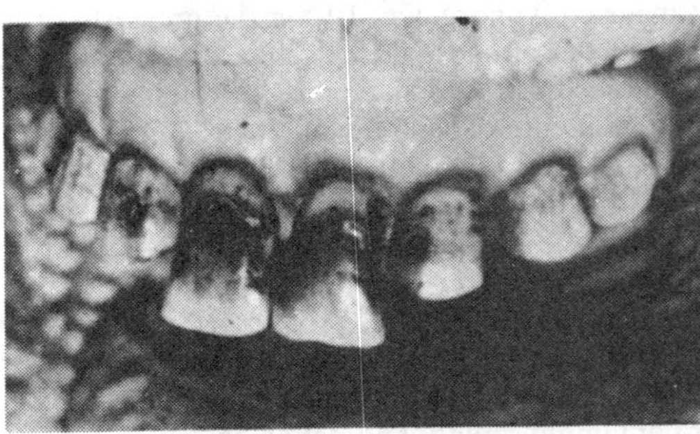

Figure 33.2 Teeth of cow (*above*) fed ration containing 7 ppm fluorine. Teeth of cow (*below*) fed ration containing 107 ppm fluorine; note excess chalkiness, staining, deep erosions, and hypoplasia of enamel and teeth. (From Hobbs et al. 1954, *U. Tenn. Ag. Exp. Sta. Bull.* 235.)

No single symptom of fluorosis is proof of the toxicity. The results of chemical analysis of the bone, teeth, and urine, in conjunction with evidence of chalkiness, mottling, erosion of enamel, enamel hypoplasia, and excessive wear of the teeth, as well as evidence of anorexia, inanition, and bone changes, are all important in recognizing fluorine toxicosis.

SELENIUM

The recognition of the nutritional significance of selenium is of recent origin and is still somewhat confounded by its potential toxic effects. The beneficial level for animals is approximately 0.1 ppm of the diet; levels of 5–8 ppm are toxic.

Certain plants grown on soils containing high levels of selenium (0.5–40 ppm) concentrate selenium and are potentially hazardous to animals. Where soil is low in selenium, the incidence of white muscle disease of lambs and calves is high. In areas where soil is high in selenium, white muscle disease is not a serious problem (Fig. 33.3). Selenium is incorporated into the plant primarily by replacement of sulfur in the amino acids methionine and cystine. Toxic levels in plants result in blind staggers in horses and the sloughing of hair and hoofs in horses and cattle. The animals develop lameness, and death in such cases is mainly due to starvation resulting from the locomotive impediment.

Organic and inorganic selenium compounds function in preventing certain disease conditions that have in the past been associated with vitamin E deficiency. Selenium will prevent liver necrosis in rats, white muscle disease in lambs, and exudative diathesis in chicks. It will not protect against certain other manifestations of vitamin E deficiency, for example, muscular dystrophy in rabbits or reproductive failure in rats, turkeys, and chickens.

Selenium is a component of glutathione peroxidase. A selenium deficiency in rats, chicks, and sheep causes a marked reduction in the activity of this enzyme in various tissues (Hoekstra 1975). Selenium protects the organism from oxidative damage to cell membranes through its role in glutathione peroxidase by destroying H_2O_2, whereas vitamin E protects against damage by preventing the formation of the lipid hydroperoxides.

The activity of selenium appears to be closely related to the antioxidative properties of α-tocopherol (vitamin E) and coenzyme Q (ubiquinone). It enhances the overall activity of the α-ketoglutarate oxidase system, probably by affecting the decarboxylation reaction. Further, selenium may be involved in the transduction of photons to electrical signals in the photoreceptor mechanism of the eye (Siren 1964). Supporting this theory is the observation that the retinas of terns and roedeer, which are known to have good visual acuity, contain 600–800 ppm of selenium, whereas the retina of the guinea pig, known for its poor visual acuity, contains only 8–10.

MOLYBDENUM

Molybdenum has been identified as a cofactor of several metalloenzyme systems including xanthine oxidase, aldehyde oxidase, nitrate reductase, and hydrogenase. Its occurrence in these metalloflavoproteins suggests that it is an essential nutrient. However, a definite requirement for molybdenum has been difficult to confirm as no characteristic syndrome of molybdenum deficiency has been recognized, and animals have performed normally on extremely low dietary levels of molybdenum.

Some evidence of a need for molybdenum has been found in studies involving the mineral element tungsten, which acts as an antagonist to molybdenum. Leach and Norris (1957) reported a growth response to molybdenum in chicks on a diet containing 0.5–0.8 ppm provided that tungsten was also added to the diet. Also Reid et al. (1956) reported a response to supplemental molybdenum by chicks fed a diet containing 1 ppm of molybdenum. They postulated that naturally occurring molybdenum was largely unavailable. Ellis and Pfander (1960) reported a growth response in lambs from supplemental molybdenum added to a diet containing 0.4 ppm; however, they suggested that the molybdenum was rendering its influence through a stimulatory effect on the microbial degradation of cellulose in the rumen.

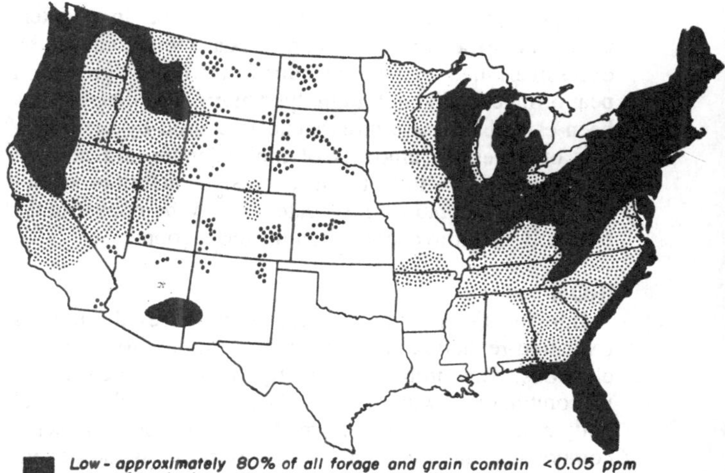

Figure 33.3. Distribution of selenium in forages and grains in the United States. (Reproduced from Kubota and Allaway, Geographic distribution of trace element problems, in Mortvedt, Giordano, and Lindsay, eds., *Micronutrients in Agriculture,* Soil Science Society of America, Madison, Wis., 1972, pp. 525–54, by permission of the Soil Science Society of America.)

Askew (1958) presented evidence that low molybdenum intake is a predisposing cause to renal xanthine calculi. A high incidence of such calculi occurred in sheep restricted to the Moutere Hills pastures of the south island of New Zealand. The pasture forages of the area contained 0.03 ppm molybdenum or less. Sheep grazing these pastures also had subnormal molybdenum levels in the liver. The incidence of calculi was lower in areas nearby in which the forages contained 0.4 ppm or more of molybdenum. The incidence was also lower in the calculi areas following fertilization of the pastures; however, changes in molybdenum concentration of the forages were accompanied by other changes in composition including an increase in protein content.

A reciprocal antagonism exists between molybdenum and copper. Molybdenum, in the presence of sulfates, limits copper retention in cattle and sheep; however, neither molybdenum nor sulfates alone affect copper retention. Chronic copper poisoning associated with high levels of copper in the liver of ruminants has been observed under conditions of moderate intake of copper but very low dietary levels of molybdenum and sulfate. Conversely, excessive levels of molybdenum and sulfate may lead to characteristic symptoms of copper deficiency even with apparently adequate intake of copper.

Supplemental copper has been beneficial in counteracting a diarrhea of cattle, teart or peat scours, caused by excessive intake of molybdenum from forages grown on peat or muck soils high in molybdenum. The diarrhea has been established as a molybdenosis caused by the ingestion of excessive amounts of molybdenum and may be reproduced by administering excessive quantities of sodium- or ammonium molybdate. It may be counteracted by orally or intravenously administered copper.

IRON

Iron functions in the respiratory processes through its oxidation-reduction activity and its ability to transport electrons. This property is greatly enhanced when iron is in combination with protein. Iron exists in the animal body mainly in complex forms bound to protein as heme compounds (hemoglobin or myoglobin), as heme enzymes (mitochondrial and microsomal cytochromes, catalase, and peroxidase), or as nonheme compounds (flavin-Fe enzymes, transferrin, and ferritin). Only negligible amounts of free inorganic iron are found in the animal body. Ionic iron tends to form complexes with six coordinate bonds, linking with oxygen or nitrogen disposed in appropriate groupings. The porphyrins, tetrapyrrole compounds, combine with iron in this way, their nitrogen atoms satisfying four of the coordinate valences (see Fig. 2.2). Heme, one such complex of protoporphyrin and iron, links with a number of different proteins to form compounds that are active in mammalian respiration: hemoglobin, myoglobin, the cytochromes, cytochrome oxidase, peroxidases, and catalases. Hemoglobin and the catalases contain four heme groups per molecule, whereas myoglobin, the cytochromes, and peroxidases contain one heme group per molecule (see Chapter 2). The protein component of these compounds determines their specific function, but heme is the functional group and iron serves as the carrier of oxygen or transporter of electrons in each.

Hemoglobin iron represents approximately 60 percent of the total body iron (Hahn 1937). Thus any factor influencing the hemoglobin level in the blood greatly affects the total iron status of the body. Myoglobin represents only about 3 percent of the total iron, but is appreciably higher in some species, e.g. horse and dog. Hahn estimated that myoglobin contains 7 percent of the total iron in the dog. Species differences in total body iron are relatively small in adults but appreciable in the newborn. Individual variation in iron content within a species can be large in the iron storage organs such as liver, spleen, and kidney, but is relatively small in other organs of the body.

Iron exists in the blood mainly as hemoglobin in the erythrocytes and as transferrin in the plasma. Small quantities of ferritin and nonheme iron also exist in the erythrocytes. Figure 33.4 outlines iron metabolism.

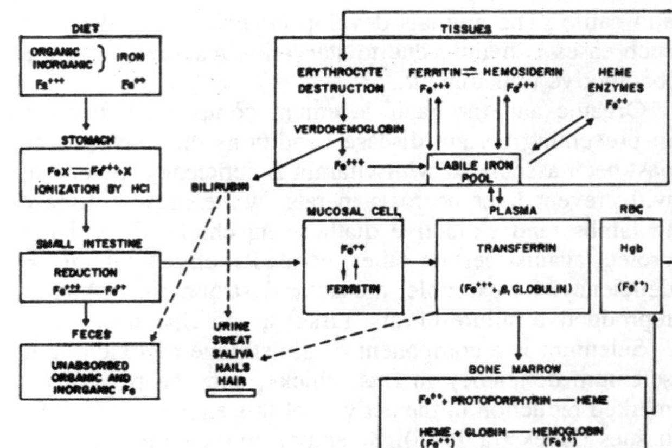

Figure 33.4. Outline of iron metabolism. (From M.M. Wintrobe, *Clinical Hematology*, 5th ed., Lea & Febiger, Philadelphia, 1961.)

The nonhemoglobin iron in blood, transferrin, is bound to β-globulin. Two atoms of ferric iron unite with the plasma protein, which serves as an iron carrier in the vascular system. There are at least three different transferrin proteins (Smithies and Hiller 1959), and normally only about 40 percent of the transferrin protein is bound with iron, the remainder being known as the latent iron-binding capacity. The plasma iron concentration is normally 100–300 μg/100 ml. In iron deficiency of pigs and other animals it may be as low as 40–50 μg/100 ml. When plasma iron is low, ferritin in hepatic and other cells is released. Adrenocortical hormones (glucocorticoids) play a part in regulating the level of plasma iron. During stress, when the hypothalamus, adenohypophysis, and adrenal cortex are activated, regardless of the source, the plasma iron decreases (Cartwright et al. 1951, Hamilton et al. 1950). Simultaneously with the lowering of the plasma iron the erythrocyte sedimentation rate increases (see Chapter 2).

In monogastric species iron is absorbed principally as the ferrous state from the duodenum (Fig. 33.4). Iron in foods occurs predominantly in the ferric form and also in combination with organic compounds. Therefore, it must be released from the organic molecule and reduced prior to absorption. The fact that ferric salts have been shown to be relatively well utilized indicates that gastrointestinal conditions are favorable to such reduction.

Reducing substances in the food, such as ascorbic acid and cysteine, may aid in the reduction of iron from the ferric to the ferrous state and enhance iron absorption. Dietary factors may also interfere with iron absorption, for example, higher levels of phosphates reduce absorption (Kenney et al. 1949). Phytates also interfere with the absorption of this element by the formation of insoluble iron-phytate, but it is questionable whether the normal phytates of feeds are of much practical significance in this respect.

Iron absorption is quantitatively controlled by body requirements (McCance and Widdowson 1938). With reduced iron stores or increased erythropoiesis, iron absorption is enhanced, whereas in the presence of adequate iron stores and normal erythropoiesis, iron absorption is diminished. Evidence suggests that an active carrier protein system carries the iron across the mucosal cell membrane (Dowdle et al. 1960).

Except for what is known about the suckling pig, much remains to be learned about the iron requirements of domestic animals. The abundance of iron in natural feedstuffs and macromineral supplements largely explains the limited interest shown in establishing iron requirements, especially for ruminants.

The pig is born with low iron stores and develops an iron-deficiency anemia if not provided with supplementary iron. The factors responsible for the onset of anemia in the baby pig are its relatively low stores of iron at birth (approximately 45–50 mg per pig), its high growth rate early in life, and the low level of iron in sow milk. Pigs reach 4–5 times their birth weight by 3 weeks of age. Such a rapid increase in body size requires a retention of 6–8 mg of iron per day. Since sow milk will provide only about 1 mg per day (Venn et al. 1947), a source of supplemental iron must be provided. The absorption rate of iron is relatively low; thus about 15 mg of oral iron must be provided daily to maintain adequate erythropoiesis and iron stores.

COPPER

Copper is an integral part of cytochrome A (Okunuki et al. 1958, Takemori 1960) and cytochrome oxidase (Griffiths and Wharton 1961). It appears that copper functions in the cytochrome system in the same way as iron, that is, through a change in valence. The enzymes tyrosinase, laccase, ascorbic acid oxidase, cytochrome oxidase, plasma monoamine oxidase, ceruloplasmin, and uricase contain copper, and their activity is dependent on this element (Allen and Bodine 1941, Dressler and Dawson 1960).

Copper is present in blood plasma as a copper-protein complex, ceruloplasmin (Holmberg and Laurell 1948). Essentially, all of the copper in plasma is in firm combination with protein, but evidence from studies with electrophoresis and sedimentation indicates that ceruloplasmin is not a homogeneous protein. Ceruloplasmin differs from the iron protein, transferrin, in that it shows oxidative activity, especially toward *p*-phenylenediamine. The activity is proportional to the copper content, which averages about 0.35 percent, and it is inhibited by substances that inhibit copper-dependent oxidative enzymes (Brown and White 1961). The function of ceruloplasmin appears to be enzymatic.

The dietary rquirement for copper is affected by the level of some other minerals in the diet, being increased in ruminants by excessive molybdenum. Excess dietary copper results in an accumulation of copper in the liver with a decrease in blood hemoglobin concentration and packed cell volume. Liver function is impaired in copper poisoning. Jaundice results from hemolysis of erythrocytes; death occurs unless treatment is begun. Treatment is based on the rationale that excess molybdenum may cause copper deficiency. And in fact molybdenum in conjunction with the sulfate ion is effective in treating copper poisoning in ruminants (Pierson and Aanes 1958).

Since liver is the main storage organ for copper, it provides a useful index of the copper status of the animal. There are variations in liver copper concentrations within and between species. The copper concentration in the liver of man, pigs, dogs, cats, and domestic fowls ranges from 10–50 ppm on a dry-weight, fat-free basis. Beck (1956) reported liver values of 100–400 ppm for sheep and cattle. However, Pierson and Aanes (1958) reported values of 15–21 ppm in normal sheep, and in those with copper poisoning 390–540 ppm on a dry-weight basis. There is no evidence of species differences in ability to absorb copper. The liver concentration is higher in the newborn than in adults, but the level may be reduced in the young if the dam is fed a deficient diet. By feeding the recommended dietary level of copper to the dam the copper concentration in the tissue of the newborn will be normal. The administration of excess copper during pregnancy will not result in excess storage of copper in the liver of the newborn (Allcroft and Uvarov 1959).

In the monogastric animal, copper is absorbed mainly in the upper part of the small intestine, where the pH of the contents is still acid. The availability of copper is influenced by the chemical form, the sulfides being less available than the carbonate, oxide, or sulfate. In general, copper is poorly absorbed, with only about 5–10 percent of the ingested copper being absorbed and retained (Bowland et al. 1961). Under normal conditions 90 percent or more of the ingested copper appears in the feces. Most of the fecal copper is unabsorbed dietary copper, but some of it comes from bile, which is the major pathway of copper excretion. Biliary obstruction increases the excretion of the copper through the kidney and intestinal wall.

Clinical disorders associated with copper deficiencies include anemia, bone disorders, neonatal ataxia, depigmentation and abnormal growth of hair or wool, impaired growth and reproductive performance, heart failure, and gastrointestinal disturbances. The incidence of these disorders varies widely among species. For example, in sheep the depigmentation and abnormal growth of wool are frequently observed first. Neonatal ataxia occurs frequently in lambs from copper-deficient ewes, but it has never been noted in pigs or dogs.

Copper functions in the utilization of iron in an early stage of hematopoiesis (Elvehjem 1935). In iron deficiency, the number of cells is not affected, but the cells are smaller (microcytic) and usually hypochromic; whereas, copper deficiency reduces the number of cells but not their hemoglobin concentration. However, the nature of copper deficiency anemias varies with species. In rabbits and pigs it is hypochromic and microcytic, and indistinguishable from iron deficiency (Lahey et al. 1952, Smith et al. 1944). In lambs it is hypochromic and microcytic (Bennetts and Beck 1942); in cattle, ewes, and chicks it is hypochromic and macrocytic (Bennetts and Beck 1942, Bennetts et al. 1946, McDougall 1947); and in dogs, normochromic and normocytic (Baxter and Van Wyk 1953). Such varied differences suggest other complicating environmental or nutritional factors in addition to species variation. Copper deficiency results in an increase in iron in the liver, whereas an excess of copper results in a decrease in iron content of the liver, reflecting the role of copper in the utilization of iron.

Spontaneous bone fractures have been observed in sheep and cattle grazing copper-deficient pastures. The fractured bones exhibit a mild degree of osteoporosis along with other defects. In pigs, copper deficiency results in a failure of deposition of calcium salts in the normal cartilage matrix (Follis et al. 1955).

Bennetts and Chapman (1937) revealed that a long-recognized nervous disorder of lambs is associated with copper deficiency. Various names, including swayback, lamkruis, renguera, and Gingin rickets, have been given to this condition. All these disorders appear to be pathologically the same as the neonatal enzootic ataxia described by Bennetts and Chapman. The changes in ataxia may include symmetrical cerebral demyelination, degeneration of motor tracts in the spinal cord, and changes in the neurons of the brain stem. The lesions are irreversible and may commence as early as 6 weeks before birth and continue until delivery. The condition is frequently observed in lambs but has also been reported in cattle and goats. It has not been reported in pigs.

Lack of pigmentation and marked changes in the growth and physical appearance of hair, fur, or wool may result from copper deficiency. The mechanism is related to the biochemical conversion of tyrosine to melanin, since this conversion is catalyzed by copper-containing oxidases (Raper 1928, Lerner and Fitzpatrick 1950). The deficiency leads to progressively less crimp in wool until the fibers emerge as straight hairlike growth that has been referred to as stringy or steely wool. The fact that straight wool has more sulfhydryl groups and fewer disulfide groups suggests that copper is required for the oxidation of -SH to -S-S- (disulfide) groups in keratin synthesis (Burley 1954).

Copper deficiency has also been associated with cardiac hypertrophy and sudden cardiac failure. These are reported to be greater than can be accounted for by the anemia resulting from the deficiency (Gubler et al. 1957).

The copper requirement varies among species to some extent but is influenced to a greater degree by its relationship with and the intake of other mineral elements such as iron, molybdenum, and sulfate. The minimum requirement is probably near 1–2 ppm of the diet for sheep and cattle and 4–6 ppm for pigs and chicks.

COBALT

The only established function of cobalt is its role as a component of the vitamin B_{12} molecule. Approximately 4.5 percent of the molecular weight of B_{12} (cyanocobalamin) is contributed by elemental cobalt (see Chapter 32).

Cobalt is readily absorbed into the blood stream and excreted primarily in the urine. It is firmly bound in the vitamin B_{12} molecule. Excessive intake results in polycythemia, which is apparently due to the inhibition by cobalt of certain respiratory enzyme systems, e.g. cytochrome oxidase and succinic dehydrogenase.

Although ruminants require a dietary source of cobalt, it appears that it is used solely as a part of the B_{12} molecule and that the animal is completely dependent on the microflora within the rumen for vitamin B_{12} biosynthesis. Deficiencies of cobalt in ruminants result in anorexia, wasting of the skeletal muscle, fatty livers, hemosiderosis of the spleen, and anemia.

A coenzyme form of B_{12} is required in the conversion of methylmalonate to succinate, an intermediate step in the metabolism of propionic acid. Thus cobalt, as a component of B_{12}, is required for a reaction which is more prevalent in the energy (propionate) metabolism of ruminants than in nonruminants. This likely accounts for the apparent high requirement for cobalt or B_{12} by the ruminant. Vitamin B_{12} also plays a role in methylating choline and thymine. The latter is required in the synthesis of DNA, which regulates cell division and growth.

Nonruminants require preformed vitamin B_{12} to meet their metabolic needs; however, in ruminants practical control of B_{12} deficiency may be achieved by supplementation of the diet with cobalt or treating the pastures with cobalt salts or ore. (See Figure 33.5 for cobalt-deficient areas.) Also, cobalt deficiency in ruminants has been successfully alleviated by use of cobalt oxide pellets, which remain in the reticulum or rumen to yield a relatively steady supply of cobalt to the rumen fluid. However, in the case of young animals the pellets may become coated with a calcium phosphate deposit rendering the cobalt unavailable to the animal.

The estimated dietary requirement of vitamin B_{12} for pigs and chicks is 0.01–0.02 ppm (10–20 μg/kg diet) which would represent only 0.0005–0.0010 ppm of cobalt. There is little evidence that chicks and pigs require cobalt in addition to that needed as B_{12}. The estimated

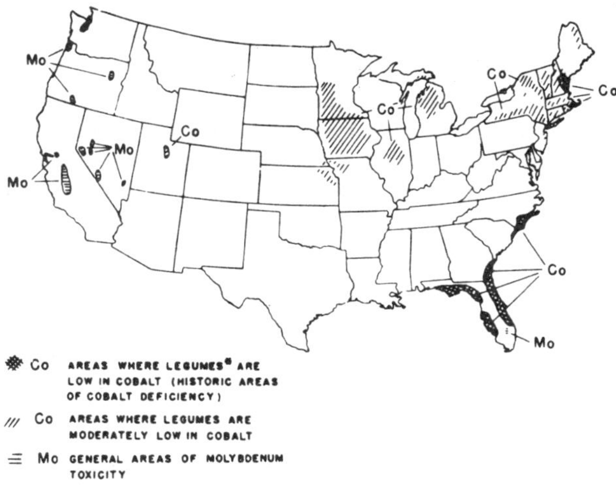

Figure 33.5. Soil status of cobalt and molybdenum in the United States. (Courtesy of J. Kubota.)

cobalt requirement for ruminants is 0.07–0.10 ppm of the diet or several times that included in the required B_{12} for nonruminants. This difference is related to the inefficiency of the biosynthesis of vitamin B_{12} in the rumen and the additional amount required for the energy metabolism of methylmalonate.

ZINC

Zinc is distributed widely in plant and animal tissues and is a functional component of several enzyme systems, including carbonic anhydrase, carboxypeptidase, alkaline phosphatase, lactic dehydrogenase, and glutamic dehydrogenase.

Carbonic anhydrase is present in erythrocytes, kidney tubules, gastrointestinal mucosa, and glandular epithelium. In erythrocytes it functions by combining carbon dioxide and water in peripheral capillary blood and then releasing carbon dioxide from pulmonary capillary blood into the alveoli. These changes are based on pressure differences of carbon dioxide.

Zinc is important in an enzymic system that is necessary for the synthesis of RNA. RNA is present in cytoplasm and in the nucleoli and chromosomes of the nuclei and is essential for the growth of germinal and somatic cells. Zinc in testes and the prostate gland in relatively large quantities is important in the maturation of spermatozoa.

Lactic dehydrogenase is most abundant in the kidney, heart, and skeletal muscle. It catalyzes the reversible reaction for the interconversions of pyruvic and lactic acid. In peptidases it is important in proteolytic digestion of foodstuffs.

Zinc occurs in all living cells. The zinc found in the pancreas exhibits an active metabolic turnover, a large proportion being secreted in pancreatic juice. The addition of zinc to insulin solutions results in a delay in the physiological action of insulin and prolongs the hypoglycemia produced when injected. Apparently zinc is not a part of the insulin molecule (Sanger 1959) but it does combine readily with insulin.

Tucker and Salmon observed (1955) that elemental zinc cures and prevents parakeratosis (thickening or hyperkeratinization of the epithelial cells of the skin and esophagus) in swine, and O'Dell et al. (1958) found that it prevents a similar malady in chicks. Excess calcium in the diet, however, hastens the onset of parakeratosis. The dietary requirement of an animal for zinc is higher with plant protein diets than with animal protein diets. This difference is associated with the phytic acid content of the plant protein source, since the addition of phytic acid to casein diets, which are known to be low in phytic acid, also increases the dietary zinc requirements.

Zinc is of relatively low toxicity to animals (Brink et al. 1959, Cox and Harris 1960). Grant-Frost and Underwood (1958) reported that 5000 ppm of zinc, as zinc oxide, depresses feed consumption, growth rate, and hemoglobin formation. Lewis et al. (1957a,b) observed no toxic effects in pigs fed 1000 ppm zinc. Klussendorf and Pensack (1958) found that 1200–1400 ppm of elemental zinc can be fed to broiler chicks without detrimental effects.

Zinc deficiency in pigs results in a marked depression of appetite and growth rate. Continued deficiency leads to parakeratosis. Zinc deficiency in the chick is similarly characterized by poor growth, severe dermatitis, especially of the feet, and poor feathering. In addition, zinc-deficient chicks exhibit abnormal respiration and a shortening and thickening of long bones (O'Dell et al. 1958). The abnormal bone development appears to arise from a failure of cartilage cell development in the epiphyseal plate region of the long bones and decreased osteoblastic activity in the thin bony collar. The severity of the lesions and the growth depression in chicks and pigs are directly related to the extent to which zinc content of the diet falls below the optimum level. Zinc deficiency has been experimentally produced in calves. The symptoms are similar to those of other species: rough and scaly skin, breaks in the skin around the hoofs, and a dull listless appearance (Miller and Miller 1960).

The absorption of zinc is inefficient. Thus the dietary requirement is much greater than the metabolic requirement. Green et al. (1962) estimated the metabolic requirement of the pig at only 3–4 ppm of the diet, whereas 30–40 ppm in the diet, or higher levels in the presence of phytic acid, are required to prevent parakeratosis and allow for normal growth. The oxide, carbonate, and sulfate forms of zinc are efficiently utilized, whereas the sulfide form is poorly utilized.

Zinc, whether ingested or injected, is excreted primarily in the feces. Zinc found in the feces consists largely of unabsorbed dietary zinc, and the balance is from pancreatic excretions. Urinary excretion of zinc and several other metals is increased if chelating agents such as ethylenediaminetetraacetic acid (EDTA) are given in combination with the mineral.

MANGANESE

Little is known of the chemical form or combinations in which manganese exists in the animal body. Manganese deficiency is associated with a number of defects including ataxia, skeletal deformities and impairments in growth, reproduction, egg shell formation, and blood clotting. Some of these defects are related to the role of the manganous ion as the most effective activator of glycosyltransferase enzymes in the synthesis of mucopolysaccharides and glycoproteins (Leach 1974).

Numerous enzyme systems are activated by manganese in vitro, a property shared in most cases by other bivalent ions, particularly magnesium. The fact that manganese is concentrated in the mitochondria has led to the suggestion that, in vivo, manganese is involved in the partial regulation of oxidative phosphorylation.

Manganese is distributed throughout the body, but the total quantity is much lower than for other elements, amounting to only about one tenth the copper content. Manganese is not concentrated in any specific organ or tissue, but it is found in higher concentrations in bone, liver, kidney, and pancreas (1–3 ppm of fresh tissue) than in skeletal muscle (0.1–0.2 ppm). The concentrations in the bone, liver, and hair can be altered considerably by varying the manganese intake (Johnson 1943, Insko et al. 1938, Leibholz et al. 1962).

Greenberg et al. (1940) estimated that only 3–4 percent of orally administered manganese is absorbed by rats. Of that, a large portion appears in the bile and is excreted in the feces. Some manganese occurs in the pancreatic secretions, but this is minor compared with the total amount excreted (Burnett et al. 1952). Even though the diet may contain a high level, very little manganese is normally excreted in the urine (Kent and McCance 1941). However, a marked increase in urinary excretion can be induced by administration of chelating agents (Maynard and Fink 1956). There is some evidence that manganese is more efficiently absorbed under deficiency conditions, and there is abundant evidence that excess calcium and phosphorus in the diet increase manganese requirements by reducing absorption (Hawkins et al. 1955, Wachtel et al. 1943, Wilgus and Patton 1939).

Manganese deficiency has been demonstrated in several species of animals including laboratory animals, pigs, poultry, and possibly in cattle. Its severity depends greatly on the degree and duration of the deficiency and on the maturity of the animal.

In pigs, lameness, enlarged hock joints, and shortened legs (Neher et al. 1956); in cattle, leg deformities with overknuckling (Grashuis et al. 1953); in chicks, poults, and ducklings, perosis or slipped tendon; and in chick embryos, nutritional chondrodystrophy (Wilgus et al. 1937); all have been attributed to manganese deficiency. Perosis in chicks is the most commonly observed manganese deficiency. It is characterized by enlarged and malformed tibiometatarsal joints, twisting and bending of the tibia and the tarsometatarsus, thickening and shortening of the long bones, "parrot beak" resulting from shortening of the lower mandible, and high embryonic mortality. Other factors such as deficiencies of choline or biotin may cause a similar condition, and an excess of calcium may aggravate the condition. In other species similar congenital defects in embryonic bone development result from manganese deficiency.

The manganese needs for growth, health, and reproduction are more precisely defined for poultry than they are for mammals. The dietary requirement is approximately 55 ppm for growth and 30 ppm for hatchability. The requirements are less precisely established for turkeys but are estimated to be similar to those for chickens. The requirements for pigs and cattle are much lower than those for birds and are approximately 10–12 ppm of the diet for growth and possibly higher for reproduction (Bentley and Phillips 1951).

Manganese deficiency is not encountered in cattle and seldom in pigs fed diets composed of natural ingredients. However, Swenson et al. (1962) showed that excess calcium added to nonlegume rations without added trace minerals inhibited the estrous cycle, including ovulation, in cattle. Excess calcium did not alter the normal estrous cycle if alfalfa hay or trace minerals including manganese were added to the ration.

Corn is extremely low in manganese (4–12 ppm); thus animals fed high-corn diets especially if supplemented with animal by-products, which are also low in manganese content, may receive inadequate amounts. The high requirement of poultry and the low levels of manganese in many of the ingredients of poultry diets make manganese supplementation of paramount importance.

Animals appear to be highly tolerant of excess dietary manganese. Growth of rats is unaffected by intakes as high as 1000–2000 ppm, but higher levels have been reported to interfere with phosphorus retention. Hens tolerate 1000 ppm without ill effects (Gallup and Norris 1939), but 4800 ppm are toxic to young chicks (Heller and Penquite 1937). Pigs tolerate 4000 ppm with only slight depressions in growth rate and no other signs of ill effects (Leibholz et al. 1962).

OTHER TRACE ELEMENTS

The mineral elements that have been unequivocally proven as essential dietary nutrients represent only a small portion of the total number that occur regularly in animal tissues. Arsenic, bromine, barium, chromium, and strontium should be included with those that have strong possibilities of being metabolically essential.

Bromine has been reported to increase the growth rate of chicks and mice (Huff et al. 1956). There is evidence that the thyroid glands of rabbits concentrate bromine during periods of dietary iodine insufficiency. This suggests that the thyroid gland does not distinguish perfectly between iodine and bromine. However, the bromine does not prevent the development of goiter, and it is rapidly replaced by iodine when the latter is restored to the diet (Baumann et al. 1941, Richards et al. 1949).

The omission of either barium or strontium from diets has resulted in growth depressions in rats and guinea pigs (Rygh 1949). The omission of strontium also resulted in an impairment of the calcification of the bones and teeth and in a higher incidence of carious teeth. These observations are yet to be confirmed. ^{90}Sr is one of the most abundant and potentially hazardous radioactive byproducts of nuclear fission. Although animals are less efficient than plants in the absorption of strontium, radioactive strontium is absorbed and deposited in tissues, especially in the bones. It is also readily transmitted to the fetus and secreted in the milk. Strontium and calcium have a similar and interrelated physiological behavior. Calcium is, however, preferentially absorbed from the intestinal tract, and strontium is preferentially excreted, especially in the urine, thereby providing a substantial factor of protection against ^{90}Sr.

Arsenic has been reported to stimulate the growth of tissue cultures. However, an arsenic deficiency in animals has not been demonstrated. On the other hand, the beneficial effect of various organic arsenicals on the performance and health of pigs and poultry has been shown. The action of these compounds closely resembles that of antibiotics and appears to be largely related to the control of harmful intestinal organisms.

There is limited evidence that other mineral elements may be of physiological significance. That an aggregation of cadmium in specific association with protein macromolecules has been fractionated from horse kidney cortex suggests a biological role for cadmium (Kägi and Vallee 1960).

Chromium has been found in nucleoproteins isolated from beef liver and also in RNA preparations (Wacker and Vallee 1959). It may play a role in the maintenance of the configuration of the RNA molecule, as chromium has been shown to be particularly effective as a cross-linking agent for collagen (Gustavson 1958). Also, chromium has been identified as the active ingredient of the glucose tolerance factor of Schwarz and Mertz (1959), a dietary factor required to maintain normal glucose tolerance in the rat. Chromium has also been shown to catalyze the phosphoglucomutase system (Strickland 1949), and to a limited extent it activates the succinic dehydrogenase-cytochrome system (Horecker et al. 1939). Evidence is accumulating on the role and essentiality of chromium, and there are indications that deficiencies may exist, particularly in children suffering from protein-calorie malnutrition (Mertz 1974).

Rubidium is also found in animal tissue and resembles potassium in its distribution and excretory pattern. Relatively high levels of rubidium occur in soft tissue, whereas skeletal tissue contains very little. Additions of rubidium or cesium to potassium-deficient diets have been reported to prevent the lesions characteristic of potassium depletion in rats (Follis 1943) and for short periods of time support near normal growth (Heppel and Schmidt 1938).

Silicon is one of the most abundant elements in plant and animal tissue. The economic losses resulting from silicon urolithiasis in grazing steers and wethers have stimulated research on the metabolism of silicon in sheep and cattle. Herbivorous animals consume relatively large quantities of silica (silicon dioxide) daily, and most of the insoluble silica passes unabsorbed through the alimentary tract, but appreciable amounts are absorbed and excreted in the urine. Normally, the silica is eliminated without ill effects, but in some animals a portion is deposited as granules in the kidney, bladder, or urethra to form uroliths or calculi. These can block urine passages, which may result in death. These calculi may be composed of various minerals, especially magnesium, phosphorus, and silicon.

Silicon has been shown to be essential for normal growth and skeletal development in rats and chicks (Schwarz 1974, Carlisle 1974). The level required is low, and one would not expect a deficiency in animals fed other than purified diets.

Aluminum, nickel, titanium, and vanadium also occur

Table 33.5. Some dietary mineral requirements of pigs and chicks (mg/kg)

Element	Pigs	Chicks
Potassium (%)	0.25	0.2
Iron	80	40
Copper	6	4
Manganese	12	55
Magnesium	400	500
Zinc	50	35
Iodine	0.2	0.35
Selenium	0.1	0.05–0.1

Data from National Research Council, *Nutrient Requirements of Domestic Animals,* Nat. Acad. Sci., Washington, 1966, 1968

in animal tissue. Satisfactory elucidation of a physiological role for any of them has as yet not been demonstrated. However, there is strong evidence that nickel (Nielsen 1974) and vanadium (Hopkins 1974) are essential for the physiological well-being of animals.

There are many metabolic and absorptive interrelationships among the mineral elements which contribute to variations in degree of physiological response to deficient or toxic levels. These relationships make it very difficult to determine the optimum dietary level for the individual elements as nutrients. Tables 33.1 and 33.5 present the estimated dietary requirements for those nutrients for which relatively reliable data are available. The recommended dietary level of any element should seldom be considered independent of the level of other essential nutrients.

REFERENCES

Aikawa, J.K., Reardon, J.Z., and Harms, D.R. 1962. Effect of a magnesium-deficient diet on magnesium metabolism in rabbits: A study with ^{28}Mg. *J. Nutr.* 76:90–93.

Allcroft, R., and Uvarov, O. 1959. Parenteral administration of copper compounds to cattle with special reference to copper glycine (copper amino-acetate). *Vet. Rec.* 71:797–810.

Allen, T.H., and Bodine, J.H. 1941. Enzymes in ontogenesis (arthroptera). XVII. The importance of copper for protyrosinase. *Science* 94:443–44.

Allman, R.T., and Hamilton, T.S. 1948. Nutritional deficiencies in livestock. *FAO Ag. Studies,* no. 5.

Askew, H.O. 1958. Molybdenum in relation to the occurrence of xanthin calculi in sheep. *New Zealand J. Ag. Res.* 1:447–54.

Baumann, E.J., Sprinson, D.B., and Marine, D. 1941. Bromine and the thyroid. *Endocrinology* 28:793–96.

Baxter, J.H., and VanWyk, J.J. 1953. A bone disorder associated with copper deficiency. I. Gross morphological, roentgenological, and chemical observations. *Bull. Johns Hopkins Hosp.* 93:1–25.

Beck, A.B. 1956. The copper content of the liver and blood of some vertebrates. *Austral. J. Zool.* 4:1–18.

Bennetts, H.W., and Beck, A.B. 1942. Enzootic ataxia and copper deficiency of sheep in Western Australia. *Austral. Council Sci. Ind. Res. Bull.* 147.

Bennetts, H.W., Beck, A.B., and Cunningham, I.J. 1946. Copper deficiency in cattle and sheep on peat lands. *New Zealand J. Sci. Technol.* 27:381–96.

Bennetts, H.W., and Chapman, F.E. 1937. Copper deficiency in Western Australia: A preliminary account of the aetiology of enzootic ataxia of lambs and an anaemia of ewes. *Austral. Vet. J.* 13:138–49.

Bentley, O.G., and Phillips, P.H. 1951. The effect of low manganese rations upon dairy cattle. *J. Dairy Sci.* 34:396–403.

Blaxter, K.L., Rook, J.A.F., and McDonald, A.M. 1954. The metabolism of calcium, magnesium, and nitrogen, and magnesium requirements. *J. Comp. Path. Ther.* 64:176–86.

Blaxter, K.L., and Sharman, G.A.M. 1955. Hypomagnesaemic tetany in beef cattle. *Vet. Rec.* 67:108–15.

Bowland, J.P., Braude, R., Chamberlain, A.G., Glascock, R.F., and Mitchell, K.G. 1961. The absorption, distribution, and excretion of labeled copper in young pigs given different quantities, as sulphate or sulphide, orally or intravenously. *Brit. J. Nutr.* 15:59–74.

Brink, M.F., Becker, D.E., Terrill, S.W., and Jensen, A.H. 1959. Zinc toxicity in the weanling pig. *J. Anim. Sci.* 18:836–42.

Brown, F.C., and White, J.B., Jr. 1961. The reduction of ceruloplasmin by the electron transport system. *J. Biol. Chem.* 236: 911–14.

Burley, R.W. 1954. Sulphydryl groups in wool. *Nature,* 174:1019–20.

Burnett, W.J., Jr., Bigelow, R.R., Kimball, A.W., and Sheppard, C.W. 1952. Radio-manganese studies on the mouse, rat, and pancreatic fistula dog. *Am. J. Physiol.* 168:620–25.

Carlisle, E.M. 1974. Essentiality and function of silicon. In Hoekstra et al.

Cartwright, G.E., Hamilton, L.D., Gubler, C.J., Fellows, N.M., Ashenbrucker, H.; and Wintrobe, M.M. 1951. The anemia of infection. XIII. Studies on experimentally produced acute hypoferremia in dogs and the relationship of the adrenal cortex to hypoferremia. *J. Clin. Invest.* 30:161–74.

Clements, F.W. 1957. A goitrogenic factor in milk. *Med. J. Austral.* 2:645–46.

Clements, F.W., and Wishart, J.W. 1956. A thyroid blocking agent in the etiology of endemic goiter. *Metabolism* 5:623–39.

Cohen, I., Hurwitz, S., and Bar, A. 1972. Acid-base balance and sodium-to-chloride ratio in diets of laying hens. *J. Nutr.* 102:1–7.

Cox, D.H., and Harris, D.L. 1960. Effect of excess dietary zinc on iron and copper in the rat. *J. Nutr.* 70:514–21.

Creek, R.D., Parker, H.E., Hauge, S.M., Andrews, F.N., and Carrick, C.W. 1954. The iodine requirement of young chickens. *Poul. Sci.* 33:1052.

Darrow, D.C., and Miller, H.C. 1942. The production of cardiac lesions by repeated injections of desoxycorticosterone acetate. *J. Clin. Invest.* 21:601–11.

Dowdle, E.B., Schachter, D., and Schenker, H. 1960. Active transport of Fe^{59} by everted segments of rat duodenum. *Am. J. Physiol.* 198:609–13.

Dressler, H., and Dawson, C.R. 1960. On the nature and mode of action of the copper-protein, tyrosinase. I. Exchange experiments with radioactive copper and the resting enzyme. *Biochim. Biophys. Acta* 45:508–15.

Duckworth, J., and Godden, W. 1941. The lability of skeletal magnesium reserves: The influence of rates of bone growth. *Biochem. J.* 35:816–23.

Ellis, W.C., and Pfander, W.H. 1960. Further studies on molybdenum as a possible component of the "alfalfa ash factor" for sheep. *J. Anim. Sci.* 19:1260.

Elvehjem, C.A. 1935. The biological significance of copper and its relation to iron metabolism. *Physiol. Rev.* 15:471–507.

Ershoff, B.H. 1948. Conditioning factors in nutritional disease. *Physiol. Rev.* 28:107–37.

Follis, R.H., Jr. 1943. Histological effects in rats resulting from adding rubidium or cesium to a diet deficient in potassium. *Am. J. Physiol.* 138:246–50.

Follis, R.H., Jr., Bush, J.A., Cartwright, G.E., and Wintrobe, M.M. 1955. Studies on copper metabolism. XVIII. Skeletal changes associated with copper deficiency in swine. *Bull. Johns Hopkins Hosp.* 97:405–14.

Follis, R.H., Jr., Orient-Keiles, E., and McCollum, E.V. 1942. The production of cardiac and renal lesions in rats by a diet extremely deficient in potassium. *Am. J. Path.* 18:29–39.

Fuhrman, F.A. 1951. Glycogen, glucose tolerance, and tissue metabolism in potassium-deficient rats. *Am. J. Physiol.* 167:314–20.

Gallup, W.D., and Norris, L.C. 1939. The effect of a deficiency of manganese in the diet of a hen. *Poul. Sci.* 18:83–88.

Gamble, A.H., Wiese, H.F., and Hansen, A.E. 1948. Marked hypokalemia in prolonged diarrhea: Possible effect on heart. *Pediatrics* 1:58–65.

Gillis, M.B. 1948. Potassium requirement of the chick. *J. Nutr.* 36:351–57.

Grant-Frost, D.R., and Underwood, E.J. 1958. Zinc toxicity in the rat and its interrelation with copper. *Austral. J. Exp. Biol. Med. Sci.* 36:339–45.

Grashuis, J., Lehr, J.J., Beuvery, L.L.E., and Beuvery-Asman, A.

1953. "De Schothorste" Inst. Moderne Veevoeding, Netherlands. Cited by E.J. Underwood in *Trace Elements in Human and Animal Nutrition,* 2d ed. Academic Press, New York, 1962. P. 197.

Green, J.D., McCall, J.T., Speer, V.C., and Hays, V.W. 1962. Effect of complexing agents on utilization of zinc by pigs. *J. Anim. Sci.* 21:997.

Greenberg, D.M., and Campbell, W.W. 1940. Studies in mineral metabolism with the aid of radioactive isotopes. *Proc. Nat. Acad. Sci.* 26:448–52.

Griffiths, D.E., and Wharton, D.C. 1961. Studies of the electron transport system. XXXV. Purification and properties of cytochrome oxidase. *J. Biol. Chem.* 236:1850–56.

Gubler, C.J., Cartwright, G.E., and Wintrobe, M.M. 1957. Studies on copper metabolism. XX. Enzyme activities and iron metabolism in copper and iron deficiencies. *J. Biol. Chem.* 224:533–46.

Gustavson, K.H. 1958. A novel type of metal-protein compound. *Nature* 182:1125–28.

Hahn, P.F. 1937. The metabolism of iron. *Medicine* 16:249–66.

Hamilton, L.D., Gubler, C.J., Cartwright, G.E., and Wintrobe, M.M. 1950. Diurnal variations in the plasma iron level in man. *Proc. Soc. Exp. Biol. Med.* 75:65–68.

Hawkins, G.E., Jr., Wise, G.H., Matrone, G., and Waugh, R.K. 1955. Manganese in the nutrition of young dairy cattle fed different levels of calcium and phosphorus. *J. Dairy Sci.* 38:536–47.

Head, M.J., and Rook, J.A.F. 1955. Hypomagnesaemia in dairy cattle and its possible relationship to ruminal ammonia production. *Nature* 176:262–63.

Heller, V.G., and Penquite, R. 1937. Factors producing perosis in chickens. *Poul. Sci.* 16:243–46.

Henrikson, H.W. 1951. Effect of potassium deficiency on gastrointestinal motility in rats. *Am. J. Physiol.* 164:263–73.

Heppel, L.A., and Schmidt, C.L.A. 1938. Studies on the potassium metabolism of the rat during pregnancy, lactation, and growth. *U. Calif. (Berkeley) Pub. Physiol.* 8:189–205.

Hobbs, C.S., Moorman, R.P., Jr., Griffith, J.M., West, J.L., Merriman, G.M., Hansard, S.L., Chamberlain, C.C., MacIntire, W.H., Hardin, L.J., and Jones, L.S. 1954. Fluorosis in cattle and sheep. *U. Tenn. Ag. Exp. Sta. Bull.* 235.

Hoekstra, W.G. 1975. Biochemical function of selenium and its relation to vitamin E. *Fed. Proc.* 34:2083–89.

Hoekstra, W.G., Suttie, J.W., Ganther, H.E., and Mertz, W., eds., 1974. *Trace Element Metabolism in Animals.* 2d ed. University Park Press, Baltimore.

Holmberg, C.G., and Laurell, C.B. 1948. Investigations in serum copper. II. Isolation of the copper containing protein, and a description of some of its properties. *Acta Chem. Scand.* 2:550–56.

Hopkins, L.L., Jr. 1974. Essentiality and function of vanadium. In Hoekstra et al.

Horecker, B.L., Stotz, E., and Hogness, T.R. 1939. The promoting effect of aluminum, chromium, and the rare earths in the succinic dehydrogenase-cytochrome system. *J. Biol. Chem.* 128:251–56.

Huff, J.W., Bosshardt, D.K., Miller, O.P., and Barnes, R.H. 1956. A nutritional requirement for bromine. *Proc. Soc. Exp. Biol. Med.* 92:216–19.

Hurwitz, S., Cohen, I., Bar, A., and Bornstein, S. 1973. Sodium and chloride requirements of the chick: Relationship to acid-base balance. *Poul. Sci.* 52:903–9.

Insko, W.M., Jr., Lyons, M., and Martin, J.H. 1938. The effect of manganese, zinc, aluminum, and iron salts on the incidence of perosis in chicks. *Poul. Sci.* 17:264–69.

Jensen, A.H., Terrill, S.W., and Becker, D.E. 1961. Response of the young pig to levels of dietary potassium. *J. Anim. Sci.* 20:464–67.

Johnson, S.R. 1943. Studies with swine on rations extremely low in manganese. *J. Anim. Sci.* 2:14–22.

Kägi, J.H.R., and Vallee, B.L. 1960. Metallothionein: A cadmium- and zinc-containing protein from equine renal cortex. *J. Biol. Chem.* 235:3460–65.

Kelly, F.C., and Snedden, W.W. 1960. Prevalence and geographical distribution of endemic goitre. In *Endemic Goiter.* World Health Organization Monograph Series, no. 44. Geneva. Pp. 27–233.

Kenney, T.D., Hegsted, D.M., and Finck, C.A. 1949. The influence of diet on iron absorption. I. The pathology of iron excess. *J. Exp. Med.* 90:137–47.

Kent, N.L., and McCance, R.A. 1941. The absorption and excretion of "minor" elements by man. II. Cobalt, nickel, tin, and manganese. *Biochem. J.* 35:877–83.

Klussendorf, R.C., and Pensack, J.M. 1958. Newer aspects of zinc metabolism. *J. Am. Vet. Med. Ass.* 132:446–50.

Kornberg, A., and Endicott, K.M. 1946. Potassium deficiency in rats. *Am. J. Physiol.* 145:291–98.

Kruse, H.D., Orent, E.R., and McCollum, E.V. 1932. Studies on magnesium deficiency in animals. I. Symptomatology resulting from magnesium deprivation. *J. Biol. Chem.* 96:519–39.

Kruse, H.D., Schmidt, M.M., and McCollum, E.V. 1933. Studies on magnesium deficiency in animals. IV. Reaction to galvanic stimuli following magnesium deprivation. *Am. J. Physiol.* 105:635–42.

Kubota, J., and Allaway, W.H. 1972. Geographic distribution of trace element problems. In J.J. Mortvedt, P.M. Giordano, and W.L. Lindsay, eds., *Micronutrients in Agriculture.* Soil Science Society of America, Madison, Wis. Pp. 525–54.

Lahey, M.E., Gubler, C.J., Chase, M.S., Cartwright, C.E., and Wintrobe, M.M. 1952. Studies on copper metabolism. II. Hematologic manifestations of copper deficiency in swine. *Blood* 7:1053–74.

Leach, R.M., Jr. 1974. Biochemical role of manganese. In Hoekstra et al.

Leach, R.M., and Norris, L.C. 1957. Studies on factors affecting the response of chicks to molybdenum. *Poul. Sci.* 36:1136.

Leach, R.M., Jr., Dam, R., Ziegler, T.R., and Norris, L.C. 1959. The effect of protein and energy on the potassium requirement of the chick. *J. Nutr.* 68:89–100.

Leibholz, J., Speer, V.C., and Hays, V.W. 1962. Effect of dietary manganese on baby pig performance and tissue manganese levels. *J. Anim. Sci.* 21:772–76.

Lerner, A.B., and Fitzpatrick, T.B. 1950. Biochemistry of melanin formation. *Physiol. Rev.* 30:91–126.

Levine, H.D., Merrill, J.P., and Somerville, W. 1951. Advanced disturbances of the cardiac mechanism in potassium intoxication in man. *Circulation* 3:889–905.

Lewis, P.K., Hoekstra, W.G., and Grummer, R.H. 1957a. Restricted calcium feeding versus zinc supplementation for the control of parakeratosis in swine. *J. Anim. Sci.* 16:578–88.

——. 1957b. The effect of method of feeding upon the susceptibility of the pig to parakeratosis. *J. Anim. Sci.* 16:927–36.

Marine, D., and Lenhart, C.H. 1909a. Further observations on the relation of iodine to the structure of the thyroid gland in the sheep, dog, hog, and ox. *Arch. Internal Med.* 3:66–77.

——. 1909b. Relation of iodine to the structure of human thyroids: Relation of iodine and histologic structure to diseases in general, to exophthalmic goiter, to cretinism and myxedema. *Arch. Internal Med.* 4:440–93.

Maynard, L.S., and Fink, S. 1956. The influence of chelation on radiomanganese excretion in man and mouse. *J. Clin. Invest.* 35:831–36.

McCance, R.A., and Widdowson, E.M. 1938. The absorption and excretion of iron following oral and intravenous administration. *J. Physiol.* 94:148–54.

McCandlish, A.C. 1923. Studies in the growth and nutrition of dairy calves. VI. The addition of hay and grain to a milk ration for calves. *J. Dairy Sci.* 6:347–72.

McDougall, E.I. 1947. The copper, iron, and lead contents of a series of livers from normal foetal and new-born lambs. *J. Ag. Sci.* 37:337–41.

Mertz, W. 1974. Chromium as a dietary essential for man. In Hoekstra et al.

Messer, H.H., Armstrong, W.D., and Singer, L. 1974. Essentiality and function of fluoride. In Hoekstra et al.

Meyer, J.H., Grummer, R.H., Phillips, P.H., and Bohstedt, G. 1950. Sodium, chlorine, and potassium requirements of growing pigs. *J. Anim. Sci.* 9:300–306.

Miller, J.K., and Miller, W.J. 1960. Development of zinc deficiency in Holstein calves fed a purified diet. *J. Dairy Sci.* 43:1854–56.

Moore, L.A., Halman, E.T., and Sholl, L.B. 1938. Cardiovascular and other lesions in calves fed diets low in magnesium. *Arch. Path.* 26:820–38.

National Research Council. 1960. *The Fluorosis Problems in Livestock Production.* Nat. Acad. Sci., Washington.

National Research Council. 1963–1968. *Nutrient Requirements of Domestic Animals:* I (1966), *Poultry;* II (1968), *Swine;* III (1966), *Dairy Cattle;* IV (1963), *Beef Cattle.* Nat. Acad. Sci., Washington.

National Research Council. 1970–1973. *Nutrient Requirements of Domestic Animals:* I (1971), *Poultry;* II (1973), *Swine;* III (1971), *Dairy Cattle;* IV (1970), *Beef Cattle.* Nat. Acad. Sci., Washington.

Neher, G.M., Doyle, L.P., Thrasher, D.M., and Plumlee, M.P. 1956. Radiographic and histopathological findings in the bones of swine deficient in manganese. *Am. J. Vet. Res.* 17:121–28.

Nielsen, F.H. 1974. Essentiality and function of nickel. In Hoekstra et al.

O'Dell, B.L., Newberne, P.M., and Savage, J.E. 1958. Significance of dietary zinc for the growing chicken. *J. Nutr.* 65:503–18.

O'Dell, B.L., and Savage, J.E. 1957. Potassium, zinc, and distillers dried solubles as supplements to a purified diet. *Poul. Sci.* 36:459–60.

Okunuki, K., Sekuzu, J., Yonetani, T., and Takemori, S. 1958. Studies on cytochrome A. I. Extraction, purification and some properties of cytochrome A. *J. Biochem.* (Tokyo), 45:847–54.

Pierson, R.E., and Aanes, W.A. 1958. Treatment of chronic copper poisoning in sheep. *J. Am. Vet. Med. Ass.* 133:307–11.

Raper, H.S. 1928. The aerobic oxidases. *Physiol. Rev.* 8:245–82.

Reid, B.L., Kurnick, A.A., Svacha, R.L., and Couch, J.R. 1956. The effect of molybdenum on chick and poultry growth. *Proc. Soc. Exp. Biol. Med.* 93:245–48.

Richards, C.E., Brady, R.O., and Riggs, D.S. 1949. Thyroid hormone-like properties of tetrabromthyronine and tetrachlorthyronine. *J. Clin. Endocr.* 9:1107–21.

Roy, J.H.B., Shillam, K.W.G., Hawkins, G.M., and Long, J.M. 1959. The effect of white scours on the sodium and potassium concentration in the serum of newborn calves. *Brit. J. Nutr.* 13:219–26.

Rygh, O. 1949. Research on trace elements. I. Importance of strontium, barium, and zinc. *Bull. Soc. Chim. Biol.* 31:1052–61.

Sanger, F. 1959. Chemistry of insulin. *Science* 129:1340–44.

Schwarz, K. 1974. New essential trace elements (Sn, V, F, Si): Progress report and outlook. In Hoekstra et al.

Schwarz, K., and Mertz, W. 1959. Chromium (III) and the glucose tolerance factor. *Arch. Biochem. Biophys.* 85:292–95.

Siren, M.J. 1964. Is selenium involved in the excitation mechanism of photoreceptors? *LKB Instrument J.* 11:37–43.

Smith, R.H. 1957. Calcium and magnesium metabolism in calves: Plasma levels and retention in milk-fed calves. *Biochem. J.* 67: 472–81.

Smith, S.E., Medlicott, M., and Ellis, G.H. 1944. The blood picture of iron and copper deficiency anemias in the rabbit. *Am. J. Physiol.* 142:179–81.

Smithies, O., and Hiller, O. 1959. The genetic control of transferrins in humans. *Biochem. J.* 72:121–26.

Streef, G.M. 1939. Sodium and calcium content of erythrocytes. *J. Biol. Chem.* 129:661–72.

Streeten, D.H.P., and Williams, E.M.V. 1952. Loss of cellular potassium as a cause of intestinal paralysis in dogs. *J. Physiol.* 118:149–70.

Strickland, L.H. 1949. The activation of phosphoglucomutase by metal ions. *Biochem. J.* 44:190–97.

Swenson, M.J., Goetsch, D.D., and Underbjerg, G.K.L. 1962. Effects of dietary trace minerals, excess calcium, and various roughages on the hemogram, tissues, and estrous cycles of Hereford heifers. *Am. J. Vet. Res.* 23:803–8.

Sykes, J.F., and Alfredson, B.V. 1940. Studies on the bovine electrocardiogram. I. Electrocardiographic changes in calves on low potassium rations. *Proc. Soc. Exp. Biol. Med.* 43:575–79.

Takemori, S. 1960. Studies on cytochrome A. V. Properties of copper in purified cytochrome A. *J. Biochem.* 47:382–90.

Tucker, H.F., and Salmon, W.D. 1955. Parakeratosis or zinc deficiency disease in the pig. *Proc. Soc. Exp. Biol. Med.* 88:613–16.

Valberg, L.S., Card, R.T., Paulson, E.J., and Szivek, J. 1965. The metal composition of erythrocytes in different species and its relationship to the lifespan on the cells in the circulation. *Comp. Biochem. Physiol.* 15:347–59.

Venn, J.A.J., McCann, R.A., and Widdowson, E.M. 1947. Iron metabolism in piglet anemia. *J. Comp. Path. Ther.* 57:315–25.

Wachtel, L.W., Elvehjem, C.A., and Hart, E.B. 1943. Studies on the physiology of manganese of the rat. *Am. J. Physiol.* 104:72–82.

Wacker, W.E.C., and Vallee, B.L. 1959. Nucleic acids and metals. I. Chromium, manganese, nickel, iron, and other metals in ribonucleic acid from diverse biological sources. *J. Biol. Chem.* 234:3257–62.

Wilgus, H.S., Jr., Norris, L.C., and Heuser, G.F. 1937. The role of certain inorganic elements in the cause and prevention of perosis. *Science* 84:252–53.

Wilgus, H.S., Jr., and Patton, A.R. 1939. Factors affecting manganese utilization in the chicken. *J. Nutr.* 18:35–45.

Wolff, J., Chaikoff, I.L., Taurog, A., and Rubin, L. 1946. The disturbance in iodine metabolism produced by thiocyanate: The mechanism of its goitrogenic action with radioactive iodine as indicator. *Endocrinology* 39: 140–48.

Wooley, J.G., and Mickelson, O. 1954. Effect of sodium, potassium, and calcium on the growth of young rabbits fed purified diets containing different levels of fat and protein. *J. Nutr.* 52:591–600.

CHAPTER 34

Bones | by Robert H. Wasserman

Because of bone's relative permanence and resistance to decay, one is tempted to consider it, even in the living animal, as "dead" tissue, a tissue relatively inert after it is formed. On the contrary, bone is dynamic throughout life, responding to internal and external stresses that modify its anatomy and behavior. It is grossly different from other types of connective tissue in its high mineral content, which is responsible for its hardness, and is characterized by the presence of unique cells: osteoblasts, osteoclasts, and osteocytes. These bone cells are influenced by various hormones, ions, and nutritional factors (e.g. parathyroid hormone, calcitonin, calcium, phosphate, and vitamin D). Through hormonal action, for example, the minerals within the intercellular matrix can be withdrawn when exogenous sources are limited and, in this way, aid in maintaining a relatively constant concentration of calcium ions in body tissues and fluids, including blood plasma.

The three main functions served by bones and the bone cells of the skeleton are: (1) helping to maintain, through homeostatic regulation, a constant ionic environment within the organism; (2) supporting and protecting soft tissues and organs, including bone marrow; and (3) with muscles and tendons, providing a means of locomotion. The skeleton also has the capacity to sequester (segregate) extraneous mineral ions such as lead, fallout radiostrontium (^{90}Sr), and radium from extracellular fluids.

ANATOMY

The anatomy of a growing long bone is diagramed in Figure 34.1. The end of the bone is termed the *epiphysis;* the long, compact shaft, the *diaphysis;* and the end of the diaphysis where it joins the epiphysis, the *metaphysis*.

The diaphysis consists of compact bone in the form of a hollow cylinder which contains the medullary (marrow) cavity and the bone marrow. The epiphysis is composed of cancellous or spongy bone surrounded by a thin cortex of compact bone. Cancellous bone is made up of delicate spicules of bone called trabeculae. In the growing animal, the epiphysis is separated from the diaphysis by the epiphyseal plate, which consists of cartilage matrix and cells, invading blood vessels, and newly forming bone. Immediately beneath the epiphyseal plate are columns of spongy bone which join with the diaphysis and are a part of the metaphysis. The epiphyseal plate and adjacent columns of spongy bone (the primary and secondary spongiosa) comprise the growth apparatus (Fig. 34.2). In mature nongrowing bone, the epiphyseal plate is absent and the cancellous bone of the epiphysis becomes continuous with that of the diaphysis and the marrow cavity.

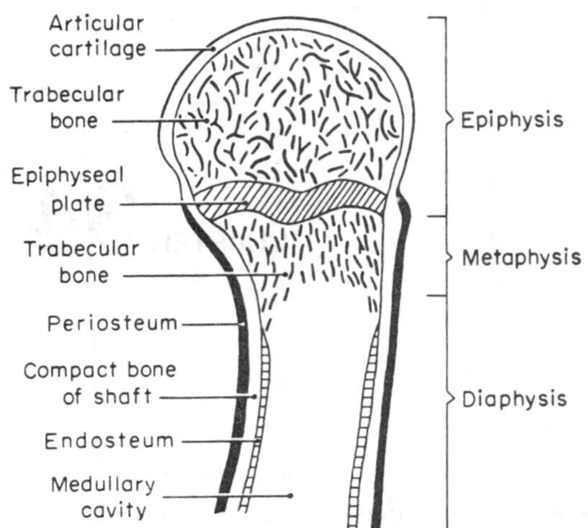

Figure 34.1. Anatomy of a growing long bone

Figure 34.2. Histological section of the proximal epiphyseal region of a tibia from a 4-month-old cat. At the top of the illustration, note the hyaline cartilage of the epiphyseal plate, with embedded chondrocytes. Below this are the proliferating cartilage cells arranged in vertical rows which subsequently hypertrophy, with the intracellular matrix becoming calcified. The hypertrophic cells are removed, leaving the primary spongiosa. At the bottom is the secondary spongiosa. ×50. (Courtesy of L. Krook, New York State Veterinary College.)

The strength and rigidity of long bones are due to the hardness of the compact bone of the shaft and epiphysis, and to the underlying scaffolding arrangement of the cancellous bony spicules, the trabeculae. These trabeculae run parallel to the lines of maximum stress and, in accordance with sound engineering principles, help the bone resist mechanical stresses. Changes in the size, number, disposition, and orientation of the trabeculae occur in response to alterations in mechanical needs.

The flat bones of the skull are composed primarily of compact bone on both surfaces with a layer of cancellous bone between them. The smaller and irregularly shaped bones consist primarily of spongiosa, circumferentially bounded by a cortex of compact bone.

Bone, except where joined to the articular cartilage, is covered by a special dense connective tissue layer, the periosteum (collagenous bundles, known as Sharpey's fibers, attach the periosteum to bone). The closeness of attachment depends on the type of bone and the location of the periosteum on a particular bone. When the periosteum is loosely connected, the attachment is mainly due to small blood vessels. In the growing bone, the periosteum has an osteogenic function by virtue of a layer of osteoblasts in the deepest layer of the periosteum. In the mature animal, the periosteum does not function osteogenically except in cases of fracture and other disease states.

Along the surfaces of the medullary cavity of bone is a layer of thin connective tissue, the endosteum. Endosteum also lines the cavities of the Haversian canals of compact bone and covers the trabeculae of spongy bone.

In the mature animal, the bone cell envelope associated with the periosteal surface remains active in bone remodeling but only at very slow rates (Rasmussen and Bordier 1974). The bone cell envelope on the endosteal and trabecular surfaces also remains active in the adult and participates to a greater degree in bone remodeling than the periosteal envelope (Rasmussen and Bordier 1974).

In postnatal life, erythropoiesis occurs primarily in the bone marrow. This myeloid tissue also produces leukocytes (granulocytes), platelets, and some lymphocytes (20% in humans). The mesenchymal cells, which give rise to myeloid, accompany the blood vessels that enter and participate in the erosion of the marrow cavity. The least differentiated bone marrow cells probably can evolve into bone-forming as well as blood-forming cells.

The compact bone of the shaft and elsewhere has an internal structure that reflects its pattern of formation. A longitudinal section from the diaphysis (Fig. 34.3) shows channels running generally parallel with the long axis of the bone; these are the Haversian canals, which contain blood vessels supported by a small amount of connective tissue. Haversian canals communicate with the external

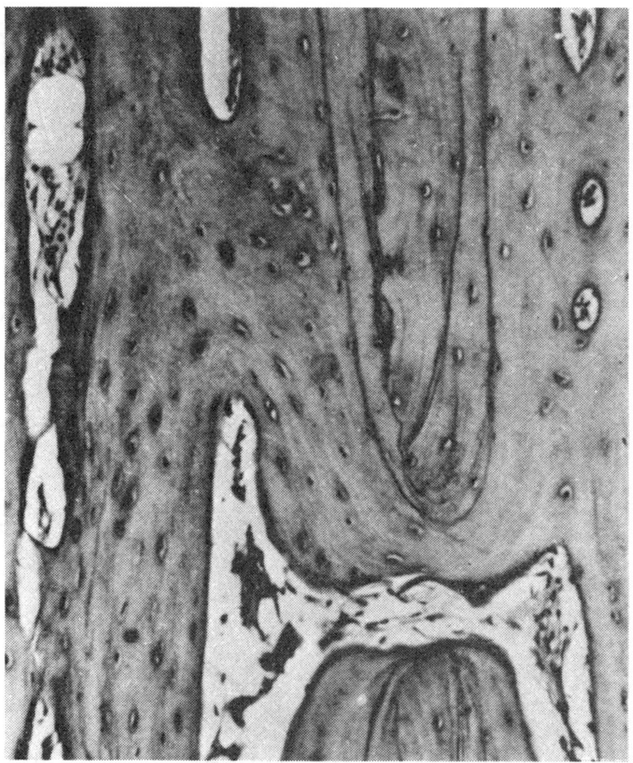

Figure 34.3. Longitudinal section of tibia cortex from a 6-month-old pig, showing Haversian canals both in cross and longitudinal sections. The two adjacent canals at the bottom are united by a Volkmann's canal. Note the osteocytes embedded in the bone matrix and the dark cement lines which delineate adjacent osteons. ×75. (Courtesy of L. Krook, New York State Veterinary College.)

Figure 34.4. Cross section of the humerus diaphysis of a 14-month-old horse under polarized light. The concentric circles are lamellae surrounding the canal of the Haversian system. The alternating dark and light lamellae are due to the spiraling configuration of the matrix fibers and, in cross section, the fibrillar structure may be longitudinal, circular, or intermediate, causing the polarized light to be transmitted with varying intensities. ×65. (From Krook and Lowe 1964, *Path. Vet.* 1(suppl.):1–98.)

surface and the medullary cavity by way of the canals of Volkmann. The unit of structure of compact bone is the Haversian system or osteon, which consists of a central Haversian canal with interconnecting channels, surrounded by concentric layers of bone, the lamellae (Figs. 34.3, 34.4). Included within the bone substance are lacunae (melon-shaped cavities) containing osteocytes, previously entrapped during the calcification process (Fig. 34.3). The lacunae intercommunicate with each other and with the Haversian canal through a branching network of canaliculae. The blood vessels within the Haversian canal are primarily capillaries and postcapillary venules; occasionally an arteriole is present. The canaliculae and lacunae are extravascular, and the tissue fluids and interstitial substances for the maintenance of the osteocytes presumably move by diffusion to and from the blood vessels in the canal, although other mechanisms to facilitate fluid transport may be present, such as the periodic contraction of the bone cells and mechanical stresses.

The trabeculae of spongy bone also contain concentric lamella with enclosed lacunae and osteocytes. As in compact bone, the lacunae intercommunicate with each other via canaliculae, but the Haversian system is absent.

CELLS

Three types of cells are associated with specific functions of bone tissue: the *osteoblast* participates in the ossification process and is readily observed when new bone is being formed; the *osteoclast* is usually found at sites where bone resorption (dissolution and removal of mineral and intercellular matrix) is taking place; the *osteocyte*, embedded in bone proper within a lacuna, participates both in osteocytic osteolysis and bone formation. The cell types are interrelated and are derived from a common ancestor. Transformations of one cell type to another occur either directly or indirectly in developing bone, and can be induced in adults by the administration of parathyroid hormone or estrogen (in mice or birds) or in response to skeletal fractures.

Osteoblasts

These columnar cells vary greatly in size, being from 15–180 μ in length, although most fall within a range of 20–30 μ. These bone-forming cells are characteristically observed as a one-cell thick pseudo-epithelium covering the surfaces of newly forming bone. The osteoblast is polarized in that its nucleus is located farthest from the bone surface; many cytoplasmic processes are seen on the cell surface that is closest to the bone. The cytoplasm contains abundant endoplasmic reticula, most of which have dense granules (ribosomes) on the outer surface. This is characteristic of cells involved in the synthesis and extrusion of proteins. The paired membranes of the endoplasmic reticulum enclose a lumen whose contents appear amorphous and more dense than the surrounding cytoplasm. Many vesicles (20–40 nm in diameter) occur throughout the cell and are closely associated with the granular endoplasmic reticulum. Numerous threadlike mitochondria with abundant cristae are dispersed through the cytoplasm and often lie in close apposition to the granular endoplasmic reticular surface. A Golgi apparatus and membrane-limited secretion-type droplets are also found. Osteoblasts are characterized histologically by their strong cytoplasmic basophilia, which varies directly with cell activity. The basophilic nature of these and other cells is due to the presence of ribonucleic acid (RNA). These granules are decreased in number when the osteoblast is in the resting stage. Alkaline phosphatase (determined histochemically with sodium β-glycerophosphate as substrate at pH 9.5) is confined to the external surface of the osteoblast plasma membrane; none is associated with intracytoplasmic membranes. Lysosomes containing acid phosphatase are also present (Doty et al. 1976).

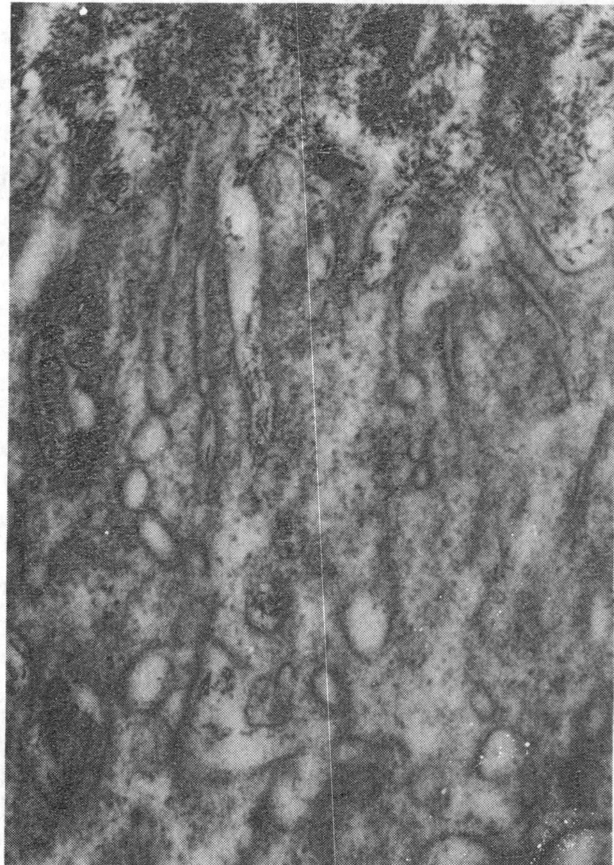

Figure 34.5. Electron micrograph of an osteoclast at the bone surface. The ruffled border consists of a complex of cytoplasmic folds and projections separated by cleftlike spaces. The dense area consists of numerous extracellular bone crystals. Some of the crystals are in five channels and in the cell proper within saclike vesicles. ×50,000. (From Hancox and Boothroyd, in Sognnaes, ed., *Mechanisms of Hard Tissue Destruction*, Pub. 75, p. 508. Copyright 1963 by the American Association for the Advancement of Science, Washington.)

Osteocytes

These cells are entrapped and embedded in growing bone. They are situated within the flat, oval lacunae and have cytoplasmic processes extending through apertures into the canaliculae of bone to connect directly with other bone cells. The cytoplasm is faintly basophilic, containing few mitochondria and a small Golgi net. Fat globules and glycogen have also been demonstrated. When the bone surrounding the osteocyte is resorbed, the cell is then released.

Unlike its osteoblastic precursor, alkaline glycerophosphatase was not detected in the cell membrane of the osteocyte. Acid phosphatase and other lysomal enzymes are present (Doty et al. 1976).

Osteoclasts

These are usually multinucleated giant cells that are observed at sites of bone resorption and in eroded cavities of bone called Howship's lacunae. Like osteoblasts, osteoclasts are polarized in that the nuclei are usually remote from the bone surface. Mitochondria are very numerous, especially in the regions near bone, and contain abundance cristae. The cytoplasm appears dense due to large numbers of small dense particles thought to be nonmembrane-bounded ribosomes. Lysosomes are found in considerable numbers adjacent to the surface where bone is being resorbed (Doty et al. 1976).

The cell membrane adjacent to an actively resorbing bone surface has a brush border comprised of cytoplasmic folds and projections with an associated system of cytoplasmic vacuoles and vesicles (Fig. 34.5) (Hancox and Boothroyd 1963, Dudley and Spiro 1961).

The osteoclast is highly mobile, capable of migrating along surfaces of resorbing bone and also of entering the blood stream.

Origin

According to classical theory, cells from an undifferentiated cell population (mesenchymal cells, reticular cells) become osteoblasts which then take part in osteogenesis. During the growth of bone matrix, the osteoblasts on the bone surface, when trapped, are transformed into osteocytes, remaining within a lacuna until released by resorption. The multinucleated osteoclast, associated with bone resorption, arises either from coalescing osteoblasts or osteocytes, or from reticular cells. Studies with tritium-labeled thymidine have shown the time sequence of these transformations. The nuclei of the unspecialized population, termed the osteoprogenitor cells, accumulated thymidine before those of the specialized bone cells. Significantly, osteoclasts became labeled *before* osteoblasts or osteocytes, indicating that osteoclasts can arise directly from the osteoprogenitor cells and possibly are also precursors of osteoblasts. The specialized bone cells may revert back to the osteoprogenitor stage or may die and disintegrate. By way of the cyclic progenitor pool, one type of bone cell may be transformed into another type (e.g. osteoblasts to osteoprogenitor cells to osteoclasts) (Young 1963, Rasmussen and Bordier 1974).

Membrane

There seems to be anatomical evidence that, in the normal state, osteons and trabeculae are separated from the vascular compartment by a membrane composed of osteoblasts, osteocytes (and their filaments), or endosteal lining cells (Dudley and Spiro 1961, Thomas and Howard 1964). There is physiological evidence that the composition of bone extracellular fluid, particularly potassium ion, differs from that of nonosseous extracellular fluid (Neuman and Ramp 1971). The K^+ ion, although rapidly exchangeable and not sequestered by bone surfaces, was considerably higher in bone fluid than would be expected if it were in equilibrium with the overall extracellular fluid. Calcium transport by chick calvaria (periosteum and endosteum intact) provides additional evidence for a functional bone membrane (Neuman et al. 1973).

This membrane may serve as a barrier to the free flow of ions and other substances between body fluids and the crystalline surfaces of bone. It also may regulate or facilitate the transfer of nutrients to and from sites of accretion and resorption.

INTERCELLULAR MATRIX

Composition

The osteogenic cells (osteocytes, osteoblasts) synthesize and release the organic components of the intercellular matrix which subsequently calcify and form bone. The main nonviable components of bone are: (1) the bone mineral; (2) collagen, a fibrillar protein; (3) amorphous ground substance, composed mainly of mucopolysaccharides (chondroitin sulfate), with fatty acids, phospholipids, and other substances being present; and (4) water. In the adult, bone contains on a wet-weight basis approximately 25 percent water, 45 percent ash, and 30 percent organic matter. Calcium constitutes about 37 percent of the ash content, and phosphorus about 18.5 percent. On a dry-weight basis, the mineral content of bone is between 65 and 70 percent and the organic fraction roughly 30–35 percent. Of the organic fraction, from 95 to 99 percent is collagen, which, upon heating in aqueous solution, is converted to gelatin.

Changes with age

The chemical composition of bone changes with embryonic development and postfetal growth and maturation. The ash (mineral) content progressively increases as the water content decreases; the organic fraction remains relatively constant (Hammett 1925). The reciprocal relationship between the mineral and water fractions suggested that, as ossification proceeds, there is a progressive displacement of water by mineral.

During gestation, the proportion of the calcium in dry, fat-free bone in the human fetus increases steadily from a fetal age of 12 weeks until birth; immediately after birth and for several months, the fraction of calcium decreases rapidly before the pattern mentioned above is established. The same situation occurs in the kitten. The low proportion of inorganic to organic during the immediate postfetal period is attributed to a local deficiency of mineral ions; that is, the rate of synthesis of collagen and other components of the calcifiable matrix supersedes the supply of calcium, phosphate, and other ions (Widdowson and Dickerson 1964). When $CaHPO_4$ was administered to kittens during the first week of life, the decline in skeletal mineralization in the postnatal stage was prevented.

Collagen

This is a fibrous protein synthesized by fibroblasts and related cells, such as osteoblasts of bone and chondroblasts of cartilage, and is found in all tissues of the body. The formation of collagen fibrils is a complex process with reactions occurring both intracellularly and extracellularly. Within the cell the following events take place: the synthesis of protocollagen molecules, the hydroxylation of some of the proline and lysine residues and the glycosylation of hydroxylysine residues to form procollagen monomers, and the extrusion of procollagen as trimers in helical configuration. External to the cell there is limited proteolytic hydrolysis of procollagen to form tropocollagen; the latter subsequently forms the matrix fibrils (Grant and Prockop 1972, Rasmussen and Bordier 1974). Vitamin C is a requirement of the hydroxylation reaction.

The amino acid composition of collagen differs from

that of other proteins. About one third is glycine, another one third consists of proline and hydroxyproline, with the rest consisting of other amino acids, including lysine and hydroxylysine (Schmitt 1959). Because collagen contains almost the entire body content of proline and hydroxyproline, these amino acids can serve, with the large glycine content, to identify collagen protein. In biochemical studies hydroxyproline labeled with ^{14}C is often employed to follow the synthesis and breakdown of collagen. Also the urinary excretion of hydroxyproline has been used as a measure of collagen destruction. However, Raisz (1976) pointed out the unreliability of hydroxyproline measurements as an index of bone resorption because: (1) hydroxyproline can originate from other sources, e.g. skin, tendon; (2) most of the hydroxyproline released from collagen is not excreted but is degraded elsewhere; and (3) hydroxyproline can arise directly from the procollagen not used for matrix formation.

Collagen is considered crystalline in nature due to the ordered aggregation of the collagen macromolecules and to the high degree of structural regularity of the collagen fibril. This feature is particularly evident with the electron microscope since the fibers have cross bands at intervals of about 64 nm. Covalent cross-linking between adjacent collagen molecules occurs during maturation and involves hydroxylysine or dihydroxylysine on one molecule and norleucine on the other (Mechanic 1975).

Ground substance

Interspersed between the collagen fibers of connective tissue is the ground substance. It was defined by McLean and Urist (1955) as the "extracellular and interfibrillar amorphous component of all connective tissue." The ground substance is continuous with the interstitial fluid and exhibits varying degrees of condensation. It consists mainly of protein-polysaccharides (chondroitin sulfate), glycoproteins, nonstructural protein, electrolytes, and water. The electrolytes and water are undoubtedly derived directly from plasma or other extracellular fluid, and the protein-polysaccharides and proteins from connective tissue cells.

Bone mineral

Bone salt, deposited within the interstitial substance, is composed of calcium, phosphorus (phosphate), hydroxyl ions, carbonate, citrate, and water. Other ions, such as sodium, magnesium, potassium, chloride, and fluoride, are also included (Table 34.1).

Table 34.1. Composition of dry, fat-free, bovine cortical bone

Constituents	Percentage	mEq/g
Cations		
Calcium	26.7	13.3
Magnesium	0.44	0.36
Sodium	0.73	0.32
Potassium	0.056	0.014
Anions		
Phosphorus	12.5	
as $PO_4^{\equiv}$		12.1
Carbon dioxide	3.5	
as $CO_3^{=}$		1.6
Citric acid	0.36	
as $Cit^{\equiv}$		0.14
Chloride	0.08	0.02
Fluoride	0.07	0.04
Molar ratio Ca/P		1.656

Adapted from W.D. Armstrong and L. Singer, as given by McLean and Budy, *Radiation, Isotopes, and Bone*, Academic Press, New York, 1964

Although there is some controversy, it is generally accepted that the crystalline structure of bone mineral is that of the apatite series and is approximated by the formula of hydroxyapatite: $3Ca_3(PO_4)_2 \cdot Ca(OH)_2$. The mineral salt in all vertebrate structures, such as endochondral and intramembranous bone, dentin, cementum, and enamel, appears to be the same and of this type. According to Neuman and Neuman (1958), hydroxyapatite is the only solid phase of a calcium-phosphate-water system stable at neutral pH.

Herman and Dallemagne (1961) suggested that bone mineral consists of more than one type of calcium salt and behaves like mixtures of hydrated tricalcium phosphate and $CaCO_3$. These mineral phases are supposedly kept separate in vivo by the organic components of bone so that the extra calcium (as carbonate) is not in close contact with the calcium phosphate phase.

More recently, attention was given to the presence in bone of amorphous calcium phosphate. The proportion of amorphous calcium phosphate to crystalline hydroxyapatite is highest in young bone, with the proportion decreasing with age (Posner 1973). This constitutes part of the evidence that the type of bone mineral first laid down is the amorphous form, which subsequently undergoes recrystallization to form hydroxyapatite.

Bone crystals may first appear at the major period lines on and within the collagen fibers (Fig. 34.6) and not necessarily in the ground substance. Initially and even after some crystal growth, these are extremely small in size, measuring about 2.5–7.5 nm in width and perhaps 20–60 nm in length (along the C axis).

Nevertheless, the large numbers of crystals yield enormous surface areas. It was estimated that the area of the bone crystals in the skeleton of a 70 kg man exceeds 100 acres (41 hectares) and that the surface area of 1 g of bone mineral is more than 100 sq m (McLean and Urist 1955). Because of these tremendous areas, reactions involving the crystalline surface provide for a rapid interchange of ions between interstitial fluid and bone.

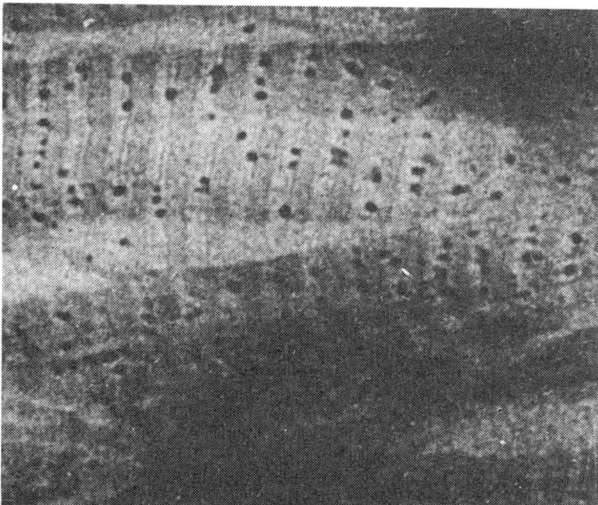

Figure 34.6. Electron micrograph of an intercellular area from a section of periosteal bone from a 16-day-old chick embryo. Collagen fibers with periodic bands are seen in longitudinal section. Small particles, presumably bone crystals, are localized in one interband of each period. ×54,000. (From Jackson 1957, *Proc. Roy. Soc.*, ser. B, 146:270–80.)

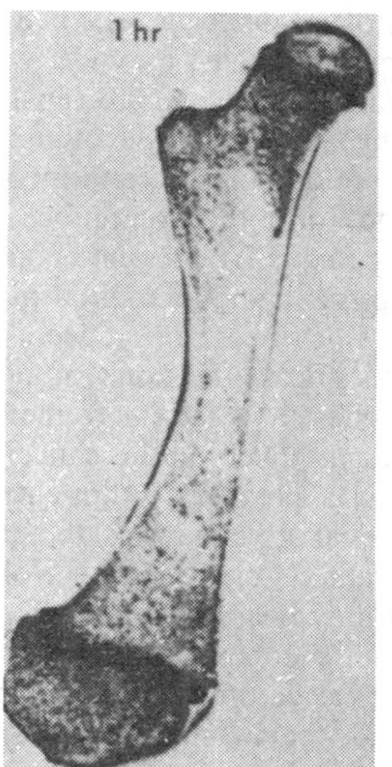

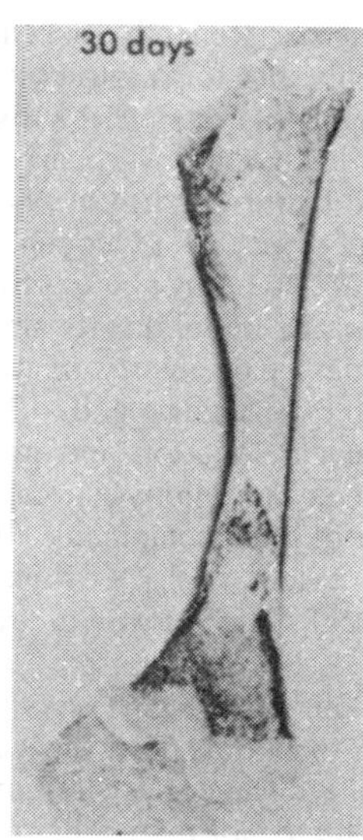

Figure 34.7. Autoradiograms of femurs of pigs injected with ^{45}Ca at 1 hour and 30 days before sacrificing. (From Plate I, C.L. Comar, W.E. Lotz, and G.A. Boyd 1952, *Am. J. Anat.* 90:113-25.)

HISTOGENESIS AND DEVELOPMENT

The development of bone occurs either by the direct transformation of connective tissue (intramembranous ossification), or by replacement of a previously formed cartilage model (endochondral or intracartilaginous ossification), or by a combination of these. In either situation, the mechanism appears to be identical and to involve the osteoblasts.

Intramembranous ossification

This type of ossification occurs in all parts of the body and is exemplified by bone formation under the periosteum of long bones and the formation of the flat bones (calvaria) of the skull. At the site where bone is to be formed, one observes mesenchymal cells that are connected by cell processes. Bundles of collagenous fibrils run between the cells in all directions, and the semifluid ground substance bathes both cells and fibrils. Just prior to ossification, the mesenchymal cells are transformed to osteoblasts, and the intercellular substance increases in density and amount and becomes more homogeneous. Through these transformations, the interstitial matrix becomes calcifiable and the mineral content of the matrix rapidly increases, forming bone. Through the activity of the osteoblasts, additional matrix is synthesized and calcified, and the bone increases in thickness. The layer of osteoblasts remains on the exterior surface although some osteoblasts become surrounded by calcified matrix and develop into osteocytes.

During the growth phase, periosteal bone of the diaphysis increases in diameter while functioning as support, housing for the bone marrow, and the means of locomotion. In general terms, the manner in which the diameter increases is as follows. The osteoblastic layer of cells lying under the periosteum continues to lay down new bone appositionally to the exterior surface of pre-existing periosteal bone. At the inner surface of the diaphysis, numerous osteoclasts remove bone at about the same rate as new bone is formed on the periosteal side. If one considers a small cross section of the diaphysis over a period of time, it appears as if compact bone is slowly moving outward with no apparent increase in width (Fig. 34.7). At early periods after a single injection of ^{45}Ca, heavy deposition is seen under the periosteum of the diaphysis. The labeled part of bone appears to progress toward the center until the resorbing, endosteal surface is reached. The labeled bone is removed by osteoclastic action.

Endochondral (intracartilaginous) ossification

The growth apparatus, the complex system or mechanism by which bones elongate during growth, illustrates this type of bone formation. Encompassing the area from the hyaline cartilage of the epiphyseal plate to the secondary spongiosa, the growth apparatus may be separated into arbitrary zones, each zone corresponding to a phase of endochondral ossification (see Fig. 34.2). At the epiphyseal front, there is a layer of hyaline cartilage formed by cartilage cells, some of which are embedded within the matrix. Beneath this, the older cartilage cells begin to multiply and form into columns separated by wide, parallel bands of interstitial substance. The cells are separated from each other vertically by a thin capsule of matrix. These then hypertrophy, becoming enlarged and incorporating stores of glycogen, to form the contiguous columns of hypertrophic cartilage cells. If adequate concentrations of mineral salts are present, the interstitial matrix calcifies, particularly in the areas between adjacent columns of cartilage cells. This forms the zone of provisional calcification and provides a structural framework between the epiphyseal cartilage plate and the cancellous bone of the metaphysis. It was previously thought that after extensive hypertrophy and glycogenesis the cartilage cells die. However, recent observations by Holtrop (1972) strongly suggest that they become bone cells.

Loops of blood vessels with accompanying connective tissue penetrate into the vertical columns, and the interstitial substances are removed, leaving the calcified vertical matrix of the primary spongiosa intact to act as scaffolding upon which bone matrix is later deposited. In this way, the newly formed endochrondral bone has a configuration similar to that of the replaced cartilage. With further growth of bone, remodeling of primary spongiosa takes place, and most of the remaining cartilage is removed. Bone trabeculae of a more permanent type, the secondary spongiosa, are formed. In the secondary spongiosa, some of the newly formed trabeculae may be either strengthened through osteoblastic activity or resorbed by osteoclasts. The remaining trabeculae become thicker, eventually assuming the form of the coarse cancellous bone of the adult skeleton.

The width of the growth apparatus remains relatively constant during the growth process. New hyaline cartilage is formed proximally at about the same rate as the secondary spongiosa is resorbed. In this way, there is an advancing front of hyaline cartilage with a continually disappearing zone of bony trabeculae behind.

As with the widening of the diaphysis, the pattern of mineralization at the growth apparatus can also be demonstrated by autoradiography (see Figure 34.7). Soon after ^{45}Ca administration, heavy deposition is seen at the epiphyseal plate and in the subjacent trabecular bone of the metaphysis. At 30 days after ^{45}Ca administration, the radioactive content of the plate is relatively low, and the image given by trabecular bone is considerably less than in the first autoradiogram. At 60 days, nearly all of the radioactivity within the trabecular bone of the metaphysis has disappeared, due to the resorption of the labeled mineral by osteoclasts and replacement with nonlabeled bone.

When growth ceases, there is no further net synthesis of bone in the adult, but the skeleton continues to be renewed and remodeled. However, skeletal turnover is quite slow, and if radiocalcium were desposited at this stage, some would not move into sites of resorption for years or perhaps over the lifetime of the individual. This fact accentuates the hazard from certain fallout radionuclides (^{90}Sr, ^{89}Sr) that selectively accumulate in the skeleton (McLean and Budy 1964, Comar and Wasserman 1964).

Modeling and remodeling

The shape of long bones is undoubtedly predetermined genetically for the function to be served and modified by the mechanical stresses of weight-bearing and of the attached musculature. In general, growth occurs at the diaphysis and epiphysis as described, but specific areas of bone have different rates of formation and destruction. A case in point is the developing femur of the growing rat, as studied with radiocalcium and autoradiographic procedures by Tomlin et al. (1953). The femur increases in mass while at the same time, retaining its original configuration and shape (Fig. 34.8). Tomlin et al. observed that little of the original mineral of the 30-day-old bone was

Figure 34.8. Three stages in the growth of the femur in the rat. (From Tomlin, Henry, and Kon 1953, *Brit. J. Nutr.* 7:235–52. By courtesy of the British Journal of Nutrition.)

present in the older, larger femurs. Most had been resorbed.

The curvatures at either end of the femur result from different rates of bone formation and resorption on the convex and concave surfaces. An increase in the width of cortical bone occurs since bone formation under the periosteum takes place at a somewhat more rapid rate than resorption under the endosteum.

Even as bone is growing in size, internal reconstruction is taking place, principally through the formation, destruction, and remodeling of the Haversian systems (osteons).

Osteoclasts associated with blood vessels erode through the endosteal surface, forming channels oriented with the long axis of the shaft. A layer of osteoblasts forms on the surface of the eroded tunnel and successive layers of lamellar bone are laid down, enclosing osteocytes within their lacunae. As the blood vessels grow and branch, new channels are made and new osteons form to surround them. These initial osteons are termed the Haversian system of the first generation. Subsequently, the first generation osteons may be eroded by similar processes, replaced by Haversian systems of the second and later generations. The newer osteons usually cut across, when seen in cross section, more than one of the older osteons, giving rise to a complicated pattern of lamellae which are generally concentric in shape but whose outer circumference may be round, oval, teardrop shaped, and so forth. A cement line separates adjacent osteons at their boundaries. When the channel is being eroded, their surface is covered with osteoclasts and, when being filled in, with osteoblasts.

According to Vincent (1957, quoted from McLean and Rowland 1963), the average resorption cavity in the dog forms in about 3 weeks, the time necessary for tunneling or excavation. Some 6–12 weeks are required to construct the new osteon, including partial mineralization. Deposition of bone mineral occurs rapidly at first (up to 70 percent mineralized) and then at a slower rate thereafter.

Osteons in various stages of formation are shown in Figure 34.9. In the forming osteon (large dark circle in A) four regions can be delineated. Central is the round, dark space (the Haversian canal) enclosing the osteoblastic layer, blood vessels, and connective tissue. The canal is immedately surrounded by a light band of preosseous osteoid tissue. A dark band separates the preosseous tissue from already ossified lamella, and this band is called the zone of demarcation (Frost 1963). The osteoid seam comprises the zone of demarcation and the inner preosseous layer. The fourth region is the bone itself. The soft X rays used in producing the microradiogram (B) readily penetrate through the preosseous tissue and the contents of the Haversian canal. The canal of the developing osteon, therefore, appears much larger than in the undecalcified section. The more mature osteons are of greater densities, indicating that the degree of mineralization varies among osteons and that some are not yet completely ossified. The autoradiogram (C) and fluorescent image (D) show that mineral deposition and tetracycline incorporation occur at the same site, the zone of demarcation.

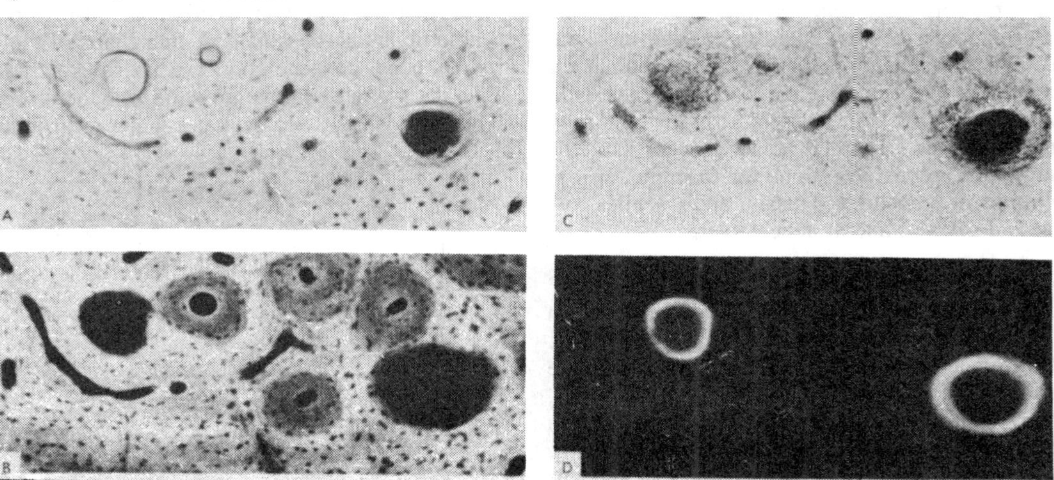

Figure 34.9. Micrographs of the same section of diaphyseal radius of an 8-month-old beagle intravenously given both tetracycline 4 days and ^{226}Ra 2 days before sacrifice. A, photomicrograph of the unstained, undecalcified section shows several osteons with central Haversian canals, circumferential lamellae, and embedded osteocytes within lacunae. Those osteons with small canals are fully or almost fully calcified. B, microradiogram made with 9 kv X-rays, shows that much of the newly forming osteon at the right is largely nonmineralized. C, α-track autoradiogram indicates the sites of ^{226}Ra deposition. D, fluorescent image with ultraviolet light shows the sites of tetracycline incorporation. ×90. (From R.E. Rowland, in McLean and Budy, *Radiation, Isotopes, and Bone*, Academic Press, New York, 1964.)

SKELETAL DYNAMICS

Net bone growth

During growth, the mass of the skeleton obviously increases, and the net change can be estimated by several methods. First, the increase in the gross height, length, and so on of the animal can be measured. Second, a typical long bone, for example, the femur, can be visualized on film by X rays and its length measured at two different times. Third, since most of the body's calcium resides in the skeleton, a conventional calcium balance can reveal net skeletal calcium retention. Fourth, from a uniform experimental animal population, individuals can be killed at different periods and the increment in skeletal mass determined. The values obtained will be either direct or indirect measurements of net bone growth and will represent the difference between two opposing processes: total bone growth or accretion and total bone loss or resorption. For example, at time period 1, a hypothetical growing bone has a mass of 16 mg. Through the complex process of bone formation 8 mg is accreted to the skeleton and at the same time 4 mg is resorbed; the net bone growth is 4 mg, and the bone at period 2 has attained a mass of 20 mg. This relationship can be expressed by the equation $\Delta S = A - R$, where ΔS is the rate of net gain or loss of skeletal calcium; A, rate of calcium accretion; and R, rate of calcium resorption. (Other units can be used, such as skeletal mass or skeletal phosphorus.) The rates of accretion and resorption change during growth and maturation and as a consequence of disease and malnutrition.

An increase in the rate of net bone growth could result from either an increase in the rate of accretion or a decrease in the rate of resorption, for example, in growing animals, during repair of a fracture, and during the curative phase after treatment of rickets and osteomalacia with vitamin D. When accretion and resorption are equal, there is of course no net bone growth, as in the nongrowing mature individual. There is a net loss of skeleton when resorption exceeds accretion, for example, in hyperparathyroidism, postmenopausal and senile osteoporosis, and severe mineral deficiencies.

Exchangeable and nonexchangeable bone

Mineral ions from the plasma and interstitial fluid can enter the skeleton by accretion or by exchange reactions. The basic difference between these processes is that there is an addition of actual mineral during accretion whereas, with exchange, there is no net gain or loss of mineral. In the latter case, for every ion that enters the skeleton, another ion of the same or similar kind leaves. The importance of exchange reactions was first noted when the rate of incorporation of bone-seeking radionuclides into the skeleton was determined. The rate of uptake of plasma ^{45}Ca by bone was more rapid than could be accounted for by accretion alone. It became apparent that some of the radiocalcium atoms entered the skeleton by an ionic exchange reaction, replacing nonradioactive stable calcium atoms. Before this process was widely recognized, serious errors in the calculation of accretion rates were made.

Not all of the skeletal mineral is exchangeable; in fact, only about 1 percent of the total bone mineral is involved. The major fraction is nonexchangeable and represents that mineral that is buried deep within the crystal interior and not in direct contact with body fluids.

Measurement

Kinetic method

Bauer et al. (1961) were among the first to propose a method, using radiocalcium, for calculating accretion, resorption, net bone growth, and exchangeable bone calcium. A group of uniform animals are parenterally injected with a tracer (carrier-free) quantity of radiocalcium (^{45}Ca). Periodically, individuals are bled and killed, and at autopsy a representative bone or the total skeleton is removed. The radioactive and nonradioactive concentrations of calcium in serum or plasma are accurately measured, and the amount of radiocalcium in the skeleton is determined (Fig. 34.10). The specific activity of serum calcium (ratio of radioactive to total calcium per unit volume of serum) falls rapidly soon after isotope injection, and the radiocalcium content of the bone first increases rapidly and then less rapidly, approaching some maximum value at 72–120 hours. With these data and using certain assumptions, Bauer et al. (1961) estimated exchangeable bone calcium and rate of bone-calcium accretion (Table 34.2). These data show comparisons between net bone growth, accretion, and resorption in the whole tibia and the tibia ends and shafts of the rat. In the whole bone, the accretion rate is several times greater than the net rate of bone growth, as is the resorption rate. This dramatically demonstrates that a measurement of net

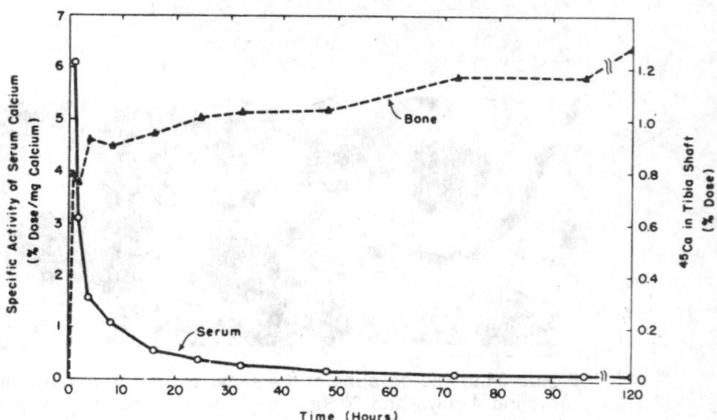

Figure 34.10. Specific activity of calcium in serum and radiocalcium in bone after a single injection of ^{45}Ca. (Data from Bauer, Carlsson, and Lindquist, in Comar and Bronner, eds., *Mineral Metabolism*, Academic Press, New York, 1961.)

e 34.2. Calcium metabolism in the tibiae of a young rat

ue	Ca content (mg)	Net bone growth rate (mg Ca/hr)	Accretion rate (mg Ca/hr)	Resorption rate (mg Ca/hr)	Exchangeable fraction (mg Ca)
le tibiae	66	0.04	0.17	0.13	2.1
s	36	0.02	0.14	0.12	1.8
fts	30	0.02	0.03	0.01	0.3

om Bauer, Carlsson, and Lindquist, in Comar and Bronner, eds., *Mineral abolism*, Academic Press, New York, 1961

bone growth alone would give only a small indication of the overall metabolic activity of the skeleton. The tabulated values, in addition, reveal that the turnover rate of the ends (epiphysis, metaphysis) greatly exceeds that of the shafts (diaphysis). They further show that the exchangeable calcium fraction in the ends is greater than that in the shafts.

Other kinetic methods have been devised for calculating accretion and the other components of overall skeletal function. In principle, calcium tracer is used primarily in the measurement of pool size and turnover of the miscible calcium pool. According to the formulation, pool turnover can be accounted for by the absorption of dietary calcium and bone resorption as calcium inputs into the pool, and by total excretion and bone mineralization as outputs from the pool (Harris and Heaney 1969, Aubert and Milhaud 1960).

Microradiographic method

An alternative method for assessing bone turnover and bone formation and resorption has been used by Jowsey (1963). Her procedure entails the microradiographic analysis of bone sections taken by biopsy. A visual distinction is made between osteons undergoing active resorption, osteons where active formation is occurring, inactive osteons, and osteons in intermediate transition stages (Fig. 34.11). Resorbing osteons have highly calcified surfaces which are highly irregular; the lamellae lay at angles to the surface rather than concentrically about the central canal. Forming osteons are distinctly different in appearance; the surfaces are smooth and have regions of low density with new lamellae running parallel to the surface. Other topographical signs point to those osteons that are resorbing very actively, those that were once resorbing but have since stopped, and those which are metabolically inactive.

The metabolic status of the bone sample is quantitated by measuring the lengths of the bone surface that are either resorbing, forming, or inactive. The data are expressed as the length of the surface undergoing resorption or formation, as a percent of the length of the surfaces of inactive osteons in the same section. There is justification for using the length of surface as the parameter of bone activity, since the processes of resorption and formation do occur at these interfaces.

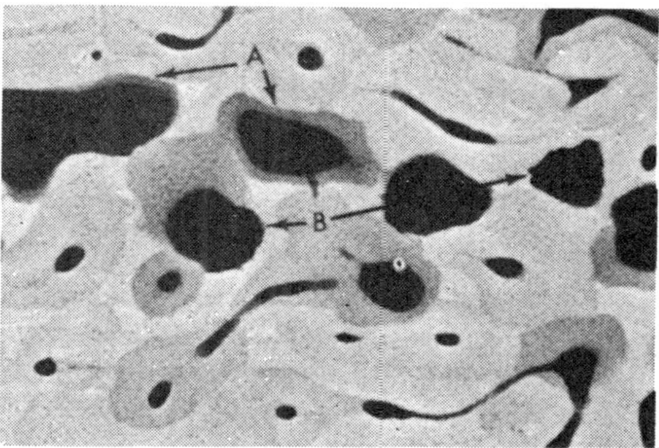

Figure 34.11. Osteons showing format on, resorption, and inactivity with intermediate stages. Arrows designate regions of bone formation (A) and resorption (B). ×25. (Courtesy of J. Jowsey, Mayo Clinic, 1963.)

Accretion in disease states

Bauer et al. (1961) made a survey of the effect of various diseases on calcium accretion, as determined by kinetic methods. High accretion rates were observed in patients with Paget's disease, fractures, tumors, hyperparathyroidism, vitamin D–resistant rickets after treatment with massive doses of vitamin D, and hyperthyroidism. Normal rates were seen in vitamin D–resistant rickets, and in vitamin D–deficient rickets after vitamin D administration. Low accretion rates were associated with hypoparathyroidism, untreated vitamin D–deficiency rickets, and hypothyroidism.

From microradiographic investigations Jowsey (1963) observed that the bone formation rates of normal individuals and osteoporotic patients of similar age were similar, whereas in the osteoporotics bone resorption was much higher than normal. This indicates that osteoporosis is a consequence of an enhanced bone destruction when, at the same time, bone formation is proceeding at a normal or near normal rate. In hyperparathyroidism, the rate of bone resorption was increased by a factor of 10 and the formation rate was also increased but to a lesser degree; the difference yields a net bone loss.

Accretion in domestic animals

With the Bauer equation, the skeletal accretion rates of some domestic animals were calculated from existing radioisotope data (Table 34.3). Accretion values, as expected, decreased with age both in sheep and cattle; the values were similar between species at comparable age levels when expressed as per kg body calcium. Also, in the goat lactation does not apparently infuence skeletal accretion; the accretion values of the mature goats were again in good agreement with the values for the other ruminants of comparable age.

Using a different approach but also based on ^{45}Ca tracer methodology, Kronfeld et al. (1976) observed that

Table 34.3. Calcium accretion rates

Species	Age (months)	Accretion rate * (g Ca/day)
Cattle	0.3	30
	6	10
	15–36	5
	60–160	3
Sheep	0.5	25
	6	15
	12	4
	aged	4
Goats (nonlactating)	mature	3.1
Goats (lactating)	mature	3

* Per kg body calcium

From Wasserman, *Second United Nations Conference on the Peaceful Uses of Atomic Energy,* Pergamon, London, 1958, p. 136. Calculations based on equations of Bauer et al. 1961.

total calcium uptake by mature nonlactating, nonpregnant cows was about 9 g of calcium per day.

CALCIFICATION MECHANISM

In general the osteoblasts appear at the centers of calcification. These cells synthesize and then elaborate in the intercellular spaces the organic components of the bone matrix. After a period of time, the matrix becomes calcifiable, and inorganic salts, ultimately arising from plasma, deposit into the bone matrix. Obviously, an adequate supply of all components and their precursors are required for normal bone formation. In vitamin D–deficiency rickets, for example, part of the syndrome is due to a deficiency of adequate amounts of calcium and phosphate to support ossification. Calcification and other related events at the zone of provisional calcification do not take place, but the preosseous cartilage continues to be synthesized by the chondroblasts; this results in the characteristic widening of the epiphyseal plate as seen in rickets.

The deposition of bone salts in matrix requires a physical change in state from ions in solution to ions aggregated into insoluble bone salts. The calcium, phosphate, and hydroxyl ions derived from the extracellular fluid combine in some manner to form the initial crystal nuclei upon which additional ions are deposited or aggregated. The physical change thus encompasses two continuous processes: first, crystal nucleation, in which the first units of the crystal are formed, and second, crystal growth, by which the size of the initial fragments are increased. There may also be recrystallization, in which larger crystals are formed at the expense of smaller ones; this involves the dissolution of some of the primary crystals, followed by redeposition of the constituent ions onto the surfaces of larger crystals.

If, as proposed by Termine et al. (1967), amorphous calcium phosphate is the bone salt initially deposited, there would then follow its transformation to hydroxyapatite.

Table 34.4. Average distribution of calcium in serum (mEq/L)

Protein-bound	
To globulin	0.34
To albumin	1.30
	1.64
Soluble complexes	
To bicarbonate	0.32
To citrate	0.14
To phosphate	0.12
To others	0.02
	0.60
Ionic	2.66
Total	5.00

Adapted from Neuman and Neuman, *The Chemical Dynamics of Bone Mineral,* U. of Chicago Press, Chicago, 1958

Calcium and phosphorus in serum

The distribution of calcium among the various serum factions has been measured or estimated (Table 34.4). The total calcium concentration in serum of many species averages about 5 mEq/L, and a considerable proportion is bound to either serum proteins or smaller molecular weight anions (bicarbonate, citrate, phosphate) such that the ionic calcium concentration is substantially less than the total, being about 2.6 mEq/L or 1.3×10^{-3} M. By multiplying this concentration by the activity coefficient (0.36), the calcium activity is found to be 4.7×10^{-4}. This value would be different in the serums of diseased or abnormal animals, since some of the many variables (pH, A/G ratio, citrate concentration) influencing calcium binding would be different.

The approximate average plasma phosphate concentration (as $HPO_4^{=}$) for several species, in mEq/L, is as follows: pig, 11.9; sheep, cattle, and goats, 8.9; horses, 3.4. Nearly all of the phosphate is present as orthophosphate ions with approximately 12 percent bound to protein (Walser 1960). Calculations indicate that 81.4 percent of the orthophosphate is in the form of the divalent anion, $HPO_4^{=}$, and 18.6 percent as the univalent anion, $H_2PO_4^-$, at 37°C and at an ionic strength of 0.165. The activities of $HPO_4^{=}$ and $H_2PO_4^-$ were estimated to be 0.19×10^{-3} and 0.12×10^{-3} respectively.

Calcium-phosphorus ion product

The calcium and $HPO_4^{=}$ activities given above yield an ion product of about 0.9×10^{-7}. How does this value compare to the solubility product of bone mineral? As discussed by Neuman and Neuman (1958), there is evidence that the ill-defined solubility product for hydroxyapatite is significantly less than the ion product of Ca^{++}

and $HPO_4^{=}$ in serum. This means that serum is supersaturated with respect to this form of bone mineral. On the other hand, serum is undersaturated with respect to amorphous calcium phosphate.

Theories of calcification

Theories of the calcification mechanism are dependent upon knowledge of the form of bone salt in contact with the extracellular fluid of bone. If it is hydroxyapatite, the bone salt could spontaneously precipitate, provided that an available nucleation site were present. If the bone salt is amorphous calcium phosphate, then the mineral ions in bone fluid would have to be concentrated by an enzymatic or a transport process to the point of precipitation.

Phosphatase theory

One of the early theories attempted to explain the function of alkaline phosphatase in calcifying areas (Robison 1923). This enzyme catalyzes the hydrolysis of phosphate esters and hypothetically could operate by the scheme given below:

$$\text{Phosphate ester} \longrightarrow PO_4^{\equiv} + \text{an alcohol}$$

$$PO_4^{\equiv} + Ca^{++} \longrightarrow [CaPO_4]_{ppt}$$

By increasing the phosphate ion concentration at the calcifying site, the solubility product of bone salt would be exceeded, and precipitation within the organic matrix would occur.

Related to the Robison theory are the findings of Gutman and Yu (1950) on the relationship of glycogen and glycogenolysis to calcification. Glycogen was earlier known to accumulate in cartilage cells and to disappear before cartilage cell degeneration took place. During glycogen breakdown, organic phosphate esters are formed which could serve as substrates for alkaline phosphatase and as sources of inorganic phosphate.

Although the theory Robison originally proposed now appears untenable, alkaline phosphatase may still have an important role in calcification, such as in the synthesis of the components of the organic matrix and the transfer of high-energy phosphate bond energy to the calcification site.

Matrix vesicles

In 1958, Irving, using a "very crude method," observed that a lipophilic dye (Sudan Black B) exclusively stained calcification sites of bones and teeth previously extracted with hot pyridine (Irving 1976). The stained material was later found to be phospholipids, mainly phosphatidyl serine and phosphatidyl inositol (Irving 1976). A relationship between Irving's lipid, alkaline phosphatase, and the calcification mechanism is suggested from recent studies. Anderson (1969) and Bonucci (1970), by ultrastructural techniques, described tiny globules in the region of calcifying cartilage of bone. These globules, now termed matrix vesicles, are membrane-bounded structures containing alkaline phosphatase and other phosphatases, and their membranes are, of course, comprised of lipid. These matrix vesicles are present not only in calcifying cartilage, but also in bone, teeth, and antlers (Anderson 1976). An important feature of these extracellular vesicles is their ability to accumulate calcium phosphate salts, both within their volume and on their surfaces. Calcium uptake is facilitated by the presence of adenosine triphosphate (ATP) and pyrophosphate. The isolated vesicles were shown to contain hydroxyapatite. The evidence suggests a significant role for these structures in the calcification mechanism, and they might constitute the initial site of calcification in the bone matrix.

The mitochondria of bone and cartilage cells also have the capacity to accumulate calcium, and this particular function of mitochondria also bears on the overall mechanism of calcification (Martin and Matthews 1970, Brighton and Hunt 1976).

Collagen and nucleation

The fibrous protein, collagen, as shown by X-ray diffraction and electron diffraction, has a crystallinelike structure and could act as a nucleating center for the deposition or precipitation of calcium phosphate salts. In fact, Glimcher (1960) was able to show that reconstituted native collagen (64 nm repeating unit) from skin and tendon induced crystal nucleation when added to metastable calcium-phosphate solutions. If the molecular structure of the isolated collagen was altered, the ability to induce nucleation or crystallization was lost. The deposition of the mineral phase appears to occur in spaces or holes located within the collagen fibers of the organic matrix (Glimcher 1968). These spaces may provide not only nucleation sites, but also a suitable microenvironment for the phase transition, i.e. solution to solid, to occur.

Other lines of evidence strongly suggest that collagen is intimately involved in the process of bone formation. Jackson (1957) showed quite clearly by electron microscopy that early deposition of apatite particles in embryonic avian periosteal bone occurs not only on the surface of collagen fibrils but also within the fibrils (see Fig. 34.6). She demonstrated further that the early deposited material is mainly localized in one interband of each period. Therefore, initial apatite crystal formation is first seen within or on the collagen fibrils in a definite spatial relationship to the molecular structure of the fibril itself, suggesting a significant role of collagen in calcification. However, in hypertrophic cartilage, the situation is not as clear. At this site, there was no obvious relationship between the deposition of crystals and the orientation of the fibers of cartilage (Robinson and Cameron 1956).

The ion, i.e. calcium or phosphate, that first associates

with the nucleating site is not known. Rasmussen and Bordier (1974) argued that phosphate first binds to collagen, either covalently or noncovalently, and that the next step is the association of Ca^{++} with the bound phosphate group. Others (Urist 1966, Urry 1971) have proposed that Ca^{++} first associates with matrix collagen, followed by phosphate.

The function of the protein-polysaccharides of bone matrix is not precisely known, but their concentration decreases in regions of calcification. It is most likely that the removal of protein-polysaccharides allows the deposition of mineral salts into collagen to occur, or that these macromolecules serve as nucleation sites for mineral ions (Rasmussen and Bordier 1974).

Cartilage will not calcify if certain factors are either absent (inducers of calcification) or present (inhibitors of calcification). Proposed as possible inhibitors are pyrophosphates (Fleish and Neuman 1961) and polysaccharides (Glimcher 1960); each would be hydrolyzed by suitable enzymes (phosphatases or sulfatases) before a site becomes calcifiable. On the other side, a specific ATP-phosphorylating system may be a factor in allowing the organic matrix to calcify. Further, there might be subtle differences between the macromolecular structure of collagen in cartilage and collagen in bone that allows only the latter to calcify.

RESORPTION

Resorption is the removal by degradation and dissolution of the entire complicated structure of bone. The components of organic matrix are degraded and released, and the bone salt is solubilized.

Enzymes such as cathepsin, collagenase, and hyaluronidase hydrolyze either collagen or protein-polysaccharides. Except for collagenase, they are thought to reside in the lysosomal particles within osteoclasts and osteocytes and are released during bone resorption (Vaes 1968a).

Bone salt dissolution involves a different problem. Hydroxyapatite must be put into solution in an environment supposedly supersaturated with respect to the mineral phase. In principle, there are two mechanisms by which this can be accomplished: the local pH at the resorbing site could be low, favoring solubilization; or organic substances could be present which form soluble complexes or chelates with calcium. Both possibilities are unified in the "acid-theory" of Neuman which was reviewed by Munson et al. (1963). The theory suggests that parathyroid hormone stimulates or alters bone cell metabolism so that the formation and release of organic acids are greatly increased. These acids, primarily lactic and citric, produce a low pH locally which favors the dissolution of bone salt. Also, the organic acids, especially citrate, could further enhance resorption by forming firm complexes with calcium and by exchanging for phosphate ions at the crystal surface. There is considerable evidence in support of this theory but additional observations are required. Specifically, the pH of the resorption sites has yet to be measured. It is clear, however, that the resorption of bone and the action of parathyroid hormone are intimately associated with intermediary cellular metabolism. This is further supported by the observation that the inhibition of glycolysis also inhibits calcium mobilization by bone fragments in vitro.

The release of organic matrix components and the inorganic salts of the mineral phase during resorption presumably occurs extracellularly and almost simultaneously. However, histological studies with the electron microscope suggest another possible sequence of events at the resorbing site adjacent to the osteoclast. Hancox and Boothroyd (1963) clearly showed that loose detached apatite crystals were present within cytoplasmic channels and vacuoles of the cell (see Fig. 34.5). The denuded collagen fibrils were observed exterior to the cell between the cytoplasmic folds of the ruffled border. This suggested that the crystals could be removed intact from the organic matrix and transferred to intracellular sites for dissolution and subsequent release of the mineral ions to extracellular fluid. The osteoid is then hydrolyzed extracellularly by lysosomal-like hydrolytic enzymes supplied by the osteoclast. Whereas Neuman and Neuman (1958) suggest that the solubilization of bone mineral occurs primarily at the crystal surface, the electron micrographs of Hancox and Boothroyd (1963) suggest that the crystals can be shifted in toto to the cell interior and acted upon there. The forces causing crystal dissolution (low pH, chelation) may be the same in both regions.

Osteocytes, situated within lacunae of bone, are also capable of resorbing bone under the appropriate stimuli; this process is termed osteocytic osteolysis. The relative significance of osteoclastic osteolysis and osteocytic osteolysis in calcium homeostasis was discussed by Rasmussen and Bordier (1974). It was proposed that the former reacts more rapidly (but to a limited extent) to hormonal regulation, whereas the osteoclastic process responds more slowly and achieves considerable magnitude with time. These dual responses are cooperatively responsible for animals' fine-tuned control of blood calcium levels.

REGULATION OF BONE METABOLISM AND HOMEOSTASIS

Several important factors influence the rate of bone turnover and renewal, bone growth, bone resorption, calcium and phosphorus concentrations in blood, the degree of intestinal calcium and phosphorus absorption, and the reabsorption of these elements by the kidney tubule. Those of significance are the gonadal hormones (estrogen, androgens), thyroid hormone, hydrocortisone, growth hormone, vitamin A, and ascorbic acid. Most of these are prominent in the normal growth and maturation of bone tissue, and their deficiency or excess can exert profound effects. For example, ascorbic acid deficiency results in impaired collagen synthesis, since it is required in the hydroxylation reaction of the proline and lysine residues of protocollagen. The hydroxylated amino acids participate in the formation of collagen cross linkings. As another example, excess vitamin A can induce excessive bone resorption; a suggested mechanism is the labilization of lysosomal membranes and thereby the release of lysosomal digestive enzymes. Vitamin A deficiency inhibits osteoclastic activity and thus results in abnormal bone resorption patterns. Growth hormone in deficient amounts leads to dwarfism and, in excess, to gigantism (in the growing individual) or acromegaly (in the adult).

Of considerable importance also is the maintenance of blood calcium levels, for which the bone represents an available reservoir. Abnormally low or high blood calcium concentrations lead to acute or chronic pathological states. The consequences of severe hypocalcemia in man are hyperirritability, tetany, and if untreated, coma and death. At the other end, hypercalcemia induces nausea, muscular weakness, oliguria, thirst, nephrocalcinosis, and mental (psychosislike) symptoms (Fourman et al. 1968).

From the viewpoint of homeostatic regulation of calcium and phosphate metabolism, the most prominent factors are parathyroid hormone, calcitonin, and vitamin D.

Parathyroid hormone and calcitonin

The parathyroid glands secrete a hormone that influences blood calcium levels. The classical effect of parathyroidectomy in most animal species is a rapid decline of blood calcium; if followed by an injection of either parathyroid extract or purified hormone, the blood calcium level rises. In addition to parathyroid hormone, another hormone first described by Copp and Cheney (1962) and Hirsch et al. (1963) also has a central role in calcium homeostasis. This hormone, calcitonin (or thyrocalcitonin), is elaborated by the parafollicular C cells of the thyroid gland of mammals. In lower vertebrates, such as the chicken, frog, and shark, calcitonin is present in high concentration in the ultimobranchial gland. The parafollicular C cells of the mammal are of ultimobranchial origin (Copp 1969). The action of calcitonin, from all evidence, is opposite to that of parathyroid hormone, functioning in much the same way as the insulin-glucagon system in the control of blood sugar. When blood calcium levels are high, calcitonin is secreted and apparently acts by inhibiting bone resorption to cause a rapid decrease in blood calcium levels, presumably to normal. (For more details on parathyroid hormone and calcitonin see Chapter 52.)

Parathyroid hormone directly affects bone resorption by stimulating osteoclastic osteolysis and osteocytic osteolysis (Bélanger et al. 1963), and increasing the number of osteoclasts on the bone surface. This hormone also has a phosphaturic effect, that is, it inhibits the reabsorption of phosphate by the kidney.

Recent evidence suggests that parathyroid hormone directly stimulates the membrane-bounded enzyme, adenylate cyclase (Chase and Aurbach 1968), which catalyzes the formation of cyclic 3′,5′-adenosine monophosphate (cyclic AMP). It was proposed that cyclic AMP acts as the direct, intracellular effector of parathyroid activity in bone and kidney. The hormone increased the urinary excretion of cyclic AMP in vivo and stimulated adenyl cyclase activity by kidney membrane fractions in vitro. Further, a derivative of cyclic AMP (dibutyryl cyclic AMP) stimulated the resorption of bone in tissue culture and induced hypercalcemia when injected into parathyroidectomized rats (Vaes 1968b, Wells and Lloyd 1969). Parathyroid hormone also increases calcium movement into responsive cells, and this cellular calcium, in conjunction with cyclic AMP, may be the immediate effector of parathyroid hormone action on osteocytes, osteoblasts, and osteoclasts (Rasmussen and Bordier 1974).

Calcitonin acts directly on bone by inhibiting bone resorption, and there is some evidence that this hormone might stimulate bone formation. Calcitonin does not appear to alter calcium absorption by the intestine, and a direct effect on the kidney has not been unequivocally demonstrated (Hirsch and Munson 1969). Capen and Young (1967) proposed that parturient paresis is due to the abrupt release of calcitonin from the thyroid gland, causing a rapid decrease in blood calcium levels. The existence of ultimobranchial tumors in breeding bulls fed an excessively high calcium diet was shown by Krook et al. (1969). This finding is consistent with the suggestion that one of calcitonin's functions is to maintain normal blood calcium levels during transient periods of hypercalcemia.

Vitamin D

Vitamin D deficiency causes rickets in the growing animal and osteomalacia in the adult. Both diseases are characterized by a depressed mineralization of the skeleton while the synthesis of uncalcified matrix, the osteoid, continues. The result is bone that has a low ash or mineral content in relation to its wet weight, dry weight, or total nitrogen content. Although the primary cause for rickets and osteomalacia is vitamin D deficiency, other disorders, such as steatorrhea (malabsorption by the intestine), renal tubular defects, and chronic uremia, produce similar pathological conditions. In rickets and osteomalacia, blood calcium is either normal or low, blood phosphate is low, and blood alkaline phosphatase is either high or normal.

Recent investigations into the metabolism of vitamin D have produced new concepts and information on mineral

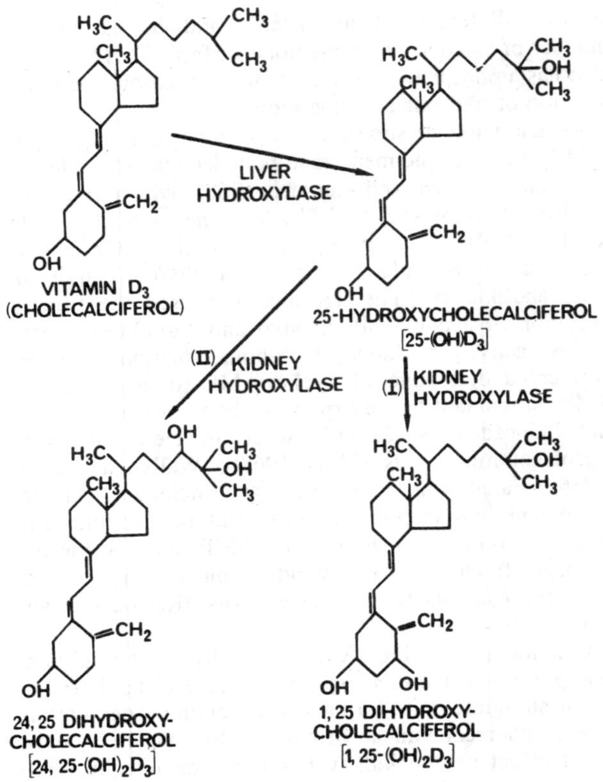

Figure 34.12. Structure and metabolism of vitamin D_3 and its important metabolites

homeostasis (Wasserman 1975b, Norman and Henry 1974, Omdahl and DeLuca 1973, Kodiček 1974, Haussler 1974). Vitamin D, derived from the diet or from ultraviolet irradiation of skin, is first hydroxylated in the liver to the 25-hydroxycholecalciferol form and subsequently to 1,25-dihydroxycholecalciferol [1,25-$(OH)_2D_3$] in the kidney (Fig. 34.12). The latter metabolite is considered to be the hormonal form of vitamin D and meets the usual criteria of a hormone, that is, it is produced at one site and causes a response elsewhere, and its production is feedback regulated. This hormonal form is synthesized in the kidney and elicits effects in the intestine, bone, and other tissues. Its rate of formation is related to the calcium, phosphate, and/or parathyroid hormone levels in blood, and the calcium and phosphorus needs of the animal. Under conditions in which 1,25-$(OH)_2D_3$ production is decreased because of an adequate mineral status, another metabolite of vitamin D_3 is formed in the kidney, 24,25-dihydroxycholecalciferol. This form can be further hydroxylated in the synthesis of 1,24,25-trihydroxycholecalciferol.

The major site of action of 1,25-$(OH)_2D_3$ is the intestine, where the absorption of calcium is increased. The mechanism for this appears to involve the stimulation of the synthesis of macromolecules that constitute essential parts of the calcium transport system. One such macromolecule is the vitamin D–dependent calcium-binding protein (CaBP) (Wasserman et al. 1969). A high correlation exists between the concentration of CaBP and the efficiency of calcium transport (Wasserman and Corradino 1973). Other intestinal macromolecules responsive to vitamin D or its metabolites are alkaline phosphatase (Holdsworth 1970, Norman et al. 1970) and a brush-border calcium-stimulated adenosine triphosphatase (Melancon and DeLuca 1970).

Vitamin D and 1,25-$(OH)_2D_3$ also have a direct effect on the intestinal absorption of phosphate.

Vitamin D and its metabolites have a direct effect on the kidney, increasing calcium and phosphate reabsorption (Puschett et al. 1972, Costanzo et al. 1974). A vitamin D–dependent CaBP is also present in this organ, exclusively in the distal tubule (Lippiello 1974).

The rate of synthesis of 1,25-$(OH)_2D_3$ is a key point in mineral homeostasis and can be modified by various factors and conditions. In animals receiving an inadequate supply of dietary calcium, calcium absorption is increased and the production of the metabolite by the kidney enzyme system is considerably greater than in normal controls. This stimulation of the kidney 1α-hydroxylase system could be a consequence of hypocalcemia and/or secondary to the increased release of parathyroid hormone; there is direct evidence that parathyroid hormone increases the formation of 1,25-$(OH)_2D_3$. In addition to calcium deficiency, an inadequacy of dietary phosphate also results in the increased formation of the metabolite, and subsequently, in the stimulation of calcium and phosphate absorption by the intestine. Other factors known or thought to affect its production are excess dietary strontium (inhibition), calcitonin, vitamin D or the metabolite itself, and certain toxic trace elements such as cadmium.

It should also be pointed out that 1,25-$(OH)_2D_3$ is an effective stimulator of bone resorption, and this and other vitamin D metabolites might have a favorable effect on bone formation (Raisz 1976, Rasmussen and Bordier 1974). Through its osteolytic action, in conjunction with parathyroid hormone, blood calcium levels could be maintained during periods of calcium deprivation by stimulating bone resorption.

Another possible point of control of vitamin D metabolism is the formation of 25-(OH)D_3 by liver enzymes. However, this reaction does not appear to be limiting under normal conditions.

DISEASES

The skeleton, like other tissues and organs, is prone to abnormal metabolism through a number of different causes. In general, these can be a consequence of genetic factors, abnormal endocrine function, nutritional deficiencies or excesses, or the presence of toxic elements (Fourman et al. 1968, Rasmussen and Bordier 1974, Prien et al. 1976).

Rickets and osteomalacia. The primary cause is inadequate vitamin D intake. There is excess formation of undermineralized bone matrix, due in large part to insufficient absorption of calcium and phosphorus.

Osteoporosis. This is characterized by a decreased bone mass. It is due to bone resorption being greater than bone formation. It is prominent in aging, and related to gonadal hormone deficiency. It also might be genetic in origin (idiopathatic osteoporosis). Inactivity causes disuse osteoporosis.

Paget's disease. Characterized by an increased bone turnover rate, i.e. accelerated bone formation and bone resorption, the bone is less well organized and of lower density than normal bone. This disease is associated with structural defects of the skeleton.

Osteogenesis imperfecta. This is an hereditary disease which appears to affect the synthesis of normal matrix by bone cells, particularly osteoblasts. Thin bones are seen, and multiple fractures occur in later life.

Primary hyperparathyroidism. Excess production of parathyroid hormone occurs even when the animal is hypercalcemic. It is commonly due to adenoma (benign tumor) of the parathyroid gland, parathyroid hyperplasia, and carcinoma. Acute hyperparathyroidism primarily stimulates osteolytic activity, and in the chronic state bone turnover is enhanced, with concomitant formation of less structured bone.

Secondary hyperparathyroidism. The excess secretion of hormone is a direct consequence of hypocalcemia due to inadequate absorption or availability of calcium, excess loss of calcium from the body, or the inability of bone to supply calcium to the extracellular fluid. Parathyroid glands are hyperplastic. Skeletal effects are similar to those in primary hyperparathyroidism.

Renal osteodystrophy. One consequence of this is decreased synthesis of 1,25-$(OH)_2D_3$ by kidney enzymes. Symptoms are osteomalacic, and favorable responses are obtained with appropriate vitamin D metabolites.

Excess adrenal corticoid secretion. The steroids secreted by the adrenal cortex elicit profound effects on skeletal and calcium metabolism. In the human, disease states associated with a hyperactive adrenal cortex, such as Cushing's syndrome, lead to a general rarefaction of the skeleton and spontaneous fractures. The hypercalcemia due to either vitamin D intoxication or sarcoidosis can often be corrected by the administration of ACTH or cortisone. Recent evidence also indicates that the hypercalcemia induced by a parathyroid adenoma can be normalized by corticosteroid administration.

In dogs, the chronic administration of cortical steroids depresses the uptake of radiocalcium by bone and increases the fecal excretion of this isotope, and in the human a slight increase in bone mineral deposition was noted (Eisenberg 1964). Adrenalectomy in rats was shown, by kinetic analysis, to decrease bone formation significantly and to decrease the exchangeable calcium pool by a factor of two (Kallfelz and Wasserman 1969).

Hypothyroidism and hyperthyroidism. Thyroid hormones elicit several effects, including increased rates of bone formation and resorption, increased plasma calcium and phosphorus levels, and increased urinary calcium and decreased urinary phosphate excretion. Excess thyroid hormone secretion leads to a type of osteoporosis with a high rate of bone turnover, and may cause a premature closure of the epiphyseal plate and cessation of growth. In hypothyroidism, the skeleton matures late and growth is delayed.

Osteopetrosis. This is an overmineralization of bone that could be due to excess mineral absorption, hypercalcemia, or hypercalcitonin secretion.

Pituitary abnormalities. The anterior lobe of the pituitary gland secretes several hormones, with one of these, growth (somatotropic) hormone, having an action directly on bone and cartilage. Other anterior pituitary hormones, such as the adrenocorticotropin, thyrotropin, and gonadotropins, influence bone indirectly through their target organs.

The removal of the pituitary gland (hypophysectomy) has a pronounced consequence on skeletal metabolism. The gross effect is retardation of bone growth, depending on the age at which the animal was hypophysectomized. When the operation is performed on 6-day-old rats, growth continues but at a reduced rate, suggesting that young animals have growth capacity independent of the stimulation provided by the pituitary hormones. If older animals are hypophysectomized, the capacity for continued growth is less; this indicates the greater dependence of the more mature individuals on the hormonal effects of the hypophysis (Asling and Evans 1956).

After hypophysectomy, the proliferation of the chondrocytes at the epiphyseal cartilage plate and their transformation from flattened to vacuolated forms cease. Because of these changes, the epiphyseal plate becomes narrower. The primary spongiosa is resorbed, and eventually the cartilage plate is sealed from the marrow by a transverse lamina (thin plate) of bone. Cortical bone becomes thinner. The administration of crystalline growth hormone to the hypophysectomized animal causes a prompt restoration of growth, and the histological appearance of the epiphyseal plate becomes characteristic of young actively growing bones. Growth hormone alone can induce growth equal to or exceeding the normal rate, but with suboptimal doses of growth hormone it is possible to show a synergistic effect with thyroxine. Thyroxine alone, however, cannot replace the pituitary hormone.

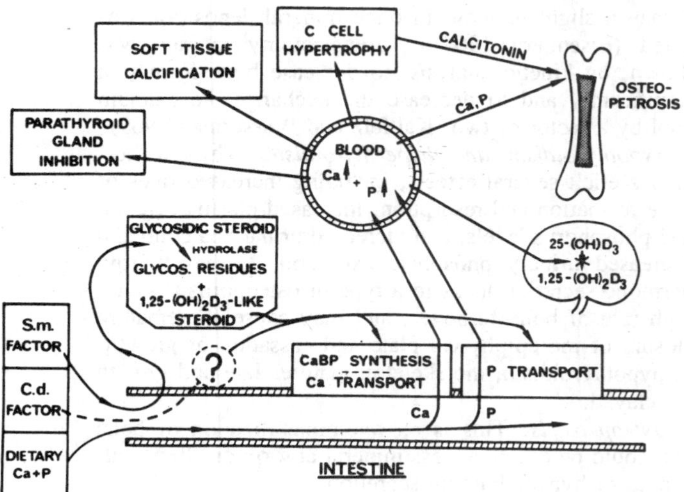

Figure 34.13. Proposed scheme by which calcinosis is produced in grazing animals due to the ingestion of calcinogenic plants. S.m., *Solanum malacoxylon;* C.d., *Cestrum diurnum.*

CALCINOSIS IN GRAZING ANIMALS

Grazing animals in several parts of the world develop calcinosis from consuming specific toxic plants. In this disease calcium salts are deposited in various soft tissues, including the aorta, kidney, tendons, ligaments, and heart. In Argentina, the plant species involved was identified as *Solanum malacoxylon* (syn. *glaucophyllum*), and more recently the plant *Cestrum diurnum* was implicated as the cause of calcinosis in the Miami, Florida, area (Wasserman 1975a, Krook et al. 1975). The active principle in both plants has biological properties similar to the hormonal form of vitamin D, 1,25-dihydroxycholecalciferol (Wasserman 1974, 1975a, Wasserman et al. 1975). In fact, the factor in *Solanum* is identical to 1,25-$(OH)_2D_3$ (Peterlik et al. 1976, Haussler et al. 1976).

As to the mechanism of calcinosis (Fig. 34.13), first, the plant containing the active principle, present as the steroidal glycoside, is ingested. Hydrolytic enzymes, either in intestinal or other tissues or in the bacterial flora, cleave the sugar residue from the glycoside, releasing the active steroidal fragment, presumably 1,25-$(OH)_2D_3$. This excess vitamin D hormone stimulates CaBP synthesis and calcium and phosphate absorption, producing hypercalcemia and/or hyperphosphatemia. The hypercalcemic state depresses parathyroid hormone secretion and stimulates calcitonin secretion from the C cells of the thyroid. The formation of endogenous 1,25-$(OH)_2D_3$ is inhibited because of the hypoparathyroidism, hypercalcemia, and/or hyperphosphatemia. The hypercalcitonism coupled with the hypercalcemia and hyperphosphatemia results in osteopetrosis. Since the excessively absorbed mineral cannot be otherwise physiologically accommodated, deposition in soft tissues results in calcinosis.

REFERENCES

Anderson, H.C. 1969. Vesicles associated with calcification in the matrix of epiphyseal cartilage. *J. Cell Biol.* 41:59–72.

——. 1976. Matrix vesicle calcification. *Fed. Proc.* 35:105–8.

Asling, C.W., and Evans, H.M. 1956. Anterior pituitary regulation of skeletal development. In G.H. Bourne, ed., *Biochemistry and Physiology of Bone.* Academic Press, New York.

Aubert, J.P., and Milhaud, G. 1960. A method of measuring the principal routes of calcium metabolism in man. *Biochim. Biophys. Acta* 39:122–39.

Aurbach, G.D., ed. 1976. *Parathyroid Gland.* Vol. 7 in *Handbook of Physiology,* sec. 7, *Endocrinology.* Am. Physiol. Soc., Washington.

Bauer, G.C.H., Carlsson, A., and Lindquist, B. 1961. Metabolism and homeostatic function of bone. In C.L. Comar and F. Bronner, eds., *Mineral Metabolism.* Academic Press, New York. Vol. 1, pt. 1B.

Bélanger, L.F., Robichon, J., Migicovsky, B.B., Copp, D.H., and Vincent, J. 1963. Resorption without osteoclasts (osteolysis). In Sognnaes.

Bonucci, E. 1970. Fine structure and histochemistry of calcifying globules in epiphyseal cartilage. *Zeitschrift Zellforsch. Mikrosk. Anat.* 103:192–217.

Brighton, C.T., and Hunt, R.M. 1976. Histochemical localization of calcium in growth plate mitochondria and matrix vesicles. *Fed. Proc.* 35:143–47.

Capen, C.C., and Young, D.M. 1967. The ultrastructure of the parathyroid glands and thyroid parafollicular cells of cows with parturient paresis and hypocalcemia. *Lab. Invest.* 17:717–37.

Chase, L.R., and Aurbach, G.D. 1968. Cyclic AMP and the mechanism of action of parathyroid hormone. In R.V. Talmage and L.F. Bélanger, eds., *Parathyroid Hormone and Thyrocalcitonin (Calcitonin).* Excerpta Med. Found., Amsterdam. Pp. 247–57.

Comar, C.L., Lotz, W.E., and Boyd, G.A. 1952. Autoradiographic studies of calcium, phosphorus, and strontium distribution in the bones of the growing pig. *Am. J. Anat.* 90:113–25.

Comar, C.L., and Wasserman, R.H. 1964. Strontium. In C.L. Comar and F. Bronner, eds., *Mineral Metabolism.* Academic Press, New York. Vol. 2, pt. 2A.

Copp, D.H. 1969. Endocrine control of calcium homeostasis. *J. Endocr.* 43:137–61.

Copp, D.H., and Cheney, B. 1962. Calcitonin: A hormone from the parathyroid which lowers the calcium level of the blood. *Nature* 193:381–82.

Costanzo, L.S., Sheehe, P.R., and Weiner, I.M. 1974. Renal actions of vitamin D in deficient rats. *Am. J. Physiol.* 226:1490–95.

Doty, S.B., Robinson, R.A. and Schofield, B. 1976. Morphology of bone and histochemical staining characteristics of bone cells. In Aurbach.

Dudley, H.R., and Spiro, D. 1961. The fine structure of bone cells. *J. Biophys. Biochem. Cytol.* 11:627–49.

Eisenberg, E. 1964. Effects of corticoids on bone. In O.H. Pearson and G.F. Joplin, eds., *Dynamic Studies of Metabolic Bone Disease.* Davis, Philadelphia. Pp. 119–22.

Fleish, H., and Neuman, W.F. 1961. Mechanisms of calcification: Role of collagen, polyphosphates, and phosphatase. *Am. J. Physiol.* 200:1296–1300.

Fourman, P., Royer, P., Levell, M.J., and Morgan, D.B. 1968. *Calcium Metabolism and the Bone.* 2d ed. Blackwell Scientific, Oxford.

Frost, H.M. 1963. Tetracycline bone labelling. In C.R. Lam, ed., *Bone Remodelling Dynamics.* Thomas, Springfield, Ill. App. 12.

Glimcher, M.J. 1960. Specificity of the molecular structure of organic matrices in mineralization. In R.F. Sognnaes, ed., *Calcification in Biological Systems.* Am. Ass. Advmt. Sci., Washington.

——. 1968. A basic architectural principle in the organization of mineralized tissues. *Clin. Orthop.* 61:16–36.

Grant, M., and Prockop, D. 1972. Biosynthesis of collagen. *New Eng. J. Med.* 286:291–300.

Gutman, A.B., and Yu, T.F. 1950. A concept of the role of enzymes in endochondral calcification. In E.C. Reifenstein, Jr., ed., *Conference on Metabolic Interrelations*. Trans. 2d Conf. Josiah Macy, Jr., Found., New York. Vol. 2, 167–90.

Hammett, F.S. 1925. A biochemical study of bone growth. I. Changes in the ash, organic matter, and water during growth. *J. Biol. Chem.* 64:409–28.

Hancox, N.M., and Boothroyd, B. 1963. Structure-function relationships in the osteoclast. In Sognnaes.

Harris, W.H., and Heaney, R.P. 1969. Skeletal renewal and metabolic bone disease. *New Eng. J. Med.* 280:193–202, 253–59, 303–11.

Haussler, M.R. 1974. Vitamin D: Mode of action and biomedical implications. *Nutr. Rev.* 32:257–66.

Haussler, M.R., Wasserman, R.H., McCain, T.A., Peterlik, M., Bursac, K., and Hughes, M.R. 1976. 1,25-dihydroxyvitamin D_3–glycoside: Identification of the calcinogenic principle of *Solanun malacoxylon. Life Sci.* 18:1049–56.

Herman, H., and Dallemagne, M.J. 1961. The main mineral constituent in bone and teeth. *Arch. Oral Biol.* 5:137–44.

Hirsch, P.F., Gauthier, G.F., and Munson, P.L. 1963. Thyroid hypocalcemic principle and recurrent laryngeal nerve injury as factors affecting the response to parathyroidectomy in rats. *Endocrinology* 73:244–52.

Hirsch, P.F., and Munson, P.L. 1969. Thyrocalcitonin. *Physiol. Rev.* 49:549–622.

Holdsworth, E.S. 1970. The effect of vitamin D on enzyme activities in the mucosal cell of the chick small intestine. *J. Memb. Biol.* 3:43–53.

Holtrop, M.E. 1972. The ultrastructure of the epiphyseal plate. II. The hypertrophic chondrocyte. *Calcified Tissue Res.* 9:140–51.

Irving, J.T. 1976. Interrelations of matrix lipids, vesicles, and calcification. *Fed. Proc.* 35:109–11.

Jackson, S.F. 1957. The fine structure of developing bone in the embryonic fowl. *Proc. Roy. Soc.*, ser. B, 146:270–80.

Jowsey, J. 1963. Microradiography of bone resorption. In Sognnaes.

Kallfelz, F.A., and Wasserman, R.H. 1969. Effect of adrenalectomy on calcium metabolism in vitamin D–treated and rachitic rats. *Calcified Tissue Res.* 3:74–83.

Kodicek, E. 1974. The story of vitamin D from vitamin to hormone. *Lancet* 1(Jan.):325–29.

Kronfeld, D.S., Mayer, G.P., Ramberg, C.D. 1976. Calcium homeostasis in cattle. In Aurbach.

Krook, L., and Lowe, J.E. 1964. Nutritional secondary hyperparathyroidism in the horse. *Path. Vet.* 1(suppl.):1–98.

Krook, L., Lutwak, L., and McEntee, K. 1969. Dietary calcium, ultimobranchial tumors, and osteopetrosis in the bull: Syndrome of calcitonin excess? *Am. J. Clin. Nutr.* 22:115–18.

Krook, L.P., Wasserman, R.H., Shively, J.N., Tashjian, A.H., Brokken, T.D., and Morton, J.F. 1975. Hypercalcemia and calcinosis in Florida horses: Implication of the shrub, *Cestrum diurnum,* as causative agent. *Cornell Vet.* 65:26–56.

Lippiello, L. 1974. Vitamin D–induced calcium binding protein: Fluorescent antibody localization in the shell gland (uterus) and kidney and related studies. Ph.D. diss., Cornell U.

Martin, J.H., and Matthews, J.L. 1970. Mitochondrial granules in chondrocytes, osteoblasts, and osteocytes. *Clin. Orthop.* 68:273–78.

McLean, F.C., and Budy, A.M. 1964. *Radiation, Isotopes, and Bone.* Academic Press, New York.

McLean, F.C., and Rowland, R.E. 1963. Internal remodeling of compact bone. In Sognnaes.

McLean, F.C., and Urist, M.R. 1955. *Bone: An Introduction to the Physiology of Skeletal Tissue.* U. of Chicago Press, Chicago.

Mechanic, G.L. 1975. Collagen structure and calcification. In F. Kuhlencordt and H.-P. Kruse eds., *Calcium Metabolism, Bone, and Metabolic Bone Diseases*. Springer-Verlag, New York. Pp. 157–63.

Melancon, M.J., Jr. and DeLuca, H.F. 1970. Vitamin D stimulation of calcium-dependent adenosine triphosphatase in chick intestinal brush borders. *Biochemistry* 9:1658–64.

Munson, P.L., Hirsch, P.F., and Tashjian, A.H., Jr. 1963. Parathyroid gland. *Ann. Rev. Physiol.* 25:325–60.

Neuman, W.F., Mulryan, B.J., Neuman, M.W., and Lane, K. 1973. Calcium transport systems in the chick calvaria. *Am. J. Physiol.* 224:600–605.

Neuman, W.F., and Neuman, M.W. 1958. *The Chemical Dynamics of Bone Mineral*. U. of Chicago Press, Chicago.

Neuman, W.F., and Ramp, W.K. 1971. The concept of a bone membrane: Some implications. In G. Nichols, Jr., and R.H. Wasserman, eds., *Cellular Mechanisms for Calcium Transfer and Homeostasis.* Academic Press, New York. Pp. 197–209.

Norman, A.W., and Henry, H. 1974. 1,25-Dihydroxycholecalciferol: A hormonally active form of vitamin D. *Recent Prog. Horm. Res.* 30:431–80.

Norman, A.W., Mircheff, A.K., Adams, T.H., and Spielvogel, A. 1970. Studies on the mechanism of action of calciferol. III. Vitamin D–mediated increase of intestinal brush border alkaline phosphatase activity. *Biochim. Biophys. Acta* 215:348–59.

Omdahl, J.L., and DeLuca, H.F. 1973. Regulation of vitamin D metabolism and function. *Physiol. Rev.* 53:327–72.

Peterlik, M., Bursac, K., Haussler, M.R., Hughes, M.R., and Wasserman, R.H. 1976. Further evidence for the 1,25-Dihydroxyvitamin D–like activity of *Solanum malacoxylon. Biochem. Biophys. Res. Comm.* 70:797–804.

Posner, A.S. 1973. Bone mineral on the molecular level. *Fed. Proc.* 32:1933–37.

Prien, E.L., Jr., Pyle, E.B., and Krane, S.M. 1976. Secondary hyperparathyroidism. In Aurbach.

Puschett, J.B., Moranz, J., and Kurnick, W. 1972. Evidence for a direct action of cholecalciferol and 25-hydroxycholecalciferol on the renal transport of phosphate, sodium, and calcium. *J. Clin. Invest.* 51:373–78.

Raisz, L.G. 1976. Mechanisms of Bone Resorption. In Aurbach.

Rasmussen, H., and Bordier, P. 1974. *The Physiological and Cellular Basis of Metabolic Bone Disease,* Williams & Wilkins, Baltimore.

Robinson, R.A., and Cameron, D.A. 1956. Electron microscopy of cartilage and bone matrix at the distal epiphyseal line of the femur in the newborn infant. *J. Biophys. Biochem. Cytol.* 2(suppl.):253–60.

Robison, R. 1923. The possible significance of hexosephosphoric esters in ossification. *Biochem. J.* 17:286–93.

Schmitt, F.O. 1959. Interaction properties of elongate protein macromolecules with particular reference to collagen (tropocollagen). *Rev. Mod. Phys.* 31:349–58.

Sognnaes, R.F., ed. 1963. *Mechanisms of Hard Tissue Destruction.* Am. Ass. Advmt. Sci., Washington.

Termine, J.D., Wuthier, R.E., and Posner, A.S. 1967. Amorphous-crystalline mineral changes during endochondral and periosteal bone formation. *Proc. Soc. Exp. Biol. Med.* 125:4–9.

Thomas, W.C., Jr., and Howard, J.E. 1964. Disturbances of calcium metabolism. In C.L. Comar and F. Bronner, eds., *Mineral Metabolism*. Academic Press, New York, Vol. 2, pt. 2A.

Tomlin, D.H., Henry, K.M., and Kon, S.K. 1953. Autoradiographic study of growth and calcium metabolism in the long bones of the rat. *Brit. J. Nutr.* 7:235–52.

Urist, M.R. 1966. Origins of current ideas about calcification. *Clin. Orthop. Rel. Res.* 44:13–39.

Urry, D.W. 1971. Neutral sites for calcium ion binding to elastin and collagen: A charge neutralization theory for calcification and its relation to atherosclerosis. *Proc. Nat. Acad. Sci.* 68:810–14.

Vaes, G. 1968a. On the mechanisms of bone resorption: The action of parathyroid hormone on the excretion and synthesis of lysosomal enzymes and on the extracellular release of acid by bone cells. *J. Cell. Biol.* 39:676–97.

——. 1968b. Parathyroid hormone–like action of N^6-2′-0-dibutyryladenosine-3′,5′ (cyclic)-monophosphate on bone explants in tissue culture. *Nature* 219:939–40.

Walser, M. 1960. Protein-binding of inorganic phosphate in plasma of normal subjects and patients with renal disease. *J. Clin. Invest.* 39:501–6.

Wasserman, R.H. 1958. Quantitative studies on skeletal accretion in laboratory and domestic animals. *Second United Nations Conference on the Peaceful Uses of Atomic Energy*. Pergamon, London.

——. 1974. Calcium absorption and calcium-binding protein synthesis: *Solanum malacoxylon* reverses strontium inhibition. *Science* 183:1092–94.

——. 1975a. Active vitamin D–like substances in *Solanum malacoxylon* and other calcinogenic plants. *Nutr. Rev.* 33:1–5.

——. 1975b. Metabolism, function, and clinical aspects of vitamin D. *Cornell Vet.* 65:3–25.

Wasserman, R.H., and Corradino, R.A. 1973. Vitamin D, calcium, and protein synthesis. *Vitam. Horm.* 31:43–103.

Wasserman, R.H., Corradino, R.A., and Krook, L.P. 1975. *Cestrum diurnum:* A domestic plant with 1,25-dihydroxycholecalciferol-like activity. *Biochem. Biophys. Res. Comm.* 62:85–91.

Wasserman, R.H., Corradino, R.A., and Taylor, A.N. 1969. Binding proteins from animals with possible transport function. *J. Gen. Physiol.* 54(suppl.):114–34.

Wells, H., and Lloyd, W. 1969. Hypercalcemic and hypophosphatemic effects of dibutyryl cyclic AMP in rats after parathyroidectomy. *Endocrinology* 85:861–67.

Widdowson, E.M., and Dickerson, J.W.T. 1964. Chemical composition of the body. In C.L. Comar and F. Bronner, eds., *Mineral Metabolism*. Academic Press, New York. Vol. 2, pt. 2A.

Young, R.W. 1963. Nucleic acids, protein synthesis, and bone. *Clin. Orthop.* 26:147–60.

CHAPTER 35

Joints and Synovial Fluid | by Ernest D. Gardner

In anatomy a *joint* is the connection in the skeleton between any of its rigid component parts, whether bones or cartilages. *Articulation,* a term which has the same Latin origin as the word *article,* is synonymous with joint. Terms such as *arthrology,* which means the study of joints, and *arthritis,* which means the inflammation of joints, are of Greek origin (*arthron*).

Vertebrate joints have certain common structural and functional features. On the basis of their most characteristic structural features, joints may be classified into three main types: fibrous, cartilaginous, and synovial. The present account deals mainly with synovial joints in mammals.

FIBROUS JOINTS

The bones of a fibrous joint (sometimes called a synarthrosis) are united by fibrous tissue. There are two types of fibrous joints—sutures and syndesmoses. In the sutures of the skull, the bones are tightly connected by several fibrous layers. The mechanisms of growth at these joints are important in accommodating the growth of the brain. A syndesmosis is a fibrous joint in which the intervening connective tissue is much greater in amount than in a suture. The joint between a tooth and the bone of its socket is termed a gomphosis and is sometimes classed as a third type of fibrous joint.

CARTILAGINOUS JOINTS

The bones of cartilaginous joints are united either by hyaline cartilage or by fibrocartilage.

Hyaline cartilage joints

In this type of joint, which is sometimes called a synchondrosis and sometimes a primary cartilaginous joint, the bones are temporarily united by hyaline cartilage. This cartilage is a persistent part of the embryonic cartilaginous skeleton, and it serves as a growth zone for one or both of the bones that it joins. Most hyaline cartilage joints have been obliterated, that is, have been replaced by bone, by the time growth ceases. Examples of hyaline cartilage joints include epiphyseal plates and the spheno-occipital and neurocentral synchondroses.

Fibrocartilaginous joints

In this type of joint, which is sometimes called an amphiarthrosis and sometimes a secondary cartilaginous joint, the skeletal elements are united by fibrocartilage during some phase of their existence. The fibrocartilage is usually separated from the bones by thin plates of hyaline cartilage. Fibrocartilaginous joints include the pubic symphysis and the discs between the bodies of the vertebrae.

An intervertebral disc consists of the annulus fibrosus and the nucleus pulposus. These form a resilient body whose superior and inferior (or anterior and posterior) aspects are each separated from the adjacent vertebral body by a thin hyaline cartilage plate, which is a growth zone for the vertebral body. The annulus fibrosus consists of a series of lamellae of collagen bundles that are anchored to the margins of the hyaline plates and to the edges of the vertebral bodies. The innermost lamellae contain fibrocartilage. The annulus fibrosus surrounds the nucleus pulposus, which consists of fine strands of collagenous fibers, connective tissue cells, cartilage cells, and amorphous ground substance. Early in its development the nucleus pulposus is mucoid and contains notochordal cells. With advancing age, the entire disc tends to become cartilaginous, and the differences between the annulus and the nucleus are often lost. Degenerative changes of the disc are common in many domestic animals, especially large ones of relatively long life. The precise nature of these changes is often unknown. When present, they predispose the disc to injury. In some animals (e.g. dachshunds), intervertebral disc disease appears to be brought about by abnormalities of the hyaline cartilage plates.

In many mammals, including humans, marked pelvic relaxation occurs late in pregnancy to facilitate the passage of the fetus. This relaxation, which consists of a separation of the pubic symphysis and, in some, a loosening of the sacroiliac joints, is brought about by the hormone relaxin operating in conjunction with other hormones, especially estrogens. The pubic symphysis is a fibrocartilaginous joint in which the fibrocartilage may contain a cleft. Separation of this joint under the influence of relaxin is especially pronounced in guinea pigs and mice. The sacroiliac joint is a synovial joint, and the relaxation of its capsule and ligaments is marked in sheep and cows. The actions of relaxin and estrogens on joint capsules and ligaments are complex, and their cellular mechanisms have not yet been determined.

SYNOVIAL JOINTS

Synovia is the fluid present in certain joints, which are consequently termed synovial. Similar fluid is present in bursae and in synovial tendon sheaths.

Synovial joints, which are often termed diarthrodial joints, possess a cavity and are specialized to permit more or less free movement. The articular or bearing surfaces of the bones comprising a synovial joint are usually covered with hyaline cartilage, but in some joints are covered with fibrous tissue, which may contain fibrocartilage. The bones are united by a joint capsule and by ligaments (Fig. 35.1). The inner aspect of the joint capsule is lined with synovial membrane, which produces the synovial fluid that fills the joint cavity and lubricates the joint. The remainder of the capsule consists of a fibrous layer (the term joint capsule is often used to refer specifically to the fibrous layer). The joint cavity is sometimes partially or completely subdivided by fibrous or fibrocartilaginous discs or menisci, and in some joints may be traversed by a tendon.

Types

Although synovial joints have complex mechanical functions, which must be appreciated in terms of spherical as well as plane geometry, they may be classified as simple or compound according to the number of articulating surfaces. A simple joint has one pair of articulating surfaces, a compound joint more than one pair. In addition, the term complex joint is sometimes applied to joints in which the cavity is partially or completely subdivided by a disc or meniscus.

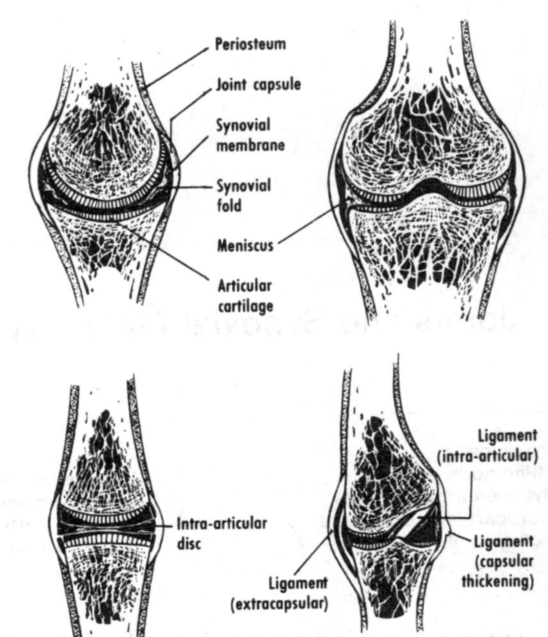

Figure 35.1. Characteristics of synovial joints. The joint cavity in each drawing is exaggerated, as is the thickness of the synovial membrane. (From E. Gardner, D.J. Gray, and R. O'Rahilly, *Anatomy*, 4th ed., Saunders, Philadelphia, 1975.)

Synovial joints may also be classified according to the shapes of the articular surfaces of the constituent bones. These shapes determine the type of movement and are partly responsible for determining the range of movement. The more common types of synovial joints are plane, hinge, and condylar. Ball-and-socket, ellipsoidal, pivot, and saddle joints are less common.

The articular surfaces of a plane joint are usually slightly curved. They permit gliding or slipping in any direction, or the twisting of one bone on the other. A hinge joint is self-explanatory. In a condylar joint, the articular area of each bone consists of two distinct articular surfaces, each called a condyle. Although resembling a hinge joint in movement, a condylar joint permits several kinds of movement. In a ball-and-socket or spheroidal joint, a spheroidal surface of one bone moves about three axes within a socket of the other bone. Flexion, extension, adduction, abduction, and rotation can occur, as well as a combination of these movements termed circumduction. In circumduction, the limb is swung so that it describes the side of a cone, the apex of which is the center of the ball. In an ellipsoidal joint, which resembles a ball-and-socket joint, the articulating surfaces are much longer in one direction than in the direction at right angles. The circumference of the joint thus resembles an ellipse. In a pivot or trochoid joint, the axis is vertical, and one bone pivots within a bony or an osseoligamentous ring. A saddle or sellar joint is shaped like a saddle and is a biaxial joint.

The range of movements at joints is limited by the muscles, the ligaments and capsule, the shapes of the bones, and the opposition of soft parts.

The movements that occur at synovial joints may be classified as active, passive, and accessory. Active movements include (1) gliding or slipping movements, (2) angular movements about a horizontal or side-to-side axis (flexion and extension) or about an anteroposterior axis (abduction and adduction), and (3) rotary movements about a longitudinal axis (medial and lateral rotation). Whether one, several, or all types of movement occur at a particular joint depends upon the shape and ligaments of that joint.

Passive movements are those produced by an external force, such as gravity or an examiner. Accessory movements (often classified with massive movements) are defined as movements for which the muscular arrangements are not suitable, but which can be brought about by the manipulation of an examiner. The production of passive and accessory movements is of value in testing and in diagnosing muscle and joint disorders.

Lubrication mechanisms

It should be emphasized that synovial joints are mechanical structures that are specialized to permit more or less free movement. The lubricating mechanisms of these joints are such that the effects of friction upon bearing surfaces are minimized. The coefficient of friction during movement is less than that of ice sliding on ice. This is made possible by the nature of the lubricating fluid, by the nature and shapes of the bearing surfaces, and by a variety of mechanisms that permit a replaceable fluid rather than an irreplaceable bearing to reduce friction.

Any mechanical system wears with time, and synovial joints are no exception. Even though the effects of friction are minimized, some wear-and-tear (also called use-destruction or attrition) is inevitable. The most common result is the wearing away of articular cartilage to varying degrees, occasionally to the extent of exposing, eroding, and polishing the underlying bone. Wear-and-tear may be exaggerated by factors such as body weight, abnormal movements or gait, trauma, and disease, and by pathological processes that change articular geometry, alter synovial fluid, and interfere with cartilage metabolism. Osteoarthritic conditions aggravated by wear-and-tear occur in many domestic animals, including birds; when a Thoroughbred is so afflicted the animal may become useless for normal activity.

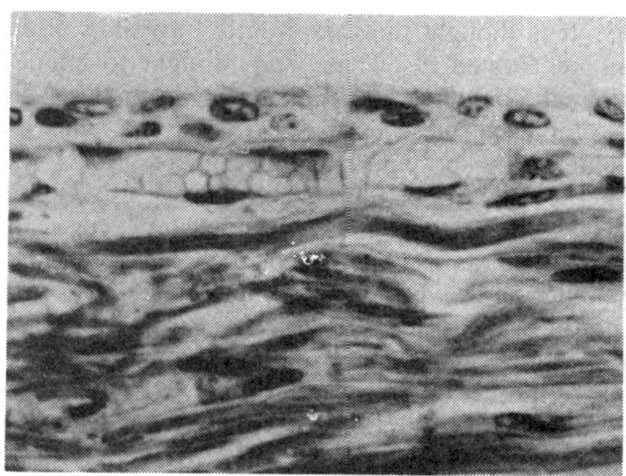

Figure 35.2. Photomicrograph of a section of human hip joint, showing, from above downward, the synovial membrane, a capillary cut longitudinally, and the joint capsule

Synovial membrane and synovial fluid

Synovial membrane is a vascular connective tissue that lines the inner surface of the capsule but does not cover the bearing surfaces. It consists of formed elements such as cells and fibers, together with intercellular material called matrix or ground substance.

The connective tissue cells (synoviocytes) that are adjacent to the joint cavity are grouped together in one to three layers to form a relatively smooth surface from which a variable number of folds, villi, and fat pads project into the joint cavity. Immediately subjacent to these surface cells is a capillary network (Fig. 35.2). Scanning electron microscopy demonstrates characteristic undulations of the surface and separation of the synoviocytes (Figs. 35.3, 35.4). Two types of synoviocytes (A and B, Fig. 35.5) have been described in a number of species. These types differ in their ultrastructure, and may represent different states of activity of the same cell type. The tissue immediately subjacent to the surface cells and capillary network may be fibrous, areolar, or fatty. It varies in thickness and contains fibroblasts, macrophages, mast cells, and fat cells, as well as blood and lymphatic vessels and a few nerve fibers. If a synovial membrane is removed, a new synovial membrane may form from this underlying tissue or from the joint capsule.

The ground substance or matrix of any connective tissue when examined under the light microscope seems to be an amorphous substance. All ground substances contain complex compounds of high molecular weight, including mucopolysaccharides, of which at least five different kinds are known, most of them being sulfated. Synovial fluid, which may be likened to a fluid ground substance, contains a single mucopolysaccharide, a sulfate-free compound termed hyaluronic acid. All mucopolysaccharides are complex asymmetric long-chain compounds that form viscous sols or even gels. They are attacked by a variety of enzymes usually called hyaluronidases. It is thought that basic units, probably disaccharides, are formed elsewhere and brought to connective tissue by the blood stream (Fig. 35.6). In joints, synoviocytes synthesize these units into hyaluronic acid, probably chiefly by polymerization, that is, by a linking together of the basic units. This is an active, energy-requiring process. It is not yet known, however, whether type A cells alone, or type B, or both, are responsible.

Synovial fluid, whose chief functions are joint lubrication and the nourishment of articular cartilage, is a sticky viscous fluid, often like egg white in consistency. It is usually slightly alkaline and ranges from colorless to deep yellow. The color and viscosity vary with species and type of joint. For example, fluid from large joints is usually less viscous and cellular than that from small joints. Synovial fluid viscosity also varies inversely with temperature, being more viscous at lower temperatures.

The viscosity of synovial fluid is due almost entirely to the hyaluronic acid, the viscosity of which increases exponentially with increasing concentration. Solutions of more than 1 percent may form gels. The viscosity of synovial fluid decreases to that of water if the hyaluronic acid is removed by precipitation with acid, if it is hydrolyzed enzymatically, or if its polymerization is destroyed by enzymes or by physical processes. Hyaluronic acid is normally bound to protein to form what is termed hyaluronate-protein. The binding is a specific function of synoviocytes. Moreover, the protein moiety is an impor-

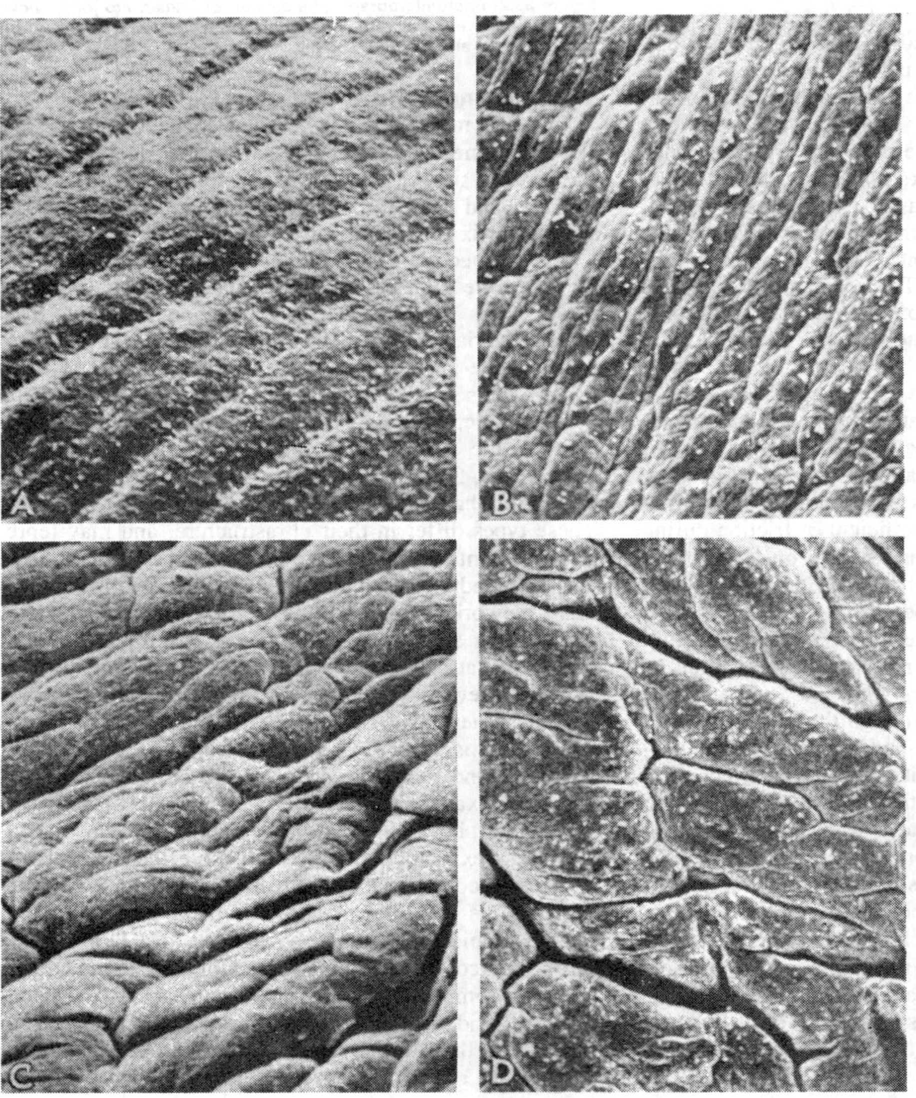

Figure 35.3. Surface topography of the synovial membrane as viewed at low magnification with the scanning microscope. A, surface shows nearly parallel shallow undulations (×54). B, as in A, surface shows many approximately parallel shallow folds (×54). C (×41) and D (×54), both show somewhat larger but still roughly parallel shallow folds. All four views suggest an arrangement designed to permit adjustment and expansion, and perhaps also related to lubrication mechanisms. (From Gardner, in Hollander and McCarty, eds., *Arthritis,* Lea & Febiger, Philadelphia, 1972.)

tant lubrication factor (trypsin digestion destroys lubricating properties).

The other constituents of synovial fluid are those that are normally present in blood plasma. In fact, synovial fluid, aside from its hyaluronic acid content, can be considered as a dialysate of blood plasma. Synovial fluid also normally contains a few cells, mostly mononuclear, derived from the lining tissue (the cells appear to be more numerous in fluid from smaller joints). Many pathological processes (infections, rheumatic disorders, autoimmune disorders, neoplasms) affect the synovial membrane, and they generally alter the cellular content of the fluid. Withdrawal of synovial fluid and determination of its cellular and chemical content and physical characteristics can be a valuable diagnostic aid.

Articular cartilage

Adult articular cartilage is usually hyaline in nature. Avascular, nerveless, and relatively acellular, it is nevertheless a highly specialized connective tissue with biochemical and biophysical characteristics that enable it to play a dual role as a shock absorber and a bearing surface. Its matrix, which is hyperhydrated, contains collagen and sulfated mucopolysaccharides. The part of articular hyaline cartilage adjacent to bone is usually calcified (Fig. 35.7). Articular cartilage, except for its

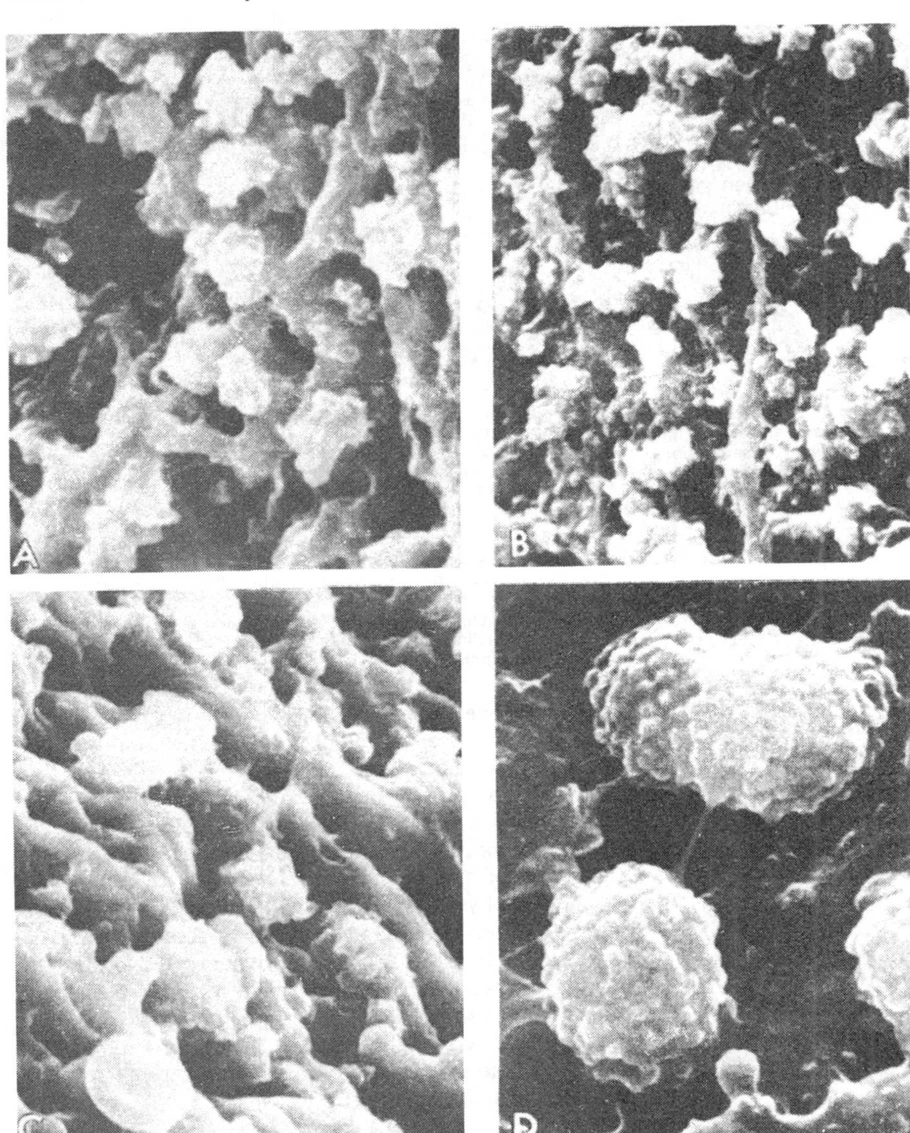

Figure 35.4. Surface of the synovial membrane at higher magnifications than in Figure 35.3. A, individual synoviocytes are clearly visualized; they are relatively uniform in size, exhibit a surface with knobby and foldlike processes, are evenly distributed, and are separated by matrix (×2630). B, from another part of the same joint, similar findings (×2630). C, similar findings from the synovial membrane of another joint; in addition, a red blood cell is visible at the lower left (×2110). D, the surface details of individual synoviocytes at higher magnification, showing that some synoviocytes are connected by narrow cytoplasmic spans that extend across the surrounding matrix (×5260). (From Gardner, in Hollander and McCarty, eds., *Arthritis*, Lea & Febiger, Philadelphia, 1972.)

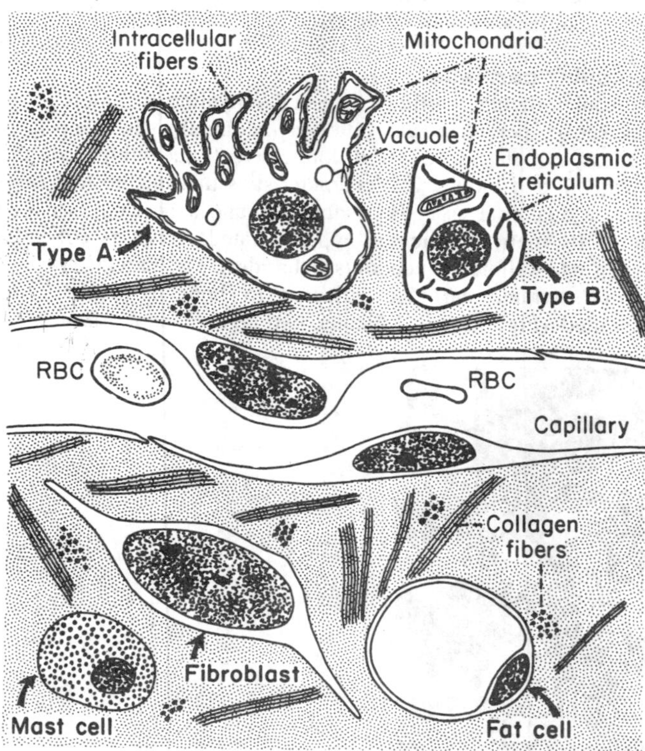

Figure 35.5. Major features of the synovial membrane and joint capsule. Type A and type B cells are shown with a capillary separating them from the joint capsule. (From Gardner, in Hollander and McCarty, eds., *Arthritis,* Lea & Febiger, Philadelphia, 1972.)

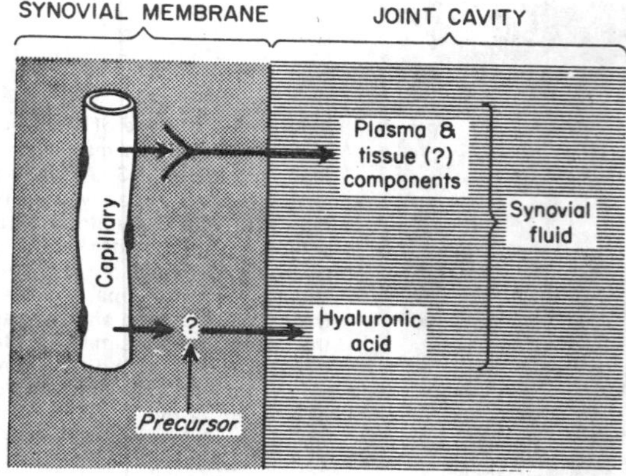

Figure 35.6. Diagram of synovial membrane and synovial fluid. Most constituents of synovial fluid diffuse through the tissue to the joint cavity; it may be that tissue components are added. It is assumed that precursors brought to synovial tissue by blood give rise to hyaluronic acid. (Modified from E. Gardner, *Instructional Course Lectures,* Am. Acad. Orthop. Surg., Chicago, 1952, vol. 9.)

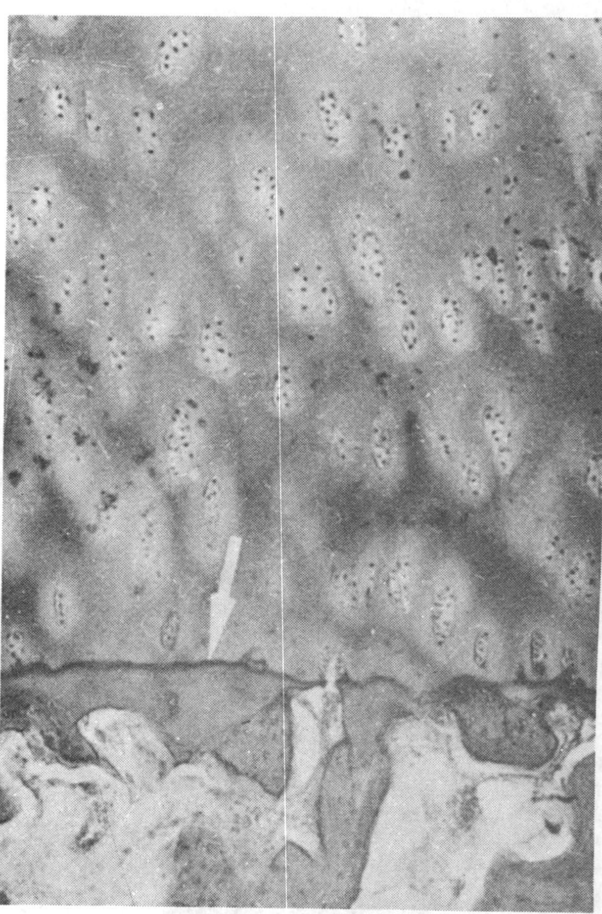

Figure 35.7. Microscopic section of articular cartilage and subchondral bone; the superficial part of the cartilage is not included. The thin layer of calcified cartilage (arrow) separates the cartilage above from the subchondral bone below. At the right the vascular marrow spaces approach the cartilage through the subchondral bone. About ×75. (From Gardner, in Hollander and McCarty, eds., *Arthritis,* Lea & Febiger, Philadelphia, 1972).

calcified zone, is not visible in ordinary radiograms. Hence, the so-called radiological joint space is wider than the true joint space.

During the growth period, articular cartilage provides the growth zone for endochondral ossification in the epiphysis and, like the epiphyseal cartilage, is under the influence of the somatotropic hormone (STH) of the adenohypophysis. During growth, articular cartilage is capable of regeneration and can repair defects. However, when growth in body length or stature ceases, articular cartilage loses much of its power of repair, especially in the higher vertebrates. Some growth is still possible, though, and is brought into play in the slow remodeling of adult joints which may result from mechanical or pathological stress.

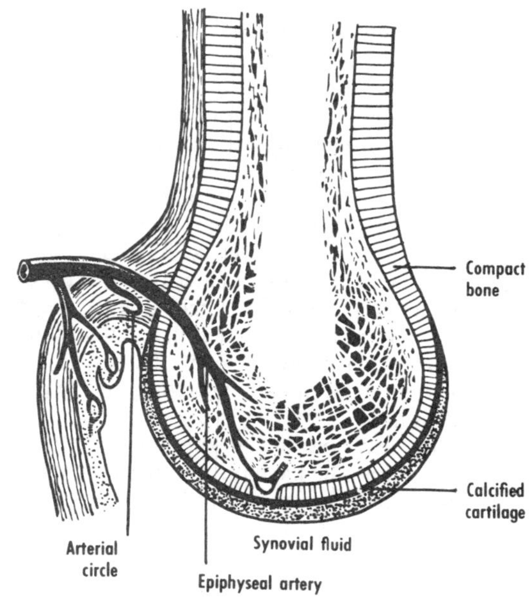

Figure 35.8. Possible sources of nutrition of articular cartilage: synovial fluid, diffusion from capillaries in adjacent bone marrow, and diffusion from capillaries from the arterial circle around the joint at the line of capsular attachment. The thickness of compact bone of the articular surface is exaggerated, as is also that of the layer of calcified cartilage. (From E. Gardner, D.J. Gray, and R. O'Rahilly, *Anatomy*, 4th ed., Saunders, Philadelphia, 1975.)

Cartilage is a resilient and elastic tissue. When it is compressed, it becomes thinner. When the pressure is released, the cartilage slowly regains its original thickness. There is also evidence that intermittent pressure causes cartilage to thicken by taking up fluid. Thus cartilage has the spongelike property of being able to absorb synovial fluid, which diffuses through the cartilage matrix. Articular cartilage probably derives its main nourishment from synovial fluid by diffusion, but other possible sources include diffusion from epiphyseal vessels that loop through subchondral bone, and diffusion from capillaries in the arterial circle at the periphery of the joint (Fig. 35.8).

The stiffness and strength of articular cartilage depend upon the orientation of surface collagen, whose fibers resist tensile stresses. The surface of cartilage is comprised of undulating, tightly woven fiber bundles that in turn exhibit microundulations. In general terms, articular cartilage resembles a stiff sponge, capable of resisting tensile stresses, exhibiting elastic deformation under load, containing a high proportion of extracellular fluid, and exuding fluid under pressure. Articular cartilage is of major importance in lubricating mechanisms, and disorders of articular cartilage are at the basis of much joint pathology.

Joint capsule and ligaments

In most joints, the capsule is composed of bundles of collagenous fibers (elastic fibers in a few joints, e.g. middle ear) which are arranged somewhat irregularly in contrast to their more regular arrangement in tendons and many ligaments. These bundles, and the bundles in some ligaments, tend to spiral. Such an arrangement renders them sensitive to tension in most positions that the joint occupies. Therefore, movement alters the tension or torsion in the bundles, and this change in tension in turn stimulates proprioceptive nerve endings in the capsule and ligaments.

Ligaments are classified as capsular, extracapsular, and intra-articular, and these serve different kinds of mechanical functions.

The relationship of the epiphyseal plate to the line of capsular attachment is important. For example, the epiphyseal plate is a barrier to the spread of infection between the metaphysis and the epiphysis. If the epiphyseal line is intra-articular, then a part of the metaphysis is also intra-articular, and a metaphyseal infection may involve the joint. Likewise, in such instances a metaphyseal fracture becomes intra-articular, always a serious matter from the standpoint of damage to articular surfaces. If the capsule is attached directly to the periphery of the epiphyseal plate, damage to the joint may involve the plate and thereby interfere with growth.

Menisci, intra-articular discs, fat pads, and synovial folds are intra-articular structures that aid in spreading synovial fluid throughout the joint and therefore aid in joint lubrication. The menisci and discs, which are composed mostly of fibrous tissue but may contain some fibrocartilage, have other important functions. They are attached at their periphery to the joint capsule, and are usually present in joints where flexion and extension are associated with gliding, a combination that requires a rounded male surface and a relatively flattened female surface. The mobility of menisci and discs is under ligament or muscle control. This prevents instability and yet allows a considerable range of gliding.

Periarticular tissues

The term periarticular tissues is a general one, and refers to fascial investments around the joint. These investments blend with the capsule and ligaments, with the musculotendinous expansions that pass over or blend with the joint capsule, and with the looser connective tissue that invests the vessels and nerves approaching the joint. The periarticular tissues contain many elastic fibers, blood vessels, and nerves. The joints and adjacent tendons and ligaments of domestic animals are often injured, for example, in a Thoroughbred during a race. The repair of such injuries involves the periarticular tissues as well as the joints themselves, and often leads to fibrosis (adhesions) of the periarticular tissues. The fibrosis may be increased if therapy involving inflammation is used. Fibrosis of periarticular tissues may limit movement almost as much as does fibrosis within a joint.

Blood and lymphatic supply

The arteries that supply a joint and adjacent bone arise more or less in common. Those that supply the bone usually enter the bone at or near the line of capsular attachment and form a prominent network around the joint. Articular vessels (Fig. 35.9) ultimately form a capillary network that is most prominent in the cellular and areolar areas of the synovial membrane. Both the joint capsule and synovial membrane bleed profusely when injured. Arteriovenous anastomoses are also present in positions that would enable them to shunt blood past the capillary networks. However, their specific functions in joints are unknown. Relatively little is known about the normal pattern of blood flow in joints and the control of such flow.

Lymphatic vessels accompany blood vessels and form plexuses in the synovial membrane and capsule. The lymphatic vessels that leave a joint drain into regional lymph nodes.

Diffusion takes place readily in either direction between the joint cavity on the one hand and the blood and lymphatic capillaries on the other. Most substances in the blood stream, normal or pathological, easily enter the joint cavity. Conversely, when true solutions are injected into the joint cavity, they diffuse rapidly through the synovial membrane and into capillaries. When colloidal solutions or fine suspensions are injected into the cavity, the rate of entrance into the synovial membrane and subsynovial tissue is inversely proportional to particle size. Small colloidal particles enter both blood and lymphatic capillaries from the cavity, but with greater difficulty than do solutions. Above a certain critical size, probably that of the globulin molecule, removal by these routes stops, except for small quantities that enter lymphatic capillaries and reach regional nodes. Particles over 100 μ in diameter remain in the synovial membrane and subsynovial tissue.

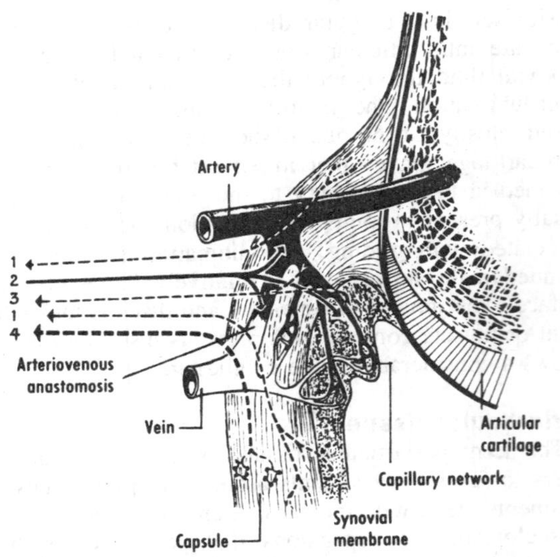

Figure 35.9. Blood and nerve supply of a synovial joint. An artery is shown supplying the epiphysis, joint capsule, and synovial membrane. Note the arteriovenous anastomosis. The articular nerve contains (1) sensory fibers (mostly pain) from the capsule and synovial membrane, (2) autonomic fibers (postganglionic, sympathetic to blood vessels), (3) sensory fibers (pain, and others with unknown functions) from the adventitia of blood vessels, and (4) proprioceptive fibers from Ruffini endings and from small lamellated corpuscles (not shown). Arrows indicate direction of conduction. (From E. Gardner, D.J. Gray, and R. O'Rahilly, *Anatomy*, 4th ed.. Saunders, Philadelphia, 1975.)

The rate of diffusion and absorption of fluids is increased if the intra-articular pressure is increased, either by injection under high pressure or by movement. Moreover, in infected joints, bacteria may enter the circulation. Infection of a joint because of material introduced from the outside (as by trauma) may be followed by septicemia.

Nerve supply

The importance of a joint nerve supply lies in two main factors: the marked subjective effects (pain) and reflex changes that may accompany joint disease; and the role of joint nerves in posture, locomotion, and the kinesthetic sense. The macroscopic anatomy of joint nerves has been studied mostly in man, but the microscopic and experimental studies have been carried out mostly in cats.

Nerves to joints arise, either directly or indirectly, from the nerves supplying the overlying skin and the muscles that move the joint. The major features of distribution, termination, and functions of articular nerves are as follows:

1. Each joint is supplied by fibers derived from several spinal nerves, the fibers being distributed by several peripheral nerves. The articular branches of the peripheral nerves show considerable variation in course and arrangements, in the number of branches from specific nerves, and in the presence or absence of specific branches. Once a nerve reaches a joint it has a widespread distribution of a rather constant pattern.

2. Some regions of joints, especially those that undergo compression during movement such as the posterior part of the knee joint, have a particularly rich nerve supply and contain large numbers of proprioceptive endings.

3. Sympathetic vasomotor fibers reach joints by way of peripheral nerves and their articular branches. The proximal joints of the limbs, such as the hip and shoul-

der, and the joints of the vertebral column also receive vasomotor fibers that leave the sympathetic trunks and travel in the adventitia (external covering) of blood vessels to the joints.

4. Articular nerves contain nonmyelinated fibers and myelinated fibers of various sizes which form sensory and motor endings (Fig. 35.9). The sensory endings present in the joint capsule and ligaments (there are relatively few in synovial membrane) include encapsulated endings (e.g. paciniform corpuscles), nonencapsulated endings (e.g. Ruffini endings), and free nerve endings. The motor endings are formed by postganglionic sympathetic fibers in relation to the smooth muscle of blood vessels.

5. The free nerve endings in the joint capsule and ligaments appear to be pain endings. The capsule and ligaments are highly sensitive to painful stimuli, especially to twisting, whereas synovial membrane is relatively insensitive. The relative insensitiveness of synovial membrane is correlated with the fact that it contains fewer pain endings. This in turn accounts for the fact that in severe sprains an intra-articular injection of a local anesthetic for the relief of pain and muscle spasm is much less effective than a periarticular injection. Likewise, synovitis is usually much less painful than inflammation of the capsule and ligaments, and is accompanied by minimal reflex muscle spasm.

Certain reflex effects are characteristic of joint pain. If the pain is sudden and severe in onset there may be marked visceral reactions, such as slowing of the pulse, fall in blood pressure, and even vomiting. The moment of disarticulation of a joint (as during surgical repair) may be accompanied by a severe though temporary fall in blood pressure.

Reflex effects on skeletal muscles are common. In the limbs they usually consist of widespread spasm of flexor (or adductor) muscles, with differences in pattern depending upon species and upon the joint. Reflex muscular spasm may be accompanied by inhibition of antagonistic muscles, which, if the spasm is maintained for long, may atrophy. For example, in an animal with a painful joint disease or a painful joint and tendon injury, spasm and limp are evident immediately, and muscle atrophy may begin within a few days.

Although the blood vessels in joints, including the arteriovenous anastomoses, are supplied by postganglionic sympathetic fibers, little is known of the nervous control of blood flow through the joints. That reflex effects do occur is known from reports that intra-articular temperature may be changed (owing to changes in blood flow) by changing the temperature of the skin over the joint.

The paciniform and Ruffini endings are highly sensitive to joint movement and position, and undoubtedly have important roles in the detection and reflex control of position and movement. However, relatively little has been done in this field as compared with the vast amount of study of the neuromuscular spindle and neurotendinous ending.

DEVELOPMENT OF JOINTS

Most studies of the development of joints have been concerned with the synovial joints of the limbs. Shortly after the limb buds appear in the embryo, the mesenchymal cells of the limb buds proliferate and form an axial mass termed a blastema. The blastema then becomes chondrified in the region of future bones, the chondrification proceeding in a proximodistal sequence. The blastema that remains between the chondrifying skeletal elements forms homogeneous cellular areas from which the joint capsule, ligaments, and synovial membrane develop. In mammals, the development of joints proceeds rapidly, and by the end of the embryonic period they closely resemble adult joints in form and arrangement. At about this time also, or early in the fetal period, the synovial membrane begins to develop and become vascularized, and synovial fluid begins to be formed.

Congenital malformations of joints, like those of bones, are important causes of morbidity and mortality. Many are genetic in nature, although for most of them the precise causes and pathogenesis remain unknown. Moreover, it is important to realize that some joint disorders that have a strong genetic background may not be manifested until well after birth (e.g. hip dyscrasias, which are common in large breeds of dogs).

REFERENCES

Barland, P., Novikoff, A.B., and Hamerman, D. 1962. Electron microscopy of the human synovial membrane. *J. Cell Biol.* 14:207–20.

Barnett, C.H., Davies, D.V., and MacConaill, M.A. 1961. *Synovial Joints*. Clowes, London.

Cutlip, R.C., and Cheville, N.F. 1973. Structure of synovial membrane of sheep. *Am. J. Vet. Res.* 34:45–50.

Freeman, M.A.R., ed. 1973. *Adult Articular Cartilage*. Pitman Medical, London.

Furey, J.G., Clark, W.S., and Brine, K.L. 1959. The practical importance of synovial fluid analyses. *J. Bone Joint Surg.*, ser. A, 41:167–74.

Gardner, E. 1972. The structure and function of joints. In J.L. Hollander and D.J. McCarty, Jr., eds., *Arthritis and Allied Conditions*. 8th ed. Lea & Febiger, Philadelphia.

Ghadially, F.N., and Roy, S. 1969. *Ultrastructure of Synovial Joints in Health and Disease*. Butterworth, London.

Hamerman, D., Rosenberg, L.C., and Schubert, M. 1970. Diarthrodial joints revisited. *J. Bone Joint Surg.*, ser. A, 52:725–74.

Jaffe, H.L. 1972. *Metabolic, Degenerative, and Inflammatory Diseases of Bones and Joints*. Lea & Febiger, Philadelphia.

Mackay-Smith, M.P. 1962. Pathogenesis and pathology of equine osteoarthritis. *J. Am. Vet. Med. Ass* 141:1246–48.

Mankin, H.J. 1974. The reaction of articular cartilage to injury and osteoarthritis. *New Eng. J. Med.* 291:1285–92.

Schubert, M., and Hamerman, D. 1968. *A Primer on Connective Tissue Biochemistry*. Lea & Febiger, Philadelphia.

Seppälä, P.O., and Balazs, E.A. 1969. Hyaluronic acid in synovial fluid. *J. Geront.* 24:309–14.

Skoglund, S. 1973. Joint receptors and kinaesthesis. In A. Iggo, ed., *Somatosensory System*. Springer, Berlin.

Van Pelt, R.W. 1962. Anatomy and physiology of articular structures. *Vet. Med.* 57:135–43.

———. Properties of equine synovial fluid. *J. Am. Vet. Med. Ass.* 141:1051–61.

Van Pelt, R.W., and Connor, G.H. 1963. Synovial fluid from the normal bovine tarsus. *Am. J. Vet. Res.* 24:112–21, 537–44, 735–42.

PART V WATER BALANCE AND EXCRETION

CHAPTER 36

Water, Electrolytes, and Acid-Base Balance

by T. Richard Houpt

Unicellular organisms originated in the sea long before multicellular animals developed. The appearance of multicellular forms and their movement onto the land were accompanied by the development of body fluids that resemble the primordial sea water and in which the tissue cells are continuously bathed. Normal tissue function and development of the higher forms of animal life depend upon the maintenance and control of the composition of that fluid. Claude Bernard pointed out over one hundred years ago that this extracellular fluid constitutes an internal environment, and W.B. Cannon early in this century coined the word homeostasis to express the existence and maintenance of stability within this environment.

WATER

All life is intimately associated with water. Most of the ions and molecules comprising living matter have chemical and physical relationships with water, and the number of chemical compounds which can be put into aqueous solution is exceptionally large. The physical properties of water are also particularly fitting. For example, water has a very high specific heat. As a result, water can hold large amounts of heat without a great rise in temperature. Thus water not only supplies the matrix in which all living processes occur, but it also participates significantly in those processes.

Distribution of body water

Total body water and fluid compartments

There is considerable variation in total body water content between different species, ages, sexes, nutritional states, and other conditions. Generally, the lean adult nonherbivore has a total body water content of about 70 percent of its body weight. Water content is highest in the newborn animal, declines rapidly at first, and then declines slowly (Fig. 36.1). Fat tissue is exceptional in its low water content (10 percent or less); thus the total water content of a fat animal will be lower than that of a lean one. Kraybill et al. (1951) found that in very lean cattle about 70 percent of body weight was water, while in very fat animals, total body water comprised only about 40 percent.

Water contained within cells is called *intracellular fluid*. All fluid lying outside of cells is called *extracellular fluid*. The extracellular fluid is in turn divided by the walls of the vascular system into the *interstitial fluid* and the *plasma*. Roughly an amount of water equal to 50 percent of the body weight lies within the cells, 15 percent in the interstitial spaces, and 5 percent in blood plasma. Water in the alimentary canal, although it strictly speaking is outside the body tissues proper, is usually included as extracellular water. The cerebrospinal fluid, aqueous humor of the eye, synovial fluids, urine, and

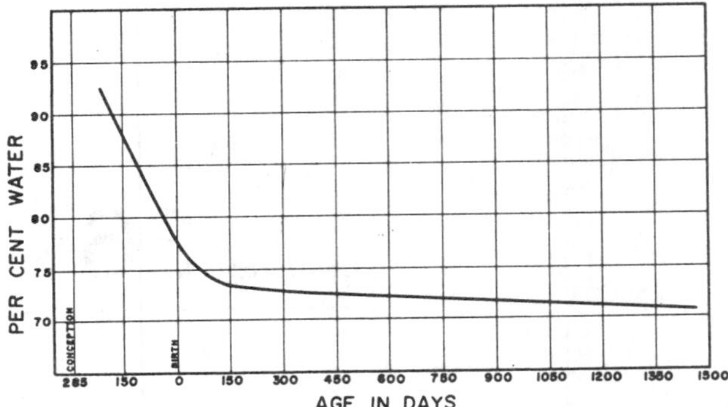

Figure 36.1. Relation between water content and age in cattle. (From Armsby and Moulton, *The Animal as a Converter of Matter and Energy*, Chemical Catalog Co., New York, 1925.)

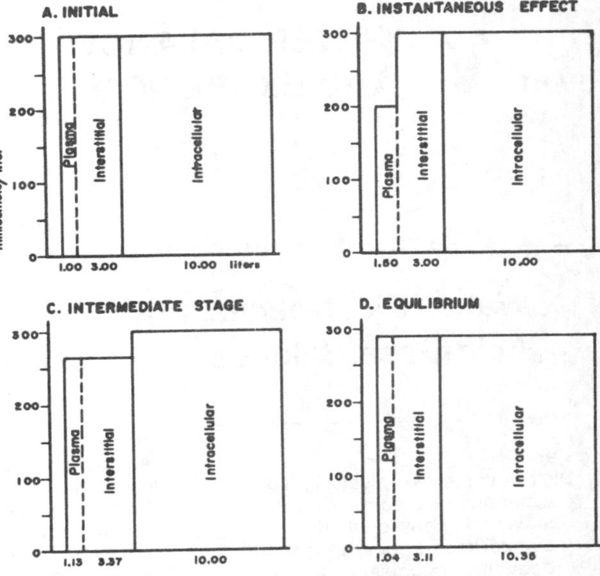

Figure 36.2. Hypothetical water shifts among fluid compartments as a result of injection of 500 ml water intravenously into a 20 kg dog. Height of each compartment represents osmoconcentration in milliosmoles per liter, width represents volume in liters.

bile also are subdivisions of extracellular fluid which may exhibit special characteristics. These fluids, which are somewhat separated from the main body of extracellular fluid, are called *transcellular fluids*.

Water movement between fluid compartments

Water molecules can rapidly penetrate most cell membranes. If an osmotic or hydrostatic pressure gradient exists between any of the body fluid compartments, a shift of water will occur. If there is no appreciable hydrostatic pressure involved, the result of the water movement will be to equalize the osmoconcentrations of the fluids. The response to an intravenous injection of water is illustrated in Figure 36.2. Initially osmoconcentration is identical in all compartments (A), but there is a rapid dilution of plasma osmoconcentration as the injection is being made. B shows the extent of plasma dilution which would occur if the distribution of the injected water was instantaneous and limited to the plasma. Actually the osmotic gradient between plasma and interstitial fluid, plus a rise of blood pressure due to the increased volume of fluid, causes water to begin its shift out of the vascular system even while the injection is occurring. This prevents the extreme dilution of plasma shown in B, and instead osmoconcentrations shortly after the injection are approximately shown in C. Of course, as soon as the interstitial fluid osmoconcentration begins to drop, water begins to move into the cells. Within a few minutes equality of osmoconcentration has been re-established for all fluid compartments at a slightly subnormal level (D). If for any reason a very large amount of water were added to the extracellular fluid, the water movement into cells might disrupt normal metabolic function and might even cause death. This condition of cellular overhydration is known as water intoxication.

Water shifts similar to those described above will occur after the addition of any hypotonic sodium chloride solution to the extracellular fluid. If an isotonic sodium chloride solution were injected, it would become evenly distributed throughout the extracellular compartment, but would have little effect upon cellular water. If a hypertonic NaCl solution were administered intravenously, water would begin to shift into the plasma; but since the capillaries are freely permeable to both water and electrolytes, the osmotic gradient would disappear as solvent and solute are distributed throughout the extracellular compartment. However, the cell membrane, unlike the capillary wall, does not permit the free movement of NaCl, and so the increased osmoconcentration of the extracellular fluid would cause a cellular dehydration.

Measurement of body fluid volumes

Total body water can be determined directly by drying the whole animal and measuring the loss of weight. Blood volume has been estimated directly, but inaccurately, by measuring the volume of blood which can be bled from the circulatory system. However, these methods are inconvenient and necessitate the death of the animal. The general method commonly used to estimate these and other fluid volumes is the dilution technique (see Chapter 2). A compound is injected which becomes distributed throughout the fluid volume in question. The compound must be restricted to that particular fluid volume. After distribution of the compound is complete, a sample of the fluid is obtained and concentration of the compound is determined. The volume of that fluid compartment then equals the weight of the compound injected divided by its concentration after distribution. Unfortunately, while the compound is being distributed throughout the fluid compartment, it may also be excreted or metabolized; and corrections must be made for these losses occurring during the distribution time. Furthermore, it is difficult to find suitable substances which are distributed only within the fluid volume under study.

The best compounds for measurement of total body water are heavy water (deuterium oxide) and radioactive water (tritium oxide). Isotopically labeled water distributes itself in a fashion identical to the normal water of the body. Other compounds used include antipyrine, sulfanilamide, thiourea, and urea. Estimation of extracellular fluid volume requires a substance which does not enter cells. Inulin, a large dextran molecule, is frequently used for this purpose, but sucrose, thiocyanate, sulfate, and others are also used. Intracellular fluid volume cannot be estimated directly, but must be calculated as the difference between total and extracellular fluid volumes. Plasma volume can be measured by injecting a substance, such as Evans blue dye (also known as T-1824), which is adsorbed to plasma proteins. An alternative way is to measure blood volume with erythrocytes labeled with radioactive phosphorus. Plasma volume can be easily calculated from blood volume if the volume of erythrocytes is also determined. The measurement of the various body fluid compartments is not precise; repetition of measurements or use of different substances often gives variations of several percent in the same animal.

Water balance

The total amount of water in the body remains relatively constant from day to day. Water is gained by ingestion or as an end product of cellular metabolism; water loss occurs in urine, from the skin, with expired gases, and in the feces. The lactating animal also loses large amounts of water in milk. Typical values for lactating and nonlactating cows under moderate environmental conditions are given in Table 36.1. Most of these routes of water loss or gain are not controlled with respect to body water content. Only ingestion of water and urinary water excretion are controlled in order to regulate body water volume.

Table 36.1. Daily water balance (L) of Holstein cows eating legume hay

Balance	Nonlactating	Lactating
Intake		
Drinking water	26	51
Food water	1	2
Metabolic water	2	3
Total	29	56
Output		
Feces	12	19
Urine	7	11
Vaporized	10	14
Milk	0	12
Total	29	56

Adapted from Leitch and Thomson 1944, *Nutr. Abstr. Rev.* 14:197–223

Thirst and ingestion of water

Much of the loss of water from the body is continuous, and over a period of time a deficit in body water develops which is corrected periodically by the ingestion of water. There appear to be several mechanisms which control the amount of water ingested so that it equals the body water deficit (Epstein et al. 1973). Water deprivation causes both the sensation of thirst and an associated behavioral drive to drink water. Thirst is characterized by a dryness of the throat and mouth due to the decrease in salivary gland secretory rate as a water deficit develops. This sensation of dryness may become so intense in man as to be acutely painful. It can only partially and temporarily be relieved by wetting the mouth and throat. Temporary inhibition of drinking can also be caused by other stimuli. If a dog equipped with an esophageal fistula is deprived of water and then permitted to drink, it will take in only a limited amount of water. However, the amount ingested may be more than twice the initial water deficit (Bellows 1939). Apparently the amount of water ingested is measured as it passes through the mouth and pharynx, but the measurement is not precise. Furthermore, after about 20 minutes the inhibition to drinking disappears, and the animal will ingest more water. If an amount of water equal to the water deficit is placed in a balloon in the stomach, drinking will likewise be inhibited for a few minutes (Towbin 1949).

Andersson and McCann (1955a) have shown that the system controlling thirst and drinking behavior is located in the medial hypothalamus. They permanently implanted electrodes in a region of the hypothalamus of goats. When electrical stimuli were applied to the conscious goat, the animal would immediately seek and drink water although no water deficit existed. In fact, the animal would continue to drink until it had ingested an excess of water equal to 40 percent of its body weight. These investigators were able also to inject minute amounts of hypertonic solutions into the same region of the hypothalamus, and they found that this also caused the animal to drink. These results suggest that certain cells of the hypothalamus or nearby in the cerebral ventricles are sensitive to changes in osmoconcentration and that such osmotic stimuli cause thirst and drinking behavior (Andersson 1971). When a dehydrated animal drinks, thirst is temporarily inhibited when an amount approximately equal to the water deficit has been ingested, but prolonged satisfaction is not attained until absorption and dilution of the body fluids remove the osmotic stimulus to the hypothalamic system.

There is considerable evidence that thirst and the ingestion of water can also be stimulated by a fall in blood pressure. It is widely believed, but not well proven, that a fall of pressure within the left atrium (possibly also the great veins and right atrium) and within the carotid sinus and aortic arch initiates thirst much as a fall in pressure results in antidiuretic hormone (ADH) release by this afferent pathway (Fitzsimons 1972). Evidence for a role of angiotensin as a stimulant of thirst by direct action on the hypothalamic system provides a second mechanism for stimulation of thirst by hypovolemia (Epstein et al. 1970). These control mechanisms also constitute part of the regulatory system for extracellular fluid (ECF) volume, since any fall in ECF volume will generally result in a fall in blood pressure.

Urinary excretion of water and its hormonal control

If an animal is deprived of water, the rate of water excretion in the urine decreases, and conversely, but there are limitations. On the one hand, a minimum urine volume is determined by the quantity of solutes to be excreted and by the ability of the kidney to concentrate urine. The maximum urine concentration possible varies greatly among animals. Some approximate values (osmol/L) are: human 1.5, dog 2.3, cat 3.3, sheep 3.2, rabbit 1.9, kangaroo rat 5.5, beaver 0.6. On the other hand, a limit can eventually be reached as urinary volume is increased; however, it is very high and ordinarily excess water will be excreted rapidly. The excretion of water by the kidney is controlled primarily by the ADH of the posterior pituitary gland (see Chapters 37 and 52). ADH (also known as vasopressin) acts upon the nephron to permit increased reabsorption of water and hence a decreased excretion in the urine. During water deprivation the concentration of ADH in the blood rises and urine volume falls. If the animal is overhydrated, less ADH will be present in the blood, urine flow rises, and the concentration of the urine may decrease until it approaches that of the plasma.

The release of ADH from the posterior pituitary gland is believed to be caused primarily by changes in the osmoconcentration of the plasma. Verney and his associates showed that, if a hypertonic saline solution is injected into the carotid artery, a decrease in urine flow results. Other evidence indicated that the hypertonic solution acted upon structures in the ventral diencephalon, and they suggested that the supraoptic nuclei of the hypothalamus contain the cells sensitive to changes in osmoconcentration of plasma (Jewell and Verney 1957). The cells of these nuclei exert their control by way of the hypothalamic-hypophyseal nerve tracts to cause release of ADH. This hypothesis states that when the osmotic concentration of plasma rises it stimulates the release of ADH and that, when osmoconcentration falls, little or no ADH is released (Verney 1947).

The hypothalamic osmoreceptor system is involved with the regulation of the ECF osmoconcentration through variation in water excretion, but ADH also functions as a control for regulation of ECF volume (Schrier and Berl 1975). A fall in ECF volume generally involves a fall in circulating blood volume. However, there appear to be no true volume receptors. Instead, the degree of distension of the left atrium and large arteries is monitored by stretch receptors located at those sites. This afferent limb of the pathway is the same as that for thirst. The resultant change in afferent nerve discharge frequency causes by way of the hypothalamus an increase of ADH release from the posterior pituitary. The consequent conservation of water by the kidney aids restoration of ECF volume. Another consequence of this hypothalamic response is the increased retention of sodium that is necessary to maintain normal osmoconcentration as water retention occurs. The release of ADH can also be stimulated by pain, exercise, and many other stresses.

Variations of glomerular filtration rate (GFR) may also be an important influence on water conservation in some domestic animals. For example, a 50 percent fall in GFR was reported in sheep deprived of drinking water for 5 days (Macfarlane 1964).

Water in food and metabolic water

Although the bulk of the water obtained by the animal is ingested as drinking water, under certain circumstances much water may be obtained in the food. Most foodstuffs contain at least a small amount of water, and lush green vegetation may contain 75–90 percent water. Nonlactating ruminants when on succulent pasture may ingest little or no drinking water. In fact, cattle on such pasture may appear to be somewhat overhydrated and as a result excrete copious amounts of urine. The oxidation of foodstuffs also yields some water. The oxidation of each gram of carbohydrate yields about 0.6 ml of water; the corresponding amounts for fats and protein are 1.1 and 0.4 ml respectively per gram metabolized. For most domestic animals this oxidative or metabolic water comprises only from 5–10 percent of the total water intake and remains constant provided metabolic rate is constant.

Metabolic water, however, can be of great importance in the water balance of many small desert rodents and may constitute 100 percent of their water intake. Best known of this group are the kangaroo rats, which may live indefinitely on dried food with no drinking water. These animals are able to maintain water balance, first, by avoiding the greatest daily heat load and hence the necessity to expend water for heat dissipation, and second by minimizing water loss to an unusual degree. These rodents remain in their relatively cool burrows during the hot day and emerge only during the night. Loss of water is minimized by a nearly water-impermeable skin, low respiratory water loss due to a low temperature of the expired air, a highly concentrated urine of small volume, and exceptionally dry feces.

Water loss by other routes

Besides excretion in the urine, water is lost from the body in feces, with respiratory gases, and from the surface of the body. These routes of water loss are not generally regulated with respect to the water content of the body. The amount of fecal water varies with the species of animal; for example, it is small in sheep but considerable in cattle. In all animals water loss in gastrointestinal disturbances may be substantial and rapid. The air inspired by an animal ordinarily has a lower water content than the air expired. This is because the incoming air is warmed and saturated with water before expiration. Loss by this route under moderate conditions is constant, but when an animal is exposed to a hot environment, evaporation of water from the respiratory tract increases as the respiratory minute volume rises. Water loss from animals which show a marked thermal polypnea, such as the dog and sheep, may become considerable under these circumstances.

Water loss from the surface of the skin occurs in two ways. Water may simply diffuse through the surface from the blood vessels and body fluids in the skin and evaporate from the surface. This diffusion of water will vary according to the temperature of the skin and circulation. Diffusion water loss through the skin and evaporation of water from the respiratory tract together are known as the insensible water loss. Sweating, which is varied with respect to body temperature, is another process by which water is lost from the body surface. Under moderate environmental conditions water loss as sweat is insignificant. However, under heat stress sweating losses may be tremendous in freely sweating animals such as man and the horse. Finally, some animals such as cats, rats, and kangaroos produce large amounts of saliva when under heat stress and then spread the saliva over the body surface.

Dehydration

Since the intake of water is intermittent and loss of water is continuous, the animal is always faced with the problem of slow dehydration. Any serious dehydration involves the loss of both water and electrolytes. The process of dehydration will vary somewhat according to whether the loss of water and electrolytes is rapid or slow and according to the relative rates of loss of water and electrolyte. Only simple dehydration due to a lack of drinking water under moderate environmental conditions will be considered here.

The first sign of dehydration is a tendency to seek and drink water. Concomitantly there is a decrease in urine volume. These changes can be observed when only 1–2 percent of the body weight has been lost as water. Dehydration to the extent of 10 percent of the body weight is considered severe. A dog deprived of water under moderate conditions will lose about 10 percent of its body weight in 5 days. Most animals will not eat during moderate or severe dehydration, and hence part of the body weight loss is loss of tissue substance used for energy metabolism. The immediate source of water lost from the body is the extracellular fluid, and if the rate of loss is very rapid, extracellular fluid volume may be severely reduced. In slow dehydration, however, there will be a shift of water from the cells into the extracellular fluid. Painter et al. (1948) found in a dog that after 5 days of water deprivation 67 percent of the water loss was from the extracellular fluid volume and 33 percent from the cells.

During water deprivation the slow loss of water from the body results in a rise of ECF osmoconcentration and a fall of ECF volume which stimulate both drinking behavior and the decreased urine flow. Electrolyte concentration does not, however, continue to rise during dehydration. Instead, electrolytes are also excreted from the body roughly in proportion to water loss, and this prevents a further rise of osmoconcentration until dehydration has proceeded nearly to the point of death. In early dehydration increased quantities of sodium chloride appear in the urine as extracellular fluid is reduced. Then as cellular water shifts to the extracellular compartment, cellular potassium also is excreted in the urine. Thus after a long period of dehydration the animal will be depleted of both water and the primary electrolytes. The proportion of body weight which can be lost as water before death occurs varies widely according to the dietary and environmental conditions. In man, for example, this limit may range from 15 to 25 percent.

Adaptation to water lack

Among domestic animals a wide range of adaptation to water lack exists. Some species, e.g. cattle, dogs, cats, and swine, exhibit little special adaptation; generally neither they nor their wild progenitors have inhabited arid regions. On the other hand, some common domestic species such as sheep, as well as certain domestic animals indigenous to arid regions such as the camel and donkey, have acquired adaptations enabling them to withstand severe water lack. Almost without exception the problem of water lack is compounded by exposure to high temperatures. During the cool season of most arid areas the small amount of rainfall is sufficient to increase the water content of the vegetation appreciably, and some herbivores are able to maintain water balance on plant water for long periods, for example, camels in the Sahara. High summer temperatures, however, necessitate expenditures of increased amounts of water in order to control body temperature, and the natural vegetation contains far less water. Under these circumstances even the camel must drink water periodically.

Cattle appear to have no special water conservation mechanisms, but there is an important difference between

European cattle and Indian cattle (Zebu or Brahman cattle). Zebu cattle are better able to regulate their body temperatures when exposed to heat stress; they can dissipate larger quantities of heat by evaporation of larger quantities of water from their body surface. Furthermore, Indian cattle have more and larger sweat glands over most of their body surface (Nay and Hayman 1956). This heat resistance, however, depends upon an ample supply of water.

It has only been recently that reliable information has been obtained on the means by which a camel dissipates body heat in the face of a severe heat stress without excessive use of water for cooling purposes (B. Schmidt-Nielsen et al. 1956, K. Schmidt-Nielsen et al. 1957).

First, it is necessary to point out that the camel can neither store water nor derive important additional amounts of water from metabolism of the fat of its hump. When severely dehydrated camels are permitted to drink they do not store water by overhydration. Only if an excessive amount of salt is ingested will the animal in effect overhydrate. Peculiar small sacs located in the wall of the rumen have given rise to the legend that the camel stores water in its rumen. Although rumen fluid may act as a source of water when the animal is deprived of water, there is no evidence that more water is present in the camel rumen than in the rumen of other ruminants. The small rumen sacs, on the contrary, contain comparatively dry ingesta when examined postmortem. The camel stores water only in the sense that it can withstand a greater degree of dehydration than can many other mammals.

It has been suggested that, whereas the metabolism of each gram of fat yields 1.1 ml of water the fatty hump of the camel should represent an important store of water. The camel, as other animals, does derive a certain amount of water from oxidation of nutrients. Presumably the special value of the hump fat would be due to a shift from the metabolism of starch and protein to that of fat, total metabolic rate remaining relatively constant. However, this additional metabolic water can be of little value. First, although the camel has remarkable ability to conserve water, its daily needs in absolute terms are sizable. Even when conserving water maximally, a medium-sized camel will expend over 10 liters of water daily during summer months. Obviously only an enormous hump could supply enough water to meet needs for more than 2–3 days. Second, in the desert a fat animal is a rarity; most camel humps there contain relatively little fat. Finally, whether energy needs are satisfied by the oxidation of fat or by the oxidation of starch and protein, about the same total amount of metabolic water will be produced. This is because, although more water will be produced per gram of fat oxidized, less than half as much fat will be required to replace the starch and proteins. The actual amounts of water formed per kcal derived from the oxidation of the nutrients are: for fat 0.12 g H_2O/kcal, for carbohydrate 0.14 g H_2O/kcal, and for protein 0.10 g H_2O/kcal. Further, as K. Schmidt-Nielsen (1964) has pointed out, the oxidation of the smaller amount of fat will require more than twice as much oxygen. Hence the animal's oxygen consumption will be nearly the same regardless of the nutrients metabolized. It follows that respiratory water loss is also nearly the same whether fat or other nutrients are oxidized. Little or no net gain of water is accrued from fat metabolism under these circumstances. Needless to say, the hump fat does constitute an energy reserve of great importance.

Under conditions of heat stress where a man could only survive a single day without drinking water, camels can easily survive for a week and in fact show little discomfort. At the end of that first day, man will have lost about 12 percent of his body weight as water, while by the end of the week the camel will have lost over 25 percent. In addition to being able to withstand greater degrees of dehydration, the camel has several means of conserving water. During the day, when the heat stress is greatest, the camel's body temperature rises thereby storing heat and saving the water which would have been required to dissipate this heat. During the cooler desert night this stored heat is dissipated and body temperature is normal or even slightly subnormal by dawn. In addition, in the camel the summer fur, which is most prominent on the dorsal surfaces, is very effective in reducing solar heat gain. Although the camel has considerable ability to concentrate its urine and to form very dry feces, the amounts of water conserved by these means are less significant in maintaining water balance. The animal does, of course, dissipate heat through the evaporation of water. Sweating may be the most important route of evaporative heat dissipation, for a marked thermal polypnea is not observed. A final remarkable attribute of the camel is its ability to rehydrate rapidly. It is not unusual for a camel to ingest more than one fourth its body weight as water in a few minutes.

There have been relatively few investigations of resistance to water lack by equids, and most of these concern the donkey (Dill 1938, B. Schmidt-Nielsen et al. 1956, Yousef et al. 1970, Maloiy 1970). It is the domestic member of this group most frequently seen in arid areas. Even deep in the Sahara it is found in regions where its equine relatives are rarely seen. The donkey matches the camel with respect to the degree of dehydration which it will withstand and the rapidity with which it can rehydrate. Although the donkey can survive up to a 30 percent loss of body weight as water under heat stress, it uses water for cooling at a rate three times that of a camel, with a corresponding reduction in the donkey's survival time. Upon rehydrating, a small donkey has been observed to drink 20.5 liters of water in 2.5 minutes.

Lee and Robinson (1941) investigated the ability of a variety of common domestic animals to withstand high environmental temperatures and concluded that sheep had the greatest tolerance. Various investigations have confirmed their conclusion. The principal adaptations are an ability to endure a degree of dehydration equal to about 30 percent of their body weight and to minimize absorption of solar heat. When exposed to intense solar radiation, the temperature of the wool surface may rise to 87°C. Apparently the insulative capacity of the wool prevents a rapid transfer of heat from the wool surface to the skin, while at the same time the high surface temperature will cause radiation of heat to the cooler environment (Macfarlane 1964). The sheep also conserves water by excreting dry feces and a relatively concentrated urine. Dissipation of heat by evaporation of water is effected primarily by panting. Sweating does occur, but the rate is considerably lower than that, for example, of the cow. Finally, the sheep is similar to the camel and donkey in being able to drink nearly one fourth of its body weight in water at one drinking without harmful effects.

ELECTROLYTES

The ionic composition of the body fluids typical of mammals is illustrated in Figure 36.3. The height of each pair of columns represents the concentration of electrolytes in terms of chemical equivalents. The necessity for electrical neutrality dictates that the height of each column representing the cations must exactly equal the height of its adjacent column representing the anions. All of the extracellular fluid is similar, consisting primarily of sodium, chloride, and bicarbonate ions. The blood plasma component in addition has an appreciable amount of protein, the plasma proteins. Furthermore, there is a slightly unequal distribution of all diffusible ions across the capillary wall in compliance with the Gibbs-Donnan phenomenon. The small block representing nonelectrolytes refers to glucose, urea, and so forth. The major cations of the fluid of the cells, on the other hand, are potassium and magnesium with only small amounts of sodium. These cellular cations are balanced by organic phosphates, proteinate, sulfate, and a small amount of bicarbonate. The ionic composition of the cells depicted in this figure is typical of many body cells, but there are important exceptions. For example, although little chloride ion is found in muscle cells, significant quantities are found in certain other cells such as erythrocytes and those of the gastric mucosa. Variations of electrolyte concentration in plasma and red blood cells are given in Chapter 33.

If the composition of the body fluids is expressed in terms of osmoconcentration instead of chemical equivalents, a somewhat similar pattern is found, except that the multivalent ions have less osmotic effect (Table 36.2). Variations from this exist in domestic animals (see

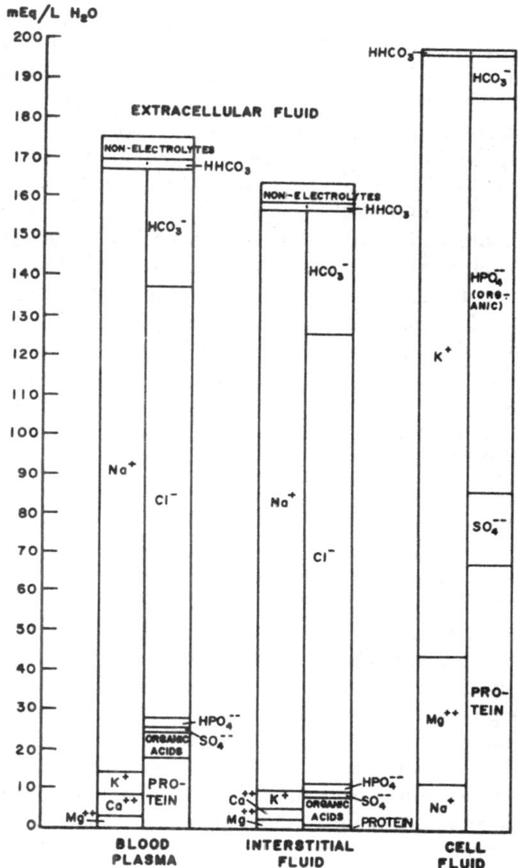

Figure 36.3. Composition of human body fluids. (From J.L. Gamble, *Chemical Anatomy, Physiology, and Pathology of Extracellular Fluid*, Harvard U. Press, Cambridge, 1954.)

Table 36.2. Osmotically active substances in human body fluids

Substances	Plasma	Interstitial (mOsmol/L H_2O)	Intracellular
Na^+	144	137	10
K^+	5	4.7	141
Ca^{++}	2.5	2.4	0
Mg^{++}	1.5	1.4	31
Cl^-	107	112.7	4
HCO_3^-	27	28.3	10
$HPO_4^=$, $H_2PO_4^-$	2	2	11
$SO_4^=$	0.5	0.5	1
Glucose	5.6	5.6	
Proteins	1.2	0.2	4
Urea	4	4	4
Other organic substances	3.4	3.4	86.2
Total	303.7	302.2	302.2
Total osmotic pressure at 37°C in mm Hg	5455	5430	5430

Adapted from A.C. Guyton, *Textbook of Medical Physiology*, 4th ed., Saunders, Philadelphia, 1971

Chapter 33). Nearly all of the osmoconcentration of the extracellular fluid is due to sodium, chloride, and bicarbonate ions, while that of the intracellular fluid is mostly due to potassium, magnesium, and organic substances. Because of intermolecular and interionic attractive forces, the actual osmotic effect of the solutes in body fluids is only about 93 percent of that which would be calculated from their chemical composition. Total osmotic pressure values given on the bottom line of the table have been corrected for this depression of osmotic effect. The osmotic activity of all body fluids is nearly equal except for the small difference between plasma and interstitial fluid. The plasma proteins create this osmotic pressure difference across the capillary wall, and, although it is small in comparison to the total osmotic pressure of the extracellular fluids, it is of great importance for maintenance of blood volume and pressure.

Sodium

This is the major cation of extracellular fluid and an important component of the skeleton. About 45 percent of the body store of sodium is found in extracellular fluid and 45 percent in bone, and the remainder is intracellular. Although most body sodium is in a readily exchangeable form, nearly half of that in bone does not exchange with sodium ions in the fluid compartments. The nonexchangeable sodium is absorbed on the surfaces of hydroxyapatite crystals deep in long bones. None of the bone sodium is osmotically active, although part of it may become available to ameliorate the osmotic effects of extracellular fluid dilution (Edelman and Leibman 1959).

Regulation of sodium concentration

A relatively constant [Na^+] of the extracellular fluid is attained by regulation of both intake and excretion of sodium so as to maintain a salt balance. Relatively little is known of the central mechanism of salt hunger or appetite, but many sodium-deficient animals have a strong behavioral drive to ingest salt and show a remarkable ability to control ingestion of sodium chloride or sodium solutions so that they just replace a body deficit of sodium. When more than minimal amounts of salt are ingested with the ration, as is usually the case, salt hunger will not be evident, and excess salt will be excreted. Presumably sodium appetite is controlled by a neuromuscular system similar to that of thirst (Denton 1967).

Excretion of sodium by the kidney involves first the filtration at the glomerulus of plasma sodium and then reabsorption from the tubule of most of the filtered sodium. The difference between the amount of sodium filtered and that reabsorbed is the amount excreted in the urine. Changes in sodium excretion can be effected in two ways. Firstly, if plasma [Na^+] or glomerular filtration rate suddenly increases, the amount of sodium filtered per unit time into the tubule will also increase. However, sodium reabsorption from the tubule will not increase proportionately in such a short period of time. Therefore, the difference between sodium filtered and sodium reabsorbed will be greater, and more sodium will be excreted in the urine. Conversely, if plasma [Na^+] or glomerular filtration rate decreases, less sodium will be excreted. Secondly a rise of plasma [Na^+] will cause decreased secretion of aldosterone by the adrenal cortex. The primary action of aldosterone is to increase sodium reabsorption from the renal tubule. Decreased amounts of aldosterone will result in less reabsorption of sodium, and consequently more sodium will escape reabsorption and appear in the urine. On the other hand, a fall in plasma [Na^+] will cause an increase of aldosterone secretion and increased reabsorption of sodium from the tubule. In severe sodium deficiency virtually all filtered sodium will be reabsorbed and a sodium-free urine will be excreted. Both mechanisms act to control sodium excretion so as to maintain the normal [Na^+] of extracellular fluids, but aldosterone is the more important where the disturbance of [Na^+] is prolonged.

The most important way in which changes in ECF [Na^+] influence the release of aldosterone is by the renin-angiotensin system (Oparil and Haber 1974). A fall of plasma [Na^+] results in the release of renin, a proteolytic enzyme, from the juxtaglomerular cells located in the afferent arterioles of the kidney glomerulus. It is not clear whether this action of [Na^+] is directly upon the juxtaglomerular cells or whether the macula densa cells of the distal convoluted tubules are also involved. A fall in renal arterial pressure has a similar effect on renin release. Renin then acts in the blood stream upon angiotensinogen, a protein of hepatic origin, with the formation of angiotensin I. The latter is enzymatically converted to angiotensin II as the blood passes through the lungs and other organs. Angiotensin II causes release of aldosterone, and urinary excretion of sodium decreases. There is also evidence that angiotensin can act centrally to stimulate salt hunger (Buggy and Fisher 1974). Renin release can also be elicited by excitation of the sympathetic nerves to the renal blood vessels. This sympathetic pathway is the efferent limb of a reflex which may originate either from stretch receptors in the left atrium or the arterial baroreceptors when a fall in blood pressure occurs.

There is considerable evidence that another hormone exists which increases sodium excretion (natriuresis) by the kidney. Supposedly a fall in ECF volume causes release of this natriuretic hormone (Wardener 1973).

The adrenocorticotropic hormone (ACTH) from the anterior pituitary has a positive influence on the release of aldosterone. ACTH is released following many general stresses and also by ADH.

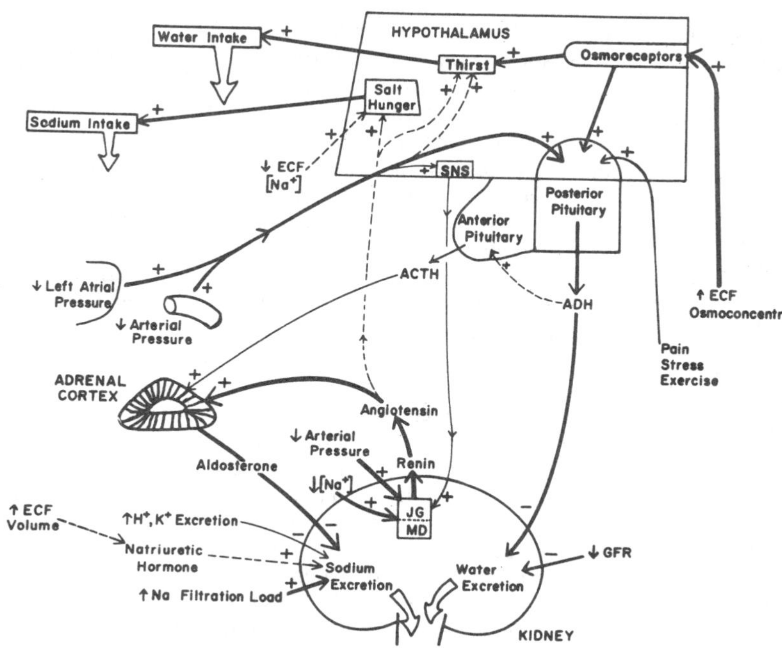

Figure 36.4. Controls of water and sodium intake and excretion. Well-established pathways are shown with solid lines; others with dashed lines. Each pathway is initiated by a deviation of an ECF variable from normal; typical deviations are indicated by an arrow before the variable. The effect of the deviation on the next structure or process in the pathway is shown as + for increase or − for decrease in its action. JG, juxtaglomerular cells; MD, macula densa. Control mechanisms indicated in the hypothalamus are not meant to represent cellular nuclei or centers but rather systems which may actually include structures in other parts of the brain. SNS, sympathetic nervous system.

Osmoconcentration versus volume regulation

The volume and osmoconcentration of the ECF are regulated together by the thirst-ADH and salt appetite–aldosterone systems, but the coordinating links between these regulatory systems are not fully understood. The two systems often work together as, for example, following a hemorrhage when both renal conservation of water with thirst and retention of body sodium occur. In many situations there is a conflict between the two systems. During simple dehydration ECF volume is falling and both conservation of water and salt might be expected. However, plasma [Na^+] is also rising. In mild or moderate dehydration the conflict is resolved in favor of defense of ECF osmoconcentration, and sodium is excreted in greater amounts to approximately match the loss of water. Osmoconcentration is thus often more vigorously defended than ECF volume; however, if the loss of ECF is great enough to seriously affect circulating blood volume and hence cardiac output, maintenance of plasma volume takes precedence, and water is conserved despite a low plasma osmoconcentration (Johnson et al. 1970).

The multiple-control systems that regulate ECF osmoconcentration and volume are summarized in Figure 36.4, including both well-established pathways as well as some still controversial.

Potassium

Potassium is the major cation of the intracellular fluid, and 89 percent of the total body content of potassium is located within the cells. Nearly all of the intracellular potassium is readily exchangeable with potassium in the extracellular fluid. The [K^+] in extracellular fluid is well regulated, but the details are incompletely known. Dietary intake is usually in excess of needs because most foodstuffs contain considerable potassium, and the kidneys seem better able to excrete this excess than to conserve it. However, dogs fed a potassium-deficient diet for several days gradually decrease the amount of potassium excreted in the urine to a very low level, and are able to re-establish potassium balance (Lemieux et al. 1964). Ruminants can vary their urinary excretion rate of potassium to meet wide and rapid changes in intake (Pickering 1965).

Renal handling of potassium is complex. The potassium that appears in the urine is the result of secretion by the distal convoluted tubules. There appears to be no specific control system as there is for sodium, but rather the rate of potassium secretion into the urine is proportional to renal tubular intracellular [K^+] and to the magnitude of the membrane potential across the luminal membrane of the tubular cells (Pitts 1975). Intracellular [K^+] will generally rise and fall with plasma [K^+], and the resulting effects on the rate of potassium diffusion from the tubular cells into the tubular fluid may be the primary control of potassium excretion. The membrane potential is negative on the tubular lumen side and positive on the interior of the cell, and so the electrical gradient favors electromigration of K^+ out of the cells into the tubular fluid. An increased rate of sodium reabsorption increases the transmembrane potential. Since aldosterone increases sodium reabsorption, there is usually an inverse relationship between sodium and potassium excretion.

Chloride and bicarbonate

Sodium ions of extracellular fluid are balanced electrically for the most part by chloride ions and bicarbonate ions. Osmotically the effect of these ions equals that of sodium ions, but the variations of osmoconcentration are usually a consequence of changes in cation concentration (or water content) rather than that of anions. The $[Cl^-]$ tends to be regulated secondarily to regulation of $[Na^+]$ and $[HCO_3^-]$. If excess sodium is excreted by the kidney, chloride usually accompanies it. If, due to an alkalotic condition, the plasma level of bicarbonate ion rises, an equivalent amount of chloride ion is excreted in order that electroneutrality be maintained in the extracellular fluid.

The bicarbonate ion is unique in that it can be formed or removed in the body with great rapidity. It is formed in solution from its anhydride:

$$CO_2 + H_2O \rightleftharpoons H_2CO_3 \rightleftharpoons H^+ + HCO_3^-$$

There is a ready supply of carbon dioxide from cellular metabolism and a rapid means for its removal by the respiratory tract.

ACID-BASE BALANCE

The hydrogen ion concentration of the extracellular fluids is one of the most vigorously regulated variables of the body. The vital limits of pH variation for mammals are usually given as from pH 7.0 to 7.8. The normal pH range in arterial blood is 7.36–7.44, and the average pH is 7.4. In terms of $[H^+]$, pH 7.8 represents 40 percent and pH 7.0 represents 250 percent of the $[H^+]$ at pH 7.4. It appears from this that tissue cells are relatively tolerant to changes in $[H^+]$. However, the amounts of hydrogen ion involved are small, and the $[H^+]$ of the fluids is easily disturbed by addition of small amounts of strong acid or base.

The relatively constant $[H^+]$ of the extracellular fluids is the result of a balance between acids and bases. Acids are substances that tend to donate hydrogen ions (i.e. protons) to a solution; bases are substances that tend to accept and bind hydrogen ions from a solution. This balance is disturbed when acids or bases are added to or removed from the body fluids: a depression of blood pH to below the normal range is known as acidemia; a value above the normal pH range is called alkalemia. The process in which excess acid is being added or base removed from ECF is known as acidosis. If excess base is being added or acid lost, the condition is called alkalosis.

Under normal conditions acids or bases are added continuously to the body fluids either because of their ingestion or as the result of their production in cellular metabolism. In disease such conditions as insufficient respiratory ventilation, vomiting, diarrhea, or renal insufficiency may cause an unusual loss or gain of acid or base. To combat these disturbances, the body utilizes three basic mechanisms: chemical buffering, respiratory adjustment of blood carbonic acid concentration, and excretion of H^+ or HCO_3^- by the kidneys. The buffers and the respiratory mechanism act within minutes to prevent a large shift in hydrogen ion concentration. If a nonvolatile acid or base is involved, renal excretion of hydrogen ions or bicarbonate ions begins immediately, but complete restoration of acid-base balance may require from a few hours to several days.

Metabolic problems

Within the body the metabolism of most organic compounds containing carbon, hydrogen, oxygen, and nitrogen atoms results in the formation of water, carbon dioxide, and urea. The carbon dioxide reacts with water to form carbonic acid, which is quantitatively the most important acid formed within the body. In a large dog about 5000 mEq hydrogen ions from carbonic acid are formed daily as compared to about 100 mEq hydrogen ions from all other acids. However, due to its volatile nature, all of the carbon dioxide is expired through the respiratory system as it is formed from metabolism. The metabolic breakdown of the sulfur-containing amino acids yields the nonvolatile sulfuric acid, which cannot be excreted by the lungs. On the average, 60 mEq of sulfuric acid are formed for every 100 g protein metabolized. This strong acid does not exist as such to any appreciable extent in the body fluids, but rather it reacts immediately with buffer bases. In this buffer reaction the weak acids of the buffer systems are substituted for the strong acid. However, the buffer bases must be restored, and this ultimately requires the excretion of an equivalent amount of hydrogen ions by the kidneys. Much smaller amounts of hydrogen ions are also formed in the hydrolysis of the phosphodiesters of phosphoproteins.

Various other compounds not normally in the diet or formed in metabolism may tend to cause an acidemia when administered to an animal, e.g. ammonium chloride. Here the ammonium ion is acidic, yielding in solution a hydrogen ion and ammonia. After absorption into the body fluids, the ammonia is rapidly removed for the synthesis of urea in the liver. The hydrogen ions remaining, electrically balanced by chloride ions, tend to cause an acidemia. Reaction with buffer base occurs, and the overall effect is identical to the addition of a strong acid to the body fluids. Ultimately hydrogen ions must be excreted by the kidneys in order to restore the buffer base.

Certain basic compounds are formed as a result of the metabolism of many foods of plant origin. Herbivorous mammals that ingest large amounts of leafy plant material have to contend with the formation of much excess base. The maintenance of the buffer systems then requires the renal excretion of considerable base, and the urine is accordingly alkaline (Blatherwick 1920). An example of such a food compound is potassium citrate. The citrate is completely oxidized in the body to CO_2 and H_2O, but apparently the oxidative breakdown pathway requires hydrogen ions. The source of hydrogen ions is carbonic acid derived from hydration of carbon dioxide:

$$CO_2 + H_2O \rightleftharpoons H_2CO_3 \rightleftharpoons H^+ + HCO_3^-$$

Thus, as citrate ions are oxidized, HCO_3^- is produced which has an alkalotic action on body fluid pH. Citrates are only one component of the typical foodstuffs of a cow or horse. In addition, grasses and other leafy plant food contain other similar organic anions, electrically balanced by potassium and other cations (Mayland and Grunes 1974). The metabolism of these organic anions within the body also results in the production of bicarbonate ions. The urine is consequently alkaline and may also contain large amounts of potassium and other cations.

The opposing tendencies of the metabolic processes to produce both acids and bases cancel one another to a certain degree. However, the rations of some animals produce a predominance of acidic products, while the diet of other animals tends to produce a predominance of basic products. Dogs, cats, and other carnivores, omnivores eating a high-protein ration (most remarkably the human), and animals which are not eating (in which case body proteins are being metabolized for energy production) have to contend with an excess of acid and excrete an acidic urine. Ruminants, equids, and other herbivores have an excess of base and excrete an alkaline urine.

Some of the major ions of the body fluids are of no importance with respect to acid-base balance. The strong cations such as sodium and potassium cannot influence $[H^+]$ directly because they are neither acids nor bases. The strong cation, ammonium, is exceptional in that it can donate an hydrogen ion and therefore is a weak acid. The anions such as chloride and sulfate are likewise of little importance with respect to $[H^+]$. However, the strong cations like potassium and sodium are vital for body function in other respects, and their excessive loss from the body would be disastrous. For this reason, the urinary excretion of hydrogen ions by substitution for sodium and potassium ions in the urine is of extreme importance for the conservation of body stores of these cations as well as for the removal of excess hydrogen ion.

Chemical buffers

A buffer system consists of a mixture of a weak acid and its conjugate base. An example would be a solution of carbonic acid and bicarbonate ion. When a buffer system is present, the addition of an acid or base will result in a much smaller shift of pH than would occur if no buffers were present. If a strong acid is added to the solution, the added hydrogen ions are bound by the buffer base forming more of the weak acid. For example, if sulfuric acid were added to the bicarbonate buffer system, the reaction would be:

$$2\ H^+ + SO_4^= + 2\ HCO_3^- \rightarrow 2\ H_2CO_3 + SO_4^=$$

In effect, the added strong acid has been replaced by the weak acid of the buffer system.

The relationship between pH and the mixture of weak acid and its conjugate base is given by the Henderson-Hasselbalch equation:

$$pH = pK + \log \frac{[base]}{[acid]}$$

The dissociation constant of the weak acid is represented by K, and pK is the negative logarithm of K. In this context pK can be defined as the pH at which the acid and base of the buffer system are in equal concentrations, that is, the pH at which the ratio of base to acid is 1. Thus the Henderson-Hasselbalch equation shows that the pH of a solution containing such a buffer system is determined by the ratio of the base to the acid. The effectiveness of most buffer systems is greatest at a pH equal to the pK of its weak acid and over a range extending one pH unit above and one pH unit below the pK value. However, the bicarbonate buffer system normally operates at a pH far from its pK′ but is still very effective, because its weak acid concentration can be maintained by respiratory action.

When an acid is added to the buffer system, a shift of pH is resisted, but the ratio of base to acid decreases, and the pH is somewhat depressed. If more acid were added, a further decrease of the base-acid ratio would occur because the base would be used up in reaction with the added hydrogen ions. Thus the protective function of buffer systems is limited; and unless the favorable ratio of base to acid is restored, the buffers will become exhausted with repeated addition of acid, and acidemia will result. The restoration of buffer base ultimately requires the formation and secretion of hydrogen ions by the kidney tubules. If instead a strong base were added to the body fluids, it would react with the acid of the buffer and so form more buffer base. This ultimately must be corrected by renal excretion of base and retention of hydrogen ions.

The principal buffer systems of the blood are the bicarbonate, plasma protein, phosphate, and hemoglobin buffers. Of these the most important are bicarbonate and hemoglobin. If a strong acid is added to blood in vitro, 53 percent of the buffer action is due to bicarbonate, 35 percent to hemoglobin, 7 percent to plasma protein, and 5 percent to phosphates (Winters et al. 1969). The total buffering capacity of the blood is considerable and is adequate to prevent a pH shift beyond the vital limit even if the entire daily metabolic output of nonvolatile acid were suddenly added. However, in reality the blood alone is never required to buffer all acid products at one time. The buffers in the ECF outside of the vascular system and the tissue buffers rapidly assume part of the load. Finally, excretion of acid by the lungs and kidneys begins immediately to reduce the total load.

The bicarbonate buffer system is the principal buffer of the blood and of the ECF. Chemically the weak acid component of the bicarbonate buffer system is carbonic acid, H_2CO_3. However, only about 1 of every 800 CO_2 molecules dissolved in body fluids is hydrated to form one H_2CO_3 molecule. In fact, measurement of true carbonic acid concentration is difficult and usually impractical. Instead, in practice the total concentration of dissolved CO_2, which includes and is proportional to true H_2CO_3, is used as the concentration of the acid component in the Henderson-Hasselbalch equation. The concentration of dissolved CO_2 can easily be calculated as the product of CO_2 tension in the fluid and the solubility coefficient, s, for CO_2. Normal P_{CO_2} in arterial blood is 40 mm Hg; s is 0.03 mMol/mm Hg; and so $s \cdot P_{CO_2} = 1.2$ mMol CO_2 dissolved per liter blood. The dissociation constant K in the Henderson-Hasselbalch equation is for the dissociation of the weak acid component. When $s \cdot P_{CO_2}$ is substituted for the weak acid, the dissociation constant is an apparent dissociation constant, indicated by the use of a prime mark, K′. The useful form of the Henderson-Hasselbalch equation is then:

$$pH = pK' + \log \frac{[HCO_3^-]}{s \cdot P_{CO_2}}$$

If pH and P_{CO_2} are measured, $[HCO_3^-]$ can be calculated ($pK' = 6.1$). The ratio of bicarbonate to dissolved CO_2 is normally about 20, far from the ideal buffer ratio of 1. However, the bicarbonate system is very effective, partly because CO_2 is in plentiful supply in the body and so P_{CO_2} can be maintained or varied rapidly by changes in the rate at which CO_2 is removed by pulmonary ventilation.

Hemoglobin is the second most important blood buffer. At normal blood pH part of the hemoglobin molecules is in the form of proteinate ions, Hb^-. These basic ions with their weak acids, HHb, form a buffer pair. When acid is added to the blood the reaction:

$$H^+ + Hb^- \rightleftharpoons HHb$$

shifts to the right and the ratio of base to acid is decreased. The buffer reactions of reduced and oxygenated hemoglobin are similar, but the reduced hemoglobin ion is a stronger base. The plasma proteins also exist to a certain extent as proteinate ions at body pH and bind hydrogen ions in a manner similar to hemoglobin. The components of the phosphate buffers at blood pH are $HPO_4^=$, the base, and $H_2PO_4^-$, the weak acid. This buffer system plays a minor role in the blood.

The cells of the body contain large amounts of buffering compounds which are in the aggregate more important than the blood buffers. These are assumed to be mainly proteinate ions and their weak acidic forms. In addition, a type of buffering is effected by exchange of hydrogen ions for cations loosely bound to the vast surface of crystallites in the skeleton. It is believed to operate primarily in chronic acidotic states.

The relative importance of the various buffers is well illustrated by experiments performed by Swan et al. (1955) on nephrectomized dogs in which renal mechanisms could not operate. When acid was infused, it was found that about one half of the hydrogen-ion binding occurred in the cells, while less than one fifth was effected in the blood, and the remainder in the extracellular fluids outside the vascular bed.

Although the reactions of the various buffer systems have been considered as though each were the only buffer present, all of the buffer systems in the ECF react in unison. When hydrogen ions are added to the ECF, each base of each buffer pair will tend to bind hydrogen ions, and hence all buffers share the imposed acid load. Since the pH involved is the same for all buffers in a solution, the buffers are related:

$$pH = pK_a' + \log \frac{[HCO_3^-]}{[H_2CO_3]} = pK_b + \log \frac{[Hb^-]}{[HHb]}$$

$$= pK_c + \log \frac{[HPO_4^=]}{[H_2PO_4^-]}, \text{ etc.}$$

Each pK is that characteristic for the weak acid of each buffer pair. This interrelation is often referred to as the isohydric principle. As a result of this principle, addition of an acid or base to a solution containing several buffers will result in a change in the ratios of all the buffer pairs.

Respiratory adjustment of P_{CO_2}

Blood P_{CO_2} can be varied extensively because the partial pressure of CO_2 in the lung alveoli generally determines the amount of CO_2 dissolved in the blood. This respiratory mechanism depends upon the exquisite sensitivity of the respiratory control systems to changes in blood P_{CO_2} and pH. A small increase in P_{CO_2} or decrease in pH stimulates pulmonary ventilation so that the rate of CO_2 expiration increases. If acid has been added to the body fluids, the first reaction is a purely chemical buffering which results in the formation of additional carbonic acid and a depletion of bicarbonate:

$$H^+ + HCO_3^- \rightarrow H_2CO_3 \rightarrow CO_2 + H_2O$$

As a result the $[HCO_3^-]/(s \cdot P_{CO_2})$ ratio falls, and pH falls slightly. However, the increase in CO_2 and decrease in pH stimulate respiration, causing a rapid expiration of the extra CO_2. Then over a period of hours P_{CO_2} in blood decreases to below the normal level; the $[HCO_3^-]/(s \cdot P_{CO_2})$ ratio is returned toward its normal value, and pH is also nearly back to 7.4. However, although the ratio of base to acid is nearly normal, the amounts of each are subnormal. This adjustment of P_{CO_2} by the respiratory system is compensatory; full correction of the acid-base abnormality can be effected only by renal excretion of hydrogen ions and production of bicarbonate. When an alkali is added to the blood, a similar but opposite respiratory response occurs and additional CO_2 is retained in ECF. This increases P_{CO_2} to balance the increase in $[HCO_3^-]$ which results from the added alkali. These respiratory adjustments of P_{CO_2} during an acid or base disturbance begin to be effective within minutes, but several hours may be required before the adjustments are maximal.

Excretion of hydrogen and bicarbonate ions by the kidney

When acids or bases are added to the body fluids, chemical buffers remove the immediate threat to the body from altered $[H^+]$, but a depletion of buffer bases or acids occurs. For example, if sulfuric acid is added, a reaction with bicarbonate ions results in the formation of carbonic acid, which can be removed largely by expiration of carbon dioxide. To excrete the sulfate ion in the urine would not correct the deficit of bicarbonate ions, and would in addition cause the loss in the urine of some strong cations such as sodium, which is necessary for electrical balance. In effect, the problem is solved within the kidney by formation of hydrogen ions through a mechanism which forms one bicarbonate ion for every hydrogen ion formed. The hydrogen ions are actively secreted into the tubular fluid in exchange for cation, while the bicarbonate ions move into the plasma. Thus hydrogen ions, equivalent in amount to those added as sulfuric acid, are excreted; and the amount of bicarbonate ions is restored to its normal level.

The basic mechanism of hydrogen ion secretion is outlined in Figure 36.5. In this scheme a hydrogen ion is derived from carbonic acid formed from carbon dioxide. The presence of carbonic anhydrase insures a sufficiently rapid formation of carbonic acid. When this enzyme is inhibited by pharmacological agents, acidification of the urine is depressed. Although some acidification may occur in the proximal tubules, the hydrogen ion concentration gradient which can be developed there is small. Most of the acidification is effected in the distal tubules and collecting ducts, where the movement of hydrogen ions is by an active transport mechanism which can operate against a high concentration gradient. This transport of hydrogen ions involves an ion-for-ion exchange with tubular sodium ions. Thus not only is the urine acidified, but sodium ions are restored to the body fluids. The bicarbonate ions formed in the tubular cell move passively into the blood and are electrically paired with the reabsorbed sodium ions. This simple hypothetical scheme may have to be modified, for recent evidence indicates that the actual source of hydrogen ions is not carbonic acid but rather a metabolic process which yields a hydroxyl ion for each hydrogen ion secreted. The strongly basic hydroxyl ion would then be neutralized by a hydrogen ion from carbonic acid. The overall result, however, is identical: hydrogen ions are secreted into the urine and bicarbonate ions in equivalent amounts are added to the blood.

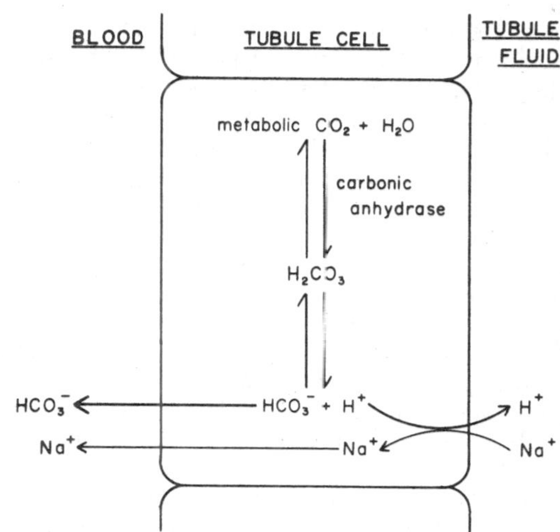

Figure 36.5. Secretion of H^+ by the renal tubule cell

The rate of hydrogen ion secretion by renal tubule cells is largely determined by intracellular pH. A high pH depresses H^+ secretion into the tubule lumen while a low intracellular pH increases the rate. Generally, intracellular pH changes as blood pH or P_{CO_2} changes, and so acidemia and hypercapnia result in increased H^+ secretion, and alkalemia and hypocapnia in decreased H^+ secretion. Intracellular $[K^+]$ also has an important effect upon acid secretion. A high $[K^+]$ results in an increase in intracellular pH and hence a decrease in H^+ secretion into the urine. A low intracellular $[K^+]$ conversely results in increased acid secretion into the urine. The cause of this effect of potassium on intracellular pH is not well understood, but one explanation is that as potassium ions enter the cells, they displace hydrogen ions as the balancing cations for anionic sites on protein and other organic molecules. The hydrogen ions leave the cells and intracellular pH rises. Since most of the cells of the body would be involved in this process, the release of hydrogen ions by cells may be sufficient to cause a fall in

ECF pH. The paradoxical situation may then exist where H^+ secretion into the urine is depressed by the high intracellular pH, yet an extracellular acidemia exists. Potassium deficient states result in low intracellular [K^+], high [H^+], and enhanced H^+ secretion into the urine. The secretion of hydrogen ions involves addition of HCO_3^- to ECF, and this may occur despite an existing alkalemia.

The secretion of hydrogen ions into the urine results in an acid urine, but the quantity of acid which can be excreted as free hydrogen ions is limited. Urine can be acidified only to a pH of about 4.5. This means that most of the hydrogen ions excreted must be bound by bases. The most important of these are $HPO_4^=$ and ammonia. Phosphate is present at pH 7.4 in the glomerular filtrate mostly in the form of $HPO_4^=$. As the tubular fluid is acidified by hydrogen ion secretion, the basic $HPO_4^=$ takes up and binds hydrogen ions to form predominantly $H_2PO_4^-$. Part of the cation which electrically balances $HPO_4^=$ in the glomerular filtrate (mostly sodium ions) is exchanged with the secreted hydrogen ion and thus is returned to the blood.

The base ammonia is formed by the renal tubular cells *de novo* from glutamine and other amino acids of the blood. The movement of ammonia from the site of synthesis in the tubular cells into the tubular lumen is by passive diffusion and occurs rapidly when a concentration gradient exists in this direction. However, if the tubular fluids are alkaline, the ammonia molecule will not bind hydrogen ions and will remain mostly as ammonia. The concentration of ammonia will then rise in the slow-flowing tubular fluid, and diffusion of ammonia in that direction will be limited. On the other hand, if the urine is acidic, ammonia will bind hydrogen ions, forming ammonium, a strong cation which penetrates membranes slowly and thus is trapped in the tubular fluid. Under these circumstances ammonia as such is disappearing from the tubular fluid and rapid diffusion from the tubular cells continues into the tubular lumen. Diffusion into the blood also occurs because the blood concentration of ammonia is kept low by the rapid flow of blood. Although ammonia is formed to a certain extent even when an alkaline urine is being formed, its rate of synthesis increases greatly when an acidemia develops, and large amounts of hydrogen ion are then excreted as ammonium.

The principal base of the plasma, bicarbonate ion, is present in the glomerular filtrate, and the amount filtered each day into the renal tubule is many times the total amount present in the body. Obviously most of this bicarbonate must be reabsorbed from the tubular fluid. The mechanism of bicarbonate reabsorption is linked to the mechanism of hydrogen ion secretion into the tubular fluid. When bicarbonate ions are present in the tubular fluid, secreted H^+ react with them:

$$H^+ + HCO_3^- \rightarrow H_2CO_3 \rightarrow CO_2 + H_2O$$

The CO_2 so formed in the tubule is readily absorbed and joins the general body pool of CO_2. However, when the hydrogen ions are formed and secreted, bicarbonate ions are also formed, and for each hydrogen ion secreted one bicarbonate ion is added to the plasma (see Fig. 36.5). Thus for every HCO_3^- removed from the tubular fluid by reaction with a H^+, a HCO_3^- is added to the blood. In effect, bicarbonate is reabsorbed from the tubular fluid and restored to the blood.

Whether or not all of the filtered bicarbonate ions will be reabsorbed depends upon the rate of hydrogen ion secretion into the tubular fluid and the amount of HCO_3^- filtered. If hydrogen ion secretion rate exceeds bicarbonate ion filtration rate, all bicarbonate ions will be reabsorbed. If hydrogen ion secretion rate is less than bicarbonate ion filtration rate, some bicarbonate ions will escape reabsorption and will appear in the urine. Generally, under an acid stress, the hydrogen ion secretion rate rises, causing reabsorption of all bicarbonate and acidification of the urine. Under a base stress, less hydrogen ion is secreted, more bicarbonate ion appears in the urine, and the urine will be alkaline. In the majority of acid-base disturbances, changes in hydrogen ion secretion rate appear to determine how much bicarbonate will be excreted in the urine, and changes in rate of glomerular filtration of bicarbonate play a minor role. However, when a large amount of base is added to the body fluids, as when sodium bicarbonate is ingested or injected, the great increase in filtration of bicarbonate ions will often exceed tubular hydrogen ion secretion rate; and much bicarbonate will be excreted rapidly in the urine.

ACID-BASE BALANCE DISTURBANCES

The pH of the ECF is determined by the ratio of conjugate bases to their weak acids as expressed for each buffer pair in the Henderson-Hasselbalch equation. The total amount of base in whole blood—including bicarbonate, hemoglobin, and the other bases of lesser importance—is called buffer base. Buffer base (BB) characteristically has a normal value of about 48 mEq/L of blood, but this varies somewhat with hemoglobin concentration. These bases constitute the metabolic component determining blood pH. The other component, the weak acids of the ECF, includes carbonic acid (represented as dissolved CO_2) and the acid form of hemoglobin (both reduced and oxygenated forms). The other acids in blood are of little quantitative importance. The changes in the amounts of these weak acids can be monitored by measuring the concentration of any one, usually carbonic acid expressed as dissolved CO_2, i.e. $s \cdot P_{CO_2}$ or simply P_{CO_2}. This is the respiratory component. The relationship between blood pH, total aggregated base, and weak acids can be represented as a proportionality:

$$\text{pH} \propto \frac{\text{metabolic component}}{\text{respiratory component}}$$

Acid-base disturbances involve either the gain or loss of strong acid or the gain or loss of base (OH^- or HCO_3^-) by the ECF. If the primary disturbance is to the metabolic component, the process is known as a metabolic disturbance—metabolic acidosis or metabolic alkalosis. If the primary defect is in ventilation of the lung alveoli with consequent changes in blood P_{CO_2}, the process is known as a respiratory disturbance—respiratory acidosis or respiratory alkalosis.

When an acid-base disturbance occurs with the development of one of these four processes, the first and immediate response is the amelioration of the effect on pH by reaction with blood buffers. A second response is compensation in which the component not primarily affected by the initial disturbance is adjusted so as to bring blood pH back toward normal. Thus, if abnormal pulmonary ventilation is the primary defect, compensation by renal action on excretion of H^+ and HCO_3^- will develop. Such compensation is called incomplete if pH is not returned to the normal range or complete if pH is returned to the normal range. Even if compensation is complete, the quantities of the metabolic or respiratory component primarily affected will not have been restored to normal. Another secondary response to the primary disturbance is one which acts to restore the acid-base component primarily affected; this is called correction. Complete correction of the disturbance has been effected when blood pH and concentration of all acid-base components have been restored to normal.

Metabolic acidosis

The gain of strong acid to or loss of base (bicarbonate) from the ECF is known as metabolic acidosis. Characteristically, an acidemia is present which if severe threatens life. Typical disease conditions causing metabolic acidosis include ketosis and diabetes mellitus in which β-hydroxybutyric acid and acetoacetic acid are produced, renal acidosis in which there is a failure of bicarbonate reabsorption and it is lost in the urine, capture myopathy following intense exercise in which metabolic acids of uncertain origin are produced, and diarrhea where pancreatic juice containing bicarbonate is not reabsorbed and is lost. In all these cases, $[HCO_3^-]$ falls either as a result of reaction with the added acid or due to direct loss from ECF—and pH falls. By the isohydric principle a fall of $[HCO_3^-]$ will result in a fall of all blood buffer base. This condition of low blood concentration of buffer base is called hypobasemia. It might be expected that plasma P_{CO_2} would rise as a result of the production of CO_2, as acid reacts with bicarbonate. However, the respiratory control systems are very sensitive to changes in P_{CO_2} and will rapidly correct any deviation from the normal of 40 mm Hg. Usually no change in plasma P_{CO_2} as a result of buffer action will be detected. However, the fall in pH persists and will act as a drive to the respiratory control systems resulting in an increase in alveolar ventilation and a fall in P_{CO_2}. This respiratory adjustment of plasma P_{CO_2} will begin within a few minutes but will not be maximally developed for up to 24 hours. Conversely, if the deficit of bicarbonate is suddenly corrected by therapeutic injection of bicarbonate, the respiratory compensation, i.e. low P_{CO_2}, will persist for some hours (overcompensation). Compensation by decreasing P_{CO_2} will bring the ratio of conjugate base to weak acid back toward the normal value, but the hypobasemia will persist until the lost bicarbonate is replaced. This requires renal corrective action: the excretion of H^+ and restoration of plasma $[HCO_3^-]$. The acidemia acts as a stimulus to the secretion of hydrogen ions by the renal tubule cells into the tubular fluid. This first ensures that all bicarbonate in the glomerular filtrate will be reabsorbed. Then excess hydrogen ions beyond those required to effect reabsorption of all bicarbonate ions will begin to acidify the urine and will largely be excreted from the body combined with urinary buffer bases. For each hydrogen ion excreted, one bicarbonate ion will be restored to the plasma. This will continue as long as the acidemia persists. In some cases renal action may be adequate to correct the hypobasemia completely. This would be the outcome of a short-term stress, e.g. following the injection of a small quantity of strong acid, the acid would be excreted by the kidney and bicarbonate would be restored. In mild continuing acid-base disturbance, e.g. preclinical ketosis, renal action may also be sufficient to restore plasma bicarbonate as rapidly as it is destroyed by the continuous release of organic acids within the body. However, in many severe diseases renal action will not be sufficient to keep up with the release of acidic products within the body, and a serious acidemia develops. Here complete correction will be attained only when the disease has been terminated or as the result of vigorous therapeutic action.

Metabolic alkalosis

This process involves the gain of base (OH^- or HCO_3^-) or loss of strong acid by the ECF. Typically an alkalemia is present. Some common conditions which usually result in metabolic alkalosis are: persistent vomiting in which gastic acid is lost from the body, potassium deficiency in which renal tubule cells secrete inappropriate amounts of hydrogen ion into the urine, oxidation of ingested or injected salts of organic acids such as lactate or citrate, and injection of bicarbonate solutions. In all these conditions there is an increase in $[HCO_3^-]$ in ECF, which then secondarily results in an adjustment of all buffer bases upward—hyperbasemia. Most of the responses of the body are the corresponding but opposite ones to those found in metabolic acidosis. The hyperbasemia is accompanied by alkalemia. The rise in pH will depress pulmonary ventilation and P_{CO_2} will rise. This respiratory compensation will bring pH back down toward the normal level, but the hyperbasemia persists. Renal correction consists of decreased secretion of hydrogen ions and hence increased excretion of bicarbonate which will continue until the alkalemia is abolished.

Respiratory acidosis

If excretion of CO_2 by the lungs falls below the rate of CO_2 production in the body, respiratory acidosis develops. Here the primary change will be an increase in blood P_{CO_2} (hypercapnia), and the primary defect will be in the ability of the lungs to expire CO_2 at a normal rate. This may be because of depression of the respiratory centers in the CNS, some abnormality of the chest wall or respiratory muscles which impedes the bellows action of the thorax, or obstructions to gas movement or diffusion within the lung. Either ventilation of the lung alveoli is diminished or diffusion between alveoli and capillary blood is impeded. The rise in P_{CO_2} represents a rise in carbonic acid, and buffer reactions occur with the nonbicarbonate bases. Hemoglobin is the most important of these bases, and the reaction with it will be:

$$H_2CO_3 + Hb^- \rightleftharpoons HCO_3^- + HHb$$

This interaction between blood buffers results in an appreciable rise of plasma $[HCO_3^-]$. The buffer action ameliorates the fall in pH caused by the rise in H_2CO_3. Within a few hours renal compensation becomes evident: the low pH stimulates increased secretion of H^+ into urine with concomitant increase in plasma $[HCO_3^-]$. This renal compensation may require several days for maximal effect and may be complete if pH is moved back into the normal range, or partial if significant acidemia persists. Complete correction of respiratory acidosis will not be possible until recovery from the pulmonary disease occurs.

Respiratory alkalosis

When alveolar hyperventilation occurs, the expiration of CO_2 may exceed the rate of its production within the body, and respiratory alkalosis may develop. This is characterized by low plasma P_{CO_2} (hypocapnia) and alkalemia. Usually the hyperventilation is caused by some abnormal stimulus to the respiratory centers, either directly as in ammonia toxicity or indirectly as when hypoxemia acts reflexly via the peripheral chemoreceptors. Initially, plasma $[HCO_3^-]$ is unchanged by the fall of P_{CO_2}, but buffer reactions with the nonbicarbonate buffers occur immediately. Using the reaction with hemoglobin as the example:

$$HHb + HCO_3^- \rightarrow Hb^- + \underset{\substack{\downarrow \\ CO_2 \text{ (removed)}}}{H_2CO_3}$$

Thus $[HCO_3^-]$ falls somewhat and Hb^- rises by an equivalent amount. Renal compensation begins in a few hours and reaches its maximal capacity after several days; alkalemia depresses the rate of hydrogen ion secretion by renal tubules and excretion of filtered bicarbonate rises. This results in a further fall of plasma $[HCO_3^-]$, and the $[HCO_3^-]/(s \cdot P_{CO_2})$ ratio moves back toward its normal value, as does blood pH. Correction of the primary change in P_{CO_2} can only be brought about by correction of the cause of the hyperventilation.

EVALUATION OF ACID-BASE STATUS

The blood or plasma variables involved in assessment of acid-base disturbances are pH, plasma $[HCO_3^-]$ or whole blood buffer base, and hemoglobin concentration. Two systems of clinical evaluation that differ in the value used as the metabolic component are common: one is based on plasma $[HCO_3^-]$ and the other on whole blood buffer base. Both systems use P_{CO_2} as the respiratory component. The first system uses the pH-bicarbonate diagram (see Fig. 36.6) on which are plotted values taken from plasma separated from oxygenated whole blood. The diagram then includes the influence of hemoglobin as a blood buffer. The other system uses whole blood values plotted either on the Siggaard-Andersen alignment nomogram (see Fig. 36.7) or the curved nomogram (see Fig. 36.8).

The pH-bicarbonate diagram

The assessment of an acid-base disturbance is aided by a diagram that expresses the relationship between P_{CO_2}, $[HCO_3^-]$, and pH of the plasma (Fig. 36.6). This diagram, based on the Henderson-Hasselbalch equation, is for plasma that was exposed to the particular P_{CO_2} before being separated from the erythrocytes of fully oxygenated blood. Therefore, any buffering effect includes that of the erythrocytes. The diagram is constructed by substituting values for pH into the equation while holding P_{CO_2} constant and then solving for $[HCO_3^-]$. The plot of pH values against $[HCO_3^-]$ for a given P_{CO_2} will form a line called a carbon dioxide isobar (Davenport 1974).

If normal whole blood is exposed to various pressures of carbon dioxide and then the pH and $[HCO_3^-]$ of separated plasma are measured, a normal buffer line results. This is in effect a titration of the blood with carbon dioxide, and represents the changes which occur in uncompensated respiratory acidosis and alkalosis (points A and B respectively). If metabolic base is added to the blood, the carbon dioxide titration curve will parallel the normal buffer line but will lie above it. The upward shift is due to the formation of additional bicarbonate ions as the

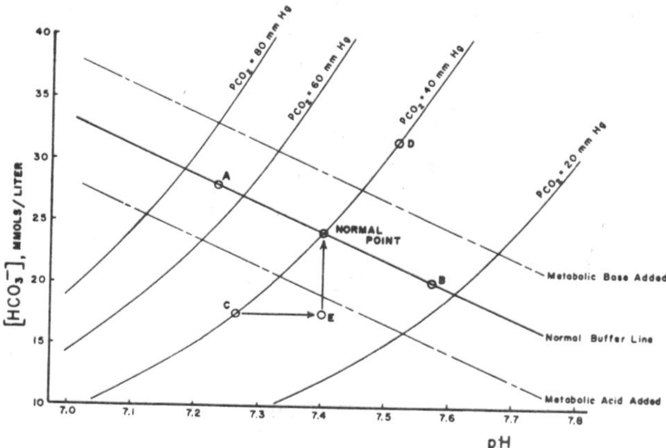

Figure 36.6. The pH-bicarbonate diagram for oxygenated human blood equilibrated with CO_2 before separation of plasma from erythrocytes

base reacts with carbonic acid. After addition of metabolic acid, a similar shift occurs but it will be downward because bicarbonate ions are used up in reaction with the added acid. A shift along the 40 mm Hg CO_2 isobar from the normal point upward as excess base is added represents uncompensated metabolic alkalosis (D). A shift along this isobar downward as excess acid is added represents uncompensated metabolic acidosis (C). The shifts of pH and $[HCO_3^-]$ in these uncompensated acid-base disturbances are the result of reaction of the added acid or base with the chemical buffers. By the isohydric principle the changes in all the buffers are reflected by changes in $[HCO_3^-]$ and pH. In the animal, however, respiratory and renal compensation would soon become effective. For example, point C represents uncompensated metabolic acidosis in which $[HCO_3^-]$ has decreased while P_{CO_2} is little changed. The decreased pH would cause an increase in respiratory ventilation and a lower P_{CO_2}. On the diagram this results in a movement to the lower carbon dioxide isobar, and pH would be restored to nearly normal (E). It has been assumed here that renal restoration of bicarbonate has already begun, otherwise the line from C to E would also show a small decrease in $[HCO_3^-]$. Over a longer time period, renal retention of bicarbonate ions and excretion of hydrogen ions would restore $[HCO_3^-]$, and there would be a shift from point E toward the normal point.

In many severe or prolonged diseases the acid-base balance disturbance would likely be only partially compensated. Furthermore, complex combinations of the forms of acidosis and alkalosis may result from separate disease processes.

Whole blood base excess and the Siggaard-Andersen nomograms

The development of electrometric methods of direct measurement of pH and P_{CO_2} have made this method the most widely used. The objective of the procedure is to determine the deviation of buffer base (BB) of a particular blood sample from the normal value. This deviation, called base excess (BE), can most specifically be defined as the amount of strong acid or base which must be added to a liter of oxygenated whole blood in order to bring its pH to 7.40. It follows that: normal [BB] = actual [BB] − [BE]. If [BB] is abnormally high, [BE] will be positive; if [BB] is abnormally low, [BE] will be negative. Sometimes the term base deficit is used to indicate the negative condition. In an animal without acid-base disturbance, normal [BB] is approximately 48 mEq/L whole blood, but this value will vary with the amount of hemoglobin present. Nomograms include a correction for variations in hemoglobin concentration. Accurate calculation of whole blood acid-base values is not possible, and instead nomograms must be used which have been developed from data derived from direct determination of such blood values in vitro when titrated with strong acid or base.

There are two procedures commonly used for the determination of BE.

1. Direct measurement of pH and P_{CO_2} of oxygenated whole blood. Arterial or free-flowing (arterialized) capillary blood samples are obtained using special precautions to prevent loss of blood gases, and pH and P_{CO_2} are measured under carefully controlled conditions at 37°C. Hemoglobin concentration is also determined. The Siggaard-Andersen alignment nomogram (Fig. 36.7) is the simplest method of applying these data. A line is drawn from the point on the P_{CO_2} scale determined by the measured value through the corresponding point on the pH scale and then extended to the bicarbonate and base excess scales. Plasma $[HCO_3^-]$ can be read directly. Base excess will vary with hemoglobin concentration: the intersection of the line drawn with the appropriate hemoglobin concentration line is also an intersection with a BE line which indicates the deviation of BB from normal. Points A and B are the measured values for P_{CO_2} (65 mm Hg) and pH (7.13). Point C gives a plasma $[HCO_3^-]$ of 21.2 mEq/L and, since in this case [Hb] was found to be 15 g/100 ml, point D leads to the value for BE of −10 mEq/L. Total CO_2 content of the plasma could be read if desired.

The Siggaard-Andersen alignment nomogram can also be used for the determination of plasma values using the scales for pH, P_{CO_2}, plasma HCO_3^-, and total plasma CO_2 content.

The Siggaard-Andersen curved nomogram (Fig. 36.8) can also be used to determine whole blood acid-base values from pH and P_{CO_2} data. For an example one can use the same blood data as above. First, point A representing the blood sample can be plotted on the graph. Next, total whole blood buffer base for normal blood with the hemoglobin concentration found can be estimated from the

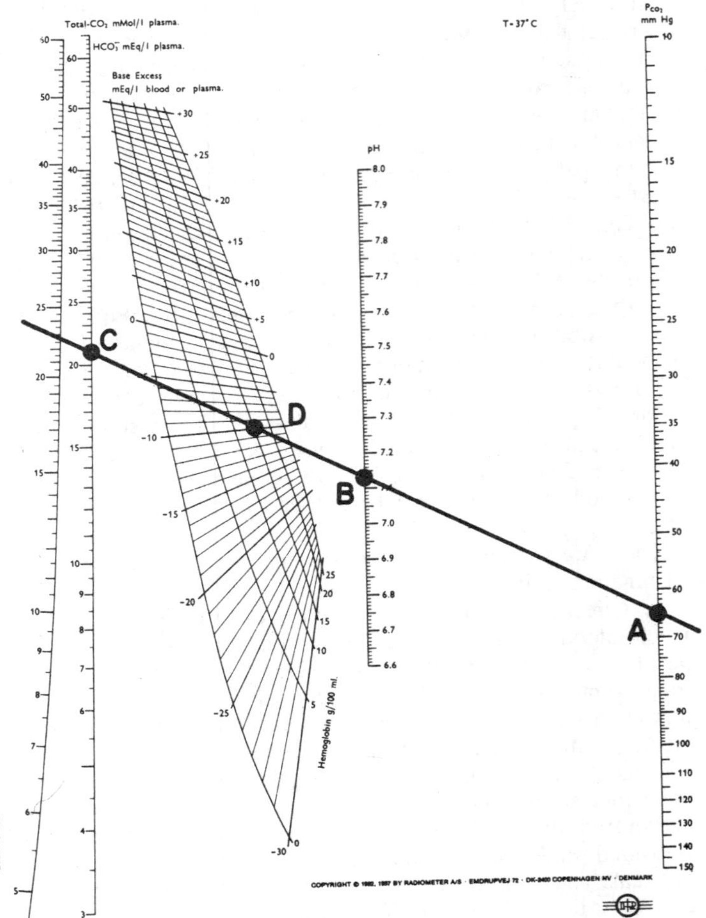

Figure 36.7. Siggaard-Andersen alignment nomogram with values plotted for whole blood sample

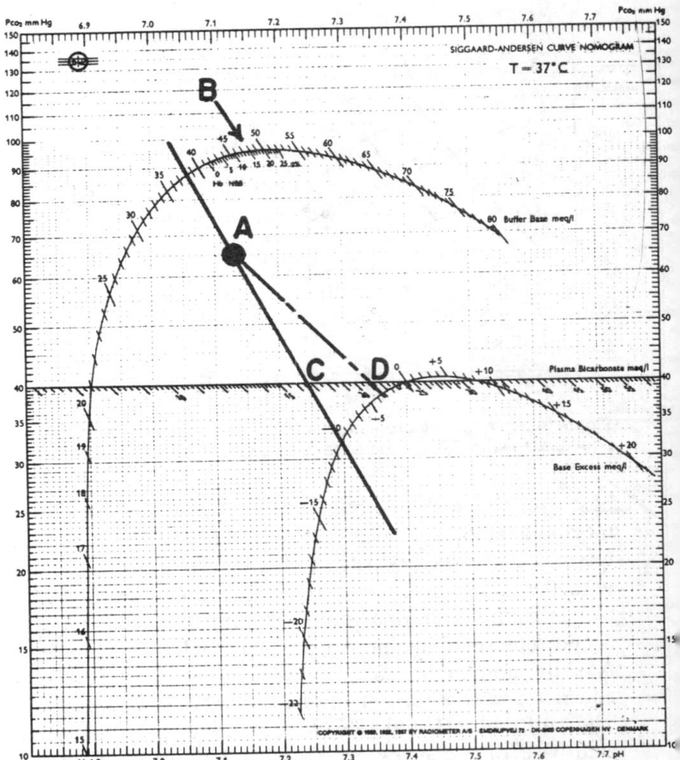

Figure 36.8. Siggaard-Andersen curved nomogram with example showing determination of [BE] of whole blood sample

upper curve by matching the hemoglobin concentration of the blood sample with the buffer base scale (indicated by arrow B). For Hb = 15 g/100 ml, normal [BB] = 48 mEq/L.

Any line drawn on this graph through point A would represent the changes of pH as Pco_2 is changed, that is, it would be a CO_2 titration curve for whole blood. The problem is to find the slope of the particular line for the blood sample under study. To find that line the [BB] and [BE] curves on the graph can be used as follows. First, under these in vitro conditions, as Pco_2 changes, the resultant H_2CO_3 will react with nonbicarbonate buffers (mostly hemoglobin) with the production of some bicarbonate:

$$H_2CO_3 + HbO_2 \rightarrow HHbO_2 + HCO_3^-$$

However, the amount of HCO_3^- produced will be matched ion for ion by the disappearance of nonbicarbonate base, and so total [BB] does not change. This total [BB], however, may not be normal for this blood sample, and, if not, will deviate from normal [BB] by the amount of base excess. It is known, however, that for this blood sample normal [BB] would be 48 mEq/L, and further that normal [BB] = actual [BB] − [BE]. Finally, the appropriate line passing through point A will intersect the BB curve and the BE curve so that actual [BB] − [BE] = 48 mEq/L. This is determined by trial and error; the edge of a ruler can be rotated about point A until the desired combination of [BB] and [BE] is found. In our example, the combination of [BB] = 38 mEq/L and [BE] = −10 mEq/L gives the desired sum of 48 mEq/L.

Standard bicarbonate is the plasma $[HCO_3^-]$ of blood at $Pco_2 = 40$ mm Hg, and it is another measure of the disturbance of the metabolic component but in the absence of respiratory compensation. The intersection of the line drawn in Figure 36.8 with the plasma $[HCO_3^-]$ line (C) gives directly the standard bicarbonate. Actual plasma $[HCO_3^-]$ can be found as the intersection of a line drawn from point A at 45° to the perpendicular with the plasma bicarbonate scale (D, 21.2 mEq/L in the example).

2. The CO_2 equilibration method. The procedure of blood sampling is similar to that described in the preceding section. The method differs in that only pH measure-

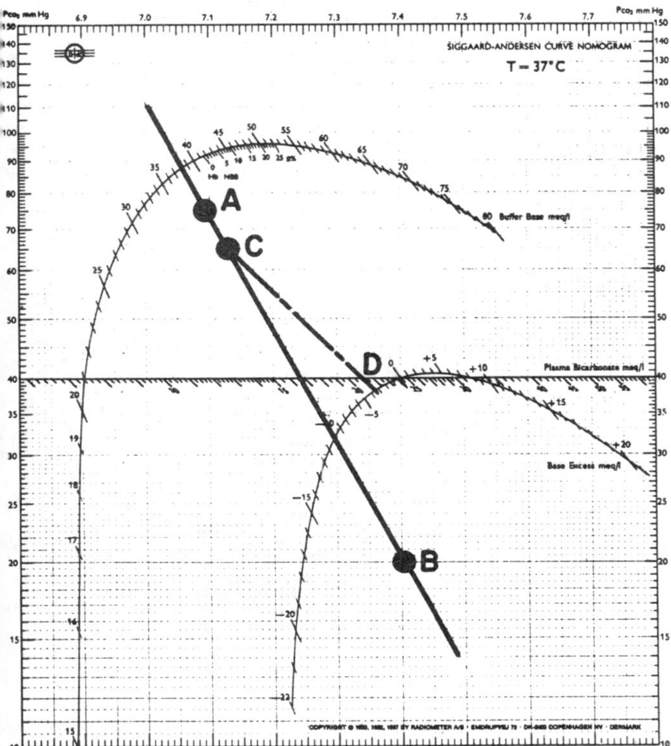

Figure 36.9. Use of the Siggaard-Andersen curved nomogram to determine [BE] by the equilibration method. Sample portions A and B were equilibrated at a Pco_2 of 75 and 20 mm Hg respectively. C is the untreated portion of the whole blood sample (pH = 7.13).

ments are made. Three portions of a blood sample are used: one is first equilibrated with CO_2 at a known high partial pressure, a second portion is equilibrated with CO_2 at a lower partial pressure, and a third is used as it comes from the patient. The pH of all three portions is carefully measured. Since Pco_2 for the two equilibrated portions of blood is known, the values for these can be plotted on the nomogram (Fig. 36.9). These two points establish the CO_2 titration curve for the blood under study. Buffering by bicarbonate and nonbicarbonate buffers is accounted for automatically in this procedure. The intersection of the CO_2 titration curve with [BB] and [BE] curves gives those values directly. A 45° line from the untreated sample point will give the plasma [HCO_3^-]. The final step is to find the pH point for the untreated portion of the blood on the line and read the Pco_2. If hemoglobin concentration is also known, the results can be checked by using the method described in the preceding section.

Note that full oxygenation of the blood used in the evaluation of acid-base status described in procedures 1 and 2 above is assumed. If the condition of the patient suggests that even arterial blood may not be fully oxygenated or if venous blood must be used, the results must be corrected for the difference in buffering capacity between oxygenated and reduced hemoglobin (Winters et al. 1969).

The Siggaard-Andersen nomograms were developed for use with human blood, and hence normal [BB] and [BE] (48 and 0 mEq/L respectively) are specifically for average oxygenated human blood at pH = 7.40, Pco_2 = 40 mm Hg, and 37°C. There are slight variations from these human values among domestic mammals due to differences in hemoglobin buffering capacity, plasma [HCO_3], and plasma protein concentration. These variations from the human are relatively small, and approximate BE can be determined for most domestic mammals using the nomograms (Siggaard-Andersen 1963). For example, the blood of normal dogs (Siggaard-Andersen 1962) and ruminants (Phillips 1970) have acid-base characteristics very similar to those of human blood. However, normal young pigs may show a consistent positive deviation of BE of about 6–8 mEq/L (Scott and McIntosh 1975). The nomograms are still suitable for use with pigs, but any deviate value for normal [BE] would have to be considered. The application of the Siggaard-Andersen nomograms to other species should be done judiciously.

REFERENCES

Adolph, E.F., Barker, J.P., and Hoy, P.A. 1954. Multiple factors in thirst. *Am. J. Physiol.* 178:538–62.

Andersson, B. 1971. Thirst—and brain control of water balance. *Am. Scientist* 59:408–15.

Andersson, B., and McCann, S.M. 1955a. A further study of polydipsia evoked by hypothalamic stimulation in the goat. *Acta Physiol. Scand.* 33:333–46.

——. 1955b. Drinking, antidiuresis, and milk ejection from electrical stimulation within the hypothalamus of the goat. *Acta Physiol. Scand.* 35:191–201.

——. 1955c. The effect of hypothalamic lesions on the water intake of the dog. *Acta Physiol. Scand.* 35:312–20.

Armsby, H.P., and Moulton, C.R. 1925. *The Animal as a Converter of Matter and Energy*. Chemical Catalog Co., New York.

Bellows, R.T. 1939. Time factors in water drinking in dogs. *Am. J. Physiol.* 125:87–97.

Bianca, W. 1955. The effect of thermal stress on the acid-base balance of the Ayrshire calf. *J. Ag. Sci.* 45:428–30.

Blair-West, J.R., Coghlan, J.P., Denton, D.A., Goding, J.R., Wintour, M., and Wright, R.D. 1963. The control of aldosterone secretion. *Recent Prog. Horm. Res.* 19:311–83.

Blatherwick, N.R. 1920. Neutrality regulation in cattle. *J. Biol. Chem.* 42:517–39.

Buggy, J., and Fisher, A.E. 1974. Evidence for a dual central role for angiotensin in water and sodium intake. *Nature* 250:733–34.

Cizek, L.J. 1959. Long-term observations on relationship between food and water ingestion in the dog. *Am. J. Physiol.* 197:342–46.

Dale, H.E., Goberdhan, C.K., and Brody, S. 1954. A comparison of the effects of starvation and thermal stress on the acid-base balance of dairy cattle. *Am. J. Vet. Res.* 15:197–201.

Davenport, H.W. 1974. *The ABC of Acid-Base Chemistry*. 6th ed. U. of Chicago Press, Chicago.

Denton, D.A. 1967. Salt appetite. In *Handbook of Physiology*. Sec. 6,

C.F. Code and W. Heidel, eds., *The Alimentary Canal.* Am. Physiol. Soc., Washington. Vol. 1, 433–59.

Denton, D.A., and Sabine, J.R. 1963. The behavior of Na deficient sheep. *Behavior* 20:364–76.

Dill, D.B. 1938. *Life, Heat, and Altitude*. Harvard U. Press, Cambridge.

Edelman, I.S., and Leibman, J. 1959. Anatomy of body water and electrolytes. *Am. J. Med.* 27:256–77.

Elkinton, J.R., and Taffel, M. 1942. Prolonged water deprivation in the dog. *J. Clin. Invest.* 21:787–94.

Epstein, A.N., Fitzsimons, J.T., and Rolls, B.J. 1970. Drinking induced by injection of angiotensin into the brain of the rat. *J. Physiol.* 210:457–74.

Epstein, A.N., Kissileff, H.R., and Stellar, E., eds. 1973. *The Neuropsychology of Thirst: New Findings and Advances in Concepts*. Winston, Washington.

Fitzsimons, J.T. 1972. Thirst. *Physiol. Rev.* 52:468–561.

Hansard, S.L. 1964. Total body water in farm animals. *Am. J. Physiol.* 206:1369–72.

Harthoorn, A.M. 1975. A relationship between acid-base balance and capture myopathy in zebra (*Equus burchelli*) and an apparent therapy. *Vet. Rec.* 95:337–42.

Hemingway, A., and Barbour, H.G. 1938. The thermal tolerance of normal resting dogs as measured by changes of the acid-base equilibrium and the dilution-concentration effect of plasma. *Am. J. Physiol.* 124:264–70.

Hix, E.L., Underbjerg, G.K.L., and Hughes, J.S. 1959. The body fluids of ruminants and their simultaneous determination. *Am. J. Vet. Res.* 20:184–91.

Jewell, P.A., and Verney, E.B. 1957. An experimental attempt to determine the site of the neurohypophysial osmoreceptors in the dog. *Phil. Trans.*, ser. B, 240:197–324.

Johnson, J.A., Zehr, J.E., and Moore, W.W. 1970. Effects of separate and concurrent osmotic and volume stimuli on plasma ADH in sheep. *Am. J. Physiol.* 218:1273–80.

Kraybill, H.F., Hankins, O.G., and Bitter, H.L. 1951. Body composition of cattle. I. Estimation of body fat from measurement in vivo of body water by the use of antipyrine. *J. Appl. Physiol.* 3:681–89.

Lee, D.H.K., and Robinson, K. 1941. Reactions of the sheep to hot atmospheres. *Proc. Roy. Soc. Queensland* 53:189–200.

Leitch, I., and Thomson, J.S. 1944. The water economy of farm animals. *Nutr. Abstr. Rev.* 14:197–223.

Lemieux, G., Warren, Y., and Gervais, M. 1964. Characteristics of potassium conservation by the dog kidney. *Am. J. Physiol.* 206:743–49.

Macallum, A.B. 1926. The paleochemistry of the body fluids and tissues. *Physiol. Rev.* 6:316–57.

Macfarlane, W.V. 1964. Terrestrial animals in dry heat: Ungulates. In *Handbook of Physiology*. Sec. 4, D.B. Dill et al., eds., *Adaptation to the Environment*. Am. Physiol. Soc., Washington. Pp. 509–39.

Maloiy, G.M.O. 1970. Water economy of the Somali donkey. *Am. J. Physiol.* 219:1522–27.

Mayland, H.F., and Grunes, D.L. 1974. Shade-induced grass-tetany–prone chemical changes in *Agropyron desertorum* and *Elymus cinereus*. *J. Range Mgmt.* 27:198–201.

McLean, J.A. 1963. The partition of insensible losses of body weight and heat from cattle under various climatic conditions. *J. Physiol.* 167:427–47.

Nay, T., and Hayman, R.H. 1956. Sweat glands in Zebu (Bos indicus L.) and European (B. taurus L.) cattle. *Austral. J. Ag. Res.* 7:482–94.

Needham, A.D., Dawson, T.J., and Hales, J.R.S. 1974. Forelimb blood flow and saliva spreading in the thermoregulation of the red kangaroo *Megaleia rufa*. *Comp. Biochem. Physiol.*, ser. A, 49:555–65.

Oparil, S., and Haber, E. 1974. The renin-angiotensin system. *New Eng. J. Med.* 291:389–401, 446–57.

Painter, E.E., Holmes, J.H., and Gregersen, M.I. 1948. Exchange and distribution of fluid in dehydration in the dog. *Am. J. Physiol.* 152:66–76.

Peters, J.P., and Van Slyke, D.D. 1931. *Quantitative Clinical Chemistry*. Vol. 1, *Interpretations*. Williams & Wilkins, Baltimore.

Phillips, G.D. 1970. The assessment of blood acid-base parameters in ruminants. *Brit. Vet. J.* 126:325–31.

Pickering, E.C. 1965. The role of the kidney in sodium and potassium balance in the cow. *Proc. Nutr. Soc.* 24:73–80.

Pitts, R.F. 1975. *Physiology of the Kidney and Body Fluids*. 3d ed. Year Book Medical, Chicago.

Prentiss, P.G., Wolf, A.V., and Eddy, H.A. 1959. Hydropenia in cat and dog: Ability of the cat to meet its water requirements solely from a diet of fish or meat. *Am. J. Physiol.* 196:626–32.

Reynolds, M. 1953. Plasma and blood volume in the cow using the T-1824 hematocrit method. *Am. J. Physiol.* 173:421–27.

Rice, H.A., and Steinhaus, A.H. 1931. Studies in the physiology of exercise. V. Acid-base changes in the serum of exercised dogs. *Am. J. Physiol.* 96:529–37.

Sampson, J., and Hayden, C.E. 1935. The acid-base balance in cows and ewes during and after pregnancy, with special reference to milk fever and acetonemia. *J. Am. Vet. Med. Ass.* 39:13–23.

Schmidt-Nielsen, B., Schmidt-Nielsen, K., Houpt, T.R., and Jarnum, S.A. 1956. Water balance of the camel. *Am. J. Physiol.* 185:185–94.

Schmidt-Nielsen, K. 1964. *Desert Animals: Physiological Problems of Heat and Water*. Oxford U. Press, London.

Schmidt-Nielsen, K., Schmidt-Nielsen, B., Jarnum, S.A., and Houpt, T.R. 1957. Body temperature of the camel and its relation to water economy. *Am. J. Physiol.* 188:103–12.

Schrier, R.W., and Berl, T. 1975. Nonosmolar factors affecting renal water excretion. *New Eng. J. Med.* 292:81–88, 141–45.

Scott, D., and McIntosh, G.H. 1975. Changes in blood composition and in urinary mineral excretion in the pig in response to acute acid-base disturbance. *Q. J. Exp. Physiol.* 60:131–40.

Sellers, A.F., Gitis, T.L., and Roepke, M.H. 1951. Studies of electrolytes in body fluids of dairy cattle. III. Effects of potassium on electrolyte levels in body fluids in midlactation. *Am. J. Vet. Res.* 12:296–301.

Sellers, A.F., and Roepke, M.H. 1951. Studies of electrolytes in body fluids of dairy cattle. II. Effects of estrogen on electrolyte levels in body fluids in late pregnancy. *Am. J. Vet. Res.* 12:292–95.

Siggaard-Anderson, O. 1962. Acute experimental blood acid-base disturbances in dogs. *Scand. J. Clin. Lab. Invest.* 14(suppl. 66):1–20.

——. 1963. The acid-base status of the blood. *Scand. J. Clin. Lab. Invest.* 15(suppl. 70):1–134.

Swan, R.C., Pitts, R.F., and Madisso, H. 1955. Neutralization of infused acid by nephrectomized dogs. *J. Clin. Invest.* 34:205–12.

Towbin, E.J. 1949. Gastric distention as a factor in satiation of thirst in esophagostomized dogs. *Am. J. Physiol.* 159:533–41.

Verney, E.B. 1947. The antidiuretic hormone and the factors which determine its release. *Proc. Roy. Soc.*, ser. B, 135:25–106.

Wardener, H.E. de. 1973. The control of sodium excretion. In *Handbook of Physiology*. Sec. 8, J. Orloff and R.W. Berliner, eds., *Renal Physiology*. Am. Physiol. Soc., Washington. Pp. 677–720.

Widdowson, E.M., and McCance, R.A. 1956. The effect of development on the composition of the serum and extracellular fluids. *Clin. Sci.* 56:361–65.

Winters, R.W., Engel, K., and Dell, R.B. 1969. *Acid Base Physiology in Medicine*. 2d ed. London Co., Cleveland.

Wolf, A.V. 1958. *Thirst: Physiology of the Urge to Drink and Problems of Water Lack*. Thomas, Springfield, Ill.

Yousef, M.K., Dill, D.B., and Mayes, M.G. 1970. Shifts in body fluids during dehydration in the burro, *Equus asinus*. *J. Appl. Physiol.* 29:345–49.

CHAPTER 37

The Kidneys | by Joseph H. Gans and Paul F. Mercer

The primary function of the kidney is the formation of urine. In this the kidney performs a number of functions which help maintain the physiological integrity of the extracellular fluid volume. These processes are (1) conservation of water, fixed cations, glucose, and amino acids, conservation being used in the broad sense to imply the return to the body fluids of the amount of the substance required by the body's needs, the excess being excreted into urine; (2) elimination of nitrogenous end products of protein metabolism, primarily urea (uric acid in birds), creatinine, and ammonia; (3) elimination of excess hydrogen ions and the maintenance of physiological pH of the body fluids; and (4) elimination of complex organic compounds both endogenous and exogenous. Two important endocrine substances are secreted by the kidney, erythropoietin (see Chapter 2), which assumes a role in normal hematopoiesis, and renin, which is involved in the regulation of aldosterone secretion by the adrenal cortex.

The integration of renal excretory and endocrine functions is accomplished by interrelationships with the central nervous and endocrine systems. The CNS contributes to renal integration through a number of pathways. Maximum urine concentration requires the secretion of antidiuretic hormone, ADH (also called vasopressin), by the hypothalamo-neurohypophyseal complex. Reflexes from peripheral receptors, e.g. the postulated volume receptors, may influence renal function by central nervous integration through the hypothalamus and autonomic nervous system. Hypothalamic mediation of the adenohypophyseal secretions represents another pathway through which the CNS may alter the output of hormones which modify renal function.

The thyroid hormones and the adenohypophyseal

growth hormone exert tropic effects on the kidney; however, the hormones which assume major importance in the regulation of kidney function are the steroid secretions of the adrenal cortex and the hormone of the parathyroid gland. For example, the permissive action of the cortisol-type steroids is essential for maximal rates of water excretion, while aldosterone regulates the transport of potassium into urine and the retention of sodium within the body fluids. The hormone of the parathyroid gland influences the rate of calcium and phosphate excretion into urine.

The normal kidney, adequately perfused with blood, demonstrates considerable functional autonomy. Only small percentage decreases in any given process can be produced by removing a specific neurohumoral or endocrine mediator. The volumes of fluid which pass through the kidney each day are of such magnitude, however, that small percentage decreases in any given function usually represent a major crisis in terms of maintaining the physiological integrity of the body fluid compartments.

ANATOMICAL RÉSUMÉ

Mammalian kidneys contain two types of nephrons which are distinguished by (1) the locus of the origin, that is, the area of the cortex in which the glomeruli are found, and (2) the extent to which the loops of Henle penetrate the medulla. The *cortical* or *corticomedullary* nephrons arise from glomeruli located in the peripheral area of the kidney cortex; their loops of Henle extend into the corticomedullary junctional area but rarely penetrate to the outer level of the medulla. The *juxtamedullary nephrons* originate from glomeruli situated in the deeper portion of the cortex adjacent to the corticomedullary junctional area. Henle's loops, particularly the thin segments of these juxtamedullary nephrons, extend into the medullary substance, and many of the longer-looped nephrons penetrate to the medullary crest or renal papilla.

The glomerulus is composed of a capillary tuft, which lies between two arterioles, and the epithelium of the proximal end of the nephron (Figs. 37.1, 37.2, 37.3). The tubular epithelium, Bowman's membrane or capsule, is invaginated and forms folds which invest the endothelium of the glomerular capillaries. A basement membrane separates the capillary endothelium from the tubular epithelial cells. The cells of Bowman's membrane form small projections called foot processes or podocytes, which rest against the basement membrane. In diseases characterized by increased permeability and loss of protein into urine, the podocytes become less distinct, swollen, and vacuolized, and often are totally lost. A third cell type (in addition to capillary endothelium and tubular epithelium), the mesangial cell, also may be seen in the glomerulus.

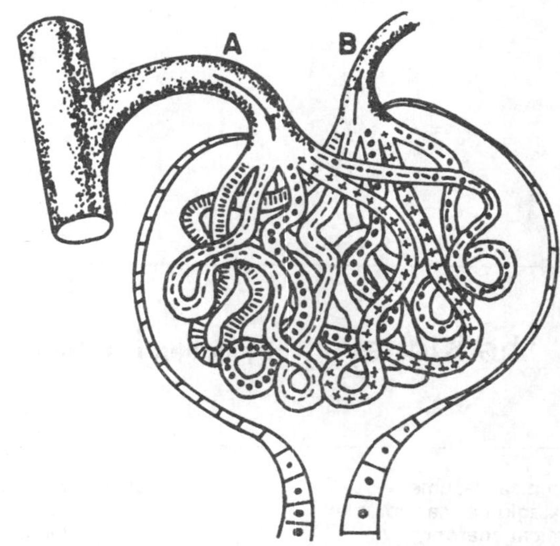

Figure 37.1. Glomerulus showing the arrangement of twisted capillary loops and the absence of anastomoses. Note that the afferent vessel (A) is larger than the efferent vessel (B). The change in vessel size emphasizes the passage of fluid from the capillary bed to the expanded portion of the proximal convoluted tubule. (From B. Vimtrup 1928, *Am. J. Anat.* 41:123–51.)

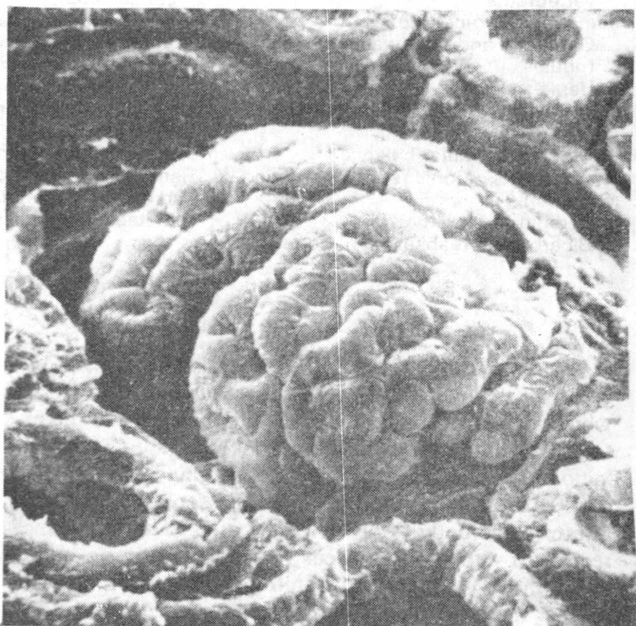

Figure 37.2. Scanning electron microscopy of a glomerulus surrounded by truncated tubules. Part of Bowman's capsule has been removed in the cutting procedure, leaving the capillary tuft exposed. The transected portions of the parietal leaf of Bowman's capsule are clearly visible both on the left and below on the right. Several flattened spherical podocytes are seen nestled together in the spaces between the capillaries. The primary processes radiating from the cell body twine around the individual capillary. Usually, one podocyte supplies either several loops or both limbs of the same loop. ×1020. (From Spinelli 1974, *Internat. Rev. Cytol.* 39:345–81.)

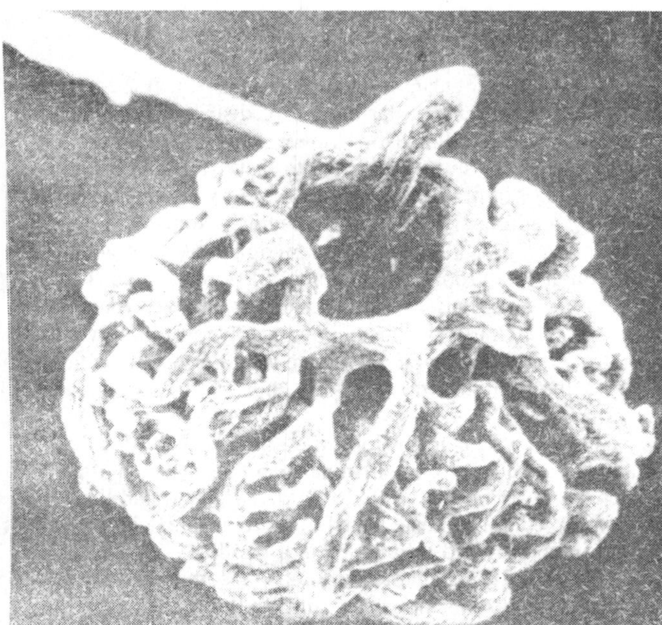

Figure 37.3. Silicon rubber cast of a juxtamedullary glomerulus of a dog kidney. The afferent arteriole empties into a semicircular vessel, which is the origin of the lobular capillaries. Multiple anastomoses between the descending limb and the returning limb follow a course parallel to the surface of the spherical glomerular tuft in such a way that the ultrafiltering surface of the first segments of the capillaries is augmented, while the returning segments, where filtration equilibrium is nearly reached, run more centrally. No direct connection between afferent and efferent arterioles can be seen. ×510. (From Spinelli 1974, *Internat. Rev. Cytol.* 39:345–81.)

The cuboidal or irregularly columnar cells of the proximal convoluted tubule rest upon a basement membrane which separates the tubular cells from the endothelium of the peritubular capillaries. The basement membrane is continuous and invests the entire nephron. Proximal tubular cells are characterized by a brush border on the luminal surface. Electron microscopy has shown that on the luminal surface the cellular membrane is thrown into many long microvilli which project into the tubule and vastly increase the surface area available for the reabsorptive functions of these cells. Mitochondria are numerous in the cytoplasm, and their numbers correlate well with the highly oxidative metabolism of the kidney cortex. The cytoplasm also contains a prominent, granular endoplasmic reticulum.

Henle's loop is composed of two well-defined segments, each having its characteristic cell type. The descending limb of Henle's loop in its progression through the corticomedullary junction and part of the outer medullary zone is composed of cells which have microvilli on their luminal surfaces. In comparison with the cells of the thin portions of the loop, the cells of this first segment of the descending limb are relatively complex, having cellular organelles, a greater thickness, and complex interdigitations with adjacent cells. Continued penetration into the medulla is accompanied by progressively decreased thickness of the cells of the descending limb and loss of interdigitations. Henle's loops in the middle of the inner medulla and through to the medullary crest are composed of thin-walled cells, and it is difficult to differentiate the descending from the ascending portions of the loop.

The cells of the thick ascending portion of Henle's loop are cuboidal or columnar, and their luminal border contains numerous short microvilli. Projections of the basal surface of the plasma membrane extend deeply into the cytoplasm, in which densely packed, elongated mitochondria are prominent.

The cells of the first portion of the distal convoluted tubule are similar to those of the thick ascending segment of Henle's loop. They contain many mitochondria, and the cytoplasm is densely packed with the ribonucleoprotein particles. With progression toward the collecting duct, the cells show fewer mitochondria and nucleoprotein particles, and the invaginations of the basal plasma membrane become less frequent and less prominent.

Two cell types are recognized in the collecting duct. The more numerous light cell is characterized by a light-staining cytoplasm, few cellular organelles, and small amounts of ribosomes. The intercalated or dark cells can be differentiated by the presence of greater numbers of mitochondria and ribosomes.

The postglomerular blood supply is divided into two types of vessels. One portion of the efferent arteriole breaks into a very dense capillary network which surrounds the proximal and distal convoluted tubules in the kidney cortex. The capillaries converge again to drain into the venous system of the kidney. The second group of postglomerular vessels passes into the medulla in close approximation to the thin segments of Henle's loops and the collecting ducts. These channels are known as the vasa recta; they dip deeply into the medullary crest and then form ascending branches, thus resembling the course of Henle's loops.

The vasa recta give rise to capillary plexuses at various levels in their passage from cortex to medullary crest. One prominent plexus is in the corticomedullary junction. Other plexuses are found at descending levels in the medulla. The vasa recta do not form the hairpinlike loops in the medullary crest that are so characteristic of the thin segment of Henle's loop. The descending limbs of the vasa recta form a capillary plexus from which the ascending limbs take their origin. As a consequence of this peculiar arrangement, there are progressively fewer descending capillary branches from cortex to medulla, and therefore there is a progressive decrease in medullary blood flow.

The kidney medulla contains not only nephronal elements and blood vessels but also three distinctive types of interstitial cells. The first is found throughout the medullary substance and contains osmophilic droplets in its cytoplasm. These cells may be the elaborators of the specific prostaglandins that are secreted by the kidney medulla. The second type is considered to be a collagen-forming cell, and the third type possesses properties suggestive of contractile activity.

Juxtaglomerular complex

The juxtaglomerular complex is composed of specialized cells, in the walls of the afferent glomerular arterioles, which are in intimate contact with a distinctive portion of the distal convoluted tubule known as the macula densa. The specialized cells in the arteriolar walls are designated as granular or agranular cells because of the presence or absence in their cytoplasm of secretory granules. That endoplasmic reticulum with ribosomes is present in the cytoplasm of both cell types suggests the presence of active protein formation. The agranular cells may represent less active cell types. Cells of the macula densa may be differentiated from the other cell types of the distal convoluted tubule by specific staining characteristics. Electron microscopy has shown that the cells of the macula densa contain fewer mitochondria than the other cells of the distal convoluted tubule.

CHEMICAL ANATOMY

The marked differences between the morphology of the cortex and the medulla are accompanied by equally profound differences in their chemical composition. In addition, the composition of both cortex and medulla will vary, depending upon whether the kidney is forming dilute or concentrated urine.

The composition of some chemical constituents in the kidney on a wet basis is summarized in Table 37.1. On a mg/g basis the cortex contains more lipid and apparently more protein than the medulla. Histochemical studies have shown that the cortex contains a greater concentration of nucleic acids, both DNA and RNA, than does the medulla. Glycogen concentrations in the dog kidney are the same in both cortex and medulla; in rabbits and sheep, however, the glycogen concentrations in the medulla are approximately two times greater than in the cortex.

Table 37.1. Chemical composition of the dog kidney (mg/g)

Zone	TCA extractable protein	Total lipid	Cholesterol	Glycogen	Glycosamino-glycan
Cortex	98.5	26	3.8	1.5	0.33
Medulla	45	18	2	1.2	1.27

Similar data have been obtained from sheep kidney with the exception of glycogen concentration. Sheep kidney cortex and medulla contain on the average 2.2 and 3.8 mg/g wet weight of glycogen respectively. These figures compare closely with glycogen concentrations in the rabbit kidney reported by Lee et al. 1962. Glycosaminoglycan figures are from Castor and Green 1968. TCA, trichloroacetic acid.

Glycosaminoglycans (mucopolysaccharides) occur in the kidney with a singular pattern of distribution between cortex and medulla. Dog kidney cortex contains primarily heparan sulfate and hyaluronate, the glycosaminoglycan concentration being 0.33 mg/g wet weight. Dog kidney medulla, by contrast, contains a fourfold greater concentration, 1.27 mg glycosaminoglycan/g wet weight, of which hyaluronate constitutes 70 percent (see Table 37.1). A quantitatively similar relationship is found in the rabbit kidney, but the dominant glycosaminoglycans in the cortex are heparan sulfate and dermatan sulfate, while those of the medulla are chondroitin sulfate and hyaluronate.

The kidneys of most domestic animals, e.g. dog, cat, and sheep, do not contain renal papillae. The papilla of each renal pyramid is fused with adjacent papillae to form a medullary crest. In the cow, as in man, however, each renal pyramid terminates in a papilla.

The medulla is characterized by a somewhat greater water content than the cortex and by the presence of the corticomedullary osmotic gradient, particularly when concentrated urine is being formed (Fig. 37.4). This gra-

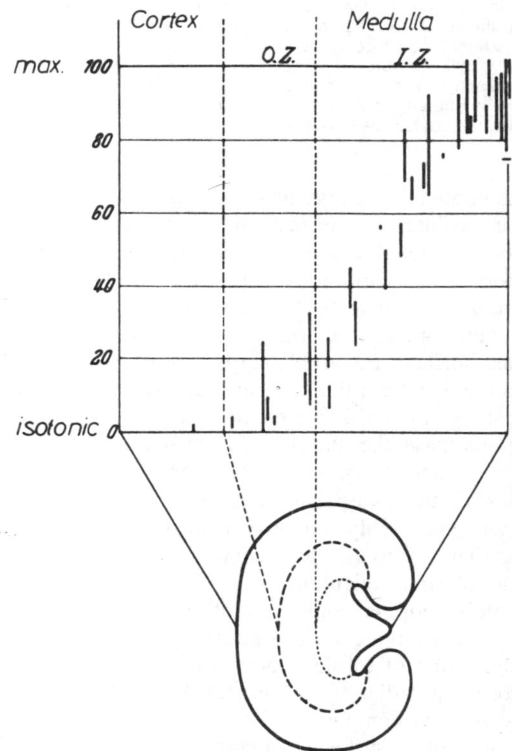

Figure 37.4. Variation of osmotic pressure along the axis of the papilla. O.Z., outer zone; I.Z., inner zone. (From Wirz, Hargitay, and Kuhn 1951, *Helv. Physiol. Pharmac. Acta* 9:196–207.)

Table 37.2. Concentration of electrolytes, urea, and osmolality of urine, cortex, medulla, and papilla of kidneys taken from hydropenic dogs and from dogs undergoing water diuresis

	Urine	Cortex	Medulla	Papilla
	24 hr dehydration			
Osmolality	1,725 ± 361			
Na (mMol/kg H_2O)	153 ± 60	80.8 ± 8.9	258 ± 18.7	320 ± 48.8
K (mMol/kg H_2O)	162 ± 70	80.5 ± 7.9	44.5 ± 14.2	52.7 ± 5.5
NH_4 (mMol/kg H_2O)	76.2 ± 59.5	7.5 ± 0.3	14.2 ± 3.2	21.3 ± 2.3
Urea (mMol/kg H_2O)	991 ± 228	21 ± 4.6	532 ± 127	855 ± 160
Sum of osmol	1,771 ± 328	358 ± 27.5	1,165 ± 127	1,645 ± 255
	Water diuresis			
Osmolality	70.6 ± 16.6			
Na (mMol/kg H_2O)	2.8 ± 2.5	68.1 ± 5.7	134 ± 17.7	118 ± 23.1
K (mMol/kg H_2O)	5.8 ± 3.7	77.2 ± 4	45.8 ± 5	48.6 ± 4.4
NH_4 (mMol/kg H_2O)	5.3 ± 2.5	7.6 ± 0.71	3.9 ± 0.51	6.8 ± 2.8
Urea (mMol/kg H_2O)	42.1 ± 16.4	10 ± 2.5	31.1 ± 9.9	33.4 ± 9.1
Sum of osmol	69.9 ± 16.5	315 ± 13.9	401 ± 32.5	381 ± 50.7

From Levitin, Goodman, Pigeon, and Epstein 1962, *J. Clin. Invest.* 41:1145–51

dient in the osmolality of tissue water increases from the cortex, where the tissue water osmolality is approximately equal to the osmolality of plasma, to the medullary crest (papilla); during antidiuresis the osmolality of tissue water at the medullary crest may be five times greater than the osmolality of plasma, thus approximating the osmolality of urine. The corticomedullary osmotic gradient is composed essentially of increasing concentrations of sodium and urea from the corticomedullary junction to the medullary crest (Table 37.2).

RENAL CIRCULATION

The formation of urine begins as an ultrafiltrate of plasma passes across the glomerular capillary walls and Bowman's capsules into the glomerular ends of the nephrons. Energy for this filtration process is provided by the heart in the form of blood pressure within the glomerular capillaries and is opposed by the colloid osmotic pressure (COP) of plasma proteins plus the intrinsic tissue pressure of the kidney:

$$\text{Net filtration pressure} = \text{Capillary blood pressure} - (\text{COP of plasma proteins} + \text{tissue pressure})$$

Under normal circumstances, in which renal arterial pressures vary between 90 and 100 mm Hg with mean pressures as blood enters the glomerular afferent arterioles of 75 mm Hg, the net filtration pressure would be approximately 45 mm Hg: $75-(25+5)$. Decreases in blood pressure below a level consistent with the maintenance of adequate pressure within the glomeruli result in progressive reduction in filtration rate. If the blood pressure within the afferent arteriole decreases to 45 mm Hg, filtration of the plasma ceases.

The net filtration pressure represents the measurement of pressures across the glomerulus. Within the glomerulus there is an additional redistribution of pressure. The hydrostatic pressure drops as blood flows from the afferent arterioles into the glomerular capillaries, and the colloid osmotic pressure increases in the efferent portions of the glomerular capillaries as fluid is lost during the filtration process. The ultrafiltration pressure, the net pressure available to force an ultrafiltrate of plasma into Bowman's space, will be greatest in afferent portions of the glomerular capillaries. The following data from micropuncture studies illustrate the changes in ultrafiltration pressures within the glomerulus:

$$P_{UF} = (P_{GC} - \pi_{GC}) - (P_T - \pi_T)$$

in which P_{UF} = ultrafiltration pressure in glomerular capillaries, P_{GC} = hydrostatic pressure in glomerular capillaries, π_{GC} = COP in glomerular capillaries, P_T = hydrostatic pressure of fluid in Bowman's capsule, π_T = COP in fluid of Bowman's capsule (under normal circumstances no protein is filtered and this would be zero). $P_{UF} = (45-20)-(10-0)$ in the afferent arterioles or 15 mm Hg. And $P_{UF} = (45-35)-(10-0)$ in the efferent arterioles or 0 mm Hg. Changes in glomerular filtration rate, therefore, can occur by shifting the point at which filtration equilibrium is reached.

Increasing the tissue pressure within the kidney also decreases filtration rate by decreasing the net filtration pressure. Clamping the ureter permits fluid to accumulate within the nephrons. Assuming no change in blood pressure and continued filtration, the pressure within the nephrons increases until intratubular pressures reach 45 mm Hg. At this point net filtration pressure should be abolished. Ureteral obstruction decreases the filtration rate, but continued absorption of tubular fluid into the peritubular blood flow generally prevents complete cessation of the plasma filtering process.

Regional blood flow

Estimates of regional blood flow indicate that at least 85 percent of the effective renal blood flow perfuses the cortex. Quantitative determinations in unanesthetized dogs have shown that the total renal blood flow was 642 ml/100 g/min. This represents approximately 20 percent of the cardiac output, and indicates the magnitude of blood flow to an organ which comprises 0.3 percent of the total body mass. The intrarenal distribution of blood is as follows: cortical flow 472 ml/100 g/min, outer medulla 132, inner medulla 17, hilar and perirenal fat 21. Medullary blood flow not only differs quantitatively from the cortical flow, but also shows qualitative changes which reflect both the composition of the area which it perfuses and the singular arrangement of the vasa recta into a countercurrent exchange system. Blood taken by micropuncture from vasa recta near the medullary crest has an osmolality approximating the osmolality of the medullary interstitium. In general, blood samples taken at varying levels of the medulla have osmolalities indicative of the corticomedullary osmotic gradient.

Determinations of the renal arteriovenous difference in the partial pressure of oxygen (Po_2) have shown that oxygen extraction is somewhat less than that anticipated on the basis of renal blood flow measurements and renal metabolism. The Po_2 of urine, however, is less than the calculated value, if it is assumed that there is some equilibrium between Po_2 in the renal blood flow and Po_2 in urine. Apparently, the final equilibration of urine in the collecting ducts occurs within a region of low oxygen tension, the deeper medullary areas. The low Po_2 in the medullary area therefore results from the smaller blood flow to the medulla than that to the cortex and from countercurrent diffusion of oxygen from the descending to the ascending limbs of the vasa recta. Hemoglobin saturation of blood perfusing the medulla may be as low as 45 percent while cortical blood shows hemoglobin saturation of 80–85 percent.

Autoregulation

One of the intriguing characteristics of the renal vasculature is its ability to maintain a relatively stable blood flow despite large changes in the arterial blood pressure. Although other vascular beds show this tendency, autoregulation is most highly developed in the kidney. The most effective experimental procedures lend strong support to the concept that the autoregulation of the renal blood flow is due to the inherent myogenicity of the smooth muscle of the renal vascular bed (Fig. 37.5).

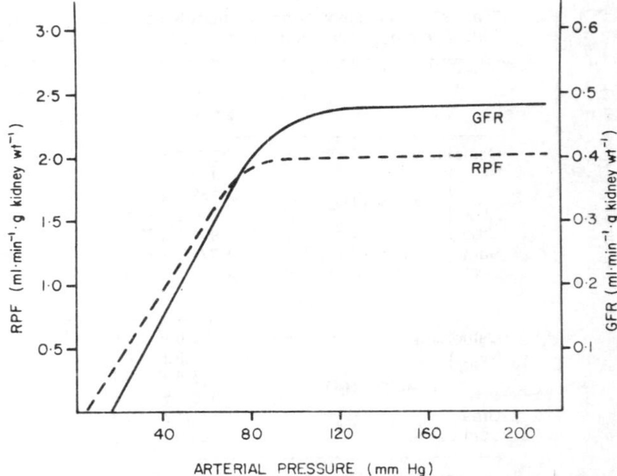

Figure 37.5. Autoregulation of renal blood flow and glomerular filtration rate (GFR) for arterial pressures of 80–180 mm Hg. RPF, renal plasma flow.

METHODS OF STUDYING NEPHRON FUNCTIONS

Micropuncture

Localization of tubular functions has been accomplished most successfully by micropuncture techniques in which micropipettes are inserted into the nephrons at various levels and small quantities of tubular fluid are removed and analyzed. Micropuncture techniques originally were used to obtain patterns of nephron function in amphibians. In recent years these techniques have been applied to the mammalian kidney. A modification of these procedures, using microelectrodes, has been adapted to measure the transcellular and transmembrane electrical potentials in various segments of the nephrons.

Comparative studies on lower vertebrates

Comparative studies of renal function in vertebrates other than mammals have provided information which may be applicable to the mammalian kidney. For example, some species of fish have aglomerular kidneys; the tubular elements appear to be physiological analogues of the proximal convoluted tubules of the mammalian kidney. Experiments with these kidneys have been of considerable value for the study of renal transport processes.

Clinical research has been utilized most effectively for the study of renal function. The correlation of changes in renal function with the morphological manifestations of kidney disease has provided much important information regarding quantitative aspects of renal physiology as well as indications of functional localization within the nephrons.

FUNCTIONS OF RENAL TUBULES

Glomeruli and proximal convoluted tubules

The glomeruli function primarily as filters. A membrane of differential permeability, composed of the endothelium of the glomerular capillaries, a basement membrane, and the invaginations of Bowman's capsule, permits the passage of the aqueous, ionic, and crystalloid components of blood into Bowman's space. The erythrocytes and most of the plasma proteins do not filter through the glomerular membrane. The glomerular fluid may be characterized as an ultrafiltrate of plasma containing only trace amounts of protein, primarily albumin. In other respects the glomerular filtrate prior to its entrance into the proximal convolutions is almost identical in composition and osmolality to plasma.

Tubular fluid collected by micropipettes near the end of the proximal convoluted tubules still shows a fluid-plasma osmolal ratio of 1 (Figs. 37.6, 37.7), but marked changes in its composition can be demonstrated. This fluid is devoid of glucose and amino acids, and most of the filtered protein is no longer present. Quantitative estimates indicate that only 20 percent of the original glomerular filtrate remains after its passage through the proximal tubules. Thus the primary function of the cells of the proximal tubule is to return approximately 80 percent of the glomerular filtrate into the peritubular blood, and hence into the systemic circulation. When plasma glucose concentrations are normal, all of the filtered glucose is transported from the tubular fluid of the proximal convoluted tubules into the plasma. Amino acids also are almost entirely removed from the proximal tubular fluid.

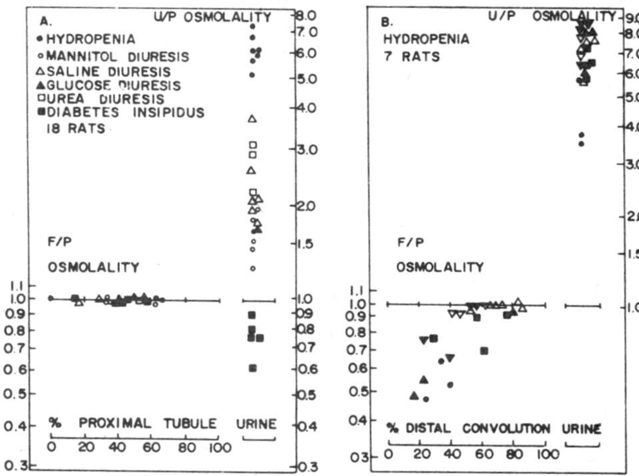

Figure 37.6. Osmolality ratios. A, proximal tubular fluid and urine in rats; B, fluid from the distal convolution and urine during hydropenia. F/P, tubular fluid/plasma; U/P, urine/plasma. (From Gottschalk and Mylle 1959, *Am. J. Physiol.* 196:927–36.)

The primary determinants of proximal reabsorption apparently are (1) the active transport of sodium, against an electrochemical gradient, from the tubular fluid into the peritubular interstitial fluid and capillary blood, (2) hydrogen ion-sodium ion exchange processes, and (3) reabsorption of glucose. Chloride either diffuses along with sodium to maintain electrical neutrality or may also be transported by some carrier system.

The nitrogenous components of the glomerular filtrate other than the amino acids, primarily creatinine and urea, are differentially affected by events in the proximal convoluted tubule. Creatinine, which is not reabsorbed by the nephrons, becomes more concentrated as reabsorption proceeds. Urea, on the other hand, diffuses readily across most biological membranes. Approximately 30–40 percent of the filtered urea is reabsorbed in the proximal tubules.

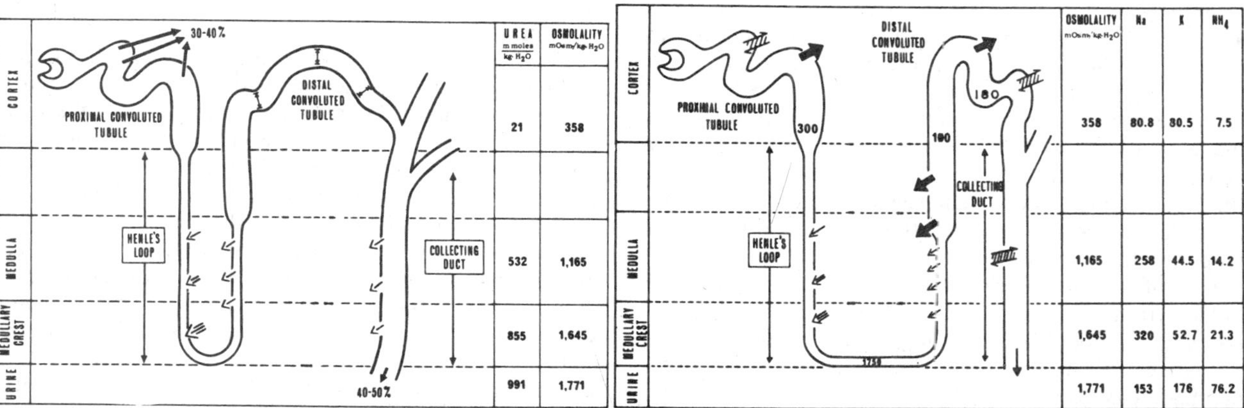

Figure 37.7. Juxtamedullary nephron. A. Renal handling of urea during the formation of concentrated urine. Approximately 30–40 percent of the filtered urea is reabsorbed as the filtrate passes through the proximal convoluted tubule. In its transit through Henle's loop, urea undergoes a countercurrent distribution between the ascending and descending limbs of the loop. The concentration of tubular fluid in the collecting ducts permits back-diffusion of urea into the medullary fluid in the direction of its concentration gradient. The countercurrent diffusion of urea is augmented by the singular arrangement of the vasa recta which results in a progressively smaller blood flow from corticomedullary junction to medullary crest. The distal convoluted tubule and possibly the thick ascending limb of Henle's loop are impermeable to urea. Data on osmolality and urea concentrations are from Levitin et al. (1962). B. Sodium chloride transport and establishment of the corticomedullary concentration gradient. The active transport of sodium (or chloride) is designated by heavy arrows, diffusion by thin arrows, and ion exchange processes by hatched arrows. Data on osmolality, sodium, potassium, and ammonium concentrations from Levitin et al. (1962). The figures within the tubules represent the approximate osmolality of tubular fluid (Clapp et al. 1963, Clapp and Robinson 1966).

Henle's loops

The tubular fluid in transit through Henle's loop must pass through the hyperosmotic medulla. Micropuncture studies have shown that the tubular fluid becomes increasingly hypertonic as it passes into the medulla. The descending limb of Henle's loop apparently is permeable to the passage of ions and crystalloids. Both sodium chloride and urea are added by passive diffusion to the tubular fluid in this segment from the medullary interstitium. Fluid from the tip of Henle's loop resembles both in composition and osmolality the medullary interstitial fluid. The initial segment of the ascending limb of Henle's loop may be less permeable than the descending, but some equilibration occurs between tubular fluid and medullary interstitium. Henle's loop therefore functions as a countercurrent diffusion system in concert with the vasa recta, as sodium chloride and urea diffuse circuitously from the ascending segments into the medullary interstitium and into the descending segments (see Fig. 37.7).

Tubular fluid then passes through the thick portion of the ascending limb of Henle's loop in the corticomedullary junctional area and subsequently into the distal convoluted tubule. Despite its recent transit through the hyperosmotic medulla, the fluid entering the distal convoluted tubule is hypo-osmotic to plasma (see Fig. 37.6). Clearly, some portion of the ascending limb performs a critical function in urine formation. This segment of the ascending limb apparently is relatively impermeable to water but is the site of the processes that carry sodium (chloride) from the tubular fluid into the interstitial fluid of the junctional area. The very high concentration of Na^+-K^+ ATPase in the cells of the thick ascending limb of Henle's loop indicates that these cells transport sodium chloride out of the tubular fluid.

It is clear that water excretion, that is the elimination of dilute urine, is not a passive process solely related to the absence of ADH. The active transport of sodium chloride from the relatively water-impermeable ascending limbs of Henle's loops represents an essential energy-dependent process in the formation of dilute urine. Potent loop diuretics such as furosemide which inhibit this component of sodium chloride transport not only prevent the kidney from excreting a concentrated urine, but also diminish the kidney's capacity to excrete a dilute urine.

The establishment and maintenance of the corticomedullary osmotic gradient can now be summarized. The energy for the system that provides sodium chloride in excess of water comes from metabolically linked sodium transport across a relatively water-impermeable segment of the ascending limb of Henle's loops. In conjunction with the closely approximated vasa recta, Henle's loops act as a countercurrent multiplier and diffusion system to keep sodium chloride (and urea) recirculating within the medulla (see Figs. 37.6, 37.7). This process, enhanced by the relatively meager medullary blood flow, tends to trap sodium chloride and urea within the medulla, thereby maintaining the high concentration of solute in the medullary interstitium.

Distal convoluted tubules and collecting ducts

The distal convoluted tubules receive a hypotonic fluid from the medullary region. Micropuncture studies in the rat have shown that isosmotic equilibration occurs in the first one third of the distal convolution (assuming that the kidney is elaborating a concentrated urine) as water leaves the tubular fluid in the direction of its concentration gradient. Further isosmotic reabsorption occurs in the remaining portions of the distal convoluted tubules secondary to sodium transport from the tubular fluid into plasma. The osmolality of the fluid at the end of the distal convoluted tubule is equal to the osmolality of plasma, but quantitatively the tubular fluid now represents approximately 5 percent of the original glomerular filtrate.

Isosmotic equilibration of tubular fluid does not occur in the distal convoluted tubules of dog nephrons (see Fig. 37.7). Rather, the tubular fluid at the end of the distal convoluted tubules is still hypotonic to plasma. Some portion of the ascending limb of Henle's loop in the dog kidney appears to be involved in the processes which regulate urine concentration and dilution. Fluid entering the distal convoluted tubule shows a fluid-plasma osmolal ratio of 0.5–0.6 when the dog kidney is elaborating a concentrated urine. Under conditions of water diuresis, that is, when the kidney excretes a hypotonic urine, the fluid-plasma osmolal ratio may be as low as 0.2.

Final concentration of the urine takes place in the collecting ducts, as these terminal segments of the nephron system carry the urine through the medulla to the renal pelvis. The permeability of the collecting duct to water and to urea is variable, depending upon the presence of ADH. In the presence of ADH that is, when the kidney is excreting a concentrated urine, the collecting duct becomes increasingly permeable to water and to urea. Water, free of solute, then passes in the direction of its concentration gradient, from the lumen of the collecting duct into the hypertonic medullary interstitium. As the fluid in the collecting duct becomes concentrated, urea concentration in the collecting duct fluid increases until it exceeds the urea concentration in the medulla. Urea then diffuses from the collecting fluid into the medullary interstitium, thus obligating the reabsorption of water from the collecting duct fluid (see Fig. 37.7). The collecting duct appears to be relatively impermeable to nonurea solute—for example, sodium and potassium salts of chloride, sulfate, bicarbonate—and to creatinine, and these solutes become increasingly concentrated. The net result of these processes is the excretion of urine which may be five to seven times the concentration of plasma.

Dilute urine is excreted when the release of ADH is inhibited. The primary target organs of ADH are the collecting ducts, but the distal convoluted tubules and the ascending limb of Henle's loop, in the dog at least, share to some extent as sites of action of this hormone. In the absence of ADH the distal convoluted tubules, the collecting ducts, and the ascending limb of Henle's loop in the dog become relatively impermeable to water and to urea. Sodium reabsorption still takes place from the fluid in the distal convoluted tubule, but water movement is decreased; concurrently water reabsorption in the collecting ducts is markedly inhibited. The absence of ADH, therefore, results in water diuresis, that is, the excretion of large volumes of urine hypotonic to plasma.

The specialized morphology and metabolism of the medulla permit the mammalian kidney to concentrate urine and thereby conserve water. There is evidence, however, that the hyperosmoticity of the medulla may also be detrimental. It has been shown that chronic infectious diseases of the kidney may be closely associated with the maintenance of the corticomedullary osmotic gradient. The hyperosmotic environment of the medulla apparently inhibits the migration of leukocytes to the site of infection, thus depriving the area of one of the primary defense mechanisms against bacteria. Additionally the relatively small medullary blood flow would limit the amount of antimicrobial drugs which could be carried into the medulla. These two factors complicate the therapeutic management of renal infections.

The urine concentrating process functions most effectively when protein intake is sufficient to maintain positive nitrogen balance. Protein-deficient diets result in an impairment in the capacity of the kidneys to conserve water. There may be subtle changes in permeability characteristics as protein turnover in the kidney responds to an unfavorable nitrogen equilibrium. Enzyme synthesis in the kidney may be similarly affected. Urea, however, assumes an important role in the renal responses to changes in protein intake. The urea component of the corticomedullary osmotic gradient is virtually eliminated by protein deficiency, and urea excretion falls to low levels. As the urine is concentrated in the collecting ducts, there is a minimal reabsorption of urea, and the amount of water reabsorption obligated by urea diffusion also is greatly reduced. A decrease in the corticomedullary osmotic gradient also is anticipated since the quantity of filtered urea is decreased. Water conservation, therefore, depends to some extent upon urea reabsorption and is decreased as the result of the decrease in the osmolality of the medullary interstitium.

Glomerulotubular balance

In the dog, and probably in many other species as well, the glomerular filtration rate (GFR) varies markedly with diet. It has been reported that the filtration rate in the dog may be increased nearly 100 percent 4–5 hours after a meal of raw beef. Changes in GFR of this magnitude would result in a very large increase in sodium load presented to the tubules. If the tubules were unable to adjust their sodium reabsorptive ability accordingly, a severe loss of sodium in the urine would occur which could not be tolerated. In order to prevent such wide fluctuations the tubules are able to adjust their sodium reabsorption proportionally. Thus if GFR increases, tubular reabsorption of sodium increases proportionally and less sodium is lost in the urine than would have occurred if sodium reabsorption were fixed. This proportionality between sodium reabsorption by the tubule and glomerular filtration rate has been termed glomerulotubular balance.

Changes in sodium reabsorptive capacity occur primarily in the proximal tubule. The distal convoluted tubules and collecting ducts can only partially alter their reabsorptive rates for sodium, and the modest changes in sodium excretion which result from changes in GFR may be due at least in part to this incomplete adjustment at the more distal nephron sites. Glomerulotubular balance appears to be intact over a range of filtration rates, but during acute reductions or elevations in GFR some slight deviations from perfect balance can occur.

How the tubules are informed of the necessity to read-

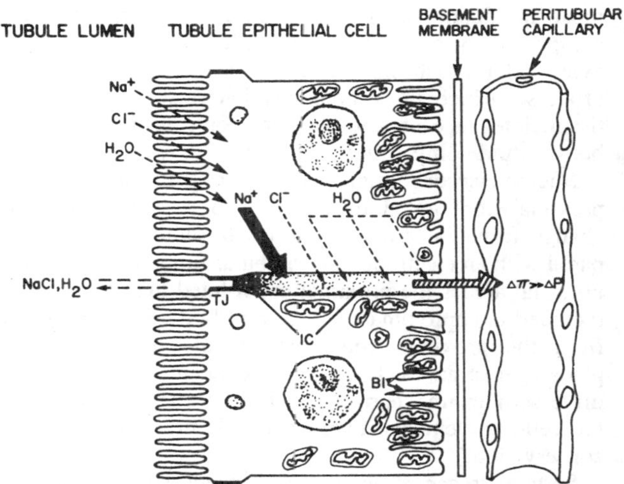

Figure 37.8. Reabsorption of sodium, chloride, and water across an idealized proximal tubule. TJ, tight junction; BI, basilar infoldings; IC, lateral intercellular channel; $\Delta\pi$, mean peritubular transcapillary colloid osmotic pressure difference; ΔP, mean peritubular transcapillary hydrostatic pressure difference. Solid arrows represent active sodium transport. Interrupted arrows represent passive transport. Hatched arrows represent the path for fluid movement as a function of the peritubular transcapillary forces, $\Delta\pi$ and ΔP.

just their reabsorptive ability when the filtration rate changes has been the subject of intensive investigation in recent years. The proposal for which there is some evidence suggests that the interactions of the hydrostatic and colloid osmotic pressures at the peritubular capillaries surrounding the proximal tubules are of primary importance. A change in these forces may be brought about by a change in GFR relative to the renal blood flow (Fig. 37.8).

For example, if GFR increases but the renal blood flow did not change or changed less than the GFR (that is, the filtration fraction increased) the colloid osmotic pressure of the peritubular capillaries would increase, and reabsorption into the capillary from the interstitial compartment would be facilitated. This movement of fluid from the interstitial compartment would increase fluid movement from the intercellular spaces and basal infoldings of the proximal tubular cells. This in turn could permit more sodium chloride transport and hence more water movement from the proximal tubular cell and ultimately from the tubular fluid. Decreased filtration fraction would presumably cause the opposite effects.

MECHANISMS OF IONIC REABSORPTION AND EXCRETION

Sodium transport

Sodium reabsorption occurs at several nephronal levels; in the proximal convoluted tubules, the thick ascending segment of Henle's loops, and the distal convoluted tubules and collecting ducts. Quantitatively the most significant component of sodium reabsorption is accompanied by an attendant chloride reabsorption. However, sodium reabsorption also is linked to ion-exchange processes which are of great physiological significance in the maintenance of acid-base and ionic equilibria of the body's fluid compartments (see Fig. 37.7).

Microelectrodes implanted within the lumen of the proximal convoluted tubule in vivo record a negative change from the luminal side of the tubule when compared with an electrode in peritubular fluid. The electrical potential across the proximal convoluted tubule has been recorded at approximately −20 mv. Sodium reabsorption from the proximal convoluted tubule therefore takes place against an electrochemical gradient. The energy to drive sodium transport comes from metabolic energy of the cellular elements involved in this process of sodium conservation.

Sodium transport against its concentration gradient is limited in the proximal tubules and can be inhibited by diluting its concentration in the fluid of the proximal convoluted tubule. If a nonreabsorbable solute, mannitol, is included within the tubular fluid, initial sodium reabsorption fails to obligate the reabsorption of water because the osmotic effects of the mannitol hold water within the tubule. Sodium is diluted within the tubular fluid until the concentration gradient created becomes great enough to exceed the capacity of the tubule to transport sodium. Sodium reabsorption from the distal convoluted tubule can proceed against a much greater concentration gradient. The hypotonic urine excreted during a water diuresis is virtually free of sodium, indicating that sodium in the distal tubular fluid has been conserved despite an increasingly unfavorable concentration gradient. Electrophysiological studies have shown that the potential across the distal convoluted tubules may be greater than −50 mv (−35 to −60 mv), emphasizing further the great capacity of sodium reabsorption to overcome this electrochemical gradient.

Bicarbonate reabsorption, urine acidification, and potassium transport

Ion exchange processes linked to sodium reabsorption include systems which exchange either hydrogen ion or potassium for sodium. Hydrogen ion transport into urine takes place in the proximal convoluted tubules, in the distal convoluted tubules, and in the collecting ducts, and it is also involved with the reabsorption of bicarbonate ions from the tubular fluid. The source of hydrogen ion is the metabolism of the renal tubular cells and the hydration of carbon dioxide to carbonic acid and dissociation of this acid into hydrogen and bicarbonate ions. The secretion of hydrogen ions by the renal tubular cells may account for their relatively high intracellular pH. Hydrogen ions when transferred into urine may react with urinary constituents (Diagrams 1, 2, 3).

Under normal conditions, plasma bicarbonate concentration in the dog is 24–26 mEq/L. The quantity of bicarbonate reabsorbed per minute varies with the GFR (Fig. 37.9); assuming a constant GFR, tubular maximal bicarbonate reabsorption in the dog ($TmHCO_3^-$) is about 2–3 mMol/min/100 ml filtrate (Fig. 37.10). Bicarbonate reabsorption also depends upon the partial pressure of carbon dioxide in plasma. Increased arterial Pco_2 increases the maximal rate of bicarbonate reabsorption, and conversely decreases in arterial Pco_2 reduce the kidney's capacity to reabsorb bicarbonate (Fig. 37.11).

Micropuncture studies have given some estimate of the amount of bicarbonate absorbed from the various segments of the nephrons. Bicarbonate concentrations in the glomerular filtrate are comparable to those of plasma, 24–26 mEq/L, but in fluid taken from the end of the accessible portion of the proximal convoluted tubule of the dog kidney the bicarbonate concentration is 17 mEq/L. These data show clearly that bicarbonate reabsorption and acidification of the urine in the nephrons of the dog kidney are initiated in the proximal convoluted tubule. Continued bicarbonate reabsorption and urine acidification (hydrogen ion secretion) occur in the distal convoluted tubule and probably also in the collecting duct.

The reactions of hydrogen ion with bicarbonate and

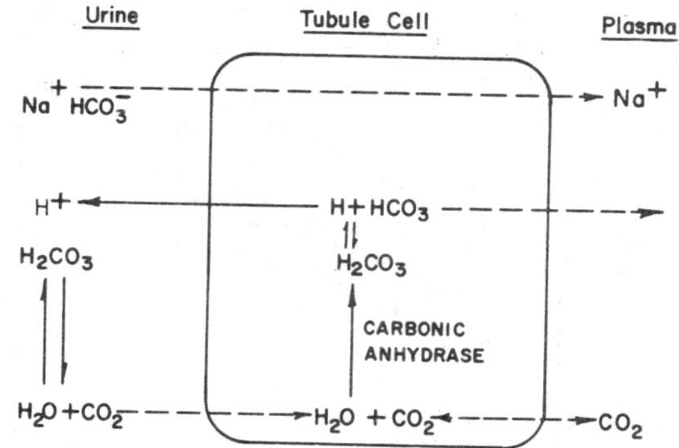

Diagram 1. Hydrogen ion reacting with bicarbonate

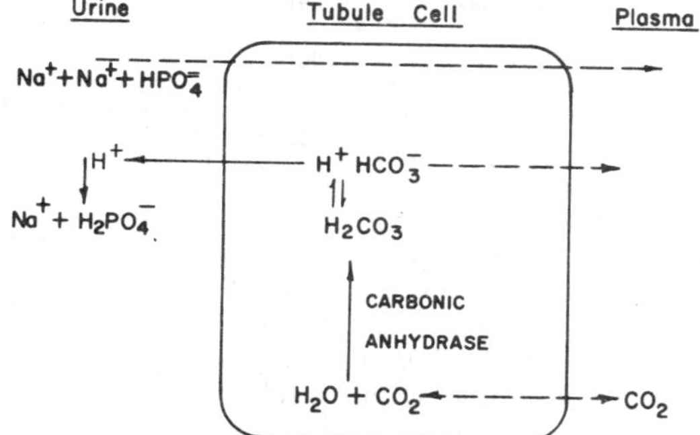

Diagram 2. Hydrogen ion reacting with disodium phosphate

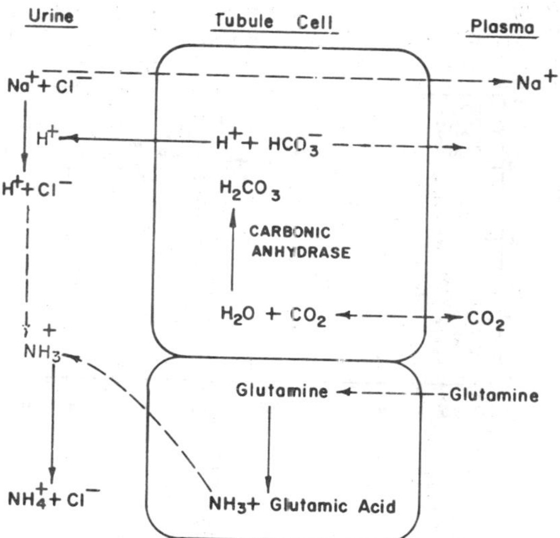

Diagram 3. Hydrogen ion reacting with sodium chloride

anions such as phosphate and chloride occur in both the proximal and distal convoluted tubules and in the collecting ducts. The ultimate pH of urine is determined, however, by the rate of hydrogen ion transport into the distal tubular fluids. During the formation of an acid urine, the concentration of hydrogen ions into either the proximal or the distal tubular fluids would limit continued acidification of the urine. Continuing acidification is made possible by ammonia diffusion into the tubular fluid, thereby buffering the acid as ammonium salts (Diagram 3). The enzymatic hydrolysis of glutamine to form glutamic acid and ammonia is catalyzed by a carbamase system named glutaminase. Ammonia enters the tubular fluid by diffusion, the adequate stimulus for its release into urine being an acid urine, that is, a pH gradient favoring the diffusion of ammonia into urine and formation of ammonium ions.

Potassium ions, filtered across the glomeruli into the tubular filtrate, are almost completely reabsorbed by the proximal convoluted tubules. An active transport process has been indicated in potassium reabsorption. The appearance of potassium in urine may result from either a transport process in the distal convoluted tubules and collecting ducts, which functions primarily as an ion ex-

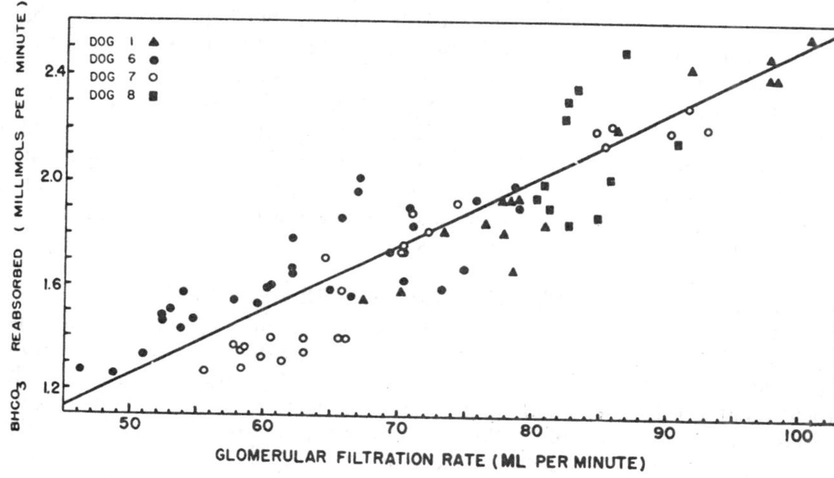

Figure 37.9. Renal reabsorption of bicarbonate in the dog as a function of the rate of glomerular filtration. All reabsorptive capacities were determined at plasma bicarbonate concentrations well above the renal threshold. Filtration rate in a given animal was varied by fasting and by feeding meat. (From Pitts and Lotspeich 1946. *Am. J. Physiol.* 147:138–54.)

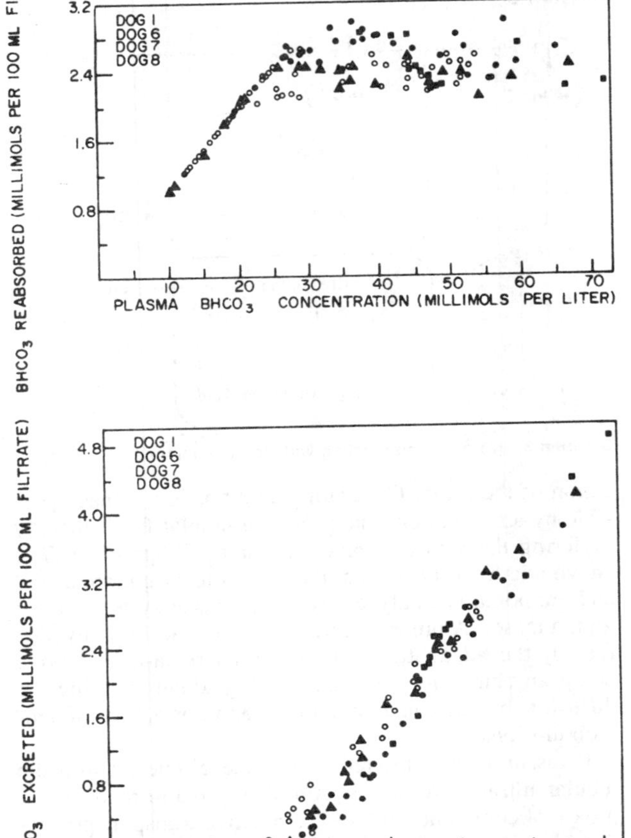

Figure 37.10. Renal reabsorption and excretion of bicarbonate in the dog as a function of plasma concentration. (From Pitts and Lotspeich 1946, *Am. J. Physiol.* 147:138–54.)

change process, or from the diffusion of potassium down a favorable electrochemical gradient from the interior of the tubular cells into the tubular fluid. The physiological stimulus from initiating potassium secretion is the transport of sodium from the tubular fluid, particularly if hydrogen ion secretion is suppressed. Secretion of potassium into urine also may be markedly increased by the intravenous infusion or oral ingestion of potassium salts, although the plasma concentration of potassium remains unchanged. Under these circumstances, an increase in the concentration of potassium within the renal cells probably serves as the stimulus to secretion. Potassium and hydrogen ions may utilize a common transport or diffusion pathway, and in general a reciprocal relationship exists between the secretion of these two ions. The secretory patterns of potassium and hydrogen are compatible

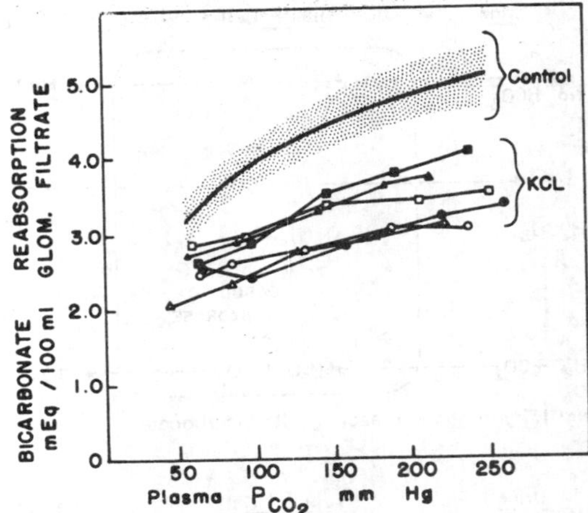

Figure 37.11. Effect of K^+ administration on the relationship between HCO_3^- reabsorption and plasma P_{CO_2} in the presence of intact carbonic acid anhydrase. The shaded area represents the range of HCO_3^- reabsorption at different plasma CO_2 tensions in control dogs not fed KCl. (From F.C. Rector, Jr., H. Buttram, and D.W. Seldin 1962, *J. Clin. Invest.* 41:611–17.)

with the concept that there is reciprocity between the two ions for the transport or diffusion system (see Fig. 37.11). The metabolic state of the organism determines whether potassium or hydrogen ions will be preferentially transported into urine by this mechanism.

The urinary excretion of ions, particularly sodium and potassium, does not always conform to a stoichiometric relationship which would be anticipated on the basis of ion exchange mechanisms. The administration of excess potassium salts to the dog is followed by the rapid excretion of the excess potassium into urine without corresponding increases in sodium reabsorption. The adequate stimulus for potassium excretion into urine would appear to be the increased concentration of potassium in the intracellular fluid of the tubular cells. Potassium may be transported by some carrier system from the tubular cell into the lumen of the tubules, but it is more likely that potassium diffuses along a favorable electrochemical gradient from the intracellular to the tubular fluid.

Calcium and magnesium are reabsorbed primarily from the glomerular filtrate in the proximal convoluted tubules. Transport of calcium also occurs in the ascending limb of Henle's loop and in the distal tubules. Calcium transport is an active process and may be linked to the sodium transport system.

MEASUREMENTS OF RENAL FUNCTION

The simplest method of quantitating renal function is to measure the total output of urine over a 24 hour period and to relate it to the amount of water ingested. Such methods can be utilized effectively to estimate the capacity of the kidneys to concentrate urine or, on the other hand, to excrete either a water or a solute load. These procedures, however, do not provide any information about the rate of filtration, the total blood flow through the kidney, and the relationship between filtration and solute excretion and between water reabsorption and excretion. The concept of renal clearance has been employed for the analyses of the more discrete aspects of renal function.

Renal clearance

Estimations of GFR may be performed under the following conditions. Assume that a chemical, I, is available which can be shown to be excreted into urine by filtration only, regardless of the status of renal function, that is, whether the kidney is elaborating a dilute or concentrated urine. This substance would neither be added to the tubular fluid by some transport mechanism nor would it be reabsorbed from the tubular fluid. If a stable concentration of the chemical is maintained in blood by constant infusion, all of the drug appearing in the urine will have resulted from filtration through the glomeruli. Monitoring the rate of urine flow will provide a measure of the rate of excretion of the drug. If U_I = concentration of drug I in urine (mg/ml) and V = flow rate of urine (ml/min), then $U_I \times V$ = mg drug I per ml urine × ml urine/min = mg drug excreted/min. Since the drug was eliminated by filtration only, the amount excreted into urine per minute equals the amount filtered through the glomeruli per minute. If one knows the plasma concentration, the filtration rate can be calculated:

$$\text{GFR} = \frac{\text{mg drug excreted/min}}{\text{mg drug/ml plasma}} = \text{ml plasma/min}$$

$$= \frac{U_I\,(\text{mg/ml urine}) \times V\,(\text{ml urine/min})}{P_I\ (\text{mg/ml plasma})}$$

Example: A dog weighing 20 kg was moderately hydrated to give a urine flow of 3.5 ml/min. About 1 hour prior to the actual study, a priming dose of chemical I was given intravenously followed immediately by the administration of chemical I by constant intravenous infusion. A 1-hour period was allowed for equilibration. Urine samples were then collected for four 15-minute periods, and blood samples were taken between the eighth and tenth minute of each urine collection. The urine flow rate remained steady at 4 ml/min. The concentration of chemical I in plasma was 0.2 mg/ml and in urine 2.8 mg/ml.

$$\text{GFR} = \frac{U_I \times V}{P_I} = \frac{2.8\ \text{mg/ml} \times 4\ \text{ml/min}}{0.2\ \text{mg/ml}} = 56\ \text{ml/min}$$

The rate of filtration in this experiment was 56 ml/min, that is, 56 ml plasma had to be filtered in 1 minute in order to provide the amount of chemical I (inulin) excreted into urine each minute. Another interpretation is that 56 ml of plasma were cleared of chemical I in each minute—this is referred to as the clearance of the chemical, designated as C_I. Since the chemical was excreted by filtration only, the clearance of the chemical was a measure of the rate of glomerular filtration; that is, C_I = GFR.

A number of compounds have been used to estimate GFR. The most popular and most applicable is the fructose polymer, inulin. Creatinine also has been employed in the dog. Exogenous creatinine may be infused intravenously, or endogenous true creatinine (ETC) may be determined, since the rate of formation of creatinine and its concentration in plasma usually remain relatively constant. Creatinine may be subject to some degree of tubular secretion in the male dog; the creatinine clearance (C_{cr}) in the male dog therefore would be an overestimation of the GFR. However, the ratio of creatinine clearance to inulin clearance does not deviate from 1 to any considerable extent, and creatinine continues to be used as a reasonable indicator of the GFR in the dog.

Clearance techniques may also be employed to estimate the effective renal plasma flow, that is, the amount of plasma which perfuses functioning renal tissue. Certain substances are not only filtered but also may be added to the tubular fluid from plasma by active transport systems. Many of these compounds, when maintained at low concentrations in plasma, are virtually completely extracted from the renal circulation. (They are completely extracted from blood perfusing the functional transport elements; a small amount of the renal plasma flow perfuses nonfunctional, i.e. nonextracting tissue, and complete extraction cannot be anticipated—hence the use of the term effective renal plasma flow.) Under these circumstances, the rate of excretion is a measure of the renal plasma flow. The most commonly used chemical for estimating the effective renal plasma flow is *p*-aminohippurate (PAH).

For example, assume that in the experiment discussed above for the estimation of the GFR, PAH also was included in the infusion. During the 15-minute periods in which urine flow was monitored and blood samples taken, the following concentrations of PAH were recovered: U_{PAH} = 1.1 mg/ml urine and P_{PAH} = 0.02 mg/ml plasma. Then

$$C_{PAH} = \frac{U_{PAH} \times V}{P_{PAH}} = \frac{1.1\ \text{mg/ml} \times 4\ \text{ml/min}}{0.02\ \text{mg/ml}} = 220\ \text{ml/min}$$

The PAH clearance (C_{PAH}) was 220 ml plasma/min, i.e. 220 ml of plasma were cleared of PAH per minute or the effective renal plasma flow (ERPF) was 220 ml/min. ERBF may be calculated from the PCV (packed cell volume):

$$\text{ERBF} = \frac{\text{ERPF}}{1 - \text{PCV}}$$

The ratio of the inulin clearance to the clearance of PAH indicates the percentage of the effective renal plasma flow which was filtered by the glomeruli and is referred to as the filtration fraction.

Renal clearance is used to indicate the manner of disposition of a given substance known to be excreted into urine. If the clearance of a given substance is determined concurrently with the inulin clearance, the ratio of the individual clearance provides a measure of the degree to which renal excretion resulted from filtration and a combination of reabsorption or tubular secretion.

$\frac{C_X}{C_I} = 1$; substance x was excreted solely by filtration.

$\frac{C_X}{C_I} < 1$; substance x was both filtered and to some extent reabsorbed.

$\frac{C_X}{C_I} > 1$; substance x was both filtered and secreted into urine.

Quantitative estimates of solute and water excretion into urine may be obtained from the general formulas for renal clearances. The osmolality of urine and plasma may be determined conveniently with a freezing-point depression osmometer, and the osmolal clearance (C_{osm}) would be obtained from these data.

Example: A dog is excreting concentrated urine. The urine flow rate is 0.3 ml/min, plasma osmolality is 310 mOsm/kg H_2O, and urine osmolality 1860 mOsm/kg H_2O.

$$C_{osm} = \frac{U_{osm} \times V}{P_{osm}}$$

$$= \frac{1860 \text{ mOsm/kg } H_2O \times 0.3 \text{ ml/min}}{310 \text{ mOsm/kg } H_2O} = 1.8 \text{ ml/min}$$

The osmolal clearance indicates that 1.8 ml of plasma were cleared of solute per minute; that is, this is the volume of plasma water in which the excreted solute would have to be dissolved in order to be isosmotic with plasma. It is also evident that in order to produce urine which was six times as concentrated as plasma ($U_{osm}/P_{osm} = 1860/310 = 6$), a quantity of solute-free water had to be extracted from the tubular fluid. This quantity of solute-free water would represent the difference between the amount of plasma cleared of solute per minute (C_{osm}) and the amount of fluid ultimately excreted per minute as urine (V):

$$T^C_{H_2O} = C_{osm} - V = 1.8 - 0.3 = 1.5$$

Solute-free water reabsorption ($T^C_{H_2O}$) was 1.5 ml/min, that is, 1.5 ml of solute-free water was extracted from the tubular fluid per minute in order to concentrate the urine to 1860 mOsm/kg H_2O. It is often desirable to compare $T^C_{H_2O}$ in groups of experimental animals which may be of varying sizes and have different surface areas. Such comparisons are made by performing simultaneous inulin clearances and then determining the percentage of the glomerular filtrate that was reabsorbed as solute-free water. If $T^C_{H_2O} = 1.5$ ml/min and $C_I(GFR) = 56$ ml/min, the ratio

$$\frac{1.5 \text{ ml/min}}{56 \text{ ml/min}}$$

indicates 2.68 percent of the glomerular filtrate was reabsorbed as solute-free water.

The extent of solute-free water excretion (more generally termed solute-free water clearance, C_{H_2O}) during water diuresis also may be estimated from the osmolal clearance. For example, if a dog is hydrated to produce a urine flow of 17 ml/min with a plasma osmolality of 298 mOsm/kg H_2O and a urine osmolality of 40 mOsm/kg H_2O, the osmolal clearance would be:

$$C_{osm} = \frac{U_{osm} \times V}{P_{osm}}$$

$$= \frac{40 \text{ mOsm/kg } H_2O \times 17 \text{ ml/min}}{298 \text{ mOsm/kg } H_2O} = 2.28 \text{ ml/min}$$

Thus 2.28 ml of plasma were cleared per min of solute, but the urine flow was 14.72 ml/min in excess of the amount of plasma cleared of solute:

$$C_{H_2O} = V - C_{osm} = 17 - 2.28 = 14.72$$

Therefore, 14.72 ml of solute-free water were excreted per minute in order to dilute the urine to an osmolality less than 15 percent that of plasma:

$$U_{osm}/P_{osm} = \frac{40 \text{ mOsm/kg } H_2O}{298 \text{ mOsm/kg } H_2O} = 0.134$$

If the GFR in this experiment had been determined simultaneously and was found to be 56 ml/min, 26.3 percent of the glomerular filtrate (14.72/56) would have been excreted as solute-free water.

The urea clearance often is employed as an indirect measure of GFR. However, the physical properties of urea complicate its passage through the nephrons and alter to some extent the interpretation which may be applied to the urea clearance. Urea is a relatively small nonionic substance, is very soluble in an aqueous medium, and diffuses readily across most biological membranes. For example, the concentrations of urea in plasma and in the erythrocytes are identical because of the rapid and uninhibited diffusion of urea between the interior of the erythrocytes and their environment. The glomerular membranes offer no barrier to urea, and it readily diffuses into the nephron with other constituents of plasma which make up a glomerular filtrate. Approximately 30–40 percent of the filtered urea is reabsorbed as the tubular fluid passes through the proximal convoluted tubules.

The fate of urea in the more distal segments of the nephrons depends upon the rate of urine flow. Some urea is added to the filtrate as the fluid enters the medullary interstitium in the descending limb of Henle's loop. If the kidney is excreting a concentrated urine, a considerable portion of the urea will be returned by diffusion from the collecting ducts into the medullary interstitium (see Fig. 37.7). Under these circumstances, the urea clearance will be considerably less than the inulin clearance.

Example: Simultaneous inulin and urea clearances are determined in a 40 kg dog deprived of water for 30 hours:

$$V = 0.3 \text{ ml/min} \qquad U_I = 42 \text{ mg/ml}$$
$$P_I = 0.2 \text{ mg/ml}$$
$$U_{urea} = 28 \text{ mg/ml}$$
$$P_{urea} = 30 \text{ mg/100 ml}$$

$$C_I = \frac{42 \text{ mg/ml} \times 0.3 \text{ ml/min}}{0.2 \text{ mg/ml}} = 63 \text{ ml/min}$$

$$C_{urea} = \frac{28 \text{ mg/ml} \times 0.3 \text{ ml/min}}{0.3 \text{ mg/ml}}$$
$$= 28 \text{ ml/min (observed clearance)}$$

$$\frac{C_{urea}}{C_I} = \frac{28}{63} = 0.44$$

Thus 44 percent of filtered urea was excreted into urine, or 28 ml of plasma were cleared of urea per minute.

Increased urine flow rates are accompanied by an increase in the urea clearance, that is, an increase in the amount of urea excreted into urine (Fig. 37.12). This increased output of urea occurs as the fluid in the collecting ducts fails to become concentrated and the concentration of urea in the collecting duct fluid becomes less than the concentration of urea in the medullary interstitial fluid. Smaller quantities of urea therefore diffuse from the tubular fluid into the medullary interstitium and urea is excreted at an augmented rate.

Example: Simultaneous inulin and urea clearances are determined in a 40 kg dog that has been adequately hydrated:

$$V = 4 \text{ ml/min} \qquad U_I = 3.2 \text{ mg/ml}$$
$$P_I = 0.2 \text{ mg/ml}$$
$$U_{urea} = 3.2 \text{ mg/ml}$$
$$P_{urea} = 30 \text{ mg/100 ml}$$

$$C_I = \frac{3.2 \text{ mg/ml} \times 4 \text{ ml/min}}{0.2 \text{ mg/ml}} = 64 \text{ ml/min}$$

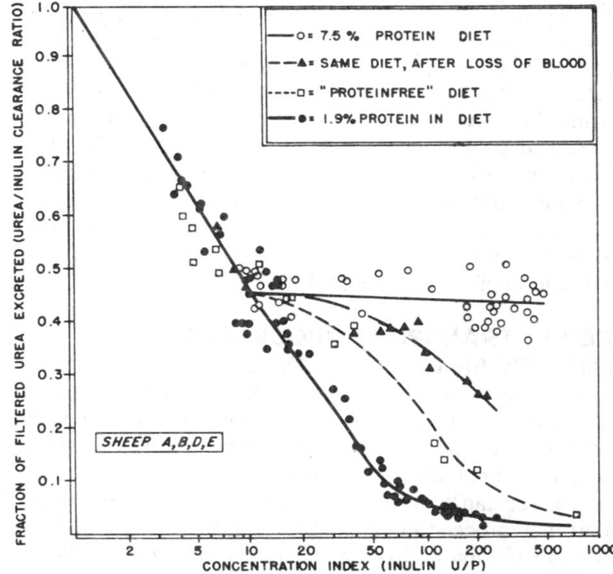

Figure 37.12. Effect of urine flow upon urea excretion during normal and low protein intake. All data on constant or slowly falling urine flow have been included. (From Schmidt-Nielsen, Osaki, Murdaugh, and O'Dell 1958, *Am. J. Physiol.* 194:221–28.)

$$C_{urea} = \frac{3.2 \text{ mg/ml} \times 4 \text{ ml/min}}{0.3 \text{ mg/ml}} = 43 \text{ ml/min}$$

$$\frac{C_{urea}}{C_I} = \frac{43}{64} = 0.67$$

Under these conditions 67 percent of the filtered urea was excreted into urine. The urea clearance, when determined at urine flow rates greater than 2 ml/min also has been called the maximum urea clearance, and the urea clearance under these circumstances represents 65–70 percent of the GFR.

The urea clearance often is used clinically as an estimate of GFR, the assumption being that the urea clearance represents between 70 and 75 percent of GFR. At low urine flows, the observed urea clearance, therefore, would underestimate the GFR. Reasonably adequate corrections can be made by calculating the standard clearance which becomes a function of $\sqrt{V}$ at urine flow rates less than 2 ml/min. In the experiment noted above, the calculations would be:

$$C_{urea} \text{ (standard)} = \frac{U \times \sqrt{V}}{P}$$

$$= \frac{28 \text{ mg/ml} \times \sqrt{0.3 \text{ ml/min}}}{0.3 \text{ mg/ml}} = 51 \text{ ml/min}$$

$$\frac{C_{urea}}{C_I} = \frac{51}{63} = 0.81$$

These results indicate that the estimated urea clearance was 81 percent of the GFR.

The relationship between urea clearance and urine flow rates is shown in Figure 37.12. Even at considerable urine dilutions, that is, $U/P_I < 10$, the ratio between the urea and creatinine clearances does not equal 1. These data emphasize the role of urea reabsorption from the proximal convoluted tubules in determining the ultimate rate of urea excretion at high urine flow rates. They should also indicate that the urea clearance at best is only a rough approximation of GFR.

RENAL TRANSPORT PROCESSES FOR ORGANIC COMPOUNDS

The routes by which complex organic compounds pass through the kidney depend largely upon the physical properties of the compounds and the capacity of the kidney to channel some of its metabolic energy for transport of the substance across the tubular barriers. Renal transport may proceed in either direction, that is, from tubular fluid to plasma or from plasma into the tubular fluid. In addition, a large number of compounds are subject to bidirectional fluxes, and the ultimate quantity excreted into urine will result from the total effects of glomerular filtration, tubular secretion, and reabsorption.

Highly polar substances generally are excreted into urine by glomerular filtration. Because of their polarity, these substances exist in urine in their ionic or dissociated forms. The nephrons, in common with most biological membranes, are relatively impermeable to ions, and reabsorption cannot take place without the involvement of some metabolically linked transport system. Examples of highly polar substances which are eliminated into urine by filtration only include such drugs as the bisquaternary ammonium compound hexamethonium.

The urinary excretion rate of many weak proton donors or acceptors is determined by the dissociation constants (pK) of the compounds, the pH of the tubular fluid, and the lipid solubility of the undissociated compounds. A weak proton donor having a pKa of 7.8 would exist largely in the undissociated form in the fluid of the proximal convoluted tubule (and also the distal convoluted tubules if the kidney is excreting an acid urine) as the result of hydrogen ion secretion into the tubular fluid. If the undissociated form of the chemical is highly lipid soluble, considerable quantities of the filtered load would diffuse from the tubular fluid into plasma, as concentration of the chemical in the fluid of the proximal and distal convoluted tubules provided a favorable gradient for diffusion. The clearance of this substance therefore would be less than the clearance of inulin. Alkalinization of the urine, by administering large quantities of sodium bicarbonate, would increase the pH of the filtrate in the distal convoluted tubules and more of the chemical would remain in its dissociated form, thus enhancing its excretion into urine; that is, the clearance of the chemical would approach the clearance of inulin. Weak proton acceptors having pKb's of 1 or less would behave in a reciprocal fashion; an acid urine would favor their excretion into urine, while an alkaline urine would enhance reabsorption.

Active transport

A number of organic compounds are concentrated in urine or reabsorbed from the tubular fluid to an extent which indicates that the tubular cells performed work in accomplishing their transport. The active participation of tubular cells has been termed active transport. A transport system is active when it meets the following requirements: (1) the chemical involved is moved against its concentration or electrochemical gradient, (2) the process has an obligatory requirement for metabolic energy, (3) the chemical structure of the compound is not altered by the transport system, and (4) the system exhibits a maximum rate at which the compound may be transported.

Glucose

Glucose reabsorption from the tubular filtrate in the proximal convoluted tubules is a classic example of an active transport system. Glucose is transported against a concentration gradient (at normal plasma levels of approximately 100 mg/100 ml plasma, all of the filtered glucose is reabsorbed) by a process which requires metabolic energy. Glucose is not chemically altered; for example, it is not phosphorylated during reabsorption. The hexose can be reabsorbed up to a maximal rate, and when glucose load exceeds this reabsorptive limit it is excreted into urine.

Quantitative aspects of glucose transport are shown in Figure 37.13. As the filtered load of glucose in the dog is increased by increasing its concentration in plasma, the amount reabsorbed also increases, and the urine remains free of hexose. At plasma glucose concentrations in excess of 250 mg/100 ml, the fraction of the filtered glucose which is reabsorbed is less than 100 percent, and glucose is excreted into urine. Further increments in plasma glucose concentrations result in additional increases in the amount excreted, indicating that the maximum rate of glucose transport has been attained.

Quantitatively, these two relationships may be calculated as follows, assuming a GFR (inulin clearance) of 50 ml/min: Glucose excreted into urine = glucose filtered − glucose reabsorbed. $U_{Gl} \times V = P_{Gl} \times GFR - Tm_{Gl}$. The tubular or transport maximum capacity for glucose, Tm_{Gl}, occurred when the plasma concentration was 250 mg/100 ml or greater. The Tm_{Gl} was 140 mg/min in a dog with GFR of 50 ml/min.

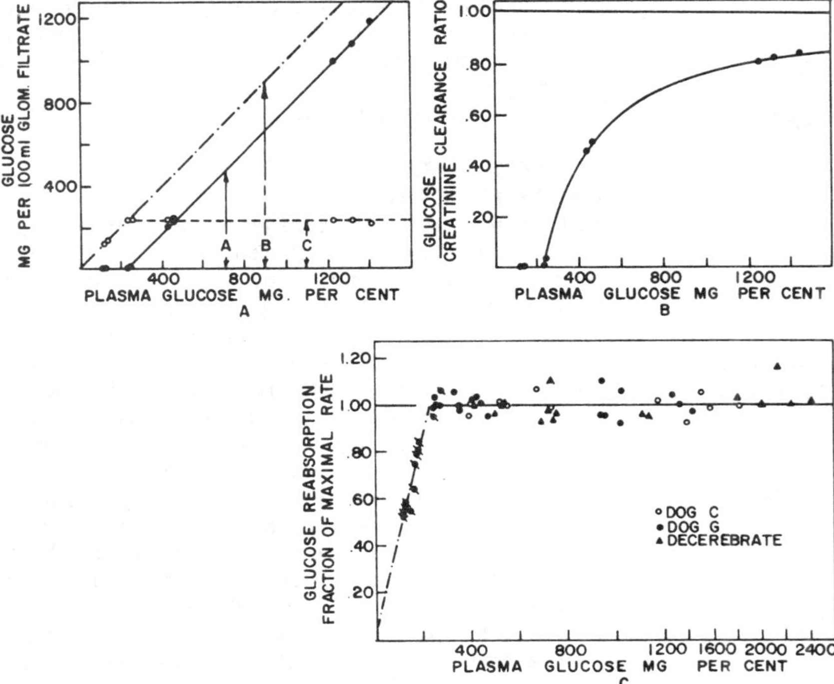

Figure 37.13. Glucose transport. A. Glucose filtration (line B), reabsorption (line C), and excretion (line A) (mg/min). B. In consequence of the relationship shown here, the glucose/creatinine clearance ratio (the fraction of filtered glucose which is excreted) rises as the plasma level is increased and approaches 1 as a limiting value. The curve is calculated on the assumption that 234 mg of glucose (per 100 ml of glomerular filtrate) can be reabsorbed. C. Relationship between glucose reabsorption and plasma concentration and the genesis of the glucose threshold. The maximal rate of glucose reabsorption in each of seven experiments has been taken as the mean of the individual observations at plasma concentrations above the level of frank glycuresis. The rate of glucose reabsorption in each period of the experiment has then been expressed as the fraction of this mean value. The broken line shows the relationship to the expected in dog G, taking into account the mean rate of filtration and maximal reabsorption in this dog, and assuming that all filtered glucose is reabsorbed up to the maximal rate. The crossed symbols indicate observations where more than 99 percent of the filtered glucose has been reabsorbed. (From J.A. Shannon and S. Fisher 1938, *Am. J. Physiol.* 122:765–74; Shannon 1938, *Am. J. Physiol.* 122:782–87.)

Amino acids

Amino acids filtered through the glomeruli are reabsorbed by several discrete active transport systems. The basic amino acids, lysine, arginine, and histidine, share a common transport system and competition among them can be shown. Two other amino acid transport systems have been identified, one which reabsorbs leucine and isoleucine, and another involved with the reabsorption of proline, hydroxyproline, and glycine. Amino acid reabsorption requires the presence of pyridoxal phosphate, and it has been suggested that a complex is formed by the amino acid pyridoxal phosphate and a metallic ion (Mg^{++}). This complex probably facilitates the transport of amino acids from the tubular filtrate into the intracellular pool of amino acids and subsequently into the peritubular blood flow.

Para-aminohippurate

Tubular transport from plasma into urine is the mechanism by which a large group of organic acids are primarily eliminated into urine. The transport of PAH (*p*-aminohippurate) has been well defined both in vitro and in vivo and serves as a model for the active transport systems which concentrate organic chemicals in urine. PAH transport into the tubular fluid is a function of the proximal convoluted tubules and can be competitively inhibited by compounds such as iodopyracet and penicillin which utilize the same transport process. Although PAH is a relatively weak acid, its undissociated form is poorly lipid soluble. Therefore, all of the PAH transferred into the tubular fluid is excreted even when the urine is acid. At low plasma concentrations, all of the PAH is extracted from the plasma perfusing the cortex, and the PAH clearance may be used as an estimate of the effective renal plasma flow. Increasing the concentration of PAH in plasma results in increased urinary output of PAH which approximates the transport rate of PAH. When concentrations of PAH exceed 15–18 mg/100 ml of plasma, the excretion of PAH into urine becomes parallel to the amount filtered, which indicates saturation of the transport system (Fig. 37.14). The Tm_{PAH} in a dog having a GFR of 50 ml/min and ERPF of 290 ml/min would be 15 mg PAH/min.

At high plasma concentrations, a portion of the plasma PAH may be bound to plasma proteins and therefore is nonfilterable. The clearance formula must be corrected to account for protein binding:

$$Tm_{PAH} = U_{PAH} \times V - f(P_{PAH} \times GFR)$$

when f is the percentage of the total plasma PAH concentration that is filterable. The fact that in the dog f is approximately 92 indicates that even at high plasma concentrations more than 90 percent of the PAH is filterable.

Other weak organic acids also may be transported by

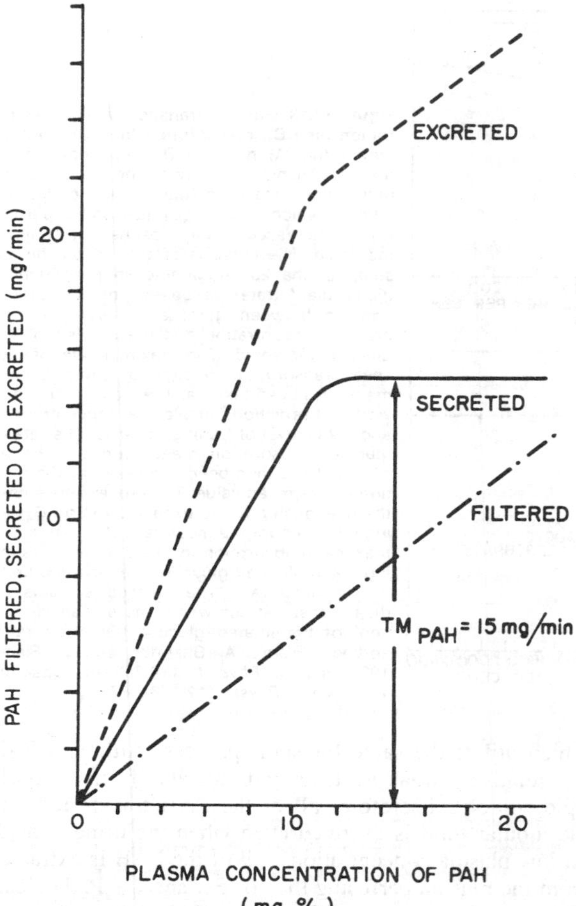

Figure 37.14. Relationship between the plasma concentration and the amount of PAH filtered, secreted, and excreted in the dog. GFR and RPF are assumed to be constant.

the proximal convoluted tubules from plasma into urine and yet have clearances which approximate or even are less than the inulin clearances. These acids—e.g. probenecid—are lipid soluble in the undissociated form and may diffuse back into plasma from the tubular fluid of the more distal segments of the nephrons.

Organic anions such as N-methylnicotinamide also are actively transported into urine. Other quaternary ammonium compounds share this system and also compete for transport with N-methylnicotinamide. This system, however, is functionally distinct from the PAH transport system.

Uric acid

Uric acid is formed from the degradation of purines, adenine, and guanine. With the exception of man and higher apes mammals convert uric acid to allantoin by action of the enzyme uricase. The end products of purine metabolism are eliminated in urine by a combination of filtration, secretion, and reabsorption. In the Dalmatian a secretory component is dominant and often results in the accumulation of urate calculi, which may produce obstructive pathology in the urinary tract.

HORMONAL REGULATION OF RENAL FUNCTION

Antidiuretic hormone and water conservation

Water conservation is regulated by the hypothalamo-neurohypophyseal system through the mediation of one of its hormones, ADH. The dog, in common with most mammals, synthesizes arginine ADH. This hormone, alone with oxytocin, is synthesized in hypothalamic nuclei and is carried, apparently by axoplasmic flow, to the neurohypophysis, where it is stored in specialized cells, the pituicytes. ADH release occurs as increases in plasma osmolality, for example, during water deprivation, stimulate osmoreceptors that are located in the hypothalamus and possibly in other areas of the CNS. Neural pathways carry the impulses from these osmoreceptors through the median eminence and into the neurohypophysis. Other stimuli that reflexly stimulate ADH release include decreases in the extracellular fluid volume, fear, and pain. ADH alters the permeability of the distal segments of the nephrons favoring the diffusion of solute-free water and urea from the tubular fluid of the distal convoluted tubules into the peritubular blood and from the fluid in the collecting ducts into the hypertonic medullary interstitium. ADH release is inhibited by overhydration and reduction in plasma osmolality, thus permitting the kidneys to excrete excess water as hypotonic urine. Destruction of the hypothalamo-neurohypophyseal system results in a syndrome known as diabetes insipidus, which is characterized by the excretion of large volumes of hypotonic urine and the compulsive ingestion of equally large quantities of water.

Specific ADH-sensitive receptors located in renal medullary cells are linked to membrane-bounded adenylate cyclase. Stimulation of the receptors by ADH results in increased activity of the cyclase, accelerating the formation of cyclic AMP. Increased amounts of the cyclic nucleotide then activate by phosphorylation a protein kinase which, in turn, probably initiates a series of enzymatic activations resulting ultimately in the increased permeability of the collecting ducts to water and urea. The sequential effects initiated by cyclic AMP in kidney medullary cells resemble the cyclic AMP-induced cascade effect in the liver which leads to activation of phosphorylase and to glycogenolysis.

Adenohypophyseal hormones

Adenohypophyseal hormones also influence renal function. Growth hormone (somatotropin) exerts a tropic effect on the kidney; when given to the hypophysectomized animal, growth hormone results in increases in GFR, ERPF, and TM_{PAH}. Thyroid-stimulating hormone (TSH) indirectly produces effects similar to those of growth hormone, the mediation of these changes being a function of the thyroid hormones, triiodothyronine, and thyroxine. Adrenocorticotropic hormone (ACTH) produces effects on renal function which are mediated directly by the steroid hormones secreted by the adrenal cortex.

Adrenal cortex

Aldosterone

Adrenal insufficiency in the dog is characterized by a loss of sodium chloride and water into urine and the retention of potassium and urea in plasma. The administration of cortisol (hydrocortisone), deoxycorticosterone, or aldosterone promptly reverses these disturbances and simultaneously increases both GFR and ERPF. Aldosterone is now recognized as a primary mediator of the renal regulation of sodium and potassium equilibrium. This function is due to a direct tubular effect of the hormone that permits normal rates of sodium reabsorption and potassium excretion.

As with other steroid hormones, the initial event in aldosterone activity is its binding to specific receptors in the cytoplasm of renal cells. The receptor-hormone complex apparently provides the means by which aldosterone is carried into the cell nucleus where it influences transcription leading to the production of messenger RNA (mRNA).

Renin-angiotensin system

The kidney not only is the target organ of aldosterone but also participates in the regulation of aldosterone secretion by the adrenal cortex. The juxtaglomerular cells of the kidney produce the proteolytic enzyme renin, which is liberated into the systemic circulation. This enzyme reacts with an α_2-globulin to produce a decapeptide known as angiotensin I. An ubiquitous peptidase referred to as converting enzyme releases two amino acid residues from the decapeptide to form the octapeptide angiotensin II, which in the dog has the following amino acid sequence: aspartyl-arginyl-valyl-tyrosyl-isoleucyl-histadyl-prolyl-phenylalanine. Angiotensin II, a powerful vasoconstrictor, stimulates aldosterone secretion by the zona glomerulosa of the adrenal cortex. Renal regulation of aldosterone secretion is further modulated by the presence in the kidney of a peptidase, angiotensinase, which destroys the biological activity of angiotensin II.

Sodium reabsorption and potassium excretion proceed under normal circumstances through the "permissive" influence of aldosterone. Changes in sodium reabsorption and potassium excretion in response to changes in body position and to periodic alterations in dietary sodium or potassium are accommodated without alterations in the rate of aldosterone secretion. The imposition of more severe stress on the maintenance of ionic equilibria or the volume of the extracellular fluid is generally accompanied by increases in aldosterone secretion. For example, the chronic ingestion by the dog of a salt-free diet results in an increase in aldosterone secretion, and concurrently almost 100 percent of filtered sodium is reabsorbed from the tubular fluid. Decreases in total body exchangeable sodium may be adequate stimulus for aldosterone secretion by the glomerulosa cells in salt-depleted dogs, although stimulation by the renin-angiotensin system also may be involved.

The renin-angiotensin system is prominently activated by constriction of the vena cava, hemorrhage, and other circumstances which decrease the effective circulating blood volume. Another intrarenal regulator of renin secretion appears to be the rate of sodium or total solute entry into the fluid of the distal convoluted tubules. Increasing the amount of sodium or total solute which traverses the distal convoluted tubules appears to be a stimulus for renin secretion. Possibly the cells of the macula densa act as chemoreceptors in the initiation of renin secretion.

The sympathetic nervous system has been implicated in the release of renin from the kidney. Stimulation of the renal nerves is capable of altering the output of renin by the kidney independently of changes in arterial pressure. Enhanced secretion of renin by sympathetic stimulation appears to be mediated by β-adrenergic receptors.

Cortisol and water excretion

Cortisol produces effects on renal sodium reabsorption and potassium excretion which in general are similar to the effects of aldosterone. Under normal circumstances these effects are quantitatively of no physiological significance. Pathological increases in cortisol secretion, for example, the result of a functional (ACTH-secreting) adenoma of the adenohypophysis, produce marked increases in urinary potassium secretion and metabolic alkalosis in addition to widespread muscular atrophy, which reflects the catabolic effects of excess cortisol on muscle proteins. However, cortisol secreted in "permissive" quantitites assumes an important role in the maintenance of water equilibrium. The adrenalectomized animal shows a deficit in its capacity to excrete a water load, and this impairment is reversed by the administration of cortisol. The permissive presence of the gluconeogenic steroids such as cortisol enables the body to mobilize water for excretion or for translocation among body water compartments.

Parathyroid hormone

Calcium and phosphate excretion into urine is regulated by the hormones parathormone (from the parathyroid gland) and thyrocalcitonin (from the thyroid gland) (see Chapter 52). Parathormone from the parathyroid glands causes a decrease in phosphate reabsorption and an increase in phosphate excretion in urine. These changes are due to direct tubular effects. The administration of parathormone is accompanied by increases in calcium excretion in urine, but this effect may not indicate any specific responses in renal tubular transport of calcium. The primary effect of the parathyroid hormone on calcium metabolism is the result of mobilization of calcium from bone and enhanced absorption of calcium from the intestinal tract. As the result of parathyroid stimulation, plasma concentrations and consequently the filtered load of calcium are increased to an extent which exceeds the tubular reabsorptive capacity for calcium.

The relationship between ADH and adenylate cyclase of the kidney medulla has been discussed. A somewhat similar process is involved in the effects of parathyroid hormone (PTH). In this case specific receptors are located in the kidney cortex. When activated by PTH they increase the activity of renal cortical adenylate cyclase with subsequent increases in the formation of cyclic AMP. At least two significant kidney functions are mediated by PTH, presumably by PTH-induced cyclic AMP formation: regulation of phosphate excretion, and the hydroxylation of 25-hydroxycholecalciferol to 1,25-dihydroxycholecalciferol, the active form of vitamin D.

Prostaglandins

The kidney exerts significant influence over a number of endocrine functions. Renal production of erythropoietin represents an important regulator of erythropoiesis. Renin controls the production of angiotensin and aldosterone. The kidney, specifically certain medullary components, also produces an acidic lipid which possesses vasodepressor properties. This blood pressure–lowering substance probably is a prostaglandin of the E series.

Renal prostaglandins may be formed by one of the three types of interstitial cells which are located within the ground substance (the proteoglycans) of the kidney medulla. These kidney-derived prostaglandins not only decrease systemic blood pressure but, perhaps more significantly, alter intrarenal hemodynamics and net sodium balance. Prostaglandins of the E series are natriuretic, that is, they increase urinary sodium excretion and they increase blood flow through the medullary regions.

REFLEXES INFLUENCING RENAL FUNCTION

The intrinsic autonomy of the renal circulation maintains renal blood flow at a constant rate within the physiological range of blood pressure changes. However, certain reflex patterns include a sympathetic efferent pathway that alters the pattern of blood flow within the kidney. Decreases in blood pressure that activate the sympathetic nervous system result in a redistribution of the blood flow through the kidney. Cortical flow is diminished, and concurrently blood flow through the corticomedullary junctional area is augmented. Intense sympathetic stimulation of the renal vasculature results in (1) ischemia of the kidney cortex, (2) a washout of sodium chloride from the area in which sodium (chloride) transport participates in the production of the corticomedullary osmotic gradient, and (3) a decrease in the ability of the kidney to concentrate urine (Pomeranz et al. 1968).

The presence of volume receptors capable of sensing changes in the extracellular fluid volume has never been conclusively demonstrated, although considerable evidence supports this concept. For example, increasing acutely the extracellular fluid volume results in an increase in GFR and salt excretion. And a saline diuresis occurs in response to expansion of the extracellular fluid volume when the GFR is kept constant or even reduced (Levinsky and Lalone 1963). Expansion of the extracellular fluid volume therefore initiates a reflex which results in decreased NaCl reabsorption by the kidney, producing saline diuresis.

RENAL RESPONSES TO CHANGES IN pH, FLUID, AND ELECTROLYTE EQUILIBRIA

Metabolic acidosis

This derangement is characterized by a decrease in the bicarbonate buffer capacity of the extracellular fluid, and it occurs as hydrogen ion (acid) production exceeds the body's capacity to excrete hydrogen ions. When metabolic acidosis is compensated, the total carbon dioxide content of plasma is reduced, but the ratio $[HCO_3^-]/[H_2CO_3] + [CO_2]$ in the Henderson-Hasselbalch equation

$$pH = pKa + \log \frac{[HCO_3^-]}{[H_2CO_3] + [\text{dissolved } CO_2]}$$

$$= pKa + \log \frac{[HCO_3^-]}{s \cdot P_{CO_2}}$$

is maintained near 20; carbon dioxide is lost in proportion to the loss of bicarbonate, and the pH of plasma remains within normal limits. (S is the solubility coefficient of carbon dioxide.) Uncompensated metabolic acidosis supervenes as the loss of bicarbonate exceeds the loss of carbon dixoide and the ratio of plasma bicarbonate concentration to the carbonic acid-carbon dioxide concentrations decreases below 20. Under these circumstances the pH of plasma decreases.

The kidney responds to metabolic acidosis by increasing hydrogen ion secretion into urine and secondarily by enhancing bicarbonate reabsorption. Increased hydrogen ion secretion in exchange for sodium also provides a mechanism through which the kidney conserves fixed cation. Metabolic acidosis is usually accompanied by the increased formation of acetoacetate and β-hydroxybutyrate which are filtered into the tubular fluid but are poorly reabsorbed. These relatively impermeable salts obligate the excretion of sodium and to a smaller extent of potassium in the tubular fluid. As long as the production of these compounds does not exceed the kidney's capacity to secrete hydrogen ions, the loss of sodium into urine will be minimal. Hydrogen ion secretion in uncompensated metabolic acidosis is not sufficient to conserve sodium, and a considerable fraction of the filtered sodium is excreted into urine. In addition, the presence of the sodium salts of relatively impermeable anions in the fluid of the distal nephronal segments is accompanied by the excretion of potassium into urine, possibly in exchange for sodium. Potassium excretion under these circumstances may be of such magnitude as to result in hypokalemia.

Respiratory acidosis

The retention of carbon dioxide in the body at a rate which exceeds the formation of bicarbonate decreases the ratio

$$\log \frac{[HCO_3^-]}{[H_2CO_3] + [CO_2]} \text{ or } \log \frac{[HCO_3^-]}{s \cdot P_{CO_2}}$$

(s equals 0.03) and results in a decrease in the pH of extracellular fluid. The kidney compensates by increasing hydrogen ion secretion and the return of bicarbonate to the extracellular fluid. The increased P_{CO_2} of plasma tends to increase the $TmHCO_3^-$, thereby enhancing bicarbonate reabsorption. Compensation by the kidney usually does not return bicarbonate to plasma at a rate commensurate with the accumulation of carbon dioxide; the pH of plasma is not restored to normal.

Respiratory alkalosis

Hyperventilation results in a primary deficit of carbon dioxide which increases the ratio $[HCO_3^-]/[H_2CO_3] + [CO_2]$ and the pH of plasma. In response to the decrease in the P_{CO_2} of arterial blood, the kidney decreases the reabsorption of bicarbonate. Both respiratory loss of carbon dioxide and increased renal excretion of bicarbonate reduce the total bicarbonate buffer capacity and thereby aid the development of a secondary metabolic acidosis.

Metabolic alkalosis

Two primary factors result in the production of metabolic alkalosis: excessive ingestion of bicarbonate or loss of hydrochloric acid. Depletion of potassium plays a role in developing metabolic alkalosis. Excessive ingestion of sodium bicarbonate reduces the amount of hydorchloric acid in gastric juice for neutralization of bicarbonate ions secreted into the intestine by the pancreas. As increased amounts of bicarbonate are absorbed from the intestine, the bicarbonate concentration of the extracellular fluid is increased. The kidney, presented with a greater filtered load of bicarbonate, increases the secretion of hydrogen ions to maximal rates and secondarily increases the reabsorption of bicarbonate. The urine becomes alkaline because the amount of bicarbonate filtered into the tubular fluid is greater than the rate of hydrogen ion secretion.

Hydrochloric acid is lost from the body as the result of uncontrolled vomiting. The loss of both hydrochloric acid and water decreases the extracellular fluid volume, and there results a relative increase in bicarbonate concentration. The kidney reacts to this disturbance in water and electrolyte equilibrium by secreting a paradoxically acid urine. If vomiting has been of short duration, the administration of sodium chloride solution usually restores to normal the plasma concentrations of chloride and bicarbonate and decreases the acidification of the urine. However, the gastric juice, particularly under basal conditions, contains substantial quantities of potassium, as much as 30 mEq/L. Continued vomiting results in considerable loss of potassium and exaggeration of the alkalosis by potassium depletion.

Metabolic alkalosis accompanies potassium depletion whether negative potassium balance is produced by increased aldosterone secretion (the primary hyperaldosteronism of man), by the administration of aldosterone or deoxycorticosterone, or by the experimental feeding of potassium-free diets. There is, however, a relationship between concurrent chloride loss and the degree of metabolic alkalosis which develops. As long as adequate chloride is supplied, severe potassium depletion does not produce a prominent alkalosis. The kidney cells are affected, as are all cells of the body by the loss of potassium, but the manner in which the kidney compensates tends to exaggerate an existing alkalosis. The kidney increases hydrogen ion secretion into urine, and this in turn provokes increased reabsorption of bicarbonate.

Potassium depletion also reduces the kidney's capacity to concentrate urine. This defect is characterized by a decrease in solute-free water reabsorption and failure to concentrate urine to osmolality in excess of 800–900 mOsm/kg H_2O.

Renal acidosis and secondary hyperparathyroidism

Chronic nephritis in the dog is accompanied by dehydration, excessive salt loss, anemia, acidosis, and ammonia retention. The derangements in fluid and electrolyte equilibrium result from distortions in function and from the loss of functional renal tissue as connective tissue invades the interstitium of the kidney. The nephrons remaining in the fibrotic, contracted kidneys are incapable of maintaining hydrogen ion excretion in urine. This failure to excrete hydrogen ions is accompanied by a decrease in ammonia secretion by the kidney. The urine, under normal circumstances, is an important exit for ammonia, and in chronic nephritis ammoniacal end products of protein catabolism accumulate not only in urine but also in extracellular fluid.

Chronic renal failure in the dog and in man often is accompanied by the development of osteodystrophy. Loss of kidney tissue and function is accompanied by a decrease in the absorption of calcium from the intestine. As renal mass decreases, there is a comparable decrease in the renal hydroxylation of 25-hydroxycholecalciferol to 1,25-dihydroxycholecalciferol, the active form of vitamin D. The well-known phenomenon of resistance to even massive doses of vitamin D in chronic renal disease is a reflection of the decreased metabolism by the kidney of vitamin D to its active form. The decrease in plasma calcium concentrations is the stimulus for increased parathyroid secretion, which mobilizes calcium from bone. The secondary hyperparathyroidism actually decreases phosphate reabsorption by the nephrons, that is, increases the excretion of phosphate into urine. Hyperphosphatemia is not seen until the later stages of the disease when GFR has been reduced to 15–20 percent of the normal filtration rate.

COMPARATIVE RENAL PHYSIOLOGY

Two prominent characteristics distinguish the kidneys of lower vertebrates from the mammalian kidney: the presence of a renal portal system, and the absence of the thin segment of Henle's loop, that is, the absence of a medulla. The lower vertebrates therefore cannot concentrate urine much above the osmolality of plasma. Water balance among these animals depends not only upon the kidney but also other body systems, e.g. the gills of fish, the skin of amphibia, the cloaca of birds.

Sea water has an osmolality considerably higher than that of avian or mammalian plasma. The elasmobranchs have survived in this environment by retaining urea in plasma and in interstitial fluid and thereby raising the osmolality of plasma to that of sea water. The teleosts, however, ingest sea water, but an apparently well-developed sodium chloride transport system in the gills returns salt to the ocean, leaving an increment of solute-free water for urine formation. An unusual circumstance among the bony fishes is the occurrence of species of fish which have aglomerular kidneys. The tubules which make up these aglomerular kidneys are analogous to the middle and distal protions of the proximal convoluted tubules of the mammalian kidney and are well adapted for excretory functions.

The succession to a partially terrestrial habitat presented the amphibians with the problem of obtaining sufficient water to maintain renal excretory functions as well as the integrity of the fluid compartments of the body. This requirement is met by hormonally regulated diffusion of water across the amphibian skin. The neurohypophyseal hormone of the amphibians, vasotocin, influences the amphibian skin in a manner analogous to the effect of ADH on the mammalian nephron; that is, the hormone increases the rate of diffusion of water from the environment across the skin. Neurohypophyseal hormones also stimulate sodium transport from the environment into the extracellular fluid compartment by the amphibian skin.

Reptiles and birds

Water conservation is accomplished in these animals by a change in the pathway of protein catabolism and by the ability of the cloaca to serve as a site for water reabsorption. Both reptiles and birds form uric acid rather than urea as the end product of nitrogen metabolism. Uric acid is a relatively insoluble substance, and during the isosmotic reabsorption of the glomerular filtrate by the renal tubules, the solubility of uric acid is exceeded. Hence, urates precipitate from the tubular fluid, leaving a net increment of solute-free water. The urine and the precipitated urates are carried to the cloaca, and the liberated water is reabsorbed across the cloacal epithelium, leaving a concentrate of urate and fecal material for excretion. Some reptiles such as alligators and crocodiles excrete ammonia into urine in the form of ammonium bicarbonate.

Reptilian kidneys contain no medullary structures and therefore cannot elaborate a concentrated urine. Their nephrons, arranged in long parallel rows, are composed of glomeruli, proximal convoluted tubules, and elements comparable to the mammalian distal convoluted tubule.

The avian kidney contains two types of nephrons, a reptilian type with no Henle's loop, and a nephron resembling that of mammalian kidneys, containing a well-defined Henle's loop. In some birds, the loops of Henle of the mammalian-type nephrons are grouped into a medullary cone in which a corticomedullary osmotic gradient exists. These birds may excrete urine, which has an osmolality greater than the osmolality of plasma. In order to insure maximum water conservation, these kidneys may divert a major fraction of the renal blood flow from the reptilian to the mammalian type nephrons.

The renal portal system of birds has been used to study tubular transport systems. In experiments using chickens, the saphenous vein of one side is cannulated and test materials are infused. They reach the tubular segments of the ipsilateral kidney and secondarily reach the glomeruli of both kidneys only after entrance into the systemic circulation. Urine is collected from each ureter separately as the test substance is infused into the saphenous vein. If the material is excreted into urine by a tubular transport system, it will appear rapidly in the urine from the ipsilateral kidney, and after a delay, in the urine from the kidney of the opposite side. Substances eliminated into urine primarily by glomerular filtration will appear simultaneously and in equal concentration in the urine from both kidneys. With these techniques it has been shown that the nephrons of the chicken possess transport systems analogous to those of the mammalian nephrons.

Simple-stomached mammals

Differences in renal structure among mammals are due to varying types of nephrons and the relative thickness of the medulla (Table 37.3). The human kidney contains essentially two types of nephrons. The glomeruli of one group of nephrons, the cortical nephrons, are located in the central and more peripheral layers of the cortex; these nephrons have short thin segments which do not extend beyond the corticomedullary junctional area. The glomeruli of the second group, the juxtamedullary nephrons, lie within the deeper layers of the cortex and send long thin loops into the medulla. Juxtamedullary nephrons comprise about 14 percent of the nephron population of the human kidney. The sheep kidney contains three nephron types, a long-looped nephron comprising about 20 percent of the tubular elements and resembling the juxtamedullary nephrons of the human kidney, cortical nephrons analogous to the human type, and a third group the segments of which are confined solely to the cortex and possess a very small thin segment. Other species contain kidneys that are composed of all long-looped nephrons.

The relative depth of the medulla (the depth being measured from corticomedullary junction to the papilla or medullary crest) of the mammalian kidney is related to the kidney's capacity to concentrate urine (see Table 37.3). A greater medullary depth permits the kidney to concentrate urine to a greater osmolality. One of the most efficient urine-concentrating systems is found in the desert rodents—e.g. the kangaroo rat and the hamster—which have extremely long thin loops and a crest formed into a papilla which protrudes prominently into the renal pelvis. Surgical papillectomy markedly reduces the capacity of hamsters to concentrate urine.

Table 37.3. Relationship of structure to concentrating capacity in mammalian kidneys

Animal	Size (mm)	Long-looped nephrons (%)	Relative medullary thickness	Max. freez. pt. depression in urine (°C)
Beaver	36	0	1.3	0.96
Pig	66	3	1.6	2
Man	64	14	3	2.6
Dog *	40	100	4.3	4.85
Cat	24	100	4.8	5.8
Rat	14	28	5.8	4.85
Kangaroo rat	5.9	27	8.5	10.4
Jerboa	4.5	33	9.3	12
Psammomys	13	100	10.7	9.2

* Beeuwkes and Bonventre (1975) showed, however, that the dog kidney does contain short-looped or corticomedullary nephrons.

From Schmidt-Nielsen and O'Dell 1961, *Am. J. Physiol.* 200:1119–24

Monkeys of the genus *Macaca* represent an unusual departure from the relationship between medullary thickness and urine-concentrating capacity shown in Table 37.3. The macaque kidney has a poorly developed renal medulla; the outer medullary region is either rudimentary or virtually nonexistent. The relative thickness of the macaque kidney medulla is comparable to that of the beaver, and additionally, like the beaver, its corticomedullary osmotic gradient contains little urea. However, the macaque kidney, in contrast to that of the beaver, can concentrate its urine to an osmolality at least threefold greater than plasma osmolality and in some species, urine concentrations of 1800 mOsm/kg H_2O have been recovered. Structurally, the macaque kidney contains few if any long-looped nephrons with the thin descending and ascending segments. The entire ascending limb of the remnant of Henle's loop is composed of cuboidal cells with many mitochondria resembling those of the thick ascending limb of Henle's loop seen in other mammalian kidneys, e.g. the dog kidney.

Renal function in carnivorous and omnivorous animals shows considerable adaptability to diet. For example, the dog maintained on the usual dry food with a high ash content will excrete a neutral or even alkaline urine. When placed on a meat diet, the kidney increases the rate of hydrogen ion secretion, as the acidic end products of a meat diet require excretion. The members of the various canine genera in their natural habitat are phasic feeders, and renal function can vary considerably to accommodate a sudden influx of proteinaceous material and the secondary increase in urea formation. Within a few hours after the dog has eaten a meat meal, the glomerular filtration increases by 50–100 percent, thereby permitting a correlative increase in urea excretion.

Hydrogen-ion and ammonia secretion into urine and bicarbonate reabsorption from the tubular fluid are processes which are qualitatively similar in all mammalian species studied. However, quantitative differences of considerable magnitude have been observed. For example, the bicarbonate concentration in the tubular fluid near the end of the proximal convoluted tubules is 17 mEq/L in the dog and 7.5 mEq/L in the rat, indicating a substantially greater hydrogen-ion secretory rate in the proximal convoluted tubules of the rat. The rat also exhibits a greater $TmHCO_3^-$ than the dog, 40–45 μmol/min in the rat in contrast to approximately 30 μmol/min in the dog. Experimental acidosis in the rat is accompanied by an inductive increase in the amount of the enzyme glutaminase in the kidney.

Ruminants

Herbivorous animals excrete into urine a portion of the dietary intake of potassium. This usually is coupled to extensive sodium conservation, particularly under range conditions where the diet is devoid of salt. On the other hand, the availability of adequate salt in the diet is accompanied by considerable excretion of sodium into the urine. Sodium concentrations of 300 to even 500 mEq/L have been found in the urine of sheep given constant access to salt. Potassium concentrations in these urine samples were between 400 to 200 mEq/L, giving a total urinary cation concentration of approximately 650–700 mEq/L. In the author's laboratory, urine potassium concentrations approaching 700 mEq/L have been observed in sodium-free urine from sheep maintained without salt supplementation of the diet. The sheep kidney is also capable of remarkable concurrent sodium and potassium conservation. By exteriorizing one of the parotid salivary ducts, a portion of the voluminous parotid secretion of the sheep is drained from the digestive tract. The saliva of sheep contains sodium, chloride, bicarbonate, and potassium ions in concentrations of 178, 17, 140, and 16 mEq/L respectively, and the loss of this fluid results in negative sodium balance and increased aldosterone secretion. As the parotid fistula is maintained, the sodium concentrations in saliva decrease and salivary potassium concentrations increase. The urine also becomes depleted of both sodium and potassium, its solute composition being primarily urea and ammonium chloride.

The quantitatively important anions in the urine of ruminants are chloride and bicarbonate. Urine from ruminants is usually alkaline (pH 7.5–8.5) and the bicarbonate concentrations may be as high as 300 mEq/L. There is the suggestion of a reationship between renal function and the fermentative and motor functions of the rumen. Carbon dioxide with other rumen gases, when eructated, is forced into the tracheobronchial space. This peculiar circumstance results in undulating increases in plasma bicarbonate concentrations (and also presumably in arterial P_{CO_2}). The increase in arterial P_{CO_2} should stimulate hydrogen ion secretion, and augmented hydrogen ion secretion may occur in the proximal convoluted tubules. The increased filtered load of bicarbonate, however, would result in greater amounts being delivered to the more distal nephronal segments. Potassium secretion into the tubular fluid in the distal convoluted tubules and collecting ducts would result in the formation of an alkaline urine.

Ruminants generally excrete an alkaline urine with a relatively high potassium content, a reflection of their herbivorous diet. That this large urinary potassium excretion is usually associated with sodium conservation conforms to the accepted relationship between sodium and potassium exchange in the renal tubules. However, even in simple-stomached mammals the stoichiometry of urinary potassium and sodium excretion does not indicate a mole-for-mole exchange between the two ions.

The situation becomes more complex in ruminants, because the requirements for maintaining the constancy of the ionic content of the rumen dominate the systemic regulation of fluid and electrolyte equilibria. For example, when excess potassium is added to the diet of sheep there occurs an initial increase in urinary excretion of both potassium and sodium, leading to negative sodium balance before a steady state is restored. Sudden reductions of potassium intake are followed by intense sodium conservation. In both circumstances the priorities of the ruminant are adjusted so that in the first instance excess cation is removed from the ruminal fluid into the extracellular water and in the second circumstance cations are diverted from the extracellular water into the rumen. There is evidence that these adjustments are aided by changes in adrenal cortical secretion.

The continued administration of adrenal cortical steroids with mineralocorticoid activity to simple-stomached animals such as the dog or man results in continued urinary potassium excretion long after escape from sodium retention has occurred. The hypokalemia which accompanies mineralocorticoid administration can be directly attributed to intense urinary potassium loss. A hypokalemic response occurs in sheep when mineralocorticoid activity is increased during ACTH administration, but this is not accompanied by an increase in urinary potassium excretion. The administration of a potent mineralocorticoid drug to sheep induces severe hypokalemia and does not provoke an increase in urinary potassium output. These results point to a prominent effect of mineralocorticoid activity on ion transport across the ruminal membrane, emphasizing the dominance of the rumen in electrolyte metabolism.

Although the ruminant kidney usually elaborates an alkaline urine, it is also capable of secreting hydrogen ions. Ruminants grazing on pastures that contain much sulfate and phosphate residues excrete an acid urine and also maintain urinary potassium excretion. Experimentally, the addition of acid to the rumen of sheep or feeding sheep a concentrated diet which results in acid production markedly decreases urinary bicarbonate excretion and enhances the excretion of protons as ammonium ions. A comparable response occurs in calves given an increased acid intake, but in addition to an increased urinary excretion of ammonium ions there occurs an increased urinary excretion of acid phosphate and calcium.

The dominance of rumen function on fluid and electrolyte metabolism also influences endocrine reflexes in ruminants. The ingestion of hay or grain by sheep results in the release of ADH which in turn promotes water retention. The profuse secretions of the salivary glands in response to food ingestion by sheep apparently divert sufficient body water into the rumen, making water conservation mandatory.

Protein metabolism in the ruminant involves the participation of a urea cycle between the blood and the rumen. In the presence of adequate or excess dietary proteins, the microorganisms of the rumen form ammonia which is carried to the liver and detoxified by incorporation into urea. Thus plasma urea concentrations are directly related to the partial pressure of ammonia in the rumen gases. Feeding sheep a high-protein diet results in increased plasma urea concentrations and increased urea excretion into the urine. Severe curtailment of protein intake results in decreased P_{NH_3} in rumen gas, decreased plasma urea concentrations, and the diffusion or transport of urea from plasma into the rumen with hydrolysis of urea to form carbon dioxide and ammonia. If sufficient carbohydrate is available, the ammonia resulting from the hydrolysis of urea may be incorporated into bacterial or protozoal protein, thus becoming available to the host. The kidney in severe dietary protein restrictions conserves urea by markedly decreasing urea excretion. The ratio of urea clearance to endogenous true creatinine clearance may fall to less than 5 percent under conditions of prolonged negative nitrogen balance (Table 37.4 and Fig. 37.12). These adaptations suggest the presence of an active urea transport system in the ruminant which becomes operative during conditions requiring maximum urea conservation.

The animal with normal renal function excretes into urine only meager quantities of protein in such a low concentration as to be undetectable by the usual procedures of urinalyses. The adult sheep, however, may excrete into urine an average of 500 mg of protein/day/50 kg body weight, within a range of 100–2000 mg protein/day. Proteinuria of this magnitude in man would indicate glomerulonephritis. The glomeruli of sheep kidneys show a much greater cellularity than do the glomeruli of other mammalian kidneys, e.g. those of dog and man, and it has been proposed that all adult sheep are glomerulonephritic. However, there is no evidence of hypertension in adult sheep, and all aspects of renal function studied fail to demonstrate any gross distortions. This pattern of increased glomerular cellularity and proteinuria has been observed in goats and cattle and may be characteristic of all ruminants.

Large variations in glomerular filtration rate in sheep have been shown to be seasonably dependent. The GFR in range sheep in the summer is 2.0–2.5 times greater than in the winter months.

Table 37.4. Urea excretion characteristics on different diets

Diet	Digestible protein (%)	Plasma urea conc. (mM)	Urea clearance: ETC * clearance av.	Maximum urea U/P
Omolene and hay	7.5	5.26	0.42	App. 200
Hay and molasses	2–3	1.49	0.14	App. 40
Wheatstraw, molasses, and omolene	1.9	1.2	0.03	App. 6
Cellulose and molasses	0	0.84	0.1	App. 20

* Endogenous true creatinine
From Schmidt-Nielsen and Osaki 1958, *Am. J. Physiol.* 193:657–61

RENAL METABOLISM

A 10 kg dog will filter approximately 35 liters of blood plasma per day through the glomeruli. Variable amounts of water will be excreted into urine depending upon the state of hyrdration, but more than 99 percent of the sodium and all of the glucose and amino acids in the filtrate will be reabsorbed. The stoichiometry between ionic and crystalloid reabsorption and ATP utilization is not known. It is obvious, however, that the metabolic cost of renal function is high. The appropriate substrates for renal metabolism should be those which provide the highest yield of energy per mole.

Glucose

The reabsorption of glucose by the proximal convoluted tubules occurs as hexose is transported as an intact molecule from the tubular fluid across the nephron into the extracellular fluid and plasma. Glucose reabsorption does not involve any metabolic transformations, and glucose during reabsorption does not mix with the glucose pool of the kidney cells. For example, the administration of glucose-1-^{14}C or glucose-6-^{14}C into the renal artery resulted in the recovery, in the renal venous effluent, of almost the entire dose of radioactivity in the form in which it was administered. Approximately 2 percent of the radioactivity was recovered as $^{14}CO_2$ (Chinard et al. 1964).

These studies suggest that the kidney does not utilize plasma glucose to any considerable extent for its energy requirements. However, in vitro experiments have shown that the kidney possesses the metabolic machinery to metabolize glucose.

Gluconeogenesis by the kidney cortex has been demonstrated both in vivo and in vitro. It accounts for approximately 10 percent of the glucose produced by nonpregnant sheep and 15 percent in sheep fasted for 3 days. Metabolic acidosis in the rat enhances renal gluconeogenesis, specifically the utilization of glutamate for glucose production.

Lactate and pyruvate

The kidney has both a high oxygen consumption and an active carbohydrate metabolism. Lactate and to a lesser extent pyruvate are extracted by the kidney from plasma perfusing the kidney and are utilized as sources of energy and as carbohydrate precursors. There are differences in the patterns of metabolism between cortex and medulla which in general reflect the differences in blood flow between the two areas of the kidney. The cortex, perfused by a large volume of arterial blood, carries on a highly oxidative metabolism. Medullary tissue not only receives a much smaller portion of the renal blood flow, but oxygen supply to the deeper medullary regions may be further reduced as the result of countercurrent diffusion of oxygen across the vasa recta. Thus the medulla exists in a relatively anaerobic environment, and its metabolism is glycolytic to a large extent. Glycogen turnover is much more rapid in the medulla than the cortex, thereby supplying hexose phosphate for glycolysis. Under aerobic conditions the medulla is capable of oxidizing the acetyl moiety of acetyl coenzyme A to carbon dioxide and water.

The respiratory quotient (RQ) of the kidney has been the subject of few investigations, and the results have been conflicting. It has generally been assumed that the renal RQ was approimately 0.78–0.88, resembling the RQ of the other body organs. Experiments utilizing anesthetized dogs have provided estimates of the renal RQ, which average 1.14 to as high as 1.33. This unusually high figure would indicate either an area whose metabolic pattern is primarily anaerobic or a disproportionate rate of pyruvate decarboxylation accompanied by incomplete oxidation of acetyl CoA to carbon dioxide and water. These results have not been confirmed; for example, studies in unanesthetized human subjects have given renal respiratory quotients averaging 0.88 (Barker et al. 1963). However, in both series of experiments (i.e. in both dogs and humans) there was considerable variation, the range of the kidney RQ being from 0.45–2.5.

Lipids

The RQ of the kidney indicates that lipids also serve as fuel for the kidney's oxidative processes. Experiments in vivo have confirmed this observation by showing that unesterified fatty acids in the renal blood flow are taken up and oxidized by the kidney. Fatty acids serve as an important substrate for energy metabolism primarily in the cortex. The medulla, on the other hand, does not utilize fatty acids to any significant extent. This relatively meager rate, even under aerobic conditions, may result either from an inability of the medullary elements to extract fatty acids from the renal perfusate or from a disparity in the quantity of oxidative enzyme systems in the medulla. Fatty acid synthesis has been demonstrated in the kidney; both the synthesis and turnover of sterols in the kidney have been shown to be slow processes. An interesting group of lipid compounds that have been isolated from the renal medulla is the prostaglandins, which may regulate intrarenal blood flow or function as natriuretic factors.

Amino acids

Amino acid metabolism is a complex process involving (1) the utilization of some amino acids for ammonia synthesis, (2) the utilization of amino acids by the kidney for its own metabolic requirements, and (3) the conservation of amino acids by transport processes which return the amino acids from the tubular fluid to the blood. Glutamine and the basic amino acids arginine and asparagine are taken from renal blood plasma, and their nitrogen atoms are incorporated into ammonia. Metabolic acidosis with attendant increases in hydrogen ion secretion into the tubular fluid is accompanied by a significant increase in the extraction of these amino acids from the plasma perfusing the kidney. Other amino acids may be extracted from, or added to, the renal perfusate in very small quantities.

The kidney cortex concentrates amino acids within the intracellular fluid, and a variable portion of the amino acids may be incorporated into protein. The major quantity of amino acids taken up by the cortex is returned to the extracellular fluid, but a significant amount of some amino acids, for example, glutamic acid and glutamine, may be oxidized to carbon dioxide and water. The primary difference between cortex and medulla is the inability of the medullary cells to transport (i.e. concentrate) most amino acids into the intracellular fluid. Basic amino acids such as glutamine and lysine may be concentrated within the intracellular fluid of medullary cells; their uptake does not occur by active transport but rather by some form of diffusion. Other amino acids in small amounts enter the medullary cells, apparently by diffusion, and incorporation of amino acids into medullary protein occurs at rates equal to incorporation into cortex protein. In both cortical and medullary zones of the kidney, transamination of tricarboxylic acid cycle intermediates to amino acids represents a quantitatively significant pathway for the synthesis of kidney protein.

Carbon dioxide

Carbon dioxide metabolism in the kidney is qualitatively similar to its metabolism in other tissues, but there are important quantitative and physiological differences. Pyruvate, lactate, and fatty acids constitute the major substrates for endogenously produced carbon dioxide. A significant quantity of renal carbon dioxide production is derived from the carboxyl group of pyruvic acid. (The kidneys of all mammalian species studied oxidize propionate and acetate to carbon dioxide; the considerable production of volatile fatty acids in ruminants makes these substances quantitatively important substrates for oxidation by the ruminant kidney.)

The enzyme pyruvate carboxylase, which catalyzes the formation of oxalacetate from pyruvate and CO_2, has been found in a number of tissues, the most active preparation being from the kidney. Carbon dioxide fixation therefore could result in the net synthesis of tricarboxylic acid cycle intermediates and may be of considerable physiological significance. For example, the kidney extracts lactate (and to a lesser extent pyruvate) from blood, and the flow of substrate through CO_2 fixation could maintain a level of oxalacetate formation sufficient for the requirements of glucose formation from the reversal of glycolysis.

MICTURITION

The function of the urinary bladder is to provide an expandable reservoir for the urine, which is continuously passed from the pelvis of the kidney through the ureters to the bladder. It is of course essential that the bladder be capable of discharging its contents at an appropriate time and that it completely empty. The emptying process must be maintained for a relatively long period despite the continued reduction in the size and tension of the bladder. Normal micturition therefore depends upon neural reflexes which first permit the bladder to fill, and second permit the bladder to completely discharge its contents.

Two types of muscle are involved in the micturition reflex. The external sphincter is skeletal muscle and is innervated by somatic nerve fibers. The detrusor muscle of the bladder and the internal sphincter are smooth muscle and are innervated by fibers from the autonomic nervous system. In addition, the smooth muscle of the bladder maintains its own inherent myogenicity which is manifested by changes in tone. The tone of the bladder muscle is maintained in response to changes in pressure despite the elimination of extrinsic nerve supply and blockade of intramural ganglionic transmission. Bladder tone, however, is affected by the physical state of the bladder, and this in turn is dependent upon the integrity of the extrinsic innervation.

Motor nerve fibers to the bladder and sphincter are found in the pudic nerve, the pelvic nerve, and the hypogastric nerve. The pudic nerve contains somatic nerve fibers which innervate the external sphincter. The function of this neuromuscular device is to maintain tonic contraction and closure of the orifice from the bladder into the urethra. Motor fibers in the pelvic nerve are characteristic of the parasympathetic division of the autonomic nervous system. The preganglionic fibers originate from neurons in the sacral portion of the spinal cord and pass to ganglia of the hypogastric plexus or vesical plexus on the bladder wall. Postganglionic cholinergic fibers innvervate the detrusor muscle of the bladder. Motor nerves from the sympathetic division of the autonomic nervous system arise from neurons in the lumbar portion of the spinal cord. The postganglionic adrenergic fibers reach the bladder from the hypogastric plexus via the hypogastric nerve.

Sensory fibers from the bladder and from the sphincters pass to the spinal cord in all three nerves; hence, the pudic, pelvic, and hypogastric nerves are mixed nerves. Fibers from the sensory nerves synapse with neurons at the same level of the cord. In addition, sensory fibers pass rostrally to the brain via ill-defined tracts in the funiculus lateralis.

The motor neurons in the sacral portion of the spinal cord that innervate the bladder are subjected to both facilitatory and inhibitory fibers from the brain. Nerve centers in the mesencephalon, pons, and medulla send fibers via the lateral reticulospinal tract which mediate and enhance reflex contraction of the bladder. Fibers from pontine neurons also course through the medial reticulospinal tract and provide facilitation for the motor neurons which innervate the external sphincter. The ventral reticulospinal tract contains fibers from neurons located in the dorsal and the medial reticular formation, and these nerve cells provide for relaxation of the bladder. Thus the brain stem contains neuronal groupings which function as either vesicoexcitatory or vesicorelaxation centers. These brain-stem centers have connections with the hypothalamus, the limbic system through the amygdaloid nuclei, and the cerebral cortex.

The filling of the urinary bladder occurs as the detrusor muscle relaxes to accommodate the influx of urine from the ureters. The accommodation results from both changes in tone of the bladder musculature and central inhibition of neurons which provide facilitation to the parasympathetic nerves that contract the bladder. Additionally, bladder filling also involves increased facilitation to the somatic motor neurons which contract the external sphincter.

Accommodation by the smooth muscle of the urinary bladder permits it to expand without any significant increases in pressure to a certain critical point. At this critical level of filling (150 mm of water for man) there is a sudden increase in pressure both in the bladder and to a lesser extent in the perineal area in general. Impulses then pass to the excitatory centers in the brain to provide facilitation to the contractile system. Sensory impulses also provide inhibition of the vesicorelaxation areas of the brain stem. The primary efferent pathway which mediates contraction of the detrusor muscle involves the sacral parasympathetic nerves. Bladder contraction also is aided by contraction of the diaphragm, muscles of the abdominal wall, and levator ani. Simultaneous relaxation of the external sphincter takes place, thus permitting the urine to be voided into the urethra.

Complete emptying of the bladder depends upon the maintenance of detrusor contraction and sphincter relaxation. This is accomplished by at least two reflex systems. Receptors in the bladder wall, apparently placed in series with muscle fibers, contract during the contraction of the detrusor muscle and send impulses to the higher facilitatory centers. This sensory input maintains excitation of the vesicoexcitatory centers and secondarily maintains contraction of the bladder muscle. A second reflex arises from sensory fibers located in the wall or in the mucosa of the urethra. These receptors are stimulated by the flow of urine through the urethra, and the reflexes initiated by these receptors provide additional recruitment of reflexes to maintain bladder contraction and to relax the external sphincter. Reflexes originating from the urethral wall are integrated at both the pontine and spinal levels.

Little is known of the reflexes which mediate the cessation of micturition. The tone of the bladder decreases as the vesicle becomes emptied of its contents, and this is accompanied by contraction of the sphincters. The origins of impulses which initiate these changes are in doubt; they may arise either from the urethra, from the bladder, or from both areas. The reflex mechanism for cessation of micturition is a complex one involving volitional control as well as involuntary regulation from lower brain centers.

URINE

Urine is essentially a solution of the products of nitrogen and sulfur metabolism, of inorganic salts, and of pigments. It is usually yellowish in color; however, wide normal variations may occur. The odor is characteristic for the different species. In most animals the consistency is watery; but in the horse it is thickish and more or less syrupy, owing to the secretion of the mucous glands in the pelvis of the kidney and the upper part of the ureter. In most animals the urine is clear when voided; in the horse it is turbid, chiefly by reason of suspended crystals of calcium carbonate, which settle out upon standing. The urine of ruminants becomes turbid upon standing because of the precipitation of the same salt.

Specific gravity

The specific gravity of urine varies with the relative proportion of dissolved matter and water. In general, the greater the volume, the lower the specific gravity (Table 37.5).

Table 37.5. Volumes and specific gravities of urine

Animal	Volume (ml/kg body wt./day)	Specific gravity mean and range
Cat	10–20	1.030 (1.020–1.040)
Cattle	17–45	1.032 (1.030–1.045)
Dog	20–100	1.025 (1.016–1.060)
Goat	10–40	1.030 (1.015–1.045)
Horse	3–18	1.040 (1.025–1.060)
Sheep	10–40	1.030 (1.015–1.045)
Swine	5–30	1.012 (1.010–1.050)
Man	8.6–28.6	1.020 (1.002–1.040)

Data from Ellenberger and Scheunert 1923, Altman and Dittmer 1961

Molecular concentration

The depression of the freezing point is a measure of the molecular concentration of a solution. The following freezing-point values for urine from different species have been obtained: horse, −1.77° to −2°C; dog, −1.573° to −3.638°C; cat, −5°C (Ellenberger and Scheunert 1923). In all cases the molecular concentration of urine is much higher than that of blood plasma (average freezing point, −0.59°C). This means that the kidney performs work in the formation of urine.

Amount

The amount of urine excreted daily varies with the food, work, external temperature, water consumption, season, and other factors. Marked pathological variations may occur. Table 37.5 lists normal daily amounts.

REFERENCES

Altman, P.L., and Dittmer, D.S. 1961. *Blood and Other Body Fluids*. Fed. Am. Soc. Exp. Biol., Washington.

Aukland, K. 1962. Hemoglobin oxygen saturation in the dog kidney. *Acta Physiol. Scand.* 56:315–23.

Bahlmann, J., Ochwadt, B., and Schroder, E. 1965. Uber den Glucose-und Lactat-Stoffwechsel von isolierten Hundenieren. *Pflüg. Arch. ges. Physiol.* 286:207–19.

Barker, E.S., Crosley, A.P., Jr., and Clark, J.K. 1963. Respiratory quotients of human kidney *in vivo*. *J. Appl. Physiol.* 18:815–17.

Beeuwkes, R., and Bonventre, J.V. 1975. Tubular organization and vascular tubular relations in the dog kidney. *Am. J. Physiol.* 229:695–713.

Bennett, C.M., Clapp, J.R., and Berliner, R.W. 1967. Micropuncture study of the proximal and distal tubule in the dog. *Am. J. Physiol.* 213:1254–62.

Bergman, E.N., Brockman, R.P., and Kaufman, E.C. 1974. Glucose metabolism in ruminants: Comparison of whole-body turnover with production by gut, liver, and kidneys. *Fed. Proc.* 33:1849–54.

Berliner, R.W., Kennedy, T.J., Jr., and Orloff, J. 1951. Relationship between acidification of the urine and potassium metabolism. *Am. J. Med.* 11:274–82.

Berliner, R.W., Levinsky, N.G., Davidson, D.G., and Eden, M. 1958. Dilution and concentration of the urine and the action of antidiuretic hormone. *Am. J. Med.* 24:730–44.

Bernanke, D., and Epstein, F.H. 1965. Metabolism of the renal medulla. *Am. J. Physiol.* 208:541–45.

Blaine, E.H., Davis, J.O., and Prewitt, R.L. 1971. Evidence for a renal vascular receptor in control of renin secretion. *Am. J. Physiol.* 220:1593–97.

Blair-West, J.R., Coghlan, J.P., Denton, D.A., Goding, J.R., Winton, M., and Wright, R.D. 1962. The control of aldosterone secretion. *Rec. Prog. Horm. Res.* 19:311–83.

Bohman, S.D. 1974. The ultrastructure of the rat renal medulla as observed after improved fixation methods. *J. Ultrastruc. Res.* 47:329–60.

Braun, E.J., and Dantzler, W.H. 1974. Effects of ADH on single-nephron glomerular filtration rates in the avian kidney. *Am. J. Physiol.* 226:1–8.

Brenner, B.M., and Troy, J.L. 1971. Post-glomerular vascular protein concentration: Evidence for a causal role in governing fluid reabsorption and glomerulotubular balance by the renal proximal tubule. *J. Clin. Invest.* 50:336–49.

Burg, M., and Stoner, L. 1974. Sodium transport in the distal nephron. *Fed. Proc.* 33:31–36.

Castor, C.W., and Green, J.A. 1968. Regional distribution of acid mucopolysaccharides in the kidney. *J. Clin. Invest.* 4:2125–32.

Chang, L.C.T., Splawinski, J.A., Oates, J.A., and Nies, A.S. 1975. Enhanced renal prostaglandin production in the dog. II. Effects on intrarenal hemodynamics. *Circ. Res.* 36:204–7.

Chinard, F.P., Nolan, M.F., and Enns, T. 1964. Renal handling of exogenous and metabolic carbon dioxide. *Am. J. Physiol.* 206:362–368.

Clapp, J.R., and Robinson, R.R. 1966. Osmolality of distal tubular fluid in the dog. *J. Clin. Invest.* 45:1847–53.

Clapp, J.R., Watson, J.F., and Berliner, R.W. 1963. Osmolality, bicarbonate concentration, and water reabsorption in proximal tubule of the dog nephron. *Am. J. Physiol.* 205:273–80.

Cohen, J.J. 1960. High respiratory quotient of dog kidney *in vivo*. *Am. J. Physiol.* 199:560–68.

Dantzler, W.H. 1967. Stop-flow studies of renal function in conscious water snakes (Natrix sapedon). *Comp. Biochem. Physiol.* 22:131–40.

Davis, J.O., Hartroft, P.M., Titus, E.O., Carpenter, C.C.J., Ayres, C.R., and Spiegel, H.E. 1962. The role of the renin-angiotensin system in the control of aldosterone secretion. *J. Clin. Invest.* 41:378–89.

Deen, W.M., Robertson, C.R., and Brenner, B.M. 1973. Transcapillary fluid exchange in the renal cortex. *Circ. Res.* 33:1–8.

Denton, D.A. 1956. The effect of Na^+ depletion on the Na^+:K^+ ratio of parotid saliva of the sheep. *J. Physiol.* 131:516–25.

Diamond, J.M. 1971. Standing-gradient model of fluid transport in epithelia. *Fed. Proc.* 30:6–13.

Dougherty, R.W., Stewart, W.E., Nold, M.M., Lindahl, I.L., Mullenax, C.H., and Leek, B.F. 1962. Pulmonary absorption of eructated gas in ruminants. *Am. J. Vet. Res.* 23:205–12.

Edelman, I.S., Bogoroch, R., and Porter, G.A. 1963. On the mechanism of action of aldosterone on sodium transport: The role of protein synthesis. *Proc. Nat. Acad. Sci.* 50:1169–77.

Emery, N., Paulson, T.L., and Kinter, W.B. 1972. Production of concentrated urine by avian kidneys. *Am. J. Physiol.* 223:180–87.

Farber, S.J., and Van Praag, D. 1970. Composition of glycosaminoglycans (mucopolysaccharides) in rabbit renal papillae. *Biochim. Biophys. Acta* 208:219–26.

Gans, J.H. 1975. Effects of triamcinolone and of desoxycorticosterone on renal function in sheep. *Proc. Soc. Exp. Biol. Med.* 150:244–48.

Gans, J.H., Bailie, M.D., and Biggs, D.L. 1966. *In vitro* metabolism of ^{14}C-labelled amino acids by sheep kidney cortex and medulla. *Am. J. Physiol.* 211:249–54.

Giebisch, G., Boulpaep, E.L., and Whittembury, G. 1971. Electrolyte transport in kidney tubule cells. *Phil. Trans. Roy. Soc.*, ser. B, 262:175–96.

Gottschalk, C.W., and Mylle, M. 1959. Micropuncture study of the mammalian urinary concentrating mechanism: Evidence for the countercurrent hypothesis. *Am. J. Physiol.* 196:927–36.

Huber, G.C. 1917. On the morphology of the renal tubules of vertebrates. *Anat. Rec.* 13:305–40.

Jaenike, J.R. 1961. The influence of vasopressin on the permeability of the mammalian collecting duct to urea. *J. Clin. Invest.* 40:144–51.

Jamison, R.L. 1973. Intrarenal heterogeneity. *Am. J. Med.* 54:281–89.

Jamison, R.L., Bennett, C.M., and Berliner, R.W. 1967. Countercurrent multiplication by thin loops of Henle. *Am. J. Physiol.* 212:357–66.

Keech, D.B., and Utter, M.F. 1963. Pyruvate carboxylase. II. Properties. *J. Biol. Chem.* 238:2609–14.

Knox, F.G., Schneider, E.G., Willis, L.R., Strandhoy, J.W., and Ott, C.E. 1973. Site and control of phosphate reabsorption by the kidney. *Kidney Internat.* 3:347–53.

Kokko, J.P. 1972. Urea transport in the proximal tubule and the descending limb of Henle. *J. Clin. Invest.* 51:1999–2008.

——. 1973. Sodium chloride and water transport in the medullary thick ascending limb of Henle. *J. Clin. Invest.* 52:612–23.

Kuru, M. 1965. Nervous control of micturition. *Physiol. Rev.* 45:425–94.

Laragh, J.H., and Sealey, J.E. 1973. The renin-angiotensin-aldosterone hormonal system and regulation of sodium, potassium, and blood pressure homeostasis. In *Handbook of Physiology*. Sec. 8, J. Orloff and R.W. Berliner, eds., *Renal Physiology*. Am. Physiol. Soc., Washington.

Lee, J.B. 1974. Prostaglandins and the renal antihypertensive and natriuretic endocrine function. *Recent Prog. Horm. Res.* 30:481–532.

Lee, J.B., Vance, V.K., and Cahill, G.F., Jr. 1962. Metabolism of ^{14}C-labelled substrates by rabbit kidney cortex and medulla. *Am. J. Physiol.* 203:27–36.

Lerner, R.A., Dixon, F.J., and Lee, S. 1968. Spontaneous glomerulonephritis in sheep. II. Studies on natural history, occurrence in other species, and pathogenesis. *Am. J. Path.* 53:501–12.

Levinsky, N.G. 1974. Natriuretic hormones. *Adv. Metab. Disorders* 7:37–71.

Levinsky, N.G., and Lalone, R.C. 1963. The mechanism of sodium diuresis after saline infusion in the dog. *J. Clin. Invest.* 42:1261–76.

Levitin, H., Goodman, A., Pigeon, G., and Epstein, F.H. 1962. Composition of renal medulla during water diuresis. *J. Clin. Invest.* 41:1145–51.

Levy, M.N. 1962. Uptake of lactate and pyruvate by intact kidney of the dog. *Am. J. Physiol.* 202:302–8.

Maddox, D.A., Deen, W.M., and Brenner, B.M. 1974. Dynamics of glomerular ultrafiltration. VI. Studies in the primate. *Kidney Internat.* 5:271–78.

Malnic, G., Klose, R.M., and Giebisch, G. 1966. Micropuncture study of distal tubular potassium and sodium transport in rat nephron. *Am. J. Physiol.* 211:548–59.

Marshall, S., Miller, T.B., and Farah, A.E. 1963. Effect of renal papillectomy on ability of the hamster to concentrate urine. *Am. J. Physiol.* 204:363–68.

Massry, S.G., and Coburn, J.W. 1973. The hormonal and non-hormonal control of renal excretion of calcium and magnesium. *Nephron* 10:66–112.

McDonald, J., and Macfarlane, W.V. 1958. Renal function of sheep in hot environments. *Austral. J. Ag. Res.* 9:680–92.

Mercer, P.F., Maddox, D.A., and Brenner, B.M. 1974. Current concepts of sodium chloride and water transport in the mammalian nephron. *Western J. Med.* 120:33–45.

Mudge, G.H., and Taggart, J.V. 1950. Effect of acetate on the renal excretion of p-aminohippurate in the dog. *Am. J. Physiol.* 161:191–97.

Oparil, S., and Haber, E. 1970. The renin-angiotensin system. *New Eng. J. Med.* 291:389–401, 446–57.

Parsons, V. 1973. Divalent ion metabolism and the kidney. *Nephron* 10:157–73.

Passo, S.S., Assaykeen, T.A., Otsuka, K., Wise, B.L., Goldfein, A., and Ganong, W.F. 1967. Effect of stimulation of the medulla oblongata on renin secretion in dogs. *Neuroendocrinology* 7:1–10.

Pennell, J.P., Lacy, F.B., and Jamison, R.L. 1974. An in vivo study of the concentrating process in the descending limb of Henle's loop. *Kidney Internat.* 5:337–47.

Pennell, J.P., Sanjana, V., Frey, N.R., and Jamison, R.S. 1975. The effect of urea infusion on the urinary concentration mechanism in protein depleted rats. *J. Clin. Invest.* 55:399–409.

Pitts, R.F. 1944. The effects of infusing glycin and of varying the dietary protein intake on renal hemodynamics in the dog. *Am. J. Physiol.* 142:355–65.

Pitts, R.F., and Lotspeich, W.D. 1946. Bicarbonate and the renal regulation of acid-base balance. *Am. J. Physiol.* 147:138–54.

Pomeranz, B.H., Birtch, A.G., and Barger, A.C. 1968. Neural control of intrarenal blood flow. *Am. J. Physiol.* 215:1067–81.

Rhodin, J.A.G. 1963. Structure of the kidney. In M.B. Strauss and L.G. Welt, eds., *Diseases of the Kidney*. Little, Brown, Boston.

Rosenberg, L.E., Berman, M., and Segal, S. 1963. Studies of the kinetics of amino acid transport, incorporation into protein, and oxidation in kidney cortex slices. *Biochim. Biophys. Acta* 71:664–75.

Schmid, U., Schmid, J., Schmid, H., and Duback, V.C. 1975. Sodium- and potassium-activated ATPase: A possible target for aldosterone. *J. Clin. Invest.* 55:655–60.

Schmidt-Nielsen, B., and O'Dell, R. 1959. Effect of diet on distribution of urea and electrolytes in kidneys of sheep. *Am. J. Physiol.* 197:856–60.

———. 1961. Structure and concentrating mechanism in the mammalian kidney. *Am. J. Physiol.* 200:1119–24.

Schmidt-Nielsen, B., and Osaki, H. 1958. Renal responses to changes in nitrogen metabolism in sheep. *Am. J. Physiol.* 193:657–61.

Schmidt-Nielsen, B., Osaki, H., Murdaugh, H.V., Jr., and O'Dell, R. 1958. Renal regulation of urea excretion in sheep. *Am. J. Physiol.* 194:221–28.

Schmidt-Nielsen, B., and Skadhauge, E. 1967. Function of the excretory system of the crocodile. *Am. J. Physiol.* 212:973–80.

Scoggins, B.A., Coghlan, J.P., Denton, D.A., Fan, J.S.K., McDougall, J.G., Oddie, C.J., and Shulkes, A.A. 1974. Metabolic effects of ACTH in the sheep. *Am. J. Physiol.* 226:198–205.

Scott, D., Whitelaw, F.G., and Kay, M. 1971. Renal excretion of acid in calves fed either roughage or concentrate diets. *Q. J. Exp. Physiol.* 56:18–32.

Shalhoub, R., Webber, W., Glabman, S., Canessa-Fischer, M., Klein, J., deHass, J., and Pitts, R.F. 1963. Extraction of amino acids from and their addition to renal blood plasma. *Am. J. Physiol.* 204:181–86.

Shannon, J.A. 1938. Urea excretion in the normal dog during forced diuresis. *Am. J. Physiol.* 122:782–87.

Spinelli, F. 1974. Structure and development of renal glomerulus as revealed by scanning electron microscopy. *Internat. Rev. Cytol.* 39:345–81.

Stacy, B.D., and Brook, A.H. 1965. Antidiuretic hormone activity in sheep after feeding. *Q. J. Exp. Physiol.* 50:65–78.

Stacy, B.D., and Warner, A.C.I. 1966. Balances of water and sodium in the rumen during feeding: Osmotic stimulation of sodium absorption in the sheep. *Q. J. Exp. Physiol.* 51:79–93.

Tannenbaum, J., Splawinski, J.A., Oates, J.A., and Nies, A.S. 1975. Enhanced renal prostaglandin production in the dog. I. Effects on renal function. *Circ. Res.* 36:197–203.

Thorburn, G.D., Kopald, H.H., Herd, J.A., Hollenberg, M., O'Morchoe, C.C.C., and Barger, A.C. 1963. Intrarenal distribution of nutrient blood flow determined with Krypton^{85} in the unanesthetized dog. *Circ. Res.* 13:290–307.

Tisher, C.C. 1971. Relationship between renal structure and concentrating ability in the rhesus monkey. *Am. J. Physiol.* 220:1100–1106.

Tisher, C.C., Schrier, R.W., and McNeil, J.S. 1972. Nature of the urine concentrating mechanism in the Macaque monkey. *Am. J. Physiol.* 223:1128–37.

Van Praag, D., Stone, A.L., Richter, A.J., and Farber, S.J. 1972. Composition of glycosaminoglycans (mucopolysaccharides) in rabbit kidney. II. Renal cortex. *Biochim. Biophys. Acta* 273:149–56.

Welt, L.G., and Orloff, J. 1951. The effects of an increase in plasma volume on the metabolism and excretion of water and electrolytes by normal subjects. *J. Clin. Invest.* 30:751–61.

Wheeler, K.P., and Whittam, R. 1964. Structural and enzymic aspects of the hydrolysis of adenosine triphosphate by membranes of kidney cortex and erythrocytes. *Biochem. J.* 93:349–63.

Windhager, E.E., and Giebisch, G.H. 1965. Electrophysiology of the nephron. *Physiol. Rev.* 45:214–44.

Wirz, H., Hargitary, B., and Kuhn, W. 1951. Lokalisation des Konzentrierungs-prozesses in der Niere durch direkte Kryoskopie. *Helv. Physiol. Pharmac. Acta* 9:196–207.

Wright, L.D., Russo, H.F., Skeggs, H.R., Patch, E.A., and Beyer, K.H. 1947. The renal clearance of essential amino acids: Arginine, histidine, lysine, and methionine. *Am. J. Physiol.* 149:130–34.

CHAPTER 38

The Skin * | by H.S. Bal

GENERAL ANATOMY

Skin is the largest organ in the body, not in surface area, but in bulk. It protects the animal organism from dessication and from the environment while maintaining communication with the outside. Two of the main components of the skin are the epidermis (Fig. 38.1), consisting of keratinized stratified squamous epithelium, and the dermis (corium), made up of intricately woven collagenous, elastic, and reticular fibers with cellular elements, smooth muscle fibers, and the amorphous ground substance. These two skin components are mutually dependent. Epidermis with its keratin is affected by cellular and humoral dermal factors (Jarret 1973). Hair growth is dependent on the dermal papillae, and their integrity is essential for the continued existence of the hair follicle. Oliver indicated (1966) that a follicle can regenerate its papillary cells.

The structure and thickness of the skin of domestic animals vary according to breed, age, and sex in certain species. Average skin thickness of general body areas of the adult sheep is 2.7 mm (Kozlowski and Calhoun 1969), swine 2.2 mm (Marcarian and Calhoun 1966), cattle 6 mm (Goldsberry and Calhoun 1959), and goats 2.9 mm (Sar and Calhoun 1966). The dog skin is 1 mm or more in thickness in the head and neck regions where it is the thickest (Webb and Calhoun 1954). The horse skin varies in thickness from 1 to 5 mm and is thickest on the dorsal surface of the tail and at the attachment of the mane (Getty 1975).

Wilson (1941) reported that the skin of the domestic animal becomes more uniform in structure, smoother, tighter, and more dense after castration.

Epidermis

The epidermis consists of an upper horny layer of dead keratinized cells (stratum corneum) and a lower viable layer of cells (stratum Malpighii). The cells of the viable epidermis, which are produced by proliferation of basal cells, are called keratinocytes.

Stratum Malpighii is further subdivided into stratum basale or germinativum, stratum spinosum (prickle-cell layer), and stratum granulosum (Fig. 38.2). Stratum basale is a layer one or two cells thick (Jarret 1973). Stratum basale (basal layer, Fig. 38.2) is in contact with the basement membrane of the dermis below and with stratum spinosum (prickle-cell layer) of variable thickness above. These basal cells are low columnar or cuboidal with their long axis aligned vertical to the skin surface. Cell division, necessary for the replacement of the superficial cells, occurs in this layer only when the animal is sleeping, unlike that of the hair follicle which continues 24 hours a day (Ryder 1973).

Stratum spinosum or the prickle-cell layer was named because the cell junctions of this layer look like spines which were first described as intercellular bridges. They

* Part of this chapter has been taken from the chapter in the Eighth Edition written by Milton Orkin and Robert M. Schwartzman.

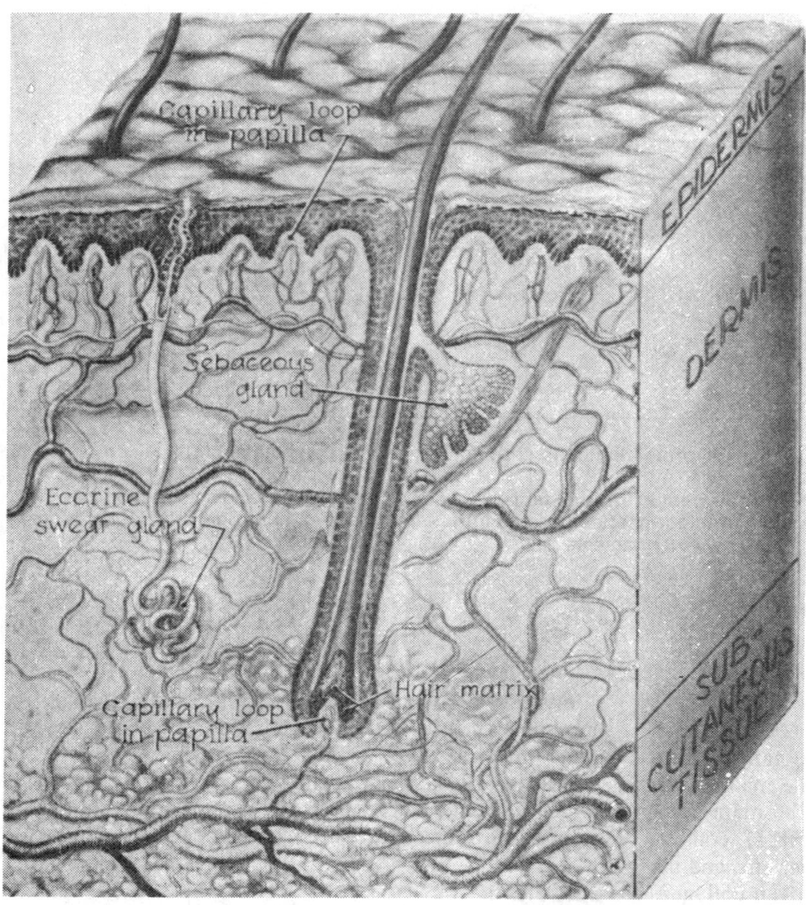

Figure 38.1. Human skin. (From D.M. Pillsbury, W.B. Shelley, and A.M. Kligman, *Dermatology*, Saunders, Philadelphia, 1956.)

are now called desmosomes or maculae adherentes (Montagna and Parakkal 1974). In malignant and proliferative conditions of the epidermis, the cells of this layer also divide by mitosis.

Stratum granulosum or the granular layer is a transitional zone between the viable epidermal cells below and the dead keratinized material above. Its nuclei are absent or abnormal, and keratohyaline granules appear in the cell cytoplasm (Jarret 1973). Absence of the keratohyaline granules in this layer is associated with the production of parakeratotic keratin in psoriasis and exfoliative dermatitis, when the cells of the stratum corneum retain their nuclei and appear as scales.

In cattle, the stratum granulosum is only in the perianal region and occasionally over the extremities (Goldsberry and Calhoun 1959). In dogs, the stratum in these areas has about 15 layers of cells and consists of a single layer in the ventral region of the neck, the abdominal, sternal, axillary, and shoulder regions, and the flank, tail, and back. It is absent in the mandibular, temporal, and dorsal portions of the head and outer covering of the ear (Webb and Calhoun 1954). In swine, 1–5 layers of flat polygonal cells constitute this stratum in the thicker skin regions, but there is only a single layer or the cells are sporadic in thin skin (Macarian and Calhoun 1966). In goats, this stratum is represented by 5 layers of diamond-shaped cells in some body areas and is rarely noticeable in others (Sar and Calhoun 1966).

Cytoplasmic contents of the cells of the stratum granulosum are hydrolyzed prior to the formation of the keratin layer. Basophilia of this layer is due to mineralization there, predominantly of calcium and magnesium, as well as to the mordanting action of the metallic ions. Many metallic ions are attached to the keratohyaline granules (Jarret 1973).

Stratum lucidum (a thin hyaline layer above the stratum granulosum) is generally absent in the skin of the domestic animal except in specialized areas such as the perianal region, the hoof margins, the teat, and over the Achilles tendon insertion in cattle, in the ovine lip and muzzle, and in the planum nasale of the dog and cat.

The cellular stratification is the reflection of various

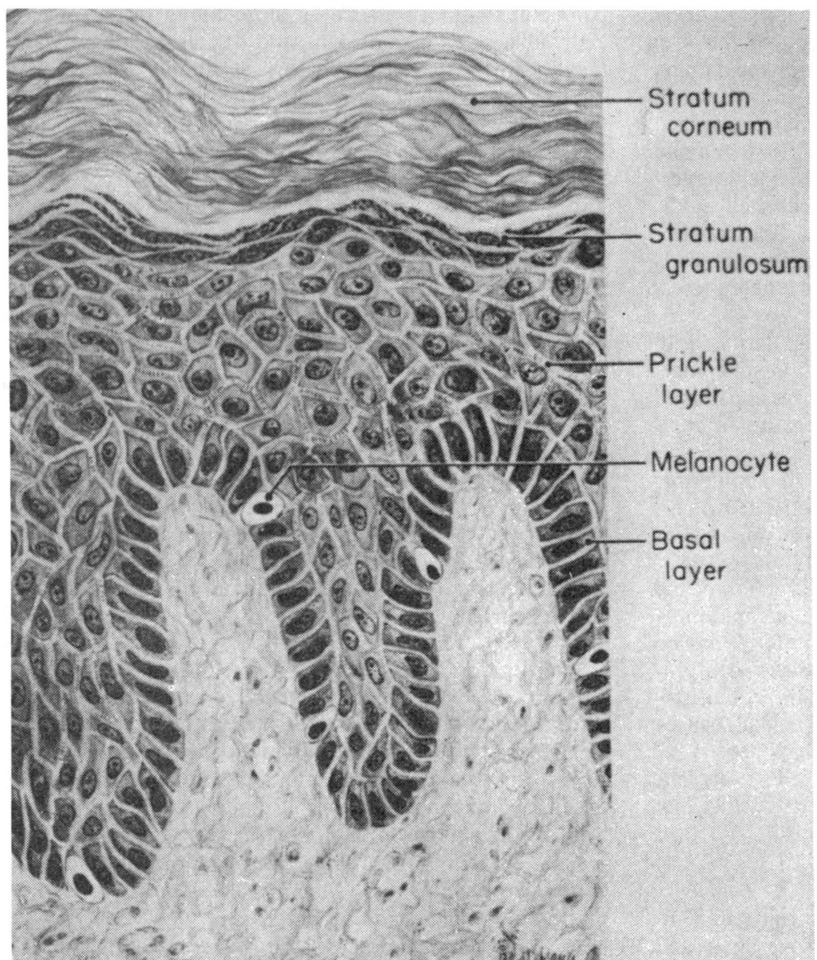

Figure 38.2. Human epidermis. (From D.M. Pillsbury, W.B. Shelley, and A.M. Kligman, *Dermatology,* Saunders, Philadelphia, 1956.)

stages through which the basal cells pass in their gradual conversion to the horny material of the stratum corneum. Horny cells are continuously shed from the skin surface. Cell division definitely takes place in the basal layer; the reproductive participation of the more superficial layers is problematic (Medawar 1953).

The epidermis consists of two entirely distinct lineages of cells. About 85–95 percent of the cells derive from the embryonic ectoderm and constitute the Malpighian system, principally concerned with the production of keratin. But there are a number of cells in the epidermis other than keratinocytes.

Melanocytes. The melanocytes differentiate from the neural crest cells of neuroectodermal origin. They are recognized by the presence of the pigment melanin (melanosomes) in their cytoplasm; they may bear many dendritic processes, appear as bipolar cells, or even be amorphous, depending upon their location and functional state (Montagna and Parakkal 1974). Keratinocytes acquire melanin by phagocytosis of the dendritic processes of the melanocytes laden with melanosomes (Mottag and Zelickson 1967). Other distinguishing features of the melanocytes are the scarcity of tonofilaments and absence of desmosomal attachments. The main function of melanocytes appears to be synthesis of melanosomes (Montagna and Parakkal 1974). Melanocytes give a DOPA (dihydroxyphenylalanine) reaction.

Mast cells. According to Okun (1965) and Okun and Zook (1967), mast cells and melanocytes have the same lineage, and under certain conditions mast cells represent a transitional phase in the formation of melanocytes. Increased pigmentation of the skin occurs in the urticaria pigmentosa and in mast cell tumors of dogs. Mast cells are also positive to the DOPA reaction, which provides intermediates in the metabolism of phenylalanine and tyrosine, and the production of norepinephrine, epinephrine, and melanin (see Fig. 52.11).

Langerhans cells. These cells were first described by

Langerhans in 1868 and were named after him. Langerhans cells have been found in the epithelia of the oral mucosa, gingiva, and vagina, as well as in the lamina propria of the trachea. In vitamin A–deficient rats and in histiocytosis X (histiocytic proliferation of undetermined type), they abound in the urinary bladder (Montagna and Parakkal 1974). Masson (1951) considered the Langerhans cells to be effete melanocytes. Breathnach et al. (1968) observed these cells in the mouse skin experimentally deprived of neural crest; thus Langerhans cells and melanocytes which differentiate from the neural crest cells cannot have the same lineage.

Merkel cells. Merkel cells are found in epidermis with hairy surfaces, in nail matrix, in palms, and in subepidermal mesenchyme (FitzGerald 1968). They are considered to be sensory receptors or transducers because of their close association with nerve terminals.

Some dermatologists refer to the cells of the epidermis other than the keratinocytes as dendritic cells. However, under pathological conditions, the epidermis may be invaded by a variety of dermal cells.

Basement membrane. The structure and function of the baement membrane between the dermis and epidermis have been described best by Jarret (1973). It should be regarded as a chemical interface which appears as a precise and continuous structure under certain conditions where an exchange of fixation and staining that causes precipitation takes place. Nutrition and the integrity of the epidermis are maintained by the nutrients, oxygen, and humoral and cellular components of the dermis that move across this interface into the epidermis.

Dermis

Dermis is the fibrous connective tissue of skin. Epidermis and the cutaneous appendages grow upon and within it and sustain their nourishment from it. Collagen makes up the bulk of connective tissue; elastic and reticular fibers constitute relatively small segments. The dermis may be divided into a superficial papillary layer and a thick, deep reticular layer. Aside from the hoofs, lips, and snout of the ox, pig, and other animals, however, it is only in man that the dermis of the general body surface is clearly definable into two segments (Montagna 1963). The ground substance is the semifluid amorphous material which fills the spaces between fibers.

Hypodermis

This layer consists of loose fibrous connective tissue infiltrated with fat or adipose tissue and connects the skin to the underlying structures of the body such as the muscles and bones. The hypodermis is the subcutaneous tissue shown in Figure 38.1. The distribution of fat in the hypodermis is influenced by estrogenic hormones. Large masses of fat that make up a cushion or pad are called panniculus adiposus, such as those found in pork bacon and fatback, or in foot pads and digital cushions where they serve as shock absorbers (Calhoun and Stinson 1976). Fat which is stored in the hypodermis insulates the body while maintaining its contour. Hypodermic injections of medicinal agents may be deposited in this layer.

GENERAL PHYSIOLOGY

Mechanical protection

Hair, hoofs, nails, feathers, and the horny layer of the epidermis afford mechanical protection to underlying parts. The horny layer is thickest where chances of injury by external factors are greatest.

Hair

Because of its fibrous and bulky nature, hair affords great protection against cuts, abrasions, thermal and radiation injury, and chemical irritation (Kligman 1964). Hair is also an efficient filter and insulator. Few substances actually contact the skin of hairy animals. Physical traumata are usually blunted before they reach the cutaneous surface.

Stratum corneum

From a phylogenetic point of view, keratinization came about when the vertebrates attempted to adapt themselves to life on land (Biedermann 1926, Rothman 1964). In larval forms of amphibia a tegument is found which is similar to that of fishes and has cilia on the surface. In the adult form amphibia develop a kind of keratinizing epidermis. The epidermis of reptiles develops an impressive horny layer. Mammals and birds have very similar epidermal shedding processes.

In many mammals there is an inverse relationship between the thickness of epidermis and hairiness (Kligman 1964). An extreme example is the sheep, whose epidermis is about three cells thick and whose stratum corneum is trivial. Wherever fur is dense and thick, as in the rabbit, mouse, dog, cat, and so forth, the stratum corneum is minute. In many animals, such as deer, cattle, horse, and rabbit, it is so fragile that it cannot be separated into a sheet.

Having lost most of its hair, human skin is exposed to many noxious environmental influences. Thus the epidermis has become much thicker; it has become tough and durable, yet is flexible and plastic. It is remarkably efficient as a chemical- and water-proofing membrane. The exclusive function of the epidermis is the protection which it affords by virtue of its dead-end product, the horny layer.

The major portion of hair, horn, hoof, feather, nail, and the stratum corneum of the skin is composed of albuminoid proteins.

Permeability

The epidermis is an effective barrier to the penetration of a wide variety of substances, the absorption of which depends upon their properties as well as upon the state of the skin (Malkinson 1964). In general the skin has a higher order of impermeability than do other biological membranes. Overall cutaneous permeability is largely determined by the least penetrable layer, that is, stratum corneum.

Passage of materials into mammalian skin occurs through two main pathways: transepidermal and transappendageal (essentially through the pilosebaceous apparatus). Transepidermal absorption is thought to be limited by a superficial barrier between the stratum corneum and the uppermost layers of living epidermis. This barrier is particularly effective in preventing passage of water and some water-soluble substances such as electrolytes. Substances unable to penetrate the superficial barrier may be absorbed in varying quantities through the more permeable cells of the sebaceous gland, the sebaceous gland duct, and the follicular epithelium. Once a substance has passed through the superficial barrier, there is apparently no significant impedance for its penetration into the remaining layers of the epidermis and the corium, following which there is ready entry into capillaries and lymph vessels and then into the general circulation.

Membrane permeability is thought to be determined largely by the lipid-protein structure of cellular membranes (Overton 1924, Davson and Danielli 1952). This theory proposes that materials that are lipid soluble (alcohols, ketones, and so forth) penetrate the cell wall because of its lipid content, while uptake of water by cell membrane protein provides entry for water-soluble substances. Substances soluble in both lipids and water penetrate most rapidly of all (Rothman 1943). Permeability rates are generally lower at anatomical sites where the stratum corneum is thickest. The skin-surface lipid film probably plays a relatively small role in opposing percutaneous (through unbroken skin) absorption.

Factors that promote physiological absorption include the following. Increasing temperature, short of producing cellular damage, tends to increase penetration. Increased blood flow or hyperemia is an important factor in facilitating percutaneous absorption, particularly via the transepidermal route. It is probably most significant for gases and vapors, to which skin, like most other tissues, is highly permeable. With gases there is definite evidence that increasing concentration will yield increasing penetration.

Factors that promote absorption by barrier injury include the following. Mechanical trauma sufficient to produce breaks in barrier continuity increases permeability. Injurious agents such as mustard gas, acids, and alkalies damage the barrier membrane, thus increasing permeability. Absorption of either predominantly lipid- or water-soluble compounds may be aided by prior application of organic solvents such as benzene or chloroform. Absorption is also facilitated by inflammatory changes which impair barrier permeability and are accompanied by hyperemia. Finally, cell permeability is increased following persistent hydration of the stratum corneum.

Specific substances

1. *Water*. There is evidence to suggest the transepidermal inward movement of water (Rothman 1954). The continuous outward movement of water through the epidermis is well known.

2. *Electrolytes*. In animals there is evidence for percutaneous penetration of electrolytes, but in man it is debatable.

3. *Lipid-soluble substances*. These substances are absorbed through the skin fairly rapidly and completely. Compounds which are soluble in both lipids and water penetrate so rapidly that the rate of absorption approaches that of gastrointestinal or even parenteral absorption, for example, subcutaneous injections (Rothman 1954). This rapidity suggests that the route of absorption is transepidermal.

(a) Phenol. The percutaenous absorption of phenol is well known; it has led to many deaths in humans following the application of carbolic acid to large areas of the skin.

(b) Sex hormones. Estrogenic hormones, testosterone, and progesterone penetrate the intact skin rapidly and with ease. In general, provided a volatile solvent vehicle is used, the percutaneous and subcutaneous administration of these hormones produces effects which are quantitatively of the same order (Calvery et al. 1946).

(c) Vitamins. The lipid-soluble vitamins A, D, and K penetrate the skin with ease. The biological significance of vitamin D formation in the skin by ultraviolet light and its subsequent absorption are well established.

(d) Heavy metals. Mercury has received a great deal of attention because of its historical significance in the treatment of syphilis by cutaneous inunction. Metallic mercury incorporated in ointments penetrates the intact skin through hair follicles and sebaceous glands. It then may be found in tissues, body fluids, and excreta. Lead penetrates the skin to a much lesser degree. The percutaneous absorption of arsenic—as well as certain other heavy metals, e.g. mercury, tin, copper, bismuth, and antimony—depends upon the transformation of the original lipid-insoluble compound into a lipid-soluble metal oleate. This may occur in or on the horny layer by combination of the salt of the heavy metal with fatty acids of sebum, or outside the body when incorporated in ointment bases containing fatty acids.

4. *Gases*. All gases and many vaporized and volatile

substances easily penetrate the skin, with the remarkable exception of carbon monoxide. The process appears to be one of simple diffusion across the entire skin, which behaves like an inert membrane (Calvery et al. 1946). Ease of percutaneous absorption has been demonstrated for oxygen, nitrogen, helium, carbon dioxide, hydrogen sulfide, hydrogen cyanide, and vapors of ammonia, nitrobenzene, dinitrotoluene, and volatile aromatic oils.

Actinic irradiation

Sunlight may be divided arbitrarily into ultraviolet, visible (see Table 2.5), and infrared spectral regions. The intensity and spectral distribution of sunlight vary greatly with season, latitude, time of day, and changes in the earth's atmosphere. Visible light is defined as that radiation perceived by the human eye; radiation of shorter wavelengths is referred to as ultraviolet and that of longer wavelengths as infrared.

The main sites of biological action of light rays are the skin and superficial tissues. Infrared rays are absorbed in the upper layers of the skin where they may produce marked thermal effect; action at greater depth is insignificant (Kovacs 1950). Visible light penetrates to a much greater extent than infrared. Intense irradiation with visible light may raise tissue temperature by several degrees to a depth of centimeters, while the surface of the skin is relatively little affected. Increased blood flow and enhanced sweat-gland activity may follow. Ultraviolet rays differ significantly from other rays in their ability to produce chemical changes in superficial tissues.

Effects of sunlight

The formation of vitamin D and the resultant antirachitic action are the most clear-cut effects produced by sunlight.

Sunburn appears to be the result of direct injury of the cells of the epidermis by ultraviolet irradiation with the subsequent elaboration from these cells of substances that bring about the specific physiological response (Blum 1945). This may account for the long latent period between exposure and the development of clinical features. Ultraviolet light may exert its injurious action by altering proteins and/or nucleic acids. Sunburn is much less common in animals than man because animal skin is better protected by hair and pigment.

There is a wealth of convincing evidence that sunlight is one of the major causes of cancer of the skin in man (Blum 1945). The major lines of evidence are that cancer of the skin (a) occurs principally on the parts of the body most exposed to sunlight; (b) is more common among outdoor than indoor workers; (c) is much more common in southern regions of the United States than in northern; (d) is much less prevalent in Negroes than in white races, presumably because the skin of the fomer is more resistant to the harmful effects of sunlight; and (e) can be induced in laboratory animals (mice and rats) by exposure to ultraviolet irradiation.

Photosensitization may occur in man or animals due to toxic or allergic mechanisms, with or without the intervention of photosensitizing agents. These agents may be chemicals, such as drugs or coal-tar derivatives, or plant products (Allington 1956, Kral and Schwartzman 1964). They may reach the skin either by contact, ingestion, or injection. Endogenous substances, such as abnormal metabolites or toxins or other products absorbed from infection, also may act as photosensitizers. Photosensitivity occurs in erythropoietic porphyria in cattle and man and in certain types of hepatic porphyrias in man (Jorgenson and With 1965, Goldberg 1965). Liver damage may be associated with other forms of light sensitivity in animals.

Protective mechanisms

There are five pigments that play a role in the origin of skin color: melanin, melanoid (degradation product of melanin), oxyhemoglobin, reduced hemoglobin, and carotene (Edwards and Duntley 1939). Of these five, melanin is the most important. It is a yellow to black pigment produced in the cytoplasm of melanocytes, which form a horizontal network at the dermoepidermal junction. In mammals the amino acid tyrosine is the starting point for the production of melanin; the copper-containing enzyme tyrosinase catalyzes the entire sequence in which tyrosine is converted to melanin. Differences in color between Caucasian and Negro skin and variations between colored areas of particolored animals are functions of the pigmentary activity of individual melanocytes and not differences in their number, distribution, or structure (Billingham 1949, Billingham and Medawar 1953).

One of the direct or indirect targets of ultraviolet exposure of the skin is the melanocyte. Ultraviolet radiant energy is a highly effective agent for stimulating melanin formation. Suntanning is the result of the effects of ultraviolet light upon melanin; three mechanisms are thought to be operative: melanin darkening, melanin migration, and melanin formation (Blum 1945).

Melanin acts as a biological ultraviolet filter. Negroes have much greater protection against ultraviolet light than Caucasians. This may be accounted for by the presence of dustlike melanic particles flecking the stratum corneum of Negroes (Thomson 1955). The stratum corneum of Caucasians is not ordinarily melanized.

In the domesticated water buffalo of India, Singh (1962) observed that the dorsal and lateral regions of the skin which were more exposed to sunlight exhibited greater pigmentation of melanin than the ventral or less exposed regions. This phenomenon appears to occur in all breeds of the water buffalo whether in temperate, subtropical, or tropical zones.

As with mechanical protection, hair and stratum corneum, particularly when thick, also are effective biological ultraviolet filters. Albino or vitiligo skin of humans can develop increased resistance to ultraviolet irradiation by graded exposures, presumably by thickening of the stratum corneum (Fitzpatrick and Szabo 1957).

Sweat glands

Two types of glands may be described: apocrine and eccrine. Apocrine glands elaborate membrane-bound secretions while the excretions of the eccrine glands are of the serous type. According to Montagna and Parakkal (1974), apocrine glands have been wrongly designated because they do not slough off their apical cytoplasm. These so-called apocrine glands in humans rarely respond to thermal stimulation, but secrete slowly and sparsely. Except in the horse, their secreted product should not be called sweat. The mode of secretion from merocrine to holocrine seems to be present in apocrine glands.

Apocrine

Among the domestic animals, apocrine sweat glands are found in cattle, sheep, horses, swine, dogs, and cats. Apocrine glands make up the majority of tubular skin glands that produce watery but nonfatty proteinaceous secretion, as in the horse, in response to heat stimulation (Trautman and Febiger 1957). In the horse, the apocrine glands perform a thermoregulatory function and secrete under the influence of epinephrine. The adrenal medulla in response to impulses received from the thermoregulatory center in the hypothalamus releases epinephrine into the circulation.

According to Jenkinson (1969), apocrine glands aid evaporative heat loss in the horse and cow. Only the hooved animals and marsupials have thermoregulatory apocrine glands. Rodents do not have either eccrine or apocrine thermoregulatory sweat glands. The hippopotamus when excited secretes a pink apocrine sweat, well known as "bloody sweat" (Hurley and Shelley 1960).

The detailed structure of these glands has been described in human subjects. In other animal species, the structure is likely to vary because of their diverse mechanism of secretion. In man, the apocrine glands have a secretory coil embedded in the dermis and a duct that conveys the secretory product to the pilosebaceous canal. The secretory coil of these glands is lined by epithelial cells of varying shape depending upon the secretory activity. Myoepithelial cells, functionally contractile, surround the secretory cells. A basement membrane is found outside the myoepithelial cells. Secretory cells may have a single large rounded nucleus or may be binucleated. With basic dyes, basophilia at the base of the secretory cells is seen. The basophilic material in the cytoplasm of the secretory cells is inversely proportional to the number of granules and apparently directly proportional to the number of mitochondria (Montes et al. 1960).

In stained preparations, mitochondria were numerous in cells with few granules and scarce in cells replete with granules (Ota 1950). A prominent Golgi complex is seen between the nucleus and the distal border of the secretory cells. Lipid granules and substances positive to PAS (periodic acid–Schiff) stain that could be phospholipids, glycoproteins, or mucopolysaccharides are seen in the Golgi apparatus (Montagna and Parakkal 1974). The ducts of these glands are lined with two layers of cells, the superficial or the luminal layer being composed of flattened squamous-type cells. The terminal part of the duct is funnel shaped with cells becoming multilayered. The duct is surrounded by the myoepithelial cells.

Spearman (1973) describes two distinct types of apocrine glands, thermoregulatory and accessory sexual scent glands. The thermoregulatory type produce watery secretion, probably involving the merocrine as well as the apocrine secretion seen in hooved animals. The scent glands, which secrete very actively in both sexes during the breeding season, elaborate a scanty viscous secretion containing volatile substances and mucopolysaccharides and are most developed in species with a strong olfactory sense. The function of scent glands is to enable males and females to locate one another during the breeding season, a matter of particular importance in normally solitary animals. The volatile scent can be detected by other members of a species over long distances.

Scent glands are not confined to the urogenital skin—the elephants have musth glands behind their eyes. Glands in the belly of the male musk deer secrete musk, used in the manufacture of all high-quality perfume (Spearman 1973). Scent glands of the goat, however, are sebaceous (Bal and Ghoshal 1976). Pheromones give to human beings characteristic as well as specifically individual and topographical odors. They also play a significant and subtle role in communication between microsmatic animals (animals with a feeble sense of smell), a significance they may once have had in human communications (Montagna and Parakkal 1974). The apocrine glands seem to develop under the influence of gonadal hormones, but once developed they function independently.

The nature of secretions varies according to the gland and the region of the body: apocrine glands in the axillary region of the human body elaborate a malodorous substance; the secretion of the ceruminous glands mixes with the sebum secreted by the sebaceous glands of the external ear canal to form cerumen; a venomous poison is secreted from the skin glands of the duckbill platypus through an opening in the spine in each hindfoot.

Apocrine glands in the dog and horse possess dual autonomic innervation; that is, they may respond to intradermal epinephrine and acetylcholine (Aoki and Wada 1951, Hurley and Shelley 1960). In the human, intradermal injections of epinephrine or norepinephrine in concentrations of 10^{-4} or 10^{-5} induce apocrine secretion (Aoki 1962, Goodall 1970).

Eccrine

Eccrine sweat glands are simple tubular glands that develop like other skin glands as invaginations from the surface epithelium of the skin. They extend down into the dermis as well as the epidermis. In mammals other than the primates the sweat glands are nearly torpid or represent a whole array of different mechanisms for dissipating body heat. Horses, cows, and some dogs rely partially on their apocrine glands for this function. In general only primates possess large numbers of true eccrine glands in their hairy skin. The sweat glands of primates do not respond appreciably to either cholinergic or adrenergic stimulation.

Kozlowski and Calhoun (1969) observed sweat glands of various sizes in different regions of the skin in sheep. They found large coiled glands in the region of the scrotum, interdigital pouch, infraorbital pouch, and in the prepuce and inguinal area. They did not give a separate description of the eccrine and apocrine glands. The goat has compound tubular sweat glands in the planum nasale (Sar and Calhoun 1966). For cattle, Goldsberry and Calhoun (1959) have classified the sweat glands into three categories: saccular noncoiled in the general body area, saccular coiled around natural openings and skin margin areas, and compound tubular confined to the nasolabial region. In the dog merocrine sweat glands are embedded in the adipose tissue of the foot pads. The excretory ducts of these glands become continuous with the epidermis at the very depths of the epidermal pegs where their epithelium joins with the stratum basale of the epidermis. The lumen of the excretory duct then follows a tortuous path through the epidermal cells to the surface where the glandular secretion is expelled (Lovell and Getty 1957).

The major function of eccrine sweat glands in man is thermoregulation. Thermal sweating takes place more acutely and intensely and the body temperature can be more accurately regulated in man than in any other mammal (Kuno 1956). Eccrine sweat may be copious yet dilute despite the small size of the gland.

Other animals may control body temperature effectively by evaporation through respiratory passages. This may be augmented by panting, a type of shallow respiration specifically adapted for elimination of heat. Evaporation from mucous membranes of the mouth and tongue can successfully control body temperature when these organs are large in proportion to body size, as in the dog (Kuno 1956). In animals possessing a small mouth, for example, horse, sheep, goat, monkey, and man, body temperature may be controlled by evaporation from well-developed sweat glands.

A number of species of small-mouthed mammals, however, have no sweat glands and do not pant. In some of these animals saliva substitutes for sweat. In hot weather the body of the mouse is entirely wet; salivation is profuse. The mouse first wets the frontal portion of its chest and abdomen, then rubs saliva all over the body with its legs. The evaporation of the saliva removes heat. In hot countries, cattle are known to salivate continually.

During panting the increase in salivation is significant, and large amounts of water are evaporated. Panting and salivation are the two most important processes for controlling body temperatures in animals who do not have sweat glands. An increase in body temperature in hot weather is a common phenomenon in animals, while that of man is kept normal by his superbly developed sweat mechanism.

The elephant has an enormous body with a small mouth. It appears to show neither panting nor intense salivation; no sweat glands can be detected. Kuno (1956) has observed that elephants frequently suck water into their trunk and spray it over their heads, backs, and sides. If water is not available they appear to attain temperature control by inserting their trunks into their mouths and using saliva in much the same way.

In thermoregulatory sweating, general sweat outbreak is effected in two ways: warmed blood from the periphery, arriving at the brain, stimulates the hypothalamic thermoregulatory centers; and afferent nerve impulses from the periphery stimulate the same centers via a long reflex mechanism (Rothman 1954).

Perspiration on the palms and soles, as contrasted to the general body surface, is not increased at all by ordinary thermal stimuli but is easily stimulated by mental or sensory agents. Insensible perspiration at these sites is very large. In animals mental stress is almost always accompanied by muscular work, such as encountered in self-defense and battle for food (Kuno 1956). It is therefore of great advantage to animals for the pads of their feet to become wet when excited, since this provides an adhesive surface to facilitate physical work. In human beings mental stress is not necessarily accompanied by muscular activity; however, this may still be an atavistic trait.

Because of the qualities of its constituents, sweat has been considered similar to urine. Sweat, however, is the most dilute animal fluid; most of its solid constituents are exceedingly small in quantity, and therefore it would seem unlikely for sweating to play a significant role in excretion.

Innervation

Although eccrine glands of man, as well as those of the paw of cat and dog, are anatomically sympathetic, they are physiologically and pharmacologically cholinergic. Adrenergic sweating has been reported. Adrenergic agents may contact the myoepithelium of the sweat glands, pressing out preformed sweat droplets (Rothman 1954).

Sebaceous glands

Generally the sebaceous glands in the domestic animals are associated with the hair follicles and open via the pilosebaceous canal into the upper part of the follicle. They secrete sebum, a fatty lubricant.

The perianal or circumanal glands of the dog are modified sebaceous glands that exist as solid alveolar masses, the alveoli consisting of small darkly staining peripheral cells and large cytoplasm-rich central cells; their ducts usually open into hair follicles. They are present in both sexes at birth but are best developed after puberty, forming a ring around the anus. Tumors of the circumanal glands, seen exclusively in the males, may occur anywhere around the anus or above it, at the base of the tail or the side of the prepuce as a result of metastasis. Perianal or circumanal glands are one and the same thing.

Sebaceous glands of dogs appear to be similar to the human glands. In the cat, the sebaceous gland complexes are dispersed in the connective tissue of the wall of the anal sac at fairly regular intervals (Greer and Calhoun 1966). In newborn pigs the sebaceous glands are rudimentary but may still contain functional cells. In sheep the sebaceous glands are associated with the upper third of the wool or the hair follicle. Glandular epithelium is lobulated and the lobules are separated by connective tissue trabeculae (Kozlowski and Calhoun 1969). In cattle the size of the sebaceous glands is inversely proportional to the hair density. They are more highly developed in the perianal region and at the horn, hoof, and muzzle margins but absent in the hairless areas (Goldsberry and Calhoun, 1959). In the goat, the sebaceous glands open independently of the hair follicles in the perianal region and on the eyelids. At the junctions of the hoof with the skin, the base of the horn, the base of ear, and in the perianal region the sebaceous glands appear as large branched alveolar glands (Sar and Calhoun 1966).

The scent glands of the goat, which are modified sebaceous glands, are located around the caudomedial aspect of the base of the horn. Found in both sexes, they are usually smaller in castrated males and pregnant females. During breeding season, they become hypertrophied and very odorous in the male, and the odor is attributed to the presence of capric or caproic acids secreted by the glands. As the activity of these glands is dependent upon the mating season, it can be correlated with gonadal function (Bal and Ghoshal 1976).

Some mammals, such as whales and porpoises, are relatively free of sebaceous glands. In laboratory animals aggregates of glands like the preputial and inguinal glands in rats, mice, rabbits, and gerbils become encapsulated to form specialized organs. Sebaceous glands can also differentiate or form in other organs. They are often found in the parotid and submaxillary glands of humans (Hamperl 1931, Hartz 1946, Andrew 1952, Meza Chavez 1949). Sebaceous metaplasia occurring in the salivary glands is surprising because it happens so often. Sebaceous metaplasia have been found in the cervix uteri (Donnelly and Navidi 1950), larynx (Geipel 1949), and esophagus.

Secretion of sebum

A number of factors contribute to the secretion of sebum. The contraction of the arrectores pilorum muscles may have some effect (Kligman and Shelley 1958, Pontein 1960). The viscosity of the sebum and its spread on the skin and hair may be affected by the skin temperature. According to Montagna and Ford (1969), there is no nervous control of the sebaceous secretion except in the Meibomian glands. Growth and differentiation of the sebaceous glands are not affected by the complete denervation of the skin areas (Doupe and Sharp 1943, Pontein 1960). The flow of sebum from the sebaceous glands is a continuous process (Kligman and Shelley 1958). The quantity of sebum released in a given time per unit area is proportional to the total glandular volume. This function is attributed to the entire mass of the differentiated secretory cells.

Hormonal effects

According to Straus et al. (1962) and Takayasu and Adachi (1970), hormones regulate the size and rate of maturation of the sebaceous glands. At birth the sebaceous glands are large; they become smaller in infancy and childhood, and grow larger at puberty and adulthood; sebum production in women drops after menopause. Hamilton (1941) showed the influence of androgens on the human sebaceous glands. Testosterone has a direct effect on the sebaceous glands which respond by enlarged growth in areas where the hormone is locally injected after a week's interval. Eunuchs normally produce very little sebum and its production is increased by testosterone administration.

Large doses of progesterone injected into laboratory animals cause glandular enlargement, but physiological doses of progesterone (50 mg/day) administered intramuscularly to women produced no response in the sebaceous glands (Montagna and Parakkal 1974). There is no increase in sebum production during the luteal phase of the menstrual cycle, which is too short to stimulate sebaceous glands.

Estrogens administered in large doses over a prolonged period suppress sebum production, although, unlike testosterone, injections of estrogens have no local effect on the growth or enlargement of the sebaceous glands. Regardless of the amounts of estrogens administered locally, sebum production can be reactivated by androgen.

Adrenalectomy decreases sebum production in male rats. Glucocorticoids on the other hand do not stimulate sebum secretion. Adrenal androgens may play a significant role in the pituitary-adrenal and androgen–sebaceous gland stimulatory cycle (Thody and Shuster 1971a,b,c). In male animals and men, testicular testosterone is the controlling factor, whereas in women it is the ovarian and adrenal androgens. The specific tropic hormone that stimulates the secretion of sebum is dihydrotestosterone, which is produced by the catalytic action of the enzyme α-reductase in its conversion from testosterone and other androgens.

Characteristic odors in ranting boars emanate from the preputial glands. The agent responsible for the body odor is lipophilic and probably a muscone (an oily cyclic ketone that is the chief odoriferous constituent of musk and is used in perfumes). Dutt et al. (1959) reported that preputial glands dependent upon the male sex hormone for secretory activity produce a fat diffusible material which is responsible for sexual odor in boar carcasses.

Functions of sebum

An important function of sebum in domestic animals is to provide luster to the hair coat, as well as to be an emolient to the keratinized superficial layer of the skin. Sebum may act as a bacteriostatic and fungistatic agent.

The real function of sebum seems to be as a pheromone or olfactant signal. Sebums secreted by the different glands of various animal species have characteristic odors. Sometimes olfactory perceptions in birds are manifested in changes in breathing rate, blood pressure, heart beat, and widening of pupils (Wenzel 1967). Ability to produce scent signals varies with species and season depending on sex, social status, age, density of population, and other factors (Mykytowycz 1970).

REFERENCES

Allington, H.V. 1956. Eczematous and polymorphous hypersensitivity to light. In R.B. Baer, ed., *Allergic Dermatoses Due to Physical Agents*. Lippincott, Philadelphia. Pp. 25–47.

Andrew, W. 1952. A comparison of age changes in salivary glands of man and the rat. *J. Geront*. 7:178–90.

Aoki, T. 1962. Stimulation of human axillary sweat glands by cholinergic agents. *J. Invest. Derm*. 38:41–44.

Aoki, T., and Wada, M. 1951. Functional activity of the sweat glands in the hairy skin of the dog. *Science* 114:123–24.

Bal, H.S., and Ghoshal, N.G. 1976. The "scent glands" of the goat (Capra hircus). *Zentralblatt Veterinärmedizin,* ser. C, 5(1):104.

Biedermann, W. 1926. Vergleichende Physiologie des Integumentes der Wirbeltiere. *Ergeb. Biol*. 1:120–36.

Billingham, R.E. 1949. Dendritic cells in pigmented human skin. *J. Anat*. 83:109–15.

Billingham, R.E., and Medawar, P.B. 1953. A study of the branched cells of the mammalian epidermis with special references to the fate of their division products. *Phil. Trans. Roy. Soc*. 237:151–69.

Blum, H.F. 1945. The physiologic effects of sunlight on man. *Physiol. Rev*. 25:483–530.

Breathnach, A.S., and Robins, E.J. 1970. Ultrastructural observations on Merkel cells in human fetal skin. *J. Anat*. 106:4110.

Breathnach, A.S., Silver, W.K., Smith, T., and Heyner, S. 1968. Langerhans cells in mouse skin experimentally deprived of its neural crest component. *J. Invest. Derm*. 50:147–60.

Calhoun, M.L., and Stinson, A.W. 1976. Skin. In H.-D. Dellmann and E.M. Brown, eds., *Textbook of Veterinary Histology*. Lea & Febiger, Philadelphia. Pp. 463.

Calvery, H.D., Draize, J.H., and Laug, E.P. 1946. The metabolism and permeability of normal skin. *Physiol. Rev*. 26:510–40.

Davson, H., and Danielli, J.F. 1952. *The Permeability of Natural Membranes*. Cambridge U. Press, London, New York.

Donnelly, G.H., and Navidi, S. 1950. Sebaceous glands in the cervix uteri. *J. Path. Bact*. 62:453–654.

Doupe, J., and Sharp, M.E. 1943. Studies in denervation: (G)-Sebaceous secretion. *J. Neurol. Psychiat*. 6:133–35.

Dutt, R.H., Simpson, E.C., Christian, J.C., and Barnhart, C.E. 1959. Identification of preputial glands as the site of production of sexual odour in the boar. *J. Anim. Sci*. 13:1557.

Edwards, E.A., and Duntley, S.R. 1939. The pigments and color of living human skin. *Am. J. Anat*. 65:1–33.

FitzGerald, M.J.T. 1968. The innervation of the epidermis. In D.R. Kenshalo, ed., *The Skin Senses*. Thomas, Springfield, Ill. Pp. 61–83.

Fitzpatrick, T.B., and Szabo, G. 1957. The melanocyte: Cytology and cytochemistry. *J. Invest. Derm*. 32:197–209.

Geipel, P. 1949. Talgdrüse im Kehlkopf. *Zentralblatt Allg. Path. Anat*. 83:69–71.

Getty, R. 1975. *Sisson and Grossman's The Anatomy of the Domestic Animals*. 5th ed. Saunders, Philadelphia. Pp. 728–35.

Goldberg, A. 1965. The hepatic porphyrias. In A. Rook and G.S. Walton, eds., *Comparative Physiology of the Skin*. Blackwell Scientific, Oxford. Pp. 345–50.

Goldsberry, S., and Calhoun, M.L. 1959. The comparative histology of the skin of Hereford and Aberdeen Angus cattle. *Am. J. Vet. Res*. 20:61–68.

Goodall, McC. 1970. Innervation and inhibition of eccrine and apocrine sweating. *J. Clin. Pharmac*. 10:235–46.

Greer, B., and Calhoun, M.L. 1966. Anal sacs of the cat (Felis domesticus). *Am. J. Vet. Res*. 27:773–81.

Hamilton, J.B. 1941. Male hormone substance: A prime factor in acne. *J. Clin. Endocr*. 1:570–92.

Hamperl, H. 1931. Beiträge zür normalen pathologischen histologie menschlicher Speicheldrüsen. *Zeitschrift Mikrosk. Anat. Forsch*. 27:1–55.

Hartz, P.H. 1946. Development of sebaceous glands from intralobular ducts of the parotid gland. *Arch. Path*. 41:651–54.

Hashimoto, K. 1972. Fine structure of Merkel cells in human mucosa. *J. Invest. Derm*. 58:381–87.

Hurley, H.J., and W.B. Shelley. 1960. *The Human Apocrine Sweat Gland in Health and Disease*. Thomas, Springfield, Ill. Pp. 23–26, 51–55.

Jarret, A. 1973. *The Physiology and Pathophysiology of the Skin*. Academic Press, London, New York. Vol. 1, 3–44.

Jenkinson, D.M. 1969. Sweat gland function in domestic animals. In S.Y. Botelho, F.B. Brooks, and W.B. Shelley, eds., *Exocrine Glands*. Proc. Internat. Cong. Physiol. Sci. 14th Satellite Symp. U. of Pennsylvania Press, Philadelphia. Pp. 201–16.

Jorgenson, S.K., and With, T.K. 1965. Congenital porphyria in animals other than man. In A. Rook and G.S. Walton, eds., *Comparative Physiology and Pathology of the Skin*. Blackwell Scientific, Oxford. Pp. 317–31.

Kligman, A.M. 1964. The biology of the stratum corneum. In W. Montagna and W.C. Lobitz, Jr., eds., *The Epidermis*. Academic Press, New York. Pp. 387–430.

Kligman, A.M., and Shelley, W.B. 1958. An investigation of the biology of the human sebaceous gland. *J. Invest. Derm.* 30:99–125.

Kovacs, R. 1950. *Light Therapy*. Thomas, Springfield, Ill. Pp. 14–17.

Kozlowski, G.P., and Calhoun, M.L. 1969. Microscopic anatomy of the integument of sheep. *Am. J. Vet. Res.* 30(8):1267–79.

Kral, F., and Schwartzman, R.M. 1964. *Veterinary and Comparative Dermatology*. Lippincott, Philadelphia. Pp. 8, 122–29.

Kuno, U. 1956. *Human Perspiration*. Thomas, Springfield, Ill.

Lovell, J.E., and Getty, R. 1957. The hair follicle, epidermis, dermis, and skin glands of the dog. *Am. J. Vet. Res.* 38(69):873–85.

Malkinson, F.D. 1964. Permeability of the stratum corneum. In W. Montagna and W.C. Lobitz, Jr., eds., *The Epidermis*. Academic Press, New York. Pp. 435–48.

Marcarian, H.Q., and Calhoun, M.L. 1966. Microscopic anatomy of the integument of adult swine. *Am. J. Vet. Res.* 27:765–72.

Masson, P. 1951. My conception of cellular naevi. *Cancer* 4:9–38.

Medawar, P.B. 1953. The micro-anatomy of the mammalian epidermis. *Q. J. Microsc. Sci.* 94:481–503.

Meza Chavez, L. 1949. Sebaceous glands in normal and neoplastic parotid glands: Possible significance of sebaceous glands in respect to the origin of tumors of the salivary glands. *Am. J. Path.* 25:627–45.

Montagna, W. 1963. Comparative aspects of sebaceous glands. In W. Montagna, R.A. Ellis, and A.F. Silver, eds., *Advances in Biology of Skin*. Vol. 4, *Sebaceous Glands*. Pergamon, New York, London. Pp. 32–45.

Montagna, W., and Ford, D.M. 1969. Histology and cytochemistry of human skin. XXXIII. The eyelid. *Arch. Derm.* 100:328–35.

Montagna, W., and Parakkal, P.F. 1974. *The Structure and Function of Skin*. 3d ed. Academic Press, New York. Pp. 75–95, 280–331, 332–59, 371–406.

Montes, L.F., Baker, B.L., and Curtis, A.C. 1960. The cytology and the large axillary sweat glands in man. *J. Invest. Derm.* 35:273–91.

Mottag, J.H., and Zelickson, A.S. 1967. Melanin transfer: A possible phagocytic process. *J. Invest. Derm.* 49:605–10.

Mykytowycz, R. 1970. The role of skin glands in mammalian communication. In J.W. Johnson, D.G. Moulton, and A. Turk, eds., *Advances in Chemoreception*. Appleton-Century-Crofts, New York. Vol. 1, 327–60.

Okun, M.R. 1965. Histogenesis of melanocytes. *J. Invest. Derm.* 44:285–99.

Okun, M.R., and Zook, B.C. 1967. Histological parallels between mastocytoma and melanoma. *Arch. Derm.* (Chicago) 95:275–86.

Oliver, R.F. 1966. Regeneration of dermal papilla in rat vibrissae. *J. Invest. Derm.* 47:496–97.

Ota, R. 1950. Zytologische und histologische Untersuchungen der apokrinen Schweissdrüsen in den normalen, keinen Achselgeruch (Osmidrosis axillae) gebenden Achselhäuten von Japanern. *Arch. Anat. Jap.* 1:285–308.

Overton, E. 1924. *Studien über die Narkose*. Fischer, Jena.

Pontein, B. 1960. Grafted skin: Observations on innervation and other qualities. *Acta Chir. Scand.* 257(suppl.):1–78.

Rothman, S. 1943. The principles of percutaneous absorption. *J. Lab. Clin. Med.* 28:1305–21.

——. 1954. *Physiology and Biochemistry of the Skin*. U. of Chicago Press, Chicago.

——. 1964. Keratinization in historical perspective. In W. Montagna and W.C. Lobitz, Jr., eds., *The Epidermis*. Academic Press, New York. Pp. 172.

Ryder, M.L. 1973. *Hair*. Edward Arnold, London. Pp. 1.

Sar, M., and Calhoun, M.L. 1966. The microscopic anatomy of the integument of the common American goat. *Am. J. Vet. Res.* 27:444–56.

Schiefferdecker, P. 1922. Die Hautdrüsen des Menschen und des Säugetieres, ihre Bedeutung sowie die Muscularis sexualis. *Zoologica* 72:1–154.

Singh, A. 1962. Skin pigmentation in buffalo calves. *Can. Vet. J.* 3:343–46.

Spearman, R.I.C. 1973. *The Integument*. Cambridge U. Press, Cambridge. Pp. 134–38.

Straus, J.S., Kligman, A.M., and Pochi, E.E. 1962. The effect of androgens and estrogens on human sebaceous glands. *J. Invest. Derm.* 39:139–55.

Takayasu, S., and Adachi, K. 1970. Hormonal control of metabolism in hamster costovertebral glands. *J. Invest. Derm.* 55:13–19.

Thody, A.J., and Shuster, S. 1971a. Sebotrophic activity of B-lipotrophin. *J. Endocr.* 50:533–34.

——. 1971b. The effect of hypophysectomy on the response of the sebaceous gland to testosterone propionate. *J. Endocr.* 49:329–33.

——. 1971c. Effect of adrenalectomy and adrenocorticotrophic hormone on sebum secretion in the rat. *J. Endocr.* 49:325–28.

Thomson, M.L. 1955. Relative efficiency of pigment and horny layer thickness in protecting the skin of Europeans and Africans against solar ultraviolet irradiation. *J. Physiol.* 127:236–46.

Trautman, A., and Febiger, J. 1957. *Fundamentals of the Histology of Domestic Animals*. 9th ed. McGraw-Hill, New York. Pp. 346–57.

Webb, A.J., and Calhoun, M.L. 1954. The microscopic anatomy of the skin of mongrel dogs. *Am. J. Vet. Res.* 15(55):274–80.

Wenzel, B.M. 1967. Olfactory perception in birds. In T. Hayashi, ed., *Proceedings of the Second International Symposium on Olfaction and Taste*. Pergamon, Tokyo, London. Pp. 203–17.

Wilson, J.A. 1941. *Modern Practice in Leather Manufacture*. Reinhold, New York.

PART VI SKELETAL MUSCLE, NERVOUS SYSTEM, TEMPERATURE REGULATION, AND SPECIAL SENSES

CHAPTER 39

Skeletal Muscle

by Darrel E. Goll, Marvin H. Stromer, and Richard M. Robson

The three different kinds of muscle tissue found in mammals can be distinguished by their structure, innervation and control, and function. Skeletal muscle (so called because it attaches to the skeleton) is by far the most abundant; it composes approximately 40 percent of the total body weight of mammals and is under voluntary nervous control. Skeletal muscle is sometimes called striated muscle because it contains alternating light and dark bands that have a cross-striated appearance in the light microscope. Striated muscle is a less specific term, however, because both skeletal and cardiac muscles are striated.

The second type of muscle tissue, cardiac muscle, is found only in the heart and appears similar in some ways to skeletal muscle when observed in the light microscope. Like skeletal muscle, cardiac muscle is cross-striated, but in contrast to skeletal muscle, it is under involuntary nervous control. The third type of muscle tissue is called smooth muscle. Although smooth muscles contain contractile proteins that are very similar to those found in skeletal and cardiac muscle, smooth muscle is not cross-striated and appears completely different from skeletal or cardiac muscle in the light microscope. Smooth muscle is found in a variety of places in the mammalian organism, including walls of the blood and lymphatic vessels, the walls of the digestive, urinary, reproductive, and respiratory tracts, the muscular walls of the uterus, and the dermal layer of the skin. The gizzard found in chickens and turkeys, for example, is almost entirely smooth muscle. Smooth muscle is also under involuntary nervous control.

This chapter is devoted largely to skeletal muscle tissue; at the end of this chapter, however, some of the physiological properties of cardiac and smooth muscles are briefly compared with the properties of skeletal muscle.

GROSS ANATOMY

Nomenclature

Skeletal muscles are usually named for one or more of their characteristics. For example, muscles may be named on the basis of their physiological action (adductor, supinator), location (quadriceps, subscapularis, supraspinatus, rectus abdominus), size (magnus), attachments (sternomastoid), shape (trapezius, triceps brachii, biceps femoris), structure (semimembranosus), or a combination of these features (e.g. shape and location—longissimus dorsi, externus abdominus obliquus). Muscles may also be classified as prime movers, antagonists, fixation muscles, or synergists, depending on their physiological action. Prime movers are those muscles primarily responsible for particular movements. Antagonists are those muscles that must relax to allow prime movers to act. Antagonists are important in coordinated and controlled muscular movements. Fixation muscles fix or set the base upon which movement by the prime movers occurs. For example, during movements of the forelimb in domestic animals, the scapula is steadied by the serratus ventralis. Synergists are muscles that act in conjunction with prime movers to perform movement. For example, a synergist may control movement at some proximal joint and thereby permit the prime mover to act upon a distal joint.

Origin, insertion, and belly are other terms sometimes used to describe skeletal muscles. The origin of a muscle refers to the stationary or less movable end of a muscle's attachment. Conversely, the insertion is the mobile or more movable end of a muscle's attachment. The belly is the center of a muscle and in general refers to the part of the muscle between its origin and insertion.

A muscle contraction may be either /isotonic or isometric. In an isotonic contraction, a muscle shortens against a constant load and therefore performs work. In an isometric contraction, the muscle is attached to a load that is too large for it to move; hence it does not shorten or contract at all, even though it develops tension. Because the muscle does not actually move a load in an isometric contraction, it does no work. Isometric contractions are often used experimentally to study muscle physiology.

Lever systems

Skeletal muscles are attached to the skeleton in a variety of ways to produce different types of lever systems. Some of these systems are adapted for rapid and large displacements, often at a loss of mechanical advantage; others are useful for holding heavy weights with little or no displacement. Muscles used for locomotion are examples of the former systems, whereas postural muscles are examples of the latter. Some of the lever systems that exist in mammals are illustrated in Figure 39.1. In type I levers (left), the fulcrum is located between the load and the applied force. The dorsal-cervical muscle system and the atlanto-occipital joint form an example of this kind of lever system. The head is the load, and the muscular force is applied behind the atlanto-occipital joint, which serves as the fulcrum.

In a type II lever system (middle), the load is placed between the fulcrum and the applied force. The interphalangeal joints, the gastrocnemius muscle, and the digital flexor muscles are examples of this type of system. In a type III lever system (right), the force is applied between the load and the fulcrum. Type III, which is the most common lever system found in mammals, permits a large displacement of a load with relatively little shortening of the muscle, but the gain in mobility is accomplished at the expense of mechanical advantage. The branchialis muscle and elbow joint form an example of a type III system.

The stifle joint, which must support a heavy load, is an example of an end-loaded compound lever system. This system produces a large mechanical advantage and consists of an articulated lever in which the fulcrum is at one end, the force is applied at the articulation (in this instance between the femur and the tibia), and the load is applied at the other end. Hence, when the leg is straight, the load is imposed longitudinally (i.e. end-loaded). With this arrangement relatively little force is required to support body weight when the joint is extended; in addition the muscle has a large mechanical advantage.

Structure

Examination of a cross section through an entire muscle such as the semitendinosus muscle of the leg (Fig. 39.2) shows that muscles are surrounded by a sheet of connective tissue called the epimysium. The epimysium is often fairly thick and tough and is a site of fat deposition (intermuscular fat) in animals. At irregular intervals, smaller sheets of connective tissue called the perimysium pass into the muscle and divide it into bundles of muscle fibers or fasciculi. Perimysial connective tissue layers also contain and envelope blood vessels and nerves, and muscle spindles are commonly found in the perimysial spaces. The size of muscle fasciculi determines muscle

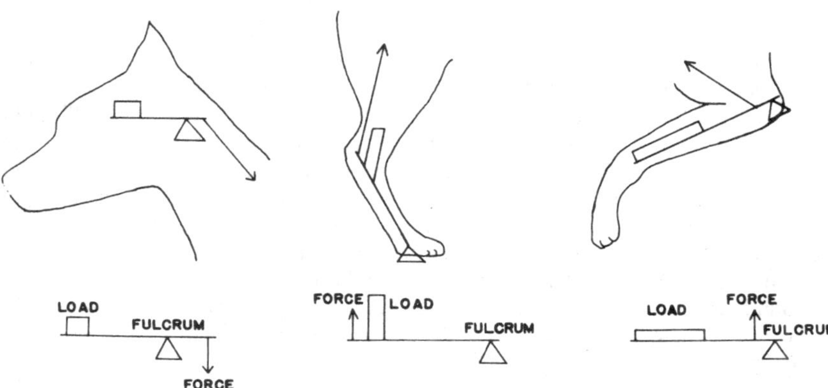

Figure 39.1. Lever systems of musculoskeletal structures. (Adapted from R.S. Stacy, D.T. Williams, R.E. Worden, and R.O. McMorris, *Essentials of Biological and Medical Physics*, McGraw-Hill, 1955.)

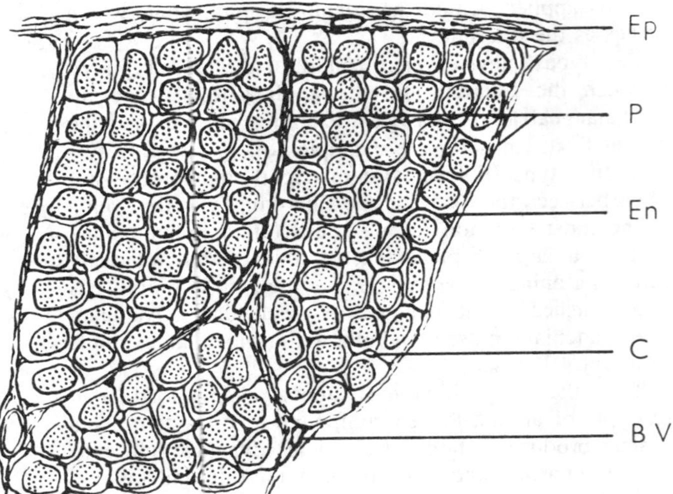

Figure 39.2. Diagram of a cross section through an entire muscle, showing its connective tissue framework. Ep, epimysium; P, perimysium; En, endomysium; BV, blood vessels; C, capillaries. (From Gould, in Bourne, ed. *The Structure and Function of Muscle,* Academic Press, New York, 1973.)

texture: the larger the fasciculi, the coarser the texture. In general, powerful muscles that perform large movements (e.g. leg or arm muscles) have larger fasciculi and therefore a coarser texture than smaller muscles that must perform very finely judged movement (e.g. ocular muscles). Adipose cells may also be deposited in the perimysial connective tissue layer.

Very delicate, fine sheets of connective tissue called the endomysium extend from the perimysium to surround each individual muscle fiber (Fig. 39.2). The endomysium lies immediately adjacent to the sarcolemma or outer muscle cell membrane, and is sometimes difficult to distinguish from it. There are usually 50 to 200 or 300 muscle fibers in each fasciculus. These muscle fibers can barely be distinguished with the unaided eye. Although muscles used for power usually have large fasciculi, they also usually have large fibers; therefore, the number of fibers per fasciculus may actually be less in such muscles than in muscles that perform fine movements. The endomysial connective tissue sheath only rarely contains large numbers of adipose cells.

MICROANATOMY

Muscle cells

The term muscle fiber is synonymous with muscle cell; therefore, muscle fibers are the physiological units of muscles. Muscle fibers are long, cylindrical, tubular cells with tapering ends and are not perfectly round in cross section. In general, skeletal muscle cells do not branch. Muscle cells can exist in three different anatomical configurations within a muscle, but cells in each of these three configurations have identical functions. The three configurations are: (1) extending completely from one end of a muscle to the other—cells of this configuration are rare in large muscles; (2) extending from one end of the muscle to the center of the muscle and terminating there; (3) beginning and terminating in the center or belly of the muscle. Skeletal muscle cells may range from 1–340 mm in length. Long muscle cells are rare, however, and most muscle cells are 1–40 mm long with an average of 20–30 mm.

Because skeletal muscle cells taper at either end, their diameter varies along their length. At their center it ranges from 10 to 100 μ. Diameter depends also on animal class, type of muscle, location within a muscle, amount of exercise, maturity, level of nutrition, and type of fiber. Diameter of muscle cells among different animal classes varies in the order: fishes>amphibians>reptiles>mammals>birds. Within the same animal, shorter thicker muscles generally have fibers with larger diameters than do long slender muscles. Within the same muscle, cells near the center generally have larger diameters than those near the ends. Muscle cell diameter also increases with exercise, maturity, and plane of nutrition. Muscle cells can be grouped into at least three categories based on their metabolism: (1) fast-twitch, glycolytic cells, (2) fast-twitch, oxidative-glycolytic cells, and (3) slow-twitch, oxidative cells. Among these three types of cells, the slow-twitch, oxidative cells generally have smaller diameters than the other two types. There is no relation between size or weight of animal and muscle cell diameter. For example, muscle cells in the mouse are over one half the diameter of muscle cells in the elephant.

Subcellular components

Muscle fibers or cells perform many of the same functions as cells in other tissues, and muscle cells therefore possess many of the same subcellular organelles that cells in other tissues do. For example, muscle cells contain an outer cell membrane or sarcolemma, mitochondria, Golgi apparatus, endoplasmic reticulum, peroxisomes, lysosomes, and ribosomes, just as other cells do. In many instances, these organelles in muscle cells are given the prefix *sarco* (from *sarkos,* Greek for flesh); for example, mitochondria are sometimes called sarcosomes (although this practice is becoming infrequent). In addition to the subcellular organelles commonly found in animal cells, muscle fibers also contain an organelle that adapts them for their special function of contraction. These contractile organelles are called myofibrils.

The outer cell membrane or sarcolemma of muscle cells differs in several ways from the plasma membrane of nonmuscle cells. Structurally, the sarcolemma is about 100 nm thick and consists of two distinguishable parts. The innermost part is the plasmalemma, which is 7.5–10 nm thick and is similar to the plasmalemma of nonmuscle cells. Chemically, the plasmalemma is composed of protein (60%), phospholipids (20%), and cholesterol (20%). The outer part of the sarcolemma is 70–90 nm thick and is called the basement membrane. The basement membrane itself is composed of three morphologically different parts: (1) an outer layer, 10 nm thick, containing noncollagenous fibrils; (2) a middle layer, 30 nm thick, containing collagen fibers; and (3) an inner amorphous layer, 30–50 nm thick, containing polysaccharides among other constituents. In addition, the sarcolemma can propagate an action potential and therefore differs physiologically from outer cell membranes of all nonmuscle cells except nerve cells. Because the sarcolemma lies immediately under the endomysium and is contiguous with it, the outer layer of noncollagenous fibrils of the basement membrane can be difficult to distinguish from the endomysium in some areas.

Skeletal muscle cells are multinucleated and average 100–200 nuclei per cell. This multinucleated nature occurs because skeletal muscle cells in mature muscles originate from fusion of 100–200 different embryonic muscle cells (myoblasts), with each myoblast contributing one nucleus. Although nuclei lie in the interior of skeletal muscle cells in immature muscles or in invertebrate muscles, they all lie peripherally just under the sarcolemma in mature vertebrate skeletal muscle. Once a nucleus has been incorporated into a multinucleated skeletal muscle cell, it ceases mitotic division. In contrast to skeletal muscle cells, smooth and cardiac muscle cells contain only one nucleus which is located in the interior of the cell. Structurally, muscle cell nuclei are ellipsoidal, about 8–10 μ long, and resemble nuclei in nonmuscle cells.

Mitochondria, ribosomes, and the Golgi complex in muscle cells are structurally and functionally similar to their counterparts in nonmuscle cells. In general, the Golgi complex and ribosomes are seen less frequently in muscle cells than in nonmuscle cells. The prevalence of mitochondria in muscle cells varies widely among different types of muscles. Cardiac muscle cells and slow-twitch, oxidative types of skeletal muscle cells contain numerous mitochrondria; these types of muscle cells are capable of prolonged and sustained contractions, and the aerobic metabolism that occurs in mitochondria is necessary to supply energy for such sustained contractions. Mitochondria may be rare, however, in fast-twitch, glycolytic skeletal muscle cells. Muscle cells also contain small spherical glycogen granules, 20–45 nm in diameter. Glycogen granules are much more numerous in muscle cells from well-fed rested animals than in muscle cells of starved or exhausted animals.

Lysosomes in mature, healthy, skeletal muscle cells are evidently part of the sarcoplasmic reticular (endoplasmic reticulum) system (Seiden 1973, Smith and Bird 1975). Structures that resemble lysosomes seen in liver or kidney cells are observed in muscle cells only in pathological states and never in cells from mature healthy muscle, although lysosomal-like particles can be prepared biochemically from both pathological and healthy muscle cells. Muscle cells generally have a much lower lysosomal enzyme content than liver or kidney cells.

Cytoplasm in muscle cells is called sarcoplasm and generally has the same function and protein composition as cytoplasm from nonmuscle cells, except that sarcoplasm contains myoglobin, an oxygen-storage protein not found in other cell types, and also has a slightly different glycolytic enzyme content than most nonmuscle cells. Because myoglobin has a higher affinity for oxygen than hemoglobin, myoglobin in the muscle cell is able to bind oxygen from oxygenated hemoglobin in the blood stream. This oxygen is then used in aerobic metabolism by mitochondria. Mitochondria are the main oxygen consumers of the cell, and it is not surprising that cells that contain many mitochondria and that are adapted for prolonged and sustained contraction also contain large amounts of myoglobin. Oxygenated myoglobin is red, and muscles that contain large amounts of myoglobin often appear darker red than myoglobin-poor muscles. Whales, which must store enough oxygen to permit them to dive to great depths, have very large amounts of myoglobin in their muscle (50 mg/g of muscle compared with 1–4 mg/g in pigs).

Myofibrils, the organelles responsible for the contractile properties of muscle cells, are elongated protein threads, 1–3 μ in diameter in vertebrate skeletal muscle, that lie with their axes parallel with the long axis of the muscle cell (Fig. 39.3). Myofibrils extend completely from one end of the muscle cell to the other. In contrast to muscle cells, myofibrils occasionally branch. Branching evidently is a growth mechanism, and as a branching point "moves" along a single myofibril, two new myofibrils are produced (Goldspink 1972, Stromer et al. 1974). In contrast to most other subcellular organelles, myofibrils are not surrounded by a membrane; they exist as structural entities simply because they are insoluble at the ionic strength of the cell. The interior of muscle cells is literally packed with myofibrils; experiments show that 80–87 percent of the interior of skeletal muscle cells and approximately 50 percent of the interior of cardiac muscle cells are occupied by myofibrils. Although myofibrils are responsible for the complex biological function of movement, they contain relatively few proteins; only nine (or possibly ten) have been discovered thus far (Table 39.1), and it seems unlikely that many more will be found.

Myofibrils are cross-striated, that is, they consist of alternating light and dark bands (see Fig. 39.3). In skeletal and cardiac muscle cells, adjacent myofibrils lie with their light and dark bands in register, and this confers a

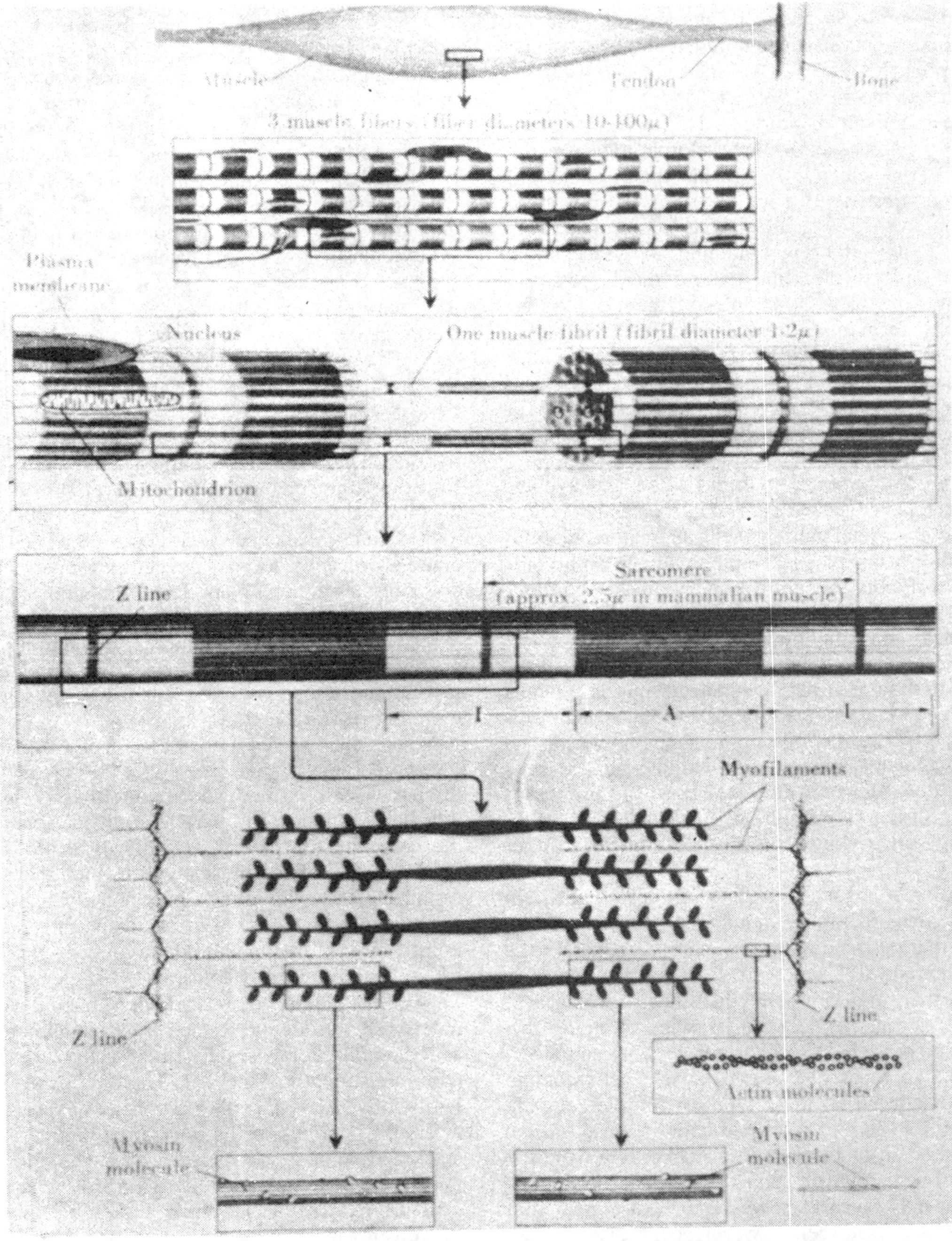

Figure 39.3. Diagram of a mature vertebrate skeletal muscle, such as the biceps femoris or semitendinosus, at different levels of organization ranging from an entire muscle with tendon attachments (top panel) to the molecular architecture of the myofilaments (bottom panel). Three muscle cells or fibers are shown in the second panel, which also shows the cross-striated structure and peripheral location of nuclei just under the sarcolemma. Small lines represent mitochondria. The third panel portrays a single muscle cell and its myofibrils at an intermediate light microscope magnification. The fourth panel shows the cross-striated structure of the myofibril at very high light microscope magnification. What appear to be single filaments at the light microscope level (fourth panel) are seen to be an interdigitating array of two kinds of filaments at very high electron microscope magnification (fifth panel). Thin filaments contain two strands of actin molecules coiled around one another, whereas thick filaments contain myosin molecules packed in a very specific way (bottom of figure). (From A.B. Novikoff and E. Holtzman, *Cells and Organelles,* Holt, Rinehart and Winston, New York, 1970. Reproduced by permission of Holt, Rinehart and Winston, Inc.; and H.E. Huxley.)

able 39.1. Properties of the myofibrillar proteins

rotein	Percentage of myofibril by weight	Mol wt (g/mol)	Mass (dalton) and no. of subunits per molecule *
yosin	50–58	475,000	200,000—two 20,700—one † 19,050—two † 16,500—one †
ctin	15–20	41,785	41,785—one †
ropomyosin	4–6	68,000	35,000—one 32,758—one † or 32,758—two †
roponin	4–6	72,000	30,503 (TN-T)—one † 20,864 (TN-I)—one † 17,846 (TN-C)—one †
-protein	2.5–3	140,000	140,000—one
-actinin	2–3	206,000	103,000—two
-actinin	<1	70,000	
-protein ‡	3–5	160,000	160,000—one
aramyosin §	3–30	220,000	110,000—two

* Subunit polypeptide mass and composition of myosin, tropomyosin, and roponin differ in slow-twitch, oxidative and fast-twitch, glycolytic muscle cells. igures are for fast-twitch, glycolytic cells.

† Complete amino acid sequence has been determined.

‡ Some reports suggest that a second M-protein with a 42,000 dalton subunit xists in addition to the M-protein described.

§ Found only in invertebrate muscles.

cross-striated appearance on the entire cell (hence the name striated muscle). The dark band is anisotropic or birefringent and is called the A-band. The light band is isotropic or weakly birefringent and is called the I-band. Because of their birefringence properties, the A-band will appear bright or light and the I-band will appear dark in a polarizing microscope. The A-band is dark and the I-band is light, however, if the myofibril is viewed in the phase microscope or in the electron microscope after staining with ordinary electron microscope stains. The light or I-band is bisected by a dark disk called the Z-disk (called the Z-line in the figures). The distance from one Z-disk to the next is called a sarcomere and is 2.5–2.8 μ in resting mammalian muscle. During muscle contraction, sarcomere lengths decrease to 2 μ or even less, depending on the extent of the contraction, but it is unlikely that sarcomere lengths ever decrease beyond 1.8 μ during physiological contraction of a living muscle cell. The sarcomere is the physiological contractile unit of the myofibril, and a myofibril may be viewed as a series of sarcomeres (several hundred to a thousand or more depending on length of the muscle cell) joined end to end. Although not shown in Figure 39.3, a light zone, called the H-zone, can also be seen in the middle of the dark A-band in mammalian myofibrils.

Myofibrils consist of two kinds of yet smaller filaments organized in an interdigitating array (see Fig. 39.3). Because one kind of filament has a diameter twice that of the other, they have been named simply thick and thin filaments. In mammalian skeletal and cardiac muscle. thick filaments are 14–16 nm in diameter and 1.5 μ long, tapering at both ends. Thin filaments are 6–8 nm in diameter and 1 μ long. Thin filaments are anchored at one end to the Z-disk, and interdigitate between the thick filaments at their other end. Thick filaments contain protrusions or cross-bridges that extend outward from their surfaces at regular intervals. These cross-bridges are 4–5 nm in diameter and approximately 10–14 nm long.

Thick filaments contain all the myosin in the myofibril and thin filaments contain most if not all the actin. Approximately 94–96 percent of the protein in thick filaments from vertebrate skeletal or cardiac muscle is myosin and the remaining 4–6 percent is probably C-protein. Thick filaments from invertebrate muscles may contain a protein called paramyosin in addition to myosin and C-protein (see Table 39.1). Thin filaments contain tropomyosin, troponin, and β-actinin in addition to actin. And α-actinin probably constitutes the darkly staining amorphous part of the Z-disk (dotted band in Fig. 39.3), whereas the filaments in the Z-disk may be made of either actin or tropomyosin or both. The M-line, which is a transverse structure that connects thick filaments at their centers and which is not shown in Figure 39.3, is made of M-protein.

The interdigitating thick and thin filament structure is easily and directly related to the cross-striated appearance of myofibrils as seen in the phase or electron microscope (Figs. 39.3, 39.4). The dark bands in the phase or electron microscope are those areas of the myofibril that contain thick filaments, whereas the light bands in the phase or electron microscope are those areas that have no thick filaments. The H-zone, which is the light zone in the center of the dark A-band, corresponds to the area where the thin filaments do not meet in the center of the sarcomere. As indicated in Figure 39.4, the pseudo-H-zone in electron micrographs is that area in the center of the thick filaments that has no cross-bridges. The M-line is readily seen in electron micrographs of longitudinal sections (see Fig. 39.4), but it is very difficult to show the details of the M-line schematically in longitudinal sections. The M-line originates from protein bridges seen nearly end-on in longitudinal sections.

It is frequently difficult to resolve thick and thin filaments in electron micrographs of striated muscle (see the micrograph in Fig. 39.4). This difficulty often is not due to lack of magnification, but rather to thickness of the section. Thick and thin filaments in the plane immediately under those on the surface of a section are not stacked in register with the filaments on the surface. Consequently, individual filaments become difficult to resolve in thick sections because of interference from adjoining, slightly displaced filaments. The thick and thin filament structure is readily seen in micrographs of thin sections that contain only one or two layers of filaments (Fig. 39.5). That two thin filaments are interdigitated be-

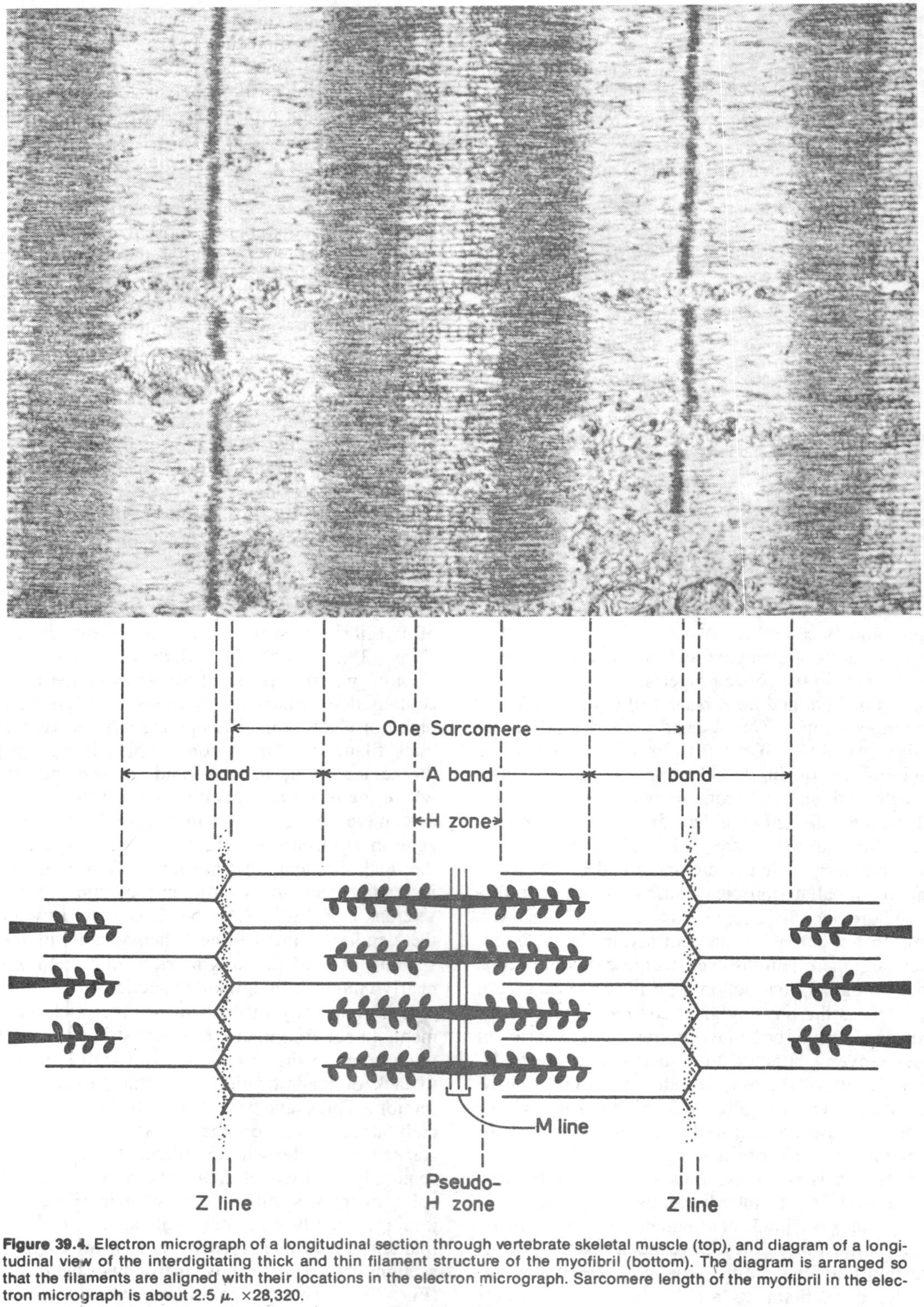

One Sarcomere
I band
A band
I band
H zone
M line
Z line
Pseudo-H zone
Z line

Figure 39.4. Electron micrograph of a longitudinal section through vertebrate skeletal muscle (top), and diagram of a longitudinal view of the interdigitating thick and thin filament structure of the myofibril (bottom). The diagram is arranged so that the filaments are aligned with their locations in the electron micrograph. Sarcomere length of the myofibril in the electron micrograph is about 2.5 μ. ×28,320.

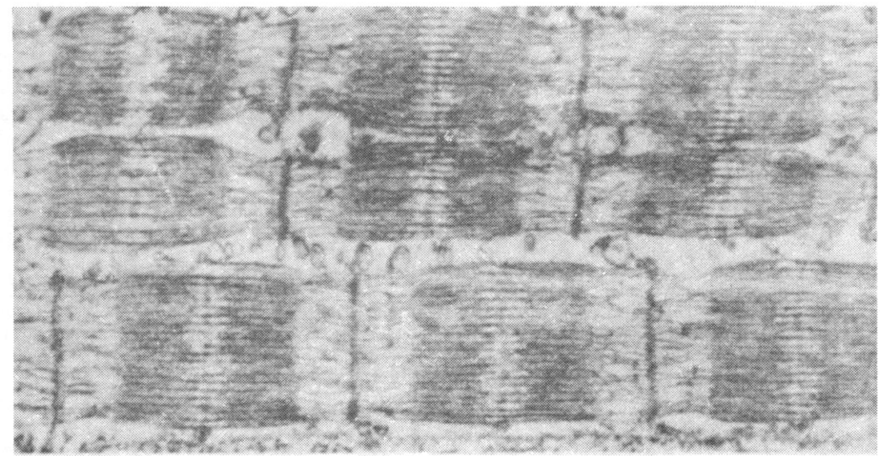

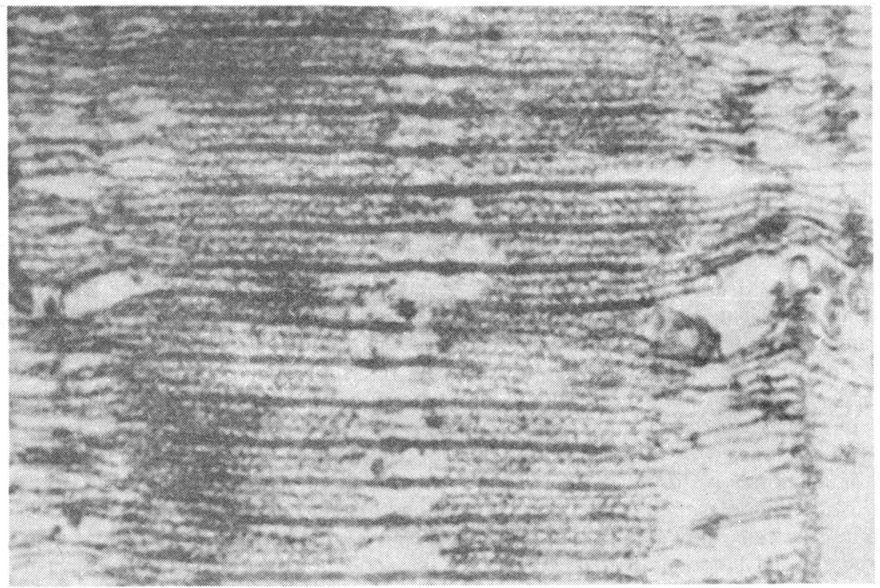

Figure 39.5. Electron micrographs of a longitudinal section of glycerinated rabbit psoas muscle cut sufficiently thin so that only single layers of filaments lie in the plane of the section. The thick and thin filaments can be seen clearly under these conditions. Above, lower magnification micrograph. ×16,000. Below, higher magnification micrograph of the same myofibrils shown above. Only a single sarcomere is seen in this high magnification micrograph and Z-disks bounding this sarcomere are seen on either edge of the figure. Cross-bridges extending between the thick and thin filaments are also visible. ×46,500. (From Huxley, in Bourne, ed., *The Structure and Function of Muscle*, Academic Press, New York, 1972.)

tween each pair of thick filaments in Figure 39.5 rather than one thin filament between each pair of thick filaments as depicted in Figures 39.3 and 39.4 is a consequence of the plane of sectioning (see Fig. 39.6).

Myofibrils from vertebrate striated muscle have a highly organized cross-sectional structure in addition to the very characteristic longitudinal structure discussed thus far. Cross sections through the region of thick and thin filament overlap in vertebrate striated muscles show that each thick filament is surrounded by six thin filaments that form a regular hexagon with the thick filament at its center (Fig. 39.6A). Each thin filament in turn is surrounded by three thick filaments. Hence, in vertebrate striated muscle, the ratio of thin filaments to thick filaments in a given plane is 2:1. Invertebrate muscles may contain anywhere from six to twelve thin filaments around each thick filament and have thin to thick filament ratios ranging from 3:1 up to 6:1. Cross sections through the H-zone in the middle of the A-band show that thick filaments are also arranged in a hexagonal lattice (Fig. 39.6B). Thick filaments are held in this lattice by protein bridges that join thick filaments at their centers (Fig. 39.6B). These protein bridges are called M-bridges and when viewed nearly end-on in longitudinal sections, the M-bridges form the M-line. Center-to-center distances between thick filaments in mammalian skeletal muscle range from approximately 35 nm in relaxed muscle to 45 nm in contracted muscle. A cross section through the I-band is shown in Figure 39.6C. Thin filaments change from a hexagonal lattice to a square lattice as they pass

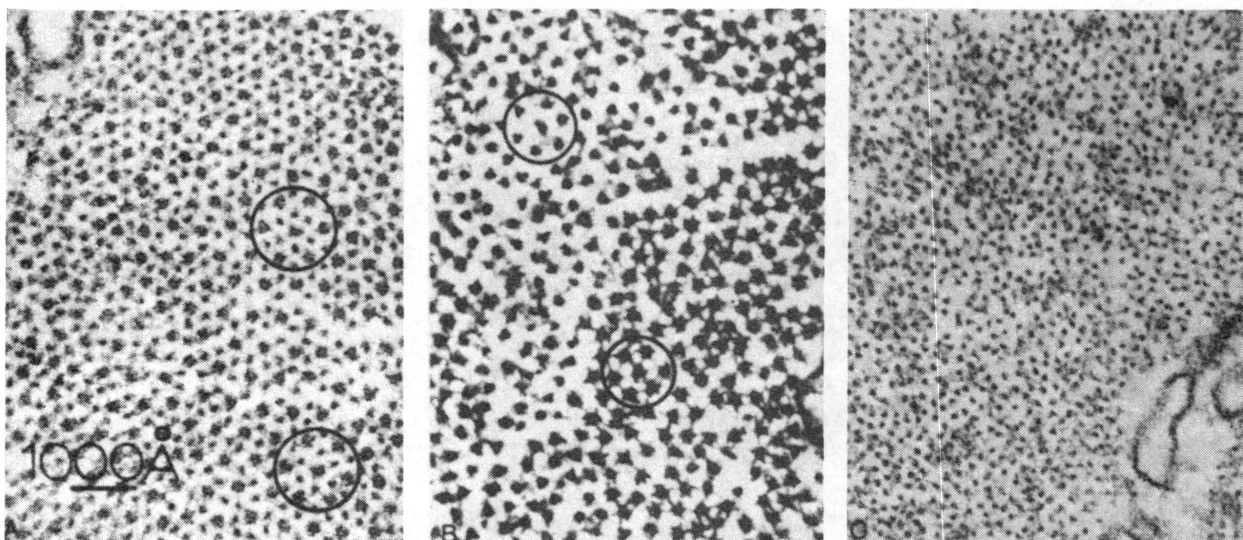

Figure 39.6. Electron micrographs of cross sections through different regions of a mammalian muscle sarcomere. A, region of thick and thin filament overlap in the A-band that shows both thick and thin filaments. Circles show instances of single thick filaments surrounded by six thin filaments, which are in turn each surrounded by three thick filaments. ×90,000. B, H-zone in the center of the A-band. Only thick filaments are seen and their hexagonal array is evident. Faint outlines of M-bridges extending from one thick filament to the adjacent thick filament can sometimes be seen. ×90,000. C, I-band region where only thin filaments are present. Because thin filaments change from a hexagonal array in the region of thick and thin filament overlap to a square lattice just before entering the Z-disk, three-dimensional order is sometimes difficult to detect in the I-band. ×90,000.

from the thick and thin overlap region to the Z-disk. The Z-disk holds thin filaments in the proper three-dimensional array and is therefore analogous to the M-line in this respect. Surface-to-surface distances between thin filaments as they enter the Z-disk range from approximately 23 nm in relaxed muscle to 28 nm in contracted muscle. Hence, center-to-center distances between thick and thin filaments in the region of overlap vary from approximately 19 nm (relaxed) to 31 nm (contracted).

Muscle cells also contain a series of membranous tubules that are structurally analogous to the endoplasmic reticulum of other vertebrate cells. In muscle cells, however, these tubules have a special structure and function and are called the sarcotubular system. The sarcotubular system may be divided into two sets of membranous tubules that do not open into one another, although the cell must be able to pass signals from one to the other. These two sets of tubules are called the transverse system (T-system) and the longitudinal system (L-system). The L-system is also called the sarcoplasmic reticulum (Fig. 39.7). The T-system consists of a set of tubules formed by invaginations of the plasmalemma. These tubules run perpendicular to the long axis of the muscle cell. Because T-tubules are invaginations of the plasmalemma, the lumen of the T-tubule is actually extracellular. T-tubules occur at very regular intervals along the length of the muscle cell. In some muscles, they are found at the level of every Z-disk (see Fig. 39.7); there is one T-tubule for every sarcomere in such muscles. In other muscles, T-tubules are found at the level of every A-I junction; this arrangement results in two T-tubules for every sarcomere and is usually found in fast-acting muscles. The function of T-tubules is to conduct a signal from a nerve impulse to the interior of the muscle cell. In this way, myofibrils located in the center of a muscle cell receive the signal to contract at almost the same time as myofibrils located on the periphery.

The sarcoplasmic reticulum consists of an extensive system of membranous tubules that extend from one T-tubule to the next and that surround each individual myofibril (see Fig. 39.7). As sarcoplasmic reticular membranes approach the T-tubule, they coalesce to form two large sacs called the lateral cisternae, one on each side. When cut in cross section, the T-tubule and associated lateral cisternae appear as three closely apposed tubules; this structure is called a triad. At the end opposite the lateral cisternae, sarcoplasmic reticular tubules meet and anastomose in the center of the space between T-tubules.

Sarcoplasmic reticular tubules have a remarkable ability to accumulate Ca^{++} against a concentration gradient. A large proportion of the total protein in sarcoplasmic reticular membranes is composed of an enzyme (mol wt 105,000) that has the ability to split ATP (adenosine triphosphate). Release of energy due to splitting of one molecule of ATP by this enzyme is coupled to transport of two molecules of Ca^{++} from the interior of the muscle cell into the lumen of the sarcoplasmic reticular tubule. By this mechanism, the ATPase keeps the free intracellular Ca^{++} concentration in resting muscle cells at a very low level (approximately 10^{-8} M), and most of the Ca^{++} in resting muscle cells is actually localized in the lateral cisternae. Passage of a signal from a nerve impulse along the T-tubule causes some of this Ca^{++} in the lateral cisternae to be disgorged into the interior of the muscle cell and results in the free intracellular Ca^{++} concentration rising momentarily to 10^{-5} or 10^{-6} M. This increase in free intracellular Ca^{++} triggers muscle contraction.

CHEMICAL COMPOSITION

Proximate composition

The proximate composition of mammalian skeletal muscle is given in Table 39.2. Muscle is almost entirely protein and a dilute aqueous salt solution. A small part of the lipid found in muscle tissue (about 1.0–1.5% of total muscle weight) originates from phospholipids and cholesterol found in membranes of the plasmalemma, the sarcotubular system, and other membranous subcellular organelles. This lipid is relatively invariant and exists at this level in all muscle tissue. Any lipid in addition to this

Table 39.2. Proximate composition of mammalian skeletal muscle *

Constituent	Percentage by weight	Comments
Water	55–78	Fat-free muscle is 72–78% water. Water content varies inversely with lipid content.
Protein	15–23	Fat-free muscle is 20–23% protein. Smooth muscle has a slightly lower protein content.
Lipid	1–20	About 1.0–1.5% phospholipid. Varies widely depending on neutral lipid content.
Carbohydrate	1–2	Mostly glycogen in living rested muscle. Some lactate in exhausted or postmortem muscle. Also includes some mucopolysaccharides.
Ash	1	100–140 mM K^+, 60–80 mM phosphate, 15–40 mM Na^+, 5–10 mM Cl^-, 15–25 mM Mg^{++}
Nucleic acid	<1	In porcine muscle, 25–30 mg DNA/100 g, 100 mg RNA/100 g.
Other soluble organic compounds	1	8–15 mM ATP, 20 mM phosphocreatine, 4–5 mM creatine, 350 mg carnosine/100 g, 140 mg anserine/100 g

* Muscle tissue is defined as muscle cells plus associated extracellular tissue that would be found in a whole muscle.

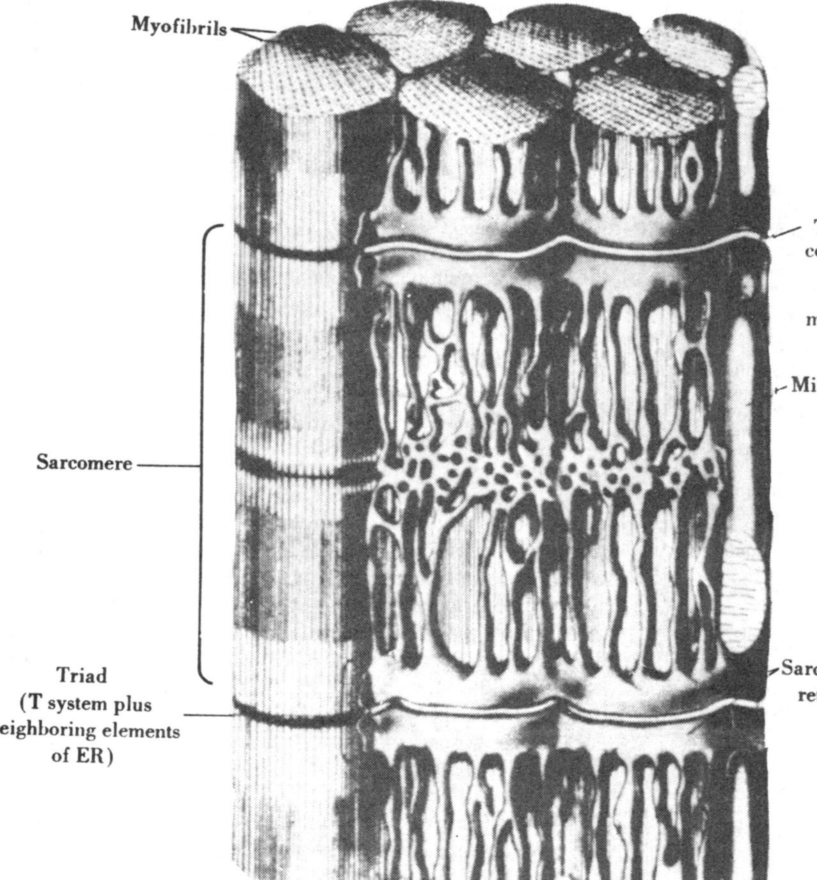

Figure 39.7. Diagram of the sarcotubular system of vertebrate skeletal muscle. T-tubules are shown at the level of every Z-disk and the sarcoplasmic reticular membranes form an extensive three-dimensional network around each myofibril. Lateral cisternae of the sarcoplasmic reticulum are shown as large pockets on either side of the T-tubules, forming triads. ER, endoplasmic reticulum. (From A.B. Novikoff and E. Holtzman, *Cells and Organelles*, Holt, Rinehart and Winston, New York, 1970. Reproduced by permission of Holt, Rinehart and Winston, Inc., and L.D. Peachey and D.W. Fawcett. Modified from *J. Cell Biol.*, vol. 25, no. 3, pt. 2, pp. 209–31, 1965.)

basal level, however, originates largely from neutral lipid deposited in epimysial and perimysial connective tissue layers. The amount of this neutral lipid obviously varies widely depending on metabolic condition. Muscle cells contain relatively high concentrations of K^+ and phosphate, and relatively low concentrations of Na^+ and Cl^-. DNA and RNA concentrations in muscle are lower than in most other animal cells. The dipeptides, anserine and carnosine, are found in large amounts in muscle cells, but their physiological role is still unclear. Some investigators suggest that they act as buffers.

Protein classification

The proteins in mammalian muscle may be grouped into three categories on the basis of their solubility in aqueous solvents (Table 39.3). The sarcoplasmic protein fraction is the most soluble of the three classes and generally includes those proteins found in the cytoplasm of the muscle cell. It therefore contains many of the enzymes associated with carbohydrate, lipid, and amino acid metabolism as well as those used for synthesis of cell constituents. Consequently, the sarcoplasmic protein fraction is very complex. Studies of muscle protein composition during development and growth have shown that, when expressed as a percentage of total muscle weight, sarcoplasmic protein content increases during prenatal development and also increases postnatally until the animal is approximately half mature. When expressed as a percentage of total muscle protein, however, sarcoplasmic protein content of muscle cells is highest early in the prenatal period, when it may make up as much as 70 percent of total muscle protein, and decreases during both prenatal and postnatal development.

Table 39.3. Protein composition of mammalian muscle *

Protein class	Properties
Sarcoplasmic proteins	Soluble at ionic strength of 0.1 or less at neutral pH. Constitute 30–35% of total protein in skeletal muscle and slightly more in cardiac muscle. Contain at least 100–200 different proteins. Sometimes called myogen.
Myofibrillar proteins	Constitute the myofibril. Make up 52–56% of total protein in skeletal muscle but only 45–50% in cardiac muscle. Ionic strengths above 0.3 are generally required to disrupt the myofibril, but many of the myofibrillar proteins are soluble in H_2O once they have been extracted from the myofibril.
Stroma proteins	Insoluble in neutral aqueous solvents. Constitute 10–15% of total protein in skeletal muscle and slightly more in cardiac muscle. Include lipoproteins and mucoproteins from cell membranes and surfaces as well as connective tissue proteins. Exact percentages vary widely, but collagen generally makes up 40–60% of total stroma protein and elastin may make up 10–20%.

* Muscle tissue is defined as muscle cells plus associated extracellular tissue that would be found in a whole muscle.

The myofibrillar or contractile proteins are the largest fraction of proteins in muscle cells. Although the myofibrillar proteins have frequently been defined as those muscle proteins insoluble in water but soluble in dilute salt solutions (also the classical definition of a globulin), all known myofibrillar proteins except one are soluble in water once they have been extracted from the myofibril. Therefore, it is most accurate to define the myofibrillar proteins as those proteins that constitute the myofibril. The content of myofibrillar protein in muscle tissue increases during both prenatal and postnatal development whether expressed as a percentage of total muscle weight or as a percentage of total muscle protein.

The stroma proteins are the least soluble class of proteins in muscle tissue. Like the sarcoplasmic protein fraction, the stroma protein fraction contains a large number of different proteins. Most of this fraction is collagen and elastin that originate from the epimysial, perimysial, and endomysial connective tissue layers. Hence, most of the stroma protein fraction is extracellular in origin, although some lipoproteins from the subcellular organelles in muscle cells may also fall into the stroma protein fraction because of their insolubility. In contrast to what is often supposed, stroma protein content (and hence connective tissue content) of muscle tissue decreases during both prenatal and postnatal development when expressed either as a percentage of total muscle weight or as a percentage of total muscle protein.

Myofibrillar proteins

There are surprisingly few myofibrillar proteins considering the fact that they are solely responsible for converting the chemical energy of ATP into biological movement. The 9 or 10 proteins used to accomplish biological movement are especially remarkable when compared with the number of proteins required for other biological processes; for example, muscle cell ribosomes, which contain only part of the proteins required for biosynthesis of muscle proteins, are composed of 67–74 different proteins. The subunit polypeptide chains of the myofibrillar proteins all have different molecular masses (see Table 39.1), and it is possible to separate all myofibrillar protein polypeptides by a single polyacrylamide-gel electrophoresis experiment run in the presence of sodium dodecyl sulfate.

Myosin and actin together are both necessary and completely sufficient for an in vitro contractile response. The other seven or eight myofibrillar proteins either regulate the myosin-actin interaction so that contraction can be either initiated or stopped in the presence of ATP (tropomyosin, troponin, and possibly α-actinin), or they assist in assembly of the myofibril into the proper three-dimensional structure (C-protein, α-actinin, β-actinin, M-protein, and paramyosin). For this reason, these seven or eight myofibrillar proteins are sometimes referred to collectively as the regulatory proteins.

Myosin is a very large protein molecule that has been studied extensively and that contains six different polypeptide chains. Evidence from direct electron microscope observation, selective cleavage by proteolytic enzymes (trypsin and papain), and separation of subunit polypeptide chains has shown that the myosin molecule consists of a long rod with two globular heads at one end (Fig. 39.8). The entire molecule is 155–160 nm long. The rod portion of the molecule is 135–140 nm long and approximately 1.5 nm in diameter; biochemical measurements have shown that it contains two polypeptide chains that are 100 percent α-helical. The two globular heads are actually ellipsoidal and are approximately 4.5 nm in diameter and 15–18 nm long (note similarity in dimensions between the myosin heads and the cross-bridges extending from the thick filaments). The myosin molecule

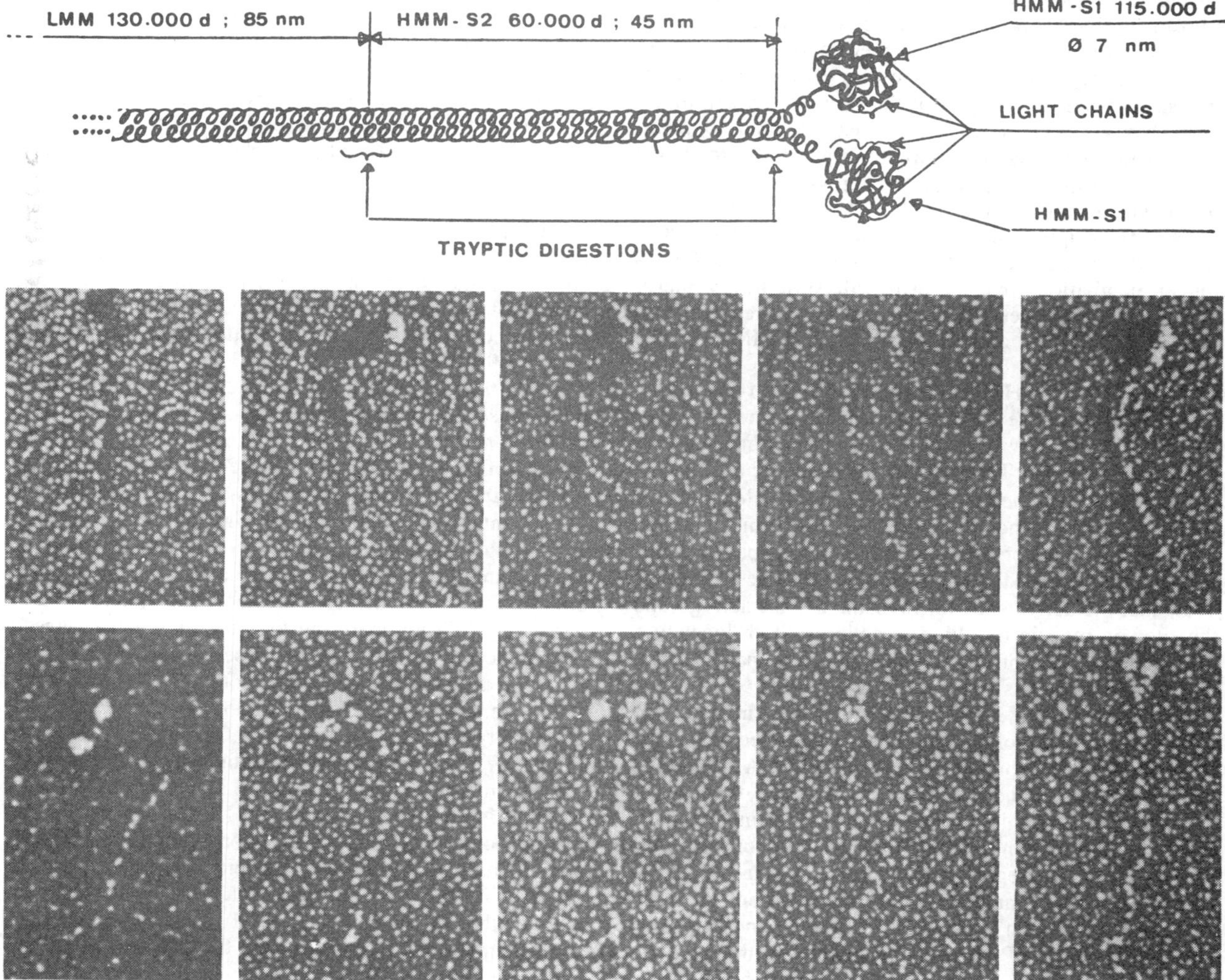

Figure 39.8. Diagram and electron micrographs of the myosin molecule. Top, diagram of the myosin molecule. Part of the long, rodlike portion of the molecule is not shown at the left so that the remainder could be shown in proper proportion. The α-helical nature of the polypeptide chains in the rod part of the molecule is shown and approximate lengths and molecular weights of the tryptic fragments are indicated. Although the diameter of HMM-S1 is given as 7 nm, recent evidence shows that HMM-S1 is ellipsoidal with axes of 4 and 15–18 nm. (From J.E. Morel and I. Pinset-Harstrom 1975, *Biomédicine* 22:88–96.) Bottom, electron micrographs of unidirectionally shadowed (first row) and rotary shadowed (second row) myosin molecules. The doublet heads of myosin are evident. ×236,500. (From H.S. Slayter and S. Lowey 1967, *Proc. Nat. Acad. Sci.* 58:1611–18.)

has at least three physiologically important properties: (1) it has the enzymic ability to split ATP and release energy; in the absence of actin, myosin ATPase activity is inhibited by Mg^{++}, but when myosin is combined with actin, its ATPase activity is activated by Mg^{++}; (2) myosin binds strongly to actin; the actin-myosin complex is specifically dissociated by ATP, pyrophosphate, and a few other polyanions when Mg^{++} is present; and (3) myosin spontaneously aggregates to form dimers, which can aggregate to form thick filaments that are structurally indistinguishable from native thick filaments.

Much of our detailed knowledge about myosin has emanated from the discovery that the proteolytic enzyme, trypsin, will split the myosin molecule near its center to form two fragments called light meromyosin (LMM) and heavy meromyosin (HMM) (see Fig. 39.8). Light meromyosin is from the tail part of the original myosin molecule, has no ATPase activity, does not bind to actin, and forms thick filaments structurally similar to native thick filaments but having no cross-bridges. Heavy meromyosin contains the head and part of the tail portions of the original myosin molecule, has ATPase activity, binds to actin, but does not form filaments. With a longer incubation time, trypsin will split heavy meromyosin into two yet smaller fragments called subfragment 1 (HMM-S1) and subfragment 2 (HMM-S2) (see Fig. 39.8). This cleavage produces two HMM-S1 molecules for each HMM-S2 molecule. HMM-S2 is from the short stub of the myosin tail on heavy meromyosin, has no ATPase activity, does not bind to actin, and does not form filaments. The two HMM-S1 molecules are the globular heads on the original myosin molecule; each has ATPase activity, binds to actin, does not form filaments, and contains two of the four small polypeptide chains found in the original myosin molecule. These findings show that the active sites for myosin ATPase activity and the sites on myosin that bind to actin are both located in the globular heads of the myosin molecule and that each myosin molecule has two each of these sites.

Actin is a much smaller molecule than myosin and contains only one polypeptide chain per molecule. Every molecule of actin contains one molecule of ATP and, as usually prepared, one molecule of Ca^{++}; the function of this ATP and Ca^{++} is unknown. A large number of different conditions, including 100 mM KCl or 1–5 mM Mg^{++}, cause aggregation of actin to form a double-stranded, helical filament. During aggregation, the ATP associated with actin is hydrolyzed to ADP and inorganic phosphate; the ADP remains associated with the actin aggregated in the filament, but the inorganic phosphate does not. Because vertebrate muscle cells contain at least 100 mM KCl and 5 mM Mg^{++} (see Table 39.2), actin exists almost entirely in the aggregated, filamentous form in these cells.

Molecular anatomy of thick and thin filaments

Huxley (1963) first showed that it was possible, by incubating myosin solutions at ionic strengths of 0.1–0.2 and in the pH range of 6.5–7.0 (i.e. under nearly physiological conditions) to produce thick filaments that were structurally similar to native thick filaments. Additional study has shown that two myosin molecules will spontaneously aggregate head-to-tail to produce dimers and that these dimers will then aggregate tail-to-tail to produce a short filament having a smooth central region flanked on either side by projections (Fig. 39.9A). M-protein may be involved in the tail-to-tail aggregation of these myosin dimers. Note that the projections extending from these short filaments are the doublet heads of myosin and represent the cross-bridges observed in electron micrographs of striated muscle cells. Hence, each cross-bridge is derived from a single myosin molecule having two heads. That thick filament cross-bridges contain the heads of the myosin molecule and that these heads contain the actin-binding ability of the myosin molecule means that the actin-binding site is in the cross-bridges, where it is free to interact with actin in the thin filament rather than buried in the shaft of the thick filament. Additional growth of the thick filament then occurs by head-to-tail addition of myosin dimers to the nucleated filament (Fig. 39.9B).

Thick filaments have a very specific geometrical structure. A set of three myosin cross-bridges, arranged at trigonal points, arise every 14.2–14.4 nm along the length of the filament. Because thick filaments are 1.5–1.6 μ long, it can be calculated that one thick filament contains 300–310 myosin molecules. C-protein is located in bands that evidently completely encircle the thick filament, like staves around a barrel. These bands are 43 nm apart, center-to-center. The innermost two bands are 492 nm apart and the outermost bands are approximately 300 nm from the tapered ends of the thick filament, so each thick filament contains 14–18 bands of C-protein, 7–9 on each side of the M-line. Each band contains two to four molecules of C-protein.

Just as solutions of myosin can be induced to form thick filaments that are structurally indistinguishable from native thick filaments, solutions of actin can be induced by addition of KCl or $MgCl_2$ to form double-stranded filaments that, except for heterogeneity of length, are structurally similar in the electron microscope to the backbone of thin filaments (Fig. 39.10). The double-stranded actin filament has a helical repeat distance of 35–38 nm, contains 13 actin monomers per strand per turn, and makes one complete turn every 70–76 nm. Actin monomers are almost spherical with a radius of 5.5 nm. Because thin filaments are 1 μ long, it can be calculated that each thin filament in vivo contains 340–380 actin

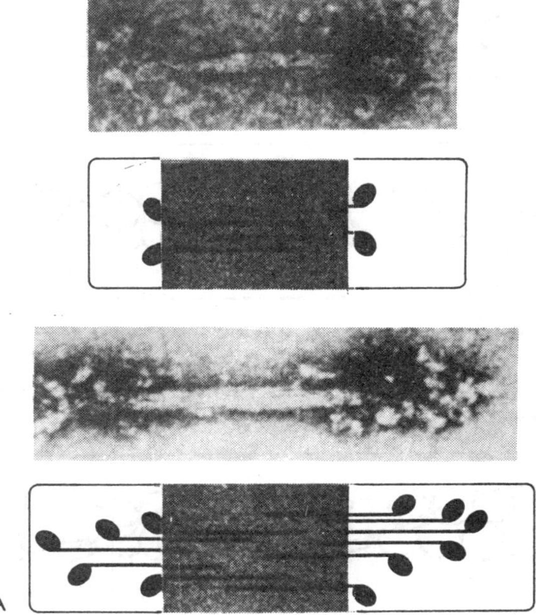

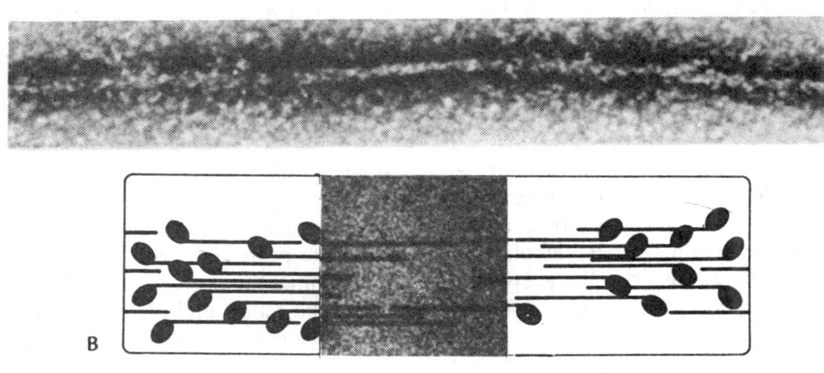

Figure 39.9. Electron micrographs and corresponding diagrams showing aggregation of myosin molecules to form thick filaments. For simplicity, the double-headed myosin molecule is represented by a single sphere attached to a rod. A, initial stages of myosin aggregation. B, complete thick filament; only the central part is shown in the micrograph. (From A.G. Loewy and P. Siekevitz, *Cell Structure and Function,* Holt, Rinehart and Winston, New York, 1969. Reproduced by permission of Holt, Rinehart and Winston, Inc., and H.E. Huxley.)

monomers. Vertebrate striated muscle contains twice as many thin filaments as thick filaments in cross section and each thick filament in a given sarcomere interacts with thin filaments from both ends of the sarcomere; therefore the molar concentration of actin in muscle is about four times the molar concentration of myosin.

The tropomyosin molecule is simply a rod shaped molecule 42.3 nm long. These rod-shaped molecules lie in the two grooves of the double-stranded actin filament and aggregate end-to-end to produce two strands of tropomyosin running the entire length of the thin filament. Troponin is an ellipsoidal or more globular molecule than tropomyosin and binds to tropomyosin at a particular site on the tropomyosin molecule. Because each tropomyosin molecule has one binding site for troponin, troponin is located at periodic intervals, 38.5 nm apart, along the thin filament (see Fig. 39.10).

Troponin has an important role as the switch for muscle contraction. It is a complex protein molecule that has three different subunit polypeptide chains named troponin-T, troponin-I, and troponin-C. Each subunit polypeptide has a particular physiological function. Troponin-T is the subunit containing the principal binding site that attaches the troponin complex to tropomyosin (T for tropomyosin). Troponin-I binds to both troponin-T and troponin-C and also binds to actin in the absence of Ca^{++}. It inhibits the actin-activated ATPase activity of myosin (i.e. the ATPase activity of myosin that is activated by Mg^{++} in the presence of actin). Hence, I for inhibitor. Troponin-C binds both to troponin-T and troponin-I but

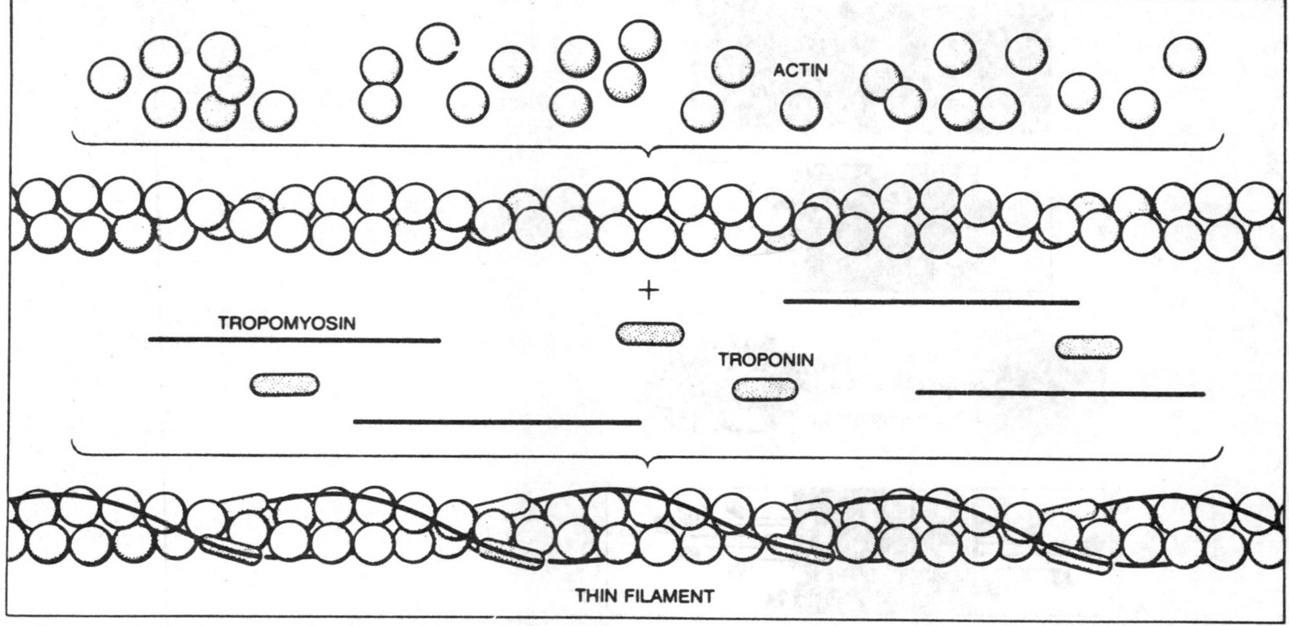

Figure 39.10. Diagram showing assembly of thin filaments from actin, tropomyosin, and troponin, and the molecular architecture of the assembled thin filament. Actin, tropomyosin, and troponin monomers are portrayed approximately to scale as indicated by physicochemical measurements. (From J.M. Murray and A. Weber 1974, The cooperative action of muscle proteins, *Scien. Am.* 230:58–71. Copyright © 1974 by Scientific American, Inc. All rights reserved.)

not to actin. Troponin-C has four high-affinity binding sites for Ca^{++} per molecule (C for Ca^{++}).

MUSCLE CONTRACTION

Motor end-plate depolarization and action potential

Two general classes of muscle cells can be distinguished on the basis of their innervation and speed of contraction. Many vertebrate skeletal muscles and almost all mammalian skeletal muscles (extraocular eye and tympanic muscles are two known exceptions) contain cells with relatively fast contraction times (less than 50 msec); these fibers are called phasic or twitch fibers, and show a propagated action potential and twitch response after nerve stimulation. Muscle fibers that can respond to a nerve stimulus with a prolonged contracture and that usually exhibit no propagated action potential are called slow or tonic fibers. Tonic skeletal muscle cells are more prevalent in certain muscles of amphibians, fish, and reptiles. The anterior latissimus dorsi of the chicken is an example of a muscle that contains exclusively slow or tonic muscle fibers. Phasic fibers are generally innervated by a single, relatively large motor neuron (or infrequently by two motor neurons) that impinge on the cells at a given area; this area is called the motor end-plate region of the muscle cell, and this type of nerve ending is called an *en plaque* innervation. The motor end-plate region on skeletal muscle cells is a very small, discrete area on the sarcolemmal surface. Tonic muscle fibers, on the other hand, are innervated by multiple, relatively small nerve endings that usually arise from a smaller motor neuron. This type of nerve ending is called an *en grappe* (grape-like) innervation. Application of acetylcholine to the surface of a muscle cell causes contraction of that cell if the acetylcholine is applied at the proper location. In phasic cells, acetylcholine elicits contraction only if applied at a single location on the cell, the motor end-plate. In tonic muscles, acetylcholine elicits contraction if applied at several different locations along the surface of the muscle cell. Presumably, these areas of acetylcholine sensitivity in tonic cells correspond to the areas that the multiple nerve endings impinge on these cells. Because most mammalian skeletal muscles are of the phasic or fast type, the discussion in this chapter will focus on this type of cell.

As it approaches a muscle, a nerve fiber containing a number of neuronal axons divides into a number of smaller, myelinated motor neurons, each of which impinges on a single muscle cell. Hence, one motor nerve fiber serves a number of muscle cells in a single muscle. The group of muscle cells innervated by a single motor nerve fiber is called a motor unit. The number of muscle cells in a motor unit varies among different muscles. In muscles where delicate control is required, the innervation ratio (number of muscle cells served by one motor nerve fiber) may be as low as 3. On the other hand, innervation ratios in muscles of the limb, where fine control is not as necessary, may be as high as 1000. As a branch of a motor neuron approaches a muscle cell, it loses its myelin sheath, and the nerve axon is covered only by perineural epithelial cells. The plasmalemma at the motor end-plate has a specialized structure consisting of numerous large infoldings, 0.5–1.0 μ deep and 50–100 nm wide. The nerve axon arborizes and sends fingerlike processes into these infoldings, but the perineural epithelium and the muscle cell plasmalemma remain separated by a 40–60 nm space. A nerve impulse, propagated along the motor nerve axon, reaches the terminus of the neuromuscular junction. The terminus of the neuron contains numerous presynaptic vesicles that ostensibly contain the chemical compound acetylcholine. The action potential propagated along the neuron evidently causes the release of acetylcholine from these presynaptic vesicles, and the liberated acetylcholine causes depolarization of the motor end-plate region. The motor end-plate does not propagate an action potential itself, but if depolarization of the motor end-plate is sufficiently extensive, it depolarizes the adjacent plasmalemmal membrane. The plasmalemma resembles neuronal membranes in its ability to propagate an action potential; at rest, the inner surface of the plasmalemma is approximately -80 mv with respect to the outer surface, and the conduction of an action potential along the plasmalemma occurs by a process essentially identical to that for neurons. Rate of propagation of the action potential along the plasmalemma is approximately 5 m per second, and this action potential quickly spreads to the many openings of T-tubules that exist in the skeletal muscle cell membrane. The mechanism by which this action potential passing along the plasmalemma eventually initiates contraction is called excitation-contraction coupling.

Excitation-contraction coupling

The action potential propagated along the plasmalemma is received and propagated along the T-tubules that pass across the muscle cell. Electron micrographs have shown that the lateral cisternae are located very close (within approximately 5 nm) to the T-tubules. These lateral cisternae contain up to 90 percent of the total Ca^{++} in the resting muscle cell. Although the nature of the signal that passes from the T-tubules to the lateral cisternae is unknown, the result of this signal is the release of Ca^{++} from the lateral cisternae into the medium immediately surrounding the myofibrils. Hence, free Ca^{++} concentration around the myofibrils rises from approximately 10^{-8} M to 10^{-6} or 10^{-5} M. This increase initiates contraction.

Molecular mechanism

Muscle contraction is accomplished by a sliding together or telescoping of the interdigitating thick and thin filament array without any detectable shortening of the filaments themselves (Fig. 39.11, Huxley 1972). Structurally, muscle contraction causes a narrowing and eventual disappearance of the H-zone as thin filaments slide into this area, and a narrowing of the I-band as the thick filaments pass into the I-band region. It seems unlikely that shortening proceeds much beyond the stage of loss of the H-zone (i.e. just beyond stage 2 in Fig. 39.11) in living vertebrate muscle. It is possible, however, in in vitro experiments to induce much more extensive shortening so that thin filaments overlap in the center of the sarcomere (stage 3), and eventually thick filaments crumple against the Z-disk (stage 4).

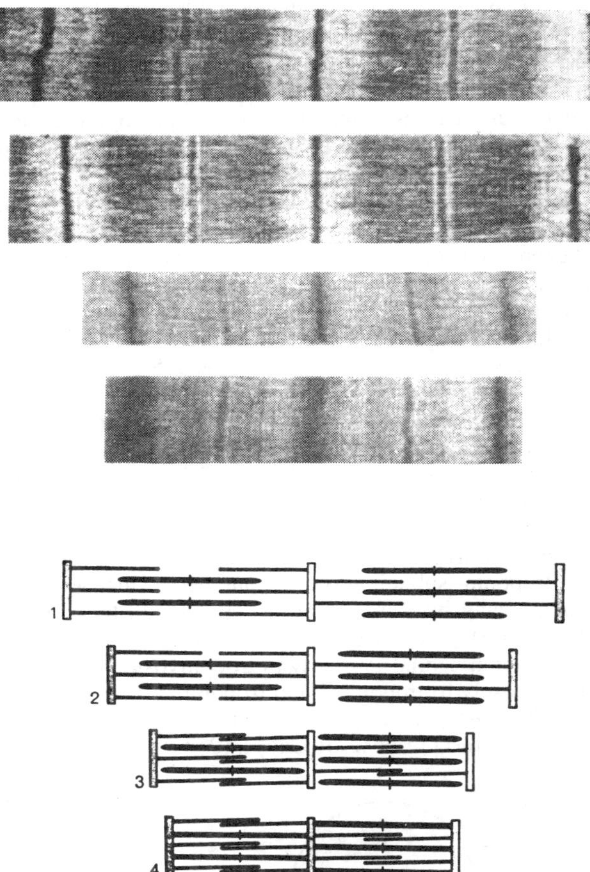

Figure 39.11. Electron micrographs showing banding changes in vertebrate skeletal muscle at different states of contraction, and diagrams showing corresponding changes in the thick and thin filament structure. The central Z-disk of the two sarcomeres shown in the electron micrographs is aligned with those shown in the diagrams. (From Huxley, in Bourne, ed., *The Structure and Function of Muscle,* Academic Press, New York, 1972.)

The force causing thick and thin filaments to slide past one another is generated by the cross-bridges or myosin heads that project outward from the surface of the thick filament (see Fig. 39.3). During contraction these cross-bridges attach to actin in the thin filament. Interaction with actin causes the myosin head to swivel or angle with respect to the shaft of the myosin filament. This swiveling pushes the actin filament toward the center of the sarcomere and causes contraction. Consequently, the force for muscle contraction is generated when the myosin head interacts with actin.

It is convenient to divide the events that occur during muscle contraction into (1) those that occur in the thin filament, and (2) those that occur in the thick filament. The events that occur in the thin filament are concerned with turning muscle contraction on and off, so this discussion will begin with a review of these events. Because troponin-C has a binding constant near 5×10^6 M^{-1} for Ca^{++}, it can bind Ca^{++} from the surrounding medium whenever the release of that ion from the sarcoplasmic reticular membranes causes free intracellular Ca^{++} concentration to rise to 10^{-6}–10^{-5} M. Biochemical studies have shown that binding of Ca^{++} to troponin-C causes conformation of the troponin-C subunit to change, and this change triggers a series of changes in the binding of the troponin subunits to one another. This series of changes may be summarized as follows. In the absence of Ca^{++} (10^{-8} M or less so there is no Ca^{++} on troponin-C), troponin-T binds strongly to tropomyosin, troponin-C binds loosely to troponin-I and troponin-T, and troponin-I binds loosely to troponin-T but firmly to actin (Fig. 39.12). In the presence of Ca^{++} (10^{-6}–10^{-5} M, or high enough to permit troponin-C to bind Ca^{++}), troponin-T binds strongly to tropomyosin (this linkage seems unaffected by Ca^{++}), troponin-C binds strongly to troponin-I and troponin-T, and troponin-I binds to troponin-T but loses its affinity for actin (it is unclear whether Ca^{++} affects the troponin-I–troponin-T linkage). The important change among this series of complex interactions is that binding of Ca^{++} to troponin-C causes troponin-I to lose its affinity for actin.

X-ray diffraction measurements have shown that in resting muscle the tropomyosin strand is located out of the groove of the double-stranded actin helix, in a position where it would block the site on actin that binds myosin (see Fig. 39.12). It seems that troponin is necessary to maintain the tropomyosin strand in this position, which is at a radius of 4.4 nm from the center of the double-stranded actin filament. It is possible that the firm interaction between troponin-I and actin enables troponin-I to act as a prop that holds the tropomyosin strand in this blocking position. When troponin-C binds Ca^{++}, however, the firm linkage between troponin-I and actin is weakened, and troponin can no longer hold the tropomyosin strand in the out or blocking position. The tropomyosin strand rolls back into the groove of the double-stranded actin helix (to a radius of 2.4 nm, see Fig. 39.12), and the myosin binding site on actin is exposed. Myosin can then bind to actin, and contraction ensues and continues until Ca^{++} is removed from troponin-C and

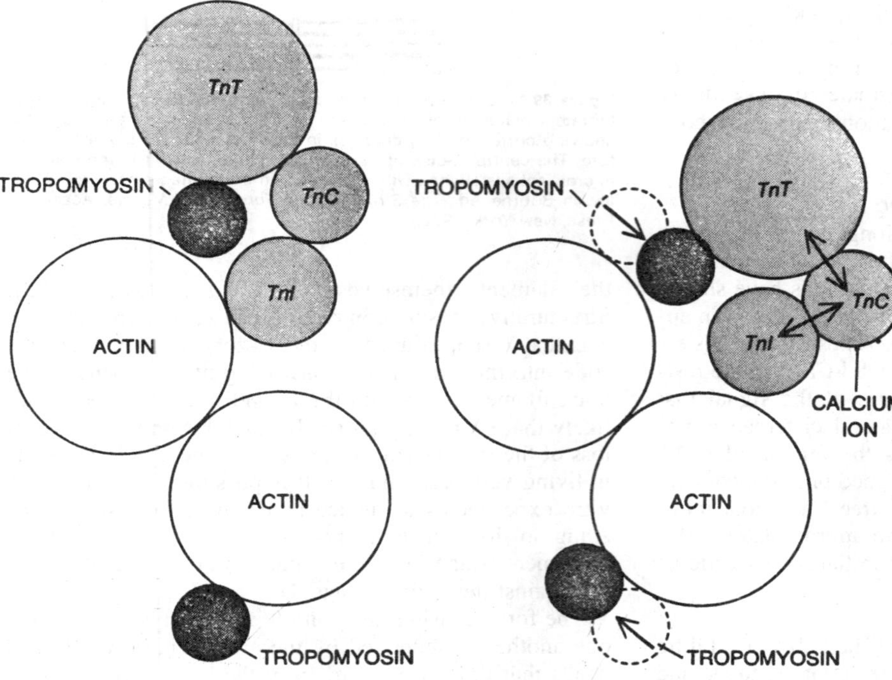

Figure 39.12. Diagrams of thin filament cross sections showing how interactions among the troponin subunits, tropomyosin, and actin regulate ability of the thin filament to participate in contraction. Although troponin-I does not contact troponin-T in this diagram, recent evidence indicates that they are very close. (From Cohen 1975, The protein switch of muscle contraction, *Scien. Am.* 233:36–45. Copyright © 1975 by Scientific American, Inc. All rights reserved.)

troponin-I binds to actin and forces the tropomyosin strand back out of the groove of the actin filament to block the myosin-binding site of actin.

Events in the thick filament during muscle contraction principally involve changes in the cross-bridges (Fig. 39.13). During a single twitch of a muscle fiber, each myosin cross-bridge may perform many cycles of attaching to actin, swiveling, and then dissociating from the actin filament, but only 10–20 percent of the total cross-bridges in a single sarcomere are attached to the

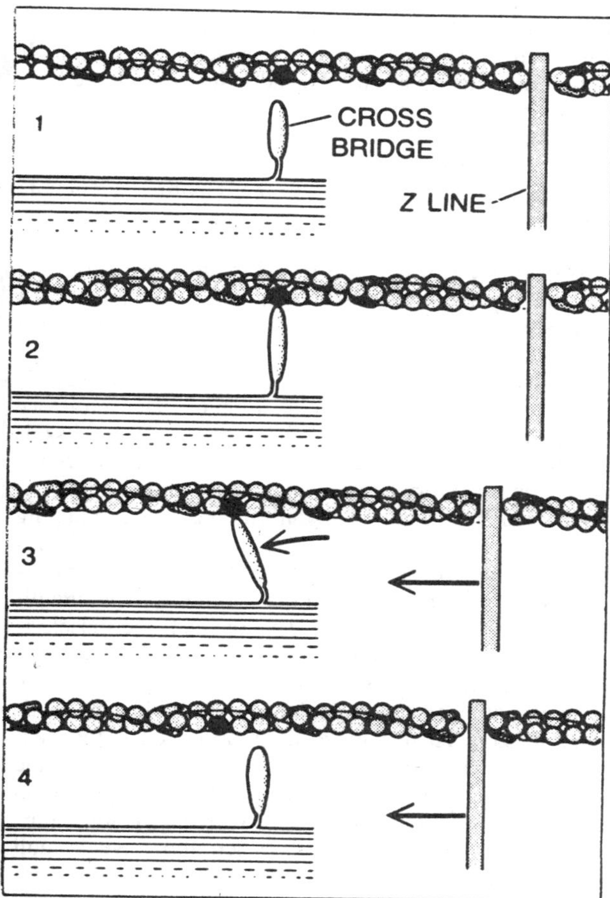

Figure 39.13. Diagram of the cross-bridge cycle in striated muscle. In resting muscle, myosin cross-bridges cannot attach to thin filaments because the myosin binding site on actin is blocked by tropomyosin (1). A nerve impulse releases Ca^{++}, and Ca^{++} causes a series of conformational changes in the thin filament (see Fig. 39.12) so that the myosin-binding site on actin is unblocked. The myosin cross-bridge attaches to the actin filament (2), then swivels or rotates to push the actin filament to the center of the sarcomere (3), and finally, after binding a new molecule of ATP, is detached and reoriented to the resting position ready to repeat the cycle (4). (From J.M. Murray and A. Weber 1974, The cooperative action of muscle proteins, *Scien. Am.* 230:58–71. Copyright © 1974 by Scientific American, Inc. All rights reserved.)

thin filament at any given instant during contraction. Because cross-bridges interact asynchronously with actin (i.e. they do not all attach to the thin filament simultaneously, then swivel simultaneously, etc.), the thick and thin filaments slide past each other at a uniform rate rather than with the jerky ratchetlike motion that would be produced by synchronous cross-bridge action. The range of movement of an individual myosin cross-bridge is about 10–15 nm, and the time required for one cross-bridge cycle in the contracting muscle at room temperature is approximately 0.1 msec.

It has been difficult to relate the ATPase of myosin to this cross-bridge cycle, partly because ATP has two roles in muscle contraction that until recently have seemed dichotomous. First, ATP hydrolysis is clearly involved in providing energy for muscle contraction. Second, at physiological concentrations, ATP prevents the actin-myosin interaction and even dissociates the actin-myosin complex necessary for contraction. This ostensible dichotomy has been at least partly resolved by recent transient-state kinetic studies of myosin ATPase activity, and the following scheme summarizes current thinking in this area.

In living resting muscle, almost every myosin cross-bridge is energized and contains one molecule each of ADP and inorganic phosphate, the hydrolysis products of ATP. (Energized here refers to some unknown conformational state of myosin in which the energy of ATP is stored.) The energized myosin cross-bridge is unable to bind to actin because the thin filament is turned off, that is, tropomyosin is blocking the myosin-binding site on actin. Release of Ca^{++} from the sarcoplasmic reticulum turns on the thin filament. Because the ATP bound to myosin has already been split to ADP and inorganic phosphate, and because neither ADP nor inorganic phosphate is a very effective dissociator of the actin-myosin complex, the myosin cross-bridge interacts with actin immediately after the actin is unblocked in the switching-on process. Interaction with actin triggers the swiveling or rotating of the myosin cross-bridge, so that the actin filament is pushed toward the center of the sarcomere (step 3 in Fig. 39.13). The exact nature of actin's participation in cross-bridge swiveling or force generation is unclear.

Once the myosin cross-bridge has rotated or swiveled, ADP and inorganic phosphate, the hydrolysis products of ATP bound to myosin, are quickly released. Only after ADP has been released from the spent cross-bridge can the myosin head bind a new molecule of ATP. Because ATP is a potent dissociator of the actin-myosin complex, binding a new molecule of ATP immediately dissociates the myosin cross-bridge from the actin filament. Dissociation of the angled cross-bridge is followed very quickly by reorientation of the cross-bridge back to the state shown in step 4 and by hydrolysis of the bound ATP to

ADP and inorganic phosphate. Consequently, ATP is hydrolyzed by myosin while it is dissociated from actin, and the energy of ATP is used to reorient angled myosin cross-bridges. Hydrolysis of ATP to ADP and inorganic phosphate removes the dissociating influence of ATP, so the myosin cross-bridge can rebind to actin and repeat the cycle. This series of events continues until Ca^{++} is rebound by the sarcoplasmic reticular membranes and the thin filament is turned off so that actin is no longer available to bind myosin cross-bridges, or until no ATP is available to bind to the spent cross-bridge and dissociate it from actin. In the latter instance, all myosin cross-bridges stop attached to actin at an angled position; this occurs only in muscle after death and results in rigor mortis.

Macroscopic phenomena

Latency

The time course of tension development in a single muscle cell following an electrical stimulus can be divided into three phases. The brief period between the arrival of the stimulus and the initiation of tension is called the latent period. This period is typically 3–4 msec in vertebrate skeletal muscles at room temperature *if* the lag in the mechanical apparatus used to make such measurements is removed. The first 1.5 msec of the latent period seems to be a quiescent period; this period is followed by a 1.5 msec period in which tension actually decreases. This decrease in tension is called latency relaxation and is followed immediately by the rising phase of tension. The quiescent part of the latent period may represent the period of time required for conduction of the impulse signal to the lateral cisternae and release of Ca^{++} from the lateral cisternae. The contractile apparatus is evidently active during the latency-relaxation part of the latent period, however, and latency relaxation has been ascribed to the necessity for muscle to stretch a series elastic component before tension can be recorded externally.

The latent period is followed by the contraction period or the period of rising tension, and then by a period of gradually declining tension or the relaxation period. Length of the contraction and relaxation periods varies among different muscles but is typically 20–50 msec for each period in vertebrate skeletal muscles.

All-or-nothing law

Electrical stimulation of a motor nerve fiber elicits no contractile response until the strength of the stimulus exceeds a certain level, the threshold level. Above this level, increasing the intensity of the stimulus causes an increase in the amount of tension developed until a second level of electrical intensity called the maximal stimulus is reached. Above this level, increasing intensity of electrical stimulation produces no additional increase in tension. These phenomena are a direct result of the fact that a single motor nerve fiber innervates more than one muscle fiber. Up to a given intensity of electrical stimulus, the nerve action potential is too weak to produce a depolarization of the motor end-plate that is large enough to initiate an action potential in the surrounding sarcolemmal membrane. As intensity of the stimulus increases, however, some neurons obtain an action potential strong enough to cause a sarcolemmal action potential. All muscle cells in the motor unit innervated by that neuron contract maximally. As intensity of the electrical stimulus increases yet further, additional neurons are able to initiate sarcolemmal action potentials and additional muscle cells contract. At the maximal stimulus, all muscle cells innervated by that nerve fiber are developing tension. It should be understood that the individual muscle cell responds in an all-or-none fashion; that is, it either contracts maximally or not at all. The increasing tension elicited with increasing intensity of electrical stimulation between the threshold level and the maximal stimulus is due simply to recruitment of additional muscle cells.

Refractory period, summation, and tetanus

A brief period exists following the stimulation of a muscle cell during which the cell is unresponsive to a second stimulus. This time is called the refractory period and is the interval during which the motor end-plate is still depolarized from the initial stimulus. The refractory period varies from 5–50 msec in different vertebrate skeletal muscles. If a second stimulus is given just after the end of the refractory period when the motor end-plate has repolarized but when the myofibrils are still contracting from the initial stimulus, the tension developed in response to this second stimulus is added to the tension developed in response to the initial stimulus, so a significantly greater total tension is developed. If the muscle is stimulated repeatedly in this manner, successively greater tension development is elicited until finally maximum tension is attained, and additional stimuli elicit no additional tension. At this stage, the muscle cell is fully activated and all myosin cross-bridges are producing the maximum tension. The additional tension developed in response to repetitive stimuli is called summation, staircase phenomenon, or treppe. When repetitive stimuli elicit no additional tension, the muscle is in tetanus. Tension development in tetanus may be nearly ten times greater than tension development during a single twitch. Although different muscles differ in their tension-developing capacities, most vertebrate skeletal muscles are capable of developing 3–4 kg of tension per square centimeter of cross section during maximal tetanic contraction.

Muscle tonus or resting tension

Skeletal muscle that has been neither stimulated nor stretched continues to develop a small amount of tension.

This resting tension is revealed in a number of different ways; for example, if a tendon is cut in vivo, its associated muscle shortens. This muscle tonus has been postulated to originate from the presence of a few myosin cross-bridges that attach to thin filaments and cycle very slowly. Motor nerve impulses are evidently also important in resting muscle tonus.

Gradation of contraction

A strong contraction of a skeletal muscle requires participation of many motor units in that muscle. Different motor units in a muscle are stimulated to contract asynchronously by the asynchronous volleys of impulses passing along the different axons. Moreover, different motor units within a given muscle also contract at different velocities. The en masse action of different motor units contracting and relaxing asynchronously and at different velocities produces a smoothly integrated, macroscopic muscle contraction.

Mechanical changes

Velocity of muscle contraction is inversely related to the muscle's load. As the load increases, the velocity of shortening decreases. When the maximum load that a muscle can move is exceeded, the muscle does not shorten at all. The mathematical relationship between force and velocity that is applicable to all vertebrate skeletal muscles was first deduced by Hill (1938):

$$(P + a)v = (P_0 - P)b$$

where P_0 is the maximal tetanic force that a muscle can develop; P is force developed at any given velocity of shortening, v; a is a constant with dimensions of force; and b is a constant with dimensions of velocity. When the quantity $(P_0 - P)/v$ is plotted against P, a straight line with slope b and intercept $-a$ results. This is the experimental procedure used to determine the constants, a and b, which differ for different muscles. The maximal tetanic force for several different muscles is given in Table 39.4. The power developed by a muscle is the product of force and velocity and is maximal at approximately 0.3 v_0 and 0.3 P_0 where v_0 is the maximum velocity that a muscle can attain. Mechanical efficiency of a muscle is the work done divided by the energy used and is maximal at approximately 0.2 v_0 and 0.5 P_0. Hence, maximum power output of a muscle does not occur under the same conditions of load and shortening velocity as maximum efficiency does.

Because a in Hill's force-velocity equation has the dimensions of force, the quantity $(P + a)v$ is force times velocity and equals energy. Moreover, because the quantity $(P_0 - P)b$ increases as the load or force, P, decreases, Hill's force-velocity equation also states that the energy output of a muscle increases as the load decreases.

Huxley (1974) indicated that myosin cross-bridges behave mechanically like a stretchable spring in series with a parallel combination of a spring and a dashpot. The stretchable spring is the series elastic component. The parallel combination of the spring and dashpot may be the tension-generating component of the cross-bridge. The series elastic component may be located in subfragment-2 of the myosin molecule, whereas the parallel combination of a spring and a dashpot may be in subfragment-1.

Table 39.4. Maximum tetanic force developed by different muscles

Muscle	Maximum force (kg/sq cm)
Rat extensor digitorum longus	3
Rat gastrocnemius	1.8
Rat soleus	0.28
Rat heart	0.02
Cat longissimus	1.4

Thermal changes

Muscles are only 20–25 percent efficient, and a large part of the energy derived from the hydrolysis of ATP is liberated as heat rather than converted to mechanical energy. Measurements of heat production by muscle have shown that three kinds of heat production are associated with muscle activity: (1) resting heat, (2) initial heat including both activation heat and shortening heat, and (3) recovery heat, including relaxation heat if the shortened muscle is stretched by a load.

Unstimulated, resting muscle produces about 0.0002 cal/g/min of heat. This heat is called resting heat and is due to aerobic biochemical reactions within the muscle cell. If oxygen is excluded from a resting muscle cell so that aerobic metabolism ceases, resting heat production decreases.

About 0.003 cal/g of heat are produced during a single muscle twitch. This heat, called initial heat, can be divided into two parts: (1) a very rapid heat production that occurs before muscle shortening starts; its size is independent of extent of shortening, load, temperature, velocity of shortening, oxygen supply, and work done; and (2) heat liberated during muscle shortening; its size is directly proportional to the amount of muscle shortening. The first kind of heat production is called activation heat and is associated with the events that occur during excitation-contraction coupling (i.e. movement of Ca^{++}, etc.). The second kind of heat production is called shortening heat, is associated with movement of myosin cross-bridges, and is zero in an isometric contraction. It is possible to produce a negative shortening heat by stretching a muscle already at rest length so that the muscle absorbs heat rather than liberates it.

If a shortened muscle is relaxed by having a load stretch it back to rest length, an amount of heat equal to the work done by the muscle during the shortening is liberated; this heat is called relaxation heat. Additional heat is liberated from a muscle for as long as 30 minutes after shortening. This heat is called recovery heat and is associated with the aerobic metabolism necessary to restore the glycogen and creatine phosphate used during the contraction. The recovery heat is usually approximately equal to the sum of the initial heat and the energy used for work.

Fenn observed many years ago that the total energy (work plus heat) liberated by a muscle increases as muscle work increases (Fenn effect). This seemingly simple observation has far-reaching implications because it indicates that a muscle adapts the total energy available for a contraction in response to the load it is to move. Hence, the work demand of a muscle seems to exert some control over the chemical reactions in the muscle.

MUSCLE METABOLISM

Although it was widely assumed for many years that ATP provides the energy for muscle contraction, it was impossible to demonstrate any decrease in ATP concentration accompanying muscle contraction until the work of Davies and coworkers (see Curtin and Davies 1973). They used 2,4-dinitrofluorobenzene to inhibit creatine kinase and thereby prevent any ADP produced during muscle contraction from immediately being rephosphorylated back to ATP. By using 2,4-dinitrofluorobenzene, it was possible to demonstrate that ATP concentration decreased during contraction in direct proportion to the tension developed.

Living skeletal muscle cells contain large amounts of creatine kinase, which acts rapidly to re-establish the equilibrium between ATP and creatine phosphate. Because skeletal muscle cells contain two to three times more creatine phosphate than ATP (see Table 39.2), any ADP formed as the result of breakdown of ATP during muscle contraction is very rapidly rephosphorylated back to ATP at the expense of creatine phosphate. Indeed, before the use of 2,4-dinitrofluorobenzene, the only chemical change that could be identified during a single twitch of a muscle strip was a decrease in creatine phosphate content, regardless of how rapidly the muscle was frozen after the twitch. Moreover, the rapid rephosphorylation of ADP back to ATP greatly reduces the degradation of ADP to AMP and the resulting loss of adenine nucleotides available to the muscle cell. Skeletal muscle cells, however, do contain myokinase, which can degrade ADP to AMP by the following reaction:

$$2\text{ADP} \xrightarrow{\text{myokinase}} \text{ATP} + \text{AMP}$$

Any AMP produced by this reaction is usually deaminated to inosine monophosphate (IMP) by adenylic deaminase, and the IMP is then further degraded to uric acid, which is excreted.

Although ATP is replenished very rapidly from creatine phosphate in skeletal muscle cells, slightly longer times are required to replenish the creatine phosphate in this chain of reactions, because metabolic formation of ATP from glycolysis or other energy-yielding reactions is required. ATP produced by metabolism is then used to rephosphorylate the creatine produced when creatine phosphate is consumed in a muscle contraction. Hence the enzyme creatine kinase is used both to restore creatine phosphate when it is used to replenish ATP and to restore ATP when it has been consumed in a muscle contraction:

$$\text{Creatine phosphate} + \text{ADP} \underset{\text{after metabolism}}{\overset{\text{after contraction}}{\rightleftharpoons}} \text{creatine} + \text{ATP}$$

The most important metabolic route for replenishing creatine phosphate involves carbohydrates and the process of glycolysis (i.e. lysis of glycogen). Depending on the physiological state of the animal, 50 percent of total glycogen may be in muscle cells and 50 percent in liver cells; these are the only two kinds of cells that contain glycogen in the animal organism. About 0.5–1.5 percent of total wet weight of vertebrate skeletal muscle is glycogen (see Table 39.2). The type of metabolism used to restore creatine phosphate in skeletal muscle cells depends on the type of skeletal muscle cell. Fast-twitch, glycolytic muscle cells rely largely on anaerobic glycolysis; that is, the breakdown of glycogen in the absence of oxygen. Degradation of one mole of glucose from glycogen via anaerobic glycolysis produces two moles of lactic acid and three moles of ATP. Complete oxidation of one mole of glucose to CO_2 and H_2O in an experimental device such as a bomb calorimeter produces 686,000 cal (calories). One mole of ATP represents about 8000 cal, so production of three moles of ATP from one mole of glucose by anaerobic glycolysis means that only 24,000 cal out of the potential 686,000 cal in one mole of glucose is saved by anaerobic glycolysis. Although anaerobic glycolysis is an inefficient use of glucose (only 3.5 percent of total possible energy), it has the advantages of producing energy relatively rapidly and in the complete absence of oxygen.

In contrast to fast-twitch, glycolytic muscle cells, slow-twitch, oxidative muscle cells rely on aerobic metabolism of fatty acids and amino acids in addition to aerobic and anaerobic metabolism of glycogen and glucose. Aerobic metabolism of 1 mole of glucose from glycogen requires 6 moles of O_2 and produces 6 moles of CO_2, 6 moles of H_2O, and 39 moles of ATP. Thus complete aerobic metabolism of one mole of glucose from glycogen produces 39×8000 or 312,000 cal from the potential 686,000 cal (approximately 45 percent). Although aerobic or oxidative metabolism is considerably more efficient than anaerobic glycolysis, it requires longer to obtain ATP from aerobic metabolism than from anaerobic glycolysis, and aerobic metabolism ceases completely if oxygen is not available. Consequently, muscle cells capable of oxidative or aerobic metabolism can sustain activity for long periods of time (such as in the heart, which has only brief rest periods) if the activity is not too rapid or too severe. Rapid or severe contractions, however, deplete energy supplies more rapidly than they can be replenished in such cells and they quickly become exhausted and have to stop. Therefore, myosin in muscle cells that rely on oxidative metabolism for energy supply is adapted so that it contracts slowly and its use of ATP is unlikely to exceed the cell's capacity to restore ATP.

Muscle fatigue

Muscle fatigue occurs when muscle glycogen supplies decrease to zero and the muscle is no longer able to produce energy metabolically by anaerobic glycolysis. In those muscle cells that use aerobic metabolism to replenish the creatine phosphate and ATP depleted by contraction, anaerobic use of glycogen occurs only when the muscle cell's energy demands exceed the rate at which oxygen can be carried to the cell. Hence, anaerobic glycolysis occurs as a last resort in these cells, and exhaustion of glycogen in slow-twitch, oxidative muscle cells heralds fatigue in these cells just as it does in fast-twitch, glycolytic cells. It is still unclear how depletion of glycogen in a muscle cell is translated into a signal for that cell to stop contracting, but chemical measurements have indicated that muscle exhaustion occurs about the time glycogen is depleted. Muscle fatigue occurs before ATP concentrations decrease, and it seems unlikely that these concentrations are ever permitted to decrease significantly in a living muscle cell.

Because muscle fatigue seems to occur when muscle glycogen is exhausted, a fatigued muscle generally contains appreciable quantities of lactic acid, the end product of anaerobic glycolysis.

Lactic acid produced during muscle contraction generally passes into the blood stream and is transported to the liver for further metabolism because the muscle cell contains only small amounts of the enzymes necessary to convert lactic acid back to glucose. Consequently, during contraction or activity, muscle cells use glucose from the blood stream and break down the glycogen they contain to form lactic acid. The lactic acid is passed into the blood stream. During rest, the muscle cell removes glucose from the blood stream and uses this glucose to rebuild its glycogen stores. The liver removes lactic acid from the blood stream, converts it back to glucose, and passes the glucose into the blood stream for use by the muscle cell. This cycle is called the Cori cycle.

Muscle fatigue is also accompanied by changes in end-plate depolarization and ability of the muscle cell plasmalemma to propagate action potentials. The latent and relaxation periods are both greatly prolonged in fatigued muscle cells, and less acetylcholine seems to be released at the neuromuscular junction of fatigued muscle cells, so it becomes more difficult to obtain a depolarization of the motor end-plate that is large enough to initiate an action potential.

Types of muscle cells

The phasic muscle fibers that constitute most vertebrate skeletal musculature can be subdivided into three groups (Peter et al. 1972) depending on their contraction times and metabolism: (1) fast-twitch, glycolytic cells, (2) fast-twitch, oxidative-glycolytic cells, and (3) slow-twitch, oxidative cells. This subdivision pertains only to phasic or twitch muscle fibers and does not include the tonic muscle fibers discussed earlier. The fast-twitch, glycolytic and slow-twitch, oxidative cells represent the two extremes in this subdivision. In general, fast-twitch, glycolytic muscle cells are adapted for rapid contraction for short periods of time, whereas slow-twitch, oxidative muscle cells are adapted for slow contractions for long periods of time. Fast-twitch, glycolytic cells obtain energy almost exclusively by anaerobic metabolism, whereas slow-twitch, oxidative cells obtain much of their energy from aerobic metabolism. Many of the biochemical and physiological differences between these two types of muscle cells exist simply because of this basic difference in the way the cells obtain their energy. When compared with slow-twitch, oxidative cells, fast-twitch, glycolytic cells in general have shorter contraction times (approximately 5–20 msec compared with 70–90 msec), much less myoglobin (some fast-twitch, glycolytic muscle cells in chicken breast muscle have almost no myoglobin; because myoglobin stores oxygen for aerobic metabolism it is not needed in fast-twitch, glycolytic fibers), more phosphorylase (needed to degrade glycogen), larger cell diameters, fewer mitochondria (not needed because mitochondria are the sites of aerobic metabolism), more glycogen (for use in anaerobic glycolysis), much less lipid (lipid is metabolized aerobically and so is not used in fast-twitch, glycolytic cells), less blood flow, a slower rate of protein turnover, narrower Z-disks (66 nm wide compared with 144 nm), a more extensive and more highly organized sarcotubular system, and less resistance to fatigue.

In addition, myosin, α-actinin, tropomyosin, and troponin molecules and the ATPase enzyme in the sarcoplasmic reticular membranes in fast-twitch, glycolytic muscle cells differ from the corresponding proteins in slow-twitch, oxidative cells. The ATPase activity of myosin from fast-twitch, glycolytic cells is generally two to three times higher than that of myosin from slow-twitch, oxidative cells. Indeed, ATPase activity of the myosin in a muscle cell is very highly correlated with the contractile speed of that cell; the higher the myosin ATPase activity, the greater the contractile speed. Hence, the myosin molecule, which hydrolyzes ATP to release energy for muscle contraction, also serves as a control to insure that slow-twitch, oxidative fibers do not contract so rapidly that they exceed their capacity to supply energy via aerobic metabolism. The sarcoplasmic reticular membranes from fast-twitch, glycolytic cells also accumulate and release Ca^{++} faster than these membranes from slow-twitch, oxidative cells. This property, together with the more extensive nature of the sarcoplasmic reticulum in fast-twitch, glycolytic cells, adapts these cells for their faster rates of contraction. One study has reported that troponin from fast-twitch, glycolytic fibers binds Ca^{++} more rapidly than troponin from slow-twitch, oxidative cells. This property would also predispose fast-twitch, glycolytic cells to contract more rapidly than slow-twitch, oxidative muscle cells.

Fast-twitch, oxidative-glycolytic muscle cells are a heterogeneous group of cells that have properties intermediate between the other two cell types. As their name implies, fast-twitch, oxidative-glycolytic muscle cells generally have short contraction periods similar to the fast-twitch, glycolytic cells and much less than the slow-twitch, oxidative cells. The metabolic capabilities of fast-twitch, oxidative-glycolytic fibers, however, can vary over a wide range from almost totally committed to anaerobic glycolysis (i.e. very similar to fast-twitch, glycolytic cells) to almost totally committed to aerobic glycolysis (i.e. very similar to the metabolism—but not the contraction speed—of slow-twitch, oxidative fibers). Because fast-twitch, oxidative-glycolytic muscle cells contain the fast type of myosin ATPase activity and because those fast-twitch, oxidative-glycolytic cells committed to aerobic metabolism contain large amounts of myoglobin and mitochondria, it is possible to find muscle cells that have short contraction periods and yet appear dark red. Consequently, although it is tempting to categorize muscle cells into red and white or dark and light cells on the basis of their general appearance, and to categorize red cells as slow and white cells as fast, the existence of the fast-twitch, oxidative-glycolytic group of muscle cells makes this practice subject to serious error. These cells have sometimes been called intermediate fibers, but they are not actually intermediate in most of their features; they are fast-twitch, not intermediate between fast-twitch and slow-twitch, etc. One of the few characteristics in which fast-twitch, oxidative-glycolytic muscle cells are actually intermediate is Z-disk width; average width in fast-twitch, oxidative-glycolytic cells is 88 nm compared with 66 nm for fast-twitch, glycolytic cells and 144 nm for slow-twitch, oxidative cells.

It is also hazardous to characterize all cells in a muscle by muscle color. Most mammalian skeletal muscles contain all three types of phasic muscle cells. Hence, even muscles with relatively slow contraction speeds and dark color may contain an appreciable number of fast-twitch, glycolytic cells. The presence of these cells contributes to the smoothly integrated, macroscopic gradation of contraction.

The preceding subdivision includes only the phasic or twitch muscle cells that are innervated with single, discrete en plaque nerve endings and does not include the tonic fibers innervated with the en grappe multiple nerve endings. It is not possible to subdivide the tonic muscle cells into groups, although tonic muscle cells in general have lower levels of resting potential (50–70 mv compared to 70–80 mv), longer latent periods (6–8 msec compared to 3–4 msec), and smaller motor nerve fibers (axons 5–8 μ in diameter compared to 10–12 μ) that conduct impulses more slowly (2–8 m/sec compared to 20–35 m/sec) than any of the phasic or twitch muscle cells.

The motor nerves themselves evidently are partly responsible for differentiation of phasic or twitch muscle cells into three types. Studies have shown that fast-twitch, glycolytic cells can be changed into slow-twitch, oxidative cells by severing the nerve leading to the fast-twitch, glycolytic cell and reinnervating this cell with a nerve that normally serves a slow-twitch, oxidative cell. Slow-twitch, oxidative cells can also be changed into fast-twitch, glycolytic cells by using this same nerve-switching process, although this change is not as complete as the opposite one. Not only does general metabolism of the cross-reinnervated cells change, but myosin and the other myofibrillar proteins in these cells are also replaced with a myofibrillar protein appropriate for the new type of cell (e.g. myosin with high ATPase activity is replaced with myosin having low ATPase activity when a fast-twitch, glycolytic cell is reinnervated with a nerve from a slow-twitch, oxidative cell).

CARDIAC AND SMOOTH MUSCLE

Although cardiac muscle is cross-striated like skeletal muscle, it differs structurally from skeletal muscle in that its cells are mononucleated and the nuclei lie in the interior of the cell. Cardiac muscle cells rely heavily on aerobic metabolism for their energy supply, and they therefore contain large numbers of mitochondria and a large amount of myoglobin. Moreover, cardiac muscle cells have relatively long contraction periods and have a differently developed and organized sarcotubular system. Hence, cardiac muscle cells metabolically resemble a form of a slow-twitch, oxidative fiber.

One of the most striking differences between cardiac and skeletal muscle is the presence of structures called intercalated disks (Fig. 39.14A). An intercalated disk is defined as the entire, continuous, stepwise boundary joining the end regions of adjacent cardiac muscle cells. The intercalated disk, therefore, is composed of highly specialized transverse portions and of longitudinal sections connecting these transverse portions, and is structurally

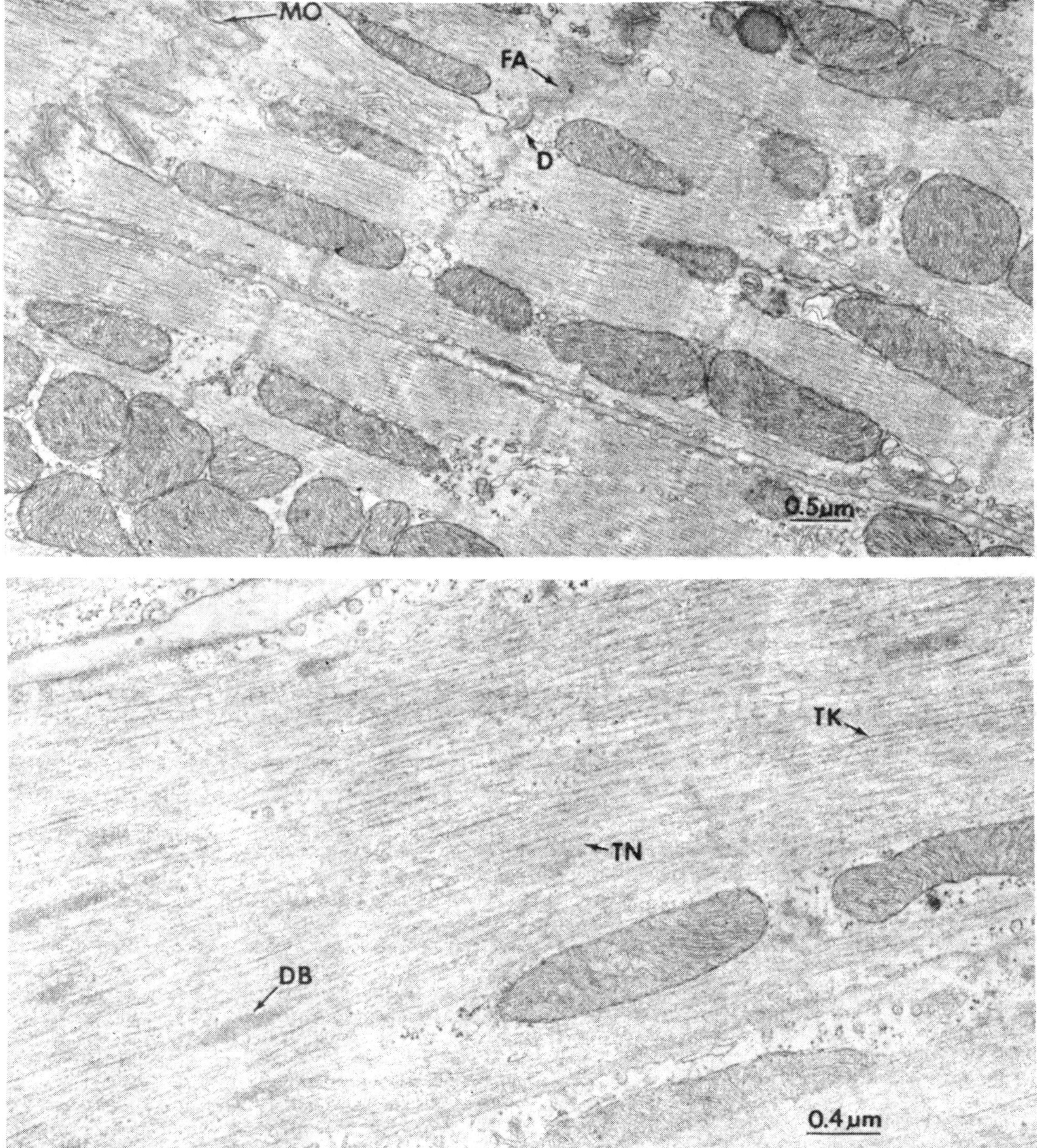

Figure 39.14. Electron micrographs of cardiac and smooth muscle cells. Above, electron micrograph of a rat cardiac muscle cell. Part of an intercalated disk is shown and the fascia adherentes (FA), desmosome (D), and macula occludens (MO) are indicated. ×19,500. Below, electron micrograph of a chicken gizzard smooth muscle cell. Thick, 120–160 nm filaments (TK), thin, 6–8 nm filaments (TN), and an intracellular dense body (DB) are designated. ×29,850.

differentiated to include three kinds of specialized cell junctions or contact regions. These are (1) the fasciae adherentes or zonulae adherens, which make up most of the transverse portion of the intercalated disk and which contain dense material into which thin filaments from terminal sarcomeres insert (hence, they are analogous to the Z-disk in skeletal muscle cells); (2) the maculae adherentes or desmosomes, which are also located in the transverse portion of the intercalated disk between areas of fasciae adherentes and which consist of a dense layer of uniform thickness closely applied to the inner surface of two apposing plasmalemmas; and (3) the zonulae occludens (or nexus or tight junctions). The fasciae adherentes and desmosomes evidently are responsible for maintaining intercellular adhesion between adjacent cardiac muscle cells, and the nexus may provide low resistance pathways for transmission of excitation through the myocardium. The intercalated disk contains the myofibrillar protein, α-actinin. Little else is known about composition of the intercalated disk although this structure may be involved in spread of excitation and as an area for insertion of new sarcomeres into cardiac myofibrils (i.e. in muscle cell growth).

The structure of smooth muscle cells is completely different from the highly organized myofibrillar structure observed in cardiac and skeletal muscle cells (Fig. 39.14B). Smooth muscle cells are smaller than skeletal muscle cells and are long spindle-shaped cells, thickened in the middle and tapering at both ends. Smooth muscle cells range from 15–500 μ in length (average length of 60 μ) and from 1–12 μ in diameter (average diameter of 4 μ). Like cardiac muscle cells, smooth muscle cells contain a single nucleus located centrally.

Smooth muscle cells contain three different kinds of filaments: (1) those 6–8 nm in diameter that contain actin and tropomyosin and that are analogous to thin filaments in skeletal or cardiac muscle cells; (2) those about 10 nm in diameter (sometimes called intermediate filaments) that have an unknown protein composition (may contain a protein with subunit molecular weight of 55,000–60,000) and function; and (3) those 120–160 nm in diameter that contain myosin and that are analogous to thick filaments in skeletal or cardiac muscle. Unlike skeletal or cardiac muscle, adjacent myosin and actin filaments do not lie in register in smooth muscle cells, so smooth muscle cells are not cross-striated in appearance. The 6-nm, actin-containing filaments insert into densely staining regions called dense bodies (see Fig. 39.14B), which seem to be analogous to Z-disks in skeletal and cardiac muscle cells.

Current evidence indicates that the elementary processes that accompany the actin-myosin interaction and that are responsible for contraction in skeletal and cardiac muscle cells also produce contraction in smooth muscle cells. Control of the initiation and cessation of contraction is probably different in smooth muscle and skeletal muscle cells because smooth muscle may not contain troponin and because smooth muscle myosin may have a Ca^{++}-regulatory function. The less organized structure of smooth muscle cells adapts these cells to their special functions, which may involve producing uterine contractions and decreasing the size of circular channels such as blood vessels or intestines, rather than the simpler two-dimensional displacement characteristic of skeletal muscle cells.

MUSCLE PATHOLOGIES

The Research Group on Neuromuscular Disorders of the World Federation of Neurology has delineated three classes of skeletal muscle pathologies: (1) neural muscular atrophies that derive from diseases of the anterior horn cells, motor nerve roots, or peripheral nerves; (2) disorders of neuromuscular transmission, including myasthenia gravis, poisoning with various anticholinesterase compounds, botulism, and tick paralysis; and (3) disorders of the muscle cell itself. The third category is further subdivided into seven groups: (a) genetically determined myopathies; (b) muscle damage by external agents, including physical damage, toxins, and drugs such as steroids and chloroquine; (c) inflammatory reactions due to viral or bacterial infections, parasite infestations, and autoimmune disease (polymyositis may be in the latter category); (d) muscle disorders associated with endocrine or metabolic disease; (e) myopathies associated with malignant diseases such as rhabdomyeloma; (f) other myopathies of unknown origin such as amyloidosis and paroxysmal myoglobinuria; and (g) tumors of muscle.

Myotonia and myasthenia are two classic symptoms of many muscle diseases. Myotonia is a condition in which the affected muscles continue to contract after nerve stimulation has ceased, that is, the muscle seems unable to relax. Hence, muscle diseases that include the name myotonia have the inability to relax as one of their symptoms. Myotonic diseases usually involve some malfunction of the muscle cell membrane. Myasthenia, on the other hand, indicates a state of abnormal muscle fatigability in response to exercise. Hence, muscle pathologies that include the name myasthenia are characterized by muscle fatigue. The disease myasthenia gravis is caused by an abnormality of the neuromuscular junction.

Etiology of several of the muscle pathologies that involve abnormalities in metabolism is well understood. Several diseases involving inability of the muscle cell to degrade glycogen to produce energy and characterized by accumulation of abnormally large amounts of glycogen in the muscle cell have been grouped together under the title glycogen storage diseases. These diseases are all genetically determined myopathies. Muscles are weak and frequently painful due to large numbers of glycogen particles between myofibrils. At least four different glycogen storage diseases have been described in man. Pompe's disease (type II glycogenesis) is due to a deficiency of acid maltase, a lysosomal enzyme that degrades glycogen. McArdle's disease (type V glycogenesis) is due to a deficiency of phosphorylase, the enzyme that degrades glycogen metabolically. Forbe's disease (type III glycogenesis) is due to a deficiency of debranching enzyme so that glycogen degradation cannot proceed past α-(1→6)-branch points. Type VIII glycogenesis is due to a deficiency of the enzyme phosphofructokinase. This enzyme catalyzes an important control reaction in glycolysis, and its absence also results in accumulation of glycogen. A congenital, familial muscle disease that is characterized by nonprogressive muscle weakness is nemaline myopathy. In addition to an overall decrease in the number of muscle cells, examination of this muscle in either the light or the electron microscope shows prominent rod bodies that ostensibly are hypertrophied Z-disks (Fig. 39.15). Muscle weakness may be severe enough to result in death.

Chronic alcoholics may be afflicted with a form of muscle abnormality called alcoholic myopathy. This condition is characterized by severe pain, cramps, muscle tenderness, and weakness, especially in the lower limbs. Myoglobinuria (myoglobin in the urine) is present in severe cases, and death can result from renal damage. Phosphorylase activity frequently is low, and Z-disks are often convoluted and disrupted. The condition responds positively to abstinence from alcohol.

There are many different types of muscular dystrophy that are of genetic origin. Most recent findings show that these muscular dystrophies affect muscle cells directly rather than affecting the motor nerve supplying the muscle cell. These muscular dystrophies are characterized by muscle atrophy and weakness and by loss of myofibrillar protein from muscle cells. Z-disks are frequently disrupted, and thick and thin filaments are disordered in necrotic areas of dystrophic muscle. No cures are known for these muscular dystrophies, and the prognosis depends on the type of dystrophy. The Duchenne type is one of the most common. It is inherited as a sex-linked recessive, so males are most commonly afflicted. The disease is inexorably progressive, and death results from respiratory failure or cardiac involvement, usually in adolescence.

Denervation of a muscle cell occurs when the cell body of the motor neuron degenerates or when the axon is severed in a peripheral nerve injury. Muscle degeneration begins almost immediately after denervation. Many of the changes in denervated muscle cells resemble those in dystrophic muscle cells. Cells atrophy, myofibrils disappear, Z-disks are disrupted, and thick and thin filaments become disordered. The space vacated by atrophying muscle cells is filled with connective tissue and adipose cells, just as it is in dystrophic muscle. Dener-

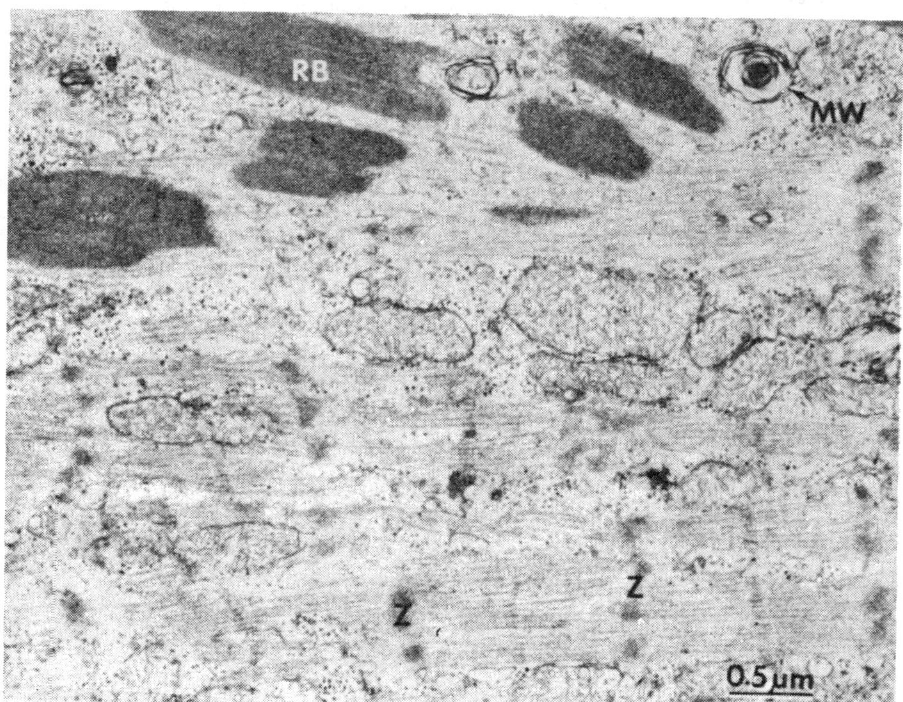

Figure 39.15. Electron micrograph of human skeletal muscle from a nemaline myopathy case. Note the characteristic rod bodies (RB), discontinuous Z-disks (Z), and membrane whorls (MW). ×22,200. (From M.H. Stromer, L.B. Tabatabai, R.M. Robson, D.E. Goll, and M.G. Zeece 1976, *Exp. Neurol.* 50:402–21.)

vated muscle also gradually develops increasing sensitivity to acetylcholine, and acetylcholine sensitivity is not limited to the motor end-plate region but is spread over the surface of the cell.

One of the common features of all muscle pathologies that involve degeneration and atrophy of muscle cells and loss of myofibrils is a variable disruption of the Z-disk. This disruption may vary from convoluted or hypertrophied, overgrown Z-disks to complete disappearance of the Z-disk.

REFERENCES

Bourne, G.H., ed. 1972–1973. *The Structure and Function of Muscle.* 2d ed. Academic Press, New York. 4 vols.

Cohen, C. 1975. The protein switch of muscle contraction. *Scien. Am.* 233:36–45.

Couteaux, R. 1973. Motor end plate structure. In Bourne. Vol. 2, 483–530.

Curtin, N.A., and Davies, R.E. 1973. ATP breakdown following activation of muscle. In Bourne. Vol. 3, 471–515.

Ebashi, S. 1976. Excitation-contraction coupling. *Ann. Rev. Physiol.* 38:293–313.

Fuchs, F. 1974. Striated muscle. *Ann. Rev. Physiol.* 36:461–502.

Goldspink, G. 1972. Postembryonic growth and differentiation of striated muscle. In Bourne. Vol. 1, 179–236.

Gordon, A.M., Huxley, A.F., and Julian, F.J. 1966. The variation in isometric tension with sarcomere length in vertebrate muscle fibers. *J. Physiol.* 184:170–92.

Gould, R.P. 1973. The microanatomy of muscle. In Bourne. Vol. 2, 186–241.

Hanson, J., and Lowy, J. 1963. The structure of F-actin and of actin filaments isolated from muscle. *J. Mol. Biol.* 6:46–60.

Henson, R.A. 1973. Clinical aspects of some diseases of muscle. In Bourne. Vol. 4, 433–73.

Hill, A.V. 1938. The heat of shortening and the dynamic constants of muscle. *Proc. Roy. Soc.*, ser. B, 126:136–95.

Holloszy, J.O., and Booth, F.W. 1976. Biochemical adaptations to endurance exercise in muscle. *Ann. Rev. Physiol.* 38:273–91.

Huxley, A.F. 1974. Muscular contraction. *J. Physiol.* 243:1–43.

Huxley, H.E. 1963. Electron microscope studies on the structure of natural and synthetic protein filaments from striated muscle. *J. Mol. Biol.* 7:281–308.

——. 1972. Molecular basis of contraction in cross-striated muscles. In Bourne. Vol. 1, 301–87.

Huxley, H.E., and Brown, W. 1967. The low-angle X-ray diagram of vertebrate striated muscle and its behavior during contraction and rigor. *J. Mol. Biol.* 30:383–434.

Lowey, S., Slayter, H.S., Weeds, A.G., and Baker, H. 1969. Substructure of the myosin molecule. I. Subfragments of myosin by enzymic degradation. *J. Mol. Biol.* 42:1–29.

MacLennen, D.H., and Holland, P.C. 1975. Calcium transport in sarcoplasmic reticulum. *Ann. Rev. Biophys. Bioengin.* 4:377–404.

Mannherz, H.G., and Goody, R.S. 1976. Proteins of contractile systems. *Ann. Rev. Biochem.* 45:427–65.

Parry, D.A.D., and Squire, J.M. 1973. Structural role of tropomyosin in muscle regulation: Analysis of the X-ray diffraction patterns from relaxed and contracting muscles. *J. Mol. Biol.* 75:33–55.

Peter, J.B., Barnard, R., Edgerton, V.R., Gillespie, C.A., and Stempel, K.E. 1972. Metabolic profiles of three fiber types of skeletal muscle in guinea pigs and rabbits. *Biochemistry* 11:2627–33.

Prosser, C.L. 1974. Smooth muscle. *Ann. Rev. Physiol.* 36:503–35.

Seiden, D. 1973. Effects of colchicine on myofilament arrangement and the lysosomal system in skeletal muscle. *Zeitschrift Zellforsch.* 144:467–73.

Smith, A.L., and Bird, J.W.C. 1975. Distribution and particle properties of the vacuolar apparatus of cardiac muscle tissue. I. Biochemical characterization of cardiac muscle lysosomes and the isolation and characterization of acid, neutral, and alkaline proteases. *J. Mol. Cell. Cardiol.* 7:39–61.

Spudich, J.A., Huxley, H.E., and Finch, J.T. 1972. Regulation of skeletal muscle contraction. II. Structural studies of the interaction of the tropomyosin-troponin complex with actin. *J. Mol. Biol.* 72:619–32.

Stromer, M.H., Goll, D.E., Young, R.B., Robson, R.M., and Parrish, F.C., Jr. 1974. Ultrastructural features of skeletal muscle differentiation and development. *J. Anim. Sci.* 38:1111–41.

Taylor, E.W. 1972. Chemistry of muscle contraction. *Ann. Rev. Biochem.* 41:577–616.

CHAPTER 40

Design and Basic Functions of the Nervous System | by William R. Klemm

The nervous system is the body's chief coordinating agency, exerting control over almost all functions. For example, the endocrine system, which regulates metabolism and growth, is not only controlled by the nervous system, but also is to a large extent part of it; one part of the brain, the hypothalamus, releases secretions that regulate the master endocrine gland, the pituitary. Hormones from the endocrine system also act upon the nervous system, suggesting that it is a control system with feedback not only from the impulse conducting nerve channels but also from hormones.

Other body structures have supportive functions for the nervous system. The CNS (brain and spinal cord) is wrapped in multiple membranes and floated in liquid which is contained inside a bony armor—all giving protection against mechanical damage. Pressure and chemical sensors in the aortic and carotid arteries help ensure that a constant supply of blood of proper composition reaches the brain. The brain itself controls certain features of the blood that bathes it, such as osmotic pressure and temperature. A special permeability barrier in the brain, the blood-brain barrier, greatly restricts the kind and amount of chemicals that can gain access to nerve cells (neurons).

Because the CNS has such important roles in regulating body functions, chemicals that act upon this system can have profound effects, even in small amounts. For example, in a 7 kg dog, 0.5 g of the stimulant pentylenetetrazol will produce convulsions; 0.2 g of pentobarbital can produce surgical anesthesia, and 0.25 μg of botulinus toxin can lead to fatal paralysis. The most generally accepted explanation is that only certain molecules in neurons are acted upon by a given chemical, and in turn these neuron molecules, or receptor sites, affect the function of the entire nerve cell.

OVERALL FUNCTION

Input "information" (from sensory receptors) into the nervous system results in output "instructions" (to muscles, glands). The "processing" of input data, when needed, sometimes requires reference to "memory" (Fig. 40.1).

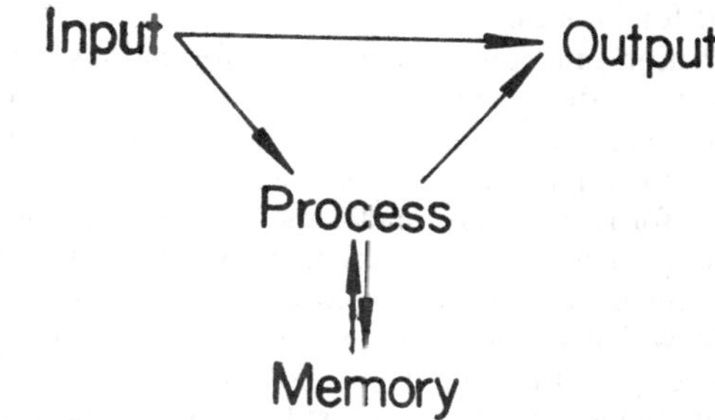

Figure 40.1. Overall functions of the nervous system

Input information for the CNS originates in the external environment as well as within the body. This information is received by peripheral sensory organs such as the eye and ear, which depend on the harmonious function of several kinds of tissue. Other sensory receptors, such as those for pain, touch, pressure, temperature, and smell, are actual processes of nerve cells, either bare endings or highly specialized structures.

Changes in physical environment are "transduced" (converted to another form) by sensory receptors, and this transduction must be coded. The initial coding is achieved by a relatively steady change in the voltage across the membrane of the receptor; the relation between stimulus intensity and magnitude of change in receptor voltage is often logarithmic.

For most sensory receptors the next stage of coding occurs as the steady receptor voltage change triggers the discharge of impulses—quite brief transmembrane voltage changes (about 1 msec)—which move from the receptor via the attached neuronal process into the CNS. Impulses code information in various ways: by latency between stimulus and impulse discharge, by the number of impulses in a burst, by the interval between impulses in a burst, or by rate of change in impulse frequency.

The next stage of information transfer, or processing, occurs when the impulses from receptors reach other neurons. The message transfer begins with the release of chemical secretions which diffuse across the intercellular gap (the synapse) to react with the membrane of the neuron that contacts the receptor. The chemical then causes a relatively slow change in transmembrane voltage, somewhat analogous to the change physical stimuli induce in receptors. Finally, this slow voltage change, if of the right polarity, may trigger the neuron to discharge impulses to the next neurons in line or to the effector organs (glands and muscles). The slow voltage change must reach a certain magnitude, or threshold, before impulses can be triggered. This scheme allows a great deal of processing to occur at this level. Because a given neuron receives information from many other neurons, the slow voltage changes contributed by each can interact, adding or subtracting to determine whether or not threshold for impulse discharge is reached.

Information undergoes many transformations within the nervous system, and these basic processing mechanisms, although complicated, work quite well in helping an animal to adapt to its environment.

Input information may lead almost directly to output instructions; such simple function is usually confined to simple reflexes in the spinal cord, such as the "knee jerk," in which the neuron carrying sensory input connects directly to the output (or motor) neuron. Even at this level, however, processing still occurs in the receptor's membrane voltage, in the chemical release in the one synapse, in the membrane voltage of the motoneuron, and even at the neuromuscular junction.

More commonly, many nerve cells are required to process input signals before they generate output signals. For example, the routing of sensory impulses is well regulated by inherited functional pathways for such signals, and the various interconnections of the neurons making up these pathways can be very complicated. Also, the brain compares incoming information with stored information of previous experiences, called memory, before processing and generating output signals.

CELLS OF THE NERVOUS SYSTEM

Neurons

The neuron, the basic unit of the nervous system, consists of a large cell body, with a nucleus and the usual organelles, and often with a long process called an axon (Fig. 40.2).

Neuron organelles function similarly to those of any cell: chromosomes carry "ancestral wisdom," mitochondria regulate energy flow, microsomal particles control biochemical synthesis, and cell membranes surround the cytoplasm and regulate transport of solutes (Hydén 1960). Neurons are unusual, however, in having long neurotubules and shorter and smaller neurofibrils in their axons. In the cell body, or soma, clumps called

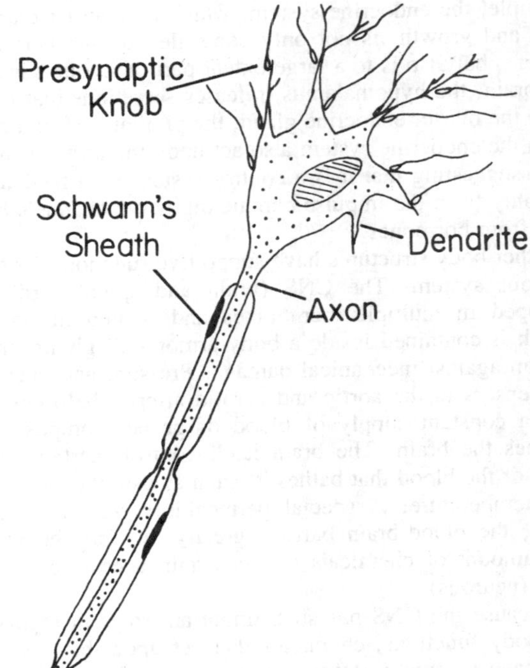

Figure 40.2. A neuron, showing a myelinated Schwann's sheath and presynaptic knobs of an adjacent neuron

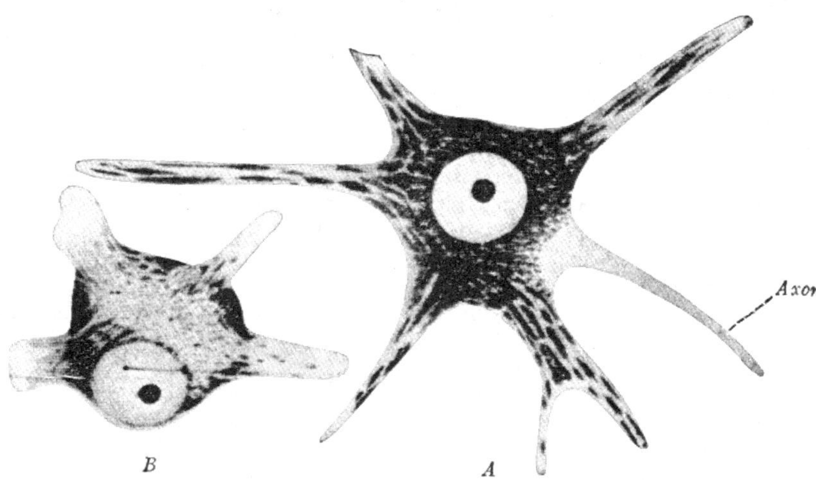

Figure 40.3. Nissl bodies in the cytoplasm of nerve cells. A, cell from ventral gray column of the spinal cord of a monkey. B, cell from the facial nerve of a dog in which Nissl bodies are disappearing because the nerve has been cut. (From S.W. Ranson, *Anatomy of the Nervous System*, 7th ed., Saunders, Philadelphia, 1943.)

Nissl bodies (Fig. 40.3) contain ribosomes and endoplasmic reticulum (Palay and Palade 1955). A special pigment, lipofucsin, accumulates in the cytoplasm as the neuron ages or if its mitochondria or lysosomes are damaged. Mature neurons are unusual also in that they do not normally divide.

Axons terminate in branches that interact with branches of other neurons. These synaptic contacts permit impulse transmission between neurons, often from one neuron's axonal branches to the short dendrites of an adjacent neuron body. In some neurons, however, impulses in one axon can directly affect transmission in other axons (see Chapter 41). The active region of a synaptic membrane is presumed to be the isolated dark patches near the membrane which are seen in electron micrographs.

The cell synthesizes many chemicals that are constantly transported to the periphery, as was initially demonstrated in experiments in which ligation of an axon caused bulging on the side proximal to the cell body. Simple diffusion and hydrostatic gradients alone cannot account for this transport; time-lapse photography has indicated that peristaltic motions of axons may assist in propelling material down the axon (Weiss et al. 1962). The rate of transport depends on the nature of transported materials. Some chemicals move slowly, about 1–6 mm/day, perhaps being oriented in their direction of flow along the 10 nm neurofibrils that are parallel to the long axis of the axon. Also in the same axis are the neurotubules of about 24 nm, which are considered transport ducts for the chemicals that have been observed to move at such very fast rates as 100–1000 mm/day (Schmitt 1968).

The term nerve signifies a group of fibers made up of many neurons, closely enveloped in tough connective tissue, which connects the brain with the periphery. Nerve cell bodies that are grouped in clusters in the brain and spinal cord are sometimes called nuclei. Some nuclei also occur outside of the brain and spinal cord; these have connective tissue sheaths and are called ganglia.

Although neurons appear in many forms, and many atypical forms occur, they may be classified by the number and arrangement of their processes.

Unipolar cells, having a single process, are rare in higher animals. They are somewhat more common in lower vertebrates and invertebrates. The physiological relation of the single process to the cell body is not clear.

Bipolar cells have two processes, one axon and one dendrite. In vertebrates these cells are well exemplified in the retina by sensory cells with a short axon and dendrite. Similar cells are found elsewhere. In higher vertebrates the nerve cells in spinal nerve ganglia are embryologically bipolar. The two processes later fuse near the cell body into one process with a T-shaped appearance. One branch becomes an axis cylinder of a peripheral afferent nerve fiber; the other branch passes into the CNS by way of the dorsal root of a spinal nerve. Although both branches are anatomically axons, the peripheral branch is physiologically a dendrite that conducts impulses centrally.

Multipolar cells have numerous branching dendrites and an axon, which may be long or short. Typical multipolar cells with long axons are the motor nerve cells (motoneurons) in the ventral gray column of the spinal cord. The axons of these neurons emerge from the CNS in spinal nerves to become peripheral motor nerve fibers. The axons of other multipolar cells, instead of leaving the gray matter are very short and break up into numerous branches in the vicinity of the cell body. By means of these cells, an afferent neuron may be placed into relation with a great many motor neurons. They are therefore designated as internuncial neurons or interneurons.

Special neuronal functions

Generation of electricity

The nervous system's electrical activity is the most conspicuous aspect of nervous tissue function; much of what is known about the nervous system has been inferred from study of its electrical activity.

Electrophysiological data are usually expressed as voltage, or the potential force generated by the separation of electrically charged ions. The most fundamental biological potential is the steady cell voltage that exists between the inside and the outside of the resting, or unstimulated neuron (see Chapters 6 and 41). Although the resting potential of neurons is similar to that of other cells, neurons are different in that their membrane potential is constantly being modified by interactions with other neurons.

Activity in adjacent neurons alters the direction and magnitude of this polarization of postsynaptic neurons. If the membrane polarity tends to reverse, a nerve impulse is discharged when a critical threshold level of depolarization is achieved. Such membrane potential changes are called postsynaptic potentials. They form a background pattern of various levels of neuronal excitability, upon which is played the pattern of impulse discharge in the nervous system. A neuron receives not only excitatory postsynaptic input but often also inhibitory (hyperpolarizing) input, which can be added to determine the net level of polarization and excitability.

Electrodes placed in the brain or on the scalp record a composite sum of the voltages caused by extracellular currents near the electrodes, compounded from postsynaptic voltages, impulses, and even glial cell depolarizations. This sum of electrical activity is the electroencephalogram, which has been a useful diagnostic tool in human medicine for years and is now beginning to be used in veterinary medicine (Klemm 1976).

Secretion of chemicals

The electrical impulse current usually is unable to influence the postsynaptic neuron directly. The electrical disturbance releases a chemical transmitter from the presynaptic neuron which diffuses across the synapse, reacts with molecular receptors on the postsynaptic membrane, and initiates a new electrical disturbance in the neuron (or target muscle or gland). This neurochemical transducer system includes means for synthesizing, storing, and releasing the transmitter. Moreover, the system can destroy the released transmitter, thus ensuring only transient activation of postsynaptic membranes. Some neurons, instead of releasing an excitatory transmitter, release a substance that actually inhibits postsynaptic activation (Eccles 1964). No exception has yet been found to Dale's law, that a neuron releases only one kind of transmitter, although a neuron may receive more than one kind of transmitter input.

Some neurosecretions are actually hormones (i.e. transported in the blood), for example epinephrine, released from modified neurons in the adrenal medulla (see Chapter 52).

Growth

Neurons stop dividing shortly after birth, but their axons and dendrites grow extensively during the preadult period (Jacobson 1970). Some scientists believe that some growth occurs also in the adult animal. Maturation of behavior is paralleled by proliferation of neuronal processes; presumably this growth creates new contact areas among neurons and new information processing networks.

One aspect of growth has particular medical importance. Since the brain grows at a much faster rate than the body, its growth depends critically on a proper supply of nutrients; deficiencies during the growing time can cause permanent damage. Animal experiments also indicate that sensory and learning experiences help stimulate neuronal and glial growth (Rosenzweig 1966). A chemical known as nerve growth factor was discovered years ago, but much remains to be learned about it.

Growth of axonal processes is especially important in regenerating cut nerves. When an axon is cut, a process known as Wallerian degeneration begins, in which the part distal to the cut starts fragmenting within 3–4 days; centrifugal degeneration continues until all the distal axon is gone (about 3–4 weeks).

The cell body of a cut axon also undergoes changes known as chromatolysis. Within about the first week after a cut, the cell body swells, organelles are displaced, and, most obvious of all, the Nissl substance dissolves (see Fig. 40.3). A marked shift in protein synthesis occurs as the ribosomes attached to endoplasmic reticulum disperse.

Functional differences among neurons

Even among neurons which are anatomically similar functional differences exist. Chemicals have different effects on different parts of the nervous system (Gerard 1960). Carbon disulfide exerts its greatest effect in destroying a portion of the brain involved in motor functions (the caudate nucleus). Vitamin deficiencies initiate degenerations in specific portions of the nervous system. Some cells are especially sensitive to the osmotic balance in surrounding fluid, others to carbon dioxide concentrations, others to blood glucose, and still others to hormones.

Differences among nerve cells are illustrated by the different chemical neurohumors released by various neurons. Another, more subtle, indication of chemical differences among neurons is in the specificities exhibited during development and regeneration of cut nerves. The "wiring" of many neural networks is predetermined, and during embryonic growth, neuronal processes grow and somehow "recognize" their appropriate targets so that a final, appropriate connection is made and growth stops. This is not to say that the processes are attracted to a certain site; they may simply be able to recognize a compatible physical and chemical environment when it is presented. This specificity of cells has been demonstrated to exist in neuron-to-neuron relations and in neuron-to-muscle fiber relations (Weiss 1966).

Glial cells

The connective tissue cells of the brain are called glial cells or neuroglia. Depending on the counting technique used, they outnumber neurons as much as tenfold. The dense packing of so many neurons (total estimated at 10^{10} in the human brain) and the even more numerous glia cause nervous tissue to have less extracellular space than other tissue (Van Harreveld et al. 1966). Glial cell function is poorly understood in comparison with our understanding of neurons, but neuroglia are considered to interact with neurons in a supportive and symbiotic way (De Robertis and Carrea 1965, Galambos 1966, Bunge 1970). However, glia are not essential for all neuron functions, as indicated by the absence of glia in certain coelenterates and by the fact that neurons survive well by themselves in tissue culture.

Glia form loose ensheathments around neurons, except when myelin is formed by the systematic spiralization and compaction of glial cytoplasmic processes (Fig. 40.4). Cells that form myelin in peripheral nerves are called Schwann cells. The myelin-forming cells in the CNS are called oligodendrocytes. The cytoplasm and membrane of both these cells wrap around neuronal processes; the junctions between adjacent glial cells form the nodes of Ranvier, which are relatively uninsulated patches of neuronal membrane (Fig. 40.5). Because nerve impulses can skip from node to node, impulse conduction is much faster in myelinated nerves (see Chapter 41). Another consequence of glial ensheathment is that the extremely sensitive neuronal membranes are more or less shielded from straying neurotransmitters, neurohumors, toxins, and the like. Such chemicals can only react with neuronal membranes by moving through narrow extracellular spaces between the sheaths and membranes.

Another very common type of glial cell is the astrocyte. These have cytoplasmic processes, many of which attach to blood vessels to help form the so-called blood-brain barrier (see Chapter 14). Astrocytes differ also from oligodendrocytes in having a more lucent cytoplasm, fewer organelles, and microfilaments gathered into bundles.

Membrane potentials of glial cells have been recorded with microelectrodes (Bunge 1970). Such studies reveal that glia are depolarized by impulse discharge in adjacent nerve fibers; the excitation is due to K^+ release from the neuron. The glial cell response is long-lasting and graded; it can summate to very large voltage shifts (up to 48 mv), provided neuron discharges are rapid.

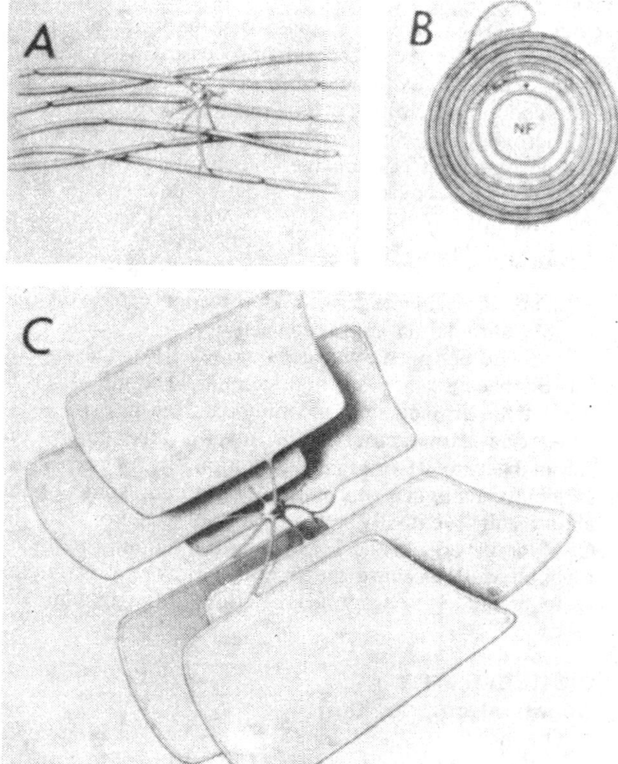

Figure 40.4. CNS glial cell body. A, with its cytoplasmic extensions wrapped around several axons. B, cross section of a wrapped nerve fiber (NF). C, the cell with the cytoplasmic extensions unwrapped. (From Bunge 1970, in Schmitt, ed., *The Neurosciences: Second Study Program,* Rockefeller U. Press, New York.)

A third kind of cell, the microglia, is considered to be glial by some authorities, but it is not nervous tissue. These are ameboid, phagocytic cells that invade the ner-

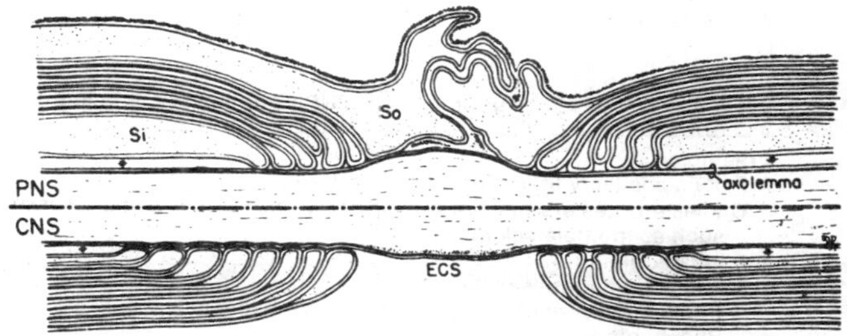

Figure 40.5. Node formed by junction of two glial cells of a myelinated nerve fiber. In the PNS (peripheral nervous system) the Schwann cell provides an internal collar (Si) and an outer collar (So) of cytoplasm for the compact myelin. Contact with extracellular space (ECS) is more intimate in the CNS nodes. (From Bunge 1970, in Schmitt, ed., *The Neurosciences: Second Study Program,* Rockefeller U. Press, New York.)

vous system from the blood; they originate from leukocytes. Microglia are very small, with dark nuclei, sparse cytoplasm, and irregular, short processes. They contain many dense bodies (assumed to be lysosomes), but have little endoplasmic reticulum or ribosomes.

Microglia are important in the degeneration reactions that accompany CNS damage (Jacobson 1970). They invade damaged areas and phagocytize debris; later they may transform into macrophages. Other glial reactions to damage include a reactive hyperplasia of astrocytes and of oligodendrocytes. Such increases have been observed in many diseases, and even as a response to increased sensory stimulation and motor activity.

The cutting of nerves does not destroy the myelin sheaths because they are multicellular. The glia distal to the cut remain and will accommodate the growth of regenerating axon sprouts. The myelin tube guides the sprout back to its original destination. If cut nerves are surgically realigned and carefully sutured, some of the axons will eventually restore normal function. In the CNS, however, cuts such as spinal transection, are never repaired well, because the microanatomy is so complex as to preclude axon sprouts "finding" the right myelin tubes.

BIOCHEMISTRY

Chemical composition

The nervous system, like all tissues, is composed mostly of water, 70–85 percent (Fig. 40.6). Most of this water (85%) is intracellular. The solutes, such as glucose, electrolytes, and amino acids, are only about 1 percent of the total mass in cerebrospinal fluid (Holmes and Tower 1955) and about 2 percent in intracellular compartments (Rossiter 1955).

Most nervous system solids (40–65%) are complex lipids (Table 40.1). These lipids are usually quite different from lipids in other body regions (LeBaron and Folch 1957). Phospholipids constitute about 25 percent of the total dry weight; all but sphingomyelin contain phosphatidic acid, a base (choline or ethanolamine), and an amino acid (serine) or inositol. Sphingomyelin has

Table 40.1. Classification of lipids in CNS of normal adult mammals

- Free lipids
  - Fatty acids (very little present in free form)
  - Cholesterol (esters present only in the young and in some diseases such as multiple sclerosis)
- Conjugated lipids
  - Phospholipids (phosphatides)
    - Phosphoglycerides (lecithin, various cephalins)
    - Phosphoinositides
    - Phosphosphingosides (sphingomyelin)
  - Glycolipids (hexose + fatty acid + sphingosine)
    - Cerebrosides
    - Gangliosides
  - Lipoproteins
  - Proteolipids

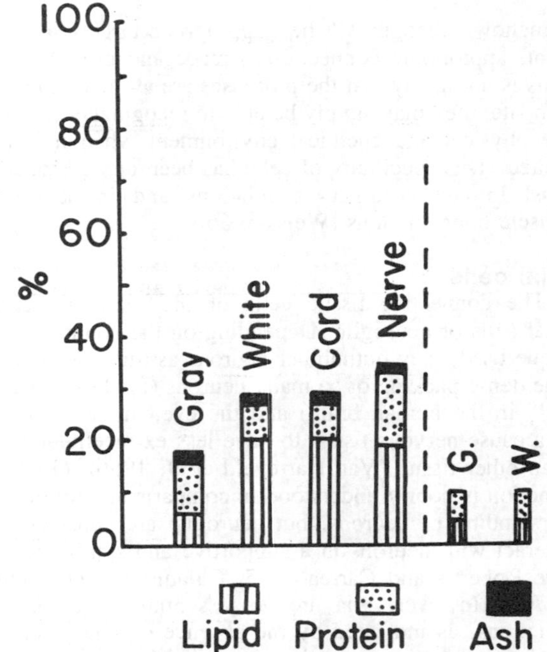

Figure 40.6. Chemical constituents of gray matter (mostly neurons), white matter (mostly lipid-insulating material), spinal cord, and peripheral nerves. Solid matter is indicated by the bars; the rest is water. Values to the left of the dashed line are from adults, to the right are neonatal. (Modified from D.B. Tower, in H.F. Harlow and C.N. Woolsey, eds., *Biological and Biochemical Bases of Behavior,* U. of Wisconsin Press, Madison.)

phosphorylcholine and sphingosine. Among the glycolipids, gangliosides are composed of sialic acid, hexoseamine, and two or more sugar molecules. Phospholipids and glycolipids are not well understood, but they are principal components of myelin and neuronal membranes. Their composition is conspicuously altered in such genetic diseases as cerebral lipidoses. Neutral fat is not present.

Proteins in the nervous system generally occur in complexes with lipids. Lipoproteins behave chemically as proteins but contain lipid. Proteolipids behave as lipids but contain protein; they are especially concentrated in myelin. These lipid-protein complexes constitute the vast bulk of total lipid (Schmitt and Davison 1967, Dickerson 1968); they differ from related complexes in plasma in that they are not soluble in water.

Proteins of the nervous system were once considered to be relatively inert, but that notion has been dispelled by radioactive isotope studies indicating extensive and even rapid turnover (Lajtha 1970), comparable to secreting glandular tissue. Most of the synthesis occurs in Nissl granules. The carbon originates from glucose, and incorporation apparently occurs first in the smaller proteins. The immunological properties of nervous system proteins are not well understood, but they may be a factor in autoimmune allergic encephalidides and also in memory processes.

Many important peptides have been identified in the brain; some are released by hypothalamic neurons to regulate hormonal output of the pituitary (Schally et al. 1973); others, called endorphins, mimic the action of morphine and other opiates (Goldstein 1976). Still other peptides seem associated with learning and memory (Ungar 1974). One peptide, substance P, is found in the spinal cord, where it excites neurons (Leeman and Mroz 1975).

Oxidative metabolism

Nerve tissue requires considerable metabolic activity to sustain impulse conduction and to synthesize, store, and release its secretions (see also Chapter 41). For normal functioning, the brain must have a steady supply of blood. Stasis of brain circulation for 8 minutes in dogs causes severe and permanent damage, including "loss of function of the cerebral cortex, loss of auditory reflexes, of the ability to stand and walk, of emotional reactions and vocalization, as well as dysfunction suggestive of strial involvement" (Kabat et al. 1941). From 5–10 minutes of anoxia can injure cells in higher brain areas so severely that they will not recover (Alvarez 1928). The respiratory and cardiovascular regulatory centers are more resistant and can be revived after complete interruption of their blood supply for as long as 30 minutes.

Since hypoxia causes such rapid loss of cerebral functions, the brain evidently derives the bulk of its energy from aerobic sources. The tolerance of the adult to hypoxia is much less than that of the newborn (Fazekas et al. 1941), perhaps because the metabolic rate of the newborn's brain is low and relatively more energy can be derived anaerobically. In fact, newborn puppies and kittens tolerate an exposure of about 24 minutes to an oxygen-free atmosphere.

The respiratory quotient of brain tissue is approximately 1, which indicates primarily carbohydrate metabolism (see Chapters 15 and 31). The importance of glucose as a fuel for the brain is indicated by the loss of about 10 mg glucose per 100 ml of blood as blood passes through the brain. The brain does not require insulin for the oxidation of carbohydrate (Himwich 1951), which suggests that the cell barriers presented by most cells to glucose are not present in most nerve cells. Although the brain normally utilizes only glucose as an energy substrate, it can use ketone bodies during certain disease states such as starvation. Transport of sugar into the brain from both blood and cerebrospinal fluid results from a membrane transport system, which facilitates diffusion independent of energy and leads to equilibration of sugar across the membrane, mediating equally a rapid flux in and out of the cell (Elbrink and Bihler 1975).

The amount of oxygen consumed by nervous tissue is considerable, especially during periods of hyperactivity such as muscular convulsions. Conversely, during depressed states of function the oxygen consumption is considerably reduced. The CNS (in man) accounts for about 20 percent of the oxygen consumption of the body at rest, yet the CNS comprises only about 2 percent of the body weight. In the metabolism of the perfused brain of the dog approximately 50 percent of the oxygen supplied to the head is used by the brain, and the brain accounts for about 8 percent of the total oxygen consumption of the body at rest (Handley et al. 1943). The brain weighs less than 1 percent of the total body weight of a medium-sized dog.

Blood flow to various parts of the nervous system varies widely, with only slight circulation to white areas and marked circulation to gray areas such as the cortex. During depression of neural functions with anesthetics, the blood flow in nervous tissue is reduced (Landau et al. 1955).

The blood supply to the brain, carried by carotid and vertebral arteries, is regulated intrinsically by local changes in oxygen and carbon dioxide content. Many substances cannot cross from the blood into brain cells, giving rise to the postulated blood-brain barrier (see Chapter 14). Cerebrospinal fluid supplies little nutrition to the brain, having as its main function the mechanical cushioning of the CNS.

Neurosecretions

Most neurons have the ability to secrete certain chemicals into their immediate environment. These chemicals act on postsynaptic membranes either to excite or to inhibit the discharge of impulses. Which response is produced to a given transmitter seems to depend on the properties of the postsynaptic membrane.

There is some debate over which neurochemicals actually have a transmitter function. The standard criteria are that the candidate transmitter must be normally present, synthesized, stored, released, reacted with postsynaptic membranes to alter polarization, and destroyed or otherwise removed from the site of action. An example of these overall reactions is given in Figure 40.7. The compounds that are generally considered to be transmitters are acetylcholine, norepinephrine, dopamine, and serotonin. Some amino acids may also function as transmitters in addition to their normal function in protein metabolism. Two amino acids are generally regarded as inhibitory transmitters, glycine and gamma amino butyric acid (Cooper et al. 1970).

Transmitters affect postsynaptic membranes by reacting reversibly with certain sites or receptors, which they "recognize" on the basis of compatible size, three-dimensional shape, and electric charge distribution. Similar to the "lock and key" reactions of enzymes and sub-

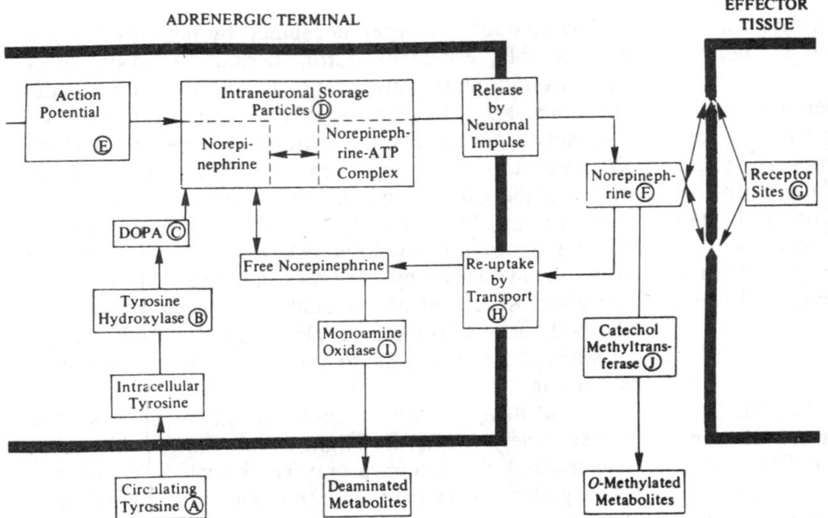

Figure 40.7. Mechanisms associated with neurotransmitter function, with norepinephrine as an example. Steps A through D show the uptake of tyrosine and its conversion by tyrosine hydroxylase into DOPA (dihydroxyphenylalanine). This is then converted into norepinephrine which is bound in storage particles at the axon terminal. Action potentials moving down into the terminal (E) release some of the bound transmitter into the synapse, or in case of axons ending in visceral organs, onto effector tissue (glands or muscle). The transmitter can react with postsynaptic or effector cell membrane receptors (G), be destroyed by catechol-O-methyltransferase (J), or taken back up into the terminal (H), whereupon it is redeposited in storage or destroyed by the intracellular enzyme, monoamine oxidase (I). (From R.G. Grenell, in P.L. Altman and D.S. Dittmer, eds., *Biology Data Book,* 2d ed., Fed. Am. Soc. Exp. Biol., Bethesda, Md., 1973, vol. 2.)

strates, the transmitter is thought to react only with receptors, destructive enzymes, and drugs that have comparable physical characteristics of the binding site of the molecule.

There is growing evidence that some neurotransmitters may act indirectly, via stimulating synthesis of a cyclic nucleotide, cAMP or cGMP, which then causes the typical postsynaptic response (Stone et al. 1975).

ANATOMICAL DIVISIONS

Sensory receptors

A receptor cell initiates sensory input into the nervous system by responding to a change in energy in its environment, inducing appropriate patterns of nerve impulses in its axons. Receptors vary greatly in structure and function, being highly specialized and usually modality specific (see Chapters 43, 50, 51).

Peripheral nerves

In the peripheral system many fibers are grouped into trunks which connect with the CNS. The connecting fibers course in spinal and cranial nerves, many of which contain both afferent (input) and efferent (output) fibers.

At various places outside the CNS are collections of neurons called ganglia. Axons or nerves that send impulses into ganglia are called presynaptic or preganglionic; those that send impulses out of a ganglion are called postsynaptic or postganglionic. The peripheral ganglia, together with their pre- and postsynaptic nerves, are often called the autonomic nervous system, which functions in maintaining homeostasis of viscera, glands, and cardiac and smooth muscle.

Spinal cord

The spinal cord contains many nerve tracts which connect the brain stem and higher centers with the spinal nerves. To a large degree, different sensory and motor tracts are segregated in the cord. For example, proprioceptive impulses arising from the periphery ascend in the fasciculus cuneatus and fasciculus gracilis (dorsal cord) and in the spinocerebellar tract (lateral cord). Other sensory impulses, such as those for pain, temperature, and touch, ascend in various tracts located in lateral and ventral portions of the cord (see Chapter 42). Descending motor tracts, such as the corticospinal, rubrospinal, and tectospinal, occur in the lateral cord; the vestibulospinal tract and another branch of the corticospinal tract occur in the ventral cord. In addition to communicating with higher centers, the cord also has many neurons which process reflexes locally, so that higher centers are only slightly involved.

Brain

Fiber tracts

The white matter of the cerebral hemispheres, situated beneath the cerebral cortex, consists of three types of myelinated nerve fibers: association, commissural, and projection fibers. Association fibers connect different cortical regions; they are most evident in the brains of primates. The commissural fibers form the connecting links between the two cerebral hemispheres. They comprise mainly the corpus callosum, the anterior commissure, and the hippocampal commissure. The projection fibers, motor and sensory, connect the cerebral cortex with the brain stem and spinal cord. The sensory projection fibers connect the thalamus with the visual, auditory, and somesthetic cortex areas, and the olfactory center at the base of the olfactory bulb with the olfactory area of the cerebral cortex. Accompanying the thalamocortical radiations are corticothalamic fibers, which conduct in the opposite direction.

Specific structures

The brain (Fig. 40.8) is composed of a stem that contains fiber tracts and many neuronal centers for regulating, automatically and without volition, many visceral functions, particularly emesis, coughing, respiration, blood pressure, and heart rate. These centers are located in that portion of the brain stem which is continuous with the spinal cord—the medulla oblongata.

The cephalad connection of the medulla is with the pons, which lies directly underneath the cerebellum and contains many relays with motor systems. The pons has a dorsal (tegmental) part and a ventral (basilar) part. The dorsal part resembles the medulla anatomically and physiologically and may be regarded as its forward extension. The ventral part of the pons contains the fibers of the corticospinal tract, fibers from the cerebrum to the pontine nuclei, and fibers from these to the cerebellum. The cerebellum functions in regulating body posture and movement (see Chapter 44).

Emerging from the various portions of the brain stem are the cranial nerves. All the cranial nerves, except the first two (olfactory and optic), are connected with the medulla oblongata, pons, or midbrain (Table 40.2). The spinal nerves are arranged segmentally, and this was the primitive condition in the cranial nerves also, but in the adult mammal the segmental arrangement has been greatly altered on the afferent side, which allows afferent fibers possessing similar physiological functions to discharge into a single center of the brain stem. Segmental arrangement is still fairly evident in the motor roots and nuclei.

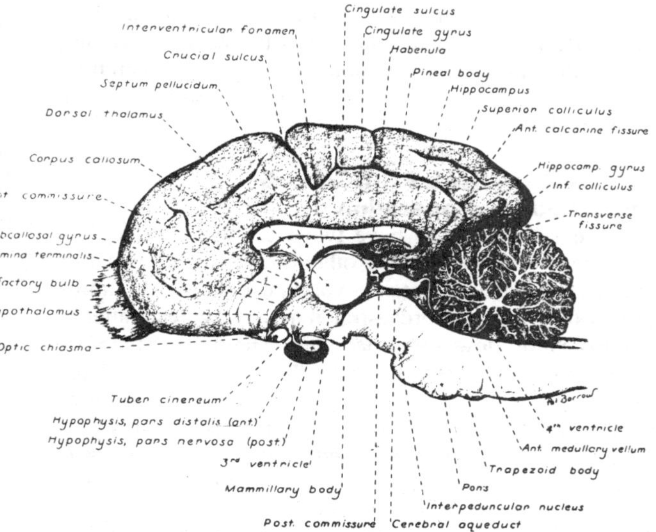

Figure 40.8. Midsagittal section of a dog brain. (From M.E. Miller, *Guide to the Dissection of the Dog*, 3d ed., Edwards, Ann Arbor, 1952.)

Table 40.2. Cranial nerves

Number	Name	Function	Location
I	olfactory	sensory	bulb at anterior of brain
II	optic	sensory	anterior to pituitary
III	oculomotor	motor	posterior to pituitary
IV	trochlear	motor	posterior to colliculi
V	trigeminal	mixed	ventral pons
VI	abducent	motor	posteroventral pons
VII	facial	mixed	posteroventral pons
VIII	acoustic	sensory	posteroventral pons
IX	glossopharyngeal	mixed	lateral medulla
X	vagus	mixed	lateral medulla
XI	spinal accessory	motor	lateral medulla
XII	hypoglossal	motor	lateral medulla

Adjacent to the pons is the midbrain or mesencephalon. The midbrain has two parts: the dorsal, consisting of the corpora quadrigemina or colliculi (4 rounded prominences, 2 anterior and 2 posterior) and the ventral, consisting of the cerebral peduncles. The anterior pair of colliculi is chiefly a visual reflex center; the posterior pair, chiefly an auditory reflex center. Cross sections show that each cerebral peduncle is made up of three parts, which from the top down are the tegmentum, substantia nigra, and basis pedunculi. The tegmentum is structurally and functionally a forward continuation of the dorsal part of the pons. It contains the red nucleus (nucleus ruber) and the nuclei of the trochlear and oculomotor nerves. The substantia nigra is composed chiefly of deeply pigmented nerve cells. The basis pedunculi consists of descending fibers including the corticospinal, corticobulbar, and corticopontine tracts. In the ventral and lateral tegmentum regions is a mass of greatly branching neurons, referred to as the midbrain reticular formation, which serve important relay and integrative functions in both sensory and motor functions (see Chapters 43, 44).

The reticular formation extends within the central core of the brain stem from the medulla, through the tegmentum of the pons and midbrain, to the anterior end of the thalamus. Although superficially homogeneous, the reticular formation contains assorted nuclear aggregates. In the caudal portion are the well-known centers for controlling respiration and cardiac activity. Likewise, in the caudal regions are centers that inhibit spinal motoneurons. Centers in the pontine reticular formation tend to be sleep promoting; centers in the midbrain reticular formation promote wakefulness (see Chapter 45). Many regions of the reticular formation facilitate motor activity.

The midbrain leads directly to the diencephalon, or interbrain, which consists, from the bottom up, of the pituitary gland, hypothalamus, subthalamus, thalamus, and epithalamus. A cerebrospinal fluid–filled third ventricle separates the thalamus into two symmetrical portions.

The pituitary, or hypophysis, is an endocrine gland (see Chapter 52). The hypothalamus contains the paired mammillary body (posterior) and the tuber cinereum (anterior). It integrates functions carried out through the autonomic nervous system. In the hypothalamus are other areas that regulate such functions as temperature, hunger, thirst, and sexual drive. The centers of the hypothalamus are subject to regulation by many other areas of the brain.

The subthalamus is a small area that functions in the regulation of motor activity.

The thalamus, the largest component of the diencephalon, consists of a great number of nuclei which may be divided into three main groups: (1) those that relay impulses to the cerebral cortex from the somatic afferent systems and from the paths of special sense, (2) association and projection nuclei, having connections with other regions of the interbrain or with the cerebral cortex, and (3) nuclei with purely subcortical connections.

The epithalamus contains the habenula, which is an olfactory center, and the pineal gland, which is a neurosecretory organ that regulates gonadal hormones and certain daily rhythms.

The thalamus and the rest of the brain anterior to it are paired. The major portion of the paired systems is the telencephalon, the most conspicuous components of which are the cerebral hemispheres. Each cerebral hemisphere contains a mantle of cells—the cerebral cortex. The cortex's evolutionary development is related to the function of its parts. The only parts present in primitive animals have mainly olfactory and emotional functions. A later development in reptiles, birds, and mammals added the neocortex, which displaced more primitive cortex medially and became the most dominant structure of the brain's surface. Neocortex development parallels evolutionary rank and is best developed in primates and man. Certain discrete portions of the neocortex control precise sensory and motor activities. The large amount of remaining cortex functions less specifically in sensory-motor regulation and in memory and problem solving (Fig. 40.9).

The cerebral cortex of some small mammals, particularly the more primitive ones, is smooth; that of most mammals, including ungulates, carnivores, and primates, shows convolutions (gyri) and fissures (sulci), which are more or less characteristically arranged in each higher mammalian order. In primates the cortex of each hemisphere is divided, somewhat arbitrarily, into frontal, parietal, temporal, and occipital lobes. In man, the frontal lobe is exceedingly well developed. Sections through the cerebral cortex show that it has six layers parallel to the surface of the gyri and consisting of nerve cells and nerve fibers.

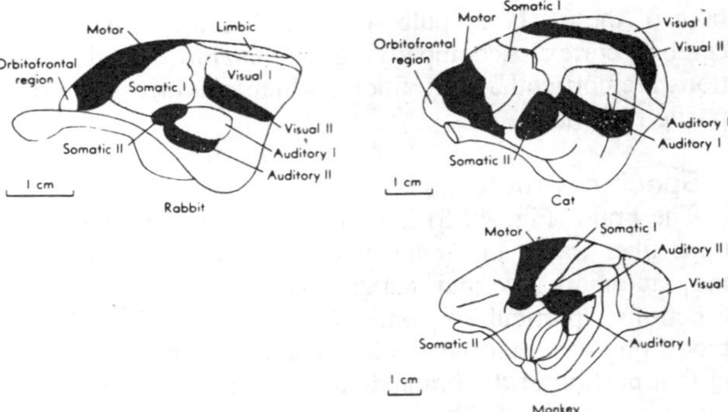

Figure 40.9. Sensory and motor areas of the cerebral cortex of representative species. In the mammalian series, relatively less and less cortex is devoted to sensory and motor functions and more and more to associational functions. (From J.E. Rose and C.N. Woolsey 1949, Organization of the mammalian thalamus and its relationships to the cerebral cortex, *Electroenceph. Clin. Neurophysiol.* 1:391.)

Under the cortex of the telencephalon and anteriolateral to the thalamus are the basal ganglia—clusters of nerve cells and the fiber tracts involved in motor activity (see Chapter 44). Two masses, the putamen and the globus pallidus, are often collectively referred to as the lenticular nucleus. Anterior and dorsal to the lenticular nucleus is the caudate nucleus.

Cerebrospinal fluid in the ventricles bathes inner structures of the brain. In the telencephalon the lateral ventricles are paired extensions of the single third ventricle, which separates the paired thalamus. A narrow channel in the mesencephalon joins the third ventricle with the fourth ventricle, which lies underneath the cerebellum. The roof of the fourth ventricle contains a small opening into the cisterna magna, which in turn is continuous with the subarchnoid space that surrounds the whole outer surface of the brain. Thus the brain is bathed with cerebrospinal fluid all over its outside surface and over many of its internal structures.

ORGANIZATIONAL PRINCIPLES

Basic modes of operation

Nerve cells can only have two main actions: they either excite or they inhibit other nerve cells. Because neurons are organized into networks, excitatory and inhibitory effects can be orchestrated into complex patterns of information flow and processing. The most simple organization is illustrated by the reflex, such as spinal reflexes (see Chapters 42, 44, 46). A reflex is a specific, usually stereotyped response to stimulation. Most reflexes are genetically determined by the anatomical organization of neurons that mediate the reflex. For example, in the withdrawal reflex in which a dog withdraws his foot in response to toe pinch, each sensory neuron that is activated sends input into the spinal cord which automatically relays excitation back into nerves that excite muscles of that leg. Some reflexes may also have inhibitory

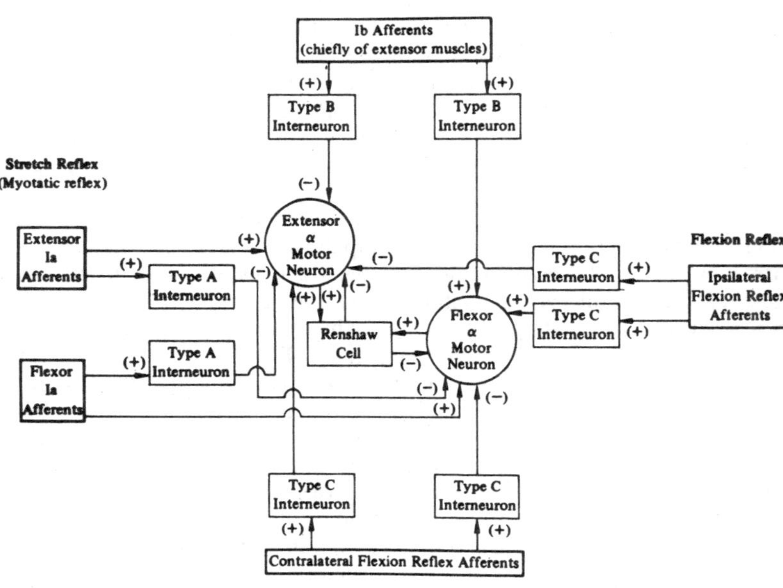

Figure 40.10. Spinal reflex organization illustrating the basic modes of nervous system operation. In the center, an extensor and a flexor motoneuron receive a variety of inputs; if they are activated, their respective muscles will contract. The Ia afferents of the stretch reflex originate from sensors of muscle stretch, the spindles. The Ib afferents of the tension feedback arise from sensors of tension in tendons, the Golgi tendon organs. Ia afferents excite type A interneurons, Ib afferents excite type B interneurons, and flexion afferents from cutaneous, muscular, and joint receptors excite type C interneurons. Flexion afferents also can excite type A and B interneurons, but that is not shown for simplicity. Each given neuron has only one output function, to either excite or inhibit. The paths of reflex action in response to stimulation of any one of the four input paths can be traced readily. For a given input path, the motoneurons are reciprocally innervated, with one being excited while the other is inhibited. If more than one input path is activated, the net result of excitatory and inhibitory action on motoneurons determines which motoneuron will discharge impulses and cause muscular contraction. Mutual regulation is evident between the two motoneurons; when either one is discharging impulses, collateral branches of their axons excite a Renshaw cell, which is inhibitory and is so "wired" as to inhibit the other motoneuron. (From W.D. Willis, Jr., in P.L. Altman and D.S. Dittmer, eds., *Biology Data Book*, 2d ed., Fed. Am. Soc. Exp. Biol., Washington, 1973, vol. 2.)

components. In the flexion reflex, for example, sensory input excites some neurons in the cord that inhibit the antagonists (extensors) of the flexor muscles of that limb. This organization of neurons is called reciprocal innervation, and it is found in many kinds of reflexes.

Another basic mode of nervous system operation is mutual regulation, where two pools of neurons have reciprocal influences on the same function or behavior. In a sense, this organization provides checks and balances that have the effect of regulating functions within reasonable limits. Some of the functions and behaviors that are regulated in this way are respiration, blood pressure, heart rate, various visceral secretions and movements, temperature control, eating, drinking, sleep, and approach and avoidance drives. Paired control centers are often reciprocally inhibitory, but in some cases, such as sleep and approach-avoidance centers, the mutual regulation may be more complex.

In a neural network, excitation, inhibition, reflex action, and, in a simplified way, mutual regulation all operate to control a behavioral act (Fig. 40.10).

Mechanisms of information processing

While there are many elegant and mathematical ways of explaining information processing, it can be regarded at the neuronal level as consisting of the specific transformations, chemical and physical, that occur when the nervous system detects, analyzes, and responds to changes in environment. That analysis may involve filtering or averaging of information so that some is lost. Information may be transformed or erased, especially as it is contrasted and compared with the stored information that we call memory. Ultimately, information may be added to existing memory or may emerge from the analysis system in the form of output for appropriate operation of glands and muscles.

Processing reactions take place at all levels of the nervous system, from the coding in sensory receptors, to synaptic reactions and associated patterns of impulse generation, to the routing through neuronal networks, to profuse interactions of widespread neuronal subsystems.

Many interesting analogies can be drawn between certain principles of computer and engineering technology and information processing phenomena in the nervous system. Such properties as triggering, gating, switching, and synchronizing have been found in the nervous system. Also observable are amplitude discrimination, filtering, amplification, linear-to-logarithmic signal transformation, waveform generation and frequency modulation. Basic arithmetical operations have been documented, such as counting, averaging, integration, differentiation, sign inversion, correlation, coincidence detection, delay, phase, shift, and interval measurement.

Sensory receptor cells first record the information, coding it in the form of nerve impulses. Some degree of processing occurs during the coding in that the number of impulses discharged is proportional to stimulus intensity (see Chapter 43). In addition, intensity is also obviously coded in terms of the number of responding sense cells, and in the spatial and temporal pattern of the impulse discharge.

Coding for the quality of a stimulus depends largely on how neurons are organized into networks. A network refers to the pathways through which nerve impulses are propagated. Some of these paths are "hard-wired," built-in under genetic control during embryonic development. The simplest network is the spinal reflex arc; information arising from sensory receptors in the skin is led directly back to contract muscles from that area. In a flexion reflex, for example, strong stimulation causes withdrawal of the stimulated limb, and information is usually interpreted as pain at that limb because of the hard-wired circuitry. Likewise animals "see" because axons from the retina propagate impulses to a specific zone of neurons in the cortex at the back of the brain. Sound is not "seen," for example, because sound receptors do not send impulses to the visual receiving areas of the brain.

At least four basic types of circuits are found in the CNS: divergent, convergent, parallel, and reverberating (Fig. 40.11).

In a divergent circuit, one neuron ultimately affects many neurons. A typical example of such circuitry is found in certain nerves in the cortex which initiate voluntary motor activity. Connections of a given cortical cell fan out so that an initial impulse in the brain results in many impulses reaching many muscle fiber units.

In a convergent circuit, the process is reversed; impulses from many nerves ultimately impinge on a single neuron. This has the effect of enabling a neuron to receive information from a wide range of receptors. An example can be found in the spinal cord where a neuron

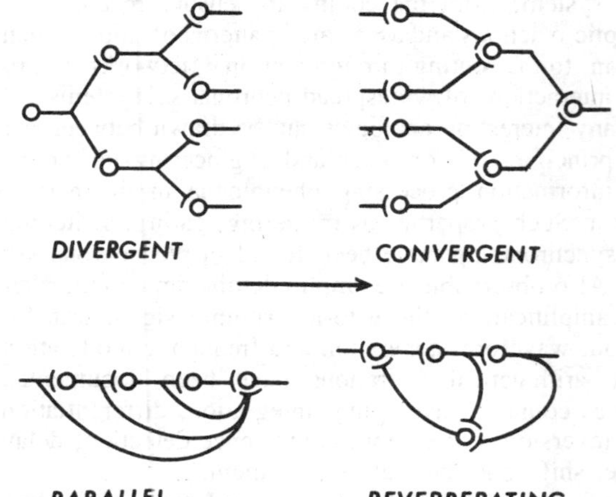

Figure 40.11. Common types of circuits in the nervous system. Arrow indicates direction of impulse propagation. (Modified from A.C. Guyton, *Function of the Human Body,* 2d ed., Saunders, Philadelphia, 1964.)

may receive sensory input from the skin and from viscera (see Chapter 43).

The parallel circuit provides for special functions not obtainable in the first two circuits: a single impulse can initiate a series of impulses in other neurons (see Fig. 40.11). Those impulses that must "cross" synapses before reaching the target are delayed because synaptic transmission is slower than axonal. Thus the arrival of impulses at the target is protracted but not self-perpetuating.

The fourth type of circuit not only provides for the protracted receipt of impulses at the target but also is self-perpetuating, and electrical disturbances in the circuit can be continuous. One input impulse can drive an oscillatory network in which impulses are continually generated around the circuit. Two obvious examples of this type of circuit are in the nervous control of respiration (see Chapter 15) and in the cycling of impulses between the cerebral cortex and certain subcortical centers.

Irrespective of the circuit design, information about a stimulus may be coded by variations in the pattern of impulse discharge. For example, the onset of stimulation can be signalled by receptors that discharge when a stimulus comes on; some receptors, at least in the retina, are "off" receptors, discharging only when stimulation ends. The duration of a train of impulses can also code some temporal aspects of a stimulus. For example, some receptors for touch are phasic, with impulse discharge gradually diminishing even though the stimulation persists; some pain receptors, however, discharge impulses continuously. More subtle codes for stimulus information are possibly contained in such parameters as the rate of activity after stimulus onset and offset, and in the pattern of intervals between and among impulses.

Once information about stimuli enters the CNS, chemical and electrical changes in the synapses provide enormous capacity for processing that information as it passes from neuron to neuron. Release of transmitter chemical can produce a graded change in the membrane voltage of the postsynaptic neuron. If the polarity of that change is in the proper direction, the cell becomes excited and begins to discharge impulses; this change is called an excitatory postsynaptic potential (EPSP) (see Chapter 41). Cells are inhibited if the voltage change is of the opposite polarity, a so-called inhibitory postsynaptic potential (IPSP). Because the discharge threshold across a synapse is a function of the presynaptic volleys that act upon it, and because a given synapse may receive branches from many axons, the passage of impulses in a network of such synapses can be highly varied. The versatility of the synapse arises from a great ability to modify information, by adding input signals. The subsequent change in stimulation threshold of the postsynaptic membrane can be enhanced or inhibited, depending upon the transmitter chemical involved and the ion permeabilities. Thus the

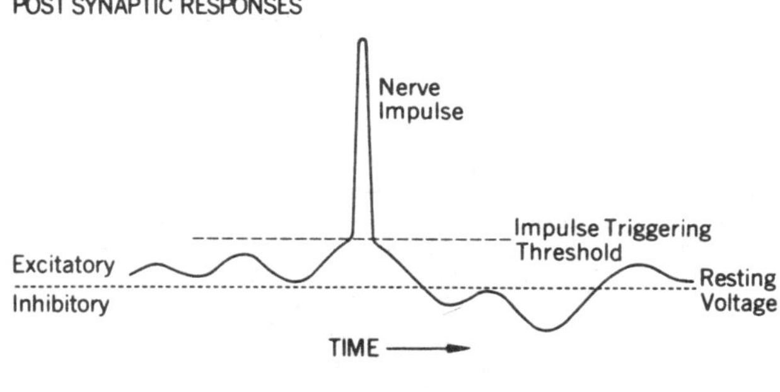

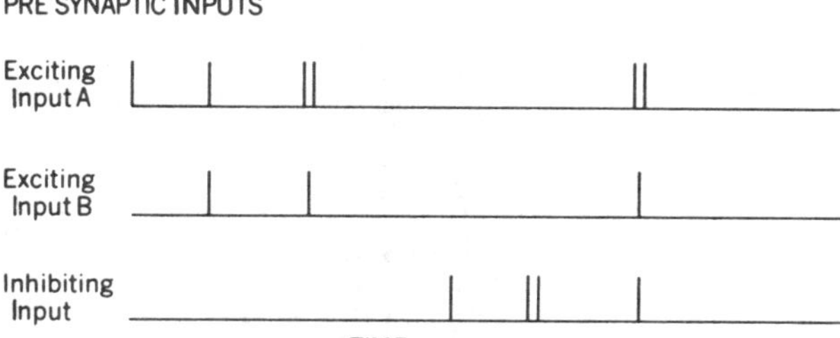

Figure 40.12. Interaction of excitatory and inhibitory postsynaptic responses. *Above,* postsynaptic membrane voltage changes in response to excitatory and inhibitory input influences, occurring either alone or (at far right) simultaneously. *Below,* correlation of the above postsynaptic voltage changes with impulses arriving in presynaptic terminals (vertical bars on lower traces), containing either excitatory or inhibitory transmitter. If two excitatory terminals have enough impulses in a short enough time span, they will release enough transmitter to move the postsynaptic membrane voltage to the impulse-discharging threshold. Conversely, this excitatory trend can be offset by simultaneously occurring impulses in input terminals that release inhibitory transmitters. (From W.R. Klemm, *Science, the Brain, and Our Future,* Bobbs-Merrill, Indianapolis; copyright 1972 by the Regents of the University of Colorado.)

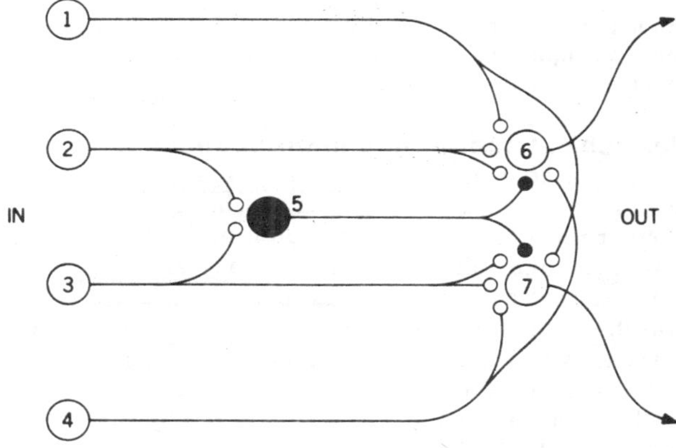

INPUT NEURONS ACTIVATED	OUTPUT NEURONS ACTIVATED			
	NONE	6 ONLY	7 ONLY	6 AND 7
1	X			
1&2		X		
1&3			X	
1&4				X
2		X		
2&3	X			
2&4		X		
3			X	
3&4			X	
4	X			

Figure 40.13. Pool of excitatory neurons and an inhibitory neuron (solid circle), illustrating the effect of circuit design and threshold for excitation on routing of information. Assume that impulses begin in the four input neurons on the left and that a net of at least two excitatory terminals must be active to release enough transmitter chemical to reach the threshold for exciting subsequent neurons. Input from neuron 2, for instance, would excite neuron 6 because two axon terminals are active. Input from 2 and 3, however, would not have an output because the inhibitory neuron would also be activated, and its inhibitory transmitter would cancel part of the effect of the two active excitatory terminals at 6 and 7. Note from the summary table that a variety of output possibilities exist. Still further complexity could be achieved, as it is in brain circuits, by drawing in branches that feed back excitatory or inhibitory effect on other neurons in the circuit. (From W.R. Klemm, *Science, the Brain, and Our Future,* Bobbs-Merrill, Indianapolis; copyright 1972 by the Regents of the University of Colorado.)

synapse acts as a decision point at which information converges, and is modified by algebraic processing of EPSPs and IPSPs (Fig. 40.12).

Variations in impulse patterns permit very sophisticated discrimination and evaluation of stimulus information when the networks are not hard-wired but rather can change their functional organization in response to inputs. Often this flexibility depends on the existence of inhibitory neurons; these can act as a gate to regulate the paths through which information flows (Fig. 40.13).

Relative localization of function

Throughout the chapters involving the nervous system in this text, there are many examples of specific functions being governed by an anatomically defined pool of neurons (''centers''). Examples include specific reflexes, arousal, sleep, dreaming, reward and aversive responses, regulation of viscera, and specific sensory and motor functions of the neocortex. However, the idea of centers for certain functions needs to be evaluated with some perspective, and this can be illustrated by the neocortex.

The pioneer physiologists took the view that the cortex functions as a whole. When it was found, in 1870, that electrical stimulation of certain parts of the exposed cortex produced contraction of some skeletal muscles, an era of cortical localization theory was inaugurated. But the pendulum has started back, and modern opinion finds motor and sensory localization in the cortex but not rigidly circumscribed centers; the various parts, though mediating different functions, are often mutually interdependent, so that injury to one part may cause dysfunction of distant parts. On the other hand, a lesion of one part does not always abolish the function that is represented in that part, but rather may only disturb it.

The consequences of cortical lesions are most conspicuous when damage occurs in the specific sensory and motor regions. In other cortical areas the deranged function after injury may depend more on how much cortex is affected rather than on where the lesion is.

Hierarchical control and interdependence

Some invertebrates have special central "command" neurons that release coordinated behavior (Kennedy 1969). Excitation of one such neuron in crayfish causes activity in more than 200 motoneurons affecting five body segments; for a given category of movement patterns there are a small number of command neurons. The extent to which this command principle operates in the more complex vertebrate nervous system is not known, but the behaviors most likely to be released by command neurons would be simple and stereotyped.

When considering the gross organization of more advanced nervous systems, it is tempting to view them as a hierarchy of subsystems with the brain in charge. In humans, for instance, neurons in the spinal cord can carry out mundane control functions for their respective body segment while the brain neurons are "free to think higher thoughts." But the assignment of rank order to the spinal cord and subsystems in the brain is not as obvious as it may seem. Although that part of the brain which provides intelligence, the neocortex, ranks above the reflex systems in the brain stem and spinal cord, there are practical limits on the degree of control exerted by the neocortex. If control were absolute, animals would not succumb to the dizziness and ataxia associated with motion sickness and the vestibular system of the brain stem. Animals would be able to suppress the pain that is mediated in the thalamus. They could stave off sleep indefinitely by keeping the reticular activating system active.

It thus seems more reasonable to regard the nervous system as a hierarchy of semi-autonomous subsystems whose rank order is variable; any subsystem may take part in many types of interrelationships. Whichever subsystem happens to dominate a situation, each subsystem is independent only to a certain extent, being subordinate to the unit above it and modulated by the inputs from its own subordinate subsystems. This design feature of the mammalian nervous system provides maximum flexibility and is probably the basis for the brain's marvelous effectiveness.

MAJOR FUNCTIONAL SYSTEMS

Motor

Motor function can be classified into two types according to the system from which the function arises: (1) from the pyramidal system, (2) from the extrapyramidal system (Fig. 40.14; see also Chapter 44). The pyramidal system consists of pyramidal-shaped cells in the cortex and their efferent pathways to skeletal muscles. Impulses arising from other areas of the cortex and subcortex initiate discharge of these pyramidal cells, which then send

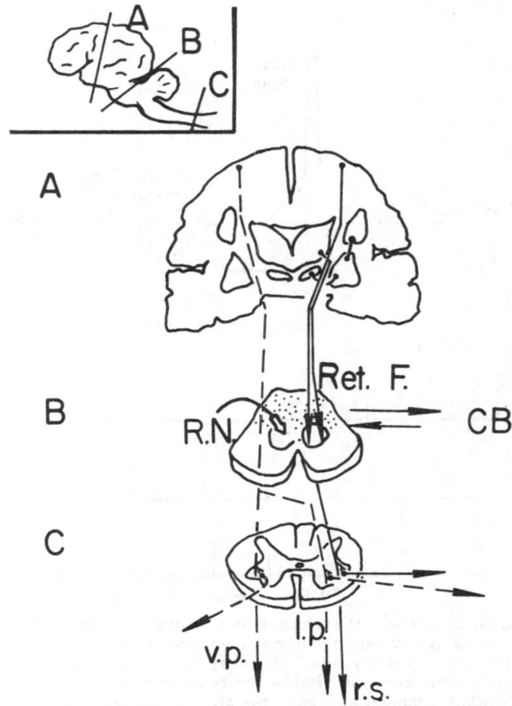

Figure 40.14. Major motor pathways in the CNS, showing one half of the bilaterally symmetrical pyramidal and extrapyramidal systems. The pyramidal system (left) arises in layer V of the cortex (Betz cells) and is composed of fiber tracts in the spinal cord (ventral and lateral pyramidal tracts: v.p. and l.p.) which make contact with lower motoneurons in the cord. The extrapyramidal system (right) has fibers in the cortex which act on subcortical areas, especially the reticular formation (Ret. F.) and the red nucleus (R.N.). Thalamic and basal ganglia influences are also exerted. The cerebellum (CB) exerts its servomechanism functions primarily by way of the brain stem structures. The inhibitory and facilitatory functions of the motor portions of the reticular formation are mediated by way of the reticulospinal tract (r.s.).

impulses down a long bundle of nerve fibers (pyramidal tract or corticospinal tract) that traverses the internal capsule of the brain. The tract splits at the level of the pons into a ventral and lateral bundle which course in the spinal cord. Along various points in the ventral horn of the spinal cord, synaptic junctions are made with neurons that go to muscles. Motor activity of this pyramidal system is voluntary, and, because of the high degree of localized function in the motor cortex, can be very precise and discrete. Specific neurons of the motor cortex activate specific muscles.

The extrapyramidal system includes all portions of the CNS that are not in the pyramidal system. Most important are the basal ganglia (caudate nucleus, putamen, globus pallidus, subthalamus, red nucleus, substantia nigra, brain-stem reticular formation) and some portions of the thalamus and cortex. These brain nuclei actually play the dominant role of motor regulation in lower animals such as birds, which have a poorly developed motor cortex. Even in the cat and the dog these brain areas dominate motor activity, as shown by studies in which removal of the motor cortex does not have serious effects on motor ability (Bard and Macht 1958).

The cerebellum monitors states of inertia and momentum of muscles through a feedback mechanism by which signals are sent to the cerebral cortex to make necessary adjustments (Bell and Dow 1967, Fox and Snider 1967). The cerebellum receives impulses from all proprioceptive receptors in joints and muscles, which signal the physical state of the muscles and joints. It also receives stimuli from the equilibrium apparatus in the inner ear. Finally, the cerebellum also receives impulses from the motor cortex. The efferent signals of the cerebellum go primarily to motor centers in the brain stem and to the motor cortex.

To summarize motor function, one can say that the extrapyramidal system maintains an organized background of muscle tone, posture, and gross movements upon which the pyramidal system can direct discrete and precise movements.

Sensory

The primary sensory pathway, in an oversimplified view, contains a chain of three neurons (Fig. 40.15). The first neuron conveys impulses from the periphery into the spinal cord or cranial nerve nuclei. The second neuron projects to cells in lateral and posterior areas of the thalamus; some second neurons terminate on motor neurons in the spinal cord and thus form a basis for spinal reflexes. Thalamic cells are arranged topographically (somatotopically); that is, specific cells receive input from specific points on the body. The thalamic third neuron projects to sensory portions of the cerebral cortex, also topographically arranged. Excitability of neurons in this chain is partially regulated by the sensory cortex, which exerts excitation and inhibition on ascending paths (Calma 1965).

Proprioceptive impulses are a special case in that some first-order neurons terminate in the nucleus gracilis and nucleus cuneatus in the medulla. The second neuron passes to the thalamus, and the third from thalamus to cortex; additional paths exist where the second neuron relays in the brain stem, from which third neurons pass to the cerebellum.

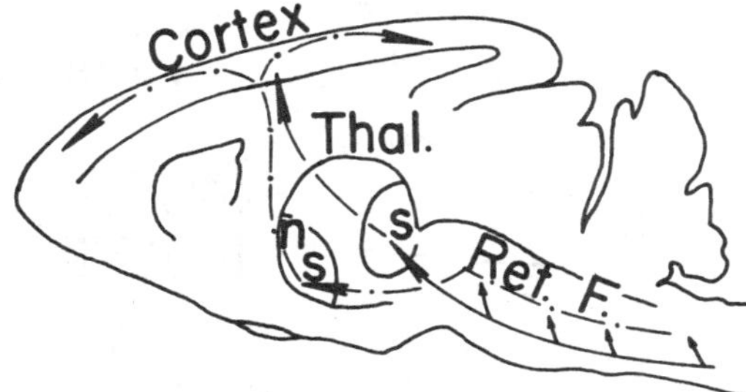

Figure 40.15. The major sensory pathways in the brain: s, "specific" thalamic sensory nuclei; ns, "nonspecific" thalamic sensory nuclei. Spinothalamic afferents enter specific thalamic nuclei, whereas nonspecific thalamic areas receive indirect innervation from polysynaptic pathways in the reticular formation.

The second sensory route is via the brain-stem reticular formation, which receives collateral innervation from ascending primary paths (see Chapter 45). At the same time impulses are arriving over primary pathways; branches from those pathways feed into the highly synaptic reticular region, where the impulses are projected cephalad to medial and anteroventral regions of the thalamus, and then to diffuse regions of the cortex. Clearly, topographic specificity for sensations cannot be preserved in this reticular net. The apparent function of this secondary sensory system is to cause a generalized activation of the cortex rather than to preserve information about the quality of a specific sensation.

Consciousness

The brain's function can be described as a continuum of states ranging from alert wakefulness to sleep. The spectrum of states of consciousness is regulated in large measure by function of the reticular sensory system.

When the brain-stem reticular formation is active, it provides a tonic excitatory drive for the whole cortex. In a sense, the reticular formation can be said to "arouse" cortical cells to be more receptive to sensory information arriving over the primary pathways. These events are accompanied by behavioral alertness. Conversely, when reticular activity is depressed, behavioral sedation ensues. Destruction of the reticular formation causes permanent unconsciousness and coma.

Depression of the brain-stem reticular formation facilitates sleep, but sleep is more than a passive phenomenon. Sleep also appears to be promoted by activity in such areas as the diffuse thalamic projection system (DTPS), the preoptic region of the hypothalamus, and the solitary tract region of the medulla. The dream stages of sleep appear to be produced actively by regions in the pontine reticular formation (see Chapter 45).

Emotion

In the more primitive animals, behavior is dominated by the olfactory sense, and the olfactory portions of the brains of such animals are relatively large. The higher brain centers associated with olfactory sensations are often referred to as the rhinencephalon or the limbic system. In higher animals the components of the limbic system (the septum, hippocampus, amygdala, and cingulate portion of cortex) have evolved into regulation of many aspects of emotion and behavior. In fact the animal disease rabies, which damages the hippocampus and results in profound emotional disorders, originally suggested the role of the limbic system in emotional behavior (Papez 1937).

Although many details of the limbic system are not understood, much research effort has revealed that such emotions as appetite, thirst, rage, fear, and sexual drive are controlled by this system (Adey and Tokizane 1967). Moreover, the limbic system exerts control over hypothalamic autonomic centers (Ruch 1961, Nauta 1960). One of the first insights resulted from early experiments with decorticate cats, which eventually localized the neural mechanisms of rage to the hypothalamus (Bard and Macht 1958).

Study of the self-stimulation phenomenon, where animals operate levers to deliver electric current through electrodes implanted in certain limbic areas, show that animals will work to the point of exhaustion to provide stimulation of these areas (Olds 1956, 1960). The limbic system also appears to have a crucial role in the consolidation of temporary memories into permanent form (Nauta 1966, John 1967).

Some anatomical relationships between portions of the limbic system have been determined (Fig. 40.16). The physiological relationships are much less certain (see Chapter 46), but it has been shown that the amygdala and areas of limbic cortex facilitate function in the hypothalamus (Ruch 1961), while the hypothalamus in turn controls autonomic outflow and can exert a tonic excitatory effect on the midbrain reticular formation (Adey and Lindsley 1959).

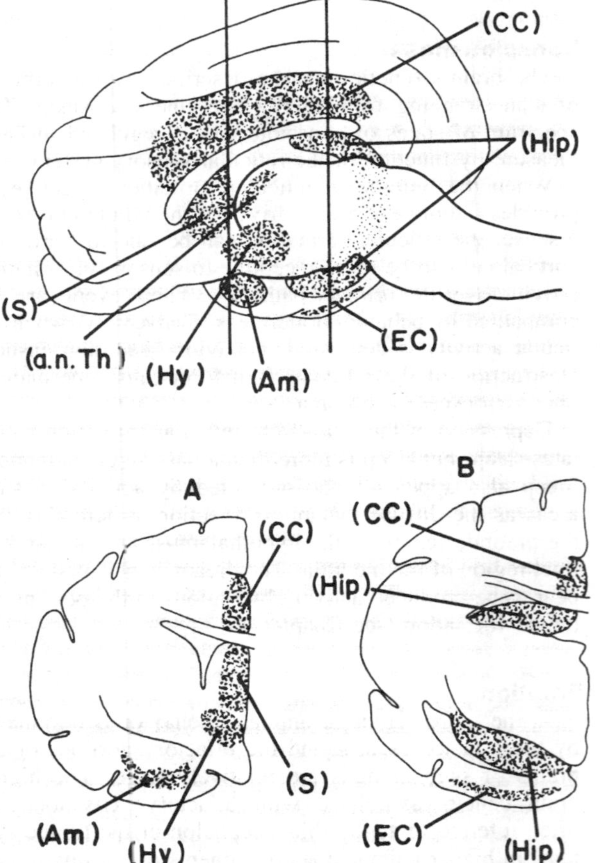

Figure 40.16. Major components of the limbic system and their relative positions. *Above*, vertical slice through middle of the brain. *Below*, cross sections at two different anterior-posterior levels. Am, amygdala; a.n. Th, anterior nucleus of thalamus; CC, cingulate cortex; EC, entorhinal cortex; Hip, hippocampus; Hy, hypothalamus; S, septum. (From T.R. Lane, ed., *Life, the Individual, the Species*, Mosby, St. Louis, 1976.)

Visceral control

A major subsystem of the brain regulates visceral functions, such as the activity of the cardiovascular, gastrointestinal, and urinogenital systems (Fig. 40.17). These functions are monitored and modulated by the autonomic nervous system (see Chapter 48). This system has dual components, one enhancing organ function, the other opposing it. Activation of the sympathetic portion of this system results in a fast heart rate and increased blood

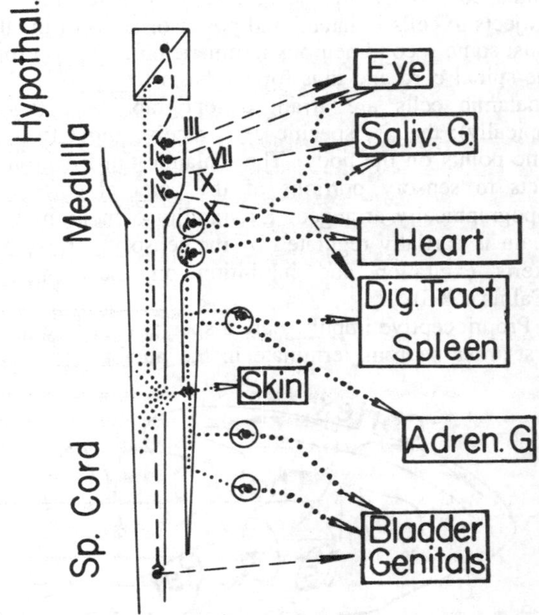

Figure 40.17. Simplified autonomic nervous system. Dotted lines, sympathetic nervous system; dashed lines, parasympathetic nervous system. Sympathetic fibers are shown emerging from thoracolumbar regions of the spinal cord and making synaptic junctions in the sympathetic trunk or in cervical, celiac, or mesenteric ganglia (exception: innervation of adrenal gland). Parasympathetic fibers are shown emerging from the cranial and sacral nerves and making synaptic junctions in the target organs.

pressure; activation of the parasympathetic portion has opposite effects. The dual innervation of the various organs also arises from rather ill-defined dual centers in the hypothalamus, which in turn are influenced by the action of other brain areas. For example, in the posterior portion of the hypothalamus are centers which control emergency sympathetic responses that prepare the animal for "fight or flight." Other centers in the anterior hypothalamus and in the septal area apparently control parasympathetic functions such as rest, recovery, digestion, and elimination (Ingram 1960).

Although autonomic functions generally have been considered to be automatic and not subject to voluntary control, recent conditioning studies have indicated that "visceral learning" is possible. Therapeutic training techniques may develop that will help correct visceral disorders (Miller 1969).

REFERENCES

Adey, W.R., and Lindsley, D.F. 1959. On the role of subthalamic areas in the maintenance of brain stem reticular formation excitability. *Exp. Neurol.* 1:407–26.

Adey, W.R., and Tokizane, T., eds. 1967. *Progress in Brain Research.* Vol. 27, *Structure and Function of the Limbic System.* Elsevier, Amsterdam.

Alvarez, W.C. 1928. *The Mechanics of the Digestive Tract.* 2d ed. Hoeber, New York.

Bard, P., and Macht, M.B. 1958. The behavior of chronically decerebrate cats. In G.E.W. Wolstenholme and C.M. O'Connor, eds., *Ciba Foundation Symposium on the Neurological Basis of Behavior.* Churchill, London. Pp. 55–75.

Bell, C.C., and Dow, R.S. 1967. Cerebellar circuitry. In *Neurosciences Research Symposium Summaries.* Vol. 2, F.O. Schmitt, T. Melnechuk, G.C. Quarton, and G. Adelman, eds. M.I.T. Press, Cambridge. Pp. 515–616.

Bunge, R.P. 1970. Structure and function of neuroglia: Some recent observations. In F.O. Schmitt, ed., *The Neurosciences: Second Study Program.* Rockefeller U. Press, New York. Pp. 782–97.

Calma, I. 1965. Thalamo-cortical relations in the sensory nuclei of the cat. *Nature* 205:394–96.

Cooper, J.R., Bloom, F.E., and Roth, R.H. 1970. *The Biochemical Basis of Neuropharmacology.* 2d ed. Oxford U. Press, London.

DeRobertis, E.D.P., and Carrea, R., eds. 1965. *Progress in Brain Research.* Vol. 15, *Biology of Neuroglia.* Elsevier, Amsterdam.

Dickerson, J.W.T. 1968. The composition of nervous tissues. In A.N. Davison and J. Dobbing, eds., *Applied Neurochemistry.* Davis, Philadelphia. Pp. 48–115.

Eccles, J.C. 1964. Ionic mechanisms of post-synaptic inhibition. *Science* 145:1140–47.

Elbrink, J., and Bihler, I. 1975. Membrane transport: Its relation to cellular metabolic rates. *Science* 188:1177–84.

Fazekas, J.F., Alexander, F.A.D., and Himwich, H.E. 1941. Tolerance of the newborn to anoxia. *Am. J. Physiol.* 134:281–87.

Fox, C.A., and Snider, R.S., eds. 1967. *Progress in Brain Research.* Vol. 25, *The Cerebellum.* Elsevier, Amsterdam.

Galambos, R. 1966. Glial cells. In *Neurosciences Research Symposium Summaries.* Vol. 1, F.O. Schmitt and T. Melnechuk, eds. M.I.T. Press, Cambridge.

Gerard, R.W. 1960. Neurophysiology: An integration (molecules, neurons, and behavior). In *Handbook of Physiology.* Sec. 1, J. Field, H.W. Magoun, and V.E. Hall, eds., *Neurophysiology.* Am. Physiol. Soc., Washington. Vol. 3, 1919–65.

Goldstein, A. 1976. Opioid peptides (endorphins) in pituitary and brain. *Science* 193:1081–86.

Goth, A. 1961. *Medical Pharmacology.* Mosby, St. Louis.

Handley, C.A., Sweeney, H.M., Scherman, Q., and Severance, R. 1943. Metabolism of the perfused dog's brain. *Am. J. Physiol.* 140:190–96.

Himwich, H.E. 1951. *Brain Metabolism and Cerebral Disorders.* Williams & Wilkins, Baltimore.

Hodgkin, A.L. 1964. The ionic basis of nervous conduction. *Science* 145:1148–54.

Holmes, J.H., and Tower, D.B. 1955. Intracranial fluids. In K.A.C. Elliott, J.H. Page, and H.H. Quastel, eds., *Neurochemistry: The Chemical Dynamics of Brain and Nerve.* Thomas, Springfield, Ill. Pp. 262–93.

Huxley, A.F. 1964. Excitation and conduction in nerve: Quantitative analysis. *Science* 145:1154–59.

Hydén, H. 1960. The neuron. In J. Brachet and A.E. Mirsky, eds., *The Cell.* Academic Press, New York. Vol. 4, 215–323.

Ingram, W.R. 1960. Central autonomic mechanisms. In *Handbook of Physiology.* Sec. 1, J. Field, H.W. Magoun, and V.E. Hall, eds., *Neurophysiology.* Am. Physiol. Soc., Washington. Vol. 1, 951–78.

Jacobson, M. 1970. *Developmental Neurobiology.* Holt, Rinehart and Winston, New York.

John, E.R. 1967. *Mechanisms of Memory.* Academic Press, New York.

Kabat, H., Dennis, C., and Baker, A.B. 1941. Recovery of function following arrest of the brain circulation. *Am. J. Physiol.* 132:737–47.

Kennedy, D. 1969. The control of output by central neurons. In M.A.B. Brazier, ed., *The Interneuron.* U. of California Press, Los Angeles. Pp. 21–36.

Klemm, W.R. 1976. Electroencephalography. In W.R. Klemm, ed., *Applied Electronics in Veterinary Medicine and Animal Physiology.* Thomas, Springfield, Ill. Pp. 287–351.

Lajtha, A., ed. 1970. *Protein Metabolism of the Nervous System.* Plenum, New York.

Landau, W.M., Freygang, W.H., Roland, L.P., Sokoloff, L., and Kety, S.S. 1955. The local circulation of the living brain: Values in the unanesthetized and anesthetized cat. *Trans. Am. Neurol. Ass.* 80:125–29.

LeBaron, F.N., and Folch, J. 1957. Structure of brain tissue lipids. *Physiol. Rev.* 37:539–61.

Leeman, S.E., and Mroz, E.A. 1975. Substance P. *Life Sciences* 15:2033–44.

Miller, N.E. 1969. Learning of visceral and glandular responses. *Science* 163:434–45.

Nauta, W.J.H. 1960. Some neural pathways related to the limbic system. In E.R. Ramey and D.S. O'Doherty, eds., *Electrical Studies on the Unanesthetized Brain.* Hoeber, New York. Pp. 1–16.

Nauta, W.J.H. 1966. Some brain structures and functions related to memory. In *Neurosciences Research Symposium Summaries.* Vol. 1, F.O. Schmitt and T. Melnechuk, eds. M.I.T. Press, Cambridge. Pp. 73–107.

Olds, J. 1956. Pleasure centers in the brain. *Scien. Am.* 195(4):105–16.

Olds, J. 1960. Differentiation of reward systems in the brain by self-stimulation techniques. In E.R. Ramey and D.S. O'Doherty, eds., *Electrical Studies on the Unanesthetized Brain.* Hoeber, New York. Pp. 17–51.

Palay, S.L., and Palade, G.E. 1955. The fine structure of neurons. *J. Biophys. Biochem. Cytol.* 1:69–88.

Papez, J.W. 1937. A proposed mechanism of emotion. *Arch. Neurol. Psychiat.* 38:725–43.

Rosenzweig, M.R. 1966. Environmental complexity, cerebral change, and behavior. *Am. Psychologist* 21:321–32.

Rossiter, R.J. 1955. Chemical constituents of brain and nerve. In K.A.C. Elliott, J.H. Page, and J.H. Quastel, eds., *Neurochemistry: The Chemical Dynamics of Brain and Nerve.* Thomas, Springfield, Ill. Pp. 11–52.

Ruch, T.C. 1961. Neurophysiology of emotion and motivation. In T.C.

Ruch, H.D. Patton, J.W. Woodbury, and A.L. Towne, eds., *Neurophysiology*. Saunders, Philadelphia. Pp. 483–99.

Schally, A.V., Arimura, A., and Kastin, A.J. 1973. Hypothalamic regulatory hormones. *Science* 179:341–50.

Schmitt, F.O. 1968. Fibrous proteins: Neuronal organelles. *Proc. Nat. Acad. Sci.* 60:1092–1101.

Schmitt, F.O., and Davison, P.F. 1967. Brain and nerve proteins: Functional correlates. In *Neurosciences Research Symposium Summaries*. Vol. 2, F.O. Schmitt, T. Melnechuk, G.C. Quarton, and G. Adelman, eds. M.I.T. Press, Cambridge. Pp. 329–98.

Stone, T.W., Taylor, D.A., and Bloom, F.E. 1975. Cyclic AMP and cyclic GMP may mediate opposite neuronal responses in the rat cerebral cortex. *Science* 187:845–47.

Ungar, G., 1974. Molecular coding of memory. *Life Sciences* 14:595–604.

Van Harreveld, A., Collewijn, H., and Malhotra, S.K. 1966. Water, electrolytes, and extracellular space in hydrated and dehydrated brains. *Am. J. Physiol.* 210:251–56.

Weiss, P., Taylor, A.C., and Pillai, P.A. 1962. The nerve fiber as a system in continuous flow: Microcinematographic and electron-microscopic demonstrations. *Science* 136:330.

Weiss, P.A. 1966. Specificity in the neurosciences: Work session report. In *Neurosciences Research Symposium Summaries*. Vol. 1, F.O. Schmitt and T. Melnechuk, eds. M.I.T. Press, Cambridge. Pp. 179–212.

CHAPTER 41

Activity of Peripheral Nerves and Junctional Regions | by Ainsley Iggo

Peripheral nerves are formed from the axons of neurons with cell bodies in (1) dorsal root ganglia and cranial nerve ganglia (these are afferent or sensory axons), (2) the ventral horn of the spinal cord or corresponding cranial nerve nuclei in the brain stem (these are efferent or motor axons), and (3) autonomic nuclei of the brain stem and spinal cord or the peripheral ganglia of the autonomic system (these are the efferent fibers of the autonomic nervous system). The cell bodies of neurons in the CNS and in autonomic ganglia have dendrites that ramify in the tissues adjacent to the cell body, where they may make synaptic contact with the dendrites or axons of other neurons. Contact at greater distances is made through the axons, which may form synapses with the cell body, dendrites, or axons of other neurons, or in the case of motoneurons with skeletal muscle fibers.

The peripheral nerves act as communication channels between the CNS and the peripherally placed effectors and receptors. They also have significant effects on the development of the tissues in which they end. Each individual nerve cell or neuron is formed from several elements (see Figs. 40.2, 40.3). During nervous activity nerve impulses travel intermittently along the axon at a speed (conduction velocity) ranging from less than 1 to 120 m/sec in mammalian nerves. Ionic mechanisms underlie these impulses or action potentials; each impulse is associated with changes in electrical activity in the axon (Fig. 41.1).

RECORDING METHODS

The method of electrical recording influences the shape of the record obtained. The activity of a single axon may be recorded either extracellularly, with both electrodes outside, or intracellularly, with one electrode inside the cell and the other outside.

When extracellular methods are used, the type of recording obtained depends on the positions of the recording electrodes (Fig. 41.2 I). When this method of recording is applied to a nerve trunk containing many different fibers conducting at different velocities, the shape of the action potential (called a compound action potential) is extremely difficult to analyze. The situation can be simplified by changing the recording conditions (Fig. 41.2 II). When a monophasic compound action potential is recorded from a whole nerve, the contribution of fibers with different conduction velocities can be seen (see Fig. 41.14).

Intracellular records are obtained by inserting one elec-

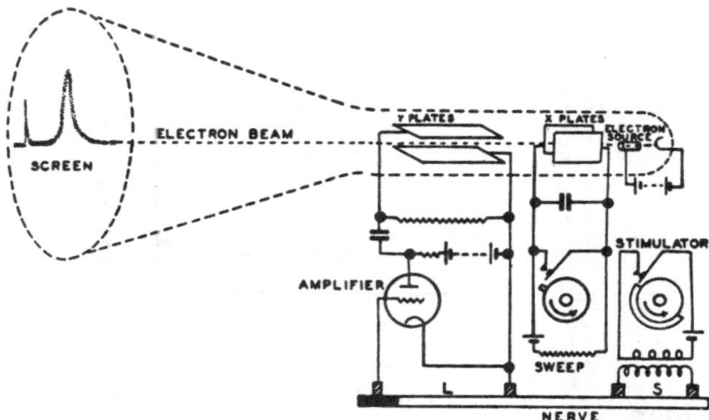

Figure 41.1. Cathode ray oscilloscope for studying electrical activity of nerve, muscle, and CNS. The electron beam emitted from a cathode strikes the fluorescent screen and forms a spot that responds to the electrical changes impressed upon the X and Y deflecting plates. Permanent records are made by photographing the movements of the spot on the fluorescent screen. The tissue is stimulated by discharge from the stimulator, and the electrical changes caused by tissue activity are led to an amplifier by means of recording electrodes. The amplified potential changes are then impressed upon the Y plates to cause vertical movements of the spot. The sweep potential is rhythmically applied to the X plates to provide a time axis. (From Erlanger and Gasser, *Electrical Signs of Nervous Activity*, U. of Pennsylvania Press, Philadelphia, 1937.)

trode into the axon (Ling and Gerard 1949). With this method, which records the potential difference across the membrane close to the intracellular electrode, the resting membrane potential can be registered and monophasic potential recording conditions are obtained. This method's use is limited by the difficulty of inserting electrodes into very small cells or axons and by the damage the electrode may cause when it penetrates a cell.

The nerve impulse forms the basis of activity in the nervous system. It is the sign of action and hence is called the action potential, and the degree of activity in a nerve cell is indicated by the frequency of discharge. Individual impulses in any axon are constant in amplitude, and succeeding impulses have the same size, except at high frequency. This property is called the all-or-nothing response; if the axon is active, then the propagated response occurs at full size. This basic concept was established by Adrian in Cambridge, England, and has been the foundation of our present concept of the operation of the nervous system (Adrian 1914, Adrian and Forbes 1922). In peripheral nerve trunks, which contain many thousands of axons, the response of the whole nerve is not all-or-nothing, since it is only the individual nerve fibers that have this property.

CHEMICAL COMPOSITION OF NERVE CELLS

The composition of a nerve cell is strikingly different from that of the extracellular fluid. The inside of mammalian nerve cells contains a relatively high concentration of potassium ions and large inorganic anions, but low concentrations of sodium and chloride ions. More exact information about the composition of axoplasm is obtained from invertebrates such as the squid, which possesses giant axons up to 1 mm in diameter from which the axoplasm can be extruded.

The membrane at the surface of the cell is a barrier that prevents the free mixing of the internal axoplasm and the external extracellular fluid. If a cell is made anoxic, the high internal concentration of potassium ions falls and potassium ions appear in greater amounts in the extracellular fluid; conversely, the sodium ion concentration in the cell rises. Measurements with radioactive potassium (^{42}K) show that potassium can diffuse within the cell with nearly the same freedom as it can in a free solution (Hodgkin and Keynes 1955b). This ion is almost completely unbound in the cell, whereas other ions, such as calcium and sodium, move less easily (calcium about one thirtieth and sodium about one tenth) than in free solution, probably because they form complexes in the cell.

This relative freedom of potassium to move about inside the cell is in striking contrast to its difficulty in passing through the resting membrane.

The rate of movement, that is, the permeability, of ions through the cell membrane is expressed as the ionic flux across the membrane (Table 41.1). The most surprising feature of this flux is the relatively high movement rate of sodium ions in both directions across the resting membrane, although the sodium concentration in axoplasm is only one tenth the sodium concentration outside. This low internal sodium concentration in the resting axon is due to its *sodium-potassium ion pump,* which actively extrudes the sodium that leaks into the cell. The membrane is *effectively impermeable* to sodium ions. The pump also carries some of the potassium that enters the cell.

Metabolic energy is used to pump out the sodium ions—this process depends on oxidative metabolism in nerve, and on glycolysis in skeletal muscle and in mammalian red cells. Energy is expended by the resting nerve

Table 41.1 Ionic fluxes in resting axons dissected from cuttlefish (*Sepia*) and suspended in artificial sea water. The fluxes establish that ions are continually passing through the resting membrane.

	Flux (pmol/sq cm/sec)	
	Normal nerve	Nerve poisoned with DNP
Na influx	32	32
Na efflux	39	1.5
K influx	15–30	2–3
K efflux	20–40	27

pmol = 10^{-12} mol or $\mu\mu$mol
Data from Hodgkin and Keynes 1955, *J. Physiol.* 128:28–60, 61–88

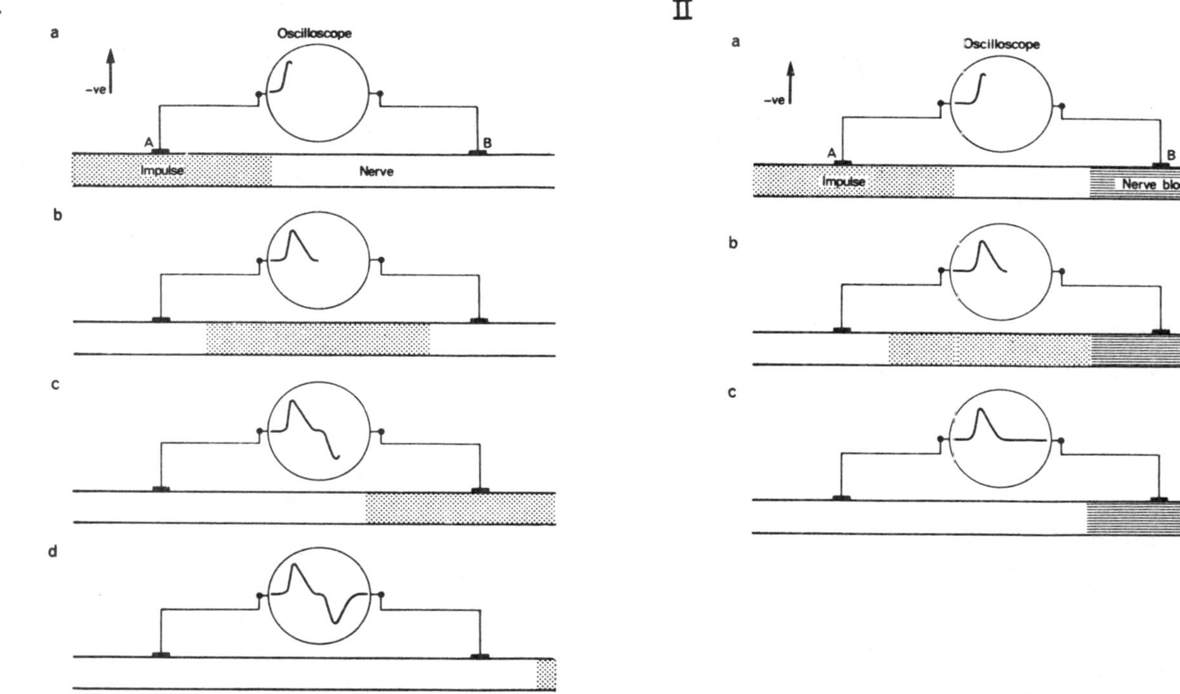

Figure 41.2. How the method of recording from a peripheral nerve affects the shape of the potential record. In both I and II the potentials are detected by the electrodes A and B and the difference between them is displayed on the oscilloscope, with a deflection of the oscilloscope beam upward (-ve↑) when A is negative to B. The diagrams show the build-up of a record as the impulse travels along the nerve, as indicated by the stippled region in the nerve and by the tracing on the oscilloscope. I. *Biphasic action potential*. The impulse travels past both electrodes: (a) when it is passing electrode A, this electrode goes negative with respect to B and the oscilloscope spot moves upward; (b) when the impulse is between A and B the oscilloscope shows no displacement; (c) as the impulse passes B this electrode goes negative with respect to A; and finally in (d) the action potential has passed B and once again the spot is at the zero potential level. The path taken by the oscilloscope spot thus has both a negative and positive deflection from zero. II. *Monophasic action potential*. The impulse is prevented from passing electrode B by a nerve block. The oscilloscope trace therefore shows only a negative deflection as the impulse passes electrode A but does not reach B.

to maintain electrochemical gradients which themselves represent a large reserve of potential energy available for immediate release on excitation of the nerve. The extrusion of sodium ions from a nerve can be blocked by dinitrophenol (DNP) (Fig. 41.3). DNP acts by uncoupling oxidative phosphorylation so that the formation of adenosine triphosphate (ATP) is arrested. The addition of ATP (or some other source of energy-rich P bonds) enables the axon to extrude sodium ions again.

The movements of ions and their dependence on metabolic energy or existing concentration differences are shown in Figure 41.4. Two separate mechanisms move sodium and potassium across the membrane: the sodium-potassium pump, which is active in the resting membrane; and the sodium and potassium carriers that are active during an impulse. The activity of the sodium pump is loosely coupled to the transfer of potassium ions. If sodium movement is depressed, less potassium is transferred; and vice versa. One potassium ion is absorbed for every 2–3 sodium ions pumped out.

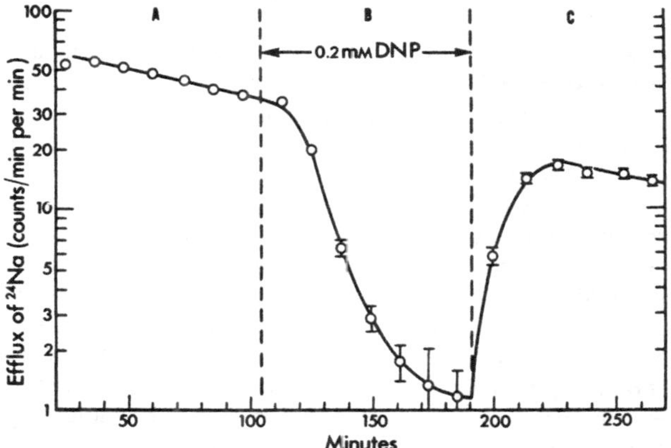

Figure 41.3. Effect of dinitrophenol (DNP) on the sodium pump of a Sepia axon, as measured by the rate of loss of radioactive sodium from the axon. In A and C the axon was in artificial seawater and there was a steady extrusion of radioactivity. In B, during treatment with DNP, the loss of ^{24}Na was almost completely arrested. Recovery of the extrusion process occurred as the DNP effect wore off. (From Hodgkin and Keynes 1955a, *J. Physiol.* 128:28–60.)

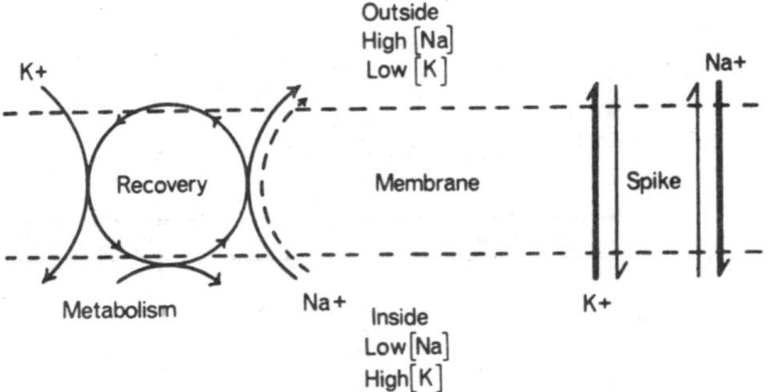

Figure 41.4. Diagram of the nerve membrane illustrating the separate mechanisms for movement of ions: in the sodium-potassium pump, recovery depends on an immediate source of metabolic energy and causes the uphill movement of ions (against the gradient); the sodium and potassium carriers that are active during the action potential (spike) depend on the established concentration gradients and cause the downhill movements of ions (with the concentration gradient). (From Hodgkin and Keynes 1955a, *J. Physiol.* 128:28–60.)

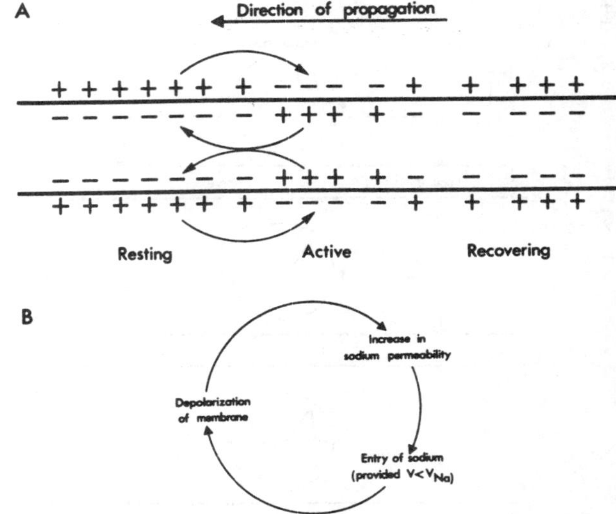

Figure 41.5. Membrane potentials. A: distribution of charges on the membrane at rest and during the action potential. At rest the nerve is positively charged on the outside; the charge is reversed at the height of the action potential. The flow of action currents is indicated—in the extracellular fluid, from the resting membrane into the active region of the membrane; in the axoplasm, from the active region to the adjacent resting membrane inside the axon. B: cycle of changes in membrane affecting sodium permeability. V, potential across cell membrane; V_{Na}, sodium equilibrium potential.

BIOELECTRICITY AND MEMBRANE POTENTIALS

Theory of membrane potentials

The steady state equilibrium in the distribution of sodium and potassium ions that results from the action of the sodium pump leads to a voltage difference, or potential, across the cell membrane. This potential appears in a purely physical system when charged ions are separated by a semipermeable membrane. Such a system is called a concentration cell; and the amplitude and sign of the voltage potential are given by the Nernst equation

$$V = \frac{RT}{F} \log_e \frac{[C]_o}{[C]_i}$$

where V is the transmembrane voltage (emf), R is the gas constant, T is the absolute temperature, F is the Faraday, and $[C]_i$ and $[C]_o$ are the concentrations of the diffusible ion on either side of the membrane. The voltage potential is also known as the concentration cell potential, or the *equilibrium potential* for the ion. At the stated potential, the ion is in equilibrium, that is, there is no net movement from one side of the membrane to the other. To predict the voltage difference existing across a cell membrane that is permeable to more than one ion, the Nernst equation must be extended to include consideration of all permeable ions. Since cell membranes are not equally permeable to different ions, factors indicating membrane permeability to each ion must be included. Thus the constant field equation was formulated by Goldman:

$$E_m = \frac{RT}{F} \log_e \frac{P_K[K^+]_o + P_{Na}[Na^+]_o + P_{Cl}[Cl^-]_i}{P_K[K^+]_i + P_{Na}[Na^+]_i + P_{Cl}[Cl^-]_o}$$

where E_m is the equilibrium potential across the resting cell membrane and P is the permeability coefficient for the ion.

The most exact quantitative explanation for the biological potentials, at rest and during activity, is the Hodgkin-Huxley theory: the electrical behavior of an excitable membrane is determined by its ionic permeabilities (Hodgkin 1964).

During an action potential the membrane for a brief period becomes highly permeable to sodium ions (due to activation of the sodium carrier), and the membrane potential is then largely determined by the equilibrium potential for sodium.

The potentials across membranes can be depicted as in Figure 41.5. (It should be noted that in biological tissues the electrical current flow is in the form of ions, not of electrons.) At the active region the current is carried across the membrane by sodium ions moving inward. Action potentials can be measured with intracellular electrodes (Fig. 41.6). During an impulse the membrane potential of an axon changes from the normal resting value of −70 mv (inside negative), at first slowly and then more rapidly. During the rapid swing the potential reverses and reaches +45 mv. Next it rapidly swings back again toward the resting value. These rapid changes make up the action potential or the *action potential spike*. They are followed by a slow return of the potential back

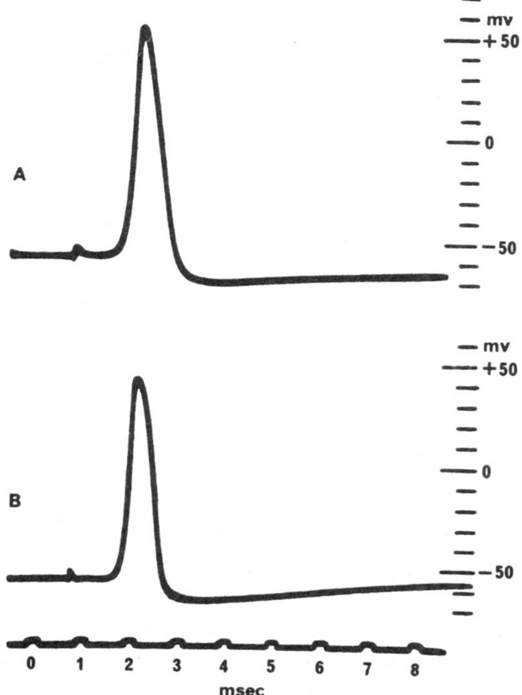

Figure 41.6. Action potentials recorded from giant axons of the squid, using internal electrodes. The amplification and time scales are identical in each record. A, action potential of an axon from which the axoplasm was extruded and which had been filled with isotonic potassium sulfate solution. B, an intact axon. (From Baker, Hodgkin, and Shaw 1961, *Nature* 190:885–87.)

to the resting value. These slow changes are called after-potentials.

The principal lines of evidence for this membrane theory of conduction can be summarized under five headings.

Local currents for propagation

The theory states that propagation depends on depolarization of the resting membrane by a flow of current in the extracellular space. If current flow is decreased, so is the velocity of propagation, and vice versa.

Changes in ionic composition

Until recently most tests of the ionic membrane hypothesis have relied either on changing the external electrolyte concentrations, or on the electrophoretic injection of ions into the cell, causing large but unmeasurable changes in ionic composition. A newer method is to replace the axoplasm of a squid giant axon with artificial solutions.

Several kinds of test solutions have been used to examine their effects on the resting potential and action potential (Baker et al. 1961). These experiments, based on changes in the potassium concentration, all substantiate the hypothesis that the resting potential is determined by membrane permeability for potassium ion, and that the potassium ion is the only internal ion that is essential to maintain the excitability of the axon (Fig. 41.7).

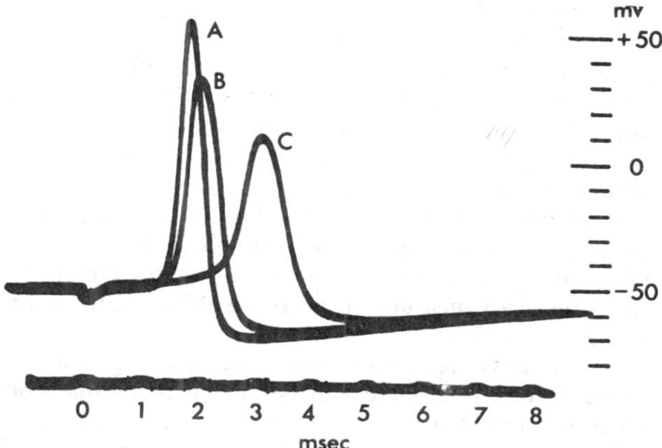

Figure 41.7. Effect on the action potential, recorded from a perfused squid giant axon, of replacing the internal potassium ions with sodium ions. A, isotonic potassium sulfate inside; B, one quarter of the potassium ions replaced by sodium ions; C, half the potassium replaced. The records were taken from a long experiment and were obtained in the order B, A, C. (From Baker, Hodgkin, and Shaw 1961, *Nature* 190:885–87.)

Ionic movements in resting and active axons

The membrane hypothesis states that there is a relatively free diffusion of potassium across the membrane at rest, that this movement is greatly increased during activity, and that there is an increased movement of sodium during activity. The movements of these ions have been measured using radioactive tracers. The results (Table 41.2) show the expected movements in the appropriate directions, that is, sodium entering and potassium leaving the cell during activity.

Table 41.2. Net movements of sodium and potassium ions with the passage of one impulse at 15–20°C

Preparation	Fiber diameter (μ)	Na entry (pmol/sq cm)	K loss (pmol/sq cm)	Calc. Na entry *
Carcinus axon	30		2	1.2
Sepia axon	200	3–4	3–4	1.2
Squid axon	500	3–4	3–4	1.2
Frog muscle fiber	100	15	10	6

* The quantity of sodium that entered the fiber was in each case more than sufficient to account for the action potential. This column shows the quantity calculated to be required.

Data from Hodgkin, *Conduction of the Nervous Impulse*, Liverpool U. Press, 1964

Permeability changes in axons

So far the membrane theory of conduction has been presented from the viewpoint of the permeability changes associated with the resting and active state of the axon. Next the quantitative measurement of changes in permeability will be considered during stages of the action potential. The method used, known as the voltage clamp, was introduced by Cole in 1949. It allows the membrane potential to be fixed at any desired voltage by controlling the quantity of current flowing across the membrane and gives an exact measure of the permeability of the membrane.

When the voltage to an axon held in a voltage clamp is suddenly changed, there will be an initial instantaneous surge of current as the membrane condensers discharge followed by a prolonged flow of current through R_{Na} and R_K (Fig. 41.8) carried by the respective ions. A change of 91 mv (from approximately −70 mv to +21 mv) causes first an outward membrane current with an early sudden rise. This outward current is absent at 117 mv displacement and is therefore carried by sodium ions. Second, there is a slower rise in an inward current that continues for longer time. This is still present at 117 mv and is carried by the potassium ions (Hodgkin et al. 1952). The sodium conductance decreases about 10 times as rapidly as the potassium conductance when the potential is restored to the resting value. If the potential is not restored to the resting value, the sodium conductance nevertheless declines exponentially—this process is known as inactivation. A second voltage pulse is ineffective in re-exciting sodium conductance when inactivation has occurred, unless the membrane is repolarized for a few milliseconds (in squid nerve) after the first voltage pulse. This process is responsible for the refractory period phenomena (see below).

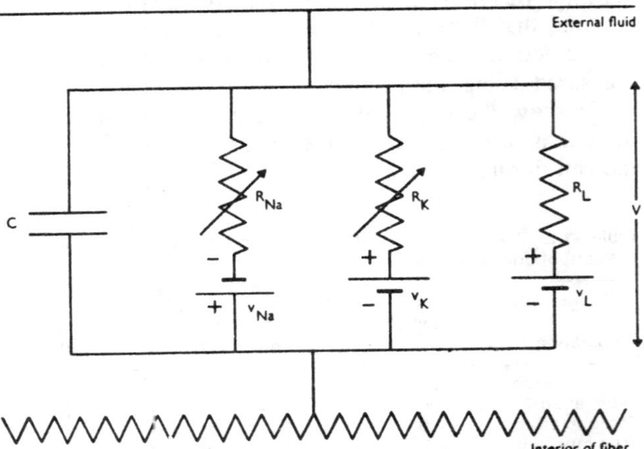

Figure 41.8. Electrical analogue of the circuit diagram of an element of the excitable membrane. C is membrane capacity; R_{Na}, R_K, and R_L are resistances of the membrane for sodium, potassium, and leakage current respectively; V_{Na}, V_K, and V_L are the respective "batteries" supplying the Na, K, and L current (R_L and V_L are small and can be ignored). The membrane of an axon can be regarded as a continuous cable made of a large number of these elements connected together. (From Hodgkin 1958, *Proc. Roy. Soc.*, ser. B, 148:1–37.)

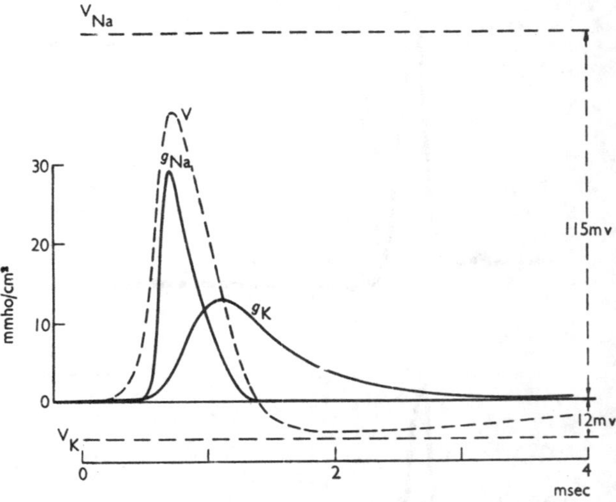

Figure 41.9. Action potential (---) computed from the Hodgkin-Huxley equation and the calculated sodium (^gNa) and potassium (^gK) conductances. V_{Na}, sodium equilibrium potential; V, computed membrane potential. (From Hodgkin and Huxley 1952, *J. Physiol.* 117:500–544.)

Application of voltage-clamp data. The conductances determined experimentally agree remarkably well with predictions based on the Hodgkin-Huxley equations (Fig. 41.9). The number of ions that cross the membrane can be calculated. The theoretical figures (4.33 pmol Na^+ per sq cm, and 4.26 pmol K^+ per sq cm) are in excellent agreement with measurements made with radioactive tracers (see Table 41.2). These results place the Hodgkin-Huxley theoretical interpretation of the genesis of resting and action potentials on a sound experimental basis.

MYELINATED AXONS

This account of the biophysics of the cell membrane has been largely confined to invertebrate axons, principally because their larger size, up to 500 μ diameter, makes them easier experimental material. In vertebrate animals similar nonmyelinated axons are always thin, 0.25–1.0 μ diameter (Gasser 1955), and are usually covered by a single Schwann cell membrane (Fig. 41.10a).

Thicker axons, 1–20 μ in diameter, are surrounded by a fatty layer, the myelin sheath, which is interrupted at intervals by the nodes of Ranvier (Fig. 41.11A). The myelin sheath is formed by Schwann cells that wind themselves around the axon (Fig. 41.10b) (Geren 1954). In electron micrographs the myelin sheath is seen to be composed of concentric layers, and each layer is formed by Schwann cell membranes.

This myelin sheath is a very effective insulator and

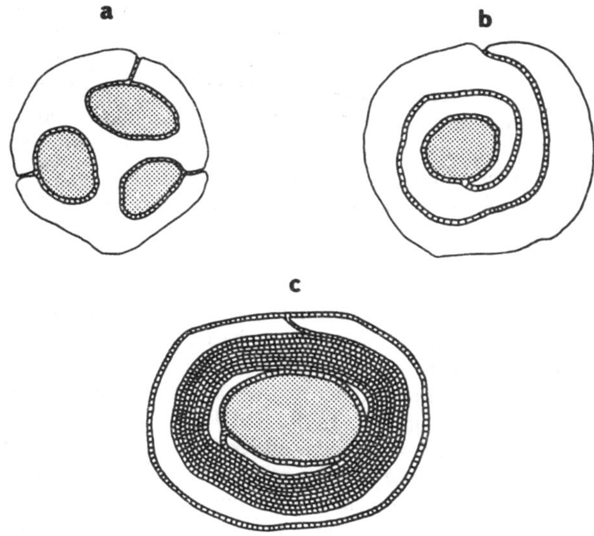

Figure 41.10. Structure of the intimate sheaths of axons: (a) three nonmyelinated axons embedded in a Schwann cell; (b) early stage in the development of a myelin sheath, produced by the winding of a Schwann cell around a single axon; (c) more fully developed myelinated axon in which the lamellation of the myelin is conspicuous and in which the Schwann cell cytoplasm has disappeared from the lamellae. Stippled areas show the axon, cross hatching shows extracellular space.

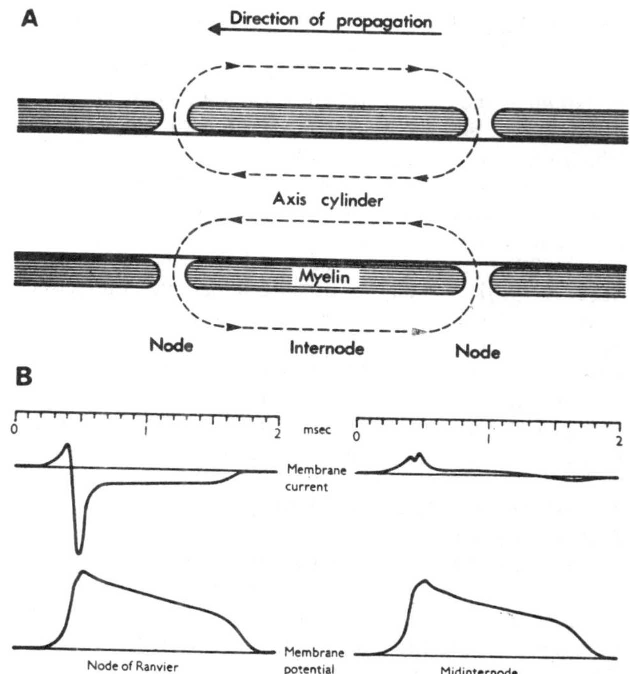

Figure 41.11. Myelinated nerve fiber. A, arrangement of nodes of Ranvier and internodes. The axon is continuous. The lines show the path taken by current flow. B, membrane current and membrane potential changes during an action potential, outward current upward. (From Huxley and Stämpfli 1949, *Arch. Sci. Physiol.* 3:435–49.) There is an inward flow of current (carried by sodium ions) only at the node, whereas the potential also appears at the midinternode. Initially there is an outward flow of current at the node; this is passive and is associated with the local-circuit current flow. It is followed by a large inflow of current, which begins after the membrane potential has fallen slightly, as would be predicted from the local-circuit hypothesis.

isolates the parts of the axon it covers from the extracellular fluid. The axon is exposed only at the nodes for about 0.5–1.0 μ. The distance apart of nodes of Ranvier depends on axon diameter.

The existence of the myelin sheath broken by these nodes alters the behavior of a propagated action potential. The excitability of a myelinated fiber is greatest at the nodes of Ranvier (Tasaki 1953) because the myelin acts as an effective insulator and forces the current to depolarize the axonal membrane only at the nodes.

These results have led to the hypothesis that in myelinated axons the action potential jumps from node to node—that is, it is *saltatory* (*salire,* leap). This means that as the sodium permeability changes and sodium entry is restricted to the membrane at the nodes, the action currents associated with this increased permeability are forced to act at the next node instead of on the immediately adjacent resting membrane, as in nonmyelinated axons. Although the permeability changes occur only at the nodes, the potential also appears across the myelin sheath in the internode.

The hypothesis that current flow is largely through the nodes has been tested by measuring the current flowing in the external fluid along short lengths of the myelinated fiber. Huxley and Stämpfli (1949) found a large current flow only when they recorded across a node, there being first an outward flowing current (the action current flowing out and depolarizing the membrane) followed by a large inward flowing current (the sodium current) (Fig. 41.11).

Influence of myelination on conduction velocity

The consequences of myelination in altering the propagation method of action potentials lead to an important change in the relation between conduction velocity and diameter of an axon. In nonmyelinated axons the wave of increased sodium permeability affects all parts of the axonal membrane in turn, so the action currents always depolarize the resting membrane adjacent to the active region. The rate of spread of this wave of depolarization—that is, the conduction velocity of the action potential—is proportional to the length constant (λ) of the membrane. The magnitude of a stationary voltage signal decreases exponentially along an axon, and the length constant is the distance over which the amplitude drops to $^1/_e$ of its value ($e = 2.718$ and is the base of the natural logarithm).

In the nonmyelinated axons of the squid the length

constant of a 500 μ diameter fiber is 0.25 cm, and the conduction velocity is 20 m/sec. A myelinated frog axon 20 μ in diameter has a conduction velocity of 20 m/sec. In mammals the conduction velocity of a 20 μ nerve fiber is 120 m/sec, largely because of the higher temperature at which the mammalian nerve operates.

This enhancement of conduction velocity by myelination is of considerable benefit to the animal. In the frog, for example, it enables the volume occupied by one squid axon (500 μ diameter) to be filled by several hundred fibers of 20 μ diameter, all with comparable conduction velocities. This great economy allows many thousands of axons with high conduction velocities to be contained in relatively small nerves. Myelination also reduces energy expenditure since the sodium and potassium ion movements are limited to the nodes, with a consequent restriction in the activity of pumps and carriers to the nodes.

THRESHOLD AND SUBTHRESHOLD PHENOMENA

Threshold membrane potential

When an axon is excited electrically the stimulating current has to reach a particular value before an action potential is initiated—the threshold value for excitation. Any stimulus weaker than the threshold value will not set up a propagated action potential. A stronger stimulus may make the impulse appear slightly earlier, but will not otherwise change it. The property of a threshold reaction is typical of excitable biological tissue and is an all-or-nothing response. In many excitable tissues with a resting potential of 50–90 mv, the depolarization required is 10–20 mv.

Subthreshold membrane potentials

At threshold the sodium conductance exceeds the outward potassium current. If a stimulating current is just below threshold and fails to initiate an all-or-nothing action potential, it will nevertheless increase the sodium conductance, which will decay exponentially when the stimulating current is withdrawn. While it is decaying, it can be revealed by a second test shock. The threshold for a second shock is lower when it has been preceded within a few milliseconds by another subthreshold shock.

Accommodation

If the subthreshold stimulus is prolonged or if a very slowly rising current is used to stimulate the nerve, it may fail to set up a conducted action potential. This failure can be ascribed to the activation and inactivation rates of sodium and potassium permeabilities. The rapid effect of depolarization is to increase sodium permeability; the slow effects are to inactivate the sodium-carrying system and to enhance the potassium permeability. During accommodation to slowly rising or to prolonged subthreshold currents where there is a slow depolarization, the slow effects are dominant and the regenerative increase in sodium permeability is blocked. As a result, the membrane passes into a state of refractoriness without having been excited. In this way an axon can be blocked by applying a weak cathodal current (Hodgkin 1964). Sustained rapidly rising suprathreshold currents will also induce block, after initiating one or a few impulses. Muscle relaxants that block at the neuromuscular junction may also cause depolarization block. Their action in depolarizing the muscle membrane at the junction, due to persistent depolarization, causes inactivation of the sodium carrier in the surrounding membrane. Synonyms for this kind of block are inactivation block or depolarization block. Local anesthetics that block without causing depolarization are thought to act by increasing the inactivation of sodium permeability (Taylor 1959).

The converse of cathodal block is anodal block, in which the membrane is hyperpolarized by the passage of an outwardly directed current. In this situation the safety factor is reduced, since the action current intensity of an impulse entering the hyperpolarized part of the axon is not sufficient to depolarize the hyperpolarized membrane and initiate the regenerative increase in sodium permeability that is needed for propagation.

Refractory period

When an axon has discharged an impulse, it enters a period of depressed excitability or raised threshold. For a short time after the first shock, the second shock fails to excite the nerve, no matter how strong it is. This interval of inexcitability is called the absolute refractory period. It is followed by a longer interval during which the nerve can be excited, but only by shocks of greater than normal threshold intensity. This is the relative refractory period (Fig. 41.12).

The phenomenon of the refractory period is accounted for by the membrance hypothesis as follows. After an action potential is discharged, the sodium-carrying system in the membrane is inactivated and potassium permeability is enhanced. A second stimulus occurring at this time must fail, since the sodium carrier cannot be activated and the potassium carrier is already activated and is holding the membrane near the potassium equilibrium potential.

During the period of recovery the excitability slowly returns to normal; that is, the nerve is in a state of relative refractoriness. One consequence of the refractory period is that action potentials initiated at one or other end of the axon travel in only one direction, because the membrane in the wake of the action potential is temporarily incapable of being excited by action currents.

The absolute refractory period lasts about as long as the action potential spike. In cardiac muscle, for example, the action potential lasts nearly as long as the contraction of the muscle. Consequently a tetanic con-

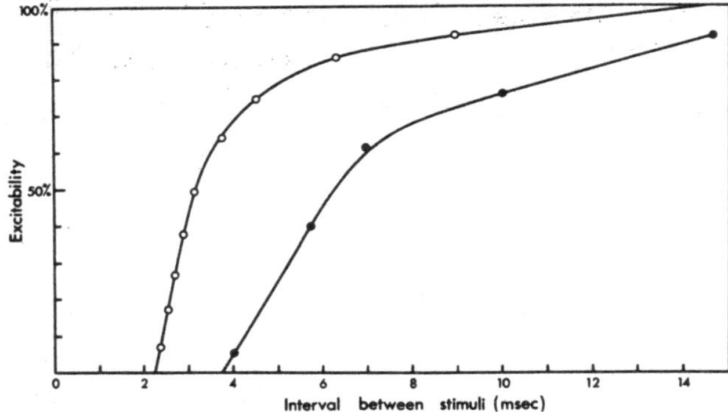

Figure 41.12. Recovery of excitability in the sciatic nerve (left) and sartorius muscle (right) of the frog after the passage of an impulse. Two shocks were sent into the tissue, the first at threshold of the resting tissue. The strength of the second shock needed to excite a response was plotted as the reciprocal of the first and expressed as a percentage. For about 2 and 4 msec, respectively, after the first shock the nerve or muscle was inexcitable (the absolute refractory period). Thereafter excitability gradually returned to normal (relative refractory period). The rate of recovery of excitability was slower in the muscle than in the nerve. (After Adrian 1921, *J. Physiol.* 55:193–225.)

traction cannot normally be produced. In skeletal muscle, on the other hand, the action potential in the muscle membrane may be over before the muscle begins to contract. Several action potentials may pass along the muscle fiber membrane while the contractile processes are being activated, and a summation of contractions can therefore occur.

ACTIVITY IN NERVE TRUNKS

Composition of peripheral nerve trunks

The nerve trunks that connect the brain and spinal cord to peripheral structures are formed from many individual axons, often thousands, or as in the optic nerve, millions. The individual axons are always surrounded and supported by Schwann cells. Several nonmyelinated axons may be associated with one Schwann cell, the membrane of which is folded around each axon so that the nerve fibers, although surrounded, are not completely enclosed (Fig. 41.13B). Contact with extracellular space is via the mesaxon. In myelinated vertebrate axons, on the other hand, each Schwann cell surrounds a single axon, and the tightly wound, closely apposed Schwann cell membranes constitute the myelin sheath. These elements are in turn supported by connective tissue containing collagen (manufactured by fibroblasts), permeated by blood vessels and lymphatics, and bound by tough connective tissue sheaths.

Different peripheral nerves have characteristic axonal compositions. All nerves contain both afferent and efferent axons that arise from the dorsal and ventral roots, respectively, of the spinal cord. The sciatic nerve contains about equal numbers; the muscular branches of the sciatic have proportionally more efferent axons, and the

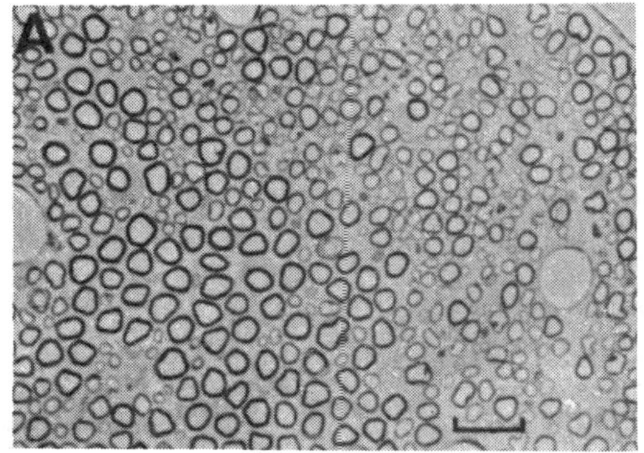

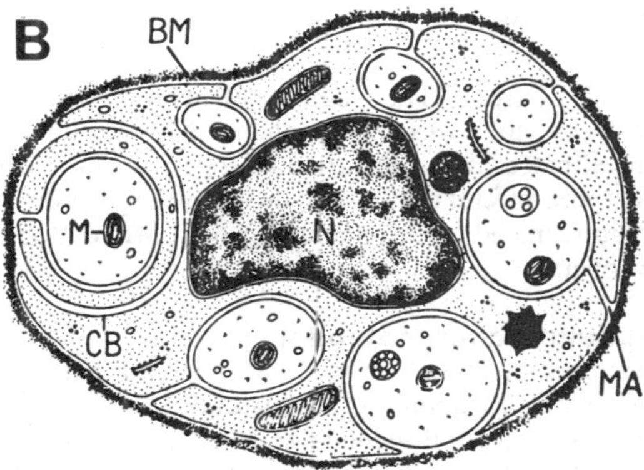

Figure 41.13. Fine structure of peripheral nerve trunks. A, section of part of an osmic acid–stained sciatic nerve from the hind limb of a rat (light microscope), ×365. The myelinated axons vary in diameter from 1–10 μ. The nerve is bounded by a connective tissue sheath. (From Webster and Collins 1964, *J. Neuropath. Exp. Neurol.* 23:109–26.) B, diagram, based on an electronmicrograph of a splenic nerve, of a single Schwann cell that surrounds seven nonmyelinated axons. N, nucleus of Schwann cell; M, mitochondrion in nonmyelinated axon; MA, mesaxon; BM, basement membrane; CB, common border between two Schwann cells. Note that the cytoplasm of the two cells is quite separate. (From Elfvin 1958, *J. Ultrastruct. Res.* 1:428–54.)

cutaneous branches are almost exclusively afferent, except for some sympathetic postganglionic axons. The visceral nerves, e.g. the vagus and splanchnic nerves, are also mixed. The large axons in dorsal roots pass predominantly into the skeletal muscles, where they terminate either as annulospiral endings in the muscle spindles, or in the Golgi tendon organs. The largest efferent or motor axons also go to skeletal muscles, where they supply the extrafusal muscle fibers. The smaller motor axons separately innervate the intrafusal muscle fibers in the muscle spindles. In cutaneous nerves the largest axons are smaller than the large muscle afferent fibers. There are also numerous fine myelinated and nonmyelinated axons. Visceral nerves contain few large myelinated axons, and

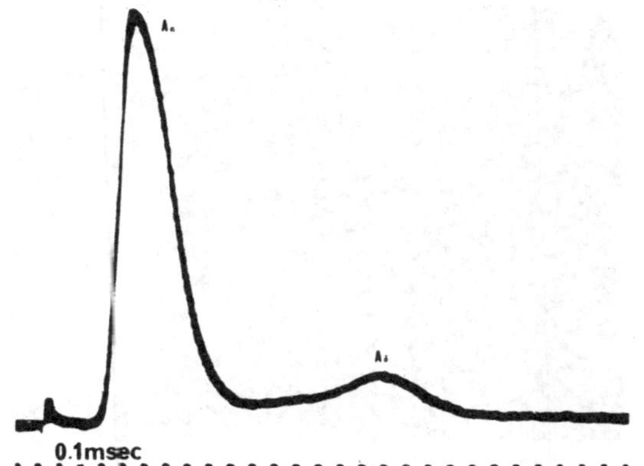

Figure 41.14. Compound action potential recorded from the excised saphenous nerve of the cat, with apparatus similar to that shown in Fig. 41.1. Two prominent waves or elevations, labeled Aα and Aδ, are produced by group II and III nerve fibers. (From Gasser 1960, *J. Gen. Physiol.* 43:927–40.)

these are afferent. The vagus, splanchnic, and pelvic nerves have no axons thicker than 12–14 μ, but many fine myelinated axons 1–4 μ in diameter, including both afferent and efferent axons, and a very large proportion of nonmyelinated axons, including both afferent and efferent fibers.

Compound action potential

The action potential set up in a peripheral nerve trunk by an electrical stimulus (compound action potential) lasts for several milliseconds and has a complex shape (Fig. 41.14). This potential, recorded with extracellular electrodes, is composed of the action potentials of all the myelinated axons in the nerve. Several distinct elevations or waves in the action potential are evident (labeled Aα and Aδ in the figure). In addition there are B and C waves, the B waves generated by preganglionic autonomic axons that are absent from the saphenous nerve, and the C waves by nonmyelinated axons. The sizes of the waves in the compound action potential depend on the relative proportions of the axon diameters in the nerve trunk.

Classification of axons in peripheral nerves

Several systems have been used to classify the nerve fibers in peripheral nerve trunks. There are two main criteria: (1) electrophysiological, based on conduction velocity, and (2) histological, based on fiber diameter.

(1) The electrophysiological system of Erlanger and Gasser divides the axons into three main groups, A, B, and C (with subdivisions in each group), based on the existence of waves or elevations in the compound action potential. The A group, subdivided into α, β, γ, and δ, is produced by the myelinated axons of dorsal or ventral root origin. It is not easy to give precise conduction velocities for the subgroups because of variations in the axonal composition of nerve trunks; in the cat, velocities for α are 40–120 m/sec and for δ, 4–25 m/sec. The B group is produced by the preganglionic autonomic efferent axons. Since no visceral nerve consists exclusively of these fibers, they are more difficult to study; their conduction velocities range from 3 to 16 m/sec. The C group is produced by the nonmyelinated axons with conduction velocities of less than 2.5 m/sec (Grundfest 1940).

(2) Histological classification based on fiber diameters avoids difficulties that may arise in electrical recording and its interpretation. The system of Lloyd (1943) is in general use for afferents. Four groups of axons are recognized: group I, 12–21 μ; II, 6–12 μ; III, 1–6 μ (all myelinated); and IV (nonmyelinated), 0.25–1.25 μ in diameter.

The two systems are interchangeable, and the corresponding groups are $I + II = A\alpha$, $III = A\delta + B$, and $IV = C$.

The relative proportions of groups of axons in corresponding nerves vary among species. Rats and rabbits have proportionally more C fibers, and large animals such as ruminants relatively few (Duncan 1934). The proportions may also show species variations because of changes in the functional complexity of the structures supplied by a nerve. For example, the abdominal vagus of the rabbit, which is a monogastric animal, contains almost no myelinated group III fibers; the same nerve in ruminant animals, which have large compound stomachs, contains several thousand group III fibers (Agostoni et al. 1957, Iggo 1956).

DEGENERATION AND REGENERATION IN NERVOUS TISSUE

The number of neurons in the body of mammals is fixed at or near birth, after which a neuron, if destroyed, cannot be replaced. Under certain circumstances, however, a degenerated peripheral nerve fiber can be quickly and completely replaced. For this to occur, its parent nerve cell body must be intact. The cell body, if destroyed, cannot be replaced.

In peripheral nerves

When a nerve is transected, the peripheral portion soon alters in appearance and in 3–4 days loses its ability to conduct nerve impulses when stimulated. The central portion undergoes no grossly apparent change, and when stimulated is still able to conduct nerve impulses, as is indicated by the production of pain and reflex contraction of muscles.

Histological studies of degeneration in fibers of peripheral nerves show that the immediate effect of the section is to cause comparatively mild degenerative changes in both the central and peripheral ends of the fiber, known as traumatic degeneration. Later, the entire peripheral portion of the nerve will undergo severe degeneration. It takes place because the nerve fiber is completely separated from the cell body. The degeneration finally becomes complete, involving not only the axon but also the myelin sheath, if present. After 30 days or more all that is left of the nerve fiber is the syncytial neurilemma, known as a protoplasmic or band fiber, which has helped remove the products of degeneration.

If conditions are favorable, complete regeneration may occur in the degenerated nerve fiber. Under the influence of the cell body, the portion of the axon connected with the cell body sends out a process along the protoplasmic fiber which finally reaches the termination of the old nerve fiber. This outgrowth becomes the axon of the regenerated fiber. The protoplasmic fiber serves the important function of guiding the new axon to its termination, but it cannot develop a new axon. This can be done only by the cell body and the attached portion of the axon.

The time required for regeneration of nerve fiber varies with the distance between the severed ends. If the ends are brought close together, regeneration occurs relatively quickly; if they are widely separated, regeneration may require years or may not occur at all. If regeneration does not occur, the cell body and its attached stump of axon degenerate. A functionally complete fiber, capable of carrying effective impulses, is obviously required before regeneration is completely accomplished. Much time may elapse between the arrival of the axon tip at its destination and the establishment of functional connection, and during reinnervation there is a complex sequence of interactions between the regenerating nerve and the tissue being reinnervated (Guth 1968), by which the nerve exerts a tropic influence.

After a nerve is cut, the neuromuscular junction loses its ability to transmit impulses before the axon becomes unable to conduct impulses. The specialized junctional muscle membrane is also altered and a hypersensitivity to ACh (acetylcholine) develops; with this occurs an increase in sensitivity of all the muscle membrane to ACh. The hypersensitivity disappears when new neuromuscular junctions are formed during regeneration (Thesleff 1960). This hypersensitivity is the cause of paralytic secretions; for example, in a cat after the chorda tympani are cut, the salivary glands may secrete spontaneously.

The receptors for afferent fibers degenerate along with the axon after nerve section, but some elements of the receptor structure may persist (Smith 1968). If the receptor is reinnervated by an outgrowth from its old axon, the specialized terminals and associated cells may reappear. The selective sensitivity and other characteristic features of the afferent discharge return only after the specialized receptor terminals and associated cells have re-formed (Brown and Iggo 1963).

Under practical conditions, where nerves have been severed it is essential to reunite the stumps if regeneration is to be assured.

In the CNS

Evidence from a number of sources indicates that the nerve fibers of the CNS are capable of regenerating but that the regeneration is usually abortive. Recent work, however, shows that under some conditions functional regeneration in the CNS of mammals is possible, as after transection of the spinal cord in rats. Various explanations have been offered for the rarity with which functional connections are reestablished in the CNS (Young 1942). The formation of scar tissue in the region of transection is probably a factor. Other mechanical difficulties might be present.

In nerve cells

When a peripheral nerve fiber is separated from its nerve cell, more or less severe lytic changes take place in the nerve cell. The chromatin substance tends to become liquefied, and the cell shows other evidences of injury. The ribonucleic acid metabolism of nerve cells is stimulated after cutting their axons (Watson 1965). RNA precursors are incorporated first in the nucleus and later in the cytoplasm, probably due to a transfer of RNA from the nucleus to cytoplasm during axonal regeneration.

If the axon is divided close to the cell body, or if the axon stump cannot establish connection with its protoplasmic fiber, or if the neuron is subjected to severe fatigue, the cell body may undergo complete degeneration from which recovery is impossible.

JUNCTIONAL TRANSMISSION

The neuron theory, which states that the nervous system is formed of individual nerve cells or neurons, immediately raises the problem of how an impulse in one nerve cell affects the next in a chain of neurons or how a nerve acts on an effector. In a muscle cell, for example, this transmission takes place at specialized junctional regions termed synapses, at which an action potential in the prejunctional axon is able to modify the behavior of the postjunctional cell; it may cause either excitation, and lead to the discharge of an impulse by the postjunctional cell, or inhibition, the suppression of discharge by the postjunctional cell (Eccles 1964).

At all junctional regions between excitable cells there is a morphological specialization of both the pre- and postjunctional membranes. Several kinds of nerve to nerve junctions are known: *axosomatic,* between axons and nerve-cell bodies, as in autonomic ganglia or in the spinal cord; *axoaxonic,* as the junction between the axons of interneurons and primary afferent fibers in the mammalian spinal cord; *axodendritic,* between axons and dendrites as in the dorsal horn of the spinal cord; or *dendrodendritic* as in the cerebellum. The precise structure of these synapses depends on their type, but the axosomatic synapse shows properties common to all. First, there is no continuity of the cytoplasm across the synapse. In electronmicrographs the membrane of each cell is clearly defined and separated by a synaptic cleft, 20–30 nm wide. Second, at the junctional region both the pre- and postsynaptic membranes are thickened and modified. Third, the cytoplasm, especially of the prejunctional axon, is densely packed with mitochondria. Fourth, the presynaptic terminal contains synaptic vesicles 30–60 nm in diameter, which contain the stores of chemical transmitter released during synaptic activity. These vesicles are not present in the postsynaptic cell. Fifth, the myelin sheath is lost from the axon shortly before it forms the synaptic junction.

As much as 65 percent of the surface of a neuron (including soma and dendrites) may be covered by synapses. One part of a neuron, the axon hillock from which the axon arises, is usually entirely free of synapses, and there may be a spatial separation of morphologically and functionally different kinds of synapses, excitatory and inhibitory, on various parts of the dendrites and soma (Furshpan and Furukawa 1962, Diamond 1968).

The junctional region between nerve and muscle (neuromuscular junction, nerve-muscle junction) shows a similar specialization, with a larger area and a folding of the postjunctional membrane to form a series of invaginations (Fig. 41.15).

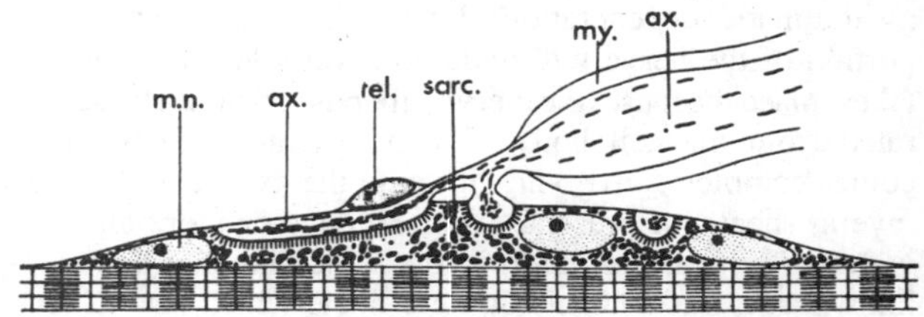

Figure 41.15. Diagram of a frog neuromuscular junction. The axon (ax.) loses its myelin (my.), divides near the muscle, and ends in grooves. The underlying muscle membrane is folded into grooves. m.n., muscle nucleus; tel., terminal Schwann cell; sarc., sarcoplasm. (From Couteaux, in Bourne, ed., *The Structure and Function of Muscle*, Academic Press, New York, 1960.)

Neuromuscular transmission

When an impulse in a motor axon supplying a skeletal muscle arrives at the neuromuscular junction, it is normally transmitted across the junctional region and causes an action potential to be set up in the membrane of the muscle fiber. This process of transmission can be blocked by curare (a plant extract, used by South American Indians on the tips of their blowpipe arrows). With a suitable concentration of *d*-tubocurarine, transmission of excitation is blocked, but a change in potential of the muscle membrane localized to the junction (the end-plate potential) can be recorded (Fig. 41.16). This change is caused by the action of acetylcholine, released from the motor nerve terminal, on special receptive sites on the postjunctional membrane. At these sites the acetylcholine causes a nonspecific increase in membrane cation permeability and starts a flow of current that is carried by the sodium ions entering the cell down their concentration gradient, which in turn causes a depolarization of surrounding normal muscle membrane. Several other chemicals structurally similar to acetylcholine (e.g. carbamylcholine) have a similar action at the nerve-muscle junction.

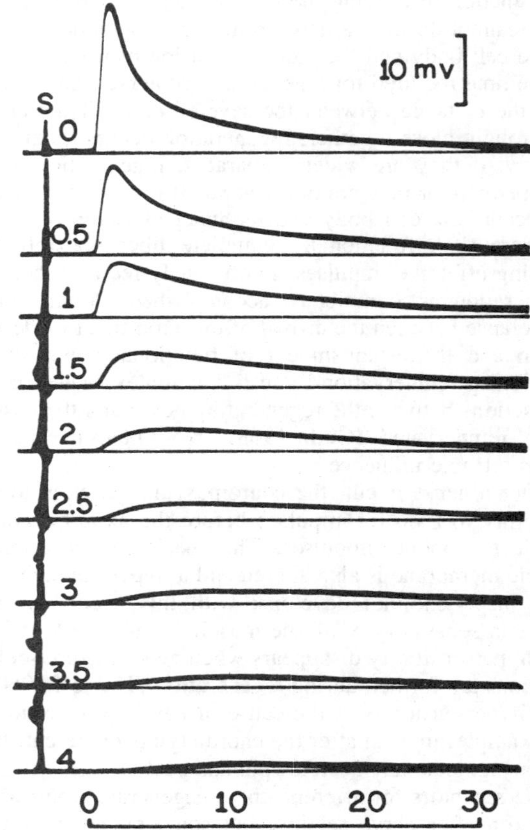

Figure 41.16. End-plate potentials recorded from a curarized frog skeletal muscle with intracellular electrodes. The motor nerve was stimulated electrically at S in each record. From above downward the recording electrode was inserted at progressively greater distances from the neuromuscular junction. The potential was largest at the junction and spread about 4 mm along the muscle fiber. The acetylcholine released from the motor nerve terminals has a direct action that is closely limited to the junction. (From Fatt and Katz 1951, *J. Physiol.* 115:320–70.)

The action of ACh released by the nerve terminal is restricted to the outside of the postjunctional muscle mem-

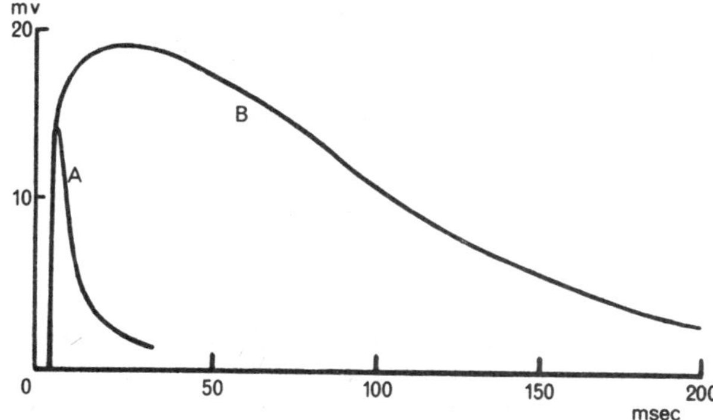

Figure 41.17. Effect of an anticholinesterase (prostigmine) on the size and duration of the end-plate potential. The normal potential (A) was larger and lasted much longer when the cholinesterase was inhibited (B), thus allowing the ACh to have a prolonged action. (From Fatt and Katz 1951, *J. Physiol.* 115:320–70.)

brane, and lasts for only a few milliseconds because it is rapidly destroyed by an enzyme, cholinesterase. The action of ACh can be prolonged if the muscle is treated with chemicals such as physostigmine or prostigmine (Fig. 41.17). These chemicals inhibit the cholinesterase, which is present in the junctional cleft, and so prevent the normally rapid hydrolysis of ACh. Thus junctional transmission may be improved; for example, in the curare-blocked muscle, the addition of prostigmine may restore transmission.

The various stages in neuromuscular transmission can be summarized as follows: (1) formation in the axon of ACh by choline acetylase and its storage in synaptic vesicles; (2) depolarization of the nerve terminal by motor-nerve action potential, entry of Ca^{++} into the nerve terminal, and the release of ACh (in small packets or quanta each containing 1000–10,000 molecules); (3) diffusion of ACh across the narrow cleft between pre- and postjunctional membranes; (4) interaction of ACh with receptor sites on the specialized muscle membrane; (5) increase in nonspecific cation permeability of muscle membrane by action of the ACh-receptor complex resulting in a large net inward current flow; (6) destruction of ACh by cholinesterase (coincident with 4 and 5); (7) collapse of the membrane potential toward zero, as the adjacent muscle membrane is depolarized by the current flow in 5; (8) excitation of muscle action potential, if the increase in sodium-carrier activity is sufficient to cause a regenerative increase in sodium permeability; and (9) restoration of resting potential and return of permeability to normal.

Junctional transmission differs in several important ways from the propagation of the action potential. First, the junctional region has a much greater sensitivity to interference by anoxia, anesthetics, or drug action. Second, the mechanisms are different: (1) The propagated action potential is all-or-nothing, whereas the end-plate potential can be graded in size. (2) The alterations in membrane permeability are quite different. At the neuromuscular junction, the ACh causes a *nonspecific* increase in cation permeability to potassium ions, sodium ions, and calcium ions. In the normal membrane during an action potential there is a cyclical series of *specific changes in permeability,* first for sodium and later for potassium. (3) The end-plate potential can only be recorded near the nerve-muscle junction because the action of ACh is localized and the length constant of the muscle (2.5 mm in frog) prevents the spread of the potential. (4) Finally, the link between prejunctional impulse and the end-plate potential is a chemical, ACh, while the link between the end-plate potential and the muscle action potential is the flow of current caused by the permeability changes.

Role of calcium

Extracellular calcium ions in a minimum concentration of about 10^{-4} M are absolutely necessary for the release of ACh during neuromuscular transmission (Hubbard 1974). The calcium ions enter the prejunctional membrane while it is invaded by an action potential and cause a powerful acceleration of the release of ACh. The entry of Ca^{++} lasts only a short time and therefore the duration of Ca-evoked ACh release is short. If the extracellular calcium ion concentration falls, or if the extracellular magnesium ion concentration rises, the amount of ACh released will be less and may be insufficient to cause normal neuromuscular transmission—so neuromuscular block may occur.

In hypocalcemia or hypermagnesemia of dairy cows, a state of semiparalysis may develop due to partial neuromuscular block. It can be relieved dramatically and rapidly by the administration of calcium ions in a suitable form.

Postganglionic autonomic transmitters

Transmission across an autonomic nerve-effector organ junction, as across the somatic nerve-muscle junction, occurs by release of a chemical at the nerve endings and its diffusion across the cleft to react with special receptive sites on the postjunctional membrane. This transmitter action is more prolonged than at the somatic nerve-muscle junction because the transmitter chemicals are much more slowly destroyed or removed. Thus the electrical and mechanical activity recorded from an autonomic effector, for example the cat nictitating membrane, long outlasts the duration of the stimulus.

Two chemicals are released from postganglionic autonomic nerve endings. Individual axons form and use only one of them, and are classified as *cholinergic* if the transmitter is acetylcholine, or as *adrenergic* if it is norepinephrine. The specificity of action of these substances is determined by the properties of the receptor sites in the postjunctional membrane; for example, norepinephrine reduces activity in intestinal smooth muscle, but excites cardiac muscle. The receptor sites also react with certain chemical compounds bearing a structional relationship to the transmitter substances; thus epinephrine, carried in the blood from its site of release in the adrenal medulla, will react with the adrenergic receptors.

Adrenergic receptors

The classical work of Dale (1906) established the variability of response to adrenergic stimulation in different tissues. Epinephrine or sympathetic nerve stimulation causes relaxation of many smooth muscles (e.g. intestine, bronchioles), but causes contraction of other types (e.g. vascular smooth muscle, sphincters of the gastrointestinal tract, ureter, cat nictitating membrane). Evidence obtained by studying the effects of various types of synthetic blocking agents, mainly on vascular and cardiac muscles, led to the conclusion that different types of receptors existed, now called α-receptors and β-receptors.

Alpha (α-) *receptors*. These are at junctions where norepinephrine acts. The reaction between the transmitter and the receptor can be prevented by adrenergic blocking drugs—e.g. ergot alkaloids, dibenamine, and phenoxybenzamine (Dibenyline). The release of the transmitter from the postganglionic nerve endings can be prevented by bretylium and guanethidine (short-term effect). Reserpine depletes the stores of norepinephrine normally found at the postganglionic terminals, preventing transmission until fresh stores are synthesized or replenished by infusion of norepinephrine (long-term effect).

Beta (β-) *receptors*. These are at junctions where norepinephrine causes relaxation or inhibitory responses (and also the excitor responses of cardiac muscle). In vascular smooth muscle the β-receptors react to circulating epinephrine and, weakly, to norepinephrine, and also react with the synthetic catecholamine, isopropylnorepinephrine (isoproterenol), which inhibits vascular smooth muscle and is presumed to have no reaction with α-receptors. These vascular inhibitory responses and the cardiac excitor effects of catecholamines are all blocked by dichloro-isopropylnorepinephrine (DCI) and nethalide.

Adrenergic receptors may be located in the cell membrane or inside cells and may in fact be enzymes for which the catecholamine acts as an activator or substrate.

The formation of norepinephrine commences with the hydroxylation of the amino acid phenylalanine to tyrosine, which in turn is hydroxylated to dihydroxyphenylalanine (DOPA). DOPA is decarboxylated by the enzyme dopa-decarboxylase to dopamine. Side-chain hydroxylation then leads to the formation of norepinephrine, whose methylation gives rise to epinephrine (Figure 52.11).

Gillespie and Kirpekar (1965), as a result of norepinephrine recovery experiments in the cat's spleen, found that enzymatic inactivation accounts for only 15 percent of the total transmitter released from the nerve endings. They suggested that reincorporation of the released transmitter into the nerve endings is the most important mechanism for the removal of norepinephrine.

Cholinergic receptors

Parasympathetic. Acetylcholine is released at two kinds of postganglionic parasympathetic nerve endings. At the first type ACh is excitatory (e.g. in the stomach or bladder). It causes depolarization of the postjunctional membrane and excitation of the smooth muscle cells.

At the second type of ending, ACh is inhibitory, as in postganglionic vagal nerve action on the pacemaker region of the heart. Here the transmitter receptor complex alters the electrical stability of the membrane by increasing its permeability to potassium ions and the membrane becomes hyperpolarized (Harris and Hutter 1956). This makes it difficult to excite by other depolarizing influences, and the heart rate slows.

These actions are blocked by atropine, which competes with ACh for the available receptor sites. Atropine's combination with the receptors is long lasting, and as long as it persists ACh is unable to combine with the receptors and is therefore blocked.

Sympathetic gamma (γ-) *receptors*. Acetylcholine is also the transmitter at the endings of certain postganglionic sympathetic nerves, including the dilator fibers running in the sympathetic outflow to the blood vessels in skeletal muscle. The γ-receptors form complexes with ACh that probably cause hyperpolarization of the smooth muscle cells leading to dilatation of the blood vessel. This action of acetylcholine is also blocked by atropine (see Chapter 48).

Other receptors

Delta (δ-) *receptors*. Other receptors have been postulated to account for the actions of other chemicals on structures innervated by the autonomic nervous system. In vascular smooth muscle, particularly in skeletal muscle, the dilator action of metabolites cannot be accounted for by the action of these substances at the α- or β- or γ-endings—suggesting there is a separate group of receptors with which these substances combine. These have been called δ-receptors.

Epsilon (ϵ-) *receptors*. Again in vascular smooth muscle the constrictor actions of polypeptides—e.g. anitdiuretic hormone, angiotensin, and other substances such as 5-hydroxytryptamine (5-HT)—have led to a suggestion that receptor sites must exist with which these substances react. These have been called ϵ-receptors. For example, the action of 5-HT in raising blood pressure is blocked by the 5-HT blocking agent, 1-benzyl-2-methyl-5-hydroxytryptamine, whereas a similar action of the parent substance tryptamine, which releases norepinephrine from α-endings, is not. This is highly suggestive of a specific receptor for 5-HT.

SYNAPTIC TRANSMISSION

The general principles for neuromuscular transmission also hold for transmission in the mammalian CNS and in peripheral autonomic ganglia. There are two main categories. In the first, *chemical transmission,* the presynaptic nerve on stimulation releases a chemical transmitter that alters the permeability of the postsynaptic membrane. The kind of alteration depends on the function of the synapse. Three types of chemical transmitter action are known: postsynaptic excitation, postsynaptic inhibition, and presynaptic inhibition (Fig. 41.18). In the second category, *electrical transmission,* the presynaptic nerve operates by the process of electrical coupling on the postsynaptic elements.

Chemical transmission

At the junctions an essential link between the nerves is a chemical that is released from the prejunctional terminal, which diffuses across the synaptic cleft and alters the permeability of the postsynaptic membrane (Eccles 1964).

Postsynaptic excitation

At the excitatory junctions the arrival of the presynaptic impulse is followed after a short delay by a depolarization of the postsynaptic membrane caused by a chemical released from the presynaptic nerve. The chemical diffuses across the synaptic cleft and forms a transmitter-receptor complex on the postsynaptic membrane. The transmitter-receptor complex causes a nonspecific increase in ionic permeability of the postsynaptic membrane, and the movement of ions across the membrane causes an inward current flow that leads to a depolarization of the surrounding neuronal membrane (Fig. 41.19).

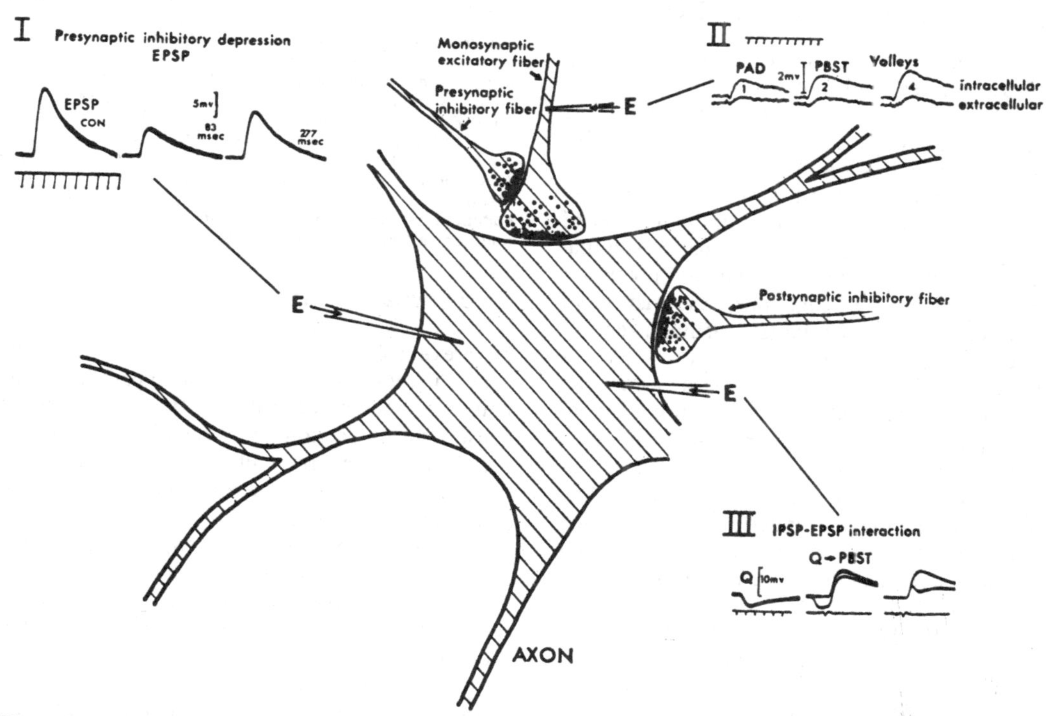

Figure 41.18. Diagram illustrating three kinds of chemical synaptic transmission at motoneurons. The large diagonally marked cell is a motoneuron. Two synaptic junctions are shown on its surface; one is excitatory (monosynaptic excitatory fiber), the other is inhibitory (postsynaptic inhibitory fiber). A third synapse is shown between a presynaptic inhibitory fiber and the monosynaptic excitatory fiber. The recording electrodes (E) have lines pointing to the records obtained with them. I. These three records show excitatory postsynaptic potentials (EPSPs) recorded from the motoneuron; the first record is a control and the second and third records show the effect of presynaptic inhibition in reducing the amplitude of the EPSP. II. The three records are from a primary afferent fiber and show the depolarization (PAD) caused by 1, 2, and 4 volleys of impulses in the posterior biceps semitendinous nerve (PBST) presynaptic inhibitory fiber. This activity depolarizes the synaptic excitatory fiber terminals. III. The three intracellular records from the motoneuron show first an inhibitory postsynaptic potential (IPSP) caused by a volley of impulses in a quadriceps (Q) nerve and then its interaction with an EPSP caused by a volley of impulses in a PBST nerve. Time marks are at 1 msec intervals in I and III and 10 msec in II. (After Eccles 1965, *Brit. Med. Bull.* 21:19–25.)

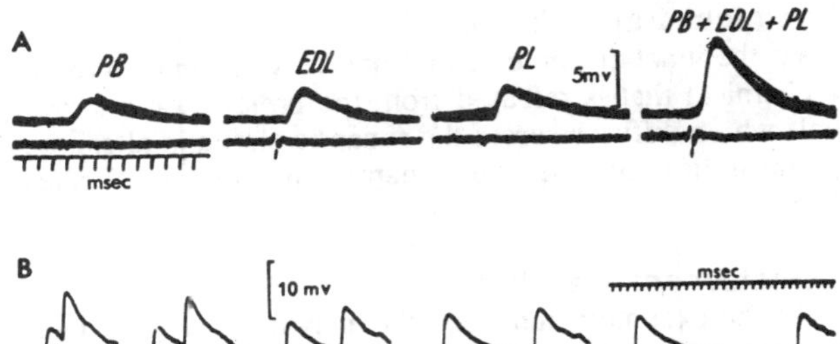

Figure 41.19. Excitatory postsynaptic potentials (EPSPs), recorded with intracellular electrodes from motoneurons in the cat. A, summation caused by the arrival, along several afferent paths, of impulses that arrive simultaneously at their respective synapses. The EPSPs caused in a single motoneuron by volleys in three afferent nerves are first shown separately (PB, EDL, PL) and then the spatial summation caused when they arrive together (PB + EDL + PL). (From Eccles, *The Physiology of Synapses*, Springer, Berlin, 1964.) B, in each record two presynaptic volleys of impulses were sent along the same afferent nerve fibers but at different time intervals. The widely spaced volleys in the right-hand record caused EPSPs that were almost identical in shape and size. At shorter intervals the two EPSPs were added together to cause a larger potential change; this is temporal summation. (From Curtis and Eccles 1960, *J. Physiol.* 150:374–98.)

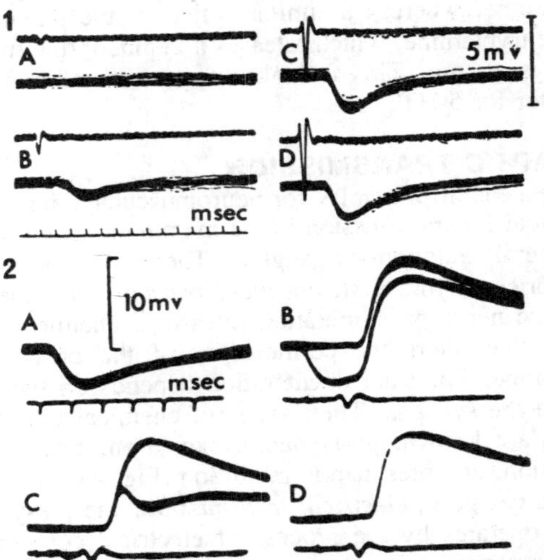

Figure 41.20. Postsynaptic inhibition recorded with an intracellular electrode as in Fig. 41.18. 1: IPSPs caused by stimulating an inhibitory pathway to a motoneuron. The number of active presynaptic fibers was increased progressively from A to D—spatial summation. (From Coombs, Eccles, and Fatt 1955, *J. Physiol.* 130:396–413.) 2: The interaction in a single motoneuron of inhibitory and excitatory synaptic action. A, the inhibitory potential (IPSP) alone; D, the excitatory potential (EPSP) alone. In B and C the two potentials are set up together, but with the interval between them less in C than in B. B and C show the EPSP as the large wave and then the effect of adding in the IPSP. As C shows, the two actions can almost cancel each other out. The result is that the neuron can be prevented from discharging by the suitably timed arrival of an inhibitory volley of impulses. (From Curtis and Eccles 1959, *J. Physiol.* 145:529–46.)

The membrane potential returns slowly to its resting value due to passive recharging of the membrane, at a rate determined by the resistance and capacity of the membrane. This excitatory postsynaptic potential (EPSP) lasts 1–120 msec, depending on the neuron.

The synaptic potential is graded in size (Fig. 41.19A) and can be varied in amplitude by altering the number of active presynaptic fibers—this is called spatial summation, the adding together of the small synaptic potentials arising at individual synaptic junctions. Summation of EPSPs can also occur when two volleys of impulses follow each other in the same presynaptic axons—this is called temporal summation (Fig. 41.19B). It occurs because the postsynaptic potentials last several times longer than the presynaptic impulses, so the transmitter released by the second presynaptic impulse is able to add its effects to the synaptic potential caused by the preceding impulse. These two phenomena underlie the summation that is evident in reflex activity. The synaptic transmitter is released in quanta or packets, as described for neuromuscular transmission.

Initiation of spike discharge. When the EPSP reaches a critical level (the threshold), it causes the neuron to discharge an impulse. In many kinds of neurons the impulse is initiated at the axon hillock. In motoneurons of the cat the axon hillock has a lower threshold for excitation (10mv) than the membrane of the cell body or dendrites (25 mv), so impulses start at the hillock and spread both down the axon and back over the cell body into the dendrites. After a neuron has discharged an impulse it is temporarily inexcitable. The length of this period varies: in motoneurons it restricts the rate of repetitive discharge to 50–100 per second; interneurons on the other hand can discharge at frequencies as high as 1500 per second.

Postsynaptic inhibition

The discharge of a neuron in response to an EPSP can be prevented by excitation of other presynaptic fibers. This inhibition is caused by a hyperpolarization of the neuronal membrane. When this hyperpolarization is caused by the action of a chemical liberated from the presynaptic fiber, the inhibition is called postsynaptic and the hyperpolarization is termed an inhibitory postsynaptic potential (IPSP) (Fig. 41.20, 1). IPSPs are in many respects similar in latency and time-course to EPSPs, but reversed in sign. The chemical transmitter, either glycine or GABA (gamma amino butyric acid), has a specific action on the postsynaptic membrane; it enhances the permeability for potassium and for chloride ions. The result is that the membrane potential moves closer to the equilibrium potential for these ions and the cells are more difficult to depolarize. When EPSPs and IPSPs are set up together in the same cell, the response of the neuron will be determined by the relative strengths of the excitatory and inhibitory action. In this way the discharge of a cell caused by excitatory impulses from one source can be controlled by the intervention of inhibitory effects from impulses in other fibers, an essential part of the regulation of reflex activity within the CNS.

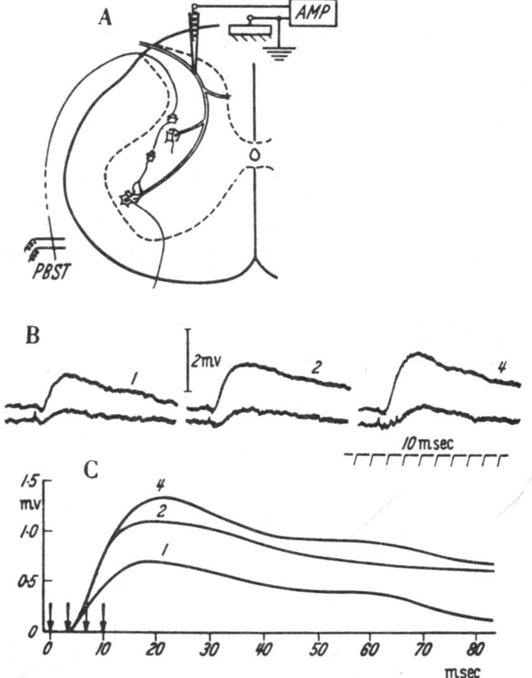

Figure 41.21. Presynaptic inhibitory action. Potentials in B are recorded intracellularly from a primary afferent fiber (as shown in Fig. 41.18 and A). The depolarization shown in B and C (PAD) weakens the excitatory synaptic action of the depolarized synaptic terminals. The PAD can be graded in size—C shows the effects of 1, 2, and 4 volleys in the inhibitory pathway. The inhibitory volley is in the posterior biceps semitendinosus nerve (PBST). The potential is long lasting. AMP is the amplifier, recording from a large afferent nerve fiber. (From Eccles, *The Physiology of Synapses,* Springer, Berlin, 1964.)

Presynaptic inhibition

The discharge of a neuron can be inhibited, even when no IPSP can be detected, by the depression of the excitatory presynaptic terminals. The terminals are depolarized by a transmitter that is liberated from axoaxonic synapses formed on them by interneurons—this is called primary afferent depolarization (PAD) (Fig. 41.21). The depolarized terminals release less of their excitatory transmitter when they are excited; the EPSPs are smaller, and the neuron is inhibited (Fig. 41.18, I). Presynaptic inhibition has a long time span (up to 300 msec). It is powerfully effective on the synapses made by the primary afferent nerves, and may control the inflow of sensory information into the CNS. It may prevent the sudden excessive incursion of new information from peripheral receptors and so smooth out any sudden fluctuation in sensory input.

Interference with junctional transmission

The specialized chemical sensitivity of the junctional regions, compared with the axons, makes them especially vulnerable to interference. The effectiveness of a synapse may be enhanced or depressed by certain chemicals that modify, often in a specific way, the effectiveness of the junctions. Considerable therapeutic use is made of these properties in many pharmaceutical compounds and the list grows steadily.

Electrical transmission

There are some synapses in invertebrates and fish where transmission is accomplished electrically, rather than through the mediation of chemicals. In these junctions the influence of the prejunctional nerve is mediated by the flow of electric currents through the postjunctional membrane. The source of these currents is the prejunctional nerve.

Excitatory synapses

Probably the simplest electrical-coupling system is found in the giant axons of earthworms and crayfish, in which the axon is divided into segments by septa. Electrical transmission also occurs at synapses between neurons in the spinal electromotor neurons of the electric fish—*Mormorydes*. It is not known whether a similar type of mechanism operates in the CNS of vertebrates other than the electric fish.

Inhibitory synapses

In many species of fish there are large cells in the brain (Mauthner cells) with their axon hillock region surrounded by nervous and glial structures. When the fine nerve fibers in the cap are active they apply a hyperpolarizing current (designated external hyperpolarizing current, EHP) to the hillock. The EHP increases the membrane potential and raises the threshold for the generation of an impulse by the cell. There are also chemical transmitter synapses elsewhere on the Mauthner cells, both excitatory and inhibitory, and these operate by chemical transmitter mechanisms (Diamond 1968; see also Eccles 1964 for comparison of chemical and electrical transmission mechanisms).

RECEPTOR POTENTIALS

The peripheral ends of afferent fibers are also highly specialized to form receptors (see Chapter 43). At the receptors nonnervous physical, thermal, and chemical stimuli are converted into nervous activity. The receptors are said to *transduce* the stimuli. Each mechanical pulse is converted by the receptor into a stream of impulses, and the intensity of stimulation is signaled by the frequency of discharge of afferent impulses. Electrical recording at a receptor shows that the first electrical sign of a response to the stimulus is a depolarization of the nerve ending in the receptor (Figure 41.22). An important property of this generator potential is that it is graded in size, according to the intensity of mechanical stimula-

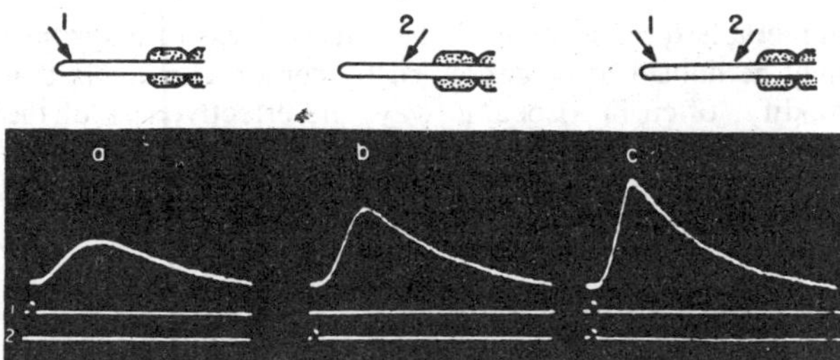

Figure 41.22. Generator potentials recorded from a Pacinian corpuscle in cat mesentery. The outer lamellae were dissected away and two mechanical probes (1 and 2) were arranged so that brief mechanical pulses could be applied to the specialized nonmyelinated nerve ending. Electrical records were made from the surface of the dissected core of the exposed corpuscle and show the generator potentials caused by each mechanical pulse alone (a to spot 1 and b to spot 2) and then applied simultaneously in c. The generator potential is graded in size, according to the intensity of stimulation. (From Loewenstein and Ishiko 1959, *Nature* 183:1724–26.)

tion. In some receptors the conversion of a maintained "natural" stimulus into a persistent depolarization allows the afferent nervous system to signal long-lasting changes in the environment, even though the individual afferent impulses last only 0.5 msec (Katz 1950). In some receptors an accessory cell is interposed between the stimulus and the nerve ending, and some kind of transmitter mechanism transfers the action from the transducer cell to the nerve. In other receptors the transducer is formed by a modification of the terminals of the afferent nerve (see Chapter 42).

The generator potential initiates impulses in the afferent fiber through the depolarization caused by the flow of current from the adjacent axon into the terminal of the axon. This kind of linkage is common to three mechanisms: (1) in the propagation of an impulse, where it is called the action current, (2) at the synaptic junctions, the transmitter current, and (3) in receptors, the generator current. At each site it switches on the regenerative sodium-carrier mechanism in the membrane of the nerve fiber and maintains or initiates the conduction of an impulse. The selective sensitivity of afferent fibers that allows them to respond in a discriminative way to a variety of stimuli is attributed to their endings (that are modified to form receptors), not to the conducting part of the axon (Davis 1961).

INTERCELLULAR COUPLING

In addition to the specialized junctional regions, there is evidence for regions of special contact between cells, for example in epithelial tissues (Loewenstein 1967). In such tissues the electrical resistance between cells is lower than the electrical resistance across the outer, free borders of the cell. The lower resistance is due to patches of junctional membrane, *gap junctions* (also called tight junctions), that are morphologically distinct from the synaptic junctions operated by chemical transmitters.

These junctions are regions of special and high ionic permeability and may also be places at which larger molecules are exchanged between cells. In the developing embryo regions of high permeability, revealed by measurement of intercellular resistance, are formed when, at critical stages in development or in tissue culture, cells make contact with each other. Cancer cells appear to lack the ability to form these junctions in the normal way. These gap junctions may therefore play an important part in providing an avenue by which developing cells can influence each other.

REFERENCES

Adrian, E.D. 1914. The 'all-or-none' principle in nerve. *J. Physiol.* 47:460–74.

——. 1921. The recovery process of excitable tissues. *J. Physiol.* 55:193–225.

Adrian, E.D., and Forbes, A. 1922. All-or-nothing response of sensory nerve fibres. *J. Physiol.* 56:301–30.

Agostoni, E., Chinnock, J.E., Daly, M. de B., and Murray, J.G. 1957. Functional and histological studies of the vagus nerve and its branches to the heart, lungs, and abdominal viscera in the cat. *J. Physiol.* 135:182–205.

Baker, P.F., Hodgkin, A.L., and Shaw, T.I. 1961. Replacement of the protoplasm of a giant nerve fibre with artificial solutions. *Nature* 190:885–87.

Brown, A.G., and Iggo, A. 1963. The structure and function of cutaneous 'touch corpuscles' after nerve crush. *J. Physiol.* 165:28–29P.

Cole, K.S. 1949. Dynamic electrical characteristics of the squid axon membrane. *Arch. Sci. Physiol.* 3:253–59.

Coombs, J.S., Eccles, J.C., and Fatt, P. 1955. The inhibitory suppression of reflex discharges from motoneurones. *J. Physiol.* 130:396–413.

Couteaux, R. 1960. Motor end-plate structure. In G.H. Bourne, ed., *The Structure and Function of Muscle*. Academic Press, New York. Vol. 1, 337–80.

Curtis, D.R., and Eccles, J.C. 1959. The time courses of excitatory and inhibitory synaptic actions. *J. Physiol.* 145:529–46.

——. 1960. Synaptic action during and after repetitive stimulation. *J. Physiol.* 150:374–98.

Dale, H.H. 1906. On some physiological actions of ergot. *J. Physiol.* 34:163–206.

Davis, H. 1961. Some principles of sensory receptor action. *Physiol. Rev.* 41:391–416.

Diamond, J. 1968. The activation and distribution of GABA and L-glutamate receptors on goldfish Mauthner neurones: An analysis of dendritic remote inhibition. *J. Physiol.* 194:669–723.

Duncan, D. 1934. A relation between axone diameter and myelination determined by measurement of myelinated spinal root fibers. *J. Comp. Neurol.* 60:437–62.

Eccles, J.C. 1964. *The Physiology of Synapses*. Springer, Berlin.

——. 1965. Pharmacology of central inhibitory synapses. *Brit. Med. Bull.* 21:19–25.

Elfvin, L.G. 1958. The ultrastructure of unmyelinated fibers in the splenic nerve of the cat. *J. Ultrastruc. Res.* 1:428–54.

Erlanger, J., and Gasser, H.S. 1937. *Electrical Signs of Nervous Activity*. U. of Pennsylvania Press, Philadelphia.

Fatt, P., and Katz, B. 1951. An analysis of the end-plate potential recorded with an intracellular electrode. *J. Physiol.* 115:320–70.

Furshpan, E.J., and Furukawa, T. 1962. Intracellular and extracellular responses of the several regions of the Mauthner cell of the goldfish. *J. Neurophysiol.* 25:732–71.

Gasser, H.S. 1955. Properties of dorsal root unmedullated fibers on the two sides of the ganglion. *J. Gen. Physiol.* 38:709–28.

——. 1960. Effect of the method of leading on the recording of the nerve fiber spectrum. *J. Gen. Physiol.* 43:927–40.

Geren, B.B. 1954. The formation from the Schwann cell surface of myelin in the peripheral nerves of chick embryos. *Exp. Cell Res.* 7:558–62.

Gillespie, J.S., and Kirpekar, S.M. 1965. The inactivation of infused noradrenaline by the cat spleen. *J. Physiol.* 176:205–27.

Grundfest, H. 1940 Bioelectric potentials. *Ann. Rev. Physiol.* 2:213–42.

Guth, L. 1968. Trophic influences of nerve on muscle. *Physiol. Rev.* 48:645–87.

Harris, E.J., and Hutter, O.F. 1956. The action of acetylcholine on the movement of potassium ions in the sinus venosus of the heart. *J. Physiol.* 133:58–59.

Hodgkin, A.L. 1958. Ionic movements and electrical activity in giant nerve fibers. *Proc. Roy. Soc.*, ser. B, 148:1–37.

——. 1964. *The Conduction of the Nervous Impulse*. Sherrington Lectures. Liverpool U. Press.

Hodgkin, A.L., and Huxley, A.F. 1952. A quantitative description of membrane current and its application to conduction and excitation in nerve. *J. Physiol.* 117:500–544.

Hodgkin, A.L., and Keynes, R.D. 1955a. Active transport of cations in giant axons from *Sepia* and *Loligo*. *J. Physiol.* 128:28–60.

——. 1955b. The potassium permeability of a giant nerve fibre. *J. Physiol.* 128:61–88.

Hubbard, J.I. 1974. *The Peripheral Nervous System*. Plenum, New York.

Huxley, A.F., and Stämpfli, R. 1949. Saltatory transmission of nervous impulse. *Arch. Sci. Physiol.* 3:435–49.

Iggo, A. 1956. Central nervous control of gastric movements in sheep and goats. *J. Physiol.* 131:248–56.

Katz, B. 1950. Depolarization of sensory terminals and the initiation of impulses in the muscle spindle. *J. Physiol.* 111:261–82.

Ling, G., and Gerard, R.W. 1949. The normal membrane potential of frog sartorius fibers. *J. Cell. Comp. Physiol.* 34:383–96.

Lloyd, D.P.C. 1943. Neuron patterns controlling transmission of ipsilateral hind limb reflexes in cat. *J. Neurophysiol.* 6:293–315.

Loewenstein, W.R. 1967. On the genesis of cellular communication. *Devel. Biol.* 15:503–20.

Loewenstein, W.R., and Ishiko, N. 1959. Spatial summation of electric activity in a nonmyelinated nerve ending. *Nature* 183:1724–26.

Pinsker, H., and Kandel, E.R. 1969. Synaptic activation of an electrogenic sodium pump. *Science* 163:931–35.

Smith, K.R. 1968. The structure and function of Haarscheibe. *J. Comp. Neurol.* 131:459–74.

Tasaki, I. 1953. *Nervous Transmission*. Thomas, Springfield, Ill.

Taylor, R.E. 1959. Effect of procaine on electrical properties of squid axon membrane. *Am. J. Physiol.* 196:1071–78.

Thesleff, S. 1960. Supersensitivity of skeletal muscle produced by botulinum toxin. *J. Physiol.* 151:598–607.

Watson, W.E. 1965. An autoradiographic study of the incorporation of nucleic-acid precursors by neurones and glia during nerve regeneration. *J. Physiol.* 180:741–53.

Webster, H. De F., and Collins, G.H. 1964. Comparison of osmium tetroxide and glutaraldehyde perfusion fixation for the electron microscopic study of the normal rat peripheral nervous system. *J. Neuropath. Exp. Neurol.* 23:109–26.

Young, J.Z. 1942. The functional repair of nervous tissue. *Physiol. Rev.* 22:318–74.

CHAPTER 42

Spinal Cord and Brain Stem Function | by James E. Breazile

Spinal cord
- Anatomical review
- Sensory systems in the gray matter
- Motor systems in the gray matter: intermediolateral nucleus
- Fiber tracts: ascending, descending
- Physiology: spinal animal, spinal shock, reflex activity
- Pathophysiology

Medulla and pons
- Anatomical review
- Fiber tracts that traverse the medulla oblongata and pons: dorsal funiculus—medial lemniscus system, external arcuate system; spinotectal, spinothalamic, and lateral lemniscus tracts; spinoreticular tracts; spinocerebellar tracts; spino-olivary tracts; corticospinal and corticopontomedullary tracts; vestibulospinal tracts; medial longitudinal fasciculus; central tegmental fasciculus; fasciculus solitarius; central pathways of the trigeminal nerve; cerebellar peduncles
- Nuclei and their connections: cranial nerve nuclei
- Physiology: salivary reflexes; reflex deglutition; mastication reflexes; suckling reflex; vomiting reflex; cough reflex; sneeze reflex; oculocardiac reflex (trigeminovagal reflex); blink reflex
- Postural reflexes: central mechanisms, vestibular organ
- Reticular formation of the brain stem: descending reticular formation

SPINAL CORD

Anatomical review

The spinal cord in cross section is shown in Figure 42.1. (Unless stated otherwise the anatomical and physiological information presented in this chapter is based upon literature dealing primarily with the cat and dog.) The gray matter, located centrally, forms a cellular column which extends throughout the length of the spinal cord. This portion of the spinal cord is composed of the cell bodies of neurons, supportive tissues, and nerve fibers. Surrounding the gray matter and comprising the remainder of the spinal cord is the white matter. This portion of the spinal cord is comprised of nerve fibers and supportive tissues which make up large tracts of fibers projecting rostrally and caudally within the cord. The size and shape of the spinal cord vary at different levels because of its internal structure. The neurons of the gray matter are arranged into distinct columns of cells (often referred to as nuclei), each of which subserves somewhat different functions.

The gray matter contains numerous multipolar cells of varying size and shape which are of two main classes, root cells and tract cells. Root cells, located in the ventral and lateral portion of the gray matter, are efferent neurons which project their axons out of the spinal cord

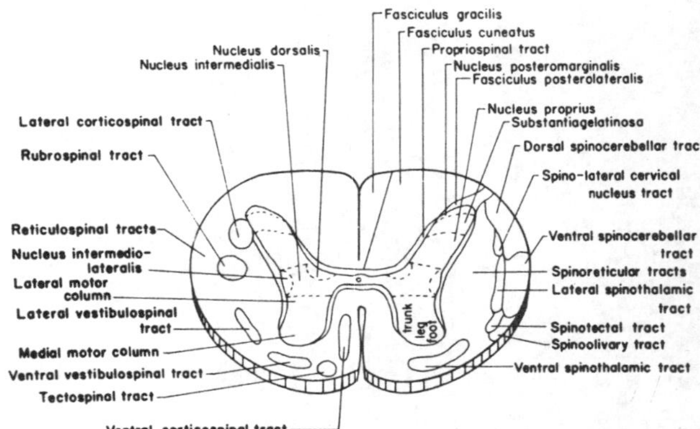

Figure 42.1. Spinal cord of domestic animals, principal ascending fiber tracts on the right, principal descending fiber tracts on the left. The nuclei of the gray matter are illustrated with the motor pools.

as ventral root fibers to innervate the somatic and visceral effector structures. Tract cells and their processes, on the other hand, are entirely confined to the CNS. The majority of these cells project their fibers into the white matter, where they may ascend or descend to form the fiber bundles of the white matter. Some of the neurons project their fibers only to other portions of the gray matter and are referred to as association or internuncial neurons. Many of the neurons project their fibers into the white or gray of the ipsilateral side of the spinal cord, whereas others project their fibers to the opposite side of the spinal cord. The latter are referred to as commissural cells.

Sensory systems in the gray matter

The cells of the spinal cord that contribute to the sensory systems are located in the dorsal columns of the gray matter. These cells and their processes are confined entirely to the CNS. They receive collaterals and direct terminations of dorsal root fibers. They send their axons either to the ventral horn for reflex connections or to the white matter where, by bifurcation, they may ascend and/or descend, forming intersegmental tracts of varying length. The longest of these fibers pass cranially to terminate in the brain.

The nucleus posteromarginalis forms a column of cells which extends throughout the length of the spinal cord. It receives afferents from several sensory systems and projects its axons into the lateral funiculus of the white matter, where they may ascend and/or descend to form intersegmental pathways.

The substantia gelatinosa extends throughout the length of the spinal cord. It forms the chief associative center of the dorsal horn for sensory systems. These cells form an important part of the pathways for reflexes and perception of pain, temperature, and tactile sensory information.

The nucleus proprius forms a column which extends throughout the length of the spinal cord and serves as an important relay for pain and temperature sensory pathways.

The nucleus dorsalis (dorsal nucleus of Clark) is limited in its extent within the spinal cord. In primates this nucleus extends from upper lumbar to lower cervical levels as a continuous column. In the bovine, however, it is limited to lower thoracic and upper lumbar levels (Goller 1963). The neurons of the nucleus dorsalis receive afferents from stretch receptors of muscle and project their axons to the cerebellum by way of the dorsal spinocerebellar tract.

The dorsal roots of spinal nerves are composed of thick myelinated fibers and of fine fibers, many of which are nonmyelinated (Fig. 42.2). The thick fibers are axons of the spinal cord afferents that conduct impulses from stretch receptors of muscle. The small myelinated and nonmyelinated fibers are axons of the spinal cord afferents that conduct impulses primarily from pain, temperature, and tactile receptors. The dorsal roots of each spinal nerve break up into a number of rootlets, each of which upon entering the cord separates into a small-fibered lateral bundle and a large-fibered medial bundle before entering the gray matter of the spinal cord. Each root fiber bifurcates into a long ascending and a short descending branch upon entrance into the cord. The small fibers pass along the tip of the dorsal horn to form Lissauer's tract. The large fibers pass into the dorsal funiculus, where they ascend and descend to make connections with neurons of the gray matter.

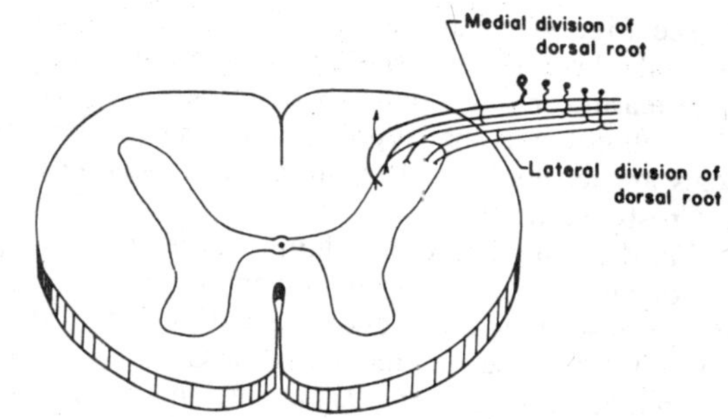

Figure 42.2. Dorsal root fibers. The large medial fibers possess a larger soma within the dorsal root ganglion than do the small lateral fibers.

Motor systems in the gray matter

The nuclei serving the motor systems of the spinal cord are limited to the ventral horn and the intermediolateral cell column. The motor systems are clearly divided into somatic efferent and visceral efferent systems. The visceral efferent system is limited to the intermediolateral cell column throughout the thoracic upper lumbar levels and sacral levels of the spinal cord. The remainder of the ventral horn primarily controls somatic motor activity. This portion of the gray matter is clearly divisible into medial and lateral nuclear groups.

Intermediolateral nucleus

This nucleus is limited to spinal cord levels T1 to L3. It is comprised of preganglionic neurons of the sympathetic nervous system. The sacral autonomic preganglionic neurons are located in an analogous region of the spinal cord, but they do not form a separate column in the lateral portion of the gray matter. The latter neurons are localized in the spinal cord of the cat (Schnitzlein et al. 1963). They form a wedge-shaped column of cells in the peripheral area of the intermediate gray matter adjacent to the lateral white funiculus.

The medial nuclear group extends throughout the entire length of the cord. It contains large motoneurons which innervate the muscles of the axial skeleton.

The lateral nuclear group innervates the remainder of the somatic musculature. It is greatly enlarged in thoracic and lumbar levels, where it innervates the muscles of the limbs. It contains very large neurons, particularly in the regions of the limb innervation. The exact innervation of the various muscles of the body has not been completely mapped out in the motor column, but there is an indication that in passing from medial to lateral in the ventral horn (see Fig. 42.1) the nerve cell bodies project their axons to the lateral trunk, shoulder or hip muscles, upper arm, forearm or leg, and foot, respectively (Goller 1963). Cell columns that supply nerve fibers to the flexor muscles are located dorsal to those that innervate extensors (Crosby et al. 1962).

Within the somatic motor columns there are two types of motoneurons, large or alpha ventral horn cells, so called because their conduction velocities fall in the α-group, 40–120 m/sec in the Erlanger-Gasser classification (Erlanger and Gasser 1937), and another group of cells which are small and are called γ-cells because their conduction velocities are from 20 to 44 m/sec. The γ-cells comprise about 30 percent of the total number of motor cells in the spinal cord. The large α-cells innervate ordinary or extrafusal muscle fibers and the small γ-cells innervate small specialized muscle fibers which form an inherent part of muscle spindles. These muscles are often referred to as intrafusal muscle fibers, and the nerve fibers innervating them (the γ-fibers) are termed fusimotor nerve fibers.

Fiber tracts

The ascending and descending fibers of the spinal cord are organized into more or less distinct bundles which occupy particular areas in the white matter (see Fig. 42.1). Fiber bundles having the same origin, course, and termination are known as tracts or fasciculi. Several fasciculi usually make up a funiculus. It is customary to divide the white matter of the spinal cord into three funiculi: dorsal, lateral, and ventral. The dorsal funiculus lies between the midline and the dorsal horn; the lateral funiculus is located lateral to the gray matter, bounded ventromedially by the ventral horn; and the ventral funiculus lies between the midline and the ventral horn.

Ascending tracts

The fasciculus gracilis and fasciculus cuneatus occupy the major portion of the dorsal funiculus of the spinal cord. The fasciculus gracilis, lying medially, runs the length of the spinal cord, but the more lateral fasciculus cuneatus is limited to thoracic and cervical levels. The fibers comprising these fasciculi have their cell bodies in the dorsal root ganglia. These fibers pass into the spinal cord with the heavily myelinated medial branch of the dorsal rootlets and turn cranially to terminate in the nuclei gracilis and cuneatus of the brain stem. Both these fiber tracts are somatotopically organized; that is, they represent the body surface in a topographically organized fashion. The fasciculus gracilis contains fibers from receptors in the rear limbs and caudal part of the trunk, and the fasciculus cuneatus contains fibers from the cranial part of the trunk, the forelimb, and the cervical regions. Therefore, sensory neurons serving tactile and kinesthetic systems are contained in these fasciculi, with the fibers from the caudal part of the body located medially and the fibers from the cranial part of the body located laterally. Although these fasciculi are well represented in all domestic animals, the fasciculus gracilis is quite small in most animals, leaving the fasciculus cuneatus (representing the cranial portion of the body) to comprise the greatest portion of the dorsal funiculus. The division into two fasciculi is somewhat artificial in that they represent only one tract with fibers serving different parts of the body. The two fasciculi also contain fibers that project into these fasciculi only to ascend or descend within the spinal cord itself, and such fibers synapse upon association neurons to initiate reflex activity or form association systems within the white matter.

The ventral and lateral spinothalamic tracts, although well defined in primates, are less clearly developed in other animals. The two tracts arise from neurons of the nucleus proprius and in primates project to the thalamus. In these species the ventral tract serves tactile and pressure sensory systems and the lateral tract serves pain and temperature systems.

In subprimate species these tracts also project to the thalamus but serve primarily as association pathways within the spinal cord and as spinoreticular pathways. Their role in sensory mechanisms for tactile, pressure, pain, and temperature sensation is not clear.

The spinotectal tract has much in common with the lateral and ventral spinothalamic tracts in that it subserves the pain, temperature, and tactile sensory systems in animals and man. This tract receives its axons from cells located within the nucleus proprius. These fibers cross to the opposite side of the spinal cord and ascend to terminate in the rostral colliculus of the midbrain.

The dorsal spinocerebellar tract is a large, uncrossed fiber system that projects directly to the cerebellum. It receives many of its afferents from the nucleus dorsalis. Since the dorsal nucleus of Clark is limited in its distribution to the thoracic and lumbar levels, those nerve fibers entering the spinal cord at lower levels must ascend within the dorsal funiculus before synapsing (Grant and Rexed 1958). These are for the most part large myelinated fibers of neurons serving muscle stretch receptors, such as muscle spindles and Golgi tendon organs. This nucleus receives a predominance of fibers from muscle spindles and can be considered primarily as a muscle spindle pathway to the cerebellum. In addition to these sensory systems, however, the dorsal spinocerebellar tract carries information to the cerebellum from tactile, pressure, and pain sensory systems. In many instances a single neuron contributing to this tract may be activated by several of these sensory systems.

The ventral spinocerebellar tract is mainly a crossed ascending tract that terminates within the cerebellum. The tract fibers have their origin in the nucleus proprius. These fibers cross to the opposite side of the spinal cord and ascend to the midbrain level, where they are reflected back upon themselves to enter the rostral cerebellar peduncle. The ventral spinocerebellar tract subserves primarily the Golgi tendon organ afferent system. The neurons giving rise to the ventral spinocerebellar tract also carry activity arising from cutaneous receptors, joint receptors, and other muscle afferents which are active when muscle is stretched or contracts.

Recent investigations of spinoreticular tracts indicate that fiber systems of the spinal cord project to widespread regions of the brain-stem reticular formation. These fibers arise from all spinal levels from cells located within the dorsal horn. They do not form a compact fiber bundle within the spinal cord, but are most prominent within the ventral portion of the lateral funiculus. Functionally these fiber systems represent an important component of a phylogenetically old system which plays a significant role in the maintenance of consciousness and perception. This system is discussed more fully as the ascending reticular formation.

The spino-olivary tract arises from cells of the dorsal horn. The fibers of these cells ascend contralaterally within the spinal cord in the ventral funiculus. These fibers arise from all levels of the spinal cord, terminate within the caudal olivary complex, and from there neural activity is relayed to the cerebellum ipsilateral to their spinal origin. Anatomical studies indicate that the spino-olivo–cerebellar pathway is somewhat analogous to the dorsal spinocerebellar tract (Morin 1955).

The spinocervical tract is a fiber system located within the dorsal portion of the lateral funiculus; its cell bodies are located within the dorsal horn of the gray matter. The fibers of these cells ascend ipsilaterally to terminate upon the neurons of the lateral cervical nucleus. This fiber system appears to be mainly a route to the cerebral cortex for the tactile system fibers, but it is known to subserve pressure and pain sensory systems as well (Morin 1955, Oswaldo-Cruz and Kidd 1964).

Descending tracts

The corticospinal tracts have their origin from cell bodies located in the cerebral cortex. These fibers, which for the most part are small in diameter, pass through the brain stem to form the pyramids on the ventral surface of the pons and medulla. At this level the tracts divide into two unequal portions. The larger portion crosses over to the opposite side (forming the pyramidal decussation), and the smaller portion descends on the ipsilateral side of the spinal cord. In this manner two corticospinal tracts are formed, a crossed or lateral corticospinal tract and an uncrossed or ventral corticospinal tract. The ventral corticospinal tract is located in the ventral funiculus of the spinal cord in most species and descends only to lower cervical or upper thoracic levels of the cord. Fibers of this tract cross over to the contralateral side of the cord before synapsing. The lateral or crossed corticospinal tract descends in the lateral funiculus in most species. In most rodents and a number of other mammals, however, it is located in the dorsal funiculus (Linowiecki 1914). In ungulates, the rabbit, and some other species it does not extend beyond the cervical region (Swank 1936), but in primates and carnivores it extends throughout the length of the spinal cord. Both of these tracts terminate upon internuncial neurons which control the activity of α- and γ-motoneurons. Only in primates, where fine motor control is required, do these fiber systems terminate directly upon α-motoneurons.

The rubrospinal tract arises from cells within the midbrain which comprise the red nucleus (nucleus ruber). The fibers, immediately upon leaving the nucleus, cross to the opposite side and descend through the reticular formation of the pons and medulla to enter the lateral funiculus of the spinal cord. In domestic animals this tract appears to be more prominent than in primates. This tract is a part of the extrapyramidal motor complex which plays a prominent role in the control of motor activity of animals.

The vestibulospinal tracts arise from the vestibular complex of the brain stem and descend into the spinal cord. The ventral vestibulospinal tract has its origin predominantly from the medial vestibular nucleus but receives fibers from the caudal and rostral as well. This tract is the spinal cord continuation of the medial longitudinal fasciculus of the brain stem. It extends the entire length of the spinal cord, presumably to function in the coordination of body musculature with head turning and eye movements. The lateral vestibulospinal tract originates in the lateral vestibular nucleus (Deiter's nucleus) and descends in the lateral funiculus of the spinal cord; in the cat about one third of the fibers cross to the opposite side to descend, the remainder descending ipsilaterally to terminate upon interneurons of the spinal cord which supply motoneurons. This tract has its greatest excitatory effect upon extensor muscles of the limbs.

The tectospinal tract is comprised of neurons with cell bodies located within the contralateral rostral colliculus. The fibers descend only into the upper cervical levels of the spinal cord to terminate upon internuncial neurons for the control of cervical muscular activity (Nyberg-Hansen 1964). This tract functions in the production of reflex head movements initiated by visual stimuli.

The reticulospinal tracts constitute a system of fibers originating from the pontine and medullary reticular formation and descending in the ventral and lateral funiculi. These fibers descend the full length of the spinal cord to terminate upon internuncial neurons of the gray matter. The function of these tracts is varied. They (1) modify reflex and voluntary motor activity, (2) control respiration, (3) exert pressor and depressor effects on the cardiovascular system, (4) control micturition reflexes, and

(5) control the central transmission of impulses within the sensory systems.

Physiology

The spinal cord, besides serving as a passageway for activity moving to and from the brain, contains a very complex reflex mechanism. It is through the modification of the reflex machinery of the spinal cord that high levels of the CNS exert an effect upon skeletal and visceral motor activity. The spinal cord of domestic animals comprises a much greater percentage of the total CNS than in man. It is estimated that 10 times more of the total CNS activity takes place in the spinal cord of the dog than in man (Gelfan 1963). In primates the spinal cord is no less complex than in domestic animals, but many of its functions have been relegated to control by higher structures.

Spinal animal

The reflexes that are inherent to the spinal cord can be studied in a spinal preparation. This preparation is made by removing the brain, either by transection at the spinomedullary junction or by ischemic destruction of the brain. Such an animal must be maintained by artificial respiration because the respiratory centers of the brain stem have been removed; disturbances occur in the cardiovascular system and in acid-base balance, however, which cannot be easily controlled. Because of these difficulties, the reflexes of the spinal cord are not maintained in their normal environment and therefore may be somewhat abnormal. Regardless of this difficulty, the study of reflex activity in a spinal animal is helpful in elucidating the capacity of the spinal cord to function in motor control. The following reflexes can be studied in the spinal animal: myotatic reflex, flexion reflex, crossed extensor reflex, scratch reflex, and extensor thrust reflex.

Spinal shock

Immediately following spinal cord transection in all mammalian species, all somatic and visceral reflex activity is abolished caudal to the lesion for a variable period of time. This severe depression of intrinsic spinal cord function is known as spinal shock. Reflex activity within the isolated portion of the cord usually begins to return, from within a few minutes (frog, chicken) to a few hours in most animals, and to increase in efficiency for some weeks. The myotatic reflex and flexion reflex are among the first to return to normal. Crossed extensor reflexes and long spinal reflexes such as the scratch reflex do not reappear for several days. The loss of reflex activity during this period is apparently not due to injury to the isolated portion of the spinal cord, but is due to functional disorganization resulting from the sudden removal of stabilizing influences from the brain.

Immediately after section of the spinal cord there is complete atony of the musculature of the urinary bladder wall, with a loss of tone in the sphincter muscles. Urine accumulates within the bladder until it escapes in small amounts at irregular intervals. This is referred to as overflow incontinence. Within a few days (7–10), tone returns to the bladder muscles and reflex micturition occurs. The bladder is not emptied at micturition, however, for a considerable amount of residual urine remains after each bladder contraction. Reflex emptying is usually facilitated or may be initiated by cutaneous stimulation applied to the abdomen, lower extremities, or perineum. The development of reflex bladder activity differs little among carnivores, pigs, sheep, and primates except in its time course. In carnivores, pigs, and sheep a reflexogenic bladder is usually established within the first week following cord transection. In primates 3–4 weeks may be required.

Little is known of the activity of the gastrointestinal tract following spinal cord transection. In dogs and pigs a diarrhea may be observed during the first week that is usually of a transient nature. The recovery of nearly normal gastrointestinal activity usually accompanies the establishment of a reflexogenic bladder, but defecation continues to be somewhat depressed. A reflex defecation can usually be facilitated or initiated by cutaneous stimulation of the skin supplied by the sacral nerves.

Vasomotor activity below the transection is profoundly depressed in carnivores, swine, and sheep. Cutaneous vessels are dilated and extremities are warm to the touch. Within a week, however, the marked vasodilatation has subsided, and local vasomotor reflex control can be demonstrated.

Reflex activity

A reflex is an involuntary activity in an effector organ (muscle, gland) elicited by the stimulation of a receptor organ. There are five component parts to most reflexes: (1) the receptor organ, which may be located either in the soma or in the viscera, (2) the afferent neuron, which has its cell body located in the dorsal root ganglion or an equivalent structure (such as the semilunar ganglion), (3) internuncial neurons of the spinal cord or brain stem, (4) efferent neurons which supply the effector organ, and (5) the effector organ, which may be skeletal muscle, smooth muscle, cardiac muscle, or gland. These structures form an arc through the CNS which is known as the reflex arc (Fig. 42.3). The only reflex arc which does not contain these five components is that of the myotatic reflex. This reflex does not utilize internuncial neurons; instead the afferent neurons synapse directly upon the efferent neurons. This is a monosynaptic reflex arc, because only one synapse is necessary for neuronal activity to be transmitted from the receptor to the effector organ. Other reflexes are polysynaptic, because one or more in-

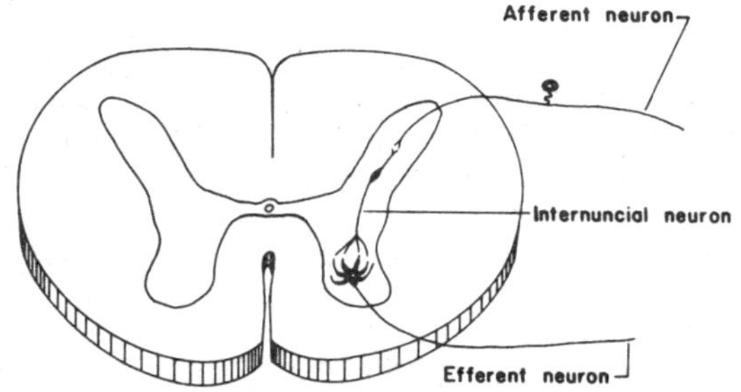

Figure 42.3. Typical reflex arc comprised of the afferent neuron which conducts information from a receptor organ to the CNS, an internuncial neuron which has various connections within the spinal cord, and the motoneuron which evokes activity within an effector organ

ternuncial neurons are interposed in the reflex arc, resulting in a minimum of two synapses for neuronal activity to pass from the receptor to the effector.

The organization of afferent neurons in their projection to internuncial neurons or to the motoneurons demonstrates several patterns of distribution. All afferent neurons may contribute to all types of distribution within the spinal cord. It is in this manner that coordinated patterns of reflex motor activity are elicited.

The simplest reflex arc is the monosynaptic reflex consisting of two neurons. This type of arc is used by the myotatic reflex (Fig. 42.4, 1).

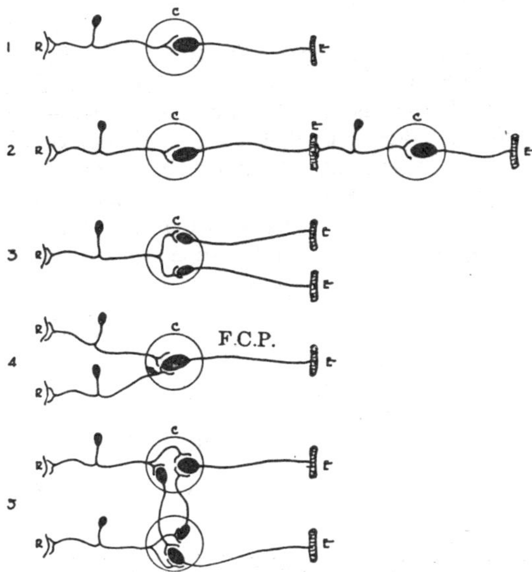

Figure 42.4. Ways in which afferent and internuncial neurons may be organized in the formation of reflex arcs. 1, monosynaptic reflex; 2, series reflex system; 3, divergence in a reflex pathway; 4, convergence in a reflex pathway; 5, interrelations of various internuncial neurons to give rise to a coordinated response involving more than one effector organ. (Modified from Herrick, *An Introduction to Neurology,* 4th ed., Saunders, Philadelphia, 1928.)

Several simple reflex arcs may be united in series so as to give a chain of reflex arcs (Fig. 42.4, 2). Activity in the first arc stimulates activity in the second, which in turn stimulates the third and so on. Such an organization is seen in the production of a series of myotatic reflexes alternating between flexors and extensors (see below).

Neurons may be organized in a diverging pathway so that more than one effector organ is stimulated by activity in one afferent neuron (Fig. 42.4, 3).

Neurons may be organized in a converging pathway so that more than one afferent neuron stimulates the same effector organ (Fig. 42.4, 4).

Internuncial neurons may be organized in their projections so that patterns of activity result which may involve both excitation and inhibition of various effector organ activity (Fig. 42.4, 5). Such reflex organization is present within the spinal cord for the production of smoothly coordinated motor activity.

Figure 42.5 demonstrates a sixth pattern of organization which is characteristic of many reflex arcs. It results in a closed-chain, recurrent pathway which may result in either self-reexcitation or inhibition of the reflex activity.

In examining reflexes, one must bear in mind that a reflex arc is not rigorously isolated from the general network of the nervous system, but is a single pathway among many. If a reflex arc is strongly stimulated, impulses will spread to neighboring pathways not usually involved. It should also be kept in mind that no reflex arc (not even the monosynaptic arc) is a separate chain of individual neurons. Arcs are often diagramed for illustrative purposes as being composed of neurons which devote their entire function to the operation of the reflex. In reality the monosynaptic reflex, as well as other reflexes, is only a small part of the CNS activity initiated by an afferent volley of neuronal activity. The interneurons of polysynaptic reflex arcs may be the same neurons that

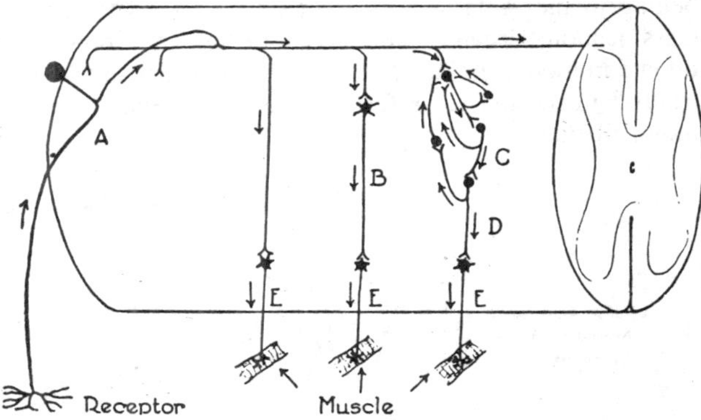

Figure 42.5. Monosynaptic, polysynaptic, and recurrent circuits for self-reexcitation or inhibition of the reflex arc. (From Larsell, *Anatomy of the Nervous System,* 2d ed., Appleton-Century-Crofts, New York, 1951.)

contribute to integration of sensory information to be transmitted to higher levels of the nervous system, or they may contribute to the integration of neuronal activity descending from higher levels for the control of motor and sensory systems within the spinal cord. It should be emphasized also that simple, unilateral reflexes rarely occur as the only function elicited by stimulation of a receptor system. In most instances when a muscle group (such as extensors of the stifle joint) is excited by a reflex activity, the antagonists to these muscles (the flexors of the stifle joint) exhibit a decrease in tone. This is a result of the phenomenon of reciprocal innervation. Reciprocal innervation is a reflection of synaptic inhibition within the motoneuron pool supplying the antagonistic muscles. It is exhibited in all motor activity, whether reflex or voluntary. The mechanism of reciprocal innervation allows antagonistic muscles to relax as synergists are contracting so that smooth flexion and extension of joints can occur.

Myotatic reflex. This reflex is sometimes referred to as the stretch reflex, but since other reflexes are initiated when muscle is stretched, it should be designated as the myotatic reflex to differentiate it from other activities of similar nature. The receptor organ for this reflex arc is located within skeletal muscle. These organs are called muscle spindles because of their overall shape (Fig. 42.6). These receptors are found in all skeletal muscles but more abundantly in antigravity muscles and in other muscles where control of muscle tone is of considerable importance.

Muscle spindles contain specialized striated muscle fibers called intrafusal fibers; these fibers are smaller than those of the skeletal muscle or extrafusal fibers and usually appear paler (see Chapter 43). The intrafusal fibers are oriented parallel to the extrafusal fibers and are indirectly attached to the sarcolemma by tapered ends.

There may be several motor nerve fibers to a muscle spindle. These fibers are small in diameter (3–8 μ) and belong to the A-gamma class of Erlanger and Gasser's classification (Erlanger and Gasser 1937). The fibers terminate in motor endings in the striated portions of the intrafusal fibers and are referred to as γ-efferents or fusimotor fibers.

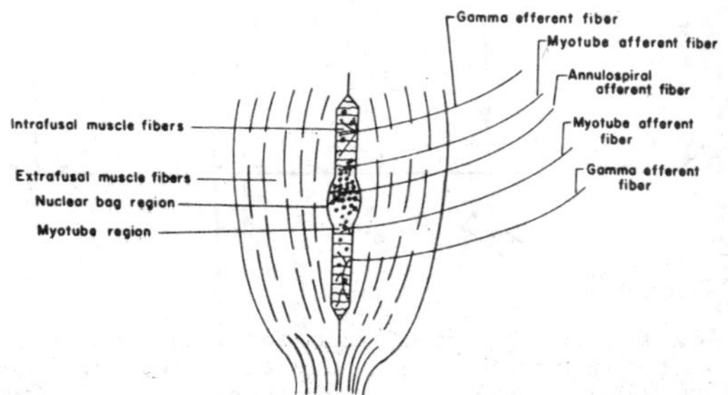

Figure 42.6. Muscle spindle fiber (greatly enlarged), demonstrating its orientation within a skeletal muscle and its innervation

The adequate stimulus for muscle spindle receptor organs is stretch of the myotube and nuclear bag regions. Such a stretch can be brought about through stretch of the entire muscle in which the spindle is located and thus expansion of the muscle spindle, or by stimulation of the fusimotor nerve fibers which elicits a contraction of the intrafusal muscle fibers (see Fig. 42.6). The application of the adequate stimulus through sudden stretch applied to the muscle or its tendon (as in tapping the patellar tendon) is an appropriate method for initiation of the myotatic reflex. Such a stretch applied to any tendon initiates a reflex activity which causes contraction of the extrafusal muscle fibers that were stretched. The afferent limb of the reflex is comprised of the annulospiral neurons with their cell bodies located within the dorsal root ganglia. These neurons project fibers into the spinal cord which pass into the dorsal funiculus and ascend to synapse in the dorsal nucleus of Clark which in turn contributes to the dorsal spinocerebellar tract. Collaterals from these nerve fibers project into the gray matter at the level of entrance into the spinal cord to synapse directly upon the α-motoneurons of the ventral horn (Fig. 42.7). The α-motoneurons supplying the extrafusal muscles which were stretched are discharged, and the motoneurons supplying the muscles which are synergistic to those that were stretched are facilitated, but may not be discharged. Therefore, if the lateral head of the triceps muscle were stretched and its muscle spindles were excited, the resulting reflex activity would cause a contraction of the muscle fibers of the lateral head of the triceps and a facilitation of the α-motoneurons supplying the remainder of the triceps complex. Thus the myotatic reflex is organized to initiate muscle contraction that resists stretching of skeletal muscle. When a joint is forcibly flexed, muscular activity is elicited by the myotatic reflex, which resists the displacement. This reflex serves as the basis for muscle tone and keeps the muscles in a proper state of contraction for the maintenance of posture.

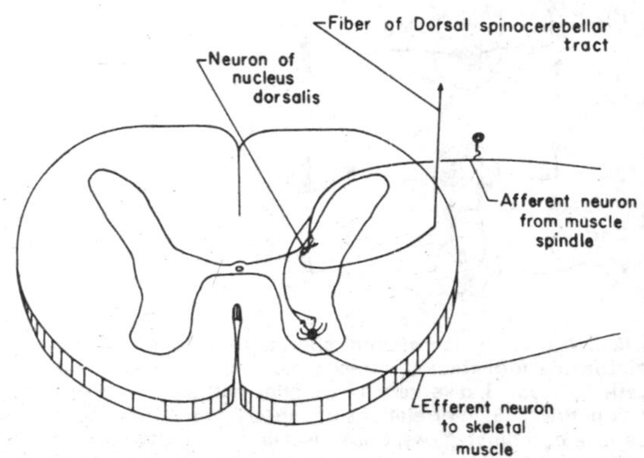

Figure 42.7. Connections of an afferent fiber from a muscle spindle, with neurons giving rise to the dorsal spinocerebellar tract and efferent neurons to skeletal muscle

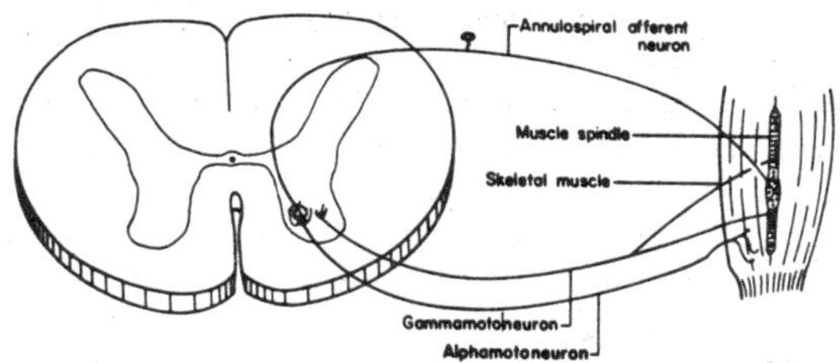

Figure 42.8. The γ-loop mechanism, including a γ-motoneuron to an intrafusal fiber of a muscle spindle, an annulospiral afferent neuron, and α-motoneurons to extrafusal muscle fibers forming the skeletal muscle

The intrafusal muscle fiber innervation controls the sensitivity of the muscle spindle to stretch applied to the extrafusal muscle fibers. If the fusimotor system is active, the nuclear bag regions of the intrafusal fibers are placed under tension and the myotatic reflex is easily elicited. The neuromuscular mechanism that allows the fusimotor neuron to alter activity within the α-motoneuron pools supplying extrafusal muscle fibers is referred to as the γ-loop mechanism (Fig. 42.8).

A myotatic reflex initiated within extensor muscles is accompanied by a decrease in muscle tone within flexor muscles. This is an example of a reciprocal innervation that is inherent in the organization of most reflex activity. The muscle spindle afferents which synapse monosynaptically upon the extensor motoneuron pools give off collaterals which terminate upon interneurons of the spinal cord gray matter that are inhibitory to motoneurons of antagonistic muscles.

The intensity of contraction of the skeletal muscles that is elicited by the myotatic reflex is graded to be commensurate with the intensity and rate of the stretch applied to the muscle. If a mild stretch is applied to the muscle, a slight contraction occurs. If a strong stretch is applied, a strong contraction occurs. A minimal amount of stretch is required to initiate the myotatic reflex. This stimulus is referred to as the threshold stimulus for reflex activity, and the response obtained is referred to as the liminal response. As stretches of increasing strength are applied to the muscle, a stimulus strength is reached above which no further increase in strength of contraction is obtained. This stimulus is called the maximal stimulus for reflex activity, and the response obtained is called the maximal response. However, before a liminal response is obtained impulses are being conducted along the afferent nerve fibers from the muscle spindle, and the threshold for reflex activity is a central phenomenon and is not entirely limited by the sensitivity of the receptor organs.

Inverse myotatic reflex. If a limb is forcibly flexed. muscle tone is increased in the extensors and decreased in the flexors (myotatic reflex). If the flexion is continued, however, a point is reached at which the tone of the extensors is suddenly decreased and the flexors increased; thus the limb is actively flexed, or it collapses under the flexing force. This is the inverse myotatic reflex, sometimes called the clasp-knife reflex (because of its characteristics in a decerebrate animal). The receptor organ for this reflex is the Golgi tendon organ. This is a stretch sensitive receptor organ located at the myotendinous junction or within the tendon. These receptors are activated whenever the tendon is stretched, by contraction of the muscle attached to the tendon. In the absence of muscle contraction, these stretch receptors exhibit a much higher threshold for activation than do muscle spindles and serve a reflex (inverse myotatic) which is antagonistic to the reflex served by muscle spindles (myotatic). This reflex is important in the control of somatic movement and is best demonstrated in a decerebrate animal, in which the myotatic reflex is hyperactive. The reflex, however, is operative in the intact animal.

Withdrawal reflex (flexion reflex). If a noxious stimulus is applied to the distal portions of a limb, the limb is quickly withdrawn from the stimulus. This is the withdrawal or flexion reflex. The motor activity elicited by this reflex is not always flexion of a limb, but it is always adequate to remove the body or affected part from the stimulus. Thus if a stimulus is applied to the proximal part of a limb, extension of the limb may be obtained. This phenomenon is referred to as local sign of reflex activity. Local sign phenomenon is dependent upon the organization of the projection of afferent neurons into internuncial pools and the organization of the latter in their projection to motoneuron pools so that the reflex activity is appropriate for removal of the initiating stimulus.

The receptors for reflex withdrawal are those which are part of the pain sensory system. The afferent neurons are small myelinated or nonmyelinated nerve fibers with their cell bodies located within the dorsal root ganglia. These neurons project their fibers into the spinal cord, where they terminate upon interneurons for projection into ascending pathways and for reflex connections. The α-motoneurons supplying muscles whose contraction would remove the affected part from the stimulus are excited and neurons to their antagonists are inhibited. This is another example of reciprocal innervation, which allows for an efficient reflex motor activity. This reflex uses one or more interneurons and is therefore a multisynaptic reflex.

Crossed extensor reflex. When the withdrawal reflex is elicited in a limb by a noxious stimulus at its extremity, the opposite limb extends. This results from excitation of the extensor muscles and inhibition of the motoneurons to flexors of the contralateral limb. This reflex is generally not easily elicited in the intact nonanesthetized animal, but is easily elicited in the spinal animal. In clinical neurology, this reflex is commonly an indicator of removal of descending influences that usually prevent its occurrence.

Reflex action which is quite similar to the crossed extensor reflex occurs in an animal for the maintenance of posture. As a limb is lifted from the ground, the limb of the opposite side is extended for balance. This, however, is not considered to be a crossed extensor reflex, because the adequate stimulus for elicitation of the motor activity does not result in a withdrawal of the opposite limb.

Scratch reflex. This reflex is elicited in the dog by the application of cutaneous stimuli to the skin over the dorsal and lateral surfaces of the thorax. When the stimulus is applied to the skin, the animal will stand on one rear limb and will scratch near the stimulated area in a manner appropriate to remove the stimulus. The scratch reflex can be elicited in both the intact and spinal animal, indicating that the mechanisms underlying its organization are located within the spinal cord. If the stimulus is moved to a new area, the scratching is directed there; thus the scratch reflex exhibits local sign, similar to that seen in the withdrawal reflex. The spinal cord pathways linking the cutaneous afferents with the motoneuron pools supplying the rear limbs are the propriospinal systems.

Extensor thrust reflex. If pressure is applied to the palmar or plantar surface of a dog's paw, the limb is extended into a rigid column due to simultaneous contraction of both extensors and flexors of the limb. This reflex is useful in providing a supporting response in the limb when it is placed upon the ground. The receptors serving this response are a combination of stretch receptors in the muscles and cutaneous pressure receptors in the paw. It should be emphasized that this reflex is the myotatic reflex, modified by afferent activity from cutaneous receptors. This reflex is important in the maintenance of the posture of the animal.

There are many other reflex actions which involve the spinal cord. These reflexes will be considered in subsequent discussions of the CNS control of somatic and visceral motor activity.

Pathophysiology

The physiology of the spinal cord is dependent upon the function and coordination of many different types of neuronal systems. Many of these neuronal systems are located within the spinal cord itself, but others are located within the brain or in the peripheral nervous system. A dysfunction of any of these systems may be reflected in the dysfunction of the spinal cord. The cells of the spinal cord may be hyperexcitable due to excessive excitation or insufficient inhibition from other regions of the nervous system, or due to a change in the metabolic state of the neurons within the cord. In such a situation the reflexes of the spinal cord may be hyperactive or the animal is said to be hyperreflexic. On the other hand, the neurons of the spinal cord may be depressed in their activity by excessive inhibition imposed by other regions of the nervous system or by a change in the metabolic state of the animal. In this situation the animal is said to be hyporeflexic, or to be in a state of areflexia if no reflexes can be elicited at all.

Normally the α-motoneurons are bombarded asynchronously by impulses arriving over interneurons or directly from dorsal root fibers and thus are discharging asynchronously. If, however, a dysfunction of the CNS causes the α-motoneurons to receive synchronous volleys of impulses, tremors or convulsions of the skeletal muscular system are seen. Such conditions exist in grand mal epilepsy, myoclonia congenita, distemper convulsions, and other conditions in domestic animals.

MEDULLA AND PONS

Anatomical review

The brain stem is defined anatomically to include the medulla oblongata, pons, midbrain, thalamus, hypothalamus, and epithalamus. This discussion will, however, be limited to the medulla oblongata and pons because the functions of the others are discussed in other chapters.

The medulla oblongata is the rostral continuation of the spinal cord into the brain. It is related dorsally to the fourth cerebral ventricle and the cerebellum, and rostrally is continued as the pons. The caudal boundary of the medulla is rostral to the most cranial rootlets of the first cervical nerve.

The pons is the continuation of the medulla and extends rostrally to the midbrain. It is defined best on its ventral surface by a large transversely oriented fiber system which projects into the cerebellum.

The internal organization of the medulla oblongata and the pons is much more complex than that seen in the spinal cord. The fiber tracts are not limited to the periphery of these structures, but are dispersed throughout the gray matter. The gray matter is organized into columns of cells which may be considered as continuations from the spinal cord, but it has lost its compact nature, and even though the nuclei are well organized, they are in most instances separated from adjacent gray areas by the intervention of fiber tracts.

Fiber tracts that traverse the medulla oblongata and pons

Dorsal funiculus—Medial lemniscus system

The dorsal funiculus of the spinal cord contains fibers which terminate in the caudal portion of the medulla oblongata within the nuclei gracilis and cuneatus. These fibers synapse within these nuclei in a somatotopically organized fashion. The cells of the nucleus gracilis and nucleus cuneatus give rise to axons which enter the medulla, arching ventromedially to cross the midline as the internal arcuate fibers. On the contralateral side of the brain stem these fibers collect into a compact bundle which ascends to thalamic levels as the medial lemniscus. This fiber tract represents the brain-stem pathway for tactile and kinesthetic sensory systems from the body. In its trajectory through the medulla, the medial lemniscus is joined by trigeminal tract fibers which represent these sensory systems of the head.

Dorsal funiculus—External arcuate system

A portion of the dorsal funiculus of the spinal cord terminates within the accessory cuneate nucleus. This nucleus and its projections via the external arcuate fibers to the cerebellum resemble very closely, both anatomically and physiologically, the cells of the dorsal nucleus of Clarke of the spinal cord and the dorsal spinocerebellar tract. This nucleus receives afferents from muscle stretch receptors of the cranial thoracic and cervical levels of the body and projects the activity arising from these receptor organs to the cerebellum. It therefore serves the same function as the dorsal spinocerebellar tract, with the difference that it serves the cranial portion of the body while the latter serves the caudal portion.

Spinotectal, spinothalamic, and lateral lemniscus tracts

The lateral and ventral spinothalamic and the spinotectal tracts of the spinal cord pass through the ventrolateral portion of the medulla and pons in their trajectory to the tectum and thalamus. Within the medulla and caudal pons, they join with the ascending vestibular and auditory tracts to form the lateral lemniscus. The auditory and vestibular pathways accompany these tracts only as far as the caudal colliculus of the midbrain. The spinotectal tract ends in the rostral colliculus, and the spinothalamic tracts continue on to the ventrobasilar complex of the thalamus or to project by way of the central tegmental fasciculus to the intralaminar nuclei of the thalamus.

Spinoreticular tracts

The spinoreticular fibers of the spinal cord ascend in the ventral portion of the lateral funiculus and terminate within the reticular formation of the medulla in a predominantly uncrossed fashion. These fibers terminate predominantly upon the nucleus gigantocellularis and the lateral reticular nucleus. The lateral reticular nucleus is a relay nucleus for spinocerebellar impulses conducting information from the tactile sensory system (Brodal 1949). These fibers project to the cerebellum of the ipsilateral side, somewhat analogous to the projection of the dorsal spinocerebellar tract for the stretch receptor system. The medullary reticular formation projects a major part of its efferents back into the spinal cord as a part of the reticulospinal tracts.

Spinoreticular fibers also project to the reticular nuclei of the pons, where they are distributed bilaterally and less numerously than in the medulla. Most of these fibers terminate in the caudal portion of the pons. The pontine reticular formation contributes to both the reticulospinal tracts for control of motor activity and the ascending reticular system which is important in the maintenance of consciousness in animals.

Spinocerebellar tracts

The dorsal spinocerebellar tract ascending in the lateral funiculus enters the dorsolateral portion of the medulla and forms the greater part of the caudal cerebellar peduncle (restiform body) as it enters the cerebellum. The ventral spinocerebellar tract passes through the medulla and pons to midbrain levels, where it is reflected back upon itself to pass through the rostral cerebellar peduncle to terminate within the cerebellum.

Spino-olivary tracts

The spino-olivary tracts, ascending in the lateral funiculus of the spinal cord, enter the caudal olivary complex of the ipsilateral side. Fibers arising from the cells of the caudal olivary complex arch mediodorsally to the contralateral side to enter the caudal cerebellar peduncle of the cerebellum.

Corticospinal and corticopontomedullary tracts

Fibers that have their cell bodies located within the cerebral cortex pass through the internal capsule and cerebral peduncles to form the pyramid that is seen on the ventral surface of the brain stem. This tract at the pyramidal level contains predominantly corticospinal tract fibers which decussate and enter the spinal cord for control of α- and γ-motoneurons. In its passage through the pons and medulla this tract gives off fibers to the pontine gray (corticopontine fibers) and to the gray matter of the medulla (corticomedullary fibers). A portion of the pontine terminations synapse upon neurons which project their axons across the brain stem to form the middle cerebellar peduncle and enter the cerebellum. The remainder of the pontine and medullary terminals synapse upon cells of the reticular formation or upon internuncial neurons for control of α- and γ-motoneurons to skeletal muscle supplied by the cranial nerves. In the cat and monkey a portion of these fibers terminate within sensory relay nuclei for cortical control of sensory phenomena (Kuypers 1958, 1960; Kuypers et al. 1961; Jabbur and Towe 1960).

Vestibulospinal tracts

The lateral vestibulospinal tract arises from the lateral vestibular nucleus and descends within the ventral funiculus of the spinal cord for alteration of α- and γ-motoneuron activity. The ventral vestibulospinal tract is a portion of a large fiber complex having its origin primarily from the medial vestibular nucleus. This fiber system is the medial longitudinal fasciculus.

Medial longitudinal fasciculus

This fiber system has its primary origin in the vestibular nuclear complex described above. The fibers are both crossed and uncrossed, and many bifurcate into ascending and descending branches. The descending fibers form the ventral vestibulospinal tract. The ascending fibers terminate within the nuclei containing α-motoneurons that control the extraocular muscles (cranial nerves III, IV, and VI). The medial longitudinal fasciculus is also comprised of fibers which have their origin from other regions of the CNS than the vestibular nuclear complex. All of these fibers are descending toward the spinal cord or from higher levels to the pons and medulla. These include: fibers from the interstitial nucleus of Cajal (in the midbrain) to upper cervical levels of the spinal cord, tectobulbar, and tectospinal tracts; reticulospinal tracts from pontine and medullary reticular formation; and fibers from rostral brain stem nuclei projecting to the caudal olivary complex.

Central tegmental fasciculus

This tract descends into the pons and medulla from higher levels to terminate within the caudal olivary complex. The fibers comprising this fasciculus at these levels have their origin from the cerebral cortex, the globus pallidus, the caudate nucleus, the red nucleus, and the midbrain tegmentum (Walberg 1956, 1960). These nuclei form an important part of the somatic motor system. The fibers of the central tegmental tract terminate upon parts of the caudal olivary complex from which fibers are projected to the contralateral cerebellum via the caudal cerebellar peduncle.

The central tegmental tract receives many fibers that have their origin within the reticular formation and ascend to higher levels as a portion of the ascending reticular formation.

Fasciculus solitarius

This tract, also known as the descending tract of the glossopharyngeal, facial, and vagus nerves, is comprised of the central fibers of these nerves. Their cell bodies are located within the petrosal ganglion of the glossopharyngeal nerve, the geniculate ganglion of the facial nerve, and the nodosal ganglion of the vagus nerve, respectively. The fibers of this fasciculus terminate within the nucleus of the fasciculus solitarius for relay to other regions of the CNS. Projections of the nucleus of the fasciculus solitarius form a part of the gustatory sensory system, as well as contribute to important visceral and somatic reflex activities originating from the brain stem.

Central pathways of the trigeminal nerve

The CNS projections of the neurons of the trigeminal nerve are of enough significance to be considered under a separate heading. The afferent neurons of the trigeminal nerve have their cell bodies within the trigeminal ganglion (semilunar ganglion). The central processes of these neurons enter the brain stem at the level of the pons and divide into a short ascending and a long descending tract. Most of the afferent fibers of the trigeminal nerve contribute to both tracts by bifurcation; a few fibers, however, either ascend or descend without bifurcation. The ascending fibers terminate within the rostral sensory nucleus of the trigeminal nerve, while the descending fibers terminate within the nucleus of the descending tract of the trigeminal nerve. The ascending tract projects for only a short distance within the brain stem before synapsing upon the neurons of the rostral sensory nucleus, but the descending tract may descend into the cervical levels of the spinal cord before terminating within the nucleus of the descending tract. Neurons of the nucleus of the descending tract of the trigeminal nerve are located as far caudally as the third cervical level of the spinal cord in the cat (Kerr 1961) and the fifth cervical level of the cord in the bovine (Gudden 1891). At these levels the cells of the nucleus of the descending tract are intermingled with those of the sensory systems from the cervical region. Throughout the length of the medulla and caudal pons this structure occupies a large part of the brain stem. These fiber systems serve the sensory systems from the head and in doing so contribute to reflex activity within the brain stem that is analogous to that seen in the spinal cord.

A small afferent component of the trigeminal nerve does not have its cell bodies located within the trigeminal ganglion. These fibers enter the brain stem and pass to cell bodies in the mesencephalon. These cells, which extend throughout the length of the rostral pons and the entire midbrain, are connected to stretch receptors of the masticatory muscles and pressure receptors associated with the teeth (Jerge 1963).

Cerebellar peduncles

Three very large fiber tracts that have been mentioned briefly are the rostral, middle, and caudal cerebellar peduncles. These form the pathways for afferent and efferent connections to the cerebellum.

There are several other fiber tracts that traverse the medulla and pons and are associated with sensory systems. They will be discussed with these sensory systems.

Nuclei and their connections

Cranial nerve nuclei

The nuclei associated with the cranial nerves form a large portion of the nuclei of the brain stem. These extend from the cranial spinal cord levels through midbrain levels of the brain stem. They are organized into five cellular columns parallel to the long axis of the brain stem. The columns represent the somatic, branchial, and

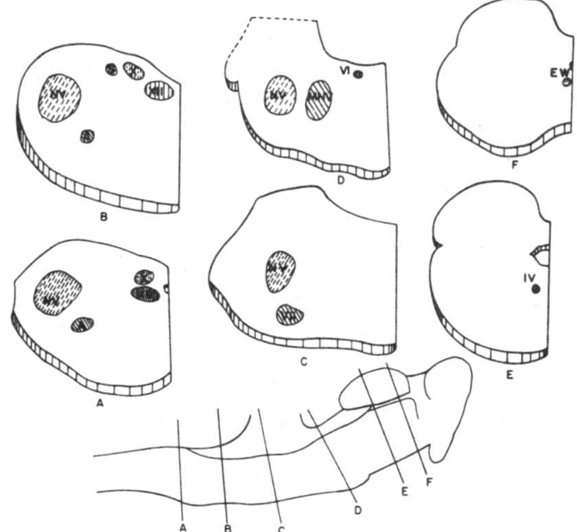

Figure 42.9. Sensory and motor columns within the brain stem, demonstrating the disposition of various functionally related nuclei. The somatic motor column contains the hypoglossal (XII), trochlear (IV), abducent (VI), and oculomotor nuclei (III, not shown). The branchial motor column contains the motor nucleus of the trigeminal nerve (MNV), the facial nucleus (VII), the nucleus ambiguus (A), and the spinal accessory nucleus (not shown). The visceral motor column includes the Edinger-Westphal nucleus (EW), the dorsal motor nucleus of the vagus (X), and the rostral and caudal salivatory nuclei (not shown). The visceral sensory column contains the nucleus of the fasciculus solitarius (S). The somatic sensory column contains the sensory nuclei of the trigeminal complex (NV).

visceral motor columns and the visceral and somatic sensory columns. Within these nuclear columns are 14 nuclei on each side of the brain stem (Fig. 42.9).

The somatic motor column supplies all skeletal muscle of the head that is derived from the somites. This includes the extrinsic muscles of the eye and the muscle of the tongue. This column of cells occupies a dorsomedial position within the brain stem and includes four nuclei: the hypoglossal, trochlear, abducent, and oculomotor nuclei. The neurons comprising these nuclei are similar to those of the ventral horn of the spinal cord.

The branchial motor column is comprised of four nuclei which supply skeletal muscles derived from the branchial arches in the embryo. These include the motor nucleus of the trigeminal nerve, the facial nucleus, the nucleus ambiguus, and the spinal-accessory nerve nucleus. The neurons of this column are similar to those found in the somatic motor column.

The visceral motor column supplies parasympathetic innervation to smooth muscle and glands of the head and to cervical, thoracic, and abdominal viscera as far caudal as the left colic flexure. This column includes the rostral and caudal salivatory nuclei, the Edinger-Westphal nucleus, and the dorsal motor nucleus of the vagus. The Edinger-Westphal nucleus supplies the intrinsic eye muscles; the rostral salivatory nucleus supplies all the major glands of the head except the parotid salivary gland; the caudal salivatory nucleus supplies the parotid salivary gland; and the dorsal motor nucleus of the vagus supplies the cervical, thoracic, and abdominal viscera. This column is analogous to the intermediolateral cell column of the spinal cord.

The visceral sensory column is comprised of one nucleus, the nucleus of the fasciculus solitarius. This nucleus receives taste afferents and general visceral afferents from the mouth, pharynx, larynx, thoracic, and abdominal viscera.

The somatic sensory column receives general somatic afferents from the face and meninges. This column consists of the sensory nuclei of the trigeminal complex. It is continuous with and is analogous to the dorsal horn gray matter of the spinal cord.

Ten of these fourteen nuclei are located within distinct columns. The facial nucleus and the nucleus ambiguus have, however, migrated ventrally into the brain stem and are not in line with the remaining nuclei of their column. The Edinger-Westphal nucleus has migrated to lie rostral to the somatic motor column, and the spinal accessory nucleus has migrated caudally into the cervical spinal cord. These migrations occur during embryogenesis because of a process known as neurobiotaxis, whereby nuclei are attracted toward their innervating nerve fibers during development. The facial nucleus, the spinal accessory nucleus, and the nucleus ambiguus are under considerable control from the cerebral cortex and have migrated toward the corticobulbar and corticospinal tracts from which this control is derived.

The cells of the special somatic afferent nerves do not form distinct columns within the brain stem. These nuclei are associated with the auditory and vestibular sensory systems.

Other nuclei that comprise a portion of the medulla, pons, and midbrain are the nucleus gracilis, nucleus cuneatus, caudal olivary complex, pontine gray nucleus, and the reticular formation.

Physiology

Functionally the medulla and pons are not basically different from the spinal cord. These structures form a reflex center with controls imposed from higher centers of the brain and from the spinal cord.

Salivary reflexes

Materials placed in the mouth stimulate receptors of general sense as well as taste and produce activity in the glossopharyngeal, facial, and trigeminal nerves. Action potentials conducted over these nerves are distributed to internuncial neurons in the reticular formation of the medulla which alter activity in turn in either the dorsal or ventral salivatory nuclei or both. Through these nuclei and their efferent fibers, which are distributed via the glossopharyngeal nerve to the mandibular and lingual salivary glands and the facial nerve to the parotid salivary gland, a reflex salivary flow is initiated. The type of reflex activity elicited is dependent upon the substance placed in the mouth. Taste afferents elicit the production of a salivary flow that is abundant in enzymes and mucin so that the material being eaten is lubricated for easy swallowing and digestion. If nonedible material is placed in the mouth, such as crushed rock, a liquid saliva low in organic matter is produced so that the material is washed away (see Chapter 20).

Reflex deglutition

If the soft palate, the dorsal surface of the epiglottis, or the posterior wall of the oral pharynx below the soft palate is stimulated in the dog or cat, a swallowing reflex will be initiated. The afferent limb of this reflex uses the glossopharyngeal, trigeminal, and vagus nerves. Fibers that project into the brain stem terminate within the reticular formation near the nucleus tractus solitarius. Located in this region, but distinct from the internuncials activating skeletal muscles in the swallowing reflex, are neurons that control respiration. These neurons are influenced by activity in the swallowing center, so that respiration is interrupted during deglutition (Hukuhara and Okada 1956, Sumi 1963). The internuncial neurons forming the swallowing center control activity in certain nuclei of the hypoglossal, vagus, and glossopharyngeal nerves. These nerves control the muscles of the pharynx, larynx, hyoid apparatus, and tongue. In the swallowing reflex, there is an organized sequence of muscular activity to propel material from the oral cavity caudally into the upper esophagus. The vagus nerve supplies the upper end of the esophagus and initiates peristalsis which sweeps distally along the esophagus toward the stomach (see Chapter 20).

Mastication reflexes

Normally mastication is under conscious control, but it is always modified to a great extent by reflexes which protect oral structures from trauma. The afferent limb of these reflexes involves the sensory receptor organs of the oral and lingual mucosa and the fibers of the trigeminal, facial, and glossopharyngeal nerves. These fibers enter the brain stem and influence the activity of the motor nucleus of the trigeminal nerve through the intervention of internuncial neurons located within the reticular formation.

Suckling reflex

In newborn animals a mechanical stimulus applied to the lips, tongue, and oral mucosa initiates a suckling reflex. This is a normal feeding response in immature animals and is carried out entirely by medullary and pontine structures. The afferent limb of this reflex involves the trigeminal and facial nerves, and the efferent limb involves the facial, hypoglossal, and trigeminal nerves. The resulting motor activity is adequate for suckling of milk.

Vomiting reflex

Emesis is a reflex action which removes irritating materials from the stomach and upper intestinal tract. The usual adequate stimulus for initiating this reflex is the presence of irritating material within these organs, but there are many other types of stimuli that give rise to this reflex, for example, stimuli from other abdominal organs, such as the kidney, uterus, and bladder, or from the vestibular receptor system. In fact, general visceral afferents all over the body can under the proper conditions give rise to the vomiting reflex. Psychic influences, particularly in man, may at times give rise to this reflex. Vomiting may be initiated in the dog by an irritative lesion within the external auditory canal. The afferents from this region which give rise to the reflex are believed to be in the vagus nerve and its projection to CNS structures which receive visceral afferents initiating the reflex. Vomiting induced by recurrent motion (as in car sickness) is produced by a rhythmic stimulation of the vestibular sensory system.

Within the medulla, in the region of the nucleus tractus solitarius and involving it and a portion of the surrounding reticular formation, is a region which upon stimulation produces vomiting. This region is referred to as the vomiting center (Fig. 42.10). When this region is stimulated, either by an electrical stimulus or by stimulation of the peripheral nerves (such as the vagus, glossopharyngeal, facial, and vestibular nerves), vomiting will be produced. These nerves project their fibers directly to this region before synapsing within the brain stem. The vestibular nerves project fibers first to the vestibular nuclear complex of the medulla and pons, and from there fibers are projected to the vomiting center.

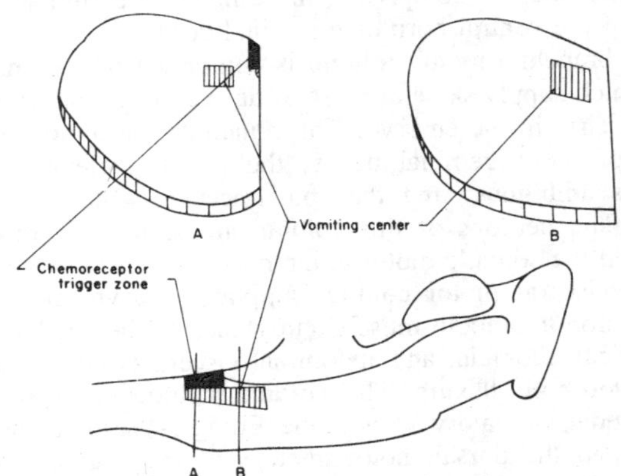

Figure 42.10. Location of the chemoreceptor trigger zone and the vomiting center within the medulla

A chemoreceptor trigger zone, located within the area postrema of the medulla (see Fig. 42.10), is sensitive to apomorphine, morphine, ergot alkaloids, and digitalis glycosides. Activity within this zone can initiate vomiting through its neural connections with the vomiting center.

The internuncial pathways and the efferent limb of the vomiting reflex are quite complex. The efferent pathways that lead from the vomiting reflex are as follows. Fibers project from neurons of the vomiting center to the rostral and caudal salivatory nuclei to initiate efferent activity within the facial and glossopharyngeal nerves. This activity results in profuse salivation which may precede the act of emesis. Other fibers project to neurons which control respiration and cardiovascular systems so that respiration is altered and blood pressure drops. The efferents giving rise to these effects involve the reticular formation of the brain stem (respiratory and cardiovascular centers), the phrenic nucleus (in lower cervical spinal cord), the intermediolateral cell column of the spinal cord, and the vagus nerve. Efferent connections from the vomiting center project to the nucleus ambiguus for control of the pharynx, larynx, and hyoid muscles during the act of emesis.

The motor activity that occurs during the vomiting reflex is very well organized and involves constriction of the pylorus of the stomach, relaxation of the cardia, contraction of the abdominal skeletal muscles, cessation of respiration, and constriction of the nasopharynx. This well-coordinated skeletal and smooth muscle activity is due to precise CNS control.

Cough reflex

A mechanical stimulus applied to the tracheal or laryngeal mucosa results in a cough. A well-coordinated complex of muscular activity forces air out of the lungs through the tracheal and laryngeal passageway. This reflex is initiated by a rapid inspiration followed by closure of the glottis. An expiration is begun with the glottis closed, and the glottis is suddenly opened (by relaxation of the muscles involved) and air is forced out of the respiratory passageways. The afferent limb of this reflex involves the vagus nerve from the viscera concerned. These afferents enter the brain stem to synapse in the nucleus of the fasciculus solitarius or in the surrounding reticular formation. From here fibers are projected to the spinal cord (via reticulospinal tracts) to control respiration and to the nucleus ambiguus to control muscular activity within the larynx.

Sneeze reflex

This reflex is very much like the cough reflex, but it removes foreign material from the nasal passageways rather than from the larynx or trachea. The afferent limb of this reflex is the nerve fibers of the trigeminal nerve that supply the mucosa of the nasal passageways. The central connections of these fibers involve the sensory nuclei of the trigeminal nerve rather than the nucleus of the fasciculus solitarius. From here fibers project to various regions of the brain-stem reticular formation and to the nucleus ambiguus so that appropriate respiratory activity is initiated to remove the stimulus from the nasal mucosa.

Oculocardiac reflex (trigeminovagal reflex)

If a stimulus applied to the eye or the orbit excites receptors of the ophthalmic division of the trigeminal nerve, a reflex slowing of the heart is observed. This is the result of a multisynaptic reflex involving the trigeminal nerve. Trigeminal fibers synapse within the sensory nuclei of the trigeminal nerve, and from these nuclei neural connections are made with the cardiovascular centers of the brain-stem reticular formation. The cardioinhibitory center of the medulla is most strongly excited by this activity and results in a slowing of the heart through excitation of the vagus nerve.

Similar reflexes may be initiated by afferent activity within other cranial nerves. Excitation of the carotid sinus initiates activity within the glossopharyngeal nerve which results in reflex slowing of the heart. This reflex is thought to be organized in a similar fashion to the oculocardiac reflex.

Blink reflex

This reflex results in a protective response that prevents damage to the cornea by foreign objects. When the ophthalmic division of the trigeminal nerve is stimulated, a multisynaptic reflex arc involving the trigeminal nerve and the facial nerves is activated. The resulting skeletal muscular activity results in a closure of the eyelid. This reflex is used many times a day to remove small particles of material from the eye and to keep the cornea bathed with lacrimal secretion. If the foreign material is not removed, lacrimation is increased through the intervention of the lacrimal reflex. The afferent limb of the lacrimal reflex is the same as for the blink reflex; the efferent limb involves the rostral salivatory nucleus of the brain stem and the facial nerve fibers to the lacrimal gland.

Postural reflexes

Each species of animal maintains a normal orientation in space which is referred to as a normal posture and attitude. The maintenance of this posture is accomplished through the continuous activity of a complex of interrelated reflexes which are referred to as postural reflexes. These reflexes can be divided into two general types: supporting responses and attitudinal responses. Supporting responses involve reflex activity that initiates coordinated muscular activity converting the limbs into pillars to support the body against the pull of gravity. Attitudinal responses alter skeletal muscle tone so as to maintain the body in an attitude which is appropriate to various positions of the head.

Supporting responses involve two classes of reflexes, based upon the complexity of the muscular activity involved. Local supporting reflexes limit their activity to the segments of the spinal cord that contribute to the afferent limb of the reflexes. Segmental supporting reflexes may produce alterations in muscular activity in all limbs even when the afferent limb of the reflex is limited to only lumbar or cervical levels.

Local supporting reflexes (local static reflexes) are primarily reflections of myotatic reflexes, but they may be supported by reflex activity subserved by cutaneous receptors. When the paw is placed on the ground, the flexor muscles of the digit and carpus are stretched and the toes are spread apart, activating the myotatic reflex which causes a contraction of these muscles. Similarly the extensor muscles of the stifle joint or the elbow are stretched and in turn increase their tone. In this way, the limb is placed in extension and the animal is supported against the pull of gravity. With the animal thus supported, if the center of gravity shifts so as to stretch the muscles antagonistic to those mentioned above, the myotatic reflex involving these muscles is activated and the center of gravity is readjusted.

Withdrawal and cross-extension reflexes are segmental and modify the activity initiated by the local supporting reflexes. These reflexes are supporting in nature during the response initiated by the application of a noxious stimulus to the extremities of an animal.

Segmental supporting reflexes (segmental static reflexes) involve the activity initiated in all the limbs by myotatic reflex activity due to stretch of muscles in a single limb. When a rear limb is extended in the local supporting response described above, the opposite forelimb is also extended. Likewise, if a forelimb exhibits such a supporting response, the opposite rear limb is also extended. Thus it is evident that reflex activity within the lumbar spinal cord alters activity within the cervical spinal cord, and similarly, reflex activity within the cervical spinal cord alters α-motor activity within the lumbar spinal cord. The pathways used by these reflexes in the cat are twofold (Gernandt and Megirian 1961, Gernandt and Shimamura 1961, Shimamura and Livingston 1963). One pathway is a slow-conducting, multisynaptic pathway that ascends the spinal cord bilaterally within the propriospinal system. The other is a rapidly conducting pathway with few synapses, which utilizes spinoreticular and reticulospinal pathways within the spinal cord. The latter system, termed the spinobulbospinal pathway, involves the reticulospinal tracts with a synapse in the reticular formation of the medulla oblongata. Fibers from the reticular formation project to the spinal cord by way of the reticulospinal tracts to synapse upon internuncial neurons which control α- and γ-motor activity.

Attitudinal reflexes, often referred to as general supporting reflexes (general static reflexes), involve modification of posture as a result of varying positions of the head. These reflexes are served by stretch receptors of the neck muscles and by a portion of the membranous labyrinth of the vestibular apparatus. The stretch receptors of the neck muscles initiate reciprocal influences upon extensor muscle tone of the various limbs, that is, an increase in extensor tone in the forelimb and a decrease in the rear limbs or vice versa. The reflexes initiated by the labyrinth initiate a similar influence upon extensor tone of all forelimbs, that is, an increase or a decrease in extensor tone of both forelimbs and rear limbs. These reflexes are usually referred to as tonic neck reflexes and tonic labyrinthine reflexes respectively.

Tonic neck reflexes can be studied in their pure form only if the labyrinths have been surgically destroyed, but they can be observed in the intact animal if they are well understood. Rotation of the jaw to the right around the longitudinal axis of the head when the head is extended initiates activity within the stretch receptors of the left cervical muscles, which results in a reflex extension of the left forelimb and the left rear limb. A decrease in muscle tone is observed in the extensors of the opposite side. Dorsal flexion of the head causes extension of both forelimbs and relaxation of the extensors of the rear limbs; ventral flexion of the head produces the opposite effect, that is, extension of the rear limbs and flexion of the forelimbs.

Tonic labyrinthine reflexes can be studied in their pure form only if the cervical muscles have been denervated, but these reflexes are active in the intact animal and should be understood in relation to their coordination with other postural reflexes. The vestibular labyrinth contains two distinct receptor organs, the otolith organs and the semicircular canals. The otolith organs subserve the tonic labyrinthine reflexes, and the semicircular canals subserve reflexes initiated by angular acceleration. Tonic labyrinthine reflexes are initiated by alteration of the position of the animal's head within the earth's gravitational field. When the animal is placed on its back with the nose at a 45° angle above horizontal, all four extremities exhibit increased extensor tone. When the nose is in a position of 45° below the horizontal gravitational field with the animal in a prone position, extensor tone is minimized.

If the animal is placed on its side, the head is raised to an erect position and righting of the body occurs. These responses are referred to as righting reflexes, a complex series of reflexes initiated by the tonic labyrinthine reflexes: the tonic labyrinthine reflex initiates righting of the head; righting of the head initiates tonic neck reflexes; which brings about righting of the body. These responses can also be exhibited in a cat that is blindfolded and dropped in a supine position: the cat turns very rapidly and lands on its feet. The time required for the completion of these reflex activities is in the order of milliseconds, so that the cat is righted very rapidly and avoids injury in the fall.

Righting reflexes in the normal unrestrained animal involve the visual and cutaneous sensory systems as well as the vestibular system. If an animal is placed on its side and the head is not allowed to right, the caudal portion of the animal will right itself independent of the forelimbs. The reflex is apparently initiated by an uneven cutaneous stimulation of the two sides of the animal. This response is inhibited, though, if a uniformly distributed weight is applied to the upper surface of the animal.

The visual system is operant in the control of righting reflexes in the intact animal. If the labyrinthine receptors are destroyed, however, the animal will not attempt to right itself in the usual manner.

Placing reflexes initiate coordinated muscular activity that results in supporting responses of the animal. These responses differ from the above supporting responses in that the afferent limbs of these reflexes involve vestibular, visual, or cutaneous sensory systems and in the fact that the visual and cutaneous responses are dependent upon the integrity of the sensory and motor areas of the cerebral cortex and are therefore "cortical" reflexes.

The tactile placing reflexes are easily studied in the blindfolded animal. If a part of a blindfolded animal's body, such as the dorsum of the paw, the vibrissae, or the ventral surface of the chin is brought into contact with a supporting surface with the limbs free in the air, the limbs are immediately placed on the surface in a supporting manner.

The visual placing reflexes are exhibited in an animal which is lowered toward a visible supporting surface. The limbs will be extended so that the animal is supported when contact is made with the surface.

Vestibular placing reflexes are exhibited in a blindfolded animal (to eliminate visual placing) which is lowered rapidly through the air. The forelimbs will be extended and the toes will spread to ready the animal for contact with the supporting surface. In the normal animal, these reflexes are integrated with the visual placing reflexes so that a more appropriate response is obtained.

Hopping reflexes are dependent upon the myotatic reflexes of a given limb as well as tactile placing responses. If an animal is supported upon one fore- or hindlimb and is then displaced laterally, medially, rostrally, or caudally, the supporting limb will hop rapidly in the direction of displacement so as to maintain a supporting column for the body.

Central mechanisms

Many CNS structures contribute to the normal functioning of the postural reflexes. The most important, however, are the cerebral cortex, pons, medulla, and cervical spinal cord. The cerebral cortex is essential to the visual and tactile placing reflexes and to the hopping reflex. The pons and medulla are essential for the labyrinthine reflexes since the vestibular nuclear complex is located within these structures. The cervical levels of the spinal cord are essential to the tonic neck reflexes in that the afferents from stretch receptors of cervical muscles enter at these levels.

Other CNS structures that alter the neuronal activity of the structures directly involved in these reflex activities also serve a role in the normal functioning of these reflexes. The cerebellum is very important in this capacity. It not only controls the activity of many of the primary reflex structures, but also controls the excitability of the α-motoneurons that carry out the reflex motor activity. The latter role is served also by the reticular formation, the red nucleus, and other descending motor pathways of the brain. An abnormal function of these structures will modify the excitability of the spinal cord α-motoneuron pools so that normal reflex activity may be disturbed.

Vestibular organ

This organ is an important receptor in the postural reflex mechanisms. The bony labyrinth of the internal ear, lying within the temporal bone, contains the membranous labyrinth. Surrounding the membranous labyrinth and separating it from the bony labyrinth is a liquid known as perilymph. In the cavities of the membranous labyrinth is another fluid known as endolymph. The membranous labyrinth is composed of two parts, which differ greatly in both structure and function: (1) the nonacoustic labyrinth or vestibular organ, and (2) the acoustic labyrinth or cochlear duct on the latter (see Chapter 51).

The vestibular organ comprises two membranous sacs, known as the saccule and the utricle, and the membranous semicircular canals (Fig. 42.11). The saccule communicates with the cochlear duct, and the utricle with the semicircular canals. Connecting the saccule with the utricle is the short ductus utriculosaccularis.

The membranous labyrinth contains the receptor organs of the VIIIth cranial nerve. This nerve, like the labyrinth, is comprised of two components, a vestibular component and a cochlear component. The receptor organs of the vestibular component consist of specialized receptor organs within each of the semicircular canals and one each of the saccule and utricle. The receptor organs of the saccule and utricle are called maculae and those of the semicircular canals, cristae.

The maculae are referred to as otolith organs because

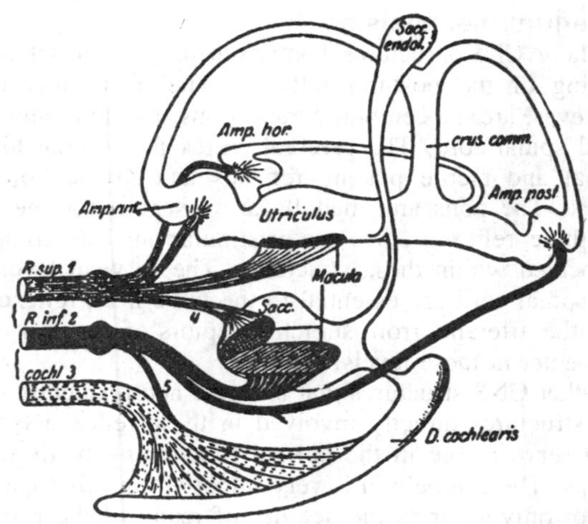

Figure 42.11. Membranous labyrinth, illustrating the relationships of the semicircular canals, the utriculus, and the sacculus. (From De Burlet, in Camis, ed., *The Physiology of the Vestibular Apparatus*, trans. R.S. Creed, The Clarendon Press, Oxford, 1930.)

of their structure. They are comprised of a plaque of hair cells covered by a gelatinous material. Within the gelatinous material are concretions of calcareous substance that are called otoliths. These receptor organs are involved in most of the labyrinthine postural reflexes referred to above. The adequate stimulus for these receptors is a displacement of the otoliths due either to gravity or to positive or negative linear acceleration.

The cristae, the receptor organs of the semicircular canals, are located within an enlargement of each of the canals called ampulla. The receptor cells of this organ, like those of the maculae, are hair cells covered by a gelatinous material. Here, however, the gelatinous mass forms a definite structure called the cupula which obstructs the ampulla of the semicircular canal. The semicircular canals are oriented in planes approximately at right angles to each other and are called respectively lateral (horizontal), rostral (vertical), and caudal (vertical). With this orientation, at least one of the canals will be rotated in the direction of the head when it is turned. Each of these canals, like the entire membranous labyrinth, is filled with endolymph. When the canal rotates with the head, the endolymph, due to inertia, lags behind the movement of the canal and produces a deflection of the cupula of the crista within the canal involved. This is the adequate stimulus for the receptor cells of the cristae. Therefore, the cristae can be thought of as receptor organs sensing changes in the position of the head but not indicating the final position. An indication of the final position of the head is given by the maculae of the saccule and utricle. Because of their orientation within the head and the nature of their adequate stimulus, the receptors of the semicircular canals are excited only by rotary acceleration of the head while the otolith organs (the maculae) are stimulated by position in the gravitational field and linear acceleration of the head. It can be deduced from the nature of the adequate stimulus that in order to maintain a prolonged stimulus to the cristae, the head rotation must continue to accelerate or decelerate. If the rotation is maintained at a given velocity, the inertia of the endolymph will soon be overcome, and the adequate stimulus to the cristae will be removed.

The reflexes initiated by the otolith organs have been adequately described above as a part of the tonic postural reflexes. The reflexes initiated by the semicircular canals are referred to as acceleratory reflexes. However, in this sense the term acceleratory refers only to rotary acceleration.

Nystagmus. When the semicircular canals are stimulated continuously for a period of time, one of the most obvious responses is nystagmus. This refers to a rhythmic to and fro movement of the eyes consisting of two components: a slow deviation in the direction opposite to the rotation, followed by a rapid deviation in the direction of rotation. By convention, the direction of nystagmus is said to be in the direction of the fast component; that is, if the head is rotated to the left, the fast component will be to the left and the nystagmus would be to the left. The CNS structures responsible for this reflex are the vestibular nuclear complex, the medial longitudinal fasciculus, and the motor nuclei of the extraocular muscles (cranial nerves III, IV, and VI).

Nystagmus is commonly observed in animals under the influence of anesthetic agents. Nystagmus under these conditions is not, however, due to adequate stimulation of vestibular receptor organs but is due to central neural mechanisms which have not been adequately determined.

Methods of stimulating the semicircular canals. The cristae of the semicircular canals can be stimulated by any force that will cause the endolymph to move in a different direction or at a different rate. Thus rotation produces a good adequate stimulus for the receptor organs. Differences in temperature between different regions of a semicircular canal will also stimulate the cristae, through the production of convection currents in the endolymph. This method of stimulation is often used as a clinical test for the functioning of the vestibular apparatus and nerve. Called a caloric stimulation, it is produced clinically by flushing the external auditory canal with hot (45°C) or cold (12°C) water. This type of stimulation will give rise to the same reflex motor activity as rotary stimulation.

Motion sickness is a condition that develops in animals subjected to a prolonged intermittent stimulation of either the otolith organs (linear acceleration and/or deceleration) or the semicircular canal receptor (rotary acceleration and/or deceleration). Such a stimulation is presented by a moving automobile and may result in what is commonly known as car sickness. Airsickness and seasickness in man are similar conditions. The development of this condition is dependent upon the vestibular receptor organs and their neural connections within the CNS. The syndrome is characterized in dogs by salivation, swallowing, a drop in blood pressure, and vomiting, all of which are characteristic of the vomiting reflex. The vestibular nerve terminates within the vestibular nuclear complex of the brain stem which in turn projects fibers to the vomiting center of the medulla. A prolonged series of synchronous vestibular afferent activity to the vomiting center of the medulla is apparently adequate to initiate the vomiting reflex.

Since ablation of the nodulus and uvula of the cerebellum renders an animal refractory to motion sickness, the cerebellum must play an important role in the development of motion sickness, but the extent of this role has not been determined.

Reticular formation of the brain stem

The reticular formation comprises a considerable portion of the mass of the brain stem. It is a phylogenetically old structure which occupies a part of all levels of the brain stem. It extends from the spinal cord–medullary junction throughout the length of the medulla, pons, and midbrain. Rostral to the midbrain, the reticular formation is continuous with the medial thalamus and the lateral hypothalamus.

The reticular formation derives its name from its cytoarchitectonic structure. It is comprised of a reticulum of nerve fibers passing in all directions. Within this network are many nerve cells of various sizes and shapes. These nerve cells, somewhat unlike those of the spinal cord and the remainder of the brain stem, are not organized into sharply localized nuclear groups.

The reticular formation receives its afferents from all sensory systems. These afferents enter either as terminal fibers or as collaterals of parent fibers that project to other CNS structures. Afferents are also received from nearly all other structures of the CNS such as the cerebellum, cerebral cortex, basal ganglia, thalamus, and hypothalamus.

The efferent fibers of the reticular formation are organized into three groups: ascending fibers, which project to other structures of the brain stem and cerebrum and form the ascending reticular formation; descending fibers, which project to structures of the spinal cord and form the descending reticular formation; and fibers which project to the cerebellum and serve both ascending and descending reticular formation projections.

Descending reticular formation

The major functions of the descending reticular formation are the control of skeletal muscle motor activity; control of cardiovascular, respiratory, and other autonomic activity; and control of activity within the sensory pathways of the CNS (see Chapter 44).

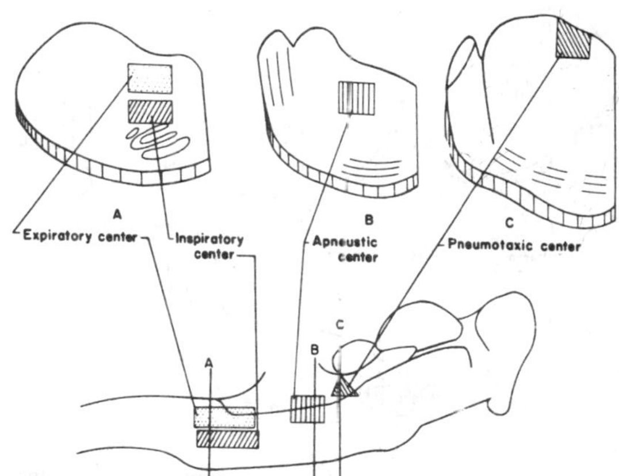

Figure 42.12. Location of respiratory centers within the brain stem

The descending reticular formation alters skeletal muscle motor activity through the termination of the reticulospinal tracts which form a functional part of the extrapyramidal motor system.

The CNS control of respiration involves many structures. The brain-stem reticular formation, however, plays a central role in this control (Breckenridge and Hoff 1950, Breckenridge and Hoff 1953, Hoff and Breckenridge 1949, Brodie and Borison 1957, Tang 1953). As a result of electrophysiological and stimulation-ablation experiments, a series of respiratory centers have been defined within the brain-stem reticular formation (Fig. 42.12) (see Chapter 15).

The reticular formation of the medulla oblongata exerts a considerable control upon the cardiovascular system. This control is exerted through the influence of neurons of this region upon the autonomic nervous system, which serves as a direct control of the cardiovascular system.

The vasomotor centers have been defined within the medulla: a pressor center located within the lateral reticular formation and a depressor center within the medial reticular formation (Fig. 42.13). Both of these centers are bilaterally located within the medulla oblongata (Amoroso et al. 1954, Salmoiraghi 1962). They exert their control upon the vasomotor system by altering the excitability of the vasoconstrictor neurons within the spinal cord that contribute to the autonomic nervous system (see Chapter 9).

The presence of reticular formation centers that control micturition reflexes has been demonstrated by several investigators. These centers are distributed through the mesencephalic, pontine, and medullary reticular formation.

A mesencephalic micturition area has been described; it is composed of two centers that are very close together but slightly separated from each other (Kuru et al. 1961) (Fig. 42.14.). A mesencephalic vesicoconstrictor center is located slightly rostral to a mesencephalic vesicorelaxer center within the dorsal and lateral regions of the

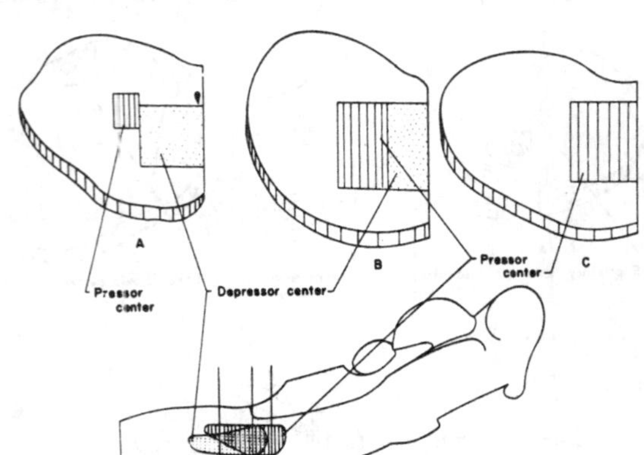

Figure 42.13. Location of vasomotor centers within the brain stem

mesencephalic reticular formation. From these regions two separate descending pathways arise. One tract descends in the contralateral brain stem with the tectospinal tract to form a tectobulbar tract. The other tract is called the mesencephalobulbospinal tract and descends with the rubrospinal tract, to terminate within the medulla and sacral spinal cord. The tectobulbar tract connects the mesencephalic micturition center with the micturition centers of the pons and medulla of the contralateral side. The mesencephalobulbospinal tract connects its fibers to both the medullary micturition centers and to the spinal cord for control of spinal micturition reflexes.

A pontine micturition center has been defined within the reticular formation of the rostral position of the pons (Tang 1955) (see Fig. 42.14.) This center facilitates the micturition reflex of the spinal cord. The pathways leading from this center include bilateral reticulospinal tracts to the spinal cord and projections to the micturition centers of the medulla (Kuru et al. 1961).

Medullary micturition centers have been defined within the medullary reticular formation. They are comprised of

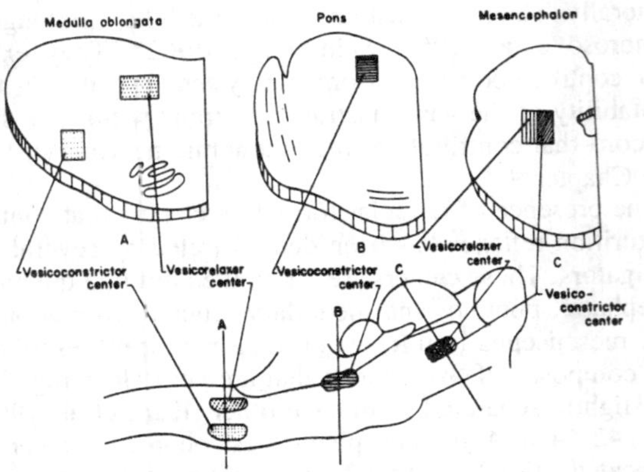

Figure 42.14. Location of micturition centers within the brain stem

two antagonistic areas, the medullary vesicoconstrictor center and the medullary vesicorelaxer center (Tokunaga and Kuru 1951) (see Fig. 42.14.) These centers receive afferents from the mesencephalic and pontine micturition centers, and visceral afferents from the urinary bladder reach these centers via the spinoreticular pathways. The efferents of the medullary micturition centers project bilaterally to the sacral spinal cord for modification of micturition reflexes.

Micturition responses are also obtained by stimulation of the hypothalamus and the cerebral cortex (see Chapter 37).

REFERENCES

Amoroso, E.C., Bell, F.R., and Rosenberg, H. 1954. The relationship of the vasomotor and respiratory regions in the medulla oblongata of the sheep. *J. Physiol.* 126:86–95.

Breckenridge, C.G., and Hoff, H.E. 1950. Pontine and medullary regulation of respiration in the cat. *Am. J. Physiol.* 160:385–94.

——. 1953. Ischemic and anoxic dissolution of the supramedullary control of respiration. *Am. J. Physiol.* 175:449–57.

Brodal, A. 1949. Spinal afferents to the lateral reticular nucleus of the medulla oblongata in the cat: An experimental study. *J. Comp. Neurol.* 91:259–95.

Brodie, D.A., and Borison, H.L. 1957. Evidence for a medullary inspiratory pacemaker: Functional concept of central regulation of respiration. *Am. J. Physiol.* 188:347–54.

Camis, M., ed. 1930. *The Physiology of the Vestibular Apparatus.* Clarendon, Oxford.

Crosby, E.C., Humphrey, T., and Lauer, E.W. 1962. *Correlative Anatomy of the Nervous System.* Macmillan, New York.

Erlanger, J., and Gasser, H.S. 1937. *Electrical Signs of Nervous Activity.* U. of Pennsylvania Press, Philadelphia. P. 221.

Gelfan, S. 1963. Neurone and synapse population in the spinal cord indicates the role in total integration. *Nature* 198:162–63.

Gernandt, B.E., and Megirian, D. 1961. Ascending propriospinal mechanisms. *J. Neurophysiol.* 24:364–76.

Gernandt, B.E., and Shimamura, M. 1961. Mechanisms of interlimb reflexes in cat. *J. Neurophysiol.* 24:665–76.

Goller, H. 1963. Kerngebiete des Rinderruckenmarkes. *Zentralblatt Veterinärmedizin* 10(1):51–66.

Grant, G., and Rexed, B. 1958. Dorsal spinal root afferents to Clarke's column. *Brain* 81:567–76.

Gudden, H.V. 1891. Beitrag zur Kenntnis der Wurzeln des Trigeminusnerven. *Allgemein Zeitschrift Psychiat.* 48:16–33.

Herrick, C.J. 1928. *An Introduction to Neurology.* 4th ed. Saunders, Philadelphia.

Hoff, H.E., and Breckenridge, C.G. 1949. The medullary origin of respiratory periodicity in the dog. *Am. J. Physiol.* 158:157–72.

Hukuhara, T., and Okada, H. 1956. Effects of deglutition upon the spike discharges of neurons in the respiratory center. *Jap. J. Physiol.* 6:162–66.

Jabbur, S.J., and Towe, A.L. 1960. Effect of pyramidal tract activity on dorsal column nuclei. *Science* 132:547–48.

Jerge, C.R. 1963. Organization and function of the trigeminal mesencephalic nucleus. *J. Neurophysiol.* 26:379–92.

Kerr, F.W.L. 1961. Structural relation of the trigeminal spinal tract to upper cervical roots and the solitary nucleus in the cat. *Exp. Neurol.* 4:134–48.

Kuru, M., Makuya, A., and Koyama, Y. 1961. Fiber connections between the mesencephalic micturition facilitatory area and the bulbar vesico-motor centers. *J. Comp. Neurol.* 117:161–78.

Kuypers, H.G.J.M. 1958. Pericentral cortical projections to motor and sensory nuclei. *Science* 128:662–63.

——. 1960. Central cortical projections to motor and somato-sensory cell groups. *Brain* 83:161–84.

Kuypers, H.G.J.M., Hoffman, A.L., and Beasley, R.M. 1961. Distribution of cortical "feedback" fibers in the nuclei cuneatus and gracilis. *Proc. Soc. Exp. Biol. Med.* 108:634–37.

Larsell, O. 1951. *Anatomy of the Nervous System*. 2d ed. Appleton-Century-Crofts, New York.

Linowiecki, A.J. 1914. The comparative anatomy of the pyramidal tract. *J. Comp. Neurol.* 24:509–30.

Morin, F. 1955. A new spinal pathway for cutaneous impulses. *Am. J. Physiol.* 183:245–52.

Nyberg-Hansen, R. 1964. The location and termination of tectospinal fibers in the cat. *Exp. Neurol.* 9:212–27.

Oswaldo-Cruz, E., and Kidd, C. 1964. Functional properties of neurons in the lateral cervical nucleus of the cat. *J. Neurophysiol.* 27:1–14.

Salmoiraghi, G.C. 1962. "Cardiovascular" neurons in brain stem of cat. *J. Neurophysiol.* 25:182–97.

Schnitzlein, H.N., Hoffman, H.H., Hamlett, D.M., and Howell, E.M. 1963. A study of the sacral parasympathetic nucleus. *J. Comp. Neurol.* 120(3):477–94.

Shimamura, M., and Livingston, R.B. 1963. Longitudinal conduction systems serving spinal and brain-stem coordination. *J. Neurophysiol.* 26:258–72.

Sumi, T. 1963. The activity of brain-stem respiratory neurons and spinal respiratory motoneurons during swallowing. *J. Neurophysiol.* 26:466–77.

Swank, R.L. 1936. The pyramidal tract: An experimental study of the corticospinal and other components of the rabbit. *Arch. Neurol. Psychiat.* 36:530–41.

Tang, P.C. 1953. Localization of the pneumotaxic center in the cat. *Am. J. Physiol.* 172:645–52.

——. 1955. Levels of brain stem and diencephalon controlling micturition reflex. *J. Neurophysiol.* 18:583–95.

Tokunaga, S., and Kuru, M. 1951. Vesico-constrictor center and vesico-relaxer center in the medulla. *Jap. J. Physiol.* 9:365–74.

Walberg, F. 1956. Descending connections to the inferior olive: An experimental study in the cat. *J. Comp. Neurol.* 104:77–174.

——. 1960. Further studies on the descending connections to the inferior olive: Reticulo-olivary fibers, an experimental study in the cat. *J. Comp. Neurol.* 114:79–87.

CHAPTER 43

Somesthetic Sensory Mechanisms | by Ainsley Iggo

The afferent input to the nervous system enters via the dorsal roots or via the afferent divisions of certain cranial nerves (I, II, V, VII, VIII, IX, and X). Not all of these ingoing impulses enter consciousness as a sensation, nor are any of them exclusively sensory. For this reason a distinction should be made between afferent input and sensory input, and the latter term should be restricted to input along the sensory pathways.

The peripheral nervous system is divided functionally into two main parts. The *afferent* division detects changes in the environment of the animal and signals these to the CNS. Through the operation of its *efferent* division the CNS regulates the effectors, for example, muscles and glands, in some appropriate way.

Receptors can be divided physiologically into three principal groups (Sherrington 1906): (1) the exteroceptors, which detect stimuli that affect the outer surface of the body and which include the receptors for warmth, cold, touch, and pressure in the skin and the special receptor organs for hearing and vision (also classed as distance or teleceptors); (2) the interoceptors, which lie inside the body (the taste and the olfactory receptors form part of this system); and (3) the proprioceptors, which are located in the internal mass of the body, for example, the muscles, joints, and other deep tissues.

PRINCIPLES OF AFFERENT NERVOUS ACTIVITY

The main principles of afferent nervous activity were established by Adrian and his colleagues in Cambridge. The receptive field, that is, the area from which a response can be aroused, is supplied by afferent nerve fibers, each of which if excited by the stimulus will carry a stream of identical nerve impulses (Fig. 43.1). The receptive fields of individual afferent fibers often overlap, so that any natural stimulus usually excites a number of afferent fibers. The more exactly the receptive field of an afferent fiber coincides with the position of the stimulus the higher will be its frequency of discharge.

Selective sensitivity

The receptors at the ends of afferent fibers have the important function of lowering the threshold of the axon for a particular mode or kind of stimulus. Thus the photoreceptors in the retina of the eye are excited by quantities of energy that do not act directly on the axons in the optic nerve.

The thresholds of different receptors are lowered to varying degrees for different kinds of energy; for example, there are mechanoreceptors that are particularly sensitive to mechanical changes, thermoreceptors with a

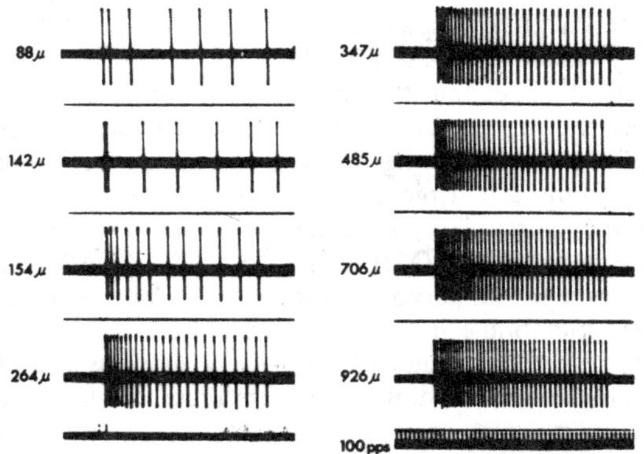

Figure 43.1. Discharge of afferent impulses in the axon of a cutaneous mechanoreceptor in the hairy skin of a cat, in response to mechanical stimulation. The mechanical pulses were identical except in displacement, shown in μ. This afferent unit adapts slowly and shows clearly the initial high frequency discharge during the dynamic phase, followed by the more gradual decrease of frequency during the static phase of adaptation. (From Werner and Mountcastle 1965, *J. Neurophysiol.* 28:359–97.)

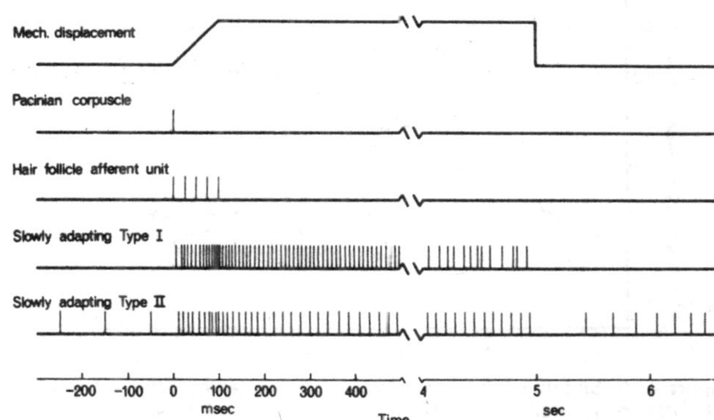

Figure 43.2. Differences in the responses of cutaneous afferent units to an identical mechanical stimulus. The movement of the mechanical probe is indicated in the upper trace. The unit responses are: Pacinian corpuscle, very rapidly adapting; hair follicle afferent unit, rapidly adapting; type I slowly adapting unit, with no resting discharge; type II slowly adapting unit, with a resting discharge.

heightened sensitivity to temperature, and chemoreceptors that are sensitive to substances in solution. This selective sensitivity is not absolute. The cutaneous thermoreceptors in the monkey, for example, can be excited by mechanical stimuli, but the force required is about 2000 times as great as that needed to excite the sensitive mechanoreceptors (Iggo 1964).

Adaptation

When the natural stimulus to a peripheral receptor is changed from one steady value to a new steady value, the discharge of impulses in the afferent fiber lasts for an interval that is characteristic of the afferent unit (defined as the receptor and afferent nerve fiber). The length of the interval gives an index of the rate of adaptation. Usually when a stimulus is applied, the frequency of discharge rises rapidly to a peak and then declines (the dynamic phase of the response) (see Fig. 43.2). There may then follow a longer period during which the frequency falls slowly (static phase). An afferent unit is said to adapt rapidly if the discharge is brief, as in the Pacinian corpuscle. An afferent unit adapts slowly if the discharge of afferent impulses persists and has a long static phase. It is characteristic of these very slowly adapting units that very often there is a resting discharge in the absence of an applied stimulus.

There is a biological advantage in different receptors adapting at different rates. Those afferent units which adapt rapidly are well suited to signaling sudden changes in the environment. The slowly adapting receptors, on the other hand, signal more persistent changes.

Adaptation should be distinguished from fatigue. Fatigue, or weariness after exertion, is associated with prolonged work, especially if the metabolic conditions are impaired or if the blood supply is inadequate. A fatigued receptor cannot be excited by withdrawal and reapplication of the stimulus at high frequencies. The behavior of a receptor may change during the development of fatigue; receptors that normally adapt slowly begin to adapt rapidly as fatigue develops.

Stimulus-response relations

Over a limited range of intensities of stimulation there is, for slowly adapting receptors, a logarithmic relation between the stimulus load and the frequency of afferent discharge. This relation was first established in human sensory studies by Weber (1846) and has been expressed mathematically as the Weber-Fechner Law

$$R = a \cdot \log S + b,$$

where R is the response or sensation, S is the intensity of the stimulus, a is a constant, and b is the constant of integration. This law states that the response or sensation is linearly related to the logarithm of the stimulus. This linear relation has been shown for the response of the slowly adapting muscle spindle afferent units to stretch (Matthews 1933) and for response of the Limulus eye to light (Granit 1955). Werner and Mountcastle (1965) have shown, for the slowly adapting cutaneous *touch corpuscles,* that there is a power function relationship (Fig. 43.3) between the stimulus and response, as would be predicted from Stevens' power law in psychophysics.

Structural basis for selective sensitivity

The hypothesis that there is a correlation between the structure of a receptor organ and its function was formulated by von Frey in 1895, and has been reaffirmed by the combined use of electrophysiological and histological methods. In the hairy skin of monkeys, cats, and rabbits,

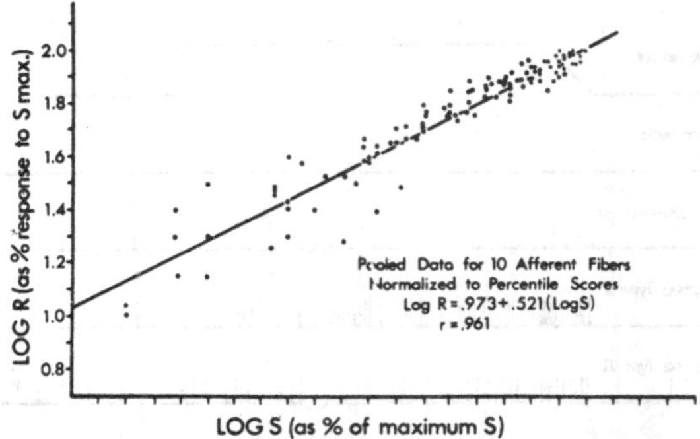

Figure 43.3. Stimulus-response relation for mechanical stimulation of 10 cutaneous touch corpuscles in the hairy skin of cats, plotted on logarithmic coordinates. There is a very good fit of the data to the straight line. These results demonstrate a power function relation between stimulus intensity and rate of discharge in the afferent fiber. (From Werner and Mountcastle 1965, *J. Neurophysiol.* 28: 359–97.)

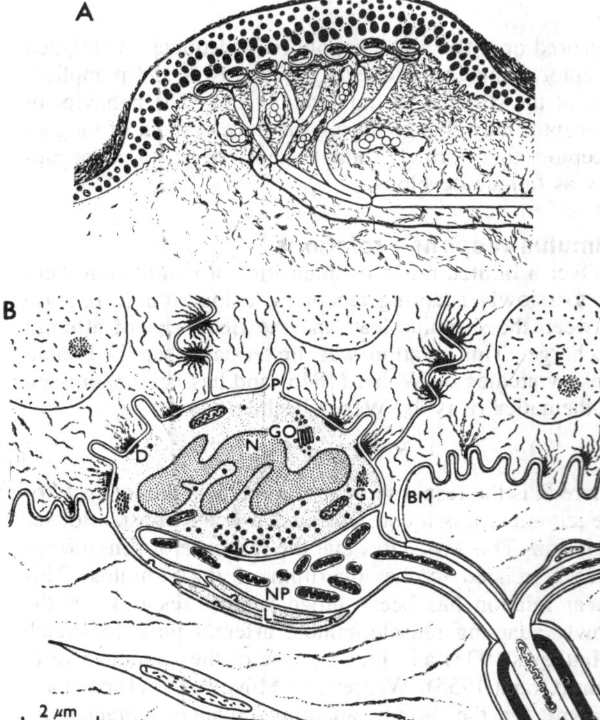

Figure 43.4. Structure of the slowly adapting type I cutaneous mechanoreceptor in hairy skin of the cat. A: cross section of skin showing a cutaneous touch corpuscle (SA type I mechanoreceptor), which is formed by a dome-shaped swelling of the epidermis within the basal layer off which the myelinated afferent nerve fiber branches to end in expanded discs (Merkel's discs). B: detailed structure of one Merkel cell and disc, based on electromicrographs. A, myelinated axon; BM, basement membrane; D, desmosome; E, nucleus of epidermal call; G, osmiophilic granules; GO, Golgi apparatus; GY, glycogen; L, laminae on the dermal side of the disc; N, nucleus of Merkel cell; NP, Merkel disc, which is an expanded terminal of the afferent nerve; P, rodlike process of Merkel cell (From A. Iggo and A.R. Muir 1969, *J. Physiol.* 200:763–96.)

there are four receptor structures with specific functions. First, the Pacinian corpuscle in the dermis is excited by vibratory mechanical stimuli, is very sensitive, and adapts rapidly. Second, the hair follicle is innervated in a characteristic manner and is excited by hair movements. Third, the slowly adapting mechanoreceptor, type I (Fig. 43.4A), forms a conspicuous elevation of the epidermis among the hairs. The nerve terminals in this receptor form expanded discs (Merkel's discs; Fig. 43.4B) that are enclosed in nonnervous structures and lie inside the basement membrane in a regular array. Fourth, the Ruffini ending is the receptor of the slowly adapting type II mechanoreceptor. In addition to these receptors there are other afferent units, such as thermoreceptors and nociceptors, in the skin.

In other receptors, e.g. taste buds in the tongue, there is convincing histological evidence that the transducer function is due to the taste cells that enclose the afferent nerve fibers (Fig. 43.5). Presumably chemicals in the solution react with the microvilli on the free outer border of the taste cells. This reaction alters the taste cell in such a way that the cell excites the afferent nerve fibers embedded in it.

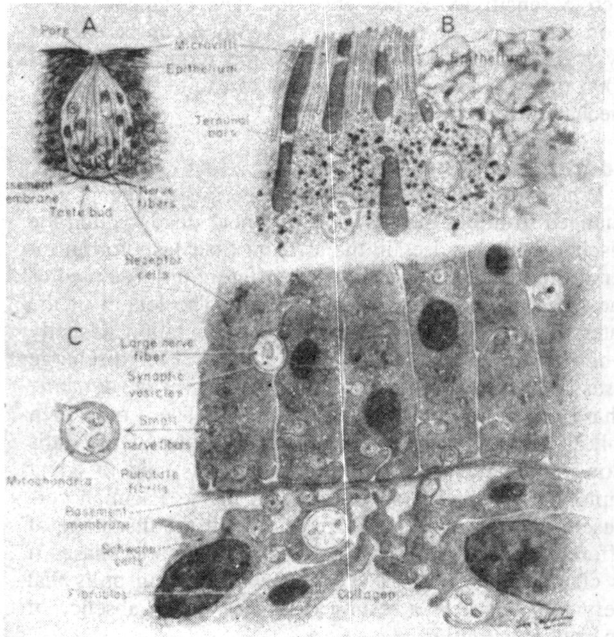

Figure 43.5. Diagram of the taste bud, based on electron microscopic examination of taste buds in the foliate papillae of rabbits. A, taste bud, buried in the epithelium and opening to the buccal cavity at the pore; B, the structures in the pore; the individual taste cells end in microvilli, which project slightly above the surrounding epithelium; C, the base of a taste bud, with the taste cells resting on the basement membrane. The terminals of the afferent nerve fibers are embedded in or enclosed by the taste cells, but are separated from them by cell membranes. (Reprinted with permission from de Lorenzo, in Zotterman, ed., *Olfaction and Taste*, Pergamon Press Ltd., London, 1963.)

FUNCTIONAL PROPERTIES OF RECEPTORS (AFFERENT UNITS)

Exact information about the physiological properties of receptors is obtained by recording from single afferent fibers reacting to quantitative mechanical, chemical, or thermal stimulation of the receptive field of the receptors.

The following account of the functional properties of receptors is based on results obtained from this method and follows the physiological classification of Sherrington.

Exteroceptors

The skin is richly supplied with afferent nerve fibers of many sizes, and the dermis and epidermis contain several histologically distinct receptor structures. At least 10 kinds of afferent units (that is, afferent fiber and receptor) have been described in the hairy skin of mammals. The nonhairy, or glabrous, skin has a more orderly arrangement of its afferent innervation.

These afferent units in skin can be classified into three main groups: mechanoreceptor, thermoreceptor, and nociceptor (high threshold receptor), on the basis of their sensitivity to mechanical and thermal stimuli. The central connections of the afferent fibers determine the kind of sensation perceived, and clinical studies have provided good evidence for a separation of the sensory pathways for touch, pressure, temperature, and pain. This evidence supports the receptor classification that is used below.

Cutaneous mechanoreceptors

Hair follicle afferent units. In the hairy skin of animals the majority of the afferent fibers innervate receptors in the hair follicles. All these afferent units give a brief discharge to movement of the hair, especially in experiments with rigorous control of the mechanical conditions. In the cat and rabbit there are three kinds of hair follicle afferent units with myelinated afferent fibers.

(1) Type T units. Each of these large axons supplies large guard hairs that project well above the general hairy coat in cats and rabbits. Moving one hair produces little response; moving several hairs in succession, as by brushing, gives a more prolonged and high-frequency discharge of impulses.

(2) Type G units. Each axon supplies as many as 50 guard hairs, and these hairs are usually shorter than those supplied by Type T units.

(3) Type D units. These are more sensitive to slight movement of the hairs than either types T or G, and there may often be a persistent irregular discharge of impulses when the hair is moved and held in a new position. All three kinds of afferent units are silent when the skin is undisturbed.

(4) Nonmyelinated units. A fourth type of unit is supplied by nonmyelinated afferent fibers, in which a discharge of impulses can be elicited by moving the tips of the hairs.

Slowly adapting mechanoreceptors. Two types are present in the hairy skin. In type I, the receptive fields are small spots scattered among the hairs. The mechanical threshold is a load of less than 2 mg wt and the discharge of impulses adapts very slowly and may persist for 5–10 minutes or longer. The receptor has the structure shown in Figure 43.4. In type II, the slowly adapting mechanoreceptors also have spotlike receptive fields and the receptors are Ruffini endings in the dermis. Their mechanical thresholds are higher than the type I. Particular differences are that the receptors can be excited by stretching the skin and that they adapt more slowly.

High threshold mechanoreceptors. Afferent units with a high mechanical threshold are present in the skin. Some of the fibers end in small receptive fields, and firm pressure on the skin is required to excite them. Other high threshold units are innervated by nonmyelinated fibers.

Thermal sensitivity of mechanoreceptors. All the mechanoreceptors can be excited by suddenly lowering the temperature of the skin. At skin temperatures below 20°C the receptors become less sensitive and at 10°C may actually fail to be excited by a mechanical stimulus. Normally these thermal effects are masked by the response to mechanical stimuli.

Cutaneous thermoreceptors

The cutaneous thermoreceptors have an enhanced sensitivity to both the temperature and the rate of change of temperature of the skin (Iggo 1960). There are two main classes of thermoreceptors: cold receptors, excited by a fall in skin temperature and depressed by a rise, and warm receptors, which respond in the opposite manner.

The common properties shared by both classes are: (1) a steady discharge at constant temperatures, (2) an accelerated discharge when the temperature changes (that is, increase for a fall in temperature for cold receptors and for a rise with warm receptors), (3) a relative insensitivity to mechanical stimulation, and (4) small receptive fields. Figure 43.6 shows the discharge in a cold receptor unit. The steady discharge under static thermal conditions

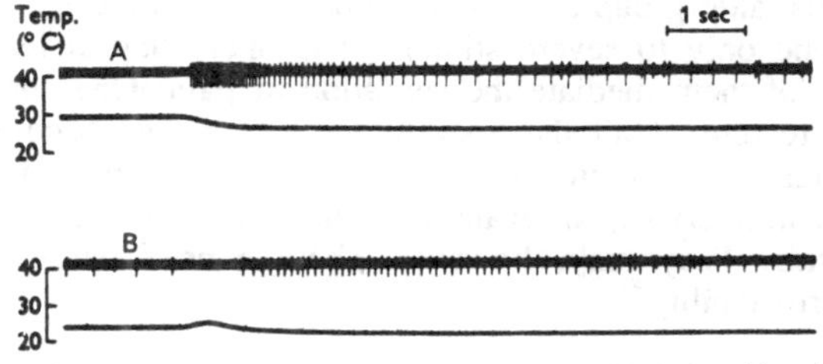

Figure 43.6. Cutaneous cold thermoreceptor in the hairy skin of the cat, responding to a fall in skin temperature. Before each record was taken, the temperature had been constant for 3 minutes. In A, the temperature was changed from a steady 29°C to 25.5°C and caused a brisk discharge, which adapted slowly. There was no resting discharge at 29°C. In B, at a steady temperature of 22°C, there was a steady background discharge that was enhanced when the temperature fell to 20.5°C. (After Hensel, Iggo, and Witt 1960, *J. Physiol.* 153:113–26.)

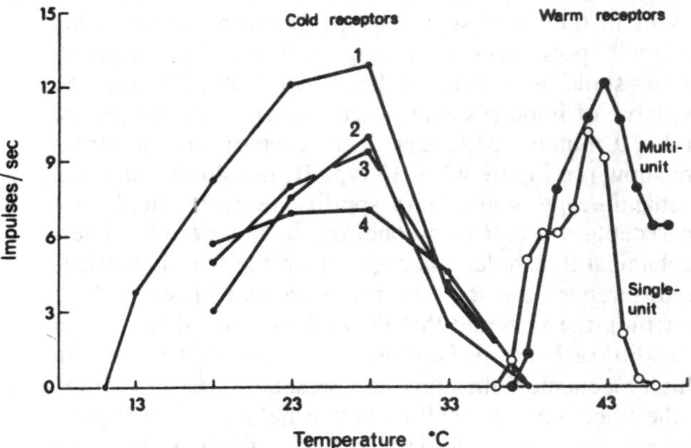

Figure 43.7. Temperature sensitivity curves for four cold receptors and one warm receptor in the scrotal skin of the rat. Each point indicates the mean rate of firing of impulses after the skin had been held at the given temperature for at least 3 minutes. (From Iggo 1969, *J. Physiol.* 200:403–30.)

is a characteristic property of the thermoreceptors. As Figure 43.7 shows, the cold receptors and warm receptors have a maximal sensitivity at different temperatures. about 15°C apart.

Cutaneous nociceptors

Some afferent units are excited only by high intensity stimulation, that is, by mechanical, thermal, or chemical stimuli that are many times greater than are required to excite the mechano- and thermoreceptors. In the cat and rabbit the majority of these units have nonmyelinated afferent fibers. Four types of afferent units have been found: (1) those responding only to mechanical deformation of the skin, such as pressing firmly with a blunt probe, squeezing, or pinching the skin; (2) those excited by high skin temperatures (>43°C) and also by severe mechanical deformation; (3) those excited by low skin temperatures (<20°C); and (4) units excited by both high and low temperatures, as well as severe mechanical stimuli.

This latter group is classed as nociceptors because they respond only to severe stimuli; it is likely that at least some of them mediate the sensation of pain. One common feature of all the nociceptors is that they become less responsive if the stimulus to the skin is repeated at frequent intervals, for example at intervals of less than 30 seconds. They may, however, show a brief phase of hyperirritability.

Interoceptors

This group is rather heterogeneous and includes several different classes of receptors, some of which are very highly specialized, for example, olfactory receptors and taste buds. Some develop from endoderm, e.g. taste buds and intestinal mucosal receptors; others from ectoderm, e.g. the olfactory receptors; while still others are mesodermal in origin, e.g. receptors in the urethra.

Olfactory receptors

These receptors are in the olfactory epithelium, particularly in the mucosa of the ethmoturbinal region and the nasal septum. Each olfactory neuron is a bipolar cell, with an olfactory rod at its peripheral end. The central end of the olfactory neuron gives rise to a fine nonmyelinated nerve fiber (0.2 μ diameter) that joins other similar fibers to make up the olfactory nerve (de Lorenzo 1963, Fig. 43.8).

The adequate stimuli of the receptors in the olfactory region are minute odorous particles usually brought in with the inspired air. However, not all particles stimulating the olfactory organ reach it by way of the anterior nares. Foods during mastication give off odorous particles which reach the olfactory organ by way of the posterior nares.

When an odorous substance is blown over the olfactory receptors in the olfactory mucosa, it causes their depolarization as depicted in the electro-olfactogram

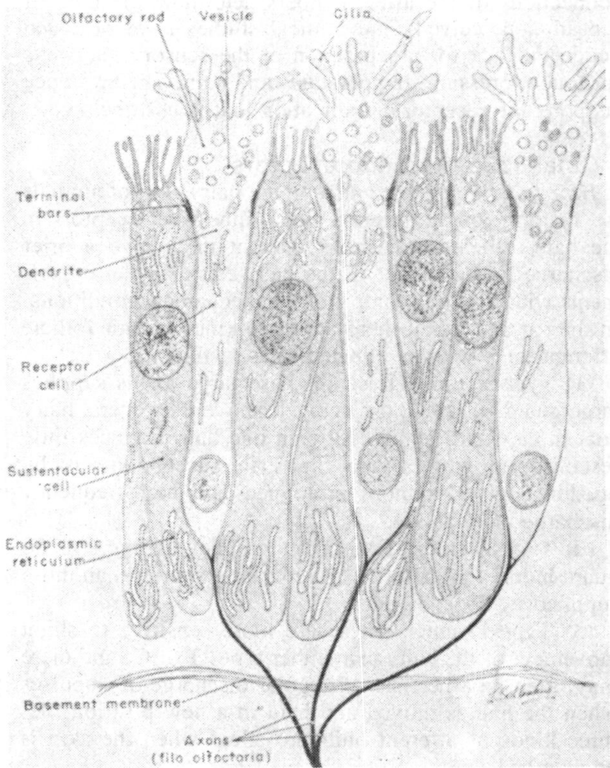

Figure 43.8. Diagram of the olfactory mucosa of the rabbit, based on an electron micrograph. The only part of the olfactory receptor that is exposed to odorants is the olfactory rod, which terminates in a number of cilia. (Reprinted with permission from de Lorenzo, in Zotterman, ed., *Olfaction and Taste*, Pergamon Press Ltd., London, 1963.)

(EOG). More precise information about the behavior of indiviual olfactory neurons can be obtained by recording from fibers in the olfactory nerve. The discharge of olfactory fibers is related both to the concentration of an odorant in the air stream that is flowing over the mucosa and to the rate of flow of air.

It is a well-known fact that many animals have a much keener sense of smell than man. The dominant position occupied by the olfactory sense in these keen-scented animals is indicated by the great development of their olfactory apparatus, both peripheral and central. Such animals are designated as macrosmatic. Most of the domestic animals belong to this group. Animals in which the olfactory apparatus is poorly developed are designated as microsmatic. Man, monkeys, and some aquatic mammals belong to this group. There is a third group, including a number of aquatic mammals, in which olfaction is apparently absent. They are said to be anosmatic.

According to Negus the epiglottis plays an important role in olfaction in many animals by forming with the soft palate a partition that prevents the breathing of air by the mouth. During eating, and at other times when the mouth is open, air is thus made to flow through the nasal passages, and in this way keen olfaction is attained. This arrangement is best seen in macrosmatic animals, and among domestic animals it is well exemplified in the horse.

An important function of olfaction is to aid animals in the search for food. Grazing animals may avoid grass contaminated with urine or feces, probably as a result of olfactory cues. Some ingested material may be rejected by an animal, and taste may be an important factor for this. Also, since some of the odors released by mastication reach the olfactory mucosa, olfaction plays a part in the acceptance or rejection of food once it is in the mouth.

Taste receptors

The taste receptors are found on the dorsal surface of the tongue, and in buccal mucosa, soft palate, epiglottis, and the posterior wall of the pharynx. They have distinctive morphological features and form part of taste buds (see Fig. 43.5). The taste cells form the body of the taste bud, and their free ends form microvilli (de Lorenzo 1958). The taste cells in the taste bud display a growth cycle. New cells are continually being formed at the margins of the bud and move slowly to its center. The mature cells in the center then degenerate and disappear.

The anterior two thirds of the tongue is innervated by the lingual nerve. The gustatory fibers leave this nerve to run in the chorda tympani to join the VIIth cranial nerve, whereas the mechanoreceptor fibers continue in the Vth cranial nerve. The glossopharyngeal nerves supply afferent fibers to the posterior third of the tongue, and the vagus supplies the epiglottis and other nearby structures.

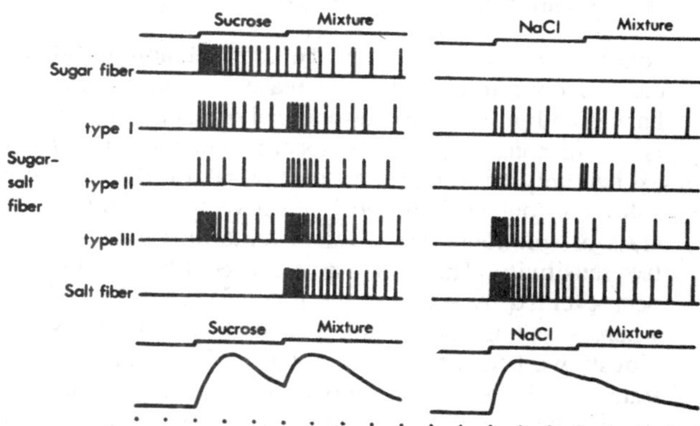

Figure 43.9. Diagram of the discharge in taste afferent units recorded from fibers in the chorda tympani of dogs. Three types of unit are tested by three solutions: sugar, 0.5 M sucrose; salt, 0.5 M NaCl; and a mixture containing both sugar and salt. The sweet unit is excited only by the sucrose solution and the salt unit is excited only by NaCl. The intermediate units are excited in varying degrees by both sucrose and NaCl. The prior application of NaCl reduces the response of the sugar and the mixed units to sucrose. The lowest tracings are integrated responses from the whole chorda tympani. (From Funakoshi and Zotterman 1963, *Acta Physiol. Scand.* 57:193–200.)

Detailed knowledge of the reactions of the taste cells and taste fibers is obtained by recording electrophysiologically from the afferent fibers in the gustatory nerves (Fig. 43.9). There are at least five kinds of taste afferent units:

(1) Water fibers, excited by distilled water (<0.03 M NaCl) but not by a salty solution.

(2) Salt fibers, excited by solutions containing NaCl, KCl, LiCl, NH_4Cl, and others. The essential components of a solution are the anion and cation of a soluble salt. Thus sodium chloride excites, whereas sodium acetate may not, or at least is much less effective.

(3) Acid fibers, excited by hydrogen ions in high concentration. The threshold pH is between 3 and 4. Sensitivity is related to pH, and an equimolar solution of strong acid, e.g. hydrochloric acid, is more effective than a similar solution of a weak acid, e.g. acetic acid, since the latter is less dissociated.

(4) Bitter fibers, excited by bitter substances, such as quinine, caffeine, and strychnine, which are all alkaloids.

(5) Sweet fibers, excited by solutions containing organic compounds, such as the simpler carbohydrates of which D-fructose is the most effective in 0.5 M solution. Other effective chemicals include aldehydes, ketones, amino acids, and synthetic sweetening agents such as saccharin. The more complex molecules may also excite other classes of fibers; for example, saccharin may excite bitter fibers.

(6) Additional classes containing mixed fibers can be made, that is, afferent units excited equally by several different kinds of solutions, e.g. sweet and salt.

For each of these groups of fibers there is a threshold

concentration below which the afferent unit is not excited. Above threshold an increase in concentration enhances and prolongs the response. For none of the groups is the response completely specific—that is, no fiber is excited only by water, or by acid or salt or bitter or sweet solutions, but each is most sensitive to one or another class of solutions. The afferent units thus exhibit selective sensitivity. The response of a sweet fiber to sugar can be prevented by washing the tongue with 0.5 M NaC1, whereas salt fibers are unaffected if the tongue is previously washed with a sugar solution. This example illustrates the degree of complexity and interaction that may occur when natural foodstuffs are eaten and goes some way toward accounting for the complex gustatory sensations that arise with various combinations of foods and sauces.

Finally, the response of the afferent units may be inhibited selectively. Gymnemic acid, a glycoside from the Indian plant *Gymnema sylvestre,* reduces or blocks the excitation of sweet fibers by sugar solutions, but does not affect the behavior of salt or acid fibers (Pfaffman 1963).

Species differences. There are wide species differences in the kinds of taste fibers present (Table 43.1). All species have taste fibers in the salt and acid categories, although the relative effectiveness of different ions may vary. In rodents (rat, guinea pig, and hamster) sodium chloride is more effective than potassium chloride in exciting salt fibers, whereas the converse is true in the carnivores (cat and dog). Bitter fibers are present in all mammals tested, but the threshold is lowest in cats and is high in the goat. They are present in the chicken but absent from the pigeon. In Japanese carp they have much lower thresholds than similar units in Swedish carp. There is even more variation for water fibers. These are absent from man, rat, ruminants, and fish. Water in these species therefore has no positive taste. Sweet fibers are absent from the cat and may be relatively insensitive in the pigeon and chicken. Allied to sweet fibers are those excited by saccharin. The sweet fibers in the dog, rabbit, and rat are not excited by saccharin, whereas the cat, which lacks sweet fibers, has other fibers that are excited by saccharin.

Taste sensations. Four primary modalities of taste are recognized in psychophysical work in man—salt, sour, bitter, and sweet. The sensation presumably arises from excitation by chemicals in solution of the different classes of taste fiber described above. The different tastes' sensibilities are distributed over the tongue in a characteristic way in man. The salty taste is best developed on the tip and at the edge, the sour or acid taste at the lateral margins, the bitter taste at the base, and the sweet taste at the tip. The electrophysiological evidence is in agreement in reporting a concentration of receptors at the tip and margins of the tongue and among the circumvallate papillae at the base of the tongue, but shows that at all regions there is an admixture of receptors, with variation in the proportions of the different kinds.

The tongue, in addition to this important role in taste, is also richly supplied with mechanoreceptors and thermoreceptors. The properties of these afferent units are comparable to similar receptors in the skin (Zotterman 1959).

Nociceptors are also present in the tongue and, as with all the other lingual receptors, the dorsal and lateral surfaces of the tongue are most richly supplied.

Afferent units in the viscera

Another main class of interoceptors lie in the walls of the alimentary tract. By definition this class should comprise only the afferent units with receptors or endings in the epithelial or mucosal lining of the gut. This restriction will, however, be disregarded and all classes of receptors in the alimentary tract and in other abdominal and pelvic viscera will be included in this section.

Receptors in the mucosa. One kind of afferent unit examined electrophysiologically is the gastric pH receptor (Iggo 1957b). When an acid or an alkaline solution is allowed to flow over the exposed gastric mucosa or is placed in the intact stomach, a discharge of impulses in vagal afferent fibers is evoked. Two subclasses are found: (1) units that are excited only by acidic solutions, pH 3 or less; the discharge adapts slowly and will continue for minutes if the acid solution is left in contact with the mucosa; (2) units excited by alkaline solutions,

Table 43.1 Presence of gustatory afferent fibers

Type of stimulus	Monkey	Cat	Dog	Sheep	Goat	Pig	Rabbit	Rat	Pigeon	Hen
Distilled water	+	+	+	−	−	+	+	−	+	+
Ringer solution (0.15 M NaC1)	−	−	−	+	+	−	−	−	−	−
NaC1 (0.5 M)	+	+	+	+	+	+	+	+	+	+
Quinine HC1 (0.02 M)	+	+	+	+	+	+	+	+	−	+
Acetic acid (0.1 M)	+	+	+	+	+	+	+	+	+	+
Sucrose (0.5 M)	+	−	+	+	+	+	+	+	−	−

+, present; −, absent
Based on Zotterman 1956, Appelberg 1958, Kitchell 1963, Iggo and Leek 1967

pH 8 or above, which also adapt slowly to a maintained stimulus.

The gastric pH receptors can also be excited by rapidly stroking the mucosa with a smooth blunt object, e.g. a glass rod. These properties, in addition to their location in the mucosa, distinguish the pH receptors from the other main classes of gastric and intestinal receptors.

Evidence from reflex experiments in sheep indicates that there are probably receptors in the reticuloruminal epithelium that are excited by the acetate anion and reflexly inhibit ruminal movements (Ash 1959) and others that initiate or inhibit eructation.

Distension receptors. When any of the hollow abdominal or pelvic viscera is distended there is a discharge of impulses in distension-sensitive afferent units in the visceral nerve that innervates it (Iggo 1955, 1957a). The receptors are in the muscularis externa. Distension of some viscera may evoke a series of contractions, for example, the peristaltic reflex of the intestine. During such contractions the frequency of discharge in the afferent unit is enhanced. This is an important property of these afferent units. They are excited *both* by distension and by contraction of the hollow viscus in whose wall they lie.

The rate of distension has an important effect on the response of the receptors. The higher frequency of discharge in these "in series" distension receptors upon rapid distension is thus accounted for by response of the receptor to the rate of change of the stimulus and by the plastic properties of smooth muscle, which first resists a change in length and then slowly readjusts to it.

A particularly vigorous discharge from the in-series distension receptors is provoked if a distended hollow viscus contracts strongly (Fig. 43.10). The frequency of discharge during a contraction may be higher than that caused by severe distension. In either event, the afferent inflow carries no information that permits the CNS to distinguish the cause of the discharge, that is, to discriminate between distension and contraction. This property of the receptors increases the difficulty of diagnosing abdominal disorders.

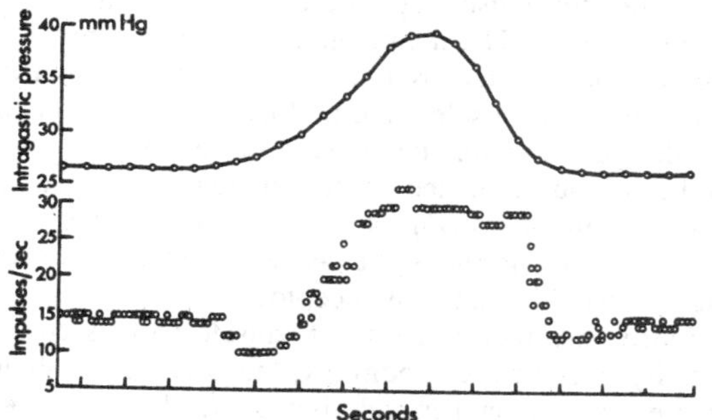

Figure 43.10. Response of a slowly adapting tension receptor, in the wall of the esophageal groove region in a goat, to maintain reticular distension and during a reticular contraction elicited by the distension. The frequency of discharge was about 15 impulses per second initially and doubled at the peak of contraction. These afferent units do not discriminate between distension and contraction of a viscus. Similar receptors are found all along the alimentary canal and in the urinary bladder. (From Iggo and Leek 1966, *Acta Neuroveg.* 28:353–59.)

There is evidence from reflex experiments for a receptor mechanism that distinguishes between gas and fluid distension, but the afferent units have not been identified. One example is the eructation reflex in ruminants, which is evoked by gaseous distension of a region around the cardia. If this region is distended with a fluid, then the reflex opening of the cardia is abolished. Dougherty et al. (1958) considered that the receptors which reflexly inhibit opening of the cardia are superficially placed in the gastric epithelium.

Flow receptors. Some visceral receptors function as flow detectors. When fluid is flowing rapidly along the urethra, a discharge of impulses is elicited in pudendal afferent nerve fibers. The frequency of discharge (5–40/sec) depends on the rate of flow (Todd 1964). These receptors, which lie in the substance of the urethra, probably initiate reflex contraction of the bladder and relaxation of the urethra (Barrington 1931).

Receptors in the mesentery. Pacinian corpuscles are present in the mesentery, where they can be seen as small (0.5–2.0 mm) ovoid objects lying alongside the blood vessels. The responses of these receptors (a very rapidly adapting discharge) have already been described. Other less rapidly adapting receptors, which lie around the mesenteric arteries, are innervated by small (1–4 μ) myelinated fibers (Bessou and Perl 1966).

Proprioceptors

The mesodermal structures of the body are supplied by afferent nerves which are continually signaling to the CNS the state of affairs deep within the body.

Muscle receptors

There are three main classes of muscle afferent units: muscle spindle receptors (primary and secondary endings), Golgi tendon organs, and high threshold receptors (Barker 1962, Matthews 1964).

Muscle spindles. They are embedded among the large contractile muscle fibers in skeletal muscles (Fig. 43.11), and have a characteristic fusiform shape and a distinctive structure. There are stretch receptors in the muscle spindle (Fig. 43.12): (1) the primary endings (synonyms—nuclear bag, annulospiral) that wind around the intrafusal fibers in the equatorial region of the spindle, and (2) the secondary endings (synonyms—nuclear chain, myotube, flower-spray) that surround or end on the intrafusal muscle fibers out toward the poles of the spindles. The afferent fibers supplying the primary endings are the largest axons in peripheral nerves (12–20 μ diameter, group Ia) and are thicker than the axons supplying the secondary receptors (6–12 μ diameter, group II).

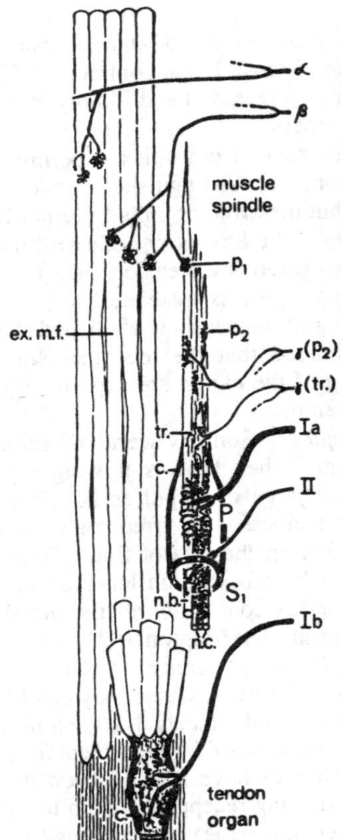

Figure 43.11. Innervation of skeletal muscles in the cat. The muscle spindle (right), contains one nuclear bag (n.b.) intrafusal muscle fiber and three myctube fibers (n.c.) within the capsule (c.). The spindle is parallel to large extrafusal muscle fibers (ex.m.f.). Several kinds of nerve fibers are shown entering from the right. They are, in order, α- and β-axons which are motor fibers in the extrafusal muscles (including β-branches to nuclear bag intrafusal fibers); γ-axons that are motor fibers to and form end plates on the intrafusal muscle fibers; group II axons that end as secondary endings (S_1) in the spindle; group Ia axons that form primary endings (P) in the spindle, and group Ib axons that end in Golgi tendon organs. The group III and group IV have been omitted from the figure. P1, P2, and tr. are types of intrafusal end plates. (Modified from D.C. Barker, in A.V.S. de Reuck and J. Knight, eds., *Myotatic, Kinesthetic, and Vestibular Mechanisms,* Ciba Found. Symp., Churchill, London, 1967.)

Both kinds of receptors are excited by stretch of the muscle and adapt very slowly to maintained stretch. They respond differently to rhythmical stretching and relaxation of the muscle (Matthews 1964). The primary endings may be particularly important in reflex adjustments to changes in length of the skeletal muscles. The secondary endings give a more accurate indication of the length of the spindle since they have a weak dynamic response. When the intrafusal muscle fibers contract, the secondary endings have an enhanced sensitivity to maintained stretch (static response). A discharge in the fusimotor nerve fibers causes the intrafusal muscle fibers to contract, and the spindle receptors are excited because of the shortening of the intrafusal fibers. This shortening may be sufficient to offset the overall shortening of the spindle due to extrafusal fiber contraction, so that the spindle receptor discharge continues (or even increases) in frequency if both extrafusal and intrafusal motor nerve fibers are active simultaneously. In this way the discharge of the spindle receptors can be maintained during contraction of the muscles. There are important reflex consequences of this mechanism (see Chapter 42).

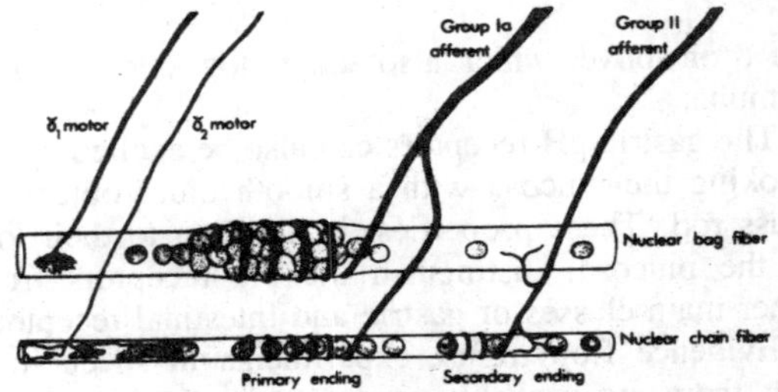

Figure 43.12. Very simplified diagram of the intrafusal muscles and their innervation. The nuclear bag fibers have a central accumulation of nuclei, which is absent from the narrower nuclear chain fiber. Each kind of fiber is separately innervated by fusimotor (γ-efferent) axons. (From Matthews 1964, *Physiol. Rev.* 44:219–88.)

Golgi tendon organs. The receptors are found near the tendinous ends of the skeletal muscles (see Fig. 43.11). They respond with a slowly adapting discharge when the muscle is stretched, and this discharge is further increased if the muscle contracts. The thresholds of the receptors are higher than the stretch receptors in the spindles so that during stretch of a muscle a discharge will appear first from the stretch receptor afferent units and only later from the tendon organ afferent units (Granit 1955).

High threshold receptors. Excitation of the high-threshold muscle receptors requires a much more vigorous mechanical stimulation of the muscle than is needed for either the muscle spindle or tendon organ receptors. (Paintal 1960). The nonmyelinated afferent units in muscles are not excited by either severe stretch or a tetanic contraction of muscles. Direct localized pressure, for example, pressing on the muscle or tendon with a blunt probe or squeezing the muscle or tendon, evokes a discharge of impulses (Fig. 43.13). The intensities of stimulation are about the same as are needed to excite the high-threshold cutaneous receptors.

Since an effective cause of muscle pain is contractile activity in ischemic conditions, the nociceptors should be excited if a skeletal muscle is made ischemic by occluding the blood supply, and then made to contract tetanically for several minutes. Ischemia in the absence of muscle work is not effective. The discharge of impulses caused by ischemic work disappears within 30 seconds of restoring the arterial blood supply (see Fig. 43.13).

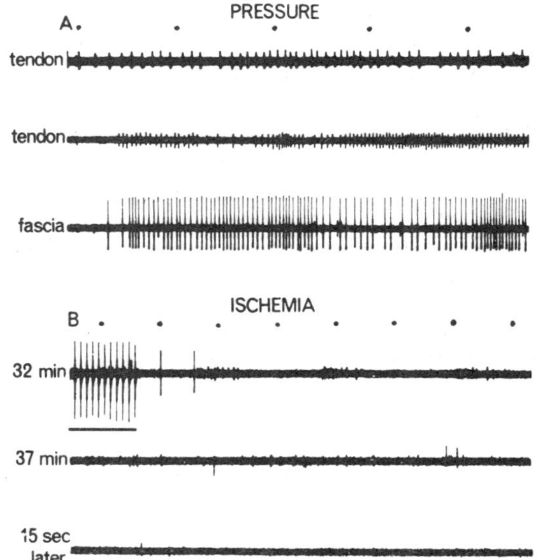

Figure 43.13. Muscle nociceptors; nonmyelinated (group IV) afferent fibers in skeletal muscle. A, response of three afferent units to direct mechanical pressure (squeezing between finger and thumb); two units were in the gastrocnemius tendon and the third was in the superficial fascia. B, effect of muscle ischemia. Thirty-two minutes after occluding the blood supply, the muscle was made to contract tetanically by electrical stimulation (artifacts above solid bar in B_1) of the muscle nerve. Following the contraction there were rhythmical bursts of impulses in small axons. Five minutes later there was a persistent, irregular discharge which disappeared 15 seconds after the blood supply was restored. Time marks are at 1 second intervals.

Joint receptors

The joints are richly supplied with afferent nerve fibers. Individual slowly adapting afferent units are very sensitive to the position or angle of the joint; the frequency of discharge in the afferent fiber is maximal at one angle and less at all other positions. Unlike the muscle spindle receptors the joint receptors are not innervated by efferent fibers that alter their sensitivity, and accordingly they act as accurate detectors of limb position. Rapidly adapting receptors with larger axons (10–15 μ) are also present in the joint capsule.

Joint nociceptors

These form a different category of afferent unit than the previous group. The physiological properties have been little studied.

DISTRIBUTION OF DORSAL ROOT AFFERENT FIBERS

All dorsal root afferent fibers, regardless of their function, branch after they have entered the spinal cord and end within it or in the medulla; nearly all end on the side of entry (ipsilateral) except in the sacral region, where they may end on both sides. The branching disseminates the incoming afferent impulses to diverse end stations. A functional pattern is, however, preserved in the distribution of the branches or collaterals.

The dorsal root afferent fibers which enter at a particular segmental level send many collaterals into the dorsal horn gray matter at the level of entry. In addition to these segmental collaterals the large afferent fibers, from skin and joints especially, send long collaterals up the dorsal columns (dorsal fasciculi) that end in the cuneate and gracile nuclei at the rostral end of the spinal cord and in the medulla. Other collaterals pass down in the dorsal columns to enter the gray matter at lower levels (Fig. 43.14).

The segmentally distributed collaterals of the afferent fibers are important for local reflex actions in the spinal cord, but also end on cells that give rise to ascending spinal pathways. The consideration of these tracts can be simplified by making a major distinction between the functions of ascending spinal pathways: (1) those that in man result in conscious sensations; these in general end

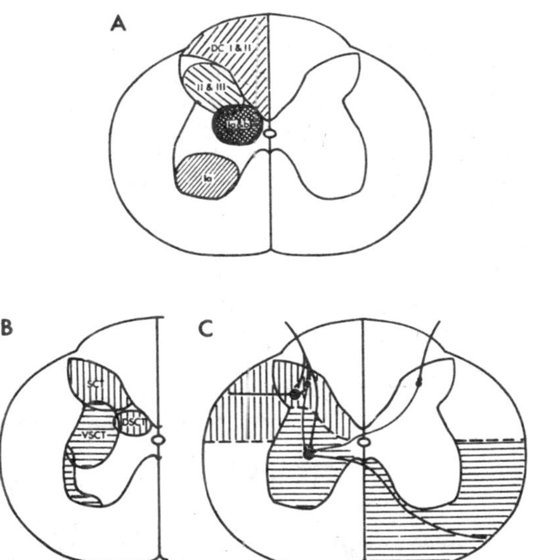

Figure 43.14. Distribution of dorsal root afferent fibers in the lumbar spinal cord of the cat (A); B and C, ascending tracts that arise from cell columns in the lumbar spinal cord. The group I and II afferent fibers send collaterals to dorsal columns (DC); the large cutaneous (group II) fibers end in the dorsal horn, dorsal to the group III cutaneous and muscle fibers. The large group Ia and b muscle fibers end at the lower part of the dorsal horn. The group Ia (primary ending fibers from the muscle spindles) also send collaterals into the ventral horn, to end on motoneurons. The ascending tracts, apart from the dorsal columns, arise from cell bodies as shown. The ipsilateral tracts (DSCT and SCT, vertical hatching) come from dorsomedial cells in the gray matter, whereas the contralateral or crossed tracts (VSCT) in the ventral quadrant of the cord arise from cells in the ventrolateral region of the gray matter, horizontal hatching. (Based on O. Oscarsson, B. Rexed, and J.M. Sprague and Hongchien Ha, in J.C. Eccles and J.P. Schadé, eds., *Progress in Brain Research*, Elsevier, Amsterdam, 1964, vols. 2, 11, 12.)

in the thalamus and make synaptic connections with neurons that send axons to the sensory areas of the cerebral cortex; and (2) those that do not result directly in sensation. Important end stations for these latter tracts are the cerebellum and the brain stem, where they play a vital part in the reflex regulation of posture and movements. Some of the afferent systems, particularly those from the skin and joints and the secondary spindle receptors, make important contributions to both systems, whereas those from the primary muscle spindle receptors and Golgi tendon organs are directed principally into tracts not resulting in sensation. These latter tracts may contribute indirectly to perception.

Ascending spinal pathways directly concerned with sensation

There are two principal pathways in this group. Through these channels flow the afferent information that enters consciousness.

Dorsal column pathways

Branches of the large primary afferent fibers enter the dorsal columns of the white matter and travel up or down the cord (Fig. 43.15). The group I afferent fiber collaterals from the hind limbs, on the other hand, leave the dorsal columns at lower levels of the spinal cord and make synaptic connections directly with the neurons that give rise to the spinocerebellar tracts and so do not contribute to muscle sensations (Mountcastle and Powell 1959).

In addition, collaterals of group I afferent fibers from the forelimb also end in the cuneate nucleus. The dorsal column nuclei are therefore able to perform some of the analysis of afferent information that is carried out by the CNS. This kind of analysis presumably also occurs in other nuclei in the afferent pathways (e.g. spinothalamic, spinocerebellar), so that these nuclei are more than simple switchboards or relay stations. The afferent information leaves the dorsal column nuclei along second-order afferent fibers. The largest path goes via the medial lemniscus to the contralateral thalamus. The crossing over in the pathway occurs in the decussation of the lemnisci.

The dorsal columns are the principal paths for the sensations of cutaneous touch and for joint, muscle, and tendon sensations. In man all these sensations are disturbed, at least temporarily, by dorsal column lesions. One consequence of such lesions is ataxia, which is an inability to control voluntary movements. In the monkey, which has well-developed dorsal columns, there is a loss of weight discrimination but this is only temporary. The other spinal cord paths, such as the spinothalamic tract, carry sufficient information to allow at least partial recovery from dorsal column lesions.

Spinothalamic tract

This tract arises in cell bodies in the gray matter of the dorsal horns within a segment or two of the level of entry of the afferent fibers. The second-order fibers cross the midline and enter the white matter of the ventrolateral quadrant, in which they ascend to the medulla (see Fig. 43.15). In primates, including man, the spinothalamic tract is well developed and ends in the thalamus, probably in the ventrobasal complex and the posterior nuclear group (Mountcastle 1961). In other animals, although it

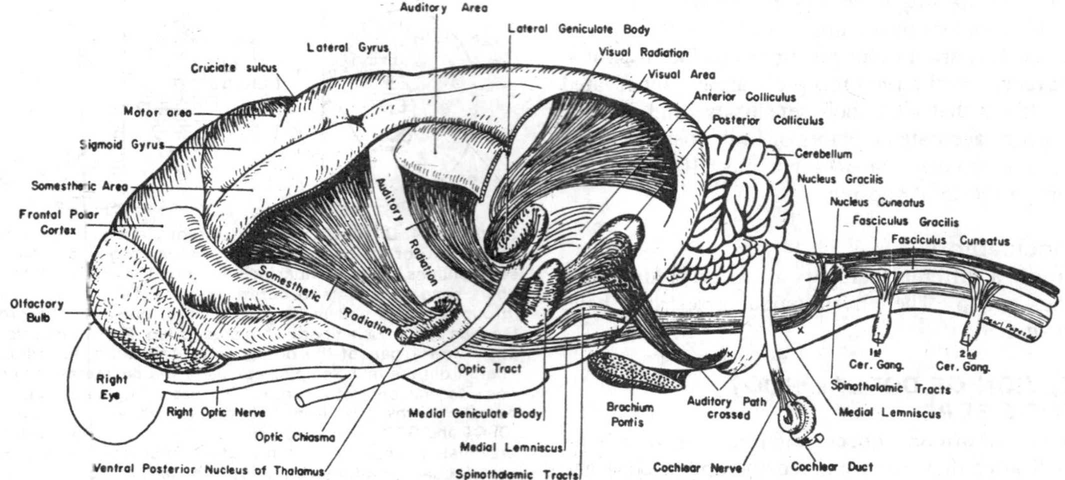

Figure 43.15. Afferent paths to the thalamus and cerebral cortex in the brain of the dog. The four paths represented are cutaneous (and visceral pain), proprioceptive, auditory, and visual. Two cervical segments of the spinal cord are also shown. The thalamic nuclei and the paths have been simplified. The decussations of the auditory path and the medial lemniscus are indicated by X. (Designed and drawn by Dr. James W. Papez, Cornell University.)

exists, it is less well developed and its exact termination in the thalamus is uncertain, partly because the tract is made up of thin myelinated fibers. This small size of the ventrolateral (spinothalamic) fibers increases the difficulty of tracing their paths.

The spinothalamic tract is probably an important pain pathway, but the central paths taken by ascending pain tracts can be tortuous (Gaze and Gordon 1955) and for this reason are difficult to interrupt surgically.

The sensations of pain and temperature in man are mediated exclusively by fibers in this tract, whereas touch and pressure sensations are also subserved by the dorsal column paths. A hemisection of the spinal cord will therefore cause loss of pain and temperature sensations on the side of the body about two segments below the level of the lesion (crossed spinothalamic tract), and of position, touch, pressure, and vibration on the same side as the lesion (uncrossed dorsal column path). This is the Brown-Séquard syndrome. Surgical interruption of the spinothalamic tract is used in man to relieve severe or intractable pain. The operation, known as cordotomy, involves the transection of the white matter in the ventrolateral quadrant of the spinal cord.

Spinocervical tract

This tract originates in the large cells in the head of the dorsal horn in the upper thoracic and lower cervical region of the spinal cord (Morin 1955) (see Fig. 43.15). The neurons are excited by cutaneous afferent fibers but probably not by muscle afferent fibers. They are readily excited by mild cutaneous stimuli such as blowing on hairs, and the receptive fields are small. This pathway therefore shows a high spatial discrimination for cutaneous tactile stimuli. The tract terminates ipsilaterally in the lateral cervical nucleus. This nucleus sends axons that cross in the anterior commissure to the ventral quadrant of the cord. From there the tract runs until it joins the medial lemniscus and ends in the thalamus.

Trigeminal tract

The very rich sensory innervation of the skin of the face is provided by the trigeminal nerve. Afferent fibers in this nerve end in the trigeminal nucleus in the medulla oblongata. The large afferent fibers make synaptic connections with cells in the rostral part of this nucleus, whereas the finer afferent fibers travel caudally to the descending part of the trigeminal nucleus. These latter fibers include the nociceptor afferent units.

Ascending spinal pathways not concerned with conscious sensation

One of the largest of these pathways that carries information from the spinal cord is the spinocerebellar pathway, which ends in the cerebellum. It is made up of several parts, each of which travels in a different region of the white matter (see Fig. 43.14). Other tracts are the spinoreticular and the spinotectal.

Dorsal spinocerebellar tract (DSCT)

This arises from cell bodies in the dorsomedial gray matter (Clarke's column) in the thoracic and lumbar spinal cord, and enters the cerebellum through the restiform body (the inferior peduncle). The DSCT is well developed in mammals but less so in birds (Oscarsson 1965). The forelimb homologue is the cuneocerebellar tract which arises from cells in the external cuneate nucleus. These tracts are probably concerned chiefly with the adjustment and coordination of movement of the ipsilateral limbs in which the primary afferent fibers end.

Ventral spinocerebellar tract (VSCT)

This tract arises from neurons situated in the gray matter of the cord ventral and lateral to the DSCT cell bodies. The fibers cross to the opposite side of the cord and, entering via the superior cerebellar peduncle, reach the hind limb area on both sides of the anterior cerebellum. The VSCT is well developed in the cat, rabbit, phalanger, and duck but is relatively small in the monkey and dog. The forelimb homologue is the rostral spinocerebellar tract (RSCT).

The information carried by these two tracts (VSCT and RSCT) is probably concerned with both the stage of movement and the position of limbs. Since the RSCT ends in both forelimb and hind limb areas, it may in addition be concerned with the coordination of fore- and hind limb movements.

Spinoreticular connections

The fibers ascend in the ventrolateral funiculus of the spinal cord at all levels and end, for the most part ipsilaterally, in the medullary reticular formation and bilaterally in the pontine reticular formation, according to anatomical studies. Brodal (1957) suggested that this tract is important in altering the activity of the reticular formation.

The reticular formation is very complex and, in view of recent evidence that it plays an important part in the control of the general level of activity in the cerebral cortex (see Chapter 45), these spinoreticular connections may have important functions in contributing to the regulation of consciousness.

Spinotectal tract

This arises from cells in the dorsal horn of gray matter in the spinal cord. The fibers, after crossing in the ventral white commissure, ascend in the lateral funiculus together with the lateral spinothalamic tract fibers. The tract ends in the colliculi of the tectum. It is probable that these fibers are concerned in the integration and coordination of movements reflexly associated with the visual and acoustic stimuli.

Descending control of spinal afferent nuclei

In a preceding section some aspects of the functional organization of the dorsal column nuclei were considered, and it was pointed out that the nuclei were modifying the information they received. There is a further important way in which the afferent information from receptors entering a sensory nucleus can be modified on its way to higher centers in the brain. The discharge of a cell in the gracile nucleus of the cat, for example, evoked by a peripheral stimulus, can be inhibited or facilitated by descending impulses that arise in more cranial parts of the CNS. These actions may arise from impulses in fibers which come from the sensorimotor area of the cerebral cortex and travel down to the gracile nucleus in the pyramidal tract. Descending inhibitory effects could cause a 100 percent reduction in the discharge of the sensory nucleus cells. The descending inhibition is characteristically long lasting. These powerful actions may be part of the mechanism that underlies *attention*, that is, the ability to concentrate or focus on some particular sensory stimulus to the exclusion of others.

In addition to these well-established actions there may also be recurrent inhibitory or excitatory actions within a sensory nucleus. The discharge of a cell may by this mechanism alter its own excitability by feedback from axon collaterals.

The role of these nuclei interposed on the pathway from the peripheral receptors to the cerebral cortex is thus complex. There may be (1) convergence from a large receptive field or from a restricted small receptive field, (2) surround inhibition or facilitation from the area surrounding the excitatory receptive field of an individual cell, (3) descending control from a higher center that either enhances or depresses transmission, and (4) recurrent actions that arise from the activity of the nuclear projection cells.

Thalamus

The thalamus is the great sensory ganglion of the brain stem and lies at its upper end (see Fig. 43.15). It has large and important connections with the cerebral cortex, basal ganglia, hypothalamus, cerebellum, brain stem, reticular formation, and spinal cord. Some of the connections are direct, often through long tracts, whereas others are by polysynaptic paths. The thalamus contains many nuclear masses which can be divided into several groups on anatomical (Table 43.2) or physiological grounds.

Anatomically the thalamus can be considered as three parts (Crosby et al. 1962): (1) the epithalamus, which does not degenerate after removal of the forebrain, con-

Table 43.2. Thalamic subdivisions and nuclei, with abbreviations used in text and Figure 43.17

Division	Nuclei		Forebrain connections
Epithalamus	n. habenularis		do not degenerate
	n. paraventricularis	PVA	
	pretectal area		
Dorsal thalamus			
Intralaminar	n. centromedianus	CM	nonspecific system *
	n. centralis lateralis	CL	
	n. centralis medialis	NCM	
	n. ventralis medialis	VM	
	n. paracentralis		
Midline	n. reuniens	RE	
	n. parataenialis	Pt	
Medial	n. parafasicularis		specific system *
	n. medialis dorsalis	MD	
Posterior	n. geniculatis lateralis	LG	
	n. geniculatis medialis	MG	
Anterior	n. anterodorsalis		
	n. anteroventralis		
	n. anteromedialis		
Lateral	pulvinar		
	n. lateralis posterior	LP	
	n. lateralis dorsalis	LD	
	n. suprageniculatus	SG	
Ventral	n. ventralis lateralis	VL	
	n. ventralis posterior	VP	
	n. ventralis posterolateralis	VPL } VB	
	n. ventralis posteromedialis	VPM } VB	
	n. ventralis anterior	VA	
Ventral thalamus	n. reticularis †	R	nonspecific system *
	zona incerta		
	subthalamic nucleus		

* Degenerate after cortical ablation † Sometimes included in dorsal thalamus

tains the habenular and paraventricular nuclei and pretectal area—its functions are not completely known; (2) the dorsal thalamus, which degenerates after removal of the forebrain, contains the sensory relay nuclei; (3) the ventral thalamus, which partly degenerates on removal of the cortex. The degeneration of cells in a nucleus following removal of another part of the brain establishes the existence of direct connections from the former to the latter (Rose and Woolsey 1949).

The nuclei of the dorsal thalamus, which is the largest part of the thalamus, can be grouped as follows: the medial, midline, and intralaminar complexes; the anterior nuclei; the lateral group; the ventral nuclei: lateroventral (VL), posteroventral of two parts—n. ventralis posteromedialis (VPM) and n. ventralis posterolateralis (VPL), also known as the ventrobasal complex (VB), and the anteroventral (VA); and the posterior group (including the medial and lateral geniculate bodies, MG and LG). This grouping is based on anatomical and embryological criteria. All the nuclei degenerate after removal of the entire forebrain but only VL, VB, LG, MG, and the anterior nuclei degenerate after removal of the neocortex. These latter are the cortical relay nuclei.

The dorsal thalamus can be subdivided on a physiological basis into three parts. First are those parts that project to specific sensory areas of the cerebral cortex (specific projection system for cortical relay nuclei). These are (1) the lateral geniculate body, which receives fibers from the optic tract and projects to the visual area of the cortex; (2) the medial geniculate body that has connections from the cochlea via the lateral lemniscus and projects to the auditory area of the cortex; (3) the ventrobasal complex (VPL and VPM) which receives an input from the medial lemniscus, spinothalamic tract, and trigeminal tract and projects to the primary and secondary somatic areas of the cortex; (4) the posterior (PO) nuclear group (parts of LP and MG, and lying between the ventrobasal complex and the medial geniculate body), which receives an input from the spinothalamic tract and medial lemniscus and projects to the cortex in a less precise way than the ventrobasal complex (Darian-Smith 1964); (5) the lateroventral (VL) nuclei which receive afferent fibers from the cerebellum (via brachium conjunctivum) and project to the motor cortex; and (6) the anterior nuclei which have connections with the mammillary bodies and project to the cingulate gyrus (limbic cortex).

The second major physiological group of nuclei in the dorsal thalamus includes those which are without direct cortical connections and which are not sensory relay nuclei. The nuclei can be further subdivided into (1) a nonspecific cortical projecting group (nonspecific projection system) which includes medial, midline, and intralaminar nuclei (e.g. center median, centralis medialis, and centralis lateralis); and (2) nuclei with a cortical projection but no established function (pulvinar, dorsomedial, and lateral and posterior nuclei of the dorsolateral group).

The ventral thalamus comprises the ventral lateral geniculate body, of unknown function, and the reticular nucleus (R), which extends the full length of the thalamus and has a very widely spread projection to the cortex. It forms part of the nonspecific or diffuse projection system, together with nuclei in the dorsal thalamus.

In summary, the thalamic nuclei can be divided anatomically into three groups—epithalamus of obscure function, dorsal thalamus with direct anatomical dependence on the forebrain, and ventral thalamus—or physiologically, based on the cortical actions and connections of the nuclei, into three divisions: (1) the specific projection system nuclei which transmit precise information to and from the cortex and include the thalamic sensory relay nuclei; (2) the nonspecific or diffuse projecting system nuclei, which are not sensory relay nuclei and which have a diffuse or widespread action on the cortex; (3) other nuclei of obscure action and probably with diverse functions.

Specific projection system

The specific cortical projection is from the nuclei in the thalamus which send fibers to restricted regions of the cerebral cortex. The sensory surfaces of the skin, joints, eye, and ear project to the specific sensory areas of the cerebral cortex through relay nuclei in the thalamus via the specific cortical projection (see Fig. 43.14). (There is also a specific projection from the cerebellum to the motor cortex.)

The ventrobasal complex has a very precise point-to-point relationship both with its receptive fields and with the somatic sensory areas of the cerebral cortex (Mountcastle and Henneman 1952). Tactile and kinesthetic activity from the contralateral side of the body is relayed via this region to the somatic sensory area of the cerebral cortex (Darian-Smith 1964). These ventrobasal cells preserve the identity of the stimulus.

The response of these specific units is quantitatively related to the intensity of the natural stimulus, and so the quantitative aspects are preserved along with modality and place specificity. This region of the thalamus is thus fully capable of transmitting precise and accurate information about events occurring on the contralateral side of the body to the somatic sensory cortex.

The representation of the body in the ventrobasal complex of the thalamus is not linear, but is related to the innervation density of the various parts. As a result there is a distortion of the body image even though the entire body surface is represented (Fig. 43.16). Animals like the rabbit have a relative dominance of the trigeminal representation which is presented in detail in the posteromedial part (VPM) of the ventrobasal complex. The cat has a more balanced spinal and trigeminal projection and a corresponding enlargement of the ventrolateral

Figure 43.16. Representation of the body surface in the ventrobasal nucleus of the thalamus. In the rabbit, the trigeminal representation is dominant. There is a relative increase in the size of the limb and trunk areas in cat and monkey. Similar maps can be prepared for the somatosensory areas of the cerebral cortex. (From Rose and Mountcastle, in *Handbook of Physiology,* sec. 1, H.W. Magoun, ed., *Neurophysiology,* Am. Physiol. Soc., Washington, 1959, vol. 1, 387–429.)

(VPL) nucleus to accommodate the projection from the trunk and limbs. In the monkey, the hands and feet have a very rich afferent innervation and are more highly developed as tactile and prehensile organs; a larger share of the representation is given to these structures in this animal with a corresponding still greater enlargement of the ventrolateral part of the ventrobasal complex (Rose and Mountcastle 1959).

Posterior (PO) group of nuclei

This group of nuclei is posterior to the ventrobasal complex and medial to the geniculate bodies in the caudal portion of the dorsal thalamus in the cat (Poggio and Mountcastle 1960). Afferent fibers from the somatic system (bilaterally via the spinothalamic tract without any clear-cut topographical arrangement) and the auditory system end in this posterior nuclear group. The efferent connections do not project directly to the primary or secondary somatic sensory cortex (Darian-Smith 1964). The majority of the neurons in the posterior group in the cat can only be activated by stimuli that excite nociceptors (such as pinpricks or shallow cuts in the skin, or heavy pressure on the periosteum).

Many of the PO cells are excited by noxious stimuli delivered to the skin, and this pathway from the periphery to the cortex may play a role in the conscious perception of pain. The ventrobasal complex does not contain such cells.

Nonspecific cortical projection

Morison and Dempsey in 1942 described a cortical projection from thalamic nuclei that lacked the precise point-to-point, short latency projection from the specific thalamic nuclei (Fig. 43.17).

Electrical stimulation of the nonspecific thalamic nuclei causes a widespread alteration in the electrical activity of the cerebral cortex. Single shocks have only a small effect, but repetition at rates of 8–10 per second causes a progressively larger potential change, until rhythmic potential waves of large amplitude develop. This gradual growth is called the recruiting response. It can be elicited by stimulation of any part of the nonspecific thalamic nuclear complex and may spread widely in

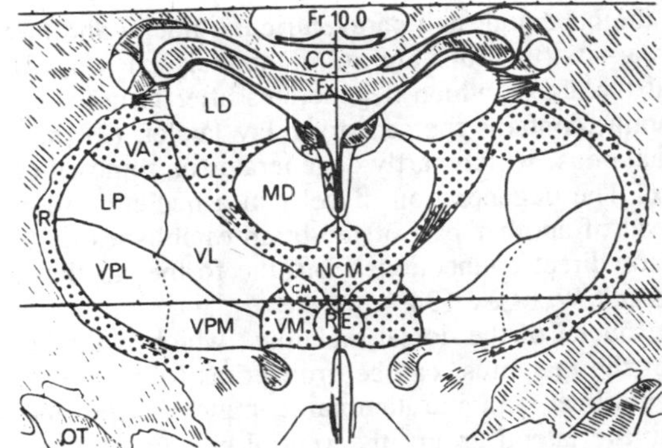

Figure 43.17. Cross section near the middle of the thalamus of a cat to show the nonspecific cortical projecting nuclei (stippled). At this plane of section these are the medial (RE) and intralaminar complexes (CL, NCM), and n. reticularis (R). The specific nuclei include VPL, VPM, VL, MD, LD. This section is cut in the Horsley-Clark stereotaxic coordinate frontal 10.0 (Fr 10.0). CC, corpus callosum; Fx, fornix; OT, optic tract; (From Jasper, in *Handbook of Physiology,* sec. 1, H.W. Magoun, ed., *Neurophysiology,* Am. Physiol. Soc., Washington, 1960, vol. 2, 1307–21.)

the cerebral cortex (Hanbery and Jasper 1953). This nonspecific cortical projection may play an important part in the regulation of cortical activity and of consciousness (see Chapter 45).

Sensory areas in the cerebral cortex

The principal sensory systems (visual, auditory, gustatory, and somesthetic) thus relay through different nuclei in the thalamus. This separation of the sensory tracts is preserved in their projection to the cerebral cortex. Each goes to a different part of the cortex and within each of these regions there is a topographical or point-to-point representation of the sense organ or the body surface.

Somatosensory

The thalamocortical radiation from the ventrobasal region of the thalamus goes to the somatosensory region of cerebral cortex (see Fig. 43.15). Detailed electrophysiological recording from the sensory cortex shows a detailed topographical representation of the body. The tongue and face are represented at the most medial end of the sensory cortex, while the hind leg is represented on the lateral convexity of its surface. The precise location and extent of the sensory areas depend on the degree of development of the cerebral cortex. In the primates, which have a very elaborate and highly developed forebrain, the sensory motor cortex is in the parietal region. In the cat, dog, and sheep it is more frontally placed. The area of the sensory cortex to which a part of the body surface projects is related to the sensory importance of the part in question, and there is a wide species variation (Adrian 1943).

The general picture in the somatosensory cortex corresponds with the representation of the body surface in the thalamus (see Fig. 43.16), which in the rabbit shows a relatively greater preponderance of the lips and face.

The trunks and limbs project to the somatosensory cortex on the opposite (contralateral) side of the body. The projection of the face shows some interesting species differences. In the horse, cat, dog, rat, rabbit, ferret, and monkey it is contralateral, whereas in the sheep and goat it is ipsilateral. Adrian (1943) has suggested that this is related, first, to the contralateral representation of the eyes and second, to the relative importance of the sense of smell in feeding. Since the eyes project to the contralateral cortex, it is probably advantageous for the afferent information from the limbs, face, and mouth to cross to the opposite cortex. In this way the coordination of sight and muscular movements is more readily achieved. In ungulates, by contrast, sight is relatively less important for feeding, whereas the coordination of smell and of touch from the upper and lower lips is of greater significance than the coordination of sight and of touch from the mouth. The coordination of selective grazing with the sense of smell (which has an uncrossed projection to the cerebral cortex) can therefore be obtained most simply if both smell and labial touch afferent inputs go to the same side of the cortex, as in fact they do in the ungulates. The horse, like the sheep and goat, has an extensive cortical representation of the skin around the nostrils and upper lips but differs from them in that the representation is contralateral. The nostrils are important tactile organs in the horse, and it is probably advantageous to have their cortical representation on the same side as the eyes, so that the tactile information goes to the same side of the cerebral cortex as the visual information.

The relative importance of the representation of the body on the sensory cortex is reflected in the results of damage to it. After ablation of the sensory cortex, the principal defect in a sheep is its inability to control the movements of its lips in feeding and rumination. This disparity in the representation of different parts of the body may also account for the apparent insensitivity of these animals to severe wounds on the trunk. A sheep recovering from the surgical insertion of a ruminal cannula appears to be quite indifferent to the wound in its flank. On the other hand, injuries to the face or feet are more distressing.

In addition to the large primary somatosensory cortical areas just described there are other cortical receiving areas which are smaller in area. These secondary sensory areas are less well organized topographically and receive information from both sides of the body, and afferent information takes longer to reach them. In the cat the somatic secondary sensory area extends from the bottom of the post central gyrus to the bottom of the sylvian fissure on the lateral surface of the cortex.

Ablation experiments in monkeys, cats, and dogs establish that tactile discrimination is impaired if the first somatic sensory area is removed. Recovery will take place. Bilateral ablation of the primary somatic sensory area in dogs only slightly reduced discrimination of a tactile stimulus (stroking the hair with and against the grain once a second) on conditional reflex experiments in three dogs, and left one animal unaffected, when tested 2 weeks after the operation. All the dogs recovered during the first day's training (Allen 1947). More severe deficits in tactile discrimination were caused by bilateral removal of primary and secondary somatic sensory areas. Operated dogs were unable to distinguish stroking with the grain from stroking against the grain of the hair during 5000 trials over a 6 month period.

Several channels are open for the transmission of impulses (i.e. information) from the peripheral receptors to the somatosensory cortex. The classical path is via the spinothalamic tract or the dorsal columns and the ventrobasal complex and PO group of the thalamus. Additional paths are via (1) the cerebellum, which like the cerebral cortex has a somatotopic representation of the body and important connections with the proprioceptors; (2) a fast short latency projection to the motor cortex from the group I muscle afferent fibers, especially from the forelimbs; and (3) a diffuse projection from the thalamus.

Visual

The optic radiation from the lateral geniculate body of the thalamus ends in the primary visual receiving area at the occipital pole of the cerebral cortex (striate area). A detailed map of the retina, and therefore of the visual field, is preserved in the visual area, although the extensive folding of the cortex in this region may obscure the relationships in some species. In lower vertebrates such as the fish, amphibia, and birds, in which the eyes are on the opposite sides of the head, there is complete crossing over of the optic tract fibers in the optic chiasma, and all the optic nerve fibers from the left eye go to the right lateral geniculate and so to the right visual cortex. In mammals the crossover is incomplete. In the horse and rabbit probably less than 10 percent of the optic fibers are uncrossed. In intermediate forms, such as the cat and dog, about 80 percent of the fibers cross, whereas in the primates only 50 percent do so. In primates, therefore, the left half of the visual field is represented in the right visual cortex and vice versa. As a result, the left cerebral hemisphere receives information from the left visual field of both eyes, that is, from nasal retina of the right eye and the temporal retina of the left eye, and conversely for the right hemisphere.

In the visual cortex there is a point-to-point representation of the visual field. Coincidence of the visual fields seen from each eye is an important feature of the visual system in animals with binocular vision.

In the primary visual cortex (striate area) there is once

again a point-to-point representation, but in the cat and monkey there is a high degree of binocular convergence onto individual cortical cells. Nearly 90 percent of cells show binocular effects in the cat, but individual cells are unequally affected by the two eyes (Hubel and Wiesel 1962). In other mammals there is binocular vision but for a much more restricted part of the visual field. In the rabbit there is an ipsilateral projection of about 20° of the visual field (from the temporal retina, therefore the nasal visual field) and the remainder of the field (about 140°) goes to the contralateral cortex. If the animal converges its eyes there is therefore binocular vision for about 40° of field in front of the head (Thompson et al. 1950).

The processing of visual information by the cerebral cortex has been the subject of intensive study by Hubel and Wiesel (1962), and the results obtained give some indication of the operation of the sensory cortex in general.

The functions of the visual cortex have been determined by experiments in which the visual cortex has been removed, in whole or in part. The lower vertebrates (fish, amphibia, and birds) are largely unaffected by removal of the cortex; the remarkable visual feats of which birds are capable are carried out by subcortical structures. In the mammals the visual cortex is much larger and more important and has become dominant in controlling visual activity. Blindness follows damage to or removal of the visual cortex in man, monkey, cat, and dog (Marquis 1934). The cat, dog, and rat can still learn to discriminate between a bright and dark light after removal of the visual cortex, but are unable to distinguish patterns or make fine discrimination between small differences in light intensity.

Auditory

The acoustic pathway from the cochlea in the ear to the auditory areas of the cerebral cortex contains at least four neurons and is bilateral. It passes via the cochlea nuclei in the pons to the inferior colliculi, to the medial geniculate bodies in the thalamus, and then to the auditory receiving area in the ectosylvian gyrus in the temporal lobe of the cortex (cat and dog, see Fig. 43.15). The primary auditory cortex receives an orderly projection from the medial geniculate and therefore from the cochlea. The basal region of the cochlea (corresponding to high tones) evokes a discharge in the most forward region of the auditory cortex, whereas the apical region projects to the caudal part.

Unilateral destruction of the auditory cortex does not cause deafness, whereas bilateral destruction in the cat causes tone discrimination to be permanently lost. Different regions of the acoustic area are concerned with pattern discrimination and with tone discrimination.

Olfactory

The olfactory receptors in the nasal cavity send axons in the olfactory nerve that end in the secondary olfactory centers in the olfactory bulb. The fibers leaving the bulb go to the anterior part of the pyriform lobe of the cerebral cortex (paleopallium) and to parts of the amygdaloid nuclear complex (Clark and Meyer 1947). These authors were unable to demonstrate any direct connections to the hippocampus, which was formerly regarded as an important olfactory center, or to the posterior half of the pyriform lobe. These anatomical findings are also supported by physiological experiments in which evoked potentials have been recorded, in response to odorants on the olfactory mucosa, from the olfactory tract and from the anterior pyriform lobe of the dog (Allen 1943).

The olfactory pathway is distinctive, since unlike the other sensory pathways it does not pass to the cerebral cortex via the thalamus.

Gustatory

The cortical taste areas and pathways through the thalamus have only recently been examined electrophysiologically. In the thalamus of the rat and monkey the taste receptors project to an area in the ventrobasal complex that is medial to the area for touch and temperature. Taste is represented ipsilaterally. In the cerebral cortex the taste area is at the medial end of the face area in the somatosensory receiving area (Benjamin 1963). Bilateral removal of this region of the cortex in rats leads to an impairment of taste discrimination. Such a lesion also causes degeneration in the thalamic area described above. The cortical taste center in the monkey is not so clearly defined, and there may be a second area outside the somatosensory cortex. Ablation experiments in monkeys are also less definite in allowing taste discrimination to be assigned to a particular part of the sensory cortex (Benjamin 1963).

SENSATION

The information about the body that is available to the CNS is derived from afferent nervous activity that has its origin in receptors. Different kinds of stimuli and different types of receptors give rise to unique sensations. Some sensations are simple, e.g. touch and warmth; whereas others are very complex, e.g. nausea and sexual sensations. In each case there is a subjective reaction to the stimulus, and for this reason it is argued that the only sensations one knows about are human sensations, since each individual can experience them. The discussion of cerebral mechanisms elsewhere in this chapter should make it clear that although the peripheral receptor mechanisms may be similar in mammals generally, nevertheless there are big differences in the development of the cerebral cortex, and there are probably equally large differences in the degree and kind of sensation that is experienced.

Somatic sensation

Four basic qualities or distinctive sensory responses to stimulation of the skin are recognized: touch, warmth, cold, and pain. Touch is aroused by mechanical contact of an object with the skin. Two subdivisions can be recognized—first, a fleeting sensation that lasts less than a second, and second, a persistent sensation that may continue for as long as the stimulus is maintained. Information about the different kinds of receptors excited by mechanical stimuli indicates that there are at least five kinds of receptors with a high sensitivity to mechanical stimuli. Psychological experiments reveal less complexity of touch sensation, and no receptor has yet been experimentally established as giving rise uniquely to a particular kind of sensation. The rapidly adapting hair follicle receptors may subserve the fleeting sensation of touch, and the slowly adapting epidermal and dermal receptors may subserve the sensation of pressure.

Thermal sensations

Psychophysical experiments in man have established that temperature sensation from the skin arises from small spots. A small probe at above skin temperature arouses a sensation of warmth from discrete spots. Conversely, a probe cooler than the skin arouses a sensation of cold from other distinct spots. At each spot an enduring sensation can be set up. The temperature spots may vary in number according to the temperature of the skin, but the character of the sensation they elicit does not change.

The quality of the sensation caused by altering skin temperature depends both on initial temperature of the skin and on the rate of change of temperature. This is because the thermoreceptors adapt to the prevailing temperature, and when the temperature is changed they discharge at frequencies which depend both on the initial temperature and on the rate of change of temperature (see Fig. 43.6).

There are wide species variations in the reflex responses to thermal stimuli and presumably also in the sensations. The cat, for example, cannot be conditioned to respond if the skin of the back is heated, whereas warmth sensations can be elicited from this part of the body surface in man (Kenshalo 1964). Part of this difference may arise from species differences in the receptors.

Certain areas of the body surface in the cat, dog, rat, and rabbit are, however, known to evoke powerful thermoregulatory reflexes, although whether they also evoke correspondingly powerful thermal sensations is not known. When the scrotal skin of a ram or the udder of a ewe is heated to 40°C, breathing becomes rapid and shallow; that is, the animal begins to pant and deep body temperature falls. The respiratory rate may rise to 300 per minute. Similar heating of an equivalent area of the shorn skin of the flank is without effect (Waites 1962). Electrophysiological analysis of the scrotal skin of the rat shows that there is a much larger number of thermoreceptors in this skin than elsewhere on trunk or limbs (Iggo 1969). The tongue is another region of the body richly supplied with thermoreceptors. Both cold and warm receptors have been described in it (Zotterman 1959), and the afferent fibers are myelinated.

Pain

The sensation of pain is aroused by damaging or noxious stimulation of nearly all parts of the body, excluding only the CNS itself, unless damage is done to the pain pathways. Several qualities of painful sensation are recognized. Superficial or cutaneous pain is highly localized and is sharp and pricking in quality. It can be aroused by many different forms of stimulation, for example, by burning or by pinching the skin or pulling on hairs. Careful analysis has revealed two kinds of superficial pain. The first has a short latency and is mediated by myelinated (group III) afferent fibers and has a "bright" quality. The second pain has a longer latency and is mediated by nonmyelinated fibers; it is more diffuse and has an aching, throbbing quality.

A particular feature of pain is that it can be called forth by a range of thermal, chemical, and mechanical stimuli with only one feature in common, that is, high intensity. Accordingly, it has been postulated that pain receptors are not specialized to react to any particular kind of energy change.

Electrical recording from cutaneous afferent fibers establishes that impulses may arise from a cut and damaged nerve, even when the receptor has been cut off and impulses can no longer be aroused by natural stimuli that were effective when applied to the receptive field of the fiber before the injury. An osmotic stimulus will excite impulses in most kinds of the afferent fibers when the damaged nerve is exposed to it, not only those that end in nociceptors. The sensation, however, is always pain because this sensation dominates all others. Pain is aroused by the stimulation of specific nociceptors, but the stimulus may also excite many other afferent fibers in a nerve trunk in addition to those that end in nociceptors. In the latter case, although all the afferent fibers in the nerve may discharge, the sensation is of pain only. Pain does not arise from overstimulation of receptors that normally subserve a different sensation.

The discharge of other receptors, in addition to the nociceptors, may color or alter the sensations associated with a painful stimulus. For example, the description "burning pain" is often given to the sensation caused by an object at high temperature (>45°C) applied to the skin. Such a stimulus will make the warm receptors discharge as well as the nociceptors, and the sensation may thus be modified or enriched by this additional afferent inflow.

Tickle and itch

These sensations, although not necessarily painful, are very irritating. They can both be aroused from the skin and, with greatest ease, from certain parts of the body. Tickle can readily be evoked in man by moving individual hairs around the nostrils, the ears, and the mouth. The sensation characteristically persists after withdrawal of the stimulus and can be relieved by rubbing the skin.

Visceral sensations

The range of sensations that can be elicited from visceral structures is very limited. A great deal of afferent nervous activity is caused by both mechanical and chemical changes in the viscera. Most of this is concerned with the reflex regulation of visceral activity and does not enter consciousness. The abdominal and thoracic viscera can be handled in conscious human subjects (e.g. the classical gastric fistula subjects, Alexis St. Martin, Mr. V, and "Tom" in the United States, and the young man whose heart was touched by King Charles II) without any sensation being evoked. It is also common experience that ruminants are largely indifferent to the manual exploration of the fistulated reticulum and rumen, even when reflex gastric movements are caused by the examination.

The sensations which can be elicited include the "sense of fullness or distension," a limited range of thermal sensations and pain. Fullness or distension is caused by the filling of a hollow abdominal or pelvic viscus, but not the thoracic viscera. Hurst (1911), from an extensive study of human clinical material, established that gastric and esophageal sensations are associated with rapid filling and strong contractions of the stomach. The normal propulsive movements of the alimentary canal are not perceived, and it is only if the contractions become very strong that they give rise to any sensation, and then it is usually pain (Payne and Poulton 1927). The sensations from the bladder (Denny-Brown and Robertson 1933) caused by progressive distension from the inflow of fluid vary from the sense of fullness, which may be variable, to a sensation of extreme fullness associated with an irrepressible desire to micturate. During filling, the bladder contracts intermittently, and these contractions enhance the sensation of fullness. This is explicable if the appropriate receptors are the in-series distension receptors described earlier These afferent units are excited both by distension and contraction of the viscus. The sense of fullness may therefore arise both from overdistension or from a strong contraction of the viscus, and the CNS appears to be unable to discriminate between the two conditions. Consequently, the diagnosis is more difficult.

Organic sensations are those that arise from the viscera (with the exception of pain) and cause behavior of the animal directed to satisfying some organic need (hunger, thirst, sexual sensations, etc.). Hunger sensations arise from the alimentary canal, and are associated with powerful gastric contractions (Cannon and Washburn 1912) that may last from one half to one and a half minutes and recur at short intervals. This association of gastric contractions and hunger pains is not universal (James 1957), and in animals such as sheep, where there are very well-developed gastric movements, the contractions actually increase during feeding, and it is unlikely that there are any sensations of hunger associated with them.

The gastrointestinal afferent fibers in the vagus may have a role in satiety, that is, the satisfaction of hunger associated with a full stomach. The ingestion of food by a sham-fed dog (that is a dog with an esophagostomy) may be reduced if a balloon, inserted through a gastric fistula, is inflated in the stomach while the animal is feeding (Share et al. 1952). This effect should be distinguished from the more prolonged satiety that follows the absorption of food or water that may be associated with a satiety center in the medial hypothalamus and with a feeding center in the lateral hypothalamus (Brobeck 1960).

Visceral pain

Pain does arise from the viscera. The most sensitive parts are the peritoneal linings, and inflammatory changes in the peritoneum (e.g. peritonitis) can be extremely painful. Some of the thoracic viscera can be the source of pain (e.g. the heart), whereas others (e.g. the lungs) are not.

Pain from the hollow viscera is evoked by severe distension or powerful contractions, such as intestinal colic, or by the passage of solid objects, such as urinary calculi, or by high levels of hydrogen ion concentration, or by inflammatory conditions. Very frequently the last may enhance the sensitivity of the viscera to any one of the previous stimuli, so that distention that normally is innocuous becomes painful.

The pain fibers reach the viscera with the sympathetic and parasympathetic efferent fibers. The cell bodies of the afferent fibers are, however, in the dorsal root ganglia. The viscera receive afferent fibers both in the sympathetic (thoracolumbar outflow) and the parasympathetic (craniosacral outflow) divisions of the autonomic nervous system, but most of the pain fibers enter via the sympathetic route. For this reason surgical division of the sympathetic nerve is more effective in relieving abdominal visceral pain than is cutting the vagus, even though most of the nerve fibers in the latter are afferent. Because there is a modified segmental distribution of afferent fibers to the thoracic and abdominal viscera, it is possible to denervate general regions without total sympathectomy, and so obtain localized relief of pain. For the same reason a restricted surgical division of dorsal roots may give relief from intractable visceral pain.

Referred pain

This sensation arises from stimulation of the viscera or other deep structures, although it is felt on the surface of the body. The site of reference for this type of pain is related to the dermatomal distribution of the afferent fibers. The pain of angina pectoris is felt on the chest or upper arm although it arises in the heart. The phenomenon of reference can be very misleading in veterinary cases. A bitch with a denuded tail, due to the animal gnawing it, was not relieved by surgical removal of the distal half of the tail. Relief followed the discovery and treatment of a subcutaneous sinus (cyst lined with a pyogenic membrane) on the thigh (Humphreys and Randall 1964). The situation can be still more difficult with visceral lesions.

Referred pain probably arises because of convergence of cutaneous pain afferent fibers and visceral afferent fibers upon the same neuron at some point in the sensory pathway. Because of this convergence the path becomes identified or labeled in sensation as cutaneous, since it is more likely to be activated by stimuli which can be seen to be cutaneous. Any activity of visceral origin is therefore mistakenly referred to the site of the relevant cutaneous fibers. The convergence also accounts for a modification of the pain by cutaneous stimulation.

Relief from pain

Pain is a sensation that is not experienced by an unconscious individual, and indeed fainting can be regarded as a defense against very severe pain. In an unconscious person, however, the peripheral disturbances that evoked the pain will continue, as will many of the reflex consequences of the painful stimulus, such as flexion of an injured limb. The spinal reflexes will also persist even if the cerebral cortex is permanently damaged, or if the spinal cord itself is damaged above the level of entry of the afferent fibers. For this reason apparently purposive movements of an animal are not reliable indicators of a painful condition. Pain in animals is more difficult to diagnose than in man because of the lack of verbal expression, although a conscious animal can usually manage to convey at least an indication of the unpleasant nature of a stimulus, by biting, snarling, growling, and so forth, accompanied by the withdrawal of the affected part. These external signs have to be used, and experience, skill, and judgment have to be developed to interpret them as well as to judge how effectively they are relieved by treatment.

Local anesthesia may relieve pain, by blocking the pain afferent fibers. It does not afford permanent relief nor does it remove the source of the pain. More central interference of the pain pathway is also used, such as surgical interruption or chemical block. Surgery may be restricted to peripheral nerves, or it may involve division of the dorsal roots, partial transection of the spinal cord (anterolateral cordotomy), or destruction of the thalamic relay nuclei by stereotaxic surgery (Hankinson 1962).

Pain can also be relieved by the use of analgesics and narcotics. Aspirin (acetylsalycilic acid), codeine, or morphine act by raising the pain threshold. At least part of the action of aspirin is peripheral; it blocks the pain-inducing action of bradykinin injected in visceral arteries. Narcotic analgesics, on the other hand, act centrally (Lim et al. 1964).

Electroanalgesia, or electrical stimulation of the skin, peripheral nerves, or certain regions of the CNS (e.g. dorsal columns, midline of the brain stem), can give relief from pain in human patients (see Long and Hagfors 1975). The methods and technology are still in a developmental state, and it is not yet established whether these procedures will become useful in veterinary medicine. Acupuncture is another, in some respects similar, clinical procedure which has been reported as causing analgesia. The physiological mechanisms that underly both procedures depend in part on inhibitory suppression of the excitability of nerve cells in the spinal cord. This inhibition of pain pathway neurons can be produced by impulses in mechanoreceptor afferent fibers, whether they are initiated by electrical stimulation of nerve trunks or by mechanical stimulation of the skin.

REFERENCES

Adrian, E.D. 1943 Afferent areas in the brain of ungulates. *Brain* 66:89–103.

Allen, W.F. 1943. Distribution of cortical potentials resulting from insufflation of vapors into the nostrils and from stimulation of the olfactory bulbs and pyriform lobe. *Am. J. Physiol* 139:553–55.

——. 1947. Effect of partial and complete destruction of the tactile cerebral cortex on correct conditioned differential foreleg responses from cutaneous stimulation. *Am. J. Physiol.* 151:325–37.

Appelberg, B. 1958. Species differences in taste qualities mediated through the glossopharyngeal nerve. *Acta Physiol. Scand.* 44:129–37.

Ash, R.W. 1959. Inhibition and excitation of reticulo-rumen contractions following the introduction of acids into the rumen and abomasum. *J. Physiol.* 147:58–73.

Barker, D.C., ed. 1962. *The Structure and Distribution of Muscle Receptors*. Hong Kong U. Press. Pp. 227–40.

Barrington, F.J.F. 1931. The component reflexes of micturition in the cat. *Brain* 54:177–88.

Benjamin, R.M. 1963. Some thalamic and cortical mechanisms of taste. In Y. Zotterman, ed., *Olfaction and Taste*. Pergamon, London. Pp. 309–29.

Bessou, P., and Perl, E.R. 1966. A movement receptor of the small intestine. *J. Physiol.* 182:404–26.

Brobeck, J.R. 1960. Regulation of feeding and drinking. In *Handbook of Physiology*. Sec. 1, H.W. Magoun, ed., *Neurophysiology*. Am. Physiol. Soc. Washington. Vol. 2, 1197–1206.

Brodal, A. 1957. *The Reticular Formation of the Brain Stem*. Oliver & Boyd, Edinburgh.

Cannon, W.B., and Washburn, A.L. 1912. An explanation of hunger. *Am. J. Physiol.* 29:441–54.

Clark, W.E. Le Gros, and Meyer, M. 1947. The terminal connections of the olfactory tract in the rabbit. *Brain* 70:304–28.

Crosby, E.C., Humphrey, T., and Lauer, E.W. 1962. *Correlative Anatomy of the Nervous System*. Macmillan, New York.

Darian-Smith, I. 1964. Cortical projections of thalamic neurones excited by mechanical stimulation of the face of the cat. *J. Physiol.* 171:339–60.

Denny-Brown, D., and Robertson, E.G. 1933. The physiology of micturition. *Brain* 56:149–90.

Dougherty, R.W., Habel, R.E., and Bond, H.E. 1958. Esophageal innervation and the eructation reflex in sheep. *Am. J. Vet. Res.* 19:115–28.

Frey, M. von. 1895. Beiträge zur Sinnesphysiologie der Haut III. *Leipsig Math. Phys. Ber.* 47:166–84.

Funakoshi, M., and Zotterman, Y. 1963. Effect of salt on sugar responses. *Acta Physiol. Scand.* 57:193–200.

Gaze, R.M., and Gordon, G. 1955. Some observations on the central pathway for cutaneous impulses in the cat. *Q. J. Exp. Physiol.* 40:187–94.

Granit, R. 1955. *Receptors and Sensory Perception*. Yale U. Press, New Haven.

Hanbery, J., and Jasper, H. 1953. Independence of diffuse thalamocortical projection system shown by specific nuclear destructions. *J. Neurophysiol.* 16:252–71.

Hankinson, J. 1962. Neurosurgical aspects of relief of pain at the cerebral level. In C.A. Keele and R. Smith, eds., *The Assessment of Pain in Man and Animals*. Churchill Livingstone, Edinburgh, London.

Hensel, H., Iggo, A., and Witt, I. 1960. A quantitative study of sensitive cutaneous thermoreceptors with C afferent fibres. *J. Physiol.* 153:113–26.

Hubel, D.H., and Wiesel, T.N. 1962. Receptive fields, binocular interaction, and functional architecture in the cat's visual cortex. *J. Physiol.* 160:106–54.

Humphreys, P.N., and Randall, P.M. 1964. A case of tail-worrying due to referred pain in a wire-haired terrier. *Vet. Rec.* 76:97–98.

Hurst, A.F. 1911. *The Sensibility of the Alimentary Canal*. Oxford U. Press, London.

Iggo, A. 1955. Tension receptors in stomach and urinary bladder. *J. Physiol.* 128:593–607.

———. 1957a. Gastrointestinal tension receptors with unmyelinated afferent fibres in the vagus of the cat. *Q. J. Exp. Physiol.* 42:130–43.

———. 1957b. Gastric mucosal chemoreceptors with vagal afferent fibres in the cat. *Q. J. Exp. Physiol.* 42:398–409.

———. 1960. Cutaneous mechanoreceptors with afferent C fibres. *J. Physiol.* 152:337–53.

———. 1964. Temperature discrimination in the skin. *Nature* 204:481–83.

———. 1969. Cutaneous thermoreceptors in primates and sub-primates. *J. Physiol.* 200:403–30.

Iggo, A., and Leek, B.F. 1966. Reflex regulation of gastric activity. *Acta Neuroveg.* 28:353–59.

———. 1967. The afferent innervation of the tongue of the sheep. In T. Hayashi, ed., *Olfaction and Taste*. Pergamon, Oxford, New York. Pp. 493–507.

James, A.H. 1957. *The Physiology of Gastric Digestion*. Edward Arnold, London.

Jasper, H.H. 1960. Unspecific thalamocortical relations. In *Handbook of Physiology*. Sec. 1, H.W. Magoun, ed., *Neurophysiology*. Am. Physiol. Soc., Washington. Vol. 2, 1307–21.

Kenshalo, D.R. 1964. The temperature sensitivity of furred skins of cats. *J. Physiol.* 172:439–48.

Kitchell, R.L. 1963. Comparative anatomical and physiological studies of gustatory mechanisms. In Y. Zotterman, ed., *Olfaction and Taste*. Pergamon, London. Pp. 235–55.

Lim, R.K.S., Guzman, F., Rodgers, D.W., Goto, K., Braun, C., Dickerson, G.D., and Engle, R.J. 1964. Site of action of narcotic and non-narcotic analgesics determined by blocking bradykinin-evoked visceral pain. *Arch. Internat. Pharmacodyn.* 152:25–58.

Long, D.M., and Hagfors, N. 1975. Electrical stimulation in the nervous system: The current status of electrical stimulation of the nervous system for relief of pain. *Pain* 1:109–23.

Lorenzo, A.J. de. 1958. Electron microscopic observations on the taste buds of the rabbit. *J. Biophys. Biochem. Cytol.* 4:143–50.

———. 1963. Studies on the ultrastructure and histophysiology of cell membranes, nerve fibres, and synaptic junctions in chemoreceptors. In Y. Zotterman, ed., *Olfaction and Taste*. Pergamon, London. Pp. 5–17.

Marquis, D.G. 1934. Effects of removal of visual cortex in mammals, with observations on the retention of light discrimination in dogs. *Ass. Res. Nerv. Ment. Dis. Proc.* 13:558–92.

Matthews, B.H.C. 1933. Nerve endings in mammalian muscle. *J. Physiol.* 78:1–53.

Matthews, P.B.C. 1964. Muscle spindles and their motor control. *Physiol. Rev.* 44:219–88.

Morin, F. 1955. A new spinal pathway for cutaneous impulses. *Am. J. Physiol.* 183:245–52.

Morison, R.S., and Dempsey, E.W. 1942. A study of thalamocortical relations. *Am. J. Physiol.* 135:281–92.

Mountcastle, V.B. 1961. Some functional properties of the somatic afferent system. In W.A. Rosenblith, ed., *Sensory Communications*. M.I.T. Press, Cambridge.

Mountcastle, V.B., and Henneman, E. 1952. The representation of tactile sensibility in the thalamus of the monkey. *J. Comp. Neurol.* 97:409–39.

Mountcastle, V.B., and Powell, T.P.S. 1959. Central nervous mechanisms subserving position sense and kinesthesis. *Bull. Johns Hopkins Hosp.* 105:173–200.

Oscarsson, O. 1965. Functional organization of the spino- and cuneocerebellar tracts. *Physiol. Rev.* 45:495–522.

Paintal, A.S. 1960. Functional analysis of Group III afferent fibres of mammalian muscles. *J. Physiol.* 156:498–514.

Payne, W.W., and Poulton, E.P. 1927. Experiments on visceral sensation. I. The relation of pain to activity of the human oesophagus. *J. Physiol.* 63:217–41.

Pfaffman, C. 1963. Taste stimulation and preference behaviour. In Y. Zotterman, ed., *Olfaction and Taste*. Pergamon, London. Pp. 257–73.

Poggio, G.F., and Mountcastle, V.B. 1960. A study of the functional contributions of the lemniscal and spinothalamic systems to somatic sensibility. *Bull. Johns Hopkins Hosp.* 106:266–316.

Rose, J.E., and Mountcastle, V.B. 1959. Touch and kinesthesis. In *Handbook of Physiology*. Sec. 1, H.W. Magoun, ed., *Neurophysiology*. Am. Physiol. Soc., Washington. Vol. 1, 387–429.

Rose, J.E., and Woolsey, C.N. 1949. Organization of the mammalian thalamus and its relationships to the cerebral cortex. *Electroenceph. Clin. Neurophysiol.* 1:391–404.

Share, I., Martyniuk, E., and Grossman, M.I. 1952. The effect of prolonged intragastric feeding on oral food intake in dogs. *Am. J. Physiol.* 169:229–35.

Sherrington, C.S. 1906. *The Integrative Action of the Nervous System*. Silliman Memorial Lectures. Scribner's, New York.

Sprague, J.M., and Hongchien Ha. 1964. The terminal fields of dorsal root fibers in the lumbosacral spinal cord of the cat and the dendritic organization of the motor nuclei. In *Progress in Brain Research*. Elsevier, Amsterdam. Vol. 11, 120–54.

Thompson, J.M., Woolsey, C.N., and Talbot, S.A. 1950. Visual areas I and II of the cerebral cortex of the rabbit. *J. Neurophysiol.* 13:277–88.

Todd, J.K. 1964. Afferent impulses in the pudendal nerve of the cat. *Q. J. Exp. Physiol.* 49:258–67.

Waites, G.M.H. 1962. The effect of heating the scrotum of the ram on respiration and body temperature. *Q. J. Exp. Physiol.* 47:314–23.

Weber, E.H. 1846. Der Tastsinn und das Gemeingefühl. In R. Wagner, ed., *Handworterbuch der Physiologie*. Bieweg, Braunschweig. Pp. 481–562.

Werner, G., and Mountcastle, V.B. 1965. Neural activity in mechanoreceptive cutaneous afferents: Stimulus-response relations, Weber functions, and information transmission, *J. Neurophysiol.* 28:359–97.

Zotterman, Y. 1956. Species differences in the water taste. *Acta Physiol. Scand.* 37:60–70.

——. 1959. Thermal sensations. In *Handbook of Physiology*. Sec. 1, H.W. Magoun, ed., *Neurophysiology*. Am. Physiol. Soc., Washington. Vol. 1, 431–58.

CHAPTER 44

Brain Regulation of Motor Activity | by James E. Breazile

Skeletal muscle activity is controlled by α-motoneurons of the brain stem and spinal cord. The regulation of skeletal muscular activity into a coordinated complex which gives rise to reflex or voluntary motor activity is therefore dependent upon the influences that determine the excitability of the α-motoneurons. A study of the CNS control of motor activity, therefore, is a study of α-motoneuron physiology and its reflection in the activity of skeletal muscle. The α-motoneurons are said to be the *final common pathway* for CNS activity exerting an influence upon motor activity.

MUSCLE TONE

The term muscle tone refers to a continuous state of partial contraction of the skeletal muscles in the relaxed, awake animal. (Unless stated otherwise, the anatomical and physiological information in this chapter is based upon literature dealing primarily with the cat and dog.) This tonic state of contraction is important in the maintenance of the normal posture (see Chapter 42). Muscle tone is maintained continuously in the awake, normal animal but is lost when an animal is deeply anesthetized or is in a state of deep sleep. Transection of either the dorsal or the ventral roots of the spinal nerves supplying a given muscle will abolish muscle tone, which indicates that both peripheral sensory and CNS mechanisms are responsible for its maintenance. Muscle tone is greater in muscles utilized for tonic activity (maintenance of posture) than for those that are functional in phasic motor activity (locomotion).

Evidence

If a muscle is transected, the two cut ends retract from each other toward the origin and insertion of the muscle. Sectioning of the dorsal and/or the ventral roots of the spinal nerves causes the muscles that have been denervated to become flaccid or atonic. In a deeply anesthetized animal, in which the mechanisms supporting muscle tone have been depressed, the muscles also exhibit atonia. Electrical recording from skeletal muscle (electromyography) indicates that in the normal state continuous electrical activity is present. Upon the production of atonia, by transection of the nerves or by deep anesthesia, the recorded electrical activity ceases, indicating that such activity is a reflection of the ongoing electrical activity of the muscle and its nerve (action potentials) which are responsible for the maintenance of a state of contraction.

Reflex mechanisms for maintenance and regulation

These mechanisms are segmental in their distribution. Since muscle tone is increased when the muscles are stretched, it must be dependent upon a reflex arc that includes as its receptor a stretch-sensitive organ. Localized stretching of a tendon and thus activation of the Golgi tendon organ stretch receptor does not result in an increase in muscle tone. Thus the muscle spindle must be the receptor. There are some important differences between these two receptor organs:

(1) Muscle spindles are distributed among fibers of the

muscle in which they are located and therefore are *in parallel* with extrafusal muscle fibers. Golgi tendon organs are located in fibers of the tendon and therefore are *in series* with the muscle. This difference in location gives rise to differences in response during muscular activity. The muscle spindle receptor organs are stretched only when the muscle is stretched, and thus are silent when the muscle is contracting. Golgi tendon organs, on the other hand, are stretched whenever the tendon is stretched and thus are active when the muscle is contracting. Both receptors are activated when the muscle is passively stretched.

(2) Muscle spindles are complex receptor organs that contain muscle fibers (intrafusal fibers) possessing different properties and different innervations from those of the muscle (extrafusal fibers) in which these organs are located. This innervation alters the sensitivity of the receptor organ and makes it more or less sensitive to stretch. The Golgi tendon organs possess no inherent mechanism for altering their sensitivity to stretch.

(3) Muscle spindles exhibit a low threshold to stretch, whereas Golgi tendon organs exhibit a low threshold to stretch of the tendon only if the associated muscle is contracting

These differences allow one to make a few assumptions concerning the receptor organ that is responsible for the maintenance of muscle tone: (a) Muscle spindles appear to be the receptor of choice for the maintenance of muscle tone because they are responsive only when the muscle is stretched (as in an antigravity muscle in the maintenance of posture). This stretch need not be severe, but may be of a mild nature similar to that imposed by the pull of gravity. (b) Muscle spindles are the receptor organs that subserve the myotatic reflex. This reflex is responsible for the increase in contraction strength of a muscle when it is stretched. (c) Golgi tendon organs are the receptor organs subserving the inverse myotatic reflex (clasp-knife reflex) which promotes a braking action on a contracting muscle and its synergists. (d) Muscle spindles possess an inherent mechanism for adjusting the sensitivity of the receptor organ during muscular activity, so that muscle tone may be maintained while motor activity is being carried out. One of the most important functions of muscle tone is that of providing a positive state of muscle contraction, from which motor activity may be initiated by either increasing or decreasing the activity of skeletal muscle. A study of the central regulation of motor activity is best understood if it is approached from the standpoint of mechanisms that alter muscle tone.

Physiological role

Muscle tone maintains posture, provides a background of contraction upon which reflex and voluntary motor activity may be initiated, and aids in the maintenance of body temperature by continuous contraction of muscle.

Muscle tone functions in the maintenance of posture and attitude by alterations in intensity of contractions of flexor and extensor muscles so that the limbs and trunk are oriented into various positions. These alterations are brought about by various reflex activities discussed in Chapter 42. Postural alterations during locomotor activity are also sustained by changes in muscle tone. These changes are brought about by alterations in the γ-loop mechanism by fiber systems that descend from cerebral structures such as the corticospinal, rubrospinal, reticulospinal, and other tracts. These fiber systems are referred to as cerebral motor systems.

MOVEMENT

Movement is initiated by the contraction of skeletal muscles in an organized fashion so that the limbs are alternately shifted and the animal is propelled along the ground. The smoothness of locomotion in domestic animals indicates the fine degree of organization of muscular activity that is responsible for this achievement. In the flexion of a limb for the initiation of a motor act, the extensor muscles relax and the flexor muscles contract. This indicates that within the spinal cord there are mechanisms that result in the excitation of flexor motoneurons and inhibition of extensor motoneurons. As the limb is carried forward, there is a fine balance of phasic contraction of the muscles responsible for this movement and tonic relaxation of their antagonists. As the limb is placed on the ground, the myotatic reflexes are activated, which initiates appropriate muscle activity to produce a supporting column with the limb. The maintenance of muscle tone while the limb is off the ground is due to activity of γ-motoneurons; γ-motoneurons are usually activated in accord with the α-motoneurons to a given muscle and cause the intrafusal fibers to contract with the extrafusal fibers. This allows the muscle spindle to discharge afferent activity during contraction of the muscle. Muscles that are relaxing (due to depressed activity in their respective α-motoneurons) in a given locomotor movement have their muscle spindles stretched. This is the adequate stimulus for the myotatic reflex, which results in the maintenance of tone in the relaxing muscle (tonic relaxation). In this way a smooth, well-coordinated movement of the limb takes place. The agonist muscles move the limb, and their antagonists maintain just enough tone to prevent the limb from being moved too rapidly or too far for adequate locomotion.

Motor activity always involves complex interrelationships between various muscles, including (1) those muscles that are active in creating the movement, (2) those muscles that are antagonistic to the muscles creating and thus controlling the rate of movement, and (3) those muscles that do not take part in initiating the movement, but stabilize various joints so that a limb is placed in an appropriate manner for support of the body. The precision of these interrelationships determines the smoothness of locomotor activity. The mechanisms that determine this precision are located within the spinal cord.

Locomotor activity in domestic animals involves rhythmic alteration of skeletal muscle activity so that the limbs are alternately moved in sequence. In this manner the animal is maintained on one or two limbs while the remainder are off the ground. The rhythmic alteration that occurs in stepping can be exhibited in a spinal animal when appropriately stimulated (Sherrington 1961). This indicates that the neural mechanisms which give rise to rhythmic motor activity are located within the spinal cord. Rhythmic, alternating motor activity influences all four limbs, which move in precise spatial and temporal relationships with each other. The mechanisms for coordination of all four limbs in this type of motor activity are in part inherent in the spinal cord, but this coordination is controlled to a great extent by neural mechanisms of the brain.

Motor activity is commonly classified into two types, involuntary or reflex motor activity and voluntary or willed motor activity. In many instances it is difficult to distinguish between the two. In the following discussions those motor acts that have been discussed in Chapter 42 as being reflex in nature will be referred to as involuntary or reflex activity and those that appear to depend upon cerebral structures for their initiation will be referred to as voluntary. This does not mean that there is any basic difference between the types of motor activity elicited, but the complexity of CNS pathways is usually greater for the initiation of voluntary motor activity.

DECEREBRATE RIGIDITY

Muscle tone is exaggerated in an animal in which the brain stem has been transected through the midbrain. In such a preparation an extensor rigidity is exhibited that is dependent upon an intact myotatic reflex arc. Decerebrate rigidity is characterized by strong tonic contraction of both extensor and flexor muscles, but extensor muscles are more powerful than their antagonists, so that an extensor rigidity results. The reflex nature of the hypertonus may be shown by section of the dorsal roots of the nerves supplying the muscle. This results in a disappearance of the rigidity. Decerebrate rigidity is sometimes referred to as exaggerated reflex standing.

In the dog and cat the rigidity is evident almost immediately, or within a few minutes, after the transection of the brain stem, but additional time is usually required for it to reach its greatest intensity. If the animal is kept alive, the rigidity may persist for an indefinite time.

Decerebrate rigidity is a release phenomenon and is caused by the withdrawal of normal descending inhibitory activity to the segmental myotatic reflex; it is not due to irritation at the level of the lesion, for it persists indefinitely in the chronic preparation. It is likely, though not yet completely substantiated, that decerebrate rigidity is caused by the loss of activation of the inhibitory centers in the medullary reticular formation that are controlled by the cerebral cortex. Facilitation of the stretch reflex is produced by other centers in the medulla that are activated by the collaterals of ascending tracts. Stimulation of these zones causes an increased discharge from muscle spindles and thus facilitates the myotatic reflex. The vestibulospinal tracts also exert a strong excitatory influence upon muscle tone, particularly of antigravity muscles. Normally muscle tone is maintained by a balance of inhibitory and facilitatory influences from various sources within the CNS. If a portion of the inhibitory influences are removed, the effect of the facilitatory influences is displayed much more clearly. This is the mechanism which is functional in the production of decerebrate rigidity.

The rigidity produced by decerebration is dependent primarily upon the facilitation of γ-motoneuron activity which increases the rate of discharge of muscle spindles; this in turn influences the discharge of α-motoneurons to maintain the exaggerated tonic state. This type of rigidity is referred to as γ-rigidity. Gamma rigidity is abolished by the transection of any portion of the γ-loop mechanisms and thus disappears when the dorsal roots supplying the muscles in question are transected. A type of rigidity which is initiated by hyperactivity of α-motoneurons is referred to as α-rigidity. Alpha rigidity is not relieved by transection of the dorsal roots of the nerves supplying the muscles in question; γ-rigidity can be transformed into an α-rigidity by removal of the anterior lobe of the cerebellum. Thus the cerebellum functions in part to correlate α- and γ-motor activity.

Regions of the CNS that exert facilitatory and inhibitory influences upon the α- and γ-motoneurons are illustrated in Figure 44.1. Electrical stimulation of the inhibi-

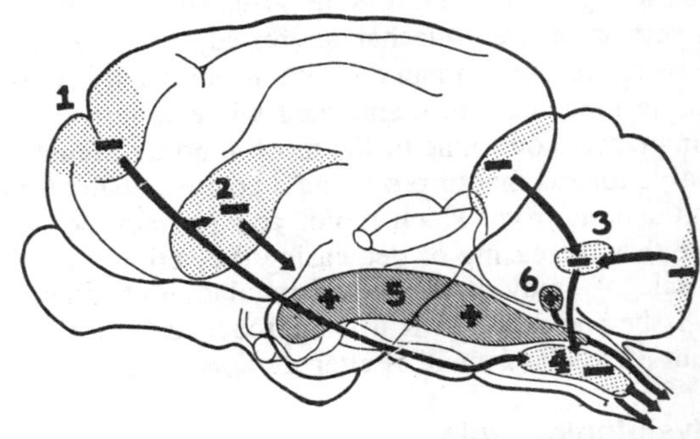

Figure 44.1. Suppressor or inhibitory (−) and facilitatory (+) effects on the spinal reflexes. Suppressor pathways: 1, corticobulboreticular; 2, caudatospinal; 3, cerebelloreticular; 4, reticulospinal. Facilitatory pathways: 5, reticulospinal; 6, vestibulospinal. (From Lindsley, Schreiner, and Magoun 1949, *J. Neurophysiol.* 12:197–205.)

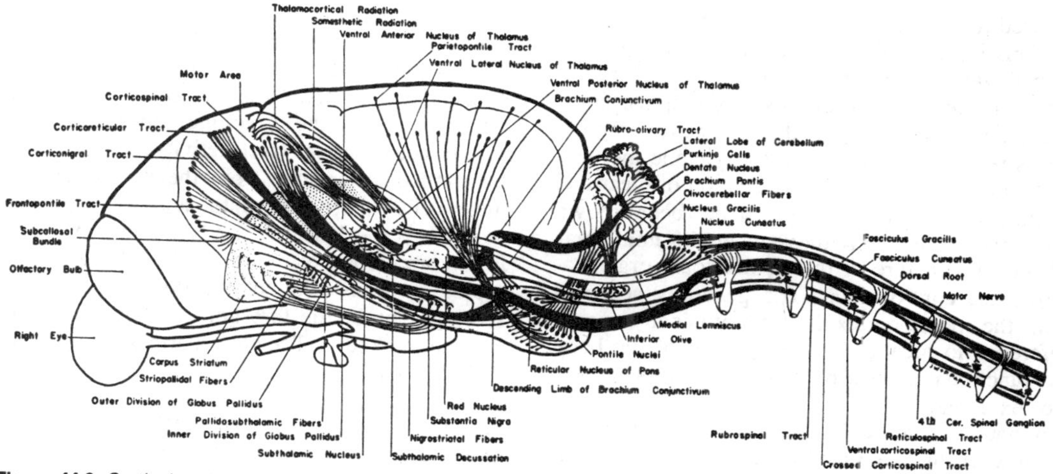

Figure 44.2. Cortical motor system of the dog. Represented are the descending paths to the substantia nigra, pontine (pontile) nuclei, opposite lateral lobe of the cerebellum, and motoneurons of the spinal cord. Descending paths from the corpus striatum, outer division of the globus pallidus, subthalamic nucleus, and red nucleus (nucleus ruber) are shown. Ascending paths from the proprioceptors to the somesthetic area, from the cerebellum to the cortical motor area, and from the substantia nigra to the corpus striatum are shown. An X indicates that the tract is derived from or crosses to the opposite side. (Designed and drawn by Dr. James W. Papez, Cornell University.)

tory areas reduces muscle tone in antigravity muscles, while stimulation of the facilitatory areas increases tone in these muscles.

CEREBRAL CONTROL OF MOTOR ACTIVITY

Many regions of the brain control motor activity (Figs. 44.2, 44.3). For convenience these regions have been grouped into two systems, the pyramidal and extrapyramidal motor systems, but this classification should not imply a differential or separate function. These two systems do not function independently and in fact are not even separate anatomically, but serve in the control of motor activity as a single motor system that coordinates skeletal muscle activity.

Pyramidal system (corticospinal tract)

The corticospinal tract is comprised of neurons with descending axons that form the bulbar pyramids. These fibers have their origin from cells of the cerebral cortex. Though these fibers arise from pyramidal cells of the cerebral cortex, the name of the tract was acquired because of its pyramidal shape at medullary levels. The axons that form the corticospinal tract arise from several regions and several cell types. A study in the cat indicates that nearly all the fibers of the pyramid originate in the rostral third of the cerebral cortex (Crevel and Verhaart 1963). These results support much of the earlier work on this problem.

The region of the frontal cortex from which the corticospinal tract fibers arise (motor cortex) contains many large pyramid-shaped cells called Betz cells. In early studies of the corticospinal tract, these cells were thought to be the origin of all the axons forming the pyramid. When the number of fibers within the pyramid is counted, however, it is seen that there are many more fibers than there are Betz cells. From this it must be accepted that other pyramidal cells of the cerebral cortex give rise to the axons that pass through the pyramid. Many of the fibers arising from the motor cortex terminate within motor nuclei of the brain stem before reaching the level of the pyramid. It is for these reasons that a discussion of the corticospinal tract as a separate motor system is somewhat artificial.

The fibers that comprise the corticospinal tract are for the most part small in diameter; many are nonmyelinated. It is estimated that only about 2 percent of the tract is comprised of large myelinated fibers which are suspected to arise from Betz cells in the cortex (Lassek and Rasmussen 1939, Brookhart and Morris 1948, Haggqvist 1937).

The corticospinal tract passes from the cortex through the internal capsule, the cerebral peduncle, and the pyramid of the brain stem to project caudally into the spinal cord. The corticospinal fibers decussate before their termination within the spinal cord; a majority decussate within the medulla to form the pyramidal decussation, and the remainder decussate within the spinal cord, presumably near their level of termination.

A characteristic of the function of the corticospinal tract is the great amount of facilitation that is required to produce a motor act (Patton and Amassian 1960). In stimulating either the cerebral cortex or the corticospinal tract at the medullary level, repetitive electrical stimulation is required to produce gross movements of a limb or body part. This is due to the intervention of interneurons within the pathway between the pyramidal cells of the cerebral cortex and the α-motoneurons of the spinal cord. With more than one synapse in the pathway, temporal summation is required to overcome the synaptic inertia.

Since the first studies with the application of electrical stimuli to the cerebral motor cortex, it has been known that different parts of the body move when different areas are stimulated. The nature of this somatotopic organization is, however, controversial. The generally accepted view is that the motor cortex is somatotopically organized in reference to location of the muscles of the body and not to functional groups of muscles (flexors vs. extensors, for example).

The termination of the corticospinal tract in domestic animals is always by means of interneurons. In no instance have corticospinal tract fibers been found to terminate directly upon α-motoneurons except in primates. Both electrophysiological and anatomical evidence indicates a direct cortical–α-motoneuron pathway for control of digital movement in primates (Kuypers 1960). It is probable that for the fine motor control required in the forelimbs of primates a direct corticospinal α-motoneuron linkage is necessary. In the cat, however, it has been shown both electrophysiologically and anatomically that the corticospinal tract terminates upon interneurons of the spinal cord (Nyberg-Hansen and Brodal 1963, Lloyd 1941). These interneurons are the same interneurons that function in the flexion reflex; that is, they are excitatory to the flexor muscles and inhibitory to the extensors. Corticospinal tract activity facilitates the monosynaptic reflex of ankle flexor muscles and inhibits the monosynaptic reflex of extensors in the cat (Agnew et al. 1963). The mode of termination of the corticospinal tract in other animals has not been studied. The predominance of flexor motor activity over extensor motor activity is obvious when the motor cortex is electrically stimulated (Sherrington 1905, Livingston and Phillips 1957). The functional significance of a motor cortex–initiated flexor facilitation and extensor inhibition may be explained as follows. Any cortically evoked phasic movement would by necessity have to overcome the postural set of the animal. Since standing posture in quadrupeds is largely extensor in character and since the initial phasic movements of walking are primarily flexor in nature, the motor cortex influence to overcome supporting posture appears to be an important function in the initiation of locomotor activity.

The corticospinal tract produces motor activity in a somewhat indirect manner. The fibers of the corticospinal tract terminate within the spinal cord upon interneurons that facilitate both α- and γ-motoneurons. The α-motoneurons have a higher threshold for activity than do the γ-motoneurons and are thus facilitated by the corticospinal activity, while the γ-motoneurons are discharged. The discharge of the γ-motoneurons produces a contraction of the intrafusal muscle fibers which in turn gives rise to monosynaptic activation of the α-motoneurons. Since the α-motoneurons have been facilitated by the corticospinal tract activity, the additional excitatory influence coming from the muscle spindles causes these cells to fire and motor activity is produced. Thus the γ-loop mechanism "leads" α-motoneuron discharge in the production of motor activity. If the γ-loop is interrupted by transection of the dorsal roots of the nerves serving a limb, the threshold for motor activation is increased markedly. The close correlation of α- with γ-motor activity is controlled by the extrapyramidal motor system, most specifically by the cerebellum. A similar mechanism is probably operant in the production of motor activity arising from either the pyramidal or the extrapyramidal motor system.

The function of the corticospinal tract in the overall scheme of motor activity is somewhat difficult to ascertain. It has been shown that it mediates tremor and certain other dysfunctions which arise following lesions of certain of the extrapyramidal motor structures (Carpenter et al. 1960, Carpenter and Correll 1961). Therefore, it is necessary to consider the pyramidal tract as simply a cortically mediated motor tract that is integrated into the activity of a single motor system including all extrapyramidal and pyramidal structures.

Extrapyramidal system

The extrapyramidal motor system includes all motor mechanisms of the brain exclusive of the pyramidal system. Since it is impossible to define the pyramidal system precisely, either anatomically or physiologically, this differentiation is quite artificial. In a broad sense, all brain structures influence motor activity either directly or indirectly (through reflex connections or chains of several neurons). Our discussion here will deal primarily with the physiology of those structures of the telencephalon and brain stem that are conventionally considered to be a part of the extrapyramidal system. These include the caudate nucleus, putamen, globus pallidus, substantia nigra, red nucleus (nucleus ruber), subthalamic nucleus, thalamus, rostral colliculus, and the reticular formation (Fig. 44.3). The cerebellum serves as a complex control center for motor activity and is considered separately.

Several of the nuclei listed above receive fibers from the cerebral cortex. Most of these fibers arise from the anterior one third of the cortex, that is, from areas giving rise to the pyramidal system; other areas of the cortex contribute only a small portion of these fibers. The cortical fibers to these extrapyramidal structures descend in the internal capsule together with those of the pyramidal tract.

Cortical fibers to the reticular formation arise from the

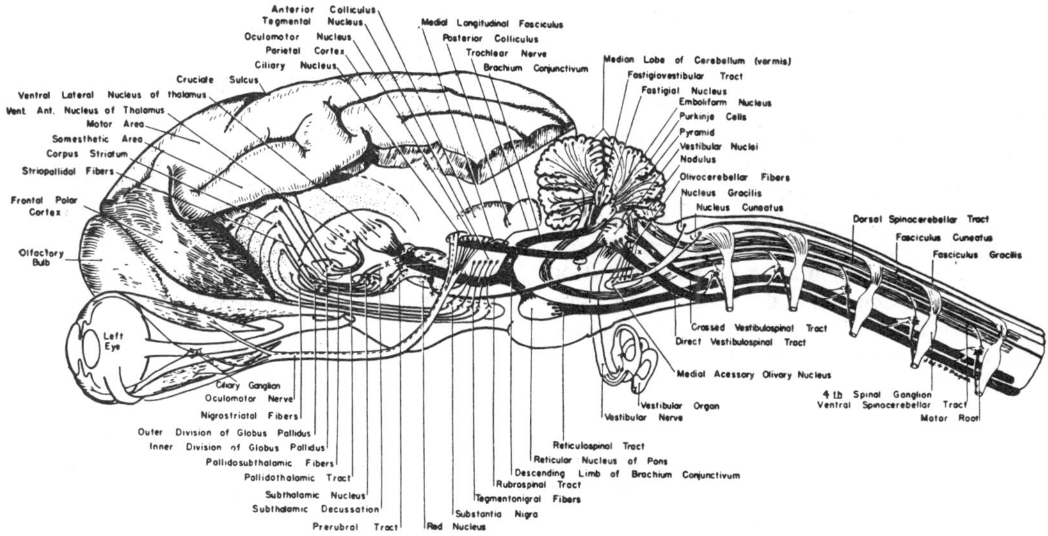

Figure 44.3. Subcortical motor system of the dog showing the connections of the vestibular system, median lobe of the cerebellum, reticular nucleus of the pons, and red nucleus. The subcortical connections of the substantia nigra, corpus striatum, the two divisions of the globus pallidus, the subthalamic nucleus, and red nucleus are also shown. The oculomotor and ciliary nuclei in the region of the anterior colliculus are included, and their innervation of some of the muscles of the eye and ciliary muscle is shown. 6 is the nucleus of the abducens nerve. X indicates decussation of a tract. The vestibular organ is drawn in a ventral position for diagrammatic reasons. (Designed and drawn by Dr. James W. Papez, Cornell University.)

region of the motor area with small components from other regions of the cortex. In the cat these fibers terminate within the medulla and pons in fairly well-circumscribed regions, which in part give rise to reticulospinal fibers (Rossi and Brodal 1956). There is thus a relatively direct corticoreticulospinal pathway.

Cortical fibers to the red nucleus appear to be derived largely from the region of the motor cortex (Levin 1936, Mettler 1945, Rinvik and Walberg 1963). Like the corticoreticular fibers, they descend, intermingled with the corticospinal fibers, in the internal capsule and terminate predominantly in the ipsilateral red nucleus. The rubrospinal tract projects contralaterally to the spinal cord. This fiber system, the corticorubrospinal system, is somatotopically organized (Rinvik and Walberg 1963). Fibers from the forelimb area of the motor cortex in the cat end in the forelimb area of the red nucleus; fibers from the forelimb area of the red nucleus project to the lower cervical and upper thoracic levels of the spinal cord to alter the excitability of α-motoneurons supplying muscles of the forelimb. Thus there is in the cat a pathway apart from the corticospinal, which mediates somatotopically localized messages from the cerebral cortex to the spinal cord. For this reason there is little loss of discrete motor performance with impairment of pyramidal tract activity (Brodal 1963).

Cortical fibers to the putamen, caudate nucleus, globus pallidus, substantia nigra, and subthalamic nucleus arise from other cortical regions (Mettler 1943, 1945). These structures do not project directly to the spinal cord, but contribute to other portions of the CNS that do have spinal cord projections or to regions, such as the cerebellum, that serve as a controlling influence upon the motor activity of the animal.

The rostral colliculus receives fibers from the occipital cortex (Crosby and Henderson 1948). There is a topographical arrangement of this projection that helps explain the conjugate movements of the eyes according to the cortical focal area stimulated (Brodal 1963). The occipital cortex has, via the rostral colliculus and the tectospinal tract, a relatively direct route for impulses to the spinal cord.

It appears from the above that the cerebral cortex, especially the region of the motor cortex, has several pathways through which it may influence the peripheral motoneurons, either fairly directly (corticorubral, corticoreticular, and corticotectal) or more indirectly (projections to the putamen, caudate, globus pallidus, subthalamic nucleus, and substantia nigra).

Most of the extrapyramidal system nuclei receive afferent fibers from various sensory systems. The information received by way of these fibers is integrated within the nuclei with information received from other sources. In this way, the appropriate motor activity is initiated.

The cortical areas that serve the extrapyramidal motor system receive many afferents from the sensory cortex in the form of association fibers. The cortical area in the occipital region that gives rise to fibers passing to the rostral colliculus overlaps with the visual sensory cortex and therefore has its activity very intimately correlated with sensory information entering the brain over the pathways of the visual system.

Among the subcortical nuclei, several receive fibers from sensory systems or are an integral part of ascending sensory systems. The vestibular nuclei, which give rise to the lateral and ventral vestibulospinal tracts and thus are a part of the extrapyramidal system, receive afferent information by way of the vestibular nerve, as well as from sensory fiber systems ascending in the ventrolateral funiculus of the spinal cord. The spinotectal and spinoreticular tracts carry information from various sensory systems; of particular interest is the termination of spinal afferents in certain parts of the medullary and pontine reticular formation. The intralaminar nucleus of the thalamus receives afferents from the reticular formation areas upon which the spinoreticular fibers terminate. This portion of the thalamus also receives afferents from the superior colliculus, red nucleus, substantia nigra, and cerebellum. These thalamic nuclei project efferents to the putamen, caudate nucleus, and the globus pallidum and thus provide a direct route for influence of the reticular formation on these extrapyramidal nuclei (Brodal 1963). It can be seen from these relationships that the intralaminar thalamus plays an important role in the correlation of sensory information and motor activity.

There is a very close association between the activity of the putamen, caudate nucleus, thalamus, substantia nigra, and subthalamic nuclei. There are reciprocal connections between many of these structures, so that they all participate in the integration of neuronal activity that is necessary to assure an adequate motor function.

It is well known that the integrated activity of all the structures included in the extrapyramidal system is important in the control of movement and posture in animals. The specific role played by any single structure, however, is difficult to ascertain.

Substantia nigra

If the substantia nigra is destroyed in the cat or dog, rigidity and immobility result. It is thought that this is a release phenomenon resulting from the removal of a tonic inhibitory influence of the substantia nigra upon γ- and α-motor activity within the spinal cord. The immobility appears to be due to an interference in the relationship of the γ- and α-motoneuron excitability. If the γ-motoneuron does not discharge in a motor act (or the γ-loop is interrupted) the threshold for discharging the α-motoneurons is increased. If the γ-discharge does not occur in the proper temporal relationship with the α-motoneuron facilitation (due to synaptic bombardment from higher centers), the additional facilitation from the γ-loop mechanisms needed to discharge the α-neurons may not occur at the proper time. The substantia nigra appears to influence this α-γ linkage in the performance of normal motor activity. According to some authors, the destruction of the substantia nigra in older animals does not produce notable motor deficits, but in young animals abnormal motor activity and rigidity are marked (Jung and Hassler 1960). Thus the age and therefore the motor competence of the animal may help determine the role played by the substantia nigra in motor activity. Destruction of the substantia nigra occurs in the horse as a result of yellow star thistle poisoning. These animals exhibit an inability to prehend food with their lips.

Subthalamic nucleus

This nucleus appears to control rhythmic alternate movement of the contralateral limbs. Control is elicited through the influence of this nucleus upon the globus pallidus and its projection systems. The patterning of rhythmic, alternate limb movement in walking may be dependent upon the interrelation of this nucleus with other extrapyramidal nuclei.

Red nucleus (nucleus ruber)

The red nucleus serves as a relay station for fairly direct cortical control of α- and γ-motoneuron activity. Activation of this nucleus elicits excitation of α-motoneurons to flexor muscles of the rear limb and simultaneously elicits a contraction of the intrafusal muscle fibers of flexor muscle spindles. These responses occur with a reciprocal inhibition of the α- and γ-motoneurons to extensor muscles. Activation of the portion of the red nucleus which projects fibers to lower cervical and upper thoracic levels of the spinal cord results in inhibition of α- and γ-motoneurons of both extensor and flexor muscles (Appelberg and Kosary 1963). Thus the red nucleus exerts an excitatory influence on flexor muscle tone of the rear limbs and an inhibitory influence on tone of the extensors of the rear limbs and both extensors and flexors of the forelimbs. Rubrospinal control of α- and γ-motoneurons exhibits threshold differences which are quite similar to those of the pyramidal motor system. Threshold for activation of γ-motoneurons is lower than for activation of α-motoneurons. It appears, therefore, that the γ-system "leads" the α-system in the performance of both pyramidal and extrapyramidal motor activity.

The red nucleus is influenced by activity in many of the other extrapyramidal structures and the cerebellum, so that the information projected to the spinal cord along the rubrospinal tract serves to coordinate motor responses in accord with various CNS activities.

Caudate nucleus, putamen, and globus pallidus

These nuclei form the highest level of integration of motor activity below the cerebral cortex. In lower animals such as birds and reptiles they form the major portion of the higher control of motor activity. These animals possess a very rudimentary cerebral cortex, and their behavior and locomotor activity are primarily controlled by these nuclei. Their function in domestic animals has not been clearly ascertained. It is likely that they retain many of the functions they possess in lower animals, but many of these functions appear to have been taken over by the cerebral cortex. Rhythmic locomotor activity is controlled by these nuclei. The precise, sequential, synchronous alteration of limb activity, as occurs in a trotting horse or in the dog, is also controlled in some way by them. By comparing the activity which is initiated by these nuclei with that which is initiated by the cerebral cortex, one can see that cortically initiated motor activity is very flexible and can be easily adjusted to fit rapid changes in the environment, whereas activity initiated by the subcortical nuclei of the extrapyramidal system is stereotyped, synchronous, and rhythmic.

Reticular formation

The reticular formation alters the activity of α- and γ-motor systems by several routes. Reticulocortical projections alter the activity of the cerebral cortex, which in turn has an influence upon the pyramidal system and upon other nuclei of the extrapyramidal system. The reticular formation is in close anatomical and functional relation with the cerebellum, which coordinates motor activity of both the pyramidal and extrapyramidal motor systems. The reticulospinal tracts give the reticular formation a rather direct pathway for altering the activity of spinal cord mechanisms.

The reticular formation is capable of exerting marked facilitation and inhibition upon spinal motor activity (Magoun and Rhines 1946, Rhines and Magoun 1946). The regions of the reticular formation that inhibit spinal cord motor mechanisms were originally defined to lie within the medioventral portion of the brain stem, and the facilitatory areas were defined dorsolaterally. Later investigations, however, have indicated that the reticulospinal systems exhibit reciprocal innervation and that thus each point giving rise to facilitation of a group of muscles inhibits the α-motoneurons of antagonist muscle groups (Sprague and Chambers 1954).

Reticulospinal fibers terminate upon interneurons and therefore exert an indirect influence upon the α- and γ-motoneurons of the spinal cord similar to that of the corticospinal tract. The reticulospinal tract is, however, a more rapidly conducting pathway than the corticospinal tract and sets the stage for precise locomotor activity initiated by either tract.

The reticular formation receives afferent fibers from the cerebral cortex, the cerebellum, other extrapyramidal motor system structures, the spinal cord and brain-stem somesthetic sensory systems, and the vestibular, visual, auditory, gustatory, and olfactory sensory systems. Thus this structure serves as a center of convergence for many influences that alter motor activity. This allows an integration of a wide variety of information into the sphere of motor activity and plays a key role in the determination of the type of motor activity initiated by cerebral motor systems.

CEREBELLUM

The cerebellum is a portion of the metencephalon. It is located dorsal to the pons and medulla and caudal to the mass of the cerebral hemispheres. The cerebellum is attached to the brain stem by three peduncles: the rostral cerebellar peduncle (brachium conjunctivum), the middle cerebellar peduncle (brachium pontis), and the caudal cerebellar peduncle (brachium restiformis). Fibers passing through these peduncles connect cerebellar structures with other structures of the brain stem and spinal cord.

The cerebellum is characterized by numerous small folds on its surface referred to as folia. The cerebellum is divided into several parts by deep fissures that separate the cortex into several lobes having different functional capacities (Fig. 44.4). The most caudal and ventral lobe is the flocculonodular lobe which functions in close relationship with the vestibular system of the medulla and pons. The flocculonodular lobe is separated from the remainder of the cerebellum by the posterolateral fissure. This lobe forms the archicerebellum, the oldest phylogenetic division of the cerebellum. The archicerebellum primarily modulates spinal control of muscle tone.

The remainder of the cerebellum is divided into a central portion referred to as the vermis (because of its wormlike appearance), and two lateral portions called the hemispheres. These three parts are further divided by the deep primary fissure. Rostral to the primary fissure is the anterior lobe of the cerebellum which comprises the paleocerebellum; caudal to the primary fissure is the neocerebellum.

The cerebellar cortex differs from the cerebral cortex in that all regions have a similar cytoarchitectonic organization and thus appear equipotential for a given type of

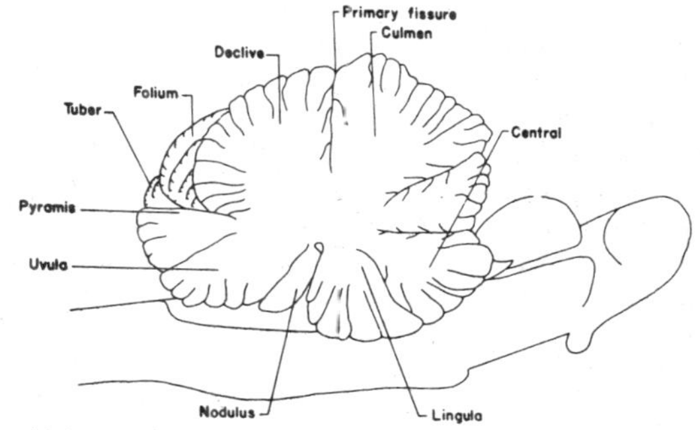

Figure 44.4. Midsagittal section of the cerebellum and brain stem demonstrating the principal lobes and fissures

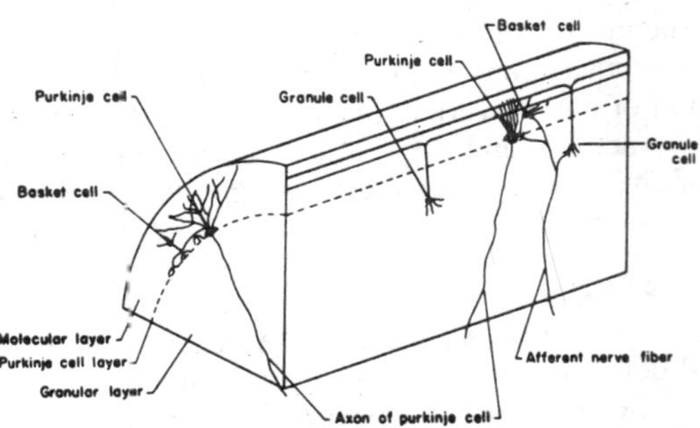

Figure 44.5. Folium of the cerebellum, demonstrating the organization of the cerebellar cortex into the molecular layer, Purkinje cell layer, and granular layer. The possible connections of afferent cerebellar fibers are also illustrated.

function. The cerebellar cortex is organized into three layers: an outer molecular layer, a middle layer of Purkinje cells, and a deep layer of granule cells (Fig. 44.5). The molecular layer is comprised of small cells that project their fibers transversely to the long axis of the folia and serve as a neural connection between cells of the underlying layer. These cells of the molecular layer are called basket cells because of their characteristic basket-like terminations at their synaptic endings. The second layer is comprised of Purkinje cells. These cells possess a large, pear-shaped cell body that projects its dendrites in a tree-shaped pattern into the molecular layer. The synaptic terminals of the basket cells terminate upon the soma of the Purkinje cells. The third layer of the cerebellar cortex is comprised of granule cells. These are small cells that project their axons into the molecular layer to synapse upon either the basket cells or upon the Purkinje cells. An afferent nerve fiber entering the cerebellar cortex may terminate upon granule cells, Purkinje cells, or basket cells. Efferent fibers of the cerebellar cortex all originate from the Purkinje cells. These efferents for the most part terminate within nuclei of the white matter of the cerebellum, but a few pass directly to the vestibular nuclei of the brain stem. A major part of the efferent fibers of the cerebellum arise from the deep cerebellar nuclei.

Deep in the cerebellar cortex, within the white matter of the cerebellum, are three pairs of nuclei: laterally is located the dentate nucleus, intermediate in position is the interpositus nucleus, and medially is the fastigial nucleus. The dentate nucleus is related primarily to the neocerebellar cortex and projects its fibers to regions of the cerebrum that control voluntary motor activity. The nucleus interpositus receives afferent fibers from the neocerebellum and paleocerebellum and projects its fibers to regions of the CNS that control both voluntary motor activity and the maintenance of muscle tone. The fastigial nucleus receives afferents from the paleocerebellum and archicerebellum and projects its fibers into the brain stem to regions that function primarily to control muscle tone. Thus the neocerebellum (the latest portion developed) serves as a modulator of voluntary motor activity, the paleocerebellum (intermediate in age) serves as a modulator of both voluntary motor activity and muscle tone, and the archicerebellum (oldest) serves as a modulator primarily of muscle tone. Since the control of muscle tone is the basic mechanism for smooth locomotor activity, all regions of the cerebellum play a significant role in this locomotive capacity.

The cerebellum exerts its control of motor activity in three ways: through its influence upon postural tone by way of its connections with the vestibular system, through its influence upon reflex responses of the spinal cord and brain-stem motoneurons, and through its influence upon voluntary responses through its cerebral connections. Total ablation of the cerebellum influences all of these systems by removing its modulating influence. The relative extent to which any of these functions is disrupted depends upon the dependence of a given function upon the modulatory influence of the cerebellum.

These functions developed phylogenetically, beginning with spinal cord mechanisms for muscle tone controlled by the archicerebellum and paleocerebellum, followed by spinal cord and brain-stem reflex activity controlled by the paleocerebellum, and finally by voluntary motor activity controlled by the paleocerebellum and neocerebellum. Because of this differential development, the influence of cerebellar removal depends upon the position of the species within the phylogenetic scale. Cerebellar ablation in birds results in a continuous state of spasticity resulting from overexcitability of α-motoneurons. Cerebellar ablation in dogs results in periodic seizures of extensor rigidity that are quite similar to those seen in the decerebrate animal. This rigidity is due to removal of cerebellar inhibitory influences upon the vestibular nuclear complex, as destruction of the labyrinth results in an alleviation of the rigidity (Pollock and Davis 1927). In later stages following decerebellation in dogs some recovery of ridigity is seen, but incoordination of both reflex and voluntary motor activity persists. Cerebellar ablation in primates results in an acute picture that is quite similar to that seen in dogs. Recovery from the rigidity and the onset of incoordination of locomotor activity are, however, more rapid. These animals exhibit a marked tremor when they attempt to move. This tremor has been shown to be dependent upon the corticospinal tract, which demonstrates the close relationship between the cerebellum and the cerebral structures that control motor activity.

The function of the cerebellum has been elucidated largely through stimulation studies. Sherrington in 1898 (Sherrington 1961) demonstrated that stimulation of the anterior lobe (paleocerebellum) of the cerebellum resulted in a loss of decerebrate rigidity, illustrating that this portion of the cerebellum exerts a powerful inhibitory influence upon the spinal motoneurons, either directly or through vestibular and other brain stem nuclei. The complex control of motoneuron activity by the cerebellum has been demonstrated by Moruzzi (1950) in the decerebrate cat. He demonstrated that when the anterior lobe is stimulated at a low frequency (2–30/sec), the rigidity of decerebration was increased. When the frequency was increased, facilitation gradually was converted into inhibition. These results indicate that the cerebellum serves as a powerful modulator of the activity of myotatic reflex arcs. This control may be exerted either upon the α-motoneuron of the reflex arc or upon the muscle spindle receptor organ, by alteration of activity of γ-motoneurons (Terzuolo and Terzian 1953).

The cerebellum apparently possesses the mechanisms necessary to switch from γ- to α-motoneuron facilitation and vice versa. If one recalls that decerebrate rigidity is an enhanced myotatic reflex activity, the fact that the cerebellum can inhibit this rigidity demonstrates its control of α- and γ-motor activity. If the cerebellum is ablated in a decerebrate animal, the rigidity is not lost; instead it may be more intense and changed in character in that it cannot be abolished by sectioning of the dorsal roots of the spinal nerves. Thus removal of the cerebellum converts a γ-rigidity (due to hyperactivity in γ-motoneurons) into an α-rigidity (due to hyperactivity in α-motoneurons). This conversion is brought about by the removal of excitatory influences upon the γ-motoneurons and of inhibitory influences upon the α-motoneurons.

The afferent fibers to the cerebellum can be segregated roughly into three categories: those that project to the archicerebellum, those that project to the paleocerebellum, and those that project to the neocerebellum. Afferents to the archicerebellum arise primarily from the vestibular nuclear complex. A few of these fibers may enter the cerebellum directly from the vestibular nerve without a brain stem synapse. Afferents to the paleocerebellum represent the dorsal and ventral spinocerebellar tracts and fibers from the accessory (lateral) cuneate nucleus. These fibers carry information concerning the activity of muscle and tendon stretch receptors and provide the paleocerebellum with the information needed for modulation of various reflex activity. The neocerebellum receives afferents from the pontine and medullary structures which are concerned with control of cerebrally initiated motor activity. These include, among others, the pontine gray matter and the reticular formation which supply the neocerebellum with information necessary for the modulation of voluntary motor activity.

There are also afferent fibers that project to the cerebellar cortex from the auditory, visual, and tactile sensory systems. It is possible that they inform the cerebellum of the necessity of specific motor activity modulation.

The function of the cerebellum in the control of activities of the CNS other than those subserving skeletal muscle motor mechanisms has been indicated by many studies. Evidence indicates that the cerebellum plays some role in the maintenance of consciousness in the normal animal and in the regulation of various autonomic motor activities.

If the afferent and efferent connections of the cerebellum are viewed simultaneously, it can be seen that the cerebellum forms an important part of an extensive chain of feedback connections all of which serve to control in some way the coordination of locomotor activity (see Figs. 44.2, 44.3). With this view in mind, the cerebellum can be said to form an integral part of both the pyramidal and extrapyramidal motor systems.

REFERENCES

Agnew, R.F., Preston, J.B., and Whitlock, D.G. 1963. Patterns of motor cortex effects on ankle flexor and extensory motoneurons in the "pyramidal" cat preparation. *Exp. Neurol.* 8:248–63.

Appelberg, B., and Kosary, I.Z. 1963. Excitation of flexor fusimotor neurons by electrical stimulation in the red nucleus. *Acta Physiol. Scand.* 59:445–53.

Brodal, A. 1963. Some data and perspectives on the anatomy of the so-called "extrapyramidal system." *Acta Neurol. Scand.* 39(suppl. 4):17–38.

Brookhart, H.M., and Morris, R.E. 1948. Antidromic potential recordings from the bulbar pyramid of the cat. *J. Neurophysiol.* 11:387–98.

Carpenter, M.B., and Correll, J.W. 1961. Spinal pathways mediating cerebellar dyskinesia in Rhesus monkey. *J. Neurophysiol.* 24:534–51.

Carpenter, M.B., Correll, J.W., and Hinman, A. 1960. Spinal tracts mediating subthalamic hyperkinesia: Physiological effects of selective partial cordotomies upon dyskinesia in Rhesus monkey. *J. Neurophysiol.* 23:288–304.

Crevel, H. van, and Verhaart, W.J.C. 1963. The 'exact' origin of the pyramidal tract. *J. Anat.* 97:495–515.

Crosby, E.C., and Henderson, J.W. 1948. The mammalian midbrain and isthmus regions. II. Fiber connections of the superior colliculus. B. Pathways concerned in automatic eye movements. *J. Comp. Neurol.* 88:53–92.

Haggqvist, G. 1937. Faseranalytische Studien uber die Pyramidenbahn. *Acta Psychiat. Neurol.* 12:457–66.

Jung, R., and Hassler, R. 1960. The extrapyramidal motor system. In *Handbook of Physiology*. Am. Physiol. Soc., Washington. Sec. 1, vol. 2, 863–927.

Kuypers, H.G.J.M. 1960. Central cortical projections to motor and somato-sensory cell groups: An experimental study in the Rhesus monkey. *Brain* 83:161–84.

Lassek, A.M., and Rasmussen, G.L. 1939. The human pyramidal tract. I. A fiber and numerical analysis. *Arch. Neurol. Psychiat.* 42:872–76.

Levin, P.M. 1936. The efferent fibers of the frontal lobe of the monkey, *Macaca mulatta*. *J. Comp. Neurol.* 63:369–419.

Lindsley, D.B., Schreiner, L.H., and Magoun, H.W. 1949. An electromyographic study of spasticity. *J. Neurophysiol.* 12:197–205.

Livingston, A., and Phillips, C.G. 1957. Maps and thresholds for the sensorimotor cortex of the cat. *Q. J. Exp. Physiol.* 42:190–205.

Lloyd, D.P.C. 1941. The spinal mechanism of the pyramidal system in cats. *J. Neurophysiol.* 4:525–46.

Magoun, H.W., and Rhines, R. 1946. An inhibitory mechanism in the bulbar reticular formation. *J. Neurophysiol.* 9:165–71.

Mettler, F.A. 1943. Extensive unilateral cerebral removals in the primate: Physiologic effects and resultant degeneration. *J. Comp. Neurol.* 79:185–245.

——. 1945. Fiber connections of the corpus striatum of the monkey and baboon. *J. Comp. Neurol.* 82:169–203.

Moruzzi, G. 1950. Effects at different frequencies of cerebellar stimulation upon postural tonus after deafferentation and labyrinthectomy. *J. Neurophysiol.* 16:551–61.

Nyberg-Hansen, R., and Brodal, A. 1963. Sites of termination of cortico-spinal fibers in the cat: An experimental study with silver impregnation methods. *J. Comp. Neurol.* 120:369–91.

Patton, H.D., and Amassian, V.E. 1960. The pyramidal tract: Its excitation and functions. In *Handbook of Physiology*. Am. Physiol. Soc., Washington. Sec. 1, vol. 2, 837–61.

Pollock, L.J., and Davis, L. 1927. The influence of the cerebellum upon the reflex activities of the decerebrate animal. *Brain* 50:277–312.

Rhines, R., and Magoun, H.W. 1946. Brain stem facilitation of cortical motor response. *J. Neurophysiol.* 9:219–29.

Rinvik, E., and Walberg, F. 1963. Demonstration of a somatotopically arranged corticorubral projection in the cat: An experimental study with silver methods. *J. Comp. Neurol.* 120:393–407.

Rossi, G.F., and Brodal, A. 1956. Corticofugal fibers to the brain stem reticular formation: An experimental study in the cat. *J. Anat.* 90:42–62.

Sherrington, C.S. 1905. On reciprocal innervation of antagonistic muscles: Eighth note. *Proc. Roy. Soc.*, ser. B, 76:269–97.

——. 1961. *The Integrative Action of the Nervous System*. Yale U. Press, New Haven.

Sprague, J.M., and Chambers, W.W. 1954. Control of posture by reticular formation and cerebellum in the intact, anesthetized, and unanesthetized and in the decerebrate cat. *Am. J. Physiol.* 176:52–64.

Terzuolo, C., and Terzian, H. 1953. Cerebellar increase postural tonus after deafferentation and labyrinthectomy. *J. Neurophysiol.* 16:551–61.

CHAPTER 45

Alertness, Sleep, and Related States | by William R. Klemm

Certain behavioral states, such as alertness and sleep, are commonly called "states of consciousness." However, since consciousness, like beauty, is in the mind of the beholder, it is semantically awkward to talk about the physiology of such an abstraction.

OBJECTIVE MEASURES

Behavior

Various states are commonly defined in terms of the observed behavior. For example, a hunting dog is *alert* when, upon detecting the scent of birds, it stops, becomes tense, perks its ears, and points its tail. It is *asleep* when it lies down, curls up, closes its eyes, and does not move for a time. More precise definitions will become evident for each of the states that are subsequently discussed.

Electrographic correlates

The electrical activity from various body organs measures the behavioral state by providing information on functions such as heart rate, muscle tone, and neuron activity. Such measures not only provide a more precise definition of behavioral states, but more importantly they enable us to learn about the mechanisms that cause the various states.

Information on brain electrical activity is usually derived from electrodes placed on the head or within the brain and is displayed by pen and ink recorders; the written record thus obtained is called the electroencephalogram or EEG. The EEG is actually a plot of voltage changes as a function of time. The magnitude of the voltage in animals is quite variable, but in general ranges up to about 200 μv. The wave form of the EEG is irregular, because the waves have been compounded from a mixture of different voltages and frequencies that were generated by partially independent neuronal generators. The duration of the more prominent waves ranges from about 20 milliseconds to 1 second.

The physiological origin of the EEG is not completely understood, but most evidence indicates that it comes from algebraic summation of slow membrane potential changes (EPSPs and IPSPs) of individual neurons (see end of chapter for abbreviations). It is also possible that some of the EEG comes from membrane potential fluctuations of glial cells and from compounding of nearly synchronous impulses.

In an oversimplified way, the EEG can be said to appear in one of two forms: (1) low voltage, fast activity (LVFA), in which most waves are of low voltage and have short durations; and (2) high voltage, slow activity (HVSA), in which most waves are of high voltage and have long durations.

Usually, brain electrical activity correlates with behavior over a wide range of normal phenomena (Lindsley 1952). In general, LVFA is associated with alert states and HVSA is associated with sedated states such as sleep and anesthesia. These correlations may not apply in certain disease or drug states.

Since LVFA occurs during alert states, the EEG is sometimes said to be *activated;* another synonym is *desynchronized,* a term intended to reflect a presumed desynchrony of neuronal generators. Conversely, because HVSA is associated with sedated states, the EEG is sometimes said to be *deactivated;* another synonym is *synchronized,* reflecting perhaps more synchronous discharge of neurons.

NEUROPHYSIOLOGICAL BASES

Key Discoveries

As commonly happens in physiology, investigations on behavioral states were stimulated by medical problems in dealing with abnormalities, in particular certain lethargic syndromes. Analysis of some of these human clinical cases by Gayet in 1875 in France and Mauthner in 1890 in Austria disclosed the importance of lesions in the rostral midbrain in the pathogenesis of such syndromes. Further pathological study by von Economo (1929) revealed that lethargic patients often had lesions in the midbrain reticular formation (MBRF) and in the posterior hypothalamus, while patients with insomnia often had lesions around the basal forebrain.

Bremer (1935) provided a key breakthrough by demonstrating that transection of the cat's brain at the anterior MBRF produced behavioral and EEG signs of somnolence, whereas transection at the first cervical segment produced a state of alternating EEG activation and deactivation. Bremer concluded that transection anterior to the MBRF caused sleep because sensory input to the forebrain was stopped.

Animal experimentation on cats and monkeys by Ranson in 1939 helped confirm the idea that there was also a wakefulness mechanism located in the posterior hypothalamus.

Research on wakefulness mechanisms culminated in the synthesis by Moruzzi and Magoun in 1949, who showed that electrical stimulation of the MBRF produces hyperarousal in alert animals and awakens sleeping animals.

The demonstration of the MBRF's arousing power led naturally to the notion that sleep could be promoted by diminution of MBRF influence, either passively or actively. Some active inhibitory influences are suspected on the basis of several studies. Hess in 1944 showed that electrical stimulation in certain thalamic regions of cats prompted them to become drowsy and even go to sleep. Nauta in 1946 advanced evidence for an active hypnogenic system in the preoptic region of the hypothalamus. Additionally, Moruzzi (1958) and Italian colleagues demonstrated an active hypnogenic system in the caudal brain stem of cats; transection of the brain stem in the middle of the pons caused permanent EEG activation, showing that some area caudal to the cut normally inhibited the arousal influence of the MBRF. The same arousal response was demonstrated by blocking caudal brainstem function with locally applied anesthetic. In 1962 Sterman and Clemente confirmed the active sleep-promoting function of the preoptic hypothalamus; they demonstrated sleep induction in cats by electrical stimulation of this structure.

Another major discovery was that of dream sleep in man by Dement and Kleitman in 1957, and its animal counterpart by Dement (1958).

In recent years, much provocative research has been conducted on the biochemistry of behavioral states, especially concerning the function of neurochemical transmitter systems. (See Bremer 1974 for more detail on the history of all these areas of research.)

Cerebral cortex

The cerebral cortex receives many of the stimuli that cause changes in behavioral state. Neural activity within the cortex, moreover, often determines the state and degree of response to stimuli. If one ablates a specific sensory portion of cortex, for example, the cells that receive sound input, then the appropriate stimulus (sound in this case) would fail to change the behavioral state.

The cortex helps to regulate those subcortical structures that affect it. For example, electrical stimulation at many points on the cortex can evoke neural responses in the brain stem activating system which in turn stimulates the cortex into awareness and responsiveness (see below). Thus, while the cortex is necessary for some behavioral states, it cannot be the sole determinant because of the profound influences of subcortical areas.

Brain-stem reticular activating system (RAS)

The central core of the brain stem, the reticular formation (BSRF), plays a key role in a variety of behavioral states. These cells receive collateral sensory input from all levels of the spinal cord, including such diverse sources as cutaneous receptors of the body and head, Golgi tendon organs, aortic and carotid sinuses, several cranial nerves, olfactory organs, eyes, and ears, in addition to extensive inputs from other brain stem areas, the cerebellum, and the cerebral cortex (Klemm 1976a).

When RAS neurons are stimulated by sensory input of any kind, they relay excitation through numerous reticular synapses (French et al. 1953) and finally activate widespread zones of the cerebral cortex. In contrast, sensory information that arrives in the cortex via the main sensory paths passes through relatively few synapses and arrives at specific and relatively discrete zones of the cortex.

The RAS responds in the same way to any sensory stimulus, whether from the skin, eyes, ears, or whatever, to "awaken" the cerebral cortex so that it can respond to and process stimuli. The RAS is a kind of general alarm system, sending out signals that activate the entire cortex rather than any one center of sensation. Moreover, tonic background activity in this system sustains wakefulness and alertness. RAS signals activate not only the cortex, but also the hypothalamus, pituitary gland, and possibly other structures. Also, via direct reticulospinal connections, this system controls not only certain effectors but also the reactivity of receptors (Akert 1965).

The emphasis here on the sensory functions of the reticular formation should not obscure the fact that many other functions reside in the BSRF; there are also descending motor functions that regulate postural tone, respiration, and vasomotor responses (Moruzzi 1958). These functions are controlled by different neurons intermingled and scattered throughout the formation; the BSRF is noted for its lack of topographical segregation of functions.

Any comprehensive concept of RAS function must take into account the neurohumoral transmission in the region. Unfortunately, however, our understanding is still very limited, in spite of a great deal of investigation.

The activation of the cerebral cortex that results from RAS activity is cholinergic (Kanai and Szerb 1965, Jasper 1966). During behavioral arousal in cats, acetylcholine release by cortical cells is greatly increased. Injection of the acetylcholine blocker, atropine, prevents excitation of cortical cells by the released acetylcholine.

Limbic system

The limbic system, consisting of such brain areas as the hypothalamus, hippocampus, septum, amygdala, and parts of the cortex, has many functions (see Chapter 46), including an influence on activated behavioral states. For example, activation of the BSRF in turn excites the hypothalamus to generate the so-called fight-or-flight visceral activities of the autonomic nervous system (see Chapter 48).

Other probable influences are less well understood. Of particular interest has been the observation that aroused behavioral states are often associated with a very rhythmic oscillation in the EEG of the hippocampus (Fig. 45.1). This rhythm is often so large that it can be detected from other nearby areas. It has been correlated with many behaviors and physiological functions, such as arousal, orienting, body movements, motivation, and even learning and memory (Klemm 1976a). A variety of ideas have been advanced to explain the involvement of the hippocampus and allied limbic structures in activated behaviors, but none is generally accepted.

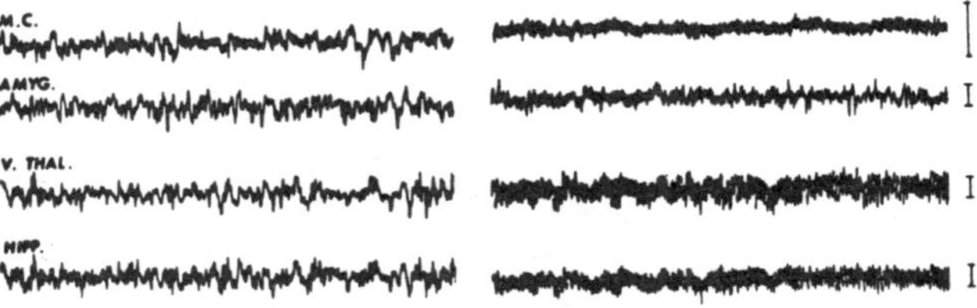

Figure 45.1. Typical records of brain electrical activity in cortical and subcortical areas during relaxation (on the left) and alertness (on the right). During alertness the activity is of lower voltage and faster frequencies in the motor cortex (M.C.) and the amygdala (AMYG.). In the ventral thalamus (V. THAL.) and the hippocampus (HIPP.) there is a regular rhythm of six per second (theta rhythm). Calibration marks, 100 μv and 1 second.

Deactivating systems

There are thalamic areas rostral to the BSRF that are known to have certain effects antagonistic to the activity of the RAS. These areas, known collectively as the diffuse thalamic projection system (DTPS), are separate and largely independent of the topographically specific thalamic relay nuclei (Hanbery and Jasper 1953). The thalamic nuclei that are generally regarded as members of the DTPS are mainly located medially (Bureš et al. 1967).

The projection of the DTPS is, as the name implies, quite diffuse, projecting ascendingly to the cortex and descendingly to the MBRF (Schlag and Faidherbe 1961).

The significance of the DTPS seems to be its role as a pacemaker that can regulate cortical activity. The most conspicuous known feature of the DTPS was discovered in classical experiments by Dempsey and Morison (1942, 1943). They showed that slow stimulation of the DTPS (8–12 per second) produced rhythmically recurrent potentials, primarily in the frontal and parietal association cortex, which they termed recruiting potentials (Fig. 45.2).

These potentials are mainly electronegative, and they increase in size with successive discharges. The increasing size results from successive recruiting of more cortical neurons into activity. Similar potentials can be evoked by rhythmic electrical stimulation of specific thalamic nuclei; these responses are termed augmenting responses (Buser 1964). Such potentials can also be evoked

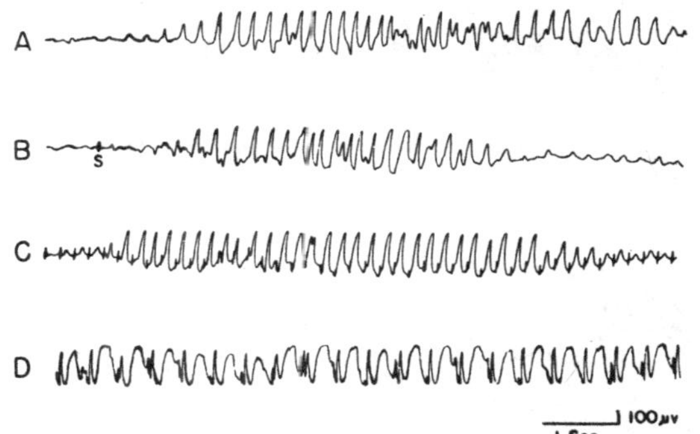

Figure 45.2. Effects of DTPS stimulation in the centralis medialis of the cat upon electrical activity in the cortex. The animal was under light pentobarbital anesthesia. A, spontaneous spindle burst; B, a single 1 msec shock (S) triggering a spindle burst; C, repetitive stimulation at five per second showing waxing and waning of recruiting response; D, spike and wave, epileptiform response to stimulation at 2.5 per second. (From Jasper, in *Handbook of Physiology*, sec. 1, Magoun, ed., *Neurophysiology*, Am. Physiol. Soc., Washington, 1960, vol. 2.)

reciprocally between thalamus and hippocampus, in association with similar responses in skeletal muscle (Palmer and Klemm 1977).

One intriguing aspect of the interpretation of recruiting is the similarity of recruiting potentials to the spontaneous spindles of drowsy animals in both morphology and topography. Among the other facts that suggest a close relationship is that spindles can be triggered by a single stimulation of the DTPS.

Recruiting potentials and spontaneous spindles have a common neural origin in the cortex, as indicated by their occlusive interaction; when recruitment is induced during spontaneous spindling, the spindles become smaller than normal.

During spontaneous cortical spindling or during evoked recruiting, the pacemaker thalamic cells owe their timing to unusually large IPSPs that alternate regularly with EPSPs (Andersen and Sears 1964). The timing of these thalamic discharges controls the timing of the cortex spindles.

In addition to the recruiting and RAS-inhibiting functions, the DTPS is also the thalamic extension of the RAS and can participate in behavioral and EEG arousal. Fast frequency stimulation of the DTPS results not in recruiting but in LVFA (Starzl et al. 1951); possibly this effect is indirect, acting via descending connections to the RAS (Schlag and Chaillet 1962, Grantyn et al. 1971).

Several other parts of the brain are antagonistic to the RAS and promote behavioral drowsiness and EEG spindling-synchrony, especially if the animal is in a pre-existing relaxed state.

Low frequency stimulation of the caudate nucleus can produce spindling, HVSA, and sleep (Kleitman 1963); similar results have been reported for stimulation of the anterior preoptic regions of the hypothalamus (Sterman and Clemente 1962a,b). The preoptic region seems particularly important for the genesis of sleep (Bremer 1974).

Several areas in the caudal pons and rostral medulla, upon appropriate stimulation promote electrographic and behavioral signs of sleep. These areas include the pontine reticular formation, solitary nucleus, and ventral nucleus of the medulla (Magnes et al. 1961, Bueno et al. 1968). These deactivating systems have not been studied as extensively as has the DTPS, but they clearly have profound effects and may even be more important than the DTPS for the promotion of sleep (Moruzzi 1974).

ALERT BEHAVIOR

An animal's basic response to biologically meaningful stimuli involves a succession of stages. First there is attention or startle, depending on stimulus intensity. Then there is orientation, followed by either approach, withdrawal, or habituation.

The initial arousing and orienting responses are more reflexive than later stages, and the behavior is associated with conspicuous activation of the EEG (Fig. 45.3). Initial responses are triggered by a major *change* in sensa-

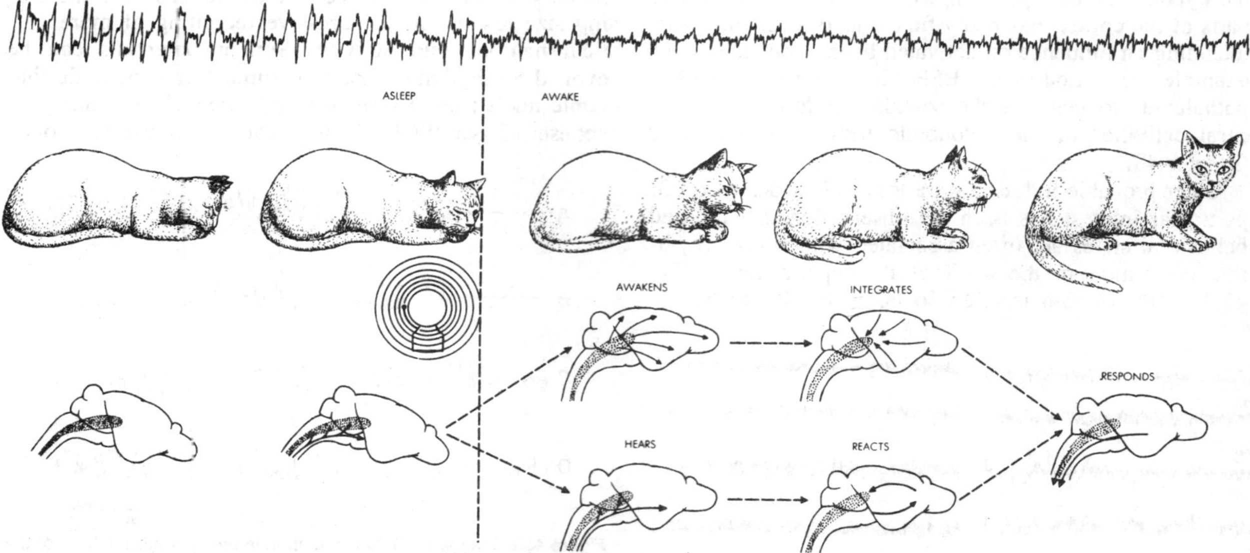

Figure 45.3. EEG and behavioral effects of an auditory stimulus upon the RAS. The brain diagram illustrates sound stimuli (incoming arrows) reaching the BSRF (stippled area) by way of collateral branches of the axons that lead to a restricted auditory region of the cortex. At this stage, the animal has received the sensory information and thus hears without necessarily processing the information. The RAS then "awakens" the cortex diffusely so that it integrates and processes the auditory information. Associated with the RAS effect is a behavioral arousal and a desynchronization of the EEG. Interactions of RAS and cortical activity then prepare the cat to make an appropriate motor response to the sound stimulus. (From French 1957, The reticular formation. Copyright © 1957, 1958, 1961 by Scientific American, Inc. All rights reserved.)

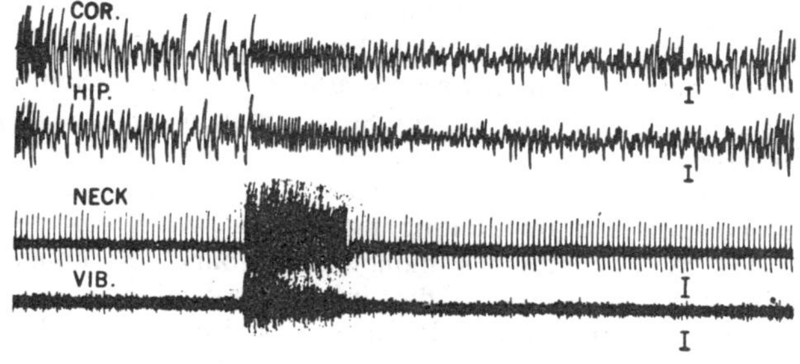

Figure 45.4. Stimulation of areas in the rat BSRF, showing the widespread nature of RAS activation of bodily functions. A focal point of the BSRF was stimulated mildly (2.8 v, 300 per second pulses), as indicated by thickened portion of the 1-second time line at the bottom. Both cortex (COR.) and hippocampus (HIP.) were activated, as indicated by the initial theta rhythm followed by LVFA in the EEG. Simultaneously there was activation of both ascending and descending muscle activities, as revealed in the electromyogram of vibrissal (VIB.) and nuchal muscles (NECK, contaminated with electrocardiographic spikes). The spinal cord was transected cervically in order to restrict feedback variables and to achieve substantial deafferentation (note deactivated EEG prior to BSRF stimulation). Voltage calibrations, 100 μv. (From W.R. Klemm 1972, *Brain Res.* 41:331–44.)

tion; for example, sudden cessation of continuous stimulation can be just as arousing as can sudden stimulation during continuous absence of stimulation (Weinberger and Lindsley 1964).

The role of the RAS in these arousing responses can be demonstrated by direct electrical stimulation at many points within the BSRF. Such stimulation activates the neocortex (indicated by LVFA in the EEG), the limbic system (rhythmic theta activity in the hippocampus), and postural tone (increased electromyographic activity of muscles) (Fig. 45.4). Additionally, many visceral activities are activated via spread of BSRF excitation into the hypothalamus.

The RAS gets extensive input from various brain regions, particularly the neocortex and limbic system, and such input can be a major factor in causing certain behavioral states. For example, the cortical and limbic-system activities that are associated with the distress of a newly weaned puppy probably supply a continuous barrage of impulses to the RAS, which in turn continually excites the cortex to keep the pup awake and howling all night.

Some control or braking system must exist if the brain is to prevent excessive BSRF activation and arousal. Intracellular recordings indicate that rostral BSRF neurons have mainly an inhibitory action (i.e. production of IPSPs) on caudal BSRF neurons and that these in turn have mostly an inhibitory action on the rostral BSRF neurons. Perhaps this is the basis for a negative feedback braking system to prevent excessive arousal (Mancia et al. 1974).

The brain can, through previous experience, learn to discriminate against certain stimuli that are of no consequence to the animal. This habituation or accommodation is indicated in the EEG by failure of the stimulus to elicit desynchronization (Oswald 1962). If an arousing stimulus is given repeatedly, the arousal response may gradually disappear. It can reappear only when some change is made in the stimulus, such as in frequency or amplitude. Studies on this topic indicate that the chief feature of arousing stimuli is their strangeness to the animal. Once an animal learns that a given stimulus is biologically insignificant, it ignores the stimulus. Arousal habituation is very relevant to the study of sleep, since it means that uniform stimulation will be followed by decreased RAS activity.

The general view of wakefulness is that it exists whenever the tonic flow of impulses of the RAS is above the critical level for sustaining consciousness. Animals lapse into sleep or similar states whenever this activity diminishes. Reduction of RAS activity, either normal or abnormal (by barbiturates, tranquilizers, experimental injury, or disease), can lead to various degrees of sedation, sleeplike states, and coma. For example, Lindsley et al. (1950) showed that BSRF lesions which spared the lateral sensory paths produced a state of sleep that was extremely resistant to sensory stimulation. Lesions in the lateral sensory paths that spared the BSRF produced no such unresponsive state. Likewise, drug-induced sedation and anesthesia result from the drug's affinity for the RAS (Root and Hofmann 1963).

The general view of sleep as a sequel to RAS depression, although extremely convenient, is an oversimplification in that it requires sleep to be a strictly passive phenomenon.

SLEEP

Deactivated sleep

Only a brief description of the physiology of sleep can be given here, but the great amount of recent research has been comprehensively reviewed elsewhere (Chase 1972, Petre-Quadens and Schlag 1974).

General characteristics

Sleep is recognized most obviously as a reversible unconsciousness and relative immobility of an animal. Behavior during sleep is characterized by (1) reduced ability to analyze changes in the environment, (2) increased threshold to sensory stimulation, and (3) relative muscular inactivity. The environmental influences that usually modify behavior are relatively ineffective. Likewise, in all animals except birds, the tonic proprioceptive, labyrinthine, and visual reflexes that are responsible for righting the body and maintaining normal posture are no longer operative.

Since one of the primary characteristics of sleep is a synchronized, HVSA-type of EEG, typical sleep is sometimes called slow-wave sleep. Also conspicuous are cortical EEG spindles. However, by themselves these electrical correlates are not specific indicators of sleep, for they can also occur in certain drug sedation states, during natural drowsiness, during anesthesia, and in certain disease conditions.

Here we will refer to the typical stage of sleep as deactivated sleep (DS) to contrast it from another, qualitatively different, stage of sleep that will be discussed later.

The threshold for response to sensory stimulation is increased during DS. Some sensory input processing occurs, as indicated by conditioning studies in humans (Beh and Barratt 1965). Discrimination and conditioning performance were greatly improved when the stimuli were specially significant or meaningful to the sleeper.

Absence of movement is conspicuous during sleep; spinal reflexes are also depressed. Although muscle tone is generally reduced, some muscles may be more active during sleep. Typical examples include the curling up by dogs and cats, the standing sleep in horses, the upside-down position of bats, and the perching behavior of birds.

Visceral functions are usually depressed during typical sleep, which is achieved by the dominance of the parasympathetic nervous system. The usual parasympathetic effects are seen, such as slower heart rate and lower blood pressure. Pupils are constricted, and in fact subtle changes in pupil size can be monitored as an index of the degree of drowsiness (Lowenstein and Loewenfeld 1964). Studies involving direct recording of sympathetic nerve impulses in cats revealed that phasic changes in impulse activity could occur independently of behavioral or EEG changes. During typical sleep, any arousal, either spontaneous or induced, was accompanied by increased impulse discharge that outlasted the EEG arousal (Baust et al. 1968).

It had long been believed that anemia and hypoxia of the brain occurred during sleep, but this view is no longer tenable. Breathing movements are slower, alveolar CO_2 levels drop, blood pH becomes slightly more acid, overall metabolic rate decreases, and body temperature drops. However, no parallel signs of metabolic depression in the brain are seen. Cerebral blood flow and oxygen consumption remain about the same as during alert wakefulness (Nauta et al. 1967). Moreover, electrical recording of individual neuron activity has revealed that some neurons actually become more active during sleep than during wakefulness (Evarts 1962, Evarts et al. 1962).

Sleep is necessary for health, and animals deprived of sleep will eventually become ill. Animals that are experimentally forced to stay awake become irritable and engage in vicious fights (Kleitman 1963).

Theories on mechanisms

A number of theories have been proposed to explain sleep, but no one theory seems sufficient by itself. Some insight is provided by the normal requirements for inducing sleep.

Sleep is best induced by restricting excessive sensory stimulation and by limiting movement, which can be aided by a continuous monotonous sound. Kleitman (1963) reviewed many studies in which monotony or absence of external stimulation promoted sleep in animals. Reducing the proprioceptive drive with muscle relaxants is also known to promote sleep (Hodes 1961). Under natural conditions, fatigue of postural tonus markedly decreases the number of proprioceptive impulses (Matsumoto et al. 1968). The highest cerebral centers, thus partly isolated from afferent stimulation, are able to lapse into inactivity, resulting in sleep. Although fatigue is the usual cause of muscle relaxation, it is not necessary for induced sleep. Many times sleep and wakefulness cycles are largely controlled by conditioned responses.

There are several humoral theories of sleep. They all share the premise that certain body chemicals, usually metabolic end-products, accumulate and excite the neurons that cause sleep. One of the first humoral theories was the hypnotoxin theory of Piéron; it was reinvestigated by Schnedorf and Ivy (1939), who found that cerebrospinal fluid (CSF) from fatigued dogs would induce profound sleep when injected intracisternally into normal dogs. The major objection to the hypnotoxin theory is the fact that injection of the suspected agents can result in wakefulness as well as sleep. In addition, sleep can occur independently in parabiotic "monsters" and in animals experimentally sharing the same circulation (Kleitman 1963).

The subject has been recently reinvestigated; dialysate from cerebral venous blood of sleeping rabbits, upon injection in awake rabbits, induced sleep within 15 minutes. Contrarily, dialysate from alert animals induced EEG signs of arousal when injected into other animals. This study tended to rule out respiration, pH, inorganic phosphates, and certain electrolytes (Na, K, Ca) at the cause. Similar results have been obtained in cross-circulation studies in cats and rabbits wherein electrosleep induced in one animal was accompanied by sleep in the other animal that shared the same circulation (Monnier and Hösli 1965).

There is substantial evidence to suggest that at least one of the humors is serotonin (Koella 1967, Jouvet 1969). Serotonin does excite sinoaortic pressoreceptors, which are known to be sleep-promoting. And intracarotid injection of serotonin (in cats with denervated sinus receptors) induces physiological signs of sleep; brain transection studies localized this effect to the posterior brain stem. Further studies defined the serotonin-sensitive area as the area postrema, which forms the floor of the posterior part of the fourth ventricle. Nerve impulses may travel from the area postrema to the nearby solitary tract nucleus region, which, along with other more rostral areas, seems to be involved in the active neural induction of sleep. In addition, destruction of the serotonergic neurons in the brain stem causes insomnia, as does drug-induced suppression of serotonin synthesis. Paradoxically, sleep returns in a few days, even though drug suppression of serotonin is continued (Dement 1972).

Another possibility, not mutually exclusive of the serotonin theory, is the possible role of acetylcholine. Acetylcholine injections into the hypothalamus also produce sleep, whereas a drug which interferes with acetylcholine action, pilocarpine, causes excitement (Dikshit 1935). Cholinergic substances injected in parts of the limbic system, preoptic region, the DTPS, and the pontine reticular formation can also induce sleep (Hernández-Peón et al. 1963, Hernandez-Peon 1965).

The parasympathetic nervous system has been suggested as one of the possible neural causes of DS because of the dominance of this system during typical sleep. This, however, does not prove a parasympathetic cause of sleep. For example, during extreme alertness, there is activation of the sympathetic system; but sympathetic activity is not the *cause* of the alertness. Although sympathetic activity can help sustain alertness, its activation is initially the *result* of alertness. Likewise, parasympathetic activity may be just the result of sleep.

Since decorticate animals sleep, the basic sleep-wakefulness mechanisms must be subcortical. These subcortical mechanisms include the activating role of the RAS and the deactivating role of diencephalic and medullary structures. The RAS accomplishes wakefulness by supplying (perhaps indirectly) a powerful tonic drive in the form of nerve impulses to the cortex. Diminution of this activity is an important predisposing factor of sleep, inasmuch as the capacity for alertness is lost after the brain is sectioned above the level of the RAS (*cerveau isolé*) (Bremer 1935). The basic question of why RAS activity diminishes naturally has not been satisfactorily answered.

Most evidence favors an active inhibitory process in specific hypnogenic systems as the cause of sleep. The most significant early work in this field was that of Hess et al. (1953) who showed that low-rate electrical current stimulation of the DTPS produced sleep. From their studies, they concluded that this region of the thalamus was a sleep center that was normally involved in the production and maintenance of sleep.

As previously mentioned, other brain areas involved in the production of sleep are the preoptic region of the hypothalamus and the soltiary tract nucleus and adjacent area in the pontine and medullary reticular formation. Electrical stimulation of these areas induces sleep in a relaxed animal. Destroying or otherwise disrupting the function of these areas produces lasting insomnia.

In addition, many investigators suspect that another sleep center is the *raphe*, a small group of cells in the center of the BSRF.

Koella (1967) considered the DTPS to be the primary hypnogenic system, based on several observations during electrical stimulation of the DTPS: (1) sleep is induced more easily than with other systems; (2) the duration of induced sleep is longer, more like that in normal sleep; (3) sleep is preceded by the normal behavioral changes that precede natural sleep; (4) recruiting responses, which are generated by the same mechanism as sleep spindles, are best obtained by DTPS stimulation.

One can only speculate on the mechanisms that initiate inhibitory center activity. Discharge patterns in afferent proprioceptive and autonomic nerves may trigger inhibitory centers directly, or indirectly by release of excitatory drive. Chemical action, at the area postrema, for example, remains an important possibility.

It is clear, however, that the antagonistic relations of the RAS and the deactivating centers are the major known mechanisms of sleep and wakefulness. Sleep could result from overactivity of the deactivating centers or from reduction of activity in the RAS excitatory center. The major unanswered question about the deactivating systems is how they are triggered into activity and orchestrated into performing their influence on the RAS.

Activated sleep

General characteristics

In 1957, EEG studies in man revealed that during sleep there were alternating periods of EEG activity in which the waves were not synchronized, but were actually desynchronized and associated with stereotyped rapid eye movements (REM). When people were awakened in the midst of these episodes, they usually remembered a dream being interrupted. Subsequently, these same physiological changes of EEG activation and REM were observed to occur periodically during the sleep of animals.

This stage of sleep is considered to be qualitatively different from DS. The physiological changes are such that activated sleep (AS) is an appropriate name.

AS has many characteristics that distinguish it from DS, including activation of the cortical EEG, a hippocampal theta rhythm, spikelike EEG waves in several vision-related brain areas (pons, lateral geniculate nuclei, and occipital cortex), bursts of REM, and postural muscle atonia with superimposed phasic twitching. Other changes during AS include dilatation of peripheral vessels and lower blood pressure (Rossi 1963), slower heart rate, decreased sympathetic activity (Baust et al. 1968), and increased brain temperature (Kawamura and Sawyer 1965), presumably reflecting increased oxygen consumption in the brain (Brebbia and Altshuler 1965).

The various aspects of muscle activity during AS may seem confusing; nuchal activity declines at the same time that face and eye muscles are phasically activated. Moreover, phasic myoclonic jerks have been noted in many hind limb muscles during AS; in between these twitches were periods of inactivity. These twitches contrast sharply with the tonic inhibition of nuchal and limb muscles. Studies involving dorsal-root sections and spinal cord lesions indicate that these twitches result from phasic barrages of nerve impulses arriving at spinal motoneurons from supraspinal levels and overwhelming the tonic inhibitory influences of other supraspinal centers (Gassel et al. 1964, Giaquinto et al. 1964).

Spinal reflexes during normal sleep are only slightly modified from those of the waking state, but during AS both monosynaptic and polysynaptic reflexes are markedly depressed, except for those periods when phasic twitching occurs.

These body-function changes are somewhat unexpected in a sleeping animal, and for that reason AS is often referred to as paradoxical sleep.

Another unusual feature is that AS is a *deep* stage of sleep, in that the threshold for arousing stimuli is greater than during DS.

The phylogenetic distribution of AS indicates that it is a relatively recent evolutionary development. AS does not occur in fish or amphibians, and is poorly developed in reptiles, birds, and lower mammals (Jouvet 1969, Klemm 1974).

AS represents an ontogenetically older condition than slow-wave sleep. Valtax et al. (1964) have shown that in week-old kittens, typical slow-wave sleep seldom occurs; AS constitutes 90 percent of the total sleep time. During the second week, more variability appears in the EEG, with some arousal during wakefulness, and some spindles during slow-wave sleep. At 3 weeks the EEG resembles that of the adult, with more distinct slow waves and a greater incidence of slow-wave sleep. Thus slow-wave sleep develops with maturation, at the expense of AS (Roffwarg et al. 1966).

In man, arousals from the AS state are followed by reports of vivid dreaming to a much greater extent than are arousals from DS (Hess 1964). In addition, the neural activity of the brain during AS is at levels equal to that of aroused waking (Evarts 1967, Hobson and McCarley 1971).

Since AS is associated with dreaming in man, the question arises as to whether a similar association exists in animals. It is very difficult to establish whether or not animals dream, but many instances seem to indicate this. Sleeping dogs, for example, often pedal their feet, twitch their lips and nose, and even bark. Hediger (1945) documents a series of anecdotes of apparent dreams in a variety of different animals.

Theories on mechanisms

The brain area that seems to be most concerned with producing AS is the pons. Neither surgical removal of the cerebellum nor complete transections of the brain stem at the midbrain level prevent the peripheral physiological signs of AS. Similarly, transection of the brain stem caudal to the pons fails to prevent EEG signs of AS (Jouvet 1963). As confirmation of the role of the pons, AS is abolished by lesions in the pons of intact animals (Jouvet 1963, Candia et al. 1967). And low-level electrical stimulation of the midbrain or pontine reticular formation during DS can trigger AS (Jouvet 1963, Lissák et al. 1963, Rossi 1963). High-level stimulation during DS causes awakening.

There is much present interest in the neurochemical transmitter functions that might cause and sustain AS. Recent work, reviewed by Jouvet (1969), indicates that numerous drugs that alter concentrations of monoamines (serotonin and norepinephrine) act in a rather predictable way on sleep states. Some of this evidence has been mentioned before in connection with a serotonergic theory for typical sleep. Other evidence includes the fact that reserpine, which depletes brain serotonin and norepinephrine, produces tranquility while suppressing the onset of both DS and AS. Injection of the serotonin precursor, 5-hydroxytryptophan, into a reserpine-treated animal produces an immediate EEG pattern like that of typical sleep; on the other hand, injection of dihydroxyphenylalanine, which restores norepinephrine levels in reserpine-treated animals, promotes the onset of AS.

In untreated animals, injection of a drug that depletes brain serotonin selectively (*p*-chlorophenylalanine) produces a marked insomnia after a latency of about a day; this insomnia is reversed by injection of 5-hydroxytryptophan. Destruction of neurons in the pontine raphe (shown by histofluorescence methods to contain large amounts of serotonin) likewise causes insomnia.

Histofluorescence studies have also revealed that the other common neurotransmitter candidate in the brain stem is norepinephrine. The locus coeruleus region of the pons is rich in norepinephrine, and discrete bilateral lesions confined to that area suppress AS without corresponding inhibition of typical sleep; discrete lesions in the nearby areas do not have this effect. Drugs which prevent norepinephrine synthesis (alpha-methyl-*p*-tyrosine) selectively inhibit AS.

The serotonin-containing raphe cells and the norepinephrine-containing locus coeruleus cells both project terminals into the basal forebrain area and to widespread regions of the neocortex. Additionally, the locus coeruleus sends fibers into the pons and cervical spinal cord

(Chase 1972). Although both systems are generally regarded as important in the genesis of DS and AS, considerable anatomical and physiological complexity makes it difficult to secure unequivocal data and a simple explanation of their function.

Finally, AS also seems to be directly affected by cholinergic influences. Topical application of cholinergic substances into the locus coeruleus triggers AS in normal cats. Systemic injection of atropine, a CNS cholinergic blocker, selectively suppresses AS.

The evidence implicating these three transmitter systems also raises provocative questions about the possibility that two or more transmitter systems interact to cause and sustain AS (Stein et al. 1974).

Another category of biochemical influences on AS involves possible hormone effects. Naturally occurring hormonal changes in the internal environment appear to modulate AS. For example, adrenocorticotropic hormone (ACTH) strongly inhibits AS in rabbits. This inhibition is not associated with glucocorticoid release from the adrenal gland; the ACTH action on AS is independent of the adrenals (Kawakami et al. 1965). In addition, AS is promoted by injections of epinephrine, vasopressin, and oxytocin, while it is inhibited by injections of insulin.

Some insight into AS mechanisms can be gleaned from the demonstration of a biological need for AS. This has been shown in cats, for example, by awakening them every time they exhibited physiological signs of AS (but not DS). On successive days of deprivation, a successively increasing number of awakenings were needed. On the first day of recovery after deprivation, when sleep was not interrupted, the AS phase occupied 53 percent of the total sleep time (Siegel and Gordon 1965).

The biological significance of AS is not known, but evidence exists for several possibilities, namely, that AS (1) serves as an endogenous source of stimulation to promote maturation (Roffwarg et al. 1966), (2) is needed to establish neuronal pathways serving binocular vision (Berger 1969), (3) is an internal reward mechanism (Steiner and Ellman 1972), (4) promotes consolidation of memories for recently learned events (Empson and Clarke 1970, Fishbein et al. 1974), (5) is essential for maintaining emotional stability (Clemes and Dement 1967), and (6) is required for sustaining norepinephrine and dopamine neurotransmitter systems (Stern and Morgane 1974).

Comparisons of domestic species

Conspicuous species differences exist in activity cycles, which can be classified as monophasic or polyphasic, although the distinction is sometimes tenuous. Monophasic animals, generally adults of higher species, are ones that tend to have a long rest period each day, usually at night. Many domestic animals tend to be monophasic, being most active during daylight (Curtis 1937). Most birds, which are largely responsive to optical stimuli, are also monophasic. Primates have a distinct diurnal cycle, being more active during daylight (DeVore 1965).

Polyphasic animals show several alternating periods of rest and activity in a 24 hour period. Many wild mammals and the young of domestic animals are of this type (Kleitman and Camille 1932).

Activity cycles are subject to modification by environmental changes; many domestic animals adjust to man's activity cycles. Cats experimentally kept in the dark have been observed to remain quiescent for 18–20 hours out of 24 (Rioch 1954). In another study in which time cues were eliminated by constant lighting, cats slept about 57 percent of the time, mostly during the day (Sterman et al. 1965). A herd of monkeys has been observed to sleep 8.5 hours per night in the summer and 14.5 hours in the winter (Slonim and Shcherbakova 1954). Other environmental changes, such as food scarcity, endocrine arousal of mating instincts, and danger situations, can also modify the usual sleep-wakefulness cycles.

Animals can sleep in various positions. Among livestock species, horses are the most likely to sleep standing up (Ruckebusch 1972), an ability that is due to the bracing support of sesamoidean ligaments. Pigs are the most likely to lie down. Ruminants lie down in sternal recumbency to prevent aspiration of regurgitated rumen contents. Cattle can also exhibit DS during standing (Ruckebusch 1972), and birds exhibit both DS and AS while perching (Klein et al. 1964, Karmanova and Churnoson 1972). Photographs of sleeping positions in a great variety of vertebrates have been published by Hediger (1959).

The most species-related visceral effect is on the rumen-reticulum activity of ruminants (Fig. 45.5). Rumination does not usually occur during AS, and contraction rates and strength are decreased in both DS and AS (Ruckebusch 1975). No causal relations between sleep and rumen activity have been found; in goats, tranquilization promotes sleep without a major effect on contraction rate, and atropine blocks contraction without preventing DS or AS (Klemm 1966).

The depth of sleep varies greatly with species. Cats are notoriously deep sleepers, but cattle are very easily aroused from sleep.

The amount of time that animals spend sleeping seems to be a species-specific function of the animal's life style, phylogenetic rank, and age. The amount of sleeping also reflects the degree of adaptation to the physical and social environment. Many conditions can interfere with sleep: new surroundings, lack of security, food quality and quantity, weather changes, and so on. The amount of sleep can be changed as much as 30 percent by adjusting the environment to allow complete habituation (Ruckebusch 1972).

Normally, predator species sleep more than nonpreda-

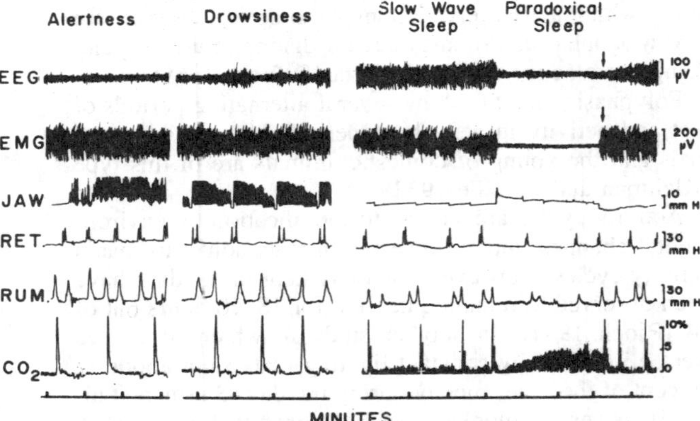

Figure 45.5. Electrographic correlates of various stages of sleep and wakefulness in cattle. As cow becomes drowsy, the EEG deactivates, muscle tone (EMG) and chewing (JAW) decrease, and some slowing of reticular (RET.) and ruminal (RUM.) contractions occurs. These changes progress in DS (slow-wave sleep). During AS (paradoxical sleep), ending at the right-hand arrows, the EEG becomes activated, nuchal muscle tone (EMG) is abolished, and RET. and RUM. rate and strength of contraction decrease further, with rumination being arrested (peaks of CO_2 trace reflect eructation). (From Ruckebusch, in McDonald and Warner, eds., *Digestion and Metabolism in the Ruminant,* New England Pub. Unit, Armidale, Austral., 1975.)

Table 45.1. Sleep and wakefulness during 24 hour day (%)

Species	Alert wakefulness	Drowsiness and DS	AS	References
Fox	38.9	51.1	10	Dallaire and Ruckebusch 1
Cat	44.9	41.7	13.4	Ursin 1968
Pig	46.3	46.4	7.3	Ruckebusch and Morel 196
Rat	48	45	7	Matsumoto et al. 1967
Cow	52.3	44.5 *	3.1	Ruckebush and Bell 1970
	67.2	32.8 †	0	Merrick and Scharp 1971
Sheep	66.5	31.1	2.4	Ruckebusch 1972
Rabbit	71.3	25.5	3.1	Narebski et al. 1969
Guinea pig	71.6	24.5	3.9	Pellet and Beraud 1967
Horse	80	16.7	3.3	Ruckebush et al. 1970

* About 30% in drowsiness, 14.5 in DS
† Considered as all drowsiness, no DS

tors, presumably because natural selective forces discriminated against the evolution of long-sleeping prey species. For example, cats sleep a great deal—more than half of their time—and they have a high incidence of AS. Prey species, such as ruminants, rabbits, and guinea pigs, sleep very little; they also have little AS, which, because it is a deep stage of sleep, would reduce the ability of a prey animal to awaken and escape capture by a predator (Table 45.1).

The basic phylogenetic relationship is that sleep occurs in higher species only. EEG signs of sleep, for example, are not found in the amphibians that have been tested. There are conflicting reports on sleep in reptiles, but in birds EEG signs of both DS and AS can be observed. Among primitive mammals, it seems that most species exhibit signs of both DS and AS, except for the most primitive species, the anteater, which exhibits DS only. Primitive mammals also tend to have incompletely developed AS, in that some of the physiological correlates may be absent (Allison and Van Twyver 1970, Prudom and Klemm 1973).

The basic age relationship is that young animals sleep more than do older ones of the same species. Moreover, most of the sleep time is spent in AS, and the amount of AS time gradually decreases with maturation. In sheep, for example, 8-day-old lambs spend about half the time sleeping, with about 15 percent of that time in AS. By 1 month, total sleep time has decreased some, but AS time drops to 3–5 percent; both DS and AS continue gradual decrements until the adult pattern is reached at 6 months (Ruckebusch 1962).

The high incidence of AS in the young probably begins in the fetal stage. Fetal calves within 30 days of parturition have almost half of their total sleep time in AS; EEG signs of nonsleeping were present only about 15 percent of the time (Ruckebusch and Barbey 1971).

Horses, cows, and sheep seem to sleep mostly at night, whereas pigs also sleep a lot during the day (Table 45.2). All these species have polyphasic DS and AS, with pigs showing the most episodes of sleep. Horses have the least amount of drowsiness, but have the greatest percentage of their sleep time in AS. A given DS epi-

Table 45.2. Analysis of drowsiness (DR) and activated sleep (AS) during a 24 hour period (mean values for three subjects of each species)

	Incidence (%)		Ratio (%)		Duration (min)	
Species	Wakefulness	Sleep	DR/total wakefulness	AS/total sleep	DR	AS
Horse	88	12	9.06	27.32	33	9
	(71.4) *	(28.6)	(26.63)	(27.32)	(29) †	(9)
Cow	83.5	16.5	37.37	18.9	25	11
	(67.9)	(32.1)	(96.14)	(19.48)	(19)	(10)
Sheep	84	16	20.84	14.71	25	7
	(72.7)	(27.3)	(31.54)	(17.25)	(16)	(7)
Pig	67.4	32.6	31.3	22.38	52	33
	(53.7)	(42.7)	(36.31)	(24.42)	(23)	(25)

* For night time only † In last two columns parentheses contain number of periods.
From Ruckebusch 1972, *Anim. Behav.* 20:637–43

sode averages about one-half hour, except in the pig where it is longer. Duration of the average AS period is about 10 minutes or less except for pigs which average about one-half hour.

In most species, sleep deprivation is followed by a compensatory rebound increase in sleeping when the opportunity becomes available. But not all stages of sleep are equally affected. The deepest stage of DS is made up for first, followed by a compensatory increase in amount of time spent in AS. Cattle, however, and perhaps other ruminants, can be deprived of AS if they are not allowed to lie down. They tend to show DS more readily while standing, and although both DS and AS increase in the early postdeprivation period, cattle are more tolerant of AS deprivation than other species (Ruckebusch 1974).

DRUG-ALTERED BEHAVIORAL STATES

Analgesia

Proper understanding of the action of analgesics or pain-relieving drugs such as aspirin requires that we understand the physiology of pain. Unfortunately, that understanding eludes us.

Pain of course is a conscious perception. Whether or not a given pattern of sensory input is perceived as painful depends on many variables. First, the sensory receptors that supply the impulses are important. Which receptors are responsible for pain are not clearly identified; some of them are probably free nerve endings. Moreover, intensity of stimulation is a factor; many receptors will mediate pain if the stimulus is very great.

The afferent fibers that carry pain-producing stimuli are small in diameter. Those that are myelinated probably account for sharp, rapidly produced pain, while the small unmyelinated (C) fibers probably account for the slow-onset, long-lasting (aching) kind of pain (Casey 1973).

These small fibers form tracts in the ventrolateral quadrants of the spinal cord and project into specific thalamic nuclei which in turn project fibers into the cerebral cortex. Additionally, many of these small fibers project into the BSRF and other thalamic areas.

Various kinds of stimuli excite impulse activity in the ventrolateral fibers, but discharge becomes more vigorous if noxious stimuli are used (Casey 1973). Alleviation of pain could thus be accomplished by drugs or other input stimuli that attenuate the impulse discharge in ventrolateral pathways. Descending neural influences from the cortex might also have that effect.

Once the impulses enter the CNS, they become subject to a great deal of modification, either by drug or by interaction with the influences of other kinds of stimuli. This interaction can occur at all levels of the CNS, and may be especially important in those parts which do not have topographical representation of the body nor stereotypical relay functions. Such areas include the so-called substantia gelatinosa of the spinal cord, the reticular formation and central grey area of the brain stem, the nonspecific thalamic nuclei, and many areas of the cerebral cortex.

Some clues are provided by studies that show that chronic, intractable pain in humans is sometimes, but not always, alleviated by surgical cutting of fibers in ventrolateral quadrants of the spinal cord, or by lesions in certain parts of the thalamus.

Considerable emphasis has been given to various theories that pain is determined by the *gating* or routing of sensory information within the CNS. Certain synaptic paths are opened or closed by receipt of other kinds of input. Veterinarians use this principle when they hit a cow's leg with the edge of their hand just prior to turning the hand to throw in an injection needle—which does not cause pain under these circumstances. Perhaps acupuncture and the various kinds of electrical stimulation therapy for pain are also influencing the gating of pain-producing stimulation. While we glibly talk of gating mechanisms, we must admit that we have virtually no data to prove their existence or to elucidate specifically how they operate to govern whether or not pain is perceived.

The common analgesics are aspirin and narcotics. There has not been much modern study of aspirin, but recent experiments with narcotics show that at least part of the analgesic action is on the BSRF and central grey area (Bramwell and Bradley 1974, Herz et al. 1973, Jacquet and Lajtha 1974, Pert and Yaksh 1974, Tsou and Jang 1964). More recently, there is evidence that such effects are mimicked and perhaps mediated by a class of endogenous peptides (Kosterlitz 1976).

Anesthetics, of course, also abolish pain, but they do so by eliminating consciousness. Impulse patterns that are normally perceived as painful are generally unimpaired or even augmented in their propagation through spinothalamic pathways during anesthesia; but associated evoked responses in the RAS are greatly attenuated during anesthesia (French and King 1955). In other words, painful stimuli must be perceived as well as received.

Anesthesia

The most commonly used injectable agents are barbiturates; the most common inhalant anesthetic is ether, although newer agents such as methoxyflurane and halothane are popular.

Although no one theory explains why anesthetics cross the blood-brain barriers so effectively, the marked lipophilia of anesthetics and the large amount of lipoprotein in the brain are certainly important factors. The extensive blood supply to the brain, as opposed to the relatively poor blood supply of fat depots, permits sufficient drug to be carried to the brain to produce anesthesia.

Anesthetics have an effect on blood flow, tending to depress it. Pentobarbital has been reported to have a selective reduction in blood flow to the basal ganglia, midbrain, and frontal and occipital cortex (Goldman et al. 1973).

The neurophysiology of anesthesia is not completely understood. The action of anesthetics at the cellular level is often initial stimulation followed by a progressive depression of synaptic transmission and reduction of unit activity. Dosage is often the critical factor. The depression may result from interference of neurohumoral transmission or from stabilization of the postsynaptic membrane (Winters et al. 1967). Ether produces a depolarization block and barbiturates produce a nondepolarization block (Dunkin 1965). In both situations, impulse generation and propagation are prevented. Some evidence suggests that anesthetics disorder components within the cell membrane, thereby depressing paths for facilitated diffusion of sodium and potassium ions (Seeman 1972).

One of the first neurophysiological studies involving anesthesia was the discovery that barbiturate anesthesia did not block evoked responses in the sensory cortex from sciatic nerve stimulation (Derbyshire et al. 1936). Moreover, the presence of such evoked responses can be made strikingly conspicuous in deepest surgical anesthesia when spontaneous cortical electrical activity is suppressed, while the evoked response is not.

Subsequently, other workers discovered that there were two evoked responses to a single sciatic stimulation in the deeply anesthetized animal (Brazier 1963). The primary response was of short latency and restricted to the localized cortical receiving area of the hind limb. The secondary response was of long latency, suggesting cephalad transmission along multisynaptic pathways, and was more widely distributed in the cerebral cortex. It can also be elicited, in masked form and of lower amplitude and shorter latency, in the spontaneous activity of unanesthetized animals. Since barbiturates preferentially depress multisynaptic areas, the discovery that they enhance the secondary discharge seems paradoxical. However, the drug seems to act on certain polysynaptic inhibitory centers that release those centers responsible for the conduction of the secondary discharge. The polysynaptic areas of the RAS are known, for example, to contain both inhibitory and facilitatory areas; barbiturates are actually more effective on inhibitory centers than facilitatory areas. The evidence for this conclusion includes the observation that cortical inhibition of spinal motoneurons is abolished by small doses of barbiturates that are unable to affect facilitatory influences (Preston and Whitlock 1960). Another example is that injection into the vertebral artery blood supply of an EEG synchronizing system of the medulla results in depression of this inhibitory area and consequent EEG activation. A similar injection into the carotids results in typical EEG synchrony (Magni et al. 1959). Recently, evidence has been presented for preferential anesthetic action on inhibitory neurons of the reticulospinal system (Frank and Ohta 1971).

A common clinical experience with anesthetics is that during injection there is a transient excitement stage in which the animal seems very excited and is difficult to restrain. Sometimes anesthetics even trigger epileptiform seizures in diseased animals (Klemm 1976b). Since anesthetics are definitely depressants, this seeming paradox has been explained as indicating disinhibition.

Anesthetics, although they are distributed widely and relatively uniformly throughout the CNS, probably exert their most profound effect on the RAS and neocortex, presumably because anesthetics act at synaptic junctions and because these areas are composed of so many synapses.

Anesthetics produce profound unconsciousness by selective depression of the RAS in the central core of the brain stem, rather than by deafferentiation of the more lateral spinothalamic sensory paths. The consequence of this RAS-blocking is, as might be expected, decreased function of many other parts of the brain. With both volatile and injectable anesthetics, the EEG during a surgical plane of anesthesia is dominated by HVSA. Some exceptions to this rule should be noted, however. During the early stages of ether anesthesia, the EEG may be activated. Also, in young puppies, barbiturates cause a paradoxical flattening of the EEG instead of the usual HVSA (Fox 1964).

In all situations of very deep anesthesia, there is a progressive decrease in activity, and finally a complete absence of brain waves (Root and Hofmann 1963). This absence of EEG activity is a cardinal sign that death is imminent or has already occurred.

The loss of muscle tone produced by anesthetics probably results from a depression of the motor facilitatory portions of the BSRF. Neuromuscular transmission is interfered with by some anesthetics, but not by all.

Respiration depth and rate are depressed in deep anesthesia. The decreased responsiveness of the medullary respiratory centers to carbon dioxide concentrations in blood allows carbon dioxide buildup and consequent acidosis. Some anesthetics enhance sympathomimetic activity, while others apparently do not. All anesthetics, except cyclopropane, decrease the usual pressor response to either exogenous or endogenous catecholamines. All anesthetics decrease cardiac contractility, with a consequent decrease in circulation effectiveness. This direct cardiac depression can be counteracted to some extent by those anesthetics that stimulate sympathetic activity. On the other hand, catecholamines increase the possibility of ventricular fibrillation. Effects on heart rate are mediated by action on autonomic centers. Cardiac arrhythmias, such as ventricular extrasystoles and ventricular tachycardia, can develop during anesthesia and can lead to serious complications such as fibrillation.

Many anesthetics depress the tone and contractions of the gastrointestinal tract. On the other hand, anesthetics commonly cause reflex emesis, either during induction or during recovery.

Oxidative metabolism is greatly depressed by anesthetics. Inability to utilize lactate and pyruvate can lead to metabolic acidosis. Disturbances in liver function can be a considerable problem with most anesthetics, but in normal patients recovery occurs in about a week. Kidney function is impaired during anesthesia, primarily as a result of renal vasoconstriction and a decrease in renal blood flow.

Tranquilization

A variety of drugs are used medically to produce tranquilization, a state of relative depression of emotionality without corresponding sedation. Compared with sedative drugs, tranquilizers have a milder effect in dulling of senses, ataxia, soporific action, and addictiveness.

The biochemical mode of action of one class of tranquilizers, reserpine derivatives, is due to depletion of neural stores of serotonin and norepinephrine. However, other classes of tranquilizers do not have this effect, and therefore generalizations are not possible.

The selective behavioral effects of these drugs suggest a certain degree of localized function within the brain, but our understanding is incomplete. Some depression of the RAS and/or neocortex is suggested by the observation that these drugs tend to block the EEG arousal response (Fig. 45.6). In some species, such as cats and horses, certain tranquilizers can cause a paradoxical hyper-reactivity, due presumably to disinhibitory phenomena such as were discussed for anesthetics.

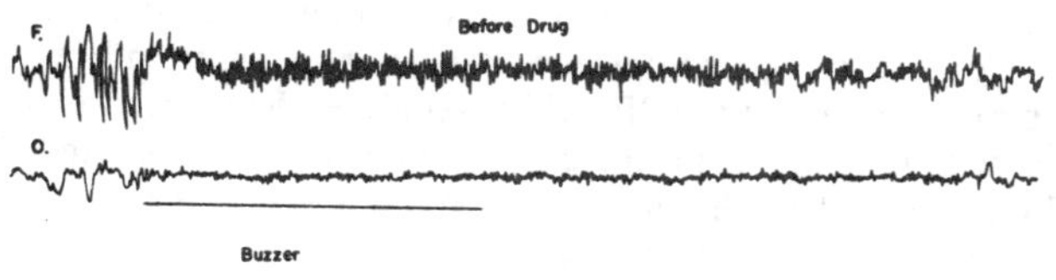

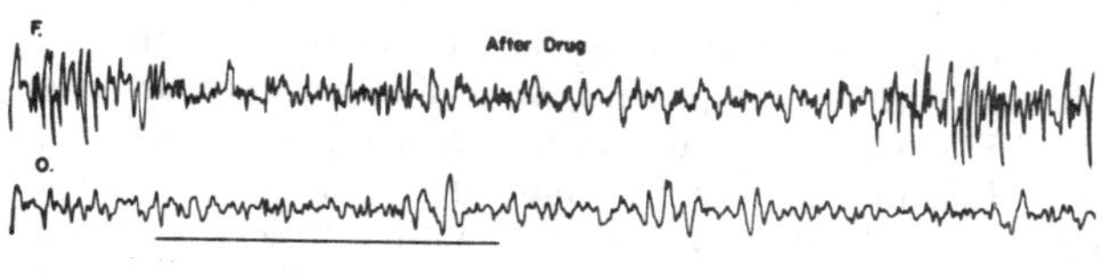

Figure 45.6. EEGs (F., frontal; O., occipital) illustrating a normal arousal response to a sound stimulus. After treatment (below) with a tranquilizing drug (chlorpromazine, 5 mg/kg, intravenous) the usual arousal response is not elicited.

ELECTRICAL ANESTHESIA

Electroanesthesia is an anestheticlike state induced by applying relatively large amounts of pulsating or alternating current across the head. Only recently has there been a great deal of interest in the subject, and a group of investigators has formed an international society. The research literature has been reviewed by Geddes (1965), Smith et al. (1967), and Herin (1968).

Electroanesthesia differs from electrosleep in several important ways. For one, much higher current densities are employed with electroanesthesia (10–40 milliamperes, depending upon the species and stimulation values). The stimulus frequencies are high (100, 700, and even thousands of cycles per second). The immobilization produced is not interrupted by arousing painful stimuli; and it does not outlast the current, although there is some persistence of analgesia. Indeed, one of the main practical advantages of electroanesthesia over chemical anesthesia is that animals recover full consciousness almost immediately after the current is turned off (Smith 1963, Van Poznak 1963).

Another unusual aspect of electroanesthesia is that there is considerable variability in pain reflexes, at least in cats. Pain reception in the toes can sometimes be present when all other pain reflexes are abolished, even responses to such drastic stimuli as strong pressure on the tail and surgery (Klemm and O'Leary 1964).

The question often arises as to whether animals feel pain but just cannot respond to it. Animals do, however, respond to pain with current levels just below the anesthetic level; and, at the same level of current, pain responses can be elicited in certain regions but not others. A definitive answer to this question has not yet been provided, although Sances and coworkers (1963) have developed a proper approach wherein responses evoked in sensory areas such as the thalamus were usually not attenuated much during electroanesthesia, except with higher current densities. Motor responses to motor cortex stimulation were completely blocked. Another proper approach, not yet tested, would involve classical conditioning studies. Thus one could learn whether an animal can learn and remember sensory input during electrical anesthesia. In other words, does the animal "perceive" information as well as receive it?

There are several problems with electroanesthesia that limit its usefulness. These generally involve severe induction reactions and some side effects after anesthesia has been developed. The side effects include relatively poor muscle relaxation, laryngospasm and cyanosis, cardiac arrhythmias, and skin burns at the electrode sites (Van Poznak 1963).

HIBERNATION

True hibernation should not be confused with the prolonged winter sleep that some species such as the bear exhibit. Unlike prolonged sleep, hibernation is a more profound biological adjustment that enables some homeothermal animals to survive a season of cold and of food scarcity by setting their thermostatic controls at very low levels and by practically abolishing activity. Presumably, species with this ability have unique thermoregulatory functions in the portion of the hypothalamus that controls body temperature by adjustments of the autonomic nervous system.

Hibernating animals become like temporary poikilotherms, with their body temperatures close to that of the environment in cold weather. Unlike genuine poikilotherms, hibernating animals recover their ability to regulate high body temperatures during favorable environments and periods of activity. During periods of hibernation, the most characteristic physiological changes include a marked depression of metabolism, heart and respiratory rates, blood pressure, and brain electrical activity (Lyman and Chatfield 1955, Kayser 1961, Kleitman 1963, Hock 1965, Fisher 1968).

Hibernation, which evolved independently in several lines of mammals, is an adaptational advantage in that it permits an animal to conserve food. Yet freezing to death is avoided because the animals awaken and generate body heat if their body temperature approaches freezing.

The common domestic animals do not hibernate. Those species that do include dormouse, gopher, ground squirrel, pocket mouse, hamster, hedgehog, marmot, squirrel, woodchuck, bat, and several species of birds.

The factors that trigger the onset of hibernation and arousal from it are apparently related to environmental temperatures. In a study of ground squirrels, for example, the duration of hibernation was proportional to the induced body temperature. Moreover, after long hibernation at a constant environmental temperature, animals were more responsive to sound or environmental warming, suggesting perhaps that metabolism changes induce hibernation and that thresholds of metabolites may be involved in terminating it (Twente and Twente 1965). Many species, however, anticipate impending cold and food scarcity by hibernating in advance (Hock 1965).

Two aspects of behavior, feeding before hibernation and sleep, are associated with the body temperature drop of hibernation. All three functions are modulated by activity in different hypothalamic nuclei (Satinoff 1967).

Hypothermia, as distinguished from true hibernation, can be induced in the nonhibernating species of domestic animals. It is entirely safe, provided certain techniques are employed, and is a useful aid in experimental surgery (Koella and Ballin 1954, Fisher et al. 1955).

REFLEX IMMOBILITY (HYPNOSIS)

Hypnosis is a unique state of profound immobility and relative unresponsiveness that can be triggered by several kinds of stimulation. The state is reversible, terminating either spontaneously or upon visual, auditory, or tactile stimulation. The most useful reviews of the subject are by Gilman and Marcuse (1949), Völgyesi (1966), Ratner (1967), Chertok (1968), and Klemm (1971, 1976c).

Although the condition is usually called animal hypnosis, the term is somewhat anthropomorphic. The term immobility reflex (IR) seems better because it describes the state in terms of its physiology; the most conspicuous feature is an immobility that seems to be a reflex because it is a specific, stereotyped, involuntary, and unconditioned response to specific stimuli.

The usual induction methods involve either fixation of vision or manual restraint. The immobilization method for rabbits requires that all animal movements be prohibited for a few seconds. Rabbits can be placed on their back and the limbs held immobile for a few seconds; then careful removal of the hands is required so that sensory input does not disrupt the trance.

Species differences in susceptibility to IR can be quite marked, and even within a species susceptibility varies. Most IR research has been conducted in guinea pigs, rabbits, and chickens, because they are especially susceptible. Cats, although not usually considered good subjects, have been immobilized by an optic fixation method (Gerebetzoff 1941). Dogs are not good subjects, although Vaksleiger (1958) reported success in puppies immobilized on their side between the ages of 4–7 days and 20–30 days after birth. Chickens can be immobilized by the commonly known technique of drawing a line in front of the beak and briefly enforcing immobility. Goats (Moore and Amstey 1960) and sheep (Ruckebusch 1965) have been immobilized by manual restraint methods.

Concerning physiological values such as heart and respiratory rates during IR, all possibilities have been reported, ranging from decrease to increase (Gilman and Marcuse 1949). The variation may be due to whether or not an animal was excited during induction.

EEG activity during IR is somewhat paradoxical, in that both activated and deactivated EEGs can be seen, even in a given session with the same animal. When synchronized EEGs are present, arousal stimuli can activate the EEG without disrupting the immobility. In general, the EEG immediately after induction is activated, and it may or may not convert at a later time to a deactivated EEG (Gerebetzoff 1941, Liberson et al. 1961, van Reeth 1963, Klemm 1971).

Studies on mechanisms of animal hypnosis were virtually nonexistent until recently. From these experiments, a working hypothesis has been developed (Fig. 45.7, Klemm 1976c).

Fundamentally, the IR is considered a reflex in which

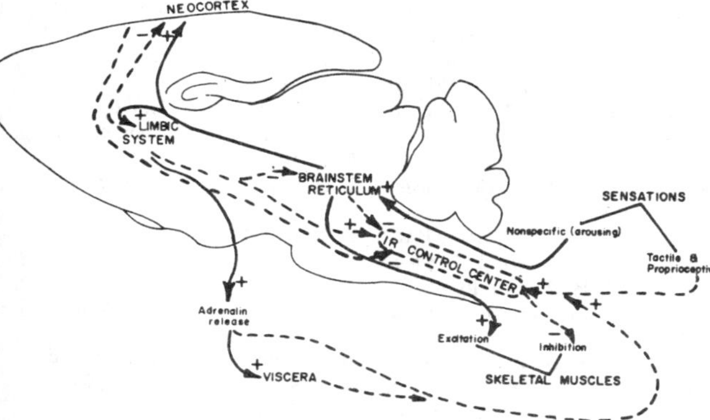

Figure 45.7. Sensory and motor mechanisms of the IR and their interrelations with other systems that affect overall behavioral state. Dashed lines refer to exclusively IR-related influences: +, excitatory action; −, inhibitory action. The IR control system (which is much smaller than indicated) is a specific group of neurons in the BSRF that is presumed to inhibit skeletal muscle reflexly when the neurons are activated by a certain pattern of tactile and proprioceptive input. Among the rostral brain structures that modulate activity in the control system is the limbic system, which under fear-producing conditions potentiates the IR, either by a direct inhibition of neocortex or of certain brain stem neurons, a direct excitation of the IR center, or a release of epinephrine that excites the IR center directly or via visceral efferents to the center. Inhibition of the IR control center appears to come from the neocortex, as well as ascending arousal portions of the BSRF when they are activated by nonspecific, arousing sensations to excite the neocortex, limbic system, and skeletal muscle. (From Klemm 1976c, *J. Neurosci. Res.* 2:57–69.)

induction stimuli activate a pool of interneurons in the BSRF, which in turn sends diffuse descending inhibitory influences to spinal motoneurons. The relevant sensory pathways, especially the tactile, have extensive input into the caudal brain stem reticulum (Lymans'kyi 1966), and no doubt activate reflexly many of its neurons. Some of the caudal reticular neurons, under specific conditions, can cause a profound, generalized inhibition of skeletal muscles (Magoun and Rhines 1946, Sprague and Chambers 1954) by causing inhibitory postsynaptic potentials on spinal motoneurons (Jankowska et al. 1968, Llinás and Terzuolo 1964). The inhibitory reticular neurons presumably produce the IR if other influences do not interfere.

No reflex system operates in isolation from other systems of the brain. One modulating influence that promotes IR comes from the limbic system, which mediates affective behavior, especially fear. Fear's apparent potentiation of IR may involve some direct action on the reticulum since that area does receive some of the main output of the limbic system (Nauta 1960). Under fear-producing conditions, the limbic system causes release of epinephrine, which by itself seems to enhance IR. More speculative is the idea that the limbic system, as well as the diffuse thalamic projection system, may potentiate IR by inhibition of the neocortex, which in turn has an inhibitory influence on IR.

Several lines of evidence indicate that the neocortex inhibits the IR control center: (1) phylogenetically advanced species have better developed neocortex, and they also are poorly susceptible to IR (Chertok 1968, Ratner 1967); (2) susceptibility decreases in the young animal at about the time that the neocortex matures (McGraw and Klemm 1969); (3) surgical decortication of insusceptible animals can make them susceptible (McGraw and Klemm 1969); and (4) KCl-induced spreading depression of neocortex likewise potentiates the IR (Bureš and Burešová 1956, Teschke et al. 1975).

Another clearly disruptive influence comes from the RAS, whose neurons intermingle with the IR control-center neurons but are much more widely distributed throughout the BSRF. Intense peripheral stimulation (other than that which causes the stereotyped pattern of afferent impulses that in turn causes IR) can disrupt IR by activating the overriding influence of the RAS.

It is impossible at this time to ascertain the exact relations of IR to sleep stages. IR is qualitatively different; it differs from typical sleep in that it (1) can be associated with EEG desynchrony, (2) is enhanced by manipulation, (3) occurs less frequently in phylogenetically advanced species and with ontogenetic development. IR differs from AS in that it has (1) no REM, (2) no persistent phasic limb twitches, (3) no absence of nuchal muscle tone, (4) periods of EEG synchrony, (5) increased incidence with tranquilizing drugs and with manipulation, and (6) decreased incidence with phylogenetically advanced species (Klemm 1971).

The relationship of IR to human hypnosis is obscure, primarily because so little is known about the physiology of human hypnosis. Although there is no evidence that proves a similarity, the two states do share certain physiological features: relative analgesia, a lack of specific EEG correlates, little change in visceral function, and most importantly, reduced patterned motor activity (Draper and Klemm 1967).

ABBREVIATIONS

ACTH	adrenocorticotropic hormone
AS	activated sleep
BSRF	brain stem reticular formation
CSF	cerebrospinal fluid
DS	deactivated sleep
DTPS	diffuse thalamic projection system
EEG	electroencephalogram
EMG	electromyogram
EPSP	excitatory postsynaptic potential
HVSA	high voltage, slow activity
IPSP	inhibitory postsynaptic potential
IR	immobility reflex
LVFA	low voltage, fast activity
MBRF	midbrain reticular formation
RAS	reticular activating system
REM	rapid eye movements

REFERENCES

Akert, K. 1965. The anatomical substrate of sleep. In *Progress in Brain Research*. Vol. 18, K. Akert, C. Bally, and J.P. Schadé, eds., *Sleep Mechanisms*. Elsevier, Amsterdam. Pp. 9–19.

Allison, T., and Van Twyver, H. 1970. The evolution of sleep. *Natur. Hist*. 79:56–65.

Andersen, P., and Sears, T.A. 1964. The role of inhibition in the phasing of spontaneous thalamo-cortical discharge. *J. Physiol*. 173:459–80.

Baust, W., Weidinger, H., and Kirchner, F. 1968. Sympathetic activity during natural sleep and arousal. *Arch. Ital. Biol*. 106:379–90.

Beh, H.C., and Barratt, P.E.H. 1965. Discrimination and conditioning during sleep as indicated by the electroencephalogram. *Science* 147: 1470–71.

Berger, R.J. 1969. Oculomotor control: A possible function of REM sleep. *Psychol. Rev*. 76:144–64.

Bramwell, G.J., and Bradley, P.B. 1974. Actions and interactions of narcotic agonists and antagonists on brain stem neurones. *Brain Res*. 73:167–70.

Brazier, M.A.B. 1963. The electrophysiological effects of barbiturates on the brain. In W.S. Root and F.G. Hofmann, eds., *Physiological Pharmacology*. Academic Press, New York. Pp. 219–38.

Brebbia, D.R., and Altshuler, K.Z. 1965. Oxygen consumption rate and electroencephalographic stage of sleep. *Science* 150:1621–23.

Bremer, F. 1935. Cereau "isolé" et physiologie du sommeil. *Comptes Rend. Séances Soc. Biol*. 118:1235–41.

——. 1974. Historical development of ideas on sleep. In O. Petre-Quadens and J.D. Schlag, eds., *Basic Sleep Mechanisms*. Academic Press, New York. Pp. 3–11.

Bueno, J.R., Bost, K., and Himwich, H.E. 1968. Lower brain-stem EEG synchronizing mechanisms in the rabbit. *Electroenceph. Clin. Neurophysiol*. 24:25–34.

Bureš, J., and Burešová, O. 1956. The influencing of reflex acoustic epilepsy and reflex inhibition ("animal hypnosis") by spreading depression. *Physiol. Bohemoslov*. 5:395–400.

Bureš, J., Petráň, M., and Zachar, J. 1967. *Electrophysiological Methods in Biological Research*. 3d ed. Academic Press, New York.

Buser, P. 1964. Thalamic influences on the EEG. *Electroenceph. Clin. Neurophysiol*. 16:18–26.

Candia, O., Rossi, G.F., and Sekino, T. 1967. Brain stem structures responsible for the electroencephalographic patterns of desynchronized sleep. *Science* 155:720–22.

Casey, K.L. 1973. Pain: A current view of neural mechanisms. *Am. Scientist* 61:194–200.

Chase, M.H., ed. 1972. *The Sleeping Brain*. U. California Press, Los Angeles. Vol. 1.

Chertok, L. 1968. Animal hypnosis. In M.W. Fox, ed., *Abnormal Behavior in Animals*. Saunders, Philadelphia. Pp. 129–58.

Clemes, S.R., and Dement, W. 1967. Effect of REM sleep deprivation on psychological functioning. *J. Nerv. Ment. Dis*. 144:485–91.

Curtis, Q.F. 1937. Diurnal variation in the free activity of sheep and pig. *Proc. Soc. Exp. Biol*. 35:566–67.

Dallaire, A., and Ruckebusch, Y. 1974. Sleep and wakefulness in the housed pony under different dietary conditions. *Can. J. Comp. Med*. 38:65–71.

Dement, W. 1958. The occurrence of low voltage, fast, electro-encephalogram patterns during behavioral sleep in the cat. *Electroenceph. Clin. Neurophysiol*. 10:291–96.

——. 1972. The effects of the chronic administration of parachlorophenylalanine on sleep parameters. In M.H. Chase, ed., *The Sleeping Brain*. U. of California Press, Los Angeles. Pp. 153–58.

Dempsey, E.W., and Morison, R.S. 1942. The production of rhythmically recurrent cortical potentials after localized thalamic stimulation. *Am. J. Physiol*. 135:293–300.

——. 1943. The electrical activity of a thalamocortical relay system. *Am. J. Physiol*. 138:283–96.

Derbyshire, A.J., Rempel, B., Forbes, A., and Lambert, E.F. 1936. The effects of anesthetics on action potentials in the cerebral cortex of the cat. *Am. J. Physiol*. 116:577–96.

DeVore, I., ed. 1965. *Primate Behavior: Field Studies of Monkeys and Apes*. Holt, Rinehart and Winston, New York.

Dikshit, B.B. 1935. The physiology of sleep. *Lancet* 228(1):570.

Draper, D.C., and Klemm, W.R. 1967. Behavioral responses associated with animal hypnosis. *Psychol. Rec*. 17:13–21.

Dunkin, L.J. 1965. Mechanisms of anesthetic sleep. *Anesthesia* 20:157–63.

Empson, J.A.C., and Clarke, P.R.F. 1970. Rapid eye movements and remembering. *Nature* 227:287–88.

Evarts, E.V. 1962. Activity of neurons in visual cortex of the cat during sleep with low voltage, fast, EEG activity. *J. Neurophysiol*. 25:812–16.

——. 1967. Activity of individual cerebral neurons during sleep and arousal. In S.S. Kety, E.V. Evarts, and H.L. Williams, eds., *Sleep and Altered States of Consciousness*. Williams & Wilkins, Baltimore. Pp. 319–36.

Evarts, E.V., Bental, E., Bihari, B., and Huttenlocher, P.R. 1962. Spontaneous discharges of single neurons during sleep and waking. *Science* 135:726–28.

Fishbein, W., Kastaniolis, C., and Chattman, D. 1974. Paradoxical sleep: Prolonged augmentation following learning. *Brain Res*. 79:61–75.

Fisher, B., Russ, C., Fedor, E., Wilde, R., Engstrom, P., Happel, J., and Prendergast, P. 1955. Experimental evaluation of prolonged hypothermia. *Arch. Surg*. 71:431–48.

Fisher, K.C., ed. 1968. *Mammalian Hibernation*. Elsevier, New York.

Fox, M.W. 1964. Effects of pentobarbital on the EEG of maturing dogs and a review of the literature. *Vet. Rec*. 76:768–70.

Frank, G.B., and Ohta, M. 1971. Blockade of the reticulospinal inhibitory pathway by anesthetic agents. *Brit. J. Pharmac*. 42:328–42.

French, J.D. 1957. The reticular formation. *Scien. Am*. 196(5):54–60.

French, J.D., and King, E.E. 1955. Mechanisms involved in the anesthetic state. *Surgery* 38:228–38.

French, J.D., Verzeano, M., and Magoun, H.W. 1953. A neural basis for the anesthetic state. *Arch. Neurol. Psychiat*. 69:519–29.

Gassel, M.M., Marchiafava, P.L., and Pompeiano, O. 1964. Phasic changes in muscular activity during desynchronized sleep in unrestrained cats. *Arch. Ital. Biol*. 102:449–70.

Geddes, L.A. 1965. Electronarcosis. *Med. Electron. Biol. Engin*. 3:11–26.

Gerebetzoff, M.A. 1941. Etat fonctionnel de l'écorce cérébrale au course de l'hypnose animale. *Arch. Int. Physiol*. 51:365–78.

Giaquinto, S., Pompeiano, O., and Somogyi, I. 1964. Descending inhibitory influences on spinal reflexes during natural sleep. *Arch. Ital. Biol*. 102:282–307.

Gilman, T., and Marcuse, F.L. 1949. Animal hypnosis. *Psychol. Bull*. 46:151–65.

Goldman, H., Sapirstein, L.A., Murphy, S., and Moore, J. 1973. Alcohol and regional blood flow in brains of rats. *Proc. Soc. Exp. Biol. Med*. 144:983–88.

Grantyn, A., Mancia, M., Broggi, G., and Margnelli, M. 1971. Intralaminar thalamic influences on bulbo-pontine and mesencephalic neurones as revealed by intracellular recording. *Brain Res*. 33:223–26.

Hanbery, J., and Jasper, H. 1953. Independence of diffuse thalamocortical projection system shown by specific nuclear destruction. *J. Neurophysiol*. 16:252–71.

Hediger, H. 1945. Vom Traum der Tiere. *Ciba Z*. 9:3558.

——. 1959. Wie Tiere schlafen. *Med. Klin*. (Berlin) 54:938–46.

Herin, R.A. 1968. Electroanesthesia: A review of the literature (1819–1965). *Acta Neuroveg*. 10 (suppl.):439–54.

Hernández-Peón, R. 1965. Central neurohumoral transmission in sheep and wakefulness. In *Progress in Brain Research*. Vol. 18, K. Akert, C. Bally, and J.P. Schadé, eds., *Sleep Mechanisms*. Elsevier, Amsterdam. Pp. 96–117.

Hernandez-Peon, R., Chávez-Ibarra, G., Morgane, P.J., and Timio-Iaria, C. 1963. Limbic cholinergic pathways involved in sleep and emotional behavior. *Exp. Neurol.* 8:93–111.

Herz, A., Teschemacher, H.J., Albus, K., and Zieglansberger, S. 1973. In H.W. Kosterlitz, H.O.J. Collier, and J.E. Villarreal, eds., *Agonist and Antagonist Actions of Narcotic Analgesic Drugs*. University Park Press, Baltimore. Pp. 104–5.

Hess, R., Jr. 1964. The electroencephalogram in sleep. *Electroenceph. Clin. Neurophysiol.*, 16:44–55.

Hess, R., Jr., Koella, W.P., and Akert, K. 1953. Cortical and subcortical recordings in natural and artificially induced sleep in cats. *Electroenceph. Clin. Neurophysiol.* 5:75–90.

Hobson, J.A., and McCarley, R.W. 1971. Cortical unit activity in sleep and waking. *Electroenceph. Clin. Neurophysiol.* 30:97–112.

Hock, R.J. 1965. The care and use of hibernating animals. In W.I. Gay, ed., *Methods of Animal Experimentation*. Academic Press, New York. Vol. 2, 273–331.

Hodes, R. 1961. Electrocortical synchronization (ECS) in cats from reduction of proprioceptive drive caused by a muscle relaxant (Flaxedil). *Fed. Proc.* 20:332.

Jacquet, Y.F., and Lajtha, A. 1974. Paradoxical effects after microinjection of morphine in the periaqueductal gray matter in the rat. *Science* 185:1055–57.

Jankowska, E., Lund, S., Lundberg, A., and Pompeiano, O. 1968. Inhibitory effects evoked through ventral reticulospinal pathways. *Arch. Ital. Biol.* 106:124–40.

Jasper, Herbert H. 1960. Unspecific thalamocortical relations. In *Handbook of Physiology*. Sec. 1, J. Field, H.W. Magoun, and V.E. Hall, eds., *Neurophysiology*. Am. Physiol. Soc., Washington. Vol. 2, 1307–21.

——. 1966. Brain mechanisms and states of consciousness. In J.C. Eccles, ed., *Brain and Conscious Experience*. Springer, Berlin. Pp. 256–82.

Jouvet, M. 1963. The rhombencephalic phase of sleep. In *Progress in Brain Research*. Vol. 1, G. Moruzzi, A. Fessard, and H.H. Jasper, eds., *Brain Mechanisms*. Elsevier, New York. Pp. 406–24.

——. 1969. Biogenic amines and the states of sleep. *Science* 163:32–40.

Kanai, T., and Szerb, J.C. 1965. Mesencephalic reticular activating system and cortical acetylcholine output. *Nature* 205:80–82.

Karmanova, I.G., and Churnoson, E.V. 1972. Electrophysiological investigation of natural sleep and wakefulness in tortoises and chickens. *J. Evol. Biochem. Physiol.* 8:47–53.

Kawakami, M., Negoro, H., and Terasawa, E. 1965. Influence of immobilization stress upon the paradoxical sleep (EEG afterreaction) in the rabbit. *Jap. J. Physiol.* 15:1–16.

Kawamura, H., and Sawyer, C.H. 1964. D-C potential changes in rabbit brain during slow-wave and paradoxical sleep. *Am. J. Physiol.* 207:1379–86.

——. 1965. Elevation in brain temperature during paradoxical sleep. *Science* 150:912–13.

Kayser, C. 1961. *The Physiology of Natural Hibernation*. Pergamon, New York.

Klein, M., Michel, F., and Jouvet, M. 1964. Etude polygraphique du sommeil chez les oiseaux. *Comptes Rend. Séances Soc. Biol.* 158:99–103.

Kleitman, N. 1963. *Sleep and Wakefulness*. U. of Chicago Press, Chicago.

Kleitman, N., and Camille, N. 1932. Studies of the physiology of sleep. VI. Behavior of decorticated dogs. *Am. J. Physiol.* 100:474–80.

Klemm, W.R. 1966. Study of normal and paradoxical sleep in ruminating goats. *Proc. Soc. Exp. Biol.* 121:635–38.

——. 1971. Neurophysiologic studies of the immobility reflex ("animal hypnosis"). In S. Ehrenpreis and O.C. Solnitzky, eds., *Neurosciences Research*. Academic Press, New York. Vol. 4, 165–212.

——. 1974. Typical electroencephalograms: Vertebrates. In P.L. Altman and D.S. Dittmer, eds., *Biology Data Book*. 2d ed. Fed. Am. Soc. Exp. Biol., Bethesda, Md. Vol. 2, 1254–60.

——. 1976a. Physiological and behavioral significance of hippocampal, rhythmic, slow activity ("theta rhythm"). *Prog. Neurobiol.* 5:1–25.

——. 1976b. Electroencephalography. In Klemm, ed., *Applied Electronics for Veterinary Medicine and Animal Physiology*. Thomas, Springfield, Ill. Pp. 287–351.

——. 1976c. Identity of sensory and motor systems that are critical to the immobility reflex ("animal hypnosis"). *J. Neurosci. Res.* 2:57–69.

Klemm, W.R., and O'Leary, T. 1964. Comparison of electrical parameters and the quality of electrical anesthesia. *Anesthesiology* 25:776–80.

Koella, W.P. 1967. *Sleep: Its Nature and Physiological Organization*. Thomas, Springfield, Ill.

Koella, W.P., and Ballin, H.M. 1954. The influence of environmental and body temperature on the electroencephalogram in the anesthetized cat. *Arch. Internat. Physiol.* 62:369–80.

Kosterlitz, H.W. 1976. *Opiates and Endogenous Peptides*. North-Holland, Amsterdam.

Liberson, W.T., Smith, R.W., and Stern, A. 1961. Experimental studies of the prolonged "hypnotic withdrawal" in guinea pigs. *J. Neuropsychiat.* 3(1):23–34.

Lindsley, D.B. 1952. Psychological phenomena and the electroencephalogram. *Electroenceph. Clin. Neurophysiol.* 4:443–56.

Lindsley, D.B., Schreiner, L.H., Knowles, W.B., and Magoun, H.W. 1950. Behavioral and EEG changes following chronic brain stem lesions in the cat. *Electroenceph. Clin. Neurophysiol.* 2:483–98.

Lissák, K., Karmos, G., and Grastyán, E. 1963. A study of the so-called "paradoxical" phase of sleep in cats. In *Progress in Brain Research*. Vol. 1, G. Moruzzi, A. Fessard, and H.H. Jasper, eds., *Brain Mechanisms*. Elsevier, New York. Pp. 424–28.

Llinás, R., and Terzuolo, C.A. 1964. Mechanisms of supraspinal actions upon spinal cord activities. *J. Neurophysiol.* 27:579–91.

Lowenstein, O., and Loewenfeld, I.E. 1964. The sleep-waking cycle and pupillary activity. *Ann. N.Y. Acad. Sci.* 117:142–56.

Lyman, C.P., and Chatfield, P.O. 1955. Physiology of hibernation in mammals. *Physiol. Rev.* 35:403–25.

Lymans'kyi, Yu.P. 1966. Responses of neurons of the medullary reticular formation to afferent impulses from cutaneous and muscle nerves. *Fed. Proc. Trans. Suppl.* 25:T15–T17.

Magnes, J., Moruzzi, G., and Pompeiano, O. 1961. Synchronization of the EEG by low-frequency electrical stimulation of the region of the solitary tract. *Arch. Ital. Biol.* 99:33–67.

Magni, F., Moruzzi, G., Rossi, G.F., and Zanchetti, A. 1959. EEG arousal following inactivation of the lower brain stem by selective injection of barbiturate into the vertebral circulation. *Arch. Ital. Biol.* 97:33–46.

Magoun, H.W., and Rhines, R. 1946. An inhibitory mechanism in the bulbar reticular formation. *J. Neurophysiol.* 9:165–71.

Mancia, M., Marioti, M., and Spreafico, R. 1974. Caudo-rostral brain stem reciprocal influences in the cat. *Brain Res.* 80:41–51.

Matsumoto, J., Nishisho, T., Suto, T., Sadahiro, T., and Miyoshi, M. 1967. Normal sleep cycle of male albino rats. *Proc. Jap. Acad. Sci.* 43:62–64.

——. 1968. Influence of fatigue on sleep. *Nature* 218:177–78.

McGraw, C.P., and Klemm, W.R. 1969. Mechanisms of the immobility reflex ("animal hypnosis"). III. Neocortical inhibition in rats. *Commun. Behav. Biol.* 3:53–59.

Merrick, A.W., and Scharp, D.W. 1971. Electroencephalography of resting behavior in cattle, with observations on the question of sleep. *Am. J. Vet. Res.* 32:1893–97.

Monnier, M., and Hösli, L. 1965. Humoral regulation of sleep and wakefulness by hypnogenic and activating dialysable factors. In *Progress in Brain Research*. Vol. 18, K. Akert, C. Bally, and J.P. Schadé, eds., *Sleep Mechanisms*. Elsevier, Amsterdam. Pp. 118–26.

Monnier, M., Kalberer, M., and Krupp, P. 1960. Functional antagonism between diffuse reticular and intrathalamic recruiting projections in the medial thalamus. *Exp. Neurol.* 2:271–89.

Moore, A.L., and Amstey, M. 1960. Animal hypnosis (tonic immobility) considered as a parameter of behavior in distinguishing between a group of normal and abnormal (experimental) lambs and kids (abstr.). *Anat. Rec.* 138:371.

Moruzzi, G. 1958. The functional significance of the ascending reticular system. *Arch. Ital. Biol.* 96:17–28.

——. 1974. Neural mechanisms of the sleep-waking cycle. In O. Petre-Quadens and J.D. Schlag, eds., *Basic Sleep Mechanisms.* Academic Press, New York. Pp. 13–31.

Narebski, J., Tymicz, J., and Lewesz, W. 1969. The circadian sleep of rabbits. *Acta Biol. Exp.* 29:185–200.

Nauta, W.J.H. 1960. Some neural pathways related to the limbic system. In E.R. Ramey and D.S. O'Doherty, eds., *Electrical Studies on the Unanesthetized Brain.* Hoeber, New York. Pp. 1–16.

Nauta, W.J.H., Koella, W.P., and Quarton, G.C. 1967. Sleep, wakefulness, dreams, and memory. In *Neurosciences Research Symposium Summaries.* Vol. 2, F.O. Schmitt, T. Melnechuk, G.C. Quarton, and G. Adelman, eds. M.I.T. Press, Cambridge. Pp. 1–90.

Oswald, Ian. 1962. *Sleeping and Waking.* Elsevier, Amsterdam.

Palmer, M.R., and Klemm, W.R. 1977. Reciprocal thalamo-hippocampal EEG augmenting and muscle responses in rabbits. *Brain Res. Bull.* In press.

Pellet, J., and Beraud, G. 1967. Organisation nycthemerqle de la veille et du sommeil chez cobaye (*Cavia porcellus*): Comparisons interspecifiques avec le rat et la chat. *Physiol. Behav.* 2:131–37.

Pert, A., and Yaksh, T. 1974. Sites of morphine-induced analgesia in the primate brain: Relation of the pain pathways. *Brain Res.* 80:135–40.

Petre-Quadens, O., and Schlag, J.D., eds. 1974. *Basic Sleep Mechanisms.* Academic Press, New York.

Preston, J.B., and Whitlock, D.G. 1960. Precentral facilitation and inhibition of spinal motoneurons. *J. Neurophysiol.* 23:154–70.

Prudom, A.E., and Klemm, W.R. 1973. Electrographic correlates of sleep behavior in a primitive mammal, the armadillo, *Dasypus novemcinctus*. *Physiol. Behav.* 10:275–82.

Ratner, S.C. 1967. Comparative aspects of hypnosis. In J.E. Gordon, ed., *Handbook of Clinical and Experimental Hypnosis.* Macmillan, New York. Pp. 550–87.

Rinaldi, F., and Himwich, H.E. 1955. Cholinergic mechanism involved in function of mesodiencephalic activating system. *Arch. Neurol. Psychiat.* 73:396–402.

Rioch, D. McK. 1954. Discussion of paper by W.R. Hess. In J.F. Delafresnaye, ed., *Brain Mechanisms and Consciousness.* Thomas, Springfield, Ill. Pp. 133–34.

Roffwarg, H.P., Muzio, J.N., and Dement, W.C. 1966. Ontogenetic development of the human sleep-dream cycle. *Science* 152:604–19.

Root, W.S., and Hofmann, F.G., eds. 1963. *Physiological Pharmacology.* Academic Press, New York. Vol. 1.

Rossi, G.F. 1963. A study of the signs of sleep in the cat. In *Progress in Brain Research,* Vol. 1, G. Moruzzi, A. Fessard, and H.H. Jasper, eds., *Brain Mechanisms.* Elsevier, New York. Pp. 404–6.

Ruckebusch, Y. 1962. Evolution post-natale du sommeil chez les ruminants. *Comptes Rend. Séances Soc. Biol.* 156:1869–73.

——. 1965. The normal and pathological electroencephalogram of ruminants. *Proc. Roy. Soc. Med.* 58:551–52.

——. 1972. The relevance of drowsiness in the circadian cycle of farm animals. *Anim. Behav.* 20:637–43.

——. 1974. Sleep deprivation in cattle. *Brain Res.* 78:495–99.

——. 1975. Motility of the ruminant stomach associated with states of sleep. In I.W. McDonald and A.C.I. Warner, eds., *Digestion and Metabolism in the Ruminant.* U. of New England Pub. Unit, Armidale, Austral.

Ruckebusch, Y., and Barbey, P. 1971. Les états de sommeil chez le foetus et le nouveau-né de la vache (*Bos taurus*). *Comptes Rend. Séances Soc. Biol.* 165:1176–84.

Ruckebusch, Y., Barbey, P., and Guillemot, P. 1970. Les états de sommeil chez le cheval (*Equus caballus*). *Comptes Rend. Séances Soc. Biol.* 164:658–64.

Ruckebusch, Y., and Morel, M.T. 1968. Etude polygraphique du sommeil chez le porc. *Comptes Rend. Séances Soc. Biol.* 162:1346–54.

Sances, A., Jr., Larson, S.J., and Jacobs, J.E. 1963. Electronarcosis and evoked cortical responses. *Science* 141:733–35.

Satinoff, E. 1967. Disruption of hibernation caused by hypothalamic lesions. *Science* 155:1031–33.

Schlag, J.D., and Chaillet, F. 1962. Thalamic mechanisms involved in cortical desynchronization and recruiting responses. *Electroenceph. Clin. Neurophysiol.* 15:39–62.

Schlag, J., and Faidherbe, J. 1961. Recruiting responses in the brain stem reticular formation. *Arch. Ital. Biol.* 99:135–62.

Schnedorf, G., and Ivy, A.C. 1939. An examination of the hypnotoxin theory of sleep. *Am. J. Physiol.* 125:491–505.

Seeman, P. 1972. The membrane actions of anesthetics and tranquilizers. *Pharmac. Rev.* 24:583–655.

Siegel, J., and Gordon, T.P. 1965. Paradoxical sleep: Deprivation in the cat. *Science* 148:978–80.

Slonim, A.D., and Shcherbakova, O.P. 1954. Observations of night sleep in monkeys. In S.I. Bogorad, ed., *The Sleep Problem.* Medgiz, Moscow. Pp. 312–19.

Smith, R.H. 1963. Electrical anesthesia. Thomas, Springfield, Ill.

Smith, R.H., Tatsuno, J., and Jouhar, R.L. 1967. Electroanesthesia: A review, 1966. *Anes. Analg.* 46:109–25.

Sprague, J.M., and Chambers, W.W. 1954. Control of posture by reticular formation and cerebellum in the intact, anesthetized, and unanesthetized and in the decerebrated cat. *Am. J. Physiol.* 176:52–64.

Starzl, T.E., Taylor, C.W., and Magoun, H.W. 1951. Ascending conduction in reticular activating system with special reference to the diencephalon. *J. Neurophysiol.* 14:461–77.

Stein, D., Jouvet, M., and Pujol, J.-F. 1974. Effects of α-methyl-*p*-tyrosine upon cerebral amine metabolism and sleep states in the cat. *Brain Res.* 72:360–65.

Steiner, S.S., and Ellman, S.J. 1972. Relation between REM sleep and intracranial self-stimulation. *Science* 177:1122–24.

Sterman, M.B., and Clemente, C.D. 1962a. Forebrain inhibitory mechanisms: Cortical synchronization induced by forebrain stimulation. *Exp. Neurol.* 6:91–102.

——. 1962b. Forebrain inhibitory mechanisms: Sleep patterns induced by basal forebrain stimulation in the behaving cat. *Exp. Neurol.* 6:103–17.

Sterman, M.B., Knauss, T., Lehmann, D., and Clemente, C.D. 1965. Circadian sleep and waking patterns in the laboratory cat. *Electroenceph. Clin. Neurophysiol.* 19:509–17.

Stern, W.C., and Morgane, P.J. 1974. Theoretical view of REM sleep function: Maintenance of catecholamine systems in the central nervous system. *Behav. Biol.* 11:1–32.

Teschke, E.J., Maser, J.D., and Gallup, G.G., Jr. 1975. Cortical involvement in tonic immobility ("animal hypnosis"): Effect of spreading cortical depression. *Behav. Biol.* 13:139–43.

Tsou, K., and Jang, C.S. 1964. Studies on the site of analgesic action of morphine by intracerebral micro-injection. *Scientia Sinica* 13:1100–1108.

Twente, J.W., and Twente, J.A. 1965. Effects of core temperature upon duration of hibernation of *Citellus lateralis*. *J. Appl. Physiol.* 20:411–16.

Ursin, H. 1968. The two stages of slow-wave sleep in the cat and their relation to REM sleep. *Brain Res.* 11:347–56.

Vaksleiger, G.A. 1958. Yavleniya zhivotnogo gipnoza u shchenkov v postnatal'nom periode. *Biokhim. Farmakol.* 1:43–48.

Valtax, J.L., Jouvet, D., and Jouvet, M. 1964. Evolution électroencéphalographique des différents états de sommeil chez le chaton. *Electroenceph. Clin. Neurophysiol.* 17:218–33.

Van Poznak, A. 1963. Electrical anesthesia. *Anesthesiology* 24:101–8.

van Reeth, P.C. 1963. Analysé electrophysiologique et comportementale de l'hypnose animale. *J. Physiol.* (Paris) 55:354.

Völgyesi, F.A. 1966. *Hypnosis of Man and Animals*. 2d ed. Williams & Wilkins, Baltimore.

Von Economo, C. 1929. Schlaftheorie. *Ergeb. Physiol.* 28:312–39.

Weinberger, N.M., and Lindsley, D.B. 1964. Behavioral and electroencephalographic arousal to contrasting novel stimulation. *Science* 144:1355–57.

Winters, W.D., Mori, K., Spooner, C.E., and Bauer, R.O. 1967. The neurophysiology of anesthesia. *Anesthesiology* 28:65–80.

CHAPTER 46

Neurophysiological Bases of Behavior | by M.G.M. Jukes

Conscious animals display an ever-changing sequence of highly complex forms of behavior. Previous chapters have described basic neural elements of behavior, starting from single nerve cells, progressing to reflexes, and finishing with combinations and sequences of movements that are involved in complex behavior. Behavior is often taken to refer only to elaborate patterns of movements that contain many reflexes such as those underlying locomotion, balance, and orientation, but in principle there is no sharp dividing line between simple reflexes and complex behavior, and one of the aims of physiology is to explain both in the same terms. In addition to the nervous system the other great control system of the body, the system of hormones, plays a complementary role in the synthesis of behavior. The two integrating systems act together to ensure both the day-to-day survival of individual members of a species and the survival of the species itself. Physiological and behavioral reactions to environmental change act in a harmonious way to ensure the appropriate homeostatic responses; for example, the survival of mammals in hot dry deserts depends as much or more on their burrowing and shade-seeking behavior as on their physiological means of heat loss. Similarly, the processes of reproduction and thus of survival of species depend both upon the physiological cycles of hormone changes in females and males and also upon the related and coordinated male and female behavior that results in successful mating.

REFLEXES AND BEHAVIOR

A study of the reflex responses of an animal to its environment shows a hierarchy from apparently simple reflexes, such as the withdrawal of a limb in response to a noxious stimulus (the flexor reflex) to the more elaborate reflex combinations seen for example in feeding, where the food placed in the mouth is first chewed, then swallowed, and then passed to the stomach via the esophagus, the sequence being accompanied by reflex secretion of saliva and reflex suppression of respiration during swallowing. This chain of events emphasizes that different types of effector tissue may be activated in a particular sequence; the reflex activity of somatic muscle is harmoniously integrated with that of glandular tissue, of esophageal striated and smooth muscle, and of the smooth muscle of blood vessels in all these tissues. Yet even the apparently simple spinal flexor reflex is complex: the amount of flexion at each joint of the limb depends upon the site of the stimulus, and limb flexion is accompanied by postural adjustments of the other limbs which help to maintain balance and may be followed in turn by rhythmic movements of the limbs, enabling the animal to escape the damaging stimulus. This example illustrates not only the complexity of spinal reflexes but also their purposiveness and importance in behavior: "The effect of any reflex is to enable the organism in some particular respect to better dominate the environment" (Sherrington 1906).

Study of the postural adjustments made by animals under different experimental conditions demonstrates how supraspinal influences may be exerted. The spinal cat has weak postural reflexes, and they are mostly secondary to other reflexes. A decerebrate animal has a wider range of postural reflexes, due in part to additional receptors, e.g. vestibular receptors, connected with the spinal cord. A decorticate cat, on the other hand, has a much greater range of righting reflexes and other postural adjustments but has no additional receptors. Thus one can see a hierarchy of reflex abilities; all are purposive, but the flexibility and range of movements increase as more and more of the higher CNS comes into functional relation with the spinal cord.

There is a similar range of complexity in the behavior of animals. At one end of the scale are the actions seen in newly born animals, like those that enable them to obtain food by suckling or to escape detection by predators; such actions appear to be inborn or instinctive, to be very similar for each member of a species, to be similar on each occasion (stereotyped), and to be responses to relatively simple stimuli. At the other end of the scale are those flexible behavior patterns that develop during an animal's life, that vary from individual to individual depending upon past experience, and that are called learned behavior. Yet, as with reflexes, there is no sharp distinction between these different behavioral responses or between their functional bases. Learned behavior appears to be due to a refinement and modification of instinctive responses shown in the neonatal period, and in any case the potential for learning must be inherent in the genetic material in the fertilized ovum.

It is often thought that spinal reflexes depend upon inbuilt neural circuits in the spinal cord which develop in the embryo and are subsequently thrown into activity in a predetermined way. Yet there is good evidence that some basic reflexes, such as bladder emptying in the neonatal rat, cannot occur for the first time except after tactile stimulus to the genital region normally provided by the licking of the mother rat; thereafter the reflex operates in response to fullness of the bladder, having been learned from experience in the same way as behavior.

SENSORY STIMULI

During its life an animal is subjected to a continual barrage of changes both in its external environment and within its own body. These changes do not all provoke either immediate or delayed behavior, and so some selection of stimuli must occur. How is this brought about?

At one level this concerns the evolution of the behavior of species, since appropriate behavior will have been selected to enable a species to exist in a particular environment. At another level one can consider the present sensory capacities of various species, which respond selectively to their environment (see Chapters 43, 50, 51), and note how this selectivity detects only a limited number and range of environmental changes. Some examples of variations in sensory capacity are the excellent twilight vision of the cat, the color vision of birds, and the ability of dogs to respond to high-frequency sounds.

However, the selective properties of sense organs do not provide a whole answer; for instance, it is clear that some stimuli have differing importance, e.g. in the dog some odors have a particular significance for feeding, other odors for territorial behavior, and yet others for sexual behavior. There appear to be two aspects to the problem; one must define first what features of a particular stimulus are important in producing acts of behavior, and second what particular sensory patterns are recognized by the brain as being especially important while other patterns are filtered out and discarded.

Analysis of the important features of stimuli can be illustrated by Tinbergen's study of young herring gulls, whose pecking at the bills of their parents provokes parents to feed them (Tinbergen and Perdeck 1950). The red patch on the yellow bill of the parent seems to be the stimulus, and the redness of the patch and the contrast of the patch with its background are among its most important aspects. Such relatively simple stimulus patterns, which evoke stereotyped instinctive behavior, are called sign-stimuli. In this example there is good reason to suppose that the retina and brain of the herring gull are capable of detecting many other colors and shapes, so the selective response of the gull chick raises the question: How does the herring gull's brain recognize this pattern as significant for feeding?

It seems that particular stimuli, derived from an animal's structure or behavior, provoke specific behavior in other animals, e.g. in their young, in their sexual partners, in their competitors, and in their predators, that is to say, the response to stimuli has evolved as a form of communication. Sign-stimuli that provoke specific behavior have been called *releasers* by Lorenz. In the herring gull the releaser is a feature in the anatomical structure of the adult, but in communication between animals the stimulus may be a more variable factor such as the general appearance and/or behavior of the animals, as shown by Charles Darwin (1872) in his classic book *The Expression of the Emotions in Man and Animals*. For example, an enraged cat has a characteristic posture and appearance that are the external results of the activity of the somatic and autonomic nervous system, the latter producing the fight-or-flight reactions; other characteristic appearances occur in fear, in sexual behavior, etc. The response of a second animal to these displays may be aggression, flight, or ritual submission, so that the whole becomes an elaborate system of nonverbal communication. A general feature in mammalian interactions seems to be that inputs from several different sense organs act together to produce the appropriate response, as Beach (1942) has shown in his study of the inputs necessary to produce full copulatory behavior in rats: normally olfactory, visual, and tactile patterns are all needed.

In explaining this selective response of animals to their environment, sensory physiology can go some way beyond merely pointing out the limitations imposed by the sensory receptors of a particular animal.

First, animals do not just passively respond to their environment but can regulate to some extent the information received. This regulation may depend upon centrifugal control of sensory receptors, as in the regulation of muscle spindles or pupillary diameter, or may occur more centrally as in the descending control exerted by areas of the cerebral cortex over various sensory relay nuclei. The function of these regulatory mechanisms, while not yet clear, may be to direct attention to particular sensory organs at the expense of others or to particular features within the input from an individual sense organ.

Second, analysis of sensory inputs such as vision has shown that in the response of nerve cells at successive stages in the visual pathway from the retina to the visual cortex, outlines and shapes are abstracted from visual stimuli, a finding that correlates well with behavioral studies that show the ability of many animals to discriminate accurately between different shapes or between the same shape oriented in different ways in the visual field. However, such explanations do not yet show why certain shapes or patterns are recognized as important when seen for the first time.

BEHAVIORAL RESPONSES

Behavioral responses to sensory stimuli may be conveniently classified into three groups: arousal, specific, and orienting. At first sight these seem to correspond neatly to physiological mechanisms. Almost any stimulus activates the nonspecific paths to the reticular formation that cause physiological arousal, resulting in general activation of the cerebral cortex and general alertness and responsiveness of the animal. Such stimuli also activate specific sensory paths and thus the specialized sensory receiving areas of the cerebral cortex. Orienting responses result in specific responses being accurately directed toward their own goals: in physiological terms these responses seem to correspond to the postural adjustments that accompany phasic reflexes, for example, in the scratch reflex they ensure that the scratching paw is directed to the itchy area of skin, or in the startle response that the eyes, ears, head, and body are reflexly turned toward a sudden stimulus.

In the behavioral sense, however, the term arousal is often used to describe the fact that the same external stimulus may give variable behavioral responses on different occasions, and also is used to account for spontaneous behavior, that is, behavior in the absence of known external stimuli. Arousal has also been applied, first, to a hierarchy of responses, with sleep at the lowest level; feeding, drinking, and sexual behavior at an intermediate level; and aggression or defense at the highest level; and second, to many different types of behavior that become more likely to occur as arousal is increased. When arousal is used in these ways, it is not yet clear that any physiological explanation is valid, and even in behavioral terms the concept may not be sound. A more useful approach is to consider specific items of behavior, such as feeding, drinking, or sexual behavior, and to deal with what are called specific motivations or drives rather than to consider arousal in its wider use. (For more details see Chapter 47.)

MOTIVATION AND DRIVE

In behavioral study it is supposed that specific drives or motivations can be created by manipulating biogenic needs, for example, by deprivation of food or water. These drives are defined as a high probability that the animal will feed or drink if given the opportunity; thus they lead to the appropriate goal-oriented behavior directed toward satisfaction of the original need. Goal-oriented behavior usually falls into several consecutive phases: first, exploration for the goal, called appetitive behavior, leading to recognition and approach; then consummatory behavior, such as feeding or drinking, which are generally fixed action patterns and which center on the immediate satisfaction of the need; and finally a period of quiescence where the animal no longer shows the particular consummatory behavior, for example, an animal which has recently eaten its fill will not feed again even if presented with more food.

With this hypothesis one can explain both the fluctuation of response to constant stimuli and the spontaneous behavior that occurs without change in the environment. Thus the response of a dog to a bowl of water will depend upon how recently it has drunk, how hot are its surroundings, how dry was its recent meal, and so on, while a dog deprived of food and water for several days will have a high level of drive and will actively seek out food and water ''spontaneously'' to satisfy its need. In the case of both feeding and drinking there are good physiological correlates with this behavioral analysis, and drinking may be taken as an example.

The homeostatic mechanisms of the body regulate the osmolarity of the body fluids by balancing the intake and output of water, salt, and other electrolytes (see Chapter 36). A rise in osmolarity is detected by hypothalamic osmoreceptors which activate regulatory mechanisms that reduce the loss of water, promote drinking, and lead to the sensation of thirst in man and supposedly in other animals. It is also known from both physiological and behavioral experiments that receptors other than central osmoreceptors play a part in regulating drinking and thus in the short term regulate water intake. Dryness of the mouth creates a powerful drive to drinking, while conversely both wetting the mouth or throat and distension of the stomach with water will temporarily abolish the drive to drink caused by a true deficit of water. In behavioral studies stimuli that indicate satisfaction of the biogenic drive are called consummatory stimuli; in physiological terms they include in this example removal of osmotic stimulation to central receptors and stimulation both of water receptors in the taste buds and of gastric stretch receptors.

The role of the hypothalamus as a center that integrates the physiological and behavioral mechanisms in drinking has been shown by the techniques of ablation and stimulation. Destruction of the lateral hypothalamus experimentally or by disease causes a decreased water intake or even aversion to water, while stimulation of an anteromedial area electrically or by chemical means causes excessive drinking. Such findings suggest two reciprocally related control centers, one promoting drinking and water conservation, the other causing water loss and reduced drinking. Experiments on feeding give similar results and suggest the existence of reciprocally linked feeding and satiety centers.

The hypothalamus is concerned with more than just the physiological mechanisms of regulation of water loss and the fixed action patterns of drinking; artificial stimulation also leads to exploratory behavior and can be used as a basis for learned behavior. One may conclude therefore that the hypothalamus acts as an important link in the coordination of responses at both the physiological and the most complex behavior levels. Through the actions of the autonomic and somatic nervous systems and the actions of hormones, other parts of the brain also play a part in the full expression of behavior, as will be seen in the later section on the limbic system.

Behavioral measurements of drive have taken various forms. For example, in drinking one can quantitate the amount of water consumed or the amount of physical work done by an animal to obtain water or the level of unpleasant stimulation, such as bitterness or electrical shock, that the animal will accept to gain access to the water. Unfortunately, when several such behavioral measurements are made simultaneously, they often produce inconsistent results, indicating that the true stimulus is not being measured directly. Indeed, in the case of feeding or drinking, it seems that even the present incomplete physiological explanations are more useful in explaining the associated behavior.

It is now necessary to consider how far the concept of specific drives can be taken as a general explanation of the cause of behavior. The concept seems to apply quite well to feeding, drinking, and sexual behavior but appears to be less successful for attack, escape, parental, and other behavior; there are several difficulties.

First, there are important interactions and sometimes conflicts between the specific drives of feeding, drinking, and sexual behavior, so that even these drives are not completely isolated. Second, even within feeding and drinking it is possible to identify subdivisions, e.g. behavioral mechanisms for satisfying the need for particular items in the diet such as sodium or calcium; if one item is deficient, animals will positively discriminate in favor of foods or fluids rich in that item. In describing the causes of such behavior there is a clear danger in suggesting a specific drive for each different act of behavior, since the consequent number of drives would become enormous and the hypothesis would lose its value as a simplifying aid to understanding; further physiological investigation is particularly desirable here.

Additionally, some behavior may be caused by external rather than by internal stimuli; an interesting discussion has taken place about aggression, with Lorenz (1966) championing the view that there is an in-built specific drive for aggression, while others such as Scott (1958) have considered aggression to be largely the result of external stimuli and of past experience.

Finally, although most of the present discussion has centered on specific drives, it should be remembered that many stimuli, arising either externally or from within an animal's body, have general effects on behavior and on the physiological mechanism of arousal mediated by the reticular ascending system. For all these reasons it seems that the concept of specific drives, although very useful in some contexts, is not universally applicable.

Emotions

Conscious humans feel emotions such as hunger and thirst in situations that the behaviorist describes in terms of drives and the physiologist in terms of altered chemistry of body fluids and of stimulation of neural receptors. We infer that animals have similar emotions to man, perhaps chiefly because they have the same external appearances of fear or rage as humans have in similar situations. The parallel that is usually drawn between the feelings of man and animals usually embodies, however, a double assumption: first, that the stimuli of a particular situation give rise in animals to conscious sensations similar to those in man, and second, that these sensations in turn cause emotions in animals which resemble human emotions. Although these assumptions are generally accepted, and indeed form the basis of much animal welfare legislation, the fact that they are assumptions ought to be kept in mind.

The brain mechanisms underlying the expression of the

emotions of rage and fear have been investigated particularly by Bard (1950), who showed that chronically decorticate cats and dogs were notably liable to explosive attacks of rage or sometimes of terror, and by Hess (1954), who produced the characteristic behavior of rage and fear by electrical stimulation of defined areas of the hypothalamus and of the midbrain in conscious cats. Lower levels of the brain also play a part, as shown by the limited, short-lasting, and ineffective displays that can be provoked in decerebration experiments where the hypothalamus has been entirely removed.

From these and other experiments using local ablations and stimulation it has been concluded that neural mechanisms exist in the caudal hypothalamus which coordinate the behavior normally associated with the expression of the emotions of rage and fear. It is true that such coordinated behavior falls short of that seen in the intact animal; it is not usually directed accurately at a particular target, often seems out of proportion to the circumstances, and sometimes appears without obvious stimulation. It has therefore been deduced that brain stem structures rostral and dorsal to the hypothalamus, such as the thalamus and the limbic system, normally act with the cerebral cortex to moderate and direct the behavior synthesized by the hypothalamus. The cerebral cortex is presumably also necessary for the conscious appreciation of emotions although it is probably not necessary for their physical expression. In man and primates the frontal lobes of the cerebral cortex are thought to play a crucial role in the conscious appreciation of the emotions of pain, fear, and stress. Their removal or disconnection from the rest of the brain produces placidity in subjects previously incapacitated by worry, and removes the unpleasant emotional consequences of pain without abolishing the underlying sensation, so that after such an operation patients will notice tissue damage but do not feel pain. It is a short step to assume that many other human emotions have parallels in animals and that these are similarly dependent upon the activity of particular parts of the brain.

Emotionality is a term used to describe behavior that is thought to indicate the emotional reactivity of animals. Most studies have been made on laboratory rodents, who react to novel or stressful situations by immobility or reduced exploration and by urination and defecation. Using these criteria, abnormally low levels of sensory stimulation in newborn rats result in greater emotionality in later life and reduced ability to learn. The features used to define emotionality in rodents may correspond to the better recognized behavior and appearance of cats and dogs subjected to stress, e.g. the fight-or-flight reaction, but little work has been done on the physiological basis of emotions in rodents; certainly these criteria cannot be used in a simple way in other domestic species generally.

Conflict behavior

In their everyday lives, animals are subjected to many situations where stimuli to different and opposing behavior may be present at the same moment; for example, in herds or flocks there is a tendency for animals to come into close proximity, yet proximity itself leads to aggression and a tendency to disperse. Such conflict in opposing drives often results in one sort of behavior inhibiting others and becoming dominant, so that either feeding or flight may result. Sometimes behavior patterns such as feeding and flight alternate, but both cannot occur fully at the same time. There are, however, a number of behavioral patterns that seem to be special responses to conflicting drives; they also appear when animals are denied the reward of some behavior and become frustrated, for example, if an animal is allowed to see or smell food but access to the food or eating is prevented.

The term threat is given to one sort of behavior resulting from conflicting drives. Studies of cats show not only that their behavior and appearance in aggression and fear have their own characteristics, but that situations which tend to produce both responses result in a hybrid behavior which contains some elements from each of the two types. Such threat displays are presumably important in animal communication, as are those of simple fear and aggression. Another response in these situations is displacement activity, where episodes of seemingly irrelevant behavior occur, interrupting what appear to be the appropriate responses; pawing of ground in the larger domestic animals is an example.

Where conflict of drives occurs in encounters between animals, the conflicts are often resolved by submission of one animal. Submission is signaled by its own characteristic display called appeasement which has the function of inhibiting further attack. The submissive animal reduces the aggressive drive in the opponent by postures that reduce the exposure of its own threat releasers and also by making submissive gestures; for example, dogs expose their necks, an area particularly vulnerable to attack. Victory appears to be reinforced by special patterns of behavior where the victor asserts his dominance, in some animals by ritualized sexual behavior such as a brief attempt at mounting.

Animal courtship provides a most interesting example of potential conflict. The initial approaches of the male and female arouse the conflicting drives of aggression, fear, and sex, yet the drives of fear and aggression must be overcome for sexual behavior to become dominant in each animal and for the sexual behavior of both to be properly synchronized so that mating occurs. In part these drives become redirected toward other members of the species so that both members of a pair defend their territories and their young. In part they seem to find their outlet in elaborate courtship displays, particularly in birds.

Physical conflict in the lives of wild animals, particularly between members of the same species, seems to be limited by the behavior patterns mentioned above which reduce the likelihood of actual fighting and physical damage. In laboratory experiments animals can be subjected to situations of prolonged conflict and may then develop physical signs of stress, such as enlargement and later exhaustion of the adrenal or pituitary glands; or gastric ulcers or other intestinal disorders may develop. They may also show gross disorders of behavior such as persistent overactivity, or they may at the other extreme become dull and unresponsive to their surroundings.

The underlying physiology of conflict behavior is still poorly understood. It has been argued that the characteristic behavior of defensive threat in the cat and other animals may be due to a single neuronal mechanism, or that it may be caused by simultaneous activation of two neuronal mechanisms which give the appearances of rage and fear respectively. However, the real contrast may not be between the drives or responses of attack and escape but between activity at one extreme and immobility or hiding at the other extreme (Andrew 1972). In Andrew's classification, the fight-or-flight response of the autonomic nervous system anticipates activity and, together with an extended posture of the limbs and trunk, has many of the same features as the body's cooling responses to raised body temperature. Immobility and hiding, on the other hand, are characterized by decreases in heart rate and in respiration, vasoconstriction, shivering, piloerection, and the huddled-up posture of limbs and trunk that are characteristic of warming responses seen in a cold environment. When behavior is analyzed in this way, the relatively simple behavior concepts of drives seem inadequate, yet physiological knowledge cannot yet provide a more coherent explanation.

BEHAVIORAL RESPONSES FROM THE RHINENCEPHALON (LIMBIC SYSTEM)

The rhinencephalon (from rhino, nose) is the deeply situated region of the cerebral cortex that is concerned, at least partly, with the olfactory input from the nose. It includes the pyriform and entorhinal cortex, the hippocampus, parts of the amygdala, and some other subcortical nuclei. Important connections pass between the rhinencephalon and the hypothalamus, the thalamus, and the midbrain reticular formation. The region has a very complex anatomical structure. The medial forebrain bundle (MFB) arises in the hippocampus and septum and contains fibers that end in the hypothalamus (Fig. 46.1).

Both lesions and electrical stimulation of the rhinencephalon produce well-organized patterns of offensive and defensive behavior as well as stereotyped reflex movements and autonomic responses. In the cat, the behavioral responses (many of which can be interpreted as part of the cat's emotional and sexual behavior) appear

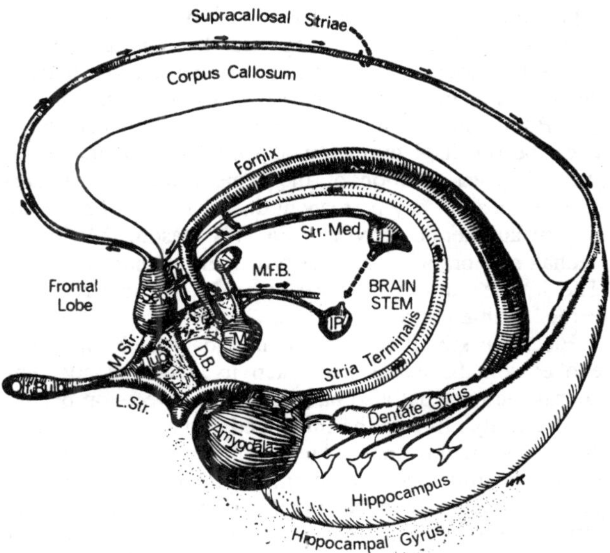

Figure 46.1. Idealized diagram to illustrate the relationship of the main subcortical structures and connections of the mammalian rhinencephalon, viewed from the right hemisphere, medial aspect. Arrows indicate the direction of the connections. AT, anterior thalamic nucleus; D.B., diagonal band of Broca; H, habenula; IP, interpeduncular nucleus; L.Str., lateral olfactory stria; M, mammillary body; M.F.B., medial forebrain bundle; M.Str., medial olfactory stria; Olf.Bulb, olfactory bulb; Sep., septal region; Str.Med., stria medullaris; Tub, olfactory tubercle. (From P.D. MacLean 1949, *Psychosomatic Med.* 11:338–53.)

during and immediately after electrical stimulation through implanted electrodes. In these experiments, the cats were observed for prolonged periods (up to 10 hours) in group situations, where one cat with implanted electrodes shared a small room with several normal cats.

Several patterns of behavior were seen: walking or standing; aggressiveness, indicated by snarling, flattening of the ears, and assumption of the fighting position; playful activity; and contactual activity, shown by sniffing, licking, or rubbing. The complex patterns of behavior were also associated with stereotyped reflex movements such as closing of the eye and rhythmic movements of the lips. All the responses were strictly associated with stimulation and rarely persisted for more than one minute after stimulation ceased; this is reflex behavior. Electrical stimulation of the amygdala led in particular to an increase in playfulness. However, electrical stimulation of the same point might on one occasion induce an increase of aggressiveness and on another a decrease. In more recent experiments Ursin and Kaada (1960) reported anatomically separate fear-yielding and anger-yielding regions of the amygdala in cats. Stimulation of lesions in the rhinencephalon may also lead to conspicuous changes in or to elicitation of sexual or reproductive behavior.

While powerful effects on visceral, cardiovascular, and respiratory systems were noted as a consequence of electrical stimulation of the limbic cortex, no obvious topographical localization was found. Because of the visceral effects it has been suggested that this area of the cortex functions as a visceral cortical center, in a manner analogous to the somatosensory cortex or the motor cortex. Rather similar and more powerful effects can, however, be obtained by electrical stimulation of the hypothalamus, yet ablation of the rhinencephalic structures does not lead to any permanent disturbance of the regulation of autonomic activities. For this reason, the rhinencephalon is probably not the principal autonomic center. The limbic cortex, however, may be particularly concerned with emotion.

Electrical stimulation of the amygdala nuclei not only evokes somatic and visceral activity and may alter endocrine activity but also has significant effects on behavioral activity. In cats the integrated behavioral responses are of two main kinds: (1) Feeding behavior—sniffing, biting, licking, and salivation, together with searching activity—may be evoked. Food may be eaten ravenously after a period of stimulation. (2) Emotional behavior is the most common type of response, and the kinds of emotional reactions aroused depend on the intensity of the electrical stimulation. The first response is usually attention, that is, the animal's ongoing behavior is arrested. The other responses are fear or rage, with their associated postural and autonomic readjustments. The rage, in contrast to sham rage in decorticate animals, is very well directed, and tame rats may be converted by electrical stimulation into wild unmanageable animals that attack their attendants.

Bilateral ablation of the amygdaloid and septal nuclei modifies behavioral activity. Ablation of the amygdala region has a profound effect on emotional behavior, but only a transitory action on many of the somatic, autonomic, and endocrine systems that can be altered by electrical stimulation of the amygdala. It has therefore been concluded that the amygdala region does not integrate these functions but only modifies them. The integration probably occurs in the hypothalamus. Emotional behavior, on the other hand, may be profoundly affected by bilateral amygdaloid lesions. Two types of changes have been reported. Some animals exhibit a taming effect in which they become more docile, less aggressive, lose fear, and may develop hypersexuality. Other animals become more aggressive, and placid animals become easily enraged. These differences are probably due to the lesions involving different parts of the amygdaloid complex—specifically, either the fear-yielding or the anger-yielding regions described above.

The relation between rhinencephalon and hypothalamus was examined in dual stimulation experiments (Egger and Flynn 1963). Electrodes were placed in the hypothalamus in a position that caused the cats to make a well-directed attack. Other electrodes were put in the amygdala region of the rhinencephalon. Stimulation in the medial region of the amygdala suppressed the attack provoked by hypothalamic stimuli, whereas electrodes in the dorsolateral amygdala regions enhanced the attacking behavior. It is thus possible that some of the behavioral consequences of rhinencephalic stimulation operate through hypothalamic systems, but in experiments such as these the precise neural mechanisms are not established.

HORMONES AND BEHAVIOR

Behavior depends as much upon hormonal activity as upon the actions of the nervous system. An example of this appears in the response of the adrenal gland medulla in stress, a result of stimulation of the autonomic nervous system. The adrenal cortex is also involved in this response (see Chapter 52), being stimulated by the anterior pituitary hormone, ACTH, released under the influence of the hypothalamus. The complex interactions between hormones, the CNS, and peripheral tissues are particularly well illustrated in male and female sexual behavior, a subject of great importance to the veterinarian. Only certain aspects will be considered here, including the behavior of adult males and females in the events leading up to and resulting in successful mating, together with the development of sexual behavior. Behavior associated with parturition, maternal and paternal care of the young, and nursing are also very important but less well understood in physiological terms (see Chapter 47).

Female behavior

It has long been recognized that most wild and some domestic female animals show characteristic sexual behavior and are sexually receptive only at certain seasons of the year, varying with different species: autumn in sheep but spring in horses for example.

Superimposed upon this general seasonal periodicity there are shorter cycles of sexual behavior and receptivity, so that within the breeding season females are receptive for only a few days at a time, these periods recurring at intervals of a few weeks if the animals do not become pregnant. This cyclic sexual behavior is accompanied by cyclic changes in the reproductive tract and in the activity of endocrine glands, chiefly the anterior pituitary and gonads, causing characteristic fluctuations in hormone levels in the blood (see Chapter 53).

Seasonal changes in ovarian and uterine activity and in hormonal activity are thought to be initiated in domestic animals primarily through neural stimuli acting eventually on the hypothalamus and provided by changing day length, although other environmental and internal factors, such as ambient temperature, altitude, and nutrition, may play a part. The precise timing of hormonal cycles can also be influenced by external factors such as the presence of other animals, male or female. In some species, such as the cat and rabbit, ovulation itself depends upon the nervous stimuli generated by the act of copulation.

Cats ovariectomized before puberty do not develop secondary sexual characteristics or show female behavior as adults, but nevertheless after suitable treatment with progesterone and estrogen they exhibit typical cyclic female behavior, showing that feedback from the peripheral sex organs is not necessary for the appearance of adult female sexual behavior. There is evidence that cyclic hormonal changes and behavior may depend upon different neural centers in the hypothalamus, but they would normally be economically and effectively coordinated through the changing blood levels of estrogen and progesterone. Once developed, adult female behavior may persist even after ovariectomy, although its intensity depends both upon the species and the extent of previous experience.

Progesterone, in addition to being necessary for normal adult cyclic sexual behavior, also appears to be responsible for suppressing sexual behavior when present in high concentrations, e.g. after estrus and in most species throughout pregnancy.

Male behavior

Research on laboratory mammals into the control of spermatogenesis has shown that testicular activity in the adult depends upon gonadotropins released from the anterior pituitary gland under hypothalamic control (see Chapter 54), while the accessory organs which are also important for the storage and ejaculation of viable spermatozoa depend upon androgens secreted by the testes. This research stressed the relative constancy of testicular activity compared with the conspicuous ovarian and behavioral cycles in the female. But seasonal alterations of male activity and appearance have been long recognized in wild birds and mammals, and there is now accumulating evidence that this same principle applies to domesticated species, particularly the ram and male goat, and less noticeably to the bull, boar, and stallion. The same seasonal factors, such as day length, nutrition, and temperature, that influence female seasonal behavior also seem to be responsible for male seasonal behavior.

Castration in the adult male generally produces a decrease or even abolition of sexual behavior, but experienced males are less affected. Sexual behavior in castrated males can be fully restored by systemic injections of testosterone. In rats this is due to the separate actions of two types of testosterone metabolites. Aromatization of testosterone to estrogenic products stimulates sexual behavior, while nonaromatized derivatives stimulate peripheral sex organs: both actions must occur if full sexual behavior is to be restored, since the feedback to the brain from peripheral sex organs, particularly from the penis, seems to be very important.

The hypothalamus is the area of the brain that normally controls testicular activity and reacts to estrogenlike compounds to produce male behavior. The male rat however, unlike the female, shows sexual behavior only if the cerebral cortex is intact. Besides the hypothalamus, other brain areas also influence sexual behavior in the male, perhaps by modifying the basic patterns of sexual activity organized by the hypothalamus; one of the most striking illustrations of this is the gross hypersexuality shown by cats with bilateral lesions of the limbic cortex.

Synchronization of male and female sexual behavior

Seasonal influences ensure that both males and females are in the correct reproductive state at the same time of the year. However, it is useful if sexual behavior is even more closely synchronized so that attempts of males to mount and copulate are more likely to occur on those days when females are in estrus. To promote this synchronization there is an elaborate system of interactions between the male and female at the time of estrus and a variety of sensory cues are used.

First, estrous cycles become more regular in the presence of a male, and in a flock of sheep the cycles of individuals tend to become synchronized. This effect is due to olfactory stimuli in ewes and is caused by chemicals known as pheromones, which are released especially by dominant and sexually active males and are generally present in urine. Second, pheromones released by females reduce aggression in the male and thus play a part in resolving the conflict of drives described above. In addition a complex of stimuli such as pheromones released by both sexes, characteristic visual appearances such as soliciting behavior and vulval swelling, and vocalization by either sex appear to be important in sexual arousal immediately before mating. All these stimuli and responses act at a distance and combine to encourage male and female to approach one another, with arousal of sexual behavior and inhibition of aggressive behavior brought on by proximity. Approach and contact then lead to the next stage where full receptivity in the female and full copulatory performance in the male are enhanced by the tactile stimuli provided by the sexual partner. Thus intromission and ejaculation are the culmination of physiological and behavioral changes that build up through a process of mutual stimulation acting as a positive feedback mechanism. The sequence is also effectively ended by behavioral mechanisms; the female becomes unreceptive and resists further attempts at intromission and the male shows a disinclination to mount, although in each case this may not occur until many bouts of copulation have occurred. It is also a well-documented fact that a male, having apparently become sexually refractory after copulation with one female, can be freshly aroused by introduction to a new receptive female, the so-called novelty effect.

Development of sexual behavior

The hypothalamus of the mammal just before birth has an inherently female rhythm which is manifested after puberty in the typical cyclic patterns of gonadotropin release from the pituitary gland and of estrous behavior. This pattern develops unless the hypothalamus is subjected to the action of androgens during a critical few days at about the time of birth; in the latter case the more continuous patterns of male gonadotropin release and of male behavior develop in the adult. Androgens are aromatized to estrogenic products in the brain to exert this organizing influence on the neonatal hypothalamus, but important peripheral effects are also due to androgens. These are necessary for adequate maturation of spinal sexual reflexes, for development of accessory organs producing pheromones, and for full development of the penis, without which the positive feedback necessary for full sexual performance cannot occur during copulation.

The action of androgens on the neonatal hypothalamus illustrates an important type of relation between hormones and the CNS in the synthesis of behavior. Hormones here organize the neural substrate of behavior along a particular line, switching neural circuits from the cyclic female pattern to the more continuous male pattern. The interaction of hormones and the hypothalamus in the adult by contrast is permissive, allowing the basic neural circuits that have differentiated after birth to be revealed. The situation in the adult, however, is more complex, for full sexual behavior depends upon more general sensory experiences during development; animals raised in isolation or in contact only with other species show deficiencies both in sexual behavior and in development of secondary sex organs. Once full sexual behavior has been established, moreover, it may then take on the character of purely neural-learned behavior since it may persist after castration and thus after removal of those hormones that were essential for its original appearance.

LEARNING AND MEMORY

A feature of higher animals is the ability of individuals to modify their behavior in the light of experience, so that behavior becomes better adapted to ensure survival: this process is called learning. Thorpe (1963) stressed the useful distinction between the processes of learning and the changed state of the brain which occurs as the result of learning and which is called memory. A separate process of retrieval is necessary to show that something has been learned, that is, a memory has been stored. Thus experiments on learning are sometimes difficult to interpret since memories may sometimes only be retrieved under special circumstances, and failure to retrieve can be easily confused with failure to learn.

Types of learning

There is a close relation between instinct and learning, since learning consists of a modification of inborn motor reactions which become refined and selective in the light of experience and thus better adapted. It is not known whether all learning depends upon essentially the same physiological machinery, but from the behavioral point of view Thorpe's classification of different types of learning is useful:

(1) Habituation is learning *not* to respond to stimuli that are of no significance to the animal; it is well illustrated by the alarm responses of birds to the sight of predators flying overhead. Initially, almost any moving object overhead produces the response, but those such as leaves or branches which are frequently repeated, or those such as nonpredatory birds which are not associated in any way with danger, gradually cease to evoke responses. On the other hand infrequent and irregular appearances of a hawklike shape continue to provoke the response which thus becomes appropriately selective. The lack of any significance of the stimulus in terms of reward or punishment appears to be crucial in habituation; it would be extremely inappropriate for habituation to occur to stimuli indicating the presence of food or water, for example.

(2) Conditioned reflexes type I are the classical conditioned reflexes of the Russian physiologist Pavlov, who studied these in an extended series of experiments. By a simple medullary reflex a dog will normally secrete saliva in response to food in its mouth. If another unrelated stimulus, such as ringing a bell, is given over a period of days, either immediately before or at the same time as each presentation of food, secretion of saliva can subsequently be produced if the bell is rung without the food being given. The unconditioned stimulus (UCS) of food in the mouth, which first produced the unconditioned reflex response (UCR) of salivary secretion, has become conditioned so that the conditional stimulus (CS) of the bell now gives the conditioned response (CR) of salivation. The learned behavior of the CR will, however, decline, a process called extinction, unless the CR is positively reinforced by the reward of food from time to time. Conditioning will also occur in response to punishment (negative reinforcement) so that, for example, reflex withdrawal of a foot to an electrical shock may be conditioned by the sound of a buzzer, which later becomes a sufficient stimulus by itself to cause withdrawal.

(3) Conditioned reflex type II, also called operant or instrumental conditioning, is particularly associated with the American behaviorist Skinner whose apparatus, the Skinner box, has been extensively used in experiments on this type of learning. Typically, an animal that is hungry is rewarded for some voluntary activity that is *not* related in a simple reflex fashion to the consummatory act of feeding; for example, the reward might be given for running a maze successfully or for pressing a lever. Eventually, as the number of times rises at which the animal is rewarded for lever pressing, the animal learns to press the lever to obtain food whenever it is hungry.

As in classical conditioned reflexes, the important factor causing learning is the association in time between the movement and the reward; repetition of the association is also important. Both reward and punishment can be used in operant conditioning to modify behavior, and both are frequently used in a deliberate way when domestic animals are trained as pets or when animals are trained to perform in circus acts.

Wild animals do not experience the artificial laboratory situations which best demonstrate the two types of conditioning but learn in a trial and error way which combines elements of both types of learning. One of the main differences is that animals naturally explore their environment actively and thus repeatedly create the possibility of chance associations between voluntary movements and the rewards of food, drink, etc. Active exploration will thus inevitably lead to the development of learned behavior that adapts the individual to its own environment.

(4) Latent and insight learning are closely related, and in each case learning occurs without immediate reward. Latent learning is shown where rats are given access to a maze and explore it even if not rewarded in any way; if later conditioned to use the maze to obtain food they will show evidence of having learned the maze previously, since their performance reaches maximum much more quickly than rats whose conditioning started at the same time but who had no prior access to the maze. The learning was latent in the sense that only subsequent testing in the appropriate way showed that something had been remembered. Insight learning has been shown in experiments on chimpanzees who were presented with bananas placed out of reach and who were able on the first occasion to use sticks or other tools to get them. This occurred where the sticks had been available previously but where their use had never been rewarded before. The chimpanzees apparently extrapolated from their previous experience of playing with sticks.

(5) Imprinting is an example of the way in which early experience modifies later behavior. Lorenz was one of the first to make a detailed study of the way in which some species of birds, e.g. ducks and geese, become attached to whatever moving object they encounter during the first few days of life. Normally the object would be their parent, but experimentally they may become attached to other species, such as man, or even to inanimate objects. The phenomenon appears to be shown in mammals as well as birds. One of the important behavioral consequences is the choice of sexual partner in adult life.

The principles of imprinting are of considerable importance in veterinary work; animals reared in isolation do not later respond normally to other members of their own species and so may not mate readily with them, a considerable disadvantage for farmers, animal breeders, and zoos, but sometimes an advantage in training dogs as nonbreeding companion animals, since early contact with a human family results in a well-domesticated animal.

Study of imprinting seems to show a critical period in the early life of an animal that determines later behavior. Critical periods may also occur in later life. A good example is the mother/young relationship which is established in a crucial way during the first few postpartum days; this is a two-way process that involves both the neonate responding to stimuli provided by the mother and the mother reacting to stimuli from her newborn, usually to taste and smell derived from licking and nuzzling her young. Failure to establish such a relationship accounts for the nonacceptance by ewes of foster lambs more than a few hours old, although there are long-standing farming practices that try to circumvent this, such as tying the skin of one of the ewe's dead lambs to the foster lamb.

Generalization and discrimination

Generalization can be tested by training a rat to respond to a black triangle on a white background as an essential precondition for obtaining food by bar pressing. Subsequently, triangles and other shapes of differing size, orientation, and angles are tested to see how far the rat abstracts the property of triangularity from the other features of the stimuli, that is, the rat is tested for its ability to pick out common features of the differing stimuli. Rats are quite good at this sort of generalization. Rather surprisingly, both birds and mammals appear to have a limited concept of number, abstracting this property from the varied nature of objects presented to them in such tests.

Discrimination is the reverse of generalization and can be tested in a similar way. A dog is first rewarded for pressing a lever when a 1000 Hz (hertz, or cycles per second) tone is sounded but is punished for lever pressing when a 600 Hz tone sounds. After a relatively limited number of trials the dog will learn to discriminate correctly between the two tones, only pressing the lever when the 1000 Hz tone sounds. The dog's capacity for maximum discrimination can now be tested by increasing the frequency of the tone associated with punishment in steps towards 1000 Hz and finding the smallest difference in tone that is correctly distinguished. Such tests of discrimination depend upon the whole learning/memory/retrieval complex of the animal, not just the sensory capacity of the sense organs as is sometimes claimed. It is to be expected that discrimination varies for different types of learned response and with differing intensities of the drive at the time of testing.

Neural substrates for reward and punishment

Reward and punishment clearly play a crucial role in establishing learning by conditioning. Experiments by Olds (1962) showed that electrical stimulation of certain areas of the brain could be either rewarding or aversive. Rats were fitted with chronically implanted electrodes whose tips were sited in the basal or lateral parts of the diencephalon: the rats could control the self-stimulation by pressing a lever that turned on or off the electrical pulses. With certain electrode placements rats apparently found the stimulation extremely rewarding, for they continued to press the lever at high rates for hours. At some sites self-stimulation replaced the natural rewards of satisfying biogenic drives, so that hungry or thirsty rats would press the lever for electric stimulation rather than eat or drink even when severe deficits and strong drives were present. Self-stimulation can also be used to establish conditioned responses, to motivate trial and error learning, and to potentiate learning associated with natural rewards and punishments.

Stimulation at other sites causes consummatory behavior such as eating or drinking, even in satiated animals. This appears to be due to an increase of the respective drives, but the responses are stimulus bound, that is, the effects last only as long as the stimulation.

All these effects are particularly obtained from the region of the medial forebrain bundle (MFB) that has extensive connections with the hypothalamus, limbic system, and frontal cortex.

While precise interpretation is still lacking—for instance it is uncertain whether there is a common reward system or a separate system for each of the drives—clearly this type of electrical stimulation breaks into the neural circuits normally concerned with motivating behavior and learning through reinforcement and drive enhancement.

Short- and long-term memory

People who receive a blow on the head may lose their memory for events immediately before the blow (retrograde amnesia) but not for much earlier events. Other procedures, such as electroconvulsive shock and anesthesia, that similarly alter the electrical activity of the brain have the same effect on memory for very recent events. These observations led to the idea that there may be two types of memory, a short-term labile memory (STM) dependent upon continuing activity in neuronal circuits, and a long-term memory (LTM) that is much more stable and is dependent upon some permanent structural change. Some workers, however, believe that there is only one type of memory storage with perhaps more than one process of retrieval.

The processes of consolidation of memory into either STM or LTM have caused much discussion. There is good evidence that sensory inputs from a changed environment are immediately stored in a very short-term register for a period of perhaps a minute or so, but can be perpetuated for longer by persistence of the same external stimulus or by re-creation of the stimulus internally by rehearsal, a sort of mental playback. However, if the subject is distracted by new inputs, the preceding storage is rapidly erased, and the register is filled by new information.

Consolidation from the immediate sensory register into STM takes place selectively and relatively slowly, the storage in STM usually lasting for an hour or so at maximum and being labile. Consolidation into LTM also occurs, the input being encoded in a more permanent form that may last the lifetime of the animal. At some stage the sensory input is analyzed and apparently compared to the individual's own model or artificial abstraction of the external world, since those features which are both novel and significant in terms of past experience are particularly likely to enter the memory.

In most human patients, lesions of the hippocampus and medial parietal cortex cause gross impairment of acquisition of new memories with relatively slight effects on memories already stored, suggesting an important role for this part of the brain in consolidation of memory. In other human patients, STM is markedly reduced but there is no impairment of LTM. These two conditions not only strongly support the idea of separate short- and long-term memories but also suggest that learned material enters STM and LTM by separate and parallel paths, rather than being passed from STM to LTM as had been thought previously.

The quest for a precise location of memories in the brain has been fruitless. Lashley (1950) clearly showed that lesions could be made in a variety of places in the cerebral cortex of the rat but that loss of learning ability was only related to the mass and not the location of the cortical tissue destroyed. Although later studies of human patients have shown that destruction of the cortex in the dominant and nondominant hemispheres respectively may differentially affect verbal and nonverbal learning, and that the corpus callosum is important in the transfer of information from one hemisphere to the other so that it is later stored in duplicate, all these findings relate to the processes of learning and recall rather than demonstrating a specific location for certain memories.

Electrical changes during learning

Two principal changes have emerged that could relate memory to the ongoing electrical activity of the brain. First, self-exciting or reverberating circuits probably account for some forms of prolonged neural activity triggered by a sudden stimulus, for example in long-lasting spinal and medullary reflexes. But attempts to explain memory on this basis rest largely on argument by analogy and direct experimental evidence is still lacking. Second, long-lasting changes in synaptic excitability follow transmission, particularly in invertebrate preparations such as the giant neurons of various mollusks. Such changes can be caused by both pre- and postsynaptic alterations and may last tens of minutes, but again it has not yet been clearly shown that specific changes occur at specific synapses and encode particular memories.

Chemical changes during learning

Investigations of changes in the chemical composition of neurons during learning stem from the fact that ribonucleic acids (RNA) are concerned with the genetic memory of cells and the expression of this memory in the synthesis of particular protein molecules. Neurons are rich in RNA, and perhaps during learning the synthesis of specific protein molecules leads to a change in the chemical composition of neuron membranes, which might lead in turn to specific alterations of function.

Early experiments sought to prove that memory acquired during training of planaria or rats for a particular discrimination could be transferred to other animals by grinding up the brains and extracting the RNA of the trained animals and injecting the extract into previously untrained animals. These animals should then acquire the memory established in the originally trained animals and perform the discrimination better than uninjected controls. Results from such experiments have usually been very inconsistent, and there have been arguments as to whether RNA or protein or other complex molecules are important in the postulated transfer, so that many regard the basic phenomenon as still not proven.

Nevertheless, increased activity of neural tissue is undoubtedly accompanied both by structural changes, such as increase in size of synaptic knobs and increased numbers of dendritic spines, and by changes in chemical activity, with increases in RNA content and in synthesis of new protein. Hydén (1970) found evidence that the changes in RNA content and in protein synthesis are not simply due to increased neural activity as such but are linked to the processes of learning. He suggested that new and specific proteins are made under these conditions and are incorporated into the cell membrane.

The importance of protein synthesis as part of learning is confirmed by the action of certain antibiotics, such as puromycin, that block protein synthesis. When these antibiotics are injected into animals during training, learning is reduced or abolished, but not if the injection occurs too early or too late. This suggests that protein synthesis plays some part in the consolidation of memory.

These results all provide tantalizing pointers toward the basic chemical mechanism of memory, but it is worth recalling that a whole host of metabolic pathways are directed by enzymatic proteins and that general interference with protein synthesis is like using a blunderbuss to hit a small target.

REFERENCES

Andrew, R.J. 1972. The information potentially available in animal displays. In R.A. Hinde, ed., *Non-Verbal Communication*. Cambridge U. Press, Cambridge.

Bard, P. 1950. Central nervous mechanisms for the expression of anger in animals. In M.L. Reymert, ed., *Feelings and Emotions*. McGraw-Hill, New York. Chap. 18.

Beach, F.A. 1942. Analysis of the stimuli adequate to elicit mating behaviour in the sexually inexperienced male rat. *J. Comp. Psychol.* 33:163–207.

Darwin, C. 1872. *The Expression of the Emotions in Man and Animals*. John Murray, London.

Egger, M.D., and Flynn, J.P. 1963. Effects of electrical stimulation of the amygdala on hypothalamically elicited attack behaviour in cats. *J. Neurophysiol.* 26:705–20.

Hess, W.R. 1954. *Diencephalon, Autonomic, and Extrapyramidal Functions*. Grune & Stratton, New York.

Hydén, H. 1970. The question of a molecular basis for the memory, In K.H. Pribram and D.E. Broadbent, eds., *Biology of Memory*. Academic Press, New York.

Lashley, K.S. 1950. In search of the engram. *Symp. Soc. Exp. Biol.* 4:454–82.

Lorenz, K.Z. 1966. *On Aggression*. Methuen, London.

Olds, J. 1962. Hypothalamic substrates of reward. *Physiol. Rev.* 42:554–604.

Scott, J.P. 1958. *Aggression*. U. of Chicago Press, Chicago.

Sherrington, C.S. 1906. *The Integrative Action of the Nervous System*. Yale U. Press, New Haven.

Skinner, B.F. 1938. *The Behavior of Organisms*. Appleton-Century-Crofts, New York.

Thorpe, W.H. 1963. *Learning and Instinct in Animals*. 2d ed. Methuen, London.

Tinbergen, N., and Perdeck, A.C. 1950. On the stimulus situation releasing the begging response in the newly-hatched herring gull chick (Larus a. argentatus Pont.). *Behaviour* 3:1–38.

Ursin, H., and Kaada, B.R. 1960. Functional localization within the amygdaloid complex in the cat. *Electroenceph. Clin. Neurophysiol.* 12:1–20.

CHAPTER 47

Physiology of Behavior | by E.S.E. Hafez

Animal behavior is the expression of an effort to adapt or to adjust to different internal and exteroceptive conditions; that is, behavior is a response to stimuli. A stimulus is a change of energy outside or inside an animal that leads to a large change of energy output by the animal's effectors. Several separable stimuli act concurrently or sequentially and exert their maximum effectiveness as a complex. The sensory capacities play an important role in the expression of behavioral patterns. For example, sound localization and odor detection, which are well developed in the dog, play a significant role in ingestive, sexual, social, and tracking behavior.

Just as morphological characteristics are inherited, so are behavioral characteristics. By selective breeding, domestic animals have been bred for particular behavioral patterns—for example, fighting bulls, rodeo horses, game cocks, and dogs suited for tracking humans, herding sheep, guiding the blind, or hunting. Many animals exhibit regular patterns of locomotor activity that appear to be controlled by endogenous rhythms (biological clocks). Environmental factors that are controlled cyclically and with some degree of regularity govern these endogenous rhythms and are termed *Zeitgebers* (Aschoff 1958). This phenomenon has not been studied in farm animals.

Domestic animals can be classified into two major groups according to the available living space: free-ranging animals, such as cattle herds and sheep flocks, and confined animals, such as the laboratory rabbit and house pets. A home range is established by free-ranging mammals within a particular locality where the animal lives and wanders. The size of the home range varies considerably with different species. Sheep, for example, do not usually extend their home range more than 120 acres (Hunter and Davies 1963). In domestic animals, living space is limited artificially by fences, except in stock farms and ranges. Even in unfenced areas, herd animals move around only within their own home range, keeping to set routes at certain times of the day. For recognition of home range the large herd animals depend upon their visual capacities and dogs and rabbits on their olfactory sense.

Since grazing, feeding, and sexual behavior are directly related to the economics of animal husbandry, these systems of behavior have been studied more extensively than other systems.

Table 47.1. Behavioral patterns and thermoregulation in mammals and birds

	Ambient temperature			
	High		Low	
	Mammals	Birds	Mammals	Birds
Activities	Wallowing Rooting Licking body surfaces Night grazing Eating succulent feeds Aestivation	Extending wings Sitting on cool soil Keeping feet off soil Throwing water on comb Splashing water Moistening incubated eggs	Hibernation	Fluffing feathers Placing head under wing Covering feet and legs Torpidity Burying incubated eggs Incubating and brooding Basking
Patterns	Anorexia Body extension Group dispersion Extra drinking Decreasing locomotor activities Moistening body surface with water, saliva, or nasal secretions Seeking microclimates with lower temperature		Body flexing Huddling Increasing locomotor activities Nest building Seeking microclimates with higher temperature	

THERMOREGULATORY BEHAVIOR

Thermoregulation in domestic animals is accomplished by physical and physiological adjustments. The latter entail involuntary activation of somatic responses and voluntary behavioral adjustments. The former include postural changes, qualitative and quantitative changes in water consumption, and changes in nocturnal habits (Table 47.1). Thermoregulatory behavioral changes are controlled by the CNS and hypothalamic centers. The anterior hypothalamus is believed to be the sensory receptor organ for thermoregulation (Benzinger 1960). There is also evidence to indicate that cutaneous temperature is more important than brain temperature in instigating adequate response to ambient temperature. The skin, respiratory surfaces, and endocrine glands influence both behavioral and physiological adjustment. However, the distinction between the behavioral and physiological processes of thermoregulation is an arbitrary one made mostly for the purposes of study.

Behavioral adjustments in hot weather

Animals tend to seek the microenvironment in which they find themselves most comfortable. They seek any shade that is available; for example, sheep look for shade particularly for the head, but if none is available, they face away from the sun and cease walking or grazing. Swine frequent wet spots in the shade and often wallow in the mud, water, or areas wet with urine and feces; and if they have access to soil, pigs root up the ground and lie on the cooler subsoil. If a water pool is present, they root around in it and wallow to cool themselves by evaporative loss; they turn over from time to time exposing their moist side to the air. Pigs adopt a sleeping position with their snouts against the cool wind. During hot weather unshorn sheep become lethargic and lie stretched out on their sides. When the thermal and solar load is high in the desert, camels orient themselves while sitting so that minimum surface is presented to the sun. The behavioral adjustment to thermal stress varies with different breeds of cattle of the same species. The exposure of European breeds to thermal stress causes panting, drooling, sweating, and increased water consumption. However, Brahman cattle can withstand hot, wet climates.

In the tropics, ruminants reduce their heat production by voluntary anorexia. This reduction in feed intake as a means of reducing the heat load is reflected in the grazing pattern. Animals usually graze during the hours of comfortable temperature; during extreme heat animals tend to increase nocturnal grazing.

In general, water intake is fundamentally a function of water loss, which in turn depends upon ambient temperature and other factors. The restriction of water in cattle reduces dry-matter intake, more so in Brahman cattle than in European breeds. Small desert mammals avoid high temperatures by feeding at night and by remaining underground during the day. Due to the scarcity of accessible drinking water in the desert, the kangaroo rat (*Dipodomys*) utilizes metabolic water with great physiological efficiency; evaporative water loss is reduced to a minimum and the urine is highly concentrated. The pack rat (*Neotoma*) derives its water from succulent plants.

Behavioral adjustment and heat conservation

The newborn animal thermoregulates poorly, especially in species with altricial young, such as cats and rats. Baby pigs are dependent on heat from their mother and are unable to regulate their own temperature until a few days old. Conservation of heat by huddling is a basic factor in social behavior in several polytocous species at birth.

The inclination in pigs to huddle is common in cold climates. Pigs may lie on top of one another in subzero temperature when shelter is limited. Animals covered with hair or fur face into the cold wind so that the blanket of warm air held in the coat is not driven out by the wind.

GRAZING BEHAVIOR

Patterns

The pattern of prehension of forage varies with the species and is related to the anatomy of the jaw and teeth and the capacity of the stomach. Horses grasp the herbage between their incisors and tear it off. Cattle depend mostly on their mobile tongue which emerges from the mouth to encircle a mouthful of grass and to draw it into the mouth. Thus cattle cannot graze closer than one-half inch from the soil. Sheep overcome this difficulty with their cleft upper lip which permits very close grazing. With their lower incisor against the dental pad, they can sever the grass by jerking the head slightly forward and upward. Because of the anatomy of their snout and the structure of their simple stomach, pigs cannot graze efficiently.

As the animal gathers the preferred forage, it progresses slightly to the right, left, or forward. The time during which the animal bites uninterruptedly varies greatly (Hancock 1950): on a sward 4–4½ inches in height cattle may graze up to 30 minutes. The total grazing time increases when the quantity or quality of forage is low (Hancock 1955).

The pattern of grazing and rumination behavior in cattle and sheep is summarized in Table 47.2. The daily grazing time, grazing distance, total rumination time, number of boluses regurgitated per day, and number of chews per bolus were higher for sheep than for cattle.

Cattle and sheep graze during 4 to 7 periods each 24 hours. Intensive grazing begins around sunrise and stops about sundown, and the longest periods of grazing occur in the early morning and between late afternoon and dusk. Thus the onset of early morning grazing is correlated with the season of the year (Fig. 47.1). In dairy cattle 3–4 grazing periods occur between the morning and evening milkings and 1–2 grazings after the evening milking. The grazings immediately following the milkings are generally the major ones. When the daytime temperature is high the animals tend to increase their night grazing. The grazing periods are well defined on pastures with highly palatable plants, whereas grazing on pastures with unpalatable plants is very irregular. Periods of grazing alternate with periods of exploring, idling, and ruminating. In general, the herd functions as a unit. All herd members engage in the same activity at the same time.

Table 47.2. Comparative grazing behavior in cattle and sheep

	Pattern	Average values* (24 hr period) Cattle	Sheep
Grazing	Number of grazing periods	4–7	4–7
	Total grazing hours	4–9	9–11
	Grazing distance (miles)	2–3	3–8
	Dry matter grazed/head (kg)	5.9–12.3	0.5–1.3
	Dry matter grazed/45.4 kg body wt. (kg)	0.6–2.7	0.3–0.9
Rumination	No. of rumination periods	15–20	15
	Total rumination time (hr)	4–9	8–10
	No. of boluses regurgitated	360	500
	No. of chews/bolus	50	80

* Subject to variations according to type, breed, and age of animal; climate; botanical and chemical composition of pasture; and managerial factors.

Data from Hafez, Schein, and Ewbank, in Hafez, ed., *The Behavior of Domestic Animals*, Baillière, Tindall & Cassell, London, 1969

Animals graze selectively: they eat specific parts of individual plants or particular species at different stages of growth. Two phases are recognized: progressive defoliation, the selection of only the most succulent parts of the plant; and creaming, the selection of only certain plant species. Selective grazing has been studied by comparing the chemical composition of forage samples obtained by harvesting to that taken from esophagus-fistulated animals that have foraged on a wide variety of pasture.

Several psychological, physiological, and mechanical factors are involved in selective grazing. Goats, which

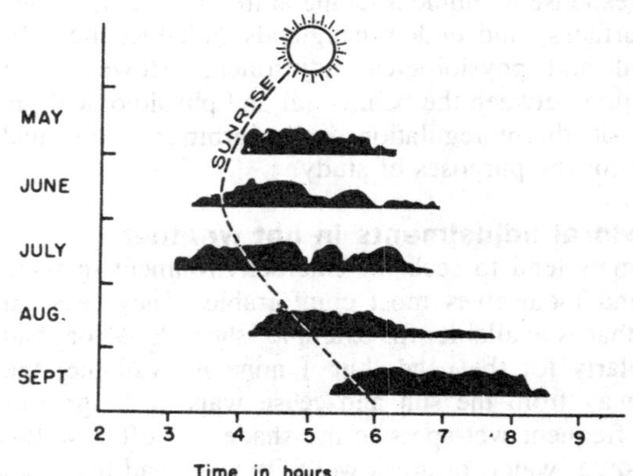

Figure 47.1. Seasonal variation in the time of first daylight grazing. Note the close relationship with sunrise. The heights of the black curves represent the intensities of herd grazing. (By permission from Hughes and Reid 1951, *J. Ag. Sci.* 41:350–66.)

are browsing animals, have bitter taste receptors, so they enjoy a wide variety of bitter plants that are distasteful to other animals. Goats have a higher threshold for bitter tastes than do cattle, but probably a lower threshold than do camels. The threshold of taste discrimination is partly genetic, since the threshold of discrimination for quinine in cattle was similar among monozygotic twins and different among fraternal twins (Bell and Williams 1959). Some plants develop chemical substances with distasteful flavor at late stages of growth and are then rejected by the animal.

Palatability of the plant species may affect the degree of selective grazing. Palatability is influenced by the properties of the forage, such as aroma, morphology, botanical composition, succulence, harshness, hairiness, leaf-to-stem ratio, manurial treatment, and physical and chemical properties of soils. Cattle readily eat orchard grass, but sheep only do so if the grass is very immature. Sheep are relatively more fond of meadow fescue than are cattle.

Distance traveled

The grazing distance varies with the climate, topography, and availability of forage, as well as with the species and breed of animal. In countries where the seasonal variations in rainfall are extreme, the plant growth also shows extreme seasonality and the animal is forced to migrate for long distances in search of food. On an average, cattle travel 3 miles a day on the range. Sheep travel longer distances than cattle and goats. Cheviot sheep travel farther than the Romney Marsh when both are kept on hill country (Cresswell 1960). Breed differences in ranging behavior are related to the habitat in which the animals developed. In Canada, Cattalo (a hybrid between bison and domestic cattle) graze more frequently during the winter than do cattle (Smoliak and Peters 1955). Brahman cattle graze longer and travel farther than do the European breeds.

Grazing intake

The daily intake of fresh forage and dry matter of the grazing animal varies with the species and live weight. In three breeds of dairy cattle (Flechvieh, Braunvieh, and Hinterwälder, weighing 564, 518, and 386 kg respectively) the daily quantity of fresh forage consumed was 10 percent of their live weight. On an average, the daily dry-matter intake of herbage is 8.2–12.3 kg for dairy cattle, 5.9 kg for beef cattle, and 0.45–1.36 kg for sheep. Sheep appear to select and eat forage higher in total digestible nutrients (TDN) than do cattle. Breed differences in grazing intake may be due to anatomical and genetic characteristics causing differences in number of bites per minute, intake per bite, and efficiency of selective grazing.

Transmission of parasites

The grazing behavior of the animal controls the transmission of external parasites. Cattle usually avoid herbage contaminated by feces; thus they may deliberately avoid nematode larvae. Young lambs normally develop parasite resistance by ingesting larvae of common parasites. The trifoliate leaf of clover is likely to carry many strongylid larvae, whereas the upper leaves of grasses are relatively free. By selecting the clover leaves, sheep may collect most of the nematode larvae. The relationship between the life cycle of common parasites and the grazing behavior of their hosts awaits further investigation.

FEEDING BEHAVIOR

In ungulates, the prehension of grains, pellets, and roughage involves the use of the tongue, lips, and teeth. The rabbit nibbles its feed with its sharp front incisors and draws its head back to chew from side to side and also from back to front; the tongue seldom protrudes during eating. Unlike the teeth of ungulates, those of carnivores do not permit lateral grinding movements. The domestic carnivores normally eat only once per day and spend very little time in the process since they gulp their meal in large mouthfuls. They crack and swallow bones in pieces but cut meats and soft feeds into large chunks.

Specialized feeding patterns characterize certain species. Examples are rooting in swine, geophagia in cattle, coprophagia in rabbits, and primitive feeding habits in dogs. Pigs root and spend much time turning over the surface soil; some breeds root more vigorously than others. Since its olfactory sense is acute, the pig learns to seek earthworms and other subsurface feeds. In the Périgord county of France, pigs are trained to search for subterranean mushrooms (truffles).

Geophagia (earth eating), which is widespread in certain cattle breeds, does not seem to be due to a low sodium content in the herbage. The rabbit is a coprophagous species; it reingests its feces rapidly. The animal sits and bends its head down between its legs, or sometimes around its flank, to procure the fecal pellets directly from the anus. The fecal pellets differ in physical consistency from the familiar hard, round pellets that are voided onto the ground. The former are lined with mucus and contain secretory material from the cecum. Their reingestion may enable the rabbit to obtain certain of the B-complex vitamins synthesized in the cecum and large intestine by microbial flora (Baker 1944). Coprophagy is often called pseudorumination. The dog, which is descended from carnivorous stock, may show some primitive feeding habits, such as chasing poultry, burying bones, or carrying food from one place to another. The shape and size of different breeds of dogs have been modified by selective breeding, but the dentition remains suited for chewing meat and bone.

One of the fundamental concepts in group physiology

is social facilitation; this refers to any increment in the frequency, intensity, or skill in the behavior of an animal resulting from the presence of another animal. Group-fed animals eat more and gain more weight than isolated animals. In puppies, however, the effects of social facilitation are temporary: group-fed puppies center their dominance relationships about the food pan. The dominant animals overeat, and the subordinates become undernourished (James 1949). Social facilitation may also affect the feed preference as distinct from the feed intake. Laboratory rats in groups eat more than those in solitary rearing, but if offered both a standard solid diet and a glucose solution, the rats in groups eat more of the former but drink less of the solution than the solitary ones. The net result is still a greater caloric intake for the rats fed in groups (Soulairac and Soulairac 1954).

RUMINATION BEHAVIOR

The age at which rumination starts in young animals depends on the nature of the diet, and in calves rumination may begin in the first week of life. The bolus of ruminal ingesta is regurgitated and rechewed with lateral grinding of the jaw. Recording devices have been used to measure the frequency and intensity of jaw movement by an air manometer system or an ink-writing continuous recorder. Chewing the bolus during rumination is characterized by regular intervals of short pauses for swallowing and regurgitation; chewing during eating, however, is irregular. During rumination the animal often lies slightly to one side with the forelegs bent under the chest and the hind limbs brought forward to lie partly under the body. Rumination may also occur while the animal is either standing quietly or walking slowly.

The average daily rumination time ranges from 4 to 9 hours (see Table 47.2); this includes the time spent in regurgitation, mastication, swallowing of ingesta, and the brief intervals between boluses. The daily rumination time is approximately three quarters of the time spent in grazing. The relationship of rumination time to grazing time is influenced by climate and the quality and quantity of herbage.

The stimuli responsible for the onset and cessation of rumination have not been elucidated; physical factors in the rumen and several neural stimuli are involved. Regurgitation is brought about by the fall in esophageal pressure that occurs with the decrease in intrathoracic pressure caused by deep inspiration with the glottis closed. The positive pressure produced by ruminal contraction might also play a part in the regurgitation phase of rumination. The peripheral receptors situated in the reticulum and distal esophagus may be activated by contact with fibrous ingesta, and their afferent inflow may subsequently induce rumination. The posterior medulla oblongata is a region of the CNS that controls rumination (Ruckebusch 1963). Iggo (1951) postulated that a reticuloruminal motor center, caudal of the intercollicular plane in the brain, maintains the coordinated activity of the reticulum and the rumen. The reticuloruminal center shows an inherent rhythm similar to that of the respiratory center, and like it, receives modulation from the reticulum itself as a feedback controlling mechanism. The reflex masticatory movements of rumination do not require the stimulus of ingesta in the mouth.

The electrical stimulation of lateral regions of the hypothalamus of unanesthetized goats caused them to become calm and drowsy and after a few minutes to start ruminating. The fact that milking often induces rumination in goats suggests a common afferent channel with anatomical pathways in the hypothalamus (Andersson et al. 1958) or through the ascending reticular formation of the brain stem. Rumination is inhibited by a variety of circumstances, such as hunger, fear, pain, curiosity, or maternal anxiety. During estrus, rumination is reduced in intensity and extent but does not cease.

SEXUAL BEHAVIOR OF MALES

Sexual behavior (in both males and females) is influenced by social environment, sensory capacities, and sexual stimuli.

Patterns

Patterns of sexual behavior can be classified into three groups: precopulatory patterns or courtship, copulatory patterns, and postcopulatory patterns or orgasmlike reactions. The duration of precopulatory behavior is long in swine, horses, and dogs, intermediate in cattle and sheep, and brief in rabbits. The male detects proestrous females and remains in their general vicinity. Bulls and stallions often show partial erection, protrusion, and dribbling of some accessory fluid. The male often displays masculinity patterns; bulls may paw and horn the ground, throw dirt over their backs, and rub their necks. All wild and domestic *Artiodactyla* except pigs exhibit a characteristic pattern called lipcurl. The male stands very rigidly and holds his head in a horizontal position with the neck extended and the upper lip raised (Fig. 47.2). The head may move slowly from side to side. The duration of lipcurl is quite variable and ranges from 10 to 30 seconds. The stimulus to lipcurl seems to be the smell of urine, although some males show lipcurl after sniffing the female's genitalia. Some males lower the head to the ground, then go into lipcurl, probably having smelled a place where a female had urinated. Prior to mounting, the male rests his chin on the estrous female which in turn responds by standing still or even exerting some back pressure. Species differences in precopulatory behavior are shown in Table 47.3.

Vocalization associated with courtship is well marked in swine and sheep. The boar emits mating songs (*chant*

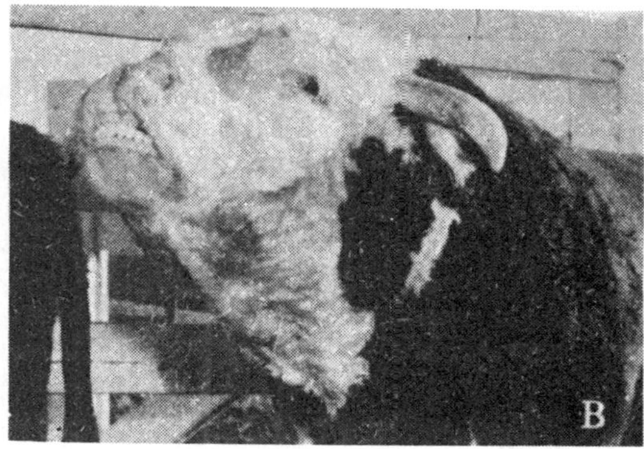

Figure 47.2. Lipcurl (*Flehmen* or *la moue*). In the stallion, the corners of the mouth and ears appear to be drawn backward and the facial muscles are tense. (Photo A from Wierzbowski 1959, *Roczn. Nauk Roln.*, ser. B, 73:753; Photo B from E.S.E. Hafez and M.W. Schein, in Hafez, ed., *Behavior of Domestic Animals*, 2d ed., Baillière, Tindall & Cassell, London, 1969.)

de cour), a regular series of soft, guttural grunts, about 6–8 per second at an intensity of 85–95 db (decibels).

Intromission in horses takes place after several pelvic oscillations which stimulate the engorgement of the penis with blood. At full erection and after intromission, the glans penis forms the shape of a basin. Before ejaculation, the penis is kept quite still and tight against the vaginal wall for some seconds; the semen is then ejaculated with great pressure, entering the uterus directly. In cattle and sheep, intromission is achieved when the muscles (particularly the rectus abdominis muscle) contract suddenly and the forelegs are fixed on the female's pelvis. In the boar, the penis is fully unsheathed only when the penis tip penetrates either the vaginal or rectal orifice. After a rectal intromission there may be a series of pelvic thrusts, but the penis is usually withdrawn without ejaculation.

Among farm animals, the stallion and boar have the longest ejaculation time and the greatest ejaculate volume (see Chapter 54). During ejaculation, the haunches of the male are clenched together and pressed forward, and a muscular wavelike movement of the perineum is visible as anal winking. One of the testes may be retracted, causing a visible contraction of one side of the scrotum. In horses and swine, two or three separate waves of semen may be ejaculated before the male dismounts and slides limply from the back of the female. Ejaculation is followed by relaxation of muscular tension and dismounting.

Intensity

The intensity of sexual behavior is usually assessed as the latency of ejaculation (reaction time), the number of ejaculations during a given period of time, the maximum number of ejaculations until exhaustion (depletion test), or the recovery period after sexual exhaustion.

The intensity varies with the species, degree of sexual rest, age, and climate. Hale and Almquist (1960) re-

Table 47.3. Species differences in precopulatory behavior

Species	Female	Male	
		Locomotor patterns	Vocalization
Cattle	Mounts or solicits mounts from another female; raises and switches her tail; may become separated from other females	Guards female (stands with female head to tail); paws and horns the ground; throws dirt over his back and withers	Snorts with head lowered and nostrils distended
Sheep	Rubs neck and body against male; roams around male and sniffs his genitalia; shakes tail vigorously	Sniffs urine of estrous female; runs tongue in and out; nudges and steps back; moves along side of female rubbing her wool	Gives several series of staccato grunts
Swine	Attains mating stance (rigid limbs and cocked ears) when pressure is exerted on her rump by chin of male or hands of attendant; licks male's sheath	Noses female's sides and flanks; pokes snout between hind legs of female with a sudden jerk; lifts her hind quarters; grinds teeth; moves jaws from side to side; frothy saliva at mouth	Gives regular series of soft guttural grunts (mating song)
Horse	Allows male to smell and bite her; extends hind legs; lifts tail sidewise; lowers croup; shrinks labia and exposes clitoris (some mares show no signs)	Smells groin of mare; grasps the folds of skin near the mare's rump with his teeth	Snorts
Dog	Initiates spurts of running; postures; noses male genitals; wrestles; turns tail sidewise	Faces female with forelegs lowered, hindquarters elevated, then bounces upward to normal position; urinates; noses vulva; paws female's back	Some breeds howl

ported that they have collected 6 or more ejaculations per week from bulls for 22 or more weeks with no deleterious effects. They also collected an average of 70 ejaculations per week for 6 weeks from a mature bull. At regular periods of sexual rest, stallions can copulate 2–3 times in several minutes. A maximum of 12 copulations was obtained during a 24 hour period.

Lindsay (1963) tested the seasonal variation in the intensity of sexual behavior of several breeds of rams. In order to eliminate the effect of seasonality of sexual behavior of the ewe, Lindsay tested the rams by placing them with estrogen-progesterone-treated spayed ewes. Border Leicester rams were least active in the summer and most active in the fall, whereas Merino rams showed a reverse seasonal trend. Great similarities in the levels of expression between identical twin pairs have been reported in bulls (Fig. 47.3). This observation shows the genetic effect on the intensity of sexual behavior.

The males of some species become apprehensive about

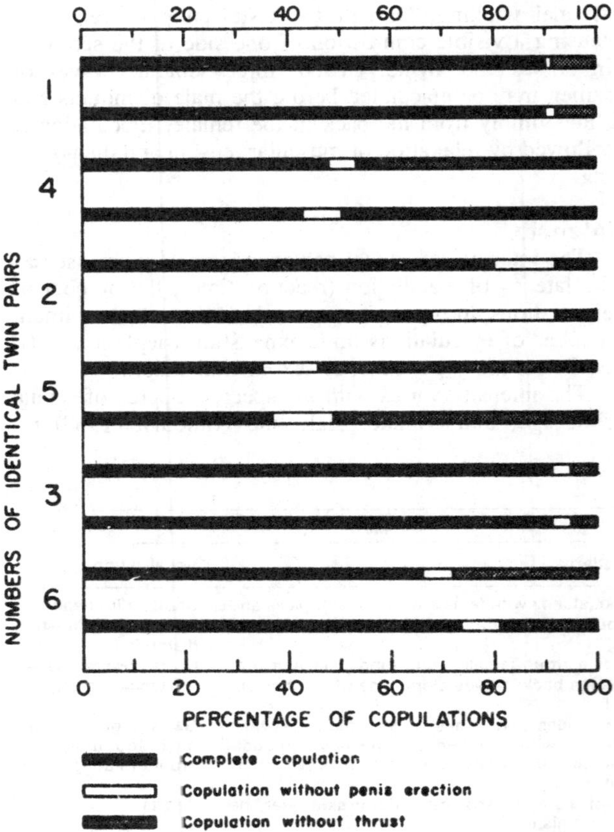

Figure 47.3. Ejaculatory behavior in identical twin dairy bulls in Sweden. Note the great similarities in the ejaculatory pattern of the twin brothers and the great variability among the twin pairs. (Adapted from Bane 1954, *Acta Ag. Scand.* 4:95–208.)

sudden changes in the environment, such as changing the farm, barn, cage, attendant, or locality. Since fear and apprehension inhibit sexual expression, the intensity of sexual behavior may decline when males are transported to a new environment. The period required for adaptation in a new environment varies with the species and age, and is longer in old animals than in young ones. In rabbits and dogs, breeding is facilitated when the female is brought to the male's quarters as compared with the reverse. Some males are inhibited in the presence of a human observer. Other males are aided by the presence of a familiar person, particularly if the female is overactive.

Stimuli eliciting sexual behavior

The stimuli by which the male detects females in estrus have been the subject of conjecture. It has been claimed that the odor of vaginal secretions and of the perineal region are important cues. The characteristic pattern of lipcurl after smelling voided urine from estrous females has also been claimed as evidence of the importance of olfactory cues in detecting estrus. Although rams deprived of the sense of smell cannot immediately determine which ewes are in estrus, they readily adopt a trial-and-error system involving actual attempts to copulate. Young stallions usually show poor or no response to a dummy, yet sexual behavior is elicited when the dummy is sprinkled with urine from the estrous mare. However, Wierzbowski (1959) inhibited olfactory stimuli of adult stallions with nose masks soaked with trichloroethylene, and he found no inhibition in sexual behavior. When both olfactory and visual stimuli were inhibited, the stallion manifested erection and mounting even when a cow was used as a sexual stimulus. The detection of females in estrus is a complex process involving several sensory modalities, as well as the previous sexual experience of the male.

The development of sexual behavior is influenced by the social environment. Valenstein and Young (1955) found that guinea pigs raised in social groups developed more sexual activity than those raised in isolation. When castrated, both groups dropped to the same minimal level. Androgen replacement therapy, however, caused the sexual activity level of each group to rise to the level that had characterized it before castration. Such results indicate that early experience of the male helps determine the type of effect that exogenous hormones will have on behavior. The deleterious effects of solitary rearing seem to be permanent. Also these effects are quantitative in nature; some males are much more seriously affected than others.

The expression of sexual behavior of males in close competition for estrous females depends on the relative social dominance of individual males; this effect is reduced in large herds and under range conditions where the males can keep apart and gather about them small groups of estrous females.

Physiological mechanisms

Hormonal factors

Copulation can be performed successfully after hypophysectomy, but gonadal hormones are more directly important for sexual behavior. In most farm animals, castration reduces or abolishes sexual behavior, whether the operation is performed before or after puberty. In contrast, male Rhesus monkeys castrated at 3 months showed normal development of sexual behavior; the capacity for erection was retained and characteristic masculine patterns continued to develop normally in the complete absence of testicular androgen. The injection of androgens is effective in restoring sexual behavior following castration when sexual activity is reduced. Individual differences in sexual behavior follow castration. Individual differences in sexual behavior of male guinea pigs before castration continued to be displayed when the animals received equivalent amounts of testosterone after castration (Grunt and Young 1952).

The effects of castration on sexual behavior also depend in part on the animal's previous experience. A male cat that has not copulated before is likely to be sexually unresponsive after castration, but in an experienced male the mating pattern will probably persist (Rosenblatt and Aronson 1958). Once organized through experience, the sexual pattern becomes partly independent of hormones. The relative importance of gonadal hormones for sexual behavior in farm animals is still controversial, but it seems that sexual behavior is independent of the influence of the gonadal hormones if the animal is castrated in adult life and after sexual experience.

Precoital stimulation affects both composition of the ejaculate and androgen secretion. Sexual stimulation of bulls causes an immediate release of luteinizing hormone (LH) followed by a peak of testosterone, if the blood level of this hormone is low at the time of stimulation (Katongole et al. 1971). Erection is primarily under the control of the parasympathetic system.

Neural factors

It has long been held that the neural mediators of sexual behavior in male mammals are different from those in females. The neocortex is more involved in the mating performance of the male than the female. Copulatory patterns of the male are controlled by complex pathways from the autonomic nervous system. Both erection and ejaculation involve muscular contractions and cortical coordination primarily triggered through the sacral autonomic (parasympathetic) nerves. The secretions of the accessory glands are attributed to the sympathetic system. Ejaculation is also elicited by tactile stimuli (warmth of vagina and slipperiness of mucus) acting on the receptors in the penis. The penis of the bull and ram is quite sensitive to temperature, whereas that of the stallion is more sensitive to pressure exerted by the vagina.

Sexual arousal is initiated by the secretion of steroid hormones, released in the blood stream to be bound to receptor sites in the CNS. In the sow and ewe, blood estrogens reach a peak some 24 hours after onset of estrus.

Several hypothalamic centers control certain components of sexual behavior independently of those involved in the regulation of the pituitary-gonadal axis. Extensive investigations have been undertaken to identify a possible sexual center in the hypothalamus. Electrolytic lesions in the anterior preoptic area prevented copulatory activity but did not inhibit the secretion of gonadotropins in the male.

Abnormal sexual behavior

Several abnormal patterns of sexual behavior have been observed: expression of all the chain of events of copulation except ejaculation; courtship and mounting without erection and/or protrusion; failure to mount, but licking the vulvar region and hind quarters of an estrous female; no apparent interest other than standing near or following the estrous female; failure to detect an estrous female; avoidance of or disinterest in an estrous female. Also, incomplete intromission and lack of pelvic oscillations after intromission, which are partly hereditary, may appear in young stallions at the onset of their sexual life and may persist during subsequent years.

Males reared in isolation from females will often display sexual behavior toward inanimate objects of suitable size and simple shape. Boars reared in pairs or all-male groups often form stable homosexual relationships; this behavior persists even though both members repeatedly copulate with females. Pillows or furniture may elicit sexual responses in dogs and become habitual objects for self-stimulation. Masturbation is common in cattle and horses. The bull arches his back, performs pelvic movements, and passes his penis in and out of the preputial orifice, which provides the tactile stimulation for ejaculation. In some cases, contraction of the abdominal muscles is so strong that the front and hind legs cross each other and the bull loses his balance. Masturbation is very common among show bulls; high-protein diets probably raise the sensitivity of the penis to tactile stimulation. The stallion rhythmically rubs his rigid erected penis against his hypogastrium, then lowers the croup, makes forward movements of the pelvis, and ejaculates.

Sexual behavior and semen collection

The expression of sexual behavior and the ability to produce viable spermatozoa do not appear to be correlated. Under hot conditions (110°F), Australian Merino rams continue to copulate freely, but their semen quality declines markedly (Lindsay 1963). On the other hand, Dorset Horn rams retain the ability to produce reasonable-quality semen but show a low intensity of sexual behavior. Such breed differences are partly due to the degree of adaptability to the prevailing environment and to breed differences in the cooling efficiency of the scrotum.

The concept of stimulus pressure has been used to explain the total sexual stimulation impinging on the male (Hale and Almquist 1960). Various methods have been used for precoital stimulation to increase the stimulus pressure during semen collection, such as a period of restraint (2–20 min), false mounts, pursuit of a teaser female, presence of another male, or changing the teaser female. A false mount or a period of restraint causes an increase in semen volume, concentration, and the number of spermatozoa in bulls. High stimulus pressures associated with changing the stimulus animal or the settings increase the ejaculation per unit time in the bull. The recovery period after sexual satiety varies among species, breeds, and individuals. If the recovery is slow, the male shows steadily increasing reaction time to ejaculation and may eventually fail to respond for a prolonged time.

In artificial breeding centers the sexual behavior of males may be inhibited by repeated frustration, faulty management, wrong techniques during semen collection, distraction during copulation, and too rapid withdrawal of the animal after copulation. Incomplete erection, incomplete ejaculation, or abortive ejaculation often occurs as a result of psychological disturbances, for example, shipping stress, changing the barn, or changing the herdsman.

SEXUAL BEHAVIOR OF FEMALES

Patterns of behavioral estrus

Three distinct behavioral patterns can be recognized during estrus: malelike mounting, increased spontaneous activity, and copulatory responses. The manifestation and intensity of these behavioral responses vary with the species (see Table 47.3).

Estrous females may mount other females; this pattern is observed in swine and dogs but is most common in cattle.

Behavioral estrus in horses and swine is often associated with gross changes in the external genitalia. Estrous mares are characterized by erect clitorises, elongated vulvas, and swollen and partly everted labia. Estrous sows show swollen vulvas and mucous discharges from the vagina; they also mount other females. They frequently attempt to urinate in the presence of the boar. During late estrus there is a marked increase of spontaneous activity in swine, cattle, and dogs; this behavior is not present in the estrous ewe.

The onset of estrus is more gradual in the mare than in other domestic animals. The duration of estrus is influenced by the geographical locality, breed, age, season of the year, and possibly the total digestible nutrients in the ration. The duration of estrus is longer in light mares than in draft mares. The intensity of behavioral estrus is affected by genetic and environmental factors. Breed differences also exist: estrus in European breeds of dairy cattle is more intense than in beef or Brahman cattle.

During copulation the female displays specialized postural adjustments to facilitate or accommodate intromission by the male. These adjustments are commonly known as lordosis or sexual presentation. This pattern is quite marked in the female rat, which adopts a characteristic position with the coccygeal region raised and the tail to one side. The female shows little or no sign of postcopulatory behavior. Mares and cows may exhibit an orgasmlike reaction, since some females maintain a characteristic posture for several seconds after copulation. In this respect, Cordts (1953) measured the galvanic skin response of cows during copulation and found that the electrical resistance of the skin dropped suddenly at the time of ejaculation. Female captive elks show intense spasms following copulation; they assume a defecating posture and excrete a large quantity of vaginal fluids. The spasms usually terminate within 5 minutes.

Stimuli eliciting sexual behavior

The onset, intensity, and cessation of estrus are influenced by the stimulus pressure impinging on the female, for example, the presence of a teaser male, frequency and persistence of courtship activity, and presence of another estrous female. The stimulating effect of the presence of another estrous female may be partly due to social facilitation. In this respect, Hafez (1952) observed the onset of the breeding season of ewes of different breeds of sheep on the same pasture for 3 successive years. For the most part, he found that individual ewes came into heat sooner if other ewes were in heat.

The stimulatory effect of the presence of the male on the manifestation of estrus has been used to improve sheep fertility. Australian scientists introduced a ram to ewes during the transition from anestrus to the sexual season. The intermittent association with the ram increased the number of ewes exhibiting estrus and the lambing percentage. The effects of continuous association with rams throughout the year on the onset of sexual season in ewes is not entirely clear. Schinckel (1954) showed that intermittent association stimulated quiet ovulation (ovulation unaccompanied by estrus) in ewes that had not already begun cyclic estrous activity. The stimulation provided by the ram's presence is more marked in certain breeds and in certain localities than in others.

It would appear that visual, auditory, and olfactory cues play a role in the expression of estrus. The majority of estrous sows show a characteristic mating stance (rigidness in the hind legs) when pressure is applied to their backs by a herdsman. Signoret et al. (1961) have experimentally partitioned the stimuli that elicit this mating stance and have shown that the rhythm of the boar's courting song is an important cue. They tested estrous gilts that did not respond to hand pressure alone. When a recording of the courting song was broadcast during the test (as hand pressure was applied), 50–60 percent of these females assumed the mating stance. The number of positive responses decreased to 9 percent when the frequency of the boar's grunts was reduced by one half; 26 percent of the gilts responded positively to an artificial courting song only.

The substances responsible for olfactory stimulation of sexual behavior have not been identified in any species. The perineal glands of the boar secrete a lipophilic substance, probably muscone, that has an extremely penetrating odor. Since sows distinguish males from females without first smelling the genitalia, the olfactory cue might arise from salivary gland secretions. And different feeds seem to produce different odors in pigs; boars fed on garbage may be rejected by estrous sows fed on grains, suggesting that olfactory cues may be involved in mate preference.

Physiological mechanisms

Behavioral estrus is under the influence of sensory stimulation, hormone secretion, and central neural organization. These mechanisms serve independently as target areas for the ovarian and possibly the gonadotropic hormones in the manifestation of behavioral estrus and in the feedback regulation of the anterior pituitary gland.

In general, the female utilizes less complex locomotor adjustments than the male during copulation, and the sensory control of female sexual behavior appears more restricted to tactile stimuli. The display of spontaneous activity, malelike mounting, and copulatory responses are attributed to the gonadal hormones. Estrogen pellets implanted in castrated or spayed rats resulted in a considerable amount of voluntary exercise in both males and females. Mounting behavior in the cow is also increased by adrenocortical hormones. If a young female is spayed, normal sexual behavior does not appear; in a mature female spaying is followed by permanent anestrus and invariably by rejection of the male. Female rabbits, however, show irregular sexual receptivity following gonadectomy. Responsiveness is restored if suitable amounts of both estrogen and progesterone are injected. The hormonal factors essential for restoring sexual behavior in ovariectomized females vary among species. In sheep, the action of either endogenous or exogenous estrogen is greatly facilitated by previous treatment with progesterone (Robinson et al. 1956). A reverse relationship occurs in rodents; a primary dose of estrogen

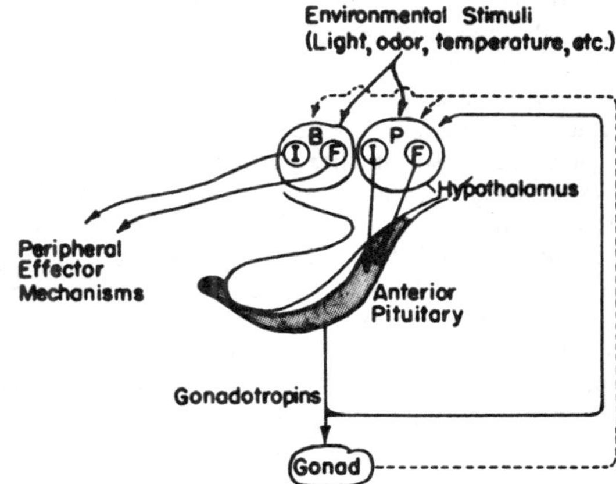

Figure 47.4. Facilitative (F) and inhibitory (I) hypothalamic mechanisms that influence sexual behavior (B) as well as pituitary function (P). The particular regions involved vary greatly among species. (From J.R. Johnson, Jr., R.W. Goy, and K.M. Michels, in E.S.E. Hafez, ed., *Behavior of Domestic Animals*, 2d ed., Baillière, Tindall & Cassell, London, 1969.)

should be followed by a small amount of progesterone. In dogs and cats, estrogens alone are sufficient to induce sexual receptivity.

The hypothalamus serves as a target organ for the gonadal and pituitary hormones. Thus the hypothalamus functions as an integrator of exteroceptive stimuli and as a feedback mechanism controlling the release of pituitary gonadotropin (Fig. 47.4). Certain hypothalamic loci participate in the display of sexual behavior independently of those involved in the regulation of the pituitary-gonadal axis. Evidence for a hypothalamic sexual facilitation mechanism has been obtained consistently in a variety of mammalian species. Lesions in the anterior hypothalamus abolish estrus in the estrous ewe without, at least in some cases, changing the cyclical endocrine rela-

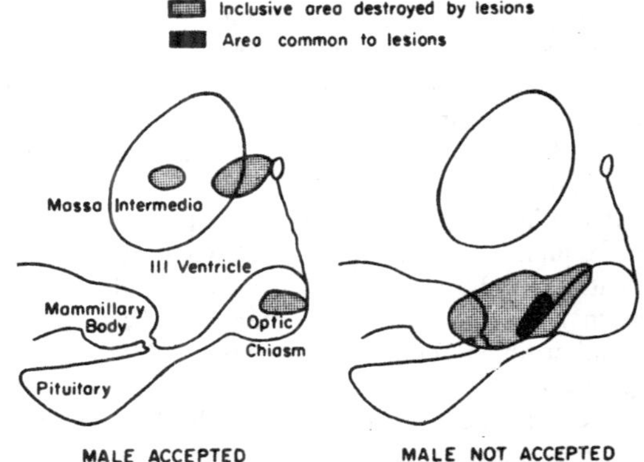

Figure 47.5. Effect of hypothalamic lesions of estrous behavior of the ewe. The lesions are projected on a midsagittal section of the hypothalamus. (From Clegg, Santolucito, Smith, and Ganong 1958, *Endocrinology* 62:790–97.)

tionship between the pituitary and ovary. Destruction limited to the massa intermedia or optic chiasma has no effect on cycles, but lesions in the ventral hypothalamus, with a common area just above the anterior median eminence, abolish estrus (Fig. 47.5).

The breeding season in sheep coincides with the shortest days of the year; this photoperiodic control is mediated by hormonal and neurohumoral mechanisms via the adenohypophysis. The relationship between environmental stimuli and pituitary-gonadal activities is confined to seasonal breeders such as sheep and some breeds of horses. In the female of other domestic species, endogenous rhythms (biological clocks) of control have evolved which replace dependence on environmental changes. The rabbit, cat, and ferret depend on the stimulus of copulation for the final pituitary surge of gonadotropins that cause ovulation.

Abnormal estrous patterns

Domestic animals may show several abnormal patterns of estrous behavior, such as nymphomania, split estrus, quiet ovulation, and weak estrus. Nymphomania is a hereditary disorder common in dairy cattle. The affected cows show signs of persistent estrus at frequent but irregular intervals; the voice, behavior, and general body conformation tend to become malelike. Cystic follicles frequently occur, although not all cows with cystic ovaries are nymphomanic. In fact, cystic follicles in cattle cause three types of abnormalities: nymphomania, anestrus, and anovulatory estrus. In anovulatory estrus, the ovarian follicle develops in cycles then regresses; behavioral estrus is manifested when the cyst reaches a certain stage of development. The continuation of the cystic condition and the cyclic nature of behavioral estrus are believed to be due to the degree of luteinization of the follicular wall which in turn alters the estrogen-progesterone ratio.

Split estrus and prolonged estrus are common in mares. In split estrus, the manifestation of estrus ceases for a short period followed by recurrence of sexual receptivity for what is evidently one full estrous period. Prolonged estrus in mares may last from 1 to 6 weeks. Split estrus is also common in cattle treated with gonadotropins such as pregnant mare serum.

Quiet ovulation (ovulation unaccompanied by estrus) occurs frequently before the onset of postpartum estrus in dairy cattle, at the onset and cessation of the breeding season in sheep, or on submaintenance diets. In large herds, subordinate females may show quiet ovulations. Ulberg (1968), checking the records of herds with high frequencies of quiet ovulation, noted that single cows in estrus were often not detected unless they came into estrus with another cow, in which case the two animals mounted each other and both were detected.

Weak estrus causes a decline in conception rate, but improved management during the sexual season will increase the chances that females with short or weak estrous periods will be bred by the male. Frequently, it is necessary to try several males before such females are bred successfully. However, the intensity of estrous behavior is so variable in any animal that selective breeding for this characteristic seems to be of little value in increasing conception rate.

MATERNAL BEHAVIOR

Maternal behavior includes the building of maternal nests, cleaning and care of the young at the time of parturition, retrieving of young that stray from the nest, and nursing and nurturing of the young. The preparturient female, which normally lives gregariously in a closely integrated herd, leaves the herd and seeks isolation and shelter. Lehrman (1961) pointed out that the postures taken by animals of different species during parturition are related to the manner in which they establish care of the young, and may be of considerable importance for the analysis of the development of maternal care. Rodents characteristically give birth sitting or crouching on the hind legs. The rabbit during parturition crouches with the back arched, the hind limbs flexed ventrally, and the head bent down between the front legs. Thus the vagina is oriented so that a fetus during birth is propelled forward and downward between the hind limbs of the doe and close to her mouth. The domestic ungulates and the elephant give birth in a standing position, whereas the pig, American elk, and guanaco may give birth in a reclining position. The sequence of events during parturition and related phenomena is shown for sheep in Table 47.4.

Postpartum placentophagy and licking

In most domestic mammals, the mother licks herself, the neonate, and the placental fluid. She tears the fetal membranes, bites through the umbilical cord, and eats

Table 47.4. Normal time variation in parturition and related phenomena in sheep

Pattern	Minimum	Maximum
Interval between onset of uneasiness and birth of lamb (hr)	1	3
Interval between bursting of placenta and birth of lamb (hr)	0.5	2
Interval between onset of labor and birth of lamb (hr)	0.5	2
Interval between first appearance of lamb and final expulsion (min)	15	60
Interval between birth of lamb and lamb's first standing on four feet (min)	15	30
Interval between birth of lamb and first suckling of teat (hr)	0.5	2
Interval between birth of lamb and expulsion of placenta (hr)	1	4

From Wallace 1949, *Proc. New Zealand Soc. Anim. Prod.* 9:85–96

the placenta and sometimes the bedding contaminated by the placental fluids. Placentophagy is widespread in both herbivores and carnivores. However, the camelids (camels, llamas, etc.) neither lick the young nor appear to be attracted to the fetal membranes or fluids. The pattern of placentophagy varies with the species. The sow seldom licks her neonate and usually pays little attention to the young until the last one is delivered; she roots the neonates along her belly toward the udder or pushes them back with a front foot. The bitch chews through the umbilical cord, cleans her own hindquarters, dries the puppy and directs it to her side; then she curls herself protectively around the puppy and rests until the next birth begins.

Licking of the neonate has a thermoregulatory function, especially under cold, wet, and windy conditions. If a newborn lamb is left without stimulation for as little as 1 hour, it may fail to stand and subsequently die. The lamb expends up to 70 Cal each hour; this energy is utilized to maintain body temperature, which drops at birth but normally rises again within a few hours. After 2–3 hours the total energy used may amount to a substantial proportion of the estimated initial energy reserve (Alexander 1958). The licking of the neonate by the mother also facilitates the beginning of urination and defecation. Baby rats isolated at birth die within a few days because they do not urinate. The survival of the young can be assured by stroking the genitals, which reflexly elicits urination; after such handling, urination occurs normally without further manual stimulation.

Postpartum licking and cleaning seem to be controlled by neural mechanisms, since such cleaning can be inhibited by destroying the neocortex or by hypophysectomy (Obias 1957).

Nest building

Maternal nest building is common in polytocous species, especially in swine, rabbits, and rodents. The nesting material, the onset of building, the choice of location, and the hormonal and neural mechanisms involved vary with the species, breed, and strain. Swine start nest building 1–3 days before farrowing. The sow carries the nesting material, such as green or dry grass, and roots and scratches the dirt of bare soils into a pile. The nesting area is usually kept clean, dry, and free of defecation or urination.

The quality and size of the nest are affected by ambient temperature; the activity is initiated by peripheral body cooling and inhibited by peripheral heating.

Nursing

Nursing is the behavior of the mother that fosters access to the nipples by the young; suckling is the behavior of the young sucking the nipples. Species vary in the pattern, frequency, and duration of nursing. Cattle, sheep, and horses stand during nursing; swine spend an equal amount of time lying down on the right and left sides. Once the sow lies on one side, she does not turn over during the same nursing period. Some sows always lie on one particular side and others favor the standing position. The tall mother moose (*Alces alces*) may squat or even lie down for nursing. The mother dog or cat spends most of the day with the young during the first week after delivery. One month after whelping, some bitches begin regurgitating their food, which is quickly consumed by the puppies; the response is stimulated if the mother is separated from her litter for several hours, then returned soon after eating. Rabbits seem to visit their young only once a day and allow suckling for only a few minutes. Species differences in the duration of the nursing period are in part correlated with the conditions of the neonate's habitat and the gregariousness of the species in adulthood.

The maintenance of nursing behavior depends on the presence of external stimuli from the young. Removal of the young causes cessation of lactation. By making the young available at regular intervals, both lactation and nursing can be greatly prolonged. This effect does not seem to be mediated by the pituitary or the ovaries. Female rats normally nurse for 25–30 days, but nursing behavior can be maintained for a year by providing a succession of foster litters. Throughout this protracted interval of motherhood, the females show estrous cycles at 18 day intervals and become pregnant without abandoning their foster litters.

Milk ejection refers to the sudden flow of milk which occurs 1–2 minutes after the beginning of suckling. The ejection of milk from the mammary gland is primarily controlled by the oxytocic hormone released by the posterior pituitary. The suckling stimulus consists of mechanical and tactile stimuli applied to the nipple; this stimulates the production of oxytocin. In dairy animals the level of oxytocin rises some minutes before the beginning of milking, presumably in response to stimuli associated with the preparations for milking. The effect of the suckling or milking stimulus is not directly on the mammary glands but on the CNS via afferent nerves from the nipples.

Milk ejection can be inhibited by many factors, such as emotional stress, discomfort, or pain. Physiological factors can also contribute. Malfunction of the mechanisms responsible for maintaining milk secretion or disturbances of the milk-ejection reflex that leads eventually to inhibition of milk formation may also be contributing factors (Cross 1961). Whittlestone (1951) carried out experiments in cows using faradic shocks as the emotional stimulus and suggested that a central inhibition of the reflex was more probable than a peripheral influence of epinephrine. Both central and peripheral mechanisms may participate in emotional inhibition of milk ejection.

Milk ejection is controlled by neural mechanisms involving the hypothalamus. The removal of the posterior pituitary abolishes the milk-ejection response; after hypertrophy and reorganization of the cut end of the neural stalk the response is restored. Direct stimulation of the anterior hypothalamus also affects other animals. Andersson (1951) reported that it induced milk ejection in sheep and goats. Cross and Harris (1951, 1952) also showed that electrical stimulation of the supraopticohypophyseal tract in rabbits induces milk ejection. Electrolytic lesions in the dorsal and posterior hypothalamus do not have this effect.

Suckling

The neonate is equipped with a few well-developed behavioral patterns, such as suckling and play, but most other patterns are developed under the influence of stimulation from the mother and subsequent learning. Neonates vary widely with respect to level of development at birth. In ungulates, the neonate is very precocious, standing and walking shortly after birth, and learning the source of its food quite rapidly and efficiently. The rodent neonate, although blind and deaf, can crawl under the mother's body, position itself, find a nipple, and suckle. The time needed from birth to first suckling varies among species and breeds from a few minutes to several hours.

Maternal behavior plays an important part in the suckling experience of the neonate. The mother guides the neonate to the location of the teat (until this is done the neonate will suckle any protuberance on her body). She accomplishes this by appropriately positioning her body or by licking, nuzzling, and nudging the young. In cattle, sheep, and horses, the mother will stand so that the young stands alongside, facing caudally. In swine, the mother's lying position attracts the suckling young. During the first days after birth, young pigs fight for individual teats until they begin to assume a definite order on the udder. The most anterior pectoral and most posterior inguinal teats are appropriated earliest. By the end of the second week an order is established for the middle teats.

Suckling is also a factor in the success of nursing. The oral suction exerted by the young is mainly important for retaining the nipple, not for withdrawing milk. This tactile stimulus causes greater rigidity and protrusion of the nipple. Suckling rabbits are very active for 1–2 minutes after the beginning of suckling, then suddenly become motionless, simultaneously with the beginning of a characteristic gulping sound that indicates that substantial milk flow has begun. During this period, afferent excitation is being built up which causes the release of oxytocin from the maternal neurohypophysis. The lips of the young clamp around the base of the teats to trap the milk in the sinuses. Then the tongue is forcibly elevated to raise the pressure in the sinuses and force the milk to the mouth. In cattle, the number of pulsations during suckling ranges from 60 to 100 per minute.

The suckling young frequently wag their tails, a movement that appears to stimulate the mother to sniff under the wagging appendage. The sniffing seems to serve as a primary mechanism for recognition. Suckling in dogs is accompanied by rhythmic movements of the forelegs, which usually continue until the puppy has become satiated. In ungulates, the young suckle from either right or left sides of the udder and occasionally from the rear of the mother, with no apparent preference for front or hind teats. Some lambs may show a definite preference for suckling from a particular side of the udder. Others use both sides of the udder at random. In twins during late lactation, each twin generally suckles only from one side of the ewe's udder. Also, twins apparently suckle more often than singles during the first 4 weeks of lactation; by the fifth week the suckling rate is about the same; thereafter the rate of suckling tends to fall approximately equally for both twins and singles (Ewbank 1964). The increased suckling rate of twins may be due to allelomimetic behavior or to social facilitation.

The rate of suckling and the amount of milk consumed by the young vary with the species, breed, age, and size of the young. The suckling period lasts from 5 to 20 minutes. During the first few days of life the puppy remains on the nipple for about 20 minutes in each nursing period. In general, each suckling period is shorter as the young get older and is shorter at night than during the day. The number of sucklings per 24 hours is 1 for the rabbit, 3–4 for cattle, and 20–30 for sheep and swine. Breed differences in the frequency and duration of sucklings have been observed in beef cattle.

The urge to suckle is satisfied as the young suckles the mother's teat, but if the need is not satiated during nursing, nonnutritional suckling behavior will appear. Two groups of puppies were bottle fed on the same amount of milk; one group was fed from a nipple with very small holes so that they drank slowly, the other group was fed from a large-hole nipple so that they drank rapidly (Levy 1934). The puppies that were fed rapidly exhibited suckling movements after feeding time, made suckling noises while asleep, and tended to suckle their own bodies and those of other animals as well as to lick inanimate objects. None of these characteristics appeared in the animals that had longer suckling periods. Swanson (1956), using identical twins, estimated that calves suckling their mothers drink more milk than those bucket fed. Meanwhile, the rate of milk intake from a bucket is more rapid than from a nipple feeder when calves are sham fed. Bucket-fed calves tend to suckle each other after drinking and even during adult life, which poses a problem for the herdsman.

Mother-young interaction

The establishment and maintenance of relations between the mother and the young comprise a series of processes of great complexity and involve reciprocal interactions. The protection of the young is handled in many ways. The cow may hide the young until she returns from grazing with the herd. Sometimes a group of calves (calf pool) is deposited close together in a favorable location well secluded and protected from the wind. Mother elk (*Cervus canadensis*) visit the calf pools at intervals, each one keeping the yearlings at a distance. At times, one or two ewes will act as nursemaids to several resting or playing lambs while the other ewes are off grazing by themselves. Altmann (1956) observed that an aging bison cow may act as a guardian for the calves of other herd members; also, she may participate in herd leadership and safety activities. Little is known about such social organization in domestic animals.

Other manifestations of mother-young relationships are heeling, living separate from the group, and punishing. When heeling, the young follows its mother during grazing. The time when this response appears and disappears in neonatal life varies with the species. Separate living is enjoyed only by some species. The mother moose and her young form a small unit, living apart from the rest of the herd for a long time; yet the elk mother and young return to the herd very soon after parturition. Punishing occurs often in dogs. During the early stages of neonatal life, mother dogs exhibit intensive contact, nursing, and licking; these activities decrease as the litter grows older, apparently in orderly fashion (Rheingold 1963). The development of a mother-young relationship depends on constant contact, a possibility under undisturbed farm conditions. However, the relative importance of nursing per se and physical contact (comfort contact) on the formation of these attachments has not been determined for farm animals. In a given herd, the young tend to form young-with-young groups in addition to young-with-mother subgroups. After weaning, the young no longer depend upon the mother for protection; they assume their own place in the dominance order within the group and their ties with the mother are gradually broken.

Recognition of young

During the nursing period, the mother can distinguish her own young from others. As little as minutes or hours of contact during the neonatal period is sufficient for the mother to establish the identity of her own young. The reaction of the mother to alien young within the same species varies considerably among different animals. The mother sheep or goat rejects alien young more violently than do cattle and swine. This discriminating behavior results in stable mother-young units even within very large herds. Bison cows bred to domestic bulls, however, often fail to recognize and nurse their hybrid calves. Also, newly shorn ewes are often mistaken for other ewes by their lambs because of the mother's change in color and conformation.

Fostering

Immediately after parturition there is a critical period during which the attachment of the mother to any young animal is very strong. This drive declines rapidly after parturition, and the mother remains strongly attached only to her own young and strongly aggressive toward all other young. However, long after the sensitive postpartum period has passed, some mothers can be induced to accept alien young as their own. Goats and sheep establish the identity of their own young immediately after birth and can be induced to accept alien young only if given the aliens immediately after birth. Thereafter they vigorously repel any alien young that approach them. Fostering is especially successful with goats because goat dams separated from their young for one hour immediately after parturition fail to show normal, individual-specific maternal care. Since the mother's ability to recognize her own young increases with the age of the young, the time element in fostering alien young is very significant. Fostering is most successful when it is initiated within 2–3 days after parturition. However, fostering was successful with Beagle puppies 2–4 weeks old.

Various techniques to encourage mothers to adopt alien young have been tried. Hersher et al. (1963a) placed mother sheep and goats, 2–12 hours after parturition, in a restraining harness and forced them to remain continuously in closed proximity to an alien young. When released from the harness after 10 days, the mothers permitted the alien young to nurse and refrained from butting them. There was a positive correlation between the length of time necessary for an adoption to be established and maternal reaction to separation, but no relationship between adoption time and amount of nursing. In another experiment, an infant kitten was placed with a postparturient monkey deprived of her own infant. The female monkey accepted the kitten, cradled it, groomed it, and attempted to nurse it. These responses persisted for a few days, but the young was finally abandoned. The inability of the kitten to cling to the mother monkey in a manner similar to the behavior of the normal monkey infant seemed to be the basis for this abandonment.

Effect of separation

If the young are separated from the mother early in neonatal life but after the attachment has developed, the separation may have a severe effect on both mother and young. If the separated mother is approached by other young animals, she vigorously pushes them away. Puppies separated from their mother search ineffectively, crawl in circles, swing the head from side to side, and emit characteristic sharp cries. In sheep and goats the separation of the neonates from their mothers for a short period results in initial rejection of the young when they are returned to the mothers. If the young are nursed by the mother before separation, then the re-establishment of their relationship occurs much more quickly after the kid is returned than if the two are separated before the kid is nursed. Experienced ewes are accustomed to having their young follow close behind and become disturbed when the young fail to do so. Since kids tend to wander away, ewes rearing kids are often in a high state of disturbance, spend much time seeking the kid, and therefore tend to separate from the flock more than do ewes rearing lambs (Hersher et al. 1963b).

In spite of its academic and practical importance, little is known about the effect of maternal behavior on the development of subsequent maternal behavior of the young itself. For example, monkeys raised from birth by foster mothers exhibit maladaptive mating behavior and, in the few instances when pregnancies have occurred, defective maternal behavior.

Abnormal maternal behavior

Behavior that results in the death or injury of the neonate is clearly abnormal. Such behavior may result from disturbances to the mother during parturition or lactation. Abnormal maternal behavior in sheep includes early prepartum maternal care, temporary and permanent adoptions of alien young after birth, delay in the start of postpartum cleaning, desertion of young, and the butting of young by the ewe. Prepartum mothers may steal alien young, driving off the true mother from her own young. Young-stealing mothers are very persistent and will attempt the same behavior year after year. After their own young arrive, however, they no longer show interest in the young of other mothers.

SOCIAL BEHAVIOR

Social behavior refers to any reciprocal interaction between two or more animals and the resulting modifications. Thus social behavior includes sexual and maternal behavior, which were discussed in separate sections above for convenience.

Social organization

Social organization refers to the cohesion of a herd or flock into a fairly well-integrated and established group in which the unity is based upon the interdependence of the individual animals and upon responses to one another. The intensity of cohesion varies with the species, breed, environmental conditions, and psychological factors. Some species and breeds tend to graze in large groups, whereas others split into subgroups. Different breeds vary in gregariousness; the Merino and Rambouillet breeds of sheep are more gregarious than the Cheviot and Scottish Blackface Highland breeds.

Under range conditions, domestic animals show a high degree of social organization and strong social relationships. The different patterns of social behavior tend to draw the animals together, although the agonistic behavior tends to keep them apart. As a rule the older the animal at the time it is introduced into a new herd, the less integrated it becomes in the group; this pattern should be kept in mind in designing experiments. Also, in group feeding, dominant animals have higher priority than subordinates, and it is advisable to have adequate feed trough space in such experiments.

Dominance order

Dominance order (also called social hierarchy, rank order, or social rank) refers to the priority rating of a given individual in feeding and sexual opportunities as compared with others of the same species. Hierarchical social systems have an evolutionary advantage in that they reduce the amount of agonistic behavior; soon subordinate animals learn to avoid their superiors as much as possible. The dominance order is evaluated by direct observation of initial encounters: a contest between two animals is staged in an unfamiliar surrounding. In addition to recording the winner, other values have been used, for example, latency of fighting response, accumulated attacking time, and number of attacks. In domestic mammals there is little evidence of dominance order when adequate feeder space is provided. However, with inadequate feeder space, a dominance order is manifested by biting and pushing in pigs and by pushing or butting in cattle, sheep, and goats.

The dominance order is affected by several factors, such as age, weight, seniority, sex, and breed. Age is associated with seniority. However, body weight, locomotor abilities, and experience are closely related to age. Seniority seems to be an important factor in the attainment of a high degree of social order. In herds and flocks of mixed sexes several social ranks are established: one among the adult males, another among the adult females, and a third among the young. In most species, all adult males dominate all adult females since males are more aggressive than females; also adults usually dominate the juveniles. In the wirehaired fox terriers and Basenjis, the males usually dominate the females; whereas in the cocker spaniels and beagles, sex appears to have less influence on dominance (Pawlowski and Scott 1956). Different breeds of animals also exhibit a varying degree of dominance. For example, in the dog family, wirehaired fox terriers exhibit rigid dominance hierarchies, whereas beagle and cocker spaniels are less competitive (Fuller and Fox 1969).

The dominance order exerts a marked influence on fertility levels and possibly on population densities. In large herds and flocks, the males establish a social order, with the strongest, most aggressive male performing the majority of copulations. Such a male may prevent other males from copulation if the estrous females are limited in number. Since social dominance is not related to male fertility, a boss male that is infertile or diseased may depress conception rate.

Leadership

Leadership is the ability to initiate a new activity that will be followed by the other members of the group. This phenomenon is quite distinct from a dominance-subordination relationship in which an animal may drive another rather than lead it. It was believed that the dominant animal in the herd is also the leader, but this is not always true. Scott (1964) observed a naturally formed flock of sheep (closed flock) and found that the oldest ewes lead, followed immediately by their young lambs. Each ewe is followed less closely by her descendants of previous years. Thus the leader in such a flock is usually the oldest female with the largest number of descendants. In herds of cattle and horses the leader is usually a male, but in all-female herds one of the females must take over leadership.

Agonistic behavior

Agonistic behavior is conflict, fighting, and combative physical contact between two animals, usually of the same species. Joint attacks on an individual animal are uncommon.

Species differences in the pattern of agonistic behavior can be ascribed to anatomical differences in the skull, horns, and teeth as well as agility and locomotor capacities. Pigs bite, cattle paw the ground and bellow, sheep back off and charge headlong, goats butt with a sideways hooking action, and horses kick with their hind feet. Cattle have a characteristic threat posture: head lowered, eyes directed at opponent, and hind legs drawn forward perpendicular to the ground. Boars strut with hair bristled vertically along the dorsal midline, ears cocked, and head raised in an alert, threatening attitude. They may paw the ground, throwing loose soil in the air and champing throughout the fight. Individual animals differ greatly in the intensity with which they fight and in the extent to which they perform the separate locomotor patterns.

Males are generally more aggressive than females, and aggressiveness increases during sexual development as well as during the breeding season. In several species the mother shows increased aggression and defensive reactions while caring for her young. Fighting also increases when the feed or the feeder space is inadequate.

The intensity of agonistic behavior can be manipulated by various treatments. The injection of androgens tends to increase fighting in most species. The effect of castration on the intensity of agonistic behavior varies among species and age. Physiologically, the intensity of this behavior is associated with changes in the adrenal cortex. For example, the adrenal cortex is smaller in the domestic laboratory rat than in the wild rat. The neural regulation of fighting depends on a selective facilitation or inhibition of final effector systems, the neural mechanisms being located within the diencephalon. Neural factors in the forebrain are also involved in the expression of fighting. The removal of the amygdalar complex and the pyriform cortex reduces agonistic behavior in dogs, monkeys, and cats. Such influence may be mediated by the ventromedial nucleus of the hypothalamus.

COMMUNICATION

Communication between animals is important to convey their social status and intentions, to coordinate the activities and location of the herd members, to give warning of danger, to notify established territories, and to initiate courtship and copulation. Communication among subhuman mammals consists of acoustical, visual, tactile, and olfactory signals or various combinations of these. Small mammals are usually nocturnal, and so a nonvisual method of locating objects at a distance is appropriate for them. Except for seals and primates, most mammals have a strong sense of smell; dogs communicate by marking scent posts with urine or feces. Among domestic animals vocalization and changing the gait and body posture are the most common methods of communication.

Vocalization (acoustical signals)

In general, acoustical signals may function in (1) feeding, as in cries of hunger by young, food finding, and hunting; (2) warning and alarm calls that announce the approach or presence of an enemy, and the all-clear signal following the departure of a predator; (3) sexual behavior and related fighting, such as territorial defense vocalization; (4) parent-young interrelations to establish contact and evoke maternal care; and (5) echolocation for maintaining the cohesion or movements of the group (Collias 1960). Vocalization can be studied by recording the calls on a tape recorder and analyzing the sound spectrograms with a sonograph.

Acoustical signals are vocalizations with a tonal structure, within a narrow range of pitch, that characterize certain species at a special age and under certain circumstances. Often, the more vigorous the expiration, the better the higher overtones are developed (Andrew 1963). The type of vocalization varies among species, breeds, and strains. Calves bawl, lambs bleat, and puppies yelp or whine. Cocker dogs give a high-pitched yap, Chows seldom whine, bark, or howl, whereas Basenjis utter a low woof. Scott (1964) recorded the frequency of barking in cockers, Basenjis, and several of their crosses; he concluded that vocalization is genetically controlled according to Mendelian laws of inheritance.

Six types of calls can be recognized: suckling calls and location calls in suckling young; nursing calls by nursing mothers; distress calls and warning calls by adults; and sexual songs by the male during courtship. The nursing call of the mother is generally given in response to the vocalization of the hungry young. The location call, common in baby pigs, is given to indicate their location to the mother; the mother, in turn, responds by a similar and more powerful nursing call which generally has the effect of attracting some other young (McBride 1963). Sheep and goats will answer the call of any young lamb or kid, including those not their own or of the other species even though they will reject the alien young if it attempts to suckle. The young emit distress calls when they are hungry, hurt, or if they are separated from their mother; the type of distress call is related to the situation producing it. Puppies emit a characteristic cry when exposed to cold air, a cold cry that is distinctly different from the hot cry. Young rodents may squeal when they are hungry or when their body temperature falls below their comfort zone. American bison mother and young communicate by the initiation or intensification of grunts between the two in several circumstances, such as natural or artificial separation of mother and young (McHugh 1958). Distress calls are of special significance for neonatal survival when the young stray or fall from the nest.

Adult animals direct a distress call to the herdsman when hungry or separated from their young. In the horse a neigh is a distress call, a snort is a warning call. When two horses meet for the first time, they give the familiar whinny with the lipcurl similar to that of courtship. In sheep the sexual call is a hoarse interrupted B-a-a (grumble), the nursing call is a low M-m-m, and the distress call is a snort accompanied by stamping of one foot. Rheingold (1963) distinguished four classes of vocalizations in dogs: murmurs, nonprotest low vocalizations, including squeals, squeaks, and clucks; whimpers, protest low vocalizations, including whines, protests, complaints, and fussing; cries and yelps, louder protest vocalizations; and growls and barks. Some of these vocalizations develop in the first few days of life, others appear at later stages.

Body posture (visual signals)

Although vocalizations are the most apparent form of communication, postures with or without accompanying vocalization play a role in conveying specific information. In some wild ungulates communications are of the contact type: the young are managed and disciplined by crude contact handling, butting, biting, and pushing. In dogs an erect and rigid posture with raised tail, associated with low growls, serves as a threat signal, whereas tail wagging expresses pleasure. The role of tail wagging, commonly observed in sheep and dogs, is not completely understood. In dogs it may serve to distribute characteristic body odors which encourage recognition, but it also appears to function as a visual cue of peaceful intentions.

TEMPERAMENT AND EMOTIONAL BEHAVIOR

The terms tameness and wildness pertain to the reaction of an animal toward man. Tameness is defined as the absence of conflict behavior, and wildness as the tendency to escape. The tameness of domestic animals is partially the result of selection by research workers and animal breeders. Thus domestic animals differ genetically from their wild counterpart, and it is possible that the docility of tame animals is due in part to departures from the wild type. Also, horses, dairy cattle, and house pets have closer relations to man than beef cattle and swine because they are in daily contact with man. The former species become socialized during certain critical periods and become tamer. The tameness of the young seems to be influenced by that of the mother.

Temperament

The term temperament denotes a general consistency in the performance of specific actions in specific types of situations. It depends on physiological and genetic factors as well as experience and learning, and it can be selected for by inbreeding.

The temperament of the animal can be judged when the animal is subjected several times to physical restraint. Ewbank (1961) recognized four types of temperament in cattle according to their behavior in squeeze chutes (crushes). Submissive animals stand in the chute with their heads lowered and push forward, adopting a kneeling submissive state. Docile animals stand quietly in the chute and may even put their head into the trap. Alarmed animals try to back out of the chute and shake their heads from side to side. Greatly alarmed animals struggle, bellow, shake their heads, and defecate. As a consequence, alteration in the design of chutes should be based on the behavior of the animals to be handled. This will increase the efficiency in handling and make conditions more humane for the animals.

The temperament of animals is important in the handling of animals and in improving their productive and reproductive abilities. The temperament of the mother at parturition exerts an influence on neonatal mortality. Sows that are highly emotional and restless during farrowing cause high mortality of young by trampling. Cattle rated as considerably nervous had lower conception rates than less nervous cattle, but very placid animals also had a lower conception rate. However, uterine motility at copulation, normally under the influence of an oxytocinlike hormone, may be inhibited by the release of epinephrine if the animals are frightened.

Emotional behavior

Domestication has caused a marked decline in the degree of emotionality as measured by vagotonicity. Electrocardiographic records taken while rats were being physically restrained showed, in the case of wild rats that probably had tachycardia, a marked increase in heart rate, while there was little or no change in domestic rats (Richter 1954). Thus the reaction of wild animals to stress may vary from that of their domestic counterparts.

The degree of emotionality of the animal could be judged by subjecting the animal to some sort of social stress such as separating the young from the mother, combining strange animals in one group, isolation, overcrowding in the living space, or exposure to artificial sounds. The frequency and type of vocalization of animals under social stress may provide an objective measure of the emotional state of certain species. In general, the reaction of the animal to alarm situations is partly affected by the temperament of the animal, presence or absence of young, and experience during early life.

Animals exposed to artificial sounds show an alarmed reaction on initial exposure but quickly become conditioned to the sounds. Pigs were exposed to the following sounds: a fixed frequency at 104–120 db, varying frequency at 100–115 db, alternating sound at 115–120 db, and relative quietness (Bond et al. 1963). The typical reaction of a nursing sow to those sounds was initial alarm during which she arose to her feet and appeared to search for the source of sound, followed by resumption of suckling and apparent indifference to the sound. When baby pigs were exposed in the absence of the dam, they were alarmed and crowded together. No differences were detected in the responses to the various sounds of frequencies ranging from 200 to 5000 cps at 100–120 db intensity. Elliot and Scott (1961) tested the emotional reactions of young puppies and found that the most severe emotional reaction, when preceded by brief separation in a strange place, occurred at 6–7 weeks of age. This was near the end of the critical period for primary socialization and just before the period of final weaning to solid food.

Tranquilization

Tranquilization indicates a sedative or calming effect and a diminution in the intensity of nerve function without the enforcement of sleep. Various psychopharmacological drugs have been used to produce behavioral modifications by exerting their action on some part of the CNS. These effects vary from the mildest forms of sedation through profound narcosis to anesthesia and the loss of consciousness. Tranquilizer drugs (ataractic, neuroleptic, or neuroplegic) have been used as chemical restraints in wound treatment, grooming, removal of bandage or cast, castration, dehorning, collection of cerebrospinal fluid samples, shoeing, leading of nervous animals, and prior to surgery in a variety of zoo animals (Williams and Young 1958, Scheidy and McNally 1958). Such drugs are used too for quieting animals prior to semen collection or for nervous aggressive sows during farrowing. Range cattle under the influence of these drugs can be removed from their native pastures and can be shipped and placed in strange feed lots with less stress. Tranquilizers may also help prevent the development of shipping fever.

In vicious dogs chlorpromazine and related drugs injected intramuscularly or intravenously produced docile animals within 5–15 minutes. Various species of animals respond differently to the same drugs. The horse is apparently excited by the tranquilizer drug perphenazine (Trilafon), which causes a typical sedative action in some other large animals.

REFERENCES

Alexander, G. 1958. Behaviour of newly born lambs. *Proc. Austral. Soc. Anim. Prod.* 2:123–25.

Altmann, M. 1956. Patterns of herd behavior in free-ranging elk of Wyoming. *Zoologica* 41:65–71.

Andersson, B. 1951. The effect and localization of electrical stimulation of certain parts of the brain stem in sheep and goats. *Acta Physiol. Scand.* 23:8–23.

Andersson, B., Kitchell, R.L., and Persson, N. 1958. A study of rumination induced by milking in the goat. *Acta Physiol. Scand.* 44:92–102.

Andrew, R.J. 1963. The origin and evolution of the cells and facial expressions of the primates. *Behaviour* 20:1–109.

Aschoff, J. 1958. Tierische Periodik unter dem Einfluss von Zeitgebern. *Zeitschrift Tierpsychol.* 15:1–30.

Baker, F. 1944. Stability of the microbial populations of the caecum of guinea pigs and rabbits. *Ann. Appl. Biol.* 31:121–23.

Bane, A. 1954. Studies on monozygous cattle twins. XV. Sexual functions of bulls in relation to heredity, rearing intensity, and somatic conditions. *Acta Ag. Scand.* 4:95–208.

Bell, F.R., and Williams, H.H. 1959. Threshold values for taste in monozygotic twin calves. *Nature* 183:345–46.

Benzinger, T.H. 1960. The sensory receptor organ and quantitative mechanism of human temperature control in warm environment. *Fed. Proc.* 19, pt. 2 (suppl. 5):32–43.

Bond, J., Winchester, C.G., Campbell, L.E., and Webb, J.C. 1963. Effects of loud sounds on the physiology and behavior of swine. *USDA Tech. Bull.* no. 1280.

Clegg, M.T., Santolucito, J.A., Smith, J.D., and Ganong, W.F. 1958. The effect of hypothalamic lesions on sexual behavior and estrous cycles in the ewe. *Endocrinology* 62:790–97.

Collias, N.E. 1960. An ecological and functional classification of animal sounds. In W.E. Lanyon and W.N. Tavolga, eds., *Animal Sounds and Communication.* Am. Inst. Biol. Sci., Washington. Publ. no. 7, pp. 368–91.

Cordts, H. 1953. Zur Kenntniss der Sexuellen Erregung bei Haustieeren. *Zeitschrift Tierzuckt* 61:305–52.

Cresswell, E. 1960. Ranging behaviour studies with Romney Marsh and Cheviot sheep in New Zealand. *Anim. Behav.* 8:32–38.

Cross, B.A. 1961. Neural control of lactation. In S.K. Kon and A.T. Cowie, eds., *Milk: The Mammary Gland and Its Secretion.* Academic Press, New York. Vol. 1, 229–77.

Cross, B.A., and Harris, G.W. 1951. The neurohypophysis and "letdown" of milk. *J. Physiol.* 113:35.

——. 1952. The role of the neurohypophysis in the milk ejection reflex. *J. Endocr.* 8:148–61.

Elliot, O., and Scott, J.P. 1961. The development of emotional distress reactions to separation in puppies. *J. Genet. Psychol.* 99:3–22.

Ewbank, R. 1961. The behaviour of cattle in crushes. *Vet. Rec.* 73:853–56.

——. 1964. Observations of the suckling habits of twin lambs. *Anim. Behav.* 12:34–37.

Fuller, J.L., and Fox, M.W. 1969. The behaviour of dogs. In E.S.E. Hafez, ed., *The Behaviour of Domestic Animals*. 2d ed. Baillière, Tindall & Cassell, London. Pp. 438–81.

Grunt, J.A., and Young, W.C. 1952. Differential reactivity of individuals and the response of the male guinea pig to testosterone propionate. *Endocrinology* 51:237–48.

Hafez, E.S.E. 1952. Studies on the breeding season of the ewe. *J. Ag. Sci.* 42:189–255.

Hafez, E.S.E., Schein, M.W., and Ewbank, R. 1969. The behaviour of cattle. In E.S.E. Hafez, ed., *The Behaviour of Domestic Animals*. 2d ed. Baillière, Tindall & Cassell, London. Pp. 235–95.

Hale, E.B., and Almquist, J.O. 1960. Relation of sexual behaviour to germ cell output in farm animals. *J. Dairy Sci.* 43(suppl.):145–69.

Hancock, J. 1950. Grazing habits of dairy cows in New Zealand. *Emp. J. Exp. Ag.* 18:249–63.

——. 1955. Studies in grazing behaviour of dairy cattle. II. Bloat in relation to grazing behaviour. *J. Ag. Sci.* 45:80–95.

Hersher, L., Richmond, J.B., and Moore, A.U. 1963a. Modifiability of the critical period for the development of maternal behaviour in sheep and goats. *Behaviour* 20:311–20.

——. 1963b. Maternal behaviour in sheep and goats. In H.L. Rheingold, ed., *Maternal Behavior in Mammals*. Wiley, New York, London. Pp. 203–32.

Hughes, G.P., and Reid, D. 1951. Studies on the behaviour of cattle and sheep in relation to the utilization of grass. *J. Ag. Sci.* 41:350–66.

Hunter, R.F., and Davies, G.E. 1963. The effect of method of rearing on the social behaviour of Scottish Blackface hoggets. *Anim. Prod.* 5:183–94.

Iggo, A. 1951. Spontaneous reflexly elicited contractions of reticulum and rumen in decerebrate sheep. *J. Physiol.* 115:74–75.

James, W.T. 1949. Dominant and submissive behavior in puppies as indicated by food intake. *J. Genet. Psychol.* 75:33–43.

Johnson, J.I., Jr., Hatton, G.I., and Goy, R.W. 1969. The physiological analysis of animal behaviour. In E.S.E. Hafez, ed., *The Behaviour of Domestic Animals*. 2d ed. Baillière, Tindall & Cassell, London. Pp. 131–91.

Katongole, C.B., Naftolin, F., and Short, R.V. 1971. Relationship between blood levels of luteinizing hormone and testosterone in bulls and the effects of sexual stimulation. *J. Endocr.* 50:457–66.

Lehrman, D.S. 1961. Hormonal regulation of parental behavior in birds and infrahuman mammals. In W.C. Young, ed., *Sex and Internal Secretions*. Williams & Wilkins, Baltimore. Pp. 1268–1382.

Levy, D.M. 1934. Experiments on the suckling reflex and social behavior of dogs. *Am. J. Orthopsychiat.* 4:203–24.

Lindsay, D.R. 1963. The fertility and behaviour of Merino, crossbred, and British breeds of sheep. Ph.D. thesis, U. of Sydney. Vol. 1.

McBride, G. 1963. The "teat order" and communication in young pigs. *Anim. Behav.* 11:53–57.

McHugh, T. 1958. Social behavior of the American buffalo (*Bison bison bison*). *Zoologica* 43(1):1–40.

Obias, M.D. 1957. Maternal behavior of hypophysectomized gravid albino rats and the development and performance of their progeny. *J. Comp. Physiol. Psychol.* 56:313–17.

Pawlowski, A.A., and Scott, J.P. 1956. Hereditary differences in the development of dominance in litters of puppies. *J. Comp. Physiol. Psychol.* 49:353–58.

Rheingold, H.L. 1963. Maternal behavior in the dog. In H.L. Rheingold, ed., *Maternal Behavior in Mammals*. Wiley, New York, London. Pp. 169–202.

Richter, C.P. 1954. The effects of domestication and selection on the behavior of the Norway rat. *J. Nat. Cancer Inst.* 15:727–38.

Robinson, T.J., Moore, N.W., and Binet, F.E. 1956. The effect of the duration of progesterone pretreatment on the response of the spayed ewe to oestrogen. *J. Endocr.* 14:1–7.

Rosenblatt, J.S., and Aronson, L.R. 1958. The influence of experience on the behavioural effect of androgen in prepuberally castrated male cats. *Anim. Behav.* 6:171–82.

Ruckebusch, Y. 1963. Récherches sur la regulation centrale du comportement alimentaire chez les ruminants. Thesis, Faculté des Sciences de L'Université de Lyon, France.

Scheidy, S.F., and McNally, K.S. 1958. Tranquilizing drugs in veterinary practice. *Cornell Vet.* 43:331–47.

Schinckel, P.G. 1954. The effect of the presence of the ram on the ovarian activity of the ewe. *Austral. J. Ag. Res.* 5:465–69.

Scott, J.P. 1964. Genetics and the development of social behavior in dogs. *Am. Zool.* 4:161–68.

Signoret, J.P., du Mesnil du Buisson, F., and Busnel, R.G. 1961. Etude du comportement de la truie en oestrus. *Proc. 4th Internat. Cong. Anim. Reprod.* (The Hague), Physiol. sec. 40.

Smoliak, S., and Peters, H.F. 1955. Climatic effects of foraging performance of beef cows on winter range. *Can. J. Ag. Sci.* 35:213–16.

Soulairac, A., and Soulairac, M.L. 1954. Effects du groupement sur le comportement alimentaire du rat. *Comptes rend. séances Soc. Biol.* 148:304–7.

Swanson, E.W. 1956. The effect of nursing calves on milk production of identical twin heifers. *J. Dairy Sci.* 39:73–80.

Ulberg, L.C. 1968. The reproduction of cattle. In E.S.E. Hafez, ed., *Reproduction in Farm Animals*. 2d ed, Lea & Febiger, Philadelphia. Pp. 255–64.

Valenstein, E.S., and Young, W.C. 1955. An experiential factor influencing the effectiveness of testosterone propionate in eliciting sexual behavior in male guinea pigs. *Endocrinology* 56:173–77.

Wallace, L.R. 1949. Observations of lambing behaviour in ewes. *Proc. New Zealand Soc. Anim. Prod.* 9:85–96.

Whittlestone, W.G. 1951. Studies on milk ejection in the dairy cow: The effect of stimulus on the release of the "milk ejection" hormone. *New Zealand J. Sci. Tech.*, ser. A, 32(5):1–19.

Wierzbowski, S. 1959. The sexual reflexes of stallions. *Roczn. Nauk Roln.*, ser. B, 73:753.

Williams, R.C., and Young, J.E. 1958. Professional and therapeutic rationale of tranquilizers. *Vet. Med.* 53:127–30.

CHAPTER 48

Autonomic Nervous System | by William J. Tietz and Peter Hall

The autonomic nervous system is responsible for the visceral (or vegetative) control of the animal's body, and traditionally it has been thought to provide motor innervation to glands, to the heart, and to organs having smooth muscle. However, the overall program of the autonomic system is to maintain the internal environment of the body within carefully defined limits. This internal control function is called homeostasis, or more descriptively, homeokinesis. The latter term incorporates many dynamic processes, the equilibrium of which is so highly controlled that under normal circumstances they appear to be static. As a mechanism for control, the autonomic nervous system must be considered to include not only the visceral motor neurons but in addition peripheral afferent neurons. The latter are nerve cells that conduct impulses to the CNS and provide the information upon which the system acts. The integrating centers utilize this information and activate the appropriate visceral motor neurons. The classic autonomic "system," the peripheral motor portion, is in reality merely the branch of the total autonomic program that executes its functions and as such is efferent in nature; that is, it conducts impulses away from the CNS.

The peripheral motor projections of the central autonomic areas are the parasympathetic (craniosacral) and sympathetic (thoracolumbar) efferent systems. Their combined activity is a modified reciprocal innervation, or it may be said that they act as visceral flexors and extensors; both are necessary for efficient execution of the central integrative programs. Similarly, the detection of changes and the conduction of information to the central integrative stations are as essential to the total mechanism as the integration itself and the subsequent peripheral execution. This basic principle of interdependence must be kept in mind in the study of the autonomic nervous system, since the division of the system into constituent parts, necessary for the sake of clarity, is quite artificial.

Associated with the efferent portions of the autonomic nervous system are various drugs that, when administered at dosages that produce effective blood levels, cause activity mimicking stimulation by either the sympathetic or the parasympathetic system. Such activity, the result of direct interaction between the blood-borne agent and the effector, but without neurological participation, is called either sympathomimetic or parasympathomimetic.

ANATOMICAL DIVISIONS

Central division

The core of the central portion of the autonomic system is the hypothalamus. This area receives specific afferent input and, through appropriate connections, exercises motor functions that produce modifications necessary for maintenance of the homeokinetic state. Superimposed upon the visceral functions of the hypothalamus is the influence of the cerebrum and the cerebellum. In the following discussions the hypothalamus will be considered first, and then the areas of the cerebral cortex and the cerebellum which functionally influence it. Studies made of these areas in man necessarily provide the basis for much of the following, but where information about other species is available, it is cited.

Hypothalamus

It is generally held that the parasympathetic system is served by the rostral and medial portions of the hypothalamus, including the preoptic areas, the anterior, dorsal, and dorsomedial hypothalamic nuclei, and the mammillary bodies. Sympathetically aligned structures are the posterior and lateral hypothalamic nuclei. The ventromedial nucleus is shared by the parasympathetic and the sympathetic systems. The sympathetic centers are more strongly influenced by the cerebral cortex, principally the frontal areas and the rhinencephalon, whereas visceral afferent input from the thalamus influences the parasympathetic nuclei.

Pathways that carry impulses away from the hypothalamus can be divided into three main groups: (1) those that conduct impulses to the higher centers, e.g. the thalamus and the cerebral cortex; (2) those involved with the neurosecretory process and the posterior lobe of the pituitary gland; and (3) those forming the descending tracts, the characteristics of which are more often clearly sympathetic or parasympathetic.

The primary route for descending fibers of hypothalamic origin is the dorsal longitudinal fasciculus, the periventricular system of the diencephalon. These fibers terminate in one of two ways. Some predominantly parasympathetic fibers end in the midbrain tegmental nuclei, the secondary neurons passing in the reticulospinal tracts to the preganglionic medullary or cord neurons. The alternative to the interrupted course is a direct fiber contact between predominantly sympathetic hypothalamic nuclei and the preganglionic or other afferent centers in the medulla. As an example of the latter condition, Okinaka and Kuroiwa (1952) reported that fibers from the lateral hypothalamic nucleus have been traced directly to the dorsal motor nucleus of the vagus nerve.

For a more detailed description of hypothalamic origins and tegmental and reticular terminations, see the comprehensive comparative work of Ariëns Kappers et al. (1960).

Cerebrocortical controls

The areas of the cerebral cortex that influence visceral function are not always strictly aligned with either the sympathetic or parasympathetic divisions. Rather, the particular responses elicited by electrical stimulation depend upon the quality of the stimulus (Sachs et al. 1949) and upon the overall autonomic tone of the animal at the time of stimulation. In general, it is agreed that the cortical areas exert an inhibitory control over lower autonomic centers, particularly those in the hypothalamus.

Because the cerebral cortex is the seat of higher neurological functions, it may be expected that the psychological state of the animal will have autonomic or visceral effects. The anxiety state in both man and animals affects gastric motility, producing stimulation that can lead to muscular spasm of the organ. The gastric vasculature is also affected, and hyperemia may result from anxiety. In man, neurosis and other mental illnesses are not uncommonly accompanied by ulcerative or spastic colitis, and surgical or accidental trauma of the cerebral cortex can cause gastrointestinal hemorrhage and perforation. Also in man, high blood pressure and atherosclerosis, among other visceral problems, may apparently be precipitated or aggravated by the psychic state.

The autonomic response elicited from a given cortical area differs with the species of animal. Comparative studies have shown the cat and monkey to respond to cortical stimulation in a sympathetic manner, whereas the dog's responses are predominantly parasympathetic (Crouch and Thompson 1939). Studies of responses in other domestic species have not been made.

Cerebellar controls

The cerebellum apparently does not contain centers that originate specific autonomic functions. The influence of the cerebellum on visceral activities is dependent upon the tonic state of those activities at the time the influence is exerted. It could be said, therefore, that the cerebellum is not the primary site for any autonomic functions but is important in the modifiction of existing tonic states through numerous indirect connections to autonomic centers. For example, in rabbits, cats, dogs, and monkeys, the anterior lobe of the cerebellum and, more specifically, the vermis and its caudal portion, the uvula, are generally accepted as being inhibitory to specific autonomic functions when these functions are in a state of centrally induced excitement (Moruzzi 1940, Ban et al. 1956). Such inhibition tends to return to normal an elevated blood pressure or an increased respiratory rate. Apparently, blood pressure and respiration in the normotonic state are not affected by the cerebellum.

Peripheral efferent division

The peripheral efferent portions of the autonomic nervous system, those fibers leading impulses away from the CNS, are classified as either parasympathetic or sympathetic. Initially, this separation was based on pharmacological activity, and when anatomical studies supported the separation, the synonyms craniosacral for the

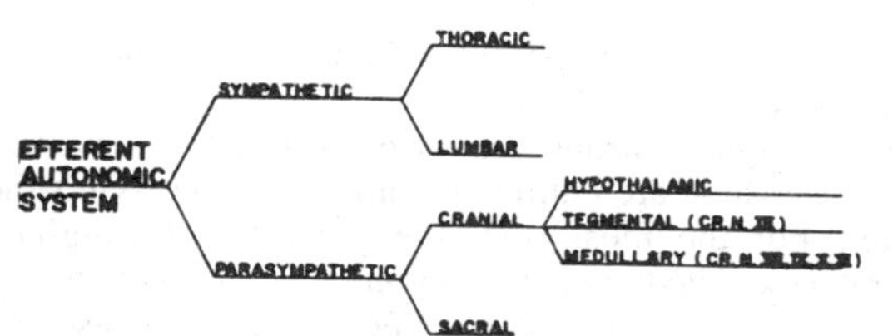

Figure 48.1. Organization of the efferent system. (From fig. 1, E.H. Polley 1955, *J. Comp. Neurol.* 103:253–68.)

parasympathetic and thoracolumbar for the sympathetic were introduced. The organization of the efferent system is presented in Figure 48.1.

The basic anatomical scheme underlying the efferent autonomic system is a two-neuron pathway with the cell bodies of the first leg of the pathway located in the CNS. The axons of these neurons leave the brain stem or spinal cord to terminate on ganglionic neurons located at varying distances from the CNS. The ganglionic neurons of the sympathetic system tend to be concentrated in grossly visible aggregates called ganglia, whereas the ganglionic neurons of the parasympathetic system are more likely to be dispersed in the wall of the innervated organ. Since the ganglion cell is a point of anatomical reference for the pathway, the neuron leading from the spinal cord or brain to the ganglion is called a preganglionic neuron and its fiber a preganglionic fiber. An axon of the ganglionic neuron itself is a postganglionic fiber. In the ganglionic synapse, the presynaptic terminal (or membrane) is actually the terminal of the preganglionic neuron, and the postsynaptic membrane is the dendritic zone of the ganglionic neuron.

One exception to the two-neuron pattern has been found. The glandular cells that compose the medullary portion of the adrenal gland are, in reality, modified postganglionic neurons. Autonomic innervation of the adrenal medulla, then, is from preganglionic fibers only.

Craniosacral (parasympathetic) division

Cranial division. The cranial efferent division is composed of axons within cranial nerves III (oculomotor), VII (facial), and IX (glossopharyngeal), which innervate structures of the head, and nerve X (vagus), whose projections supply parasympathetic innervation to the thoracic and abdominal viscera.

The autonomic preganglionic elements of the oculomotor nerve (III) leave the brain to contact ganglionic neurons in the ciliary ganglion or in the episcleral ganglia of the eye. Numerous inputs affect the autonomic oculomotor responses, including both pupillary constriction and accommodation for near vision.

Parasympathetic contributions to the facial nerve (VII) are distributed in three pathways. Some pass to the sphenopalatine (pterygopalatine) ganglion, from which postganglionic fibers innervate the lacrimal glands, nasal and oral glands, and their associated smooth muscle. A second fiber distribution is with the chorda tympani to provide vasodilatory and secretory innervation for the submandibular and sublingual salivary glands. The third group of preganglionic fibers passes directly to the sublingual and submandibular salivary glands and ganglionic neurons in the glands' surface.

Afferent fibers from taste buds in the anterior portions of the tongue provide some of the important nervous stimuli influencing the activity of these salivary glands.

The preganglionic neurons of the glossopharyngeal nerve (IX) pass to the otic ganglion or the tympanic plexus, from which the postganglionic fibers project secretory and vasodilatory fibers to the parotid and orbital salivary glands.

Afferent fibers to the salivatory nuclei originate in visceral afferent contributions from cranial nerves VII, IX, and X. These pathways provide the autonomic centers with gustatory impulses and are closely allied with the gagging and vomiting reflexes.

The principal parasympathetic origin of the vagus nerve (X) is the dorsal efferent nucleus of the medulla oblongata (dorsal nucleus of the vagus in the dog). The fibers emerge as the parasympathetic cardiac and respiratory visceral efferents and the abdominal visceral efferents.

The preganglionic fibers leave the medulla together in the vagus nerve, which provides parasympathetic innervation to all visceral structures from the caudal pharyngeal region to the upper portions of the colon. In the cervical region of several species, notably the dog, the vagus runs in direct contact with the cervical sympathetic trunk, the fibers of the two structures being intermingled. Preganglionic fibers generally terminate in neurons distributed in the walls of the organs to be innervated. Before terminating, the preganglionic fibers may ramify on the surface of organs to form plexuses. (These assume the name of the organ, for example, the cardiac plexus or aortic plexus.)

Afferent connections to the nuclei of origin of the vagus include fibers from the hypothalamus and projections from bulbar and medullary visceral control centers (e.g. respiratory centers, cardiac centers).

Sacral division. The sacral parasympathetic efferents leave the spinal cord with the ventral roots of the sacral nerves. The contributing sacral nerves vary from 5 in the horse and cow and 4 in sheep and pig, to 2 or 3 in the dog. It is generally accepted that the first 3 or 4 roots in the horse and cow and the first 2 in the dog make up the bulk of the sacral division in these species. These preganglionic parasympathetic fibers leave the spinal cord and with the sympathetic hypogastric nerves form the pelvic plexus, where some of the fibers contact postganglionic neurons while others apparently pass on through to make ganglionic contacts in the walls of pelvic organs.

Distribution of the pre- and postganglionic fibers is by way of various subsidiary plexuses and nerves to the specific organs (e.g. urethral plexus, nervus erigens).

Control of pelvic viscera is to some degree a function of the preoptic and anterior regions of the hypothalamus. The connections to the sacral preganglionic neurons from the higher centers are provided by fibers in the ventral portions of the spinal cord. The segmental afferent (dorsal root) fibers also distribute to the preganglionic neurons of the sacral division. Pelvic innervation is apparently well interconnected, and in experimental preparations a single sacral root can provide sufficient innervation to maintain normal parasympathetic function in such reflex activities as micturition, defecation, and sexual function.

Thoracolumbar (sympathetic) division

In the thoracolumbar efferent division, the two-neuron pathway also appears, with the preganglionic neurons located in the intermediolateral gray column of the thoracic and lumbar spinal cord. The preganglionic axon, which is generally myelinated, leaves the cord substance and subsequently the spinal canal with the ventral root of the segmental spinal nerve. A short distance from the canal the preganglionic fibers leave the spinal nerve to enter the vertebral (or paravertebral) sympathetic trunk. This collection of nerve fibers and ganglionic neurons is located bilaterally on the ventral surface of the vertebrae. Although the sympathetic trunk extends from the upper cervical region to the base of the tail, it receives preganglionic fibers only from the thoracic and upper lumbar spinal cord segments. The number of preganglionic axon bundles, rami communicantes, entering the trunk varies with the species and depends upon the numbers of vertebrae in each region. The number of thoracic rami depends upon the number of thoracic vertebrae, which ranges from 18 in the horse to 13 in the dog. In the lumbar region, where the upper segments are the main source of preganglionic fibers, species variation also occurs. In man, only the first 2–3 lumbar segments provide preganglionic fibers, whereas in the dog, horse, and cow there are 4–6 lumbar contributions.

The sympathetic trunk of domestic animals extends from the cervical region to the lower sacral or first coccygeal vertebra. The cervical trunk receives its preganglionic fibers from the upper thoracic spinal cord. The preganglionic fibers terminate in the caudal, middle, or cranial cervical ganglia, the last named being the largest and most frequently present. In domestic animals more obviously than in man, the caudal cervical ganglion and the first few thoracic ganglia combine to form the stellate ganglion. The sacral and coccygeal ganglia receive their preganglionic fibers from lower thoracic and lumbar segments. The ganglia themselves vary greatly in number and location among species and among individuals of the same species.

Ganglionic neurons are also located in prevertebral ganglia, which are entities separate from the sympathetic trunk. For the most part, the prevertebral ganglia are found associated with the autonomic innervation to the abdominal and pelvic viscera. For a complete description of the prevertebral and chain ganglia of the abdominal and pelvic region, see Mizeres (1955).

A given preganglionic fiber emerging from the thoracic or lumbar cord follows one of several possible courses (Fig. 48.2). All preganglionic fibers leave their respective spinal nerve roots as rami communicantes to enter and form the sympathetic trunk. From this point the course of the fiber depends upon the location of its ganglionic termination. The simplest course is for the preganglionic fiber to terminate on ganglionic neurons at the same level at which it entered. More commonly, however, the preganglionic fiber or a branch of the fiber ascends or descends some distance in the trunk before terminating on ganglion cells at other segmental levels. This course is taken by those fibers that provide preganglionic innervation to the cervical, sacral, and coccygeal ganglia. As a final alternative, the preganglionic axon may join the sympathetic trunk, pass through the trunk, often after ascending or descending a few segments, and contact a ganglion cell in one of the prevertebral ganglia.

Each preganglionic neuron exercises control over many ganglionic neurons by virtue of the terminal branching of its axon. The branches not only terminate on neurons in one ganglion but, in following an ascending or descending path, may contact neurons in several ganglia along the way. The terminal ramifications of these preganglionic fibers often number 25 or 30, thereby providing for divergence of the impulse.

The ganglionic neurons extend their axons, which are predominantly unmyelinated, directly to the organ to be innervated. The course of the postganglionic fibers varies with the location of the effector organ. From the neurons in the sympathetic trunk, the postganglionic sympathetic fibers to be distributed to cutaneous structures return in segmental bundles to the somatic spinal nerves and pass with the respective cutaneous branches to the smooth muscles of cutaneous vessels, to hair follicles, and to the cutaneous glands. In addition, sympathetic fibers accompany somatic nerves to skeletal muscle where they provide innervation to the blood vessels. As mentioned above, the axon bundles that connect the sympathetic trunk with the somatic spinal nerve are called rami communicantes. In man, the myelinated preganglionic bundles and the unmyelinated postganglionic bundles enter and leave the sympathetic trunk as discrete bundles and are called, respectively, white and gray rami communicantes. The rami of domestic animals are generally

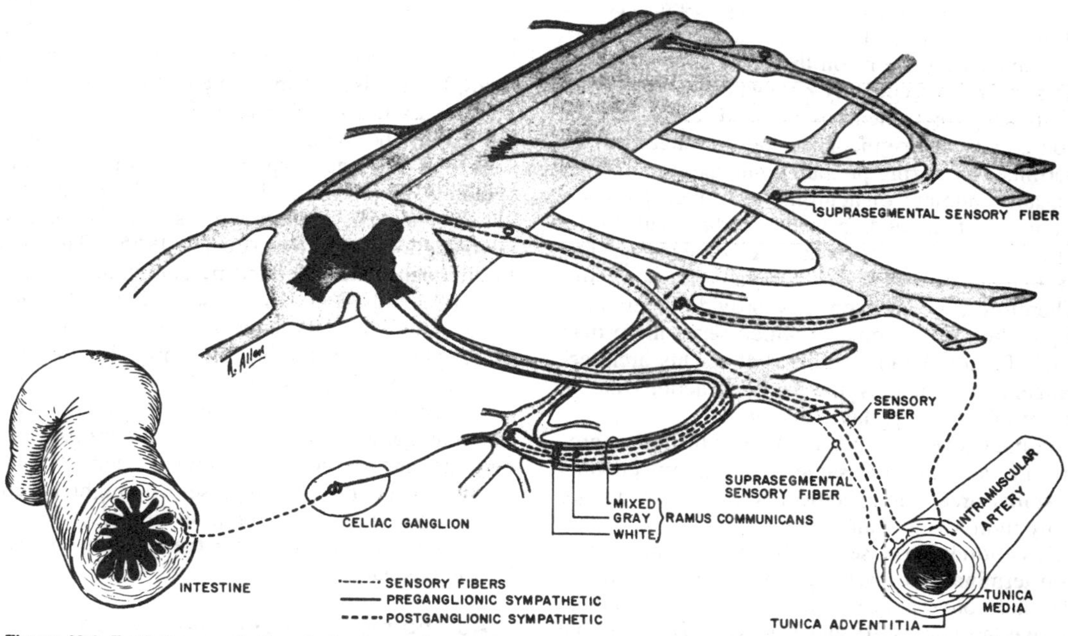

Figure 48.2. Typical sympathetic spinal reflex pathways. The afferent (sensory) limb is shown as a visceral sensory fiber. The several possibilities for efferent outflow are shown. In general, preganglionic fibers that provide central innervation to vessels of the skin and skeletal muscles terminate in the chain ganglia, and preganglionic fibers that provide central innervation to peritoneal structures pass through the chain ganglia and terminate in prevertebral ganglia.

mixed, containing both myelinated and unmyelinated fibers, and the white and gray designations are significant only to the extent that they imply pre- or postganglionic function.

Postganglionic sympathetic fibers to other visceral structures generally run together as specific visceral nerves, or they may join somatic nerves and run with them to the effector organs. Examples of specific visceral nerves are the splanchnic nerves, which provide sympathetic innervation to the abdominal viscera, and the hypogastric nerves, which carry sympathetic influence to the pelvic organs. Postganglionic axons from the cranial cervical ganglion join the trigeminal (V), facial (VII), glossopharyngeal (IX), vagus (X), accessory (XI), and hypoglossal (XII) cranial nerves and often contribute to the first, second, and third cervical nerves. In addition, each spinal (segmental) nerve carries a complement of sympathetic fibers.

Central pathways to the preganglionic sympathetic neurons in the spinal cord are of two types. First, descending facilitatory or inhibitory impulses originate in the reticular formation and the tegmental gray matter of the brain stem and descend in the reticulospinal tracts to the thoracic and lumbar gray matter. The second source of impulses is the somatic and visceral sensory system. Sensory fibers enter from the dorsal roots of the spinal nerves and through intercalated neurons contact the preganglionic sympathetic neurons. The sensory axons from the dorsal root ganglia also ascend the cord, providing the central integrating centers with somatic and visceral information.

FUNCTIONS

General function

Autonomic reflex arc

The autonomic reflex arc consists, as does its somatic counterpart, of an afferent (sensory) limb and an efferent (motor) limb (see Fig. 48.2). Visceral and somatic sensory fibers entering the dorsal horn send branches ascending in spinal sensory columns, and also send synaptic terminals to nearby interneurons. The interneurons transmit impulses to the preganglionic neurons in the cord or brain stem. Preganglionic axons make up the efferent limb and carry the visceral motor stimuli to ganglion cells, from which postganglionic axons innervate visceral effectors. In the parasympathetic efferent system, the more frequent finding is long preganglionic fibers serving a relatively few ganglionic neurons in the wall of a specific organ. The degree of divergence in the parasympathetic system is limited by the diffuse arrangement of the postganglionic neurons and the degree to which a given postganglionic axon can arborize at its effector terminal. Such limited distribution is compatible with the discrete action attributed to the parasympathetic system.

In the sympathetic system, on the other hand, the preganglionic axon most frequently contacts relatively large numbers of ganglionic neurons located close to the preganglionic cells of origin. The chain arrangement of ganglia permits an entering preganglionic axon to contact not only a large number of neurons in a given ganglion but also, through its ascending or descending path in the chain, a large number of neurons in other ganglia. The result is a marked divergence of sympathetic motor impulses. Therefore a given axon may provide innervation to 25–30 ganglion cells, some of which serve more than one type of effector organ (Patton 1948). This architectural arrangement promotes the broader action that is characteristic of the sympathetic division.

At the cranial level, simple multisynaptic reflex arcs may exist, and although the same basic pattern prevails as in the spinal area, the specific internal pathways are considerably more diverse and complex.

Ganglia as entities serve several functions. They act as distribution terminals for preganglionic-to-postganglionic divergence and convergence of impulses. As a result, a degree of overlap occurs so that a given postganglionic neuron may receive axon terminals from more than one preganglionic neuron. In addition, a given preganglionic neuron will contact many postganglionic neurons in the same or in different ganglia; that is, impulse divergence occurs. Interestingly, the degrees of divergence of the various ganglia are appropriate for the postganglionic innervation provided. There is minimal divergence of impulses in the cranial cervical ganglion, which provides rather discrete innervation to specific structures of the head; the celiac and mesenteric ganglia, on the other hand, provide a more generalized output to the gastrointestinal tract, and in these ganglia the divergence of impulse is maximal.

The convergence of several preganglionic fibers on a given ganglionic neuron provides the structural relationships for spatial summation. Should impulses from but one of the groups of converging fibers arrive at the ganglionic neuron, its membrane potential might be lowered, but not enough to cause the neuron to discharge. Such a partial depolarization of a postsynaptic neuron membrane is called an excitatory postsynaptic potential (EPSP). If impulses from several of the converging fibers arrive simultaneously, however, their individual EPSPs tend to be additive, and the sum is sufficient to cause the ganglionic neuron to discharge (Bronk 1939). Spatial summation, then, requires the convergence of two or more axons on a neuron, with impulses from each arriving at the neuron at essentially the same time. Another type of summation, temporal summation, is also demonstrable in ganglion cells. In this instance a single impulse volley from a preganglionic fiber might excite a subthreshold EPSP in the ganglionic cell, but a train of impulses would bring about discharge of the neuron. Therefore the stimulus for ganglionic discharge would be multiple impulses from a given axon arriving at the ganglion cell within a short period of time.

Finally, the sympathetic ganglia exercise a degree of selection over the frequency of incoming impulses, responding most efficiently to those frequencies under 40 per second. Higher frequencies quickly desensitize the postganglionic neurons (Eccles 1955). The majority of the frequencies transmitted by autonomic ganglia fall between 12 and 30 cycles per second. In addition, sympathetic ganglion cells show a late inhibitory effect from preganglionic stimulation, the slow inhibitory postsynaptic potential (IPSP) (Krnjevic 1974).

It is apparent, then, that the neuron relationships in autonomic ganglia have some of the properties of CNS neurons, and as such they exercise a degree of integrative power on the flow of impulses. It might be considered that the ganglia modify the nerve impulses to provide optimal stimulus conditions for the effector organs supplied by the postganglionic fibers.

Autonomic reciprocal innervation

The functioning autonomic nervous system is the internal control mechanism of the body. Sensory nerve endings of varying degrees of specialization and sensitivity are strategically located in proximity to glands or regions of critical activity. They feed information concerning changes in specific organ function or overall metabolic activity to the integrative centers (e.g. hypothalamus or spinal cord). Motor impulses to bring about the corrective alterations are then carried by the efferent parasympathetic and sympathetic systems. Together, these two systems provide both driving force and braking mechanism; for any given organ one division may provide acceleration, while the other executes deceleration. To use the terminology of Stanley-Jones and Stanley-Jones (1960), one can say that the sympathetic system most often represents the dynamic factor, whereas the parasympathetic usually represents the control factor. With but few exceptions, each visceral organ is provided with both types of innervation.

Definition of a control system becomes essential at this point. The true control is considered to be a feedback system, even more specifically a negative feedback system. In such a control the initial deviation from normal is considered to be in a positive direction. For example, if in a given situation heart rate increased and simultaneously blood pressure fell, both changes would be considered to have occurred in a positive direction. Through appropriate detectors and afferent (sensory) pathways, integrative centers would be notified of the potentially dangerous alterations and would initiate activity to counteract them. Vagal activity would slow the heart, and vasomotor activity would tend to raise the blood pressure. The reactions, then, are in a direction opposite to the original actions and are spoken of as negative. The corrective changes cause the change detectors to quiet their activity, the integrative centers are no longer excited, and functions return to a normal level. Such a complex of reactions is spoken of as a negative feedback control system, the only type of control system that can exercise corrective measures. A positive feedback system, in which any change would be amplified each time feedback occurred, could lead only to physiological disaster.

Following the Stanley-Jones analogy, the sympathetic system, as the dynamic factor, represents a positive feedback system. More diffuse actions and strong emergency reactions with epinephrine secretion both tend to push the organism toward an extreme physiological state. The parasympathetic system, representing the control factor and functioning as a negative feedback mechanism, applies the physiological brakes to the sympathetically driven changes as they approach intolerable levels. The two systems in a sense represent reciprocal innervation or the visceral counterpart of somatic flexion and extension.

Neurotransmitters and synaptic function

The first description of chemical transmission of neuron synapses was offered in 1921 by Loewi, who gave the name *vagusstoff* to a chemical released into the surrounding fluid as a result of vagal stimulation of the perfused heart. In the same year, Cannon and Uridil described the release of sympathin following stimulation of the nerves of the sympathetic system. Previously, Elliott (1905) had shown that injected epinephrine produced effects similar to stimulation of the sympathetic nerves. Subsequently, Dale and Feldberg (1933) gave the names cholinergic and adrenergic to synapses at which acetylcholine and epinephrine (adrenaline) respectively were released as chemical mediators. For some time it was generally accepted that either epinephrine or sympathin was the sympathetic mediator. Then Cannon and Rosenblueth (1933) explained certain anomalies observed in sympathetic activity by designating sympathin I as an inhibitory factor and sympathin E as an excitatory factor in sympathetic transmission.

In 1946 von Euler defined the adrenergic neurotransmitter as noradrenaline (norepinephrine), and in 1948 Ahlquist identified receptor sites in adrenergically innervated tissue as being predominantly excitatory (α-) or inhibitory (β-). Specific discoveries clarifying many of the actions of the sympathetic nervous system will be discussed in the section on adrenergic synapses.

In summary then, it is generally accepted that acetylcholine is the neurotransmitter released by nerve terminals at parasympathetic postganglionic effector junctions and that norepinephrine is the transmitter at sympathetic postganglionic effector junctions. Acetylcholine is considered to be the transmitter at ganglionic synapses in both the parasympathetic and sympathetic systems. Thus both ganglionic and postganglionic junctions in the parasympathetic system are cholinergic, whereas in the sympathetic the ganglionic synapses are generally cholinergic and the postganglionic junctions adrenergic.

Cholinergic synapses

Classically, the synaptic junctions for which acetylcholine is the transmitting agent (cholinergic synapses) are described as functionally related to nicotinic activity or muscarinic activity. These designations were made at the time the neurological activity of acetylcholine was being described, and they stem from comparisons made to drug actions then well known. The action of the alkaloid muscarine (from the fly mushrooms) was known to involve excitement of terminals of the postganglionic fibers of the parasympathetic nervous system, and consequently these neuroeffector junctions were described as muscarinic (Dixon and Hamill 1909, Dale 1914). Also, the synapses at the ganglion cells of the entire autonomic nervous system, as well as the somatic myoneural junctions, were known to be excited by nicotine; hence these junctions were referred to as nicotinic (Dixon and Hamill 1909). In terms of inhibition these two sets of synapses are also differentiable. The muscarinic terminals are blocked by the drug atropine, whereas the nicotinic sites are not susceptible to atropine but are blocked by large doses of nicotine or by the curare drugs. The curare drugs and high doses of nicotine do not inhibit the muscarinic sites. These conditions are summarized in Table 48.1.

The release of acetylcholine at autonomic cholinergic sites is, so far as is known, identical to its release by the nerve terminals at skeletal muscle. Although the process is described in detail elsewhere in this text, a few general considerations will be reviewed here. Acetylcholine is believed to be maintained in close attachment to membrane structures in the nerve fiber, with particular concentration near the terminal (De Robertis 1964). Although small quantities may be released continuously, it is not until an impulse arrives that acetylcholine is released in amounts adequate to cross to the effector cells and cause membrane depolarization. Coincident with the arrival of the impulse, calcium ions rush into the axon, where they are believed to be involved with the acetylcholine-releasing mechanism. An unidentified plasma constituent and dissolved carbon dioxide, both of which affect the ionization and physiological mobility of calcium, are cofactors in the microenvironment that increase the efficiency of acetylcholine release (Birks and MacIntosh 1961).

Degradation of the transmitter occurs for the most part in immediate proximity to the site of transmitter release.

Table 48.1. Effects of stimulating agents and blocking agents on the cholinergic synapses and neuroeffector junctions of the body

Neuronal junctions	Transmitting agents	Blocking agents
Muscarinic		
Smooth muscle Cardiac muscle Exocrine glands	Acetylcholine (in normal concentration) Muscarine	Atropine Other belladonna alkaloids
Nicotinic *		
Autonomic ganglia Skeletal muscle	Acetylcholine (in normal concentration) Nicotine (in low concentration)	Nicotine (higher concentrations depolarize ganglia cells principally) Curare (blocks skeletal muscle primarily)

* Nicotine acts in low concentrations as a stimulator, depolarizing the postsynaptic or effector membrane. In higher concentrations it blocks the same sites by preventing repolarization.

In ganglia the active enzymes are released from storage sites primarily in the presynaptic terminal, whereas in myoneural junctions the acetylcholinesterase appears concentrated in the effector membrane (Paton 1954). Further, the nonspecific acetylcholinesterase activity in the blood is sufficiently high that excess transmitter overflowing into the circulatory system will be immediately hydrolyzed.

Adrenergic synapses

When von Euler defined the transmitting agent at adrenergic nerve endings as norepinephrine (noradrenaline), epinephrine was relegated to the role of a humoral transmitter in the sympathetic nervous system. The presently accepted view is that norepinephrine is the primary secretion of adrenergic nerve cells in the peripheral autonomic system and in the CNS, whereas epinephrine is the primary secretion of chromaffin cells in the mammalian adrenal medulla.

The metabolism of the catecholamines (dopamine, norepinephrine, and epinephrine) is described by the equations in Figure 48.3. Primary raw materials are the amino acids phenylalanine and tyrosine. Intermediate steps involve the formation of 3,4-dihydroxyphenylalanine (DOPA, or dopa) which seems to have some primary adrenergic activity in the CNS. Generally speaking, however, the active products of this metabolic scheme are epinephrine and norepinephrine.

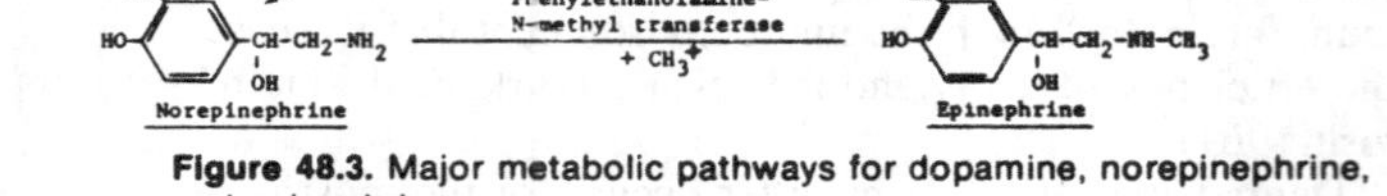

Figure 48.3. Major metabolic pathways for dopamine, norepinephrine, and epinephrine

The conversion from phenylalanine or tyrosine to dopa is mediated by tyrosine hydroxylase, and the next step from the amino acid dopa to dopamine by dopa decarboxylase. These enzymes are in the cytoplasm of adrenergic neurons and adrenal medulla chromaffin cells. The accumulation of dopamine in the cytoplasm is limited by intracellular monoamine oxidase (MAO) which converts catecholamines to inactive compounds. However, dopamine can be taken up by an active process into storage vesicles and converted to norepinephrine by the action of dopamine-β-hydroxylase. Thus in adrenergic nerve terminals norepinephrine is finally synthesized at the site in which it is stored.

The rate-limiting step in the biosynthesis of norepinephrine is the tyrosine hydroxylase reaction. The feedback inhibition of this step by the catecholamines that are produced may be an important regulatory mechanism in the formation of these compounds (Weiner et al. 1972).

Epinephrine is formed in the mammalian adrenal medulla by phenylethanolamine-N-methyltransferase (PNMT). The enzyme is activated by the very high levels of glucocorticoids present in an intra-adrenal portal vascular system. The adrenal medulla normally receives the undiluted venous effluent from the adrenal cortex (as well as its own arteries), in which the concentration of glucocorticoids is 100 times the levels in systemic arterial blood.

In hypophysectomized rats replacement doses of glucocorticoids did not restore PNMT activity, whereas adrenocorticotropic hormone (ACTH) or large doses of dexamethasone (a synthetic corticosteroid) did restore that activity.

The release of norepinephrine from adrenergic nerve terminals is a function of the frequency of impulse arrival at the nerve terminal. In general, frequencies of 20–30 per second produce optimal responses. Some organ variability is evident, and extremes are represented by pilomotor activity (optimum at 15/sec) and submandibular salivary gland secretion (35/sec). The amount of norepinephrine released per volley of impulses is considered to be constant over the physiological range, but the amount inactivated at the receptor site is greater at the lower than at the higher frequencies.

Workers attempting to localize sites of concentration of norepinephrine have found that injected tagged transmitter material is actively taken up by the adrenergic terminals themselves, as well as by the tissues they innervate. Denervation ends the absorption abruptly. Study of the disposition of tagged norepinephrine within the body and of the excretion of norepinephrine in adrenalectomized animals has led to the conclusion that the most important mechanism for the removal and inactivation of norepinephrine released by adrenergic nerves is its uptake by the adrenergic nerve terminals themselves. The norepinephrine is actively transported back across the membrane of the nerve ending and returned to the granules of the storage vesicles.

In the process, the monoamine oxidase in the cytoplasm metabolizes a portion of the norepinephrine. Catechol-O-methyltransferase (COMT) in the surrounding tissues also causes some breakdown of norepinephrine but COMT is apparently more important in the liver and kidney, where it breaks down circulating catecholamines. The end products of catecholamine metabolism are excreted in the urine.

It is difficult to distinguish norepinephrine receptor sites from a membrane catechol-binding protein that may be related to the enzyme COMT (Cuatrecasas et al. 1974), but it is widely believed that the initial mechanism of β-receptor action is mediated by activation of a membrane adenyl cyclase and the consequent conversion of ATP (adenosine triphosphate) to cyclic AMP (Krnjevic 1974).

Adrenergic receptor sites have been classified as α-sites or β-sites, according to the effects of stimulation (Ahlquist 1948, Furchgott 1960). The α-receptors cause excitement of smooth muscle, resulting in, for example, pupillary dilatation, vasoconstriction, and pilomotor activity. An exception is the relaxation of smooth muscle caused by stimulation of α-receptors in the intestinal wall. On the other hand, β-receptors are associated principally with inhibitory actions such as bronchodilatation and vasodilatation, the primary exception being excitation of cardiac muscle. Ahlquist (1948) noted that the α-receptors were highly sensitive to epinephrine and norepinephrine but much less so to the synthetic catecholamine isoproterenol, whereas the β-receptors responded most to isoproterenol, less to epinephrine, and least to norepinephrine.

Central synapses

The synapses of the brain and spinal cord do not lend themselves to analysis as readily as do autonomic terminals in peripheral areas. (For a general consideration of this topic see Chapter 40.)

Hypothalamic function

Experimental approaches

The central integrating mechanism of the autonomic nervous system is the hypothalamus, located in the floor and walls of the third ventricle, at the core of the limbic (or visceral) nervous system. Phylogenetically very old, the hypothalamus in all vertebrates is a major contributor to the central control of visceral function. Such control is exercised by neurological mechanisms, endocrine mechanisms, and combinations of the two. Although the cerebral cortex provides a degree of influence, it can be removed (decortication) without materially affecting the animal's ability to maintain a homeokinetic state. Such an animal maintains its internal environment within normal ranges, and specific autonomic reflexes, such as those associated with vascular activity or sexual function, are unaltered. A disease of cattle called polioencephalomalacia or forage poisoning is characterized by loss of cerebral cortical gray matter. Although dull and often blind, these animals are able to survive in the restricted environment of a feedlot after loss of surprisingly large amounts of cortical tissue.

A peculiar behavioral change appears in the decorticate dog and cat, specifically when the rhinencephalon is removed. In this state, very minor sensory input will throw the animal into a violent defense reaction known as sham rage. The sensory threshold responsible for the appearance of the reaction is exceedingly low, and the reaction is described as a coordinated pattern of massive sympathetic activity. When those areas whose removal produces the sham rage condition in the dog and cat are removed in man, monkeys, and rats, the result is docility. In fact, the surgical procedure of prefrontal lobotomy has been used in the treatment of certain neurological disorders in man to establish a more tractable personality.

Although the decorticate animal retains integrated control of visceral function, section of the brain stem behind the hypothalamus between the superior and inferior colliculi destroys neurogenic visceral integration. This preparation, the decerebrate animal, retains hypothalamic endocrine function, but hypothalamic afferent and efferent neurological influence is lost. The animal has a tenuous grip on life and survives for a limited time, at most a few weeks, and only with meticulous care. Characteristically, it is unable to maintain body temperature, there are alterations in the micturition reflex (in the cat a lowering of the threshold for micturition is seen), and no defense reactions in heart rate or blood pressure can be elicited. The condition of sham rage disappears with intercollicular brain stem section or with destruction of the posterior hypothalamus. Some vestiges of the rage reactions may remain as the "pseudoafferent" condition in that some fragmented portions of the rage reaction may appear, but only after extremely strong stimulation. The postural effects of decerebration, decerebrate rigidity, are well known and described elsewhere.

Specific functions

Temperature regulation. The heat sensitive centers of the hypothalamus are located in the rostral and caudal areas. Heat-dissipation activities are associated with the areas around the preoptic and supraoptic nuclei, and heat-generating and conserving activities with the caudal hypothalamic areas. The stimulus that appears to activate either of the areas is the temperature of the perfusing blood; high blood temperature calls heat-dissipating mechanisms into action, whereas cool blood entering the hypothalamus brings about heat-generating and conserving activities. These same reactions can be achieved by experimentally heating or cooling the hypothalamus. The caudal nuclei can also be neurologically activated prior to actual cooling of the hypothalamus by the peripheral sensation of cold.

Heat-conserving measures mediated by the hypothalamus may be vascular, pilomotor, metabolic, or behavioral. As an example of vascular adaptation, the blood volume is reapportioned in favor of core areas by constriction of cutaneous vessels but dilatation of vessels within heat-generating organs such as muscles and viscera. In furred animals, the pilomotor reaction to cold elevates the hair, creating an increased layer of dead air near the skin. This dead air space is an excellent insulator. Changes in hair coat density and hair color are longer-term cold adaptations controlled by the hypothalamus.

Some animals have the ability to reduce the thermal gradient by permitting their body temperature to fall. This ability, a metabolic heat-conversion mechanism, is well developed in camels and man (certain aboriginal tribes and the Laplanders) and involves the resetting of the hypothalamic "thermostat" to a lower temperature. A similar protective tolerance to low body temperature may also be characteristic of the newborn. Neonatal lambs subjected to cold can apparently survive low body temperatures for a considerable period of time, 48–72 hours, a tolerance having distinct survival value in spring or late winter lambing under range conditions. The ultimate in adaptation to lowered temperature is hibernation, during which the animal on occasion may maintain a core temperature only slightly above freezing.

Behavioral patterns related to heat conservation, believed to be mediated through the hypothalamus, include mammalian and avian migrations, huddling in groups during inclement weather, curling up to reduce exposed surface area, turning to face away from strong winds, and seeking out protected or warmer places during severe weather.

In addition to its heat-conserving reflex activities, the caudal hypothalamus also has heat-generating capabilities. Two principal mechanisms are involved. First, hypothalamic cooling brings about an increase in the tonic activity (facilitation) of the lower motor neuron pool in the spinal cord. A feedback system involving the γ-motor neurons, the annulospinal endings, and the α-motor neurons is eventually activated, and shivering results. Shivering is a synchronous, high frequency, isometric contraction of skeletal muscle resulting in a high heat output. It is, however, a short-term adaptation. A second, longer-term system involves excitement of the hypothalamic-adrenal-thyroid axis, the result of which is an overall increase in metabolic activity of most of the tissues of the body. If the demands are not extreme, such increased metabolism can exist indefinitely.

In general, then, the functions of the caudal hypothalamic center are those of the sympathetic nervous system: vasoconstriction, pilomotor stimulation, and increased metabolic rate.

Heat-dissipating activity appears to be localized above the optic chiasma and between that structure and the anterior commissure. Generally, it is felt that heat-dissipation mechanisms are superimposed on the primary heat-conservation mechanisms. The stimulus for activation of heat-dissipation systems is, apparently, the increased temperature of the hypothalamic centers. Heating the hypothalamus by diathermy causes heat-dissipation activity even if the body of the animal is cooled.

The principal mechanisms of heat dissipation involve cutaneous vasodilatation, evaporation of water, and avoidance of excessively hot environments. Cutaneous vasodilatation serves to bring deep body heat to the surface with increased efficiency. Heat loss by this method depends upon the physical processes of radiation and convection and requires an environment that is cooler than body surface temperatures. Water for evaporative cooling may be acquired from the body or from the environment. Bodily water sources include sweat glands in the skin of animals such as man and the horse, or oral and respiratory secretions, as in the cat, dog, and birds. Environmental water sources include wallows or ponds, and animals such as the pig are quite dependent upon these sources of water for cooling during hot weather.

Behavioral mechanisms help the animal avoid excessive heat by causing it to seek shade or to severely restrict activity during the heat of the day. In the extreme form such inactivity is called estivation. Estivation is the summer counterpart of winter hibernation, and represents a summer sleep.

Destructive lesions of the anterior hypothalamus often result in excessively high body temperatures. Such lesions may be traumatic, and local pressure or direct impact or penetrating injury can terminate activity of the heat-dissipation centers, in which case heat generation and conservation centers operate unopposed. A similar situation may occur in central nervous infections, and the high temperatures that accompany many types of encephalitis or meningitis can probably be explained by failure of the heat-dissipating mechanism. Injuries to the caudal hypothalamus are known to deprive the individual of the ability to generate and conserve heat. Injuries to this area also result in glucosuria, apparently because of a lowered renal threshold to blood glucose.

Water balance. The influence of the hypothalamus on water metabolism is a combination of neurogenic and humoral activities. Cells whose specialization permit them to detect changes in osmotic pressure are located within the supraoptic nuclei. Increases in osmolarity of the blood perfusing the hypothalamus bring about excitation of the osmoreceptors, which in turn cause the release of antidiuretic hormone (ADH) (see Chapters 36, 37, and 52). Increasing the amounts of ADH in the circulation decreases the amount of urine excreted and therefore increases the amount of water retained.

The hyperosmotic condition fosters the reclamation of water and increases water intake also, by activating a drinking center through osmoreceptors in the lateral hypothalamus (Anand 1961). In the goat, microinjection of hypertonic solutions into the lateral hypothalamus will cause the animal to drink (Andersson et al. 1958). Drinking can also be induced by electrical stimulation of the lateral hypothalamic area or by microinjection of acetylcholine into the same area (Miller 1961). The latter observation suggests that there is central cholinergic synaptic transmission in the autonomic system.

Feeding and gastrointestinal activity. Within the hypothalamus are areas that mediate feeding activities and satiety, that is, the sensation of being full. The two central areas have been investigated in the usual laboratory species and also extensively studied by Larsson (1954) in the sheep and goat. Use of stereotaxic methods has permitted localization of a feeding center in the anterior portion of the lateral hypothalamic nucleus. Stimulation of this area by microinjection of adrenergic substances produces feeding activity even if the animal has just eaten. Also, Schwarte (quoted by Dukes 1955) found that rumen motility increases along with feeding activity. Destructive lesions of the anterior part of the lateral nucleus produce hypophagia or aphagia.

Associated reciprocally with the feeding center is a satiety center, located in the ventromedial nucleus of the hypothalamus, that arrests feeding when fullness is achieved. When it is stimulated eating is stopped by the neurons of the area, and when the center is destroyed or masked as by an inhibitory drug, the animal continues eating (hyperphagia) and becomes obese. Special strains of mice are particularly susceptible to the administration of gold thioglucose, which concentrates in the ventromedial nucleus and abolishes the control of eating. The result is a characteristically obese mouse. Simultaneous influence upon fat metabolism in the afflicted mice has been postulated but remains to be positively established.

Threshold stimuli for the feeding and satiety centers are believed to be either changes in blood glucose levels, the glucostatic theory, or changes in body temperature, the thermostatic theory, or both. The glucostatic theory (Mayer 1955) holds that as blood sugar levels fall the feeding center is activated and the satiety center is depressed. During feeding the blood sugar levels increase, and at a critical level the center is excited and feeding suppressed. The thermostatic theory (Brobeck 1955) postulates that feeding is initiated by a fall in body temperature. As the animal eats the specific dynamic action of the ingested food gradually raises the body temperature until a threshold temperature is reached, at which point the satiety center, being activated, suppresses feeding. This theory suggests that the amount of food required may be related to its specific dynamic action rather than to its bulk, and in many cases this is true.

Not only does the hypothalamus initiate or suppress feeding, but it also influences the motor and secretory activity of the gastrointestinal tract. The effect of stimulation of the anterior hypothalamus on rumen motility was mentioned above. Also, the rostral hypothalamic regions when stimulated rapidly increase the flow of stomach acid (French et al. 1953), a response that is abolished when the vagus nerve is cut. Stimulus for the increase in gastric-acid secretion is a fall in blood sugar. Emotional upset has been associated with increased gastric acidity and is frequently cited as a cause in the formation of peptic ulcers.

The caudal hypothalamic areas can also cause an increase in gastric acidity. The increase occurs through humoral means, and peak acidity is reached about 3 hours after electrical stimulation of the caudal area (French et al. 1953). The reaction is mediated through the anterior pituitary and the adrenal glands and requires the same external stimuli as does its neurogenic counterpart. It is very likely involved with psychically induced increases in gastric motility.

Endocrine activity. Full discussion of the role of the hypothalamus as an endocrine organ and of its relationships with the pituitary and other glands of internal secretion is to be found in Chapter 52.

EFFECTS ON SPECIFIC STRUCTURES

The autonomic nervous system innervates smooth muscle, cardiac muscle, and gland cells, inducing two ef-

Table 48.2. Functions of the autonomic nervous system

	Parasympathetic	Sympathetic	
Organ	Effects	Effects	Receptor types
Heart	Decreased activity	Increased activity	β
Blood vessels			
Skin and mucosa		Constriction	α
Skeletal muscle		Dilatation	α<β
Coronary		Dilatation	α<β
Abdominal		Constriction	α>β
Pulmonary		Constriction or dilatation	α=β
Eye			
Pupil	Constriction	Dilatation	α
Ciliary muscle	Contraction (near vision)	Relaxation (far vision)	β
Third eyelid		Retraction	α
Bronchiole	Constriction	Dilatation	β
Glands			
Sweat		Secretion	α (ox)
Apocrine		Secretion	
Salivary	Secretion and vasodilatation	Constriction of myo-epithelial cells and vasoconstriction	
Lacrimal gland	Secretion		
Gastric	Secretion	Inhibition	
Pancreas	Secretion		
Liver		Glycogenolysis	
Adrenal cortex		Secretion	
Mammary		No known secretory effect	
Smooth muscle			
Skin (pilomotor)		Contraction	
Stomach and intestines			
Lumen	Increased tone and motility	Decreased tone and motility	α, β
Sphincters	Relaxation	Contraction	α
Uterus (cat and dog)			
Pregnant		Contraction (epinephrine)	
Nonpregnant		Inhibition (epinephrine)	
Milk letdown		Inhibition	
Urinary bladder	Contraction	Relaxation	β
Sphincter	Relaxation	Contraction	α
Gallbladder	Contraction	Relaxation	β
Spleen		Contraction	α
Blood coagulation		Increased rate	
Sex organs	Erection	Ejaculation	Neuro-genic
Blood glucose		Increased	

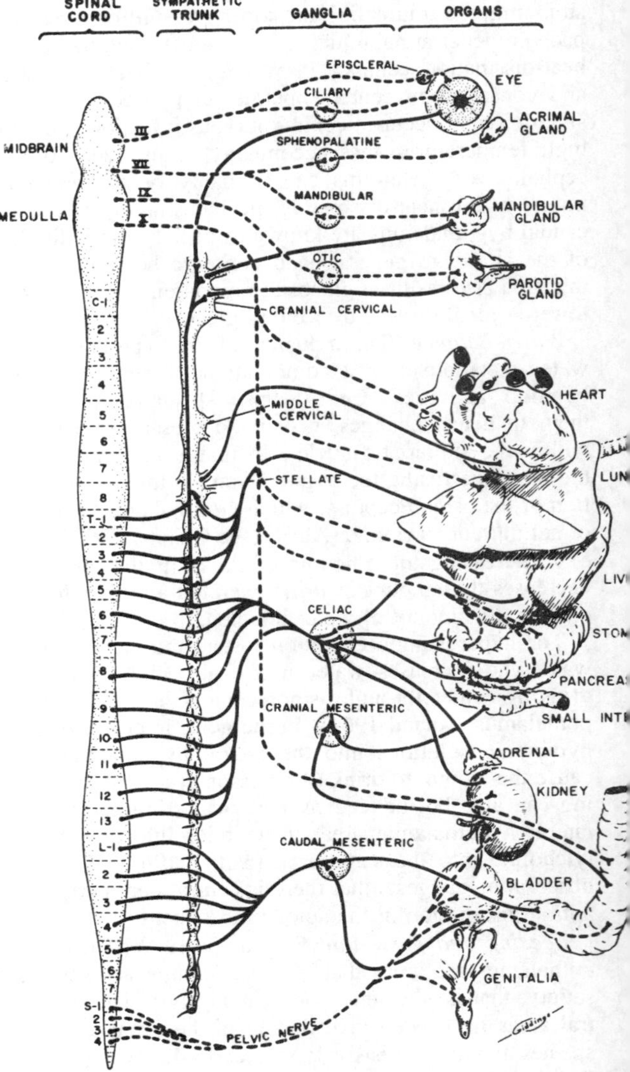

Figure 48.4. Generalized diagram of the efferent autonomic nervous system of a domestic animal. The spinal cord segmentation is characteristic of the dog, but the lumbar and sacral contributions incorporate the possibilities found in cattle and horses. The lines showing sympathetic flow are solid; parasympathetic, broken.

fector reactions: excitation and inhibition. Generally, when a given organ is innervated by both sympathetic and parasympathetic fibers, the effects are reciprocal; that is, if the sympathetic excites, the parasympathetic inhibits. However, sympathetic innervation alone may provide reciprocal innervation through α- (generally excitatory) and β- (generally inhibitory) nerve endings. An exception is the smooth muscle of the intestinal tract, which possesses α- and β-sympathetic endings both of which are inhibitory.

Following is a brief description of the autonomic effects on specific structures. It must be remembered that innervation and function vary from species to species. Some of the more important exceptions will be noted, but good comparative work is lacking for many of the species and for many of the organs. A summary of the innervations described appears in Figure 48.4 and Table 48.2.

Structures of the head

Lacrimal glands

Parasympathetic fiber stimulation causes vasodilatation and secretion from the gland cells.

Sympathetic fiber stimulation causes vasoconstriction,

has little secretory effect, but may cause an increase in the mucous content of the secretion.

Iris musculature

Parasympathetic activity causes pupillary constriction (myosis).

Sympathetic activity causes pupillary dilatation (mydriasis).

Ciliary muscle

Parasympathetic stimulation causes contraction of the ciliary muscle and thus accommodation of the lens for near vision.

Sympathetic excitation causes relaxation of the ciliary muscle and accommodation for distant vision.

Nictitating membrane

Parasympathetic innervation has not been demonstrated.

Sympathetic stimulation causes the membrane to be retracted.

Eyelid (Miller's or tarsal muscle)

Sympathetic nerve stimulation aids in raising the eyelid.

Submandibular and sublingual salivary glands

Parasympathetic stimulation produces vasodilatation and causes secretion of comparatively large volumes of saliva.

Sympathetic fibers conduct impulses that will decrease a previously augmented circulation. It may be inferred that observed increases in basal secretion rates due to sympathetic stimulation are the result of myoepithelial contraction and expulsion of saliva rather than true secretion (Coates et al. 1956, Kay 1958).

Parotid salivary gland

Parasympathetic innervation causes vasodilatation and augmented secretion. In ruminants the parotid gland secretes continually; although it is possible that the parasympathetic provides secretory tone to the gland, basal secretion continues in spite of both parasympathetic and sympathetic neurotomy (Coates et al. 1956).

Sympathetic stimulation causes vasoconstriction, and in the dog a marked increase in the organic matter of the saliva. Observations of increased saliva flow following sympathetic stimulation can be attributed to expulsion of saliva due to myoepithelial contraction (Coates et al. 1956, Kay 1958).

Brain

Innervation is exclusively vasomotor (White et al. 1952). The function of the autonomic vasomotor nerves is minimal since other vascular beds in the body act to keep the blood pressure remarkably constant, thereby assuring an equally constant rate of perfusion to the head and brain.

Thoracic viscera

Heart

Parasympathetic nerves originate in the dorsal motor nucleus of the vagus (X) nerve and pass with the nerve to the cardiac plexus, then to muscles of the atria, the vessels, the S-A (sinoatrial) and A-V (atrioventricular) nodes, and the conducting tissue.

Sympathetic nerves originate in the first to fifth thoracic cord segments and enter the chain and stellate ganglia. Postganglionic fibers then reach the heart in the cardiac plexus to terminate in the S-A node, the vessel walls, and the atrial and ventricular muscle.

As to parasympathetic stimulation, there is no agreement about the effects on coronary hemodynamics. Katz and Jochim (1939) reported that the coronary vessels of the dog dilate when the parasympathetics are stimulated, whereas Folkow et al. (1948) reported that the vessels constrict in both the dog and cat.

Sympathetic nerves accelerate and strengthen the heart. In the dog, the coronary vessels are initially constricted and subsequently dilated by sympathetic nerve stimulation and by administration of epinephrine or norepinephrine (Berne 1958, Denison and Green 1958).

Lung

The respiratory movements themselves are served by somatic nerves and skeletal muscle.

Parasympathetic innervation causes bronchial constriction and vasodilatation. Presumably the parasympathetic is also secretory (Crosby et al. 1962). There is some doubt about the universality of vasodilatation by parasympathetic nerves (White et al. 1952, Widdicombe 1963).

Sympathetic nerves produce bronchodilatation and vasoconstriction. It is believed that sympathetic nerves inhibit the glands. According to White et al. (1952), there is a difference of opinion about vasomotor effects.

Esophagus

The autonomic nervous system innervates only smooth muscle, not striated muscle. The type of muscle in the esophagus varies greatly among species. In the dog and in ruminants the esophageal musculature is entirely striated; in the pig there is only a short section of smooth muscle near the gastric cardia; and in the cat and horse the caudal one third of the esophagus has a smooth muscle coat.

Parasympathetic nerves produce smooth muscle contraction and peristalsis.

Sympathetic function is poorly defined, but presumably it is inhibitory for esophageal smooth muscle.

Abdominal viscera

Parasympathetic stimulation produces the following effects. Smooth muscle of the walls of the gastrointestinal tract, including the rumen and gallbladder, is stimulated to contract. The smooth muscle of the sphincters of the gastrointestinal tract is affected, the manner depending to some extent upon the species: in the dog and cat the pyloric sphincter is stimulated (Daniel 1964); in the cow, parasympathetic nerves inhibit the pyloric sphincter and the reticulo-omasal sphincter (Habel 1956). In the liver, the smooth muscle of the sphincter of the bile duct is relaxed. Glandular secretion is stimulated.

Sympathetic innervation produces the following effects. Constriction occurs in abdominal vessels. There is inhibition of the smooth muscle in the walls of the gastrointestinal tract including the rumen (Habel 1956) and the gallbladder and in the pyloric sphincter of the dog and cat. Smooth muscle contracts in the trabeculae, capsules, and vessels of the spleen (Kuntz 1953) and in the pyloric and reticulo-omasal sphincters (of the cow) and the sphincter of the bile duct (Crosby et al. 1962). Glycogenolysis is stimulated in the liver. There is increased secretion by the adrenal medulla but inhibition of secretion of the stomach and probably of the intestinal tract in general.

Pelvic viscera

Parasympathetic innervation mediates the following effects in pelvic viscera. Smooth muscle of the urinary bladder and colon wall is contracted. Anal sphincter and smooth muscle of the sphincter of the urinary bladder are relaxed. Vasodilatation and erection of the penis and clitoris occur. Vasodilatation takes place in the uterus, oviducts, and vagina. In the prostate, vasodilatation and secretion occur. There is no known parasympathetic innervation to the kidney or testis (Mitchell 1935).

Sympathetic innervation mediates the following effects in pelvic viscera. Constriction of vessels in general takes place. Smooth muscle of the bladder wall, colon, and rectum is inhibited. Anal sphincter and smooth muscle of the stomach, intestine, and bladder are contracted. Kidney and testis vessels are constricted (Rogers 1964). Smooth muscle of the vagina, oviduct, and their vessels is contracted. Prostate vessels are constricted and gland cells stimulated. Sympathetic nerves cause ejaculation in the male.

Cutaneous vessels, smooth muscle, and glands

Parasympathetic fibers to these structures have not been shown to exist, with the possible exception of fibers to the vessels of the face in man. This parasympathetic innervation may cause vasodilatation (blushing).

Sympathetic innervation produces the following effects: (1) Cutaneous vessels are constricted. (2) Skeletal muscle vessels are dilated. (3) Pilomotor muscles contract and elevate the hair. (4) Sweat glands are stimulated to secrete. In cattle, α-receptors are involved, with epinephrine the principal mediator (Findlay and Robertshaw 1965). The subject of control of sweating in horses has been controversial (see Chapter 49). (5) Mammary gland smooth muscle is excited to contract (Kuntz 1953, Linzell 1959). In the dog, cat, sheep, goat, and rat, mammary vessels are constricted (Linzell 1956, 1959). The effects on the secretory cells are not known. There apparently is no parasympathetic innervation to the mammary gland (Linzell 1956).

EMERGENCY REACTION

The mobilization of the systems of the body to combat a life-threatening condition has been called the emergency or fight-or-flight reaction. It is the coordinated result of increased output of adrenal medullary secretions and of increased activity of the sympathetic nervous system. The reaction establishes in the body the optimal condition for defense of the animal's life, whether this be to stand and fight or to run away. There occurs a constriction of the vessels of the skin and of the intestinal tract, but a dilatation of the vessels of skeletal muscle. This combination of vasoconstriction and vasodilatation shifts the blood volume into a compartment somewhat smaller than the at-rest blood vascular space. Accompanying the volume shift is an increased cardiac rate and output and coronary vascular dilatation. As a consequence, there is an overall improvement of circulatory efficiency. Other notable changes include an elevated blood sugar and metabolic rate, mydriasis and upper eyelid retraction, decreased gastrointestinal motility but contraction of the gastrointestinal and urinary sphincters, expulsion of red cells from the spleen, and bronchodilatation, piloerection, decreased coagulation time, and increased pain threshold. The utility of each of these changes when combat is imminent or when escape from combat is necessary is apparent. Bronchodilatation and the rise in red cell numbers provide for a more highly efficient respiratory function. Mydriasis and upper eyelid retraction improve the light-gathering power of the eye, an effect of more use to nocturnal than to diurnal animals. Piloerection, peripheral vasoconstriction, decreased coagulation time, and increased pain threshold are all modifications that help prevent wounding or offset the effects of wounds; the ultimate in defensive use of piloerection is achieved in the quills of the porcupine. Decreased gastrointestinal motility and contraction of the sphincters prevent loss of the contents of the gastrointestinal tract and bladder at inconvenient times. An exception would be the evacuation of the crop by the frightened vulture or the anal glands of the skunk, acts which are at once defensive and offensive. Finally, a rise in metabolic rate and in blood sugar provides an energy optimal for violent exercise, usually a requisite for either fight or flight.

REFERENCES

Ahlquist, R.P. 1948. A study of the adrenotropic receptors. *Am. J. Physiol.* 153:586–600.

Anand, B.K. 1961. Nervous regulation of food intake. *Physiol. Rev.* 41:677–708.

Andersson, B., Jewell, P.A., and Larsson, S. 1958. An appraisal of the effects of diencephalic stimulation in conscious animals in terms of normal behavior. In *Neurological Basis of Behavior*. Ciba Found. Symp. Churchill, London.

Ariëns Kappers, C.U., Huber, G.C., and Crosby, E.C. 1960. *The Comparative Anatomy of the Nervous System of Vertebrates including Man*. Hafner, New York.

Ban, T., Inoue, K., Ozaki, S., and Kurotsu, T. 1956. Interrelation between anterior lobe of cerebellum and hypothalamus in rabbit. *Med. J. Osaka U.* 7:101–5.

Bell, F.R., and Evans, C.L. 1956. Sweating and the innervation of sweat glands in the horse. *J. Physiol.* 133:67P.

Berne, R.M. 1958. The effect of epinephrine and norepinephrine on the coronary circulation. *Circ. Res.* 6:614–55.

Birks, R.I., and MacIntosh, F.C. 1961. Acetylcholine metabolism of a sympathetic ganglion. *Can. J. Biochem. Physiol.* 39:787–827.

Brobeck, J.R. 1955. Neural regulation of food intake. *Ann. N.Y. Acad. Sci.* 63:44–55.

Bronk, D.W. 1939. Synaptic mechanisms in sympathetic ganglia. *J. Neurophysiol.* 2:380–401.

Cannon, W.B., and Rosenblueth, A. 1933. Sympathin E and sympathin I. *Am. J. Physiol.* 104:557–74.

Cannon, W.B., and Uridil, J.E. 1921. Studies on the conditions of activity in endocrine glands. VIII. Some effects on the denervated heart of stimulating the nerves of the liver. *Am. J. Physiol.* 58:353–54.

Coates, D.A., Denton, D.A., Goding, J.R., and Wright, R.D. 1956. Secretion by the parotid gland of the sheep. *J. Physiol.* 131:13–31.

Crosby, E.C., Humphrey, T., and Lauer, E.W. 1962. *Correlative Anatomy of the Nervous System*. Macmillan, New York.

Crouch, R.L., and Thompson, J.K. 1939. Autonomic function of the cerebral cortex. *J. Nerv. Ment. Dis.* 89:328–34.

Cuatrecasas, P., Tell, G.P.E., Sica, V., Pariku, I., and Chang, K. 1974. Noradrenaline binding and the search for catecholamine receptors. *Nature* 247:92–97.

Dale, H.H. 1914. The action of certain esters and ethers of choline and their relation to muscarine. *J. Pharmac.* 6:147–90.

Dale, H.H., and Feldberg, W. 1933. The chemical transmitter of effects of the gastric vagus. *J. Physiol.* 80:16P.

Daniel, E.E. 1964. Effect of drugs on contraction of vertebrate smooth muscle. *Ann. Rev. Pharmac.* 4:189–222.

Denison, A.B., Jr., and Green, H.D. 1958. Effects of autonomic nerves and their mediators on the coronary circulation and myocardial contraction. *Circ. Res.* 6:633–43.

De Robertis, E.D.P. 1964. *Histophysiology of Synapses and Neurosecretion*. Pergamon, New York.

Dixon, W.E., and Hamill, P. 1909. The mode of action of specific substances with special reference to secretion. *J. Physiol.* 38:314–36.

Dukes, H.H. 1955. *Physiology of Domestic Animals*. 7th ed. Cornell U. Press, Ithaca, N.Y.

Eccles, R.M. 1955. Intracellular potentials recorded from a mammalian sympathetic ganglion. *J. Physiol.* 130:572–84.

Elliott, T.R. 1905. The action of adrenalin. *J. Physiol.* 32:401–67.

Findlay, J.D., and Robertshaw, D. 1965. The role of the sympathoadrenal system in the control of sweating in the ox (*Bos taurus*). *J. Physiol.* 179:285–97.

Folkow, B., Frost, J., Haeger, K., and Uvnäs, B. 1948. Cholinergic fibers in the sympathetic outflow to the heart in the dog and cat. *Acta Physiol. Scand.* 15:421–26.

French, J.D., Longmire, R.L., Porter, R.W., and Movius, H.J. 1953. Extravagal influences on gastric hydrochloric acid secretion induced by stress stimuli. *Surgery* 34:621–32.

Furchgott, R.F. 1960. Receptors for sympathetic amines. In *Adrenergic Mechanisms*. CIBA Found. Symp. Churchill, London.

Habel, R.E. 1956. A study of the innervation of the ruminant stomach. *Cornell Vet.* 46:555–627.

Katz, L.N., and Jochim, K. 1939. Observations on the innervation of the coronary vessels of the dog. *Am. J. Physiol.* 126:395–401.

Kay, R.N.B. 1958. The effects of stimulation of the sympathetic nerve and of adrenaline on the flow of parotid saliva in sheep. *J. Physiol.* 144:476–89.

Krnjevic, K. 1974. Chemical nature of synaptic transmission in vertebrates. *Physiol. Rev.* 54:481–540.

Kuntz, A. 1953. *The Autonomic Nervous System*. Lea & Febiger, Philadelphia.

Larsson, S. 1954. On the hypothalamic organisation of the nervous mechanism regulating food intake. I. Hyperphagia from stimulation of the hypothalamus and medulla in sheep and goats. *Acta Physiol. Scand.* 32(suppl. 115):1–40.

Linzell, J.L. 1956. Evidence against a parasympathetic innervation of the mammary glands. *J. Physiol.* 133:66P.

——. 1959. The innervation of the mammary gland in the sheep and goat, with some observations on the lumbo-sacral autonomic nerves. *Q. J. Exp. Physiol.* 44:160–76.

Loewi, O. 1921. Über humorale Übertragbarkeit der Herznervenwirkung. I. Mitteilung. *Pflüg. Arch. ges. Physiol.* 189:239–42.

Mayer, J. 1955. The regulation of energy intake and body weight: The glucostatic theory and the lipostatic theory. *Ann. N.Y. Acad. Sci.* 63:15–43.

Miller, N.E. 1961. Analytical studies of drive and reward. *Am. Psychologist* 16:739–54.

Mitchell, G.A.G. 1935. The innervation of the kidney, ureter, testicle, and epididymis. *J. Anat.* 70:10–32.

Mizeres, N.J. 1955. The anatomy of the autonomic nervous system in the dog. *Am. J. Anat.* 96:285–318.

Moruzzi, G. 1940. Paleocerebellar inhibition of vasomotor and respiratory carotid sinus reflexes. *J. Neurophysiol.* 3:20–32.

Okinaka, S., and Kuroiwa, Y. 1952. A contribution to the study of the histological relationship between hypothalamus and peripheral autonomic nervous system. *Folia Psychiat. Neurol. Jap.* 6:45–46.

Paton, W.D.M. 1954. Transmission and block in autonomic ganglia. *Pharmac. Rev.* 6:59–68.

Patton, H.D. 1948. Secretory innervation of the cat's footpad. *J. Neurophysiol.* 11:217–27.

Polley, E.H. 1955. The innervation of blood vessels in striated muscle and skin. *J. Comp. Neurol.* 103:253–68.

Rogers, W.A. 1964. Autonomic nervous system: Man. In P.L. Altman and D.S. Dittmar, eds., *Biology Data Book*. Fed. Am. Soc. Exp. Biol., Washington.

Sachs, E., Jr., Brendler, S.J., and Fulton, J.F. 1949. The orbital gyri. *Brain* 72:227–40.

Stanley-Jones, D., and Stanley-Jones, K. 1960. *The Kybernetics of Natural Systems*. Pergamon, New York.

von Euler, U.S. 1946. A specific sympathomimetic ergone in adrenergic nerve fibres (sympathin) and its relations to adrenaline and noradrenaline. *Acta Physiol. Scand.* 12:73–97.

Weiner, N., Clautier, G., Bjur, R., and Pfeffer, R.I. 1972. Modification of norepinephrine synthesis in intact tissue by drugs and during short-term adrenergic nerve stimulation. *Pharmac. Rev.* 24:203–21.

White, J.C., Smithwick, R.H., and Simeone, F.A. 1952. *The Autonomic Nervous System*. 2d ed. Macmillan, New York.

Widdicombe, J.G. 1963. Regulation of tracheobronchial smooth muscle. *Physiol. Rev.* 43:1–37.

CHAPTER 49

Temperature Regulation and Environmental Physiology | by Bengt E. Andersson

POIKILOTHERMISM AND HOMEOTHERMISM

Organic life depends upon reactions by which chemical energy is transformed into heat. The rate of these reactions is affected by temperature, so that heat production of living cells will increase two to three times if the temperature is raised by 10°C. The degree of acceleration with rising temperature, however, varies with different chemical reactions. A change in temperature therefore also changes the character of more complicated biological processes. This makes a relatively constant temperature a necessity for the efficient functioning of the complicated brain of adult higher animals. During evolution, higher animals (birds and mammals) have developed a heat-regulating device that enables them to maintain, under ordinary conditions, a constant deep body temperature regardless of the temperature of the surroundings. These *homeotherm* or warm-blooded animals can carry on their usual activities under a wide range of external temperature, whereas *poikilotherm* or cold-blooded animals, whose temperature varies directly with that of the environment, are dependent on the external temperature. In the cold they pass into a state of sleeplike inactivity, and in hot weather they may have to burrow into the mud to avoid disastrous overheating.

Very young mammals in which the integrative function of the brain is not yet developed show a great tolerance to changes in body temperature (Adolph 1951). This supports the idea that it is the complexity of organization that makes homeothermy necessary.

The increase of chemical activity that is achieved at the higher temperature may be the reason why the deep body temperature of homeotherms is set so high (within the range of 36°C for the elephant to 41°C for birds). But this also means that heat production must be continuously at a high level in a cold environment, which demands that the animals consume more food and spend more time obtaining it. The difference in metabolism between a poikilotherm and a homeotherm animal of the same body weight (2.5 kg) and at 37°C is illustrated by the following values from Benedict (1938): rattlesnake, 7.7; rabbit, 44.8 (Cal/kg/24 hr).

HIBERNATION

Some mammals maintain a high body temperature mainly under conditions of favorable environmental temperature but abandon homeothermy in the cold. Among these hibernants are the European marmot, the American ground hog, the hamster, and the hedgehog. The bear, on the other hand, is not a true hibernant since it remains warm blooded during its winter sleep. The temperature of the hibernants shows great variations even in the warm-blooded state and is very much dependent upon the activity of the animal. During winter sleep it falls to and remains at a level only slightly above the environmental temperature. But there is present even in the winter-sleeping hibernant a protective mechanism against profound cooling. If the body temperature falls to levels near freezing the animal wakes up and rapidly rewarms. Most hibernators arouse periodically in a rhythmic manner, where each brief arousal involves considerable energy expenditure (Bligh 1973). The ability of all mammalian hibernators to awake from hibernation using only heat from their own sources distinguishes them from true poikilotherm animals. Fundamental differences apparently exist between the biochemical processes during hibernation and in the warm-blooded state. The blood sugar in some hibernators is considerably lower during winter sleep, and in all hibernators studied the serum magnesium is markedly elevated during the hibernation (Suomalainen 1939). However, no single endocrine factor has so far been shown to be directly involved in the control of hibernation.

BODY TEMPERATURE

Many conditions are capable of causing normal variations in the body temperature of homeotherms, among which are age, sex, season, time of day, environmental temperature, exercise, eating, digestion, and drinking of water. Further, there are temperature differences to be found between different parts of the body, and these differences may vary considerably.

Gradients of temperature

In man and animals there are gradients of temperature in the blood, tissues, and rectum with the lower temperatures being toward the exterior of the body. There are also considerable variations in the different parts of the deep core. The temperature of the liver may be 1–2°C higher than the rectal temperature, and the brain temperature is usually somewhat higher than that of the carotid blood (Horvath et al. 1950). These regions are thus cooled rather than warmed by arterial blood. In ruminants the intraruminal temperature is higher than the rectal temperature due to extra heat produced by the ruminant microorganisms. The temperature of peripheral parts of the body like the limbs may in a cold environment be 10°C or more below core temperature.

Rectal temperature

An index of deep body temperature is most easily obtained in animals by insertion of a thermometer into the rectum. Although rectal temperature does not always represent an average of deep body temperature, it is better to measure the temperature at this selected site than to use various sites and call it body temperature. Further, because rectal temperature reaches equilibrium more slowly than temperatures in many other internal sites (e.g. central vessels), it is a good index of a true steady state. Since a temperature gradient exists in the rectum (Mead and Bommarito 1949), it is important to insert the thermometer to a constant depth in each species or breed of animal. Table 49.1 shows the normal rectal temperatures of certain domestic animals.

Table 49.1. Rectal temperatures

Animal	Average		Range	
	°C	°F	°C	°F
Stallion	37.6	99.7	37.2–38.1	99.0–100.6
Mare	37.8	100	37.3–38.2	99.1–100.8
Donkey	37.4	99.3	36.4–38.4	97.5–101.1
Camel	37.5	99.5	34.2–40.7	93.6–105.3
Beef cow	38.3	101	36.7–39.1	98.0–102.4
Dairy cow	38.6	101.5	38.0–39.3	100.4–102.8
Sheep	39.1	102.3	38.3–39.9	100.9–103.8
Goat	39.1	102.3	38.5–39.7	101.3–103.5
Pig	39.2	102.5	38.7–39.8	101.6–103.6
Dog	38.9	102	37.9–39.9	100.2–103.8
Cat	38.6	101.5	38.1–39.2	100.5–102.5
Rabbit	39.5	103.1	38.6–40.1	101.5–104.2
Chicken (daylight)	41.7	107.1	40.6–43.0	105.0–109.4

Diurnal variations

The thermoregulatory mechanisms are probably linked to the mechanisms controlling sleep and wakening. In animals that are active during daytime, temperature maxima are usually found in early afternoon and minima early in the morning, while those that are active at night have a reversed temperature rhythm. Variations related to the time of day are designated as diurnal variations. The extent of such temperature changes varies in different species. In the cow, the rectal temperature is regularly higher in the afternoon than in the morning with a difference of about 0.5°C (Gaalaas 1945). Radiotelemetric recordings of deep body temperature in sheep over long periods and under field conditions (Bligh et al. 1965) have demonstrated diurnal variations of about 1°C with no discernible seasonal trends in its extent. During the shortest and longest days, the duration of the rising and falling phases of body temperature appeared to be proportional to the hours of daylight and darkness respectively. The studies of Schmidt-Nielsen et al. (1957) of diurnal temperature variations in the camel are of particular interest. The rectal temperature of the dehydrated camel at rest during summer may vary from 34°C to more than 40°C, whereas the diurnal variation in the winter is usually in the order of 2°C. When camels in the hot summer are permitted to drink *ad libitum* once a day, the daily variations in rectal temperature do not exceed those found during the winter months. The usual diurnal temperature variation in the donkey during the summer was found to be between 34.6° and 38.4°C (Fig. 49.1). The observations on the rectal temperature of the camel show that a very high rectal temperature, found under

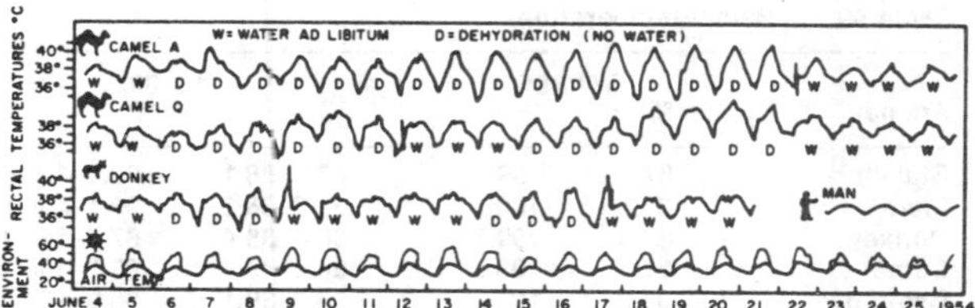

Figure 49.1. Diurnal variations in rectal temperature in two camels and one donkey for a three week period. Note the increase in diurnal fluctuations during dehydration. Air temperature corresponds closely to standard meteorological observations. The fine line above the heavy line refers to the integrated temperature of the environment. (From Schmidt-Nielsen, Schmidt-Nielsen, Jarnum, and Houpt 1957, *Am. J. Physiol.* 188:103–12)

conditions of heat stress and water deprivation, is not necessarily a sign of failure of heat regulation, although this seems to be true for man and some other animals. Schmidt-Nielsen et al. concluded that "many present attempts to use a broader basis and better physiological understanding in the selection and breeding of livestock are strongly supported by the finding that a high body temperature under heat stress may mean just the opposite of what has earlier been assumed."

HEAT BALANCE

A thermal steady state exists only when the net effect of heat gain is balanced by the net effect of heat loss.

Heat is produced in the body by metabolic activities but may also enter from the exterior by radiation, conduction, and convection. In some organs like the liver and the heart, heat production is normally relatively constant. Skeletal muscle, on the other hand, makes a variable contribution to heat production: during muscular work more than 80 percent of the heat of the body is produced in skeletal muscle; during rest the figure is much lower.

Heat is lost from the body by radiation, conduction, and convection; evaporation of water from the skin and respiratory passages; and excretion of feces and urine.

In homeotherms the various thermoregulatory mechanisms consist of a series of physiological adjustments which serve to establish a thermal steady state at the level of normal body temperature and which consequently struggle to maintain equality in heat gain and heat loss. To what extent such adjustments are required is highly dependent on the external temperature. In general it can be stated that there exists a thermoneutral zone of constant metabolism in which variable insulation (mainly due to circulatory adjustments) is sufficient to maintain a thermal steady state. Above and below this thermoneutral zone, circulatory adjustments are no longer enough for the maintenance of heat balance. In high temperatures, they must be supplemented by an increase of evaporative heat loss (sweating and panting), and in cold temperatures by increased metabolism.

PHYSIOLOGICAL RESPONSES TO HEAT

Circulatory adjustments

Cutaneous vasodilatation causes a rise in skin temperature which steepens the thermal exchange gradient for environmental temperatures below skin temperature. This increases heat loss. The cutaneous vasomotor reactions in response to thermal changes are mediated mainly by sympathetic vasoconstrictor nerves. Peripheral vasodilatation is therefore obtained by an inhibition of sympathetic vasoconstrictor tone. Warmth may decrease vasoconstrictor tone either via a rise in hypothalamic temperature or reflexly by the mediation of thermoreceptors in the skin. Local skin vasodilatation may also occur by a direct effect of warmth on the blood vessels or due to the presence in the skin of bradykinin, a powerful vasodilator substance which is released from activated sweat glands in man (Fox and Hilton 1958).

Above an environmental temperature of about 31°C skin vasodilatation no longer increases heat dissipation, and a rise in body temperature will result unless heat loss can be augmented by other means.

Evaporative heat loss

Evaporation of water is an effective way of cooling the body. The amount of heat lost by evaporation of one gram of water is approximately 0.58 Cal (Calorie, or 1000 calories). Generally speaking, at ordinary temperature and humidity, about 25 percent of the heat produced in resting mammals is lost by evaporation of water from the skin and respiratory passages. In the chicken the loss is somewhat less: on the average about 17 percent (Dukes 1937). This insensible water loss, cutaneous and respiratory, is rather constant under basal conditions. An increased flow of blood through the skin causes it to increase somewhat, but the mechanisms of sweating and panting offer much more efficient ways for increasing the evaporative heat loss.

Sweating

There are two kinds of sweat glands: eccrine glands which are supplied by cholinergic fibers present in sympathetic nerves, and apocrine glands which develop from hair follicles. The latter glands are generally considered not to be supplied by secretory nerves and are sensitive to epinephrine carried in the blood stream. Evidence has been produced, however, that at least in the goat and the sheep the apocrine sweat glands are under direct nervous control (Waites and Voglmayr 1963). In man the eccrine sweat glands alone are responsible for thermal sweating, but in many domestic animals apocrine sweat glands are of importance for evaporative heat loss.

Thermoregulatory sweating is elicited in two ways: (1) reflexly by stimulation of warmth receptors in the skin, and (2) by a rise of the hypothalamic temperature. Although reflex sweating may occur in the absence of an increased central temperature, a high skin temperature cannot elicit full-scale sweating without simultaneous hypothalamic facilitation. The horse and other equines were once regarded as exceptions from this generalization. Earlier it was thought that equine sweat glands had no direct innervation and that sweat gland activity was controlled solely by epinephrine from the adrenal medulla. But later work shows that adrenomedullary denervation, which stops the physiological release of epinephrine by the adrenal medulla, does not alter heat-induced sweating in equines. If a skin area is sympathetically denervated, heat-induced sweating no longer takes place in that area (Robertshaw and Taylor 1968). It can be concluded, therefore, that in equines sweating in response to heat is controlled by sympathetic nerves with epinephrine as the transmitter substance.

The relative importance of sweating as a heat-dissipation mechanism varies between species. In the dog sweating is insignificant in heat regulation, whereas panting is all the more important. In cows maximum evaporation from the skin surface amounts to about 150 g/sq m/hr at an external temperature of 40°C. The respiratory evaporation under the same condition is only about one third of that amount (Kibler and Brody 1950, Fig. 49.2). In the sheep sweat secretion is less important than in the cow. Maximum sweat secretion obtained in shorn sheep during heat stress is 32 g/sq m/hr, which means that a sheep may dissipate about 20 Cal per hour by

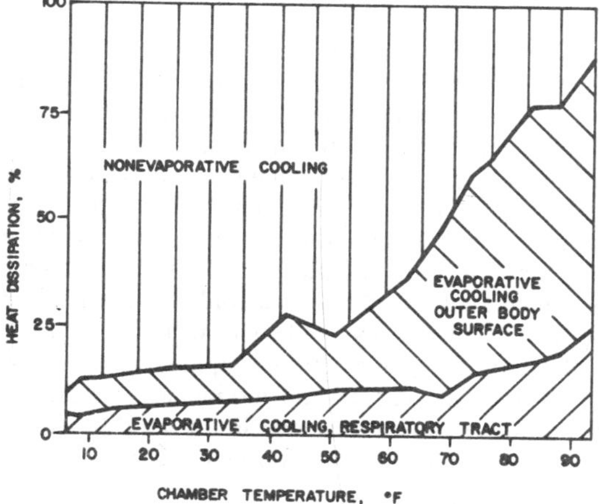

Figure 49.2. Percentages of total heat loss (averaged for Jersey and Holstein cows) by evaporation from the respiratory tract, evaporation from the body surface, and nonevaporative means (radiation, conduction, and convection) at different environmental temperatures in a climatic chamber. The respiratory evaporation rises slowly with rising ambient temperature, accounting for 4–30 percent of the total heat loss. Between ambient temperatures of 5° and approximately 50°F (−15° and +10°C), the skin evaporation is about the same as that from the respiratory tract, but from 50°F (10°C) on, surface evaporation rises markedly. The sharper rise in skin evaporation between 65° and 80°F (18 and 27°C) may correspond to the breaking out in sweat of man at 80°–90°F (27–32°C). (From Kibler and Brody 1950, *U. Mo. Ag. Exp. Sta. Res. Bull.* 461.)

sweating. Consequently, evaporative heat loss via the respiratory passages is more important in the sheep than in the cow (Brook and Short 1960). In the camel the problem of the relative importance of evaporation from the skin in comparison with that from the respiratory tracts has been solved by Schmidt-Nielsen et al. (1957). Even when the camel is exposed to the full heat load of the desert, the increase in respiratory frequency is insignificant, but sweating is considerable. One characteristic of sweating in the camel in the dry desert is that there is no copious flow of sweat or conspicuous wetting of the fur. This may explain earlier erroneous reports that the camel does not sweat. Since the evaporation takes place at the surface of the skin under the fur, and not at the surface of the fur, there is a great advantage in water economy.

In general, the function of sweat glands in domestic animals falls short of the remarkable activity of the human sweat glands. In man heat loss obtained by sweating may be as high as 1000 Cal per hour.

Panting

A heat load will in many species evoke polypnea (rapid breathing) and, in some, polypneic panting, that is, breathing at a frequency between 200 and 400 per minute with an open mouth. Panting is usually accompanied by increased salivary secretion and may cause a considerable increase in respiratory evaporative cooling if the humidity of the inspired air is not too high. Studies of the panting mechanism in cattle (Bligh 1957a,b) have shown that evaporative cooling occurs in the upper respiratory passages and not from cooling in the lungs. It is equally clear that in the calf and in the sheep, panting, in response to a raised environmental temperature, may start before there is an increase in the temperature of the blood supplying the brain. But panting may also be induced at a constant external temperature by a rise in body temperature or by local warming of the anterior hypothalamus. This shows that the panting mechanism, like sweating, may be stimulated both reflexly and centrally.

PHYSIOLOGICAL RESPONSES TO COLD

When the environmental temperature falls, some means must be taken by the homeotherm animal to prevent a drop in its body temperature. This regulation against cooling is primarily brought about by a reduction of heat loss—physical regulation. If physical regulation is not sufficient to maintain body temperature, heat production has to be increased as a second line of defense—chemical regulation.

Reduction of heat loss

Behavioral responses and increased fur insulation

A reduction of heat loss can be accomplished by the adoption of a posture which reduces the surface area exposed to cold to a minimum, such as the curled-up position of animals. During acute exposure animals may further increase the effective insulation of the fur by piloerection. Increased fur growth and subcutaneous fat deposition are other means.

Circulatory adjustments

Vasoconstriction, mediated by vasoconstrictor nerves, occurs in the skin and superficial tissues of homeotherms exposed to cold. This accomplishes two main reductions in heat loss. (1) The decreased peripheral blood flow causes a drop in skin temperature, reducing the temperature gradient between the skin and the environment. (2) The functional insulation of the skin increases due to a reduction in the convected heat loss of perfusing blood. An increased peripheral vasoconstrictor tone may be elicited reflexly by the stimulation of skin cold receptors or centrally by a lowered hypothalamic temperature.

A very important improvement in heat economy is gained by the arrangement of deep arteries and veins running close together. Cold venous blood is transported centrally adjacent to warm arterial blood coursing peripherally. By continuous heat exchange, the returning venous blood is warmed, whereas the arterial blood is cooled, which effectively minimizes heat losses to a cold environment. This countercurrent heat exchange system permits adequate blood supply to the limbs in spite of large temperature gradients. In a cold environment the temperature of radial artery blood in man may be about 20°C without the subject feeling unendurably cold and with the rectal temperature remaining at the normal 37°C (Schmidt-Nielsen 1963). Countercurrent heat exchange also helps to keep the temperature of the testes at the lower level necessary for spermatogenesis (Dahl and Herrick 1959). Due to skin vasoconstriction in the cold there is a shift of returning venous blood from superficial to deep channels increasing the efficiency of the countercurrent heat-exchange system. During skin vasodilatation in a hot environment the shift goes in the opposite direction.

Increase of heat production

The external temperature at which the heat-retaining mechanisms are no longer adequate to maintain a constant body temperature and at which heat production has to be increased is known as the critical temperature (t_c). This varies a good deal in different animals. Among farm animals, cattle and sheep have the lowest critical temperature and are therefore most able to withstand the cold. Rubner (1902) classified the cold-induced increase in metabolism of body tissues of all varieties as "chemical regulation." Since so much of the heat of the body is produced in the skeletal muscles, these structures are of first importance in the increased metabolic rate that occurs below the critical temperature. The principal way in which the enhancement of metabolism is brought about is by shivering, which consists of rhythmic muscular contractions. An increase in heat production in animals exposed to cold may also occur in the absence of detectable muscular activity (so-called nonshivering thermogenesis).

Shivering

During sudden exposure to cold, shivering is the major contributor to the enhanced heat production. It may increase oxygen consumption by 400 percent, whereas the contribution of nonshivering thermogenesis is far less. Shivering is an involuntary function of the body and consists of a muscular tremor with a frequency of about 10 per second. The muscle oscillations are usually preceded by an increased muscular tone. The circuit consisting of γ-motoneurons, muscle spindles, and muscle afferent fibers is apparently of great importance in the control of shivering (Stuart et al. 1963). From the thermodynamic point of view shivering is much more effective than voluntary muscle contractions.

Like other thermoregulatory mechanisms, shivering may be initiated and influenced by peripheral and central temperatures. Peripheral cooling may induce shivering with no change occurring in brain temperature, and local cooling of the anterior hypothalamus may elicit shivering at an external temperature that remains constant. The termination of peripherally elicited shivering by brain warming and that of centrally induced shivering by skin warming demonstrate the close association between the two mechanisms.

Nonshivering thermogenesis

Recent work has demonstrated beyond doubt that there exists a cold-stimulated thermogenesis without shivering. Cold-acclimated animals, in which muscular activity is blocked by curare, may double their heat production during cold exposure (see Carlson 1960). This nonshivering thermogenesis is due predominantly to the calorigenic effect of epinephrine and norepinephrine which are both released in increased amounts in the cold. Thyroxine secretion is also stimulated by cold. The fact that thyroxine potentiates the calorigenic action of epinephrine indicates that there exists a complex and modulated interplay between various endocrine factors in the bodily defense against cold. Adrenocortical hormones may also be of importance.

Brown multilobular adipose tissue (brown fat) is an important site of nonshivering thermogenesis in small mammals, particularly the rat. Cold-induced sympathetic stimulation of brown fat markedly increases lipid metabolism and hence the heat production of this tissue (Cottle 1973).

TEMPERATURE PERCEPTION

Temperature perception is mediated by peripheral thermoreceptors and thermosensitive units in the CNS. Their

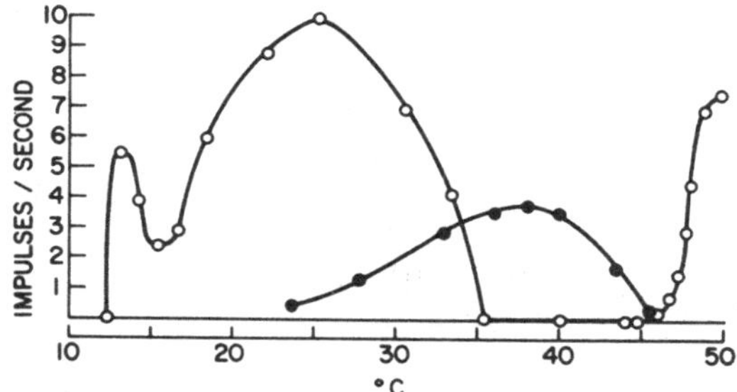

Figure 49.3. Frequency of the steady discharge of a single cold fiber (open circles) and of a single warm fiber (solid circles) when the temperature receptors of the cat's tongue are exposed to constant temperatures within the range of 10°–50°C. (From Zotterman 1953, *Ann. Rev. Physiol.* 15:357–72.)

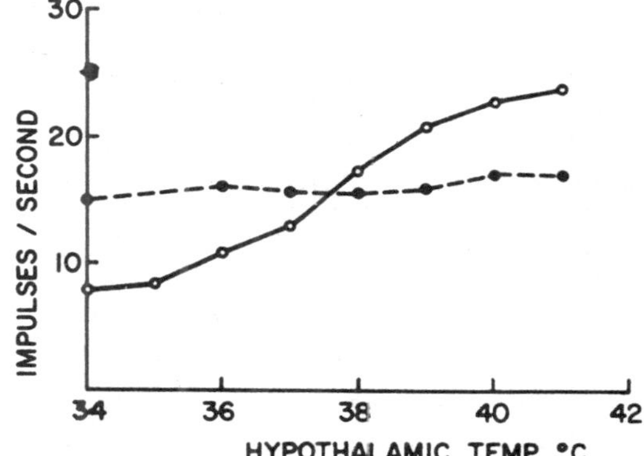

Figure 49.4. Average discharge rates of warmth-sensitive (solid line) and insensitive (dashed line) neurons in the preoptic region of the cat. (From Nakayama, Hammel, Hardy, and Eisenman 1963, *Am. J. Physiol.* 204:1122–26.)

joint action seems to be necessary to obtain the maximal temperature regulation against heat or cold.

Peripheral thermoreceptors

The sensations of warmth and cold in man originate from thermoreceptors in the skin and certain mucous membranes. It is not known for sure that animals experience peripheral warmth or cold in the same manner. Nevertheless, most of the knowledge about the properties of the thermoreceptors derives from electrophysiological studies in animals (Hensel 1974). There are two kinds of thermoreceptors—warmth receptors and cold receptors. At constant temperatures they show a steady discharge (a static response), the frequency of which is dependent on the absolute temperature (Fig. 49.3). On a sudden temperature rise the warmth receptors react with a transient increase in frequency (a phasic response) but soon adapt to a new static discharge rate. The cold receptors behave in the opposite way, showing a transient increase in discharge on a sudden temperature drop. Certain areas of the skin seem to be of greater importance than others in the peripheral control of body temperature. For example, local warming of the scrotal skin in the ram elicits polypnea much more readily than heating any other skin area (Waites 1961).

Central thermosensitivity

Central thermosensitivity obviously plays an important role in temperature regulation. The local warming of the anterior hypothalamus (the preoptic region) in conscious mammals activates all available physiological and behavioral heat-loss mechanisms, and local cooling of the same part of the brain stem evokes the thermoregulatory responses for heat gain. The recording of single neuron activity has confirmed the presence of cells in the anterior hypothalamus that act as thermal receptors. Some are activated by warming (Fig. 49.4), and others by cooling. Similar thermal receptors are present in the spinal cord. The latter pass information about the spinal temperature to the thermoregulatory center in the anterior hypothalamus (Hellon 1973).

REGULATION OF BODY TEMPERATURE

Peripheral versus central factors

A problem much debated is the relative importance of peripheral, spinal, and hypothalamic thermoreceptors for determining the set-point of the body thermostat. In general central heat counteracts the effect of peripheral cold, and vice versa. This is indicated by the effects of local cooling and warming of the anterior hypothalamus at different external temperatures.

Local cooling of the anterior hypothalamus causes marked peripheral vasoconstriction and may further cause shivering even in a thermally neutral environment (Hammel et al. 1959). This leads to an elevation of core temperature. The shivering response, however, is highly dependent on the external temperature. It is strong in a cold environment and weak or absent in a warm one.

Local warming of the hypothalamic thermoregulatory center has the reverse effect to cooling. It inhibits the cold-defense mechanisms and activates the heat-loss mechanisms. However, the heat-loss response to central warming is highly dependent on the external temperature. It is strong in the warmth and weak in the cold. Nevertheless, by blocking the cold defense, prolonged local warming of the anterior hypothalamus may cause almost a 10°C drop in rectal temperature of goats placed in the cold (Andersson 1970).

Interaction between neural and hormonal mechanisms

As epinephrine, norepinephrine, and thyroxine are of major importance in cold-stimulated nonshivering thermogenesis, an increased secretion of these hormones

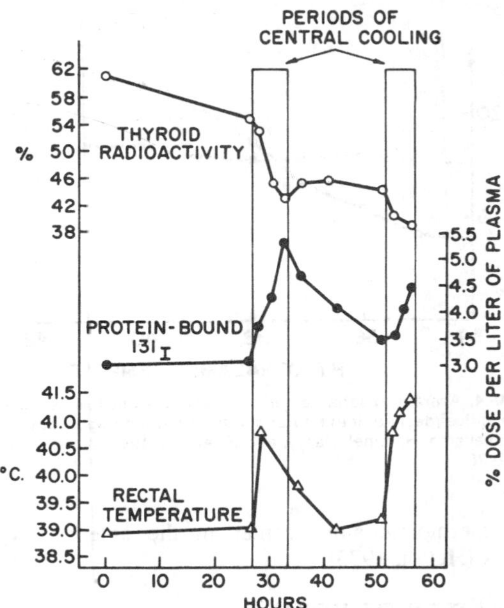

Figure 49.5. Thyroid activation elicited by local cooling of the hypothalamic thermoregulatory center of a goat (central cooling). The animal had been given 40 microcurie of ^{131}I as KI three days prior to the experiment. The increased release of thyroxine from the thyroid gland during central cooling is evidenced by a rapid fall in thyroid radioactivity and a steep rise of protein-bound radioiodine (PB^{131}I) in the blood plasma. Note the rise in rectal temperature during local cooling of the anterior hypothalamus. (From Andersson, Ekman, Gale, and Sundsten 1962, *Acta Physiol. Scand.* 54:191–92.)

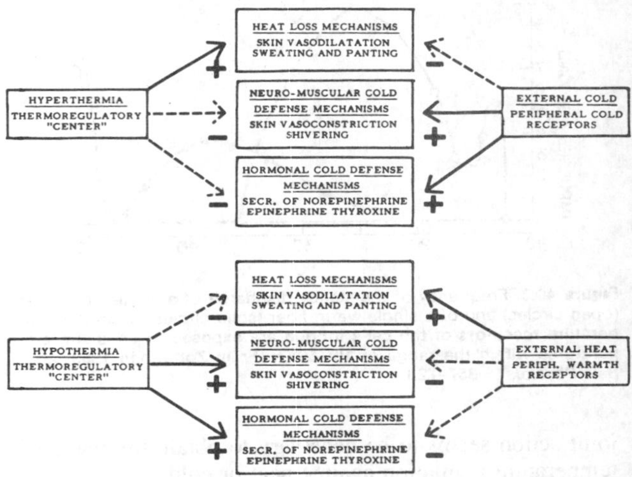

Figure 49.6. A tentative summary of temperature regulation in homeotherms. The upper part shows how an elevated body temperature (hyperthermia) may counteract the thermoregulatory effect of peripheral cold through the intermediation of the hypothalamic thermoregulatory center. The lower part illustrates the reverse effect of a subnormal body temperature (hypothermia).

occurs in mammals during cold stress. The anterior hypothalamus participates in the control of these hormonal cold-defense mechanisms (Gale 1973). Local warming of this part of the brain inhibits the activation of the sympathicoadrenomedullary system and the thyroid activation normally occurring during a general cold stress. Local cooling of the anterior hypothalamus, on the other hand, causes sympathicoadrenomedullary activation and increased secretion of thyroxine (Fig. 49.5). The latter response is mediated by the release of thyrotropic hormone (TSH) from the anterior pituitary. It is therefore evident that changes in deep body temperature influence both neural and hormonal thermoregulatory mechanisms by altering the activity of thermosensitive cells in the anterior hypothalamus.

A tentative summary of the regulation of body temperature is given in Figure 49.6.

REACTION TO EXTREME ENVIRONMENTAL TEMPERATURES

Heat tolerance

Many experimental studies have established the ability of various domestic animals to withstand external heat. The remarkable ability of the camel has been mentioned. Lee et al. (see Robinson and Lee 1946) have investigated the reactions to heat in several domestic animals. In the sheep the rectal temperature starts to rise above normal at an air temperature of 32°C, and open-mouth panting begins at a rectal temperature of 41°C. Unless the relative humidity is high (above 65%), the sheep is able to withstand for hours an external temperature as high as 43°C. Both sweating and panting are important heat regulatory devices in this species. The same applies to cattle. In the cow, sweat gland activity increases in relation to the rise in temperature, and polypnea often occurs at rectal temperatures above 40°C. At an average air temperature of 10°C the mean rectal temperature of Jersey cows was found to be 38.3°C and the respiratory rate about 20 per minute. At an average air temperature of 35°C the corresponding mean values were 39.6°C and 90 per minute (Gaalaas 1945).

The rectal temperature of the pig begins to rise above normal at an environmental temperature of 30°–32°C. If the relative humidity is 65 percent or more, the pig cannot tolerate a prolonged exposure to a temperature of 35°C. At 40°C the pig is unable to stand an atmosphere of any humidity. A rectal temperature of 41°C is near the danger point and collapse easily occurs.

The rectal temperature of the dog tends to rise above normal at a room temperature of 27°–30°C. As the environmental temperature rises, the rate of breathing increases, but the depth of breathing (tidal volume) is markedly reduced. This helps to protect the carbon dioxide content of the blood against reduction. At a rectal temperature of 41°C the dog is in danger of a breakdown in its thermal equilibrium, and at a rectal temperature of

42.5°C severe nervous symptoms develop, with danger of immediate collapse.

The rectal temperature of the cat begins to be elevated at an air temperature of 32°C, and at a relative humidity above 65 percent the cat is unable to withstand prolonged exposure to an environmental temperature of 40°C. As in the dog, polypnea and panting are the main ways to increase heat loss during heat stress. In addition, a cat may increase its evaporative heat loss by spreading saliva on its coat.

In birds, evaporation occurring as air passes through the air sacs has a cooling effect. When body temperature rises, they pant and drink more water. At external temperatures above 27°C the hen begins to show a rise in rectal temperature and respiratory rate. Prolonged exposure of a hen to an air temperature of 38°C is unsafe unless the relative humidity is below 75 percent. A rectal temperature of 45°C (113°F) appears to be the upper limit of safety in the hen. In the mourning dove panting was found to start at a rectal temperature of about 42.5°C, and at an air temperature of 39°C water consumption was four times that observed at 23°C (Bartholomew and Dawson 1954).

Adjustments during prolonged cold exposure

The environmental critical temperature (t_c) varies among species, but may also vary considerably among individuals of the same species dependent upon climatically induced changes in body insulation. Increased insulation causes a lowering of t_c, and decreased insulation has the reverse effect.

The physiological adjustments to prolonged cold exposure can be separated into three categories: (1) changes occurring during cold exposure for a few weeks when other environmental factors remain unchanged (cold acclimation), (2) modifications developing during the slow seasonal change from summer to winter (cold acclimatization), and (3) genetic alterations over several generations as a result of natural selection of the individuals best suited for survival in the cold climate (climatic adaptation). The principal difference between the first two is that animals acclimated to cold show persistent elevation of metabolism as a result of enzyme reactions but usually no significant lowering of t_c, whereas cold-acclimatized animals generally show no increase in metabolism but have a markedly lowered t_c as the result of improved insulation.

Cold acclimation

The phenomenon of cold acclimation has been studied mainly in small animals under laboratory conditions. It involves primarily a shift from shivering to nonshivering thermogenesis occurring during the first 2–3 weeks of cold exposure. The increase in nonshivering thermogenesis enables the animals to survive longer than nonacclimated animals in severe cold. The nature of the physiological adjustments in the cold-acclimated animal is still largely unknown. However, definite changes in carbohydrate and fat metabolism occur, and the calorigenic effect of epinephrine and norepinephrine is potentiated during cold acclimation (Hsieh and Carlson 1957). Maintenance of the increased nonshivering metabolism requires the presence of the thyroid and the adrenal glands. The effect of cold acclimation is lost when the animals are placed in an environmental temperature of 30°C for 4 days.

Cold acclimatization

For animals living in a cold climate, compensation by increased heat production similar to that occurring during cold acclimation would be highly uneconomical. Mammals living under winter conditions maintain a normal body temperature mainly by adjustments involving improved insulation. Consequently, they have a lower t_c than individuals of the same species not acclimatized to cold. Measurements of the insulative value of the fur show marked increases in winter over summer values. Vasomotor adaptations may also be of great importance. Heat production, on the other hand, is usually not elevated in cold-acclimatized animals. In many arctic animals the metabolism in the winter is actually less than that during summer when measured at a given external temperature.

Climatic adaptation

The body temperature of homeotherms does not show adaptive changes. Thus the rectal temperature does not vary significantly between tropic and arctic mammals although the latter have to live in the extreme cold. Arctic animals maintain their body temperature at a high level due to a most efficient insulation, and they do not increase their metabolism until the environmental temperature is very low (Scholander 1955). The critical environmental temperature for the Eskimo dog is between 0° and −10°C, and for the Arctic fox −30°C, whereas man and large tropical animals have critical temperatures as high as 25°–27°C. The extreme temperature gradients that exist between peripheral and central parts of the body in arctic animals do necessitate certain chemical changes in the tissues. The melting point of the marrow fat of the phalanges of the Eskimo dog has, for example, been found to be 30°C lower than that from the upper part of the femur (Irving et al. 1957).

HYPOTHERMIA

Hypothermia means a reduction of deep body temperature below the normal in nonhibernating homeotherms. In nature hypothermia usually develops slowly due to an exhaustion of the metabolic cold mechanisms. Shivering may persist for a long time, causing a depletion of the skeletal muscle and liver glycogen reserves, and also a fall in the glycogen content of cardiac muscle. Concomitant with the fall in deep body temperature there is gradual slowing of the heart and a hemoconcentration as the result of a fluid shift from the blood to tissues. The lethal low level of body temperature varies among species and among individuals of the same species. In man and in the dog cardiac arrest followed by respiratory depression and death usually occurs at a rectal temperature of about 25°C (77°F). However, considerably lower levels of rectal temperature have sometimes been observed in surviving man and dog. Due to reduced brain metabolism, mental effects are detected in man when the rectal temperature has fallen to about 35°C, and in dogs and cats consciousness is lost at a rectal temperature of about 26°C.

In order to facilitate cardiac and brain surgery in man the use of artificially induced hypothermia has become common in recent years. Concomitantly much experimental work has been performed on the effect of deliberate lowering of the body temperature in animals. A rapid body cooling is facilitated by initial use of anesthesia, which is no longer necessary when the rectal temperature falls below 25°C. Since cardiac arrhythmias and cardiac arrest are likely to occur at this rectal temperature, the usual level of surgical hypothermia is in the range of 25° to 30° (so-called moderate hypothermia). Much experimental work in both large and small animals has been performed, however, in the range of 15° to 25°C. With the information obtained from these studies it has been possible to perform cardiac surgery in man during deep hypothermia, that is, at body temperatures near 15°C. Under such circumstances a certain degree of circulation is maintained by the use of an artificial heart-lung pump, and the heart may be arrested for periods of an hour. With similar precautions taken, a dog survived one hour of cardiac arrest when the rectal temperature was reduced to 0°C (Gollan 1964).

By a special method of prewarming the heart during recovery, Andjus (1955) has been able to lower the body temperature below 0°C in rats and obtain survival without the use of an artificial circulation pump. The main danger at temperatures below 0°C is ice formation in the tissues. Extensive ice crystallization appears to damage the tissues by dehydration. These experiments open interesting possibilities for the use of deep hypothermia during space travel to reduce oxygen and food requirements and to prolong life.

FEVER

Fever is a rise in deep body temperature that develops during pathological conditions. It may be caused by damage to the brain itself or by toxic substances that affect the central control of body temperature. During the development of fever the heat balance is positive, due to a reduction in heat loss (skin vasoconstriction) and due to increased heat production. Later, when the body temperature reaches a certain height, the balance between heat loss and heat production is restored, and the temperature is again precisely regulated at the new high level. Under these conditions there is still an increased heat production, but this may be only secondary to the elevated temperature, since the velocity of the biochemical reactions follows van't Hoff's law and increases 2–3 times for a temperature rise of 10°C. A rise of 1°C in body temperature should therefore cause an increase of 10–20 percent in the basal metabolism. Actual measurements in man show an average increase of about 13 percent for each rise in body temperature of 1°C. The elevated metabolic rate during the steady state of fever may therefore be more the result of than the cause of the high temperature. With termination of fever, various heat-loss mechanisms are activated and heat balance is restored to its normal level.

The cause of and the mechanisms underlying fever caused by infectious agents have been extensively studied in recent years (Bligh 1973). Bacteria and other microorganisms contain and produce lipopolysaccharide and other substances. These exogenous pyrogens induce a febrile response in man and animals one-half to one hour after injection. They are apparently removed from the blood and inactivated by the reticuloendothelial system. On repetitive injections of exogenous pyrogen animals develop a tolerance which markedly reduces the febrile response. This tolerance may be due to a more efficient removal of the pyrogen from the blood by the reticuloendothelial system. The exogenous pyrogens do not seem to elicit fever by a direct action on thermoregulatory structures of the brain. Rather, they induce a release of another agent (endogenous pyrogen) from the granulocytes, which in turn seems to act directly on central thermoregulatory mechanisms to facilitate cold defense mechanisms and inhibit the heat loss mechanisms. Endogenous pyrogen may also be released from granulocytes under certain noninfectious conditions (i.e. in surgical fever).

Although the role played by fever in the defensive processes of the body is largely unknown, there are many indications that fever is beneficial in many diseases. It has been suggested that the rise in body temperature increases the formation of antibodies, and it has been reported that in animals infected with certain microorganisms the disease becomes less severe if the temperature is raised artificially.

REFERENCES

Adolph, E.F. 1951. Responses to hypothermia in several species of infant mammals. *Am. J. Physiol.* 166:75–91.

Andersson, B. 1970. Central nervous and hormonal interaction in temperature regulation of the goat. In J.D. Hardy, A.P. Gagge, J.A.J. Stolwijk, eds., *Physiological and Behavioral Temperature Regulation*. Thomas, Springfield, Ill. Pp. 634–47.

Andersson, B., Ekman, L., Gale, C.C., and Sundsten, J.W. 1962. Activation of the thyroid gland by cooling of the preoptic area in the goat. *Acta Physiol. Scand.* 54:191–92.

Andjus, R.K. 1955. Suspended animation in cooled, supercooled, and frozen rats. *J. Physiol.* 128:547–56.

Bartholomew, G.A., and Dawson, W.R. 1954. Temperature relations in mourning dove. *Ecology* 35:181–87.

Benedict, F.G. 1938. *Vital Energetics in Comparative Metabolism.* Carnegie Inst. Pub. no. 503. Washington. 215 pp.

Bligh, J. 1957a. A comparison of the temperature in the pulmonary artery and in the bicarotid trunk of the calf during thermal polypnea. *J. Physiol.* 136:404–12.

——. 1957b. The initiation of thermal polypnea in the calf. *J. Physiol.* 136:413–19.

——. 1973. Temperature regulation in mammals and other vertebrates. In A. Neuberger and E.L. Tatum, eds., *Frontiers in Biology.* North-Holland, Amsterdam.

Bligh, J., Ingram, D.L., Keynes, R.D., and Robinson, S.G. 1965. The deep body temperature of an unrestrained Welsh mountain sheep recorded by a radiotelemetric technique during a 12-month period. *J. Physiol.* 176:136–44.

Brook, A.H., and Short, B.F. 1960. Regulation of body temperature of sheep in a hot environment. *Austral. J. Ag. Res.* 11:402–7.

Carlson, L.B. 1960. Non-shivering thermogenesis and its endocrine control. *Fed. Proc.* 19 (pt. 2, suppl. 5):25–30.

Cottle, M.K.W. 1973. Acclimation to cold and the effect of drugs. In E. Schönbaum and P. Lomax, eds., *The Pharmacology of Thermoregulation.* S. Karger, Basel. Pp. 342–58.

Dahl, E.V., and Herrick, J.F. 1959. A vascular mechanism for maintaining testicular temperature by counter-current exchange. *Surg. Gynecol. Obstet.* 108:697–705.

Dukes, H.H. 1937. Studies of the energy metabolism of the hen. *J. Nutr.* 14:341–54.

Fox, R.H., and Hilton, S.M. 1958. Bradykinin formation in human skin as a factor in heat vasodilatation. *J. Physiol.* 142:219–32.

Gaalaas, J. 1945. Effect of atmospheric temperature on body temperature and respiration rate of Jersey cattle. *J. Dairy Sci.* 28:555–63.

Gale, C.C. 1973. Neuroendocrine aspects of thermoregulation. *Ann. Rev. Physiol.* 35:391–430.

Gollan, F. 1964. Cardiac arrest of one hour duration in dogs during hypothermia of 0°C followed by survival. *Fed. Proc.* 13:57.

Hammel, H.T., Fusco, M., and Hardy, J.D. 1959. Responses to hypothalamic cooling in conscious dogs. *Fed. Proc.* 18:63.

Hellon, R.F. 1973. Central thermoreceptors and thermoregulation. In *Handbook of Sensory Physiology.* Vol. 3, pt. 1, E. Neil, ed., *Enteroceptors.* Springer, Berlin. Pp. 161–86.

Hensel, H. 1974. Thermoreceptors. *Ann. Rev. Physiol.* 36:233–49.

Horvath, S.M., Rubin, A., and Foltz, E.L. 1950. Thermal gradients in the vascular system. *Am. J. Physiol.* 161:316–22.

Hsieh, A.C.L., and Carlson, L.D. 1957. Role of adrenaline and noradrenaline in chemical regulation of heat production. *Am. J. Physiol.* 190:243–46.

Irving, L., Schmidt-Nielsen, K., and Abrahamson, N.S. 1957. Melting points of animal fats in cold climates. *Physiol. Zool.* 30:93–105.

Kibler, H.H., and Brody, S. 1950. Environmental physiology with special reference to domestic animals. X. Influence of temperature, 5° to 95°F, on evaporative cooling from the respiratory and exterior body surfaces in Jersey and Holstein cows. *U. Mo. Ag. Exp. Sta. Res. Bull.* 461.

Mead, J., and Bommarito, C.L. 1949. Reliability of rectal temperature as an index of internal body temperature. *J. Appl. Physiol.* 2:97–109.

Nakayama, T., Hammel, H.T., Hardy, J.D., and Eisenman, J.S. 1963. Thermal stimulation of electrical activity of single units of the preoptic region. *Am. J. Physiol.* 204:1122–26.

Robertshaw, D., and Taylor, C.R. 1968. The control of sweat gland function in equines. *Proc. Internat. Union Physiol. Sci.* XXIV Internat. Cong., Washington. Vol. 7, 370.

Robinson, K.W., and Lee, D.H.K. 1946. *Animal Behavior and Heat Regulation in Hot Atmospheres.* U. of Queensland Press, Brisbane.

Rubner, M. 1902. *The Laws of Energy.* Deuticke, Leipzig. P. 105.

Schmidt-Nielsen, K. 1963. Heat conservation in counter-current systems. In *Temperature: Its Measurement and Control in Science and Industry.* Vol. 3, M. Herzfeld, ed., pt. 3, J.D. Hardy, ed. Reinhold, New York. Pp. 143–46.

Schmidt-Nielsen, K., Schmidt-Nielsen, B., Jarnum, S.A., and Houpt, T.R. 1957. Body temperature of the camel and its relation to water economy. *Am. J. Physiol.* 188:103–12.

Scholander, P.F. 1955. Evolution of climatic adaptation in homeotherms. *Evolution* 9:15–26.

Stuart, D.G., Eldred, E., Hemingway, A., and Kawamura, Y. 1963. Neural regulation of the rhythm of shivering. In *Temperature: Its Measurement and Control in Science and Industry.* Vol. 3, M. Herzfeld, ed., pt. 3, J.D. Hardy, ed. Reinhold, New York. Pp. 545–57.

Suomalainen, P. 1939. Hibernation in the hedgehog. VI. Serum magnesium and calcium: Artificial hibernation. *Ann. Acad. Sci. Fenn.*, ser. A, 10:1–68.

Waites, G.M.H. 1961. Polypnea evoked by heating the scrotum of the ram. *Nature* 190:172–73.

Waites, G.M.H., and Voglmayr, J.K. 1963. The functional activity and control of the apocrine sweat glands of the scrotum of the ram. *Austral. J. Ag. Res.* 14:839–51.

Zotterman, Y. 1953. Special senses: Thermal receptors. *Ann. Rev. Physiol.* 15:357–72.

CHAPTER 50

The Eye and Vision

by Jack H. Prince

Anatomy

The eye is composed of the eyeball or globe, the optic nerve, and certain accessory structures: the eyelids, conjunctiva, lacrimal apparatus, and ocular muscles. The eyeball is a spheroidal body consisting of three tunics or coats enclosing the aqueous humor, crystalline lens, and vitreous humor (Fig. 50.1).

The fibrous tunic or external coat gives strength and rigidity to the eyeball. It consists of an anterior part, the cornea, and a posterior part, the sclera. The cornea is a transparent, colorless, nonvascular connective tissue with an index of refraction so nearly the same throughout that it is practically homogeneous optically. The sclera forms the greater part of the fibrous tunic. It joins the cornea at the sclerocorneal junction. It is composed largely of dense white fibrous connective tissue and is opaque to light.

The vascular tunic or middle coat comprises the choroid, ciliary body, and iris. The choroid consists mainly of blood vessels, pigment cells, and some connective tissue. Three layers are evident: the suprachoroid layer, the cells of which contain a brownish pigment; the vascular layer or choroid proper, which contains the branches of the ciliary arteries and veins; and the capillary layer, which contains a rich capillary network. Between the vascular and capillary layers, in the posterior part of the eye, a peculiar, lustrous, opaque structure, the tapetum, is found in all domestic animals except the pig. Its color varies greatly in different species and is often strikingly beautiful. Light passing through the transparent retina is collected by the tapetum and reflected back to the retinal receptors, thus providing a double stimulation. The chief function of the choroid is to supply nutrition to the outer layers of the retina.

The ciliary body is a ring of tissue continuous with the choroid behind and the iris in front. Its main components are the ciliary processes and the ciliary muscle. The numerous ciliary processes form a circle of radial folds surrounding the lens and giving attachment to its suspensory ligament. They are highly vascularized. The ciliary muscle is a ring of smooth muscle fibers, some of which are arranged meridionally and others circularly.

The iris is a muscular diaphragm arising from the ciliary body. It presents a central opening, the pupil, the shape of which varies in different species and with different degrees of dilatation. Corpora nigra, or granula iridis, are found at the upper and lower margins of the pupil of horses and ruminants. They are described as "cystic protrusions of the pigmented retinal layers." The iris presents three layers: an external epithelial layer; a middle, usually pigmented, fibrous layer; and an internal, pigmented, epithelial layer. The muscle fibers of the iris are arranged in two ways. Some surround the pupil and constitute a sphincter pupilla; others are radially disposed

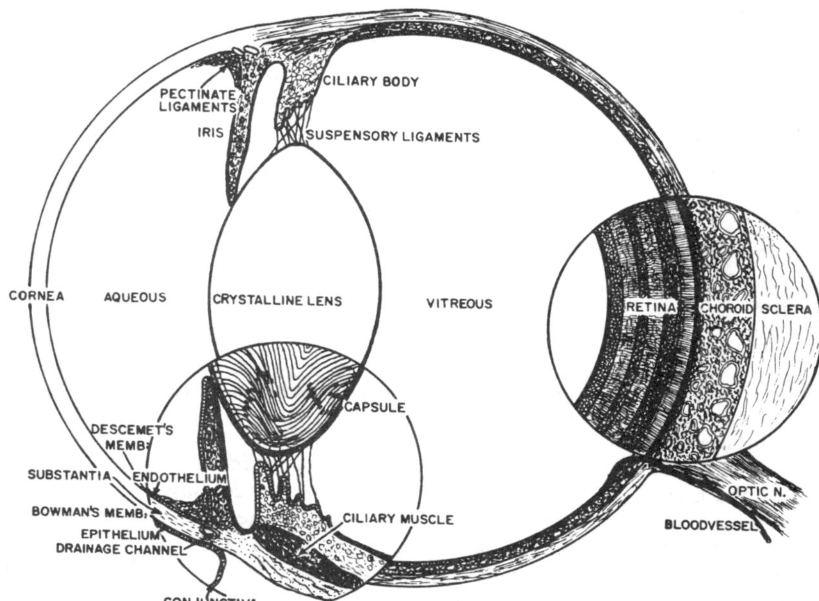

Figure 50.1. Section of the eye of a cat. The two circles enclose magnified sections of the macroscopic drawing. Not to scale.

in the iris and form a dilator pupilla. These muscle fibers are smooth in mammals, striated in birds.

The retina or nerve tunic is the light-sensitive coat of the eye. It is connected to the brain by the optic nerve, and its receptors are the rods and cones. Embryologically the retina is a part of the brain and the optic nerve is a cerebral tract.

The crystalline lens is a biconvex transparent mass situated between the vitreous body and the iris. Its anterior surface is bathed by the aqueous humor and is in partial contact with the iris. Its posterior surface, more strongly curved than the anterior, fits into the vitreous body. The lens, although apparently optically homogeneous, is not actually so, its refractive power increasing from the periphery to the center. This fact helps to correct spherical aberration. The lens is enclosed in an elastic, transparent membrane known as the capsule. Supporting the lens are its annular suspensory ligaments, which extend from the ciliary processes to the capsule of the lens, where they are inserted on each side of the equator of the lens. The spaces between the fibers of the suspensory ligaments connect with one another and with the posterior chamber and are filled with aqueous humor. Posteriorly the suspensory ligaments are intimately related to the hyaloid membrane enclosing the vitreous humor.

The vitreous humor is a transparent, jellylike substance found in the cavity of the eye behind the lens. The aqueous humor is a watery liquid found in the spaces between the lens and the cornea and in the interstices of the suspensory ligaments.

REFRACTION

When light travels through a homogeneous transparent medium such as air, it moves at a uniform velocity and in a straight line; but when it falls obliquely on the surface of another transparent medium, part of it is reflected, while the rest travels through the new medium at a different velocity and in a different direction. This alteration is known as refraction. When light passes from a rarer medium into a denser, the direction of refraction is toward the normal (perpendicular), whereas when it passes from a denser medium into a rarer, the direction of refraction is away from the normal. Light passing into a medium as a normal to its surface is not refracted. Because a denser medium bends and slows light passing into it from a rarer medium, the denser medium is said to have a greater index of refraction than the rarer.

When parallel rays of light fall upon the surface of a biconvex lens, they are converged to a focus or point beyond the other surface. For parallel rays this point is known as the principal focus of the lens. The distance between the lens and the principal focus is the focal length of the lens. It is determined by the curvature and refractive index of the lens. The power or strength of a lens is expressed by the reciprocal of its focal length. In physiological optics the unit of power of a lens is the diopter (D), a lens with a focal length of 1 m having a power of 1 D. A lens with a focal length of 0.5 m has a power of 2 D; one with a focal length of 2 m, a power of 0.5 D, and so on.

Conversely, if a luminous point is situated at the principal focus of a lens, the rays leaving the other surface of the lens will be parallel.

If a luminous point is situated at a distance from a lens greater than its focal length but not so great that the rays are parallel when they reach the lens, these divergent rays will be brought to a focus, on the other side of the lens, at a distance greater than the principal focus. This is the conjugate focus.

A line passing through the centers of curvature of the surfaces of a lens is known as the optic axis. Situated on this axis is a point, the nodal point, through which a ray of light may pass without undergoing refraction.

PHYSIOLOGICAL OPTICS

The production of visual images within the eye is somewhat different from the production of optical images by cameras and other instruments, even though these can be used to demonstrate certain eye functions. The reception of light, its translation into an image, and the transmission of that image can certainly be produced mechanically. But control of the system to accommodate to changing conditions and to meet the demands of a highly evolved cerebral complex is not yet possible with instruments.

Image formation

If one reduces the many refracting elements of the eye to a single theoretical refracting curve at the corneal surface, an image will be formed on the retina in reverse and inverted (Fig. 50.2).

When the image is not formed at the plane of the retinal receptors, as is occasionally found, then a refractive error exists, and this is named according to whether the image falls before or behind the retina. Such errors exist in animals just as they do in man, e.g. horses when they reach maturity. Most domestic animals are more subject to these conditions than are wild animals, which perhaps would have less chance of survival.

On whichever side of the retina the image is formed, the retina receives only a blurred impression of the image. While it is convenient to consider the formation of images in this way, it is really not so simple, as will be seen in Figure 50.3, which depicts some of the more obvious refracting surfaces. Even this diagram is oversimplified (Fig. 50.4). The cornea and the crystalline lens both have numerous refracting surfaces where tissues of

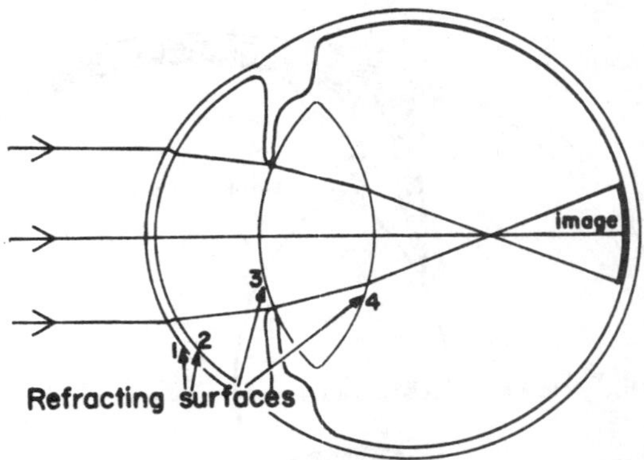

Figure 50.3. Corneal and lenticular surfaces. All of them bend the light according to the differences in refractive index between them and the fluids adjacent to them.

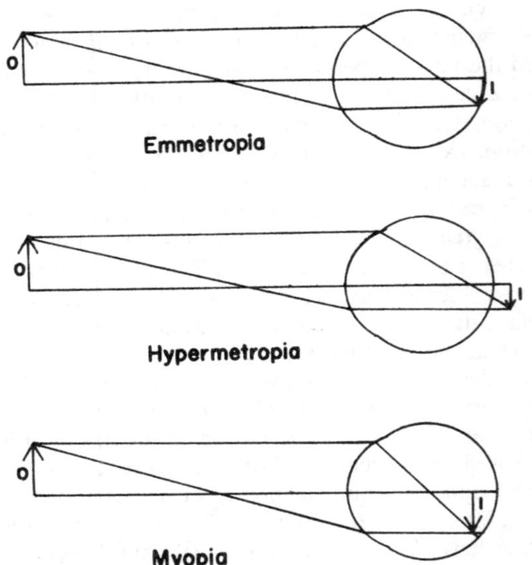

Figure 50.2. Paths of primary light rays into the eye to form an image of an object at infinity in emmetropia (normal vision), hypermetropia (long sight), and myopia (short sight)

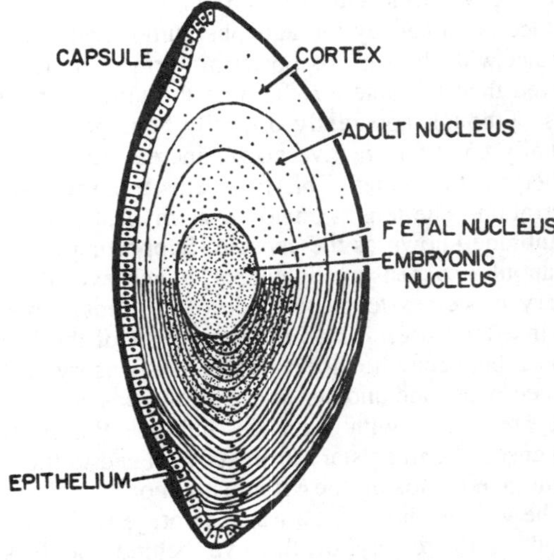

Figure 50.4. Zones of density within the crystalline lens. These change the direction of the light rays according to their density. (From Prince, Diesem, Eglitis, and Ruskell, *Anatomy and Histology of the Eye and Orbit in Domestic Animals*, Thomas, Springfield, Ill., 1960.)

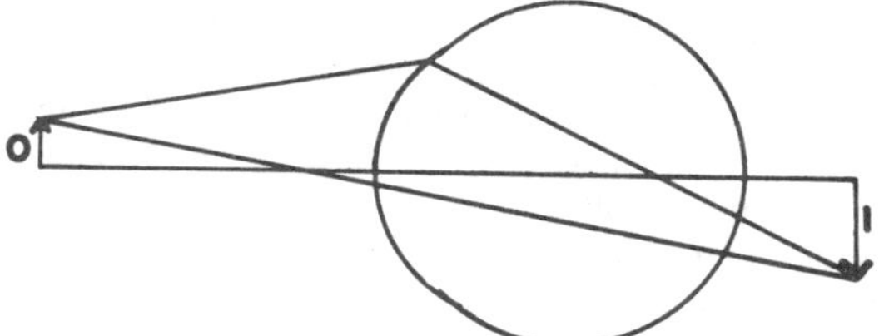

Figure 50.5. The forward and back focal lengths, or object (O) and image (I) distances, also known as conjugate foci

different refractive indices are either adjacent to each other or adjacent to humors having lower refractive indices.

Accommodation

Figure 50.2 holds good only when the object is at infinity. If the object is closer, the focal plane of the image recedes beyond the retina, and there is an artificial hypermetropia which can only be overcome by an adjustment of the refractive condition of the eye (Fig. 50.5). This change, known as accommodation, is achieved in most instances by an alteration in the curvature of the crystalline lens (Fig. 50.6). There is a very limited capacity for accommodation in domestic animals, except perhaps in the cat.

The alteration in lens curvature is brought about by an unstriated ciliary muscle which encircles the eye within the ciliary body and takes three directions. There are flat bundles of fibers against the sclera, running anteroposteriorly; radial fibers; and sphincterlike bundles encircling the ciliary processes from which the crystalline lens is suspended. When these muscles contract, especially the sphincter, this reduces the tension on the suspensory ligaments holding the lens. This permits the natural elasticity

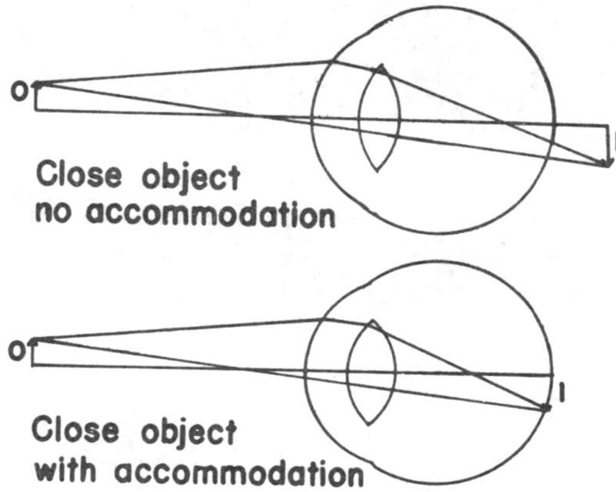

Figure 50.6. Accommodation. When an object (O) approaches an eye, the image (I) from that object will recede behind the eye unless the refractive power of the eye increases. This can be done by increasing the curvature and power of the crystalline lens as shown in the lower diagram.

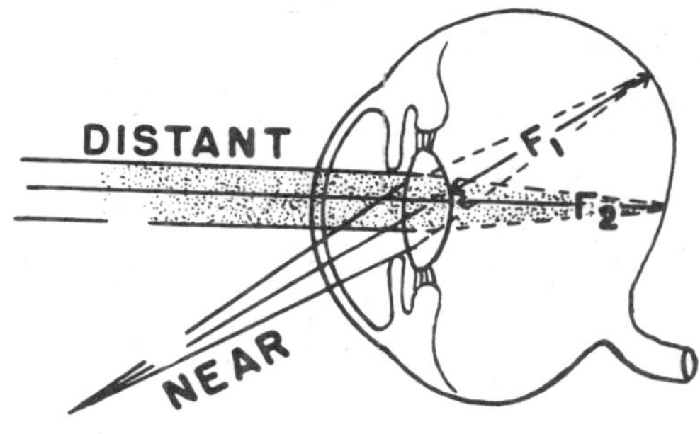

Figure 50.7. Horse's ramp-shaped retina, which provides a longer focal length for viewing downward (F_1) than for viewing along the axis of the eye (F_2). This means that lower, nearer objects are automatically in focus without the use of accommodation—within limits. (From Prince, Diesem, Eglitis, and Ruskell, *Anatomy and Histology of the Eye and Orbit in Domestic Animals,* Thomas, Springfield. Ill., 1960.)

of the latter to increase its anteroposterior dimension, which in turn increases the surface curvature and shortens its focus. Different animals have different degrees of accommodation. Some of them also supplement their system with some auxiliary feature. The horse has an eye specially shaped to augment its natural accommodation. Shaped like an oblate spheroid (Prince et al. 1960) it provides multiple focal distances, and objects at different distances can be in focus at the same time (Fig. 50.7).

The crystalline lens becomes denser with age, and its resilience and curvature variability are eventually eliminated, with an accompanying loss of accommodation. In the dog, this loss varies even within breeds, and this animal probably utilizes nasal investigation and the observation of movement in small close objects for its cues.

The cat may be better endowed with accommodation than other domestic animals, but it still does not command any extensive range, for in it also some of the muscle fiber patterns are poorly developed. The ciliary muscle in cattle is poorly developed, especially the sphincter. The same applies to the sheep, pig, goat, and rabbit.

The rabbit has perhaps half the focal range the cat has, but this is supplemented by blood engorgement of the ciliary processes, which may change the lens position slightly, and therefore change its focal plane. This in turn shortens the distance from the eye at which an object can be focused. There is a variation in accommodation with changes in blood flow after superior cervical sympathectomy, while stimulation of the sympathetic nerve supply via the long ciliary nerves appears to reduce lens curvature by relaxation of the ciliary muscle. Both mechanisms are involved in some animals.

Light absorption

When light passes into the eye and is refracted to form an image at the retina, much of it is also absorbed by the

Table 50.1. Average absorption by the various eye media of the light that reaches them (%)

Wavelength (nm)	Cornea	Aqueous	Lens	Vitreous
320	22	5	99.5	23.7
330	20	4.25	99.3	13.5
350	14	4.07	99.78	11
360	12	4	95.03	9.5
370	10	3.33	86.1	9.1
380	8.8	3.29	68.03	8.55
390	7.2	1.53	46.94	8.04
400	6	1.07	26.34	7.3
450	4		12.5	4.17
500	4		8.86	1.74

numerous transparent membranes, tissues, and fluids through which it passes. Table 50.1 and Figure 50.8 show how the blue end of the spectrum particularly suffers great absorption before reaching the retina, and this will obviously affect the color responses of that membrane in larger, more absorbent eyes. With the retina being transparent also, only a fraction of the light reaching it is absorbed. The balance of the light passes on to be absorbed by the choroidal tissues and blood without contributing to retinal stimulation.

Some animals possess a tapetum for reflecting this otherwise wasted light back onto the receptors, so that these receive almost twice the amount of stimulation they would receive without a tapetum. What is not absorbed by the retina in this second impingement then passes out through the transparent tissues on a forward path through the pupil and out of the eye. This returned light is seen as the familiar eyeshine when eyes glow in the presence of light at night. These tapeta are composed of choroidal layers of reflecting cells in the predatory carnivores and layers of collagenous fibers in herbivores. Where they occur, there is an absence of pigment epithelium coloring between the receptors and the choroid, for this would obstruct by absorption the passage of the light to the tapetum and back (Fig. 50.9).

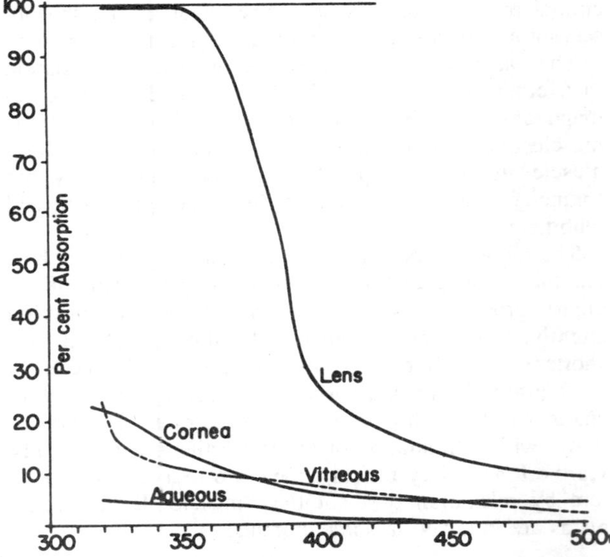

Figure 50.8. Percent absorption curves of the light reaching the anterior surfaces of the eye media in a rabbit. Beyond 500 nm, very little light is absorbed. Although some light of low wavelengths reaches the retina, it is doubtful if much actual stimulation of most retinas occurs from wavelengths below 380.

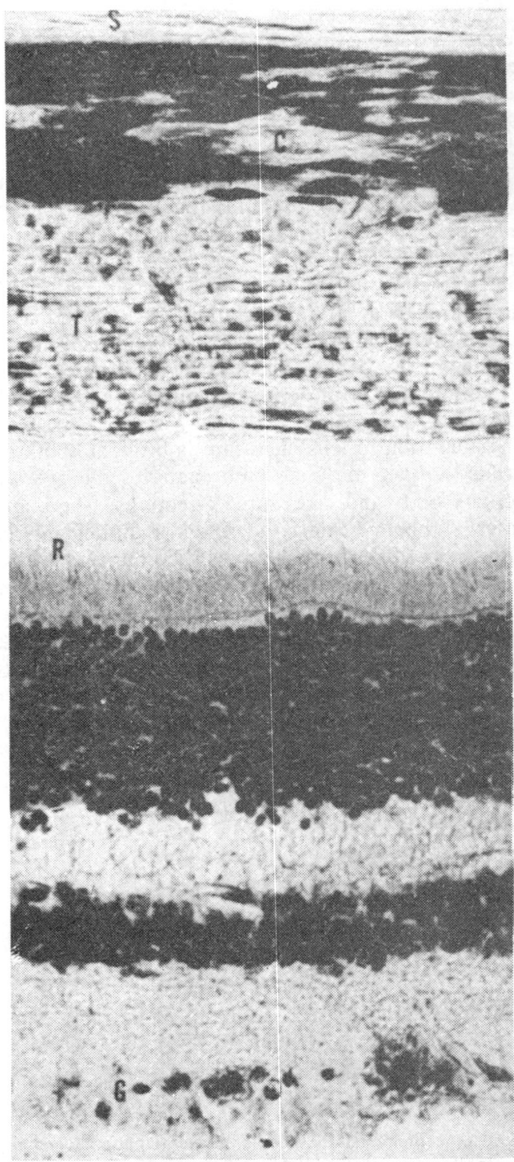

Figure 50.9. Tapetum of a cat seen as a broad band of cell layers (T) between the pigmented choroid (C) and the retina. S, sclera; R, receptors; G, ganglion cells.

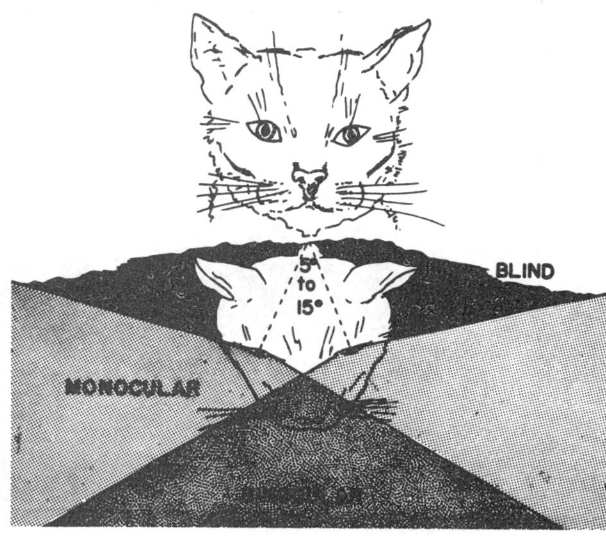

Figure 50.10. Field of vision of a cat, showing a large binocular area resulting from the forward position of the eyes

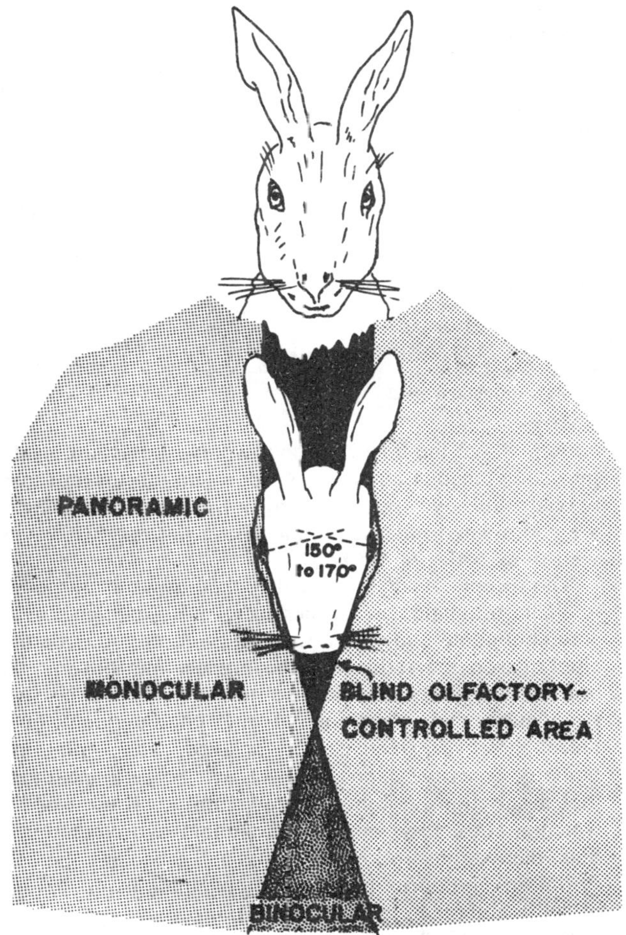

Figure 50.11. Field of vision of a rabbit, showing a very small binocular area, but a wide panoramic view resulting from lateral positioning of the eyes

Binocular vision

The entire spatial area from which the complete visual image of an eye is formed is known as its field of vision. In all domestic animals, no matter how far apart their eyes may be situated laterally, there is an area in which the visual fields overlap centrally. In the cat and some dogs, a very large part of each field overlaps the other (Fig. 50.10); in the rabbit, only a small nasal area in each field overlaps (Fig. 50.11). Quite obviously, where these two areas overlap, the impressions of the images must superimpose perfectly in the cerebral cortex or there will be double vision and consequent confusion.

This area of image overlap forms a zone of simultaneous binocular vision which is involved with depth perception and judgment of position. The larger areas of binocular vision in the cat and dog are responsible for their ability to leap on fast-moving prey accurately. The wider-set eyes of the herbivores enable them to enjoy a much larger panoramic field of vision, even to the extent of seeing everything around them through slight head movements. What is immediately behind their hindquarters is all that is outside their field of view. The rabbit even has a small binocular field behind it when it raises its head.

Thus the position of the eyes in the head is very much related to the habits of the animal. It is also related in some animals to the efficiency of the olfactory sense. Those animals with eyes well to the sides of the head and with large snouts often have more efficient scent detection, while those with the eyes well forward and with shorter snouts depend more on vision than on smell for their hunting.

Another factor in the field of vision available to an animal is the prominence of the eyes. It will be noticed that most animals with laterally situated eyes also have prominent ones. The calculation of either a panoramic or a binocular field of vision is therefore not just a simple product of the angles between the midline and the optic axes. Those which have been calculated within reasonable limits are shown in Table 50.2.

OCULAR PHYSIOLOGY

Once light is absorbed by the receptors, a complex series of reactions takes place which is still not fully understood. The visual pigment or photochemical in a receptor undergoes a change (bleaching) which produces an electrical transmission along its axon to the site of synaptic relationships with bipolar cells. Thence it travels similarly to the synaptic junctions with the ganglion cells, on through their axons via the lateral geniculate body to the

Table 50.2. Fields of vision (figures are subject to variation even between breeds)

Animal	Divergence between visual axes	Panoramic field	Binocular field
Cat	5°–20°	250°–280°	100°–130°
Dog	20°–50°	250°–290°	80°–110°
Rabbit *	150°–170°	360° or less	10°–35° (9° at rear)
Horse *	up to 130°	330°–350°	30°–70°
Cattle *	90°–115°	330°–360°	25°–50°
Sheep *	90°–100°	330°–360°	25°–50°
Pig	70°±	310°?	30°–50°
Goat *	100°–120°	320°–340°	20°–60°
Guinea pig	100° up		up to 70°

* More prominent eyes.

cortex, where the images of the two eyes are coordinated into simultaneous binocular vision. This occurs in those animals with eyes well forward in the head. The images are coordinated into panoramic vision in those with eyes well to the sides of the head.

The receptor visual pigment broken down in response to light stimulation is regenerated rapidly enough to ensure continuous function at balance, and this may be the chief reason the retina has the highest metabolism per unit of weight of any known tissue. When excessive stimulation and bleaching of the photopigment take place, however, recovery is delayed, and with sufficiently excessive exposure there will be permanent retinal destruction (as by a nuclear bomb explosion, or by watching an eclipse or arcweld without eye protection). Such thermal absorption by the tissues, especially the cell cytoplasm, produces boiling and coagulation, disruption of cell membranes, and rapid generalized degeneration.

It is possible that the cones (photopic receptors) and rods (scotopic receptors) contain different visual pigments, for they are different in their responses to a given quantity and/or quality of light. The rods are low threshold elements that are sensitive in low illumination but not responsive to color as are the brighter threshold cones. The mechanism of rhodopsin (rod photopigment) recovery or dark adaptation is well known. A dietary deficiency of vitamin A will inhibit it.

The synaptic areas are perhaps the most complex zones of the retina. The manner in which numbers of rods and cones are related to each other by the bipolar cells, and in which some cones and the bipolar cells are related to each other by the ganglion cells before the response pattern resulting from this complicated circuitry passes on to the lateral geniculate body, is only partially understood (Figs. 50.12, 50.13). The pattern is not identical even among mammals.

One reason why the retinal patterns are different in different animals is that there are varying proportions of rod and cone populations in keeping with the habits of the animals. Some animals are more nocturnal, some purely diurnal, and others arhythmic. These differences also produce variation in the quality of vision, as will the size of the eye and the size and number of receptors.

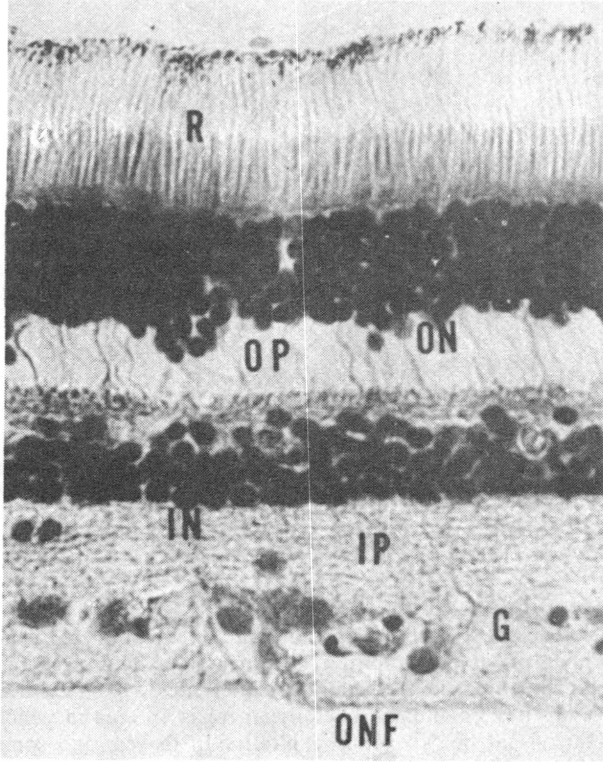

Figure 50.12. Section of a cat's retina. R, receptors; ON, outer nuclei; OP, outer plexiform; IN, inner nuclei; IP, inner plexiform; G, ganglion cells; ONF, optic nerve fibers.

Area centralis

Few animals have uniformly sensitive retinas. Those that are diurnally active usually have a greater concentration of cones, and therefore a higher image resolution in the region of the posterior pole of the eye. This region is known as the area centralis, but as this term really only describes its position, some authorities prefer the term macula. Blood vessels of a caliber large enough to be seen with the ophthalmoscope seldom invade the area, and because of this its position can be identified in animals such as the cat, dog, goat, and sheep which have holangiotic fundi (that is, show a direct blood supply from main arteries), but somewhat less easily in the pig (Fig. 50.14).

The area centralis is usually slightly dorsal to the optic nerve head, and a little to one side, depending on the lateral disposition of the eyes. In the horse, whose absence of almost all retinal blood vessels makes this area dif-

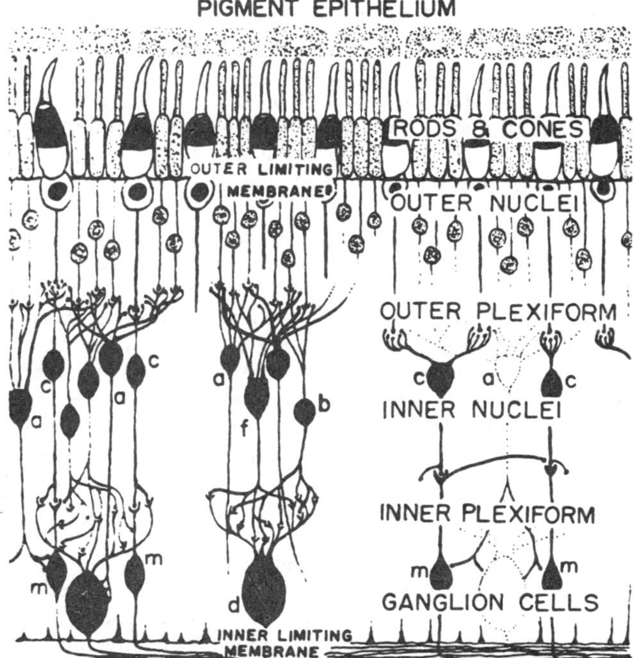

Figure 50.13. Diagram of retina to match Figure 50.12. This is oversimplified but gives an idea of the complex summation of receptors' responses to light. a, mop bipolars (tufted cells with treelike appearance, see Polyak 1941), diffuse cells which summate both rods and cones; b, brush bipolars, different from mop bipolars only in the relation of their terminal endings to the receptors; c, cone bipolars, which summate only cones; d, diffuse ganglion cells, which synapse with all forms of bipolar cells; f, flat bipolars, similar to brush bipolars; m, midget ganglion cells, which are monosynaptic and relate to only one cone bipolar cell each. Other cells are not shown for the sake of clarity. Where cones only are present in the retina, mop bipolars are absent, and ganglion cells include a third diffuse kind. Amacrine cells in the bipolar layer summate cones only, and horizontal cells connect ganglion cells with each other. (From Prince, Diesem, Eglitis, and Ruskell, *Anatomy and Histology of the Eye and Orbit in Domestic Animals*, Thomas, Springfield, Ill., 1960.)

ficult to identify, histological examination shows it to be about 15 mm dorsal to the optic nerve head, slightly nasally situated to this point, and broader than it is high. In cattle also it is a little dorsal to the level of the optic nerve head, perhaps 7 mm, and slightly nasal to that point, but because cattle eyes are generously endowed with retinal blood vessels, the area is more easily recognized due to its relative freedom from these vessels.

The receptors in the macular area of any eye are usually summated differently from the rest of the retina. This summation can perhaps be best described as simpler and more direct in the connections between the receptors and the lateral geniculate body. This, and the fact that the cones are usually finer and more closely packed here, provides the greater image resolution found in the macular area.

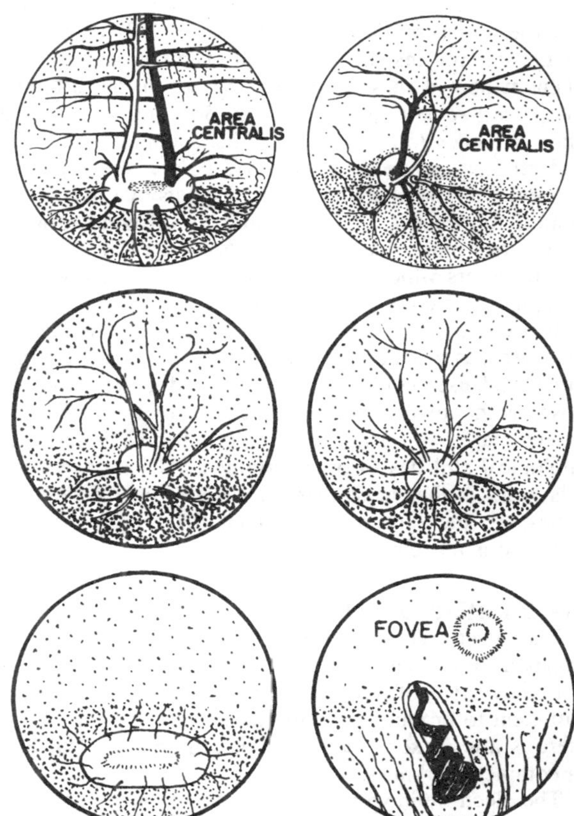

Figure 50.14. Fundus drawings of the steer (top left), sheep (top right), dog (middle left), cat (middle right), horse (bottom left), and bird (bottom right). The optic nerve head and the so-called area centralis (macular area) are shown in the steer and sheep.

Color vision

To what extent mammals other than man experience color vision is still debated. It is known that their retinas respond differently to light of different wavelengths, and careful measures have been adopted to ensure that it is only color and not brightness or any other quality to which the response is made at a particular wavelength. As the cones are the receptors that mediate color vision, it is also known that there are limitations to the animal's experience which are related to the cone population of its retina.

Some mammals have virtually all-rod retinas, and so they must either be devoid of color vision or experience it by a mechanism not yet identified. Others have almost all-cone retinas; while it might be assumed that these enjoy color vision, there is no absolute proof beyond the electrophysical responses to chromatic stimuli that one can observe, plus a number of subjective tests that are suggestive of color appreciation (and these are not universally convincing).

Experiments by Daw and Pearlman (1969) suggest that in the cat for instance, color discrimination may be a phenomenon of mesopic vision, based on the difference in spectral sensitivity of the rods (500 nm) and a single class of cones (556 nm). Some fish, amphibians, birds, and reptiles use color, even vivid color, for protection, recognition, and courtship. This suggests that they appreciate it for what it is. They also have different forms of retinas from mammals (Prince 1956, Prince et al. 1960), and receptors which lend themselves more readily to the acceptance of color-vision theories.

However, man, with a typical duplex mammalian retina, also has a wide appreciation of color and color mixtures, and uses color very effectively for the same purposes as the lower vertebrates mentioned earlier. To what extent man's appreciation of color may be purely psychological still has to be determined. All one can say at this point is that most mammals have some cones, and cones are the receptors to which the quality of color response is attributed.

Electroretinal activity

The electroretinogram and direct coupling of electrodes to individual cells have together greatly enhanced our knowledge of visual function. Metabolism alone is sufficient to produce potential in the retinal elements, so there is always some activity that can be recorded, even in complete darkness.

The electroretinogram seems to be initiated some time after birth, coinciding with the functional development of the ganglion cells, and increasing in its capacity with the increase of glycolytic activity. This is also the time of greatest growth of the receptors, and the b-wave particularly seems to be tied to receptor growth and the increase in retinal rhodopsin content.

Pupil control

The actions of the various pupil forms (round, horizontal oval or slit, vertical oval or slit) are protective in that they contract to exclude light so bright it will bleach photopigments excessively, and adaptive in that they dilate widely in low illumination so that the maximum amount of light may enter the eye and stimulate those receptors with the lowest response thresholds. Slit pupils close more effectively than circular ones because the two sides of a slit can virtually touch each other and effect almost complete closure.

There is another action besides this reflex contraction to light, a much less marked contraction with concentrated attention and accommodation, but mammals do not have any voluntary pupil control. Pupil control has always been considered to be by direct muscular action in the iris, but this is less certain now in some of the animals which show poorly developed musculature but good pupil action. Pupil constriction and dilation can be mediated in some animals by turgescence and detumescence of the rich iris blood-vessel network. Just how there can be such localized variations of pressure is not yet clear, but they have even been seen to equalize the pupils in the two eyes of a rabbit after unilateral superior cervical ganglionectomy has created an inequality of pupil size (Prince 1964).

The muscle fibers of the iris are well supplied with nerve fibers. In fact unmyelinated fibers considered to be parasympathetic appear to reach every smooth muscle fiber, and all appear to be endowed with end plates capable of spreading the stimulus over a wide area for rapid action. The arteries and capillaries also receive larger myelinated fibers which are closely related to the endothelial cells in the blood vessel walls.

Such myelinated fibers would appear to be sensory were it not for their close connection with the blood vessels through swellings which differ from the endings in the muscle and stromal fibers, and from those on the finer fibers reaching the chromatophores. Much work still has to be done to trace all the fibers, and some confusion has arisen on the action of some of them because in certain animals, e.g. the rabbit, some of the myelinated fibers which arise from the trigeminal nerve via the long ciliary nerves pass close enough to the oculomotor nerve and the ciliary ganglion to have been severed in ciliary ganglionectomy. Then too the ciliary nerve distribution within the orbits varies greatly in its arrangement, from very simple to exceedingly complex.

Pupil control is neurological, probably by two mediators, neuromuscular and neurovascular, perhaps acting concertedly, but capable of acting independently when one or the other is suppressed. It is probable that additional work will reveal somewhat differing mechanisms in the herbivores, the carnivores, and the rodents.

Glands

Domestic animals differ considerably in their orbital glandular patterns, and some have more glands than others. Furthermore, similar glands may have different secretions in different animals (Tables 50.3, 50.4).

Table 50.3. Types of lacrimal glands

Animal	Mixed tubuloalveolar	Serous tubuloalveolar	Mucous tubuloalveolar
Dog	X		
Cat		X	
Rabbit	?	X	
Pig		X	
Sheep	X		
Goat	?		X
Horse		X	
Steer		X	

Lacrimal

While every mammal appears to have a lacrimal gland, which in the domestic animals is a large double-lobed modified skin gland, this is invariably less active than in man. Similarly there is always a nictitans gland if a nictitating membrane is present, but only a relatively few of those listed have Harder's gland. In some, the Harder's gland and the nictitans gland are confluent, and at some ancestral period these two glands probably constituted a single one, possibly the Harder's gland, because this can be found in the orbits of both blepharid and ablepharid animals such as amphibians, reptiles, birds, monotremes and all mammals except primates, although vestiges of it are sometimes encountered in the latter.

Table 50.3 shows that those animals listed have a great preponderance of the serous tubuloalveolar glands. Even the goat, with a mucous tubuloalveolar gland, has some slight serous element which, with those animals having mixed tubuloalveolar elements, gives all of them some serous properties. Ordinarily, lacrimal secretion consists of a relatively large amount of the proteins albumin and globulin, plus nitrogen, urea, glucose, sodium chloride, potassium, chlorine, and other ions. The hydrogen ion concentration is important in its influence on the enzyme lysozyme which dissolves airborne saprophytes.

The functions of these three glands (lacrimal, Harder's, and nictitans) are similar and complementary in that they all remove desquamated cellular tissue and lubricate the globe within the palpebral cavity and behind the nictitating membrane, the Harder's and nictitans gland both draining into the fornix of the bulbar surface of the nictitating membrane. They also appear to combine their forms of secretion to produce a resulting mixed serous and mucous flow in proportions which are most suited to the particular animal's ancestral habits, and which are well regulated for viscosity, wetting potential, and optical clarity.

Most work has been done on the rabbit, but as Tables 50.3 and 50.4 suggest, what is known of the rabbit could apply to several other animals. Loss or deactivation of the lacrimal gland is not devastating but will nevertheless result in some corneal damage, recoverable when the gland regenerates or becomes functional again. Functional loss of this gland will occur after trigeminal section, and conversely hypersecretion occurs after trigeminal, lacrimal, or facial nerve stimulation. All the animals have a high protein content in their lacrimal secretion, and the rabbit has an unusually high albumin concentration. Ordinarily there is no lysozyme of measurable quantity in the tears, but when irritation or infection arises, it is clearly demonstrable.

Harder's

Harder's gland is not present in all animals, but as it and the nictitans gland appear always to have a common function and may even be derivatives of one common gland, this may not be very important to those animals which have only the latter. Where both glands are present, they combine functionally to produce a mixed secretion, and the secretion from either or both added to that from the lacrimal gland often is the vehicle for ensuring a mixed or seromucoid palpebral and corneal lubricant (Table 50.4). It is even obvious in a few animals that there is a reciprocity of volume for lacrimal and Harder's glands, the one being larger whenever the other is smaller.

Sometimes Harder's gland has two lobes, each of which will secrete differently (see the steer, Table 50.4). If the gland is lipid secreting as in the rabbit, the two lobes will usually show different sizes of secretory cells and of lipid droplets, uniformity of size of the droplets being retained within each lobe and within each endpiece. No single description of Harder's glands is possible, even among mammals.

In the rabbit, the secretion of Harder's gland is complex. The cells and secretion of both lobes contain sudanophilic material, neutral fats, Fischler-positive material, phospholipid alkaline phosphatase, and a neutral glycoprotein, with acid phosphatase in the white lobe only and small amounts of acetal lipid in the ducts and blood vessels (Schneir and Hayes 1951). Signs of holocrine secretion have been reported, as have signs of apocrine, but the degeneration of the cells and the resulting detritus do not conform to that of holocrine secretion in sebaceous glands. Similarly, no apocrine secretion has been observed with the electron microscope.

Nictitans

The nictitans gland has been confused so frequently with Harder's gland that very little work has been done on it under its own identity. Thus the information on what has so often mistakenly been called Harder's gland has had to be confirmed and reassigned to the nictitans gland whenever necessary. Table 50.4 shows the forms of secretion found in the domestic animals. The impor-

Table 50.4. Types of Harder's and nictitans glands

	Harder's				Nictitans		
Animal	Seromucoid	Mucous	Serous	Lipid	Mucous	Serous	Seromucoid
Dog						+	X
Cat						+	X
Rabbit				X			X*
Pig			X		+	+	+
Sheep					+	X	+
Goat					+	X	+
Horse					+	X	
Steer	X (ant. lobe)	X (post. lobe)			+	X	

X means present; + means acini of this type present also
* May also contain albumin

tant characteristic of this gland is that its secretion complements that of the lacrimal gland and that of the Harder's gland when it is present.

Other

Supplementing the secretions of the three large glands are other less prominent but still important ones in the conjunctiva and eyelids. The largest group is the meibomian glands found in even, vertical rows in each eyelid. Their many outlets give vent to a sebaceous secretion which, because of its viscous nature, forms a fine barrier at the lid margins and prevents the lacrimal and other secretions from flowing over the edges of the eyelids.

In addition to these there are modified sweat glands (glands of Moll) and rudimentary sebaceous glands (glands of Zeis) which open into the cilia follicles or on the lid margin near the cilia. Accessory lacrimal glands (Krause glands) within the conjunctiva secrete into the upper and lower fornices. All these supplementary glands play some part in balancing the secretion that bathes the cornea and inner palpebral surfaces.

METABOLISM

The provision of oxygen and nutrients and the elimination of waste products in the ocular tissues are entirely chemical or by blood transport except for the small amount of exchange that takes place at the surface of the cornea and conjunctiva. The crystalline lens particularly is quite separated from any vascular source or tissue-to-air surface and must therefore obtain its oxygen chemically from substances reaching it through the aqueous and possibly the vitreous humors. The cornea, on the other hand, is in contact with both the aqueous humor and the air, and at its periphery with a vascular (perilimbal) sinus.

The retina is in contact with the vitreous humor and the highly vascular choroid, and in addition has its own vascular tree. All the remaining ocular tissues are well endowed with blood vessels.

Cornea

The cornea exchanges oxygen and carbon dioxide mostly within the fluids that permeate the tissues, but carbon dioxide is also eliminated extensively from the corneal surface. The first characteristic recognized in the respiratory process is its essentialness to corneal hydration, and therefore to corneal transparency. Any oxygen reduction will encourage imbibition of fluid and consequent edema, with loss of transparency. Closure of the eyelids for a protracted period will cause increased hydration, for instance, reducing the oxygen uptake and the carbon dioxide elimination to the air. Although carbon dioxide seemingly will only pass in the direction of the outer corneal surface and then dissipate with surface evaporation, oxygen is probably able to pass in both directions with equal ease. Water also passes in both directions when under osmotic force, but the sodium and chloride contents encounter a powerful barrier in the epithelial and endothelial membranes.

Glycolysis within the cornea is by both aerobic and anaerobic pathways and is apparently confined to the epithelium, which may be able to alternate the two methods of producing lactic acid according to the atmospheric oxygen tension. In some animals any increase or decrease of atmospheric oxygen tension is accompanied by a corresponding fall or rise respectively in the lactic acid concentration.

Storage of glycogen seems virtually unnecessary in some corneas. Small quantities of it are found only intracellularly in the epithelium. There is a high intake of glucose from the aqueous humor, however, and this can penetrate through to the stroma. Its rapid breakdown to lactate provides the energy for other physiological processes and for the maintenance of hydration balance.

An active lactic dehydrogenase mechanism exists in the corneal epithelium. This enzyme system appears to hold the level of lactic acid steady. There is a great variation between animals, however, which does not seem in any way related to corneal size, environment, or an animal's habits. It is 20 times higher in the rabbit, for instance, than it is in the cat or rat (Kuhlman 1959). The cornea is very rich in mucopolysaccharides, and most of its lipid content is found in the epithelium.

Aqueous humor

The main tasks of the aqueous humor, apart from participation in the retention of intraocular pressure, are to act as a carrier for nutrients to the cornea through its posterior surface and to the crystalline lens, and to remove waste products from the interior of the eye.

The passage into the posterior chamber of the aqueous humor from the ciliary epithelium has been the subject of much investigation. Some experimental results suggest it is formed intracellularly, then passes across the cell membrane. Others have supported the idea that it is secreted at the surface of the cell across its membrane. It is known that active transport of sodium across the ciliary epithelium accompanied by other solutes transfers water osmotically into the posterior chamber, and oxidative phosphorylation is involved too.

Berggren (1964) has shown with reasonable conclusiveness that there is a pump mechanism involved in the transfer or secretion of aqueous humor from the ciliary processes and that this is dependent on potassium. Kinsey and Reddy (Prince 1964), in their work on the rabbit, have estimated the net influx of water to the aqueous humor to be 2.5–4.0 μl per minute, and its turnover from 10–20 percent per minute. Thus they calculate that between 25 and 50 μl of water exchanges each minute between the blood and the anterior aqueous humor, most of it across the anterior surface of the iris and perhaps a little across the cornea. The major exit for the aqueous fluid is via the trabecular meshwork in the anterior chamber angle.

It is not entirely clear to what extent the aqueous humor derives oxygen from the blood vessels in the ciliary processes before it enters the posterior chamber, because the capillaries carry blood which has already given up much of its oxygen to the surrounding tissues and therefore may be very near in oxygen content to the aqueous humor itself. Ordinarily the oxygen tension of the aqueous humor is little more than a quarter of that of the blood, but a rabbit breathing pure oxygen accumulates this in the anterior aqueous humor chamber until a new steady state is reached at 200 mm Hg (Adler 1951). Thus there is evidently a fairly direct relationship between the oxygen content of the ciliary blood vessels and that of the aqueous humor whatever the normal relative tensions.

Besides the inorganic ions—sodium, potassium, chloride, phosphate, hydrogen, calcium, magnesium, and sulfate—found in aqueous humor, there are many organic constituents. Small amounts of protein, a number of enzymes, quantities of ascorbic acid, lactic acid, glucose, urea, many amino acids, hyaluronic acid, and so forth are present. With all these, the aqueous humor remains 99 percent water. Estimates for various animals vary no more than 1 percent, the horse perhaps being the highest published, with 99.7 percent water (Wolff 1948).

Aqueous outflow

The outflow of aqueous humor through the trabecular meshwork of the angle between the cornea and iris depends greatly on the condition of the endothelium and its surrounding mucopolysaccharides which make up the meshwork. Undue hydration of this tissue has the ability to reduce the pores or openings through which drainage takes place. Different animals have different numbers and systems of drainage channels (Prince et al. 1960, Prince 1964) and the volume of outflow differs between them also.

As the meshwork pores only pass fluid containing substances of limited molecular weight, obstruction or reduction of flow is possible if the aqueous humor acquires excess proteins which will lodge in the meshwork pores. Obstruction is also possible anatomically by the iris sagging and covering part of the trabecular angle, and there is considerable evidence that neurological influence on the meshwork will affect aqueous outflow. These factors are exceedingly important in possible disturbances of the internal pressure of the eye (the intraocular pressure or IOP).

Intraocular pressure

Intraocular pressure (or tension) keeps the external coats of the eye rigid and closely positioned to each other. It also keeps the tissues in fluid balance. It is dependent upon the influx and efflux of water and is somewhat variable in the lower mammals. If one uses manometry, laboratory animals will demonstrate from 20–25 mm Hg (Adler 1951). The nictitating membrane exerts some pressure on the globe, and the retractor bulbi muscle aids this. When under tension, this muscle can raise the intraocular pressure to 100 mm Hg (Prince 1964).

While there are diurnal (high in the morning and low in the evening) and other physiological variations in the intraocular tension, any extensive or extended variations lead to pathological changes. An abnormally high IOP produces glaucoma (a disease that may result in optic atrophy), which is becoming increasingly recognized in some domestic animals.

Any change in the venous pressure is reflected in the IOP, but at best the venous pressure only accounts for 10 mm Hg. The effects of arterial pressure are less well understood, pulsation changing the IOP no more than 1–2 mm Hg, although respiration changes it up to 5 mm Hg (Adler 1951). Any increase in aqueous humor due to obstructed outflow can increase IOP to phenomenal heights.

Undoubtedly the IOP is at least partially under some kind of neurological or hormonal control, or perhaps both. Neurological control has been confirmed by experiments with cats, dogs, rabbits, and monkeys. The epithelium adjacent to the capillaries of the ciliary processes, from which the aqueous humor originates, and the trabecular meshwork through which it leaves the eye, both respond to neurological influence that can cause slight imbalance between inflow and outflow. This imbalance in flow can cause a change of IOP.

A slight change in osmotic pressure in the aqueous humor permitting entry of water but not of dissolved substances, or a slight change in the protein concentration of the blood, will affect the IOP, the former very greatly.

Crystalline lens

As the crystalline lens is enclosed in a continuous capsular membrane, its oxygen uptake, which is very modest, depends on the permeability of that capsule. This becomes obvious when the capsule is ruptured, the oxygen uptake soaring to a very high level. There is disagreement on the specific site of this uptake, but it seems to be mostly in the anterior epithelium, the outer cortex being next in importance. As the respiratory enzymes are more concentrated in the epithelium, one would expect this to be the main site. The permeability of the capsule is greater in young animals, and it is selective to molecular size.

Neither the oxygen uptake nor the water content of the lens is ordinarily high. These values are further reduced with age and with increased weight of the animal. Age changes reduce the permeability of the capsule and its selectivity for molecular size, harden the nucleus, produce a progressive increase in density, and decrease metabolic activity, leaving only the epithelium and outer cortex to take up the bulk of the oxygen and hold most of the water. The epithelium and outer cortex may be the only zones of the lens to utilize oxygen adequately, and this, with other physiological deficiencies, may encourage the changes in the nucleus mentioned above.

The respiratory enzymes located in the anterior epithelium appear to share the main site for aerobic glycolysis. Anaerobic glycolysis probably constitutes two thirds of the energy requirement taking place elsewhere and this helps to offset the low oxygen uptake. It would seem that the aqueous humor must be the major path by which metabolites reach the lens. The aqueous humor is rich in glucose, and most of this is rapidly transformed into lactate by the lens, its movement into the lens being proportional to its concentration in the aqueous humor. Diffusion alone is evidently not sufficient to promote its entry. There must be some form of active transport as well.

Although damage to the capsule will increase oxygen uptake, it will usually reduce the glucose uptake. It is possible that the capsule contains some of the glycolytic enzymes. The formation of lactic acid decreases and the metabolic activity and glucose content of the lens appear to be reduced with age. Not only does the lens take up less glucose but changes take place in the carbohydrate metabolism. Since any change of the glucose concentration in the lens will produce a functional disturbance, there could be a degenerative cycle set up either at the capsule or within the lens stroma.

Some chemicals, such as phosphate, once they enter the lens are stored in sites distant from those which use them. Phosphate enters the lens from all directions and quickly participates in metabolism. In usable form it is found in highest concentration in the epithelium, but it is stored mainly in the posterior cortex. This is in keeping with the fact that most of that phosphate entering through the anterior surface of the lens is soon used, while of that entering through the posterior surface probably half is stored.

Of the total lipids of the crystalline lens, up to 80 percent are likely to be phospholipids, which differ in composition and distribution in each species. These differences may be related to the fact that there are also wide differences between the lipid contents of various parts of any eye.

There are very wide quantitative differences among species in the ascorbic acid content of the lens (listed below). Content is higher in the herbivores than in the carnivores. According to Adler (1951), almost all animals show more ascorbic acid in the lens than in the aqueous humor, but the rabbit is a notable exception to this, some analyses showing the aqueous humor to have three times as much as the lens (Prince 1964). In all animals, the ascorbic acid content of the lens is reduced with age, and as with so many other constituents it is present in the cortex in greatest concentration. The ascorbic acid contents of the lens and aqueous humor as given by Davson (1949) are as follows (mg/100 g):

Animal	*Aqueous*	*Lens*
Horse	18–24	26–57
Sheep	12–25	17–46
Rabbit	13–61	4–38
Man	3–15	5–49
Dog	4–6	3–8
Cat	5	

Smythe (1958) felt that ascorbic acid may take the place of oxygen in lens metabolism in combination with sulfur compounds and one of the lens proteins.

Protein, both soluble and insoluble, shows a higher percentage in the lens than in many other organs in the body and is uniformly distributed throughout the lens. It constitutes most of the dry weight. It increases with age and is proportionate with the weight of the lens. Kinsey and Reddy have found that the maintenance of protein level is dependent on the entry of free amino acids from the aqueous humor (Prince 1964) by active transport and possibly other mechanisms. This transport and the loss of amino acids, which is by diffusion, are associated with the capsule and the epithelium (Kinsey and Reddy 1963).

Reduction of the water-soluble proteins, which are found mostly in the cortex of the lens, takes place with those changes that produce reduced transparency of the lens, which are usually associated with aging. Almost all metabolic activity in the lens slows down as the animal ages. The oxygen and water contents are reduced, the growth rate slows, the chemical constituents are quantitatively reduced, and the curvature becomes finally stabilized.

Any of these chemical changes can probably be produced by systemic disturbance also. The most commonly recognized pathological condition of the lens is cataract. This is an opacity brought about both by reduction of soluble proteins and reduced oxygen uptake. Structural changes of the lens cells and consequent opacification also accompany alterations in the hydration balance and the uptake of sodium, which is ordinarily found outside the lens, while potassium is found inside.

Traumatic cataract is probably due to penetration of the metabolic barrier formed by the lens capsule, thus permitting disturbances of hydration, ionic exchange, and protein level. Radiation cataract, especially that produced by a thermal agent, is also the result of reduction of soluble proteins. Other forms of radiation which produce enzyme disturbance, nuclear fragmentation, reduction of glycolysis, and the suppression of aqueous formation result in similar opacification.

The lens physiology is further disturbed by some drugs and by certain chemicals introduced intravenously. Sodium iodoacetate is one of those which will reduce aqueous secretion and produce a cataract closely resembling those formed by radiation. Disturbance of lens chemistry or metabolism in any way whatsoever will tend to produce opacification.

Vitreous humor

While a great deal is known of the water movement and chemical composition of the vitreous humor, there is less information regarding the actual pathway of oxygen. It is known, however, that oxygen tension responds readily to hypoxia or inspired high-oxygen air (Adler 1951). There is a diffusion barrier between the retina and the vitreous humor and between the posterior aqueous and the vitreous humors. From both choroidal and retinal vessels there is some exchange with the vitreous humor, there being evidence of active transport in and unidirectional movement out by some substances.

The gel structure of the vitreous humor is probably derived mostly from collagen, which increases with age, and from hyaluronic acid, which together with the soluble protein glycoprotein is close to the retina. The ascorbic acid content of the vitreous humor also increases with age and, as this acid is essential for collagen formation, it could be the explanation for lessening transparency and increasing light scatter within the vitreous in older animals.

All the substances that enter the vitreous humor take up an uneven distribution. There is little glucose, the crystalline lens and retina probably utilizing most of what is available, but it increases proportionally to any increase in the aqueous humor or the blood. This suggests its free diffusion into the vitreous humor across the aqueous-vitreous surface. There is probably four times as much lactate as glucose. Large quantities of nonprotein nitrogen are present. There is, however, a much lower concentration of all amino acids than in the aqueous humor or plasma.

In almost all the domestic animals, the phosphate content of the vitreous humor is much lower than that of the aqueous humor, and its highest concentration is at the aqueous-vitreous barrier. The nonprotein nitrogen, amino acids, sodium, and phosphate are all generally lower than in the aqueous humor, but the potassium, chloride, and lactate are higher.

Reddy and Kinsey (Prince 1964) considered that aqueous and vitreous chemical balance permits the vitreous humor to act as a source for the aqueous humor of substances in which the vitreous is rich, and as a sink for those substances with which the aqueous is better supplied or which the vitreous has in lower concentration, such as carbon dioxide. The pathway by which carbonic anhydrase reaches the vitreous humor is from the retina, for it is found in its greatest concentrations in the peripheral retina and the adjacent tissues.

One usually thinks of the vitreous humor as a viscous medium of greater peripheral density. It is surprising, then, to discover that there is a very active water movement and turnover, the entire content being replaced several times daily, perhaps more frequently than in the aqueous humor. Where this water comes from and then goes is not entirely known; some comes from the aqueous humor and more perhaps from the retinal and uveal blood vessels.

Ordinarily there is a very well-balanced hyaluronic acid–hyaluronidase relationship in the vitreous humor, and disturbance of this balance changes its viscosity. Hemoglobin will liquefy it and so will ultrasonic vibration. Possibly most iron compounds with a low molecular weight will do this in rabbits, but not necessarily in other animals.

Retina

The retina has the highest metabolic rate per unit of weight of any tissue in the body, and the consumption of oxygen varies with the size of the receptors as they develop (Prince 1964). It also responds to trauma and surgical interference. Oxygen must be available to the retina from both the retinal and choroidal blood vessels, and the maintenance of oxygen balance is absolutely vital to retinal function; retinal structure will be damaged by either excess or insufficiency. The degree of damage and the time required vary in different species and with age. This variation can be an important factor in experiments involving circulation obstruction. Frayser and Hickam (1964), while confirming that most of the retinal energy is provided through glycolysis (the retina has high glycolytic activity) and glucose oxidation, have suggested that there may also be a compensatory mechanism between glycolysis and oxygen consumption. Certainly the retina has a unique ability to split glucose into lactic acid without the presence of oxygen.

While the receptors appear to contain the main concentrations of respiratory enzymes, other elements of the retina may also be involved in respiration although to a lesser extent. The pigment epithelium appears to be a suitable site.

The retina's high rate of glycolysis makes it very sensitive to glucose deficiency. There are, however, considerable glucose reserves within the tissues. Glycolysis is by both the aerobic and anaerobic pathways, the latter being very much greater than the former. The process increases the maturation of the retina. As with oxygen consumption, there is a decrease in glycolytic activity after stress, and the utilization of glucose is also reduced as the retinal cells degenerate.

Glycolysis in some form appears probable in almost all the layers of the retina including the pigment epithelium, where it may even be related in some complex manner to the degree or speed of rhodopsin regeneration. There is still uncertainty regarding the actions of the glycolytic enzymes in some layers, especially the pigment epithelium, because of the involvement of vitamin A and retinene. There is also considerable citric acid metabolism present in most of the layers.

Visual pigments

The retinal chemistry as a whole is exceedingly complex. Much of it is related to the process of breaking down and resynthesis of visual pigments in the visual process, that is to light and dark adaptation. McConnell found that the pigment epithelium not only contains considerable quantities of vitamin A utilized in the resynthesis of rhodopsin; it also contains some highly organized lipoprotein structures (Prince 1964). If there is a deficiency of vitamin A, the regeneration of the visual pigments is greatly delayed (poor dark adaptation), and a degree of night blindness may result.

Rhodopsin and other visual pigments are formed by combinations of one of two forms of retinene with a protein (opsin), and at least four combinations have been identified in the vertebrates. Some experts will acknowledge only two, but others accept the possibility that there are quite a number of them, each responsive to different wavelengths. Rhodopsin, the photochemical of the rods, is the visual pigment on which most information is available (Fig. 50.15).

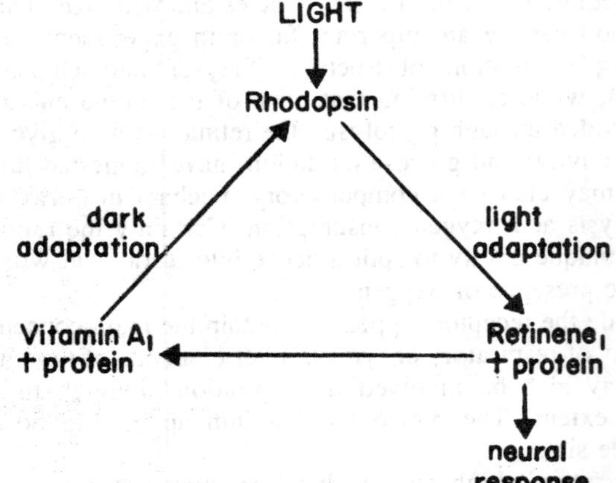

Figure 50.15. Breakdown and resynthesis of rhodopsin, the rate of each process being well balanced in normal circumstances (i.e. at all tolerable levels of illumination). In the event of vitamin A_1–deficiency, the dark-adaptation process is slowed or inhibited, the steady state being restored with renewal of vitamin A_1 stores.

Rhodopsin bleaches rapidly in the presence of light. The degree of bleaching is related to the intensity of the light. The process is quite visible in the freshly enucleated frog eye, and so is the experimental regeneration and rebleaching of the pigment. It does not absorb all wavelengths, and those not absorbed are reflected back so that one can identify a color for the pigment. Visual pigments in different classes of animals present different appearances. These differences, together with the various absorption peaks of the pigments, have been a strong factor in the contention that there are many visual pigments with only slightly different chemical properties.

The absorption peak of rhodopsin (for light reaching the retina after traversing the clear media) is in the region of 500 nm, with only slight variations between orders. In man it is 497, in the rabbit 500–502 (McConnell, in Prince 1964), in the rat 497, in the monkey 500, in freshwater fish (porphyropsin) 524–532. Other visual pigments have been identified (or postulated) with absorption maxima at 260, 330, 400, 405, 450–490, 498, 500–502, 507, 510, 520, 523, 530, 533, 540, 543, 560, and 610 nm. Those with the higher wavelengths are related to photopic (cone) receptors, but just what is the purpose of those with peaks in the two lowest wavelengths remains to be discovered.

A cone photopigment has not been successfully isolated from the human eye, or from the eyes of the domestic animals, in which the cones are greatly outnumbered by rods anyway; but it has been separated from the all-cone retina of the chicken. This photopigment is called iodopsin and its absorption peak is 560 nm (Prince 1949, Adler 1951). The chemistry of iodopsin is similar to that of rhodopsin, the main difference being in the protein present.

By using monochromatic light and recording responses at the lateral geniculate nucleus in light-adapted rabbits, Hill (1962) identified seven wavelength responses, five excitatory and 2 inhibitory, with sensitivity maxima from 435 to 635 nm. Single cells exhibited several combinations, usually one inhibitory and one excitatory, often with mutually antagonistic qualities. Most of the responses registered were confined to the blue and green regions of the spectrum (Prince 1964).

VISUAL RESPONSE

A given quanta of light of a specified wavelength striking a receptor will produce a certain level of photopigment bleaching, but equal quanta of light of another wavelength will not necessarily have the same effect. The quantum level required to produce a visual response to light of 510 nm is less than for any other wavelength. According to Adler (1951) a quantum of 500 nm wavelength light has a quantum value of 4.01×10^{-12} ergs, whereas a quantum of 600 nm light has a quantum value of 3.27×10^{-12} ergs. When these factors are introduced into light perception data, the sensitivity peak of the eye coincides exactly with the absorption peak in the rhodopsin spectrum, that is, 500 nm.

The absorption of light by the media not only filters out some of the incident wavelengths before these reach the retina (see Fig. 50.8), but it also reduces the quantum values available for retinal stimulation. Hecht once suggested that to initiate the reduction of rhodopsin, the maximum quanta required to enter the receptor is six, but from 58 to 148 quanta must be incident on the cornea to achieve this (Prince 1949).

The action of light on the retina produces a response to both the quanta of energy involved and the wavelength, in that the energy level depends entirely on the part of the spectrum from which the light is derived. The shorter wavelengths have a greater energy value and vice versa: "The energy of the quantum varies inversely to the wavelength, and the smallest amount of light energy which can be emitted from any source of light equals its frequency times a constant, that is, the energy of the quantum" (Adler 1951).

Because the brightness of a monochromatic light is determined by its energy level, threshold measurements of eye responses at various wavelengths must naturally include calculations for this fact, or the different wavelengths of light must be controlled to give equal brightness values after passing through the ocular media. Visual acuity, color response, and threshold measurement have all been carried out on a number of animals at retinal, lateral geniculate, and cortical levels.

Many retinal receptors, if not all, have some directional sensitivity, responding to a stimulus in one direction but not in the opposite direction. The selected direction differs in different cells (Prince 1964) and is in no way related to any other stimulus quality such as intensity or color, black or white. This may aid the analysis of retinal summation, for it occurs in some degree or another in all retinas investigated.

TEMPERATURE

Undoubtedly the metabolism of the eye is influenced by temperature, which increases from the surface of the cornea to the depths of the orbit (Fig. 50.16). The evaporation from the front surface of the cornea keeps the temperature down several degrees from that behind the eye. The air temperature, especially when it is low, influences that of the anterior chamber considerably. It is not yet proven that this in turn has any influence on intraocular pressure, but some opinions lean toward this possibility, especially as glaucoma, a disease which depends on increased intraocular pressure for its production, is more prevalent in cold climates.

Eye temperature in animals always appears to be less with the head lowered to the ground than when it is upright, a somewhat contradictory situation which needs

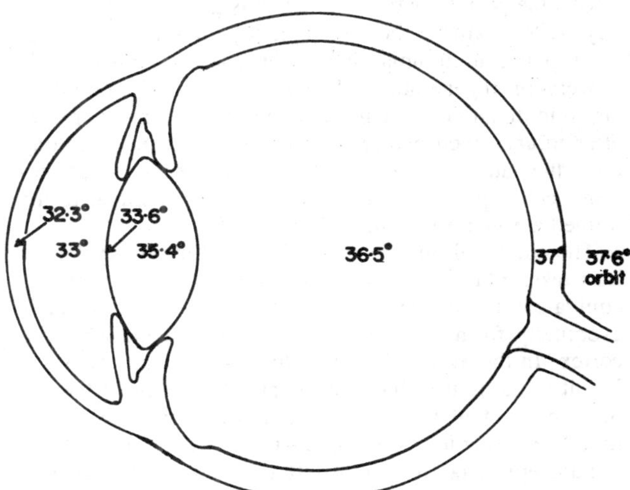

Figure 50.16. Temperatures (°C) found by Schwartz and Feller (Prince 1964) in the eyes of rabbits. Penetration to the deep orbit is necessary to record approximations to body temperature.

clarifying. When the eyelids are closed, the temperature gradient is abolished entirely. The anterior surface of the cornea and all intraocular zones rise to 37.7°C, confirming the part played by surface evaporation in temperature control. Schwartz (1964a) has also established a pH-temperature coefficient in the rabbit anterior-chamber aqueous humor and claimed that these two factors have a linear relationship.

REPARATORY AND CONTINUOUS MITOSIS

Once the eye has reached adult development, mitosis in the corneal epithelium is only in response to desquamation and trauma, while that of the endothelium is almost exclusively in response to trauma. In the epithelium of the crystalline lens, however, it is a somewhat continuous process.

One of the interesting features of the corneal epithelium is that after mitosis the basal and intermediate cells move toward the anterior surface, changing not only their shape but also their cytoplasmic content from a granular to a fibrillar pattern. As they reach the surface, they undergo fragmentation. When the eye is growing, most epithelial mitosis is at the periphery, but this appears to be reversed in the adult animal.

The regenerative power of this tissue is phenomenal, and replacement of damaged or stripped epithelium will be aided by mitotic activity all around the area concerned, and out to relatively distant zones. Epithelial mitosis responds very positively to sympathetic denervation. At first there is increased activity, but within a short time this is followed by a permanent decrease. With trigeminal denervation there is only a decreased activity. Neural stimulation has a somewhat opposite effect.

During development, most of the endothelial mitosis is also at the periphery of the eye and is greatest early in the day. After maturity there is no endothelial mitosis except in response to trauma, but the tissue has considerable powers of regeneration. There is a minute amount of amitotic division under normal conditions. This increases after injury, even preceding mitosis, and continues long after the latter has ceased. Unlike the repair of epithelium, cell replacement in endothelium is confined to the immediate vicinity of the injury.

The epithelial mitosis normally found in the crystalline lens takes place close to the equator, which is probably equivalent to the periphery in the cornea. These cells eventually form those of the main body of the lens, the cortex. In the event of trauma, the greatest activity is adjacent to the injury, but later it spreads widely. If the entire lens content is removed from within the capsule, at times remarkable tissue regeneration takes place from minute epithelial remnants left clinging to the anterior capsule, even to the point where there is eventually complete replacement of the lens. Several experiments have been conducted on rabbits to establish this finding, some utilizing the implantation of fetal tissue to hasten the process. Implantation certainly gives a little greater regeneration over a given period of time, but if one averages a large number of control animals and a large number of those implanted with cytolyzing tissue, the difference in some experimental series is by no means as great as has been claimed (Pettit 1963, Prince 1964).

REFERENCES

Adler, F.H. 1951. *Physiology of the Eye*. Mosby, St. Louis.

Berggren, L.B. 1964. Direct observation of secretory pumping in vitro of the rabbit eye ciliary processes. *Invest. Ophth.* 3:266–72.

Davson, H. 1949. *Physiology of the Eye*. 11th ed. Blakiston, Philadelphia.

Daw, N.W., and Pearlman, A.L. 1969. Cat colour vision: One cone process or several? *J. Physiol.* 201:745–64.

Elgin, S.S. 1964. Arteriovenous oxygen difference across the uveal tract of the dog eye. *Invest. Ophth.* 3:417–26.

Frayser, R., and Hickam, J.B. 1964. Retinal vascular response to breathing increased carbon dioxide and oxygen concentrations. *Invest. Ophth.* 3:427–31.

Hill, R.M. 1962. Unit responses of the rabbit lateral geniculate nucleus to monochromatic light on the retina. *Science* 135:98–99.

Kinsey, V.E., and Reddy, D.V.N. 1963. Studies on the crystalline lens. X. Transport of amino acids. *Invest. Ophth.* 2:229–36.

Kuhlman, R.E. 1959. Species variation in the enzyme content of the corneal epithelium. *J. Cell. Comp. Physiol.* 53:313–26.

Pettit, T.H. 1963. A study of lens regeneration in the rabbit. *Invest. Ophth.* 2:243–51.

Polyak, S.L. 1941. *The Retina*. U. of Chicago Press, Chicago.

Prince, J.H. 1949. *Visual Development*. Churchill Livingstone, Edinburgh.

———. 1956. *Comparative Anatomy of the Eye*. Thomas, Springfield, Ill.

Prince, J.H., ed. 1964. *The Rabbit in Eye Research*. Thomas, Springfield, Ill.

Prince, J.H., Diesem, C.D., Eglitis, I., and Ruskell, G.L. 1960. *Anatomy and Histology of the Eye and Orbit in Domestic Animals*. Thomas, Springfield, Ill.

Reddy, D.V., and Kinsey, V.E. 1960. Composition of the vitreous humor in relation to that of plasma and aqueous humors. *Am. Med. Ass. Arch. Ophth.* 63:715–20.

Schneir, E.S., and Hayes, E.R. 1951. The histochemistry of the Harderian gland of the rabbit. *J. Nat. Cancer Inst.* 12:257.

Schwartz, B. 1964a. The pH-temperature coefficient of rabbit anterior chamber aqueous humor. *Invest. Ophth.* 3:96–99.

———. 1964b. The effect of lid closure temperature gradients in the rabbit eye. *Invest. Ophth.* 3:100–106.

Schwartz, B., and Feller, M.R. 1962. Temperature gradients in the rabbit eye. *Invest. Ophth.* 1:513–21.

Smythe, R.H. 1958. *Veterinary Ophthalmology*. 2d ed. Williams & Wilkins, Baltimore.

Wolff, E. 1948. *Anatomy of the Eye and Orbit*. Lewis, London.

CHAPTER 51

Taste, Smell, and Hearing

by Morley R. Kare and Gary K. Beauchamp

THE CHEMICAL SENSES

The animal body is a network of chemical receptors (chemoreceptors). All cell membranes respond to chemical stimulation. Some cells have become specialized to respond only to chemical stimuli from the external environment, whereas others, such as those in the carotid sinus, respond only to internal chemical stimuli. The former are collectively referred to as the chemical senses. This arbitrary division is bridged by the chemical receptors in the gut (Sharma and Nasset 1962).

Fish have chemoreceptors distributed over the body surface. In amphibians, reactions to chemicals applied to the surface of the skin are observed; however, other specialized chemical receptors are concentrated in the oral cavity. For all air-breathing animals, chemoreception is primarily associated with the orally located taste buds or with the olfactory epithelium.

The chemical senses are commonly divided into three classes: (1) olfaction or smell, (2) gustation or taste, and (3) the common chemical sense. Olfaction is characterized by a sensitivity to volatile substances in extreme dilution. This accounts for its description as a distance receptor. The gustatory receptors usually require more gross contact with the chemical stimulant. The common chemical sense is reserved for the nonspecific stimulants, which are often irritants. The divisions among smell, taste, and the common chemical sense are arbitrary and can overlap, for a single chemical may affect all three categories. In some species, particularly in the less complex forms, it is difficult if not impossible to distinguish among the chemical receptor systems.

COMMON CHEMICAL SENSE

Moncrieff (1951) suggested that the common chemical sense is probably primitive, and that taste and olfaction are later differentiations. The prevalence of the common chemical sense in the lower vertebrates and invertebrates and the diffuse and relatively unspecialized nature of the receptors support this contention. Irritants, such as ammonia and acids, stimulate the free nerve endings of numerous surfaces, for example, those in the nasal chambers, mouth, and eyelids of vertebrates.

TASTE

The function of taste is generally associated with the ingestion of food. Some investigators suggest that it encourages nutritional prudence, that is, taste provides a cue to the animal as to the value of a food. Taste will stimulate the flow of saliva. There is some evidence that selection behavior based upon taste is complementary to physiological need. For example, in a choice situation (water vs. saline) the adrenalectomized rat will select the salt necessary to maintain life (Richter 1943, Harriman and Kare 1964). There are a number of reports, many

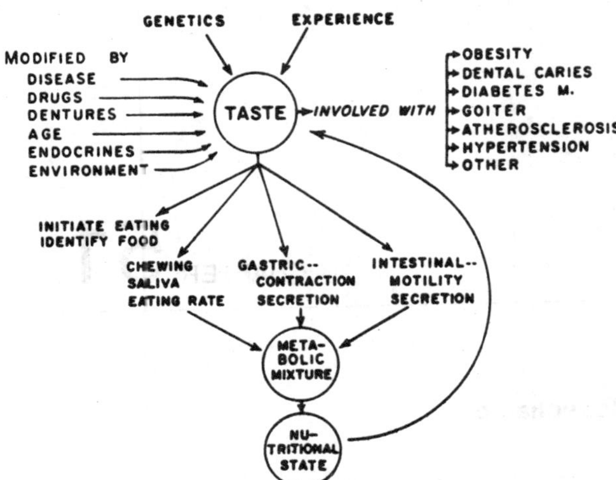

Figure 51.1. Taste and nutrition. The sense of taste can both directly and indirectly have a multifaceted relationship to the nutritional state of the animal. In turn, the nutritive state can modify taste. A major role of this sense is its influence on the activity and secretions of the digestive tract.

pseudoscientific, which imply that taste has evolved to permit an animal to reject toxic substances and accept nutritious materials.

Perhaps the most important function of taste is its effect on the digestive system (Fig. 51.1). Taste stimuli can increase gastric contractions and reduce intestinal motility. Further, gastric and pancreatic secretion have been directly related to the nature of the stimulus (Kare 1969).

Commonly, a diet is characteristic of the species. It would be expected that the taste system in a particular animal would complement the metabolic and dietary requirements of that species. But this seemingly obvious relationship has not been systematically investigated.

Taste receptors

The taste organs of mammals have their seat in the mucosa of the oral and pharyngeal cavities. The maximal concentration of receptors is in the mucosa of the tongue, particularly the dorsum.

All mammals and birds that have been studied have taste organs commonly referred to as taste buds. The distribution of taste buds varies greatly among species. Taste buds are usually concentrated on the circumvallate and fungiform papillae. In some animals, including the cow, a search was made on the filiform papillae but none were found. The taste buds in cows and sheep are generally oval in shape; their length is approximately 100 μ and the width varies from 20 to 45 μ. The taste buds of the horse are slightly smaller and melon shaped, while those of goats are still smaller, irregular ovals of about 30 by 60 μ. The pig has spindle-shaped buds 20 by 90 μ. In the cat and the dog, the taste buds are circular with a diameter of approximately 30 μ. Avian taste buds have shape characteristics which are intermediate between those of fish and mammals and which resemble those of reptiles. Chicken taste receptors are approximately 30 μ wide and 70 μ long.

While taste buds are characteristically found on the tongue, they have also been found on various structures related to the oral cavity, such as upper margins of the gullet, epiglottis, soft palate, pharynx, and larynx.

The tip of the tongue of cows is well supplied with taste buds; the middle has relatively few; and the back, which contains the circumvallate papillae, has by far the greatest number. There are, in fact, approximately ten times as many taste buds on the relatively few circumvallate papillae as there are on the fungiform.

In the dog, the reverse is true; the greatest concentration of taste buds is on the anterior portion of the tongue. In the chicken, there are no taste buds on the highly cornified anterior portion of the tongue; further, the few buds that are present are located on the base of the tongue and on the floor of the pharynx (Lindenmaier and Kare 1959).

Beidler (1960), using autoradiographic techniques, demonstrated that the cells in the outer layer of the taste buds are continually undergoing mitotic divisions. The relationship of age to numbers of taste buds is not uniform among species. While Arey (1954) found the maximum number in 5- to 7-month human fetuses, there are, in contrast, no taste buds in the rat until the ninth day postpartum, with the maximum being reached at 12 weeks (Torrey 1940).

The taste buds degenerate when the taste nerves to them are cut. They will reappear very quickly when the nerve regenerates. Poritsky and Singer (1963) found that taste buds transplanted to eyeless orbits in the adult newt regenerate after extensive invasion of the transplant by nerve fibers of the orbit.

De Lorenzo (1958) studied the rabbit taste bud with the electron microscope. The cytological evidence suggests that many types of cells are present. The so-called hair cells commonly associated with microvilli in the mouth of the bud were found to be minute apical extensions of the plasma membrane of the gustatory receptor cells.

Early studies (Oppel 1900) provided extensive information on the size and precise distribution of taste buds on the papillae and on the number of taste receptors in the various domestic animals. However, no simple relation between the total numbers or type and taste threshold or spectrum exists. The chicken, with its few dozen buds (Table 51.1), responds to chemical solutions to which the cow, with a thousand times as many buds, is unresponsive. Nonetheless, in general the cow responds behaviorally to many more taste stimulants than the bird.

Table 51.1 Numbers of taste buds

Animal	Taste buds	Authority
Chicken	24	Lindenmaier and Kare 1959
Pigeon	37	Moore and Elliot 1946
Starling	200	Bath 1906
Duck	200	Bath 1906
Parrot	350	Bath 1906
Kitten	473	Elliot 1937
Bat	800	Moncrieff 1951
Dog	1,706	Holliday 1940
Human	9,000	Cole 1941
Pig and goat	15,000	Moncrieff 1951
Rabbit	17,000	Moncrieff 1951
Calf	25,000	Weber et al. 1960
Catfish	100,000	Hyman 1942

Anatomy

In the typical mammal, taste receptors in the posterior one third of the tongue are supplied with nerve fibers from the IXth cranial nerve (glossopharyngeal). Receptors located on the anterior two thirds of the tongue receive nerve fibers from the chorda tympani branch of the VIIth cranial nerve (facial). The Xth cranial nerve (vagus) services taste receptors in the pharynx and larynx. All three of these neural pathways, after passing through their respective cranial ganglia, terminate in the medulla or pons of the brain. At the medulla, these nerve fibers are collected through a tract (tractus solitarius) which extends to the second order neurons of the solitary nucleus. The fibers from the solitary nucleus extend forward in the tract called the medial lemniscus, which leads to the posteroventral and arcuate nuclei of the thalamus. From the thalamus, projection fibers penetrate the cortex in the vicinity of the central fissure.

There is, of course, considerable species variation in the importance of specific nerves for taste information transmission. Bernard (1964) reported a posterior receptive field for the chorda tympani in the calf. He related this unique placement to the possibility that chemoreception plays a significant role in the mechanism of rumination. In the fowl, taste buds are limited to the posterior portion of the tongue which is served by the lingual branch of the glossopharyngeal nerve (Kitchell et al. 1959, Halpern 1962). Kitchell (1963) offered detailed observations on the anatomy and physiology of the gustatory mechanisms in the dog, pig, cow, and horse. He described the neural responses recorded from the chorda tympani and the lingual branch of the glossopharyngeal following the application of various test solutions.

Methods of study

The sense of taste of domestic animals has not, until this last decade, been the subject of extensive scientific investigation. Folklore and casual observations are the basis for many of the current opinions as to what taste sensations can be perceived.

The most common method used to evaluate the sense of taste in an animal is the preference test. Typical of this approach is the two-choice situation where the material to be tested is added to one of two otherwise identical food or fluid choices, and the animal's preference and intake are then recorded. This type of testing is difficult to reproduce since the chemical and physical context in which a taste stimulant might be tested can substantially modify the taste quality. Thus, although an animal may preferentially ingest salt in solution, the same concentration of salt in feed may have no influence on intake. There is further complication because variables that modify taste reception can be different for each species. For example, odor is of no consequence to the fowl; yet odor may confound results in a taste preference trial with cats.

Electrophysiological studies involve the application of substances to the tongue of the anesthetized subject and the measurement of consequent changes in electrical activity on the related taste nerve (Fig. 51.2). The results will indicate whether or not the chemical evoked a peripheral discharge but not whether the chemical had an appealing or offending taste to the animal (Figs. 51.3, 51.4). While there are examples of good relationships between behavioral and electrophysiological responses, there are also abrupt contradictions. For example, concentrations of sucrose solutions that will elicit avid selection and ingestion responses in calves are not detectable electrophysiologically. Furthermore, sucrose octaacetate at concentrations that evoke no behavioral response in the fowl is an effective electrophysiological stimulant. The behavioral response commonly measures preference thresholds, and the electrophysiological recordings can be related to discrimination thresholds. Considerable emphasis in current electrophysiological research has been on single-fiber as opposed to whole-nerve recordings. Also, recording after taste stimulation has been pursued from various areas of the CNS, e.g. the thalamus. A comprehensive discussion of electrophysiological findings is reported by Sato (1971).

Operant conditioning techniques have been used to a limited extent on taste research in domestic animals. Koh and Teitelbaum (1961) used conditioning techniques to compare thresholds in the rat with those obtained from preference tests and found them comparable. Andreev used this approach with the cow. His work, as well as other techniques, including measurement of salivary flow, vasodilatation, and electroencephalograms which are most commonly used in the Soviet Union, have been reviewed by Pick (1961).

A common assumption is that animals share the human taste world. This is usually qualified to indicate varying degrees of taste deficiency in animals. The basis may be the fact that so much of the behavioral taste research has been carried out on the laboratory rat, which, by chance, happens to have a sense of taste similar in many aspects to that of man. Recent evidence, however, clearly es-

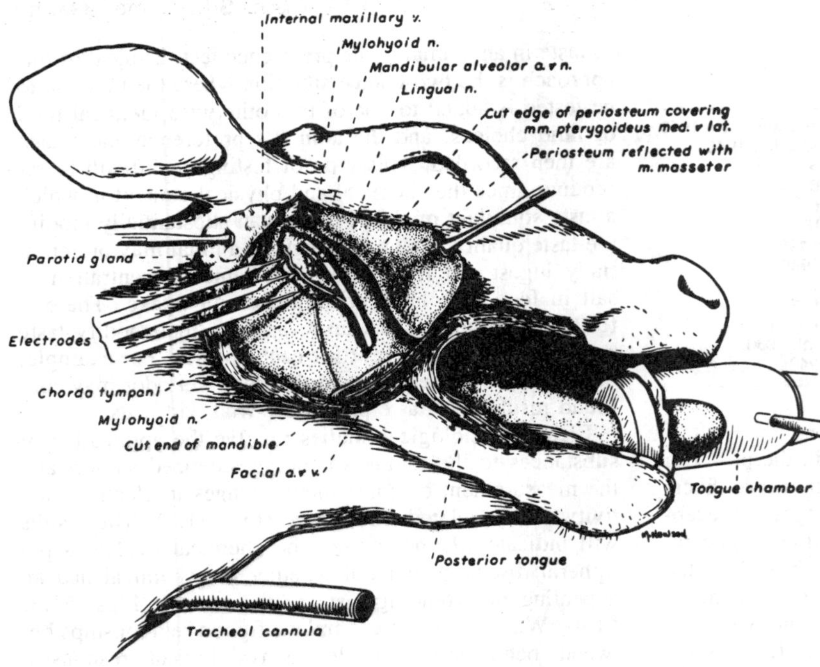

Figure 51.2. Preparation of the head of a calf, showing anatomical landmarks, position of electrodes, and tongue chamber used for flowing the stimulating solutions over the anterior part of the tongue. The right cheek is cut open and sutured, to provide access to the posterior part of the tongue (From Bernard 1964, *Am. J. Physiol.* 206:827–35.)

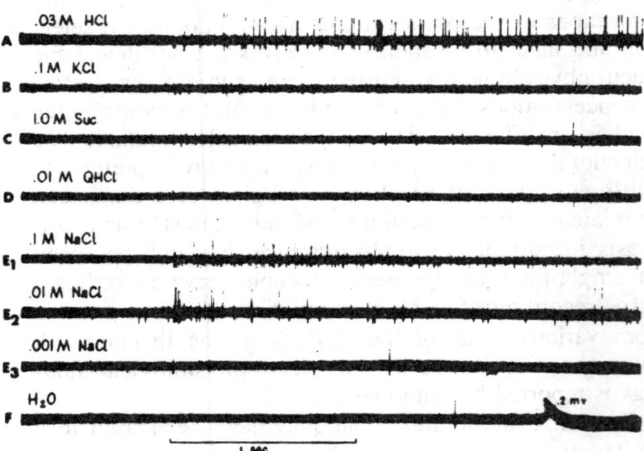

Figure 51.3. Responses of a single neuron in the gustatory system of a white rat, obtained in the medulla from the cell body of a neuron extending from medulla to thalamus, the second in the chain of three neurons from tongue to cortex. These responses are qualitatively similar to those of the neurons of the gustatory systems of all mammals so far investigated. The all-or-nothing principle of nerve action is seen in the similarity of the size of these voltage changes or spikes. The slight variations in spike amplitude between records are due to small displacements in electrode position relative to the neuron, while within each record some short-term "fatigue" is seen in spike height. This neuron responds to many stimuli; this is probably true of all gustatory neurons of all animals. It is quite sensitive to NaCl and HCl, but not very sensitive to sucrose (Suc.) or quinine hydrochloride (QHCl); other neurons have different patterns of sensitivity, providing a basis for discrimination among stimuli. $E_1 - E_3$ show that spike frequency, here as in most sensory neurons, is a function of stimulus intensity. F shows that this neuron does not respond to water; some species (dog, cat, rabbit, chicken) have neurons sensitive to water. (Unpublished data of Dr. R.P. Erickson, Duke University.)

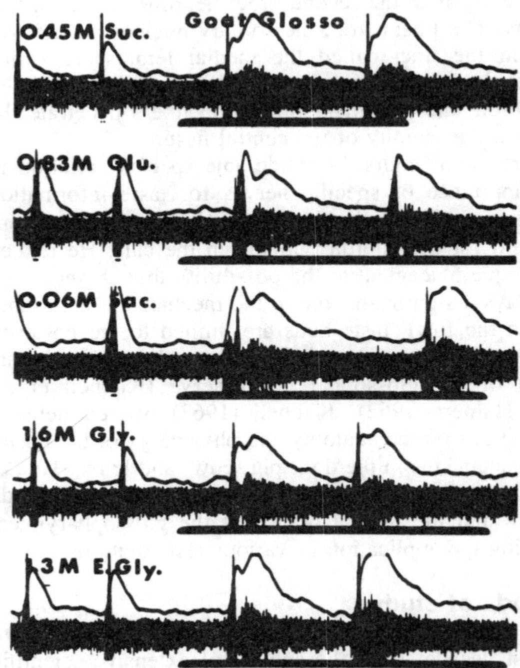

Figure 51.4. Records from the whole lingual branch of the glossopharyngeal nerve of a goat. Sac., sodium saccharinate; Gly., glycerine; E.Gly., ethylene glycol. (From Bell and Kitchell 1966, *J. Physiol.* 183:145–51.)

tablishes that each animal lives in a separate taste world. It is more realistic to accept that each species has a sense of taste complementary to its own ecological needs, and that similarities with man are instances of overlapping rather than more complete development. For humans, taste sensations are classified by means of verbal reports into the categories of sweet, sour, bitter, and salty. With animals, it is more appropriate to divide responses into pleasant, unpleasant, and indifferent. Nevertheless, comparison of the responses of various animal species to those of man necessitates reference to the classical divisions.

Individual variability

Every species studied thus far has exhibited considerable individual variability. As an example, calves varied in their response to the common sugars from indifferent to pronounced preference (Kare 1961). In a litter of pigs that were tested with a wide range of concentrations of saccharin solutions, some were found to prefer markedly the synthetic sweetener and others to reject it (Kare et al. 1965). Many dogs actively rejected saccharin in low concentrations in their food, but a small minority were indifferent and a few preferred it.

Individual variation was studied with chickens and quail. Using a single stimulus procedure, several chlorides at various concentrations were tested. Different individuals had markedly different thresholds (the lowest concentration at which the intake differed significantly from that of water). No individual was found to be completely taste blind, since all birds responded if the concentration reached a sufficiently high level. Chemical specificity was apparently involved, since an individual that could taste one chloride at a low concentration did not necessarily respond to other chlorides at equally low concentrations. In fact, a bird that was indifferent to one chloride often showed good taste sensitivity for another. The response of the individual animals was chemical specific and concentration dependent.

A breeding program was carried out in which birds sensitive to ferric chloride were selected and mated and also those insensitive to the chemical were mated. After five generations, there was a statistically significant difference between those with high- and those with low-threshold parents. The findings suggest that the taste for ferric chloride has a genetic basis.

Fowl

The domestic fowl does have a sense of taste, but it is characterized by a general indifference to the categories man recognizes as sweet and bitter. The chicken and many other species of birds (Kare and Rogers 1976) are indifferent to the common sugars; xylose, however, is offensive to the chicken. The fowl exhibits an indifference, then aversion, to increasingly concentrated salt solutions. This is in contrast to many mammals which prefer hypotonic salt concentrations to pure water. Fowl will not voluntarily ingest salt solutions in concentrations beyond the capacity of their eliminating system. However, they exhibit unexplainable responses to some salts. For example, heavy metal compounds are relatively offensive (Kare and Ficken 1963); yet fowl indifferently accept lithium and cadmium chlorides which are lethal. Birds have a wide range of tolerance for acidity and alkalinity in their drinking water. Fuerst and Kare (1962) observed that chicks would accept strong mineral acid solutions over extended periods of time.

Sucrose octaacetate at a concentration bitter to man is readily accepted by the fowl and by many other avian species. However, quinine sulfate, which is used extensively as a standard bitter stimulus for man and rat, is also rejected by many species of birds. Some of the defensive secretions of insects have a uniquely offensive taste for birds (Yang and Kare 1968). Taste apparently can be important in this predator-prey relationship.

Dimethyl anthranilate, which is used in the human food industry, is uniquely offensive to the fowl and to many other members of the class *Aves* at one part in 10,000. Particularly with regard to sweet and bitter, human sensory judgment is thus not a reliable guide to how the bird will respond. In fact, the bird has never been demonstrated to prefer any taste compound in solution over pure water.

A review of the physiological and behavioral aspects of taste, smell, and hearing in birds can be found in Kare and Rogers (1976).

Ruminants

Most of the work on taste in ruminants has been carried out with calves. Added caution must be assumed then because this species undergoes an abrupt dietary change early in life, switching from milk to a typically herbivorous diet.

Calves, when offered a choice between pure water and even a 1 percent sucrose solution, which is insipid to man, will select the sucrose almost exclusively. Further, this sucrose solution brings about a doubling of daily fluid intake. The calf is indifferent to lactose, which is a preferred sugar by the opossum (Figs. 51.5, 51.6). Further, the calf selects xylose, which is the only sugar reported to be offensive to the fowl. The calf is indifferent to saccharin solutions at levels which are sweet or pleasant to man and rats. A screening of several other synthetic sweeteners used by man failed to reveal any marked preferences. Bell (1959) reported that both calves and goats exhibited pronounced preferences for glucose.

The calf has a wide pH tolerance. However, in contrast to the fowl, there is a greater degree of acceptance on the alkaline side and less on the acid side. Further,

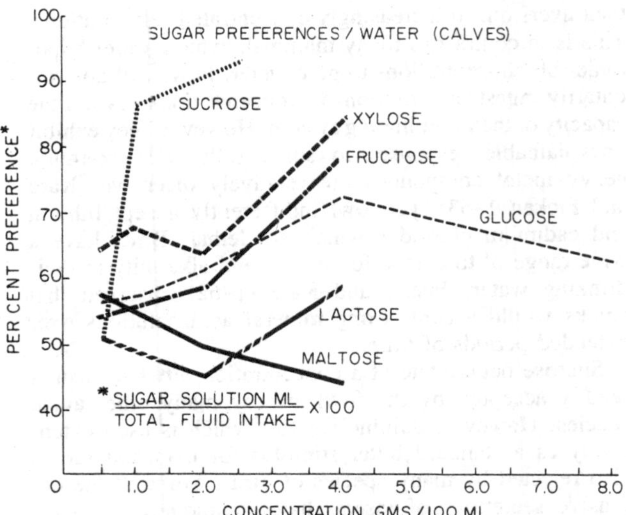

Figure 51.5. Response of the calf to various sugar solutions in a two-choice preference test. With the exception of maltose and lactose, marked preferences for the sugars are indicated. (Reprinted with permission from Kare and Ficken, in Zotterman, ed., *Olfaction and Taste*, Pergamon, Oxford, 1963.)

calves are less responsive to mineral acids than they are to organic acids.

Bell and Williams (1959) and Bell (1959) reported on the substantial tolerance for sodium chloride by calves and goats. This taste response has been used in situations where salt is added to a protein supplement for the purpose of regulating intake. Although goats are unusually tolerant of quinine hydrochloride, calves reject solutions at the 0.0001 M level. However, dairy cows are not offended by sucrose octaacetate at levels which are repugnant to man.

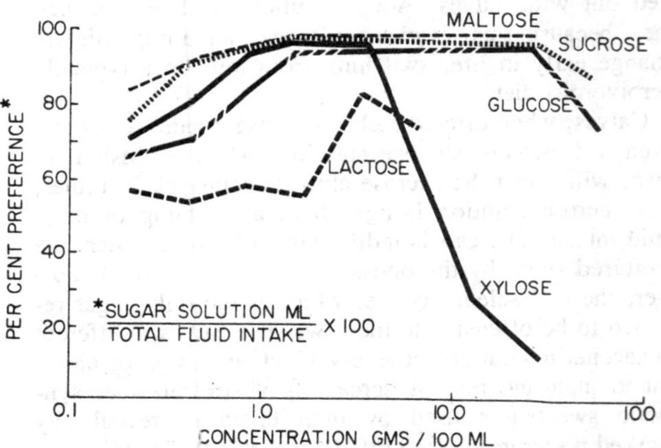

Figure 51.6. Response of the rat to various sugar solutions in a two-choice preference test. (Reprinted with permission from Kare and Ficken, in Zotterman, ed., *Olfaction and Taste*, Pergamon, Oxford, 1963.)

Goatcher and Church (1970) reported species and strain differences among sheep, goats, pigmy goats, and cattle in behavioral responses to a variety of taste substances. Of particular interest were the findings that mature sheep apparently exhibited no preference for sucrose, and goats exhibited only a very mild preference at relatively low concentrations. These responses are in marked contrast to the responses of calves (see Fig. 51.5).

A wide variety of aromatic oils have been used as additives for ruminant feed. The most common is anise. Miller et al. (1958), however, found it actually reduced the palatability of calf starter rations.

Cats

Mature cats on an adequate diet exhibit no preference for sucrose, lactose, maltose, fructose, glucose, or mannose (Beauchamp et al., in press). In fact, large intake of at least one sugar, sucrose, can cause vomiting, diarrhea, and even death in cats. Cats avoid saccharin and cyclamate at high concentrations (Bartoshuk et al. 1975). Quinine and citric acid are also avoided at high concentrations. The cat's response to sodium chloride in solution is unsettled; there is one report (Carpenter 1956) of a slight preference at one concentration. Thus cats are indifferent to or avoid most common taste substances. Both wild and domestic cats prefer solutions of hydrolyzed protein and several individual amino acids to water (Beauchamp et al., in press; White and Boudreau 1975). It is not known whether taste and/or olfactory components induce ingestion. Thus the flavor preference profile of this strict carnivore corresponds to the natural food preferences.

Dogs

Mature dogs were presented with glucose, fructose, sucrose, maltose, or saccharin incorporated into standard biscuits. Although there was substantial individual variation, all the sugar-containing biscuits were selected or at least tolerated indifferently. Some of the dogs were markedly offended by the saccharin. Sucrose octaacetate at levels offensive to rats and humans was accepted indifferently by dogs. Using conscious dogs with gastric and intestinal fistulae, Behrman and Kare (1968) observed that the nature and volume of pancreatic secretions were influenced by taste stimuli.

Pigs

Pigs respond to sucrose solutions. The preference for glucose and lactose is more modest. In a test with saccharin, Kare et al. (1965) observed a minority of pigs that were offended at every concentration offered. However, a majority of pigs selected saccharin solutions even at concentrations excessively sweet (2.5%) to humans. Pigs appear to show no preference for sodium cyclamate, a substance sweet to man (Kennedy and Baldwin 1972). Salt intoxication of pigs is periodically reported. Nevertheless, where pure water was available, test animals would not consume lethal quantities of salt. The pig is offended by some quinine salts.

Both the rabbit and the horse are credited with a sweet tooth; however, the tangible evidence is limited to tests with sucrose. The horse does not differentiate between solutions of pure water and sucrose octaacetate at concentrations offensive to man. Porcupines (Bloom et al. 1973) avoid higher concentrations of hydrochloric acid and quinine sulfate, but are indifferent to salt and saccharin. They apparently show a preference for sucrose at some concentrations. Both wild and domestic guinea pigs prefer glucose to water but the wild species exhibits this preference at lower and higher concentrations than does the domestic animal (Jacobs and Beauchamp, in press).

Nutrition

The function of taste in the physiological economy of the vertebrate animal body has not been established. The cat and the fowl on an adequate diet are both indifferent to sucrose solutions. Where caloric intake in feed is restricted, a chick will select a sucrose solution and will increase fluid intake to make up the deficiency (Kare and Ficken 1963). A similarly "correct" nutritional choice was not made when the sugar was replaced with an isocaloric solution of fat or protein. In fact, the domestic fowl acutely depleted of protein will avoid a casein solution and will select only water, apparently because of the taste.

Feed that had been rendered so distasteful to the fowl that it was totally avoided in a choice situation did not influence intake when there was no alternative (Kare and Pick 1960). The response to the taste quality was modified by hunger. In fact, the offensiveness had to be increased almost tenfold in a no-choice situation to effect a reduced intake over an extended period.

Many species, especially herbivores, often need extra salt to maintain sodium balance. When an animal is salt deficient, it responds immediately if salt is available by ingesting quantities sufficient to make up the deficit (Denton 1965). Taste is an important mediator of this behavior. A similar specific appetite for sweets appears to exist for rats since food-deprived and insulin-treated animals respond with an increase in intake of sweet solutions. To what degree this holds for other mammals is not known. There appear to be no specific hungers for vitamins (Scott and Verney 1947); instead when animals are made thiamin deficient and then presented with a choice between two differently flavored diets, one thiamin sufficient and the other thiamin deficient, they must learn to associate the flavor of the thiamin-sufficient diet with recovery from the deficiency. Once this association is made, they will preferentially ingest the diet containing thiamin.

Aggressive and exploratory behavior develops in animals after depletion of calcium or of other minerals (Wood-Gush and Kare 1966). The degree to which this behavior is taste directed has not been established. Further, the overall food-preference behavior of domestic animals is not a reliable guide to nutritional adequacy of a diet (Kare and Scott 1962). Nachman and Cole (1971) have reviewed the role of taste in specific hungers.

The nutritional "wisdom" of jungle fowl was compared with domestic chickens (Kare and Maller 1967), and also wild Norway rats with laboratory rats (Maller and Kare 1965). In both instances, the wild animals were found to be more precise in their caloric regulation or correction. Further, they tended to be more responsive to the nutritional and physiological consequences of their diet than to the sensory qualities. The laboratory rat was particularly "self-indulgent." It may well be that with domestication acute sensory mechanisms would be disadvantageous. For this reason, experimental work with highly selected populations may be less than ideal for discerning function of the chemical senses.

Water sense

Zotterman (1956) reported neurons in the pig and the cat that respond to pure water. Kitchell et al. (1959) also found water fibers in the fowl. Similar neurons apparently are absent in man and the rat. While man finds that pure water approaches a tasteless category, for those species with water fibers water might convey a characteristic taste. This interpretation is borne out in the fowl, where the addition of a wide variety of chemicals to water has failed to improve its acceptability; on the contrary, in most instances intake was reduced.

Temperature

Temperature can substantially modify the reaction to taste stimulation in man; for example, the acceptability of various beverages is dependent upon their temperature. The domestic fowl is acutely sensitive to the temperature of water. Acceptability decreases as the temperature of water increases above ambient levels. In fact, fowl will discriminate between choices with a temperature difference of only a few degrees C, rejecting the higher temperature. The chicken will suffer from acute thirst rather than drink water 5°C above its body temperature. At the other extreme, the chicken will readily accept water down to the level of freezing. A sizable minority of chickens lack this sensitivity to temperature; however, when it is present, response to it takes precedence over the chemical stimulants. These findings are important when one is trying to induce animals to take medicine.

Mechanism of taste stimulation

Theories on how the taste receptors are stimulated are primarily based upon loose bonding. Baradi and Bourne (1959) described enzyme distributions in receptor areas and proposed their involvement in taste. Beidler (1954) presented an analytical theory based upon nonenzymal transitory adsorption, this causing a depolarization of the receptor surface which excites the nerve. Vitamin A has been demonstrated to be necessary for a functional taste system (Bernard et al. 1961).

Kare et al. (1969) demonstrated that nutrients can move rapidly and directly from the oral cavity to the brain. This raised the possibility that gustatory information obtained from extraneural pathways could be of consequence to the total taste sensation. Recent biochemical work by Cagan (1971) suggests that receptor sites obtained from taste buds of cows are capable of discriminating among sugars. Thus at least some of the specificity in the differential response to different taste substances may be based on peripheral events.

No pattern, whether chemical, physical, or nutritional, explains all the comparative results. An explanation in terms of detailed function has been sought. However, there are no suggestions to separate the taste behavior of the carnivore from that of the herbivore. The chicken, which is indifferent to sugars, has a relatively high blood glucose level, while the ruminant, which responds so dramatically to sugar solutions, has a low circulating glucose level. A possible theory based on this suggestion is challenged by observations derived from work with the cat and the armadillo, which are indifferent behaviorally to sugars but which have blood glucose levels similar to the level found in man.

Some food habits of animals are seasonal in nature. Perhaps taste directs or follows the abrupt feeding changes of birds which are insectivorous part of the year and granivorous for the remainder. The diet of ruminants also changes abruptly, from the high protein of the suckling calf to the low-protein herbivorous diet. Taste might also take part in the intensive feeding prior to hibernation or migration. Whether taste changes direct or follow these altered eating patterns and whether structural changes in taste receptors have occurred are unresolved questions.

SMELL

Olfaction in animals is commonly associated with securing and selecting food, avoiding predators, and with social behavior, especially reproduction. Whether or not smell is critical for these functions is difficult to assess under conditions of domestication. Most domestic animals have a limited opportunity to exercise their sensory faculties, and further, animal breeders have not selected for the characteristic of sensory acuity.

With the exception of birds, all of the domesticated animals exhibit sniffing behavior. Domesticated birds exhibit no apparent responsiveness to the odors of their environment. However, the presence of neuroanatomic structures suggests that olfactory information can be transmitted even if it is not behaviorally meaningful. Although the observed olfactory behavior varies greatly among domestic animals, the morphology of the olfactory organs are basically similar in all vertebrates.

Anatomy

The olfactory system consists of paired nostrils (external nares), internal nares (choanae), nasal cavities or chambers, the receptor cells found in specialized epithelium (which lines portions of the cavities), olfactory nerves, and olfactory lobes of the brain. The comparative anatomy of the nose and the nasal air streams, including that of the chicken, has been described by Bang and Bang (1959) and by Parsons (1971).

The paired nasal cavities are divided by an epithelium-covered medial septum which is supported by partially ossified cartilage. Their lateral walls consist of turbinate bones named for the facial bones of which they are a part. It is on the ethmoid turbinate that the specialized olfactory epithelium is found (Fig. 51.7). In all animals the nasoturbinate remains a fairly simple elongated structure; the maxilloturbinate, however, varies considerably in its complexity. In the horse, pig, sheep, and cow, the maxilloturbinate is similar to the nasoturbinate in its simplicity. By contrast, in the rabbit, numerous folds run from anterodorsal to posteroventral in the maxilloturbinate. This condition of complexity also occurs in the cat, and to an even greater extent in the dog (see Fig. 51.7). The olfactory areas in keen-scented animals have been in-

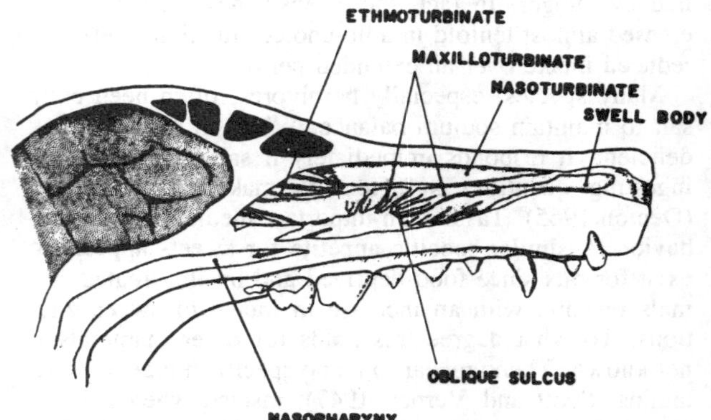

Figure 51.7. Normal anatomy of midsagittal section of a dog head with septum removed. (From Becker and King 1957, *Am. Med. Ass. Arch. Otolaryngol.* 65:428–36.)

creased through evolution by a lengthening of the nose and a folding of the turbinates. Furthermore, this development has involved excavation of the frontal and sphenoid bones with an extension of the olfactory ethmoturbinates into recesses or sinuses. The respiratory epithelium is present in a proportionally larger extent than is the olfactory epithelium to provide greater filtration and warming of inspired air.

The surface area of the microvilli and cilia of the olfactory mucosa is enormous and may often exceed that of the entire body surface. The mobility of the external nares during sniffing suggests that this organ's structure is important to olfaction. Lucas and Douglas (1934), who studied air currents in several species, concluded that the location and angle of the external nares to the cavity were of special importance in determining the direction that air currents follow. Posteriorly, there exists a bony subethmoidal shelf which is found below the ethmoidal turbinates and is so situated that it forces inspired air into the olfactory epithelium. A washing out of the region upon expiration does not occur, by virtue of the recess it creates (Negus 1954). The recess permits the accumulation of odor molecules which would be unrecognizable in a single sniff. Such a shelf is not seen among primates. Negus (1927) suggests that the epiglottis serves as an accessory olfactory organ. It forms with the soft palate a partition which permits those animals in which it is best developed to inspire air through the nose while eating. Thus, with the mouth open, the animal is alert for predators and also can effect an olfactory screening of its forage.

In normal inspiration by awake dogs, air enters the vestibule and traverses through all meatuses (passages) as far back as the anterior tips of the ethmoidal turbinate. The mainstream, however, takes a downward path anterior to this to enter the nasopharynx. Expired air flows primarily through the ventral meatus with a small flow through the middle meatus. There is no air flow in the dorsal meatus or over the ethmoid region. This observation adds some support to the hypothesized function of the ethmoid shelf. Sniffing, on the other hand, fills the entire nasal chamber (Becker and King 1957).

The lining of the anterior part of the nasal cavity (the vestibule) is continuous with that of the nostrils and may contain hair as in the horse or pig, or it may be bare as in the cow and dog. The role of the cilia in clearing nasal passages has been detailed in the cow, sheep, rabbit, cat, and other mammals (Lucas and Douglas 1934). The nasal vascular pattern has been described by Davies and Prichard (1953) for the cat, dog, rabbit, sheep, goat, and pig.

The olfactory portion of the nasal mucous membrane is largely confined to the region of the ethmoidal turbinate and to the opposing portion of the septum. The olfactory cells extend throughout the whole layer of olfactory epithelium. These are bipolar nerve cells which consist of a small oval cell body containing a nucleus and a scant amount of cytoplasm. The distal process or dendrite is termed the olfactory rod, and it projects beyond the free surface and bears olfactory hairs. The latter are assumed to be the receptor elements (De Lorenzo 1963, Moulton and Beidler 1967). Comparative studies of the olfactory epithelium reveal no substantial difference among animals with a keen sense of smell (macrosmatic) and those with one apparently less developed (microsmatic).

The central processes of the bipolar olfactory cells become the olfactory nerve fibers. Each of the fibers is a direct continuation of the axon of a single olfactory receptor and remains separate, without synapse, until it reaches the olfactory bulb. The nerve fibers then form a dense external layer of olfactory nerve fibers around the olfactory bulb. From this point, they turn inward to end in the glomeruli. A glomerulus is an encapsulated group of synaptic connections of the fine terminal branches of the olfactory fibers and the dendrites of both the mitral and tufted cells whose cell bodies are located more deeply in the bulb.

Olfaction and the CNS

Olfactory function, particularly of the more evolved portions of the brain, has been the subject of a number of ablation and recording studies. Impulses have been traced to some of the central structures. However, the available information is still insufficient to describe the role of the central mechanisms in olfaction (MacLeod 1971). Of particular interest is the observation of quite direct connections between olfactory receptors and the hypothalamus, a brain area of importance in regulating eating, drinking, and sexual behavior.

Olfactory pigments

The pigmentation of the olfactory mucosa has been implicated by many investigators in the olfactory response. Some evidence has been presented to support the contention that albino animals by virtue of limited pigmentation have poorly developed chemical senses. In fact, it has been suggested that white pigs or sheep have an impaired ability to recognize and avoid poisonous plants while foraging or grazing. Moulton (1960), however, reports no significant difference in olfactory acuity between colored and albino animals. Furthermore, the coat color of an animal is not an index of olfactory pigmentation.

Organ of Jacobson

The vomeronasal organ, or organ of Jacobson, is an elongated sac which opens into the mouth or nose. It is lined with olfactorylike epithelium and is connected to the CNS by nonmyelinated fibers which run in the vomeronasal nerves and enter the cranium through the cribriform plate. The nervous connections terminate in the olfactory bulb (Adrian 1955).

The organ is absent or vestigial in birds, cetaceans, and some primates, but it is present in virtually all other classes of vertebrates. It is most highly developed in snakes and lizards; however, even in man it can be identified in the early embryonic stages. Some workers have suggested that it serves an olfactory and gustatory function, particularly in snakes. Estes (1972) has suggested that this organ is a specific receptor for mammalian sexual signals.

Methods of study

Behavioral tests are difficult to design, and the results from these tests do not lend themselves to simple assessment. Part of the problem is the difficulty of quantifying stimuli and responses. In addition, an odor may be meaningful only in a specific food context. The delivery of a stimulus restricted solely to the olfactory receptor can also be a major problem. To meet these and other objections some investigators have developed specially built chambers which permit the introduction of the odor isolated from auditory, visual, or pressure cues.

Conditioning techniques have been employed with several species. Allen (1941) conditioned dogs to avoid shock by lifting a forelimb when presented a specific odor. The animals were retested after ablation of various brain areas. Conditioned responses and discriminatory abilities were retained except when the pyriform-amygdaloid areas were destroyed. A review of the early Russian work in this area has been made by Razran and Warden (1929).

Conditioned responses have been used in a variety of investigations. Ashton et al. (1957) trained dogs to sniff at three or more stations and to make a motor response if an odor were detected. However, there is a question whether all extraolfactory cues such as those provided by a solvent or the presence of the animal handler had been eliminated.

An experimental method of wide use has been the recording of the electrical activity which follows stimulation of the olfactory system. These electrophysiological recordings are made in some cases from the olfactory epithelium or from the nerve fibers, but most commonly from the olfactory bulb. Ottoson (1956) recorded a slow negative potential from the olfactory mucosa and observed that response was largest at the surface and diminished as the microelectrodes were placed more deeply into the epithelial tissue. He suggested that the olfactory epithelium is therefore the source of the potential. While olfactory information has only a short distance to traverse through the conduction pathways to the brain, the olfactory nerve fibers conduct more slowly than any other afferent system in the body.

Most of the electrical measurements reported represent activity from a collection of receptors. Recently, techniques that allow records to be made of the action potentials in a single primary olfactory receptor have been described (Gesteland et al. 1963). A further substantial advance in this area would result from the use of unanesthetized and unrestrained animals that would sniff the stimulant by themselves. Moulton and Tucker (1964) have described the use of chronically implanted electrodes in measuring olfactory response. Subsequently Moulton (1967) used this approach in reporting on spatiotemporal patterning. Recently, there have been a variety of attempts, using electrophysiological methods, to follow olfactory transfer of biologically relevant information (e.g. urine odors) into the CNS (Pfaffmann 1971).

Little electrophysiological work has been carried out using domestic animals. This may be in part because the olfactory nerve is extremely short in mammals and in a difficult location. Furthermore, since electrophysiology does not distinguish between the pleasant and unpleasant, the results have limited practical application.

Behavior

Nutrition

The extent to which the sense of smell is necessary to locate and discriminate among foods is difficult to measure. Maller and Kare (1965) reported that the domesticated animal is less sensitive to the nutritional and toxic consequences of a food choice and more responsive to the sensory qualities of food than is its wild counterpart. This conclusion could complicate the selection of animals for the study of the function of smell.

Harris et al. (1933) and Scott and Verney (1947) found that rats depleted of a specific vitamin would correct their deficiency in a food choice situation. The observed sniffing behavior in these studies supports the conclusion that olfaction is involved. Le Magnen and Rapaport (1951) observed a reduction in olfactory acuity among vitamin A–deprived rats.

Mugford (1977) has reported that cats select dry chow suffused with the odor of meat in preference to the same chow suffused with air only. Further, if cats were poisoned with lithium chloride soon after eating the odor-laden dry food, the animals avoided the odor-laden chow during subsequent trials; that is, it was possible to develop a conditional aversion to the meat odor.

Kovach (1971) has described several Russian ethological studies which suggest that behavioral responses to meat odors are innately determined. Dogs begin responding with salivation to meat odors at approximately the age at which weaning would normally occur even though they had no prior experience eating meat. One cannot eliminate the possibility that there are similar chemicals in milk to which salivation has been conditioned.

A variety of aromatic mixtures have been recommended for animal feeds. Typical ingredients of these mixtures are anise, fenugreek, or onion. The inference is that these odors render food more appealing and hence increase food intake. Nonetheless, there is no evidence to justify this. Furthermore, preference tests indicate that many of these flavors are actually offensive to the animal for which they are sold. Even if they were appealing, there is no evidence to indicate that long-term control of intake would be altered by these flavors.

In formal studies with heifers, dogs, and pigs, attempts have been made to cater to their chemical senses. Short, transitory increases in food intake were observed; however, they were approximately equal to the modest depression in intake recorded when the additive was removed. Enhancing the smell or taste appeared to be warranted only when food intake was depressed due to abnormal circumstances, for example, by a strange environment or a substantial change in the diet. Here, a return to normal intake has been affected more rapidly by increasing the sensory appeal.

No behavioral function of smell is apparent in the domestic fowl (Kare, unpublished). The olfactory lobes in chicks were eliminated by cautery, and the birds were given food discrimination tests with a variety of compounds which are odiferous to man. No change in preference behavior could be attributed to the surgery. Normal chicks were presented with two identical waterers, resting above screen-covered pans, only one of which contained an odorant. The presence of the odor failed to exert a measurable effect on the preference between waterers. This work is subject to the criticism that the odorants were not typical of what the bird would encounter in nature. Furthermore, perhaps a bird must be in flight for the stimulus to be carried to the receptors.

Social behavior

The chemical senses, mainly olfaction and perhaps the vomeronasal system, play an important role in regulating social and especially reproductive behavior of many mammalian species. Commonly males and/or females are attracted to and sexually stimulated by chemical signals (often called pheromones) in urine, vaginal secretions, glandular secretions, or saliva. Individual recognition, a prerequisite for maintenance of group structures such as dominance hierarchies, may also be coded by olfactory signals. Olfactory signals may also play a role in maintaining the mother/young dyad (e.g. in the goat, Klopfer and Gamble 1966), in stimulating aggression, and in territorial maintenance (Mykytowycz 1970).

In pigs it has been shown that a steroid metabolite in boar saliva is capable of enhancing the lordosis response to back pressure in receptive females (Melrose et al. 1971). Urine appears to play a role in stimulating mounting of a dummy in young stallions (Wierzbowski 1959, Hafez et al. 1969b), while the role of chemical signals in bovine reproductive behavior is unclear (Hafez et al. 1969a). In dogs, urine from estrous bitches is very attractive to intact males as long as the males have had sexual experience; inexperienced males are not as attracted (Doty and Dunbar 1974). In most species, chemical signals probably act in concert with visual, tactile, and auditory cues to insure reproduction. Even when one sense is eliminated, the others may be able to insure appropriate behavior. Further, domestication may have diminished the specificity of response to precise chemical signals.

There is now a large body of research with rodents which shows that chemical signals from conspecifics may also influence reproductive physiology. For example, urine-based signals may affect the regularity of estrus cycles and even the age at which reproductive maturation occurs (Bronson 1971). Phenomena such as synchronization of estrus periods may in part be mediated by chemical signals.

While olfaction plays a role in the behavior of some birds (Grubb 1974, Wenzel 1971), there is no evidence that this sense regulates social behavior in most birds including domestic fowl. Visual and auditory cues appear primary in these species.

The ability of many mammals to identify individuals on the basis of extremely small amounts of secretions is probably the basis for the tracking ability of some species, especially dogs. Much of the information on the tracking ability of dogs is anecdotal, and olfactory thresholds are not separated from discrimination among odors or from training. King et al. (1964) studied the ability of dogs to detect human odor under laboratory conditions. They reported dogs were capable of detecting human traces, indoors, for as long as six weeks. McCartney (1968) presents a fascinating historical account of the controversies over the tracking abilities of dogs.

Theories of olfaction

Many attempts have been made to explain odor in terms of the chemical structure of the stimulant. Even if such a classification, based upon human description, were established, there is no evidence to suggest that it would be applicable across animal species.

Moncrieff (1951) has reviewed, and contributed to, the concept that configuration of the molecule is involved in determining the quality of an olfactory sensation. He reports instances of agreement between the external shape of the molecule, or the position and nature of functional groups, and odor. However, the theory is applicable only to a select group of compounds and of course only to humans.

Currently, the major emphasis has been on characterizing the electrical nature of the stimulus arising from the peripheral receptors. Many of the reported experiments are limited to electrophysiological techniques on microsmatic amphibians. How meaningful these results are to keen-scented domestic mammals (macrosmatic) has not yet been established. Furthermore, electrophysiological thresholds have not been translated into terms that are meaningful in a behavioral context. In most of these experiments, chemicals of reagent-grade purity have been applied singly as stimuli. It is improbable that in the natural environment members of these animal species would encounter such isolated chemicals separate from a sexual or dietary context. It still remains impossible on the basis of chemical or physical qualities to reliably predict how wild or domestic animals, even humans, will react to an odor. Theories to explain olfaction are reviewed by Davies (1971).

HEARING

All of the domestic animals are capable of hearing sounds in their environment and of using sound to communicate. Hearing in the mammal and in the bird is generally recognized to be more highly developed than in any other classes of animals. While the hearing apparatus is not identical in all domestic species (the bird's ear differs substantially from that of mammals), the basic structures and modes of functioning share a common pattern. The ear in all domestic animals efficiently converts acoustical information from the environment to nerve impulses which are transmitted to the CNS.

Anatomy

The ear is made up of three divisions: the external ear, consisting of the pinna or auricle and the external auditory meatus; the middle ear, consisting of the tympanic cavity, with its contents, and the Eustachian tube, with its diverticulum, the guttural pouch (in the Equidae); and the internal ear or labyrinth, consisting of an acoustic part, the cochlea, and a nonacoustic part, the vestibular organ (Fig. 51.8). The functional significance of the vestibular organ is considered in Chapter 42. The cochlea, supplied by the cochlear branch of the acoustic nerve,

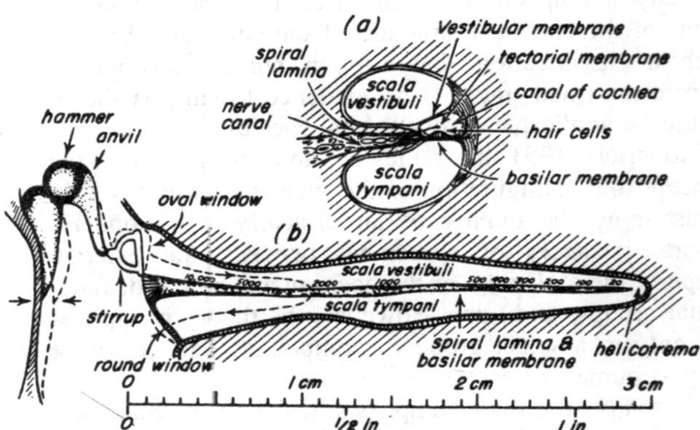

Figure 51.8. The cochlea: (a) cross section; (b) represented as if uncoiled to illustrate the different regions of the basilar membrane sensitive to sounds of different frequencies. (Slightly modified from White, *Classical and Modern Physics*, Van Nostrand, New York, 1940.)

contains the receptors for the sense of hearing. The essential function of the external ear is to receive sound waves and that of the middle ear to amplify them and to facilitate their passage to the perilymph of the internal ear and thence to the sound receptors in the cochlea.

Auricle

The function of this structure is to collect sound waves, which are then transmitted to the tympanic membrane by way of the external auditory meatus. The mobility of the auricle in most mammals enhances its value as a collector of sound waves by enabling it to be turned in the direction of the sound. The pinnae of man contribute little to the collection of sound, and they are totally absent in birds.

Tympanic membrane

Completely separating the external auditory meatus of the external ear from the tympanic cavity of the middle ear is a thin septum known as the tympanic membrane or eardrum. It is composed of three layers: the external layer, which is continuous with the skin lining the external auditory meatus; the middle layer, which is composed of radially and circularly arranged connective tissue fibers; and the internal layer, which is continuous with the mucous membrane of the tympanic cavity. Attached to the internal surface of the membrane is the manubrium or handle of the malleus, the first of the auditory ossicles. In this way, vibrations of the tympanic membrane are transmitted to the chain of bones, and by them, to the perilymph of the inner ear. An important feature of the tympanic membrane is that it is aperiodic, that is, it has no inherent resonant frequency and therefore can transmit any frequency without modifying it except for attenuation. There is no selective emphasis or attenuation with regard to the frequency of incoming sound.

Auditory ossicles

These are three small bones (the malleus, incus, and stapes) in the tympanic cavity. They comprise a chain extending from the tympanic membrane to the oval window (fenestra ovalis) which opens into the inner ear. Through them the vibrations of the tympanic membrane are transmitted to the perilymph, the fluid of the labyrinth. The head of the malleus articulates with the head of the incus. Several ligaments help to hold the malleus in place. The incus head also articulates with two processes. A ligament attaches the shorter process to the wall of the tympanic cavity. The long process articulates with the head of the stapes. The foot plate of the stapes is inserted into the oval window and is attached to the margin of the window by a membrane. In transmitting the vibrations of the tympanic membrane to the perilymph, the auditory ossicles act as a reduction lever. Since the manubrium of the malleus is longer than the long process of the incus, the vibrations of the tympanic membrane are transmitted to the perilymph with increased force but with decreased amplitude. Although the total force at the oval window is almost the same as at the tympanic membrane, the pressure is greater per unit area since the area of the window is much smaller. Actually at the time of movement the ossicular chain works as one unit with a pistonlike action.

In birds, unlike mammals, the eardrum connects to the inner ear by means of a bony columella. The foot plate which attaches to the oval window is unusually large.

Eustachian tube and guttural pouch

Connecting the tympanic cavity with the pharynx is the Eustachian tube, whose presence ensures that the air pressure in the tympanic cavity shall be the same as that outside the body. Ordinarily closed, at least in man, the pharyngeal aperture of the tube is opened during swallowing. Therefore, should an inequality of atmospheric pressure on the two sides of the tympanic membrane result, it can quickly be corrected by deglutition.

The guttural pouch, found among domestic animals only in Equidae, is a remarkable diverticulum of the Eustachian tube. Sisson states that the average capacity of each pouch in the horse is about 300 ml. The function of the guttural pouch is not known. Experiments show that in the horse, air enters the guttural pouch through the relaxed aperture of the Eustachian tube during expiration and leaves mainly during the expiratory pause. During inspiration the aperture of the Eustachian tube is closed.

Stimulus for hearing

Physically, sounds differ as to frequency, intensity, and wave form. Frequency refers to the number of vibrations per second and primarily determines perceived pitch. The intensity of a sound wave also depends on both the frequency and amplitude of the vibration; however, intensity principally determines the loudness of the sound. Wave form refers to the presence or absence of overtones, which determine subjectively the quality, or timbre, of a sound. Thus, although a violin string and a piano string may be vibrating at the same amplitude and frequency, it is possible to distinguish between the sounds emitted.

Cochlea

The acoustic labyrinth or cochlea contains the receptors for the sense of hearing. It consists essentially of a spiral bony tube, wound several times around a central core of bone (modiolus), and a much smaller membranous canal known as the cochlear duct, contained within the bony tube. Inside the cochlear duct is the organ of Corti with its sensory hair cells and the terminations of the cochlear nerve (Fig. 51.9). The cells of origin of the cochlear nerve fibers are bipolar nerve cells in

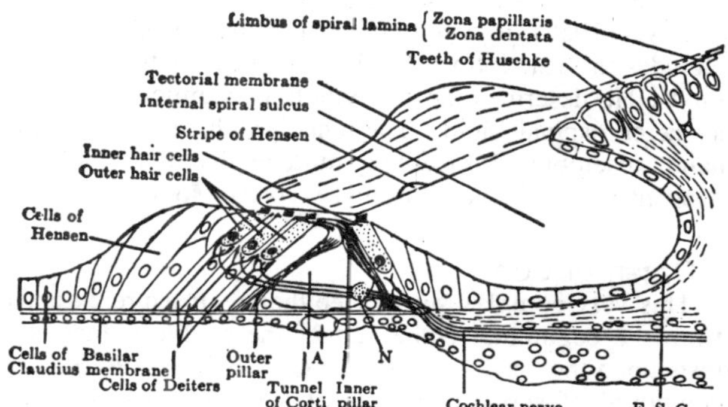

Figure 51.9. Cross section of the organ of Corti. A, artery; N, nerve; E.S.C., epithelial sensory cell. (From Herrick, *An Introduction to Neurology*, 4th ed., Saunders, Philadelphia, 1928.)

the spiral ganglion located in the bony modiolus. The peripheral branches of these nerve cells end in relation to the hair cells of the organ of Corti. The central branches end in the ventral and dorsal cochlear nuclei of the pons.

The avian cochlea differs from the corresponding organ in mammals in being shorter and uncoiled. An interesting exception among mammals is the egg-laying monotreme in which the cochlea is similar to that in birds.

The cochlear duct, somewhat triangular in cross section, begins in the vestibule, extends the length of the bony canal, and is attached to the base and apex of the canal. Forming one side of the cochlear duct and separating its cavity from that of the scala vestibuli is the delicate Reissner's or vestibular membrane. Forming the other side of the duct and separating its cavity from that of the scala tympani is the much firmer basilar membrane. Situated on the inner side of the basilar membrane and running its entire length is the highly specialized organ of Corti. The basilar membrane is composed of a large number of fibers which increase in length but apparently decrease in tension from the base to the apex of the cochlea. This membrane is believed to be the structure that receives the sound waves in the perilymph and thus cause stimulation of the hair cells and their associated nerve endings in the organ of Corti.

The cochlear duct, filled with endolymph, communicates with the saccule through the canalis reuniens. The scala vestibuli and the scala tympani, filled with perilymph, communicate with each other at the apex of the cochlea, the helicotrema. At the base of the cochlea the scala vestibuli communicates with the vestibule. The scala tympani ends at the fenestra rotunda, which is closed by a membrane, the secondary tympanic membrane. By its elasticity this membrane compensates for pressure changes in the perilymph as a result of the impact delivered to the latter by the stapes at the fenestra ovalis. This, however, may not represent its sole function.

Davis (1959), in a comprehensive chapter on audition, includes a description of the chemical nature of ear fluids. He describes the perilymph as chemically similar to cerebrospinal fluid. The endolymph, on the other hand, resembles intracellular fluid in that it has a high concentration of potassium and is low in sodium.

Organ of Corti

This very complex sensory epithelial structure extends from the beginning to the end of the cochlear duct and rests upon the basilar membrane (von Békésy 1960). It is composed of supporting cells of several kinds, sensory epithelial cells known as the auditory hair cells, and the fibers of the cochlear nerve. An associated structure is the tectorial membrane. The hair cells are the structures by which sound waves are converted into nerve impulses. The free ends of these cells possess stiff cilia, whereas the basal ends are connected to the terminal fibrils of the cochlear nerve. It is estimated that there are more than 20,000 hair cells in the organ of Corti, and that there are about as many fibers in the cochlear nerve. The cilia of the hair cells project, near their free margin, into the tectorial membrane, a gelatinous pad which covers the outer surface of the organ of Corti. At its other margin, this membrane is attached to the wall of the cochlea at the spiral lamina. It is thought that the bending of the hair triggers the release of energy which excites the auditory nerve.

Central auditory pathways

The auditory nerve runs down the center of the organ of Corti. The nerve enters the medulla at the inferior border of the pons at the cochlear portion of the VIIIth cranial nerve. The neurons terminate amid a mass of cell bodies, the dorsal and ventral cochlear nuclei. There is a substantial diminution of fibers, and the tract extends to the inferior colliculus. There is some interconnection with the neurons from the opposite ear prior to the passage to the medial geniculate body in the thalamus. The axons then proceed to the auditory area of the cortex. Most of the research has been limited to the cat. Ades (1959), in a comprehensive discussion of central auditory mechanisms, includes a description of the limits of the cortex which are currently known to be activated by acoustic stimulation.

Mechanism of hearing

Sound waves entering the external auditory ear throw the tympanic membrane in vibration. With relatively little energy loss the waves so generated are transmitted mechanically across the tympanic cavity by action of the auditory ossicles. The movements of the foot plate of the stapes set up waves in the perilymph of the labyrinth which cause the basilar membrane to vibrate. This membrane moves with a shearing motion, both across and lengthwise. These fine movements cause changes of pressure on the cilia of the hair cells, probably by bending them, and the nerve impulses are presumably set up in the nerve terminations at the bases of the cells. Nerve impulses thus aroused are transmitted to the CNS.

The cochlea shows potential changes, known as the microphonic effect, which may be involved in stimulation of the nerve terminations. The potential changes follow closely, up to a limit, the pressure variations caused by the sound waves. The relationship suggests the action of a microphone. They should not be confused, however, with the spike potentials shown by the nerve fibers. The cochlear microphonic effect may be produced at the cuticular surface of the hair cells.

Vinnikov and Titova (1963) offered a cytochemical theory of hearing. They suggested that wave motions in the fluids of the cochlea cause a series of localized biochemical changes, and that reversible denaturation of protein components of the cytoplasm of the hair cells occurs with excitation. They support their position with complementary observations on the distribution of enzymes in the hairs of the cells. Other ideas as to how the nerve endings are stimulated are that mechanical vibrations are transmitted to them and that a chemical mediator is released by the bending of the hair cells.

Just how the basilar membrane behaves in response to waves in the perilymph is not known. The classical resonance theory of hearing by Helmholtz (1885) holds that the basilar membrane is a resonator whose different parts respond by vibration to sound waves in the perilymph. Different frequencies cause vibrations in the membrane at different places, thus stimulating different nerve fibers. Because the basilar membrane is a continuous structure, vibrations of one part can never be entirely independent of vibrations of an adjacent part. Perception of intensity, or loudness, of sound depends largely upon the frequency of the nerve impulses generated in the cochlear nerve fibers. A loud sound causes a response of greater amplitude in the fibers of the basilar membrane which calls forth impulses of a higher frequency in the nerve fibers by the action of the hair cells.

There are many objections to this theory, including the absence of clear-cut anatomical corroboration. Birds, cats, and rabbits have a basilar membrane made up of two layers of fibers, rather than only one layer as in man. Von Békésy (1960) has suggested that different frequencies are represented along the basilar membrane. However, on an anatomical basis he questions that it involves a resonator mechanism. An extension of the resonance theory is the resonance-volley theory (Wever 1949).

How the sound is converted into a nerve impulse at the receptor level or how this impulse is translated into meaningful sound in the CNS is largely unknown (Harris 1972).

Range of hearing

There are several methods of obtaining sensitivity distributions to sound in animals. Recording of cochlear potentials of the inner ear has been done on a wide variety of species including cats, bats, opossums, hedgehogs and rodents (Harris 1972). Sensitivity curves can also be obtained by recording the inferior collicular response. Peaks of these curves showed good correspondence in frequency with ultrasounds produced by several rodent species (Brown 1973). A more readily accessible method is the use of behavioral tests with trained animals. Some reflex movement produced with training is a very successful index to the auditory capacity of the animal. An example of this is the pairing of an aversive stimulus such as electric shock to a sound. The sound comes to have a biological value to the animal, and after a number of repetitions the animal will respond to the sound alone. Food can be used rather than shock.

The range of frequencies through which sound can be perceived varies in different species. In man the average pitch limits are 20 and 20,000 vibrations or cps (cycles per second) (Fletcher 1929). Some animals can perceive frequencies much higher than 20,000 cps. The upper pitch unit of dogs is generally thought to be about twice that of man. The silent dog whistle emits some frequencies too high for man to hear but below the upper pitch limit for dogs. The frequency most audible to the rat appears to be 40,000 (Gould and Morgan 1941, Brown 1973). Frequencies as high as 98,000 cause potential changes in the cochlea of bats. In terms of sensitivity (the least loud sound perceivable at a given frequency) dogs and man are about equal at low frequency, but dogs appear markedly superior at frequencies between 1000 and 8000 (Lipman and Grassi 1942). Studies of the range of hearing in adult birds indicate that they are about equal to man (Schwartzkopff 1955).

Location of sound

Ability to judge the direction from which sound is coming depends largely on the fact that sound is heard louder and sooner in the ear nearer the source. Movements of the pinnae should greatly assist animals in locating the source, the sound being heard loudest and earliest when the pinna points in the direction from which it is coming. In man, movements of the head in listening serve a similar purpose.

Deafness

Loss of hearing encountered in domestic animals is of two general types. Nerve deafness involves pathology of the cochlea or the cochlear branch of the auditory nerve; conduction deafness occurs where the sound waves cannot be transmitted to the inner ear. In the latter instance the causes include occlusion of the exterior meatus, rupture of the ear drum, and malfunction of the ossicles.

In domestic animals the major causes of nerve deafness have been attributed to trauma, congenital anomalies of the cochlear system, and toxicity related to drug administration. The degeneration of the cochlea which occurs with old age has been studied in the horse, the cat, and other animals.

Systematic genetic studies on hereditary deficits in audition of white cats were conducted by Wolff (1942). A number of investigations have reported that while deafness is fairly common in both white and albino cats it does not constantly occur in either (e.g. Innes and Saunders 1962). Hereditary deafness in cocker spaniels (Snyder 1946) and bull terriers (Jubb and Kennedy 1963) has been described.

Antibiotics have been reported to be ototoxic in dogs, cats, pigs, and other animals (Hawkins 1959). The drugs quinine, ascaridole, and salicylates administered over extended periods have also been observed to produce deafness (Lurie 1955).

Behavior

Sound plays an important role in communication in all species of domestic animals. The kinds of messages which can be transferred between members of a species are probably similar to those in olfaction: species, sex, age, sexual status, emotional state, and individual identity. Since many mammals can perceive frequencies beyond man's ability, there may be a whole range of sound communication of which man is unaware. Recent research indicates this is the case with rodents (Sales and Pye 1974). The Canidae have an especially large repertoire of sounds. Tembrock (1968) lists four classes, (1) warning sounds (barking), (2) approach-eliciting sounds (howling), (3) withdrawal-eliciting sounds (explosive sounds with onset at the highest amplitude), and (4) infantile sounds. Any or all of these sound classes may transmit individual, sex, and physiological information as well.

In pigs, sounds produced by the young have an apparent role in nursing, and the rhythmic *chant de coeur* or mating song produced by the boar may play a role in inducing female receptivity (Hafez and Signoret 1969). Similar examples could be cited for other domestic mammals but it is in birds that auditory communication has probably reached its most complex level, excluding human speech. Birdsong and bird calls transmit an amazingly complex range of information. Among domestic birds, such as the chicken and the duck, calls provide important signals in maintaining parent-young contact. For example, an excited chick under a bell jar will not attract the attention of the mother hen. Yet even when it is out of sight of the mother, calls of distress from the offspring will immediately draw the hen to the point where the sound of the chick originates (Bruckner 1933). Chicks hear almost nothing above 400 cps (which corresponds to the calls in the hen); however, the hen responds to the calls (above 300 cps) of the chick (Collias and Joos 1953). Schwartzkopff (1955) suggests that the inaudibility of sounds above 400 cps in chicks results from incomplete development of the middle ear.

Recorded alarm calls of starlings have been used to try to repel these birds from feed lots and airports. The initial success was impressive but unfortunately transitory. In this regard, the report of Frings et al. (1958) reflects the limits of our understanding of animal communication. They observed different calls with distinct meanings among crows; the alarm call of a crow would scare off crows exposed to a recording. However, the recorded distress call of American crows evoked no response from French crows.

Klopfer (1962) discussed auditory imprinting in Peking ducklings. The exposure of a duckling to a particular sound could lead to subsequent partial preferences for that sound. The preference occurs, however, only where the exposure takes place during a specific and limited period within the critical period after hatching.

REFERENCES

Ades, H.W. 1959 Central auditory mechanisms. In *Handbook of Physiology*. Sec. 1, J. Field, H.W. Magoun, and V.E. Hall, eds., *Neurophysiology*. Am. Physiol. Soc., Washington. Vol. 1, 585–613.

Adrian, E.D. 1955. Synchronized activity in the vomeronasal nerves with a note on the function of the organ of Jacobson. *Pflüg. Arch. ges. Physiol*. 260:188–92.

Allen, W.F. 1941. Effect of ablating pyriform amygdaloid areas and hippocampi on positive and negative olfactory conditioned reflexes and on conditioned differentiation. *Am. J. Physiol*. 132:81–92.

Arey, L. 1954. *Developmental Anatomy*. Saunders, Philadelphia.

Ashton, E.Y., Eayrs, J.T., and Moulton, D.G. 1957. Olfactory acuity in the dog. *Nature* 179:1069–70.

Bang, B.G., and Bang, F.B. 1959. A comparative study of the vertebrate nasal chamber in relation to upper respiratory infections. *Bull. Johns Hopkins Hosp*. 104:107–49.

Baradi, A.F., and Bourne, G.H. 1959. New observations of the alkaline glycerophosphatase reaction in the papilla foliata. *J. Biophys. Biochem. Cytol*. 5:173–74.

Bartoshuk, L.M., Jacobs, H.L., Nichols, T.L., Hoff, L.A., and Ryckman, J.J. 1975. Taste rejection of nonnutritive sweeteners. *J. Comp. Physiol. Psychol*. 89:971–75.

Bath, W. 1906. Die Greschmacksorgane der Vögel und Krokodile. *Arch. Biontol*. 1:1–47.

Beauchamp, G.K., Maller, O. and Rogers, J.G., Jr. Flavor preferences in cats (*Felis catus* and *Panthera* sp). *J. Comp. Physiol. Psychol.*, in press.

Becker, R.F., and King, J.E. 1957. Delineation of the nasal air streams in the living dog. *Am. Med. Ass. Arch. Otolaryngol*. 65:428–36.

Behrman, H.R., and Kare, M.R. 1968. Canine pancreatic secretions in response to acceptable and aversive taste stimuli. *Proc. Soc. Exp. Biol. Med*. 129:343–46.

Beidler, L.M. 1954. A theory of taste stimulation. *J. Gen. Physiol*. 38:133–39.

——. 1960. Physiology of olfaction and gustation. *Ann. Otolaryngol. Rhinolaryngol. Laryngol*. 69:398–410.

Bell, F.R. 1959. Preference thresholds for taste discrimination in goats. *J. Ag. Sci*. 52:125–28.

Bell, F.R., and Kitchell, R.L. 1966. Taste reception in the goat, sheep, and calf. *J. Physiol*. 183:145–51.

Bell, F.R., and Williams, H.L. 1959. Threshold values for taste in monozygotic twin calves. *Nature* 183:345–46.

Bernard, R.A. 1964. An electrophysiological study of taste reception in peripheral nerves of the calf. *Am. J. Physiol*. 206:827–35.

Bernard, R.A., Halpern, B.P., and Kare, M.R. 1961. Effect of vitamin A deficiency on taste. *Proc. Soc. Exp. Biol. Med*. 108:784–86.

Bloom, J.C., Rogers, J.G., Jr., and Maller, O. 1973. Taste responses of the North American porcupine (*Erethizon dorsatum*). *Physiol. Behav*. 11:95–98.

Bronson, F.H. 1971. Rodent pheromones. *Biol. Reprod*. 4:344–57.

Brown, A.M. 1973. High levels of responsiveness from the inferior colliculus of rodents at ultrasonic frequencies. *J. Comp. Physiol*. 83:393–406.

Bruckner, G.H. 1933. Untersuchungen sur Tiersoziologie, in besonder zur Auflösing der Familie. *Zeitschrift Psychol*. 128:1–105.

Cagan, R.H. 1971. Biochemical studies of taste sensation. I. Binding of ^{14}C-labeled sugars to bovine taste papillae. *Biochim. Biophys. Acta* 252:199–206.

Carpenter, J.A. 1956. Species differences in taste preferences. *J. Comp. Physiol. Psychol*. 49:139–44.

Cole, E.C. 1941. *Comparative Histology*. Blakiston, Philadelphia.

Collias, N., and Joos, M. 1953. The spectrographic analysis of sound signals of the domestic fowl. *Behaviour* 5:175–87.

Davies, J.D., and Prichard, M.M. 1953. Studies on the vascular arrangements of the nose. *J. Anat*. 87:311–22.

Davies, J.T. 1971. Olfactory theories. In *Handbook*. Pt. 1, 322–50.

Davis, H. 1959. Excitation of auditory receptors. In *Handbook of Physiology*. Sec. 1, J. Field, H.W. Magoun, and V.E. Hall, eds., *Neurophysiology*. Am. Physiol. Soc. Washington. Vol. 1, 565–84.

De Lorenzo, A.J. 1958. Electron microscopic observations on the taste buds of the rabbit. *J. Biophys. Biochem. Cytol*. 4:143–48.

——. 1963. Studies on the ultrastructure and histophysiology of cell membranes, nerve fibers, and synaptic junctions in chemoreceptors. In Y. Zotterman, ed., *Olfaction and Taste*. Pergamon, Oxford. Pp. 5–17.

Denton, D.A. 1965. Evolutionary aspects of the emergence of aldosterone secretion and salt appetite. *Physiol. Review* 45:245–95.

Doty, R.L., and Dunbar, I. 1974. Attraction of beagles to conspecific urine, vaginal, and anal sac secretion odors. *Physiol. Behav*. 12:825–33.

Elliott, R. 1937. Total distribution of taste buds on the tongue of the kitten at birth. *J. Comp. Neurol*. 66:361–73.

Estes, R.D. 1972. The role of the vomeronasal organ in mammalian reproduction. *Mammalia* 36:315–41.

Fletcher, H. 1929. *Speech and Hearing*. Van Nostrand, New York.

Frings, H., Frings, M., Jumber, J., Busnell, R.G., Giban, J., and Gramet, P. 1958. Reactions to American and French species of *Carvus* and *Larus* to recorded communications signals tested reciprocally. *Ecology* 39:126–32.

Fuerst, W.F., Jr., and Kare, M.R. 1962. The influence of pH on fluid tolerance and preference. *Poul. Sci*. 41:71–77.

Gesteland, R.C., Lettvin, J.Y., Pitts, W.H., and Rojas, A. 1963. Odor specificities of frog's olfactory receptors. In Y. Zotterman, ed., *Olfaction and Taste*. Pergamon, Oxford. Pp. 19–34.

Goatcher, W.D., and Church, D.C. 1970. Taste responses in ruminants. *J. Anim. Sci*. 30:777–90, 31:373–82.

Gould, J., and Morgan, C. 1941. Hearing in the rat at high frequencies. *Science* 94:168.

Grubb, T.C. 1974. Olfactory navigation to the nesting burrow in Leach's petrel (*Oceanodroma leucorrhoa*). *Anim. Behav*. 22:192–202.

Hafez, E.S.E., Schein, M.W., and Ewbank, R. 1969a. The behaviour of cattle. In Hafez, ed., *The Behaviour of Domestic Animals*. 2d ed. Williams & Wilkins, Baltimore. Pp. 235–95.

Hafez, E.S.E., and Signoret, J.P. 1969. The behavior of swine. In Hafez, ed., *The Behavior of Domestic Animals*. Williams & Wilkins, Baltimore. Pp. 349–90.

Hafez, E.S.E., Williams, M., and Wierzbowski, S. 1969b. The behavior of horses. In Hafez, ed., *The Behavior of Domestic Animals.* Williams & Wilkins, Baltimore. Pp. 391–416.

Halpern, B.P. 1962. Gustatory nerve responses in the chicken. *Am. J. Physiol.* 203:541–44.

Handbook of Sensory Physiology. Vol. 4, L.M. Beidler, ed., *Chemical Senses.* 1971. Pt. 1, *Olfaction.* Pt. 2, *Taste.* Springer, Berlin.

Harriman, A.E., and Kare, M.R. 1964. Preference for sodium chloride over lithium chloride by adrenalectomized rats. *Am. J. Physiol.* 207:941–43.

Harris, J.D. 1972. Audition. In P.H. Mussen and M.R. Rosenzweig, eds., *Annual Review of Psychology.* Annual Reviews, Palo Alto, Calif. Vol. 23.

Harris, L.J., Clay, J., Hargreaves, F.J., and Ward, A. 1933. Appetite and choice of diet: The ability of the vitamin B deficient rat to discriminate between diets containing and lacking the vitamin. *Proc. Roy. Soc.*, ser. B, 113:161–90.

Hawkins, J.R. 1959. Antibiotics and the inner ear. *Trans. Am. Acad. Ophth. Otolaryngol.* 63:206–18.

Helmholtz, H.L.F. 1885. *Sensations of Tone.* 2d ed. Longmans, Green, London.

Herrick, C.J. 1928. *An Introduction to Neurology.* 4th ed. Saunders, Philadelphia.

Holliday, J.C. 1940. Total distribution of taste buds on the tongue of the pup. *Ohio J. Sci.* 40:337–44.

Hyman, L.H. 1942. *Comparative Vertebrate Anatomy.* 2d ed. U. of Chicago Press, Chicago.

Innes, J.R.M., and Saunders, L.Z. 1962. Congenital deafness of white animals. In *Comparative Neuropathology.* Academic Press, New York. Pp. 316–17.

Jacobs, W.W., and Beauchamp, G.K. Glucose preferences in wild and domestic guinea pigs. *Physiol. Behav.*, in press.

Jubb, K.V.F., and Kennedy, P.C. 1963. *Pathology of Domestic Animals.* Academic Press, New York. Pp. 475–93.

Kare, M.R. 1961. Comparative aspects of the sense of taste. In M.R. Kare and B.P. Halpern, eds., *Physiological and Behavioral Aspects of Taste.* U. of Chicago Press, Chicago. Pp. 6–15.

——. 1969. Digestive functions of taste stimuli. In C. Pfaffmann, ed., *Olfaction and Taste.* Rockefeller U. Press. Pp. 586–92.

Kare, M.R., and Ficken, M.S. 1963. Comparative studies on the sense of taste. In Y. Zotterman, ed., *Olfaction and Taste.* Pergamon, Oxford. Pp. 285–97.

Kare, M.R., and Maller, O. 1967. Taste and food intake in domesticated and jungle fowl. *J. Nutr.* 92:191–96.

Kare, M.R., and Pick, H.L., Jr. 1960. The influence of the sense of taste on feed and fluid consumption. *Poul. Sci.* 39:697–706.

Kare, M.R., Pond, W.C., and Campbell, J. 1965. Observations on taste reactions in pigs. *Anim. Behav.* 13:265–69.

Kare, M.R., and Rogers, J.G., Jr. 1976. The special senses. In P.D. Sturkie, ed., *Avian Physiology.* Springer, Berlin.

Kare, M.R., Schecter, P.J., Grossman, S.P., and Roth, L.S. 1969. Direct pathway to the brain. *Science* 163:952–53.

Kare, M.R., and Scott, M.L. 1962. Nutritional value and feed acceptability. *Poul. Sci.* 41:276–78.

Kennedy, J.M., and Baldwin, B.A. 1972. Taste preferences in pigs for nutritive and non-nutritive sweet solutions. *Anim. Behav.* 20:706–18.

King, J.E., Becker, R.F., and Markee, J.E. 1964. Studies on olfactory discrimination in dogs. III. Ability to detect human odor trace. *J. Anim. Behav.* 12:311–15.

Kitchell, R.L. 1963. Comparative anatomical and physiological studies of gustatory mechanisms. In Y. Zotterman, ed., *Olfaction and Taste.* Pergamon, Oxford. Pp. 235–55.

Kitchell, R.L., Strom, L., and Zotterman, Y. 1959. Electrophysiological studies of thermal and taste reception in chickens and pigeons. *Acta Physiol. Scand.* 46:133–51.

Klopfer, P.H. 1962. *Behavioral Aspects of Ecology.* Prentice Hall, Englewood Cliffs, N.J.

Klopfer, P.H., and Gamble, J. 1966. Maternal "imprinting" in goats: The role of the chemical senses. *Zeitschrift Tierpsychol.* 23:588–92.

Koh, S.D., and Teitelbaum, P. 1961. Absolute behavioral taste thresholds in the rat. *J. Comp. Physiol. Psychol.* 54:223–29.

Kovach, J.K. 1971. Ethology in the Soviet Union. *Behavior* 39:237–65.

Le Magnen, J., and Rapaport, A. 1951. Essai de détermination de rôle de la vitamin A dans le mécanisme de l'olfaction chez le rat blanc. *Comptes rend. séances Soc. biol.* 145:800–804.

Lindenmaier, P., and Kare, M.R. 1959. The taste end-organs of the chicken. *Poul. Sci.* 38:545–50.

Lipman, E.A., and Grassi, J.R. 1942. Comparative auditory sensitivity of man and dog. *Am. J. Psychol.* 55:84–89.

Lucas, A.M., and Douglas, L.C. 1934. Principles underlying ciliary activity in the respiratory tract. II. Comparison of nasal clearance in man, monkey, and other mammals. *Arch. Otolaryngol.* 20:518–41.

Lurie, M.H. 1955. The ototoxicity of drugs. *Trans. Am. Acad. Ophth. Otolaryngol.* 59:111–17.

MacLeod, P. 1971. Structure and function of higher olfactory centers. In *Handbook.* Pt. 1, 182–204.

Maller, O., and Kare, M.R. 1965. Selection and intake of carbohydrates by wild and domesticated rats. *Proc. Soc. Exp. Biol. Med.* 119:199–203.

McCartney, W. 1968. *Olfaction and Odours.* Springer, Berlin.

Melrose, D.R., Reed, H.C.B., and Patterson, R.L.S. 1971. Androgen steroids associated with boar odour as an aid to the detection of oestrus in pig artificial insemination. *Brit. Vet. J.* 127:497–502.

Miller, W.J., Carmon, J.L., and Dalton, H.L. 1958. Influence of anise oils on the palatability of calf starters. *J. Dairy Sci.* 41:1262–66.

Moncrieff, R.W. 1951. *The Chemical Senses.* Leonard Hill, London.

Moore, C.A., and Elliott, R. 1946. Numerical and regional distribution of taste buds on the tongue of the bird. *J. Comp. Neurol.* 84:119–32.

Moulton, D.G. 1960. Studies in olfaction acuity. V. The comparative olfactory sensitivity of pigmented and albino rats. *Anim. Behav.* 8:129–33.

——. 1967. Spatiotemporal patterning of response in the olfactory system. In T. Hayashi, ed., *Olfaction and Taste.* Pergamon, New York. Pp. 109–16.

Moulton, D.G., and Beidler, L.M. 1967. Structure and function in the peripheral olfactory system. *Physiol. Rev.* 47:1–52.

Moulton, D.G., and Tucker, D. 1964. Electrophysiology of the olfactory system. *Ann. N.Y. Acad. Sci.* 116:380–428.

Mugford, R.A. 1977. External influences upon the feeding of carnivores. In M.R. Kare and O. Maller, eds., *The Chemical Senses in Nutrition.* Academic, New York.

Mykytowycz, R. 1970. The role of skin glands in mammalian communication. In J.W. Johnston, Jr., D.G. Moulton, and A. Turk, eds., *Advances in Chemoreception: Communication by Chemical Signals.* Appleton-Century-Crofts, New York. Pp. 327–60.

Nachman, M., and Cole, L.P. 1971. Role of taste in specific hungers. In *Handbook.* Pt. 2, 337–62.

Negus, V.E. 1927. Function of the epiglottis (in smell). *J. Anat.* 62:1–8.

——. 1954. The function of the paranasal sinuses. *Acta Otolaryngol. Laryngol.* 44:408–26.

Oppel, A. 1900. *Lehrbuch der vergleichenden mikroskopischen Anatomie der Wirbeltiere.* Gustav Fischer, Jena. Vol. 3.

Ottoson, D. 1956. Analysis of the electrical activity of the olfactory epithelium. *Acta Physiol. Scand.* 35:1–83.

Parsons, T.S. 1971. Anatomy of nasal structures from a comparative viewpoint. In *Handbook.* Pt. 1, 1–26.

Pfaffmann, C. 1971. Sensory reception of olfactory cues. *Biol. Reprod.* 4:327–43.

Pick, H.L., Jr. 1961. Research on taste in the Soviet Union. In M.R. Kare and B.P. Halpern, eds., *Physiological and Behavioral Aspects of Taste.* U. of Chicago Press, Chicago. Pp. 117–26.

Poritsky, R.L., and Singer, M. 1963. The fate of taste buds in tongue transplants to the orbit of the urodele, Triturus. *J. Exp. Zool.* 153:211–18.

Razran, H.S., and Warden, C.J. 1929. Sensory capacities of the dog, as studied by the conditioned reflex method (Russian Schools). *Psychol. Bull.* 26:202–22.

Richter, C.P. 1943. Total self-regulatory functions in animals and human beings. *Harvey Lectures* 38:63–103.

Sales, G., and Pye, D. 1974. *Ultrasonic Communication by Animals.* Chapman & Hall, London.

Sato, M. 1971. Neural coding in taste as seen from recordings from peripheral receptors and nerves. In *Handbook*. Pt. 2, 116–47.

Schwartzkopff, J. 1955. On the hearing in birds. *Auk* 72:340–47.

Scott, E.M., and Verney, E.L. 1947. The nature of appetite for B vitamins. *J. Nutr.* 34(5):471–80.

Sharma, K.N., and Nasset, E.S. 1962. Electrical activity in mesenteric nerves after perfusion of gut lumen. *Am. J. Physiol.* 202:725–30.

Snyder, L.H. 1946. *The Principles of Heredity.* 3d ed. Heath, Boston.

Tembrock, G. 1968. Land mammals. In T.A. Sebeok, ed., *Animal Communication*. Indiana U. Press, Bloomington. Pp. 338–404.

Torrey, T.W. 1940. The influence of nerve fibers upon taste buds during embryonic development. *Proc. Nat. Acad. Sci.* 26:627–34.

Vinnikov, J.A., and Titova, L.K. 1963. Cytophysiology and cytochemistry of the organ of Corti: Cytochemical theory of hearing. *Internat. Rev. Cytol.* 14:157–91.

von Békésy, G. 1960. *Experiments in Hearing*. McGraw-Hill, New York.

Weber, W., Davies, R.O., and Kare, M.R. 1960. Distribution of taste buds and changes with age in the ruminant. Unpublished data.

Wenzel, B.M. 1971. Olfaction in birds. In *Handbook*. Pt. 1, 432–48.

Wever, E.G. 1949. *Theory of Hearing*. Wiley, New York.

White, H.E. 1940. *Classical and Modern Physics*. Van Nostrand, New York.

White, T.D., and Boudreau, J.C. 1975. Taste preferences in cats for neurophysiologically active compounds. *Physiol. Psychol.* 3:405–10.

Wierzbowski, S. 1959. The sexual reflexes of stallions. *Roczn. Nauk Roln.* 73-B-4:753–88.

Wolff, D. 1942. Three generations of deaf white cats. *J. Hered.* 33:39–42.

Wood-Gush, D-G.M., and Kare, M.R. 1966. The behavior of calcium-deficient chickens. *Brit. Poul. Sci.* 7:285–90.

Yang, R.S.H., and Kare, M.R. 1968. Taste response of a bird to constituents of arthropod defensive secretions. *Ann. Entom. Soc. Am.* 61:7810.

Zotterman, Y. 1956. Species differences in the water taste. *Acta Physiol. Scand.* 37:60–70.

PART VII | ENDOCRINOLOGY, REPRODUCTION, AND LACTATION

CHAPTER 52

Endocrine Glands | by William M. Dickson

INTRODUCTION

The development of animals into complex structures with thousands of diverse specialized cells involved the formation of systems whereby cellular functions are unified and coordinated. The smoothness and exquisite gradation of muscle movement is an easily observed example of such coordination. Equally important but less apparent is the integration of diverse biochemical changes. Classically, the integrative organization of the body has been divided into two distinct entities—the nervous system and the endocrine system. While this distinction is roughly valid with respect to the pathways utilized and the speed of coordination, it has become increasingly evident that the two are intimately interrelated, both morphologically and functionally. Until recently the endocrine system was regarded as a primitive, slow, and relatively inefficient means of integration that during the course of evolution has been replaced by the nervous system in the more important integrative areas. It now is realized that the two systems complement each other and are equally important.

The endocrine glands differ from other glands in that their secretions, the hormones, pass directly into the circulatory system rather than through a special duct network. Our knowledge of hormones has vastly increased during the past four decades, but a completely satisfactory definition of these compounds is lacking.

General nature of hormones

There are a few characteristics shared by all hormones. Chemically, hormones can be roughly divided into two classes: steroids, and protein or protein derivatives. Hormones secreted by the adrenal cortex and the gonads characterize the first group, while the pituitary gland, thyroid, parathyroid, pancreas, and adrenal medulla secrete the latter type. Even this classification does not hold completely true, as the ovary appears to be the major secretory source for relaxin, a protein-type hormone. The fact that hormones fall into two general chemical categories may have functional significance. A few general observations on function are possible: (1) hormones appear to regulate rather than initiate reactions; (2) hormones are effective in minute quantities—for example, a perceptible antidiuretic effect can be produced in humans with 2 ng of pure arginine vasopressin; and (3) hormones are not secreted at uniform rates. This latter quality is vital to integrating systems that must meet the diverse requirements posed by growth, differentiation, reproduction, and adaptation to environmental change.

A generalized mechanism by which several hormones act on effector cells has been proposed by Sutherland et al. (1965). Certain polypeptide hormones (catecholamines, glucagon, ACTH, LH, ADH, parathormone) interact with target tissues to activate adenyl cyclase, resulting in increased levels of cyclic 3′,5′-AMP in the cytoplasm.

Cyclic AMP (cAMP), termed the second messenger, stimulates changes in various cellular particulates; increased permeability of the mitochondria to calcium, phosphorylation of microtubules and microtubule polymerization, enzyme activation in ribosomes and endoplasmic reticulum, and so on. Specificity of action of the hormone or first messenger results from the presence of specific binding proteins in the membranes of the target cells. In some cases (thyroid hormones, prolactin) cAMP does not appear to be involved, while in others (steroids) activation of adenyl cyclase occurs together with other intracellular reactions. Figure 52.1 illustrates a general scheme of hormone mechanism of action, based largely on a hypothesis advanced by Szego (1974), which proposes that steroid hormones interact with a specific membrane protein, are transported to the nucleus in lysosomes, and exert such intranuclear effects as gene derepression. There is considerable evidence that in vivo protein binding is vital for extracellular and intracellular transport, specificity of action, and mechanism of action. Szego (1974), Tata (1974), and Liao and Fang (1969) give further details.

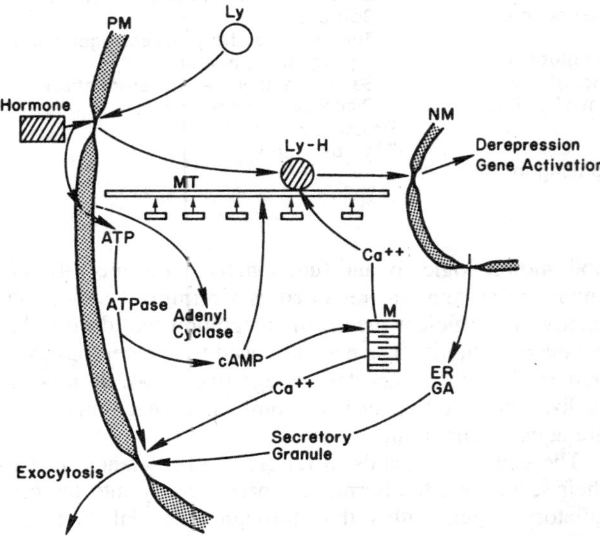

Figure 52.1. Some elements of hormone mechanism of action. PM, plasma membrane; NM, nuclear membrane; ER, endoplasmic reticulum; Ly, lysosome; Ly-H, bound hormone-lysosome; MT, microtubule; M, mitochondrion; GA, Golgi apparatus

General function of hormones

The endocrine glands play an especially important part in the regulation of such body activities as growth, differentiation, reproduction, maintenance of the internal environment, and adaptation to changes in the external environment. With the possible exception of growth and differentiation, each of these activities can be regarded as a type of adaptation. Reproduction constitutes an adaptation of the organism in that the entire body is redirected toward this end. Internal regulatory adjustments such as the control of blood sugar levels by the pancreas and the maintenance of blood calcium through parathormone secretion, on the other hand, are short-term adaptations to frequently recurring internal changes.

Adaptation to external environmental influences is an important function for both the nervous and endocrine systems (in fact, environmental change usually activates both systems). Nerve impulses are particularly useful in evoking fast, short-term reactions to sporadic environmental change. Hormones, on the other hand, are more involved in adaptive reactions of longer duration in response to environmental stimuli to which the body is likely to be exposed for a longer time. For example, one may consider the role of the two systems in the organism's reaction to an emergency or stress situation that endangers the health of the animal. Ultrashort responses, primarily motor, are effected by the somatic or voluntary nervous system. Autonomic nerves bring about rapid internal adjustments, reinforced by epinephrine from the adrenal medulla, while adrenocortical hormones institute changes designed to enable the animal to withstand prolonged stress. Other endocrine glands participate in realigning and coordinating the body chemistry in response to these new demands. Endocrine activity not only aids in long-term body defense but initiates recovery processes—an example of what Cannon chose to call "the wisdom of the body."

Another example of the interplay of the two integrative systems is the response of the body to temperature change. A lower temperature causes increased thyroid and adrenal medullary activity, which results in increased heat production, while peripheral vasoconstriction occurs as a result of autonomic nerve impulses. Voluntary adaptive reactions can be included too: the animal usually withdraws, if possible, to a warmer site. Thus biology and change are inseparable, and biological integrative systems are dynamic. It matters little if one speaks of adaptation or dynamic integration. The endocrine glands, in concert with the nervous system, redirect, coordinate, and unify diverse organ functions to accomplish optimal conditions under a given set of circumstances. These changes constitute adaptation.

Regulation of endocrine activity

The reflex arc is often considered to be the unit of function of the nervous system. It is possible to consider endocrine integrative activity in the same way. It is particularly useful to do so in those instances when the two systems are interwoven. In these cases, one speaks of *neuroendocrine reflexes,* which are those in which the afferent or regulatory component is neural while the efferent arm is endocrine. The best example of peripheral neural regulation of endocrine function is found in the adrenal medulla, where endocrine secretion is wholly under the direction of preganglionic sympathetic nerve fibers. The secretion of the posterior pituitary also appears to be under the control of peripheral afferent impulses. However, the situation in this instance is not clear-cut; it is probable that the afferent pathway is partly blood-vascular. The regulation of anterior pituitary secretion resembles that of the posterior pituitary in that both neural and blood-vascular afferent inputs can be demonstrated. The central integrative pathways for pituitary regulation are primarily neural, but humoral "regulating hormones" from the hypothalamus control anterior pituitary activity. The efferent output (i.e. secretion) of the posterior pituitary is unique in that these hormones pass from the hypothalamus to the posterior pituitary *within the axons* before being released into the general circulation.

Among the endocrine glands that are sensitive to concentrations of a particular chemical are the pancreas and parathyroid glands. This type of regulation is somewhat analogous to the spinal reflex in the nervous system. It must be recognized that other endocrine glands, through their efferent function, will affect the concentration of the aforementioned chemical. Thus the pancreas and parathyroid are not isolated from other regulatory influences. For example, an afferent neural pathway may activate the adrenal medulla, which then increases blood glucose concentration, which in turn calls for increased insulin secretion from the pancreatic islets.

Another type of humoral regulation of endocrine activity occurs when the efferent pathway from one endocrine gland serves as the afferent input for another. This type of regulation is best exemplified by the relation of the anterior pituitary to its target glands. The tropic hormones of the pituitary gland regulate the activity of other endocrine glands, and the secretions from the latter glands feed back or serve as afferent humoral controls of the specific pituitary hormone that stimulated their production. Such feedback may be exerted on the adenohypophysis itself or upon the hypothalamic regulating hormones. It is also probable that circulating hormones affect higher centers in the CNS, which in turn influence the secretion of the tropic hormones.

A unique means of control of endocrine activity is found in the prostaglandins. These compounds are secreted by many tissues in the body in response to various stimuli and have powerful systemic effects. It is likely, however, that when they respond to a specific stimulus their regulatory influence is relatively localized, since they are rapidly and effectively deactivated by the lung and liver and do not appear in the arterial circulation.

Antihormones

Long-continued injections of protein or polypeptide hormones give rise to a state of lowered reactivity or no reactivity. While antihormone research was conducted during the years following the initial observations of Collip and his colleagues in the 1920's, the impurity of the hormone preparations available at that time prevented the full potential of this phenomenon from being realized. Advances in protein purification and improved immunological techniques have led to revived interest in antibody production following hormone injection.

Antibodies against insulin, parathormone, calcitonin, glucagon, and all six anterior pituitary hormones have been produced and evaluated. In the experimental production of antibodies, endogenous hormone action has not commonly been inhibited in the animal in which the antiserum has been produced. Thus antihormones are produced by the organism only when it is confronted with a hormone antigen from another species. However, it is possible to produce or encounter antibodies against a hormone precursor (proinsulin, proparathormone, iodothyroglobulin) that is not normally found in the circulation. Such is the case in certain types of thyroiditis in humans (Hashimoto's disease, Riedel's thyroiditis, acute nonsuppurative thyroditis). In these diseases, acinar destruction results in the liberation of microsomal particles and colloid that act as antigens; the subsequent antigen-antibody reaction may cause further thyroid destruction.

Protein hormone antibodies have proved to be of great value in the development of highly sensitive hormone assays. Yalow and Berson (1961) were able to detect 0.1 microunit of human insulin using such an assay. When the specificity of such an assay has been reasonably well established, immunoassay is a precise, sensitive, and accurate technique that has proved invaluable. Such problems as species specificity, antigen purity, and cross-reactions with antigenically similar prohormones or hormone metabolites have been encountered and emphasize the need for careful evaluation of results.

In addition to the previously mentioned autoimmune diseases, antihormones are interesting from a clinical standpoint in that animals treated with protein hormones derived from another species may become unresponsive to further treatment. This has been observed in cattle given human chorionic gonadotropin.

HYPOPHYSIS CEREBRI AND HYPOTHALAMUS

The hypophysis cerebri (or pituitary gland) and the hypothalamus are so intimately related both morphologically and functionally that it is necessary to discuss them together. Here the zenith of endocrine and neural coordination is reached.

Morphology and nomenclature

The pituitary is formed early in embryonic life from the fusion of two ectodermal processes. An evagination from the roof of the embryonic buccal area (Rathke's pouch) extends upward toward the brain and is met by an outpouching of the floor of the third ventricle. This outpouching becomes the neurohypophysis, and the region derived from oral epithelium becomes the adenohypophysis. Figure 52.2 is a diagram of neurovascular connections between hypothalamic nuclei and the pituitary gland.

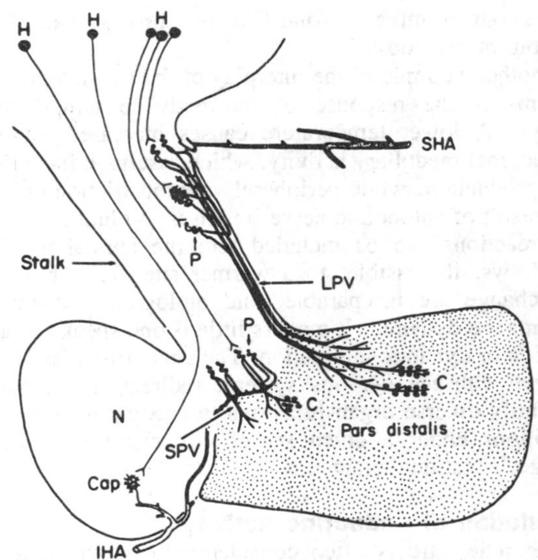

Figure 52.2. Some of the possible neurovascular connections between hypothalamic nuclei and the pituitary gland: nerve cells (H), parenchymal cells (C), primary capillary bed (P), long portal vessels (LPV), short portal vessels (SPV), posterior lobe (N), posterior lobe capillary bed (Cap), dorsal (superior) hypophyseal artery (SHA), ventral (inferior) hypophyseal artery (IHA). (From Hume-Adams, Daniel, and Prichard 1964, *Endocrinology* 75:120–26.)

Hypothalamus

The hypothalamus is that part of the diencephalon lying ventral to the thalamus and forming the floor of the third ventricle. Usually the hypothalamus is considered to include the optic chiasma, the tuber cinereum, the mammillary bodies, the median eminence, the infundibulum, and the neurohypophysis. The latter two parts are also included in descriptions of pituitary morphology. However, since the infundibulum and neurohypophysis constitute ventral projections of the neural tissue of the hypothalamus, they are logically included with this element.

Hypothalamic and hypophyseal tissue is composed of connective tissue, nonmedullated axons, and neuroglia. Between the median eminence and the neurohypophysis proper, the axons run more or less parallel to one another, and most of them pass through the neural stalk to end in the neurohypophysis. For the most part, axons arise from two pairs of nuclei in the hypothalamus: the supraoptic and the paraventricular nuclei. Neurosecretory material within the axons can be discerned throughout their course. This neurosecretory material is visible in electron micrographs as numerous spherical bodies 100–180 nm in diameter having the typical structure of the secretory granules seen in the pancreas or in the adenohypophyseal cells.

Adenohypophysis

The adenohypophysis lies anterior to the neurohypophysis and is divided into three parts: the pars distalis, the pars tuberalis, and the pars intermedia. The pars intermedia is formed by a layer of cells contiguous to the neurohypophysis, while the pars tuberalis consists of a layer of cells surrounding the neural stalk, or as in the human, lying only on the anterior surface of the stalk. The pars distalis comprises the bulk of the adenohypophysis and consists of branching cords of cells separated by sinusoids. On the basis of older histological techniques, adenohypophyseal cells were classified as acidophil, basophil, or chromophobe, depending upon the presence or absence of granules having an affinity for certain dyes. Modern techniques of electron microscopy and selective staining have enabled cytologists to identify six types of cells in the adenohypophysis. No true chromophobes exist, only cells with more or fewer granules.

Blood supply

The pituitary gland receives both arterial and venous blood. The arterial blood arises from the dorsal hypophyseal and ventral hypophyseal arteries, which carry nutrients and oxygen to the adenohypophysis and neurohypophysis respectively. Venous blood enters the adenohypophysis from two capillary beds: one in the median eminence, the other in the lower pituitary stalk and neural lobe of the neurohypophysis. This venous blood is collected in two series of parallel veins running down the anterior surface of the pituitary stalk and draining into the sinusoidal capillaries of the pars distalis. The ventral and central part of the pars distalis receives blood from the long portal vessels, whereas the sinusoids receiving blood from the short vessels are restricted to the more dorsal and peripheral regions. This constitutes the hypophyseal-portal system, which is the humoral link between the hypothalamus and higher brain centers and the adenohypophysis.

Hormones of the neurohypophysis

The first demonstration of posterior pituitary hormonal activity was made by Oliver and Schafer in 1895. They found that the intravenous injection of whole pituitary extracts produced a prolonged rise in blood pressure. Soon afterward, this effect was shown to be identifiable with the pars nervosa. Subsequent studies, culminating in the work of DuVigneaud and his collaborators, have resulted in the isolation, purification, and synthesis of the neurohypophyseal hormones.

Chemistry

The compounds isolated from the pars nervosa are octapeptides containing cystine. Though several octapeptides having biological activity have been studied, only four occur naturally: oxytocin (Fig. 52.3), arginine vasopressin, lysine vasopressin, and arginine vasotocin. Those compounds with phenylalanine substituted for isoleucine are vasopressins. The two vasopressins have arginine or lysine in the position occupied by leucine in the oxytocin molecule. Arginine vasotocin is intermediate in that arginine substitutes for leucine but isoleucine is present as in oxytocin.

Antidiuretic function

If hypertonic saline is given intravenously into the carotid artery, concentration of the urine and decreased urine volume are observed. Conversely, if an animal is water-loaded, an increased volume of watery urine is excreted. This latter effect can be obliterated by the injection of a small amount of posterior pituitary extract. Purification and fractionation led to the term antidiuretic hormone (ADH) for the fraction that exhibited this activity. Further research established that ADH and vasopressin are identical in mammals. The natural hormone in most mammals is arginine vasopressin, but the pig and some related species utilize lysine vasopressin. In birds, arginine vasotocin exerts the primary antidiuretic effect. The search for the afferent pathways and sensory receptors that signal the release or inhibition of ADH is still not entirely completed. According to one theory, specific osmoreceptors in the brain respond to changes in the osmotic pressure of blood plasma. However, hemorrhage has been observed to be a very powerful stimulus for ADH release. The effect of hemorrhage appears to be part of a general reaction to conserve blood volume. Recent evidence has shown that circulating angiotensin stimulates increased ADH secretion.

Hemorrhage is the only situation in which sufficient vasopressin is released into the blood to give a pressor response. Further, arginine vasotocin is a vasodepressor in birds and a weak vasopressor in rats. These and other observations have led to general agreement that the vasopressor action of the neurohypophysis is pharmacological and not an important function under normal conditions. Trauma, pain, anxiety, and certain drugs will also cause the release of ADH, while cold environmental temperature inhibits it.

The target organ for ADH is the kidney. As the glomerular filtrate passes through the proximal tubule, sodium, chloride, and water pass into the blood stream simultaneously. Thus the filtrate remains isosmotic. In the loops of Henle, a countercurrent multiplier mechanism enables the reabsorption of large quantities of sodium chloride in excess of water; thus urine entering the distal tubule is hypotonic with respect to plasma. In the absence of ADH, the distal tubule and collecting duct are impermeable to water, and a highly dilute urine is excreted. However, in the presence of ADH, these tubules become permeable to water and the osmotic gradient existing between plasma and this hypotonic urine leads to water reabsorption. Therefore, the driving force for urine concentration is osmotic. Two explanations of the effect of ADH on the permeability of the distal tubule and collecting duct have been offered: (1) vasopressin, by forming S-S bridges with tubule cell protein, might disrupt the permeability characteristics of the tubular membrane and widen the pores through which water can flow; and (2) on the basis of histochemical observations, Ginetzinsky (1958) has suggested that ADH accelerates water flow through the wall of the kidney tubule by an effect on the intercellular cement substance.

ISOLEUCINE - TYROSINE - CYSTEINE(NH_2) - S
| |
GLUTAMINE(NH_2) - ASPARAGINE - CYSTEINE - S
|
PROLINE
|
LEUCINE
|
GLYCINE(NH_2)

Figure 52.3. The amino acid arrangement in the oxytocin molecule

Oxytocic function

Oxytocin exerts its functional activity entirely upon reproduction. Cannulation of the teat canal of a lactating cow or goat results in the collection of only a minor portion of the total amount of milk in the gland. The greater portion of milk in the alveoli becomes available only upon contraction of the myoepithelial cells surrounding the alveoli. These cells act during milking or sucking. Gaines postulated in 1915 that the action of posterior pituitary extracts on the mammary gland resulted in a constriction of the alveoli and subsequent milk ejection. In 1941, Ely and Peterson observed milk ejection in a denervated mammary gland perfused with blood to which posterior pituitary extract had been added. Milk ejection or ''letdown'' serves as an excellent example of a neuroendocrine reflex. The afferent stimulus, suckling, is neural in nature, travels to the hypothalamic nuclei, and stimulates the release of oxytocin from the neurohypophysis.

It is generally agreed that oxytocin exerts a stimulatory effect upon the myometrium provided the myometrium is under estrogen dominance. This occurs during the follicular phase of the ovarian cycle and during the latter part of gestation. During the follicular phase of the cycle, uterine contractions stimulated by oxytocin aid in the transport of the spermatozoa to the oviduct, while in late pregnancy they are of obvious utility in parturition. The assumption that oxytocin participates in the process of labor is supported by evidence that stretching the cervix induces a release of oxytocin and that the oxytocin activity of the blood of some mammals increases substantially during parturition. However, Assali et al. (1958) were unable to stimulate the uterus of the pregnant ewe or bitch with this hormone unless spontaneous labor had commenced. The hypothesis that spermatozoa transport is aided by oxytocin release is supported by the observation that, during mating, oxytocin is secreted and uterine motility increases; however, contradictory data exist. In the laying hen, arginine vasotocin causes an increase in intrauterine pressure and may be functionally involved in oviposition.

Oxytocin has also been proposed as a factor influencing adenohypophyseal secretion. Injection of oxytocin in the cow during the follicular phase results in a marked shortening of the ovarian cycle. The corpora lutea formed following treatment are cystic and fail to attain normal size. However, the fact that oxytocin effects are not seen in hysterectomized cows indicates that the luteal response may arise from endometrial activity rather than from a direct oxytocic effect. The observations that (1) oxytocin injection prolongs lactation in female rats from which the young have been removed, and (2) that full lactation can be maintained after complete denervation of the udder, provided that oxytocin is regularly given, suggest that oxytocin is involved in prolactin release. A possibility remains, however, that the same neural afferent pathways activate both humoral agents.

Table 52.1 summarizes the activities of the four known natural octapeptides from the neurohypophysis.

Hormones of the adenohypophysis

There are seven well-established hormones secreted from the adenohypophysis: follicle-stimulating hormone (FSH), luteinizing hormone (LH), prolactin, adrenocorticotropic hormone (ACTH), thyroid-stimulating hormone (TSH), growth hormone, and intermedin. The first six of these are secreted by the pars distalis, while the seventh, intermedin, is derived from the pars intermedia. The cytological source of secretion of the hormones of the pars distalis has been a subject of controversy. The evidence appears to favor the secretion of growth hormone and prolactin from the acidophil cells, and TSH and the gonadotropins (FSH and LH) from the basophil cells. In many species there are two types of acidophil cell and three clearly different basophils. A sixth cell type, a relatively agranular cell, has been identified as the source of ACTH.

Role in reproduction

The two active principles of the adenohypophysis that maintain gonadal function are FSH and LH. These two tropic hormones are often collectively referred to as go-

Table 52.1. Comparative potency of neurohypophyseal octapeptides as measured by various bioassay methods (units/mg) in terms of the U.S.P. Standard (A, B, and C are natural products, and D is a synthetic analogue)

Products	In vivo (intravenous route)			In vitro		
	Antidiuresis (dog)	Milk ejec. (rabbit)	Vasopressor (rat)	Uterus (rat)	Oviduct (fowl)	Bladder permeability (frog)
A. Arginine vasopressin	300	51	300	9	240	20
B. Lysine vasopressin	34	34	200	5	15	5
C. Oxytocin	4	360	7	420	29	360
D. Arginine vasotocin	50	80	60	37	640	10,000

From Munsick, Sawyer, and van Dyke 1960, *Endocrinology* 66:860–71

nadotropins or, properly, pituitary gonadotropins. Prolactin is sometimes included in this category since it is luteotropic (stimulates corpus luteum progesterone production) in rats, mice, and possibly ewes. In the female, FSH acts upon ovarian follicles. After a follicle has developed to the stage where several layers of cells envelop an oocyte, FSH stimulates the maturation of the oocyte, the secretion of follicular fluid, the proliferation of granulosa cells, and the development of the thecal layer, resulting in overall follicular growth. It is probable that FSH does not in itself initiate or stimulate estrogen secretion, nor is FSH able to complete follicle maturation. This requires the concerted action of FSH, LH, and possibly the sex hormones. In the male the action of FSH appears to be upon the Sertoli cells within the seminiferous tubules in the stimulation of spermatogenesis. Again there is evidence that FSH cannot achieve full spermatogenesis without the cooperation of LH (ICSH, or interstitial cell stimulating hormone, in the male) and/or testosterone.

Immunological assay of FSH has proved difficult due primarily to the lack of species-specific purified antigen. L'Hermite et al. (1972) reported peripheral circulating blood concentrations of 100–160 ng/ml in cycling ewes, increasing just before estrus to 180–200 ng/ml. These workers found 60–119 ng/ml in rams. Slightly lower concentrations have been reported in the bovine (Akbar et al. 1973).

The physiological effects of LH are most clearly seen upon the ovarian follicle that has previously been under the influence of FSH. In such a follicle, LH intensifies growth and initiates the secretion of estrogen from the thecal cells. The culmination of this spurt of follicular growth is of course ovulation. Radioimmunoassay of circulating LH has revealed a transient and dramatic increase from concentrations of 1 ng/ml during most of the cycle to over 100 ng/ml about 10 hours before ovulation (bovine). This ''LH surge'' occurs within 4–6 hours and constitutes a good example of positive feedback in that it appears to be stimulated by increasing estrogen concentration. LH, in addition to promoting estrogen secretion, ovulation, and luteinization, is instrumental in stimulating the secretion of progesterone from the corpus luteum in many mammalian species. In the male, ICSH promotes the secretion of testosterone from the interstitial cells (cells of Leydig) of the testis.

Initiation and maintenance of lactation are complex phenomena involving many hormones, including estrogen, progesterone, corticoids, growth hormone, ACTH, and prolactin. Prolactin appears to be necessary for mammary growth and for the initiation and maintenance of lactation. Increased circulating prolactin concentrations have been observed at proestrus, at parturition, and following suckling. The latter neural stimulus is also associated with increased ACTH secretion. In common with growth hormone and ACTH, circulating prolactin is elevated by various stresses. It has been suggested that increased prolactin secretion at proestrus and perhaps at parturition, as well as at puberty, results from estrogen stimulation (Meites and Clemens 1972).

In the male, no function for prolactin has been elucidated. Convey et al. (1971), however, reported a postejaculation increase from 10.8 ng/ml to 59.0 ng/ml followed by a decrease to 38.3 ng/ml within 30 minutes. That this may have been a stress effect was indicated by a concurrent increase in growth hormone.

The terms prolactin and LTH (luteotropic hormone) have been used synonymously for some time, but there is no definitive evidence, except in rodents and perhaps sheep, that prolactin is luteotropic. It appears that in most species, LH or a combination of LH and FSH provides the stimulus for progesterone secretion from luteal tissue.

For a more complete description of FSH, LH, and prolactin physiology see Chapters 53–56.

Function of adrenocorticotropic hormone

The administration of ACTH to normal or hypophysectomized animals results in increased adrenocortical activity. There is an increased secretion of adrenocortical steroids into the adrenal vein, a loss of lipid from the adrenocortical cells, decreased adrenal cholesterol and ascorbic acid concentrations, adrenal hypertrophy and hyperplasia, and an increase in adrenal blood flow. The fact that this hypertrophy and hyperplasia of the adrenal gland are limited to the zona reticularis and zona fasciculata and the marked increase in the secretion of cortisol and corticosterone led to the conclusion that ACTH was of no importance in the control of aldosterone secretion. However, ACTH will stimulate the production of aldosterone, and there is evidence that aldosterone secretion is initiated by ACTH following acute blood loss or a similar severe stress. Injected ACTH is more effective in stimulating aldosterone output if the dietary content of sodium has been low.

It has become increasingly apparent that the effects of ACTH are not limited to the adrenal gland. The following changes have been observed when ACTH has been administered to adrenalectomized animals: mobilization of nonesterified fatty acids and neutral fats from the fat depots, enhanced ketogenesis, increased muscle glycogen, hypoglycemia, and decreased plasma amino acid concentration. ACTH also prolongs the biological half-life of cortisol injected in adrenalectomized animals. These effects and those of growth hormone are interrelated in the so-called diabetogenic action of crude pituitary extracts.

Function of thyroid-stimulating hormone

When thyroid-stimulating hormone (TSH) is administered to experimental animals, both morphological and functional changes are seen in the thyroid gland. The height of the alveolar epithelium is increased, and the stored colloid becomes vacuolated and depleted. Following hypophysectomy, there is a decrease in all the functional aspects of thyroid physiology, including accumulation of iodine, the organic binding of iodine, the formation of thyroxine, and the release of thyroxine into the circulation. Administration of TSH reverses these effects. While TSH affects all aspects of thyroid hormone synthesis and release, its principal action appears to be colloid endocytosis and hormone release. There is no convincing evidence of the existence of normal extrathyroidal activity for TSH.

Function of growth hormone

The important and characteristic role of growth hormone is stimulation of an increase in body size. There is no doubt that growth hormone and other pituitary hormones are important in the processes of true growth, that is, protein synthesis and increased metabolic mass. In the intact animal, pituitary hormones join with other endocrine secretions to achieve coordinated body growth. However, in the hypophysectomized animal, in which adrenal, thyroid, and gonadal function is markedly impaired, growth hormone is the most potent agent in increasing the markedly reduced growth rate. Furthermore, growth hormone is the only hormone capable of stimulating increased and abnormally rapid growth in the intact animal. The effects of growth hormone are observed particularly in bone, muscle, kidney, liver, and adipose tissue. The epiphyseal discs of long bones are particularly sensitive to growth hormone. In fact, the most popular bioassay method for growth hormone involves measuring an increase in the width of the epiphyseal disc of the rat tibia. Mitotic activity is stimulated in growing bones, and elevated osteoblastic activity can be observed. It appears that growth hormone does not act directly on bone, but through a peripheral factor that has been termed sulfation factor or somatomedin. Several somatomedins have been identified and exert actions similar to those of insulin and growth hormone. The source of these compounds is uncertain.

Cellular effects of growth hormone deficiency and administration are observed readily in the liver cells. Hypophysectomy causes a decrease in cell size, nuclear RNA, nuclear protein, cytoplasm RNA, and cytoplasm protein. Growth hormone reverses these changes. In the normal animal, if one kidney is removed there is a compensatory hypertrophy of the other kidney. This will not occur in the absence of growth hormone. In addition, growth hormone appears to affect the kidney in a manner not entirely related to growth alone. Hypophysectomy causes a decreased glomerular filtration rate, a diminished renal blood flow, and reduced tubular secretion. These defects are corrected by the administration of growth hormone and thyroid hormone, but not by thyroid hormone alone. In muscle and adipose tissue, growth hormone acts as an antagonist to insulin; hypophysectomized animals are quite sensitive to insulin administration. This antagonism assumes increased importance in view of the observation that hypoglycemia acts as a potent stimulus for growth hormone secretion. Growth hormone, together with ACTH, also has the ability to mobilize fat from adipose tissue and increase the blood level of the so-called ketone bodies. The diabetogenic properties of ACTH and growth hormone are similar to changes seen in starvation and may represent an adaptation to reduced food intake. In addition, at least in the dog and cat, excessive growth hormone results in damage to the insulin-secreting β-cells of the pancreatic islets, which further enhances ketogenesis through insulin deprivation.

Growth in the CNS appears to be relatively independent of growth hormone, as is the growth of the thyroid, adrenals, and gonads. Studies of the lactating cow reveal an interesting galactopoietic effect following the injection of growth hormone. A highly significant and linear relationship has been demonstrated between the logarithm of the dose of growth hormone and an increase in milk yield. This effect is probably due partially, if not entirely, to an increase in mammary gland growth.

The incorporation of radioactive-labeled amino acids into protein and the intracellular accumulation of a nonutilizable amino acid (α-amino-isobutyric acid) are stimulated by the addition of growth hormone to an in vitro diaphragm preparation. It is possible that the rate-limiting step in growth is the availability of intracellular raw material and that the primary mechanism of action of growth hormone may be to provide a high intracellular concentration of amino acids.

Function of intermedin

Many species of reptiles, amphibians, and fish show a marked color change in response to changes in illumination, temperature, or humidity. This color change results from the dispersion or concentration of pigment granules in the melanophores. This phenomenon is at least partially due to a hormone secreted by the pars intermedia of the adenohypophysis and named intermedin or melanophore-stimulating hormone (MSH). Curiously, these studies were carried out with extracts of mammalian pars intermedia, but no function for this hormone has been established in warm-blooded animals.

Chemistry of adenohypophyseal hormones

During the last decade in the study of adenohypophyseal hormone chemistry complete amino acid sequences have been reported, and complete synthesis of all seven appears to be a possibility in the near future. The subunit nature of the adenohypophyseal glycoproteins, LH, FSH, and TSH, has been clearly demonstrated (Pierce et al.

1971); this structure involves a noncovalent bonding of an α (common, nonspecific) and β (hormone-specific) subunit to constitute the biologically active molecule. The α subunit of ovine LH consists of 96 amino acids with 5 disulfide bonds and 2 oligosaccharide units, while the β subunit includes 119 amino acids, 6 disulfide bonds, and 1 oligosaccharide unit (Papkoff et al. 1973).

The two hormones secreted by acidophils, growth hormone and prolactin, are large polypeptides (about 200 amino acids in growth hormone) with no sugar residues. The two are chemically similar and may contain an active core similar to ACTH. There is a possibility that these three hormones are secreted as inactive prohormones and exert their action only when the active core is released during metabolism. ACTH is a smaller molecule and its chemistry has been well studied. ACTH is related to α-MSH (one of two known intermedins) in that the first 13 amino acids of ACTH constitute the structure of α-MSH.

Regulation of adenohypophyseal secretion

The afferent input that regulates the quality and quantity of hormone output from the adenohypophysis is both humoral and neural. The neural element of this afferent system, however, includes a short humoral pathway consisting of the hypophyseal-portal system, which unifies the hypothalamus and the adenohypophysis. The primary afferent humoral element consists for the most part of the feedback of hormones secreted from a target gland that has been stimulated by the tropic hormone of the adenohypophysis. However, it has become increasingly apparent that this humoral control is not always a simple feedback mechanism, and other humoral afferent agents have been postulated.

Humoral pathways

The best examples of relatively uncomplicated feedback in the control of efferent hypophyseal secretion are found in the secretions of the thyroid gland and the adrenal cortex. Suppression of the thyroid gland or adrenal cortex either by chemical means or by removal leads to an increased output of TSH and ACTH respectively. Conversely, the administration of thyroxine or cortisol leads to a decreased output of these tropic hormones. One manifestation of feedback is the phenomenon of compensatory hypertrophy, which is exemplified by the tumorous growth of the thyroid gland in response to a simple iodine deficiency. In such a case, the gland is unable to manufacture thyroxine, the pituitary gland is uninhibited, and increased TSH is secreted. As a result, the thyroid gland continues to undergo hypertrophy and hyperplasia, and goiter results. The opposite effects can be demonstrated by sustained thyroxine administration, which results in continued inhibition of pituitary TSH and atrophy of the thyroid gland.

With respect to the gonadotropins, feedback is not so clear-cut. The striking elevation of blood gonadotropin concentration following castration has been long established, and it is well known that the injection of sex hormones will depress pituitary gonadotropin output. The most active sex steroids in this regard are estrogens. Estrogen can act as a positive feedback agent as well as a negative one; conversion of the inhibitory effect of estrogen on gonadotropin secretion to a stimulatory action is not completely understood, but may involve a complex interaction between low concentrations of progesterone and increases in estrogen and FSH. There is little doubt that progesterone is a potent inhibitor of ovulation during the luteal and gravid phases of the reproductive cycle. Exogenous administration of progesterone in high doses will inhibit ovulation in rats, guinea pigs, sheep, and cattle.

Though the androgen-LH relationship might be expected to yield a more clear-cut picture of negative feedback, such has not been the case. Androgens increase pituitary FSH in the castrate whereas pituitary LH falls.

The regulation of growth-hormone secretion or release has been the object of considerable investigation. Roth et al. (1963) and Glick et al. (1965) presented evidence that carbohydrate deficit acts as a potent stimulus for growth-hormone secretion. Using immunoassay, these investigators observed increased blood plasma HGH (human growth hormone) following hypoglycemia induced by insulin injection or by prolonged fasting. Increased HGH also occurred after the administration of 2-deoxy-D-glucose, an inhibitor of intracellular glucose utilization. The stimulation of HGH secretion following insulin injection or fasting could be inhibited by the prior infusion of glucose. Moderate exercise, however, stimulates HGH secretion despite hyperglycemia, and major abdominal or chest surgery is frequently followed by an elevation in plasma HGH even after glucose infusion (Glick et al. 1965). Several amino acids, particularly arginine, will also trigger HGH release, and hyperglycemia fails to affect the response (Rabinowitz et al. 1966). There is now convincing evidence that several adenohypophyseal hormones inhibit their own secretion. This "short loop" feedback has been demonstrated for LH, growth hormone, FSH, and prolactin (McCann et al. 1968). This type of regulation appears to be particularly important for prolactin (Meites and Clemens 1972). Adenohypophyseal short-loop feedback may operate directly or through the hypothalamic regulating hormones.

Neural pathways

Neural afferent stimuli that result in adenohypophyseal secretion operate through a short humoral component. Sensory impulses from the periphery terminate in the hypothalamus, activating neurosecretory axons in this area. These axons release humoral "regulating hormones" into the capillary loops of the median eminence.

The capillaries converge into the portal trunks of the neural stalk, travel to the adenohypophysis, and break up into venous sinusoids, where the regulating hormones stimulate adenohypophyseal hormone synthesis and release.

This unique and efficient system of neuroendocrine integration enables the organism to deliver an afferent humoral impulse selectively and in high concentration to the pituitary gland. Conformation of the importance of this pathway is provided by transplantation experiments. If the anterior pituitary gland is removed and transplanted under the kidney capsule, there is marked decline of adrenocortical, thyroid, and gonad function. Transplantation of the gland back into the sella turcica results, after a suitable period of time, in a return to normal function. The fact that adrenal and thyroid function does not decrease as markedly following transplant as it does after adrenalectomy or thyroidectomy is interpreted as evidence that the regulating hormones are effective but diluted. Until recently it was thought that the regulating hormones stimulated hormone release in every case but one; the fact that transplantation of the hypophysis resulted in increased prolactin release indicates that this particular factor was inhibited in the intact animal. It now appears that there are both stimulatory and inhibitory hypothalamic agents for growth hormone (the inhibitory factor is termed somatostatin) and for MSH. In birds, the control of prolactin release differs in that the hypothalamic factor is stimulatory rather than inhibitory.

The chemistry of the hypothalamic regulating hormones (sometimes called releasing or inhibiting factors) has been extensively studied, and most have been purified (Harris et al. 1966). Despite many efforts, investigators have been unable to find a distinct FSH-RH. LH-RH (alternately called LRF, LH-RH/FSH-RH, and GnRH) is a decapeptide with an amino acid formula of pGlu-His-Trp-Ser-Tyr-Gly-Leu-Arg-Pro-GlyNH_2. Injection of this polypeptide results in release of both LH and FSH, but the response slope of FSH is much flatter. Thyroid-regulating hormone (TRH or TRF) is a tripeptide with the sequence (pyro)Glu-His-Pro-amide. An interesting relationship between oxytocin and melanocyte releasing and inhibiting factors has been observed: Pro-Leu-GlyNH_2, the terminal tripeptide of oxytocin, has melanocyte inhibiting factor activity while the initial pentapeptide has melanocyte releasing activity.

Hypothalamic regulating hormones appear to be influenced by long-loop and short-loop feedback control by target gland and adenohypophyseal hormones and by other humoral agents as well as by neural inputs.

The exteroceptive stimuli acting upon the nervous system and producing tropic hormone secretion of the adenohypophysis are widely documented. Such afferent signals as intense light, sound, restraint, changes in activity, pain, and certain emotional disturbances cause an immediate increase in the output of ACTH. The increase in thyroid activity associated with exposure to cold and the decrease associated with high environmental temperatures are dependent upon the functional integrity of the hypothalamic-hypophyseal pathway. The seasonal sexual cycle in many mammals and birds, the occurrence of ovulation following copulation in the rabbit and cat, the suckling reflex, and the prevention of implantation by uterine denervation are also examples of neuroendocrine reflex arcs.

That there is some localization in the hypothalamic control of anterior pituitary secretion is indicated by experiments in which lesions have been placed in various hypothalamic areas, with resultant inhibition of individual target gland function.

PINEAL GLAND

While the existence of the pineal body (epiphysis cerebri) has been known since the second century A.D., its function has remained obscure. In the frog it appears to be a photoreceptor, and bovine pineal glands contain a factor that blanches pigment cells in tadpoles. This skin factor, melatonin (N-acetyl-5-methoxytryptamine), has been isolated and identified (Lerner et al. 1960); only the pineal gland possesses the enzyme (hydroxyindole-O-methyltransferase) necessary for melatonin synthesis (Wurtman and Axelrod 1965).

The delayed sexual development associated with pineal tumors in children (Kitay and Altschule 1954) led to the speculation that the pineal gland was inhibitory to the gonads. During the past few years, evidence that supports this concept has accumulated. The increased ovary weight and shortened estrous cycles that result when rats are exposed to continuous illumination can be duplicated by pinealectomy, while conversely, the injection of pineal extracts or melatonin results in decreased ovarian weight and lengthened cycles. Further, sectioning of the sympathetic nerves to the pineal counters the effect of constant lighting. On the basis of these findings and experiments in which the methoxylating enzyme content of the pineal was studied under different lighting schedules, Wurtman and Axelrod (1965) suggested that light impinging on the retinas causes a change in the sympathetic output of the anterior cervical ganglion, which results in decreased melatonin synthesis and release. These workers have also demonstrated a daily rhythmic activity in melatonin synthesis which is entirely dependent on environmental lighting.

THYROID GLAND

The thyroid gland is unique among endocrine glands in that its secretion, the thyroid hormone(s), includes in its structure a specific chemical element, iodine. Essentially, the function of the thyroid gland involves the concentration of iodide and the synthesis, storage, and secretion of the thyroid hormone. Quantitatively, the iodine accumulated by other tissues is of little significance compared with that which is trapped in the thyroid gland. Over 90 percent of administered iodine can be accounted for by thyroid uptake and urinary excretion.

Morphology

The thyroid gland is one of the first endocrine glands to appear in the developing individual. In the human, pig, and rabbit, the embryonic thyroid gland is functional at approximately midterm. In the chick, function begins on the seventh to ninth day of incubation. In most mammals, the thyroid lies just caudal to the larynx on the first or second tracheal ring and consists of two lateral lobes connected by a narrow isthmus. In birds, the thyroid consists of two lobes lying on either side of the trachea at the level of the clavicle.

Microscopically, the thyroid gland contains numerous closely packed small sacs filled with a clear, viscous fluid. The sacs or follicles are lined by simple epithelium that varies from low squamous in inactive glands to tall, columnar epithelium in more active thyroids. On fixation and staining with hematoxylin and eosin, the material within the follicle is seen as a noncellular, homogenous, acidophilic mass, sometimes vacuolated. Cytological features are sometimes used as criteria of the functional state of the gland. In active glands the colloid is nonuniform, may be somewhat basophilic, and usually contains numerous vacuoles; the height of the lining epithelium increases; and the number of secretory droplets in the follicular cells is increased. Electron microscopy has revealed numerous filamentous villi projecting from the follicular cells into the lumen. These microvilli afford a great increase in the inner surface area of the follicles.

Metabolism of iodine

Iodide trap

Iodine occurs throughout the animal body, but a very high percentage of the total amount is concentrated in the thyroid gland (Fig. 52.4) despite the fact that this gland constitutes only 0.2 percent of the body weight. Iodine is present in animal tissue in two forms—inorganic iodide and organically bound iodine. Iodide occurs in extremely low concentration, around 1–2 μg/100 ml of serum. The levels of organically bound iodine vary greatly and may reach 500 mg/100 g in the desiccated thyroid gland. Many forms of organic-bound thyroid iodine are found, including monoiodotyrosine, diiodotyrosine, triiodothyronine, and thyroxine (Fig. 52.5).

Iodide accumulation in the thyroid gland is expressed in terms of the thyroid uptake (the percentage of administered iodine accumulating within the gland) or by the T/S ratio, which is the ratio of concentration of iodide in the thyroid to that in the blood serum. The normal T/S ratio is about 25 and may increase to as much as 500 when the

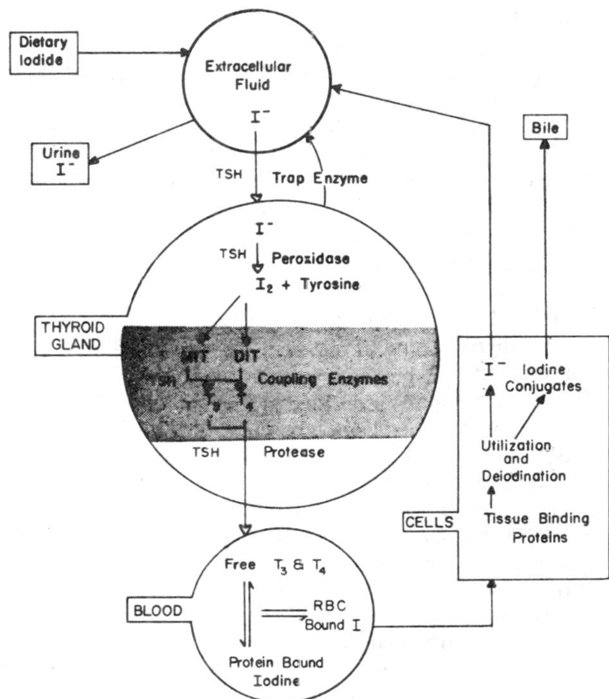

Figure 52.4. Major pathways of iodine metabolism (shaded area indicates thyroglobulin)

gland is being stimulated by TSH or decrease to 1 if thyroid inhibitors are administered. Certain chemical radicals, thiocyanate, perchlorate, or nitrate, selectively inhibit the operation of the thyroid iodide trap (see Fig. 52.4). Since this inhibition can be reversed by large doses of iodide, it is thought that these radicals compete with iodide for some component of the trapping mecha-

MONOIODOTYROSINE

DIIODOTYROSINE

3,5,3′ TRIIODOTHYRONINE

THYROXINE

Figure 52.5. Structural formulas of the iodinated amino acids in the thyroid gland

nism. Thyroid accumulation of iodine is measured by the administration of radioactive iodine and subsequent counting of radioactivity over the thyroid area. Results with this technique are somewhat variable and depend on the time that has elapsed since administration and the counting geometry; neither has been sufficiently standardized for domestic species. In addition, previous administration or ingestion of iodine-containing compounds greatly affects uptake. In humans, 15–45 percent of the administered dose is accumulated in 24 hours (Hamolsky et al. 1957), while in the dog, 10–40 percent is accumulated in 72 hours (Kaneko 1963).

Extrathyroidal iodide traps occur in mammals, but it is doubtful if these sites are able to carry on the synthesis of thyroid hormone beyond the stage of monoiodotyrosine.

Synthesis of thyroid hormones

After the iodide is trapped in the colloid of the thyroid gland, it is oxidized to iodine in a reaction that is probably mediated by a peroxidase enzyme. The amino acid tyrosine is then iodinated to form monoiodotyrosine (MIT) and diiodotyrosine (DIT). The coupling of the iodotyrosines to form iodothyronines has two possible routes—the combination of two DIT molecules to form thyroxine (T_4) or the combination of one DIT with one MIT to form triiodothyronine (T_3) (see Fig. 52.5). The likelihood that these reactions are enzymatically controlled is indicated by the fact that the cell-free supernatant fluid of centrifuged homogenized thyroid tissue is unable to promote protein iodination beyond the MIT stage; however, the enzymes involved have not been identified. The organic binding of iodine into compounds that have thyroid hormone activity is also inhibited by certain chemical agents described later. These iodinated amino acids that occur during synthesis of thyroid hormones are found in the colloidal protein thyroglobulin. Thyroglobulin is a glycoprotein with a molecular weight of about 680,000.

Release and transport of thyroid hormones

Two of the iodinated amino acids found in colloid thyroglobulin, T_3 and T_4, are secreted into the bloodstream. In contrast, the two iodotyrosines are deiodinated within the gland by an enzyme that has been termed deiodinase. This cycle, which can be regarded as intrathyroidal, reclaims the iodide from tyrosine for use in the manufacture of the more active iodinated thyronine compounds. Of the two iodinated thyronines, thyroxine is predominant in all animals; approximately one third of the total iodine in the thyroid is in the form of T_4, and usually less than 10 percent is in the form of T_3. If radioactive iodine is injected into an animal and a blood sample is assayed for iodine activity after a suitable period of time, this activity is found to reside for the most part in the blood proteins. If blood plasma is then subjected to electrophoresis, the radioactivity is found, in most species, to be carried principally by a serum globulin migrating in the α-region (TBG, or thyroid-binding globulin). In primates and horses, a small amount of activity is found related to a protein migrating with albumin (TBPA, thyroid-binding prealbumin), and in other mammals albumin itself is a thyroid hormone carrier. Collectively, the iodine that is bound to serum proteins is known as protein-bound iodine or PBI. Protein binding is not only vital for hormone transport, but has also been exploited as a means of assaying blood hormone concentration. Such an assay, known as a competitive protein binding assay (CPB), involves adding a minute quantity of radioactive hormone to a mixture of the binding protein and the sample (usually extracted or subjected to some separation process such as chromatography to remove competing substances), separating bound from free radioactivity, and counting either the bound or the free. If a considerable quantity of hormone is present in the sample, less radioactive hormone is found in the bound fraction, whereas if low concentrations are present, a higher percentage of added radioactive hormone is bound. Table 52.2 lists normal values of total thyroxine in the serum of various domestic animals determined by this procedure. T_4 has 3–4 times more affinity for the binding proteins than T_3, whereas T_3 in free form is considerably more active as a thyroid hormone. This fact has led to the hypothesis that T_4 is a type of prohormone, a buffered source of T_3, or a specialized transport form of hormone, while T_3 is the actual metabolically active agent. Both T_4 and T_3 are also bound to erythrocytes.

Table 52.2. Total serum thyroxine values

Animal	n	T_4(μg/100ml±SD)	Source
Dog	29	1.10±0.59	Kelley et al. 1974b
Horse	9	1.47±0.21	Kelley et al. 1974a
Cat	40	0.95±0.5	Ling et al. 1974.
Cattle	6	4.10±0.7	Sutherland and Irvine 1973
Sheep	12	3.70±0.6	Sutherland and Irvine 1973
Goat	4	5.25±2.08	Kallfelz and Erali 1973
Pig	6	3.50±0.5	Sutherland and Irvine 1973

Distribution and fate of thyroid hormones

Thyroxine and triiodothyronine have been detected in almost every tissue of the body. Because of its large size, skeletal muscle represents the major extrathyroidal and extravascular store of body thyroxine and triiodothyronine. Little is known concerning the transfer of thyroid hormones from the blood into the extracellular space except that the rate of distribution of thyroxine is a function of the free hormone concentration and the total number of binding sites in the extracellular fluid. Tata et al. (1962) demonstrated thyroxine binding by a soluble cellular protein (C-TBP) and by liver and muscle mitochondria, microsomes, and submitochondrial particles. They reported that thyroxine and triiodothyronine were bound equally at these sites. It appears that the rate of transfer of the thyroid hormone from the blood into the cell depends to a great extent upon the relation between protein-binding sites in the blood and those in the soluble cytoplasm and particulate fractions of the cytoplasm.

Intracellular metabolic conversions of T_3 and T_4 include the following: (1) deiodination, (2) deamination, alone or in conjunction with oxidation or decarboxylation, and (3) glucuronide or sulfate conjugation. Not all of these transformations occur in all tissues; for example, skeletal muscle can only deiodinate thyroid hormones, whereas all of the conversions mentioned can take place in the liver. Glucuronide and sulfate conjugation of thyroid hormones is regarded as a detoxifying mechanism and occurs primarily in the liver. These esters are excreted principally in the bile. The subsequent intestinal degradation of the glucuronide and sulfate esters and the reabsorption of inorganic iodine into the bloodstream is termed the *enterohepatic cycle*. The propionic acid, pyruvic acid, and acetic acid derivatives of T_4 that result from deamination aroused considerable interest when it was reported that these analogs were more active than thyroxine and did not have the latent period typical of the natural hormone. Further investigations indicate that these relatively high potencies of the deaminated derivatives are probably due primarily to better absorption. Many workers feel that the same situation exists with respect to the computed higher potency of T_3 as compared to T_4, and have suggested that the difference lies more in the faster onset of action than in the total activity. The most important metabolic pathway for the thyroid hormones is deiodination. This conversion appears to be related to the action of the hormone.

Effects of thyroid hormones

Thyroid hormones influence practically every organ in the body. The effects of these hormones can be roughly divided into two sections: morphological and functional.

Morphological changes

One of the most striking effects of thyroid hormones is their effect on metamorphosis in amphibian larvae. If thyroxine is administered to tadpoles, they will become miniature frogs, whereas thyroidectomy will produce giant tadpoles. While thyroid-induced metamorphosis is restricted to amphibians, thyroid hormones will cause maturational changes in other vertebrates. In young birds and mammals, removal of the thyroid gland is followed by a slowing or stoppage of growth, and the administration of thyroxine counteracts this effect. If growth hormone is given to thyroidectomized animals, there is an increased growth rate, largely through the stimulation of the epiphyseal cartilages, but little differentiation occurs. If, however, thyroxine is given to an animal deprived of its pituitary at a young age, there will be rapid differentiation and ossification of the epiphyses with no appreciable effect on length. Though the effects of thyroid hormone are primarily on differentiation, it should be pointed out again that the maximum growth rate of hypophysectomized animals is obtained by the injection of both growth hormone and thyroxine rather than of growth hormone alone. The growth and eruption of the teeth are also under thyroid control as are the horns of sheep and the antlers of deer. Hypothyroidism severely retards the eruption of permanent teeth.

Thyroidectomy will usually inhibit the molting of feathers, whereas thyroxine injection favors it. It appears as if, insofar as this function is concerned, the thyroid operates in conjunction with the sex steroids. The regeneration of feathers after the molt is again stimulated by thyroxine in synergism with the steroid hormones. It is possible that the two hormones act in sequence, so that one causes the feather germ cell to be receptive to the action of the other ("permissive action"). Another example of cooperation between sex steroids and the thyroid is seen in the thyroidectomized rooster, in which there are regressive changes in the comb that cannot be repaired by the administration of testosterone. In mammals, both skin and hair are affected by thyroid changes. Thyroidectomized cattle and sheep have thinner hair and the individual hairs are coarse and brittle. In humans, and sometimes in dogs, the subcutaneous edema of mucopolysaccharide-rich material is responsible for the name myxedema which is given to the hypothyroid condition. Myxedema and alopecia have also been observed in calves and pigs born to iodine-deficient mothers. It appears that the normal development of the wool-producing follicles of sheep requires thyroxine in excess of that needed for growth; thus a thyroid deficiency in the growing lamb may severely impair the quality of the adult fleece.

The relationship between the thyroid and the gonads in both male and female is of particular interest. Reproductive failure is often a major sign of deficiency, and the birth of excessive numbers of weak or dead young has been noted in goitrous areas (iodine-deficient soils) for many years. Abortion, stillbirth, and the live birth of weak young are the major results of hypothyroidism. Less severe deficiencies will result in delayed puberty, irregular estrus, anestrus, and reduced fertility in the female. In the male, thyroidectomy results in decreased testicular growth, impaired spermatogenesis, and lowered libido. In rams, a seasonal reduction in semen quality has been associated with hypothyroidism. The accessory reproductive gland that appears to be most sensitive to the effect of the thyroid hormone is the mammary gland. Thyroxine is a powerful galactopoietic agent, and the use of thyromimetic agents as a means of increasing milk production has aroused interest. For example, artificially iodinated casein (0.5 percent crystalline thyroxine) has been fed to dairy cattle at a rate of 1–1.5 g per 45 kg of body weight daily, resulting in an increase in milk production of 10–30 percent. However, addition of these thyroactive substances must be accompanied by an increase of approximately 20 percent in the daily energy intake. Despite this additional intake, body weight decreases have been noted when thyroprotein was fed. Thomas and Moore (1953) presented evidence that control cows fed at 125 percent TDN (total digestible nutrients) achieved lactation levels as high as those given thyroprotein. A disadvantage of feeding thyroprotein in an effort to increase milk production is the increased susceptibility of these animals to high environmental temperatures; instances of severe heat exhaustion have been reported in such situations.

The nervous system is also morphologically affected by a severe alteration in thyroid function. Thyroidectomy in immature rats results in a reduction in the number of axons in the cerebral cortex, reduced myelin deposition, and decreased brain weight.

Functional effects

The best-known function of thyroid hormones in the mammal is their ability to increase the rate of oxygen consumption. This and the increased thyroid activity following low environmental temperature support the hypothesis that the thyroid hormones are involved in thermoregulation by increasing internal heat production. Tissues removed from hypothyroid individuals have low oxygen consumption, while those from a hyperthyroid animal are high in this respect. This calorigenic effect of the thyroid hormones has been classically regarded as the primary action of the hormone and attempts have been made to interpret other changes on this basis. There is considerable evidence that conflicts with this hypothesis, however: (1) there is a considerable latent period between the injection of thyroxine and changes in the metabolic rate; (2) the calorigenic effect is not noted if thyroxine is added to tissues in vitro; (3) certain tissues (e.g. brain, testes, and retina) do not exhibit decreased or increased metabolism when obtained from animals with altered thyroid function; (4) surgical or pharmacological blockade of the adrenergic nerves prevents the calorigenic effect resulting from the injection of thyroxine into dogs. Brewster et al. (1956) suggested that permissive amounts of epinephrine are necessary if thyroid hormones are to exert their action upon metabolism.

Nervous function at all levels is influenced by the thyroid. Injection of thyroxine causes increased spontaneous electrical activity in the brain, a decreased threshold of sensitivity to a variety of stimuli, decreased reflex time, and increased neuromuscular irritability. Hypothyroidism and hyperthyroidism are both characterized by disturbances in muscle tissue. In hyperthyroidism, there is a negative nitrogen balance and creatinuria, which suggest a rapid metabolism of muscle protein and an impairment of creatinine production from creatine. The evident muscular weakness of hyperthyroidism is a combination of circulatory failure, decreased creatine in the muscle, and decreased neuromuscular control. It is important to realize that the "energy" of the hyperthyroid animal is apparent rather than real, and that these animals require twice the usual amount of oxygen and nutrients to accomplish a given quantity of muscular work. Muscular hypotonus is characteristic of low thyroid activity.

There is a very important interrelationship between thyroxine and the pressor amines, epinephrine and norepinephrine. Thyrotoxic rats can only tolerate 3 percent of the normal dose of epinephrine. This is partially explained by the fact that thyroxine appears to inhibit the degradation of epinephrine and norepinephrine by blocking monoamine oxidase. Cardiovascular physiology is highly influenced by the thyroid hormones, and the effects are almost entirely attributable to the previously mentioned muscular, neural, and pressor amine changes. The initial calorigenic effect following exposure to cold temperature may not be a direct thyroid effect but rather the result of thyroxine potentiation of norepinephrine.

Metabolic effects

Thyroxine enhances the cellular absorption and peripheral utilization of glucose and leads to increased glycogenolysis. While an oral glucose tolerance test shows a high and prolonged curve in hyperthyroidism, the intravenous tolerance curve is usually normal. This suggests, and other direct experiments have confirmed, that the thyroid hormones increase the absorption of glucose from the intestine.

One of the major metabolic results of thyroid deficiency is a marked increase in the serum cholesterol level. This finding is often used by clinicians as a "suggestive" indicator for hypothyroidism. However, cholesterol synthesis is markedly increased in thyroxine excess and reduced in thyroxine deficiency. These contradictory observations have been attributed to decreased biliary excretion of cholesterol in hypothyroid individuals, causing increased blood cholesterol despite reduced synthesis.

It has been assumed that thyroid deficiency is a major factor in obesity, particularly in humans; however, it has been observed that the total fat content of the body is eventually decreased in individuals with a marked thyroid deficiency, and there is little evidence to support the concept of hypothyroid obesity. The relationship of the thyroid to fat deposition has been of great interest to livestock producers in their search for a means of improving meat quality and increasing efficiency of weight gain.

Feeding trials following partial thyroidectomy or the administration of thyroid inhibitors have not resulted in sufficient improvement to justify these practices in livestock production.

In the myxedematous hypothyroid individual, the administration of thyroxine results in increased protein synthesis and marked diuresis, which apparently results from the mobilization of the extracellular myxedema fluid. In normal animals, the administration of thyroxine in high doses for a sustained period will accelerate protein catabolism and result in a negative nitrogen balance accompanied by diuresis. Since this diuresis is accompanied by increased urinary potassium, it is probably secondary to the protein catabolism.

Mechanism of action

The most accessible and studied indicator of thyroid function is the effect of thyroid hormones on tissue oxygen consumption. Studies in this area have led to the popular belief that the thyroid hormones exert their effect by uncoupling oxidation and phosphorylation. The mechanism of this uncoupling effect is not known, but the swelling of the mitochondria after the addition of thyroxine has suggested that this hormone alters the internal spatial relationship of the mitochondria and impedes phosphorylation. However, the uncoupling effect can be produced only by very high concentrations of thyroid hormones in vitro (10^{-5} M) or after the administration of toxic doses to the animal (1–2 percent thyroid powder in the diet); no uncoupling, loss of respiratory control, or mitochondrial swelling can be produced when hypermetabolism is induced with small amounts of hormone.

Tata (1974) has presented evidence suggesting that the calorigenic action of thyroid hormones is secondary to a general stimulation of cytoplasmic protein synthesis. Small amounts of thyroid hormones fail to stimulate increased calorigenesis when the protein synthesis of the cells is inhibited. In addition, the increased capacity for protein synthesis and the increased metabolic rate following thyroid hormone administration are preceded by an enhanced turnover of nuclear RNA and a rise in the DNA-dependent RNA polymerase activity. Thyroid hormones stimulate protein synthesis in cytoplasmic ribosomes or mitochondria; this is accompanied by the appearance of new ribosomes and additional microsomal RNA. After a lag period, there is increased synthesis of urea cycle enzymes and mitochondrial respiratory enzymes. Tata (1974) summarized thyroid hormone action as a preferential synthesis of proteins involved in adaptation with minimal effect on uninvolved proteins.

Antithyroid compounds

Enlargement of the thyroid, or goiter, can be associated with either hyper- or hypothyroidism (Fig. 52.6). Though the greatest single cause of goiter in man

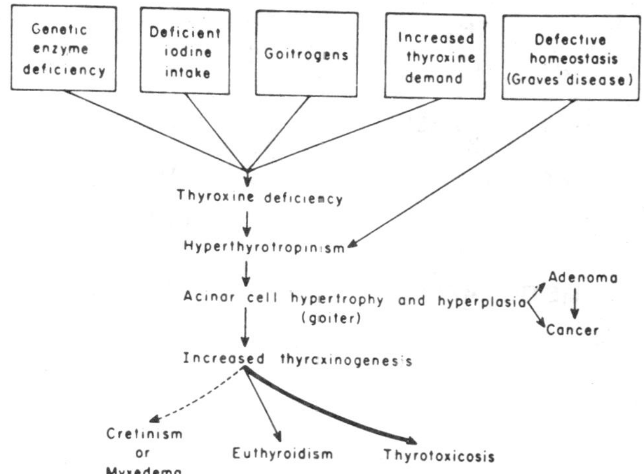

Figure 52.6. Mechanism of goitrogenesis. (From R.H. Williams and J.L. Bakke, in Williams, ed., *Textbook of Endocrinology*, 3d ed., Saunders, Philadelphia, 1962.)

and farm animals is a simple dietary iodine deficiency, certain foodstuffs contain substances that inhibit thyroid activity. Goitrogenic activity was first observed following the feeding of cabbage; subsequently other vegetables, including virtually all the cruciferous plants, soybeans, lentils, linseed, peas, and peanuts, have been incriminated. Extensive studies, particularly in New Zealand, have resulted in the isolation of a potent goitrogenic compound, goitrin (Fig. 52.7), which is probably responsible for most of the thyroid activity of the Brassica family of plants (rutabaga, rapeseed, black and white mustard seed). However, the goitrogenicity of many plants, including the Brassica family, is partially due to the presence of other goitrogens such as thiocyanate. In some parts of the world, notably Australia and Finland, plant goitrogens are of considerable importance in animal goiter, and, because of their secretion into the milk, are also of interest in respect to the human goiter that is endemic to these areas. Certainly the ingestion of goitrogenic plant material increases the iodine requirement.

Since thiocyanate and other chemical radicals interfere with the trapping of iodine (see Fig. 52.4) by the thyroid gland, the goitrogenicity of these radicals can be overcome by feeding excess iodide. It is more difficult to overcome the effect of goitrin and related compounds, however, since they interfere with the organic binding of iodine but not with the iodine trap. An important outcome of studies of antithyroid activity in plants has been the development of a series of potent antithyroid drugs with therapeutic value in the treatment of hyperthyroidism. The compounds exerting the most potent antithyroid activity are the thiocarbamides (see Fig. 52.7). The thiourea and thiouracil compounds all inhibit either the conversion of iodide to iodine or the organic binding

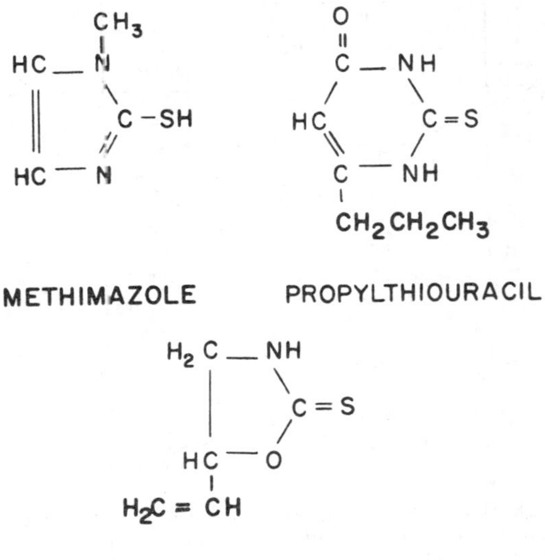

METHIMAZOLE

PROPYLTHIOURACIL

GOITRIN

Figure 52.7. Chemical structure of two commonly used antithyroid agents (methimazole and propylthiouracil) and that of the most important natural goitrogen (goitrin)

of molecular iodine with tyrosine, and perhaps the conversion of T_4 to T_3. Other antithyroid drugs include the sulfonamides, *p*-aminosalicylic acid, amphenone, phenylbutazone, and chlorpromazine.

An interesting antithyroid activity is shown by iodide itself. The administration of iodide or free iodine (Lugol's solution) to hyperthyroid individuals results in a decrease in thyroid activity, as evidenced by a decrease in basal metabolic rate, reduced blood thyroxine, and remission of clinical signs. This treatment is only effective for a few weeks, and iodide will not depress thyroid activity in euthyroid individuals. The specific iodide sensitivity of the hyperthyroid patient has possibilities as a diagnostic aid (Feinberg et al. 1959, Thorpe 1953).

HORMONES ASSOCIATED WITH CALCIUM AND SKELETAL HOMEOSTASIS

Although calcium is usually associated with the skeleton, the calcium ion concentration in the blood and extracellular fluid is important in many critical body activities. The maintenance of a constant calcium environment in these fluids and the regulation of dynamic bone remodeling is the responsibility of three hormones: parathormone from the parathyroid gland, calcitonin from the thyroid, and 1,25-dihydroxycholecalciferol, a derivative of vitamin D.

PARATHYROID GLAND

The parathyroid glands were first adequately described in 1880 by Sandstrom, and in 1891 Gley proved that a complete thyroidectomy was not fatal if the parathyroids were left intact. In 1909 MacCallum and Voegtlin related the parathyroid to calcium metabolism by alleviating the symptoms of this operation with the administration of calcium salts.

Morphology

In mammals (man, horse, carnivore), parathyroid glands consist of one or two pairs of beanlike organs located at or within the thyroid gland. In ruminants and pigs, the external parathyroid glands lie cranial to the thyroid near the carotid bifurcation; ruminant internal parathyroids are usually found imbedded in the thyroid gland, while pigs have no internal parathyroids. In birds, there are either two or four parathyroids located posterior to the thyroid on either side of the trachea. Parathyroid glands are lighter in color than the surrounding thyroid tissue and can also be distinguished by their definite tissue capsule.

Microscopically, the epithelial cells of the parathyroid have been divided into various types. In general, however, there are two cell types in most species (e.g. cow, horse, dog, cat, human, monkey)—chief cells and oxyphil cells. Other types are thought to represent differing degrees of secretory activity; for example, the "water-clear cell," a commonly described cell type, is now believed to be a variant of the chief cell. Although it is generally thought that the chief cells represent the source of parathormone secretion, the evidence is not conclusive.

Chemistry of parathyroid hormone

Parathormone (PTH), in common with other polypeptide hormones, is initially synthesized within the parathyroid cells as a larger molecule termed proparathormone (100–105 amino acids) (Kemper et al. 1972). The biologically active circulating molecule includes 84 amino acids with an alanine amino terminal and a glutamine carboxy end.

Regulation of parathyroid secretion

The parathyroid glands, together with the pancreatic islets, exemplify direct humoral control of endocrine activity by a specific blood constituent. Low-calcium diets lead to hypertrophy and hyperplasia of the parathyroid glands, and perfusion of the parathyroids with calcium-free blood results in the appearance of parathormone in the glandular effluent.

Effect of parathormone on bone

The work of Barnicot (1948) and Gaillard (1959) leaves no doubt that parathormone acts directly upon bone. If a fragment of bone is placed immediately adjacent to a parathyroid gland, after several weeks the part of the bone next to the graft dissolves, and the part away from the gland proliferates. Tissues other than parathyroid do not produce this effect. If an animal is injected with radioactive calcium during a rapid growth period and immediately thereafter is given an injection of parathormone, there is little influx of radioactivity into the circulation. On the other hand, if the parathormone injection is delayed until the radioactive calcium is stabilized in old bone, considerable radioactivity is released into the blood in the form of ^{45}Ca. This experiment clearly indicates that parathormone is able to mobilize calcium from bone. The increase in mucopolysaccharides in the blood following parathormone treatment suggests that parathormone affects the ground substance of bone as well as the mineral components. This would help explain the observation that parathormone acts on old bone. In vitro histological changes that occur in bone grown in tissue culture next to parathyroid tissue include (1) the disappearance of typical osteoblasts, (2) the formation of multinuclear osteoclasts, (3) the dissolution of bone matrix, and (4) proliferation of connective tissue on the side of the bone graft opposite the parathyroid tissue. These changes are very similar to those observed in vivo in osteitis fibrosa cystica, which may result from a functional parathyroid adenoma. Rasmussen and Bordier (1974) divided the action of parathormone on bone into two stages: (1) osteocytic osteolysis, occurring within the Haversian system and concerned primarily with mineral homeostasis; calcium released by this process travels via the bone minicirculation to the endosteal surface, where, together with parathormone, it stimulates (2) osteoclastic osteolysis. This is the stage that accomplishes bone remodeling, and thus it is primary to skeletal homeostasis. Parathormone will stimulate the conversion of osteoprogenitor cells to osteoclasts only in the presence of high calcium concentration. There is ample evidence that PTH also acts as a first messenger to activate adenyl cyclase and stimulate the production of cAMP. This second messenger affects the cell membrane and the mitochondrial membrane, particularly the latter, to increase cytosolic calcium.

Effect of parathormone on the kidney

The injection of parathormone results in increased phosphate excretion, which may reach levels as much as 20 times the normal rate. Since ionic calcium and phosphate in the blood and extracellular fluid behave in a reciprocal manner ($Ca \times PO_4 =$ a constant), an increased diuresis of phosphate lowers the serum phosphate and an increased serum calcium level results. This was the basis of the "renal phosphate theory" of parathyroid function. Parathyroid-induced renal phosphate diuresis was long thought to be inhibitory; that is, parathormone was thought to inhibit the absorption of phosphate in the renal tubules. However, evidence that the kidney is capable of secreting phosphate has cast some doubt on this premise.

In addition to its effect on phosphate, PTH enhances the renal retention of calcium. A further renal effect of PTH is its ability to stimulate renal hydroxylation of 25-(OH)-cholecalciferol.

Other effects

If parathormone is injected into a parathyroidectomized rat and an intestinal loop is isolated, an increased transport of calcium from the loop can be demonstrated. Decreased calcium absorption has also been observed from Thiry-Vella fistulas constructed in parathyroidectomized dogs. Absorption could be returned to normal by the injection of parathyroid extract. A further parathyroid effect is illustrated by the decreasing calcium concentration in the milk of lactating rats injected with parathormone.

Marked excess or deficiency of parathyroid hormone

In the dog, complete extirpation of the parathyroid glands is followed within 24 hours by severe neuromuscular dysfunction that eventually terminates in death. There are increased involuntary muscle spasms and periodic contractions of large groups of muscles, constituting what is known as *parathyroid tetany*. That these signs result from lowered ionic calcium in the extracellular fluid is clear since (1) administration of calcium will bring neuromuscular function back to normal, (2) hypocalcemia of any cause leads to similar signs, and (3) alkalosis will lead to neuromuscular disturbances due to decreased calcium ionization. In general, carnivorous animals are more severely affected by parathyroidectomy than herbivorous animals. It is possible that herbivorous animals possess accessory parathyroid tissue that is difficult to locate and remove surgically. Hypocalcemia in cows is well documented, but attempts to relate these syndromes (milk fever, grass tetany) to decreased parathyroid activity have been unsuccessful.

Primary hyperparathyroidism usually results from a functional adenoma. This condition is relatively rare in humans, but the increased use of appropriate chemical tests and a better understanding of the clinical signs of the condition have led to an increase in its diagnosis. Hyperparathyroidism is characterized by an elevated serum calcium level and decreased serum phosphate concentration. Severe forms of the disease involve bone changes and/or kidney calculi. A more common hyperparathyroidism occurs secondary to kidney damage. Certain renal diseases often result in calcium diuresis or phosphate retention, either of which lowers the serum calcium level. The resultant activation of the parathyroid gland, if continued for a long time, leads to skeletal demineralization. In dogs, this condition has been called rubber-jaw syndrome.

CALCITONIN

In parathyroidectomized dogs, plasma calcium levels are very slow in returning to normal after the injection of calcium or EDTA; in the former case, the inhibition of parathormone could not account for the slow response. These observations led Copp et al. (1962) to postulate a hypocalcemic factor, calcitonin, secreted in response to hypercalcemia. Subsequently, Foster et al. (1964) confirmed this factor and demonstrated its origin in the thyroid gland. The source of thyrocalcitonin, as it is now commonly termed, is the parafollicular cells found immediately outside the cells bordering the thyroid follicles. These cells represent ultimobranchial tissue that, in mammals, is incorporated within the thyroid gland. In the chicken, in which the thyroid and ultimobranchial glands are separate, no calcitonin can be extracted from the thyroid, whereas the ultimobranchial tissue contains 100 times the hormone content of a similar weight of porcine thyroid (Copp et al. 1967). Thus it appears that both hormones involved in calcium regulation arise from tissue of similar embryological origin. Structural analysis (Potts et al. 1968) of porcine calcitonin has shown that it is a simple polypeptide containing 32 amino acids with 2 half-cystine residues. Apparently a dual feedback system controls calcium homeostasis with continuous secretion of both calcitonin and parathormone. Hypercalcemia causes elaboration of calcitonin and inhibition of parathormone secretion, while hypocalcemia induces opposite effects.

Several studies indicate that calcitonin opposes parathormone in that it inhibits bone resorption (Aurbach et al. 1969). For example, when calcitonin was given to rats injected with radioactive calcium, there was a sharp interruption in the rate of fall in specific activity of calcium in the blood plasma. This would suggest decreased resorption rather than increased bone mineral accretion, which would have been reflected by an increased rate of disappearance of calcium from plasma. The major effect of calcitonin is exerted on bone; however, it appears that this hormone also inhibits the conversion of 25-hydroxycholecalciferol to 1,25-dihydroxycholecalciferol in the kidney (Fig. 52.8). The effects of calcitonin are much more apparent in young animals than in older ones; there is some doubt as to its physiological role in the adult.

1,25-DIHYDROXYCHOLECALCIFEROL

Within the last decade the hydroxylation of vitamin D or cholecalciferol to 25-hydroxycholecalciferol in the liver, and subsequently a second hydroxylation to 1,25-dihydroxycholecalciferol [1,25-$(OH)_2D_3$] in the kidney, have established this compound as an important regulator of bone and mineral homeostasis (De Luca 1971a). This hormone stimulates increased body calcium by enhancing intestinal calcium absorption (through an increase in calcium-binding protein as well as calcium

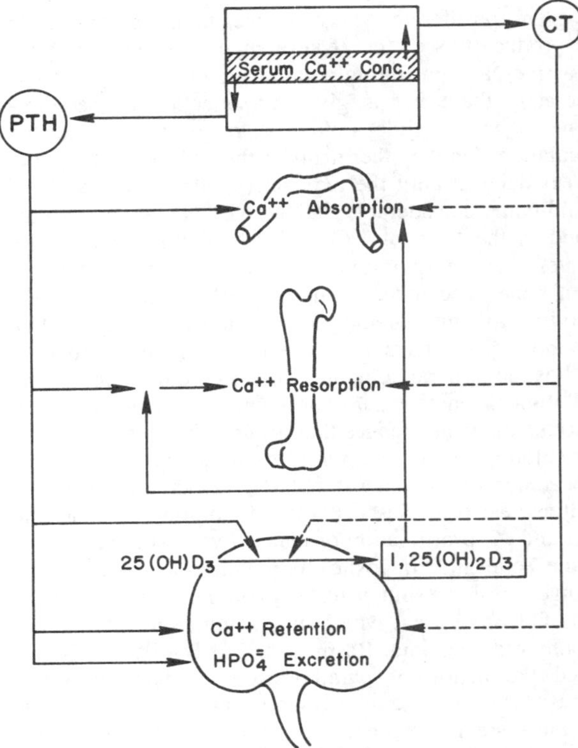

Figure 52.8. Parathormone, calcitonin, and 1,25-dihydroxycholecalciferol and calcium homeostasis. PTH, parathormone; CT, calcitonin; 1,25$(OH)_2D_3$, dihydroxycholecalciferol. Solid line indicates stimulation; broken line shows inhibition.

transport) and kidney calcium retention; aids in bone formation by enhancing maturation of bone matrix; and interacts with PTH in that 1,25-$(OH)_2D_3$ is necessary for full PTH activity (Norman and Henry 1974, Rasmussen and Bordier 1974).

ENDOCRINE SECRETIONS OF THE PANCREAS

In 1788 Cawley associated diabetes with the pancreas, and in 1869 Langerhans described islets of tissue within the pancreas. In 1921 Banting and Best discovered insulin. Since that time, the physiological importance of the internal secretions of the pancreas in regard to protein, fat, and carbohydrate metabolism has received a large amount of attention. It is now agreed that the two hormones of the pancreas, insulin and glucagon, are secreted into the blood stream from the islets of Langerhans.

The hypoglycemic activity of plasma is not a direct reflection of the insulin concentration. The presence of counterinsulin substances as well as material with insulinlike action (i.e. somatomedin) confuses the situation. Counterinsulin material includes hormones such as STH, cortisol, epinephrine, and glucagon; insulin antagonists (synalbumin, β_1-lipoprotein in the rat, α_2-β-globulin in man); and in individuals previously treated with insulin, antibodies to this hormone. The insulinlike material found in blood plasma resembles the actual hormone to a great degree but is not inhibited by insulin antibodies when the fat-pad assay is used.

Morphology

The pancreas is a V-shaped organ lying along the duodenum and is composed primarily of pancreatic acini which secrete the pancreatic enzymes important in digestion. These enzymes constitute the exocrine section and are liberated through the pancreatic duct system into the duodenum. Scattered throughout the pancreas are small (0.3 mm in diameter in humans) islets of cells that are structurally quite different from those in the acini. Islet tissue is arranged as branching irregular cords of cells among a rich capillary plexus. Two types of cells are recognized: the insulin-producing β-cells, which contain alcohol-soluble granules, and the glucagon-producing α-cells, which contain alcohol-insoluble granules. The α-cells are usually somewhat larger. In mammals the majority of the cells are β, while in birds and reptiles the α-cells predominate. Glands in which the β-cells have been destroyed either by sustained hyperglycemia or by the injection of alloxan contain no extractable insulin. Chemical agents such as cobaltous chloride have been discovered which selectively destroy the α-cells; treatment with such agents results in reduced glucagon content. Additional evidence that α-cells produce glucagon is provided by the higher glucagon content of those parts of the canine pancreas that contain greater numbers of α-cells.

Chemistry of insulin and glucagon

The determination of the exact structure of insulin by Sanger and his colleagues in 1955 (Sanger 1959) stands as a landmark not only in pancreatic and endocrine research but also in protein biochemistry. The chemical structure of ox insulin is given in Figure 52.9. The elementary insulin molecule contains one of each of two amino acid chain units and has a molecular weight of about 6000. The two chains are joined to each other by disulfide bridges, and a disulfide ring occurs in the A chain. There are differences in chemical structure between the insulins prepared from the glands of different species. Insulins from ox, sheep, horse, pig, dog, and whale differ only in positions 8, 9, and 10 of the A chain. In human insulin the terminal alanine in the B chain is replaced by threonine, and in rabbit insulin the amino acid in this position is serine. Insulin from one species is antigenic when injected into another, and some human diabetic patients become unresponsive to cattle or sheep insulin. These structural differences should be kept in mind when interpreting experiments on the functional activity of insulin, particularly since rat heart, liver, and diaphragm preparations are often used for in vitro investigations of bovine insulin activity. Rat insulin differs from ox insulin at four points in the A chain and two or three points in the B chain (two different insulin molecules have been isolated from the rat). Guinea pig insulin, which differs from bovine insulin in 18 of the 51 amino acid residues, is only one fourth as potent when assayed in the mouse (Smith 1966). The initial synthesis of insulin within the β-cell is a single-chain polypeptide that in the bovine is larger than insulin by 30 amino acids. The additional amino acid chain (C chain), which connects the A and B chains and is thought to ensure proper disulfide linkage, is normally removed within the gland before insulin secretion. But proinsulin, as the precursor molecule is termed, may escape into the circulation and be a source of error in immunological assays.

Glucagon has been isolated from swine and cattle pancreas. The two products appear to be similar but their identity has not been completely proven. Bromer et al. (1957) have determined the amino acid sequence and find glucagon to be a small polypeptide with 29 amino acids and a molecular weight of about 3500. In contrast to insulin, glucagon contains no disulfide bridges and consists of a single chain.

Function of insulin

In mammals, complete insulin deprivation results in diverse effects involving the entire metabolism of the organism, including that of fat, protein, carbohydrate, electrolytes, and water. The depancreatized dog exhibits glycosuria, and the blood sugar concentration is elevated to 300–500 mg/100 ml (normal is 80–120 mg/100 ml). Other important signs are polyphagia, polydipsia, polyuria, ketonemia, and hypercholesterolemia. A severe negative nitrogen balance occurs and the animal rapidly becomes emaciated. The dog becomes dehydrated and

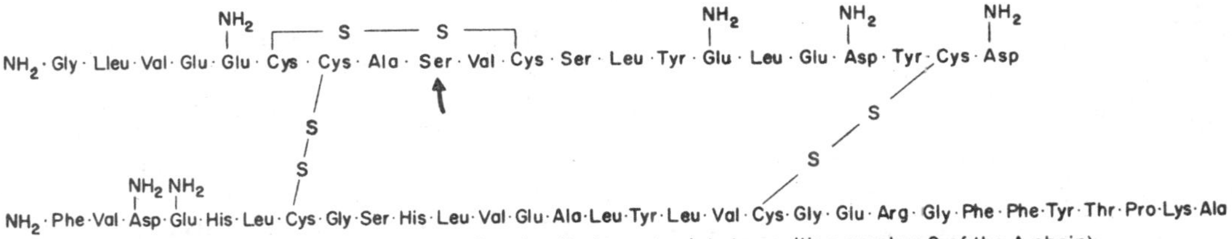

NH_2 · Gly · Lleu · Val · Glu · Glu(NH_2) · Cys · Cys · Ala · Ser · Val · Cys · Ser · Leu · Tyr · Glu(NH_2) · Leu · Glu · Asp(NH_2) · Tyr · Cys · Asp(NH_2)

S — S (A6–A11); S — S (A7–B7); S — S (A20–B19)

NH_2 · Phe · Val · Asp(NH_2) · Glu(NH_2) · His · Leu · Cys · Gly · Ser · His · Leu · Val · Glu · Ala · Leu · Tyr · Leu · Val · Cys · Gly · Glu · Arg · Gly · Phe · Phe · Tyr · Thr · Pro · Lys · Ala

Figure 52.9. Amino acid sequence of ox insulin (arrow points to position number 9 of the A chain).

comatose, and dies within a few days. In many omnivorous and herbivorous animals pancreatectomy, or the injection of alloxan, induces a relatively mild condition that is easily controlled by small doses of insulin. Although pancreatectomy induces hyperglycemia and glycosuria in carnivorous birds, in many herbivorous bird species, particularly the duck, this operation is followed by hypoglycemia. The difference has been attributed to the predominance of α-cells in the pancreas of the duck. These metabolic interrelations are summarized in Figure 52.10.

There is considerable variation in the response of different tissues to insulin. Brain, kidney, intestines, and erythrocytes show little response to insulin in comparison with muscle, adipose tissue, and leucocytes. The viewpoint that insulin acts only indirectly on liver tissue has resulted from in vitro experiments in which the period of observation was probably too short. If isolated perfused liver is observed over a sufficiently long time, effects similar to those that have been reported for muscle will be noted. Since insulin and glucagon are secreted into the hepatic portal veins, it would appear that the liver is the most important target organ for these secretions.

Effect of insulin deficiency

In insulin deficiency the ability of the peripheral tissues to utilize glucose either for oxidation or, in the case of the liver and muscle, for the synthesis of glycogen is greatly impaired. This leads to hyperglycemia from increased glycogenolysis and increased gluconeogenesis, and as a result sugar is excreted in the urine. Since the loss of glucose through the urine necessarily involves the concomitant loss of water and electrolytes, polyuria, dehydration, and hemoconcentration result. The marked dehydration, hemoconcentration, and reduced circulating blood volume result in shock, and eventually anuria ensues due to a marked decrease in kidney blood flow.

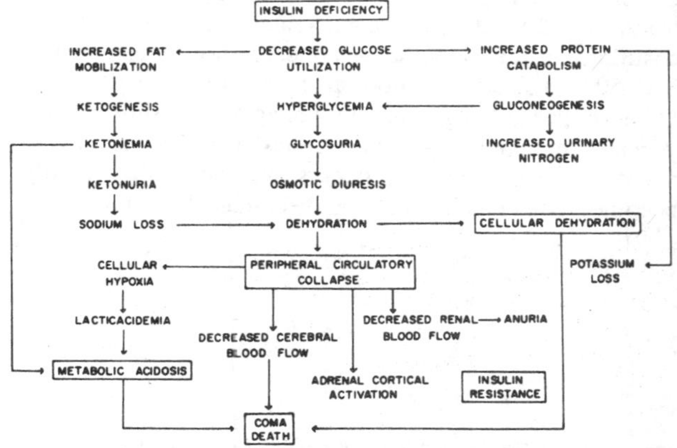

Figure 52.10. Metabolic and physiological sequellae to pancreatectomy

The importance of glucose in the intermediary metabolism of the animal body lies not only in its use as a source of energy but also in the fact that the metabolism of glucose furnishes the cell with many chemical compounds important to various vital reactions. For example, in fat tissue, glucose metabolism provides acetyl CoA and glycerophosphate, which act as substrates for the synthesis of triglycerides as well as NADH and NADPH, which are necessary for fatty acid synthesis (see Chapters 27, 28).

Insulin deficiency affects fat metabolism in two ways. Fat is utilized by the normal animal as a means of storing food energy; the liver and adipose tissue convert carbohydrate into fat for storage. In the insulin-deprived animal, glucose utilization is depressed and the organism is forced to mobilize fat from the storage depots to provide energy for cellular function. There is increased fat in the bloodstream in the form of free fatty acids and triglycerides. These fatty acids are oxidized, primarily in the liver, to the two-carbon acetyl-CoA stage, at which point, if sufficient oxalacetate is available, oxidation is completed through the tricarboxylic acid cycle. However, in the insulin-deficient animal, the lack of glucose utilization results in an inadequate supply of oxalacetate and a diminished ability to oxidize acetyl CoA. Since the synthesis of fatty acids from acetyl CoA is also linked to the metabolism of carbohydrate, this pathway is closed and the accumulating acetyl CoA is converted to acetoacetic or β-hydroxybutyric acid. These compounds together with acetone constitute the ketone bodies. The resultant ketonemia and ketonuria deplete the body of fixed base, causing acidosis, and contribute to urinary sodium loss which enhances dehydration.

Decreased glucose utilization resulting from insulin deficiency leads to a marked increase in gluconeogenesis, which must in turn involve an increase in protein catabolism. The increase in protein catabolism is further increased by intracellular dehydration and is accompanied by a serious potassium diuresis. In addition, insulin deprivation results in enzyme defects, e.g. liver glucokinase, pyruvate dehydrogenase, and acetyl CoA carboxylase. Further, insulin appears to depress the formation of enzymes necessary for gluconeogenesis, so that deficiency of this hormone contributes to increased gluconeogenesis.

Mechanism of action of insulin

The utilization of glucose by the cell involves the diffusion of glucose from the capillary onto the cell surface, the transport of glucose through the cell membrane, and the intracellular phosphorylation of glucose. Though extracellular glucose concentrations are high in comparison to the concentration within the cell, the membrane transport system appears to be distinct from simple diffusion and probably involves a membrane carrier system.

It is now generally agreed that it is this membrane transport system that is influenced by insulin. Since this view was first advocated by Levine and Goldstein (1955), the acceleration of monosaccharide transport by insulin has been demonstrated in many species and in various isolated muscle preparations. This phenomenon is not specific for glucose, and in fact much of the support for this hypothesis has been derived from experiments with nonmetabolized analogues of glucose. Though the mechanism by which insulin facilitates the entry of glucose into the cell is still unknown, Randle and Smith (1958) suggested a glucose barrier in muscle cells which is maintained by the constant application of energy; insulin is thought to interfere with this barrier. This hypothesis is supported by the fact that anoxia and various metabolic poisons enhance the entry of glucose from the extracellular fluid into the cell. The action of insulin in removing the barrier to glucose entry may be related to its inhibitory action on adenyl cyclase. There is some indication that magnesium may act as an intracellular "second messenger" in the action of insulin.

An earlier theory of the mechanism of action of insulin implicated the enzyme hexokinase, which catalyzes the conversion of glucose to glucose-6-PO_4. There is a marked depression of phosphorylation in muscle from alloxan-diabetic animals, and this depression can be reversed by the administration of insulin to the animal before it is sacrificed. Since the inhibition of phosphorylation in the diabetic can be prevented by hypophysectomy and then regained by treatment with either growth hormone or hydrocortisone, the effect of insulin is presumed to be due to the removal of an inhibition imposed by one or both of these hormones.

The enzymes involved in the various metabolic reactions of glucose occur in the cell in sufficiently great amounts to handle large quantities of glucose. It is probable that the membrane transport system is rate-limiting and that the action of insulin on this site is of more importance than any effect it may have on phosphorylation. A nonglucose-linked effect of insulin has been observed in experiments in which the injection of insulin has resulted in a lower blood amino acid concentration and the appearance of injected radioactive amino acids into tissue protein. The effects of insulin in promoting synthesis can be obtained in the absence of growth hormone but are optimal when the tissue is under the influence of both hormones.

Function of glucagon

Glucagon is much more effective if injected into a hepatic portal vessel than into a systemic vessel, and in the latter instance this hormone is completely ineffective if the hepatic portal vessels are blocked. The isolated perfused liver is extremely susceptible to the glycogenolytic action of glucagon and the addition of glucagon to the perfusing fluid results in enhancement of protein catabolism, which can be neutralized by insulin. With respect to metabolism, proof has been offered that chronic treatment with glucagon will prevent fat storage. The predominance of glucagon in the pancreas in some species of birds suggests that this hormone may be physiologically more important in this vertebrate class than in the mammal; however, these animals are not nearly as dependent on glucagon as most mammals are on insulin.

Control of insulin and glucagon

In view of the many and diverse pathways of glucose utilization, and the number of hormone agents that influence glucose metabolism, the variation in systemic blood glucose concentration is remarkably small. Among the endocrine organs that influence glucose concentration, the internal secretions of the pancreas are of primary importance since their secretion is directly controlled by the blood glucose level. Cross-circulation experiments have been used to demonstrate this control. If pancreatic venous blood from an insulin-injected animal is cross-circulated into a second, untreated animal, the blood sugar of the recipient will increase. Conversely, if the donor has been previously given glucose rather than insulin, the blood sugar of the recipient will be reduced. These observations are attributed to increased secretion of glucagon or insulin by the donor in response to altered blood glucose concentration.

Although the blood glucose concentration has generally been considered the control for insulin secretion, other means of increasing the secretion of this hormone have been observed (Frohman 1969). Protein ingestion or the intravenous injection of amino acids will stimulate insulin secretion that is not inhibited by agents (epinephrine, benzothiadiazine) that inhibit glucose-stimulated secretion. In the sheep, a species in which short-chain fatty acids are important as an energy source, butyrate and propionate cause release of insulin. Octanoate administration will result in insulin release from rat pancreas in vitro and after duodenal installation in man. Long-chain fatty acids stimulate insulin release in the dog. Further, experiments with inhibitors such as 2-deoxyglucose and glucosamine, as well as studies with human patients suffering from a deficiency of glucose-6-phosphatase, suggest that some intermediate in the glycolytic cycle is responsible for insulin secretion rather than the glucose molecule itself. Renewed interest has been directed toward a possible CNS control of insulin secretion; CNS stimulation of insulin secretion, via the vagus nerve, has been demonstrated, and cholinergic nerve fibers have been observed surrounding the islet cells. Finally, intestinal hormones, principally gastrin, stimulate the release of insulin.

In common with some other secretory processes of the body, the secretion of insulin is dependent on the presence of sufficient extracellular calcium. Littledike et al. (1968) observed a diabetic glucose tolerance curve and depressed circulating immunoreactive insulin in hypocalcemic cows; normal lactating cows had 78.9 ± 7.2 $\mu U/ml$, while cows with mild hypocalcemic paresis had a mean value of 47.8 ± 9.6 $\mu U/ml$. Depressed insulin secretion following hypocalcemia has also been reported in pigs (Witzel and Littledike 1973).

ADRENAL GLAND

With the possible exception of pituitary secretions, the secretions of the adrenal glands are the most diverse in their effects. In mammals the adrenal glands are embryologically, morphologically, and functionally separable into two distinct organs: the adrenal cortex and the adrenal medulla. Cortical hormones are steroids and exert their primary activity on carbohydrate and electrolyte metabolism, while those secreted from the medulla are amines with effects similar to those of postganglionic sympathetic neurons (see Chapter 48). Both parts of the gland appear to be important in the adaptation of the animal to adverse environmental influences.

Morphology

In birds and mammals, the adrenal glands are small ellipsoid organs found bilaterally at the anterior poles of the kidneys. The distance from the kidney and proximity to the posterior vena cava vary from species to species and from right to left gland. On cross section the mammalian adrenal is seen to be separated into an external cortex surrounding internal medullary tissue. In birds, the medullary tissue is scattered throughout the cortical tissue.

In 1865, Henle observed that a brownish coloration resulted when adrenal medullary tissue was subjected to potassium bichromate. This reaction led to the name "chromaffin cells" for cells containing catecholamines (adrenal medulla and peripheral sympathetic ganglia). Critical review of this and similar reactions (green color with ferric chloride, blue color with ferric ferricyanide, blackening with osmium tetroxide) has not confirmed the early confidence in the specificity of these methods for the pressoramines. Adrenal medullary tissue is relatively homogeneous, contains secretory granules, and is often arranged in lobules. This part of the adrenal gland arises from the neural crest, and the chromaffin cells differentiate from neuroblasts. For this reason, and because the nerve supply to the medulla consists of preganglionic sympathetic neurons, the cells of the adrenal medulla are regarded as modified postganglionic sympathetic neurons.

The adrenal cortex is derived from the mesodermal coelomic epithelium. Thus this part of the gland is embryologically associated with the other important steroidogenic endocrine glands, the gonads. The mammalian adrenal cortex is typically divided into three zones: zona reticularis, zona fasciculata, and zona glomerulosa. The inner zona reticularis lies adjacent to the medulla and consists of randomly arranged cells with densely staining cytoplasm and a high percentage of pycnotic nuclei. In the zona fasciculata, cells are arranged in columns, while in the outermost portion of the cortex, the zona glomerulosa, there is a looped or whorled arrangement resulting in an acinar appearance. The zonation of the mammalian adrenal cortex varies somewhat among species. For example, in the cow and sheep the zona fasciculata is divided into an inner and outer portion, and an intermediate zone can be distinguished between the zona fasciculata and the zona glomerulosa. In the juvenile mouse and rabbit there is an inner cortical zone where the zona reticularis is usually found, consisting of healthy cells with large vesicular nuclei. This is called the x-zone and is replaced by the zona reticularis at puberty in the male mouse and during the first pregnancy in the female.

The histological appearance of adrenocortical cells varies considerably with the stage of activity of the gland because of the depletion of certain substances upon stimulation. The cells of the inactive gland are vacuolated and have a spongy appearance due to the presence of large amounts of lipid. Increased secretory activity results in the depletion of lipid, cholesterol, and ascorbic acid and results in a more compact cell. Following hypophysectomy, the zona fasciculata undergoes degeneration, whereas the zona glomerulosa remains virtually unchanged. In addition, there is considerable evidence that the injection of ACTH results in a more marked lipid depletion of the zona fasciculata. Baniukiewicz et al. (1967) confirmed that zona glomerulosa cells produced aldosterone; its immediate precursor, 18-hydroxycorticosterone; and a small amount of corticosterone. Decapsulated adrenals (zona fasciculata and reticularis) produce 18-OH-deoxycorticosterone and corticosterone in the rat, and cortisol and corticosterone in higher vertebrates.

Chemistry and metabolism of the adrenal medullary hormones

The hormones of the adrenal medulla consist of two amines derived from tyrosine which differ only in the presence or absence of a terminal methyl group (Fig. 52.11). The amino acid tyrosine is converted to dihydroxyphenylalanine (DOPA), which is converted to dopamine by a decarboxylase. β-hydroxylation of dopamine results in norepinephrine, and the terminal methylation of this substance forms epinephrine. The secretion of epinephrine appears to be virtually limited to the adrenal medulla, whereas norepinephrine is secreted both by this organ and by the postganglionic sympathetic neurons. The ratio of epinephrine to norepinephrine secreted by the adrenal medulla varies considerably among species (Table 52.3) and with age. Epinephrine usually

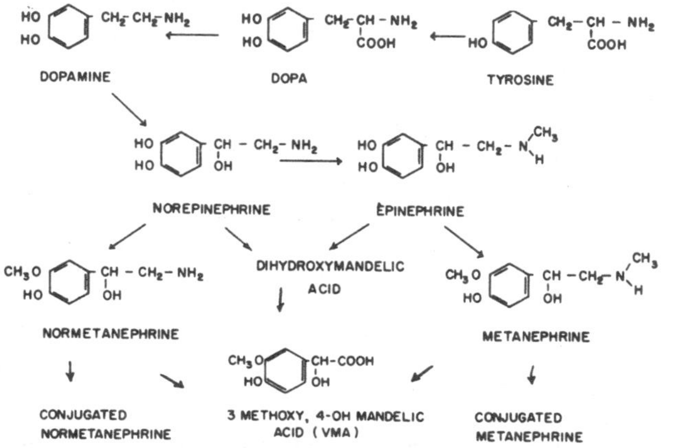

Figure 52.11. Biosynthesis and metabolism of the catecholamines

predominates over norepinephrine in the secretion from the adult mammalian gland, and in some mammals (rabbits and guinea pigs) norepinephrine is a very minor constituent. In contrast, the adrenal medullary output of the whale and of chickens is about 80 percent norepinephrine. Fetal adrenal tissue appears to contain predominantly norepinephrine in all species. At birth the rabbit adrenal medulla contains approximately 70 percent norepinephrine, compared with a 2 percent concentration in adult tissue. There is considerable speculation and no real agreement as to the differential release of the two amines in response to varying physiological demand. Malmejac (1964) was not able to vary the ratio of epinephrine to norepinephrine in the secretion from the canine medulla by any of various stimuli. On the other hand, histochemical studies have revealed the presence of norepinephrine-containing and epinephrine-containing cells, and differential release has been observed in the human, cat, rabbit, and rat. There is some evidence that the steroids of the adrenal cortex affect the conversion of norepinephrine to epinephrine in the adrenal medulla.

Inactivation of the hormones from the adrenal medulla occurs through three pathways: (1) physical diffusion away from the receptor site, (2) enzymatic degradation, (3) reentry into the neuron. Reentry into the neuron is probably the major route of initial inactivation. Enzymatic degradation occurs through O-methylation brought about by the enzyme catechol-O-methyltransferase, and also by oxidative deamination through monoamine oxidase (see Fig. 52.11). Following the administration of labeled epinephrine, 45 percent of the radioactivity appearing in the urine was found to be 3-methoxy, 4-hydroxymandelic acid, while 34.3 percent was found in free or conjugated metanephrine (Axelrod 1959). Metanephrine and normetanephrine appear in the urine either as free compounds or conjugated with sulfuric or glucuronic acid. Inactivation of the catecholamines is rapid, as evidenced by the half-life of epinephrine, which has been estimated at 20–40 seconds.

Table 52.3. Catecholamines in adrenal glands from various adult mammalian species

Species	Norepinephrine (%)	Total catecholamines (mg/g whole gland)
Pig	49	2.2
Cat	41	1
Sheep	33	0.75
Cow	29	1.8
Dog	27	1.5
Horse	20	0.84
Man	17	0.6
Rabbit	2	0.48

Modified from West 1955, *Q. Rev. Biol.* 30:116–37

Function and control of the adrenal medulla

The chromaffin cell hormones do not appear to be essential for life, as removal of the adrenal medulla does not result in marked physiological change. This is at least partially due to the fact that the sympathetic nervous system remains intact following this operation, and the function of the adrenal medulla appears to be largely reinforcement of this system. Historically there have been two contrasting theories regarding the general function of adrenal medullary secretion. The first of these, the *emergency theory,* was articulated by Cannon (1932) and is commonly referred to as the fight-or-flight hypothesis. Advocates of the opposing theory held that the nerve endings were maintained in a continual state of responsiveness by epinephrine and/or norepinephrine. This theory became known as the *tonus theory*. As is often the case in such controversies, there is increasing realization that both points of view may be correct. There is convincing evidence that adrenal medullary secretion is a continuous process that may increase to a striking degree during an emergency.

The diverse and similar effects of epinephrine and norepinephrine are in large part explained by the hypothesis of two adrenergic receptors. α-receptors are stimulatory, with the exception of those in the intestinal smooth muscle, while β-receptors are inhibitory, with the exception of those in cardiac muscle. Epinephrine and norepinephrine stimulate both receptors, but the α-effect of norepinephrine is more potent than that of epinephrine, while epinephrine may have a more potent β-action.

Moderate to small doses of epinephrine decrease total peripheral resistance due to stimulation of the β-inhibitory receptors (dilatation) in the skeletal muscle; epinephrine, on the other hand, constricts cutaneous vessels and those of the hepatic mesenteric and uterine vasculature. Norepinephrine increases peripheral resistance and is a generalized vasoconstrictor with the possible exception of the coronary vessels. The catecholamines accelerate the rate of depolarization and enhance transmission in the cardiac muscle and cardiac transmission fibers, increasing the speed and force of contraction and hastening relaxation in cardiac muscle; thus heart rate increases (chronotropic effect) and the force of contraction is enhanced (inotropic effect). A combination of the cardiac and peripheral vasculature effects results in a difference in their action on blood pressure; epinephrine causes increased systolic blood pressure and decreased diastolic pressure, with little effect on mean blood pressure, while norepinephrine increases systolic, diastolic, and mean pressures. Both amines produce bronchiolar dilatation and an increased rate and depth of respiration. Adequate tissue oxygen supply is further guaranteed by the epinephrine-induced contraction of the spleen, increasing the peripheral concentration of erythrocytes. The ciliary muscle of the eye, bronchial musculature, esophageal muscle, stomach wall muscle, and bladder detrusor muscle are relaxed by the catecholamines through the β-receptors, while the smooth muscles of the radial iris muscle in the eye, the pylorus of the stomach, the intestinal sphincters, and the trigone and sphincter muscles of the bladder are constricted through an α-effect. The smooth muscle of the intestine is also inhibited but apparently contains both α- and β-receptors. There is some species variation in the bladder response. Species variation as well as reproductive state is apparent in the effects of the catecholamines on the reproductive organs. In the nonpregnant cat, epinephrine generally inhibits uterine motility, but in the pregnant cat its injection is followed by contraction. In the rabbit, epinephrine causes contraction, while in the dog the uterus first contracts and then relaxes.

Catecholamines have pronounced metabolic effects: hyperglycemia, increased calorigenesis, lipolysis, elevated blood lactate, and increased serum potassium. Hyperglycemia results from enhanced liver glycogenolysis and inhibition of insulin release, while increased blood lactate ensues from stimulation of muscle glycogenolysis. The latter may be responsible for the increased metabolic rate together with the interaction of thyroid hormones and catecholamines. Increased activity of the sympathetic nervous system and the adrenal medulla may be the most important physiological stimulus for the mobilization of adipose tissue and the subsequent release of free fatty acids into the bloodstream. Interestingly norepinephrine is relatively ineffective as a hyperglycemic agent in fasted rats, whereas both amines act in the fed rat.

In experiments in which the reaction time to a stimulus is measured, the transmission of information in and out of the CNS appears to be facilitated by the catecholamines. The question of the importance of adrenergic pathways in the CNS has aroused intense interest, particularly since such pathways appear to be important to the secretion of hypothalamic regulating hormones.

A feedback mechanism appears to operate through hypertension and its effect on the carotid sinus and vasomotor center to limit the maximum secretion rate of these hormones. In the cat, a maximum secretion rate of 10 μg/min has been observed; this corresponds to a dose of 0.02 ml of a 1:1000 solution of epinephrine.

The mechanism of action of epinephrine has been studied most using hepatic glycogenolysis. Epinephrine stimulates or activates adenyl cyclase, resulting in increased intracellular cAMP. In the presence of ATP, cyclic AMP activates the enzyme phosphorylase kinase, which converts inactive phosphorylase to active phosphorylase, which catalyzes the breakdown of glycogen. Glucagon is thought to act in the same manner.

Other pressor substances

An increasing number of substances that have an effect on smooth muscle are being isolated from animal tissues. These include the kinins (bradykinin, angiotensin, substance P), various physiologically active lipid anions, histamine, and 5-hydroxytryptamine (5-HT). The latter substance, which is also known as serotonin, is found in certain special silver-staining cells that are particularly common in the mucosa of the gastrointestinal tract and in association with the bile ducts. These cells represent the enterochromaffin tissue. Serotonin is also found in high concentration in certain parts of the CNS and in the blood platelets. The latter represent a storage or transport site and can accumulate large quantities of this substance. Serotonin exerts interesting and diverse effects, including contraction of intestinal smooth muscle, dilatation of the coronary vascular bed, constriction of the afferent glomerular arterioles, and depression of activity in the CNS. Serotonin has a complicated effect on blood pressure; depending upon the dose and the species, its effects may be either hypertensive or hypotensive.

Histamine, serotonin, substance P, and γ-aminobutyric acid have all been suggested as neurotransmitters in addition to the well-known transmitters, acetylcholine and norepinephrine. Certain vertebrate nerve endings appear to release histamine, and the so-called adrenergic fibers of some invertebrates release serotonin. According to one hypothesis (Brodie and Shore 1957), serotonin is a chemical transmitter in the parasympathetic nervous system, while Marazzi (1957) regards it as an adrenergic cerebral neurohumor. Evidence has been presented that γ-aminobutyric acid is a likely candidate for the long-sought synaptic inhibitor substance.

Chemistry of the adrenocortical hormones

A large number of biologically active and inactive steroids have been isolated from mammalian adrenocortical tissue. However, most of these represent intermediates or metabolites rather than true adrenocortical hormones. The adrenocortical hormones are derivatives of the 21 carbon pregnane nuclei, and the true secretions

Table 52.4. Naturally occurring adrenal cortical steroids *

Chemical name	Common names
4-pregnene-11β,21-diol-3,20-dione-18-al	Aldosterone, electrocortin
4-pregnene-21-ol-3,20-dione	Deoxycorticosterone
4-pregnene-17α,21-diol-3,20-dione	Compound S, 11-deoxycortisol
4-pregnene-11β,21-diol-3,20-dione	Corticosterone, compound B
4-pregnene-11β,17α,21-triol-3,20-dione	Cortisol, hydrocortisone, compound F, 17-hydroxycorticosterone
4-pregnene-17α,21-diol-3,11,20-trione	Cortisone, compound E 17-hydroxy-11-dehydrocorticosterone
4-pregnene-21-ol-3,11,20-trione	Compound A, 11-dehydrocorticosterone

* For details see Dorfman and Ungar 1953, Klyne 1957

have a double bond between C-4 and C-5. There are seven generally recognized adrenocortical hormones (corticosteroids) (Table 52.4), differing in structure in only three positions, C-11, C-13, and C-17. Six of these hormones can be considered as and are sometimes designated as modifications of one of their number, with the common name corticosterone (4-pregnene-11β,21-diol-3,20-dione). The seventh hormone, aldosterone, is unique in that the angular methyl group on C-13 is replaced by an aldehyde; this aldehyde group is in equilibrium with a hemiacetal ring structure between C-11 and C-13. Figure 52.12 gives the structural formulas for cortisol and the two forms of aldosterone.

Soon after the chemical structure of the corticosteroids was established, it was noted that corticoids with a hydroxyl or ketone group on C-11 had greater physiological activity in respect to carbohydrate metabolism than corticoids with no substituents at this position; such steroids, exemplified by corticosterone, cortisol, cortisone, and 11-dehydrocorticosterone, are termed *glucocorticoids*. Adrenocortical steroids with no substituents at C-11 have an enhanced effect on electrolyte metabolism and are termed *mineralocorticoids;* 11-deoxycorticosterone and 17-hydroxy-11-deoxycorticosterone are examples of this type. Aldosterone proved to be an exception to this system; in addition to its powerful effect on electrolyte metabolism, aldosterone has glucocorticoid activity. The glucocorticoid activity of 11-hydroxy and 11-carbonyl compounds is further enhanced by 17α-hydroxylation.

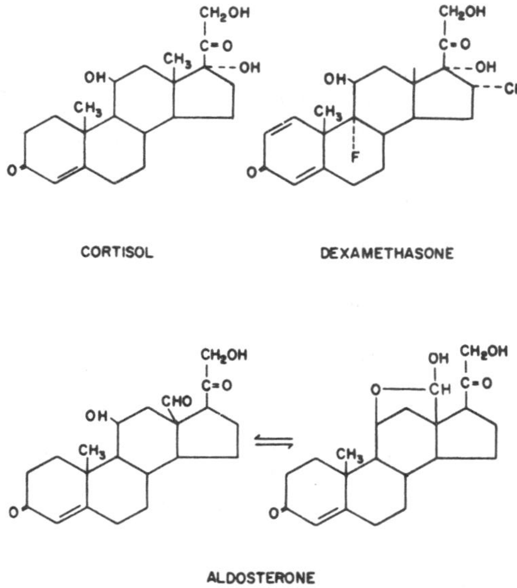

The biosynthesis of the adrenocortical steroids is a complex process involving many steps (see Fig. 53.5). Although cholesterol is probably the basic substrate for steroid synthesis within the adrenal gland, the synthesis of cholesterol from two-carbon acetyl fragments must be considered an important part of steroid synthesis. Upon stimulation of the adrenal cortex with ACTH, adrenocortical cholesterol and ascorbic acid are immediately depleted and the adrenal venous steroid concentration is increased. While the cholesterol depletion of the adrenal cortex has obvious purpose, the ascorbic acid depletion is less well understood. The exact effect of ACTH on the adrenal is not completely known, but it has been established that ACTH promotes adrenocortical glycogenolysis through the activation of phosphorylase and that ACTH is important in 17-hydroxylation.

Steroid hormones are catabolized and inactivated principally in the liver, the kidney, and the target organs themselves. The liver is most important in this regard because of its well-developed ability to form sulfates by esterification and glucuronides by conjugation; the fact that these compounds are inactive and water-soluble facilitates their elimination in the bile or urine. Many corticoid metabolites have been found in the urine; many of these are 17-ketosteroids. In the dog, the principal metabolites of cortisol are cortol, 3-epiallocortol, and cortolone, all of which have a trihydroxy side chain; the dihydroxy, 20-ketone compounds, tetrahydrocortisol, and tetrahydrocortisone are excreted in lesser quantities.

CORTISOL DEXAMETHASONE

ALDOSTERONE

Figure 52.12. Chemical structure of the most important mineralocorticoid (aldosterone), the most important glucocorticoid (cortisol), and a highly active anti-inflammatory synthetic steroid (dexamethasone)

Physiology of aldosterone

One of the most striking physiological changes observed following the removal of both adrenal glands in mammals and birds is marked sodium diuresis. Electrolyte changes in the blood after adrenalectomy include decreases in blood sodium, chloride, and bicarbonate and a rise in blood potassium. Continued sodium and fluid loss leads to dehydration, hypotension, reduced renal blood flow, and increased blood levels of nonprotein nitrogen and phosphate. In many species, death can be delayed or completely averted by a high dietary sodium intake.

In adrenal insufficiency mineralocorticoids are capable of reducing sodium diuresis, and aldosterone is the most effective (Table 52.5). Although the kidney appears to be the primary site of sodium retention following the release of aldosterone into the circulation, the same process is operative in sweat glands, salivary glands, and intestinal mucosa, and in sodium exchange between intra- and extracellular fluid. In the kidney, the effect of aldosterone appears to be on reabsorption of sodium from the hypotonic urine which enters the distal convoluted tubule. While aldosterone affects carbohydrate metabolism, its concentration in the blood (0.08 μg/100 ml whole blood in humans) indicates that this hormone is secreted in amounts too small to contribute to this aspect of adrenocortical function. However, the relatively large amounts of cortisol and/or corticosterone that are secreted into the bloodstream become a factor in sodium retention, although their sodium-retentive ability is small compared with that of aldosterone. Excess mineralocorticoid activity, whether from increased secretion of aldosterone or from excess corticoid therapy, gives rise to an increased serum sodium, a fall in serum potassium, hypochloremic alkalosis, and excess extracellular fluid volume. The opposite effect, sodium diuresis, and a subsequent decrease in blood pressure, may be mediated by prostaglandin.

At present the evidence seems to favor the concept that aldosterone secretion is controlled through two agents:

(1) In 1960 it was discovered that the kidney is the source of a potent aldosterone-stimulating factor and that removal of the kidneys in hypophysectomized dogs was followed by a 50 percent reduction in the rate of aldosterone secretion. In addition, acute hemorrhage, a potent stimulus for aldosterone production, did not augment the secretion of this hormone in dogs that were nephrectomized and hypophysectomized. Since then, fractionation studies with kidney extracts have indicated that the only fraction with aldosterone-stimulating activity was that containing renin. Further, intravenous infusions of renin or angiotensin II stimulate the secretion of aldosterone. The afferent stimulus for this "endocrine reflex" is probably a decrease in renal blood flow or renal arterial pressure which results in the release of renin from the juxtaglomerular apparatus. Renin acts upon a circulating blood globulin to form angiotensin I, which is further split by a circulating enzyme to angiotensin II.

(2) It has been known for some time that hypophysectomy decreases the rate of secretion of aldosterone and that ACTH can prevent the depressing effect of hypophysectomy on secondary hyperaldosteronism. On the other hand, maximal aldosterone secretion has been observed in dogs with low plasma levels of ACTH and a low output of glucocorticoids. From these findings, it appears that in some instances (i.e. laparotomy) ACTH initiates aldosterone secretion, while in other cases, such as acute hemorrhage, ACTH augments the secretion that has been initiated by angiotensin II.

A variety of stimuli cause increases in aldosterone secretion: laparotomy, hemorrhage, vena caval constriction, congestive heart failure, sodium depletion, and potassium excess. The effects of these stimuli, with the exception of the latter two, can be explained on the basis of decreased renal blood flow or increased ACTH output; the mechanism of increased aldosterone output following a decrease of blood sodium or an increase in blood potassium has not been determined, but angiotensin II has little effect on steroid synthesis in sodium-loaded animals (Davis et al. 1967). In addition, Ganong et al. (1967) noted increased renin levels during sodium depletion. Farrell (1959) suggested that aldosterone secretion is regulated by a hormone secreted from the pineal gland called adrenoglomerulotropin. However, experiments with decapitated and pinealectomized animals have failed to confirm this hypothesis.

Table 52.5. Relative potencies of selected natural and synthetic adrenal corticoids

	Sodium retention	Anti-inflammatory	Carbohydrate activity
Cortisol	slight	1	1
Cortisone	slight	0.8	0.8
Deoxycorticosterone	1	0*	minimal
Aldosterone	30	0.3	0.3
Prednisolone	minimal	4	3
Dexamethasone	0	25	minimal †
2-methyl, 9-fluorocortisol	100	10	10

* Usually classed as proinflammatory.
† Manufacturer indicates nitrogen loss at high dosage.
Data from P.Y. Forsham, in R.W. Williams, ed., *Textbook of Endocrinology,* Saunders, Philadelphia, 1962; F.T.G. Prunty, in H. Gardiner-Hill, ed., *Modern Trends in Endocrinology,* Hoeber, New York, 1958

Physiology of the glucocorticoids

The metabolic consequences of a complete loss of adrenocortical activity are far-reaching and include almost every organ, system, and tissue in the body. When deoxycorticosterone became available for experimental use, it was recognized that, while this hormone could reverse many of these changes, many metabolic defects continued to be seriously impaired. In all species in which a complete removal of the adrenal cortex has been effected (dog, human, rat, sheep, pig, cow, and horse), the results of this operation include weakness, easy fatigability, hypotension, marked intolerance to fasting, exaggerated response to insulin, and decreased ability to withstand stresses.

While it is difficult to distinguish between effects resulting from a deficiency in mineralocorticoids and those resulting from a deficiency from glucocorticoids, replacement therapy in adrenalectomized animals has clearly indicated that a deficiency in glucocorticoid function has serious and widespread results in general body metabolism. For example, the adrenalectomized animal shows a striking inability to excrete a large water load, and this defect is present even after the administration of deoxycorticosterone. Cortisol, on the other hand, will correct this deficiency in water metabolism and, if administered in large enough amounts, possesses sufficient salt-retentive activity to maintain life in adrenalectomized animals.

The primary effect of the glucocorticoids on carbohydrate metabolism is an enhancement of gluconeogenesis. The typical hypoglycemia and liver glycogen depletion that follow adrenalectomy are corrected by the administration of a potent glucocorticoid such as cortisol. Following this administration, the urinary nitrogen concentration is increased. It is probable that the noncarbohydrate source from which new glucose is synthesized is largely protein even though these hormones have a definite effect upon fat metabolism. Chronic administration of glucocorticoid hormones leads to hyperlipemia and hypercholesterolemia and, in the human, to an increase in the total amount of fat together with a centripetal redistribution of body fat. Though some of the hyperglycemic action of the glucocorticoids can be ascribed to peripheral insulin antagonism, radioactive labeling techniques have indicated that this is minor in comparison to the increase in gluconeogenesis. Cortisol exerts a permissive effect in that glucagon and epinephrine require it in order to release significant amounts of glucose from liver glycogen. Within the cell, cortisol induces enzymes involved in deamination and transamination.

Glucocorticoids cause lysis of lymphoid tissue, and thus lymphopenia and 17-hydroxylated glucocorticoids depress circulating eosinophils through destruction and sequestration in the lungs and spleen. Following the injection of either ACTH or cortisol, the decrease in peripheral blood lymphocytes and blood eosinophils may amount to as much as 45–50 percent for the former and up to 90 percent for the latter. In man, dog, horse, and pig, this decrease will reach a peak in about 4 hours; in the cow, however, the maximum decrease is seen between 8 and 10 hours. The physiological role of this process is not well understood but may be at least partly a mechanism for making available to the organism a quantity of protein that can be used immediately for gluconeogenesis.

As previously indicated, the glucocorticoid hormones enhance water diuresis; this may be explained by the observation that cortisol prevents the shift of water into the cell and thus maintains the extracellular fluid volume. Though cortisol and other glucocorticoids possess considerable sodium retentive activity, this diuretic effect may result in an actual loss of sodium from the body following the administration of one of these hormones.

Of all the diverse ways in which the glucocorticoids have been exploited in clinical practice, they have been used to the greatest extent for the inhibition of inflammation. When tissue is injured, the typical inflammatory response includes extravasation of fluid into the tissue spaces, leukocytic infiltration, hyperemia, and connective tissue synthesis. Following the administration of cortisol or another glucocorticoid, there is a decrease in hyperemia, diminished cellular response, a decrease in exudation, and an inhibition of fibroblast formation. In all phases of glucocorticoid activity, but most particularly with respect to the one just described, it is difficult to separate physiological effect of the agent from the response to the exogenous administration of large doses, which is more realistically referred to as a pharmacological effect. For example, the administration of reasonably normal doses of cortisol does not reduce the circulating antibody level, while large doses eventually reduce both antibody production and release. Early in cortisol therapy there may be an increase in circulating antibodies in the blood due to lysis of fixed plasma cells and lymphocytes. The anti-inflammatory action of glucocorticoids may also account for their ability to diminish an allergic response, as these hormones do not interfere with histamine formation or prevent the interaction of antigen and antibody. The clinical usefulness of certain glucocorticoid effects has led to the development of a large number of "pharmacological steroids." These compounds are steroids in which various alterations have been made in the molecule to enhance certain of the physiological actions while diminishing others. As an example, one of the more popular anti-inflammatory agents, dexamethasone (see Fig. 52.12), has 25 times the anti-inflammatory potency of cortisol and very little effect on sodium retention. Table 52.5 compares the potencies of several of the normal and synthetic steroids.

Many other body functions are affected by glucocorticoid depletion or excess. Chronic overdosage with cortisol leads to a decrease in muscle protein, edema, and fibrosis of muscle tissue, whereas adrenalectomized animals suffer from extreme muscle weakness that can be reversed only by the administration of a glucocorticoid. The protein-mobilizing or catabolic effect of cortisol is quite apparent in its effect on bone metabolism; there is decreased development of cartilage, interruption of growth, and an inhibition of the formation of new bone. Because of the insulin antagonism exhibited by cortisol and the hyperglycemia produced by large doses of this compound, chronic overdosage can lead to a metabolic syndrome known as steroid diabetes. Reid in Australia (1960) has suggested that pregnancy toxemia in sheep is a diabeticlike syndrome resulting from adrenocortical hyperfunction coupled with severe undernutrition. In this disease, the typical diabetic hyperglycemia is only potential, the ewe being hypoglycemic as a result of high fetal demand for glucose. In adrenal insufficiency, electroencephalography reveals a slowing of the electrical discharges of the CNS while cortisol injection lowers the brain threshold for electrical excitation. Some steroids given in large doses act as anesthetics.

One of the most important and little understood functions of cortisol has been described as a *permissive effect*. Many cells that are responsive to a variety of stimuli will respond to these stimuli only if they are exposed to a certain base-line concentration of adrenocortical steroids. This permissive action is demonstrated by the lack of response of the arterioles to the pressor effect of norepinephrine in adrenalectomized animals.

In adrenalectomized animals there is a diminished absorption of glucose and calcium from the gastrointestinal tract. Thus the oral glucose tolerance test can be easily misinterpreted in the adrenal-deficient animal. It is possible that adrenocorticoids are equally important in the transport of glucose across other membranes such as the placenta. This would explain the observation that the blood glucose concentration of adrenalectomized fasted pregnant ewes does not fall as rapidly as that of intact fasted pregnant controls (Dickson and Seekins 1963). The importance of the fetal hypothalamus and pituitary in initiating parturition has been suspected for many years (Kennedy et al. 1957, Binns et al. 1960). Liggins et al. (1973), on the basis of evidence from their studies and from other laboratories, have proposed a mechanism that implicates the fetal adrenal cortex. Cortisol in the fetal blood acts on the placenta to reduce progesterone and increase estrogen. Reduced progesterone and elevated estrogen concentrations promote the synthesis and release of prostaglandin-$F_2\alpha$, which sensitizes the uterus to oxytocin. Whether the fetal cortisol "surge" arises from hypothalamic, pituitary, or adrenal maturation or from fetal "stress" stimuli is not known. Elevated fetal cortisol has also been proposed as the stimulus for lung surfactant formation.

Control of glucocorticoid secretion

The secretion of the adrenal glucocorticoids from the zona fasciculata of the adrenal cortex is controlled by ACTH. In the absence of ACTH, the production of glucocorticoids falls to very low levels and the adrenal cortex undergoes atrophy. The fact that adrenal atrophy will also result from the continued exogenous administration of glucocorticoids indicates that ACTH and the adrenal glucocorticoids are reciprocally related in a negative feedback mechanism. Many stimuli, however, are capable of eliciting the release of ACTH from the anterior pituitary, even when the plasma corticoid levels are elevated. Included in this category are many types of noxious agents or stimuli that require an adaptation of the organism to meet a potential danger; in some species, epinephrine can elicit ACTH release. In animals not subjected to stress, there is a definite diurnal variation in ACTH release and blood corticoid concentration. This diurnal cycle is related to the activity pattern of the species; in the mouse, maximal corticoid secretion occurs during the night, when the animal is active; in species that are active in the daylight hours, the maximal corticoid secretion occurs during the day (Table 52.6).

Table 52.6. Peripheral plasma concentration of corticoids, progesterone, and estradiol

Species	Corticoids ng/ml	Progesterone ng/ml	Estradiol pg/ml
Canine	28, A.M.[1]	2.6, estrus[2] 20.3, diestrus	3–8, estrus[3]
Equine	26.7, A.M.[4] 5.5, P.M.	0.09, estrus[5] 5.49, diestrus	141, estrus[6] 20, diestrus
Porcine	24, A.M.[4] 6, P.M.	0.5, estrus[7] 27, diestrus	60–70, estrus[8] 10–20, diestrus
Bovine	7.6[9]	0.5, estrus[10] 6.6, diestrus	25, estrus[11] <7, diestrus
Ovine	14[12]	1.6, estrus[12] 5.4, diestrus	

1. Schechter et al. 1973
2. Christie et al. 1971
3. Jones et al. 1973
4. Bottoms et al. 1972
5. Plotka et al. 1972
6. Pattison et al. 1974
7. Stabenfeldt et al. 1969
8. Hendricks et al. 1972b
9. Miller and Alliston. 1974
10. Stabenfeldt et al. 1969b
11. Hendricks et al. 1972a
12. Dunn et al. 1972

Adrenal cortex and adaptation

One of the most striking results of adrenalectomy is the inability of the animal to resist adverse conditions that require the reintegration of the internal metabolism of the organism for defense against injury. In 1936 Selye published the first of a long series of observations on the stereotyped response of the organism to a variety of noxious stimuli.

Selye termed this response the "general adaptation syndrome" and divided it into three phases: the alarm reaction, the stage of resistance or adaptation, and the stage of exhaustion. According to his hypothesis, adverse stimuli or "stressors" have *nonspecific* as well as *specific* damaging effects on the organism, and the organism likewise responds in nonspecific as well as specific ways. Although the nervous system, the kidney, and many endocrine glands are involved in the various body responses termed nonspecific, the adrenal cortex is assigned the leading role in body adaptation. In a sense, the role of the adrenal cortex in adaptation represents an extension and reinforcement of what Cannon originally termed the fight-or-flight response of the adrenal medulla. For example, the organism's immediate need for glucose is satisfied through glycogenolysis resulting from the effect of epinephrine, while at the same time the glucocorticoids promote the formation of glucose from noncarbohydrate precursors. This hypothesis has stimulated a considerable amount of research, and it has been considerably modified since 1946, when Selye formulated it in detail. The permissive action of the corticoid hormones in adaptation has been demonstrated by Engel (1957), who observed the triphasic response in adrenalectomized rats provided with exogenous hormones. While there is substantial evidence of the importance of the adrenal cortex in the adaptation of the organism to adverse stimuli, adaptation is a complex process with many facets, and various response patterns result from different combinations of general reactions and specific responses. Figure 52.13 diagrams some of the reactions that occur in response to hypotension resulting from hemorrhage.

Many examples of animal adaptation involving adrenal participation have been described. Domestic chickens subjected to crowding exhibit adrenal hypertrophy, and the adrenal weights of wild mammals appear to be a reasonably accurate measure of the population density. It has been speculated that these overactive adrenals produce sufficient androgen to inhibit pituitary gonadotropin production with a subsequent reduction in reproductive potential. Hibernation and estivation have also been cited as possible instances of adrenocortical-mediated adaptation.

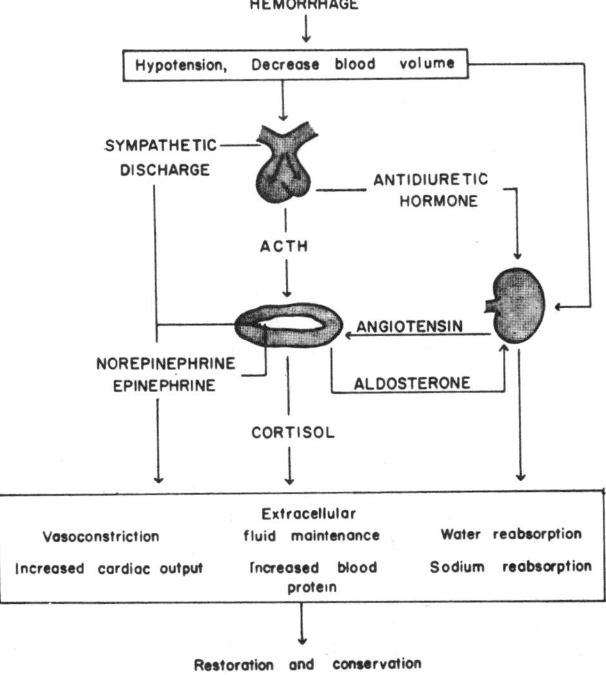

Figure 52.13. Endocrine responses to hemorrhage

Glucocorticoid concentration in peripheral blood

Since hormones function as regulators of adaptation to environmental or internal change and initiate physiological changes at appropriate times, their secretion and thus their peripheral circulating concentration vary widely. Consequently, it is difficult to list "normal" values. The values listed in Table 52.6 reflect reasonable concentrations for resting animals. In clinical evaluation, a generally more useful technique is a procedure known as a perturbation test, in which the physiological condition of the patient is manipulated to see if the hormone response is appropriate.

Detailed discussion of hormone assay is well beyond the scope of this chapter, but the physiological as well as methodological importance of protein binding deserves emphasis. As noted before, the transport of hormones in the blood to their sites of action is highly dependent on protein binding. In addition, hormone release at the target cell may depend on relative binding affinities, and there is good evidence that the intracellular mechanism of action is equally linked to a specific binding protein. With respect to hormone assay, the presence of specific binding proteins in the plasma (competitive protein binding assay, e.g. of thyroxine, corticoid, progesterone) and in the receptor site (radioreceptor assay, e.g. of estrogen, aldosterone) and the genesis of specific proteins (radioimmunoassay, e.g. of adenohypophyseal peptides, insulin, parathormone) have revolutionized experimental and clinical endocrinology. With respect to adrenal glucocorticoids, the plasma binding protein is a globulin referred to as transcortin or CBG. It should be noted that free, not protein-bound, cortisol is effective as a negative feedback to pituitary ACTH.

Physiology of the adrenal sex hormones

In human females, certain adrenal tumors give rise to a syndrome characterized by masculinization, including abnormal hair growth, atrophy of the mammary tissue, an enlarged clitoris, and atrophy of the accessory sex organs. In addition, it has been reported that the adrenal gland of castrated rodents can produce androgen in response to ACTH administration. These and other observations have led to the conclusion that the adrenal cortex is capable of producing weak androgenic steroids. In domestic animals, masculinizing adrenal hyperplasia has been reported in a female mink (Dickson and Kainer 1954), and Garm (1949) has suggested that anestrus in the cow may result from adrenal masculinization.

SEX HORMONES

The term *sex hormones,* as customarily used, includes those hormones that are primarily secreted by the ovary or testis. It is now recognized that these physiological compounds are also secreted from nongonadal sources and have effects that are not directly concerned with the reproductive process. With respect to their chemical structure and to some extent their physiological activity, these hormones are usually classified into four divisions: androgens, estrogens, progestins, and relaxin.

Chemical structure and metabolism

Three of the four sex hormone divisions are steroids and represent the three major modifications of the basic steroid nucleus. The androgens are derivatives of the 19-carbon androstane nuclei; the estrogens are phenolic or naphtholic 18-carbon compounds with the basic estrane nucleus, while the progestins share the 21-carbon pregnane nuclei structure with the adrenocortical steroids.

The predominant and most potent androgenic steroid in most species is testosterone (4-androstene-17,α-ol-3-one; see Fig. 53.5). In the rat, no testosterone is secreted, and androstenedione (4-androstene-3,17-dione) is the active androgen. (Androstenedione has also been isolated from the testes of many mammalian species and from the ovaries of some.) The three principal urinary excretion products of testosterone are androsterone (5α-androstane-3α-ol-17-one), epiandrosterone (4-androstene-3β-ol-17-one), and etiocholanolone (4-androstene-3α-ol-17-one). Since these metabolites all have a ketone group at carbon 17, the total urinary excretion of 17-ketosteroids (17-KS) has been used as a measure of testicular activity; however, a considerable percentage of the 17-KS compounds found in the urine result from the catabolism of adrenocortical steroids.

Estradiol-17β (estratriene-3,17β-diol; see Fig. 53.4) appears to be the major ovarian estrogen in the cow, mare, pig, bitch, and human. Estrone (estratriene-3β-ol-17-one) is present in small amounts. Examination of the hormone content of an endocrine gland as well as the venous effluent from this gland will reveal many compounds of similar structure possessing different degrees of activity; these compounds may represent intermediates in the synthesis of the predominant hormone as well as metabolites resulting from catabolism within the gland itself. It is neither possible nor necessary to attempt to designate one true endocrine secretion from a given gland. Thus Short (1960) has examined the ovarian follicular fluid of the mare and found not only estradiol-17β and estrone, but also 6α-hydroxyestradiol-17β, androstenediol, epitestosterone, and other unidentified steroids.

In most species the estrogenic secretion from the placenta and the testes is similar to that from the ovary; however, the estrogen isolated from sheep and goat placenta appears to be predominantly estradiol-17α, while that isolated from porcine placenta consists of estrone. Although many different estrogens have been isolated from the urine of various species, the principal metabolite of estradiol-17β is probably estradiol-17α, at least in the cow, sheep, and bitch. In the pig, mare, and human, estrone is found in greater amounts. The most extensive investigations of the chemistry of the estrogen metabolites have been conducted in the pregnant human and in the pregnant mare, and many other estrogenic compounds have been isolated. The metabolites found in mare urine (equilin, equilenin, and others) are interesting in that they contain a series of steroids with an unsaturated B-ring.

The principal sex hormone with progestational activity (progestins, gestogens, luteoids) is progesterone (4-pregnene-3,20-dione), and for many years it was reputed to be the only naturally secreted hormone of this class. However, bioassay of luteal tissue, follicular fluid, or placenta has always indicated a higher activity than could be accounted for by chemical assay of the progesterone present in such tissues. This has been resolved, in part, by the isolation of two other progestins of high biological activity from these sources: 20α- and 20β-hydroxy-4-pregnene-3-one.

The central role of progesterone in the biosynthesis of all steroid hormones results in a large number of metabolic possibilities. In the human female and in the mare, but not in other domestic animals, pregnanediol (5β-pregnene-3α,20α-diol) is the principal excreted metabolite of progesterone. In ruminants and rodents, the fact that radioactive carbon dioxide appears in the expired air following the administration of progesterone with radioactive carbon at C-21 indicates a significant splitting of the C-17 side chain during inactivation.

Though the kidney and other organs inactivate or catabolize steroids, the liver appears to be of primary importance in this regard. This function of the liver is a specific example of its general role in the inactivation of potentially toxic compounds, and, in the case of steroid hormones, includes not only metabolism or chemical degradation but also esterification of steroids to form sulfates and conjugation to form glucuronides. The liver handles estrogens and progestins most effectively and androgens and corticoids to a lesser extent. A further advantage in hepatic steroid inactivation is the ready availability of bile as an excretory pathway. There are indications that this pathway is of considerable significance in the ruminant.

Less is known concerning the chemistry of relaxin; however, this compound appears to be a straight-chain polypeptide with a molecular weight in the neighborhood of 7500–9000.

Sources

It has become increasingly obvious that the organs capable of synthesizing biologically active steroids, are able to secrete steroids of the estrogenic, androgenic, and progestational category under normal as well as abnormal circumstances. While the secretion of estrogens by the testis, and conversely the secretion of androgens from the ovary or female adrenal cortex, is probably of physiological significance, it is more useful to consider the predominant or principal sites of secretion of these compounds.

The interstitial cells of the testis (cells of Leydig) are the principal secretory source of testosterone. The activity of these cells is under the control of ICSH from the anterior pituitary; in the domestic animals and man, there does not seem to be a cyclic change in the secretion rate, but in birds and wild mammals there is a male cycle that corresponds to the estrous cycle in the female.

While it is clear that in the nonpregnant female the principal source of both progestins and estrogens is the ovary, there is controversy concerning the cellular site of secretion for these sex steroids. Short (1960) has suggested that the cells of the theca interna are responsible for the secretion of estrogen, while the granulosa cells secrete progesterone and other progestins. (Figure 52.14 shows the theca interna as a narrow layer of cells just outside the basement membrane surrounding the granulosa cells.) This theory is compatible with the evidence that estrogens are not secreted by the corpus luteum of the cow, mare, or ewe; in the human, however, luteal estrogen secretion is strongly indicated. Further evidence for the two-cell theory are the observations that the progesterone content of ovarian venous blood decreases to the same extent following ovariectomy or corpus luteum enucleation. In pregnant animals of many species, the placenta appears to be an important secretory source for both progestins and estrogens. Estrogens have been detected in human, mare, cow, pig, sheep, and goat placentas, while progestins have been isolated from those of the human, mare, and sheep. In those species in which ovariectomy at any stage of pregnancy results in abortion (pig, goat, rabbit, rat, mouse), extraovarian progestin sources may not exist, but in those cases in which pregnancy continues following ovariectomy, an extraovarian source is necessary.

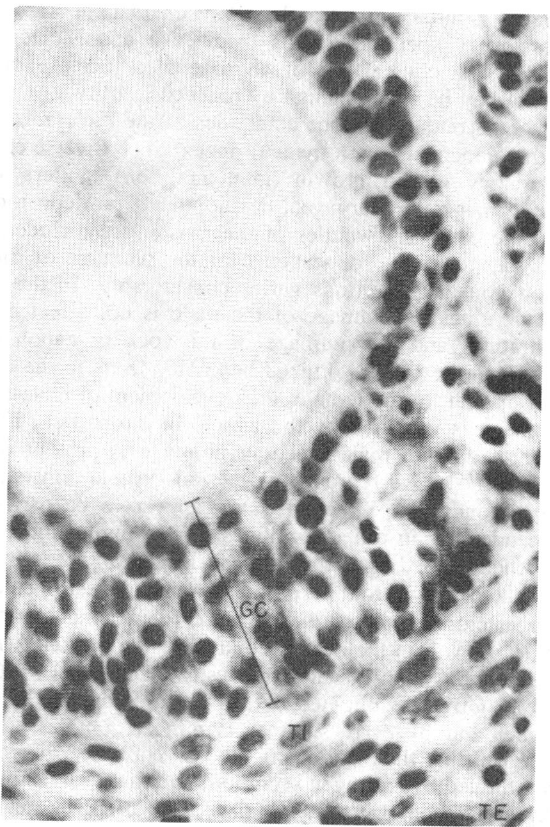

Figure 52.14. Photomicrograph of the canine Graafian follicle showing the granulosa cells (GC), theca interna (TI), and theca externa (TE). ×500.

Relaxin has been found in the ovary of the nonpregnant sow and rat, in the serum of dogs in estrus, and in the testis of the rooster as well as in the ovaries and placentas of various species during pregnancy. This hormone appears to be produced by the ovaries in those species, previously mentioned, that require ovaries throughout pregnancy, and in the placentas of those that do not require this organ.

Curiously, forage plants of the legume family are a potent source of compounds that have a high degree of estrogenic activity. These compounds are not steroids but are similar in structure to the well-known synthetic estrogen diethylstilbestrol (see Fig. 53.4). Most of these plant estrogens have low activity but are present in the plant in considerable quantity and may cause a serious infertility problem in certain areas (Moule et al. 1963). Many synthetic estrogens similar to diethylstilbestrol have been produced; while these compounds do not have the estrogenic potency of estradiol-17β, their activity is surprisingly close to that of estrone.

Though many synthetic protgestins have been developed, this situation differs in that the progestational synthetics usually represent modifications of the parent pregnane nucleus and have been designed to intensify certain properties of the progestins while minimizing others. An interesting group of synthetic relatives of progesterone are those that prevent ovulation and delay estrus.

The peripheral blood concentration of the sex steroids is extremely low. Table 52.6 lists peripheral blood concentrations for progesterone and estradiol during two phases of the estrous cycle in five domestic animals. As would be expected, estradiol values are low during late diestrus and rise throughout proestrus to reach a peak during early estrus. Often a second peak is seen in early or mid-diestrus. Progesterone, on the other hand, increases during diestrus, reaching a peak plateau during mid- and late diestrus (days 12–14 in the sow) and then abruptly decreasing to very low concentrations. In the bitch, an early-estrus ovulator, blood progesterone increases sharply throughout estrus, peaks in early metestrus, then declines steadily to low values by the fortieth to fiftieth day. In the pregnant animal, the concentration of urinary estrogens increases steadily throughout gestation, reaching a peak just before parturition. Nett et al. (1973), however, found rapidly increasing estradiol values in the plasma of the pregnant mare from days 90 to 210 with a slight decline thereafter. Hendricks et al. (1972a,b) observed an increase of blood estradiol from 500 to 2660 pg/ml during the last 14 days of gestation in the cow. In sows, in addition to the late-pregnancy increase in estrogens, there is an early peak reflected by increased urinary estrogen from days 23 to 31. In the cow, progesterone declines slightly from diestrus values, remains at about 4.6 ng/ml from days 140 to 200 of pregnancy, increases to 6.8 ng/ml by day 250, declines to 4 ng/ml 10 days before parturition, then sharply decreases to less than 1 ng/ml on the day before parturition (Stabenfeldt et al. 1970). In animals in which placental progesterone secretion takes place, the decline in blood progesterone occurs at or just after parturition.

Circulating plasma testosterone values have been reported in the ram (3.8 ng/ml, Ginther et al. 1974) and bull (4.3–9.3 ng/ml, increasing with age; Smith et al. 1973). In the latter species, increases occurred at 5 and 30 minutes after ejaculation.

Functions

In recent years, many of the classic concepts of sex hormone function have been either abandoned or considerably modified as more species have come under investigation and experiments have been conducted under physiological rather than artificial circumstances. The diverse effects of the sex hormones on nonreproductive as well as reproductive function are complicated by the various interactions among them as well as by the extreme species variability. Thus when injected or secreted simultaneously, sex hormones may act synergistically, permissively, or antagonistically; the type as well as the degree of action depends upon the stage of the reproductive cycle and the concentrations of the individual compounds. Further, there are strong indications that under certain circumstances, the sex hormones may exert a local diffusion action quite different from that which is obtained when these agents are injected under experimental conditions.

Androgens

The effects of castration of the male have been known since antiquity. Following castration, the accessory sex organs (seminal vesicles, prostate, bulbourethral glands, penis, scrotum, vas deferens, epididymis) undergo a marked decrease in both size and function. (If this operation is performed on very young animals, these organs fail to develop.) If testicular tissue is transplanted into such animals, the organs recover. The injection of testosterone, particularly in immature animals, results in hypertrophy of these accessory sex organs to a degree which may be considerably greater than normal. While the accessory sex organs of the nonmammalian vertebrates are less prominent than those of the mammal, they are also strongly influenced by the androgens. Some of the accessory sex organs appear to be responsive to either androgens or estrogens; for example, the preputial gland of the male responds similarly to both classes and the uterine glands of the bitch are more responsive to androgen than to estrogen.

There are contradictory reports concerning the effect of androgens upon spermatogenesis; however, in hypophysectomized rats, the process of spermatogenesis can be maintained by injected testosterone. This hormone prevents the degeneration of the seminal epithelium which usually follows this operation. However, the injection of testosterone in high doses to intact males depresses the anterior pituitary gland and may result in temporary regression of spermatogenesis (Meinecke and McDonald 1961). The clinical use of androgens to increase male libido may be accompanied by reduced fertility.

The secondary sex characteristics of the male are also highly dependent upon the androgens. Such diverse characteristics as hair growth (man and lion), antlers and horns, hair color, laryngeal development, fat deposition, and the comb and wattles of the rooster are included in this category. The dependence of the plumage of birds upon gonadal secretions varies considerably. In the domestic chicken, plumage of the male is not affected by castration, and the plumage of the cock or capon develops in the ovariectomized hen. This leads to the conclusion that, in the female, the development of male-type plumage is inhibited by the ovary. In the ostrich, however, a definite male breeding plumage is present only during the active reproductive period. In many instances the secondary sex characteristics appear to be partially dependent upon other hormones; for example, the head appendages of Leghorn cocks and hens are under the influence of the thyroid hormone as well as of estrogen and progesterone, and there is good evidence that periodic antler growth in the deer is controlled by hormones from the adenohypophysis and the testes (Hall et al. 1960). Antler growth is initiated by the adenohypophysis in late winter and by early summer is almost complete. It is believed that the "antler growth" hypophyseal hormone is inhibited by androgen secretion, and that as a result the velvet is shed. Finally, when activity of the testes declines in the fall, antlers are shed. Aggressiveness in the male and sex behavior are also secondary sex characteristics and as such are under androgenic influence. Castrated male animals continue to show copulatory behavior for long periods of time to a diminished degree; however, most authorities agree that androgens exert an important influence on the psychic mating reactions. The influence of testosterone on aggressiveness can be particularly noted in birds. In a group of hens in which a social hierarchy or "peck order" exists, testosterone injections into the hens of lower rank will result in an improvement of rank of these hens within the group. It has been suggested that rank in hens results from the quantity of testosterone secreted by the ovaries of each bird.

There appears to be both a direct and an indirect antagonism between the male and female hormones. Both androgens and estrogens inhibit the gonadotropic action of the anterior pituitary gland; thus there is usually a regression of the accessory sex organs and female sex characters following the injection of a relatively large dose of androgen into the female. The presence of a direct antagonism is indicated by the fact that testosterone inhibits the ovarian weight gain induced by diethylstilbestrol in the hypophysectomized rat. In addition, testosterone will diminish the local effect of estrogen on vaginal cornification in the rodent. A degree of synergism and/or similarity between androgens and estrogens has also been demonstrated. Testosterone is capable of enlarging the uterus and increasing the weight gain induced by estrogens. A combination of testosterone and estradiol produces larger seminal vesicles in the immature rat than either steroid by itself. Gaarenstroom and deJongh (1946) postulated that antrum formation in the follicles of the rat ovary occurs under the influence of testosterone secreted by the interstitial cells of the ovary.

Individual sex hormones are apparently not specific in their action on sexual behavior. For example, androgens may induce estrus in castrated female rats, and estrogens can be used to intensify male copulatory behavior in this species. However, large doses of heterologous hormone are required to elicit mating behavior in either sex.

The nonreproductive nitrogen anabolic effect of testosterone and other androgens is well known. Many balance experiments have revealed that androgens cause nitrogen, potassium, and phosphorus retention and an increased mass of skeletal muscle. This effect has been exploited by the synthesis of androgens in which the ratio of anabolic activity and androgen activity is 20:1, compared to 1:1 for testosterone. This effect has also interested investigators working on the mechanism of action of the sex steroids.

Estrogens and progestins

The predominance of estrogen secretion during proestrus and estrus and progestin secretion during the luteal phase of the estrous cycle has led to the oversimplification that the estrogens are primarily responsible for the preparation of the female genital passage for copulation and a successful union between the male and female gamete, while the progestins are necessary for implantation and the maintenance of pregnancy. While this is a useful and partially valid concept, these two classes of female sex hormones act either synergistically or antagonistically upon all aspects of female reproduction. Few if any actions can be attributed to either class alone. In addition, there is a considerable degree of permissiveness between these two types of female sex steroids. For example, vaginal mucification resulting from progesterone administration will not occur unless the animal is pretreated or "primed" with estrogen.

The female accessory sex organs consist of the oviduct, uterus, cervix, and vagina; in contrast with the male, the female accessory sex glands are diffused throughout the genital passage rather than being segregated in discrete organ structures. The outstanding effect of estrogen on the uterus is growth; the involuted uterus of the castrated female can be restored to its normal size by adequate amounts of estrogen, and there is an increase in vascularity and the secretion of luminal fluid as well as an increase in tissue fluid. If this estrogen treatment is followed by progesterone, the uterus will grow larger still. In addition, there is a pronounced increase in glandular convolutions and secretion is greatly increased. Progesterone by itself exerts little growth effect upon the uterus of the castrated female. In birds there is a marked response to estrogen administration by the oviduct. Proliferative growth of this organ can be brought about by estrogen alone, but additional effects are noted when either progesterone or an androgen is given simultaneously.

Both estrogens and progestins affect the motility and contractility of the female reproductive tract as well as the growth and secretion of these organs. The characteristic effect of estrogen on uterine and oviductal motility is increased frequency of contraction. Progesterone inhibits increased frequency of contraction in both uterus and oviduct, but appears to increase the amplitude of contraction in the oviduct. Blandau and Boling (1973) proposed that oviductal motility is increased by waning estrogen levels together with increasing progesterone. Perhaps more important, estrogen may sensitize the uterus to oxytocin, which is particularly important at estrus as an aid to sperm transport and at parturition. While oxytocin increases motility in uteri pretreated with estrogen and progesterone in a wide range of ratios, the effect appears to be enhanced in the estrogen-primed uterus.

Estrogen and progesterone exert synergistic actions on the oviduct cilia: estrogen is important in ciliogenesis while progesterone stimulates the frequency of cilia beats. This synergism is probably important in the transport of the ovum from the infundibulum to the ampullary-isthmus junction.

While the effects of estrogen and progestin on uterine motility exemplify positive and negative permissiveness to oxytocin, and uterine growth illustrates a synergism among the sex steroids, a third type of interaction is seen with respect to cervical and vaginal growth. If estrogen is given to a castrated female, the uterus, cervix, and vagina grow as large as those of the normal estrous female; if the estrogen treatment is followed by progesterone, the uterine size increases still further while the cervix and vagina shrink to the size they were before treatment. Early experiments with rodents suggested that the vagina was highly sensitive to the action of estrogens and that vaginal cornification was a characteristic response. Cornification does not occur in all mammalian species following estrogen administration, however, and appears to be secondary to the primary proliferating and metaplastic response in the vagina. Progesterone induces an entirely different vaginal response, characterized by increased activity of the mucous cells. This mucification reaction is also seen following androgen administration.

In sufficient doses, estrogens administered to the intact animal will produce ovarian atrophy through suppression of the gonadotropic secretion; however, when immature rats are given estrogen, there is a definite increase in ovarian weight, an increase in the number of follicles, and a marked increase in the mitotic activity of the granulosa cells. There is evidence that estrogen secretion results in a persistence of the corpus luteum either by protecting it from degeneration or by making it more sensitive to pituitary luteotropic activity. The removal of the corpus luteum results in an early resumption of follicular activity; the administration of progestins will suppress this reaction. It is generally believed that this effect is obtained through inhibition of the secretion of LH. In contrast to this antagonistic effect of progestin on follicular development, there is good evidence that if progesterone is administered in small doses at the proper time, it significantly advances the time of ovulation. Thus ovulation, as well as other aspects of female reproduction, results from a precisely timed interplay among progesterone, estrogen, and the pituitary gonadotropins.

The effects of estrogens and progestins on the female mating behavior or psychic estrus differ in various animals. In the ewe, psychic estrus does not occur in the absence of a waning corpus luteum from the previous cycle, and thus the first ovulation of the season may show no psychic signs of heat. While continuous estrus can be produced in rodents by frequent estrogen administration, more normal estrus behavior occurs when progesterone follows estrogen. In the cow, estrogen injections cause behavioral estrus for only a short time. Broodiness in hens and turkeys is probably caused by the secretion of prolactin from the adenohypophysis, and the effects of estrogen and progesterone on this phenomenon may be entirely due to their action on the pituitary gland.

The importance of the progestins in the maintenance of pregnancy is unquestioned; in animals in which ovariectomy induces abortion, it is possible to maintain pregnancy with adequate exogenous progesterone. If the progestational mammalian uterus is traumatized by the presence of a foreign body, a hyperplastic localized growth response will occur. This experimentally induced growth is referred to as a deciduoma and represents a modified version of the endometrial response to the blastocyst; it will not occur in a uterus under the influence of estrogen. On the other hand, an estrogen surge occurs at about the time of implantation in some species and is thought to be necessary for normal implantation. In lactating mice and rats in which blastocyst development is arrested, estrogen injection results in a resumption of RNA synthesis, trophoblast proliferation, and implantation of the ovum.

Mammary development and lactation are important phases of female reproductive function and are controlled and influenced by various hormones. In general, the sex steroids of the ovary exert their major action on the developmental stage of this process and, in a sense, act synergistically to ensure mammary growth. Although it is generally agreed that the estrogens are primarily concerned with the growth and development of the mammary ducts, while the progestins complete mammary development through their action on the alveoli, the relative importance of the two steroids varies considerably from species to species. In domestic ruminants and in guinea pigs, estrogens appear to be primary, while in the bitch little mammary development results from this group of hormones. However, in all species that have been studied, a combination of hormones, including estrogen, progesterone, and prolactin, is necessary to attain full and normal mammary development. Many theories have been advanced to explain the hormonal role in the initiation of milk flow following parturition. In most species there is no lactation during gestation, and it has been suggested that in the pregnant nonlactating animal estrogens and progestins promote mammary growth, and that there is competition between growth and lactation. At the end of pregnancy the estrogen levels have risen to a level which stimulates prolactin secretion, and at term the marked decline in estrogen and progestin concentration leaves the mammary gland receptive to the action of prolactin. Lactation is then initiated and maintained through an interaction between the milking stimulus (suckling) and pituitary prolactin secretion.

Possibly the most important extragenital effect of the estrogens is found in bone metabolism. The injection of high doses of estradiol into mammals may result in bone deposition within the marrow cavity to the point where hematopoiesis is inhibited, with resultant anemia. In birds, the effect of estrogen may be so marked as to result in solid mammal-like long bones rather than in the normal avian hollow structures. Striking changes in blood and tissue composition take place during periods of ovarian activity and following estrogen administration in birds. These include lipemia and a significant elevation in blood calcium concentration. The responses are contrary to those seen in mammals, in which estrogens appear to depress both blood calcium and blood lipid concentrations. In human females, estrogen deficiency may contribute to postmenopausal osteoporosis. Other extragenital effects of estrogen are growth retardation at puberty and increased synthesis of thyroid-binding globulin and transcortin. While the increase in blood flow attributable to estrogens is particularly evident in reproductive organs, these hormones also cause increased cardiac output and systemic hyperemia, which is particularly evident in cutaneous tissue. In lower primates, cutaneous hyperemia and edema resulting from elevated estrogen account for the so-called sex skin seen at estrus. Progesterone has few extragenital effects not associated with secondary sex characteristics, but the nitrogen diuresis following its injection indicates that it is slightly catabolic.

Although no function for either estrogen or progestin has been established in the male, estrogen stimulates certain accessory male tissues and may cause fibromuscular hypertrophy and/or metaplasia. In general, estrogen acts as an antagonist to the male sex hormone while progestin has been described as a weak androgen.

The mechanism of action of the estrogens has been much studied. Though the anabolic effects of this hormone are reasonably restricted to the target organs, many physiologists are of the opinion that the induction of protein synthesis is the primary action. Estrogen-specific receptor protein has been isolated from the uterus and it has been shown that estrogen-receptor protein binding is necessary to its action. The intranuclear effects (gene derepression, RNA synthesis) are also accompanied by increased intracellular cAMP.

Relaxin

The polypeptide hormone relaxin was isolated from ovarian extracts by Hisaw (1959) and has been most extensively studied in the guinea pig and mouse. In these species prolonged treatment with an estrogen (23 days) or an estrogen and progesterone (13 days) may induce relaxation of the pubic symphysis, but this is much more quickly accomplished by relaxin (6 hours). Histological studies reveal that estrogen treatment causes resorption of bone, proliferation of loose connective tissue, and an increase in water content, while relaxin treatment results in a breakdown of the collagenous fibers into thin threads together with a depolymerization of the ground substance. In the sheep and cow, this hormone induces relaxation of the sacroiliac joints, which widens the birth canal. The induction of cervical dilatation by relaxin has been confirmed in the rat, human, cow, and sow, and probably occurs in other species. Cervical dilatation probably occurs as a result of a synergism between progesterone and relaxin and will take place only in estrogen-primed animals. The effect of relaxin on myometrial activity is controversial. While it is generally accepted that relaxin will inhibit estrogen-induced uterine contractions, this hormone does not appear to interfere with the action of oxytocin on the uterus. The function of relaxin in nonpregnant females and in males has not been established, although this hormone has been isolated from both sources.

Sex steroids in sex differentiation

Sex differentiation consists of the retention of one sex duct, with the development of its derivatives, while the other duct either disappears or survives only as a vestige. In female subjects, the female hormones (estrogens) accelerate sexual differentiation and usually induce a precocious hypertrophy of the Müllerian ducts, while in males these hormones stimulate persistence of the Müllerian ducts to a degree which depends on the species, hormone dosage, and timing of the treatment. Androgenic hormones have not produced as clear-cut results, and in most experiments Müllerian duct inhibition has not been obtained. Early castration of avian embryos results in the persistence of the Müllerian ducts in both sexes; in the females, in which the right duct normally regresses, both ducts persist and are well developed, while in the male both ducts persist and develop rather than regressing, as they normally would. In mammals, castration of the female has little effect, while in male castrates, the Müllerian ducts persist and develop till they are as large as those of castrate females. The administration of female hormones to the embryo appears to have little influence on the development of the male Wolffian duct system, but as expected, the administration of male hormones results in marked hypertrophy of these ducts. The effects of castration indicate that in all species the presence of the embryonic testis is necessary for sexual differentiation of the Wolffian duct.

During early embryonic life, every animal passes through a sexually undifferentiated period of development during which all of the embryonic structures necessary for the development of either sex are present. If sex hormones are administered during this period, various degrees of gonadal sex reversal can be obtained. In young birds before sexual development is complete, the administration of estrogens to males causes the development of the left testis into an ovotestis, and the administration of male hormones to females can cause conversion of the left ovary into an ovotestis, while the right ovary is superficially changed into a testislike gonad. After hatching there is a tendency for experimentally modified gonads to revert toward the original genetic sex. Sex-reversal experiments have not been as rewarding in mammals as in birds, but X-irradiation experiments have indicated that in the mammal the neutral pattern is of the female type and is modified by the presence of the testis, in direct contrast to the situation in avian species. The classic intersexual condition in mammals is known as *freemartinism*. In this condition, the anastomosis of the embryonic circulation in the bovine animal leads to a masculine modification of the female twin in a female-male twinning (Lillie 1916). Though this phenomenon has stimulated a great deal of research, no adequate explanation has resulted. In dogs, perinatal administration of testosterone to female pups prevented overt sex receptivity and attractiveness to males when the pups reached the age of sexual maturity, and in rats, early postnatal administration of androgens to females prevented the cyclic LH surge when they reached adulthood.

Placental gonadotropins

The secretion of placental gonadotropins has been established in primates, mares, and rats. The gonadotropins secreted from these three groups of mammals differ from each other considerably. Rat placental gonadotropin has no effect on follicular growth or ovulation and appears to function exclusively in a luteotropic capacity. Mare placental gonadotropin (PMS) is very active in producing follicular growth and in this respect resembles FSH, whereas human placental gonadotropin (HCG) has little effect on follicular growth and, like LH, can be used to induce ovulation. Further evidence reflecting the close similarity between HCG and LH is the immunological cross-reactivity between the two hormones. Substantial amounts of placental gonadotropin appear in the blood of the pregnant mare and in the blood and urine of the pregnant human early in the gestation period. In the human, HCG appears in the blood at about the twenty-fifth day of pregnancy, reaches a peak on the forty-ninth or fiftieth day, and disappears at about day 150. In the mare, PMS appears in the bloodstream at around the fortieth day, increases rapidly to a peak concentration on day 60, and declines to undetectable levels by the 170th day of gestation. Although the function of these gonadotropins during pregnancy is not entirely clear, their appearance coincides with the time of implantation and their disappearance corresponds to the time when ovariectomy no longer causes abortion in these species. While it is clear that the chorion is responsible for the secretion of HCG in the human, there is strong evidence that in the mare the hormone is secreted by the allantochorion girdle cells of the fetal trophoblast. The apperance in the blood and urine of these potent substances at a relatively early stage of pregnancy has been used as a basis for the laboratory diagnosis of early pregnancy. Many such tests have been described, starting with the Ascheim-Zondek procedure in 1927 and culminating in the immunological test for HCG; most of these tests are equally applicable to the diagnosis of pregnancy in the mare.

While there is a close physiological and immunological similarity between pituitary LH and HCG and a close physiological resemblance between FSH and PMS, there are considerable chemical differences between the pituitary and placental gonadotropins.

PROSTAGLANDINS

In 1934 von Euler found that human semen and extracts of sheep seminal vesicles contained a lipid-soluble material that lowered arterial blood pressure and stimulated isolated intestinal and uterine smooth muscle, and in 1960 Bergstrom purified and isolated the active principles. Presently, four fundamental types of natural prostaglandins have been described: E, F, A, and B, corresponding to differences in the five-membered ring (Fig. 52.15). The degree of unsaturation of the side chains is designated by a subscript numeral. These compounds have been isolated from a wide variety of tissues (lungs, skin, brain, reproductive organs, intestine, iris, kidney) and have potent effects on many systems. The principal basic substrates for prostaglandin synthesis appear to be the unsaturated fatty acids, such as arachidonic acid.

The metabolism of the prostaglandins represents another possible mechanism whereby the action of humoral regulating compounds is restricted to certain target organs. Prostaglandins, due to rapid and almost complete deactivation in the liver and lung, exert their effects either within the organ in which they are produced or on an organ reached by the venous drainage from that organ (e.g. renal cortical blood flow affected by renal prostaglandin produced in the medulla, and ovarian luteolysis stimulated by prostaglandin produced by the endometrium).

The area that has received the most attention and therapeutic exploitation in prostaglandin (PG) research has been reproduction. $PGF_{2}\alpha$ is particularly potent in ter-

PGE_1 $PGF_{2\alpha}$ PGA_1 PGB_2

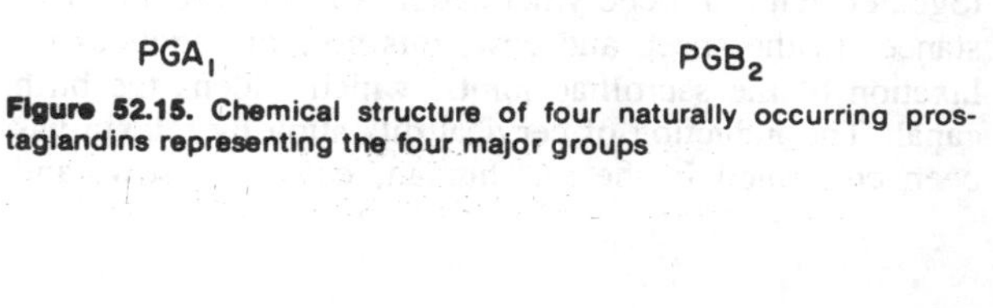

Figure 52.15. Chemical structure of four naturally occurring prostaglandins representing the four major groups

minating early pregnancy, and convincing evidence has been presented that this PG is the natural luteolytic agent that terminates the luteal phase and allows the initiation of a new estrous cycle in the absence of fertilization (McCracken et al. 1971). It is suggested that $PGF_2\alpha$ is secreted from the uterus into the uterine venous blood and transferred directly to the ovarian artery by a countercurrent exchange mechanism. It has also been hypothesized that PG's act through a vasoconstrictive action on the utero-ovarian veins or by stimulating uterine contractions. In veterinary medicine, the luteolytic action of $PGF_2\alpha$ has led to its use as an effective agent in estrous synchronization.

The circulatory effects of prostaglandins vary considerably among compounds and somewhat among species. In general, PGE_1 and PGE_2 are peripheral vasodilators, while in many species PGF_2 is a vasopressor. It has been proposed that PGE_2 and PGA_2 are released by the renal medulla following increased arterial blood pressure, causing vasodilatation in the renal cortex with resultant diuresis and increased sodium excretion.

Other proposed actions of the prostaglandins include inhibition of gastric secretion, relaxation of the bronchial musculature (PGE relaxes, PGF constricts), enhancement of inflammation (aspirin and indomethacin, anti-inflammatory agents, are both potent PG inhibitors), and inhibition of sympathetic neuroeffector transmission.

THYMUS GLAND

It has long been recognized that the thymus gland of mammals atrophies at about the time of adolescence, and the studies of Selye (1950) revealed that this lymphoid organ is particularly sensitive to the action of adrenal glucocorticoids. In 1941 (Cole and Furth) the relationship of the thymus to leukemia was demonstrated in the mouse, and in 1961 Miller found that if thymectomy was performed in newborn mice, these animals survived for only a few months. Various experiments have demonstrated that the thymus is essential for the normal development and maintenance of immunological competence. Mice that have been thymectomized at birth do not succumb to the so-called wasting disease if they receive an implant of thymus tissue; this was the case even when the implant was enclosed in a cell-tight diffusion compartment (Levey 1964). Levey proposed that normally a thymic hormone reacts with the lymphoid cells from the thymus and other lymphoid tissues to produce cells that are capable of reacting with antigens. Whenever one of these competent but uncommitted lymphoid cells encounters and reacts with an antigen, it begins to multiply and gives rise to plasma cells which synthesize the appropriate antibodies. In adult animals, the effects of thymectomy are considerably delayed. Metcalf (1965) and Miller (1965) reported that adult thymectomized mice behaved much like neonatally thymectomized mice 3 months after the operation.

Various protein substances varying in molecular weight from less than 1000 to 200,000 have been isolated from the thymus and proposed as thymic hormones. Wasting disease can be prevented by injections of HTH (homeostatic thymic hormone, Comsa 1965), thymosin (White and Goldstein 1968), or THF (thymic humoral factor, Trainin et al. 1966). HTH or LSH (lymphocyte-stimulating hormone, Luckey et al. 1973) are capable of increasing the lymphocyte-polymorphonuclear cell ratio, and either thymosin or THF stimulate cell-mediated immunity.

Actions not directly related to the immune response and the lymphoid system have been ascribed to thymic extracts. A neuromuscular blocking agent, thymin, is thought to be released in excess in autoimmune thymitis and cause depression of neuromuscular transmission (Goldstein 1968). Comsa (1965) has reviewed the hormonal interactions of the thymus and suggests that the thymic hormones act in opposition to the adrenal glucocorticoids. Finally, thymosterin, a thymic steroid substance isolated by Potop and Milcu (1973), inhibits lymphocytopoiesis and inhibits tumor growth both in vitro and in vivo.

REFERENCES

General

Bondy, P.K., and Rosenberg, L.E., eds. 1974. *Duncan's Diseases of Metabolism*. Saunders, Philadelphia. Vols. 1, 2.

Dorfman, R.I., ed. 1962. *Methods in Hormone Research*. Academic Press, New York. Vols. 1, 2.

Gray, C.H., and Bacharach, A.L., eds. 1967. *Hormones in Blood*. 2d ed. Academic Press, New York. Vols. 1, 2.

Marshall, A.J., ed. 1961. *Biology and Comparative Physiology of Birds*. Academic Press, New York.

Martini, L., and Ganong, W.F. 1966. *Neuroendocrinology*. Academic Press, New York. Vols. 1, 2.

McDonald, L.E. 1976. *Veterinary Endocrinology and Reproduction*. Lea & Febiger, Philadelphia.

Turner, C.T., and Bagnara, J.T. 1971. *General Endocrinology*. 5th ed. Saunders, Philadelphia.

Von Euler, U.S., and Heller, H. 1963. *Comparative Endocrinology*. Academic Press, New York. Vols. 1, 2

Williams, R.H., ed. 1974. *Textbook of Endocrinology*. 5th ed. Saunders, Philadelphia.

Zarrow, M.X., Jochim, J.M., McCarthy, J.L., and Sanborn, R.C. 1964. *Experimental Endocrinology*. Academic Press, New York.

Introduction

Cannon, W.B. 1932. *The Wisdom of the Body*. Norton, New York.

Collip, J.B. 1935. Recent studies on antihormones. *Ann. Internal Med.* 9:150–61.

Kirkham, K.E., and Hunter, W.M., eds. 1971. *Radioimmunoassay Methods*. Churchill Livingstone, Edinburgh.

Kornel, L. 1973. On the mechanism of action of corticosteroids in normal and neoplastic target tissues: Findings and hypotheses. *Acta Endocr.*, suppl. 178, 5–45.

Liao, S., and Fang, S. 1969. Receptor proteins for androgens and the mode of action of androgens on gene transcription in ventral prostate. *Vitam. Horm.* 27:17–90.

Sutherland, E.W., Øye, I., and Butcher, R.W. 1965. The action of epinephrine and the role of the adenyl cyclase system in hormone action. *Recent Prog. Horm. Res.* 21:623–46.

Szego, C.M. 1974. The lysosome as a mediator of hormone action. *Recent Prog. Horm. Res.* 30:171–233.

Tata, J.R. 1974. Growth and developmental action of thyroid hormones at the cellular level. In *Handbook of Physiology*. Sec. 7, M.A. Greer and D.H. Solomon, eds. Am. Physiol. Soc., Washington. Vol. 3.

Yalow, R.S., and Berson, S.A. 1961. Immunoassay of plasma insulin in man. *Diabetes* 10:339–44.

The hypophysis cerebri and hypothalamus

Akbar, A.M., Reichert, L.E., Jr., Dunn, T.G., Kaltenbach, C.C., and Niswender, G.D.. 1973. Bovine FSH in serum measured by radioimmunoassay. *J. Anim. Sci.* 37:299.

Assali, N.S., Dasgupta, K., Kolin, A., and Holmes, L. 1958. Measurement of uterine blood flow and uterine metabolism. V. Changes during spontaneous and induced labor in unanesthetized pregnant sheep and dogs. *Am. J. Physiol.* 195:614–20.

Caldeyro-Barcia, R., and Poseiro, J.J. 1959. Oxytocin and contractility of the pregnant human uterus. *Ann. N.Y. Acad. Sci.* 75:813–30.

Convey, E.M. 1973. Neuroendocrine relationships in farm animals: A review. *J. Anim Sci.* 37:745–57.

Convey, E.M., Bretschneider, E., Hafs, H.D., and Oxender, W.D. 1971. Serum levels of LH, prolactin, and growth hormone after ejaculation in bulls. *Biol. Reprod.* 5:20–24.

DeBodo, R.C., and Altshuler, N. 1958. The metabolic effects of growth hormone and their physiological significance. *Vitam. Horm.* 15:205–58.

DuVigneaud, V. 1956. *Hormones of the Posterior Pituitary Gland: Oxytocin and Vasopressin.* Harvey Lectures, Academic Press, New York.

Ely, F., and Peterson, W.E. 1941. Factors involved in the ejection of milk. *J. Dairy Sci.* 24:211–23.

Everett, J.W. 1964. Central neural control of reproductive functions of the adenohypophysis. *Physiol. Rev.* 44:373–431.

Farner, D.S. 1964. The photoperiodic control of reproductive cycles in birds. *Am. Scientist* 52:137–56.

Folley, S.J. 1956. *The Physiology and Biochemistry of Lactation.* Oliver & Boyd, Edinburgh.

Fortier, C. 1962. Adenohypophysis and adrenal cortex. *Ann. Rev. Physiol.* 24:223–58.

Gaines, W.L. 1915. A contribution to the physiology of lactation. *Am. J. Physiol.* 38:285–312.

Ginetzinsky, A.G. 1958. Role of hyaluronidase in the reabsorption of water in renal tubules: The mechanism of action of the antidiuretic hormone. *Nature* 182:1218–19.

Glick, S.M., Roth, J., Yalow, R.S., and Berson, S.A. 1965. The regulation of growth hormone secretion. *Recent Prog. Horm. Res.* 21:241–70.

Green, J.D., and Harris, G.W. 1947. The neurovascular link between the neurohypophysis and adenohypophysis. *J. Endocr.* 5:136–46.

Harris, G.W., and Donovan, B.T. 1966. *The Pituitary Gland.* U. of California Press, Berkeley. Vols. 1, 2, 3.

Harris, G.W., Reed, M., and Fawcett, C.P. 1966. Hypothalamic releasing factors and the control of anterior pituitary function. *Brit. Med. Bull.* 22:266–72.

Hume-Adams, J., Daniel, P.M., and Prichard, M.L. 1964. Distribution of hypophysial portal blood in the anterior lobe of the pituitary gland. *Endocrinology* 75:120–26.

L'Hermite, M., Niswender, G.D., Reichert, L.E., Jr., and Midgley, A.R., Jr. 1972. Serum follicle stimulating hormone in sheep as measured by radioimmunoassay. *Biol. Reprod.* 6:325–32.

Li, C.H. 1959. The relation of chemical structure to the biologic activity of pituitary hormones. *Lab. Invest.* 8:574–87.

McCann, S.M., Dhariwal, A.P.S., and Porter, V.C. 1968. Regulation of the adenohypophysis. *Ann. Rev. Physiol.* 30:589–640.

Meites, J., and Clemens, J.A. 1972. Hypothalamic control of prolactin secretion. *Vitam. Horm.* 30:165–221.

Munsick, R.A., Sawyer, W.H., and van Dyke, H.B. 1958. The antidiuretic potency of arginine and lysine vasopressins in the pig with observations on porcine renal function. *Endocrinology* 63:860–71.

——. 1960. Avian neurohypophysial hormones: Pharmacological properties and tentative identification. *Endocrinology* 66:860–71.

Oliver, G., and Schaefer, E.A. 1895. On the physiological action of extracts of pituitary body and certain other glandular organs. *J. Physiol.* 18:277–79.

Papkoff, H., Sairam, M.R., Farmer, S.W., and Li, C.H. 1973. Studies on the structure and function of interstitial cell-stimulating hormone. *Recent Prog. Horm. Res.* 29:563–90.

Pierce, J.G., Liao, T.H., Howard, S.M., Shome, B., and Cornell, J.S. 1971. *Recent Prog. Horm. Res.* 27:165–212.

Rabinowitz, D., Merimee, T.J., Burgess, J.A., and Riggs, L. 1966. Growth hormone and insulin release after arginine: Indifference to hyperglycemia and epinephrine. *J. Clin. Endocr. Metab.* 26:1170–72.

Rasmussen, H., Schwartz, I.L., Schuessler, M.A., and Hochester, G. 1960. Studies on the mechanism of action of vasopressin. *Proc. Nat. Acad. Sci.* 46:1278–87.

Roth, J., Glick, S.M., Yalow, R.S., and Berson, S.A. 1963. Hypoglycemia: A potent stimulus to secretion of growth hormone. *Science* 140:987–88.

Schally, A.V., Kastin, A.J., and Arimura, A. 1972. FSH-releasing hormone and LH-releasing hormone. *Vitam. Horm.* 30:84–164.

Van Wyk, J.J., Underwood, L.E., Hintz, P.L., Clemmons, D.R., Voina, J., and Weaver, R.P. 1974. The somatomedins: A family of insulin-like hormones under growth hormone control. *Recent Prog. Horm. Res.* 30:259–318.

Yalow, R.S. 1974. Heterogeneity of peptide hormones. *Recent Prog. Horm. Res.* 30:597–634.

The pineal gland

Kitay, J.I., and Altschule, M.D. 1954. *The Pineal Gland.* Harvard U. Press, Cambridge.

Lerner, A.B., Case, J.D., and Takahashi, Y. 1960. Isolation of melatonin and 5-methoxy-indole-3-acetic acid from bovine pineal glands. *J. Biol. Chem.* 235:1992–97.

Wolstenholme, G.E.W., and J. Knight, eds. 1971. *The Pineal Gland.* Churchill Livingstone, Edinburgh.

Wurtman, R.J., and Axelrod, J. 1965. The pineal gland. *Scien. Am.* 213:50–60.

The thyroid gland

Brewster, W.R., Isaacs, J.P., Osgood, P.F., and King, T.L. 1956. The hemodynamic and metabolic interrelationships in the activity of epinephrine, norepinephrine, and the thyroid hormones. *Circulation* 13:1–20.

Feinberg, W.D., Hoffman, D.L., and Owen, C.A. 1959. The effects of varying amounts of stable iodide on the function of the human thyroid. *J. Clin. Endocr. Metab.* 19:567–82.

Hamolsky, M.W., Stein, M., and Freedberg, A.S. 1957. The thyroid hormone-plasma protein complex in man. II. A new in vitro method for study of "uptake" of labelled hormone by human erythrocytes. *J. Clin. Endocr. Metab.* 17:33–44.

Kallfelz, F.A., and Erali, R.P. 1973. Thyroid function tests in domesticated animals: Free thyroxine index. *Am. J. Vet. Res.* 34:1449–55.

Kaneko, J.J. 1963. Selected organ function tests: Thyroid function. In J.J. Kaneko and C.E. Cornelius, eds., *Clinical Biochemistry of Domestic Animals.* Academic Press, New York. Pp. 310–13.

Kelley, S.T., Oehme, F.W., and Brandt, G.W. 1974a. Measurement of thyroid gland function during the estrous cycle of nine mares. *Am. J. Vet. Res.* 35:657–60.

Kelley, S.T., Oehme, F.W., and Hoffman, S.B. 1974b. Evaluation of selected commercial thyroid function tests in dogs. *Am. J. Vet. Res.* 35:733–36.

Ling, G.V., Lowenstine, L.K., and Kaneko, J.J. 1974. Serum thyroxine and triiodothyronine uptake values in normal adult cats. *Am. J. Vet. Res.* 35:1247–49.

Sutherland, R.L., and Irvine, C.H.G. 1973. Total plasma thyroxine concentration in horses, pigs, cattle, and sheep: Anion exchange resin chromatography and ceric arsenite colorimetry. *Am. J. Vet. Res.* 34:1261–70.

Tata, J.R., Ernster, L., and Lindberg, O. 1962. Control of basal metabolic rate by thyroid hormones and cellular function. *Nature* 193:1058–60.

Thomas, J.W., and Moore, L.A. 1953. Thyroprotein feeding to dairy cows during successive lactations. *J. Dairy Sci.* 36:657–72.

Thorpe, B.R. 1953. Thyroid enlargement in a dog, treated with iodine and methyl thiouracil. *Austral. Vet. J.* 29:75–78.

Werner, S.C., and Ingbar, S.H. 1971. *The Thyroid.* 3d ed. Harper & Row, New York.

Hormones associated with calcium and skeletal homeostasis

Aurbach, G.D., Potts, J.T., Jr., Chase, L.R., and Melson, G.L. 1969. Polypeptide hormones and calcium metabolism. *Ann. Internal Med.* 70:1243–65.

Barnicot, N.A. 1948. The local action of the parathyroid and other tissues on bone in intracerebral grafts. *J. Anat.* 82:233–48.

Brewer, H.B., Jr., and Ronan, R. 1970. Bovine parathyroid hormone: Amino acid sequence. *Proc. Nat. Acad. Sci.* 67:1862–69.

Copp, D.H., Cameron, E.C., Cheney, B.A., Davidson, A.G.F., and Henze, K.G. 1962. Evidence for calcitonin: A new hormone from the parathyroid that lowers blood calcium. *Endocrinology* 70:638–49.

Copp, D.H., Cockcroft, D.W., and Kueh, Y. 1967. Calcitonin from ultimobranchial glands of dogfish and chickens. *Science* 158:924.

DeLuca, H.F. 1971a. The role of vitamin D and its relationship to parathyroid hormone and calcitonin. *Recent Prog. Horm. Res.* 27:479–516.

——. 1971b. Vitamin D: A new look at an old vitamin. *Nutr. Rev.* 29:179–81.

Foster, G.V., Baghdiantz, A., Kumar, M.A., Slack, E., Soliman, H.A., and MacIntyre, I. 1964. Thyroid origin of calcitonin. *Nature* 202:1303.

Galliard, P. 1959. The influence of parathormone on cartilage and bone in vitro. *Acta Physiol. Pharmac. Neerl.* 8:287–89.

Gley, E. 1891. Sur les fonctions du corps thyroide. *Comptes rend. Soc. Biol.* 43:841–47.

Kemper, B., Habener, J.F., Potts, J.T., Jr., and Rich, A. 1972. Proparathyroid hormone: Identification of a biosynthetic precursor to parathyroid hormone. *Proc. Nat. Acad. Sci.* 69:643–47.

Krook, L., Barrett, R.B., Usui, K., and Wolke, R.E. 1963. Nutritional secondary hyperparathyroidism in the cat. *Cornell Vet.* 53:224–40.

MacCallum, W.G., and Voegtlin, C. 1909. On the relation of tetany to the parathyroid glands and to calcium metabolism. *J. Exp. Med.* 11:118–51.

Norman, A.W., and Henry, H. 1974. 1,25-dihydroxycholecalciferol: Hormonally active form of vitamin D_3. *Recent Prog. Horm. Res.* 30:431–73.

Potts, J.T., Jr., Brewer, H.B., Jr., Reisfield, R.A., Hirsch, P.F., Schlueter, R., and Munson, P.L. 1968. Isolation and chemical properties of porcine thyrocalcitonin. In R.V. Talmage and L.F. Belanger, eds., *Parathyroid Hormone and Thyrocalcitonin* (*Calcitonin*). Excerpta Medica Foundation, Amsterdam.

Rasmussen, H., and Bordier, P. 1974. *The Physiological and Cellular Basis of Metabolic Bone Disease.* Williams & Wilkins, Baltimore.

Sandstrom, I. 1880. Über eine neue Druse menschen und bei verschiedenen Saugethieren. *Üpsala Läkarefören. Forh.* 15:635–39.

Vassale, G., and Generali, G. 1896. Sugli effetti dell 'estirpazione delle ghiandole paratiroidee. *Riv. Path. Nerv. E. Ment.* 1:95–99, 249–52.

Endocrine secretions of the pancreas

Banting, F.G., and Best, C.H. 1921. Pancreatic extracts. *J. Lab. Clin. Med.* 7:464–72.

Bromer, W.W., Sinn, L.G., Staub, A., and Behrens, O.K. 1957. The amino acid sequence of glucagon. *Diabetes* 6:234–38.

Frohman, L.A. 1969. The endocrine function of the pancreas. *Ann. Rev. Physiol.* 31:353–82.

Krahl, M.E. 1974. The endocrine function of the pancreas. *Ann. Rev. Physiol.* 36:331–60.

Langerhans, P. 1869. *Beitrage zur Mikroskopischen Anatomie der Bauch Speicheldruse.* Gustav Lange, Berlin.

Levine, R., and Goldstein, M.S. 1955. On the mechanism of action of insulin. *Recent Prog. Horm. Res.* 11:343–75.

Littledike, E.T., Witzel, D.A., and Whipp, S.C. 1968. Insulin: Evidence for inhibition of release in spontaneous hypocalcemia. *Proc. Soc. Exp. Biol. Med.* 129:135–39.

Manns, J.G., and Martin, C.L. 1972. Plasma insulin, glucagon, and nonesterified fatty acids in dogs with diabetes mellitus. *Am. J. Vet. Res.* 33:981–85.

Randle, P.J., and Smith, G.H. 1958. Regulation of glucose uptake by muscle. I. The effects of insulin, anaerobiosis, and cell poisons on the uptake of glucose and release of potassium by isolated rat diaphragm. *Biochem. J.* 70:490–500.

Sanger, F. 1959. Chemistry of insulin. *Science* 129:1340–44.

Smith, L.F. 1966. Species variation in the amino acid sequence of insulin. *Am. J. Med.* 40:662–66.

Steiner, D.F., Clark, J.L., Nolan, C., Rubenstein, A., Margoliash, E., Atea, B., and Oyer, P.E. 1969. Proinsulin and the biosynthesis of insulin. *Recent Prog. Horm. Res.* 25:207–82.

Sutherland, E.W., and Robison, G.A. 1969. The role of cyclic AMP in the control of carbohydrate metabolism. *Diabetes* 18:797–819.

Witzel, D.A., and Littledike, E.T 1973. Suppression of insulin secretion during induced hypocalcemia. *Endocrinology* 93:761–66.

The adrenal gland

Axelrod, J. 1959. Metabolism of epinephrine and other sympathomimetic amines. *Physiol. Rev.* 39:751–76.

Baniukiewicz, S., Brodie, A., Flood, G., Motta, M., Okamoto, M., Tait, J.F., Tait, S.A.S., Blair-West, J.R., Coghlan, J.P., Denton, D.A., Goding, J.R., Scoggins, B.A., Wintour, M., and Wright, R.D.. 1967. Adrenal biosynthesis of steroids in vitro and in vivo using continuous superfusion and infusion procedures. In D. McKerns, ed., *Functions of the Adrenal Cortex.* Appleton-Century-Crofts, New York.

Binns, W., Anderson, W.A., and Sullivan, D.J. 1960. Further observations on a congenital cyclopian type malformation. *J. Am. Vet. Med. Ass.* 137:515–21.

Blair-West, J.R., Coghlan, J.P., Denton, D.A., Goding, J.R., Wintour, M., and Wright, R.D. 1963. The control of aldosterone secretion. *Recent Prog. Horm. Res.* 19:11–383.

Bottoms, G.D., Roesel, O.F., Rausch, F.D., and Akins, E.L. 1972. Circadian variation in plasma cortisol and corticosterone in pigs and mares. *Am. J. Vet. Res.* 33:785–90.

Brodie, B.B., and Shore, P.A. 1957. A concept for a role of serotonin and norepinephrine as chemical mediators in the brain. *Ann. N.Y. Acad. Sci.* 66:631–42.

Carrier, O. 1972. *Pharmacology of the Peripheral Autonomic Nervous System.* Year Book Medical, Chicago.

Christie, D.W., Bell, E.T., Horth, C.E., and Palmer, R.F. 1971. Peripheral plasma progesterone levels during the canine oestrous cycle. *Acta Endocr.* 68:543–50.

Davis, W.W., Burwell, L.R., and Bartter, F.C. 1967. Loss of stimulation of aldosterone secretion by angiotensin in the sodium-loaded dog. *Clin. Res.* 15:258.

Dickson, W.M., and Kainer, R.A. 1954. Adrenogenital syndrome in a female mink. *J. Am. Vet. Med. Ass.* 125:45–46.

Dickson, W.M., and Seekins, J. 1963. Blood plasma 17-hydroxycorticosteroid, blood glucose, and blood ketone body concentrations in intact and adrenalectomized pregnant ewes subjected to reduced food intake. *Am. J. Vet. Res.* 25:955–62.

Dorfman, R.I., and Ungar, F. 1953. *Metabolism of Steroid Hormones*. Burgess, Minneapolis.

Dunn, T.G., Hopwood, M.L., House, W.A., and Faulkner, L.C. 1972. Glucose metabolism and plasma progesterone and corticoids during the estrous cycle of ewes. *Am. J. Physiol.* 222:468–73.

Engel, F.L. 1957. Some unexplained metabolic action of pituitary hormones with a unifying hypothesis concerning their significance. *Yale J. Biol. Med.* 30:201–23.

Farrell, G.L. 1959. The physiological factors which influence the secretion of aldosterone. *Recent Prog. Horm. Res.* 15:275–310.

Ganong, W.F., Boryczka, A.T., and Shackelford, R. 1967. Effect of renin on adrenocortical sensitivity to ACTH and angiotensin II in dogs. *Endocrinology* 80:703–6.

Ganong, W.F., and Martini, L. 1973. *Frontiers in Neuroendocrinology*. Oxford U. Press, London.

Garm, O. 1949. A study on bovine nymphomania. *Acta Endocr.* 2(suppl. 3):1–144.

Hagen, P. 1959. The storage and release of catecholamines. *Pharmac. Rev.* 11:361–73.

Hendricks, D.M., Dickey, J.F., Hill, J.R., and Johnston, W.E. 1972a. Plasma estrogen and progesterone levels after mating and during late pregnancy and postpartum in cows. *Endocrinology* 90:1336–42.

Hendricks, D.M., Guthrie, H.D., and Handlin, D.L. 1972b. Plasma estrogen, progesterone, and luteinizing hormone levels during the estrous cycle in pigs. *Biol. Reprod.* 6:210–18.

Jones, G.E., Boyns, A.R., Cameron, E.H.D., Bell, E.T., Christie, D.W., and Parkes, M.F. 1973. Plasma oestradiol, luteinizing hormone, and progesterone during the estrous cycle in the beagle bitch. *J. Endocr.* 57:331–32.

Kennedy, P.C., Kendrick, J.W., and Stormont, C. 1957. Adenohypophyseal aplasia, an inherited defect associated with abnormal gestation in Guernsey cattle. *Cornell Vet.* 47:160–78.

Klyne, W. 1957. *The Chemistry of the Steroids*. Methuen, London.

Liggins, G.C., Fairclough, R.J., Grieves, S.A., Kendall, J.Z., and Knox, B.S. 1973. The mechanism of initiation of parturition in the ewe. *Recent Prog. Horm. Res.* 29:111–59.

Lyman, C.P., and Chatfield, P.O. 1955. Physiology of hibernation in mammals. *Physiol. Rev.* 35:403–25.

Malmejac, J. 1964. Activity of the adrenal medulla and its regulation. *Physiol. Rev.* 44:186–218.

Marazzi, A.S. 1957. The effects of certain drugs on cerebral synapses. *Ann. N.Y. Acad. Sci.* 66:496–507.

Miller, H.L., and Alliston, C.W. 1974. Plasma corticoids of Angus heifers in programmed circadian temperatures of 17–21°C. and 21–34°C. *J. Anim. Sci.* 38:819–22.

Pattison, M.L., Chen, C.L., Kelley, S.T., and Brandt, G.W. 1974. Luteinizing hormone and estradiol in peripheral blood of mares during the estrous cycle. *Biol. Reprod.* 11:245–50.

Plotka, E.D., Witherspoon, D.M., and Foley, C.W. 1972. Luteal function in the mare as reflected by progesterone concentrations in peripheral blood plasma. *Am. J. Vet. Res.* 33:917–20.

Reid, R.L. 1960. Studies on the carbohydrate metabolism of sheep. *Austral. J. Ag. Res.* 11:364–82, 530–38.

Schechter, R.D., Stabenfeldt, G.H., Gribble, D.H., and Ling, G.V. 1973. Treatment of Cushing's syndrome in the dog with an adrenocorticolytic agent (o,p' DDD). *J. Am. Vet. Med. Ass.* 162:629–39.

Selye, H. 1936. A syndrome produced by diverse noxious agents. *Nature* 138:32.

——. 1946. The general adaptation syndrome and diseases of adaptation. *J. Clin. Endocr. Metab.* 6:117–230.

——. 1971. *Hormones and Resistance*. Springer-Verlag, New York.

Stabenfeldt, G.H., Akins, E.L., Ewing, L.L., and Morrissette, M.J. 1969a. Peripheral plasma progesterone levels in pigs during the oestrous cycle. *J. Reprod. Fert.* 20:443–49.

Stabenfeldt, G.H., Ewing, L.L., and McDonald, L.E. 1969b. Peripheral plasma progesterone levels during the bovine estrous cycle. *J. Reprod. Fert.* 19:433–42.

Thomas, P.J. 1973. Review: Steroid hormones and their receptors. *J. Endocr.* 57:333–59.

von Euler, U.S. 1959. The physiological role of adrenalin and noradrenalin. Internat. Cong. Physiol. Sci. 21st, Buenos Aires, Symp. Spec. Lectures. Pp. 127–32.

West, G.B. 1955. The comparative pharmacology of the suprarenal medulla. *Q. Rev. Biol.* 30:116–37.

Yates, F.E., and Urquhart, J. 1962. Control of plasma concentrations of adrenocortical hormones. *Physiol. Rev.* 42:359–443.

The sex hormones

Bengtsson, L.P. 1973. Hormonal effects on human myometrial activity. *Vitam. Horm.* 31:257–303.

Berthold, A.A. 1849. Transplantation der Hoden. *Arch. Anat. Physiol. wiss Medicin* 16:42–46.

Blandau, R.J., and Boling, J.L. 1973. An experimental approach to the study of egg transport through the oviducts of mammals. In S.J. Segal, R. Crozier, P.A. Corfman, and P.G. Condliffe, eds., *The Regulation of Mammalian Reproduction*. Thomas, Springfield, Ill. Pp. 400–418.

Dickson, W.M., Bosc, M.J., and Locatelli, A. 1969. Effect of estrogen and progesterone on uterine blood flow of castrate sows. *Am. J. Physiol.* 217:1431–34.

Dunn, T.G., Hopwood, M.L., House, W.A., and Faulkner, L.C. 1972. Glucose metabolism and plasma progesterone and corticoids during the estrous cycle of ewes. *Am. J. Physiol.* 222:468–73.

Gaarenstroom, J.H., and deJongh, S.E. 1946. *A Contribution to the Knowledge of the Influences of Gonadotropic and Sex Hormones on the Gonads of Rats*. Elsevier, New York. P. 87.

Ginther, O.J., Mapletoft, R.J., Zimmerman, N., Meckley, P.E., and Nuti, L. 1974. Local increase in testosterone concentration in the testicular artery in rams. *J. Anim. Sci.* 38:835–37.

Grumbach, M.M., and Ducharme, J.R. 1960. The effects of androgens on fetal sexual development: Androgen-induced female pseudohermaphrodism. *Fert. Steril.* 11:157–80.

Hall, T.C., Ganong, W.F., Taft, E.B., and Aub, J.C. 1960. Endocrine control of deer antler growth. *Acta Endocr.* 35(suppl. 51):525–26.

Hendricks, D.M., Dickey, J.F., Hill, J.R., and Johnston, W.E. 1972a. Plasma estrogen and progesterone levels after mating and during late pregnancy and postpartum in cows. *Endocrinology* 90:1336–42.

Hendricks, D.M., Guthrie, H.D., and Handlin, D.L. 1972b. Plasma estrogen, progesterone, and luteinizing hormone levels during the estrous cycle in pigs. *Biol. Reprod.* 6:210–18.

Hisaw, F.L. 1959. Endocrine adaptations of the mammalian estrous cycle and gestation. In A. Gorbman, ed., *Comparative Endocrinology*. Wiley, New York. Pp. 533–52.

Hunter, J. 1792. *Observations on the Glands Situated between the Rectum and Bladder, Called Vesiculae Seminales*. Nicol, London.

Jost, A. 1961. *The Role of Fetal Hormones in Prenatal Development*. Harvey Lectures, Academic Press, New York. Pp. 201–26.

Jost, A., Vigier, B., Prepin, J., and Perchellet, J.P. 1973. Studies on sex differentiation in mammals. *Recent Prog. Horm. Res.* 29:1–41.

Lillie, F.R. 1916. The theory of the freemartin. *Science* (n.s.) 43:611–13.

Mann, T. 1956. Male sex hormone and its role in reproduction. *Recent Prog. Horm. Res.* 12:353–76.

McLaren, A. 1973. Blastocyst activation. In S.J. Segal, R. Crozier, P.A. Corfman, and P.G. Condliffe, eds., *The Regulation of Mammalian Reproduction.* Thomas, Springfield, Ill. Pp. 321–36.

Meinecke, C.F., and McDonald, L.E. 1961. The effects of exogenous testosterone on spermatogenesis of bulls. *Am. J. Vet. Res.* 22:209–16.

Mintz, B. 1972. Implantation: Initiation factor from mouse uterus. In K.S. Moghissi and E.S.E. Hafez, eds., *Biology of Mammalian Fertilization and Implantation.* Thomas, Springfield, Ill. Pp. 343–56.

Moore, N.W., Barrett, S., Brown, J.B., Schindler, I., Smith, M.A., and Smyth, B. 1969. Oestrogen and progesterone content of ovarian vein blood of the ewe during the oestrous cycle. *J. Endocr.* 44:55–62.

Moule, G.R., Braden, A.W.H., and Lamond, D.R. 1963. The significance of estrogens in pasture plants in relation to animal production. *Anim. Breeding Abstr.* 31:139–57.

Mueller, G.C., Vonderhaar, B., Kim, U.H., and LeMahieu, M. 1972. Estrogen action: An inroad to cell biology. *Recent Prog. Horm. Res.* 28:1–44.

Nett, T.M., Holtan, D.W., and Estergreen, V.L. 1973. Plasma estrogens in pregnant and postpartum mares. *J. Anim. Sci.* 37:962–70.

Psychoyos, A. 1973. Hormonal control of ovoimplantation. *Vitam. Horm.* 31:201–56.

Short, R.V. 1960. Steroids present in the follicular fluid of the mare. *J. Endocr.* 20:147–56.

Smith, O.W., Mongkonpunya, K., Hafs, H.D., Convey, E.M., and Oxender, W.D. 1973. Blood serum testosterone after sexual preparation or ejaculation or after injections of LH or prolactin in bulls. *J. Anim. Sci.* 37:979–84.

Stabenfeldt, G.H., Osburn, B.I., and Ewing, L.L. 1970. Peripheral plasma progesterone levels in the cow during pregnancy and parturition. *Am. J. Physiol.* 218:571–75.

Prostaglandins

Channing, C.P. 1973. The interrelationship of prostaglandins, cyclic 3′,5′ AMP, and ovarian function. *Res. Prostaglandins* 2(5):1–4.

Karim, S.M.M., and Hillier, K. 1973. Prostaglandins and the induction of labor. *Res. Prostaglandins* 2(6):1–2.

Lee, J.B. 1974. Prostaglandins and the renal antihypertensive and natriuretic endocrine function. *Recent Prog. Horm. Res.* 30:481–532.

McCracken, J.A., Baird, D.T., and Goding, J.R. 1971. Factors affecting the secretion of steroids from the transplanted ovary in the sheep. *Recent Prog. Horm. Res.* 27:537–82.

Pharriss, B.B., and Shaw, J.E. 1974. Prostaglandins in reproduction. *Ann. Rev. Physiol.* 36:331–60.

Thymus gland

Cole, R.K., and Furth, J. 1941. Experimental studies on the genetics of spontaneous leukemia in mice. *Cancer Res.* 1:957–65.

Comsa, J. 1965. Action of the purified thymus hormone in thymectomized guinea pigs. *Am. J. Med. Sci.* 250:79–85.

Goldstein, G. 1968. The thymus and neuromuscular function: A substance in thymus which causes myositis and neuromuscular block in guinea pigs. *Lancet* 2:119–23.

Good, R.A., and Gabrielsen, A.E. 1964. *The Thymus in Immunobiology.* Harper & Row, New York.

Levey, R.H. 1964. The thymus hormone. *Scien. Am.* 211:66–77.

Luckey, T.D. 1973. Perspective of thymic hormones. In Luckey, ed., *Thymic Hormones.* University Park Press, Baltimore. Pp. 275–314.

Luckey, T.D., Robey, W.G., and Campbell, B.J. 1973. LSH, a lymphocyte-stimulating hormone. In Luckey, ed., *Thymic Hormones.* University Park Press, Baltimore. Pp. 167–82.

Metcalf, D. 1965. Delayed effect of thymectomy in adult life on immunological competence. *Nature* 208:1336.

Miller, J.F.A.P. 1961. Immunological function of the thymus. *Lancet* 2(7205):748–49.

——. 1965. Effect of thymectomy in adult mice on immunological responsiveness. *Nature* 208:1337–38.

Potop, I., and Milcu, S.M. 1973. Biologic activity, isolation, and structure of thymic lipids and thymosterin. In T.D. Luckey, ed., *Thymic Hormones.* University Park Press, Baltimore. Pp. 205–71.

Rowntree, L.G., Clark, J.H., and Hanson, A.M. 1934. The biologic effects of thymus extract. *J. Am. Med. Ass.* 103:1425–30.

Selye, H. 1950. *The Physiology and Pathology of Exposure to Stress.* Acta, Montreal.

Trainin, N., Bejerano, A., Strahilevitch, M., Goldring, D., and Small, M. 1966. A thymic factor preventing wasting and influencing lymphopoiesis in mice. *Israel J. Med. Sci.* 2:549–59.

White, A., and Goldstein, A.L. 1968. Is the thymus an endocrine gland? Old problem, new data. *Perspec. Biol. Med.* 11:475–89.

CHAPTER 53

Female Reproductive Processes | by William Hansel and Kenneth McEntee

Physiology of reproduction is one of the most rapidly developing biological sciences and pressures for further rapid developments in the field remain great. On one hand, there is pressure to find socially acceptable ways of reducing the reproductive capacity of the world's exploding population; on the other hand, there is a great need to maintain reproductive performances in our domestic animals at maximum capacities to provide adequate nutrition for this population. These goals can be achieved only to the extent that detailed knowledge of all phases of reproduction is developed and applied in practical ways. For example, treatments for infertility based on incomplete knowledge are useless and at times can even be detrimental. New techniques in artificial insemination, semen freezing, and estrous cycle synchronization cannot be fully exploited until the basic principles on which they are based are completely and widely understood.

REPRODUCTIVE PHYSIOLOGY

Pituitary gonadotropins

Removal of the adenohypophysis before puberty causes the accessory reproductive organs to remain infantile. The interstitial tissue in the ovaries remains sparse, while ovarian follicles fail to ovulate and undergo atresia. Corpora lutea are not formed and estrous cycles do not occur. If hypophysectomy is performed in an adult female, the uterus and vagina involute; small vesicular follicles continue to differentiate but ovulation does not occur.

All these changes can be reversed by injections of crude aqueous extracts of anterior pituitary tissue. Such extracts contain three protein hormones involved in the regulation of ovarian functions. The first of these, follicle-stimulating hormone (FSH), causes ovarian follicles to grow and produce increased amounts of estrogenic hormones. The second, luteinizing hormone (LH), causes rupture of follicles and liberation of ova (ovulation) and initiates the formation of temporary endocrine organs (corpora lutea) in the ovaries. Relatively small amounts of LH may synergize with FSH to produce follicle growth and estrogens in normal animals (Fig. 53.1). The third hormone, prolactin, maintains the corpus luteum in hypophysectomized rats (Astwood 1941), but attempts to show that it is luteotropic in cattle, swine, goats, guinea pigs, and monkeys have been unsuccessful or unconvincing (Donaldson et al. 1965). However, prolactin may have a luteotropic function in the ewe (Denamur et al. 1973).

Highly purified preparations of FSH produce follicular growth but not ovulation in hypophysectomized animals. LH given alone has little effect on the ovaries unless the follicles have been developed to a proper degree by FSH

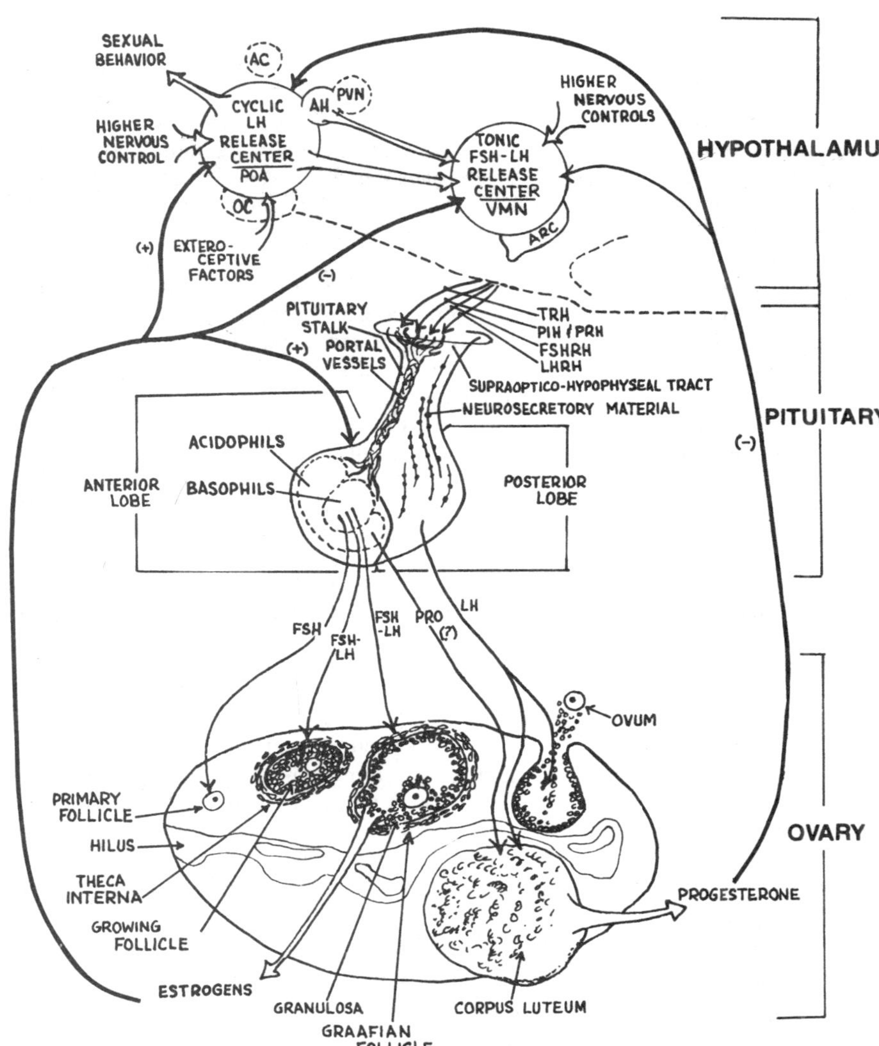

Figure 53.1. Interrelationships among the hypothalamus, anterior pituitary, and ovary in domestic animals. The diagram of the ovary represents successive stages in follicle development and corpus luteum formation as they occur during a normal estrous cycle. OC, optic chiasma; AC, anterior commissure; AH, anterior hypothalamus; ARC, arcuate nucleus; POA, preoptic area; PVN, paraventricular nucleus; VMN, ventromedial nucleus; FSH, follicle-stimulating hormone; LH, luteinizing hormone; PRO, prolactin; TRH, thyrotropin-releasing hormone; PIH, prolactin-inhibiting hormone; PRH, prolactin-releasing hormone; FSHRH, follicle-stimulating-hormone–releasing hormone; LHRH, luteinizing-hormone–releasing hormone.

stimulation. This synergism between FSH and LH in promoting follicle growth and ovulation has been demonstrated in numerous experiments carried out with rats and other laboratory animals (Simpson 1959). The addition of small amounts of LH to any given level of FSH almost invariably causes marked increases in follicular growth and ovarian weight. Levels of LH insufficient to cause ovulation and corpus luteum formation when given alone will do so when small amounts of FSH are added.

This synergism represents an important concept in reproductive physiology, and it appears to function in much the same way in the large domestic animals. The injection of pituitary hormone preparations devoid of LH activity into cattle causes the development of numerous small- and medium-sized follicles, but ovulation does not occur. In contrast, injection of pituitary preparations containing both FSH and LH causes ovulation and corpus luteum formation, and in some cases luteinization of large follicles (Malven and Hansel 1964).

The gonadotropins, as well as thyrotropin, are produced in the basophil cells in the medullary area of the adenohypophysis. The hormones appear to be contained in characteristic granules found in these cells. These granules stain an intense magenta color when reacted with periodic acid–Schiff reagent (PAS), and it is generally believed that the glycoprotein hormones (FSH and LH) contribute significantly to the staining reaction.

Purves and Griesbach (1954, 1957) described three types of basophils in rats and dogs and identified them as thyrotropin-, FSH-, and LH-secreting cells. Jubb and McEntee (1955) were able to identify only two basophil types in cattle pituitaries. The large basophils (β-cells) are clearly thyrotropin producers in this species, since they undergo marked vacuolation and degeneration following thyroidectomy. The small PAS-positive basophils (Δ-cells) often found closely apposed to blood sinusoids in the medullary portion are clearly gonadotropin producers, but it has not been possible to identify specific FSH- and LH-secreting cells. A remarkably rapid degranulation of these cells occurs at the beginning of estrus (Fig. 53.2). It begins in the medulla adjacent to the zona tuberalis and sweeps on a broad front through the whole pars distalis proper. The degranulation probably represents release of LH or of combined FSH and LH, since a large preovulatory LH peak occurs in the plasma during the first 6 hours of estrus (Fig. 53.3).

The granules begin to reaccumulate in the small basophils at approximately 3 days after ovulation, but pronounced changes do not occur until the last days of the luteal phase. At this time a rapid accumulation of PAS-positive material begins, and the process accelerates during the proestrual phase of follicular development.

The complete structures of ovine, bovine, and human LH have been determined (Liu et al. 1972) and the structure of human FSH has been described (Shome and Parlow 1974). Each consists of α- and β-subunits; the α-subunits are identical but the β-subunits differ and thus are responsible for the specific actions of the two hormones.

Ovarian hormones

The complex series of events occurring in a single estrous cycle cannot be fully appreciated without some understanding of the nature and effects of the ovarian hormones secreted in response to the gonadotropins. The major hormones of ovarian origin are steroids having either estrogenic or progestational effects. The estrogens, mainly 17β-estradiol and estrone, are produced by the theca interna and granulosa cells surrounding the growing follicles, and progesterone is produced by the corpora lutea (see Fig. 53.1). A third hormone, a nonsteroid called relaxin, may be produced by ovarian tissues, although its exact site of origin remains uncertain. It relaxes the pelvic ligaments, enlarging the birth canal at the time of parturition (see Chapter 52).

When the ovaries are removed, the animal is deprived of its source of germ cells as well as of the ovarian hormones, and a condition of permanent anestrus results. If ovariectomy is performed before puberty, the genitalia remain infantile; the oviducts, uterus, and vagina fail to develop as do the mammary glands, teats, and other secondary sex organs. The skeletal development and hair and fat distribution patterns characteristic of the female also fail to develop. If ovariectomy is performed after puberty, a regression of the genitalia occurs, the mammary glands involute, and menstruation ceases in primates.

The administration of estrogens to castrate animals reverses these changes, particularly those affecting the vagina and uterus. The vagina of the immature rat can also be made to open prematurely by estrogen administration. After ovariectomy, the vaginal epithelium of most species becomes thin and inactive. The administration of estrogen causes the cells in the vaginal wall to grow and divide; as the vaginal epithelium thickens under the influence of estrogens, the old epithelium is pushed

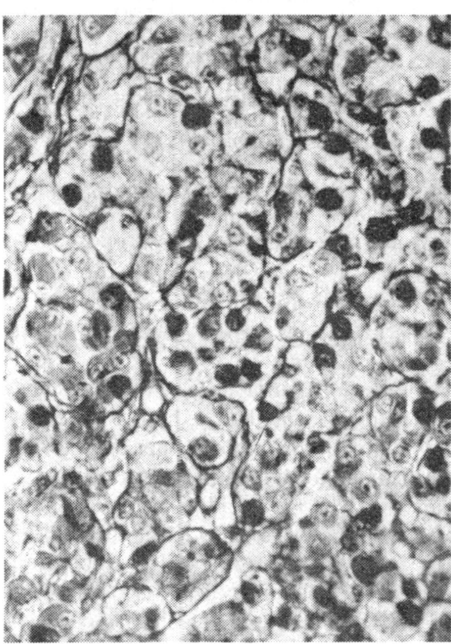

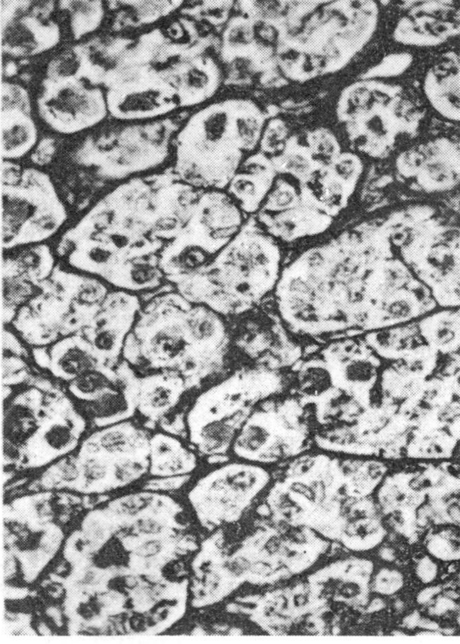

Figure 53.2. Heavily granulated small basophils in the adenohypophysis of a heifer during the nineteenth day of the estrous cycle (left); completely degranulated small basophils in the adenohypophysis of a heifer in estrus (right). PAS-Orange G. ×340. (From McEntee 1958, *Internat. J. Fert.* 3:120–28.)

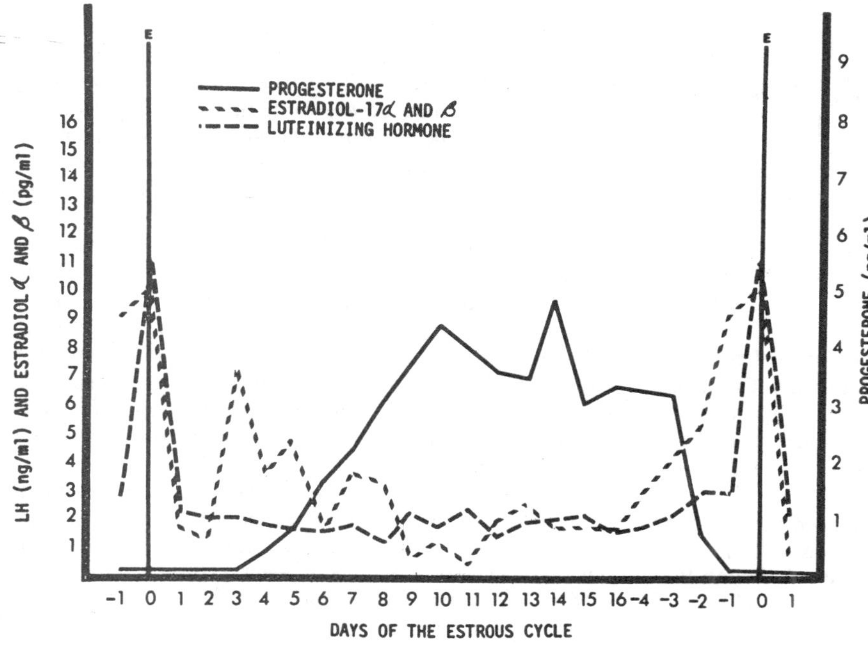

Figure 53.3. Peripheral plasma levels of progesterone, estradiol, estrone, and luteinizing hormone (LH) in Holstein cows. LH values are expressed in terms of NIH-LH-B-7 (1.16 × NIH-LH-S-1). (From Hansel and Echternkamp 1972, *Am. Zoologist* 12:225–43.)

toward the lumen, and the outer cells become granular and are finally keratinized and desquamated into the lumen of the vagina. As the effect of the injected estrogen wears off, the vagina passes into a metestrous stage, and then into the castrate condition.

These changes resemble those occurring in a normal estrous cycle in rodents and some other animals. Microscopic examination of vaginal smears from these animals enables the stage of the cycle to be ascertained with considerable accuracy. Typically, smears taken from the bitch during mid-proestrus, when follicle growth and estrogen production are maximal, contain many cornified epithelial cells with pyknotic nuclei, many erythrocytes, few leukocytes, and abundant debris (Gier 1960). Smears taken during mid-estrus contain many cornified epithelial cells and many erythrocytes; leukocytes are absent. After ovulation occurs, leukocytes invade the vaginal wall, and many of them, along with degenerated epithelial cells, appear in vaginal smears. The reappearance of leukocytes in the vaginal smear denotes the end of estrus. Estrus merges into metestrus, during which time estrogen levels are low and corpora lutea are forming. Vaginal smears taken during metestrus contain many leukocytes, many noncornified epithelial cells, and a few cornified epithelial cells. In anestrus the epithelial cells are noncornified and later give way to cornified cells in proestrus. Vaginal smears are also useful in estimating the stage of the cycle for rats, mice, guinea pigs, and sheep. Vaginal smears are of little use in determining the stage of the cycle in cattle, because the vaginal epithelium tends to undergo mucification rather than cornification. The mucification reaction is probably due to the combined action of estrogen and progesterone; it can be produced in castrate rats by injecting a combination of estrogen and progesterone. The clear, watery vaginal mucus characteristically seen in cattle at estrus is primarily due to the high level of estrogen at this time.

The uterus becomes atrophic and relatively inactive after ovariectomy; the endometrial glands involute, blood supply is diminished, and the myometrium loses tone. Estrogen administration, however, causes a remarkable increase in size and vascularity of the uterus. This reaction forms the basis of the most commonly used bioassays for estrogens. The increase in weight, which is linear over a wide dose range, is due to a great increase in the water content of the tissue and later to an enhanced protein synthesis. The vasodilator effects of estrogens probably account for their marked ability to cause water retention in the tissue; the endometrial glands increase in size and become filled with fluid. Estrogen-stimulated glands are relatively straight when viewed in cross section, and the convoluted glands characteristic of the fully developed endometrium are seen only after combined estrogen-progesterone treatments. The contractility of the myometrium is also increased by estrogen administration. Estrogens are mainly responsible, though, for regulating the rate of passage of ova through the oviduct.

Estrogens have many other physiological effects, and some of these occur to varying degrees in different species. Estrogens produce estrus in all species, however,

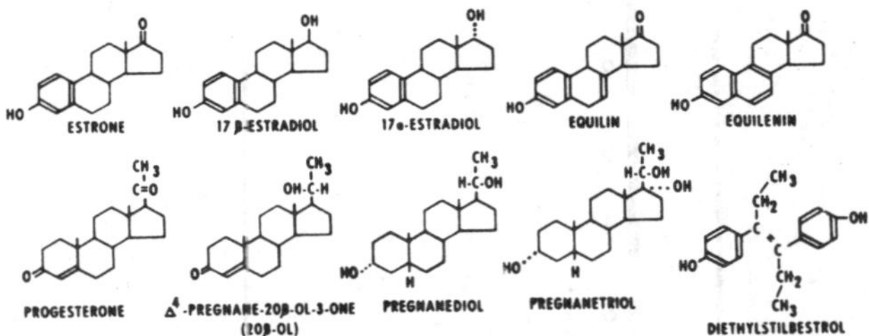

Figure 53.4. Major steroids found in domestic animals, and diethylstilbestrol, a nonsteroid synthetic estrogenic substance

although small amounts of progesterone may also play a role in the induction of estrus in some animals. Cattle are remarkably sensitive to estrogens; two daily injections of as little as 0.25 mg of the synthetic estrogen diethylstilbestrol (Fig. 53.4) will produce estrus in ovariectomized heifers weighing as much as 400 kg.

Estrogens are generally thought to hasten the ossification of the epiphyseal plates in the long bones of the skeleton and in this way limit skeletal growth. Although this explanation is often given for the smaller skeletal size of the female of most species, it is obviously only a partial explanation of a very complex phenomenon. Actually, estrogens stimulate bone growth in young ruminants and exhibit other anabolic effects. Lambs and steers fed diethylstilbestrol or receiving implants of the naturally occurring hormone estradiol have increased growth rates, increased nitrogen retention, and improved feed utilization. Carcasses from estrogen-treated lambs contain less fat, more protein and water, more bone, and more ash.

Estrogenic hormones control the development of all of the female secondary sex characteristics and play a major role in mammary gland development. They suppress the secondary sex characters when given to males of most species and cause atrophy of the genital tract and sterility. Spermatozoa production is inhibited by estrogen treatments in bulls, rams, boars, and most laboratory animals. Estrogens also play important roles in modifying production and release rates of hypophyseal gonadotropins.

Progesterone is the most important hormone of pregnancy. It plays important roles in preparing the uterus to receive the embryo and in maintaining pregnancy. It accomplishes the former by acting synergistically with estrogens to develop the extremely complex endometrial glands characteristic of the luteal phase of the cycle and early pregnancy. When viewed in cross section, fully developed endometria have a lacelike appearance.

Implantation of the fertilized ovum in the uterus cannot occur in the absence of progesterone. As long ago as 1908 Loeb performed a classical series of experiments providing clear-cut evidence for this function of the corpus luteum. He allowed guinea pigs to copulate with vasectomized males, and later, at about the time implantation would normally have occurred, inserted glass beads into the uteri. The beads simulated implanting blastocysts and induced the formation of overgrowths of uterine cells. These formations are called deciduomata and can be induced only when an actively secreting corpus luteum is present or when progesterone is supplied from some other source.

Progesterone is antagonistic to estrogens in two respects. It inhibits uterine motility and when given in relatively large amounts inhibits the manifestations of estrus and ovulation. In cattle, daily injections of 50–100 mg delay the occurrence of estrus and ovulation until 4–5 days after the last injection. However, it has also been shown that very small amounts of progesterone facilitate the induction of estrus in ovariectomized, estrogen-treated cattle.

Although progesterone appears necessary for the maintenance of pregnancy in all species, the corpus luteum can be removed in some species during pregnancy without causing abortion. The placenta appears to produce sufficient progesterone to maintain pregnancy. The roles played by estrogen and progesterone in mammary gland development are considered in Chapters 52 and 56.

The major estrogenic hormones found in biological fluids of cattle, sheep, and swine are 17β-estradiol, 17α-estradiol, and estrone. The urine of pregnant mares also contains equilin and equilenin (see Fig. 53.4) in relatively large amounts. These and other estrogens are isolated from pregnant mares' urine on a commercial basis. The amounts of estrogens in the blood and urine of cattle and sheep are very small, and radioimmunoassays capable of identifying and measuring changes in levels of these hormones during the estrous cycle, pregnancy, and various pathological states have been developed.

The major progestational hormones in cattle and sheep corpora lutea and blood are progesterone itself and its 20-hydroxy derivatives, 20β-hydroxypregn-4-ene-3-one (20β-ol) in cattle (see Fig. 53.4) and 20α-hydroxypregn-4-ene-3-one (20α-ol) in ewes.

All these compounds are relatively insoluble in water and soluble in organic solvents such as ethanol, ethyl ether, vegetable oils, and animal fats. They are not absorbed from the gastrointestinal tract to any appreciable extent and must be injected intramuscularly or subcutaneously for effective utilization. The naturally occurring ovarian hormones are often administered as micro- or macrocrystalline suspensions and in ester forms (propionate or benzoate) in order to prolong the period during which they are effective. Orally active progestational and estrogenic compounds of potential use have been developed. Several of the orally active progestogens have been used to synchronize the estrous cycles of cattle, sheep, and swine (Sierk 1965).

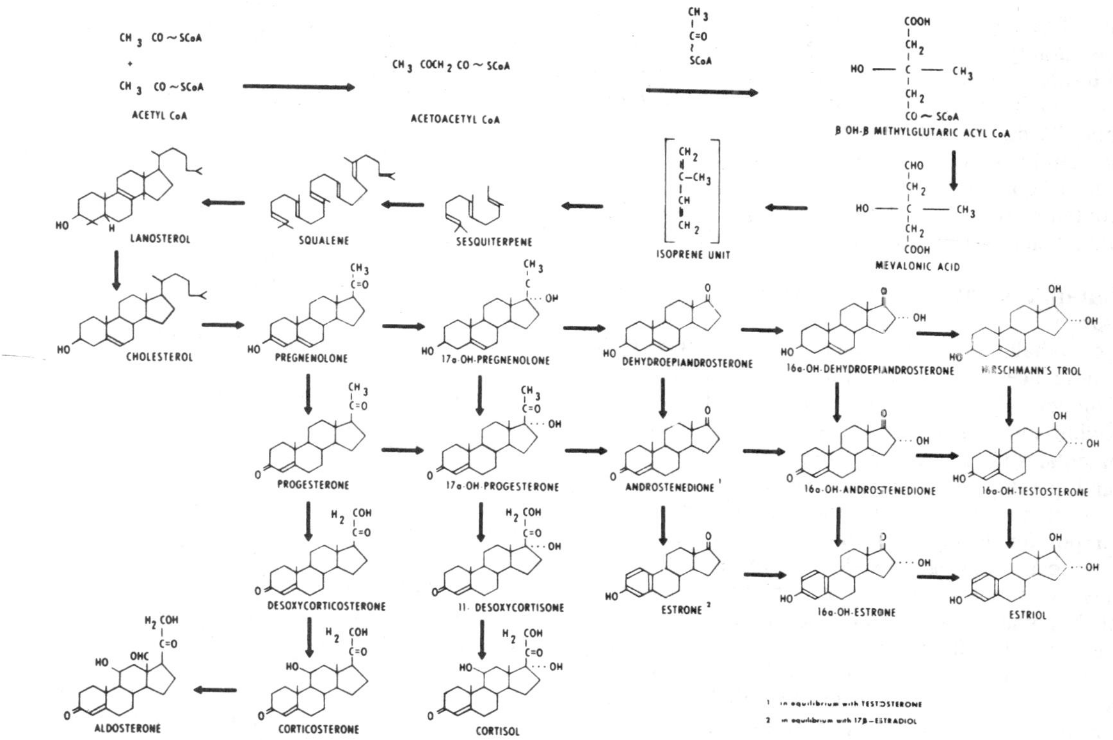

Figure 53.5. Biosynthetic pathways involved in production of the major steroid hormones from acetate. (Adapted from Diczfalusy 1964, *Fed. Proc.* 23:791–98; Villee 1961a, in Young, ed., *Sex and Internal Secretions*, vol. 1, Williams & Wilkins, Baltimore, 1961.)

The biosynthetic pathways by which the major steroid hormones are produced are shown in Figure 53.5. It is convenient to consider this process in three parts: (1) the synthesis of cholesterol from acetate, (2) the conversion of cholesterol to progesterone, and (3) the formation of estrogens, androgens, and corticoids from progesterone. The key position of progesterone in the entire process is obvious; this hormone is a common precursor of estrogens, androgens, and the adrenocorticoids. It should be emphasized at this point that none of the steroid hormones are produced exclusively by one gland. The corpus luteum is the major site of progesterone synthesis, but the adrenal cortices and placenta in some species also contribute to the total body pool of the hormone; the testes produce mainly testosterone, but stallion testes, for example, are a rich source of estrogens. And bovine adrenals and fetal cotyledons appear to produce estrone. Many of the enzyme systems involved in steroidogenesis appear to be common to several glands. The differences among steroid-secreting glands are thus more quantitative than qualitative. It is for this reason that abnormalities in steroid-secreting glands often result in the secretion of unusually large amounts of hormones most characteristic of other glands. Examples are the production of estrogens by Sertoli cell tumors in dog testes and the production of large amounts of androgen by certain adrenocortical tumors.

The liver plays a major role in the inactivation of steroids. Estrogen pellets implanted beneath the capsule of the spleen fail to produce the characteristic vaginal cornification in rats because the hormone absorbed into the blood is carried directly to the liver, where it undergoes reductive inactivation and conjugation with sulfate or glucuronic acid. The reductive processes involve reduction of ketone groups to hydroxyl groups and the hydrogenation of double bonds. The conjugations generally occur at carbon atom 3.

The bile appears to be an important pathway for estrogen excretion in all domestic animals. The urine contains lesser amounts. Estrone is the major urinary estrogen in the sow and its level reaches a peak near the onset of estrus; 17α-estradiol is the main urinary estrogen in the cow, although considerable amounts of estrone are also excreted. In primates progesterone is excreted as conjugates of pregnanediol or pregnanetriol (see Fig. 53.4), but these compounds do not appear in the urine of ruminants. The metabolic fate of the hormone in these animals is largely unknown. The 20-hydroxy compound (20β-ol) has less physiological activity than progesterone and occurs in appreciable amounts in bovine corpora lutea only during the latter part of the estrous cycle, when the gland is regressing, and during pregnancy. Sow and gilt urines contain pregnanediol, and pregnant mare's urine contains relatively large amounts of a 16α-hydroxylated steroid (allopregnane-3β,16α,20β-triol).

Hypothalamic control of gonadotropin secretion

The hypothalamus and higher nerve centers exert marked influences on the secretion of several hypophyseal hormones. The importance of these findings is that they provide some understanding of the way changes in environmental stimuli are converted into changes in the nature and quantity of pituitary hormones secreted.

In a sense, it is surprising to find that the nervous system is important in regulating the rates of gonadotropin secretion because the pars distalis, which produces these hormones, does not have any direct neural connections with the hypothalamus, except possibly the neural elements associated with blood vessels. Two large nerve tracts, the supraopticohypophyseal and the tuberohypophyseal, extend from nuclei in the hypothalamus to the posterior lobe (pars nervosa). It appears, then, that the hypothalamus must exert its influence over anterior pituitary hormone secretion through blood-borne factors carried by the portal vessels. These vessels transport venous blood from the hypothalamus to the pars distalis and are present in all domestic and laboratory animals studied. Cattle and sheep have secondary portal systems as well. (These features are presented in Figure 53.1.) Most evidence indicates that the sinusoidal bed of the epithelial tissue of the pars distalis is supplied solely by the hypophyseal portal vessels.

The return of ovarian functions after pituitary stalk sectioning in several species is very closely correlated with regeneration of the portal vascular system (Harris 1961). As an example, exposure of normal anestrous ferrets to additional illumination during winter months induces a precocious estrus, but estrus does not occur in response to additional artificial illumination in hypophysectomized or blinded animals. The response is also abolished if the pituitary stalk is sectioned and portal vessel regeneration prevented by placing plates of waxed paper between the cut ends of the stalk. Similar experiments demonstrating the essentiality of portal vessels for gonadotropin secretion have been carried out in rats, chicks, rabbits, dogs, and monkeys.

Sawyer et al. (1949) reported that the release of LH and consequently ovulation could be blocked in the rabbit by the administration of either atropine or the sympatholytic drug dibenamine immediately after coitus. Coitus normally activates LH release in the rabbit, and ovulation occurs about 11 hours later. Hansel and Trimberger (1951) were able to block ovulation in the cow by atropine injections given at the very beginning of estrus and found that the blockade was overcome when exogenous LH was administered along with the atropine. In the rat, another "spontaneously" ovulating species with estrous cycles 4–5 days in length, ovulation was blocked by the injection of atropine or dibenamine before 2 P.M. on the day of proestrus. Injection of either drug later than 4 P.M. was ineffective in blocking ovulation, presumably because LH release had already occurred (Everett et al. 1949). Later it was found that pentobarbital, phenobarbital, chlorpromazine, and several other drugs have similar ovulation-blocking properties in several species.

These experiments and many others have given rise to a concept of the mechanism of ovulation and corpus luteum formation having these basic features: (1) the production of one or more neurohumoral substances in hypothalamic nuclei or higher nerve centers, (2) the release of these substances into the hypophyseal portal system under the influence of various exteroceptive stimuli, and (3) the transport of these substances to the pars distalis, where gonadotropin release is effected (see Fig. 53.1).

The releasing factors appear to be peptides of relatively small molecular weight. The hypothalamus is also involved in a similar way in the release of adrenocorticotropic hormone (ACTH), thyrotropin or thyroid-stimulating hormone (TSH), and somatotropin or somatotropic hormone (STH). Thyrotropin-releasing hormone (TRH) and LH-releasing hormone (LHRH) have been isolated, identified, and synthesized. TRH is a tripeptide [L-(pyro)-Glu-L-His-L-Pro-(NH_2)] and LHRH is a decapeptide [(pyro)-Glu-His-Trp-Ser-Tyr-Gly-Leu-Arg-Pro-Gly-NH_2]. Exogenous TRH also causes prolactin release in several species, including the cow.

Numerous experiments involving the production of lesions and stimulation of various hypothalamic and CNS areas have led to the concept of dual hypothalamic control of pituitary gonadotropin secretion. An area within the ventromedial arcuate nuclear region is responsible for maintenance of a tonic secretion of gonadotropins sufficient to cause estrogen production at a low level. However, the preovulatory cyclic LH surge that is responsible for the very high plasma LH levels seen at the onset of estrus in the cow and other species (see Fig. 53.3) is controlled by the preoptic area of the hypothalamus. This properly timed cyclic LH release, which is necessary for ovulation, does not occur in the male, where only the tonic hypothalamic influence seems necessary to maintain testosterone secretion and spermatogenesis. Although most evidence suggests that intrinsic control of hypothalamic activation and the ovulatory discharge of LH resides in the medial preoptic area, the pathways by which information is conveyed to the ventromedial-arcuate area of the hypothalamus are less well defined (see Fig. 53.1). A direct pathway from the preoptic area to the arcuate nucleus may exist. There is also evidence that the final step in activation of the release of LHRH, and ultimately of LH, involves the release of a catecholamine, possibly dopamine, by the ventromedial-arcuate area.

Clearly many environmental stimuli act through the release-regulating system and hypophyseotropic area to influence pituitary gonadotropin secretion. Knowledge of the nature and effects of these exteroceptive stimuli in various species is increasing rapidly.

Classic examples of the operation of this mechanism are found in ferrets, as previously discussed, and in ducks. Increasing daily amounts of light causes increased secretion of gonadotropins and activation of the testes in young male ducks. The portal vessels of the duck can be destroyed without damage to a second blood supply to the anterior pituitary. Severing the portal vessels abolished the ability of the gonadotropin-dependent testes to respond to increasing light (Benoit and Assenmacher 1953). Illumination also activates the gonads of many other birds, including the junco, starling, and sparrow.

Results of numerous experiments attest to the fact that alterations of the light-dark ratio alter the estrous cycles of rats. Reversal of the rhythms of activity and estrous behavior occurs about 2 weeks after day-night lighting conditions have been reversed. There is also a clearly defined 24 hour rhythm in the LH release mechanism of rats. Rats subjected to continuous illumination develop persistent estrus and persistent follicles.

Most economically important breeds of sheep in the northern hemisphere are anestrous during the late spring and early summer. Decreased daily amounts of light initiate estrous cycles in the early fall. However, estrus can be induced in ewes and goats during the normally anestrous summer months by an artificial decrease in the amount of light each day.

The effects of light on reproduction in cattle are not so clearly established. Improved fertility has been reported in cattle subjected to additional hours of light under conditions of limited natural daylight. And several workers have noted a hastening of the onset of estrus in barren pony mares subjected to artificial light and a correlation between the initiation of ovarian activity and shedding of hair.

Olfactory stimuli, probably acting through the hypothalamus, appear to play an important role in gonadotropin release in mice and swine. Placing a strange male in the cage with bred females results in a block to pregnancy in mice. This results from a failure of implantation and a return to estrus due to inadequate secretion of luteotropin, resulting in turn in a failure of the corpora lutea to develop and produce adequate amounts of progesterone. Removal of the olfactory bulbs prevents this phenomenon (Bruce and Parrott 1960), as do injections of prolactin. Female mice under crowded conditions become anestrous, but a high percentage come into estrus on the third night after the introduction of a male into the cage under conditions in which physical contact is prevented. These effects are mediated by pheromones produced by the male and transmitted through the air to the female. In addition, surgical removal of the olfactory bulbs causes anestrus in gilts, and the onset of the breeding season in sheep and goats is hastened by the presence of the male.

Steroid and gonadotropic hormone interactions

The interactions of pituitary and gonadal hormones are complex. A given sex steroid may exert either a stimulatory or an inhibitory effect on gonadotropin secretion depending on dose, duration of treatment, age of the animal, and stage of the estrous cycle. Generally, large doses of steroids given for long periods are inhibitory, while small doses given at precise times can be stimulatory. For example, progesterone from ovarian or placental sources is generally considered responsible for the inhibition of ovulation that occurs during pregnancy and pseudopregnancy. Nevertheless, exogenous progesterone can either prevent estrus and ovulation or facilitate them, depending on the stage of the estrous cycle at which it is administered, the amount and duration of treatment, and whether or not a priming action of estrogen has occurred.

Results obtained with cattle illustrate this point. Daily subcutaneous injections of relatively large amounts (50–75 mg) of progesterone beginning at about mid-cycle inhibit estrus and ovulation until 3–4 days after withdrawal of the hormone; yet single injections of small amounts of progesterone (10–15 mg) given at the beginning of estrus hasten ovulation (Hansel and Trimberger 1952).

The inhibitory effects of prolonged treatment by either injected or orally effective progestational preparations have also been demonstrated in sheep, swine, guinea pigs, and rats under appropriate experimental conditions. The facilitating action of progesterone on ovulation has been demonstrated in women and in monkeys, rabbits, rats, and hens.

Recent studies emphasize the positive feedback effect of rising plasma estrogen levels on the preovulatory release of LH. This phenomenon has been clearly demonstrated in the cow and the ewe and in most other species in which appropriate studies have been made (Hansel and Echternkamp 1972). Hobson and Hansel (1972) showed that estradiol benzoate injections into cows ovariectomized at days 13–15 of the cycle, or into cows from which the corpora lutea were removed at days 13–15, uniformly caused the appearance of large plasma LH peaks 39–42 hours later. In contrast, the same doses of estrogen had no effect on plasma LH levels when given to intact animals at this stage of the cycle, while plasma progesterone levels were high. These and many similar results suggest that high plasma levels of progesterone prevent the stimulatory effect of estrogens on the preovulatory LH surge.

Plasma LH levels in the cow, ewe, sow, and bitch rise and become more variable after ovariectomy. When estradiol 17β is administered to ovariectomized cows, the large plasma LH peak elicited is usually preceded by a depression of plasma LH concentration lasting 3–10 hours. This initial depressing effect of estradiol on plasma LH appears to be exerted at the hypothalamic level. Some experiments, however (Hobson and Hansel 1974), suggest that at least a part of the LH-releasing effect of estrogen may be exerted at the pituitary level. These findings suggest that administration of estrogens to cattle at times when progesterone levels are low can result in premature or inadequate release of LH and cause development of cystic ovarian conditions. Indeed, cystic ovaries have been produced experimentally by this method as well as by the administration of antibovine LH serum at the onset of estrus.

PUBERTY

Puberty in the female is commonly considered as the time at which cyclic gonadal functions begin. It is brought about by the secretion of gradually increasing amounts of gonadotropins, particularly FSH, and by a concomitant increase in the ability of the ovaries to respond to the gonadotropins. The fact that first ovulation is not always accompanied by estrus suggests that a small amount of progesterone from a declining corpus luteum may normally play a part in the induction of estrous behavior, although it has been repeatedly demonstrated that ovulation and corpus luteum formation occur in prepuberal rats after estrogen injections alone.

Nutritional effects on age and weight at puberty

Age and weight at first estrus are so markedly influenced by factors such as breed and level of nutrition that average figures are of limited value unless some additional information is available. Age at first estrus in cattle is hastened by heavy feeding and delayed by underfeeding. It was found, for example, that first estrus occurred at an average age of 49.1 weeks in Holstein heifers reared at a medium feeding level consisting of 93 percent of the total digestible nutrients normally recommended for growing heifers. In contrast, heifers reared on 129 percent of the medium level came into estrus at 37.4 weeks of age, and those fed only 61 percent of the medium level did not show first estrus until 72 weeks of age. These data and the weights at which these heifers attained first estrus are shown in Figure 53.6. Comparable data are not available for other breeds, but Jerseys, Guernseys, and Ayrshires can be expected to reach puberty at earlier ages and lighter weights, while Brown Swiss mature more slowly. Weight at first estrus, especially in well-fed heifers, is likely to be rather variable. In Figure 53.6 the weights at first estrus of the heifers on the high level of feeding range from 180 to 424 kg.

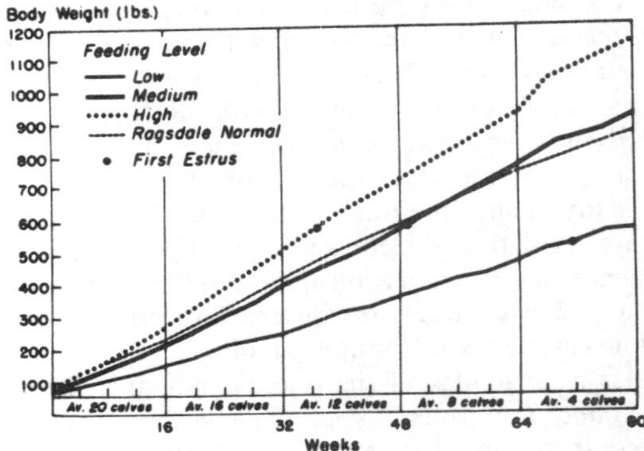

Figure 53.6. Growth rates, weights, and ages at first estrus for Holstein heifers fed at low, medium, and high planes of nutrition. A standard growth rate for heifers (Ragsdale normal) is included for comparison. (From Sorensen et al. 1959, *Cornell U. Ag. Exp. Sta. Bull.* 936.)

Lambs and kids born in the spring will come into estrus during the fall of the same year provided they are well fed. Ewes are usually bred to lamb at about 2 years of age.

The age at which puberty is attained in gilts is much less sensitive to changes in energy intake. In fact, most data indicate that gilts fed low-energy rations will reach puberty at about the same age as those fed high-energy rations, although extreme limitation of feed intake (40 percent of full feed) has been shown to delay puberty. Average ages at puberty range from 200 to 210 days for most breeds. The weights at first estrus are invariably greater in gilts on high planes of nutrition than in gilts on low planes. Average weights at first estrus range from 73 to 87 kg. Ovulation rates are increased by high levels of feed, but a higher percentage of embryo mortality usually follows.

Mares usually reach puberty during their second year, but detailed studies on the effects of nutrition, season, and climate such as those that have been carried out in cattle, sheep, and swine have not been made.

Great breed and individual differences exist in the age of puberty in dogs. Beagles and most breeds of a similar size show signs of estrus at 9–14 months of age, but large breeds may not attain estrus until 18 months. Cats reach puberty at about 7 months.

Other factors

One of the most intriguing new concepts in reproductive physiology suggests that events occurring in utero or at the time of birth can exert profound influences on reproductive performance at puberty and even in adult life. It has been clearly shown that single injections of relatively large amounts of testosterone propionate at birth result during later life in a condition of constant vaginal cornification, a failure of ovulation, and the absence of mating behavior in female rats. Smaller doses result in frequent mating or "constant estrus." Even lower doses cause the rats to be in constant estrus after having several normal estrous cycles. Estrogens and other steroids have similar effects.

It is thought that the hypothalamus undergoes a period of sexual differentiation, either shortly after birth in the case of animals such as the rat that are normally born in an immature state, or in utero in other animals. If this period of differentiation occurs in the presence of androgen, a male pattern of gonadotropin secretion emerges characterized by a steady or tonic release of amounts of LH too small to cause ovulation. In contrast, a cyclic pattern of LH release necessary for ovulation develops in the normal female (Villee 1961b).

The importance of these phenomena in domestic animals is unknown, but they may be related to the development of cystic ovarian conditions, such as nymphomania in cattle; altered growth rates, especially in species in which the male grows more rapidly than the female; and variations in the attainment of puberty.

SPECIES DIFFERENCES IN ESTROUS CYCLES

The changes occurring in the uterus, vagina, and ovaries during an estrous cycle are much the same in all animals, but the times and conditions under which they occur vary greatly from species to species. The basic mechanisms for follicle growth, ovulation, and corpus luteum formation are probably similar for most mammals; the striking differences that occur in the estrous cycles most likely reflect differences in the way in which exteroceptive stimuli are translated into hormone production and release. The rat, for example, ovulates spontaneously toward the end of estrous periods that recur at 4–5 day intervals. The rabbit is an induced ovulator and ovulates only 10–11 hours after copulation. Although these species seem most dissimilar, both have mechanisms for LH release that can be blocked by appropriate treatments at the proper time. The differences between the two may be mainly differences in the nature of the effective exteroceptive stimuli, and in the positive feedback of 20α-ol on LH release in the rabbit.

The rat and rabbit also differ in the mechanisms for corpus luteum maintenance. If the rat becomes pregnant, or if copulation is allowed with a vasectomized male, or if the cervix is stimulated electrically, the corpora lutea become functional. In the absence of pregnancy functional corpora lutea produce a period of pseudopregnancy lasting about 13 days. The rabbit does not require any stimulus after ovulation for corpus luteum function, and pseudopregnancy lasts 14–16 days.

All the large domestic animals except the Camelidae are spontaneous ovulators like the rat, but their corpora lutea function in the absence of any obvious additional stimulation as in the rabbit. Members of the camel family are induced ovulators. Plasma hormone levels during the estrous cycles of the cow, ewe, and sow have been described by Hansel and Echternkamp (1972) and Hansel et al. (1973).

Cow

The average estrous cycle in cattle lasts about 21 days (Table 53.1). It is slightly shorter in heifers than in mature cows, and cycles within the range of 18–24 days are usually considered normal.

The length of estrus is arbitrarily defined as the interval during which a cow will accept mounting by another cow or a bull. The average length of estrus for both dairy and beef cattle is 18 hours, and periods of 12–24 hours are usually considered normal. Heifers have slightly shorter periods than mature cows. The average length of estrus is as short as 12–13 hours in cows of European breeds in a subtropical climate (Branton et al. 1957).

Ovulation occurs 10–11 hours after the end of estrus in both beef and dairy breeds, and intervals of 5–15 hours are considered normal. Late ovulations do not appear to occur very frequently, and attempts to improve fertility in repeat breeder cows by ovulation-hastening treatments during estrus have met with little success.

Corpus luteum weights and progesterone contents increase rapidly between days 3 and 12 of the cycle and remain relatively constant until days 16–18 of the cycle, after which rapid regression occurs. The exact time of corpus luteum regression is individually variable. These changes are reflected in peripheral plasma progesterone levels (see Fig. 53.3). Levels are very low on days 1–3, rise rapidly between days 4 and 12, and then remain relatively constant until days 16–18; a rapid decline occurs 2–4 days prior to estrus.

Follicles appear to develop continuously during the bovine estrous cycle. One or more large follicles 7–12 mm in diameter are characteristically seen at midcycle, when plasma progesterone levels are high (Rajakoski 1960); but these follicles usually undergo atresia in the course of the normal cycle. The follicle destined for ovulation is less than 10 mm in diameter at the time of corpus luteum regression and expands to 16–20 mm during the ensuing four days. Approximately 70 percent of the follicles of any one size are atretic at any specific time in the cycle, and Marion and Gier (1971) have estimated that a cow must produce as many as 2000 oocytes in order for one to be normally ovulated after estrus. There are two distinct peaks in peripheral plasma estrogen levels, one reflecting the growth of the defini-

Table 53.1. Average reproductive cycles

Species	Length of estrous cycle (days)	Length of estrus	Time of ovulation	Time fertilized ova enter uterus (days)	Time implantation begins (days)	Type of placenta	Length of pregnancy (days)
Cow	21	18 hr	11 hr after end of estrus	4, postestrus	35, postestrus	Epitheliochorial	282
Ewe	17 (most breeds seasonally polyestrous)	29 hr	Near end of estrus	4, postestrus	15, postestrus	Syndesmochorial	148
Sow	21	45 hr	24–36 hr after beginning of estrus	3–4, postcoitus	10, postestrus	Epitheliochorial	115
Mare	21 (most seasonally polyestrous)	5.3 days	3d–6th day of estrus		56, postestrus	Epitheliochorial	335
Doe (goat)	20 (seasonally polyestrous)	40 hr	33 hr after beginning of estrus	4, postestrus	20, postestrus	Syndesmochorial	148
Bitch	In estrus at 4–8 mo intervals depending on breed	proestrus 9 days, estrus 7–9 days	2d–3d day of estrus	5–6, postcoitus	15, postcoitus	Endotheliochorial	63
Cat	Seasonally polyestrous —spring and fall (pseudopregnancy lasts 36)	4 days	Induced, 27 hr postcoitus	4, after ovulation	13, postcoitus	Endotheliochorial	63
Rabbit	Polyestrous (pseudopregnancy lasts 14–16)	No clearly defined period	Induced, 10.5 hr postcoitus	4, postcoitus	8, postcoitus	Hemoendothelial	32
Rat	4–5 (pseudopregnancy lasts 13)	14 hr	10 hr after beginning of estrus	4, postcoitus	6, postcoitus	Hemochorial	22
Rhesus monkey	Menstrual cycle 28	No clearly defined period	9th–20th day of menstrual cycle	4, postcoitus	9, postcoitus	Hemochorial	164
Guinea pig	16	8 hr	10 hr after beginning of estrus	4, postcoitus	7, postcoitus	Hemochorial	68

tive follicle late in the cycle and one reflecting follicle growth early in the cycle (see Fig. 53.3). The peak that occurs late in the cycle represents growth of the preovulatory follicle and provides the positive estrogen feedback for the preovulatory plasma LH peak. The early peak declines as the plasma progesterone level rises. In addition to the data shown in Fig. 53.3, there is some evidence for a series of smaller midcycle estrogen peaks occurring just before the onset of regression of the corpus luteum (Hansel et al. 1973). The preovulatory plasma LH peaks occur at the onset of estrus and usually last only 6–8 hours. Some workers have claimed that smaller midcycle peaks of plasma LH may also occur before regression of the corpus luteum. Unfortunately, few data are available concerning plasma FSH levels during the cycle. Akbar et al. (1974) found average serum FSH levels of 66 ng/ml during the follicular and luteal phases of the cycle and an average level of 78 ng/ml in estrous animals. There was a trend for FSH levels to be elevated on the day of estrus.

The corpora lutea persist throughout pregnancy and apparently produce progesterone until late in the gestation period. Indications are that the bovine placenta does not produce large amounts of progesterone and that the corpora lutea are probably essential throughout most of pregnancy. The average length of pregnancy is about 280 days; small differences due to breed, genotype of the sire and the dam, sex of the fetus, and season of the year occur.

The corpus luteum of pregnancy declines rapidly at parturition (McNutt 1924). The length of the average postpartum interval to first estrus is quite variable; estimates in dairy cattle range from 32 to 69 days. Endometritis and underfeeding clearly prolong the interval. However, the first ovulation occurs much earlier in young, well-fed animals than reports might indicate. A recent study found that 31 of 35 primiparous Holsteins had ovulated at least once by 30 days postpartum. Similar observations have been made in young, well-fed Hereford cows. Postmortem examinations indicate that the first ovulation, unaccompanied by estrus, may occur in some animals between 2 and 3 weeks following parturition and that the following cycle is often shortened. The latter result is probably due to a failure of the corpus luteum to produce a normal amount of progesterone. The postpartum interval may be somewhat longer in older cattle, and particularly in range cattle under suboptimal conditions. Most studies indicate that optimum fertility is obtained in dairy cattle bred artificially 50–60 days after calving. Subcutaneous administration of LHRH (100 μg) at day 14 postpartum results in LH release, ovulation, and corpus luteum formation (Britt et al. 1974).

Ewe and doe (goat)

British breeds of sheep are seasonally polyestrous; that is, cycles are normally initiated in early fall in nonpregnant animals. Merinos and Dorsets are exceptions in that they will breed during the spring and summer. Many factors, such as light-dark ratios, temperatures, nutritional status, and presence of the ram, influence the time of onset. The ovaries of anestrous ewes are not inactive, as might be supposed; relatively large follicles may be present and subdued cycles of ovarian activity have been reported. FSH is probably being secreted, but ovulatory surges of LH secretion do not occur. The first ovulation of the season, which usually occurs in late July or early August in the northern part of the United States, is often a silent one unaccompanied by the usual overt signs of estrus.

The duration of the cycle is 16–17 days in most breeds (see Table 53.1). Cycles shorter than 14 and longer than 19 days are usually considered abnormal. The length of estrus is generally considered to be 24–36 hours, but exact figures such as those cited for cattle are not available. The duration of estrus is reported to be shorter in young ewes than in old. Accurate data are also lacking on the time of ovulation in relation to the beginning or end of estrus; many reports indicate that it occurs at about the end of estrus. Whereas cattle usually have single ovulations, two and three ovulations often occur in ewes. The number of ova shed can be increased by "flushing," or placing ewes on a high plane of nutrition for a short time before breeding.

The pattern of plasma estrogen, progesterone, and LH levels in the ewe is similar to that in the cow. Large preovulatory plasma LH peaks occur between the fifth and twelfth hour of estrus. Peak levels of LH seem to be higher in the ewe (20–100 ng/ml) than in the cow (10–50 ng/ml). Progesterone levels are low during the first few days of the cycle, rise rapidly between days 3–11, and decline precipitously about day 14. Three peaks of plasma estrogens occur: one before the onset of estrus, presenting growth of the preovulatory follicle(s); one between the end of estrus and the onset of progesterone secretion by the developing corpora lutea; and the third during the luteal phase of the cycle.

Pregnancy lasts 144–152 days. Breed differences in the length of pregnancy exist; fine-wooled breeds such as Merino and Rambouillet have gestation lengths of 148–152 days, while the mutton breeds, such as Southdown, Hampshire, and Shropshire, have shorter periods of 144–148 days.

The corpora lutea are maintained during pregnancy, although the placenta of the ewe also produces progesterone then. As in the cow, the corpora lutea regress rapidly before parturition. The ovaries are usually inactive during the lactation period, so that cycles are not resumed until the following fall.

The cycle in the doe (goat) is similar to that of the ewe, in that she is seasonally polyestrous and the peak of activity occurs in the fall. However, the length of the cycle (19–20 days) is longer than in the ewe. The duration of estrus is 40 hours, and ovulation occurs 30–36 hours after the onset of estrus. The length of pregnancy varies from 146 to 153 days in different breeds.

Sow

The average length of estrous cycles in gilts and sows is about 21 days (see Table 53.1). Estrus normally lasts an average of 40–46 hours. With the advent of artificial breeding techniques for swine the difficulty of accurate diagnosis of estrus in the absence of the boar has become evident. Vulvar swelling and redness are useful criteria, but the most useful test is to determine if the sow will stand when heavy pressure is placed on the loins.

Some workers have observed breed differences in the length of estrus, but they appear to be slight. Ovulation occurs during the latter part of estrus; estimates of the exact time vary from 24–55 hours from the beginning of estrus. Gestation lengths range from 113–127 days for various breeds.

Plasma hormone levels during the porcine estrous cycle differ in several respects from those seen in the cow and ewe. Plasma progesterone levels rise earlier in the cycle (day 2) and are considerably higher at midcycle (20–30 ng/ml) than in the cow (4–6 ng/ml) or ewe (1–3 ng/ml). Plasma LH peaks occur during estrus as in the ewe and cow, but peak levels are lower (4–7 ng/ml) and concentrations remain elevated for a somewhat longer time. Preliminary data indicate that serum FSH levels are lowered on the day before estrus and elevated 2–3 days following estrus (Rayford et al. 1974). Plasma estrogen levels increase sharply about 48 hours before the preovulatory LH peak; midcycle estrogen peaks have not been reported.

Sows differ from the other domestic animals in that some of them undergo estrus a few days after giving birth. Although ovulation may occur in some sows during postpartum estrus, they rarely conceive when bred at this time. Estrus is normally inhibited during lactation, although some sows show estrus before the young are weaned. The average interval between the end of lactation and the onset of estrus is 7–9 days, but considerable individual variation exists.

Mare

The reproductive cycle of the mare is subject to the greatest variability of all the domestic animals. Some individual mares appear to be truly polyestrous; they can produce offspring at any time of the year. However, the great majority of the mare population is seasonally polyestrous. Although many mares in the northern hemisphere show behavioral estrus in February, March, and April, estrus during this time is often unaccompanied by ovulation, and conception rates in mares bred during the period are low. In the northern hemisphere the best conception rates usually occur in mares bred from May to July. The same trends occur in mares in the southern hemisphere for the corresponding seasons.

The mean length of the estrous cycle is 21 days (see Table 53.1), but the variation is great; approximately 60 percent of the cycle lengths fall between 17 and 24 days, but a considerable proportion of the cycles are long (29 days) or extremely short (10–16 days).

The duration of estrus is similarly variable. Most data indicate that the mean length of estrus is about 5.3 days and that about 60 percent of the periods are 4–6 days. Many periods, however, are 2–3 days or 7–9 days. Several reports indicate that long estrous periods (18 days or more) tend to occur in the early spring months, and that as the lengths of the periods decrease from May through July, the conception rates improve. The time of ovulation is also quite variable; mean times of about 4–5 days after the onset of estrus have been reported. Most mares go out of estrus 24–72 hours after ovulation.

Plasma progesterone concentrations are low during estrus and rise significantly about 24 hours after ovulation. The average life span of the corpus luteum is about 12 days, and plasma progesterone levels decline precipitously about 14 days after ovulation. Peak progesterone levels of 10–22 ng/ml have been reported (Stabenfeldt et al. 1972, Squires et al. 1974). Plasma LH levels appear to increase gradually during estrus and begin to decline shortly after ovulation.

Most mares experience a foal heat between 5 and 18 days after parturition. The commonly accepted practice of breeding mares on the ninth day after foaling does not appear to result in a high conception rate; initial conceptions are lower, the abortion rate is higher, and more cases of dystocia and stillbirths occur. The length of the foal heat is similar to the length of cyclic estrous periods.

The length of the estrous cycle and the duration of estrus in the jennet are similar to those in the mare.

Pregnancy in the mare averages 322–339 days depending on the breed, and its length is influenced by the same factors involved in the other species. The mare is unique among the domestic animals in that the corpus luteum of pregnancy is not maintained; it regresses between days 140 and 210 of pregnancy. Ovulations occur and new corpora lutea are formed between days 40 and 60 of pregnancy. These corpora lutea are formed under the influence of a placental gonadotropin (PMS), which also contributes to increased progesterone production by the original corpus luteum at this time.

Bitch

The average interval between the manifestations of estrus in the bitch is about 7 months, but considerable individual variation exists. Smaller breeds generally have shorter cycles (4 mo) and larger breeds longer cycles (8 mo). The intervals between estrus increase as animals grow older, and aged females may have extended periods of anestrus.

The bitch has a characteristically long period of proestrus lasting about 9 days, and an unusually long estrous period of about the same length. If pregnancy does not occur, a period of metestrus 80–90 days in length follows estrus. Proestrous bleeding usually occurs 2–4 days after the first swelling of the external genitalia and subsides during estrus.

Ovulation normally occurs during the first 3 days of estrus. Corpora lutea form after ovulation and reach maximal size (5–10 mm) by day 13 of metestrus. Regression begins by day 25 and continues slowly over an extended period. Many dogs show a chocolate-colored vaginal discharge after ovulation, and many exhibit slight mammary development about 50 days later, even though they are not pregnant.

As in other animals, plasma total estrogen concentrations rise to peak levels (50–60 pg/ml) just before the preovulatory plasma LH peak. Plasma LH levels remain elevated for about 24 hours and ovulation occurs 40–50 hours after the LH peak. Plasma progesterone concentrations rise immediately during the LH surge and reach very high levels (20–30 ng/ml) within about 10 days. Progesterone levels remain high until about day 25 and then decline slowly during the next 30 days.

Considerable individual variation exists in the rate at which the corpora lutea regress during metestrus, and this variation is reflected in the plasma progesterone levels during late metestrus. The overall pattern of progesterone secretion during metestrus is similar to that seen during pregnancy; the major difference is the very rapid decline in plasma progesterone levels in the pregnant bitch just before parturition. Symptoms of pseudopregnancy, including mammary gland development, fat deposition, and nesting between days 50 and 70, are sometimes seen during metestrus. The gestation period ranges from 58 to 65 days. The corpora lutea of pregnancy appear to regress more slowly than in other species, and this may be a factor in the prolonged postparturient uterine bleeding sometimes seen in bitches.

Data concerning the cycles of many other mammalian species have been compiled by Asdell (1964).

CYCLIC CHANGES IN REPRODUCTIVE ORGANS

Once the basic mechanisms of ovarian, pituitary, and hypothalamic functions are established, it becomes important to see how they interact.

The female reproductive organs consist of the ovaries, oviducts, uterus, cervix, vagina, and vulva. The anatomical features of the tracts of all animals have been described elsewhere (Roberts 1971), but a few general concepts should be re-emphasized. The cow and the mare usually shed only one ovum; sheep often shed 2–3, and swine have multiple ovulations (av., 14; range, 10–25). Each ruptured follicle usually releases one ovum, but polyovular follicles may contain double or multiple oocytes. Polyovular follicles are particularly numerous in the dog, monkey, and opossum. The right ovary functions more often than the left (in about 60 percent of the cycles) in the cow and the ewe, while the left ovary is slightly more active in the mare and the sow. At the time of ovulation the ova are picked up by the fimbriated (ovarian) end of the oviduct, and fertilization normally occurs in the ovarian third of the oviduct. Ova are rarely lost into the abdominal cavity, and fertilization seldom fails in normal animals. Fertilized ova have been recovered from the oviducts 3 days after breeding in high percentages of heifers, ewes, and sows studied.

After fertilization, the oviduct transports the dividing ovum to the uterus, a process usually requiring about 4 days in most species. The dog may be an exception, since ova can often be found in the oviducts on the fifth day after breeding.

The uterus must perform many complex functions in supplying nutrients and removing waste products from the developing fetus, particularly in the cow, where placentation does not occur until after the thirtieth day of pregnancy. Ruminant uteri are characterized by caruncles on the luminal surfaces of the uterine horns, which serve as sites of attachment for the fetal placenta. The uterus is attached to the abdominal wall by the broad ligament or mesometrium; it receives its blood mainly from the middle uterine arteries.

The uterine cornua merge into the relatively short body of the uterus and the cervix uteri in the cow and the ewe. The cervix consists of four rings of dense connective tissue covered by tall mucus-secreting epithelial cells. The opening of the cervix into the anterior vagina is called the os uteri.

The external urethral orifice opens into the ventral surface of the vulva at the junction with the vagina. A blind sac, the suburethral diverticulum, is found just anterior to this point. Gartner's ducts open into the vulva just lateral to the urethral orifice, and the ducts of the vestibular glands open into the vulva posterior and lateral to the urethral orifice. The clitoris, homologue of the male penis, is located in the ventral part of the vulva.

Follicle growth

The ovary of an immature domestic animal consists of a cortex of connective tissue stroma, in which primary follicles containing the primary oocytes surrounded by a single layer of epithelial cells are found, and a medulla containing connective tissue and numerous blood vessels and nerves. The surface of the ovary is covered by a layer of cells known as the germinal epithelium. There has been considerable debate as to whether the germinal epithelium can give rise to germ cells in the adult animal, but modern evidence indicates that such is not the case.

As the oocyte develops, the cells surrounding it proliferate and form several layers of granulosa cells. As the granulosa cells proliferate, the surrounding connective tissue differentiates into the theca. The theca develops into two layers, externa and interna. The early growth of the follicle apparently does not require gonadotropins since it occurs in hypophysectomized rabbits and guinea pigs. The granulosa cells secrete follicular fluid, which results in the formation of an antrum in the follicle. All subsequent stages of folliculogenesis are gonadotropin-dependent. The cells surrounding the oocyte, the cumulus oophorus, eventually become separated from the granulosa cells lining the cavity of the follicle. Both thecal and granulosa cells have steroidogenic capabilities, and granulosa cells have the specific ability to aromatize testosterone and convert it to estrogen.

The terms primordial, growing, and Graafian are often applied to follicles. A primordial follicle consists of an oocyte surrounded by flattened cuboidal epithelium. A growing follicle has two or more layers of epithelium, but has not developed an antrum and has no thecal layer. A Graafian follicle has an antrum and a thecal layer that differentiates into interna and externa. Maturation changes in the oocyte occur during the later stages of follicle growth (Fig. 53.7).

Follicle growth during the estrous cycle appears to be a continuous process, but rapid growth of the preovulatory follicle late in the cycle can be associated with the marked preovulatory rise in plasma estradiol concentration (see Fig. 53.3). Typical preovulatory swelling occurs between days 18 and 21 of the cycle. All layers of the follicle become thin, and the follicle swells beyond the surface of the ovary. In cattle, the follicle reaches a diameter of about 2 cm before ovulation, but follicular size at ovulation is quite variable in all domestic animals.

The follicular phase of the cycle in the ewe lasts 3–4 days and the luteal phase about 13 days. Waves of follicular growth that do not culminate in ovulation occur in anestrous ewes prior to initiation of regular cycles. Numerous follicles (10–25) mature in swine, but otherwise the general process is the same as in other animals. The average diameter of the follicles increases until day 18, reaching a maximum of approximately 9 mm. Two or three days before estrus the definitive follicles enlarge rapidly, the theca interna hypertrophies, and the cumulus oophorus partially dissolves, so that the ovum is nearly free in the follicular fluid.

Follicular changes in the mare are similar, but the follicles grow toward an ovulation fossa as they mature, and they rupture in this area. Follicle size at the beginning of estrus in the mare is quite variable (1–7 cm in di-

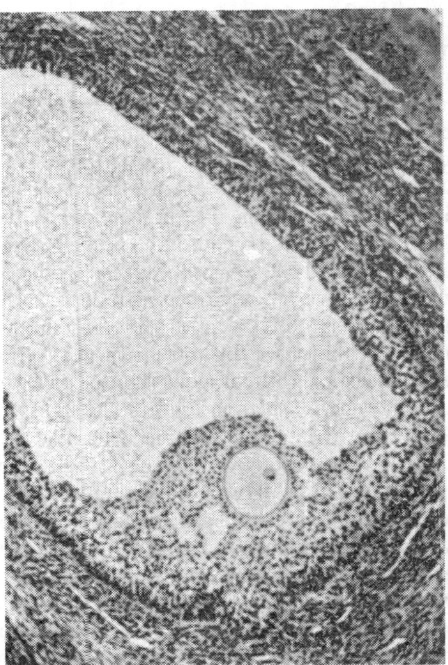

Figure 53.7. Bovine Graafian follicle. Note the oocyte, antrum, granulosa cells, and thecal layers. ×340.

ameter). As estrus advances, the size of the follicle increases, but ovulation may occur from follicles as small as 2 cm and as large as 8 cm.

Follicle growth occurs rapidly during proestrus in the bitch. A pronounced folding and luteinization of the granulosa are noted in the mature follicle, and these folds contain well-vascularized cones of invaginated theca interna. At the time of mating the ova are free-floating, or have only small connections to the follicle wall by the discus proligerus. In the dog the first polar body is not formed until after ovulation.

Obviously many of the oocytes present at birth will be destroyed before ovulation. This occurs through a process of follicular atresia both before and after puberty. It has been estimated that normal heifers have an average of 50,000 primordial follicles in their ovaries (Settergren 1964). Several times this number are present at birth, and the number declines with advancing age. Similar losses occur in all species. When vesicular follicles become atretic, the granulosa disintegrates, and the theca later regresses. Large numbers of atretic follicles are seen in the ovaries of calves up to 3 months of age. As the degenerative process develops, connective tissue elements invade the antrum and trap the oocyte. The degenerating ovum is characterized by hyalinization of the zona pellucida and cytoplasmic fragmentation. The exact cause of follicular atresia is unknown.

Ovulation and corpus luteum formation

Although ovulation occurs in all species in response to LH, little is known of the mechanism. The outer layers of the follicle rupture first, and the inner cells protrude through the opening to form a papilla, which ultimately breaks down and releases the follicular fluid and the ovum.

After ovulation in the cow, a small amount of blood escapes into the collapsed follicle. The granulosa folds inward as the follicle collapses, and thecal elements can be seen within each fold. Strands of connective tissue from the theca invade the developing corpus luteum. It is generally believed that these thecal cells eventually develop into fully functional luteal cells. Mitotic figures are numerous in developing bovine corpora lutea even as late as day 12 of the cycle. The corpus luteum increases in weight and progesterone content until day 16 and the first obvious signs of regression and a decrease of progesterone content occur on days 17 and 18 (see Fig. 53.3, 53.8).

The development of corpora lutea follows similar patterns in the mare, ewe, doe, and sow. The fact that the corpus luteum of the sow has a relatively high content of relaxin suggests that it may produce this hormone in addition to progesterone. Irregular columns of luteinized cells fill the follicular cavity of the dog by early metestrus. Regression begins in the nonpregnant bitch at about 25 days, but it proceeds at an unusually slow rate.

Development and regression of the corpus luteum

Recent research suggests that mechanisms for stimulating growth and progesterone secretion by the corpus luteum differ greatly among the domestic animals. Practically all available evidence suggests that LH, in addition to promoting ovulation, is the major hormone responsible for growth of the corpus luteum as well as progesterone secretion in the cow (Hansel and Seifart 1967). The most highly purified preparations of bovine LH currently available stimulate progesterone synthesis by bovine luteal tissues incubated in vitro. In vivo, daily injections of LH prolong the estrous cycle and overcome the inhibitory effects of concurrently injected oxytocin on the size and progesterone content of the gland. In contrast, prolactin injections fail to prolong the estrous cycle or overcome the inhibitory effects of oxytocin injections in cattle (Donaldson et al. 1965, Simmons and Hansel 1964).

In contrast to the cow, which apparently requires continuous or repeated releases of pituitary LH for maintenance of the corpus luteum, a single release of pituitary gonadotropin at the time of ovulation is capable of maintaining the corpora for an entire estrous cycle in the sow. Corpora develop and are maintained for approximately

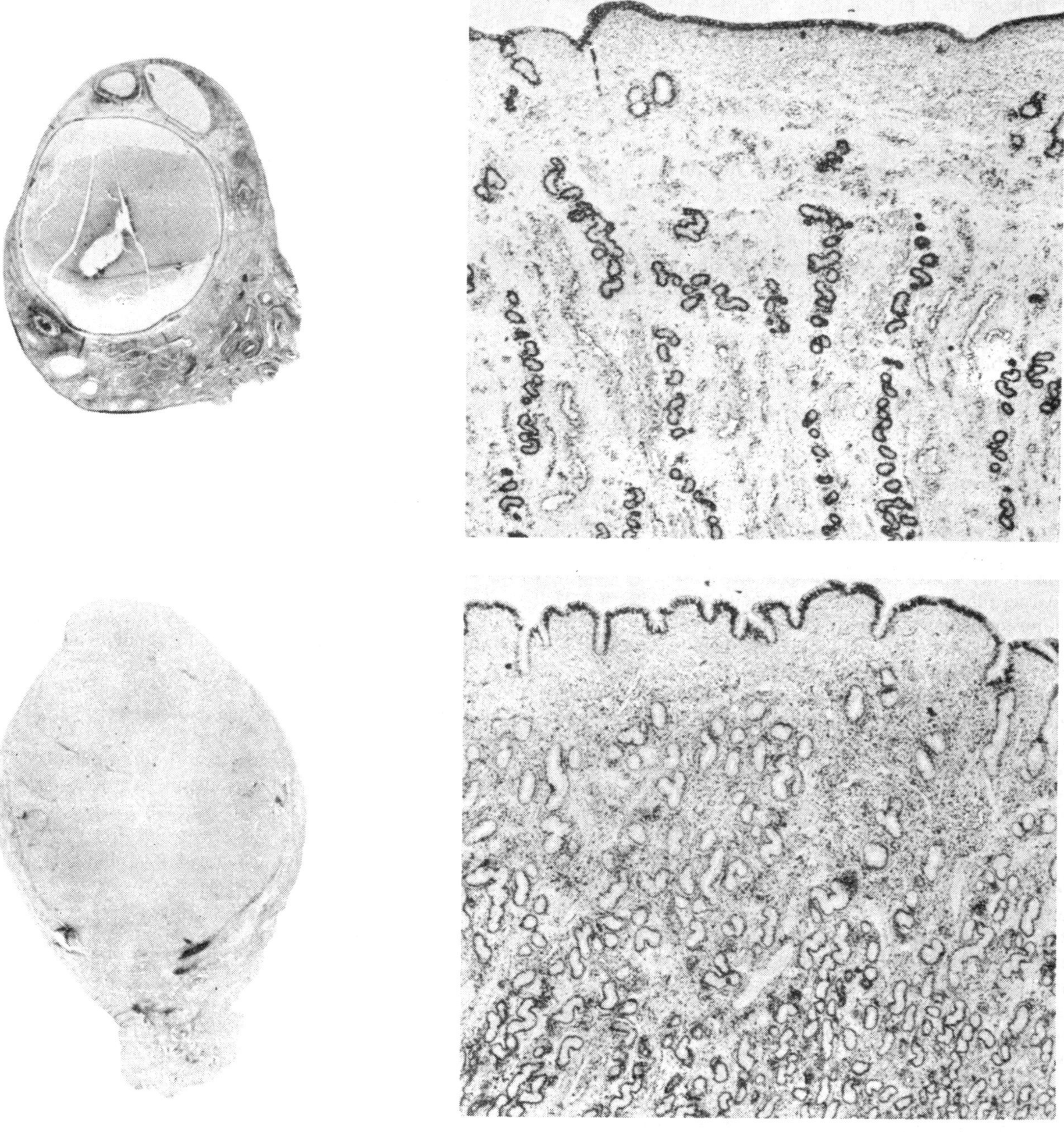

Figure 53.8. Cross section of the ovary (upper left) and endometrium (upper right) of a Holstein heifer at estrus. Note the large ovarian follicle and relatively straight endometrial glands. Cross section of the ovary (lower left) and endometrium (lower right) of a similar heifer at day 15 of the estrous cycle. Note the large corpus luteum and the highly developed endometrial glands. Ovaries ×2.6, endometria ×77.

one cycle length in sows hypophysectomized at the onset of estrus. Swine corpora lutea also differ from cattle corpora lutea in their response to exogenous estrogen; daily estradiol injections begun at day 11 of the cycle maintain swine corpora lutea beyond their normal life span, while similar injections cause luteal regression and decreased concentrations of progesterone in the luteal tissue of cattle. Estrogen appears to be luteotropic in the rabbit as well. Several studies indicate that LH plays an important role in maintaining corpus luteum function in the ewe, but Denamur et al. (1973) found that both LH and prolactin were required to maintain corpora lutea in hysterectomized, hypophysectomized ewes.

It is clear that the uterus plays an important role in regulating the function of the corpus luteum in many species. Corpora lutea are maintained in a functional state for long periods following hysterectomy of guinea pigs, rabbits, sheep, cattle, and swine. If small amounts of uterine tissue remain in situ, luteal regression occurs and cycles are resumed after variable periods. Following unilateral hysterectomies, corpora lutea adjacent to the excised uterine horn are usually better maintained than those adjacent to the remaining horn.

Conversely, uterine dilatation and irritation inhibit the normal development and function of the cyclic corpora lutea of cows and ewes. This mechanism may play a role in infertility under many practical conditions. Infusions of large numbers of nonspecific bacteria into the uterus and insemination of heifers with semen containing a virus cause luteal inhibition and induce precocious estrus (Kendrick 1964, Hansel and Wagner 1960).

These facts suggest that the uterus produces or participates in the production of some luteolytic substance, and several studies (see Hansel et al. 1973) suggest that this uterine luteolysin may be selectively transferred from the utero-ovarian vein to the closely adherent ovarian artery, and thus reach the ovary in much greater concentrations than found in peripheral blood (Ginther 1974).

Prostaglandin $F_2\alpha$ ($PGF_2\alpha$) administered into the uterus or intramuscularly in relatively large doses causes complete luteal regression in the cow and ewe. Infusions of $PGF_2\alpha$ into the utero-ovarian vein in ewes also causes rapid regression of the corpora lutea and a decline in plasma progesterone levels. These and other findings have led to the suggestion (Goding 1974) that $PGF_2\alpha$ is the uterine luteolysin in the ewe and that it is transmitted by way of a venoarterial pathway directly from the uterus to the corpus luteum, where it causes luteal regression.

Further evidence is needed before this concept can be accepted as a complete explanation of the mechanism of luteal regression in the cow (Shemesh and Hansel 1975). Nevertheless, administration of $PGF_2\alpha$ has proved useful in artificially regulating the bovine estrous cycle. Intrauterine doses of 5–6 mg or intramuscular doses of 25–30 mg cause a rapid decline in plasma progesterone levels and a return to estrus in 48–72 hours in a high proportion of treated animals. Conception rates of cattle bred at the artificially induced estrus appear to be equal to rates obtained in control animals. However, the treatment is ineffective in causing luteolysis when given during the first 5 days of the estrous cycle.

Tubular genitalia

The uterus of every domestic animal consists of a thin outer layer, the perimetrium, a thick myometrium composed of inner circular and outer longitudinal smooth muscle layers, and an inner layer, the endometrium. The changes occurring in the endometrium during the cycle are designed to prepare the uterus to receive the blastocyst and therefore play vital roles in successful reproduction.

The endometrial glands of cattle are branched, coiled, tubular structures lined with columnar epithelium. They open onto the endometrial surface, except in the caruncular areas. The glands are relatively straight at the time of estrus; they grow, secrete, and become more coiled and complex as the level of progesterone produced by the developing corpus luteum rises (see Fig. 53.8). They begin to regress at about the sixteenth day, when the first signs of luteal regression are also noted. The glandular epithelial cells reach their maximum height at about the eighth day of the cycle.

The endometrial surface epithelial cells are relatively tall during estrus; following a period of active secretion during estrus they become low and cuboidal at 2 days postestrus. As the cycle progresses they again grow, reaching a maximum height at days 9–12 of the cycle. The nuclei are notably elongated and basally situated during estrus.

As in all domestic animals, the stromal elements undergo vascular congestion and edema beginning several days before the onset of estrus. A second wave of vascular congestion occurs at days 8–10 of the cycle, but little or no extravasation occurs at this time. This increase in vascularity may be associated with the first wave of follicular growth and subsequent atresia described by Rajakoski (1960).

The spontaneous motility of the uterine musculature is greatest from 1 day proestrus to 1 day postestrus, while the levels of estrogen are highest. Motility declines until day 16, while progesterone levels are high, and then increases as estrus is approached. Frequent contractions of small amplitude characterize the estrogen-dominated portion of the cycle, and less frequent contractions of greater amplitude are present during the progestational phase.

During proestrus the superficial layer of epithelial cells on the cervix consists of wide goblet cells. Compressed nuclei are often seen between these cells. Active mucous secretion occurs during estrus, and the cells are tallest at this time; their nuclei are elongated with their long axes perpendicular to the basement membrane. The height of the cells decreases to low cuboidal at 8–11 days, at which time the nuclei are oval and basal; the cells no longer contain mucus and have a ragged appearance. The cervix is open during estrus, but rather tightly contracted at other times in the cycle.

A fern pattern formed by the bovine cervical mucus on drying is characteristic of estrus and other phases of the cycle in which estrogen levels are high. The fern pattern is associated with the high chloride content of the mucus found at estrus. The pattern does not occur on drying of mucus obtained at stages of the cycle when progesterone levels are high or during pregnancy. The phenomenon may have some value, when combined with other observations, for early pregnancy diagnosis. Estrous cervical mucus of the mare and the ewe also undergoes fern-pattern crystallization.

The cyclic uterine changes in the ewe are quite similar to those in the cow, except that the period of progestational influence is shorter. The surface epithelium of the sow's uterus is pseudostratified during estrus, but by day 7 of the cycle it changes to high columnar. By late diestrus (days 10–15) the surface epithelium reverts to a low-columnar type. The glandular changes and the changes in spontaneous motility of the uterine musculature appear to parallel those seen in the cow. The diameter of the uterine glands of the mare and the height of the glandular epithelium are greatest between day 3 of estrus and day 5 of interestrus, and least during the 6–7 days before the onset of estrus. The height of the surface epithelium is greatest during the latter stages of estrus and the first 5–8 days of interestrus; minimal height is seen at the days 10–15 of interestrus. The cervix of the mare undergoes secretory changes during estrus and proestrus similar to those described for the cow. In addition, it shifts posteriorly during estrus and becomes erectile, so that on palpation it changes from a state of complete relaxation with rather loose folds around the os uteri into a firmly constricted cone.

Cyclic changes in the canine uterus are basically the same as those described for other species. The vascular congestion during proestrus is particularly marked and results in the extravasation of erythrocytes from vessels in a hyperemic zone surrounding the uterine lumen. These erythrocytes migrate through the epithelium into the lumen and account for the proestrous bleeding. Endometrial glandular growth is extensive at the end of estrus and continues into metestrus. Glandular atrophy begins at about day 20 of metestrus and is complete by 80–90 days. The cervical canal increases in size during estrus and early metestrus but is virtually sealed by the end of metestrus.

Because of the complex functions they perform in sperm and ovum transport, the oviducts or Fallopian tubes have been studied in considerable detail. The ovarian or fimbriated portion has thin walls and the mucosa forms many projecting folds. In contrast, the uterine portion of the oviduct has a thick muscular wall and resembles a miniature uterus. The parts of the oviduct are: the isthmus, a constricted portion proximal to the tubouterine junction; the ampulla or middle section, comprising about half of the length of the tube; and a dilated ovarian portion, the infundibulum. The fimbrial processes on the infundibulum help transfer the ovum into the oviduct, and the isthmus also appears to play a major role in ovum transport.

The mucosa of the bovine oviduct is almost entirely covered by cilia, which play an important role in the transport of ova into the tube. These cilia, which beat toward the uterus, are longest (7–10 μ) during estrus and shorter (5–8 μ) during the remainder of the cycle. The epithelium of the mucosa at the fimbriated end of the oviduct is at maximal height at estrus and minimal height at 8–9 days. These cells undergo remarkable changes in which the nuclei are extruded into cytoplasmic projections, the maximal extrusion being at about 9 days.

The musculature of the oviduct, particularly in the isthmus, is remarkably responsive to estrogens and consequently is responsible for regulating the rate of passage of ova into the uterus. The oviduct produces relatively large amounts of fluid at the time of estrus and ovulation; surprisingly, the direction of flow of a large part of this fluid is toward the ovary. The isthmus blocks or partially blocks the flow of fluids into the uterus. Ligation of the fimbriated end of the tube at this time results in marked tubal distention in rabbits, ewes, and cattle. The blockage, which is primarily due to estrogen, disappears 72–84 hours after ovulation, and fluids enter the uterus.

The changes in the ciliated columnar cells of the oviduct of the ewe during the cycle differ from those reported for the cow. The greatest cell height and ciliary height are coincident with maximal luteal development and not with estrus, as in the cow. The cytoplasmic nuclear extrusions, however, appear to occur at the same time in the cycle (midcycle). The mucosa of the bitch oviduct becomes convoluted and thickened during proestrus and estrus. The ciliated epithelial cells of the mucosa are most numerous at the anterior end of the oviduct and appear to increase in height at estrus.

Differences also exist in vaginal changes during the cycles of the domestic animals. These differences probably reflect different secretion rates for estrogen and progesterone and ultimately for the gonadotropins.

The anterior vagina and cervix of the cow consist largely of mucous-secreting cells, and true cornification of these cells does not occur. These cells are mainly responsible for the flow of thin, watery mucus characteristic of proestrus and estrus. They become cuboidal by day 2, and by days 8–11 are vacuolated and degenerating.

Changes in the vaginal epithelium near the urethra are similar but occur slightly later. Small compact cells and many lymphocytes are seen in this area at proestrus. The cells increase in height until 2 days postestrus; subsequently they regress and become squamous by day 10, without undergoing true cornification. Vaginal smears are not useful in diagnosing the stage of the cycle or hormonal abnormalities.

In contrast, growth of the vaginal epithelium of the ewe is accelerated during estrus, and marked desquamation occurs in late estrus and early metestrus. The incidence of leukocytes is greatest during diestrus, when progesterone secretion is maximal. Corresponding changes are seen in vaginal smears. The mucus is thin and copious during estrus and contains few cells and no leukocytes. Smears taken one day later contain many nucleated epithelial and cornified cells. On the second day, smears consist almost entirely of squamous and cornified cells. Many leukocytes appear in smears taken at day 4 and throughout the diestrous period. Cellular debris and a few squamous cells characterize smears taken during late diestrus. Similar changes occur in the sow: the vaginal epithelium increases in height to a maximum at estrus and decreases to a low point at days 12–16. The superficial layers of vaginal epithelium slough away between days 4 and 12.

During diestrus and anestrus the vaginal epithelium of the mare is covered by a sticky, grayish secretion. As estrus approaches, the vascularity of the vaginal wall increases and the vaginal mucus becomes thinner. The changes in the vaginal smear of the dog parallel those in rodents. During proestrus the smear consists of increasing numbers of disintegrating cornified squamous epithelial cells with pyknotic nuclei, along with numerous erythrocytes resulting from uterine bleeding and an increasing amount of dense mucus. During estrus the mucus clears and the smear consists almost entirely of keratinized superficial squamous cells with distinct nuclei and intact cell membranes; erythrocyte numbers usually decrease. Leukocytes appear toward the end of estrus and during a 1–2 day period the keratinized superficial cells are almost entirely replaced by nonkeratinized cells. These changes are reflected in the vaginal epithelium; the height of epithelial activity during early estrus is followed by a reduction in the squamous epithelium and desquamation of epithelial cells.

FERTILIZATION AND OVUM TRANSPORT

The fimbria of the oviduct closely invest the ovary at the time of ovulation, when the ova are transferred to the infundibulum. Cilia on the mucosal surface of the oviduct probably play a role in the transfer, but the exact mechanism is poorly understood. The cilia uniformly beat toward the uterus, but the flow of fluid within the oviduct at this time is toward the abdominal ostium. The ova remain viable for about 12 hours in most domestic animals if they are not fertilized. Fertilization normally occurs in the ampullary portion of the oviduct. The dog, fox, and mare differ from the ewe, cow, and sow in that the eggs are released as primary oocytes and pass through maturation in the oviduct. In the latter species the first polar body has been abstricted, and the second maturation division has reached metaphase at the time of ovulation. The second division is not completed until fertilization occurs. The ovum (secondary oocyte) at this time consists of the nucleus surrounded by the vitellus, which is limited by the vitelline membrane and closely invested with a thick transparent membrane, the zona pellucida. The space between the zona pellucida and the vitellus is called the perivitelline space. The cumulus cells are rapidly lost and the egg is denuded following ovulation in domestic animals (Fig. 53.9).

Spermatozoa transport

Under normal conditions the spermatozoa reach the site of fertilization some hours before the ova. Their transport to the ampullary portion of the oviduct, where fertilization occurs, is very rapid in all species in which it has been studied. In the cow, for example, the first spermatozoa reach the ovarian portion of the oviduct within a few minutes after insemination. Transport in the ewe and the bitch is nearly as rapid. The mechanism by which this transport occurs is imperfectly understood, but it is obvious that the motility of the sperm cell itself is of little significance. The spermatozoa are rapidly mixed with the fluids in the cervix and uterine lumen, and contractions of the uterine and oviduct walls are probably the major factors involved in propelling the sperm toward the site of fertilization. The spermatozoa become progressively less concentrated as they ascend the tract, so that relatively few of the enormous numbers normally ejaculated reach the upper regions of the oviduct. Most data indicate that sperm retain their fertilizing capacity in the female tract for about 24 hours. The mare and the bitch are again exceptions; spermatozoa can survive for as long as 5 days in the mare's tract and as long as 90 hours in the bitch. Fertilization capacity may, however, be somewhat reduced by these times.

Capacitation

Spermatozoa must undergo some change after they are deposited in the female reproductive tract in order to acquire the ability to penetrate the zona pellucida and fertilize ova. This process is commonly referred to as capacitation. The initial demonstrations of this phenomenon showed that when spermatozoa were placed in the oviduct at or near the site of fertilization they did not penetrate the eggs immediately but only after several hours. The time required appears to be 5–6 hours in the rabbit

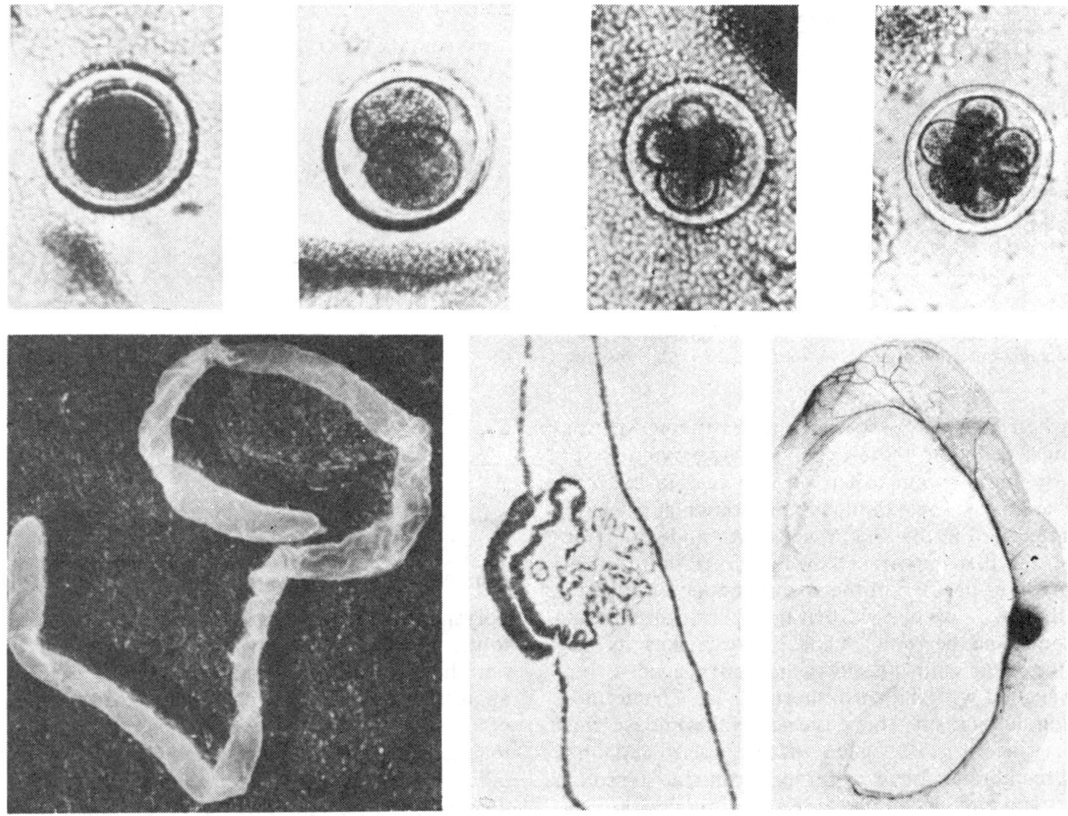

Figure 53.9. Development of cow embryo. *Top, left to right:* unfertilized ovum and 2-, 6-, and 8-cell embryos removed from oviduct at 2–3 days postestrus. Note the zona pellucida, vitellus, and vitelline membrane. Outside diameters range from 146 to 165 μ. *Bottom left:* 336 hr embryo, overall length 70 mm. *Bottom center:* section through the embryonic disc of the 336 hr embryo. Note beginning mesoderm formation. The embryo disc is 0.58 mm in diameter. *Bottom right:* 35 day embryo removed at the beginning of implantation. The embryo is 12 mm long; the entire vesicle (dilated) is 45 cm in length.

and 4 hours in the rat. Chang (1955) transferred spermatozoa into the uterus of incubator rabbits and later recovered them. He found that 6 hours of incubation were required for the spermatozoa to acquire fertilizing capacity.

Furthermore, some component of seminal plasma can reversibly inhibit the capacitated state. This decapacitation factor does not seem to be species-specific, since stallion, boar, bull, and monkey seminal plasma all decapacitate rabbit spermatozoa after its removal from the uterus (Williams et al. 1967). Spermatozoa become penetrating cells after capacitation, and it has been suggested that the presence of the decapacitation factors in the fluids of the male tract may serve to prevent the sperm from penetrating other cells and tissues of the male.

Capacitation confers on the sperm the ability to undergo a coordinated acrosome reaction involving intermittent fusion and breakdown of plasma and outer acrosome membranes (see Chapter 54) to form ports through which the acrosome enzymes, including a trypsin-like enzyme, acrosin, may escape. Acrosin allows the sperm to penetrate the substance of the zona pellucida. Thus destabilization of the outer acrosome membrane and the overlying plasma membrane appears to be an important step in capacitation (Bedford 1974).

Low doses of estradiol stimulate the capacitation process in spermatozoa within the uteri of ovariectomized rabbits (Soupart 1967). Bedford (1967) has shown that capacitation does not occur in spermatozoa placed in the progesterone-dominated uterus of the pseudopregnant rabbit.

There is as yet no *direct* evidence for the essentiality of capacitation of the semen of farm animals other than the ram. However, the sharp decline in the fertility of cows bred near the time of ovulation (Fig. 53.10) suggests that such a phenomenon is important.

Fertilization

The eggs of some mammals are surrounded by the cumulus oophorus at the time of ovulation and during

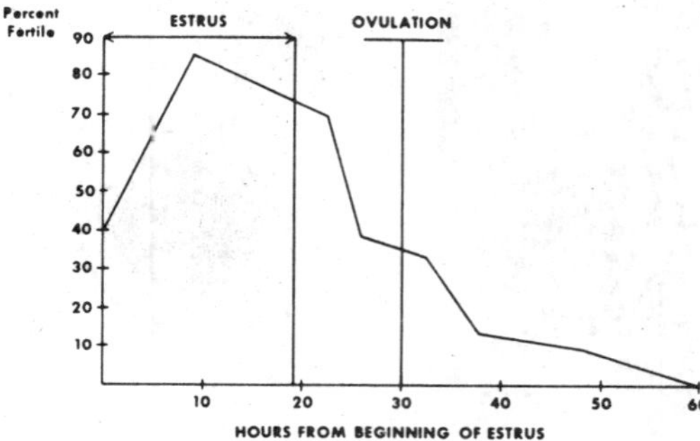

Figure 53.10. The effect of time of insemination on conception rate in cattle. (Adapted from Trimberger 1948, *Neb. Ag. Exp. Sta. Res. Bull.* 153.)

most of their fertile life so that the fertilizing spermatozoon must penetrate these cells. The dog ovum is surrounded by cumulus but this is not the case in the other domestic animals. The cumulus breaks down at ovulation or soon afterward in the cow, ewe, mare, and sow. Consequently, the first important step in fertilization in these species involves passage of the spermatozoon through the zona pellucida. It is believed that the sperm, after losing its acrosome and becoming capacitated, makes its way through the zona with the aid of an active agent or enzyme associated with the perforatorium (see Chapter 54). In addition to acrosin, the enzyme hyaluronidase may play a role since it is associated with the sperm and since the zonal membrane consists of a hyaluronic acid–protein complex. Having penetrated the zona pellucida, the sperm attaches itself to the vitellus and soon becomes absorbed within it. When the sperm becomes attached to the vitellus the second meiosis is resumed and the second polar body is extruded; the egg is "activated." Spermatozoon penetration of the dog ovum is accomplished before the first polar body is formed, and no further activity occurs until the second polar body is extruded.

Simultaneously with formation of the second polar body, the chromosomes in the ovum form the female pronucleus (Fig. 53.11). The sperm head begins to enlarge and is converted into the male pronucleus. The pronuclei, each containing several nucleoli, enlarge many times and move toward each other through the cytoplasm. The gamete membranes come in contact with each other and eventually fuse, incorporating sperm and egg nuclei into a single cell. This process, known as syngamy, signals the completion of fertilization. The two chromosome groups then move together and the first cleavage begins.

Several observations indicate that DNA concentrations increase in the pronuclei just before syngamy, and DNA duplication may occur at this time. Since DNA is the essential genetic material to be passed on to the embryo, this synthesis prior to syngamy is essential.

The ova of domestic animals are notably resistant to

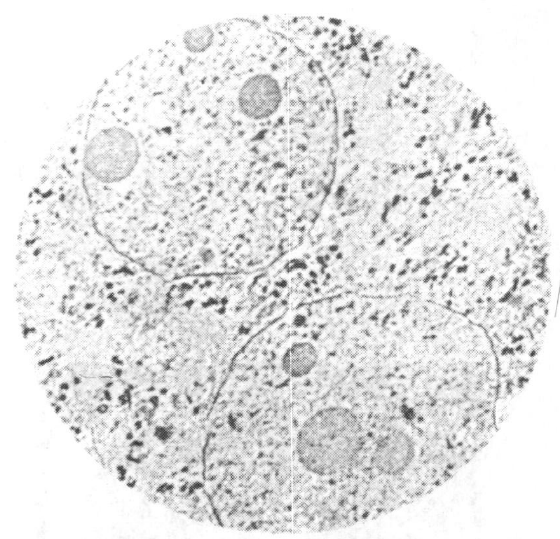

Figure 53.11. Electron micrograph of the pronuclei in a golden hamster egg. ×1100. (Reprinted with permission from Austin, in Hartman, ed., *Mechanisms Concerned with Conception*. Pergamon Press, Oxford, 1963.)

polyspermy; numerous sperm can be observed adhering to the outer surface of the zona pellucida of fertilized ova but they cannot penetrate the vitellus. This protection against polyspermy, which might well be lethal to the embryo, is due to a protective mechanism called the zona reaction. When the spermatozoon head attaches to the vitellus, some propagated change occurs in the zona that decreases its penetrability. The reaction may be due to the release of some substance from the vitellus that diffuses into the zona pellucida.

Embryo transport

Pronuclei are formed 11–39 hours after ovulation in the cow and the ewe. The first cleavage has usually occurred in an embryo recovered from the oviduct on the second day after estrus and insemination. On the third day 8–16 cells are commonly seen. Embryos of these species normally enter the uterus on the fourth postestrous day.

Embryos recovered from the oviduct of the sow 48 hours after insemination are usually in the 2- to 4-cell stage, and indications are that they enter the uterus at a slightly earlier time than the ova of the ewe and cow. Little is known of the rate of embryo transport in the mare; first cleavage has been reported to occur 24 hours after ovulation. Embryos of the bitch require a longer time to reach the uterus; they can usually be recovered from the oviducts on the fifth day after coitus.

Embryos pass quickly through the ovarian half of the oviduct and arrive at the junction of the ampulla and isthmus within a few hours. They remain at this halfway point during the next 48 hours and then gradually pass through the isthmus and enter the uterus about 72–80 hours postcoitus. This general pattern of transport appears to hold for the rabbit, ewe, and cow, and probably for many other species.

The rate of passage of embryos through the oviduct is under endocrine control. Ligation of the ovarian end of the oviduct results in fluid accumulation in and distention of the tubes until about 72–80 hours after estrus. At this time the fluids normally pass into the uterus, but they can be prevented from doing so by the administration of adequate daily amounts of estrogen beginning on the day of mating. Progesterone administration during the same period has not been found effective in hastening the time at which the fluids enter the uterus. The results suggest that the withdrawal of the estrogenic influence rather than the initiation of progestational influence is the major factor in releasing the tubal blockade to fluids and ova.

Rabbit ova can be retained at the ampullary-isthmic junction for as long as 6 days after ovulation by the administration of relatively large doses of estrogen, another suggestion that the mechanism controlling the retention of ova is estrogen-dominated. However, very small doses of estrogen may actually hasten the passage of ova and cause their rapid expulsion through the vagina. Normally, the level of estrogen declines after about 48 hours and the ova pass into the lower portions of the isthmus.

Early embryo development

After fertilization and the union of the paternal and maternal chromosomes, the embryo begins to develop by a special form of cell division called cleavage. The chromosomes become arranged on the first cleavage spindle and proceed through metaphase, anaphase, and telophase, after which the cytoplasm divides into two blastomeres. The second cleavage usually occurs first in the larger of the two blastomeres, resulting in the formation of a 4-cell embryo. The third, fourth, and fifth cleavage divisions result in 8-, 16-, and 32-cell embryos (see Fig. 53.9). The compact group of resulting cells is commonly referred to as a morula. The cleavage divisions actually reduce the total protoplasmic volume of the ovum, perhaps as a result of utilization of nutrients stored in the cytoplasm. Hamilton and Laing (1946) stated that the cytoplasmic volume of a one-cell cow ovum is reduced 22 percent by the time it becomes an 8-cell embryo.

Cavitation of the cell mass (blastocoele formation) results in formation of the early blastocyst. The blastocysts of all domestic animals soon fill with fluid, and cells differentiate into those from which the fetus will develop and those from which the fetal membranes will form. The formative cells, the inner cell mass, are surrounded by the trophoblast, or extraembryonic cells. Later, a layer of cells arising from the inner cell mass proliferates along the inner layer of the trophoblast, making up the endoderm (see Fig. 53.9). They become intercalated in the trophoblast and later form the embryonic disc. Greenstein and Foley (1958) described these early changes in the bovine embryo in considerable detail. The blastocyst stage is reached in the cow at about the eighth day; in the ewe, goat, and sow at about the sixth day.

In litter-bearing animals, complex adjustments resulting in proper spacing of the blastocysts occur after the embryos enter the uterus. These adjustments often involve intrauterine migration. Dziuk et al. (1964) studied the extent of intrauterine migration in swine by transferring genetically marked eggs to each uterine horn. Migration of one or more eggs from one horn to the other occurred in all of the pregnant animals studied.

Eventually the embryos undergo implantation, a process involving the development of a placenta and the establishment of firm contact with the endometrium. Before this time the nutritive requirements of the embryo are supplied by the yolk material and the uterine and tubal secretions; afterward the placenta performs this function. Implantation occurs at a remarkably late date in the cow (about 35 days) and the mare (about 56 days). It occurs at about 15–18 days in the ewe and at about 10–12 days in the sow. The first implantation sites are visible in the bitch at 15 days postcoitus. Developing embryos are referred to as fetuses after the major tissues, organs, and systems are formed.

Early embryo mortality

A relatively high proportion of fertilized ova perish early in embryonic life. This seems to occur in all species of domestic animals in which the problem has been studied, and it even occurs when all known diseases are eliminated and when management and nutritional factors are carefully controlled. These facts are illustrated by the experiment of Bearden et al. (1956), who studied the problem in 110 virgin Holstein heifers that were free of all known reproductive diseases and bred artificially to bulls of high or low fertility, as determined by their performance in a large artificial breeding stud. Ninety-seven percent of the ova recovered from heifers 3 days after insemination to bulls of high fertility were fertilized and appeared normal when examined microscopically. Only 86 percent of the heifers bred to these same bulls had normal embryos 30 days after insemination. A much lower percentage of fertilized ova (77) was recovered from heifers bred to bulls of low fertility, and only 58 percent of the heifers bred to these bulls had embryos at 30 days. The difference in embryo mortality attributable to the low-fertility bulls fell short of statistical significance, but other work suggests that such a difference may in fact exist.

Earlier studies (Tanabe and Casida 1949, Laing 1949) carried out with repeat-breeder cattle showed that embryo mortality rates may reach 36–43 percent in these animals.

Studies with swine indicate that 20–40 percent of embryos may die, with the greatest wastage during early stages of gestation. Embryonic losses of approximately 30 percent have been estimated to occur by the twenty-fifth day after breeding in ewes. Similarly high rates occur in rats, guinea pigs, mice, and ferrets (Ayalon 1964).

HORMONAL CONTROL OF GESTATION AND PARTURITION

During gestation a new individual develops from the blastocyst within the uterus, and the uterus is called upon to perform many complex functions. It must supply the growing embryo with nutrients and oxygen and remove the excretory products. As pregnancy progresses, the uterus must enlarge to permit the growth of the fetus, and at the same time the musculature must remain quiescent enough to prevent premature expulsion of the fetus. At the time of parturition the uterine musculature must expel the fetus. In addition, the mammary glands must be developed and induced to secrete milk for the postpartum nutrition of the young. It has often been said that it is not remarkable that a few pregnancies fail; the remarkable thing is that so many of them succeed.

Uterine accommodation

In addition to spacing the blastocysts so that each will have a maximal opportunity of survival, the uterus must accommodate the growing products of conception. It does so in two ways: by growing and by stretching. Two factors, hormonal influences and distension, promote uterine growth during gestation (Reynolds 1955). The amount of uterine growth is small when litter size is small, and larger when litter size is larger. The size of the uterus, in turn, is an important factor in determining the extent to which it can be stretched. The interaction of these factors plays an important role in determining the length of gestation and the maturity of offspring at birth.

Within a species, the smaller the number in a litter, the larger the individuals and the more mature they are at birth. The converse is also true. Nutritional and genetic factors also influence the size of the fetus at birth. A marked maternal influence on birth weights is evident. The weights of fetuses born to dams of small breeds and sires of large breeds are likely to be smaller than the mean of the weights of fetuses for the two breeds.

Placenta as endocrine organ

Since the placenta assumes major importance as an endocrine organ during pregnancy in most species, it is necessary to consider a few of the major differences in placental development among the domestic animals (for more detail see Wislocki and Padykula 1961, Harvey 1959).

The chorioallantoic placentas of mammals are usually arranged schematically in ascending order according to the successive disappearance of tissue layers intervening between maternal and fetal bloodstreams. This scheme is generally considered to have evolutionary significance; in the more primitive species more barriers are interposed between the two circulatory systems, and these successively disappear so that the placental barrier becomes more permeable in species higher in the evolutionary scale. Six tissue layers separate maternal and fetal blood in the most primitive placentas: (1) the uterine vascular endothelium, (2) the uterine stroma, (3) the uterine epithelium, (4) the fetal trophoblast (allantochorionic epithelium), (5) the fetal stroma, and (6) the fetal capillary endothelium. This type of placenta, called the *epitheliochorial,* is found in the cow, mare, and sow (see Table 53.1). Using electron microscopy, Björkman (1964) found that the cow placenta should be classified epitheliochorial. In the sow the allantochorion remains external to the endometrium and is apposed to it in a simple way; no erosion is involved. The corrugated surfaces of the chorion and uterine mucosa interdigitate. The gross form of the placenta is diffuse and the endometrial relationship nondeciduate. The placenta of the mare is also of epitheliochorial type and diffuse. It is further characterized by a unique endometrial development, the endometrial cups, which are formed in a semicircular area of the uterus between the sixth and twentieth weeks of gestation. Secretions from the endometrial cups accumulate and cause pouches to form in the allantochorion.

In the ewe and doe (goat) the uterine epithelium disappears in restricted areas due to the invasive action of the trophoblast. Thus five tissue layers separate fetal and maternal blood in these species, and this type of placenta is called *syndesmochorial*. However, the fetal-maternal structures in the cow, ewe, and doe are more properly designated as placentomes. The allantochorionic trophoblast forms villi in these areas which later invade the caruncle, of which the cow has 80–120 arranged in regular rows. The arterioles supplying the caruncles are remarkably coiled.

In the next type of placenta, the *endotheliochorial,* the maternal connective tissue is lost and the allantochorionic epithelium is in apposition to the endothelium of the maternal vessels. This placenta is characteristic of the dog, cat, and other carnivores. The gross form of the placenta is zonary or discoid. In the dog and cat, invasion of the uterine mucosa by allantochorionic villi is restricted to a band in the middle of the implantation site. In this region primary villi of the chorion penetrate deeply into the uterine mucosa, in which all but the capillary endothelium disappears. Hematocysts formed by the extravasation of maternal blood at the border of the placenta are characteristic features of the dog placenta.

The *hemochorial* type of placenta found in primates

results from the additional loss of maternal endothelium. It is the most advanced evolutionary type, and transmission across it is presumably most rapid and complete.

A further concept of paramount importance in considering the endocrine role of the placenta is that as gestation advances and the placenta ages, it becomes progressively more permeable to hormones and other compounds.

The placentas of many species become endocrine organs during pregnancy and secrete estrogens, progesterone, and gonadotropic hormones. The evidence that the placenta produces estrogens hinges on three major points: (1) estrogen can be extracted from placental tissue, (2) estrogen excretion increases in the urine of pregnant women and mares until the end of pregnancy and then disappears, and (3) the infant and foal excrete estrogen in the first few days of life, indicating that estrogen has entered their blood from the placenta. In addition, the urinary excretion of estrogens is not abolished by ovariectomy of pregnant mares or women.

There is also considerable evidence that the placenta produces progesterone. Pregnanediol, one of the metabolic products of progesterone metabolism in primates, is present in the urine of pregnant women whose ovaries have been removed. And typical progestational effects, such as endometrial proliferation and mammary gland growth, can be demonstrated in pregnant animals from which the ovaries, and in some cases the fetuses, have been removed (Courrier 1945).

There is also considerable evidence that the placenta produces gonadotropins. In fact, fragments of human placenta have been shown to elaborate gonadotropins when grown in tissue cultures in vitro.

The fetal trophoblast, composed of cells lining the chorionic villi, is believed to be the source of placental hormones in all species. Thus the chorionic gonadotropins provide the basis for most of the tests for pregnancy currently in use. In these tests extracts of urine are injected into immature rats or rabbits, and if pregnancy has occurred, the ovaries will be activated by the gonadotropin from the urine.

The placental gonadotropins fall into two classes. The first type has relatively more FSH activity than LH activity, and is found in the serum of pregnant mares (PMS). The second type has mainly LH activity and is found in the blood and urine of women during early pregnancy. It originates from the chorion and hence is called human chorionic gonadotropin (HCG).

Both PMS and HCG are secreted in large amounts relatively early in pregnancy and consequently have been widely used as sources of gonadotropins. The maximum concentration of PMS occurs at day 70 of gestation, after which it declines rapidly. Amounts of HCG sufficient to give positive pregnancy tests appear in human urine within the first 30 days of pregnancy. The presence of gonadotropin in pregnant mare serum is the basis for a widely used pregnancy test for mares. Clinically, PMS is used mainly in situations where stimulation of follicular growth is desired and HCG in cases where ovulation failure appears to be involved.

Ovarian and pituitary hormones

The ovary, pituitary, and placenta play major roles in the hormonal regulation of pregnancy. The ovary and anterior pituitary are of major importance in preparing the uterus for pregnancy. The placental hormones exert their major effects at varying times during pregnancy depending on the species.

The role of the ovary in promoting endometrial development and early maintenance of pregnancy has already been considered. The corpus luteum persists throughout pregnancy in all domestic animals except the mare. Its decline at the end of pregnancy usually signals the onset of parturition. Even though the corpus luteum normally persists in most species, it may be removed from some animals at certain stages of pregnancy without causing abortion. Ovariectomy in the mare after day 200 of pregnancy and in the ewe after day 55 is not followed by abortion. Corpus luteum removal in cattle between days 92 and 236 is followed by abortion (McDonald et al. 1953). Similar results have been obtained with goats in which the corpus was removed at between 100 and 125 days of pregnancy, and in the bitch ovariectomized before day 56. The ovaries of primates may be removed early in pregnancy (40–60 days) without causing abortion or fetal resorption.

The third ovarian hormone, relaxin, assumes major importance during pregnancy. Relaxation of the pelvic ligaments, which serves to enlarge the birth canal, occurs at or slightly before parturition. This effect is especially pronounced in the guinea pig but occurs to some extent in all animals, and it is attributed to relaxin (see Chapter 52). Unlike the other ovarian hormones, relaxin is water-soluble. It may be extracted from corpora lutea, whole ovaries, placental tissues, and the blood serum of pregnant rabbits. The ovaries of the pregnant sow are a particularly rich source. It also appears at times in the blood and tissues of cattle, sheep, dogs, rats, rabbits, and women. Despite some earlier controversy, it is now generally agreed that relaxin is a distinct hormone, and it has been partially characterized.

The adenohypophysis certainly plays a dominant role in the early maintenance of pregnancy by virtue of its effects on ovarian hormone secretion rates, but its role in the later stages is less clearly established. Hypophysectomy prior to mid-pregnancy is followed by fetal resorption in rats, mice, and guinea pigs, but removal at later stages is not followed by abortion. On the other hand, hypophysectomy at any time causes abortion in the dog and the rabbit.

In some species the corpus luteum regresses quickly after hypophysectomy, while in others, including the sow and the guinea pig, it appears to be maintained for about the length of a normal estrous cycle before regressing. Ewes hypophysectomized after day 44 of gestation did not abort, but goats hypophysectomized at the same period did (Cowie et al. 1963).

Development of accurate methods of monitoring fetal and maternal plasma, urine, and tissue levels of glucocorticoids, progesterone, estrogens, ACTH, prolactin, and LH has greatly increased our knowledge of the hormonal control of pregnancy and parturition in the domestic animals.

In the cow the level of total progestins (progesterone plus 20β-ol) in the corpus luteum increases during the estrous cycle until it reaches a maximum of approximately 250–300 μg at day 16, after which it declines rapidly unless pregnancy intervenes. Total luteal progesterone declines slowly in the pregnant animal from the 16 day maximum to about 125 μg at day 125. After this time it rises gradually to about 180 μg at day 240. The minimal amount of progesterone in the luteal tissue necessary to maintain pregnancy to day 15 and to prevent a return to estrus is about 100 μg, and corpora lutea of normal cows contain approximately three times this amount. The metabolite 20β-ol appears in the bovine corpus luteum in measurable quantities after day 15 of the estrous cycle and is present throughout pregnancy. Replacement studies (Tanabe 1970) indicate that the progesterone requirement for maintenance of pregnancy after enucleation of the corpus luteum declines from about 1.75 mg/kg body weight at day 30 to about 0.3 mg/kg body weight at day 190.

Peripheral plasma levels of progesterone average 4–5 ng/ml between days 140 and 200 of pregnancy, then increase to about 7 ng/ml by day 250; thereafter levels decline to about 4 ng/ml at about 10 days before parturition. It appears that the cow is dependent to some degree on ovarian progesterone during a large part of the gestation period.

In contrast, concentration of both urinary and peripheral plasma estrogens rises rapidly during the last 35–40 days of pregnancy in the cow. For example, plasma estrone levels remain below 0.1 ng/ml between days 140 and 245, then increase gradually to 1–5 ng/ml during the last week of gestation. Prolactin levels tend to decline during pregnancy in lactating cows, but diurnal and seasonal effects cause greater changes in basal levels. Levels of about one guinea pig unit (GPU) per ml of relaxin have been found in the blood of cows during the first month of pregnancy (Wada and Yuhara 1955). This level rises gradually to about 4 GPU at 6 months and remains at this level until parturition.

In the doe, the pattern of progesterone secretion during pregnancy is quite similar to that seen in the cow, and like the cow's, the doe's placenta seems to produce little progesterone. Plasma estrogen levels rise (400–1300 pg/ml) as early as 25 days before parturition, and as in the cow increase until the time of parturition. The 17α-estradiol is the major estrogen in goat plasma.

In the ewe, ovarian venous blood contains a maximum level of progesterone (2 μg/ml) at the fourteenth day of the estrous cycle. In the pregnant ewe it remains high (1–2 μg/ml) until the eighteenth week of pregnancy and then declines rapidly (Edgar and Ronaldson 1958). Peripheral blood levels, however, rise from about 4 ng/ml at day 80 to 10–15 ng/ml prior to parturition (Bedford et al. 1972). These facts suggest that some nonovarian source of progesterone may be responsible for the maintenance of pregnancy in ewes ovariectomized after day 55. Significantly, the placenta of the ewe has been reported to contain appreciable amounts of progesterone.

In marked contrast to the situation in the cow and doe, the ewe's peripheral plasma estrogen levels remain at low basal levels (approximately 20 pg/ml of unconjugated 17β-estradiol) until about 24 hours before parturition, and then increase sharply (Thorburn et al. 1972). Quantitatively, estrone is the major estrogen in ewe plasma, and 17β-estradiol is the main isomer.

In the sow, the total progesterone content of luteal tissue declines slowly from an average of 246 μg at day 14 of pregnancy to 115 μg at day 110, just before parturition. Similarly, ovarian venous plasma progesterone levels decline slowly from a mean value of 2.8 μg/ml at day 14 to 1.4 μg/ml at day 110 (Masuda et al. 1967). Peripheral plasma levels remain relatively high (8–12 ng/ml) until about 15 days before parturition. Thus the sow seems to resemble the cow and doe in that the ovary continues to provide a major amount of progesterone until near the time of parturition. Peripheral plasma estrogen levels in the sow rise steadily during the last 6 days of pregnancy, reaching levels as high as 2300 pg/ml of estrone and 75 pg/ml of 17β-estradiol. Numerous studies suggest that this abrupt rise is the result of estrogen production by the placenta.

In the mare, peripheral plasma progesterone levels tend to decrease slowly between days 7 and 19, and then rise between days 32 and 44, apparently even prior to formation of the secondary corpora lutea of pregnancy (Squires et al. 1974). This rise corresponds with the first appearance of PMS in the serum. Progesterone levels appear to increase between days 32 and 90 and decline during days 150–180. There is considerable evidence that the mare placenta produces progesterone after day 150. Plasma estrogens (estrone, equilin, equilenin, and estradiol) rise steadily from days 80–210 of gestation and then decline gradually until parturition (Nett et al. 1973).

In the pregnant bitch, the pattern and absolute levels of

plasma progesterone concentrations are remarkably similar to those seen in the nonpregnant bitch during the first 65 days after ovulation. However, the progesterone levels in the pregnant bitch would be somewhat higher if corrections were made for the apparent hemodilution that occurs during the last half of pregnancy. Peripheral plasma total estrogen levels in the pregnant bitch are maintained at about 15 pg/ml during the first 25 days, and then rise to about 22 pg/ml by day 35. Concentrations are maintained at this level until parturition. Peripheral plasma estrogen concentrations are considerably higher in the pregnant than in the nonpregnant bitch between days 30 and 65 after ovulation.

Parturition

Parturition is an obviously complex phenomenon that cannot be satisfactorily explained by existing knowledge. Aside from hormonal influences, the degree of distension of the uterus per se is a critical factor in its initiation. Among litter-bearing animals at the end of pregnancy a very constant relationship exists between the size of the uterus and the size of its contents, despite variations in litter size and the size of individuals within a litter. The amount of distension is about equal for animals with small and large litters at the termination of pregnancy. In addition, a period of uterine ischemia occurs at the end of pregnancy, when the fetus is gaining weight at its greatest rate.

A remarkable series of hormonal changes occurs in all of the domestic animals prior to and during parturition. Changes occurring in peripheral plasma hormone levels in the cow are shown in Fig. 53.12. Progesterone begins to decline 24–48 hours before parturition. Estrogen levels continue to rise until a few hours before delivery, then decline rapidly. Prolactin levels peak just before delivery, while LH levels remain consistently low (Hoffmann et al. 1973). All workers agree that corticoid levels rise as progesterone levels fall during the 48 hours preceding

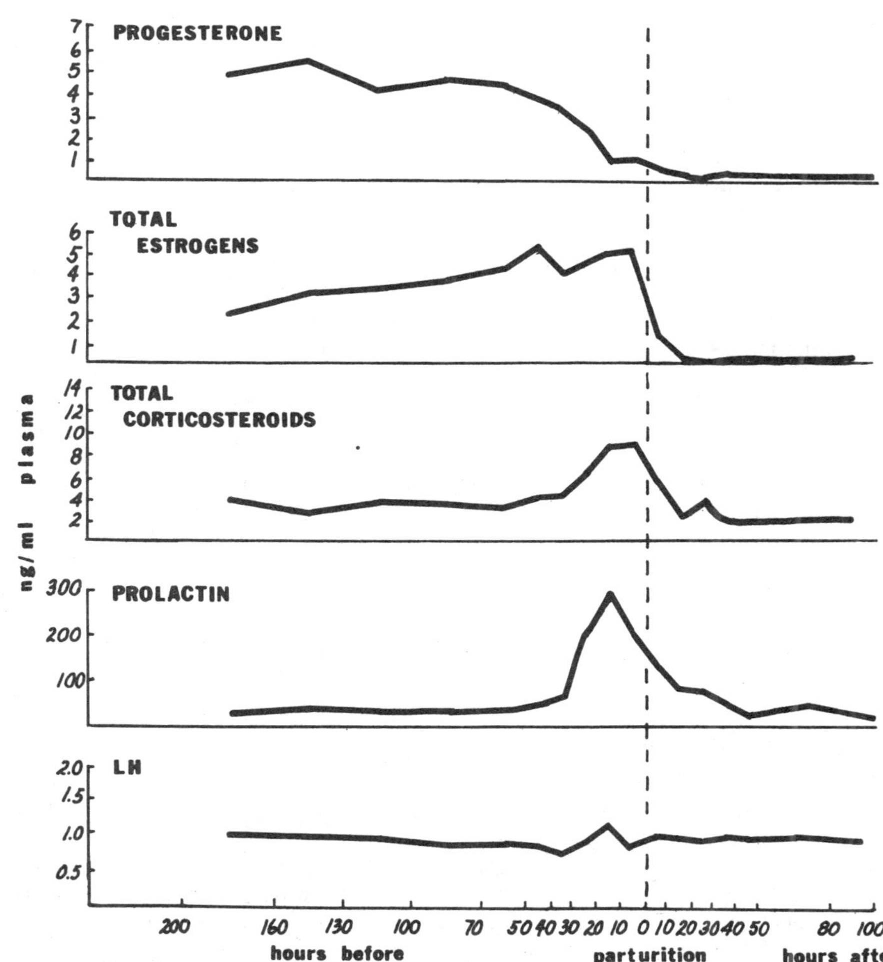

Figure 53.12. Changes in peripheral plasma hormone levels at parturition in the cow. (From Hoffmann et al. 1973, *Acta Endocr.* 73:385–95.)

parturition. However, there is at least one report of a rise in corticoids beginning 4 days before parturition (Wagner et al. 1974). Relaxin levels remain high until parturition.

Again, changes in plasma hormone levels associated with parturition in the doe are similar to those occurring in the cow; plasma 17α-estradiol levels are high as early as 25 days before parturition and show a further increase on the day of parturition, while progesterone levels decline sharply beginning about 48 hours before delivery (Thorburn et al. 1972).

In the ewe, changes in plasma hormone levels associated with parturition follow a somewhat different pattern. The relatively low unconjugated plasma estrogen levels found during the latter part of gestation increase dramatically during the 24 hours prior to delivery. Plasma progesterone levels decline before parturition, as in the cow. The decline, however, is reported to begin several days earlier than in the cow, and parturition sometimes occurs in the presence of fairly high levels (1.5–2.0 ng/ml) of progesterone. As in the cow, plasma corticoids rise during the last 24 hours of gestation. A plasma prolactin peak occurs on the day before parturition. LH is not released at parturition.

In the sow, peripheral plasma progesterone begins to fall from levels of 10–12 ng/ml at 4 or 5 days before farrowing, and then declines abruptly to less than 1 ng/ml during the last 48 hours. Peripheral plasma estrogen levels rise during the last week of pregnancy; estrone levels increase from 1.2 to 2.4 ng/ml at 2 days before parturition and are maintained at this level through farrowing. Levels of both estrone and estradiol decline rapidly by 24 hours postpartum. Peripheral plasma corticoids rise from about 60 to 100 ng/ml during the last 48 hours of gestation.

In the bitch, plasma total estrogen levels decline from an average of 22 pg/ml at 4 days before parturition to an average of 12 pg/ml at the time of parturition and 10 pg/ml at 4 days postpartum. Plasma progesterone levels decline from about 4 ng/ml at 2 days before parturition to less than 1 ng/ml at parturition. As in the other species described, plasma corticoid peaks coincide with the fall in progesterone.

In the mare, plasma estrogen levels decline slowly during the last 30 days of pregnancy, then fall precipitously at the time of parturition. Progesterone levels increase from 1–2 ng/ml to 4.5 ng/ml during the last 30 days and then decline precipitously to less than 0.5 ng/ml at one day postpartum.

The mechanism responsible for triggering these abrupt hormonal changes and initiating myometrial contractions has been most intensively studied in the ewe (Liggins et al. 1972, Thorburn et al. 1972). Many experiments suggest that the initial stimulus to parturition is an increased output of fetal corticoids in response to increased release of ACTH from the fetal pituitary. Fetal plasma corticosteroid levels increase greatly during the final 4 days of gestation in the ewe. Hypophysectomy, adrenalectomy, or pituitary stalk section of the fetus leads to prolonged pregnancy in the ewe, and premature delivery can be evoked by administering either ACTH or glucocorticoids, which elevates fetal corticosteroids. Elevated fetal corticosteroid levels stimulate the synthesis and release of prostaglandin $F_{2}\alpha$ ($PGF_{2}\alpha$) by the maternal cotyledons, and later by the myometrium. However, these elevated levels of $PGF_{2}\alpha$ appear to occur after plasma progesterone levels have already declined. It is possible that $PGF_{2}\alpha$ acts directly on the myometrium of the ewe to initiate uterine contractions after progesterone levels are lowered and estrogen levels are elevated. $PGF_{2}\alpha$ also has the ability to cause oxytocin release from the posterior pituitary and could initiate parturition in this way. It has been difficult, however, to clearly demonstrate a rise in plasma levels of oxytocin prior to parturition, even though marked increases in oxytocin levels occur during delivery.

The placenta is the major site of progesterone production in the ewe in late pregnancy, but the increasing level of fetal corticosteroids depresses placental progesterone production. In the doe, however, and possibly in the cow and sow, the corpus luteum appears to continue to secrete progesterone in late pregnancy. Experiments with the doe suggest that rising levels of fetal corticosteroids cause luteal regression in these species. The mechanism is unknown. A decrease in maternal plasma progesterone levels seems essential to the initiation of parturition in these species.

As might be expected, parturition can be induced late in pregnancy in the cow, sow, and ewe by administration of either $PGF_{2}\alpha$ or potent glucocorticoids such as dexamethasone. The induction of parturition in cattle by corticosteroid administration has been widely practiced in areas such as New Zealand, where it is important for cows to calve at an optimal time of the year. Labor usually begins within 72 hours after intramuscular injections of 20 mg dexamethasone. These injections cause an increase in maternal plasma estrogen levels and a decline in progesterone levels, such as normally occurs before parturition. The treatments have caused increases in calf mortality in some experiments and an increased incidence of retained placentas in others; the procedure is most effective when used after day 255 of pregnancy.

Very large intramuscular doses (10–20 mg) of dexamethasone given late in pregnancy (days 140–142) also cause lambing within 72 hours in ewes. Extremely large doses of dexamethasone (75 mg) appear to be required to induce premature parturition in the sow.

Intravenous doses of 5–40 ng $PGF_{2}\alpha$ induce parturition in cows in the third trimester of pregnancy but apparently not in the second. The mean interval between injection and parturition is 2.9 days. Premature parturition has been induced in sows at day 111 by intramuscular injections of 2.5 mg $PGF_2\alpha$. Parturitions followed the injections by about 30 hours.

REFERENCES

Akbar, A., Reichert, L.E., Dunn, T.G., Kaltenbach, C.C., and Niswender, G.D. 1974. Serum levels of follicle stimulating hormone during the bovine estrous cycle. *J. Anim. Sci.* 39:360–65.

Asdell, S.A. 1964. *Patterns of Mammalian Reproduction.* 2d ed. Cornell U. Press, Ithaca, N.Y.

Astwood, E.B. 1941. The regulation of corpus luteum function by hypophysial luteotropin. *Endocrinology* 28:309–13.

Austin, C.R. 1952. The 'capacitation' of the mammalian sperm. *Nature* 170:326.

——. 1963. Fertilization and transport of the ovum. In C.G. Hartman, ed., *Mechanisms Concerned with Conception.* Pergamon, Oxford.

——. 1964. Behaviour of spermatozoa in the female genital tract and fertilization. *Proc. Vth Internat. Cong. Anim. Reprod. Artificial Insem.* (Trento Italy) 3:7–23.

Ayalon, N. 1964. Sterility not clinically diagnosable. *Proc. Vth Internat. Cong. Anim. Reprod. Artificial Insem.* (Trento, Italy) 5:47–80.

Barraclough, C.A. 1973. Sex steroid regulation of reproductive neuroendocrine processes. In *Handbook of Physiology.* Sec. 7, R.O. Greep and E.B. Astwood, eds., *Endocrinology.* Am. Physiol. Soc., Washington. Vol. 2, pt. 1, 29–56.

Bearden, H.J., Hansel, W., and Bratton, R.W. 1956. Fertilization and embryonic mortality rates of bulls with histories of either low or high fertility in artificial breeding. *J. Dairy Sci.* 39:312–18.

Bedford, C.A., Challis, J.R.G., Harrison, F.A., and Heap, R.B. 1972. The role of oestrogens and progesterone in the onset of parturition in various species. *J. Reprod. Fert.,* suppl. 16, pp. 1–23.

Bedford, J.M. 1967. Experimental requirements for capacitation and observations on ultrastructural changes in rabbit spermatozoa during fertilization. *J. Reprod. Fert.,* suppl. 2, 35–48.

——. 1974. Report of a workshop: Maturation of the fertilizing ability of mammalian spermatozoa. *Biol. Reprod.* 11:346–62.

Benoit, J., and Assenmacher, J. 1953. Rapport entre la stimulation sexuelle préhypophysaire et la neurosecretion chez l'oiseau. *Arch. Anat. Microsc. Exp.* 42:334–86.

Björkman, N. 1964. Ultrastructural features of placenta in ungulates. *Proc. Vth Internat. Cong. Anim. Reprod. Artificial Insem.* (Trento, Italy) 5:259–63.

Branton, C.J., Hall, G., Stone, C.J., Lank, R.B., and Frye, J.B., Jr. 1957. The duration of estrus and the length of estrous cycles in dairy cattle in a sub-tropical climate. *J. Dairy Sci.* 40:628.

Britt, J.H., Kittok, R.J., and Harrison, D.S. 1974. Ovulation, estrus, and endocrine response after GnRH in early postpartum cows. *J. Anim. Sci.* 39:915–19.

Bruce, H.M., and Parrott, D.M.V. 1960. Role of olfactory sense in pregnancy block by strange males. *Science* 131:1526.

Bryans, F.E. 1951. Progesterone of the blood in the menstrual cycle of the monkey. *Endocrinology* 48:733–40.

Chang, M.C. 1955. Development of fertilizing capacity of rabbit spermatozoa in the uterus. *Nature* 175:1036–37.

Courrier, R. 1945. *Endocrinologie de la gestation.* Masson, Paris.

Cowie, A.T., Daniel, P.M., Prichard, M.M.L., and Tindal, T.S. 1963. Hypophysectomy in pregnant goats and section of the pituitary stalk in pregnant goats and sheep. *J. Endocr.* 28:93–102.

Denamur, R., Martinet, J., and Short, R.V. 1973. Pituitary control of the ovine corpus luteum. *J. Reprod. Fert.* 32:207–20.

Diczfalusy, E. 1964. Endocrine function of the human fetoplacental unit. *Fed. Proc.* 23:791–98.

Donaldson, L.E., Hansel, W., and Van Vleck, L.D. 1965. The luteotropic properties of luteinizing hormone and the nature of oxytocin induced luteal inhibition in cattle. *J. Dairy Sci.* 48:331–37.

Donovan, B.T., and Harris, G.W. 1956. The effect of pituitary stalk section on light-induced oestrus in the ferret. *J. Physiol.* 131:102–14.

Dziuk, P.J., Polge, C., and Rowson, L.E. 1964. Intrauterine migration and mixing of embryos in swine following egg transfer. *J. Anim. Sci.* 23:37–42.

Edgar, D.G., and Ronaldson, J.W. 1958. Blood levels of progesterone in the ewe. *J. Endocr.* 161:378–84.

Everett, J.W. 1964. Central neural control of reproductive functions of the adenohypophysis. *Physiol. Rev.* 44:374–418.

Everett, J.W., Sawyer, C.H., and Markee, J.E. 1949. A neurogenic timing factor in control of the ovulatory discharge of luteinizing hormone in the cyclic rat. *Endocrinology* 44:234–50.

Gier, H.T. 1960. Estrous cycle in the bitch: Vaginal fluids. *Vet. Scope* 5(2):2–9.

Ginther, O.J. 1974. Internal regulation of physiological processes through local venoarterial pathways. *J. Anim. Sci.* 39:550–64.

Goding, J.R. 1974. The demonstration that $PGF_2\alpha$ is the uterine luteolysin in the ewe. *J. Reprod. Fert.* 38:261–71.

Gomes, W.R., and Erb, R.E. 1965. Progesterone in bovine reproduction: A review. *J. Dairy Sci.* 48:314–30.

Greenstein, J.S., and Foley, R.C. 1958. Early embryology of the cow. I. Gastrula and primitive streak stages. *J. Dairy Sci.* 41:409–21.

Hamilton, W.J., and Laing, J.A. 1946. Development of the egg of the cow up to the stage of blastocyst formation. *J. Anat.* 8:194–204.

Hansel, W. 1961. The hypothalamus and pituitary function in mammals. *Internat. J. Fert.* 6:241–59.

Hansel, W., Concannon, P.W., and Lukaszewska, J.H. 1973. Corpora lutea of the large domestic animals. *Biol. Reprod.* 8:222–45.

Hansel, W., and Echternkamp, S.E. 1972. Control of ovarian function in domestic animals. *Am. Zoologist* 12:225–43.

Hansel, W., and Seifart, K.H. 1967. Maintenance of luteal function in the cow. *J. Dairy Sci.* 50:1948–58.

Hansel, W., and Trimberger, G.W. 1951. Atropine blockage of ovulation in the cow and its possible significance. *J. Anim. Sci.* 10:719–25.

——. 1952. The effect of progesterone on ovulation time in dairy heifers. *J. Dairy Sci.* 35:65–70.

Hansel, W., and Wagner, W.C. 1960. Luteal inhibition in the bovine as a result of oxytocin injections, uterine dilatation, and intrauterine infusions of seminal and preputial fluids. *J. Dairy Sci.* 43:796–805.

Harris, G.W. 1961. The pituitary stalk and ovulation. In C.A. Villee, ed., *Control of Ovulation.* Pergamon, Long Island City, N.Y. Pp. 56–78.

Harvey, E.R. 1959. Implantation, development of the fetus, and fetal membranes. In H.H. Cole and P.T. Cupps, eds., *Reproduction in Domestic Animals.* Academic Press, New York. Vol. 1, 433–66.

Hobson, W.C., and Hansel, W. 1972. Plasma LH levels after ovariectomy, corpus luteum removal, and estradiol administration in cattle. *Endocrinology* 91:185–90.

——. 1974. Increased *in vitro* pituitary response to LH-RH after *in vivo* estrogen treatment. *Proc. Soc. Exp. Biol. Med.* 146:470–74.

Hoffman, B., Schams, D., Gimenez, T., Ender, M.L., Hermann, C., and Karg, H. 1973. Changes in progesterone, total estrogens, corticosteroids, prolactin, and LH in bovine peripheral plasma around parturition with special reference to the effect of exogenous corticoids and a prolactin inhibitor, respectively. *Acta Endocr.* 73:385–95.

Jubb, K.V., and McEntee, K. 1955. Observations on the bovine pituitary gland. II. Architecture and cytology with special reference to basophil cell function. *Cornell Vet.* 45:593–641.

Kendrick, J.W. 1964. The effect of infectious pustular vulvovaginitis on the uterus of the cow. *Proc. Vth Internat. Cong. Anim. Reprod. Artificial Insem.* (Trento, Italy) 5:161–65.

Laing, J.A. 1949. Infertility in cattle associated with death of ova at early stages after fertilization. *J. Comp. Path. Ther.* 59:97–108.

Liggins, G.C., Grieves, S.A., Kendall, J.Z., and Knox, B.S. 1972. The physiological roles of progesterone, oestradiol-17β, and prostaglandin $F_2\alpha$ in the control of ovine parturition. *J. Reprod. Fert.*, suppl. 16, 85–103.

Liu, W., Nabim, H.S., Sweeney, C.M., Holcomb, G.N., and Ward, D.N. 1972. The primary structure of ovine luteinizing hormone. *J. Biol. Chem.* 247:4365–81.

Loeb, L. 1908. The production of deciduomata and the relation between the ovaries and the formation of decidua. *J. Am. Med. Ass.* 50:1897–1901.

Malven, P.V., and Hansel, W. 1964. Ovarian function in dairy heifers following hysterectomy. *J. Dairy Sci.* 47:1388–93.

Marion, G.B., and Gier, H.T. 1971. Ovarian and uterine embryogenesis and morphology of the non-pregnant female mammal. *J. Anim. Sci.* 32(suppl. 1):24–47.

Masuda, H., Anderson, L.L., Hendricks, D.M., and Melampy, R.M. 1967. Progesterone in ovarian venous plasma and corpora lutea of the pig. *Endocrinology* 80:240–46.

McDonald, L.E., McNutt, S.H., and Nichols, R.E. 1953. On the essentiality of the bovine corpus luteum of pregnancy. *Am. J. Vet. Res.* 14:539–41.

McEntee, K. 1958. Cystic corpora lutea in cattle. *Internat. J. Fert.* 3:120–28.

McNutt, G.W. 1924. The corpus luteum of the ox ovary in relation to the estrous cycle. *J. Am. Vet. Med. Ass.* 65:556–97.

Mellin, T.N., and Erb, R.E. 1965. Estrogens in the bovine: A review. *J. Dairy Sci.* 48:687–700.

Nett, T.M., Holton, D.W., and Estergreen, V.L. 1973. Plasma estrogens in pregnant and postpartum mares. *J. Anim. Sci.* 37:962–70.

Purves, H.D., and Griesbach, W.E. 1954. The site of follicle stimulating and luteinizing hormone production on the rat pituitary. *Endocrinology* 55:785–93.

——. 1957. A study on the cytology of the adenohypophysis of the dog. *J. Endocr.* 14:361–70.

Rajakoski, E. 1960. The ovarian follicular system in sexually mature heifers with special reference to season, cyclical and left-right variation. *Acta Endocr.* 34(suppl. 52):1–68.

Rayford, P.L., Brinkley, H.J., Young, E.P., and Reichert, L.E. 1974. Radioimmunoassay of porcine FSH. *J. Anim. Sci.* 39:348–54.

Reynolds, S.R.M. 1955. Gestation mechanisms. In *Reproduction and Infertility*. Proc. 2d Bien. Symp. Reprod. Infert. Michigan State U. Centennial Symp. East Lansing. Pp. 71–78.

Roberts, S.J. 1971. *Veterinary Obstetrics and Genital Diseases*. 2d ed. J.W. Edwards, Ann Arbor, Mich.

Samuels, L.T. 1958. Biosynthesis of steroid hormones. In F.X. Gassner, ed., *Reproduction and Infertility*. Proc. 3d Bien. Symp. Reprod. Infert. Fort Collins, Colo., 1957. Pergamon, Long Island City, N.Y. Pp. 119–28.

Sawyer, C.H. 1964. Control of secretion of gonadotropins. In H.H. Cole, ed., *Gonadotropins: Their Chemical and Biological Properties and Secretory Control*. Freeman, San Francisco.

Sawyer, C.H., Markee, J.E., and Townsend, B.F. 1949. Cholinergic and adrenergic components in the neurohumoral control of the release of LH in the rabbit. *Endocrinology* 44:18–37.

Settergren, I. 1964. The number of primordial follicles in clinically normal and hypoplastic heifer ovaries. *Proc. Vth Internat. Cong. Anim. Reprod.* (Trento, Italy) 1:188–92.

Shemesh, M., and Hansel, W. 1975. Levels of prostaglandin F (PGF) in bovine endometrium, uterine venous, ovarian arterial, and jugular plasma during the estrous cycle. *Proc. Soc. Exp. Biol. Med.* 148:123–26.

Shome, B., and Parlow, A.F. 1974. Human follicle stimulating hormone: First proposal for the amino acid sequence of the hormone specific β subunit (FSHB). *J. Clin. Endocr. Metab.* 39:203–5.

Sierk, C.F. 1965. *Proceedings of the Conference on Estrous Cycle Control in Domestic Animals*. U.S.D.A. Misc. Pub. 1005.

Simmons, K.R., and Hansel, W. 1964. The nature of the luteotropic hormone in the bovine. *J. Anim. Sci.* 23:136–41.

Simpson, M.E. 1959. Gonadotropins in reproduction. In H.H. Cole and P.T. Cupps, eds., *Reproduction in Domestic Animals*, Academic Press, New York.

Sorensen, A.M., Hansel, W., Hough, W.H., Armstrong, D.T., McEntee, K., and Bratton, R.W. 1959. Causes and prevention of reproductive failures in dairy cattle. I. Influence of underfeeding and overfeeding on growth and development of Holstein heifers. *Cornell U. Ag. Exp. Sta. Bull.* 936.

Soupart, P. 1967. Studies on the hormonal control of rabbit sperm capacitation. *J. Reprod. Fert.*, suppl. 2, 49–63.

Squires, E.L., Wentworth, B.C., and Ginther, O.J. 1974. Progesterone concentration in blood of mares during the estrous cycle, pregnancy, and after hysterectomy. *J. Anim. Sci.* 39:759–67.

Stabenfeldt, G.H., Hughes, J.P., and Evans, J.W. 1972. Ovarian activity during the estrous cycle of the mare. *Endocrinology* 90:1379–84.

Szentagothai, J., Flerko, B., Mess, B., and Halasz, B. 1968. *Hypothalamic Control of the Anterior Pituitary*. 3d ed. Akademiai Kiado, Budapest.

Tanabe, T.Y. 1970. The role of progesterone during pregnancy in dairy cows. *Penn. State U. Ag. Exp. Sta. Bull.* 774. University Park.

Tanabe, T.Y., and Casida, L.E. 1949. The nature of reproductive failures in cows of low fertility. *J. Dairy Sci.* 32:237–46.

Thorburn, G.D., Nicol, D.A., Bassett, J.M., Schutt, D.A., and Cox, R.I. 1972. Parturition in the sheep and goat: Changes in corticosteroids, progesterone, oestrogens, and prostaglandin F. *J. Reprod. Fert.*, suppl. 16, 61–84.

Trimberger, G.W. 1948. Breeding efficiency in dairy cattle from artificial insemination at various intervals before and after ovulation. *Neb. Ag. Exp. Sta. Res. Bull.* 153. Pp. 1–26.

Villee, C.A. 1961a. Some problems of the metabolism and mechanism of action of steroid sex hormones. In W.C. Young, ed., *Sex and Internal Secretions*. Williams & Wilkins, Baltimore. Vol. 1, 643–65.

——, ed. 1961b. *Control of Ovulation*. Pergamon, Long Island City, N.Y.

Wada, H., and Yuhara, M. 1955. Relaxin in ruminants. I. Relaxin content of the blood serum of pregnant dairy cows. *Japan. J. Zootech. Sci.* 26:215–20.

Wagner, W.C., Thompson, F.W., Evans, L.E., and Molokwu, E.C.I. 1974. Hormonal mechanisms controlling parturition. *J. Anim. Sci.* 38(suppl. 1):39–57.

Williams, W.L., Abney, T.O., Chernoff, H.N., Dukelow, W.R., and Pinsker, M.C. 1967. Biochemistry and physiology of decapacitation factor. *J. Reprod. Fert.*, suppl. 2, 11–23.

Wislocki, G.B., and Padykula, H.A. 1961. Biochemistry of placenta. In W.C. Young, ed., *Sex and Internal Secretions*. Williams & Wilkins, Baltimore. Vol. 2.

CHAPTER 54

Male Reproductive Processes | by William Hansel and Kenneth McEntee

The major functional parts of the male genital system of domestic animals include the scrotum and testes, rete tubules, efferent tubules, epididymides, penis, and several accessory glands, including the prostate, seminal vesicles, and bulbourethral glands (Fig. 54.1). These organs have been described for several species by Roberts (1971). The spermatozoa are produced within the seminiferous tubules in the testes (Fig. 54.2) by processes called spermatogenesis and spermiogenesis. During these processes, the number of chromosomes characteristic for each species is halved, so that each new individual receives half of its genes as a random sample from its sire, and a similar contribution from its dam. The spermatozoa pass into the epididymides, where they mature until they are ejaculated. Many of them degenerate and are resorbed by the epididymal epithelium and ductus deferens; many are also lost in the urine. The secretions of the accessory glands (seminal vesicles, bulbourethral glands, and prostate) are added to the spermatozoa at the time of ejaculation.

The reproductive organs of the ram have several unique features. The prostate gland is diffused, and the penis is characterized by a filiform appendage containing the urethra. The reproductive organs of the boar are characterized by relatively large seminal vesicles and bulbourethral glands that contribute in a major way to the remarkably large volume of semen produced. The boar has

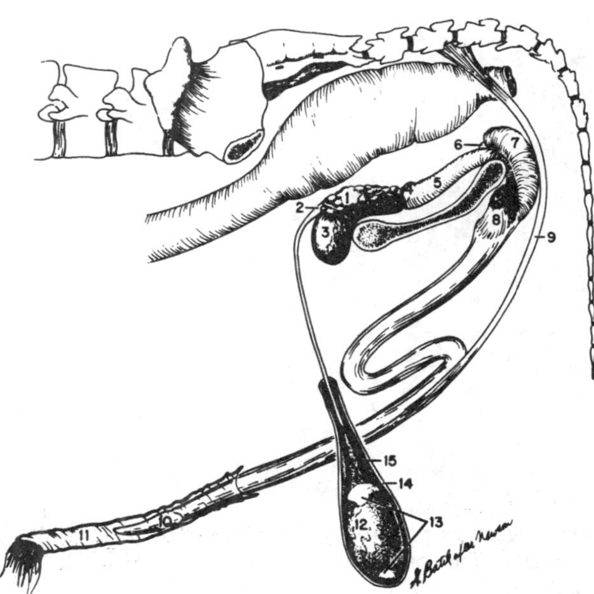

Figure 54.1. Reproductive organs of the bull: 1, seminal vesicle; 2, ampulla; 3, urinary bladder; 4, prostate; 5, urethral muscle surrounding the pelvic urethra; 6, bulbourethral gland; 7, bulbocavernosus muscle; 8, ischiocavernosus muscle; 9, retractor penis muscle; 10, glans penis; 11, preputial membrane and cavity; 12, testis; 13, epididymis; 14, scrotum; 15, spermatic cord.

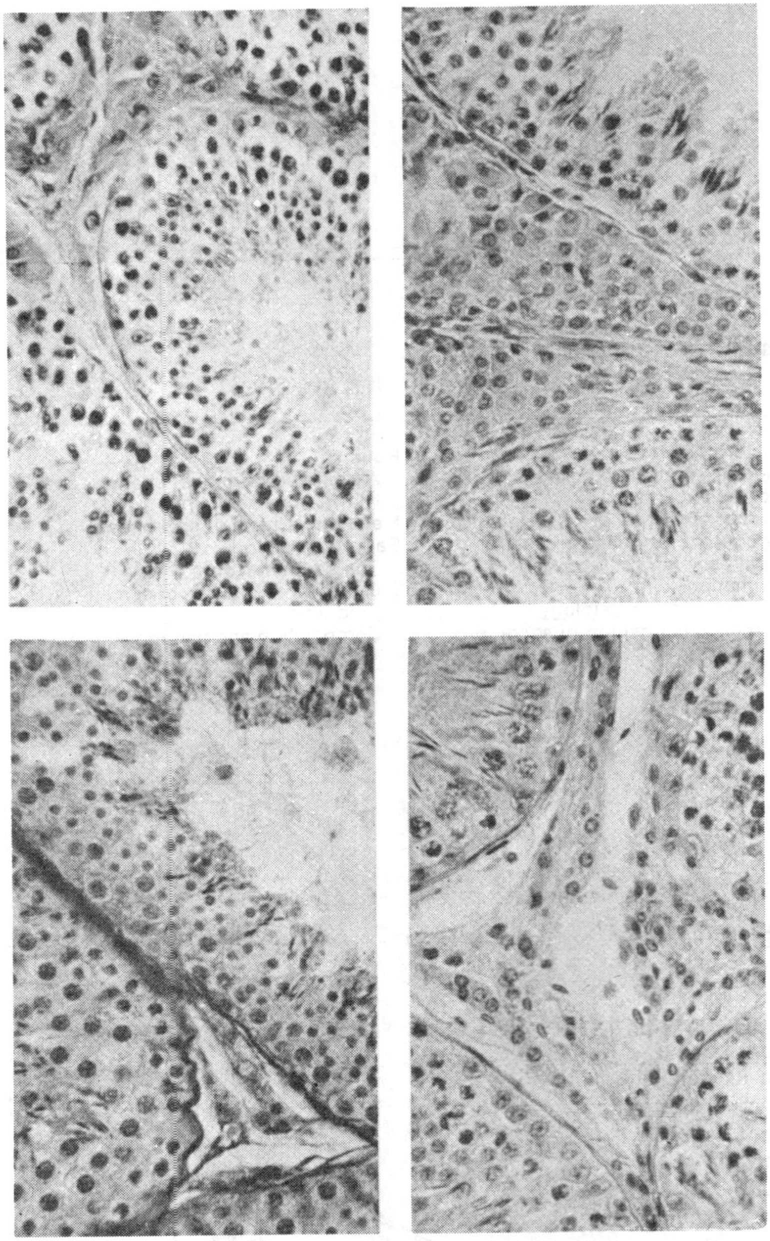

Figure 54.2. Cross sections of testes from a stallion (upper left), boar (upper right), dog (lower left), and bull (lower right). Note the relatively large amount of interstitial tissue in the boar testis. ×320.

the largest testes per unit of body weight of the domestic animals. The preputial diverticulum is well developed and usually contains degenerating epithelial cells and urine. The penis of the stallion is extremely vascular and does not have the sigmoid flexure of that of the bull, ram, and boar. The urethra protrudes several centimeters from the surface of the glans penis. The most remarkable features of the male dog reproductive tract are the os penis and the absence of all accessory glands except the prostate.

Under the influence of the pituitary gonadotropins, the testes produce the male or androgenic hormones. The interstitial cells—sometimes called the Leydig cells, and interspersed among the seminiferous tubules—are the major source of the androgenic hormones (see Fig. 54.2). The testes of the boar contain a higher proportion of interstitial cells than those of any of the other large domestic animals.

HYPOTHALAMUS, PITUITARY, AND TESTES INTERRELATIONSHIPS

Spermatogenesis

The term spermatogenesis represents the total of all the changes that result in the transformation of the stem cells or spermatogonia lining the seminiferous tubules into free spermatozoa within the lumen. These changes in the seminiferous epithelium all occur in proximity to a second cell type, the Sertoli cell (Fig. 54.3). These large cells are attached to the basement membrane and have numerous long processes that may contact all other cells within the tubules. They are believed to serve as nurse cells for the developing spermatids.

Cycle of seminiferous epithelium

The process of spermatogenesis consists of a complex series of events in all of the domestic animals. The seminiferous epithelial cycle has been carefully studied in the ram (Ortavant 1959); the pattern is similar in the bull (Amann 1962) and in the boar (Swierstra 1968). The primordial germ cells or gonocytes are contained in the seminiferous tubules during the fetal period and at birth. These multiply and give rise to spermatogonia, which undergo a series of mitotic divisions resulting in primary spermatocytes. These divisions are similar in the ram,

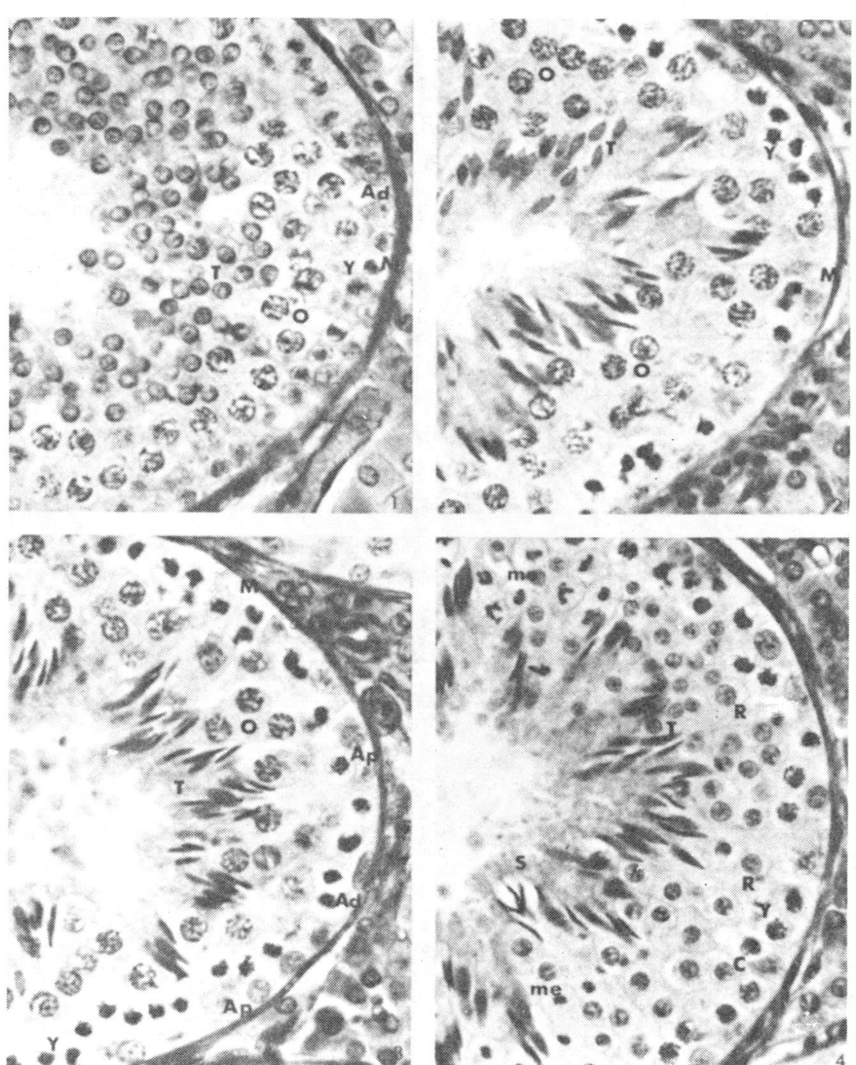

Figure 54.3. Cross sections of seminiferous tubules of the boar, representative of stages 1 and 2 (top) and 3 and 4 (bottom). ×460. Ad, dark type A spermatogonium; Ap, pale type A spermatogonium; B, type B spermatogonium; C, Sertoli cell; M, basement membrane; me, metaphase configuration; O, old primary spermatocyte; R, secondary spermatocyte; T, spermatid; S, spermatozoa; Y, young primary spermatocyte. (From Swierstra 1968, *Anat. Rec.* 161:171–86.)

bull, and rabbit, and result in the production of 16 primary spermatocytes. The process has been divided into eight stages by Ortavant (1959) as illustrated in Figures 54.3, 54.4, and 54.5.

Three types of spermatogonia are present in most animals. The type A spermatogonia divide to yield intermediate spermatogonia and dormant type A cells. The intermediate cells further divide to yield type B spermatogonia, which divide to yield 16 primary spermatocytes. Thus four divisions yield 16 primary spermatocytes from one type A spermatogonium. The dormant type A cell later behaves as its parent, thus ensuring the continuity of spermatogenesis (Fig. 54.5). The primary spermatocytes later undergo the long evolution known as meiotic prophase through leptotene, zygotene, pachytene, and diakinesis, resulting in secondary spermatocytes. These secondary spermatocytes divide, forming spermatids, each containing half of the chromosomes characteristic of the species. Thus 64 spermatids are theoretically produced from each stem cell. Actually, some cells degenerate during normal spermatogenesis. The remainder then undergo a long series of developmental changes resulting in spermatozoa. In the rat, hamster, and mouse, 24 primary spermatocytes, and thus 96 spermatids, are formed, rather than 16 as in the bull and ram. This results from an additional division in which one type A spermatogonium produces three type A spermatogonia and one stem A, which divide successively to produce 6 intermediate spermatcgonia, 12 type B cells, and 24 primary spermatocytes (Amann 1962, Ortavant 1959).

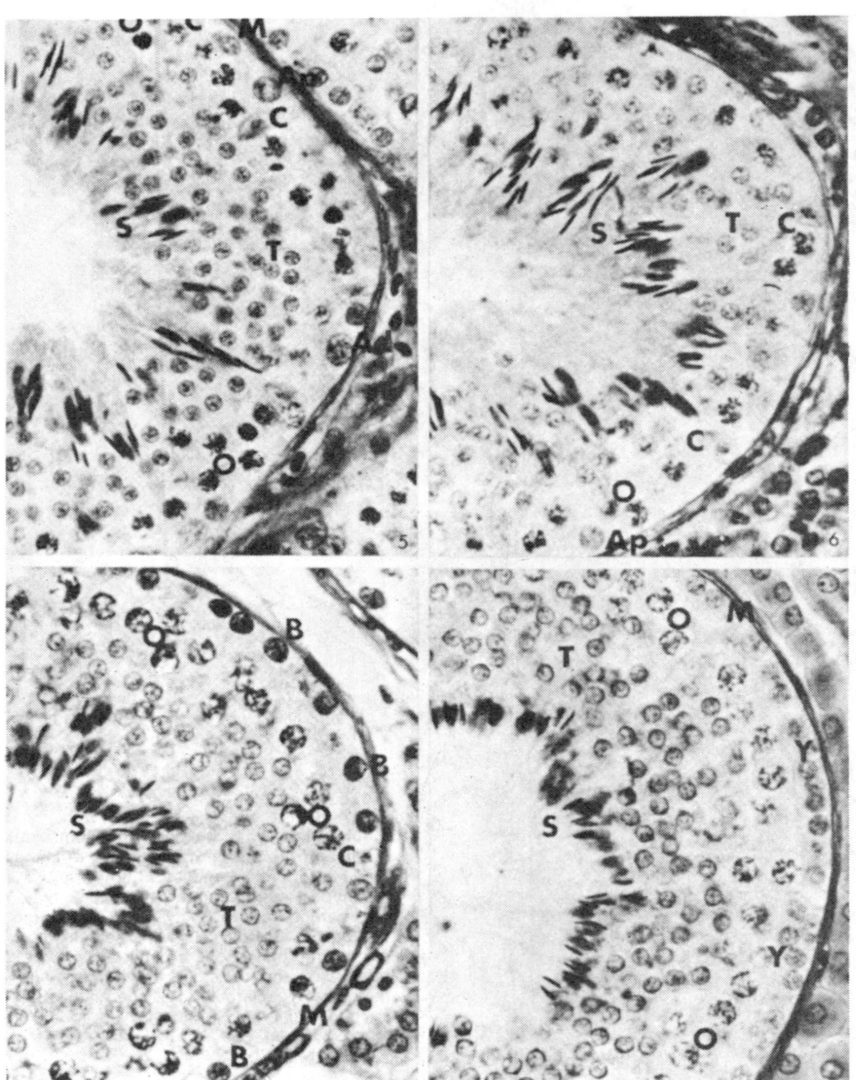

Figure 54.4. Cross sections of seminiferous tubules of the boar representative of stages 5 and 6 (top) and 7 and 8 (bottom). ×460. Cells are identified as in Figure 54.3. (From Swierstra 1968, *Anat. Rec.* 161:171–86.)

Table 54.1. Seminiferous epithelial cycle with cells of the spermatogenic series characteristic of each stage

Stage 1	Stage 2	Stage 3	Stage 4	Stage 5	Stage 6	Stage 7	Stage 8
		1 Spg A_1	A_1	A_1	A_1	A_1	A_1
A_1	x A_1	1 A_2	x A_2	2 In	x In	4 B_1	x 8 B_2
x 16 Spc I	16 L	16 (L + Z)	16 Z	16 (Z + P)	16 P	16 P	16 P
16 P	16 D	16 D	x 32 Spc IIx	64 Spi R	64 R	64 R	64 R
64 R	64 Spi L	64 L	64 L	64 L	64 L	64 L	64 Spz

One horizontal row is equivalent to one seminiferous epithelial cycle. The evolution of one spermatogonium A_1 (at the top of the table) until the release of the spermatozoa produced from it (at the bottom of the table) takes place in 4 complete horizontal rows plus a fraction (0.68) of the upper row, or 4.68 seminiferous epithelial cycles. Spg, spermatogonia; Spc I, primary spermatocyte; L, leptotene; Z, zygotene; P, pachytene; D, diplotene; Spc II, secondary spermatocyte; Spi R, round spermatid; Spi L, elongated spermatid; Spz, spermatozoa; x, division.

From Ortavant, in Cole and Cupps, eds., *Reproduction in Domestic Animals*, Academic Press, New York, 1959

The exact number of spermatogonial divisions is species-specific and stable. Roosen-Runge (1969) stated that there are five of these premeiotic divisions in the rat, four in the Rhesus monkey, and three in man. The rabbit, ram, and bull all have four spermatogonial divisions, but the pattern for the boar has not been clearly established.

Data in Table 54.1 and Figure 54.5 suggest that certain cell associations exist at various stages in the evolution of the germinal cells. The cells evolve in homogeneous groups, all cells in each group at the same stage of development. These groups are usually referred to as cell generations. Examinations of cross sections of tubules reveal distinct groups comprising concentric layers of cells, all cells in each layer at the same stage of development. In examining such a cross section from basement membrane to lumen one finds: (1) spermatogonia of the several types described above, (2) spermatocytes of two generations, the old generation comprising the layer nearest the lumen, and (3) spermatids of either the round or elongated type representing two stages of their development (spermiogenesis). Spermatids at a given stage of development are always associated with the same type of spermatocytes and spermatogonia; consequently a certain number of cellular associations arise. The successive cellular associations evolve with time, and the sequence of events by which a complete series of cellular associations follow one another is called the cycle of the seminiferous epithelium. The duration of the cycle is the time between cellular associations in a given area of the tubule.

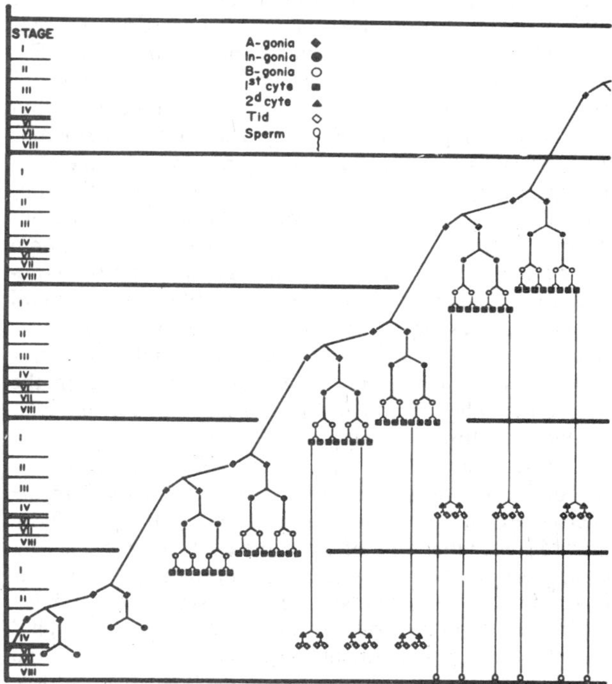

Figure 54.5. Pattern of spermatogenesis in bulls. It starts with the formation of a stem A-spermatogonium in stage 3 and terminates approximately 4.6 cycles of the seminiferous epithelium later with the release of 64 spermatozoa at the end of stage 8. (From fig. 4, R.P. Amann 1962, *Am. J. Anat.* 110:69–78.)

In the spermatogenic cycle, stage 1 extends from a time at which spermatozoa are absent from the lumen to the time of onset of elongation of spermatids. Light and dark type-A spermatogonia and Sertoli cells are present along the basement membrane. Two generations of primary spermatocytes, young and old, are present. The young primary spermatocytes are in the preleptotene phase and are located near the basement membrane. The cells of the old generation are in the pachytene phase and are scattered between the basement membrane and the lumen of the tubule. The young primary spermatocytes have round nuclei, and the older ones have large pachytene nuclei and indistinct nuclear membranes. All the spermatids have spherical nuclei.

Stage 2 extends from the beginning to the end of elongation of the spermatid nuclei. Two generations of primary spermatocytes are present, each having an indistinct nuclear membrane. Sertoli cells and both light and dark type-A spermatogonia, which have increased in number from stage 1, line the basement membrane.

Stage 3 extends from the end of spermatid elongation to the beginning of the first maturation (meiotic) division of the primary spermatocytes. Sertoli cells and type A spermatogonia line the basement membrane, and two generations of primary spermatocytes are present. The spermatid nuclei are elongated.

Stage 4 extends from the beginning of the first maturation (meiotic) division to the end of the second maturation (meiotic) division. Two generations of primary spermatocytes are present in the early part of stage 4: the old primary spermatocytes undergo the first maturation division and then give rise to secondary spermatocytes. These cells have spherical nuclei with distinct nuclear membranes; the chromatin is evenly distributed and appears as granules connected by filaments. The life span of the secondary spermatocytes is relatively short. They are seen only in stage 4, and soon after their formation they undergo the second maturation division and yield spermatids. These spermatids have spherical nuclei with distinct nuclear membranes. Other cells seen at stage 4 include Sertoli cells and type A spermatogonia near the basement membrane. Metaphase configurations of dividing primary and secondary spermatocytes are often observed.

Stage 5 extends from the end of the second maturation division to the time the spermatid nuclei show a characteristic dusty appearance. The primary spermatocytes enter pachytene during this stage; this is a long phase during which the chromatin forms a characteristic netlike pattern. The nuclei increase in size during pachytene and move away from the basement membrane. The spermatid nuclei contain 5–5 karyosomes bound together by fine filaments of chromatin. The spermatozoa are grouped in bundles. Sertoli cells and type A spermatogonia line the basement membrane.

Stage 6 extends from the time the spermatid nuclei show a dusty appearance to the time at which all spermatozoa leave the Sertoli cells and move to the lumen. Both dark and pale type-A spermatogonia are present, and type B spermatogonia appear near the end of the stage. The spermatid nuclei retain their dusty appearance, but the karyosomes are fewer and less pronounced.

Stage 7 extends from the beginning to the end of movement of spermatozoa to the lumen. Type B spermatogonia undergo mitosis at the end of this stage and give rise to young primary spermatocytes. Sertoli cells and spermatogonia line the basement membrane.

Stage 8 extends from the time the spermatozoa line the lumen until they completely disappear from it. Most of the spermatozoa are still in the lumen in the photograph shown in Figure 54.4. Type B spermatogonia may be seen in the early phases of stage 8; the remaining spermatogonia are mostly pale type A's. The young primary spermatocytes are in preleptotene and the old ones are in pachytene. The spermatid nuclei are spherical and an acrosome is present.

It is important to realize that these stages represent changes in time. They represent the pictures that would be seen successively in a given cross section of a tubule during a complete cycle of the seminiferous epithelium, that is, between two successive appearances of the same cellular association. Approximately 4.6 successive cycles (see Fig. 54.5) are required for complete evolution of 64 free spermatozoa from a dormant type A spermatogonium (formed in stage 3) in the ram (Ortavant 1959) and bull (Amann 1962). However, spermatozoa are released into the tubule lumen at the end of each stage 8.

Some of these potential germ cells degenerate during the process; Amann (1962) estimated that in mature bulls the losses amount to 19 percent, of which 7 percent occur during spermatogonial multiplication, 7 percent during the first cycle of the seminiferous epithelium in which the primary spermatocytes are in prophase, and the remaining 5 percent during the cycle of the seminiferous epithelium containing the two meiotic divisions. Losses of about the same magnitude have been estimated for other species.

The nuclear and cytoplasmic changes involved in converting spermatids to spermatozoa are collectively referred to as spermiogenesis. The nuclei of the spermatids of domestic animals contain several large granules of chromatin surrounded by a double nuclear membrane. At stage 2 the nucleus elongates and flattens, and its chromatin contents are condensed into very large dense granules. A postnuclear cap differentiates from the nuclear membrane. Sperm nuclei assume the characteristic spatula shape seen in all domestic animals at this time. The formation of the acrosome system begins with the appearance of two or three proacrosomic granules within the Golgi complex in the cytoplasm of the spermatid. These coalesce to form a single acrosomic granule contained in an acrosomic vesicle. The vesicle and the contained granule move toward the anterior part of the nuclear membrane. The acrosomic vesicle, flattened onto the nucleus, forms the head cap encompassing the granule; it grows during the seminiferous epithelial cycle until it encompasses nearly two thirds of the nucleus in the ram and the boar, and slightly less in the bull. The acrosomic granule undergoes modifications resulting in the acrosome. The combination, acrosome and head cap, forms the acrosome system (Fig. 54.6).

During stage 2 of the seminiferous cycle the mitochondria of the spermatids begin to collect within the caudal sheath, a tubule that appears in the cytoplasm around the caudal pole of the nucleus. This caudal sheath disappears in the final stages of spermiogenesis, and its exact function is unknown. Between stages 5 and 7 the spermatid mitochondria assemble into a double spiral around the axial filament to form the mitochondrial sheath of the middle piece between the proximal centriole and the distal ringlike centriole (Fig. 54.7). The locomotive apparatus, or tail, develops from the axial filament, which originates from the proximal centriole as it migrates toward the posterior part of the nucleus. (Struc-

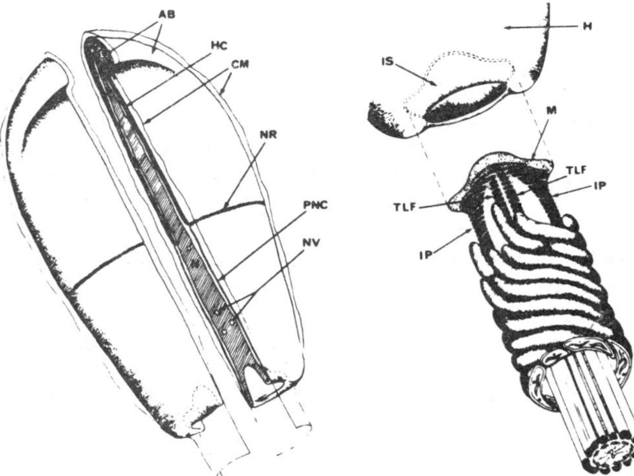

Figure 54.6. Ultrastructural features of the bovine sperm head and neck region. The cell membrane is removed and the tail separated from the head in the right illustration to show the articulation mechanism. AB, apical body; HC, head cap; CM, cell membrane; NR, nuclear ring; N, nucleus; PNC, postnuclear cap; NV, nuclear vacuoles; H, head; IS, implantation socket; M, matrix; IP, implantation plates; and TLF, thin laminated fibers. (From fig. 1, R.G. Saacke and J.O. Almquist 1964, *Am. J. Anat.* 115:143–61, and fig. 3, 115:163–84.)

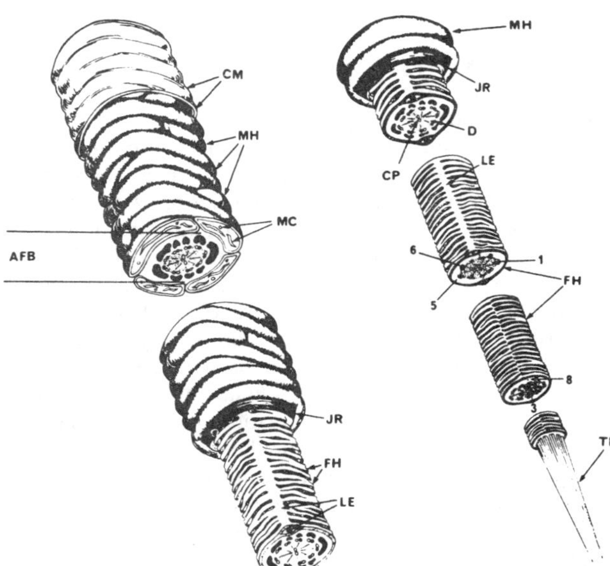

Figure 54.7. Ultrastructural features of the middle, principal, and terminal pieces of the bovine spermatozoon. The cell membrane has been partially removed and the flagellum cut at several levels to show the internal structure. CM, cell membrane; MH, mitochondrial helix; MC, mitochondrial cristae; JR, Jensen's ring; FH, fibrous helix; LE, longitudinal element; AFB, axial fiber bundle, consisting of nine outer coarse fibers, nine inner fibers or doublets (D), and a center pair of fibers (CP); LE, longitudinal element; and TP, terminal piece. (From figs. 1 and 2, R.G. Saacke and J.O. Almquist 1964, *Am. J. Anat.* 115:163–84.)

tural details of mature spermatozoa are considered later.)

The times required for completion of each of the phases outlined above have been accurately determined for rams, bulls, rabbits, and several other species by the use of tracer substances to label the germ cells. Radioactive phosphorus (^{32}P) and more recently tritium (^{3}H) labeled thymidine have been particularly useful in these studies, since they become incorporated into the deoxyribonucleic acid (DNA) of the primary spermatocytes at the preleptotene stage. Thirty days elapse in the ram and 25 days in the boar before spermatozoa produced by the labeled spermatocytes are released into the lumina of the tubules. The time required for this part of spermatogenesis in the bull is about 10 days longer (40–42 days). From these and similar results it is possible to calculate that the duration of spermatogenesis—that is, the elapsed time between the appearance of the spermatogonial stem cell and liberation of the resulting spermatozoa into the lumen of the tubule—requires about 49 days in the ram, 60 days in the bull (Amann 1962), and 52 days in the rabbit (Swierstra and Foote 1965). Swierstra (1968) considered 34.4 days a reasonable approximation of the duration of spermatogenesis in the boar, based on the assumption that it extends over four consecutive cycles of the seminiferous epithelium.

Sertoli cells

The Sertoli cells are large, are basally situated, and have prominent nucleoli. They have multiple long processes that surround the spermatocytes and spermatids, and their cytoplasm contains glycogen, glycoproteins, many lipid droplets, and certain steroid compounds. The number of Sertoli cells remains constant during the seminiferous cycle.

The nuclei of Sertoli cells are irregular in shape and the nuclear membrane shows deep indentations. Most of the nuclei are perpendicular to the basement membrane of the tubules before the spermatozoa are released into the lumen; later they tend to parallel this membrane (Ortavant 1959). These cells apparently supply nutrition and allow maturation of the spermatids and release them under the influence of anterior pituitary hormones; they may also perform an essential role in the transport of androgens to the germinal epithelial cells.

Hormonal control of seminiferous epithelium

Hypophysectomy in some species results in disappearance of all tubular cells except the spermatogonia and Sertoli cells. And spermatogenesis can no longer occur in a normal manner in any animal after hypophysectomy. The effects in the rat differ somewhat from those in other species; spermatocytes, as well as spermatogonia and Sertoli cells, remain for considerable periods, although the spermatids degenerate, tubular fluid is lost, and the germinal epithelium atrophies to varying degrees. The androgen-producing interstitial cells also atrophy after hypophysectomy. Administration of crude extracts of adenohypophyseal tissue reverses these changes in all species.

The effects of the individual gonadotropins in hypophysectomized laboratory animals have been exhaustively studied, but similar studies have not been carried out for any of the domestic animals except the dog.

The administration of relatively small doses of androgens decreases testicular weights of mature rats by depressing gonadotropin secretion through the feedback mechanism discussed in Chapters 52 and 53. Similarly, solid testosterone implanted in the basal tuberal posterior median eminence in the rat or in the arcuate nucleus of the dog induces atrophy of the testes. However, relatively large amounts of androgens have a direct stimulatory effect on testes, and are even capable of maintaining spermatogenesis at a low level in hypophysectomized rats. Steinberger and Duckett (1967) stated that there is an absolute requirement for testosterone for the reduction division of primary spermatocytes (see Fig. 54.5); the formation of primitive type A spermatogonia from gonocytes and the early phases of spermatid maturation may also require testosterone. The final maturation of spermatids also requires FSH (follicle-stimulating hormone). Of course, these requirements for spermatogenesis are qualitative and tell us nothing about the hormonal requirements for quantitative maintenance of normal spermatogenesis.

Since testosterone secretion in the normal animal is under pituitary LH (luteinizing hormone) control, it might be inferred that, contrary to our earlier concepts, FSH plays no important role in the qualitative aspects of spermatogenesis. Recent studies (French and Ritzén 1973), however, show that Sertoli cells within the seminiferous tubules in the testes of several species produce an androgen-binding protein that is secreted into the testicular fluid and concentrated in the caput epididymis. This protein has a high affinity for both testosterone and 5α-dihydrotestosterone. FSH clearly provides the stimulus to production of this androgen-binding protein by the Sertoli cells. The androgen-binding protein is thought to provide a mechanism for transport of androgens into the germinal epithelium, and the rate of transport is regulated by FSH. Yet another receptor protein system is apparently involved in transporting testosterone and 5α-dihydrotestosterone from the cytoplasm into the nuclei of the tubular epithelial cells. A role of FSH, alone or in combination with LH, in maintaining longitudinal growth of the seminiferous tubules in rats was demonstrated by Leidl and Hansel (1972). Thus it appears that FSH is important in both qualitative and quantitative aspects of spermatogenesis in the rat. Prolactin also appears to have a synergistic effect with LH in maintaining testosterone production in the rat (Hafiez et al. 1972).

Experiments with parabiotic rats show that less LH is required to maintain the male interstitial cells than is required to produce ovulation in the female. For example, if a castrate male rat is united parabiotically with a hypophysectomized female on one side and a hypophysectomized male on the other, the pituitary secretions of the castrate, which contain mostly FSH and little LH, are capable of maintaining normal interstitial cells and spermatogenesis in the hypophysectomized male. However, the ovaries of the hypophysectomized female parabiont do not ovulate and become cystic, a result characteristic of excessive FSH and too little LH (Finerty 1952). These and other experiments (see Chapter 53) indicate that the tonic gonadotropin secretion sustained by the center in the ventromedial arcuate area of the hypothalamus is sufficient to maintain adequate levels of testosterone in the male.

Detailed studies of the hormonal control of spermatogenesis in domestic animals are badly needed. Some attempts to improve spermatogenesis in farm animals by hormonal treatments have been based on misconceptions of the nature of spermatogenesis and its hormonal control. In many cases, the results of the treatments have not been evaluated for a long enough time to permit really valid conclusions.

Steroidogenesis

Hormonal control of interstitial cells

The male hormones are produced mainly by the interstitial cells of the testes, although smaller amounts may be produced by the adrenals, and in females by the ovaries. Most evidence indicates that the seminiferous tubules do not produce androgens, although the Sertoli cells do produce estrogenic hormones in several species.

Histochemical techniques have frequently been used to demonstrate the production of steroids by interstitial cells. When sections of testicular tissue are treated with phenylhydrazine and observed under the microscope, characteristic yellow phenylhydrazones are seen in the interstitial cells but not in the tubular elements. Previous treatment of the sections with acetone, which dissolves the lipid-soluble steroids, results in failure of phenylhydrazones to form in the interstitial cells. The formation of hydrazones is dependent upon the presence of compounds having a ketone radical, and most of the major androgens are 3-keto compounds. Similarly, when sections of testes are examined microscopically, the blood vessels do not appear to enter the tubules. Consequently, any hormones produced within the tubules could not readily pass into the circulation. In contrast, the interstitial cells have an abundant blood supply.

Many observations indicate that androgen production by the interstitial cells is controlled by the pituitary and that LH is the hormone primarily involved. Four types of testicular alterations have been used to differentiate the spermatogenic and steroidogenic functions of the testes and to elucidate the hormonal control of each: (1) castration, (2) vasectomy, (3) cryptorchidism, and (4) testicular transplantations.

If an animal is castrated, it becomes sterile, and involution of the secondary sex characteristics occurs. Castration of the cockerel is followed by atrophy of the comb and wattles with a loss of red color, a loss of courtship behavior, and a loss of pugnacity. In mammals the accessory ducts and glands involute following castration. If castration is performed prepubertally, the secondary sex characteristics do not develop. In men, the larynx remains small and the voice high-pitched; hair growth on the face and body is suppressed and there is a lack of libido. After castration the body conformation typical of the male of various species does not develop. Castration retards closure of the epiphyses in the long bones. If castration is performed after the age of puberty, the male secondary sex characteristics persist to variable degrees depending on age, species, and other factors.

Cryptorchidism may occur naturally, or it may be produced surgically. In this condition one or both testes remain or are placed in the abdominal cavity. If one testis remains in the abdominal cavity, the condition is referred to as unilateral cryptorchidism, while the retention of both results in bilateral cryptorchidism. When the testes are placed in the abdominal cavity, spermatozoa and other constituents of the germinal epithelium rapidly degenerate. Hormone production, however, remains normal or nearly so for a considerable period, so that the seminal vesicles and prostate are maintained at nearly normal weights. In some species androgen production of cryptorchid testes is somewhat reduced; the longer the condition exists, the greater the deficiency of androgens noted in these species. The testes are normally retained in the abdominal cavity during the nonmating season in some species.

The effects of cryptorchidism point out the heat-regulating function of the scrotum. A temperature difference of several degrees exists between the scrotum and the abdominal cavity. Spermatogenesis cannot occur in a normal manner in most mammals at the higher temperature of the abdominal cavity.

The scrotum regulates testicular temperature by two specialized mechanisms. The arterial blood entering the testes is precooled by heat exchange with the cooler venous blood returning through the remarkably convoluted pampiniform plexus. Blood passing onto the surface of testes is several degrees cooler than when it enters the spermatic artery from the aorta; blood leaving the pampiniform plexus is several degrees warmer than the blood in veins on the surface of the testes. These temperature changes occur in the spermatic cord, where the internal spermatic artery is in close contact with veins of the pampiniform plexus. The scrotum can also regulate the temperature of the testes to some degree by contraction and relaxation of the external cremaster and tunica dartos muscles in response to changes in environmental temperature. Exposure to cold causes these muscles to draw the testes nearer the body wall.

The close and extensive contact between the spermatic artery and veins in the pampiniform plexus may serve yet another important physiological function. Transfer of testosterone, and possibly other substances, from the spermatic vein to the spermatic artery has been demonstrated in several species (Ginther 1974). The venoarterial pathway could be part of a mechanism for maintaining higher concentrations of testosterone and 5α-dihydrotestosterone within the seminiferous tubules than in peripheral blood.

Vasectomy (section of the ductus deferens) is of course an effective sterilization measure. At one time it was claimed that vasectomy was also effective in restoring vigor to the senescent. It was thought that the number of interstitial cells increased after vasectomy and that this restored sexual vigor. Such does not appear to be the case, and no important endocrine changes seem to result from this sterilization measure. Amann (1962) found that vasectomy had no effect on spermatogenesis or testes histology in bulls. Some reports indicate that alternate degeneration and repair of the seminiferous tubules occur after vasoligation in laboratory rodents, but this has been a variable finding. Hafs et al. (1974) reported a temporary interruption of spermatogenesis after vasectomy in bulls.

There are three kinds of testicular transplants: auto-, homo-, and heterotransplants. Autotransplants involve the removal of the testis from its normal site in the scrotum to another site elsewhere in the body of the same animal. Homotransplantation is the transfer of the testes from one animal to another of the same species, and heterotransplantation is the transplantation of the testes from an animal of one species to an animal of another species. Heterotransplants are rarely successful, although some exceptions to the general rule have been noted. For example, tissues from other species can sometimes be successfully transplanted into the cheek pouch of the hamster.

Testes may be successfully transplanted to subcutaneous or intramuscular sites or into the peritoneal cavity. After transplantation, the germinal epithelium in the seminiferous tubules diminishes rapidly; no spermatozoa are produced. The only exception to this result is found in grafts into the anterior chamber of the eye, where some sperm may actually be produced, perhaps because the temperature at that site more nearly approaches the normal temperature within the scrotum. Testicular transplantation repairs the deterioration of the secondary sex characters that follows castration, indicating that transplanted testes continue to produce the male hormone for a considerable time even though the spermatogenic function has ceased.

Male sex steroids

The first effective lipoid extract of bull testes was prepared in 1927; it was effective in causing growth of the atrophied comb and wattles of the capon. Since that time, several potent androgens have been isolated from testicular tissues and from urine. Orally active androgens have been prepared synthetically. Androsterone was isolated from male urine in 1931 by Butenandt. Testosterone, the major androgen secreted by the testes, was isolated in 1935 by David et al. 5α-dihydrotestosterone, a potent metabolite of testosterone, is found in many androgen target tissues and appears to be an active compound at the cellular level.

The biosynthetic pathways leading to androgen production are outlined in Figure 53.5. Oxidative cleavage of the cholesterol side chain yields pregnenolone, which is converted to progesterone by dehydrogenation in ring A and a spontaneous shift of the double bond from the 5-6 to the 4-5 position. Progesterone undergoes hydroxylation at carbon-17 to yield 17α-hydroxyprogesterone, the immediate precursor of the androgens. Oxidative cleavage of its side chain yields Δ^4-androstenedione, which is reduced to testosterone. Hydroxylation of Δ^4-androstenedione at carbon-11 yields 11β-hydroxy-Δ^4-androstenedione, an androgen that has been isolated from human urine and certain tumors of the adrenal cortex. Dehydroepiandrosterone is another androgen found in the urine; it probably serves as an intermediate in a second pathway for testosterone formation in the testes. This second pathway is thought to include 17α-hydroxypregnenolone, dehydroepiandrosterone, and Δ^4-androstenedione; Δ^4-androstenedione and testosterone may also serve as precursors of estrone and estradiol. The synthesis of ^{14}C-labeled acetate into testosterone after its infusion into the spermatic artery has been demonstrated in the bull. Eik-Nes (1967) measured steroid production in vivo by a technique in which the testes of anesthetized, heparinized dogs were infused through the spermatic artery with the animal's own arterial blood under controlled conditions. Addition of human chorionic gonadotropin (HCG) to the blood perfusing the testis caused an increase in testosterone secretion within 8–12 minutes. The spermatic venous blood levels of progesterone, 17α-hydroxyprogesterone, Δ^4-androstenedione, Δ^5-pregnenolone, and dehydroepiandrosterone were also increased, indicating that both metabolic pathways described above were responsive to the gonadotropin treatment. Either bovine LH or HCG injected into bulls increases plasma testosterone levels for about 4 hours; prolactin injections have no effect.

The first step in the catabolism of the androgens as well as estrogen and progesterone is usually the reduction of the ketone group in ring A, resulting in 3α-OH compounds. Testosterone and dehydroepiandrosterone are converted to Δ^4-androstenedione, which is reduced to androsterone and etiocholanone, both compounds having 3α-OH configurations. In addition to reductive inactivation of the steroids, the liver is responsible for their conjugation as sulfates and glucuronides. These water-soluble conjugates are more readily excreted through the urine and bile. The bull, however, seems to differ from several other animals studied in that it conjugates testosterone metabolites exclusively with glucuronic acid for excretion in both urine and bile. Epitestosterone (17α-hydroxy-4-androstene-3-one) and its reduction product, 17α-hydroxy-5-β-androstene-3-one, are the most abundant metabolites of testosterone found in the feces of the bull. Neither androsterone nor etiocholanone has been found in the feces, but etiocholanone and epitestosterone have been found in the bile.

The testes of several species produce estrogenic substances as well as androgens. Bull, deer, and stallion testes contain estrogens, and the urine of the stallion contains high levels of estrogen, which disappear after castration. Some workers feel that Sertoli cells or other tubular elements produce estrogenic substances under certain conditions, but in most species the interstitial cells are probably the major source of these estrogens.

Factors influencing spermatogenesis and steroidogenesis

Since spermatogenesis and steroidogenesis are controlled by FSH and LH, the mechanisms that affect ovarian function may be expected to apply in a general way to the testes as well. The basic environmental factors affecting adenohypophyseal function through the hypothalamus have been discussed in Chapter 53. The importance of the hypothalamus and exteroceptive factors affecting it in regulating pituitary gonadotropin secretion was illustrated by an example: the inability of the young male duck to respond normally to increased daily amounts of light by increasing spermatogenesis following section of the portal vessels.

Chapter 53 showed that both the behavioral responses to estrogen and its feedback effects on pituitary gonadotropin secretion in the female are mediated by the hypothalamus. Apparently, a similar situation exists with respect to testosterone in the male; both the negative gonadotropin-inhibiting response and the behavioral responses are controlled by the hypothalamus. Different hypothalamic areas are involved in the two types of response (Davidson and Bloch 1969). The negative feedback effect is produced only by testosterone implants in the basomedial area. On the other hand, testosterone implants in a wide area of the hypothalamus are effective in restoring male sex behavior, although implants in the anterior hypothalamic-preoptic area are most effective. Behavioral activation is apparently achieved with very low levels of testosterone, while feedback inhibition of LH secretion seems to require relatively high levels of the hormone.

Exteroceptive factors

Light is probably the most important environmental factor influencing the hypothalamus, pituitary, and testes in most species. Additional daily illumination has been shown to cause activation of the testes and spermatogenesis during the normal nonbreeding seasons in many species of birds, including the starling, sparrow, duck, and junco. In some birds the development of male plumage is regulated by androgens: in others gonadotropic and gonadal hormones are involved in regulating feather growth patterns (see Chapter 53).

Males of some species undergo a distinct rutting season, during which androgen secretion and spermatogenesis occur at maximal rates. The rutting season can be induced during the normally quiescent seasons by administration of androgen. The Virginia deer is an excellent example. In the northern hemisphere antler growth begins in the spring and the velvetlike tissue covering the antler is shed in September. The antlers are heavily calcified during November and December and are shed in midwinter. The testes and male accessory glands are inactive during the spring months, when antler growth is initiated; they enlarge in the fall, when the antlers become calcified and mating occurs, and decline in size after the mating season, at the time the antlers are shed. Antler growth may be induced in females that do not normally grow antlers or in prepubertally castrated males by androgen administration. Testosterone administered to antlered adult males causes prompt shedding of the velvet and calcification of the antlers. Testosterone apparently controls the shedding of the velvet and calcification of the antlers (Wislocki et al. 1947), but initiation of antler growth is a more complex phenomenon involving both androgens and one or more pituitary principles. Decreasing daily amounts of light may well be involved in causing the increased gonadotropin production necessary to activate the testes and to bring about the increased androgen production and spermatogenesis; decreasing temperatures may also play a role.

The domestic animals may be classed into three groups with respect to their responses to light: (1) those in which the pituitary is activated by periods of short or decreasing daylight (sheep and goats), (2) those in which the pituitary is activated by long or increasing light periods (horse and donkey), and (3) those in which sensitivity to photoperiodic stimulation is difficult to characterize (cattle and pigs).

The effects of light on testes and pituitary functions in the ram and male goat are clear-cut. Although these animals can reproduce during the entire year, the total number of spermatozoa and spermatogenic activity reach a maximum during the normal breeding season in the fall and then gradually decline until a minimum is reached during the summer months. Semen quality, as measured by motility and percentage of live spermatozoa in the ejaculate, is lowest in summer. The fructose content of the seminal plasma, generally considered to be a reflection of pituitary gonadotropin and testicular androgen production, is also highest in the ram in early autumn and lowest during late winter and spring.

Semen volume, spermatozoon concentration, and total spermatozoa collected are markedly increased when rams are subjected to artificially controlled short photoperiods. Exposure to long photoperiods (16 hr) results in decreased testicular weights and spermatic reserves. Some studies (Ortavant et al. 1964) show that the gonadotropin content of pituitary glands of rams subjected to short photoperiods is much higher than the content of glands from rams subjected to long photoperiods. The pituitaries of rams slaughtered after 8 hours of illumination daily contained twice as much LH and nearly four times as much FSH as glands from rams slaughtered after being exposed to periods of illumination of 16 hours daily.

Spermatogenesis and steroidogenesis in the bull are less affected by variations in the daily photoperiod. Most workers, but not all, have found that semen quality is lowest in summer and highest in winter or spring. Fertility of cattle bred artificially is generally lowest in summer and highest in autumn, but temperature appears to play a major role. The concentration of fructose in bull semen is lowest in May, June, and July and again in December and January; peak levels occur in March and September. Roussel et al. (1964), working in a semitropical climate, observed that progressive motility and concentration of bull spermatozoa declined appreciably for a 20 week period beginning in May, and that the decline was significantly less in bulls subjected to 14 hours of incandescent illumination daily. However, Ortavant et al. (1964) were unable to find marked differences in spermatogenic activities in testes of bulls slaughtered after exposure to 8 and 16 hour photoperiods.

The stallion produces an increased volume of semen containing a gelatinous component during the breeding season in April. Additional daily illumination in November activates the testes prematurely, while decreasing the photoperiod in April decreases semen volume (Nishikawa and Horie 1952). The effects of varying photoperiods on testis function do not appear to have been studied in the boar or the dog. The testes of the fox are small and inactive until December, when they begin to enlarge rapidly. Spermatogenesis and testicular size are maximal in February, when the vixens come in estrus, and they decline again in April and May. The increase in testicular size begins early in December, though, before the days begin to lengthen, suggesting that gonadal activity is not entirely regulated by light.

Although there is ample evidence that heat applied directly to the scrotum causes testicular damage and interrupts spermatogenesis in several species, the role of environmental temperature is less clearly understood. High ambient temperatures have been associated with lowered fertility in rams. Dutt and Simpson (1957) demonstrated improved motility ratings and a decreased percentage of abnormal cells in semen of rams kept in an air-conditioned room at 7–9°C during the hot summer months. Semen from treated rams had higher sperm cell concentrations than semen from rams kept at uncontrolled environmental temperatures. The lowered fertility in both cattle and swine bred artificially during the summer suggests that elevated temperatures may have adverse effects on sperm production in the boar and the bull. Casady et al. (1953) reported that spermatogenesis in young bulls may be impaired by continuous exposure to temperatures exceeding 30°C for more than 5 weeks.

These results may represent direct effects of temperature on the testes or they may represent effects mediated through the hypothalamus. Most studies indicate that the direct effects of heat on the testis are most important and that the efficiency of the heat-dissipating properties of the scrotum determines the magnitude of the adverse effects of elevated air temperature on the quality of semen produced. It has also been suggested that these adverse effects may be secondary to the hypothyroidism induced by high ambient temperatures, but thyroidectomy does not interfere with spermatogenesis or libido in rams, and thyroxine therapy during periods of heat stress does not consistently improve semen quality. Indeed, excessive amounts of thyroxine may even exaggerate the effects of heat stress.

Although it has been stated that the tonic secretion of FSH and LH sustained by the ventromedial-arcuate nuclei of the hypothalamus is sufficient to maintain testosterone secretion and spermatogenesis in the male, it should not be inferred that secretion of these hormones occurs at a constant rate. Indeed, recent studies show that plasma LH and testosterone levels fluctuate greatly in individual bulls. Peaks in plasma LH levels are normally followed within an hour by peaks in plasma testosterone. The causes of these temporal fluctuations are not completely understood, but diurnal variations and differences in age and in sexual stimulation have been found (Gombe et al. 1973, Smith et al. 1973). Samples collected during the morning and early afternoon generally contain more LH than those collected at night, and mean plasma LH concentrations increase from levels of 4.3 ng/ml in bulls 12–14 months old to levels of 7–10 ng/ml in bulls 3 years old. Sexual stimulation and ejaculation do not appear to cause increases in plasma LH and testosterone in young bulls, but may in mature bulls. However, these factors do not account for all of the episodic fluctuations seen in plasma LH and testosterone levels in bulls, which suggests that undetermined external factors influence LH secretion.

Nutritive deficiencies

The effects of nutrition on semen production in farm animals have been studied in detail in young animals, but less information is available on adult animals. Although underfeeding delays the onset of puberty in all animals, probably as a result of interference with gonadotropin production or its release at a normal rate, it has been difficult to influence spermatogenesis or androgen production adversely in adult animals by imposing nutritive deficiencies. The feed intake of adult bulls can be restricted until body weight is reduced as much as 25 percent without causing changes in spermatozoon concentration, motility, semen volume, or libido (Mann and Walton 1953). However, the fructose and citric acid levels in the semen, indicators of androgen secretion in the bull, are drastically reduced.

Meacham et al. (1963) found that low protein rations caused significant decreases in semen volume and total number of sperm per ejaculate when fed to young bulls for prolonged periods. Libido was also adversely affected by the protein deficiency. However, VanDemark et al. (1964) found that a rather severe reduction of total digestible nutrient intake at 46 months of age in bulls previously fed at a normal level had little effect on semen-producing ability. Similarly, the total number of sperm produced, sperm motility, and fertility appeared not to be decreased as a result of feeding mature rams or boars low-energy rations for considerable periods (Tilton et al. 1964, Stevermer et al. 1961). Inanition causes reductions of semen volume and concentrations of citric acid, fructose, ergothionene, and inositol in boars. Ergothionene concentration in particular is closely related to feed intake. Both inanition and protein deficiencies of long duration have been reported to cause testis hypofunction in mature laboratory animals (Leathem 1961), and very severe reductions of protein intake result in decreases in the total number of sperm per ejaculate in young beef bulls.

Unlike the immature animal that is highly dependent on dietary protein, the adult can probably shift protein reserves so as to maintain gonadotropin production and spermatogenesis for a considerable time after nutritional stress is imposed. Decreased androgen production, as measured by reduced seminal vesicle weights and reduced levels of fructose and citric acid in the semen, is usually noted before spermatogenesis is adversely affected in underfed animals.

Prolonged vitamin A deficiency causes reduced sperm production in bulls, but other clinical symptoms of the vitamin deficiency usually become evident before sperm production declines (Bratton et al. 1948). Vitamin A deficiency also causes degeneration of the germinal epithelium of the ram, which occurs even before the deficient animals begin to lose weight. Vitamin E deficiency causes atrophy of the germinal epithelium in rats, but similarly deficient rations have no effect on spermatogenesis in bulls (Gullickson et al. 1949).

Noxious agents

Many chemicals, some metals, ionizing radiations, and heat affect spermatogenesis adversely in several species. These include agents such as triethylenemelamines (TEM), bis (dichloroacetyl) diamines, 1,4-dimethanesulfonoxybutane, and related alkyl sulfonates, nitrofurans, thiophens, and cadmium salts (Leblond et al. 1963).

Single injections of TEM, 1,4-dimethanesulfonoxybutane, and isopropyl methanesulfonate result in aspermia 10–11 weeks after injection into rabbits (Fox et al. 1963). All of these compounds inhibit early spermatogonial development, but their effects are at least partially reversible for variable periods of time in different species. In contrast, subcutaneous or intraperitoneal injections of cadmium salts often result in complete testicular necrosis and a permanent cessation of spermatogenesis in rabbits, rats, guinea pigs, and goats (Pařízek 1960). The concurrent administration of zinc tends to prevent the necrotizing effects of cadmium.

Many other compounds interfere with normal spermatogenesis, spermiogenesis, or testes development. These include highly chlorinated naphthalene in bulls (Vlahos et al. 1955), an orally active progestin, 6-methyl-17-acetoxyprogesterone, in ram lambs (Dutt and Falcon 1964), amphotericin B in rabbits (Swierstra et al. 1964), numerous metallic salts in rabbits (Kamboj and Kar 1964), and an orally active androgen, methyl testosterone, in boars (Noland and Burris 1956). The effects of all of these substances are reversible.

Practically every stage of spermatogenesis is susceptible to one or more of these agents, and selected dose levels of some of them—e.g. the alkylating agents—destroy a definite group of cells, while permitting the remainder of the germinal epithelium to develop normally. Amphotericin B, for example, has no effect on the duration of the stages of the seminiferous cycle but decreases the rate at which spermatozoa migrate from the Sertoli cells to the lumen. The effects of the nitrofurans depend on the presence of gonadotropins. Results such as these suggest that it may be possible to find agents that have specific effects on spermatozoa or spermatogenesis but no other major effects on the whole organism. It seems unlikely, however, that any of the compounds mentioned completely fulfill this criterion. Cadmium salts cause vascular and CNS lesions and liver, kidney, and spleen damage; and 1,4-dimethanesulfonoxybutane has thrombocytopenic effects (Foster and Cameron 1963, Pařízek 1964).

Another noxious agent, α-chlorohydrin (3-chlor-1,2-propanediol), causes temporary infertility when administered daily to rats, hamsters, guinea pigs, rams, and boars. It has no effect on mating behavior, and the spermatozoa recover their fertilizing ability within 5 days after withdrawal of the drug. This compound acts in the epididymis, and short-term treatments have no effects on the testes (Lubicz-Nawrocki and Chang 1974).

MALE ACCESSORY ORGANS

In addition to the testes, which produce the spermatozoa, and the system of ducts that transport them to the epididymides and finally to the exterior, the male genital system consists of various glands that add their secretions to the spermatozoa at the time of emission. These include the ampullary glands, seminal vesicles, prostate, and bulbourethral glands. The only known function of these glands is the secretion of the seminal plasma. Each of them consists of a secretory epithelium, connective tissue, and smooth muscle fibers.

The size and location of these glands and the chemical nature of their secretions vary considerably among the domestic animals. The prostate, for example, is disseminated in the ram and the goat, while in the boar and the bull the gland has a disseminated region as well as a discrete body. The prostate is a compact gland in the dog, and in fact is the only accessory gland found in this species. It is a compound tubuloalveolar gland in all domestic animals, and distinct dorsal, ventral, and lateral lobes are present in some species.

The bulbourethrals are also compound tubuloalveolar glands; they are remarkably large, cylindrical structures in the boar. The seminal vesicles are elongated glands with complex internal villous projections; they are relatively large in domestic animals and especially so in the boar. The ampullary glands are enlargements arising from the ampullae of the ductus deferentia.

Androgen dependence and estrogen effects

The accessory glands are all remarkably dependent on androgen; following castration their weights decrease and the heights of the secretory epithelia decrease. Testosterone injections reverse these changes. When testosterone is injected into castrate rats, the increase in weights of the seminal vesicles and ventral lobe of the prostate bear a linear relationship to the level of testosterone injected. This relationship provides a convenient method of determining the amount of male sex hormones present. Other bioassay methods for androgens are based on growth of the capon's comb and increases in fructose and citric acid in the accessory glands. Immunoassays and competitive protein-binding assays (Shemesh and Hansel 1974) are commonly used to determine plasma levels of testosterone in domestic animals.

Cytological changes in the prostates and seminal vesicles are even more sensitive indicators for androgenic hormones. The normal epithelial cells in these glands are characterized by basal nuclei, conspicuous nucleoli, and a supranuclear clear area in the cytoplasm representing the Golgi zone. Mitochondria are seen in all parts of the cell. The basement membrane rests on a connective tissue stroma containing smooth muscle fibers. A reduction in cell height occurs after castration and the cytoplasmic clear zone soon disappears; the nuclei become small and pyknotic and the basement membrane disappears. Androgen injections reverse all of these changes and promote mitotic activity within 24–48 hours.

Spermatozoa are stored in the epididymides, where they undergo certain maturational changes and develop the ability to fertilize eggs. Spermatozoa taken from the caput region of the epididymis fertilize few eggs, while those removed from the cauda region are highly fertile (Fig. 54.8). During passage of the spermatozoa through the epididymis, the protoplasmic droplet moves posteriorly from the head until it reaches the midpiece, where it detaches. The function of this lipid-containing droplet is unknown, but its retention in ejaculated sperm is often associated with reduced fertility. Sperm taken from regions anterior to the cauda epididymis of the bull are immotile until exposed to air, and it is thought that high carbon dioxide tension in the epididymis plays a major role in inhibiting their motility. However, such factors as pH, low oxygen tension, and sodium and potassium concentrations in the fluids may also contribute to immotility. Ram spermatozoa are reported to be motile in the epididymis (Risley 1963).

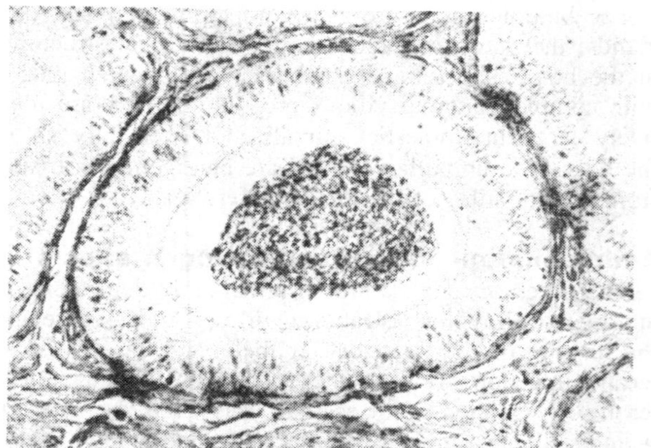

Figure 54.8. Cross section of the epididymis of a bull showing the spermatozoa and epithelial elements within the lumen. x 100.

Many spermatozoa are resorbed from the epididymides; the number resorbed is roughly proportional to the number present in the caput epididymis, the region from which most resorption occurs. Amann and Almquist (1962) estimated that 50–60 percent of the spermatozoa produced in bulls may be resorbed by the epididymides, the exact figure depending somewhat on the frequency of ejaculation and other factors. The epididymal epithelial cells may reutilize the DNA resulting from the breakdown and absorption of the dead sperm (Orgebin-Crist 1964). The functions of the epididymis have been summarized as follows: (1) to transport sperm from the testis to the ejaculatory duct, (2) to bring about sperm maturation and fertilizing capacity, (3) to store the sperm formed, (4) to foster the dissolution of aging sperm in proportion to the fullness of the epididymis and dependent on the frequency of collection, and (5) to resorb both fluids and the products from sperm breakdown (Orgebin-Crist 1969). The time required for passage of sperm through the epididymis has been estimated as 14–20 days in the ram, 8–11 days in the bull, and 10 days in the boar (Swierstra 1968).

The epididymides are dependent on the androgenic hormones; castration results in decreased weights, epithelial cell heights, and tubule diameters, while androgen therapy restores all these figures to normal values. Glycerylphosphorylcholine, one of the major chemical constituents of epididymal fluid, declines after castration and increases under the influence of exogenous testosterone propionate. Sperm tail abnormalities and poor sperm motility have been associated with epididymal dysfunction in the bull (Gustafsson et al. 1972). Metabolic changes occurring in ram and bull sperm as they pass through the epididymis have recently been reviewed by Bedford (1974).

The enlarged accessory glands usually found in steers and wethers fed the synthetic estrogen diethylstilbestrol in order to increase their rates of gain, and the production of excessive amounts of estrogen by certain tumors in domestic animals, have aroused interest in the effects of the female sex hormones on the male accessory glands. Both of the above cases reflect the combined effects of decreased androgen production resulting from the ability of estrogen to inhibit pituitary gonadotropin production, and the direct effect of the particular estrogenic substance involved on the glandular tissue. The immediate effect of excess estrogens in intact males is likely to be atrophy of the accessory glands. However, after prolonged treatment, animals are likely to show fibromuscular hypertrophy and metaplastic transformations of the epithelial elements of the accessory glands. Changes in the male accessory glands of ruminants after diethylstilbestrol feeding mainly involve epithelial metaplasia, resulting from the ability of estrogens to stimulate mitotic activity directly.

Spermiation

The release of the spermatozoa from the Sertoli cells, often referred to as spermiation, appears to be brought about by the action of gonadotropins. It has been suggested that gonadotropins release the sperm by activating a mucolytic enzyme in the region of the apical cytoplasm of the Sertoli cells. The spermatozoa are then transported into the rete testis, apparently tail first, by rhythmic surface contractions of certain epithelial cells in the region of the tubuli rectis (Risley 1963). Muscular activities of the seminal tubules and the rete system may also aid in the process, and some workers postulate that periodic contractions of the testicular capsule aid in propelling the sperm out of the testes.

Smooth muscle physiology

Contractile activity of the smooth muscle elements of the ductus efferentes and ductus epididymides is dependent upon the pituitary-gonadal hormone system. Contractility disappears 12–15 days after hypophysectomy in the rat and is restored after 7–10 daily injections of HCG. The fact that castration of hypophysectomized, gonadotropin-treated animals prevents the restoration of contractile activity by gonadotropin suggests that the effect is mediated by testosterone (Risley 1963). Testosterone propionate injections restore contractile activity in the vasa efferentia and ductus epididymides of castrate rats. Epinephrine injections increase the contractility of tubules, while oxytocin has no effect on contractility of the rabbit epididymis.

In contrast, androgens appear to inhibit the musculature of the duct system more distal to the testes (the vas deferens and seminal vesicles), while estrogens are stimulatory. Gassner (1952) reported an increase in sperm concentration in bull semen within a short period of time after estrogen administration, a finding that may have been related to the stimulatory effect of this hormone on the musculature of the vas deferens.

Numerous studies indicate that the parasympathetic division of the autonomic nervous system plays an active role in regulating the secretions of the accessory glands and in influencing the passage of spermatozoa through the vas deferens and epididymis at the time of ejaculation. Treatment of either boars (Dziuk and Mann 1963) or bulls (Baker et al. 1964) with atropine results in reduced semen volume, spermatozoa per ejaculate, and chloride concentration, and an increased concentration of fructose in the semen. Administration of parasympathomimetic drugs such as pilocarpine has opposite effects in the bull, except for fructose concentration, which is unaffected. Pilocarpine stimulates secretion of seminal fluids from the accessory glands, particularly the prostate and bulbourethral glands, and promotes the passage of sperm through epididymides and vasa deferentia.

Hodson (1964) studied the role of the hypogastric nerves in seminal emission in the rabbit and concluded that emission (expulsion of seminal fluid into the pelvic urethra) is brought about by contraction of smooth muscles in the accessory organs innervated by predominantly sympathetic fibers. However, removal of the hypogastric nerve and posterior mesenteric ganglion has no effect on ejaculation (expulsion of fluid from the external urethral orifice); erection and orgasm occur normally and subsidence of erection is only slightly delayed. Fibers controlling ejaculation and subsidence of erection are probably contained in the internal pudendal nerve. Histological studies of the seminal vesicles, prostate gland, and ductus deferentes indicate that removal of sympathetic innervation does not prevent secretion in these organs, but merely prevents expulsion of the secretory products. Function of the urinary bladder sphincter is lost following removal of the hypogastric nerves and posterior mesenteric ganglion.

Chemical composition of secretions

Fructose is the major source of energy for spermatozoa of the bull, ram, goat, and rabbit under both aerobic and anaerobic conditions. It is derived mainly from the seminal vesicles and metabolized to lactic acid by the spermatozoa. The production of fructose by the seminal vesicles is androgen-dependent; the levels in the seminal plasma fall rapidly after castration, and the fall is prevented in castrate animals by testosterone implants (Mann and Parsons 1950, Gassner et al. 1952).

Fructose is absent from seminal plasma of the dog, and only a trace is present in the seminal fluid of the stallion. A closely related sugar alcohol, sorbitol, which is readily reduced to fructose, is present in the semen of stallions as well as of several other species. Sorbitol is derived from the accessory glands and has been identified in the seminal vesicles of the ram. Dog seminal plasma, however, contains no sorbitol. The seminal vesicles of the boar produce large amounts of a nonreducing carbohydrate, inositol. Much smaller amounts of the same substance are present in bull, ram, and stallion seminal plasma. The seminal vesicles are the major source of inositol in most species, although it has also been found in ampullary secretions of the stallion. The physiological significance of this substance is unknown.

Boar seminal vesicles secrete a large quantity of ergothioneine, a sulfur-containing base thought to protect the spermatozoa from the toxic effects of oxidizing agents. Ampullary secretions of the stallion also contain ergothioneine. Both boar and stallion semen possess characteristics that make them particularly vulnerable to oxidizing agents. These include large volume, low sperm concentration, and low levels of glycolyzable sugars. Ergothioneine is a strong reducing substance. Ascorbic acid produced by the seminal vesicles of most other species is also a strong reducing substance.

The seminal vesicles of most species produce citric acid; it is present in bull semen in particularly large amounts. Like fructose, it disappears from the semen after castration and reappears when androgens are administered.

Seminal vesicle secretions contain many other substances, such as phosphorylcholine, which produces choline by the action of acid phosphatase, amino acids, proteins, sodium, potassium, lipids, and numerous proteolytic enzymes (White and MacLeod 1963, Price and Williams-Ashman 1961).

The prostate glands are similarly responsible for the secretions of several characteristic substances. The nitrogenous base spermine, present in human semen but apparently absent in the semen of domestic animals, is contributed by the prostate. A conjugated protein called sperm antiagglutinin, which prevents head-to-head agglutination of sperm, is also produced by the prostate.

Another group of compounds, the prostaglandins, was first isolated from ram prostate glands. These substances are produced by many other tissues; the possible role in ovarian function of prostaglandin $F_2\alpha$ from the uterus is discussed in Chapter 53. Ram seminal vesicles are particularly rich sources of the enzymes needed to convert the long-chain, highly unsaturated fatty acids (dihomo-α-linolenic and arachidonic) to prostaglandins. Prostaglandins E_1, E_2, E_3, $F_1\alpha$, and $F_2\alpha$ have been isolated from semen. Prostaglandin E_1 inhibits contractions of the rabbit testicular capsule in vitro, while prostaglandin $F_1\alpha$ stimulates capsular contractions (Johnson et al. 1971). The testes of mature animals synthesize prostaglandins, and these compounds may play a role in testosterone synthesis.

The dorsolateral lobe of the prostate has a remarkably high content of zinc. The uptake of zinc by the gland is hormonally controlled; castration causes a marked decrease and the administration of either testosterone or LH causes a dose-dependent increase. Zinc is an integral part of the enzyme carbonic anhydrase, and is also associated with lactic dehydrogenase in the semen, but its exact role in prostatic secretions is unknown. Prostatic secretions also contain fructose, citric acid, cholesterol, proteins, and in some species free amino acids. Numerous enzymes, including acid and alkaline phosphatases, proteolytic enzymes, glycosidases, and glutamic oxalacetic transaminase, occur in seminal plasma and probably originate at least in part from the prostate gland (White and MacLeod 1963).

The choline derivative glycerylphosphorylcholine is a normal constituent of the seminal plasma of all domestic animals. The epididymis is the principal source of this compound. Several studies show that ^{32}P injected subcutaneously is incorporated into the compound by epididymal tissues both in vivo and in vitro.

PUBERTY

The testes of all domestic animals normally descend into the scrotum before birth. The action of androgens of fetal origin appears to be the major factor involved. From birth to maturity the testes and accessory glands grow at a rather uniform rate, generally following the pattern of body weight. In fact, the correlation between body and testes weights in the bull is remarkably high.

Sperm production in Holstein bulls raised on medium levels of feeding begins at an average age of 47 weeks and an average weight of 273 kg (Bratton et al. 1961). Secretory function in the seminal vesicles begins several months earlier, however, resulting in the appearance of fructose and citric acid in semen from electrically ejaculated bulls before the first spermatozoa are produced (Davies et al. 1957). These findings imply that androgen production is at a rather high level for several months before the appearance of the first spermatozoa. In fact, it has been shown that premature appearance of both fructose and citric acid in electrically discharged semen of 5-month-old bull calves can be brought about by administering HCG for relatively short periods.

Rams reach puberty at about 209 days of age and 32 kg of body weight, boars at about 200 days, and the stallion at 16–17 months (Rowson 1959). The boar testes and epididymides develop rapidly between the fourth and seventh months, probably as a result of increased androgen secretion.

Associated hormonal changes

On the basis of what has been said about the hormonal control of spermatogenesis, it should be clear that puberty results from the secretion of increased amounts of both FSG and LH from the adenohypophysis. Several studies indicate that male pituitaries generally contain considerably more FSH and LH than glands from females. The gonads may well increase their ability to respond to increasing amounts of gonadotropins with age, since many reports suggest that gonads of very young animals are partially refractory to injected gonadotropins. The androgens produced by the testes of the maturing animal may also suppress pituitary gonadotropin production.

Courot (1967) studied the effects of hypophysectomy and subsequent gonadotropin replacement therapy in impubertal lambs. Hypophysectomy stopped testis growth and prevented the onset of spermatogenesis. LH injections reversed the effects of hypophysectomy on testes weights and the number of supporting cells. Either FSH or LH initiated spermatogenic activity, as indicated by the presence of meiotic prophases in the testes.

Only two types of cells are found in the testes of the lamb until about 60 days after birth: the gonocytes and the supportive cells that are precursors of the Sertoli cells. Serum testosterone levels begin to increase between 60 and 80 days of age, and primary spermatocytes are present by 69 days. Spermatids and occasional spermatozoa are present in the tubules at 120 days. Adult levels of serum testosterone and normal spermatogenesis are finally achieved by 180 days (Schanbacher et al. 1974).

Nutrition and puberty

Many studies have shown that underfeeding delays and overfeeding hastens the onset of spermatogenesis in bulls and rams. Significantly different growth rates were found to result from different feeding levels in all of these studies. Bratton et al. (1961) found that Holstein bulls fed about 130 percent of currently recommended total digestible nutrients came into semen production at an average age of 39 weeks and an average weight of 311 kg. Bulls raised on a low level of feeding did not come into semen production until an average age of 56 weeks and an average weight of 228 kg. Bulls raised on an intermediate plane of nutrition (100 percent of recommended allowances) came into semen production at an average age of 47 weeks and an average weight of 273 kg. The total digestible nutrients required to develop Holstein bulls to semen-producing age approaches a constant, the magnitude of which is about 773 kg. However, breed differences exist in rates of maturity, and caution must be exercised in applying these recommendations to other breeds.

Although total sperm output is reduced in underfed bulls because of the retarded development of the testes, young animals are able to increase spermatozoa output gradually when feed intake is increased to a normal level. VanDemark et al. (1964), however, were unable to correct the detrimental effects of underfeeding on total sperm production, bone development, and endocrine gland and testicular growth when the low level of feeding was maintained until the bulls were 46 months of age before a normal ration was supplied. At this age the endocrine glands and reproductive tract are apparently no longer responsive to increased nutrient intake. In contrast, the same workers found that a rather severe reduction of total digestible nutrient intake in 46-month-old bulls previously fed at a normal level had little effect on semen-producing ability.

The fertility levels of spermatozoa produced by bulls fed on low, medium, and high levels as measured by nonreturns to first service in artificially inseminated cattle are nearly identical (Bratton et al. 1961, Flipse and Almquist 1961). Bulls fed on a high plane of nutrition in early life tend to develop weaknesses of the feet and legs and become slower in their sexual reactions during their adult life (Flipse and Almquist 1961).

Severe protein deficiencies interfere with both spermatogenesis and steroidogenesis in young bulls. Fructose, citric acid, and 5-nucleotidase activity are markedly reduced in the semen of young bulls fed very low levels of protein (1.35–1.65 percent) for 187 days beginning at about 240 days of age (Shirley et al. 1963). Libido, semen volume, and total sperm per ejaculate are also reduced by protein deprivation severe enough to cause marked body weight loss and weakness (Meacham et al. 1963).

Boars growing at subnormal rates because of reduced feed intake have reduced semen volumes and develop ejaculatory capacity at slightly older ages than well-fed boars (Niwa 1954). However, Dutt and Barnhart (1959) found no effects of underfeeding on total number of spermatozoa, motility, or percentage of abnormal sperm. The average ages at puberty for boars fed 100, 70, and 50 percent of recommended total digestible nutrients were 203, 212, and 219 days respectively, and weights at puberty were 101, 78, and 61 kg respectively.

METABOLIC EFFECTS OF ANDROGENS

In addition to the roles androgens play in spermatogenesis, the male sex hormones function in maintaining the accessory glands and the secondary sex characteristics and in bringing about the changes associated with puberty. Perhaps the most important of these is the protein anabolic effect of testosterone and other androgens. The androgens increase the synthesis of proteins and decrease the rate at which amino acids are broken down, resulting in a general increase in muscle mass. Some muscles are stimulated much more than others; results are most noticeable when androgens are administered to castrated males in which such muscles as the levator ani of the rat have atrophied. The muscles of the head, neck, shoulder, back, and abdominal wall of castrated guinea pigs are stimulated by androgen administration out of proportion to the increase in body weight (Kochakian and Tillotson 1957).

Growth rate may or may not increase in response to testosterone treatment, depending on dose, species, and nutritional status. Large doses generally inhibit growth in laboratory animals while small doses may be stimulatory. Several interesting experiments have attempted to influence growth rates and carcass characteristics of domestic animals by injecting testosterone or feeding orally active androgens such as methyl testosterone. The increasing consumer preference for leaner cuts of meat has stimulated interest in the possible use of compounds having protein anabolic effects in animal feeding. Burris et al. (1953) produced marked increases in daily rates of gain of both heifers and steers by weekly intramuscular injections of 1 mg testosterone per kg of body weight. Heifers gained 0.53 kg per day more than untreated control animals and steers 0.29 kg. The total digestible nutrients required per unit of gain were less in the treated animals, and they had a higher percentage of round and a lower percentage of loin in their carcasses. Administration of lower doses of testosterone, either as implants or as subcutaneous injections, has been generally ineffective.

Testosterone implants also produce slight, but not always statistically significant, increases in the growth rates of lambs when used alone or in combination with diethylstilbestrol implants (see Chapter 53). Andrews et al. (1958) found that a combined estrogen-androgen treatment produced more rapid rates of gain than either one alone and also resulted in the most efficient feed utilization. The carcass grades of the testosterone-treated lambs were superior to those of the estrogen-treated animals. Growth rates of swine were depressed by either oral or injected androgens, but leaner carcasses resulted (Perry et al. 1956).

The levels of glycogen in muscles are reduced following castration and are returned to normal or higher concentrations after the administration of testosterone (Leonard 1952). Muscles affected in the rat include the rectus femoris, cremaster, abdominal, and perineal. The effect is apparently a direct one, since testosterone injections prevent glycogen levels from declining during fasting in hypophysectomized rats. Several other hormones, including insulin, gonadotropins, corticotropins, glucocorticoids, and estrogens, can also stimulate glycogen deposition in skeletal muscles. Creatine, usually not present in the urine of normal men, appears in rapidly increasing amounts after castration. Testosterone prevents this increase, probably by causing an increased storage of creatine in the muscles.

SEMEN PHYSIOLOGY

In a sense, the artificial insemination industry is devoted to the collection, storage, and dissemination of DNA, an essential chromosomal constituent that is an integral part of the genetic material. The quantity of DNA in nondividing normal cells is remarkably constant and the amount in diploid somatic cells is twice that found in the haploid spermatozoa of any given species. Salisbury et al. (1961) suggested that DNA levels in bull spermatozoa decline with age during storage, and this decline could be related to the reduced fertility that occurs.

The remarkable growth of the artificial insemination industry has contributed a great deal to the improvement of the productivity of domestic animals, particularly dairy cattle. Nearly 100 percent of the cattle in some areas of the world are now bred artificially, and a large percentage of cattle bred artificially are inseminated with frozen semen. In large dairy areas it is common for more than 30,000 cows a year to be bred with semen provided by a single outstanding sire. Calves have even been born to cows inseminated with semen that had been frozen for more than 10 years. Artificial insemination techniques for sheep, swine, dogs, goats, and horses have also been developed.

These achievements make it essential that all veterinarians and animal scientists understand some of the essential facts concerning the spermatozoon and its physiology. For detailed accounts of semen collection techniques, the processing and distribution of semen, and insemination techniques see Almquist (1959), Rowson (1959), and Pickett and Berndtson (1974).

The spermatozoon

Integrating information on metabolism, structure, and behavior of the spermatozoon is particularly difficult because both its structure and biochemistry are remarkably complex. The ultrastructure of the spermatozoa of domestic animals, particularly the bull, has been the subject of intensive investigations ever since thin-sectioning techniques and electron microscopy became available (Saacke and Almquist 1964, Nicander and Bane 1962).

The bovine sperm head consists of a homogeneous, flattened nucleus covered anteriorly by a three-layered head cap and posteriorly by a loose, thin, dense postnuclear cap (see Fig. 54.6). The nucleus is 0.2–0.3 μ thick, tapering anteriorly to a point along the frontal part of the head and thickening posteriorly to provide an implantation socket for the tail. A basal plate, separate from the nucleus, lines the implantation recess formed by the nucleus in boar and bull sperm. The nucleus is covered by a porous, double nuclear membrane.

The head cap, which covers the anterior 55–60 percent of the nucleus, consists of inner and outer membranes that envelop an electron-dense middle layer. The outer and inner layers are continuous with one another at the posterior margin of the head cap in bull and boar sperm. The inner and outer membranes represent the wall of the acrosomic vesicle seen during spermiogenesis, while the midde layer is of acrosomal origin. The head cap thickens across the frontal part of the head forming a ridge on one side of the nucleus; this thickening is due to the fact that the head cap bends back upon itself at this point. The postnuclear cap extends from the base of the head to the posterior margin of the head cap. It is a single dense cover and is often found in very close association with the cell membrane.

When whole sperm are examined with the light microscope, a third area differing in light intensity from both the head cap and the postnuclear cap is evident. This area has been designated the equatorial segment; it results from the fact that degenerative changes associated with aging or death of the cell cause alterations in the anterior portion of the head cap but not in the posterior portion. The three layers of the posterior portion of the head cap remain intact and distinguishable from the postnuclear cap, resulting in the equatorial segment. The acrosomal material in the anterior portion of the head cap increases in volume, the outer membrane of the head cap deteriorates, and at a latter stage the acrosomal material is lost.

The tail of the spermatozoon consists of a thick middle piece, a long thin principal piece, and a short terminal piece (see Fig. 54.7). The middle piece is joined with the head by a shorter, easily disrupted segment called the neck or implantation region. The length of the neck ranges from 0.3 to 1.5 μ and is characterized by two large laminated fibers, often called implantation plates, entering the head at either extremity of the head recess. Each of these implantation plates is formed by the merger of two (possibly more) thick coarse fibers found on each side of the axial fiber bundle. These laminated fibers are thought to make a 180° arch at the top of the head recess and pass back into the neck. A homogeneous matrix across the tops of the laminated fibers forms a common base for insertion of the fibers into the head recess. The common base is held in the head recess by a lip on either side of the recess; there is no evidence that any of the fibers attach directly to the head (Saacke and Almquist 1964).

The bovine sperm tail consists of 20 fibers arranged concentrically in a 9+9+2 pattern, bound anteriorly by the mitochondrial helix and posteriorly by the fibrous helix, except for the terminal 2–3 μ (see Fig. 54.7). This arrangement of fibrils is found in all mammalian sperm, and the 9+2 pattern is in fact characteristic of many flagella and cilia. The inner ring of 9 fibers, or doublets, and the central pair extend through the middle, principal, and terminal places. They originate in the anterior region of the middle piece. The central pair are hollow tubes, and each of the 9 doublets consists of one hollow subfiber and one electron-dense subfiber. Fine radial spokes extend from the central pair to the dense subfiber of each doublet. The outer ring of 9 coarse fibers consists of 3 large, 5 small, and 1 intermediate-sized fiber in the area of the middle piece. They taper as they pass into the principal piece. These coarse fibers originate as laminated columns, beginning from a common base located in the recess at the base of the head.

The middle piece of the sperm tail is characterized by the mitochondrial helix (see Fig. 54.7). It is formed by numerous elongated mitochondria fitted end to end, and may be formed by several strands of mitochondria. The helix makes 65–75 turns from the neck to the posterior end of the middle piece (Jensen's ring); the pitch of the spiral is 20–25°. The mitochondrial wall and internal membranes (cristae) are double.

Jensen's ring is an electron-dense structure surrounding the axial fiber bundle at the junction of the middle and principal pieces. Posterior to this point the axial fiber bundle is bound by the fibrous helix (see Fig. 54.7), except for the terminal 2–3 μ which are unbound. The fibrillar windings are thin, dense strands of variable size and shape. Two thickenings on opposite sides of the fibrous helix have been interpreted to represent longitudinal rods that pass down on both sides of the principal piece. Both the circumferential strands and the longitudinal elements become thinner as they progress posteriorly.

Saacke and Almquist (1964) suggested that alternate contraction and expansion of the laminated segments of the coarse fibers in the neck may be the mechanism responsible for initiating the flagellar wave in the spermatozoon.

Quantitative aspects of semen production

As quantitative geneticists improved their ability to select truly outstanding sires, the artificial insemination industry grew. The demand for semen from these sires intensified, making it obvious that reproductive physiologists needed to turn their attention to the quantitative aspects of sperm production. Many cattle are now inseminated with frozen semen packaged in plastic straws. Although widely varying numbers of sperm and volumes of extender have been used, doses of 10 million motile spermatozoa in 0.5 ml straws give satisfactory results. Approximately 25 percent of the sperm lose their motility on freezing. Many factors, such as freezing and thawing rates, size of straw, and selection of ejaculates, influence the conception rates obtained with frozen semen (Pickett and Berndtson 1974).

The number of spermatozoa required for insemination of other species is less clearly defined, but most estimates suggest that it is about 125 million motile sperm for ewes, 2 billion for sows, and an approximately equal number for mares.

Proper sexual excitement of bulls results in increased semen volume and increased numbers of sperm in the ejaculate. In practice, this sexual preparation is usually accomplished by restraining the bull for some time before mounting is allowed, followed by one or more false mounts before the ejaculate is collected by the artificial vagina. A combination of one false mount, 2 minutes of restraint, and two additional false mounts is commonly used. The introduction of a new teaser animal (either male or female), moving the teaser backward or to another part of the collection area, presenting two teaser animals side by side, and moving the bull and teaser to a new collection site have proved useful in obtaining the greatest volume of semen in the shortest period of time and with as few ejaculations as possible.

The second factor of major importance in harvesting the maximum percentage of the sperm produced by a sire is the frequency of ejaculation. Although sperm concentration and sperm numbers per ejaculate are greater with infrequent collections, the number of sperm obtained per day or week is increased when collections are made at more frequent intervals with bulls, rams, boars, and rabbits. Bulls ejaculated daily for long periods are capable of producing about 5 billion sperm per day, or 30 or more billion per week (Hafs et al. 1959, Amann and Almquist 1961). In contrast, bulls ejaculated once a week produce only about 10 billion sperm per week. No adverse effects from frequent ejaculations of bulls have been noted, although libido may be reduced in some cases.

These differences are due largely to resorption of the stored sperm by the epididymides and to losses in the urine. Amann and Almquist (1962) estimated that 57 percent of the sperm produced are resorbed in the epididymides in bulls whose semen is collected as frequently as eight times weekly; the rate of resorption in unilaterally vasectomized bulls (vasectomized side only) amounts to more than 96 percent. Results such as these suggest that the rate of resorption is dependent on the number of spermatozoa present in the cauda epididymis.

Thus it is clear that careful evaluation of reproductive function in any male requires repeated ejaculations, and that sperm production and sperm output may differ greatly. Nevertheless, it should be possible to estimate total sperm production from sperm output under carefully controlled conditions in which semen is collected frequently after proper sexual preparations for a length of time sufficient to deplete the epididymal reserves to a steady state. Formulas have been proposed for estimating total daily spermatozoon production based on information concerning the number of spermatids (or primary spermatocytes) per unit volume of testes reaching a certain stage in spermatogenesis, the duration of one cycle of the seminiferous epithelium, and certain other factors. Although these approaches have certain limitations, estimates obtained for both boars and bulls are highly correlated with daily sperm outputs (0.80 and 0.87 respectively), suggesting that daily sperm production can be estimated in individual animals by frequent collection of semen (Amann and Almquist 1962, Kennelly and Foote 1964). Testis weight is highly correlated with daily sperm output, a fact that has led many workers to study the correlation between various testes measurements and sperm output. The relationship found between testis size and sperm output suggests that an estimate of sperm output can be made when testis size is measurable in situ. Measurements of scrotal circumference and sperm output per week are positively correlated in bulls up to 53 months of age. Sperm output per week per gram of testes declines with increasing age (Hahn et al. 1969).

Composition and metabolism of semen

Semen is composed of the spermatozoa and fluids from the testes and the secretions of the accessory glands and ducts, particularly the prostate and seminal vesicles. The bulbourethral glands also contribute to the fluid portion of the ejaculate; their secretions are believed to be preejaculatory, thus serving primarily as a lubricant. The fluid portion of semen is referred to as seminal plasma. The volume of the ejaculate in domestic animals ranges from about 1 ml in the ram to 250 ml or more in the boar. Species differences in the accessory glands and their secretions have been described.

A remarkable diversity exists in the chemical composition of semen from the several species of domestic animals. The differences are both quantitative and qualitative; unfortunately the physiological significance of many of them is unknown (Mann 1964, White and MacLeod 1963).

The component parts of the spermatozoon differ greatly in chemical makeup. The head, consisting mainly of the nucleus, contains a large amount of deoxyribonucleoprotein. DNA, when separated from the nuclear protein, is found to consist of the sugar deoxyribose, phosphoric acid, and the purine and pyrimidine bases, adenine, guanine, cytosine, and thymine, arranged in a configuration resembling a ladder that has been twisted to form a helix. The rails of the ladder are formed by deoxyribose units bound together by phosphoric acid molecules; the rungs are combinations of bases, either adenine-thymine or cytosine-guanine linkages. All of the genetic information contributed by the spermatozoon is thought to be encoded in its DNA. The amount of DNA in the spermatozoon is half that in somatic cells of the same species.

The proteins conjugated with DNA in the nucleus are mainly of the basic type, histones and protamines, although other residual proteins are also present. The acrosome contains protein-bound carbohydrates in the form of fructose, mannose, galactose, and hexosamine.

Bovine semen contains 3.75 percent total lipids on a dry-weight basis, most of which is within the cells (Dietz et al. 1963). Saturated acids containing 14, 16, and 18 carbon atoms account for over 80 percent of the fatty acids present. Phospholipids in spermatozoa and seminal plasma are of particular interest since they serve as components of the highly organized membrane systems in the sperm, and as nutrients they may supply the sperm with an oxidizable substrate. Several studies (Darin-Bennett et al. 1973, Clegg and Foote 1973) have provided a great deal of information on the phospholipid composition of sperm heads, tails, midpieces, and cytoplasmic droplets, and on the nature of the phospholipid-bound fatty acids in spermatozoa of domestic animals. In bull spermatozoa, 30, 24, and 36 percent of the total phospholipids are contributed by the head, midpiece, and tail respectively. Choline phosphatide is the major sperm phospholipid. The phospholipid composition of the cytoplasmic droplets is similar to that of the seminal plasma. Very high levels of unsaturated fatty acids are found in the phospholipids of ram, bull, and boar spermatozoa. Docosahexanoic acid (22:6) is quantitatively the most important of these unsaturated acids, but arachidonic acid, the precursor of prostaglandin E_2 and $F_2\alpha$, is present in appreciable amounts in the sperm of all three species. Under aerobic conditions ram and bull sperm display an endogenous respiration in the absence of fructose that is capable of maintaining motility. This respiration is said to be due to the breakdown of plasmalogen, a lipid that contains choline, phosphorus, and a fatty aldehyde in a molecular ratio of 1:1:1, and to the oxidation of the resultant fatty acids to carbon dioxide. However, washed ram spermatozoa do not appear capable of using intracellular phospholipids as sources of oxidizable substrates in a sugar-free medium (Darin-Bennett et al. 1973).

The exact nature of the sperm fibrils is unknown, but the fibrillar proteins appear to resemble those found in the protein contractile system of muscle. Adenosine triphosphate (ATP) is present in sperm and is thought to furnish the energy necessary for the contraction of the sperm fibrils, as it does in muscle fibers. With the exception of hyaluronidase, which is confined to the head and thought by some to play a role in fertilization, most of the enzymes controlling both aerobic and anaerobic metabolism of semen are found in the midpiece and tail.

The carbohydrate constituents of the seminal plasma include fructose, sorbitol, inositol, and in some species traces of glucose. Fructose acts as the source of energy for motility of the sperm in most species. Blood glucose is the precursor of seminal fructose, and sorbitol is probably an intermediate in the conversion of glucose to fructose. Fructose concentration ranges from a few mg/100 ml in the boar to 500 mg/100 ml in the bull. Several workers have shown that the rate of fructose breakdown (fructolysis) in bull semen is correlated with the number of motile spermatozoa, but the correlation is not high enough to be useful in predicting the fertility of individual bulls used in artificial insemination. Sorbitol occurs in bull, boar, ram, and stallion semen; it is readily oxidized to fructose by sorbitol dehydrogenase, so that it can act as a substrate for fructose. Stallion semen lacks fructose. Sorbitol probably provides a substrate for glycolysis in this species.

Inositol occurs in high concentrations in boar semen, but it is not utilized by mammalian spermatozoa and its function is unknown. Inositol can be formed in vitro from glucose by slices of rat seminal vesicle and prostate, indicating that it may be an intermediate in conversion of glucose to fructose. The source of readily metabolizable energy in dog semen is unknown; it contains no reducing sugar and has a very short survival time after ejaculation if no substrate is added. Dog spermatozoa will rapidly utilize fructose added in vitro.

There is good evidence that fructose in semen is broken down to lactic acid by the Embden-Myerhof phosphorylated pathway. Under anaerobic conditions spermatozoa of different species produce lactic acid at relatively constant rates of 0.1–0.2 mg per 10^8 cells per hour. Sperm with poor motility seldom produce appreciable amounts of lactic acid, and under anaerobic conditions fructose is probably the only naturally occurring substrate utilized by spermatozoa that is capable of maintaining motility for long periods. Spermatozoa can utilize other carbohydrate sources, however; bull sperm will preferentially utilize glucose if it is presented to them along with fructose, and they can also form lactic acid and fructose from glycerol.

Boar spermatozoa convert fructose to lactic acid under anaerobic conditions at a much slower rate than bull or ram sperm; consequently their motility is lower. However, under aerobic conditions their motility is high, presumably due to their ability to oxidize lactic acid with a high efficiency and to utilize glycerol, pyruvic, and acetic acids and other substrates under these conditions.

The major nitrogenous bases in semen are ergothioneine, spermine, and glycerylphosphorylcholine. Ergothioneine, a sulfhydryl-containing compound, is present in relatively large amounts in stallion and boar semen, but its function is unknown. Spermine is found only in human semen.

Glycerylphosphorylcholine is present in ram and bull semen in relatively large amounts. It is added to the seminal plasma by the epididymis, and it may replace some of the sodium and chloride ions to maintain osmotic pressure as sperm pass from the rete testis to the vas deferens. Spermatozoa are unable to metabolize glycerylphosphorylcholine, however, and its function is not known. The uterine secretions of the ewe contain an enzyme capable of splitting choline from the molecule. Since ram and bull spermatozoa can utilize free glycerol, it has been suggested that glycerylphosphorylcholine may act as a source of energy for the spermatozoa in the female tract, even though the sperm themselves are incapable of breaking down the molecule (White and MacLeod 1963).

Bull and ram semen contain relatively high levels of protein and free amino acids, including glutamic acid, alanine, glycine, and aspartic acid. Bull spermatozoa are able to metabolize glycine and to transaminate glycine and pyruvate to alanine and glyoxylate (Flipse and Anderson 1959). The amino acids and proteins in seminal plasma are thought to exert a protective action on spermatozoa by combining with heavy metals and by preventing sperm agglutination. The conjugated protein sperm antiagglutinin produced by the prostate was mentioned previously.

Many important enzymes are found in semen. Bull and ram semen have relatively little acid phosphatase activity. Other enzymes present include phosphomonoesterases, a pyrophosphatase, several adenosine triphosphatases, 5-nucleotidase, and several glycosidases. A glutamic-oxalacetate transaminase has also been found in bull semen (Gregoire et al. 1961). Carnitine acetyltransferase is present in high concentrations in rat testes and it has been suggested that this enzyme plays some role in the processes by which lipids serve as substrates for spermatozoa during their maturation in the epididymis. Testicular carnitine acetyltransferase levels increase in growing lambs and are highly correlated with serum testosterone levels (Schanbacher et al. 1974).

The major organic acids in semen are citric and lactic, and in the case of bull semen, the volatile fatty acids, chiefly acetic. Citric acid levels are particularly high in bull semen. This acid is contributed by the accessory glands, and like fructose its production is androgen dependent. It is used only at a very slow rate by the sperm and probably contributes little as a source of energy. Lactic acid is present in variable amounts; some is found in semen at ejaculation and the amount increases to very high levels as fructose is broken down. Bull sperm can oxidize lactic acid to carbon dioxide and water under aerobic conditions.

Bull semen contains appreciable amounts of acetic acid. Bull and ram semen preferentially oxidize acetate at a higher rate than glucose. Conversely, dog semen oxidizes acetate at a slower rate than glucose when presented with a mixture of the two. The ruminant is equipped to metabolize large amounts of acetate, a normal product of ruminant digestion. The existence of a different pattern of acetate and glucose metabolism in spermatozoa of ruminants and nonruminants may be related to the relative availability of these substrates to the tissues of each species. Thus ram and probably bull spermatozoa are said to obtain energy for motility by at least three methods: (1) anaerobic breakdown of fructose to lactic acid, (2) aerobic breakdown of fatty acids produced by the breakdown of plasmalogen, and (3) aerobic oxidation of lactic acid through the citric acid or Krebs cycle (White and MacLeod 1963).

The major inorganic ions in seminal plasma are sodium, chloride, phosphate, potassium, magnesium, and calcium. The osmotic pressure of the seminal plasma of all mammals is approximately equivalent to 0.9 percent sodium chloride. Removal of potassium from the seminal plasma depresses sperm motility and glycolytic activity. Conversely, the addition of potassium to washed ram and bull spermatozoa incubated in vitro stimulates their motility. Dott and White (1964) suggested that the adverse effect of potassium depletion is on the ability of the spermatozoa to produce or use energy from the oxidation of exogenous substrates through the citric acid cycle. However, addition of potassium during cooling from 30°C to 5°C adversely affects ram spermatozoa (O'Shea and Wales 1964). Wallace and Wales (1964) studied the effects of potassium, magnesium, calcium, and phosphate ions added to ejaculated and epididymal ram spermatozoa in all combinations. Potassium and phosphate ions significantly increased both respiration and fructolysis, and there were few interactions between these and other ions. Potassium stimulated both aerobic fructolysis and the oxidation of fructose, but had no effect on the oxidation of other substrates. Phosphate ions also stimulated fructolysis and fructose oxidation. Similar studies with bull spermatozoa (Lodge et al. 1963) showed that added phosphate depressed respiration in washed ejaculated bull sperm. Calcium ions appear to depress oxygen uptake and fructose oxidation in both ram and bull spermatozoa, while variations of magnesium concentration within the physiological range have little effect on metabolism.

REFERENCES

Almquist, J.O. 1959. Insemination techniques. In H.H. Cole and P.T. Cupps, eds., *Reproduction in Domestic Animals*. Academic Press, New York. Vol. 2, 135–64.

Amann, R.P. 1962. Reproductive capacity of dairy bulls. III. The effect of ejaculation frequency, unilateral vasectomy, and age on spermatogenesis. IV. Spermatogenesis and testicular germ cell degeneration. *Am. J. Anat.* 110:49–67, 69–78.

Amann, R.P., and Almquist, J.O. 1961. Reproductive capacity of dairy bulls. V. Detection of testicular deficiencies and requirements for experimentally evaluating testis function from semen characteristics. *J. Dairy Sci.* 44:2283–91.

——. 1962. Reproductive capacity of dairy bulls. VIII. Direct and indirect measurement of testicular sperm production. *J. Dairy Sci.* 45:774–81.

Andrews, F.N., Perry, T.W., Stob, M., and Beeson, W.M. 1958. The effects of diethylstilbestrol, testosterone, and reserpine on growth and carcass grade of lambs. *J. Anim. Sci.* 17:157–63.

Baker, R.D., VanDemark, N.L., Graves, C.N., and Norton, H.W. 1964. Effects of pilocarpine and atropine on copulatory behavior, ejaculation, and semen composition in the bull. *J. Reprod. Fert.* 8:297–303.

Bedford, J.M. 1974. Report of a workshop: Maturation of the fertilizing ability of mammalian spermatozoa in the male and female reproductive tract. *Biol. Reprod.* 11:346–62.

Bratton, R.W., Musgrave, S.D., Dunn, H.O., and Foote, R.H. 1961. Causes and prevention of reproductive failures in dairy cattle. III. Influence of underfeeding and overfeeding from birth through 80 weeks of age on growth, sexual development, and fertility of Holstein bulls. *Cornell U. Ag. Exp. Sta. Bull.* 964.

Bratton, R.W., Salisbury, G.W., Tanabe, T., Branton, C., Mercier, E., and Loosli, J.K. 1948. Breeding behavior, spermatogenesis, and semen production of mature dairy bulls fed rations low in carotene. *J. Dairy Sci.* 31:779–91.

Burris, M.J., Bogart, R., and Oliver, A.W. 1953. Alteration of daily gain, feed efficiency, and carcass characteristics in beef cattle with male hormones. *J. Anim. Sci.* 12:740–46.

Butenandt, A. 1931. Über die chermische Utersuchung der Sexualhormone. *Zeitschrift Angewandt Chem.* 44:905–8.

Casady, R.B., Myers, R.M., and Legates, J.E. 1953. The effect of exposure to high ambient temperature on spermatogenesis in the dairy bull. *J. Dairy Sci.* 36:14–23.

Clegg, E.D., and Foote, R.H. 1973. Phospholipid composition of bovine sperm fractions, seminal plasma, and cytoplasmic droplets. *J. Reprod. Fert.* 34:379–83.

Courot, M. 1967. Endocrine control of the supporting and germ cells of the impuberal testis. In G.W. Duncan, R.J. Ericsson, and R.G. Zimbelman, eds., *Capacitation of Spermatozoa and Endocrine Control of Spermatogenesis. J. Reprod. Fert.*, suppl. 2, 89–101.

Darin-Bennett, A., Poulos, A., and White, I.G. 1973. A reexamination of the role of phospholipids as energy substrates during incubation of ram spermatozoa. *J. Reprod. Fert.* 34:543–46.

David, K., Dingemanse, E., Freud, J., and Laquer, E. 1935. Über krystallinisches männliches Hormon aus Hoden (Testosteron), wirksamer als aus Harn oder aus cholesterin bereitetes Androsteron. *Zeitschrift Physiol. Chem.* 233:281–82.

Davidson, J.M., and Bloch, G.J. 1969. Neuroendocrine aspects of male reproduction. *Biol. Reprod.*, suppl. 1, 67–92.

Davies, D.V., Mann, T., and Rowson, L.E.A. 1957. Effect of nutrition on the onset of male sex hormone activity and sperm formation in monozygous bull calves. *Proc. Roy. Soc.*, ser. B, 147:332–51.

Dietz, R.W., Pickett, B.W., Komarek, R.J., and Jensen, R.G. 1963. Fatty acid composition of bovine semen. *J. Dairy Sci.* 46:468–71.

Dott, H.M., and White, J.G. 1964. Effect of potassium on ram spermatozoa studied by a flow dialysis technique. *J. Reprod. Fert.* 7:127–38.

Dutt, R.H., and Barnhart, C.E. 1959. Effect of plane of nutrition on the reproductive performance of boars. *J. Anim. Sci.* 18:3–13.

Dutt, R.H., and Falcon, C.J. 1964. Progestogens and development of sex glands in lambs. *J. Anin* 23:904.

Dutt, R.H., and Simpson, E.C. 1957. Environmental temperature and fertility of Southdown rams early in the breeding season. *J. Anim. Sci.* 16:136–43.

Dziuk, P.J., and Mann, T. 1963. Effect of atropine on the composition of semen and secretory function of the male accessory organs in the boar. *J. Reprod. Fert.* 5:101–8.

Eik-Nes, K.B. 1967. Factors controlling the secretion of testicular steroids in the anesthetized dog. In G.W. Duncan, R.J. Ericsson, and R.G. Zimbelman, eds., *Capacitation of Spermatozoa and Endocrine Control of Spermatogenesis. J. Reprod. Fert.*, suppl. 2, 125–41.

Finerty, J.C. 1952. Parabiosis in physiological studies. *Physiol. Rev.* 32:277–302.

Flipse, R.J., and Almquist, J.O. 1961. Effect of total digestible nutrients intake from birth to four years of age on growth and reproductive development and performance of dairy bulls. *J. Dairy Sci.* 44:905–14.

Flipse, R.J., and Anderson, W.R. 1959. Metabolism of bovine semen. VII. Pyruvate-alanine conversion. *J. Dairy Sci.* 42:637–41.

Foster, C.L., and Cameron, E. 1963. Observations on the histological effects of sub-lethal doses of cadmium chloride in the rabbit. I. The effect on the kidney cortex. *J. Anat.* 97:281–88.

Fox, B.W., Jackson, H., Craig, A.W., and Glover, T.D. 1963. Effects of alkylating agents on spermatogenesis in the rabbit. *J. Reprod. Fert.* 5:13–22.

French, F.S., and Ritzén, E.M. 1973. A high affinity androgen binding protein (ABP) in rat testis: Evidence for secretion into efferent duct fluid and absorption by epididymis. *Endocrinology* 93:88–95.

Gassner, F.X. 1952. Some physiological and medical aspects of the gonadal cycle of domestic animals. *Recent Prog. Horm. Res.* 7:165–208.

Gassner, F.X., Hill, H.J., and Sulzberger, L. 1952. Relationships of seminal fructose to testis function in the domestic animal. *Fert. Steril.* 3:121–40.

Ginther, O.J. 1974. Internal regulation of physiological processes through local venoarterial pathways: A review. *J. Anim. Sci.* 39:550–64.

Gombe, S., Hall, W.C., McEntee, K., Hansel, W., and Pickett, B.W. 1973. Regulation of blood levels of LH in bulls. *J. Reprod. Fert.* 35:493–503.

Gregoire, A.T., Rakoff, A.E., and Ward, K. 1961. Glutamic-oxaloacetic transaminase in semen of human, bull, and rabbit seminal plasma. *Internat. J. Fert.* 6:73–78.

Gullickson, T.W., Palmer, L.S., Boyd, W.L., Nelson, J.W., Olson, F.C., Calverly, C.E., and Boyer, P.D. 1949. Vitamin E in nutrition of cattle. I. Effect of feeding vitamin E–poor rations on reproduction, health, milk production, and growth. *J. Dairy Sci.* 32:495–508.

Gustafsson, B., Crabo, B., and Rao, A.R. 1972. Two cases of bovine epididymal dysfunction. *Cornell Vet.* 62:392–402.

Hafiez, A.A., Lloyd, C.W., and Bartke, A. 1972. The role of prolactin in regulation of testis function: The effects of prolactin and luteinizing hormone on the plasma levels of testosterone and androstenedione in hypophysectomized rats. *J. Endocr.* 52:327–32.

Hafs, H.D., Hoyt, R.S., and Bratton, R.W. 1959. Libido, sperm characteristics, sperm output, and fertility of mature dairy bulls ejaculated daily or weekly for thirty-two weeks. *J. Dairy Sci.* 42:626–36.

Hafs, H.D., Oxender, W.P., Noden, P.A., and Amann, R.P. 1974. Testicular function in bulls 10 weeks after unilateral vasectomy. *J. Anim. Sci.* 38:117–20.

Hahn, J., Foote, R.H., and Seidel, G.E., Jr. 1969. Testicular growth and related sperm output in dairy bulls. *J. Anim. Sci.* 29:41–47.

Hodson, N. 1964. Role of the hypogastric nerves in seminal emission in the rabbit. *J. Reprod. Fert.* 7:113–22.

Johnson, J.M., Hargrove, J.L., and Ellis, L.C. 1971. Prostaglandin $F_1\alpha$ induced stimulation of rabbit testicular contractions in vitro. *Proc. Soc. Exp. Biol. Med.* 138:378–81.

Kamboj, V.P., and Kar, A.B. 1964. Antitesticular effect of metallic and rare earth salts. *J. Reprod. Fert.* 7:21–28.

Kennelly, J.J., and Foote, R.H. 1964. Sampling boar testes to study spermatogenesis quantitatively and to predict semen production. *J. Anim. Sci.* 23:160–67.

Kochakian, C.C., and Tillotson, C. 1957. Influence of several C-19 steroids on the growth of individual muscles of the guinea pig. *Endocrinology* 60:607–18.

Leathem, G.H. 1961. Nutritional effects on endocrine secretions. In W.C. Young, ed., *Sex and Internal Secretions*. 3d ed. Williams & Wilkins, Baltimore. Pp. 666–94.

Leblond, C.P., Steinberger, E., and Roosen-Runge, E.C. 1963. Spermatogenesis. In C.G. Hartman, ed., *Mechanisms Concerned with Conception*. Macmillan, New York. Pp. 1–72.

Leidl, W., and Hansel, W. 1972. Longitudinal growth of the seminiferous tubules in rats and its hormonal control. *Adv. Biosci.* 10:117–25.

Leonard, S.L. 1952. The effect of castration and testosterone propionate injection on glycogen storage in skeletal muscle. *Endocrinology* 51:293–97.

Lodge, J.R., Salisbury, G.W., Schmidt, R.P., and Graves, C.N. 1963. Effect of phosphate and of related co-factors on the metabolism of bovine spermatozoa. *J. Dairy Sci.* 46:473–78.

Lubicz-Nawrocki, C.M., and Chang, M.C. 1974. The onset and duration of infertility in hamsters treated with α-chlorohydrin. *J. Reprod. Fert.* 39:291–95.

Mann, T. 1964. *Biochemistry of Semen and the Male Reproductive Tract*. Wiley, New York.

Mann, T., and Parsons, U. 1950. Studies on the metabolism of semen. VI. Role of hormones; effect of castration, hypophysectomy and diabetes; relation between blood glucose and seminal fructose. *Biochem. J.* 46:440–50.

Mann, T., and Walton, A. 1953. The effect of underfeeding on the genital functions of a bull. *J. Ag. Sci.* 43:343–347.

Meacham, T.N., Cunha, T.J., Warnick, A.C., Hentges, J.F., Jr., and Hargrove, D.D. 1963. Influence of low protein rations on growth and semen characteristics of young beef bulls. *J. Anim. Sci.* 22:115–20.

Nicander, L., and Bane, A. 1962. Fine structure of boar spermatozoa. *Zeitschrift Zellforsch.* 57:390–405.

Nishikawa, Y., and Horie, T. 1952. Studies on the effect of day length on the reproductive function in horses. II. Effect of day length on the function of testes. *Bull. Nat. Inst. Ag. Sci.* (Japan), ser. G., 3:45–52.

Niwa, T. 1954. Studies on the spermatogenic function in swine. I. Relationship between body growth and spermatogenetic function. *Bull. Nat. Inst. Ag. Sci.* (Japan), ser. G, 8:17–29.

Noland, P.R., and Burris, M.J. 1956. The effect of oral administration of methyltestosterone on swine growth and development. *J. Anim. Sci.* 15:1014–19.

Orgebin-Crist, M.C. 1964. Delayed incorporation of thymidine ^{3}H in epithelial cells of the ductus epididymis of the rabbit. *J. Reprod. Fert.* 8:259–60.

——. 1969. Studies on the function of the epididymis. *Biol. Reprod.*, suppl. 1, 155–75.

Ortavant, R. 1959. Spermatogenesis and morphology of the spermatozoon. In H.H. Cole and P.T. Cupps, eds., *Reproduction in Domestic Animals*. Academic Press, New York. Vol. 2, 1–50.

Ortavant, R., Mauleon, P., and Thibault, C. 1964. Photoperiodic control of gonadal and hypophyseal activity in domestic mammals. *Ann. N.Y. Acad. Sci.* 117:157–73.

O'Shea, T., and Wales, R.G. 1964. Effects of potassium on ram spermatozoa during chilling to and storage at 5°C. *J. Reprod. Fert.* 8:121–32.

Pařízek, J. 1960. Sterilization of the male by cadmium salts. *J. Reprod. Fert.* 1:294–309.

——. 1964. Vascular changes at sites of oestrogen biosynthesis produced by parenteral injection of cadmium salts: The destruction of placenta by cadmium salts. *J. Reprod. Fert.* 7:263–65.

Perry, T.W., Beeson, W.M., Mohler, M., Andrews, F.N., and Stob, M. 1956. The effect of various levels of orally administered methyltestosterone on growth and carcass composition of swine. *J. Anim. Sci.* 15:1008–13.

Pickett, B.W., and Berndtson, W.E. 1974. Preservation of bovine spermatozoa by freezing in straws: A review. *J. Dairy Sci.* 57:1287–1301.

Price, D., and Williams-Ashman, H.G. 1961. The accessory reproductive glands of mammals. In W.C. Young, ed., *Sex and Internal Secretions*. 3d ed. Williams & Wilkins, Baltimore. Pp. 366–435.

Risley, P.L. 1963. Physiology of male accessory organs. In C.G. Hartman, ed., *Mechanisms Concerned with Conception*. Macmillan, New York. Pp. 73–133.

Roberts, S.J. 1971. *Veterinary Obstetrics and Genital Diseases*. 2d ed. J.W. Edwards, Ann Arbor, Mich.

Roosen-Runge, E.C. 1969. Comparative aspects of spermatogenesis. *Biol. Reprod.*, suppl. 1, 24–39.

Roussel, J.D., Patrick, T.E., Kellgren, H.C., and Guidry, A.J. 1964. Influence of incandescent light on reproductive and physiological responses of bulls. *J. Dairy Sci.* 47:175–78.

Rowson, L.E.A. 1959. Libido in the male. In H.H. Cole and P.T. Cupps, eds., *Reproduction in Domestic Animals*. Academic Press, New York. Pp. 75–90.

Saacke, R.G., and Almquist, J.O. 1964. Ultrastructure of bovine spermatozoa. I. The head of normal, ejaculated sperm. II. The neck and tail of normal, ejaculated sperm. *Am. J. Anat.* 115:143–61, 163–84.

Salisbury, G.W., Birge, W.J., de la Torre, L., and Lodge, J.R. 1961. Decrease in nuclear Feulgen-positive material (DNA) upon aging in in vitro storage of bovine spermatozoa. *J. Biophys. Biochem. Cytol.* 10:353–59.

Schanbacher, B.D., Gomes, W.R., and VanDemark, N.L. 1974. Developmental changes in spermatogenesis, testicular carnitine acetyltransferase activity, and serum testosterone in the ram. *J. Anim. Sci.* 39:889–92.

Shemesh, M., and Hansel, W. 1974. Measurement of bovine plasma testosterone by radioimmunoassay (RIA) and by a rapid competitive protein binding (CPB) assay. *J. Anim. Sci.* 39:720–24.

Shirley, R.L., Meacham, T.N., Warnick, A.C., Hentges, J.F., Jr., and Cunha, T.J. 1963. Effect of dietary protein on fructose, citric acid, and 5-nucleotidase activity in the semen of bulls. *J. Anim. Sci.* 22:14–18.

Smith, O.W., Mongkonpunya, K., and Hafs, H.D. 1973. Blood serum testosterone after sexual preparation or ejaculation, or after injections of LH or prolactin in bulls. *J. Anim. Sci.* 37:979–84.

Steinberger, E., and Duckett, G.E. 1967. Hormonal control of spermatogenesis. In G.W. Duncan, R.J. Ericsson, and R.G. Zimbelman, eds., *Capacitation of Spermatozoa and Endocrine Control of Spermatogenesis*. *J. Reprod. Fert.*, suppl. 2, 75–87.

Stevermer, E.J., Kovacs, M.F., Jr., Hoekstra, W.G., and Self, H.L. 1961. Effect of feed intake on semen characteristics and reproductive performance of mature boars. *J. Anim. Sci.* 20:858–65.

Swierstra, E.E. 1968. Cytology and duration of the cycle of the seminiferous epithelium of the boar: Duration of spermatozoan transit through the epididymis. *Anat. Rec.* 161:171–86.

Swierstra, E.E., and Foote, R.H. 1965. Duration of spermatogenesis and spermatozoan transport in the rabbit based on cytological changes, DNA synthesis, and labeling with tritiated thymidine. *Am. J. Anat.* 116:401–12.

Swierstra, E.E., Whitehead, J.W., and Foote, R.H. 1964. Action of amphotericin B (Fungizone) on spermatogenesis in the rabbit. *J. Reprod. Fert.* 7:13–20.

Tilton, W.A., Warnick, A.C., Cunha, T.J., Loggins, P.E., and Shirley, R.L. 1964. Effect of low energy and protein intake on growth and reproductive performance of young rams. *J. Anim. Sci.* 23:645–50.

VanDemark, N.L., Friz, G.R., and Mauger, R.E. 1964. Effect of energy intake on reproductive performance of dairy bulls. II. Semen production and replenishment. *J. Dairy Sci.* 47:898–904.

VanDemark, N.L., and Mauger, R.E. 1964. Effect of energy intake on reproductive performance of dairy bulls. I. Growth, reproductive organs, and puberty. *J. Dairy Sci.* 47:798–802.

Vlahos, K., McEntee, K., Olafson, P., and Hansel, W. 1955. Destruction and restoration of spermatogenesis in a bull experimentally poisoned with highly chlorinated naphthalene. *Cornell Vet.* 45:198–209.

Wallace, J.C., and Wales, R.G. 1964. Effect of ions on the metabolism of ejaculated and epididymal ram spermatozoa. *J. Reprod. Fert.* 8:187–203.

White, I.G., and MacLeod, J. 1963. Composition and physiology of semen. In C.G. Hartman, ed., *Mechanisms Concerned with Conception*. Macmillan, New York. Pp. 135–72.

Wislocki, G.B., Aub, J.C., and Waldo, C.M. 1947. The effects of gonadectomy and the administration of testosterone propionate on the growth of antlers in male and female deer. *Endocrinology* 407:202–24.

CHAPTER 55

Avian Reproduction | by William H. Burke

This chapter will deal primarily with the domestic chicken (*Gallus domesticus*) and to a lesser degree with the domestic turkey (*Meleagris gallopavo*). Because of their economic importance, these two species have been subjected to heavy selection for increased reproductive potential. It should be kept in mind that the reproductive characteristics of these two species do not reflect the wide variety of reproductive habits of the thousands of wild avian species adapted to diverse environments. Many of the anatomical and physiological characteristics described here are found to greater or lesser degree in many wild birds, but details of reproductive characteristics vary greatly among species.

Reproduction in birds is characterized by ovoviviparity. While this mode of reproduction is found in several mammalian species and in many reptilian species, it is ubiquitous among Aves. The potential offspring leaves the mother's body after a very short period of embryonic development and undergoes the major portion of its development outside her body. The egg, as it is laid, consists of nutrient materials in the yolk and in the albumen, water, several protective membranes, and a hard protective shell. In addition, the fertilized egg, at the time it is laid, contains an embryo in the gastrula stage of development.

REPRODUCTIVE ENDOCRINOLOGY

The anterior pituitary glands of birds and mammals secrete the same six hormones: follicle-stimulating hormone (FSH), luteinizing hormone (LH), prolactin, growth hormone (STH or somatotropic hormone), adrenocorticotropic hormone (ACTH), and thyroid-stimulating hormone (TSH). Although the anterior pituitary hormones of birds and mammals have some common biological activities, there appear to be major differences in their chemical composition. Some immunological cross-reactions have been reported between antibodies produced against mammalian anterior pituitary hormones and avian hormones (Hayashida 1970, McKeown 1973), but these appear to be exceptions; in general, major cross-reactions have not been found.

Secretion of anterior pituitary hormones in birds is regulated by hypothalamic-releasing factors, as in other species (Ma and Nalbandov 1963). Removal of the chicken anterior pituitary gland from its vascular connections to the hypothalamus causes hypofunction of the gonads but surprisingly little change in activity of the thyroids and adrenal glands.

Release of avian gonadotropins is regulated by one or more hypothalamic factors. Extracts of avian hypothalami cause the release of LH and FSH. The hypothalamic substance that elicits gonadotropin release is chemically and immunologically identical to the pure decapeptide that regulates gonadotropin secretion in mammals. This pure synthetic material is biologically active in birds, causing LH release, ovulation, and gonadal growth.

Removal of the mammalian pituitary gland from its hypothalamic connections leads to increased prolactin secretion. Experiments of this kind have led to the hypothesis that the mammalian hypothalamus secretes a material that chronically inhibits prolactin secretion (prolactin-inhibiting factor, or PIF). However, hypothalamic compounds that release prolactin from mammalian pituitaries have also been found. The best described of these is the thyrotropin-releasing hormone (TRH), a tripeptide named for its TSH-releasing activity. Removal of the pituitary glands of birds of several species from their hypothalamic connections has led to decreased prolactin secretion (Nicoll 1964), suggesting a major difference in the prolactin-regulating mechanisms in birds and mammals. These studies indicate that avian prolactin secretion is regulated by a releasing factor (PRF) rather than by PIF. The duck pituitary gland, however, continues to secrete prolactin in the absence of hypothalamic stimulation (Tixier-Vidal and Gourdji 1965), in contrast to the pituitary glands of other birds studied. Prolactin secretion is increased by the administration of TRH in birds as in mammals.

TSH release is also regulated by a hypothalamic secretion (TRH), and administration of pure TRH increases TSH output by the avian pituitary gland. Thus TRH is capable of releasing two avian pituitary hormones, as in mammals. In addition, TRH administration causes gonadal growth in Coturnix quail, which may indicate that it also causes gonadotropin release.

The posterior pituitary hormones of avian species are oxytocin (as in mammals) and arginine vasotocin (rather than arginine vasopressin which is found in mammals) (see Chapter 52).

Avian gonads produce steroid hormones that act on the tubular genitalia and on secondary sex characteristics such as head furnishings (Fig. 55.1), feathers, and voice. The ovary produces estrogens and progestogens and avian testes produce testosterone. The ovary also produces androgenic compounds, and progesterone has been found in the blood of males.

While the details of endocrine interaction in birds are even less well understood than in mammals, the following generalizations can be made with regard to reproductive function. Hypothalamic secretions act on the anterior pituitary gland to cause the release of the gonadotropins, LH and FSH. These in turn stimulate gametogenesis and steroid hormone production by the gonads. The gonadal steroids then act on the tubular genitalia to stimulate their growth and secretion. In addition, there is a negative feedback by these steroids to the hypothalamus and pituitary gland to further regulate gonadotropin secretion.

PHOTOPERIODISM

Reproductive activity in many avian species is controlled by environmental stimuli that synchronize breeding seasons with the optimum time of year for survival of offspring. Day length regulates breeding seasons of many wild and domestic species; sexual activity increases with longer days and decreases with shorter ones. Thus artificial light regulation is widely used in commercial poultry breeding operations to both retard and initiate gonadal activity.

Light acts on the bird through some unknown mechanism to regulate secretion of hypothalamic-releasing hormones, which in turn regulate the secretion of pituitary gonadotropins. Certainly the response to light is mediated by brain centers that have input into the hypothalamus, and much current work is devoted to the elucidation of the role of brain neurotransmitters in the control of hypothalamic-releasing hormones. Many observations suggest that light restriction limits gonadotropin production by the pituitary and that long photoperiods (more than 12 hours) stimulate it.

While chickens and turkeys are responsive to light stimulation, they are not absolutely dependent on it for gonadal activity. Chickens will lay in continuous darkness, and some turkeys will lay eggs when exposed to light for as little as 6 hours per day. However, the ability to produce some eggs and the ability to produce at maximum rates are two quite different things, and light stimulation is required for the latter.

Blinded birds are fully able to develop sexually in response to light stimulation. Early work (Benoit 1964) showed that light directed onto the hypothalamus of the duck could elicit testicular growth. More recently it has been demonstrated that eyes are not necessary for the photosexual response of house sparrows, and in fact play no role in the response. According to this work all light involved in the photosexual response is perceived by extraretinal light receptors. Direct light stimulation of certain brain areas has been shown to induce gonadal growth in some birds. Gonadal activity also continues in pinealectomized blinded chickens. The extensive literature on avian pineal-gonadal relationships has been reviewed by Menaker and Oksche (1974). There is little evidence to suggest that the pineal gland of birds is the photoreceptive organ involved in the photosexual response.

Another interesting facet of the photosexual response is the phenomenon of light refractoriness. Many avian species require prepubertal exposure to a nongonad-stimulating light regime before they are able to respond to stimulatory photoperiods. A nonstimulatory light regime of short days (real or simulated winter) must follow each reproductively active period if a second period of reproductive activity is to occur. The physiological basis of refractoriness is unknown, but it may be a mechanism to prevent egg laying at inappropriate times of the year (i.e. late summer, when photoperiods are long but offspring hatched then would have little chance of maturing sufficiently before migration time). Many other aspects of avian photoperiodism are extensively discussed by Follett (1973) and Lofts and Lam (1973).

ANATOMY OF THE OVARY

In all domestic species of birds only the left ovary and oviduct are normally functional, although occasional individuals are found with left and right functional ovaries or oviducts. The functional left ovary is tightly attached

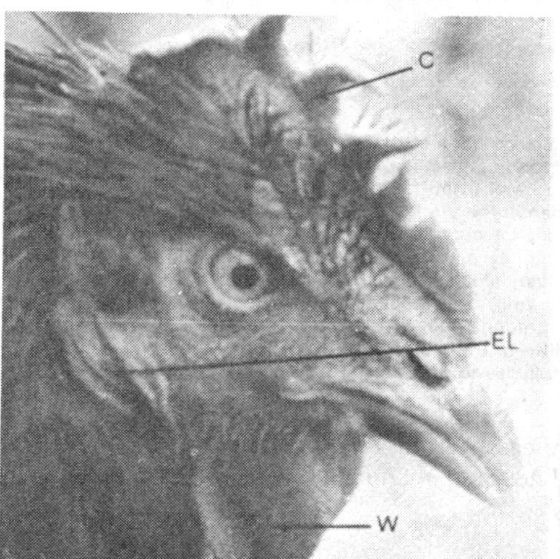

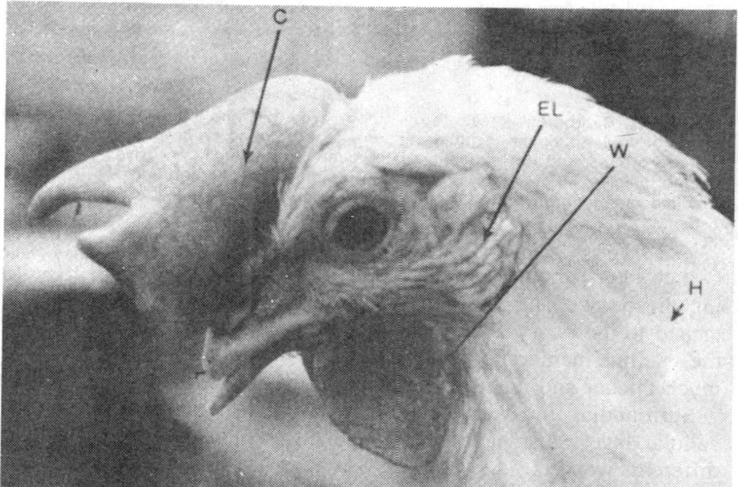

Figure 55.1. Head furnishings of chickens: *left,* sexually active male; *lower left,* mature male with inactive testes; *below,* mature female with active ovary. C, comb; W, wattles; EL, ear lobes; H, hackle feathers. These structures are responsive to androgenic hormones. The large, well-developed head furnishings of the sexually active male and female are indicative of androgen secretion by these individuals, whereas the shrunken comb and wattles of the male with inactive testes show the effect of androgen withdrawal. The active male and female also demonstrate the effect of estrogen on neck (hackle) feathers. The female has shorter, more rounded neck feathers due to the presence of estrogenic hormones. The typical male pattern of long pointed hackle, saddle, and tail feathering is not due to testosterone but to the absence of estrogenic hormones.

to the dorsal body wall just anterior to the left kidney and posterior to the left lung, and adheres closely to the posterior vena cava.

The mature, functional ovaries of birds are relatively large. For example, the ovary of a 2 kg chicken may weigh 40–50 g. The largest 3–5 follicles account for all but about 6 g of this. When one views the functional ovary, the most striking parts are the 3–5 large structures that look like egg yolks (Fig. 55.2). These are the mature or nearly mature ovarian follicles.

In addition to the relatively few rapidly developing follicles that are readily visible, the ovary contains many intermediate-sized follicles and many more that are microscopic (Fig. 55.3). Estimates of the total number of follicles in the chicken ovary vary. Early workers counted 2500 with the naked eye and 12,000 with the microscope. In the life of an individual, only a small fraction of these will develop to the point of ovulation.

All of the ovarian structures described to this point comprise the cortex of the ovary. Beneath the cortex is a region rich in vascular, neural, and connective tissue termed the medulla. In addition to nerves associated with the ovarian vasculature, the maturing follicles receive sympathetic innervation. Interruption of these nerves by pharmacological means blocks ovulation.

The mature avian follicle consists of the oocyte itself

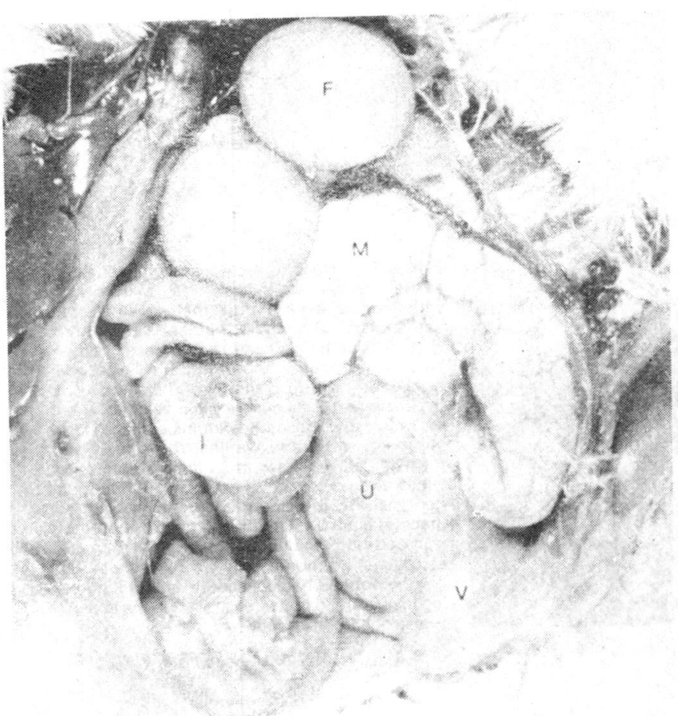

Figure 55.2. Reproductive tract in the body cavity of a hen, showing coiling of the long (80 cm) oviduct, the large amount of space devoted to these organs, and the proximity of the ovary and oviduct. F, large ovarian follicles; M, magnum; U, uterus, containing a developing egg; V, coiled vagina tightly bound to the uterus by connective tissue; I, intestine.

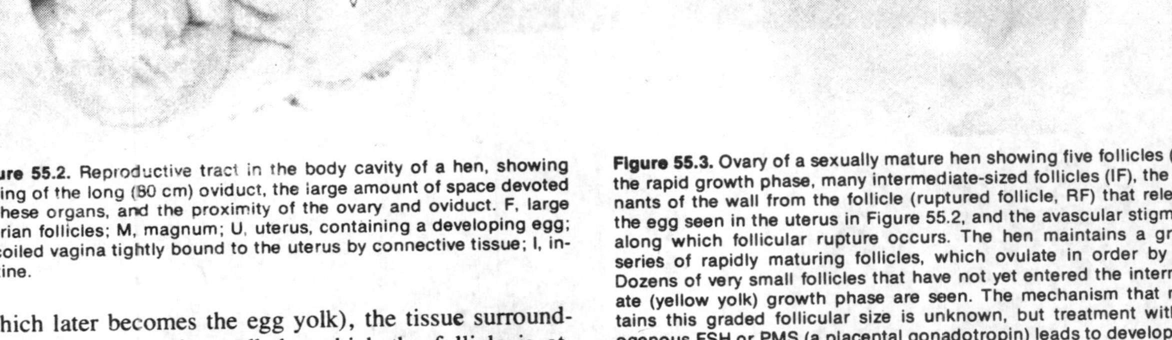

Figure 55.3. Ovary of a sexually mature hen showing five follicles (F) in the rapid growth phase, many intermediate-sized follicles (IF), the remnants of the wall from the follicle (ruptured follicle, RF) that released the egg seen in the uterus in Figure 55.2, and the avascular stigma (S) along which follicular rupture occurs. The hen maintains a graded series of rapidly maturing follicles, which ovulate in order by size. Dozens of very small follicles that have not yet entered the intermediate (yellow yolk) growth phase are seen. The mechanism that maintains this graded follicular size is unknown, but treatment with exogenous FSH or PMS (a placental gonadotropin) leads to development of 10–20 follicles to about two thirds of full size, although they fail to ovulate.

(which later becomes the egg yolk), the tissue surrounding the oocyte, and a stalk by which the follicle is attached to the ovary. The outer membrane of the oocyte, the vitelline membrane, is not a true cell membrane but is much thicker and made up of coarse fibers.

Surrounding the vitelline membrane are a number of cellular layers that have been given different names by different workers. A complex vascular system exists throughout these tissues, and the venous drainage is readily discernible to the naked eye. One region of the follicle, the stigma (see Fig. 55.3), appears relatively avascular, and follicular rupture occurs along this region when the oocyte is released.

In addition to follicles in many stages of development, the ovary of actively ovulating birds contains the remnants of follicles that have ruptured (see Fig. 55.3). These structures, which appear much like grape skins after the contents have been squeezed out, regress rapidly, but they appear to function for a short time in regulating ova transport through the oviduct. The details of this regulatory mechanism remain unclear, but removal of the ruptured follicle causes delayed oviposition of the ovum released from it. No structure analogous to the corpus luteum of mammals forms in these postovulatory follicles.

OOGENESIS

It has often been stated that all of the potential ova that a female bird will ever have are present in her ovary by the time she is hatched, but recent work has shown that oogenesis persists for 2–3 days thereafter. The chromosomal material of each potential egg, however, is present in each follicle at hatching. As the ovary matures and individual follicles begin to grow, a small, round, white disc is seen on the surface of each follicle, under the vitelline membrane. This disc, the blastodisc, contains the chromosomal material of the ovum. The disc sits atop a column of white yolk, the latebra, which extends to the center of the oocyte. Before ovulation the oocyte completes the first meiotic division, but meiosis is not completed until the blastodisc is penetrated by a spermatozoon. After fertilization the blastodisc is termed a blastoderm, and by the time the egg is laid the blastoderm has developed to the point where it can be identified with the naked eye in about 90 percent of eggs that have been opened.

The smallest visible follicles appear white, while intermediate-sized follicles are yellow, indicating that yolk deposition has begun. Studies of the chicken show that the initial phase of yellow yolk deposition is relatively slow, occurring over a period of some 60 days. During this time follicles achieve a diameter of about 6 mm. Some individual follicles then undergo a rapid growth phase during which they grow to 30–40 mm in 9–11 days. The mechanism that selects individual follicles to undergo the rapid growth phase, which may culminate in ovulation or occasionally in atresia and regression, is unknown.

Yellow egg yolk is a complex mixture of water, lipid, protein (Table 55.1) and numerous other microcomponents including vitamins and minerals. Most of the lipid exists in lipoprotein form, and these compounds are often complexed with Ca or Fe. Phospholipids such as lecithin and cephalin are also found in substantial quantities in yolk (Gilbert 1967). Yolk proteins and lipoproteins are formed in the liver under the influence of estrogens, transported to the ovary, and deposited in developing follicles. Total serum lipids are markedly increased in estrogenized birds (i.e. laying females, females just before sexual maturity, immature estrogen-treated females, and estrogen-treated males), and their sera often appear white or creamy as a result.

Yolk is not a physically homogeneous substance, but consists of granular fractions suspended in a continuous phase. The composition of egg yolk has been extensively studied, and various names have been given to its fractions. Much of the free protein in yolk is clearly identical to blood proteins and probably is derived from them. For example, the water-soluble proteins in egg yolk, called livetins, contain serum albumin, serum γ-globulin, and transferrins (Gilbert 1971).

The yellow color typical of egg yolk is due to xanthophyll pigments in the diet. Diets low in xanthophyll result in light-yellow or white egg yolks.

Table 55.1. Composition of the hen's egg

Composition	Yolk	Albumen layers: Outer thin	Middle thick	Inner thin	Chalaziferous	Shell
Weight (g)	18.7	7.6	18.9	5.5	0.9	6.2
Water (%)	48.7	88.8	87.6	86.4	84.3	1.6
Solids (%)	51.3	11.2	12.4	13.6	15.7	98.4
		All layers				
Proteins (%)	16.6	10.6				3.3
Carbohydrates (%)	1	0.9				
Fats (%)	32.6	trace				0.03
Minerals (%)	1.1	0.6				95.1

Modified from A.L. Romanoff and A.J. Romanoff, *The Avian Egg*, Wiley, New York, 1949

ANATOMY OF THE OVIDUCT

In bird anatomy the term oviduct is used to describe the complete tubular genitalia of the female. It is large, weighing about 60 g in a sexually mature chicken and extending from the ovary to the cloaca. The oviduct is highly coiled (see Fig. 55.2), but when removed from the animal it can be straightened out to a length of 70–80 cm (Fig. 55.4). The oviduct presents the typical hollow tubular organ structure—that is, a mucosal layer surrounded by a tunica muscularis that is bounded by serosa. The

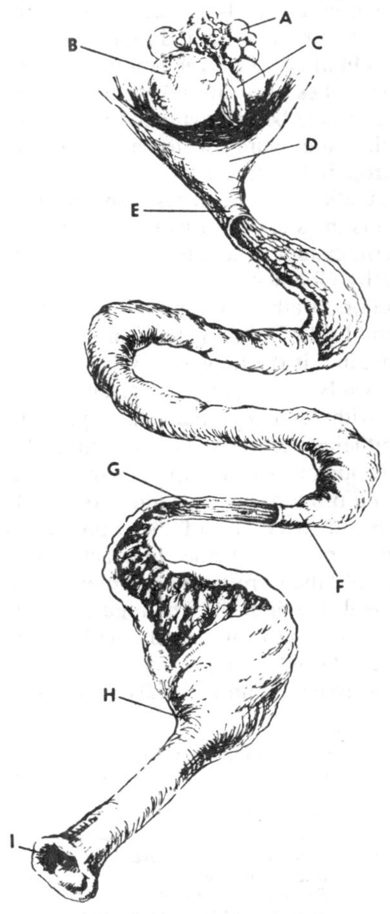

Figure 55.4. Reproductive tract of the laying hen. A, immature ovum of ovary; B, mature ovum; C, ruptured ovarian follicle; D, infundibulum or funnel of oviduct; E, beginning of albumen-secreting region or magnum; F, end of magnum and beginning of isthmus; G, end of isthmus and beginning of uterus; H, end of uterus and beginning of vagina; I, opening of oviduct into cloaca. (From P.D. Sturkie, in M.J. Swenson, ed., *Dukes' Physiology of Domestic Animals*, 8th ed., Cornell U. Press, Ithaca, N.Y., 1970.)

muscularis layer contains inner circular and outer longitudinal fibers. The oviduct can be subdivided into five functional regions. From the ovarian end they are the infundibulum, magnum, isthmus, uterus (shell gland), and vagina. The vagina attaches to the cloaca, a region through which pass digestive wastes, kidney wastes, and genital tract products. Each of the five regions is easily identified by gross appearance and microscopic structure, and each has specific functions.

The infundibulum is about 8 cm long. At its funnel-shaped anterior extremity it is a thin membranous tissue with scanty smooth muscle. In the posterior tubular-shaped region it becomes more heavily muscled and glandular. There is a gradual transition from posterior infundibulum to anterior magnum. The infundibulum is aglandular except in its posterior regions, where a gradual transition to glands characteristic of the magnum occurs. Visual observation and motion pictures have shown the infundibulum to be very motile as the time of ovulation approaches. The infundibulum has been observed to engulf a follicle before ovulation and to be well around it by the time the ovum is released. Thus the concept of an ovum dropping from the ovary and then being picked up after ovulation is not necessarily accurate. The infundibulum is the site of fertilization, and it is often assumed that sperm cannot penetrate the ovum after it begins to be covered by albumen.

Secretion of albumen (egg white) is the function of the magnum (Table 55.2). As the name implies, this segment of the oviduct is the longest (33 cm), and it has thickened whitish walls. The mucosa of the magnum is densely packed with tubular glands that open onto its surface. The epithelial cells consist of ciliated and secretory types. Albumen is made up of many protein components in varying proportions. Specific biological properties can be attributed to certain of these proteins when they are tested in vitro, but whether they actually serve any more specific role than providing a protein reserve for embryonic growth is not clear. The regulation of magnal secretion involves estrogenic, androgenic, and progestogenic hormones. Growth of the oviduct and development of secretory tissue are undoubtedly dependent on estrogens,

Table 55.2. Formation of the hen's egg

Oviduct segment	Function	Time spent
Infundibulum	Pickup of ovulated ova Site of fertilization	15 min
Magnum	Secretion of albumen	3 hr
Isthmus	Secretion of shell membranes	1½ hr
Shell gland	Addition of fluid to egg (plumping) Stratification of albumen Shell production Secretion of shell pigments (if present)	20 hr
Vagina	Sperm storage Egg transport	1 min

but estrogens alone will not bring the magnum to a fully functional state. Epithelial goblet cells, which secrete the biotin-binding protein avidin, are dependent on progesterone for their function. Under certain experimental conditions, testosterone synergizes with estrogen in causing magnal development, while progesterone is sometimes antagonistic. Other work has shown that progesterone can either synergize with or antagonize estrogenic stimulation, depending on the dose. Progesterone antagonizes estrogen-induced cytodifferentiation of magnal cells, but it synergizes with estrogen to evoke secretion from previously differentiated secretory glands. The relative importance and dynamic interactions of these three hormones in normal laying females have not been clarified; they are obviously complex.

The isthmus, about 10 cm long, is separated from the magnum by a narrow (1 mm) nonglandular band that is clearly distinguishable to the eye. The isthmus secretes the two keratinous, fibrous shell membranes that form an enclosing sac that holds in the egg contents and serve as a support upon which the hard shell is deposited.

The shell gland (uterus) is about 12 cm long and is adjacent to the isthmus. This thick-walled, pouchlike, muscular region has long narrow mucosal folds consisting of ciliated and nonciliated epithelial cells and tubular glands underlying the epithelium. Schraer and Schraer (1970) suggested that the ciliated epithelial cells are primarily involved in calcium secretion while the underlying tubular glands are responsible for bicarbonate secretion.

The uterus is separated from the vagina by a constricting muscle sometimes called the uterovaginal sphincter. Just beyond this in the vagina are tubular glands capable of prolonged storage of spermatozoa. The vaginal mucosa contains few glands other than these. The vagina, approximately 12 cm long, is the terminal portion of the oviduct and is attached to the cloaca. Its function appears to be the transport and storage of sperm and the transport of eggs; it adds nothing to the eggs that move through it.

EGG FORMATION

Approximately 25–26 hours elapse from the time an oocyte is released from the ovary until the finished product, an egg, is released from the body. It is the function of the oviduct to store and transport sperm, to pick up ova, to provide a site for fertilization and early embryonic growth, and to add nutritive and protective layers around the embryo. The time spent in each segment of the oviduct and their functions are shown in Table 55.2.

The infundibulum has not generally been considered to play a role in egg formation, other than that of transport and serving as the site of fertilization.

The magnum secretes and stores albumen prior to egg formation and releases the proteinaceous material as the ovum passes. The stimulus for release of this material has often been assumed to be mechanical distension due to the passage of a yolk. But distension by a yolk is not absolutely necessary, since small eggs are sometimes laid which have no yolk at all, and small foreign objects placed in the infundibulum can pass down the oviduct and become coated with albumen, shell membranes, and shell. The volume of albumen surrounding an ovum as it leaves the magnum is only about half of that in a finished egg. At this time the albumen is thicker and more viscous than in a finished egg, and is not separated into layers. Fluids added later increase albumen volume.

Two shell membranes are laid down around the albumen as it passes through the isthmus. These layers are closely apposed except at the blunt end of the egg, where they usually separate, forming an air cell after the egg is laid. Since surgical extirpation of portions of the isthmus results in deformed eggs (Asmundson and Jervis 1933), it seems that the characteristic egg shape is due to factors in the isthmus. While deposition of the bulk of the egg shell undoubtedly occurs in the uterus, recent evidence suggests that initial calcification of specific sites on the shell membrane occurs in the isthmus.

During the first 5 hours that the developing egg spends in the shell gland, fluid is added to the albumen, approximately doubling its volume (Burmester 1940). This added fluid plus the mechanical effects of turning result in stratification of the egg white into four recognizable regions. Extending out from the yolk toward both ends of the egg are white twisted strands of protein called the chalazae. The inner albumen layer extends around the yolk, and the chalazae represent extensions of this layer. Just outside this layer is a watery white layer, then a thick white layer, and then another thin white layer. The formation of such a highly organized structure suggests that it has some importance in embryonic development. It is often suggested that the chalazae serve to hold the yolk and developing embryo in the center of the egg to prevent embryonic adhesion to the shell membranes. Eggs with poor albumen quality (i.e. thin and watery) tend to hatch more poorly than those with albumen of good quality.

Shell is secreted most actively during the last 15 hours that the egg spends in the uterus. It is predominantly made up of calcium carbonate (98%) and a glycoprotein matrix (2%). The crystalline part of the shell consists of columns of material embedded in the outer shell membrane. These columns are separated by pores that extend from the outside of the egg to the shell membranes and allow for gas exchange by the embryo. Outside of the shell is a thin proteinaceous layer, the cuticle, which may block the entrance of bacteria. If the shell is pigmented, the pigment is secreted by the uterine glands late in shell formation. When newly laid eggs are still wet, the pigment is easily rubbed off.

The source of calcium for shell formation is a subject of much interest. Of course the origin of the hen's calcium is dietary, but female birds have mechanisms for making large amounts of calcium available over a relatively short time. As Hertelendy and Taylor (1961) pointed out, the hen deposits about 2 g of calcium on the egg in 15 hours. This is equivalent to removing the total amount of circulating calcium every 15 minutes during shell formation. As puberty approaches, ovarian estrogen secretion brings about marked changes in calcium handling in birds. Under the influence of this hormone, circulating calcium levels rise from about 10 mg/100 ml of plasma to about 25, the rise being in the protein-bound (nondiffusible) fraction. In addition, estrogen stimulates the deposition of 4–5 g of calcium in the hollow medullary region of bones, and with the onset of reproductive activity, calcium absorption from the gut becomes much more efficient. All of the calcium secreted into the uterine lumen during shell formation is derived from the blood, and the blood calcium is obtained from feed and from the bones. In the laying hen, medullary bone is in a dynamic state, continuously being deposited and broken down. A sizeable fraction of each shell's calcium is derived from this source. Actual shell formation involves the secretion of calcium into the shell gland lumen by uterine epithelial cells, the secretion of a carbonate (bicarbonate ions) source by the subepithelial tubular glands, and the interaction of these components to form calcium carbonate. Insufficient calcium can lead to faulty shell formation, as can inhibition of the enzyme carbonic anhydrase, which catalyzes the conversion of CO_2 and H_2O to H_2CO_3. Hot environments, associated with panting and low blood CO_2, can result in thin egg shells.

Major changes in uterine fluid composition occur during the ovulatory cycle. Experimentally, significant changes in uterine fluid composition have resulted from administration of the adrenal steroids, corticosterone, and aldosterone. Furthermore an aldosterone antagonist, spironolactone, can affect the composition of this fluid. These findings suggest an involvement of mineralocorticoid hormones in the regulation of uterine fluid composition.

FEMALE REPRODUCTIVE CYCLES

The ovulatory cycle of the domestic hen is about 25–26 hours long, and cycles may occur for many days without interruption. Eventually, a series of ovulatory days is interrupted by one or more anovulatory days, after which ovulation is resumed. The best laying hens have ovulatory cycles of 24 hours or slightly less. The time relations between events in the ovulatory cycle of the hen have been extensively studied and described (Figs. 55.5, 55.6, Table 55.2), but the internal regulatory mechanisms are not understood. The eggs laid day after day without interruption are commonly called a clutch, although some reserve this term for the group of eggs that wild birds incubate at one time.

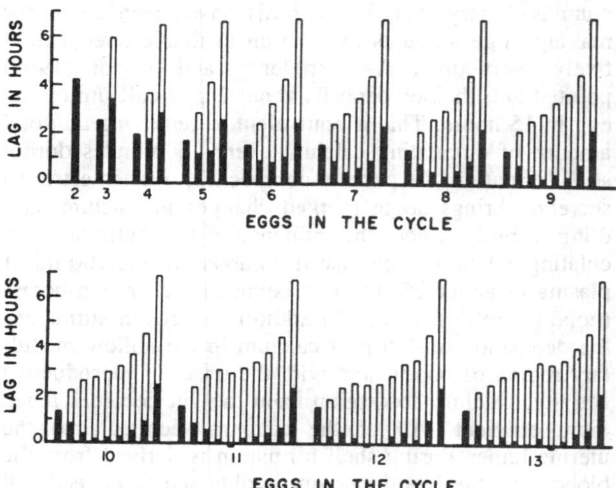

Figure 55.5. Delay between the laying of successive eggs in a cycle. A two-egg cycle is represented by one bar, a three-egg cycle by two bars, etc. A lag of 0 hours means an interval of 24 hours between eggs. A lag of 4.2 hours occurs between the laying of the first and second eggs of a two-egg cycle (black bar). For the three-egg cycle, the lag between the first and second eggs is about 2.5 hours, and between the second and third, about 3.4 hours (second black bar). The cumulative lag (black bar plus white bar) is about 5.9 hours. In a sequence, the lag between the last egg and the preceding one is always greatest. (Courtesy of Dr. R.M. Fraps, based on data of B.W. Heywang 1938, *Poul. Sci.* 17:240–47.)

Chicken clutches range from 1 to 30 or more eggs. While clutch size is based on ovarian activity, the most obvious manifestation of this activity is the production of a complete egg. Ovulation and oviposition (the act of laying) are not absolutely related, but these events are usually very highly correlated. As many as 11–20 percent of the ovulated ova are released into the abdominal cavity; since they do not enter the oviduct, no eggs result. This tendency is more pronounced in hens at the onset of ovarian activity, but some individuals are permanent "internal layers." This condition can often be attributed to some oviducal abnormality. Large fast growing breeds of chickens and turkeys are often poor egg producers, but recent work has indicated that they may actually produce more yolks than better layers. This apparent contradiction might be due to lower rates of oviducal capture of ovulated ova in the large breeds, or greater atresia rates of partially developed follicles. Ova that do not get picked up by the oviduct are reabsorbed, but eggs that escape from the oviduct after the shell membrane or shell is formed tend to be retained, and many may accumulate in the abdominal cavity.

The times between ovipositions within clutches of various sizes are shown in Table 55.3. These are actual records from 10 hens over an arbitrarily chosen 10 day period. Usually each egg in a clutch is laid somewhat

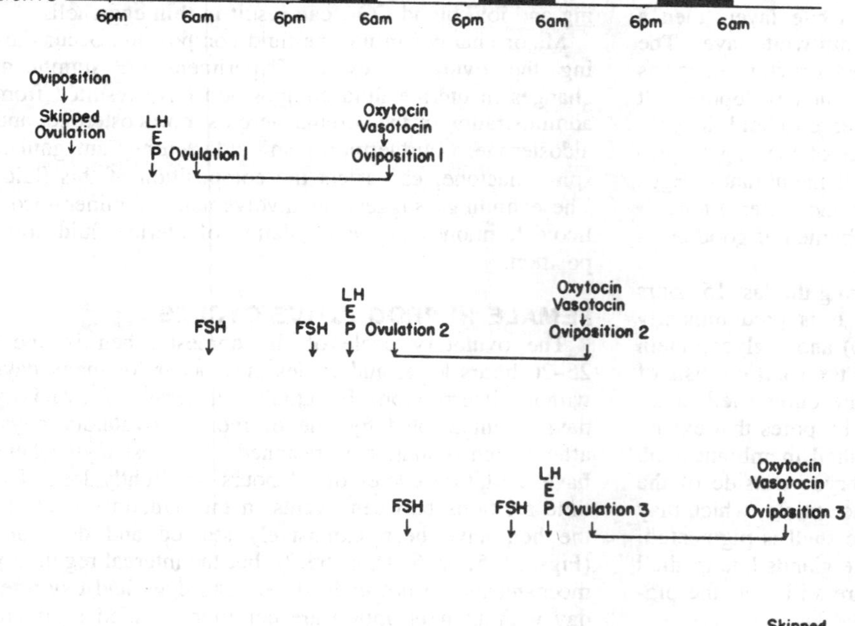

Figure 55.6. Time relations among hormonal events, ovulation, and oviposition in a hypothetical three-egg clutch. Lights were on from 6 A.M. to 8 P.M. each day. One clutch ended when ovulation was skipped following an oviposition. The next clutch was initiated by an ovulation about 6 A.M. the following day. The ovum ovulated at this time was laid approximately 26 hours later. This oviposition was quickly followed by ovulation 2. The hormonal events shown are based on references cited in the text, but in some cases they represent an extrapolation of original data and should be regarded as probable rather than absolute. The release of FSH, LH, estrogen (E), and progesterone (P) does not occur abruptly, as indicated by the arrows, but rises slowly to peak levels, then declines slowly. The arrows indicate average time that peak levels of the hormone are attained.

Table 55.3. Oviposition times

Hen	Day 1	2	3	4	5	6	7	8	9	10
5585	10:30	11:22	*1:16* *	*3:39*		6:52	9:19	10:05	11:04	*12:35*
1429	*1:19*	11:32	12:00n	*12:50*	*3:10*		6:47	7:54	8:40	9:09
1430	*3:25*		10:11	11:28	*1:30*	*4:33*		8:58	10:50	*1:07*
5586		6:42	10:50	*12:20*	*3:31*		7:29	10:18	*3:18*	*4:57*
5582	*3:30*		10:08	*1:05*	*3:32*		8:49	11:28	*2:43*	
1438	*3:01*		8:40	9:30	9:45	9:56	10:12	10:50	11:30	*2:14*
1439	*2:45*		10:05	*12:07*	*3:05*		11:53	9:54	*1:43*	
1442	11:47		*4:20*	*1:07*	8:05	10:37	11:37	*3:31*	*3:35*	8:00
1443	8:50		11:32	*3:46*		8:00	9:40		10:52	*1:10*
5555	8:11	11:01	*12:44*	*3:16*		9:32	9:25	10:16	11:43	*2:20*

* Times in italic are P.M. Lights on 7 A.M. to 9 P.M. daily.

later in the day than the egg laid on the previous day, but not always; hen 1442 presents an atypical laying pattern. The first egg in a clutch is usually laid in the morning hours, shortly after the onset of light, but again this is not always the case (note hen 5585 on day 6, hen 1429 on day 7, and hen 1443 on days 3, 6, and 9). The data in Table 55.3 also show that the last egg in the clutch tends to be laid in late afternoon; only rarely are eggs laid after dark. In this sample of hens, no eggs were laid later than 4:57 P.M. Figure 55.5 shows the delay in hours between successively laid eggs in a cycle. The interval is greater in short clutches than in long ones, and is longer between the first two and last two eggs of a sequence than between intervening eggs (Fraps 1954).

Usually, but not invariably, an oviducal egg will be laid before the next ovulation occurs. Within a clutch, the interval from oviposition to the following ovulation averages about 35 minutes, with a range of 15–75 minutes (Warren and Scott 1935).

The productivity of a laying hen will be determined by the length of her clutches and the length of time she continues to lay (persistency). Obviously, the longer the clutches are, the fewer days she will fail to lay. Egg-laying hens today will average 240 or more eggs per year. Other domestic birds generally lay far fewer eggs than this, but some breeds of ducks are very good layers. Turkeys, particularly the large modern broad-breasted breeds, may average 80–90 eggs per hen in a breeding season of 20–25 weeks. Average production generally is too low to justify keeping a turkey flock longer than this, but certain individuals in a flock will still be laying well at this time.

REGULATION OF THE OVULATORY CYCLE

The mechanisms responsible for ovulation and for its failure, which lead to skipped days in the cycle, have been much studied but little clarified. Many studies have shown that LH of mammalian origin will induce ovulation in hens. Several experiments have shown that FSH can act in concert with small amounts of LH to cause ovulation when both are administered to laying hens.

In recent years it has become possible to measure circulating levels of some hormones in the blood of birds by using radioimmunoassays. One peak of LH, one of progesterone, and one of estradiol occur each ovulatory cycle. All three of these hormones appear to rise simultaneously and peak 4–7 hours before ovulation. Testosterone also rises in relation to ovulation and this rise is reported to precede the rise in the other hormones. No increases in these hormones are noted on days in which no ovulation occurs. FSH has not yet been measured in individual birds in relation to the ovulatory cycle. Large pools of blood have been obtained from many birds and then extracted and subjected to bioassay. From this study it appears that there are two peaks of FSH in each ovulatory cycle, one 25 hours before ovulation and one about 11 hours before ovulation. The second peak is higher and more sustained than the first. Figure 55.6 shows a composite picture of events in a hypothetical three-egg clutch.

The regulation and interaction of these four hormones in the ovulatory cycle are still unclear, but some relevant facts are available. Injection of either LH or FSH causes marked increases in serum estradiol and progesterone levels in turkeys within minutes and increases the follicular levels of progesterone and testosterone in the chicken. Thus one could predict that rises in either of these gonadotropins would be followed by increased serum steroid levels. Also, injection of either progesterone or testosterone can induce ovulation. In the case of progesterone, and probably testosterone as well, the ovulation is due to LH, which is released in response to the elevated serum steroids. Estradiol injection neither releases nor inhibits gonadotropin release. Inhibition of normal progesterone or testosterone peaks by injection of specific antihormone antisera blocks ovulation, but similar blockade of the estradiol peak does not. These studies suggest that progesterone or testosterone may be involved in evoking the ovulatory LH surge. The question then is what terminates LH release. Again the ovarian steroids can be suggested since high blood levels of either testosterone or progesterone will inhibit gonadotropin release and if prolonged will cause gonadal regression.

Inherent in the hypothesis advanced by Fraps (1954) concerning the control of ovulation is the concept of a neural diurnal sensitivity to an excitation hormone. Fraps believed that the excitation hormone was released at different times on successive days until it eventually failed to reach a high enough level to cause LH release during the sensitive time of the day. Evidence cited above, however, shows a very close or simultaneous release of the ovarian steroids and LH and no increase in ovarian steroids on anovulatory days. These facts suggest that if an excitatory hormone exists it is not one of the main ovarian steroids. The ability of the avian pituitary gland to release LH in response to LH-releasing hormone (LHRH) does vary however at different stages of the ovulatory cycle. In laying turkeys only those hens carrying hard-shelled eggs showed a marked increase in LH in the response to the LHRH injection. Chickens respond at most stages of the ovulatory cycle, except in the hours just preceding ovulation. In both of these species much greater responses are obtained in females with inactive ovaries than in laying birds, suggesting an ovarian steroid modulation of the response.

A neural relationship between the oviduct and the hypothalamic-pituitary axis was suggested by reports that a thread in the oviduct would block ovulation (and presumably LH secretion). Other attempts have failed to replicate this finding, and in fact one study suggested an increased ovulation rate in hens with a surgical thread in the uterus. On the basis of nesting behavior, which is reported to be causally related to ovulation 24 hours earlier, it has been reported that chickens from which the oviducts had been removed ovulated at increased rates. Oviduct removal in Coturnix quail causes an increase in ovarian weight and increased diameter of the largest follicle, but no increase in ovulation rate as measured by the numbers of ruptured follicles at autopsy. These findings all suggest an oviducal-hypothalamic-pituitary interaction in birds.

Another factor to be considered in the study of ovarian cycles is the "ruptured follicle hormone." Removal of the remnants of a recently ruptured follicle causes prolonged retention in the oviduct of the ovum that originated from it. Thus while the avian ovary has no counterpart of the mammalian corpus luteum, the postovulatory structure does seem to play a role in the reproductive cycle.

Interference with adrenergic neurons in the follicular wall can block ovulation, but injection of LH-FSH mixtures into the follicular wall can reverse this block. These findings indicate that local neural as well as hormonal factors control ovulation in birds.

BROODINESS

Broodiness, that is, the incubation behavior of birds, has virtually disappeared from chickens selected for egg production, but it is common in chickens used for meat, in turkeys, and in other domestic species of birds. Turkeys, particularly the modern broad-breasted strains selected for meat production, retain much of their ancestors' reproductive patterns even in confinement. After a few weeks of laying eggs, many turkeys exhibit a desire to incubate them. While this trait is indispensable for the survival of most species of wild birds, it is undesirable in modern poultry operations. This situation arises because of an apparent incompatibility between ovarian activity and incubation. When hens become broody, their ovaries regress and egg production ceases. Since it is more efficient to incubate eggs artificially than to allow the hens to do it, broodiness is undesirable.

Many management techniques are used to prevent or discourage broodiness, but basically they all involve placing the hen in strange, uncomfortable surroundings. This may be done by removing nests or nesting material (i.e. using a wire floor), adding intense 24-hour lights, shifting from one pen into a new pen or barn, or shifting from an inside pen to an outside pasture. All these techniques may work to some degree, but the key to success is early recognition of incipient broodiness and early treatment. Decreased serum LH, estradiol, and progesterone levels precede the behavioral signs of broodiness by some days, indicating that pituitary and ovarian function are decreasing before broodiness is apparent. Since the behavioral signs of broodiness follow the changes in internal function, it is not possible to prevent the endocrine changes with current broody control techniques, but it is possible to reverse them after they are well underway. Invariably this results in some loss in egg production, even when the best-known broody treatments are used. If broodiness is allowed to persist for some days before treatment begins, ovarian regression will have set in and several weeks may elapse before ovulation resumes. If no treatment is given, hens will persist in their broody behavior indefinitely.

Incubation behavior of chickens and turkeys is usually said to be caused by increased prolactin secretion from the anterior pituitary gland. It is further stated that prolactin is antigonadotropic, presumably either blocking secretion of pituitary gonadotropins or blocking their action on the gonad. Prolactin injection has been shown to block the ability of both LH and FSH to elicit increases in serum estradiol and progesterone in turkeys, suggesting that it acts at the ovarian level to antagonize the gonadotropins.

Dopamine, a brain neurotransmitter, is intimately involved in the regulation of prolactin secretion in mammals. Studies with turkeys have shown that the metabolic turnover rate of this compound is greatly increased in the hypothalamus just at the time behavioral broodiness is detected. It is not known if dopamine affects prolactin secretion in birds.

A number of studies show increased pituitary prolactin levels in broody gallinaceous birds, but current techniques are not sensitive enough to show if blood levels of the hormone are increased. Further evidence of the role of prolactin in broodiness is provided by the ability of this hormone to induce incubation behavior, although quite high levels (about 2 mg per day) are needed to produce an effect.

CONTROL OF OVIPOSITION

A great deal of research has been conducted on ovulation, but little on oviposition. Although certain hormones are known to influence ovulation, considerably less is known about hormones that affect oviposition. The uterus must contract to expel the egg through the vagina and cloaca. There is some evidence that the hormone from the posterior pituitary, vasotocin, initiates the contraction of the uterus that leads to oviposition. Work by Munsick et al. (1960) demonstrated conclusively that the posterior lobe of the chicken pituitary contains arginine vasotocin and that the chicken uterus is very sensitive to this hormone. Tanaka and Nakajo (1962) demonstrated that the posterior pituitary of chickens contains the least vasotocin at the time of laying, and they suggested that the pituitary releases the hormone into the blood just before an egg is laid. More recent work by Douglas and Sturkie (1964) and Sturkie and Lin (1966) indicates that the posterior pituitary releases oxytocin as well as vasotocin, and that the blood concentration of these hormones increases manyfold just before the egg is expelled. Opel (1966) has also reported an apparent causal relationship between vasotocin release and oviposition by inducing premature laying by brain puncture with a stainless steel electrode and by showing high plasma levels of vasotocin coincident with laying. Furthermore, oxytocin, vasotocin, and vasopressin all can induce oviposition.

Other stimuli also can induce oviposition, e.g. certain prostaglandins. And treatment of hens with prostaglandin inhibitors can block normal oviposition or oxytocin-induced oviposition. These findings suggest that normal ovipositions, which are induced by the release of endogenous posterior pituitary hormones, are mediated by prostaglandins. In addition, acetylcholine injection increases uterine contractions and causes expulsion of the egg. Ephedrine and epinephrine cause relaxation of the uterus and retardation of laying. Some stimuli that cause premature expulsion of the egg do not do so by causing the release of vasotocin, e.g. acetylcholine or sodium pentobarbital administration.

The oviduct and particularly the uterus receive sympathetic and parasympathetic innervation, but there is little evidence that these nerves play a dominant role in the control of oviposition. Transection of the hypogastric nerve (Freedman and Sturkie 1962) or the pelvic nerves (Sturkie and Freedman 1962) did not influence oviposition. Though vasotocin may trigger the contraction that results in oviposition, the question remains as to what causes the cyclic release of the hormone. Electrical stimulation of the preoptic area of the brain causes premature oviposition in a high percentage of chickens, probably through release of vasotocin (Opel 1964), but other studies are needed.

NESTING

Accumulation of eggs in a nest is obviously a prerequisite for incubation; a group of eggs must be gathered in one spot so the female can sit on all of them simultaneously. Domestic birds still retain strong nesting behavior and the urge to deposit eggs in a nest. This urge can apparently be modified in chickens by prepubertal environment, since birds reared in outdoor pasture lay fewer floor eggs and more nest eggs than those raised in confinement. Experience with turkey hens indicates that some must be trained to lay in nests rather than on the floor by repeatedly being placed in the nest early in the laying period.

The assumption might be made that a hen nests when it has an egg ready to be laid, but this is not necessarily so. The stimulus for nesting appears to be related to the ovulation which occurred about 24–25 hours earlier, rather than to the actual presence of an egg in the uterus. Usually both nesting and a nearly complete egg coincide 24–25 hours after ovulation. If these events are separated—for instance, by stopping oviducal engulfment of the ovum or transplanting the ovary to another site in the body—nesting behavior still proceeds at the expected time after ovulation. Wood-Gush and Gilbert (1970) have suggested that not less than 95 percent of nestings are associated with a prior ovulation, and nesting is a much better indicator of prior ovulation than is oviposition. The ovarian signal evoking nesting behavior cannot be neural, since normal nesting is observed in hens whose ovaries have been severed from normal nervous connections. Thus an unknown hormonal mechanism may be responsible.

ANATOMY OF THE MALE REPRODUCTIVE TRACT

The following description of male anatomy is based primarily on the rooster. Males of all avian species have internally placed rather than scrotal testes. In domestic birds they are located just anterior to the kidneys and are attached to the dorsal body wall (Fig. 55.7). The testes of birds are larger, relative to body weight, than those of mammals, and in many species there is bilateral asymmetry, with the left gonad larger than the right. Whether the mechanisms that are responsible for testicular asymmetry are the same as those that cause the marked ovarian asymmetry in birds is unknown. The testes are often whitish, although darkly pigmented gonads are seen in some breeds and species, and functional olive-green testes have been observed by the author in the ruffed grouse. The testes are soft, lacking the connective-tissue septa commonly found in mammals. The great mass of testicular tissue is composed of seminiferous tubules, with relatively few Leydig cells visible in microscopic sections. As a consequence of their intra-abdominal loca-

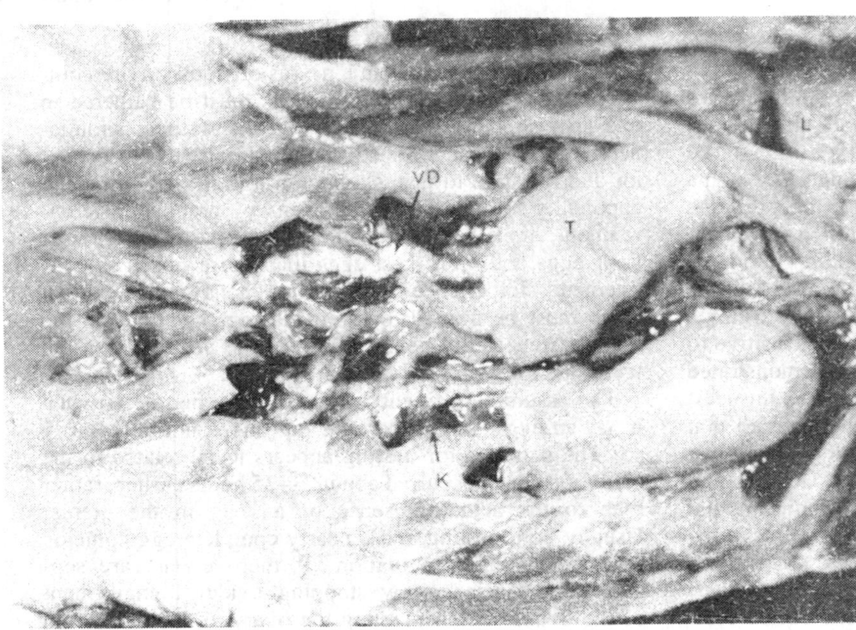

Figure 55.7. Internal reproductive organs of the rooster, showing the testes (T) and coiled vas deferens (VD) which carries sperm to the ejaculatory apparatus in the cloaca. The proximity of the gonads to the lungs (L) and kidneys (K) can be noted. The epididymal region is not apparent.

tion, avian testes function at body temperature (about 41–42°C for domestic species), a feat that would be impossible for most mammals. It has been suggested that the testes are cooled by airflow in the abdominal air sacs. This hypothesis is unsupported by experimental evidence.

The accessory tubular organs associated with the testes are relatively undeveloped in birds; birds have no seminal vesicles, bulbourethral glands, or prostate glands. Tightly apposed to each testis is a small structure that has often been termed an epididymis (Fig. 55.8). The epididymal region consists of efferent tubules carrying sperm from the testis to a single epididymal duct, which is apparent on the epididymal surface. This duct is short (about 2–4 cm) and is quite unlike the mammalian structure of the same name. Leading from each epididymis is a coiled tube, the vas deferens (see Figs. 55.7, 55.8) which traverses posteriorly, is attached to the dorsal body wall, and terminates at a small phallus in the cloaca. Just before its termination the vas deferens becomes somewhat enlarged and serves as a storage site for spermatozoa, as does the entire duct. Each vas deferens penetrates a small papilla and ejects the semen through it into the cloaca. At the time of sexual excitation several small folds in the ventral cloaca become engorged with lymphatic fluid and protrude, forming a troughlike structure to direct the flow of semen (Fig. 55.9). The phalluses of the rooster and the tom and many other birds are small and do not function as intromittent organs. Semen is transferred to the female by touching the rudimentary phallus to the everted vagina. Ducks and geese, however, have sizeable penises (Fig. 55.10) and mating is accomplished by intromission. The vasa deferentia and cloacal ejaculatory apparatus probably receive both sympathetic and parasympathetic innervation (Lake 1971). External stroking of this region around the base of the tail

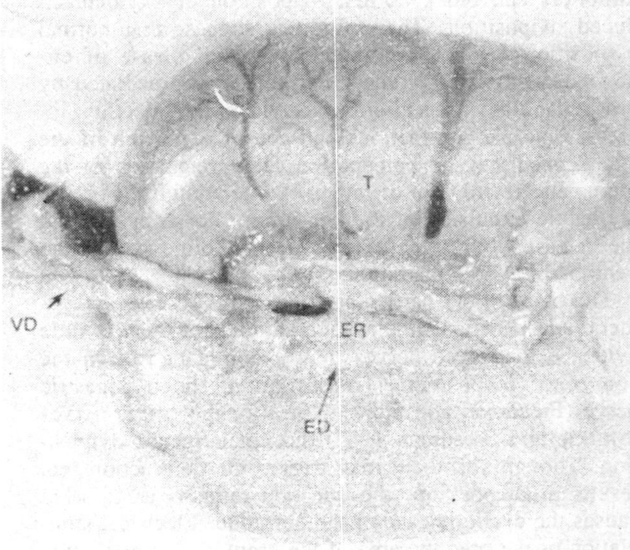

Figure 55.8. Rooster testes (T) removed from the body and viewed from the dorsal aspect. The whitish epididymal duct (ED) in the small epididymal region (ER) collects sperm leaving the testis and joins with the vas deferens (VD). Sperm taken from this region of the vas deferens (upper third) are already capable of fertilization.

Figure 55.9. The small phallic region (Ph) of a rooster everted for semen collection by manual stroking of the abdominal and tail head regions. After eversion is obtained the fingers are moved to the cloacal region to maintain the eversion and squeeze semen from the terminal segment of the vas deferens. Semen (S) can be seen running from the troughlike structures formed by engorgement of cloacal tissues with lymphatic fluid during sexual excitation. Semen can be seen emanating high up on the cloacal wall where one of the bilateral papillae (Pa) is visible. Each vas deferens terminates in one of these papillae.

causes protrusion of the genitalia and often forceful expulsion of semen from the rooster, suggesting that nerves in this region are involved in ejaculation. In the female the same sort of manipulation evokes vaginal eversion.

The physiological role that the various juxtatesticular structures play in maturation of spermatozoa is relatively unstudied in birds. Applying names used for mammalian tissues to structures in the avian tract may cause misleading conclusions regarding functional similarities. The mammalian epididymis is clearly a site of great importance in sperm maturation, but the importance of the avian epididymis in sperm maturation is not clear. It is relatively minuscule compared to that of the mammal, and transit time through it is on the order of a day or so. In fact, estimates of total transit time from the testes to the terminal region of the vasa deferentia range from 1 to 4 days. Munro (1938) determined that sperm taken from the testis and epididymis were capable of fertilization, but the fertilization rate was much higher with semen from the vas deferens. Since semen manually squeezed

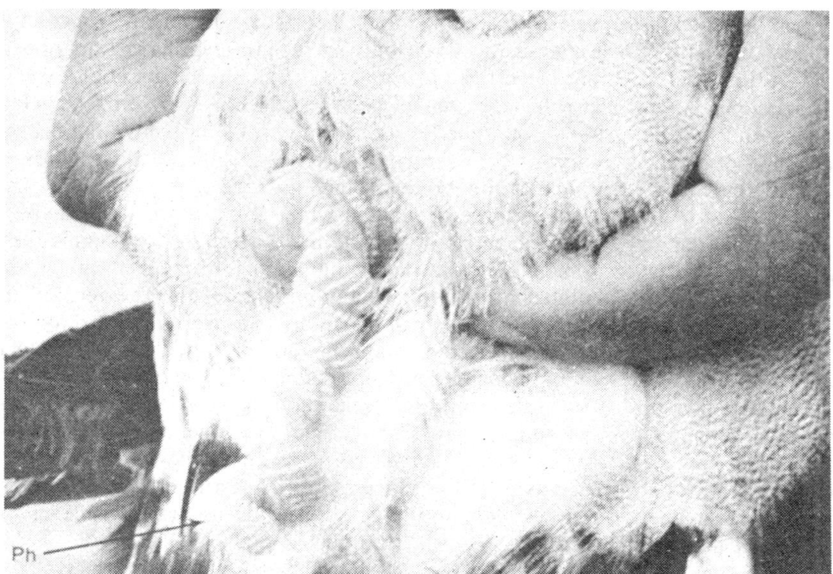

Figure 55.10. Long coiled phallus (Ph) of a mallard drake. This structure, about 3 in long, coils into the cloaca when the duck is not sexually aroused. To evert the phallus for semen collection the duck was held with its abdominal region up and digital pressure was applied around the cloaca. This type of penis is found in both ducks and geese.

from the testes and epididymides is mixed with considerable debris, any comparison of the fertility of this adulterated semen with that of semen obtained from the vas deferens or by ejaculation is unwise. The key observation here is that testicular and epididymal sperm both can fertilize eggs. Quantitative comparison of the relative maturity of sperm from these three regions, in a manner unconfounded by other experimental variables, remains to be done. Unpublished work has shown that sperm from upper, middle, and lower regions of the vas deferens of the cock have about equal fertilizing ability. It has also been shown that the vasa deferentia of the cock have the ability to preserve sperm trapped in them.

SEMEN

Semen is a mixture of sperm cells and carrying fluids. In domestic birds the ejaculate is characteristically highly concentrated and of low volume. Artificial collection of semen from chickens and turkeys is widely practiced and relatively simple. Nearly all of the information available regarding physical and chemical characteristics of avian semen has been obtained from semen collected in this manner. The composition of semen so obtained is quite variable, the sperm cells being mixed with secretory fluids from the engorged phallic apparatus and with digestive and urinary tract wastes. The contributions of these factors are not easily controlled, and consequently considerable variation in semen composition has been reported. The average volume of cock ejaculate is about 0.5 ml, but amounts considerably above and below this are commonly obtained. The sperm cell concentration of such an ejaculate averages around 4 billion per ml of semen. Semen volume of turkey toms tends to average around 0.25–0.35 ml, with concentrations of 8-12 billion sperm per ml. Thus the number of sperm released at each ejaculation in these two species does not differ markedly, both being in the range of 2–4 billion cells. Striking differences do exist in the chemical composition of seminal fluids of birds and mammals, and indeed among mammals, the physiological meanings of which remain obscure. Lake (1966) has reviewed the biochemical aspects of avian semen.

Spermatozoa of the chicken and turkey are similar in shape, but differ from mammalian sperm. In these avian species the sperm head is narrow and long ($0.5\ \mu \times 12.5\ \mu$) with a small acrosome overlying the apical end of the nucleus. The middle piece and main piece of the tail together are about 94 μ long, for a total sperm length of about 110 μ. The diameter of the tail is about 0.5 μ or slightly less, giving the sperm an overall filiform shape.

SPERM STORAGE IN VIVO

Females of many avian species can store sperm in specialized oviducal glands for prolonged periods and can produce fertile eggs for days, weeks, or even months after a single mating or artificial insemination. Early studies suggested that sperm were stored in mucosal crypts of the infundibulum. While these structures do have the ability to store sperm, the most important normal sperm storage tissue is probably located in the vagina, very near its junction with the uterus. Sperm are found in these uterovaginal sperm storage glands shortly after mating or artificial insemination (Bobr et al. 1964) and persist there for the fertile period of the female. Sperm are seldom found in the infundibular storage sites unless semen is introduced into the oviduct in such a manner that it bypasses the uterovaginal glands. There is evidence that sperm move from the uterovaginal area to the infundibulum following oviposition and there await the arrival of the next ovulated ovum, which may take place within minutes. Other work (Burke et al. 1969) has shown that the passage of an egg through the uterovaginal area is not essential for sperm release, but the mechanism that does bring about their release is not known. It may well be that the uterovaginal and infundibular storage areas act in concert. The biochemical basis for these glands' ability to store sperm is unknown. It is often hypothesized that they provide a microenvironment that nourishes the sperm, or that they induce reversible sperm quiescence; they may function in both ways.

SPERM STORAGE IN VITRO

Attempts at prolonged storage of avian sperm in vitro have not been successful. Under most conditions fertility is drastically decreased if semen is stored more than 1–2 hours in the unfrozen state and it suffers even more if the semen is frozen. The inability of avian sperm to remain fertile after freezing is not understood, but freeze preservation of mammalian semen is not universally successful either, and in fact only in recent years have litters been produced from frozen swine semen (Graham et al. 1971). Fertile eggs have been produced from frozen avian semen, but the level of fertility falls far below that necessary for commercial use. Strangely, the fertility of frozen chicken and turkey semen is increased when it is introduced directly into the uterus or magnum, by bypassing the uterovaginal storage sites. Chicken and turkey semen have drastically impaired fertilizing ability when diluted in glycerol-containing extenders. The fertility of this semen too can be improved by intrauterine or intramagnal insemination. Glycerol is often used to protect mammalian sperm from damage during freezing and appears also to preserve the motility of avian sperm during freezing, but unfortunately it is detrimental to the fertilizing ability of avian sperm, even in the unfrozen state. Removal of the glycerol from sperm cells after storage renews their fertilizing ability, but no practical means of accomplishing this has been found.

ARTIFICIAL INSEMINATION

Even though prolonged preservation of avian spermatozoa has not been practical, artificial insemination (A.I.) of chickens and turkeys is widely practiced. In the United States, artificial insemination of chickens is usually done only in a research setting, but it is carried out commercially in other parts of the world and is becoming more common here as well. Nearly all turkey breeding hens are artificially inseminated in the United States. Broad-breasted turkey toms have resulted from generations of intense selection for size and conformation. Along with the extreme development of the pectoral muscles has come a diminished libido and ability to mate. Modern toms lack the coordination and dexterity to complete sufficient matings to assure high fertility. In addition, partial completion of the mating act, even without transfer of semen to the female, can result in variable periods of sexual refractoriness during which turkey hens will not remate.

A.I., as it is practiced commercially in the turkey industry, proceeds as follows. Semen from many toms is collected in a common pool and mixed, and the semen is protected from temperature extremes. This pool of semen from unidentified toms is used to inseminate an indeterminate group of unidentified hens, with no attention to individual matings or parentage of resulting offspring. Each hen is inseminated with about 0.025 ml of semen dispensed from a plastic straw 10 cm long. To accomplish this one worker causes the vagina to protrude or evert by placing pressure around the cloacal and abdominal region. When the vagina is everted, a second worker inserts the inseminating straw 5–7 cm into the vagina, abdominal pressure is relaxed, and the semen, containing about 200×10^6 sperm, is expelled into it. Most studies show that placement of the semen close to the uterovaginal storage glands, but not beyond them in the uterus, results in maximum fertility. Though turkey hens will produce fertile eggs 40 or more days after a single A.I., it is common practice to inseminate them at 7–14 day intervals to assure maximum fertility. Although lower fertility does result from inseminations carried out when hens are carrying hard-shelled eggs (i.e. near the time of oviposition), turkey hens are inseminated commercially without regard to ovulatory stage.

If the semen is to be kept for some time, the least damage results when it is held at about 15°C (Bajpai and Brown 1963). Burke et al. (1973) have shown that good-quality semen diluted with two parts of a commercial diluent can be stored at 15°C for 90 minutes with only moderate loss in fertilizing ability. Other workers have shown that sperm can retain fertilizing ability for somewhat longer periods when stored in hypertonic diluents.

Many diluents for avian semen have been developed, and some of these have been widely used with turkeys. These diluents allow fewer toms to be used for a given hen flock, but only moderate success has been obtained in extending the viable life of sperm in vitro with them. Possible dilution rates are on the order of 1 part semen to 2 parts diluent. Even with this dilution rate, hens still are inseminated with only 0.025–0.03 ml of semen, or about 70×10^6 sperm. Semen of low concentration or poor viability should not be diluted, since the number of fertile sperm may then be inadequate. Brown (1970) has indicated that as many as 92×10^6 live sperm may be required each week for maximum fertility, but more recently (1974) he has suggested that 70 million sperm administered every 14 days is sufficient. The fertility of a flock of hens depends in large part on unknown factors within the females. While some flocks have good fertility with relatively infrequent A.I., others require more frequent insemination for moderate fertility. A general recommendation for insemination of turkey flocks is therefore hard to make. By using A.I., it is not uncommon to obtain 85 percent fertile eggs from a flock of turkeys during their 20–25 week laying season. It is also common for other flocks to average 60 percent fertile eggs for the same period. The reasons for such differences are not fully known. Poor results are sometimes attributable to insemination technique and sometimes to problems within the flock. Unraveling the causes of these differences is difficult because records of individual hens in commercial flocks are seldom available.

EMBRYO DEVELOPMENT

The fertile egg at the time it is laid is already carrying an embryo at the gastrula stage of development. Fertilization has occurred some 24–26 hours earlier, and the nuclear region of the fertilized egg has undergone repeated divisions. After oviposition, embryonic development can be arrested by cooling the egg. In fact, development can be arrested, started again by heating, rearrested by cooling, and later reinitiated and carried to completion by proper incubation. The percentage of embryos that live through the incubation period and hatch decreases with the length of time the eggs have been stored. Prolonged storage of sperm in the female tract also tends to decrease the viability of embryos resulting from such sperm. Often the last several fertile eggs laid in a hen's fertile period die early in incubation, presumably because the sperm have grown stale or weak.

Under normal or optimal conditions of artificial incubation, the chicken embryo will hatch after 21 days and the turkey after 28. These are average figures; considerable variation in emergence time exists between individuals. Vince (1966) demonstrated that in several species, such as the bobwhite quail and the Coturnix quail, which show only a few hours variance in hatching time, the rate of embryonic development is influenced by signals transmitted from egg to egg. This communication synchronizes hatching time, a feature that might be of considerable survival value in the wild. In these quail, with an incubation period of about 16–18 days, embryo development can be accelerated by a full day and the young will still hatch fully mature.

Many factors influence the development of avian embryos (Landauer 1967). Some are environmental and others are associated with characteristics of the egg itself. The environmental factors most often considered are temperature, humidity, concentration of oxygen and carbon dioxide, and turning of the eggs. While there are rather wide ranges of these factors within which some eggs will hatch, the ranges over which maximum hatches can be obtained under artificial conditions are much narrower. Recommendations for these factors vary somewhat with stage of incubation and type of equipment, but temperatures around 37.2–37.8°C and relative humidity of 50 percent are satisfactory. If humidity is too low, the developing embryo loses excessive water and chance of survival is decreased. Oxygen is obviously necessary; carbon dioxide levels above 1 percent should be avoided. The addition of oxygen to incubators at altitudes of 5000 feet and above is beneficial.

Dietary deficiencies in hens' rations can be reflected in deficiencies of specific nutrients in eggs. Since the embryo depends upon egg constituents for all of its nutrients, deficiencies in certain vitamins and minerals can result in embryonic abnormalities and death.

Embryo mortality in chicken eggs tends to follow a well-defined pattern, with the greatest peaks of death occurring about day 3 and day 19 of incubation. The basis for these two peaks is not known, but similar peaks are seen at comparable stages of embryonic development in other avian species. Many specific genetic factors have been identified that produce gross physical abnormalities and death at various stages of development.

Parthenogenesis, the development of unfertilized eggs, is a well-documented phenomenon in turkeys. By genetic selection the incidence of parthenogenesis has been increased to over 40 percent in eggs of experimental flocks. Most of the parthenogenetic embryos die, but about 1 percent of them complete development and hatch. All of these have been diploid males, but testis weights are low and only about 20 percent of them produce semen (Olsen 1973).

REFERENCES

Asmundson, V.S., and Jervis, J.G. 1933. The effect of resection on different parts of the oviduct on the formation of the hen's egg. *J. Exp. Zool.* 65:395–420.

Bajpai, P.K., and Brown, K.I. 1963. The effect of some diluents on semen characteristics of turkeys. *Poul. Sci.* 42:882–88.

Benoit, J. 1964. The role of the eye and the hypothalamus in the photostimulation of gonads in the duck. *Ann. N.Y. Acad. Sci.* 117:204–15.

Bobr, L.W., Lorenz, F.W., and Ogasawara, F.X. 1964. Distribution of spermatozoa in the oviduct and fertility in domestic birds. I. Residence sites of spermatozoa in fowl oviducts. *J. Reprod. Fert.* 8:39–47.

Brown, K.I. 1970. Effect of sperm numbers and interval of insemination on fertility in turkeys. Res. Summary 47. Ohio Ag. Res. Devel. Ctr. Wooster.

——. 1974. Effects of sperm number on onset and duration of fertility in turkeys. Res. Summary 80. Ohio Ag. Res. Devel. Ctr. Wooster.

Burke, W.H., Graham, E.F., and Yu, W.C.Y. 1973. Effect of storage temperature and time on the fertilizing ability of turkey spermatozoa. Misc. Rept. 121. Minn. Ag. Exp. Sta., St. Paul.

Burke, W.H., Ogasawara, F.X., and Fuqua, C.L. 1969. Transport of spermatozoa to the site of fertilization in the absence of oviposition and ovulation in the chicken. *Poul. Sci.* 48:602–8.

Burmester, B.R. 1940. A study of the physical and chemical changes of the egg during its passage through the isthmus and uterus of the hen's oviduct. *J. Exp. Zool.* 84:445–500.

Douglas, D.S., and Sturkie, P.D. 1964. Plasma levels of antidiuretic hormone during oviposition in the hen. *Fed. Proc.* 23:150.

Follett, B.K. 1973. Circadian rhythms and photoperiodic time measurement in birds. *J. Reprod. Fert.*, suppl. 19, 5–18.

Fraps, R.M. 1954. Neural basis of diurnal periodicity in release of ovulation-inducing hormone in fowl. *Proc. Nat. Acad. Sci.* 40:348–56.

Freedman, S.L., and Sturkie, P.D. 1962. Disruption of the sympathetic innervation of the fowl's uterus. *Poul. Sci.* 41:1644.

Gilbert, A.B. 1967. Formation of the egg in the domestic chicken. In A. McLaren, ed., *Advances in Reproductive Physiology*. Logos, London. Vol. 2.

——. 1971. The ovary. In D.J. Bell and B.M. Freeman, eds., *Physiology and Biochemistry of the Domestic Fowl*. Academic Press, London. Vol. 3.

Graham, E.F., Rajamannan, A.H.J., Schmehl, M.K.L., Maki-Laurila, M., and Bower, R.E. 1971. Fertility studies with frozen boar spermatozoa. *A.I. Digest* 19:6.

Hayashida, T. 1970. Immunological studies with rat pituitary growth hormone (RGH). II. Comparative immunochemical investigation of GH from representatives of various vertebrate classes with monkey antiserum to RGH. *Gen. Comp. Endocr.* 15:432–52.

Hertelendy, F., and Taylor, T.G. 1961. Changes in blood calcium associated with egg shell calcification in the domestic fowl. I. Change in the total calcium. *Poul. Sci.* 40:108–14.

Lake, P.E. 1966. Physiology and biochemistry of poultry semen. In A. McLaren, ed., *Advances in Reproductive Physiology*. Logos, London. Vol. 1.

——. 1971. The male in reproduction. In D.J. Bell and B.M. Freeman, eds., *Physiology and Biochemistry of the Domestic Fowl*. Academic Press, London. Vol. 3.

Landauer, W. 1967. The hatchability of chicken eggs as influenced by environment and heredity. Monograph 1 (rev.). U. Conn. Ag. Exp. Sta., Storrs.

Lofts, B., and Lam, W.L. 1973. Circadian regulation of gonadotrophin secretion. *J. Reprod. Fert.*, suppl. 19, 19–34.

Ma, R.C.S., and Nalbandov, A.V. 1963. The transplanted hypophysis: Discussion. In A.V. Nalbandov, ed., *Advances in Neuroendocrinology*. U. of Illinois Press, Urbana.

McKeown, B.A. 1973. Comparative radioimmunological investigation of prolactin from various species of vertebrates. *Biochem. System.* 1:163–67.

Menaker, M., and Oksche, A. 1974. The avian pineal organ. In D.S. Farner and J.R. King, eds., *Avian Biology*. Academic Press, New York.

Munro, S.S. 1938. Functional changes in fowl sperm during their passage through the excurrent ducts of the male. *J. Exp. Zool.* 79:71–92.

Munsick, R.A., Sawyer, W.H., and Van Dyke, H.B. 1960. Avian

neurohypophysial hormones: Pharmacological properties and tentative identification. *Endocrinology* 66:860–71.

Nicoll, C.S. 1964. Neural regulation of adenohypophysial prolactin secretion in tetrapods: Indications from in vitro studies. *J. Exp. Zool.* 158:203–10.

Olsen, M.W. 1973. Longevity and organ weights of Beltsville Small White parthenogens and normal turkeys. *Poul. Sci.* 52:666–70.

Opel, H. 1964. Premature oviposition following operative interference with the brain of the chicken. *Endocrinology* 74:193–200.

——. 1966. Release of oviposition-inducing factor from the median eminence-pituitary stalk region in neural lobectomized hens. *Anat. Rec.* 154:396.

Schraer, R., and Schraer, H. 1970. The avian shell gland: A study in calcium translocation. In H. Schraer, ed., *Biological Calcification.* Appleton-Century-Crofts, New York.

Sturkie, P.D., and Freedman, S.L. 1962. Effects of transection of pelvic and lumbosacral nerves on ovulation and oviposition in the fowl. *J. Reprod. Fert.* 4:81–85.

Sturkie, P.D., and Lin, Y.C. 1966. Release of vasotocin and oviposition in the hen. *J. Endocr.* 35:555–56.

Tanaka, K., and Nakajo, S. 1962. Participation of neurohypophysial hormone in oviposition in the hen. *Endocrinology* 70:453–58.

Tixier-Vidal, A., and Gourdji, D. 1965. Evolution cytologique ultrastructurale de l'hypophyse du canard en culture organotypique: Elaboration autonome de prolactine par les explants. *Compte rend. Acad. sci.* 261:805–808.

Vince, M.A. 1966. Artificial acceleration of hatching in quail embryos. *Anim. Behav.* 14:389–94.

Warren, D.C., and Scott, H.M. 1935. The time factor in egg formation. *Poul. Sci.* 14:195–207.

Wood-Gush, D.G.M., and Gilbert, A.B. 1970. The rate of egg loss through internal laying. *Brit. Poul. Sci.* 11:161–63.

CHAPTER 56

The Mammary Gland and Lactation | by Norman L. Jacobson

The mammary gland, like sebaceous and sweat glands, is a cutaneous gland. Histologically, in the more advanced mammals it is a compound tubuloalveolar type that originates from the ectoderm. Although the mammary gland is basically similar in all mammals, there are wide species variations in the appearance of the gland and in the relative amounts of the components secreted.

The most primitive of present-day mammals is the egg-laying monotreme, of which one representative is the duckbilled platypus. The formation of the egg in the platypus requires about 2 weeks, and the incubation period is approximately 10 days to 2 weeks (Smith 1959). The platypus is very immature when hatched and does not move about for several months. The primary difference between the mammary gland of the platypus and that of higher mammals is the absence of a nipple. The milk is expressed from 100 or more ducts (or glands) located in two lines lateral to the ventral midline of the animal. The milk accumulates on the abdominal fur, which is licked by the young.

A somewhat more advanced type of mammal is the marsupial, whose young are born in a very immature state. The newborn marsupial, if it is to survive, must find its way quickly to a nipple, which in most marsupials is located in a pouch. If there are more young than nipples, the latecomers perish.

The most advanced mammals are those with true placentas. About 95 percent of the mammals existing today belong to this group (Smith 1959).

FUNCTIONAL ANATOMY OF THE MAMMARY GLAND

External

The mammary glands of cattle, sheep, goats, horses, and whales are located in the inguinal region; those of primates and elephants in the thoracic region; and those of pigs, rodents, and carnivores along the ventral surface of both the thorax and abdomen.

Normally, cattle have four functional teats and glands, whereas sheep and goats have two; each teat has one streak canal and drains a separate gland area. The glands and teats of domestic animals are known collectively as the udder. Pigs and horses usually have two streak canals per teat, with each canal serving a separate secretory area. In rodents, carnivores, and primates the number of streak canals per teat ranges up to 10 or 20.

Because more is known about the mammary glands of cattle than about those of other mammals, more attention will be given here to that species. A cow's udder is composed of two halves, each of which has two teats, and each teat drains a separate area (quarter). Each quarter is separated from the others by connective tissue and has a separate milk-collecting system (Fig. 56.1).

In addition to the four normal teats, there may be supernumerary teats, each of which is associated with a small gland, with a normal gland, or with no secretory area. About 40 percent of all cows have supernumerary teats, although there is considerable variation among reports. One and two extra teats occur with about equal

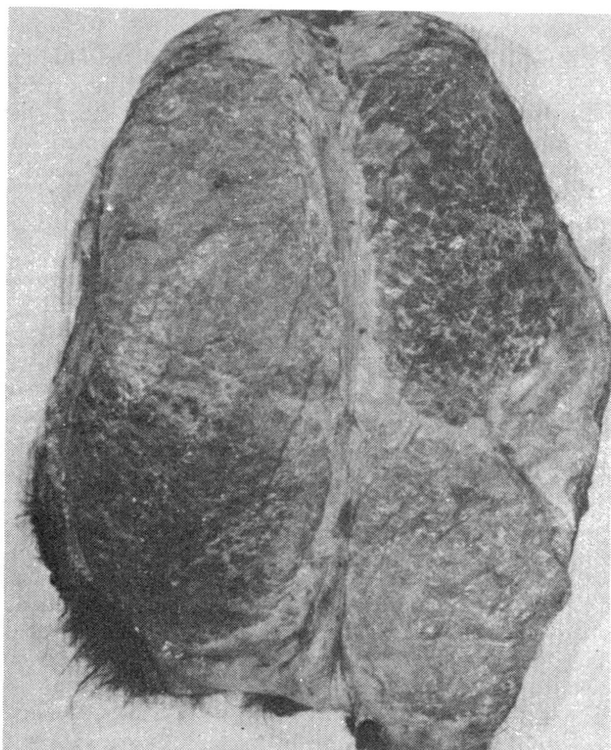

Figure 56.1. Horizontal section through a bovine udder. The milk-collecting systems of the right front (upper right) and left rear (lower left) quarters have been injected through the respective teats with a dye.

frequency, with a lesser number of animals having three or four. The supernumerary teats usually are oriented similarly to normal teats and may be caudad to (most common), between, or fused with the normal teats. Supernumerary teats also are found in sheep, goats, swine, and horses. In these species, with the exception of the horse, rudimentary teats are usually found in the male.

The empty weight of the lactating bovine udder usually is 14–32 kg, but weights from about 1 to 114 kg have been reported. Capacity likewise is extremely variable but not necessarily closely correlated with empty weight of the udder, since the ratio of parenchyma (secretory tissue) to stroma (connective tissue) varies widely. The weight and capacity of the udder usually increase until the cow reaches maturity, at about 6 years of age.

The whale represents an interesting adaptation of the mammary gland to the environment. The two glands are located in the inguinal region on either side of the vulva; the teats are located in depressions but are exposed during lactation. The gland is long and narrow. It is believed by some that the milk is ejected by a compressor muscle into the mouth of the calf, thus facilitating underwater nursing.

Internal

Supporting structure

The two halves of the bovine udder are separated by the median suspensory ligament, which is formed by two lamellae of yellow elastic connective tissue originating from the abdominal tunic (see Fig. 56.1). The posterior extremity of this ligament is attached to the prepubic tendon. On the lateral surface of the mammary gland are the lateral suspensory ligaments, composed largely of fibrous, nonelastic strands, from which arise numerous lamellae that penetrate the gland and become continuous with the interstitial tissue of the udder. The lateral suspensory ligaments are attached to the prepubic and subpubic tendons, which in turn are attached to the ischium and pubis. The lateral and median suspensory ligaments are the primary structures supporting the bovine udder. The skin is of relatively little significance for support but does protect the udder. On the ventral surface of the udder the lamellae of the median suspensory ligament and the lateral suspensory ligaments are in close relationship, providing a saclike support for the mammary gland.

Milk-collecting system

The bovine teat has a small cistern terminating at its distal extremity in the streak canal, which is the opening to the exterior of the teat (Figs. 56.2, 56.3). Radiating upward from the streak canal into the teat is a structure known as Fürstenberg's rosette, which is composed of about seven or eight loose folds of mucous membrane; each fold has a number of secondary folds. The rosette helps to retain milk in the teat. The primary structure in cattle responsible for retention of milk, however, is a sphincter muscle surrounding the streak canal. In sheep, though, closure of the streak canal is due largely to strong, dense, elastic connective tissue rather than to circular smooth muscle fibers. In swine, which usually have two streak canals per teat (each canal draining a separate gland area), the streak canal is tightly closed by longitudinal folds originating in the teat cistern. Each streak canal also has a circular elastic connective tissue band. Only a few muscle fiber bundles are found.

Above each teat is located a gland cistern into which numerous large ducts empty (see Fig. 56.2). These ducts branch profusely, ultimately ending in the secretory units called alveoli or acini (Figs. 56.4, 56.5).

There is a gradual change in the nature of the epithelium from the outside of the udder and teat to the inside. The skin epithelium is stratified squamous; the streak canal epithelium is transitional; and the teat and gland cisterns are lined by a two-layer epithelium, a layer of cuboidal cells overlaid with high cylindrical cells. There is a gradual change in the epithelium in the ducts from the type noted for the teat and gland cisterns to the single layer of epithelium characteristic of the alveoli.

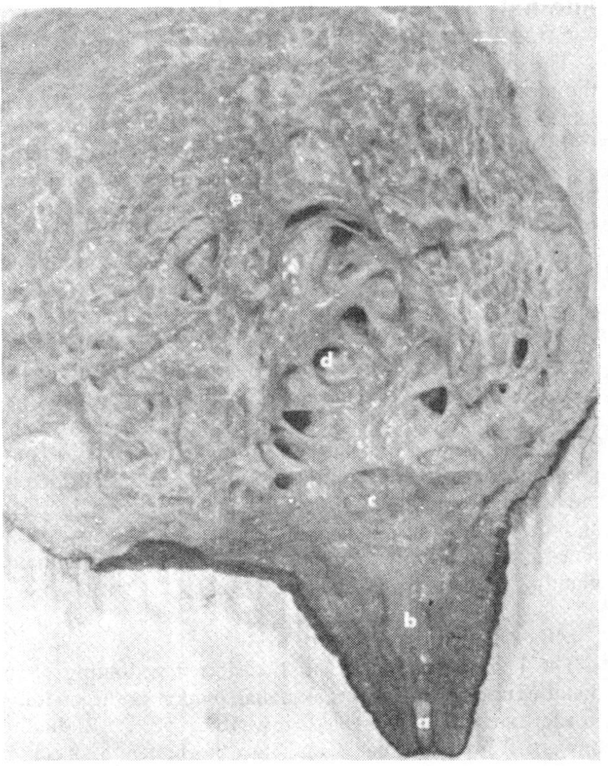

Figure 56.2. Vertical section through one quarter of a bovine udder: a, streak canal; b, teat cistern; c, gland cistern; d, large duct at point of entry into gland cistern; and e, secretory tissue.

Alveoli

Milk is formed in the epithelial cells of the alveolus (Figs. 56.6, 56.7). The alveolus when filled with milk is approximately 0.1–0.3 mm in diameter. The size of the alveolus is affected by many factors, one of the more important of which is the amount of milk in the lumen. When the alveolus is filled with milk, the width of the alveolar cells is exceedingly small in comparison to the diameter of the entire alveolus.

The alveoli are grouped together in units known as lobules, each of which is surrounded by a distinct connective tissue septum. The lobule in the bovine is somewhat less than 1 cu mm in volume. Lobules in turn are grouped together into larger units called lobes, which are surrounded by more extensive connective tissue septa. On visual examination of the fresh udder, the parenchyma, which is orange-yellow, can easily be differentiated from the white connective tissue.

The alveoli are surrounded by myoepithelial cells that are involved in the milk ejection (or milk letdown) reflex. Myoepithelial cells also are located along the ducts. Apparently these cells are widely distributed among mammals, since they have been identified in the cat, dog, goat, pig, rabbit, rat, sheep, and human (Cross, in Kon and Cowie 1961; Linzell 1952).

Blood supply

The main route followed by the blood in passing from the heart to mammary glands in the inguinal region is by way of the posterior aorta, the right and left common

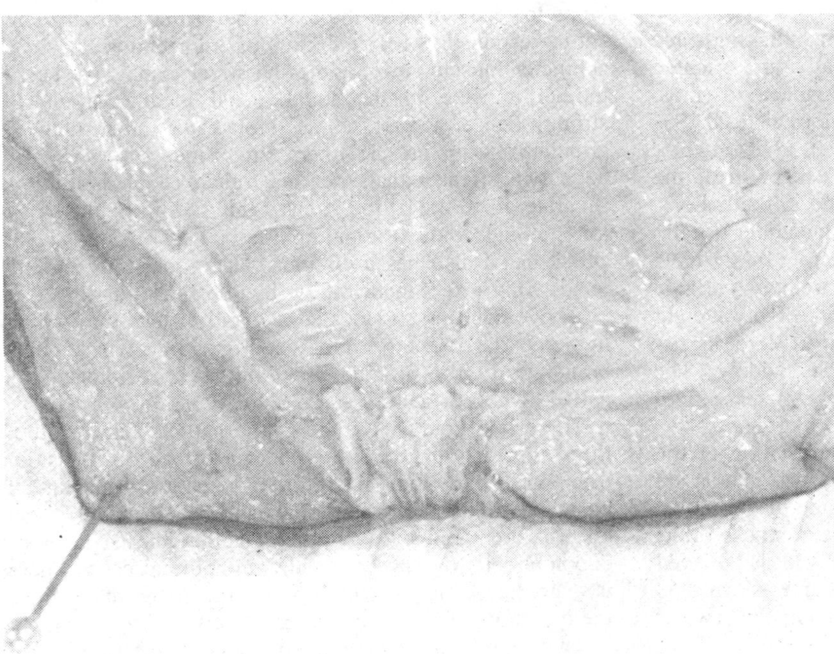

Figure 56.3. Vertical section through the distal portion of a bovine teat, bisected through the streak canal and adjacent teat cistern

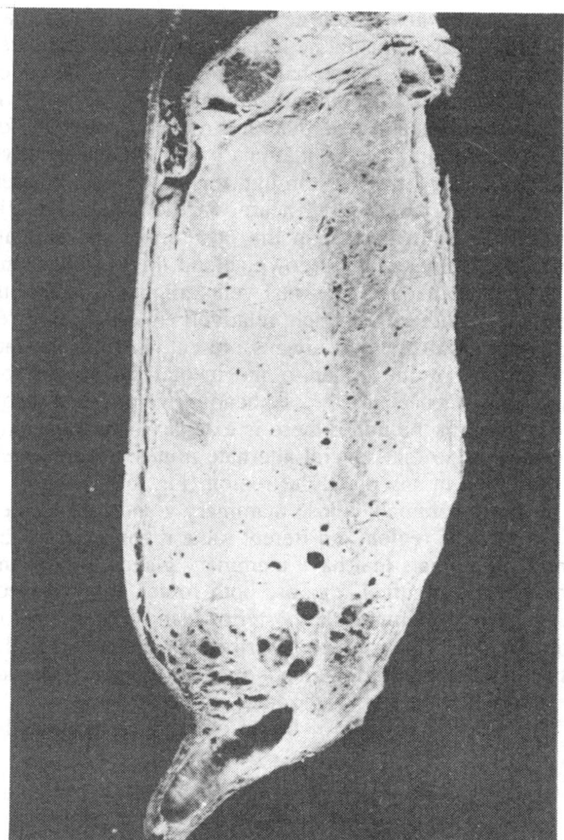

Figure 56.4. Vertical section through a rear quarter of the high-quality udder of a nonlactating Holstein cow. (From Swett et al. 1937, *J. Ag. Res.* 55:239–87.)

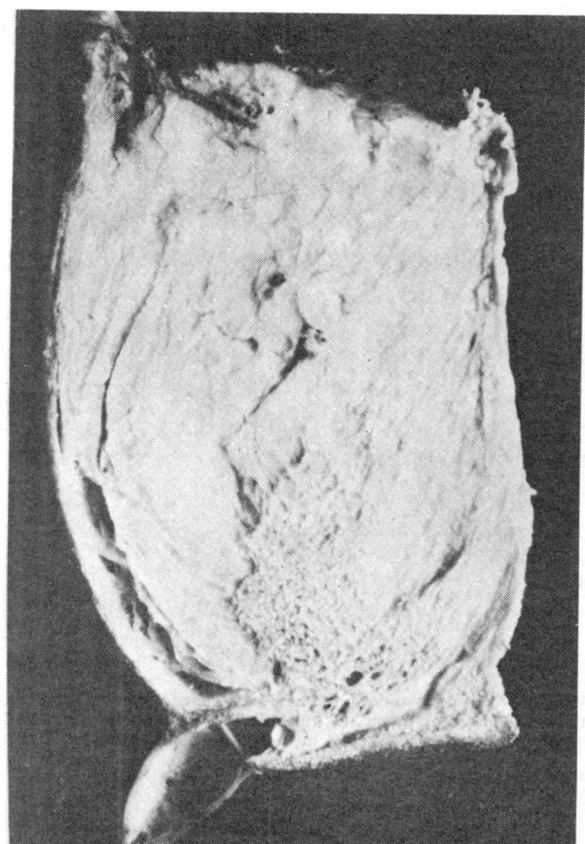

Figure 56.5. Vertical section through a rear quarter of the udder of a nonlactating Aberdeen Angus cow. It is composed largely of fat except for a small area dorsal to the teat. (From Swett et al. 1937, *J. Ag. Res.* 55:239–87.)

iliac arteries (from this point the route is bilateral), the external iliac arteries, and the external pudic arteries. The mammary arteries that originate from the external pudics form cranial and caudal branches, which supply respectively the anterior and posterior portions of the udder. The internal pudic arteries, which arise from the internal iliacs, give rise to the perineal arteries, which supply a small amount of blood to the posterior portion of the mammary glands. A major route for the return of blood from the udder to the heart is via veins traversing much the same route as the arteries just described. The blood passes through the external pudic veins, the external iliac veins, and the posterior vena cava. The perineal veins are of little significance; in fact, valves in these veins direct the blood toward rather than away from the udder (Swett and Matthews 1949).

The subcutaneous abdominal veins (caudal superficial epigastric veins) provide a potential route for passage of blood from the udder to the heart by way of the anterior vena cava. It has been observed that the valve structure in virgin female and male cattle, sheep, and goats is such that most of the blood posterior to the umbilical region is directed toward the udder (Linzell 1960a). A similar situation apparently exists in the pig and horse. As the ani-

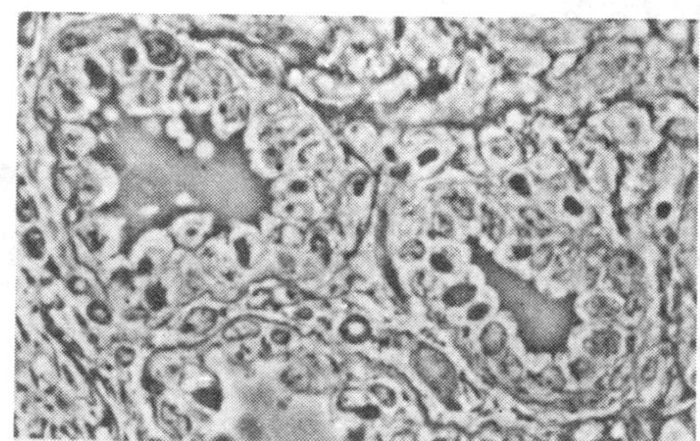

Figure 56.6. Phase contrast micrograph (section 1 μ thick) of two small acini (alveoli) and portions of others from a cow's udder 60 days after calving. ×820. (From Feldman 1961, *Lab. Invest.* 10:238–55.)

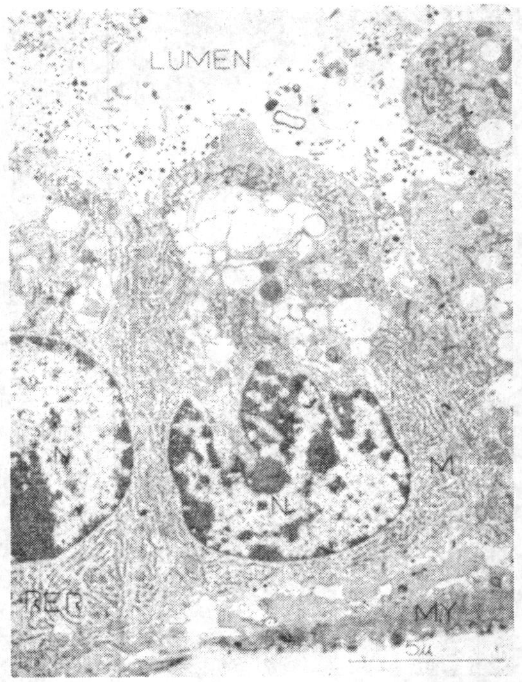

Figure 56.7. Electron micrograph of several acinar cells from a lactating bovine mammary gland. N, nucleus; RER, rough endoplasmic reticulum; M, mitochondrion; MY, myoepithelial cell. ×4300.

mal ages the valves become ineffective and blood may flow either way. Thus in the lactating animal an appreciable amount of blood is probably removed from the udder through the subcutaneous abdominal veins, although it has not been established that this route is essential for proper functioning of the mammary glands. The relative amount of blood passing through this route as compared with that returning to the heart via the external pudic veins depends in part upon the position of the animal. When the animal is lying down, blood flow through one of the subcutaneous abdominal veins might easily be obstructed. Another, although relatively insignificant, return route, which is not always present, is from the lateral surface of the udder to the medial surface of the thigh and thence to the saphenous vein (Emmerson 1941). Within the udder there is extensive anastomosing of the veins so that several alternate routes are presented to the blood in any particular region (Fig. 56.8).

In those mammals whose mammary glands are located in the thoracic region, a different route is followed by the blood. In animals that have mammary glands in both the thoracic and inguinal regions, both routes are involved. In swine, for example, the posterior glands receive blood from the posterior aorta as described for the cow. On the other hand, the anterior glands receive blood by way of the internal and external thoracic arteries.

The ratio of volume of blood circulating through the

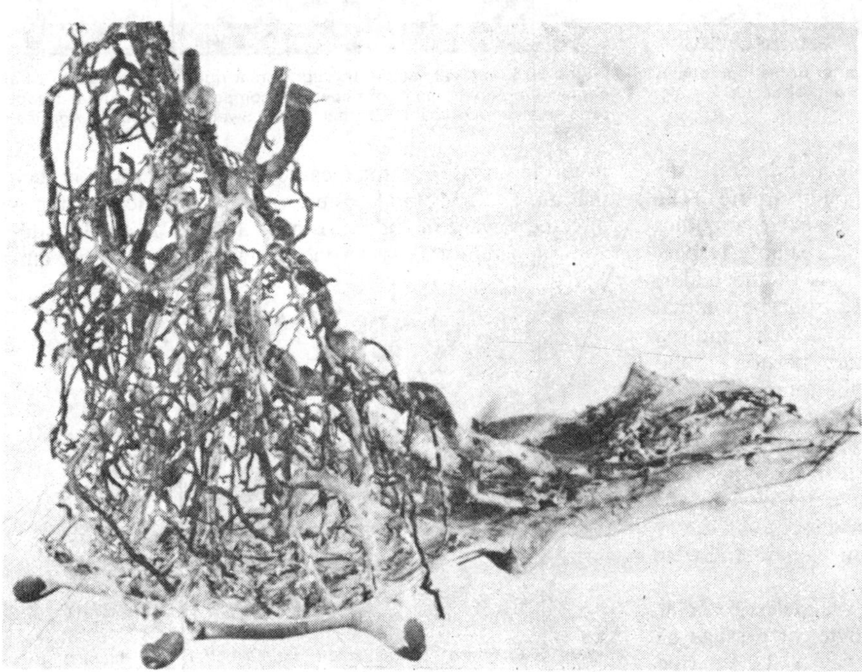

Figure 56.8. Latex-filled arteries and veins of a 24 kg udder of a lactating cow. The molds of the arteries are lighter in color than those of the veins. (From Swett and Matthews 1949, *U.S.D.A. Tech. Bull.* 982.)

mammary gland to volume of milk produced has been the subject of many studies. In the dairy cow producing at a moderate level the ratio is about 670:1 as calculated from the data of Barry (in Kon and Cowie 1961) and Kronfeld et al. (1968).

Lymph

In the body, fluids and solutes are continuously being exchanged between the blood plasma and the interstitial fluid. The latter apparently gives rise directly to the lymph flowing from that particular region. The mammary glands have an extensive network of lymph vessels, which in the bovine leave the udder by way of the supramammary lymph nodes (round dark areas in fatty tissue at top of the gland in Figure 56.4); there usually are two but sometimes there are more. The efferent vessels from the supramammary lymph nodes pass through the inguinal canal to the external iliac (or deep inguinal) lymph glands and then by way of the deep lumbar trunk through the cisterna chyli, and via the thoracic duct into the venous system near the origin of the anterior vena cava. Emmerson (1941) reported the weight of the average supramammary lymph gland in the cow to be about 44 g.

The flow of lymph from the mammary ducts is much greater in animals that are lactating than in those that are not. Rate of flow in cows, as calculated from data of Lascelles et al. (1964), ranged from 14 to 240 ml per hour in dry cows to as high as 2600 ml per hour in cows just prior to parturition and in early lactation. Lascelles and Morris (1961) reported about a 10-fold increase in lymph flow in the mammary ducts of ewes due to lactation, with the highest rates occurring in ewes producing the most milk. Some of the lymph flowing from the mammary ducts may not originate in the mammary glands, but the extramammary portion probably is comparatively small in the lactating animal. There are marked diurnal variations in flow rate. Mild exercise increases rate of flow sharply; this change apparently is due in part, but not entirely, to an increase in rate at which lymph (which is already formed) is propelled through the ducts. Rate of flow in sheep was found to be increased markedly by suckling or massaging of the glands (Lascelles and Morris 1961), but machine milking of cows and goats has not produced a consistent effect.

Lascelles and Morris (1961) estimated that the mammary lymph ducts in the lactating ewe contribute as much as 20–30 percent of the total thoracic lymph flow. In the lactating cow, however, Lascelles et al. (1964) estimated that perhaps 50–70 percent of the lymph in the thoracic duct may come from the mammary glands, if it is assumed that lactation does not appreciably alter the output of intestinal and thoracic lymph.

The concentrations of various constituents in lymph and in plasma from the jugular vein and subcutaneous abdominal vein blood have been determined by Lascelles et al. (1964). The protein content of lymph of dry cows was 56–59 percent of plasma values, and the relative amount in lymph decreased markedly shortly before parturition and continued to be low through early lactation. Ratios of albumin to globulin were higher in lymph than in plasma. In general, lymph from the mammary glands of cows is similar in composition to that from sheep and goats.

Nerve supply

The bovine udder is supplied with sensory (afferent) and motor (efferent) nerves. The afferent nerves consist of ventral branches of the first and second lumbar nerves; the inguinal nerve, consisting of ventral branches of the second, third, and fourth lumbar nerves; and the perineal nerve, which is a branch of the pudic nerve (St. Clair 1942).

The ventral branches of the first and second lumbar nerves supply a small area of the anterior part of the udder, principally the skin. The inguinal nerve is located anterior to the external iliac blood vessels as they descend to the internal inguinal ring, where the inguinal nerve divides into anterior and posterior nerves. The anterior nerve supplies the fold of the flank and the anterior part of the forequarter and foreteat (including the apex) but innervates the glandular tissue only to a minor degree. Outside the external inguinal ring the posterior inguinal nerve divides. The anterior branch (or branches) supplies primarily the skin of the lateral part of the forequarter and the posterior portion of the foreteat, and to a lesser degree the glandular tissue. The posterior branch of the posterior inguinal nerve innervates the lymph node area, the glandular tissue of the rear quarter and the posterior part of the front quarter, the rear teat, and the skin of the rear quarter except the posterior portion above the base of the teat. The skin of the posterior part of the udder above the teat is innervated by the perineal nerve. These afferent nerves are significant in the milk-ejection process. Neither secretion nor ejection of milk in the bovine, however, requires efferent nerve fibers. The efferent fibers of the bovine udder originate from the lumbar sympathetic plexus and pass through the inguinal canal. They are vasoconstrictors to the peripheral blood vessels; if the inguinal nerve is cut there is a temporary vasodilatation in the udder. The mammary gland apparently is not innervated by parasympathetic fibers, which would be expected since it is of cutaneous origin. The nerves of the mammary gland are in the connective tissue and are not in direct contact with the alveolar cells (St. Clair 1942). Moreover, the nerves of the mammary gland apparently have no direct effect on rate of milk secretion or on milk composition.

GROWTH AND DEVELOPMENT OF THE MAMMARY GLAND

Turner (1952) has reviewed the prenatal and postnatal development of the mammary gland. When the bovine embryo is about 35 days old, a mammary line forms from the stratum germinativum (in the Malpighian layer) on either side of and parallel to the ventral midline. Subsequently the development is concentrated in areas where the future mammary glands will be located. At about 2 months the mammary bud sinks deeper and the teat begins to form. Up to this point development in the male and female is about the same, although the development of the teat proceeds somewhat more slowly in the male. The proliferating ectoderm moves deeper into the mesenchyme, forming what is known as a primary sprout. At about 100 days canalization begins; this is caused by widening of the diameter of the sprout and production of a cavity within. The canalization begins at the proximal end of the sprout and proceeds gradually toward the distal end, eventually producing an opening to the exterior. Secondary sprouts develop from the proximal end of the primary sprout, and canalization begins at the end adjacent to the primary sprout. The cavity within the primary sprout eventually develops into the gland and teat cisterns, and the cavities in the secondary sprouts develop into the major ducts.

At birth the bovine udder has distinct teat and gland cisterns, but the major ducts are developed only to a limited extent. The difference between male and female is relatively small. The vascular and lymphatic systems are organized essentially as they will be in the mature udder. The adipose and other connective tissues are well organized and a large fatty pad makes up a large part of the udder. With some modifications, development of the mammary glands in other species proceeds in a similar manner.

From birth until shortly before puberty the mammary gland undergoes relatively little development. Its increase in size is due to an increase in connective tissue and fat and to some extension of the duct system. As puberty nears, growth of the duct system is stimulated.

During a cow's first pregnancy the mammary gland develops rapidly. Duct growth proceeds during early pregnancy; by the fifth month lobules are formed but they are small. Lobuloalveolar development is extensive by the end of the sixth month. Secretory activity develops gradually during the last several months. In the sow, the lobuloalveolar development has been reported to be essentially complete by midpregnancy (Turner 1952). Studies by Griffith and Turner (1959, 1961a) in which DNA and RNA/DNA ratios were employed as criteria, however, indicated that the mammary glands of rats do not attain maximum cellular activity until 5–10 days after the end of pregnancy. Growth at the end of pregnancy was only about 60 percent of maximum. Apparently there also is substantial development of the mammary glands in the mouse during early lactation. Probably this occurs in other species as well (Munford 1964).

Following parturition, rate of milk secretion usually increases for a short period (about 2–4 weeks in dairy cows) and then slowly declines. Despite generation of some new cells, there is a gradual decrease in total number (due to degeneration and death) of mammary epithelial cells as lactation progresses. Studies with rats (Tucker 1969) indicate that involution also involves a decline in metabolic activity of individual cells. When lactation ceases, the epithelial cells of the alveoli disappear but the myoepithelial cells remain. Retention of milk in the gland hastens involution whereas removal of milk retards the process. It is possible that the frequent release of oxytocin retards mammary involution. Distension of the alveoli causes an increase in pressure in the secretory areas and reduces circulation in the capillaries. Periodic contraction of the alveoli and removal of milk may enhance circulation (Cross, in Kon and Cowie 1961).

RELATIONSHIP OF ENDOCRINES TO THE MAMMARY GLAND AND LACTATION

Secretions of the endocrines are intimately involved in the development of the mammary gland. Hormones of the anterior lobe of the hypophysis that are related directly or indirectly to development of the mammary gland and lactation are thyrotropic or thyroid-stimulating hormone (TSH), growth or somatotropic hormone (STH), adrenocorticotropic hormone (ACTH), follicle-stimulating hormone (FSH), luteinizing hormone (LH), and lactogenic hormone (prolactin) (see Chapter 52). All of the hormones of the anterior pituitary appear to be under the direct control of the hypothalamic region of the brain. The hypothalamus produces neurohormones that act directly on the anterior pituitary to stimulate or inhibit release of hormones. Thyroxine, STH, and the corticosteroids are involved in general growth and development of the animal and thus are related to mammary development also.

At sexual maturity the effect of the gonadotropic hormones becomes evident. Under the influence of FSH the follicle develops and is a source of estrogen. LH, in conjunction with FSH, produces ovulation; the resulting corpus luteum is a source of progesterone, the production of which is stimulated by LH. In general, an estrogen alone causes duct development, and progesterone and estrogen together cause lobuloalveolar growth. There are, however, variations among species. In the intact cat, mouse, rat, and rabbit moderate doses of estrogen produce mainly duct growth, but in the intact guinea pig and monkey this hormone produces extensive lobuloalveolar growth as well. In the goat, estrogen causes abnormal development of the mammary gland and production of some milk. The same is true to a degree in the bovine but the results are erratic. Estrogen alone in these species produces markedly dilated alveoli. In the dog estrogen alone will not cause development of the ducts. For complete development of the mammary gland in the various species, both estrogen and progesterone are necessary as well as pituitary hormones. The ratio of estrogen to progesterone is important and varies with species, but usually much more progesterone is required than estrogen. The absolute amounts of the two steroids given also are important. Estrogen or estrogen and progesterone will not produce development of the mammary gland in the hypophysectomized animal. Apparently both STH and prolactin are required. There is a synergism between pituitary hormones (particularly STH and prolactin) and the ovarian hormones. The placenta serves as a source of estrogen and progesterone in some species and also of pituitarylike hormones.

Prolactin and ACTH (acting through the adrenals) are necessary for the initiation and maintenance of lactation. Apparently there is a marked increase in prolactin content of the pituitary just prior to parturition. It has been proposed that this increase is related to the relative amounts of estrogen and progesterone in the blood. An increase in ACTH and adrenocortical function has also been observed at parturition. Administration of adrenocortical hormones to pregnant cattle, rats, rabbits, and mice can initiate lactation without disturbing pregnancy. Either prolactin or cortical hormones can evoke lactation in the pregnant rabbit, and the two hormones synergize when given together. Using in vitro organ cultures, Topper (1968) has shown that insulin stimulates proliferation of new mammary epithelial cells, that hydrocortisone promotes development of synthetic mechanisms (e.g. rough endoplasmic reticulum) in the new cells, and that prolactin causes elaboration of milk protein synthesis. Other hormones (STH, thyroxine) can influence the quantity of milk produced but are not essential for lactation. Caruolo and Mochrie (1968) showed that injection of estradiol-testosterone suppresses lactation in cattle, goats, and sheep. Small injections produced a colostrum-like milk; larger doses produced a watery, clotted secretion.

The hormone of the neurohypophysis that is of primary interest in lactation is oxytocin. In the lactating animal, oxytocin is concerned with the milk-expulsion mechanism; it causes contraction of the myoepithelial cells surrounding the alveoli and lying along the small ducts, thereby forcing milk out of these areas as milk is removed from the sinuses in the udder and teat. Milk expulsion can be initiated in several ways. Under natural conditions it is effected by nursing, probably by way of the afferent nerve endings in the teat, which cause a release of oxytocin, which in turn is carried by the blood to the mammary glands and stimulates contraction of the myoepithelium. Many other circumstances, however, will initiate the reflex. In the bovine, at least, such a reaction is caused by washing or massaging of the udder before milking, the sound of the milking machine, approach to the milking area, and sight of the calf. Thus the reflex need not be mediated through the nerve endings in the teat or udder. In fact, even when the nerves to the mammary glands are severed in the goat, milk secretion and excretion can continue. In goats also, lactation occurred in glands transplanted to the rib area and to the ventral surface of the neck (Linzell 1960b).

Excitation of the animal interferes with milk expulsion. One explanation that has been offered is that the increased release of epinephrine causes a constriction of the arterioles and precapillaries in the udder and thereby reduces the amount of oxytocin that passes through the capillaries of the udder. There is reason to believe, however, that a central inhibition of the reflex is a more important factor than a peripheral influence of epinephrine.

The effect of orally administered thyroxine has been studied extensively, particularly in dairy cattle. By appropriate treatment of casein a product containing thyroxine can be produced. This material commonly is referred to as thyroprotein or iodinated casein. When fed to animals in appropriate amounts it increases the basal metabolic rate and, if the animals are sufficiently well nourished, often increases milk production. The magnitude and duration of the effect, the response in efficiency of milk production, and other physiological reactions are highly variable. Injections of STH also increase milk production in dairy cattle.

PHYSIOLOGICAL AND BIOCHEMICAL ASPECTS OF LACTATION

The components of milk are produced either directly or indirectly from blood. Although the osmotic pressure is the same for milk and blood, there is a striking difference in composition. Milk contains much more sugar, lipid, calcium, phosphorus, and potassium but less protein, sodium, and chlorine. Moreover, the protein in milk is primarily casein (with small amounts of albumins and globulins), whereas albumins and globulins are the principal proteins of blood plasma. Also, quantitatively, most of the lipid in milk is triglyceride, whereas phospholipids and cholesterol represent a major portion of the blood lipids.

Milk composition

Table 56.1 gives the average composition of milk of various species of animals. In general, milk of marine mammals has a very high fat content, as is evidenced by the analyses shown for the dolphin, seal, and whale. The polar bear also produces milk of high fat content. Many of the more rapidly growing species, such as the rabbit and rat, have a very high protein content, but the rela-

Table 56.1. Composition of milk from various species (%)

Species	Fat	Protein	Lactose	Ash	References
Anteater	20.0	11.0	0.3	0.8	Altman and Dittmer 1961
Antelope					
Black buck	9.3	6.9	4.3	0.4	Dill et al. 1972
Eland	9.8	6.8	3.9	1.3	Treus and Kravchenko 1968
Gazelle	19.4	11.1	2.9	1.5	Ben Shaul 1962
Impala	20.4	10.8	2.4	1.4	Ben Shaul 1962
Pronghorn	13.0	6.9	4.0	1.3	Einarsen 1948
Ass (donkey)	1.3	1.8	6.2	0.4	Altman and Dittmer 1961, Smith 1959
Baboon	5.0	1.6	7.3	0.3	Buss 1968
Bear					
Black	24.5	14.5	0.4	1.8	Jenness et al. 1972
Grizzly	22.3	11.1	0.6	1.5	Jenness et al. 1972
Polar	33.1	10.9	0.3	1.4	Jenness et al. 1972
Beaver	19.8	9.0	2.2	2.0	Ben Shaul 1962
Bison	1.7	4.8	5.7	0.9	Altman and Dittmer 1961, Shutt 1932
Buffalo					
Chinese	12.6	6.0	3.7	0.9	Altman and Dittmer 1961
Egyptian	7.7	4.3	4.7	0.8	Altman and Dittmer 1961
Philippine	10.4	5.9	4.3	0.8	Altman and Dittmer 1961
Camel	4.2	3.5	4.8	0.7	Altman and Dittmer 1961, Bestuzheva 1958, Heraskov 1962, Siddiqui and Bari 1959, Smith 1959
Cat	7.1	10.1	4.2	0.5	Altman and Dittmer 1961
Cattle					
Ayrshire	4.1	3.6	4.7	0.7	Armstrong 1959
Brown Swiss	4.0	3.6	5.0	0.7	Armstrong 1959
Guernsey	5.0	3.8	4.9	0.7	Armstrong 1959
Holstein	3.5	3.1	4.9	0.7	Armstrong 1959
Jersey	5.5	3.9	4.9	0.7	Armstrong 1959
Shorthorn	3.6	3.3	4.5	0.8	Ling et al. 1961
Red Steppe	3.9	3.3	4.6	0.8	Abol 1956
Kurgan	4.0	3.7	4.9	0.7	Chernova 1956
Aulie-Ata	3.6	2.9		0.6	Mironenko and Mossorova 1956
Tagil	4.1		4.7	0.8	Konovalov 1956
Latvian Black Pied	3.3		4.4	0.7	Lazauskas 1956
Zebu	4.9	3.9	5.1	0.8	Bakulin 1954, Verdiev and Veli-Zade 1960
Cheetah	9.5	9.4	3.5	1.3	Ben Shaul 1962
Chimpanzee	3.7	1.2	7.0	0.2	Ben Shaul 1962
Chinchilla	12.5	8.0	1.7	1.0	Volcani et al. 1973
Collared peccary	3.6	5.4	6.6		Sowls et al. 1961
Coyote	10.7	9.9	3.0	0.9	Ben Shaul 1962
Deer	19.7	10.4	2.6	1.4	Spector 1956
Dog	9.5	9.3	3.1	1.2	Altman and Dittmer 1961
Dolphin	41.5	10.9	1.1	0.7	Altman and Dittmer 1961, Eichelberger et al. 1940
Elephant	16.6	4.2	5.1	0.7	Altman and Dittmer 1961, Simon 1959, Steuer 1957
Fox	6.3	6.3	4.7	1.0	Young and Grant 1931
Giraffe	13.5	5.8	3.4	0.9	Aschaffenburg et al. 1962
Goat	3.5	3.1	4.6	0.8	Lythgoe 1940
Gorilla	2.2				Ben Shaul 1962
Guinea pig	3.9	8.1	3.0	0.8	Nelson et al. 1951
Hamster	12.6	9.0	3.4	1.4	Ben Shaul 1962
Hedgehog	10.1	7.2	2.0	2.3	Ben Shaul 1962
Hippopotamus	4.5		4.4	0.1	Spector 1956
Horse	1.6	2.4	6.1	0.5	Holmes et al. 1947, Linton 1931, Ullrey et al. 1966
Human	4.3	1.4	6.9	0.2	Altman and Dittmer 1961, Bassir 1956, Fomon et al. 1960, Osmond 1954, Smith 1959, Williams 1961
Jackal	10.5	10.0	3.0	1.2	Ben Shaul 1962
Kangaroo	5.4	7.9	0.3	1.7	Bolliger and Pascoe 1953
Kangaroo rat	23.5	(solids-not-fat, 26.1)			Kooyman 1963
Leopard	6.5	11.1	4.2	0.8	Ben Shaul 1962
Lion	18.9	12.5	2.7	1.4	Ben Shaul 1962
Llama	3.2	3.9	5.6	0.8	Altman and Dittmer 1961
Lynx, European	6.2	10.2	4.5	0.8	Ben Shaul 1962
Mink	8.0	7.0	6.9	0.7	Jørgensen 1960
Monkey					
M. mulatta	3.9	2.1	5.9	0.3	Van Wagenen et al. 1941
Squirrel	5.1	3.5	6.3	0.3	Buss and Copper 1972
Moose	7.0	13.5	3.6	1.6	Ben Shaul 1962
Mouse	12.1	9.0	3.2	1.5	Ben Shaul 1962
Mule	1.8	2.0	5.5	0.5	Altman and Dittmer 1961, Spector 1956
Musk ox	11.0	5.3	3.6	1.8	Evans 1959, Tener 1956
Nutria (coypu)	27.9	13.7	0.6	1.3	Ben Shaul 1962

Species	Fat	Protein	Lactose	Ash	References
Okapi	2.0	9.9	5.1	1.4	Ben Shaul 1962
Opossum	6.1	9.2	3.2	1.6	Gross and Bolliger 1959
Orangutan	3.5	1.4	6.0	0.2	Altman and Dittmer 1961
Otter	24.0	11.0	0.1	0.8	Ben Shaul 1962
Porcupine	13.2	12.4	1.8	2.3	Ben Shaul 1962
Puma	18.6	12.0	3.9	1.0	Ben Shaul 1962
Rabbit	12.2	10.4	1.8	2.0	Bergman and Turner 1937
Raccoon	3.5	8.0	6.6	1.0	Evans 1959
Rat	13.0	9.7	3.2	1.4	Altman and Dittmer 1961
Reindeer	20.9	10.0	2.5	1.4	Altman and Dittmer 1961
Rhinoceros	Trace	1.5	6.1	0.3	Aschaffenburg et al. 1961
Sea lion, California	34.9	13.6	0.0	0.6	Pilson and Kelley 1962
Seal					
Gray	53.2	11.2	2.6	0.7	Amoroso et al. 1951
Harp	42.6	10.4		0.8	Ben Shaul 1962
Hooded	40.4	6.6		0.9	Ben Shaul 1962
Sheep	10.4	6.8	3.7	0.9	Perrin 1958a,b
Shrew					
Short-tailed	6.5	11.0	3.2	0.8	Ben Shaul 1962
Water	20.0	10.0	0.1	0.8	Ben Shaul 1962
Squirrel, gray	12.6	9.2	3.4	1.4	Ben Shaul 1962
Swine	7.9	5.9	4.9	0.9	Lodge 1959, Perrin 1958b
Thar	9.8	5.8	3.3		Rammell and Caughley 1964
Whale	33.2	12.2	1.4	1.4	Altman and Dittmer 1961, Gregory et al. 1955, Ohta et al. 1953, White 1953
Wolf, European	9.6	9.2	3.4	1.4	Ben Shaul 1962
Yak	7.0	5.2	4.6		Ling et al. 1961
Zebra	4.8	3.0	5.3	0.7	Altman and Dittmer 1961

tionship between rate of maturity and level of protein is not consistent. The lactose content is probably the most constant, varying in most cases between 3 and 7 percent, although it is apparently very low in some mammals. Kangaroo milk is rather atypical in composition, since it is reported to contain pentoses (instead of lactose) as well as proteins and other nitrogenous compounds not usually associated with mammalian milk (Bolliger and Pascoe 1953).

It must be recognized that many of the values shown in Table 56.1 are based on relatively few analyses, whereas there is a considerable amount of information on milk composition of domestic animals, particularly the bovine. Not only are the data on many wild species very meager, but frequently little is known about the stage of lactation and the time when milk previously was removed from the gland. Even under standard conditions of removal of milk from the gland, there are substantial short-term (diurnal and day-to-day) variations in composition. Furthermore, there may be significant differences in the milk withdrawn from different glands in the same animal.

There are major differences in milk composition among and within breeds of cattle; these differences can be accentuated by genetic selection. There is a rather high correlation between fat and other solids in cow's milk; changes in protein account for a major part of the changes in solids other than fat. There is a slight increase in fat percentage with age up to about 3 years, after which there is a modest decline, usually not exceeding 0.2 percent. The decline with age in milk solids other than fat is approximately twice the decline in fat. There is little decline in total protein, but the casein fraction declines and the whey proteins increase. Most of the decline in solids other than fat is due to a decrease in lactose with age.

During the first few weeks after parturition, fat percentage of cow's milk is high; then it declines for 3–4 months and thereafter gradually increases. If a cow or sow is in good condition at parturition, fat percentage of the milk usually is higher for a time than if the animal is thin. The percentage of other solids begins to increase at about the second month after parturition, with a rather sharp rise occurring near the seventh month. In nonpregnant cows the change is less. Lactose rises to a maximum at about the forty-fifth day and then declines slowly. The percentage of whey protein is relatively high in early and late lactation.

In the bovine the fat content of the milk drawn last from the udder at a single milking contains more fat than the first-drawn milk. The fat content may be 4–8 times as high in the last pound of milk as in the first. A higher fat content in the last-drawn milk also has been observed in the human and goat. The reason for this phenomenon is not clear, although there are several reasons why it cannot be due to a simple "creaming" effect (rise of fat globules) within the udder. Such a change does not occur in the sow (Whittlestone 1952).

The nutrient requirements of domestic animals, including needs during lactation, are summarized in a series of publications by the National Research Council (1971–1976). Reid (in Kon and Cowie 1961) has discussed the nutrition of lactating farm animals.

The caloric intake by the cow affects milk composition. Feeding about 30 percent fewer calories than recommended by the commonly accepted standards usually reduces the actual percentage of solids other than fat by 0.3–0.5, the major portion of this reduction being due to a decrease in protein content. Feeding 30 percent above normal increases solids other than fat modestly (about 0.2 percent); this increase is likewise due primarily to a change in protein. Altering protein intake does not greatly affect the protein content of the milk, although a drastic reduction will reduce the protein content slightly. The amount of fat in the diet of the cow has relatively little effect on the fat content of the milk. Reducing the fat content of the cow's diet to a very low level will have no appreciable effect on milk-fat percentage but will depress milk production slightly. A high level of fat intake sometimes causes a small increase in the fat content of the milk. Ingestion of highly unsaturated vegetable oils will increase the unsaturated fatty acid content of milk of nonruminants. Similarly, the unsaturated fatty acid content of ruminants' milk has been greatly increased when the oil has been treated to prevent hydrogenation in the rumen (Bitman et al. 1973, Scott et al. 1970).

An excessively high-calorie diet during a cow's early life (before first parturition) has an adverse effect on milk yield. The productive life of the animal is reduced, and there is excessive fat deposition in the udder, less proliferation of secretory tissue, and lowered milk production (Swanson 1957). On the other hand, marked underfeeding of high-energy feed in early life delays sexual maturity and consequently age at first calving. Thus it would seem desirable to avoid both extremes. Usually, however, cows fed sparingly in early life and fed well after first parturition will produce a quantity of milk not far below that of animals fed more liberally prior to lactation. Likewise, modest underfeeding before parturition probably does not substantially reduce the milk production of sows and ewes if they are fed in accordance with needs during lactation.

Ruminants appear to utilize metabolizable energy for maintenance, fattening, and milk production somewhat less efficiently than nonruminants, which is not surprising in view of the higher fermentative losses in the ruminant. The horse probably is less efficient than the pig and more efficient than cattle and sheep. Ruminants use metabolizable energy more efficiently for milk production and maintenance than for fattening, but there are indications that fattening is more efficient in the lactating than in the nonlactating animal.

Milk secretion

In recent years considerable progress has been made in identifying the components of milk, particularly of the cow, and of the precursors of the milk components. Rose et al. (1970) listed the following protein fractions that have been isolated in substantial quantity from bovine skim milk: α_s-casein, β-casein, γ-casein, κ-casein, α-lactalbumin, β-lactoglobulin, blood serum albumin, immunoglobulins, and a proteose-peptone fraction. The caseins constitute the major part of the milk proteins with α_s-casein predominating. Immunoglobulins are present in very small amounts except in colostrum. Those proteins synthesized in the mammary gland from amino acids are α_s-, β-, and κ-casein; α-lactalbumin; and the β-lactoglobulins. Gamma casein, blood serum albumin, and immunoglobulins of milk apparently are largely synthesized elsewhere. Barry (in Kon and Cowie 1961), however, stated that the amino acid composition of the immunoglobulins of colostrum is different from that of immunoglobulins of blood and that the major portion of the immunoglobulin fraction of colostrum is probably synthesized in the mammary gland from free amino acids of the blood. It is likely that the general mechanisms for protein synthesis, involving DNA and RNA, in the cells of the mammary gland are similar to those systems related to protein synthesis in other cells. Beitz et al. (1969) synthesized milk proteins in a cell-free system, primarily on the basis of components isolated from bovine mammary tissue. The synthesis was dependent on the presence of microsomes and an energy source; synthesis was enhanced by addition of tRNA and an amino-acyl-tRNA synthetase preparation.

There are many minor proteins such as enzymes in milk, but the total amount is very small. Also there are many nonprotein nitrogen compounds such as urea, creatine, creatinine, uric acid, ammonia, and (especially in bovine milk) orotic acid. Some, perhaps, are products from blood and others are waste products or metabolites from the mammary gland. The protein components of milk vary significantly from species to species; for example, human milk contains relatively less of the casein and relatively more of the noncasein fractions than cow's milk.

The principal carbohydrate of milk, lactose, is synthesized in the mammary gland. The primary precursor of the glucose and galactose moieties in the lactose molecule is blood glucose. Propionic acid is also readily utilized, via glucose, in the synthesis of lactose. Lactose is normally found in appreciable amounts only in the mammary gland, but small amounts may appear in the blood and urine during lactation (Leloir and Cardini, in Kon and Cowie 1961). Galactose, on the other hand, is found elsewhere, such as in galactolipids, cerebrosides, and galactoproteins. Synthesis of galactose can occur not only in the mammary gland but in certain other tissues as well. Since the normal fermentative process in the rumen converts a major portion of the carbohydrate to volatile fatty acids, it is likely that these acids, especially propionic acid, are more important precursors of lactose in ruminants than in nonruminants. Studies with compounds containing ^{14}C have demonstrated that propionate preferentially appears in the lactose, whereas much of the acetate carbon appears in milk fat. Butyrate carbon, on the other hand, is more evenly distributed among the lactose, casein, and fat. One of the proteins synthesized in the mammary gland, α-lactalbumin, has been shown to be a part of the lactose synthetase complex. Thus this protein has a role other than simply being a component of milk. Perhaps other milk proteins also are so involved.

Milk lipids consist primarily of triglycerides, although there are very small amounts of phospholipids, cholesterol, fat-soluble vitamins, squalene, free fatty acids, monoglycerides, and many other compounds (Garton 1963, Jack and Smith 1956). The fat is present in milk in small globules with an average size of about 3–4 μ in diameter. The interior of the globule is essentially glyceride, whereas the outer membrane contains phospholipid, cholesterol, vitamin A, protein, and many other components. Apparently the outer membrane is formed from the outer membrane of the alveolar cell when the fat globule is secreted from the cell into the lumen of the alveolus.

Milk fat from herbivores, particularly ruminants, has relatively high levels of fatty acids with carbon-chain lengths from 4 to 14. Milk of nonherbivorous animals contains very little butyric, caproic, and caprylic acids. It appears that the fatty acids from butyric to palmitic are synthesized largely in the mammary gland, starting with either acetate or β-hydroxybutyrate and proceeding by stepwise condensation with acetyl-CoA units to form the longer-chain acids (Palmquist et al. 1969). Part of the palmitic acid and all of the C-18 acids arise from sources other than mammary synthesis, although stearic acid can be desaturated to oleic acid in the alveolar cell. It has been demonstrated also, by in vitro studies, that mammary gland slices from nonruminants are capable of utilizing glucose both as a source of energy and as a source of carbon for lipogenesis, whereas mammary gland slices from ruminants apparently are not able to provide two-carbon units from glucose for fatty acid synthesis (Folley and McNaught, in Kon and Cowie 1961). Thus in the nonruminant, glucose probably is a major contributor of two-carbon units for synthesis of fatty acids containing 16 carbon atoms or less. Glycerol, the other component of the triglyceride molecule, is derived primarily from glucose.

Normally acetic acid is the predominant fatty acid in the rumen, representing about 60–70 percent on a molar basis. Under certain circumstances, however, the ratios can be changed significantly. For example, when cows are fed a high-concentrate, low-roughage ration, the relative proportion of acetate decreases and propionate increases, due principally to an increase in total amount of propionate. In the lactating cow (and goat), this alteration in rumen acids often causes a sharp reduction in the milk-fat percentage, possibly due not only to the relative amounts of the acids available for metabolism, but also to a reduction in the activity of certain enzymes (e.g. fatty acid synthetase) in the mammary tissue (Opstvedt et al. 1967, Varman and Schultz 1968). As the ability of the mammary gland to synthesize milk fat declines, fat synthesis in the adipose tissue increases.

The major mineral components of milk, with the approximate percentage in bovine whole milk shown in parentheses, are calcium (0.12), phosphorus (0.10), sodium (0.05), potassium (0.15), and chlorine (0.11). The amounts of magnesium and sulfur have been reported to be approximately 120 and 300 ppm respectively (Macy et al. 1953). In addition, there are small amounts, usually less than 1 ppm, of aluminum, boron, bromine, cobalt, copper, fluorine, iodine, iron, manganese, molybdenum, silicon, silver, strontium, and zinc (Ling et al. 1961). There are significant variations among species in the amount of certain mineral components of milk; a part, but not all, of these differences is due to variations in total ash content.

Probably all of the known vitamins can be found in milk, but some are present in abundance whereas others occur only in relatively small amounts. The levels of many of them may vary considerably among and within species. The microorganisms in the rumen synthesize B-complex vitamins; therefore, the amounts of these vitamins in the milk of ruminants are less dependent on diet than is the case with nonruminants. Vitamin K is synthesized not only in the rumen but also in the intestine of most animals. Consequently, the content of this vitamin in milk, which is rather low, is not greatly affected by dietary intake. Vitamins A, D, and E are not synthesized in the rumen, and therefore the amount in the milk reflects more closely the amount in the diet. This is especially true for vitamin A and its precursors, the carotenoids. Vitamin D, which is normally present in milk in only small amounts, cannot be increased greatly except when exceedingly high levels are fed. An exogenous source of ascorbic acid is not needed for most mammals. The amount of this vitamin in milk is not greatly influenced by diet.

The relative proportions of carotenoids and vitamin A in the milk reflect the amount of these substances in the blood. Some species, such as the sheep, goat, and pig, convert essentially all of the carotenoids to vitamin A and very little of the former is found in milk. On the other hand, there is a considerable amount of the carotenoids in milk of the bovine. Even in bovines, however, there is variation among breeds. The Holstein, for example, is an efficient converter of carotene to vitamin A and therefore has proportionately less of the former in the milk than Guernseys and Jerseys, which are less efficient in this respect.

Many drugs pass readily from blood to milk, ether and chloroform being typical examples. Antibiotics are eliminated in part by way of the milk, especially when administered parenterally. Alcohol also passes into the milk but in relatively small amounts.

It long has been recognized that many substances that inadvertently contaminate feed will cause off-flavors and undesirable odors in milk. It has been demonstrated that many volatile substances causing off-flavors are detectable much more quickly in cow's milk when these materials are introduced by way of the lungs than when introduced by way of the digestive tract (Dougherty et al. 1962). A large part of the eructated gas is inhaled before expulsion, thus facilitating absorption of volatile materials that cause off-flavors in milk.

BIOLOGICAL SIGNIFICANCE OF MILK TO THE YOUNG

Colostrum, the first milk produced after parturition, is of primary significance to the young. It is highly nutritious and in some species contains components essential for survival during the neonatal period (Table 56.2). The dry-matter content is considerably higher in colostrum than in normal milk. This is due primarily to the great increase in protein, particularly the whey proteins (albumins and globulins). Many of the vitamins are present in substantially higher levels in colostrum. Lactose content, however, is much lower. Colostrum of the sow also is markedly higher in solids and in protein and is lower in lactose than normal milk.

Transfer of vitamin A from maternal to fetal tissue via the placenta is quite inefficient in many mammals. Newborn calves and pigs, for example, usually have very low reserves of vitamin A. Consequently, the high levels of vitamin A (and carotenoids in some species) in colostrum are of primary importance in correcting this deficiency. Likewise the colostrum has a high level of antibodies or immunoglobulin (γ-globulin) in which the newborn of many species is deficient. Placental transmission of antibodies occurs in some species, e.g. humans, guinea pigs, and rabbits. On the other hand, sheep, goat, pig, dog, horse, and cattle neonates are dependent upon colostrum as a source of antibodies. This passive immunity is necessary for the young until they are able to develop active immunity.

Table 56.2. Amounts of selected components of bovine colostrum as percentage of level in normal milk

	Days after parturition		
Constituent	0	3	5
Dry matter	220	100	100
Lactose	45	90	100
Lipids	150	90	100
Minerals	120	100	100
Proteins			
Casein	210	110	110
Albumin	500	120	105
Globulin	3500	300	200
Vitamins			
A	600	120	100
Carotene	1200	250	125
E	500	200	125
Thiamin	150	150	150
Riboflavin	320	130	110
Pantothenic acid	45	110	105

Since the antibodies are proteins and since proteins normally are hydrolyzed in the gastrointestinal tract, this ability of the young to absorb antibodies intact is an unusual phenomenon. The period during which this absorption normally can occur extends for only 1–2 days after birth in the pig, horse, dog, and cattle (see Chapter 17). Likewise, it has been estimated to be 4 days or less in sheep and goats under normal circumstances. Shannon and Lascelles (1968) observed a marked increase in rate of flow and γ-globulin content of thoracic duct lymph during the 8 hours following the first feeding of colostrum to the young calf. There was a subsequent decline with values becoming relatively constant by 24 hours, at which time absorption of γ-globulin apparently had virtually ceased. Asplund et al. (1962) observed that oral administration of insulin to pigs within 18–24 hours after birth caused a measurable hypoglycemia. Thus it appears that materials other than γ-globulin can be absorbed from the gut of the young. Insulin, like γ-globulin, is a protein. Payne and Marsh (1962) observed that the length of time during which γ-globulin could be absorbed was affected by diet. It was found that pigs fed milk for 12 hours after birth were unable to absorb γ-globulin subsequent to that time. On the other hand, pigs that received only water or that were starved for 106 hours after birth retained the ability to absorb γ-globulin. The maximum blood levels of antibodies usually are reached about 24 hours after birth and decline gradually over a period of several weeks or months.

Although colostrum is undoubtedly the most important liquid feed for the young mammal, whole milk or a whole milk replacer is needed until the young consumes enough dry feed to satisfy its nutritional requirements. In ruminants, the esophageal groove provides a means of directing the milk past the ruminoreticulum into the abomasum and intestine, where the milk nutrients are digested and efficiently absorbed. Despite its outstanding nutritional contribution and near-essentiality in the nourishment of the young mammal, milk has certain inadequacies. In relation to the needs of the young, milk normally is very low in vitamin D, iron, and copper. Also a diet restricted to milk for an extended period is not adequate to prevent hypomagnesemia in the calf.

PHYSIOLOGY OF MILKING

It is now generally agreed that essentially all of the milk yielded at a given milking is present in the mammary gland at the onset of milking or nursing. Although it had been thought that the intramammary pressure in the dairy cow's udder before milking may range up to about 40 mm Hg, Witzel and McDonald (1964) suggested that a more realistic range is 0–8 mm Hg. These researchers also found that washing the udder stimulated milk letdown within 20–90 seconds, resulting in markedly higher intramammary pressure (35–55 mm Hg). Graf and Lawson (1968) reported rather similar post-stimulation pressures (28–43 mm Hg). The increased pressure resulting from milk letdown slowly declines even if no milk is removed from the gland. Termination of the letdown, after about 10–20 minutes, apparently is due to dissipation or inactivation of the oxytocin. If it were due to fatigue of the myoepithelial cells, one would not expect to get more milk (as in fact one does) when additional oxytocin is injected.

Witzel and McDonald (1964) found that pressures within the teat and gland sinuses were similar when milk was present in both. The pressure declined during milking, and near the termination of milking there was a slight vacuum (0 to −5 mm Hg) within the udder. The milking machine employed in this study had a pulsator ratio of 50:50, was equipped with narrow-bore rubber inflations, and maintained a vacuum of −312 mm Hg. These authors found that, upon cessation of milk flow, the vacuum in the teat sinus increased markedly to a maximum of −216 to −316 mm Hg with each dilatation of the inflation (expansion phase) of the milking machine. When the inflation was collapsed, a vacuum of −48 to −120 mm Hg persisted. The authors postulated that pressure changes within the teat cistern are the result of the action of the teat cup of the milking machine upon the teat wall and the extension of the vacuum of the milk line through the teat canal. Vacuum within the gland sinus was much lower, possibly because of closure at the annular ring. When the teat canal was ligated, the vacuum within the teat cistern pulsated between 0 and −20 mm Hg.

It seems logical to assume that the maximum amount of milk would be obtained from a dairy cow if she were milked at equal intervals (12-hour intervals in twice-a-day milking or 8-hour intervals in 3-time-a-day milking). The reduction that occurs with the use of unequal intervals, however, is much less than might be expected. With cows producing (on a mature equivalent basis) over 13,000 lb (5889 kg) of milk per year, Schmidt and Trimberger (1963) found that the use of intervals of 14 and 10 hours reduced milk production only about 0.3 percent below that which was obtained with equal intervals (12 and 12 hours). Moreover, the reduction when the intervals were changed to 16 and 8 hours was only about 1.3 percent. No significant differences due to milking interval were observed in the percentage of milk fat or total solids. The unequal intervals appeared to have no deleterious effects on udder health or incidence of ketosis. Morag and Fox (1967) found no difference in milk yield of ewes when milking intervals were varied from 12 and 12 to 8 and 16.

Wheelock et al. (1965b) observed that injection of oxytocin into the cow and removal of residual milk in the udder affected composition of milk obtained at several subsequent milkings, perhaps through an effect on permeability of mammary epithelium. Lactose content was decreased and sodium, chloride, and whey proteins were increased.

In cows milked continuously throughout pregnancy, milk yield decreases until 3 weeks or less before parturition, then gradually increases (Wheelock et al. 1965a). A sharp increase in proteins in late pregnancy in continuously milked cows suggests that colostral protein is secreted several days before parturition. In such cows, lactose content of the colostrum is only slightly subnormal in contrast to the low level in cows that are not milked for several weeks before parturition. Continuous milking during pregnancy decreases milk yield in the subsequent lactation, apparently because of an effect within the gland rather than a more general effect, since this depression has been observed when half the udder was given a normal dry period and the other half was milked continuously (Smith et al. 1967).

Wheelock et al. (1967) showed that suspension of milking of two quarters of the udder of the cow for 2 weeks does not cause complete involution. When milking was resumed, the concentrations of sodium and chloride in the milk were elevated and concentrations of lactose and potassium were depressed. Milk composition gradually returned to normal over a period of 8 weeks.

METABOLIC DISTURBANCES RELATED TO LACTATION

One of the most common disturbances associated with lactation in dairy cows is *milk fever* (parturient paresis). This disease, which occurs during parturition and beginning lactation, is characterized by a generalized paresis, circulatory collapse, and gradual loss of consciousness. The temperature may be elevated early but later it is normal or subnormal. When the disease is not treated, it often terminates in death. The milk fever syndrome is characterized by a sharp drop in calcium and inorganic phosphorus levels in the blood plasma. Calcium declines from a normal 5 mEq/L to 1.5–3.5 mEq/L. Serum inorganic phosphorus levels ordinarily are depressed, whereas serum magnesium levels sometimes are elevated. In most cases prompt recovery will follow the introduction of calcium into the blood (usually in the form of calcium borogluconate); however, relapses requiring a repetition of the treatment are rather common. This syndrome seldom occurs at first parturition and is much more common in high-producing animals. It is most prevalent in the Jersey breed. Prepartum milking has no significant effect on the incidence or severity of the disease. Milk fever is not restricted to dairy cattle, but it is of lesser significance in other animals.

Incidence of milk fever can be reduced sharply by oral administration of approximately 20 million IU of vitamin D daily, starting about 5 days before the expected date of parturition. Hibbs and Conrad (1960) indicated that the protection afforded by this dosage of vitamin D increases for the first 3 days but will decline precipitously after vitamin D has been discontinued for 1 day. Since feeding the vitamin D for longer than 7 days may result in calcification of soft tissue, it is obvious that the date of parturition must be predicted with great accuracy if this method of prevention is to be effective.

It has been shown that vitamin D is metabolized in the liver to 25-hydroxycholecalciferol; this in turn is converted in the kidney to 1,25-hydroxycholecalciferol, which increases intestinal absorption and bone mobilization of calcium. Olson et al. (1973) have shown that intramuscular injection of 4 or 8 mg of 25-hydroxycholecalciferol prevented milk fever when cows calved 3–10 days after injection.

Low-calcium but otherwise adequate diets for about 2 weeks before parturition have been shown to prevent milk fever in dairy cows. Apparently the low-calcium diet sensitizes the calcium homeostatic mechanism (Goings et al. 1974).

Grass tetany, a magnesium-deficiency disease that is aggravated by high levels of milk production, is discussed in Chapter 33. *Ketosis,* a third metabolic disease associated with lactation in dairy cows, as well as with pregnancy in ewes, is discussed in Chapter 30.

REFERENCES

Abol, T.P. 1956. Chemical composition of the milk of Red Steppe cows in Omsk province. *Dairy Sci. Abstr.* 18:440.

Ackman, R.G., and Burgher, R.D. 1963. Component fatty acids of the milk of the grey (Atlantic) seal. *Can. J. Biochem. Physiol.* 41:2501–5.

Altman, P.L., and Dittmer, D.S., eds. 1961. *Blood and Other Body Fluids*. Fed. Am. Soc. Exp. Biol., Washington.

Amoroso, E.C., Goffin, A., Halley, G., Matthews, L.H., and Matthews, D.J. 1951. Lactation in the grey seal. *J. Physiol.* 113:4P–5P.

Ardran, G.M., Cowie, A.T., and Kemp, F.H. 1957. A cineradiographic study of the teat sinus during suckling in the goat. *Vet. Rec.* 69:1100–1101.

Armstrong, T.V. 1959. Variations in the gross composition of milk as related to the breed of the cow: A review and critical evaluation of literature of the United States and Canada. *J. Dairy Sci.* 42:1–19.

Aschaffenburg, R. 1965. Variants of milk proteins and their pattern of inheritance. *J. Dairy Sci.* 48:128–32.

Aschaffenburg, R., Gregory, M.E., Rowland, S.J., Thompson, S.Y., and Kon, V.M. 1961. The composition of the milk of the African black rhinoceros (*Diceros bicornis;* Linn.). *Proc. Zool. Soc. Lond.* 137:475–79.

——. 1962. The composition of the milk of the giraffe. *Proc. Zool. Soc. Lond.* 139:359–63.

Asplund, J.M., Grummer, R.H., and Phillips, P.H. 1962. Absorption of colostral gamma-globulins and insulin by the newborn pig. *J. Anim. Sci.* 21:412–13.

Baker, B.E., Bertok, E.I., and Symes, A.L. 1963. The protein and lipid constitution of guinea pig milk. *Can. J. Zool.* 41:1041–44.

Baker, B.E., Harington, C.R., and Symes, A.L. 1963. Polar bear milk. I. Gross composition and fat constitution. *Can. J. Zool.* 41:1035–39.

Bakulin, I.I. 1954. Zebu in Azerbaijan. *Priroda* 43:108–10.

Baldwin, R.L. 1969. Development of milk synthesis. *J. Dairy Sci.* 52:729–36.

Bassir, O. 1956. Nutritional studies on breast milk of Nigerian women: Some biochemical features of breast milk of Lagos women during the first year of lactation. *J. Trop. Med. Hyg.* 59:139–44.

Becker, R.B., and Arnold, P.T.D. 1942. Circulatory system of the cow's udder. *Fla. Ag. Exp. Sta. Bull.* 379.

Beitz, D.C., Mohrenweiser, H.W., Thomas, J.W., and Wood, W.A. 1969. Synthesis of milk proteins in a cell-free system isolated from lactating bovine mammary tissue. *Arch. Biochem. Biophys.* 132:210–22.

Ben Shaul, D.M. 1962. The composition of the milk of wild animals. *Internat. Zoo Yearbook* 4:333–42.

Berge, S. 1963. New analyses of reindeer milk. *Tidsskr. norske Landbr.* 70:27–34.

Bergman, A.J., and Turner, C.W. 1937. The composition of rabbit milk stimulated by the lactogenic hormone. *J. Biol. Chem.* 120:21–27.

Bestuzheva, K.T. 1958. Composition of the colostrum and milk of camels. *Dairy Sci. Abstr.* 20:1039–40.

Bitman, J., Cecil, H.C., Gilliam, D.R., and Wrenn, T.R. 1963. Chemical composition of sheep mammary gland. *J. Dairy Sci.* 46:941–46.

Bitman, J., Dryden, L.P., Goering, H.K., Wrenn, T.R., Yoncoskie, R.A., and Edmondson, L.F. 1973. Efficiency of transfer of polyunsaturated fats into milk. *J. Am. Oil Chem. Soc.* 50:93–98.

Blakemore, F., and Garner, R.J. 1956. The maternal transference of antibodies in the bovine. *J. Comp. Path. Ther.* 66:287–89.

Blaxter, K.L. 1964. Protein metabolism and requirements in pregnancy and lactation. In H.N. Munro and J.B. Allison, eds., *Mammalian Protein Metabolism*. Academic Press, New York.

Boda, J.M. 1956. Further studies on the influence of dietary calcium and phosphorous on the incidence of milk fever. *J. Dairy Sci.* 39:66–72.

Boda, J.M., and Cole, H.H. 1954. The influence of dietary calcium and phosphorous on the incidence of milk fever in dairy cattle. *J. Dairy Sci.* 37:360–72.

Bolliger, A., and Pascoe, J.V. 1953. Composition of kangaroo milk (Wallaroo, *Macropus robustus*). *Austral. J. Sci.* 15:215–17.

Broderick, G.A., Satter, L.D., and Harper, A.E. 1974. Use of plasma amino acid concentration to identify limiting amino acids for milk production. *J. Dairy Sci.* 57:1015–23.

Buss, D.H., 1968. Gross composition and variation of the components of baboon milk during natural lactation. *J. Nutr.* 96:421–26.

Buss, D.H., and Copper, R.W. 1972. Composition of squirrel monkey milk. *Folia Primatologica* 17:285–91.

Caruolo, E.V., and Mochrie, R.D. 1968. Effects of temporary hormonal suppression of lactation on milk constituents, clinical mastitis, colostrum, and the estrous cycle. *J. Dairy Sci.* 51:1436–44.

Chernova, A.Kh. 1956. Composition of milk of Kurgan Cows. *Dairy Sci. Abstr.* 18:440.

Cmelik, S.H.W. 1962. Fatty acid composition of the milk fat of the Eland antelope (*Taurotragus oryx*). *J. Sci. Food Ag.* 13:662–65.

Convey, E.M. 1974. Serum hormone concentrations in ruminants during mammary growth, lactogenesis, and lactation: A review. *J. Dairy Sci.* 57:905–17.

Crichton, J.A., Aitken, J.N., and Boyne, A.W. 1960. The effect of plane of nutrition during rearing on growth, production, reproduction, and health of dairy cattle. III. Milk production during the first three lactations. *Anim. Prod.* 2:159–68.

Dill, C.W., Tybor, P.T., McGill, R., and Ramsey, C.W. 1972. Gross composition and fatty acid constitution of blackbuck antelope (*Antilope cervicapra*) milk. *Can. J. Zool.* 50:1127–29.

Dougherty, R.W., Shipe, W.F., Gudnason, G.V., Ledford, R.A., Peterson, R.D., and Scarpellino, R. 1962. Physiological mechanisms involved in transmitting flavors and odors to milk. I. Contribution of eructated gases to milk flavor. *J. Dairy Sci.* 45:472–76.

Edmondson, L.F., Yoncoskie, R.A., Rainey, N.H., Douglas, F.W., Jr., and Bitman, J. 1974. Feeding encapsulated oils to increase the polyunsaturation in milk and meat fat. *J. Am. Oil Chem. Soc.* 51:71–76.

Eichelberger, L., Fetcher, E.S., Jr., Geiling, E.M.K., and Vos, B.J., Jr. 1940. The composition of dolphin milk. *J. Biol. Chem.* 134:171–76.

Einarsen, A.S. 1948. *The Pronghorn Antelope and Its Management.* Wildlife Management Inst., Washington.

Elliott, G.M., and Brumby, P.J. 1955. Rate of milk secretion with increasing interval between milking. *Nature* 176:350–52.

Emmerson, M.A. 1941. Studies on the microscopic anatomy of the bovine udder and teat. *Vet. Ext. Q.* 41:1–36.

Ensor, W.L., Shaw, J.C., and Tellechea, H.F. 1959. Special diets for the production of low fat milk and more efficient gains in body weight. *J. Dairy Sci.* 42:189–91.

Espe, D. 1947. Some observations on nerve regeneration in the udder. *J. Dairy Sci.* 30:9–12.

Espe, D., and Cannon, C.Y. 1942. The anatomy and physiology of the teat sphincter. *J. Dairy Sci.* 25:155–60.

——. 1943. Reestablishment of the arterial supply to the udder. *J. Dairy Sci.* 26:841.

Evans, D.E. 1959. Milk composition of mammals whose milk is not normally used for human consumption. *Dairy Sci. Abstr.* 21:277–88.

Feldman, J.D. 1961. Fine structure of the cow's udder during gestation and lactation. *Lab. Invest.* 10:238–55.

Fomon, S.J., Clement, D.H., Forbes, G.B., Fraser, D., Hansen, A.E., Lowe, C.U., May, C.D., Smith, C.A., and Smith, N.J. 1960. Composition of milks. *Pediatrics* 26:1039–49.

Foust, H.L. 1941. The surgical anatomy of the teat of the cow. *J. Am. Vet. Med. Ass.* 98:143–49.

Ganguli, N.C., Prabhakaran, R.J.V., and Iya, K.K. 1964. Composition of the caseins of buffalo and cow milk. *J. Dairy Sci.* 47:13–18.

Garton, G.A. 1963. The composition and biosynthesis of milk lipids. *J. Lipid Res.* 4:237–54.

Gillette, D.D., and Filkins, M. 1966. Factors affecting antibody transfer in the newborn puppy. *Am. J. Physiol.* 210:419–22.

Gilmore, H.C., and Gaunt, S.N. 1963. Variations in per cent of protein, milk fat, and solids-not-fat between milkings and during the milking process. *J. Dairy Sci.* 46:680–85.

Goings, R.L., Jacobson, N.L., Beitz, D.C., Littledike, E.T., and Wiggers, K.D. 1974. Prevention of parturient paresis by a prepartum calcium-deficient diet. *J. Dairy Sci.* 57:1184–88.

Graf, G.C., and Lawson, D.M. 1968. Factors affecting intramammary pressures. *J. Dairy Sci.* 51:1672–75.

Gregory, M.E., Kon, S.K., Rowland, S.J., and Thompson, S.Y. 1955. The composition of the milk of the blue whale. *J. Dairy Res.* 22:108–12.

Griffith, D.R., and Turner, C.W. 1959. Normal growth of rat mammary glands during pregnancy and lactation. *Proc. Soc. Exp. Biol. Med.* 102:619–21.

——. 1961a. Normal growth of rat mammary gland during pregnancy and early lactation. *Proc. Soc. Exp. Biol. Med.* 106:448–50.

——. 1961b. Normal and experimental involution of rat mammary gland. *Proc. Soc. Exp. Biol. Med.* 107:668–70.

Gross, R., and Bolliger, A. 1959. Composition of milk of the marsupial *Trichosurus vulpecula*. *Am. J. Dis. Child.* 98:768–75.

Hartman, A.M., and Dryden, L.P. 1965. The vitamins in milk and milk products. In B.H. Webb and A.H. Johnson, eds., *Fundamentals of Dairy Chemistry.* Avi, Westport, Conn.

Hendriks, H.J. 1964. Neutrality regulation in normal cows and in cows suffering from hypomagnesaemia and hypomagnesaemic tetany ("grass tetany"). *Tijdschr. Diergeneesk.* 89:487–98.

Heraskov, S.G. 1962. Composition, properties, and nutritive value of camel's milk. *Nutr. Abstr. Rev.* 32:383.

Hibbs, J.W. 1950. Milk fever (parturient paresis) in dairy cows: A review. *J. Dairy Sci.* 33:758–89.

Hibbs, J.W., and Conrad, H.R. 1960. Studies of milk fever in dairy cows. VI. Effect of three prepartal dosage levels of vitamin D on milk fever incidence. *J. Dairy Sci.* 43:1124–29.

Hindery, G.A., and Turner, C.W. 1964. Effect of repeated injection of estrogen on milk yield of nulliparous heifers. *J. Dairy Sci.* 47:1092–95.

Holmes, A.D., Spelman, A.F., Smith, C.T., and Kuymeski, J.W. 1947. Composition of mare's milk as compared with that of other species. *J. Dairy Sci.* 30:385–95.

Jack, E.L., and Smith, L.M. 1956. Chemistry of milk fat: A review. *J. Dairy Sci.* 39:1–25.

Jenness, R., Erickson, A.W., and Craighead, J.J. 1972. Some comparative aspects of milk from four species of bears. *J. Mammal.* 53:34–47.

Jørgensen, G. 1960. Composition and nutritive value of mink's milk. *Nutr. Abstr. Rev.* 30:1218.

Jorgensen, N.A. 1974. Combating milk fever. *J. Dairy Sci.* 57:933–44.

Jylling, B., and Sørensen, P.H. 1960. Investigations on the composition of sow milk. *Den Kong. Veterinaer-og landbohøjskole Årsskrift,* pp. 20–36.

Kon, S.K., and Cowie, A.T., eds. 1961. *Milk: The Mammary Gland and its Secretion.* Academic Press, New York. 2 vols.

Konovalov, V.F. 1956. Composition and properties of milk of Tagil cows. *Dairy Sci. Abstr.* 18:440.

Kooyman, G.L. 1963. Milk analysis of the kangaroo rat, *Dipodomys merriami*. *Science* 142:1467.

Kronfeld, D.S., Raggi, F., and Ramberg, C.F., Jr. 1968. Mammary blood flow and ketone body metabolism in normal, fasted, and ketotic cows. *Am. J. Physiol.* 215:218–27.

Larson, B.L. 1969. Biosynthesis of milk. *J. Dairy Sci.* 52:737–47.

Larson, B.L., and Gillespie, D.C. 1957. Origin of the major specific proteins in milk. *J. Biol. Chem.* 227:565–73.

Larson, B.L., and Smith, V.R. 1974. *Lactation: A Comprehensive Treatise.* Academic Press, New York.

Lascelles, A.K., Cowie, A.T., Hartmann, P.E., and Edwards, M.J. 1964. The flow and composition of lymph from the mammary gland of lactating and dry cows. *Res. Vet. Sci.* 5:190–201.

Lascelles, A.K., and Morris, B. 1961. The flow and composition of lymph from the mammary gland in Merino sheep. *Q. J. Exp. Physiol.* 46:206–15.

Lazauskas, M. 1956. Changes in the composition of milk of Latvian Black Pied cows during lactation. *Dairy Sci. Abstr.* 18:512.

Lecce, J.G., Morgan, D.O., and Matrone, G. 1964. Effect of feeding colostral and milk components on the cessation of intestinal absorption of large molecules (closure) in neonatal pigs. *J. Nutr.* 84:43–48.

Ling, E.R., Kon, S.K., and Porter, J.W.G. 1961. The composition of milk and the nutritive value of its components. In S.K. Kon and A.T. Cowie, eds., *Milk: The Mammary Gland and Its Secretion.* Academic Press, New York. Vol. 2.

Linton, R.G. 1931. The composition of mare's milk. *J. Ag. Sci.* 21:669–88.

Linzell, J.L. 1952. The silver staining of myoepithelial cells, particularly in the mammary gland, and their relation to the ejection of milk. *J. Anat.* 86:49–57.

——. 1955. Some observations on the contractile tissue of the mammary glands. *J. Physiol.* 130:257–67.

——. 1956. Evidence against a parasympathetic innervation of the mammary glands. *J. Physiol.* 133:66P.

——. 1959. The innervation of the mammary glands in the sheep and goat with some observations on the lumbosacral autonomic nerves. *Q. J. Exp. Physiol.* 44:160–76.

——. 1960a. Valvular incompetence in the venous drainage of the udder. *J. Physiol.* 153:481–91.

——. 1960b. Transplantation of mammary glands. *Nature* 188:596–98.

Lodge, G.A. 1959. The composition of sow's milk during lactation with particular reference to the relationship between protein and lactose. *J. Dairy Res.* 26:134–39.

Lukas, V.K., Albert, W.W., Owens, F.N., and Peters, A. 1972. Lactation of Shetland mares. *J. Anim. Sci.* 34:350.

Lythgoe, H.C. 1940. Composition of goat milk of known purity. *J. Dairy Sci.* 23:1097–1108.

Macy, I.G., Kelley, H., and Sloan, R. 1953. *The Composition of Milks*. Nat. Res. Coun. Pub. 254. Nat. Acad. Sci., Washington.

McCullagh, K.G., and Widdowson, E.M. 1970. The milk of the African elephant. *Brit. J. Nutr.* 24:109–17.

Mironenko, M.S., and Mossorova, R.V. 1956. Composition of milk in Aulie-Ata cows. *Dairy Sci. Abstr.* 18:440.

Mohammed, K., Brown, W.H., Riley, P.W., and Stull, J.W. 1964. Effect of feeding coconut oil meal on milk production and composition. *J. Dairy Sci.* 47:1208–12.

Morag, M., and Fox, S. 1967. The effect of equal and unequal intervals in twice-daily milking on the milk yield of ewes. *J. Dairy Res.* 34:163–67.

Munford, R.E. 1964. A review of anatomical and biochemical changes in the mammary gland with particular reference to quantitative methods of assessing mammary development. *Dairy Sci. Abstr.* 26:293–304.

Nandi, S. 1959. Hormonal control of mammogenesis and lactogenesis in the C3H/He Crgl mouse. *U. Calif. Pub. Zool.* 65:1–128.

Narendran, R., Hacker, R.R., Batra, T.R., and Burnside, E.B. 1974. Hormonal induction of lactation in the bovine: Mammary gland histology and milk composition. *J. Dairy Sci.* 57:1334–40.

National Research Council. 1971–1976. *Nutrient Requirements of Domestic Animals*. No. 2, *Swine*, 1973; no. 3, *Dairy Cattle*, 1971; no. 4, *Beef Cattle*, 1976; no. 5, *Sheep*, 1975; no. 6, *Horses*, 1973. Nat. Acad. Sci., Washington.

Nelson, W.L., Kaye, A., Moore, M., Williams, H.H., and Herrington, B.L. 1951. Milking techniques and the composition of guinea pig milk. *J. Nutr.* 44:585–94.

Ohta, K., Watarai, T., Oishi, T., Ueshiba, Y., Hirose, S., Yoshizawa, T., Akikusa, Y., Sato, M., and Okano, H. 1953. Composition of Fin whale milk. *Proc. Imper. Acad. Jap.* 29:392–98.

Olson, W.G., Jorgensen, N.A., Bringe, A.N., Schultz, L.H., and DeLuca, H.F. 1973. 25-hydroxycholecalciferol (25-OHD_3). I. Treatment for parturient paresis. *J. Dairy Sci.*, 56:885–88.

Olson, W.G., Jorgensen, N.A., Schultz, L.H., and DeLuca, H.F. 1973. 25-hydroxycholecalciferol (25-OHD_3). II. Efficacy of parenteral administration in prevention of parturient paresis. *J. Dairy Sci.* 56:889–95.

Opstvedt, J., Baldwin, R.L., and Ronning, M. 1967. Effect of diet upon activities of several enzymes in abdominal adipose and mammary tissues in the lactating dairy cow. *J. Dairy Sci.* 50:108–9.

Osmond, A. 1954. The composition of mature human milk in Southern Tasmania. *Dairy Sci. Abstr.* 16:150.

Otagaki, K.K., Black, A.L., Bartley, J.C., Kleiber, M., and Eggum, B.O. 1963. Metabolism of uniformly labeled glucose-C^{14} introduced into the rumen of a lactating cow. I. Transfer of C^{14} to respired air, volatile fatty acids, and major milk constituents. *J. Dairy Sci.* 46:690–95.

Palmquist, D.L., Davis, C.L., Brown, R.E., and Sachan, D.S. 1969. Availability and metabolism of various substrates in ruminants. V. Entry rate into the body and incorporation into milk fat of D(-)β-hydroxybutyrate. *J. Dairy Sci.* 52:633–38.

Payne, L.C., and Marsh, C.L. 1962. Gamma globulin absorption in the baby pig: The nonselective absorption of heterologous globulins and factors influencing absorption time. *J. Nutr.* 76:151–58.

Perrin, D.R. 1958a. The chemical composition of the colostrum and milk of the ewe. *J. Dairy Res.* 25:70–74.

——. 1958b. The calorific value of milk of different species. *J. Dairy Res.* 25:215–20.

Pilson, M.E.Q., and Kelley, A.L. 1962. Composition of the milk from Zalophus Californianus, the California sea lion. *Science* 135:104–5.

Rammell, C.G., and Caughley, G. 1964. Composition of Thar's milk. *New Zealand J. Sci.* 7:667–70.

Reid, J.T. 1961. Problems of feed evaluation related to feeding of dairy cows. *J. Dairy Sci.* 44:2122–33.

Rook, J.A.F. 1961. Variations in the chemical composition of the milk of the cow. *Dairy Sci. Abstr.* 23:251–58, 303–8.

Rose, D., Brunner, J.R., Kalan, E.B., Larsen, B.L., Melnychyn, P., Swaisgood, H.E., and Waugh, D.F. 1970. Nomenclature of the proteins of cow's milk. 3d rev. *J. Dairy Sci.* 53:1–17.

St. Clair, L.E. 1942. The nerve supply to the bovine mammary gland. *Am. J. Vet. Res.* 3:10–16.

Schmidt, G.H. 1971. *Biology of Lactation*. Freeman, San Francisco.

Schmidt, G.H., Chatterton, R.T., Jr., and Hansel, W. 1964. Mammary gland growth and the initiation of lactation in dairy goats. *J. Dairy Sci.* 47:74–78.

Schmidt, G.H., and Trimberger, G.W. 1963. Effect of unequal milking intervals on lactation milk, milk fat, and total solids production of cows. *J. Dairy Sci.* 46:19–21.

Scott, T.W., Cook, I.J., Ferguson, K.A., McDonald, I.W., Buchanan, R.A., and Hills, G..L. 1970. Production of polyunsaturated milk fat in domestic ruminants. *Austral. J. Sci.* 32:291–93.

Shahani, K.M., Harper, W.J., Jensen, R.G., Parry, R.M., Jr., and Little, C.A. 1973. Enzymes in bovine milk: A review. *J. Dairy Sci.* 56:531–43.

Shannon, A.D., and Lascelles, A.K. 1968. Lymph flow and protein composition of thoracic duct lymph in the newborn calf. *Q. J. Exp. Physiol.* 53:415–21.

Shirley, J.E., Emery, R.S., Convey, E.M., and Oxender, W.D. 1973. Enzymic changes in bovine adipose and mammary tissue: Serum and mammary tissue hormonal changes with initiation of lactation. *J. Dairy Sci.* 56:569–74.

Shutt, F.T. 1932. Milk of the American buffalo. *Analyst* 57:454.

Siddiqui, R.H., and Bari, M.A. 1959. Examination of milk and fat of camel. *Chem. Abstr.* 53:18322C.

Simon, K.J. 1959. Preliminary studies on composition of milk of Indian elephants. *Indian Vet. J.* 36:500–503.

Smith, A., Wheelock, J.V., and Dodd, F.H. 1967. The effect of milking throughout pregnancy on milk secretion in the succeeding lactation. *J. Dairy Res.* 34:145–50.

Smith, V.R. 1959. *Physiology of Lactation*. 5th ed. Iowa State U. Press, Ames.

Sowls, L.K., Smith, V.R., Jenness, R., Sloan, R.E., and Regehr, E. 1961. Chemical composition and physical properties of the milk of the collared peccary. *J. Mammal.* 42:245–51.

Spector, W.S., ed. 1956. *Handbook of Biological Data*. Saunders, Philadelphia.

Steuer, H. 1957. Diseases of elephants. *Med. Weterynar.* 13:427–30 (*Chem. Abstr.* 52:3124b, 1958).

Storry, J.E., and Rook, J.A.F. 1964. Plasma triglycerides and milk-fat synthesis. *Biochem. J.* 91:27c–29c.

Stott, G.H. 1965. Parturient paresis related to dietary phosphorus. *J. Dairy Sci.* 48:1485–89.

Swanson, E.W. 1957. Fat heifers give less milk. *Hoard's Dairyman* 102:550–51.

Swett, W.W., and Matthews, C.A. 1949. Some studies of the circulatory system of the cow's udder. *U.S.D.A. Tech. Bull.* 982.

Swett, W.W., Miller, F.W., Graves, R.R., Black, W.H., and Creech, G.T. 1937. Comparative conformation, anatomy, and udder characteristics of cows of certain beef and dairy breeds. *J. Ag. Res.* 55:239–87.

Swett, W.W., Underwood, P.C., Matthews, C.A., and Graves, R.R.

1942. Arrangement of the tissues by which the cow's udder is suspended. *J. Ag. Res.* 65:19–43.
Tener, J.S. 1956. Gross composition of musk-ox milk. *Can. J. Zool.* 34:569–71.
Thompson, M.P. 1964. Phenotyping of caseins of cow's milk: Collaborative experiment. *J. Dairy Sci.* 47:1261–62.
Tobon, H., and Salazar, H. 1974. Ultrastructure of the human mammary gland. I. Development of the fetal gland throughout gestation. *J. Clin. Endocr. Metab.* 39:443–56.
Topper, Y. 1968. Multiple hormone interactions related to the growth and differentiation of mammary gland in vitro. *Trans. N.Y. Acad. Sci.* 30:869–74.
Treus, V., and Kravchenko, D. 1968. Methods of rearing and economic utilization of eland in the Askaniyanova Zoological Park. In M.A. Crawford, ed., *Comparative Nutrition of Wild Animals*. Academic Press, London.
Tucker, H.A. 1969. Factors affecting mammary gland cell numbers. *J. Dairy Sci.* 52:721–29.
Turner, C.W. 1952. *The Mammary Gland.* Lucas, Columbia, Mo.
——. 1959. The experimental induction of growth of the cow's udder and the initiation of milk secretion. *U. Mo. Ag. Exp. Sta. Res. Bull.* 697.
Ullrey, D.E., Struthers, R.D., Hendricks, D.G., and Brent, B.E. 1966. Composition of mare's milk. *J. Anim. Sci.* 25:217–22.
Van Soest, P.J. 1963. Ruminant fat metabolism with particular reference to factors affecting low milk fat and feed efficiency: A review. *J. Dairy Sci.* 46:204–16.
van Wagenen, G., Himwich, H.E., and Catchpole, H.R. 1941. Composition of the milk of the monkey (*M. mulatta*). *Proc. Soc. Exp. Biol. Med.* 48:133–34.
Varman, P.N., and Schultz, L.H. 1968. Blood lipid changes in cows of different breeds fed rations depressing milk fat test. *J. Dairy Sci.* 51:1597–1605.
Varo, M., and Varo, H. 1971. The milk production of reindeer cows and the share of milk in the growth of reindeer calves. *J. Sci. Ag. Soc. Finland* 43:1–10.
Venzke, C.E. 1940. A histological study of the teat and gland cistern of the bovine mammary gland. *J. Am. Vet. Med. Ass.* 96:170–75.
Verdiev, Z., and Veli-Zade, D. 1960. Physicochemical properties of milk of Azerbaijan Zebu cattle. *Dairy Sci. Abstr.* 22:471.
Volcani, R., Zisling, R., Sklan, D., and Nitzan, Z. 1973. The composition of chinchilla milk. *Brit. J. Nutr.* 29:121–25.
Vorherr, H. 1974. *The Breast: Morphology, Physiology, and Lactation.* Academic Press, New York.
Walker, E.P., Warnick, F., Lange, K.I., Uible, H.E., Hamlet, S.E., Davis, M.A., and Wright, P.F. 1964. *Mammals of the World.* Johns Hopkins Press, Baltimore. Vols. 1, 2, 3.
Weber, A.F., Kitchell, R.L., and Sautter, J.H. 1955. Mammary gland studies. I. The identity and characterization of the smallest lobule unit in the udder of the dairy cow. *Am. J. Vet. Res.* 16:255–63.
Wheelock, J.V., Rook, J.A.F., and Dodd, F.H. 1965a. The effect of milking throughout the whole of pregnancy on the composition of cow's milk. *J. Dairy Res.* 32:249–54.
——. 1965b. The effect of intravenous injections of oxytocin during milking and the removal of residual milk on the composition of cow's milk. *J. Dairy Res.* 32:255–62.
Wheelock, J.V., Smith, A., and Dodd, F.H. 1967. The effect of a temporary suspension of milking in mid-lactation on milk secretion after the resumption of milking and in the following lactation. *J. Dairy Res.* 34:151–61.
White, J.C.D. 1953. Composition of whales' milk. *Nature* 171:612–13.
Whittlestone, W.G. 1952. The distribution of fat-globule size in sow's milk. *J. Dairy Res.* 19:127–32.
Wickersham, E.W., and Schultz, L.H. 1964. Response of dairy heifers to diethylstilbestrol. *J. Anim. Sci.* 23:177–82.
Williams, H.H. 1961. Differences between cow's and human milk. *J. Am. Med. Ass.* 175:104–7.
Williams, W.F., Weisshaar, A.G., and Lauterbach, G.E. 1966. Lactogenic hormone effects on plasma nonesterified fatty acids and blood glucose concentration. *J. Dairy Sci.* 49:106–7.
Witzel, D.A., and McDonald, J.S. 1964. Bovine intramammary pressure changes during mechanical milking. *J. Dairy Sci.* 47:1378–81.
Young, E.G., and Grant, G.A. 1931. The composition of vixen milk. *J. Biol. Chem.* 93:805–10.

PART VIII RADIOBIOLOGY

CHAPTER 57

Radiation and Radionuclides (Radioisotopes) | by A. Robert Twardock

The value of radionuclides in physiological research stems primarily from the facts that (1) radionuclides or radionuclide-labeled compounds react chemically the same way as the stable nuclides or compounds they are used to trace, and (2) they can be measured with extreme sensitivity and accuracy and often with considerable ease by the radiation they emit. Radionuclides provide a most versatile means of introducing tracer quantities of physiological substances into biological systems, and later of identifying those atoms or molecules that were introduced.

Radionuclides can also be used, like X-ray machines, nuclear reactors, and particle accelerators, as sources of radiation for studying the effects of radiation upon biological systems, a field of study known as radiation biology. Certain interests of the physiologist and the radiation biologist are practically identical. By selectively depositing energy from ionizing radiation within the entire animal body, within organs, or even within cell organelles, the radiation biologist can study the function of organs and subcellular systems much as the classical physiologist uses surgery and microdissection for the same purpose.

The techniques, skills, and knowledge of animal experimentation are extremely important in radionuclide and radiation research, and animal physiologists are contributing significantly to these fields.

IONIZING RADIATION

Radiation is usually defined as the emission and propagation of energy in the form of waves or particles through space or matter. The key word in this definition is *energy*. *Ionizing* radiation is radiation having sufficient energy to cause ion pairs to be formed in the medium through which it passes. To define energy in units upon which an intuitive understanding can be based, a sequence of definitions is necessary. Energy is the capacity to do *work*, and it may exist as potential energy or kinetic energy. Kinetic energy is the energy of motion, such as occurs in ionizing radiation. Work, in turn, is *force* acting through distance. Force is required to accelerate mass through distance. Thus work can be defined in terms of its basic units: time, mass, and distance.

Radiation energy

Quantities of energy may be expressed in different units, such as the calorie (heat), coulomb (electrical), and erg (mechanical). For ionizing radiation the commonly used unit is the electron volt (ev), which is defined as the energy gained by a particle of unit charge (+ or −) in passing through a potential difference of one volt. One electron volt is equal in energy to 1.6×10^{-12} ergs. Ionizing radiations have energies measured in terms of thousands (Kev), millions (Mev), or billions (Bev) of electron volts, whereas ordinary chemical reactions involve energy exchanges between atoms of only 10–30 ev.

Types of ionizing radiation

The different kinds of ionizing radiation can be characterized according to their mass, their charge, and whether their basic properties allow them to be considered primarily as particles or waves. The nature of the wave forms (electromagnetic radiation) can be most perplexing to the nonphysicist because they can be considered simultaneously as having no mass and yet as possessing the properties of particles with mass. In this text they will be considered as having no mass. Although many kinds of ionizing radiation have been discovered, knowledge of the properties of α-particles, β-particles, γ-rays, and X rays is quite sufficient for most radiobiological applications.

A γ-ray is an electromagnetic wave (photon) having no mass, no charge, the velocity of light, and the atomic nucleus as its source. From different radionuclides, γ-rays with energies as low as 37 Kev and as high as 2.8 Mev are emitted. X rays are physically identical to γ-rays except that they originate from the extranuclear portions of the atom. By considering the relationship of X and γ-rays to the entire electromagnetic spectrum, one can gain a further understanding of their nature (Fig. 57.1). Radio waves and infrared, visible, and ultraviolet light differ from ionizing electromagnetic radiation only in having longer wavelengths and consequently lower energies. X rays generated by most diagnostic and therapeutic machines have lower energies than most γ-rays, although supervoltage machines that produce very high energy X rays do exist.

An α-particle is a high-speed particle having the same composition as a helium nucleus (2 protons and 2 neutrons), a mass of 4 a.m.u. (atomic mass units), a charge of +2, and an initial velocity as great as 1/16 that of light. These particles originate from the atomic nuclei of elements having atomic numbers greater than 83. A β-particle is a high-speed particle with properties identical to those of an electron, except that it originates from the nucleus rather than one of the electron shells of the atom. It has a mass of 1/1840 a.m.u., a charge of −1, and a variable velocity that can approach the speed of light. *Electrons,* when removed from their atomic orbits and accelerated to high velocities by magnetic and electrical fields, become ionizing particles and are used in medicine for therapeutic purposes, in electron microscopy, and in radiation physics.

The energy of particulate radiation is directly related to its mass and velocity. The energy of a photon is inversely related to its wavelength. Low-energy ionizing radiation having low penetrability, such as the 0.019 Mev β-particle of tritium, is referred to as soft or weak radiation; high-energy ionizing radiation, such as the 1.7 Mev β-particle of ^{32}P or the 2.8 Mev γ-ray of ^{24}Na, is referred to as hard, strong, or penetrating radiation. For reasons considered below, electromagnetic radiation of a given energy is much more penetrating than particulate radiation of the same energy.

SOURCES OF IONIZING RADIATION

The primary sources of ionizing radiation are (1) radioactive decay, (2) X-ray machines and accelerators, (3) nuclear fission, and (4) outer space. The first three sources are most important to radiobiologists and physiologists.

X-ray production

An X-ray tube consists of two electrodes enclosed by an evacuated tube and supplied with a voltage source (Fig. 57.2). The cathode serves as a source of electrons, which, when accelerated toward the anode by the voltage

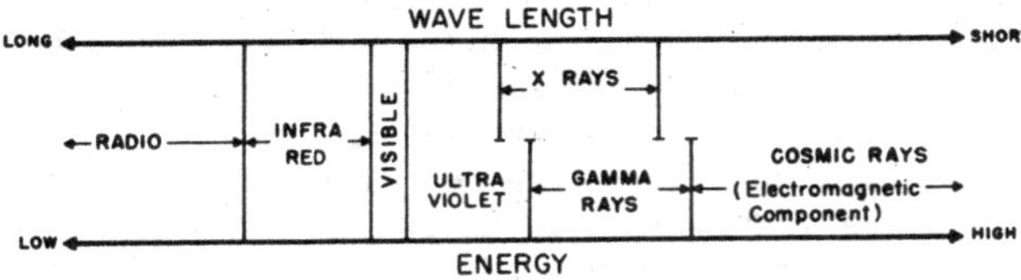

Figure 57.1. The electromagnetic radiation spectrum

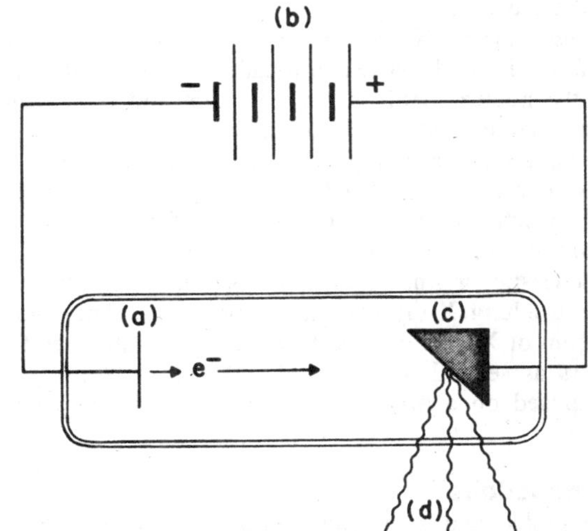

Figure 57.2. Schematic X-ray tube. Electrons released from cathode (a) are accelerated by high voltage potential (b) into target (c), and interact with atoms of target element to produce X rays (d).

potential difference, interact with atoms of the anode material to produce X rays. The anode is referred to as the target of the X-ray tube and is made of metal, usually tungsten. Before a flow of electrons from cathode to target can be established, some of the cathode electrons must be raised to an excited energy state. In modern X-ray tubes, this is done by heating the cathode, and gas molecules are evacuated from the tubes as completely as possible to reduce interference with the electron stream.

Electrons accelerated to high velocity by the tube potential strike the target and interact with atoms of the target material in two ways, causing the emission of two kinds of X rays. *Characteristic* X-rays are produced when a cathode electron interacts with an orbital electron of a target atom and ejects it from the target atom. The vacancy in the atom's electron shell cannot be tolerated and is filled by an electron from one of the outer shells. Thus a series of vacancies occurs from inner to outer shells, and electrons drop in stepwise fashion from outer to inner shells to fill them. Electrons in outer shells have greater potential energy than those in inner shells, and consequently they must release energy during their inward movement. The energy released appears in the form of characteristic X rays. The electron shells of the atom are labeled from K (the innermost) to L, M, and N, whichever is the outermost. X rays produced by electron transitions from the L shell to the K shell are termed K-series or K-line X rays, and transitions from M to L shells, N to M shells, and so on are labeled according to the innermost shell. Thus the target element emits K-, L-, and M-line X rays, each having a discrete energy characteristic of that element. X-ray wavelength increases with distance between nucleus and electron orbit, K-series X rays having the shortest wavelength and therefore the greatest energy.

A *continuous* X ray, otherwise known as *bremsstrahlung,* is produced when a cathode electron interacts with the nuclear field of a target atom and is deflected and decelerated, with a resultant loss of kinetic energy that appears as an X ray. The energy of the X ray depends upon the angle of deflection and degree of deceleration, which may vary continuously from zero to some maximum value. In contrast to the discrete energies of characteristic or line X rays, a continuous spectrum of bremsstrahlung X-ray energies is produced. The energy spectrum of X rays emitted from an X-ray tube therefore appears as several well-defined spikes (line X rays) superimposed on a broad base (continuous X rays) (Fig. 57.3).

Radionuclides

To understand radionuclides and radioactive decay, one must comprehend the basic aspects of atomic structure. Although the atomic nucleus consists of many par-

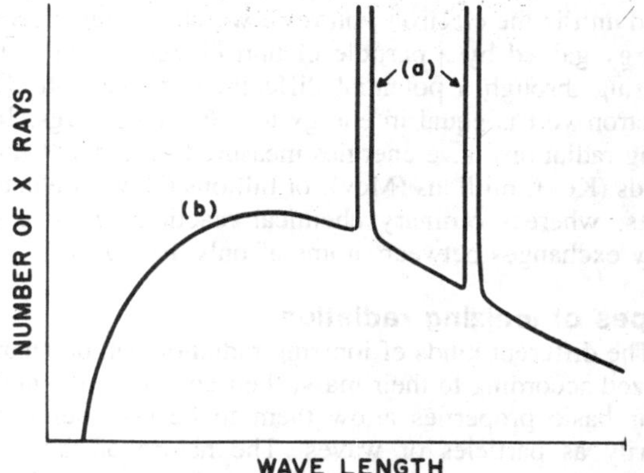

Figure 57.3. Typical X-ray spectrum showing characteristic X-ray peaks (a) superimposed upon continuous X-ray (bremsstrahlung) base (b).

ticles, a model of the atom consisting of only three fundamental particles is adequate for our consideration. The Bohr-Rutherford model of the atom consists of an extremely dense nucleus made up of protons and neutrons (collectively termed nucleons), around which electrons spin in elliptical orbits. The electron orbits or shells are located at fixed distances from the nucleus. There is a limit to the number of electrons that can be contained in each shell: 2 in the K shell, 8 in L, 18 in M, 32 in N, and 50 in the O shell. The electrons in the outermost shell, called valence electrons, determine the chemical reactivity of the atom and therefore the element to which the atom belongs. The neutron has no charge, the proton a unit positive charge, and the electron a unit negative charge; the normal atom is therefore neutral, having equal numbers of protons and electrons. Almost the entire mass of the atom is concentrated in the nucleus, which has a radius of about 10^{-12} cm; the radius of the entire atom, including its electron shells, is about 10^{-8} cm. Thus the atom has an effective volume (the volume enclosed by the outermost electron shell) that is 10^{12} times the real volume of the nucleus and orbital electrons, which shows that most of matter is in reality empty space. Because of this, ionizing radiations are capable of penetrating significant distances through matter before they lose all of their energy as a result of interactions with the widely separated nuclei and electrons.

An atom can be symbolized as ${}^{A}_{Z}X$, where X represents the element, Z the atomic number (the number of protons in the nucleus), and A the mass number, or number of nucleons (protons + neutrons) in the nucleus. Because the number of protons (Z) determines the element, Z and X are redundant and Z is usually omitted.

The mass number, A, can be changed by adding or subtracting neutrons without changing Z (Fig. 57.4). *Isotopes* may therefore be defined as nuclear configurations

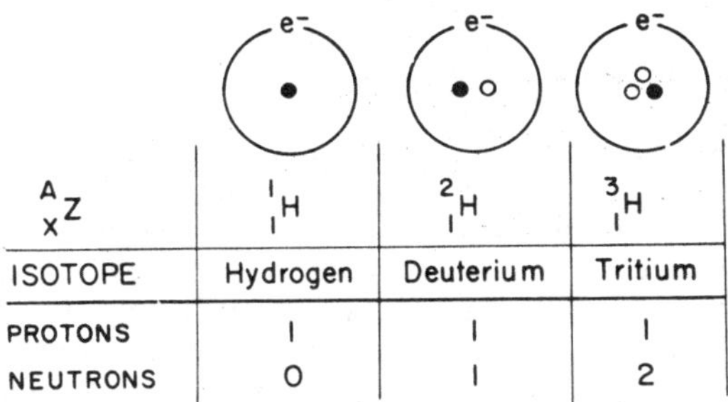

Figure 57.4. The isotopes of hydrogen. The black circles represent protons, the white circles neutrons.

having the same number of protons but different numbers of neutrons. Isotopes can be looked upon as members of a family, with the name of the element as the family name. Another term that requires explanation is *nuclide* or *radionuclide*. This term is often used synonymously with isotope, with or without the prefix *radio-* (which denotes the emission of radiation), even though such usage is technically incorrect. An *individual* nuclear configuration such as ^{16}O, ^{32}P, or ^{40}Ca is properly referred to as a nuclide or radionuclide, depending upon its stability. Isotope, on the other hand, is more properly used to refer to nuclear configurations of the same element, such as ^{128}I and ^{131}I, which are radioisotopes.

Radioactivity

The three isotopes of the element hydrogen—hydrogen, deuterium, and tritium—serve well as a basis for discussing radioactivity. Hydrogen and deuterium are stable, whereas tritium is not and emits β-particles during radioactive decay. The only difference between the three hydrogen isotopes is the number of neutrons in their nuclei, and therein lies the basis of nuclear instability and decay. Nuclear stability depends upon the neutron-proton (n/p) ratio of the nuclide, and radioactive decay is a process whereby an unstable n/p ratio is shifted toward a more stable configuration. Radioactivity, then, is the process by which unstable nuclides spontaneously disintegrate (decay), releasing energy partially in the form of ionizing radiations, and generally resulting in the formation of new nuclides. Certain principles of nuclear stability and radioactive decay become apparent when one considers a graph on which stable nuclides are plotted in terms of neutron number versus proton number (Fig. 57.5). The stable nuclides fall closely around a line that, for the light elements, represents an n/p ratio of 1:1, and which gradually rises above this ratio among the heavier elements until it reaches the heaviest stable nuclide, ^{209}Bi, with an n/p ratio of 1.5:1. Obviously nuclear stability is possible only within a narrow range of n/p ratios, and an increasing proportion of neutrons is required as nuclear mass increases.

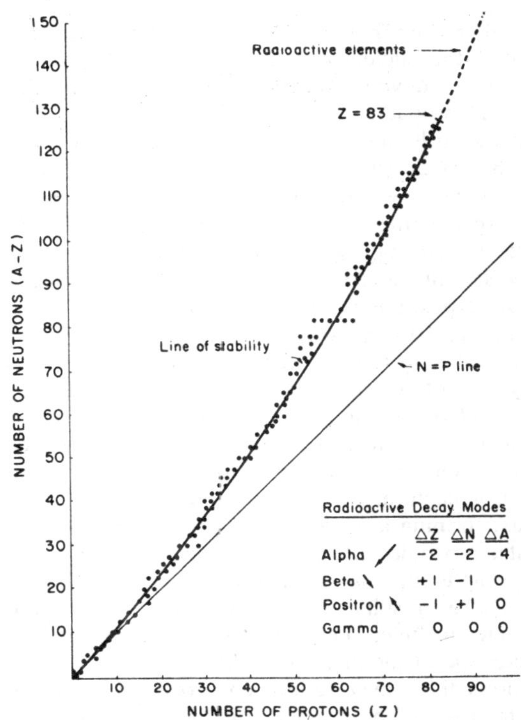

Figure 57.5. Neutron-proton plot of stable nuclides having relative isotopic abundances greater than 20 percent

There is no *stable* nuclide with an atomic number above 83. There are over 50 nuclides with atomic numbers greater than 83, but they are all radioactive. One may ask why radioactive elements heavier than ^{208}Pb and ^{209}Bi still exist. Since they are radioactive, why have they not decayed completely during the billions of years of the earth's existence? The answer is that they belong to one of four radioactive decay series at the heads of which are parent radionuclides whose half-lives approach or exceed the age of the earth. Beginning with the decay of the parent radionuclide, a series of new radionuclides called *decay products* or *daughters* are formed in stepwise fashion by successive decays. These decay series account for almost all of the earth's naturally occurring radioactivity, although there are five naturally occurring radionuclides with Z's under 83. Members of the natural decay series include such well-known radionuclides as radium, radon, plutonium, and uranium. All α-emitters are members of such decay series.

Radioactive decay modes

Radioactive decay represents the rearrangement of nucleons in an unstable atomic nucleus to a nuclear configuration having greater stability; the mode (type) of decay that it undergoes depends upon its relationship to the line of stability (see Fig. 57.5): *α-emission* causes a net change in the nucleus of −2 protons and −2 neutrons, resulting in a downward shift of the daughter toward the stable end product, ^{208}Pb or ^{209}Bi. *β-emission* may be considered to be the conversion of a neutron to a proton and a β-particle ($n \rightarrow p^+ + \beta^-$), which causes a net nuclear change of +1 proton and −1 neutron. β-emitters are above the line of nuclear stability and shift toward stability by β-decay. Radionuclides also exist below the line of stability and shift toward stability by means of *positron* (a positive electron) *emission* ($p^+ \rightarrow n + \beta^+$).

γ-emission occurs when an atomic nucleus reverts from a higher to a lower energy level. Such changes in energy state often accompany β- or α-decay. Emission of the particulate radiation leaves the product nucleus in an excited state, and it then emits a γ-ray. X rays are emitted by radionuclides that undergo a decay mode known as electron capture. An orbital electron is captured by the nucleus, forming a neutron ($e^- + p^+ \rightarrow n$) and raising the daughter n/p ratio. Electrons from the K shell are most readily captured; this is called K capture. Loss of a K shell electron results in a series of electron transitions from outer to inner shells and the production of X rays characteristic of the daughter radionuclide.

Radionuclides may follow only one decay mode or more than one. For example, while ^{32}P decays to ^{32}S with the emission of a single β-particle, ^{64}Cu decays to ^{64}Zn with a single β-emission or to ^{64}Ni by positron emission or electron capture. The radiations emitted by ^{64}Cu include β-particles, positrons, X rays, and γ-rays. Thus knowledge of the decay scheme of a radionuclide is important in considering methods for detecting it or its significance as a radiation hazard.

Curie

The unit quantity of radioactivity is the curie (Ci). Derived originally from the disintegration rate of one gram of radium, the curie was defined at the 1954 International Congress of Radiology as that amount of a radionuclide in which 3.7×10^{10} atoms disintegrate per second (dps). Subunits of the curie include the millicurie (mCi), which is one thousandth of a curie (3.7×10^7 dps), and the microcurie (μCi), one millionth of a curie (3.7×10^4 dps); the megacurie, a multiple of the curie, represents one million curies (3.7×10^{16} dps).

The curie measures only the number of atoms disintegrating per unit of time; it indicates nothing about the kind or energy of radiation emitted, or the effects the radiation might produce in living organisms. Only by specifying the radionuclide and the conditions of exposure can the biological effects of a given quantity of radioactivity be predicted. For example, 2 mCi of tritium, a weak β-emitter, requires no shielding other than the glass bottle in which it is contained, whereas the same amount of cobalt-60, a strong γ-emitter, must be shielded by lead bricks if work is to be done in close proximity to it.

Energy release

The "energy of the atom" is a phrase often used in describing the multitudinous benefits made possible by the discoveries of radioactive decay and nuclear fission. Energy in quantities and kinds previously unknown constitutes the foundation of the atomic age. The source of this energy is contained in the mass of the atom. In radioactive decay, nuclear fission, and nuclear fusion, mass is converted to energy.

In the decay of ^{235}U to ^{231}Th, energy is liberated in the form of the kinetic energy of α-particles, about 4.5 Mev being released per disintegration. The combined mass of the ^{231}Th daughter and the α-particle is less than the mass of the parent ^{235}U, the mass difference being converted to the energy required to release the α-particle from the nucleus and accelerate it to high velocity.

Similarly, fission of a ^{235}U nucleus results in two radionuclides (fission products), the combined mass of which is less than the mass of the ^{235}U atom. The mass loss during fission, however, is much greater than the mass loss during radioactive decay of the same nuclide. It is equivalent to an energy release in excess of 200 Mev, a magnitude that can be appreciated by comparing it with the 10–30 ev energy exchange involved in most chemical reactions. The fission reaction must be initiated by the addition of a neutron to a ^{235}U or ^{239}Pu nucleus and can be maintained because additional neutrons are released by each atom that fissions. Fission energy is released initially in the form of the kinetic energy of fission products, particulate radiation, and electromagnetic radiation, and is eventually degraded to heat. Nuclear reactors are used to take advantage of the original energy release as neutron sources for artificial radionuclide production and as power plants utilizing the large amounts of heat produced.

INTERACTIONS OF IONIZING RADIATION WITH MATTER

Any substance placed between a source of ionizing radiation and a detector will reduce the number of radiations registered by the detector, the degree of reduction depending upon the thickness of the intervening substance. Since radiation intensity is reduced as it passes through matter, and since radiation is energy, energy has been deposited in matter. This energy deposition occurs in two basic ways: (1) excitation, in which molecular bonds or orbital electrons of atoms are raised to higher energy levels, and (2) ionization, in which orbital electrons are completely ejected from atoms in the absorbing medium. The end result of ionization is the formation of an *ion pair,* the negative electron and the positively charged atom from which the electron is ejected. The amount of energy required to produce an ion pair varies with the absorbing medium, but in soft tissue and air an average of 35 ev is deposited for each ion pair formed. Thus an ionizing particle or photon with an initial energy of 1 Mev will form approximately 28,600 ion pairs (1×10^6 ev per 35 ev per ion pair) while depositing its energy in soft tissue or air.

The electrons ejected in the process of ion-pair formation are called *secondary electrons,* and they often have enough energy to cause ionizations themselves and produce additional secondary electrons in chainlike fashion. The numbers and energies of secondary electrons depend on the primary ionizing particle—its mass, charge, and velocity—and on the conditions of its impact with the initial electron.

Ion-pair formation by X rays or γ-rays occurs as a result of three kinds of interaction: (1) the photoelectric effect, (2) the Compton effect or Compton scatter, and (3) pair production (Fig. 57.6). In the photoelectric effect, a photon of relatively low energy ionizes an atom in the absorbing medium. The entire energy of the photon is used to eject and accelerate the electron. In the Compton effect, a medium-energy photon gives up only part of its energy in ionizing an atom in the absorbing medium, the photon continuing in a new direction (scatter) and at a low energy. In pair production, a high-energy photon passing close to the nucleus of an atom in the absorbing medium results in conversion of the photon energy to a positron (e^+)–electron (e^-) pair. The incident photon energy must exceed 1.02 Mev for this interaction to occur. Care must be taken to distinguish pair production from ion-pair production.

The secondary electrons produced by these interactions are responsible for practically all of the ionizations caused by X and γ-rays; hence the photons themselves are said to cause ionization only in a secondary fashion.

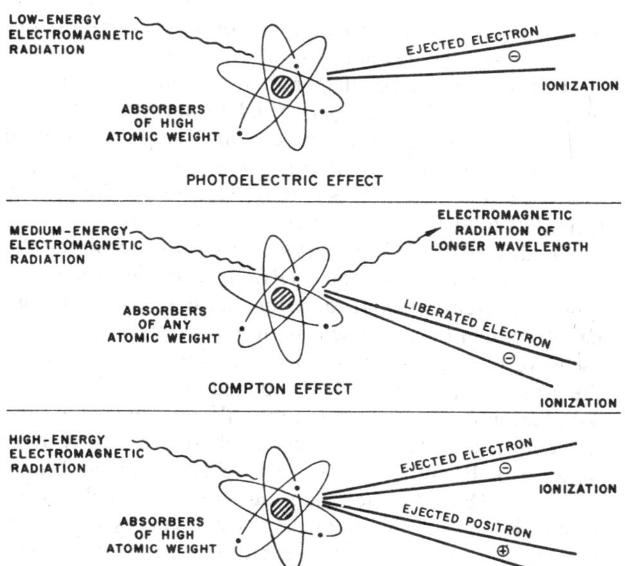

Figure 57.6. Interactions of X rays and γ-rays with matter. (From RCA Service Co., *Atomic Radiation,* Camden, N.J., 1962.)

Penetrability and linear energy transfer

Ionizing radiations vary considerably in their ability to penetrate matter, a property called *range.* Range can be measured in terms of distance traveled through a specified absorbing medium or in terms of density thickness in any medium. First, consider *distance traveled* as a measure of range. Table 57.1 illustrates differences in the penetrability of α-particles, β-particles, and photons. The particles or photons have the same initial energy (1 Mev) and will deposit that energy in matter, but (1) in the same absorbing medium, air for instance, different kinds of radiation deposit energy over greatly varying distances; (2) all kinds of radiation have much greater ranges in air than in lead; and (3) particulate radiations have finite ranges, whereas electromagnetic radiations have no maximum at which all photons are stopped.

Consider next the range difference in air for the three kinds of radiation. Because they all deposit 1 Mev of energy, the rate of energy deposition (ion-pair formation) per unit of distance traveled must be much higher for α- than for β-radiation, and is lowest for X or γ-radiation. This distance-rate of energy deposition is called the linear energy transfer (LET) of the ionizing particle, and is defined as the energy deposition per unit path length of the original particle or photon. The LET of a given kind of radiation is directly proportional to its mass and the square of its charge and inversely proportional to its velocity. The influence of mass and charge on ion-pair formation should be apparent; reduced velocity increases the time an ionizing particle spends in the vicinity of an orbital electron, and thus the time during which it can interact with it. An α-particle, which has a mass 7360 times that of a β-particle and twice the charge, therefore has a much greater LET than a β-particle.

Another expression for the energy deposition rate of

Table 57.1. Penetrability of different types of ionizing radiation having equal energies of 1 Mev

Type of radiation	Range: Air	Range: Lead	Range: Soft tissue
α	5 mm	a few microns	6 μ
β	3.7 m	0.3 mm	4.2 mm
X or γ	meters to infinity	HVL* of 9 mm	HVL of 10 cm

* Half-value layer

ionizing radiation is specific ionization, the number of ion pairs formed per unit path length. The specific ionization of a particle is the LET of the particle divided by the average energy required to form an ion pair (W); that is, specific ionization = LET/W.

In air, the range of all three types of radiation is much greater than in lead, a fact explained by the density difference between the two media. Because the mass density and electron density of matter are directly related, the rate at which ionizing radiations encounter electrons and lose energy is directly related to the density of the absorbing medium, while their ranges are in inverse relation to it. An ionizing particle must thus travel much farther through air in order to interact with a given number of electrons than it does through lead. In each medium, however, it travels through masses that are approximately equal, since the path is so much longer through air than through lead. A unit of range common to all media, therefore, is a unit based on mass and known as *areal density* or *density thickness*. Expressed in units of g/sq cm or mg/sq cm, density thickness is the actual thickness through which the particle travels multiplied by the density of the medium. One-Mev β-particles have a maximum range of about 400 mg/sq cm in any medium.

Range is an appropriate measure of penetrability for particulate radiation because there is a maximum range (R_{max}) beyond which no particles will penetrate. X rays and γ-rays, however, have no R_{max}; there is no specific thickness of material that will stop all of the photons incident upon it. A graph of the percentage of photons passing through an absorber (% transmission) versus absorber thickness reveals that photon absorption can be described, like radioactive decay, in exponential terms (see Fig. 57.14). The properties of exponential behavior will be discussed later; at this point it is necessary to know only that an exponential function is one that continues to infinity. Regardless of the thickness of shielding used, therefore, it is possible that one or more photons will penetrate the entire thickness. Because no absorber thickness stops all photons, photon penetrability must be measured in terms of the half-value layer (HVL), which is the thickness of a particular material that will reduce the intensity of an X-ray or γ-ray beam to one half its original value.

Radiation dose

Radiation dosimetry is the measurement of energy deposition by ionizing radiation in matter. The most commonly used unit of radiation dose is the roentgen (R), which represents a certain number of ion pairs produced by electromagnetic radiation within one ml of air under standard conditions of temperature and pressure. The roentgen was the first and still is the most widely used unit of radiation dose, because the most convenient and most accurate methods of radiation dosimetry are based on the detection of ionization in gases. However, use of the roentgen is limited since it is applicable only to electromagnetic radiation (X and γ) and cannot be measured in absorbing media other than air. For this reason, additional units have been developed. Of these, the radiation absorbed dose (rad) is the most recent and the most versatile. One rad represents an energy deposition of 100 ergs per gram in any absorbing medium by any type of ionizing radiation. In radiation dosimetry the usual procedure is to measure the exposure dose in roentgens with a detector located at the same position relative to the radiation source as the object to be irradiated. Absorbed dose is then calculated according to the composition of the exposed object by the use of experimentally determined factors to convert roentgens to rads. For example, an exposure to ^{60}Co γ-rays of 1 R represents approximate energy depositions of 87 ergs per gram in air, 98 ergs per gram in soft tissue, and 87 ergs per gram in bone. The R is used to measure exposure to ionizing radiation and the rad is used to measure the absorbed dose that results from that exposure.

Because a total radiation exposure is seldom delivered instantaneously, radiation exposure or absorbed dose must be described in terms of exposure rate or dose rate and total exposure time. The units can be any unit of exposure or dose and any unit of time: mR/hr, R/yr, megarads/min, and so on.

Two other units that have been used to express radiation dose are the roentgen equivalent physical (rep) and the roentgen equivalent mammal (rem). The rep was designed before the development of the rad to measure radiation dose from particulate radiations and for materials other than air. The rem was used to account for variations in the magnitude of a given biological effect caused by equal exposures to different types of radiation. Neither the rep nor the rem is extensively used at the present time, but both are encountered in the literature.

Another term that has served a useful purpose is relative biological effectiveness (RBE). The efficiency with which different types of radiation cause a certain biological effect can be expressed in an approximate fashion by the RBE of each radiation for that effect. As an example, the rate of cataract formation induced by a certain dose of γ-radiation can be duplicated by only one tenth that dose of neutron exposure; neutrons are therefore said to have an RBE of 10 and γ-rays an RBE of 1 for cataract formation. The RBE of an ionizing radiation is related directly to its LET and to the manner in which energy deposition is concentrated in the exposed biological material. These relationships are highly dependent upon experimental conditions, however. Relative biological effectiveness is therefore most useful as a descriptive term; its application in a quantitative fashion can be misleading (Hine and Brownell 1956, ICRU 1962).

Physical radiation protection

Radiation protection can be accomplished by (1) increased source-to-subject distance, (2) decreased exposure time, and (3) shielding between source and subject. Because of its short range even in air, α-radiation is hazardous only when the α-emitting radionuclide enters the body. Laboratory glassware or clear plastic shields provide adequate protection from the usual quantities of β-emitters used in tracer laboratories. X-ray and γ-ray shielding is thus the primary problem.

Distance reduces the intensity of electromagnetic radiation from a small (point) source according to the equation

$$\frac{I_1}{I_2} = \frac{(d_2)^2}{(d_1)^2}$$

where I_1 is the radiation intensity at distance d_1 from the source and I_2 is the radiation intensity at distance d_2. The intensity varies inversely with the square of the distance from the source, a relationship known as the inverse square law.

Total radiation exposure depends upon the exposure rate at the site of exposure and the total time of exposure. In a radiation field with an exposure rate of 600 R/hr, a total exposure of 50 R would be received by limiting the exposure time to 5 minutes. If the calculated dose for a certain manipulation is excessive and one can neither increase the distance nor decrease the exposure time, shielding must be used. A useful equation for calculating γ-ray shielding requirements is

$$N = 3.32 \log X$$

where N is the number of half-value layers (HVL) required to reduce the radiation intensity by a factor of X. In practice, one calculates or measures the radiation intensity at the source-to-subject distance. Then one decides what factor X should be on the basis of experience with time requirements for the manipulation to be carried out and radiation protection guides for laboratory workers. Having determined N, one can obtain the HVL thickness for the photon energy and shielding material being used from standard references. The total thickness required can also be found in tables of percent transmission for certain γ-emitters and specific shielding materials (International Atomic Energy Agency 1973b, Kinsman 1970).

Radiation protection guides

National and international committees have been active in evaluating and establishing radiation protection standards. These standards have been revised downward through the years as more sensitive experimental techniques have demonstrated biological effects at lower exposures and as increasing numbers of people are being exposed. The organizations involved include the International Commission on Radiological Protection (ICRP), the National Committee on Radiation Protection and Measurements (NCRP), the Federal Radiation Council (FRC, advisory to the U.S. Government), and most recently the Nuclear Regulatory Commission (NRC).

The FRC issued a series of reports describing its philosophy of radiation protection and providing radiation protection guide (RPG) values for external radiation exposures and daily consumptions of certain fallout radionuclides (FRC, 1960, 1961). Presently recommended RPG values include (1) for radiation workers, whole-body exposure for lifetime of $5(N-18)$ rem in excess of background and required medical exposure, where N is age in years; (2) for individuals in the general population, 0.5 rem per year; and (3) for large groups in the general population, 0.17 rem per year in excess of background and medical exposure. Values are also given for exposures to specific organs and parts of the body.

The numerical values assigned as RPG's assume added significance when their influence on the development and application of nuclear technology is considered. The risks that follow from a certain increase in radiation exposure must be constantly balanced against the benefits gained by society. In making such judgments, such groups as the NRC are heavily dependent on radiobiological research, especially in the area of long-term, low-level exposure effects. But experiments approximating the very low exposure rates and large populations of interest are very costly and difficult to design. Although new scientific information will be available in the future, human judgment must play a major role in determining the exact values at which radiation protection guides are set. The first report of the FRC states: "The radiation dose to the population which is appropriate to the benefits derived will vary widely depending upon the importance of the reason for exposing the population to a radiation dose. . . . The guides recommended herein are appropriate for normal peacetime operations" (pp. 37–38).

BIOLOGICAL EFFECTS OF IONIZING RADIATION

The processes by which ionizing radiation deposits energy in living tissue are the same as in inert matter, and the result is the same: excitation and ionization of atoms and molecules. In living tissue, however, the disrupted molecules may be essential to the metabolism of the organism, and their loss may result in observable biological effects. The amount of energy deposited in tissue by a lethal dose of radiation is extremely small. A dose of 500,000 R is required to raise the temperature of irradiated tissue 0.25°C, whereas short-term exposure of only 1000 R is lethal to most mammals within 30 days of exposure. Approximately one molecule is ionized by a lethal dose for each 100 million molecules in a cell. Why should biological effects result from so little energy absorption? The answer is related at least partially to the highly localized nature of energy deposition and the abrupt, violent manner in which it occurs. Although the total chemical change in a cell may be small, biologically important molecules and cell organelles near the track of the ionizing particle are disrupted as a result of its passage. Ion-pair formation along the path of the radiation results in high concentrations of charged particles, something that occurs under no other circumstances in living tissue. Electrically polarized molecules react violently to this instantaneous charge deposition, with resultant bond breakage and the disruption of normal molecular arrangements. In addition, ion pairs react among themselves and other molecules, especially hydrogen, oxygen, and water, to form free radicals, which are highly reactive, uncharged atoms or molecules having electronic configurations differing from the usual molecular or ionic species. For example, the usual molecular and ionic forms of hydrogen are H_2 and H^+; the free radical is the hydrogen atom, H. Other products of the radiolysis of water include H_2O_2 and the free radicals OH and HO_2. Free radicals may diffuse as far as 5 nm around the path of the ionizing particle, disrupting normal chemical substances in the cell.

Direct and indirect action

Radiation effects have been studied at all levels of chemical and biological organization. At the molecular level two mechanisms by which effects are produced have been demonstrated: the direct and indirect action theories. The direct action theory, also known as the target or hit theory, states that radiation acts directly upon essential molecules and organelles. The indirect action theory takes into consideration the fact that approximately 75 percent of the cell is water and that most of the energy deposition occurs in water. As previously described, water molecules are ionized and free radicals are formed which react in destructive fashion with cellular enzymes, nucleoproteins, and other essential molecules. Although the direct and indirect action theories were once considered opposing viewpoints, it is now known that both mechanisms are important in the production of biological effects. The phase of radiation damage that ends with the interactions of free radicals is called the physicochemical stage, which lasts approximately 10^{-5} seconds and terminates in the production of biochemical lesions. If unrepaired, biochemical lesions may be magnified by the metabolism of the organism to functional or morphological lesions during a span of minutes, days, or years known as the biological stage of radiation damage. As the complexity of the irradiated system increases, the mechanisms by which radiation effects are produced are more poorly understood. The symptoms, lesions, and sequential development of radiation damage in mammals are well defined. It is very difficult, however, to define the chain of events occurring between energy deposition and appearance of a lesion or death because of the interactions between organs, organ systems, and repair processes of the body.

Injury at the biochemical level

Immediately after a mouse is given a 1000 R short-term whole body X- or γ-ray exposure there is no gross or microscopic evidence of exposure, even though the mouse will probably die within 4 days. There is a latent period that must pass before effects can be observed. A certain amount of damage may be repairable by the organism; the response may not appear unless the size of the dose is increased until it causes damage that cannot be hidden by recovery. Radiation effects exhibiting this kind of dose-response relationship are known as *threshold effects;* they have a threshold dose below which no effect can be discerned (Fig. 57.7). An example would be the dose required to cause death in mice within 30 days. Below a threshold of 200–300 R short-term exposure, no mice die in less than 30 days; their life span, however, may be significantly shortened. Threshold effects may therefore be artificially defined by imposing time and dose limits, but the existence of true threshold effects from very small exposures during the lifetime of an individual is open to question. Whether or not certain radiation effects are threshold or nonthreshold effects assumes real significance when questions regarding low-level exposure of human populations to background and medical radiation, reactors, and nuclear weapons are explored.

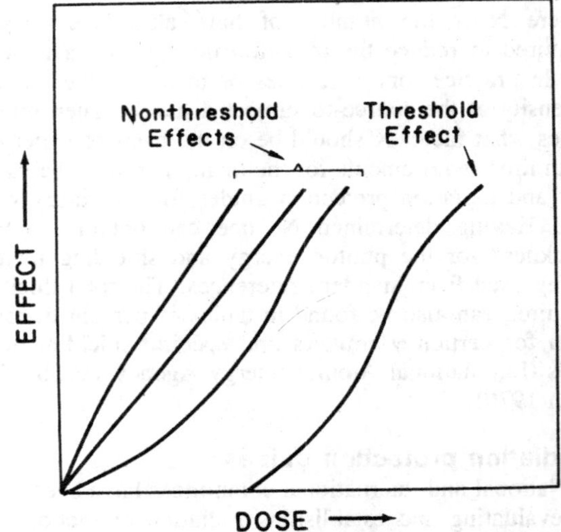

Figure 57.7. Radiation dose-effect relationships illustrating threshold and nonthreshold effects. The shapes of dose-effect curves may vary considerably as shown for nonthreshold effects.

Effects on specific molecules and pathways

The primary biochemical effects produced by radiation in vivo must be studied within seconds or minutes after exposure, before they are masked by the response of the organism. Many compounds, including members of all of the major biochemical groups, have been examined for altered concentrations and tissue distributions. Because such a small proportion of all molecules in a given volume of tissue is affected, interest has centered on large molecules present in small quantities that play key roles in cell function and metabolism, particularly enzymes, coenzymes, and nucleoproteins. For example, both DNA synthesis and to a lesser extent RNA synthesis are reduced within hours after irradiation in vivo. DNA molecules are highly sensitive to radiation damage and their disruption is considered the primary cause of mammalian cell death. Alterations in base sequences disrupt normal coding for messenger RNA, and consequently disrupt cell enzyme synthesis and function.

There is no interference with nucleotide synthesis, but phosphorylation of nucleotides and the activity of the polymerase enzyme may be inhibited. Oxidative phosphorylation is impaired in rats and mice as soon as 30 minutes after 25–100 R whole-body exposure. Induced protein synthesis (antibody formation) is inhibited. The general metabolism of the organism, however, is little affected shortly after exposure to the minimum 100 percent lethal dose. Protein, lipid, and carbohydrate metabolism are not seriously disturbed. Sulfhydryl enzymes have received special attention because compounds bearing free SH groups are particularly effective inactivators of free radicals in systems in vitro. No reduction in sulfhydryl enzymes has been observed after in vivo exposure, however. Changes in membrane permeability, evidenced by increased weights of extremities after radiation exposure and altered ionic fluxes from isolated organs, indicate effects on membrane structure and ion transport mechanisms (Dalrymple and Baker 1973, Prasad 1974, Spinks and Woods 1964).

Chemical radiation protection

The indirect effects of ionizing radiation can be influenced by changing the availability of water and oxygen for free radical formation or by introducing chemicals that interfere with free radical reactions. In lower organisms, radiation damage can be decreased by desiccation, freezing, and irradiation under reduced oxygen tension. The effect of such treatments cannot be attributed entirely to reduced free radical formation because they are also known to cause reduced cellular metabolic rates. The efficacies of chemical radioprotectants have been investigated in chemical systems, lower organisms, and mammals, with apparent discrepancies existing between mechanisms of action in vitro and in vivo. According to the radical scavenger theory, chemicals such as thiourea, cysteamine, and AET (aminoethylisothiuronium bromide hydrobromide) have a high affinity for and an ability to inactivate free radicals before they destroy target molecules in the cell. Radical scavenging *is* an important mechanism of radioprotection in vitro and may be in certain instances in vivo, but it does not explain in vivo protection entirely. The mixed disulfide theory suggests that compounds of the cysteine-cysteamine group exist in tissues in the form of mixed disulfides with -S-S- and -SH groups of tissue constituents, protecting such active enzyme groups from oxidation by free radicals. Similar protective action may be exerted by the substrate of an enzyme or its coenzyme. Production of hypoxia with consequent reduced free radical formation is also an action of certain radioprotectants. Thiol compounds and amines (epinephrine, serotonin) act to reduce tissue oxygen. Whatever the mechanism, chemical radioprotectants are capable of increasing the radioresistance of laboratory animals as much as twofold. Their use in human beings is not yet considered practical because they are toxic in the concentrations required for significant protection. They must be present in tissue in adequate concentrations at the time of radiation exposure, and their effect is short lived (Bacq 1965, Kollmann 1973, Prasad 1974).

Injury at the cellular level

The first step in the biological stage of radiation damage takes place in the cell, where physicochemical effects are translated from biochemical lesions to biological lesions. Differences in the radiosensitivities of tissues are related to cellular activity, as are recovery and repair mechanisms. The fact that much of our knowledge about radiation damage in cells is derived from experiments on single-cell systems and tissue cultures of mammalian cells raises the question of the validity of results extrapolated from lower organisms and in vitro systems to mammals. However, homogeneous cell cultures offer the only means of studying the relative radiosensitivities of cell structures and the direct effects of radiation on cells uninfluenced by surrounding tissues and the homeostatic mechanisms of the body (Bond et al. 1965, McAfee 1975).

Cellular radiosensitivity

In 1906 Bergonie and Tribondeau, from studies of radiation effects on the germinative tissues of the male rat, postulated: "The sensitivity of cells to irradiation is in direct proportion to their productive activity and inversely proportional to their degree of differentiation," a statement that soon became known as the Law of Bergonie and Tribondeau. Like most biological "laws" it has exceptions; certain fully differentiated, nondividing cells such as mature lymphocytes are extremely radiosensitive. But as a rule cells *are* more radiosensitive during active periods of growth and division. As stated previously, biological lesions develop from physicochemical damage as a result of metabolism. Evidence for this fact can be found in irradiated hibernating mammals. Irradiation during hibernation delays the appearance of radiation damage and results in a longer mean survival time after irradiation in comparison with nonhibernating controls.

Radiosensitivity during the cell cycle

Mammalian cells grown in tissue culture vary in their radiosensitivity according to stage of cell cycle, being most sensitive during mitosis and least sensitive during interphase. Acute exposures of 50 to a few hundred R cause some cells in the culture to delay division (mitotic delay), resulting in a lowered mitotic index (the fraction of cells dividing at any given time). At this exposure level the delayed cells eventually divide at the same time as cells not delayed, causing an increased mitotic index called a compensatory wave of mitosis (Fig. 57.8). As the exposure is increased, the mitotic index is further reduced and the compensatory wave is delayed and increased in magnitude.

As radiation exposure is increased to around 1000 R, the compensatory wave disappears and increasing numbers of dead and degenerating cells are observed. This phenomenon, called mitosis-linked degeneration, has been attributed to nuclear damage insufficient to prevent division but great enough to cause cell death when division is attempted. Exposures of several hundred to several thousand R cause mitotic arrest (sterilization, reproductive failure) in increasing numbers of cells. Cells no longer attempt to divide, and because metabolic processes remain active, giant cell formation is common. To

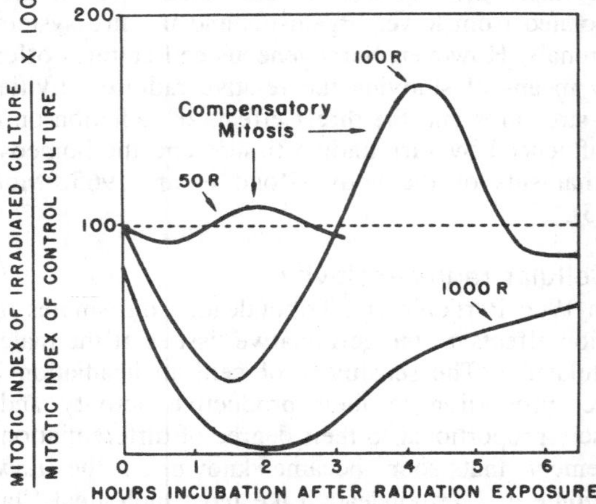

Figure 57.8. Effect of ionizing radiation on mitosis in cells grown in tissue culture. The mitotic index of irradiated cultures is expressed as a percentage of the mitotic index of control cultures and graphed as a function of time after radiation exposure.

kill mammalian tissue culture cells outright during the exposure period, a minimum of 10,000 R and as much as 100,000–200,000 R is required.

Knowledge of mitotic delay, arrest, and cell degeneration as related to radiation dose and timing can be usefully applied to radiotherapy of neoplasms. Biopsy specimens obtained at selected intervals after exposure can provide guidance for the timing and number of doses needed for optimum effect. Nevertheless, most radiotherapy schedules are determined by empirical evidence gained through years of experience and by hospital routines.

Results from irradiation experiments on cell cultures obviously cannot be extrapolated to tissues in situ. Cultured cells are atypical in several ways; for one thing, they multiply much more rapidly than their counterparts in the whole organism. Even the media in which they are grown are frequently quite different from body fluids. Intercellular factors influencing growth and division rates are absent, and so are hormonal and neural control mechanisms of the body. However, the radiation dose levels that affect cell cultures are quite similar to those that affect cells in situ, and the basic mechanisms and patterns of injury are undoubtedly the same in many respects (Arena 1971, Casarett 1968, McAfee 1975).

Cellular pathology of radiation damage

The cellular pathology of radiation damage is not unique. The most common lesions are swelling and increased volume of the cell and its organelles (probably associated with disrupted membrane function), vacuolation and fragmentation of nuclei and nucleoli, pyknotic nuclei, and chromosome abnormalities such as breakage, bridging, adherence, and swelling. Chromosome aberrations provide visible evidence of a key radiation effect: DNA damage resulting in somatic cell sterilization and death and in abnormal germ cells and genetic effects on future generations. Radiation damage to chromosomes, cells, and tissues in general produces lesions that can be caused by many other harmful agents and diseases. In other words, there is no lesion at any level, biochemical, functional, or morphological, that is pathognomonic of radiation injury. Damage from ionizing radiation acts as a stress, and the body reacts accordingly.

Radiosensitivity of cell organelles

Much research has been centered on the comparative radiosensitivities of the nucleus and the cytoplasm. Ingenious methods for selectively irradiating either the nucleus or the cytoplasm have been devised. These and other types of experiments have shown that the nucleus is much more sensitive than cytoplasm to ionizing radiation, an expected result in view of the high susceptibility of DNA. Furthermore, there are large numbers of cytoplasmic organelles in a cell that provide reserve capacity when a few are damaged, whereas nuclear structures are infrequently replicated.

Mammalian response

The mammalian physiologist will readily recognize that the response of the whole organism to ionizing radiation cannot be explained entirely on the basis of known mechanisms at the physicochemical, biochemical, and cellular levels. Interactions between organ systems via the endocrine and nervous systems and the capacity of the body for repair result in patterns of injury and response much more complex than those observed at lower organizational levels. A few of the many variables known to influence mammalian response are:

1. Conditions of radiation exposure. For human beings, the high-energy X-ray or γ-ray exposure required to produce 50 percent lethality in 30 days (LD 50/30) is estimated to be about 450 R if the exposure is short term; that is, if given within a period of a few hours. However, if the same exposure were given at a rate extended over the lifetime of the individual, it would be difficult to demonstrate any effect. Exposure-rate effects are dependent on the repair and recovery capacities of the organism. Radiation exposures delivered over short-time intervals (seconds to hours) are termed short-term, acute, or brief, in contrast to protracted exposures (days to years).

The total exposure may be delivered in several small exposures at specific intervals rather than all at once (exposure fractionation).

In addition, the biological effect will be influenced by the penetrability and specific ionization of the radiation used.

2. Extent of body irradiated. The degree of response is approximately proportional to the fraction of the body irradiated. An exposure that would be lethal if given to the whole body is easily tolerated when delivered to just the foot or hand.
3. Specific part of body irradiated. Certain organs or portions of the body such as the spleen and stomach are more radiosensitive than others.
4. Species and strain. The LD 50/30 ranges from about 250 R for the dog to 900 R for the chicken. Different strains of mice and rats are known to vary significantly in radiosensitivity.
5. Age. The very young and very old tend to be more susceptible than others.
6. Sex. Female mice are more resistant than males.
7. Diet. Diets supplemented with essential fatty acids have been shown to reduce the life-span shortening effect of radiation exposure in mice.
8. Stress. The animal's capacity for recovery and repair will be reduced by any stress imposed in addition to that of irradiation.
9. Hibernation. As we have seen, hibernation temporarily reduces the biological effects of radiation exposure.

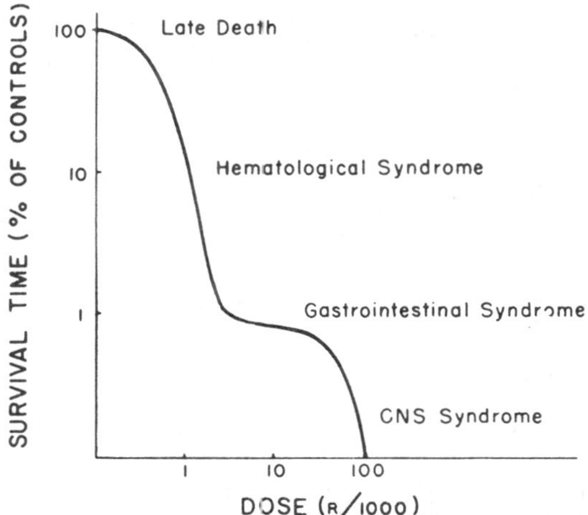

Figure 57.9. Dose-response curve for mammalian death after short-term, whole-body X-ray or γ-ray exposure

The relationship between total radiation exposure (brief whole-body exposure to X- or γ-rays) and survival time of mammals (expressed as a percentage of the lifetime of nonirradiated controls) is illustrated in Figure 57.9. Although mammalian response varies considerably, Figure 57.9 and the following discussion are intended to provide a general description without regard to species peculiarities.

CNS death

Very large exposures cause death within minutes or hours after exposure, primarily as a result of CNS disturbances (Haley and Snider 1962).

Radiation sickness

The gastrointestinal and hematological syndromes, which occur between 2 days and 1–2 months after exposures of a few hundred to several thousand R, comprise what is known as radiation sickness or the radiation syndrome. The primary cause of death is injury to the progenitive tissues of the body, the blast or stem cells that are precursors to those fully differentiated cells that are relatively short lived and must be constantly replaced. Stem cells as a rule are more radiosensitive than their mature successors. Therefore, lesions develop when adult cells live their normal span, die, and are not replaced. Mature cells of the intestinal epithelium and blood in particular have lives measured in days, and the predominant lesions of radiation sickness are observed in these tissues.

Gastrointestinal syndrome

Death at 2–7 days after about 1000–10,000 R exposure is largely a result of damage to the gastrointestinal tract. The life span of mature intestinal epithelial cells is about

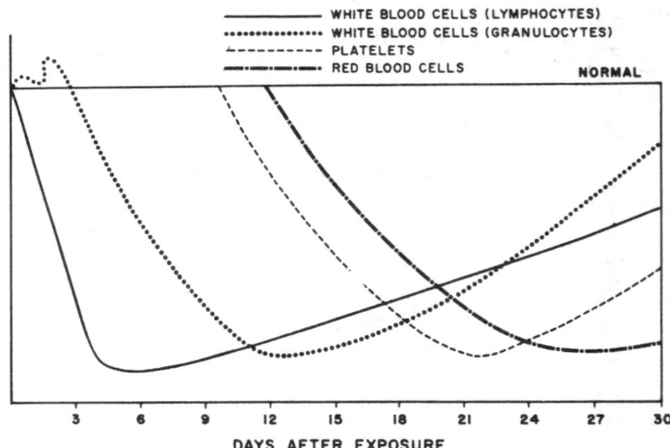

Figure 57.10. Effect of short-term, whole-body γ-ray exposure on the cellular elements of blood. (From RCA Service Co., *Atomic Radiation*, Camden, N.J., 1962.)

2 days. Their degeneration and lack of replacement result in intestinal denudation accompanied by numerous sequelae, including weight loss, diarrhea, dehydration, toxemia, and reduced resistance to bacterial invasion.

Hematological syndrome

Death between 1 and 4 weeks after exposures of about 1000 R or less is associated mainly with destruction of hemopoietic tissue. The numbers of circulating cellular elements of the blood decrease in patterns related to adult cell life spans (Fig. 57.10). With the exception of mature lymphocytes, there is no evidence that adult blood cells are affected by exposures as high as 1000 R. Lesions of the hematological syndrome include hemorrhage, edema, leukopenia, and anemia.

The hematological and gastrointestinal syndromes should not be viewed as separate and distinct entities. Rather, each is present to a greater or lesser degree in radiation sickness, and depending upon the amount of radiation exposure, one may contribute more to the death of a mammal than the other. Both syndromes reduce the individual's resistance to disease through loss of the intestinal barrier and reduced immunogenic and phagocytic responses. Since these syndromes are accompanied by a general debility associated with electrolyte loss, malnutrition, toxemia, and anemia, it is easy to understand that death is usually caused by secondary complications and that "pure" radiation death is seldom observed.

Late death

Radiation sickness will not always cause death if the exposure is low and the individual's defense mechanisms are strong. Survivors may exhibit delayed effects long after irradiation, which, in a large population of irradiated subjects, results in a significantly reduced average life span in comparison with controls. Delayed effects may also be caused by protracted low-level exposures and are characterized by long and variable latent periods. Delayed effects include:

1. Premature aging and life-span shortening. Although it is not known that physiological aging and the accelerated senescence caused by irradiation are identical, there is undoubtedly much to be gained from comparative studies of these processes. Premature aging may lead to a shortened life span because of the appearance of lesions and the development of diseases found more often in older organisms (Brown 1966, Harris 1963, Jones 1968, Kinsell 1961, Lindop and Sacher 1966).
2. Neoplasia. Leukemia, osteogenic sarcoma, and pulmonary and skin carcinoma are among the more commonly observed radiation-induced cancers (Harris 1963, United Nations 1964).
3. Cataract formation. The latent period for cataract development varies from months to years. This is a function, in part, of the long life span of the lens cells of the eye.
4. Genetic effects are truly delayed, affecting not only the irradiated population but succeeding generations. Artificial induction of mutations was first demonstrated by Müller (1927), who showed that X rays can cause an increased incidence of lethal mutants in *Drosophila*. Because mutations are usually deleterious and are not completely repairable, they have perhaps caused the greatest concern among those who deal with problems associated with increases in radiation in the environment. Because they are replicated and perpetuated, mutations are often referred to as the genetic burden of society. When applications of atomic energy are likely to contribute to the genetic burden, the benefits to be expected must be carefully weighed against the risks associated with their use. Limitations in our knowledge of the extent to which various natural causes contribute to the genetic burden, and even the present magnitude of the burden, make accurate predictions of the risk associated with a given increase in the radiation environment almost impossible. It is known, however, that current and past uses of atomic energy, including nuclear weapons testing, have increased the ionizing radiation environment by only a small fraction of the natural background radiation (Arena 1971, McAfee 1975, Russell 1968, United Nations 1964).

RADIONUCLIDES IN PHYSIOLOGICAL RESEARCH

There are two basic reasons why radionuclides are such valuable investigatory tools in physiological research. First, their chemical and physiological behavior before they decay is generally identical to that of the stable nuclides or labeled molecules that they are used to trace. Obviously, such a relationship must exist for radionuclide procedures to be valid. Second, radionuclides can be measured with great accuracy, sensitivity, and ease in comparison with most conventional analytical techniques. As little as 10^{-11} to 10^{-14} grams of many elements can be detected. Furthermore, radionuclides provide the most versatile means of studying, under experimental conditions that are entirely physiological, the rates of movement of ions and molecules and the biochemical pathways through which the body obtains energy and synthesizes and degrades molecules. It is important to realize, however, that radioactive tracer methods must often be accompanied by routine chemical analyses, that they do not always offer the easiest approach to all problems, and that they are no substitute for meticulous, accurate laboratory techniques.

Radiation detection and measurement

The amount of radiation passing through a given point cannot be measured directly, but only indirectly by the effects it produces. Quantitative methods of detection include (1) methods based upon ionization in gases (G-M counters, ion chambers), (2) scintillation counting, (3) photographic film and emulsion, (4) solid-state dosimeters, and (5) chemical dosimeters.

Gas-filled detectors

Geiger-Müller (G-M) counters and ion chambers are gas-filled devices that record ionizations caused by radiation passing through their sensitive volume (Fig. 57.11). In the absence of ionizing radiation, no electricity is conducted between the electrodes unless the applied potential is so great that a spark is produced. If radiation passes through the chamber with no voltage potential between electrodes, ion pairs recombine and no current is recorded. As a potential is introduced and gradually increased, positive and negative members of each ion pair move toward opposite electrodes and a current pulse is recorded, the magnitude of which depends on the number

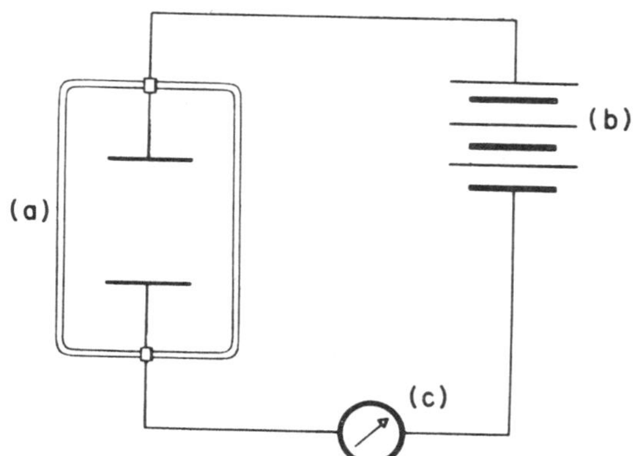

Figure 57.11. Schematic radiation detector consisting of electrodes enclosed by a gas-filled chamber (a), connected to a circuit that includes a source of applied voltage (b) and a current-measuring device (c)

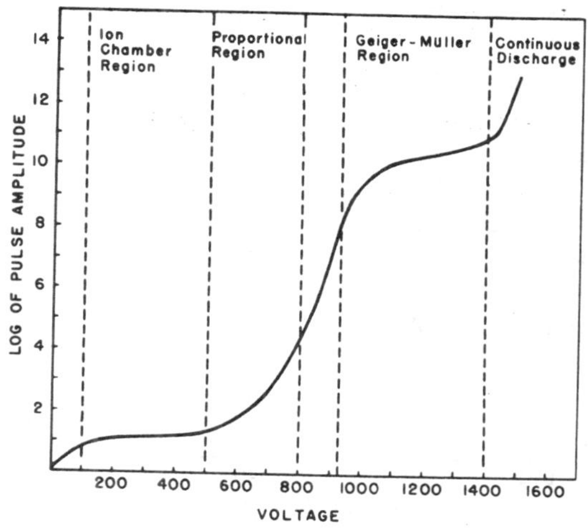

Figure 57.12. Pulse amplitude produced by a gas-filled radiation detector as a function of applied voltage

of charged particles collected (Fig. 57.12). Ion-pair recombination decreases as the potential is increased until no recombination occurs; all charged particles are collected, and pulse size remains almost constant as voltage increases. This voltage region, from approximately 100 to 500 volts, is the ion chamber region. As the applied voltage is increased above 500 volts, electrons from primary ionizations are accelerated to velocities at which they are capable of producing additional ionizations, from which additional electrons are released, causing a chainlike multiplication of ion-pair formation toward the anode known as a Townsend avalanche or Townsend cascade. Between 500 and 800 volts the Townsend avalanche increases in magnitude and the length of the collecting electrode involved in the avalanche increases until, at about 900–1000 volts, avalanche occurs along the entire length of the anode. At this point, further increases in applied voltage do not change pulse size until the protential reaches approximately 1500 volts. The region between 500 and 800 volts is called the proportional region because the pulse size is proportional to the number of primary ion pairs formed by the ionizing particle or photon as it passed through the chamber. Proportional counters are particularly useful for counting α- and β-particles in the presence of one another.

Geiger-Müller counters operate in the region of 800–1500 volts. A typical counter consists of a G-M tube, a high-voltage supply, and a scaler that registers the number of pulses coming from the tube. Scalers for G-M counting are provided with electronic discriminators that prevent the scaler from registering a pulse unless it has a certain amplitude, usually at the upper end of the proportional region. The G-M region of Figure 57.12 is illustrated in greater detail in Figure 57.13. When pulse magnitude exceeds the discriminator setting, each ionizing

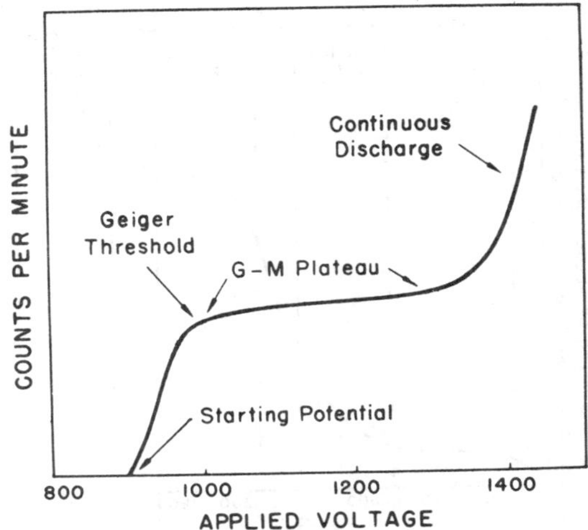

Figure 57.13. Count rate from a G-M tube as the voltage applied to the tube is increased

particle that interacts with gas in the tube produces a single pulse that is registered by the scaler as a count. The starting potential for a G-M tube is the voltage at which counts are first observed (pulse size exceeds discriminator setting). The count rate increases as voltage increases until the Townsend avalanche is complete along the entire anode. Above this voltage, the Geiger threshold, the number of pulses registered per minute increases only slightly as applied voltage is increased, a region known as the Geiger plateau. Operating an ionization detector in this region has two distinct advantages: the gas amplification factor (avalanche) is large, producing a pulse that can be used by the scaler with minimal amplification, and small changes in applied voltage have little effect on the count rate. Counting errors caused by changes in line voltage or inadequate power supply regulation are thereby minimized.

Most tracer-level radionuclide laboratories contain instruments of the ion chamber and G-M type. Ion chamber devices such as the cutie pie and pocket dosimeter are used to monitor exposures from radiation sources at selected laboratory sites and to laboratory workers. Because these devices have no gas amplification factor, their sensitivity to radiation is low and they can be used in radiation fields of relatively high intensity (20–2500 mR/hr). Geiger counters, because of their high gas amplification factor, are very sensitive to radiation and are most useful as low-level survey meters (0–20 mR/hr) and can be used as counters for measuring radioactivity quantitatively in tracer experiments. Scintillation counters have replaced ionization detectors for most routine radionuclide assays, however.

Scintillation detectors

A scintillation counter consists of a phosphor—which may be an organic or inorganic substance—a photomultiplier tube, a pulse amplifier, and a scaling device. Ionizing radiation deposits energy in the phosphor, which instantaneously emits a portion of that energy as photons (scintillations) having energies in the visible and ultraviolet regions. The photomultiplier tube is used to convert scintillation light energy to electrical pulses that can be amplified and recorded by the scaler. A direct relationship exists between the magnitude of energy depositions (by photoelectric or Compton interactions) and the magnitude of scintillation light output. By the use of electronic devices called pulse-height analyzers or γ-ray spectrometers, the energies of γ-rays interacting with the detector can be determined and mixtures of γ-emitting radionuclides can be assayed for their individual components. The most frequently used inorganic phosphor is thallium-activated sodium iodide, NaI(T1), in the form of a large, single crystal that can be obtained in a shape and dimension best suited for the counting application at hand. Inorganic phosphors are most useful as γ-detectors. Because of the density of this crystal, the opportunity for highly penetrating γ-rays to interact is much greater within its detecting volume than within the gas of a G-M tube. Scintillation counters, therefore, are 6–10 times more sensitive to γ-radiation than Geiger counters.

Two different types of NaI(T1) detectors are well-type crystals and external scintillation probes. Well-type crystals are cylindrically shaped, 4–7.5 cm in diameter, with a central hole drilled partially through the long axis to accommodate a test tube containing the sample. External scintillation probes are used to detect γ-radiation at some distance from the object being counted, usually a live human being or animal containing a radionuclide. Scintillation probes are often mounted on movable carts and are easily positioned over the area where a radionuclide is localized. When a lead collimator is placed in front of the crystal, a probe is extremely directional in its detecting ability. Such directional probes are used in conjunction with special recording devices to "picture" concentrations of radioactivity in organs and lesions, a technique known as scintiscanning (see below). Very thin, large-diameter (25 cm) crystals joined to arrays of photomultiplier tubes are rapidly replacing scanners in human medical facilities. Called γ-cameras, these instruments have crystals of sufficient diameter and area to view the organ of interest without requiring a scanning mechanism.

Although organic phosphors are also used for γ-counting, they are most useful for liquid scintillation counting of low-energy β-emitters such as ^{14}C and tritium. Because of their short range and low penetrability, weak β-particles are difficult to detect with ordinary Geiger counters. Special ion chambers that permit introduction of the sample in solid or gaseous form directly into the detecting volume are more sensitive and efficient, but the sample preparation that is necessary may be time consuming and difficult. In many instances liquid scintillation counters provide equal sensitivity and require much less sample preparation. The detector is a scintillation fluid consisting of an organic phosphor dissolved in a solvent in which the sample can be dissolved to provide excellent sample-detector geometry. Many biological materials can be prepared for liquid scintillation counting by the use of varying combinations of solvents and solubilizing agents (Birks 1964, Bransome 1970, Kobayashi and Maudsley 1974, Parmentier 1969).

Solid-state detectors

The most recently developed method of radiation detection uses solid-state devices. Such devices depend upon electron excitation or the production of free electrons in solid materials by ionizing radiation. When free electrons are produced, the resulting electric conductivity can be measured and related to radiation dose rate. Detecting substances include silicon, germanium, and cadmium sulfide. By the use of conductivity devices, dose rates can be monitored continuously.

Solid-state dosimeters that accumulate the total dose for a given length of exposure (integrating dosimeters) are also available. Free electrons trapped in excited energy states may increase the luminescent response of the solid to ultraviolet light exposure (photoluminescence); or heating the solid may release trapped electrons with an accompanying emission of light (thermoluminescence). In each case, electronic instruments are used to measure light emission, the intensity of luminescence being directly proportional to ionizing radiation exposure.

Solid-state devices are especially useful for in vivo radiation dose measurements. A photoluminescent dosimeter, for example, can be made in the form of a silver-activated phosphate glass cylinder 6 mm long and 1 mm in diameter. Such dosimeters are readily implanted surgically at sites within the body. Small thermoluminescent dosimeters made of encapsulated calcium fluoride or lithium fluoride can also be implanted in vivo. Radiation doses measurable with solid-state dosimeters range as low as 10 mR and as high as 10^4 R (Fowler 1963, Hayes et al. 1960, Hollander and Perlman 1966, Naylor 1967).

Artificially produced radioactivity

Prior to the advent of nuclear reactors and particle accelerators, there were only 5 radionuclides with atomic numbers below 83. Today there are more than 800 radionuclides that can be produced by artificial means, including isotopes of the light elements that are of most importance in biological and medical research. Neutron bombardment of stable nuclides is an efficient means of producing many radionuclides in large quantities. Nuclear reactors provide the high neutron fluxes needed for this purpose. Accelerators are used when bombardment with protons or other heavy, charged particles is necessary. In addition to their value as neutron sources, reactors also provide many useful radionuclides as a result of the fission process. Nuclear fission occurs when a very heavy nucleus, such as ^{235}U, splits into two separate nuclides of roughly equal mass called fission products, with an accompanying release of neutrons and energy in the form of electromagnetic radiation and heat. The apportionment of the ^{235}U nuclear mass among its fission products is quite variable, and the fission products include some 200 nuclides, all radioactive, belonging to 34 elements. Radioactive tracers such as ^{131}I, ^{89}Sr, ^{90}Sr, and ^{85}Kr are fission products that are used in biological research.

Radioactive decay equations

The time at which a single unstable atomic nucleus decays is entirely random and there is no known means of influencing its decay. One does not ordinarily deal with single atoms, however. When billions of atoms are involved, radioactive decay can be described in precise quantitative terms. Rutherford and Soddy in 1902 (cited by Glasstone 1967) first observed that the rate of decay of a single radionuclide can be described as an exponential function of time. To fully understand exponential behavior requires some knowledge of differential and integral calculus, but an adequate understanding is possible from the following equations.

Exponential reactions, also called first order or logarithmic reactions, are those reactions that occur at a rate proportional to the amount of reacting substance present. Reactions of this type are quite common in both the physical and biological sciences, including radioactive decay. If N atoms of a radionuclide are present at a given instant in time, and dN atoms decay during the next infinitely small interval of time, dt, then, according to the definition of an exponential function, the decay rate, dN/dt, is proportional to N. The decay rate dN/dt is negative because

$$-\frac{dN}{dt} = kN$$

N decreases with time in radioactive decay. The proportionality constant k, in this case the disintegration constant or decay constant of the radionuclide, has a specific, constant value for a given radionuclide. Determining the value of the decay constant of an unknown radionuclide, therefore, is one means of identifying it. The above equation as such is not usable and must be rearranged:

$$\frac{dN}{N} = -kdt$$

and integrated:

$$\ln (N/No) = -kt$$

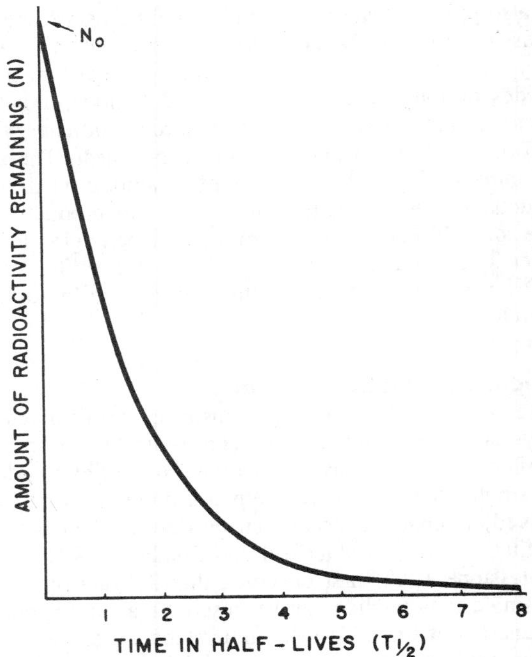

Figure 57.14. Radioactive decay

This equation states that the natural logarithm (to base e) of the number of atoms present at zero time (No) divided into the number of atoms (N) remaining after an elapsed time (t) equals the negative decay constant times t. One of the most useful derivations of this equation for purposes of calculating radioactive decay is:

$$\log (\mathrm{No/N}) = \frac{0.3\ t}{T½}$$

where No = amount of radioactivity at zero time, N = amount of radioactivity at time t, and T½ = half-life of radionuclide in the same unit as t. Other derivations include:

$$2.3 \log (\mathrm{N/No}) = -kt$$
$$\mathrm{N} = \mathrm{No} \times e^{-kt}$$

The exponential behavior of radioactive decay is shown in Figure 57.14. Note that N will never reach zero; theoretically, one or more atoms will never decay. For this reason the lifetime of a radioactive atom cannot be defined, whereas its *half-life* can be measured and is one of the units commonly used to characterize a radionuclide. Half-life can be calculated from the fourth equation above, or from the following:

$$T½ = \frac{0.693}{k}$$

Radionuclide administration, sampling, and data expression

Radionuclide experiments differ from other experiments only in the procedures required to safeguard personnel and equipment from contamination with radioactivity. Such procedures include the use of gloves, smocks, manual pipetting devices, and absorbent paper and trays to contain radioactive solutions within well-defined areas (Comar 1955; Hansard and Comar 1953; International Atomic Energy Agency 1965, 1973a,b; Silver 1968; Wang et al. 1975).

Radionuclides are most often used in the form of solutions that can be introduced into biological systems (such as animals or in vitro systems) in quantities accurately measured by volume or weight. Samples withdrawn from the system at selected times after introduction of the tracer are then subjected to standard chemical and biochemical analysis, if desired, and to radiochemical analysis such as scintillation counting. If γ-emitters are used, scintillation detectors can be positioned externally to count photons emitted from either the entire animal or specific organs such as the thyroid gland, liver, and kidney. In each instance, the raw data are recorded from a scaler or count-rate meter in terms of counts per unit time, usually counts per minute (cpm). Almost all radionuclide counting in biology is relative counting; that is, samples from the biological system and the dose solution (the solution originally introduced into the system) are counted at the same time under the same conditions. The amounts of radioactivity in the two samples can then be directly compared, or the activity can be related to the total activity introduced in the dose solution as a percentage of the dose per unit mass or volume of sample, a commonly used means of data expression which is nothing more than a measure of the concentration of radioactivity in a specimen.

For many purposes it is useful to express data as radioactivity per quantity of the substance being traced. This unit, known as *specific activity,* can be expressed in many subunits, such as cpm, percentage of dose or μCi per gram, mM or mEq of the total (stable plus labeled) element or molecule being traced. To determine specific activity, one must measure the radioactivity of the sample and also analyze the sample chemically for the stable substance. It is important that both the radiochemical and chemical analyses be performed to determine the same chemical state of the substance being studied. As Comar (1955) pointed out, a specific activity based upon chemical analysis of plasma inorganic phosphorus and radioassay of total plasma ^{32}P would be meaningless because the radioassay includes two distinct chemical compartments and the chemical assay only one.

Radionuclide movement and rates

Radionuclides can be used to answer such apparently simple questions as: "Are biological membranes freely permeable to certain ions?" "Is a certain substance absorbed by the intestine or do conventional balance techniques lack the sensitivity required to measure its absorption?" "How rapidly does blood flow through specific organs or parts of the body?" "How are labeled elements or molecules distributed within the body?" A qualitative answer is often sufficient. For example, erythrocytes are incubated in a medium containing ^{42}K. After a time they are removed and washed, and ^{42}K is shown to have penetrated into the cells. The cells are then placed in a nonradioactive incubating medium. The fact that ^{42}K is observed passing into the medium demonstrates the rapid exchange between intra- and extracellular potassium. As simple as this experiment is to perform, there is no way to obtain comparable information without the use of a radioisotope of potassium. This simple experiment exemplifies the means by which the concept of the "dynamic state of body constituents" was obtained; that is, largely by the use of stable and radionuclide tracers, beginning with the use of deuterium and ^{15}N by Schoenheimer (1949).

By recording the time during which movement is observed, one determines rates of movement. The arrival at the femoral vein of ^{51}Cr-labeled erythrocytes injected into the saphenous vein of a dog can be recorded by an external scintillation probe. The circulation time between the points of injection and detection is readily determined. The rate at which colloidal ^{198}Au is accumulated in the liver from circulating blood can be used to estimate liver blood flow. Cardiac output can be determined by the movement of ^{131}I-serum albumin through the heart and aorta, as measured by external counting. These and other organ function tests are based upon the measurement of rates and the observation of patterns of radionuclide movement (Ashkar et al. 1975, Boyd and Dalrymple 1974, Early et al. 1969).

Labeled ceramic microspheres and macroaggregated albumin are used to measure blood flow distribution in the body. After injection into a major blood vessel, the particles mix rapidly with the blood and are distributed in the same proportion as the blood to the organs supplied by the vessel. Because of their size (10–50 μ) they are trapped in the capillary beds. Comparative measurements of tissue radioactivities reveal the proportion of the vessel's blood flow delivered to each organ. Microspheres have been used to study arteriovenous shunting in sheep (Hamlin et al. 1962), blood flow in the fetal lamb (Rudolph and Heymann 1967), and distribution of cardiac output in the rabbit (Neutze et al. 1968).

Radionuclide dilution

Dilution techniques employing dyes and other chemicals have long been used to estimate the size of fluid and chemical spaces within the body. Conventional dilution techniques necessarily rely on the use of substances that can be assayed because they are nonphysiological in character. Therefore, these substances may disturb the physiological state of the experimental subject and tend to be lost at excessive rates from the physiological space by leakage or metabolism. Radionuclide dilution minimizes difficulties of this kind because atoms, molecules, and cells normally present in the space of interest are

Table 57.2. Radionuclides and radionuclide-labeled compounds used for volume and space determinations, organ function studies, and organ imaging

Determinations	Radionuclide or labeled compound
Volume or space	
Erythrocyte volume and life span	^{51}Cr-labeled erythrocytes, ^{59}Fe-labeled erythrocytes
Plasma volume	RISA *, ^{99m}Tc-serum albumin
Calcium (total body)	^{48}Ca activation analysis
Chloride space	^{82}Br, ^{36}Cl, ^{38}Cl
Magnesium space	^{28}Mg
Potassium space	^{42}K, ^{86}Rb
Sodium space	^{22}Na, ^{24}Na
Extracellular water	^{82}Br
Total body water	Tritiated H_2O
Organ function	
Cardiac function, coronary circulation	RISA *, ^{99m}Tc-serum albumin, ^{125}I- or ^{99m}Tc-MAA †
Gastrointestinal and pancreatic function	
B_{12} absorption	^{57}Co-cyanocobalamin
Fat absorption	RIFA ‡
Plasma protein loss	RISA *
Kidney function	^{131}I-Hippuran, ^{197}Hg-chlormerodrin
Liver function	^{131}I- or ^{125}I-Rose Bengal
Lung	^{133}Xe, ^{13}N
Organ blood flow (liver lung, heart, brain, placenta)	Colloidal ^{198}Au, labeled microspheres, MAA † with radioiodine or ^{99m}Tc label, ^{99m}Tc-Na pertechnetate, RISA*, ^{99m}Tc-serum albumin
Organ imaging	
Bone	^{47}Ca, ^{18}F, ^{85}Sr, ^{87m}Sr, ^{99m}Tc- or Sr-polyphosphate and -diphosphonate
Bone marrow	^{59}Fe
Brain (CSF flow, lesion localization)	RISA *, ^{99m}Tc-serum albumin, ^{99m}Tc-inulin, ^{197}Hg-chlormerodrin, ^{99m}Tc-Na pertechnetate
Heart	^{137m}Ba, RIFA ‡, RISA *, ^{131}I- or ^{99m}Tc-MAA †, ^{99m}Tc-Na pertechnetate
Kidney	^{131}I- or ^{125}I-Hippuran, ^{197}Hg- or ^{203}Hg-Neohydrin §, ^{99m}Tc-pertechnetate
Liver, lymph nodes	Radioiodinated or ^{99m}Tc-MAA †, colloidal ^{198}Au, ^{99m}Tc-sulfur colloid, ^{131}I-Rose Bengal, ^{99m}Tc-Na pertechnetate
Lung	Radioiodinated or ^{99m}Tc-MAA †, labeled microspheres
Pancreas	^{75}Se-methionine
Placenta	RISA *, ^{99m}Tc-Na pertechnetate, ^{99m}Tc- or ^{51}Cr-serum albumin
Parathyroid gland	^{75}Se-methionine, ^{57}Co-cyanocobalamin, ^{131}I- or ^{125}I-toluidine blue
Salivary glands	^{99m}Tc-Na pertechnetate
Spleen	Radioiodinated or ^{99m}Tc-MAA †, colloidal ^{198}Au, ^{99m}Tc-sulfur colloid, ^{51}Cr-labeled denatured erythrocytes, ^{113m}In-colloid, ^{197}Hg- or ^{203}Hg-BMHP ‖
Thyroid	^{131}I, ^{125}I, ^{132}I, ^{99m}Tc-Na pertechnetate

* Radioiodinated serum albumin
† Macroaggregated serum albumin
‡ Radioiodinated fatty acids
§ 3-chloromercuri-2-methoxy-propyl-urea
‖ 1-bromomercuri-2-hydroxypropane

labeled and diluted into that space. Besides, radionuclide measurement has the advantages of sensitivity, accuracy, and ease. Many volumes and spaces, particularly chemical, can be measured only by radionuclide dilution.

As in all dilution procedures, the known quantity of diluted substance remains constant regardless of the volume or mass into which it is diluted. When one knows the total amount of a substance diluted into an unknown volume and the concentration of the substance in a portion of that volume following complete mixing, one can calculate the volume (V):

$$V = \frac{\text{Total diluted substance}}{\text{Substance/Unit volume}}$$

Physiological spaces measurable by radionuclide dilution include erythrocyte volume (using ^{51}Cr- or ^{59}Fe-labeled red cells), plasma volume (^{131}I-serum albumin), body water (tritiated H_2O), and chlorine, potassium, and sodium spaces (using radioisotopes of these elements) (Table 57.2) (Bergner and Lushbaugh 1967, Boyd and Dalrymple 1974, Early et al. 1969, Morgan et al. 1967, Silver 1968).

Radionuclide dilution can also be applied to determination of mass, making possible quantitative chemical analysis without the necessity of quantitative separations. Specific activity is a particularly valuable unit for this purpose and can be viewed as a mass concentration unit of radioactivity when the mass is that of the substance being assayed. As in volume dilution, the activity added (A) is the same before and after dilution, and

$$A = M \times SA, \text{ or } M = \frac{A}{SA}$$

where M is the unknown mass and SA the specific activity of the mass after dilution. For example, 1000 cpm of radioactive iron is thoroughly mixed into a solution containing an unknown quantity of iron. The iron is precipitated as ferric hydroxide, and only a portion of the precipitate, which has a specific activity of 50 cpm/mg of iron, is recovered. The unknown mass of iron in the solution can be easily calculated by means of the above equation:

$$\frac{1000 \text{ cpm}}{50 \text{ cpm/mg}} = 20 \text{ mg}$$

If a significant quantity of mass accompanies the label added to the unknown mass, the equation becomes:

$$\frac{\text{Total activity}}{\text{before dilution}} = \frac{\text{Total activity}}{\text{after dilution}}$$

$$M_1 \times SA_1 = (M_1 + M_2)SA_2$$

where M_1 = known mass accompanying label, M_2 = unknown mass, SA_1 = known specific activity of label, and SA_2 = measured specific activity of mixture following dilution. Solving for the unknown mass, M_2:

$$M_2 = M_1\left(\frac{SA_1}{SA_2} - 1\right)$$

Modifications of radionuclide dilution allow the technique to be used when the substance to be measured is not readily available in labeled form but can be labeled biosynthetically within the animal or plant (inverse isotope dilution), and when the specific activity of the biosynthetically labeled substance cannot be directly determined (double isotope dilution) (Boyd and Dalrymple 1974, Chase and Rabinowitz 1967, Comar 1955).

Kinetic analysis

Radionuclides provide the primary means of approaching many of the basic questions of current physiological research. For example, the mechanisms of muscle contraction and nerve conduction are closely associated with membrane permeabilities and ion diffusion and transport, usually under circumstances in which ion concentrations in tissues and fluids remain relatively constant even though dynamic exchange processes are in progress. Under such conditions, ion fluxes and exchange rates can be determined only by tracer methods. Experimentally, one determines the rate at which a tracer moves from one "phase" or "compartment" to another—from a nerve fiber or muscle to a bathing medium, for example—by measuring the radioactivity of samples taken from one compartment at selected times after the introduction of the tracer. The rate at which the tracer enters or leaves the compartment can be graphed and equations can be formulated to describe the behavior of the tracer. In biological systems, mathematical models of an exponential form will often best fit to data from tracer experiments. The mathematical relationships developed in describing radioactive decay also apply to such data.

To illustrate the application of mathematical models to biological data, two relatively simple examples will be discussed. In the first example, a radioactive tracer is injected intravenously into an animal and a number of blood samples are taken (Table 57.3, column 1). At the end of the experiment the radioactivity of the blood samples is measured (Table 57.3, column 2). The investigator theorizes that the labeled substance leaves the blood at an exponential rate; that is, at a rate proportional to the amount of labeled substance remaining in the blood. To test the theory, he or she plots the data as the logarithm of each count rate versus time, or, to accomplish the same purpose, as count rate versus time on semilogarithmic paper. If the removal rate is exponential, the

Table 57.3. Hypothetical data illustrating removal of a label from a physiological space by single and double exponential (logarithmic) processes

Time after tracer administration (min)	Removal by a single exponential process (cpm/ml blood)	Removal by two exponential processes (cpm/ml blood)
2	1739	3137
4	1313	2630
6	1003	2231
10	573	1651
15	288	1197
20	143	919
30	35	593
40	9	409
50		288
60		207

data points will form a straight line (Fig. 57.15). (If the data were plotted on linear graph paper it would look like Figure 57.14.) Once it has been determined that the data can be represented as an exponential process, the investigator proceeds to formulate the equation that describes the data. The equation used to describe radioactive decay can also be represented as:

$$2.3 \log \frac{A}{Ao} = -kt$$

where A = cpm/ml of blood at time t, Ao = cpm/ml of blood at zero time, and k = the fraction of A leaving the blood per unit time. To solve for k, this equation can be rearranged:

$$k = \frac{2.3\ (\log Ao - \log A)}{t}$$

Substituting values from Table 57.3:

$$k = \frac{2.3\ (\log 1739 - \log 35)}{28\ \text{min}} = 0.139/\text{min}$$

The half-time of removal of the labeled substance from the blood is:

$$t\tfrac{1}{2} = \frac{0.693}{0.139/\text{min}} = 5\ \text{min}$$

The basic principle of exponential (logarithmic) behavior is that for every equal interval of time a constant fraction of the labeled substance enters or leaves the compartment. The rate constant, k, denotes the fraction removed per unit time. In this case, 14 percent of the labeled material remaining in the blood is removed each minute; 50 percent of the remaining material is removed every 5 minutes. The equation that describes the removal of the labeled substance from the blood can now be written as: $A = 2300e^{-0.139t}$ (since $N = No \times e^{-kt}$). The data can be interpreted to mean that the label is disappearing from the blood as a result of one physiological mechanism, or as a

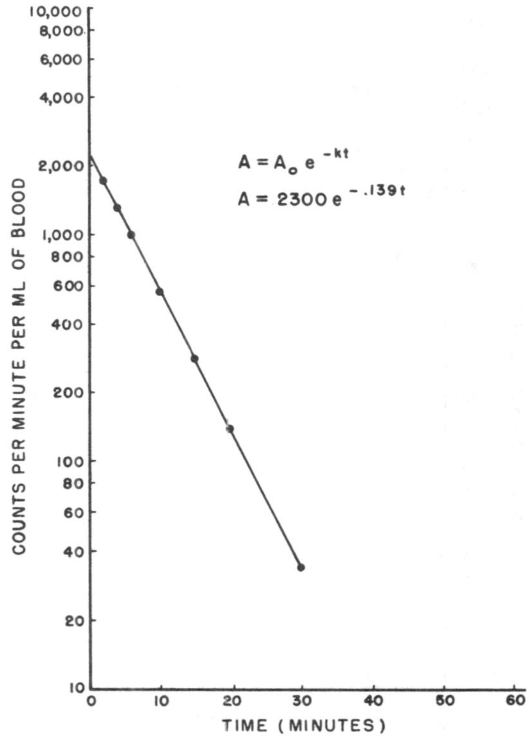

Figure 57.15. Semilogarithmic graph of the removal of a tracer from a physiological compartment by a process represented by a single exponential equation

result of more than one physiological mechanism, each having the same rate constant, k.

Substances may be removed from the blood by several processes, including dilution into extravascular spaces, clearance by the kidneys, intestinal excretion, sequestration by bone, and catabolism. If the rate of disappearance is a function of two or more removal mechanisms, each of which is exponential, then disappearance can be represented by the sum of the exponentials. A two-component exponential system is illustrated by the data in column 3 of Table 57.3 and Figure 57.16. Administration of the tracer, blood sampling, and radioanalysis are the same as for the first example. In this case, however, a semilogarithmic plot of the data yields a line that initially is curved and then becomes straight near the end of the experiment. The straight portion represents a single exponential process that can be isolated from the combined curve by fitting a line to the last few data points and extrapolating back to zero time (dotted line). The equation for this line can be determined in the same manner as previously described for a single exponential function, and is:

$$A_2 = 1500e^{-0.033t}$$

The count rate of A_2 at the times when blood samples were taken can be calculated and subtracted from the

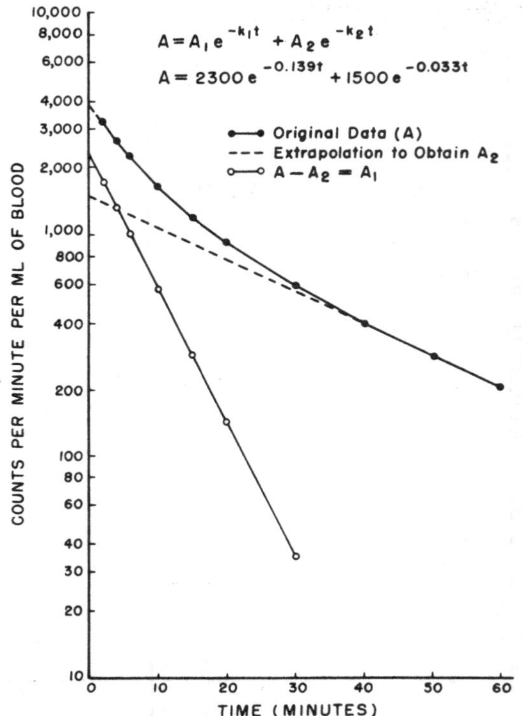

Figure 57.16. Semilogarithmic graph of the removal of a tracer from a physiological compartment by processes that can be represented as the sum of two exponential equations

total count rate, A; the differences, when plotted on the same graph (Fig. 57.16, open circles), form a straight line representing the second exponential removal mechanism, which has the equation $A_1 = 2300e^{-0.139t}$, chosen for convenience to be the same as the single exponential mechanism of the first example. The sum of the two exponential functions, then, forms the equation describing the original data in column 3 of Table 57.3: $A = 2300e^{-0.139t} + 1500e^{-0.033t}$. The labeled substance is removed from the blood by at least two separate processes. The first removes 60 percent of the label $(2300/3800 \times 100)$ at a rate of 14 percent of the remainder per minute with a half-time of 5 minutes. The second removes 40 percent of the label $(1500/3800 \times 100)$ at a rate of 3.3 percent of the remainder per minute with a half-time of 21 minutes. If the disappearance of the label were a function of three or more exponential processes, the constants for the additional processes could be obtained by repeating the process of extrapolation and subtraction just described. The accuracy of results obtained will decrease with each additional process so defined and is highly dependent on the quality of the original data. Computer techniques are commonly used for curve fitting and analyzing data of this type.

The examples of kinetic analysis just described are relatively simple compared with others that can be found in the literature (Bergner 1964, Boyd and Dalrymple 1974, Hart 1963, Sheppard 1962), and represent idealized situations tailored for illustrative purposes. Mathematical models permit calculations of compartment numbers and sizes and of transfer rates between compartments, which may then be interpreted in terms of physiological mechanisms known to influence the behavior of the tracer. Turnover rates, the rates at which biochemical substances of the body are synthesized and degraded, can also be calculated. It must be understood that the applicability of such calculations depends on the validity of certain assumptions regarding the nature of the system being studied.

Metabolic pathways

The use of radionuclides in biochemistry has been most rewarding. The difficult tasks of defining reaction sequences by which cells obtain and use energy, synthesize structural and functional molecules, and dispose of waste products have often been accomplished with the aid of radionuclides. Carbon-14 and tritium have been especially useful, and a wide variety of techniques has been developed for synthesizing, degrading, and counting ^{14}C- and ^{3}H-labeled molecules. Entire carbon chains of molecules can be uniformly labeled, or specific positions of the molecular structure can be selectively labeled by using methods of organic chemistry. In the case of naturally occurring compounds not readily synthesized artificially, biosynthesis can be employed. Techniques include selective degradation procedures, chromatography, ion exchange, and liquid scintillation counting. By following the positions of ^{14}C atoms in molecules and their reaction products, biochemists can determine sites of enzyme action and outline the sequence of reactions within metabolic pathways.

External counting procedures

Organ function

The estimation of thyroid function by the measurement of radioiodine uptake by the gland was the first radionuclide organ-function test widely used with domestic animals. Although the availability of other tests such as the serum T_4 assay has decreased the frequency of radioiodine uptake measurement for clinical purposes, it remains a useful research tool. A number of measurement techniques have been described, but they differ mostly in detail rather than in principle. At a specified time after parenteral $Na^{131}I$ administration, measurements with an external detector are made of the count rates of the thyroid gland and of a volume of $Na^{131}I$ dose solution (standard solution) equal to the volume administered to the subject, under conditions as similar as possible. To simulate the tissues surrounding the thyroid gland, plastic or water *phantoms* are used to surround the standard solution during counting so that γ-ray absorption and scattering will be as similar as possible for subject and standard. It is essential that the distance between the scintillation probe and the subject's neck be the same as the distance between the probe and the phantom, and that it be constant during measurement. Finally, the thyroid count rate must be corrected for counts caused by γ-rays emitted by nonthyroidal ^{131}I; this can be done by taking counts with and without the thyroid shielded by lead, or by using a collimating device on the scintillation probe that allows it to detect only photons coming from a small area that includes the thyroid. Uptake is then calculated as:

$$\% \text{ thyroid } ^{131}\text{I uptake} = \frac{\text{Net thyroid count rate}}{\text{Net standard count rate}} \times 100$$

Results are interpreted on the basis of information obtained from animals assumed to have normal thyroid activity and from experimentally induced hypo- and hyperthyroid subjects. Most investigations of thyroid ^{131}I uptake in animals have been in dogs, sheep, and swine. The results have shown good relationships between radioiodine uptake and thyroid activity. However, factors known to influence iodine and thyroid metabolism must be taken into account, such as breed, age, renal disease, diet, and pregnancy (Goyings et al. 1962, Griffin et al. 1962, Howes et al. 1962, Kaneko and Cornelius 1971, Lombardi et al. 1962, Quinlan and Michaelson 1967, Silver 1968).

Additional information on thyroid activity can be obtained by measuring the amount of hormone-bound ^{131}I released into the blood by the thyroid gland. One technique is to pass blood plasma (from an animal given Na^{131}I) through an ion exchange column, removing free ^{131}I and collecting protein-bound ^{131}I (PB^{131}I) in the eluate. By calculating a conversion ratio (C.R.):

$$\text{C.R.} = \frac{\text{PB}^{131}\text{I}}{\text{Total plasma } ^{131}\text{I}} \times 100$$

one can obtain an estimate of the amount of hormone-bound ^{131}I and, if serial samples are taken, the rate of its release. A second technique depends upon competition between triiodothyronine (T_3) and thyroid hormone (T_4) for binding sites on serum protein, which binds T_4 in preference to T_3. Normally T_4 does not occupy all the sites, the remainder being available for T_3. When T_3-^{131}I is added to whole blood or to blood serum containing an exchange resin, T_3 is bound first by protein sites unoccupied by T_4, and the remainder binds to erythrocytes or the resin. Hence erythrocyte or resin uptake of labeled T_3 is directly related to, and is used as an index of, serum T_4 content. Resin uptake has been found to be more reproducible than erythrocyte uptake and is the preferred method. Also, changes in serum protein composition or content will influence and complicate interpretation of the results (Greve and Gaafar 1964, Kallfelz 1968, Rabinowitz et al. 1964, Silver 1968).

Kallfelz (1969) has used ^{125}I-thyroxine to measure thyroid gland function in the dog. His results suggest that this test is more sensitive and reliable than the T_3 uptake method. Both tests have the advantage of avoiding exposure of the patient to radioactivity. Blood serum can be collected and sent to a laboratory where the necessary equipment and personnel are available. If T_3 uptake and/or serum thyroxine (T_4) concentrations suggest thyroid deficiency, the animal's response to thyroid-stimulating hormone (TSH) can be measured. If thyroid function is the primary problem, serum T_4 will not increase after TSH administration (Kallfelz 1973).

Other external counting techniques for measuring organ function depend on rates and patterns of appearance and disappearance of a label in the organ or area of interest (see Table 57.2). Figure 57.17 depicts rate-meter readings for one such label. Similar recordings are made

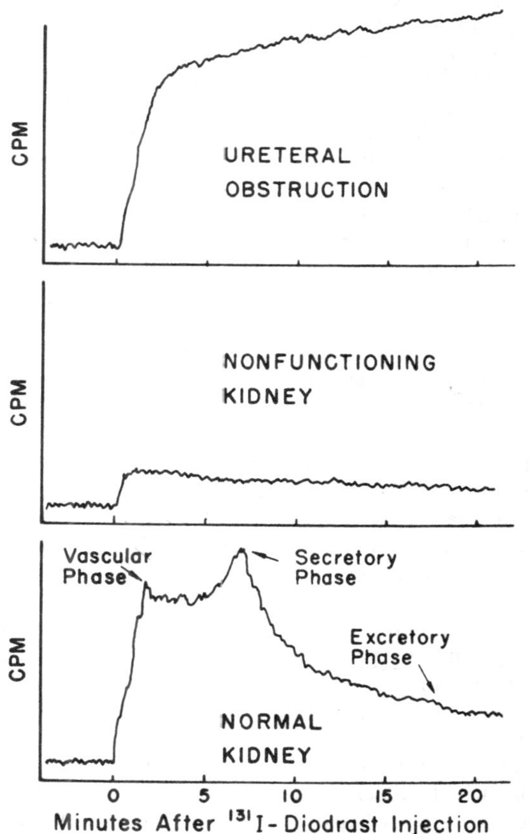

Figure 57.17. Chart recordings of ^{131}I-Diodrast radioactivity measured by a scintillation detector positioned over the kidney

for observation of ^{131}I-labeled rose-bengal concentration and release by the liver, and for measurement of cardiac output by detection of the movement of ^{131}I-labeled serum albumin through the heart (Holmes 1960, Casey et al. 1963, Kaneko and Cornelius 1971). Most of these procedures were first developed for use in human beings and have not been widely employed in animal physiology even though they should be quite applicable. Kallfelz et al. (1968) have shown that tests for intestinal malabsorption and pancreatic insufficiency using ^{131}I-labeled triolein and oleic acid in human beings can also be used in dogs.

Scintiscanning

Another external counting procedure, scintiscanning, produces maps of the location of radionuclides within the body. A scintillation probe, mechanically devised to sweep back and forth over the area of interest, is connected through a scaler to a solenoid, which tracks over a sheet of paper in the same pattern as the probe over the subject, marking the paper each time the scaler accumulates a certain number of counts. The scan appears as a pattern of light and dark areas corresponding to regions of low and high concentrations of radioactivity. This is only one of many electromechanical systems that are used. Scintiscanning has been especially useful for locating neoplasms that concentrate γ-emitting radionuclides or molecules. Radioisotopes of iodine are used to diagnose thyroid carcinoma and to locate metastatic lesions. Other scanning techniques include the use of ^{197}Hg-labeled neohydrin or chlormerodrin and ^{131}I- or ^{125}I-labeled fibrinogen to locate malignancies, ^{75}Se-labeled methionine to scan the pancreas, and ^{131}I-labeled serum albumin aggregates to scan the liver, spleen, and lungs.

In recent years ^{99m}Tc has been used increasingly as a label for a wide variety of organ function and scanning tests. The parent-daughter combination ^{99}Mo-^{99m}Tc is stored in an ion exchange generator, or "cow." For labeling purposes, one can "milk" ^{99m}Tc (6 hr half-life) from the generator by eluting it from its ^{99}Mo parent (60 hr half-life), which is held by the resin. Advantages of ^{99m}Tc scanning are its low γ-energy (0.14 Mev) and short half-life, which enhance scanning resolution and decrease radiation exposure.

Scintiscanning does, however, have a serious disadvantage in the time required for the probe to make the required number of sweeps over the area of interest; scanning times for most applications range from a few minutes to half an hour. Animal subjects require anesthetization to prevent movement during scanning, and the dynamics of processes that occur over a span of minutes (such as renal or hepatic clearance of a radiolabeled dye from the bloodstream) are difficult or impossible to observe. To minimize these problems, γ-scintillation "cameras" have been developed capable of visualizing entire organs or areas of the body at one time without scanning. The unique feature of the camera is a thin sodium iodide crystal of large diameter (typically 25 cm); scintillation light from γ-ray interactions in the crystal is collected by a large number of photomultiplier tubes that are electronically matrixed to permit localization of the precise site of the interaction in the crystal. Images of radionuclide distributions within the area "viewed" by the 25 cm crystal are displayed on an oscilloscope and can be obtained at intervals of a few seconds, allowing visualization of the time distribution pattern of the label. The greater counting efficiency of these cameras also allows the use of a smaller radionuclide dose than is required by the single-crystal scanner. Unfortunately, these cameras cost 5–10 times as much as standard scintillation probes, so their present use in animal medicine and research is limited (Boyd and Dalrymple 1974; Lange 1973; Maynard 1969; Sodee and Early 1972; Wang 1967, 1968).

Whole-body counting

Whole-body counting is a specialized form of external counting. As the term implies, radiation emitted from all parts of the body is measured, so far as possible. Such measurements can be made either by positioning the subject so that all parts of the body are approximately equidistant from the detector or by surrounding the subject with the detector. The first approach is used when NaI(Tl) crystals, some as large as 10 cm thick and 30 cm in diameter, are used as detectors. Organic scintillators large enough to surround the subject can be constructed of liquid scintillation solutions enclosed in metal tanks or plastic block scintillators. Whole-body counters are used to measure radioactivity in human beings and in domestic animals, including species as large as cattle (International Atomic Energy Agency 1962; Twardock et al. 1964, 1966).

Whole-body counting has two primary advantages: (1) radionuclide retention and excretion can be measured directly, and (2) the large sample volume that such detectors will accommodate permits the measurement of radionuclides that are present in very low concentrations. Anyone who has performed a nutritional balance study will appreciate the value of measuring the amount of a substance retained in the body directly rather than subtracting excretion from intake. The latter method, in addition to being time consuming and difficult, offers many opportunities for errors in collection and sampling, especially when only a small fraction of the substance is being retained. Whole-body counters can be used to measure retention of any γ-emitting radionuclide, including radioisotopes of such biologically essential elements as Ca, Cl, Co, Fe, I, K, Mg, Mn, Na, and Zn (Table 57.4).

The second advantage of whole-body counters, their

ability to measure small amounts of radioactivity in large samples, has led to their use in studies of body composition and as quantitative monitors of fission products in foodstuffs and in human and animal populations. The γ-emitters found in human and animal tissues include ^{40}K, a naturally occurring radionuclide, and the products of nuclear reactors and weapons testing, ^{137}Cs, ^{54}Mn, and ^{65}Zn. The relationship between ^{40}K radioactivity and lean body mass has been heavily researched. Most of the potassium in the body is located in lean tissue, and the potassium content of lean tissue remains reasonably constant in the absence of disease. Whole-body counters, by measuring γ-radiation from ^{40}K, can be used to estimate the total potassium content of the body with an accuracy of about 3 percent. ^{40}K measurements have also been applied to studies of growth patterns as related to sex and age, and to the effects of diet, athletic activity, aging, and disease upon body potassium.

In addition to their applications in medical and physiological research, whole-body counters are used to monitor existing quantities of radioactivity in the environment and the extent to which such radioactivities are retained

Table 57.4. Biologically useful radionuclides

Element	Isotope	Half-life *	Emissions (Mev) †		
			β	γ	Other
Arsenic	^{74}As	17.5 d	(2) 1.36–0.69	(2) 0.60–0.63	EC; 0.92, 1.53 positron
	^{76}As	26.8 h	(3) 1.76–2.96	(3) 0.549–1.21	
	^{77}As	38.7 h	(2) 0.44, 0.70	(1) 0.525	
Bismuth	^{207}Bi	30 y	none	(2) 0.57, 1.06	
	^{210}Bi	5 d	(1) 1.17	none	
Bromine	^{82}Br	35.9 h	(1) 0.465	(7) 0.547–1.312	
Calcium	^{45}Ca	165 d	(1) 0.254	none	
	^{47}Ca	4.5 d	(4) 0.46–1.90	(4) 0.157–1.29	
Carbon	^{14}C	5,570 y	(1) 0.155	none	
Cesium	^{137}Cs	30 y	(2) 0.51–1.17	(1) 0.662	
Chlorine	^{36}Cl	3.08×10^5 y	(1) 0.714	none	
Chromium	^{51}Cr	27.8 d	none	(1) 0.32	EC
Cobalt	^{57}Co	270 d	none	(3) 0.014–0.136	EC
	^{58}Co	71.3 d	none	(1) 0.81	EC; 0.47 positron
	^{60}Co	5.24 y	(1) 0.306	(2) 1.17–1.33	
Copper	^{64}Cu	12.9 h	(1) 0.571	(1) 1.34	EC; 0.657 positron
Fluorine	^{18}F	112 m	none	none	0.65 positron
Gold	^{198}Au	2.7 d	(1) 0.97	(1) 0.411	
	^{199}Au	3.14 d	(3) 0.251–0.460	(3) 0.050–0.208	
Hydrogen	^{3}H	12.46 y	(1) 0.01795	none	
Indium	^{113m}In	1.7 h	none	(2) 0.398, 0.606	EC
Iodine	^{125}I	57.4 d	none	(1) 0.0354	EC; 0.0274 X ray
	^{131}I	8.05 d	(2) 0.335–0.608	(3) 0.284–0.637	
Iron	^{59}Fe	45.1 d	(2) 0.271, 0.462	(2) 0.098, 1.289	
Krypton	^{79}Kr	1.45 d	(1) 0.60	none	EC
	^{85}Kr	10.3 y	(1) 0.67	(1) 0.514	
Magnesium	^{28}Mg	21.3 h	(1) 0.42	(4) 0.32–1.35	
Manganese	^{54}Mn	313 d	none	(1) 0.840	EC
Mercury	^{197}Hg	65 h	none	(2) 0.077, 0.191	EC
	^{203}Hg	45.4 d	(1) 0.208	(1) 0.279	
Molybdenum	^{99}Mo	2.85 d	(2) 0.54, 1.23	(5) 0.140–0.780	
Nickel	^{56}Ni	6.4 d	none	(6) 0.163–1.56	EC
	^{63}Ni	100 y	(1) 0.067	none	
Phosphorus	^{32}P	14.3 d	(1) 1.701	none	
Potassium	^{42}K	12.47 h	(2) 2.04, 3.58	(1) 1.51	
Rubidium	^{86}Rb	18.7 d	(1) 1.78	(1) 1.078	
Selenium	^{75}Se	119.9 d	none	(3) 0.136–0.281	EC
Silver	^{111}Ag	7.5 d	(1) 1.05	(1) 0.342	
Sodium	^{22}Na	2.58 y	none	(2) 1.28	0.58 positron
	^{24}Na	15.05 h	(1) 1.39	(2) 1.368, 2.754	
Strontium	^{85}Sr	64.0 d	none	(1) 0.51	EC
	^{89}Sr	50.5 d	(1) 1.463	none	
Sulfur	^{35}S	89.0 d	(1) 0.167	none	
Technetium	^{99m}Tc	6 h	none	(1) 0.140	
Thallium	^{204}Tl	3.8 y	(1) 0.766	Hg X rays	EC
Xenon	^{133}Xe	5.27 d	(1) 0.346	(1) 0.081	
Zinc	^{65}Zn	246.4 d	none	(1) 1.12	EC; 0.325 positron

* m, minutes; h, hours; d, days; y, years

† Only those radiations with frequencies greater than 5% [illegible] total disintegrations are listed (total no. in parentheses), unless the nuclide emits only radiation with a [illegible] yield or less, in which case the value is listed. EC refers to electron capture; the nucleus captures an electron from the K-shell, resulting in a series of electron transitions and soft X-ray emission.

in the bodies of animals and human beings (National Academy of Sciences 1968, Ward 1970).

Autoradiography

Photographic film represents one of the earliest and one of the most useful modern methods of detecting ionizing radiation. Becquerel accidentally discovered the existence of natural radioactivity in 1896 as a result of exposing film to radiation from uranium salt, a technique that has been highly developed in recent years and is known as autoradiography. Photographic film can be exposed by ionizing radiation in the same manner as by light. When placed in contact with an object containing radioactivity for a length of time, a film when developed will show the location of the radioactivity in the object. Autoradiography has been used to visualize concentrations of radionuclides in objects as large as entire animals and organs (gross autoradiography) and as small as cell organelles (microscopic autoradiography).

The work of Ullberg (1958) provides a good example of gross autoradiographic technique. He studied the distribution of labeled atoms and molecules within the body by means of whole-body autoradiography of small laboratory animals such as mice, rats, and cats. The labeled substance was administered to the animal and a period of time allowed for its uptake and distribution. The animal was anesthetized and further movement of the label stopped by quick freezing in a carbon dioxide and acetone mixture at $-78°C$. Sections 5–20 μ thick were cut through the whole body, dehydrated, and apposed to X-ray film for periods of 1–14 days; sectioning and exposure were carried out in a cold room at $-10°C$. Following exposure, the film and section were treated separately; the film was developed, and darkened areas corresponding to localizations of the radionuclide were compared with anatomical landmarks on the whole-body section. Ullberg centered his interest on the actions of membranes in facilitating or inhibiting the movement of molecules, the accumulation of substances by tissues, and routes of excretion. Subtances he studied included antibiotics (penicillin-^{35}S, dihydrostreptomycin-^{3}H, tetracycline-^{3}H), chemotherapeutic agents (*p*-aminosalicylic acid-^{14}C), ^{198}Au, ^{18}F, and radioiodine.

In microscopic autoradiography, slides of tissue sections or dried cell suspensions are prepared by the usual histological techniques. A photographic emulsion is apposed to the specimen by any of several procedures. In the dipping or coating method, liquid photographic emulsion is applied to the slide and allowed to dry. In the stripping film method, a dry emulsion is stripped from its base and wrapped around the specimen and slide. Exposure times vary from hours to months, depending on the kind and amount of radionuclide in the specimen. The emulsion remains in contact with the specimen during development. Conventional histological stains penetrate the emulsion and show structural detail in the specimen; histological structure and location of radioactivity are correlated by observation of the numbers of reduced silver grains at different sites on the specimen.

Low-energy β-emitters (^{14}C, ^{35}S, ^{45}Ca, tritium) are particularly valuable for microscopic autoradiography. Weak β-particles deposit their energy within a short distance of the atom or molecule from which they originate. This permits better correlations between labeled structures and reduced silver grains than strong β-particles, which can cause grain formation at long distances from the point of origin. Pure γ-emitters are of little use in autoradiography.

By means of densitometric measuring devices or by specialized procedures for grain counting, autoradiography can be employed to determine amounts of radioactivity at different locations on a specimen. Autoradiography has been used to demonstrate distributions of labeled mineral elements, drugs, metabolites, and hormones in the body. At the cellular level, new insight into nucleic acid metabolism and chromosome structure and division has been obtained. Advances in adapting autoradiography to electron microscopy have permitted observation of the distribution of labeled substances among organelles. However, the techniques and data analyses are most painstaking and should be undertaken only after careful evaluation of the benefits to be gained from the effort expended (Bélanger et al. 1959, Gahan 1972, Gude 1968, Rogers 1973).

Activation analysis

Activation analysis, or radioactivation analysis, is a very useful technique for the quantitative measurement of many elements in biological materials, particularly trace elements. The sample to be analyzed is bombarded with heavy nuclear particles, usually neutrons, which cause nuclear transmutations among isotopes of many of the elements in the sample, changing stable nuclides to radionuclides. The amount of the element of interest in the sample is determined by measuring the radiation emitted by its neutron-activation daughter product. The applicability of the technique to a specific element or specimen depends on the nature of neutron reactions with its isotopes, the kind and energy of radiation emitted by its activation products, the amount of the element present in the sample, and the presence or absence of other elements whose activation products emit interfering radiation. Radiochemical separations are used to remove interfering radionuclides when necessary, but chemical treatment may often be avoided by use of instrumental techniques to resolve γ-ray spectra.

One of the main advantages of activation analysis is its sensitivity. For certain trace elements, analytical sensitivities 100 times greater than those of conventional techniques can be obtained, making possible investigations of certain aspects of trace element function and metabolism that were previously unfeasible. Trace elements measurable by activation analysis include As, Co, Cu, Mn, Se, Sr, and Zn. Techniques have also been described for the analysis of Au, I, K, and Na, among others. In addition to its sensitivity, activation analysis is often much faster than standard chemical methods (International Atomic Energy Agency 1967, 1972; Koch 1960; Lyon 1964; Wainerdi 1964).

Radioimmunoassay

The combination of immunological and radionuclide techniques has produced an extremely sensitive assay procedure known as radioimmunoassay (RIA). By means of this procedure, substances of physiological and pharmaceutical importance that formerly were incapable of direct measurement (as contrasted to biological assay) can now be readily assayed in extremely small quantities down to the picogram level. A wide variety of hormones, peptide and nonpeptide, and nonhormonal substances are presently assayable—including cyclic AMP and GMP, prostaglandins, and hypothalamic, pituitary, thyroid, parathyroid, gastrointestinal, gonadal, adrenal, placental, and vasoactive hormones—and the list is expanding rapidly.

Radioimmunoassays are based on the isotope dilution principle and depend on the availability of a specific antibody to the substance being measured, and the availability of that substance in radiolabeled form. In the case of a hormone RIA, a fixed amount of labeled hormone (H*) is mixed with varying quantities either of nonlabeled hormone (H) in known amounts to prepare a standard curve, or in unknown amounts from the sample to be assayed. The specific activity of the mixture (H*/H) varies inversely with the quantity of H added. The mixture is then reacted with a fixed amount of antibody (Ab) specific to the hormone, the amount of antibody being insufficient to complex all the hormone in the sample. The H*/H-Ab complex is then separated from uncomplexed H*/H by any of a variety of techniques, including charcoal absorption, electrophoresis, column chromatography, and antibody precipitation. When the radioactivity of the H*/H-Ab is measured, it will vary inversely with the amount of H that is present to compete with H* for Ab binding sites; hence the technique is known as competitive binding or competitive inhibition. Comparison of H* in the unknown sample to a standard curve yields the amount of H in the sample. Precautions must be taken to ensure that the hormone is pure and that the antibody is specific to the hormone in order to prevent cross reactions (Boyd and Dalrymple 1974, Jaffe and Behrman 1974, Miller 1972).

REFERENCES

Arena, V. 1971. *Ionizing Radiation and Life.* Mosby, St. Louis.

Ashkar, F., Miale, A., Jr., and Smoak, W., eds. 1975. *A Study Guide in Nuclear Medicine.* Thomas, Springfield, Ill.

Bacq, Z.M. 1965. *Chemical Protection against Ionizing Radiation.* Thomas, Springfield, Ill.

Bélanger, L.F., Boyd, G.A., Fitzgerald, P.J., Lamerton, L.F., Leblond, C.P., Levi, H., and Pelc, S.R. 1959. Conference on autoradiography. *Lab Invest.* 8:59–333.

Bergner, P.E.E. 1964. Tracer dynamics and the determination of pool sizes and turnover factors in metabolic systems. *J. Theor. Biol.* 6:137–58.

Bergner, P.E.E., and Lushbaugh, C.C., eds. 1967. *Compartments, Pools, and Spaces in Medical Physiology.* Clearinghouse for Federal Scientific and Technical Information, National Bureau of Standards, U.S. Dept. of Commerce, Springfield, Va.

Bergonie, J., and Tribondeau, L. 1906. Interpretation de quelques résultats de la radiotherapie et essai de fixation d'une technique rationnelle. *Compte rend. Acad. sci.* 143:983–85, trans. *Radiat. Res.* 11:587. 1959.

Birks, J.B. 1964. *The Theory and Practice of Scintillation Counting.* Macmillan, New York.

Bond, V.P., Fliedner, T.M., and Archambeau, J.O. 1965. *Mammalian Radiation Lethality.* Academic Press, New York.

Boyd, C.M., and Dalrymple, G.V., eds. 1974. *Basic Science Principles of Nuclear Medicine.* Mosby, St. Louis.

Bransome, E.D., Jr. 1970. *The Current Status of Liquid Scintillation Counting.* Grune & Stratton, New York.

Brown, B. 1966. *Long-Term Radiation Damage: Evaluation of Life-Span Studies.* Rand Corp., Santa Monica, Calif.

Brown, D.G., Gramly, W.A., and Cross, F.H. 1964. Response of 3 breeds of swine exposed to whole-body cobalt-60 gamma radiation in daily doses of 100 roentgens *Am. J. Vet. Res.* 25:1347–53.

Casarett, A.P. 1968. *Radiation Biology.* Prentice-Hall, Englewood Cliffs, N.J.

Casey, H.W., McClellan, R.O., Clarke, W.J., and Bustad, L.K. 1963. Iodine-131-labeled rose bengal blood clearance as a liver function test in sheep. *Am. J. Vet. Res.* 24:1189–94.

Chase, G.D., and Rabinowitz, J.L. 1967. *Principles of Radioisotope Methodology.* 3d ed. Burgess, Minneapolis.

Comar, C.L. 1955. *Radioisotopes in Biology and Agriculture.* McGraw-Hill, New York.

Dalrymple, G.V., and Baker, M.L. 1973. Molecular biology. In Dalrymple, M.E. Gaulden, G.M. Kollmorgen, and H.H. Vogel, Jr., eds., *Medical Radiation Biology.* Saunders, Philadelphia.

Early, P.J., Razzak, M.H., and Sodee, D.B. 1969. *Nuclear Medicine Technology.* Mosby, St. Louis.

Federal Radiation Council. 1960, 1961. *Background Material for the Development of Radiation Protection Standards.* Reports 1 and 2. Supt. of Documents, U.S. Govt. Printing Office, Washington, D.C.

Fowler, J.F. 1963. Solid-state dosimeters for in-vivo measurements. *Nucleonics* 21(10):60–65.

Gahan, P., ed. 1972. *Autoradiography for Biologists.* Academic Press, New York.

Glasser, O., Quimby, E.H., Taylor, L.S., Weatherwax, J.L., and Morgan, R.H. 1961. *Physical Foundation of Radiology.* 3d ed. Harper & Row, New York. Pp. 8–9.

Glasstone, S. 1967. *Sourcebook on Atomic Energy.* 3d ed. Van Nostrand, Princeton, N.J.

Goyings, L.S., Reineke, E.P., and Schirmer, R.G. 1962. Clinical diagnosis and therapy of hypothyroidism in dogs. *J. Am. Vet. Med. Ass.* 141:341–47.

Greve, J.H., and Gaafar, S.M. 1964. Radiotriiodothyronine for the evaluation of experimentally induced hypothyroidism in dogs. *Am. J. Vet. Res.* 25:1191–94.

Griffin, S.A., Henneman, H.A., and Reineke, E.P. 1962. The thyroid secretion rate of sheep as related to season, breed, sex, and semen quality. *Am. J. Vet. Res.* 23:109–14.

Grigg, E.R.N. 1965. *The Trail of the Invisible Light*. Thomas, Springfield, Ill.

Gude, W.D. 1968. *Autoradiographic Techniques*. Prentice-Hall, Englewood Cliffs, N.J.

Haley, T.J., and Snider, R.S., eds. 1962. *Response of the Nervous System to Ionizing Radiation*. Academic Press, New York.

Hamlin, R.L., Marsland, W.P., and Smith, C.R. 1962. Absence of arteriovenous anastomoses in anesthetized sheep. *Am. J. Physiol.* 202:961–62.

Hansard, S.L., and Comar, C.L. 1953. Radioisotope procedures with laboratory animals. *Nucleonics* 11(7):44–47.

Harris, R.J.C., ed. 1963. *Cellular Basis and Aetiology of Late Somatic Effects of Ionizing Radiation*. Academic Press, New York.

Hart, H.E., ed. 1963. Multi-compartment analysis of tracer experiments. *Ann. N.Y. Acad. Sci.* 108:1–338.

Hayes, R.L., Nold, M.M., Comar, C.L., and Kakehi, H. 1960. Internal radiation dose measurements in live experimental animals. *Health Physics* 4(2):79–85.

Hine, G.J., and Brownell, G.L., eds. 1956. *Radiation Dosimetry*. Academic Press, New York.

Hollander, J.M., and Perlman, I. 1966. The semiconductor revolution in nuclear radiation counting. *Science* 154:84–93.

Holmes, J.R. 1960. A preliminary report on the use of I^{131}-labeled rose-bengal as a liver function test in sheep. *Cornell Vet.* 50:308–18.

Howes, J.R., Feaster, J.P., and Hentges, J.F., Jr. 1962. Comparison of the thyroid release of I-131 by Hereford and Brahman cattle maintained under identical environmental conditions. *J. Anim. Sci.* 21:210–13.

International Atomic Energy Agency. 1962. *Whole-Body Counting*. Proc. Symp. Whole-Body Counting, Vienna, June 12–15, 1961. International Publications, New York.

——. 1965. *Symposium on Radioisotope Sample Measurement Techniques in Medicine and Biology*. Vienna.

——. 1967. *Nuclear Activation Techniques in the Life Sciences*. Vienna.

——. 1972. *Nuclear Activation Techniques in the Life Sciences*. Vienna.

——. 1973a. *Safe Handling of Radionuclides*. Safety Series no. 1. Vienna.

——. 1973b. *Radiation Protection Procedures*. Safety Series no. 38. Vienna.

International Commission on Radiological Units and Measurements (ICRU). 1962. *Radiation Quantities and Units*. Report 10a. National Bureau of Standards Handbook 84. Supt. of Documents, U.S. Gov. Printing Office, Washington.

Jaffe, B.M., and Behrman, H.R., eds. 1974. *Methods of Hormone Radioimmunoassay*. Academic Press, New York.

Jones, H.B. 1968. A concept of lifetime tolerance to radiation. *Pediatrics* 41:271–77.

Kallfelz, F.A. 1968. The triiodothyronine-^{131}I test as an indicator of thyroid function in dogs. *J. Am. Vet. Med. Ass.* 152:1647–50.

——. 1969. Comparison of the ^{125}T-3 and ^{125}T-4 tests in the diagnosis of thyroid gland function in the dog. *J. Am. Vet. Med. Ass.* 154:22–25.

——. 1973. Observations on thyroid gland function in dogs: Response to thyrotropin and thyroidectomy and determination of thyroid secretion rate. *Am. J. Vet. Res.* 34:535–38.

Kallfelz, F.A., Norrdin, R.W., and Neal, T.M. 1968. Intestinal absorption of oleic acid ^{131}I and triolein ^{131}I in the differential diagnosis of malabsorption syndrome and pancreatic dysfunction in the dog. *J. Am. Vet. Med. Ass.* 153:43–46.

Kaneko, J.J., and Cornelius, C.E., eds. 1971. *Clinical Biochemistry of Domestic Animals*. Academic Press, New York.

Kinsell, L.W. 1961. Physiologic aging and radiologic life-shortening. *Fed. Proc.* 20(suppl. 8):14–21.

Kinsman, S., ed. 1970. *Radiological Health Handbook*. Office of Tech. Services, U.S. Dept. of Commerce, Washington.

Kobayashi, Y., and Maudsley, D.V. 1974. *Biological Applications of Liquid Scintillation Counting*. Academic Press, New York.

Koch, R.C. 1960. *Activation Analysis Handbook*. Academic Press, New York.

Kollman, G.J. 1973. Chemical protective agents. In G.V. Dalrymple, M.E. Gaulden, G.M. Kollmorgen, and H.H. Vogel, Jr., eds., *Medical Radiation Biology*. Saunders, Philadelphia.

Lange, R.C. 1973. *Nuclear Medicine for Technicians*. Year Book Medical, Chicago.

Lindop, P.J., and Sacher, G.A. 1966. *Radiation and Ageing*. Taylor & Francis, London.

Lombardi, M.H., Comar, C.L., and Kirk, R.W. 1962. Diagnosis of thyroid gland function in the dog. *Am. J. Vet. Res.* 23:412–21.

Lyon, W.S., Jr., ed. 1964. *Guide to Activation Analysis*. Van Nostrand, New York.

McAfee, J.G. 1975. The biological effects of radiation. In F. Ashkar, A. Miale, and W. Smoak, eds., *A Study Guide to Nuclear Medicine*. Thomas, Springfield, Ill.

Maynard, C.D. 1969. *Clinical Nuclear Medicine*. Lea & Febiger, Philadelphia.

Miller, W.H. 1972. Radioimmunoassay. In D.B. Sodee and P.J. Early, eds., *Technology and Interpretation of Nuclear Medicine Procedures*. Mosby, St. Louis.

Morgan, A.P., Boyden, C.M., and Moore, F.D. 1967. Radioisotope dilution techniques for measurement of body composition in health and disease. *Radiol. Clinics N. Am.* 5:193–204.

Müller, H.J. 1927. Artificial transmutation of the gene. *Science* 66:84–87.

National Academy of Sciences. 1968. *Body Composition in Animals and Man*. NAS Printing Office, Washington.

Naylor, G.P. 1967. The application of thermoluminescent phosphors in dosimetry problems in radiotherapy and radiobiology. *Brit. J. Radiol.* 40:170–76.

Neutze, J.M., Wyler, F., and Rudolph, A.M. 1968. Use of radioactive microspheres to assess distribution of cardiac output in rabbits. *Am. J. Physiol.* 215:486–95.

Parmentier, J.H. 1969. Developments in liquid scintillation counting since 1963. *Internat. J. Appl. Radiat. Isotopes* 20:305–34.

Prasad, K.N. 1974. *Human Radiation Biology*. Harper & Row, Hagerstown, Md.

Quinlan, W., Jr., and Michaelson, S.M. 1967. Iodine-131 uptake and protein-bound iodine in normal adult beagles. *Am. J. Vet. Res.* 28:179–82.

Rabinowitz, J.L., Banks, W.C., and Greenberg, C.M. 1964. Confirmation of a new, rapid, reliable test of thyroid function in dogs. *Am. J. Vet. Res.* 25:1314–16.

RCA Service Company. 1962. *Atomic Radiation*. Camden, N.J.

Rogers, A.W. 1973. *Techniques of Autoradiography*. 2d ed. Elsevier, New York.

Rubin, P., and Casarett, G.W. 1968. *Clinical Radiation Pathology*. Saunders, Philadelphia.

Rudolph, A.M., and Heymann, M.A. 1967. The circulation of the fetus in utero: Methods for studying distribution of blood flow, cardiac output, and organ blood flow. *Circ. Res.* 21:163–84.

Russell, W.L. 1968. Recent studies on the genetic effects of radiation in mice. *Pediatrics* 41:223–30.

Schoenheimer, R. 1949. *The Dynamic State of Body Constituents*. Harvard U. Press, Cambridge.

Sheppard, C.W. 1962. *Basic Principles of the Tracer Method*. Wiley, New York.

Shively, J.N., Andrews, H.L., Warner, A.R., Miller, H.P., Kurtz, H.J., and Woodward, K.T. 1964. X-ray exposure of swine previously exposed to a nuclear detonation. *Am. J. Vet. Res.* 25:1128–33.

Silver, S. 1968. *Radioactive Nuclides in Medicine and Biology*. 3d ed. Lea & Febiger, Philadelphia.

Sodee, D.B., and Early, J.E., eds. 1972. *Technology and Interpretation of Nuclear Medicine Techniques*. Mosby, St. Louis.

Spinks, J.W.T., and Woods, R.J. 1964. *An Introduction to Radiation Chemistry*. Wiley, New York.

Taliaferro, W.H., Taliaferro, L.G., and Jaroslow, B.N. 1964. *Radiation and Immune Mechanisms*. Academic Press, New York.

Twardock, A.R., Georgi, J.R., and Comar, C.L. 1964. Cisco: A whole-body counter for domestic animals and man. *Am. J. Vet. Res.* 25:270–73.

Twardock, A.R., Lohman, T.G., Smith, G.S., and Breidenstein, B.C. 1966. Symposium on atomic energy in animal science. I. The Illinois animal science counter: Performance characteristics and animal radioactivity measurement procedures. *J. Anim. Sci.* 25:1209–17.

Ullberg, S. 1958. Autoradiographic studies on the distribution of labelled drugs in the body. *Second UN Conf. Peaceful Uses Atomic Energy* 24:248–54.

United Nations. 1964. *Report of the Scientific Committee on the Effects of Atomic Radiation*. New York. Suppl. 14.

Wainerdi, R.E. 1964. Activation analysis finds its place in the life sciences. *Nucleonics* 22(2):57–60.

Wang, C.H., Willis, D.L., and Loveland, W.D. 1975. *Radiotracer Methodology in the Biological, Environmental, and Physical Sciences*. Prentice-Hall, Englewood Cliffs, N.J.

Wang, Y. 1967. *Clinical Radioisotope Scanning*. Thomas, Springfield, Ill.

Wang, Y., ed. 1968. *Advances In Dynamic Radioactive Scanning*. Thomas, Springfield, Ill.

Ward, G.M. 1970. Radioisotope techniques for the in vivo determination of body composition (mammals). *Wein. Tierärztl. Monatschr.* 57:204–10.

Demonstrations in Physiology | by H. Hugh Dukes

These demonstrations are not designed to replace laboratory work. They illustrate, supplement, and extend the lectures but are in no way a substitute for practical work done by the student. The demonstrations might, of course, have additional value to students who do not have an opportunity to take a laboratory course.

The percentage of successful demonstrations is very high. Many of the demonstrations are brief, being only a few minutes in duration. The demonstrations do take time to set up before class (everything should be ready when the students arrive), but the time factor is not at all prohibitive. Much of the equipment can be kept assembled in a storeroom for use from year to year. By simple projection methods most of the demonstrations that require visibility and are not readily seen otherwise can be made visible even to large classes. While a certain amount of equipment is required, much of this is already on hand in a good physiology laboratory. The cost of living material is not very great, as many of the experiments do not require that the animal be killed. Many of the demonstrations require no help at all, but a number of them require one assistant. Only on rare occasions is more than one assistant needed, and then only for a short time.

Extensive surgical procedures are generally not used in the demonstrations. Nor are graphic records, or tracings, commonly made. This work is generally reserved for the laboratory experiments.

In the demonstrations I emphasize the physiological facts and principles illustrated and generally touch rather lightly on the techniques used. The demonstrations are given right along with the lectures and discussions, the experiments paralleling closely the readings assigned in the text. A number of the demonstrations have or can be given pharmacodynamic interest.

PROJECTION TECHNIQUES

In classes of medium-to-large size it is desirable or essential to project many of the experiments onto a screen. Several kinds of projectors are useful.

A *vertical projector* (overhead) can be used not only for slide projection but also for the showing of such things as the isolated beating heart, muscle and nerve-muscle preparations, intestinal segments, chemical reactions, and hemolysis and coagulation experiments. The object to be projected is placed in a suitable container, such as a glass dish containing saline, on the stage of the projector. Opaque objects project largely in silhouette. This is usually not a serious disadvantage. Several kinds of large vertical projectors are available. They allow the projection of a great variety of material, inanimate and animate, including intact small animals such as frogs, rats, and guinea pigs.

A *horizontal projector* has even greater usefulness in physiological demonstrations. A conventional slide projector, considerably modified, may be used. I have taken the lamp housing including the condensing lenses from an old projector and clamped it to a heavy stand. To another stand the projecting lens is fixed by means of a clamp. The bellows is discarded and any interfering rods are removed, the space between the condensing and projecting lenses being entirely open. The object to be projected goes in this space. A prism is placed in front of the projecting lens to erect the image. In the absence of a prism a first-surface mirror may be used. Lacking that, an ordinary mirror will do. The uses to which such a projector may be put are very numerous. Levers, tambours, manometers, electrodes, signal magnets, drop recorders, circulation and respiration models, isolated organs and tissues, intact small animals, and chemical reactions may be projected.

Probably an optical bench with suitable accessories would serve very well as a horizontal projector for physiological demonstrations.

The familiar *opaque projector* has many uses other than the projection of graphs, charts, pages of books, and the like. If regions of intact (anesthetized) animals are placed under the projector, it is possible to show vasomotor changes, cardiac and jugular pulsations, respiratory movements, and so forth. Intestinal motility in a laparotomized guinea pig or rabbit projects well. An isolated beating heart makes a beautiful projection. The action of the heart and lungs in an anesthetized small mammal with open thorax is easily projected. The experiments should be short, lest the preparation become too hot. Overheating can be diminished by placing two glass plates with intervening air space over the opening below the lamp. By removing the under parts of the projector (platen, legs, etc.) and supporting it on long legs on top of a table, free access to the field of the lantern can be obtained.

Shadow projection with a carbon arc lamp is very useful. The room need not be dark. Many experiments may be sharply outlined on the screen in this way. An entire animal may be projected. If the lamp is run on A.C., cored carbons should be used. Shadow projection with the arc lamp is quite easy once a few simple requirements are learned, and in many instances it is very effective. This type of projection is not suitable for showing transparent objects: they also tend to project as shadows. The lens projector is better here.

When using the carbon arc lamp, one should avoid undue exposure to its radiation.

Optical projection may be accomplished in a number of instances by fixing a small mirror to the surface or object whose movement is to be observed. A band or spot of light is projected upon the mirror, which reflects the light onto a screen. The movements of the light are then observed. A concave (galvanometer) mirror makes unnecessary the use of lenses for focusing. The movements of tambour membranes, "spoon" manometers, and isometric levers may readily be seen in this way.

If a *microprojector* is available, demonstrations can include the circulation in the web of a frog's foot or other thin membrane and rumen protozoa.

Probably some of the demonstrations here described could be presented better by closed-circuit television.

SOUND AMPLIFICATION

A good microphone, amplifier, and loudspeaker have wide usefulness. A number of cardiac changes and reflexes, alimentary and respiratory activities, and muscle phenomena can be shown in this way. The sounds of Korotkov are readily demonstrated. A contact microphone especially designed for heart sounds is used. Since most of the sounds to be amplified are of low frequency, the amplifier and loudspeaker will give better results if selected with this point in mind.

ANIMAL EXPERIMENTATION

All demonstrations involving the use of living animals must be done with full regard for the principles of animal experimentation. It is the duty of the teacher to inform the students about the necessity for, and the moral basis of, animal experimentation in the physiological, medical, veterinary medical, and other biological sciences.

ANESTHESIA

When an anesthetic is required in these demonstrations, the one generally used (for dogs) is sodium pentobarbital. The dose is about 40 mg per kg, given intravenously. (This is larger than the usual clinical dose.) The injection may be made rather rapidly if due attention is given to the heart action and the respirations. It is more important to watch the former than the latter.

INTRAVENOUS INJECTION

This technique is required in a number of demonstrations. It is not difficult to use. In the dog the cephalic and lateral saphenous veins are readily available. The former vein is preferable. Clipping of the hair is recommended. The vein is raised by occlusion, and the needle, already on the syringe, is inserted into it. When blood appears in the syringe, the occlusion is discontinued and the injection made. A syringe with an eccentric tip is preferable. A 20-gauge needle with short bevel is satisfactory. An even smaller needle may be used. The needle is so placed on the syringe that the bevel is up when the puncture is made.

Since the experiments in which the animals are subjected to venous, arterial, cardiac, cisternal, pleural, and other punctures do not result in the animal's death, the punctures should be done with suitable cleanliness. Strict asepsis is generally unnecessary.

EUTHANASIA

Those experiments in which the animals should be euthanized either before or after are: 33, 37, 40, 41, 47, 80, 81, 83, 84, 85, 88. To reduce cost, several of these experiments may be combined.

BLOOD

1. *Plasma and cells.* Project a graduate containing uncoagulated horse blood to show the color of plasma and relative volumes of plasma and cells. Hold the graduate in the field of the horizontal projector.

2. *Serum and clot.* Project a graduate containing coagulated horse blood to show serum, clot, and probably the buffy coat.

3. *Plasma carbon dioxide.* Equilibrate a sample of plasma with alveolar air in a flask. Introduce some of the

plasma into an oiled syringe provided with a stopcock. Close the stopcock and evacuate by pulling on the plunger, projecting with either the vertical or horizontal lantern. The evolution of gases (mainly CO_2) will be evident. Discuss carbon dioxide capacity.

4. *Packed cell volume*. Project a PCV tube containing heparinized dog blood. Show "leukocyte cream." Use either projector.

5. *Color of plasma*. Project samples of dog, cow, and horse plasma to show the colors.

6. *Sedimentation rates*. Fill sedimentation tubes with horse and dog bloods. Clamp the tubes in the field of the horizontal projector. Compare sedimentation rates.

7. *Hemolysis*. Place on a glass plate on the stage of the vertical projector two small amounts (a few drops) of blood diluted with physiological saline. Add water to one quantity of blood (for hemolysis) and saline to the other (for control).

8. *Agglutination of erythrocytes*. Place on a glass plate on the stage of the vertical projector a few drops of blood diluted with saline. Add a saline extract of ground-up beans to produce agglutination of the red cells.

9. *Hemagglutination*. Place on a glass plate on the stage of the vertical projector a few drops of cow serum or plasma. Add horse erythrocytes suspended in saline. Note hemagglutination (heterohemagglutination).

10. *Color of arterial and venous bloods*. Obtain from a gentle unanesthetized dog, before class or in class, samples of venous and arterial blood by venous and femoral arterial puncture, using oiled, heparinized syringes with stopcocks attached to the tips. Close the stopcocks and project the syringes by placing them in the field of the opaque projector to show the difference in color of the two blood samples.

11. *Carbon monoxide poisoning*. Place a guinea pig in a glass dish on the stage of the large vertical projector and cover the dish. Run in automobile exhaust fumes (through soda lime to remove CO_2 if desired) and observe the quickly developing signs of carbon monoxide poisoning (hypohemoglobinemic hypoxia). With the onset of unconsciousness and convulsions, remove the animal and give artificial respiration.

12. *Absorption spectra*. Convert the horizontal projector into a projection spectroscope by placing a vertical slit in focus in front of the condensing lenses and a prism with good dispersion in front of the projecting lens. Use the erecting prism to raise the resulting spectrum to the desired position on the screen. Put blood diluted with distilled water (1:100) in an absorption cell with parallel sides and place this in front of the slit. The absorption spectrum of oxyhemoglobin will be seen on the screen.

Add a reducing agent to the oxyhemoglobin solution. The spectrum of reduced hemoglobin will appear. Agitate the hemoglobin solution in the air. Oxyhemoglobin will be formed.

Bubble carbon monoxide through hemoglobin solution to produce carboxyhemoglobin or obtain blood from a small animal just poisoned with carbon monoxide and hemolyze it. In either case note the spectrum of carboxyhemoglobin. Add a reducing agent. The spectrum remains unchanged.

13. *Spleen experiment*. From a gentle unanesthetized dog standing on the lecture table obtain a small amount of venous blood in a heparinized syringe. Inject intravenously 0.5–1.0 ml epinephrine. After 2–3 minutes, obtain a blood sample from the opposite vein. Place the samples in PCV tubes and spin in the centrifuge. Project the tubes by placing them on the stage of a vertical projector. There is generally a significant increase in red cell volume in the second tube. The results *may* indicate the ejection of concentrated blood from the spleen—reservoir function of the spleen in the dog—but other interpretations are possible.

14. *Blood coagulation*. Anesthetize a dog in class by intravenous injection of sodium pentobarbital and obtain in a syringe a large sample of blood by heart puncture. Quickly divide the blood into small quantities for coagulation studies. Small cylindrical vials or small beakers, appropriately labeled, are convenient for receiving the blood. Whether or not coagulation occurs can be demonstrated by placing each vial on the stage of a vertical projector and tipping it over if necessary. Following is a suggested series of tubes: (a) blood only; (b) blood and thromboplastin; (c) blood and thrombin; (d) blood and oxalate, to which preparation calcium is later added; (e) blood and citrate; (f) blood and fluoride; (g) blood and heparin; (h) plasma (previously obtained) and thrombin; (i) defibrinated blood.

Wash the fibrin obtained from (i) and project it.

15. *Absorption*. As a part of the study of lymph formation, perform the following demonstrations on absorption. Before class anesthetize four dogs with sodium pentobarbital. Place the dogs on high tables in such a way that their heads will hang over the table edge and can be projected with the arc lamp. Give the animals pilocarpine (5–10 mg) or some other cholinergic substance as follows: dog 1, intravenously; dog 2, intramuscularly; dog 3, intraperitoneally; dog 4, subcutaneously. Saliva will be secreted in all instances, generally in the order indicated. Project the salivary secretion with the arc lamp. Note the lapsed time in each case.

16. *Cerebrospinal fluid (CSF)*. Needle the cisterna magna of an anesthetized dog and connect the needle, by means of a three-way stopcock and rubber tubing, with a vertical glass tube of small diameter in the field of the horizontal projector. Before the demonstration fill the tubes with colored saline by means of a syringe attached to the stopcock, locate the point of atmospheric pressure, and place a transparent millimeter scale alongside the manometer tube, with the zero at atmospheric pressure.

Then run some additional saline into the tubes so that there will be a minimum movement of CSF into the system of tubes or of saline out of it when the needle is connected to it.

Produce variations in CSF pressure by (a) occlusion of the jugular veins, (b) injection of epinephrine, (c) raising the hind parts of the dog.

From the same or another anesthetized dog, obtain CSF in an oiled syringe provided with a stopcock. Place the syringe on the stage of a vertical projector. Note the clear fluid. Evacuate the fluid to show the evolution of gases (mainly CO_2). Run some of the fluid into a dish and test for chloride with silver nitrate.

Shadow the head of the dog and note the drops of fluid falling out of the needle.

CIRCULATION

17. *Pacemaker of the frog heart.* Tie off the sinus venosus of a frog heart in the field of the horizontal projector. Let the frog lie on a small platform clamped to a stand and have the heart attached by a thread to a lever (suspension method). Stimulate the quiescent ventricle with single shocks to show summation of subminimal stimuli, all-or-nothing contractions, and so forth.

18. *Exposed turtle heart.* Make various experiments on the exposed beating heart of a decapitated turtle in the field of an opaque projector.

19. *Electrical changes of muscle and heart.* (a) Grasp metal electrodes in the hands. Use salt jelly to lower skin resistance. Connect the electrodes to an amplifier and loudspeaker. Contract the arm and hand muscles to produce electrical changes, which are converted into audible sounds. The intensity of sound is roughly proportional to the force of the muscle contraction. (b) Show the electrical changes of muscle and heart with the cathode ray oscilloscope. (c) Show the changes with a direct-writing electrocardiograph. Project (with the opaque projector) an electrocardiogram.

20. *Cardiac pulsation.* Show this pulsation in an anesthetized dog by means of a cardiograph placed over the heart and a recording tambour. Project the movements of the tambour lever.

21. *Heart sounds.* Demonstrate laryngeal (talking) and pharyngeal (drinking of water) sounds on oneself by the use of a heart-sound microphone, amplifier, and loudspeaker. Then demonstrate heart sounds in animals and birds of all sizes (mouse, rat, guinea pig, rabbit, pigeon, chicken, cat, dog, man, sheep, cow, horse). No anesthesia is required.

22. *Muscle sounds.* Show that contracting skeletal muscle produces sound by placing a microphone over the biceps muscle and contracting it isometrically with varying force.

23. *Cardiac cycle.* A correlation of electrical changes, heart sounds, and intraventricular pressure variations can be made. An anesthetized dog is used as the subject. The electrical changes are observed on the screen of the cathode ray oscilloscope. Cardiac sounds are heard by means of a microphone, amplifier, and loudspeaker. The intraventricular pressure changes are observed by inserting through the chest wall into a ventricle a long needle connected by rigid tubing to a glass "spoon" manometer (Fig. A.1). The entire manometric system should be previously filled with liquid containing an anticoagulant and the level of atmospheric pressure determined and marked on the screen. Projection of the pressure changes is accomplished by transmitting a band of light to a concave mirror fixed on the manometer. The mirror reflects the focused light onto a screen where its movements are observed. A slit in front of a suitably housed lamp serves very well as the band of light transmitted to the mirror.

If the needle is properly placed in the ventricle and the manometric system is in good order, the intraventricular pressure will fall to atmospheric during diastole. It is not difficult to arrange a calibration device (aneroid manometer) in the manometric system. It can be included or excluded by means of a suitably placed stopcock.

The presence of the needle in the ventricle will probably produce premature beats, with compensatory pauses followed by louder sounds (caused by the operation of the Frank-Starling law). (It is easy to show simultaneously the electrical changes and the sounds. It is more difficult to get a satisfactory demonstration of the pressure changes. But the results, when good, are worth the effort.)

24. *Syringe model for cardiac output.* Fix a glass sy-

Figure A.1. A glass "spoon" manometer, which works on the principle of the Bourdon gauge. A concave galvanometer mirror (left) is cemented to the glass. A metal adapter (right) facilitates connection of the manometer to the pressure-transmission tube.

ringe (10 ml) with suitable valves in the field of the horizontal projector. Pump colored water through the syringe. Show stroke volume at constant rate. Use a metronome to keep the rate constant. Double the stroke volume, but leave the rate the same. Double the rate, but go back to the original stroke volume. Double both rate and stroke volume to give a 4-fold increase in syringe output. (A simple experiment but quite worthwhile.)

25. *Auto-rhythmicity of heart.* Place a frog or turtle heart in a dish of Ringer's solution on the stage of a vertical projector. Note the auto-rhythmic beat. Cut it up and note auto-rhythmicity of the different parts.

26. *Properties of cardiac muscle: Poikilotherm.* Isolate a turtle heart and suspend it (ventricle) between two bent pins in the field of the horizontal projector. The upper pin should be stationary, the lower fixed to a heart lever. Insert electrodes into the ventricle (small fishhooks attached to fine wires serve very well) and connect them to a stimulator. If necessary, slow the heart with cold Ringer's solution dropped on it. Show (a) auto-rhythmicity, (b) refractory period, (c) premature beats and compensatory pause, (d) driving of ventricle by repetitive stimulation but no tetanus, (e) van't Hoff effect (heat of lantern or warm Ringer's solution). Then cut off the atria to stop the ventricle and show the all-or-nothing law.

27. *Properties of cardiac muscle: Mammal.* Amplify the heart sounds of an anesthetized dog lying on the lecture table. Quickly thrust a sharp stylet through the chest wall over the heart. With the stylet, mechanically stimulate the heart and show (a) refractory period, (b) premature beats, (c) compensatory pause, and (d) Frank-Starling law.

28. *Skeletal muscle contraction (frog).* Show that this contraction is not all-or-nothing and that skeletal muscle can be tetanized. Project the muscle, lever, stimulator, and so on with the arc lamp.

29. *Nervous regulation of the heart.* Place a microphone over the heart of a quiet dog. Inject the following substances intravenously: (a) Sodium pentobarbital. With the induction of anesthesia cardiac acceleration occurs. This is caused by depression of the inhibitory center as well as a temporary fall of blood pressure—the fall diminishing reflex inhibition from the aortic arch and carotid sinuses. Sinus arrhythmia, if present, disappears. (b) Arecoline or acetylcholine, in amount sufficient to slow or stop the heart. If the heart stops, ectopic beats will soon occur because of shifting of the pacemaker to the A-V (atrioventricular) node. (c) Atropine, given quickly and in considerable dilution. (The blood pressure is now quite low and the venous return poor.) Cardiac acceleration soon occurs. (d) Epinephrine. Dramatic acceleration and augmentation of the beat occur.

30. *Aortic and carotid sinus reflexes.* Inject amphetamine into an anesthetized dog with heart microphone in place. Note the recurring acceleration and reflex slowing of the heart. Then block the vagi with an injection of atropine. The reflexes initiated from the baroceptors no longer slow the heart.

31. *Carotid sinus reflex.* Press on the carotid sinuses of a selected unanesthesized dog. Reflex slowing of the heart may occur. Use microphone.

32. *Reflex slowing of heart.* Let an unanesthetized rabbit inhale ammonia. Reflex slowing of the heart will occur. Use microphone.

33. *Perfusion of mammalian heart.* Using the Langendorff procedure, show the effect of ions, neurohumoral substances, drugs, and temperature. Very good projection of the action of the heart may be made by placing the heart during perfusion in a transparent dish on the stage of the large vertical projector.

34. *Action of ions and neurohumoral substances on the heart.* Place a turtle or frog heart in a dish of Ringer's solution on the stage of a vertical projector and drop the solutions on the heart. The heart should be rinsed and the solution changed when necessary.

35. *Temperature effect.* Place an isolated frog or turtle heart in a dish of cold Ringer's solution on the stage of a vertical projector. Note the increase in rate of beat as the preparation heats up. Add warm Ringer's solution to hasten the effect if desirable.

36. *Sinus arrhythmia.* Amplify the heart sounds of a quiet dog showing respiratory sinus arrhythmia. Inject atropine intravenously. Cardiac acceleration and disappearance of the arrhythmia follow.

37. *Action of the mammalian heart in situ.* Anesthetize a mammal (small size), open the chest, and give artificial respiration. This may be conveniently done by connecting a rubber bag containing oxygen to the trachea. A small amount of soda lime may be placed in the bag, or otherwise introduced into the rebreathing system, to absorb the carbon dioxide. Insert fishhook electrodes (see 26) into the heart. Place the preparation under the opaque projector. Show features of the physiology of the heart and respiration: stimulate a vagus, inject epinephrine, stop artificial respiration, stimulate a phrenic nerve, induce premature ventricular beats mechanically or electrically, fibrillate the ventricle. Defibrillate if apparatus is available. (Avoid overheating the preparation.)

38. *Flow of a liquid through rigid and elastic tubes.* Using an intermittent pump (rubber bulb with valves), compare flow from (a) long rigid tube, (b) long rigid tube with added resistance, (c) long elastic tube without added resistance, (d) long elastic tube with added peripheral resistance. Project the outflow with the arc lamp. Different-sized hypodermic needles placed on the ends of the tubes by means of adapters allow the resistance to be changed easily.

39. *Model of the circulation.* A simple model may be made of a rubber bulb with valves, rubber tubing, clamps, hypodermic needles of various calibers for pe-

ripheral resistance, mercury manometer for arterial pressure, narrow rubber balloon or finger cot for vena cava, etc. If the model is arranged on a stand, appropriate parts of it may be placed in the field of the horizontal projector. By use of a contact microphone the sounds produced by the valves and turbulent flow may be heard, and these may be correlated with the visible pulses.

40. *Blood pressure*. Cannulate the carotid artery of an anesthetized dog and show in succession (a) Stephen Hales' experiment by allowing blood to run up a long vertical glass or clear plastic tube (somewhat longer than 2 m), (b) blood pressure with a mercury manometer and transparent millimeter scale in the field of the horizontal projector, and (c) blood pressure with an optical manometer (see 23). Use an anticoagulant in each case.

41. *Blood pressure*. As a part of the preceding demonstration, or as another experiment, place a mercury manometer, connected to a carotid artery, in the field of the horizontal projector and show the effects of vagus stimulation, hemorrhage, infusion, acetylcholine, atropine, epinephrine, and so forth.

42. *Indirect or clinical method of determining blood pressure*. Place an aneroid manometer in the field of an opaque projector, or a mercury manometer in the field of a horizontal projector, or both. Listen to the sounds of Korotkov by means of a microphone placed over the artery, an amplifier, and a loudspeaker. Place a blood pressure cuff on the arm of a person and let the entire class simultaneously take the blood pressure. (A very effective demonstration.)

43. *Rabbit in upright position*. Hold a female rabbit in the vertical head-up position to show lack of tone of abdominal muscles. Relate this to blood flow. The hair over the abdomen may be clipped and the animal projected with the arc lamp.

44. *Venous pulse*. Anesthetize a dog and clip the hair off the lower part of the neck. Cement a concave galvanometer mirror to the skin over the jugular pulse. Project the pulsation by transmitting a band or spot of light to the mirror. (Considerable wobbling of the reflected light will occur.)

45. *Arterial pulses*. Receive the carotid and radial pulses with appropriate devices and transmit them to tambours. Project the levers with the arc lamp or place them in the horizontal projector. Note the delay of the radial pulse.

46. *Arterial pulse*. Receive an arterial pulse (carotid, radial, or femoral) and transmit it to a tambour with a concave mirror fixed to the periphery of the rubber membrane. Project the movements as a band or spot of light onto a screen.

47. *Vasomotor mechanisms*. Observe the blood pressure from a cannulated artery of a dog by means of a mercury manometer in the field of a horizontal projector. Amplify the heart sounds. Produce various vasomotor responses: stimulate central ends of the vagus and anterior laryngeal nerves; inject various autonomic blocking agents, histamine, and so on.

48. *Plethysmograph*. Have a subject insert an arm into a glass or plastic cylinder with a tubulature at the other end. Make the junction between the arm and cylinder airtight with the wrist of a rubber glove. Connect the other end with a tambour as described in 46 and project the volume changes of the arm. Observe the effects of (a) obstructing the venous return by means of a tourniquet applied to the upper arm, (b) deep breathing and holding the breath, (c) a mental calculation, (d) inhaling amyl nitrite, and (e) contraction of arm muscles. (Changes in heart rate, pulse volume, and arm volume are readily detected.)

RESPIRATION

49. *Model of the thorax*. Make this out of a bell jar with an opening at the top and preferably an opening on the side near the bottom. Use a rubber balloon for lungs and a rubber glove as a diaphragm. The rubber stopper at the top should have two glass tubes running through it—one to serve as the trachea, the other to connect with the pleural cavity. The lower opening can be used to illustrate the aspiratory action of the thorax on the venous return and in regurgitation; another balloon serves as the vena cava or the esophagus. At appropriate times show (a) mechanism of inspiration and expiration, (b) effect of partial and complete closure of the glottis, (c) intrathoracic pressure by means of a bromoform manometer, (d) pneumothorax, (e) abdominal press, (f) effect of inspiration on venous return, and (g) mechanism of regurgitation.

50. *Mechanism of inspiration and expiration*. Place an anesthetized dog on a high table and illustrate (a) the mechanism of inspiration and expiration, (b) abdominal and costal types of breathing, and (c) eupnea and dyspnea. The entire animal may be projected with the arc lamp. Where desirable to stimulate respiration, let the animal inhale carbon dioxide from a bag.

51. *Respiratory volumes*. Show tidal volume, pulmonary minute volume, vital capacity, etc., on oneself by use of the Benedict-Roth apparatus (without CO_2 absorber) or other suitable device.

52. *Accessory respiratory movements*. Show movements of the nostrils of a rabbit during respiration by projection of the head of the animal held in the hands. Use a vertical projector.

53. *Purring*. Place a microphone over the chest of a purring cat and listen to the sounds produced.

54. *Intrathoracic pressure*. Needle the pleural space of an anesthetized dog and connect the needle to a bromoform manometer for measuring of intrathoracic pressure. The manometer may be placed in the field of the horizontal projector. Produce a mild degree of pneumo-

thorax by injection of air into the pleural cavity by means of a syringe. A three-way stopcock can be used to facilitate connections and injections.

55. *Expired air.* Breathe through lime water in a beaker on the stage of a vertical projector.

56. *Carbon dioxide of expired air.* Collect expired air in a rubber bag and analyze it for CO_2. A simple method of analysis over water may be used.

57. *Blood gases.* Place a small amount of blood in a gas sampling tube, lay it on the stage of a vertical projector, and evacuate it by means of a vacuum pump. Note the evolution of the blood gases and the change in color of the blood.

58. *Plasma carbon dioxide.* Evacuate a sample of plasma (in equilibrium with alveolar air) in a gas sampling tube. Run in acid to cause further evolution of carbon dioxide. Repeat with a solution of sodium bicarbonate in another gas sampling tube.

59. *Arterial hypoxia.* Place a guinea pig in a glass container on the stage of the large vertical projector as in 11. Produce arterial hypoxia by running nitrogen into the container. Then run in oxygen and give artificial respiration if necessary.

60. *Arterial hypoxia.* Place a guinea pig in a bell jar or other suitable container connected to a mercury barometer calibrated in mm Hg and thousands of feet of elevation and to a vacuum pump. Use stopcock grease where necessary to make the system airtight. Produce arterial hypoxia by evacuation. Then return the animal to atmospheric pressure.

The upper part of a bell jar may be cut off and the upper open end of the resulting cylinder closed with a heavy glass plate in the same way as the lower end. The truncated bell jar with the animal in it may be placed on the stage of the large vertical projector and shown on the screen. (Use heavy glass to prevent implosion.)

61. *Hypohemoglobinemic hypoxia.* Repeat 11 if desirable.

62. *Hyperoxygenation.* Place a guinea pig in a jar and run in oxygen to produce hyperoxygenation at atmospheric pressure. Note absence of effect on the animal. Project if necessary.

63. *Hypercapnia.* Place a guinea pig in a jar of oxygen. Run in carbon dioxide. Project.

64. *Experiments on arterial hypoxia, hypercapnia, and hypoxia and hypercapnia combined (asphyxia)* can readily be made with the Benedict-Roth or similar metabolism apparatus connected to an endotracheal tube with inflated cuff in place in an anesthetized dog. To show hypoxia, let the animal rebreathe air with the absorption of carbon dioxide. To show hypercapnia, let the animal rebreathe oxygen with the accumulation of carbon dioxide (CO_2 absorber removed). To show hypoxia and hypercapnia combined, let the animal rebreathe air with the accumulation of carbon dioxide.

65. *Regulation of respiration.* Intubate the trachea of a dog under sodium pentobarbital anesthesia, using an endotracheal tube with inflatable cuff. Show effects of (a) breathing carbon dioxide, (b) closing the tube at the end of inspiration—inspiratory inhibitory reflex, (c) closing the tube at the end of expiration—no reflex effect, (d) quick pressure on the chest wall—inspiratory reflex, (e) passive movement of a leg, (f) pressure on carotid sinuses, (g) epinephrine intravenously (after atropine to block the vagi)—epinephrine apnea, and (h) amphetamine.

DIGESTION

66. *Secretion of saliva.* Cannulate the parotid duct of an anesthetized dog via the oral cavity. Use a lachrymal duct cannula and tie it securely in the duct by means of a suture placed with a fine curved needle. Remove the suture and cannula after the demonstration. Connect the cannula through tubing with a mercury manometer, as well as with a fine bent glass tube for observation of drops, in the field of the horizontal projector. A three-way stopcock in the course of the tube from the cannula enables one easily to change from observation of drops to observation of pressure. The entire system should previously be filled with water and the point of atmospheric pressure on the manometer located. A transparent millimeter scale may be placed alongside the manometer tube. A three-way stopcock at the cannula end of the tube is convenient for filling the manometric system and the drop-observation tube as well as for connecting the main tube to the cannula. With the distal stopcock set for drops, inject pilocarpine or other cholinergic substance intravenously and (a) observe the drops from the tube, (b) switch to presssure observation and note the salivary secretory pressure, (c) return to drops and inject atropine intravenously. Secretion stops at once.

67. *Conditioned salivary response.* Many dogs that have had repeated injections of sodium pentobarbital will develop a salivary conditioned response. The unconditioned stimulus is presumed to be the bitter taste of the drug as it reaches the taste receptors via the blood stream. The conditioned stimulus is the sight of the syringe and the other procedures accompanying the injection. In some animals profuse salivation occurs when the conditioned stimulus is presented.

68. *Salivary amylase.* Test for this in saliva of a cow or sheep, dog, and man. Use starch solution and iodine in culture dishes on the stage of the large vertical projector. Add the salivas to the several dishes. One dish may serve as a negative control. Amylase of bacterial or plant origin may cause some amylolytic action by the ruminant saliva. It is convenient to collect the ruminant saliva before class, but the human and dog salivas are easily collected in class.

69. *Deglutition.* Demonstrate swallowing sounds (caused by drinking of water) on oneself by means of a heart-sound microphone, amplifier, and loudspeaker. If after the pharyngeal sounds are heard, the microphone is quickly transferred to a location near the xiphoid region, sounds caused by the entry of water into the stomach are readily heard. The elapsed time is several seconds. The sounds at the cardia are more evident if some air is swallowed with the water.

70. *Effect of anesthesia on deglutition.* Anesthetize a dog with sodium pentobarbital. Show the complete absence or the depression of the swallowing reflex by testing the posterior part of the mouth and the pharynx by means of (a) water sprayed in from a syringe, and (b) a stomach tube inserted into the cavities.

71. *Gastric juice.* Some days previously make a gastric pouch in a dog. Drain the pouch by means of a Pezzer catheter permanently placed in it. Connect the pouch to a sphygmomanometer arm bag fixed like a saddle bag to a many-tail bandage on the animal. Collect juice overnight, bring the dog into class, and empty the bag. Project a sample of the juice. Measure the pH and test for chlorides in the field of a projector.

72. *Action of pepsin.* Prepare two beakers of gastric juice the night before, one specimen boiled, the other unboiled. To each add some protein (a skinned frog leg works well). The next day project the beakers in class by placing them on the stage of a vertical projector. Remove the solid contents, place them in culture dishes, and project.

73. *Secretion of gastric juice.* Place a dog with a gastric pouch on a table having a Pavlov frame. Connect the Pezzer catheter of the pouch by means of tubing with a fine glass tube in the field of the horizontal projector for the observation of drops. The system is then filled with water injected through a stopcock placed at a suitable location in the course of the connecting tube. To make the secretion audible, the drops may be allowed to fall on a microphone covered with a piece of rubber dam. Another method of observing the rate of secretion is simply to project the catheter and drops with an arc lamp. Inject histamine subcutaneously. In some minutes a copious secretion of gastric juice will result.

74. *Stomach motility.* Connect the Pezzer catheter of a gastric pouch to a vertical glass tube in the field of a horizontal projector. Fill the system with colored water and study pouch motor activity by observing the movements of the water in the manometer tube. Try for various effects on motility.

75. *Thirst.* Place a gentle dog on a table having a Pavlov frame. Induce thirst and drinking by intravenous injection of hypertonic saline. A suitable amount for a large dog is 50 ml of a 20 percent solution of NaCl. (Occasionally the animal will show excitement.)

76. *Rumen fistula.* Show a cow or sheep with a large rumen fistula.

77. *Rumen motility.* Needle the rumen of a sheep in a sheep crate on a table and connect the needle to a tambour or other recorder. Make a tracing of motility. Tease the hungry animal with food and note the increased rate of contraction. Test other effects on rumen motility. The movements of the recording lever may be calibrated in mm water. Other methods of receiving rumen contractions may be used.

78. *Rumen gases.* Needle the rumen of a sheep and connect the needle to the inlet of a glass water trap placed in the field of a horizontal projector. Connect the outlet of the trap with a rubber or plastic bag for collection of gas. Note motility; gas evolution; pressure changes, positive and negative, etc. Analyze some of the gas for carbon dioxide and burn some of it to show methane. (To ensure enough gas for the latter purposes, a previous collection of gas should be made in another bag. To show combustion well, it is advisable to pass the gas through soda lime or other carbon dioxide absorber on its way to the burner, which may be a hypodermic needle on the end of a rubber tube.)

79. *Regurgitation.* Show the essential features of regurgitation in ruminants by use of a model of the thorax (see 49).

80. *Pancreatic secretion.* Cannulate the pancreatic duct of an anesthetized dog. Place a glass tube in the field of a horizontal projector and connect it by means of rubber tubing to the cannula. Using a three-way stopcock, fill the tubes with water. Allow the drops to fall on a microphone if desired (see 73). Show the effects of HCl injected into the duodenum, secretin injected intravenously, and so on.

81. *Bile secretion.* This experiment may be done as a part of 80 or as a separate demonstration. Stimulate bile secretion by intravenous injection of (a) bile salts and (b) secretin.

82. *Intestinal secretion.* Show several types of intestinal fistula if chronic preparations are available. Anesthetize an animal having a Thiry-Vella fistula and insert through the fistula a catheter with perforations along its wall. Place the animal on a high stand and project the ends of the catheter with the arc lamp. Note any secretion. Inject tetraethylammonium (TEA). This generally causes an increased rate of secretion, presumably as a result of sympathetic blockade. Then transfer the animal to the opaque projector and withdraw the catheter.

83. *Action of an isolated intestinal segment.* Place a parallel-sided jar (small museum jar) containing warm Locke's solution in the field of a horizontal projector and suspend in it an intestinal segment of a rabbit, the lower end being fixed and the upper end being connected to a light lever. Observe the normal contractions and note the

effects of (a) epinephrine, (b) arecoline or other cholinergic substance, (c) atropine, and (d) a change of temperature of the solution.

84. *Intestinal motility.* Place a long loop of rabbit intestine in a transparent dish containing warm Locke's solution on the stage of the large vertical projector. Note the various types of motility and show the effects of adrenergic and cholinergic substances added to the solution or sprayed on the intestine.

85. *Intestinal motility.* Place an anesthetized laparotomized guinea pig or rabbit in the field of the opaque projector and observe motor activity of the small and large intestine.

86. *Alimentary tract of chicken.* Remove the entire alimentary tract of a recently killed chicken and place it in warm Locke's solution in a dish on the stage of the large vertical projector. Identify the different parts. Note motility at various levels.

87. *Absorption.* If animals with stomach pouch and intestinal fistulas are available, study absorption from these locations by introducing a solution of pilocarpine or other cholinergic substance into the pouch or fistula. Let the salivary glands signal absorption. Anesthesia is desirable for restraint.

URINE SECRETION, ENERGY METABOLISM, TEMPERATURE REGULATION

88. *Urine secretion.* Anesthetize a dog, cannulate a ureter, and lead the urine flow to the outside. Project the drops with an arc lamp or a horizontal projector. Follow circulatory changes by placing a microphone over the region of the heart. Observe the effects on urine flow of injection of (a) strong glucose solution, (b) sodium sulfate, (c) a cholinergic substance, (d) atropine, (e) epinephrine, and (f) saline.

89. *Energy metabolism.* Demonstrate measurement of the metabolic rate by the oxygen-consumption method, using a Benedict-Roth or similar metabolism apparatus. A man or a dog may be used as the subject.

90. *Insensible water loss.* Place the arm in a pharmaceutical percolator or the finger in a Harvard muscle warmer. Close the small end and make the other end tight around the arm or finger with a rubber cuff. Place the glass vessel on the stage of a vertical projector. Note the accumulation of water on the inner surface of the chamber.

91. *Temperature regulation* (see also 109). Illustrate radiation, convection, conduction, and evaporation. A familiar type of portable electric heater works by radiation. Others heat by convection. Convection in water can be illustrated by means of a glass tube in the shape of a rectangle filled with water through an opening at the top. A few drops of dye are also introduced through the opening. Convection currents are set up by heating one of the lower angles of the tube. An air thermometer can be used to illustrate conduction from the hand to the glass bulb. Evaporation can be illustrated by placing a piece of wet cloth on the bulb and blowing air on it.

MUSCULAR ACTIVITY AND THE NERVOUS SYSTEM

92. *Muscle and nerve-muscle experiments.* Tracings may be made, but are not necessary. For better visibility the muscle and lever may be projected with the arc lamp. Some experiments can be demonstrated very well by placing the preparation on the stage of a vertical projector. The slight movement of an isometric lever may be observed by means of optical projection. Demonstrations include: isotonic contraction, isometric contraction, genesis of tetanus shown isotonically and isometrically, graded response, temperature effect, and fatigue.

93. *Genesis of tetanus.* Demonstrate this on the muscles of one's own arm by stimulation of the median nerve at the elbow with single shocks from a suitable stimulator. Use unipolar stimulation, at first at low frequency, and gradually increase the frequency until tetanic contraction of the arm muscles results. Project the entire arm with the arc lamp throughout the demonstration.

94. *Muscle sounds.* See 22.

95. *Electrical changes.* See 19.

96. *Receptors.* Use a suspended spinal frog (projected with the arc lamp if desirable) to illustrate the working of several classes of receptors: touch, pressure, and pain receptors (pinch toe); chemoreceptors (acid to skin); warmth receptors (hot water); cold receptors (cold water). Illustrate auditory receptors with sound, visual receptors with light, touch receptors by bending hairs on the forearm (projected from the stage of a vertical projector), and proprioceptors by tapping the patellar tendon (man or animal).

97. *Synaptic functions or conduction in reflex arc.* Illustrate depression of central conduction by anesthetizing a frog with ether in a covered dish on the stage of a large vertical projector. Illustrate increased synaptic activity with strychnine in a spinal frog on the stage of the large vertical projector. Show summation, after-discharge, etc., in a suspended spinal frog projected with the arc lamp or placed in the field of a horizontal projector.

98. *Reflex action.* Show reflexes in a suspended spinal frog (if they have not been adequately demonstrated previously). Destroy the spinal cord. Project with an arc lamp or horizontal projector if desirable.

99. *Reflex action in a mammal.* Show in a quiet dog or cat, or both, the following reflexes: (a) knee-jerk, (b) flexor reflex, (c) crossed-extensor reflex, (d) extensor thrust, (e) head-shake reflex—elicited by a jet of air into ear, (f) scratch reflex—not easily elicited in the normal

animal but sometimes well shown in the dog *just* after the induction of anesthesia with sodium pentobarbital.

100. *Reflex action in man.* Show a number of reflexes including (a) the knee-jerk and its reinforcement by tightly clasping the hands, (b) the flexor reflex (leg), and (c) the plantar reflex, elicited by stroking "the lateral aspect of the sole of the foot with a pin from the heel toward the toes."

101. *Spinal shock.* Decapitate a frog and place it on the stage of the large vertical projector. Observe the disappearance of spinal shock.

102. *Cerebellar functions.* The decerebellate pigeon is excellent for demonstrating cerebellar functions. Anesthetize a normal pigeon (with a string tied to a leg!) by placing it in a jar containing ether vapor. Remove the pigeon from the jar and allow it to come out of the anesthesia. Observe the reactions. This serves as a control. Anesthetize another pigeon and quickly destroy the cerebellum by inserting a small flattened probe through the bone, just above the foramen magnum, into the posterior fossa and moving it around gently. Avoid injury to the medulla oblongata. Allow the bird to recover from the anesthesia; dramatic signs of cerebellar lack will quickly appear. (If preferred, a decerebellate pigeon may be prepared before class.)

103. *Agenesis of the cerebellum.* This condition is fairly common in cats. A veterinary clinic might serve as a source of such animals. They are valuable for illustrating cerebellar functions. With care they can be kept indefinitely. The extent of the anatomical defect can be confirmed later at autopsy. (Of course, decerebellate mammals may be prepared in survival experiments.)

104. *Postural reflexes and reactions.* With a cooperative normal cat or dog, demonstrate a number of postural reflexes and placing and hopping reactions. In a gentle dog abolish the standing reflex (muscle tonus) by injection of an anesthetic dose of sodium pentobarbital.

105. *Decerebrate rigidity and walking reflex.* Partly anesthetize (with ether in a chamber) a small dog or cat and show alternating rigidity and walking reflexes.

106. *Investigatory and righting reflexes.* Without warning have someone make a loud noise in the back of the room. Many members of the class will turn the head to investigate. Righting of the head will promptly follow.

107. *Cerebral cortex: What a decorticate pigeon can do.* A few days before they are needed in class, prepare several decorticate pigeons. The operation is simple, but the mortality and the number of partially successful or unsatisfactory preparations are fairly large. With experience both of these losses can be reduced. The perfect preparations often obtained justify the losses. A simple procedure is to anesthetize a pigeon in a jar containing vaporized ether. Remove the bird from the jar and quickly clip the feathers off the top of the head. Make a midline skin incision with a sharp scalpel. (Ordinary cleanliness will suffice; asepsis is unnecessary.) Using the point of the scalpel as a trephine, make an opening on each side over the cerebrum (at about the level of greatest curvature of the skull). Insert a probe and destroy the cortex by a gentle stirring motion in all directions from the opening. Avoid too deep insertion of the probe as well as injury to the cerebellum. Repeat on the other side. Close the skin incision with sutures. Allow the bird to recover from the anesthesia and do not disturb it for an hour or so lest severe intracranial bleeding occur. With a little experience one can tell if the preparation will be satisfactory. Muscle tonus should be good and the bird should stand symmetrically. It should not move when the hand is quickly advanced toward it (without touching it). A characteristic ruffling of the feathers occurs, especially if the environment is cool. Regurgitation may occur. When undisturbed, the pigeon usually appears sleepy, although it may walk a good deal. When taken in the hand or otherwise stimulated, it arouses and appears almost normal. It must be fed and watered by hand and kept in a protected environment.

This preparation can carry on perfect reflex activity (projection with the arc lamp may be used where desirable): (a) The standing reflex is unimpaired. (b) Place the pigeon on the hand or on a board and tip it. A new attitude is struck—attitudinal reflex. (c) Place the pigeon on its back. Prompt righting of the body occurs. (d) Hold the pigeon horizontally between the hands and rotate the body around the long and transverse axes. Righting of the head occurs. (e) With the pigeon standing on a stick held in one hand, bring another stick held in the other hand in contact with the sternum. Placing occurs. (f) Suddenly lower the bird while it is standing on a stick held horizontally. A statokinetic reflex occurs. (g) Suddenly lower the bird held with its feet free. The toes fan out in preparation for landing—statokinetic reflex. (h) Lower the bird faster than in (f). It will fly away and light gracefully. (i) The head-shake reflex, elicited by a jet of air into the ear, works well. (j) Autonomic reflexes are essentially normal. (Probably the striatum, which is a large mass in the bird, is damaged or destroyed in this operation. Perhaps this preparation would more properly be designated as "decorticate-destriate." In this sense the pigeon would be essentially "hemispherectomized.")

108. *Cerebral cortex: What a decorticate pigeon will not do.* (a) It will not eat or drink unless fed or watered. (b) It shows no fear. (c) It will not get off a hot plate but will simply step up and down in place (flexor and extensor reflexes). (d) It lacks cortical vision (but reflex vision is present, for it will fly without hitting objects and will light with precision). (e) It will not respond to a loud sound (except by feel).

109. *Temperature regulation* (see also 91). The decor-

ticate pigeon shows good temperature control, but it will not seek out a warm place. In a cold environment the pteromotor reflex shows up well

110. *Vision and hearing*. Demonstrations include (a) stimulation of the retina electrically; (b) image formation with a lens; (c) Purkinje images with a watch glass for the cornea and a reading glass for the lens; (d) divergence of the optic axes in a pigeon, rabbit, cat, and dog; (e) auditory ossicles as a bent lever (physical model); (f) ''silent'' dog whistle.

Index

Page numbers indicate where discussion of the subject begins.

DUKES' PHYSIOLOGY OF DOMESTIC ANIMALS

Designed by R. E. Rosenbaum.
Composed by Vail-Ballou Press, Inc.,
in 10 point VIP Times Roman, 1 point leaded,
with display lines in VIP Helvetica and Helvetica Bold.
Printed offset by Vail-Ballou Press on
Allied Laural Text, 50 pound basis.
Bound by Vail-Ballou Press
in Joanna book cloth
and stamped in All Purpose foil.

Library of Congress Cataloging in Publication Data
(For library cataloging purposes only)

Dukes, Henry Hugh, 1895–
Dukes' physiology of domestic animals.

Bibliography: p.
Includes index.
1. Veterinary physiology. I. Swenson, Melvin J., 1917– II. Title. III. Title: Physiology of domestic animals. [DNLM: 1. Animals, Domestic—Physiology. 2. Physiology, Comparative. SF768 D877p]
SF768.D77 1977 636.089'2 77-255
ISBN 0-8014-1076-2